S0-CFZ-058

The Official

PROCEEDINGS

Conference Co-Chairs

Margaret C. Campbell
Jeff Inman
Rik Pieters

International Standard Book Number (ISBN): 0-915552-65-5

International Standard Serial Number (ISSN): 0098-9258

Margaret C. Campbell, Jeff Inman and Rik Pieters, Editors

Advances in Consumer Research, Volume 37

(Duluth, MN: Association for Consumer Research, 20109)

Preface

The Fortieth Annual conference of the Association for Consumer Research (ACR) was held at the Westin Hotel in Pittsburgh, PA over four terrific days, October 22 to October 25, 2009. This volume is comprised of research presented during the meetings. The volume is organized by type of research submission and includes: Full Competitive Papers; Extended Abstracts; Special Session Summaries; Working Paper Abstracts; Roundtable Summaries; and Film Festival Abstracts.

The conference theme, A World of Knowledge at the Point of Confluence, represented both the vibrant, diverse research presented at the conference, and the geographic beauty of the three rivers that join together in Pittsburgh. ACR2009 had the highest number of submissions and attendees to date. ACR2009 provided a point of confluence for researchers from 32 different countries. Out of over 900 submissions, there were 417 pieces of research accepted for presentation at the conference. The large amount of research necessitated–for the first ACR ever–13 concurrent sessions. It was well worth it to have the exposure to so much strong research representing a broad variety of paradigms and an amazing array of topics on consumers and consumer behavior.

Another first for ACR2009 was the inaugural ACRun. Actually, we had two runs, one for early birds, guided by Joann Peck, and one for those ready to run after a day of sessions, guided by Susan Jung Grant. These three-mile runs along the rivers "at the point of confluence" were well-attended and quite enjoyable. The runs offered time for participants to interact with each other outside of the hotel environment.

We are grateful to many people. The ACR community is hard-working and generous with time and effort. Fifteen Associate Editors guided the acceptance of competitive papers; 67 ACR members served on the Program Committee, providing valuable input on special session proposals; and over 750 members helped review. The names of all these people appear in the ACR2009 Program. We are also very grateful to the past conference chairs, Ann McGill and Sharon Shavitt, and the executive director, Rajiv Vaidyanathan, for their willingness to share their experience and to answer many questions. While we were not feeling particularly thankful last October—just depleted of all executive and other resources—we do sincerely thank ACR President Chris Janiszewski for trusting us with the conference and for supporting us throughout the process.

Lastly, we thank all of you who helped to make ACR2009 a reality by contributing your work, reviewing papers and session proposals, and chairing key components like working papers, roundtables, the film festival and the doctoral symposium. With all of your help, the conference was a success. Now, based on the conference, this volume summarizes the confluence of the very best consumer research to serve as a stepping stone for additional knowledge to come. Happy reading!

Margaret C. Campbell, University of Colorado, Boulder
Jeff Inman, University of Pittsburgh
Rik Pieters, Tilburg University
2009 ACR Conference Co-Chairs and Proceedings Editors

Conference Committees and Reviewers

President
Chris Janiszewski, University of Florida, USA

Conference Chairs
Margaret C. Campbell, University of Colorado, Boulder
Jeff Inman, University of Pittsburgh
Rik Pieters, Tilburg University

Associate Editors
Hans Baumgartner, Pennsylvania State University, USA
Susan Broniarczyk, University of Texas at Austin, USA
Pierre Chandon, INSEAD, France
Eileen Fischer, York University, Canada
Gerald Häubl, University of Alberta, Canada
Doug Holt, Oxford University, UK
Amna Kirmani, University of Maryland, USA
Davy Lerouge, Tilburg University, the Netherlands
C. Page Moreau, University of Colorado at Boulder, USA
Joseph Nunes, University of Southern California, USA
L. J. Shrum, University of Texas at San Antonio, USA
Vanitha Swaminathan, University of Pittsburgh, USA
Patti Williams, University of Pennsylvania, USA
Richard Yalch, University of Washington, USA
Carolyn Yoon, University of Michigan, USA

Program Committee–Special Session Reviewers

Joseph Alba, University of Florida, USA
Dana Alden, University of Hawaii, USA
Jennifer Argo, University of Alberta, Canada
Rajeev Batra, Ross School of Business, University of Michigan, USA
Jonah Berger, The Wharton School, University of Pennsylvania, USA
Barbara Bickart, Boston University, USA
Lauren G. Block, Baruch College, CUNY, USA
C. Miguel Brendl, Northwestern University, USA
James Burroughs, University of Virginia, USA
Julien Cayla, Australian School of Business, University of New South Wales, Australia
Amitava Chattopadhyay, INSEAD, Singapore
Amar Cheema, Washington University / University of Virginia, USA
June Cotte, University of Western Ontario, Canada
Elizabeth Cowley, University of Sydney, Australia
Marcus Cunha Jr, University of Washington, USA
Peter Dacin, Queen's University, Canada
Kalpesh Desai, State University of New York at Binghamton, USA
Siegfried Dewitte, K.U. Leuven, Belgium
Kristin Diehl, University of Southern California, USA
Adam Duhachek, Indiana University, USA
Rosellina Ferraro, University of Maryland, USA
Robert Fisher, University of Alberta, Canada
Ayelet Gneezy, University of California at San Diego, USA
Noah J. Goldstein, University of California at Los Angeles, USA
Gerald Gorn, Hong Kong University of Science and Technology, Hong Kong, China
Rebecca Hamilton, University of Maryland, USA
Deborah Heisley, California State University, Northridge, USA
Wayne D. Hoyer, University of Texas at Austin, USA
Susan Jung Grant, University of Colorado at Boulder, USA
Ajay Kalra, Rice University, USA
Tina Kiesler, California State University, Northridge, USA
Juliano Laran, University of Miami, USA
Loraine Lau-Gesk, University of California at Irvine, USA
Richard Lutz, University of Florida, USA
John G. Lynch jr., Leeds School of Business, University of Colorado at Boulder, USA
Karen Machleit, University of Cincinnati, USA
Naomi Mandel, Arizona State University, USA
Arul Mishra, University of Utah, USA
Vikas Mittal, Rice University, USA
Maureen Morrin, Rutgers University-Camden, USA
Anirban Mukhopadhyay, Hong Kong University of Science and Technology, Hong Kong, China/University of Michigan, USA
Albert Muniz, DePaul University, USA
A V Muthukrishnan, Hong Kong University of Science and Technology, Hong Kong, China
Gergana Nenkov, Boston College, USA
Richard Netemeyer, University of Virginia, USA
Vanessa Patrick, University of Houston, USA
Joann Peck, University of Wisconsin-Madison, USA
Cait Poynor, University of Pittsburgh, USA
John Pracejus, University of Alberta, Canada
Linda Price, University of Arizona, USA
Priya Raghubir, New York University, USA
Raj Raghunathan, University of Texas at Austin, USA

Ratti Ratneshwar, University of Missouri, USA
Americus Reed II, The Wharton School, University of Pennsylvania, USA
Dennis Rook, University of Southern California, USA
Terry Shimp, University of South Carolina, USA
Baba Shiv, Stanford University, USA
David Sprott, Washington State University, USA
Debora Thompson, Georgetown University, USA
Rao Unnava, Ohio State University, USA
Peeter Verlegh, Erasmus University Rotterdam, the Netherlands
Joachim Vosgerau, Carnegie Mellon University, USA
Christian Wheeler, Stanford University, USA
Katherine White, University of Calgary, Canada
Lawrence Williams, University of Colorado, USA
Catherine Yeung, National University of Singapore, Singapore
Rui (Juliet) Zhu, University of British Columbia, Canada

Competitive Paper Reviewers

Lisa Abendroth, University of St. Thomas, USA
Praveen Aggarwal, University of Minnesota Duluth, USA
Nidhi Agrawal, Northwestern University, USA
David Alexander, University of St. Thomas, USA
Mark Alpert, University of Texas at Austin, USA
Jim Alvarez-Mourey, University of Michigan, USA
Clinton Amos, Augusta State University, USA
Laurel Anderson, Arizona State University, USA
Alan Andreasen, Georgetown University, USA
Demetra Andrews, University of Houston, USA
J. Craig Andrews, Marquette University, USA
Lalin Anik, Harvard Business School, USA
Christina I. Anthony, University of Sydney, Australia
Eric Arnould, University of Wyoming, USA
Zeynep Arsel, Concordia University, Canada
Søren Askegaard, University of Southern Denmark, Odense, Denmark
Jill Avery, Simmons School of Management, USA
Yana Avramova, Tilburg University, the Netherlands
Shahar Ayal, Duke University, USA
Rajesh Bagchi, Virginia Tech, USA
Aysen Bakir, Illinois State University, USA
Fleura Bardhi, Northeastern University, USA
Sema Barlas, McGill University, Canada
Michael Barone, University of Louisville, USA
Debra Basil, University of Lethbridge, Canada
Michael Basil, University of Lethbridge, Canada
Stacey Baxter, University of Newcastle, Australia
Enrique Becerra, Texas State University at San Marcos, USA
Colleen Bee, Oregon State University, USA
Mickey Belch, San Diego State University, USA
Steven Bellman, Murdoch University, Australia
Christine Bennett, University of St. Thomas, USA
Michelle Bergadaa, University of Geneva, Switzerland
Matt Bernthal, University of South Carolina, USA
Mariam Beruchashvili, California State University, Northridge, USA
Namita Bhatnagar, University of Manitoba, Canada
Baler Bilgin, Koc University, Turkey
Darron Billeter, Brigham Young University, USA
Abhijit Biswas, Wayne State University, USA
Dipayan Biswas, Bentley University, USA
Iain Black, University of Sydney, USA
Janneke Blijlevens, Delft University of Technology, the Netherlands
Paul N. Bloom, Fuqua School of Business, Duke University, USA
Onur Bodur, Concordia University, Canada
Wendy Boland, American University, USA
Lisa Bolton, Pennsylvania State University, USA
Samuel Bond, Georgia Institute of Technology, USA
Rick Bonsall, McKendree University, USA
Derrick Boone, Wake Forest University, USA
Adilson Borges, Reims Management School, France
Stefania Borghini, Bocconi University, Italy
Mousumi Bose Godbole, Louisiana State University, USA
Simona Botti, London Business School, UK
Lisanne Bouten, Delft University of Technology, the Netherlands
Tonya Williams Bradford, University of Notre Dame, USA
S. Adam Brasel, Boston College, USA
Rafael Bravo, University of Zaragoza, Spain
Julie Edell Britton, Fuqua School of Business, Duke University, USA
Aaron Brough, Northwestern University, USA
Katja H. Brunk, Université Libre de Bruxelles, Belgium
Sabrina Bruyneel, K.U. Leuven, Belgium
Eva Buechel, Carnegie Mellon University, USA
Alvin Burns, Louisiana State University, USA
Katherine Burson, University of Michigan, USA
Jennifer Burton, Bradley University, USA
Dave Bussiere, University of Windsor, Canada
Oliver B. Büttner, Zeppelin University Friedrichshafen, Germany
Kurt Carlson, Georgetown University, USA
Les Carlson, University of Nebraska, USA
Lorena de la Paz Carrete Lucero, Tec de Monterrey Campus Toluca, Mexico
Ryall Carroll, St. John's University, USA
Sergio Carvalho, University of Manitoba, Canada
Monica Casabayo, ESADE, Spain
Harold Cassab, University of Auckland, New Zealand
Jesse Catlin, University of California at Irvine, USA
Priscilla Y. L. Chan, Hong Kong Polytechnic University, Hong Kong, China
Chiu-chi Angela Chang, Shippensburg University, USA
Chun-Tuan Chang, National Sun Yat-sen University, Taiwan
Hannah Chang, Singapore Management University, Singapore
Joseph Chang, Vancouver Island University, Canada
Patrali Chatterjee, Montclair State University, USA
Promothesh Chatterjee, University of South Carolina, USA
Subimal Chatterjee, Binghamton University, USA
Suzanne Chehayeb Makarem, Temple University, USA
Piotr Chelminski, Providence College, USA
Haipeng Chen, Texas A&M University, USA
Yu-Jen Chen, University of Maryland, USA
Shirley Y. Y. Cheng, University of Illinois at Urbana-Champaign, USA
Cecile Cho, Moscow School of Management, Skolkovo, Russia
Hyejeung Cho, University of Texas at San Antonio, USA
James Cho, Lunghwa University of Science and Technology, Taiwan

Tilo G. Chowdhury, Quinnipiac University, USA
Athinodoros Chronis, California State University, Stanislaus, USA
Alice Chu, Hong Kong Polytechnic University, Hong Kong, China
Shih-Chieh Chuang, National Chung Cheng University, Taiwan
HaeEun Helen Chun, Cornell University, USA
Magdalena Cismaru, University of Regina, Canada
Bart Claus, K.U. Leuven, Belgium
Angeline Close, University of Nevada at Las Vegas, USA
Kevina Cody, Dublin Institute of Technology, Ireland, UK
Rita Coelho do Vale, FCEE-UCP, Catholic University of Portugal, Portugal
Catherine A. Cole, University of Iowa, USA
Larry Compeau, Clarkson University, USA
Paul M. Connell, Stony Brook University, USA
Alan Cooke, University of Florida, USA
Gert Cornelissen, Pompeu Fabra University, Spain
Carolyn Costley, University of Waikato, New Zealand
Deborah Cours, California State University, Northridge, USA
Georgiana Craciun, Loyola College in Maryland, USA
Adam Craig, University of South Carolina, USA
Margaret Craig-Lees, Auckland University of Technology, New Zealand
David Crockett, University of South Carolina, USA
Maria L. Cronley, Miami University of Ohio, USA
Cynthia Cryder, Carnegie Mellon University, USA
Keisha Cutright, Duke University, USA
Xianchi Dai, Chinese University of Hong Kong, Hong Kong, China
Vassilis Dalakas, California State University, San Marcos, USA
Kim Daniloski, Virginia Tech, USA
Peter Darke, Schulich School of Business, York University, Canada
Neel Das, Appalachian State University, USA
Prakash Das, University of Calgary, Canada
Hugh Daubek, Purdue University at Calumet, USA
Brennan Davis, Baylor University, USA
Teresa Davis, University of Sydney, Australia
Ilona De Hooge, Erasmus University Rotterdam, the Netherlands
Bart De Langhe, Erasmus University Rotterdam, the Netherlands
Benet DeBerry-Spence, University of Illinois at Chicago, USA
Marjorie Delbaere, University of Saskatchewan, Canada
Benedict Dellaert, Erasmus University Rotterdam, the Netherlands
Sameer Deshpande, University of Lethbridge, Canada
Hélène Deval, University of Cincinnati, USA
Berna Devezer, Michigan State University, USA
Radu-Mihai Dimitriu, Norwegian School of Management BI, Norway
Claudiu Dimofte, Georgetown University, USA
Susan Dobscha, Bentley College, USA
Eric Dolansky, Brock University, Canada
Jan Drengner, Chemnitz University of Technology, Germany
Jenna Drenten, University of Georgia, USA
Kent Drummond, University of Wyoming, USA
Jeffrey Durgee, Rensselaer Polytechnic Institute, USA
Sujay Dutta, Wayne State University, USA
Toni Eagar, Australian National University, Australia
Mary Ann Eastlick, University of Arizona, USA
Jane Ebert, University of Minnesota, USA
Giana Eckhardt, Suffolk University, USA
Kristine Ehrich, University of San Diego, USA
Eric Eisenstein, Fox School of Business, Temple University, USA
Stefan Elsner, University of Trier, Germany
Basil Englis, Berry College, USA
Amber M. Epp, University of Wisconsin-Madison, USA
Eyal Ert, Harvard Business School, USA
Francine Espinoza, ESMT Berlin, Germany
Douglas Ewing, University of Cincinnati, USA
David Faro, London Business School, UK
Alexander (Sasha) Fedorikhin, Kelley School of Business, Indiana University, USA
Reto Felix, University of Monterrey, Mexico
Florian Fessel, University of Illinois at Urbana-Champaign, USA
Arne Floh, Vienna University of Economics and Business (WU Wien), Austria
Suzanne Fogel, DePaul University, USA
Susan Fournier, Boston University, USA
Ellen Foxman, Bentley College, USA
Marieke Fransen, University of Amsterdam, the Netherlands
Lorraine Friend, University of Waikato, New Zealand
David Gal, Northwestern University, USA
Jeff Galak, Carnegie Mellon University, USA
Leilei Gao, Chinese University of Hong Kong, Hong Kong, China
Zhihong Gao, Rider University, USA
Ellen Garbarino, University of Sydney, Australia
Stephen Garcia, University of Michigan, USA
Nitika Garg, University of Mississippi, USA
Andrew Gershoff, University of Michigan, USA
Maggie Geuens, Ghent University, Belgium
Kelly Geyskens, University of Maastricht, the Netherlands
Mary Gilly, University of California at Irvine, USA
Richard Godfrey, Aberystwyth University, Wales, UK
Kelly Goldsmith, Northwestern University, USA
Dilney Goncalves, INSEAD, France
Miranda Goode, University of Western Ontario, Canada
Joseph K. Goodman, Washington University in St. Louis, USA
Ronald Goodstein, Georgetown University, USA
Caroline Goukens, University of Maastricht, the Netherlands
Stephen Gould, Baruch College, CUNY, USA
Eric Greenleaf, Stern School of Business, New York University, USA
Yany Gregoire, Washington State University, USA
Ulrike Gretzel, Texas A&M University, USA
Merlyn Griffiths, University of North Carolina at Greensboro, USA
Martin Grimmer, School of Management, University of Tasmania, Australia
Andrea Groeppel-Klein, Saarland University, Germany
Bianca Grohmann, John Molson School of Business, Concordia University, Canada
Barbara Gross, California State University, Northridge, USA
Aditi Grover, Plymouth State University, USA
Zeynep Gurhan-Canli, Koc University, Turkey
Patricia Gurviez, AgroParisTech, France
Young Won Ha, Sogang University, Republic of Korea
Henrik Hagtvedt, Boston College, USA
Eric Hamerman, Columbia University, USA
Kathy Hamilton, University of Strathclyde, Scotland, UK
Ryan Hamilton, Emory University, USA
Jay Handelman, Queen's University, Canada
Haiming Hang, Lancaster University, UK
Vijay Hariharan, State University of New York at Buffalo, USA

Tracy Harmon, University of Dayton, USA
Douglas Hausknecht, University of Akron, USA
Angela Hausman, University of North Carolina, Pembroke, USA
Kelly Haws, Texas A&M University, USA
Xin He, University of Central Florida, USA
Yi He, California State University, East Bay, USA
Timothy Heath, Miami University of Ohio, USA
William Hedgcock, University of Iowa, USA
Andrea Hemetsberger, University of Innsbruck, Austria
Paul Henry, University of Sydney, Australia
Paul Herr, University of Colorado, USA
Michal Herzenstein, University of Delaware, USA
Patrick Hetzel, Universite Pantheon-Assas Paris II, France
Paul Hewer, Strathclyde University, Scotland, UK
Donna Hill, Bradley University, USA
Mark E. Hill, Montclair State University, USA
Elizabeth Hirschman, Rutgers University, USA
Candy K. Y. Ho, Hong Kong Baptist University, Hong Kong, China
JoAndrea Hoegg, University of British Columbia, Canada
Susan Hogan, Emory University, USA
Margaret K. Hogg, Lancaster University, UK
Susan Holak, College of Staten Island/CUNY, USA
Soonkwan Hong, University of Texas-Pan American, USA
Chris Horbel, University of Bayreuth, Germany
Monali Hota, Lille Catholic University, France
Jianwei Hou, Minnesota State University, Mankato, USA
Rika Houston, California State University, Los Angeles, USA
Lei Huang, Dalhousie University, Canada
Bradford Hudson, Boston University, USA
Kyle Huggins, James Madison University, USA
Ashlee Humphreys, Northwestern University, USA
Jim Hunt, Temple University, USA
Gary Hunter, Illinois State University, USA
Kenneth F. Hyde, Auckland University of Technology, New Zealand
Mathew Isaac, Northwestern University, USA
Jesse Itzkowitz, University of Florida, USA
Elif Izberk-Bilgin, University of Michigan-Dearborn, USA
Shailendra Jain, University of Washington, USA
Narayan Janakiraman, University of Arizona, USA
Jing Jiang, Renmin University of China, China
Yuwei Jiang, The Hong Kong Polytechnic University, Hong Kong, China
Seung-A Jin, Boston College, USA
Leslie John, Carnegie Mellon University, USA
Camille Johnson, San Jose State University, USA
Chris Joiner, George Mason University, USA
Bill Jolley, Norwich University, USA
Joshy Joseph, Indian Institute of Technology Madras, India
Kwon Jung, KDI School of Public Policy & Management, Korea
Luke Kachersky, Fordham University, USA
Karen Kaigler-Walker, Woodbury University, USA
Andrew Kaikati, University of Minnesota, USA
Velitchka Kaltcheva, Loyola Marymount University, USA
Uma Karmarkar, Stanford University, USA
Jan Katz, Cornell University, USA
Carol Kaufman-Scarborough, Rutgers University-Camden, USA
Katie Kelting, Indiana University, USA
Keri Kettle, University of Alberta, Canada
Adwait Khare, Quinnipiac University, USA
Eunice Kim, Yale University, USA
Junyong Kim, Purdue University, USA
Moon-Yong Kim, Dongguk University, Korea
Junko Kimura, Hosei University, Japan
Tracey King, American University, USA
Jill Klein, Melbourne Business School, Australia
Rob Kleine, Ohio Northern University, USA
Susan Kleine, Bowling Green State University, USA
Maria Kniazeva, University of San Diego, USA
Bruno Kocher, Baruch College, CUNY, USA
Monika Koller, Vienna University of Economics and Business (WU Wien), Austria
Yuliya Komarova, University of South Carolina, USA
Scott Koslow, University of Waikato, New Zealand
Nevena Koukova, Lehigh University, USA
Thomas Kramer, Baruch College, CUNY, USA
Didem Kurt, University of Pittsburgh, USA
Kyoung-Nan Kwon, Ajou University, Korea
Yoo Jin Kwon, Washington State University, USA
Jessica Y. Y. Kwong, Chinese University of Hong Kong, Hong Kong, China
Monica LaBarge, Queens University
Lauren Labrecque, University of Massachusetts, Amherst, USA
Aparna Labroo, University of Chicago, USA
Joseph Lajos, HEC Paris, France
Alexander Jan Lakotta, ESCP-EAP European School of Management, Germany
Arun Lakshmanan, University at Buffalo, State University of New York, USA
Jan R. Landwehr, University of St. Gallen, Switzerland
Michel Laroche, Concordia University, Canada
Kathryn LaTour, University of Nevada, Las Vegas
Benjamin Lawrence, Boston University, USA
Robyn LeBoeuf, University of Florida, USA
JungKook Lee, Indiana University-Purdue University Columbus, USA
Leonard Lee, Columbia University, USA
Seung-Hee Lee, Kent State University, USA
Sooyeon Nikki Lee-Wingate, Fairfield University, USA
Renaud Legoux, HEC Montreal, Canada
Donald Lehmann, Columbia University, USA
Hillary Leonard, University of Rhode Island, USA
Siew Meng Leong, National University of Singapore, Singapore
Ada Leung, University of Nebraska at Kearney, USA
Jonathan Levav, Columbia University, USA
Sidney Levy, University of Arizona, USA
Mark Ligas, Fairfield University, USA
Heejin Lim, University of Tennessee, USA
Ab Litt, Stanford University, USA
Jia Liu, University of Groningen, the Netherlands
Maggie Wenjing Liu, University of Toronto, Canada
Wendy Liu, UCLA Anderson School of Management, USA
Alison Lo, University of Washington, USA
Caezilia Loibl, Ohio State University, USA
Sylvia Long-Tolbert, University of Toledo, USA
Sherry L. Lotz, University of Arizona, USA
Carlos Lourenco, Erasmus University Rotterdam, the Netherlands
Tina M. Lowrey, University of Texas at San Antonio, USA
Michael Luchs, The College of William and Mary, USA
Marius K. Luedicke, Innsbruck University, Austria
Renaud Lunardo, Troyes Champagne School of Management, France
Nicholas Lurie, Georgia Institute of Technology, USA
Jane Machin, Virginia Polytechnic Institute and State University, USA
Boris Maciejovsky, Imperial College Business School, London, UK
Scott MacKenzie, Indiana University, USA
Robert Madrigal, University of Oregon, USA

Satish Maheswarappa, Doctoral Student, IIT Madras, Chennai, India
Humaira Mahi, San Francisco State University, USA
Kelley Main, University of Manitoba, Canada
Igor Makienko, University of Nevada at Reno, USA
Prashant Malaviya, Georgetown University, USA
Keven Malkewitz, Oregon State University, USA
Selin Malkoc, Washington University in St. Louis, USA
Alan Malter, University of Illinois at Chicago, USA
Anne-Flore Maman, ESSEC, France
Andreina Mandelli, Bocconi University, Italy
Ken Manning, Colorado State University, USA
Antonia Mantonakis, Brock University, Canada
Huifang Mao, University of Central Florida, USA
Ingrid Martin, California State University, Long Beach, USA
Pragya Mathur, Baruch College, CUNY, USA
Takeshi Matsui, Hitotsubashi University, Japan
Shashi Matta, Ohio State University, USA
Leigh McAlister, University of Texas at Austin, USA
Deborah McCabe, Arizona State University, USA
John McCarty, The College of New Jersey, USA
A. Peter McGraw, University of Colorado at Boulder, USA
Laurie Meamber, George Mason University, USA
David Mick, University of Virginia, USA
Kathleen Micken, Roger Williams University, USA
Camelia Micu, Fairfield University, USA
Elizabeth Miller, Boston College, USA
Milica Milosavljevic, Caltech, USA
Hyun Jeong Min, University of Utah, USA
Kyeong Sam Min, University of New Orleans, USA
Yuko Minowa, Long Island University-Brooklyn Campus, USA
Mauricio Mittelman, Universidad Torcuato Di Tella, Argentina
Daniel Mochon, Yale University, USA
Risto Moisio, California State University, Long Beach, USA
Alokparna Monga, University of South Carolina, USA
Ashwani Monga, University of South Carolina, USA
Nicole Montgomery, College of William and Mary, USA
Detra Montoya, University of Washington, Seattle, USA
Rex Moody, University of Colorado, USA
Sangkil Moon, North Carolina State University, USA
David J. Moore, University of Michigan, USA
Elizabeth Moore, University of Notre Dame, USA
Andrea C. Morales, Arizona State University, USA
Vicki Morwitz, Stern School of Business, New York University, USA
Jill Mosteller, Portland State University, USA
Mehdi Mourali, University of Calgary, Canada
Ruth Mugge, Delft University of Technology, the Netherlands
Ashesh Mukherjee, McGill University, Canada
Jyotsna Mukherji, Texas A&M University, USA
Anish Nagpal, University of Melbourne, Australia
Kent Nakamoto, Virginia Polytechnic Institute and State University, USA
Myungwoo Nam, INSEAD, Singapore
Rebecca Naylor, Ohio State University, USA
Sharon Ng, Nanyang Business School, Singapore
Hieu Nguyen, California State University, Long Beach, USA
Thuc-Doan Nguyen, California State University, Long Beach, USA
Leonardo Nicolao, Texas Christian University, USA
Jesper Nielsen, University of Arizona, USA
Hayden Noel, University of Illinois at Urbana-Champaign, USA
Valeria Noguti, University of Technology Sydney, Australia
Marret Noordewier, Tilburg University, the Netherlands
Patricia Norberg, Quinnipiac University, USA
Christie Nordhielm, University of Michigan, USA
Leigh Novak, Marshall School of Business, University of Southern California, USA
Nathan Novemsky, Yale University, USA
James Oakley, University of North Carolina, USA
Chezy Ofir, Hebrew University, Israel
Madeleine Ogilvie, Edith Cowan Univsity, Australia
Shintaro Okazaki, Universidad Autonoma de Madrid, Spain
Barbara Olsen, State University of NY, Old Westbury, USA
Lars Erling Olsen, Oslo School of Management, Norway
Jacob Ostberg, Stockholm University, Sweden
Per Ostergaard, University of Southern Denmark, Odense, Denmark
Massimiliano Ostinelli, University of Wisconsin-Milwaukee, USA
Shweta Oza, University of Miami, USA
Neeru Paharia, Harvard University, USA
Mario Pandelaere, Ghent University, Belgium
Ameet Pandit, University of Melbourne, Australia
Cheol Park, Korea University, Korea
Jungkun Park, Purdue University, USA
Jeffrey Parker, Columbia University, USA
Elizabeth Parsons, University of Keele, UK
Anthony Patino, Loyola Marymount University, USA
Teresa Pavia, University of Utah, USA
Collin Payne, New Mexico State University, USA
Connie Pechmann, University of California at Irvine, USA
Laura Peracchio, University of Wisconsin-Milwaukee, USA
Theodoro Peters, FEI University, Brazil
Bruce Pfeiffer, University of New Hampshire, USA
Barbara Phillips, University of Saskatchewan, Canada
Anastasiya Pocheptsova, University of Maryland, USA
Jeffrey Podoshen, Franklin and Marshall College, USA
T. Andrew Poehlman, Southern Methodist University, USA
Greta Polites, Bucknell University, USA
Kawpong Polyorat, Khonkaen University, Thailand
Frank Pons, Laval University, Canada
Monica Popa, University of Alberta, Canada
Constance Porter, University of Notre Dame, USA
Paulo H M Prado, Federal University of Parana, Brazil
Melea Press, University of Wyoming, USA
Sonja Prokopec, ESSEC Business School, France
Andrea Prothero, University College Dublin, Ireland, UK
Sanjay Puligadda, Miami University of Ohio, USA
Girish Punj, University of Connecticut, USA
Stefano Puntoni, Erasmus University Rotterdam, the Netherlands
Pascale Quester, University of Adelaide, Australia
Kaleel Rahman, American University in Dubai, United Arab Emirates
Priyali Rajagopal, Southern Methodist University, USA
Sekar Raju, Iowa State University, USA
Vithala Rao, Cornell University, USA
Brian Ratchford, University of Texas at Dallas, USA
Rebecca Ratner, University of Maryland, USA
Sarita Ray Chaudhury, New Mexico State University, USA
Dan Rice, Louisiana State University, USA
Scott Rick, University of Michigan, USA
Nancy Ridgway, University of Richmond, USA
Hila Riemer, Ben-Gurion University, Israel
Shannon Rinaldo, Texas Tech University, USA
Diego Rinallo, Bocconi University, Italy
Torsten Ringberg, University of Wisconsin-Milwaukee, USA
Scott Roberts, St. Edward's University, USA
Jennifer Robinson, Murdoch University, Australia

Joseph Rocereto, Monmouth University, USA
Amy Rodie, University of Nebraska at Omaha, USA
Michelle Roehm, Wake Forest University, USA
Anne Roggeveen, Babson College, USA
Jenni Romaniuk, University of South Australia, Australia
Mark Rosenbaum, Northern Illinois University, USA
Bill Ross, Pennsylvania State University, USA
Caroline Roux, McGill University, Canada
Rajat Roy, Curtin University of Technology, Australia
Salvador Ruiz, University of Murcia, Spain
Cristel Russell, University of Auckland, New Zealand
Namika Sagara, University of Oregon, USA
John Sailors, University of St. Thomas, USA
Ritesh Saini, University of Texas at Arlington, USA
Laura Salciuviene, Lancaster University, UK
Linda Court Salisbury, Boston College, USA
Sridhar Samu, Indian School of Business, India
Raquel Sánchez Fernández, University of Almería, Spain
Ozlem Sandikci, Bilkent University, Turkey
João Felipe Sauerbronn, ECSA-Unigranrio, Brazil
Dorothea Schaffner, Lucerne University of Applied Sciences, Switzerland
Hope Jensen Schau, University of Arizona, USA
Ann Schlosser, University of Washington, USA
Tanja Schneider, University of Oxford, UK
Hanna Schramm-Klein, University of Siegen, Germany
Rom Schrift, Columbia University, USA
Jonathan Schroeder, University of Exeter, UK
Janet Schwartz, Princeton University, USA
Maura Scott, University of Kentucky, USA
Aner Sela, Stanford University, USA
Anne-Laure Sellier, New York University, USA
Selime Sezgin, Bahcesehir University, Turkey
Edith Shalev, New York University, USA
Hao Shen, Chinese University of Hong Kong, Hong Kong, China
Paurav Shukla, University of Brighton, UK
Shakeel Siddiqui, Dublin City University, Ireland, UK
David H. Silvera, University of Texas at San Antonio, USA
Peter Simcock, Liverpool John Moores University, UK
Joseph Simmons, Yale University, USA
Itamar Simonson, Stanford University, USA
Noel Y.M. Siu, Hong Kong Baptist University, Hong Kong, China
Bharadhwaj Sivakumaran, Great Lakes Institute of Management, India
Anu Sivaraman, University of Delaware, USA
Henrik Sjödin, Center for Consumer Marketing, Stockholm School of Economics, Sweden
Dirk Smeesters, Erasmus University Rotterdam, the Netherlands
Michael Smith, Temple University, USA
Pamela Smith, University of California at San Diego, USA
Rana Sobh, Qatar University, Qatar
Harmeen Soch, Guru Nanak Dev University, India
Jane Sojka, Ohio University, USA
Hyunjin Song, University of Michigan, USA
Susan Spiggle, University of Connecticut
Rajendran Sriramachandramurthy, Southern Illinois University at Carbondale, USA
Antonios Stamatogiannakis, INSEAD, France
Yael Steinhart, University of Haifa, Israel
Sascha Steinmann, Institute of Marketing and Retailing, University of Goettingen, Germany
Andrew Stephen, INSEAD, France
Amy Stokes, University of Arkansas, USA
Saroja Subrahmanyan, St. Mary's College of California, USA
Raji Sugumar, Bharathidasan Government College for Women, India
Harish Sujan, Tulane University, USA
Kwanho Suk, Korea University, Korea
Jill Sundie, University of Houston, USA
Magne Supphellen, Norwegian School of Economics and Business Administration, Norway
Scott Swain, Northeastern University, USA
Steven Sweldens, Erasmus University Rotterdam, the Netherlands
Aner Tal, Duke University, USA
Sarah Tanford, University of Nevada at Las Vegas, USA
Felix Tang, Hang Seng School of Commerce, Hong Kong, China
Rob Tanner, University of Wisconsin-Madison, USA
Berna Tari, TOBB University of Economics and Technology, Turkey
David Taylor, University of North Texas, USA
Maneesh Thakkar, Radford University, USA
Dominic Thomas, Monash University, Australia
Manoj Thomas, Cornell University, USA
Kelly Tian, New Mexico State University, USA
Carlos Torelli, University of Minnesota, USA
Zakary Tormala, Stanford University, USA
Olivier Toubia, Columbia University, USA
Marlene Towns, University of Southern California, USA
Claudia Townsend, UCLA Anderson School of Management, USA
Remi Trudel, University of Western Ontario, Canada
Chia-Ching Tsai, National Yunlin University of Science and Technology, Taiwan
Claire Tsai, University of Toronto, Canada
Yelena Tsarenko, Monash University, Australia
Rodoula Tsiotsou, Higher Technological Education Institution of Crete, Greece
Gulnur Tumbat, San Francisco State University, USA
Darach Turley, Dublin City University, Ireland, UK
Mine Üçok Hughes, Woodbury University, USA
Gülden Ülkümen, University of Southern California, USA
Sofia Ulver, Foretagsekonomiska Institutionen, Lund University, Sweden
Nancy Upton, Northeastern University, USA
Joe Urbany, University of Notre Dame, USA
Oleg Urminsky, University of Chicago, USA
Ana Valenzuela, Baruch College, CUNY, USA
Beth Vallen, Loyola College, USA
Niels van de Ven, Tilburg University, the Netherlands
Bram Van den Bergh, K.U. Leuven, Belgium
Erica van Herpen, Wageningen University, the Netherlands
Femke van Horen, Tilburg University, the Netherlands
Koert Van Ittersum, Georgia Institute of Technology, USA
Guda van Noort, University of Amsterdam, the Netherlands
Stijn van Osselaer, Erasmus University Rotterdam, the Netherlands
W. Fred van Raaij, Tilburg University, the Netherlands
Wouter Vanhouche, University of Central Florida, USA
Richard Varey, Waikato Management School, New Zealand
Rohit Varman, Indian Institute of Management, Calcutta, India
Ann Veeck, Western Michigan University, USA
Martijn Veltkamp, University of Twente, the Netherlands
Alladi Venkatesh, University of California at Irvine, USA
Meera Venkatraman, Suffolk University, USA
Vinod Venkatraman, Duke University, USA
Joost W. M. Verhoeven, University of Twente, the Netherlands
Nicole Verrochi, University of Pennsylvania, USA
Nanda Viswanathan, Delaware State University, USA
Kathleen Vohs, University of Minnesota, USA
Monica Wadhwa, Stanford University, USA

Martin Waiguny, University of Klagenfurt, Germany
Fang Wan, University of Manitoba, Canada
Lisa C. Wan, Lingnan University, Hong Kong, China
Jeff Wang, City University of Hong Kong, Hong Kong, China
Jing Wang, University of Iowa, USA
Kai-Yu Wang, Brock University, Canada
Paul Wang, University of Technology, Sydney, Australia
Qing Wang, University of Warwick, UK
Ze Wang, University of Kansas, USA
Michaela Wanke, University of Basel, Switzerland
James Ward, Arizona State University, USA
Kittichai (Tu) Watchravesringkan, University of North Carolina at Greensboro, USA
Stevie Watson, Rutgers University, USA
Kimberlee Weaver, Virginia Polytechnic Institute and State University, USA
Clare Weeden, University of Brighton, UK
Fei Weisstein, University of Illinois at Urbana-Champaign, USA
Daniel Wentzel, University of St. Gallen, Switzerland
Caroline Wiertz, Cass Business School, City University London, UK
Robert Wilken, ESCP-EAP European School of Management, Germany
Jerome Williams, University of Texas at Austin, USA
Sarah Wilner, Schulich School of Business, York University, Canada
Andrew Wilson, Schulich School of Business, York University, Canada
Karen Winterich, Texas A&M University, USA
Jorge A. Wise, Tecnologico de Monterrey, Mexico
Amy Wong, Universitas 21 Global, Singapore
Susanna Y. N. Wong, Chinese University of Hong Kong, Hong Kong, China
Natalie Wood, Saint Joseph's University, USA
Christine Wright-Isak, Florida Gulf Coast University, USA
Eugenia Wu, Duke University, USA
Lan Wu, California State University, East Bay, USA
Kang-Ning Xia, Yuan Ze University, Taiwan
Lan Xia, Bentley University, USA
Jing Jian Xiao, University of Rhode Island, USA
Chunyan Xie, Stord/Haugesund University College, Norway
Guang-Xin (Vincent) Xie, University of Massachusetts, USA
Alison Jing Xu, University of Illinois at Urbana-Champaign, USA
Huimin Xu, State University of New York at Oneonta, USA
Dengfeng Yan, Hong Kong University of Science and Technology, Hong Kong, China
Ruoh-Nan Yan, Colorado State University, USA
Kenneth C. C. Yang, University of Texas at El Paso, USA
Lifeng Yang, Ohio State University, USA
Linyun Yang, Duke University, USA
Sybil Yang, Cornell University, USA
Zhiyong Yang, University of Texas at Arlington, USA
E. Tacli Yazicioglu, Bogazici University, Turkey
Hurrem Yilmaz, State University New York at Oneonta, USA
Kyung-Hyan Yoo, Texas A&M University, USA
Sukki Yoon, Bryant University, USA
Alessandra Zammit, University of Bologna, Italy
Lia Zarantonello, Bocconi University, Italy
Yael Zemack-Rugar, Virginia Tech, USA
Jiao Zhang, University of Miami, USA
Meng Zhang, Chinese University of Hong Kong, Hong Kong, China
Shuoyang Zhang, Indiana University, USA
Ying Zhang, University of Texas at Austin, USA
Yinlong Zhang, University of Texas at San Antonio, USA
Guangzhi Zhao, University of Kansas, USA
Min Zhao, University of Toronto, Canada
Xin Zhao, University of Hawaii at Manoa, USA
Meng Zhu, Carnegie Mellon University, USA
Stephan Zielke, University of Goettingen, Germany
Natalina Zlatevska, Bond University, Australia
Rami Zwick, University of California at Riverside, USA

Working Paper Reviewers

Hee-Kyung Ahn, Rotman School of Management, University of Toronto, Canada
Hongmin Ahn, University of Texas at Austin, USA
Maria Aladjem, McGill University, Canada
Jim Alvarez-Mourey, University of Michigan, USA
Eduardo Andrade, University of California at Berkeley, USA
Demetra Andrews, University of Houston, USA
Manon Arcand, Université du Québec à Montréal, Canada
Sukriye Atakan, University of Michigan, USA
A. Selin Atalay, HEC Paris, France
Stephen Atlas, Columbia University, USA
Caroline Graham Austin, University of Georgia/Montana State University, USA
Shahar Ayal, Duke University, USA
Audrey Azoulay, HEC Paris, France
Rajesh Bagchi, Virginia Tech, USA
Ilaria Baghi, University of Modena and Reggio Emilia, Italy
Domen Bajde, University of Ljubljana, Slovenia
Gary Bamossy, Georgetown University, USA
Wided Batat, University of Poitiers, France
Jennifer Bechkoff, San Jose State University, USA
Jean-Francois Belisle, McGill University, Canada
Steven Bellman, Murdoch University, Australia
Julia Belyavsky Bayuk, University of Delaware, USA
Aronte Bennett, New York University, USA
Mariam Beruchashvili, California State University, Northridge, USA
Shona Bettany, Bradford University, UK
Amit Bhattacharjee, The Wharton School, University of Pennsylvania, USA
Sandeep Bhowmick, Louisiana State University, USA
George Bizer, Union College, USA
Iain Black, University of Sydney, USA
Simon J. Blanchard, Pennsylvania State University, USA
Janneke Blijlevens, Delft University of Technology, the Netherlands
Jeff Blodgett, North Carolina A&T State University, USA
Courtney Boerstler, University of Oregon, USA
Aaron Brough, Northwestern University, USA
Melissa Bublitz, University of Wisonsin-Milwaukee, USA
Eva Buechel, Carnegie Mellon University, USA
Erik Bushey, University of Illinois, USA
Oliver B. Büttner, Zeppelin University Friedrichshafen, Germany
Dennis Cahill, AdWriter, Inc., USA
Zhen Cai, University of Rhode Island, USA
Marylouise Caldwell, University of Sydney, Australia

Yuri Cameron, Rackspace, USA
Jesse Catlin, University of California at Irvine, USA
Lisa Cavanaugh, University of Southern California, USA
Elaine Chan, Hong Kong University of Science and Technology, Hong Kong, China
Eugene Chan, University of Toronto, Canada
Jennifer D. Chandler, University of Hawaii, USA
Chun-Tuan Chang, National Sun Yat-sen University, Taiwan
Connie Chang, Coventry University, UK
Promothesh Chatterjee, University of South Carolina, USA
Etta Y. I. Chen, Yuan Ze University, Taiwan
Yin-Hui Cheng, National Penghu Uniersity, Taiwan
Sunaina Chugani, University of Texas at Austin, USA
Sunghun Chung, KAIST Business School, Korea
Catherine Coleman, University of Illinois at Urbana-Champaign, USA
Gert Cornelissen, Pompeu Fabra University, Spain
Peter Corrigan, University of New England, Australia
Patrice Cottet, University of Reims, France
Adam Craig, University of South Carolina, USA
Margaret Craig-Lees, Auckland University of Technology, New Zealand
Heather Crawford, University of New South Wales, Australia
David Crockett, University of South Carolina, USA
Elizabeth Crosby, University of Illinois at Urbana-Champaign, USA
Cynthia Cryder, Carnegie Mellon University, USA
Aron Darmody, Schulich School of Business, York University, Canada
Prakash Das, University of Calgary, Canada
Matteo De Angelis, LUISS University, Italy
Bart De Langhe, Erasmus University Rotterdam, the Netherlands
Stephanie Dellande, University of New Orleans, USA
Susan Dobscha, Bentley College, USA
Kivilcim Dogerlioglu-Demir, Washington State University, USA
Jenna Drenten, University of Georgia, USA
Courtney Droms, Valdosta State University, USA
Brittany Duff, University of Illinois at Urbana-Champaign, USA
Toni Eagar, Australian National University, Australia
Sue Eccles, Bournemouth University, UK
Ryan Elder, University of Michigan, USA
Alet C Erasmus, University of Pretoria, South Africa
Jie Feng, University of Wisconsin-Milwaukee, USA
Florian Fessel, University of Illinois at Urbana-Champaign, USA
Stephanie Finnel, The Wharton School, University of Pennsylvania, USA
Aubrey Fowler III, Valdosta State University, USA
Eliane Francisco-Maffezzolli, Universidade Federal do Parana (UFPR), Brazil
Lorraine Friend, University of Waikato, New Zealand
Anne Fries, University of Cologne, Germany
Chen-Su Fu, National Cheng Kung University, Taiwan
Rajani Ganesh Pillai, North Dakota State University, USA
Alexandra Ganglmair-Wooliscroft, University of Otago, New Zealand
Leilei Gao, Chinese University of Hong Kong, Hong Kong, China
Stephen Garcia, University of Michigan, USA
Meryl Gardner, University of Delaware, USA
M Geetha, Doctoral Candidate
Claas Christian Germelmann, Saarland University, Germany
Richard Godfrey, Aberystwyth University, Wales, UK
Pierrick Gomez, Reims Management School, France
Miranda Goode, University of Western Ontario, Canada
Joseph K. Goodman, Washington University in St. Louis, USA
Kendall Goodrich, Florida Atlantic University, USA
R. Justin Goss, University of Texas at San Antonio, USA
Judy Graham, St. John Fisher College, USA
Ulrike Gretzel, Texas A&M University, USA
Pamela Grimm, Kent State University, USA
Aditi Grover, Plymouth State University, USA
Haodong Gu, University of New South Wales, Sydney, Australia
Veronique Guilloux, Universite Paris XII, France
Michael Guiry, University of the Incarnate Word, USA
Eda Gurel Atay, University of Oregon, USA
Erin Younhee Ha, University of Illinois at Urbana-Champaign, USA
Georgios Halkias, Athens University of Economics & Business, Greece
Ryan Hamilton, Emory University, USA
Xiaoqi Han, University of Cincinnati, USA
Haiming Hang, Lancaster University, UK
Håvard Hansen, University of Stavanger, Norway
Vijay Hariharan, State University of New York at Buffalo, USA
Philip Harris, University of Melbourne, Australia
Angela Hausman, University of North Carolina, Pembroke, USA
Daniel Heinrich, University of Mannheim, Germany
Kelly Herd, University of Colorado at Boulder, USA
Elizabeth Hirschman, Rutgers University, USA
Monica Hodis, Southern Illinois University at Carbondale, USA
Susan Hogan, Emory University, USA
Susan Holak, College of Staten Island/CUNY, USA
Melanie Hoppe, Innsbruck University, Austria
Meng-Hua Hsieh, University of Washington, USA
Hazel Huang, Durham Business School, UK
Yanliu Huang, Chinese University of Hong Kong, Hong Kong, China
Kyle Huggins, James Madison University, USA
Bruce Humbert, Florida Atlantic University, USA
Iris Hung, National University of Singapore, Singapore
Yu-chen Hung, National University of Singapore, Singapore
Martina Hutton, University College Dublin, Ireland, UK (Student Member of the ACR)
Kenneth F. Hyde, Auckland University of Technology, New Zealand
Behice Ece Ilhan, University of Illinois at Urbana-Champaign, USA
Caglar Irmak, University of South Carolina, USA
Jesse Itzkowitz, University of Florida, USA
Aarti Ivanic, University of Southern California, USA
Mazen Jaber, Louisiana State University, USA
Aliakbar Jafari, University of Strathclyde, Scotland, UK
Ahmad Jamal, Cardiff University, Wales, UK
Peter Jarnebrant, Columbia University, USA
Laknath Jayasinghe, Melbourne Business School, Australia
Ji-Hoon Jhang, University of Colorado at Boulder, USA
Lan Jiang, University of British Columbia, Canada
Ying Jiang, University of Ontario Institute of Technology, Canada
Yuwei Jiang, The Hong Kong Polytechnic University, Hong Kong, China
Lokesh Jindal, Maharaja Agrasen Institute of Technology (Affiliate of GGSIP Univeristy), Delhi, India
Napatsorn Jiraporn, State University of New York at Binghamton, USA
Micael-Lee Johnstone, Victoria University, New Zealand
Jaewoo Joo, University of Toronto, Canada
Andrew Kaikati, University of Minnesota, USA
Arti Kalro, Indian Institute of Technology Madras, India
Velitchka Kaltcheva, Loyola Marymount University, USA
Bernadette Kamleitner, Queen Mary, University of London, UK

Jun Kang, University of Massachusetts, USA
Uma Karmarkar, Stanford University, USA
Samy Keffi, IEMN-IAE de Nantes, France
Pelin Kesebir, University of Colorado at Colorado Sprins , USA
Selin Kesebir, University of Virginia, USA
Sajid Khan, American University of Sharjah, United Arab Emirates
Eunice Kim, Yale University, USA
Hae Joo Kim, University of Toronto, Canada
Hye-Young Kim, University of Minnesota, USA
John Kim, Oakland University, USA
Jungkeun Kim, University of Minnesota, USA
Moon-Yong Kim, Dongguk University, Korea
Soyean Kim, Boston University, USA
Dan King, University of Florida, USA
Ingeborg Kleppe, Norwegian School of Economics and Business, Norway
Christos Koritos, Athens University of Economics and Business, Greece
Anjala Krishen, University of Nevada at Las Vegas, USA
Ann Kronrod, Tel-Aviv University, Israel
Owen Kulemeka, University of Illinois at Urbana-Champaign, USA
Atul Kulkarni, University of Illinois at Urbana-Champaign, USA
Didem Kurt, University of Pittsburgh, USA
Ellie Kyung, New York University, USA
Marie J. Lachance, Université Laval, Canada
Sandra Laporte, HEC Paris, France
JungKook Lee, Indiana University-Purdue University Columbus, USA
Leonard Lee, Columbia University, USA
Seung Hwan (Mark) Lee, University of Western Ontario, Canada
Seung-Hee Lee, Kent State University, USA
Yun Lee, University of Iowa, USA
Sooyeon Nikki Lee-Wingate, Fairfield University, USA
Renaud Legoux, HEC Montreal, Canada
Eric Levy, University of Washington, USA
Eric P. H. Li, York University, Canada
Xiuping Li, National University of Singapore, Singapore
Jianping Liang, School of Business, Sun Yat-sen University
Chin-Feng Lin, National Pingtung Institute of Commerce, Taiwan
Jeppe Linnet, University of Southern Denmark, Odense, Denmark
Jen-Yuan Martin Liu, University of Portsmouth, UK
Jia Liu, University of Groningen, the Netherlands
Xuefeng Liu, University of Illinois at Urbana-Champagin, USA
Jordi Lopez, Universitat Autonoma Barcelona, Spain
Peggy Sue Loroz, Gonzaga University, USA
Sara Loughran, University of Pittsburgh, USA
Katherine Loveland, Arizona State University, USA
Yuliya Lutchyn, University of Minnesota, USA
Pauline Maclaran, Royal Hollway, University of London, UK
Natalia Maehle, Nofima Market, Norway
Satish Maheswarappa, Doctoral Student, IIT Madras, Chennai, India
Michal Maimaran, Northwestern University, USA
Vincent Mak, Hong Kong University of Science and Technology, Hong Kong, China
Prashant Malaviya, Georgetown University, USA
Anne-Flore Maman, ESSEC, France
Emmanouela Manganari, Athens University of Economics and Business, Greece
Antonia Mantonakis, Brock University, Canada
Danielle Mantovani, Universidade Federal do Parana, Brazil
Ted Matherly, University of Maryland, USA
Charla Mathwick, Portland State University, USA
Brent McFerran, University of British Columbia, Canada
Nicole Mead, Tilburg University, the Netherlands
Juan (Gloria) Meng, Minnesota State University, Mankato, USA
Tomasz Miaskiewicz, University of Colorado, USA
Gina Miller, Mercer University, USA
Kobe Millet, K.U. Leuven, Belgium; Free University Amsterdam, the Netherlands
Hyun Jeong Min, University of Utah, USA
Melissa Minor, University of Florida, USA
Juan-Antonio Mondejar, Castilla-La Mancha University, Spain
Alokparna Monga, University of South Carolina, USA
Sarah G. Moore, University of Alberta, Canada
Sayantani Mukherjee, California State University, Long Beach, USA
Jun Myers, University of Minnesota, USA
Mohammed Nadeem, National University, USA
Anish Nagpal, University of Melbourne, Australia
Iana Nelson, Arizona State University, USA
Michelle R. Nelson, University of Illinois at Urbana-Champaign, USA
Wilson Neto, University of Arizona, USA
Casey Newmeyer, University of Pittsburgh, USA
Leonardo Nicolao, Texas Christian University, USA
Valeria Noguti, University of Technology Sydney, Australia
Leigh Novak, Marshall School of Business, University of Southern California, USA
Krittinee Nuttavuthisit, Chulalongkorn University, Thailand
D. Selcen O. Aykac, Ozyegin University, Turkey
Sahver Omeraki, Bilkent University, Turkey
Ayse Onculer, ESSEC Business School, France
Nailya Ordabayeva, INSEAD, France
Massimiliano Ostinelli, University of Wisconsin-Milwaukee, USA
Cele C. Otnes, University of Illinois at Urbana-Champaign, USA
Nacima Ourahmoune, ESSEC Business School, France
Shweta Oza, University of Miami, USA
Yesim Ozalp, York University, Canada
Stefano Pace, Universita Bocconi, Italy
Grant Packard, University of Michigan, USA
M. G. Parameswaran, FCB Ulka Advertising, India
Cheol Park, Korea University, Korea
Ji Kyung Park, University of Minnesota, USA
Young-Hoon Park, Cornell University, USA
Marie-Agnès Parmentier, HEC Montreal, Canada
Elizabeth Parsons, University of Keele, UK
Vladimir Pashkevich, Marymount Manhattan College, USA
Kirsten Passyn, Salisbury University, USA
Alessandro M. Peluso, LUISS University, Italy
Beatriz Pereira, University of Michigan, USA
Maria Eugenia Perez, Tecnologico de Monterrey, Mexico
Paula Peter, San Diego State University, USA
Ethan Pew, University of Colorado at Boulder, USA
Todd Pezzuti, University of California at Irvine, USA
Barbara Phillips, University of Saskatchewan, Canada
T. Andrew Poehlman, Southern Methodist University, USA
Gratiana Pol, University of Southern California, USA
Maxim Polonsky, University of Connecticut, USA
Frank Pons, Laval University, Canada
Monica Popa, University of Alberta, Canada
Sanne Poulsen, University of Otago, New Zealand
Paulo H M Prado, Federal University of Parana, Brazil
Andrea Prothero, University College Dublin, Ireland, UK
Pingping Qiu, University of Manitoba, Canada
Jeffrey Radighieri, Washington State University, USA
Mark Ratchford, University of Colorado at Boulder, USA

Sarita Ray Chaudhury, New Mexico State University, USA
Joseph Redden, University of Minnesota, USA
William Rhyne, Golden Gate University, USA
Dan Rice, Louisiana State University, USA
Brendan Richardson, University College Cork, Ireland, UK
Hila Riemer, Ben-Gurion University, Israel
Joonas Rokka, Helsinki School of Economics, Finland
Stefanie Rosen, University of South Carolina, USA
Sara Rosengren, Stockholm School of Economics, Sweden
Caroline Roux, McGill University, Canada
Abhijit Roy, University of Scranton, USA
Ayalla Ruvio, Temple University, USA
Aaron Sackett, University of Chicago, USA
Christina Saenger, Kent State University, USA
Mukunthan Santhanakrishnan, Idaho State University, USA
Kumar Sarangee, University of Illinois at Urbana-Champaign, USA
Gülen Sarial Abi, Koc University, Turkey
Daiane Scaraboto, Schulich School of Business, York University, Canada
Dorothea Schaffner, Lucerne University of Applied Sciences, Switzerland
Gaby Schellekens, Erasmus University Rotterdam, the Netherlands
Rom Schrift, Columbia University, USA
Irene Scopelliti, Bocconi University, Italy
Satheeshkumar Seenivasan, University at Buffalo, USA
Joon Yong Seo, University of Utah, USA
Piyush Sharma, Hong Kong Polytechnic University, Hong Kong, China
Jeremy Sierra, Texas State University at San Marcos, USA
Lawrence Silver, Southeastern Oklahoma State University, USA
David H. Silvera, University of Texas at San Antonio, USA
Jayati Sinha, University of Iowa, USA
Nancy J. Sirianni, Arizona State University, USA
Lionel Sitz, EM Lyon Business School, France
Anu Sivaraman, University of Delaware, USA
Craig Smith, INSEAD, France
Michael Smith, Temple University, USA
Youngseok Son, Hallym University, Korea
Robin Soster, University of South Carolina, USA
Stephen Spiller, Duke University, USA
Lara Spiteri Cornish, University of Keele, UK
Katherine Sredl, University of Notre Dame, USA
Sascha Steinmann, Institute of Marketing and Retailing, University of Goettingen, Germany
Jennifer Stewart, Ohio State University, USA
Amy Stokes, University of Arkansas, USA
Shirley Stretch-Stephenson, California State University at Los Angeles, USA
Yuliya Strizhakova, Rutgers University, USA
Isabelle Sueur, Université de La Rochelle, France
Raji Sugumar, Bharathidasan Government College for Women, India
Kwanho Suk, Korea University, Korea
Steven Sweldens, Erasmus University Rotterdam, the Netherlands
Ataollah Tafaghodi Jami, University of Utah, USA
Sarah Tanford, University of Nevada at Las Vegas, USA
Felix Tang, Hang Seng School of Commerce, Hong Kong, China
Marilyn Terzic, McGill University, Canada
Veronica Thomas, Kent State University, USA
Julie Tinson, University of Stirling, Scotland, UK
Claudia Townsend, UCLA Anderson School of Management, USA
Luiz Valerio Trindade, Universidade Nove de Julho, Brazil
Sanjeev Tripathi, IIM Ahmedabad, India
Rebecca Trump, University of Arizona, USA
Gulnur Tumbat, San Francisco State University, USA
Linda Tuncay, Loyola University Chicago, USA
Meltem Ture, Bilkent University, Turkey
Gaelle Ulvoas-Moal, ESC BRETAGNE Brest, France
Oleg Urminsky, University of Chicago, USA
Rajiv Vaidyanathan, University of Minnesota Duluth, USA
Hester Van Herk, Free University Amsterdam, the Netherlands
W. Fred van Raaij, Tilburg University, the Netherlands
Rohit Varman, Indian Institute of Management, Calcutta, India
Vinod Venkatraman, Duke University, USA
Julian Vieceli, Deakin University, Australia
Valter Vieira, UTFPR-Technological Federal University of Parana, Brazil
Luca Visconti, Universita Bocconi, Italy
Hilde Voorveld, University of Amsterdam, the Netherlands
Monica Wadhwa, Stanford University, USA
Michael Walsh, West Virginia University, USA
Carla Walter, Missouri Southern State University, USA
Echo Wen Wan, University of Hong Kong, Hong Kong, China
Heather Wan, University of Southern California, USA
Jing Wang, Singapore Management University, Singapore
Morgan Ward, University of Texas at Austin, USA
Caleb Warren, University of Colorado at Boulder, USA
Ray Weaver, Harvard University, USA
Clare Weeden, University of Brighton, UK
Fei Weisstein, University of Illinois at Urbana-Champaign, USA
Daniel Wentzel, University of St. Gallen, Switzerland
Keith Wilcox, Babson College, USA
Robert Wilken, ESCP-EAP European School of Management, Germany
William Wilkie, University of Notre Dame, USA
Andrew Wilson, Schulich School of Business, York University, Canada
Jimmy Wong, University of Illinois at Urbana-Champaign, USA
Kachat Andrew Wong, University of Southern California, USA
Michael Wood, Hunter College, City University of New York, USA
Natalie Wood, Saint Joseph's University, USA
Christine Wright-Isak, Florida Gulf Coast University, USA
Eugenia Wu, Duke University, USA
Jiayun Wu, University of Arizona, USA
Kang-Ning Xia, Yuan Ze University, Taiwan
Chunyan Xie, Stord/Haugesund University College, Norway
Alison Jing Xu, University of Illinois at Urbana-Champaign, USA
Cagri Yalkin, King's College, London, UK
Lifeng Yang, Ohio State University, USA
Natalia Yannopoulou, Nottingham University, UK
E. Tacli Yazicioglu, Bogazici University, Turkey
Lilly Ye, Frostburg State University, USA
Nai-Chi (Nike) Yeh, National Cheng-Chi University, Taiwan
Baskin Yenicioglu, Henley Management College, USA
Lia Zarantonello, Bocconi University, Italy
Yael Zemack-Rugar, Virginia Tech, USA
Charles Zhang, University of Michigan, USA
Dan Zhang, Temple University, USA
Yinlong Zhang, University of Texas at San Antonio, USA
Yuhuang Zheng, Tsinghua University, China
Meng Zhu, Carnegie Mellon University, USA
Mohammadali Zolfagharian, University of Texas-Pan American, USA
Rami Zwick, University of California at Riverside, USA

Table of Contents

PROGRAM OVERVIEW

Thursday, 22 October 2009
ACR DOCTORAL SYMPOSIUM

Friday, 23 October 2009
FILM FESTIVAL I-V
8:00am–5:00pm

Black Friday: A Video-Ethnography of an Experiential Shopping Event
Blogs - Consumption, Behaviour, Interaction
Fashion, Consumption and Identity
VINILEIROS – Those Crazy Guys that Love Their Vinyl Records
Brothers in Paint: Practice-Oriented Inquiry into a Tribal Marketplace Culture
Pirates of the Web: The Curse of Anti-piracy Advertising
Restrained Pursuit of Luxury: Wealthy Shanghainese Attitudes towards Upscale Consumption
POV: Point of View... Consumers and Ethnographers in Perspective...
"Does Green?"
Remade China: The Re-production of Chineseness in a Multi-Cultural Society

Friday, 23 October 2009
FRIDAY SESSION 1
8:00am–9:15am

FRI 1.1 *Paper Session:* Saving Money in a Tough Economy: How to Succeed?
FRI 1.2 *Paper Session:* We are not all the Same: New Issues, Confluence, and Divergence in Consumer Acculturation Studies
FRI 1.3 *Paper Session:* Attitude Strength and Consistency Between Attitude and Behavior
FRI 1.4 *Paper Session:* On Being Better (or Worse) Than Others: Illuminating and Eliminating Biases in Social Comparison
FRI 1.5 *Paper Session:* Positive Emotions Are Like a Box of Chocolates: Without Identifying the Different Flavors You Never Know What Behavior You're Going to Get
FRI 1.6 *Paper Session:* Mixed Emotions in Service Experiences
FRI 1.7 *Paper Session:* Contemporary Topics in Regulatory Focus Research
FRI 1.8 *Paper Session:* Drivers of Consumer Decision Making
FRI 1.9 *Paper Session:* Exploring the Links between Stigma and Consumption
FRI 1.10 *Paper Session:* "Self-ish" Consumer Behavior
FRI 1.11 *Paper Session:* Who You Are Influences How You Behave: Exploring The Interplay of Personality and Consumer Behavior
FRI 1.12 *Paper Session:* Talk the Green Talk, Shop the Green Walk?
FRI 1.13 *Film Festival:* Film Festival Session 1

Friday, 23 October 2009
Friday Session 2
9:45am–11:00am

FRI 2.1 *Paper Session:* Money and People Make Strange Bedfellows
FRI 2.2 *Paper Session:* The Pitfalls of Fame: Insights from Human Brands
FRI 2.3 *Paper Session:* On the Fly: Impression Formation and Updating
FRI 2.4 *Paper Session:* On Being the Same and Different: The Dynamics of Interpretation and Comparison in Consumer Judgment
FRI 2.5 *Paper Session:* How Environmental Cues Impact Consumer Judgments
FRI 2.6 *Paper Session:* Saving for Later or Wasting: A Transformative Research Perspective
FRI 2.7 *Paper Session:* Information Integration in Judgment and Decision Making: New Directions
FRI 2.8 *Paper Session:* Expanding the Research Boundaries of Emotions
FRI 2.9 *Paper Session:* Plates, Smiley Faces and Price Tags: How Contextual Factors Bias Consumption
FRI 2.10 *Paper Session:* Constraints and Consequences: Psychological Reactance in Consumption Contexts
FRI 2.11 *Paper Session:* The Effects of Process and Outcome Simulations on Decision Making
FRI 2.12 *Paper Session:* Unhealthy Behaviors and Outcomes: Personal and Public Policy Implications
FRI 2.13 *Paper Session:* How Pricing Impacts Preferences and Satisfaction
FRI 2.14 *Film Festival:* Film Festival Session 2

Friday, 23 October 2009
Friday Session 3
11:15am–12:30pm

FRI 3.1 *Paper Session:* Multiple Systems for Choice and Valuation: New Perspectives from Decision Neuroscience
FRI 3.2 *Paper Session:* Other People's Things: Perspectives on Ownership Transfer and Sharing
FRI 3.3 *Paper Session:* Social Sources of Persuasion
FRI 3.4 *Paper Session:* Customization and Consumer Choice
FRI 3.5 *Paper Session:* Crossing Thresholds: Research in Life's Transitions
FRI 3.6 *Paper Session:* Charity Begins at Home: Increasing Charitable Donations
FRI 3.7 *Paper Session:* Mind Your Primes and Cues
FRI 3.8 *Paper Session:* Nudging Consumers Towards Healthier Food Choices
FRI 3.9 *Paper Session:* The Interplay between Goal Categories and Effort
FRI 3.10 *Paper Session:* Is Identity Signaling so Great? Limitations and Negative Consequences
FRI 3.11 *Roundtable Session:* Advancing the Production/Consumption Dialectic in Consumer Culture Theory
FRI 3.12 *Paper Session:* It's a Bundle! New Directions for Pricing and Promotion
FRI 3.13 *Film Festival:* Film Festival Session 3

Friday, 23 October 2009
Friday Session 4
2:00pm–3:15pm

FRI 4.1 *Paper Session:* Choices, Judgments and Temperature: From Visceral States to Metaphors
FRI 4.2 *Paper Session:* Having It All: Marketplace Negotiations of Feminism and Women's Roles
FRI 4.3 *Paper Session:* Persuasion, Confusion, and Sponsorship
FRI 4.4 *Paper Session:* Frontiers of Affect and Choice
FRI 4.5 *Paper Session:* Are Crowds Always Wiser?
FRI 4.6 *Paper Session:* Aging Consumers: Perceptions, Attitudes and Choice
FRI 4.7 *Paper Session:* Overconsumption and the Morality of Health
FRI 4.8 *Paper Session:* Choice in Context: The Yin and Yang of Societal and Personal Goals
FRI 4.9 *Paper Session:* The Other Side of the Story: New Perspectives on Word of Mouth
FRI 4.10 *Paper Session:* Beyond Functionality: Aesthetic Considerations in Consumer Behavior
FRI 4.11 *Paper Session:* Improving, Protecting, or Redefining the Self
FRI 4.12 *Roundtable Session:* Towards a Theoretical Vocabulary for Consumer Research on Sustainability
FRI 4.13 *Paper Session:* Preference Reversals and Counterfactuals in Choice
FRI 4.14 *Film Festival:* Film Festival Session 4

Friday, 23 October 2009
FRIDAY SESSION 5
3:45pm–5:00pm

FRI 5.1 *Paper Session:* Deep Determinants of Value: New Perspectives on the Endowment Effect
FRI 5.2 *Paper Session:* What is the Intelligent Choice? Performance on the CRT and Preferences
FRI 5.3 *Paper Session:* The Constructive Role of Effort in Consumer Choice
FRI 5.4 *Paper Session:* Affective Advertising Effects: Where the Rubber Meets the Road
FRI 5.5 *Paper Session:* The Malleability of Choice Processes
FRI 5.6 *Paper Session:* The Many Faces of Social Influence
FRI 5.7 *Paper Session:* The Buzz about Buzz: Drivers and Consequences of Word-of-Mouth
FRI 5.8 *Paper Session:* For What It's Worth: Valuation of Price and Time
FRI 5.9 *Paper Session:* Looks Matter! Aesthetics, Design, and Consumer Judgments
FRI 5.10 *Film Festival:* Film Festival Session 5

Friday, 23 October 2009
WORKING PAPER SESSION
5:00pm–7:00pm

Saturday, 24 October 2009
FILM FESTIVAL VI-VIII
AND
AWARD WINNING FILMS
8:00am–5:00pm

Black Friday: A Video-Ethnography of an Experiential Shopping Event
Blogs - Consumption, Behaviour, Interaction
Fashion, Consumption and Identity
VINILEIROS – Those Crazy Guys that Love Their Vinyl Records
Brothers in Paint: Practice-Oriented Inquiry into a Tribal Marketplace Culture
Pirates of the Web: The Curse of Anti-piracy Advertising
Restrained Pursuit of Luxury: Wealthy Shanghainese Attitudes towards Upscale Consumption
POV: Point of View... Consumers and Ethnographers in Perspective...
"Does Green?"
Remade China: The Re-production of Chineseness in a Multi-Cultural Society

Saturday, 24 October 2009
SATURDAY SESSION 1
8:00am–9:15am

SAT 1.1 *Paper Session:* The Role of the Past and Present on Persuasion and Influence
SAT 1.2 *Paper Session:* Greasing the Skids: Fluency and Ease of Processing Impacts
SAT 1.3 *Paper Session:* The Role of Emotions in Self-control Dilemmas
SAT 1.4 *Paper Session:* A Touch of Imagination: The Role of Imagery in Hedonic Consumption
SAT 1.5 *Paper Session:* It's a Two-Way Street: The Influence of Communicators and Recipients in Word-of-Mouth Contexts
SAT 1.6 *Paper Session:* From Ear to Brain, From Heart to Pocket: Branding Challenges and Possibilities in the Music Industry
SAT 1.7 *Paper Session:* Time is More Precious than Money
SAT 1.8 *Paper Session:* Underpinnings of Risky Behavior: Non-health Motives for Health-related Behaviors
SAT 1.9 *Paper Session:* Continuing to Sin or a Reformed Sinner: Examining Sequential Self-Regulation Choices
SAT 1.10 *Paper Session:* Packaging and Sensory Effects on Consumption
SAT 1.11 *Paper Session:* The Shifting Sands of Consumer Culture
SAT 1.12 *Film Festival:* Film Festival Session 6

Saturday, 24 October 2009
Saturday Session 2
9:45am–11:00am

SAT 2.1	*Paper Session:*	I'm Afraid, But Am I Persuaded? How to Make Fear Appeals More Effective
SAT 2.2	*Paper Session:*	Metacognitive Experiences in Number Processing
SAT 2.3	*Paper Session:*	Finding the Uncompromising Consumer: A Deeper Understanding of Context Effects on Choice
SAT 2.4	*Paper Session:*	All Things New: Originality, Innovation Adoption, and Creative Behavior
SAT 2.5	*Paper Session:*	Examining Individual and Situational Drivers of Prosocial Behaviors
SAT 2.6	*Paper Session:*	Let the Games Begin: Evaluating Fun Experiences
SAT 2.7	*Paper Session:*	Dynamic Influences on Investors' Decisions
SAT 2.8	*Paper Session:*	The Role of Stereotypes in Changing Consumers' Attitudes and Behaviors
SAT 2.9	*Paper Session:*	Exploring Self-Control: Moving Beyond Depletion Hypothesis
SAT 2.10	*Paper Session:*	Visualization, Imagination, and Product Choice: Affective Forecasting of Future Product Consumption and Utilization Experiences
SAT 2.11	*Paper Session:*	Virtual Worlds: Balancing Creativity and Motivation
SAT 2.12	*Paper Session:*	Self-Identity Across Possessions and Places
SAT 2.13	*Film Festival:*	Film Festival Session 7

Saturday, 24 October 2009
Saturday Session 3
11:15am–12:30pm

SAT 3.1	*Paper Session:*	Setting the Stage: How Frames of Reference May Be Influencing Your Behavior
SAT 3.2	*Paper Session:*	When (and How) Does Metacognitive Experience Affect Consumer Behavior?
SAT 3.3	*Paper Session:*	Pre-Purchase Planning and Post-Purchase Learning: The Role of Internal and External Factors
SAT 3.4	*Paper Session:*	Social Comparison and Negative Emotions: Understanding Regret, Envy, and Schadenfreude in a Consumer World
SAT 3.5	*Paper Session:*	The Wellbeing of Subsistence Consumers
SAT 3.6	*Paper Session:*	Looking on the Bright Side: The Effects of Optimism on Goals and Behavior
SAT 3.7	*Paper Session:*	Multidisciplinary Approaches to Communicating Health Risks
SAT 3.8	*Paper Session:*	Deviating from or Resetting Consumers Ethical Standards
SAT 3.9	*Paper Session:*	Assimilation and Contrast: Comparison Processes in Judgments and Evaluations
SAT 3.10	*Paper Session:*	Cue Substitution: Inferential Processes in Judgements and Experiences of Time
SAT 3.11	*Paper Session:*	New or Different Product Evaluation
SAT 3.12	*Paper Session:*	Consumer Culture and Branding
SAT 3.13	*Film Festival:*	Film Festival Session 8

Saturday, 24 October 2009
Saturday Session 4
2:00pm–3:15pm

SAT 4.1	*Paper Session:*	Effects of Minor Language Variations on Consumer Persuasion
SAT 4.2	*Paper Session:*	Psychological Distance and Metacognitive Experience
SAT 4.3	*Paper Session:*	New Insights into Consumers' Inherent Preferences
SAT 4.4	*Paper Session:*	Where's My Bailout? A New Look at Factors Affecting Consumer Fairness Perceptions in the Age of Vengeful Populism
SAT 4.5	*Paper Session:*	A Voter Among Voters: Political Decisions in the Social Context
SAT 4.6	*Paper Session:*	Long-term Decisions and Focusing on the Future
SAT 4.7	*Paper Session:*	The Influence of Lay Beliefs on Consumers' Food Consumption Decisions
SAT 4.8	*Paper Session:*	Consuming in Self-Defense: Consumer Responses to Self Threat
SAT 4.9	*Paper Session:*	In Pursuit of the Prime Suspects: Insights from Second Generation Research on Nonconscious Influences of Consumer Behavior
SAT 4.10	*Paper Session:*	Goals' Roles in Consumer Behavior
SAT 4.11	*Paper Session:*	Deep Measurement in Consumer Research: The Next Step
SAT 4.12	*Paper Session:*	Transcending Culture: Religion and Politics in Consumption
SAT 4.13	*Paper Session:*	The Rosy Side of Negative Emotions
SAT 4.14	*Roundtable Session:*	Navigating the Networked Rivers of the Social Web: Emerging Themes for Consumer Behavior Research on Web 2.X

Saturday, 24 October 2009

Saturday Session 5

3:45pm–5:00pm

SAT 5.1	*Paper Session:*	Morality, Suspicion, and Modification: New Directions After 15 Years' Persuasion Knowledge Research
SAT 5.2	*Paper Session:*	The Distinct Effects of Hope in Consumption
SAT 5.3	*Paper Session:*	Why Reproduction Involves More Than Sex: The Diverse Effects of Mating Motivation on Consumer Behavior
SAT 5.4	*Paper Session:*	It's Not What You Think it Is: Insights into Consumers' Perceptual Biases in Response to Brand Strategies
SAT 5.5	*Paper Session:*	Effects of Social Influence on Consumer Spending Decisions
SAT 5.6	*Paper Session:*	The Consequences of Being Naughty
SAT 5.7	*Paper Session:*	Consumer-Generated Advertising: Creators and Spectators
SAT 5.8	*Paper Session:*	Emotional and Motivational Drivers of Our "Want" and "Should" Desires
SAT 5.9	*Paper Session:*	Consumer Strategies to Track Spending
SAT 5.10	*Paper Session:*	Tough Choices and Comparisons
SAT 5.11	*Film Festival:*	2009 AWARD WINNING FILMS

Table of Contents

Special Session Summaries

Wanting What I Shouldn't Have and Finding a Way to Get It: When Guilt Increases Hedonic Consumption

Yael Zemack-Rugar, Virginia Tech, USA

Lisa A. Cavanaugh, University of Southern California, USA

Gavan J. Fitzsimons, Duke University, USA

Competitive Papers

Full Papers

Competitive Papers

Extended Abstracts

Film Festival

Roundtable Summaries

Working Paper Abstracts

Presidential Address

The Consumer Experience

Chris Janiszewski, University of Florida, USA

Over the years, I have participated in a number of consortia, symposia, and meetings with graduate students. One of the most common questions has been, "What is hot?" My stock answer has always been, "Whatever is 'hot' today will be cold by the time you complete a research project in the area, so don't chase current trends." I then follow up with, "Find something interesting and make it 'hot'." This advice often results in a glazed look that I used to interpret as appreciation. Now that I am older, and less vain, I understand my advice contained little information. The graduate students could have gained as much information from a conversation with Sarah Palin.

My uninformative answer to the question, "What is hot?" was a consequence of my failure to understand the intent of the question. The real question was, "Can you explain the market place of academic ideas?" The graduate students knew they were entering a business where their job was to market ideas, but their current marketing plan lacked a customer and a competitive analysis. The students knew that if they could understand the needs of the target market, and the strengths and weaknesses of their competition, they could identify marketable projects. They could then make personal tradeoffs between pursuing these marketable projects versus projects that might be less marketable, but more intrinsically interesting.

Over the next twenty minutes, I hope to provide some insight into this issue. I will organize my comments around the broader issue of how academics typically identify interesting ideas, the competition you will face as you attempt to market ideas, and the types of research that are likely to allow you, and by extension the discipline of consumer behavior, to experience success. I will provide examples of promising areas of research, with the understanding that I intend to illustrate as opposed to advocate.

MAKING A CONTRIBUTION

There are two common approaches to identifying potentially interesting consumer research ideas. The first is to be an active participant in a basic social science discipline. Whether one is a disciple of anthropology, economics, psychology, or sociology, the prescription is the same. Try to reach a level of excellence and insight that allows you to understand and apply state-of-the-art theory. Use this knowledge to (1) extend theory and make a contribution to the core discipline, (2) gain insight into how and why consumers behave the way they do, or (3) both. This is an effective strategy that has been executed by consumer behavior researchers over the past 40 years. Yet, I perceive two problems with the core discipline approach. First, many of us do not have the resources to compete. For example, a successful psychology professor has post-docs, many Ph.D. students, and a cadre of undergraduate research assistants in his or her lab.

Academic progress is quicker in this environment. Second, consumer behavior research is by definition, an interdisciplinary endeavor. We make progress though shared interdisciplinary insights. Thus, as a consumer researcher becomes more expert in a core area, the person's ideas are likely to become less interesting to the consumer research community as a whole. To put it plainly, enhancing discipline-specific expertise leads to an increased appreciation for one's ideas in the core area, but less appreciation for one's ideas among the consumer research audience.

The second approach to identifying potentially interesting research ideas is to focus on a substantive domain. There is a long history of this type of research in consumer behavior. For example, advertising response, branding, collecting, gift giving, health behavior, impulsive buying, new product adoption, and nutritional labeling are some of the substantive areas that have received research attention over the past four decades. Again, a subset of consumer behavior researchers have executed this strategy successfully. Yet, a substantive focus does not guarantee that research is marketable. A substantive focus often involves an application of an existing theory that has been "borrowed" from a base social science discipline. When insight into a substantive domain is based on "borrowed" theory, there is always the danger that the insight will be perceived as redundant. This makes the publication of the idea more difficult.

So, we are faced with two approaches to making a contribution: (1) make a theoretical advance in a core discipline, using a consumer behavior context as a setting for the research, or (2) provide insight into a substantive domain. And, as I have argued, each of these approaches has potential disadvantages. The question is how to mitigate these disadvantages. The answer is not simple. My solution? I propose that you select substantive domains where existing social science theory is not easily applied or where social scientists from the core disciplines are reluctant to go. To put it another way, we need to work in areas where there is limited competition from the core social sciences, but where our insights are likely to capture market share somewhere down the road.

CAN AN APPLIED DISCIPLINE LEAD?

My advice that our discipline should focus on research topics that are somewhat removed from the mainstream of social science research implies isolationism and the potential of irrelevance. To allay these criticisms, I would like you to consider three areas in which consumer researchers were the driving force behind theory development.

1. 1970's: Consumer satisfaction / dissatisfaction. Consumer satisfaction and dissatisfaction are consequences of consumption or service experiences. Consumer satisfaction and dissatisfaction research began during the 1970's as a response to the concerns of government regulators and consumer advocates. The initial research focused on the measurement of consumer satisfaction (Pfaff 1972) and the role of expectation disconfirmation in dissatisfaction (Anderson 1973; Olshavsky and Miller 1972). Subsequently, research indentified the antecedents and consequences of consumer satisfaction and dissatisfaction. Antecedents include performance expectations and the pleasantness of prior consumption experiences. Consequences include changes in price sensitivity, brand loyalty, and changes in the frequency of purchase. These findings led to expectation-confirmation theory of customer satisfaction (Oliver 1980) and to a discussion of the role satisfaction plays in a consumer's life (Fournier and Mick 1999). To date, there have been over 3000 publications on consumer satisfaction, many of them motivated by the original research conducted in the consumer behavior domain.
2. 1980's: Attitude toward the Advertisement. Attitude toward the advertisement refers to the "pleasant or unpleasant feelings evoked by advertising" (MacKenzie, Lutz,

and Belch 1986, p. 131). Although the Aad concept has a long history (see Lutz 1985; Silk and Vavra 1974), research began in earnest in the 1980's. The initial research focused on documenting that the feelings evoked by an advertisement could influence feelings toward the advertised product (Mitchell and Olson 1981), brand consideration (Moore and Hutchinson 1983), brand choice (Shimp 1981; Shimp and Yokum 1982), and the rate at which an advertisement lost its effectiveness owing to repeated use (Calder and Sternthal 1980). Subsequently, Aad research focused on the factors that influenced the attitude toward the ad and the likelihood that these feelings would impact relevant downstream behaviors including choice and purchase execution (MacKenzie and Lutz 1989). The Aad construct is interesting because it encouraged consumer behavior researchers to focus on how the feelings evoked by an advertisement interacted with the more cognitively-based beliefs the ad was designed to communicate (e.g., Brown and Stayman 1992; Madden, Allen, and Twible 1988).

3. 1990's: Brand relationships. In her 1998 JCR article, Susan Fournier proposed that consumers form relationships with their brands. Her analysis was based on relationship theory. Her insights were threefold. First, brand relationships come in many forms, including buddies, friendships, committed partnerships, and marriages of convenience. Second, these relationships evolve over time. Third, marketing actions can influence the quality and stability of these consumer-brand relationships. The key insight was that product usage not only provides a benefit experience, but also an experience related to the brand and the meanings it has come to represent. To my knowledge, this is the most cited piece of research in consumer behavior over the past ten years.

What is common across these three examples? These are examples of substantive domains that were initially of special interest to consumer researchers and of lesser interest to social scientists that seek to generate knowledge in their core areas. As a consequence, our discipline took a leadership position among social scientists in developing these areas of thought. In fact, I would argue that there was a collective recognition, by the intellectual producers and the gatekeepers of consumer behavior research, that these topics were interesting consumer behavior experiences that were worthy of investigation.

OUR OPPORTUNITY: CONSUMER EXPERIENCE

So, what is our opportunity? In what substantive areas do we, as a discipline have a special interest and a competitive advantage? The answer is "consumer experience." CCT researchers have a long history of calling for, and focusing on, consumer experiences (Arnould and Thompson 2005; Holbrook and Hirschman 1982; Hirschman and Holbrook 1982; cf. Holt 1995). There has also been growing interest in consumer experience among information processing and decision science researchers. In the past few years, I have seen papers on aesthetic experience (Joy and Sherry 2003; Veryzer and Hutchinson 1998), authenticity (e.g., Rose and Wood 2005), consumer socialization (John 1999), emotional responses (e.g., Andrade and Cohen 1997; Ramanathan and Williams 2007), excitement (Ding et al. 2005), extraordinary experiences (Arnould and Price 1993), hedonic experience (e.g., Nelson and Meyvis 2008; Ratner, Kahn, and Kahneman 1999), prestige and status (e.g., Ivanic and Nunes 2009; Ordabayeva and Chandon 2009), processing fluency (e.g., Allen 2002), retail experience (Verhoef et al. 2009), self-identity (e.g., Wood, Chaplin, and Solomon 2009), tactile experience (e.g., Peck and Wiggins 2006), taste experience (e.g., Elder and Krishna 2009; Hoegg and Alba 2007), and visceral experience (e.g., Celsi, Rose, and Leigh 1993; Chang and Pham 2009).

Although consumer researchers may not have been the initiators of many of these research streams, our discipline certainly has the potential to develop innovative insights into these consumption experiences. Yet, in order to do this, we will have to focus on the richness of the consumer experience and the consumer's role in the management of this experience (e.g., Fournier and Mick 1999). In doing this, we must focus on the mental and physiological states that accompany information acquisition, product choice, consumption, and post-consumption activities. In the next part of my talk, I would like to illustrate what a discipline wide program on consumer experience might entail. I will focus on consumption utility because it is a concept that is relevant to researchers that represent the breadth of approaches to consumer research.

CONSUMPTION UTILITY

The utility of any object . . . pleases the master by perpetually suggesting to him the pleasure or conveniency which it is fitted to promote.

Adam Smith

Two foundational social sciences have informed the study of utility in consumer behavior (cf. Hsee and Tsai 2008). The economic approach to utility assumes that consumers have an underlying set of preference functions that allow them to anticipate the value of any product or experience. These preference functions are assumed to be relatively stable and enduring. Psychologists and decision making theorists accept that some portion of utility is stable, but add that context can alter the relative preferences for choice options. The literatures on preference reversals, constructed preferences, and local and global context effects all provide testimony to the malleability of utility. Economists and psychologists have shown that preferences are not time consistent, frame consistent, or context consistent. More importantly, we are not the dominant players in these literatures. We certainly have superstars that contribute to the research on utility, but I would argue that utility is studied in economics first, psychology second, and consumer behavior third.

So the question becomes, "What utility-based research could we own?" Where do we have a differential advantage with respect to our interest, our expertise, and our areas of application? I contend that it is not in the "utility of choice" (expected utility), but the "utility of consumption" (experienced utility or *subjective value*) (see Holbrook and Hirschman 1982). Although this change in emphasis sounds subtle, it is not. Our current focus in the "utility of choice" makes choice the seminal event. The antecedent and consequences of choice all must be understood through the investigative frame we have adopted. If our focus were to shift to the utility of consumption, then we would worry more about how people experience utility than how they anticipate utility. We would put less emphasis on the events that are external to the individual, such as product features and contextual events, and more emphasis on the consumption experiences and, by extension, events that are internal to the individual such as a consumer's mood (e.g., happiness, eagerness, calmness, relief, anger, sadness, embarrassment, anxiety) or mental state (e.g., pleasure, pain, confidence, uncertainty, desire, contentment). Even more importantly, we would look at how the external and internal factors interact to determine the consumer's experienced utility (e.g., Chen 2009). This leads to the following research issues:

This leads to the following research issues:

1. Where does experienced utility come from? A typical approach to answering this question comes from the information processing perspective. Utility is a function of the features of a product. This viewpoint is predicated on the assumption that there is a one-to-one mapping between the level of a product's features and the benefits of consumption. Yet, we know this is not true. Benefits are not in the products. Benefits are in the consumer experience. Experienced benefits not only vary significantly across consumers, but across time for the same consumer, because internal factors such as emotional states, psychological states, and physiological states vary over time. Give the same person the same food or beverage on five different occasions and the experienced utility will vary by occasion. In fact, it can vary quite dramatically. A similar claim about the inconsistency of experience has been made with respect to time perception, pain perception, hedonic experiences, etc. Thus, internal states matter for experienced utility.
2. What events are responsible for experienced utility? One could posit that experienced utility is a consequence of direct and indirect sources. For example, baseball fans are prone to say that hot dogs taste better at the ball park. Many people also believe that beer taste better when it is consumed with friends. These examples are meant to illustrate that utility is derived from the consumption of the product itself (a direct source) and the social situations in which it is consumed (an indirect source). More interesting is what happens the next time the person consumes a hot dog or beer. Does the indirect utility from the prior social consumption episode influence the utility derived in the next consumption episode, even though the social cues are absent? If this is so, one might wonder about the conditions that are favorable to this form of utility expansion and/or contraction?
3. What are consumers trying to achieve with experienced utility? Do consumers simply seek to maintain a mood or are there other objectives? To illustrate, consider the consumption of a meal that consists of a single course with multiple food items. We could assess the utility associated with each individual bite, with a series of bites, with a series of bites interspersed with beverage consumption, or with bites, beverages, and conversation. Does the consumer manage this sequence of utility? This is not an issue of expectations (e.g., von Neumann and Morgenstern) or retrospective evaluations (e.g., Ratner, Kahn, and Kahneman 1999), but an issue of managed experiences. Rather than thinking about utility experiences as temporally distinct, we can of them as inter-temporally managed. Thus, if we were to extrapolate from the food example to a day's worth of events, we could research how consumers manage experienced utility throughout the day. We might even discover that there are different types of experienced utility that are being managed.
4. If consumers are trying to string together a set of experiences that provide utility, how does this process work? An obvious starting point for this conversation is the literature on adaptation. The literature on adaptation shows that an experience becomes less intense with repetition (Nelson and Meyvis 2008). Yet, at some level, this process explanation is much too simplistic. Most adaptation level findings are local, not global. For example, I can quickly adapt to repeatedly listening to my favorite song, but not to repeated listening to a favorite collection of songs and even less to a mix of songs, conversation, and food (e.g., a party). The interesting question is why people satiate to a series of hedonic experiences when they come from the same source but not when they come from different sources? After all, utility is utility, right? Similarly, how do different types of intervening experiences influence adaptation and experienced utility? In effect, this is a question of variety seeking on a grand level, but with the emphasis on experience as opposed to prospective evaluation or retrospection assessment.
5. Has the focus on expectations about product performance led us ignore experiences that accompany the act of purchasing? The traditional focus on the "utility of choice", as opposed to the "utility of consumption", leads to the implicit assumption that expectations are focal and experiences are secondary. It's all about the choice. Yet, we could argue the opposite. Purchases do nothing more that create opportunities for experiences. In fact, it could be argued that the act of purchasing is sufficient to create the desired experience. To illustrate, consider food acquisition and consumption. In the U.S., 13% of income is spent on food. The average American consumer eats 1750 pounds of food per year and discards about 250 pounds of it. What is even crazier is that 20 percent of the food U.S. consumers discard food that hasn't even been removed from the package! This fact can lead to two very different research questions. First, we could adopt a traditional expected utility choice paradigm and wonder why consumers are being suboptimal. Why can't consumers learn to purchase and consume food properly? Alternatively we could adopt an experience perspective and seek to understand how utility is derived from the purchase, storage, and failure to consume the food. Maybe wilting one's lettuce in the refrigerator creates more utility than consuming it. This example illustrates the importance of understanding how consumers derive utility from a wide range of consumption-related experiences.

I have just made a case for investigating utility as an experience. If we can unlock the door into consideration, acquisition, and consumption experiences, we can gain insight into what people buy, when they buy, how much they buy, and why all of this buying influences, or fails to influence, their happiness. This is an area of inquiry that is closely aligned with consumer researcher interests, provides an opportunity for theory development, and can benefit from interdisciplinary study.

NARRATIVES, BELIEFS, AND UTILITY

Thus far, I have argued that consumers derive utility from experience. Yet, I have failed to discuss what makes an experience pleasurable or painful. For the marketing faculty in the audience, this is akin to asking, "Where do benefit segments come from?" Why do some people derive utility from a product whereas others do not? My contention is that utility is a function of an individual's beliefs, and by extension, the meanings that support these beliefs. Beliefs create utility during the acquisition of a product, the consumption of a product, and the communication about these experiences. Thus, insight can be gained by understanding the events that lead to belief structures that allow a person to extract utility from an experience.

The idea that belief structures support utility extraction from experiences should sound like Marketing 101 because, in many ways, it is. Yet, what is interesting is the variability in the effectiveness of belief structures. For example, consider the belief structure that supports the use of dental floss. Everyone knows that flossing is important. It promotes healthy teeth and gums. In the U.S., we are taught this from our very first visit to the dentist. Yet, the American Dental Association reports that only 12% of American floss daily. Contrast this will another health behavior. Over the past 30 years, the U.S. market share of world pharmaceutical consumption has increased from 20% to 50%. A significant portion of this increased consumption is non-essential drug use. One could use observations about drug consumption and the use of dental floss to conclude that pharmaceutical manufacturers are much better marketers than dental hygiene product manufactures. Alternatively, one could conclude that marketers are generally effective and that there must be something about how beliefs are organized or supported that creates differences in the utility for these two types of behavior.

There are two potential solutions to this problem of belief–behavior inconsistency. First it may be that consumption beliefs have to be supported by the appropriate foundational beliefs or values in order for utility to accrue from an experience. For example, Western cultures believe that man can control nature, that science can solve problems, and that life is sacred. Given these core beliefs, the promise of a pill is more believable and valuable than the promise of a piece of waxed string. Second, the narratives that accompany or organize beliefs lead to utility (Thompson and Haytko 1997; Thompson and Troester 2002). Certainly, the magic potion narrative associated with pill popping is more valuable than the manual labor narrative associated with plaque removal. This view of how belief structures contribute to utility lends itself to an interdisciplinary research effort. Relevant research questions include:

1. First, is there an optimal procedure for communicating information to consumers so that beliefs are perceived as consistent with an existing consumption utility narrative? Alternatively, why do certain people resist adopting certain beliefs about consumption experiences? In other words, to what extent do the characteristics of an existing utility narrative, the characteristics of proposed beliefs, or a combination of the two contribute to the formation of a belief structure that supports the creation of utility in a consumption experience?
2. Second, if consumption utility narratives are organizational schemes that structure beliefs and determine their influence on consumption utility, then there must be a process by which these narratives are adopted, used, and updated. I say this because narratives are largely culturally determined. We need research that identifies how a specific consumption utility narrative is chosen for a particular situation and the extent to which the narrative or the accompanying beliefs are updated as a consequence of the experience. Insight into this issue will help us understand the intensity, frequency, and persistence of consuming specific types of products.
3. Third, how are consumption utility narratives diffused (e.g., Sirsi, Ward, and Reingen 1995)? One possibility is that narrative acceptance happens in accordance with economic market principles (Glaeser 2004; 2005). If this is so, three conditions should support acceptance of the consumption utility narrative. First, business or government must be able to extract value when consumers accept a consumption narrative. This encourages a supply of narratives that can be "marketed" to the public. Second, the consumer must experience value from adopting the narrative. Third, there must be limited negative personal consequences to adopting the narrative. In effect, this third condition limits the cost of adoption for the individual. If these conditions are met, businesses can peddle consumption utility narratives, consumers can adopt them, and social networks can reinforce them (e.g., Moore, Wilkie, and Lutz 2002).

Thus far, I have treated consumption utility narratives and their accompanying belief systems as a frame that influences the utility derived from a product acquisition or consumption experience. This is an appropriate framework given our field's focus on consumerism. Yet, my remarks would not be complete if we did not consider two other major sources of utility: thought and social interaction (Ariely and Norton 2009). Thought clearly creates utility (e.g., Zauberman, Ratner, and Kim 2009). One simply has to think of one's parents, spouse, or children to appreciate the power of thought. Relationships also have utility (Saffer 2008). We would not interact with others if there was no utility associated with the experience. What intrigues me is how consumers coordinate thought utility and social interaction utility with utility from consumption. If thought itself can generate utility, why do we acquire and consume so many products? And if John Lennon was right, isn't the world filled with enough love to put some limits on excessive consumption?

Insight into how consumers might coordinate alternative sources of utility over time may be traced to the relative availability of utility producing narratives. The truth is that consumption utility narratives are much more available than narratives that allow us to derive utility from interpersonal interaction or thought (e.g., anticipation, recollection, creative ideas, etc.). To appreciate this fact, consider the consumption maturation of most children (cf. Chaplin and Roedder John 2007). Babies derive the most utility from interactions with their family. Toddlers derive utility from play and the thoughts that accompany it. Yet, as children maturate, consumption utility narratives are learned and practiced. Growing up in Western culture teaches children many more consumption utility narratives than interpersonal interaction or thought utility narratives. Moreover, advertising and culture makes the consumption utility narratives much more salient than the competing narratives. Thus, altering the way humans consume the earth will never be accomplished by telling people to conserve, to be less superficial, or to live within their means. Instead, the mix of narratives must be changed. Someone has to market interpersonal interaction or thought narratives that can generate utility. Unfortunately, this is not something that capitalist cultures have been designed to do.

In the end, maybe insight can be gained by understanding how to increase the utility associated with any one narrative or how to create variations of interpersonal or thought utility narratives so that they can become more prevalent. Alternatively, we need to understand how to squeeze more utility out of an experience, or to create more utility experiences, per unit of consumption. Increasing the amount of utility derived from savoring, remembering, and interacting should allow people to live more satisfying lives. Of course, understanding how people coordinate these experiences, adapt to these experiences, and come to appreciate new experiences is one of the great mysteries of consumption (Hsee et al. 2009; Wilson and Gilbert 2008).

CONCLUSION

In summary, I have tried to make the case that we have a competitive advantage when it comes to the study of consumer experience. I expect we have competitive advantages in other substantive domains as well. I hope you will consider a research strategy that focuses on developing theory in these areas. Who knows, this research strategy might help you become famous.

REFERENCES

Allen, Douglas E. (2002), "Toward a Theory of Consumer Choice as Sociohistorically Shaped Practical Experience: The Fits-Like-A-Glove (FLAG) Framework," *Journal of Consumer Research*, 28 (March), 157-179

Anderson, Rolph E. (1973), "Consumer Dissatisfaction: The Effect of Disconfirmed Expectancy on Perceived Product Performance," *Journal of Marketing Research*, 10 (February), 38-44.

Andrade, Eduardo B. and Joel B. Cohen (2007), "On the Consumption of Negative Feelings," *Journal of Consumer Research*, 34 (October), 283-300.

Ariely, Dan and Michael I. Norton (2009), "Conceptual Consumption," *Annual Review of Psychology*, 60, 475-499.

Arnould, Eric J and Linda L. Price (1993), "River Magic: Extraordinary Experience and the Extended Service Encounter," *Journal of Consumer Research*, 20 (June), 24-45.

Arnould, Eric J. and Craig J. Thompson (2005), "Consumer Culture Theory (CCT): Twenty Years of Research," *Journal of Consumer Research*, 31 (March), 868-882.

Brown, Steven P. and Douglas M. Stayman (1992), "Antecedents and Consequences of Attitude toward the Ad: A Meta-analysis," *Journal of Consumer Research*, 19 (June), 34-51.

Calder, Bobby J. and Brian Sternthal (1980), "Television Commercial Wearout: An Information Processing View," *Journal of Marketing Research*, 17 (May), 173-186.

Celsi, Richard L., Randall L. Rose, and Thomas W. Leigh (1993), "An Exploration of High-risk Leisure Consumption through Skydiving," *Journal of Consumer Research*, 20 (June), 1-23.

Chang, Hannah H. and Michel Tuan Pham (2009), "Differential Reliance on Feelings in the Present vs. the Future (or Past): Affect as a Decision Making System of the Present," working paper, Columbia University.

Chaplin, Lan Nguyen and Deborah Roedder John (2007), "Growing Up in a Material World: Age Differences in Materialism in Children and Adolescents," *Journal of Consumer Research*, 34 (December), 480-493.

Chen, Yu (2009), "Possession and Access: Consumer Desires and Value Perceptions Regarding Contemporary Art Collection and Exhibit Visits," *Journal of Consumer Research*, 35 (April), 925-940.

Ding, Min, Jehoshua Eliashberg, Joel Huber, and Ritesh Saini (2005), " Emotional Bidders—An Analytical and Experimental Examination of Consumers' Behavior in a Priceline-Like Reverse Auction," *Management Science*, 51 (March), 352-364.

Elder, Ryan and Aradhna Krishna (2009), "The Effect of Advertising Copy on Sensory Stimulation and Perceived Taste," *Advances in Consumer Research*, 36, ed. Ann L. McGill and Sharon Shavitt, San Francisco, 127-128.

Fournier, Susan (1998), "Consumers and Their Brands: Developing Relationship Theory in Consumer Research," *Journal of Consumer Research*, 24 (March), 343-373.

Fournier, Susan and David Glen Mick (1999), "Rediscovering Satisfaction," *Journal of Marketing*, 63 (October), 5-23.

Glaeser, Edward L. (2004), "Psychology and the Market," *American Economic Review Papers and Proceedings*, 94 (2), 408-413.

Glaeser, Edward L. (2005), "The Political Economy of Hatred," *Quarterly Journal of Economics*, 120 (February), 45-86.

Hirschman, Elizabeth C. and Morris B. Holbrook (1982), "Hedonic Consumption: Emerging Concepts, Methods and Propositions," *Journal of Marketing*, 46 (Summer), 92-101.

Hoegg, JoAndrea and Joseph W. Alba (2007), "Taste Perception: More (and Less) than Meets the Tongue," *Journal of Consumer Research*, 33 (March), 490-498.

Holbrook, Morris B. and Elizabeth C. Hirschman (1982), "The Experiential Aspects of Consumption: Consumer Fantasies, Feelings, and Fun," *Journal of Consumer Research*, 9 (September), 132-140.

Holt, Douglas B. (1995) "How Consumers Consume: A Typology of Consumption Practices," *Journal of Consumer Research*, 22 (June), 1-16.

Hsee, Chris K and Claire I. Tsai (2008), "Hedonomics in Consumer Choice," in *Handbook of Consumer Psychology*, eds. Curtis P. Haugtvedt, Paul M. Herr, and Frank R. Kardes, New York: Lawrence Erlbaum Associates, 639-657.

Hsee, Chris K., Yang Yang, Naihe Li, and Luxi Shen (2009), "Wealth, Warmth and Wellbeing: Whether Happiness is Relative or Absolute Depends on whether it is about Money, Acquisition, or Consumption," *Journal of Marketing Research*, 46 (June), 396-409.

Ivanic, Aarti and Joseph C. Nunes (2009), "The Intrinsic Benefits of Status," working paper, University of Southern California.

John, Deborah Roedder (1999), "Consumer Socialization of Children: A Retrospective Look at Twenty-Five Years of Research," *Journal of Consumer Research*, Vol. 26, (December), 183-213.

Joy, Annamma; Sherry, John F. Jr. (2003), "Speaking of Art as Embodied Imagination: A Multisensory Approach to Understanding Aesthetic Experience," *Journal of Consumer Research*, 30 (September), 259-282.

Lutz, Richard J. (1985), "Affective and Cognitive Antecedents of Attitude toward the Ad: A Conceptual Framework." in *Psychological Processes and Advertising Effects: Theory, Research and Application*, ed. Linda Alwitt and Andrew Mitchell, Hillsdale. NJ: Lawrence Erlbaum Associates, 45-65.

MacKenzie, Scott B. and Richard J. Lutz (1989), "An Empirical Examination of the Structural Antecedents of Attitude toward the Ad in an Advertising Pretesting Context," *Journal of Marketing*, 53 (April), 48-65.

MacKenzie, Scott B.; Lutz, Richard J.; Belch, George E. (1986), "The Role of Attitude Toward the Ad as a Mediator of Advertising Effectiveness: A Test of Competing Explanations," *Journal of Marketing Research*, 23 (May), 130-143.

Madden, Thomas J., Chris T. Allen, Jacquelyn L. Twible (1988), "Attitude toward the Ad: An Assessment of Diverse Measurement Indices under Different Processing 'Sets,'" *Journal of Marketing Research*, 25 (August), 242-252.

Mitchell, Andrew A. and Jerry C. Olson (1981), "Are Product Attribute Beliefs the Only Mediator of Advertising Effects on Brand Attitude?" *Journal of Marketing Research*, 18 (August), 318-332.

Moore, Danny L. and J. Wesley Hutchinson (1983), "The Effects of Ad Affect on Advertising Effectiveness," in *Advances in Consumer Research, Vol. 10*, ed. Richard Bagozzi and Alice Tybout, San Francisco: Association for Consumer Research, 526-531.

Moore, Elizabeth S., William L. Wilkie, and Richard J. Lutz (2002), "Passing the Torch: Intergenerational Influences as a Source of Brand Equity," *Journal of Marketing*, 66 (April), 17-37.

Nelson, Leif and Tom Meyvis (2008), "Interrupted Consumption: Disrupting Adaptation to Hedonic Experiences," *Journal of Marketing Research*, 45 (December), 654-664.

Oliver, Richard L. (1980), "A Cognitive Model of the Antecedents and Consequences of Satisfaction Decisions," *Journal of Marketing Research*, 17 (November), 460-469.

Olshavsky, Richard W. and John A. Miller (1972), "Consumer Expectations, Product Performance, and Perceived Product Quality," *Journal of Marketing Research*, 9 (February), 19-21.

Ordabayeva, Nailya and Pierre Chandon (2008), "Leapfrogging over the Joneses: Effects of Inequality on Conspicuous and Inconspicuous Consumption," working paper, INSEAD.

Peck, Joann and Jennifer Wiggins (2006), "It Just Feels Good: Customers' Affective Response to Touch and Its Influence on Persuasion," *Journal of Marketing*, 70 (October), 56-69.

Pfaff, Anita B. (1972), "An Index of Consumer Satisfaction," *Proceedings. Third Annual Conference, Association for Consumer Research*, ed. M. Venkatesan, 713–737.

Ramanathan, Suresh and Patti Williams (2007), "Immediate and Delayed Emotional Consequences of Indulgence: The Moderating Influence of Personality Type on Mixed Emotions," *Journal of Consumer Research*, 34 (August), 212-223.

Ratner, Rebecca K., Barbara E. Kahn, and Daniel Kahneman (1999), "Choosing Less-preferred Experiences for the Sake of Variety," *Journal of Consumer Research*, 26 (June), 1-15.

Rose, Randall L. and Stacy L. Wood (2005), "Paradox and the Consumption of Authenticity through Reality Television," *Journal of Consumer Research*, 32 (September), 284-296.

Saffer, Henry (2008), "The Demand for Social Interaction," *The Journal of Socio-Economics*, 37 (June), 1047-1060.

Shimp, Terence (1981), "Attitude toward the Ad as a Mediator of Consumer Brand Choice," *Journal of Advertising*, 10 (2), 9-15.

Shimp, Terence A. and J. Thomas Yokum, "Advertising Inputs and Psychophysical Judgments in Vending Machine Retailing," *Journal of Retailing*, 58 (Spring), 95-113.

Silk, Alvin J. and Terry G. Vavra (1974), "The Influences of Advertising's Affective Qualities on Consumer Response," *Buyer/Consumer Information Processing*, ed. G. David Hughes and Michael L. Ray, Chapel Hill: University of North Carolina Press, 157-186.

Sirsi, Ajay K., James C. Ward, and Peter H. Reingen (1995), "Microcultural Analysis of Variation in Sharing of Causal Reasoning about Behavior," *Journal of Consumer Research*, 22 (March), 345-372.

Thompson, Craig J. and Diana L. Haytko (1997), "Speaking of Fashion: Consumers' Use of Fashion Discourse and the Appropriation of Countervailing Cultural Meanings," *Journal of Consumer Research*, 24 (June), 15-42.

Thompson, Craig J. and Maura Troester (2002), "Consumer Value Systems in the Age of Postmodern Fragmentation: The Case of the Natural Health Microculture," *Journal of Consumer Research*, 28 (March), 550-571.

Verhoef, Peter C., Katherine N. Lemon, A. Parasuraman, Michael Tsiros, Leonard A. Schlesinger, and Anne Roggeveen (2009), "Customer Experience Creation: Determinants, Dynamics and Management Strategies," *Journal of Retailing*, 85 (March), 31-41.

Veryzer, Robert W. and J. Wesley Hutchinson (1998), "The Influence of Unity and Prototypicality on Aesthetic Responses to New Product Designs," *Journal of Consumer Research*, 24 (March), 374-394.

von Neumann, John and Oskar Morgenstern (1944), *Theory of Games and Economic Behavior*. Princeton University Press, Princeton.

Wilson, Timothy D. and Daniel T. Gilbert (2008), "Explaining Away: A Model of Affective Adaptation," *Perspectives on Psychological Science*, 3 (September), 370-386.

Wood, Natalie, Lan Nguyen Chaplin, and Michael Solomon (2009), "Virtually Me: Youth Consumers and Their Online Identities," *Advances in Consumer Research*, 36, ed. Ann L. McGill and Sharon Shavitt, San Francisco 23-25.

Zauberman, Gal, Rebecca K. Ratner, and B. Kyu Kim, (2009), "Memories as Assets: Strategic Memory Protection in Choice over Time," *Journal of Consumer Research*, 35 (February), 715-728.

Special Session Summary

Planning to Save Money Seems to be a Good Thing: But is it Always?

Julia Belyavsky Bayuk, University of Delaware, USA

EXTENDED ABSTRACTS

"Framing Goals to Increase or Decrease Personal Savings: The Effect of Specific Goals and Construal Level"

Amar Cheema, University of Virginia, USA
Gülden Ülkümen, University of Southern California, USA

Although the importance of saving is indisputable, left to themselves, consumers don't save enough (e.g., Shefrin and Thaler 1988). Therefore, consumers are prone to deviate from their optimal saving levels. Thaler and Bernartzi (2004) suggest that these deviations may be due to errors in calculation or due to lapses in self-control, and consumers could benefit from mechanisms that help overcome these deviations.

Is it possible to influence consumers' saving behavior simply by changing the way they think about their savings? In the present research, we explore whether and how goal framing influences saving success. Imagine a consumer who wants to save money for an upcoming trip. There are several different ways to think about this saving goal. For example, when thinking about how much to save, consumers can be more or less specific. Consumers can decide to save some money without specifying an amount (e.g., "I need to save as much as I can"), therefore setting a non-specific goal. Alternatively, consumers can choose to specify the amount they need to save (e.g., "I need to save $500"), thereby setting a specific goal. A second factor that influences how a consumers think about saving goals is the level at which this goal is represented. In particular, consumers can either focus on why to save (high level construal), or how to save (low level construal; Trope and Liberman 2003).

We study the how these two factors, namely, goal specificity, and the level of construal together influence several saving-related outcomes, such as anticipated success, commitment, and most importantly, goal achievement. We examine the conditions under which specific (vs. non specific goals) goals facilitate and impede goal attainment, by exploring how the effect of specificity varies across low versus high levels of construal (Vallacher and Wegner 1987).

The Effects of Goal Specificity

Previous literature has conflicting findings on the effectiveness of goal specificity. Numerous studies demonstrate the beneficial effects of goal specificity. For example, specific (vs. non-specific) goals increase goal commitment, are associated with lower performance variability, allow children to better resist temptation, and can increase persistence (e.g., Wright and Kacmar 1994).

In contrast, some literature suggests that goal specificity can have detrimental effects on goal pursuit. Kirschenbaum, Humphrey, and Malett (1981) find that people perform better with less (vs. more) specific goals, and speculate that specific goals may lead to "disengagement in self-regulation when the task at hand is difficult or perceived as difficult." These results suggest that specific goals may be more discouraging than non-specific goals in some instances.

Moderating Role of Construal Level

According to the theory of action identification (Vallacher and Wegner 1987), construing a goal-directed action at a high level allows attention to be focused on why the goal is important. In contrast, when the same action is construed at a low level, a consumer focuses more on how to do a task (Trope and Liberman 2003).

We propose that construal level influences how consumers interpret the meaning of the specificity of a saving goal. Since at high level of construal the individual is focused on why a goal is important, specificity of a saving goal can be interpreted as a signal of its importance. Consequently, among high-level construers, specific (vs. non-specific) goals may engender greater anticipation of success, commitment, and lead to higher amount of savings. In contrast, specific goals may be perceived as more difficult when the act is construed at a low level. As low-level construers are focused more on how to achieve a goal, specific (vs. non-specific) goals may appear rigid and discouraging, leading to lower commitment and disengagement, and consequently, lower amount of actual savings.

Overview of Results

Across four studies, to manipulate goal specificity we first ask participants to consider a saving occasion, and then to either indicate the dollar amount they would like to save for this occasion (specific), or we don't prompt them to specify the amount (non-specific). We either manipulate construal level via elaboration instructions (studies 1 and 2), or we measure chronic individual differences in construal (studies 3 and 4).

In study 1 we find that consumers who specify how much to save (vs. those who do not specify an amount) anticipate higher saving success if they construe this saving goal at a high level. In contrast, consumers who do not specify an amount anticipate higher success (vs. those who specify how much to save) if the saving goal is construed at a low level. Illustrating the process, study 2 reveals that high-level construers (who focus on why to save) perceive specific goals to be more important than non-specific goals, and therefore anticipate higher success. In contrast, low-level construers (who focus on how to save) perceive specific goals to be more difficult than non-specific goals, and therefore anticipate lower success. Moreover, we find that the level at which a saving goal is construed, and its specificity influence not only anticipated success, but also goal commitment, and actual success in saving. Study 3 demonstrates that anticipated success mediates the effect of specificity and construal level on goal-commitment. Importantly, study 4 explores extend these findings to actual savings, by examining consumers' actual savings over one month. Chronic high (low) level construers save more when they have specific (non-specific) goals.

References

Kirschenbaum, Daniel S., Laura L. Humphrey, and Sheldon D. Malett (1981), "Specificity of Planning in Adult Self-control: An Applied Investigation," *Journal of Personality and Social Psychology*, 40, 941-950.

Shefrin, Hersh M. and Richard H. Thaler (1988), "The Behavioral Life-Cycle Hypothesis," *Economic Inquiry*, 26 (Oct), 609-643.

Thaler, Richard H. and Shlomo Benartzi (2004), "Save More Tomorrow(TM): Using Behavioral Economics to Increase Employee Saving," *The Journal of Political Economy*, 112 (1), 164-88.

Trope, Yaacov and Nira Liberman (2003), "Temporal Construal," *Psychological Review*, 110, 403-421.

Vallacher, Robin R. and Daniel Wegner (1987), "What Do People Think They're Doing? Action Identification and Human Behavior," *Psychological Review*, 94, 3-15.

Wright, Patrick M., and K. Michele Kacmar (1994), "Goal Specificity as a Determinant of Goal Commitment and Goal Change," *Organizational Behavior and Human Decision Processes*, 59, 242-260.

"Letting Good Opportunities Pass Us By: Examining the Role of Mindset during Goal Pursuit"

Julia Belyavsky Bayuk, University of Delaware, USA
Chris Janiszewski, University of Florida, USA
Robyn LeBoeuf, University of Florida, USA

Consider the following scenario: your bank account is quickly approaching empty, and you acknowledge that dining out at restaurants, especially upscale ones, adds up quickly. Thus, you create a plan to increase your savings account that involves dining out less at restaurants and cooking more at home. You follow this plan religiously. Now imagine that the price of gas has skyrocketed, so carpooling to work and combining errands might also help you save a lot of money. How will the fact that you already have a plan to save money influence your propensity to adjust your lifestyle to drive less? In comparison to someone who has not yet formed a money-saving plan, are you more or less likely to take advantage of the public transportation and carpool options?

Although planning, or forming an implementation intention, is generally thought to promote goal achievement (Gollwitzer 1999), it is not yet known how forming an implementation intention (e.g., dining out less) might alter a consumer's evaluation of goal consistent, out-of-plan behaviors (e.g., driving less). On the one hand, an implementation intention makes a goal more salient (Gollwitzer 1999). Salient goals are more likely to be pursued (Bargh et al. 2001), and means associated with these goals are more likely to be valued (Chartrand et al. 2008). Thus, implementation intentions could enhance the value of all means (in- or out-of-plan) that are relevant to goal pursuit. On the other hand, an implementation intention involves mentally simulating the steps that must be taken to achieve a goal (Gollwitzer 1993, 1996, 1999). Specifying when, where, and how one will achieve a goal creates a readiness to respond to specific behavioral opportunities (Gollwitzer 1999). Yet, this readiness to respond to specific behavioral opportunities may encourage a narrow-mindedness that leads to a devaluation of out-of-plan opportunities to achieve a goal. Thus, there is reason to think that implementation intentions may increase or decrease the evaluation of goal consistent, out-of-plan behaviors.

We show that the influence of an implementation intention is moderated by the concreteness/abstractness of thought at the time a person evaluates goal consistent, out-of-plan behaviors. If a person is likely to be thinking concretely when exposed to goal-consistent, out-of-plan behaviors, then the person should not be encouraged to form an implementation intention: Forming an implementation intention will encourage the person to develop a specific plan, and a concrete mindset will reinforce thinking at a specific level. Thus, a concrete mindset following the formation of an implementation intention seems to simply reinforce commitment to a specific means, making goal consistent, out-of-plan behaviors seem less valuable. If, however, a person is likely to be thinking abstractly when exposed to goal-consistent, out-of-plan behaviors, then an implementation intention should be encouraged: Forming an implementation intention encourages a person to develop a specific plan, but an abstract mindset refocuses thinking at the goal level, as opposed to the plan level. Thus, an abstract mindset following the formation of an implementation intention should reinforce commitment to the goal, making goal consistent, out-of-plan behaviors seem more valuable.

These hypotheses are investigated in a set of four studies using the important consumer goal of saving money. Study 1 investigates the influence of forming an implementation intention to save money on a consumer's willingness to resist an impulse purchase when in a concrete or abstract mindset. Studies 2a and 2b investigate the influence of forming an implementation intention on a consumer's willingness to take advantage of a wide variety of money-saving opportunities when in a concrete or abstract mindset. Study 3 extends this research by altering the time frame in which money-saving, out-of-plan behaviors can be pursued, using the insight that people will think more concretely (abstractly) when contemplating events that are in the near future (distant future) (e.g., Trope and Liberman 2000). Study 4 further extends this research by encouraging a prevention focus (i.e., a concrete mindset) or promotion focus (i.e., an abstract mindset) while people assess the appeal of money-saving, out-of-plan behaviors. Combined, these studies show that forming an implementation intention can have detrimental consequences for taking advantage of out-of-plan opportunities and for goal achievement if individuals consider these opportunities while in a concrete mindset.

To conclude, although implementation intentions are generally thought to be beneficial, we show that forming an implementation intention can lead individuals to be less likely to take advantage of goal-consistent, out-of-plan opportunities. These results suggest that even when a goal such as saving money is extremely important, as it is in today's economy, specifying a plan to achieve it can negatively affect open-mindedness to consider goal-consistent out-of-plan means, and thus, can negatively affect goal achievement.

References

Bargh, John A., Peter M. Gollwitzer, Annette Lee-Chai, Kimberly Barndollar, and Roman Troetschel (2001), "The Automated Will: Nonconscious Activation and Pursuit of Behavioral Goals," *Journal of Personality and Social Psychology*, 81 (December), 1014–27.

Chartrand, Tanya L., Joel Huber, Baba Shiv, and Robin J. Tanner, R. (2008), "Nonconscious Goals and Consumer Choice," *Journal of Consumer Research*, 35 (August), 189–201.

Gollwitzer, Peter M. (1993), "Goal Achievement: The Role of Intentions," *European Review of Social Psychology*, 4 (January), 141–185.

______ (1999), "Implementation Intentions: Strong Effects of Simple Plans," *American Psychologist*, 54 (July), 493–503.

Trope, Yaacov and Nira Liberman (2000), "Temporal Construal and Time-Dependent Changes in Preference," *Journal of Personality and Social Psychology,* 79 (December), 876–889.

"When Seeing is Believing: Visualization Effects on Regulating Savings Behavior"

Eunice Kim, Yale University, USA
Ravi Dhar, Yale University, USA

A major challenge facing many American households is how to save and plan for the future. Many people express the desire to save but find that they lack the needed self-control. Not surprisingly, the question of how to encourage consumers to exercise self-control and save for the future is an important one from both a theoretical and real-world perspective. Thus, one key to increasing savings may be in addressing the psychological variables that might make it easier to self-regulate behaviors for future outcomes and benefits.

Prior research has focused mainly on showing how visualizing the pursuit of a goal (e.g. goal to study for an exam) or engaging in a specific goal-related behavior (e.g. going to the library) can increase the performance of that behavior and the eventual successful attainment of goals (Bator and Bryan 2008; Gregory et al. 1982). While visualization in prior research has been limited to circumstances in which individuals are visualizing the specific steps needed to reach a particular goal, our research examines how the simple task of visualizing the performance of everyday activities at an old age in the future, unrelated to the specific goal, can lead to the attainment of that same goal. We propose that the mere visualization of the self at an old age in the future can increase self-regulation and help individuals save today.

We posit that those who visualize routine activities at an old age will demonstrate an increased willingness to save because they feel less anxiety and more peacefulness than when they do not. Zeelenberg and Pieters (2006) proposed that one of the primary motivators of goal-directed behavior is emotions. Prior research suggests that emotions such as anxiety and stress hinder goal pursuit (Pham and Taylor, 1999; Taylor and Schneider, 1989), whereas an increase in emotions of peacefulness, which is the opposite of anxiety, can encourage goal pursuit. Therefore, decreasing emotions related to anxiety and increasing emotions related to peacefulness will allow individuals to feel as though the pursuit of long-term goals, whose consequences are attained in the distant future, (e.g. savings) is manageable. It follows, then, that the extent to which these relevant emotions can be felt via visualization of the self at an old age, is the key driving factor in affecting savings attitudes and decisions today.

We further show that the effect of visualization of old age is not based solely on priming any goal related to age. We compare the effects of visualization with those due to the semantic priming of concepts related to the elderly. While semantic primes of the elderly activate stereotypical associations of the elderly (e.g. walking slower; Bargh, Chen and Burrows, 1996), they do not facilitate the experience of emotional states as visualization does. Thus, the semantic priming of old age will not have the same impact on savings when it is not accompanied by instructions to visualize the future. We test these hypotheses in a series of three experiments.

Study 1 shows that visualization of the self at an old age leads to greater self-regulation and motivation to engage in savings behavior as evidenced by increased importance of attitudes towards a savings goal. Participants in the visualization condition visualized themselves engaging in various activities such as attending a family reunion at the age of 70 and wrote a few sentences describing thoughts, feelings, and details of each scenario. Those in the control condition completed simple mathematical calculations whose answers were close to the number "70". Then all participants completed various measures indicating the importance of long-term financial planning and saving money for retirement. As predicted, participants who had visualized themselves at age 70 reported significantly greater importance of future financial planning than those in the control condition.

Study 2 extends the influence of visualization to behaviors that reflect an increase in self-regulation toward the pursuit of long-term goals, and further demonstrates that visualization results in greater self-regulation compared to the semantic priming of old age or the elderly. Participants first either visualized themselves at the age of 70 engaging in various scenarios as in Study 1, or were semantically primed with old age by answering questions such as "At what age does the average person retire?" or "Is someone who is 70, too old to be president of the US?" Then all participants were told to allocate $5,000 into either a checking account for immediate use, or a savings account for a future purchase. As predicted, participants who had visualized themselves at the age of 70 were more inclined to spend less now and put aside more money for future use compared to those primed with the concept of the elderly.

Study 3 tests the mechanism underlying the effect of visualization by demonstrating how visualization, compared to non-visualization, increases the desire to save because it not only decreases feelings of anxiety but also increases feelings of peacefulness. Participants first visualized themselves in everyday activities at an older age or at their current age. Then, in what they believed to a separate and unrelated task, they reported their attitudes regarding savings for the future, as well as various emotions that they were feeling at the time. Consistent with our hypothesis, participants visualizing themselves at an older age were more likely to report having a greater desire to save than those visualizing themselves at their current age. Furthermore, a mediation analysis indicated that an increase in feelings of peacefulness and a decrease in feelings of anxiety mediated the effects of visualization of the self at an old age on savings attitudes.

These findings contribute to the existing literature on visualization by demonstrating that merely visualizing about engaging in non-goal activities at an old age can increase the motivation for long-term goals with distant future consequences, such as saving. Furthermore, the visualization of everyday activities can be a more effective means of encouraging goal pursuit because this occurs naturally without external prompting.

References

Bargh, John A., Mark Chen, and Lara Burrows (1996), "Automaticity of social behavior: Direct effects of trait construct and stereotype activation on action," *Journal of Personality and Social Psychology*, 71, 230-244.

Bator, Renee J. and Angela Bryan (2008), "Increasing the motivation to practice safer sex through imagery," *Social Influence*, 3, 154-170.

Gregory, W. Larry, Robert B. Cialdini, and Kathleen M. Carpenter (1982), "Self-relevant scenarios as mediators of likelihood estimates and compliance: Does imagining make it so?" *Journal of Personality and Social Psychology*, 43, 89-99.

Pham, Lien B. and Shelley E. Taylor (1999), "From thought to action: Effects of process- versus outcome-based mental simulation on performance," *Personality and Social Psychology Bulletin*, 25, 250-260.

Taylor, Shelley E. and Sherry K. Schneider (1989), "Coping and the simulation of events," *Social Cognition*, 7, 174-194.

Zeelenberg, Marcel and Rik Pieters (2006), "Feeling is for doing: A pragmatic approach to the study of emotions in economic behavior," in *Social Psychology and Economics*, D. De Cremer, M. Zeelenberg & K. Murnighan, eds. Mahwah, NJ: Erlbaum, 117-137.

Special Session Summary

We Are Not All the Same: New Issues, Confluence, and Divergence in Consumer Acculturation Studies

Søren Askegaard, University of Southern Denmark, Odense, Denmark

SESSION OVERVIEW

The theme of this year's ACR conference is "A World of Knowledge At the Point of Confluence." In congruence with this theme, this session explores various angles of consumer acculturation as they relate to their heterogeneous identity constructs. Identity is seen as a confluence of cultural, social, temporal and contextual influences. The social and cultural aspects of consumption and consumption's relation to identity construction have been well documented in consumer culture theory (Arnould and Thompson, 2005). What has not been sufficiently considered so far was their relation to consumer acculturation of immigrants in combination with other variables, such as gender, temporal evolution, in-group differences or generational factors. In this session, we focus on the mechanisms with which these factors operate in the formation of identity for immigrants and their descendants. The four presentations together attempt to explore the immigrant consumer acculturation and examine it in contexts and from perspectives that have been understudied.

The first paper examines the relationship between the immigrant women's gender roles and the power discourse in the society. Romanian female immigrants in Italy were interviewed and observed in relation to their food consumption practices. The researchers identify two identity positionings of these female migrants that correspond to two spatial contexts and temporal reference points. They identify four contextual situations that imply different power relations that move between a traditional woman and a modern one. The second paper also takes Italy as the context of study and questions the application of the interpretative model of cultural adaptation—originally elaborated for first generations—to the children of migrants (Portes 1996, p. x). The author discusses the different levels of cultural consciousness that second generations show according to ethnic, local and global consumption, and describes four ways to deploy such consumption to navigate the borders between families and the group of peers. In the next presentation, Peñaloza elaborates additional differences between first generation immigrants and their descendants, documenting changes in consumers' identity over time. Based on oral history interviews with a heterogeneous group of Mexican Americans, her cultural genealogy dissects these identity inflections across a realm of social situations and market conditions. The final paper combines the themes of immigrant consumer acculturation, temporal changes, consumption differences within an immigrant community in relation to identity positionings from the previous papers and analyzes a group of immigrants' changing consumption practices in an attempt to differentiate themselves from the rest of the immigrant community and integrate into the host society. Turkish immigrants in Denmark are chosen as the context of the study.

All the session papers are completed projects and combined offer differing theoretical perspectives. Methodologically, they all adhere to the interpretivist approach and provide empirical knowledge based on ethnographic data. This session thus provides a platform for scholars who are interested in different aspects of immigrant consumer research and would like to familiarize themselves with the latest theory and empirical work in the field.

EXTENDED ABSTRACTS

"She, Who Has the Spoon, Has the Power: Immigrant Women's Use of Food to Negotiate Power Relations"

Zuzana Chytkova, University of Pisa, Italy
Nil Özçaglar-Toulouse, Université de Lille 2, France

Immigration has been in the centre of scholarly attention for some time now and several studies have investigated consumer acculturation of immigrants. Recently, in the consumer culture tradition (Arnould and Thompson, 2005), the postassimilationist theory has made an important contribution to our understanding of immigrants' use of marketplace in their movement between home, host and transnational consumer culture (Askegaard et al., 2005). However, it does not consider the effect of hegemonic discourses in the home and host society, as well as the singular power relations the immigrants encounter in their everyday experience. Yet, these elements also play a significant role in their use of marketplace offerings in the everyday pursuit of a satisfying identity. The focus of this research is the intersection of these areas, a lens that would see consumer acculturation as a network of power relations in the immigrants' lived experience. In accordance with the goal of the research, we concentrate on gender roles as a part of a power discourse in society. This is particularly apparent in societies based on patriarchal values. The women migrating from such a society had been socialized to a traditional gender role. Upon their arrival to the country of destination, they are faced with another concept of womanhood, which, in the case of immigration to an "advanced capitalist country" (Holt, 1997) is based on the host society's construction of gender roles, but also on the transnational "modern woman" discourse featured in the marketplace as the desirable ideal of womanhood. We argue that such power relations can be studied through the analysis of female immigrants' everyday food consumption choices. Food is known to act as a key element in power relations (Lupton, 1996) and the responsible for food preparation are usually women. Women also tend to figure more clearly as the dominated part in heterogeneous power relations.

Fourteen in-depth interviews (from one and a half to three and a half hours) have been carried out with Romanian women in Italy by the first author. These interviews have been complemented by observation at multiple sites of community gathering, such as parks, the Romanian Adventist Church and the Romanian Orthodox Church in Florence, which were either video registered or written up in field notes. The field work also comprised four cooking sessions with the respondents, all video registered. The interviews were integrally transcribed. We analyzed the interviews by alternating between the specific case of each interview and the interviews taken as a whole, and by making use of observation and literature.

The analysis reveals two distinct discourses corresponding to the two spatial and temporal references of the migration experience: the country of origin and of destination and the temporal setting before and after emigration. Such discourses emerged from the respondents' narratives of migration, which presented a common structure: the emergency situation (economical crisis or the experience of the unknown upon arrival) felt as disempowering, is solved with great efforts and suffering resulting in an inner peace of the respondent, enlightened state of mind and sense of power achieved through the suffering/self-transformation. The narrative involves general understanding of womanhood in the culture of origin, which is based on a hegemonic patriarchal discourse of the traditional woman's role. This results in a disempowering relationship network and the consequent loss of the women's control over their bodies and lives. The central host culture discourse is that of a modern woman, mostly based on a marketplace myth and its liberatory power (Firat and Venkatesh, 1995), within a frame of which the woman is depicted as independent, powerful, seizing-the-day. This discourse allows the women to resist their ascribed identity as a traditional woman, providing them with concepts to redefine their understanding of womanhood and to regain the control over their body and life.

These two discourses on womanhood point out the two extreme positions in the power relations of an immigrant's everyday life. However the resistant acts are performed within heterogeneous power relations that situate the women at neither of the two extremes. The resistance must be played out in accordance with the various contextual relations that exist alongside a continuum between the two extreme situations, each one of them implying a different structure of power between its actors.

In the proposed model, four contextual situations implying different power relations were identified. Such contexts move along the imagined line of control over the self, that we call "regime of control" to illustrate its different structure in the relationship. On the one extreme of the continuum, we collocate situations, in which the actor is in relative control over his/her self. Such situations imply a relative autonomy in the decisions regarding one's body and life, including those concerning food choices. The contexts positioned on the opposite extreme are characterized by the presence of hegemonic discourses defining the role ascribed to the actor, and implicitly shaping his/her decisions concerning his/her body and life, including the food consumption decisions. The movement between these contextual situations implies a movement closer to or further from the ideal of modern or traditional woman, as well as closer or further from the symbols of these two discourses: the ideal of fast, easy, light cuisine or time-consuming, heavy, and elaborated cuisine. The proposed model permits to uncover a layer in the understanding of immigrants' consumer behavior that has not yet been explored. It demonstrates that their food preferences are not based solely on their level of acculturation from one culture to another, but are also functional to the heterogeneous power relations formed in their everyday lives and vice versa that these power relations can be studied through the analysis of food practices.

"Cross Generation: Cultural (In)visibility in the Consumption of Second Generations"

Luca Massimiliano Visconti, Bocconi University, Italy

Defining the "children of migration" (Portes, 1996, p. x) is not easy task. Subjectively, second generations (2Gs, in short) are characterized by different strategies of self identification (Rumbault, 1997) and patterns of segmented assimilation that vary with personal and family conditions (Portes and Rumbaut, 2001). The arduousness of 2Gs' self definition is due to the inapplicability of the interpretative categories that first generations and others deploy to categorize them. On the one hand, human beings are prone to use the "linear bipolar model" of ethnic identity (Schaninger, Bourgeois, and Buss, 1985). The postulated zero sum game thus implies that what is gained in one culture is symmetrically lost in the rival one. On the other hand, the social context imposes ethnic categories from the outside instead of looking for more germane, subjective definitions of the self (the so-called self-designated ethnicity, Stayman and Deshpande, 1989). It is no wonder, that consumer identity projects of 2Gs reflect the complexity, the social and psychological pressures, and the variety of personal and shared narratives originated by the aforementioned scenario.

From an epistemological viewpoint, ethnic studies—both in their traditional and postassimilationist elaboration (Askegaard, Arnould and Kjeldgaard, 2005)—have grounded a model of cultural adaptation dealing with first generation immigrants (Berry 1980), yet it is not clear that this applies to 2Gs. The constructs of original and host culture are not strictly applicable to 2Gs and also modify according to the age of arrival in the host country (Rumbault, 1994). 2Gs are often grown up and identify with the culture of destination of their parents and mostly maintain an imagined connection with the culture of origin of the parents. Frequently, their ethnic culture becomes an ethnoscape constructed by the stereotypical social and market discourse about the origins incorporated in the dominating mediascape (Appadurai 1990, 9).

As such, the adaptation processes characterizing 2Gs not only include ethnic and local cultures—however defined—but also the global and transnational culture (Glick Schiller, Basch, and Szanton Blanc, 1992). In making daily reconnection between the local and the global, 2Gs break the boundaries of the national state, and thus constitute a transnational basis where multiple systems of meanings live together regardlessly of their territorial rooting.

The paper is based on a three year field investigation of the 2Gs residing in the North of Italy. Data include 412 questionnaires and 32 depth interviews run afterwards to better investigate 2Gs' symbolic consumption and religious ties. Questionnaire data were elaborated in terms of descriptive statistics for quantitative information and content analyzed for the qualitative answers. Depth-interviews were fully transcribed and analyzed according to the criteria of interpretative ethnography.

First, findings illustrate the different level of cultural (in)visibility (i.e., salience) in the consumption of 2Gs when moving back and forth ethnic and local consumption. 2Gs tend to alternate higher and lower levels of awareness about the cultural basis of their consumption. When consuming global (e.g., jeans, English music, etc.) or local (e.g., pasta, television, etc.) artifacts, these teens are less conscious about the cultural rooting of their consumption but easily acknowledge the cultural loading of ethnic consumptions. Four main explanations about the alternating level of cultural (in)visibility are offered: i) cultural embeddedness; ii) iterated ethnocentrism; iii) unquestioned dominating culture; and iv) cultural appropriability.

Second, when visible to the eyes of the consumer, cultural meanings embedded in consumer goods can be manipulated and deployed to "navigate the border crossings between household and societal contexts" (Lindridge, Hogg, and Shah, 2004, p. 211). Field investigation confirms the intentional, transactional, and dialogic use of 2Gs' consumption when facing the requirements expressed by family members and the group of peers. Further, four main uses of consumption for 2Gs are detailed: i) consumption as trade; ii) consumption as gift; iii) consumption as opposition; and, iv) consumption as mediation.

By questioning the applicability of the traditional models of cultural adaptation, the paper identifies local, ethnic, global and transnational culture impacting 2GS' identity structures. Findings unpack the motivations of cultural (in)visibility and show the use of consumption to cope with the double structural violence (Farmer, 2006) exerted by families and peers.

"Deciphering the Socio-Temporal Dimensions of Consumer Identity Development: A Cultural Genealogy"

Lisa Peñaloza, EDHEC Business School, France

Identity is one of the most basic constructs in consumer behavior. The existential question, "who one is" finds noteworthy expression in contemporary consumer behavior as a key domain of activity in which people continually reinscribe and constitute their identity in relation to others (Arnould and Thompson, 2005). Previous work has documented how persons alter their consumption to commune with particular groups (Deshpandé, Hoyer and Donthu, 1986) and diverge from them (Berger and Heath, 2007) in expressing important aspects of their identity. Notably, this previous work points to the importance of in-out group relations in consumption. Yet because it is based on rather static, snap shot glimpses, it leaves open a number of important questions such as the changing nature of identity over the course of consumers' lives, how identity is expressed in consumption in relation to others over time, and the long term impacts on identity of selectively displaying consumption in relation to majority/minority groups and of target marketing and segmenting efforts. Such socio-temporal dimensions of identity development are particularly important for immigrants (Oswald, 1999; Peñaloza, 1994; Visconti, 2006), ethnic minorities (Askegaard, Arnould, and Kjeldgaard, 2005) and migrants (Ustuner and Holt, 2007), although they are also relevant to the growing body of work on mainstream consumers (Burton, forthcoming; Peñaloza and Barnhart, 2009)

This research extends previous work on the sociology of consumption by adding temporality to the study of identity projects. Of particular interest is dissecting changes in consumers' identities over time, as impacted by minority and majority group relations and marketing practices targeting group members. The research design features oral history interviews with 15 Mexican Americans who vary by generation in the U.S., age, gender, social class, color, residential area, language, and political sentiments. Findings trace a cultural genealogy of consumption identity across first cultural experiences; identity terminology; day to day consumption of specific products/services/brands at home, work, in neighborhoods, stores, and tourist areas; leisure/holiday activity; language development and utilization; interactions with family and friends, both subcultural group members and members of other subcultural groups; thoughts and reactions to the segmenting and target marketing efforts of firms, community development concerns, and personal hopes and dreams. Analysis proceeds to identify economic, social, and cultural dimensions of capital (Bourdieu, 1984) in the genealogy and map disjunctions and overlaps between these various types of capital. These disjunctions and overlaps are useful in highlighting the dynamic and highly charged nature of in-out group relations and tracking their impacts on consumption and identity over time, as this cultural consumption genealogy focuses on the subcultural group rather than a specific brand (Holt, 2004). Specific changes over time feature the "hostile," "welcoming," and "neutral" zones where informants have been blocked by others in their expression of their culture or received neutral treatment versus those where they have nurtured their identity in consumption and interacted favorably with members of other cultural groups. Finally, I draw attention to the transformation of these various dimensions of capital from cultural to social and economic in making sense of observed changes in identity, consumption, social relations, and marketing activities over time. Notably, the negative stigma older informants experienced decreased over time, in contrast to the more positive valuation of younger informants. The more positive valuation of both cohorts corresponded temporally with the advent of cultural tourism in the area and the segmenting and target marketing efforts by firms. Yet despite some increasing power in the ownership, representation, and exchange of cultural artifacts, a paradoxical social valuation for their subculture is juxtaposed with the economic deterioration of their neighborhoods, pointing to important limitations of consumption in identity maintenance and negotiation of social relations, Theoretical contributions provide a more comprehensive, dynamic, and nuanced account of identity development that expands understandings of consumption as an important domain through which individuals and groups negotiate cultural difference over time and elaborates the social legitimizing role of market targeting.

"From Resistance to Integration: Changing Consumer Acculturation Practices of Immigrants"

Mine Üçok Hughes, Woodbury University, USA

Consumer acculturation and identity have been two of the most popular topics studied by immigrant consumer researchers. Berry (1980), a highly referenced source on the topic of acculturation, classifies the varieties of acculturation as assimilation, integration, rejection and deculturation. Berry's classification has provided a schema for many researchers (e.g. Peñaloza, 1989 & 1994) who studied immigrant consumer acculturation. Peñaloza (1989) adapts the acculturation concept to consumer behavior in which consumer acculturation is described as "the acquisition of skills and knowledge relevant to engaging in consumer behavior in one culture by members of another culture" (p. 110). The study of consumer acculturation primarily focuses on cultural adaptation as manifest in the marketplace and examines the cultural bases of consumption behavior and the processes of consumer learning that are affected by the interactions of two or more cultures (ibid.). Peñaloza (1994) acknowledges that "immigrants may have two conflicting sets of consumer acculturation agents: one corresponding to their culture of origin and one corresponding to the existing culture" (p. 35). Reminiscent of Berry's (1980) modes of acculturation she suggests the following possible acculturation outcomes: assimilation, maintenance, resistance, and segregation. Subsequently, other post-assimiliationist researchers (Askegaard et al., 2005) have argued that immigrant consumer acculturation is a more complex phenomenon which rather than lying on a linear continuum, embraces elements from both the home and host cultures, as well as a transnational consumer culture.

The main research question that is addressed in this presentation is what happens when the resistance takes place within the cultural group? More specifically, what are the factors that trigger a sub-group within the greater immigrant community to differentiate itself from that community, what are the practices that lead to this differentiation and how is this achieved?

The findings presented in this paper are part of a bigger study that investigates the Turkish (trans)migrants in Denmark (Üçok, 2007) based on data collected from 13 Turkish immigrant families. This research can be described as a multi-sited ethnography (Marcus, 1995), which included in-depth interviews and in situ observations in multiple locations. Historically the Turkish immigrants arrived in Europe as guest workers, hired to work in factories as blue-collar laborers. Their integration into their host societies were minimal as their main intention was to save money and return to their homelands wealthier and with higher social status. The size of this population rapidly grew due to family reunification. Today, there are 54,000 Turkish immigrants in Denmark. However, they do not constitute a homogeneous group.

The focus of this paper is a subgroup within this community that tries to differentiate itself from the above-mentioned type of Turkish immigrants and attempts to integrate into the host society by consciously adopting differentiating consumption practices. Some examples of these practices are: moving out of the immigrant neighborhoods into neighborhoods populated by the host society, giving importance to higher education and encouraging their children to further their education, buying a brand new car as opposed to a second-hand one, decorating their homes in a style less reminiscent of the other Turkish immigrants' style, adopting consumption practices like wine drinking which is not typical of the Turkish immigrant community, going to vacation to places other than the home country.

The point in which this study departs from previous research on immigrant consumers is that the focus of study here moves away from the identity positionings between the home and host cultures to the one that is acquired in relation to the greater immigrant community. The resistance becomes not to the culture of origin or to the host culture but to the other members of the immigrant community. Integration becomes the desired immigrant consumer acculturation outcome. These immigrants strive to improve their social status and in relation to that their social and cultural capital in their host societies by means of their consumption practices (Üçok & Kjeldgaard, 2006).

This research contributes to the field of immigrant consumer research by providing empirical data on the in-group differences. Furthermore, I argue that these in-group differences stem from a desire to integrate better into the host culture and improve one's social status within this society. This is achieved through the transfer of various types of capital from one type to another (Bourdieu, 1984). The results extend the findings of previous research on immigrant consumer acculturation patterns by accentuating the in-group differences through fleshing out the identity positionings and the factors that influence the consumption decisions that shape these identity positionings.

REFERENCES

Appadurai, Arjun (1990), "Disjuncture and Difference in the Global Cultural Economy," *Public Culture*, 2 (2):1-24.

Arnould, Eric J., and Craig Thompson (2005), "Consumer Culture Theory (CCT): Twenty Years of Research," *Journal of Consumer Research*, 31: 868-882.

Askegaard, Søren, Eric J. Arnould, and Dannie Kjeldgaard (2005), "Postassimilationist Ethnic Consumer Research: Qualifications and Extensions," *Journal of Consumer Research*, 32 (June): 160-170.

Berger, Jonah and Chip Heath (2007), "Where Consumers Diverge from Others: Identity Signaling and Product Domains," *Journal of Consumer Research*, 34 (August): 121-134.

Berry, John W. (1980), "Acculturation as Adaptation," in *Acculturation: Theory, Models, and Some New Findings*, ed. Amado M. Padilla, Boulder: Westview Press, 9-26.

Bourdieu, Pierre (1984), *Distinction: A Social Critique of the Judgment of Taste*, translation Richard Nice, Cambridge, MA: Harvard University Press, p. 169-225.

Burton, Dawn (2009), "Reading Whiteness in Consumer Research," *Consumption, Markets, Culture*, 12:2, forthcoming.

Deshpandé, Rohit, Wayne Hoyer and Naveen Donthu (1986), "The Intensity of Ethnic Affiliation: A Study of the Sociology of Hispanic Consumption," *Journal of Consumer Research*, 13 (September), 214-220.

_(1990), "Finding an Identity in the Social Status Scene," in *Learning Capitalist Culture*, Philadelphia, PA: University of Pennsylvania Press, 63-100.

Farmer, Paul (2006), "Sofferenza Sociale e Violenza Strutturale. Diritti Sociali ed Economici nell'Era Globale," *Antropologia Medica. Gli Scritti Fondamentali*, ed. I. Quaranta, Milano: Raffaello Cortina editore.

Firat, Fuat A. and Alladi Venkatesh (1995), "Liberatory Postmodernism and the Reenchantement of Consumption," *Journal of Consumer Research* 22, 3: 239-267.

Holt, Douglas (2004), *How Brands Become Icons: The Principles of Cultural Branding*, Boston, MA: Harvard Business School Press.

______ (1997), "Post-structuralist Lifestyle Analysis: Conceptualizing the Social Patterning of Consumption," *Journal of Consumer Research*, 23, 4: 326-350.

Lupton, D. 1996. *Food, the Body and the Self.* London: Sage Publications.

Glick Schiller, Nina, Linda Basch and Cristina Szanton Blanc (1992), *Towards a Transnational Perspective on Migration. Race, Class, Ethnicity, and Nationalism Reconsidered*, New York: New York Academy Series.

Lindridge, Andrew M., Margaret K. Hogg and Mita Shah (2004), "Imagined Multiple Worlds: How South Asian Women in Britain Use Family and Friends to Navigate the "Border Crossings" Between Household and Social Contexts," *Consumption, Markets and Culture*, 7 (3): 211-238.

Marcus, George. E. (1995), Ethnography in/Of the World System: The Emergence of Multi-Sited Ethnography. *Annual Review of Anthropology*, 95-117.

Oswald, Laura (1999), "Culture Swapping: Consumption and the Ethnogenesis of Middle Class Haitian Immigrants," *Journal of Consumer Research*, 25:4, 303-318.

Peñaloza, Lisa. N. (1989), "Immigrant Consumer Acculturation," in L. McAlister & M. L. Rothschild (Eds.), *Advances in Consumer Research*, Vol. 16, (pp. 110-118). Provo, UT: Association for Consumer Research.

______ (1994), "Atravesando Fronteras/Border Crossings: A Critical Ethnographic Exploration of the Consumer Acculturation of Mexican Immigrants," *Journal of Consumer Research*, 21:1, (June) 32-54.

______ and Michelle Barnhart (2009), "Living Capitalism Upside Down: Mapping Cultural Production in the Credit/ Debt of the U.S. White Middle Class," Working paper, EDHEC Business School.

Portes, Alejandro (1996), "Preface," in *The New Second Generation*, ed. Alejandro Portes, Russell Sage Foundation, New York, ix-x.

Portes, Alejandro, and Ruben G. Rumbaut, eds. (2001), *Ethnicities. Children of Immigrants in America*, New York: Russell Sage Foundation, University of California Press.

Rumbaut, Ruben G. (1994), "The Crucible Within. Ethnic Identity, Self Esteem, and Segmented Assimilation Among Children of Immigrants," in *The New Second Generation*, ed. Alejandro Portes, Russell Sage Foundation, New York, 119-170.

______ (1997), "Assimilation and its Discontents: Between Rhetoric and Reality," *International Migration Review*, 31 (4): 923-960.

Schaninger, Charles M., Jaques B. Bourgeois and Christina W. Buss (1985), "French-English Canadian Subcultural Consumption Differences," *Journal of Marketing*, 49: 82-92.

Stayman, Douglas M. and Rohit Deshpande (1989), "Situational Ethnicity and Consumer Behavior," *Journal of Consumer Research*, 16 (December): 361-371.

Üçok, Mine and Dannie Kjeldgaard (2006), "Consumption Practices in Transnational Social Spaces: A Study of Turkish Transmigrants", in *European Advances in Consumer Research*, vol. 7, eds. Karin Ekström and Helene Brembeck.

Üçok, Mine (2007), "Consumption Practices of Transmigrants: A Multi-Sited Ethnographic Study of Turkish Immigrants in Denmark", University of Southern Denmark, Odense, unpublished PhD dissertation.

Üstüner, Tuba and Douglas B. Holt (2007), "Dominated Consumer Acculturation: The Social Construction of Poor Migrant Women's Identity Projects in a Turkish Squatter," *Journal of Consumer Research*, 34:1, 41-56.

Visconti, L.M. (2006), "Border Crossing Consumers and Postassimilationist Studies: Cultural Alternation in the Marketplace," Working Paper, Milan, Italy: Bocconi University.

Special Session Summary

Attitude Strength and Consistency Between Attitude and Behavior

Kalpesh Kaushik Desai, State University of New York at Binghamton, USA

SESSION OVERVIEW

Social psychologists and marketers have long been interested in understanding the conditions under which attitudes influence behaviors, decisions, and information processing (Fabrigar, Petty, Smith, and Crites (2006). According to Crano (1997), "The current position in social psychology is that strong attitudes do affect behavior, although social, contextual, and intrapsychic sources of variation can affect the strength of such relationships (Krosnick 1990; Krosnick et al. 1993; Petty & Krosnick, 1995)." In marketing, Sengupta and Fitzsimons (2002, 2004) and others (e.g., Dholakia and Morwitz 2002; Sengupta and Johar 2002; Simonson and Nowlis 2000) have examined the issue of attitude–behavior consistency when respondents are asked to analyze reasons underlying their attitude before reporting their evaluations. Competing explanations of weakening of attitude strength vs. greater distraction have been proposed for the disruption in the attitude-behavior consistency in the condition of analyzing reasons.

The objective of this special session is to introduce four current lines of research that offer new perspectives for improving our understanding of the link between consumers' attitudes and behaviors. Together, they focus upon attitude strength, its antecedents, and uncover new factors that moderate the attitude-behavior consistency (e.g., internal vs. external source of information underlying attitude certainty; brand ambivalence). We believe that these papers shall stimulate interesting discussion which will raise new questions and suggest new directions for future research on the topic. *The data collection for all four papers is complete and they all are either in the manuscript preparation or working paper stage.*

Of the four papers, paper # 2 and 4 adopt a managerial bent to the topic of attitude-behavior consistency whereas paper # 1 & 3 have more of a theoretical orientation. Given this mixed orientation, the likely audience of this special session will be practitioners and researchers in attitude strength, resistance, attitude-behavior consistency, brand equity, and consideration sets. The specific topics that will be covered in the special session pertain to attitude certainty/attitude strength and consistency between attitude and behavior.

Paper # 1, 2, and 4 focus upon attitude strength/attitude certainty and its influence on attitude-behavior consistency. Specifically, paper # 1 by Dubois, Rucker, and Petty argues that consumers with sensitivity to external (internal) factors display greater attitude-behavior consistency when the sources of their certainty were external (internal). Paper # 2 by Desai, Hariharan, Inman, and Talukdar argues that the attitude–behavior consistency is moderated by (other factors along with) attitude strength such that greater commitment to the target brand accentuates the relationship between brand equity and brand loyalty. Paper # 4 by Nayakankuppam, Priester, and Sinha shows that strength of attitude towards an alternative influences its choice and inclusion in the consideration set. In contrast, paper # 3 by Litt and Tormala focuses upon the fragility of liking the chosen alternative from a difficult choice task i.e., behavior–attitude consistency.

The four papers make the following important contributions: i) examine the antecedents and behavioral consequences of adopting an external vs. internal attitude certainty focus; ii) identify important caveats to the presumed durability and strength of thoughtful and involving attitude formation; iii) propose an empirically tested parsimonious measure of brand equity based on comprehensive search of prior literature and identify moderators of brand equity–brand loyalty relationship; iv) reveal the influence of attitude strength on inclusion in a consideration set and choice by impacting consideration set size.

EXTENDED ABSTRACTS

"Internal versus External Informational Sources: Causes and Consequences for Attitude Certainty and Attitude-Behavior Consistency"

David Dubois, Northwestern University, USA
Derek D. Rucker, Northwestern University, USA
Richard E. Petty, Ohio State University, USA

A key factor that has become of increasing importance in understanding attitude-behavior correspondence is the certainty individuals place in their attitudes. In this work we examine how people's sensitivity to external vs. internal information affects attitude certainty. While past research provides ample evidence that individuals rely on multiple informational sources when forming their certainty (Tormala and Rucker 2007), surprisingly little is known about the role of internal (i.e., information from oneself) vs. external (i.e., information from one's environment) factors on its formation. This work proposes and finds that consumers' sensitivity to external vs. internal informational cues leads to two types of certainty foci: while "external" certainty stems from information associated with environmental factors, "internal" certainty results from individuals' focus on personal, experience-based factors.

We first hypothesized that these two certainty foci have distinct psychological antecedents depending on individuals' sensitivity to external vs. internal information. Drawing on past research documenting chronic (Snyder 1974) and momentary (Trafimow et al., 1991) differences in individuals' sensitivity to external vs. internal information, we examined the effects of such differences on the formation of certainty based on information from external versus internal sources.

Second, we hypothesized that the adoption of a specific certainty focus would generate distinct behavioral consequences depending on people's intentions. Specifically, based on past work suggesting that realizing a goal entails consecutively going through different mindsets (e.g., Gollwitzer, 1990), we proposed that an external certainty focus would mostly impact the behavior of individuals deliberating about a goal, while an internal focus would mostly impact the behavior of individuals implementing this same goal.

Three experiments tested these hypotheses. Results were analyzed using ANOVAs and t-tests, when appropriate. In all experiments, attitudes are stable across conditions ($F<1$).

Experiment 1: Examining consumers' self monitoring orientation on the formation of external and internal certainty. Using a 2-cells design (informational cue: external, internal and control; N=82), we tested the hypothesis that one's propensity to rely on external or internal factors when forming certainty is driven by one's self-monitoring orientation. After completing the self-monitoring scale (Snyder 1974), participants were invited to participate in an ostensibly unrelated purchasing scenario that either contained internal (e.g., perceived knowledge, repeated purchase), external (e.g., social consensus, source credibility) informational cues about a product, or unrelated information (control). Finally, participants' certainty and attitudes toward the product was assessed. Results showed that high (low) self-monitors' certainty was significantly greater after they encountered an external (internal) informational cue than an internal (external) one (p<.01), suggesting that certainty formation is differentially sensitive to external or internal information, as a function of individuals' chronic self-monitoring orientation.

Experiment 2: Examining consumers' self orientation on the formation of external and internal certainty. A 2 (self-orientation: self vs. others) x 2 (certainty focus: internal vs. external; N=73) examined whether a momentary shift in one's sensitivity to external vs. internal information, rather than a chronic orientation, could similarly affect certainty formation. After completing a self-orientation manipulation (Trafimow et al., 1991), participants read a newspaper excerpt about college students' knowledge of cameras, which was either high, or low (Internal focus) and subsequently received a WOM communication from either an expert or a novice (External focus) about a camera. Last, participants' attitudes, certainty and purchase intentions were assessed. Individuals with a self (other) orientation tended to rely on internal (external) sources of certainty when judging a product (p<.01). In addition, the type of certainty formed (external vs. internal) mediated individuals' behavioral intentions, suggesting the dual nature of certainty is consequential for attitude-behavior consistency.

Experiment 3: Examining consumers' mindset on the formation of external and internal certainty. A 2 (mindset: implemental vs. deliberative) x 2 (certainty focus: internal vs. external) (N=112) aimed at suggesting that individuals rely on a particular type of certainty–external or internal–as a function of their mindset. After being presented with a purchasing scenario in which their mindset was manipulated, participants encountered an external or internal informational cue. Results suggested that individuals in a deliberative (implemental) mindset were more certain after being presented with an external (internal) cue than with an internal (external) one (p<.01).

Conclusion and Contributions. These findings suggest distinct antecedents and consequences of external and internal certainty. From a theoretical standpoint, the present research sheds light on our understanding of how certainty can emanate from different sources, and provides further evidence that each type of certainty foci investigated generates unique consequences for behavior. Given the governing role of certainty in attitude-behavior consistency, these experiments further enrich our understanding of attitude-behavior correspondence.

References

Gollwitzer, P. M. (1990), "Action Phases and Mind-Sets," in E. T. Higgins and R. M. Sorrentino (Eds.), *The Handbook of Motivation and Cognition: Foundations of Social Behavior* (Vol. 2, pp. 53-92). New York: Guilford Press

Snyder, M. (1974), "Self Monitoring of Expressive Behavior," *Journal of Personality and Social Psychology*, 30, 526-537.

Tormala, Z.L., and D. D. Rucker (2007), "Attitude Certainty: A Review of Past Findings and Emerging Perspectives," *Social and Personality Psychology Compass*, 1, 469-492

Trafimow, D., H. C. Triandis, and S. G. Goto (1991), "Some Tests of the Distinction between the Private Self and the Collective Self," *Journal of Personality and Social Psychology*, 60, 649-655

"A Field Examination of the Influence of Brand Equity on Behavioral Loyalty and Factors that Moderate this Relationship"

Kalpesh Kaushik Desai, SUNY-Binghamton, USA
Vijay Hariharan, SUNY-Buffalo, USA
Jeffrey Inman, University of Pittsburgh, USA
Debabrata Talukdar, SUNY-Buffalo, USA

Prior research in brand equity (or BE) has primarily focused upon its leveraging influence on brand and line extensions and feedback effects (e.g., Aaker and Keller 1990; Park, Milberg, and Lawson 1991). However, the relationship between brand equity and brand loyalty (or BE–BL) has been less than perfect (Keller and Lehmann 2004). Specifically, brands encounter four possible scenarios: i and ii) positive BE–BL relationship could see brands with high (low) equity correspondingly enjoy high (poor) loyalty; iii) brands enjoying high equity experience poor loyalty; and iv) brands with low equity could enjoy high brand loyalty.

Research Questions, Motivation, and Contribution

Managers, especially for brands in groups (ii)–(iv) above, would like to know how to enhance brand attitude–choice behavior consistency i.e., how to get more consumers on the high BE–high BL track. Which factors mitigate versus accentuate the BE–BL relationship? Based on prior work in several research streams, we identify 12 "contextual" factors relating to the target brand, product category, and consumers as important moderators. For example, we hypothesize that while target brand commitment and importance of brand decision accentuate the BE–BL relationship, brand ambivalence and perceived equity of other brands mitigate that linkage. We similarly hypothesize, for example, that BE–BL linkage will be accentuated for private (vs. national) label brands and for households with higher (vs. lower) income but the relationship will be mitigated by education of the primary shopper of the household and by category differentiation. By empirically showing the influence of BE on BL to be limited in several contexts, we argue that strengthening BE cannot be a solution to branding problems in all situations, contrary to the assumption of prior BE research and practitioners.

A related question that prior research has not examined is if there are distinct segments of consumers whose profile differences (e.g., maximizer vs. satisficers) make them more likely to engage in high attitude–choice consistency behavior. Dominance of the high equity–high loyalty customers (vs. high BE-low BL or low BE-high BL) among the target segment requires no change in the target marketing strategy of the brand. In addition, by focusing on profile differences, brand managers can devise appropriate marketing strategies to move "inconsistent" consumers to become high BE–high BL consumers.

A major challenge in the BE research is that prior research has proposed distinct measures of BE (e.g., Aaker 1996; Keller 1993; Yoo and Donthu 2001). Just being advised to strengthen BE without being told which variables to focus upon is not very helpful. Researchers and managers will benefit from a comprehensive but parsimonious measure of BE. Finally, we also investigate if the relative importance of the different variables that constitute the composite BE construct is stable to changes in the context engendered by moderators listed above (e.g., private label or age of consumers)? Answers to these questions for example, can help managers of private label vs. national brands to focus on distinct BE variables to strengthen BE–BL relationship and emphasize distinct BE variables in their marketing if they were targeting their brands to younger vs. older consumers.

Method and Findings

After comprehensive investigation of prior research, we identified the following nine variables as measures of brand equity: brand personality, perceived value, brand differentiation, brand trust, strength of brand's favorable associations, brand quality, brand satisfaction, brand justifiability, and in-store presence. Factor analysis using principal component extraction method revealed that all nine variables (measured by 18 items) fall into a single construct of brand equity (amount of variance explained=44.7%).

To test our hypotheses, we mailed surveys in February 2007 to 5000 bonus card shoppers of a leading grocery chain operating in the northeastern US. As incentive, participants were offered the opportunity to participate in a lottery drawing. The response rate was 75%. To ensure that we account for bulk of the grocery purchases of the participants, the 5000 bonus card holders were randomly selected from more than a million panel members such that the target grocery chain was the primary shopping outlet for these consumers accounting for more than 80% of their grocery purchases. Using established scales developed by prior research, the survey measured all the variables listed above and the hypotheses were tested using various multivariate regressions on the choice data of 52-weeks prior to the receipt of the survey i.e., April 2006-April 2007. The results were consistent across both categories (toothpaste and tortilla chips) and all our hypotheses except for the ones on age, income, annual category purchase, category differentiation, and maximizing vs. satisficing moderators were supported.

References

Aaker, David A. (1996), *Building Strong Brands*, New York: Free Press

______ and Kevin Lane Keller (1990), "Consumer Evaluations of Brand Extensions," *Journal of Marketing*, 54 (Winter), 27-41.

Keller, Kevin L. (1993), "Conceptualizing, Measuring, and Managing Customer-Based Brand Equity," *Journal of Marketing*, 57 (January), 1-22.

______ and Donald R. Lehmann (2004), "Brands and Branding: Research Findings and Future Priorities," *MSI Report.*

Park, C. Whan, Sandra Milberg, and Robert Lawson (1991), "Extension Boundaries of Two Types of Brand Names: Role of Product Feature Similarity and Brand Concept Consistency," *Journal of Consumer Research*, 18 (September), 185-193.

Yoo, Boonghee and Naveen Donthu (2001), "Developing and Validating a Multidimensional Consumer-Based Brand Equity Scale," *Journal of Business Research*, 52 (1), 1-14.

"Fragile Enhancement of Attitudes and Intentions Following Difficult Choices"

Ab Litt, Stanford University, USA

Zakary L. Tormala, Stanford University, USA

It is well-documented that, following difficult choices from sets of similarly attractive options, consumers show increased post-choice liking of chosen items, relative to choices between more easily differentiated options (e.g., Brehm 1956). Although others have been proposed, a prevailing explanation is that such choice-enhancement is driven by motivated rationalization, whereby consumers seek to reduce dissonance aroused by selecting one option while rejecting similarly attractive others. This entails an active and high-involvement process of changing attitudes and behavioral intentions post-hoc to align them with one's choice.

Despite considerable attention paid to understanding post-choice attitudinal enhancement, little has focused on examining its stability. For example, once changed to support a choice, how do difficulty-enhanced attitudes and intentions withstand subsequent attack? If dissonance-driven attitude shifting is indeed an active and thoughtful (though biased) process, then from past research showing strong attitudes fostered by increased thought (Petty, Haugtvedt, & Smith 1995), it could be surmised that post-choice attitudinal enhancement would be quite durable in the face of persuasive attack. Across three purchase scenario free-choice studies, however, we find such enhancement to be fragile, yielding to even minor and superficial attacks. Moreover, rather than bolstering attitude durability and resistance to persuasion (e.g., Petty et al. 1995), we find that heightened involvement augments this fragile enhancement and vulnerability to attack.

Study 1: Difficulty and Fragile Enhancement. In a hypothetical product-purchasing scenario, participants ranked six digital cameras (based on pictures and image-quality, weight, and price information), and were then presented with a subset from which to choose. In line with the free-choice paradigm, choice-difficulty was manipulated by presenting either the 2nd and 5th ranked options ("Easy-Choice" condition) or the 2nd and 3rd ranked options ("Difficult-Choice" condition). Following this decision, all participants reported attitudes towards their chosen camera and behavioral intentions such as product recommendation, purchase deferral, and re-purchase likelihood. Finally, participants read a single negative customer review of their chosen camera criticizing only peripheral dimensions (e.g., strap-thickness, technical support), and were again asked about their attitudes and behavioral intentions regarding their chosen camera.

Consistent with past research, in the initial post-choice/pre-attack stage we observed more favorable attitudes and intentions towards products chosen in the Difficult-Choice condition. Compared to the Easy-Choice condition, these participants were more satisfied with their camera, more likely to recommend it to others, more inclined towards future re-purchase of the same camera, and less inclined to defer purchase. However, this enhancement did not afford Difficult-Choice participants any additional resistance to the negative customer review. After the attack, participants across choice conditions did not differ in attitudes and intentions, and within-participant comparisons showed greater collapse on these dimensions by Difficult-Choice participants, though both groups were affected. Moreover, whereas pre-attack positivity in attitudes and intentions strongly predicted post-attack resilience in the Easy-Choice condition, this was not true in the Difficult-Choice condition. In short, we observed a fragile enhancement effect in the Difficult-Choice condition: participants enhanced attitudes and intentions post-choice, but in a manner proving highly vulnerable to even minor attack. Choice rationalization may thus create the appearance of strong choice-consistent attitudes, but those attitudes can be quite susceptible to change when tested.

Studies 2-3: The Role of Choice Involvement. Two additional studies replicated fragile enhancement with different stimuli (Study 2: car-stereos; Study 3: customer review attacking central rather than peripheral product-dimensions). They also provided insight into mediation (by choice-discomfort, consistent with a dissonance-based motivated rationalization account) and moderation. Most notably, we observed increased fragile enhancement as a function of increased choice-involvement. In Study 2, attitudes and intentions showed significant interactions between choice-difficulty and measured choice-involvement: both initial enhancement and later collapse in the Difficult-Choice condition were greater among participants reporting high rather than low involvement. Study 3's replication manipulated choice-involvement by varying the perceived importance of the choice itself. Thus, following difficult and important decisions, for which it would be most desirable to have a strong and defensible position, attitudes and intentions showed both greater post-choice enhancement and greater vulnerability to later persuasion.

Conclusions. Results support an involved rationalization process underlying difficulty-driven choice enhancement. In contrast to both implicit and explicit assumptions in past research, however, these motivated post-choice enhancements of attitudes and behavioral intentions turn out to be exceptionally fragile, collapsing in the face of even minor persuasive attack. Moreover, choice-involvement appears to amplify both initial post-choice enhancement and subsequent post-attack deflation. Thus, factors traditionally believed to foster increased resistance to attack by inducing thoughtful attitude change may foster increased susceptibility to attack in the free-choice paradigm. Overall, it appears that at least some forms of dissonance-based attitude change can be easily undone, and that involvement might have a more dynamic role in conferring attitude strength than is apparent from past research.

References

Brehm, J. W. (1956), "Post-Decision Changes in the Desirability of Choice Alternatives," *Journal of Abnormal and Social Psychology*, 52, 384-389.

Petty, R. E., C. P. Haugtvedt, and S. M. Smith (1995). "Message Elaboration as a Determinant of Attitude Strength, in R. E. Petty, & J. A. Krosnick (Eds.), *Attitude Strength: Antecedents and Consequences* (pp. 93-130). Hillsdale, NJ: Lawrence Erlbaum.

"The Influence of Attitude Strength on Consideration Set Size: Strong Liking Results in Smaller Consideration Sets"

Dhananjay Nayakankuppam, University of Iowa, USA
Joseph R. Priester, University of Southern California, USA
Jayati Sinha, University of Iowa, USA

Introduction

How individuals come to choose one alternative over another has lain at the heart of consumer psychology, indeed the entire field of marketing, since its very inception. This paper follows in this tradition, exploring a hypothesis that both builds upon past research and helps to understand prior findings. To do so, we adopt theory from both the literatures of attitudes (e.g., Petty and Cacioppo, 1986) and choice (e.g., Roberts and Latin, 1997): From attitudes we use the construct of attitude strength and from choice we use the construct of a consideration set.

Consideration set formation has proved to be important in consumer choice processes–much variance in choice is attributable to inclusion in a consideration set (Hauser and Wernerfelt, 1990). Prior research has shown that inclusion in a consideration set is influenced by attitudes but is moderated by attitude strength in that it is particularly true for strong, rather than weak attitudes (Priester et al., 2004). This research examines how attitude strength might moderate attitudinal influence on consideration.

Hypothesis Development

Why is it that attitude strength plays such a role in consideration? Recall that attitude strength confers greater accessibility, such that strongly held attitudes come to mind faster than weakly held attitudes (see Priester and Petty, 2003; Priester et al., 2004). If a strongly liked attitude comes to mind quickly in the formation of a consideration set, it is possible that its earlier arrival will truncate search and result in a smaller consideration set. We base this hypothesis on two distinct streams of research. First, Feldman and Lynch (1988) find that the more accessible and diagnostic an alternative is, the more likely that it will be used, and subsequent search will be terminated. Second, Alba and Chattopadyay (1986) find that brand salience inhibits recall of other brands. Together, these results suggest that the extent to which an alterative is held with greater strength, the more likely that other alternatives will not be brought into consideration. We propose a simple, yet potentially powerful hypothesis: This hypothesis is both consistent with, and may well help to understand the psychological processes underlying, prior literature. We test the hypothesis in two Experiments.

Experiment 1

Mitra and Lynch (1995) found that differentiating ads led to smaller consideration sets than reminder ads. Our interpretation of this finding is that it may have emerged because of differences in attitude strength resulting from the different ad types. Experiment 1 was designed to examine whether attitude strength can account for the Mitra and Lynch (1995) findings.

Specifically, experiment 1 examines whether differentiating ads led to smaller consideration sets than reminder ads because the differentiating ads set up conditions under which participants could elaborate, and thus form strong attitudes, whereas the reminder conditions did not foster such elaboration, and thus led to weak attitudes.

Participants were provided with mock advertisements for three brands (in three different product categories–burgers, granola bars and pizza). They processed these advertisements under conditions of either high or low elaboration, in order to form strong and weak attitudes respectively. Elaboration was manipulated between participants in a manner similar to Priester et al. (2004)–that is, participants were asked to pay attention to their thoughts and feelings as they read the ads (HiEl) or we imposed a secondary cognitive load on them by asking them to count the number of polysyllabic words in the ad as a way to reduce the resources that could be allocated to elaboration (thus LoEl). After exposure to the brands, we assessed attitudes and attitude strength, in addition to collecting their impressions of the ads.

The participants in the HiEl likelihood conditions report smaller consideration set sizes than those in the LoEl likelihood condition.

Experiment 2

The second study re-analyzes the results of two previously published studies that investigated the influence of attitude strength on consideration and choice. Participants provided attitude and attitude strength data towards a variety of soda and toothpaste brands (familiar brands). They also provided consideration sets and choice decisions in the two product categories.

This reanalysis provides further evidence that the greater the extent to which a chosen alternative is more strongly liked than the others in the consideration set, the more likely that the consideration set is smaller.

Experiment 3

In experiment three we tested the idea of search truncation i.e., the attitude strength associated with a retrieved alternative serves as a signal for search truncation. Participants were exposed to an ad for a target brand (unfamiliar brand) under conditions of high or low elaboration (same as experiment 1). After performing unrelated filler tasks, they were shown a sequence of brands with some information about each brand–one of the brands they encountered was the target brand. The position of the target brand was varied–they appeared at second, fourth or sixth position for different participants. After viewing each brand, participants made two judgments–first, whether they would like to set this brand aside for further consideration and second, whether they would like to proceed to view more brands or make a choice from the brands set aside for consideration.

Results show that participants in the high elaboration condition were more likely to truncate search earlier compared to participants in the low elaboration condition. Also results show that the position of the target brand had no impact on the low elaboration participants. However, the target brand had a significant impact on the high elaboration participants. Encountering the target brand earlier resulted in smaller set sizes as compared to encountering it later.

Discussion

This paper advances and provides support for a rather simple, but potentially powerful, hypothesis: Choices associated with strong attitudes result in smaller consideration sets than choices associated with weak attitudes. At the most basic, this research contributes to our understanding of the determinants of consideration set size. In addition, this research provides a possibly more parsimonious explanation for previous research.

References

Alba, J. W., and A. Chattopadhyay (1986), "Salience Effects in Brand Recall," *Journal of Marketing Research*, 23 (4), 363-369.

Hauser, J. R., and B. Wernerfelt (1990), "An Evaluation Cost Model of Consideration Sets," *Journal of Consumer Research*, 16(4), 393-408.

Mitra, Anusree and J. G. Lynch (1995), "Toward a Reconciliation of Market Power and Information Theories of Advertising Effects on Price Elasticity," *Journal of Consumer Research*, 21 (4), 644-659.

Petty, R. E., and J. T. Cacioppo (1986), "The Elaboration Likelihood Model of Persuasion," in Leonard Berkowitz (Ed.), *Advances in Experimental Social Psychology*. Vol.19. New York: Academic Press.

Priester, J. R., D. Nayakankuppam, M. A. Fleming, and J. Godek (2004), "The ASC Model: The Influence of Attitudes and Attitude Strength on Consideration and Choice,' *Journal of Consumer Research*, 30(March), 574-87.

Roberts, J. H., and J. M. Lattin (1997), "Consideration: Review of Research and Prospects for Future Insights," *Journal of Marketing Research*, 34, 406-410.

Special Session Summary

On Being Better (or Worse) Than Others: Illuminating and Eliminating Biases in Social Comparison

Ellie Kyung, New York University, USA

SESSION OVERVIEW

Consumers make sense of their place in the world by comparing themselves to those around them. But as research in social comparison illustrates, these comparisons are typically rife with systematic biases–biases with documented effects on consumers' product choices (Burson 2007), health risk perception (Raghubir and Menon 1998), and shopping behavior (Moorman et al. 2004). In the vast majority of documented cases, people believe they are better than others (summarized in Dunning, Heath, and Suls 2004), and on some rarer occasions, they believe they are worse than others (Kruger 1999; Moore 2007). In general, people tend to believe they are better than average on easy tasks and worse than average on difficult tasks (Kruger 1999; Moore and Healy 2008).

Each of the papers in this special session examines better-than-average and worse-than-average effects in consumer judgments to collectively (a) further clarify the mechanism behind these biases, (b) illustrate ways of overcoming them, and (c) demonstrate the impact of such biases on real decisions.

The first paper by Menon, Kyung, and Agrawal examines how perceived similarity between self and others in an unrelated domain can influence social comparison judgments. The studies illustrate the role that perceived controllability over outcomes can play in determining whether people believe they are better or worse than average, and how increasing perceived similarity between self and other–versus changing the target of comparison as in previous work–attenuates both biases. However, when motivating people to act, attenuating these biases is not always desirable.

Building on this theme of considering similarities between self and others, the second paper by Gershoff and Burson examines the flawed assumptions about the distribution of reference groups. The studies demonstrate that people consider the characteristics of others when making judgments, but that people tend to overestimate the dispersion of that distribution of others. This error can result in both better-than-average and worse-than-average effects, which have been shown to influence consumption decisions. Furthermore, simple manipulations of scale granularity or exemplar availability can influence the construction of these distributions, serving to magnify or attenuate these biases when making judgments.

The third paper by Cain, Moore, and Chen investigates the generalizability of some of these effects and examines why we tend to see a prevalence of overconfidence in the real world when underconfidence is also demonstrated in laboratory studies. Focusing on self-selection, they find that people tend to choose to participate in tasks where they believe they are better than others. When choosing to participate in tournaments involving real money, people were more likely to opt to participate when the task was easy versus difficult, even though their odds of winning were the same for tasks of both types. Imperfect information about self and others drives this effect.

Thus this special session examines different antecedents and consequences of better-than-average and worse-than-average effects in consumer contexts. The first paper examines consumer motivation to act while the second investigates performance and usage estimates and the third evaluates market entry decisions. These papers and the discussion that following can raise interesting theoretical questions such as: What is the underlying mechanism behind these biases? When and why do they occur in the "real world"? How can they be attenuated? Is it always desirable to do so? In short, we aim to discuss both theoretical insights and practical applications that stem from social comparison and related theories to deepen our understanding of when and why these biases occur and how to improve consumer decision making.

EXTENDED ABSTRACTS

"Biases in Social Comparisons: Optimism or Pessimism?"

Geeta Menon, University of Pennsylvania, USA
Ellie Kyung, New York University, USA
Nidhi Agrawal, Northwestern University, USA

The tendency for people to be comparatively optimistic or pessimistic about themselves, to the point of being unrealistic, has been well-documented. But under what circumstances do these better-than-average and worse-than-average biases occur? Recent work suggests that for easy tasks, people believe they are better than average and for difficult tasks they believe they are worse than average (Moore and Healy 2008.) We delver further into understanding this dichotomous bias by examining specifically how beliefs about one's own perceived control over an outcome and inferences about an other's can influence whether a better versus worse than average bias manifests. We also illustrate that merely increasing perceived similarity between self and others in an unrelated domain can attenuate both of these biases and when it might (or might not) be desirable to do so.

In a series of four studies, we show the following: (a) Better than average effects are likely to occur when one perceives more control over the outcome and worse than average effects are likely to occur when one perceives less control over the outcome; (b) Both these biases can be attenuated by increasing perceptions of similarity between oneself and a comparison target person (e.g., the average undergraduate) in an unrelated domain; (c) The mechanism for these effects is a change in perception of one's own control in a domain and not a change in perception of another person's control; (d) Under specific conditions, people are motivated to work harder in order to attain a positive outcome, thus helping managers and educators to provide the right work environment and means to do better and succeed. We illustrate these effects while controlling for outcome valence (positive outcomes), comparison target (average undergraduate at the school), as well as event domain (kept constant in each study) unlike previous research that varies these constructs to demonstrate these biases.

In Study 1, participants were asked to think of a course important to them and presented them with two grading scheme scenarios–one in which the outcome was highly controllable (e.g. final exam based primarily on class lectures) and one in which it was less so (e.g. final exam based primarily on ability to apply material to real world situations). They then rated the likelihood that they and the average undergraduate at the school were likely to get a good grade in the course (employing indirect comparative measures) and the extent to which getting a good grade in the course was in their control. The results revealed that in situations of high control, a better-than-average bias manifests while in situations of low control, a worse-than-average bias manifests. Additionally, perceptions of one's own control vary by situational context while those of the average undergraduate do not.

In Studies 2a and 2b, we examined the attenuating effect of perceived similarity between the self and the target other on these two biases. Rather than varying the target to be more or less similar to the self as in many previous studies, participants were all asked to think about the average undergraduate and consider either ways in which they were similar or different. Similar to Study 1, results indicate that better-than-average biases manifest in situations of higher control (Study 2a: trivia contest on pop culture) and worse-than-average biases manifest in situations of lower control (Study 2b: raffle). More importantly, we find that an increased in perceived similarity, even when the comparison target is kept constant, attenuates both biases.

In Study 3, we employed an experimental design similar to Study 1, but included a series of dependent measures related to motivation in the context of preparing for the course (hours spent preparing for class, likelihood of visiting professor during office hours, effort and motivation to work hard.) In lower control situations, where worse-than-average biases pervade, highlighting similarities leads to greater motivation to act while in higher control situations, where better-than-average biases pervade, highlighting differences leads to greater motivation to act. Mediation analysis revealed that perceptions of one's own control over these situations, and not the other's, drive this result.

Thus our studies integrate a variety of findings in extent literature by identifying outcome controllability as a variable that determines whether a better-than-average versus worse-than-average bias manifests, illustrating that in the face of uncertain information about others, highlighting perceived similarity can attenuate these biases. Furthermore, information about similarity or differences with others leads to changes in the perception of one's own control rather than that of the other person–people appear to use information by others to update information about themselves. Clarifying the roles of outcome controllability and perceived similarity in these comparative biases allows us to specify how situations can be framed to motivate desired behavioral action, such as in domains of education, employee incentive schemes, and beneficial public behaviors.

"It's Not Just Me: The Role of Inferences about Reference Distributions on Estimates of One's Own Comparative Performance"

Andrew Gershoff, University of Texas at Austin, USA
Katherine A. Burson, University of Michigan, USA

Research exploring how people make estimates about themselves compared to others has found systematic biases. For instance, easy tasks produce better-than-average (BTA) effects while difficult tasks produce worse-than-average (WTA) effects. Researchers have generally argued that these biases are due to participants' errors in combining the information about themselves and others into percentile estimates: People focus primarily on information about themselves and fail to incorporate information about the reference group (i.e. Kruger and Burrus 2004).

In three studies, we show that judges do attend to others when evaluating their relative standing, but that they tend to believe that others are distributed dispersly across the possible outcomes. Especially for easy or difficult tasks, the true distributions of performance are actually skewed. The first study illustrates how this simple misestimation can explain BTA and WTA effects. We then demonstrate that participants do indeed incorporate these beliefs about others into their comparative assessments. In studies 2-3, we are also able to show that participants' perceptions of the reference group are labile. We demonstrate that simple availability or response scale manipulations can change the perceived dispersion of others and subsequently change estimates of relative standing.

In study 1, we gave participants one difficult, one moderate, and one easy quiz about everyday knowledge. Participants estimated their own score, provided us with their perception of distribution of others' performances on each quiz, and estimated their own relative standing. As predicted, participants believed they were WTA on the difficult quiz, were unbiased on the moderate quiz, and BTA on the easy quiz. However, inspection of the estimated distributions revealed that they were significantly more disperse than the actual distributions of performance. To examine whether participants showed BTA and WTA biases because they ignored others' when forming their relative perceptions, we created a new variable we call "should standing": Given each participant's estimated score and estimated distribution of others, we calculated the percentile that each participant should have estimated. This variable contained both information about the participant's expected score and the distribution of performance in which that score lay. As predicted, regressions showed that BTA and WTA effects were explained by both participants' beliefs about their own scores and the distribution of scores. Specifically, this information fully mediated the relationship between estimated score and estimated percentile.

The next two studies also show that participants incorporate beliefs about others into their relative assessments. However, these studies also extend the results of the previous study to show how trivial manipulations can influence perceptions of the reference group and hence whether people believe they are better or worse than others.

In study 2, we asked participants how far they could putt in golf, how many Trivial Pursuit questions out of 20 they could answer correctly, and how many cell phone minutes they used per month. This time, the perception of the distribution of others for each of the three domains was manipulated. We varied the granularity of the scales. For instance, for trivial pursuit, one condition estimated the scores of the reference group on a scale that highlighted poor performance (0 correct, 1 correct, 2 correct, ...6-10 correct, 11-15, etc.) while the other condition estimated others' performances on a scale that highlighted good performance (0-5 correct, 6-10 correct, 11-15 correct, 16 correct, 17 correct, 18 correct, etc.). Similar scale-granularity manipulations were used in the other two domains. As predicted, percentile estimates were significantly shifted by the scale manipulation. When low numbers on the scale were highlighted, participants tended to estimate that more of their reference group fell in this area of the scale than when the high numbers were highlighted. Furthermore, it was participants' incorporation of these distributional beliefs that explained the occurrence of both BTA and WTA effects.

Study 3 manipulated perceptions of the distribution by manipulating the availability of distributional extremes. We showed participants a website for products for short or tall consumers. Participants examining the "short" website believed they were taller than those viewing the "tall" website. Once again, inspection of the perceived distributions of others showed that the manipulations produced a significant shift in these perceptions and it was these perceptions that explained relative estimates.

These experiments show that participants can incorporate beliefs about others into their percentile estimates and strongly suggest that inaccurate estimated distributions are to blame for relative miscalibration. If these perceptions of relative standing are inaccurate, so may be purchases. But, if marketers anticipate that people are likely to imagine referent distributions as normal, they may be able help them make better decisions.

"Overconfidence and Entry into Competitions: Reconciling Discrepant Results"

Daylian M. Cain, Yale University, USA
Don A. Moore, Carnegie Mellon University, USA
M. Keith Chen, Yale University, USA

Numerous research results attest to the robustness of people's belief that they are better than others. The strength of this evidence was sufficient for the most popular social psychology text in the United States to claim that "for nearly any subjective and socially desirable dimension...most people see themselves as better than average" (Myers 1998). Griffin and Varey (1996) went further, claiming that "Overconfidence is not only marked but nearly universal." So it is noteworthy that recent studies have found strong evidence of instances in which people, on average, believe that they are worse than others (Kruger 1999; Moore 2007). We attempt to reconcile these discrepant findings.

Our reconciliation focuses on self-selection and argues that people naturally choose tasks on which they believe they are better than others. Therefore, wherever people can choose whether to take part, we should expect to find that competitors generally think they are better than others, even when they are not. We introduce a lab experiment–a market-entry game of skill–with both hard and easy tasks and allow participants to choose where to compete. We expected that people would be more likely to believe that they had performed better than others on the easy task than the hard one.

Hypotheses. We devised a market-entry game in which participants had to choose which of two tournaments they would enter. We randomly varied both the size of the prize associated with each tournament and the difficulty of the quiz, where scores determined entrants' chances of winning the prize. Each entrant's probability of winning the prize for a given tournament was proportional his or her relative quiz performance. For half of our participants, the hard quiz was associated with a $90 prize and the easy quiz was associated with a $45 prize. For the other half of our participants, the prize sizes were reversed.

Given prior experimental findings (Rapoport, Lo, and Zwick 2002), we predicted our experimental participants would respond to increased prizes with increased entry. The Nash equilibrium would predict that two-thirds of participants in each condition would choose the prize with the larger size. This implies the expected value of entry in each tournament would be equal.

These predictions stand in contrast to prior findings that people believe they are better than average on easy tasks and worse than average on hard tasks, which led us to predict excess entry in tournaments of easy tasks and insufficient entry in tournaments of hard tasks. Finally, we also predicted that those who most overestimate their performances on any particular task relative to others would disproportionately choose to compete in it. Consequently, we predicted that, subjects would, on average, believe that they were better than average at that task where chose to compete.

Method. The 160 participants in our experiment took two ten-item tests, one easy and one hard. Each test was associated with a cash prize. Participants had to choose which prize to compete for.

Results. On average, participants were more likely to believe that they were better than others on the easy quiz (M=0.30, SD=1.76) and worse than others on the hard quiz (M=-0.12, SD=2.14), $t(159)=2.41$, $p<0.02$. The majority of participants (67 percent) chose to compete for the prize associated with the easy quiz. This difference overwhelmed the effect of our manipulation of prize size. Similar proportions of participants chose to compete for the easy prize, regardless of whether it was the $90 prize (70 percent) or the $45 prize (64 percent). However, looking only at the contests where participants chose to compete, they reported themselves to be, on average, above average (M=.36, SD=1.92), t (159)=2.35, p=.02.

Discussion. Most of our participants chose to compete in the easy tournament. Of those, 68% would have been better off individually competing in the hard tournament; and all but one would have been better off switching when the hard tournament held the large prize. So, participants correctly anticipated more competition in the easy tournament, yet flooded into the easy test tournament. No doubt this is because the easy test is where participants tended to underestimate others and therefore tended to believe that they were better than others.

This paper also illustrates how it is that self-selection produces a situation in which people systematically believe that they are better than others at the tasks in which they have chosen to engage. When people are free to choose where to compete, they self-select into domains where they think they have relative advantage. It is also interesting that this effect can result from individuals making rational choices with imperfect information. In other words, people make errors because they have imperfect information regarding their own and others' performances. However, many of these errors are consistent with Bayesian logic (which underlies differential regression). The final result, however, is that sensible people making sensible choices can produce an outcome that appears irrationally myopic, biased, and is collectively inefficient.

REFERENCES

Burson, Katherine A. (2007), "Consumer-product skill matching: The effects of difficulty on relative self-assessment and choice," *Journal of Consumer Research*, 34(1), 104-110.

Dunning, David, Chip Heath, and Jerry M. Suls (2004), "Flawed self-assessment," *Psychological Science in the Public Interest*, 5(3), 69-106.

Griffin, Dale W., and Carol A. Varey (1996), "Towards a consensus on overconfidence," *Organizational Behavior and Human Decision Processes*, 65(3), 227-231.

Kruger, Justin (1999), "Lake Wobegon Be Gone! The 'Below-average Effect' and the Egocentric Nature of Comparative Ability Judgments," *Journal of Personality and Social Psychology*, 77(2), 221-232.

Kruger, Justin and Jeremy Burrus (2004), "Egocentrism and Focalism in Unrealistic Optimism (and Pessimism)," *Journal of Experimental Social Psychology*, 40(3), 332-340.

Larrick, Richard P., Katherine A. Burson, and Jack B. Soll (2007), "Social Comparison and Confidence: When Thinking You're Better Than Average Predicts Overconfidence (and When It Does Not)," *Organizational Behavior & Human Decision Processes*, 102(1), 76-94.

Moore, Don A. (2007), "Not So Above Average After All: When People Believe They Are Worse Than Average and Its Implications for Theories of Bias in Social Comparison," *Organizational Behavior and Human Decision Processes*, 102(1), 42-58.

Moore, Don A. and Paul J. Healy (2008), "The Trouble With Overconfidence," *Psychological Review*, 115(2), 502-517.

Moorman, Christine, Kristin Diehl, David Brinberg, and Blair Kidwell (2004), "Subjective Knowledge, Search Locations, and Consumer Choice," *Journal of Consumer Research*, 31(3), 673-680.

Myers, David G. (1998), *Social Psychology* (5th ed.), New York: McGraw-Hill.

Raghubir, Priya and Geeta Menon (1998), "AIDS and Me, Never the Twain Shall Meet: the Effects of Information Accessibility on Judgments of Risk and Advertising Effectiveness," *Journal of Consumer Research*, 25(1), 52-63.
Rapoport, Amnon, Alison K. C. Lo, and Rami Zwick (2002), "Choices of Prizes Allocated by Multiple Lotteries With Endogenously Determined Probabilities," *Organizational Behavior & Human Decision Processes*, 87, 180-206.

Special Session Summary

Positive Emotions Are Like a Box of Chocolates: Without Identifying the Different Flavors You Never Know What Behavior You're Going to Get

Lisa Cavanaugh, University of Southern California, USA
Barbara Fredrickson, University of North Carolina, USA

SESSION OVERVIEW

How might different types (flavors) of positive emotions differentially influence consumption behavior? Many consumption decisions are driven primarily by a desire to cultivate positive emotional experiences for ourselves and for others. Despite the importance of positive emotions to marketing, researchers know relatively little about how or why specific positive emotions may influence behavior in different ways. For example, previous research shows that positive emotions can influence consumers in both favorable ways (e.g., increased helping and improved problem-solving; see Isen 2001; Isen 2008 for reviews) and unfavorable ways (e.g., increased stereotyping and shallow processing; see Cohen, Pham, and Andrade 2008 for a review). But to date little attention has been given to whether these effects may vary systematically across different positive emotions. The papers presented in this symposium investigate how and why different positive emotions influence consumer behavior in distinct ways.

This symposium bridges theoretical perspectives on positive emotions (i.e., appraisal, broaden-and-build, and evolutionary) to argue that positive emotions are more complex than consumer researchers have assumed to date. Together they present evidence and develop theory to explore why specific positive emotions uniquely impact consumers' judgments and behaviors across a range of consumption contexts important to marketing researchers.

Cavanaugh, Bettman, and Luce demonstrate that dimensions of positive emotional appraisal help to explain how specific positive emotions broaden consumers' thought-action repertoires in unique ways. They demonstrate dissociations among positive emotions characterized by problem-solving (e.g., hope), social connection (e.g., love and gratitude), and control (e.g., pride) appraisals using both manipulated and measured emotions. These specific types of positive emotions differentially influence effortful behaviors (e.g., considering more choice options and engaging in environmental actions) as well as socially conscious behaviors (e.g., behaviors benefiting distant others and donations to international relief).

Building on this theme, Algoe, Haidt and Gable examine other-praising positive emotions (e.g., gratitude, elevation, admiration). The authors present new data on the distinct situational appraisals and cognitive consequences of other-praising emotions. Across lab and field studies, this research demonstrates the importance of eliciting appropriate positive emotions for particular consumer contexts (e.g., gift-giving) and for producing desired effects for firms and service providers (i.e., promoting lasting relationships with both new and established consumers).

Griskevicius, Shiota, and Neufeld draw on an evolutionary approach to examine discrete positive emotions. They examine how specific positive emotions influence cognitive processing in the context of advertising and persuasion. In particular, they predict and find that certain positive emotions (e.g., amusement) lead to more heuristic processing while other positive emotions (e.g., awe) lead to more systematic processing of messages. This research helps to elucidate discrepancies in the literature regarding the relationship between positive emotion and consumer processing.

In keeping with the conference theme "A World of Knowledge At the Point of Confluence," the papers in this session bring together distinct theoretical perspectives on emotion (i.e., appraisal, broaden-and-build, and evolutionary theories), which are likely to inspire much interest and debate. A rich discussion of these findings on the differential effects of positive emotions will be led by Barbara Fredrickson. As the Principal Investigator of the Positive Emotions and Psychophysiology Lab at the University of North Carolina and author of a 2009 book entitled *Positivity*, Dr. Fredrickson is a leading expert on positive emotions. Fredrickson has suggested that positive emotions serve a unique function—broadening thought and action tendencies and building enduring resources (Fredrickson 1998; 2001; 2009). In this symposium, she will share her expertise and unique insights on the role of positive emotions in consumer behavior research and facilitate discussion in a twenty-minute segment. This symposium is likely to appeal to researchers interested in emotion and decision-making as well as transformative consumer research. The research presented contributes to our understanding of how and why consumers behave the way they do in the domains of brand relationships, gift-giving, donation behavior, socially conscious consumption, advertising and persuasion. These findings have important implications for marketers, individual consumers, and society.

EXTENDED ABSTRACTS

"Feeling Good and Doing Better: How Specific Positive Emotions Differentially Influence Consumer Behavior"

Lisa A. Cavanaugh, University of Southern California, USA
James R. Bettman, Duke University, USA
Mary Frances Luce, Duke University, USA

Many consumption decisions are driven by a desire to cultivate positive emotional experiences for ourselves and others. Marketers, likewise, go to great lengths to engineer positive emotional experiences for consumers. However, researchers lack a clear understanding of the distinct behavioral consequences of different positive emotions.

We build on appraisal theory (Lerner and Keltner 2000, 2001; Raghunathan and Pham 1999; Smith and Ellsworth 1985) and the broaden-and-build theory of positive emotions (Fredrickson 1998, 2001) to understand the influence of different positive emotions on consumption behaviors. The broaden-and-build theory suggests that all positive emotions function similarly to broaden momentary thought-action repertoires. Instead, we argue that specific positive emotions broaden in distinct ways based on differences in appraisals. In particular, we use both manipulated and measured (dispositional) emotions to show that certain positive emotions may broaden a consumer's sense of self while others may broaden a consumer's efforts or consideration set.

In study 1, we characterize positive emotions in terms of new appraisal dimensions. The results show that positive emotions can be reliably distinguished along multiple appraisal dimensions, including two new dimensions: social connection (sense of connection to others) and temporal focus (focus on past, present, future). Notably, the dimensions that explain the greatest amount of variance among these positive emotions are different from the dimensions used previously to understand important differences in negative emotions. Specifically, we find that problem-solving (sense of needing to expend energy or effort) and social connection (sense of connectedness to others) best distinguish among the positive emotions considered.

Studies 2–5 were designed to test whether the patterns of appraisals established in Study 1 enable prediction of differential effects of positive emotional experience, using specific emotions that are manipulated (studies 2 and 3) and positive emotional blends that are both measured (study 4) and manipulated through television commercials (study 5). We hypothesize that two different forms of broadening—broadened sense of self versus broadened consideration—will be triggered by different positive emotions, namely emotions high in social connection (e.g., love and gratitude) for broadened sense of self and emotions high in problem-solving (e.g., hope and interest) for consideration and effortful actions. We also introduce a new methodology accounting for the extent to which a consumer regularly experiences an array of positive emotions to develop appraisal dispositions characterizing the chronically active appraisal dimensions for that consumer. Thus, the appraisals underlying specific positive emotions can be used not only to predict consumers' momentary emotional states but also to predict patterns of behavior linked to the specific emotions that a consumer experiences regularly.

In study 2, we test our hypothesis that a high social connection positive emotion (love) but not a low social connection positive emotion (hope) will lead to a broadened sense of self and hence more socially conscious consumption behaviors benefiting distant others, with this difference dampened or eliminated for behaviors benefiting close others. As predicted, we find an emotion by social distance interaction on likelihood of engaging in socially conscious consumption behaviors. Specifically, momentary love increases intentions to engage in socially conscious behaviors benefiting distant others significantly more than hope. In contrast, love and hope have identical effects on behavior benefiting close others, i.e. above those in the neutral emotion condition. Significant moderated mediation demonstrates that appraisals of social connection mediate the relationship between emotion and behavior for distant but not close others.

In study 3, we test our hypothesis that specific positive emotions can lead to opposite effects within the same consumption context, i.e. in response to a fundraising appeal. We predict and find that a high perceived control emotion (e.g., pride) will lead donors to prioritize restricted (vs. unrestricted) monetary gifts more than a social connection emotion (e.g., love) and that a high social connection emotion (e.g., love) will lead donors to prioritize international (vs. domestic) relief more than a high perceived control emotion (e.g., pride).

Since emotional blending (i.e., experiencing multiple positive emotions concurrently) is particularly common among positive emotions, studies 4 and 5 examine positive emotional blends based on dimensions of appraisal. In study 4, we examine how combinations of dispositional positive emotions form appraisal dispositions which chronically influence consumption behavior and lead to distinct forms of broadening. In study 4, we predict and find evidence of a double dissociation such that positive emotions characterized by problem-solving (but not social connection) lead to broadened consideration (considering more options and more information seeking) and those characterized by social connection (but not problem-solving) lead to more socially conscious consumption behaviors benefiting distant others—two distinct forms of broadening. Simultaneous regression models based on the social connection and problem-solving appraisal disposition scores showed that different appraisal dispositions lead, as hypothesized, to these different types of broadening.

Study 5 predicts and finds that momentary positive emotional blends (based on positive emotional appraisal types) can similarly influence behavior. Participants who viewed a television commercial characterized by a problem-solving emotional blend (hope and interest) subsequently committed to more effortful environmental actions (e.g., bringing canvas bags to the grocery store; unplugging appliances not in use) than those who viewed a commercial depicting a social connection blend (love and gratitude). Mediation analysis shows that appraisals of problem-solving explain the relationship between positive emotional blend type and engagement in such actions.

In sum, five studies show that different positive emotions broaden in different ways and that different types of broadening foster different types of consumption behaviors. These results are among the first to characterize the different effects of distinct positive emotions. They provide the first empirical demonstration of differential broadening. We also introduce new appraisal dimensions useful for distinguishing among positive emotions and the new concept of appraisal dispositions as a means for characterizing chronic patterns of emotion and appraisal tendencies that influence consumption.

"Opportunity Knocks: Other-Praising Positive Emotions in Action"

Sara B. Algoe, University of North Carolina, USA
Jonathan Haidt, University of Virginia, USA
Shelly Gable, UC Santa Barbara, USA

Emotions mark moments and reliably coordinate humans' adaptive responses to common environmental situations that have arisen across millennia. New research and theory suggests that this characterization of emotions applies equally well to positive and negative emotions (e.g., Fredrickson & Branigan 2005). However, whereas scientists have a robust understanding of the form and function of distinct negative emotions like fear, anger, and disgust, relatively little is known about the form and functions of distinct positive emotions. This is despite the fact that positive emotions are experienced more frequently than negative emotions in daily life (e.g., Fredrickson 2009; Fredrickson and Losada 2005), and despite the fact that consumers crave, seek, and shape their lives to find positive emotional experiences.

A critical environmental factor in the experience of human emotion involves our social nature. Humans are often inspired and touched by the actions of others, triggering a range of positive emotional responses that have implications for behavior (Algoe and Haidt 2009). Drawing on theory from emotion and relationship science, we present data to document the distinct form and function of three positive emotions from the "other-praising" family: elevation, admiration, and gratitude. We then focus on specific positive emotions (e.g., gratitude) to illustrate the importance of eliciting the right appraisals (i.e., in gift-giving) to produce the desired effects promoting relationships with new and established consumers.

We first provide data to highlight key theoretical differences between moral elevation, admiration, and gratitude. These data document spontaneously-generated behavioral intentions that make each other-praising emotion distinct from joy, and each distinct from the other. As "other-praising" emotions, each emotion may help to enhance the reputation of the target (i.e., the praiseworthy other), but each appears to have unique form and function (Algoe and Haidt 2009).

Next, we present data from two experiments (studies 1 and 2) designed to demonstrate the distinct appraisal and motivational patterns of two other-praising emotions: moral elevation and admiration. Participants were randomly assigned and exposed to the emotion manipulation (elevation/ admiration/ amusement) in each of two ways: a standardized video clip viewed in the lab, and then for a three-week period they completed reports each time they experienced the type of situation to which they were assigned. As predicted, results from each study showed distinct appraisals for each other-praising emotion, distinct patterns of emotional response, and distinct patterns of motivation.

In Studies 3 and 4, we hone in on a specific other-praising emotion particularly relevant to firms and service providers (e.g., relationship marketing) and consumer choice (i.e., gift-giving): gratitude. In these studies, we illustrate how understanding the situational appraisals that produce a given emotion help us better understand subsequent consumer beliefs and behavior. Simply receiving a gift is not enough to produce the emotion of gratitude. The actual emotional response is what matters in the coordination of the desired behavior.

In study 3, we present a field study suggesting that experienced gratitude has important and long-term implications for building loyalty and lasting relationships between new consumers and firm employees (Algoe, Haidt, Gable 2008). In this study, we explore the dynamics and implications of gift-giving among new brand initiates (i.e., sorority sisters) during an annual tradition on college campuses. In this study, new members of a sorority, who received a variety of benefits (i.e., a series of gifts) from a specific benefactor over the course of four days, reported their appraisals and emotional response to receiving each benefit (i.e., gift). The results show that beyond liking for and cost of the benefit, the perception that the benefactor was responsive to the needs and wishes of the recipient in the provision of the benefit robustly predicted gratitude. For the first time, these data show that, beyond cost/benefit analyses, gratitude entails perceptions of a benefactor's understanding, validation, and caring. Mostly notably, these findings have remarkable long-term implications for the relationship with the benefactor. In fact, follow-up measures show that the recipient's gratitude experienced during gift-giving predicted the benefactor's feelings about the relationship <u>one month later</u> regardless of time spent together.

In study 4, we provide evidence that effective expression of gratitude predicts consumers' feelings of relationship satisfaction and connection in long-term relationships as well (Algoe, Gable, and Maisel in press). To illustrate how essential other-praising emotions are to meaningful real-world outcomes, we examine their role in long-term relationships as well. Study 4 measured emotions and change in relationship quality in people with already established relationships. Specifically, we wanted to see what experienced gratitude could add in an already established relationship. Members of couples independently reported their emotional responses to interactions with their partners that day and then provided daily ratings of relationship quality for two weeks. Using multilevel modeling to pair couple-members' responses and assess change over time, a participant's gratitude predicted a partner's increased feelings of satisfaction with and connection to the relationship from the previous day. These finding held for men and for women, and controlled for several alternative explanations. As a contrast, the emotion of indebtedness, which is also associated with repayment behavior and so theoretically could build a relationship, was not associated with increased relationship quality when included in the same models. Thus, everyday gratitude appears to work as a booster shot for these relationships. In sum, a costly benefit is not enough; you need to get the appraisals and the specific positive emotion right to produce desirable relationship effects.

In just the past few years, evidence has accumulated that all positive emotions are not "happiness." Instead, emotions like admiration, gratitude, and elevation have distinct forms and functions. These studies demonstrate that these emotions are differentiated in everyday life, and that they work in specific ways to change beliefs about the praiseworthy characteristics of the target, shape motivations to interact with the target and the world, and can have lasting impact on relationships, with implications for building customer loyalty and mutually beneficial relationships. Understanding the basic functions of specific positive emotions and specific types of positive emotions is important to unlocking their potential.

"Why Different Positive Emotions Have Different Effects: An Evolutionary Approach to Discrete Positive Emotions and Processing of Persuasive Messages"

Vladas Griskevicius, University of Minnesota, USA
Michelle N. Shiota, Arizona State University, USA
Samantha Neufeld, Arizona State University, USA

Imagine you're watching a pleasant television program. The program may be a travel show featuring awe-inspiring natural wonders, or an animal program about baby animals; it may be a sitcom that makes you laugh, or a highly anticipated sporting event. At some point during the program, you're likely to encounter a commercial message intended to persuade you. Given that any of these programs will elicit positive feelings, are you likely to process the persuasive message more carefully or more carelessly than if you felt no emotion at all?

The answer to this question might initially appear simple: Much research already shows that positive affect leads people to process messages in a more heuristic or careless manner. In the present series of experiments, we examine the complexity layered upon this general effect and address some of the mechanisms behind this complexity. Whereas traditional approaches have examined the influence of affective valence on cognition, our approach emphasizes differences among the likely evolutionary, fitness-enhancing functions of discrete emotions of the same valence, and suggests that emotions of the same valence can have quite different consequences.

Although positive emotion was long considered a single construct, researchers have begun to offer functional definitions of specific varieties of positive emotion, whereby different positive emotions facilitate fitness-enhancing responses to distinct types of opportunities (e.g., Keltner et al. 2006; Kenrick and Shiota 2007; Fredrickson 1998; Griskevicius et al. 2009). In the current research, we assessed the impact on processing of persuasive messages of four functionally distinct positive emotions described in previous literature (e.g., Keltner et al. 2006): amusement, enthusiasm, nurturant love (i.e., compassion), and awe.

Amusement is the positive emotion experienced during social or cognitive play, including humor. Play behavior and the experience of humor are both associated with a distinctive "drop-jaw" smile and/or laughter, expressions that promote social bonding by letting down one's guard and signaling social support. Enthusiasm serves primarily to facilitate the acquisition of material resources and rewards such as food. For example, consider the feeling experienced when smelling the preparation of a delicious dinner, or the feeling of excitement after overhearing that you might be getting a raise. Enthusiasm draws attention to predictable associations among cues of reward, the experience of reward, and behavioral strategies for acquiring rewards.

Nurturant love (sometimes referred to as compassion) is the feeling of love and concern for another's well-being, typified by one's emotions when seeing an infant, small child, or baby animal. This positive emotion serves to motivate nurturant and care giving behavior, such as attending closely to the target's needs and protecting the target from possible harm. Awe is the feeling of wonder and astonishment experienced in the presence of something novel and difficult to grasp. Prototypical elicitors of awe include panoramic views, works of great art, and others' remarkable accomplishments. This positive emotion serves to facilitate new schema formation in unexpected, information-rich environments. Accordingly, awe leads people to shift their awareness away from day-to-day concerns and toward current incoming information.

The first goal of the current research was to investigate the effects of these four positive emotions on the processing of persuasive messages. This question was addressed by developing and validating two different methods to elicit the positive emotions, and by assessing the emotions' influence on persuasive message processing using two well-established paradigms. In Study 1, emotions were elicited by having participants write about a personal emotional experience with a prototypical elicitor of a specific positive emotion and processing was assessed via the classic "comprehensive exams" paradigm. In Study 2, emotions were elicited by reading a short story depicting prototypical elicitors of a specific positive emotion, and processing was assessed via another method involving a different type of attitude topic and heuristic cue (see Tiedens and Linton 2001).

In both experiments, we found that the positive emotions of enthusiasm and amusement enhanced heuristic processing, consistent with traditional findings on the influence of positive affect. Participants induced to feel either of these two emotions were more easily persuaded by a weak argument that had persuasive heuristic cues than those in a neutral control condition. In fact, a closer look at previous studies indicates that researchers have generally used "positive affect" manipulations targeting one or more of these emotions: watching a funny video clip, which elicits amusement; receiving a gift of candy, which likely elicits enthusiasm.

In contrast, when individuals were in the positive emotional state of awe (e.g., seeing a breathtaking panorama for the first time) or nurturant love (e.g., seeing a cute, vulnerable child), they were significantly less persuaded by weak arguments than people in an emotionally neutral state—an effect that suggests systematic processing (e.g., Tiedens and Linton 2001). Overall, we found that positive affect can produce more heuristic or more systematic processing than an emotionally neutral state, depending on the specific positive emotion that is elicited in the person.

We additionally examined whether the effects of different positive emotions were accounted for by a common mediator or by different mediators. To address this goal, we investigated whether several of the positive emotions were associated with different cognitive appraisals (Tiedens and Linton 2001), or with different patterns of thoughts about the persuasive message. We did not find that certainty–or any other single appraisal dimension–adequately explained our pattern of findings. Also, no single aspect of thoughts about the persuasive message adequately explained the pattern of positive emotion effects. Instead, meditational analyses suggest that enthusiasm, amusement, nurturant love, and awe each affect persuasion through a somewhat different mechanism, some of which are yet to be established empirically. This is consistent with the evolutionary perspective driving our research, which defines each emotion as a fitness-enhancing package of cognitive, physiological, and behavioral responses to a prototypical eliciting situation. Different emotion packages may include some overlapping elements, but no single element (such as an appraisal dimension) is expected to account for the effects of all emotions.

REFERENCES

Algoe, Sara B. and Jonathan Haidt (2009), "Witnessing Excellence in Action: The 'Other-Praising' Emotions of Elevation, Gratitude, and Admiration," *Journal of Positive Psychology*, 4, 105-127.

Algoe, Sara B., Jonathan Haidt, and S. L. Gable(2008), "Beyond Reciprocity: Gratitude and Relationships in Everyday Life," *Emotion*, 8, 425-429.

Algoe, Sara B., Shelly L. Gable, and Natalya Maisel (forthcoming), "It's the Little Things: Everyday Gratitude as a Booster Shot for Romantic Relationships," *Personal Relationships.*

Fredrickson, Barbara L. (1998), "What Good Are Positive Emotions?" *Review of General Psychology*, 2 (3), 300-19.

______ (2001), "The Role of Positive Emotions in Positive Psychology: The Broaden-and-Build Theory of Positive Emotions," *American Psychologist*, 56 (3), 218-26.

______ (2009), *Positivity: Groundbreaking Research Reveals How to Embrace the Hidden Strength of Positive Emotions, Overcome Negativity, and Thrive*, New York, NY: Crown.

Fredrickson, Barbara L. and Christine Branigan (2005), "Positive Emotions Broaden the Scope of Attention and Thought-Action Repertoires," *Cognition & Emotion*, 19 (3), 313-32.

Fredrickson, Barbara L. and Marcial F. Losada (2005), "Positive Affect and the Complex Dynamics of Human Flourishing," *American Psychologist*, 60, 678-686.

Griskevicius, Vladas, Noah J. Goldstein, Chad R. Mortensen, Jill M. Sundie, Robert B. Cialdini, and Douglas T. Kenrick (2009), "Fear and Loving in Las Vegas: Evolution, Emotion, and Persuasion," *Journal of Marketing Research*, 46, 384-395.

Keltner, Dacher, Jonathan Haidt, and Michelle N. Shiota (2006), "Social Functionalism and the Evolution of Emotions," in *Evolution and Social Psychology*, ed. M. Schaller, J. Simpson, and D. Kenrick.

Kenrick, Douglas T. and Michelle N. Shiota (2008), "Approach and Avoidance Motivation(s): An Evolutionary Perspective," in *Handbook of Approach and Avoidance Motivation*, ed. A. J. Elliot, New York, NY: Psychology Press, 271-285.

Lerner, Jennifer S. and Dacher Keltner (2000), "Beyond Valence: Toward a Model of Emotion-Specific Influences on Judgement and Choice," *Cognition & Emotion*, 14 (4), 473-93.

______ (2001), "Fear, Anger, and Risk," *Journal of Personality and Social Psychology*, 81 (1), 146-59.

Raghunathan, Rajagopal and Michel Tuan Pham (1999), "All Negative Moods Are Not Equal: Motivational Influences of Anxiety and Sadness on Decision Making," *Organizational Behavior and Human Decision Processes*, 79 (1), 56-77.

Smith, Craig A. and Phoebe C. Ellsworth (1985), "Patterns of Cognitive Appraisal in Emotion," *Journal of Personality and Social Psychology*, 48 (4), 813-38.

Tiedens, Larissa Z. and Susan Linton (2001), "Judgment Under Emotional Certainty and Uncertainty: The Effects of Specific Emotions on Information Processing," *Journal of Personality and Social Psychology*, 81, 973-988.

Exploring the Links between Stigma and Consumption

Elizabeth Crosby, University of Illinois at Urbana-Champaign, USA
Cele C. Otnes, University of Illinois at Urbana-Champaign, USA

SESSION OVERVIEW

Goffman (1963) describes stigma as the possession of an attribute that has a negative connotation, and that deviates from what is considered normal in a specific category of people. Whether a particular attribute is considered a stigma varies depending largely on environmental and situational factors. Furthermore, what may be regarded as a stigma in one situation may be considered normal in another. Nevertheless, people cope with perceived stigmas in a variety of ways. Stigma management consists of the strategies employed by the stigmatized consumer or some other person on his or her behalf to cope with the stigma (Goffman 1963). Stigma is a well-researched phenomenon in sociology and psychology. Scholars have examined stigma management strategies such as resignation, confrontation, concealment, and enclave withdrawal (Miller and Kaiser 2001). Researchers have also explored the psychological effects of stigmatization, which include despondency and helplessness (Abramson et al. 1989). However, some stigmatized individuals view their stigmas as "blessings in disguise," which can reap positive effects such as increased self-esteem (Ainlay et al. 1986).

Stigma and stigma management have emerged as important constructs within consumer research. Stigma has been examined in relation to senior citizen discounts (Tepper 1994), subcultures (Kozinets 2001), low-literate consumers (Adkins and Ozanne 2005, Viswanathan, Rosa, and Harris 2005), and coupon redemption (Argo and Main 2008). Unfortunately, however, these constructs are often regulated to the background as other constructs take center stage or are context-specific. Yet stigma and stigma management deserve study in their own right, because of their implications for consumer behavior and consumer welfare. This special session places the study of stigma front and center, by exploring the complex relationships among stigma, stigma management, and consumption. Elizabeth Crosby and Cele C. Otnes (University of Illinois at Urbana-Champaign) explore how consumers use consumption to manage stigma in a wide variety of contexts. Bige Saatcioglu (HEC Paris) and Julie Ozanne (Virginia Tech) examine stigma within the context of poverty. Daiane Scaraboto (York University) and Eileen Fischer (York University) examine how groups of stigmatized consumers collectively manage their stigma online. Madhu Viswanathan (University of Illinois at Urbana-Champaign) compares the stigmas and coping strategies for low-literate and poor consumers across two different cultures.

EXTENDED ABSTRACTS

"Consumption as a Strategy for Stigma Management"

Elizabeth Crosby, University of Illinois, Urbana-Champaign, USA
Cele C. Otnes, University of Illinois, Urbana-Champaign. USA

In his seminal book on stigma and stigma management, Goffman (1963) argues that consumers can be stigmatized because of their social class. A stigma "refers to an attribute that is deeply discrediting" (Goffman 1963, 3). There are many different sources of stigmas in society, from age to a physical handicap. A consumer's stigma "makes him different from others in the category of persons available for him to be, and of a less desirable kind" (Goffman 1963, 3). Stigmatization affects not only how people perceive themselves, but also how they feel others perceive them (or will perceive them if others know about their stigmatized attribute) (Crocker, Major, and Steele 1998). Research finds that stigmatization can result in positive and negative psychological effects. Stigmatized individuals may also suffer from low self worth and depression (Abramson et al. 1989) while others may experience increased self-esteem (Ainlay et al. 1986). Much of the psychological effects of stigma depend on how the individual manages the stigmatization (Ainlay et al. 1986). As such, it is important to understand how individuals cope with stigma. Numerous studies have looked at how individuals cope with a particular stigma, such as social class (Granfield 1991), racially stigmatized individuals (Crandall, Tsang, Harvey, and Britt 2000), and HIV stigmatized consumers (Emlet 2007). Furthermore, consumer researchers also have explored the concept of stigma in particular contexts including senior citizen discounts (Tepper 1994), subcultures (Kozinets 2001), low-literate consumers (Adkins and Ozanne 2005, Viswanathan, Rosa, and Harris 2005), and coupon redemption (Argo and Main 2008).

This study explores how individuals use consumption to manage stigma across contexts. For this study, I collected 102 consumer narratives from young adult informants who detailed their experiences with being stigmatized. The narratives describe many different stigmas based on such characteristics as gender, race, religion, and social class. In analyzing the text, I sought out emergent themes while also engaging in dialectical tacking (Strauss and Corbin 1998). I read all narratives multiple times to identify salient and emergent themes (McCracken 1988).

The preliminary analysis reveals that informants employ four consumption-related strategies to manage stigma: (1) concealment, (2) reduction, (3) redirection, and (4) disclosure. With Concealment, individuals consume certain products that will hide their stigma. Consumers deliberately choose products that conceal their stigma. For example, one informant, William, felt stigmatized by his social class, and bought clothing accessories that he believed would conceal his lower social class. Consumers may feel pressured to make these consumption choices, fearing if they do not, their stigma will be revealed. This strategy has consumer welfare implications, because consumers may be pressured to spend beyond their means or consume products that are harmful to their health.

With Reducing, people attempt to decrease their stigma by limiting the consumption of products that might exacerbate their stigma. Informant Molly is often stigmatized because of her multiple tattoos. Others have told her that "tattoos make you look like a criminal." Even though she would like to have more, Molly has limited her tattoos to four so that the effects of her stigmatization are within certain boundaries.

With Redirection, consumers manage their stigma by shifting attention away from it. They consume products that highlight some other attribute they have to make their stigma less noticeable. Consumers thus shift others' attention away from the stigmatized attribute to some other attribute that better represents how they want others to view them. Another informant Mark was stigmatized for not being an athlete. In order to combat this characterization, he carried his drumsticks "prominently" on the outside of his backpack, directing people's attention away from his lack of athleticism to his musical talents.

Finally, with Disclosure, individuals can also manage their stigma by making consumption choices that intentionally draw attention to it. In doing this, consumers make the statement that they are not ashamed of whatever attribute for which they are stigmatized. Furthermore, consumers may also seek out consumption opportunities where they can meet with other individuals who are stigmatized by the same attribute (Kozinets 2001, Muniz and Schau 2005). Informant Michael notes that he enjoyed skateboarding, but felt that others stigmatized him for it, considering him to be a juvenile delinquent because it. He dealt with the stigma by immersing himself more fully in the activity. Michael started spending considerable time at the skate park with other skateboarders. He also changed his style of dress to match the other skateboarders, so that he could easily be identified as a skateboarder. This paper will fully unpack each of these strategies, as well as their implications for consumer welfare and consumer research.

"The Voices of Trailer Park Residents: Towards a Multidimensional Understanding of Stigma"

Bige Saatcioglu, HEC Paris , France
Julie L. Ozanne, Virginia Tech, USA

Since Goffman's (1963) seminal work on stigma theory, a profusion of research has explored the sources, nature, and consequences of stigma. However, much consumer research on stigma focuses on stigma management strategies from a psychological perspective investigating micro-level interactions within marketplace encounters (see, for exceptions, Hill 2001; Hill and Gaines 2007). Fewer studies take into account the deeply embedded socio-cultural stigmas that permeate particular contexts. Thus, a need exists for more research involving socio-cultural accounts that explore the development of stigmas through not only marketplace behaviors but also consumers' dialectical relationships with the macro social structure (Link and Phelan 2001). Furthermore, the relationships between stigma and its related components (e.g., different forms of deprivation and exclusion) need to be taken into account in order to arrive at a richer understanding of the social construction of stigma.

Poverty is one such state through which multiple co-existing social, cultural, motivational, and material dynamics emerge. Poverty is not only about economic and material shortage but it also involves a lack of socio culturally perceived necessities (Sen 2000) and social exclusion from meaningful interactions and exchanges (Bauman 2000). However, traditionally, poverty is treated as merely an economic problem; the poor suffer from material deprivation. Implicit in this approach known as the 'absolute poverty' is a one-dimensional deprivation in which individuals lack economic capital to meet their primary material and physical needs (Lister 2004). Consistent with this tradition, much consumer research on poverty focuses on the economic aspects of resource-constrained consumers' lives while overlooking social, cultural, and motivational dynamics (see, for exceptions, Hill and Stamey 1990; Chakravarti 2006). Alternatively, a more multidimensional perspective takes into consideration different types of deprivations and stigmatizations experienced by poor consumers. Here, poverty is not merely economic and material shortage of resources; rather, it is a multidimensional, relational, dynamic, and complex phenomenon that encompasses many different realities of the poor. It is the lack of "consumer adequacy," defined as "the continuous availability of a bundle of goods and services that are necessary for survival as well as the attainment of basic human dignity and self-determination" (Hill 2002, p. 20).

The present research builds on these nuanced relationships that exist between the impoverished consumers and multiple social constituents. We demonstrate five distinct social constructions of poverty deriving from five fragmented social identities adopted by the poor to manage and cope with multiple social stigmas. Our research shows that, even within the same bounded geographical setting, there exist various meanings and flavors of stigma. For example, within the institutionalized and cultural norms, poor people are assigned multiple labels and, as consumers, they are categorized as "flawed, blemished, and defective consumer manquées" (Bauman 2005, p. 38). Poverty is also seen as a "manifestation of moral defect"; that is, a blemish of the individual character since it is assumed that the poor are generally responsible for their socio-economic status (Lewis 1970). Moreover, poor people are stigmatized as groups or communities, indicating a tribal-like social stigma as advanced by Goffman (1963). Taking an ethnographic approach within the context of a mobile home park, we investigate how the poor negotiate their social identity and manage multiple stigmas in everyday life. Consistent with a multi-dimensional approach to poverty, we first untangle different types of stigmatizations experienced by mobile home residents. We then explore a wide range of stigma management strategies they employ.

Mobiles homes, once a low-cost opportunity for blue-collar workers to realize the middle-class American dream of home ownership and upward social mobility, have turned into degraded forms of housing since the 1960s. Their unusual appearance and potential mobility represent a threat to conventional American housing ideals and norms. Moreover, the negative social stereotyping of mobile home residents as dirty, lazy, and criminal-minded individuals further contributes to the stigmatization of mobile home parks as "white trash icons" (Bérubé and Bérubé 1997). Consequently, our findings suggest that mobile home residents are stigmatized on various dimensions and experience different forms of social devaluation. Within such proliferation of co-existing stigmas, our informants employ a variety of stigma management strategies to either manage or transform those cultural representations and practices that stigmatize. For example, many informants fight back against the stigma of 'trailer park trash' by expressing their pride in their homes through artistic and creative home projects. Others take a more consumption-oriented approach to poverty management and reject the label of poor and inadequate consumers through middle-class consumption aspirations. Those park residents with a stronger sense of belonging and affiliation to the mobile home park engage in collective community revitalization projects. At times, this active civic engagement extends beyond the confines of the trailer park and includes wider social settings such as the town council and religious communities. Such participation into meaningful social interactions and civic activities help park residents cope with feelings of isolation, exclusion, and alienation from mainstream consumer society. In contrast with these active stigma managers, some mobile home residents take a more subtle approach to stigma management. They emotionally distance themselves from similar others, engage in downward social comparison, and become outsiders within the "ghetto of similarly deficient consumers" (Bauman 2005, p. 41). Finally, other poor consumers who actually own the stigma of poverty reconstruct the meaning of stigmatization through horizontal social comparison and bonding capital (Putnam 2003).

Thus, this research approaches social stigma of poverty as a relational, multi-faceted, and dynamic process whereby individuals with different levels of agency and aspirations and multiple social constituents interact in an intertwined web of power relations (Waxman 1983). Combining individual-psychological and macro-social research traditions on stigma and exploring multiple co-existing social stigmas within a mobile home park community, this research extends our understanding of stigma creation and management.

"From Individual Coping to Collective Action: Stigma Management in Online Communities"

Daiane Scaraboto, York University, Canada
Eileen Fischer, York University, Canada

Current perspectives on stigma define it as a persistent predicament with widespread consequences for stigmatized individuals (Henry and Caldwell 2006). This conception of stigma implies that to promote effective change, a multifaceted and multilevel approach is necessary. To combat stigma, it is necessary to address issues related to the many mechanisms that can emerge in the context of disadvantaged outcomes. Consumer researchers have mainly focused on understanding the consequences of stigmatization for consumers and on identifying individual passive strategies of stigma coping, as opposed to active strategies to change stigma. Similarly, other social science research has paid limited attention to active responses to stigma (Miller 2006). Despite a recent move towards a more contextualized, less pathological view of stigmatization (Dovidio, Major, and Crocker 2000, Miller and Major 2000), active responses to stigma have received limited consideration. In particular, collective responses have yet to be considered.

We propose that because they tend to challenge the legitimacy of an existing status situation and involve the elaboration of alternative meanings for individual and collective behavior while fighting the economic and social aspects that underlie the stigma, collectives fighting a stigma can be studied as a form of social movement. On the macro level, the focus is on the role of culture in giving rise to challenges to entrenched features of social structures, such as those that support particular stigma. On the micro level, the focus in on how individual identities and behaviors lead them to challenges to specific features of such structures (Pichardo 1997). The new social movement perspective and consumer culture literature lend support to our investigation of a collective of stigmatized consumers. We are interested in identifying and explaining how collectives attempt to deal with marketing practices that they view as reinforcing aspects of a particular stigma. We are also interested in how these collectives attempt to influence marketers to mitigate stigma in society more broadly. Our research is conducted in an online context by a qualitative investigation of the "Fat Acceptance Movement" (FAM) which fights the stigma associated with fat. This choice of context also contributes to extend our understanding of stigma in consumption domains. Prior studies on stigmatized consumers exclusively address domains where the stigma is concealable or not readily apparent, as for low literacy (Adkins and Ozanne 2005, Wallendorf 2001), subculture membership (Henry and Caldwell 2006, Kozinets 2001), and senior age (Tepper 1994). In face-to-face encounters, fat people cannot easily pass for "normal" (Goffman 1974) or conceal their stigma. Besides, heavy-weight individuals are generally considered blameworthy, unlike other physically stigmatized people, like the handicapped (Page 1984). Weight bias has existed for a long time, but only recently it has received the attention of researchers, legislators, and advocates (Brownell 2005).

The FAM is mostly an online phenomenon. Offline activities associated with the movement are infrequent, while the online group spreads globally over a net of interconnected blogs and social networking websites (Samuel 2007). This online community denounces the "weight loss industry," questions the notion of an obesity epidemic, advocates "Health at Every Size," and fights weight-based discrimination (Rabin 2008). It constitutes a site of documented interactions that can provide insight into key aspects of how a community manages the stigma. Consistent with the nature of the phenomenon, we employ "netnography" (Kozinets 2002) to orient data collection and analysis. The study also involves interviewing individuals associated with the FAM movement and includes participant observation in offline settings. This methodological approach takes us closer to the meanings attributed by members to their actions, and provides an understanding of issues related to intersectionality (Gopaldas et al. 2008) and representativeness within the community.

A primary contribution of this investigation will be to explore how the actions of collectives fighting a stigma impact on cultural and marketplace practices, and, conversely, will illuminate the evaluation of market practices' impact on stigma-related issues. In addition, this study will shift significantly our theoretical understanding of stigma management from an individual, passive, to a collective, active perspective. This study will also have significant implications for social scientists engaged in stigma related research by addressing the stigma associated with fat, an important source of debate and concern to public policy makers and to legions of consumers who struggle with the embodied experience of being fat in a society that reveres thinness. Our preliminary findings indicate that, as a consequence of taking part in collective advocacy against their stigma, these individuals become more critical of the social scene, and highly conscious of human relations. In this sense, they are more inclined to notice and discuss market practices that represent their group in a positive or biased way. Furthermore, we find support to prior research (e.g. Henry and Caldwell 2006, 1035) suggesting that "in contrast to withdrawing into an enclave, the stigmatized individual may respond by challenging the stigma label by attempting to participate in the mainstream domains." Our study offers empirical evidence that endorses this assumption and also identifies how a collective of stigmatized individuals interact with the market to develop workable ways to fight the stigma and achieve mainstream insertion.

"Understanding Stigma and Coping Strategies across Resource and Literacy Barriers: A Cross-Cultural Comparison"

Madhu Viswanathan, University of Illinois at Urbana-Champaign, USA

This presentation will examine stigma and stigma management among low-literate, low-income consumers in the US and subsistence consumers and entrepreneurs in South India. Our research has focused on understanding marketplace behaviors of individuals living across literacy and resource barriers in the US and in South India. We draw from 15 shopping observations and 35 in-depth interviews of students at adult education centers in the US and from 75 in-depth interviews of low-income, low to moderately literate buyers and sellers in South India.

Research on low-literate consumers in the US has highlighted stigma and related coping strategies (Adkins and Ozanne 2005, Viswanathan, Rosa, and Harris 2005). Adkins and Ozanne (2005) employ dimensions of identity management strategies and acceptance or rejection of stigma arising from low literacy to identify types of low-literate consumers. Researchers have noted that seemingly straightforward events such as having insufficient money at the checkout counter can be cause for despair for low-literate consumers, attributed to not something as mundane as forgetfulness but to the state of low literacy and the stigma attached to it (Gau and Viswanathan 2008). Viswanathan et al. (2005) report a number of coping strategies including avoidance, dependence on others, and social deception. The contrast with even poor but literate consumers who are not stigmatized by their literacy level is striking, in terms of the willingness of such consumers to complain and seek redress in the marketplace when compared to the relatively passive reactions of low-literate consumers (Gau and Viswanathan 2008).

On the other hand, the nature of stigma associated with being poor in an advanced country needs to be disentangled from the stigma associated with low literacy. The social stigma of being barely literate may heavily influence purchase decision-making, such as giving up on functional attributes to avoid embarrassment. In shopping contexts in the US where a certain level of literacy is assumed, the presentation will examine the nature of stigma attached to low literacy and low income as well as associated coping strategies. Large retail settings, with advanced technology for computation and symbolic package information assume certain levels of literacy. Low-literate consumers negotiate shopping encounters apprehensive about being "caught" or "exposed" for their lack of literacy. A sharp contrast is provided by a different setting across the world where poverty and low literacy are both more widespread. Our research on subsistence consumers and entrepreneurs in South India provides comparative insights on stigma and its management. This intensely relational marketplace is characterized by 1-1 interactions and oral communications, with consumers sharing adversity with small entrepreneurs. Much of the marketplace for the large population of poor, low-literate consumers is relatively distinct from those for the middle and upper strata of society. Subsistence consumers and entrepreneurs learn to evaluate generic products, bargain, count money, and develop related marketplace skills despite their lack of literacy and low income. As a result, we have described these marketplaces as being resource-poor but network rich (Viswanathan 2007), and a stepping stone for developing consumer skills.

With widespread poverty and low literacy, there is almost camaraderie in an otherwise extremely harsh world among the poor and social networks that provide support. The nature of stigma in these settings may be quite different, arising to a lesser extent from poverty or low literacy, but nevertheless existing at more extreme levels of these dimensions. For example, with extreme poverty, households have no choice but to renege on family traditions and associated expenses relating to weddings, birth or death, often leading to stigmatization and being ostracized from family circles. Similarly, public humiliation, the method through which non-collateral loans of astronomic interest are enforced, works by stigmatizing the family for being unable to pay back money they owe. Thus, the very same rich social networks that play a facilitating role can also amplify stigma and the need for its management. Compared to poverty, low literacy leads appears to lead to distinctly different and arguably more acute stigma, an issue that will be explored in the presentation. Despite subsistence marketplaces that do not rely on or assume a high level of literacy, low-literate individuals view themselves as possessing an attribute with a negative connotation, i.e., as a stigma, often an explanation for their being in the state of poverty. Low literacy can lead to fear of conversation and enquiry in s shopping context, feelings of futility even when cheated, and an acceptance of conditions as they are–often justified by the stigma of low literacy. Significant events such as learning a specific trade can act to lessen the stigma of lacking formal education. In summary, this presentation will take a cross-cultural journey toward understanding the nature of stigma in strikingly different marketplaces with distinctly different levels of poverty and low literacy, while emphasizing the interplay between low income and low literacy.

References available from the authors.

SPECIAL SESSION SUMMARY

Talk the Green Talk, Shop the Green Walk?

Gary Bamossy, Georgetown University, USA
Basil Englis, Berry College, USA

SESSION OVERVIEW

While the environmental movement in the United States is not new, its history is characterized by a series of stops and starts. Many view Carson's *Silent Spring* as the beginning of the modern environmental movement. In exposing the toxic hazards many widely-used pesticides and herbicides posed for non-targeted organisms, Carson's work raised awareness and prompted a new public discourse. American consumers began to re-conceptualize everyday decisions as affecting the interconnecting environmental web. Disturb the web in one area and the entire web trembles from the impact (Carson 1962). In their growing concern about pollution, suburbanization, and pesticides, American consumers began to understand, or at least to develop incipient awareness that their consumption choices have a broader, sometimes far-reaching impact on the environment. Yet this begs the question of how much has changed since the 1960s.

In 1989, just months prior to the 20th anniversary of Earth Day, a nationally representative survey of 1000 American consumers found that 89% of shoppers claimed to be concerned about the environmental impact of the products and services they purchased. Nearly as many (78%) said they would be willing to pay a premium for a product packaged with recyclable or biodegradable materials (Makower, 2009). And the beat goes on...Numerous commercial market research efforts provide consistent evidence that American consumers are aware of and concerned about environmental issues (MINTeL, 2008; American Environics, 2008; Bonini and Oppenheim/McKinsey, 2008; Karel and Neufeld/Yankelovich, 2007; Pike et.al./Earth Justice, 2008; LOHAS, 2009). While all these surveys report high levels of awareness and concern for issues that are variously described as "Environmentalism," "Sustainable Consumption," "The Environment," or in its simplest and most generic term, "Green," these studies also consistently report that few consumers translate their concerns into action. Most American consumers will not go out of their way to find "green" products and about one-half say that price premiums prevent them from buying "green." American consumers "Talk the Green Talk," but do not "Shop the Green Walk." This chronically weak relationship between Green Awareness/Attitudes and Green Behavior provides both the rationale and the focus of this Special Session proposal.

For decades, scholars have studied the relationships between attitudes, social norms, cultural context(s), rational decision making processes, and behaviors. With respect to Green in particular, a key challenge becomes applying such research. Thus, the challenge is to create a paradigm shift in how consumers' think about and act with respect to the environment. How can consumer behavior research play a role in moving "green behaviors" (however broadly defined) from being a set of values and behaviors that is present in only small segments of American society to one of green(er) values and behaviors that are part of the mainstream marketplace?

This special session offers theoretical perspectives and empirical support that challenge us to take up and apply our discipline's talents for transformative research on an issue that has meaning, and does matter on the ground, in the market, right now (Mick, 2006; 2007). The likely audiences for this session includes researchers with an interest in transformative consumer research as a general domain, those with specific interests in green marketing and consumption, consumer reactivity, consumer resistance and practice theory, as well as colleagues with interests in applying theoretical perspectives in the public interest.

Our focus is on proposing research perspectives to better understand the multitude of reasons as to why consumers have been so reluctant to move from high levels of awareness and concern for the environment towards behaviors of sustainable consumption. We argue that green consumption behaviors must be understood within the context of a process of increasing individualization, where consumers can find ways to feel both responsible and empowered in dealing with environmental risks to both the wider global planet and themselves. The papers in this session recognize that Green is multi-layered and complex; that "Green-Washing" makes consumers feel cynical and confused; that Green is imbued with social status and is seen by many as divisive as opposed to uniting; and that consumer's feelings are accompanied by reactivity, resistance, doubts and insecurities about the consumer choices we all face (Dolan, 2002; Connolly and Prothero, 2008; Kilbourne and Carlson, 2008; Englis and Bamossy, 2009; Lorenzen, 2009; LOHAS 2009).

EXTENDED ABSTRACTS

"Green Dilemma: Libertarian Values Trump Communal Values"

Basil G. Englis, Berry College, USA
Gary Bamossy, Georgetown University, USA

We report the results of a large scale survey of American consumers which segments the market on the basis of consumers' attitudes toward the environment and how these different consumer segments engage (or, more often, don't engage) in pro-environmental consumer behaviors. As noted earlier, various industry studies estimate that 80-90% of American consumers are aware of and concerned about environmental issues, but far fewer translate their concerns into action. However, most consumers will not go out of their way to find "green" products and about one-half say that price premiums prevent them from buying "green" (Mintel 2008). A key question that consumer researchers should address is how (or perhaps, "can"?) we create a paradigm shift in how consumers' think about and act with respect to the environment. To contextualize this research within the framework of Transformative Consumer Research, how can we re-position sustainable consumption from being a niche behavior to become a more widespread behavior adopted in a more consistent manner by the majority of consumers?

There is some industry research which gives us insights on segments of green consumers. One study found that approximately 12% of the U.S. population (about 35 million people) were "True Green" consumers (Mintel 2008)—consumers who not only regularly buy green products, but also incorporate green behaviors such as reducing consumption, re-using products when possible, and recycling. Another study identifies a population segment characterized by a "Lifestyle Of Health And Sustainability" (French and Rogers 2008), and there is even a website devoted to the LOHAS lifestyle (www.lohas.com). With a few exceptions (e.g., Diekmann and Preisendorfer 2003; Ger 1999; Thorson, Thomas and Moore 1995; Meijer and Schuyt 2005), we find far less emphasis in the current consumer research or marketing literatures on studying consumers attitudes toward environmental issues and how these attitudes do (or do not) impact consumers' behavior. Our research explores how the U.S. population is segmented according to their attitudes toward environmental issues and how these attitudes map onto pro-environmental behaviors.

We conducted a large-scale survey using a sample of 4,082 adults drawn from a commercially maintained online consumer panel and matched to the demographic profile of the U.S. population (income, gender, age, geography, and ethnicity). We asked participants to fill out the New Ecological Paradigm Scale, an instrument designed to capture respondents' general orientations toward the environment (see Dunlap et al. 2000 for a review of this scale's development). We also asked respondents to complete an extensive battery of items about their pro-environment behaviors (adapted from Barr 2006; Cordano, Welcomer and Scherer 2003; McDonald and Oates 2006).

Using factor, cluster, and discriminant analyses to identify consumer segments and provide various forms of evidence regarding validity of the results, our analyses of this extensive attitudinal and behavioral data reveal several interesting findings: consistent with prior research (Mintel 2008) we found that nearly 70% of consumers hold pro-environmental attitudes, although the correlations between environmental attitudes and environmental behaviors vary greatly across segments, and for many types of behaviors, within segments. Further, more than 30% of the population is largely indifferent to environmental issues despite the large amount of recent media coverage concerning global warming (e.g., An Inconvenient Truth) and pollution (e.g., prior to the Beijing Olympics). In addition to reporting on the underlying attitudinal and behavioral differences between segments, we also have strong empirical support regarding fundamental differences in beliefs about our basic role as consumers, and the impact of our consumption on the environment. One large segment of consumers believes that there are basic limits to human growth, while another large segment believes that growth can be achieved without harming the environment. A third relatively small group (11%) expresses environmental concerns but also believes that humans should "rule over nature." This segment of consumers tends to hold a more optimistic view (e.g., that human ingenuity can overcome negative environmental consequences), while also exhibiting just modest levels of pro-environmental behavior overall.

The descriptive contribution of identifying different segments of consumers based on their attitudes and beliefs regarding the environment, and examining their (lack of) green behavior is a first step. The important second step is to recognize that within each of these existing segments which vary in their attitudes and behaviors, there is a need for new understanding into how to further cultivate and increase green behaviors. This goal is at the heart of Transformative Consumer Research, and is the key focus of this paper, and presentation.

"Change Is In the Air?"

Steven French, Natural Marketing Institute[1], USA

This paper discusses key findings taken from NMI's 2007 and 2008 Lifestyles of Health and Sustainability (LOHAS) Consumer Trends Database® (LCTD), an annual quantitative study which measures and describes the marketplace for LOHAS products, the consumers who use them, consumers' expectations of corporate behavior, and attitudes toward environmental and social issues. In this presentation, particular attention is paid to evolving consumers' attitudes, behaviors, and product/service usage patterns. Based on nationally representative surveys of 4,033 and 2,074 consumers conducted in July 2008 and July of 2007 respectively, the data clearly suggests that despite the economic crisis currently facing consumers, there continues to be high levels of concern about environmental issues and that consumers want to "act green." But at the same time, the findings point to a marketplace of consumers who are overwhelmed with green information and green dilemmas, tensions surrounding "green-washing," and confusion about just what is the best and most "green" course of action.

In just the past year, concern and discussion about environmental issues has soared by 30% (from 2007 to 2008), with more consumers reporting that "everywhere they turn people are talking about the environment" (LOHAS, 2009). At the same time, consumers increasingly do not want to make a sacrifice when buying environmentally-friendly products. Rather, consumers report feeling that manufacturers have had enough time to successfully integrate green benefits into products and that the purchase of "green" products should come without sacrifice in performance or inconvenience in acquisition. Furthermore, there is evidence that consumers are moving away from eco-friendly products that do not deliver on traditional attributes and benefits of performance. Consistent with this finding, the data also show that while consumer concern about the environment is increasing, their purchasing decisions continue to be determined mainly by price (a factor for the acquisition of almost all goods and services).

Consumers are also more likely to report feeling overwhelmed, saying that it is too difficult to consider all of the impacts of their actions. For example, upgrading old appliances to energy-efficient models means that old appliances will be sent to a landfill since appliance recycling can be inconvenient and costly. Buying Fair Trade fruit from Chile means foregoing local options that require fewer greenhouse gas emissions in transit. An issue in developing more mainstream adoption of sustainable consumption behaviors is that consumers feel it takes too much effort to consider all of the implications of their decisions, let alone make the "right" one.

Within the context of this "eco-information overload", this study also reports on the beginnings of consumer efforts to become more organized as well as consumer efforts at marketplace resistance by using a variety of tools to express their sentiments and to affect change. Increasing numbers of consumers are using social networking tools such Al Gore's "We Can Solve It" (www.wecansolveit.org) network to influence political agendas, and websites such as EnviroMedia's Greenwashing Index (www.greenwashingindex.com), which allows consumers to score the credibility of sustainability-related advertising.

NMI's research findings suggest that sustainability clearly remains on consumers' radar screen despite the economic downturn, while at the same time, their expectations about green products and information has changed. They are expecting all of the traditional and green benefits in a product/service at the right price, with no sacrifice in convenience. They also want companies to cut through the confusion and clearly spell out the environmental benefits. Confusion over divergent marketplace signals and the tensions among the myriad of "seemingly" green choices represent key areas for consumer research. This presentation offers cutting edge empirical findings that the green "rules of the game" have changed markedly in just the past few years with respect to consumer expectations—results which offer new perspectives on developing relevant, transformative consumer research efforts.

[1]Natural Marketing Institute (NMI) is a strategic consulting, market research, and business development company specializing in the health, wellness, and sustainable marketplace. NMI is the parent firm for LOHAS, with validated data from 35,000 consumers across 10 countries. For more information on NMI, and LOHAS, see: www.NMIsolutions.com and http://www.nmisolutions.com/r_lohas.html

"Dispersed Practices and Cultural Models: Implications for More Sustainable Electricity Consumption"

Eric J. Arnould, University of Wyoming, USA
Melea Press, University of Wyoming, USA

Our research aims to cast light on strategies of intervention to induce more sustainable household electrical energy consumption. Electrical energy consumption is crucial to the discussion of sustainability because it is foundational to so many other consumption practices that negatively impact the biosphere. We pay special attention to consumer tendencies for evasion and participation in the market system.

Based upon the limited research so far conducted on energy consumption and sustainable consumption generally, our argument is that classic approaches to mass behavioral change, such as pricing and public information linked to social marketing, are not likely to be effective in inducing more sustainable consumption. The reason is that electrical energy consumption is embedded in taken-for-granted dispersed behavioral practices. Practices are normative behavioral predispositions, something like the notion of habitus in Bourdieuan theory. They are comprised of discursive how-to knowledge, tacit know-how, and affective commitments and typically interact with rhetorical practices of representation. In contrast, specialized or "integrative" practices, for example, those associated with brand community participation are constitutive of particular domains or fields of social life and entail specialized behavioral expertise and jargon (Schau, Muniz and Arnould, forthcoming). In sum, practices are performative predispositions in which consumption behaviors are embedded (Schatzki, Cetina and von Savigny 2001; Warde 2005).

Dispersed practices, unlike integrative practices, are inherently more resistant to change because of their deeply tacit, rather than discursive nature. The appropriate performance of gender or composing a "proper" meal are other examples of deeply rooted, distributed practices. However, when distributed practices are challenged by market signals, powerful cultural models may be enlisted to defend them. For example, in North America, distinctive beliefs about Americans rights in nature, as well as the ideology of American exceptionalism may drive both resource intensive and luxurious "green" lifestyles that are cloaked in an ideology of frugality (Ludicke, Thompson and Giesler, n.d.). Furthermore, consumers' experience of macro-social phenomena associated with the global risk society also provides a constraint to behavioral change. Finally, misunderstandings about electric energy and a lack of household level tools for managing energy interact to inhibit the emergence of more sustainable practices. Thus, approaches to behavioral change based on a grasp of macro level social forces, including general sociological drivers of consumer behavior such as postmodern authority, consumer reactivity, social strain, and Commons tragedies, midrange cultural models like American exceptionalism, and dispersed practices associated with conforming, innovative, ritualized, and retreatist, and rebellious responses to innovation in electricity markets, are more likely to provide actionable insight.

Our findings about energy consumption are based on ongoing research conducted in energy markets in the Rocky Mountain west in collaboration with electric energy providers. Data collection and analysis will proceed during the spring and summer. Our research aims to account for 1) the range in response to price and technology innovations that cannot be explained by demographic characteristics alone; 2) to identify the cultural and social drivers of resistance to, and innovation in, demand for innovative energy solutions; and 3) to identify the informational and other tools firms may need to move market segments to more active pro-innovative practices. Our results have implications for so-called green marketing and sustainable consumption generally (Bartiaux 2008; Beck 2006; Maruyama, Nishikido and Iida 2007; Nash 1982; Owens and Driffill 2008; Shove 2003; Warde 2005; Wilhite 2005; Wüstenhagen and Bilharz 2006).

REFERENCES

American Environics, "Roadmap for a Progressive Majority," November, 2008, accessed at: http://www.americanenvironics.com/PDF/UpdatetoRoadmap2008.pdf.

Barr, Stewart (2006), "Environmental Action in the Home: Investigating the 'Value-Action' Gap," *Geography*, 91(1), 43-54.

Bartiaux, Françoise (2008), "Does Environmental Information Overcome Practice Compartmentalisation and Change Consumers' Behaviours?" *Journal of Cleaner Production*, 16, 1170-1180.

Beck, Ulrich (2006), Living in the World Risk Society," *Economy & Society*, 35 (August), 329-345.

Carson, Rachel (1962), *The Silent Spring*, Boston: Houghton Mifflin.

Connolly, John and Andrea Prothero (2008), "Green Consumption: Life-politics, Risk, and Contraditions," *Journal of Consumer Culture*, 8, 117-46.

Cordano, Mark, Stephanie A. Welcomer, and Robert F. Scherer (2003), "An Analysis of the Predictive Validity of the New Ecological Paradigm Scale," *The Journal of Environmental Education*, 34(3), 22-28.

Diekmann, Andreas and Peter Preisendorfer (2003), "Green and Greenback The Behavioral Effects of Environmental Attitudes in Low-Cost and High-Cost Situations," *Rationality and Society*, 15 (4), 441-472.

Dolan, Paddy (2002), "The Sustainability of 'Sustainable' Consumption," *Journal of Macromarketing*, 22 (2), (Dec.), 17-81.

Dunlap, Riley E., Kent D. Van Liere, Angela G. Mertig, Robert Emmet Jones (2000), "Measuring Endorsement of the New Ecological Paradigm: A Revised NEP Scale," *Journal of Social Issues*, 56(3), 425-442.

Englis, Basil and Gary J. Bamossy, (2009), "Courting America's Greens: Addressing the Gaps Between Green Attitudes and Green Behaviors," working paper, available from first author.

French, Steve and Gwynne Rogers (2008), "Understanding the LOHAS Consumer: The Rise of Ethical Consumerism," http://www.lohas.com/journal/consumertrends.htm.

Ger, Guliz (1999), "Experiential Meanings of Consumption and Sustainability in Turkey," *Advances in Consumer Research*, 26, 276-280.

Karel, Lisa and Rebecca Neufeld (2007), "'Going Green' Bandwagon Stalls Among Consumers," *Yankelovich Study*, accessed at: http://www.yankelovich.com/products/2007%20Green%20Perspective%20press%20release.pdf.

Kilbourne, William E. and Les Carlson (2008), "The Dominant Social Paradigm, Consumption, and Environmental Attitudes: Can Macromarketing Education Help?" *Journal of Macromarketing*, 28 (2), (June), 106-121.

LOHAS Consumer Trends Database (2009), *Natural Marketing Institute*, Harleysville, PA.

Lorenzen, Janet A. (2009), "Restricting Consumption: Creating and Maintaining Contrary Lifestyle Practices in the American Consumer Economy," working paper, Department of Sociology, Rutgers, the State University of New Jersey, Piscataway, NJ.

Luedicke, Marius, Markus Geisler, and Craig J. Thompson (n.d.), "Defying the Jeremiad against Consumerism: How American Exceptionalism Provides a Moral Justification for Resource-Intensive Consumption Practices," under review, *Journal of Consumer Research.*

Makower, Joel (2009), *Strategies for the Green Economy*, New York, McGraw Hill.

McDonald, Seonaidh and Caroline J. Oates (2006), "Sustainability: Consumer Perceptions and Marketing Strategies," *Business Strategy and the Environment*, 15, 157-170.

Maruyama, Yasushi, Makoto Nishikido, and Tetsunari Iida (2007), "The Rise of Community Wind Power in Japan: Enhanced Acceptance through Social Innovation," *Energy Policy*, 35 (May), 2761-2769.

Meijer, May-May and Theo Schuyt (2005), "Corporate Social Performance as a Bottom Line for Consumers," *Business & Society*, 44 (4), 442-461.

Mick, David G. (2007), "The End(s) of Marketing and the Neglect of Moral Responsibility by the American Marketing Association," *Journal of Public Policy and Marketing*, 16 (2), (Fall), 289-92.

Mick, David G. (2006), "Meaning and Matter Through Transformative Consumer Research," Connie Pechmann and Linda Price (eds), *Advances in Consumer Research*, Duluth, MN, 33, 1-4.

MINTel Report (2008), "Green Living—U.S.—2008."

Nash Roderick (1982), *Wilderness and the American Mind*, Third Edition, New Haven: Yale University Press.

Owens, Susan and LouiseDriffill (2008), "How to Change Attitudes and Behaviours in the Context of Energy," *Energy Policy*, 36, 4412–4418.

Pike, Cara, et.al. (2008), "Re: Green, The Ecological Roadmap: A Guide to American Social Values and Environmental Engagement," *EarthJustice*, http://www.earthjustice.org/index.html.

Schatzki, Theodore R., Karin Knorr Cetina, and Eike von Savigny (2001), London and New York: Routledge.

Schau, Hope Jensen, Al Muniz Jr., and Eric J. Arnould (forthcoming), "How Brand Community Practices Create Value," *Journal of Marketing*, (September).

Shove, Elizabeth (2003), "Converging Conventions of Comfort, Cleanliness and Convenience," *Journal of Consumer Policy*, 26 (December), 395-418.

Thorson, Esther, Thomas Page, and Jeri Moore (1995), "Consumer Response to Four Categories of 'Green' Television Commercials," *Advances in Consumer Research*, 22, 243-250.

Warde, Alan (2005), "Consumption and Theories of Practice," *Journal of Consumer Culture*, 5 (2), 131-153.

Wilhite, Harold (2005), "Why Energy Needs Anthropology," *Anthropology Today*, 21 (June), 1-2.

Wüstenhagen, Rolf and Michael Bilharz (2006), "Green Energy Market Development in Germany: Effective Public Policy and Emerging Customer Demand," *Energy Policy*, 34 (September), 1681-1696.

SPECIAL SESSION SUMMARY

Money and People Make Strange Bedfellows

Deborah Small, University of Pennsylvania, USA

SESSION OVERVIEW

Money often has peculiar effects on social relationships. Technically-speaking, money serves as a medium of exchange and a measure of wealth. Yet the ways that consumers feel about and behave with respect to money has implications that extend beyond money's economic purposes. Depending on the situation, money can either draw people closer together or isolate them, it can make them behave selfishly or altruistically, and it can engender relationship satisfaction or relationship conflict. The objective of this session is to discuss emerging research linking thoughts and feelings about money to social behavior. It also seeks to explore how such patterns ultimately influence relationship satisfaction and happiness more generally.

The four papers included in this session represent different perspectives on the role of money in interpersonal behavior. All papers are in late stages of completion (working paper, under review, and in press). The first two papers focus on relationships with strangers and friends, and the latter two papers focus on romantic relationships and marriage. Vohs will begin by examining the reciprocal link between thoughts of money and social exclusion. Then Norton will present research examining when spending money on others is most likely to promote happiness for both those on the spending and receiving end. Mead will move the focus to communal relationships in presenting research showing that money reduces felt moral obligations and trust in interdependent contexts. Finally, Rick will present research examining how emotional reactions toward spending money influence romantic attraction and marital satisfaction. We expect these papers will provoke productive discussions about the multifaceted impact of money in relationships. This session will appeal to a wide range of consumer behavior scholars and especially among those focused on money and other valued resources, interpersonal interactions, romantic relationships, emotions, and well-being.

ABSTRACTS

"Social Rejection and Desire for Money"

Kathleen Vohs, University of Minnesota
Xinyue Zhou, Sun Yat-Sen University
Roy Baumeister, Florida State University

Prior work showed that reminders of money led people to put more physical distance between themselves and another as well as choose activities to be enjoyed alone rather than with friends and family. These findings suggest that money reminders decrease social needs. Does this extend to being rejected by others too? Three studies tested the relationship between money reminders and social exclusion. Interpersonal rejection caused an increase in the desire for money. Counting slips of currency (compared to paper) reduced feelings of distress after social exclusion. Being reminded of having spent money, however, intensified the pain of social exclusion.

"Putting the "Social" in Prosocial Spending: Interpersonal Giving Promotes Happiness"

Michael I. Norton, Harvard Business School
Lara Aknin, University of British Columbia
Elizabeth Dunn, University of British Columbia

Recent research has demonstrated the positive impact on well-being of spending money on others. We explore the impact of increasing the "social" in prosocial spending, hypothesizing that the benefits of such spending are amplified when giving takes place in an interpersonal context. In a field study in which we gave participants Starbucks gift cards, the benefits of having coffee with a friend were particularly pronounced when participants treated their friend to that coffee. In a dictator game, the amount of money given to receivers was associated with happiness for both givers and receivers only when offers were made face-to-face.

"Reminders of Money Weaken Sociomoral Responses"

Nicole Mead, Tilburg University
Kathleen Vohs, University of Minnesota
Krishna Savini, Stanford University
Tyler Stillman, Florida State University
Roy Baumeister, Florida State University

Money reminders evoke a self-sufficient state that implies that each person take care of him/herself (Vohs, Mead, and Goode 2006). The present work tested whether money reminders produce self-sufficient behavior even within communal domains, which endorse of a code of caring for and respecting others (i.e., opposite of self-sufficiency). Even within communal contexts, money reminders reduced sociomoral responses. In India, money reminders diminished perceived moral obligations (experiment 1). In romantic relationships, money reminders reduced willingness to help (experiment 2). Experiment 3 showed that money reminders heightened perceptions that other people act in their own self-interest, which in turn reduced trust.

"Fatal (Fiscal) Attraction: Tightwads and Spendthrifts in Marriage"

Scott I. Rick, University of Michigan
Deborah A. Small, University of Pennsylvania
Eli J.Finkel, Northwestern University

Although most attraction research suggests that "birds of a feather flock together," surveys of married adults reveal that opposites attract when it comes to emotional reactions toward spending money. That is, "tightwads," who find the prospect of spending money painful and thus tend to spend less than they would like, tend to marry "spendthrifts," who find spending painless and thus spend more than they would like, consistent with the notion that people are attracted to mates who possess characteristics dissimilar to those they deplore in themselves (Klohnen and Mendelsohn 1998). Unfortunately, spendthrift/tightwad differences stimulate conflict over money, diminishing marital satisfaction.

REFERENCES

Klohnen, Eva C. and Gerald A. Mendelsohn (1998), "Partner Selection for Personality Characteristics: A Couple-Centered Approach," *Personality and Social Psychology Bulletin*, 24 (3), 268-78.

Vohs, Kathleen D., Nicole L. Mead, and Miranda R. Goode (2006), "The psychological consequences of money," *Science*, 314, 1154-56.

Special Session Summary

The Pitfalls of Fame: Insights from Human Brands

Marie-Agnès Parmentier, HEC Montréal, Canada

SESSION OVERVIEW

Consumers relate to brands of many types, but none more than human brands, "one of several operationalizations of the broader concept of a brand" (Thomson 2006: 104). Human brands (sometime equated with celebrities) are a vital part of both contemporary culture and the contemporary market economy. Given the centrality of human brands to consumers' lives, it is surprising that research that touches directly on the topic is extremely limited within our literature. The purpose of this symposium was to offer a forum for scholars interested in how consumers relate to and co-create human brands. Our aim was to provide insights on how human brands come to have the meanings they do, the implications of having powerful human brands, and the role consumers play in human brand development. In the first presentation, Hope Jensen Schau (University of Arizona) and Cristel Antonia Russell (University of Auckland) examined how the human brands developed by actors in television series matter to the relationships consumers form with these actors and the characters they portray. Next, Marie-Agnès Parmentier (HEC Montréal) and Eileen Fischer (York University), using case studies of David Beckham and Ryan Giggs, provided insights into the factors at play in the emergence and evolution of human brands with which consumers form relationships, and the practices that help maintain and restore human brand equity in the eyes of both fans and industry insiders when equity erodes. In the third presentation, Susan Fournier (Boston University) discussed the approach that has driven Martha Stewart's brand building effort while revealing the flaws of this approach, highlighting how it falls short because of its failure to take into account the full range of processes that feed the creation of human brands. Finally, Matt Thomson (University of Western Ontario), discussed the papers and offered some concluding remarks on the issues raised as well as avenues for future research.

EXTENDED ABSTRACTS

"The Ties that Bind: Consumer Engagement and Transference with a Human Brand"

Cristel Antonia Russell, University of Auckland, New Zealand
Hope Jensen Schau, University of Arizona, USA

Beginning with Fournier (1998), research on consumer-brand relationships has assumed a level of anthropomorphism and is guided by the extant literature on interpersonal human relationships, asserting that brands can be active relationship partners. Research shows that consumers develop relationships with celebrities (Thomson 2006), TV characters (Russell, Norman and Heckler 2004), and service providers (Price and Arnould 1999) because the human brand is capable of a wider range of attribute evolution than an inanimate consumption object and has an enhanced reciprocity potential. Human brands provide a vivid context to examine consumer-brand relationships because they mature and adapt to changing circumstances; or put simply they more closely mimic relationships between and among people.

This research investigates another parallel with human relationships: transference, the tendency to carry over attachment patterns from one relationship to the next. We focus on consumers' experience of the cessation of a brand's production, to identify whether and to what degree transference occurs with subsequent offerings of the human brand. The literature on human loss, and the processes of grief, mourning, and recovery, provides a conceptual basis for investigating the emotions and behaviors associated with the departure of a favored brand and the process of transference whereby new relationships are impacted by previous relationships.

According to adult attachment theory, previous relationship patterns can reemerge when people form new relationships (Andersen and Cole 1990). Past experiences and interpersonal patterns learned are superimposed onto the new relationship, including memories and affective responses. Transference is most likely triggered when previous relationships are salient (Andersen et al. 1995). In psychiatry, Freud (1917) proposed that the period following a loss is used for decathexis, the incremental divestment of libido from memories of the lost object, and that it eventually leads to recathexis, the redirection of libido from the memory of the lost person to available survivors which removes the cause of the pain and renews opportunities for pleasure. Research shows that the process of transference applies to a greater degree when there is more resemblance between the old and the new relationship objects (Brumbaugh and Fraley 2006). This process has clear implications in the domain of human brands, but, as in the brand extension area (Aaker and Keller 1990; Boush and Loken 1991), the process of transference might apply best when consumers perceive coherence between original and the extension.

The extant transference literature suggests that a brand's withdrawal might prompt the development of new consumer-brand relationships where the previous relationship pattern resurfaces. We test this proposition in the context of relationships formed with a human brand within television programs. TV programs are consumed in the intimate, domestic space, where the strongest interpersonal relationships take place, and they promote the formation and development of deep and intense attachments with characters (Russell and Puto 1999). We analyze the process consumers go through when TV programs with which they presume an active relationship are discontinued, and assess the processes of transference to subsequent programs featuring the same actor and role.

Observational and survey data were collected before, during and following the final season of one of television's most popular and long-lived programs (Friends: 10 years, 238 episodes) and at the onset of a spin-off program (Joey: 2 years, 47 episodes) that features the same actor in the same role (Matt LeBlanc as Joey Tribbiani). These data provide insights into how consumers cope with the loss of their relationship partner and whether transference occurs with the new program. Joey launched its first season with a respectable audience of 11million; however, it ended with audiences only slightly above 4 million. While Friends features an ensemble cast, this is a fragment of the Friends finale audience (52.5 million) and Joey's following decreased over time.

We examine observational data collected on three online forums centered on Matt LeBlanc and Joey (271,318 posts). Fans "forced to live without Friends" expressed loss at its end and excitement about Joey returning. Using the language of transference, fans explicitly claim to be "shifting their alliance" to Joey and "moving over with Joey" indicating that the main impetus for watching the show is to transfer their bonds to the new program and experience the continuation. Fan complaints about the show revolve around changes in continuity (Joey's family, absence of other "friends") creating impediments such that they state their transference is "less than seamless," "jarring," and "unfulfilling;" furthermore, Joey is perceived, even by his most ardent fans, as "a shadow of himself." Interestingly, prior to the cessation of Friends, these fans expressed extreme allegiance to Joey and Matt LeBlanc posting homage websites dedicated to following LeBlanc's professional and personal life. These fan tributes are often referenced in fans' signature files that follow every post on a forum.

Survey data (N=262) were collected five months after the withdrawal of Friends from a sample of viewers, ranging from occasional to avid, and including 30% who had watched Friends from the beginning. Along with participants' histories of viewing the original and spin-off series, the survey collected measures of attitude and connectedness to both series, attachment to the Joey character, as well as measures of the counteracting processes of transference and counter-transference. The results indicate that viewers maintain continuing bonds by watching re-runs and that the intensity of their bond (in this context, connectedness) is a key predictor of these continuing bonds. Connectedness is also a key predictor of the process of transference and it affects transference to viewing the spin-off series through the experience of grief. Consumers experiencing strong bonds with the original series are not only more likely to seek out the characters in their spin-off afterlife but also to develop strong bonds with the characters in the afterlife, in line with the transference process in adult attachment theory (Andersen and Cole 1990; Brumbaugh and Fraley 2006). In a manner typical of that observed in bereavement research, the newly formed bonds provide liberation from the loss and grief caused by the withdrawal of the original series.

We find that when a given program is discontinued, consumers do experience transference when they have strong bonds with human brands and when these human brands migrate from one program to another. However countertransference is also present where pre-existing strong bonds can inhibit the transference of previous bonds because the expectations for the relationship are so high they cannot be met and because the similarities with the previous experience provide a hurtful reminder of the previous relationship.

"Branded Like Beckham? An Examination of Dynamic Processes in Human Branding"

Marie- Agnès Parmentier, HEC Montréal, Canada
Eileen Fischer, York University, Canada

Given recent work on consumers' attachments to celebrity brands (Thomson 2006), we are beginning to understand that human brands are important to end consumers, to people building their brands, to the industries in which the brands emerge, and to economies as a whole. However, we have yet to develop systematic insights into how such brands emerge and evolve as people's careers progress, as they engage with distinctive target audiences, and as unforeseen or uncontrollable events occur that can challenge a person's brand equity.

In order to address this gap, our paper develops case studies of soccer stars David Beckham and Ryan Giggs as human brands. Drawing on definitions that emphasize consumers' understandings as the basis of brands (e.g., Keller 1993) we define a human brand for a person engaged in a field of practice as the sets of associations that audiences within and beyond the field identify with the individual. Drawing on our two cases, we develop theory that helps answer the following questions: What factors, including consumer fans' evolving relationships, contribute to the emergence of a powerful human brand? What challenges can undermine equity for such a human brand among consumers? And how can equity be maintained or restored?

The data used to develop our case study is archival. For each player, we collected: published biographies or autobiographies (e.g., Beckham and Freeman 2001; Beckham 2005; Milligan 2004); postings from websites (www.davidbeckham.com; www.ryangiggs.cc); and websites maintained by and for fans (e.g., davidbeckham.fans-online.com; www.start.at/giggsy). Further, we collected all articles that mentioned either Giggs or Beckham in: Sports Ilustrated; World Soccer; ESPN the Magazine; Vogue UK; and People. We also examined each player's Facebook, MySpace, and Twitter postings as well as media coverage describing fan reactions to both Giggs and Beckham (e.g. http://www.helium.com/debates/73611-does-ryan-giggs-have-david-beckham-to-thank-for-his-career). Our analytic focus has been on identifying factors that lead to equity, on categorizing challenges to equity, and on discerning practices that have helped to maintain or to re-establish equity with audiences.

In answering the first question regarding factors that contribute to the emergence of a powerful brand, the paper identifies two distinct elements of human brand equity: professional equity and celebrity equity. Our analysis suggests that while Giggs and Beckham both have the former, Giggs lacks the latter. Professional equity is earned among audiences within the field practice (e.g., professional soccer). It is earned in part through demonstrating the ability to perform well specialized activities valued within the field, but also by forming upward reaching social networks with more powerful actors in the field and by taking opportunities to achieve visibility within the field (e.g., by choosing to play for the most storied Manchester United club). Celebrity equity is earned outside the field of origin among consumers (who in this case may well not be soccer fans). And while professional equity can serve as a basis for forming celebrity equity, celebrity requires the individual to cultivate an authentic persona (cf. Thomson 2006) that is of interest to consumers relatively unfamiliar with the field (as Beckham has done through his combination of dedication to a 'manly' sport coupled with a high fashion sensibility), to develop field-spanning networks (as Beckham has done by hiring Simon Fuller, a celebrity impresario rather than a soccer agent), and to take opportunities to achieve visibility beyond the field of origin (for example by cultivating affiliations with celebrities in other fields, e.g., Tom Cruise).

In answering our second question we identified challenges to professional equity as distinct from threats to celebrity equity. Factors that promote one type of equity can challenge the other. For example, threats to professional equity can arise from publicly visible performances that are interpreted (often with critical assistance by fans and the media) as failures to demonstrate those abilities most valued in the profession (as when Beckham was sent off against Argentina in the 1998 FIFA world cup). These challenges can be compounded when it is perceived that opportunity-seeking beyond the field of practice (such as the pursuit of endorsements) is impeding performance within the profession. Celebrity equity, in contrast, is threatened when visibility beyond the field declines as may happen when individuals re-invest in their profession and withdraw from activities that attract media attention (as Giggs has done).

In addressing our third question, we identify "balancing" practices that simultaneously demonstrate the individual's ability to perform well within the standards of the profession while providing opportunities to reinforce a persona that engages fans attention and attracts media attention. Beckham's move in 2007 to the LA Galaxy team in the America, and his recent efforts to be "transferred" to AC Milan can be interpreted as (unevenly effective) efforts to rebalance his brand equity. In the conclusions of our paper, we discuss the implications of our insights for understanding both consumers' relationships to human brands, and the roles that consumers may play in shaping the evolution of human brands.

"Taking Stock in Martha Stewart: A Cultural Critique of the Marketing Practice of Building Person-Brands"

Susan Fournier, Boston University, USA

This inquiry concerns the phenomenon of the celebrity person-brand: a productized, branded entity that derives its equity from association with a celebrity that serves as creator, muse, and steward of the brand. Celebrity person-brands are at once celebrities (persons) and products (brands). They are a sub-class of celebrity brands as both are marked by recognizability, visibility, and attractiveness within the society (Gamson 1994; Turner 2004), but not all celebrity brands have been productized (e.g., Sheryl Crow, Barack Obama). In our hyper consumer culture, motivations to commercialize celebrity to capture branded product value are great (Lieb 2007).

Although recent research explores consumers' relationships with celebrity brands (Thomson 2006), insight into supply-side mechanisms through which equity is developed in person brands is lacking (for exception, see Lieb 2007). As paradigms for marketing and entertainment increasingly collide (Donaton 2004), the need for insights into celebrity brand-building grows. This research imparts a deeper appreciation of the complex workings of the process of celebrity brand creation, and the principles that guide equity development of such brands over time.

Our research focuses on one person-brand exemplar: Martha Stewart, as owned and managed under the entity Martha Stewart Living Omnimedia (MSO). Our case selection follows the logic of inquiries that inform their phenomena by focusing on that phenomenon in its extreme. While other celebrity person-brands exist—e.g., Wolfgang Puck and Emeril Lagassi—these brands are narrower in their productization, and weaker in markers of celebrity overall. It is also significant for theory development purposes that Martha Stewart experienced a lengthy, highly-visible crisis. In 2001, after thirty years in the making, the Martha Stewart brand stood as one of the world's strongest (Khermouch 2001). This situation changed entirely in 2002 when word broke of an investigation that eventually landed Stewart in jail. Though business improved with Stewart's return to MSLO as Chief Creative Officer in Fall 2006, signs of recovery are mixed. Lost equity has yet to be recovered, and analysts remain split in their forecasts. MSO's crisis serves as a critical inflection point in the trajectory of our phenomenon; the system in stress provides diagnostic learning opportunities by exposing the processes in play (Reis and Knee 1996).

This research advances the cultural branding paradigm (Holt 2004, Schroeder and Salzer-Morling 2005) by providing insight into the fallible habits of mind that brought the Martha Stewart brand to the brink of extinction. By popular accounts, MSO operated as best-in-class marketers and yet this acknowledged excellence did not prevent them from jeopardizing their brand. We argue that MSO's predicament signals fundamental shortcomings in the classic marketing principles managers apply to build, leverage, and sustain their brands.

Data for our investigation include: four MSO business case studies spanning from IPO to post-jail recovery (Fourier et al. 2001; Fournier 2001; Fournier 2006; Glynn and Mihoubi 2000); biographies of Stewart and histories of MSO (Byron 2002); company SEC filings, releases, and annual reports; MSO marketing campaigns; media coverage of MSO. Using grounded theory, we first induct a five-stage person-brand development model from the historical archives of activities at MSO. The model reflects classic brand leverage logic (Farquhar et al. 1992), whereby resources are first devoted to establishing strength in the master brand (Martha Stewart the Person) such that it can sponsor powerful extensions downstream. The model adopts a financial markets' perspective, striving toward a self-sustaining, risk-tolerant multi-brand portfolio that transitions from the parent brand. Intermediate stages in the model differ with respect to the reflexive relationships existing between the person and brand components, and the relative marketing emphasis placed on person versus brand. Second, we critique MSO's strategy from the perspective of cultural branding theory, highlighting three blind spots that compromised development of the person-brand: (a) Failure to consider multivocality of the person and brand; (b) Denial of the reciprocating, non-linear system of person-brand meaning making; and (c) Illusions of control over the collaborative cultural process of person-brand meaning making. Lastly we offer a revised framework for person-brand building that contrasts with psychologically-oriented association models that treat person-branding as a leveraging process (Keller 2003). In our model the process is one of collaborative meaning making that enables co-creation of the brand.

REFERENCES

Aaker, David A. and Kevin L. Keller (1990), "Consumer Evaluations of Brand Extensions," *Journal of Marketing*, 54 (January), 27-41.

Andersen, Susan M. and Steve W. Cole (1990), "Do I Know You? The Role of Significant Others in General Social Perception," *Journal of Personality and Social Psychology*, 59, 384-399.

Andersen, Susan M., Noah S. Glassman, Serena Chen, and Steve W. Cole (1995), "Transference in Social Perception: The Role of Chronic Accessibility in Significant-Other Representation," *Journal of Personality and Social Psychology*, 69(1), 41-57.

Beckham, Ted (2005), *David Beckham: My Son*, London: Boxtree.

Beckham, David and Dean Freeman (2001), *Beckham: My World*, London: Hodder & Stoughton.

Boush, David M. and Barbara Loken (1991), "A Process-Tracing Study of Brand Extension Evaluation," *Journal of Marketing Research*, 28 (February), 16-28.

Brumbaugh, Claudia Chloe and R. Chris Fraley (2006), "Transference and Attachment: How Do Attachment Patterns Get Carried Forward From One Relationship to the Next?" *Personality and Social Psychology Bulletin*, 32(4), 552-560.

Byron, Christopher (2002), *Martha Inc.: The Incredible Story of Martha Stewart Living Omnimedia*, New York: John Wiley & Sons.

Donaton, Scott (2004), *Madison and Vine: Why the Entertainment and Advertising Industries Must Converge to Survive*, NY: McGraw-Hill.

Farquhar, Peter, Julia Han, Paul Herr, and Yuji Ijiri (1992), "Strategies for Leveraging Master Brands," *Marketing Research*, September, 32-43.

Fournier, Susan (2005), "Martha Stewart and the ImClone Crisis," *Tuck Business School Case Study 1-0083*, Hanover, NH: Tuck Business School Press.

Fournier, Susan (2001), "Martha Stewart Living Omnimedia (B), *Harvard Business School Case 9-501-079*, Boston: Harvard Business School Publishing.

Fournier, Susan (1998), "Consumers and Their Brands: Developing Relationship Theory in Consumer Research," *Journal of Consumer Research*, 24, (March), 343-373.

Fournier, Susan, Kerry Herman, Laura Winig, and Andrea Wojnicki (2001), "Martha Stewart Living Omnimedia," *Harvard Business School Case 9-501-080*, Boston: Harvard Business School Publishing.

Freud, Sigmund (1917), "Mourning and Melancholia," in J. Strachey (Ed. & Trans.), *Standard Edition of the Complete Psychological Works of Sigmund Freud*, London: Hogarth.

Gamson, Joshua (1994), *Claims to Fame: Celebrity in Contemporary America*, Berkeley, CA: University of California Press.

Glynn, MaryAnn and Farah Mihoubi (2000), "Martha Stewart," case and video series at the Goizueta Business School, Emory University.

Holt, Douglas (2004), *How Brands Become Icons: The Principles of Cultural Branding*, Boston: Harvard Business School Press.

Keller, Kevin (2003), "Brand Synthesis: The Multidimensionality of Brand Knowledge," *Journal of Consumer Research*, 29 (March), 595-600.

Keller, Kevin Lane (1993), "Conceptualizing, Measuring, and Managing Customer-Based Brand Equity," *Journal of Marketing*, 57 (1), 1-22.

Khermouch, Gerry (2001), "The Best Global Brands," *Business Week*, August 6, 50-57.

Lieb, Kristin (2007), "Pop Tarts and Body Parts: The Imaging and Brand Management of Female Popular Music Stars," Dissertation at Syracuse University College of Communications, Dissertation #3281727, University Microfilms Inc.

Milligan, Andy (2004), *Brand It Like Beckham*, London: Cyan Books.

Price, Linda L. and Eric J. Arnould (1999), "Commercial Friendships: Service Provider-Client Relationships in Social Context," *Journal of Marketing*, 63, 38-56.

Russell, Cristel A. and Christopher P. Puto (1999), "Rethinking Television Audience Measures: An Exploration into the Construct of Audience Connectedness," *Marketing Letters*, 10 (4), 387-401.

Russell, Cristel A., Andrew T. Norman, and Susan E. Heckler (2004), "The Consumption of Television Programming: Development and Validation of the Connectedness Scale," *Journal of Consumer Research*, 31 (1), 150-61.

Schroeder, Jonathan and Miriam Salzer-Morling (2005), *Brand Culture*, London: Routledge

Thomson, Matthew (2006), "Human Brands: Investigating Antecedents to Consumers' Strong Attachments to Celebrities," *Journal of Marketing*, 70 (July), 104-119.

Turner, Graeme (2004), *Understanding Celebrity*, London: Sage.

Special Session Summary

On Being the Same and Different: The Dynamics of Interpretation and Comparison in Consumer Judgment

Femke van Horen, Tilburg University, The Netherlands

SESSION OVERVIEW

Symposium Objective. To comprehend an ambiguous product, person or brand (is the product of high quality?, will she be a good salesperson?) accessible information is used to guide evaluation which may lead to assimilation or contrast. In the past, research on accessible knowledge effects, both in social psychology and consumer behavior, has focused on the various factors that determine the direction of these effects, resulting in a host of moderators predicting either assimilation or contrast. Recently however, social cognition research has demonstrated how different types of processing may produce assimilation and contrast effects (Förster, Liberman and Kuschel 2008; Stapel 2007) and has shown that the same accessible information may lead to assimilation or contrast depending on the processing style, i.e. whether this information is used as an interpretation frame or as a comparison standard. The purpose of this symposium is to present research that builds on these recent developments in social cognition research, which are bound to have implications for our understanding of consumer behavior.

Overview. Traditionally, research on assimilation and contrast effects in social psychology and marketing has focused on the identification of moderating factors determining the direction of the effect (assimilation or contrast). Such factors include the distinctness of information (Stapel and Koomen 2000), extremity of information (Herr 1989; Smeesters and Mandel 2006) and categorical overlap (Mussweiler and Bodenhausen 2002). Instead of taking this indirect route to investigate context effects, a more direct approach has recently been taken through identification of the specific processes that determine the effects. Fresh dual process models in social cognition research, like the Interpretation Comparison Model (ICM, Stapel 2007) or the global/local processing style model (GLOMO, Förster, Liberman and Kuschel 2008), postulate a process distinction between assimilation and contrast. The ICM for instance posits that when people use information as an interpretation frame, assimilation is a likely outcome. However, when people use information as a comparison standard, then contrast is more likely to occur. GLOMO extends the inclusion/exclusion model (Bless and Schwarz 1992) and demonstrates that activating a global processing style results in assimilation, whereas activating a local processing style results in contrast. This symposium is positioned at the forefront of these new developments by showing how consumers use information (as a comparison standard or interpretative frame) in product judgment. The symposium builds on and extends the recent developments with a focus on important issues for consumer behavior, i.e. when and how feature characteristics of products and the consumer's self-concept activate specific processing mindsets, which in turn guide product evaluation and judgment.

Papers. The three papers in this set demonstrate how the type of processing may influence the direction of context effects. The first presentation focuses on the importance of interpretation processes. Specifically, Reed, Forehand and Perkins reveal that consumers who are high self-monitors, instead of low self-monitors, tend to use an interpretative frame when accessible contextual information is social but not when it is individual in nature. The second presentation of Van Horen, Pieters and Stapel addresses the evaluation of look-alike products. They show how a specific type of product imitation activates comparative mindsets in consumers, and that as a consequence the imitation of highly similar, distinct features (e.g. the color purple of the Milka chocolate brand) is liked less than the imitation of subtly similar, diffuse themes (e.g. the Alps with grazing cows of the Milka chocolate brand). The third presentation of Meyers-Levy, Zhu and Liang integrates both of the processing modes and examines the effect of distance on bodily sensations affecting product evaluation. They find that bodily sensations, elicited through floor tiling (comfort of carpet versus discomfort of tiles) are used as a comparative standard when distance is close, resulting in a contrast effect, but as an interpretative frame when distance is moderate, resulting in assimilation. In all, this symposium presents the findings of various novel research streams that both connects to the extant literature, and highlights fruitful avenues for further research on the impact of context effects on consumer behavior.

Contribution. Recent developments in social cognition theories on accessibility effects on judgment focus on the processing styles, foci or mindsets behind these effects, instead of exploring the specific factors that determine the effect. In this symposium we build on this new development and address how different types of processes (interpretation versus comparison) influence product evaluation (assimilation or contrast). Each of the three papers in this symposium presents novel and interesting results on this issue. Taken together, they constitute a new perspective on how context or priming effects determine the direction of product judgments, which can stimulate a host of research ideas. All three papers include multiple completed studies, are new and have not been submitted. None of the papers has ever been presented at ACR.

Discussion Host. The symposium's discussion host, Diederik A. Stapel (TIBER, Tilburg University, The Netherlands), is a thought leader in judgment theories in social cognition. He will introduce the symposium by shortly presenting the new developments in dual processing models on comparison and interpretation (5 minutes), and will introduce each of the speakers.

Likely Audience. We believe that this symposium will draw a large audience of researchers and PhD students interested in fundamental social cognition theories that provide new insights into consumer behavior. The presenters are at the forefront of research on the impact of interpretative or comparative effects on product judgment. We expect lively discussions that inspire new research ideas on the impact of dual processes in product evaluation.

References

Förster, J., N. Liberman, and S. Kuschel (2008), "The Effect of Global Versus Local Processing Styles on Assimilation Versus Contrast in Social Judgment," *Journal of Personality and Social Psychology*, 94, 579-599.

Herr, Paul M. (1989), "Priming Price: Prior Knowledge and Context Effects," *Journal of Consumer Research*, 16 (1), 67-75.

Mussweiler, T. and G. V. Bodenhausen (2002), "I Know You Are, But What Am I? Self-evaluative Consequences of Judging In-group and Out-group Members," *Journal of Personality and Social Psychology*, 95, 1295–1315.

Smeesters, Dirk and Mandel Naomi (2006), "Positive and Negative Media Image Effects on the Self," *Journal of Consumer Research*, 32, 576-582.

Stapel, Diederik A. (2007), "In the Mind of the Beholder: The Interpretation Comparison Model of Accessibility Effects," in *Assimilation and Contrast in Social Psychology*, Diederik A. Stapel and Jerry Suls, eds. New York: Psychology Press, 143-164.

Stapel, Diederik A. and Willem Koomen (2000), "Distinctiveness of Others, Mutability of Selves: Their Impact on Self-Evaluations," *Journal of Personality and Social Psychology*, 79 (6), 1068-1087.

EXTENDED ABSTRACTS

"The Color of the Chameleon Depends on the Prime Type"

Americus Reed II, University of Pennsylvania, USA
Mark Forehand, University of Washington, USA
Andrew Perkins, Rice University, USA

One of the most robust findings in psychology and consumer behavior is that priming constructs can have an impact on attitudes, judgments and behavior. For some time, a prime was just a prime. Research was silent on the extent to which these primes were actually relevant to a participant's self-concept or not. For example, in Bargh, Chen and Burrows's (1996) classic study, it would be hard to argue that their college student participants "had" an "elderly identity" in walking slower in response to exposure to their subtle cognitive primes (e.g., bingo, wrinkle).

Recent research however, has begun to more actively account for prime to behavior effects by more explicitly considering the self. DeMarree, Wheeler and Petty's "Active Self Account" (2005) argues that primes are more likely to affect behavior when the prime temporarily alters self-perceptions. Their evidence for this relies on the moderating role of "self monitoring" (Snyder 1974) where they find that low-self monitors—consumers who tend to rely on their internal stable beliefs, are more likely to assimilate to primed constructs. They argue that this is due not to a need to "fit in" but rather in the service of "being oneself" (DeMarree et. al 2005, page 659)—a kind of "informational influence" that drives the assimilation effect.

It seems at first glance odd that low self monitors would exhibit greater shifting of behavior as compared to high self-monitors in reaction to a cognitive prime. It is however not the case that low self monitors self-concepts exhibits no stability, rather, the stability lies in whatever internal self-representation is on top of mind. Hence, cognitive primes may be more likely to affect low self-monitors because they are more likely to react to information referring to the internal nature of the self. If primes subtly activate constructs that are perceived to be "diagnostic self-information", then one would expect these cognitive primes to have a greater effect on low-self monitors rather than high self-monitors (Wheeler and Petty 2001). However, some primes are more "social" in nature. In other words, they emanate from situational cues that have direct relevance to linking the self-concept to its connectedness to others in the immediate social environment (Forehand and Deshpande 1999). These kinds of social primes should be much less likely to be "misconstrued" as internal cues to the self. Hence, we argue that these primes will have a different effect than the work done by Wheeler and colleagues—and our research expands the view of the Active Self account—by demonstrating this empirically.

In three experiments we test whether the role of self monitoring in response to contextual triggers depends on the nature of the trigger. Although traditional stimulus primes are more influential on low self-monitors, situational or social triggers appear to me more influential on high self monitors. We demonstrate this by assessing response to social distinctiveness within low and high self-monitoring populations. In the first experiment, we used a subtle but "social" prime—the relative distinctiveness of the participants' ethnicity and gender on self-reported identification with the primed concept. Students who are members of an ethnic minority were more likely to mention ethnicity in a self-description than those who were members of an ethnic majority (19% vs. 6%)—replicating previous work (Forehand and Deshpande 2001; Deshpande and Stayman, 1994). However, as predicted, High Self-Monitors were more sensitive to the gender composition of the room in which they completed the survey. Based on a median split on the Self-Monitoring variable: when in "gender majority," 12% of high self-monitors reported their gender in self-descriptions, whereas when in "gender minority" 30% of high self-monitors reported their gender in self-descriptions. Low self-monitors demonstrated the opposite reaction to gender-minority status (22% mentioned when in majority, 13% when in minority). In the second experiment, we manipulated minority/majority standing on racial and gender dimensions and assessed activation of these components in the self-concept using an implicit measure of self-concept activation. The results showed that those exposed to the social prime of highlighting their minority status on gender were more likely to shift their working self- concepts —especially if they were high self-monitors. In the third experiment, we extend the basic moderation effect into work-group situations and assessed whether cooperative/ competitive mindsets influence both self-concept activation and whether that activation mediates other outcome measures.

The totality of our research elaborates on previous work. Our analysis shows that it is important to understand the nature of the prime under consideration. Primes that are cognitive like the ones used in prior work may trigger an assimilation effect along the lines explained by the Active Self account. However, social primes have a completely opposite effect. This finding is important because marketers will attempt to prime self-identities in different ways, and the precise effects of primes under strategic consideration must be considered to understand the likely success of using such tactics. Moreover, our findings attest to the power of identity and its flexibility in driving self-expression in response to self-concept activation that may ultimately drive consumption.

References

Bargh, John A., Mark Chen, and Lara Burrows (1996), "Automaticity of Social Behavior: Direct Effects of Trait Construct and Stereotype Activation on Action," *Journal of Personality and Social Psychology*, 71 (2), 230-244.

DeMarree, K. G., S. Christian Wheeler, and Richard E. Petty (2005), "Priming a New Identity: Self-monitoring Moderates the Effects of Non-self Stereotype Primes on Self-judgments and Behavior," *Journal of Personality and Social Psychology*, 89(5), 657-671.

Snyder, Mark (1974), "Self-monitoring of Expressive Behavior," *Journal of Personality and Social Psychology*, 30(4), 526-537.

Wheeler, S. Christian and Richard E. Petty (2001), "The Effects of Stereotype Activation on Behavior: A Review of Possible Mechanisms," *Psychological Bulletin*, 127 (6), 797-826.

Forehand, Mark R. and Rohit Deshpandé (2001), "What We See Makes Us Who We Are: Priming Ethnic Self-awareness and Advertising Response," *Journal of Marketing Research*, 38 (3), 336-348.

Deshpandé, R. and Douglas M. Stayman (1994), "A Tale of Two Cities: Distinctiveness Theory and Advertising Effectiveness," *Journal of Marketing Research*, 31 (1), 57-64.

"On Subtle Themes and Blatant Features: The Effect of Imitation-Type on Evaluation and Choice of Copycats"

Femke van Horen, Tilburg University, The Netherlands
Rik Pieters, Tilburg University, The Netherlands
Diederik A. Stapel, Tilburg University, The Netherlands

Suppose you are in Safeway for your grocery shopping. In the potato chips section you encounter Safeway's private label chips, packaged in a bright red, rectangular tube with plastic, see-through cap; features that are also used by the Pringles brand. You walk further, into the aisle with spreads, and see that the package of Safeway's spreadable butter with olive oil displays a Tuscan farm on a hill with olive- and pine trees; a theme that is used by the Bertolli brand as well. Which of the two types of imitation (imitation of the more blatant features versus imitation of the more subtle theme) would you evaluate more positively? Previous literature would predict that imitation of more blatant, distinct features would be evaluated more positively, as similarity with the leader brand is higher when blatant features, as compared to when subtle themes, are copied (Kapferer 1996). We argue, instead, that blatant imitation of distinct features may backfire and reduce the evaluation of copycats, whereas copying subtle themes can increase the evaluation of the copycat. To date little is known about how type of imitation (what is copied as compared to how much is copied) affects copycat evaluation. Further, because the focus has traditionally been on highly similar copycats, the effects of more subtle degrees of copycatting are still largely unknown.

Copycats imitate aspects of the trade-dress of leading brands to free-ride on the positive associations attached to these brands (Zaichkowsky 2006). When copycats imitate leading brands, they often choose to imitate the distinct, prototypical features (the specific colors, lettering and shapes), instead of the more subtle themes (referents to the country of origin, benefits and values). Copying the distinct features that are uniquely associated with the leading brand, will increase similarity more than imitating subtle themes, which would result in a more positive evaluation (Loken, Ross, and Hinkle 1996; Warlop and Alba 2004).

We posit however that attaining high similarity through copying the prototypical features results in contrast, as a distinct representation of the leader brand will become accessible (Stapel and Koomen 2000) which, in turn, will make consumers more aware of the practices employed by the copycat (Campbell and Kirmani 2000). Copying more subtle themes on the other hand will result in assimilation as more generic, diffuse associations will be activated, which are more likely transferred to the representation of the copycat. Support for these ideas would show that the type of imitation importantly determines copycat evaluation. Further, it would reveal that copying subtle themes is sometimes more beneficial than copying blatant features. This would point out that more subtle copycatting practices are in need of greater attention from brand management and trademark legislation, and worthy of more consumer behavior research.

Four studies were conducted to test the hypothesis if type of imitation (theme versus feature-based) affects the evaluation and choice rate of copycats. Study 1a and 1b tested the prediction that theme-based copycats are evaluated more positively than both feature-based copycats and products that show no similarity with the leader brand. Participants were asked to evaluate either a feature-based copycat in which the specific features of the Milka brand was copied (e.g. the lilac color, a Milka-like cow), or the theme-based copycat in which the theme communicated by the Milka brand was imitated (cows grazing in the Alp-mountains), or a visually differentiated product. In Study 1b a different product category was used ("Margarine with olive oil"), in order to prove the robustness of the effects. The results of Study 1a and 1b showed, as predicted that theme-based copycats were evaluated more positively than feature-based copycats and visually differentiated products. Study 2 tested whether the feature-based copycat increased awareness of insincere tactics of marketers more than the theme-based copycat. In support of the predictions, participants rated the feature-based copycat as less trustworthy, less sincere and less fair than the theme-based copycat. In Study 3 we posited and showed that the negative evaluation of the feature-based copycat as compared to the theme-based copycat is mediated by persuasion knowledge. It further showed that the effects on evaluation transferred to willingness to buy and choice. These results show the positive effects of subtle imitations of themes as compared to blatant imitation of features. The present findings show that copycat evaluation is not just determined by how much is copied, but also by what is copied, which may contribute to a better understanding of the effectiveness of copycatting.

References

Campbell, Margaret C. and Amna Kirmani (2000), "Consumers' Use of Persuasion Knowledge: The Effects of Accessibility and Cognitive Capacity on Perceptions of an Influence Agent," *Journal of Consumer Research*, 27 (1), 69-83.

Kapferer, Jean-Noel (1995), "Brand Confusion: Empirical Study of a Legal Concept," *Psychology and Marketing*, 12 (6), 551-569.

Loken, Barbara, Ivan Ross, and Ronald L. Hinkle (1986), "Consumer ''Confusion'' of Origin and Brand Similarity Perceptions," *Journal of Public Policy and Marketing*, 5, 195-211.

Stapel, Diederik A. and Willem Koomen (2000), "Distinctiveness of Others, Mutability of Selves: Their Impact on Self-Evaluations," *Journal of Personality and Social Psychology*, 79 (6), 1068-1087.

Warlop, Luk and Joseph W. Alba (2004), "Sincere Flattery: Trade-Dress Imitation and Consumer Choice," *Journal of Consumer Psychology*, 14, 21-27.

Zaichkowsky, Judith L. (2006), *The Psychology Behind Trademark Infringement and Counterfeiting*, Hillsdale, NJ: Lawrence Erlbaum Associates.

"When Bodily Sensations Elicit Context Effects: The Moderating Role of Physical Distance"

Joan Meyers-Levy, University of Minnesota, USA
Rui (Juliet) Zhu, University of British Columbia, Canada

Extending on existing research which indicates that people's incidental affective feelings are often assimilated with their assessments of unrelated items, we demonstrate that more localized bodily sensations, which emerge when people's sensory receptors come in contact with external sensory stimuli (e.g., textures), can produce either assimilation, contrast, or no effects on assessments of target products. Specifically, we show that the physical distance from which a person views a product when standing on an (un)comfortable hard tile or softly carpeted store floor can moderate the direction of the resulting context effects on people's product assessments.

Our theorizing anticipating such outcomes draws on the context effect literature. Such work indicates that the direction of context effects critically depends on how people use contextually activated data (e.g., a concept, sensation) during two stages: when encoding or interpreting the target product, and when rendering a formal judgment of it by comparing it with a standard. Further, some research shows that the clarity of the mental representation people form of a target product can influence how contextually activated data will be used at each stage, thereby determining whether assimilation or contrast effects obtain. Specifically, when one's mental representation of a product is poorly (clearly) defined, assimilation (contrast) effects should occur.

We reasoned that in most instances, the clarity of the mental representation that one forms of a product should increase as the distance between the person and the product decreases. Thus, if the texture of the flooring on which a consumer stands during product examination (i.e., the hardness of the tile or softness of the carpeting) prompts the consumer to experience bodily sensations of discomfort or comfort, the influence of these sensations on viewers' product assessments should vary as a function of the distance that separates the consumer from the product. Specifically, because a product displayed at a moderate distance is apt to prompt a somewhat ill-defined product representation, viewers should assimilate their bodily sensations with target product assessments. However, because a product displayed at a close distance should yield a clear product representation, these viewers' bodily sensations may be used as a comparison standard and prompt a contrast effect on their assessments. Finally, a product that is displayed at an extremely far distance may render its product features so blatantly ambiguous that viewers may recognize that their bodily sensation of (dis)comfort could not have emerged from the barely visible product. Thus, in this instance, we reasoned that individuals may discount their sensations, resulting in no context effects.

In Study 1 each participant stood in a specific location on either carpeted or hard tile flooring and viewed a target vase placed on the floor at a close (6 inches), moderate (5 feet), or extremely far (10 feet) distance from them. Then, participants assessed how comforting the target vase's appearance was. The results supported our predictions. When individuals viewed the product from a moderate distance, they assimilated their bodily sensations with their product assessments, but when the product was viewed from a close distance a contrast effect emerged. When individuals viewed the target product from an extreme distance no context effects emerged. Study 2 theoretically replicated these findings by using a different dependent variable, namely the firmness of the product, and demonstrated that when people are made aware of the source of their bodily sensation, these effects go away.

While these findings are encouraging, questions could arise about whether the outcomes were truly attributable to people's bodily sensations per se. It is possible that they actually reflect people's use of semantic concepts that were primed by the contextual flooring. In turn, these primed semantic concepts—not people's bodily sensations of (dis)comfort—could have served as contextual cues that shaped people's product assessments. Study 3 sought to distinguish whether our findings reflect such cognitive priming, or, as we propose, the influence of bodily sensations. It also explored whether bodily sensations elicit context effects that are confined to assessments that relate to the relevant sense, versus, overall affective assessments of the target product. To test whether our results were driven by people's internally experienced bodily sensations versus widely shared semantic concepts associated with the flooring, we examined whether differences in participants' self-monitoring would moderate our context effects. Hence, if our findings reflect people's reliance on people's internal sensations, the effects should emerge primarily among low, not high, self-monitors, as prior research has shown that they base their responses by attending to their own internal states or bodily sensations. Results from this study supported our notion that the context effects occurred because of how people used their bodily sensations (not cognitive concepts) aroused by the flooring. Further, no context effects emerged on participants' overall affect toward the target product, indicating that context effects spawned by bodily sensations may be more limited in scope. Study 4 provided further support for our theorizing by experimentally focusing people's attention on either their bodily sensations or cognitions. As anticipated, the context effects observed before only emerged when people were primed to focus on their inner sensations.

Special Session Summary

How Environmental Cues Impact Consumer Judgments

Leonard Lee, Columbia University, USA
Michel Tuan Pham, Columbia University, USA

SESSION OVERVIEW

A substantial body of research has established the critical effects that a consumer's encompassing environment has on his or her judgments and decisions. A cohesive framework that can be used to conceptualize the different ways in which environmental cues can impact how consumers think, feel, and behave is illustrated in Figure 1.

Moving from the more concrete to the more abstract, our environment can not only increase our awareness of our available choices and influence the specific goals we pursue, it can also alter how we process external stimuli as well as affect our attributions of outcomes.

This session brings together an integrated set of four recent papers that document these four dimensions. Berger, Sorensen, and Rasmussen show that, contrary to lay beliefs, negative environmental publicity (e.g. rumors and reviews) can have an unexpected upside—creating greater awareness and boosting consumption of available options (e.g. books), particularly if these options come from relatively unknown producers. Environmental cues also change the goals we pursue and influence how we evaluate brands, even brands that are irrelevant to our goals, e.g. Dalton, Fitzsimmons, Fitzsimmons, and Chartrand found that priming a creativity goal not only improved evaluations of goal-relevant options (e.g. Apple laptops) but also hurt evaluations of goal-irrelevant options (e.g. Dell or IBM laptops). More generally, adopting a dual-system model, cues in our environment can also influence whether we rely on intuitive experiential processing or deliberative cognitive processing in responding to external stimuli. For example, Lee and Thomas show that environmental music can induce greater experiential processing, which in turn, increases consumers' penchant for hedonic products and innate retrieved preferences. Finally, Pham, Goukens, Stuart, and Lehmann demonstrate the surprising power of seemingly trivial environmental artifacts (e.g. mirrors, video cameras)—heightening consumers' self-awareness and increasing their own-attributions of both positive and negative outcomes; in a retail context, for instance, these cues can increase customer satisfaction for an unfavorable service interaction but decrease satisfaction for a favorable service interaction.

Interestingly, many of these effects occur outside of consumers' conscious awareness, whether it's the potentially positive effect of negative publicity on product evaluation, or the consumption goals or processing style that external cues activate, further highlighting the counter-intuitiveness of these findings. Overall, given the fundamental relevance of these effects to consumers' daily lives, this session should be of substantial interest not only to marketing researchers and psychologists, but also to anyone who is fascinated by how environmental factors can affect consumer judgments and behavior, be it consciously or unconsciously.

EXTENDED ABSTRACTS

"Positive Effects of Negative Publicity"

Jonah Berger, University of Pennsylvania, USA
Alan Sorensen, Stanford University, USA
Scott Rasmussen, Stanford University, USA

Negative publicity often hurts. Negative rumors (e.g., a company uses worm meat in their hamburgers) decrease brand evaluations (Tybout, Calder, and Sternthal 1981) and negative reviews hurt purchase likelihood and sales (Basuroy, Chatterjee, and Ravid 2003; Huang and Chen 2006). At the same time, however, some intriguing examples seem to contradict these findings. A wine reviewed as being "redolent of stinky socks," for example, saw its sales increase by 5%, and after a popular movie made relentless fun of Kazakhstan, there was a 300% increase in requests for information about the country. Can negative publicity actually have a positive effect? And if so, when?

We argue that negative publicity can positively affect consumer choice by cueing, or priming people to think of the product. Just as environmental cues, such as advertising, can make people more aware, even negative cues can be useful by making products more top of mind. Accordingly, we suggest that whether negative publicity has positive or negative effects will depend on existing product awareness. When product awareness is already high, negative publicity should have little ability to boost awareness (see Nedungadi 1990), but should lower product evaluation, and consequently, decrease consumer choice. When product awareness is low, however, negative publicity should increase awareness and may boost choice if awareness and publicity valence become dissociated in memory. Similar to the sleeper effect (Hannah and Sternthal 1984), people may have a feeling of awareness, or remember they heard something about the product, but the valence may be forgotten. Due to decreased processing and encoding in memory of unknown product information, this dissociation should be particularly likely when product awareness is low. Three studies test these hypotheses using a combination of experimental methods and econometric analysis.

Study 1 investigates the effect of publicity valence and product awareness on actual book sales. We estimate the impact of New York Times book reviews on sales of over 200 hardcover fiction titles. To avoid potential endogeneity bias, our analysis focuses solely on reviewed books, and we examine whether positive and negative reviews have different effects on post-review sales patterns. We systematically classified reviews as positive or negative using a textual search algorithm. We then examine the post-review sales patterns among new and well established authors (i.e., those that have published more than 10 books).

As predicted, analyses revealed a review valence by product awareness interaction. While a positive review increased sales of both new and established authors (between 32% and 52%), the effect of negative publicity depended on whether the author was well known. Negative publicity decreased (-15%) sales of established authors, but it had the opposite effect on relatively unknown (new) authors, increasing sales by 45%.

Study 2 investigates these effects in a more controlled laboratory setting. We suggested that positive effects of negative publicity might be caused by the dissociation of valence in memory over time for unknown products, so to test this possibility, we manipulated whether people reported purchase likelihood either right after reading a product review, or after a delay. We also manipulated review valence and product awareness (i.e., whether an unknown or well-known product was reviewed).

As expected, analyses revealed a 3-way interaction. For well known products, there was only a main effect of review valence: Participants reported they would be more likely to purchase well

FIGURE 1

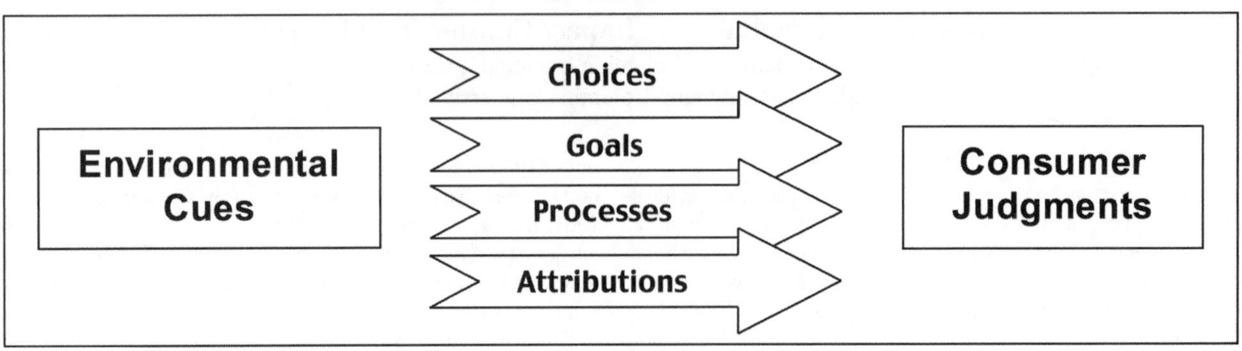

known products that were positively (vs. negatively) reviewed, regardless of whether they reported purchase likelihood right away, or after a delay. In contrast, for unknown products, delay moderated the effect of review valence on purchase likelihood: Review valence had an effect when participants reported purchase likelihood right away, but this dissipated such that after delay, purchase likelihood was similar after a positive or negative review.

Study 3 directly examined the mediating role of increased awareness. First, participants reported their awareness of a number of books. They were then exposed to either a positive or negative review about either a well known or unknown book from the set. Finally, after a long delay, participants again reported product awareness (which allowed us to calculate whether publicity affected awareness) as well as product evaluation and purchase likelihood.

Results support the expected pattern. For well-known products, being reviewed did not affect awareness. But while positive reviews increased purchase likelihood, negative reviews decreased it, and these outcomes were mediated by product evaluations (which were driven by review valence). For relatively unknown products, in contrast, review valence had little effect on product evaluations. Both positive and negative reviews boosted purchase likelihood, however, and this was mediated increased product awareness.

Overall we demonstrate that even negative cues can sometimes have positive effects. Our findings delineate conditions under which negative publicity will have positive versus negative effects on purchase likelihood and actual sales, while also shedding light on the mechanism behind these effects.

"When does Priming Cause Us to Value or Devalue a Brand?"

Amy Dalton, Hong Kong University of Science and Technology, China
Gráinne Fitzsimons, University of Waterloo, Canada
Gavan Fitzsimons, Duke University, USA
Tanya Chartrand, Duke University, USA

Activating (or priming) a mental construct can produce wide-ranging effects on choices, behaviors, and evaluations. In terms of evaluations, priming nonconsciously boosts evaluations of prime-relevant stimuli relative to prime-irrelevant stimuli. Although several studies have documented this effect, few studies have decomposed it to address whether priming is boosting evaluations of stimuli associated with a primed construct (valuation), and/or hurting evaluations of stimuli that are irrelevant to a primed construct (devaluation). Moreover, the few studies that have separated valuation and devaluation effects have not reliably yielded evidence for each, nor have they revealed when priming causes one effect or the other. It is possible that prior research has not reliably obtained both valuation and devaluation effects because these effects are associated with the priming of different types of mental constructs, i.e., priming of semantic associations versus goal associations. Along these lines, we propose that both goal priming and semantic priming can unobtrusively boost evaluations of prime-relevant stimuli (valuation), but only goal priming can reduce evaluations of prime-irrelevant stimuli (devaluation).

The purpose of Experiment 1 was to demonstrate nonconscious valuation and devaluation of consumer products as a function of brands and goals. Experiment 1 used a 2 (creativity prime vs. neutral prime) X 2 (evaluate Apple vs. IBM brand) between-subjects design. First, a scrambled sentence task was administered to supraliminally prime a creativity goal (or no goal). Participants then read a description of a new laptop that was supposedly designed by Apple or by IBM and were asked to evaluate it. We predicted that the Apple laptop would be more attractive following creativity goal priming because the Apple brand image is one of innovativeness and uniqueness. We further predicted that the IBM laptop would be less attractive following creativity goal priming because the IBM brand image is irrelevant to creativity. This pattern is precisely what we found. Thus, experiment 1 demonstrated the basic effect: that priming can simultaneously boost evaluations of a prime-relevant brand and hurt evaluations of a prime-irrelevant brand.

Experiment 2's purpose was to replicate and extend the basic valuation and devaluation effects in two ways. First, we manipulated product features in addition to brands and second, we used an entirely different product domain, automobiles. Thus, experiment 2 used a 2 (morality prime vs. neutral prime) X 2 (Prius vs. Echo brand) X 2 (fuel efficient vs. inefficient car) between-subjects design

In experiment 2, after being supraliminally primed with a morality goal (or no goal), participants evaluated one of four vehicles. Two vehicles were the brand Prius, which is associated with morality via fuel efficiency and environmental consciousness. The other two vehicles were the brand Echo, which is not associated with morality. Within each brand category, one vehicle was described as having a low environmental impact, while the other excelled on other dimensions, including performance. We predicted and found that morality goal priming caused valuation of fuel-efficient vehicles and devaluation of fuel-inefficient vehicles. But this effect was qualified by an interaction. The Prius brand gave a fuel-efficient vehicle an extra evaluative boost and buffered a blatantly fuel-inefficient vehicle against evaluative costs. These findings suggest that products are valued and devalued based on brand and features, and as a function of consumers' goals. But do valuation and devaluation occur independently?

We posit that semantic activation can produce valuation through a non-motivational process of spreading activation, but only goal activation leads to both valuation and devaluation. Experiment 3 tested this hypothesis using a satiation paradigm. Satiation should eliminate goal-based but not semantic priming effects–devaluation, but not valuation, according to our hypothesis.

Experiment 3 used a 2 (creativity prime vs. neutral prime) X 2 (evaluate Apple vs.Dell brand) X 2 (satiation vs. no satiation) between-subjects design. The methods were identical to experiment 2 except that the brand Dell was used (not IBM) and satiation was manipulated such that half the participants satisfied their creativity goal before evaluating a laptop. As we would expect, the results of the no satiation condition replicated experiment 1. Moreover, as predicted, satiation reduced devaluation but not valuation. Thus, experiment 3 showed valuation for goals and semantically-activated constructs, but devaluation only for goals.

Taken together, these studies show that product evaluations can be colored by 2 independent evaluative biases–valuation and devaluation. These effects occur nonconsciously and can be based on tangible product attributes and brand names. Moreover, valuation occurs following either goal or semantic priming, while devaluation is unique to goal priming. Devaluation, therefore, is one way to disentangle goal-based from semantic priming.

"The Effect of Music on Retrieved and Constructed Preferences"

Leonard Lee, Columbia University, USA
Manoj Thomas, Cornell University, USA

The effects of music on diverse facets of human emotion and cognition have been well documented (Kellaris 2008). As the number of headphones-wearing iPod owners sauntering through the streets continues to skyrocket, it is important to understand how music can influence how we think, feel and behave. Building upon extant research on music and preference, we examine the effects of music on retrieved and constructed preferences.

In Experiment 1 we examine the effect of music on preferences for books. Based on a pre-test, we gathered that men are more likely to prefer books on power/politics relative to those on pain/suffering. We hypothesized that listening to music will increase the propensity to retrieve these pre-existing genre-based preferences rather than constructing preferences based on the details of the book. One hundred and fifty two undergraduate and graduate students participated in this study. They were randomly assigned to one of the two conditions: music or control. Pairs of books were used as stimuli in this experiment. In each pair, one book was on power and politics while the other book was on the pain and suffering in life. In one of the pairs, participants chose between "The Federalist," a series of essays on the constitution of America, and "Candide," the adventures of a youth forced into the army, flogged, shipwrecked, and separated from his beloved. In the other pair, they chose between "An American Slave," an autobiographical account of slavery in the United States, and "Lost Illusions," on the disastrous journey of a naïve young poet who left his home to seek fortune in Parisian society. The experiment was titled "Book Evaluations" and was conducted on computers. The music was introduced subtly such that it would appear as a natural element of the study. After the audio instructions, participants saw an hourglass-wait icon, requesting them to wait for a minute as the computer sorted the books to be tested in a random order for each participant. Participants assigned to the music condition heard background music as they waited for the book evaluation task to begin. After a minute of waiting, they saw the pairs of books on the screen, one pair at a time. On each screen, they saw descriptions and posters of two books, and indicated their relative preference for these two books by clicking a button on an 11-point scale shown below the two books. Consistent with our hypothesis, we found that under conditions of music, men were more likely to prefer books on power and politics than women. Further analyses revealed that gender had a significant effect on preferences in the music condition ($p<.01$) but not in the control condition ($F<1$).

In Experiment 2, we wanted to replicate and extend these results to a different context. Further, we wanted to examine the effects of different types of music. A total of 211 participants were recruited for a study on "Foreign Movie Evaluation" and randomly assigned to one of three conditions: control, slow music, and fast music—we included two music conditions to rule out the possibility that any observed effects were caused by idiosyncratic effects (e.g. tempo or fit) due to any particular piece of music. Participants in both music conditions listened to background music on headphones during the primary task while those in the control condition did not. Participants were shown eight pairs of movies and asked to rate (on a 11-point scale) their relative rental preference between each pair. For four of the movie pairs, one movie belonged to the action/crime genre, whereas the other, the romance/comedy genre; the remaining four pairs were designed as control movies and were all documentaries. Consistent with our hypothesis, we found that in the music conditions (compared to the control condition), males and females were more likely to rent action/crime and romance/comedy movies respectively, suggesting a stronger preference for retrieved preferences when listening to music. This effect was mediated by participants' self-reported movie genre preferences and did not apply to the documentary movies.

Experiment 3 is a field study conducted in a mid-size convenience store selling a variety of common grocery products. Ninety-three customers entering the store received a $2-off coupon each and were randomly assigned to one of two conditions—approximately half of the customers were handed an iPod pre-loaded with instrumental music and asked to listen to the music while shopping (music condition), whereas the other half were not handed an iPod (control condition). Subsequently, we collected these customers' receipts when they redeemed their coupons after shopping and asked them to complete a short post-shopping survey. Consistent with our prediction, we found that participants in the music condition bought significantly more items from hedonic categories ($p=.04$) based on product ratings from two independent coders (inter-rater reliability=80%); however, customers across both conditions did not perceive any difference in changes to the amount they had spent compared to previous visits ($p=.3$), suggesting that customers in the music condition were not consciously aware of the effect that the music had on their shopping.

Together, these experiments demonstrate how music-induced experiential processing can influence consumers' preferences and shopping behavior.

"Shaping Customer Satisfaction through Self-Awareness Cues"

Michel Tuan Pham, Columbia University, USA
Caroline Goukens, University of Maastricht, The Netherlands
Jennifer Ames Stuart, Bayer Healthcare, USA
Donald Lehmann, Columbia University, USA

Improving customer satisfaction is obviously of great importance to marketers. Although satisfaction is obviously a function of the level of product/service performance vis-à-vis customers' expectations, it also depends on the outcome attributions that are made. Studies generally find that, in case of delivery failure, dissatisfaction with the provider is stronger if the failure is attributed to the provider than if it is attributed to the customer or to an external cause. On the other hand, in case of delivery success, satisfaction with the provider tends to be greater if the success is attributed to the provider than if it is attributed to the customer or to an external factor.

Findings from the social psychology literature suggest a person's state of self-awareness can influence people's attributions. In particular, high self-awareness prompts people to make more internal attributions, and does so independently of the outcome to be attributed. If customer satisfaction is a function of the perceived locus of responsibility for product/service performance, and if the perceived locus of responsibility can be shifted by states of self-awareness, it should be possible to influence customers' satisfaction by varying the customers' level of self-awareness while holding objective product/service performance constant. This prediction was tested in a series of six studies (including one field experiment) involving four different types of service interactions and four different manipulations of self-awareness.

In each study, participants whose self-awareness was manipulated were exposed to information about different service interactions and asked to rate their satisfaction with the service. The first two experiments tested the basic prediction that mere exposure to innocuous cues that heighten self-awareness can influence customers' satisfaction with a service provider. It was found, across two different service interactions and across two different self-awareness manipulations, that heightened self-awareness increased satisfaction when the outcome of the interaction was unfavorable, but lowered satisfaction when the outcome was favorable. These effects were mediated by an increased perceived responsibility of the self for the outcome under high self-awareness.

The third experiment tested whether the effects of self-awareness on customer satisfaction are driven by changes in the encoding of the service interaction or by changes in the summary interpretation of the interactions. The results favor the latter explanation. Given these results, the next experiment examined whether the same effect would hold if the service interaction occurred much earlier (e.g., several months ago). College students whose self-awareness was manipulated were asked to assess their satisfactions with college courses they were currently taking versus courses they had taken earlier. The results showed the self-awareness on satisfaction extends to current satisfaction with real service interactions that occurred much earlier. This latter finding reinforced Study 3's interpretation that the source of self-awareness effects on satisfaction lies at the moment of impression formation rather than at the encoding of the service interaction. From a substantive standpoint, the finding suggests that marketers may be able to shape not only satisfaction with recent service interactions but also satisfaction with past ones.

The fifth experiment identified a boundary condition for the above-found effects. That is, the results of this study showed that while raising self-awareness may increase the overall satisfaction with service interactions with an unfavorable outcome, it will only do so when there is mixed responsibility for the outcome. If responsibility for the outcome rests entirely with the provider, raising the customer's self-awareness may backfire and further decrease his or her satisfaction. This backfiring effect seems to be due to the triggering of ego-defense mechanisms under high self-awareness when the customer bears no responsibility for the outcome.

A sixth, field experiment, shows that the key effect—the increase in satisfaction after negative outcome interactions—also holds in a real retail setting. The study was conducted in a clothing retail store in New York City. The results show that customers who were about to return or exchange merchandize at the store's customer service desk were more satisfied (less dissatisfied) with the merchandize they were about to return when mirrors were placed in the customer service desk area than when they were no mirrors.

In sum, these six studies provide strong evidence that subtle cues that raise self-awareness can influence satisfaction with service providers, even if the objective service performance remains constant. This effect has obvious managerial implications for marketers looking for ways to improve their customers' satisfaction following delivery failures. Satisfaction-through-self-awareness tactics can be implemented relatively inexpensively (e.g., mirrors at customer service desk, addressing customers by their names, etc.), especially compared to the cost of true product/service delivery improvements.

SPECIAL SESSION SUMMARY

Plates, Smiley Faces and Price Tags: How Contextual Factors Bias Consumption

Meng Zhu, Carnegie Mellon University, USA

SESSION OVERVIEW

Decades of research in judgment and decision making (e.g., Tversky & Kahneman 1974; Chaiken, Liberman & Eagly 1989; Sloman 1996) has established the view that everyday behaviors are often guided by simple heuristics instead of deliberative reasoning. Although relatively effortless, simple heuristics can lead to systematic biases. While a great deal of research has focused on investigating heuristics and biases in judgments (e.g., Tversky & Kahneman 1974; Kahneman, Slovic & Tversky 1982) and choices (e.g., Huber, Payne & Puto 1982; Simonson 1989; Simonson & Tversky 1992), little attention has been given to how heuristic cues can bias consumption decisions. In a few notable exceptions, consumption behaviors have been shown to be influenced by package size (Wansink 1996), container shapes (e.g., Wansink & Ittersum 2003), and serving units (e.g., Cheema & Soman 2008).

Given the crucial role consumption plays in today's economy, health care, and its impact on the natural environment, it is critical to understand how people's consumption decisions can be swayed by different contextual factors. In this session, we present three papers that add to the emerging view that consumption behaviors are largely constructive and context-specific. The papers demonstrate how different subtle contextual cues (e.g., the plating and presentation of a food, the image of a smiling face, and prices of weight loss pills) can produce systematic impact on people's consumption behaviors across different domains (e.g., food, personal care products, and dieting and exercising programs), thus providing an opportunity to establish linkages between various research streams..

In the first paper, Payne and Wansink show that visual cues can induce a generalized "halo effect" and bias the consumption experience of food products. In particular, they show that the plating and presentation (e.g., presenting a brownie on a china plate, a napkin or a paper plate) significantly influence ratings of a food's taste and how much someone is willing to pay. Their results suggest that the heuristic-based "what is beautiful tastes good" association provides a better explanation of how favorable food-related visual cues (e.g., a china plate) bias post-consumption evaluations than does the conventionally used "confirmation bias" perspective.

The second paper by Zhu, Billeter and Inman illustrates how visual cues bias consumption in an advertising context. Their findings suggest that consumers rely on pictures rather than product descriptions in advertisements to infer product effectiveness and accordingly decide how much to consume. They demonstrate that pictures (e.g., a smiling face with great teeth) can increase perceived effectiveness of the advertised products (e.g., a whitening rinse) and concomitantly reduce usage amount of the featured products. They provide evidence that this negative impact of pictures on consumption mainly arises from heuristic processing and is attenuated by cognitive deliberation.

Finally, Bagchi and Cheema look at how contextual factors affect consumption of goal-relevant alternatives in consumer consumption context. They demonstrate that rather subtle cues (e.g., paid price for weight loss pills) can induce different efficacy perceptions about whether the goal is easy or hard and hence systematically impact consumption of goal-consistent (e.g., exercising to lose weight) vs. goal-inconsistent (e.g., avoiding rich foods) alternatives. Their results suggest that efficacy increases motivation to pursue goals when individuals focus on engaging in goal-consistent consumption alternatives (e.g., exercising), but hurts when the focus is on avoiding goal-inconsistent consumption alternatives (e.g., dieting).

Taken together, the three papers (all in advanced stages) in this session examine the largely underexplored relationship between contextual factors and consumption and present a consistent picture suggesting that consumption decisions are largely constructive, context-specific, and are often determined by heuristic cues rather than deliberate thoughts and stable preferences. As the session integrates diverse research, it is expected to appeal to a broad audience, including those interested in consumption, decision-making, information processing, judgment biases, advertising and goals.

EXTENDED ABSTRACTS

"What is Beautiful Tastes Good: Visual Cues, Taste, and Willingness to Pay"

Collin Payne, New Mexico State University, USA
Brian Wansink, Cornell University, USA

The plating and presentation of a food, much like the attractiveness of a person, could induce a generalized halo for it. For example, if a food is presented on an attractive plate with an attractive presentation, one might assume this food to have other related positive characteristics. Once this assumption is made, favorable assessments of the food may be generated before it is even consumed (Mela, 1999). The assumption of a direct association between favorable food-related visual cues (plating and presentation), perceived taste, and "willingness to pay" is the basis for a proposed "what is beautiful tastes good" perspective of food ratings.

In contrast to the "what is beautiful tastes good" perspective, it may be that the plating and presentation of a food may create a belief about how much one is willing to pay for it that typically would be confirmed (rather than disconfirmed) through its perceived taste ("confirmation bias" perspective) (Wason,1960). For example, if a food is presented on an attractive plate with an attractive presentation, a restaurant patron may assume that the food is "good" or high quality and initially believe that they would be willing to pay more for it. Once this belief is made, patrons will be biased in their search for positive taste evidence that confirms, rather that disconfirms, their initial belief of their willingness to pay more for it.

Where these two perspectives differ is the importance given to such taste evaluations. The confirmation bias perspective assumes the taste of a food must first be confirmed before one will be willing to pay more for it. In contrast, the "What is beautiful tastes good" perspective assumes that "there is enough information" in the plating and presentation of the food to affect not only perceived taste, but also how much one is willing to pay for it. We suggest that visual cues of plating and presentation provide enough information to influence one's willingness to pay, which is minimally influenced by an actual taste experience.

Study 1 involved 119 students (68.1% female; 19.1 years old) who were regular diners in a cafeteria. While still seated, each participant was shown a salad, sandwich, and brownie, which were all presented in one of three presentation styles (on a paper plate, on a glass plate, or on a glass plate with a garnish of parsley). Both the presentation order of the foods and its presentation style were systematically rotated. After seeing each food, participants were asked to fill out a brief questionnaire which included the question, "If this was a new menu addition in the cafeteria, what is the most you would pay for this food?"

There was a notable increase in how much people would pay for a food item based on its presentation for the sandwich [F (2, 226)=28.81, p<.001], the brownie [F (2, 225)=6.69, p=.002], and to a lesser extent, the salad [F (2, 223)=2.86, p=.059]. All possible post-hoc contrasts for sandwich were significant (all p's<.01) while—for the brownie—significant differences were found between the presentation of it on a paper plate versus glass plate with garnish (p=.001) and between its presentation on a glass plate and a glass plate with garnish (p=.029). No significant differences were found for the salad. No explicit measures were taken to check for the participants' evaluation of the appearance of the food in Study 1. The subsequent study evaluates the appearance of food as a function of its presentation and also includes an actual consumption experience.

One hundred seventy-five cafeteria diners (72% female; 26.2 years old) participated in this study. They were asked if they would like to sample a free brownie. A brownie was then presented to the seated participants in one of three ways: on a napkin, on a paper plate, or on a china plate. After consuming the brownie, participants were given a questionnaire, which assessed their perception of the brownie's taste and how much they were willing to pay for it.

A manipulation check showed plating and presentation improved appearance ratings of the brownie, F (2, 172)=39.87, p<.001. All possible post-hoc contrasts for appearance were significant and in the anticipated direction (all p's<.01). An increase in the perceived taste of the brownie as a function of plating and presentation was also found [5.22, 5.61, and 6.16; F (2, 172)=13.9, p<.001]. This result supports the idea that the plating and presentation of a food can influence subsequent taste. Post-hoc analyses indicated that the significant differences were found for "taste" between presentation of a brownie on a napkin and glass plate (p<.001) and also between a brownie presented on a paper plate and glass plate (p<.01).

To test whether plating and presentation significantly affected "willingness to pay" after controlling for taste, we conducted a Sobel test (see Baron & Kenny, 1986). This test specifically assesses whether the relationship between plating and presentation and "willingness to pay" can be accounted for by perceived taste. If the relationship is significantly reduced, the relationship is said to be accounted for by taste. The Sobel test resulted in nonsignificance (Sobel Test=1.6, p=.11). Improvements in plating and presentation influenced how much a person indicated they would be willing to pay. Improving plating and presentation in Study 1 led participants to indicate they would pay the equivalent of 22.6% more for a brownie, 14.5% more for a salad, and 60.6% more for a sandwich. In Study 2, participants given the attractively presented plate after eating their lunch were willing to pay 139.6% more for it ($0.53 vs. $1.27). It appears that a person's evaluation of willingness to pay for a food can be better explained by a person's initial impression of the appearance of the food than by their subsequent taste of it.

"Can Pictures in Advertisements Curb Consumption?"

Meng Zhu, Carnegie Mellon University, USA
Darron Billeter, Brigham Young University, USA
J. Jeffrey Inman, University of Pittsburgh, USA

Marketers often use pictures in advertisements with the hope and conviction that they would produce a positive impact on consumer preferences. Accordingly, the effect of pictures on advertising has been studied extensively by marketing researchers. Pictures have been shown to have a positive impact on advertising effectiveness, by enhancing consumer's recall of brand name (e.g., Lutz and Lutz 1977), facilitating retrieval of attribute information (e.g., Houston et al. 1987) and forming favorable attitudes towards the brand and advertisement (e.g., Mitchell 1986). However, whether the positive effect of pictures on advertising effectiveness leads to higher consumption volume remains an uninvestigated and intriguing question that has both theoretical and practical marketing implications.

The purpose of this paper is to systematically investigate the impact of pictures in advertisements on consumption. Building on an emerging stream of research showing that consumption behaviors are often guided by simple heuristics rather than deliberative thinking (e.g., Wansink 1996; Wansink and Ittersum 2003; Cheema and Soman 2008), we suggest that consumers use pictures in advertisements to simplify their consumption decision. Particularly, we suggest that the impact of pictures on consumption is mediated by perceived product effectiveness. That is, consumers infer effectiveness of the advertised product from pictures presented in the advertisement. In deciding how much of a product to consume, people rely on their perceptions of product effectiveness as an indicator for what amount is required. Because a more effective product often requires a smaller amount to accomplish the same objective, we propose that pictures that increase perceived effectiveness of the advertised products will reduce usage amount at a single occasion. As this effect mainly arises from heuristic processing, we predict that cognitive deliberation will attenuate the negative impact of pictures on consumption. Further, we predict that other marketing variables, such as brand names, can also serve as heuristic cues for inferring product effectiveness and consequently generate a similar systematic impact on consumption.

Study 1 is designed to demonstrate the proposed main effect. In particular, we study whether adding the picture of a smiling face with great teeth to an otherwise text-only rinse advertisement reduces consumption volume at a single occasion. Subjects were shown an ad for a new teeth whitening rinse, either with or without a smiling face, and then asked to estimate how much rinse they would use at one time. We found that adding the image of a smiling face with great teeth reduced the estimated consumption rate of the advertised rinse by 42.35%.

Study 2 investigates whether the negative impact of pictures on consumption occurs primarily due to heuristic processing and is attenuated by cognitive deliberation. We directly manipulate cognitive deliberation by asking half of the subjects to rate the importance of each product description presented in the advertisement (Wilson & Schooler, 1991), before estimating the consumption volume. As expected, without rationalization manipulation, subjects indicated less rinse needed for a single occasion when the image of a smiling face was added to the otherwise text-only rinse ad; in support of the proposed heuristic account, we find that the negative impact of the picture on consumption decreased in the rationalization conditions.

Study 3 demonstrates the proposed main effect in an actual consumption scenario. We presented subjects with the actual teeth whitening rinse featured in the advertisement and asked them to pour the amount of rinse they would use into a plastic cup provided by the experimenter. Our results indicate that adding the image of a smiling face reduced actual usage amount of the advertised new teeth whitening rinse by 26.54%. The results of Study 3 also provide further support for the proposed heuristic processing account by showing that pictures mainly influenced the consumption rate of individuals whose need for cognitive thinking was low, rather than individuals who had a higher natural tendency to engage in deliberative processing.

Study 4 investigates the boundaries for the proposed negative impact of pictures on consumption. We choose three different pictures found in actual advertisements of existing insect repellents, that is, a plant, a live bug and a crossed-out bug, to create advertisements for a new herbal insect repellent. Consistent with previous findings, the addition of a picture that enhanced judgment of product effectiveness (a crossed-out bug) led subjects to use less of the advertised product (insect repellent). Additionally, we find that pictures that generated worse effectiveness judgment (a live bug) and did not directly influence perceived effectiveness (a plant), led an increase and no difference respectively in consumption. The data confirmed the significant mediating role of perceived product effectiveness in the relationship between pictures and consumption. Study 5 extends the impact of pictures on consumption to brand names in another product category, toilet bowler cleaner. We find that the brand name "BalanceClean" as compared "BalanceGreen" led to increased effectiveness judgment about the featured toilet bowler cleaner and consequently decreased consumption volume.

The present research offers implications for marketing practitioners. Contrary to the common belief that pictures in advertisements generate positive influences on consumer demand, we show that pictures, particularly those images that increase perceived effectiveness of the advertised products, can inadvertently decrease sales volume due to reduced usage amount at a single occasion and lengthened repurchase cycle. Our results also indicate that pictures that decrease perceived product effectiveness can in fact increase consumption, implying that choosing pictures or brand names that do not enhance perceived effectiveness for new products and brand extensions may be a viable marketing strategy.

"The Ironic Effect of Efficacy on Consumer Consumption"

Rajesh Bagchi, Virginia Tech, USA
Amar Cheema, Washington University/University of Virginia, USA

Literature on goal-pursuit reveals that self-efficacy perceptions enhance effort and persistence of individuals pursuing a goal (Bandura 1977). Individuals also exert more effort when pursuing easy-to-achieve (vs. hard-to-achieve) goals and when the likelihood of reaching the goal is higher (Naylor and Ilgen 1984). However, other research suggests that when goals conflict (Shiv and Fedorikhin 1999), individuals sometimes decrease their effort towards one goal and focus on a competing goal. Koo and Fishbach (2008) label this as balancing and suggest that, when provided with information on how much effort remains to achieve a goal, individuals who are uncertain about their commitment towards the focal goal shift efforts to a competing goal, while those who are certain highlight the focal goal. Related research suggests that remedial products, such as a patch to quit smoking, increases incidence of smoking among existing smokers (Bolton, Cohen, and Bloom 2006). Thus, it is not evident how increased efficacy (effectiveness) influences goal-pursuit in the presence of competing goals.

We focus on situations where multiple competing goals exist, specifically in the context of losing weight. In this context, individuals try to manage goals of eating tasty (and often unhealthy) foods with a weight-loss goal, which requires exercising and dieting (avoiding rich foods). We argue that the type of action considered (engaging in goal-consistent action vs. avoiding goal-inconsistent action) will moderate the effect of efficacy on goal-pursuit. Specifically, when considering engaging in goal-consistent actions (exercising), increased efficacy will enhance goal-pursuit. However, when considering avoiding goal-inconsistent actions (dieting), increased efficacy will decrease goal-pursuit.

We expect that elaborating on goal-consistent actions will increase goal commitment. Higher efficacy will make the desirable goal easier to achieve and will enhance goal-pursuit. In contrast, elaborating on goal-inconsistent actions will decrease commitment towards the focal goal. In this context, making the focal goal easier to achieve (through increased efficacy) may encourage balancing. We demonstrate these effects in two studies.

In study 1, participants learn that they are trying to lose weight by exercising and by dieting. We measured participants' willingness to persist in actions to achieve this goal. We manipulated the type of action between subjects. Half the participants were asked how likely they were to continue working out, while the rest indicated how likely they were to continue on a diet. Participants also responded to a seven-item efficacy scale. We classified each participant as being low, medium, or high in efficacy related to the action asked. Thus, the study was a 2 (action: avoiding goal-inconsistent actions versus persisting in goal-consistent option) x 3 (efficacy: low, medium, high) mixed between-subjects design.

An ANOVA with likelihood of goal-pursuit as the dependent measure and type of action and efficacy as the predictors elicited a significant action x efficacy interaction, $F(2, 146)=3.82$, $p<.05$. Among participants considering the goal-consistent action (exercise), high- (vs. low-) efficacy led to greater likelihood of goal-pursuit (M high-efficacy=6.55 vs. M low-efficacy=5.38). Moderate-efficacy people were also more likely to pursue their goal (M moderate-efficacy=6.21) than low-efficacy people. There was no significant difference between moderate and high-efficacy participants considering the goal-consistent action.

In contrast, among participants considering avoidance of the goal-inconsistent option (diet), high-efficacy participants were significantly less likely to pursue the goal than moderate-efficacy participants (M high-efficacy=5.36 vs. M moderate-efficacy=6.28). However, consistent with a beneficial effect of efficacy, moderate-efficacy participants were more likely to pursue their goal than were the low-efficacy participants, (M moderate-efficacy=6.28 vs. M low-efficacy=5.00). While high-efficacy participants were directionally more likely to pursue their goal than low-efficacy participants, this difference was not significant. Thus, moderate levels of efficacy increase goal pursuit, while high levels of efficacy decrease goal-pursuit when the individual focuses on goal-inconsistent options. Using a continuous measure of efficacy, with a squared term for the non-linear effect, also led to similar results. In study 2, we replicate these results by manipulating perceptions of efficacy.

The scenario indicated that participants were trying to lose weight and that the university was providing free weight loss pills to help. We manipulate perceived efficacy by indicating whether the university paid full price for these pills or not. Research suggests that full-priced drugs are perceived to be more efficacious (Shiv, Carmon, and Ariely 2005). Participants then responded to likelihood of pursuing their weight-loss goal. We also manipulated type of action between subjects as in study 1. Thus, the study was a 2 (action: avoiding goal-inconsistent actions versus persisting in goal-consistent option) x 2 (efficacy: low, high) full factorial between-subjects design.

An ANOVA with likelihood of goal-pursuit as the dependent measure and type of action and efficacy as the predictors elicited the predicted action x efficacy interaction, $F(1, 136)=17.52$, $p<.0001$. Among people considering the goal-consistent action, those in the high-efficacy condition are more likely to pursue the goal (M high-efficacy=6.23 vs. M low-efficacy=5.40). In contrast, among people considering the goal-inconsistent action, increased efficacy decreased likelihood of goal-pursuit (M high-efficacy=5.11 vs. M low-efficacy=5.80). These results were consistent with those from study 1.

Thus, efficacy increases goal-pursuit when individuals elaborate on goal-consistent actions, but hinders goal-pursuit when individuals focus on goal-inconsistent actions. We believe this process occurs because elaboration of goal-inconsistent actions decreases individuals' commitment towards the goal and licenses the individual to focus on goal-inconsistent actions (Fishbach and Dhar 2005). We also discuss theoretical and managerial implications and suggest future extensions.

REFERENCES

Baron, Reuben M., and David A. Kenny (1986), "The moderator-mediator variable distinction in social psychological research: conceptual, strategic, and statistical considerations," *Journal of Personality and Social Psychology*, 51 (6), 1173-1182.

Bandura, lbert. (1977), "Self-efficacy: Toward a unifying theory of behavioral change," *Psychological Review*, 84(2), 191–215.

Bolton, Lisa E., Joel B. Cohen, and Paul N. Bloom (2006), "Does Marketing Products as Remedies Create 'Get Out of Jail Free Cards'?" *Journal of Consumer Research*, 33 (June), 71-81.

Cardello, Armand V. (1996), "The role of the human senses in food acceptance," in H.L. Meiselman and H.J.H. Macfie (Eds.), *Food Choice Acceptance and Consumption*, London: Blackie Academic.

Chaiken, Shelly, Akiva Liberman and Alice Eagly (1989), "Heuristic and Systematic Information Processing Within and Beyond the Persuasion Context," in Uleman, James. S. & Bargh, John. A. (Eds.), *Unintended Thought*, New York: Guilford Press.

Cheema, Amar and Dilip Soman (2008), "The Effect of Partitions on Controlling Consumption," *Journal of Marketing Research*, 45 (December), 665-675.

Fishbach, Ayelet and Ravi Dhar (2005), "Goals as Excuses or Guides: The Liberating Effect of Perceived Goal Progress on Choice," *Journal of Consumer Research*, 32 (3), 370-377.

Fritz, Matthew S and David P. Mackinnon (2007), "Required Sample Size to Detect the Mediated Effect," *Psychological Science*, 18 (3), 233-239.

Houston, Michael J., Terry L. Childers and Susan E. Heckler (1987), "Picture-Word Consistency and the Elaborative Processing of Advertisements," *Journal of Marketing Research*, 24 (November), 359-369.

Huber, Joel, John W. Payne, and Christopher Puto (1982), "Adding Asymmetrically Dominated Alternatives: Violations of Regularity and the Similarity Hypothesis," *Journal of Consumer Research*, 9 (June), 105-114.

Kahneman, Daniel and Shane Frederick (2005), "A Model of Heuristic Judgment" in *The Cambridge Handbook of Thinking and Reasoning*, K. J. Holyoak & R. G. Morrison (Eds.), Cambridge University Press, 267-293.

Koo, Minjung, and Ayelet Fishbach (2008), "Dynamics of Self-Regulation: How (Un)accomplished Goal Actions Affect Motivation," *Journal of Personality and Social Psychology*, 94 (2), 183-195.

Lutz, Kathy and Richard Lutz (1977), "Effects of Interactive Imagery on Learning: Applications to Advertising," *Journal of Applied Psychology*, 62 (4), 493-498.

Mela, David J. (1999), "Food choice and intake: the human factor," *Proceedings of the Nutritional Society*, 58, 513-521.

Mitchell, Andrew (1986), "The Effect of Verbal and Visual Components of Advertisements on Brand Attitudes and Attitude toward the Advertisement," *Journal of Consumer Research*, 13 (1), 12-24.

Naylor, James.C. & Daniel.R., Ilgen, (1984), "Goal-setting: A theoretical analysis of a motivational technology," in B.M. Staw & L.L. Cummings (Eds.), *Research in Organizational Behavior*, Vol. (6), Greenwich, CT: JAI Press.

Shiv, Baba and Alexander Fedorikhin (1999), "Heart and Mind in Conflict: The Interplay of Affect and Cognition in Consumer Decision Making," *Journal of Consumer Research*, 26 (December), 278-292.

Shiv, Baba, Ziv Carmon and Dan Ariely (2005), "Placebo Effects of Marketing Actions: Consumers May Get What They Pay For," *Journal of Marketing Research*, 42 (November), 383–393.

Simonson, Itamar (1989), "Choice Based on Reasons: The Case of Attraction and compromise Effects," *Journal of Consumer Research*, 16 (September), 158–74.

Simonson, Itamar and Amos Tversky (1992), "Choice in Context: Tradeoff Contrast and Extremeness Aversion," *Journal of Marketing Research*, 29 (August), 281–95.

Sloman, Steven. A. (1996), "The Empirical Case for Two Systems of Reasoning," Psychological Bulletin, 119 (1), 3-22.

Tversky, Amos and Daniel Kahneman (1974), "Judgment under uncertainty: Heuristics and biases," *Science*, 185 (4157), 1124-1131.

Wansink, Brian (1996), "Can Package Size Accelerate Usage Volume?" *Journal of Marketing*, Vol. 60, No. 3, 1-14.

Wansink, Brian and Koert van Ittersum (2003), "Bottoms Up! The Influence of Elongation and Pouring on Consumption Volume," *Journal of Consumer Research*, 30 (December), 455-463.

Wansink, Brian, Koert van Ittersum, and James Painter (2005), "How Descriptive Food Names Bias Sensory Perceptions in Restaurants," *Food Quality and Preference*, 16 (5), 393-400.

Wason, Peter C. (1960), "On the Failure to Eliminate Hypotheses in a Conceptual Task," *Quarterly Journal of Experimental Psychology*, 12 (3), 129-140.

Wilson, Timothy D. and Jonathan W. Schooler (1991), "Thinking Too Much: Introspection Can Reduce the Quality of Preferences and Decisions," *Journal of Personality and Social Psychology*, 60 (2), 181-192.

Special Session Summary

Constraints and Consequences: Psychological Reactance in Consumption Contexts

Amit Bhattacharjee, The Wharton School, University of Pennsylvania, USA

SESSION OVERVIEW

The purpose of this special session is to explore the importance of psychological freedom and reactance in consumer contexts. The marketplace is replete with promotional and social influences, persuasion attempts, advertisements perceived to be manipulative, firm and government regulations, and product unavailability or other barriers (Clee and Wicklund 1980). All of these factors may threaten the ability of consumers to make free and unconstrained choices. Psychological reactance concerns a motivation to restore a threatened freedom (Brehm 1966), and has unique and specific implications for behavior. Though researchers have suggested that psychological reactance is an important construct to study in the field of consumer behavior (e.g. Clee and Wicklund 1980), the topic has received scant empirical attention. The three papers in the proposed session illustrate the versatility and universality of reactance processes, demonstrating the influence of this understudied construct in various novel contexts.

Bertini and Dholakia investigate how common marketing promotions may undermine intrinsic motivations and arouse reactance, inducing more price-sensitive, cautious decision-making by consumers and leading to less favorable managerial outcomes. These findings provide an important counterpoint to the notion that consumers respond favorably to incentives. The second presentation, by *Bhattacharjee and Berger*, examines how identity marketing messages that are positioned too strongly, though unwittingly favored by managers, may provoke reactance in consumers. Identity marketing reactance not only results in worse managerial outcomes, but may impact the way consumers see themselves, influencing downstream identity-relevant decisions. The final presentation, by *Leander, Chartrand, Shah, and Fitzsimons*, explores how differences in chronic reactance may alter the effects of social influences, giving rise to either assimilation or contrast effects. Highly reactant individuals are likely to act in opposition to social pressures, with important implications for consequential behaviors such as underage drinking.

Together, these papers highlight some of the ways in which consumers strive to assert control over their decisions and choices by countering external influences that are perceived to diminish their freedom. Specifically, the symposium demonstrates that both firm-generated promotions and peer and social influences can threaten perceived freedom and arouse reactance. Furthermore, reactance may potentially influence managerial and purchase outcomes, consequential health behaviors, and the way in which consumers see themselves. Given the widespread applicability of the issues discussed, it is expected that the session will be attended by researchers with interests in decision-making, communication and persuasion, promotions, identity, social influence, and consumer welfare and well-being. Following Kivetz (2005), we hold that psychological reactance is a mechanism critical to consumer functioning within the marketplace. As such, we believe that psychological reactance is a crucial avenue for future consumer behavior research. We hope that the diverse approaches to consumer freedom and reactance represented in this session will generate a lively and fruitful discussion.

EXTENDED ABSTRACTS

"Financial Incentives and Consumer Product Choices"

Marco Bertini, London Business School, UK
Utpal (Paul) Dholakia, Rice University, USA

A cardinal argument in managerial economics is that individuals respond to financial incentives. This intuition follows from the assumption that money affects effort and performance such that rewards reinforce desired behaviors while penalties mitigate undesired ones. Social and cognitive psychologists, on the other hand, often claim the opposite is true. For example, they argue that behavior is primarily driven by intrinsic motivations (e.g., altruism), and that compensation, an extrinsic motivation, can crowd out the first to the point that the activity becomes less appealing (Deci, Koestner, and Ryan 1999). Similarly, researchers have also suggested that financial incentives undermine performance because they violate social norms of approval (Fehr and Falk 2002) and reciprocity (Fehr, Gächter, and Kirchsteiger 1997), or because they induce behavioral justifications that damage interpersonal judgments (Bem 1967; Kelley 1971).

The ongoing debate on the merits and shortcomings of economic concessions has important implications in the field of marketing, where consumers are constantly offered discounts in exchange for buying certain products or quantities. As recently as 2004, for example, approximately 30% of marketing mix budgets in the United States (US) was spent on promotional activities.[1] In the United Kingdom (UK), £19 billion was spent in 2007 alone, with up to 60% of the population responding to one or more campaigns in any given month (Mullin and Cummins 2008).

Building on the notion that providing incentives undermines an individual's intrinsic motivation and arouses reactance and suspicion, we propose that the mere presence of promotional instruments (all involving a lower purchase price) induces more price-sensitive, cautious consumer decision-making among existing (but not new) customers of a firm. This proposition was supported in six studies, four laboratory experiments and two field studies, conducted using a variety of different incentives in different contexts. Specifically, we studied the effects of five common marketing tactics: (1) bundling products at a lower aggregate price, (2) offering a quantity discount on larger purchases, (3) providing an initial payment to consumers that switch suppliers and become customers, (4) giving a price reduction for transactions made through a low-cost channel (e.g., the Internet), and (5) giving a referral discount to customers for signing up their family, friends, or coworkers. In each of these cases we found that the monetary incentive "backfired."

In study 1, the addition of bundled offers to a line of individual products decreased the likelihood that participants elected to purchase from this store. Moreover, participants spent significantly less money per transaction when bundles were made available. In study 2, selling two different sizes (small and large) of the same branded products led to an increase in the proportion of respondents preferring the lower priced, lower quality option. We also observed a shift in attention from quality attributes (quality ratings) to price

[1]Promotion Marketing Association (2005), 7th Annual State-of-the-Promotion Industry–2005 Report.

during decision-making. In study 3, cellular phone services with either a short (3 months) or long (2 years) contract term were offered to new customers who contacted the firm on their own initiative or were given $75 to switch providers. In the latter case, participants were more likely to choose a less expensive plan and spend less on add-on services, but only for the contract of longer duration. Finally, in study 4 we examined the effect of offering a discount for using an online channel to sign up for cable TV and Internet service. In this experiment, participants that were offered an incentive were less likely to pick a premium (more expensive) channel package and also more likely to select a lower-speed Internet connection.

Study 4 included two different tests of referral discounts. The first was conducted with 98 patrons at a café. Participants were given a screenshot of an eBay CD auction, with a picture of the CD cover, a description, a starting price of $0.99, and shipping costs of $5. The seller's feedback rating was displayed on the top right-hand corner. We manipulated whether the seller offered a referral discount or not. Specifically, only participants in the Incentive condition read the following additional message: "I offer a referral discount. Get your friend to bid and win one of my other auctions within seven days of yours and receive 10% off your winning bid." After reading their respective version of the stimulus, respondents noted the maximum amount they would be willing to bid for this CD. Participants that were offered a financial incentive (the referral discount) from the seller entered a lower maximum bid ($5.89) than those in the Control condition (M=$8.25, p<.05). A second test, involving evaluation of a pre-approved credit card offer from a bank, showed that participants in the Incentive condition were less likely to apply for the credit card (M=4.06) and liked the offer less (M=4.94) than those in the Control condition (likely to apply: M=5.16; p<.02; liking of offer: M=6.03; p<.02).

These laboratory results provide initial evidence that firms may in fact be better off not offering monetary incentives to consumers. In an effort to provide real-life evidence to support this claim, we then conducted two longitudinal field studies and found consistent results. One was conducted in cooperation with an automotive services firm and revealed that the detrimental effects of being given a coupon were limited to the firm's existing customers. In contrast, its new customers did not show any adverse effects. The last field study was conducted in cooperation with a major bank and showed that the preferences of its existing customers for incentive-based promotions foreshadowed their relational behaviors towards the firm over the course of a year afterward. Taken together, the results of these varied tests provide convergent evidence for our proposition and provide new insights into the role of reactance in customer decision making. In our presentation at the conference, we plan to present the results for a selection of these studies and discuss the theoretical and practical implications of our research.

"Escaping the Crosshairs: Reactance to Identity Marketing"

Amit Bhattacharjee, University of Pennsylvania, USA
Jonah Berger, University of Pennsylvania, USA

Researchers and practitioners alike have long acknowledged the importance and potential of marketing appeals based on identity. For decades, academics have looked beyond the functional aspects of products to examine the symbolic nature of consumption (e.g., Levy 1959). A sizeable literature has established that the identities consumers hold drive them to select constellations of products and services that maintain and strengthen those identities (e.g., Forehand Deshpande and Reed 2002).

Given that consumers are attracted to brands and products that reflect the identities that they possess (Forehand et al. 2002), brand managers and marketers presumably are smart to attempt to position brands and products in order to reflect particular social identities: fostering this sense of connection may lead to a deeper, more persistent sense of consumer loyalty (Reed 2004). Achieving a sense of congruence or fit between the product, marketing appeal, and the consumer is thus seen as mutually beneficial, helping both the company and the consumer (Sirgy 1982).

But can targeted identity marketing messages have a dark side? Research suggests that consumers are inherently motivated to avoid biasing factors such as marketing influence (Wegener and Petty 1997). Similarly, Friestad and Wright (1994) have argued that the marketplace is fraught with situations in which consumers must interpret and react to persuasion attempts and marketing messages. As such, consumers develop a store of personal knowledge of persuasion tactics, and are constantly employing these skills in negotiating the social environment (Wright 1986).

The current research examines when identity marketing may backfire. In particular, we suggest that if messages are too strongly targeted, consumers may react against them, leading to decreased evaluation and choice. Consumers often choose products and cultural tastes in order to construct their identities and communicate information to others (e.g., Berger and Heath 2007; Douglas and Isherwood 1978; Shavitt 1990), and they are motivated to protect their sense of individual agency, such that they can ensure that their expressions of identity are intrinsically motivated and not influenced by external factors (Kivetz 2005; Lepper 1981). The theory of psychological reactance concerns freedom of choice (Brehm 1966). Reactance itself is defined as "the motivational state that is hypothesized to occur when a freedom is eliminated or threatened with elimination" (Brehm and Brehm 1981 p. 37). In other words, the theory contends that when an existing freedom is threatened, people are motivated to reassert the freedom. Thus, the present research proposes that identity marketing messages that are too strongly targeted—that is, messages that infringe on the consumer's ownership of the identity, or that threaten the intrinsic nature of the expression of that identity—may threaten the freedom of consumers to freely express the targeted identity, resulting in consumer reactance. As a result, consumers may turn on the brand, leading to lower evaluation and purchase likelihood.

Three experiments begin to test this theorizing. The first study tested managerial intuition about potential reactance in identity marketing. Undergraduate business majors were shown three marketing messages (one strongly targeted: "You're not green unless you clean with Charlie's!", one moderately targeted: "Two green thumbs up for Charlie's!", and one with no targeting: "Two thumbs up for Charlie's!") for a biodegradable cleaning product identity-relevant to "green", environmentally friendly consumers, and told to choose the most effective one to reach this segment. Results revealed that the strongly targeted message was favored over the nontargeted message and the moderately targeted message, and was predicted to result in the highest consumer evaluation and purchase likelihood.

But while these results are consistent with the thrust of the identity literature, study 2 demonstrates that stronger is not always better. Participants were primed with green versus neutral identities, and viewed the advertisement for a biodegradable cleaning product from the study 1, accompanied by one of the three identity marketing messages. Results indicated that participants with activated green identities felt significantly less freedom to express their identities, and indicated lower product evaluations and purchase likelihood when they had viewed the strongly targeted advertisement, relative to participants who viewed the other messages. Furthermore, a meditational analysis showed that freedom to express identity mediated the relations between message targeting and the outcome measures of product attitude and purchase likelihood. Together, study 1 and study 2 suggest that managers may not anticipate reactance, and may unwittingly prefer those messages most likely to provoke this response in consumers.

In addition to these managerial consequences, study 2 provides initial evidence that identity marketing reactance alters the way in which consumers see themselves: consumers targeted with strong identity marketing appeals may experience a threat to the identity, subsequently de-emphasizing it and reducing its centrality. Study 3 extends these findings, demonstrating an impact on downstream identity-relevant decisions: participants who had viewed a strongly targeted message for the biodegradable cleaner indicated significantly less willingness-to-pay for an unrelated green identity-relevant item, relative to moderately targeted and nontargeted messages. This result did not hold for a neutral, non-identity-relevant item.

Taken together, the current results indicate that targeted identity marketing appeals may have a dark side. Strongly targeted messages can restrict consumer freedom, provoking consumer reactance and resulting in unfavorable outcomes for both the brand and the consumer. Consistent with research suggesting that individuals shift identities strategically in response to threat (Mussweiler, Gabriel, and Bodenhausen 2000), identity marketing reactance may have important downstream consequences. The current research underscores the importance of crafting promotions and advertisements that maintain a sense of consumer agency, particularly for products and domains relevant to the way in which consumers see themselves.

"Feeling the Pressures: Considering the Context-Dependencies of Reactance Motivation in Underage Alcohol Consumption"

N. Pontus Leander, Duke University, USA
Tanya Chartrand, Duke University, USA
James Shah, Duke University, USA
Gavan Fitzsimons, Duke University, USA

Every parent of a teenage son or daughter has struggled with how best to introduce and manage the subject of alcohol consumption with their child. Should a parent offer their sixteen year old son a beer while out fishing in the hopes of demystifying alcohol? Or should that parent suggest to their son that he not have his first beer until he turns 21, the legal drinking age, and turn a blind eye to the social realities of teenage life? In our paper, we examine the influence of the social environments in which underage potential drinkers find themselves on their drinking related attitudes. We introduce into this research domain an important psychological moderator of peer influence, namely chronic reactance (Brehm 1966).

Psychological reactance was defined by Brehm as a motivational state in which an individual seeks to restore a restricted freedom. In other words, when someone feels that you are taking away one of their choice freedoms, they will experience a desire to reassert that freedom. A typical example of such a restriction would be a parent, teacher or authority figure telling a teenager that they are forbidden from engaging in a certain activity (e.g., using drugs, drinking, unsafe sex, etc.). A reactant response to such a restriction would be a desire to be able to choose for themselves whether or not perform such a behavior. Such reactance is typically manifested in two ways. First, the restricted freedom (e.g., drinking, drugs, etc) becomes much more attractive. Second, the source of the restriction (e.g., the parent or teacher) becomes derogated.

More recently, researchers have argued that not all individuals experience reactance in similar magnitudes, but rather that some individuals are likely to experience reactance more intensely than others (Hong and Faedda 1996). In our work, we build on this basic notion and argue that the individual tendency to experience reactance is a critical moderator in determining the alcohol related attitudes and behaviors of consumers under 21 years of age. This group is particularly likely to experience reactance in this domain as prior research has found that younger consumers are more reactant than older consumers, and more importantly, that prior to 21, the law explicitly prohibits the consumption of alcohol in the United States, serving as a major restriction of a young person's freedom to consume alcohol. Across three studies, we explore situations in which trait reactance moderates underage consumers' reactions to social cues that could be perceived as restrictions to their alcohol related freedoms.

In study 1, we explore whether the choices a friend makes concerning underage drinking will impact participants. Specifically, we ask participants to imagine that a friend either made a choice to go drinking that night, or has a choice to go drinking, with the premise that a friend who has made a choice will be more of a social threat to freedom than one who simply has a choice. We later measure time spent considering alcohol related advertisements by our participants as an indirect measure of their inclination towards alcohol consumption (i.e., the more time they spend examining an alcohol related ad the more they are predisposed towards alcohol consumption). Our results show that for consumers low in trait reactance, the made/has a choice manipulation did not affect alcohol ad reading time. But as anticipated, for consumers high in trait reactance, when a friend had made a choice to go drinking (thus threatening the participants ability to choose not to go) alcohol ad reading time is significantly lower than when a friend simply has an option to go drinking, but has yet to make the choice. In other words, for reactant individuals, a choice by their friends to go drinking actually reduces the attractiveness of drinking for the participant.

In study 2, we examine an additional moderator of the effect observed in study 1, namely closeness of the other person making the drinking decision. In essence we argue that a choice by a close other should be substantially more threatening to a reactant individual than should a choice by a more distant other. This is precisely what we observe. When a close other chooses to pursue a drinking goal (i.e., to go to a party) those low in reactance also want to drink much more than if a distant other makes the same choice. However, this effect is reversed for those high in trait reactance. These consumers express more pro-drinking implicit behavior when those distant from them choose to drink than when those close to them do (as the close others choice to drink serves to threaten the high reactance consumers freedom to choose to drink, or not to drink). Study 3 extends these basic results by examining whether the context interacts with the choices of social others to influence reactant response to alcohol related choices. We find, for example, that a choice by another to have a non-alcoholic beverage in a bar serves as a highly threatening choice to consumers high (but not low) in trait reactance, and leads to more pro-alcohol related attitudes and behavior.

In summary, we find that trait reactance is a very important moderator of underage consumers' reactions to the alcohol-related choices of social others. We hope our research serves to stimulate research in the domain of teen drinking behavior, and its interaction with the desire to maintain one's freedom to choose. To date, campaigns such as "Just Say No," a famous/infamous advertising campaign against drugs that targeted a highly reactant population, suggest a deeper understanding could be highly beneficial from a public policy perspective.

REFERENCES

Bem, Daryl J. (1967), "Self-Perception: An Alternative Explanation of Cognitive Dissonance Phenomena," *Psychological Review*, 74, 183-200.

Berger, Jonah and Chip Heath (2007), "Where Consumers Diverge from Others: Identity Signaling and Product Domains," *Journal of Consumer Research*, 34 (August), 121-34.

Brehm, J. W. (1966), *A Theory of Psychological Reactance*, New York: Academic Press.

Brehm, S. S. and J. W. Brehm (1981), *Psychological Reactance: A Theory of Freedom and Control*, New York: Academic Press.

Clee, Mona A. and Robert A. Wicklund (1980), "Consumer Behavior and Psychological Reactance," *Journal of Consumer Research*, 6 (4), 389–405.

Deci, Edward L., Richard Koestner, and Richard M. Ryan (1999), "A Meta-Analytic Review of Experiments Examining the Effects of Extrinsic Rewards on Intrinsic Motivation," *Psychological Buletin*, 125, 627–668.

Douglas, Mary and Baron Isherwood (1978), *The World of Goods: Towards an Anthropology of Consumption*, New York: W.W. Norton.

Fehr, Ernst and Armin Falk (2002), "Pyschological Foundations of Incentives," *European Economic Review*, 46, 687-724.

Fehr, Ernst, Simon Gachter, and Georg Kirchsteiger (1997), "Reciprocity as a Contract Enforcement Device: Experimental Evidence," *Econometrica*, 65, 833-860.

Forehand, Mark R., Rohit Deshpande, and Americus Reed II (2002), "Identity Salience and the Influence of Differential Activation of the Social Self-schema on Advertising Response," *Journal of Applied Psychology*, 87(6) 1086-1099.

Friestad, Marian and Peter Wright (1994), "The Persuasion Knowledge Model: How People Cope with Persuasion Attempts," *Journal of Consumer Research*, 21 (1), 1–31.

Hong, S. M., and Faedda, S. (1996), "Refinement of the Hong Psychological Reactance Scale," *Educational and Psychological Measurement*, 56, 173–182.

Kelley, H.H. (1971), *Attribution in Social Interaction*, General Learning Press.

Kivetz, Ran (2005), "Promotion Reactance: The Role of Effort-Reward Congruity," *Journal of Consumer Research*, 31, 725-736.

Lepper, Mark R. (1981), "Intrinsic and Extrinsic Motivation in Children: Detrimental Effects of Superfluous Social Controls," in *Aspects of the Development of Competence*, ed. W. A. Collins, Vol. 14 of The Minnesota Symposium on Child Psychology, Hillsdale, NJ: Erlbaum, 155–214.

Levy, Sidney J. (1959), "Symbols for Sale," *Harvard Business Review*, 37(4), 117-124.

Mullin, Roddy and Julian Cummins (2008), *Sales Promotion: How to Create, Implement & Integrate Campaigns That Really Work*, London, UK: Kogan Page Publishers.

Mussweiler, Thomas, Shira Gabriel, and Galen V. Bodenhausen (2000), "Shifting Social Identities as a Strategy for Deflecting Threatening Social Comparisons," *Journal of Consumer Research*, 79, 398-409.

Reed II, Americus (2004), "Activating the Self-Importance of Consumer Selves: Exploring Identity Salience Effects on Judgments," *Journal of Consumer Research*, 31 (2), 286-295.

Shavitt, Sharon (1990), "The Role of Attitudes Objects in Attitude Functions," *Journal of Experimental Social Psychology*, 26(2), 124-148.

Sirgy, M. Joseph, (1982), "Self-concept in Consumer Behavior: A Critical Review," *Journal of Consumer Research*, 9, 287-300.

Wegener, D. T., R. E. Petty (1997), "The Flexible Correction Model: The Role of Naïve Theories of Bias in Bias Correction," In M.P. Zanna (Ed.), *Advances in Experimental Social Psychology*, Vol. 29, pp. 141-208. Mahwah, NJ: Erlbaum.

Wright, Peter (1986), "Schemer Schema: Consumers' Intuitive Theories about Marketers' Influence Tactics," in *Advances in Consumer Research*, Vol. 13, Provo, UT: Association for Consumer Research, 1–3.

SPECIAL SESSION SUMMARY

The Effects of Process and Outcome Simulations on Decision Making

Michal Herzenstein, University of Delaware, USA

SESSION OVERVIEW

Process and outcome mental simulations have been researched in psychology for over two decades; however, the marketing literature has only recently begun exploring their effects on consumer behavior. Process simulation focuses on the process of reaching a goal (or using a product) while outcome simulation focuses on the benefits of reaching a goal (or the benefits that are derived from product usage.) Which simulation is better for consumers, and under which conditions? The research presented in this session addresses these questions by examining the positive and negative effects of these simulations on effort, choice, product evaluations, and decision making.

Three papers, each with multiple studies, were presented. The first paper shows that when a product is instrumental to goal pursuit then process simulation increases its appeal, but when it is not instrumental then outcome simulation increases its appeal. The second paper shows that process-focused simulation can enhance the judgments of consumer segments that resist effortful processing, because the beneficial effects of process-focused thought can be obtained without increases in cognitive effort. Finally, the third paper examines the effect of these simulations on the evaluation of really new products (RNPs) and finds that outcome simulation under a cognitive information processing mode or process simulation under an affective information processing mode is more effective in increasing the evaluation of RNPs. The reverse is found for a distant future time frame.

EXTENDED ABSTRACTS

"The Journey to Goal Attainment: When Process Focus is Engaging"

Michal Herzenstein, University of Delaware, USA
Aparna Labroo, University of Chicago, USA

Prior research distinguishes between two types of mental simulations, outcome and process (Taylor et al. 1998). Process simulation focuses on the process of reaching a goal while outcome simulation focuses on the benefits of reaching a goal. Which simulation encourages proactivity? The literature provides mixed findings. On one hand, outcome simulation increases effort and choice. For example, Thompson, Hamilton, and Petrova (2009) show that in the face of a tradeoff between a desirable option (e.g., a camera with many features that is difficult to use) and a feasible option (e.g., a camera with less features that is easy to use), process-oriented thinking increases decision difficulty because individuals focus on the tradeoff attributes. As a result, choice was delayed and task performance was degraded. Similar results were obtained in the context of consumer saving (Baumeister 2002)—consumers perceive saving money as important when its benefits are mentioned, but find it less important when the process of savings is mentioned. This is because the process of saving money highlights its difficulty and as a result consumers yield to temptations (spending now rather than in the future.)

On the other hand, process simulation increases effort and choice. For example, Pham and Taylor (1999) show that students who simulated the process for doing well on an exam (good study habits) studied more and received better grades compared with those who simulated the desired outcome (getting a good grade). Escalas and Luce (2003, 2004) show that when advertising arguments are strong, process (vs. outcome) oriented thinking increases behavioral intentions because it delineates the path consumers should take.

The distinction between the above two streams seems to be that in the latter (process simulation is better) participants pursued a goal while in former (outcome simulation is better) they did not. Is goal pursuit the explanation for these differences? Specifically we ask: when consumers encounter a product, under which conditions process simulation (how to use the product) increases its appeal and under which conditions outcome simulation (the benefits of using the product) increases its appeal? The answer, we suggest, largely depends on the extent to which one considers the product to be relevant and instrumental to goal attainment. When a product is perceived as relevant then process simulation will increase its appeal, because it maps the path to goal attainment (the necessary steps required to use the product and achieve the goal.) However, when the product is not relevant then outcome simulation will increase its appeal because it focuses on the benefits which are important even to those who do not pursue a goal.

We support our claims in three experiments using different manipulations, products (hedonic or utilitarian), and behavioral measures, including actual behavior. In all experiments we manipulate focus by creating two ads for the same product, one highlights the process of using the product and the other, the outcome (benefits) of using it.

In experiment 1 we measured the individual inclination toward success vs. enjoyment goals, and manipulated outcome vs. process focus using two ads for a new business magazine. The process ad focused on what needs to be done in order to find a good job (with the help of the magazine), while the outcome ad focused on the benefits of finding a good job (again, with the help of the magazine.) As predicted, the magazine was more appealing to participants who saw the process focused ad and have a success (vs. an enjoyment) orientation, and to participants who saw the outcome focused ad and have an enjoyment (vs. a success) orientation. Next we explore the important role of instrumentality of the product as means to goal attainment in driving this result.

In experiment 2 participants adopted either an enjoyment or self control goal, and read one of two ads for new imported chocolate truffles. The ads either focused on the outcome of eating the chocolate (sensual, delightful, luxurious taste) or the process of eating the chocolate (opening the box, smelling the chocolate, unwrapping it while making sure not to drop even the minutest chocolate dusting). We note that the ads did not alter the importance participants assigned to their adopted goal. Results show that the chocolate was perceived as more instrumental to feeling good and more appealing to participants who saw the process focused ad and adopted an enjoyment (vs. self control) goal and to participants who saw the outcome focused ad and adopted a self control (vs. enjoyment) goal. Regression analyses show that increased instrumentality of the chocolate as means to feeling good mediated the effect of process vs. outcome focus on the chocolate's appeal.

Finally, we tested our predictions with real choice behavior in experiment 3. Participants adopted either a health or enjoyment goal, saw an ad for a health drink based on vinegar that is "really good for you but not so tasty", and rated its instrumentality to becoming healthier. Our main dependent variable is the amount participants drank from the "health drink" (they were given a mix of water and vinegar). Consistent with our previous results, those who saw the process focused ad and adopted a health goal and those who saw the outcome focused ad and adopted an enjoyment goal found the health drink more instrumental to becoming healthier and actually drank more. Regression analyses show that increased instrumentality of the health drink as means to becoming healthier mediated the effect of focus on the amount of participants drank.

The literature is inconclusive regarding the effects of process and outcome simulation on effort and choice. In goal pursuit, Pham and Taylor (1999) show that process simulation is better, but when people do not pursue a goal, Thompson et al. (2009) show that outcome simulation is better. Our research contributes by explaining why we see this difference. Instrumentality of the means (e.g., to what extent chocolate truffles are considered a means to a feel-good outcome) is the driver of this difference.

"Using Process-Focused vs. Outcome-Focused Thought to Enhance Consumer Judgment"

Jennifer Escalas, Vanderbilt University, USA
Mary Frances Luce, Duke University, USA

One of the most important goals of the marketing discipline is to assess and increase consumer decision quality. However, increasing the quality of many everyday consumer judgments is complicated by the fact that a clear cut behavioral rule is not feasible. That is, consumers cannot (and should not) be told to stop purchasing food, to avoid all use of over-the-counter drugs, or to avoid going outdoors during daylight to reduce the risk of skin cancer. However, these everyday decisions often lead to negative outcomes and the standard, normative advice to work harder or think more carefully, is often resisted in practice. In this paper, we argue that encouraging process-focused mental simulation is a creative option that will lead to more appropriate choices for consumer segments with low motivation to engage in decision effort.

Traditional consumer research approaches suggest increasing cognitive effort as the primary pathway for improving the quality of consumer decisions. However, our research suggests that decision quality can sometimes be improved through the form rather than the amount or effortfulness of decision-related thought. Specifically, process-focused (versus outcome-focused) thought can improve decision making without increasing the cognitive effort required in decision making. In two experiments, we show that process-focused thought can improve decision quality for low-motivation consumers. We believe that this is particularly important because low-motivation consumers seem particularly unlikely to respond to interventions designed to increase the amount of processing. We also show that the beneficial effects of process-focused thought do not extend to high motivation segments.

Escalas and Luce (2003, 2004) demonstrated that focusing on the process of using fictitious vitamin and shampoo products show enhanced sensitivity to argument strength, such that process-focused instructions enhance the favorable effect of strong arguments and the unfavorable effect of weak arguments. However, these beneficial effects of process-focused thought occurred only under conditions when consumers do not engage in systematic processing. Escalas and Luce (2004)'s results are consistent with the argument that relatively spontaneous planning processes are evoked by process-focused thought. When consumers engage in process-focused thought, they naturally attempt to link actions and outcomes to each other in the context of forming a plan. Thus, process-focused participants accept (or reject) the link between advertised behavior and outcomes as they spontaneously formulate (or veto) such a plan. There is also some evidence that higher elaboration actually dilutes or undermines these beneficial effects (Escalas and Luce 2004).

Given these prior findings, we predict that the advantages of process-focused thought in increasing sensitivity to argument strength will be greatest under low- to moderate-elaboration conditions. We expect that process-focused types of thought have the potential to increase decision accuracy holding constant the amount of thought; process-focused thought is naturally occurring and does not require significant amounts of cognitive elaboration. On the other hand, high levels of elaboration are necessary for outcome-focused though to elicit sensitivity to argument strength, consistent with traditional findings of dual process models such as the elaboration-likelihood model. Thus, we expect "accuracy without effort" effects for process-focused mental simulation specifically, and not for outcome-focused thought. Process-focused thought should be a relatively easy way to improve judgment quality, particularly for those segments that are resistant to increased cognitive effort. In this research, we focus on segments that are resistant to engage in effortful thought processes due to low motivation

In our first experiment, we tested the effect of mental simulation in a college exam setting to test whether the beneficial effect of process-focused thought on study behavior is moderated by both motivation to elaborate and the appropriateness of that behavior in the student's particular context (a corollary of strong vs. weak arguments in an advertising context). We found a three-way action appropriateness by thought-focus by motivation to elaborate interaction for our plan to study dependent variable ($F(1, 194)=5.74$, $p<.05$). High motivation participants differentiated between strong versus weak action appropriateness under both conditions of outcome- and process-focused thought. On the other hand, low motivation participants differentiated between strong versus weak action appropriateness only under conditions of process-focused thought. Thus, our results support our assertion that under conditions of low to moderate levels of elaboration motivation, students are more sensitive to action appropriateness when given process-focused (vs. outcome-focused) instructions. In this way, process-focused thought led to more discerning consumer judgments.

In our second study, we examined the interactive effect of process versus outcome thought-focus and argument strength on behavioral intentions (BI), in the context of print advertisements for a fictitious vitamin and a healthy bread product. Our results again supported our expectation that argument strength will differentially affect BI under process-focused thought for participants who are low in need for cognition (NFC) and thus not motivated to elaborate. We found a significant three-way argument strength by thought-focus by NFC interaction for BI ($F(1,205)=3.87$, $p=.05$). There was a differential effect of argument strength in the process condition for participants who are low in NFC, but in the case of the outcome condition, the differential effect of argument strength only existed for participants who are high in NFC.

Our research shows that focusing on the process of using a product can improve consumer decision quality in common, low-motivation to elaborate settings. Encouraging consumers to focus on the process of using a product may be a good method for improving consumer decision-making in low motivation segments, without the perhaps unattainable goal of convincing consumers to engage in effortful elaboration. This seems to be particularly promising for those consumers likely to resist the call to increase the amount of their elaboration or the complexity of their decision processes, because process-focused thought can do so without relying on appeals that consumers "think" or "work" harder. Thus, we believe it will be easier to motivate low-involvement consumers to "think better" (by encouraging them to think about the process involved, which is a relatively natural and easy thing to do) than to motivate them to "think more."

"Process- versus Outcome-focused Simulation and the Evaluation of New Products: The Temporal Effects on the Affective and Cognitive Dimensions"

Min Zhao, University of Toronto, Canada
Steve Hoeffler, Vanderbilt University, USA
Gal Zauberman, University of Pennsylvania, USA

In this research, we examine the role of process- versus outcome-focused mental simulation in the learning of really new products (RNPs). Research in psychology has identified two distinct types of mental simulation: process simulation that is focused on the process of reaching a goal versus outcome simulation that is focused on the desirable outcome of achieving the goal (Taylor et al. 1998). Process simulation has been found to be generally more effective than outcome simulation in facilitating goal attainment (e.g., Taylor et al. 1998) or behavioral intentions (Escalas and Luce 2003, 2004). However, we believe that when applied to the new product domain, process simulation is only more effective for INPs, for which people are able to figure out how to use the product (Hoeffler 2003), whereas for RNPs which evoke high learning cost association (Mukherjee and Hoyer 2001), process and outcome simulation with a traditional approach does not lead to enhanced product evaluation.

We demonstrate how manipulating the type of information processing mode (cognitive vs. affective) with a different temporal perspective elicits the unique effects within process and outcome simulation on the evaluation of RNPs. Much previous research on mental simulation has either confounded process and outcome simulation with cognitive and affective components (i.e. process simulation with a cognitive focus vs. outcome simulation with an affective focus (Taylor et al. 1998), or has incorporated both cognitive and affective components into process and outcome simulation (Escalas and Luce 2003, 2004). We attempted to tease apart the cognitive and affective processing focus and to investigate the unique effect of process and outcome simulation on the evaluation of RNPs under each type of processing when a different temporal perspective is involved. We predict that in an instant evaluation scenario where the learning cost is salient, when evaluating the RNP with a cognitive focus, outcome simulation will lead to higher product evaluations than will process simulation, whereas the reversal is true when these products are evaluated with an affective focus. However, when we introduce a distant future perspective for the product evaluation such that consumers' natural focus of the RNPs is shifted to the product benefits, we hypothesize that outcome simulation under an affective mode or process simulation under a cognitive mode will be more effective in increasing the evaluation of RNPs.

In Experiment 1, we first examined the role of traditional process and outcome simulation (i.e. combined focus on both the cognitive and affective components) on the evaluation of RNP (i.e., AudioPC) compared with INP (i.e., ThinkPad). We asked participants to practice either a process-oriented (i.e. visualizing the steps of using the product) or outcome-oriented (i.e. visualizing the benefits of using the product) simulation task after they read the ad. The results showed that the positive effect of process simulation was only replicated for the INP, whereas for the RNP, which naturally evoked high learning cost association, the effect of process and outcome simulation on product evaluation did not differ.

Experiment 2 investigated the specific effects of process and outcome simulation on the evaluation of RNPs (i.e., AudioPC) by teasing apart the effect of cognitive vs. affective processing mode in an instant evaluation scenario where consumers' natural focus of RNP is on the learning cost. Participants performed either a process-focused or outcome focused visualization task that emphasized either the cognitive or affective components. The results indicated that under a cognitive processing mode, outcome simulation increased product evaluation more than process simulation, whereas under an affective mode, process simulation was more effective than the opposite type of simulation. In addition, we found a partial mediating role of product uncertainty on this pattern.

In Experiment 3, we explicitly introduced different temporal frames by asking the participants to evaluate a RNP (a new video-editing software in this study) in a distant future scenario which enhanced participants' construal level and evoked benefit-related considerations, or in a near future scenario which evoked default usage process consideration and served as our control conditions. The results showed that when the usage process information was more salient (i.e. in the near future conditions which were similar to the settings in experiment 2), we replicated the findings of experiment 2. However, when the novel benefits became more salient, the effect of mental simulation was reversed such that process simulation led to higher product evaluation under a cognitive processing mode, and outcome simulation led to higher evaluation under an affective processing mode. In addition, product uncertainty mediated this interactive effect between time, simulation type and processing mode.

Our research centers on the role of process- and outcome simulation in the evaluation of RNPs. Our findings showed the role of affective and cognitive considerations in the different effectiveness of these two types of simulations under a different temporal perspective. We further identified performance uncertainty as a mediator. We believe that our research provides some answers to the open questions about new product preference development, and well as the open questions about the exact nature of different types of mental simulations and their effectiveness.

REFERENCES

Baumeister, Roy (2002), "Yielding to Temptation: Self-Control Failure, Impulse Purchasing, and Consumer Behavior," *Journal of Consumer Research*, 28 (March), 670–676.

Escalas, Jennifer Edson and Mary Frances Luce (2003), "Process vs. Outcome Thought Focus and Advertising," *Journal of Consumer Psychology*, 13 (3), 246–54.

Escalas, Jennifer Edson and Mary Frances Luce (2004), "Understanding the Effects of Process-Focused Versus Outcome-Focused Thought in Response to Advertising," *Journal of Consumer Research*, 31 (September), 274–85.

Hoeffler, Steve (2003), "Measuring Preferences for Really New Products," *Journal of Marketing Research*, 40 (November), 406–20.

Mukherjee, Ashesh and Wayne D. Hoyer (2001), "The Effect of Novel Attributes on Product Evaluation," *Journal of Consumer Research*, 28 (December), 462–72.

Pham, Lien B. and Shelley E. Taylor (1999), ""From Thought to Action: Effects of Process- versus Outcome-Based Mental Simulations on Performance," *Personality and Social Psychology Bulletin*, 25 (2), 250–60.

Taylor, Shelley E., Lien B. Pham, Inna D. Rivkin, and David A. Armor (1998), "Harnessing the Imagination: Mental Simulation, Self-Regulation and Coping," *American Psychologist*, 53 (April), 429–39.

Thompson, Debora Viana, Rebecca W. Hamilton, and Petia K. Petrova (2009) "When Mental Simulation Hinders Behavior: The Effects of Process Oriented Thinking on Decision Difficulty and Performance," *Journal of Consumer Research*, forthcoming.

SPECIAL SESSION SUMMARY

Multiple Systems for Choice and Valuation: New Perspectives from Decision Neuroscience

Ab Litt, Stanford University, USA

SESSION OVERVIEW

Typical consumer decisions involve the consideration and integration of a diverse range of information about the appeal of available options, decision context and situational history, and the importance and implications of making the 'right' choice. While behavioral studies have illuminated much about the nature of consumer decision making, teasing apart differences in how contributing underlying processes operate is a difficult problem for these approaches alone. Neuroscientific investigations of decision making offer direct and real-time access to these component processes, and so can crucially augment and enrich our current understanding of consumer decision making.

The objective of this session is to present an interlocking set of such insights into the multi-dimensional bases of decisions. The common thread is exploring precisely how different aspects of decision making marshal common versus dissociable underlying processing systems, and the predictive and explanatory implications thereof for central issues in consumer psychology and behavioral decision research. Bolstered by pertinent behavioral results, we employ functional magnetic resonance imaging (fMRI) to develop a more complete picture of the nature of decisions in scenarios akin to many typically faced by consumers. These findings in turn may inspire and shape further neural and behavioral investigations into how dissociable underlying choice and valuation systems may be divergently affected under specific conditions.

Hytönen, Baltussen, van den Assem, Klucharev, Smidts and Post present strong evidence for distinct neural networks active during and after experiencing gains and losses, and for how these distinguishable circuits drive path dependence in risky decision behaviors. From such prior-history effects on choices we move to future-reward discounting, where Figner, Johnson, Krosch, Steffener, Chu and Weber reveal distinguishable neural systems underlying asymmetric expressions of relative impatience across differently framed decisions regarding immediate versus future rewards. Neural circuits for affect, valuation, and action-impulse that these papers identify obtain converging support from the findings of Litt, Plassmann, Shiv and Rangel dissociating computations of motivational salience from valuation at the time of decision making. The striking divergences they observe support growing interest by behavioral decision researchers in teasing apart these components of value, and are consistent with our overarching theme of illuminating the importance of disentangling multiple distinct systems underlying valuation and decision making.

The papers in this special session feature data collected using both behavioral and neuroimaging measures. Our discussion leader, Carolyn Yoon, has conducted important behavioral studies of valuation, memory, and decision making, and is at the forefront of decision neuroscience research in consumer contexts and broader domains. While our techniques will appeal directly to those interested in (or who appreciate the growing importance of) neuroscientific and physiologically informed consumer research, our results are of broader significance to an audience interested in the nature of consumer decision making. Taken together, the findings described in this special session help to pry open the 'black-box' of the act of deciding, by revealing precise mechanisms for how dissociated and shared contributing sub-systems are engaged, interact, and lead to specific patterns of overt behavior.

EXTENDED ABSTRACTS

"Brain Processes Underlying the Influence of Prior Gains and Losses on Decisions under Risk"

Kaisa Hytönen, Erasmus University Rotterdam, The Netherlands
Guido Baltussen, Robeco, The Netherlands
Martijn van den Assem, Erasmus University Rotterdam, The Netherlands
Vasily Klucharev, Erasmus University Rotterdam, The Netherlands
Ale Smidts, Erasmus University Rotterdam, The Netherlands
G. Thierry Post, Erasmus University Rotterdam, The Netherlands

A large body of behavioral experiments has convincingly shown that the risk attitudes of consumer decision makers for a given risky choice problem generally depend on the outcomes of previous choice problems (i.e., path dependence). Most notably, Thaler and Johnson (1990) showed that the average decision-maker tends to take more risk if she has a chance to gain back a previously experienced loss, the "break even effect". Moreover, after experiencing a gain which cannot be lost, she also has a greater risk appetite, the "house money effect". These effects are pervasive outside the laboratory (Post et al., 2008), and they are expected to be common in, for example, sequential choice behavior by private investors.

In this fMRI experiment we study the behavioral changes and brain activations related to prior experiences in decision making under risk. First, we test whether removal of options from a set of possible outcomes is interpreted as a positive or negative event in the brain, relative to the overall composition of an outcome set. Second, we explore how affective neural reactions to gains and losses influence and drive future choices.

Task. Subjects (N=22) undergoing fMRI made decisions between risky lotteries and sure amounts of money (offers). Each choice problem consisted of either one or two sequential stages, depending on a subject's behavior. In the first stage, subjects selected between a lottery with three outcome options and an offer. If a subject chose the offer, they proceeded to the next choice problem. If a subject took the risk of choosing the three-outcome lottery, one outcome option was randomly removed from the lottery (outcome phase). The subject then proceeded to the second stage of the choice problem, where they chose between a lottery with the remaining two outcome options and an updated offer. The choice problems where designed so that subjects faced a fixed set of 24 lotteries and offers following a previously experienced relative gain (smallest outcome option removed), neutral outcome (middle outcome option removed), and a relative loss (highest outcome option removed). The 24 lotteries were thus replicated three times, with the same second-stage lottery evaluated after a loss, gain and neutral outcome. This within-subjects design enabled us to isolate the effects of previous relative gains and losses on future choices between lotteries and offers.

Analysis. To test the nature of subjects' risk-seeking attitudes after relative gains and losses, we compared the percentage of lottery choices for identical sets of second-stage choices across the three conditions, i.e., following a previous relative gain, neutral, or relative loss outcome. In the analysis of the brain data we concentrated on two time windows: the outcome phase, where one outcome option was removed from the lottery, and when making the second-stage choice. For both time windows we located brain areas that were sensitive to relative gains and losses in the choice problem. Using regression analyses we examined which neural regions activated during the second-stage correlated with changes in the percentages of lottery choices between the conditions.

Behavioral Results. Participants showed decreased risk aversion (i.e., an increased percentage of lottery choices), relative to following a prior neutral outcome, following both a prior relative gain ($p<0.05$) and a prior relative loss outcome ($p=0.06$). These results indicate that prior experiences influence future choices under risk in accordance with the house money and break even effects, even in a within-participants design.

Neural Results. In the outcome phase, where one of the three lottery prizes was randomly removed, we found activity in the ventral striatum and medial prefrontal cortex. These areas were most active when participants experienced a relative gain and least active when a relative loss occurred. These brain areas have been previously related to the processing of unexpected rewards (O'Doherty, 2004; Delgado, 2007). Furthermore, these regions deactivate for losses even more strongly than they activate for gains, reflecting loss aversion (Tom et al., 2007). The present findings thus indicate that the brain does indeed process lottery prize removals as relative gains and losses, even before the actual lottery win or loss is revealed. This is an important extension of existing results on reference dependence of lottery outcomes (Breiter et al., 2001).

The effects of previous outcomes during the second-stage choice were reflected by activity in the operculo-insular cortex and anterior cingulate cortex, regions known to be related to cognitive control, emotions, and pain processing (Carter et al., 1999; Frot & Mauguière, 2003). Activity was higher in these regions in the loss condition than in the gain condition. In an additional regression analysis, we found that the insular cortex activity correlated with decreased risk aversion in the loss condition as compared to the neutral condition ($b= 0.5$, $p<0.05$), which is consistent with prior findings linking insular activity to choosing high-risk options (Platt & Huettel, 2008). Another region showing increased activity after loss outcomes during the second-stage choice was the right inferior frontal gyrus, which has previously been related to suppression of responses, and linking emotional reactions and motor actions (Garavan et al., 2006; Schulz, 2009). Here we found that the smaller the difference in right inferior frontal gyrus activity between the gain and neutral conditions, the more lottery choices increased relatively after a gain ($b= -0.43$, $p<0.05$). These results suggest that prior events can lead to an increase in affect-related neural activity and a decrease in control in subjects vulnerable to biases.

In sum, these results demonstrate that removal of an option from a set of possible outcomes is processed in the brain as a positive or negative event relatively to the original outcome set, and that activity involved in processing emotions and control distinguishably drives path dependence in risky decision behaviors.

References

Breiter, H. C., I. Aharon, D. Kahneman, A. Dale, and P. Shizgal (2001), "Functional Imaging of Neural Responses to Expectancy and Experience of Monetary Gains and Losses," *Neuron*, 30, 619-639.

Carter, C. S., M. M. Botvinick, and J. D. Cohen (1999), "The Contribution of the Anterior Cingulate Cortex to Executive Processes in Cognition," *Reviews in the Neurosciences*, 10, 49-57.

Delgado, M. R. (2007), "Reward-related Responses in the Human Striatum," *Annals of the New York Academy of Science*, 1104, 70-88.

Frot, M. and F. Mauguière (2003), "Dual Representation of Pain in the Operculoinsular Cortex in Humans," *Brain*, 126, 1-13.

Garavan, H., R. Hester, K. Murphy, C. Fassbender, and C. Kelly (2006), "Individual Differences in the Functional Neuroanatomy of Inhibitory Control," *Brain Research*, 1105(1), 130-142.

O'Doherty, J. (2004), "Reward Representations and Reward-related Learning in the Human Brain: Insights from Human Neuroimaging," *Current Opinion in Neurobiology*, 14(6), 769-776.

Platt, M. L. and S. A. Huettel (2008), "Risky Business: The Neuroeconomics of Decision Making Under Uncertainty," *Nature Neuroscience*, 11(4), 398-403.

Post, T., M. J. van den Assem, G. Baltussen, and R. H. Thaler (2008), "Deal or No Deal? Decision Making Under Risk in a Large-payoff Game Show," *American Economic Review*, 98(1), 38-71.

Schulz, K. P., et al. (2009), Dissociable Neural Effects of Stimulus Valence and Preceding Context During the Inhibition of Responses to Emotional Faces," *Human Brain Mapping*, in press, DOI: 10.1002/hbm.20706.

Thaler, R. H., and E. J. Johnson (1990), "Gambling With the House Money and Trying to Break Even: The Effects of Prior Outcomes on Risky Choice," *Management Science*, 36(6), 643-660.

Tom, S., C. R. Fox, C. Trepel, and R. A. Poldrack (2007), "The Neural Basis of Loss Aversion in Decision Making Under Risk," *Science*, 315, 515-518.

"Impatient No More! Impulsivity in Choice Depends on How you Frame the Question"

Bernd Figner, Columbia University, USA
Eric Johnson, Columbia University, USA
Amy Krosch, Columbia University, USA
Jason Steffener, Columbia University, USA
Eustace Hsu, Columbia University, USA
Elke Weber, Columbia University, USA

One of the most important consumer decisions is whether to consume now, or wait until later. This willingness to trade immediate rewards for later benefits determines how much we save for retirement and whether we have that extra drink at a party (Mischel et al., 1969; Weber et al., 2007). While classical economics assumes exponential (constant per-period) discounting, people in fact discount future outcomes more steeply when they have the opportunity for immediate gratification than when all outcomes occur in the future, that is, they exhibit hyperbolic discounting (Frederick et al., 2002).

Many different explanations exist for hyperbolic discounting. A prominent example is the beta-delta model (Laibson, 1997), in which total discounting is the (quasi-hyperbolic) sum of two exponential discounting components, one (delta) that is present in all intertemporal choices, the other (beta) that is present only when immediate rewards are one of the choice options. Imaging evidence for this form of discounting decomposition was provided by McClure and colleagues (2004).

However, this approach and many other analyses ignore a robust empirical fact: people are much more impatient when delaying consumption (e.g., demanded price reduction for a downgrade from express to regular shipping) than when given the opportunity to accelerate consumption (e.g., willingness-to-pay for an upgrade from regular to express shipping; see Loewenstein, 1988). Loss aversion, as formalized by prospect theory (Kahneman & Tversky, 1979), has been used to explain such asymmetric discounting. People are assumed to encode delay of consumption as a loss and acceleration as a gain, and delays are thereby proposed to be more painful than accelerations are pleasurable. This account is silent, however, regarding the precise psychological mechanisms giving rise to any such loss aversion and consequent asymmetric discounting. Moreover, it predicts a non-existent relation between an individual's degree of loss aversion and the degree of impatience asymmetry.

An alternative, more process-specific class of explanations suggests that different kinds of valuations (acceleration vs. delay; buying vs. selling prices) shift the decision-maker's focus of attention, consistent with differences in implicit goals (Fischer et al., 1999; Weber & Kirsner, 1997). Query Theory (Johnson et al., 2007) hypothesizes that decision defaults influence the sequence of retrieval of evidence, with the expected option (immediate consumption in delay decisions, larger but later consumption in acceleration decisions) being considered first, and with initial queries generating output interference that reduces the output of subsequent queries.

Task. To explore these questions regarding the basic processes underlying asymmetric discounting and impatience, we ran an online investigation of choices made by 20 participants undergoing fMRI. Participants made binary choices between gift certificates, using stimuli based on those used by McClure et al. (2004). In each of approximately 120 trials, participants made a delay or accelerate decision between a smaller/sooner (SS) and a larger/later (LL) reward. Amounts (ranging from $15 to $85), times of delivery (either immediately, i.e., day-of-participation, 4 weeks later, or 6 weeks later), and relative time difference between SS and LL (either 2 or 4 weeks) varied across trials. After finishing the scanning portion of the experiment, one of the participant's choices was randomly selected and paid out for real, and at the designated time of delivery for that prize on that trial, participants received the gift certificate they had chosen in the selected trial. This design enabled us to investigate neural activation differences underlying observed impatience asymmetries between delay decisions and accelerate decisions, further contrasting (a) choices between an immediate and a future reward; with (b) choices between two future rewards. This allowed investigation of relative differences in hyperbolic discounting between delay and accelerate decisions.

Behavioral Results. We observed significant effects (all p's<.001) of the length-of-delay-time difference (with participants being more patient for shorter wait periods), the magnitude of the earlier reward, and the relative difference between SS and LL (indicating a trade-off between the cost of waiting and the increased reward of the LL). Moreover, and as predicted a priori based on Query Theory, we found hyperbolic discounting only in the delay condition, and not in the accelerate condition, with more impatient choices if a reward was immediately available as opposed to when both rewards were only available in the future.

Neural Results. The fMRI data revealed important differences in the two ways of measuring preference that were consistent with Query Theory. Contrasts comparing delay and accelerate decisions confirmed three hypotheses. First, as consistent with the Direction Hypothesis, greater activation in delay decisions was observed in key valuation-related brain regions: ventral striatum, medial prefrontal cortex, and orbitofrontal cortex. This suggested the distinguishable involvement of valuation circuits for each direction, delay or accelerate. Since Query Theory suggests that these judgments are constructed from recollection, our observation (particularly with immediate rewards) of activation of bilateral hippocampus and an additional network involved in prospective judgment confirmed the Memory Hypothesis. Finally, we predicted and indeed observed increased activation of anterior cingulate cortex in delay decisions, a region crucial to the monitoring of response conflict and online performance (e.g., Carter et al., 1998; Botvinick, Cohen, & Carter, 2004), and so consistent with our Conflict Hypothesis.

In ongoing additional analyses, we are relating individual differences observed in this study to (1) results of Diffusion Tensor Imaging (DTI) measurement of white matter neural-tract connectivity between key regions of interest, (2) observed activations in target regions, and (3) eye movement recordings done during imaging. These approaches provide further evidence for specific relationships between our results and similar phenomena and neural activation patterns studied in extant research on memory, choice, and valuation.

References

Botvinick, M. M., J. D. Cohen, and C. S. Carter (2004), "Conflict Monitoring and Anterior Cingulate Cortex: An Update," *Trends in Cognitive Sciences*, 8(12), 539-546.

Carter, C. S., T. S. Braver, D. M. Barch, M. M. Botvinick, D. Noll, and J. D. Cohen (1998), "Anterior Cingulate Cortex, Error Detection, and the Online Monitoring of Performance," *Science*, 280(5364), 747-749.

Fischer, G. W., Z. Carmon, D. Ariely, and G. Zauberman (1999), "Goal-based Construction of Preferences: Task Goals and the Prominence Effect," *Management Science*, 45 (8), 1057-1075.

Frederick, S., G. F. Loewenstein, and T. O'Donoghue (2002), "Time Discounting and Time Preference: A Critical Review," *Journal of Economic Literature*, 40, 351-401.

Johnson, E. J., G. Haubl, A. Keinan (2007), "Aspects of Endowment: A Query Theory of Value Construction," *Journal of Experimental Psychology: Learning Memory and Cognition*, 33(3), 461-474.

Kahneman, D., and A. Tversky (1979), "Prospect Theory: An Analysis of Decisions Under Risk," *Econometrica*, 47, 263-291.

Laibson, D. (1997), "Golden Eggs and Hyperbolic Discounting," *Quarterly Journal of Economics*, 112(2), 443-477.

Loewenstein, G. F. (1988), "Frames of Mind in Intertemporal Choice," *Management Science*, 34(2), 200-214.

McClure, S. M., D. Laibson, G. F. Loewenstein, and J. D. Cohen, (2004), "Separate Neural Systems Value Immediate and Delayed Monetary Rewards," *Science*, 306, 503-507.

Mischel, W., J. Grusec, and J. C. Masters (1969), "Effects of Expected Delay Time on Subjective Value of Rewards and Punishments," *Journal of Personality and Social Psychology*, 11(4), 363-373.

Weber, E. U., E. J. Johnson, K. F. Milch, H. Chang, J. C. Brodscholl, and D. G. Goldstein (2007), "Asymmetric Discounting in Intertemporal Choice: A Query-theory Account," *Psychological Science*, 18(6), 516-523.

Weber, E. U. and B. Kirsner (1997), "Reasons for Rank-dependent Utility Evaluation," *Journal of Risk and Uncertainty*, 14(1), 41-61.

"Distinguishable Neural Circuits for Motivation and Valuation Underlying Decision Making"

Ab Litt, Stanford University, USA
Hilke Plassmann, INSEAD, France
Baba Shiv, Stanford University, USA
Antonio Rangel, California Institute of Technology, USA

Many common consumer decisions involve considerations of value, to determine the type or nature of appropriate response; and motivational salience, influencing strength of engagement in both decision context and response implementation. Mounting research indicates important ways in which valuation and motivational components of decisions are dissociable in terms of underlying psychological processes and behavioral outcomes (e.g., Higgins, 2006). While conceptualizations of this disjunction vary—from "hedonic states" versus "hedonic stakes" (Lyubomirsky & Ross, 1999) to wanting versus liking (Winkielman & Berridge, 2003)—the notion that valuation and motivation may act in different ways and through distinct means seems of express importance to understanding the bases of consumer decision making.

Neuroscientific investigations of motivation and valuation have proven very effective in establishing the extent and limits of disjunctions between these psychological constructs, by revealing how their respective biological substrates differ, overlap, and interact (Berridge, 1996; Zink et al., 2004). This in turn sheds light on the basic psychological mechanisms influencing observed patterns of overt behavior. We conducted an fMRI study that explores dissociations in humans between specific valuation and motivational processes active and involved at the time of decision making, using an explicit and clear conceptualization of such a disjunction.

Task. During scanning, subjects (N=20) made a series of 240 choices involving different appetitive and aversive foods (60 distinct items, randomized and repeated once per session, for two sessions). Subjects were instructed, for each trial, to indicate (within a 2s interval) their willingness to eat the displayed food-item at the end of the experiment, using one of four response keys: "Strong No", "No", "Yes", or "Strong Yes". Subjects were told that at the end of the experiment, a random trial would be selected: they would actually receive that trial's food item to eat if they responded "Yes" or "Strong Yes" on the trial, but would not if they responded "No" or "Strong No". It was reiterated to subjects that "the response you gave on that [randomly chosen] trial will determine whether or not you will be asked to eat that food item at the end of the experiment." Thus, subjects faced response decisions involving valuations of food items under motivation to respond accurately in line with those valuations. Subjects were asked not to eat immediately prior to the experiment, and were pre-screened for at least occasionally eating the food stimuli generally classifiable as appealing (snack foods, chocolate, etc.).

Analysis. Valuation was captured by observing the specific response given on any trial, and taken to be increasing from "Strong No" to "No" to "Yes" to "Strong Yes". In contrast, we conceptualized motivation as the cross-valence strength of the response given on a trial: i.e., "Strong" responses were considered to be of greater motivational engagement than non-"Strong" responses. We thus coded the four possible trial responses as RESP {"Strong No"=-2, "No"=-1, "Yes"=+1, "Strong Yes"=+2}, and included RESP (valuation) and |RESP| (motivation) as modulators of food item presentation in the AR(1) GLM estimated to analyze trial events in the experiment. Single-subject and group-level contrasts were calculated to determine brain regions in which activation during decision trials was 1) modulated by valuation, but not motivation; 2) modulated by motivation, but not valuation; and 3) modulated by both motivation and valuation.

Behavioral Results. In line with our conceptualization of motivation as response strength, subjects responded significantly faster for Strong Yes/No than non-strong Yes/No ($t(77)=4.22$, $p<.00005$, computed across subjects using means pooled within-subject). Additionally, subjects' responses were correlated to a pre-scanning task in which they rated their overall liking of each food item used in the experiment, in order to test whether scanning-trial responses accurately matched valuations in both valence and intensity/strength. This correlation yielded $R^2=.9514$, supporting this contention.

Neural Results. Increased activity modulated by valuation was observed bilaterally in medial orbitofrontal and rostral anterior cingulate cortices, consistent with a wide range of findings in the cognitive neuroscience of decision making (e.g., Plassmann, O'Doherty, Shiv, & Rangel, 2008). Activity observed in dorsal posterior cingulate is consistent with work on reward-related signals in monkeys (McCoy et al., 2003). Additional valuation-modulated activity in precuneus and parahippocampal gyrus may be related to memory retrieval-related functionality previously observed for each of these regions: foods valued more highly by subjects are likely to be more familiar than the foods chosen to be generally unappealing (e.g., squash baby food, clam juice).

Increased activity modulated by motivational salience was observed bilaterally in posterior insula, dorsal anterior cingulate, supplementary motor areas, and primary motor cortex. This network of brain regions suggests several important conclusions regarding how motivational salience is represented in the brain and directs overt behavior. Insula activity correlated with cross-valence motivational salience is in contrast to a preponderance of work showing insula encoding primarily negative responses, such as disgust. These previous findings might be re-interpreted as indicative of the relatively greater motivational salience of those strong negative feelings, in a manner analogous to what has been argued for the amygdala (Anderson et al., 2003). In line with findings showing addiction and craving disruption with insula damage (Naqvi, Rudrauf, Damasio, & Bechara, 2007), our findings suggest that increased (cross-valence) motivation engages the insula, and that this representation of a high motivational state activates the planning and selection of an appropriate response action in dorsal anterior cingulate and downstream motor regions (similar to an account of ADHD by Bush et al., 1999).

Finally, different sub-regions of the nucleus accumbens (NAcc) were either distinctly or overlappingly modulated by valuation and motivation. This suggests a potential resolution to an ongoing debate over whether activity in NAcc is involved in encoding actual levels of reward or valuation, or rather representations related to the incentive salience or behavioral relevance of stimuli (Rodriguez, Aron, & Poldrack, 2006; Cooper & Knutson, 2009). Our results suggest that these divergent functionalities may be implemented in distinct but partially overlapping sub-regions of NAcc. Thus, consumer decision making seems grounded in dissociable but not disjoint sub-systems computing choice value and motivational salience.

References

Anderson, A. K., K. Christoff, I. Stappen, D. Panitz, D. G. Ghahremani, G. Glover, et al. (2003), "Dissociated Neural Representations of Intensity and Valence in Human Olfaction," *Nature Neuroscience*, 6(2), 196-202.

Berridge, K. C. (1996), "Food Reward: Brain Substrates of Wanting and Liking," *Neuroscience and Biobehavioral Reviews*, 20(1), 1-25.

Bush, G., J. A. Frazier, S. L. Rauch, L. J. Seidman, P. J. Whalen, M. A. Jenike, et al. (1999), "Anterior Cingulate Cortex Dysfunction in Attention-deficit/hyperactivity Disorder Revealed by FMRI and the Counting Stroop," *Biological Psychiatry*, 45(12), 1542-1552.

Cooper, J. C. and B. Knutson (2008), "Valence and Salience Contribute to Nucleus Accumbens Activation," *NeuroImage*, 39, 538-547.

Higgins, E. T. (2006), "Value From Hedonic Experience and Engagement," *Psychological Review*, 113(3), 439-460.

Lyubomirsky, S. and L. Ross (1999), "Changes in Attractiveness of Elected, Rejected, and Precluded Alternatives: A Comparison of Happy and Unhappy Individuals," *Journal of Personality and Social Psychology*, 76(6), 988-1007.

McCoy, A. N., J. C. Crowley, H. L. Dean, G. Haghighian, and M. L. Platt (2003), "Saccade Reward Signals in Posterior Cingulate Cortex," *Neuron*, 40, 1031-1040.

Naqvi, N. H., D. Rudrauf, H. Damasio, and A. Bechara (2007), "Damage to the Insula Disrupts Addiction to Cigarette Smoking," *Science*, 315(5811), 531-534.

Plassmann, H., J. O'Doherty, B. Shiv, and A. Rangel (2008), "Marketing Actions Can Modulate Neural Representations of Experienced Pleasantness," *Proceedings of the National Academy of Sciences of the United States of America*, 105(3), 1050-1054.

Rodriguez, P. F., A. R. Aron, and R. A. Poldrack (2006), "Ventral-striatal/nucleus-accumbens Sensitivity to Prediction Errors During Classification Learning," *Human Brain Mapping*, 27(4), 306-313.

Winkielman, P. and K. C. Berridge (2003), "Irrational Wanting and Subrational Liking: How Rudimentary Motivational and Affective Processes Shape Preferences and Choices," *Political Psychology*, 24(4), 657-680.

Zink, C. F. Pagnoni, M. E. Martin-Skurski, J. C. Chappelow, and G. S. Berns (2004), "Human Striatal Responses to Monetary Reward Depend on Saliency," *Neuron*, 42(3), 509-517.

Special Session Summary

Other People's Things: Perspectives on Ownership Transfer and Sharing

Zeynep Arsel, Concordia University, Canada

SESSION OVERVIEW

Ownership and possession practices have historically been a central interest to Consumer Culture Theory (Arnould and Thompson 2005). While there is an increased interest in boundary conditions of ownership, such as the disposal of possessions (Lastovicka and Fernandez 2005; Price, Arnould, and Curasi 2000), access in contrast to possession (Chen 2009) and sharing of possessions (Belk forthcoming), these boundary conditions still remain an under-explored territory. This session threads three empirical studies that examine boundary conditions of ownership, more specifically ownership transfer and shared ownership. We seek to address the following issues:

1. Exploring how attachment to and appropriation of objects are performed in these boundary conditions.
2. Demonstrating how emerging marketplace structures mediate these hybrid and transient forms of ownership.
3. Investigating the ways individuals manage symbolic and physical contamination of goods that are shared with or transferred from others.
4. And lastly, highlighting the ecological and political issues that arise in the context of these transient and alternative forms of ownership models.

These three papers provide a focused, but multifaceted and multi-method treatment of the topic. The specific contexts that the presenters ground their theories in are also novel: second hand clothing users, online bartering communities and shared car ownership. These marketplace contexts promise many discussion opportunities and further theory development.

This session is likely to attract three groups of ACR members: (1) researchers that are interested in ownership and identity (2) those who study emerging marketplace structures that mediate new forms of exchange, consumption and divestment (3) a broader audience that consists of Consumer Culture Theory researchers and students. We anticipate a lively dialogue facilitated by John Deighton, who will tie the session together, highlight theoretical and practical implications of the papers and offer insights for further inquiry.

EXTENDED ABSTRACTS

"Identity and Self-Territory in Second Hand Clothing Transfers"

Dominique Roux, IRG-Université Paris-Est, France

Previous studies have highlighted the emotion of disgust and the negative representations associated with possible reuse of other people's possessions (Gregson and Crewe 2003). Anthropologists and psychologists attribute this taboo to the principle of sympathetic magic and its two laws (Frazer 1950; Mauss 1902/1972; Rozin et al. 1993). The law of contagion recognizes the offensive effect that slight or incidental contact with a polluted object may have, even long after the pollution, whereas the law of similarity assumes that things that resemble each other are from the same essence. Because clothing intimately links with the body, negative contagion both through similarity and contact, may impede the reappropriation of unknown people's possessions (Gregson and Crewe 2003; O'Reilly et al. 1984). However, these principles sharply contrast with the development of second hand markets, in which clothing is an important if not central category among the wide range of goods for sale. The volume of commerce in second-hand clothes seems to contradict prevailing theories about contamination and disgust, especially when the social distance from previous owners increases.

The gap between theory and consumer practices originates in the assumptions that unfamiliarity inevitably triggers a fear of contagion but is also supported by experimental methods that tend to emphasize specific contamination cues. For example, Rozin and Fallon (1987) gather reactions to different disgust elicitors, which represent artificial situations that consumers seldom face in reality (e.g., wearing a laundered sweater that belonged to Adolf Hitler). Similarly, recent investigations of consumers' reactions to products touched by others in retail contexts (Argo et al. 2006) manipulate explicit contamination cues that might not be as salient in natural settings. When patronizing second-hand channels, consumers are perfectly aware that clothes have been previously worn. This research thus aims to understand how people, in anonymous but normal contexts of exchange, manage to reappropriate clothing from unknown owners and what distinguish them from those who reject pre-used garments.

In the literature devoted to second hand markets and exchanges, very few studies have examined appropriation or rejection processes of previously worn clothes. What they bring to light are the specific conditions that increase or reduce the perceived risks and facilitate or limit the transfers of garments. For example, O'Reilly et al. (1984) indicate that the newness and the quality of the merchandise strongly affect their resale. Gregson and Crewe (2003) confirm that specific conditions such as the absence of signs of wear, temporal distance from the former wearer, cleansing rituals and exclusion of certain types of garments are preconditions for a possible reuse of second hand clothes. As a consequence, underwear is considered as never reusable, even if washed or laundered (O'Reilly et al. 1984). The continuity of links within, and beyond, transmission has also been stressed by Lastovicka and Fernandez (2005) who emphasize the "common-identity shared self" that underlies transmission processes, even in non-family contexts.

In this study, I examine the meanings and representations that second hand buyers attached to other's possessions and contrast them with those of people who refuse to wear used clothes. More precisely, I try to uncover the reasons that are put forward to support their appropriation versus rejection processes and the underlying mechanisms that are at stake. The data come from a three-year survey conducted between 2003 and 2005 in Paris, France, that followed three steps: a first sample of eighteen second hand shoppers was recruited in different second hand outlets and settings to ensure a diversity of motives, profiles and types of clothes purchased; a second data set of 212 second hand consumers and non-consumers was built in order to get a broader knowledge of general behaviors toward previously worn clothes and to offer alternative insights; a third data set of twenty-two informants consisted in selecting respondents who could complete less common profiles such as male or older informants, enlighten unusual standpoints and provide negative cases.

The findings show that the appropriation/rejection processes of pre-used garments are both grounded in the categorization of the previous owner and in a possible or impossible negotiation of his/her territory. First, while for non-consumers the law of similarity is confirmed along the lines of "the garment makes the man", the fact that the former owner could be socially distant, totally unknown or morally unacceptable is not the only cause triggering rejection. This phenomenon is also linked to the feelings of deterritorialization and depersonalization that derive from the difficulty of re-inscribing the self into objects that remain first and foremost "inhabited". From this standpoint, reusing second hand clothing prevents these respondents from extricating themselves from a confusion of identity with the other. Second, although the law of contagion states "once in contact, always in contact" (Mauss 1902/1972), the results seem also to contradict this assertion, as several respondents testify to the possibility of wearing used clothes under particular conditions, such as a second hand evening dress or suit for a fancy dress ball or a special event. Third, a large number of respondents occasionally (20%) or regularly (2 %) purchase and/or wear second-hand clothes, even of unknown origin. The appropriation mechanism is based on a process of categorization of the seller as another oneself, someone who could be the buyer in his/her role of buyer, thus freeing the objects of their history and provenance. Clothes can thus be "emptied" of the presence of a prior owner and become re-appropriable by virtue of the exchange process. This neutral, depersonalized view of the object does not support the existence of a shared self in the sense intended by Lastovicka and Fernandez (2005), but of a shopping role community experienced in second hand buying.

"Exploring the Social Dynamics of Online Bartering"[1]

Zeynep Arsel, Concordia University, USA

Informal exchange of used commodities has been an ongoing interest of consumer culture researchers. In their influential methodological piece that introduced the naturalistic inquiry to consumer researchers, Belk, Sherry and Wallendorf (1998) depict a swap meet as an anachronistic but alternative medium of exchange. Other studies of ownership transfer (Lastovicka and Fernandez 2005; Arnould and Curasi 2000; Herrmann and Soiffer 1984; Nelson, Rademacher and Paek 2007) explore similar angles and depict socio-cultural aspects of transferring personal goods to others. While previous researchers have exemplified many ritualistic, meaning-making and identity effects of ownership transfer, the social dynamics of the process and the way emerging marketplace structures function in these dynamics is an understudied territory.

This research explores how informal marketplace structures, more specifically bartering communities, mediate ownership transfer. While bartering might be perceived as an outdated form of exchange, quite a number of online bartering communities were formed in the last few years. Through online messaging and matching systems, individuals could participate in non-monetary transactions of a gamut of consumer goods such as video games, craft supplies, clothes, books, diapers, plant seeds and even used cosmetics. In the case of cosmetics, bartering sites provide a secondary market for goods that are otherwise disproportionally depreciated, contaminated, or even deemed illegal to sell in the formal economic markets. The system theoretically provides better efficiency in trade by reducing waste and establishing exchanges that account for the use value of commodities rather than their depreciated market values.

However, the system also introduces numerous consumer vulnerabilities. For example the ability to exchange previously unmarketable goods encourage some participants to act impulsively, increase their perceptions of disposability, perpetuate compulsive variety seeking and foster the over-glorification of the treasure-hunt aspect of the medium. Furthermore, a great proportion of the products that are bartered with complete strangers are previously used cosmetics items that potentially pose health risks to their new owners. Likewise, these grassroots marketplace systems are also structurally vulnerable, in the sense that the usual safeguards of formal economy, such as consumer protection institutions, do not support them. Lastly, the social stigma of seeking returns from goods by violating the alienability and hygiene norms of the formal marketplace creates anxieties in the participants.

Drawing from multi-sited netnographic fieldwork and in-depth interviews, I explore the social dynamics of this complex marketplace system. My presentation aims to highlight four processes that sustain this otherwise risky and stigmatizing exchange behavior: humanizing (de-commercializing and de-stigmatizing), hedging (risk reducing), circulating (alienability) and vigilantism (policing). Humanizing is performed by socializing throughout the exchange and ritualizing the process akin to reciprocal gift giving. Furthermore, the participants challenge the apprehensions of using potentially contaminated products through apotheosizing the previous owners and differentiating them from the hoi polloi in terms of personal ethics and hygiene. Hedging is maintained by a complex status hierarchy where the majority of the risk is transferred to newer members of the community until they are proven reliable. Furthermore, members of swapping communities protect themselves by establishing idiosyncratic principles of exchange and shipping. Circulating corresponds to perpetual re-bartering items after a period of use, which is subjectively experienced as borrowing or sampling, rather than owning. This serves as a preventative strategy to hoarding, while satisfying variety-seeking impulses. Lastly, since there are almost no consequences of fraud within these communities, members seek justice through vigilantism, more specifically by publicizing and slandering the names of those who act dishonestly through third party web sites they establish.

Through these four processes, the participants of this online community create a self-sustaining, self-regulating and interactive marketplace system, which facilitates exchanges that customarily violate the legal, economic and hygiene norms of the formal marketplace. My findings not only theoretically advance our understanding of ownership transfer, alienability, risk and consumer communities, but also highlight issues that are of interest to marketing practitioners and policymakers and provide them with directions to make better informed decisions and policies regarding secondary markets.

"Market-Mediated Collaborative Consumption in the context of Car Sharing"

Fleura Bardhi, Northeastern University, USA
Giana M. Eckhardt, Suffolk University, USA

Rifkin (2000) suggests that in today's hypercapitalist economy, buying and owning things are outmoded ideas. Rather, consumers want access to goods, and prefer to pay for the experience of using a consumption object rather than buying it. Indeed, during the last decade, we have seen the development and popularity of alternative consumption models which involve sharing or pooling of resources/products/services (Belk 1997, forthcoming). Examples of such collective consumption models vary from time-share real-estate, to more recent developments in car-sharing programs (e.g. Zipcar.com), bag sharing programs (e.g. Bagborroworsteal.com), and jewelry renting programs (e.g. Adornbrides.com and Borrowedbling.com). While sharing has been and continues to be the norm in some cultures and social contexts, such as within the family (Belk forthcoming; Epp and Price 2008), observers argue

[1]The author thanks ACR Transformative Research Grants and Social Sciences and Humanities Research Council of Canada for their financial support for this project.

that models of collaborative consumption mediated by the marketplace, such as Zipcar, are and will continue to gain popularity fueled by the internet, as well as by a capitalist marketplace trading in cultural resources rather than material objects (Belk forthcoming, Rifkin 2000). The goal of this research is to examine this model of collective consumption when it is mediated by the marketplace.

Shared consumption has received little attention in the marketing literature. Recently Belk (2007, forthcoming) conceptualizes sharing in consumption as an alternative to the private ownership emphasized in both marketplace exchange and gift-giving. In sharing, two or more people may enjoy the benefits and costs that flow from possessing a thing. "Rather than distinguish what is mine and yours, sharing defines something as ours" (Belk 2007, p. 127). Sharing includes joint ownership, voluntary lending and borrowing, pooling and allocation of resources, and authorized use of public property. There are two types of sharing: sharing in and sharing out (Belk forthcoming), which correspond to altruistic sharing and what we call collaborative consumption. Sharing in is altruistic, involves gift-giving, and expands the extended self by expanding the domain of common property. Examples of this are the consumption of shared property or shared meals within the family by family members. Within the sharing-in consumption model, Belk (forthcoming) finds that shared consumption enables family members to create bonds/feel part of a collective, extend the self to the family, and is guided by norms of generalized reciprocity (Sahlins 1972). However, the marketplace mediated shared consumption models such as Zipcar, or collaborative consumption (Felson and Spaeth 1978), divides a resource among discrete economic interests, preserves the self/other boundary and does not involve expanding the sphere of aggregate expended self beyond the family. In this sharing out model of consumption, consumers do not own or possess the product/services, but share its consumption, which is motivated by non-altruistic concerns. While altruistic sharing is beginning to be investigated in the literature (Belk forthcoming), collaborative consumption has not been examined.

As such, in this study we examine the role of the marketplace in collaborative consumption. Belk (2007) suggests that commoditization of shared possessions doesn't change or eliminate its value. We examine this claim empirically in the context of car sharing. More specifically, we examine consumer motivations for participating in car sharing, compare and contrast the model with car ownership, and investigate the role of the company in mediating the model. The data for the study is based on 45 semi-structured interviews with Zipcar customers. Zipcar is currently the market leader in car-sharing in the US. Zipcar has 180,000 members, who pay at least $50 a year to access cars in 50 cities in US and the UK and its business hit $100 million in revenue in 2008 (Frankel 2008; Naughton 2008). For about $10 per hour, which includes gas and insurance, Zipcar customers can use any car located conveniently near them. Our results highlight the lack of brand community, the paradox of freedom within car sharing, and the lack of responsibility present in the model. We discuss the implications of our findings for theories of brand building, brand community, and gift giving/sharing.

REFERENCES

Appadurai, Arjun (1981), "Gastro-politics in Hindu South Asia," *American Ethnologist*, 8, 494-511.

Argo, Jennifer J., Darren W. Dahl, and Andrea C. Morales (2006), "Consumer Contamination: How Consumers React to Products Touched by Others," *Journal of Marketing*, 70 (April), 81-94.

Arnould, Eric J. and Craig J. Thompson (2005), "Consumer Culture Theory (CCT): Twenty Years of Research, *Journal of Consumer Research*, 31 (March), 868-882

Bardhi, Fleura and Eric J. Arnould (2005), "Thrift Shopping: Combining Utilitarian Thrift and Hedonic Treat Benefits," *Journal of Consumer Behaviour*, 4 (4), 223.

Belk, Russell W., John F. Sherry, Jr., and Melanie Wallendorf (1998), "A Naturalistic Inquiry Into Buyer And Seller Behavior at a Swap Meet," *Journal of Consumer Research*, 14 (4), 449.

Belk, Russell (2007), "Why not Share Rather than Own?" *Annals of the American Academy of Political and Social Science*, 611, 126-140.

Belk, Russell (forthcoming), "Sharing," *Journal of Consumer Research.*

Chen, Yu (2009), "Possession and Access: Consumer Desires and Value Perceptions Regarding Contemporary Art Collection and Exhibit Visits," *Journal of Consumer Research*, 35 (April), 925-940

Douglas, Mary (1966), *Purity and Danger: An Analysis of the Concepts of Pollution and Taboo*, London: Routledge & Kegan Paul.

Epp, Amber and Linda L. Price (2008), "Family Identity: A Framework of Identity Interplay in Consumption Practices," *Journal of Consumer Research*, 35 (June), 50-70.

Felson, Marcus and Joe Spaeth (1978), "Community Structure and Collaborative Consumption," *American Behavioral Scientist*, 21(4), 614-624.

Frankel, Alex (2008), "Zipcar Makes the Leap," *Fast Company*, Feb. 14.

Frazer, Sir James G. (1922/1950), *The Golden Bough*, New York: Macmillan.

Gregson, Nicky and Louise Crewe (2003), *Second-hand Cultures*, Oxford, NY:Berg.

Herrmann, G. and S. Soiffer (1984), "For Fun and Profit: an Anaylsis of the American Garage Sale," *Urban Life*, 12, 397-421.

Lastovicka, John L. and Karen V. Fernandez (2005), "Three Paths to Disposition: The Movement of Meaningful Possessions to Strangers," *Journal of Consumer Research*, 31 (March), 813–23.

Mauss, Marcel (1902/1972), *A General Theory of Magic*, New York: Norton.

Naughton, Keith (2008), "Can you Give your Car Up?" *Newsweek*, August 4.

Nelson, M. R., M. A. Rademacher, and H. Paek (2007), "Downshifting Consumer=upshifting Citizen? An Examination of a Local Freecycle Community," *The Annals of the American Academy of Political and Social Science*, 611 (1), 141-156.

O'Reilly, Lynn, Margaret Rucker, Rhonda Hughes, Marge Gorang and Susan Hand (1984), "The Relationship of Psychological and Situational Variables to Usage of a Second-Order Marketing System," *Journal of the Academy of Marketing Science*, 12 (3), 53-76.

Price, LindaL, EricJ Arnould, and Carolyn Curasi (2000), "Older Consumers' Disposition of Special Possessions," *Journal of Consumer Research*, 27 (2), 179-201.

Rifkin, Jeremy (2000), *The Age of Access: The New Culture of Hypercapitalism Where All of Life is a Paid for Experience*, New York: Penguin.

Rozin, Paul and April E. Fallon (1987), "A Perspective on Disgust," *Psychological Review*, 94 (1), 23–41.

Rozin, Paul, Jonathan Haidt, and Clark McCauley (1993), "Disgust," in *Handbook of Emotions*, Michael Lewis and Jeannette M. Haviland, eds., New York: Guilford Press, 575–94.

Sahlins, Marshall (1972), *Stone Age Economics*, Chicago: Aldine-Atherton.

Special Session Summary

Customization and Consumer Choice

Aner Sela, Stanford University, USA

SESSION OVERVIEW

Marketing is increasingly seen as an interactive process in which sellers and buyers rely on each other to co-create value (Alba et al. 1997). One of the most prominent strategies reflecting this development is offer customization, the process by which individual components of an offer are selected and modified to provide consumers with offers that match their individually stated preferences (e.g., Ansari and Mela 2003; Pine, Peppers and Rogers 1995). The assumptions underlying customization are that if consumers' preferences can only be revealed, customized offers will provide them with superior fit and satisfaction, reduce information overload, and ultimately increase perceived value, purchase likelihood, and loyalty (Simonson 2005).

However, despite the importance of customization, we still know relatively little about the conditions under which these fundamental assumptions actually hold. The present session seeks to address this topic and provide new insights into the factors that determine consumers' choices under different customization modes, their evaluation and likelihood of acceptance of the customized offer, and their ensuing satisfaction.

One of the central variables in every implementation of customization is the procedure by which preferences are elicited. This is especially true in the case of self-customization, the process by which consumers customize offerings to their own preferences. The paper by Ana Valenzuela, Ravi Dhar, and Florian Zettelmeyer examines whether and how the self-customization procedure (by-attribute versus by-alternative) influences the subjective experience of making the decision and, consequently, the construction of preferences. This research suggests that because customization by-attribute is associated with a smaller choice conflict, it tends to increase the willingness to purchase the customized option as well as the satisfaction consumers derive from it.

Another important question relates to the consequences of customization in different contexts. Providing consumers with individually customized offers is an effective strategy in general, but are there conditions under which customization can actually undermine, rather than enhance, the attractiveness of offers? The paper by Aner Sela, Itamar Simonson, and Ran Kivetz suggests that explicit customization by the marketer can undermine the perceived value of seeming "opportunities", such as offers presented as special bargains. This is because customized offers tend to be perceived as reflecting the marketer's self-interested intentions, thereby reaping any above-normal gain from the transaction. Thus, although customization is a positive signal by itself, indicating a better fit to the consumer's preferences, this research suggests that its effect on value perceptions may depend on other characteristics of the transaction.

Finally, self-customization typically involves either sequential or simultaneous evaluation of the offer's individual components. The paper by Alexander Chernev examines the impact of the evaluation mode on consumers' perceptions of the customized offer's overall value. The investigation is conducted in the important context of selecting food items from a menu to form a customized meal. Specifically, when evaluating vice and virtue combinations simultaneously, consumers tend to underestimate overall calorie content such that the combined meal can be perceived as having fewer calories than the unhealthy item alone. When a virtue item is evaluated before a vice item, however, consumers tend to overestimate the overall calorie content of the customized meal.

This session highlights the importance of understanding how specific procedures (e.g., presentation order and evaluation mode) and contexts (e.g., bargain offers) can affect consumers' perceptions and acceptance of customized offers. The session would be of interest to researchers and marketers interested in consumer judgment and decision making and choice theory.

References

Alba, Joseph, John Lynch, Barton Weitz, Chris Janiszewski, Richard Lutz, Alan Sawyer, and Stacy Wood (1997), "Interactive Home Shopping: Consumer, Retailer, and Manufacturer Incentives to Participate in Electronic Marketplaces," *Journal of Marketing*, 61 (July), 38-53.

Ansari, Asim and Carl F. Mela (2003), "E-Customization," *Journal of Marketing Research*, 40 (May), 131-45.

Pine, B. Joseph, Don Pepper, and Martha Rogers (1995), "Do You Want to Keep your Customers Forever?" *Harvard Business Review*, March-April, 103-14.

Simonson, Itamar (2005), "Determinants of Customers' Responses to Customized Offers: Conceptual Framework and Research Propositions," *Journal of Marketing*, 69 (January), 32-45.

EXTENDED ABSTRACTS

"Contingent Consumer Response to Self-Customization Procedures: Implications for Decision Satisfaction and Choice"

Ana Valenzuela, Baruch College, USA
Ravi Dhar, Yale University, USA
Florian Zettelmeyer, University of California–Berkeley, USA

The opportunity to self-customize products and services tailored to individual preferences is viewed as an important way to enhance customer relationships and reduce competitive threats. An implicit assumption for the superior value of self-customization is the notion that consumers have inherent preferences (Simonson 2008) and are able to construct the customized offer that best fits their preferences compared to a non-customized offer. This paper focuses on comparing two formats designed to help consumers self-customize a product among a large set of feasible options. We demonstrate that the two most common methods for self-customization can result in a different consumer construction processes as well as different options being chosen as most preferred.

Furthermore, consistent with the established notion that consumers have limited insight into their preferences (Simonson 2005), the construction process of self-customization may also determine consumers' post-hoc evaluations of the customized option. In particular, customers' assessment of the customized option is likely to be affected by the ease or difficulty experienced in the process of customizing (e.g. Novemsky, Dhar, Schwarz and Simonson 2007). In this paper, we differentiate between two sources of difficulty associated with the constructed choice. One source arises from choice complexity due to the sheer amount of information that requires processing as the number of available options increases (Huffman and Kahn 1998). A second source is based on an explicit consideration of between-attribute tradeoffs (Dhar 1997), that is, the extent to which the customization format makes trade-offs between competing characteristics (or quality attributes) more or less explicit. Regardless of the source of difficulty (i.e., whether it is based on processing large amount of information or based on making fewer effortful competing tradeoffs), we show that the subjective feeling of difficulty during self-customization may affect choice processes and outcomes.

Specifically, the studies in this paper highlight the effect of the two most often used self-customization procedures on consumer choice processes and preferred outcomes: i) the by-alternative customization method, which allows consumers to customize by identifying their most preferred option from a set of fully specified products; ii) the by-attribute customization method, which lets consumers decide one-by-one the desired level of each product attribute. Studies 1a and 1b show that consumers tend to choose intermediate options significantly more often when they customize a product by-attribute than when they customize by-alternative. This implies that when consumers have to make price-quality tradeoffs for each attribute in isolation, they base their choices on the ordinal position of options in the choice set. As a consequence, they perform a series of two-dimensional "compromises" between price and the particular (quality) attribute being customized. On the other hand, respondents in the by-alternative customization procedure have to perform multiple-way tradeoffs between different attributes, which makes it much harder for them to identify these "2-dimensional compromises" and, therefore, the compromise option itself.

Two additional studies support that self-customization procedures influence the construction of preferences and the subjective experience of making the decision. In particular, Study 2 shows that by-attribute customization reduces choice difficulty, enhances satisfaction and increases the probability that the customized option will actually be purchased. However, the decrease in experience difficulty in by-attribute customization is not solely due to the reduced choice complexity and information overload but is also driven by the fact that tradeoffs among competing characteristics are less explicit. By-attribute self-customization reduces emotional trade-off difficulty because of framing choice as a decision between each individual (quality) attribute level and price. In contrast, by-alternative self-customization makes consumers explicitly give up one specific (quality) attribute for another. Accordingly, if consumers were to encounter a by-attribute self-customization task which made competing (quality) attribute tradeoffs explicit, they should experience the same negative effects found in Study 2 for by-alternative self-customization. In line with this, Study 3 shows that when tradeoffs among attributes are made salient, decision conflict, satisfaction, and willingness to purchase are at a similar level to that associated with by-alternative customization.

Our findings contribute to the literature in several different ways. Customization allows consumers to exert control over shopping decisions. Our findings empirically show that differences in the experience of decision difficulty in the two self-customization modes affect consumers' decision satisfaction and their willingness to purchase the customized option. Results also support that the decrease in experienced difficulty in by-attribute customization is not solely due to the reduced choice complexity and information load but rather to less explicit tradeoffs among competing characteristics.

References

Dhar, Ravi (1997), "Consumer Preference for a No-Choice Option," *Journal of Consumer Research*, 24(September), 215-31.

Huffman, Cynthia and Barbara E. Kahn (1998), "Variety for Sale: Mass Customization or Mass Confusion?" *Journal of Retailing*, 74(4), 491-513.

Novemsky, Nathan, Ravi Dhar, Norbert Schwarz and Itamar Simonson (2007), "The Effect of Preference Fluency on Consumer Decision Making," *Journal of Marketing Research*, 44(3), 347-357.

Simonson, Itamar (2005), "Determinants of Customers' Responses to Customized Offers: Conceptual Framework and Research Propositions," *Journal of Marketing*, 69(1), 32-45.

______ (2008), "Regarding inherent preferences," *Journal of Consumer Psychology*, 18(3), 191-196.

"Negative Effects of Explicit Customization on Perceptions of Opportunity"

Aner Sela, Stanford Univeristy, USA
Itamar Simonson, Stanford University, USA
Ran Kivetz, Columbia University, USA

Marketing researchers and practitioners alike have long emphasized the benefits of customizing offers to match consumers' individual needs and preferences (e.g., Ansari and Mela 2003; Pine et al. 1995). Customization can reduce information overload, provide consumers with superior fit and satisfaction, and increase loyalty and purchase likelihood. Moreover, because consumers often do not have well-defined preferences, a "customized" label, by itself, can increase the perceived fit of the offer, thereby increasing its attractiveness (Simonson 2005).

However, are there conditions under which customization can undermine, rather than enhance, the attractiveness of offers? The present research suggests that under certain conditions, marketing offers that are presented as tailored to the consumer's individual circumstances or preferences may be perceived as less attractive than self-discovered opportunities that consumers perceive as valuable to them by coincidence.

Specifically, it is proposed that consumers seek opportunities to "beat the market" by taking advantage of offers they believe happen to be more valuable to them, due to favorable personal circumstances, than what was intended by the marketer. Thus, the allure of such perceived opportunities is based on the implicit assumption that the consumer's distinctive circumstances indeed have not been taken into account by the marketer when the parameters of the offer (e.g., price) were designed. It is suggested that consumers tend to place a large weight on whether the fact that the offer has above-normal value for them is "transparent" to the marketer. Consequently, opportunities that are self-discovered and appear to the consumer as "unforeseen" by the marketer tend to be perceived as more attractive. In contrast, when consumers believe that the circumstances that make a certain option particularly advantageous for them have been "factored-in" by the marketer, they may perceive the deal as "fairly priced" for them rather than as representing above-normal value. Over-relying on such a cue can lead consumers to prefer a dominated, non-tailored option over a superior option which has been specifically tailored for them.

Four studies, involving both real and hypothetical choices, support these propositions. Study 1 suggests that explicitly customizing a bargain offer, based on the stated preferences of the consumer, can undermine the attractiveness of the offer among people who believe they value the product more than the average person. Participants were offered to buy a subscription for The Economist magazine at 30% off the regular price. Half of them were told that the offer they received was selected randomly. The other half were told that the offer had been customized for them, based on their previously stated preferences. The results suggest that people who had indicated they were more interested in economic magazines than the average person were more likely to take advantage of the offer when they believed it matched their preferences by coincidence (23%) than when it was said to be tailored for them based on the questionnaire (3%). Importantly, the effect of customization on choice was not affected by the chronic tendency to experience psychological reactance, casting doubt on the possibility that reactance was driving the effect.

Study 2 suggests that consumers who believe they value a particular option more than the average person may find a bargain offer more attractive when it is framed as designed to attract average consumers than when it is framed as designed for people "like them". Half of the participants were offered a subscription for The Economist at 25% off the regular price, framed as "intended to get the average person excited about The Economist". The other half were offered a subscription at 30% off the regular price, framed as "intended for the classic reader of The Economist: a special offer for people who would naturally find it interesting". Participants who had indicated that they were more interested in economic magazines than the average person were subsequently more likely to take advantage of the offer when it was framed as intended for average (27%) rather than for "classic" readers (4%).

Study 3 extends these findings to a situation where the offer is tailored to consumers' distinctive circumstances rather than their preferences. Participants received an offer to join a frequent flyer program. Half of them were required to accumulate 14,000 miles to receive a free ticket. The other half were required to accumulate 15,000 miles but were told that the 700 miles just traveled on their incoming flight would qualify toward their reward. Participants who received a 700 miles head-start were willing to pay more in order to join the program ($9.5) than those who did not ($3.6). However, the effect disappeared when the offer was said to be tailored for the particular flight people came with ($5.3 vs. $7, respectively). The effect of offer customization was mediated by the extent to which consumers believed it would be easier for them to accumulate the required mileage than would normally be the case.

Study 4 examines the role of accessible concepts and norms related to competition and self-interestedness in these effects. Participants were primed with either business-related or neutral stimuli (Kay et al. 2004). They then considered a bargain offer which either seemed particularly valuable to them by coincidence or was targeted at them by a marketer who was informed about their circumstances. Participants found the offer less attractive when it had been tailored for them (M=4.2) than when it matched their preferences by coincidence (M=5.2). However, this effect was significantly stronger among participants primed with business-related stimuli (M=3.3 vs. M=5.3). This result is consistent with the notion that the effect of customization on choice is driven by consumers' lay theories about marketers' self-interested behaviors (Friestad and Wright 1994; Wright 2002).

Taken together, the studies suggest that consumers tend to associate offers with above-normal value more when they perceive them as self-discovered and "unforeseen" by the marketer, rather than as tailored especially for the consumer's individual circumstances. These findings have theoretical implications for understanding consumers' perceptions of marketing offers, as well as important practical implications for designing customized offers and targeted promotions.

References

Ansari, Asim and Carl F. Mela (2003), "E-Customization," *Journal of Marketing Research*, 40 (May), 131-45.

Kay, Aaron C., S. Christian Wheeler, John A. Bargh, and Lee Ross (2004), "Material Priming: The Influence of Mundane Physical Objects on Situational Construal and Competitive Behavioral Choice," *Organizational Behavior and Human Decision Processes*, 95 (1), 83–96.

Pine, B. Joseph, Don Pepper, and Martha Rogers (1995), "Do You Want to Keep your Customers Forever?" *Harvard Business Review*, March-April, 103-14.

Simonson, Itamar (2005), "Determinants of Customers' Responses to Customized Offers: Conceptual Framework and Research Propositions," *Journal of Marketing*, 69 (January), 32-45.

Friestad, Marian and Peter Wright (1994), "The Persuasion Knowledge Model: How People Cope with Persuasion Attempts," *Journal of Consumer Research*, 21 (June), 1-31.

Wright, Peter (2002), "Marketplace Metacognition and Social Intelligence," *Journal of Consumer Research*, 28 (March), 677-82.

"Menu Customization and Calorie Estimation Biases in Consumer Choice"

Alexander Chernev, Northwestern University, USA

Customization of offers typically involves deciding on which components to combine, as well as deciding on the sequence in which these items are presented to consumers. This research explores the impact of these decisions on consumer value judgments in the context of food consumption, where value is reflected in consumers' evaluations of the calorie content of the available items. For example, assembling a full meal from an a la carte menu might involve evaluating the caloric content of individual dishes in different categories. In particular, this research examines consumer evaluations of combinations of items classified as vices and virtues. From a conceptual standpoint, the issue of how consumers estimate the calorie content of vice/virtue combinations raises the more general question of how individuals derive numeric estimates of categorically opposite items. The goal of this research, therefore, is to investigate the decision processes leading to the formation of caloric estimates of vice/virtue combinations in a customized bundle and identify potential biases that are likely to occur in deriving such estimates.

Conventional wisdom suggests that deriving calorie estimates of combinations of food items should be fairly trivial, such that the calorie content of a meal comprising several items should be equal to the sum of the calorie estimates of the individual items. This research argues, however, that this is not always the case and that people display systematic biases in evaluating the calorie content of combinations of items. Specifically, when evaluating vice/virtue combinations, consumers tend to underestimate their calorie content, such that the combined meal can be perceived not only as having fewer calories than the sum of its individual components, but also as having fewer calories than the unhealthy item alone. This leads to the paradoxical finding that adding a virtue to a vice can lower the perceived calorie content of the combined meal.

This research further documents that the underestimation effect in evaluating vice/virtue combinations is contingent on the mode in which information is presented, and that it occurs only in scenarios in which options are presented simultaneously. When items are presented sequentially, however, the nature of the estimation bias is a function of the sequence in which options are presented, such that a virtue followed by a vice leads to an overestimation (rather than an underestimation) of their combined calorie content.

These underestimation/overestimation biases are attributed to the qualitative nature of people's information processing, stemming from categorizing food items into virtues and vices. It is argued that when evaluating combinations of vices and virtues, people use an averaging heuristic, which leads them to believe that the combination of a vice and a virtue has fewer calories than the vice alone. In contrast, when options are presented in a sequential manner, consumers tend to anchor on the virtue and overestimate the calorie content of the vice–a contrast effect resulting from the semantically opposite nature of virtues and vices. These decision biases are examined in a series of six empirical studies, which investigate their underlying mechanisms and identify boundary conditions.

The first set of three experiments examines the underestimation bias in simultaneous evaluations of vice/virtue combinations. In particular, Experiment 1 documents the existence of the bias and shows that adding a virtue to a vice can lead to an underestimation bias, whereby the vice/virtue combination is perceived to have fewer calories than the vice alone. Experiment 2 further investigates the underestimation bias by documenting that it is likely to be a function of the extremity of the virtue added to the vice and is more pronounced in the presence of more extreme virtues. Building on these findings, Experiment 3 examines the availability of alternative means for inferring calorie content, showing that the underestimation bias can be attenuated and even reversed when option size is made salient and individuals use it to infer options' calorie content.

The second set of experiments examines the overestimation bias in sequential evaluations of vice/virtue combinations. Experiment 4 documents the presence of contrast effects in sequential evaluations, showing that consumers tend to overestimate the calorie content of a vice preceded by a virtue. Experiment 5 further tests the theory by illustrating that contrast effects are a function of the type of categorization and that they are more pronounced when the vice/virtue categorization is made more salient and attenuated when an alternative (price-based) categorization is made salient. Finally, Experiment 6 lends support to the categorization theory by providing evidence that the observed contrast in numeric estimates is a function of individuals' awareness of the magnitude of the differences between the available options, such that it is attenuated in cases when the sequential evaluation is preceded by an initial overall evaluation of the options in the choice set.

Special Session Summary

Nudging Consumers Towards Healthier Food Choices

Pierre Chandon, INSEAD, France

EXTENDED ABSTRACTS

"Vicarious Goal Fulfillment: When the Mere Presence of a Healthy Option Leads to an Ironically Indulgent Decision"

Keith Wilcox, Babson College, USA
Beth Vallen, Loyola College, USA
Lauren G. Block, Baruch College, CUNY, USA
Gavan Fitzsimons, Duke University, USA

In response to mounting criticism that their offerings contribute to rising obesity rates, many fast food chains have added healthier options to their menus. While this menu expansion has been beneficial for consumers who tend to make healthier meal choices, its effect is far from ubiquitous. In fact, much of McDonald's recent financial success is not attributed to new healthy menu additions, but rather to increased sales of more indulgent options like burgers and fries (Case 2006). With the increased availability of nutritious menu options, why have more consumers not swapped their french fries for salad? In this paper, we present evidence that for many consumers, the mere presence of such alternatives can, ironically, increase the consumption of the unhealthiest item on the menu.

Recent research suggests that individuals license themselves to indulge in temptations when they have previously acted in line with a long-term goal. This research suggests that when individuals focus on their progress towards a focal goal, it allows them to temporarily disengage from that goal to pursue indulgent alternatives (Fishbach and Dhar 2005). Related research on the licensing effect shows that prior virtuous behavior–or even intentions to act in such a manner–provides individuals with the rationale for activities and choices that are not in line with long-term goals (Khan and Dhar 2007). We extend this reasoning to suggest that when individuals have the opportunity to engage in a course of action that is consistent with healthy eating goals, the consideration of this option will satisfy the goal–at least temporarily–and, in turn, license them to indulge. Moreover, we suggest that this licensing effect does not merely result in the selection of a less healthy option, but rather the most indulgent option available.

Interestingly, the goal activation processes that underlie this behavior suggests an ironic effect of sorts at the individual level; namely that the effect will be accentuated for individuals who are high in self-control. Previous research has shown that individuals high in self-control have more accessible cognitions associated with the achievement of long-term goals compared to those low in self-control, thus demonstrating a greater focus on achieving important long-term objectives (Giner-Sorolla 2001). In addition, high self-control individuals are also likely to rely more heavily on cues that justify indulgent choices (Kivetz and Zheng 2006). Thus, we predict that the mere presence of a healthy item in a choice set of less healthy food alternatives will result in a greater likelihood of choosing the least healthy item for individuals with high self-control.

In study 1, we presented respondents with side dish menus consisting of either relatively unhealthy food items (i.e., french fries, chicken nuggets and baked potato) or the same items in addition to a relatively healthy item (i.e., salad). We found that, ironically, when the healthy alternative was added to a menu, it increased the likelihood of selecting the most indulgent option for people with high self-control.

Our second study replicated the findings of study 1 in two different, food-related contexts, specifically the selection of an entrée and the choice of a within-category packaged snack food.

Study 3 provided direct evidence of goal activation/fulfillment as the underlying process. When the choice set did not include a healthy option, higher levels of self-control corresponded to faster response times to health-related words, indicating greater activation of these goals relative lower levels of self-control. Interestingly, when the choice set did include a healthy option, the response times to health-related words for high self-control individuals were slower, demonstrating less accessibility when the choice set includes a healthy option, compared to when the healthy option was not included. In other words, while high self-control individuals are better equipped to activate self-control in response to tempting stimuli, they are also highly susceptible to cues that reduce the threat imposed by tempting stimuli and, as such, are likely to fail in self-control efforts under some conditions.

Our final study provided additional support for our proposed goal activation process using a categorization approach to demonstrate vicarious goal fulfillment. Prior research (Ratneshwar et al. 2001) shows that accessible health goals lead individuals to rate food items with different levels of healthfulness as less similar to one another, while individuals with less accessible health goals rate such items as more similar to one another. In study 4, we show that the presence of the healthy item increases the perceived similarity of the items for individuals with high self-control compared to when the healthy item is not present. Importantly, we show that once healthy eating goals are fulfilled and perceived similarity among items in the choice set is high, high self-control individuals pay more attention to the most indulgent option in the choice set. Thus, we demonstrate that high self-control individuals increase the amount of attention paid to the most indulgent option in the choice set, explaining why the most indulgent option, rather than any indulgent option, is chosen.

The most obvious implication of these findings is that, despite the rush to offer healthier food alternatives, this trend may be doing little to alleviate the deeper societal issue of rising waistlines. Interestingly, while the waistlines of many consumers might be suffering as a result of the inclusion of healthier menu options, food retailers appear to be reaping substantial benefits. For instance, a recent consumer loyalty study ranks McDonald's as the front-runner in the fast food category (Hein 2008). Typically low in the rankings, McDonald's turnaround performance this year has been attributed, in part, to the inclusion of healthier alternatives that increase menu variety. Therefore, while the inclusion of healthy items is driving some consumers to make less optimal food choices, it appears to be increasing their satisfaction with food retailers and, perhaps, the choices themselves. Thus, an understanding of goal fulfilment processes is of substantial importance for understanding consumer behaviour at the individual level, as well as broader issues like the U.S. obesity epidemic.

References

Case, Tony (2006), "Fast Food," *Adweek*, 47(18) SU20.

Fishbach, Ayelet and Ravi Dhar (2005), "Goals as Excuses or Guides: The Liberating Effect of Perceived Goal Progress on Choice," *Journal of Consumer Research*, 32(3), 370-77.

Giner-Sorolla, Roger (2001), "Guilty Pleasures and Grim Necessities: Affective Attitudes in Dilemmas of Self-Control," *Journal of Personality and Social Psychology*, 80(2), 206-21.

Hein, Kenneth (2008), "McD's, Sam Adams in Line with Shifting Loyalty Drivers," *Brandweek*, 49(7), 8.

Khan, Uzma and Ravi Dhar (2006) "Licensing Effect in Consumer Choice," *Journal of Marketing Research*, 43 (2), 259-66.

Kivetz, Ran and Yuhuang Zheng (2006), "Determinants of Justification and Self-Control," *Journal of Experimental Psychology: General*, 135(4), 572-87.

Ratneshwar, S., Lawrence W. Barsalou, Cornelia Pechmann, and Melissa Moore (2001), "Goal-Derived Categories: The Role of Personal and Situational Goals in Category Representations," *Journal of Consumer Psychology*, 10(3), 147-57.

"Rejection is Good for Your Health: The Influence of Decision Strategy on Food and Drink Choices"

Jane Machin, Virginia Polytechnic Institute and State University, USA
Yong Wan Park, Virginia Polytechnic Institute and State University, USA

A hungry woman stands at a breakfast buffet deciding whether to consume an apple or a donut. Can she be nudged towards the apple simply by thinking about which option to reject, rather than which option to select? Laboratory studies provide support for this idea.

Decision strategy is the process used to make a choice: a rejection-based decision strategy occurs when the primary focus of the decision is on rejecting the undesired option(s) whereas a selection-based decision strategy occurs when the primary focus of the decision is on selecting the desired option. Prior research suggests that selection and rejection are not complementary strategies (e.g. Shafir, 1999). Of importance here is the finding that using a different decision strategy can lead to preference reversal in choice sets where one option has stronger positive attributes but also stronger negative attributes relative to another more neutral option. The positive information is weighted more heavily when using a selection-based decision strategy, but the negative information is given more attention when using a rejection-based decision strategy, resulting in the enriched option being both selected and rejected more frequently than the impoverished option.[1]

We extend findings in this literature to the area of food decisions, improving our knowledge of the food and drink decision making process and providing a simple intervention to improve dietary choices. Specifically, we propose that unhealthy foods are often spontaneously construed as enriched options. A donut, for example, is very high in calories (a strong negative attribute) but tastes great (a strong positive attribute). An apple, on the other hand is, relatively, more neutral. In support of this idea, Raghunathan, Naylor & Hoyer (2006) find that consumers rate unhealthy foods as better tasting than healthy foods. Combining these two research streams leads to the proposition that, compared to selectors, rejecters will spontaneously focus more attention on the negative attributes of the enriched option (e.g. the relatively high calorie content), leading them to reject this option and consume the alternative, relatively healthier option. Selectors, on the other hand, will focus more attention on the positive attributes of the enriched option (e.g. the superior taste), leading them to consume it.

Shafir (1993) provides some early support for this proposition in his Problem 6 (p 551). Our research extends Shafir's finding in numerous ways. First, in Shafir's vignette, rejecters received supplementary information and were also artificially endowed with both options. To demonstrate that the results replicate in more natural situations, information about the choice options was held constant between selectors and rejecters in all our studies and only decision strategy differed. For example, Study 1a presented identical information about the healthiness and taste of two types of frozen dessert to all participants. Half the participants were then asked "which do you want to eat" while the other half were simply asked "which do you not want to eat?" Consistent with the hypothesis, participants who chose by rejecting the dessert they did not want were significantly more likely to choose the healthier option. Study 1b replicated this result in a drink choice situation. Rejecters were significantly more likely to select the healthy option (mineral water) compared to selectors.

More importantly, Shafir's participants were given explicit information about both health and taste attributes. In the real world, however, such overt information is often not readily available. Building on the "unhealthy=tasty intuition" (Raghunathan, Naylor & Hoyer 2006) we expect that participants, spontaneously inferring that unhealthy options will taste better, will both select and reject the unhealthy options more frequently. Results confirm this hypothesis. Study 2 demonstrates that using a rejection-based decision strategy leads to healthier food choices when only health information is provided. Participants were given a real choice between three types of cracker, varying in the degree of fat they contained. Compared to participants who chose by selection, participants who chose by rejection were significantly more likely to choose the healthiest cracker. Study 3 removed all explicit information about the options. Participants were shown a mock drink vending machine where the brand names of various drink options were visible, but no explicit health or taste information was presented. Once again, participants who chose by rejection were significantly more likely to choose the healthier option (bottled water) compared to participants who chose by selection. Additional analyses in studies 2 and 3 demonstrate that differences in beliefs about the relative taste of the options mediate the relationship between decision strategy and choice.

Study 4 extends the findings to a situation where actual dietary information could be analyzed to provide an objective reference point regarding the healthiness of the choice. Participants were presented with a take-out menu from Arby's and asked to choose a meal for lunch that day by either selecting the items they wanted or rejecting the items they did not want. Rejecters made objectively healthier meal choices. For example, the total carbohydrate count in the meals chosen by selectors was significantly higher than that of the meals chosen by rejecters and the total grams of fat in the meals chosen by selectors was significantly higher than that in the meals chosen by rejecters.

In all the above studies, decision strategy was manipulated. While these demonstrate that consumers can be encouraged to adopt a rejection based decision strategy, leading to healthier choices, there is little understanding whether rejection-based decision making ever occurs spontaneously. Study 5 presented participants with a variety of choice situations and, using language meant to be as neutral as possible, asked participants to "indicate their decision". Compared to those who used a selection-based decision strategy, participants who spontaneously reported using a rejection-based decision strategy were significantly more likely to

[1]The term "enriched" has a specific meaning within research on nutrition (i.e. vitamins have been added to the food; Doyon and Labrecque 2008) that is not relevant here. Enriched is used only as Shafir (1999) defines it, to refer to the option with more positive as well as more negative dimensions.

choose frozen yogurt over ice cream, an apple over a donut and a medium size fast food meal over a large size.

Marketers of healthy food products could easily encourage the use of a rejection-based decision strategy through, for example, comparative advertising techniques and in-store decision aids, helping to nudge consumers to "have it their way—more healthily"–more apples, less donuts.

References

Doyon Maurice and JoAnne Labrecque (2008), "Functional Foods: A Conceptual Definition," *British Food Journal*, 110 (11) 1133-1149

Raghunathan, R., R. W. Naylor and W. D. Hoyer (2006), "The Unhealthy=Tasty Intuition and Its Effects on Taste Inferences, Enjoyment, and Choice of Food Products," *Journal of Marketing*, 70 (4) 170-184.

Shafir, E. (1993), "Choosing Versus Rejecting: Why Some Options Are Both Better and Worse Than Others," *Memory and Cognition*, 21 (4) 546-556.

"Linearize This! Why Consumers Underestimate Food Portion Changes and How to Help Them"

Pierre Chandon, INSEAD, France
Nailya Ordabayeva, INSEAD, France

Because large packages and portions lead to greater consumption, the trends towards supersized food portions and packages is considered one of the prime drivers of the obesity epidemic (Cutler et al. 2003; Nielsen and Popkin 2003). Supersizing leads to overeating because people do not realize just how big these portions are. Therefore, improving people's size estimations is essential to help consumers choose smaller, and healthier, portions sizes (Chandon and Wansink 2007). In this research, we examine how consumers estimate changes in package and portion size and what can be done to improve their estimations.

Research in psychophysics has shown that people's estimations of object size follow an inelastic power function of its actual size (Estimated size=a◊(Actual size)^b, where b<1), which means that people underestimate the magnitude of size changes (Stevens 1986). In previous research (Chandon and Ordabayeva 2009), we showed that size estimations are even less elastic when a package increases or decreases along all three dimensions (height, length, and width) rather than a single dimension in space (e.g., only in height). However, we still do not know why this happens.

As suggested by prior research (Raghubir 2007), we examine two potential causes of these psychophysical biases—information integration (i.e., incorrectly integrating dimensions) and information attention (i.e., ignoring some dimensions). We further hypothesize that the key problem is biased information integration caused by the reliance on an additive model of size change (vs. the correct multiplicative one). Specifically, we hypothesize that consumers add the increases in package dimensions instead of multiplying them. As a result, people think that a 26% increase in height, width, and length increases volume by 78% (26+26+26) when, in reality, it increases volume by 100%.

Our model leads to several testable hypotheses. First, it predicts that consumers accurately estimate size changes when they occur along a single spatial dimension but underestimate size changes when they occur along two dimensions, and even more so when they occur along three dimensions. Second, linearizing size changes by decreasing the dimensionality of changes from 3D to 2D to 1D reduces the underestimation bias and increases the preference for large packages and portions (when people prefer more food to less). Third, because it is an information integration and not an information attention bias, drawing attention to the fact that all three dimensions of a package change (i.e., by asking people to estimate the change in each of the three dimensions) does not reduce the underestimation bias or people's size preferences. However, it is possible to improve people's size change estimations by simply multiplying their (linear) estimations of the change in each of the three dimensions. We test these hypotheses in two studies.

In Study 1, we studied the effect of the two linearizing manipulations (dimensionality and decomposition estimation) on consumers' size estimations for increasing packages. The participants saw pictures of four sizes of popcorn boxes which increased either in 1D, 2D or 3D (between-subjects). Participants were given the size and the price of the smallest box (A) and were asked to estimate the sizes and prices of the remaining three boxes. Participants in the decomposition estimation condition were also provided with the sizes of the dimensions of size A and were asked to estimate the dimensions of the remaining three boxes before providing their size estimations. As expected, we found that people underestimated the magnitude of supersizing (b=.63), and more so in 3D vs. 2D vs. 1D (b=.48, .65, .73, respectively). As expected, drawing attention to the fact that all three dimensions could be changing by asking people to estimate the size of each dimension did not improve their size estimations (b=.62) and did not reduce the effect of dimensionality (b=.50, .54, .70 in 3D, 2D and 1D conditions, respectively). All these results were also obtained when looking at willingness to pay, supporting our hypotheses. In addition, the additive model of information integration fit the data significantly better than the multiplicative model, suggesting that people do indeed add % changes instead of multiplying them.

In Study 2, we looked at increasing as well as decreasing package sizes, used real products (instead of pictures), and examined the effect of the two linearizing strategies on choice (and not just on size estimations and WTP). The participants saw four increasing or four decreasing sizes (between-subjects) of a rectangular candle and a cylindrical candy box displayed on the table. We manipulated the dimensionality of size change and decomposition between-subjects as in Study 1. In addition to size estimations and WTP, we asked the participants to indicate their preferred size for each product. We found that, for both supersizing and downsizing, decreasing the dimensionality of size change improved the accuracy of size estimations. Interestingly, we found that size estimations were steeper and more linear (and hence more accurate) for downsizing than for supersizing (b=.75 vs. .85 for supersizing vs. downsizing, respectively). As in Study 1, decomposition task did not improve size estimations or reduce the effect of dimensionality. Again, the additive model predicted size estimations better than the multiplicative model.

Study 2 also showed that decreasing the dimensionality of size change increased the preference for large sizes of both products (30% vs. 43% vs. 64% chose the largest two sizes in 3D, 2D, and 1D, respectively), as expected. However, the decomposition strategy increased the preference for large size of candles (from 30% to 46%) but decreased the preference for large sizes of candies (from 55% to 49%). This suggests that drawing attention to the three dimensions, although it did not improve people's size estimations, activated more utilitarian goals and thus motivated people to choose larger (and cheaper) candle sizes but smaller (and healthier) candy sizes.

In a final study in progress, we are testing the conflicting predictions of the additive and multiplicative models when package dimensions change in opposite directions (e.g., the height of a cylinder increases, but its diameter decreases). This will allow us to test whether consumers can be fooled by downsized packages which appear bigger than they actually are (because the strong % reduction in one dimension seems to be compensated by the % increase in two other dimensions).

Understanding what drives the underestimation of size changes should suggest effective strategies to improve consumers' perceptions of supersized and downsized packages and portions. Our findings suggest that packages that linearize the estimation problem (by reducing the dimensionality of size change) should nudge consumers toward healthier choices.

References

Chandon, Pierre and Nailya Ordabayeva (2009), "Supersize in 1D, Downsize in 3D: Effects of Spatial Dimensionality on Size Perceptions and Preferences," *Journal of Marketing Research*, 46(6), 739-53.

Chandon, Pierre and Brian Wansink (2007), "Is Obesity Caused by Calorie Underestimation? A Psychophysical Model of Meal Size Estimation," *Journal of Marketing Research*, 44 (1), 84-99.

Cutler, David, Edward Glaeser, and Jesse Shapiro (2003), "Why Have Americans Become More Obese*?" Journal of Economic Perspectives*, 17 (3), 93-118.

Nielsen, Samara Joy and Barry M. Popkin (2003), "Patterns and Trends in Food Portion Sizes, 1977–1998," *The Journal of the American Medical Association*, 289 (4), 450–53.

Raghubir, Priya (2007), "*Are Visual Perceptual Biases Hard-Wired?" in Visual Marketing: From Attention to Action*, ed. Michel Wedel and Rik Pieters, New York: Lawrence Erlbaum Associates, 143-66.

Stevens, Stanley Smith (1986), *Psychophysics: Introduction to its Perceptual, Neural, and Social Prospects*, Oxford: Transaction Books.

Special Session Summary
The Interplay between Goal Categories and Effort

Antonios Stamatogiannakis, INSEAD, France

SESSION OVERVIEW

"Man is a goal seeking animal. His life only has meaning if he is reaching out and striving for his goals." (Aristotle)

Dating back to the ancient Greeks, scholars have attempted to elucidate the motivational factors underlying human goals. The importance of understanding goals and their effects on effort has been recognized by consumer researchers as well. For instance, goals increase effort and do so more strongly for difficult and specific goals (Locke and Latham 1990). Further, as people move closer to their goal they are likely to invest more effort toward that goal (Kivetz, Urminsky and Zheng 2006), and goal progress interpretations influence whether people commit to or deviate from the goal (Fishbach and Dhar 2005). The three papers in this session integrate some of these perspectives in presenting a dynamic view of goals and effort.

The broad purpose of this session is to present work that adds to the growing body of research on the interplay of goals and effort. Specifically, this session examines 1) the effect of different goal types on effort and 2) the impact of effort investment on valuation of subsequent consumption items. While the first paper examines the impact of attainment versus maintenance goal on effort, the second paper extends the focus of the first paper by examining the impact of initial success in enhancing effort on a recurring goal. Finally, the third paper complements the first two papers by examining the impact of effort investment in a meaningful goal or task on the WTP for a subsequent consumption item. A twenty minute discussion led by Ayelet Fishbach will follow the three presentations.

Stamatogiannakis, Chattopadhyay and Chakravarti pit maintenance goals against attainment goals. They find that maintenance goals are judged as harder than objectively harder modest attainment goals. For example people think that it is easier to increase one's daily working out time by five minutes than to maintain its current level. This effect is driven by biased cognitive processing of goals. Finally, the authors show circumstances under which maintenance goals can be detrimental to performance, compared to attainment goals.

Nunes and Drèze investigate recurring goals, i.e., goals for which people strive again and again, like getting a reward from a loyalty program. They find that after initial success in such goals, consumers learn about their ability to succeed in the same goal again. This results in increased perceptions of self-efficacy and therefore increased motivation in future pursuits (Bandura 1982). Importantly, as successful completions increase, so does motivation.

Wadhwa and Trudel take a different approach and examine the moderating role of task and goal characteristics on the relationship between effort investment in and willingness to pay for a consumption item. First they demonstrate the "fruit of labor effect", i.e., that investing effort in a meaningful task enhances the wanting for an associated consumption item. Further, they examine the role of meaningfulness of the task that requires effort, and the reward salience of the consumption item in moderating the proposed fruit of labor effects.

All three papers provide cutting edge counterintuitive insights into the goal processes that drive consumer behavior and decision making. In addition to attracting researchers interested in the domains of goals and motivation, we expect further interest from those who work within the application areas represented.

EXTENDED ABSTRACT

"Maintenance versus Attainment Goals: Why People Think it Is Harder to Maintain their Weight than to Lose a Couple of Kilos"

Antonios Stamatogiannakis, INSEAD, France
Amitava Chattopadhyay, INSEAD, Singapore
Dipankar Chakravarti, Johns Hopkins University, USA

The goal setting literature posits that goal distance has a positive monotonic effect on subjective goal difficulty, after controlling for self-efficacy (Locke and Latham 1990). This literature usually assumes a discrepancy between an actual and a desired state (e.g., Kruglanski 1996), but fails to acknowledge maintenance goals, i.e., goals in which the actual and the desired states coincide, but there is a time difference between the present and the goal time horizon.

The violation of the state discrepancy assumption by maintenance goals, makes doubtful the extension of the relation between goal distance and subjective difficulty to this goal category, especially since several streams of research seem to suggest otherwise. First, based on Heath, Larrick, and Wu (1999), goals are reference points and people think that the same amount of progress gives more utility and leads to greater effort in the losses than in the gains domain. Maintenance goals actors are already on or beyond the goal-reference point-and thus in the gains domain-but attainment goals actors are in the losses domain. People then could infer more effort for attainment than for maintenance goals and thus believe that attainment goals are more likely to be achieved. Second, actions interpreted as progress towards a goal make people deviate from it, but actions interpreted as commitment to a goal make people highlight the achievement of that goal (Fishbach and Dhar 2005). People might feel that they have fully progressed towards a maintenance goal, but feel committed to a modest attainment goal, because with a little more effort they can achieve it. This would make people pursuing an attainment goal try harder than people pursuing a maintenance goal. If people have this lay theory, then subjective judgment of future success will be higher for attainment goals.

Finally, Gilovich, Kerr, and Medvec (1993) find that short temporal distance from goal results in the generation of more reasons for failure, but longer temporal distance results to the generation of more reasons for success. If we extrapolate this result to goal distance, we would predict that people facing maintenance (attainment) goals would generate more reasons for failure (success). Therefore, when making a difficulty judgment, they will view maintenance goals as more difficult.

In a series of five studies, where we manipulate goal type (maintenance vs. attainment) between participants, we document that maintenance goals are judged as more difficult to attain than modest attainment goals, we examine which of the mechanisms above account for this phenomenon, and we extend our results to effects on performance. The first three studies are scenario based. Scenarios about weight, GPA, daily working out time, money, and weekly sales goals are used. The first study documents that maintenance goals are judged as more difficult than modest attainment goals, and this effect can not be attributed to differences in expected motivation between the two goal types. This suggests that the differences are likely to be driven by differences in the cognitive processing of the two goal types.

The second study confirms this prediction. It replicates the main effect of study one, and further find that when people consider maintenance goals they tend to generate more reasons for failure but less reasons for success, compared to when they consider attainment goals. Differences in reason generation mediate differences in subjective difficulty, showing that the effect is driven by differences in cognitive processing.

The third study uses a 2 X 2 between participants factorial design. Some participants judged maintenance goals and some attainment goals. Further, some participants were given a cue which aimed to make success and failure equally salient, and therefore should attenuate the effect, while others received no cues. In the no cue condition, we replicate the result that people think maintenance goals are harder than attainment goals. However, in the cued condition, which made success and failure equally salient the effect disappeared, supporting the notion that biased cognitive processing is the source of the bias. Interestingly, the neutralizing cue had an impact only on attainment goals, and not on maintenance goals.

The fourth study replicates the above effect with a self-relevant goal. Specifically, participants had to solve two word-search puzzles. They indicated that it was harder to solve the second puzzle in at most the time they solved the first, compared to improve this time by a second. The results further demonstrate that difficulty judgments of attainment and maintenance goals are impacted differently when a high performance standard is active (Bargh et al. 2001). This is important given that such standards are often active in goal directed consumption cases.

Finally, study five extends the above results to a performance measure in a laboratory word search task. The results suggest that although the two goal types have similar effects on performance, maintenance goals can act as a cue that current state is good enough, and therefore hamper performance when a high performance standard is active (Bargh et al. 2001).

"Recurring Goals and Learning: The Impact of Successful Reward Attainment on Purchase Behavior"

Joseph Nunes, University of Southern California, USA
Xavier Drèze, University of Pennsylvania, USA

"If I did it once, I can do it again," is a common mantra for those who have attained success. However, there is no indication regarding whether they will try as hard or harder the next time around. This research approaches the impact of loyalty programs and their rewards differently than previous research. Rather than model the impact of membership in a firm's loyalty program or the nature of a program's rewards on share-of-wallet, we look at the impact of successful reward redemption on future purchase behavior. More specifically, this research examines the long-term relationship between customers and the firm and whether successful reward redemption leads consumers to consolidate and/or accelerate their future purchases. While research has shown that progress toward a reward can lead consumers to accelerate their purchases, much less is known about how earning rewards can impact behavior. This research illustrates how success in a recurring goal framework allows consumers to learn something about themselves and leads them to amplify their effort in successive endeavors toward the same reward.

Kivetz et al. (2006) conducted a field study at a university café where participating customers were required to make 10 coffee purchases in order to get one free. They found consumers who accelerated their purchases faster toward their first reward exhibited a greater probability of retention and faster reengagement in the program. Reengagement was assessed by comparing the time period between the last purchase toward earning the first reward and the first purchase toward earning the second reward. More relevant for our purposes is what happened with those who reengaged. Kivetz et al. (2006) found that for customers who earned the first reward, purchase rates slowed as they began working toward their second reward. Subsequently, purchase rates accelerated as cardholders neared the second reward, just as they had for the first reward. The authors dubbed this slowdown in the inter-purchase time between the first reward and first purchase toward the second reward as post-reward resetting. They argued resetting ruled out learning as an explanation for the acceleration in purchases observed as consumers approach a reward because this deceleration would imply what was learned had been suddenly forgotten.

We argue that the increase in effort brought on by successfully reaching a goal and earning a reward is due to learning-self-learning. Our interest is in thoroughly investigating consumers' capacity to learn as a result of successful reward attainment. While post-reward resetting suggests the goal gradient phenomenon is not due to procedural learning, it does not preclude other forms of learning from taking place. We use the term self-learning to describe what Bandura (1982) called predictive learning; the reassessment of one's self-efficacy. Self-efficacy refers to an individual's perception of how well he or she can execute courses of actions to deal with prospective situations. Attaining a reward requires consumers to orchestrate their buying behavior in very specific ways. Consumers must schedule and steer purchases in a deliberate manner in order to earn rewards from select firms. Utility-maximizing individuals will modulate these efforts as a function of the perceived likelihood of success, which depends largely on judgments of how well they performed in the past.

In Study 1, we utilize real world frequent flier program data to show how success fosters reengagement; successful fliers begin the new year flying more frequently. In addition, reaching the goal of earning status impacts a flier's likelihood of success in subsequent attempts of earning status. Study 2 reveals that only in cases where the reward is challenging enough, but not too challenging, does the impact of success affect forecasts of future effort. In Study 2, we use lab data based on scenarios to show that increasing divisibility or how frequently rewards are doled out (from $1,000 to $500), reframes a larger task as several smaller tasks and can boost people's perceptions of self-efficacy. If they succeed once, albeit at reaching an easier goal, this tells them something about themselves. Conversely, too much divisibility or success arrived at too easily (rewards at every $100) was shown to be de-motivating. Therefore, loyalty programs that offer people multiple redemption opportunities must balance the attractiveness of an award with an appropriate level of difficulty in attaining success. Finally, in Study 3, we explore the underlying process. The study was presented as a game whereby the respondent's goal was to determine whether the experimenter was lying by judging his or her facial expressions. By partitioning a task differently (3 sets of 10 trials or one of 30 trials) and reframing the task as either complete or incomplete, we show how successfully reaching a pre-ordained goal enhances perceptions of self-efficacy while controlling for overall performance.

In all three studies, achieving more than one success is shown to matter. Hence, not only does goal attainment result in increased effort the second time around, but successive successes further elevate effort. We show how the successful attainment of a goal and the accompanying reward increases consumers' motivation in subsequent undertakings and that this increase in motivation can endure after more than one or two successes. From a practical perspective, all possible successes may not be entirely within the control of the firm. For example, frequent flier miles are becoming interchangeable with several other currencies and some can be redeemed at numerous second-party vendors. The result is myriad outside rewards that might qualify as successes. Earning 25,000 miles for a free roundtrip ticket is no longer the quintessential goal.

"The Fruit of Labor Effect"

Monica Wadhwa, Stanford University, USA
Remi Trudel, University of Western Ontario, Canada

Consumers often engage in experiences that require some level of effort from them. For instance, burgeoning hobby stores, such as "paint-your-own-pottery" or "make your own jewelry" stores, demonstrate consumers' desire to invest effort. The aforementioned examples raise an interesting question—Could varying the effort required in an experience impact consumer's evaluations for the associated consumption item? A pretest conducted with marketing experts indicates that the product associated with an experience that requires additional effort investment should be evaluated less favorably.

Interestingly, the implications of the findings from our pretest contradict those arising from an emerging body of research on the neurobiology of rewards. Recent research in this domain demonstrates that expending effort to earn a reward leads the ventral striatum (part of brain associated with motivational drive and reward processing) to be more intensely stimulated as compared to when no such effort is expended (Zink et al. 2004). Drawing upon this stream of research, we propose that investing a bit of effort in a task is likely to activate a motivational drive, and thereby enhance the wanting for the associated consumption item, a notion we term as the "fruit of labor" effect. Further, we argue that meaningfulness of the task that requires effort is essential for the fruit of labor effects to emerge. Specifically, when the meaningfulness of the task requiring effort is high (than when the meaningfulness is low), investing a bit of effort should enhance the wanting for the associated consumption item.

In order to examine the aforementioned propositions, in study 1, we employed a sampling task. Specifically, participants sampled a new brand of powdered energy drink purportedly meant to enhance mental acuity and intellectual performance. Effort required was manipulated by giving one group of participants premixed form of the drink (effort -absent). A second group of participants was asked to mix the drink and stir it for thirty seconds (effort -low), and a third group for three minutes (effort-high) so the crystals are properly dissolved. To manipulate the meaningfulness of the task (i.e., stirring the energy drink), prior to the sampling task, participants were either primed with an intellectual goal or were not primed with any goal. In line with the fruit of labor proposition, our results show that those primed with an intellectual goal stated higher WTP for the drink when they had invested a little bit of effort than when they had invested no effort. These participants also stated higher WTP than those not primed with the intellectual goal in the low-effort condition. Moreover, when the effort required was too high the impact of investing effort on WTP for the drink was attenuated. These results rule out alternative accounts related to cognitive dissonance and licensing, which would predict that participants in the high effort condition should have stated higher WTP than those in low effort condition.

Study 2 sought to achieve two main objectives. Besides providing further support for our fruit of labor proposition using a different manipulation for task meaningfulness, it also examines whether investing effort in one task can enhance wanting for a subsequent reward that is not related to the task. We again employed an orange juice sampling task. Participants were told that as compensation for their participation in the study, $1 would be donated to a charity. To do so, they would be provided with a coupon, which they would need to hand over to the experimenter at the sampling station. People in the high-effort condition cut out a coupon printed on a thick paper. Those in the low-effort condition were handed the same pre-cut coupon. To manipulate the task meaningfulness, we employed either a charity that participants could highly relate to—Ontario Cancer Foundation-(task-meaningfulness-high) or a charity that participants could not relate to as much—Canadian Landmine Eradication Awareness and Removal Project (CLEAR; task-meaningfulness-low). These charities were chosen based on a pretest. Subsequently, participants engaged in the orange juice sampling task and then indicated their WTP for it. As we predicted, effort investment positively impacted the WTP for the subsequently consumed orange juice, but only when task-meaningfulness was high (i.e., when participants cut the coupon for Cancer charity).

Study 3 examines the moderating role of reward salience of the consumption item. Extant motivation research suggests that when the salience of the reward is heightened prior to exerting effort in a task, the activated motivational drive is strengthened (Higgins 2006; Zink et al. 2004). Based on this logic, we argue when the reward salience of the subsequently sampled orange juice is heightened prior to investing effort in the task, the fruit of labor effect should get more pronounced. The procedure of this study closely paralleled that of study 2 with one major change. To manipulate the reward salience of the orange juice, the participants in incentive salience-high condition saw a color picture of a glass of orange juice along with the instructions for the sampling task, but those in the incentive salience-low condition saw only the instructions. In line with our predictions, we find that the participants in the effort - present condition were willing to pay more for the juice when the reward salience was high as compared to when it was low. However, when the effort investment was absent, there was no such difference in WTP between the reward salience high and the reward salience-low conditions.

In conclusion, while most of extant research on cost-benefit approach in the decision making literature considers effort as a cost (Russo and Dosher 1983), the present research suggests that the act of putting a little bit of effort in some consumption scenarios could in fact add value to the overall consumption experience. Implications for marketers are discussed.

REFERENCES

Bandura, Albert (1982), "Self-efficacy Mechanism in Human Agency," *American Psychologist*, 37 (2), 122-47.

Bargh, John A., Peter M. Gollwitzer, Annette Lee-Chai, Kimberly Barndollar, and Roman Trotschel (2001), "The Automated Will: Nonconscious Activation and Pursuit of Behavioral Goals," *Journal of Personality and Social Psychology*, 81 (6), 1014-27.

Fishbach, Ayelet, and Ravi Dhar (2005), "Goals as Excuses or Guides: The Liberating Effect of Perceived Goal Progress on Choice," *Journal of Consumer Research*, 32, 370-77.

Gilovich, Thomas, Margaret Kerr, and Victoria H. Medvec (1993), "Effect of temporal perspective on subjective confidence," *Journal of Personality and Social Psychology*, 64 (4), 552-60.

Heath, Chip, Richard P. Larrick, and George Wu (1999), "Goals as Reference Points," *Cognitive Psychology*, 38 (1), 79-109.

Higgins, Tory E. (2006), "Value from Hedonic Experience and Engagement," *Psychological Review*, Vol. 113 (3), 439-460.

Kivetz, Ran, Oleg Urminsky, and Yuhuang Zheng (2006), "The Goal-Gradient Hypothesis Resurrected: Purchase Acceleration, Illusionary Goal Progress, and Customer Retention," *Journal of Marketing Research*, 43 (1), 39-58.

Kruglanski, Arie W. (1996), "Motivated social cognition: Principles of the interface," in *Social Psychology: Handbook of Basic Principles*, Edited by E. T. Higgins, and A. W. Kruglanski. NY: Guilford, 493-522.

Locke, Edwin A., and Gary P. Latham (1990), *A Theory of Goal Setting & Task Performance*, NJ: Prentice Hall.

Russo, J. Edward, and Barbara Anne Dosher (1983), "Strategies for Multiattribute Binary Choice," *Journal of Experimental Psychology: Learning, Memory, and Cognition*, 9 (4), 676-96.

Zink, Caroline F, Giuseppe Pagnoni, Megan E. Martin-Skurski, Jonathan C. Chappelow and Gregory S. Berns (2004), "Human Striatal Response to Monetary Reward Depends on Saliency," *Neuron*, 42 (May), 509-517.

SPECIAL SESSION SUMMARY

Is Identity Signaling so Great? Limitations and Negative Consequences

Rosellina Ferraro, University of Maryland, USA

SESSION OVERVIEW

People often buy products and brands for signaling who they are or who they want to be. Prior research has provided evidence for the phenomenon of identity signaling and shown how it affects choices. The four papers in this session expand the theory related to identity signaling by exploring boundary conditions, such as negative consequences and abandonment. Two of the papers propose that engaging in identity-signaling can backfire in its purpose. One of the papers explores the functioning of identity signaling when there is a competing goal. Finally, the fourth paper explores the abandonment of culturally created tastes as a form of identity signaling.

Ferraro, et al., argue that since identity-signaling serves an important communication function, it should be perceived positively by observers. Instead, it is perceived negatively as observers view identity signaling as extrinsically motivated and a reflection of an inauthentic self. Thus perceptions of authenticity mediate how much an observer likes the signaler. The authors also show that the signaler's perceived similarity to the observer moderates this effect. Han and Nunes also examine the response to identity signaling via the interactive dynamic between the signaler and the receiver. The authors propose that while the signaler expects to feel positive from engaging in signaling, she may instead feel embarrassment under certain conditions; specifically when the signal is more conspicuous and easy to recognize and when there is explicit acknowledgement of the signal by others. Chan and Van Boven examine the tension that exists between the conflicting motives of signaling group membership and expressing uniqueness. Research suggests that people express uniqueness by opting for products that are owned by fewer others, which contrasts with identity signaling research that indicates people signal social identity by behaving similarly to in-group members. The authors propose that the conflict may be reconciled via convergence at the brand level and divergence at the product level. Finally, Berger and Le Mens examine the abandonment of cultural tastes. They propose that the speed with which a taste is adopted (i.e., its popularity) determines how quickly that taste is abandoned. The speed reflects whether the taste is a fad and thus has symbolic value. The negative signal that would come from adopting a perceived fad leads to a greater likelihood that the taste is abandoned.

Each presenter (R. Ferraro, Y. Han, C. Chan, and G. Le Mens) has agreed to serve if the proposal is accepted. Questions will be taken at the end of the session. All data have been collected. This session will have wide appeal, including to scholars of self-identity, brand relationships, and product adoption.

EXTENDED ABSTRACTS

"Signaling Identity through Brands: The Role of Perceived Authenticity"

Rosellina Ferraro, University of Maryland, USA
Amna Kirmani, University of Maryland, USA
Ted Matherly, University of Maryland, USA

Consumers frequently purchase brands for the purpose of communicating information about the qualities they possess or the categories to which they belong. In other words, people use brands for identity signaling. Prior research suggests that identity signaling can satisfy consumers' association and communication goals. This research, however, says little about how observers react to identity signaling. If identity signaling serves as an effective means of communication, recipients should interpret the signal as intended and should view the person favorably (assuming that the signaled trait is valued positively). We propose, instead, that identity signaling is perceived negatively by observers. This is because observers view identity signaling as an inauthentic means by which someone represents the self. Buying a brand for the sole purpose of conveying a particular identity may be seen to be motivated by extrinsic rewards, such as social approval, and thus a reflection of an inauthentic self. In contrast, buying a brand for intrinsic motives, such as for utilitarian benefits, is viewed as more authentic. Higher perceived authenticity is expected to translate into more favorable attitudes toward the signaler. We propose, however, that similarity to the signaler moderates the effects of purchase motives on perceived authenticity and attitude.

Study 1 examines perceptions of a target who uses a brand to signal identity compared to a target who uses the brand for utilitarian reasons or whose reason for using the brand is unspecified. Participants read about the motivation behind the target's purchase of a Toyota Prius. We expected that the target would be perceived as more authentic and likable when he bought the brand for utilitarian than for signaling reasons. The results indicate that a target engaged in identity signaling was perceived less favorably than the target whose brand usage was motivated by utilitarian reasons. Moreover, perceived authenticity appears to underlie these effects. The signaling motivation decreased perceptions of the target's authenticity, coolness, and intrinsic motivation, and increased perceptions that the target was extrinsically motivated.

Study 2 examines whether negative perceptions of identity signaling will be attenuated when the signaler is perceived to be similar to the observer. Research has found that people judge their own actions more positively than those of others, but that this asymmetry can be eliminated when the other person is perceived as similar. In our context, this is manifested in the belief that one behaves in a manner consistent with one's authentic self while others do not. We predict that this unfavorable perception of others' authenticity will be attenuated by perceptions of similarity to those others. Participants read a description of a target who recently bought an Apple computer. Motive was manipulated by varying the stated reason behind the target's purchase. Similarity was indicated via ownership of the brand. Brand users rated the target favorably regardless of his motive for buying the brand. Nonusers, however, liked the target less when he engaged in identity signaling. Authenticity, as measured by innovativeness, mediated the interactive effect of motivation and similarity on attitude.

The goal of study 3 was to test the predictions in a context in which the target's signaling motive is inferred rather than explicitly stated; specifically, in a public versus private setting. Because others can observe the target's behavior, the target is more likely to be actively managing the impression she is making when in public and as a consequence, an observer is more likely to infer an identity signaling motive. Participants read about the target, including details about the target's demographic information. This information was expected to serve as the basis for perceived similarity to the target. Motive was manipulated by varying whether the target read The New York Times in a public or private setting. Participants who felt highly similar to the target liked her equally across condition, while participants who did not feel similar to the target liked her more when she was not engaged in identity-signaling than when she was engaged in identity-signaling. A similar pattern of results emerged for the perceived intelligence of the target. Authenticity mediated the interaction effect of motive and perceived similarity on liking and perceptions of intelligence.

In sum, observers respond negatively to identity signaling, and authenticity underlies this effect. However, the data also show that as the signaler is seen as more similar, the attitude becomes positive in nature.

"Read the Signal but Don't Mention It: How Conspicuous Consumption Embarrasses the Signaler"

Young J. Han, University of Southern California, USA
Joseph C. Nunes, University of Southern California, USA

Research has shown consumers use products as communication devices when they express their desired self-identity and image to others. Among the most popular meanings consumers convey using products are wealth and status, what has been dubbed conspicuous consumption (Veblen 1899). Research on conspicuous consumption has focused on the intentions of the signaler, and has left the interaction between the signal provider and the recipient relatively unexplored. This research is a first step towards filling that gap.

When consumers engage in conspicuous consumption, they expect others to recognize and interpret their signals as they had intended. It is natural to expect that when an observer recognizes the sender's signal and provides positive feedback, the sender should feel positive, both pleased and proud. However, across several studies we find when the targets of these signals acknowledge the signal, the sender is more likely to respond negatively, specifically by feeling embarrassed. Traditionally, embarrassment arises when a person believes their demeanor has been inappropriate and judged negatively by others (Edelman 1981). Or it can occur when someone feels his behavior, or some aspects of the self, needs to be carefully monitored, hidden, or changed (Goffman 1956). In other words, embarrassment can be elicited by sensitivity to social norms. Hence, if positive feedback on leads the signaler to worry about unexpressed and potentially negative judgments, the acknowledgement of a signal should lead to embarrassment.

This occurs in two ways. First, acknowledging a signal with a compliment may lead the signaler to believe their signal was too conspicuous because it encouraged an uncommon response. Compliments typically express goodwill toward the addressee and the primary response is affective. However, compliments can convey a referential meaning in that a particular aspect of the signaler was chosen for the speaker's attention (Johnson and Roen 1992). In turn, the signaler may infer the speaker believes the signaler is being manipulative in attempting to make a particular impression. We hypothesize that the more conspicuous the signal, the more likely the signaler is to feel embarrassed when complimented by others. Second, if the signaler is communicating an inauthentic identity, explicit acknowledgement makes the false nature of the signal salient. When people are highly motivated to impress others and doubt their ability to do so, high social anxiety results, including the appearance of nervousness (Leary 1983). We explore how signalers respond to acknowledgement in four studies.

In Study 1, we test whether the false nature of signals influence a signaler's level of embarrassment upon being complimented using a thought experiment. Respondents read a scenario that either described a woman who purchased a conspicuous designer handbag, or a bag that is far more subtle. We varied the extent to which the purchase was a financial stretch. Results reveal an interaction such that respondents expected the woman to feel more embarrassed when the signal was loud and inauthentic and more proud and pleased when the signal was quiet and authentic. Study 2 is a field study focusing on the differential response by people identified and interviewed carrying either a conspicuous or an inconspicuous luxury handbag. During the interview the experimenter complimented the handbag. A recording of their emotional reaction was subsequently analyzed using Layered Voice Analysis (LVA) technology. Respondents also completed a survey designed to test the authenticity of the signal. Study 2 provides a real-world replication of Study 1–women carrying loud handbags were more embarrassed by the compliment and this effect was magnified if the signal was deemed inauthentic.

Study 3 examines the dynamic interaction between two signalers. Focusing on consumers utilizing a conspicuous signal, we focused on a signaler's response to acknowledgement from someone also signaling, either conspicuously or inconspicuously. Upon being complimented, the signaler is less likely to become embarrassed or believe the recipient is being judgmental when the recipient is signaling conspicuously. Finally, study 4 examines the connection between conspicuousness and the authenticity perception of signaling behavior. In this study, we examine whether people possess inherent beliefs about the authenticity of a signal which depends on its relative conspicuousness. People were found to be more doubtful about the authenticity of a conspicuous signal. The results help explain why conspicuous signalers become anxious when their signal is acknowledged, even when it is legitimate.

Taken together, this research documents how consumers who deliberately signal more conspicuously, respond more negatively (i.e., are more embarrassed) when their signal is acknowledged. However, we find this embarrassment is attenuated when the recognition giver was also observed signaling loudly. Furthermore, the results reveal that even consumers who signal their true identity can feel embarrassed. The extent to which they feel this way is shown to depend on their beliefs about the interpretation of the signal and the authenticity of the signal.

"Satisfying Identity-Signaling and Uniqueness Motives through Consumer Choice"

Cindy Chan, Cornell University, USA
Jonah Berger, Wharton School of Business, USA
Leaf Van Boven, University of Colorado–Boulder, USA

Consumers concerned with conveying their social identity may often experience tension between communicating their group membership and communicating what makes them unique. Different research streams have separately examined different identity motives. Work on uniqueness suggests that people want to be (at least somewhat) unique (Snyder and Fromkin 1980). People with higher needs for differentiation, for example, prefer products owned by fewer others (Tian, Bearden, and Hunter 2001). Work on identity-signaling, in contrast, suggests that people behave similarly to in-group members to effectively communicate social identity. By converging on in-group preferences (and diverging on out-group preferences), people can signal group affiliation (Berger and Heath 2007).

Because uniqueness and identity-signaling are studied independently, however, little is known about how people integrate these motives through consumer choice. Are there systematic ways in which people signal identity while still differentiating themselves? Optimal Distinctiveness (Brewer 1991) suggests that by activating social identities, people simultaneously meet needs for assimilation (by identification with an in-group) and differentiation (by comparisons to out-groups). People do not behave identically to in-group members, however, and thus we argue the need for distinctiveness continues at the intra-group level.

In particular, we focus on how choice at multiple product levels may allow consumers to satisfy both motives simultaneously. Consumers may select the same brand as their in-group, for example, but pick a slightly different product. Most research has taken a one-dimensional view of similarity and differentiation: people either select the same product as another person, or a different one. Real choice, however, is more nuanced and we explicitly allow for this. We argue that while consumers generally conform to in-group members on one level to effectively communicate social identity, they often simultaneously diverge at another level allowing them to also feel unique.

Experiments 1 and 2 provided a preliminary investigation of how consumers satisfy these different motives through choice. We asked people to identify an in-group and, across five consumer domains (e.g. shoes), to list two brands: one that was strongly associated with their in-group (Brand A), and one that was also liked by the group, but was a weaker signal of group identity (Brand B). They were next given information about the preferences of their in-group and asked to choose among four options. Specifically, they were told to imagine that out of 100 group members, 60 preferred Product 1 from Brand A, 17 preferred Product 2 from Brand A, 17 preferred Product 3 from Brand B, and 6 preferred Product 4 from Brand B. Thus, there was a majority (Product 1 and 3) and minority (Product 2 and 4) option from both a brand that would signal group identity, and a brand that would not. Participants also completed the Consumer Need for Uniqueness scale (CNFU; Tian et al. 2001).

As predicted, we found that people conformed on markers of group membership but differentiated within their group. At the brand level, people tended to choose brands that were more strongly associated with their in-group (i.e., Brand A). At the product level, however, people with higher CNFU strategically chose the less popular product from that brand (i.e., Product 2 from Brand A).

In Experiment 3, we varied the identity of the reference group by asking half of participants to list an in-group and half to list an out-group (the rest of the study was similar to Experiments 1 and 2). Consistent with an identity-signaling perspective, at the brand level, participants only tended to choose brands linked to their reference group when that group was their in-group, and this was mediated by their desire to signal that identity to others. People who had a greater desire to be associated with their reference group tended to choose options from brands linked to that group. At the product level, on the other hand, we again found that choice was driven by individual needs for differentiation. Participants with higher CNFU tended to select the minority option from the brand associated with their in-group.

Rather than measuring individual differences, Experiment 4 directly manipulated uniqueness-seeking with an image exposure task that primed half of participants with uniqueness (adapted from Maimaran and Wheeler 2008). They then completed the same choice task as in the prior studies. As predicted, uniqueness priming did not affect choices at the brand level—this was again driven by how much they wanted to be associated with that group. Instead, the uniqueness prime impacted product choice. Among participants who had conformed to the in-group at the brand level, those primed with uniqueness were more likely to select differentiating options at the product level.

Overall, these results provide insight into how people integrate identity-signaling and uniqueness motives through consumer choice. Importantly, these motives need not act in competition; by strategically conforming on one level while differentiating on another, people can effectively communicate social identity while also being unique.

References

Berger, Jonah and Chip Heath (2007) "Where Consumers Diverge from Others: Identity Signaling and Product Domains," *Journal of Consumer Research*, 34 (2), 121-34.

Brewer, Marilynn B. (1991), "The Social Self: On Being the Same and Different at the Same Time," *Personality and Social Psychology Bulletin*, 17 (5), 475-82.

Maimaran, Michal and S. Christian Wheeler (2008), "Circles, Squares, and Choice: The Effect of Shape Arrays on Uniqueness and Variety Seeking," *Journal of Marketing Research*, 45 (6), 731-40.

Snyder, Charles R. and Harold L. Fromkin (1980), *Uniqueness: The Human Pursuit of Difference*, New York: Plenum.

Tian, Kelly T., William O. Bearden, and Gary L. Hunter (2001), "Consumers' Need for Uniqueness: Scale Development and Validation," *Journal of Consumer Research*, 28 (1), 50-66.

"Why Do Products Become Unpopular? Adoption Velocity and the Death of Cultural Tastes"

Jonah Berger, Wharton School of Business, USA
Gaël Le Mens, Stanford University, USA

Products become unpopular and styles fall out of favor. But while researchers have long been interested in why cultural tastes and practices catch on and become popular, much less attention has been given to why these items are abandoned. Why do particular music artists become unpopular or popular names drop out of the cultural repertoire? More broadly, when and why do cultural tastes and practices die out?

We suggest that tastes which quickly increase in popularity die faster. In addition to functional benefits, the decision to adopt a particular product or cultural taste often depends on symbolic meaning, or what consuming the item communicates about the user. People may avoid products that are too popular, for example, or linked to dissociative reference groups) because of what that consumption would signal about them. Similarly, we argue that potential adopters may avoid items that catch on quickly because of symbolic concerns. Things not only have a particular level of popularity, but vary in how quickly that popularity has changed over time. Two styles may have each been adopted by 1000 people last year, for example, but one may have slowly increased in popularity (900 adopters the prior year) while the other shot up in quickly (100 adopters the prior year). We argue that high rates of change may lead items to die out or drop out of the cultural repertoire. Fads are often perceived negatively, and if people think that sharply increasing items will be short lived, they may avoid such items to avoid doing something that may later be seen as a flash in the pan. We test this possibility using both experimental and historical data. In particular, we focus our analysis on first names. There relatively little influence of technology or commercial effort on name choice, making it easier to tease out the effect of social dynamics. Further, data is available on the popularity of names over time, making it possible to examine the effect of popularity dynamics on cultural abandonment.

Study 1 used over 100 years of data on the number of children born each year with different names (this includes over 10,000 names). We use survival analyses (hazard modeling) to examine how adoption velocity and various control factors (e.g., time or how long a name has been around, novelty, and popularity) influence the hazard of abandonment, or likelihood that the name will no longer be used. Results demonstrate a strong positive relationship between adoption velocity and abandonment: even when controls are included, names that experience sharper increases in popularity tend to die faster. This result persists across a host of robustness checks. The effect is not simply driven by a few names that come and go very quickly (e.g., due to brief attention associated with passing celebrities). Rather, even non-extreme rates of adoption have a positive effect on the death rate. The result also holds using alternate strategies to control for time, various thresholds for defining abandonment, and data from both the United States and France, which speaks to the generalizability of the effect.

To strengthen our suggestion that adoption velocity is driving cultural abandonment, Study 2 examined this relationship at the individual level. Cultural abandonment is a collective outcome, but relies on the aggregation of individual behavior. If sharper increases in adoption really drive abandonment at the aggregate level, they should also have detrimental effects on attitudes at the individual level. To test this possibility, we gave expecting parents a sample of first names and asked them how likely they would be to give each to their child. We then computed the actual adoption velocity for each name, along with its popularity. As expected, expecting parents were more hesitant to adopt names that had sharply increased. (This persisted controlling for recent and cumulative popularity of the names).

We also investigated the mechanism behind the observed effects. We suggested that people avoid identity relevant items which spike in popularity because they do not want to adopt things that may be short lived fads. To test this possibility, we also had participants rate their perception of whether each name was a fad. As predicted, fad perceptions mediated the effect of adoption velocity on preferences. Names which were adopted more quickly were seen as more likely to be short lived fads, which decreased future parents' likelihood of adopting them.

Overall, these findings shed light on how identity and the meaning of consumption contribute to the abandonment of cultural tastes.

Special Session Summary

Choices, Judgments, and Temperature: From Visceral States to Metaphors

Hee-Kyung Ahn, University of Toronto, Canada

SESSION OVERVIEW

Session Objective: Temperature and weather are all around us, quite literally. Furthermore, temperature and weather not only permeate our atmosphere, constantly affecting our visceral states of warmth and coldness, but they metaphorically permeate our language. People, products, and ideas can all be "hot" or "cold." Given this ubiquity, it is perhaps surprising that relatively little research has systematically examined the influence of temperature on choice and judgment. This special session features current research programs that offer new perspectives on how temperature impacts judgment and choice, shed insight into new psychological processes that underlie these effects, and provide an integrative platform to discuss new research directions.

Overview: Past research on temperature in consumer behavior and social psychology demonstrated that ambient (physical) temperature can affect mood, which in turn can influence behavior (Anderson, 1989; Cunningham, 1979; Howarth & Hoffman, 1984; Parker & Tavassoli, 2000). However, recent research suggests that temperature can influence judgments and choices directly, without the person's awareness or the mediational role of incidental mood (Williams & Bargh 2008; Zhong & Leonardelli 2008). Three papers in this session attempt to investigate how temperature and its metaphoric associates can affect consumer choices and judgments, thereby expanding on recent research in qualitatively distinct ways. The present papers show how temperature can shift the perceived likelihood of future events; change preferences for impulsive, emotionally-oriented (versus more cognitive or reasoned) products; and alter one's product replacement intentions. In doing so, relevant psychological accounts are discussed.

Papers: Temperature permeates human experience, both by prompting visceral states (i.e., feeling hot or cold) and by providing useful metaphors (e.g., a "cold, calculated" decision vs. a "hot, impulsive" temper). All three papers propose that temperature—actually experienced or conceptually primed—can affect judgments and choices. Critcher and Risen suggest that temperature's influence on one's visceral states can influence the likelihood judgments of future events associated with that state (e.g., feeling hot and believing in global warming) due to visceral fit—a match between one's present visceral state and a future state of the world that would cause that visceral state. Furthermore, they demonstrate that merely priming the concepts of "warmth" did not have analogous effects. In the second paper, Ahn, Soman, and Mazar examine how variations in both physical and primed temperature can lead to different decisions due to temperature's metaphoric relation to two different psychological states (i.e., impulsive=hot, calculated=cold). Across a series of studies they show that people exposed to literal or conceptual (primed) heat are more likely to be impatient and impulsive in their judgments and decision making, whereas coldness elicits a relatively more distanced and rational approach. In the third paper, Chandler, Szczurek, and Schwarz demonstrate that when consumers are primed to think of products in anthropomorphic terms, temperature metaphors can heavily influence consumers' product replacement intentions. People feel "warmth" for other humans, but do people feel similar "warmth" for inanimate products? When first led to anthropomorphize their cars, people primed to view their car's appearance in "warm" (versus "cold") terms stated their intention not to replace their cars, regardless of its current quality.

Contribution and Likely Audience: These papers apply novel perspectives in understanding the relationship between temperature and judgment and decision making. Critcher and Risen's notion of visceral fit; Ahn et al.'s dual links between temperature concepts and mental states; and Chandler et al.'s anthropomorphic approach to consumer behavior, all reflect new approaches that both account for the findings presented here and can be used to generate a host of new hypotheses relevant to consumer behavior. Furthermore, differences between these papers also raise new questions of interest in themselves. For example, Critcher and Risen found that visceral states, but not related conceptual primes, influenced judgment. In contrast, Ahn et al. found their effects both by influencing actual visceral states and by merely priming related concepts. This discrepancy raises a heretofore underexplored topic in this literature that is crucial for predicting when these documented effects will emerge: Under what conditions can merely priming visceral states, as opposed to experiencing the visceral states, yield (dis)similar consequences on consumers' judgments and choices? Finally, Chandler et al. show that how temperature metaphors influence product evaluations depends on how much consumer have anthropomorphized the target product. This suggests an important boundary condition on these effects. Researchers and practitioners must be sensitive to how consumers construe a target consumer product to understand whether and how temperature will influence judgments of it. All papers include multiple completed studies that have not been presented at ACR before. The session is structured in an interdisciplinary manner with behavioral decision research and social psychology as backgrounds, and should appeal to researchers interested in consumer information processing and judgment and decision making more broadly.

EXTENDED ABSTRACTS

"The Influence of Visceral States on Forecasts of Future Events"

Clayton R. Critcher, Cornell University, USA
Jane L. Risen, University of Chicago, USA

Should one stock up on water in order to weather a future water shortage? Is it wise to invest in a more efficient cooling system for one's house in anticipation of global warming?

The answers to these and related questions require one to look into the future and make forecasts about the likelihood of different future states. Desertification is a growing problem, and residents of many communities must decide whether the trend is serious enough that they should take steps to preemptively avert disaster. The release and success of Al Gore's An Inconvenient Truth made the public bluntly aware of the problems associated with global warming, but skepticism still abounds about whether global warming is a veritable concern, or "just a theory."

In looking to the future to answer these questions, one would think (or hope) that people would look to experts to assess the likelihood that these consumer-impactful states would befall us. Although the dissemination of scientific knowledge no doubt informs some people, we propose that one's current visceral states may play a surprising role in guiding belief in the likelihood of these future possibilities.

Past psychological research has found that visceral states (e.g., thirst, warmth, hunger) can influence judgments by one of three pathways. First, experiencing a visceral state can be an indirect means to prime related concepts (Williams & Bargh, 2008). Second, the experience of a visceral state can moderate the effect of a conceptual prime. For example, a thirst prime only leads people to drink more when they are experiencing the visceral state of thirst (Strahan, Spencer, & Zanna, 2002, 2005). Finally, the experience of a visceral state can help one appreciate the power of a visceral state. For example, Nordgren, van der Pligt, and van Harreveld (2007) found that people were more willing to excuse the offensive behavior of a fatigued parent when the participants were fatigued themselves, presumably because they could better understand how fatigue could lead one to behave uncharacteristically.

We propose a fourth possibility, that when there is a visceral match between one's current visceral state and the visceral state that one would experience if a future state occurred, people believe it is more likely that these future states will occur. Four studies examine this hypothesis by testing whether those who experience a visceral state—warmth or thirst—are more likely to predict that there is convincing evidence in support of related phenomena—global warming or future water shortages, respectively.

Study 1 was conducted outdoors. Participants expressed their attitudes on a number of political and policy-related issues. One of the items related to global warming. The question wording was adopted from a recent CNN poll. Participants indicated to what extent participants believed that global warming was "a proven fact" or "a theory that has yet to be proven." While participants answered these questions, the experimenter recorded the outdoor temperature. Belief that global warming was a proven reality was significantly predicted by the outdoor temperature $ß=.24$, $t(63)=2.04$, $p=.05$.

Of course, it is possible that the participants were simply inappropriately inferring a long-term weather pattern from the temperature at that specific moment, and that their experience of warmth was not important. To rule out this explanation, we moved Study 2 indoors, such that we could manipulate participants' experience of warmth without providing any information about the actual weather. We found that those participants randomly assigned to state their belief in global warming in a 27°C (81°F) room expressed greater belief in global warming than did those who stated their belief in a 23°C (73°F) room.

We do not claim that our effects emerge because visceral states merely conceptually activate a related visceral state concept (e.g., Williams & Bargh, 2008), which then influences one's judgments. In other words, we do not believe that our effects are mediated by the conceptual activation of the concept warmth. To more conclusively rule out conceptual activation as a mediator of our effects in Study 3, we primed some participants conceptually with "warmth", using a sentence-unscrambling task. We found that this priming task did lead participants to complete incomplete letter strings with warmth-related words (confirming that the concept of warmth was indeed primed), but belief in global warming was unaffected.

In a final study, we moved to a new visceral state—thirst—and a new judgment—belief that the American Southwest would soon hit "peak water," which would lead to water shortages in the region. Participants were randomly assigned to a condition in which they were made thirsty by eating pretzels (visceral condition), primed subliminally with the concept thirst (prime condition), or neither (control condition). Then participants watched a video explaining the debate over whether the American Southwest would soon reach "peak water." A word-completion task found that those in the visceral and prime condition, compared to those in the control, had thirst-related concepts conceptually active. But only participants in the visceral condition actually became more convinced after watching the video that peak water would soon be reached.

These studies reflect a theoretically novel pathway by which visceral states can influence judgment. Just as the conceptual accessibility of a statement may lead it to be processed with enhanced conceptual fluency, leading to an inference of validity (see Schwarz, Sanna, Skurnik, & Yoon, 2007), we believe that the visceral fit between one's experience and a considered state of the world may lead it to be simulated with enhanced "visceral fluency," leading to a similar inference of validity (see Cesario & Higgins, 2008, for a similar "fit" argument).

Although many psychological biases are studied in contexts in which people are led astray, we have intentionally studied visceral fit in contexts in which these "biases" actually pushed people toward expert-endorsed opinions. Thus, although it is non-normative to rely on visceral states in the ways demonstrated here, these effects are not inherently helpful or harmful. Even though visceral fit may at times lead participants' judgments astray, the principle can also be harnessed to enhance the power of expert-endorsed communication.

"Being Hot or Being Cold: The Influence of Temperature on Judgment and Choice"

Hee-Kyung Ahn, University of Toronto, Canada
Nina Mazar, University of Toronto, Canada
Dilip Soman, University of Toronto, Canada

Temperature is a very familiar concept to most consumers. It not only describes our physiological degree of comfort, but it also metaphorically permeates our language. People, products, and ideas can all be "hot" or "cold." For instance, temperature-related words such as "hot" and "cold" are often used to describe impulsive and calculated behaviors, respectively. In a similar vein, our languages are replete with expressions such as "he has a hot temper," "what a cold, unfeeling person she was," and "the media, meanwhile, has blown hot and cold on the affair." In these expressions, "hot" and "cold" are interpreted through metaphoric meanings rather than as direct thermal concepts. Furthermore, even though relatively little research has systematically examined the influence of temperature on choice and judgment, psychologists as well as behavioral decision researchers often use the thermal concept "hot," (vs. "cold") to describe impulsive behaviors metaphorically (Loewenstein 1996; Metcalf and Mischel 1999; Peters et al. 2005). These metaphoric associations of thermal concepts raise the question as to whether temperature and psychological states are related to each other, and if so, how.

In this research, we examine three research questions; (1) what is the effect of temperature on choice and judgment, especially in the domain of impulsive behaviors? (2) Do these effects of temperature persist when the concept of temperature is primed rather than experienced? (3) What could be a theoretical approach that explains these effects?

To address these questions, we have conducted a series of field and laboratory experiments and have found support for a relationship between temperature and impulsivity. We operationalize impulsive behaviors by measuring a) willingness to pay [WTP] for products, b) preferences for a smaller–sooner [SS] reward over a larger–later [LL] one, c) preferences for a short term bank deposit over long term bank deposit, d) preferences for a risky gamble over a less risky gamble, and e) the errors made in answering a quiz where the intuitive answer is different from the calculated one. Across five studies, we demonstrate that the actual experiences of ambient temperature trigger decision outcomes in line with the metaphoric association between temperature and impulsivity. When people are hot, they become more impulsive than when they are cold. Moreover, these temperature effects persist when the concept of temperature is primed by temperature-related words and pictures.

In the pilot (field) study, we find evidence that temperature can influence participants' WTP judgments. WTP measures for a number of product categories were significantly higher when measured in a hot spa room than in a cold spa room. To examine whether the effect of this metaphoric link persists in the extreme temperature condition, we conducted study 1 at a spa adding one more experimental condition (i.e., an extremely hot spa room). Study 1 supported the notion that the link between temperature and impulsivity may not persist in extremely hot temperatures. We also obtained evidence to support the influence of temperature on choices. In the subsequent studies, we replicated the effects of temperature on WTP judgments and choices by using temperature primes such as slideshows of seasonal pictures (study 2) and scrambled sentence tasks (study 3). In addition, we tested the metaphorical link between hotness and impulsivity using various concepts of impulsivity including impatience (study 1, 2, and 3), risk taking (study 2), and decision time (study 4). In sum, participants in the hot (vs. cold) condition indicated a higher WTP for target products and were more likely to choose relatively impulsive options such as a 1-year bank term deposit, a risky gamble, a smaller but sooner [SS] reward, and an incorrect answer to the target problem.

Finally, we manipulate temperature by using hot and cold therapeutic packs to examine whether the simultaneous experiences (activations) of hot and cold temperatures wipe out the temperature association effect. We developed four conditions including hot packs only, cold packs only, one hot/one cold pack, and no pack (control) conditions. The results of study 4 revealed that the simultaneous experiences of hot and cold temperatures result in a similar pattern of judgments and choices as the control condition, in which temperature was not manipulated. The findings rule out a couple of alternative explanations; studies show that mood and arousal do not explain the effects of temperature on WTP and choice.

We suggest that the theories of embodied cognition provide an explanation for these findings. This theory suggests that processing of abstract concepts involves embodiment; where embodiment refers both to actual bodily states and simulations of experience in the brain's modality-specific systems for perception, action, and introspection (Barsalou 1999; Lakoff and Johnson 1999; Neidenthal et al. 2005). For example, a recent study by Zhong and Leonardelli (2008) suggests that the linguistic coupling between social isolation and coldness may reflect a person's predisposition to use concepts that are based on bodily experience (e.g., coldness) to describe complex concepts such as social rejection. Consistent with this view, the current findings demonstrate that not only actual experiences of temperature, but also temperature primes which simulate experience can influence subsequent choice and judgment.

While recent work on the effect of temperature has focused on actual temperature and its direct consequences (mood, cognition, and behaviors), our findings take this insight a step further by demonstrating that the metaphoric link between temperature concepts (temperature primes as well as actual temperature) and impulsivity can influence judgments and choices. This work demonstrates the robustness of temperature effects on judgment and choice by examining the effect across various constructs of impulsivity, product categories, and dependent variables. This research implies that the activation of the hot-impulsivity link may influence various aspects of consumer behavior varying from risk taking to excessive reliance on intuition in addition to the delay of gratification (Ainslie 1975; Metcalfe and Mischel 1999). The results also have practical implications for packaging, advertising, merchandising and pricing; as well as for public policy and awareness.

"Hot Wheels, Warm Hearts: The Effect of Temperature Metaphors on Product Replacement Intentions"

Jesse Chandler, University of Michigan, USA
Lauren Szczurek, Stanford University, USA
Norbert Schwarz, University of Michigan, USA

Judgments of interpersonal warmth produce striking and consistent differences in the perception of others. Information signaling warmth can come from many sources, including meaning laden personality descriptions (Asch, 1946), irrelevant semantic primes (Scholer & Higgins, 2008) and ambient temperature cues (Zhong & Leonardelli 2008). Despite the varied sources of temperature information, its influence is quite specific and theory-driven. Generally speaking, people described as "warm" are perceived more positively. However, the influence of temperature metaphors cannot be explained as a simple halo effect–connotations of warmth primarily influence evaluations of interpersonal characteristics and can even reduce the likelihood that some positive traits, such as strength and persistence, come to mind (Asch, 1946). Moreover, the evaluative consequences of temperature metaphors depend on other accessible information about the target such as co-occurring personality traits; under different circumstances "cold" can mean either aloof or ruthless (Asch, 1946). Together, these findings suggest that that temperature is integrated with other social knowledge to make specific inferences about the target of judgment rather than simply promoting a diffuse positive feeling.

The meaning of metaphorical warmth may depend on the domain of judgment. Outside of the social realm, metaphorical connotations of warmth and cold may not matter, or may carry different meanings entirely: connotations of warmth differ when the target of judgment is a close friend or a refrigerator. However, what belongs within the social realm is itself ambiguous, and sometimes people treat objects as if they are alive (for a review see Epley, Waytz & Cacioppo, 2007). For example, people are less willing to replace anthropomorphized objects (Chandler & Schwarz, 2008), prefer anthropomorphized objects that display prosocial cues (smiling; Aggarwal & McGill, 2007) and spontaneously apply social knowledge structures when describing or interacting with objects (Heider & Simmel, 1944; Nass & Moon, 2000). The influence of temperature metaphors on the perception of products may likewise mirror the influence of temperature metaphors on person perception when people think about objects in anthropomorphic terms. To test this hypothesis, we examine whether i) connotations of warmth and cold influence people's intentions to replace their car and ii) whether this influence depends upon the accessibility of anthropomorphic beliefs.

Participants were recruited for an online experiment about their cars. To manipulate the warm or cold connotations of the car, participants selected the color that most closely resembled their car's color from a matrix of nine colored squares and remembered the color's label as a part of a "memory task". Depending on condition, the five most common car colors were labeled with "*warm*" (e.g. "summer blue") or "*cold*" (e.g. "blizzard blue") names. Thus, both warm and cold concepts were equally accessible to all, but only one was applicable to judgments about their car. All participants saw a mixture of "warm" and "cold" color names along with four less common colors given distracter labels (e.g. "canary yellow").

Next, participants were randomly assigned to rate their car along 5 scales anchored with adjectives that implied either *psychological* (e.g. "reserved" to "enthusiastic") or *physical* features (e.g. "quiet" to "loud"); a *control* group did not provide ratings. Participants then described their car in their own words, indicated their desire to replace their car, and reported the name assigned to the color of their car (thus completing the memory task). These manipulations resulted in a 2 (warm vs. cold color labels) x 3 (psychological vs. physical features vs. control)-factorial between-participants design in which the car's temperature was purely symbolic (stripped of the physical sensation of warmth/cold), arbitrary (not dependant on the actual color of the car), and randomly assigned.

Replicating previous research, we find that participants who described their car negatively were more willing to replace it, except when psychological features of the car were accessible (Chandler & Schwarz, 2008). Although participants were more willing to replace poor quality than high quality cars in the physical feature and control conditions, this relationship vanished in the psychological feature (anthropomorphization) condition: A desire to keep their current cars was uniformly high for this group. We further find that people were particularly unwilling to replace anthropomorphized cars when their color had been associated with warm rather than cold labels. In contrast, color labels did not influence participants' replacement willingness in the physical features and control conditions.

Other experiments extend this logic by examining other contexts in which metaphorical connotations of warmth and cold influenced preferences for products. For example, we find that consumers' preferences for metaphorically warm and cold objects depend upon such products' intended use. Consumers rated notebooks with warm color names (e.g. "summer sky") as more desirable after being asked about personal uses for notebooks, and notebooks with cold color names (e.g. "blizzard blue") as more desirable after being asked about school uses for notebooks.

Taken together, these findings indicate that warm and cold metaphorical connotations influence how consumers perceive objects, but that the consequences of these connotations on judgment differ depending on both the category to which the object is assigned and its function. This line of research identifies important boundary conditions of the effects of warm and cold connotations, and has implications for how we portray objects that are imbued with agentic qualities or have social uses.

REFERENCES

Aggarwal, P. and A. L. McGill (2007), "Is that Car Smiling at Me? Schema Congruity as a Basis tor Evaluating Anthropomophized Products," *Journal of Consumer Research*, 34, 468-479.

Ainslie, G. (1975), "Specious Reward: A Behavioral Theory of Impulsiveness and Impulse Control," *Psychological Bulletin*, 82 (4), 463-495.

Anderson, C. A. (1989), "Temperature and Aggression: Ubiquitous Effects of Heat on Occurrence of Human Violence. *Psychological Bulletin*, 106 (1), 74-96.

Asch, S. E. (1946), "Forming Impressions of Personality," *Journal of Abnormal and Social Psychology*, 41, 258-290.

Barsalou, L. W. (1999), "Perceptual Symbol Systems," *Behavioral and Brain Sciences*, 22 (August), 577-660.

Cesario, J. and E. T. Higgins (2008), "Making Message Recipients 'Feel Right': How Nonverbal Cues Can Increase Persuasion. *Psychological Science*, 19, 415-420.

Chandler, J. and N. Schwarz (Feb, 2008), "Looking on the Byte Side of Life: The Cognitive and Emotional Consequences of Thinking of Computers as Alive," Poster presented at the Society for Personality and Social Psychology Annual Convention, Albuquerque, NM

Cunningham, M. R. (1979), "Weather, Mood, and Helping Behavior: Quasi-Experiments with the Sunshine Samaritan," *Journal of Personality and Social Psychology*, 37 (11), 1947-956.

Epley, N., A. Waytz, and J. T. Cacioppo (2007), "On Seeing Human: a Three-Factor Theory of Anthropomorphism," *Psychological Review*, 114, 864–886.

Heider, F. and M. Simmel (1944), "An Experimental Study of Apparent Behavior," *American Journal of Psychology*, 57, 243–249.

Howarth, E. and M. S. Hoffman (1984), "A Multidimensional Approach to the Relationship Between Mood and Weather," *British Journal of Psychology*, 75 (1), 15-23.

Lakoff, G. and M. Johnson (1999), *Philosophy in the Flesh: The Embodied Mind and Its Challenge to Western Thought*, New York: Basic Books.

Loewenstein, G. (1996), "Out of Control: Visceral Influences on Behavior," *Organizational Behavior and Human Decision Processes*, 65 (3), 272-92.

Metcalfe, J. and W. Mischel (1999), "A Hot/cool-System Analysis of Delay of Gratification: Dynamics of Willpower," *Psychological Review*, 106 (1), 3-19.

Nass, C. and Y. Moon (2000), "Machines and Mindlessness: Social Responses to Computers," *Journal of Social Issues*, 56, 81-103.

Neidenthal, P. M., L. W. Barsalou, P. Winkielman, S. Krauth-Gruber, and F. Ric (2005), "Embodiment in Attitudes, Social Perception, and Emotion," *Personality and Social Psychology Review*, 9 (3), 184-211.

Nordgren, L. F., J. van der Pligt, and F. van Harreveld (2007), "Evaluating Eve: Visceral States Influence the Evaluation of Impulsive Behavior," *Journal of Personality and Social Psychology*, 93, 75-84.

Parker, P. M. and N. T. Tavassoli (2000), "Homeostasis and Consumer Behavior Across Cultures," *International Journal of Research in Marketing*, 17, 33-53.

Peters, E., D. Vastfjall, T. Garling, and P. Slovic (2006), "Affect and Decision Making: A Hot Topic," *Journal of Behavioral Decision Making*, 19, 79-85.

Scholer, A. and E. T. Higgins (2008), "People as Resources: Exploring the Functionality of Warm and Cold," *European Journal of Social Psychology*, 38, 1111-1120.

Schwarz, N., L. J. Sanna, I. Skurnik, and C. Yoon (2007), "Metacognitive Experiences and the Intricacies of Setting People Straight: Implications for Debiasing and Public Information Campaigns," *Advances in Experimental Social Psychology*, 39, 127-161.

Strahan, E. J., S. J. Spencer, and M. P. Zanna (2002), "Subliminal Priming and Persuasion: Striking While the Iron Is Hot," *Journal of Experimental Social Psychology*, 38, 556-568.

Strahan, E. J., S. J. Spencer, and M. P. Zanna (2005), "Subliminal Priming and Persuasion: How Motivation Affects the Activation of Goals and the Persuasiveness of Messages," in F. R. Kardes, P. M. Herr, & J. Nantel (Eds.), *Applying Social Cognition to Consumer-Focused Strategy*, Mahwah, New Jersey: Lawrence Erlbaum Associates, 267-281.

Williams, L. E. and J. A. Bargh (2008), "Experiencing Physical Warmth Promotes Interpersonal Warmth," *Science*, 322, 606-607.

Zhong, C. and G. Leonardelli (2008), "Cold and Lonely: Does Social Exclusion Literally Feel Cold?" *Psychological Science*, 19, 838-842.

SPECIAL SESSION SUMMARY

Having It All: Marketplace Negotiations of Feminism and Women's Roles

Leah Carter, York University, Canada

SESSION OVERVIEW

Traditional feminist discourse challenged social structures and cultural discourses associated with the patriarchal domination of women (cf. Hollows 2000). The marketplace was identified as a negative capitalistic structure and the media was perceived as a vehicle for disseminating stereotypical, sexist portrayals of women (Linder 2004). As a result, feminists and marketing scholars have been slow to bridge marketing and feminism (cf. Catterall, Maclaran and Stevens 2000). In recent years, researchers have begun to address the positive role of the market for feminism and to challenge traditional thought (e.g., Scott 2005, Catterall, Maclaran and Stevens 2000). However, researchers have not studied the marketplace interplay between feminist discourses, consumers' feminist perceptions, and the construction of feminine identities.

One popular feminist discourse of women's identity construction focuses on the myth of "having it all" (Bordo 1989, Haussegger 2005). This idealized discourse centers on the belief that women can successfully fulfill diverse roles simultaneously: mother, wife, professional, friend, consumer, and so on, and is often represented in the media. However, "having it all" juxtaposes diverse discourses and roles of women (i.e., professional role/capitalistic discourse; mother role/nurturer discourse), creating a tension-filled, multi-discursive environment for identity work. The proposed session frames the consumption of female-targeted media as a space for negotiating the complexities of modern feminist and cultural discourses through the characters or representations of women who embody various roles and identities. By so doing, the media acts as a mirror in which women reflexively analyze and incorporate or reject cultural material into their identity and beliefs (Schroeder and Zwick 2004).

The proposed session addresses the question of how women interact with the media to identify feminist discourses and construct modern feminist beliefs and identities. The objectives of the proposed session are therefore to: (1) demonstrate responses of women to female-targeted media, (2) discuss the salient discourses in female-targeted media and characters, (3) examine the relationship between market-mediated discourses and individual notions of feminism, and (4) analyze the effects of media incorporation in the behavior, attitudes, and lifestyles of women.

To address the session objectives, the researchers demonstrate how women analyze and incorporate elements of market-mediated discourses to create personalized, multi-dimensional feminist beliefs and identities. First, Linda Tuncay discusses the ideals of femininity women create in response to advertised depictions of women, interweaving authenticity and feminist discourses. Leah Carter then explores the relationship between feminism and romance, analyzing how women construct practical feminisms of romance through consumption of "chick flicks.' Finally, Hope Jensen Schau and Kate Thompson show how the Twilight brand community is used as a marketplace tool for negotiating feminist ideas and roles based on the liminality of represented discourses. In each of these contexts, women encounter multiple discourses in the media representations of women and resolve the discursive and role tensions by active engagement with the material and identity construction.

We anticipate discussant Pauline Maclaran will encourage audience participation and direct the discussion of session themes utilizing her understanding of consumer culture and feminist literatures. We also anticipate the broad appeal of this session among consumer culture researchers as we address the popularity of female-targeted media consumption, explore manifestations and consumption of market-mediated discourses to resolve role and discourse tensions from "having it all", and investigate the identity work of the marginalized female culture in marketing research (Bristor and Fischer 1993; Ozanne and Stern 1993).

EXTENDED ABSTRACTS

"Discourses of Femininity in Advertising among Gen X Women"

Linda Tuncay, Loyola University of Chicago, USA

Much of gender research in the past followed the feminist critique tradition and sought to highlight the prevalence of gender stereotypes and sexist portrayals of women in advertising, such as the homemaker or the sexualized woman (Linder 2004). This early research serves as an important foundation for subsequent scholarly research in this area. However, as Stern (1999) points out, it is important to explore the complexities of gender across individuals, not conceptualizing women as a homogeneous group that is innately different from men.

In this vein, this study explores Gen X women's conceptualizations of femininity within the context of advertising. Gender is an important factor in not only the way consumers construct meanings in their lives, but the way in which individuals interpret text such as advertising (Stern and Holbrook 1994). Due to the fact that individuals glean much information about gender from media, advertising serves as an important milieu in which to explore the complexities of femininity among women. Defining femininity can be difficult due to a number of factors which have altered the discourses of gender in today's American society. These include the increasing earning power of women as well as a greater variety of representations of women in the media. However, little past research actually explores what consumers, themselves, define as femininity and how these notions influence the way gendered ads are interpreted. Thus, the principal research questions for this study are, 1) What ideals of femininity are held by women? and 2) How do women interpret notions of femininity in advertising?

To explore these questions, a qualitative study of 19 Gen X women was conducted. Because notions of gender can be influenced by factors such as social class, education, race/ethnicity, age (e.g., see Beynon 2002), this study examines notions of femininity from the perspective of women falling into the Gen X cohort, who are largely college educated and living in the Midwest. In-depth, semi-structured interviews using ads as projective aids (McGrath, Sherry, Levy 1993) are employed to uncover meanings of femininity in advertising. A series of ads depicting various notions of femininity were selected from some of the top circulating lifestyle magazines for the Gen X female demographic, including Vogue, Glamour, Cosmopolitan, Oprah, and Parenting Magazine. Informants were asked open-ended "grand tour" questions (McCracken 1988), as well as questions specifically probing into their ideals of femininity and their interpretations' of the ads. This research mirrors a study conducted by Tuncay (2006) on men's conceptualizations of masculinity.

Three themes dominate women's ideals of femininity in this study: the Alpha Woman, the Classic Woman, and the Centered

Woman. The ideal of the Alpha Woman emerges when women discuss confidence, strength, independence, empowerment, and a "take charge" attitude as attributes which exemplify their ideal sense of femininity. The Classic Woman is another ideal that informants identify. Women often discuss the notion that elegance, class, sophistication, and grace go hand in hand with femininity. The third salient theme is that of the Centered Woman, who is happy, relaxed, and at peace with herself. Women often comment on the desire to be happy in one's own skin, and to be drawn to women depicted in ads in a relaxed, positive atmosphere, where the models are laughing or smiling. This last theme illuminates the way women make comparisons to models in ads. When women engage in social comparison to ads, they often feel the most appealing ads are ones that they could identify with (similar to some of the informants in a study by Hirschman and Thompson, 1997) and ones that present attainable standards. Informants reveal that they feel women in advertising should be authentic and accessible and even "flawed," "not perfect." Decidedly absent from the narratives of the informants is an ideal related to domesticity, or an "other-oriented" perspective (Bordo 1989). This is surprising given this theme has been widely discussed by past scholars as central to predominant discourses of femininity.

While the themes of femininity discussed above can be seen in various forms in past research, what is most telling is that women continue to use moral judgments as a distinct lens through which they interpret feminine ideals. For instance, while having an attractive appearance or being in shape is valued, women maintain certain boundaries of what is acceptable, particularly when it comes to sexual depictions. Lamb (2001, p.43) states, "Ideals of femininity ensure that girls will not be too sexual or too aggressive…" and that it is taboo to be sexual if it is not within the context of romantic love. In fact, several informants displayed high agency negative emotions (Fisher and Dubé 2005) such as anger and disgust when they viewed an ad which depicted very thin women in scantily clad clothing (see Bower 2001). They found the ads objectifying, annoying and even calling them "disturbing " and "repulsive," and rejecting any notion of comparison (e.g. Richins 1991). Thus, while being beautiful and sexy are discussed by women, the scantily clad models depicted in the ads are conceptualized as crossing the boundary of "normal" femininity by giving a performance that is not respectable. This notion of respectability (and morality) serves as a distinct lens through which many of the women interpret gender ideals (see discussion of respectability by Skeggs 1997). Images that cross these boundaries are met with extreme outward resistance.

One limitation of this study could be the subset of ads used in this study. Further research should seek to develop a more refined understanding of what gender means today among Gen X women, as well as how notions of gender are interpreted by consumers among other groups of women and using different methodologies.

"Critically Romantic: Negotiating Feminist and Romantic Discourses in the Marketplace"

Leah Carter, York University, Canada

Early feminist discourse centered on liberating women from oppressive patriarchal systems and discourses of power (Hollows 2000). The media, in particular, was criticized for shaping women into one-dimensional, passive consumers of "false consciousness" and hindering women from freeing their "true" and natural "wild woman within" (Embree 1970; Friedan 1963; Daly 1979). In order to liberate women and encourage "true" feminine identity construction, feminists advocated recognizing and resisting the influential power of patriarchal trappings disseminated in the marketplace (Embree 1970). Female identity construction was therefore placed outside the realm of the market and in direct opposition to perceived masculine-oriented structures and discourses of power.

Romanticism was also cast as a cultural discursive villain that promoted the female surrender to male domination (Beauvoir 1953; Firestone 1970; Millet 1970; Faludi 1992). Romantic relationships, ideals, and goals were believed to constrain women to the subordinate, dependent role of the traditional "house wife" and limited the development of one's "true" identity (Friedan 1963). Contemporary cultural critics and feminist writers frequently problematized the ubiquity of romantic discourses in modern entertainment television and cinematic outlets on the basis that the consumption of these story lines and narratives reinforces longstanding gender norms and power structures (Mulvey 1975; Mintz 2003). Alternative research suggested, however, that consumption of romantic novels provided a necessary, beneficial escape from women's roles and the associated stresses of everyday life (Radway 1984). Thus, though traditional feminist discourse emphasized a dualistic worldview that reinforced binaries of romanticism/agency, market/consumer authenticity, masculine/feminine, and constraints/emancipation, consumption of romantic narratives in the media appears to create a space for active negotiation and deconstruction of feminist and romantic discourses.

In this research, I address how individual consumers integrate and enact feminism and romanticism by analyzing female consumption of mass market-mediated discourses in "chick flicks." I argue that a more nuanced theorization of the traditional relationship between feminism, romanticism, and the representations of women in the media can be derived from investigating female identity politics at the intersection of practical feminisms (the discursive and practical ways in which women construct their feminist identities in their everyday social surroundings) and the consumption of contemporary media. By so doing, I aim to deconstruct the binary boundaries in feminist discourse between feminism and romanticism, romanticism and agency, and feminism and the marketplace.

The central research question is how women engage with market-mediated products to navigate feminist and romantic discourses and construct personal, modern feminist beliefs of romance. In order to address the research question, this research focuses on consumption of female-targeted movies and television shows (i.e., "chick flicks"). These media products are specifically created for and targeted to women and are thematically centered on romantic discourses from a female's perspective. Further, they generally depict women's struggles in contemporary romantic encounters as the protagonists navigate issues such as traditional versus modern gender roles in dating contexts, relationship discord, and personal identity within a relationship situation, with the goal of achieving the idealized "happy ending." The data consist of: (1) in-depth interviews with 10 women, ages 18-30, (2) online message boards and communities connected to female-targeted media products, and (3) participant observation field notes.

From the data, the "Critically Romantic" process emerges in which women engage with and negotiate market-mediated discourses of romanticism and feminism. The media disseminates a combination of feminist and romantic discourses to the mass population in its portrayal of female stereotypes: the homemaker, the promiscuous woman, the career woman, and so on. Women identified and interacted with these market-mediated discourses as embodied and enacted by the female characters. Acting as creative agents, the respondents reflected on the symbolic meanings associated with the represented stereotypes through the lens of internalized personalized discourses (religion, ethnicity, and so on) and life experiences. For example, finding "Mr. Right" was often described as a desired fantasy ideal promoted by the media and yet tempered by real-life romantic mishaps. Real life experiences acted as criteria for assessing the truth-value of the romantic and feminist discourses depicted. Respondents also highlighted the centrality of social interactions with other women during and after the media consumption experience in analyzing represented themes and representations. Women then constructed practical, modern romantic beliefs interweaving both romantic and feminist, fantasy and "reality" elements. These beliefs shaped feminine self-concepts, personal romantic ideals and goals, and consumption preferences. Based on their own practical feminism of romance, women selected and evaluated media products, indicating certain prototypes and romantic narratives as superior to, or more resonant than, other media offerings. Respondents often cited "Sex and the City" as an exemplar of the right mix of women's roles portrayed, and of romance and feminism. Other similar shows (e.g., "Lipstick Jungle"), however, failed to portray a resonant mixture of characters, themes, and discourses, and as such, failed to connect with the respondents.

The "Critically Romantic" process develops key theoretical insights for feminist and consumer research: (1) the permeability between cultural discourses and the marketplace, (2) the intertwining of traditionally disparate romantic and feminist discourses when represented in the media and consumed by women, (3) the necessity of the market as a fluid site of discursive construction and deconstruction, (4) the agentic nature of consumers in consuming mediated discourses and constructing a practical, working concept of feministic romance, (5) the social component of discourse negotiation, and (6) the deconstruction of historically and discursively reinforced dualities in individual discourse construction. By detailing the "Critically Romantic" process, I demonstrate the necessity of the marketplace and media in the construction of practical feminisms and the interconnectedness of feminism and romanticism enacted on the consumption level.

"Betwixt and Between: Liminality and Feminism in the Twilight Brand Community"

Hope Jensen Schau, University of Arizona, USA
Kate Thompson, University of Arizona, USA

Our research revolves around representation of, and collective consumption by, females engaged in the Twilight brand community. The Twilight saga is a series of novels aimed primarily at young adult, female readers. The saga revolves around a human, Bella, and her romance with a vampire, Edward. The title Twilight captures the liminality of the heroine. Like twilight is the liminal space between day and night, Bella is riddled with liminality: child and adult, mortal and immortal, love and hate, good and evil, independence and dependence, lover and friend, present and past, mother and child, spiritual and corporeal, and offense and defense. Importantly, girls and women deeply and collectively engage with the brand. Empirically, the Twilight consumer collective offers a unique female-centered incarnation of brand community and feminine-driven consumer engagement which contrasts with previous studies favoring male-dominated brand communities, with two notable exceptions: Martin, Schouten and McAlexander (2006) who investigate modes of femininity within the Harley-Davidson brand community and Schau, Muniz and Arnould (2009) who examine value creating practices across a set of brand communities including those that skew male, are gender balanced and skew female. We reveal the manner in which feminist discourses are collectively negotiated, intertwined and reconstituted in a female-dominated brand community (Gill 2007).

Our data consist of: the Twilight saga (composed of four official novels and an unauthorized draft novel), a feature film (with another film in production and two other films planned), literary and film criticism of the Twilight media products, naturalistic and participant observation in three online fan discussion forums, fan-created videos, email and chat interviews with forum participants and videographers, and face-to-face interviews with Twilight fans. Our data were iteratively collected and thematically coded and recoded following the hermeneutic tradition.

We find this brand community is, as anticipated, composed primarily of female members ranging in age from 8 to 65. Members use Twilight as a platform to negotiate feminism and socially prescribed female roles (Mulvey 1975): good girl, independent woman, lover, wife, and mother. Twilight offers fans a paradoxical interplay of feminist and anti-feminist discourses characteristic of post-feminist media culture (Friedberg 1993). Throughout the saga, the female self is deferred in favor of the primacy of good intentions toward humanity, highlighting the "problem of femininity" as a quintessential pathology when defined in patriarchic discourses (Moscucci 1990). As in previous research tackling the intersection and interaction of gender and the marketplace (cf., Catterall, Maclaran and Stevens 2000, Costa 2000, Dobscha and Ozanne 2000, Scott 2000), this paper explores gender expressions within a media brand and specifically within the realm of brand communities (Muniz and O'Guinn 2001).The brand community members are energized by Bella's haphazard navigation of disparate role expectations and her perpetual liminality. The coven of vampires Bella (human/food) joins suppress their predatory instinct and dietary imperatives, favoring compassion, reason and defensive combat, over aggression, apathy, bloodlust and hunger. Similarly, Bella navigates her expressed ideal of eternal commitment, which is tempered by Bella's reluctance to embrace marriage and the danger motherhood poses as a "newborn vampire." In essence, we find that it is precisely Bella's liminality and her quest for equality against almost insurmountable odds that make her a compelling heroine and rallying point for the community. At the conclusion of the saga, Bella is integral in conquering seemingly omnipotent foes through enacting a protective screen on the clan that, together with a clever plan put in place by her sister-in-law, proves a triumph of the feminine defensive over the masculine offensive tactics of the foes. Fans are quick to address this gendered strategy and use it toward negotiating their own social roles and toward understanding the post-feminist perspective (Johnson 2007).

The Twilight brand community walks the line of compromise and tradeoffs as the price of being a contemporary woman through collective discourse that focuses on maximizing complex social functions: maintaining familial loyalties while pursuing romantic love, asserting independence and reveling in dependence within romance and domesticity, asserting one's self while advancing the collective good, and balancing motherhood and professional ambition. The Twilight brand community provides a media based platform to think through the complexities of femininity and of the different incarnations of feminism. Because the liminality is never fully resolved, there is ample opportunity for engagement and for continued engagement. The fan discourse is supported by the Twilight narrative, which leaves room for fans to write themselves into the story and to locate resonating themes (Derecho 2006) to extend their brand engagement. In short, our data reveal that the liminalities are key attributes of fan engagement. Furthermore, the primarily female members of the brand community grapple with fundamental issues surrounding femininity, expected roles and modes of feminist resistance (Whelehan 1995). Interestingly, the fans' discussions map rather closely onto "third wave" feminism that recognizes and asserts multi-fold gender positions (Henry 2004).

While it would be easy to dismiss the Twilight phenomenon as yet another vampire tale or Harry Potter clone, our research demonstrates that Twilight is neither of these. The brand community actively negotiates multi-fold liminality and feminism through the Twilight saga. The brand serves as a vehicle to contemplate women's potential and place in the world.

REFERENCES

Beauvoir, Simone de (1953), *The Second Sex*, New York: Knopf.

Beynon, John (2002), *Masculinities and Culture*, Philadelphia: Open University Press.

Bordo, Susan (1989), "The Body and the Reproduction of Femininity: A Feminist Appropriation of Foucault," in *Gender/Body/Knowledge: Feminist Reconstructions of Being and Knowing*, Alison M. Jaggar and Susan Bordo (eds.), New Jersey: Rutgers University Press.

Bower, Amanda (2001), "Highly Attractive Models in Advertising and the Women Who Loathe Them: The Implications of Negative Affect for Spokesperson Effectiveness," *Journal of Advertising*, 3 (Fall), 51-63.

Bristor, Julia M. and Eileen Fischer (1993), "Feminist Thought: Implications for Consumer Research," *Journal of Consumer Research*, 19(4), 518-536.

Catterall, Miriam, Pauline MacLaran, and Lorna Stevens (2000), "Marketing and Feminism: An Evolving Relationship," in *Marketing and Feminism: Current Issues and Research*, Miriam Catterall, Pauline Maclaran, and Lorna Stevens (eds.), London: Routledge.

Costa, Janeen Arnold (2000), "Gender and Consumption in a Cultural Context," in *Marketing and Feminism: Current Issues and Research*, Miriam Catterall, Pauline Maclaran, and Lorna Stevens (eds.), London: Routledge.

Daly, Mary (1979), *Gyn/Ecology: The Metaethics of Radical Feminism*, London: Women's Press.

Derecho, Abigail (2006), "Different Approaches: Fan Fiction in Context," in *Fan Fiction and Fan Communities in the Age of the Internet*, Karen Hellekson and Kristina Busse (eds.), North Carolina: McFarland and Company, Inc.

Dobscha, Susan and Julie Ozanne (2000), "Marketing and the Divided Self: Healing the Nature/Woman Separation," in *Marketing and Feminism: Current Issues and Research*, Miriam Catterall, Pauline Maclaran, and Lorna Stevens (eds.), London: Routledge.

Embree, Alice (1970), "Media images I: Madison Avenue brainwashing-the facts," in *Sisterhood is Powerful*, R. Morgan (ed.), New York: Vintage.

Faludi, Susan (1992), *Backlash: The Undeclared War against Women*, London: Chatto & Windus.

Festinger, Leon (1954), "A Theory of Social Comparison Processes," *Human Relations*, 7 (May), 117-140.

Firestone, Shulamith (1970), *The Dialectic of Sex: The Case for Feminist Revolution*, New York: Morrow.

Fisher, Robert J. and Laurette Dubé (2005), "Gender Differences in Responses to Emotional Advertising: A Social Desirability Perspective," *Journal of Consumer Research*, (March), 850-858.

Friedan, Betty (1963), *The Feminine Mystique*, London: Gollanz.

Friedberg, Anne (1993), *Window Shopping: Cinema and the Postmodern*, Los Angeles: University of California Press.

Gill, Rosalind (2007), "Postfeminist Media Culture: Elements of a Sensibility," *European Journal of Cultural Studies*, 10 (2), 147-166.

Haussegger, Virginia (2005), *Wonder Woman: The Myth of Having it All*, Australia: Allen & Unwin.

Henry, Astrid (2004), *Not My Mother's Sister: Generational Conflict and Third-Wave Feminism*, Bloomington: Indiana University Press.

Hollows, Joanne (2000), *Feminism, Femininity and Popular Culture*, New York: Manchester University Press.

Johnson, Merri Lisa (2007), *Third Wave Feminism and Television: Jane Puts it in a Box*, London: IB Tauris.

Lamb, Sharon (2001), *The Secret Lives of Girls*, New York: Free Press.

Lindner, Katharina (2004), "Images of Women in General Interest and Fashion Magazine Advertisements from 1955 to 2002," *Sex Roles*, 51 (October), 409-421.

Martin, Diane, John Schouten, and James McAlexander (2006), "Claiming the Throttle: Multiple Femininities in a Hyper-Masculine Subculture," *Consumption, Markets & Culture*, 9 (3), 171-205.

McCracken, Grant (1988), *The Long Interview*, Newbury Park: Sage.

McGrath, Mary Ann, John F. Sherry, Jr. and Sidney J. Levy (1993), "Giving Voice to the Gift: The Use of Projective Techniques to Recover Lost Meanings," *Journal of Consumer Psychology*, 2 (2), 171-191.

Millet, Kate (1970), *Sexual Politics*, New York: Doubleday.

Mintz, Susannah B. (2003), "In a word, Baywatch," in *Catching a Wave: Reclaiming Feminism for the 21st Century*, Rory Dicket and Alison Piepmeier (eds.), Boston: Northeastern University Press.

Moscucci, Ornella (1990), *The Science of Woman: Gynaecology and Gender in England 1800-1929*, Cambridge: Press Syndicate of Cambridge Press.

Mulpuru, Sucharita (2008), "Benchmark 2008: The Web Purchasing Power of Gen X," www.forrester.com, Accessed February 19, 2009.

Mulvey, Laura (1975), "Visual Pleasure and Narrative Cinema," *Screen*, 16(3), 6-18.

Muniz, Albert M. Jr. and Thomas C. O'Guinn (2001), "Brand Community," *Journal of Consumer Research*, 27 (4), 412-432.

Ozanne, Julie L., and Barbara B. Stern (1993), "The Feminine Imagination and Social Change: Four Feminist Approaches to Social Problems," *Advances in Consumer Research*, 20(1), 35-35.

Radway, Janice (1984), *Reading the Romantic: Women, Patriarchy, and Popular Literature*, Chapel Hill: University of North Carolina Press.

Richins, Martha (1991), "Social Comparison and the Idealized Images of Advertising," *Journal of Consumer Research*, 18 (June), 71-83.

Schau, Hope Jensen, Albert M. Muñiz Jr. and Eric J. Arnould (2009), "How Brand Community Practices Create Value," *Journal of Marketing*, (September).

Schroeder, Jonathan and Detlev Zwick (2004), "Mirrors of Masculinity: Representations and Identity in Advertising Images," *Consumption, Markets and Culture*, 7(1), 21-52.

Scott, Linda (2000), "Market Feminism: The Case for a Paradigm Shift," in *Marketing and Feminism: Current Issues and Research*, Miriam Catterall, Pauline Maclaran, and Lorna Stevens (eds.) London: Routledge.

______ (2005), *Fresh Lipstick*, New York: Palgrave Macmillain.

Skeggs, Beverly (1997), *Formations of Class and Gender: Becoming Respectable*, London: Sage.

Stern, Barbara (1999), "Gender and Multicultural Issues in Advertising: Stages on Research Highway," *Journal of Advertising*, 28 (1), 1-93.

Stern, Barbara and Morris B. Holbrook (1994), "Gender and Genre in the Interpretation of Advertising Text," in *Gender Issues in Consumer Behavior*, Janeen Arnold Costa (ed.) Thousand Oaks, CA: Sage Publications, 11-41.

Tuncay, Linda (2006), "Men's Responses to Depictions of Ideal Masculinity in Advertising," *Advances in Consumer Research*, (33).

Whelehan, Imelda (1995), *Modern Feminist Thought: From Second Wave to 'Post-Feminism,'* Edinburgh: University Press.

Special Session Summary
Are Crowds Always Wiser?

Andrew Stephen, INSEAD, France
Leonard Lee, Columbia University, USA

SESSION OVERVIEW

Popularized by James Surowiecki's book of the same title (Surowiecki 2004), the "wisdom-of-crowds" hypothesis states that the aggregation of information in groups can result in better reasons than any single member of the group could make. Surowiecki argues that disorganized group decisions enjoy the advantages of being faster, more reliable, less subject to political forces that can adversely impact decision quality. The popularity of this hypothesis can be attested by the throngs of applications it has spurred and endorsed, ranging from online prediction markets (e.g. NewsFuture, BetFair) to education reform (e.g. Fullan 2004).

This session brings together three recent papers that propose critical boundary conditions for the validity of the "wisdom-of-crowds" hypothesis. Simmons, Nelson, Galak, and Frederick open the session by demonstrating that point spread betting markets, an important application of this hypothesis, lead to systematically biased predictions of NFL football winnings. Even with the opportunity to learn their prediction errors over time throughout the football season, bettors did not improve due to erroneous attributions. Using a longitudinal experiment, they systematically tested the validity of four competing hypotheses and found that the estimation of point differentials, rather than point spread betting, produced significantly improved predictions.

In the same vein of refining the "wisdom-of-crowds" hypothesis, Soll, Larrick, and Mannes posit that "crowds are wise, but well-chosen small crowds are even wiser." They distinguish between the two extremes of "aggregating the masses" and "chasing the expert" on the continuum of prediction strategies and propose the middle-ground solution of using smaller crowds (e.g. of five people) to improve predictions. Using a range of methodologies—empirical, behavioral, and analytical—they demonstrate convincingly that smaller crowds can indeed be wiser.

Finally, taking things to the other extreme of the continuum, Lee, Pham, and Stephen argue that even with the sole predictor, trusting one's feelings can significantly improve one's predictions of a wide variety of crowd behavior over popular prediction markets—from important political outcomes (i.e. the recent Democratic presidential nomination race between Senators Obama and Clinton), to results in the financial (i.e. Dow Jones Index) and entertainment industries (i.e. movie box-office success).

Together, these three papers present diverse perspectives that converge towards the same conclusion—that while crowds may be reasonably wise at times, there are certain interventions or approaches that can be taken to optimize their collective wisdom. Overall, given the fundamental relevance of these papers' topics to consumers' every day lives, this special topic session should be of great interest not only to marketing researchers and psychologists, but also to anyone who is interested in the factors and strategies that can improve our prediction making.

EXTENDED ABSTRACTS

"Are Crowds Wise When Predicting Against Point Spreads? It Depends on How You Ask"

Joseph Simmons, Yale University, USA
Leif Nelson, University of California at Berkeley, USA
Jeff Galak, Carnegie Mellon University, USA
Shane Frederick, Yale University, USA

The wisdom-of-crowds hypothesis predicts that the judgments of a crowd (as measured by any form of central tendency) will be relatively accurate, even when most of the individuals in the crowd are ignorant and error-prone (Surowiecki 2004). Point spreads are often cited as an important example of the wisdom of crowds, because they are very accurate and are widely believed to reflect the "crowd's" predictions of upcoming sporting events. However, other research (Simmons & Nelson 2006) shows that bettors are biased in their predictions against point spreads: They bet on "favorites" more than "underdogs" despite the empirical observation that the two bets are equally likely to obtain. This research challenges the notion that point spreads capture crowd sentiment, leaving the "wisdom" of the crowd in question.

To test the wisdom-of-crowds hypothesis, we conducted a season-long (17-week) experimental investigation, in which a geographically diverse sample of enthusiastic NFL football fans wagered more than $20,000 on NFL football games against point spreads that were manipulated to favor the underdog (i.e., point spreads that were increased). We investigated four hypotheses. The first hypothesis constitutes the strong version of the wisdom-of-crowds hypothesis and it predicts that crowds will wisely choose against biased point spreads even when they are not told that the spreads are biased (Surowiecki 2004). Our investigation soundly rejected this hypothesis. When predicting against biased point spreads, the crowd predicted vastly more favorites than underdogs, lost more games (and money) than it won, and performed worse than the vast majority of its individual members.

The second hypothesis constitutes the weak version of the wisdom-of-crowds hypothesis, which predicts that crowds will wisely choose against biased point spreads when they are told that the spreads have been increased. Although this warning slightly increased the crowd's tendency to predict underdogs, the crowd nevertheless predicted more favorites than underdogs, lost more games (and money) than it won, and performed worse than most of its individual members. Thus, this more charitable version of the wisdom-of-crowds hypothesis was also rejected.

We investigated a third hypothesis, which asserted that even if crowds are unwise at the start of the study, they should improve over time, as the crowd's members accumulate evidence of the inferiority of favorites. This hypothesis was also rejected. Moreover, although crowds did not get more or less accurate over time, their predictions did worsen over time in the sense that they unwisely predicted more favorites as the study progressed. Analyses of participants' tendencies to attribute prediction outcomes to luck or to skill indicate that participants were more likely to attribute correct favorite (vs. underdog) predictions to skill and to attribute incorrect favorite (vs. underdog) predictions to luck. This attributional pattern may have caused people to "learn" that predicting favorites is wiser than predicting underdogs as the study progressed, despite the fact that favorites lost more than underdogs against the spread.

Finally, despite our failure to find evidence for the wisdom-of-crowds when people were asked to predict against point spreads, we did find that a different method of eliciting the same judgment (asking participants to predict point differentials rather than make choices against point spreads) produced vastly different, and vastly wiser, predictions against the spread. In this case, the crowd predicted vastly more underdogs than favorites, won more games than it lost, and outperformed the majority of its individual members. Thus, the same "crowd" of bettors can appear wise or unwise, depending on how their predictions are elicited.

"When it Comes to Wisdom, Smaller Crowds are Wiser"

Jack Soll, Duke University, USA
Richard Larrick, Duke University, USA
Al Mannes, Duke University, USA

An aggregate opinion of the masses can be more accurate than the best experts. James Surowiecki popularized this idea in his best-seller The Wisdom of Crowds. The power of aggregation is surprising because it contradicts people's intuition, when faced with a prediction task, to "chase the expert" by seeking out the one person who knows the most. One source of misapprehension is that many people incorrectly believe that an aggregate mirrors the accuracy of its average input (Larrick & Soll 2006). People also mistrust crowds because they fear being dragged down by the crowd's worst members. This is a valid concern. Aggregation may entail mixing the opinions of skilled and unskilled judges. Chasing might be better and safer, assuming that true experts can be reliably identified.

If chasing means forgoing the statistical benefits of aggregation, and using the whole crowd leaves one vulnerable to incompetence, might there be a middle-ground that employs the best of each strategy? Therein lies the beauty of small crowds. Small crowds achieve most of the benefits of aggregation (Hogarth 1978), and if well-chosen avoid being dragged down by the worst judges.

We examine the wisdom of small crowds from empirical, behavioral, and analytical perspectives for quantitative judgments. First, we compared the small crowd strategy to chasing and averaging the whole crowd in 37 experimental datasets. The chasing and small crowd strategies involve rank-ordering the judges based on their accuracy in a small sample of observations (e.g., one to ten estimates for which the correct answer is known). In the vast majority of cases, the whole crowd beats the best expert, but the small crowd does just as well or better. We also analyzed a real-world dataset—data from an economic forecasting competition sponsored by the Wall Street Journal. The dataset included semi-annual forecasts of macro-economic variables from about fifty economists representing banks, government, and academia. We replicate the wisdom of crowds, but again show that the small crowd strategy outperforms the whole crowd, even when economists are rank ordered based on performance in just one prior forecasting period.

Next, we discuss two experiments that examine beliefs and behavior. In the first experiment, the WSJ panel of economists was described to participants, who then rank ordered five potential strategies for using the forecasts. Participants clearly preferred averaging the top five economists to both chasing the most accurate economist from the previous period and averaging all fifty forecasts. The second experiment used the forecasts of eleven economists from the WSJ survey as stimuli, and required participants to make forecasts over a series of rounds. In each round participants could review summary statistics of the performance of the eleven economists on the preceding rounds. In the "All or One" condition, participants had to decide whether to go with a single expert on a given round or average all eleven forecasts. In the "Small Crowd" condition, participants could average the opinions of any subset of economists, which included the options of selecting one or averaging all. Participants in "All or One" chased a single expert on the vast majority of rounds, and their performance suffered compared to the alternative of averaging all. In contrast, the "Small Crowd" participants tended to include more than one economist in their subset. They typically averaged the forecasts of two chosen economists, which led them to perform better than the "All or One" participants, although not quite as well as they could have done with a somewhat larger small crowd (we recommend five).

Finally, we conducted simulations to investigate the generality and robustness of the small crowd strategy. To do this, we first categorized environments according to three dimensions, corresponding to dispersion in accuracy across judges, correlation in judges' forecast errors, and the validity of cues to expertise. Averaging the whole crowd performs well when dispersion and correlation are low, and chasing a single expert is ideal when dispersion is high and the better experts can be reliably identified (Soll & Larrick, in press). We find that a small crowd strategy tends to perform closer to the better of these two pure strategies regardless of the environment, and beats them both in many intermediate environments. An interesting result is that small crowds of size five, when selected based on past performance, are robust in the sense that they tend to perform reasonably well across environments, regardless of the size of the crowd from which they are drawn (assuming crowds of size ten or larger).

The fact that a "top five" strategy consistently performs well is surprising, especially in light of the fact that either pure strategy can perform very poorly in the wrong environment. Equally surprising is the fact that the rank-ordering need not be based on a large sample of available data. We find that samples of two or three estimates lead to good results, and the benefits beyond ten are very small. There is a compelling intuition for this result. When there is high dispersion in expertise the better judges are readily apparent with just a few judgments. In contrast, when there is low dispersion in expertise one would require a large sample to obtain a good rank ordering, but in this case it does not matter much which judges are included. Either way, only a small sample is needed.

Crowds are wise, but well-chosen small crowds are even wiser. People do appreciate the wisdom of small crowds, although our research shows that people tend to select crowds that are too small. Our prescription is to rank-order the judges, and then average the top five. We also discuss extensions to consumer research. For example, in choosing hedonic goods such as movies or a vacation destination, consumers can rely on either crowd ratings (available at web sites such as tripadvisor.com and IMDb.com), or on the advice of an "expert" on one's own preferences, such as a similar other. The small crowds strategy suggests that an aggregate opinion of a small group of similar others may outperform both these strategies.

"The Emotional Oracle: Predicting Crowd Behavior with Feelings"

Leonard Lee, Columbia University, USA
Michel Tuan Pham, Columbia University, USA
Andrew Stephen, INSEAD, France

On August 28, 2008, Barack Obama became the official Democratic candidate for President of the United States in the 2008 presidential election. While this might have seemed inevitable in hindsight, foreseeing it a few months earlier was difficult, especially considering the span and intensity of the contest between him and Hillary Clinton. Election outcomes, as well as events such as the success of new products (e.g., movies) and stock market movements all depend on the collective actions of masses of people. In this research, we concentrate on the challenge of predicting how such crowds will behave.

Predictions of mass behavior can be made through two distinct processes: (1) a cognitive, scenario-building process, and (2) a feeling-based process that involves the monitoring of one's subjective feelings toward the options (Dunning 2007, Loewenstein and O'Donoghue 2004). Thus, in predicting crowd behavior, affect might play a role. Whereas the cognitive system of judgment is analytical and logical, the affective system is more holistic and associative (Epstein and Pacini 1999). Consequently, the affective system fosters a more comprehensive processing of available information, distilling the situation to its gist or essential elements (Stephen & Pham 2008). It may also help predictors better relate to—or put themselves in the shoes of—the people whose behaviors they are forecasting.

We examine how reliance on feelings affects the accuracy of peoples' predictions of crowd behavior across four studies and three diverse contexts. Each study uses the same subtle procedure to induce different degrees to which participants rely on their feelings in making their predictions (Avnet & Pham 2007, Lee, Amir, & Ariely, in press, Stephen & Pham 2008). Participants were randomly assigned to either a "high-trust-in-feelings" (high-TF) or a "low-trust-in-feelings" (low-TF) condition, and asked to describe either two (high-TF) or ten (low-TF) past situations in which they trusted their feelings to make a decision and it emerged as the right decision. Participants typically find it easy to recall two examples of successful reliance on feelings and difficult to recall ten. Thus, those asked to recall two (ten) examples tend to believe that such examples are common (uncommon), and increase (decrease) their reliance on feelings when making subsequent decisions (Avnet & Pham 2007).

In study 1 (N=68; undergraduates), after completing the manipulation, we gave participants information about five movies to be released nationally in early October 2008 (the study was conducted three days before these movies' release). The task involved ranking these movies in order of predicted success, measured by opening weekend box office revenues. Using the rank-order correlation between each participant's predicted order and the actual order as a measure of prediction accuracy, high-TF participants were more accurate than their low-TF counterparts. This result held after controlling for prior knowledge and liking of the movies.

Study 2 (N=41; undergraduates) used the same procedure as study 1 and replicated this result (although here we used a set of four movies that were released in mid-December 2008). Additionally, we had participants list all the things that they thought of when making their predictions. We counted the number of items listed that were about mass behavior (and what "other people" would do). As process evidence, we found that a greater percentage of the items listed by high-TF participants were other/crowd-focused and that this was positively correlated with their prediction accuracy. Mediation analysis suggested that the positive effect of reliance on feelings on prediction accuracy was mediated by a greater focus on projections of how "other people" would feel about the movies.

In the third study (N=52; undergraduates), we asked participants (who first completed the trust-in-feelings manipulation) to predict the closing values of the Dow Jones stock market index one week in the future (this study was conducted in February 2009). The same basic result from studies 1 and 2 was replicated in this different context: high-TF participants made more accurate predictions. The dependent variable here was the prediction error (actual future value–predicted value); thus, the mean prediction error was lower for high-TF than for low-TF participants. However, we found that this effect only held for participants who possessed some expertise or knowledge of the prediction target (i.e., the economy and stock market): trust in feelings interacted with target knowledge (high for participants who were economics or finance majors, low otherwise) such that high-TF participants were only more accurate if they were knowledgeable.

Finally, in study 4 (N=229; national sample of registered voters, run in mid-February 2008), participants first completed the trust-in-feelings manipulation and then predicted the winner of the 2008 Democratic primary. We deliberately ran this study when the Democratic primary contest was far from being conclusive, with both candidates virtually tied in national opinion polls. The results revealed that six months before the Democratic National Convention, high-TF participants were more likely to correctly predict that Obama would win the nomination than low-TF participants. This result held in general, as well as separately among registered Democrats, registered Republicans, and even among participants who had already voted for Clinton.

Overall, we find that feeling-based predictions may lead to greater predictive accuracy of mass crowd behavior. This result holds across different contexts and for short- and long-range predictions. Further, regardless of one's inherent preference for the collective outcome (e.g., personally liking a particular movie or having already voted for Clinton) this result holds despite cases where the predictor's personal preference does not align with the crowd. Our results are consistent with the notion that reliance on feelings help people be less encumbered with their own personal preferences or tastes and thus better able to put themselves in the shoes of others—the crowd—to consider how others would feel and what they would do. Accordingly, this leads to more accurate predictions and the counterintuitive finding that focusing less on logic and reasoning and more on feelings enables people to better foresee the future.

REFERENCES

Avnet, T. and M. T. Pham (2007), *Metacognitive and Nonmetacognitive Reliance on Affect as Information in Judgment*, Yeshiva University, NY.

Dunning, D. (2007), "Prediction," in A. W. Kruglanski & E. T. Higgins (Eds.), *Social Psychology: Handbook of Basic Principles*, New York: The Guilford Press, pp. 69-90.

Epstein, S. and R. Pacini (1999), "Some Basic Issues Regarding Dual-Process Theories from the Perspective of Cognitive-Experiential Self-Theory," in S. Chaiken, & Y. Trope (Eds.), *Dual-Process Theories in Social Psychology*, New York: Guilford Press, pp.462-482.

Fullan, M. (2004), *Leadership & Sustainability: System Thinkers in Action*, CA: Corwin Press

Hogarth, R. M. (1978), Note on Aggregating Opinions," *Organizational Behavior and Human Performance*, 21, 40-46.

Larrick, R. P. and J. B. Soll (2006), "Intuitions about Combining Opinions: Misappreciation of the Averaging Principle," *Management Science*, 52, 111-127.

Lee, L., O. Amir, and D. Ariely (2009), "In Search of Homo Economicus: Cognitive Noise and the Role of Emotion in Preference Consistency," *Journal of Consumer Research*, 36, 173-187.

Loewenstein, G. and T. O'Donoghue (2004), *Animal Spirits: Affective and Deliberative Processes in Economic Behavior*, Carnegie Mellon University, PA.

Simmons, J. P. and L. D. Nelson (2006), "Intuitive Confidence: Choosing Between Intuitive and Nonintuitive Alternatives," *Journal of Experimental Psychology: General*, 135, 409-428.

Soll, J. B. and R. P. Larrick (in press), "Strategies for Revising Judgment: How (and How Well) People Use Others' Opinions," *Journal of Experimental Psychology: Learning, Memory, and Cognition.*

Stephen, A. T. and M. T. Pham (2008). "On Feelings as a Heuristic for Making Offers in Ultimatum Negotiations," *Psychological Science*, 19, 1051-1058.

Surowiecki, J. (2004), *The Wisdom of Crowds: Why the Many are Smarter than the Few and How Collective Wisdom Shapes Business, Economies, Societies, and Nations*, New York: Doubleday.

SPECIAL SESSION SUMMARY

The Other Side of the Story: New Perspectives on Word of Mouth

Sarah G. Moore, University of Alberta, Canada

SESSION OVERVIEW

Consumers frequently engage in word of mouth (WOM) communication, where one individual shares information about a consumption experience with another. WOM can occur face-to-face, or via spoken or written communication through various technologies (e.g. the Internet) (Godes et al. 2005). WOM has long been recognized as an important process for firms and consumers, and it remains so today, with 60% of consumers consulting friends or family about purchases (Hampton 2006). Past work on WOM has focused on how it impacts the listener (Arndt 1967) and the firm (Chevalier and Mayzlin 2006), as well as on who shares WOM and why (Wojnicki and Godes 2008). However, this work has neglected some fundamental aspects of WOM. Most importantly, there has been little attention to the question of what consumers actually say, how they say it, and how these two factors influence not only the listeners, but the speakers themselves. In this session, we hope to tell the other side of the WOM story by introducing recent work that will broaden the field's perspective on this important topic.

Our papers highlight several new aspects of WOM. We examine the specific content of WOM (Moore, Fitzsimons, and Bettman 2009; Schellekens, Verlegh, and Smidts 2009), how and why this content influences speakers (Moore et al., 2009; Cowley 2009), and how speakers think strategically about WOM (Schellekens et al. 2009; Cowley 2009). These papers "zoom in" on WOM: instead of examining the consequences of WOM for listeners or firms, we focus on the language speakers use, on the determinants of language use, and on how this language influences speakers.

First, Moore et al. (2009) examine how characteristics of experiences influence WOM content as well as how specific WOM content influences speakers' evaluations of experiences through a process of sense-making. Cowley (2009) also investigates how WOM influences the speaker, focusing on how consumers' retrospective evaluations of experiences are influenced by conversational norms and by consumers' awareness of these norms (e.g. whether they are purposely exaggerating). Finally, Schellekens et al. (2009) examine how characteristics of experiences and consumers' communication goals influence WOM content; they also examine how listeners are persuaded by different WOM content. These papers demonstrate the value of a deeper focus on WOM content and its determinants, and on how this content influences individuals who share WOM. While these papers examine similar novel aspects of WOM, each has a unique contribution: Moore et al. (2009) and Schellekens et al. (2009) both examine WOM content, but focus on different types of content, while Moore et al. (2009) and Cowley (2009) examine two different processes through which speaking can influence the speaker.

In combination, these papers provide an exciting new perspective on WOM and a solid foundation from which to begin additional research in this domain. We hope that this symposium will attract a wide audience, from WOM researchers to those who examine the roles of memory, attitudes, metacognition, and language in consumer psychology. These papers are in advanced stages of completion, and we expect this symposium to stimulate much discussion on the current work and on areas for future research. Thus, we hope to save 15-20 minutes following the presentations for Larry Feick to discuss the presentations and to receive questions from the audience.

EXTENDED ABSTRACTS

"Some Things Are Better Left Unsaid: How Word of Mouth Influences the Speaker"

Sarah G. Moore, University of Alberta, Canada
Gavan J. Fitzsimons, Duke University, USA
James R. Bettman, Duke University, USA

WOM, where individuals share information about consumption experiences with others, is an everyday occurrence. WOM spreads through various media, both traditional (face-to-face) and non-traditional (online reviews). Past research has focused on how WOM influences those who hear it (Arndt, 1967) and how this influences the firm (Chevalier and Mayzlin 2006). However, a fundamental question remains unanswered: how does WOM influence the speaker?

To answer this question, we develop a comprehensive model of how speaking affects the speaker. We argue that it is not simply the act of speaking that influences individuals sharing WOM, but that it is story content or how things are said that strongly influences storytellers. We synthesize past research from psychology and linguistics to develop a model that incorporates: 1) the process by which language influences speakers; 2) antecedent variables that influence what speakers say; and 3) the consequences of speaking, including changes in speakers' evaluations of experiences, as well as changes in speakers' intentions to repeat, recommend, and tell others about experiences.

We focus on one important type of story content and how that influences speakers. Past work suggests that individuals can understand and recover from traumatic experiences by building narratives around them and figuring out why they occurred (Pennebaker 1997). Thus, we focus on whether storytellers explain why events occurred or explain why they feel the way they do about experiences, and examine how this explaining language influences speakers. We suggest that antecedent variables such as experience valence (positive or negative) will influence how much explaining language individuals use in their stories. The use of explaining language is then hypothesized to change evaluations through a process of sense-making, where individuals come to understand experiences and consequently find them less compelling (Gilbert, Wilson, and Centerbar 2003). In short, sense-making makes positive experiences less positive and negative experiences less negative. We contribute to this literature by focusing on how specific types of language influence sense-making. In four studies, we demonstrate that explaining language does facilitate sense-making and can thereby cause paradoxical effects of WOM. Specifically, explaining positive experiences decreases the speakers' evaluations of and their willingness to repeat and recommend experiences. Conversely, explaining negative experiences increases the speakers' evaluations of and their willingness to repeat and recommend experiences. Finally, making sense of an experience makes consumers less likely to spread future WOM by telling others about the experience.

In study 1, we showed individuals two positive or negative photographs and asked them to write a story about one of the photos. First, we found that writing had an overall dampening effect on participants' photo evaluations compared to not writing. We also found that participants used more explaining language when telling stories about negative compared to positive photos. Most importantly, we found that participants who used more explaining language in their stories evaluated the positive photos less positively and the negative photos less negatively than participants who used less explaining language. These results were mediated by sense-making, where explaining language increased sense-making, and sense-making decreased evaluations of positive but increased evaluations of negative experiences. We also ruled out two alternative explanations for our findings: participants' evaluations were not altered because explaining language influenced metacognitive perceptions of difficulty in writing, nor were evaluations altered because explaining language encouraged individuals to include evaluation inconsistent information in their stories.

In study 2, we coded actual Amazon.com book reviews to ensure that our findings were not restricted to lab participants writing to an unspecified audience. We found that individuals rating books extremely, at one or five stars, used less explaining language than individuals rating books less extremely, at three stars; we observed these effects using both an across reviewer data set and a within-reviewer data set. As in study 1, then, explaining language was associated with less extreme evaluations of positive and negative experiences.

Studies 3 and 4 manipulated language use to provide experimental support for the idea that explaining language alters evaluations. In study 3, we gave individuals a Scrambled Sentence Task with explain, relive, or control prime words. We found that individuals in the explain prime conditions used more explaining language in their stories and had less extreme evaluations of positive and negative experiences than individuals in the relive prime conditions, who used less explaining language in their stories. The impact of prime on evaluations was mediated by sense-making, such that explaining language helped individuals make sense of their experiences, leading to decreased evaluations of positive but increased evaluations of negative experiences.

In study 4, we provided individuals with a constructed story for which they filled in the blanks. We had an explain, a relive, and a control condition, where the only difference between the relive and explain conditions was an explaining clause at the end of some sentences (e.g. "Dinner was _____." vs. "Dinner was _____ because ______."). Thus, this study controls for various potential differences between explaining and reliving language (e.g. evaluation inconsistent information, emotionality, detail) and varies only whether individuals provided explanations or not. This study replicated our previous findings: individuals in the explain condition had less extreme positive and negative evaluations than individuals in the relive or control conditions.

In sum, we proposed and tested a model for understanding a critical but understudied issue in WOM. While past research has indicated that WOM influences listeners (Arndt, 1967), in addition to understanding this outward ripple, it is vitally important to understand how WOM influences the speaker. We go beyond previous work to highlight WOM content and demonstrate how that content influences critical downstream consequences for the speaker. We show that some things are, indeed, better left unsaid: sharing positive stories can be bad for the speaker, while sharing negative stories can be good for the speaker, depending on their story-telling language. Explaining language dampens evaluations of positive experiences and improves evaluations of negative experiences, and these evaluative changes are linked to changes in intentions to repeat and recommend experiences.

"Selecting Snapshots from Episodic Memory's Photo Album: Sharing Experiences and Retrospective Evaluations"

Elizabeth Cowley, University of Sydney, Australia

Everyone loves a good story: hearing one is entertaining and telling one is satisfying. Stories give life to past experience and are an effective form of communication (Schank 1990). However, telling stories may adversely affect the storyteller's memory for how they felt during the event. Why? By following conversational norms such as keeping the story interesting to the listener, the storyteller may exaggerate the intensity of the most pleasant or painful moments of an experience. Since the most intense moments of an experience are used to construct a retrospective evaluation (RE) (Fredrickson and Kahneman 1993; Redelmeier and Kahneman 1996), storytelling may influence REs. Exaggeration may be particularly likely when consumers tell entertaining stories. In this case, consumers may attempt to correct for the distortions when they are subsequently remembering the experience. However, if consumers are unaware of the distortions introduced by exaggeration, then storytelling may result in biased REs (Wilson and Brekke 1994).

In two studies, we demonstrate that recounting an experience in a conversational format does polarize REs when storytellers are unaware that they may have included exaggerated affective reactions in their conversation. Study 1 also reveals that changes in REs are accompanied by changes in intentions to repeat the experience. In study 2, we find that changes to the pre-conversation peak moment of pain or pleasure do not cause shifts in REs, but that REs are influenced by a new moment which emerges as the most affectively intense as a result of the conversation.

In study 1, 94 students participated in a 2 x 2 x 2 between subject design with conversational goal (be entertaining vs. be informative), event valence (positive vs. negative), and goal instruction type (implicit vs. explicit) as independent factors. Participants thought of two recent experiences of the same valence that had occurred in two different restaurants. After providing a RE of the events, participants were provided with implicit or explicit instructions to be either entertaining or informative during an upcoming conversation. Participants then had a conversation about the least positive or negative of their two restaurant experiences, depending on condition. One day later, participants were asked to report their RE and to choose a restaurant to revisit.

In the explicit instruction conditions, REs were amplified after people recounted their experience with an informative goal, but not with an entertaining goal. The implicit instruction conditions revealed amplification of the RE in both goal conditions. The results are consistent with the assertion that it is awareness of the potentially distorting effect of the entertainment goal which eliminates the polarization of the RE. The results also provide evidence that behavioral changes accompany shifts in REs. Specifically, in the positive conditions, participants selected the restaurant they had told a story about to revisit, as opposed to the restaurant they had preferred prior to their conversation. In the negative conditions, participants selected to revisit the non-discussed restaurant, as opposed to the pre-conversation preferred (or least negative) restaurant. The only exceptions were participants in the explicit/entertaining conditions: these participants chose to revisit restaurants consistent with their pre-conversation REs and were not influenced by storytelling.

Although study 1 shows that telling someone about an experience may result in more extreme REs, the findings do not provide insight into how the shift occurs. At least three mechanisms could facilitate the adjustment: 1) Telling the story could increase the intensity of the pre-conversation peak moment. If this is the case, then information regarding the cause of the peak intensity remains intact; 2) A new, more intense, peak could be introduced during the conversation. If this is the case, then the relationship between peak intensities and moments within the experience is altered by the conversation. The moments which are inconsistent with the pre-conversation peak could be assimilated in the direction of the peak; 3) The speaker simplifies the story and makes the explanation for the events more definite by altering affectively inconsistent moments to be consistent with the affective reaction to the peak moment.

In a second study examining these mechanisms, 80 students participated in a 2 x 2 between subject design with two levels of conversational goal (be entertaining, be informative) and two levels of event valence (positive, negative). Participants thought of a positive or negative restaurant experience and provided a RE of the event. Then, they listed the moments or snapshots of the experience and rated the importance of each moment and the degree to which the moment was enjoyable. Participants were then given an explicit goal (informative vs. entertaining) to accomplish while telling a story about their experience to a conversation partner. One day later, participants were asked to report their remembered RE and to rate the importance and enjoyment of each of the moments listed before the conversation and added during the conversation. Study 2 results indicated that shifts in RE occurred because a new experience peak emerged after the conversation. The new peak was either a new moment included during the conversation which had not been identified before the conversation or was a pre-conversational non-peak moment which intensified in terms of its utility. It is interesting to note that the pre-conversation peak did not become more intense, nor was there was a general increase in the degree of pain or pleasure associated with all of the moments.

In sum, we provide evidence that REs are amplified after recounting an experience in conversation, unless the storyteller is being purposely entertaining. What difference between pre- and post-conversation REs leads to this amplification? Study 2 revealed that the post-conversation RE was constructed using a new peak. The new peak was either a pre-conversational moment which became more intense, or was a new peak, included in the conversation, but not reported before the conversation. This is an important finding because previous research has implicitly assumed that there is a peak moment from the experience which continues to be a critical determinant of REs; these studies demonstrate that storytelling can change this peak moment.

"Language Use in Word of Mouth"

Gaby Schellekens, Erasmus University, The Netherlands
Peeter Verlegh, Erasmus University, The Netherlands
Ale Smidts, Erasmus University, The Netherlands

Consumers like to share their experiences with products and services with each other. But what do consumers say during WOM conversations? For example, when your bright new "brand X" shirt has lost its color after you have washed it once or twice, you could say to your friend, "My brand X shirt has faded," or you could say, "My brand X shirt was of poor quality." In the former case, you provide a very concrete description of what actually happened. In the latter, you use more abstract wording which generalizes your experience with the shirt fading to the overall quality of the shirt. These differences in language use can also have an effect on the receiver of the WOM message. In spite of the substantial amount of prior research on WOM, there has been little attention to the question of how consumers talk about products and brands, and whether and how this influences the extent to which they persuade other consumers.

Previous research has found that abstract versus concrete descriptions of experiences influence the processing of and the inferred meaning drawn from such descriptions. To understand and study these implications, particularly in the area of person perception, Semin and Fiedler (1988) developed the Linguistic Category Model. According to the model, event descriptions that use more abstract terms (implicitly) convey that an actor's displayed behavior is more typical of the actor and is more likely to be repeated. Thus, the description is viewed as more informative of the actor and is less focused on the specific circumstances under which the behavior was performed. More concrete descriptions, on the other hand, are objective descriptions of the specific observable behavior, and are therefore verifiable and lead to less dispute (Semin and Fiedler 1988; Wigboldus et al. 2000).

The present paper first demonstrates that consumers systematically use more concrete or abstract language in descriptions of product experiences. The studies presented here are the first to examine language abstraction outside the interpersonal domain and to evaluate language use in descriptions of products. In line with earlier research (Wigboldus et al. 2000), we argue and show that consumers' a priori expectations about a brand or product determine whether they describe their experiences in abstract or concrete terms. More specifically, product experiences that are congruent with a consumer's product attitude are communicated more abstractly than incongruent experiences. We also show that consumers can use language abstraction strategically in word of mouth. Although people generally are unaware of the level of abstraction that they use to describe an event, some studies suggest that language abstraction can be used in a strategic manner (Douglas and Sutton 2003). We extend these findings by showing that consumers vary language abstraction based on a communication goal, such as the goal to persuade someone of the quality of a product. More specifically, if consumers want to persuade someone of a product, they will use a more abstract message for a favorable experience and a more concrete message for an unfavorable event.

The strategic use of language abstraction suggests that consumers consciously or unconsciously assume that there are differences in the persuasiveness of language abstraction (see Hamilton 2003 for a similar argument). To our surprise, there has been no research examining whether abstract descriptions of favorable experiences (and concrete description of unfavorable experiences) are indeed more persuasive and lead to more favorable evaluations of the actor (or, in this case, the product). In the last study of our paper, we show that the language abstraction of a message affects the purchase intentions of the receiver. Positive messages about a product are shown to be more persuasive when they are presented in more abstract language. However, the opposite effect is found for negative messages: an increase in language abstraction for a negative product referral leads to a decrease in receivers' intentions to purchase the product.

Our research extends previous work on language abstraction while providing important insights into the nature of WOM communication, which may be of use for marketers who are seeking to manage and optimize WOM marketing (Ryu and Feick 2007).

REFERENCES

Arndt, Johan (1967), "Role of Product-Related Conversations in the Diffusion of a New Product," *Journal of Marketing Research*, 4(August), 291-95.

Chevalier, Judith A. and Dina Mayzlin (2006), "The Effect of Word of Mouth on Sales: Online Book Reviews," *Journal of Marketing Research*, 43(3), 345-54.

Douglas, Karen M. and Robbie M. Sutton (2003), "Effects of Communication Goals and Expectancies on Language Abstraction," *Journal of Personality and Social Psychology*, 84(4), 682-96.

Fredrickson, Barbara L. and Daniel Kahneman, (1993), "Duration Neglect in Retrospective Evaluations of Affective Episodes," *Journal of Personality and Social Psychology*, 65, 45-55.

Gilbert, Daniel T., Timothy D. Wilson, and David B. Centerbar (2003), "Making Sense: The Causes of Emotional Evanescence," in *The Psychology of Economic Decisions: Rationality and Well Being*, Vol. 1, ed. I. Brocas, Carrillo, J., New York: Oxford University Press, 209-33.

Godes, David, Dina Mayzlin, Chen Yubo, Sanjiv Das, Chrysanthos Dellarocas, Bruce Pfeiffer, Barak Libai, Subrata Sen, Mengze Shi, and Peeter Verlegh (2005), "The Firm's Management of Social Interactions," *Marketing Letters*, 16(3-4), 415-428.

Hamilton, Rebecca W. (2003), "Why Do People Suggest What They Do Not Want? Using Context Effects to Influence Others' Choices," *Journal of Consumer Research*, 29, 492-506.

Hampton, F. (2006), "Word-of-Mouth: Heard It through the Grapevine," *Marketing Week*, 42.

Pennebaker, James W. (1997), "Writing About Emotional Experiences as a Therapeutic Process," *Psychological Science*, 8 (3), 162-66.

Redelmeier, D. A., and Daniel Kahneman (1996), "Patients' Memories of Painful Medical Treatments–Real-Time and Retrospective Evaluations of two Minimally Invasive Procedures," *Pain*, 66, 3-8.

Ryu, Gangseog and Lawrence Feick (2007), "A Penny for your Thoughts: Referral Reward Programs and Referral Likelihood," *Journal of Marketing*, 71 (1), 84-94.

Schank, R. C. (1990), *Tell Me a Story: A New Look at Real and Artificial Memory*, New York Charles Scribner and Sons.

Semin, Gün R. and Klaus Fiedler (1988), "The Cognitive Functions of Linguistic Categories in Describing Persons-Social Cognition and Language," *Journal of Personality and Social Psychology*, 54 (4), 558-68.

Wigboldus, Daniel H. J., Gün R. Semin, and Russell Spears (2000), "How Do We Communicate Stereotypes? Linguistic Bases and Inferential Consequences," *Journal of Personality and Social Psychology*, 78 (1), 5-18.

Wilson, Timothy D. and Nancy Brekke (1994), "Mental Contamination and Mental Correction: Unwanted influences on Judgments and Evaluations," *Psychological Bulletin*, 116, 117-142.

Wojnicki, Andrea C. and David Godes (2008), "Word-of-Mouth as Self-Enhancement," HBS Marketing Research Paper No. 06-01: http://ssrn.com/abstract=908999.

SPECIAL SESSION SUMMARY

Beyond Functionality: Aesthetic Considerations in Consumer Behavior

Joann Peck, University of Wisconsin-Madison, USA

SESSION OVERVIEW

"Beauty is a harmonious relation between something in our nature and the quality of the object which delights us." Blaise Pascal

The objective of this session is to highlight the role of aesthetics in consumer behavior. This session has a diversity of topics that will interest individuals interested in sensory perception, product design, web based shopping and product customization. What is especially appealing about this session is the breath of the papers included.

Peck and Klatzky investigate the attributes that invite people to reach out and touch. While we know that touch can increase impulse purchase, the feeling of ownership and other measures, we do not know anything about the visual attributes of an object that make touch irresistible

A natural paper to follow is the Townsend and Shu paper which examines the visual appeal of documents. This research uses the buying and selling of stocks to investigate the aesthetics of document design and the effects on stock valuation and investment behavior. Three studies are completed and reported in this research.

The final two papers (Deng, Hui and Hutchinson and Moreau and Herd) both address the aesthetic choices consumers make in product design. Deng, Hui and Hutchinson, in the context of designing a Nike shoe, are interested in whether assisting consumers in their self design choices is superior than providing no assistance. These researchers have completed a preliminary study with almost three hundred participants in order to determine the point at which they should offer design assistance to consumers. They expect that the assisted self-design group will be more satisfied with their aesthetic design experience than those that are unassisted.

Finally, Moreau and Herd delve into the question of *why* consumers are willing to pay a premium for self-designed products. The authors have three completed studies that examine a consumer's social comparison to the professional designers of products. Their third study uses a real online design task in which designs are created, orders are placed and product are produced and delivered to the participants. Aesthetic design is an emerging area in our field. The breath of this special session will likely have great appeal and will stimulate interesting discussion. Each paper will be presented for 15 minutes and the last 15 minutes will be a general discussion.

EXTENDED ABSTRACTS

"Please Touch: Aesthetic Features that Invite Touch"

Joann Peck, University of Wisconsin-Madison, USA
Roberta Klatzky, Carnegie Mellon University, USA

The sense of touch is important in consumer behavior for both instrumental and hedonic purposes. Instrumentally, touch can be thought of as a way to obtain specific product information in order to make a more informed purchase decision. Touch excels at obtaining texture, hardness, temperature and weight information (Klatzky and Lederman 1992, 1993). If a product category varies in a diagnostic way on one of or more of these attributes, also termed material properties, consumers will be more motivated to touch the product prior to purchase (Grohmann, Spangenberg and Sprott 2007; McCabe and Nowlis 2003; Peck and Childers 2003a). For example, books do not vary in a diagnostic manner on one these attributes so touch is relatively unimportant for purchases in this category. However, cell phones likely vary in a diagnostic way on weight which makes this category more likely to encourage touch. More recently in consumer behavior, touch that provides no diagnostic attribute information has also been found to be persuasive (Peck and Shu 2009; Peck and Wiggins 2006). Consumers may be motivated to touch solely for the sensory experience that touch provides. In summary, previous shows that consumers may be motivated to touch an object for both instrumental and/or hedonic reasons.

Being able to touch an object has been shown to increase impulse purchasing (Peck and Childers 2006) and to increase the feelings of ownership of an object (Peck and Barger working paper; Peck and Shu) and also to increase the amount an individual is willing to pay for an object (Peck and Shu). But how do we encourage consumers to reach out and touch an object? More specifically, what aesthetic features of an object encourage touch?

Evidence has been found for a "visual preview model" which states that vision provides a quick "glance" which results in coarse information about the haptic properties of an object, information that is useful in directing further processing (Klatzky, Lederman and Matula 1993).When encoding properties of some objects, vision may be sufficient because it triggers the retrieval of information about the object's properties stored in memory, eliminating the need for direct perceptual encoding by touch. However, vision may reveal that more detailed information is desired. For example, a visual glance at a sweater may encourage a consumer to touch for both instrumental reasons (to ascertain how comfortable the material would be to wear) and/or for hedonic reasons (it looks like it would feel good to touch). The goal of our research was to begin to explore which attributes encourage a consumer to reach out and touch.

We also include the individual difference in the preference for touch information (Peck and Childers 2003b) termed the Need for Touch scale (NFT). We expect that aesthetic touch judgments will be greater for those high, as compared to those low in their NFT.

Study 1 Procedure

To examine aesthetic touch, our first study uses a methodology where we show experimental participants various objects on a screen. They then rate whether the objects invite touch. The design is a 3 (shape variations) by 3 (visual texture variations) by 2 (size or graspability of an object) by 2 (object material). After the participant judges the "touchability" of each object, we also measure the individual difference need for touch.

Independent Variables: The objects used are adapted from Cooke, Kannengiesser, Wallraven, and Bulthoff (2006) and are objects in which both the macro geometry (the number of protrusions, or shape) and the micro geometry (the visual texture) of the object are varied systematically. More specifically we use three levels of macro-geometry and three levels of mirco-geometry.

We also manipulate the size of the object with two levels either graspable (the size of a ping pong ball or less graspable (the size of a cantaloupe). Finally, the material is manipulated with participants being told the object is made out of either a smoother material (marble) or a rougher material (concrete). In total each participant makes 36 judgments.

Dependent Measures

Aesthetic touch -For each object viewed, a participant completes four seven point scales with endpoints "strong agree" to "strongly disagree" including "this object invites touch," "this object would feel pleasant," "this object is aesthetically pleasing," "I want to touch this object" and, "I wouldn't be able to resist touching this object." Need for Touch–The 12 item need for touch (Peck and Childers 2003) scale will also be administered.

Thus far, it appears that the more graspable, smoother material objects are more aesthetically pleasing, especially for individuals higher in their need for touch. Fewer protrusions (macro-geometry) seem to encourage touch and a moderate amount of visual texture (micro-geometry) seem to be most attractive to touch. The study will be completed in June and results will be available for the conference.

Study 2

A second study will follow in which physical objects will be constructed for participants to evaluate. The objects will vary in size and material. Participants will evaluate the aesthetic touch appeal of the objects. The objects will be constructed in the summer/fall of 2009 and preliminary results will be available for the conference.

References

Cooke, Theresa, Sebastian Kannengiesser, Christian Wallraven, and Heinrich H. Bulthoff (2006), "Feature Validation using Visual and Haptic Similarity Ratings, *ACM Transactions on Applied Perception*, 3 (3), 239-261.

Grohman, B., Spangenberg, E. R. & Sprott, D. E. (2007). The influence of tactile input on the evaluation of retail product offerings. *Journal of Retailing*, 83 (2), 237-245.

Klatzky, Roberta L. and Susan J. Lederman (1992), "Stages of Manual Exploration in Haptic Object Identification," *Perception & Psychophysics*, 52 (6), 661-670.

Klatzky, Roberta L. and Susan J. Lederman (1993), "Toward a Computational Model of Constraint-Driven Exploration and Haptic Object Identification," *Perception*, 22, 597-621.

Klatzky, Roberta L, Susan J. Lederman and D. E. Matula,v(1993), " Haptic Exploration in the Presence of Vision," *Journal of Experimental Psychology: Human Perception and Performance*, 19 (4), 726-743.

McCabe, Deborah B. and Steve M. Nowlis (2003), "The Effect of Examining Actual Products or Product Descriptions on Consumer Preference, *Journal of Consumer Psychology*, 13 (4), 431-439.

Peck, Joann and Terry L.Childers (2003a), " To Have and to Hold: The Influence of Haptic Information on Product Judgments," *Journal of Marketing*, April 67 (2), 35-48.

Peck, Joann and Terry L.Childers (2003b), "Individual Differences in Haptic Information Processing: On the Development, Validation, and Use of the 'Need for Touch' Scale," *Journal of Consumer Research*, 30 (3), 430-442.

Peck, Joann and Terry L. Childers (2006), "If I Touch It I have to Have it: Individual and Environmental Influences on Impulse Purchasing," *Journal of Business Research,* 59, 765-769.

Peck, Joann and Jennifer Wiggins (2006), "It Just Feels Good: Consumers' Affective Response to Touch and Its Influence on Persuasion," *Journal of Marketing,* 70, October, 56-69.

Peck, Joann and Suzanne Shu (2009), "The Effect of Mere Touch on Perceived Ownership" *Journal of Consumer Research, October*.

"The Power of Aesthetic Design in Consumer Financial Decisions"

Claudia Townsend, University California, Los Angeles, USA
Suzanne Shu, University California, Los Angeles, USA

While there has certainly always been an inherent understanding that aesthetics impacts product success in the marketplace, lately the business community's appreciation for product design and its impact on the bottom line has grown (e.g. Gibney and Luscombe 2005; Postrel 2003; Schmitt and Simonson 1997). And yet our knowledge of the impact of aesthetic design on decision-making behavior is minimal. In an attempt to understand the possible limits of the impact of design, we examine it in an extreme context; we observe the influence of aesthetics on behavior involving financial products–an area where, presumably, design's impact on decision-making is at its limit as it has absolutely no rational role. In a series of three studies we find that, indeed, in hypothetical investment decisions, such as the buying and selling of stocks, the overall look of a document–even one not associated with the company's product and for a company that does not do anything design-related–impacts valuation and behavior. Our results suggests that this occurs both through an increased sense of ownership as well as through self-affirmation and, moreover, that the effects spill over into subsequent financial decisions with high design association leading to riskier investment behavior.

Our first study establishes that design does, indeed, impact hypothetical financial decisions. We find that the aesthetics of a symbolic document given at the time of purchase of company stock (e.g., a stock certificate) impacts respondents' selling price for the stock. In particular, respondents assign a higher selling price to the stock when the stock certificate is highly aesthetic versus when the stock certificate is not highly aesthetic ($M_{high\ aesthetics}$=\$38.95, $M_{low\ aesthetics}$=\$33.22, t=-2.06, p=.04). Moreover, this effect exists regardless of whether or not the decision-maker actually is to keep the stock certificate in his/her possession, thus, ruling out a "rational" explanation for this behavior based on higher utility from being able to display the aesthetically appealing certificate.

Our second study shows consistent findings but with a different document, a company's annual report which, while related to the company, is not related to its product. Again we find that respondents both rate and evaluate a company higher when the annual report is highly aesthetic versus when the annual report is not highly aesthetic. This occurs both in a context where aesthetics is evidently intrinsic to company success (e.g. for a vase manufacturer) and where aesthetics is not evidently essential to success (e.g. for a bubble wrap manufacturer). We find that a sense of ownership partially mediates the impact of aesthetics on company judgment; high aesthetics leads to a greater sense of ownership of the company than low aesthetics and this, in turn, leads to higher company valuation. This confirms the more emotion-based and less rational explanation for this impact of design.

In our third and final study we look more closely at the psychological impact of design on decision-makers and how this affects investment-related behavior. Previous research (Townsend Sood working paper) suggests that the choice of a high design option is self-affirming; in particular, they find that the choice of a high design option has the same impact on subsequent behavior (in particular, openness to counter-attitudinal arguments) as does a self-affirmation manipulation. Given that the authors found these results using a hypothetical choice context, we hypothesized that similar effects might be found by simply creating a strong association between the decision-maker and high design, even without actual choice. Using the prior literature as a starting point, in this study test whether providing the consumer with a simple personal association with high design (versus high function) impacts financial decision-making. If association with high design is self-affirming, and impacts subsequent openness to arguments, it might also impact openness to investment in a risky opportunity. Indeed, we find that association with high design (hypothetical ownership in a design-related company) leads to subsequent riskier investment activity and less risk aversion as measured through willingness to accept a risky gamble. No such effect occurs after association with high function.

Thus, the learnings from this research are two-fold. First, that aesthetic attributes impact behavior in the context of financial decisions reveals just how robust the role of aesthetics is in evaluation and decision-making. Second, we understand more about how this occurs–both through sense of ownership's partial mediation as well as through self-affirmation. Further research is needed to understand how and why respondents feel a greater sense of ownership for something that is better looking. This effect seems to imply an inherent personal connection to good looks and may be related to the illusory superiority effect (Alicke 1985, Kruger Dunning 1999, Sedikides Gregg 2003). The finding that mere association with high design leads to riskier investment activity, again, speaks to the power of aesthetics and merits further investigation and likely has implications in both consumer behavior and finance.

References

Alicke, MarkD. (1985), "Global Self-Evaluation as Determined by the Desirability and Controllability of Trait Adjectives. *Journal of Personality and Social Psychology*, 49, 1621-1630.

Gibney, Frank Jr. and Belinda Luscombe (2000), "The Redesign of America," *Time*, March 20, 66-75.

Kruger, Justin and David Dunning (1999), "Unskilled and Unaware of It: How Difficulties in Recognizing One's Own Incompetence Lead to Inflated Self-Assessments," *Journal of Personality and Social Psychology,* 77 (6), 1121–34.

Postrel, Virginia (2003), *The Substance of Style: How the Rise of Aesthetic Value is Remaking Commerce, Culture and Conscience*. New York, HarperCollins.

Schmitt, Bernd H. and Alex Simonson (1997), *Marketing Aesthetics: The Strategic Management of Brands, Identity and Image*. New York, Free Press.

Sedikides, Constantine and Aiden P. Gregg (2003), "Portraits of the Self," in M. A. Hogg & J. Cooper (Eds.), *Sage Handbook of Social Psychology*, 110-138. London: Sage Publications.

Townsend, Claudia and Sanjay Sood (2009), "Self-Affirmation Through the Choice of High Design,"(working paper).

"Assisted Aesthetic Self-Design: Application to Nike Shoe Configurator"

Xiaoyan Deng, University of Pennsylvania, USA
Sam K. Hui, New York University, USA
Wes Hutchinson, University of Pennsylvania, USA

Self-design is a form of mass customization in which consumers partly design a product by specifying certain product attributes in the product configurator provided by manufacturers.[1] For mass customization to create real value, those attributes should be ones on which consumers' preferences differ sharply and that consumers can easily manipulate and evaluate with the configurator (Zipkin 2001). *Aesthetic self-design*, a particular form of self-design in which consumers choose only the product's aesthetic specifications, meets these two conditions. "Beauty is in the eyes of the beholder." While inferring functional benefits from technical specifications often requires a high level of consumer expertise (e.g., Randall, Terwiesch, and Ulrich 2007), aesthetics is in most cases subjective, making consumers into de facto experts about what they personally find attractive. A brief examination of over 500 web-based configurators (www.configurator-database.com) reveals that about 50% are from fashion industries (e.g., apparel, footwear).

The configurators offered by manufacturers in these industries (e.g., Adidas, Converse, Lands' End, Nike, Ralph Lauren, Reebok, Timberland) are characterized by providing different color palettes for different product components and a variety of color options in each palette. For example, a consumer can use Nike's shoe configurator (www.nikeID.com) to design a Nike shoe by selecting a color from a platter of 6-12 colors for each of the 7 shoe components (e.g., base, secondary, swoosh, accent, lace, lining, and shox). Presumably the consumer wants to create an aesthetically pleasing color combination for the shoe.

Given that a consumer can select any color combinations for the 7 components, the choice space from which she can pick her most-favorite shoe is huge; a consumer can pick from more than 5 million different shoe designs (Deng and Hutchinson 2009). From a theoretical perspective, the consumer is faced with a high-dimensional optimization problem that involves numerous alternatives, which is made even more difficult because colors "interact" with each other (e.g., Matsuda 1995); for example, red may look great with green, but not with purple, and so on. We expect that consumers may become cognitively overloaded due to the huge number of possible choices (e.g., Schwartz 2004), and thus may not be able to optimally select the shoe that she likes best.

Our main goal in this research is to improve consumers' aesthetic self-design experience. Our proposed solution to the "choice overload" problem is an "assisted aesthetic self-design" paradigm. Instead of only allowing consumers free and unrestricted choice, we assist them by providing recommendations during their design processes. That is, using an algorithm similar to collaborative filtering (Bodapati 2008), we recommend completed shoes to the consumer while she is still designing her own shoes. For instance, after the consumer selects a "red" base color, we offer a few recommendations (based on how other consumers design their shoes), which also has a red base color and other colors already configured. At any time, the consumer is allowed to switch to any of the recommended design and continue her design process from there. Our hypothesis is that this assisted mode of self-design is superior to the free mode of self-design (which is used by Nike and other manufacturers) in terms of both design outcome and process.

We first conducted a pretest to determine the optimal level of prior information that we should elicit from a consumer before offering her recommendations. That is, should we recommend shoe designs after the consumer makes the 1st, 2nd … or 7th color decision? 294 participants were asked to self-design a Nike shoe (in phase 1) and later evaluate their self-designed shoe along with recommended shoes (in phase 2). The recommendations shown in phase 2 were drawn from the self-designed shoes collected in phase 1. For each participant, around 20 recommendations were made using 1-6 component colors in her self-designed shoe as anchor(s). For example, recommended shoes anchoring on the 1st color choice would have the same base color as the self-designed shoe; recommended shoes anchoring on the 1st and 2nd color choices would have the same base and secondary colors as the self-designed shoe,

[1] Self-design is also called "adaptive customization," "co-design," and "user design" and configurator is also called "co-design platform," "toolkit," and "choiceboard" in the mass customization literature.

and so on. During the study, participants were unaware of the fact that their self-designed shoe was embedded in the set of recommended shoes. The result indicates an inverted-U relationship between preference and the number of anchor (p-value for the quadratic contrast<.05). Recommendations anchoring on 3-5 component colors of a self-designed shoe were rated higher in preference than were the self-designed shoe and other recommended shoes (p's<.05). This pattern suggests that recommendations should be made using the moderate level of color preference information from consumers.

To test our hypothesis that assisted self-design via the recommendation system is better than free self-design, in our main study we will ask participants to self-design a Nike shoe using either the NIKEiD configurator (free mode) or the configurator providing recommendations (assisted mode). The later configurator has been developed by us specifically for this study. Based on the pretest result, our configurator is designed to automatically generate a few recommendations after a consumer makes the first 3, 4, and 5 color choices, respectively. Our goal is to demonstrate that the assisted self-design group has higher satisfaction, a more positive experience, and a higher purchase probability than the free self-design group.

References

Bodapati, Anand V. (2008), "Recommendation Systems with Purchase Data," *Journal of Marketing Research*, 45, 77-93.

Deng, Xiaoyan, and Wes Hutchinson (2009), "Aesthetic Self-Design: Just Do It Yourself," *Working Paper*.

Matsuda, Y. (1995), *Color Design*, Asakura Shoten.

Randall, Taylor, Christian Terwiesch, and Karl T. Ulrich (2007), "User Design of Customized Products," *Marketing Science*, 26(2), 268-80.

Schwartz, Barry (2007), *The Paradox of Choice: Why More is Less*, HarperCollins Publishers, NY: New York.

Zipkin, Paul (2001), "The Limits of Mass Customization," *MIT Sloan Management Review*, 42(3), 81-7.

"To Each His Own? How Comparisons to Others Influence Consumer Self-Design"

C. Page Moreau, University of Colorado, Boulder
Kelly Herd, University of Colorado, Boulder

In product categories ranging from running shoes, to pet beds, to ceiling fans, consumers are becoming the designers of their own products, picking aesthetic components such as colors and images, creating designs that reflect their unique preferences. Research shows that consumers are willing to pay a substantial premium for these self-designed products compared to comparable manufacturer-designed alternatives (Franke and Piller 2004), yet limited research explores *why* they are willing to pay this premium.

In this paper, three studies demonstrate that consumers' social comparisons to the designers of comparable products influence evaluations of their own creations, their behavior following the self-design experience, and their product satisfaction. Since professionally-designed, "off-the-rack" alternatives often serve as a basis of comparison for one's own designs, the first two experiments examine how social comparisons with the designers of these products influence consumers' self-evaluations. These experiments also identify two key moderators useful in overcoming the negative effects of an upward comparison to a professional designer. A third study examines how social comparisons to other self-designers influence evaluations and behavior during and after a self-design experience. This study does so by using a real online design task in which designs are created, orders are placed, and products produced and delivered to the participants.

In the first two studies, we examine the influence of social comparison by holding constant the default reference product (an LL Bean backpack) but varying whom the participants thought was its designer (a professional at LL Bean vs. an amateur who won an LL Bean-sponsored design contest). Process measures and preferences for the customized backpack were the dependent measures in all studies.

In Study 1, we manipulated both the designer of the default backpack (professional vs. amateur) and the amount of guidance provided in the self-design task (present vs. absent). The results showed that attitudes toward the *self-designed* product were higher when participants thought that the default backpack was designed by another consumer rather than by a professional ($M_{Professional}$=36.2 vs. $M_{Amateur}$=39.5, p<.05). In addition, the factors interacted such that when no guidance was provided, participants rated the self-designed backpack significantly higher when the default was designed by another amateur ($M_{No\ Guidance,\ Amateur}$=40.0 vs. $M_{No\ Guidance,\ Professional}$=34.3, p<.01); no such differences emerged in the presence of guidance. Participants appeared to process upward social comparison information non-defensively.

Study 2 provides further evidence that social comparison processing occurs in self-design situations by testing for derogation. In this study, we manipulate the order in which participants are told they will be allowed to customize their backpack (before vs. after they evaluate the default backpack). Participants who knew about the customization opportunity before they evaluated the default backpack rated it lower when the designer was a professional as compared to an amateur ($M_{Professional}$=24.1 vs. $M_{Amateur}$=27.6, (F(1, 145)=4.58, p<.05). Participants who had no knowledge of the customization opportunity when they rated the default showed no difference in their evaluations ($M_{Professional}$=27.2 vs. $M_{Amateur}$=24.7, (F(1, 145)=2.04, p>.10). Evaluations of the self-designed backpacks are also consistent with the social comparison account. For participants who had the chance to derogate the default, no differences emerged in their self-evaluations ($M_{Professional}$=35.2 vs. $M_{Amateur}$=34.8, (F(1, 119)=.29, NS). However, of the participants who did not have the chance to derogate the default, those facing an upward comparison incorporated the negative comparison information into their self-evaluations in a manner consistent with non-defensive processing ($M_{Professional}$=31.8 vs. $M_{Amateur}$=38.1, (F(1, 119)=6.88, p<.01).

In study 3, we introduce a design contest as another means for repairing threatened self-regard, manipulating the timing of the contest announcement. In this study, all participants designed customize skins for an electronic device. The results show that when a contest provides a means for repairing threatened self-regard (i.e., is announced prior to a design task), upward comparison targets (i.e., professional designers) yield higher contest participation rates than comparisons to more equivalent targets (i.e., amateur designers). When a contest does not provide a means for repairing threatened self-regard (i.e., is announced after a design task), participation rates were unaffected by type of comparison target. This decision to enter the contest lead to differences in evaluations of the self-designed skins, evaluations of perceived fit of the design, willingness to pay, time spent on design, product satisfaction, and ratings from independent judges.

The first two studies indicate that upward comparisons to professionals tend to be processed non-defensively, resulting in lower evaluations of self-designed products. Providing guidance and prompting defensive processing are both effective ways to diminish the influence of the negative information generated by these upward comparisons. The third study demonstrates that when defensive processing is prompted (e.g., by an explicit competition), the upward comparison can enhance evaluations of self-designed products when accompanied by an opportunity to repair self-regard. It does so by increasing participation in the repair opportunity, which subsequently leads to higher evaluations of self-designed products, greater willingness to pay, and higher long-run satisfaction. Ratings from independent judges confirmed these effects.

References

Franke, Nikolaus and Frank Piller (2004), "Value Creation by Toolkits for User Innovation and Design: The Case of the Watch Market," *The Journal of Product Innovation Management*, 21(6), 401.

Special Session Summary

Deep Determinants of Value: New Perspectives on the Endowment Effect

Rama Ganesan, University of Arizona, USA

SESSION OVERVIEW

Decision makers exhibit a number of systematic biases both in the lab and in the field. The endowment effect demonstrates two such biases, reference dependence and loss aversion, in the framework of economic transaction. Although the endowment effect has been applied to explaining a wide variety of small and large scale economic phenomena, its underlying mechanisms still remain obscure. Illuminating these deep *determinants of value* shaping the endowment effect and related phenomena can inform novel predictions, identify the potential scope of observed effects, and reveal the degree to which various market incentives will mitigate or enhance effects (Chen, Lakshminarayanan and Santos 2006). For instance, is the endowment effect driven by universal processes arising from evolved biological features? Emerging evidence for loss aversion in animals suggests that this may be the case (Chen et al. 2006; Marsh and Kacelnik 2002). On the other hand, loss aversion is known to be limited and influenced by complex higher-level cultural and contextual factors (Novemsky and Kahneman 2005). The papers in this session explore the endowment effect and the specific processes and systems of valuation from which it arises, employing diverse levels of analysis and taking disparate points of view.

The first two papers address the phenomenon as more fundamentally driven, respectively examining emotional reactions to anticipated losses, and anticipated (but unrealized) gain or reward. Emphasizing the loss aversion that forms the basis of the endowment effect, Ganesan and Saqib examine the temperamental variables that might predispose one to be more or less sensitive to loss. Specifically, they show that prices elicited in the endowment paradigm are dependent upon inherent differences in temperamental fear. Conversely, Litt, Khan and Shiv focus on how gain-anticipation may differentially influence distinct components of value determining the endowment effect. Drawing upon recent neuroscientific research, they examine circumstances that cause the decoupling of *wanting* (as determining prices offered by buyers) and *liking* (driving prices and sufficient-substitutions demanded by sellers). The third paper gives more emphasis to contextual factors, such as the *temporal frame* that embeds the transaction. Chatterjee and Irmak show that when pre-owned objects are presented in the past (vs. future) temporal frame (e.g., "three years of the car's lifetime have passed" vs. "nine years of the car's lifetime remain"), they are not susceptible to differential valuation by buyers and sellers.

Although the three papers apply different and complementary approaches to studying the bases of the endowment effect, they are united in their measurement and relation of the phenomenon to important individual differences in traits and tendencies. A key unifying goal of discussion will be to explore the compatibility of these approaches and results, and how each paper may illuminate different facets of the deeper processes of valuation driving the endowment effect. Guiding this discussion and audience-inspired debate will be Joel Huber, a leading researcher on the endowment effect and broader conceptualizations of choice and value.

This session will appeal both to researchers interested in the endowment effect itself, as well as those studying the underlying components and mechanisms of valuation probed by the session's papers in order to provide new insights into the effect and related phenomena. This audience includes behavioral decision researchers, those interested in emotional and motivational influences on valuation and decision making, and those employing methods ranging from behavioral study to neuroscientific investigation.

References

Chen, M.K., Lakshminarayanan, V., and Santos, L.R. (2006). How basic are behavioral biases? Evidence from Capuchin Monkey trading behavior. *Journal of Political Economy, 114 (31)*, 517-537.

Novemsky, N. & Kahneman, D. (2005). The boundaries of loss aversion. *Journal of Marketing Research*, 42 (May), 119-128.

Marsh, B., and Kacelnick, A. (2002) Framing effects and risky decisions in starlings. *Proceedings of the National Academy of Sciences*, 99(5), 3352-3355

EXTENDED ABSTRACTS

"Defending Against Loss: Temperamental Fear Predicts Endowment Effect"

Rama Ganesan, University of Arizona, USA
Najam Saqib, Ryerson University, USA

The endowment effect demonstrates one of the essential properties of Tversky and Kahneman's (1991) reference-dependent model in that the psychological effect of a loss is greater than a gain of the same magnitude. What causes this endowment effect? To answer this question, we investigate the fundamental psychological mechanism that might conceivably determine this loss aversion. We posit that the mechanism for loss aversion is *fear*. Fear is our reaction to anticipated loss, whether it is the loss of life itself at one extreme, or the loss of a consumer good in our possession at the other end. Camerer (2005) has previously suggested that the endowment effect may be a short-term fear reaction to anticipated losses and gains.

However, because the behaviors and self-reports of participants in the typical endowment paradigm do not evince fear, one needs to look for alternative methods to determine its effect. We reasoned that, if the endowment effect is essentially determined by fear, then it must be related to the inherent fearfulness of the individual. We suggest that loss aversion is related to one particular *trait variable* that relates to the threat of loss, *temperamental fear* or *trait fear*. In our first study, we show that in the standard endowment paradigm, prices elicited are highly dependent upon temperamental fear, particularly among the sellers. We find further correlational evidence in that a manipulation that reduces the endowment effect (Novemsky and Kahneman 2005) also reduces the relationship between temperamental fear and prices offered or demanded. In the second study we support our argument by manipulating fear and we find that inducing fear increases the magnitude of the endowment effect.

In the first study, we related the participant's inherent fearfulness to the price offered for buying the focal object and the price demanded for selling the focal object (set of highlighters). Participants were 228 undergraduate students who were randomly assigned to play the role of buyers or sellers. Temperament scales were administered, followed by filler tasks prior to the endowment procedure. Temperamental fear was measured by the Fear Survey Schedule II (FSS, Bernstein and Allen 1969). For FSS (alpha=0.83), the subjects reported their fear for fourteen individual objects or situations (such as *getting hurt*, *snakes*, and *public speaking*) on 7-

point scale of *none, very little, a little, some, much, very much* and *terror*. As it is important to distinguish temperamental fear from other related trait constructs, we also included other well-known and popular scales for anxiety, depression and prevention and promotion focus (NEO-PI-R, Costa and McCrae, 1992; Lockwood et al. 2002). Prior to price elicitation in either condition, current affect was measured by the PANAS scale (Positive and Negative Affect Scale, Watson et al. 1988).

The typical endowment effect was confirmed as sellers demanded twice the amount for the endowed object relative to buyers ($4.08 vs. $1.79, $F(1,224)=140.7, p<0.001$). Subsequent analyses indicated a significant relationship between the measure of temperamental fear and price demanded by sellers and price offered by buyers. Specifically, we find a strong positive relationship for sellers ($r=0.74$) and a more moderate negative relationship for buyers ($r=-0.36$). This indicates that temperamental fear is related predominantly to the increased valuation of the focal object by sellers, but also to some extent to a decreased valuation by buyers. A median split of the subjects based on the FSS score showed that the extent of the endowment effect is significantly greater among the high fear group relative to the low fear group (significant interaction between role and fear group, $F(1,144)=53.78, p<0.001$).

Other variables (NEO-PI-R anxiety and depression, PANAS current positive and negative affect) had no relationship to price in either condition. A small positive relationship found for promotion and prevention focus became nonsignificant in the follow up regression where temperamental fear score was added to the equation (control factors include age and gender). In the additional condition where subjects experienced a prior loss (losing out in a random drawing for a cup) the endowment effect was eliminated (2.77 vs. 3.08 in buyers and sellers respectively, *ns*). Here there was no correlation between FSS score and price demanded or offered. This is an important result in relation to the standard endowment condition, as it shows that the effect can be eliminated by quite simple interventions.

In the second study, we induced fear among our participants ($n=84$) by requiring them to prepare for a public presentation (a modified Trier Social Stress procedure, Childs et al. 2006). Subjects in the neutral condition ($n=84$) were required to prepare to evaluate a public presentation. Affect scores indicate an increase in current fear (relevant terms include *afraid, scared* and *nervous*) in subjects in the fear condition relative to the neutral condition, (2.03 and 1.54, $t(1,172)=3.08, p<0.001$). Price was then elicited among buyers and sellers in both affect conditions. Price demanded by fearful sellers was increased relative to neutral sellers, $4.26 vs. $3.45, $t(1,87)=2.62$, $p<0.01$. The endowment effect was enhanced in the fear condition relative to the neutral condition, $F(1,164)=3.38, p<0.07$. This result further supports the argument that fear is the mechanism underlying loss aversion, and the endowment effect (Camerer, 2005).

Taken together our findings have implications for the current global recessionary climate. As fear leads to both an increased valuation for owned objects, and a decreased valuation for objects not owned, the net effect could be a reduction in all types of buyer-seller transactions. Consumers and markets are now focused on defending against further loss than on pursuing new opportunities. In addition, our paper has implications for the resolution and management of the recessionary paralysis. Under laboratory conditions, certain interventions can eliminate the effect of fear and return participants to a more rational valuation.

References

Bernstein, D. A. & Allen, G. (1969). Fear survey schedule II: Normative data and factor analysis based on large college sample. *Behavioural Research and Therapy*, 7, 403-407.

Camerer, C. (2005). Three cheers-psychological, theoretical, empirical- for loss aversion. *Journal of Marketing Research*, 42(May), 129-133.

Childs, E. Vicini, L. & De Wit, H. (2006). Responses to the Trier Social Stress Test (TSST) in single versus grouped participants. *Psychophysiology*, 43, 366-371.

Costa, P. T. & McCrae, R. R. (1992). *Revised NEO Personality Inventory (NEO-PI-R) and NEO five-factor inventory (NEO-FFI).*

Lockwood, P., Jordan, C. H., & Kunda, Z. (2002). Motivation by positive or negative role models: Regulatory focus determines who will best inspire us. *Journal of Personality and Social Psychology*, *83*, 854-864.

Novemsky, N. & Kahneman, D. (2005). The boundaries of loss aversion. *Journal of Marketing Research*, 42 (May), 119-128.

Tversky, A. & Kahneman, D. (1991). Loss aversion in riskless choice: A reference-dependent model. *Quarterly Journal of Economics*, (November), 1039-1061.

Watson, D., Clark, L. A., & Tellegen, A. (1988). Development and validation of brief measures of positive and negative affect: The PANAS scales. *Journal of Personality and Social Psychology,* 54, 1063-1070.

"Wanting More but Liking Less: Counter-Driving Motivational and Appraisal Elements of Value"

Ab Litt, Stanford University, USA
Uzma Khan, Stanford University, USA
Baba Shiv, Stanford University, USA

Underlying many instances of the endowment effect may be qualitative differences in valuation formation processes in the presence versus absence of ownership. Value judgments in the absence of ownership may be most reflective of individuals' desire or *wanting* for a target. In contrast, valuation of owned targets may reflect actual, perceived, or forecasted *liking* of the target; that is, appraisal of its overall appeal and the pleasure it brings one. Growing work in psychology and neuroscience is establishing that wanting and liking are underserved by distinct and dissociable subsystems (Berridge, 1996; Winkielman & Berridge, 2003). This dissociability may not only underlie the valuation disparity characteristic of the endowment effect, but raise the potential for differentially influencing these systems to mitigate or reverse that disparity.

We propose that frustrating failure to obtain desired outcomes can induce such parallel counter-driving. Responses to such unpleasant "jilting" have significant implications for both peoples' subsequent desire for denied objectives (wanting), and how they feel about the targets themselves (liking). In particular, we propose that failure to achieve a desired end-state can simultaneously *increase* desire to obtain the outcome, but *decrease* its overall appeal due to tainting by the unpleasantness of failing to obtain it. Perversely, a target becomes more desired as it becomes less desirable. Thus, after experiencing initial denial, people can come to want something more and like it less, a valuation disparity opposite to that most consistent with the endowment effect.

Primary-Effect Study

Experiment. Sixty subjects were provided an allotment of 'virtual tokens', and told they would be used to purchase or play games for real prizes. They then made a series of willingness-to-pay (in tokens) judgments for various potential prize products. For half of the subjects (the "non-jilted" group), this initial series included a prize, *P*, that they subsequently won in a rigged game. The other half (the "jilted" group) were instead told that they lost this same game with the same possible prize *P*, and only after were queried regarding willingness-to-pay for *P*. These willingness-to-pay judgments were our dependent measures of "wanting" for prize *P*.

All subjects then played a second rigged game, in which the jilted group finally won prize *P* (and non-jilted subjects won tokens). All were then offered the chance to trade *P* for an alternative, *Q*, with willingness-to-*switch* taken to conceptualize "liking" for prize *P*, in terms of satisfaction (higher willingness-to-switch being akin to *lower* liking, and lower willingness-to-accept in typical endowment effect studies). Subjects also completed an Affect Intensity Measure (AIM) of individual differences in strength of emotional experience and responsiveness (Larsen & Diener, 1987), to explore the centrality of affective reactions to our proposed effects.

Results. For wanting, jilted subjects reported significantly *amplified willingness-to-pay for prize P*, both compared to non-jilted subjects (mean 7.56 vs. 5.29 tokens; $t(53)=2.289$, $p=.026$), and in within-subject comparison to a highly similar prize, *P'* (paired $t(26)=3.276$, $p=.003$) pre-tested to be similarly attractive. Importantly, this effect was driven by individuals scoring *low* in affect-intensity, based on an AIM median-split (interaction $\beta=-1.602$, $p=.043$); high-AIM jilted subjects did not show significant mean difference from non-jilted subjects in willingness-to-pay for *P*. In contrast, for liking, jilted subjects reported significantly *higher willingness-to-switch away from prize P* to alternative prize *Q* (78%) than did non-jilted subjects (43%; $p=.013$, Fisher's exact test).

A second study provided converging evidence by employing alternative wanting-liking operationalizations; tested robustness to changing product-denial attribution from a subject's own failure to a stock-out; and explored generalizability of jilting effects to based on brand-overlap alone.

Generalized-Effect Study

Experiment. Using a nested between-subjects design (n=159), in Part 1, half of subjects faced an "out of stock" denial of putative potential to obtain a pair of Guess-branded sunglasses following task completion. The other half performed the same task and were exposed to the same sunglasses, but did not expect to receive them (or anything else).

Part 2 measured wanting and liking between-subjects across Part 1 conditions. Rather than the Guess sunglasses, a pair of his-and-her Guess watches (the "jilt-proxy") was introduced. For wanting measurement, subjects *chose* one of two prize packages for a lottery draw-entry, either the Guess watches or similar Calvin Klein-branded watches. In contrast, our liking measure queried attractiveness *evaluations*, detached from wanting-influenced choice inclinations. We adapted the distortion paradigm (e.g., Russo et al., 1996), in which favoring/disfavoring of alternatives is captured by individuals' judgments of serially presented equivocal information as actually favoring one alternative over another. In particular, we measured distortions between the Guess and CK watches in evaluating equivocal and non-diagnostic attribute information (movement, watch-band, etc.). Finally, all subjects completed the AIM used in the primary-effect study.

Results. As before, we observed AIM-moderation for wanting: jilted low-AIM subjects significantly *over-chose* the jilt-proxy (83%; $B(24,0.5)$, $p=0.0015$)), whereas high-AIM subjects trended marginally towards under-choosing the jilt-proxy (30%; $B(23,0.5)$, $p=0.093$) in favor of the alternative ($p<0.0005$, Fisher's exact test).

For liking, distortion computed across nine attributes as per Russo et al. yielded near-zero distortion in favor of either Guess (jilt-proxy) or CK by non-jilted subjects, versus *+0.40 units against the Guess item by jilted subjects* ($t(582)=2.7592$, one-sided $p<0.005$), and cumulative distortion after all nine stages of 3.83 units against Guess. Paneling by AIM did not yield significant differences in anti-Guess liking-distortion ($t(286)=1.1637$, $p=0.2455$).

Implications

These findings support the notion that wanting and liking can be counter-driven by denial of desired targets; in particular, in a direction contrary to that most consistent with the endowment effect. This may aid in understanding how consumer experiences such as stock-outs could differentially affect valuation metrics that are more wanting-driven (e.g., demand, WTP) versus those more related to liking (e.g., return rate, repeat-purchase propensity, WTA). Affect-intensity interaction results may suggest tighter *coupling* of wanting and liking sub-systems in high-AIM individuals, leading to greater inter-regulation and reduced disparity. Such "hot-headed" individuals actually exhibit more *hedonically normative* desires, that is, desires and desire-driven behaviors more consistent with the ultimate evaluative feelings that would govern happiness.

References

Berridge, K. C. (1996). Food reward: Brain substrates of wanting and liking. *Neuroscience and Biobehavioral Reviews, 20*(1), 1-25.

Winkielman, P., & Berridge, K. C. (2003). Irrational wanting and subrational liking: How rudimentary motivational and affective processes shape preferences and choices. *Political Psychology, 24*(4), 657-680.

Larsen, R. J., & Diener, E. (1987). Affect intensity as an individual difference characteristic: A review. *Journal of Research in Personality, 21*(1), 1-39.

Russo, J. E., Medvec, V. H., & Meloy, M. G. (1996). The distortion of information during decisions. *Organizational Behavior and Human Decision Processes, 66*(1), 102-110.

"The Impact of Temporal Focus on the Endowment Effect"

Promothesh Chatterjee, University of South Carolina, USA
Caglar Irmak, University of South Carolina, USA

Imagine a consumer interested in buying a three-year-old, pre-owned car. The seller claims that the car is good for nine more years (future focus). On the other hand, the buyer can think of the car as one that has been used for three years (past focus). Do sellers and buyers approach such exchange occasions with pre-determined temporal foci, which diverge from each other? If so, does this variation in the temporal focus affect selling and buying prices? Given the large body of research on the endowment effect (Thaler 1980), demonstrating selling prices of objects to be considerably higher than buying prices, answers to these questions are of considerable theoretical and practical importance.

While the endowment effect has mostly been explained as a manifestation of loss aversion (Kahneman, Knetsch and Thaler 1990), some recent research investigated how sellers' and buyers' foci diverge, which sheds more light into the underlying process of this phenomenon. For example, Carmon and Ariely (2000) show that buyers and sellers focus on what they forgo in the exchange. While buyers focus on the money, sellers focus on the benefits of possessing the product and, as a result, buying prices are more affected by the change in expenditure-related aspects of the object; whereas selling prices are more influenced by the change in aspects that are related to the benefits of the object. Nayakankuppam and Mishra (2005) indicate that sellers and buyers focus on features of differing valence. Sellers' evaluations of the products are more influenced by the positive (vs. negative) features of the products, while buyers' evaluations are more affected by the negative (vs. positive) features of the products.

In the present research, we build on this body of research by investigating how temporal focus affects selling and buying prices of objects. Since time is an inherent factor in the evaluation of pre-owned products, we focus on such products in our research. Focusing on pre-owned products is not only theoretically interesting and perhaps necessary in our context, but also it is practically important given the market size of some pre-owned products (e.g., books, cars) in the U.S. is actually larger than that of the new counterparts. For example, Bureau of Transportation Statistics (2007) reports a trade volume of $339 billion for pre-owned cars and substantially greater number of old automobiles being traded than new ones.

Research on time perspective literature suggests that future-orientation entails a focus on future goals and a tendency to relate immediate choices to distant objectives (Lewin 1948). Past-orientation, on the other hand, involves a focus on similar previous situations with their accompanying positives and negatives. Importantly, Zimbardo, Keough and Boyd (1997) contend that though time perspective tends to be a functional cognitive style, it can vary as a function of situational, structural, and task demands. Based on this, and the aforementioned research on the endowment effect, we predict that, when a pre-owned product is presented in the future temporal frame, sellers, with ownership as their point of reference, will view the sale as a loss of the future benefits, while buyers will incorporate both past and future aspects of the product in their evaluation. Consequently, selling prices will be higher than buying prices. When the product is presented in the past temporal frame, however, sellers will not be able to focus solely on future benefits of the product, resulting in no significant difference between selling and buying prices, i.e., mitigation of the well-established endowment effect. We tested these predictions across three studies, summaries of these studies are described next.

In study 1 we explored how chronic temporal focus (i.e., temporal orientation) affects selling and buying prices of an object. We reasoned that sellers who are high on past-orientation would focus on the past of the product (a 3 year old car) and thus lower their valuation mitigating the endowment effect. Consistent with this, we find that endowment effect is mitigated for high past oriented people but not low past oriented people. In study 2a, 2b we manipulate the foci of buyers and sellers by a temporal framing (e.g., 3 years life used vs. 9 years life remaining) across two different domains–used cars and partly used football season tickets. Consistent with our hypothesizing we find endowment effect only in the future frame but not in the past. Study 3 again used a temporal framing but used a real stimulus of Netflix coupon instead of hypothetical scenarios as in previous studies. We also focus on the process underlying the effect. Our findings suggest that it is sellers' heightened focus on future that results in the disparity of selling and buying prices. These findings not only provide insight to the underlying process of the endowment effect by demonstrating a key moderator (e.g., temporal focus), but also have important implications for marketers of used goods (e.g., eBay, Amazon.com, car dealers).

References

Bureau of Transportation Statistics (2007): http://www.bts.gov/publications/national_transportation_statistics/html/table_01_17.html

Carmon, Ziv and Dan Ariely (2000), "Focusing on the Forgone: Why Value Can Appear So Different to Buyers and Sellers," *Journal of Consumer Research*, 27 (December), 360–70.

Lewin, Kurt (1942), "Time Perspective and Morale," In G. Lewin (Ed.), *Resolving Social Conflicts* (pp. 103-124). New York: Harper.

Kahneman, Daniel, Knetsch, Jack L. and Richard H. Thaler (1990), "Experimental Tests of the Endowment Effect and the Coase Theorem," *Journal of Political Economy*, 98, 6, 1352-1376.

Nayakankuppam, Dhananjay and Himanshu Mishra (2005), "The Endowment Effect: Rose-Tinted and Dark-Tinted Glasses," *Journal of Consumer Research*, 32 (December), 390-95.

Thaler, Richard (1980), "Toward a Positive Theory of Consumer Choice," *Journal of Economic Behavior and Organization*, 1 (March), 39–60.

Zimbardo, Philip G., Keough, K. A. and John N. Boyd (1997), "Present Time Perspective as a Predictor of Risky Driving," *Personality and Individual Differences*, 23, 1007-1023.

SPECIAL SESSION SUMMARY

What is the Intelligent Choice? Performance on the CRT and Preferences

Claudia Townsend, UCLA Anderson School of Management, USA

SESSION OVERVIEW

Typically in consumer behavior and decision-making research we examine the general trend of responses–what the majority is doing or choosing. However, it is also informative to look at the differences between individuals. The papers presented in this session examine intelligence, as measured by the Cognitive Reflection Test (CRT; Frederick, 2005), its correlates, and how this individual difference impacts various behaviors. The CRT primarily measures respondents' propensity to resist reporting the first response that comes to mind. However, its correlation with intelligence measurements allows it to substitute for such a tool as well. The works presented here utilize the CRT in both of these capacities to provide new insights both about correlates of this tendency to resist (or not) the first heuristic response, as well as the relationship between intelligence and preferences for risk, time, and aesthetically pleasing products.

In the first presentation Spunt and Lieberman examine the CRT in its primary role to discriminate "gut" first responses from slower more methodological responses. They propose that the propensity to go with one's initial response is the result of overconfidence. In three behavioral studies they find that reducing confidence in first responses, either through indirect inductions of self-doubt or by directly invalidating initial responses, can make individuals behave in what seems to be a more intelligent manner. Moreover, the results of a fourth fMRI brain imaging study corroborates this notion. Thus, this work is able to explain something further about the CRT and, subsequently, about response behavior.

The other two projects build upon this work and use the CRT as an intelligence indicator–by itself in the work by Frederick Fong, and Tsytsylin and along with vocabulary questions (Mill Hill Vocabulary Scale) in the work by Townsend, Ariely, and Sood. Both these works examine the differences in preferences between less and more intelligent individuals. Frederick, Fong, and Tsytsylin not only examine preferences, but also lay-theories about these preferences–how people expect more intelligent and less intelligent people to differ. They find that providing the less intelligent with information on the preferences of the more intelligent impacted actual choice behavior in only some domains e.g. risk preferences and not in others e.g. time preferences. Thus, as with the first work presented, Frederic, Fong, and Tsytsylin suggest one way in which to engender more intelligent choice behavior, though only in some realms. And, indeed, as the authors point out, a relation between intelligence and preference, by itself, does not necessarily identify the correct choice in all cases.

Townsend, Ariely, and Sood also examine the relationship between lay-theories about intelligent choice versus actual choice. Testing the old adage that one ought not to "judge a book by its cover," the authors examine respondents' propensity to choose good looking products–even when the choice of good looks means giving up higher functionality or a well-known brand. Contrary to popular wisdom, they find that highly aesthetic choices are more popular among the highly intelligent than the less intelligent suggesting something consequential about product design.

By looking at individual differences on the CRT, these three studies provide insights on both personal preferences as well as general trends. Specifically this research offers learnings on the propensity to respond heuristically, the role of overconfidence, and the relationship between lay-theories about intelligence and actual behavior. Moreover, these studies both suggest and find limits on interventions to encourage intelligent choice.

Therefore, the proposed session would be of interest to a broad swath of consumer researchers and anyone interested in promoting normative choice behavior. This session would be of special interest to those interested in individual differences, risk or time preferences, aesthetics and brand preferences, and/or fMRI research. We hope that a session on these essential topics will incite debate and ideas for further research.

EXTENDED ABSTRACTS

"Getting Past that First, Compelling Response: Three Behavioral Studies and an fMRI Investigation of Performance and Overconfidence on the Cognitive Reflection Test"

Robert Spunt, UCLA, USA
Matthew Lieberman, UCLA, USA

This research offers theoretical and empirical perspectives on the constructs of cognitive reflection and overconfidence as measured using the Cognitive Reflection Test (CRT; Frederick, 2005). The various forms of the CRT feature quantitative reasoning word problems, each of which tends to induce a single incorrect response which is typically reported with high confidence. The following item is illustrative: "A bat and a ball cost $1.10 in total. If the bat cost $1.00 more than the ball, how much does the ball cost?" In scores of studies, over 90% of individuals who answered this item incorrectly did so by reporting the same response—10 cents. Frederick (2005) thus defined cognitive reflection as the tendency to resist reporting the first response that comes to mind when making a judgment or decision. Moreover, this tendency was explained using a two system model (Stanovich & West, 2000), which states that judgments and decisions often induce a first response that is the product of a fast and automatic computation system (System 1), but that these responses can be overridden by a relatively slower control system (System 2), which can implement the rule-based sequential operations that permit judges and decision makers to carefully consider alternatives. It was assumed, then, that individuals who are low on cognitive reflection rely too heavily on System 1, while individuals who are high on cognitive reflection tend to spontaneously activate System 2 before committing to a response. Additionally, the tendency to cognitively reflect on the CRT is associated with measures of intelligence as well as normative preferences in the face of risk and delay.

The first three studies expand on this two system account by additionally taking an attribution substitution approach to performance and overconfidence on the CRT (Kahneman & Frederick, 2002). The framing of each problem (e.g., the bat and ball problem above) suggests an easy, heuristic operation (e.g., subtracting) on the given quantities (e.g., $1.10 and $1.00) that becomes substituted for the relatively more effort- and time-costly target operations (e.g., the algebraic relationship among the bat, ball, $1.10, and $1.10). The resulting answer is then subjectively experienced as correct because it is the correct output, but to the wrong operation. Thus, attribute substitution explains not only errors on the CRT, but also overconfidence in those errors (referred to elsewhere as intuitive confidence; Simmons & Nelson, 2006).

The two system, attribute substitution account generates the simple hypothesis that reducing confidence in or invalidating the heuristic operation should boost performance and reduce overconfidence in errors on the CRT. In three studies, we show that both of these are true. Compared to a control condition where participants complete the CRT with no special instructions, participants for whom the heuristic response (e.g., 10 cents) was indirectly invalidated performed better and exhibited realistic levels of confidence in their errors. In a third condition, participants who were explicitly cautioned against reporting the first response showed a similar improvement in performance, but those who continue to commit heuristic errors continued to exhibit overconfidence. These effects of invalidation were specific to the heuristic responses and did not occur when alternative, nonheuristic responses were directly invalidated (e.g., 20 cents). In another study, we show that describing the CRT as a confirmation of gender differences in mathematical ability (which in women is known to induce a state known as 'stereotype threat'; cf. Shapiro & Neuberg, 2007), improves performance for women but actually impairs performance for men. Given that stereotype threat is thought to induce self-doubt in women and confidence in men, this suggests that contextual variables that modulate confidence can incidentally modulate the likelihood that a given individual will seek out alternatives to their first response when making a judgment or decision. Altogether, these studies suggest that reducing confidence in first responses, either through indirect inductions of self-doubt or by directly invalidating responses known beforehand to be prepotent, can make individuals behave in what seems to be a more intelligent, self-conscious manner.

In addition to these behavioral studies, we investigated the neural correlates of performance on the CRT using functional magnetic resonance imaging (fMRI). Given that the networks for deliberative quantitative reasoning have already been mapped in the brain, comparing brain activity during the computation of correct and heuristic responses enables a novel test of the two system characterization of judgment and decision making. For this study, we developed a 48-item adapted version of the CRT that participants completed while being scanned. Preliminary results show that solving the CRT items correctly compared to heuristically is associated with regions of the lateral frontoparietal cortices believed to be involved in deliberate logical and mathematical computation. Analyses are currently underway to determine brain regions selectively associated with the computation of heuristic responses.

Taken together, these findings shed light on the psychology of naively going with one's first response versus carefully considering alternatives when making a judgment or decision. Additionally, they suggest that in addition to its utility as a brief individual differences measure of the tendency to resist reporting first responses, the CRT items present useful tools for studying the two system account of the process of attribute substitution.

References

Frederick, Shane (2005), "Cognitive Reflection and Decision Making," *Journal of Economic Perspectives*, 19, 25-42.

Kahneman, Daniel and Shane Frederick (2002), "Representativeness Revisited: Attribute Substitution in Intuitive Judgment," in *Heuristics and Biases: the Psychology of Intuitive Judgment*, (Gilovich, T. et al., eds), 49-81, Cambridge University Press

Shapiro, Jenessa R. and Steven L. Neuberg (2007), "From Stereotype Threat to Stereotype Threats: Implications of a Multi-Threat Framework for Causes, Moderators, Mediators, Consequences, and Interventions," *Personality and Social Psychology Review*, 11(2), 107-130.

Simmons, Joseph P. and Leif D. Nelson (2006), "Intuitive Confidence: Choosing Between Intuitive and Nonintuitive Alternatives," *Journal of Experimental Psychology: General*, 135(3), 409-428.

Stanovich, Keith E. and Richard F. West (2000), "Individual Differences in Reasoning: Implications for the Rationality Debate," *Behavioral and Brain Sciences*, 23, 645-665.

"Should Einstein Manage your Money? Lay Theories and Normative Force of the Relation Between Cognitive Ability and Preferences"

Shane Frederick, Yale University, USA
Nathan Fong, Sloan School of Management, USA
Eric Tsytsylin, Yale School of Management, USA

Attitudes towards time and risk affect everything from how early a person leaves to catch a 10:00 flight, to the perceived urgency of regulating carbon emissions to combat global climate change. Much evidence now suggests that smarter people both discount future rewards less and have greater risk tolerance (see, e.g., Frederick, 2005). Such results could be interpreted as support for philosophical or theoretical arguments against excessive discounting or risk aversion (Rawls, 1971; Rabin & Thaler, 2001). Some do, in fact, draw this conclusion (Stanovich & West, 2000; Frederick, 2005), while others resist this inference (Sternberg, 2000).

In this research, we study whether people are aware of the relations between cognitive ability, such preferences, and the significance they attach to these facts. Koriat and Nisan (1977) examined both of these issues with young children. Kindergarten students drew pictures for the experimenters, and were rewarded with a choice between one candy immediately and two candies the next day. While 54% chose the larger delayed reward, 86% predicted that a "smart kid" would choose the later larger reward. Surprisingly, children who were first asked what a smart kid would do did not increase their patience–although 79% predicted that the smart kid chose the delayed larger reward, only 36% did so themselves. Thus, Nisan and Koriat demonstrated that children as young as five years old anticipate the relationship between intelligence and time preferences, but gave no weight to this fact even when their attention was directed towards it.

We used a similar design with adult respondents. Respondents were told (truthfully) that previous studies had found a relation between cognitive ability and some types of preferences. Respondents then attempted to predict the direction and strength of these relations by estimating the proportion of low-scoring and high-scoring respondents who preferred the various options.

Most subjects, for example, correctly predicted that smarter people would be more inclined to choose The New Yorker magazine over People magazine, and a larger later reward ($3800 next month) over a smaller sooner reward ($3400 this month). However, for items involving choices between a sure thing (e.g., $100) and a risky option (a coin flip for $300), respondents either failed to predict the observed difference, or generally predicted the opposite effect. For instance, although high scoring respondents were much more likely to prefer the gamble (63% vs. 21%), only 29% of respondents asked to predict the difference managed to correctly predict even the direction of this effect.

When respondents were told of the true relation between cognitive ability and various preferences, the impact depended on domain. In the domain of time preference discovering (or being reminded of) the correlation between intellect and time preferences (since most predicted it correctly) did not influence respondents' time preferences, replicating Nisan and Koriat's findings with children. By contrast, for decisions involving risk, while most respondents did not anticipate the greater risk tolerance among high scorers, learning about the true correlation did influence respondents' choices, increasing the proportion of respondents choosing the gamble from 15% to 26%. In other words, the news that "Johnny chose the gamble" may have provided justification (if not the compulsion) to choose it themselves.

The relevance of a correlation between some ability and some preference clearly depends on the type of ability and the type of preference in question. It is obvious that one should imitate Gary Kasparov if deciding which chess piece to move, but equally obvious that Einstein's preference for apples over oranges has no special significance to which you should prefer. Thus, a relation between cognitive ability and preference, by itself, surely does not identify the correct choice in all cases. But such information does, apparently, have significance, in at least some domains.

References

Frederick, S. (2005), "Cognitive Reflection and Decision Making," *Journal of Economic Perspectives*, 19 (4), 25-42.

Koriat, A. and M. Nisan (1977), "Children's Actual Choices and Their Conception of the Wise Choice in a Delay-of-Gratification Situation," *Child Development*, 48, 488-494.

Rabin, M. and R. Thaler (2001), "Anomalies: Risk Aversion," *The Journal of Economic Perspectives*, 15 (1), 219-232.

Rawls, J. (1971), *A Theory of Justice*, Harvard University Press.

Stanovich, K. and R. West (2000), "Individual Differences in Reasoning: Implications for the Rationality Debate," *Behavior and Brain Sciences*, 22 (5), 645-726.

Sternberg, R.J. (2000), "The Ability is Not General, and Neither are the Conclusions," response to K. E. Stanovich and R. F. West (pp. 697-698), *Behavioral and Brain Sciences*, 23, 645-726.

"The Intelligence of Judging Products Based on Looks"

Claudia Townsend, UCLA, USA
Dan Ariely, Duke University, USA
Sanjay Sood, UCLA, USA

There is a common belief that making decisions based on the way something looks is not an intelligent way to think. There is the familiar adage that one ought not to "judge a book by its cover" and this bias against evaluation based on appearance is likely considered, either consciously or unconsciously, by people in a variety of situations–from meeting new people to selecting a new household appliance. Moreover, recent work indicates that respondents consistently under-value the importance of product aesthetics in choice and also look to other, more functional, attributes to justify the choice of more attractive products (Townsend Sood working paper A). Indeed, there seems to be some common understanding that performance and functionality ought to play a greater role in evaluation than looks. And yet, in a series of studies we find that more intelligent individuals are more likely to choose better looking options–even when selecting good looks means selecting poorer functionality or a worse brand. Along with functionality, we examine the trade-off made with brand as this is another attribute that, even more so than design, may be considered an indicator of overall quality. Moreover, in the realm of fashion-related products it functions similarly to design as a source of value and as a signal to others. And yet, the preference for good design over a well-known brand persists, despite intelligent individuals having greater overall brand knowledge. That intelligent people are more likely to allow design to drive their choices, suggests there is some value in good design that ought to be further recognized.

The Cognitive Reflect Task (CRT) was introduced to measure one specific type of cognitive ability–the propensity to question one's initial response and correct it if there is a better one (Frederick 2005). Yet, it is positively correlated (with medium correlation) with self-reports on various intelligence and performance measures including the Scholastic Aptitude Test (SAT, .44) and the Wonderlic Personnel Test (WPT, .43). Thus, we used the three question CRT, as well as ten questions from the Mill Hill vocabulary test, as an indicator of overall intelligence. Using the CRT as part of our intelligence test, in fact, worked against our hypothesis that more intelligent people would choose based on design. Previous research (Townsend Sood working paper B) provides evidence for a more system 1-based processing of design relative to the more system 2-like processing of functional attributes, finding that cognitive load increases the choice share of the more aesthetic option. Based on this finding, one would expect those who are more prone to cognitive reflection and who are less likely to give the initial or more system 1-based response are also less likely to base a decision on design and more likely to take into account the functional attributes which are, presumably, processed with more reflective system 2 thinking. Therefore, our findings that intelligence, as partially measured by CRT, and preference for good design are correlated is particularly intriguing.

In Study 1 we found that when faced with a hypothetical choice between two options where one performs better on a functional attribute and the other is better looking, those who score better on the CRT as well as our overall intelligence indicator (combination of CRT and Mill Hill vocabulary score) were more likely to select the better looking, though functionally inferior option, than less intelligent respondents. One possible explanation for these results is that, despite asking respondents to assume the products were the same on all other attributes, because we provided information on only one functional feature along with design, perhaps the selection of good looks was driven by a notion that good looks implies better performance in other domains.

In Study 2 we examined design versus brand. Moreover, we examined fashion-related goods (e.g. clothing, accessories) where functionalities are less relevant. Thus in Study 2 respondents chose between two options where one was good looking and from an unknown brand while the other was less good looking and from a well-known brand–e.g. attractive Sun Song-branded dress versus unattractive Donna Karan-branded dress. Again, we found that more intelligent respondents were more likely to select the better designed options, despite the unknown brand name.

In our third study we examined this same issue using a different probing mechanism and asked respondents to give a price at which they would be equally likely to purchase two options. Respondents were shown a branded fashion item with a price and asked at what price they would be as likely to purchase a counterfeit version. Thus, in this study we were examining more specifically the value of an authentic brand-name to consumers. Consistent with our previous results, intelligent respondents valued the authentic brand-name less, pricing the counterfeit version higher, on average, than less intelligent respondents and, again, indicating that the overall look of the product is more important to highly intelligent individuals than those less intelligent..

The research presented here reveals that, at least in consumer products, valuing looks is associated with higher intelligence. These results are counterintuitive with respect to both our lay-theories about not "judging a book by its cover" as well as research on CRT, system 1 versus System 2 processing, and design. But also, these findings build on other work on both CRT and intelligence– some of which is also presented in this session.

References

Frederick, Shane (2005), "Cognitive Reflection and Decision Making," *Journal of Economic Perspectives*, 19 (Fall), 25-42.

Townsend, Claudia and Sanjay Sood (2009), "Self Affirmation Through the Choice of Good Design," (working paper A).

Townsend, Claudia and Sanjay Sood (2009) "The Impact of Product Design on Choice: A Dual-Processing Perspective," (working paper B).

Special Session Summary

The Constructive Role of Effort in Consumer Choice

Rom Schrift, Columbia University, USA

SESSION OVERVIEW

Different streams of literature suggest that experienced effort in choice plays an important role in consumer choice and judgment. Although the sources for effort in choice are numerous and diverse (e.g. type and amount of conflict, similarity among alternatives, perceptual fluency, amount of information, etc.) the literature supports the notion that consumers are averse to effort and often engage in behaviors intended to reduce it. Such demonstrations of effort and conflict reduction behaviors can be seen in different streams of literature such as pre-decisional distortion of information (e.g., Russo, Medvec, and Meloy 1996, 1998), motivated reasoning and judgment (e.g. Kunda, 1990; Kruglanski 1990), confirmation bias (Lord, Ross, and Lepper, 1979), and also in the effort-accuracy paradigm (Payne, Bettman and Johnson 1993).

In accordance with the aforementioned effort reduction behaviors, most research has explored and reported the negative impact that effort may have on different aspects of choice. For example, research in behavioral decision theory has shown that the likelihood to defer choice is positively correlated with the intensity of conflict in choice (Tversky & Shafir 1992; Dhar 1997). In addition, research on meta-cognition has repeatedly demonstrated that effortful processing of visual stimuli (visual dissfluency) decreases the evaluations of the target object (e.g. Schwarz, 2004; see Labroo and Kim, 2009 for exception).

In contrast to existing literature, the papers in this session explore the positive aspects of effort in choice and investigate consumers' tendency to prefer and even create effortful decisions. When and why will people value more effortful decision processes? When and why will feelings of effort versus ease motivate people to work harder or make them value products more? Do we complicate our decisions? The papers in the session answer these and other related questions. Specifically, the first paper demonstrates that increased conflict in choice can actually increase the likelihood of purchase. The second paper demonstrates that consumers are not only attracted to difficult decision processes, but also endogenously seek to enhance their decision effort in order to feel that they are making an adequate choice. The third paper explores the hypothesis that feelings of effort can increase people's tendency to work harder and value products more when such effort signals higher efficacy of the particular outcome. All three papers, which are to be submitted soon for publication, include multiple studies with data that has already been fully analyzed. However, none of the three papers has ever been presented at ACR.

The proposed special session is designed to present emerging work in decision research and its implication for consumer choice. The papers in the session should help in highlighting some of the promising avenues that are emerging in this area of research. Moreover, the session's discussion leader, Drazen Prelec, will engage the audience and the authors in an analysis of the session's content as well as a discussion of the potential for future research in this area.

EXTENDED ABSTRACTS

"The Tradeoff Heuristic: The Settling Effect of Conflict"

Wendy Liu, UCLA, USA
Itamar Simonson, Stanford University, USA

Conflict is one of the most fundamental phenomena in decision making. Decisions often involve options that each has pros and cons relative to each other, creating the need to reconcile such conflicts if only (or at most) one of the options can be adopted. Generally, the consideration of conflict has been found to negatively impact people's propensity to take decisive action. For example, high conflict between competing options has been shown to lead to inaction or deferral of choice (Tversky & Shafir 1992; Dhar 1997). When people have difficulty deciding between current options, they often choose not to choose any of the options—even though each option in itself might be quite attractive. Further, in existing theory of decision making, the negative effect of conflict is assumed to be additive to the attractiveness of the options. That is, generally the perceived attractiveness of the best option within a choice set positively correlates with whether people will buy from the current set—on top of that, if there is high conflict among the options, this adds a negative effect on the probability of purchase.

In this research, we propose a more nuanced view of the role of conflict in purchase decisions by focusing on a contradiction to the two general assumptions above. First, we show that sometimes conflict can have a positive effect on purchase likelihood. Second, we show that the relationship between option attractiveness and option conflict is not additive, but rather, interactive, in determining purchase likelihood. Specifically, we propose that while conflict indeed has a negative effect on purchase likelihood when options are relatively attractive, conflict can have a positive effect on purchase when options are relatively unattractive. That is, when given two options that may not successfully exceed the threshold for purchase based on their absolute attractiveness, people can be more likely to purchase one of them (rather than search further for a better option) when the current options contain a mild conflict than when one option dominates the other option. We propose the mechanism behind this positive effect of conflict on purchase is a process we call "the tradeoff heuristic"—when people see that they have to give up some unit of one attribute in order to gain on another attribute, they are more willing to accept the current attribute levels. In other words, by considering a tradeoff, people become less optimistic about finding an absolute best option in the future, effectively lowering their sufficiency threshold for commitment. Consequently, people will be more likely to stop their search with the current choice set. We test the settling effect of conflict in 4 studies.

Study 1 establishes the basic effect that conflict (compared to dominance) can lead to greater purchase likelihood. Participants are asked to imagine themselves looking for an apartment for rent in a new city. They are randomly assigned to two conditions: in the dominance condition, one apartment is larger in size, as well as being closer to work; in the conflict condition, apartment sizes are the same as condition one, but distance to work is flipped between the two options. In both conditions, apartment size is relatively small in absolute terms. Participants are asked whether to rent one of them, or look at the next option. Results show that indeed, people are more likely to take a current option in the conflict condition (37% vs. 20%).

Study 2 demonstrates the interaction between conflict and absolute valuation using a context of shopping for a vacuum cleaner. Participants are told they are considering two vacuum cleaners at Costco, but they could also decide to go to Sears to look further. When all options are relatively attractive, dominance (69%) leads to greater purchase likelihood than conflict (58%), consistent with prior research on the attraction effect (Huber et al.

1992). However, replicating study 1 results, when both options have low attractiveness, people are more likely to purchase when there is conflict (54%) rather than dominance (35%). Of note, the tradeoff heuristic is different from merely focusing on relative rather than absolute values (Hsee 1998). Specifically, the option's relative value (compared to the other option) is worse in the condition of conflict than in dominance. Hence, if the effect is simply directing attention to relative values, purchase likelihood should be higher in the dominance condition.

In study 3, we test a boundary condition to this effect, namely, the conflict between options needs to be relatively easy to reconcile. When the conflict is large, rather than small, purchase likelihood will indeed decrease, due to choice difficulty. In study 4, we extend this effect to evaluation procedures that involve more than two options. We find that a procedure such as ranking that creates more conflict can lead to greater likelihood of purchase, compared to a procedure that involves less conflict, such as rating.

In summary, this research focuses on the question: When do people accept a current opportunity, rather than search for better opportunities? Our findings contribute to our understanding of the decision by highlighting the role of subjective sufficiency in such decisions.

"Complicating Choice"

Rom Schrift, Columbia University, USA
Oded Netzer, Columbia University, USA
Ran Kivetz, Columbia University, USA

It has been well documented that, in the pre-decisional stage, consumers often simplify their decisions by bolstering one of the alternatives and/or denigrating others (Brownstein, 2003; Janis and Mann, 1977; Mills, 1968; Montgomery, 1983; Russo Medvec and Melloy 1996, 1998; Tyszka, 1985). Such reduction of choice conflict enables consumers to make easier, more confident choices. In this research, we provide a theoretical analysis of, and empirical evidence for, the opposite behavior. We discuss conditions under which consumers complicate choices in order to feel that they invested enough effort to make the right choice. Specifically, we postulate that when faced with important decisions, such as choices between primary physicians or between career paths, consumers are motivated to engage in a diligent decision process or due diligence. When an important choice feels too easy, consumers artificially increase the choice conflict and effort by reconstruing the choice context. Consumers are shown to bolster unimportant attributes and reverse the ordinal valence of attributes (e.g., more is better becomes less is better) in a direction that counteracts the virtually-dominant alternative, which they initially prefer and eventually "choose."

We propose a unifying "effort-compatibility" principle that accounts for both simplifying and complicating decision processes. The effort compatibility principle asserts that consumers value and strive for compatibility between the degree of effort they anticipate, or think is adequate to reach a certain decision, and the level of effort they actually exert. Accordingly, when a certain decision seems harder than initially anticipated, a simplifying process ensues. However, when the decision feels easier to resolve than anticipated (e.g., important, yet easy choices), consumers artificially increase the effort they invest in making the decision. We demonstrate that the latter, complicating process is characterized by an enhancement of the conflict in choice. Such conflict enhancement, through bolstering unimportant attributes, or reversing the valence of ordinal attributes, enables consumers to attain effort-compatibility and perceive themselves as engaging in a diligent decision.

Five studies examine consumers' choice complicating processes and the effort-compatibility principle. We first demonstrate the existence of the effort enhancement behavior and its impact on consumer choice (Studies 1-3). We show that for important decisions, such as choices of primary physicians or career paths, choice sets that invoked low levels of conflict (mismatch between actual and expected effort), gave rise to pre-decisional effort enhancement behavior. Specifically, in Study 1, participants distorted the importance of different information components in a manner that facilitated greater conflict in choice. In accordance with the effort-compatibility principle, this complicating behavior was significantly attenuated after the choice was made (post-decisional stage) and in conditions where no choice was required. In Study 2, participants enhanced their pre-decisional effort by constructing positive preferences towards attributes that opposed their preferred, and ultimately chosen alternative. Study 3 demonstrated that in sequential decision process, once a complicating process is triggered, it can alter the ultimate outcome of the decision.

In Studies 4 and 5, we further investigated the underlying psychological mechanism, namely the effort-compatibility principle. We manipulated the expected and experienced effort, as well as the importance of the choice. In Study 4, we offered respondents an alternative source of experienced effort using a preference fluency manipulation. We found that the introduction of an external source of difficulty drastically reduced the need for internal effort enhancement behaviors. In Study 5, we manipulated the level of anticipated effort by cueing subjects how long the task typically lasts. Although they faced identical tasks, those participants that anticipated low effort employed simplifying processes, while those anticipating high effort increased their conflict in choice.

In summary, we hypothesize and empirically demonstrate that, in certain situations, consumers complicate their choices. Such behavior may first appear contradictory to well-documented simplifying processes, such as pre-decisional distortion of information and post-choice cognitive dissonance. However, we test and support an effort-compatibility principle that accounts for both simplifying and complicating processes, sometimes observed in the context of the same decision. Thus, consumers not only simplify and bolster the difficult choices they make, but also make harder and less appealing the obvious (or illusionary) choices they fake. We discuss how this could lead to an "illusion of choice," whereby consumers agonize over (non) decisions.

"Does Distance make your Heart Fonder or your Mind Wonder? An "Attainability-Efficacy" Framework of Preference Construction"

Sara Kim, University of Chicago, USA
Aparna Labroo, University of Chicago, USA

It is not surprising that consumers put maximum effort into obtaining products or doing things they like, however, do they also prefer products or things associated with effort (to get/ do)? For example, consider this situation. It is the holiday season, you are on your way to the grocery store, and you have been thinking about donating some money to charity. In one scenario, imagine that as you enter the store, you notice a volunteer from the Salvation Army right next to the entrance asking for a donation. In a second scenario, imagine that as you enter the store, you see a volunteer from the Salvation Army a few steps away from you at the opposite entrance asking for a donation. When are you more likely to make a donation, and why? You have been thinking about making a donation, and in the first scenario, the volunteer is close to you and it is easy to make a donation. In the second case, you will have to exert some token effort to make the donation. It appears normative that if you have been thinking about making a donation, and if you consider the Salvation Army a good cause to support, you should be more willing to make a donation when it is easy rather than effortful to do so. But are there situations when you might prefer to engage in the token effort? Further consider this situation. As you proceed inside the store, looking to purchase cookies, you find one box on the shelf right up front and another a little way behind it. Both boxes are fresh, so why exert effort to reach for the one at the back? In the current article, we examine this issue—do when and why do feelings of effort versus ease motivate people to work harder or make them value products more?

Whether it is deciding to make a donation or to buy a product, most existing research will argue that ease is good and people like to do activities or get products that are easy to do or get. A recent set of intriguing findings have additionally suggested that even when feelings of ease arise from subjective characteristics of the target and are independent of its descriptive features (Schwarz 2004), for instance, the volunteer is next to you and have your glasses on (vs. you forgot them at home) and s/he looks clear (vs. blurry), they increase value of the outcome and motivation to act. Ease is associated with positive feelings which are usually attributed to the outcome being considered and as a consequence they increase preference towards the outcome. In this paper, however, we discuss when feelings of effort, rather than ease, can motivate people to work harder and can make people value products more.

We argue that evaluating products, consumers focus either on how attainable the outcome is or if it is the best one available. When people experience illusory high control, their focus turns to product efficacy rather than product attainability. As people usually infer value from their actions (e.g., Bem 1972), and as they put most effort to pursue only the best outcomes, they mistakenly reverse this correlation when assessing efficacy of the outcome. Thus, feelings of effort also make them value the outcome more (Labroo and Kim 2009; Pochepsova et al. 2009). Only when perceived control is low, peoples focus is on successful outcome attainability. In such situations, effort signals infeasibility of attaining the outcome and they prefer outcomes associated with ease, not effort.

Across three experiments, we provide evidence for our premise. We show that people with high control (illusory or real) prefer products that are psychologically or physically effortful rather than easy to attain and they donate more to a charity when donation is effortful rather than easy. In contrast, people with illusory low control prefer products and are more likely to act if things feel easy rather than effortful. Process measures show that illusory low control results in concerns about product attainability, and ease increases perceived attainability of a successful outcome. In contrast, illusory high control increases the desire to get the best option (attainability is no longer a concern), but interestingly things that are effortful are better than things that are easy. Of additional interest are the subtle manipulations of illusory control. For example, simply writing ones own lucky number on a raffle ticket rather than being assigned one, for a box of cookies, creates illusory control, and can make us evaluate the cookies more favorably, but only when they are physically (or psychologically) distant rather than close. Or, being the first (rather than last) to make a difference to the lives of poor children, also creates illusory control, resulting in people making larger donations, but only when they have to reach out a couple of feet to the donation box (vs. it is next to them). Rolling a dice by oneself rather than having the experimenter roll it also results in preferences for products that are psychologically far rather than close. We additionally rule out mood, construal level, attention, overall goal engagement as possible alternative explanations.

In the end, all control might just be an illusion; therefore, it is particularly powerful that such subtle manipulations of controllability can alter preferences to this degree. The surprising inference is that people with high control (real or illusory) like complicated lives, and when people feel control they complicate rather than simplify their lives. Theoretical implications pertaining to the role of feelings in judgment and preference construction and managerial implications regarding what managers might be able to do to improve consumer satisfaction with products will be discussed.

REFERENCES

Bem, Daryl J. (1972), *Self-Perception Theory, Advance in Experiment Social Psychology*, New York: Academic Press.

Brownstein, Aaron L. (2003), "Biased Predecision Processing," *Psychological Bulletin*, 129 (4), 545-68.

Dhar, Ravi (1997), "Consumer Preference for a No choice Option," *Journal of Consumer Research*, 24 (September), 215-31.

Hsee, Christopher K. (1996), "The Evaluability Hypothesis: An Explanation for Preference Reversals between Joint and Separate Evaluations of Alternatives," *Organizational Behavior and Human Decision Processes*, 67 (3), 247-257.

Huber, Joel, John W. Payne, and Christopher Puto (1982), "Adding Asymmetrically Dominated Alternatives: Violations of Regularity and the Similarity Hypothesis," *Journal of Consumer Research*, 9 (1), 90-98.

Janis, Irving L. and Leon Mann (1977), *Decision making: A psychological Analysis of Conflict, Choice, and Commitment*, New York: Free Press.

Kunda, Ziva (1990), "The Case for Motivated Reasoning," *Psychological Bulletin*, 108 (3), 480-98.

Kruglanski, Arie W. (1990), "Lay Epistemic Theory in Social-cognitive Psychology," *Psychological Inquiry*, 1, 181-97.

Labroo, Aparna A. and Sara Kim (2009), "The "Instrumentality" Heuristic: Why Metacognitive Difficulty Is Desirable During Goal Pursuit," *Psychological Science*, 20 (1), 127-34.

Lord, Charles G., Lee Ross, and Mark R. Lepper (1979), "Biased Assimilation and Attitude Polarization: The Effects of Prior Theories on Subsequently Considered Evidence," *Journal of Personality and Social Psychology*, 37 (11), 2098-109.

Mills, Judson (1968), "Interest in supporting and discrepant information," in *Theories of Cognitive Consistency: A Source Book*, R. P. Abelson et al., eds. Chicago: Rand McNally, 771-76.

Montgomery, Henry (1983), "Decision Rules and the Search for a Dominance Structure: Towards a Process Model of Decision Making," in *Analyzing and Aiding Decision Processes*, P. Humphreys, O. Svenson, and A. Vari, eds. Amsterdam: North Holland, 343-69.

Pocheptsova, Anastasiya, Aparna A. Labroo, and Ravi Dhar (2009), "The Mere Luxury Effect," *Society for Consumer Psychology Proceedings*.

Russo, Edward J., Victoria H. Medvec, and Margret G. Meloy (1996), "The Distortion of Information During Decisions," *Organizational Behavior and Human Decision Processes*, 66 (1), 102-10.

_______ , Margaret G. Meloy, and Victoria H. Medvec (1998), "Predecisional Distortion of Product Information," *Journal of Marketing Research*, 35 (November), 438–52.

Schwarz, Norbert (2004), "Metacognitive Experiences in Consumer Judgment and Decision Making," *Journal of Consumer Psychology*, 14 (4), 332-48.

Tyszka, Tadeusz (1985), "Variability of Predecisional Information Seeking Behavior," *Polish Psychological Bulletin*, 16, 275-82.

Tversky, Amos, and Eldar Shafir (1992), "Choice under Conflict: The Dynamics of Deferred Decision," *Psychological Science*, 6 (November), 358-361.

Special Session Summary

The Buzz about Buzz: Drivers and Consequences of Word-of-Mouth

Jonah Berger, University of Pennsylvania, USA
Andrew Stephen, INSEAD, France

SESSION OVERVIEW

Talking and sharing are some of the most fundamental consumer motives. People tell friends about new restaurants, email relatives interesting articles, and post online reviews about books they like (or hate). But while it is clear that such behavior is frequent, and important, we know less about the causes and consequences of such behaviors.

A great deal of research in both consumer behavior and marketing science recognizes that word-of-mouth (WOM) is important, but less work has drilled more deeply to examine the psychological factors driving transmission. Research has shown that WOM can impact sales (Chevalier and Mayzlin 2006), and diffusion (Goldenberg, Libai, and Muller 2001), but what motivates consumers to spread WOM and how do aspects of conversation partners influence what people talk about? Similarly, while we know that people like to share, what types of things tend to be shared? Certain YouTube videos, ads, or New York Times articles end up being viral, but why? How do content characteristics influence what spreads? Finally, what are the consequences of transmission for consumer attitudes, choice, search, and willingness to pay?

This session addresses these, and related questions, as it integrates various research perspectives to examine drivers and consequences of WOM. Berger and Milkman use six months of data from the New York Times most emailed list to examine characteristics of content that make them more likely to be shared. Moldovan and Lehmann investigate how aspects of advertisements, such as their creativity and informational content, generate WOM and affect purchase intent. Stephen, Lehmann, and Toubia look at both sharing and listening, and consider what drives people to share WOM as well as how transmitter and item characteristics drive the decision to listen. Mayzlin and Moe focus on the impact of WOM, and investigate how customer reviews influence consumer search, willingness to pay, and outcomes for the firm.

Taken together, these talks blend psychological factors that drive transmission and reception, as well as the consequences of these processes for consumer behavior. Distinguished ACR Fellow, and renowned scholar, Donald Lehmann will integrate the papers and lead a discussion about important directions for future research. It is hoped that the discussion will generate some interesting possibilities for future work in this exciting area.

Given how fundamental transmission and sharing is to our everyday lives, we expect this session will be of substantial interest to a host of contingencies. Not only should it appeal to researchers working on social influence, attitude change, and new product adoption, but also to those who study advertising, social networks, and decision making more broadly.

EXTENDED ABSTRACTS

"Virality: What Gets Shared and Why"

Jonah Berger, University of Pennsylvania, USA
Katy Milkman, University of Pennsylvania, USA

What makes certain things more viral? Word-of-Mouth and interpersonal transmission drive social influence, purchase behavior (Godes and Mayzlin 2008), diffusion (Rogers 2003), and product success (Godes and Mayzlin 2004), but what types of things are more likely to be shared and why?

Some perspectives have argued that cultural prominence is driven by random copying, advertising, or social influence dynamics (Bentley and Shennan 2005; Salganik, Dodds, and Watts 2006). An alternate explanation of cultural selection, built on notions from the biological realm, suggests that due to shared human psychology, characteristics of items themselves can drive transmission (Schaller and Crandall 2004). Unfortunately, however, empirical tests of these predictions have been limited by the ability to examine actual transmission in the field across a host of cultural items measured on various characteristics.

We study virality and cultural transmission by examining six months of data (over 7,000 articles) on which New York Times articles make the most emailed list. The data includes everything from world news and politics to sports and travel, and its breadth and reader base makes this an ideal domain to study virality. Further, by controlling for the amount of time spent on the homepage, and where articles appeared in the print edition, we can test whether above and beyond such "advertising," item characteristics drive success.

Many theories paint transmission as an economic, value-based exchange. Linguists often assume that the function of language is to share factual information which will have immediate value (e.g., where good food is readily available or the location of predators). Similarly, social exchange theory (Homans 1958) suggests that transmission is an economic exchange of useful resources. To test such informational selection (things spread based on their utility), we examined whether content that is more broadly relevant (i.e., provides information that is relevant to more people) or provides advice (i.e., information on how to do things) is more viral.

We also take a broader theoretical perspective and argue that people also transmit information to deepen social relationships. Language can be seen as a form of social grooming (Dunbar 1996) and people may be more likely to share emotional content because it deepens social bonds (Peters and Kashima 2007). Along these lines, people may be more likely to share surprising content because it breaks existing schemas, and encourages people to confer with others to resolve the discrepancies. Consequently, we examine whether these aspects, above and beyond informational utility, increase transmission

Using a webcrawler, we collected every article that appeared on the New York Times website from August 30th, 2008 to February 15th, 2009. For each article, we collected the title, text, length, author name, publication date, section and page where it appeared, and the one sentence summary provided by the paper. We also collected snapshots every 15 minutes of where articles appeared on the New York Times website and which articles appeared on most emailed list (emailed the most in the last 24 hours). We used name lists to determine author gender, and used Google hits as a rough measure of author fame.

We used both automated and manual coding to score articles on our key independent variables. Standard word lists (General Inquirer) were used to measure the number of positive and negative words in each article and from this we computed valence and emotionality. In cases were it was not possible to use automated coding, we trained coders to rate articles of some key measures. We selected a random sample of 1,446 articles, and two independent raters coded each of the three remaining measures (surprise, broad relevance, and advice). Inter-rater reliability was high and codes were averaged to form a measure of each dimension.

Before turning to our variables of interest, we first consider controls and other factors that might drive virality. Not surprisingly, articles which should have received more attention (i.e., appeared on earlier pages of the physical paper or spent longer on more visible places on the newspapers homepage) were more likely to make the most emailed list. Articles were also more viral if they appeared in particular sections (e.g., Opinion), and were written by women or more famous authors.

Even controlling for these factors, however, our results demonstrate that content characteristics also drive transmission. Content that was more broadly relevant or contained advice was more likely to be viral. Further, even beyond more economic value, emotional selection also played a role. While more positive and surprising articles had a higher propensity to make the most emailed list, content that was more emotional, regardless of valence, was also more likely to be viral.

Overall, these results illustrate the important role that cultural selection, and shared psychology, play in cultural transmission.

"The Effect of Advertising on Word-of-Mouth"

Sarit Moldovan, Technion, Israel Institute of Technology, Israel
Donald Lehmann, Columbia University, USA

When considering the purchase of a new product, consumers often rely on word of mouth (WOM). While WOM can be important to new product success, it is not always clear how WOM can be initiated and managed. In this paper we claim that advertising can trigger WOM about the product and about the ad. Further, the spread of WOM about the ad (and not the product) may have additional effects on sales.

Previous research that explored advertising effectiveness has usually tested how different ad characteristics affect attitudes toward the ad, the brand, purchase intent, and ad recall (Brown and Stayman 1992). Although these factors may affect WOM, the common marketing models do not take into account the effect of marketing efforts on WOM (Bayus 1985). While some studies showed initial evidence that WOM can be stimulated by marketing efforts (Bayus 1985; Gelb and Johnson 1995; King and Tinkham 1990), these studies hardly discuss the valence of WOM (positive or negative), or the content of WOM (about the product or about the ad).

Based on previous findings our main hypotheses are that creative ads will have a small effect on purchase intent. However, these ads will lead to WOM about the ad. Informative ads, on the other hand, are expected to lead to greater purchase intent and positive WOM about the product, but not to WOM about the ad. While WOM about the product is expected to lead to further purchase intent, WOM about the ad is expected to increase involvement in the ad, and increase the purchase intent of the product as a result of watching the ad.

In Study 1 we asked 424 participants to rate 21 print ads (between subjects). The dependent variables were: WOM about the product (including WOM amount, positive and negative WOM, and information search), Ad WOM (intentions to talk about the ad or forward it to friends), and purchase intent. The independent variables (after factor analysis) were: creative, informative, sex appeal, status appeal, and negative. Regression results supported our hypotheses: Creativity is the main ad characteristic that leads to WOM about the ad and about the product. However, it does not lead to purchase intent. In addition, as we expected, informative ads lead to more positive WOM and increase purchase intent, but have no effect on Ad WOM.

In Study 2 we collected data of actual forwarding of 53 TV commercials in an online site. We tested how the ad characteristics (as rated by judges) affected the number of times an ad was forwarded per view, a proxy for actual spread of the ad. Ad characteristics explained 51% of the variance in actual forwarding behavior, and the results were very similar to those of Study 1.

Since creative ads were found to lead to WOM about the ad, but had little effect on purchase intent, Study 3 explores whether exposure to ad WOM prior to the ad can moderate the effect of a creative ad on purchase intent. In this study, 87 students were exposed to either a creative ad or to WOM about the ad (the WOM did not mention the product, only the ad). Later, half of all participants were then exposed (or re-exposed) to the creative ad. The dependent variable was purchase intent of the product (1-7 scale).

The results showed that the purchase intent of the product was significantly higher in the condition in which participants were exposed to the ad WOM and after that to the ad, compared with the other three conditions, indicating that exposure to WOM about the ad can moderate the effect of creative ads on purchase intent. Results confirm our hypothesis that while a creative ad had a small effect on purchase intent, exposure to WOM about the ad, prior to watching the ad, led to higher purchase intent.

Results of the three studies indicate that advertising can trigger WOM about the product and about the ad. Different characteristics of the ad lead to different types of behaviors, such as WOM and purchase intent. Although ad creativity hardly leads to purchase intent by itself, it may lead to WOM about the ad, which may in turn have an effect on purchase intent of the consumers exposed to this WOM.

"Why Do Consumers Talk, Does Anyone Listen, and What Happens?"

Andrew Stephen, INSEAD, France
Donald Lehmann, Columbia University, USA
Olivier Toubia, Columbia University, USA

Despite the large amount of research on word-of-mouth (WOM) and social contagion in marketing, sociology, physics and elsewhere, surprisingly little is known about the individual-level talking, listening, and impact processes. We know little about the underlying individual-level processes that drive WOM. Why do consumers transmit WOM about products to their peers? When do they listen to these messages? And when and in what ways are they impacted by WOM? In this research we study transmission, reception and impact. We address the following questions: (1) what are consumers' motivations or reasons for transmitting information to others, (2) what factors related to recipients affect transmitters' likelihoods of talking, (3) what factors related to transmitters affect recipients' likelihoods of listening, and (4) what types of WOM are likely to be more impactful on recipients' brand/product-related attitudes and subsequent consumption behaviors?

For transmission, in the first study (N=110) we asked participants to recall times when they actually transmitted WOM, asked them "why?" and asked them to give information on the characteristics of the people who they talked to (recipients). We found that transmission motives were predominantly self-focused and centered on needs to either express opinions or to in fact solicit (not give) information. When participants were sharing their own experiences with products the former was the only motive. However when they were passing-on information about others' experiences (retransmitting) they not only wanted to express this opinion but also sought information from the recipient (possibly to validate or verify the previously-received information).

In study 2 (N=200), participants were in a hypothetical situation where they had to select recipients who they would transmit WOM to, given knowledge of recipients' characteristics (interest in topic, track-history of being receptive, tie strength, and social connectivity). We found that transmitters preferred recipients who were likely to listen (e.g., strong topic interest, past receptivity, strong friendship tie). This was all that mattered when transmitting own information, and is consistent with just wanting to express one's opinion to people who would actually listen. However, when retransmitting information from others the social connectivity (many versus few friends) of the recipient also mattered. Well-connected people have access to more sources of information and, all else equal, should themselves be better sources. Indeed, in study 3 (N=28) we found that transmitters expected well-connected people to be sources of high quality information. Based on these studies, transmission is associated more with using the social capital embedded in one's social ties than it is for building social capital (e.g., by transmitting in order to give advice). However, transmitters use social capital in different ways: when sharing own information recipients are used as a receptive audience for one's opinions, and when passing-on others' information recipients are used for validating, verifying or elaborating the existing information.

In a fourth transmission-related study (N=920,770) we examined a different type of transmission—sharing information in an online social network—using data from a popular Facebook "app." App users can share the app itself with "friends" and can share results from quizzes that they take within the app (they take personality and psychological tests). We find the probability of sharing the app or of sharing various quiz results decreases exponentially as a person's number of friends (social connectivity) increases. Also, as a person's social connectivity (and hence their stock of social capital) increases, people become more strongly focused on using their network connections for seeking information. Related to the previous three studies, having more social capital means a stronger desire to use it for self-focused purposes.

We then consider reception/impact with three studies (participants are recipients). In the first study (N=127) we examine listening decisions as functions of transmitter characteristics (expertise, social tie strength, connectivity) and message characteristics (valence) in a hypothetical situation where participants imagined themselves exposed to WOM from certain people. Participants indicated who they would listen to. Although transmitters who are perceived to be "experts" are more likely to be listened to, we found high reception probabilities under various other combinations of transmitter and message characteristics, including cases where transmitters lack any objective credibility or expertise. In the two other studies (Ns=276 and 272; also hypothetical), participants were given uninformative product information and exposed to WOM about that product. We measured attitudes toward the product and purchase intentions pre- and post-WOM. The message varied on valence and tone (factual versus emotional), and the transmitter varied on objective credibility (category expertise) and tie strength (friend, acquaintance, or stranger). Instead of measuring only dispositional attitude, we also measured certainty (i.e., confidence in disposition toward the product). Capturing certainty changes were important: e.g., in 45% of the cases where dispositions did not change post-WOM, certainties did change (indicating that WOM had an impact, just not on disposition). Disposition and certainty changes (individual or combined) affected purchase intentions. Moreover, although objectively-credible transmitters are influential, low-credibility transmitters (e.g., strangers, novices) sometimes impact attitudes and purchasing, provided the message makes recipients feel more certain about their existing opinion. Thus, under the right conditions almost any transmitter has a good chance of being influential.

"The Impact of Consumer Reviews on Consumer Search and Firm Profits"

Dina Mayzlin, Yale University, USA
Wendy Moe, University of Maryland, USA

A number of studies have demonstrated that customer reviews affect product sales (see, for example, Chevalier and Mayzlin (2006) and Dellarocas, Zhang and Awad (forthcoming). In particular, both the valence and the quantity of reviews influence sales on a product level. But how do customer reviews impact consumer search and what they choose, as well as company profits and category-level performance? This is the focus of the current study.

In particular, consider a retailer with multiple products that implements a review tool that allows customers to post feedback on its site. The reviews can serve as a matching tool that reduces consumer uncertainty about the products. This could have two possible effects: 1) Re-allocate sales across products within a category which may result in higher utility for the consumer but not in higher profits for the retailer in the short run, and/or 2) Raise the firm's profits by increasing the probability that the consumer purchases within a category and increasing her willingness to pay for the product. Here we look at the effect of consumer reviews on category sales and traffic within a site.

To test our hypotheses, we have obtained a data set from a retailer that sells products across a large number of categories. A unique aspect of our study is that we have sales and search data before and after the review tool is introduced. This allows us to determine the effect of the introduction of the ratings tool on sales and search, as well as measuring how the volume of reviews affects search and sales within the category. Another interesting aspect of the data is a measure of search behavior: the number of times that a product is viewed within a course of the week. We argue later that the data on search behavior allows us to identify the mechanism through which reviews influence sales.

To determine the effect of the introduction of reviews onto a site, we estimate an aggregate model, where the dependent variable is category sales. First, we show that the over-all category sales increase in the period after the ratings tool was introduced. This is true even once we control for cross-category heterogeneity. Some of the increase in dollar sales seems to be due to the increase in search. That is, the total number of category page views increases in the period after the ratings are introduced. However, increase in search alone is not sufficient to explain the increase in dollar sales: even after we control for the number of page views of the category's products per week, the dollar sales per week are still significantly higher in the period after ratings were introduced. On the other hand, once we control for the number of page views of the category's products per week, the unit sales are not significantly higher in the second period. This seems to suggest that ratings increase search and make it more likely that consumers buy relatively more expensive products. This last finding leads us to investigate the effect of reviews on the relative distribution of product sales.

Next, we consider the impact of the introduction of review on the distribution of search and sales across products within a category. In particular, we investigate how the impact of reviews is moderated by the initial market share of a product as well as its price. Since reviews reduce uncertainty in consumer's expected valuation of the product, we would expect that the introduction of reviews would lead consumers to be willing to buy more expensive products. Of course, another reason why demand may shift towards more expensive products is that in the presence of correlation between price and quality, more expensive products will obtain better reviews and hence will have more sales.

We analyze the review-generating process as a function of the product's own characteristics as well as the characteristics of other products sold within a category. Our analysis also sheds light on the debate whether additional information creates a bigger marginal impact for the already successful products or for the less successful products (see Salgadnik et al (2006) and Tucker and Zhang (2008)). The findings in the previous literature have been mixed: Salganik et al (2006) find that previous download information helps the already successful products more, while Tucker and Zhang (2008) find that previous clicks information is especially useful for the niche products. We find that sales within a category become more concentrated after the introduction of the review tool. Hence, we find that reviews seem to drive consumers to more expensive, successful products.

Special Session Summary

The Role of Emotions in Self-control Dilemmas

Anastasiya Pocheptsova, University of Maryland, USA

SESSION OVERVIEW

Consumer choices often involve self-control conflict between options that are immediately tempting and options that serve long-term goals. Though prior research has examined how consumers deal with such conflict, the current session expands our understanding of this topic by examining the role of emotions evoked by self-control dilemmas that consumers face when pursuing health goals. By looking at the role of emotions in self-control conflicts, the four papers in the session raise several interesting questions that have been under-researched in the literature. Do people experience different type of emotions when they monitor pursuit of high-level goals vs. low-level temptations? Do people experience negative or positive emotions after resolving self-control conflict in favor of a higher order goal? Do people experience different levels of guilt when violating health goals during group vs. alone consumption? Finally, is there a difference in experienced affect and subsequent behavior when consumers strive to reach specific vs. abstract self-control health goals. Taken together the questions examined in this session bridge research on health consumption and emerging research in the domain of the role of the emotions in self-control conflicts to better understand consumer decision making.

The papers in this session study three important research questions. First, Fishbach & Tal show that facing a self-control conflict consumers experience abstract emotions (e.g. pride) when monitoring a pursuit of high-order goals, but concrete emotions (e.g. happiness) when monitoring the pursuit of low-order temptations. The authors further show that emotions associated with higher-order goals are more prolonged, whereas affect experienced following the pursuit of temptations is short-lived. Expanding on this theme, Gal & Liu further examine feelings that people experience as a result of resisting temptation and following long-term goals. In contrast to previous research that emphasizes positive consequences of resisting temptation, the authors show that people experience negative emotions (anger) and look at its effect on consumption choices. Next, Pocheptsova et al. examine how mere presence of others during self-control conflict affects the emotions and choices people make. They find that due to heightened feeling of guilt people tend to overestimate the calories they consume while eating in a group setting (vs. alone) which results in more health goal consistent choices later. Finally, Scott & Nowlis examine difference in consumers' health-goal pursuit based on the level of specificity of the goals. The authors find that setting more specific goals may lead to feelings of regret, guilt and over-consumption.

All papers in this session include multiple empirical studies that test both the main propositions and the underlying mechanisms of the proposed effects. Taken together, the papers examine emotions evoked by self-control conflicts and explore the consequences of such emotions on consumer choice. By looking at these issues from four different angles, the session provides a more comprehensive look at the role of emotions in self-control dilemmas. Further, all papers in the session primarily focus the attention of empirical studies in the domain of food consumption. It is well established that despite the popularity of weight-loss programs, the public focus placed on health, and the implementation of mandatory nutrition labels of packaged foods, consumers continue to make poor diet and lifestyle choices. Current session contributes to the growing body of research that examines this issue and is expected to attract audience interest at the conference for both researchers that are interested in conceptual understanding of the role of emotions in self-control dilemmas as well as researchers interested in affecting consumers' well-being in the domain of health consumption.

EXTENDED ABSTRACTS

"The Motivation-Emotion Matching Hypothesis"

Ayelet Fishbach, University of Chicago, USA
Tal Eyal, Ben Gurion University, Israel

Positive emotions signal successful goal pursuit, and the quality of the emotional experience depends on the type of goal a person pursues (Dweck and Leggett 1988; Higgins 1997). Accordingly, our research focuses on how distinct positive emotions signal the successful pursuit of conflicting motivations in a self-control dilemma. We argue that a self-control dilemma poses a conflict between two goals that vary hierarchically: high- versus low-order goals. In addition, emotions vary from abstract to concrete. These two hierarchies correspond to each other, leading to what we term as "the motivation-emotion matching hypothesis." According to this hypothesis, people associate high-order goals with abstract emotions and low-order goals (or temptations) with concrete emotions.

In support of our hypothesis, we find that individuals form implicit between high- (vs. low-) order goals and abstract (vs. concrete) emotions (study 1). Specifically, using an IAT (Nosek, Greenwald and Banaji 2005), we find faster response times for sorting affective and motivational concepts when participants use one response key for either goals or pride stimuli and the other key for either temptations or happiness stimuli, than in the incongruent pairing condition, mapping one response key for goals or happiness stimuli and the other key for either temptations or pride stimuli

Three predictions further follow from this hypothesis and received support in our studies. The first pertains to the emotional consequences of goal-pursuit. We find that regardless of the content of the self-control dilemma, abstract emotions follow from carrying out high-order goal-related behaviors, whereas concrete emotions follow from carrying out low-order goal-related behaviors. For example, consumers experience abstract emotions (e.g., pride, self-worth) after choosing to eat healthy or choosing a highbrow news magazine, and they experience concrete emotions (e.g., happiness, joy) after eating unhealthy or choosing a lowbrow news magazine (study 2). The second prediction pertains to the duration of the emotional experience. We find that abstract and concrete emotions vary in their duration. Although the elicitation of both types of emotions is an immediate response to pursuing the corresponding goal, abstract emotions are experienced for an extended period of time, whereas concrete emotions are experienced for a brief period of time. Specifically, participants who made a choice from a healthy set of options felt proud for at least 20 minutes, whereas those who made a choice from an unhealthy set felt happy for about five minutes (study 3).

The third prediction states that the activation of emotional terms cues the pursuit of the corresponding goal. We find that priming abstract emotional terms (e.g., pride, self-worth) helps people control indulgence compared with priming concrete emotional terms (e.g., happiness, joy; study 4). In addition, priming abstract emotional terms helps people persist on difficult academic tasks more than priming concrete emotional terms (study 5). Together, the results of these five studies provide evidence that distinct affective experiences monitor the pursuit of high-order goals versus low-order temptations in a self-control conflict.

We discuss the implications of the motivation-emotion matching hypothesis for self-control theory. Some previous research attests that in a self-control conflict, low-order goals are more "emotional;" that is, they involve representations that are more arousing and consummatory than high-order goals (Loewenstein, 1996; Metcalfe and Mischel 1999). In contrast with that alternative, we propose that low-order temptations are a source of concrete emotions and high-order goals are a source of another type of feeling-based experience that nonetheless "feels." Our hypothesis modifies self-control theory; it suggests the self-control conflict is a conflict between motivations that are experienced differently rather than a conflict between temptations that "feel" and goals that do not. It implies that self-control success is not tied to putting emotions aside but rather to tuning in to different emotional cues.

"What Movie Would You Watch with Your Salad? The Implicit Emotional Consequences of Exerting Self Control"

David Gal, Northwestern University, USA
Wendy Liu, UCLA, USA

A great deal of research on consumer self-control shows that yielding to temptation can lead to aversive emotions, such as feelings of guilt and regret (e.g., Baumeister 2002; Giner-Sorolla 2001; Hoch and Loewenstein 1991). Conversely, research highlights that exerting self-control by resisting temptation results in positive psychological consequences, such as an improved sense of self-worth and a heightened self-concept (Dhar and Wertenbroch 2007; Khan and Dhar 2006). In the present research, we argue that resisting temptation may also lead to aversive emotions. In particular, we argue that when individuals' freedom to fulfill their desires is thwarted by their need to act responsibly, the natural emotional response is anger. Along with happiness, sadness, fear, and disgust , anger is identified as one of the basic emotions (Ekman, Friesen, and Ellsworth 1972). In general, anger can be defined as the emotion that ensues due to a "conspicuous slight or frustration" of the individual by another (Zajonc 1998). Previous research shows that when the individual feels that his/her freedom is being restricted, reactance and hostility ensues (Brehm 1966; Wicklund 1974). Building on this conceptual framework of anger, in this research we propose that although anger manifest as psychological reactance is typically assumed to arise from the restriction of an individual's freedom by others, it can also arise from the restriction of an individual's desires by their own sense of responsibility. However, unlike when freedom of desire is restricted by another person, in the case of yielding to one's own sense of responsibility, people may not readily identify the situation as anger-inducing. Consequently, a person may not be able to consciously articulate one's emotional state as feeling angry; nonetheless, the affect of anger will be displaced to and manifest itself in the person's subsequent actions. Further, to the extent the next contexts are more readily recognized as anger-inducing, people may be able to report their displaced feelings of anger and irritation.

Based on prior research showing that angry individuals tend to evaluate anger-framed appeals particularly favorably (DeSteno et al. 2004), our first experiment examined whether anger-framed appeals would be evaluated more favorably by individuals that resisted temptation. Moreover, we examined whether this effect would apply to sadness-framed appeals and whether the effect would be more pronounced among restrained eaters. Restrained eaters are defined by their heightened sense of responsibility to delay the immediate gratification of food in order to maintain or lose weight. That is, restrained eaters have a particularly heightened sense of responsibility to constrain their desires.

We found that restrained eaters became more favorably disposed towards anger-framed messages after resisting temptation, consistent with an anger emotional state. In contrast, unrestrained eaters, for whom eating does not involve a conflict between one's desires versus sense of responsibility, did not become angry when resisting temptation. This result provided insight into the process by which anger is produced—specifically, the effect only occurs when the tempting option is construed as a "vice," and not being able to have it is construed as a restriction on one's free desire. Moreover, we did not observe similar effects for sadness-framed appeals, suggesting that the effect was specific to anger, rather than to a generalized negative mood state.

Our second experiment examined how resisting temptation affected participants irritation (a mild form of anger) at a persuasive appeal that used controlling language. Further, experiment 2 examined whether expressing anger can attenuate displaced anger evoked by resisting temptation as suggested by prior research showing that explicit anger-expression tends to attenuate suppressed anger (Gross 2006). We found that participants given the opportunity to express anger in an unrelated task after resisting temptation expressed less irritation at the persuasive appeal than those not given such an opportunity. No such difference was found among participants that yielded to temptation, suggesting that anger was evoked by resisting temptation and attenuated by the anger expression task.

Our third experiment extended the findings of the first two experiments to a consumer context where the task following the self-control task was not itself anger-provoking. In particular, experiment 3 found that participants that resisted temptation (chose an apple over a candy bar) before rather than after choosing movies, were more likely to choose anger-themed movies. A similar effect was not observed for individuals yielding to temptation, suggesting that the act of resisting temptation led to the increased choice share of anger-themed movies.

"Food Consumption in the Presence of Others"

Anastasiya Pocheptsova, University of Maryland, USA
Sara Freiberg, Yale University, USA
Ravi Dhar, Yale University, USA

Consumers frequently face self-control dilemmas when making food consumption choices: should I order a fruit salad or a chocolate cake for dessert? should I cook a healthy meal at home or go out for dinner? Oftentimes a resolution of such self-control conflicts towards temptations results in experienced feelings of guilt which affect subsequent consumption choices. Though previous research has identified a number of factors that affect consumers' resolution of self-conflict dilemmas and consequent experienced emotions, in this paper we propose a novel factor affecting such decisions: presence of others during food consumption. While the presence of others has been shown to directly contribute to consumption volume due to an increase in meal duration (de Castro & Brewer 1992, de Castro 1994, 2000) and variety-seeking (Levav & Ariely 2000), we propose that it can have an indirect effect by influencing one's consumption monitoring accuracy due to increased levels of experienced guilt.

We argue that the presence of others during food consumption prompts increased feelings of guilt due to lay belief that associates eating in groups with unhealthier food choices. This in turn leads to higher calorie consumption reports as compared to situations where individuals are dining alone. We further propose that people would rely on their lay beliefs and believe that they consumed more calories in a group setting than in individual setting even when they objectively consumed the same meal. In support of this hypothesis, across four studies we find that individuals eating alone give significantly lower calorie estimates than those eating in a group for the same meal. In Study 1, we asked participants to imagine one of three conditions: that they were eating ice cream alone, that they were eating ice cream with their family, or that they were eating ice cream with their friends. Participants were then presented with a description of an ice cream. Consistent with our proposition, participant in the group conditions reported higher consumption amounts than those in the alone condition.

We test the generalizability of our findings in Study 2, by showing that similar effects exist when people are making estimates about others' rather their own consumption. The participants we presented with either an image of a woman eating alone or an image of a woman eating in a group. Participants were then asked to estimate the calories in this individual's entrée. Consistent with our earlier findings, participants in the group condition gave significantly more exaggerated calorie estimates than those in the alone condition. We next tested our hypothesis in a real food consumption setting (Study 3), asking participants to estimate the number of calories in the bowl of M&Ms which they consumed either alone or in the presence of other. Participants in the group condition estimated more calories in their bowl of M&Ms than those in the alone condition.

In our final study we investigate the implications of such exaggerated calorie reports in a group setting on subsequent choices. Since consumer choices are rarely made in isolation, but are frequently made in sequence (Khan and Dhar 2008) systematic errors in caloric estimation of one meal could have large consequences not only for immediate consumption but for future consumer choices. To test this proposition we first asked participants to imagine one of the two scenarios: that they consumed an ice cream cone alone or that they consumed the same ice cream cone with their friends. Participants were later asked to imagine that they would be dining alone and were asked to choose either pizza or salad as their entrée. Consistent with our predictions, participants in the group condition were far less likely to choose pizza following the ice cream scenario (25.0%) than those in the alone condition (57.9%). Further the results of this study support our argument that individuals dining in groups experience increased guilt and imply that such guilt affects subsequent consumption choices. Due to increased feelings of guilt, participants dining in groups attempt to compensate for their perceived overconsumption by subsequently selecting a more healthy option.

"The Effect of Goal Setting on Consumption & Consumer Well-Being"

Maura Scott, University of Kentucky, USA
Stephen M. Nowlis, Arizona State University, USA

Many consumers set goals such as counting calories, carbohydrates, or fat grams to manage health concerns (Parker-Pope 2003), and 1 in 4 Americans is on a diet at any given time (Crossen 2003, Fetto 2002). For example, an individual may pursue a more specific (consume 1500 calories per day) or less specific goal (consume between 1400 and 1600 calories per day). In light of these issues, we examine the following research questions: Do consumers more effectively establish and reach consumption goals when the goals are more or less specific? What is impact of varying goal strategies on emotional responses, performance, success rates, and self-perception? How do consumers' goal strategies and processes differ depending on their level of dietary restraint?

Goals that are both specific and difficult lead to higher performance levels, relative to vague, non-quantitative goals such as "do your best" and more demanding goals lead to lower levels of performance satisfaction (Locke and Latham 1990). The 'Performance-Success Dilemma' predicts that as goals increase in specificity, at the more difficult end of the goal continuum, as performance increases, satisfaction decreases (Locke and Latham 1990).

Consumers vary in their ability to predict future successful self-regulation attempts (Chandon, Morwitz, and Reinartz 2005). Our experiments demonstrate that restrained eaters, those consumers who are chronically focused on managing their weight and food consumption (Herman and Polivy 1975, 1980), based on their highly emotional relationship with food (Fletcher et al. 2007, King, Herman, and Polivy 1987), experience a more difficult process to reach their objectives, and while they reach their immediate objectives (Ward and Mann 2000), they may be less successful in sustaining their efforts over the longer term.

In study 1, during the process of pursuing their stated consumption objective, restrained eaters felt more regret, guilt, embarrassment, and feelings of over-consumption about the food. In particular, restrained eaters found the process of pursuing less specific goals to be significantly more stressful. However, despite these difficulties during the consumption process and differences in choice of goal strategy relative to unrestrained eaters, the restrained consumers' performance outcomes were not significantly different than those of unrestrained consumers.

In study 2, as specificity of consumption goals increases (e.g., consume 25 of 100 M&Ms versus consume 20-30 of 100 M&Ms), consumption levels decrease (performance increases) and goal attainment decreases (success rates decrease). Hence, more specific goals result in lower levels of enjoyment, feelings of guilt, regret, and failure. Consistently experiencing lower success rates over time may be demoralizing for consumers and make it more difficult for them to sustain goal pursuit over the longer term.

These effects influence consumers' well-being two-fold. First, those consumers achieving very low levels of consumption tend to set stringent goals, so they are reaching their goals less often. These consumers tend to feel relatively less successful and do not enjoy the process of eating even pleasant products such as chocolate. Consumers taking this approach may have a more difficult time sustaining such a performance level over time, and may also tend to be less happy. Second, restrained eaters experience a significantly more stressful process relative to unrestrained eaters. Although they experience comparable levels of performance and success relative to unrestrained eaters, the strain and difficulty restrained eaters experience during the process may negatively impact their ability to sustain their performance over the long-term, which may result in those consumers being relatively more unhappy.

Our research contributes to the goal theory literature and the literature on consumption behaviors. This research predicts which approaches (specific or non-specific) yield successful short-term and sustainable outcomes. This research explains how goals and consumption behavior impact consumer well-being; we demonstrate that unrestrained consumers are generally unhappy during the process of striving to reach goals and estimates, and tend to experience guilt and regret through the goal striving process, and in general, consumers pursuing relatively more specific goals generally experience feelings of failure and lack of enjoyment.

REFERENCES

Ariely, Dan and Jonathan Levav (2000), "Sequential Choice in Group Settings: Taking the Road Less Traveled and Less Enjoyed," *Journal of Consumer Research*, 27 (3), 279-290.

Baumeister, Roy F. (2002), "Yielding to Temptation: Self-Control Failure, Impulsive Purchasing, and Consumer Behavior," *Journal of Consumer Research*, 28 (4), 670-676.

Brehm, Jack W. (1966), *A Theory of Psychological Reactance*.

DeSteno, David, Richard E. Petty, Derek D. Rucker, Duane T. Wegener, and Julia Braverman (2004), "Discrete Emotions and Persuasion: The Role of Emotion-Induced Expectancies," *Journal of Personality and Social Psychology*, 86 (1), 43-56.

Dhar, Ravi and Klaus Wertenbroch (2007), "The Costs and Benefits of Temptation in Consumer Choice, working paper, Yale University.

de Castro, John M. (1994), "Family and Friends Produce Greater Social Facilitation of Food Intake than Other Companions," *Physiology and Behavior*, 56, 445-465.

de Castro, John M. (2000), "Eating Behavior: Lessons From the Real World of Humans," *Nutrition*, 16, 800-13.

de Castro, John M. and E. Marie Brewer (1992), "The Amount Eaten in Meals by Humans is the Power Function of the Number of People Present," *Physiology and Behavior*, 51, 121-125.

Dweck, C. S. and E. L. Leggett (1988), "A Social-Cognitive Appsroach to Motivation and Personality," *Psychological Review*, 95, 256-273.

Ekman, Paul, Wallace V. Friesen, and Phoebe Ellsworth (1972), *Emotion in the Human Face: Guidelines for Research and an Integration of Findings*.

Giner-Sorolla, Roger (2001), "Guilty Pleasures and Grim Necessities: Affective Attitudes in Dilemmas of Self-Control," *Journal of Personality and Social Psychology,* 80 (2), 206-221.

Gross, James J. and Robert W. Levenson (1993), "Emotional Suppression: Physiology, Self-Report, and Expressive Behavior," *Journal of Personality and Social Psychology*, 64 (6), 970-986.

Higgins, T. E. (1997), "Beyond Pleasure and Pain," *American Psychologist*, 52, 1280-1300.

Hoch, Stephen J. and George F. Loewenstein (1991), "Time-Inconsistent Preferences and Consumer Self-Control," *Journal of Consumer Research*, 17 (4), 16.

Nosek, B. A., A. G. Greenwald, and M. R. Banaji (2005), "Understanding and Using the Implicit Association Test: II. Method Variables and Construct Validity," *Personality and Social Psychology Bulletin*, 31, 166-180.

Loewenstein, G. (1996), "Out of Control: Visceral Influences on Behavior," *Organizational Behavior & Human Decision Processes*, 65, 272-292.

Metcalfe, J. and W. Mischel (1999), "A Hot/Cool-System Analysis of Delay of Gratification: Dynamics of Willpower," *Psychological Review*, 106, 3-1.

Wicklund, Robert A. (1974), "Freedom and Reactance: (1974)," *Freedom and Reactance*.

Zajonc, Robert B. (1998), *The Handbook of Social Psychology*, Daniel T Gilbert and Susan T Fiske and Lindzey Gardner, Eds. 4th ed. Vol. 2.

SPECIAL SESSION SUMMARY

It's a Two-Way Street: The Influence of Communicators and Recipients in Word-of-Mouth Contexts

Andrew Kaikati, University of Minnesota, USA

SESSION OVERVIEW

Word of mouth (WOM) is defined as person-to-person communication concerning a brand, product, or service in the marketplace (Dichter 1966). It is a key source of information for consumers, and its importance is growing due to increases in product complexity and quantity of information, as well as increased avenues for interpersonal communications such as the internet (Godes et al. 2005). Consequently, companies are increasingly relying on WOM to promote their products (Kaikati and Kaikati 2004).

This session takes a unique and broad perspective on the topic of interpersonal WOM communication by presenting WOM research from the vantage point of message recipients, as well as from the perspective of the communicators of the message. Specifically, the first two papers attempt to understand different characteristics of the communicator (self-construal, altruism) which are likely to influence the extent as well as conditions under which WOM is likely to be generated (cf. Cheema and Kaikati 2009). These papers identify conditions under which potential communicators are likely (vs. not likely) to consider the potential message recipient, and how consideration of the potential message recipient influences their decision to talk. The third paper focuses on the recipient perspective in attempting to examine factors that are likely to influence the persuasiveness of WOM (message content and source characteristics). The three papers together provide insights relating to how individual characteristics of (potential) communicators affect both the decision to share information and also the influence of information that is shared. Across studies, these effects are examined in both face-to-face offline and also online WOM contexts.

The Zhang, Feick and Mittal paper (presented by Lawrence Feick) attempts to understand which people share negative WOM experiences, and with whom, as a function of their level of self-construal. These issues are examined in a face-to-face interpersonal setting, to various relationship ties. Their theorizing suggests that image concerns are likely to deter negative WOM transmission to weak ties (but not to strong ties) by individuals for whom an independent construal is activated. Thus, independent-construal individuals are more likely to consider the identity of the potential recipient (e.g., whether the person is a strong or a weak tie) in their decision to talk.

The Kaikati and Ahluwalia paper (presented by Andrew Kaikati) proposes a cost-benefit framework to test how people decide to share information with others, as a function of their individual differences in altruism, or their internal motivation to help others, in both online and offline settings. Their theorizing suggests that high altruists' WOM decisions are driven more by the perceived diagnostic value of information, while low altruists' WOM decisions are driven more by the perceived costs to the communicator (resource costs, social costs) of sharing the information. Thus, high (vs. low) altruists are more likely to consider the potential recipient in their decision to talk.

The Karmarkar and Tormala paper (presented by Uma Karmarkar) uses an online setting to understand when consumers are likely be persuaded by others, as a function of source credibility and expressed certainty. Persuasion is greater for low credibility communicators who express certainty, and for high credibility sources who express uncertainty. The authors propose an incongruity hypothesis, and identify involvement of the recipient as the underlying mechanism. Thus, the effect of source credibility on information recipients' acceptance of a message is dependent upon expressed certainty.

J. Peter Reingen will serve as the discussion leader. He is a well-accomplished researcher in the area of the word of mouth — in particular, as it relates to social ties, referral networks, and interpersonal influence. He will bring to bear his breadth of knowledge in this area by providing an integrative perspective on the role of communicators and recipients in WOM, and discussing future research directions.

References

Cheema, Amar and Andrew M. Kaikati (forthcoming), "The Effect of Need for Uniqueness on Word of Mouth," *Journal of Marketing Research.*

Dichter, Ernest (1966), "How Word of Mouth Advertising Works," *Harvard Business Review*, 44 (6), 147-66.

Godes, David, Dina Mayzlin, Yubo Chen, Sanjiv Das, Chrysanthos Dellarocas, Bruce Pfeiffer, Barak Libai, Subrata Sen, Mengze Shi, and Peeter Verlegh (2005), "The Firm's Management of Social Interactions," *Marketing Letters*, 16 (3-4), 415-28.

Kaikati, Andrew M. and Jack G. Kaikati (2004), "Stealth Marketing: How to Reach Consumers Surreptitiously," *California Management Review*, 46 (4), 6-22.

EXTENDED ABSTRACTS

"Negative Word-of-Mouth: Self-Construal and Image Impairment Concern"

Yinlong Zhang, University of Texas at San Antonio, USA
Lawrence Feick, University of Pittsburgh, USA
Vikas Mittal, Rice University, USA

After a negative consumption experience, are people more likely to transmit word-of-mouth (WOM) to strong rather than weak ties? The literature includes conflicting empirical results. For example, on the one hand, some research has found that consumers have a higher propensity to spread negative WOM to their strong ties than weak ties (e.g., Weenig, Groenenboom, and Wilke 2001). On the other hand, Wangenheim (2004) found that consumers are more likely to spread negative WOM to weak than to strong ties.

In this paper we articulate and test conditions that may explain at least part of this inconsistency. Specifically, we argue that after a negative purchase experience, consumers can experience two conflicting motives that affect their likelihood of transmitting WOM. On the one hand, they may feel the need to warn individuals about the product or service, but also, they may be concerned about maintaining a positive image (i.e., not revealing that they made a bad choice). The former of these motives is other-focused and the latter self-focused, and either can be more important for a given consumer in a given situation. We show in three studies that the effect of tie strength is related to the presence of either self-focused or other-focused motives.

We take a social-identity perspective that leads us to examine the role of self-construal and image-impairment concern in moderating the relationship between tie strength and (negative) WOM transmission. Study 1 focused on self-construal. The self can be seen as being more connected to others (an interdependent self-construal) or being more distinct from others (an independent self-construal) (Markus and Kitayama 1991; 1996). According to Markus and Kitayama (1991), those with activated independent self-construals are likely to be affected most by self-focused motivations. In contrast, those with activated interdependent self-construals are likely to be affected most by other-focused motivations. In our context then, consumers who are focused on the needs of others are likely to engage in negative WOM regardless of whether the ties are strong or weak. Thus, we expect that individuals with an interdependent self-construal will view weak ties altruistically and share information with them. In contrast, those with an independent self-construal will adopt this perspective only when interacting with strong ties. These arguments suggest that after a negative experience, self-construal will moderate the effect of tie strength on the likelihood of WOM transmission: we expect that under an independent self-construal, consumers are more likely to transmit negative WOM to strong ties than weak ties. In contrast, under an interdependent self-construal, consumers are equally likely to transmit negative WOM to strong ties and weak ties.

Study 1 employed a 2 (Self-Construal Priming: Independent vs. Interdependent) X 2 (Tie Strength: Weak vs. Strong) in which 78 student participants reacted to a negative consumption scenario. The results support our hypothesis: differences in WOM transmission likelihood between strong and weak ties only emerge when the independent self-construal is primed. With an interdependent self-construal, WOM is equally likely to strong and weak ties.

Study 1 results are consistent with our hypothesis, but do not address the question of how more or less self-focused thinking affects WOM transmission likelihood. We theorize that the process underlying the results involves the differential salience of image-impairment concern under independent versus interdependent self-construal. More specifically, we expect that under an independent self-construal, individuals' focus on the self allows image impairment concerns to become salient, while it is not made salient under an interdependent self-construal.

For individuals with an independent self-construal, we argued and demonstrated that a self-focused perspective dominates decision making. For such individuals, image concerns are salient (whether or not there is an additional effort to make them salient). Thus, we should expect that for such individuals we obtain results similar to those in Study 1, that is, greater WOM transmission likelihood to strong than to weak ties. On the other hand, for an interdependent self-construal, we have demonstrated that other-focused concerns are salient because an interdependent self identity motivates people to think about others and pursue relational goals. Consequently, for interdependent self-construal there was no difference between strong and weak ties in WOM transmission likelihood. However, if image impairment concerns are made salient for this group, we should see a reversal in the pattern of results. Specifically, individuals with either an interdependent or independent self-construal should be concerned with their image and should be likely to withhold negative WOM to both strong and weak ties. In summary then, we expect a three way interaction among these variables.

In Studies 2 and 3, we examine this hypothesis. Study 2 and 3 tested the same set of three variables: self-construal, tie strength, and image impairment concern. Study 2 was an experiment in which a sample of 195 students reacted to a negative consumption scenario. Study 2 used manipulated variables in a 2 (Image Impairment Concern: High salience vs. Low salience) X 2 (Self-Construal Priming: Independent vs. Interdependent) X 2 (Tie Strength: Weak vs. Strong) between-subjects design. In contrast, Study 3 was a survey of 401 adult consumers in which image impairment concern and self-construal were measured and tie strength was manipulated between subjects. A marketing research company used probability sampling from its online panel of U.S. adult consumers to obtain participants.

Results from Studies 2 and 3 support the hypothesis. Image impairment concern moderates the interactive effect of self-construal and tie strength on the likelihood of negative WOM transmission. When image impairment concern is made salient, WOM transmission is similar between self-construals. When image impairment concern is not made salient, we find greater WOM transmission for strong than weak ties for an independent self-construal and no effect of tie strength for an interdependent self-construal.

In combination, the results of our studies show that the process of managing one's image is integral to understanding the likelihood of WOM transmission. Further, our results reinforce the importance of understanding the motives—structural and psychological—that drive WOM decisions and also provide insight into the mechanisms underlying the effect of self-construal on information processing.

References

Markus, Hazal R., and Shinobu Kitayama (1991), "Culture and the Self: Implications for Cognition, Emotion and Motivation," *Psychological Review*, 98 (2), 224-253.

Markus, Hazal R., and Shinobu Kitayama (1996), "Culture and Basic Psychological Principles," in *Social Psychology: Handbook of Basic Principles*, ed. Tory E. Higgins and Ariely W. Kruglanski, New York: The Guilford Press.

Wangenheim, Florian V. (2004), "Opportunism in Interpersonal Exchange: When Dissatisfaction is Followed by Positive Word-of-Mouth," *AMA Summer Educators' Conference Proceedings*, 17.

Weenig, Mieneke W. H., Arieneke C.W. J. Groenenboom, and Henk A.M. Wilke (2001), "Bad News Transmission as a Function of the Definitiveness of Consequences and the Relationship between Communicator and Recipient," *Journal of Personality and Social Psychology*, 80 (3), 449-461.

"Word-of-Mouth Communication as Helping Behavior"

Andrew M. Kaikati, University of Minnesota, USA
Rohini Ahluwalia, University of Minnesota, USA

A person who acquires marketplace information must decide whether to share that information. WOM occurs only if a person is motivated to talk after weighing the associated costs and benefits (Cheema and Kaikati 2009; Frenzen and Nakamoto 1993). One potential benefit of sharing product-related information could be facilitating recipients' future decisions by helping them to make informed decisions and to avoid costly pitfalls. At the same time, sharing this information could result in potential costs to the communicator. There are social costs; for instance, information conveyed may reflect poorly on the communicator if others act on that information and disagree with it, or if others perceive the communicator to be a complainer. There are also resource costs. For instance, information involves a certain amount of time and effort to transmit.

We suggest that the effect of these costs and benefits on WOM behavior may differ as a function of the person's underlying values. Values are abstract representations about desired end states that are hierarchically organized in terms of their importance to the self (Bardi and Schwartz 2003). High-priority values are central to one's self concept, and serve as motivational constructs that may define as situation, elicit goals, and guide action (Torelli and Kaikati 2009; Verplanken and Holland 2002). Actions become subjectively more attractive to the extent that they lead to attainment of valued goals; thus, each person defines a situation, and weighs its associated opportunities and constraints, in terms of his or her own important values.

Specifically, the current research develops a cost-benefit framework to systematically test the effect of individual differences in altruism, which is the internal motivation to help others that is based one's personal values, on WOM. One of the primary motivations suggested in the WOM literature is the desire to help other consumers (Price, Feick, and Guskey 1995); however, there has been little systematic experimental research examining when this motivation is relevant and what its effects are on the likelihood of sharing information.

It is expected that individuals who score high (vs. low) in altruism are more focused on the needs of others, and that their behavior will be proportional to the magnitude of the perceived informational benefit (Bendapudi, Singh, and Bendapudi 1996). In a WOM context, this means that these individuals' WOM likelihood increases with information diagnosticity. Furthermore, they should be less sensitive to other factors, such as their own level of expended resources and the potential social costs of sharing information. Individuals who score low (vs. high) in altruism, on the other hand, focus less on the needs of others, and are thus less likely to be affected by the diagnosticity of information. However, they should be sensitive to the expended resources and potential costs of a situation.

Three studies were designed to test these propositions. Across three studies, participants either read a hypothetical consumer scenario or reported on a prior product experience. In each study, the relative benefits and/or costs associated with WOM were manipulated (based on pretests of these costs and benefits). After reading the study materials, participants reported their likelihood of sharing information about the product or service with others in either a face-to-face (study 1 and 2) or an online (study 3) context. They also completed a series of measures, including altruism.

In study 1, the benefits and costs of WOM communication were manipulated simultaneously via characteristics of the information (negative versus positive restaurant experience) to test the likelihood of information sharing. Pretests confirmed that compared with positive information, negative information is more useful to recipients (Feldman and Lynch 1988), but it also carries more social costs for the communicator because others may perceive him or her as a complainer (Laczniak, DeCarlo, and Ramaswami 2001). Results confirmed that high altruists were more likely to communicate negative as compared to positive information, since it offered more benefits to others, even at greater social costs to oneself. In contrast, low altruists exhibited the opposite pattern of WOM behavior–they were more likely to communicate positive versus negative experiences to others, since the latter tended to carry more social costs to the self.

In study 2, only the information value was manipulated (costs were held constant), using the context of information about an in-store special for a popular consumer product (digital cameras). The informational value (benefit) was manipulated as either moderate (store located further away) or high (store located closeby). Consistent with expectations, high altruists were more likely to talk to someone about the digital camera sale when the store was closer, due to greater information value. Low altruists, however, were unaffected by the information value of WOM, and were equally likely to engage in WOM in both conditions.

Study 3 was a computer-based study that tested the implications of the framework in an online context. In this study, only the resource cost of sharing information was manipulated (information value was held constant). Participants first reported on the most recent new movie they had seen. On the next screen, the number of existing online movie reviews for that movie was manipulated to be either very low (two reviews) or moderate (35 reviews). Pretests confirmed that WOM may take more time and effort (higher costs) when there are fewer reviews, but that the information is perceived as equally beneficial to recipients in the two conditions. Results indicated that low altruists were less likely to post a review when there were fewer existing reviews, because of the additional time and effort required. High altruists' WOM, however, was not affected by the number of reviews.

In total, three studies suggest that level of altruism, which is based on one's personal values, is an important driver of WOM motivation. Specifically, findings indicate that high altruists' WOM behavior is driven by the perceived diagnostic value of information, whereas low altruists' WOM behavior is driven by perceived communicator costs.

References

Bendapudi, Neeli, Surendra N. Singh, and Venkat Bendapudi (1996), "Enhancing Helping Behavior: An Integrative Framework for Promotion Planning," *Journal of Marketing*, 60 (July), 33-49.

Cheema, Amar and Andrew M. Kaikati (forthcoming), "The Effect of Need for Uniqueness on Word of Mouth," *Journal of Marketing Research*.

Feldman, Jack M. and John G. Lynch (1988), "Self-Generated Validity and Other Effects of Measurement on Belief, Attitude, Intention, and Behavior," *Journal of Applied Psychology*, 73 (3), 421-35.

Frenzen, Jonathan and Kent Nakamoto (1993), "Structure, Cooperation, and the Flow of Market Information," Journal of Consumer Research, 20 (December), 360-75.

Laczniak, Russell N., Thomas E. DeCarlo and Sridhar N. Ramaswami (2001), "Consumers' Responses to Negative Word-of-Mouth Communication: An Attribution Theory Perspective," *Journal of Consumer Psychology*, 11 (1), 57-73.

Price, Linda L., Lawrence L. Feick, and Audrey Guskey (1995), "Everyday Market Helping Behavior," *Journal of Public Policy and Marketing*, 14 (2), 255–66.

Torelli, Carlos J. and Andrew M. Kaikati (2009), "Values as Predictors of Judgment and Behaviors: The Role of Abstract and Concrete Mindsets," *Journal of Personality and Social Psychology*, 96 (1), 231-47.

"The Dynamic Effect of Source Certainty on Consumer Involvement and Persuasion"

Uma R. Karmarkar, Stanford University, USA
Zakary L. Tormala, Stanford University, USA

Suppose a traveler is planning a vacation through a popular travel website and reads a reviewer's recommendation for a particular beachside resort, containing several strong arguments in its favor. It seems reasonable to surmise that the more certainty the reviewer expresses about this recommendation, the more likely the traveler will be to take his or her advice. However, is it possible that by voicing certainty the reviewer will undermine his or her persuasiveness? Are there conditions under which the reviewer could gain influence by expressing uncertainty about his or her attitude? In this research, we explore the possibility that the effect of expressed certainty on persuasion can vary dependent on the expertise of the message source.

While an extensive literature speaks to the important consequences of attitude certainty for a consumer's own attitudes and behavior (see Tormala and Rucker 2007 for a review), far less attention has been devoted to exploring the impact of expressed attitude certainty on other consumers. In terms of word of mouth communications, one straightforward prediction would be that expressing certainty generally increases persuasion. Consistent with this hypothesis, research in other domains suggests that individuals who express high levels of confidence tend to be perceived as more credible than those who express lower level of confidence (e.g., Price and Stone 2004; Tenney, MacCoun, Spellman, and Hastie 2007). Thus, source certainty might have a positive effect on persuasion that is mediated by perceived source expertise.

In contrast to this main effect hypothesis, we propose that in subjective consumer contexts source certainty can have a dynamic effect on persuasion that is moderated by perceived source expertise. Under low expertise conditions (e.g., when a consumer receives a message from a nonexpert source), we predict that source certainty will have a positive effect on persuasion such that consumers are more persuaded when the source of a message expresses high compared to low certainty. Under high expertise conditions (e.g., when a consumer receives a message from an expert source), however, we predict that source certainty will have a negative effect on persuasion, such that consumers are more persuaded when the source expresses low compared to high certainty.

This interaction hypothesis is based on past research exploring the effects of informational incongruity on message processing. Most germane to our concerns, mismatches between various source attributes have been shown to increase message processing, which can boost persuasion when message arguments are strong (e.g., Ziegler, Diehl, and Ruther 2002). Thus we posit that consumers will feel greater involvement with a message when source expertise and source certainty are incongruent (low expertise/high certainty or high expertise/low certainty) rather than congruent (high expertise/high certainty or low expertise/low certainty). Furthermore, to the extent that the message itself is reasonably strong, or compelling, greater involvement should foster greater persuasion (Petty and Cacioppo 1986). In essence, we hypothesize that incongruity between perceived expertise and certainty should violate expectancies, which feels surprising and motivates involvement. Increased involvement, in turn, can enhance persuasion in response to strong arguments. However, in a situation with weak arguments, incongruities leading to greater involvement should have no appreciable benefit for persuasion and may even cause reactance against it.

In Experiment 1, we tested the impact of source certainty and source expertise on expectancy violations. A favorable restaurant review was presented from a source who varied in expertise and level of expressed certainty. Following the message, we assessed participants' perceptions of how unexpected and surprising the content of the material was. Although source expertise and certainty did not interact to influence the perceived similarity, likeability or trustworthiness of the source, they did interact to affect expectancy violations. We found that expressions of certainty induced greater surprise and unexpectedness when the source was low in expertise, whereas the converse was true for high expertise sources.

Experiment 2 examined the implications for persuasion. In this experiment, all participants received a strong and favorable restaurant review ostensibly taken from a consumer website. As in Experiment 1, the source of this review was described as either an expert or nonexpert on food and dining, and he expressed either high or low certainty about his recommendation. Following the review, we measured participants' willingness to pay (WTP) for a meal at the restaurant. Results indicated that participants who received a recommendation from a nonexpert source reported greater WTP when that source expressed certainty rather than uncertainty. Conversely, participants who received a recommendation from an expert source reported greater WTP when that source expressed uncertainty rather than certainty.

Finally, Experiment 3 sought to establish the mediating role of involvement, as measured by cognitive elaboration, in the persuasion effect revealed by the second experiment. Replicating the restaurant review paradigm with strong arguments, we found that participants generated more positive thoughts and reported more favorable attitudes and intentions when a high (low) expertise source expressed uncertainty (certainty). However, when a review with weak arguments was presented, these effects disappeared (and tended to reverse). Furthermore, the three-way interaction between source expertise, source certainty, and argument strength on attitudes and intentions was mediated by thought favorability. In short, then, incongruity between source expertise and source certainty fostered increased elaboration, which enhanced persuasion under strong but not weak argument conditions.

Discussion. Previous research exploring the effects of source certainty generally supports the existence of a confidence heuristic, whereby expressed confidence, or certainty, is interpreted as a marker of expertise (e.g., Price and Stone 2004). In the current experiments, we found that source certainty and source expertise were distinct constructs that could be manipulated without impacting other types of source perceptions. Furthermore, the current studies suggest that the effects of source certainty are dynamic, being completely contingent upon the source's level of underlying expertise. In particular, nonexperts (e.g., other consumers) can gain interest and influence by expressing certainty regarding their opinions and recommendations. In contrast, experts appear to gain interest and influence when they express uncertainty about their opinions and recommendations. Implications for interpersonal influence in word of mouth marketing contexts are discussed.

References

Petty, Richard E. and John T. Cacioppo (1986), *Communication and persuasion: Central and Peripheral Routes to Persuasion*, New York: Springer-Verlag.

Price, Paul C. and Eric R. Stone (2004), "Intuitive Evaluation of Likelihood Judgment Producers: Evidence for a Confidence Heuristic," *Journal of Behavioral Decision Making*, 17 (December), 39-57.

Tenney, Elizabeth R., Robert J. MacCoun, Barbara A. Spellman, and Reid Hastie (2007), "Calibration Trumps Confidence as a Basis for Witness Credibility," *Psychological Science*, 18 (March), 46-50.

Tormala, Zakary L. and Derek D. Rucker (2007), "Attitude Certainty: A Review of Past Findings and Emerging Perspectives," *Social and Personality Psychology Compass*, 1 (November), 469-92.

Ziegler, Rene, Michael Diehl, and Anja Ruther (2002), "Multiple Source Characteristics and Persuasion: Source Inconsistency as a Determinant of Message Scrutiny," *Personality and Social Psychology Bulletin*, 28 (4), 496-508.

SPECIAL SESSION SUMMARY

From Ear to Brain, From Heart to Pocket: Branding Challenges and Possibilities in the Music Industry

Chia-Jung Tsay, Harvard Business School, USA

SESSION OVERVIEW

The music industry faces new challenges as its nature is altered by the changing tastes of its consumers and the values of the creative industries in general. As the internet and various other mediums dominate the production, access to, and consumption of music, the perception of product quality and the objective measures of the assets are less definable and even less predictable. In three different papers, we examine the creation, development, evaluation, and communication of products through the branding perspective. Even though the three projects are grounded in an investigation of music and the music industry. The findings hold relevant insights for other, creative industries and with other important implications for businesses beyond the creative industries as well.

This Special Session on music aims to tackle the branding of music at multiple levels. The series of presentations start with a look at auditory branding, focusing on how sound may be used to create an authentic auditory identity for a brand. The experimental approach of the first paper captures the cognitive processing of the individual and offers new directions for the better use of music for higher consumer recognition and involvement. The second paper expands branding from an individual level to the product and transitions from the consumer to the organization. The experiments explore the creation of achievement as the product and the consumers' perceptions and reactions to the product, operationalized as the judgments of achievement. The third paper completes the loop by analyzing the branding of organizations as means to attract new customers. The final presentation explores how a major symphony orchestra can be re-branded via the development of their products to satisfy the varied tastes and preferences of consumers from different age groups and levels of expertise.

In order to focus on a narrower set of industries within the creative genres to develop deeper understanding of the challenges and potential solutions, we have limited this set of studies to the music industry. However, our results are very applicable to other creative industries where the strategic branding of products and organizations directly and significantly impacts consumer behavior. We foresee the issues and topics to be covered to be of interest to both academics and practitioners. We believe that by triangulating through multiple methods, including experimental methods and survey analyses, and through multiple levels of analyses, our findings will provide various opportunities for rich discussions of new directions in research and practice throughout a range of important industries that traditionally have been overlooked.

EXTENDED ABSTRACTS

"Hearing, Remembering, and Branding: Guidelines For Creating Sonic Logos"

Vijaykumar Krishnan, University of Cincinnati, USA
James J. Kellaris, University of Cincinnati, USA

A Sonic Logo, "sogo," the auditory analog of a visual logo, is a typical sonic branding device. Some interesting examples are the 5-tone Intel sogo, windows vista's 4-tone start-up chime and NBC's 3-tone sogo. Sogos vary in their design characteristics. They may have an ascending pattern (Windows Vista), descending pattern (windows XP) or a zigzagging contour (Intel). A sogo may be easier to remember because it repeats a pattern or 'chunks' (Baddeley and Hitch 1974) groups of similar tones. Thus, number of tones they comprise, their contour and their chunkability may characterize Sogos.

Per logo literature (Henderson and Cote 1998), good sogos should engender favorable consumer responses on recognition, affect, and familiarity dimensions. For instance, sogos with fewer tones should be easier to remember; thus obtain high true recognition on a subsequent encounter. On the other hand, because they are easier to process, they may engender illusions of familiarity (Wittlesea 1993) leading to high false recognition. Sogos with a zigzagging contour may be more difficult to recall but may be perceived novel and so liked more. In other words, consumers experience differing levels of ease in processing sogos based on the design characteristics.

This subjective experience of ease of processing incoming auditory information (Reber, Wurtz and Zimmerman 2004; Whittlesea 1993; Janiszewski and Meyvis 2000; Winkielman et al 2003) is misattributed to judgment at hand-Familiarity (Whittlesea 1993); Positive affect (Reber et al 1998; Winkielman and Cacioppo 2001); Judgments of truth (Reber and Schwarz 1999); Brand Evaluation (Lee and Labroo 2004). This research explores the systematic influence of three design characteristics of sogos–number of tones, contour, and chunkability across five studies on response dimensions. Study finds evidence of processing fluency mediation of these influences.

In study 1, participants were blocked into three groups. All participants heard a commercial for a hypothetical brand of bread. The commercial was identical across the three groups but for the accompanying sogo which comprised 3-tone, 6-tone or 9-tone. At test, participants rated willingness to pay for this hypothetical brand of bread. Results show that the number of tones influences the willingness to pay and this influence was fully mediated by the processing fluency of the sogo. Processing fluency was operationalized as an assessment of the ease with which an average person can hum this sogo on a seven-point scale.

In Study 2, participants heard three target sogos varying in number of tones interspersed with distraction tasks. At test, participants heard six sogos—three targets and three foils and rated recognition on a six-point scale (This sogo was in the first set too). Results show that number of tones influence false recognition. Sogos with fewer tones reveal greater perceptual fluency and a higher false recognition. A multilevel meditational analysis reveals significant fluency mediation of false recognition.

Study 3 was similar in structure to study2 except that the sogos varies only on ease of chunking—a pattern such as ABC-ABC-ABC is easy to chunk which A-B-C-D-E-F-G-H-I is not— although both have exactly same number of tones. Results show that chunking influences fluency.

Study 4 varied the contour—ascending, descending or zigzagging. Results show that contour influences affect. A multilevel meditational analysis reveals significant fluency mediation of affect—fluency is affectively positive. Contour also influences both true and false recognition.

Study 5 shows interesting interaction effects between contour and number of tones on recognition and familiarity. False recognition is for zigzag sogos is lower than that for linear sogos when the number of tones is four; this pattern flips when the number of tones in the sogo is .seven

Taken together, these results show that several response dimensions vary systematically with the sogo design characteristics, thus providing for guidelines. Leader brands would want a high true recognition and a low false recognition; brands in a low involvement product segment (e.g., bread) could profit from high false recognition and illusions of familiarity.

Huge investments are made for creation and airing of auditory branding stimuli; rights for popular songs for use in commercial jingles may top $500,000 such as for "stand by me," deployed by Citibank, (Krasilovsky and Shemel 2007). Microsoft commissioned the services of the famous musician Robert Fripe to create the 4-second Windows Vista start-up sogo, who took eighteen months to create the final version. That must surely have been a lot of investment. In conclusion, given that sogos are branding devices, guidelines from this research should reduce the precarious dependence of marketers on musicians, and provide for greater control over sonic branding.

"'She's a Natural!': From Mere Label to Actualized Consumer Preference"

Chia-Jung Tsay, Harvard Business School, USA
Mahzarin R. Banaji, Harvard University, USA

Industry leaders in marketing and public relations know well the importance of image management and branding. When the product involves an individual or an individual's output, and when assessments of such products are likely to entail much subjectivity, it often becomes important to build a narrative to best allow consumers to relate to the core attributes of the individual and products associated with such an individual. In sports, for example, several cycles of the Olympics have exemplified the success of the massive campaigns to humanize the champions whose feats defy imagination. Media pick up quickly on such human interest stories, stories of great sacrifice, of perseverance against all odds—stories where the cliché of blood, sweat, and tears is but an understatement. We see quite a different approach when it comes to the marketing and branding of classical musicians, a field that is littered with "prodigies." It is the natural talent that captures our intrigue—the youthful looks of a Joshua Bell; the nearly everyday occurrence of yet the next wunderkind; the ingénue who is featured prominently on a CD cover, her age and diminutive stature made only more striking by the elderly and robust conductor pictured standing at her side. Industry intuition would suggest that society rewards the natural, and here, we test this theory empirically.

In any domain of expertise, be it art, sports, or academia, achievement is assumed to derive from both natural and acquired sources. Of all those who undergo extensive training in any sphere of achievement, there are those who seem to shine in ways that cannot be explained by practice. On the other hand, there are those with talent, but unless that talent is put to rigorous training, nothing much can result from it. It is hardly controversial to claim that achievement in any sphere is a function of both. Our beliefs about the relative contributions of these two sources are important because they can shape our behavior toward our own talents and toward the talents of others we judge, such as with consumers' preferences towards performers and artistic products. We are interested in testing whether the evaluation of achievement, such as the assessment of performance quality, is shaped by the belief about the natural versus acquired basis of achievement. We suggest that our preferences for both early talent and the hard-working hero may co-occur, but in dissociated fashion, such that abstract, propositionally represented values about accomplishment may genuinely favor a strong work ethic, but that specific choices will reveal a preference for the natural. In other words, a dissociation between expressed values favoring hard work, or the "Striver," and actual preference for innate talent, or the "Natural," may in fact be the reality. We may say we respect and admire hard workers, but when it comes to selecting a recording or buying a concert ticket, our dollars may instead go to the natural prodigy.

In the first two experiments, we explored whether knowledge about the source of achievement influences the evaluations of target musicians (Study 1), and whether professionals differ from amateurs in vulnerability to the bias (Study 2). Our strategy was to familiarize participants with two musicians, using background descriptions that were matched for level of performance and degree of achievement described, but which differed in whether the musicians' talent appeared to be either naturally acquired, the "Natural," or rather developed primarily through hard work and training, the "Striver." Then, participants heard brief performances attributed to each musician, but which in reality were performed by the same anonymous musician, thus controlling for actual level of ability or accomplishment. After hearing each performance, participants evaluated the target musician on several dimensions intended to gauge their perceptions of the performers' musical achievement.

We observed a dissociation between reports of what mattered in the creation of achievement (hard work and training) and judgments of achievement (inborn qualities) in the field of music performance. After hearing performances that were controlled so as to be equal in quality, experts—heavy consumers of music— in Study 1 rated a musician described as having inborn ability, the "Natural," as more talented than a musician described as having worked hard to develop her ability, or the "Striver." In spite of the way they evaluated the target performers, when asked directly about their general beliefs, participants regarded effortful training as a more influential determinant of musical achievement than innate ability. Thus, the expression of the naturalness may be an implicit bias, because its manifestation in specific judgments contradicted the implications of participants' explicit general beliefs. We replicated these results in Study 2, with experts again rating effortful training as the superior determinant of musical achievement, and this difference was more pronounced for these experts than for novices, who showed a slight reversal.

As little research has thus far tackled the effect of apparent basis of achievement on our evaluations of artistic products, and since our findings in the first two studies suggest that the naturalness bias may be operating at an implicit level, we sought to triangulate through different methodologies to determine whether the naturalness bias would still be elicited. In Study 3 and Study 4, we replicated the result of a naturalness bias in the domain of music using a conjoint analysis design. Through the presentation of a set of alternatives that allowed the deduction of preferences from the tradeoffs made when choosing between sets of attributes, we tested whether the naturalness bias would emerge on a new measure of direct choice.

Much work remains to be done to clarify the processes producing the naturalness bias, and the conditions under which it is and is not likely to occur. Given the rather consequential implications of the bias for decisions involving the assessment of individual performers and their output of artistic products, a substantial investment in that mission would be well justified. Hopefully, this research will inform efforts to best allow consumers to appreciate the culmination of what is usually the combination of natural talent and hard work.

"'I Want You Back': Branding Classical Music For The New Generation"

Lalin Anik, Harvard Business School, USA
Chia-Jung Tsay, Harvard Business School, USA

Beyond the many challenges inherent in the creative industries, such as the level of subjectivity that fosters huge unpredictability in reception to products and talents and the dependence on the blockbuster hits that offset the negative revenues accrued to the large majority of products, the classical music industry poses several additional unique issues worthy of examination. While defining success and popularity for talents and brands is shaped by objective measures in many creative industries, this is far more elusive in the music industry. And although many arts organizations exist as non-profits, they still do need to keep in consideration the long-term financial sustainability of their very existence. Indeed, even the top opera houses make major artistic and strategic decisions with their donors as a priority—for example, in 2006, 41% of the revenues for the Metropolitan Opera were from contributions.

Perhaps most importantly, unlike other genres in which the target core audience can be quite large, one of the key issues for the classical industry is the aging and increasingly limited core demographic. In this paper, we collaborate with industry leaders to focus on honing a better understanding of how to best balance the varied tastes and preferences of consumers of a range of age and expertise is paramount to. Our goal has been to use the music industry as a proxy for many other creative industries that face the risk of changing demographics of customers and we make higher level suggestions for how to brand a creative organization to capture new consumers.

In the film industry, 72% of the public over 12 years old are consumers and the 12-29 age group makes up 30% of the population and half of theater admissions—while the National Endowment for the Arts reports that the average age of those attending a classical music performance in 2002 was 49. In the soccer industry, Spain's Santiago Bernabeu Stadium opened with a capacity of 75,000 back in 1947, now with further revenues from audiences through pay-per-view and internet streams—while in the classical industry, the most famous concert hall in the world, Carnegie Hall, seats a mere 2,804. The need to capture and maintain segments of the population is still important in other industries, but we note a host of additional factors that contribute to such difficulties in the classical music industry. Here, the consumption of products and the assessment of talents often involve greater levels of investment in special training or knowledge. Given that consumption of products from creative industries can often be experienced as a social activity, as social consumption of products, this again limits the range of the population that may be naturally drawn to classical music. Comparing to other genres of music, the classical segment lags far behind in sales, occupying only 2.4% of music buyer purchases in 2005.

In this paper, we worked with a major symphony orchestra to examine the outcomes of various initiatives (such as innovative uses of digital technology and social media) to attract new consumers, along with their impact on the core audience. We also explored how consumers' choices are affected by the organization's programming, including the consideration of both economic and artistic influences, such as the stature and appeal of guest artists, the inclusion of new music in repertoire, and the brand of the institution.

We also targeted strategies on both short and long term horizons. Considering the short term, we focused on issues in balancing the core missions of the organization as it develops its multiple sub-brands, with the demands of the aging core demographic. Through data from over 6,000 audience members provided by the symphony orchestra, the findings add to our understanding of the barriers to and motivators of repeat visitation, through the identification of factors that stimulate repurchase, increase frequency, and reduce churn. First of all, the data allowed us to segment the types of customers into 6 distinct groups: "unconverted trailists," who were first-timers who attended one concert and did not come back; "special occasions" who attended one concert per year for multiple years; "non-committed" who attended a couple of concerts per year but still churned at high rated; "snackers" who attended smaller concert packages and were very loyal; "high potentials" who attended a lot of concerts and were likely to purchase a subscription; "core audience" who were all subscribers. One of the most striking results was the big gap between the churn rates of the different groups. The "uncoverted trialists" attended one concert per year and churned at a rate of 91%, while the "special occasions" also attended one concert in a given year but had a much lower churn rate at 67%. On the other end of the spectrum was the "core audience" with only 8% churn rate. Our analysis indicated that the frequency of annual concert attendance and the years of 'tenure' at the symphony were the two best predictors of the churn and sub rates. Our results also revealed large gaps between the number of customers who fell into each category.

For the long term, we focused on how best to expand the core demographic given the constraints of the products in the genre, which may affect decisions to encourage the development of group rather than solo talents, and also greater versatility through crossover acts. The issue of maintaining the core audience while drawing in new audiences has been one of the greatest needs and challenges in the classical industry, perhaps best captured by the example of *bond*, the British string quartet that has its roots in classical training but marketing efforts towards wider, pop appeal—efforts that propelled the group to its status as the best-selling string quartet of all time, but at the same time, much controversy in classical circles and even removal from the UK classical chart. We found that for this symphony orchestra, the use of strategies typical of other organizations in the classical industry may have unintended effects. For example, programming decisions that include crossover repertoire actually dilute the brand of the organization and its products, such that major segments of the core demographic— young musicians and conservatory students, as well as those in the donor population who are accustomed to the inclusion of famous works and performers more traditionally associated with the classical genre—question the legitimacy of such programs.

However, the development of multiple sub-brands to which separate segments of the demographic may identify holds promise. With 5,678 valid respondents, each making twelve offer choices and yielding over 68,000 purchase decisions, we also included a conjoint analysis on the various offers, where key elements varied across the terms of package and times, the type of program, the repertoire, seating, parking as well as the availability of different pricing and ticketing options. The revealed preferences through consumers' choices and behaviors allowed us to assess the attributes that maximize utility for each cluster/group of the demographic, through the presentation of various combinations of alternatives.

These analyses were supplemented by an examination of two recent initiatives that target different segments and preferences, which have significantly increased revenues, decreased the mean age of the audience members, and even attracted a significant fraction of those who were first-time attendees. The development of individual sub-brands may also lead to greater awareness of the other alternatives. In the survey data, we find that there exists approximately a 20% crossover rate between sub-brands, despite the disparate programming and marketing between each. Another finding from analyses of survey data on another sub-brand holds implications regarding the importance of valued partners. Given the increasingly competitive landscape of not only the music industry but the entertainment industry as a whole, associations with relevant partners may provide value-added for segments of the population that may be less attracted to the music, and music alone.

SPECIAL SESSION SUMMARY

Time is More Precious than Money

Stephen A. Spiller, Duke University, USA

SESSION OVERVIEW

The allocation of time and money is fundamental to consumer behavior. Previous research comparing time and money has focused on identifying systematic differences in consumers' perceptions and has found that time and money differ in their value ambiguity (Okada and Hoch, 2004), perceived future availability (Zauberman and Lynch, 2005), and degree of personal connection (Mogilner and Aaker, 2009). The four papers in this session advance this research by considering antecedents and implications of the underlying differences between time and money and focusing on time's unique role in decision making as a particularly precious resource. We examine its unanticipated scarcity (Spiller and Lynch), its self-expressive value (Reed, Aquino, Levy, and Finnel), its implications for the pursuit of happiness (Mogilner), and its role in promoting preference stability (Lee, Lee, and Zauberman).

First, Spiller and Lynch consider why consumers have less time than expected, but not less money. They find that consumers exhibit a greater planning fallacy for time than for money because they plan more for their use of time than money. Next, Reed and colleagues examine why an active moral identity leads to a preference to donate time rather than money and find that donating time is more self-expressive than donating money. Moreover, they consider how this preference for time versus money differs depending on whether the donation is real or hypothetical. The final two papers build on the finding that the mere concept of time increases the weight consumers put on personal connection (Mogilner and Aaker, 2009). First, Mogilner shows that when time rather than money is activated, individuals are more likely to pursue consumption that leads to greater happiness. Finally, Lee and colleagues find that although time's value may be more ambiguous than money's, preferences are more stable when time (rather than money) is the resource of exchange, due to its emotional tags.

EXTENDED ABSTRACTS

"Consumers Exhibit the Planning Fallacy for Time but not Money"

Stephen A. Spiller, Duke University, USA
John G. Lynch Jr., University of Colorado, Boulder, USA

The planning fallacy has been defined as "the fact that people invariably underestimate the resources, such as time and money, that will be required to finish a project" (Taylor, Pham, Rivkin, and Armor, 1998, p. 434). Although a planning fallacy for money has been referenced by other researchers (e.g., Kahneman and Tversky, 1979; Kruger and Evans, 2004), empirical research at the personal level has focused exclusively on time plans. Given important differences in perceptions of time and money (e.g., Mogilner and Aaker, 2009; Okada and Hoch, 2004; Zauberman and Lynch, 2005), we pose the question: Does the personal planning fallacy apply to money as it does to time?

Some existing evidence suggests it does not. If individuals expect to spend less time and less money on projects than they actually spend, they will overestimate the amount of "time slack" and "money slack" they have left. Zauberman and Lynch (2005) find that although people overestimate their future time slack, they do not overestimate their future money slack, suggesting the absence of a planning fallacy for money. More direct evidence comes from Kruger and Evans (2004, Study 1), who found that decomposing a project (e.g., holiday gift shopping) into its component parts (e.g., each person on the list) increased predictions of the amount of time to be spent by more than 30% but only increased predictions of the amount of money to be spent by less than 10%. These findings lead us to hypothesize that individuals exhibit the planning fallacy for time but not for money (H1). We test H1 in Studies 1, 2, and 3.

In Study 1, 2078 members of an online panel reported how much and how frequently they exhibit the planning fallacy for time or money. In support of H1, participants reported exhibiting a greater and more frequent planning fallacy for time than for money.

In Study 2, 93 undergraduates listed short-run and long-run plans for their uses of time and money and reported when they would finish their time plans and how much money they would spend on their money plans. They later reported when they completed their time plans and how much money they spent on their money plans. In support of H1, participants completed their time plans later than planned, but spent less money than planned on their money plans.

The generally accepted explanation for the planning fallacy is that planners focus too much on how they will successfully execute their plan (they take the "inside perspective"), and neglect distributional information of past planning failures and future potential obstacles (they ignore the "outside perspective"; Kahneman and Tversky, 1979; Buehler, Griffin, and Ross, 1994). As a result, planning more leads to a greater planning fallacy. Although this inside versus outside distinction applies equally to time and money plans, people may be more likely to take the inside perspective for time than for money. Lynch, Netemeyer, Spiller, and Zammit (2009) develop and validate a measure of propensity to plan with parallel versions for time and money planning in the short-run and long-run. They find that individuals have a greater propensity to plan for time than for money, suggesting that individuals are more likely to take the inside perspective for time than for money. These findings lead us to hypothesize that individuals with a greater propensity to plan exhibit a greater planning fallacy (H2) and propensity to plan mediates the cross-resource difference in the planning fallacy (H3). We test H2 and H3 in Study 3.

In Study 3, 90 MBA students were asked when they planned to finish their holiday gift shopping, how much money they would spend on their holiday gift shopping, or both. Every day, they reported whether they went shopping the previous day and if they did go shopping, how much money they spent. In support of H1, participants exhibited the planning fallacy for time but not for money. In support of H2, participants with a greater propensity to plan exhibited a greater planning fallacy than those with a lesser propensity to plan. In support of H3, the cross-resource difference in the planning fallacy was mediated by propensity to plan; controlling for propensity to plan, there was no difference in the planning fallacy for time versus money.

This work provides the first systematic comparison of the degree to which consumers exhibit the planning fallacy for time and money and links it to existing work on the "inside perspective." Due to differences in propensity to plan, consumers exhibit a greater planning fallacy for time than for money, leaving them with less time than expected but not less money and thus making their limited remaining time all the more precious. This research also reveals a "dark-side" to the propensity to plan, which might otherwise be viewed a priori as a primarily positive trait.

"How and When the Moral Self Motivates Donations of Time versus Money"

Americus Reed II, University of Pennsylvania, USA
Karl Aquino, University of British Columbia, Canada
Eric Levy, University of Washington, USA
Stephanie Finnel, University of Pennsylvania, USA

Donating time and donating money appear equivalent, but consumers treat them differently (Liu and Aaker 2008). Consumers prefer giving time versus an equivalent amount of money when their moral identity is either consistently central to their self-concept or temporarily primed (Reed, Aquino, and Levy 2007). Reed et al. (2007) hypothesized that this effect occurs because emphasizing moral identity makes consumers choose behaviors that express that identity. Giving time (vs. money) should be seen as more expressive of the moral self because it entails greater contact with needy others and hence greater willingness to sacrifice for them. This concern for others characterizes the moral self (Aquino and Reed 2002).

However, Reed et al. (2007) did not directly test their reasoning for why consumers with an activated moral identity prefer giving time versus money; something unrelated to self-expressiveness could be driving their results. We propose the following self-expressiveness hypothesis: activating moral identity strengthens consumers' belief that giving to charity expresses who they are, and this belief makes them prefer giving time, an act more consistent with the moral identity they want to express than giving money.

But do these self-expressive benefits mean moral identity will always make consumers prefer giving time versus money in real donations? Past research cannot address this question because it considered hypothetical preferences, but we suspect the answer is no. Unlike money, time cannot be replenished through work. Thus consumers may perceive time as scarcer than money and may view giving time as costlier than giving money. They may report a hypothetical preference to give time to express their moral self but be unwilling to bear the costs of giving real time (cf. Batson and Thompson 2001). Both internal (moral identity centrality) and external (temporary moral identity priming) sources of moral motivation, rather than just one as in previous work, may be necessary to induce giving real time versus money. We call this the real donation hypothesis.

Study 1 tested the self-expressiveness hypothesis. The study was a 2 (moral identity prime: high versus low) x 2 (effort: moral versus non-moral) between-subjects design. University participants (N=183) completed two tasks. In the first task, moral identity was primed (Reed et al. 2007). Participants copied words and used them to write a story. In the high (low) moral identity prime condition, the words were traits related (unrelated) to being moral such as compassionate (carefree) (Aquino and Reed 2002). In the second task, participants imagined contributing to an organizational effort. They indicated how self-expressive contributing would be and chose from three hypothetical options: giving $5, giving $5 worth of time, or giving nothing. Following Reed et al. (2007), we manipulated the effort's perceived morality because the identity prime was expected to affect time versus money preferences for a moral but not a non-moral cause. In the moral (non-moral) effort condition, the effort's objective was to promote volunteering (sell advertising services). Manipulation checks confirmed both manipulations' effectiveness. Analyses on both dependent measures (self-expressiveness and donation preferences) revealed a moral identity prime x effort interaction such that priming moral identity led participants to view contributing as more self-expressive and to prefer giving time versus money for moral effort but not non-moral effort,. Importantly, self-expressiveness mediated the relationship between the moral identity prime x effort interaction and donation preferences, supporting the self-expressiveness hypothesis.

Study 2 tested the real donation hypothesis. The study was a two-group (moral identity prime: high versus low) between-subjects design with moral identity centrality measured. University participants (N=105) completed three tasks. The first task contained Aquino and Reed's (2002) moral identity centrality scale. The second task primed moral identity using slide shows. The high moral prime show contained photographs of historical figures acknowledged to be moral (e.g., Gandhi) and of ordinary people expressing concern for each other. The low moral prime show contained photographs of flowers. Manipulation checks confirmed the primes' effectiveness. In the third task, all participants read the moral effort description from study 1 and received a real donation opportunity. They chose from three options: give part of their $10 participation payment to the effort, spend time after the experiment aiding the effort, or do nothing. Participants were debriefed afterward and did not really donate. Our analyses of the donation decision revealed a centrality x prime interaction such that higher moral identity centrality increased preference to give time versus money in the high but not low moral prime condition. In support of the real donation hypothesis, both sources of moral motivation were needed to elicit preferences to give real time versus money.

"The Role of Time versus Money in the Pursuit of Happiness"

Cassie Mogilner, University of Pennsylvania, USA

Money is assumed to be critical for pursuit of the American Dream and our unalienable right to be happy. Indeed, when a sample of 127 American university students were asked to share their feelings related to money, "happiness" was the most frequently cited emotion. However, psychology research reveals there to be a weak relationship between money and happiness (e.g., Kahneman et al. 2006), and economists have found Americans' happiness levels to have remained constant over the past several decades despite an increase in financial wealth (Easterlin 1995). How can we reconcile the assumed association between money and happiness with empirical demonstrations suggesting the two to be largely unrelated?

Exploring the role of our other principle resource, time, may shed some light. An investigation into national allocations of time reveals that while wealth in the U.S. has increased over the last quarter of a century, so too has the number of hours Americans have spent working. In contrast, Europeans have decreased the number of hours spent at work in response to gains in economic wealth, and their happiness levels have increased (Layard 2005). This highlights the possibility that Americans' extant focus on money as the resource most critical to attaining happiness has been misdirected, and we should instead shift our focus towards time.

To explore this possibility, I conducted four lab and field experiments testing whether directing attention to time (rather than money) can improve Americans' pursuit of happiness by driving individuals to behave in ways that prior research indicates increase experienced happiness.

Prior research has found that individuals feel greater happiness having spent money to acquire an experience than having spent money to acquire a material possession (Van Boven and Gilovich 2003). Experiments 1A and 1B were conducted to test the hypothesis that increasing the relative salience of time (vs. money) would increase individuals' tendencies to choose purchases associated with greater happiness.

In experiment 1A, participants were primed with either time or money through incidental exposure to time- or money-related advertisements, and then they were presented with a series of choices between experiential and material purchases. In line with greater happiness, participants who were primed with time (vs. money) were more likely to choose experiential purchases over material purchases. Experiment 1B then demonstrated the robustness of the finding, showing that the effect occurs with an even more subtle prime of time (vs. money) and extends from tradeoffs that participants thought they would make to a choice with real consequence.

With evidence suggesting that activating time (vs. money) can lead people to spend their money in ways associated with greater happiness, experiments 2A and 2B were conducted to test whether priming time (vs. money) would also lead individuals to choose to spend their time in ways associated with greater happiness.

Prior research tracked how a national sample of Americans spent their days, as well as how they felt over the course of their days, and found people to be most happy when socializing and during intimate relations, and to be least happy when working and commuting (Kahneman et al. 2004). Participants in experiment 2A were nonconsciously primed with either time or money using a sentence scramble task, and then asked them to report the extent to which they planned to engage in various activities during the next 24 hours. The results revealed that participants primed with time (vs. money) planned to spend more time engaging in intimate relations and socializing (daily activities associated with greater happiness) and less time working and commuting (daily activities associated with less happiness).

Experiment 2B was a field experiment conducted to test whether such a subtle activation of time (vs. money) could not only impact how individuals plan to spend their time, but also how they actually spend their time. Upon entering a campus café, students were implicitly primed with either time or money while volunteering to complete a sentence scramble task. Those primed with time subsequently spent more time at the café socializing than doing schoolwork, whereas students primed with money spent more time doing schoolwork than socializing.

Together, these findings demonstrate that drawing individuals' attention to time, rather than money, increases their tendencies to spend both their money and their time in ways that are associated with greater happiness. This work contributes to the growing streams of research on time, money, and happiness.

"The Stability of Time versus Money Valuations"

Leonard Lee, Columbia University, USA
Michelle Lee, Singapore Management University, Singapore
Gal Zauberman, University of Pennsylvania, USA

Consumers make decisions about the expenditure of time and money on a daily basis. In this work, we examine the stability of consumer valuations of time versus money across different choice occasions. By stability, we specifically refer to whether there is consistency (or transitivity) in expressed valuations of time versus money—transitivity is lacking when, for instance, one prefers A to B, and B to C, but then contradictorily prefers C to A.

In two experiments, we tested two competing hypotheses. On the one hand, prior research that has examined time-money differences (e.g. Okada and Hoch 2004, Zauberman and Lynch 2005) points toward relatively greater ambiguity in time valuation versus money valuation, which may in turn translate to less stability in expressed valuations of time. On the other hand, a separate stream of research suggests that there could be less stability in expressed valuations of money, given that (1) affective processing of choice options has been found to generate greater preference consistency than more deliberate cognitive processing (Lee, Amir, and Ariely 2009); (2) money (vs. time) is likely to invoke more analytical as opposed to holistic thinking; and (3) time considerations naturally evokes more emotional responses than money considerations (Mogilner and Aaker 2009).

In experiment 1, 166 US student participants studied a set of nine different flight options for an upcoming international trip they had to make. They were subsequently shown all pair-wise combinations of these nine flight options (36 pairs) and asked to choose their preferred option within each pair. Participants were randomly assigned to one of three conditions: time, money, control. Across conditions, they were given different information about these flight options: in the control condition, each option was represented by both a service rating and an in-flight entertainment rating; additionally, the air fare of each option was also given in the money condition whereas the average one-way flight time was given in the time condition instead. The results revealed that participants in the money condition made significantly more intransitivity errors than both participants in the time condition and the control condition. Participants in the time condition, however, were equally consistent in their choices as those in the control condition. The results also indicated that the different degrees of choice consistency across conditions could not be sufficiently explained by any real or perceived differential difficulty of the choice task.

Experiment 2 conceptually replicated this basic result using a different experimental design and a different set of choice stimuli. Seventy-eight participants were asked to suppose that they had to purchase a photo essay software package for an important project. They were first shown a set of nine different software options represented by four attributes (software features, software quality, set-up time, and price) and then given all binary combinations of these nine software options (36 pairs) and asked to choose their preferred option within each pair. Participants were randomly assigned to one of three conditions: time, money, or control. Unlike experiment 1, participants were shown all four attributes, but which attribute values differed across the product options depended on the condition to which they were assigned: in the control condition, only features rating (1-5) and quality rating (1-5) differed across options while the set-up time and the price of the options were held constant; in the money condition, features rating, quality rating, and price varied across options while set-up time was held constant; in the time condition, features rating, quality rating, and set-up time varied across options while price was held constant. As such, different attributes were made relatively more salient to participants across conditions, hence inducing different degrees of consideration across attributes. To ensure similar magnitudes of attribute values for time and price, we used an implied conversion rate of 1 additional minute of set-up time for $1 of price reduction.

Again, the results demonstrated that participants in the money condition made significantly more transitivity violations than those in the control condition and those in the time condition. Additional data indicated that participants did not perceive any differences in the variability of the given product options across conditions.

Together, these results provide convergent evidence that preferences based on time are more consistent than preferences based on money. We believe that our research provides a unique test of two competing processes underlying time versus money considerations. Furthermore, it furthers our understanding of the relationship between mental representation of outcomes and type of information processing (affective versus deliberative), as well as how consumers form preferences based on two fundamental economic resources.

REFERENCES

Aquino, Karl F., and Americus Reed II (2002), "The Self-Importance of Moral Identity," *Journal of Personality and Social Psychology*, 83 (6), 1423-40.

Batson, C. Daniel, and Elizabeth R. Thompson (2001), "Why Don't Moral People Act Morally? Motivational Considerations," *Current Directions in Psychological Science*, 10 (2), 54-57.

Buehler, Roger, Dale Griffin, and Michael Ross, (1994), "Exploring the 'Planning Fallacy': Why People Underestimate Their Task Completion Times," *Journal of Personality and Social Psychology*, 67 (3) 366-81.

Easterlin, Richard A. (1995). "Will Raising the Incomes of All Increase the Happiness of All?" *Journal of Economic Behavior and Organization*, 27 (1), 35-47.

Kahneman, Daniel, Alan Krueger, David Schkade, Norbert Schwarz, and Arthur Stone (2004). "A Survey Method for Characterizing Daily Life Experience: The Day Reconstruction Method." *Science*, 306 (5702), 1776-80.

______ (2006). "Would You Be Happier If You Were Richer? A Focusing Illusion." *Science*, 312 (5782), 1908-10.

Kahneman, Daniel and Amos Tversky, (1979), "Intuitive Prediction: Biases and Corrective Procedures," *TIMS Studies in Management Science*, 39 (1), 17-31.

Kruger, Justin and Matt Evans, (2004), "If You Don't Want to Be Late, Enumerate: Unpacking Reduces the Planning Fallacy," *Journal of Experimental Social Psychology*, 40 (5), 586-98.

Layard, Richard (2005). *Happiness: Lessons from a New Science*. London: Penguin Books.

Lee, Leonard, On Amir, and Dan Ariely (2009), "In Search of Homo Economicus: Preference Consistency, Emotion, and Cognition," *Journal of Consumer Research*, 36(August), forthcoming.

Liu, Wendy, and Jennifer Aaker (2008), "The Happiness of Giving: The Time-Ask Effect," *Journal of Consumer Research*, 35 (October), 543-57.

Lynch Jr., John G., Richard Netemeyer, Stephen Spiller, and Alessandra Zammit, (2009), "The Long and Short of Propensity to Plan the Use of Time and Money," unpublished manuscript.

Mogilner, Cassie and Jennifer Aaker (2009), "'The Time vs. Money Effect': Shifting Product Attitudes and Decisions through Personal Connection," *Journal of Consumer Research*, 36 (August), 277-291.

Okada, Erica Mina and Stephen J. Hoch (2004), "Spending Time versus Spending Money," *Journal of Consumer Research*, 31 (September), 313-23.

Reed II, Americus, Karl Aquino, and Eric Levy (2007), "Moral Identity and Judgments of Charitable Behaviors," *Journal of Marketing*, 71 (January), 178-193.

Taylor, Shelley E., Lien B. Pham, Inna D. Rivken, and David A. Armor, (1999), "Harnessing the Imagination: Mental Simulation, Self-Regulation, and Coping," *American Psychologist*, 53 (4), 429-39.

Van Boven, Leaf and Thomas Gilovich (2003), "To Do or To Have: That is the Question," *Journal of Personality and Social Psychology*, 85 (December), 1193-1202.

Zauberman, Gal and John G. Lynch Jr. (2005), "Resource Slack and Propensity to Discount Delayed Investments of Time versus Money," *Journal of Experimental Psychology: General*, 134 (February), 23-37.

SPECIAL SESSION SUMMARY

Underpinnings of Risky Behavior: Non-health Motives for Health-related Behaviors

Merrie Brucks, University of Arizona, USA
Paul M. Connell, Stony Brook University, USA

SESSION OVERVIEW

Consumers often know of risks to themselves, but fail to act in ways to reduce these risks (Verplanken and Wood 2006; Thaler and Sunstein 2008). In their comprehensive review of the literature on health risk perceptions literature published in the Handbook of Consumer Psychology, Menon, Raghubir, and Nidhi Agrawal (2008) persuasively argue that there is a need to identify "antecedents other than cognitive belief-based ones." They identify a wealth of motivational, affective, individual, contextual, and disease factors that have been studied and how they relate these to consumer outcomes. Within the specific category of motivation, they discuss theoretical work on self-control, self-positivity, and social desirability. The papers in this proposed session share a focus on motivational antecedents for behaviors, but are guided by theoretical frameworks that have been under-explored in the health context: hypocrisy theory, associative processing of others' motivations, and symbolic interactionism.

This session brings together rigorous research relevant to understanding consumers' motivations for engaging in desirable and non-desirable social outcomes. More broadly, the authors in these studies take novel theoretical and methodological approaches within the context of motivation, persuasion, and consumer attitudes and behavior. Bundling these papers together is intended to stimulate discussion and to explore ideas for future research, perhaps beyond the health context. We will build in time to discuss each paper immediately after it has been presented. The audience for this session would likely include researchers interested in the self, motivation, persuasion, transformative consumer research, and public policy topics.

The first paper is co-authored by Jeff Stone (Associate Professor of Social Psychology at the University of Arizona), who has published numerous studies on cognitive dissonance in high-impact journals such as Journal of Personality and Social Psychology and Journal of Experimental Social Psychology, and his doctoral student Nicholas Fernandez, also at the University of Arizona. Their work examines the use of inducing cognitive dissonance via hypocrisy to achieve desirable health outcomes. The second paper is co-authored by Merrie Brucks (Professor of Marketing at the University of Arizona), Paul Connell (Assistant Professor of Marketing at Stony Brook University) and Dan Freeman (Associate Professor of Marketing at University of Delaware). In this paper, the authors find that children ascribe motivations to smoke or not to smoke at a very early age, even though they cannot articulate the reasoning behind these motivations. The final paper is co-authored by Connie Pechmann (Professor of Marketing at the University of California, Irvine), Dante Pirouz (Doctoral Student at the University of California, Irvine), and Todd Pezzuti (Doctoral Student at the University of California, Irvine). Across three experiments, the authors find that when teens are exposed to advertisements featuring young adult models, they actually have higher intentions to smoke than when exposed to advertisements featuring other teens, as teens see cigarettes as a means of communicating an adult identity.

EXTENDED ABSTRACTS

"The Use of Hypocrisy to Motivate Health Attitude and Behavior Change"

Jeff Stone, University of Arizona, USA
Nicholas C. Fernandez, University of Arizona, USA

This presentation examines the use of the hypocrisy strategy as a social-marketing tool for changing consumer health behaviors. Feelings of hypocrisy occur when people make a public statement about the importance of a target health behavior, such as using condoms to prevent sexually transmitted diseases like AIDS (Stone et al. 1994, 1997), quitting smoking (Peterson et al 2008), or using sunscreen to reduce the risk for skin cancer (Fernandez et al 2009). By itself, the advocacy is consistent with prevailing attitudes beliefs about the issue, and does not cause discomfort. However, when people are then made mindful that they themselves have not performed the behavior regularly in the past, the discrepancy between their advocacy and past behavior causes the discomfort associated with cognitive dissonance. To reduce their discomfort, hypocrites become motivated to "practice what they preach" and take the necessary steps toward bringing their own health behavior into line with their "preaching" about the importance of the standards for good health.

A recent review of the hypocrisy literature (Stone and Fernandez 2008) shows that there are over 20 studies of the effect of hypocrisy on motivating consumer behavior change in the domains of health, the environment and the community. The results of these studies indicate that following hypocrisy, people are most motivated to perform the target behavior when they publically advocate the target behavior and then are privately made mindful of past recent failures to perform the behavior. Studies also indicate that the hypocrisy strategy operates effectively to modify behavior in non-Western cultures (Takaku 2001, 2006).

Recent empirical research focuses on changing behaviors related to the risk for cancer (Fernandez et al 2009). A new line of study examines how much "mindfulness" of past failures is necessary to motivate behavioral change following hypocrisy. According to Festinger (1957), the magnitude of dissonance is highest when more inconsistent than consistent cognitions are present in memory. In the case of hypocrisy, this implies that after advocating the target health behavior, recalling many past failures will cause more dissonance and more behavior change. However, recent research on the role of self-validation in ease-of-retrieval processes (Tormala et al 2007) suggests that when advocates are asked to recall past instances of when they failed to perform the behavior, they may also recruit examples of when they successfully performed the behavior, especially when they are motivated and have the ability to think carefully about the past (i.e., high elaboration). The "self-validation" process predicts that if advocates carefully recall both failures and successes, it could balance the ratio of inconsistent to consistent cognitions, which would reduce the level of dissonance and need to change behavior following hypocrisy. This leads to the counter-intuitive prediction that when advocates think carefully as they recall past failures to perform the target health behavior, recalling fewer past failures may reduce the number of successes that are also recalled, such that recalling fewer past failures will cause more dissonance and more behavior change. Thus, it was predicted that under high elaboration conditions, when advocates were asked to recall many past failures to perform a health behavior, the self-validation process would reduce the magnitude of dissonance and the motivation to change behavior. However, carefully recalling few past failures would reduce the self-validation process and cause more dissonance and behavioral change following hypocrisy.

In contrast, it was hypothesized that when they are not highly motivated to think about past failures (i.e., low elaboration), advocates will focus primarily on the number of failures recalled without recruiting other relevant information (e.g., successes). As a result, under low elaboration, recalling many past failures will induce more dissonance and behavioral change following hypocrisy than recalling few past failures. In summary, we predicted that under high elaboration, advocates who think about few past failures will exhibit more behavior change, but under low elaboration, advocates who think about many past failures will exhibit more behavior change.

In a 2 (Elaboration: High vs. low) X 2 (Past failures: 2 vs. 8) experimental design, 90 female college students wrote a brief persuasive message for other college students about the importance of using sunscreen to reduce the risk for skin cancer. All were then asked to report past failures to use sunscreen. To manipulate high elaboration (Tormala, Brinol, and Petty 2007), half were told that only a few people were being asked to report information about past failures to use sunscreen; those in the low elaboration condition were told that thousands of people were reporting information about past failures to use sunscreen. Then half were asked to recall 2 past failures to use sunscreen whereas the other half were asked to recall 8 past failures to use sunscreen. All were then provided an opportunity to order a sample of sunscreen from an independent national organization, with the percentage that acquired sunscreen as the primary dependent measure.

The results revealed the predicted elaboration X past recall interaction. As hypothesized, under conditions of high elaboration, significantly more participants (82%) acquired a sample of sunscreen when they were asked to recall 2 past failures compared to those asked to recall 8 past failures. In contrast, under low elaboration, significantly more participants (68%) acquired a sample of sunscreen when asked to recall 8 past failures compared to those asked to recall 2 past failures (39%). Overall, the pattern supports the hypothesis that in hypocrisy, the effect of recalling many past failures on behavior change is a function of how carefully advocates think about their past behavior. Potential mediators of this finding and other future directions for research will be discussed.

References

Fernandez, Nicholas C., Jeff Stone, Joel Cooper, Toni Cascio, and Michael Hogg (2009), "Vicarious Hypocrisy: Using Attitude Bolstering to Restore the Integrity of the Ingroup," working paper, The University of Arizona.

Festinger, Leon (1957), *A Theory of Cognitive Dissonance*, Evanston, IL: Row, Peterson.

Peterson, Alexandra A., Graeme A. Haynes, and James M. Olson (2008), "Self-esteem Differences in the Effects of Hypocrisy Induction on Behavioral Intentions in the Health Domain," *Journal of Personality*, 76 (2), 305-22.

Stone, Jeff, Andreew W. Wiegand, Joel Cooper, and Elliott Aronson (1997), "When Exemplification Fails: Hypocrisy and the Motive for Self-integrity, *Journal of Personality and Social Psychology*, 72 (1), 54-65.

Stone, Jeff, Elliot Aronson, A. Lauren Crain, Matthew P. Winslow, and Carrie B. Fried, (1994), "Inducing Hypocrisy as a Means of Encouraging Young Adults to Use Condoms," *Personality and Social Psychology Bulletin*, 20 (1), 116-28.

Stone, Jeff and Nicholas C. Fernandez (2008), "How Behavior Influences Attitudes: Cognitive Dissonance Processes," in W. Crano & R. Prislin (Eds.), *Attitudes and Attitude Change*, New York: Psychology Press, 314-34.

Takaku, Seiji (2001), "The Effects of Apology and Perspective Taking on Interpersonal Forgiveness: a Dissonance-Attribution Model of Interpersonal Forgiveness," *Journal of Social Psychology*, 141 (4), 494-508.

Takaku, Seiji (2006), "Reducing Road Rage: An Application of the Dissonance-Attribution Model of Interpersonal Forgiveness," *Journal of Applied Social Psychology*, 36 (10), 2362-78.

Tormala, Zakary L., Pablo Brinol, and Richard E. Petty (2007), "Multiple Roles for Source Credibility Under High Elaboration: It's All in the Timing," *Social Cognition*, 25 (4), 536-52.

"Children's Ascribed Motivations for Smoking Elicited by Projective Questioning"

Merrie Brucks, University of Arizona, USA
Paul M. Connell, Stony Brook University, USA
Dan Freeman, University of Delaware, USA

Critics of increased regulation on tobacco advertising and promotion seen by children argue that such regulation would result in small, if any, effects in reducing initiation of tobacco use among minors. After all, the argument goes, eight year olds do not smoke, so cigarette advertising is personally irrelevant to them. But this perspective assumes that advertisements must be actively processed to be effective. In contrast, we note that considerable research has documented advertising effects on attitude, even under very low involvement conditions (e.g., peripheral processing, mere familiarity, evaluative conditioning). Taking this perspective, we argue that exposure to cigarette advertisements and media images are likely to be processed and encoded into memory despite the lack of individual salience of tobacco promotional activity in childhood.

Our reasoning is consistent with the associative processing model of memory, which is one of the two memory systems proposed by Smith and DeCoster (2000). Associative processing operates preconsciously and automatically (Bargh 1994) and is learned over many experiences. Hence, individuals are typically not aware of the processing itself, but only the results of it. Because tobacco advertising and media images are not likely to be self-relevant to children, we argue that they are processed through such an associative mode.

Furthermore, such associative processing of smoking imagery may produce effects that extend beyond childhood. This is because bias correction is best facilitated when individuals possess both the ability and motivation to reconsider their attitudes). If positive psychosocial associations are learned at a nonconscious and automatic level, then the individual will not likely recognize his or her own biases held in memory, thereby inhibiting the ability to metacognitively reconsider attitudes (Petty and Briñol 2008).

The goal of this study was to aid in generating a theoretical model for the psychological processes involved in children's learning of lifestyle associations with adult-themed products. Given this objective, we pursued our empirical research in the spirit of discovery-oriented research (Wells 1993). Because we suspected that children's lifestyle associations might have been learned implicitly, and because social desirability biases are a threat to validity in substance use research, we employed projective interviewing techniques.

We conducted 271 projective interviews with second and fifth grade children from three different elementary schools. Two varieties of projective stimuli were used to elicit participant responses: print advertisements and pictures of people who have various personal and lifestyle characteristics. Each child saw two ads for cigarettes, which were embedded in a series of five ads (including three unrelated products). For each ad, children were asked to choose select pictures of specific people who might be likely or unlikely to use that product. Each child was probed with follow up questions to reveal the motivations he or she attributed to these people.

In the presentation, we will show: (1) the three images that were most strongly associated with smoking, as these images were attributed with multiple motives for smoking; (2) the four images that were also associated with smoking, and were attributed with one or two motives for smoking; (3) the six images that were strongly associated with non-smoking, and were attributed with motives for non-smoking; and (4) four images that were inconsistently associated with smoking, and were attributed with motives for both smoking and non-smoking. Typically, the second graders had difficulty in articulating these motives, often with responses such as "s/he just looks like s/he would smoke." Therefore, the emergent themes were drawn largely from the fifth grade interview dataset. Nevertheless, the second graders often made many of the same lifestyle associations as the fifth graders. Chi-square analysis of the pattern of picture selections indicated that they associated the same images with smoking and non-smoking as the fifth graders did.

Qualitative data analysis revealed three broad areas of motives attributed to the characters in the images: social motives, esteem motives, and relaxation motives. Themes within the social motive included smoking for fun in social situations and smoking to impress others, whereas themes within the esteem motive primarily included issues with weight and thinness. Themes within the relaxation motive primarily included needing to escape one's troubles or smoking for leisure. Finally, for one of the images, general inactivity or lack of motivation in general was associated with smoking.

We argue that the similarity of lifestyle picture selections and attributed motivations between the second and fifth graders, in combination with the non-verbal nature of the second graders' associations, suggests that children did not purposefully and thoughtfully develop them. This pattern of data is consistent with the associative processing model of memory, in which advertisements, media images, and personal observations are encoded into memory preconsciously through associative processing.

References

Bargh, John A. (1994), "The Four Horsemen of Automaticity: Awareness, Intention, Efficiency, and Control in Social Cognition," in *Handbook of Social Cognition: Basic Processes*, eds. Robert S. Wyer and Thomas K. Srull, Hillsdale, NY: Erlbaum.

Brinol, Pablo and Richard E. Petty (2008), "Persuasion: From Single to Multiple to Metacognitive Processes," *Perspectives on Psychological Science*, 3 (2), 137-47.

Smith, Elliott R. and Jamie DeCoster (2000), "Dual-process Models in Social and Cognitive Psychology: Conceptual Integration and Links to Underlying Memory Systems," *Personality and Social Psychology Review*, 4 (2), 108-31.

Wells, William D. (1993), "Discovery-oriented Consumer Research," *Journal of Consumer Research*, 19 (4), 489-504.

"Symbolic Interactionism and Adolescent Reactions to Cigarette Advertisements"

Connie Pechmann, University of California at Irvine, USA
Dante Pirouz, University of California at Irvine, USA
Todd Pezzuti, University of California at Irvine, USA

Does restricting the age of models in cigarette advertising to 25 years or older really work in deterring adolescents from smoking? Health researchers and advocates have stressed the importance of using only adult models in cigarette ads because younger models might entice adolescents to believe that smoking is for them. As a result, there have been a number of regulatory attempts to specify the minimum age of models in cigarette ads (Richards, Tye, and Fischer 1996). For example, the Voluntary Cigarette Advertising and Promotion Code, which tobacco manufacturers claim to use as a guideline, states that "any models used in advertising be and appear to be older than 25" (The Tobacco Institute 1990, p. 1). Previous academic literature has focused on the perception of model age in cigarette advertising and has shown that people perceive many cigarette ad models to be younger than 25 (Arnett 2005; Barbeau et al. 1998; Mazis et al. 1992). However, these studies have not linked model age to persuasion nor have they studied the effect of manipulating model age.

Similarity-based theories, such as social comparison (Festinger 1954) and social identity (Tajfel and Turner 1986), predict that consumers are more influenced by similar others (White and Dahl 2006). A major implication is that ad models should mirror the target audience and teens are more likely to be persuaded by models their own age than by older or younger ones. However, these theories have focused on normative influence and have not addressed aspirational or symbolic factors. On the other hand, symbolic interactionism focuses on how people interpret, act towards, and give meaning to symbolic objects, events and situations around them (Blumer 1969; Sandstrom, Martin, and Fine 2003; Solomon 1983; Stryker 1980). Symbols acquire meaning through socialization and products that function as symbols can carry potent information about an individual's social role and status (Reynolds and Herman-Kinney 2003).

Age is a powerful indicator of social role and status (Holstein and Gubrium 2003). Across life stages, products are used as symbols to signify to the self and others the transition to a new developmental level (Peterson and Peters 1983; Piacentini and Mailer 2004). Many adolescents have a fragile and unstable self-concept which leads them to aspire to look and act older (Barker and Galambos 2005; Galambos, Turner, and Tilton-Weaver 2005). Thus, products with specific social meaning can be used to facilitate the transition but the imagery and symbolism surrounding the product must appropriately signal adulthood (Berger and Rand 2008; Solomon 1983).

Cigarettes belong to a unique class of products that are a key identity signal of adulthood (Eckert 1983). Unlike other publicly consumed products, such as music and clothing, smoking symbolizes the adult world and is taboo for adolescents and children in most cultures (Rugkasa et al. 2001). Thus many adolescents seek out conspicuous symbols of adulthood, such as cigarettes, to reinforce their pseudomature identity and help them bridge the gap to adulthood (Eckert 2007; Galambos and Tilton-Weaver 2000; Noble and Walker 1997). For adolescents, this may have an unexpected influence on their response to cigarette advertising featuring models their own age.

Our theoretical framework predicts that for an adult-signaling product category like cigarettes, young adult models would influence adolescents more positively than same age models. It also predicts that teenage or same age models might, in fact, boomerang. However, for other product categories such as clothing, teen models would be more influential than young adults. These effects would be mediated by what the model's age communicates about the product, for example, age appropriateness. Theory would also predict that because adolescence is a period of transition, only teens would be susceptible to the teenage model boomerang effect but young adults would not be.

In a series of experiments, we investigated how altering the age of models used in cigarette advertising affects whether adolescents are drawn to—or deterred from—smoking. We pretested over 1000 model images to choose a set of 16 advertising models that were equally attractive but varied on gender (2 levels), ethnicity (2 levels) and age (4 levels: child, teen, young adult and middle age). We then conducted the first study with 221 ninth grade students who rated the model images. We manipulated whether the models held cigarettes or not. As hypothesized, we found that adolescent participants identified most with teen and young adult models, suggesting that they are most likely to be influenced by these age groups.

A second study investigated how cigarette model age might affect persuasion. Participants were 479 ninth grade students who viewed a mock-up magazine containing cigarette ads or matched control ads. The ad models' age was manipulated. The teenage cigarette models boomeranged, lowering intent to smoke. The young adult cigarette models increased intent to smoke, while child and middle-aged cigarette models had no effect on intent. We repeated this experiment using 284 college students who were 18-21 years old. As predicted, the cigarette models had null effects because young adults do not need cigarettes to signal an adult identity.

A third study examined whether the age effects were moderated by product category and also explored the underlying process by identifying mediators. Participants were 278 ninth graders who were shown a magazine with cigarette ads or designer t-shirt ads. The ad models' age was manipulated. As posited, participants perceived cigarettes (vs. designer t-shirts) as more for public display, more reflective of "who the person is," and more "for adults." The cigarette ads also affected both product category (primary) and brand specific (secondary) demand. Specifically, teen versus young adult cigarette ad models lowered cigarette product and brand intent, as hypothesized. The effect of ad model age on intent to use the cigarette product and brand was at least partially mediated by age appropriateness perceptions. Teen (versus young adult) cigarette models decreased perceptions that cigarettes were an appropriate teenage product, which then lowered intent to use cigarettes.

References

Arnett, Jeffrey Jensen (2005), "Talk Is Cheap: The Tobacco Companies' Violations of Their Own Cigarette Advertising Code," *Journal of Health Communication: International Perspectives*, 10 (5), 419-31.

Barbeau, Elizabeth M, William DeJong, Douglas M. Brugge, and William M. Rand (1998), "Does Cigarette Print Advertising Adhere to the Tobacco Institute's Voluntary Advertising and Promotion Code? An Assessment," *Journal of Public Health Policy*, 19 (4), 473-88.

Barker, Erin T. and Nancy L. Galambos (2005), "Adolescents' Implicit Theories of Maturity," *Journal of Adolescent Research*, 20 (5), 557-76.

Berger, Jonah and Lindsay Rand (2008), "Shifting Signals to Help Health: Using Identity Signaling to Reduce Risky Health Behaviors," *Journal of Consumer Research*, 35 (3), 509-18.

Blumer, Herbert (1969), *Symbolic Interactionism: Perspective and Method*, Berkeley: University of California Press.

Eckert, Penelope (1983), "Beyond the Statistics of Adolescent Smoking," *American Journal of Public Health*, 73 (4), 439-41.

Festinger, Leon (1954), "A Theory of Social Comparison Processes," *Human Relations*, 7 (2), 117-40.

Galambos, Nancy L. and Lauree C. Tilton-Weaver (2000), "Adolescents' Psychosocial Maturity, Problem Behavior, and Subjective Age: In Search of the Adultoid," *Applied Developmental Science*, 4 (4), 178-92.

Galambos, Nancy L., Pamela K. Turner, and Lauree C. Tilton-Weaver (2005), "Chronological and Subjective Age in Emerging Adulthood," *Journal of Adolescent Research*, 20 (5), 538-56.

Holstein, James A. and Jaber F. Gubrium (2003), "A Constructionist Analytics for Social Problems," in James A. Holdstein and Gale Miller (eds.), *Challenges and Choices*, Hawthorne, NY: De Gruyter.

Mazis, Michael B., Debra Jones Ringold, Elgin S. Perry, and Daniel W. Denman (1992), "Perceived Age and Attractiveness of Models in Cigarette Advertisements," *Journal of Marketing*, 56 (1), 22-37.

Nobel, Charles H. and Beth a. Walker (1997), "Exploring the Relationships Among Liminal Transitions, Symbolic Consumption, and the Extended Self," *Psychology and Marketing*, 14 (1), 29-47.

Peterson, Gary W. and David F. Peters (1983), "Adolescents' Construction of Social Reality: The Impact of Television and Peers," *Youth & Society*, 15 (1), 67-85.

Piacentini, Maria and Greg Mailer (2006), "Symbolic Consumption in Teenagers' Clothing Choices," *Journal of Consumer Behaviour*, 3 (3), 251-62.

Reynolds, Larry and Nancy J. Herman-Kinney (2003), "Taking Stock: A Handbook for Symbolic Interactionsists," in Larry Reynolds and Nancy J. Herman-Kinney (eds.), *Handbook of Symbolic Interactionsim*, Lanham, MD: Rowman and Littlefield.

Richards, J.W., J.B. Tye, and P.M. Fischer (1996), "The Tobacco Industry's Code of Advertising the United States: Myth and Reality," *Tobacco Control*, 5 (4), 295-391.

Rugkasa, Jorun, Barbara Knox, Julie Sittlington, Orla Kennedy, Margaret P. Treacy, and Pilar Santos (2001), "Anxious Adults Vs. Cool Children: Children's Views on Smoking and Addiction," *Social Science & Medicine*, 53 (5), 593-602.

Sandstrom, Kent L., Daniel D. Martin, and Gary Alan Fine (2003), *Symbols, Selves, and Social Reality: A Symbolic Interactionist Approach to Social Psychology and Sociology*, Los Angeles, CA: Roxbury.

Solomon, Michael R. (1983), "The Role of Products as Social Stimuli: A Symbolic Interaction Perspective," *Journal of Consumer Research*, 10 (3), 319-29.

Stryker, Sheldon (1980), *Symbolic Interactionism: A Social Structural Version*, Upper Saddle River, NJ:Benjamin Cummings.

The Tobacco Institute 1990, *Voluntary Cigarette Advertising and Promotion Code*, www.tobaccoinstitute.com.

Tajfel, Henri and Turner, John C. (1986), "The Social Identity Theory of Inter-group Behavior," in S. Worchel and L. W. Austin (eds.), *Psychology of Intergroup Relations*, Chicago: Nelson-Hall

White, Katherine and Darren W. Dahl (2006), "To Be or Not Be: The Influence of Dissociative Reference Groups on Consumer Preferences," *Journal of Consumer Psychology*, 16 (4), 404-14.

SPECIAL SESSION SUMMARY

Continuing to Sin or a Reformed Sinner: Examining Sequential Self-Regulation Choices

Yael Zemack-Rugar, Virginia Tech, USA

SESSION OVERVIEW

In the recent decade consumer research has seen a burgeoning interest in self-regulation. A host of situational antecedents to self-regulation failures have been identified, including resource availability, emotion, regulatory focus, and justification to name just a few. Several individual difference measures have also been developed including the self-control scale, impulsivity scale, hyperopia scale, frugality scale and others. These research streams identify a wide range of individual/situational antecedents to self-regulation failure and if they teach us one thing–they teach us that such failure is bound to happen.

However, a singular self-regulation failure does not lead to the problems often cited in this research stream; having the occasional slice of cake does not an obese person make. Instead, one needs to make sequential self-regulation failures to encounter undesirable end states such as obesity and debt. This session examines sequential self control choices. We accept the widely held notion that self-regulation is no easy feat; some of us can succeed at it some of the time, but all of us cannot succeed at it all of the time. As a result, initial failures of self-regulation are bound to happen, and what determines their long-term effects is how we respond to them.

This session investigates these responses. We propose that there are essentially two response options: recommit to the goal and become a "reformed sinner", or abandon the goal and "continue to sin". In three papers we examine what might lead people to do one or the other, what actions are effective in "reforming", what actions consumers themselves might take to protect themselves against "continued sinning", and whether these responses can be related to an underlying individual difference.

In the first paper, Finkelstein and Fishbach examine the effects of feedback regarding initial failure on subsequent self-regulation. In five studies they find that experienced consumers are more sensitive to negative feedback about their lack of accomplishments. This feedback allows them to monitor their progress towards a goal and therefore supports "reform", that is, subsequent goal-congruent behavior. Experienced consumers therefore seek negative feedback as well as provide negative feedback to experienced others. These findings suggest that communication with experienced consumers should focus on past failures and "misses" to encourage future goal-congruent actions, whereas communication with inexperienced consumers should focus on prior success.

In the second paper, Mazar and Ariely examine ethical decision making and the "What-The-Hell Effect" (WTHE henceforth). The WTHE is directly related to sequential self-regulation. This effect occurs when an individuals who has failed at an initial self-regulation goal (e.g., a dieter having one cookie from the jar), then completely foregoes the goal and subsequently engages in goal-incongruent behavior (e.g., eating the contents of the entire cookie jar). Mazar and Ariely show that there is a WTHE in ethical decision making, such that people who have cheated on previous tasks and pass a certain threshold, appear to forgo their moral self-regulation, and keep on cheating. The authors identify conditions that moderate these effects such as positive reinforcers (against subsequent "sinning") and environmental control. However, this paper shows that other methods, such as confessing, do not help sinners reform.

In the third paper, Zemack-Rugar, Corus, and Brinberg develop a scale that measures individuals' propensity to enact "WTHE". The authors argue that like many other self-regulation behaviors, the tendency to respond to initial failure with reform vs. continued sinning is an individual difference factor. Moreover, this construct is distinct from the tendency to enact initial failures. The authors discuss the scale development process, identifying two cognitive/emotional factors ("sin as motivation" and "sin as permission") that differentiate between those who tend to enact WTHE and those who do not. The authors also provide three studies in which the WTHE predicts post-failure self-regulation behavior above and beyond existing measures.

We believe this session will appeal to a wide audience at ACR. The session focuses on a topic of great interest, self-regulation, but with a much needed twist–sequential choice. There is relatively little research on sequential choice, and in particular–on sequential self-regulation. In three papers we offer several different points of view on this issue, examining a variety of consumer domains (from friendship to cheating to eating) across 14 studies. We also have a discussant, Jonathan Levav, with great experience and knowledge in the domain of sequential choice. His comments are sure to add insight to the discussion during this session.

EXTENDED ABSTRACTS

"Seeking, Giving, and Responding to Negative Feedback in Self-Regulation"

Stacey Finkelstein, University of Chicago, USA
Ayelet Fishbach, University of Chicago, USA

Research on the Dynamics of Self-Regulation attests that in the course of pursuing multiple goals (e.g., the desire to enjoy one's food and be a healthy person), whether a consumer experiences commitment to or progress towards a goal influences the consumer's course of self-regulation over time. While an experience of commitment encourages goal-congruent actions due to an increased sense that one can perform the goal, the experience of not making progress towards the goal encourages goal-congruent actions when it signals that one is not doing as much as one should.

The present research applies this framework to understanding feedback seeking, feedback giving, and response to feedback with respect to goals that involve a sequence of choices that unfold over time. We propose that the emphasis on assessing commitment or monitoring progress changes as consumers become more experienced with a task. Specifically, as consumers become more experienced at pursuing a goal, they are more sensitive to negative feedback about their lack of accomplishments as this feedback allows them to monitor their progress towards a goal. Thus, experienced consumers are more likely to seek negative feedback about their lack of accomplishments, give negative feedback to experienced others, and will be more likely to subsequently perform goal-congruent actions when they consider negative feedback about their "misses."

We report five studies that tested these hypotheses. In study 1, students in a dancing class were made to feel that they are either novices or experienced, before they sought feedback about their mistakes and how they can improve. We found that compared with students who felt they have been dancing a short while ("inexperienced"), students who felt that they have been dancing a long time, sought more negative feedback about their dancing.

Study 2 extends these results to a foreign language class, where we measured how the level of experience influences students' preference for an instructor who gives them positive feedback about their performance versus an instructor who gives them negative feedback about their mistakes. Inexperienced students who were enrolled in a beginner's class preferred the instructor who provides positive feedback more than students enrolled in the advanced class. Conversely, advanced students preferred the instructor who provides negative feedback about how they could improve compared to inexperienced students enrolled in the beginner class.

Next, in study 3, we tested the hypothesis that as one becomes more experienced with a task, one moves from seeking positive feedback to seeking negative feedback. We had participants engage in an unfamiliar task where they had a chance to get feedback on their performance. Participants were told they could only get one piece of feedback and were asked to choose whether they would like to receive positive feedback about what they do well or if they would like to receive negative feedback on how they could improve. We find that as people become more experienced with the task, they seek more negative feedback about how they can improve and less positive feedback on what they do well.

In study 4, we tested for feedback giving. We hypothesized that people who infer they have been pursuing a shared friendship goal with someone for a long time will give their experienced friend negative feedback about their weaknesses. To test this hypothesis, we had participants write a toast to a friend and we analyzed the amount of positive versus negative feedback they incorporated in their toast. We found that those who thought they knew the other person for a long time gave more negative feedback to their friend than those who thought they knew their friend a short while (inexperienced) but there was no difference in positive feedback giving depending on perceived experience in the relationship

Finally, in study 5 we explored the hypothesis that after gaining some experience in a domain of goal pursuit, individuals respond more to negative feedback by increasing their efforts in that domain and making subsequent goal-congruent choices. To test this prediction, we manipulated perceived experience in the friendship using social comparison information so that friends were made to feel as if they had known each other a short while or a long time. After this experience manipulation, we asked participants to consider a time they received positive feedback about their "hits" or negative feedback about their "misses." We found that participants who were made to feel as if they had known their friend a long time and who considered negative feedback were more likely to make goal-congruent choices (e.g., indicate they wanted to spend time with their friend or contact their friend) than participants who were made to feel experienced but considered positive feedback.

These findings have important implications for how marketers can increase the motivation to adhere to different consumer goals, in particular those that involve a sequence of actions that evolves over time. For example, we suggest that a persuasive appeal for inexperienced gym users should emphasize their successes in maintaining good health in the past, whereas a message that is directed toward experienced gym users should emphasize their lack of actions toward successfully maintaining good health.

"Sequential Influences on Dishonest Behavior"

Nina Mazar, University of Toronto, Canada
Dan Ariely, Duke University, USA

In our daily lives we find ourselves continuously tempted to behave dishonestly: overstating expense reports or tax exemptions, taking credit for other people's work, picking up a zip car earlier than what we have booked it for, or copying a song. It's easy to deviate from the path of honesty from time to time, even if most of us value honesty and have very high beliefs in our own morality. But is there a tipping point? An unwelcome moment when our dishonest behavior "crosses a threshold, tips, and spreads like wildfire" (Gladwell 2002)? This paper investigates dishonesty in an episodic rather than singular context and explores mechanisms to return to the path of honesty.

People's escalation of behavior has been studied among others in the context of addiction. For example, a dieter, who, in a moment of weakness, succumbs to the temptation and has a bite of chocolate, is more likely to give up any self-control induced restriction and eat the entire bar–after all, if one's daily dieting goal has been already violated, the day is lost. This type of behavior typical for dieters has been coined the "What-the-hell" effect (Polivy and Herman 1985). One popular strategy to prevent oneself from falling into such a trap is to eliminate tempting foods from the immediate environment altogether, which requires not only to admit that indulging is unwanted, but also to foresee future self-control problems (Fishbach and Trope 2007).

When it comes, however, to ethical decision making it has been criticized that most theories and empirical evidences focus on singular events, neglecting the influence of recent behavioral histories (Zhong, Liljenquist, and Cain 2009). For example, it has been shown that when tempted to benefit financially from cheating on a test, a vast amount of people will cheat, but only by a small amount, in order to maintain their moral self-worth (Mazar, Amir, and Ariely 2008). Such research is important to understand the basic mechanism underlying the decision to be dishonest, but falls short off considering that not only current situational factors and individuals traits can influence subsequent behaviors but also past situational factors and behaviors.

Given that continuous temptations play an important role in the context of unwanted behaviors such as binge eating, we set out to explore (1) whether there exists something like the "what-the-hell" effect in the domain of dishonesty and (2) what are the measures to break a vicious cycle of dishonesty. We report three studies that document people's vulnerability to continuous temptations, which can result in unwanted escalations of dishonesty, and ways to get out of them. Study 1 shows that over 100 trials of a task, in which each trial offers a choice between being honest and dishonest, at some point 67% of participants show behavior in line with "what the hell" effect: they reach a point at which they cheat all the time. Mark Twain contemplated "there are several good protections against temptations but the surest is cowardice." In line with this notion, we find in study 2 that if given an explicit choice about the environment to which people want to be exposed to (continuing with the same tempting task as before or moving to a less tempting task), a considerable amount is willing and able to avoid subsequent temptations –even if costly. Finally, study 3 investigates the effectiveness of various measures to reform a "sinner". For this purpose we introduced a break in the middle of a tempting task and either gave no instructions, asked participants to think about their past good deeds, or to confess their regrettable actions. The good news is that we find that positive reinforcers can be effective. However, confessing one's sins to strengthen one's resolutions, and regain a pure soul appears rather harmful.

The implications of this research may be substantial for policy and education. Future studies that investigate the psychological mechanisms underlying positive reinforcers and confessions, their potential connection to moral self-regulation, and the long-term effectiveness of these approaches particularly in light of adaptation can provide valuable insights needed to design better measures to curb dishonesty.

"The 'What The Hell Effect' Scale: Measuring Post-Failure Sequential Self-Control Choice Tendencies"

Yael Zemack-Rugar, Virginia Tech, USA
Canan Corus, St. John's University, USA
David Brinberg, Virginia Tech, USA

Self-control failures lead to a variety of individual and social malaise including obesity and debt. However, one could argue that such long term outcomes require repeated consumption episodes, and repeated self-control failures. The present research examines one aspect of such sequential self-control choices.

In particular, we examine how individuals respond to initial self-control failure in subsequent choices. This question is interesting because occasional self-control failures are bound to happen; it is how we respond to these failures that determines long term implications.

Literature suggests individuals can respond in one of two ways: self correct by increasing self control or continue to indulge. The latter behavior, continued indulgence, has been dubbed the "What The Hell Effect" (WTHE henceforth). We argue that much like other self-control characteristics, the tendency to enact the WTHE is based on an individual difference; we develop a measure capturing this difference.

What limited research exists about WTHE focuses on situational antecedents such as goal framing, including short/long and gain/loss frames. However, limited attention is paid to cognitions/emotions experienced in response to goal-failure, individual differences on these factors, and their effects on subsequent behavior.

We address this gap by focusing on the thoughts/feelings that consumers have in response to initial failure, and how these help predict their responses. To this end, we developed the WTHE scale, focusing on two central consumer self-control domains, eating and spending. We briefly describe below the scale development process and 3 predictive validity studies.

Given the limited literature to support item generation, we allowed for an organic development of WTHE questionnaire through consumer experiences. In study 1, 11 scenarios describing WTHE situations were created and presented to 73 participants. Each participant saw 3 random scenarios, and was asked what they would feel/think/do in response (each separately). Participants were then asked to make a choice related to the scenario and were finally asked to evaluate how realistic each scenario was.

We created a 25-item coding scheme designed to capture the different thoughts, feelings, and actions. The diaries were then coded by two independent coders (agreement: 95%). A high correlation of responses to each item was observed across all scenarios (Cronbach's alpha>.7 for all), lending credibility to the selected thought/feeling themes.

The 7 (3 budget, 4 food) most realistic scenarios were selected, and 25 items (corresponding to the themes) were created for each. In study 2, 163 undergraduate students completed this 175-item questionnaire. Exploratory and confirmatory factor analyses were conducted leading to the identification of two factors. Factor one had six items and was consistent with an adaptive, corrective, response to goal-failure (failure as motivation). Factor 2 had three items and was consistent with a WTHE type response (failure as permission). The WTHE score was designed to be the difference between the first factor and second factor average, with lower scores indicating a higher tendency to enact the WTHE.

In study 3, this 63-item questionnaire was administered to 124 participants along with twelve other scales (e.g., self control, impulsivity, causality, perfectionism, locus of control, dieting). The scale was significantly correlated with five scales (TOSCA, dieting, two causality subscales, and impulsivity) in the expected direction, but only to a moderate degree (highest correlation 0.35), suggesting the scale was unique.

Having developed the questionnaire, we turned to examine its predictive validity. In studies 4 and 5 we provided participants with an eating/spending scenario similar to that provided in Soman and Cheema (2004), where participants had the opportunity to buy a ticket to a concert (have dessert) after either having already exceeding their budget (calorie) goal/having enough money (calories) to afford the ticket (cake).

In a separate session participants completed the WTHE scale, the four scales previously found to correlate with our scale, and several other new scales (e.g., Elaboration on Potential Outcomes, Frugality). Analysis revealed that our scale uniquely predicted whether participants indulged/not when they had already exceeded their budget (calorie) goal. The only other significant measure was the self-control scale, which predicted behavior only for those participants who had not exceeded their budget (calorie) goal. Thus, whereas the self-control scale predicts the likelihood of initial goal-failure, the WTHE scale uniquely predicts post-failure behavior, a separate construct.

Study 6 is ongoing and is a longitudinal study involving diary recording. We seek to examine in this study whether the real-life behavior of consumers following goal failure (recorded in diaries) is uniquely predicted by the WTHE scale.

In sum, the WTHE scale is extremely important and should be of interest to researchers examining self control. It not only identifies an individual difference in responding to failure, it provides insight as to the underlying cognitions/feelings (failure as permission/failure as motivation) that may underlie this difference. As sequential self-control failures are what truly underlie the long-term negative effects on consumers, it is important to identify those consumers most vulnerable to those effects as well as the reasons for this vulnerability.

REFERENCES

Fishbach, Ayelet and Yaacov Trope (2007), "Implicit and Explicit Counteractive Self-Control," in *Handbook of Motivation Science*, ed. J. Shah and W. Gardner, New York: Guilford, 281-94.

Gladwell, Malcolm (2002), *The Tipping Point: How Little Things Can Make a Big Difference*, New York: Back Bay Books, 9.

Polivy, Janet and C. Peter Herman (1985), "Dieting as a Problem in Behavioral Medicine," in *Advances in Behavioral Medicine*, ed. E. Katkin and S. Manuck, New York: JAI, 1-37.

Zhong, Chen-Bo, Katie Liljenquist, and Daylian M. Cain (2009), *Moral Self-Regulation: Licensing & Compensation*, University of Toronto.

Mazar, Nina, On Amir, and Dan Ariely (2008), "The Dishonesty of Honesty People: A Theory of Self-Concept Maintenance," *Journal of Marketing Research*, 45, 633-644.

Special Session Summary

I'm Afraid, But Am I Persuaded? How to Make Fear Appeals More Effective

Eugenia Wu, Duke University, USA

SESSION OVERVIEW

Though appealing to fear is a commonly used persuasive tactic, both practitioners and academic researchers remain divided on whether fear appeals are an effective means of conveying a message or not. While the success of some real world fear appeal campaigns suggests that fear has a positive influence on persuasion, the results of other ad campaigns indicate that fear may actually hamper message acceptance (e.g., Prevention First, 2008; Rhodes, Wolitski and Arguelles, 1989). Similarly, over fifty years of academic research on fear appeals yields mixed evidence as to how persuasive fear appeals really are, with the results of some studies showing a positive relationship between fear and persuasion and others indicating a lack of or even a negative relationship (Janis and Terwillinger, 1962; Witte and Allen, 2000). The three papers in this session all focus on exploring when fear appeals are effective and why. More specifically, each of the three papers examines a different type of factor that may influence whether consumers are persuaded by a given fear appeal or not. Broadly construed, this symposium aims to shed some light on the debate surrounding a classic persuasion technique.

To offer a fuller understanding of when fear appeals are effective and why, each paper examines a distinct factor that may influence fear appeal persuasion and offers a unique perspective. First, Morales, Fitzsimons and Wu (2009) examine how features of the appeal itself, specifically the presence or absence of a disgust-eliciting element, might influence how persuasive consumers find a given fear appeal to be. Second, Agrawal and Menon (2009) explore how factors incidental to the appeal might carry over to influence message acceptance. In particular, they investigate how incidental discrete emotions differentially determine fear appeal effectiveness. Finally, Lau, Williams and Drolet (2009) focus on how individual difference factors can moderate fear appeal persuasion. Specifically, they examine how differences in empathy neglect might impact consumer responsiveness to ads that evoke their fear of embarrassment. Together, these papers suggest that appealing to fear can be an effective persuasive technique but that there are limits and boundary conditions that may hinder persuasion.

Fear appeals have been commonly used to address a wide range of the most urgent social and public health issues ranging from domestic violence and driving while under the influence to AIDS prevention and teenage pregnancy. Given the frequency with which fear appeals are used and the significance of the messages they are attempting to convey, it becomes that much more important for marketers to understand how these appeals work, when they will get the message across and when they will backfire. This symposium aims to contribute to consumer research by providing a nuanced and detailed view of some of the factors that determine whether fear appeals will be persuasive or not.

We hope that this symposium will attract a wide ACR audience, from researchers interested in fear appeals specifically to the broad range of researchers who examine the role of emotion in consumer psychology. This symposium is also relevant for marketers interested in persuasion and emotional coping. Of note, these papers are all in advanced stages of completion. As such, we expect this symposium to stimulate much discussion. For this reason, we hope to save 20 minutes following the presentations for Lauren Block to discuss the presentations and to receive questions from the audience.

EXTENDED ABSTRACTS

"That's So Disgusting–I'll Take Two!: How Disgust Enhances the Effectiveness of Fear Appeals"

Andrea C. Morales, Arizona State University, USA
Gavan J. Fitzsimons, Duke University, USA
Eugenia C. Wu, Duke University, USA

Fear appeals have been used to promote a wide variety of consumer products and services and to address a broad range of pressing public health issues including AIDS prevention and drug use (e.g., Freimuth, Hammond, Edgar and Monahan, 1990). Despite the frequency with which fear appeals are used, practitioners and academics remain divided over whether fear appeals are an effective means of persuasion or not (e.g., National Institute on Drug Abuse, 1997; Prevention First, 2008; Beck, 1984; Rogers and Mewborn, 1976).

Research has identified a number of message features and individual difference variables that influence the effectiveness of fear appeals (e.g., Keller and Block, 1996; Rogers, 1983). We propose a previously unexamined factor that may affect fear appeal persuasiveness: the presence or absence of a disgust-eliciting element. Studies have suggested that fear appeals may evoke other emotions in addition to fear (e.g., Dabbs and Leventhal, 1966) and that these emotions may affect persuasion (Passyn and Sujan, 2006). In the current work, we focus on the role of disgust in increasing the persuasiveness of fear appeals. We focus on disgust because its role in persuasion is little understood and because many existing fear appeals seem to also include a disgusting element.

Though both fear and disgust are negative emotions, the distinct properties of each emotion should lead to divergent effects on persuasion. In terms of appraisal pattern differences, fear is characterized by maximal uncertainty whereas disgust is described by a relatively high degree of certainty. When individuals are threatened, feelings of certainty or uncertainty help determine how they will respond. Feelings of uncertainty cause individuals to question their ability to avoid an unpleasant outcome whereas feelings of certainty lead individuals to feel that they can deal with the problem. This suggests that when individuals experience fear in response to a fear (without disgust) appeal, their sense of uncertainty should make message compliance less likely, as they will be unsure whether they can actually do anything to avoid the unpleasant outcome. When individuals experience both disgust and fear in response to a disgust-eliciting fear appeal however, the sense of certainty associated with disgust (that is absent in the case of a fear-without disgust-appeal) should lead to increased message persuasion and a higher likelihood of compliance with the message's recommendations.

Similarly, the unique action tendencies that describe fear and disgust should also lead to disparate effects on persuasion. Most fear appeals are future-oriented (e.g., you will develop skin cancer if you do not use sunscreen) rather than present-oriented (e.g., you are developing skin cancer right now) so that the threat is not imminent. This characteristic of fear appeals should interact with the action tendencies of fear and disgust to influence persuasion. The action tendency in fear is avoidance or escape (Lazarus, 1991) but interestingly, fear often results in freezing or "deer in headlights" behavior. Rosen and Schulkin (1998) suggest that the fear reaction occur in two stages: threat causes individuals to freeze up initially and then to actively avoid or escape only when the danger becomes imminent. Consistent with this, consumers have been found to "seize and freeze" in response to health-related or threatening messages in fear appeals, thereby hindering persuasion (Block and Williams 2002). In contrast, disgust is characterized by a strong and pronounced impulse to move away from disgust-eliciting object in an immediate and certain manner (Lazarus, 1991). Given that fear causes individuals to freeze if the danger is not looming and that disgust causes individuals to act immediately, we expect that individuals should respond more strongly to fear appeals that also co-activate disgust relative to fear appeals that do not.

In study 1, we first explore the distinct effect that disgust has on persuasion. Though disgust's expelling properties suggest that disgusting ads may repel consumers away from the suggested behavior and advertised brand, we propose that disgust can lead to increases in persuasion if the frame of the ad fits with disgust's expelling action tendency. We test this idea in a 2 (disgust level: low vs. high) by 2 (frame: approach vs. avoid) experiment. Results reveal that participants in the high disgust/avoidance frame condition were the most persuaded relative to participants in all other conditions.

In study 2, we begin to examine how disgust might affect fear appeal effectiveness. To tease out disgust's influence on fear appeals, we pit a fear appeal that does not elicit disgust, a neutral appeal and an appeal in which disgust and fear are co-activated against each other and measure their respective effects on persuasion. Specifically, we use advertisements that attempt to persuade consumers not to use drugs. Study results show that participants were the least likely to use illegal drugs in the disgust and fear co-activation condition.

Studies 3 through 5 build on the results of study 2 and continue to examine how disgust might influence fear appeal persuasiveness. In study 3, we demonstrate that the persuasive effects of disgust-inducing fear appeals generalize across appeals that elicit disgust both through images and through ad copy. In study 4, we would like to draw on our study 1 findings and show that disgust-inducing fear appeals should be particularly effective in the context of an avoidance frame, given the fit between avoidance and how consumers naturally respond to disgust. This is exactly what we find. In study 5, we turn to the appraisal differences between disgust and fear to further examine the distinctions between disgust-inducing fear appeals and fear appeals that do not elicit disgust. Results reveal that the presence or absence of a disgust-eliciting element has a significant effect on persuasion but only for individuals who are motivated to seek a sense of certainty. For individuals who are not motivated to seek certainty, the presence or absence of disgust has little effect on persuasion.

In sum, we find that including disgust-eliciting elements in fear appeals can augment persuasion. An examination of some of the most highly cited fear appeals articles and of real world advertising campaigns suggests that many of these appeals inadvertently elicited disgust in addition to fear. Thus, disgust may be a key moderator of fear appeal effectiveness and may be able to resolve some of the controversy over them. More generally, our findings suggest that future research should examine the role of specific emotions in persuasion appeals, as discrete emotions can have unique effects on persuasion.

References

Beck, Kenneth H. (1984), "The Effects of Risk Probability, Outcome Severity, Efficacy of Protection and Access to Protection on Decision Making: A Further Test of Protection Motivation Theory," *Social Behavior and Personality*, 12, 121-125.

Block, Lauren G. and Patti Williams (2002), "Undoing the Effects of Seizing and Freezing: Decreasing Defensive Processing of Personally Relevant Messages," *Journal of Applied Social Psychology*, 32, 803-833.

Dabbs, James M., and Howard Leventhal, (1966), "Effects of Varying the Recommendations in a Fear-Arousing Communication," *Journal of Personality and Social Psychology*, 4, 525–531.

Freimuth, Vicki S., Sharon Lee Hammond, Timothy Edgar, and Jennifer L. Monahan, (1990), "Reaching Those at Risk: A Content-Analytic Study of AIDS PSAs," *Communication Research*, 17, 775-791.

Keller, Punam A. and Lauren G. Block (1996), "Increasing the Persuasiveness of Fear Appeals: The Effect of Arousal and Elaboration," *Journal of Consumer Research*, 22, 31-54.

Lazarus, Richard S. (1991), *Emotion and Adaptation*, New York: Oxford University Press.

Lerner, Jennifer S., and Dacher Keltner, (2000), "Beyond Valence: Toward a Model of Emotion-Specific Influences on Judgment and Choice," *Cognition and Emotion*, 14 (4), 473-493.

National Institute on Drug Abuse (1997), *Drug Abuse Prevention: What Works*, Rockville, MD: National Institutes of Health.

Passyn, Kirsten and Mita Sujan, (2006), "Self-Accountability Emotions and Fear Appraisals: Motivating Behavior," *Journal of Consumer Research*, 23, 583-589.

Prevention First (2008), *Ineffectiveness of Fear Appeals in Youth Alcohol, Tobacco and Other Drug (ATOD) Prevention*, Springfield, IL: Prevention First.

Rogers, Ronald W. (1983), "Cognitive and Physiological Processes in Fear appeals and Attitude Change: A Revised Theory of Protection Motivation," In J. Cacioppo and R. Petty (Eds.), *Social Psychophysiology*, New York: Guilford Press, 153-176.

Rogers, Ronald W. and C. Ronald Mewborn (1976), "Fear Appeals and Attitude Change: Effects of a Threat's Noxiousness, Probability of Occurrence, and the Efficacy of the Coping Responses," *Journal of Personality and Social Psychology*, 34, 54-61.

Rosen, Jeffrey B. and Jay Schulkin (1998), "From Normal Fear to Pathological Anxiety," *Psychological Review*, 105, 325-350.

"Harboring Hope and Avoiding Anxiety: The Role of Emotions in Determining the Effectiveness of Fear Appeals"

Nidhi Agrawal, Northwestern University, USA
Geeta Menon, University of Pennsylvania, USA

Health messages frequently try to convince consumers that they are at high risk of contracting a disease by presenting an array of risk factors and consequences that resonate with the consumers. Such messages intended to promote safe, precautionary and preventative behaviors in the context of health by creating a fear of having a disease. Such fear appeals that highlight risk factors and consequences are inherently threatening. A growing stream of research on health seeks to understand the factors that affect how people respond to fear appeals. The question that this research has asked is: When, why and how are such fear appeals effective in convincing people of their vulnerability?

Existing research has suggested that people have two responses to fear appeals: fear control or danger control. Fear control encourages people to cope with the emotion itself and process information in a way that reduces their fear. Fear control hurts the processing of fear appeals and renders them ineffective. The other response of danger control encourages people to manage the threat that lead to fear. This response encourages them to process health information and focus on actions that might help control the source of the fear (Leventhal 1971; Witte 1994). Health research has examined conditions that encourage a fear control or danger control response. Most of this past work has examined the role of message factors in determining the effectiveness of fear appeals. In this paper, we focus on role of the broader emotional context in which the appeal is presented in determining the effectiveness of the appeal. Specifically, we suggest that participants' incidental emotions, specifically those varying on valence and uncertainty (e.g., happiness, sadness, hopefulness, anxiety) will determine whether they respond to fear appeal by trying to control the fear or the danger.

To understand how incidental emotions might affect responses to fear appeals, we draw on a significant stream of research that has examined the role of specific emotions (e.g., anger, sadness, peacefulness) in processing information and forming judgments (Lerner and Keltner 2000). This literature argues that individuals' responses to given emotions are directed by the underlying appraisals (e.g., valence, uncertainty) associated with that emotions. For example, anxiety is a negatively valenced emotion with a high uncertainty appraisal whereas sadness is a negatively valenced emotion with a low uncertainty appraisal. In another contrast, hope has a high uncertainty appraisal like anxiety but is positively valenced. These distinctions in valence and uncertainty are likely to drive the systematic variations in responses across these emotions. We propose that primed emotions would only influence responses to fear appeals when they are seen as applicable or relevant to the appeal (Agrawal, Menon, and Aaker 2007). Uncertain emotions would be more applicable and hence more likely to influence the processing of uncertainty-inducing fear appeals. Certain emotions would be less applicable and hence less likely to influence the processing of fear appeals. Then, to understand how two uncertain emotions varying in valence might influence individuals' response to fear appeals, we draw on the literature on valenced affective states. We propose that positively valenced emotions would lead to a danger control response that would enhance the effectiveness of fear appeals. In contrast, negative valence would lead to an emotion-repair focused fear control response which would hinder the effectiveness of fear appeals (Raghunathan and Trope 2002). Hence, we predict that valence and uncertainty appraisals will interactively determine individual's response to fear appeals.

In all three experiments, participants are primed with one of four emotional states (i.e., happiness, hopefulness, anxiety, or sadness). Then they are exposed to a fear appeal and measures of risk perception (study 1), message processing (study 1), and health behaviors (study 2) are collected. In Experiment 1, participants experiencing anxiety exhibited a fear control response, manifesting as lower risk estimates and defensive processing of the message relative to those experiencing sadness. Those experiencing hopefulness showed a danger control response manifesting in greater risk perceptions and objective processing of the message relative to happy individuals. These findings supported our predicted interaction between valence and uncertainty. Experiment 2 followed the same paradigm but collected measures of subsequent processing of health related information. In experiment three, participants primed with one of the four emotions were shown either a high or low fear appeal. Our effects held only for high fear appeal. The processing of the low fear appeal did not vary by valence and uncertainty of the incidental emotion.

These findings add to the literature on the processing of fear appeals as well as advance our understanding of how primed emotional states might affect the processing of emotionally aversive information. These findings have implications for designing health communications as well as broader contexts in which health communications are offered.

References

Agrawal, Nidhi, Geeta Menon, and Jennifer L. Aaker (2007), "Getting Emotional About Health," *Journal of Marketing Research*, 44 (February), 100-13.

Lerner, Jennifer S. and Dacher Keltner (2000), "Beyond Valence: Toward a Model of Emotion-Specific Influences on Judgment and Choice," *Cognition and Emotion*, 14 (July), 473-93.

Leventhal, Howard (1971), "Fear appeals and persuasion: the differentiation of a motivational construct," *American Journal of Public Health*, 61 (June), 1208-1224.

Raghunathan, Rajagopal and Yaacov Trope (2002), "Walking the Tightrope Between Feeling Good and Being Accurate: Mood as a Resource in Processing Persuasive Messages," *Journal of Personality and Social Psychology*, 83 (September), 510-25.

Witte, Kim (1994), "Fear Control and Danger Control: An Empirical Test of the Extended Parallel Process Model," *Communication Monographs*, 61, 113-134.

"Why People Fear Embarrassment: The Role of Empathy Neglect"

Loraine Lau, University of California at Irvine, USA
Patti Williams, University of Pennsylvania, USA
Aimee Drolet, University of California at Los Angeles, USA

People will go to great lengths to avoid feeling embarrassed. They will sacrifice their own health (Helwig-Larsen and Collins 1994) and financial gain (Corley and Rinker 1990) to evade embarrassment. They will not help others in need if such acts prove too embarrassing (Foss and Crenshaw 1978). They will behave in many ways indicative of an underlying deep fear of embarrassment. Embarrassment is indeed a strong motivating force affecting many decisions in life. This research examines factors that determine consumers' underlying fear of embarrassment and identifies ways to manage embarrassment-avoidant behavior through persuasive ads.

The threat to the self due to embarrassing mishaps in front of others appears more imaginary than real. Recent research reveals that embarrassing pratfalls often go unnoticed and are not judged as harshly by others as expected (Gilovich, Medvec and Savitsky 2000). This suggests that actual or expected feelings of embarrassment typically prove unwarranted, for people tend to overestimate the impressions they make upon others and believe the impressions formed will be negative. Moreover, the inaccuracy of others' judgments can be attributed at least in part to empathy neglect, the tendency to not consider others' empathic orientation (Epley, Savitsky and Gilovich 2002).

The present research explores the possibility that empathy neglect may underlie embarrassment-avoidant behavior. People may steer clear from potentially embarrassing activities because of their misjudgments about others' judgments of their own actions; they assume others not only will take note of their embarrassing missteps but also will evaluate them negatively as a result of it. We examine the nuances of empathy neglect by investigating how it corresponds to people's chronic levels of public self consciousness (PUBSC). People characterized by increased levels of PUBSC tend to believe they are being noticed and negatively evaluated by others more so than people with decreased levels of PUBSC (Fenigstein, Scheier and Buss 1975). Lau-Gesk and Drolet (2008) recently showed that heightened levels of PUBSC led to increased purchase intentions for embarrassing-to-buy products designed to help fend off greater future embarrassment once consumed. This is because the more elevated in PUBSC, the more people expect to be embarrassed. However, once convinced that future embarrassment is likely for them, purchase intentions for embarrassment-prevention products tend to be elevated regardless of PUBSC levels.

The present research builds on this initial work by investigating more closely which of the two components of empathy neglect underlie these differences in expectations to feel and motivation to prevent embarrassment among people who vary in PUBSC. In sum, we test whether people's failure to realize that others do not necessarily notice them, and more crucially, if others do happen to take notice, these others tend to make less harsh judgments when empathic to the embarrassing episode can explain embarrassment-avoidant behavior.

In the first two experiments, we test our theory by examining the role of PUBSC in people's responses to real ads for an embarrassing research assistantship. The job is advertised as requiring them to walk around campus with toilet paper stuck in the zipper of their pants and count number of people who inform them of it. In experiment 1, the ads for the embarrassing research assistantship job either reminds potential applicants of the possible scrutiny of others or does not. We expected and found the latter ad to produce embarrassment-avoidant behavior as evidenced through lower intentions to apply for the job regardless of PUBSC. The control ad also generated the expected pattern of results. Increased PUBSC led to lower job application intentions. Results from the first experiment help to establish the basic idea that higher levels of PUBSC correspond to higher expectations for negative social evaluations of others.

Experiment 2 attempts to disentangle whether the effects are due to a failure to realize others do not take much notice of embarrassing outcomes versus due to the failure to realize others have empathy and won't judge embarrassing outcomes harshly. Though the control ad remained the same, two new ads were created. Specifically, one ad cautioned potential applicants that people definitely would notice and remember seeing the toilet paper person walking around campus. Note that, unlike in the first experiment, this ad did not explicitly state that onlookers would cast unfavorable judgments. The other new ad reminded potential applicants that observers would have empathy and thus not judge as harshly as they expect. Findings indicate that people with increased PUBSC automatically assume others will notice their embarrassing pratfalls. They believe themselves the focus of attention. People with lower levels of PUBSC do not appear to assume this. However, once they believe others will take notice of embarrassing social blunders, they also tend to suffer from empathy neglect as well by not taking into account others' empathic nature. Regardless of PUBSC levels, people assume others judge embarrassing outcomes harshly. The final experiment explores the possible ways to undo empathy neglect.

Experiment 3 explores whether perspective-taking can help undo empathy neglect among individuals with heightened PUBSC. These individuals should correspondently have greater empathy towards others who suffer from embarrassment. Results support this proposition. Heightened PUBSC is associated with greater empathy displayed towards an individual featured in an ad who committed an embarrassing pratfall (i.e., accidental flatulence in front of his crush), thereby producing more favorable attitudes toward him and lowering purchasing intent for a gas prevention product designed to help people avoid future embarrassment. Findings across these three experiments are discussed in light of the emerging view about the importance of understanding the interaction between individual difference and situational variables as well as that among multiple emotions including fear, embarrassment and empathy.

References

Epley, N., Savitsky, K. and T. Gilovich (2002), "Empathy Neglect: Reconciling the Spotlight Effect and the Correspondence Bias," *Journal of Personality and Social Psychology*, 83, 300-312.

Fenigstein, A., , M. F. Scheier, and A. H. Buss (1975), "Public and Private Self-Consciousness: Assessment and Theory," *Journal of Consulting and Clinical Psychology*, 43, 522-527.

Foss, R. D. and N. C. Crenshaw (1978), "Risk of Embarrassment and Helping," *Journal of Behavior and Personality*, 6, 236-243.

Froming, W. J., E. B. Corley, and L. Rinker (1990), "The Influence of Public Self-Consciousness and the Audience's Characteristics on Withdrawal from Embarrassing Situations," *Journal of Personality*, 58, 603-622.

Helweg-Larsen, M. and B. E. Collins (1994), "The UCLA Multidimensional Condom Attitudes Scale: Documenting the Complex Determinants of Condom Use in College Students," *Health Psychology*, 13, 224-237.

Gilovich, T., V. Medvec, and K. Savitsky (2000), "The Spotlight Effect in Social Judgment: an Egocentric Bias in Estimates of the Salience of One's Own Actions and Appearance," *Journal of Personality and Social Psychology*, 78 (2), 211-222.

Lau-Gesk, L. and A. Drolet (2008), "The Publicly Self-Consciousness Consumer: Prepared to Be Embarrassed," *Journal of Consumer Psychology*, 18 (2), 127-36.

Special Session Summary
Metacognitive Experiences in Number Processing

Keri Kettle, University of Alberta, Canada

SESSION OVERVIEW

Numbers are central in many decisions: consumers evaluate quantitative product attributes (Payne, Bettman, & Johnson, 1993), investors examine financial data (Slovic, 2001), and brands often include numeric values (Pavia & Costa, 1993). The objective of this symposium is to challenge the prevailing assumption that number processing is inherently cognitive. Metacognitive experiences are shown to influence people's evaluations of, and preference for, alpha-numeric brands (Paper 1) and risky gambles (Paper 2), and subjective confidence in the evaluation of precise numeric attributes (Paper 3).

Although research suggests that metacognitive experiences in information processing affect evaluations and preference in a wide range of domains (e.g., Janiszewski & Meyvis 2003; Schwarz 2004), it has been assumed that number processing is exclusively deliberative and not affected by metacognitions. The research covered in this symposium suggests that, in fact, some numbers are more fluent than others. The characteristics of particular numbers generate more or less favorable metacognitive experiences that, in turn, affect judgments and choices.

Janiszewski and King (Paper #1) show that people prefer numbers that are the sums of common addition problems (sum-numbers) and the products of common multiplication problems (product-numbers), and that this preference influences liking of alpha-numeric brand names (e.g., Resorcinol 25). The second paper, by Kettle and Häubl, demonstrates that people prefer numbers that are products of 25 and 10 (e.g., 50%, $125). People rate risky prospects comprised of those numbers as more attractive, and choose those prospects over similar prospects comprised of non-fluent numbers. Critically, each paper shows that consumers who indicate that they like a particular fluent number or gamble respond more quickly, which supports the hypothesis that processing fluency may drive this preference. The third paper, Manoj Thomas et al., suggests that precision or roundness of prices affect magnitude judgments because precise prices are less fluent than round prices. When asked to categorize products according to price, people were less confident in their response when the offer price had no zeroes (precise number) than when it had two zeroes (round number).

Aparna Labroo (University of Chicago), the discussant, will provide her own insights, and address directions for future research. Taken together, the research presented in this symposium provides additional insight into how consumers process information and form preferences, and offers the exciting potential for marketers to build more appealing numeric brand names and quantitative attributes. This research offers the exciting potential to enhance consumer decision-making in personal and business finances, budgeting and mental accounting, and product evaluation and choice.

EXTENDED ABSTRACTS

"The Affective Consequences of Alpha-Numeric Branding"

Chris Janiszewski, University of Florida, USA
Dan King, University of Florida, USA

The selection of a specific number (henceforth brand number) to be part of a brand name (henceforth alpha-numeric brand name) does not appear to be guided by a single strategy (Boyd 1985; Pavia and Costa 1993). Instead, it appears that brand numbers are selected for a variety of reasons (Boyd 1985; Pavia and Costa 1993; Robertson 1989). For example, a brand number may be phonetically consistent with other parts of the brand name (e.g., Core 2 Duo), semantically consistent with the desired brand image (e.g., 5th Avenue), semantically consistent with the product function (e.g., XBOX 360, 2000 Flushes), or highly associable (e.g., 0, 1, 7, 13, and 100) (Battig and Spera 1962; Boyd 1985; Cochran and Wickens 1963; Pavia and Costa 1993). We contend there may be an additional reason for managers to use certain brand numbers. People may like some numbers more than others (Heywood 1972; Schimmel 1993; Simon 1972). If marketers can take advantage of this fact, without violating guidelines that typically guide brand number selection, then they should be able to build more appealing alpha-numeric brand names.

We posit that one source of liking for a number is the fluency experienced when processing the number. In study 1, we have people view a randomly ordered presentation of the numbers 1 through 100 and indicate, as quickly as they can, whether they like, dislike, or are indifferent about each number. We find that people like the sum-numbers two through 20 (e.g., 1 + 1=2 through 10 + 10=20) and product-numbers (e.g., 2 x 2=4 through 10 x 10=100) more than the other numbers. In addition, when a person likes a number, the person responds to the number more quickly. This implies that fluent processing may be responsible for the number liking.

In study 2, we illustrate the importance of this finding. A choice-based-conjoint task is used to show that people prefer a brand named using a product number (e.g., Resorcinol 25) more than a brand named using a non-product number (e.g., Resorcinol 29) or no number at all (e.g., Resorcinol). Comparing the size of the brand name trade-off to the average size of a price tradeoff suggests the favorable product-number adds $ 0.43 of value to the brand name.

Study 3 is used to investigate the representation of numbers. Ashcraft (1982; 1987) proposes that declarative knowledge about arithmetic problems (e.g., 3 x 4=__) and correct responses to these problems (e.g., 12) are represented in a semantic network. The strength of association between these nodes increases with practice so that the response node (e.g., 12) is more active after encountering an arithmetic problem involving that response node (e.g., 6 + 6, 3 x 4). Campbell and Graham (1985) extend Ashcraft's ideas by arguing that the representation of arithmetic facts also includes associations from operands (e.g., 3, 4) to results (e.g., 12). The implication is that commonly practiced problems (e.g., 6 + 6=__, 3 X 4=__) are more likely to prime a product-number than uncommon problems (e.g., 67-55=__) or unrelated problems (e.g., 77 + 4). Study 3 illustrates this priming effect using addition and multiplication problems. Common problems made sum-numbers and product-numbers more accessible and more liked.

Study 4 illustrates how operand priming can operate in an advertising context. Ads are created for a product-number (e.g., 12) or a non-product number (e.g., 29). These ads include operands that can prime the product-number or not (e.g., 6, 2) (see below). Participants are asked to view one of the four ads and then report their attitude toward the ad, attitude toward the brand, and purchase intention. The ad liking, brand liking, and purchase intention measures were combined to create an affect toward the brand measure (Cronbach's ?=.85). The type of number by priming interaction was significant (F(1, 181)=3.93, p<.05). Operand priming led to more positive affect toward the brand when the product-number was in the brand name (MNo prime=5.70, MPrime=6.30; F(1, 181)=6.15, p<.01), but not when a non-product/non-sum number was in the brand name (MNo prime=5.19, MPrime=5.12; F(1, 181)=.10, p>.05). Two other ad replicates showed similar results.

"Numeric Fluency and Preference"

Keri Kettle, University of Alberta, Canada
Gerald Häubl, University of Alberta, Canada

Consumers often evaluate numbers in a decision context; they choose among products described by quantitative attributes (Payne et al., 1993), set budgets (Ülkümen et al., 2008), make investment decisions (Slovic, 2001), and decide how much to tip a waiter (Lynn et al., 1993). Although research has primarily examined the deliberate, cognitive evaluation of quantitative information (e.g., Dehaene, 1997), a growing body of literature suggests that people actually like some numbers more than others. For example, people spontaneously round off estimates of time and money (Kandel et al., 2001; Schindler & Kirby, 1997), and both stock prices and IPO offers disproportionately congregate at prices ending in "0.00", ".00", ".50" and ".25" (Huttenlocher et al., 1990; Sonneman, 2005). We propose that these numeric biases can be explained by the fluency experienced when processing the number.

Our key premise is that multiples of twenty-five and powers of ten (e.g., 10, 75, 125, 200), commonly referred to as "round numbers", are more fluent than sharp numbers of similar magnitude. According to the processing fluency model, exposure to a stimulus creates a feature- and/or meaning-based representation of that stimulus in memory that, in turn, enhances the ease with which one processes the stimulus in subsequent exposures (Lee & Labroo, 2004). Fluency is enhanced by incidental exposure and increases monotonically with repeated exposure (Janiszewski & Meyvis, 2001; Zajonc, 1968). Prior research has shown that round numbers are used in written and spoken language with greater frequency than sharp numbers (Dehaene & Mehler, 1992). We posit that the repeated use of, and exposure to, round numbers enhances their processing fluency (Lee & Labroo, 2004; Schwarz, 2004; Zajonc, 1968).

We examined numeric fluency in the context of choices between risky prospects (Kahneman & Tversky, 1979). Each prospect is described in terms of two numeric properties–a monetary payoff and the probability of attaining that payoff (as opposed to receiving nothing)–that jointly determine the expected value. Because round numbers are also easier to use in arithmetic, this context enables us to disentangle our processing fluency account from an alternative, cognitive account of the preference: effort minimization (Payne & Bettman, 2001). An effort minimization account suggests that, because people have limited cognitive capacity, they may strategically choose to exert the minimal amount of cognitive effort required to attain a satisfactory outcome. By this account, a preference for alternatives involving round numbers would reflect one's desire to avoid difficult calculations or comparisons.

To disentangle the metacognitive (fluency) and cognitive (effort minimization) explanations, we independently manipulated whether a prospect was comprised of round or sharp numbers, and the number of steps necessary to calculate the expected value. To illustrate, imagine the following choice between a prospect comprised of round numbers (Prospect A: 50% chance of $400) and a prospect comprised of sharp numbers (Prospect B: 53% chance of $378). In addition, we created prospects for which participants needed to make three additional calculations (two products and a sum) in order to estimate the expected value (e.g., Prospect B: 53% chance of 0.43 x $376 + 0.56 x $387). We refer to such prospects as being of high arithmetic complexity. The fluency and effort accounts predict contrasting effects of arithmetic complexity on preference and decision time (the time required to process the information, form a preference, and indicate that preference). First, an effort minimization account predicts that increasing the arithmetic complexity of a prospect should decrease preference for that prospect. Second, the effort account suggests that increasing the arithmetic complexity of a prospect should not lead to longer decision times (beyond an incremental increase to process the additional stimuli). That is, if the preference for round numbers reflects the desire to minimize cognitive effort, then people should not exert additional effort to estimate the expected value of a more complex prospect.

In study 1, each participant made 8 choices between pairs of prospects. Choice sets were designed such that the two prospects had nearly identical expected values, with any small discrepancies favoring the prospect comprised of sharp numbers. As predicted, participants chose the prospect comprised of round numbers 63% of the time. Participants took twice as much time to decide between two complex prospects (19.6 seconds) as they did to choose between two simple prospects (8.9 seconds), but increasing the arithmetic complexity of a prospect did not decrease preference for that prospect. Critically, decision times were significantly shorter when the fluent prospect was chosen irrespective of whether participants were choosing between two simple prospects, ($M_{roundChosen}$=8.0 seconds, $M_{sharpChosen}$=11.0 seconds), one simple and one complex prospect ($M_{roundChosen}$=14.7 seconds, $M_{sharpChosen}$=16.1 seconds), or two complex prospects ($M_{roundChosen}$=18.4 seconds, $M_{sharpChosen}$=21.9 seconds), which demonstrates that processing fluency drives the preference for round numbers. In study 2, we show that these results generalize to all sharp numbers by randomly generating the sharp numbers for each choice. The key results of study 1 were replicated. In study 3, prospects consisted either of all sharp numbers or of one sharp and one round number. The results demonstrate that the presence of even a single round number is sufficient to enhance preference by approximately 10 percentage points.

In study 4, participants were provided with the expected value of each prospect, in addition to its payoff and probability. They were first asked to choose between the same prospect pairs as in study 1. Then, they were presented with prospects one at a time, asked their willingness to pay for the prospect, and then asked to rate the attractiveness of the prospect. Numeric fluency did not affect willingness to pay. However, people rated round prospects as more attractive than sharp prospects, and they took less time to rate the sharp prospects, even though they were provided with the expected value of, and had already processed, each prospect. This pattern of results provides compelling evidence for our processing fluency account.

"The Precision Effect in Numbers: How Processing Fluency of Numbers Influence Response Confidence"

Manoj Thomas, Cornell University, USA
Vicki Morwitz, New York University, USA
Jin Seok Pyone, Cornell University, USA

Previous research has shown that precision or roundness of a price can influence magnitude judgments. For example, Janiszewski and Uy (2008) have shown that participants are willing to pay more when sellers ask for a precise list price (e.g., 799,800 or 800,200) instead of a round price (e.g., 800,000). Thomas, Kadiyali and

Simon (forthcoming) suggest that this precision effect occurs because precision or roundedness influences the magnitude perceptions of prices. They suggest that precise prices are judged to be smaller than round prices of comparable magnitudes.

This research further explores the mechanisms that underlie the precision effect. Specifically, we hypothesize that precision or roundness of prices affect magnitude judgments because precise prices are less fluent than round prices. The disfluency evoked by precise prices induces a feeling of uncertainty. This occurs because people consider the subjective experience as a metacognitive cue to assess the effectiveness of the mental processes. They try to reduce this feeling of uncertainty by heuristically attributing it to the most salient cause. The heuristic beliefs used for the attribution could be based on practices observed in the market place (e.g., sellers are more likely to round-up than to round-down prices) or the distribution of precise and round numbers in daily written and oral communication (e.g., large numbers such as the price of a car are rounded, while small numbers such as the price of gasoline are precise). The conceptual model is schematically summarized below:

Precision→Disfluency→Lower Confidence→Heuristic Attribution→Magnitude Judgment

Fundamental to this conceptualization is the premise that precision-induced processing fluency influences response confidence. Two studies that test this hypothesis are presented in this conference.

The first study shows that precision can reduce response confidence. The second study shows that direct manipulations of response confidence can moderate the effect of precision on magnitude judgments. In study 1, participants were asked to categorize various prices as high or low relative to an internal standard. They were shown a stapler and asked to guess the regular price of this stapler at a store. For each participant, the computer generated 12 offer prices, of which 6 were above the articulated internal standard and 6 were below the articulated internal standard. Participants' task was to categorize the offer prices as "HIGH" or "LOW" by clicking on one of the two response buttons. For each categorization response, we measured their confidence in the response. Participants were less confident in their response when the three digit offer price had no zeroes (78% confidence on a 50% to 100% scale), more confident when the prices had two zeroes (80% confidence), and most confident when the offer price had two zeroes (84% confidence, p<.01). Similar pattern manifested for response time. In study 2 we manipulated response-confidence and price-precision in a magnitude judgment task using between-subjects design. Participants were shown six prices of a house listed for sale. For each round price (e.g., 365000), we created a precise price that was comparable in magnitude (e.g., 365,583). It was observed that nominally larger precise prices were incorrectly judged to be smaller than round prices. However, precision affected magnitude judgments only when participants were uncertain about their ability to make magnitude judgments. Together, these results support the hypothesis that precision-induced processing fluency influences response confidence.

REFERENCES

Ashcraft, Mark H. (1987), "Children's Knowledge of Simple Arithmetic: A Developmental Model and Simulation," in Formal Methods in Developmental Psychology: Progress in *Cognitive Development Research*, eds. J. Bisanz, C. J. Brianerd, and R. Kail, New York: Springer-Verlag, 302-28.

Dehaene, Stanislas (1997), *The Number Sense,* New York: Oxford University Press.

Boyd, Colin D. (1985), "Point of View: Alpha Numeric Brand Names," *Journal of Advertising Research*, 25 (Oct/Nov), 48-52.

Campbell, Jamie, and David J. Graham (1985), "Mental Multiplication Skill: Structure, Process, and Acquisition," Canadian *Journal of Psychology*, 39 (June), 338-66.

Janiszewski, Chris and Tom Meyvis (2001), "Effects of Brand Logo Complexity, Repetition, and Spacing on Processing Fluency and Judgment," *Journal of Consumer Research*, 28, 18-32.

Janiszewski, Chris and Dan Uy (2008), "Precision of the Anchor Influences the Amount of Adjustment," *Psychological Science*, 19(2).

Lee, Angela.Y. and Aparna A. Labroo (2004), "The Effect of Conceptual and Perceptual Fluency on Brand Evaluation," *Journal of Marketing Research*, 41, 151-165.

Pavia, Teresa M. and Janeen A. Costa (1993), "The Winning Number: Consumer Perceptions of Alpha-numeric Brand Names," *Journal of Marketing*, 57 (July), 85-98.

Schwarz, Norbert (2004), "Metacognitive Experiences in Consumer Judgment and Decision Making," *Journal of Consumer Psychology*, 14, 332-348.

Thomas, Manoj, Daniel Simon, and Vrinda Kadiyali (forthcoming), "The Price Precision Effect: Evidence from Laboratory and Market Data," *Marketing Science*.

Special Session Summary

Finding the Uncompromising Consumer: A Deeper Understanding of Context Effects on Choice

Jeffrey Parker, Columbia University, USA

SESSION OVERVIEW

Time and time again, choice context has been found to dramatically affect consumer preferences (see, e.g., Huber, Payne & Puto 1982; Shafir, Simonson & Tversky 1993; Simonson 1989; Simonson & Tversky 1992). For example, choice reversals resulting from the introduction of compromise options or asymmetrically dominated alternatives are particularly robust. However, little attention has been given to how the manner in which consumers process the choices might affect their susceptibility to such biases. The question is important as different processing styles have been shown to significantly influence judgment and behavior by altering attention to and processing of information. For example, more comparative (vs. evaluative) judgments have been shown to focus consumers on more comparable (vs. enriched) attributes (Nowlis & Simonson 1997).

The current session includes three papers that examine how different processing styles influence common context effects. While all three papers explore information processing or decision strategies that influence context effects, each paper approaches this topic from a unique perspective, identifying specific influences of different evaluative processes. Specifically, the effects of non-conscious processing, affective evaluations, and abstract mindsets are investigated. This session takes the viewpoint that not only does the context surrounding the options affect consumer preference, but so too does the manner in which consumers think about those options and that context. Accordingly, the first paper, by Goldsmith, Dijksterhuis and Dhar, investigates if non-conscious processing prior to choice can attenuate the compromise effect due to an enhanced ability to resolve tradeoffs. These authors find support for this, showing that non-conscious processing reduces the compromise effect (vis-à-vis conscious elaboration or mere distraction). Correspondingly, in the second paper, Pham and Parker test the hypothesis that engaging in feelings-based processing will reduce consumer preference for compromise options. These authors find significant moderation, demonstrating that feelings-based choices shift preferences towards extreme alternatives. Finally, in the third and final paper, Khan, Zhu, and Kalra test how a consumer's level of abstraction affects their likelihood of falling prey to three classic context effects: the compromise effect, the attraction effect, and the background contrast effect. By manipulating consumer mindsets (abstract vs. concrete) the authors demonstrate that abstract mindset reduces the compromise effect, reduces background contrasts and enhances the attraction effect. All of the papers in this proposal are in their final stages of preparation.

Using multiple, yet related, theoretical perspectives these three papers extend what is currently known about when and how consumer choice may be affected by context. While some moderators of context effects have been identified (see, e.g., Dhar and Simonson 2003; Mourali, et al. 2007), no research to date has investigated how the manner in which a consumer processes their choices might affect their susceptibility to such biases. By investigating this topic, we can not only advance our theoretical understanding of the origins of these effects but can also offer practical insights for consumers and practitioners seeking to mitigate the effects of context on their choices.

We anticipate that this session will be attended by consumer researchers in general and by members of ACR who have a particular interest in context effects, consumer choice, and processing styles. Each paper in the session includes multiple completed studies with supporting results. Further, our discussant, Joel Huber, who is an expert on context effects, is expected to lead a stimulating discussion.

References

Dhar, Ravi, and Itamar Simonson (2003), "The Effect of Forced Choice on Choice," *Journal of Marketing Research*, 40(2), 146-60.

Huber, Joel, John W. Payne and Christopher Puto (1982), "Adding Asymmetrically Dominated Alternatives: Violations of Regularity and the Similarity Hypothesis," *Journal of Consumer Research*, 9(1), 90-98.

Mourali, Mehdi, Ulf Böckenhlt, and Michel Laroche (2007), "Compromise and Attraction Effects under Prevention and Promotion Motivations," *Journal of Consumer Research*, 34(2), 234-47.

Nowlis, Stephen M. and Itamar Simonson (1997), "Attribute-Task Compatibility as a Determinant of Consumer Preference Reversals," *Journal of Marketing Research*, 34(2), 205-18.

Shafir, Eldar, Itamar Simonson, and Amos Tversky (1993), "Reason-based Choice," *Cognition*, 49(1-2), 11-36.

Simonson, Itamar (1989), "Choice in Context: Tradeoff Contrast and Extremeness Aversion," *Journal of Marketing Research*, 29(3), 281-95.

Simonson, Itamar, and Amos Tversky (1992), "Choice in Context: Tradeoff Contrast and Extremeness Aversion," *Journal of Marketing Research*, 29(3), 281-95.

EXTENDED ABSTRACTS

"Non-Conscious Processing and Choice in Context"

Kelly Goldsmith, Northwestern University, USA
Ap Dijksterhuis, Radboud University Nijmegen, The Netherlands
Ravi Dhar, Yale University, USA

Most consumer choice requires making tradeoffs among the available options (e.g., should I pay $50 more for the iPod with more memory?). A major finding in choice research has been that when faced with decisions that involve making tradeoffs, consumers' choices can be inconsistent and susceptible to influence, for example, from the choice task or the decision context. This occurs as such factors can highlight different considerations, leading to different choice outcomes. These context effects have been shown to be robust across a wide variety of stimuli, and arise even when consumers are instructed to carefully process their decisions (Pocheptsova et al. 2009).

Recent research has debated whether conscious elaboration or non-conscious processing leads to better decisions (Dijksterhuis and van Olden 2005, Payne et al. 2008). We extend this research by examining how conscious vs. non-conscious processing affects a bias relevant to making tradeoffs; specifically, we examine how these different modes of processing affect consumers' propensity to demonstrate the compromise effect (Simonson 1989). The compromise effect is observed when choice of an option increases when the option is made the middle option (e.g., b in set abc) as opposed to an extreme option (e.g., b in set bc). This effect occurs due to consumers' inability to resolve tradeoffs across attributes (Dhar and Simonson 2003). Research in the domain of social psychology has demonstrated that conscious elaboration impedes our natural ability to weigh decision criteria, showing that non-conscious processing allows for superior integration and evaluation of choice attributes (Dijksterhuis and van Olden 2005, Wilson 2003). Drawing from both of these research streams, we propose that consumers who non-consciously process their options prior to making a choice will be less likely to demonstrate the compromise effect than those who consciously elaborate on the alternatives prior to choice, due to their superior ability to resolve tradeoffs.

We test our main proposition in two studies. The first study is designed to test if non-conscious processing will decrease the compromise effect as compared to conscious elaboration. For this study, participants were presented with a choice set (either ab or abc) and instructed that they would later make a choice. Following Dijksterhuis et al (2006), participants were then randomly assigned to complete either a conscious elaboration or a non-conscious processing task. Participants assigned to the conscious elaboration task were instructed to "think very carefully" about their choice and to write out their thoughts for two minutes. Participants assigned to the non-conscious processing task were instructed to "think very carefully" as they completed a two minute distraction task. This resulted in a 2 (choice set: ab vs. abc) x 2 (conscious elaboration vs. non-conscious processing) design. Finally, all participants made a choice from the set they had been shown initially. Consistent with our predictions, we observe the compromise effect only among participants who engaged in conscious elaboration. Respondents who engaged in non-conscious processing showed no evidence of the compromise effect. The interaction between processing style and the choice set was significant.

While the results of Study 1 support our hypothesis that non-conscious processing reduces the magnitude of the compromise effect, it is important to note that we do not predict this pattern of results will hold when consumers are merely distracted prior to choice. Prior research has demonstrated non-conscious elaboration is necessarily a goal directed process: the goal to make a decision is vital for the operation of non-conscious processing during an intervening task (Bos et al. 2007). Thus we argue we will observe a reduction in the compromise effect only among participants who are initially given the goal of making a choice prior to the intervening distraction.

Study 2 was intended to test this directly while providing a conceptual replication of Study 1. Half of the participants were randomly assigned to the non-conscious processing condition and asked to form an impression of a set of products, for a choice at a later stage. Remaining participants were assigned to the mere distraction condition and instructed to simply review the set of products (no mention of future choice). All participants were then shown a set of options (ab vs. abc). This resulted in a 2 (non-conscious processing vs. mere distraction) x 2 (choice set: ab vs. abc) design. All participants then completed the intervening task from the non-conscious processing condition in Study 1, then made a choice. Consistent with our predictions, we observe the compromise effect among participants who were merely distracted. In contrast, respondents who engaged in non-conscious processing showed no evidence of the compromise effect. The interaction between processing style and the choice set was significant, meaning that non-conscious processing decreased the share of the compromise option relative to the share of the extreme option. These results rule out mere distraction as an alternate explanation for the results of Study 1.

In summary, our findings demonstrate that non-conscious processing can reduce compromise effect. We believe these findings offer both theoretical and practical insights. Not only do they extend what is currently known about potential benefits of non-conscious processing for the weighing of decision criteria, they suggest that for choices involving effortful trade-offs, a decision strategy requiring non-conscious processing may be optimal.

References

Bos, Maarten W., Ap Dijksterhuis, and Rick B. van Baaren (2007), "On the Goal-directedness of Unconscious Thought," unpublished manuscript.

Dhar, Ravi, and Itamar Simonson (2003), "The Effect of Forced Choice on Choice," *Journal of Marketing Research*, 40 (2), 146-60.

Dijksterhuis, Ap, and Zeger von Olden (2005), "On the Benefits of Thinking Unconsciously: Unconscious Thought Can Increase Post-choice Satisfaction," *Journal of Experimental Social Psychology*, 42 (5), 627-31.

Dijksterhuis, AP, Maarten W. Bos, Loran F. Nordgren, Rick B. van Baaren (2006), "On Making the Right Choice: The Deliberation-Without-Attention Effect," *Science*, 311 (5763), 1005-007.

Payne, John W., Adrianna Samper, James R. Bettman, and Mary Frances Luce (2008), "Boundary Conditions on Unconscious Thought in Complex Decision Making," *Psychological Science*, 19 (11), 1118-123.

Pocheptsova, Anastasiya, On Amir, Ravi Dhar, and Roy F. Bowmeister (2009), "Deciding Without Resources: Resource Depletion and Choice in Context," *Journal of Marketing Research*, 46 (3), 344-55.

Simonson, Itamar (1989), "Choice in Context: Tradeoff Contrast and Extremeness Aversion," *Journal of Marketing Research*, 29 (3), 281-95.

Wilson, Timothy D. (2002), *Strangers to Ourselves: Discovering the Adaptive Unconscious*, Cambridge, MA: Harvard University Press.

"The Uncompromising Heart: How the Reliance on Feelings in Decisions Reduces the Preference for Compromise Options"

Michel Tuan Pham, Columbia University, USA
Jeffrey R. Parker, Columbia University, USA

While the study of human judgment and decision making has historically emphasized the role of computational, "cognitive" processes, more recent research from various disciplines has highlighted the importance of noncomputational, affective processes in judgments and decisions (Pham 1998). This research has shown that affective evaluative judgments exhibit distinct properties, when compared to cognitive evaluative judgments (see Pham 2007 for a review). For example, in addition to being produced generally faster (Pham et al. 2001), affective evaluations have repeatedly been found to be less sensitive to the quantitative magnitude of the target (Hsee and Rottenstreich 2004), and more reference-dependent in that they tend to respond not to the focal object or outcome in isolation but in relation to other objects or outcomes (Pham 2007). The purpose of this research is to examine how reliance on feelings in decision making moderates the preference for compromise options.

Consumers tend to prefer compromise options when their preferences are uncertain and when they expect their choice to be evaluated (Simonson 1989). While this effect has been found to be robust across many product categories, it has also been found to be moderated by factors such as consumers' regulatory focuses (Mourali, et al. 2007) and the availability of a no-choice option (Dhar and Simonson 2003). Less attention, however, has been paid to the effect of different decision processes (e.g., cognitive vs. affective) on this phenomenon. Accordingly, we examine how choices based on feelings (vs. objective evaluations) affect the preference for compromise options. We propose that consumers making feelings-based choices will prefer compromise options less than consumers making choices based on objective evaluations. It is argued that extreme alternatives provide a "clear picture," leading to clear feelings towards the alternatives, facilitating a feelings-based choice, whereas compromise alternatives, which are more ambiguous, lead to more ambivalent feelings, impeding feelings-based choices. We present three studies in support of our propositions.

Study 1 investigated the strength of the compromise effect across two product categories (printers and restaurants) when choices were based on feelings versus objective evaluations. The differences between choices made using feelings and choices made using objective evaluations were fully explained to the participants. Each participant was then directly encouraged to either rely on their feelings or objective evaluations when making their upcoming choices. The participants then viewed one choice set from each product category containing alternatives described on four attributes. Two of the attributes were held constant across all alternatives while the other two varied across the alternatives. Each "extreme" option was the best on one of these attributes and the worst on the other. The "compromise" option was neither the best, nor the worst on either of the attributes. To examine the compromise effect, participants were randomly assigned to receive either two or three alternatives in each category. It was predicted and found that participants encouraged to use their feelings while choosing did not exhibit the compromise effect, while participants encouraged to use their objective evaluations demonstrated a strong compromise effect. Involvement was found not to vary across conditions.

Study 2 extended Study 1 by using a more subtle manipulation. Previous research has shown consumers are more likely to rely on their feelings to make decisions guided by consummatory motives than equivalent decisions guided by instrumental motives (Pham 1998). Building on this, participants were asked to list either ten items that were purchased "purely for pleasure" or 10 items that were purchased "purely for function." It was expected that these tasks would activate the participants' consummatory or instrumental motivations, respectively. The second task of the study asked participants to choose from the same restaurant choice sets used in Study 1. The results from Study 1 were replicated. Participants whose consummatory motivations were activated did not shift their preferences toward the compromise option, while those whose instrumental motivations were activated did. Again, involvement was found to be equivalent across conditions.

Study 3 was designed to tease apart two competing explanations for the results of the first two studies. While we propose that that the reduced preference for compromise options found with feelings-based choices is caused by a desire for a "clear picture" of each alternative, it is also possible that the use of feelings to make choices inhibits the ability to make quantitative tradeoffs of the attributes (Pham 2007). We suggest that extreme options present a clear picture (e.g., the "best price alternative" or "highest quality alternative") which will result in more valenced feelings towards the alternatives, thereby facilitating feelings-based choices. Conversely, it is expected that compromise options are more ambiguous (e.g., "it's not the best or worst on anything"), which results more ambivalent feelings that do not facilitate feelings-based judgments. To test this, we examined participants' preference for the compromise option when all attributes for all alternatives were described with point data (e.g., quality="5") versus when the extreme alternatives' attributes were described with range data (e.g., quality="between 4 and 6"). Reliance on feelings was manipulated as in Study 1. Replicating Study 1's findings, when point data was used, participants making choices based on objective evaluations preferred compromise options more than participants making feelings-based choices. Importantly, it was found that among participants making feelings-based choices the compromise option was preferred more when the extreme options were described by range data. In other words, when the "clear picture" associated with extreme options was muddied by range data, the compromise option described with point data became more attractive. Thus, the evidence suggests that the need for a "clear picture" of the alternatives may be driving the reduced preference of compromise options found when choices are made using feelings.

References

Dhar, Ravi, and Itamar Simonson (2003), "The Effect of Forced Choice on Choice," *Journal of Marketing Research*, 40 (2), 146-60.

Hsee, Christopher K., and Yuval Rottenstreich (2004), "Music, Pandas, and Muggers: On the Affective Psychology of Value," *Journal of Experimental Psychology General*, 133 (1), 23-20.

Mourali, Mehdi, Ulf Böckenhlt, and Michel Laroche (2007), "Compromise and Attraction Effects under Prevention and Promotion Motivations," *Journal of Consumer Research*, 34 (2), 234-47.

Pham, Michel Tuan (1998), "Representativeness, Relevance, and the Use of Feelings in Decision Making," *Journal of Consumer Research*, 25 (2), 144-59.

Pham, Michel Tuan (2007), "Emotion and Rationality: A Critical Review and Interpretation of Empirical Evidence," *Review of General Psychology*, 11 (2), 155-78.

Pham, Michel Tuan, Joel B. Cohen, John W. Pracejus, and G. David Hughes (2001), "Affect Monitoring and the Primacy of Feelings in Judgment," *Journal of Consumer Research*, 28 (2), 167-88.

Simonson, Itamar (1989), "Choice in Context: Tradeoff Contrast and Extremeness Aversion," *Journal of Marketing Research*, 29 (3), 281-95.

"Minding the Mindsets in Context Effects"

Uzma Khan, Stanford University USA

Meng Zhu, C.M.U., USA

Ajay Kalra, Rice University, USA

Past research has shown that individuals process information differently and form different representations of the same stimuli depending on whether it is construed at an abstract de-contextualized level or at a concrete contextualized level (Trope & Liberman 2003; Fujita et al., 2006). For example, as consumers take on a more abstract rather than concrete mindset they tend to give more weight to central and global features rather than peripheral and local features of events. In other instances individuals in abstract mindsets have been shown to categorize objects in fewer and broader categories (Liberman, Sagristano & Trope 2002), classify others using traits and stereotypes (Nussbaum et al. 2003), and perform better on creative tasks but worse on analytical problem solving (Forster et al. 2004).

Despite extant research on the impact of construal levels on information processing and judgment, no research to date has examined how different mindsets impact judgment biases arising from the context in which a decision is made (Huber, Payne & Puto 1982; Simonson 1989; Simonson & Tversky 1992). In the current research we bridge this gap and investigate the effect of abstract versus concrete mindsets on three commonly reported biases in consumer decision-making –1) a bias to choose the middle option in a choice-set (compromise effect); 2) a tendency to choose an asymmetrically dominating option (attraction effect) and 3) a tendency to be influenced not only by the tradeoffs presented in the choice-set under consideration but also by a contrast generated due to the background tradeoffs.

Construal Level Theory (CLT) proposes that in abstract mindsets individuals give more weight to central and global features of events, whereas in concrete mindsets individuals center their attention on comparative and detailed features (Trope & Liberman 2003). To the extent that a compromise effect results from a focus on the relational properties of alternatives and the accompanying choice difficulty of making compensatory comparisons (Dhar, Nowlis & Sherman 2000), we propose that in comparison to a concrete mindset, an abstract mindset will reduce the compromise effect by shifting attention to global aspects of the decision and reducing the number of trade-offs and the resulting difficulty. Similarly, we predict that an abstract mindset will decrease the background contrast effect. Since the background contrast effect is driven by the influences of relevant past alternatives, diverting attention away from detailed comparative attributes across choice sets should reduce the impact of the background set on the target set. The attraction effect, however, is largely perceptual. Since an abstract mindset draws attention to global characteristics, we predict that it will further highlight the perceptually salient asymmetric-dominant relationship and hence magnifies the attraction effect.

Five experiments show support for our propositions. Study 1 demonstrates that an abstract versus a concrete mindset induced through a temporal distance manipulation (Liberman & Trope 1998) systematically impacts share of a compromise option in a subsequent choice task. Participants were asked in between-subjects conditions to either think of a goal they wanted to achieve in a week (concrete mindset) or in a year (abstract mindset). Next, they were asked to make a choice from a three-option choice-set featuring a compromise option in the middle. As predicted, we find that compared to a concrete mindset (which was similar to the control where participants did not indicate any goal prior to making the choice) an abstract mindset leads to significantly decreased choice share of the middle option. Using a different manipulation of the construal level, Study 2 found that participants were more (less) likely to choose an asymmetrically dominating option from a choice set when they were in an abstract (concrete) mindset. Consistent with our theorizing, Study 3 shows that background contrast effects have less (more) impact on participants' judgments in an abstract (concrete) mindset.

To show support for a mechanism based on difference in local tradeoffs in abstract versus concrete mindsets, Study 4 examined participants reasons for their choice and found that participants in abstract mindsets (as compared to those in a concrete mindset) indeed made fewer direct trade-offs between attributes of the different options and were more likely to base their decision on generalize preferences. Finally, we examined participants' response latencies in abstract and concrete mindsets. The results indicate that participants in an abstract mindset not only showed decreased compromise effect they also took less time to decide. The findings are consistent with the notion that the compromise effect arises due to difficulty experienced in making hard trade-offs. We propose that this difficulty can be significantly reduced in an abstract mindset that shifts consumers focus from local trade-offs to generalized global preferences.

References

Dhar, Ravi, Stephen M. Nowlis, and Steven J. Sherman (2000), "Trying Hard or Hardly Trying: An Analysis of Context Effects in Choice," *Journal of Consumer Psychology*, 9 (4), 189-200.

Förster, Jens, Ronald S. Friedman, and Nira Liberman (2004), "Temporal Construal Effects on Abstract and Concrete Thinking: Consequences for Insight and Creative Cognition," *Journal of Personality and Social Psychology*, 87 (August), 177-89.

Fujita, Kentaro, Yaacov Trope, Nira Liberman, and Maya Levin-Sagi (2006), "Construal Levels and Self-control," *Journal of Personality and Social Psychology*, 90 (March), 351-67.

Huber, Joel, John W. Payne, and Christopher Puto (1982), "Adding Asymmetrically Dominated Alternatives: Violations of Regularity and the Similarity Hypothesis," *Journal of Consumer Research*, 9 (June), 105-14.

Liberman, Nira and Yaacov Trope (1998), "The Role of Feasibility and Desirability Considerations in Near and Distant Future Decisions: A test of Temporal Construal Theory," *Journal of Personality and Social Psychology*, 75 (July), 5-18.

Liberman, Nira, Michael D. Sagristano, and Yaacov Trope (2002), "The Effect of Temporal Distance on Level of Mental Construal," *Journal of Experimental Social Psychology*, 38 (November), 523-34.

Nussbaum, Shiri, Yaacov Trope, and Nira Liberman (2003), "Creeping Dispositionism: The Temporal Dynamics of Behavior Prediction," *Journal of Personality and Social Psychology*, 84 (March), 485-97.

Simonson, Itamar (1989), "Choice Based on Reasons: The Case of Attraction and compromise Effects," *Journal of Consumer Research*, 16 (September), 158–74.

Simonson, Itamar and Amos Tversky (1992), "Choice in Context: Tradeoff Contrast and Extremeness Aversion," *Journal of Marketing Research*, 29 (August), 281–95.

Trope, Yaacov and Nira Liberman (2003), "Temporal Construal," *Psychological Review*, 110 (July), 403–21.

SPECIAL SESSION SUMMARY

Examining Individual and Situational Drivers of Prosocial Behaviors

Andrew Kaikati, University of Minnesota, USA

SESSION OVERVIEW

Prosocial behavior is the label for a broad category of actions that are defined by society as generally beneficial to other people and to the ongoing political system. Past research in this area has sought to identify the characteristics of individuals who engage in prosocial actions, and has rightly noted that prosocial behavior is a joint product of the person and the characteristics of the situation. Despite 50 years of research on prosocial drivers, most of the findings regarding personality factors and prosocial actions are correlational in nature, and there is almost no empirical work on the relationship between important individual differences in personal values and prosocial tendencies (Dovidio et al. 2006). Gaining an understanding of individual and situational factors influencing prosocial behavior is important for charities such as United Way, for instance, which need to compete vigorously for donor dollars.

The proposed session includes three papers, each aiming to further understanding of the interplay between individual-level differences (moral identity; personal values; attachment style) and situational factors (congruity between ideology and cause; abstract/concrete mindset; relationship between donor and recipient), and their combined effects on prosocial behaviors. Taken together, the papers cover three major kinds of prosocial behavior (charitable donations, volunteering one's time to close and far others, and environmental concern) and draw upon a variety of theoretical perspectives (attachment theory, construal-level theory, action identification theory, and multiple identities), to unite under a common theme of providing insights on the effects of dispositional and situational factors driving prosocial behavior.

The Winterich, Zhang, and Mittal paper (presented by Karen Page Winterich) builds upon past research on multiple identities and donations intentions. Their research provides a new perspective for understand the roles of moral identity and moral obligation, the latter of which is influenced by political ideology. They suggest that in the case of those for whom moral identity is important, alignment between political ideology and charity (e.g., characteristics of the recipient, such as pro-life/pro-choice or privately/government managed) will affect intentions to donate, and is mediated by moral obligation towards the recipient organization. Interestingly, the authors conclude that both Democrats and Republicans can be generous, depending on their moral identity and the characteristics of the donation recipient.

The Kaikati and Torelli paper (presented by Andrew Kaikati), builds upon past value-behavior research that has exhibited mixed findings on the relationship between personal values of benevolence and universalism and helping behavior. They suggest construal-level mindset as a moderating factor, such that personal values of benevolence and universalism are more likely to influence helping behaviors toward in-group members (helping a friend move), out-group members (volunteering one's time), or the environment (recycling) when people are in an abstract (vs. concrete) mindset.

The Jeong and Liu paper (presented by Genevieve Jeong) builds on past research in the area of charitable giving. Their research focuses on the role of attachment or relationship style in influencing giving to charities that do or do not emphasize close relationships between donor and recipient. They suggest that consumers for whom attachment style is chronically (or primed as) insecure (vs. secure) are more sensitive to the nature of relationship with the receiver (e.g., ingroup; outgroup), and are more likely to give in both hypothetical and real donation situations when this relationship or potential relationship is perceived to be close vs. far.

The goal of this symposium is to foster an engaging discussion on the role of individual and situational factors in prosocial behavior by bringing together researchers who are currently approaching different aspects of the topic, from different theoretical perspectives. In particular, discussion leader Mikael Strahilevitz, who is a well-accomplished researcher in this area, will attempt to involve the audience by tying these papers together and discussing future research directions.

References

Dovidio, John F., Jane Allyn Piliavin, David A. Schroeder, and Louis A. Penner (2006), *The Social Psychology of Prosocial Behavior*, Mahwah, NJ: Lawrence Erlbaum Associates

EXTENDED ABSTRACTS

"Compassionate Conservatives AND Loving Liberals?: Political Ideology, Moral Identity, and Donation Intentions"

Karen Winterich, Texas A&M University, USA
Yinlong Zhang, University of Texas at San Antonio, USA
Vikas Mittal, Rice University, USA

Political ideology represents a person's beliefs related to the underlying goals and ideals of a political system (Grove, Remy, and Zeigler, 1974). Within the United States, the Republican party represents a more conservative political ideology and the Democratic party represents a more liberal ideology (Anderson et al. 2004; Cohrs et al. 2007; Farwell and Weiner 2000). There has been some debate as to which political ideology is the more giving and compassionate of the two (Brooks 2006; MacDonald 2004; Skitka and Tetlock 1993; Sidanius et al. 1996; Wilson and DiIulio 2004). When measured as the respondent's support for government spending on social programs, liberals are more generous (Anderson et al., 2004; Brooks, 2006; Wilson and DiIulio, 2004). In contrast, when measured as the average dollar amount donated (Brooks 2006) or as the percentage of income given to charity (MacDonald, 2004) households headed by a conservative individual are more generous. Furthermore, some experimental evidence suggests no significant differences in giving based on the respondent's political ideology (Anderson et al., 2004).

The goal of the current research is to examine factors underlying the donation intentions of both conservatives and liberals. We propose that charitable donation decisions by members of either political ideology are a function of two moral dimensions inherent in a specific decision situation–moral obligation and moral identity (Creyer et al. 2004; Dunfee et al. 1999). The first of these, moral obligation, is the extent to which a person feels he or she should or ought to act in a particular manner in a particular situation (e.g., donate to a specific cause; Schwartz 1970; Zimmerman, 1996). The level of moral obligation is likely to be higher when the donation recipient, or charity, is aligned with one's political ideology (e.g., pro-life charity for conservatives; pro-choice charity for liberals). However, we predict that this alignment alone is not sufficient to predict donation intentions. The second moral dimension we examine is a person's moral identity, defined as the extent to which moral notions, such as being fair, just, and good, are central, important, and essential to one's self-understanding (Blasi 1984). Moral identity is a general "motivating force" such that placing a higher importance on moral identity results in moral actions such as greater donations (Aquino and Reed 2002). The higher the self-importance of moral identity, the more motivated one is to "do something" about a charity.

Thus, moral identity is expected to moderate the effect of political ideology on donation intentions. Amongst those for whom moral identity is important, the alignment between political ideology and charity will impact donation intentions. In contrast, among those for whom moral identity is less important, the alignment of political ideology and charity will not impact donation intentions. These ideas are tested in three studies.

Study 1 uses an experimental test to determine differences in donation intentions to victims of terrorist attacks in Iraq. In the current political milieu, we expect conservatives (Republicans) to have a higher moral obligation toward the Iraq war. However, we expect only those with high importance of moral identity to act on their moral obligation, resulting in donation intentions to terrorist victims in Iraq. Measuring moral identity (Aquino and Reed 2002) and political affiliation, we find that Republicans have significantly higher donation intentions than Democrats when moral identity is important. For those whom moral identity is less important, donation intentions do not differ between Democrats and Republicans.

Surveying a panel of U.S. adults in study 2, we expand results of study 1 by examining donation intentions to two charities with high levels of moral obligation for liberals (pro-choice charity) or for conservatives (pro-life charity; Langer 2001; Sussman 2003). Political ideology is measured with the 6-item scale by Mehrabian (1996). Supporting our theory, we find a significant three-way interaction of moral identity, political ideology, and charity type.

Specifically, among those for whom moral identity is important, conservatives have significantly higher donation intentions to pro-life than liberals, while liberals have higher donation intentions to pro-choice charities than conservatives. There is no effect of political ideology on donation intentions among those for whom moral identity is less important. Importantly, we find that amongst those high in moral identity, moral obligation toward pro-life and pro-choice organizations mediates the differential effect of political ideology on donation intentions. One alternative explanation thus far is that political ideology influenced perceptions of deservingness to the donation recipient (Farwell and Weiner 2000; Reyna et al. 2005). This is addressed in Study 3.

A third study manipulates the process by which a charity distributes its funds (i.e., privately or through government), holding perceptions of deservingness (i.e., feeding hungry children) constant across political ideology. Among those for whom moral identity is important, liberals have lower donation intentions than conservatives when the charity is privately managed whereas conservatives have lower donation intentions than liberals when the charity is managed by the government. For individuals to whom moral identity is less important, donation intentions do not differ between conservatives and liberals, regardless of how the charity is managed. Again, moral obligation fully mediated the effect of moral identity and political ideology on donation intentions.

While both public opinion surveys (Smiley 2004; Strom 2005) and academic studies (Farwell and Weiner 2000) show a widespread stereotype that liberals are more charitable than conservatives, our results take a situated perspective arguing that the question should no longer be who donates more, but rather under what conditions will one donate more to a specific charity. Examining donation intentions to various charities (terrorism victims in Iraq; pro-life/pro-choice; needy children), we find that the extent to which conservatives and liberals are generous depends on their moral identity, the donation recipient, and even fund management. We also note that religion was measured in all studies, but did not influence the pattern of results. This research not only contributes to the theoretical understanding of the role of multiple identities on decisions such as charitable giving, but it also has substantive implications for fundraising and for public policies regarding the role of political affiliation in charitable behavior.

References

Anderson, Lisa R., Jennifer M. Mellor, and Jeffrey Milyo (2004), "Do Liberals Play Nice? The Effects of Party and Political Ideology in Public Goods and Trust Games," Working Papers 07, Department of Economics, College of William and Mary.

Aquino, Karl and Americus Reed (2002), "The Self-importance of Moral Identity," *Journal of Personality and Social Psychology*, 83 (December), 1423-1440.

Blasi, Augusto (1984), "Moral Identity: Its Role in Moral Functioning," in *Morality, Moral Behavior and Moral Development*, William Kurtines and Jacob Gewirtz, ed. New York: Wiley, 128-39.

Brooks, Arthur C. (2006), *Who Really Cares*, New York: Basic Books.

Cohrs, J. Christopher, Jürgen Maes, Barbara Moschner and Sven Kielmann (2007), "Determinants of Human Rights Attitudes and Behavior: A Comparison and Integration of Psychological Perspectives," *Political Psychology*, 28 (August), 441–469.

Creyer, Elizabeth H., William T. Ross, and John Kozup (2004), "Consumer Response to a Prosocial Marketing Initiative: The Case of Discount Stores and Gun Sales," *Journal of Applied Social Psychology*, 34 (January), 206-221.

Dunfee, Thomas J., Craig N. Smith, and William T. Ross (1999), "Social Contracts and Marketing Ethics," *Journal of Marketing*, 63 (July), 13-32.

Farwell, Lisa and Bernard Weiner (2000), "Bleeding hearts and the heartless: Popular perceptions of liberal and conservative ideologies," *Personality and Social Psychology Bulletin*, 26 (7), 845–852.

Grove, D. John, Richard C. Remy, and L. Harmon Zeigler (1974), "The Effects of Political Ideology and Educational Climates On Student Dissent," *American Politics Research*, 2 (3), 259-275.

Langer, Gary (2001), "Public backs stem cell research," (accessed November 15, 2007), [available at http://www.abcnews.go.com/sections/politics/DailyNews/poll010626.html].

MacDonald, G. Jeffrey (2004), "Who are the Nation's 'Cheapstates'? Try the Blue Ones," Christian Science Monitor,(December 22), [available at http://www.cfsv.org/communitysurvey/results.html].

Mehrabian, Albert (1996), "Relations among political attitudes, personality, and psychopathology assessed with new measures of libertarianism and conservatism," *Basic and Applied Social Psychology*, 18 (4), 469–491.

Reyna, Christine, P. J. Henry, William Korfmacher and Amanda Tucker (2005), "Examining the Principles in Principled Conservatism: The Role of Responsibility Stereotypes as Cues for Deservingness in Racial Policy Decisions," *Journal of Personality and Social Psychology*, 90 (1), 109-128.

Schwartz, Shalom H. (1970), "Elicitation of moral obligation and self-sacrificing behavior: An experimental study of volunteering to be a bone marrow donor," *Journal of Personality and Social Psychology*, 15 (4), 283-293.

Skitka, Linda J. and Philip E. Tetlock (1993), "Providing public assistance: Cognitive and motivational processes underlying liberal and conservative policy preferences," *Journal of Personality and Social Psychology*, 65 (6), 1205-1223.

Sidanius, Jim, Felicia Pratto and Laurence Bobo (1996), "Racism, Conservatism, Affirmative Action, and Intellectual Sophistication: A Matter of Principled Conservatism or Group Dominance?" *Journal of Personality and Social Psychology*, 70 (3), 476–490.

Smiley, Jane (2004), "The Unteachable Ignorance of the Red States," (accessed November 15, 2007), [available at http://www.slate.com/id/2109218/].

Strom, Stephanie (2005), "What is charity?" *New York Times*, (November 14), F1.

Sussman, Dalia (2003), "Conditional support poll: Thirty years after Roe Vs. Wade, American support is conditional," (accessed November 7, 2007), [available at http://www.abcnews.go.com/sections/us/DailyNews/abortion_poll030122.html].

Wilson, James Q. and John DiIulio Jr. (2004), *American Political Institutions and Policies* (9th ed.), Boston: Houghton-Mifflin.

Zimmerman, Michael J. (1996), *The Concept of Moral Obligation*, New York: Cambridge.

"When Do Personal Values Predict Helping Behaviors? It's All in the Mindset"

Andrew Kaikati, University of Minnesota, USA
Carlos Torelli, University of Minnesota, USA

Personal values are motivational constructs involving the beliefs that people hold about desirable goals that can be applied across contexts and time (Bardi and Schwartz 2003). For instance, benevolent values are associated with the abstract goal of enhancing the welfare of in-group members with whom one is in frequent personal contact, such as friends, and universalism values are associated with protecting the welfare of out-group members or protecting the environment.

There are inconsistencies in the current literature about whether and when values guide behaviors. The main objective of the current research is to try to identify a factor that affects in the strength of the value-behavior relationship. Building upon the tenets of action identification theory (Vallacher and Wegner 1987), we argue that mindsets that facilitate defining a situation in terms of one's relevant values will affect whether behavior reflects one's values. We predict that an abstract (vs. concrete) mindset should facilitate defining a subsequent, unrelated action in terms of one's relevant values, because values are high-level constructs that are associated with abstract goals. This will consequently affect whether intentions to engage in actions are a reflection of values. Thus, we expect that the level of abstraction at which events are construed is an important moderator of the value-behavior relationship.

Across three studies, we measured the importance of values (either benevolence or universalism) at the individual level (using Schwartz's Value Survey, Schwartz 1992), where participants rate the importance of values as guiding principles in their lives (-1=opposed to my principles; 7=of extreme importance). Then following several filler tasks, we primed either an abstract or concrete mindset using manipulations in which participants were instructed to think of the "why" (abstract) or the "how" (concrete) aspects of a situation. Finally, we presented participants with real or hypothetical situations and collected measures of helping intentions or behaviors towards ingroups, outgroups, and the environment, to examine the effect of mindset on the strength of the value-behavior relation.

Study 1 tests the relationship between measured benevolence values (i.e., preservation and enhancement of the welfare of people with whom one is in frequent personal contact) and the intention to help an in-group member, a friend. Participants were instructed to imagine themselves in a situation commonly faced by students, helping a friend move to a new apartment, and then to report their intention to help the friend move. Results indicated that participants primed to think abstractly reported intentions to help a friend move that were consistent with their benevolence values, but participants primed to think concretely and those in a control condition did not.

In Study 2, we extend these findings to a different value type (universalism instead of benevolence) and measure actual behavior instead of behavioral intentions. Study 2 tests the relationship between measured universalism values (i.e., understanding, appreciation, tolerance, and protection for the welfare of all people and of nature) and signing-up to volunteer to help out-group members. At the end of the session, the experimenter introduced participants to an unrelated volunteer program involving assistance to refugee immigrants from East Africa with their reading and writing skills in English. The total number of minutes signed up to volunteer was the measure of behavior. Results confirmed our predictions that participants primed to think abstractly behaved in accordance with their universalism values in signing up to help the out-group, whereas participants primed to think concretely did not.

Study 3 explores the mechanism underlying the effect of mindset activation on the value-behavior relationship, in the context of the environmentally-friendly behavior of recycling a battery. We propose that a concrete mindset interferes with value expression by directing attention to contextual details and away from the relevant values in the situation. We expect that values will predict behavioral intentions regardless of the mindset prime when only a broad overview of the situation as related to relevant values is provided. Participants read a description of a hypothetical situation regarding the recycling of an old cell phone battery, which either included a lot of contextual information (e.g., contained several specific details) or simply described an overview of the situation as related to values. Participants rated their intention to perform the recycling behavior. Results indicate that participants primed to think abstractly reported recycling intentions that were consistent with their universalism values; however, participants in the concrete mindset condition reported intentions dissociated from their universalism values only when they were given the opportunity to construe the situation on factors other than relevant values (e.g., contextual details). These findings support our predictions that a concrete mindset interferes with defining a situation in terms of relevant values, and consequently with the expression of these values, by directing attention to contextual aspects of the situation.

In combination, results from the three experiments provide evidence for the moderating role of abstract and concrete mindsets on the strength of the value-behavior relationship. We find that personally important values predict helping behaviors and intentions after individuals are primed with an abstract (and not a concrete) mindset. We tested this in the context of multiple values and helping behaviors. These included benevolence values (context: helping a friend move) and universalism values (contexts: volunteering to help outgroup members; recycling).

References

Bardi, Anat and Shalom H. Schwartz (2003), "Values and Behavior: Strength and Structure of Relations," *Personality and Social Psychology Bulletin*, 29, 1207-20.

Schwartz, Shalom H. (1992), "Universals in the Content and Structure of Values: Theoretical Advances and Empirical Tests in 20 Countries," In M. P. Zanna (Ed.), *Advances in Experimental Social Psychology* (Vol. 25, 1-65), San Diego, CA: Academic Press.

Vallacher, Robin R. and Daniel M. Wegner (1987), "Levels of Personal Agency: Individual Variation in Action Identification," *Journal of Personality and Social Psychology*, 57, 660-71.

"When to Give? Charitable Giving as Social Relationship"

Hyewook Genevieve Jeong, UCLA, USA
Wendy Liu, UCLA, USA

Charitable giving is one of the fastest growing industries in the United States. As a result of the growth of the giving industry, consumers are exposed to an ever wider variety of charitable giving opportunities and ways to give. Among the numerous ways of giving, one of the fastest-growing methods is a charity program that emphasizes close relationships between the donor and the recipient (e.g., sponsoring one particular child in need throughout his/her development, giving to one's alma matter or church). Such emphasis on closer relationships contrasts with the other end of the relationship spectrum whereby the donor has scant ties to the recipient, in effect giving to a complete stranger (who will remain a stranger).An interesting question thus arises: Does proposing a close relationship with the recipient help to raise money for a non-profit organization? This research sheds light on when people engage in charitable giving by examining the social motivation underlying giving. In particular, we focus on giving as a form of social relationship. Drawing on attachment theory, we find that people with secure (low avoidance and low anxiety) vs. insecure (high avoidance and anxiety) relationship styles engage in giving behavior differently. Specifically, insecure individuals give more when the relationship between them and the receiver of help is close, whereas secure individuals are less sensitive to the nature of relationship with the receiver. Three studies demonstrate this effect using both chronic measures of individual relationship style and situational priming of security, and with hypothetical as well as real dollar decisions.

Attachment theory (Mikulincer and Shaver 2005) suggests that people with insecure attachment styles (high anxiety and high avoidance) have a desire for intimate interpersonal relationship. However, they are chronically concerned about acceptance and rejection from others. Therefore, we propose that insecure people would see giving as a means to establish a secure social relationship, and the promise of such a relationship motivates giving. Thus insecure individuals are more likely to donate when they perceive an interpersonal relationship with the beneficiary, than when the donation does not imply a relationship. On the other hand, people with secure attachment styles are not motivated by relationships when deciding whether to give. Therefore, they give with equal likelihood whether they have close or aloof relationship ties to the receiver.

Among the variety of ways of giving to people in need, one of the fastest growing methods is a sponsorship program (Giving USA Foundation 2007) which links a sponsor with a specific person in need on a relatively long-term basis. In Study 1 and 2, we examine the implication of such a sponsorship relationship.

Study 1 studies the basic effect of attachment style on charitable donation. All participants read a charity request letter. In the relationship condition, the charity request describes the sponsorship program which provides the continuous interpersonal interaction between the sponsor and a beneficiary. In the control condition, there is no interpersonal interaction with the receiver of help. The results show that people with insecure attachment donate more when the charity included the interpersonal relationship compared to when it did not (40% vs. 8.7%, p<.002). However, those with secure attachment do not show this differentiation (19.2 % vs. 24.1 %, p>.5).

Study 2 primes attachment security vs. insecurity situationally. In the attachment security priming condition, participants are told to imagine the situation of being loved by their romantic partner. In the attachment insecurity priming condition, participants are asked to imagine being abandoned by their romantic partner. Female participants in the insecurity condition donate more when the charity involved interpersonal relationship, compared to when it did not (70% vs. 35%, p<.04). Female participants in the secure condition, and male participants, do not show this pattern. (Presumably males react differently to romantic abandonment; e.g., rather than insecurity, they may feel anger.)

Study 3 attempts to generalize the results to real donations, and to a different operationalization of relationship. UCLA undergraduate students receive $2 as compensation for completing a survey. However, during the survey, they are also informed the opportunity to donate their compensation to a children's hospital. The key manipulation iss whether there is a relationship tie with the beneficiary (in-group: UCLA Children's Hospital vs. out-group: University of Michigan Children's Hospital). It is found that insecure people donate to the ingroup but not the outgroup (56.3% vs. 28.2%, p<.04), whereas secure people make no distinction between ingroup and outgroup (54.8% vs. 48.6 %, p>.5).

Although individual giving is always the largest single source of donation to charitable organizations (Giving USA Foundation 2007), previous studies have not extensively researched the individual differences in charitable giving behavior. Our findings contribute to the understanding of why different people donate to different causes, and have important implications for studies of charity decisions and helping behavior. The current study has also important practical implication which consumers like which types of donations. Charitable support by individual is critical to the functioning of many non-profit organizations. Thus, if marketers know certain types of consumers like specific types of donations, they can focus on target market. Our results suggest that insecure consumers donate more when there is a relationship between donor and beneficiary, while secure consumers do not care the relationship with beneficiary. Therefore, fundraising by charity organizations may be improved by allowing for a personal relationship between donor and beneficiary. Moreover, based on study 2 in which attachment security was primed, marketers may also apply relationship priming techniques to their advertisement or charity request letters in an effort to increase giving.

References

American Association of Fundraising Counsel (2007), *Giving USA*, Glenview, IL: American Association of Fundraising Counsel.

Mikulincer, Mario and Phillip R. Shaver (2005), "Attachment Security, Compassion, and Altruism," *Current Directions in Psychological Science*, 14 (1), 34–38.

Special Session Summary

Let the Games Begin: Evaluating Fun Experiences

Sayantani Mukherjee, California State University, Long Beach, USA

SESSION OVERVIEW

Consumers experience and seek fun in a variety of consumption situations, from playing videogames (Koster 2002) and sky diving (Celsi, Rose and Leigh 1993) to gambling (Hope and Havir 2002) and river rafting (Arnould and Price 1993). Fun is a key element of hedonic (Babin, Darden and Griffin 1994), playful (Grayson 1999; Kozinets et al. 2004) and experiential (Holbrook and Hirschman 1982) consumption. Consequently, fun has emerged as an important goal in product development (Norman 2004) and marketing communications (Morgan and Rao 2003).

Emerging research suggests that fun is a positive and complex experience (Celsi et al. 1993) that involves challenge (Celsi et al. 1993), goals (Draper 1999), and learning (Bandura 1997). However, very little is known about factors that influence consumer evaluations of fun consumption experiences. The three papers involved in this symposium reveal the complex nature of fun and examines how this complexity interplays with consumers' decisions regarding fun experiences.

The first paper by Mukherjee, Lau-Gesk, and Kramer investigates how consumers' episodic memories of fun experienced during a recent videogame play episode influence their global evaluations of the episode. Drawing upon research on episodic reports of past emotional experiences, they develop a relationship between moments of fun that consumers retrieve from a recent videogame play episode and their global evaluations of the episode. The second paper by Namkoong and Raghunathan examines consumers' risk seeking behavior in fun experiences. They argue that consumers' risk-seeking tendencies depend on the kind of goals that are salient in fun experiences. The third paper by Anthony and Cowley suggests that frequent (infrequent) gamblers focus on future (current) outcomes in a gambling experience. These gamblers generate mixed counterfactuals which fuels their pursuit of future better opportunities.

Two themes emerge from the current collection of works. First, the papers identify the implications of goals in fun experiences. Mukherjee, Lau-Gesk, and Kramer find that consumers' global evaluations of recent videogame episodes depend on the intensity of fun that consumers recall having experienced at the end moment of the episode. They show that final moments are memorable because they are not only accessible but also meaningful. Final moments in the current context, allow people to assess whether they have accomplished goals related to the videogame experience. These goals involve gaining levels, securing weapons, killing monsters and getting special skills and often usurp the goal of winning the game. Namkoong and Raghunathan illuminate the role of goals further, and argue that promotion (vs. prevention) oriented consumers are more risk-seeking in fun experiences. This is because, in fun contexts, consumers are more concerned about a maximal goal. When having fun, people want to enhance the chance of achieving an ideal- "hope to achieve"—goal. Relatedly, Anthony and Cowley demonstrate that when gamblers are focused on a promotion goal in the future (e.g. promoting a better situation later), they generate mixed counterfactuals (i.e. both upward and downward counterfactual) and are more willing to take increased risk in future gambles

The second theme that arises is the role of temporal focus in fun experiences. Mukherjee, Lau-Gesk, and Kramer demonstrate how consumers' episodic memories of "fun" moments in recent videogame episodes impact global evaluations of the episode. Hence, the emphasis in their paper is on past or recalled fun experiences. Namkoong and Raghunathan's paper focus on consumers' decisions and risk-seeing tendencies in fun consumption experiences that are made in the context of possible future outcomes. Complementing this is Anthony and Cowley's paper, which demonstrates that temporal focus impacts consumers' emotional experiences in gambling situations. Frequent (infrequent) gamblers focus on future (current) outcomes which cause them to have a weakened emotional reaction to gambling outcomes.

Fun experiences are growing in importance among consumers and marketers. This symposium is expected to have significant theoretical and practical implications. It is also expected to generate discussion among a wide audience, including researchers in the areas of hedonic psychology, experiential, hedonic and playful consumption, judgment and decision making, temporal issues, affect and emotion, and consumer behavior in general. The symposium is comprised of papers that are well grounded in theory and each with several completed studies.

Rebecca Ratner will synthesize the three papers. Ratner's expertise in the area of consumer decision-making and hedonic experiences is particularly valuable in providing insights into this "fun" and exciting stream of research.

References

Arnould, Eric J. and Linda L. Price (1993), "River Magic: Extraordinary Experience and the Extended Service Encounter," *Journal of Consumer Research*, 20 (June), 24-45.

Babin, Barry J., William R. Darden, and Mitch Griffin (1994), "Work and/or Fun: Measuring Hedonic and Utilitarian Shopping Value," *Journal of Consumer Research*, 20 (4), 644-56.

Bandura, Albert (1997), *Self-Efficacy: The Exercise of Control*, New York, NY: Worth Publishers.

Celsi, Richard L., Randall L. Rose, and Thomas W. Leigh (1993), "An Exploration of High-Risk Leisure Consumption through Skydiving," *Journal of Consumer Research*, 20 (June), 1-23.

Draper, Stephen W. (1999) "Analysing Fun as a Candidate Software Requirement," *Personal and Ubiquitous Computing*, 3 (3), 117-22.

Grayson, Kent (1999),"The Dangers and Opportunities of Playful Consumption," in *Consumer Value, A Framework for Analysis and Research*, ed. Morris B. Holbrook, New York, NY: Routledge.

Holbrook, Morris B. and Elizabeth C. Hirschman (1982), "The Experiential Aspects of Consumption: Consumer Fantasies, Feelings, and Fun," *Journal of Consumer Research*, 9 (September), 132-40.

Hope, Janet and Linda Havir (2002), "You Bet They are Having Fun: Older Americans and Casino Gambling," *Journal of Aging Studies*, 16 (2), 177-97.

Koster, Raph (2004), *A Theory of Fun for Game Design*, New York, NY: Ingram.

Kozinets, Robert V., John F. Sherry, Jr., Diana Storm, Adam Duhachek, Krittinee Nuttavuthisit, and Benét DeBerry-Spence, (2004), "Ludic Agency and Retail Spectacle," *Journal of Consumer Research*, 31 (December), 658-72 .

Morgan, Ivor and Jay Rao (2003), "Making Routine Customer Experiences Fun," *Sloan Management Review*, 45 (1), 93-5.

Norman, Donald A (2004), *Emotional Design: Why We Love (or Hate) Everyday Things*, Basic Books.

EXTENDED ABSTRACTS

"What Makes Videogame Experiences Fun?"

Sayantani Mukherjee, California State University, Long Beach, USA

Loraine Lau-Gesk, University of California at Irvine, USA

Thomas Kramer, Baruch College, CUNY, USA

This research seeks to understand how consumers' episodic memories of fun experienced during a recent consumption episode influence their global evaluations of the episode. Specifically, within the context of videogames, we examine how consumers construct global evaluations based on the specific moments of fun that they retrieve from a recent videogame play episode.

Previous research suggests that when people report on past emotional experiences, they rely on their episodic memory of specific moments of the episode for information (Aaker, Drolet and Griffin 2008; Robinson and Clore 2002). More memorable or distinct moments have a disproportionately greater influence on the recall of the associated affect because of their greater accessibility (Kahneman 1999). Therefore, when reconstructing the fun at various moments during the recent videogame episode, players' attention is likely to be drawn to particularly memorable moments, which will then be used to evaluate the overall experience. We expect that the most memorable moments during the videogame episode are the final ones–not just because of their relatively greater accessibility, but because of their greater personal meaningfulness and relevance (Fredrickson 2000). Specifically, people experience fun when working towards and achieving a specific goal (Draper 1999). Recent work suggests that the outcome of goal-driven experiences aligns well with end moments (Ariely and Carmon 2000) and carries personal meanings (Fredrickson 2000). End moments represent the culmination of the experience and coincide with the time at which one assesses whether goals are met (Fredrickson 2000). In videogames, goals can include gaining levels, securing weapons, killing monsters, acquiring special skills, and exploring difficult zones, which may often be more important than winning the game (Taylor 2006). Therefore, given that affect associated with memorable moments is more likely to be recalled, and that end moments tend to be the most memorable in the current context, fun associated with the end of the videogame experience may be more influential than other moments in players' retrospective evaluations. This explanation is aligned with Feldman and Lynch's (1988) accessibility-diagnosticity framework, which would predict that the likelihood that end moments of fun are used as input into global evaluations of a consumption episode is a positive function of the accessibility of the end-moment fun, a positive function of the diagnosticity of end-moment fun, a negative function of the accessibility of alternate inputs, and a negative function of the diagnosticity of the accessible alternate inputs (Feldman and Lynch 1988). In the current context, this would suggest that accessible end moments of fun should be used as input into global evaluations only to the extent that they are diagnostic, that is, meaningful.

We start to explore these issues in the first field study using individual depth interviews (Moore and Lutz 2000) with videogame players in an arcade. Depth interviews involved engaging players in open-ended dialogs about the fun they experienced in a recent videogame episode. These dialogs reveal that players exclusively recall the fun experienced at the end moment of the episode. Further, the dialogs suggest that end moments are memorable not because they are merely accessible or perceptually salient; rather end moments are memorable because these moments are personally meaningful.

Study 2 investigates the impact of recalled end moments of fun on global evaluations of a recent videogame episode through a field experiment. A confederate posing as an employee randomly approached patrons entering the arcade. Participants played a videogame of their choice. Participants were then asked to provide details associated with their recent videogame play and to report the fun they experienced during the episode. Participants also provided their global evaluations of the recent episode. Results indicate that players' global evaluations do not depend on the average of the recalled fun moments experienced during the entire game, the recalled peak moments of fun or on the outcome of the game (i.e., win-lose). Rather, it is the recalled end moment of fun that predicts consumers' global evaluations. Global evaluations were higher as the intensity of fun at the end of the videogame experience increased.

Study 3 seeks to tease apart the accessibility versus meaningfulness explanations by manipulating the meaningfulness of the end moments. If end moments are more memorable because they are meaningful, and hence used as input into global evaluations, then making them less meaningful should reduce or eliminate the impact of the end-moment fun, despite its accessibility. Similar to study 2, a field experiment was conducted in an arcade. All participants played videogames of their choice. However, in this study we included repetition of the game as a moderator, which constituted the meaningfulness manipulation. In particular, when players repeat a game, the end moment does not represent the culmination of the game and loses meaningfulness. Hence, under repetition, the impact of recalled end moments of fun on global evaluations should be lower. As predicted, the results of the third field experiment indicate that recalled end moments of fun impacts global evaluations only in the condition when players do not repeat a game.

This research contributes to the areas of affect and consumer decision-making, especially in the domain of episodic memories of emotional experiences. It also has implications for designing and advertising in "fun" videogames.

References

Aaker, Jennifer, Aimee Drolet, and Dale Griffin (2008), "Recalling Mixed Emotions," *Journal of Consumer Research*, 35 (August), 268-78.

Ariely, Dan and Ziv Carmon (2000), "Gestalt Characteristics of Experiences: The Defining Features of Summarized Events," *Journal of Behavioral Decision Making*, 13 (2), 191-201.

Draper, Stephen W. (1999) "Analysing Fun as a Candidate Software Requirement," *Personal and Ubiquitous Computing*, 3 (3), 117-22.

Feldman, Jack M. and John G. Lynch Jr. (1988), "Self-Generated Validity and Other Effects of Measurement on Belief, Attitude, Intention, and Behavior," *Journal of Applied Psychology*, 73 (August), 421-35

Fredrickson, Barbara L. (2000), "Extracting Meaning from Past Affective Experiences: The Importance of Peaks, Ends, and Specific Emotions," *Cognition and Emotion*, 14 (4), 577-606.

Kahneman, Daniel (1999), "Objective Happiness," in *Well-Being*, ed. D. Kahneman, E. Diener, and N. Schwarz, NY: Russell Sage.

Moore, Elizabeth S. and Richard J. Lutz (2000), "Children, Advertising, and Product Experiences: A Multi-Method Inquiry," *Journal of Consumer Research*, 27 (June), 31-48.

Robinson, Michael D. and Gerald L. Clore (2002), "Episodic and Semantic Knowledge in Emotional Self Report: Evidence for Two Judgment Processes," *Journal of Personality and Social Psychology*, 83 (July), 198–215.

Taylor, T. L. (2006), *Play between Worlds: Exploring Online Game Culture*, Cambridge, MA: MIT Press.

"Risk-Seeking in Utilitarian vs. Hedonic Domain: Implications for the Prospect Theory Value Function"

Jae-Eun Namkoong, University of Texas at Austin, USA
Raj Raghunathan, University of Texas at Austin, USA

How do people value monetary and other pay-offs in risky contexts, for example, how do they value a sure bet of $10 versus a 50% chance of winning $25 and a 50% chance of winning nothing? The Prospect Theory value function (cf. Kahneman and Tversky 1979) provides perhaps the most parsimonious and generalizable answer to this type of question. However, although this value function is capable of both predicting and explaining a multitude of phenomena (including mental accounting effects [Thaler 1985], loss aversion [Arkes and Blumer 1985], etc.), it actually runs contrary to some other robust real-world phenomena—like the popularity of insurance and lotteries. It is in attempting to explain these phenomena that Kahneman and Tversky (1979) proposed that people assign a subjectively higher probability to very low-probability events, like the probability that one's house will burn down, or the probability that they will win a lottery.

But what if—in addition to the (subjective) inflation of low-probabilities—there is another mechanism that boosts the popularity of insurance and lotteries? We examine such a possibility in this research. Specifically, we propose that people are more risk-averse in contexts where a utilitarian (vs. hedonic) goal is more salient and, conversely, they are more risk-seeking when a hedonic (vs. utilitarian) goal is more salient. Our proposition is based on the idea that utilitarian and hedonic contexts evoke "minimal" and "maximal" goals (Idson et al. 2000). Specifically, in contexts where a utilitarian (vs. hedonic) goal is more salient, we propose that people are more concerned about meeting a minimum "cut off" level (Chitturi et al. 2007; see also Idson et al. 2000), whereas they are more concerned about enhancing the chance of achieving an ideal—"hope to achieve"—goal in hedonic contexts. As a result, people spend on insurance to make sure that even the "worst-case scenario" (which is the occurrence of the negative event for which they are seeking insurance) is acceptable and, likewise, they spend on lotteries to increase their chances of experiencing the "best case scenario" (winning the lottery).

In order to test this hypothesis in a monetary context, we used decision making scenarios, all of which involved money–choosing between two different cell phone plans, restaurants, and lottery options–and framed them to be either hedonic or utilitarian (e.g. choosing a monthly cell phone plan either for entertainment or business use). The two options they could choose from varied in terms of both payoffs and risk (probabilities), but were identical across conditions. Specifically, participants chose between a risky (but more attractive) option and a safe (but less attractive) option. Results showed that people were more willing take the chance of obtaining a higher (vs. lower) payoff, when the situation-frame was hedonic (vs. utilitarian). We found a significant pattern consistent with our predictions in all three scenarios–cell phone plan ($F_{(1,158)}$=5.314, p=.022), restaurant ($F_{(1,159)}$=18.948, p<.0005), and lottery ($F_{(1,159)}$=6.573, p=.011). This is after we controlled for affect in all scenarios and, in addition, for monthly cell phone usage in the cell phone scenario.

In our second study, we used one of the scenarios from study 1 (lottery), in an attempt to replicate our results, with a goal of providing evidence for the underlying mechanism for our effects. Since we hypothesized that the underlying mechanism is the activation of minimal vs. maximal goal, we measured participants' chronic level of regulatory focus (Lockwood, Jordan, and Kunda 2002) to examine its role in risk-seeking tendency[1]. Our results confirmed that hedonic (vs. utilitarian) scenario renders more risk-seeking ($F_{(1,65)}$=6.71, p=.012), and also, that chronically promotion (vs. prevention) oriented participants sought more risky options ($F_{(1,65)}$=4.644, p=.035). Risk-aversion in the utilitarian scenario is expected to be prevalent, because people (regardless of their individual characteristics) tend to make sure that they meet a minimum level of functionality first, a tendency also referred to as the principle of precedence (see Chitturi et al. 2007). Hence, the difference between chronically promotion vs. prevention people is likely to be attenuated in the utilitarian (vs. hedonic) scenario, which is exactly what we found. Consistent with the idea that risk-aversion is more likely to be prevalent in utilitarian scenarios than risk-taking is in hedonic ones, a significant simple effect of chronic regulatory focus emerged in the hedonic scenario ($F_{(1,29)}$=5.637, p=.024), but not in the utilitarian scenario ($F_{(1, 34)}$=.434, p=.515). In study 3 (proposed), we aim to examine the effect of framing an identical gamble as either insurance or lottery. We expect to find more risk-seeking tendency in the context of lottery vs. when the same "lottery" is used as for insurance. This is a meaningful step as it explains some of the behaviors that are not fully explained by existing behavioral decision theories (e.g. being risk-seeking or risk-averse over large gains or losses with extremely small probabilities).

Through a series of experiments, we demonstrate the effect of framing a situation as hedonic vs. utilitarian on risk-seeking tendency, and also show its relationship with one's chronic level of regulatory focus. Further, we attempt to make theoretical contributions by providing a better picture to some of the unresolved questions in decision making literature which is why people engage in gambling and purchase insurance.

References

Arkes, Hal R. and Catherine Blumer (1985), "The Psychology of Sunk Cost," *Organizational Behavior and Human Decision Processes*, 35 (February), 124–140.

Chitturi, Ravindra, Rajagopal Raghunathan, and Vijay Mahajan (2007), "Form Versus Function: How the Intensities of Specific Emotions Evoked in Functional Versus Hedonic Trade-Offs Mediate Product Preferences," *Journal of Marketing Research*, 44 (November), 702–714.

Escalas, Jennifer Edson and James R. Bettman (2005), "Self-Construal, Reference Groups, and Brand Meaning," *Journal of Consumer Research*, 32 (December), 378–89.

---

[1]Participants were divided into high vs. low groups in each subscale of regulatory focus (promotion and prevention) through median split. Since we were interested in the independent role promotion vs. prevention on risk-taking, we only used the data from subjects who were high in one subscale, and low in the other. Those who were both high and both low in the two subscales were eliminated from the analysis, reducing the number of our subjects from 162 to 71 (see Escalas and Bettman 2005 for similar method).

Idson, Lorraine C., Nira Liberman, and E. Tory Higgins (2000), "Distinguishing Gains for Nonlosses and Losses from Nongains: A Regulatory Focus Perspective on Hedonic Intensity," *Journal of Experimental Social Psychology*, 36 (3), 252–74.

Kahneman, Daniel and Amos Tversky (1979), "Prospect Theory: An Analysis of Decision under Risk," *Econometrica*, 47 (March), 363–391.

Lockwood, Penelope, Christian H. Jordan, and Ziva Kunda (2002), "Motivation by Positive or Negative Role Models: Regulatory Focus Determines Who Will Best Inspire Us," *Journal of Personality and Social Psychology*, 83 (October), 854–64.

Thaler, Richard (1985), "Mental Accounting and Consumer Choice," *Marketing Science*, 4 (Summer), 199–214.

"Chasing Rainbows: Strategies for Promoting Future Better Outcomes"

Christina I. Anthony, University of Sydney, Australia
Elizabeth Cowley, University of Sydney, Australia

Research on counterfactual thinking demonstrates that thinking about how an outcome "could have been better" (i.e. generating Upward Counterfactual Thoughts; UCTs) allows one to prepare for future better outcomes (Epstude and Roese 2008; Markman et al. 1993; Markman, McMullen, and Elizaga 2008; Roese 1994) whereas thinking about how an outcome "could have been worse" (i.e. generating Downward Counterfactual Thoughts; DCTs) allows one to savour a good outcome or mood repair one's feelings following a bad outcome (McMullen 1997; McMullen and Markman 2000; Medvec, Madey, and Gilovich 1995; Roese and Hur 1997; White and Lehman 2005). According to this view, contrastive UCTs and DCTs, by virtue of the affect they evoke (UCTs evoke negative affect, DCTs evoke positive affect) are believed to serve distinct and competing motivations(Gleicher et al. 1995; Markman et al. 1993; Markman et al. 2008); UCTs serve a preparatory function and DCTs serve an affect regulation function. However, we propose that under certain conditions, DCTs will support the preparatory function of UCTs, given the value of the positive affect they provide. Specifically, we argue that UCTs provide the necessary cognitive information that opportunities for better outcomes exist (Epstude and Roese 2008), and that contrastive DCTs, by virtue of the positive affect they evoke, may fuel the pursuit and acquisition of future better opportunities (Carroll and Shepperd 2009). We predict that frequent gamblers are motivated to promote a good outcome later and accordingly, will strategically generate mixed counterfactuals (both UCTs and DCTs). Whereas frequent gamblers are motivated by good outcomes in the future and the anticipation of future pleasure, we propose that infrequent gamblers are motivated to enjoy a good outcome now. Therefore the presence of a win should result in enjoyment (pure DCTs), and the absence of a win (a loss) should cause disappointment (pure UCTs). We investigated this phenomenon in three studies; one in the field and two in the lab.

In study 1, real gamblers played 300 gambles on a simulated slot machine and either won or lost the game. As predicted, we found that infrequent gamblers generate pure counterfactuals (disappointing UCTs following a loss, pleasurable DCTs following a win). Alternatively, frequent gamblers generate mixed counterfactual thoughts (both UCTs and DCTs).

In study 2, we test our contention that mixed counterfactuals are generated when anticipating future pleasurable outcomes. Undergraduate students played the game in the lab and either won or lost. We then manipulated participants temporal focus (now, future) and regulatory focus (promote good outcome; prevent bad outcome) by asking participants to recall times in their life when they saved (spent) money to promote (prevent) a good (bad) situation now (later). As expected, when participants focused on promoting a better situation later they generated mixed counterfactuals. They were also more willing to take increased risk in a subsequent game. Further, we rule out the alternative explanation that mixed counterfactuals cause strategic emotional regulation. We do not find evidence of mixed counterfactuals when people were focused on preventing a bad situation later. This rules out the possibility that participants were attempting to mood repair or strategically numb their feelings in order to minimise the impact of affective interference on future goal pursuit. Thus, it appears that DCTs and the positive affect they provide are used to motivationally energise the pursuit of future better outcomes that UCTs have uncovered.

Finally, in study 3 we explore the emotion dilution found in studies 1 and 2. Again participants played the same simulated poker machine game and either won or lost credits. Counterfactual type (mixed vs. pure) and counterfactual order (better first, worst first) were then manipulated by instructing participants to consider the possibility that the outcome could have been; worse only, better only, better then worse or worse then better. As expected, mixed counterfactuals caused a weakened emotional reaction towards the outcome. Further we demonstrate that this phenomenon is not a case of emotional ambivalence.

Contrary to the common belief that frequent gamblers are addicted to the thrill of a win, it appears that they chase rainbows by imagining future wins at the expense of enjoying current wins. The frequent gamblers really are looking for the elusive pot of gold. Infrequent gamblers on the other hand are more susceptible to the highs and lows of gambling as they are more focused on the current outcome.

References

Carroll, Patrick J. and James A. Shepperd (2009), "Preparedness, Mental Simulations and Future Outlooks," in *The Handbook of Imagination and Mental Simulation*, ed. Keith D Markman, William M Klein and Julie A Suhr, New York: US: Psychology Press.

Epstude, Kai and Neal J. Roese (2008), "The Functional Theory of Counterfactual Thinking," *Personality and Social Psychology Review*, 12 (2), 168-92.

Gleicher, Faith, David S. Boninger, Alan Strathman, David Armor, John Hetts, and Mina Ahn, eds. (1995), *With an Eye toward the Future: The Impact of Counterfactual Thinking on Affect, Attitudes, and Behavior*, Hillsdale, NJ, England: Lawrence Erlbaum Associates, Inc

Markman, Keith D., Igor Gavanski, Steven J. Sherman, and Matthew N. McMullen (1993), "The Mental Simulation of Better and Worse Possible Worlds," *Journal of Experimental Social Psychology*, 29 (1), 87-109.

Markman, Keith D., Matthew N. McMullen, and Ronald A. Elizaga (2008), "Counterfactual Thinking, Persistence, and Performance: A Test of the Reflection and Evaluation Model," *Journal of Experimental Social Psychology*, 44 (2), 421-28.

McMullen, Matthew N. (1997), "Affective Contrast and Assimilation in Counterfactual Thinking," Journal of Experimental Social Psychology, 33 (1), 77-100.

McMullen, Matthew N. and Keith D. Markman (2000), "Downward Counterfactuals and Motivation: The Wake-up Call and the Pangloss Effect," *Personality and Social Psychology Bulletin*, 26 (5), 575-84.

Medvec, Victoria Husted, Scott F. Madey, and Thomas Gilovich (1995), "When Less Is More: Counterfactual Thinking and Satisfaction among Olympic Medalists," *Journal of Personality and Social Psychology*, 69 (4), 603-10.

Roese, Neal J. (1994), "The Functional Basis of Counterfactual Thinking," *Journal of Personality and Social Psychology*, 66 (May), 805-18.

Roese, Neal J. and Taekyun Hur (1997), "Affective Determinants of Counterfactual Thinking," *Social Cognition*, 15 (4), 274-90.

White, Katherine and Darrin R. Lehman (2005), "Looking on the Bright Side: Downward Counterfactual Thinking in Response to Negative Life Events," *Personality and Social Psychology Bulletin*, 31 (October), 1413-24.

Special Session Summary
Dynamic Influences on Investors' Decisions

Stephen Gould, Baruch College, CUNY, USA
Ana Valenzuela, Baruch College, CUNY, USA

SESSION OVERVIEW

Behavioral finance theory suggests that individual investments decisions will, to a certain extent, be affected by characteristics of one's personal psychology and what are said to be irrational biases (Thaler 1987). Furthermore, research on actual investment decisions shows that psychological variables do matter and actually cause individuals to make non-optimal decisions (e.g., Goldstein et al. 2008; Lee et al. 2008; Morrin et al. 2002). In that regard, investment behavior might be subject to influences and biases reflecting various cognitive traits (e.g., belief in luck), personal characteristics (e.g., gender), motivational stages (e.g. promotion or prevention focus), process responses (e.g., change in frame from gains or losses) and context characteristics (e.g., option assortment size).

Nonetheless, despite the importance of understanding the determinants of investors' decisions, and the growing interest in them in consumer research relatively little research has examined the effect of the decision maker's personal psychology, self-expressive needs and heuristic approaches on actual investment/ trading decisions. The four papers in this special session are a step forward in such an investigation since they explore the theoretical intersection between product, investor characteristics, and behavioral tendencies in the determination of trading/ investment decisions.

In the first paper, Daniel Goldstein shows that in domains involving losses, prevention-oriented individuals behave differently than predicted by the regulatory focus theory framework and, surprisingly, take greater risks. In the second paper, Stephen Gould, Ana Valenzuela, Luke Kachersky and Richard Holowczak analyze biases in traders' strategies, behaviors, and performance that result from distal personality traits. In the third paper, Priya Raghubir and Meir Statman identify 8 self-expressive benefits of financial investing and key personality constructs that distinguish between different financial products so as to provide a multi-dimensional mapping of financial instruments. Finally, in the fourth paper, Maureen Morrin and Susan Broniarczyk explore how increasing investment fund assortment size causes individuals to choose more funds for their portfolios, which is cognitively depleting, and this process results in further use of heuristic approaches to allocating one's dollars across the chosen funds.

Gita Johar briefly summarized the overlapping points across the four papers. Taken together, these papers highlight the important influence of both product characteristics and individual differences in determining consumers' investment-related evaluations and choice. With well-developed frameworks and data, all four papers provide a roadmap for how the intersection between product and investor characteristics determines trading/ investment decisions. To finalize the session, the audience participated in a discussion of areas of future research on the topic of behavioral finance and the role that different psychological variables play in consumers' investment decisions.

EXTENDED ABSTRACTS

"When Prevention-Oriented Investors Take Greater Risks: Breaking a Confound"

Daniel Goldstein, London Business School, UK
Rongrong Zhou, Hong Kong University of Science and Technology, Hong Kong, China
Michel Tuan Pham, Columbia University, USA

For those who were overinvested in stocks (relative to their taste for risk), the unfortunate consequence of incorrectly-gauged investor risk preferences is all too clear in the current market downturn. Can marketers better predict consumers' propensity for taking financial risks? Since demographic variables including age and sex are broad, and of limited predictive value (Goldstein, Johnson & Sharpe, 2008; Bajtelsmit & Bernasek, 2001), the goal of offering more individualized predictions and advice has led marketers at investment firms to devise personality scales for recommending products to investors. Unfortunately, none of these scales have been validated in a peer-reviewed article to our knowledge, and the only published journal article on the topic finds that responses from different vendors' scales have only a modest intercorrelation, even when administered in direct succession (Yook & Everett, 2003).

A promising finding of recent years was that of Zhou and Pham (2004), who investigated financial risk taking as it connects with Regulatory Focus Theory (RFT; Higgins, 1987). Zhou and Pham showed that investments products mentally coded as promotion-oriented trigger more financial risk taking compared to investments products mentally coded as prevention-oriented (Study 2). They also showed that priming of promotion or prevention through an unrelated task framed in approach or avoidance-oriented manner steers investment toward more conservative options under prevention: mutual funds rather than individual stocks, and retirement accounts rather than trading accounts. A number of other researchers in Marketing and Psychology have found a connection between RFT and risk taking outside financial services, typically finding that promotion orientation is correlated with risk taking and prevention orientation is related to risk avoidance (Liberman, Idson, Camacho, & Higgins 1999; Crowe & Higgins, 1997; Chernev, 2004; Förster, Higgins, & Bianco, 2003; Friedman & Förster, 2001; Lee & Aaker, 2004).

In the present work, we suggest that the classical relationship between financial risk taking and regulatory focus may only tell half the story, due to a confound. Typically, taking more risk is associated with potentially greater gains and greater losses. In such situations, promotion-oriented individuals take greater risks. However, when risks are framed as losses instead of gains, greater risk taking may be necessary to avoid a certain loss. We predict that, relative to promotion-oriented individuals, prevention-oriented individuals will be more concerned with avoid loss altogether and thus more likely to take greater risks in the domain of losses.

We demonstrate this counterintuitive effect using simple gambles (Zhou, 2002). In addition, to gain deeper insight into cognitive processes, we employ the Distribution Builder methodology (Goldstein, Johnson & Sharpe, 2008). The Distribution Builder allows individuals to graphically manipulate cost-constrained probability distributions of investment wealth from which they will later draw. Its advantages over simple gamble choices are many, including the ability to: detect reference dependence in addition to risk aversion, measure reaction time, test RFT-specific hypotheses about maximum and minimum outcomes, and employ click-tracking to understand which outcome levels are attended to most. Results from the Distribution Builder studies show that in the domain of gains, promotion-oriented individuals assume more downside risk in order to obtain upside gains (relative to prevention-oriented individuals). However, in the domain of losses, the relationship reverses and it is the prevention-oriented people who take greater risks in order to escape certain losses of moderate magnitude.

This research aims to clarify the relationship between promotion/prevention orientation and financial risk taking, which has important practical applications for marketers who wish to provide responsible advice (and suitable products) to their customers.

"The Behavioral Dimensions of Trading: Proximal and Distal Influences on Performance"

Stephen Gould, Baruch College, CUNY, USA
Ana Valenzuela, Baruch College, CUNY, USA
Luke Kachersky, Fordham University, USA
Richard Holowczak, Baruch College, CUNY, USA

Behavioral finance theory suggests that stock market trading performance outcomes (e.g., making or losing money) might be subject to influences and biases reflecting various cognitive traits (e.g., belief in luck), personal characteristics (e.g., gender), process responses (e.g., change in focus on gains or losses) and behaviors (e.g., trading more or less frequently). Although the influence of some of these variables has already been studied, some of traders' cognitive traits have been overlooked perhaps because they appear more distal to the trading process, and there are still other, more proximal variables yet to be studied. To this end we implemented a trading simulation in which participants were endowed with shares of a hypothetical stock and cash, and traded with each other for a period of 10 minutes. Importantly, in addition to measuring distal and proximal character traits, we measured participants' cognitive and affective states before and after the trading session.

One hundred fourteen participants recruited from a large Northeastern university participated in exchange for a cash payment and the opportunity to win a larger cash prize for the top trading performer. Trading simulations were run in groups of about 25. Participants were seated at computer terminals and given an interactive demonstration of the Rotman Interactive Trader (RIT) software. The software allows participants to interact in real-time with a central limit order book by placing market orders and limit orders to buy and sell shares of a hypothetical stock. Participants were told that they would be trading a hypothetical security with each other, and would be given 100 shares of the security and $1 million to start. As part of the simulation, participants were told that the security they were trading had five possible target prices of $20, $22, $24, $26 or $28. During the course of the simulation participants received information in their "news" window about values that the security could not be. This was done so that the market would converge toward a single price by the end of the simulation. They then participated in the real trading simulation in which the trader with the highest final value (stocks plus cash) won a real cash prize. Participants finished with a post-simulation questionnaire pertaining to the simulation, demographics, and personality traits: non-cooperative tendencies; confidence in intellectual ability; self-esteem; fatalism; desirability of control; primary-secondary control; attitudes toward risk; belief in luck; competitiveness; and regulatory focus.

A number of behavioral variables were regressed on the personality variables. One such behavior, the number of "buy" transactions the trader engaged in, was significantly related to secondary control (p=.009). The number of "sell" transactions was significantly related to risk taking (p=.045) and marginally to primary control (p=.081) and negatively to belief in luck (p=.078). We created a performance variable to reflect traders' success in buying low and selling high. The volume weighted average price (VWAP) ratio compares the VWAP of shares sold to the VWAP of shares bought. Values over 1 indicate that, on average, a trader sold his shares for a higher price than he bought them. Trading behavior and personality traits explained variation in this performance metric. Primary control (p=.019) and belief in luck (p=.056) were significant in explaining the VWAP ratio, while the number of "sell" transactions exerted a negative influence (p=.044). Finally, traders' change in value from their starting $1 million endowment was dependent on the VWAP Ratio (p=.014). Additionally, for those who made money, desirability of control (p=.004) and primary control (p=.055) were positively related with money made while belief in luck (p=.038) and regulatory focus (p=.017) were negatively related. For those who lost money, only desirability of control was significant (p=.021) and negatively related to money made.

Overall, the results indicate that personality variables can play an important role in determining trading behavior and performance along with proximal trading variables. The next study will test these traits in the same simulation by priming them in terms of opposing characterizations of traders as being lucky versus being able to control the results of their trading.

"Personalities of Financial Products"

Priya Raghubir, New York University, USA
Meir Statman, Santa Clara University, USA

Financial products, like most products, have utilitarian attributes and expressive attributes. The utilitarian attributes of financial products include their expected returns, risk, liquidity and fees. Self-expressive attributes are those that allow us to convey to ourselves and others our values, tastes and social class. Self-expressive attributes answer the question "What does the product say about me?" For example, one self-expressive attribute of a hedge fund is status. It says "I have arrived." An insurance policy says "I am responsible." A socially responsible fund says "I am a good person." An active mutual fund says "I can be a winner."

In this paper, we examine the perceptions of the utilitarian and self-expressive attributes of financial products and how these perceptions define the overall personalities of financial products. A personality is defined as a set of traits that distinguish one entity from another. We examine whether financial products have a "personality"–a set of defining characteristics and traits that are able to distinguish one financial product from the other. In doing so, we go beyond the utilitarian attributes of financial products, and examine how these affect usage benefits. Specifically, a benefit hierarchy model translates the functional attributes of a product or service into their usage benefits, laddering up to the feelings that these benefits invoke among customers, and triangulating to a set of key higher order self-expressive benefits.

In a benefit hierarchy framework, lower order functional attributes (such as fees charged, rates of return, variance around the returns, guarantee of capital remaining intact, tax advantages, presence of a market and its size, etc.) map onto a set of rational benefits. These rational benefits include utilitarian benefits such as risk, return, and liquidity. However, beyond rational benefits are emotional and self-expressive benefits that capture how a product makes people feel and what it says about them. Our approach is to map rational benefits through to these higher order self-expressive benefits that are the apex of the benefit hierarchy.

Stage 1: In the initial stage of scale development, we identified 264 words including attributes of a financial product, investor goals, descriptors of a personality, demographic descriptions, self-expressive benefits and emotions, drawing from the literatures of finance, marketing, and psychology.

Face Validity: These 264 descriptors were reduced to a set of 107 that were categorized into a set of 70 adjectives that were personality descriptors of a financial instrument; and 35 feelings and emotions that were emotional and self-expressive benefits.

Construct Validity: Study participants (n=150) rated one of twelve (savings account, checking account, stocks, time deposits, mutual funds, retirement accounts, hedge funds, private equity, stock options, life insurance, real estate and lotteries and gambles) instruments using the 70 adjectives (1=Not at all, and 5=Very) and 35 emotions (1=Not at all, and 9=Very). Exploratory factor analysis with a varimax rotation using cutoffs of .60 for factor loadings was used to reduce the data to 11 factors using 37 descriptors, and six factors using the 35 emotions.

Stage 2: Stage 2 investigated six instruments: savings accounts, stocks, retirement accounts, mutual funds, hedge funds and real estate. All participants were asked to "Think that the ___ is a person," prior to being asked to rate it on the set of 37 adjectives, and 35 emotions, using a nine-point scale. All participants (n=56) rated all six instruments on the adjectives as well as rated the feelings these elicited with the order of the instruments fully counter balanced.

Results

Personality Constructs: The 37 items tapping personality constructs were subjected to exploratory factor analysis with a varimax rotation for each of the six different financial instruments to assess which items to retain. Items whose factor loading was low overall (i.e., lacks predictive validity); that load onto a marginal factor (e.g., indicating low reliability), load onto different factors for different financial instruments (i.e., is not generalizable), and/or loads less onto a factor than other items (i.e., is not distinctive) were dropped, leading to 27 of the items being retained:

Good: positive, good, valuable (alpha=.85)
Bad: negative, bad worthless (alpha=.86)
Aesthetic: Beautiful, aesthetic and pretty (alpha=.90)
Intelligent: intelligent, up to date, latest (alpha=.77)
Boring: sleepy, shy, lethargic, and old (alpha=.83)
Fun: exciting, amusing, energetic, lively, young, entertaining, adventurous, fun, and playful (alpha=.95)
Masculine: Masculine, extroverted (alpha=.74)

Self-expressive Benefits: A similar set of analyses on the 35 items in the self-expressive benefit inventory revealed (Scales for each factor were reliable (α>.70)):

Honest: Honest, free, and common
Adventurous: fearful, reckless, adventurous, risk taker
Smart: special, smart, A winner, A sense of achievement, and responsible
Good: Intelligent, High Status, A Good person, optimistic
Hip: Playful, young, cool, hip
Connectedness: A sense of belonging, A part of a club, A member of a community
Prestige: Elite, exclusive
Power: A sense of control, A sense of dominance, A expert, Unique
Bad: Pessimistic, patriotic, and sinful.

Stage 3: To be conducted: Testing Predictive Validity: We will test this instrument with a group of adult experienced investors using a wide range of financial products and eliciting attitudinal and behavioral responses (e.g., attitude, experience, portfolio allocation, intentions). Robustness Checks: The survey will also collect information on the psychological, demographic and behavioral profiles of investors to examine differences in the perception of financial products across sub-groups of individuals and identify moderating variables.

"The Moderating Effect of Fund Assortment Size on the 1/N Heuristic"

Maureen Morrin, Rutgers University-Camden, USA
Susan Broniarczyk, University of Texas at Austin, USA
J. Jeffrey Inman, University of Pittsburgh, USA

Does offering more choices in retirement plans result in systematic decision biases? Prior research has shown that investors sometimes exhibit a naive diversification strategy whereby they evenly divide up their dollar contributions among all of the options offered, engaging in what Benartzi and Thaler (2001) term the "1/n heuristic." Interestingly, more recent research by Huberman and Jiang (2006), suggests that few investors engage in the strict definition of the 1/n heuristic. Notably, the work of Huberman and Jiang (2006) was based on a data set whose mean fund set size was about double that used by Benartzi and Thaler (2001); 13.7 versus 6.8 mean number of funds offered, respectively). Could the discrepancy in results reported by these two research teams be attributed to the different fund assortment sizes from which investors chose?

Our research explores the moderating effect of mutual fund assortment size on use of the 1/n heuristic by decomposing the heuristic into its two underlying behavioral dimensions: 1) choosing the funds from among those offered in which to invest, and 2) deciding how to allocate one's dollars across the set of chosen funds. Importantly, we argue that the two behavioral tendencies operate differently as a function of fund assortment size due to cognitive depletion. Recent investigations (Huberman and Jiang 2006) indicate that most retirement investors tend to invest in about three to five, or a handful, of funds. Thus a naïve interpretation of portfolio diversification would seem to involve the sheer number of funds consumers want to include in their portfolios. If most investors feel they should be investing in a handful of funds to be sufficiently diversified, and only a few are offered for investment in a 401k plan, then many investors are likely to include all of the available options in their portfolios in order to arrive at the desired number of investment options–even if the set of options made available does not perfectly match their preferences. If this is the case, the 1/n heuristic should be less evident as fund assortment size increases. Because Benartzi and Thaler (2001) examined smaller assortment sizes, their findings may reflect, in part, a ceiling effect due to an inadequate fund assortment.

Although we posit that choosing from a larger assortment will reduce the tendency to invest in all available funds, we do expect that the average number of funds chosen will increase (Benartzi and Thaler 2001). Choosing from a larger fund assortment will encourage investors to choose more funds for their portfolios, because they use assortment size as a normative consumption cue regarding the sheer number of funds they should choose (Kahn and Wansink 2004). When consumers do not have well-defined preferences in a choice domain, they construct their preferences using strategies that are contingent on task demands (Bettman et al. 1998). A consequence of this behavior is that investors become cognitively depleted (Pocheptsova, Amir, Dhar and Baumeister 2009), yet are faced with the daunting task of how to allocate their dollars among the large number of funds they have chosen for their portfolios. Simply dividing up one's dollars approximately evenly among the chosen alternatives represents one way to simplify this stage of the decision task. Thus, we expect that this aspect of the 1/n heuristic will be more evident as assortment size expands because of the tendency of investors to choose more funds when selecting from a larger assortment, which depletes their cognitive resources.

To date, two studies among adults have been completed, in which fund assortment size is manipulated (n=260, mail survey; n=363, online panel). In these studies mediation analyses are based on the number of funds invested in and thought listings. A third study, in which both fund assortment and cognitive load are manipulated, is in progress. As a whole, the results support our theoretical framework and help to reconcile discrepancies noted in previous research regarding asset allocation heuristics.

REFERENCES

Benartzi, Shlomo and Richard H. Thaler (2001), "Naive Diversification Strategies in Defined Contribution Plans," *The American Economic Review*, March, 79-98.

Bajtelsmit, Vickie L. and Alexandra Bernasek (2001), "Risk Preferences and the Investment Decisions of Older Americans," *AARP Public Policy Institute*, report no. 2001–11, Washington DC: American Association of Retired Persons.

Bettman, James R., Mary Frances Luce and John W. Payne (1998), "Constructive Consumer Choice Processes," *Journal of Consumer Research*, 25 (Dec), 187-217.

Chernev, A. (2004), "Goal orientation and consumer preference for the status quo," *Journal of Consumer Research*, 31 (3), 557-65.

Crowe, E. and E. Tory Higgins (1997), "Regulatory focus and strategic inclinations: Promotion and prevention in decision-making," *Organizational Behavior and Human Decision Processes*, 69 (2), 117-32.

Förster, J., E. T. Higgins, and A. T. Bianco (2003), "Speed/accuracy decisions in task performance: Built-in trade-off or separate strategic concerns?" *Organizational Behavior and Human Decision Processes*, 90 (1), 148-64.

Friedman, Ronald S. and Jens Förster (2001), "The effects of promotion and prevention cues on creativity," *Journal of Personality and Social Psychology*, 81 (6), 1001-13.

Goldstein, Daniel G., Johnson, Eric J. and William F. Sharpe (2008), "Choosing Outcomes versus Choosing Products: Consumer-Focused Retirement Investment Advice," *Journal of Consumer Research*, 35 (3), 440–456.

Higgins, E. Tory (1987), "Self-Discrepancy: A Theory Relating Self and Affect," Psychological Review, 94 (July), 319–40.

Huberman, Gur and Wei Jiang (2006), "Offering vs. Choice in 401(k) Plans: Equity Exposure and Number of Funds," *Journal of Finance*, 61 (2), 763-801.

Kahn, Barbara E. and Brian Wansink (2004), "Assortment Structure on Perceived Variety," *Journal of Consumer Research*, 30 (March), 519-533.

Morrin, Maureen, Jacoby, Jacob, Johar, Gita V., He, Xin and David Mazursky (2002), "Taking Stock of Stockbrokers: Exploring Momentum versus Contrarian Investor Strategies and Profiles," *Journal of Consumer Research*, 29 (2), 188-198.

Lee, A. Y. and J. L. Aaker (2004), "Bringing the Frame into Focus: the Influence of Regulatory Fit on Processing Fluency and Persuasion," *Journal of Personality and Social Psychology*, 86 (2), 205-18.

Lee, Carmen, Kraeussl, Roman, Lucas, Andre and Leo Paas (2009), "A Dynamic Model of Investor Decision-Making: How Adaptation to Losses Affect Future Selling Decisions," *Tinbergen Institute*, Discussion Paper No. 08-112/2.

Liberman, N., L. C. Idson, C. J. Camacho and E. T. Higgins (1999), "Promotion and Prevention Choices Between Stability and Change," *Journal of Personality and Social Psychology*, 77 (6), 1135-45.

Pocheptsova, Anastasiya, On Amir, Ravi Dhar and Roy Baumeister (2009), "Deciding Without Resources: Psychological Depletion and Choice in Context," *Journal of Marketing Research*, 46 (3), 344-355.

Thaler, Richard H. (1987), "The Psychology of Choice and the Assumptions of Economics." In Ed. Alvin E. Roth, *Laboratory Experiments in Economics: Six Points of View*, Cambridge University Press, 99-130.

Yook, Ken C. and Robert Everett (2003), "Assessing Risk Tolerance: Questioning the Questionnaire Method," *Journal of Financial Planning*, 18 (8), 48–55.

Zhou, Rongrong (2002), *Doctoral Thesis*, Columbia University Graduate School of Business.

Zhou, Rongrong and Michel T. Pham (2004), "Promotion and Prevention across Mental Accounts: How Financial Products Dictate Consumers' Investment Goals," *Journal of Consumer Research*, 31 (2), 125-35.

Special Session Summary

The Role of Stereotypes in Changing Consumers' Attitudes and Behaviors

Linyun Yang, Duke University, USA

SESSION OVERVIEW

Given their broad applicability and rich content, it is important to understand how stereotypes influence consumer's attitudes. Because individuals use stereotypes to understand their social environment, stereotypes can be activated through a wide range of cues, and this can lead to attitudes and behaviors congruent with the stereotyped group. For example, the presence of an African American individual in a record store could increase preferences for rap music or the presence of an overweight individual in a restaurant could possibly prime consumers to order and eat more food. Individuals themselves are also often targets of stereotypes and must deal with being judged based on group membership. Though depicting stereotypes in the media is generally avoided, stereotypes, particularly positive ones, can be inadvertently portrayed. For example, the use of an African American athlete can be construed as stereotyping by African American consumers and lead to detrimental consequences for the advertised product.

This collection of research seeks to understand the various ways stereotypes can shape consumer's attitudes and also identify important factors that moderate these effects. Wheeler et al. and Campbell and Mohr's papers examine how stereotypes prime attitudes and behaviors consistent with the stereotype. Wheeler et al.'s paper focuses on how individuals view themselves on traits related to a stereotype affect their susceptibility to priming. They find that individuals with consistent self-concepts on stereotype relevant traits are the most resistant to priming and demonstrate the least amount of stereotype consistent attitudes. Campbell and Mohr's paper demonstrates that priming individuals with overweight people can lead to the stereotype consistent behavior of overeating. However, this effect can be attenuated by reminding individuals of their health goals and also by reminding them that overeating leads to weight gain. Yang et al.'s research takes the perspective of the stereotype target and focuses on how they view depictions of positive stereotypes in the media. They find that group identification moderates whether individuals respond negatively or positively to an advertisement portraying a positive stereotype. These papers also emphasize the importance of individual level factors (i.e. self-concept consistency and personal goals) in understanding the effect of stereotypes on behavior.

Despite their power to shape attitudes and behavior, stereotypes have received little attention in the consumer behavior literature. This special session seeks to highlight the importance of understanding their role in shaping consumer behavior and should appeal to a wide audience. These papers demonstrate the various perspectives one can take in examining stereotypes and how they may relate to important marketing variables such as preferences, eating behavior, and persuasion.

EXTENDED ABSTRACTS

"Self-concept Consistency Fosters Resistance to Prime-induced Attitude Shifts"

Christian Wheeler, Stanford University, USA
Kenneth G. DeMarree, Texas Tech University, USA
Kimberly R. Morrison, Ohio State University, USA
Richard Petty, Ohio State University, USA

Research on stereotype priming has shown that it can have a wide array of effects on behavior and judgment. One effect of particular interest to marketers is that stereotype primes can lead to attitude shifts among prime recipients, both when they are targeted by the stereotype (Steele and Ambady 2006) and when they are not (Kawakami, Dovidio, and Dijksterhuis 2003). Specifically, following the activation of stereotypes, people report more stereotypical attitudes (e.g., racist attitudes following a skinhead stereotype prime).

There has been a great deal of recent research on the mechanism by which these types of effects occur. According to one account, the Active-Self account (Wheeler, DeMaree, & Petty, 2007), primes can have such effects via their effects on the active self-concept. A rapidly growing body of research shows that primed constructs can affect the active self-concept and lead to congruent subsequent behavior (see Wheeler, et al., 2007, for a review).

If primes affect behavior via the self-concept, factors that affect the resistance of the self-concept to change should lead to smaller priming effects. One factor associated with resistance is self-concept consistency. Paralleling research on attitude consistency, research on self-concept consistency has shown that those with consistent self-concept representations are more resistant to prime-induced self-concept shifts than are those with inconsistent self-concept representations (DeMarree, Morrision, Wheeler, and Petty 2009). We therefore predicted that people would be more resistant to priming effects on their attitude reports when there was consistency between prime-relevant aspects of their self-concepts.

In our first study, White participants were primed with either the African-American stereotype or no stereotype using a sentence unscrambling task. After the priming manipulation, participants indicated their level of agreement with four attitudinal statements that a pretest indicated were associated with the African American stereotype (e.g., "Policies aimed to reduce racial inequalities, such as affirmative action, are important to our society"). These items assessed attitudes toward affirmative action, welfare, rap music, and playing basketball and football. To minimize suspicion, these statements were interspersed with several others that were unrelated to the African American stereotype (e.g., "I like to eat apples and other fruit").

At the end of the session, all participants completed six questions designed to assess self-concept consistency along three stereotype-relevant dimensions (e.g., lazy/athletic), and we computed self-concept consistency using a formula paralleling that used to compute attitude ambivalence. In this formula, conflict within the self-concept is higher to the extent that people simultaneously strongly endorse opposing traits.

Analyses revealed the predicted prime x stereotype trait inconsistency interaction. Participants with high levels of trait inconsistency assimilated to the prime (i.e., reported more stereotypic attitudes following the stereotype prime), whereas those with low levels of trait inconsistency showed no effect of the prime.

In our second study, we replicated these effects with a different stereotype and a different measure of self-concept consistency. Research on the self has suggested that people have multiple self-representations, including representations of themselves as they actually are and representations of themselves as they desire to be (Higgins, 1987; Markus & Nurius, 1986). Actual and desired self-representations can differ in the extent to which they lead to the same overall evaluation or belief, and as such, they represent another possible measure of structural consistency. We predicted that, parallel to study 1, participants with large actual-desired self-discrepancies would exhibit larger priming effects on their attitudes.

In this study, participants first completed our actual-desired self-discrepancy measure. They indicated the extent to which each of three elderly stereotype traits–traditional, stubborn, and forgetful–characterized their actual, ideal, and ought selves. Later in the session, we primed college students with the elderly stereotype by asking them to write an essay about either an elderly woman or a young woman. Participants then indicated their level of agreement with three statements that reflected social conservatism, a component of the elderly stereotype (e.g., "There is too much violence in the media"). To minimize suspicion, these statements were interspersed with six others that were unrelated to the elderly stereotype (e.g., "I like to wear a watch").

Analyses revealed the predicted two-way condition x stereotype discrepancy interaction, whereby participants with large discrepancies assimilated to the prime (i.e., reported more conservative attitudes following the elderly prime), whereas participants with small discrepancies were not influenced by the prime.

These studies advance our understanding of both the priming literature and the attitude change literature. These findings show that structurally consistent self-concept representations foster resistance to priming effects and provide additional support for the Active-Self account of priming to behavior effects. They also lend additional insight into how attitudes can be shifted by even very subtle factors such as the accessibility of social stereotypes.

References

DeMarree, Kenneth G., Kimberly R. Morrison, S. Christian Wheeler, and Richard E. Petty (2009), "Self-ambivalence and Resistance to Subtle Self-change Attempts." Unpublished manuscript.

Higgins, E. Tory (1987), "Self-discrepancy: A Theory Relating Self and Affect," *Psychological Review*, 94(3), 319-340.

Kawakami, Kerry, John F. Dovidio, and Ap Dijksterhuis (2003), "Effect of Social Category Priming on Personal Attitudes," *Psychological Science*, 14(4), 315-319.

Markus, Hazel and Paula S. Nurius (1986), "Possible Selves," *American Psychologist*, 41(9), 954-969.

Steele, Jennifer R. and Nalini Ambady (2006), "Math is Hard! The Effect of Gender Priming on Women's Attitudes," *Journal of Experimental Social Psychology*, 42(4), 428-436.

Wheeler, S. Christian, Kenneth G. DeMarree, and Richard E. Petty (2007), "Understanding the Role of the Self in Prime-to-Behavior Effects: The Active-Self Account," *Personality and Social Psychology Review*, 11(3), 234-261.

"Effects of Priming on Instrumental Behaviors"

Margaret C. Campbell, University of Colorado at Boulder, USA
Gina S. Mohr, University of Colorado at Boulder, USA

Recent research proposes that there are person-to-person influences on weight gain such that the weight of others in individuals' social networks influences the probability of gaining weight (Christakis and Fowler 2007). While this research indicates that social factors influence weight gain, the nature of the data set precludes examination of how this influence might occur. We draw from the literature on social stereotype priming to explain how exposure to an overweight person can give rise to an increase in food consumption. We propose that social factors can influence instrumental behavior, that is, behavior such as eating that is considered to be causally linked to weight gain. We develop the idea of how instrumental behaviors are influenced by stereotype activation and explore when the effect of stereotype activation on instrumental behavior is likely to be attenuated.

Stereotypes are traits, attributes and behavioral tendencies that are associated with the members of a social category (Fiske and Taylor 1991; Hilton and Von Hippel 1996; Kunda 1999; Stangor and Lange 1994). Research shows that activation of social stereotypes can affect people's behavior, increasing behavior that is consistent with stereotypical traits, attributes and behavioral tendencies even when the behavior is somewhat negative (for reviews, see Dijksterhuis and Bargh 2001; Wheeler and Petty 2001). However, existing research in this stream has not examined instrumental behaviors. For example, whereas walking slowly is associated with the elderly, the act of walking slowly does not cause a college student to become old. In contrast, however, eating more food is associated with overweight (Barker, Tandy, and Stookey 1999) and eating is causally related to becoming overweight. What implications does instrumentality have for the effects of social stereotype primes on behavior?

We propose that the stereotype of an overweight person can lead to an increase in behavior associated with overweight people (i.e., eating more "indulgent" food), even though people are motivated to avoid membership in the "overweight" group, as evidenced by the staggering number of consumers who are trying to lose weight, and believe that eating indulgent food increases the chance of becoming overweight. We explore the process by which the instrumental behavior is increased by the stereotype. Our research assesses one mechanism by which a person may succumb to, or overcome, these behavioral priming effects. In particular, we theorize that in order for the stereotype prime to give rise to an increase in the instrumental behavior, it must first decrease motivation for the underlying, competing goal. Moreover, we propose that by making salient this underlying goal and the causal link between eating and weight gain (i.e., the instrumentality of the behavior) the priming effects can be attenuated.

We present four studies that investigate the effect of overweight primes on eating behavior and the role that the salience of competing goals and behavior instrumentality play. Study 1 establishes the prime to behavior link, showing that when people are exposed to a picture of an overweight person, they eat significantly more than people who are exposed to a picture of a healthy weight person or a neutral image (the two controls in this experiment). Study 2 further examines this relationship by testing the mediating role of health motivation. Our findings show that exposure to a picture of someone overweight led to lower ratings of health motivation and that health motivation mediated the prime-to-behavior relationship.

Together, the findings from study 1 and study 2 provide additional theoretical insight into the prime-to-behavior process. In particular, we show that an instrumental behavior associated with an active social stereotype can lead people to assimilate in behavior, but the process is mediated by an important motivational variable. To lend further support to our theory that consumer motivations are important in this process we conducted two additional studies to test the moderating role of consumer health goals and instrumentality salience.

Study 3 tests our theory that if consumers have underlying goals that are in conflict with behaviors that are associated with a stereotype and are perceived as instrumental to group membership, then making those goals salient should lead to a decrease in priming effects (i.e., food consumption). The results from study 3 reveal a significant interaction such that exposure to an overweight person led to an increase in food consumption, but that asking study participants to reflect on their health goals attenuated these affects.

We likewise theorize that increasing the salience of the instrumentality of the behavior can also attenuate the impact of a stereotype prime on an instrumental behavior. The findings from Study 4 support this hypothesis. We find that manipulating the salience of the instrumentality significantly impacts the effect of the overweight prime. Specifically, whereas participants eat more cookies in a taste test following exposure to a picture of someone overweight than someone healthy weight, this effect does not arise when the salience of the instrumentality of the behavior is increased (by seeing the overweight person eating).

Overall, this set of studies contributes to the literature on stereotype priming. This highlights the idea that some behaviors are instrumental to group membership and that motivation can play an important role in stereotype prime effects for instrumental behaviors. This research may also provide some useful insight into how social network effects may arise.

References

Barker, Margo E., M. Tandy, and J. D. Stookey (1999), "How Are Consumers of Low-Fat and High-Fat Diets Perceived by Those with Lower and Higher Fat Intake?" *Appetite*, 33 (3), 309-17.

Christakis, Nicholas A. and James H. Fowler (2007), "The Spread of Obesity in a Large Social Network over 32 Years," *The New England Journal of Medicine*, 357 (4), 370-379.

Dijksterhuis, Ap and John A. Bargh (2001), "The Perception-Behavior Expressway: Automatic Effects of Social Perception on Social Behavior," in *Advances in Experimental Social Psychology*, Vol. 33 ed. Mark P. Zanna, San Diego, CA: Academic Press, 1-40.

Fiske, Susan T. and Shelley E. Taylor (1991), *Social Cognition* (2nd Ed.), McGraw Hill Series in Social Psychology. New York, NY, England: Mcgraw Hill Book Company.

Hilton, James L. and William von Hippel (1996), "Stereotypes," Annual Review of Psychology, 47, 237-71.

Kunda, Ziva (1999), "Parallel Processing of Stereotypes and Behaviors," *Dual-Process Theories in Social Psychology*, New York, NY : Guilford Press. xiii, 314-322.

Stangor, Charles and James E. Lange (1994), "Mental Representations of Social Groups: Advances in Understanding Stereotypes and Stereotyping," in *Advances in Experimental Social Psychology*, Vol. 26. San Diego, CA : Academic Press.

Wheeler, Christian S. and Richard E. Petty (2001), "The Effects of Stereotype Activation on Behavior: A Review of Possible Mechanisms," *Psychological Bulletin*, 127 (6), 797-826.

"How Stereotype Targets Perceive Positive Stereotypes"

Linyun Yang, Duke University, USA
Tanya Chartrand, Duke University, USA
Gavan Fitzsimons, Duke University, USA

The majority of the stereotypes literature has focused on the detrimental consequences of being negatively stereotyped, but little research has focused on how stereotype targets are affected by positive stereotypes. Given the frequent portrayal of positive stereotypes (i.e. the African American athlete or the Asian math genius), it is important to understand how individuals are affected by these depictions as well as consequences for consumer behavior. Our research examines the role group identification plays in how individuals will interpret portrayals of positive stereotypes in the media.

Prior research has demonstrated that group identification determines the extent to which an individual's group membership affects a wide range of experiences and behavior (Ellemers, Spears, & Doosje 1999 for review). Most relevant to our research is the finding that those who identify highly with their group are more sensitive to threats toward their ingroup. Because highly identified individuals are more sensitive to intergroup inequalities, they are more willing to label negative incidents as threatening to their group (Sellers & Shelton 2003). For example, Operario and Fiske (2001) found that ethnic minorities highly identified with their ethnic group were more likely to interpret the ambiguous behaviors of a White confederate as discriminatory than their less identified counterparts.

Even if a stereotype is positive and endorsed with the best intentions, it can be disconcerting to the stereotype target because it is still restrictive and based solely on group membership rather than any individuating information (Czopp 2008). More importantly, positive stereotypes can also imply and bring to mind the negative component of one's group stereotype (Fiske, Cuddy, Glick, & Xu 2002). Furthermore, these complementary beliefs can contribute to the justification of enduring intergroup differences in status and power (Jost & Kay 2005). We hypothesize that those high in group identification will be particularly sensitive to these issues and be more likely to interpret portrayals of positive stereotypes as prejudiced and threatening to their group.

In Study 1, we demonstrated that images portraying individuals engaging in activities consistent with a positive stereotype can be interpreted as prejudiced. African American and White participants viewed images of African Americans engaged in either singing or running (domains in which African Americans stereotypically excel). We found that African American participants high in group identification interpreted these images as more prejudiced toward their group than those who were low in group identification. Since these images were irrelevant to their group, White participants did not demonstrate any differences in prejudice ratings with regard to group identification.

If high identifiers were responding to the potential for threat to their group in Study 1, then we should find that they will be less likely to be affected when the positive stereotype is endorsed by any ingroup member because the threat to the group is minimized. In Study 2, we examined this hypothesis and also focus on how perceived prejudice influenced persuasion and product evaluations when positive stereotypes were portrayed in advertisements. African American and White participants viewed a print advertisement for a book called "The Ultimate Running Guide." The advertisement claimed that the book would help readers "run further and faster with the training methods of the best marathon runners in Africa." In addition, either an African American or White male spokesperson was pictured running in a race with a quote endorsing the book.

Replicating Study 1, we found that African American participants high in group identification evaluated the advertisement more negatively than those low in group identification. However, we only found this effect when the spokesperson was an outgroup member. When the spokesperson was an ingroup member (i.e. African American) these effects were diminished presumably because threat to the group was not apparent when a positive stereotype was endorsed by an ingroup member. Because the stereotypes portrayed were irrelevant to stereotypes regarding White participants, we did not find any differences in their evaluations regarding group identification and advertisement spokesperson.

This line of research demonstrates that the portrayal of positive stereotypes in advertisements can have detrimental effects on the products portrayed, particularly with regard to those highly identified with the stereotyped group. Because this negative reaction to positive stereotypes is rooted in the perceived threat to one's ingroup, specifying the source of the positive stereotype as an ingroup member can reduce the perceived threat and minimize the negative impact on evaluations of the advertisement and product.

References

Czopp, Alexander M., (2008), "When is a Compliment Not a Compliment? Evaluating Expressions of Positive Stereotypes," *Journal of Experimental Social Psychology*, 44, 413-420.

Ellemers, Naomi, Russell Spears, & Bertjan Doosje, (1999), *Social Identity: Context, Commitment, Content*, Oxford, England: Blackwell Publishers.

Fiske, Susan T., Amy J.C. Cuddy, Peter Glick, & Jun Xu, (2002), "A Model of (Often Mixed) Stereotype Content: Competence and Warmth Respectively Follow from Perceived Status and Competition," *Journal of Personality and Social Psychology*, 82(6), 878-902.

Jost, John T. & Aaron C. Kay, (2005), "Exposure to Benevolent Sexism and Complementary Gender Stereotypes: Consequences for Specific and Diffuse Forms of System Justification," *Journal of Personality and Social Psychology*, 88(3), 498-509.

Operario, Don & Susan T. Fiske, (2001), "Ethnic Identity Moderates Perceptions of Prejudice: Judgments of Personal Versus Group Discrimination and Subtle Versus Blatant Bias," *Personality and Social Psychology Bulletin*, 27(5), 550-61.

Sellers, Robert M. & J. Nicole Shelton, (2003), "The Role of Racial Identity in Perceived Racial Discrimination," *Journal of Personality and Social Psychology*, 84(5), 1079-92.

Special Session Summary

Exploring Self-Control: Moving Beyond Depletion Hypothesis

Ravi Mehta, University of British Columbia, Canada

SESSION OVERVIEW

Self-control has been proposed to be one of the most important and beneficial processes in the human personality structure. Successful self-control has been linked to a broad range of desirable outcomes (e.g., healthier interpersonal relationships, greater popularity, and better mental health; see Gailliot et al. 2007). Although a large amount of research has been done on this topic, many important questions remain to be answered. For example, what is the role of self in self-control? Does resource depletion necessarily lead to more impulsivity? How do different definitions of self affect impulsive behavior? How does affect impact the self-control process? This session brings together four papers that intend to address these important questions and thus advance our knowledge of the mechanisms and boundary conditions under which consumers engage in self-control.

The first paper (Mehta et al.) aims to reconcile an existing discrepancy in the self-control literature. While traditional research on myopic behavior suggests that a high versus low construal level leads to less indulgence, more recent work on hyperopia implies the opposite. This paper demonstrates that construal level interacts with self-focus, which jointly determines an individual's indulgence level. Specifically, when self is not made salient, findings in the myopia literature are replicated, whereas when self is the central focus, effect reversal as predicted by the hyperopia literature is observed. The second paper (Ein-Gar and Johnson) further explores the role of self in self-control dilemmas. It suggests that construing the self differently influences preferences and choices such that under a "becoming" mindset consumers are more prudent whereas under a "being" mindset they are more prone to indulge. The third paper (Laran and Janiszewski) suggests that consumers' chronic self-control level affects their task perception (whether perceive as work or play) and consequently affects their self-control in subsequent tasks. Finally, the last paper (Komarova et al.) investigates the role of affect in self-regulation tasks. It demonstrates that under positive mood consumers are less likely to engage in mental accounting to justify impulsive spending.

EXTENDED ABSTRACTS

"Exploring Role of Self in Self-Control"

Ravi Mehta, University of British Columbia, Canada
Rui (Juliet) Zhu, University of British Columbia, Canada
Joan Meyers-Levy, University of Minnesota, USA

The classic literature on self-control focuses on myopic behavior, suggesting that individuals demonstrate self-control failure i.e. yield to immediate hedonic temptations when they focus on short-term benefits versus long-term goals (Trope and Fishbach 2000; Fujita et al. 2006). One way to reduce myopia is to induce a higher construal level, so that individuals focus on long-term benefits (Fujita et al. 2006; Liberman et al. 2007). However, recent research on hyperopia suggests an opposite form of self-control failure, namely many individuals have excessive farsightedness, thus they over-control themselves and constantly choose virtue over vice (e.g., Kivetz and Keinan 2006). Such a tendency is likely to evoke feelings of missing out in life and regret over time. One way to overcome hyperopia is to introduce a higher construal level (e.g., introducing greater temporal perspective; Keinan and Kivetz 2008), so that individuals will foresee their regret and consequently engage in indulgence to correct their hyperopic tendency.

The above two lines of research reveal an inconsistency. While the classic literature on myopia suggests that a higher construal level should lead to less indulgence (Fujita et al. 2006), recent work on hyperopia implies just the opposite. This research aims to offer reconciliation to the above described inconsistency.

We propose that construal level interacts with self-focus, which jointly determines an individual's present indulgence level. Specifically, when self is being explicitly primed, individuals will become aware of their chronic tendencies. Because a wide range of consumers experience some degree of tightwaddedness and perceive themselves as having insufficient indulgence (Kivetz and Simonson 2002), self prime is likely to make people realize their hyperopic tendency. Further, because a high construal level prompts people to think about their lives in the grand scheme of things, it may cause people to experience or foresee regret as they believe they have overly deprived themselves of pleasures in life. Thus, these individuals will try to correct their hyperopic tendency by engaging in more indulgence, such as spending more on hedonic products at the present moment. In contrast, when these self-focused individuals are primed with a low construal level, they should behave according to their immediately accessible chronic disposition. Thus, they would follow their hyperopic tendency, shying away from indulgence. In other words, when self is made salient, we expect to replicate findings from the hyperopia literature, i.e., a high versus low construal level should lead to more indulgence.

On the other hand, when self is not made salient, we expect that people may not become consciously aware of their chronic behavioral tendency. Consequently, the more salient manipulation of construal level will override any people's chronic tendency and determine indulgence level. Here, we expect to replicate the findings observed in the traditional research on myopia, namely a high versus low construal level should lead to less indulgence (e.g., Fujita et al. 2006; Trope et al. 2007).

A set of five experiments were conducted which offer support to our theory. Study 1 tests our above predictions directly by manipulating construal level (high vs. low) and self focus (self vs. control). The focal task involved presenting participants with a list of the hedonic and utilitarian products and asking them to indicate their highest willingness-to-pay (WTP) for each item. Higher WTP indicates greater indulgence. As expected, when self was not made salient, we replicated findings in the myopia literature, such that participants indicated higher WTP for both types of products (utilitarian and hedonic) when they were in low versus high construal level. However, when self was made salient, we observed the anticipated reversal as predicted in the hyperopia literature, but only for hedonic products (i.e., a high versus low construal level led to greater WTP). For utilitarian products, however, construal level did not affect these self-focused individuals' WTP, presumably because utilitarian products may not provide the kind of indulgence that hyperopic individuals are looking for at the high construal level. Thus, in the subsequent studies, only hedonic products were included.

While study 1 offer reconciliation to the inconsistency in the self-control literature, it does not shed light on the well-established resource-depletion model of self-control. This model posits that individuals have limited resources, and depletion in resources leads to myopia (Vohs and Schemeichel 2003). Although a large number of studies have established the resource-depletion effect, it is not entirely clear why resource depletion leads to myopia. Building on our theorizing and findings from study 1, we propose that resource availability can affect individuals' construal level, which consequently affects indulgence. Limited (ample) resources are likely to cause individuals to construe things at a lower (higher) level, thus leading to greater (less) indulgence. If the above hypothesis is true, we should also observe the moderating effect of self focus on the relationship between resource availability and indulgence level. We test these theorizing in the next two studies.

Study 2 tests the hypothesis that resource level affects construal level which subsequently influences indulgence. Resource level was manipulated via having participants remember either a two-digit (high resource level) or an eight-digit (low level) number, and participants' current construal level was measured via the 25-item BIF scale (Vallacher and Wegner 1989). The focal task involved having participants indicate their WTP for the five hedonic products as used in study1. Replicating prior research, we found that resource depletion (vs. ample resources) led to higher indulgence (i.e., WTP). More importantly this relationship was mediated by construal level.

Building on study 2, study 3 aims to replicate study 1 results by replacing construal level with resource level. Thus, this study employed a 2 (self focus: self vs. control) X 2 (resource level: high vs. low) between subjects design. Results from this study provided theoretical replication of study 1. Specifically, when self was made salient, participants revealed greater indulgence when they had high versus low resources. However, when self was not primed, we replicated the resource depletion model prediction, i.e. greater indulgence when people had low versus high resources.

Study 4 extends on our basic theorizing by identifying an important moderator, namely individuals' chronic hyperopia tendency. We propose and find that the two-way interaction between resource level and self focus as shown above is only salient among high hyperopia individuals. Finally, study 5 demonstrates that our effects are specific to hyperopia individuals, who experience regret about their self-control behavior. If for certain individuals, they do not experience regret about their self-control tendency, like those who are high on the self-control scale, the above interaction was not expected, nor observed.

In sum, this research reconciles an apparent discrepancy in the self-control literature, thus bridging two separate lines of research (i.e., myopia and hyperopia). In addition, we add to the construal level literature by demonstrating that resource availability affects construal level, which subsequently determines individuals' current indulgence.

"Being Indulgent and Becoming Prudent"

Danit Ein-Gar, Tel Aviv University, Israel
Camille Su-Lin Johnson, San Jose State University USA

It is proposed that momentary self-definitions may be associated with specific mindsets and that these mindsets can impact how consumers behave in self-control dilemmas. Specifically, we suggest that defining oneself in the future leads to prudent preferences and choices while defining oneself in the present leads to more hedonic preferences and choices. The underlying process concerns the association of the momentary self-definitions with different levels of construal.

A momentary self-definition may be characterized as defining oneself in terms of the present state and condition; the being mindset, or in terms of whom one is becoming; the becoming mindset, (Blanton , 2001; Johnson & Stapel, 2009; Markus & Nurius, 1986). We argue that the being mindset is characterized by low levels of construal in which objects are processed in terms of their concrete characteristics. In contrast, we argue that the becoming mindset is characterized by high levels of construal in which objects are processed in terms of their abstract characteristics.

Shifts in self-definition should be accompanied by shifts in construal level for a variety of reasons. First, being and becoming mindsets differ temporally and temporal factors influence construal level. That is, defining oneself in the moment may feel temporally closer than when defining oneself in the future. Hence, the being mindset should be associated with lower level construals than the becoming mindset. Second, these self-definitions are related to factors that increase psychological distance, and therefore influence construal levels (Kim, Zhang, & Li, 2008; Liberman, Trope & Waslak, 2007). Given that descriptions of the self in the present may be higher in their probability of being correct or accurate; these self-definitions should psychologically be closer than self-definitions based on future change. Thus, the being self should be accompanied by lower levels of construal and the becoming self should be accompanied by higher levels of construal, (Todorov et al., 2007).

In addition to altering levels of construal, changes in self-definitions are expected to influence behavior in self-control dilemmas, with becoming selves associated with greater self-control than being selves. These predictions are based, in part, on previous research demonstrating that shifts in temporal focus and orientation influence behavior in self-control dilemmas because they alter levels of construal (Fujita, Trope, Liberman & Levin-Sagi, 2006; Malkoc, Zauberman, & Ulu, 2005). Similarly, because, the becoming self leads to higher levels of construal and these levels of construal carryover to subsequent situations (Malkoc, Zauberman, & Bettman, 2008), people who are defining themselves in terms of the future should be better able to engage in acts of self-control than people who are defining themselves in terms of the present.

Apart from influencing preferences for products, being and becoming mindsets should be associated with differential sensitivity to product information. In general, product information that matches consumer's motivational state is valued whereas product information that mismatches consumer's goal states is devalued (Fishbach & Zhang, 2008; Hong & Lee, 2008). Accordingly, in a becoming mindset, individuals should find information regarding the practicality of a product to be more persuasive, while, in a being mindset, information regarding the indulgent qualities of a product should be more persuasive.

Study 1 (n=67, age_{mean}=36.85) examined the relation between construal levels and self-definitions. To activate becoming or being selves, participants wrote a brief self-description about "who you may become, focusing on the person you may develop into" (becoming) or about "who you are right now, focusing on the stable things that define your personality" (being). Participants in the becoming condition described themselves more abstractly (i.e. higher level construal) whereas participants in the being condition used more concrete nouns (i.e. lower level construal) (F(1,65)=9.93, p =.002).

Study 2 (n=64, age_{mean}=19.5) examined how eliciting a being or becoming self affects spending preferences in an open-ended context. Participants wrote a brief self-description (same as in Study 1) and then imagined that they had just won $1000 in a raffle. In the becoming mindset participants listed more prudent spending choices while in a being mindset they listed more indulgent choices (x^2(4, N=64)=3.83, p=.05).

In Study 3 (n=72, age_{mean}=36.92) participants were asked to imagine they were having a housewarming party. They assembled a gift registry from a selection of 20 gift items. Activation of mindsets was the same as in Study 1. Participants in a becoming mindset preferred practical to indulgent options more than participants in the being mindset (x^2(2, N=72)=6.39, p=.04).

Study 4 (n=89, age_{mean}=21.6) activated becoming or being mindsets in a more subtle way. Participants were presented with what they believed was an advertisement. The advertisement exhorted the participants to think about themselves in terms of who they are becoming, or who they are now. At the end of the study participants choose one of two snack bars (hedonic vs. prudent). Participants in the becoming mindset were more likely to choose the prudent snack, whereas those in the being mindset showed the opposite (x^2(1, N=84)=5.72, p=.01).

Study 5 (n=71, age_{mean}=48.57) Shoppers were addressed before entering a convenience store and asked to read an advertisement that elicited a being or becoming self-definition (as in Study 4). After they completed their shopping trip, they were given a choice of a snack as a reward. Shoppers in the being mindset preferred the indulgent option (i.e. chocolate bar), whereas shoppers in the becoming mindset preferred the prudent option (i.e. apple or no snack), (x^2(1, N=71)=4.12, p=.04).

Study 6 (n=103, age_{mean}=24.18) examines how lower construal level (i.e. being mindset) will lead to greater valuation of a hedonically-framed product while the higher construal level (i.e. becoming mindset) will lead to greater valuation of a prudently-framed product. Accordingly, when the advertisement and mindset matched, participants evaluated a car more positively, than when they mismatched (t(99)=2.17, p=.03).

"An Obligation to Work or an Opportunity to Play? The Influence of Task Construal and Task Completion on Regulatory Behavior"

Juliano Laran, University of Miami, USA
Chris Janiszewski, University of Florida, USA

One of the most popular explanations of self-control failures is the depletion hypothesis (Muraven and Baumeister 2000). This hypothesis posits that people control their behavior by drawing on a limited supply of regulatory resources. We propose a different approach to understanding regulatory behavior. We argue that effortful behaviors can be construed as "work" or as "play". When they are construed as an obligation to work, the person engages in the behavior in anticipation of a subsequent reward: work is a means to an end. Interruptions to the effortful behavior encourage a person to continue to work (so as to deserve the reward), whereas completing the behavior encourages the person to seek the reward. When regulatory behaviors are construed as an opportunity to play, completing the behavior is the reward in itself: the work is play (work is the reward). Interruptions to the behavior encourage a person to find alternative means of being rewarded (i.e., self-regulation declines), whereas completing the behavior provides an experience of gratification. We hypothesize that low (high) self-control people are more likely to interpret behaviors as obligations to work (opportunities to play). Completion (vs. interruption) of a self-regulatory task should encourage less (more) subsequent regulatory behavior for low (high) self-control people. Our studies featured a task that required self-control at time 1, a manipulation of this task as incomplete or completed, and a task in which participants could exert as much self-control as they wanted at time 2. We also measured self-control as an individual trait.

In study 1, participants were given M&M's and Skittles and asked to put one piece of each in their mouth and take it out. They answered questions about the candies, were asked to hold one piece of each in their finger, and answered additional questions about the candies. Participants were either told that they were done with the first study (completed task condition) or to advance in order to answer additional questions about their behavior as consumers (incomplete task condition). Time 2 involved a 20-minute filler task, which was done while the rest of the candies were in participants' work stations. We weighed how much candy participants ate and used this as a measure of regulatory behavior. Low self-control participants ate more candy in the completed task condition (M=34 grams) than in the incomplete task condition (M=22 grams). High self-control participants ate more candy in the incomplete task condition (M=40 grams) than in the completed task condition (M=29 grams), all p's<.05. A pretest indicated that low self-control participants saw the time 1 task as more of an obligation to work than high self-control participants. Because low (vs. high) self-control participants saw the task as an obligation to work, completion led them to seek more rewarding behaviors.

In study 2, we show that if a task is framed as "work", this will lead everyone to perform less self-regulation. In one condition, we replicated the results of study 1. In a second condition, we asked participants to choose the minimum amount of M&M's and Skittles they needed in order to perform the initial candy task. Making participants abide by a minimum would lead them to see the task as obligation to work. In this condition, all participants ate more candy in the completed (M=35 grams) than in the incomplete task condition (M=24 grams), all p's<.05.

In study 3, we show that a task can be framed to be "play", which will lead everyone to perform more self-regulation. When the time 1 task was said to be a fun task (the sentence "this is a fun task" was added to the instructions), all participants performed more regulatory behavior in the completed than in the incomplete task condition.

In summary, low self-control and high self-control people construe their worlds differently. Low self-control people perceive many behaviors, especially regulatory behaviors, as taxing and difficult (depleting). Upon completion of a taxing behavior, a low self-control person is more likely to exhibit regulatory failure. High self-control people perceive many behaviors as challenging and rewarding. Upon completion of a challenging behavior, the high self-control person is likely to sustain regulatory behavior. Most importantly, our manipulations show conditions under which people in general are more prone to self-regulatory failure, and conditions under which we can encourage increased regulatory behavior despite of people's natural self-control tendencies.

"The Impact of Positive Affect on Cognitive Decision Making Strategies: The Case of Mental Accounting"

Yuliya A. Komarova, University of South Carolina, USA
Kelly L. Haws, Texas A&M University, USA
Amar Cheema, University of Virginia, USA

Mental accounting is a widely adopted cognitive method of keeping track of spending and controlling consumption (e.g., Prelec and Loewenstein 1998). Individuals often use mental accounts to constrain spending by allocating budget limits (Heath and Soll 1996). Cheema and Soman (2006) demonstrate that motivated individuals may depart from mental accounting predictions when there is sufficient ambiguity in how an expense should be categorized (e.g., a restaurant experience may be categorized as either a food or an entertainment expense), via a process of malleable mental accounting. Our primary objective is to understand the role of positive affect on this process of mental accounting.

Although affect can impact judgment and decision making directly (cf. Pham 1998), in the context of financial budgeting, the associated regulation mechanisms (i.e., coping with heightened levels of affect) may reduce one's ability to engage in malleable mental accounting. In summary, we aim to: (1) investigate the influence of positive affect on spending, (2) examine the moderating role of expense ambiguity, and (3) explore the underlying mechanisms.

Predictions. In the past, the research on the role of mood regulation in self-control has focused on regulation of negative mood and generally, demonstrated the superiority of the neutral state (Tice and Bratslavsky 2000). However, in the context of mental accounting, one's cognitive resources are least taxed and available for flexible categorization when an individual is in a neutral state. Positive mood has been shown to lead to enhanced cognitive elaboration as well as greater efficiency in decision making (e.g., Aspinwall 1998; Pham 1998). More importantly, however, supporters of the hedonistic view on affect regulation (cf. Martin 2001) would predict that relative to a neutral state, when one is in a positive mood, their motivation to seek immediate hedonic pleasure should be lower. Consequently, in the presence of expense ambiguity, those in a less positive (neutral) state should be more likely to engage in motivated reasoning in order to construct justifications for spending. Hence, we predict that expense ambiguity should moderate the effect of positive mood on spending. We tested these predictions in two studies.

Study 1. Our studies adapt the procedure developed by Cheema and Soman (2006). A description of budgetary constraints was preceded by an affect manipulation. To test our prediction regarding the effect of positive affect on spending we conducted a 2 (affective states: happy, neutral) x 2 (expense ambiguity: low [comedy show—entertainment expense], high [restaurant—food or entertainment expense]) ANOVA with likelihood of spending as a dependent variable. The findings supported our prediction, as only participants in a neutral state took advantage of expense ambiguity and engaged in malleable mental accounting leading to higher likelihood of spending.

All participants also rated the restaurant expense as a 'typical food expense'. We then asked participants to imagine that they did go to the restaurant and invited them to predict pleasure from spending using three-items which were later combined into an index. We analyzed the index and the typicality ratings as two independent mediators of the relationship between affect and spending likelihood. Both mediation analyses were significant based on Sobel tests, suggesting that positive affect differentially impacted expense categorization and hedonic motivation, which subsequently influenced spending.

Next, we subjected our data to a simultaneous dual mediation analysis with both mediators in the model. While the index of anticipated pleasure from spending fully mediated the relationship, categorization of the restaurant expense as typical food became insignificant. This analysis provided initial evidence suggesting that the influence of positive affect on mental accounting and spending cannot be explained by the inhibitory role of affect in cognitive processing alone, but is also a consequence of differences in hedonic motivation.

Study 2. We designed our second study to rule out the possibility that failure on the part of individuals in a positive mood to engage in malleable mental accounting is simply a consequence of more efficient heuristic processing. We adapted our previous procedure slightly by keeping the expense ambiguous across all conditions. Here, our focal dependent variables were the time it took participants to categorize the restaurant expense as a 'typical food' expense and the time they spent completing the task. Our data revealed that participants in a positive affective (vs. neutral) state actually took longer to respond to the expense categorization question and to complete the task. These findings are consistent with a "greater-elaboration model" which predicts that "people take longer to read mood-congruent information compared to mood-incongruent information, presumably due to greater elaboration of the congruent material" (Pury 2004, p. 156).

As a part of an ongoing research effort to further investigate the impact of affect on malleable mental accounting, we are also examining the role of cognitive load in the relationship between expense ambiguity, positive affect, and spending. Here, we anticipate a three-way interaction, so that when cognitive load is high, individuals in a neutral state can no longer justify incurring a hedonic expense, whereas those in a positive affective state may actually engage in affect maintenance resulting in greater likelihood of spending.

REFERENCES

Aspinwall, Lisa. G. (1998), "Rethinking the Role of Positive Affect in Self-Regulation," *Motivation and Emotion*, 22 (1), 1-32.

Blanton, Hart (2001), "Evaluating the self in the context of another: The three-selves model of social comparison assimilation and contrast," in *Cognitive Social Psychology: The Princeton Symposium on the Legacy and Future of Social Cognition*, Gordon B. Moskowitz, ed. Mahwah, NJ, US: Lawrence Erlbaum Associates Publishers. 75-87

Cheema, Amar and Dilip Soman (2006), "Malleable Mental Accounting: The Effect of Flexibility on the Justification of Attractive Spending and Consumption Decisions," *Journal of Consumer Psychology*, 16 (1), 33-44.

Fishbach, Ayelet and Ying Zhang (2008), "Together or Apart: When Goals and Temptations Complement Versus Compete," *Journal of Personality and Social Psychology*, 94 (4), 547-59.

Fujita, Kentaro, Yaacov Trope, Nira Liberman, and Maya Levin-Sagi (2006), "Construal Levels and Self-Control," *Journal of Personality and Social Psychology*, 90(3), 351-67.

Heath, Chip and Jack Soll (1996), "Mental Budgeting and Consumer Decisions," *Journal of Consumer Research*, 23 (June), 40-52.

Hong, Jiewen and Angela Y. Lee (2008), "Be Fit and Be Strong: Mastering Self-Regulation through Regulatory Fit," *Journal of Consumer Research*, 34 (5), 682-95.

Johnson, Camille S. and Diederik A. Stapel (2009), "Threat and performance in response to social comparisons: The moderating roles of mindset and domain mutability", Working paper, under review. San Jose State University.

Kim,Kyeongheui, Meng Zhang, and Xiuping Li (2008), "Effects of Temporal and Social Distance on Consumer Evaluations," *Journal of Consumer Research*, 35 (4), 706- 13.

Keinan, Anat and Ran Kivetz (2008), "Remedying Hyperopia: The Effects of Self-Control Regret on Consumer Behavior," *Journal of Marketing Research*, 45 (December), 676-689.

Kivetz, Ran and Anat Keinan (2006), "Repenting Hyperopia: An Analysis of Self-Control Regrets," *Journal of Consumer Research*, 33 (September), 273-282.

Kivetz, Ran and Itamar Simonson (2002), "Self-Control for the Righteous: Toward a Theory of Precommitment to Indulgence," *Journal of Consumer Research*, 29 (September), 199-217.

Liberman, Nira, Yaacov Trope, and Cheryl J. Wakslak (2007), "Construal Level Theory and Consumer Behavior," *Journal of Consumer Psychology*, 17(2), 113-17.

Malkoc, Selin A., Gal Zauberman, and James R. Bettman (2008), "Unstuck from the Concrete: Carryover Effects of Abstract Mindsets in Intertemporal Preferences," Unpublished manuscript, University of Minnesota, Minneapolis.

Malkoc, Selin A., Gal Zauberman, and Canan Ulu (2005), "Consuming now or later? The interactive effect of timing and attribute alignability," *Psychological Science*, 16 (5), 411-17

Markus, Hazel and Paula Nurius (1986), "Possible selves," *American Psychologist*, 41(9), 954-69.

Martin, Leonard L. (2001), "Mood as Input: A Configural View of Mood Effects," in *Theories of Mood and Cognition: A Users Handbook*, ed. Leonard L. Martin and Gerald L. Clore, Mahwah, NJ: Lawrence Erlbaum.

Muraven, Mark and Roy F. Baumeister (2000), "Self-regulation and Depletion of Limited Resources: Does Self-control Resemble a Muscle?" *Psychological Bulletin*, 126 (March), 247-259.

Pham, Michel Tuan (1998), "Representativeness, Relevance, and the Use of Feelings in Decision Making," *Journal of Consumer Research*, 25 (2), 144-59.

Prelec, Drazen and George Loewenstein (1998), "The Red and The Black: Mental Accounting of Savings and Debt," *Marketing Science*, 17 (1), 4-27.

Pury, Cynthia L. S. (2004), "Low Positive Affect and Less Extreme Emotional Encoding," *Cognition and Emotion*, 18, 149-58.

Thaler, Richard (1985), "Mental Accounting and Consumer Choice," *Marketing Science*, 4 (3), 199-214.

Tice, D. M. and E. Bratslavsky (2000), "Giving in to Feel Good: The Place of Emotion Regulation in the Context of General Self-Control," *Psychological Inquiry*, *11*, 149-59.

Todorov, Alexander, Amir Goren, and Yaacov Trope (2007), "Probability as a psychological distance: Construal and preferences," *Journal of Experimental Social Psychology*, 43(3), 473-82.

Trope, Yaacov and Ayelet Fishbach (2000), "Counteractive Self-Control in Overcoming Temptation," *Journal of Personality and Social Psychology*, 79 (4), 493–506.

Trope, Yaacov, Nira Liberman, and Cheryl Wakslak (2007), "Construal Levels and Psychological Distance: Effects on Representation, Prediction, Evaluation, and Behavior," *Journal of Consumer Psychology*, 17(2), 83-95

Vallacher, Robin R. and Daniel M. Wegner (1989), "Levels of Personal Agency: Individual Variation in Action Identification," *Journal of Personality and Social Psychology*, 57 (October), 660–71.

Vohs, Kathleen D. and Brandon J. Schmeichel (2003), "Self-Regulation and the Extended Now: Controlling the Self Alters the Subjective Experience of Time," *Journal of Personality and Social Psychology*, 85 (2), 217-30.

SPECIAL SESSION SUMMARY

Visualization, Imagination, and Product Choice: Affective Forecasting of Future Product Consumption and Utilization Experiences

Yanliu Huang, Chinese University of Hong Kong, Hong Kong, China
Robert Meyer, University of Pennsylvania/University of Miami, USA

SESSION OVERVIEW

Many product-purchase decisions are driven less by what consumers feel about products in the present and more what they imagine they will feel about them in the future. When buying furniture, for example, consumers typically try to mentally visualize how a piece will look when placed in their home or apartment, and then forecast the pleasure they will experience upon seeing it in this new context. Likewise, the purchaser of a new cellular phone tries to imagine what it would be like to use its novel features and how difficult they will be to learn—and the affective reactions these different experiences might trigger. How do consumers go about constructing such visualizations, and how accurate are the resulting affective forecasts? The answer to this question is far from fully known. On the one hand, there is a growing body of research that shows that affective forecasts are often prone to systematic biases, such as a tendency to presume that what is felt in the present (such as a product's appeal in a showroom) will be a good predictor of what will be felt about it in the future. On the other hand, the boundary conditions of these findings—particularly when applied to consumer-judgment contexts—are not well understood, and comparatively little work has investigated how consumers construct complex mental visualizations of future product experiences that form the basis of such forecasts.

The purpose of this session is to report the findings of recent research that has sought to close this knowledge gap. The four papers touch on different aspects of the general study of product imagination and forecasting; how consumers go about building mental representations of product consumption experiences that lie in the future, the accuracy of these representations, and how correctable forecast errors are both by consumers and firms.

The opening papers by Wood and Huang and Meyer report new findings on the structure and accuracy—the internal models that consumers use to construct future preferences. In, "Change versus Comfort: How Consumers Mis-Predict Their Openness to Innovation," Wood offers evidence that consumers often are prone to hold mistaken beliefs about how some regulatory processes affect preferences. She shows that whereas consumers often believe that events that cause personal upheaval will induce an offsetting desire to avoid innovation in product choices, the opposite actually tends to be the case. In, "Tradeoffs in the Dark...," Huang and Meyer offer an analysis of the micro-level process that consumers use to form inferences about products that are unfamiliar generalizations of existing offerings. The final two papers by Zhao, Dahl, and Hoeffler and Easwar and West examine corrective issues in affective forecasting. Zhao, Dahl, and Hoeffler take up the issue of how to best design visualization aids to aid consumers overcome affective forecasting biases, while Easwar and West look at the effectiveness of perhaps the simplest of all corrective devices: educating consumers about the existence of biases.

Taken together, the session is designed to provide an integrative overview of new research aimed at enhancing our understanding the process that underlies consumer affective forecasts as well as methods by which these forecasts can be improved. The concluding discussion will then have the goal of suggesting a research agenda for future work in the area.

EXTENDED ABSTRACTS

"Change versus Comfort: How Consumers Mis-Predict Their Openness to Innovation"

Stacy Wood, University of South Carolina, USA

Many can relate to desiring dearly familiar products in an unfamiliar or changing landscape. This phenomenon is so common in culinary practice that we have a term—comfort food—that encompasses the soothing function of our long-time favorites. One can argue that this practice goes beyond food; consumers may believe that they will prefer favorite movies, familiar music, and habits (e.g., smoking, a daily jog) when surrounded by changing life factors. Like other consumer coping strategies, consumers may believe they will choose familiar things in times of change because familiar choices minimize the cognitive/emotional load engendered by a new environment; a lay theory reinforced through external norms and internal cues. However, recent research on mindsets and habits offers a competing prediction. Changing circumstances may break habitual cues that favor old favorites and promote a general 'change mindset'. This underlying openness to change may prompt choices counter to the "comfort" theory, creating a paradox in which consumers' actual choices are opposite to what they predict.

Study 1. In study 1, 203 American participants were offered the following choice during an experimental session with several unrelated studies:

"Potato chips are a favorite American snack. They are also a favorite British snack, but in England, potato chips as we know them are called "crisps." Crisps come in many of the same flavors that we have in American stores, but are also available in flavors that are not common here. Flavors like Sea Salt, Cheese & Pickle, Thai Chili & Lime, Smoky Wiltshire, Bombay Mix, and Camembert & Plum are very popular. *Two people from this study will be selected to win* a prize pack of a variety of either British crisps or American chips. If you win, which prize pack do you want? Choose below by checking one box below: [Two boxes appeared here–one box showing a selection of American (Lay's brand) chips and the other showing a selection of British (McCoy's brand) crisps. The prize pack was described in the box as a selection of 6 full-sized bags of chips/crisps.]"

Later (after several unrelated tasks, ~30-40 minutes), participants received several surveys, including five Likert items that assessed participants' perceived personal level of "life change," (e.g., "There has been more upheaval than usual in my life this month"). Responses were summed and participants were divided into two groups, High-Change and Low-Change, based on a median split of this index. It was hypothesized that consumers experiencing more change would be more likely to choose the British crisp than the American chip. Consistent with this, a significant Pearson chi-square analysis (χ^2=4.11, p=.04) showed there was higher selection of the unfamiliar British crisp option for High-Change participants (M= 57.4%) than Low-Change participants (M=42.6%) and higher selection of the familiar American chip option for Low-Change participants (M=56.8%) than for High-Change participants (M=43.2%).

Study 2. Study 2 was a prediction study. Participants were asked to consider two peers experiencing different levels of life change and to predict what choice these target others would make if given the same "chips or crisps" scenario from study 1. It was hypothesized that participants would predict (opposite to choices observed in study 1) that high-change others will choose the familiar option and low-change others will choose the unfamiliar option. Further, when given an opportunity to explain their prediction, it was hypothesized that participants would refer primarily to strategies congruent with a comfort-food lay theory. Consistent with this, 26.8% of participants predicted that Taylor (High-Change) would choose the British crisps and 73.2% predicted s/he would choose the American chips (median/modal response). Conversely, 59.8% predicted that Brook (Low-Change) would choose the British crisps (median/modal response) and 40.2% predicted s/he would choose the American chips (?2=56.26, p<.001). The cognitive response measures (coded by two independent raters) indicated that participants offered reasons consistent with coping-oriented strategies that fit with a comfort food lay theory.

Studies 3–5. Studies 3-5 replicate the effect and further explore consumers' forecasts of their future preference for comfort versus change. Study 3 demonstrates that the effect extends to non-food situations (choice of a range of new or unfamiliar products). Study 4 demonstrates that this effect occurs primarily when choices are characterized by low involvement. Study 5 demonstrates that choice of new options can be increased by manipulating perceived life change.

"Tradeoffs in the Dark: The Effect of Experience on Extrapolated Consumer Preferences"

Yanliu Huang, The Chinese University of Hong Kong, China
Robert Meyer, The University of Pennsylvania/University of Miami, USA

Many choices require consumers to extrapolate preferences formed in one domain of experience to an unfamiliar new one. Examples include decisions to adopt new goods or services, or judgments of the potential attractiveness of novel product-attribute combinations. While there has been considerable work investigating such related problems as inference formation and behavior in prediction tasks, less is known about either the process individuals use to make trade-offs among unfamiliar ranges of attributes or the algebraic structure of such trade-offs.

The goal of this work is to investigate dynamics of how consumers use preference knowledge gained over one range of product-attribute levels to predict their preferences for new attribute combinations. Prior work has suggested that given the limited direct experience in consuming products, predictive inferences may involve a blend of two processes: exemplar-based and rule-based. Exemplar-based policies are those that forecast utilities for new stimuli based on the experienced utility of similar options (Juslin, Olsson, and Olsson 2003; Meyer 1987), and rule-based policies are those that exploit generalized beliefs about the functional relationship between attribute values such as monotonicity and additivity (Delosh, Busemyer, and McDaniel 1997). In this project, we focus on two central research questions: 1) how does the use of these two processes (exemplar-based or rule-based) evolve as consumers develop judgmental experience in a product category; and 2) what does the answer to (1) imply about the likely accuracy of consumers' hedonic forecasts for unfamiliar product-attribute combinations?

Central to the work is a hypothesis that the prevalence of each process will evolve over time as experience in a core judgment domain grows. Specifically, given limited experience predictions will rely on meta-cognitive "guessing" rules that make no attempt to utilize what has been observed about product values in a core domain. As experience grows, however, knowledge gained in the core domain will be increasingly utilized, first by using exemplar-based prediction rules that draw analogies between novel products and previously-viewed ones, then by using functional prediction rules that exploited learned continuous associations between attribute levels and valuations. One of the consequences is that consumers will be prone to under-estimating the utility they will draw from novel product combinations that are objectively superior to familiar options and over-estimating the utility they will draw from inferior options. The magnitude of these errors, however, is also hypothesized in some cases to be U-shaped, where decision makers with virtually no experience at all in a judgment category may be able to provide more accurate utility predictions in novel domains than those with moderate amounts of experience.

We tested these hypotheses in six studies where participants acted as agents to learn to predict a target customer's apartment preferences based on four attributes: travel time to work, apartment appearance, security of apartment location, and rent. Three initial studies explored the nature of extrapolation judgments when decision makers have reasonably high levels of judgmental experience in a given setting, and are asked to predict that likely utility of options that have systematically superior or inferior attribute values. Here we found asymmetric support for the predicted over-and-under estimation bias: when participants were asked to predict the likely attractiveness of a novel apartment, they over-estimated the likely value of inferior options, but were accurate in their hedonic forecasts for superior ones. In contrast, when participants were asked to predict the unattractiveness of an apartment, participants under-predict the attractiveness of superior options. Studies 4 and 5 explored the boundary conditions of these prediction biases based on the amount of prior judgmental experience and the underlying "true" utility-generating rule. As predicted, the forecasting bias was most pronounced among participants with moderate amounts of judgmental experience (Study 4) but this advantage of little experience vanishes when the underlying composition rule is a complex one unlikely to be naively guessed (Study 5).

Direct evidence of the hypothesized evolution of inference strategies was provided by a sixth study where at periodic junctures of the prediction task participants were asked to type a written description of the process they had used to make the previous judgment, and these statements were content-analyzed. Consistent with the hypothesized strategy evolution, statements gave strong evidence of a use of generalized principles when direct experience was limited, exemplar-based strategies when experience was moderate, and rule-bases strategies when experience was more extensive.

"Matching Time Perspective and Visualization Aids to Enhance New Product Evaluation"

Min Zhao, University of Toronto, Canada
Darren Dahl, University of British Columbia, Canada
Steve Hoeffler, Vanderbilt University, USA

How will visualization aids impact new product evaluation under a retrospective versus an anticipatory perspective? In the new product domain, the common wisdom is that imagining the usage of a new product in a future scenario leads to higher evaluations than relating it to a past experience (Dahl, Chattopadhyay, and Gorn 1999). In our work, we draw on research on retrospection and anticipation in terms of people's natural mental construal and use these results to propose different effects of visualization aids for retrospective and anticipatory visualization.

Existing work on retrospection and anticipation has indicated that past events are generally construed as more detailed and concrete whereas future events are construed as less detailed and more abstract (Van Boven, Kane, and McGraw 2008). At the same time, existing research on consumer decision making over time has demonstrated that the type of information had the greatest impact on evaluation when it fits consumers' natural mindset in terms of construal levels (e.g., high-level information such as feature upgrade had a larger impact on consumers' purchase intention for a distant future decision where consumers' natural thoughts were at a higher level, whereas low-level information such as coupon had a larger impact on purchase intention in the near future where consumers' natural thoughts were at a lower level (Thomas, Chandran, and Trope 2007). Based on these previous findings, we predict that a match of the construal levels between visualization aids and temporal perspective would increase the evaluation of new products. Since people's natural mental construal for the past tends to be concrete, we hypothesize that concrete visualization aids will be more effective in increasing new product evaluation for retrospective visualization. However, since people's natural mental construal for the future tends to be abstract, abstract visualization aids will be more effective in increasing new product evaluation for an anticipatory visualization. In addition, we predict a reversal of this pattern when people's natural temporal perspective is reversed.

We test our hypotheses in three experiments. In all three experiments, the key constructs that we manipulated were level of concreteness of the visualization aids and temporal perspective of the visualization. To manipulate temporal perspective, we asked participants to either relate the target product to a past or future scenario. In terms of level of concreteness of the visualization aids, different operationalizations were used across the three experiments.

In experiment 1, a mock advertisement of a Tablet PC was used as our stimuli. We manipulated concreteness level by providing participants with either one or five examples about using the new product. The results showed that when participants related the new product to their past experience, concrete visualization aids increased their evaluation. However, when they related the product to the future, abstract visualization aids enhanced product evaluation.

In experiment 2, we used a new technology (Tap & Go PayPass) as our stimuli. We manipulated the concreteness of visualization aids by providing participants with either usage process-related aids (i.e., how to use this new technology) as concreter aids or benefit-related aids (i.e. why adopting this new technology) as abstracter aids (Liberman and Trope 1998; Vallacher and Wegner 1987, 1989). The results fully replicated our findings in experiment 1.

In experiment 3, we manipulated the concreteness of visualization aids by providing the same sample activity of using a Tablet PC, but describing it with lots of details in the concrete conditions, and describing it with very general wording in the abstract conditions. However, in this experiment, we shifted people's natural construal level by instructing them to think more abstractly for the past and more concretely for the future. If the match of the construal levels was the key driver of our results in experiments 1 and 2, the effects that we observed in experiments 1 and 2 should be reversed after we shifted the natural construal level. Indeed, we found that abstract visualization aids increased retrospective evaluation and concrete visualization aids increased anticipatory evaluation after the natural construal level was shifted.

Our work contributes to recent research on visualization and new product learning by demonstrating the importance of the match between the specificity of the visualization aids and temporal perspective on new product evaluation.

"The Interactive Effect of Affective Forecasting and Mood on Performance and Product Goals"

Karthik Easwar, Ohio State University, USA
Patricia West, Ohio State University, USA

Many consumer decisions involve the setting of future goals. People join gyms with the goal of losing twenty pounds, buy musical instruments hoping to learn to play them, and buy new phones expecting an easier and more pleasurable calling experience (Olshavsky and Miller 1972). These goals are driven by various motivations, including our desire to maintain a positive mood. The mood-maintenance hypothesis (Isen 1983) states that we engage in activities that ensure positivity. Given that goals divide outcomes into successes and failures, mood maintenance contends that we set goals we expect to surpass. However, people often commit affective forecasting errors (AFEs) by overestimating the future pain of failure and pleasure of success—potentially leading consumers to set inappropriate goals for themselves or during product related decisions (Kermer 2006). The following experiment examines how providing consumers with AFE knowledge influences their desire to engage in mood maintenance and goal-setting.

In study one, two factors are manipulated: AFE knowledge and mood. AFE knowledge was manipulated through passages that stated that the AFE is an overestimate of the impact of positive outcomes, an overestimate of the impact of negative outcomes, or a control passage. To manipulate mood, subjects elaborated on a good or bad experience. In the neutral mood condition subjects were given no elaboration task. Finally, in an ensuing anagram task, subjects set an anagram performance goal.

Subjects in a positive mood will engage in mood maintenance and set lower goals than those in a negative mood. However, this mood maintenance motivation can be removed with knowledge of the AFE. This knowledge removes the fear of losing positivity and frees people to set high goals. In a positive mood, we focus on preventing affective loss; therefore, knowledge of the AFE as affective gain overestimation will neither be relevant nor impact goals. Only under certain conditions will AFE knowledge enable subjects to set higher goals.

There were no significant differences between the different neutral mood conditions; therefore, they were pooled into a control condition. A 3 X 2 ANOVA revealed a significant interaction ($F(2, 262)=4.17$, $p=.016$). It was found that, in a positive mood, subjects exhibited mood maintenance, setting lower goals to ensure success ($M_{\text{positive mood, no AFE knowledge}}=25.2$, $M_{\text{negative mood, no AFE knowledge}}=30.8$, $M_{\text{control}}=30.7$, $t(391)\ 2.12$, $p=.02$ and $t(391)=2.32$, $p=.01$, respectively). However, if told the AFE was an overestimation of negative affect, subjects knew a failure would not be devastating and set higher goals than with no knowledge ($M_{\text{positive mood, negative AFE knowledge}}=34.5$, $M_{\text{positive mood, no AFE knowledge}}=25.2$, $t(391)=3.31$, $p<.001$). Subjects in the positive AFE passage condition set lower goals than the negative AFE passage condition ($M_{\text{positive mood, negative AFE knowledge}}=34.5$, $M_{\text{positive mood, positive AFE knowledge}}=25.1$, $t(391)=3.32$, $p<.001$), supporting the hypothesis that those engaging in mood maintenance focus on preventing loss.

While study one focuses on performance goals, these effects can also apply to the expectations we have for products. We often make product evaluation forecasts; how we think we will feel about the product (Zhao et al. 2009, Wood 2009). Knowing our AFE tendencies, we may realize that most products are satisfying and few overwhelm. We need neither the tiniest camera nor the loudest speakers to be happy and one weakness should not ruin product evaluations. Future studies plan to explore how the AFE influences product goals, not just performance goals.

Mood can affect our desire to engage in product exploration. One can easily imagine how exploring a product, with difficult menus, infinite settings and peripheral features can lead to frustration. In this light, the anagram task could be considered a simplified product exploration task; both are time consuming, non-linear processes. Fearing frustration, we may engage in mood maintenance and not explore our product fully. Knowing our mood state is safe, might remove this fear of exploration. And often, the nuances we find are what make us truly pleased with our products.

REFERENCES

Campbell, D. J. and Ilgen, D. R. (1976), "Additive Effects of Task Difficulty and Goal Setting on Subsequent Task Performance," *Journal of Applied Psychology*, 61, 319–324.

Dahl, Darren, Amitava Chattopadhyay, and Gerald J. Gorn (1999), "The Use of Visual Mental Imagery in New Product Design," *Journal of Marketing Research*, 36 (February), 18–28.

DeLosh, Edward L., Jerome R. Busemeyer, and Mark A. McDaniel (1997), "Extrapolation: The Sine Qua Non for Abstraction in Function Learning," *Journal of Experimental Psychology: Learning, Memory, and Cognition*, 23 (4), 968-86.

Frost, P. J. and T. A. Mahoney (1976), "Goal Setting and Task Process: An Interactive Influence on Individual Performance," Organizational Behavior and Human Performance, 17, 328 – 250.

Isen, A. M. and R. Patrick (1983), "The Effect of Positive Feelings on Risk Taking: When the Chips are Down," *Organizational Behavior and Human Decision Processes*, 31,194–202.

Isen, A. M. and N. Geva (1987), "The Influence of Positive Affect on Acceptable Level of Risk: The Person with a Large Canoe Has a Large Worry," *Organizational Behavior and Human Decision Processes*, 39, 145–154.

Isen, A. M., T. E. Nygren, F. G. Ashby (1988), "Influence of Positive Affect on the Subjective Utility of Gains and Losses: It Is Just Not Worth the Risk," *Journal of Personality and Social Psychology*, 55, 710–717.

Juslin, Peter, Henrik Olsson, and Anna-Carin Olsson (2003), "Exemplar Effects in Categorization and Multiple-Cue Judgment," *Journal of Experimental Psychology: General*, 132 (1), 133-56.

Kermer, D. A., E. Driver-Linn, T. D. Wilson, and D. T. Gilbert (2006), "Loss Aversion Is an Affective Forecasting Error," *Psychological Science*, 17, 649-653.

Meyer, Robert J. (1987), "The Learning of Multiattribute Judgment Policies," *Journal of Consumer Researc*h, 14 (September), 155-73.

Thomas, Manoj, Sucharita Chandran and Yaacov Trope (2007), "The Effects of Information Type and Temporal Distance on Purchase Intentions," Working Paper.

Van Boven, Leaf, Joanne Kane, and Peter McGraw (2008), "Temporally asymmetric constrains on mental simulation: retrospection is more constrained than prospection," In K. Markman, W. Klein, & S. Shur (Eds.), *The Handbook of Imagination and Mental Simulation.*

Special Session Summary

Setting the Stage: How Frames of Reference May Be Influencing Your Behavior

Rebecca Hamilton, University of Maryland, USA

SESSION OVERVIEW

Research on consumer decision making suggests that instead of having completely formed preferences prior to choice, consumers often construct their preferences at the time these are needed to make decisions (Bettman, Luce and Payne 1998). As a result, the context in which consumers make decisions can significantly influence their preferences among alternatives and even their willingness to pay for these alternatives.

In addition, there is a large literature showing that the way questions are asked can have a significant effect on consumers' self-reported judgments. For example, when consumers are asked to report the frequency with which they engage in a behavior such as watching TV, their responses are systematically influenced by the response scales used to provide the information (Menon, Raghubir and Schwarz 1995; Schwarz, Hippler, Deutsch and Strack 1985).

In this session, we bring together these two literatures, showing that managers may be able to influence important purchase-related variables such as confidence, affect and willingness to pay by using the right response scales. For example, although sensory scientists often assume that basic sensory evaluation is not as susceptible to bias as higher level evaluations such as product preferences, research by Mantonakis, Schwarz, Wudarzewski and Yoon (Paper 1) shows that the numeric values of the scale can bias tasters' perceptions and encoding of sensory attributes for wines. Moreover, the scales used predict willingness to pay for the wines tasted (Mantonakis is an Associate Fellow at The Cool Climate Oenology and Viticulture Institute).

Further, while most of the extant research on behavioral frequency judgments has focused on cognitive factors, Menon and Agrawal (Paper 2) investigate how consumers' emotions impact their use of response scales. Both the valence and the uncertainty of the emotions experienced predict the degree to which consumers rely on self-generated information as opposed to being influenced by contextually available information such as the response scales being used.

Consistent with Paper 2, Hamilton, Ratner and Thompson (Paper 3) examine emotions in addition to cognitive responses, and Ülkümen, Thomas and Morwitz (Paper 4) examine the role of certainty. Paper 3 shows that consumers who use a high-frequency scale to report how often they would use a product are less interested in purchasing it than those who use a low-frequency scale, even though they report higher absolute frequencies. Moreover, low-frequency scales increase perceived use of the product relative to other consumers and positive affect. Subsequent studies replicate these results using advertisements suggesting that either high- or low-frequency use is the norm. Relatedly, Paper 4 shows that the scale on which consumers are asked to report their budgets (one year vs. 12 months) significantly affects both budget estimates and confidence in these estimates, suggesting potential consequences for consumer spending.

Together, these papers extend the scope of research on response scale effects by examining how initial frames of reference shape downstream variables such as confidence, affect and willingness to pay. We expect this session to provide insights interesting to a wide range of researchers: those studying sensory perceptions, decision making, persuasion and survey design.

Norbert Schwarz (University of Michigan) served as the session discussant. Beginning with the classic paper by Schwarz et al. (1985), Norbert has published dozens of papers examining the effects of initial questions on subsequent responses. With his deep expertise on this topic, Norbert concluded the session with a rich and rewarding 10-minute discussion.

EXTENDED ABSTRACTS

"How the Numbers on Your Rating Scale Influence Taste Perception and Willingness to Pay"

Antonia Mantonakis, Brock University, Canada
Norbert Schwarz, University of Michigan, USA
Amanda Wudarzewski,!zrock University, Canada
Carolyn Yoon, University of Michigan, USA

Sensory scientists often assume that consumers are rational decision makers (Köster 2003). While much is understood about genetic differences leading to variations in taste perception (Bartoshuk, Fast and Snyder 2005), visual and verbal cues (Hoegg and Alba 2007) that impact perceptual and cognitive processes and can lead to biased judgment are only beginning to be understood. Similar to recent research demonstrating that factors undiagnostic to perception can lead to errors in judgment (Krishna 2006; Krishna and Morrin 2008), we investigate how information extraneous to sensory evaluation can lead to errors in perception.

Little is known about how factors completely unrelated to the product, such as the context, can influence utility derived from the sensation. It has been argued that perceptual systems have been optimized by evolution (Abdi 2002), and that sensory inputs are inherently evaluable (Hsee et al. forthcoming). Thus "sensory utilities" (versus prediction or memory utilities) should not be biased by contextual factors (Hsee et al. 2009). However, previous studies showing that context has no influence on sensory utility have manipulated context by creating contrasts of varying superiority (e.g., eating potato chips in the context of either a better–chocolate–or worse–sardines–alternative; Morewedge et al. 2009). Instead, we manipulate contextual factors completely unrelated to the consumption object: the format of the rating scale on which sensory reports are given.

Textbook discussions of rating scale formats usually focus on the number of scale points used and the extremity of the scale labels. What is often overlooked is that the numeric values of the rating scale can influence the interpretation of the scale labels (Schwarz et al. 1991; Schwarz 1994). Suppose, for example that you are asked to evaluate the intelligence of a public figure on a scale from "not intelligent" to "very intelligent". What does "not intelligent" stand for? Does it indicate the absence of superior intelligence or the presence of its opposite, some level of stupidity? To resolve this ambiguity, survey respondents have been found to draw on the numeric values of the rating scale (Haddock and Carrick 1999). In general, a unipolar scale (e.g., 0 to 10) pertains to different degrees of the attribute (intelligence), whereas a bipolar scale (-5 to +5) pertains to degrees of the attribute and its opposite. Accordingly, bipolar scales elicit higher ratings than unipolar scales.

We apply this logic to ratings of sensory experience. We gave participants a hedonic product to sample. Half of the participants gave their ratings on various attributes on a bipolar scale, using endpoints from -5 to +5. The other half gave ratings on a unipolar scale, using endpoints from 0 to 10. We predicted that participants who rate on a -5 to +5 scale should indicate higher hedonic evaluations of the attributes than those who rate on a 0 to 10 scale. We should see the same effect for willingness to pay, such that participants who rate on a -5 to +5 scale have a higher WTP than those who rate on a 0 to 10 scale.

The study was conducted in one session. We gave participants a glass of wine and allowed participants to taste it; they answered questions based on hedonic attributes of the wine (crispness, freshness, fruitiness and complexity), which were administered on either a 0 to 10 scale or a -5 to +5 scale. Next, we gave participants questions pertaining to the wine they had just tasted and their level of wine expertise. Of particular interest was the answer to the question, "How much would you be willing to pay for a bottle of this wine?"

Ratings on the 4 attributes (freshness, crispness, completxity and fruitness) were correlated (α=.51); ratings were combined to produce a single evaluation index. To examine whether the numerical values manipulation affected evaluation, we examined mean differences between the two groups, with expertise as a covariate. Evaluation was higher for the -5 to +5 endpoint group (M=7.14) than the 0 to 10 group (M=6.53), $F(1,77)=5.51$, $p<.03$. To examine whether the numerical values manipulation affected WTP, we examined mean differences between the groups, with expertise as a covariate. We found that WTP was higher for the -5 to +5 endpoint group than the 0 to 10 group (WTP means=$17.51 and $15.05; log(WTP) means=2.80 and 2.61; $F(1,77)=4.07$, $p<.05$).

In a follow-up study, we will use a two session procedure to replicate our results and examine the effects of scale labels on retrospective evaluations of taste (cf. Braun 1999).

"When Behavioral Frequency Judgments Depend on Incidental Emotions"

Geeta Menon, University of Pennsylvania, USA
Nidhi Agrawal, Northwestern University, USA

There is a vast literature on how consumers use self-generated (memory-based) information, or rely on contextually-available information (stimulus-based), or combine these two sources of information (mixed) in arriving at judgments (see Lynch 2004 for a review). Feldman and Lynch's (1988) Accessibility-Diagnosticity model proposes that the likelihood that an input will be used for a judgment is directly related to its accessibility and diagnosticity, and inversely related to the accessibility and diagnosticity of alternate sources of information. This model has been empirically tested in various consumer domains including brand evaluations (e.g., Lynch, Marmorstein, and Weigold 1988) and survey responses (e.g., Menon, Raghubir and Schwarz 1995, 1997). This stream of research has focused primarily on cognitive factors in information processing and judgment formation. In this paper, we present evidence for the effects of emotional factors on the formation of behavioral frequency judgments.

We examine the effects of incidental emotions varying in valence and uncertainty (i.e., happiness, hopefulness, sadness and anxiety) on whether self-generated vs. contextually-available cues are relied on more heavily to form behavioral frequency judgments. Menon et al. (1995) show that when self-generated information is not readily accessible or diagnostic, respondents rely on contextually available information. We posit that when information is accessible and diagnostic, as in the case of regular behaviors, incidental emotions do not moderate the use of this information in forming judgments; thus, regardless of the emotion experienced, we should replicate the results of Menon et al. (1995). However, we posit a moderating effect of incidental emotions on the use of self-generated vs. contextually-available information for irregular behaviors. Based on extant work, we propose that the appraisal dimension of emotional valence leads people to systematically rely on different inputs in computing behavioral frequency judgments. Positive emotions encourage a reliance on memory and pre-existing knowledge structures, while negative emotions tend to encourage a greater scrutiny of the contextual information represented by the response alternatives.

Beyond emotional valence, however, emotional uncertainty serves as an input on whether people should trust their initial inferences or not. Uncertainty casts doubt on inferences derived based on valence-driven input and leads people to rely on the alternate input (Tiedens and Linton 2001). When feeling certain, people go along with the inputs flowing out of the emotional valence appraisal dimension. But when people feel uncertain, they attribute the uncertainty to the valence-driven judgments. This doubtfulness leads them to go with the alternate process. Specifically, for positive emotions, both happy (a certain emotion) and hopeful (an uncertain emotion) people are likely to evoke self-generated inputs. The certainty accompanying happiness leads people to trust their self-generated inputs and the uncertainty accompanying hopefulness casts doubt on the self-generated inputs and drives people to consider information beyond their memory such as that gleaned from the context. Hence, happy people rely more on self-generated input and hopeful people on the response alternatives.

A similar process occurs for people experiencing negative emotions. While both sad (a certain emotion) and anxious (an uncertain emotion) people are more likely to focus on contextual factors than self-generated information, the certainty associated with sadness leads sad people to trust the contextual inputs and base judgments on response alternatives. In contrast, the uncertainty associated with anxiety leads anxious people to doubt judgments based on their default process, i.e., response alternative based judgments, so they resort to memory cues.

We demonstrate these results in two experiments in which we prime emotions varying on valence and uncertainty. In experiment 1, we prime happiness, hopefulness, sadness and anxiety in a 2 (valence: positive vs. negative) x 2 (uncertainty: certain vs. uncertain) x 2 (response alternatives: high vs. low) x 2 (regularity of behavior: irregular vs. regular) mixed design in which the first three factors were manipulated between-subjects, and the last within-subjects. In experiment 1, we demonstrate the predicted effects of the valence and uncertainty dimensions of emotions moderated by the regularity of the behavior on behavioral frequency judgments and the reliance on self-generated versus contextually-available information. In experiment 2, we replicate these results in a similar 2 x 2 x 2 x 2 design in which we include process measures of: (i) perceptions of confidence in the behavioral frequency estimate; (ii) self-reported reliance on the input used in judgment; and (iii) response latencies for forming behavioral frequency judgments. Experiment 2 provides evidence for the lower confidence and greater response times associated with uncertain emotions.

By identifying emotional antecedents to the use of self-generated versus contextually available information, we add to the literature on information processing and emotions, as well as to the substantive domain of survey methodology.

"Will I Get My Money's Worth? Inferring Product Value Based on Predictions about Relative Use"

Rebecca Hamilton, University of Maryland, USA
Rebecca Ratner, University of Maryland, USA
Debora Thompson, Georgetown University, USA

When considering the purchase of a durable product, will consumers be more likely to make the purchase if they think about using it every day or if they think about using it every week? From an economic perspective, using a durable product more frequently should increase its perceived value. However, we suggest that when considering the perceived value of a product, consumers also think about how often they will use it compared with other consumers. If consumers believe others will use the product more than they will (i.e., they are relatively light rather than relatively heavy users), they may not be willing to pay as much for the product. That is, we propose that product value is a comparative judgment rather than an absolute judgment.

In studies 1 and 2, consumers first reported their frequency of using a product with either a high- or low-frequency scale. After reporting their absolute frequency of use, they evaluated their interest in owning the product, and then they assessed whether their frequency of use was subjectively "a little" or "a lot." In study 1, half of the participants evaluated a USB drive and half evaluated a scientific calculator. Although those who initially used the high-frequency scale reported higher absolute frequency of use ($F(1, 194)=45.1$, $p<.001$), consistent with earlier research (Schwarz, Hippler, Deutsch and Strack 1985), they reported lower subjective frequency of use ($F(1, 194)=4.8, p<.05$) and were less interested in buying the product than those who saw the low-frequency scale ($F(1, 194)=6.0$, $p<.05$). A mediation analysis shows that participants' subjective perceptions of how much they would use the product mediate the observed scale label effects (Sobel test=2.06, $p<.05$).

Our second study replicated these results using a different product category, video games, and extended them by examining behavioral intentions towards specific products. Interest in the specific video game we showed participants was higher in the low- than in the high-frequency scale condition, $F(1, 121)=9.6$, $p<.01$. Notably, this study also showed that participants in the low frequency scale condition reported more positive affect than those in the high frequency condition, and that positive affect was significantly correlated with perceived frequency of use relative to others ($r=.54$, $p<.001$). This suggests that consumers may experience an affective boost when they infer a positive comparison of their own use of a product relative to others.

Our third and fourth studies extend our analysis beyond frequency scale manipulations to show that advertising a product as appropriate for weekly use as opposed to daily use can lead to higher subjective frequency of use and higher purchase intentions. In study 3, respondents either read an ad for a sandwich press or for fitness shoes. The ad described the product as providing benefits experienced daily (high-frequency) or weekly (low-frequency). As predicted, those in the week condition predicted higher relative use compared to those in the day condition, $F(1, 83)=5.57, p<.05$), even though the ad described less frequent product use. Moreover, using the words "this week" in the advertisement significantly increased participants interest in the product relative to using the words "today" ($F(1, 83)=4.29$, $p<.05$). Confirming the proposed process mechanism, perceived relative use mediated the effect of the ad on interest in the product.

In our last study, we show that whether the respondent is a light or heavy user in the product category moderates the effect. Specifically, heavy users are motivated by high frequency positioning while light users are demotivated by high-frequency positioning. Participants reviewed the fitness shoe advertisements from study 3 and then reported their interest in the shoes as well as the number of times they exercised per week. As predicted, regression analysis showed that the "day" ads created more interest in the product for heavy users than the "week" ads, but the week ads created more interest for light users, $\beta=.73$, $t(172)=4.12$, $p<.001$.

Counterintuitively, manipulations that encourage consumers to predict that they would use a product more frequently may result in less interest in the product category and lower purchase intentions. Our studies show that this effect is driven by consumers' beliefs about their own product usage relative to other consumers, and that the effect can be produced either by advertisements or by frequency scales that communicate that either a high frequency of use or low frequency of use is the norm.

"When 12 Months is Not the Same as One Year: Antecedents of Confidence in Consumer Budgets"

Gülden Ülkümen, University of Southern California, USA
Manoj Thomas, Cornell University, USA
Vicki Morwitz, New York University, USA

Consumers' plans are influenced by the confidence felt while making these plans (Ulkumen, Thomas, and Morwitz 2008). For example, consumers feel less confident, and therefore provide larger budget estimates for the next year than for the next month, even after these budgets are unitized (Ulkumen, Thomas, and Morwitz 2008). In this research, we examine how framing of the time period in a survey question (one year versus 12 months) can influence consumers' confidence in different planning domains, and consequently influence a variety of outcomes such as the magnitude of budget estimates and the likelihood of starting a diet.

We examine four antecedents of confidence in consumers' plans: (1) framing of the time period, (2) familiarity with the frame, (3) whether the sources of uncertainty are attributed to internal or external factors, and (4) perceived difficulty.

In our first study, we asked participants to provide budget estimates for time periods that differed in length or framing. Budgets for the next week, month, three months, six months and 12 months were not significantly different from each other (M_{week}=\$701, M_{month}=\$832, $M_{3months}$=\$1117, $M_{6months}$=\$986, $M_{12months}$=\$1066), and they were all significantly lower than the budgets for the next year ($M_{year=}$\$2,196). Consumers were less confident, and they provided larger budget estimates for the next year than for the next 12 months. Rather than the actual length, the framing of the budget period has an effect on confidence and budgets.

Study 2 tested whether this framing effect exists because people rarely use the period of a year (versus 12 months) to make predictions, and are less familiar with this frame. Participants estimated their budgets either for the next 12 months or the next year, and we manipulated familiarity by asking half of the participants to provide a series of estimates for the frame associated with their condition before providing their budget estimates. The results show that the familiarity manipulation did not affect confidence or budgets in the 12 month frame. However, confidence increased, and annual budgets decreased when the familiarity with the time frame increased.

The aim of study 3 was to examine whether consumers attribute the source of their uncertainty to both internal and external factors in the one year frame, but only to internal factors in the 12 month frame. Reminding consumers of one of these two components of uncertainty should make them discount this component. To test this prediction, we manipulated the source of uncertainty by providing some participants with a paragraph that emphasized events in life that are within (internal) or outside their control (external), before estimating their budgets. The results revealed that in the year frame, budgets were significantly lower when participants were reminded either of internal or external sources of confidence, than the budgets in the control condition. In the 12 month frame, there was no difference between budgets in the control or internal LOC conditions, but reminding participants of the external sources led to a significant increase in budget estimates.

In study 4, participants were first presented with a strict diet plan, which required avoiding a long list of foods. This diet plan was framed as either a 12 month plan or a one year plan. The results suggest that participants were more likely to adopt the diet when it was framed as a 12 month diet than a one year diet. Participants were more confident, and found it less difficult to follow the diet plan when it was framed as a 12 month plan than as a one year plan. Perceived difficulty fully mediated the effect of time frame on confidence, and confidence partially mediated the effect of time frame on likelihood to adopt the diet.

In summary, framing the same time period in different ways can influence consumers' plans, due to changes in confidence. We examine four factors that affect confidence: (1) framing of the time period, (2) familiarity with the frame, (3) whether the sources of uncertainty are attributed to internal or external factors, and (4) perceived difficulty. Simply framing the budget period as 12 months versus one year in the survey question can increase confidence, and lead to smaller budget forecasts. Budgets for the next year can be decreased by increasing familiarity with this frame, and budgets for the next 12 months can be increased with reminders of external factors. Consumers are more likely to adopt a strict diet plan when it is framed as a 12 month diet than a one year diet, because they perceive it to be less difficult.

SPECIAL SESSION SUMMARY

When (and How) Does Metacognitive Experience Affect Consumer Behavior?

Manoj Thomas, Cornell University, USA

SESSION OVERVIEW

A growing body of evidence demonstrates that consumers' judgments and preferences are not only based on cognitions, but are also influenced by their metacognitive experience. However, there is debate about the scope and extent of the effects of metacognitive experience. On the one hand it could be argued that all judgments are characterized by some sort of metacognitive experience. Some judgments feel easier than expected, while others feel more difficult. This view suggests that the effects of metacognitive experience will be pervasive. On the other hand, it has been argued that the effects of metacognitive experience are moderated by naïve theories and an attribution process. This view suggests that metacognitive experience will affect judgments only under specifiable situations. This symposium tries to address this debate by examining when and why metacognitive experiences affect consumers' judgments and preferences. The four papers identify hitherto unexplored factors that moderate the effects of metacognitive experience.

The first paper by Labroo and Herzenstien looks at how consumer's motivational orientation determines the impact of metacognitive difficulty on consumer preferences. The second paper by Cho and Schwarz examines when choice deferral caused by metacognitive difficulty of choice may or may not generalize to subsequent decisions. The third paper by Tormala, Henderson and Clarkson examines when easy (or fast) attitude generation positively affects attitude certainty and when it negatively affects attitude certainty. Finally, Thomas and Maitre examine whether repetition of a disfluent linguistic structure will mitigate or strengthen the effect of linguistic disfluency.

EXTENDED ABSTRACTS

"Complicated Lives of the Intrinsically Inclined: Why Some Seek Metacognitive Effort"

Aparna Labroo, University of Chicago, USA
Michal Herzenstein, University of Delaware, USA

Much research has focused on how feelings of ease are good and increase people's preferences towards associated products. This occurs because people associate ease with familiarity and personal relevance; as personally relevant and familiar objects come to mind easily, people mistakenly reverse this association, to also infer that if a product is easy to think about it must necessarily be familiar (Schwarz 2004). Thus, even when feelings of ease arise independently of the characteristics of a product, the product feels more familiar, and people infer that it is personally relevant and more likeable. More recently, research has started to consider when feelings of effort might be good, and to suggest that the impact of such feelings might depend upon the naïve theories that consumers bring to bear on their judgment. For example, when consumers consider why a product will help accomplish important goals, feelings of effort (vs. ease) associated with the product exert a positive effect on its preference—as people usually associate attaining goals with exerting effort and the most effective means and they mistakenly reverse this inference as well (Labroo & Kim 2009).

Building on this research, we argue that products that feel subjectively easy (vs. effortful) to process are preferred, as shown previously, but only if consumers are extrinsically motivated. Such consumers misattribute positive feelings of ease to product superiority and infer the product is more rewarding. However, intrinsically-motivated people, who engage in activities because they value the process rather than the outcome, ironically prefer products that feel subjectively effortful (vs. easy) to process. Easy to process is also seen as intrinsically less engaging, and lower engagement is attributed to inferior product quality. These effects are mitigated when intrinsically-motivated consumers believe the negative feelings reflect their own incompetence.

In Experiment 1, consumers evaluated a cooking cheese. Participants completed either an extrinsic or intrinsic orientation priming task, then either read an easy vs. effortful to read ad for the cheese (Novemsky et al. 2008), and finally indicated their willingness to pay for the cheese, how many things they would cook with the cheese, and how much they would enjoy cooking with the cheese. Participants with extrinsic orientation indicated higher WTP, more usability, and more enjoyment when they previously viewed the ease vs. effortful to process ad. The reverse was true for participants with intrinsic orientation. Experiment 2 replicated these effects using an individual difference measure of motivation (Amabile et al. 1994). Once motivational orientation had been measured, participants clicked on and evaluated a website for their current course book. The font was either difficult to read, easy to read, or difficult to read but participants attention was directed to font being the cause of feelings of effort. Extrinsically-oriented respondents indicated higher intent to use the website when its font was easy (vs. difficult) to read. Interestingly, and replicating experiment 1, the reverse was true for intrinsically oriented participants. When participant attention was directed to the true source of effort, these effects were mitigated. To further investigate underling process among participants who are intrinsically oriented, in Experiment 3, everyone first completed a short SAT-type analogies task, for which approximately half were given false failure feedback (the rest were not given such feedback), in an attempt to associate negative feelings to ones' incompetence (vs. not). Next, all participants were primed with intrinsic orientation, and then they were assigned to read an easy (vs. effortful) ad for Omega 3 (memory) pills. As expected, non-failure participants preferred the pills when they read an effortful (vs. easy) to read ad, and their preference was mediated by perceived product efficacy and engagement. This preference for effort was attenuated when participants previously received failure feedback.

Taken together, these findings support our premise. They suggest that people who look for intrinsic value undervalue activities that feel too easy to engage in and these feelings might be misattributed to associated products reducing liking towards them. In valuing products associated with effort, these people might unnecessarily be complicating their lives, especially when effort does not signify any real benefit of engaging in an activity.

"When Choice Deferral Does (and Does Not) Generalize to Subsequent Decisions: A Metacognitive Analysis"

Hyejeung Cho, University of Texas at San Antonio, USA
Norbert Schwarz, University of Michigan, USA

When a choice is difficult to make, consumers are likely to defer it. This effect of choice difficulty on the likelihood of deferral has been observed not only under conditions where the difficulty derives from attributes of the choice alternatives (Dhar 1997), but also when the difficulty derives from incidental manipulations of the metacognitive fluency experience. For example, presenting the information in a difficult (vs. easy) to read print font or asking consumers to provide many (vs. few) reasons for a choice has been found to increase deferral in the absence of any objective differences among the choice alternatives (Novemsky et al. 2007). Such findings highlight that the subjective experience of difficulty is the key driver of deferral. Supporting this conclusion, increased deferral is not observed when consumers attribute the experienced difficulty to an incidental source, like the print font (Novemsky et al. 2007), thus undermining its informational value for the choice at hand. These attribution effects are consistent with the logic of the feelings-as-information approach to metacognitive experiences (Schwarz 2004).

This logic further holds that any given metacognitive experience is compatible with a variety of different naïve theories of mental processes that "explain" its occurrence (Schwarz 2004). For example, a consumer who experiences a choice as difficult may attribute the experience to the nature of the choice alternatives ("This is difficult because the options are all pretty similar, making it hard to tell which one is better.") or to her own lack of expertise ("This is difficult because I know little about digital cameras."). In both cases, the consumer is likely to defer the difficult choice. However, the different explanations of the experienced difficulty have differential implications for subsequent choices. When the difficulty is attributed to the choice alternatives, it is silent on subsequent choice sets; but when it is attributed to one's own lack of expertise, it may discourage subsequent choices in the same domain as well. Hence, how consumers "explain" their difficulty is likely to determine whether deferral is limited to a given choice task or generalizes across tasks. To date, the generalization of deferral, and the generalization of inferences from metacognitive difficulty in general, has received little attention. The present research begins to fill this gap.

Specifically, participants received a shopping scenario that presented them with information about four products (binoculars) available in the market. We further told them that only two of the products were available in the store they visited. These two available products were either similarly attractive, making a choice difficult, or one was clearly more attractive than the other, making a choice easy. We then induced participants through two questions to think either about the similarity of the products or about their own expertise; a control group received no questions at this stage. Finally, participants selected one of the two available products or deferred their choice until all products are available at the store. Following this first task, participants received a second scenario that presented them with two different products from the same domain (binoculars), which were of differential attractiveness, making a choice easy. They could select one of these products or defer choice. The manipulations result in a 2 (first choice: easy vs. difficult) x 3 (attribution: product vs. expertise vs. control)-factorial design.

The results were consistent with predictions. First, replicating the usual findings, participants were more likely to defer choice on task 1 under difficult than easy conditions. Second, this effect was independent of the attribution manipulation–after all, difficult to distinguish alternatives or a lack of expertise are both good reasons for deferral. Third, and more important, how participants explained the difficulty encountered on task 1 influenced their decisions on the easy task 2. Participants who attributed the difficulty experienced on task 1 to their own lack of expertise were more likely to defer choice on the easy task 2 than participants who attributed their task 1 difficulty to the specific products presented in task 1.

These findings extend our understanding of the role of metacognitive experiences in the deferral of choice. Attributing a previous experience of difficulty to characteristics of the specific choice set of the previous task renders it irrelevant for subsequent tasks. In contrast, attributing a previous experience of difficulty to one's own lack of expertise renders it relevant to all tasks in the same expertise domain and the influence of previously experienced difficulty generalizes across related tasks.

"It's Not Just the Speed that Counts: Perceived Evaluation Duration and Attitude Certainty"

Zakary Tormala, Stanford University, USA
Marlone Henderson, University of Texas at Austin, USA
Joshua Clarkson, Indiana University, USA

People hold their attitudes with varying degrees of certainty. For example, two consumers might report liking a new product or favoring a specific brand to the same degree, but differ in how certain they are of that evaluation. Attitude certainty has stimulated considerable research interest in psychology and marketing, partly because it has been shown to have a number of important consequences for consumer-relevant outcomes. For instance, the more certain one is of one's attitude, the more predictive that attitude is of behavior and choice (e.g., Berger and Mitchell 1989; Bizer, Tormala, Rucker, and Petty 2006; Krishnan and Smith 1998) and the more resistant that attitude is to change (e.g., Bassili 1996; Tormala and Petty 2002).

Over the years, an extensive body of research has been dedicated to understanding the antecedents of attitude certainty (Tormala and Rucker 2007). One well-documented antecedent is the speed with which one's attitude comes to mind (Fazio 1995). A number of studies have shown that the faster one's attitude comes to mind, the more certain one is of that attitude (e.g., Berger and Mitchell 1989; Bizer et al. 2006; Holland, Verplanken, and van Knippenberg 2003; Petrocelli, Tormala, and Rucker 2007). Interestingly, however, other recent research suggests that slower evaluative processing can be associated with greater certainty. For example, the more time one has to form an impression of a person, the more certain one is of that impression (Willis and Todorov 2006). Presumably, more time spent evaluating indicates that one has been more thoughtful, and perceived thoughtfulness positively influences certainty (e.g., Wan, Rucker, Tormala, and Clarkson forthcoming).

The current research takes a new tack, suggesting that perceived evaluative speed (or duration) can have dynamic effects on attitude certainty that depend on numerous situational or individual difference factors. We explore three such factors in this research. First, the impact of perceived evaluative speed on attitude certainty might depend on whether consumers are focused on attitude expression or formation. Specifically, perceived evaluative speed might positively affect certainty when one is expressing one's attitude, but negatively affect certainty when one is forming one's attitude. The logic is that faster expression indicates that one has already considered the issue and decided where one stands, whereas slower formation indicates that one has been more thoughtful and rational in making one's decision. Second, the effect of perceived evaluative speed on attitude certainty might depend on the familiarity of the attitude object or issue. When an attitude object is already familiar to consumers, faster evaluation should facilitate greater certainty because it implies that one has already invested the effort to consider one's opinion. When an object is unfamiliar, however, the need for careful deliberation should be more salient, meaning consumers might be more certain after forming their evaluations more slowly. Third, the effect of perceived evaluative speed on attitude certainty might depend on consumers' lay theories that quick gut reactions or more thoughtful judgments are more accurate. We present 3 studies testing these hypotheses.

Study 1 explored the possibility that perceived evaluation duration would have different implications for attitude certainty depending on whether people were focused on attitude expression or attitude formation. In this study, undergraduate participants were asked to consider their opinion of an issue. Participants were instructed to think about this issue until they had formed their opinions, and then click "continue" on the computer screen. Participants were then presented with a single scale along which they reported their attitudes. Shortly thereafter, participants received false feedback indicating that they had taken either longer or shorter than most participants to either form or express their attitudes. Results indicated that when the feedback focused on attitude expression, participants felt more certain of their attitudes when they believed they were faster rather than slower than most participants. In contrast, when the feedback focused on attitude formation, participants felt more certain when they believed they were slower rather than faster.

In Study 2, we examined the moderating role of familiarity. Participants underwent a similar procedure as in Study 1, but in this case they were asked to consider their attitudes toward an abstract painting that, based on random assignment, was either familiar or unfamiliar to them. All participants evaluated the painting and then received false feedback concerning the amount of time it took them to do so. Among participants who were familiar with the painting, greater attitude certainty was associated with perceptions of fast rather than slow evaluation. In contrast, among participants who were unfamiliar with the painting, greater attitude certainty was associated with perceptions of slow rather than fast evaluation.

Finally, Study 3 investigated the moderating role of lay theories. This study followed the same basic procedure as Study 1, but we assessed participants' beliefs about the validity of gut reactions versus more thoughtful judgments. Among participants who believed that gut reactions were more trustworthy, we observed greater attitude certainty in the perceived fast rather than slow evaluation condition. Among participants who believed that thoughtful judgments were more trustworthy, we observed greater attitude certainty in the perceived slow rather than fast evaluation condition.

In summary, evidence from three studies highlights a dynamic link between perceived evaluation duration and attitude certainty. When consumers focus on attitude expression, evaluate familiar objects, or generally believe that gut reactions are more valid, perceived evaluative speed positively affects attitude certainty. In contrast, when consumers focus on attitude formation, evaluate unfamiliar objects, or generally believe that thoughtful judgments are more valid, perceived evaluative speed negatively affects attitude certainty. Taken together, these findings expand current understandings of the origins of attitude certainty and suggest that perceptions of evaluative speed can play an important and dynamic role in guiding people's assessments of their own attitudes.

"The Brevity Effect in New Product Labels: When Does Linguistic Fluency Affect Consumers' Responses to New Products?"

Manoj Thomas, Cornell University, USA
Thibault Maitre, Cornell University, USA

Which of the following two descriptions will evoke a more favorable response for a new brand of bubble bath-"Barbie Bubble Bath" or "Barbie Refreshing Bubble Bath for Adults and Kids"? Coming up with the appropriate description for a new product label is one of the difficult decisions that marketers often face. Several studies have shown that linguistic qualities of the new product description affect consumers' responses to new products (Lowrey and Shrum 2007; Miller and Kahn 2005; Yorkston and Menon 2004). However, most of the previous research has focused on the cognitive effects of linguistic structures. In this research we examine whether the metacognitive experience evoked by linguistic structures could affect consumers' evaluations of new products. Specifically, we address two hitherto unexplored questions that are of substantive and theoretic importance: (i) Does the length of a label on a new product influence consumers' responses to the product? (ii) When does brevity or length of label matter?

To investigate the effects of fluency induced by linguistic structures, we ran four laboratory experiments. In Experiment 1, participants were randomly assigned to one of the two between-subjects conditions–fluent vs. disfluent product descriptions. Participants saw six new product descriptions and were asked to indicate how much they disliked or liked each new product. Participants assigned to the fluent condition saw product descriptions that were short and fluent (e.g., Barbie Bubble Bath). For participants in the disfluent condition, we created a longer and less fluent product description by adding positive and/or neutral descriptive elements (e.g., Barbie Refreshing Bubble Bath for Adults and Kids). In both conditions, participants were first asked to evaluate how likely they were to try the new product, then to assess how easy or difficult the name was to pronounce, and finally how clear the benefit of the product was. The results from this study showed that perceived ease of pronunciation mediated the effect of linguistic fluency. Having established the role of linguistic fluency in new product descriptions, we then turned our attention to the second question: When does brevity or length of label matter? In Experiment 2, we examine whether repeated exposures to a disfluent linguistic structure will mitigate the unfavorable effect of linguistic disfluency on preferences? Participants were randomly assigned to one of the four conditions in a 2 (repeated prior exposures vs. no prior exposures) x 2 (fluent vs. disfluent) design experiment. The stimuli and procedure were similar to Experiment 1, except for the fact that participants assigned to the "repetition" conditions were exposed to the product descriptions several times before they evaluated the new products. We found that repeated exposure to the less fluent linguistic structures mitigated the effect of linguistic disfluency, even though it did not impact the ease of pronunciation. In Experiments 3A and 3B, we examine why repeated exposure moderated the effect of linguistic fluency on preferences. Experiment 3A shows that linguistic fluency influences preferences even for very familiar stimuli (e.g., Arabic numbers such as 3 vs. 23). Experiment 3B shows that repeated exposure does not mitigate linguistic fluency for unfamiliar stimuli (e.g., foreign names). Together, these results suggest that any factor that makes fluency seem surprising will encourage people to consider linguistic fluency as a diagnostic cue in evaluative judgments.

REFERENCES

Bassili, John N. (1996), "Meta-judgmental Versus Operative Indexes of Psychological Attributes: The Case of Measures of Attitude Strength," *Journal of Personality and Social Psychology*, 71 (4), 637-53.

Berger, Ida E. and Andrew A. Mitchell (1989), "The Effect of Advertising on Attitude Accessibility, Attitude Confidence, and the Attitude-Behavior Relationship," *Journal of Consumer Research*, 16 (3), 269–79.

Bizer Y. George, Zakary L. Tormala, Derek D. Rucker, and Richard E. Petty (2006), "Memory-based Versus On-line Processing: Implications for Attitude Strength," *Journal of Experimental Social Psychology*, 42(5), 646–53.

Fazio, Russell H. (1995), "Attitudes as Object-Evaluation Associations: Determinants, Consequences, and Correlates of Attitude Accessibility," in R. E. Petty & J. A. Krosnick (Eds.), *Attitude Strength: Antecedents and Consequences* (pp. 247–282), Mahwah, NJ: Erlbaum.

Holland, Rob W., Bas Verplanken, and Ad van Knippenberg (2003), "From Repetition to Conviction: Attitude Accessibility as a Determinant of Attitude Certainty," *Journal of Experimental Social Psychology*, 39, 594–601.

Krishnan, H. Shanker and Robert E. Smith (1998), "The Relative Endurance of Attitudes, Confidence and Attitude-Behavior Consistency: The Role of Information Source and Delay," *Journal of Consumer Psychology*, 7 (3), 273-98.

Lowrey, Tina M. and L. J. Shrum (2007), "Phonetic Symbolism and Brand Name Preference," *Journal of Consumer Research*, 34 (3), 406-14.

Miller, Elizabeth G. and Barbara E. Kahn (2005), "Shades of Meaning: The Effect of Color and Flavor Names on Consumer Choice," *Journal of Consumer Research*, 32 (1), 86-92.

Petrocelli, John V., Zakary L. Tormala, and Derek D. Rucker (2007), "Unpacking Attitude Certainty: Attitude Clarity and Attitude Correctness," *Journal of Personality and Social Psychology*, 92 (1), 30-41.

Tormala, Zakary L. and D. Rucker Derek (2007), "Attitude Certainty: A Review of Past Findings and Emerging Perspectives," *Social and Personality Psychology Compass*, 1 (1), 469-92.

Tormala, Zakary L., and Richard E. Petty (2002), "What Doesn't Kill Me Makes Me Stronger: The Effects of Resisting Persuasion on Attitude Certainty," *Journal of Personality and Social Psychology*, 83 (6), 1298-313.

Wan, Echo W., Derek D. Rucker, Zakary L. Tormala, and Joshua J. Clarkson (forthcoming), "The Effects of Regulatory Depletion on Attitude Certainty," *Journal of Marketing Research*.

Willis, Janine and Alex Todorov (2006), "First Impressions: Making Up Your Mind After 100 ms Exposure to a Face," *Psychological Science*, 17, 592-598.

Yorkston, Eric and Geeta Menon (2004), "A Sound Idea: Phonetic Effects of Brand Names on Consumer Judgments," *Journal of Consumer Research*, 31 (1), 43-51.

SPECIAL SESSION SUMMARY

Pre-Purchase Planning and Post-Purchase Learning: The Role of Internal and External Factors

Yanliu Huang, The Chinese University of Hong Kong, China
Wes Hutchinson, University of Pennsylvania, USA

SESSION OVERVIEW

For over 40 years, consumer planning has drawn considerable interest among marketing researchers (e.g., Kollat and Willett 1967). This session adds to our understanding of antecedents of consumer planning and post-purchase learning behavior. The central themes that unite the four papers in the session are (1) how internal factors or shopper characteristics influence planned vs. unplanned purchase behavior, (2) the role of external factors or interventions in determining planning performance, and (3) whether consumers learn from their prior planning and purchases and what shopper characteristics explain this learning paradigm.

Internal Factors

All four papers examine the role of internal factors in planning and learning from shopping. From the pre-purchase planning perspective, based on a dataset covering over 18,000 grocery store purchases in 58 categories, the Bell/Corsten/Knox paper demonstrates that both traditional demographics and other shopper "habit-related traits" such as "enjoyment of shopping" and "information gathering styles" affect unplanned buying. Based on a field study wherein respondents used a handheld scanner to record the order of purchases, the Stilley/Inman/Wakefield paper indicates that consumers have a mental budget that allocates some amount of money to make unplanned purchases on a specific grocery shopping trip. From the post-purchase learning perspective, in two simulated online shopping experiments, Huang and Hutchinson examine planning as a metacognitive process and show that previous planning experience increases consumers' awareness of the need to plan and forces them to think more strategically. As a result, individuals successfully transfer their planning skill from one shopping context to a new one. Finally, based on the results of a series of two-stage shopping experiments, the Chang/Cho/Lee paper demonstrates that consumers often seek out information about prior irreversible purchases they have made and this information search behavior can be explained by shopper characteristics. Particularly, cognitively-oriented consumers tend to avoid uncertainty and engage in post-purchase information search to confirm that they have indeed made the right purchase decision, whereas experientially-oriented consumers engage in such behavior for emotion enhancement purposes.

External Factors

In terms of how the external factors or interventions influence consumer planning behavior, Inman, and Wakefield examine how in-store promotional savings influence mental budgeting for planned vs. unplanned purchases. Their results suggest that many promotions do not influence basket size for the planned items, although they have an impact on unplanned purchase spending after consumers' in-store slack is depleted. Differently, the Bell, Corsten, and Knox not only replicate the classic findings on positive effect of available time and negative effect of store knowledge on unplanned buying as in Park, Iyer, and Smith (1989), but also use panel structure of their data to reconcile the positive effect of store knowledge as reported in Inman, Winer, and Ferraro (2009) — a household in a familiar store can do more unplanned buying when they have more time. Huang and Hutchinson paper indicate that requiring consumers to explicitly verbalize their plans at a "deep" level not only benefits their initial planning performance but also facilitates their planning transfer across domains (compared to control groups that do not verbalize or verbalize at a "shallow" level). Finally, Chang, Cho, and Lee successfully manipulate participants' post-purchase information processing style by asking them to either think or feel about a purchase decision.

The focus of this session is part of a larger literature on consumers' pre-purchase information processing, in-store decision making, and post-purchase knowledge learning and transfer. This is consistent with many ACR members' research interests.

EXTENDED ABSTRACTS

"Unplanned Buying by Supermarket Shoppers"

David R. Bell, University of Pennsylvania, USA
Daniel Corsten, Instituto de Empresa Business School, USA
George Knox, Tilburg University, The Netherlands

> "Supermarkets are places of high impulse buying ...–fully 60 to 70 percent of purchases there were unplanned, grocery industry studies have shown us." Paco Underhill (Why We Buy: The Science of Shopping)

Unplanned buying is a rich and ubiquitous aspect of consumer shopping behavior, yet surprisingly little academic research examines it in detail. Understanding why, how, and when it occurs has implications for consumers, managers, and researchers. In a recent study, Inman, Winer, and Ferraro (2009) explore consumer welfare — how might consumers safeguard themselves from "too much" unplanned buying? Acting in accordance with the widespread belief that unplanned buying is pervasive and environmentally-driven (see Paco Underhill quote above) managers allocate significant resources to "in-store merchandizing". Wal-Mart CMO John Fleming notes: "The store is our number one media channel"; on July 28, 2008 Advertising Age reported "... the oft-quoted statistic ... boosted shopper marketing and made other advertising seem almost pointless." Classic (e.g., Kollat and Willett 1967) and recent (e.g., Inman, Winer, and Ferraro 2009) academic articles study in-store decision making using cross-sectional shopper intercept data, or, alternatively develop field experiments (e.g., Park, Iyer, and Smith 1989). In this paper, we supplement these efforts by studying the costs and benefits of unplanned category purchases, from the perspective of the entire shopping process.

We decompose variation in unplanned buying as it results from the confluence of three factors: the shopper, the store in which the trip is taken, and context for the trip itself. We hypothesize that three classes of factors—shopper predispositions (including demographics and shopping habits), store environments, and shopping trip contexts—affect the cost-benefit calculus for unplanned buying. Within each factor we study a number of sub-factors that are expected to affect the net benefit of unplanned buying. Following Beatty and Ferrell (1998) and Rook and Fisher (1995), our measures of shopper "traits" are not confined to demographics alone, but also include measures of the household's overall shopping habits. We also include a variety of store image (e.g., Bell and Lattin

1999) and trip-specific factors (Fox and Hoch 2005; Lee and Ariely 2006). Some shoppers have a greater inclination to delay planning until inside the store than others; furthermore, different store environments could engender different rates of unplanned buying from the same shopper, as could different trips with different needs.

A multi-level random effects Poisson model calibrated on a dataset covering over 18,000 purchases in 58 categories is used to explain variation in the number of unplanned categories in the shopping basket. An important (and unique) feature of the data is that they vary over time, as well as over households and stores. This allows us to report the decomposition of variance due to trips, household-store combinations, and households. We find a high degree of within-household clustering (for two trips taken by the same household, the intra-class correlation is .579). Conversely, for any two trips taken at the same store, the intra-class correlation is extremely low (less than .010). For different trips by the same household at the same store, the intra-class correlation rises to .684, since, in addition to the household and store clustering, we add the household-store interaction clustering.

Thus, the variance decomposition implies unplanned buying is largely a household-driven phenomenon, explainable in part by traditional demographics, but more by other "traits" that reflect long-run shopping habits including "enjoyment of shopping" and "information gathering styles". Even though individual difference variables are the most important class of factors in the model, these household observables account for only 40% of the total variation. Shopping trip factors including trip antecedents, trip types, and in-store experiences are can also exert substantial shifts in the base rate of unplanned buying. While we do find evidence of persistent chain level effects, we were unable to link these to perceptual differences in prices or assortments. We replicate the classic findings on time available (more unplanned buying) and high store knowledge (less unplanned buying) in Park, Iyer, and Smith (1989) and use the panel structure of our data to reconcile the positive effect of store knowledge reported in Inman, Winer, and Ferraro (2009)—a household in a familiar store can do more unplanned buying, provided more time is available.

One implication is that researchers with an interest in unplanned buying might measure other "traits" such as proclivity for impulsivity (e.g., Rook and Fisher 1995), or the propensity to be a "spendthrift" or "tightwad" (Scott, Cryder, and Loewenstein 2008). Moreover, there is a need for more comprehensive theories of "shopping styles" and their normative relationship to unplanned buying. Promising candidates are theories of shopping goals (e.g., Lee and Ariely 2006), shopping efficiency (e.g., Chandon, Wansink, and Laurent 2000), and the "pain of payment" (Scott, Cryder, and Loewenstein 2008).

"Spending on the Fly: Mental Budgets, Promotions, and Spending Behavior"

Karen M. Stilley, University of Pittsburgh, USA
J. Jeffrey Inman, University of Pittsburgh, USA
Kirk L. Wakefield, Baylor University, USA

Grocery shopping is an example of a consumer domain where budgeting is commonly found (i.e., Heath and Soll 1996; Heilman, Nakamoto and Rao 2002). More recently, Stilley, Inman, and Wakefield (2009) take the idea of mental budgets further by demonstrating that consumers have a mental budget for the amount of money that they plan to spend on a specific grocery shopping trip and by showing that this mental budget includes room for unplanned purchases. Specifically, they introduce the idea that the trip budget consists of both an itemized portion (amount allocated to planned purchases) and in-store slack (the portion of the mental budget that remains available for in-store decisions). We argue that the amount of in-store slack remaining at a given point during the trip has important implications regarding the impact of promotional savings. We rationalize four hypotheses which focus on savings on planned items and then present two hypotheses regarding savings on unplanned items.

To test these hypotheses, we conducted a field study in which respondents used a hand held scanner to record the order of purchases. Specifically, 400 customers were systematically intercepted as they entered three different grocery stores located in a southwestern city. Respondents were offered a $10 incentive that was given to them at the end of the trip (for future use to mitigate a windfall effect). Before they entered the store, respondents were first asked what items they planned to purchase. They were then asked to estimate how much they intended to spend in total and to estimate the cost of the items they planned to purchase (i.e., their itemized budget). This approach allows us to measure the respondents' in-store slack by subtracting the itemized budget from the total planned spend. After completing these initial questions, respondents were then provided with a handheld scanner gun and instructed how to scan the barcode of each item as they placed it in their cart or basket. This methodology enables us to record the order of purchases and therefore determine which items were purchased before and after the in-store slack was exceeded. After the respondents checked out, they completed an exit interview and their receipt was copied. Respondents also provided their frequent shopper card number, which allowed us to access their shopping history.

Our research makes at least four important contributions. First, we find that savings on planned items before the in-store slack is exhausted are positively related to the amount spent on planned items, but that the amount of the increase depends on income. In fact, we find that savings on planned items before the slack is depleted have <u>no</u> impact on spending for below-average income households. The results support our thesis that the underlying mechanism is that higher income enables stockpiling of the planned items. Second, we find that savings on planned items are positively related to unplanned item spending, but that this relationship only obtains when the savings on planned items are realized after the consumer's in-store slack is depleted. Third, we show that savings on unplanned items that are purchased before the consumers' in-store slack is depleted have no impact on basket size except for high income consumers paying with a debit or credit card. This suggests that, for most consumers, the savings are simply absorbed into the in-store slack. Fourth, savings on unplanned items that are purchased after the consumer's in-store slack is depleted are positively related to basket size for consumers regardless of income or payment method. This suggests that promotions can be effective in encouraging incremental purchases if the promotion is encountered after the consumers' in-store slack is exceeded. Highlighting the importance of a mental budgeting perspective, our results have theoretical implications as well as implications for the placement of promotions in the store pattern and the nature of promoted items.

"Seeking Emotion Enhancement or Uncertainty Resolution? A Dual-System Approach to Examining Post-Purchase Information Search"

Hannah Chang, Singapore Management University, China
Cecile Cho, Moscow School of Management, Skolkovo, Russia
Leonard Lee, Columbia Business School, USA

Product information search is typically assumed to follow the recognition of a purchase need and to occur before decision making. Once a sale transaction is completed, searching for information (e.g. price) on the purchased product seems futile and even irrational. Real-life observation and prior research (e.g. Russo and Leclerc 1994), however, suggest that such post-purchase search behavior is pervasive among consumers despite having no apparent consequence.

In this research, we examine the prevalence of post-purchase information (particularly prices of already purchased products) search behavior in shopping and its underlying motivations. We propose two distinct reasons for this behavior—(1) to resolve uncertainty and ascertain that the right purchase decision has been made (Shani and Zeelenberg 2007); and (2) for emotion-enhancement particularly if consumers are confident of having made the right purchase decision. We draw upon Epstein's (1994) Cognitive-Experiential Self-Theory (CEST) as an integrative conceptual framework for these two accounts, and investigate whether the two information-processing styles (experiential or cognitive) may differentially drive post-purchase information search. Specifically, we hypothesize that, while consumers who rely more on cognitive processing during decision making would seek post-purchase product information when they are uncertain about having made the right decision, consumers who rely more on experiential processing focus on their current shopping experience and tend to seek such information for emotion-enhancement purposes, particularly when they are reasonably confident that they have made the right purchase decision. We tested our hypothesis in two experiments.

In experiment 1 (N=86), we traced participants' real-time search behavior.in a two-stage online shopping experiment using the mouselab paradigm (Payne, Bettman and Johnson 1993). Participants were endowed with $10 and asked to shop at an online-shopping website selling five desktop toys (e.g. stress ball, wood-cube puzzle), each presented in the form of a picture, a short description, size specification, and price. Participants had to purchase one item with the given cash. After making their purchase, participants were asked to shop at a second store selling ten desktop toys including the five they had already seen in the first store. (We counterbalanced which five of the ten products participants could buy in the first store.) After a short filler task, participants had to complete the Rational-Experiential Inventory (REI) as a measure of their information-processing style (Epstein et al. 1996). To manipulate participants' degree of confidence in whether they were paying a good price for their purchase in the first store, we told half the participants that the prices were discounted by 50% ("large"), and the other half, 10% ("small"). We found a significant crossover interaction between discount size and participants' information-processing style on their propensity to search within the second store for the price of the product they had already purchased in the first store (p=.05). Planned comparisons further revealed that whereas rationally-oriented participants were more likely to engage in post-purchase price search when the discount in the first store was small (57%) than when it was large (32%), experiential-oriented participants were more likely to engage in post-purchase price search when the discount was large instead (43% vs. 27%).

We replicated this result in experiment 2 (N=273) in which we manipulated participants' information-processing style prior to shopping. Participants were asked to complete two purportedly unrelated tasks. In the first task, half the participants were asked to describe a difficult decision they had to make in the past and in which they decided based on careful thinking and it turned out to be the right decision, while the other half were asked to describe a difficult decision they had to make in which they used their feelings instead. Next, participants were asked to imagine that they needed a new MP3 player and decided to buy one after looking at various models at an electronics store; they were told that the store was having a semi-annual clearance sale with the discount size being 5% ("small") or 50% ("large"). Subsequently, they saw another store that sells the same model of MP3 player they had just bought and had to indicate whether they would enter the store to check out the price of the player. Again, we found a significant crossover interaction between discount size and information-processing style on participants' likelihood to seek out the price of the MP3 player they just purchased (p=.004); while cognitively-oriented participants were more likely to search when the discount in Store A was small (61%) than when it was large (50%), experientially-oriented participants were more likely to search when the discount was large (64%) than when it was small (45%).

Together, these findings lend a first look at two contrasting motivations that spur consumers to seek post-purchase information that might appear non-consequential, suggesting disparate situations under which different types of consumers would engage in such behavior.

"There is More to Planned Purchases than Knowing What You Want: Dynamic Planning and Learning in A Repeated Multi-Store Price Search Task"

Yanliu Huang, The Chinese University of Hong Kong, China
Wes Hutchinson, University of Pennsylvania, USA

As consumers, our lives are full of planning. Understanding the strengths and weaknesses of consumer planning, how planning performance improves with experience, and the possible interventions that may help people form better shopping strategies have important implications for marketers, policy makers, and consumers. Despite the importance of this topic, there is a scarcity of research on consumer planning in marketing. Most research has focused on planned vs. unplanned purchases and defines planned purchases strictly as those items that were fully specified before entering the store (e.g., on a shopping list). These studies did not examine the process of planning itself and ignored the fact that an "unplanned" purchase made in the store can be the result of a well developed plan that intentionally stopped short of full specification. For example, a consumer who has a well-formed plan to choose the lowest priced brand in a small consideration set would be categorized as making unplanned purchases because he does not determine the specific brand before entering the store.

In the current research, planning is defined as developing a scheme or procedure for the accomplishment of an objective before the commencement of the task. Our definition emphasizes the metacognitive aspect of planning in that people intentionally and actively construct, retrieve, and update their plans to achieve their purposes. In order to identify a specific task to study planning, we first conducted two exploratory studies (N=260) in which we asked people to describe how they planned for their most recent shopping trips for different products (e.g., grocery, electronics, clothing). It was shown that both information search and learning from repeated shopping experience are two important components of consumer planning. Based on these pretest results, we selected an activity that is familiar to most consumers, incorporates both information search and learning, and also represents an important research area in marketing for many years—repeated multi-store price search. Specifically, participants were given a total budget and asked to take repeated shopping trips and make a purchase on each shopping trip. They were facing multiple stores that always included at least an EDLP (every day low price) store and a HILO store (charging a high regular price half of the time and a low sale price the other half of the time). Their goal was to minimize their total cost and they were paid based on their performance. In this task, planning consists of two parts: what consumers do at the very beginning to learn about stores and what shopping strategies they adopt based on what they learn. Based on optimal search for this task, we use the percentage of consumers who both searched exhaustively on the first shopping trip and adopted optimal cherry picking (i.e., visit the HILO store first, if the price is low, make the purchase; if the price is high, switch to the EDLP store to make the purchase) on the last two shopping trips as our dependent variable to measure planning.

We showed in two simulated shopping experiments that consumers often fail to plan optimally and do not appreciate the value of early learning. Fortunately, encouraging consumers to explicitly plan and justify their store visits can improve their performance, and merely planning without thinking about the underlying rationale of the plan is not as helpful. Furthermore, after obtaining relevant experience consumers are able to transfer their planning to shopping in a different situation successfully. Finally, both explicit planning and transfer effects do not result from consumers' increased awareness to cope with memory load and keep all the critical price information in their short term memory.

REFERENCES

Beatty, Sharon E. and M. Elizabeth Ferrell (1998), "Impulse Buying: Modeling Its Precursors," *Journal of Retailing*, 74 (2), 169-191.

Bell, David R. and Randolph E. Bucklin (1999), "The Role of Internal Reference Points in the Category Purchase Decision," *Journal of Consumer Research*, 26 (3), 128-143.

Chandon, Pierre, Brian Wansink, and Gilles Laurent (2000), "A Benefit Congruency Framework of Sales Promotion Effectiveness," Journal of Marketing, 64 (4), 65-81.

Epstein, S. (1994), "Integration of the Cognitive and the Psychodynamic Unconscious," *American Psychologist*, 49, 709-724.

Epstein, S., R. Pacini, V. Denes-Raj, and H. Heier (1996), "Individual Differences in Intuitive-Experiential and Analytical-Rational Thinking Styles," *Journal of Personality and Social Psychology*, 71, 2, 390-405.

Fox, Edward J. and Stephen J. Hoch (2005), "Cherry-Picking," *Journal of Marketing*, 69 (1), 46-62.

Heath, Chip and Jack B. Soll (1996), "Mental Budgeting and Consumer Decisions," *Journal of Consumer Research*, 23 (June), 40-52.

Heilman, M. Carrie., Kent Nakamoto and Ambar G. Rao (2002), "Pleasant Surprises: Consumer Response to Unexpected In-Store Coupons," *Journal of Marketing Research*, 34 (May), 242-52.

Inman, J. Jeffrey, Russell S. Winer, and Rosellina Ferraro (2009), "The Interplay Between Category Characteristics, Customer Characteristics, and Customer Activities on In-Store Decision Making," *Journal of Marketing*, forthcoming.

Kollat, David T. and Ronald P. Willett (1967), "Customer Impulse Purchasing Behavior," *Journal of Marketing Research*, 4 (February), 21-31.

Lee, Leonard and Dan Ariely (2006), "Shopping Goals, Goal Concreteness, and Conditional Promotions," *Journal of Consumer Research*, 33 (June), 60-70.

Park, C. Whan, Easwar S. Iyer, and Daniel C. Smith (1989), "The Effects of Situational Factors on In-Store Grocery Shopping Behavior: The Role of Store Environment and Time Available for Shopping," *Journal of Consumer Research*, 15 (December), 422-433.

Payne, J. W., J. R. Bettman and E. J. Johnson (1993), *The Adaptive Decision Maker*, Cambridge University Press, Cambridge.

Rick, Scott, Cynthia E. Cryder, and George Lowenstein (2008), "Tightwads and Spendthifts," *Journal of Consumer Research*, 34 (April), 767-782.

Rook, Dennis W. and Robert J. Fisher (1995), "Normative Influences on Impulsive Buying Behavior," *Journal of Consumer Research*, 22 (3), 305-313.

Russo, J. E. and F. Leclerc (1994), "An Eye-Fixation Analysis of Choice Processes for Consumer Nondurables," *Journal of Consumer Research*, 21, 274-290.

Shani, Y. and M. Zeelenberg (2007), "When and Why Do We Want to Know? How Experienced Regret Promotes Post-Decision Information Search," *Journal of Behavioral Decision Making*, 20, 207-222.

Stilley, Karen M., J. Jeffrey Inman, and Kirk L. Wakefield (2009), "Planning to Make Unplanned Purchases? The Role of In-Store Slack in Budget Deviation," working paper, University of Pittsburgh, Pittsburgh, PA.

SPECIAL SESSION SUMMARY

Social Comparison and Negative Emotions: Understanding Regret, Envy, and Schadenfreude in a Consumer World

Cait Poynor, University of Pittsburgh, USA

SESSION OVERVIEW

A growing body of research identifies widespread effects of social comparison on consumer behavior. For example, in the presence of others, we affiliate with them, adopt an innovation, or increase our purchase intentions for goods we see in use. Implicit in this work is the idea that social comparison can yield powerful emotions, many of which are positive for consumers and marketers. But what happens when social comparison yields powerful negative emotions? What are the consumption implications for consumers and marketers in this instance? Can this type of social outcome be managed or mitigated? Each author in this special session will report results from three empirical studies conducted to explore these questions in depth, specifically focusing on the emotions of regret, envy and schadenfreude.

Though the papers are tightly clustered around this common theme, they each also provide novel theoretical insights. Particularly, these papers not only depict these relatively understudied emotions in consumer domains, they suggest that they can be sparked by both internal and external processes. For example, Winterich, Mittal, and Inman focus on the effects of regret, which begins as a personal consumer response to their own consumption decisions. However, this individual emotion yields important external consequences, as the combination of social comparison and regret leads to distancing between the consumer and previously proximate others. Poynor and Dahl study envy, which is generated by comparing one's own personal situation to that of another consumer. As they recognize that someone else has a desired good, consumers respond with varying degrees of hostility depending on their own self-esteem levels, both in regard to the envied other and the desired product. Moving the locus of study farther outside the individual consumer, Sundie et al. highlight schadenfreude, where the driver of hostile emotion lies outside the consumer altogether, and only arises due to observation of the negative experiences of others.

Each paper also makes a compelling case that socially generated emotions are directly related to substantive marketing implications. Winterich et al., for example, show that social distancing can not only impact intentions to repeat a given behavior, but also that financial allocation decisions can be impacted by regret and consequent social distancing. Poynor and Dahl echo the impact of negative emotion on interpersonal relationships, and also demonstrate effects of envy on product value and willingness-to-pay. Sundie et al. show that schadenfreude can have important impacts on brand attitude and word of mouth.

Given the strong focus of the session, we anticipate a high degree of interest among researchers investigating issues involving social comparison, social influence, and interpersonal relationships. However, we also believe that the presentations will attract interest from a broader audience. For example, researchers exploring issues related to consumer happiness and well-being, the role of self-esteem in consumption, and importance of self-conscious emotions will see great value in this session. The range of consequences identified in this work may broaden its appeal further, as the consequences identified may be relevant for pricing, group dynamics, brand attitudes, and motivation research.

EXTENDED ABSTRACT

"The Who in Regret: How Psychological Closeness Affects Regret and Social Distancing"

Karen P. Winterich, Texas A&M University, USA
Vikas Mittal, Rice University, USA
J. Jeffrey Inman, University of Pittsburgh, USA

Regret is defined as "the emotion that we experience when realizing or imagining that our current situation would have been better, if only we had decided differently" (Zeelenberg and Pieters 2007, 3). Social comparison theory states that individuals evaluate themselves in comparison to others (Festinger 1954), suggesting that individuals not only make comparisons to forgone alternatives, but also to the chooser of the forgone alternative. We build on research examining the role of social comparison in regret (Hoelzl and Loewenstein 2005; Kumar 2004) to examine the extent to which subtle differences in psychological closeness influence regret and the relational consequences of regret, particularly social distancing.

Psychological closeness is influenced by physical proximity and/or similarities such as age or gender (Tesser and Campbell 1982). Research has found that emotional responses from social comparison are dependent on the nature of the relationship, with stronger responses when one is psychologically close (Tesser and Collins 1988). Building on this literature, we argue that regret is greater when one is outperformed by someone of high (vs. low) closeness because comparisons to less close others reduce the relevance of a forgone alternative. In doing so, this research acknowledges the "who" (chose), and not just what (was chosen), as an influential reference point for comparison affecting regret (Lin, Huang, and Zeelenberg 2006).

More importantly, we demonstrate that people may employ social strategies to regulate regret (Zeelenberg and Pieters 2007). To date, research has demonstrated distinct behavioral consequences of regret that may serve to regulate regret (Inman and Zeelenberg 2002; Kumar 2004; Tsiros and Mittal 2000). Yet, regret regulation strategies have not considered the tendency of consumers to manage their relationship with the chooser of the forgone alternative. Social distancing is viewed as informal ostracism that may occur in response to social deviance such that individuals who are distanced are not formally removed but are informally excluded from social interaction to some degree through a range of withdrawal behaviors (Westphal and Khanna 2003; Wood 1974). We argue that consumers may regulate regret by distancing themselves from those others who chose the better forgone alternative. Specifically, consumers will be more likely to engage in social distancing when the chooser is of high (vs. low) closeness because less closeness between the self and the other reduces the threat or need for regret regulation when interacting with the other.

In three studies, we prime psychological closeness to examine the effect on regret, as well as social distancing. The first study primed closeness to a cousin and examined regret regarding performance in a hypothetical stock investment scenario. The results indicated that regret was greater when participants were outperformed in a hypothetical investment scenario by a close (vs. distant) cousin. Further, participants who were outperformed by a close cousin indicated a greater desire to distance themselves from their cousin.

In the second study, each participant brought a friend to the study. Participants then completed a computer word scramble task and received feedback regarding their friends' performance or that of a random participant to manipulate closeness. Depending on condition, participants were informed that they had performed worse than or equal to the other participant and asked questions regarding their performance. At the end of the study, participants were asked their likelihood to participate in a future study with their friend. Results indicated that participants who performed worse than their friend experienced greater regret and had lower intentions to participate in a future study with their friend than those who performed worse than a random participant. We propose that choosing not to participate in a future study with their friend is a distancing mechanism, thereby regulating regret. Importantly, regret mediated the moderating effect of psychological closeness on participation intentions.

The third study primed closeness by randomly pairing participants of the same gender for three minutes to talk and get to know each other. After this time, participants were asked to think of how their partner was similar to or different from them, priming high or low psychological closeness, respectively. Then participants completed the same word scramble task used in study 2, receiving feedback on their own performance as well as that of their partner. Lastly, participants completed an ostensibly unrelated economic (i.e., dictator) game where they were given $5 to allocate between themselves and their partner. Unbeknownst to participants, each person was assigned to be the decision maker and the amount allocated to their partner served as an indicator of social distancing. Results indicated that those in the high (vs. low) closeness condition not only reported greater regret when they were outperformed in the word scramble task, but also allocated less money to their partner in a subsequent, unrelated economic game. Again, regret mediated the moderating effect of psychological closeness on partner allocation.

Together, we find that regret is influenced by psychological closeness to the chooser of the forgone alternative, and individuals may use social distancing as a strategy to regulate regret arising from social comparison. This research extends regret regulation theory demonstrating that through social distancing behaviors consumers can choose to "run and hide" from their regret or even go so far as to settle the score with the other in an unrelated task. It is important for consumers to regulate regret given that Schwartz et al. (2002) find that regret is positively correlated with depression and negatively correlated with both happiness and life satisfaction. In marketing, companies often attempt to elicit anticipated regret in potential customers by drawing comparisons to users of a competitor's brand to increase own brand sales through customers' regret avoidance, but consumers may or may not identify with the person using the target brand (i.e., Apple's campaign using distinct identities for a PC user and a MAC user). Such strategies are likely to be successful only to the extent that consumers feel psychologically close to the portrayed user of the target brand.

"Monster or Motivator? Understanding and Taming Consumer Envy"

Cait Poynor, University of Pittsburgh, USA
Darren Dahl, University of British Columbia, Canada*
Gerry Gorn, Hong Kong University, China

Envy's malignant effects have long been depicted in psychoanalysis, theology, literature, philosophy, psychology and political science (Smith and Kim 2007). Our fascination with envy may be partially driven by its ubiquity, as it springs to life as soon as individuals become capable of interpersonal comparison (Schoeck 1969). Seeing another with something we desire has been shown to prompt negative social comparisons, which in turn can yield competition, hostility, alienation, and damage to both the envier and the envied individual (Schoeck 1969, Silver and Sabini 1978, Testa and Major 1990). Indeed, in a marketing context consumers have been shown to experience envy and its negative outcomes when comparing themselves to other consumers and their purchases (Belk 1985). Envy may also drain value from the market, as it leads to a desire to demean or destroy things formerly considered good (Schimmel1993). At its most powerful, envy has been said to "lead to aggression and violence capable of destroying societies," (Foster 1972, p. 165).

Recent reviews concede that envy's antecedents and consequences remain poorly understood (Smith and Kim 2007, Zizzo 2008). A body of conflicting evidence exists on fundamental questions regarding envy and its function, particularly in a consumer context: Does envy impact consumer behavior at all (Grinblatt, Keloharju and Ikaheimo 2008)? Can we experience envy toward consumers who are dissimilar from us as well as those who are similar? Does consumer envy truly only have the malignant face portrayed in psychoanalysis, political science and theology? If so, in what circumstances is the negative outcomes of envy most likely to be realized and how can consumers be prompted to express envy in ways which are perhaps more beneficial to themselves and the marketplace?

We approach these questions by first defining envy and relating conflicting findings regarding the effects of interpersonal similarity and perceived control (defined as an individual's perceptions of their own ability to obtain an envied good on a future occasion) on envy's expression. We propose that envy, defined as the emotion generated by seeing another with a desired good (Salovey 1991) creates an "acquisition gap," that is, a sense of psychological distance that must be bridged for an individual to obtain the envied good. To the extent that the acquisition gap is narrowed by favorable combinations of trait self-esteem, perceived control, and similarity to the envied other, we argue that consumers will move away from malignant expressions of envy. Such a shift may be beneficial to consumers, who avoid the downward spiral caused by unresolved envy, to marketers, whose products can avoid devaluation, and society as a whole, which can avoid or reduce the harmful consequences of envy-driven hostility.

Results from three experiments are consistent with this framework and provide new insights into both envy and self-esteem. Study 1 considers the malignant expression of envy when an envied other is initially similar to participants. In this case, we propose that the initial acquisition gap is small. In this study, participants took part in a simulated online search "competition." In this study, a confederate, always identified as a business major allegedly wins concert tickets matched to each individual's preferences based on a survey at the beginning of the semester. Participants were then told that their search strategy was analyzed and that they could (high control) or could not (low control) have obtained the tickets, given their browsing patterns. They then provide the same product evaluation ratings as collected at the beginning of the semester. Finally, they provide their "thin slice" judgments of the confederate as part of an ostensibly unrelated task. We find that high self-esteem individuals only express less damaging envy in such cases–the feasibility of obtaining the confederate's outcome allows them to feel less hostility towards the envied individual and continue to express value for the envied product. However, low self-esteem individuals express more malignant envy (devaluing the chosen good and disparaging the envied person) if they do not clearly believe that they might be able to obtain the envied good in the future. Failing to be able to obtain what someone like them has creates a sort of "sour grapes" effect. However, low self-esteem individuals can express a less damaging form of envy (feel less hostility towards the envied person and maintain high value for the envied good, thus, acting like high self-esteem individuals) if they are explicitly told that they are able to obtain the product in the future.

A second study shows that the interaction of perceived control and self-esteem also exists when the envied other is initially dissimilar to participants but that its direction is inverted. In this study, the confederate is always identified as a consumer science major. We argue that this dissimilarity presents a large initial acquisition gap. Here we find that providing perceptions of control over the ability to subsequently obtain the envied good produces less damaging envy among high self-esteem consumers. These individuals are able to envision themselves bridging the acquisition gap and thus, express less hostility for the envied other and maintain the value of the envied good. By contrast, for low self-esteem individuals even positive beliefs about their ability to acquire the product in the future fail to narrow the gap between themselves and the envied individual enough to offset negative feelings. In light of this gap, they consistently demonstrate malignant envy, expressing hostility toward the envied other and devaluing the focal product.

Finally, a third study demonstrates that high self-esteem individuals experiencing envy demonstrate more positive responses to a "substitute" product than do low self-esteem individuals. High self-esteem individuals' acceptance of even a very poor substitute for the envied product (in this case, receiving an inexpensive mouse pad after watching a confederate win a Wii gaming system) may constitute an important means of coping with the negative experience of envy. By contrast, low self-esteem individuals' rejection of a consolation prize may serve to exacerbate negative feelings and therefore, increase the negative impacts of envy-related experiences.

"Invidious Emotions in Status-Based Social Comparison: Implications for the Status Brand"

Jill M. Sundie, University of Houston, USA
James C. Ward, Arizona State University, USA
Daniel J. Beal, Rice University, USA
Wynne W. Chin, University of Houston, USA
Stephanie Geiger-Oneto, University of Wyoming, USA

Social comparisons involving status products have the ability to evoke a variety of emotions for consumers, some of which are invidious in nature. When confronted with a similar other who possesses a status symbol superior to one's own possession, feeling envy is a likely response. Three studies examine this dark side of the emotional experience of status consumption, and explore the effects of feeling envy on downstream thoughts, feelings and consumption-relevant behaviors towards the status brand. In particular the present studies examine the effects of negative emotions such as envy and hostility on emotional and behavioral responses to status product failure.

This work contributes uniquely to the consumer literature in three ways. First, it explores a particular mediational pathway of emotions antecedent to schadenfreude in a status consumption context; a mediational pattern that has recently been conceptualized by envy researchers, but never to our knowledge tested empirically. Second, this research examines the effects of the envy-hostility-schadenfreude chain of invidious emotions on inclinations to spread negative word-of-mouth about the failed status brand, and provides a window into what the content of such word-of-mouth is likely to be. Third, this work demonstrates that brand attitudes change (become more negative) when individuals feel schadenfreude in response to the status brand's failure. This brand-level analysis also identifies the root of this brand attitude change by examining each of three foundational elements of brand attitudes (positive affect toward the brand, negative affect toward the brand, and brand cognitions). Brand attitude change associated with feeling schadenfreude after status product failure was driven by increased negative affect toward the brand.

Study 1 replicated some conceptually connected research in the emotion literature, but in a consumer context, demonstrating that feeling envy toward a similar other's status product leads to feeling schadenfreude (joy) after that person's status product fails. One novel contribution of this first study is empirical support for the recent conceptualization by envy researchers (Smith & Kim, 2007) that hostile emotions (e.g., anger, resentment) mediate the relationship between envy and schadenfreude. Consistent with other work in the emotion literature, these invidious emotions were enhanced for a higher-status product failure (a Mercedes breaking down) versus a lower-status product failure (a Ford compact breaking down). Feeling schadenfreude after product failure predicted participants' indications they would repeat the product failure story to others—spread word-of-mouth. Content coding of what participants reported they would say to others indicated this word-of-mouth would be primarily negative in nature and thus potentially damaging to the status brand.

Study 2 replicated the pattern in study 1 that hostile emotions mediate the link between feeling envy and schadenfreude in a consumption context, and built upon those findings by examining two previous unexplored but plausibly common sources of status-linked envy: envy of the status symbol itself, and envy of the social attention that possessing the status symbol affords its owner. This study also examined how the target person flaunting (versus modestly displaying) the status symbol would influence observers' emotional responses before and after the status product's failure. While envy of the social attention drawn by the status symbol did lead to hostile emotions and schadenfreude, envy of the status product itself did not predict hostile feelings, or schadenfreude post-failure. The target person's flaunting behavior did enhance schadenfreude, via enhanced envy of social attention and hostility (the positive effect of flaunting on schadenfreude was mediated by envy of social attention and hostility). Schadenfreude again predicted the likelihood to spread negative word-of-mouth about the failed brand.

Study 3 examined the downstream consequences of invidious emotions (envy, hostility) in status-based social comparison on attitudes toward the status brand post-failure. While it might be expected that witnessing a product's failure would lead unilaterally to more negative attitudes toward the failed brand, study 3 revealed that feeling schadenfreude in response to the failure uniquely predicted lower brand attitudes. By measuring brand attitudes in a pre-test and post-test design, we were able to control for prior brand attitudes and thereby assess brand attitude change after learning of the product's failure. Schadenfreude-prompted changes in brand attitudes were driven by increased negative affect toward the brand.

Our results contribute to broader work in the emotion literature by empirically testing a conceptualized mediational pathway involving envy, hostility and schadenfreude (Smith & Kim, 2007). Although some previous work on schadenfreude explored both envy and hostile emotions as predictors of feeling happiness about another person's downfall, these two groups of antecedent emotions generally were presumed to have independent effects on schadenfreude. Our results are consistent with a transmutational process for envy, and provide evidence for the crucial role that other-focused approach emotions such as anger play in the envy-induced schadenfreude.

Consumer-relevant consequences of schadenfreude studied here included word-of-mouth that is prompted by schadenfreude (studies 1 and 2), and changes in brand attitudes subsequent to experiencing schadenfreude (study 3). Although negative word-of-mouth is typically prompted by personally experienced product or service failures, studies 1 and 2 suggest that feeling schadenfreude after witnessing a product failure can also prompt the spread of negative word-of-mouth when people relate the elements of the story to others. The current data suggest this word-of-mouth will routinely contain information about the product failing, and may also be likely to contain other kinds of disparaging remarks about the product or brand. Another important downstream consequence demonstrated in study 3 is that feeling schadenfreude predicts brand attitude change, to the detriment of the failed brand. We found that when a status product failure is witnessed, those who felt greater schadenfreude in this context were more likely to experience negative affect toward the brand and change their overall attitude as a consequence. This suggests that certain emotional responses to status product failure (i.e., pleasure) can influence subsequent brand evaluations.

REFERENCES

Belk, Russell (1985), "Materialism: Trait Aspects of Living in the Material World," *Journal of Consumer Research*, 12(December), 265-280.

Festinger, Leon (1954), "A Theory of Social Comparison Processes," *Human Relations*, 7, 117-40.

Foster, George (1972), "The Anatomy of Envy," *Current Anthropology*, 13, 165-202.

Grinblatt, Mark, Matti Keloharju, and Seppo Ikaheimo (2008), "Social Influence and Consumption: Evidence from the Automobile Purchases of Neighbors," *Review of Economics and Statistics*, 90(4), 735–753.

Hoelzl, Erik and George Loewenstein (2005), "Wearing out your Shoes to Prevent Someone Else from Stepping into Them: Social Takeover and Anticipated Regret in Sequential Decisions, *Organizational Behavior and Human Decision Processes*, 98 (September), 15–27.

Inman, J. Jeffery and Marcel Zeelenberg (2002), Regret in Repeat Purchases Versus Switching Decisions: The Attenuating Role of Decision Justifiability," *Journal of Consumer Research*, 29 (June), 116-28.

Kumar, Piyush (2004), "The Effects of Social Comparison on Inaction Inertia," *Organizational Behavior and Human Decision Processes*, 95 (November), 175-85.

Lin, Chien-Huang, Wen-Hsien Huang, and Marcel Zeelenberg (2006), "Multiple Reference Points in Investor Regret," *Journal of Economic Psychology*, 27 (December), 781-92.

Salovey, Peter and Judith Rodin (1984), "Some Antecedents and Consequences of Social-Comparison Jealousy," *Journal of Personality and Social Psychology*, 50, 1100-1112.

Schimmel, Solomon (1993), *Seven Deadly Sins*, New York: Bantam Doubleday.

Schoeck, Helmut (1969), *Envy: A Theory of Social Behavior*, New York: Harcourt, Brace & World.

Schwartz, Barry, Andrew Ward, John Monterosso, Sonja Lyubomirsky, Katherine White, and Darrin R. Lehman, (2002), "Maximizing versus Satisficing: Happiness is a Matter of Choice," *Journal of Personality and Social Psychology*, 83 (November) 1178-97.

Silver, Maury and John Sabini (1978), "The Perception of Envy," *Social Psychology Quarterly*, 41, 105-117.

Smith, Richard H. and Sung Hee Kim (2007), "Comprehending Envy," *Psychological Bulletin*, 133(1), 46-64.

Tesser, Abrahoam and Jennifer Campbell (1982), "Self-evaluation Maintenance and the Perception of Friends and Strangers," *Journal of Personality*, 50 (September), 261-79.

Tesser, Abraham and James E. Collins (1988), "Emotion in Social Reflection and Comparison Situations: Intuitive, Systematic, and Exploratory Approaches," *Journal of Personality and Social Psychology*, 55 (5), 695-709.

Testa, Maria and Brenda Major (1990), "The Impact of Social Comparison after Failure: The Moderating Effect of Perceived Control," *Basic and Applied Social Psychology*, 11, 205-218.

Tsiros, Micheal and Vikas Mittal (2000), "Regret: A Model of its Antecedents and Consequences in Consumer Decision Making," *Journal of Consumer Research*, 26 (March), 401-17.

Westphal, James D. and Poonam Khanna (2003), "Keeping Directors in Line: Social Distancing as a Control Mechanism in the Social Elite," *Administrative Science Quarterly*, 48 (September), 361-98.

Wood, Arthur L. (1974), *Deviant Behavior and Control Strategies*, Lexington, MA: Lexington.

Zeelenberg, Marcel and Rik Pieters (2007), "A Theory of Regret Regulation 1.0," *Journal of Consumer Psychology*,17(1), 3-18.

Zizzo, Daniel John (2008), "The Cognitive and Behavioral Economics of Envy," in Smith, Richard H. (Ed), *Envy: Theory and Research,* New York, NY: Oxford University Press, 190-210.

Special Session Summary

The Wellbeing of Subsistence Consumers

Laurel Anderson, Arizona State University, USA

SESSION OVERVIEW

Poverty is a form of violence that arises from conflicts between competing visions of wellbeing.
(Research Group on Wellbeing in Developing Countries, University of Bath)

As transformative consumer research is further blossoming within ACR, an aspect of value that has emerged is the confluence of a number of different paradigm and methodological perspectives around this interest area. As such we see it paralleling the theme of the conference, "A World of Knowledge At the Point of Confluence."

In this session, we will illustrate different perspectives of well being and their blending. The definitions at the start of this paper give rise to the focus of this session because understandings and prescriptions for transformation/change depend on conceptions of wellbeing. Acknowledging that there are different and often competing definitions of wellbeing among stakeholders, one of the most haunting questions in transformative consumer research derives from this contestation. If change/ transformation is advocated in order to bring about well being of the consumer, how is wellbeing defined and who defines well being? The objective of session is to examine different perspectives of well being informing and deriving from our research projects.

Briefly, the discourse on well being seems to contain a number of defining, yet at times contradictory and overlapping frameworks:

1. The dominant concept has been an economic one. In this view, wellbeing is defined as the material resources consumers control, utilize, consumer, dispose of and their individual and aggregate levels of income. This view has been challenged!
2. Human Development. This perspective of wellbeing is founded on the premise of the universality of human needs and core dimensions of human wellbeing. Amartya Sen (1999) focuses on human capabilities and freedom-the extent of people's freedom or access to live the life that they value-the person's actual ability to be or do something. This approach's explicit goal is reversing power relations in a way that creates agency and voice for poor people enabling them to have more control in their lives. Others add to or constitute their own list of universal needs.
3. Livelihood/Resource Frameworks. This area is most represented by the later work of Sen, Chambers (Chambers and Conway 1992), and those at the University of Bath. Here wellbeing is predicated not only on economic vulnerability, but social and political. Research focuses on the resources and strategies that people use to mitigate their vulnerability. Various renditions of this framework identify resources such as natural, social, material, environmental, physical, financial, human, and social. The University of Bath places great emphasis on the social and is distinctive in including the cultural dimensions of the "exercise of agency in the struggle for livelihood " (Gough and McGregor 2007).
4. Subjective wellbeing. This framework recognizes that all resources, freedoms and other aspects of wellbeing are ultimately acted upon not objectively, but through the meanings to and goals of the subsistence consumers. Socio-cultural structures and agency inform this subjectivity. Thus this approach accounts for power and social identities. Consumers may have objective access to the life that they may want and the resources needed for this wellbeing, but the purpose to which these resources are assigned and power relationships circumscribe their use (Said 1985, Bourdieu 1990).

The definition of wellbeing put forth by the University of Bath incorporates four different perspectives of well being: Wellbeing is a state of being with others, where human needs are met, where one can act meaningfully to pursue one's goals, and where one enjoys a satisfactory quality of life."

These perspectives of wellbeing raise questions and controversies regarding:

1. Who is ultimately accountable for wellbeing: individual consumers or collectives that create and maintain social structures?
2. The conflict between individual freedom and social justice.
3. The universality of human needs. This question, especially with regard to developing nations and to subsistence consumers is most hotly debated by post-colonial scholarship who attest that "universals" are still caught within a particular cultural view.
4. There is an increasing stream of research in "positive psychology" focusing on subjective happiness and positive emotions. Critiques suggest that well-being has been commercialized and has become an affirmation of consumerist values. Others suggest that this perspective North American based and is a narrow, unrealistic and potentially damaging view. To be happy is an ideal consistent with a culture dominated by individualism and independence and may fit poorly with other cultures that value social relationships and interdependence (Markus and Kitayama 1997).
5. Others suggest that consumerist lifestyles are the cause of discontent, disharmony, depression and division. They cause harm to the environment and neglect the spiritual, moral, ethical aspects of life (Maxwell 2003).

Anderson's work in a Native- American subsistence community focuses on the extraordinarily high rate of diabetes. She finds considerable hopelessness and a sense of illbeing reflecting perceptions of the inevitability of diabetes for tribal members and the sense of marginalization. However, there are exceptions to this more prevalent view. Her work reflects the resource framework for wellbeing that focuses on cultural resources and the subjectivity paradigm that foregrounds consumers' perceptions of socio-cultural structures and agency within power dimensions.

Mahi's work with health literacy programs for women in India illustrates Sen's capability perspective of wellbeing. It further incorporates the socio-cultural perspective in recognizing the role of women in the family to promote/maintain health.

Viswanathan's work on the creative solutions of subsistence consumers illustrates the livelihood-resource model with a focus on the economic aspects.

References

Bourdieu, Pierre (1990), *In Other Words: Essays Towards a Reflexive Sociology*, Oxford: Polity Press.

Chambers, R. and G. Conway (1992), "Sustainable Rural Livelihoods: Practical Concepts for the 21st Century," *IDS Discussion Paper 296*, Institute of Development Studies, Brighton.

Gough, I. and J.A. McGregor (2007), *Wellbeing in Developing Countries: From Theory to Research*, Cambridge: Cambridge University Press.

Marcus, H. R. and S. Kitayama (1997), "The Cultural Construction of Self And Emotion: Implications for Social Behaviour," in Kitayama, S. and Markus, R. H. (eds.), *Emotion and Culture: Empirical Studies of Mutual Influence*, American Psychological Association, Washington, D.C.

Maxwell, T. P. (2003), "Integral Spirituality, Deep Science, and Ecological Awareness," *Zygon*, 38, 257–276.

Said, Edward (1985), *Orientalism*, Harmondsworth: Penguin.

Sen, Amartya (1999), *Development as Freedom*, Oxford: Oxford University Press.

EXTENDED ABSTRACTS

"Wellbeing Out of Hopelessness"

Laurie Anderson, Arizona State University, USA

Diabetes and related wellbeing can be envisioned as a problem involving individual consumer decision making, such as choices to eat a healthy diet and get regular exercise (Moorman et al. 2004). Alternatively, diabetes can be conceptualized as a community phenomenon in which social and cultural forces and resources have a significant impact on community wellbeing and health (Kreuter et al. 2003). For example, diabetes is at near epidemic rates in many Mexican American and Native American communities, and, in fact, in many indigenous communities throughout the world (Giachello et al. 2003). In this study, participatory community action methods are used to examine diabetes within a town where 23% of its Mexican American and Native American citizens suffer from diabetes. The community is characterized by concentrated economic disadvantage in which about 25% of the population is below the federal poverty line and two-thirds of these people are 200% below the federal poverty line. There are numerous diabetic preventive programs and services, but health care professionals in the community felt that these were ineffective in stemming the rise in diabetes.

This research involved a two year field study encompassing participant observations, visual documentation, collage led interviews, and in depth interviews with subsistence consumers, heath professionals and wellbeing advocates. This was a collaborative, participatory research project where subsistence consumers took part in the research planning, data collection, data analysis, action plans and presentation of the project results.

The definition of wellbeing impacts the way this research is understood and the transformative component/change that is suggested. Additionally, the results give rise to a certain perspective of wellbeing. As mentioned, there have been numerous efforts to transform consumer behavior in the community. There is even a town committee on diabetes. The efforts have not been deemed successful. Wellbeing definitions focused on the individual consumer and their "objective" access to goods and services appear not to have been successful as there are numerous services and goods available.

To emphasize the individual, as is most frequently the case in consumer research, means that we miss many of the social aspects that have increasingly been shown to be of major impact on health (Krieger 2001). It is most frequently the case that we expect consumers individually to be responsible for their own wellbeing. However, this begs the question of the degree of consumers' freedom and agency. The result of this study's community focus is the highlighting of ecosocial contexts that allows us to identify in a more nuanced way the structural elements that are impactful on consumers' well being but often beyond the direct control of the individual. Much sociological theory (c.f. Giddens 1984) submits that individuals are supported or constrained by larger structural and political orderings. Consequently an emphasis on the individual to the diminishment of the ecosocial contexts reflected in the focus on community would be shallow and leave larger problems unresolved. Even worse, it could lead to a narrow understanding of consumer well being such that any threat to wellbeing is attributed solely to the individual. Sontag (1978: 11) notes this in discussion about the view of illness "as the price one pays for excesses of diet…life-style–are the result of weakness of will or lack of prudence…" Thus arises the additional issue of blaming and marginalizing further those affected. Forefronting the community as the consumer unit of analysis in wellbeing and health makes it more difficult to lose sight of the socio-political and historical contexts and structures, goes beyond individual consumer's responsibilities and /or blame and highlights potential areas of social change.

Reflecting aspect of, in particular, the cultural component of the resource framework and the structural and agency informed subjectivity of these subsistence consumers, we found pervasive feelings of hopelessness about wellbeing and health. Comments such as "it is in our (tribal) blood," "why do we want to worry about that. I am already one foot and a half in the grave because of it," "who's gonna give a darn. I'm just an Indian, you know; you're insignificant" demonstrate the feelings of both hopelessness and marginalization. However, there was a group within the community that did not convey this feeling of hopelessness. These were families with children. These children through educational resources were knowledgeable about diabetes and influenced their parents' and grandparents' behavior. As one parent put it, "we would do anything for our children." Thus the children were also a positive resource influencing wellbeing and feelings of hope. Note that this change in consumers' behavior was not a reflection of access to services and programs, but in response to the socio-cultural importance and resource that the children represented.

Thus this study combines the resources available to consumers while emphasizing cultural and structural aspects that make them feel powerless and without agency. So the preventive programs and services were not being utilizing. Cultural and structural aspects emerged as dominant ones along with the subjective view of resources.

References

Giachello, A. L., J. O. Arrom, M. Davis, J. V. Sayad, D. Ramirez, N. Chandana, and C. Ramos (2003), "Reducing Diabetes Health Disparities Through Community-Based Participatory Action Research: The Chicago Southeast Diabetes Community Action Coalition," *Public Health Reports*, 118 (4), 309-323.

Giddens, Anthony (1984), *The Constitution of Society: Outline of the Theory of Structuration*, Cambridge, UK: Polity Press.

Kreuter, Matthew W., Susan N. Lukwago, Dawn C. Bucholtz, Eddie M. Clark, and Vetta Sanders-Thompson (2003), "Achieving Cultural Appropriateness in Health Promotion Programs: Targeted and Tailored Approaches," *Health Education Behavior*, 30; 133.

Krieger, Nancy (2001), "Theories for Social Epidemiology in the 21st Century: An Ecosocial Perspective," *International Journal of Epidemiology*, 30:668-677.

Moorman, Christine, Kristin Diehl, David Brinberg, and Blair Kidwell (2004), "Subjective Knowledge, Search Locations and Consumer Choice," *Journal of Consumer Research*, 31 (December) 673-680.

Sontag, Susan (1978), *Illness as Metaphor*, NY: Farrar Straus and Giroux

"Women-Oriented Health Literacy as an Asset/Capability in a Subsistence Community"

Humaira Mahi, San Francisco State University, USA

This work examines the value and effectiveness of delivery of women-oriented health literacy communication programs in a subsistence (low to no income) community by measuring changes in health outcomes over time. The research draws upon current literature in cultural sociology, public health, medicine and business to construct a programmatic research stream on underprivileged groups and how to improve health outcomes in these groups. The work focuses on women as key players in affecting change and thus examines health literacy programs as agents of social justice and empowerment in a subsistence setting.

A recent study of the evolving concept of health literacy from public health and medicine (Nutbeam, 2008) indicates that health literacy has been conceptualized so far in literature in two key ways. In the first way, health literacy is seen as a risk factor and is defined as the set of individual literacy capacities that act as a mediating factor in health and clinical decision-making (Baker, 2006). From this perspective, poor literacy skills are seen as a potential risk factor that needs to be managed in the process of providing clinical care. In the second way, it has been characterized as an asset. Health literacy in this case is seen as a means to enable individuals to exert greater control over their health and the range of personal, social and environmental determinants of health.

Nutbeam (2000) argues that the conceptualization of health literacy as an "asset" offers great promise in terms of potential impact on health and the range of actions it may enable. He also argues that ... "the potential of health education as a tool that enables action on the social determinants of health has been somewhat neglected" (Nutbeam, 2000).

Literacy is a focal issue in developing countries and is interwoven with many other transformative consumer concerns such as health, poverty, homelessness. The definition of literacy has expanded from its traditional definition as a set of skills surrounding reading and writing. "A newer stream of definition and conceptualization of literacy (the New Literacy Studies, c.f. Street 2001) firmly places literacy within a socio-cultural context. In this ideology, literacy, conceptualized as a social practice that is culturally constructed and contested, (Ozanne 2008) is of most interest rather than a specific standardized set of skills. This is manifested in the recognition of multiple literacies, varying according to social practices but also defining relations of power (Street 2001). Broadly, literacy is the ability to interpret and communicate meaning though socially constructed symbols and texts." (Anderson and Viswanathan 2009).

The recognition of this socio-cultural embeddedness, in particular the contested and power dimensions, is especially pertinent to India. In India there are prevailing gender prejudices where, especially in rural areas, there is low enrollment of girls in schools; high engagement of female children in domestic work and high school dropout rates that present major obstacles in the path to raising the rate of literacy among Indian women. UNICEF says that in India, girl children tend to be taken to health centers less frequently than boys, receive less food than boys and are given less education than boys. About 41 percent of Indian girls under the age of 14 do not attend school, according to the report. This disempowerment of women through the lack of access to education and literacy thus has far reaching implications for health when one considers that women hold the health maintenance roles in the family.

Criticisms of narrow indicators of poverty that are confined to income and consumption led to interest in asset/vulnerability approaches to understanding poverty (Moser 1998) that focus on sustainable local-level poverty reduction strategies which strengthen people's own inventive solutions. Amartya Sen argues for creation of more opportunities or capabilities as he calls it for women in particular (1979, pg 218) that would empower and provide social justice. Sen's argument is that only when barriers are removed by providing capabilities can people be truly said to act out of personal choice. This is especially true for women in subsistence communities in India where women are the main caregivers and maintainers of family health.

The "asset" model of health literacy from literature and Sen's notion of capabilities is used in this work to examine the impact of a specific women-oriented health literacy program in a subsistence community in India. The research is designed to 1) inform and educate community members on health care and its connection to wellbeing 2) to educate the community on the strong link between ill health and particular food consumption patterns in a village in South India. The health literacy program foregrounds women community members' literacy. The health outcomes are monitored at the individual and community level longitudinally to assess the changes in food consumption patterns and the changes in the level of self-management of disease and its impact on disease control. From a transformative consumer research standpoint, this study advances knowledge by bringing in very current dialogues from cultural sociology, public health and medical literature on the conceptualization of health literacy to examine and develop measures to assess health literacy oriented towards women as an asset in improving food consumption patterns and self-management of chronic diseases among subsistence communities.

References

Anderson, Laurel and Madhu Viswanathan (2009), "Socio-Culturally Embedded Literacies in an Emerging Economy," *Advances in Consumer Research–Asia Pacific*, Volume 8, eds. Sridhar Samu and Rajiv Vaidyanathan and Dipankar Chakravarti, Duluth, MN : Association for Consumer Research.

Baker, D. W. 2006, "The Meaning and Measure of Health Literacy," *Journal of General Internal Medicine*, 21 (2006), pp. 878–883.

Moser C. O. (1998), "The Asset Vulnerability Framework: Reassessing Urban Poverty Reduction Strategies," *World Development,* Volume 26, Issue 1, January 1998, Pages 1-19.

Nutbeam, D. (2000), "Health Literacy as a Public Health Goal: A Challenge for Contemporary Health Education and Communication Strategies Into the 21st Century," *Health Promotion International*, 15 (2000), 259–267.

Nutbeam, D. 2008. "The Evolving Concept of Health Literacy," *Social Science and Medicine,* 67, 2072–2078.

Ozanne, Julie, Canan Corus, and Bige Saatcioglu (2008), "Deliberative Democracy and the Poor: Developing Business Literacies to Build Capacity," Working paper.

Sen, Amartya (1979), "The Equality of What?" *Text of Talk*, Stanford University.

Street, Brian (2001), *Literacy and Development: Ethnographic Perspectives*, London: Routledge.

Unicef, "India: Empowering Women Benefit All Children," http://www.unicef.org/india/india_sowc_a.swf

"Well-Being at the Intersection of Subsistence and Sustainability"

Madhu Viswanathan, University of Illinois, Urbana-Champaign, USA

Srinivas Sridharan, University of Western Ontario, USA

Kiju Jung, University of Illinois, Urbana-Champaign, USA

A desired outcome of sustainable development is to enhance well-being among those living in subsistence. The concept of sustainability in a broad sense integrates issues relating to "Triple Bottom Line" or "Profit, Planet, and People" (Elkington 1997). As business, government, and social enterprise endeavors to create sustainable solutions, a number of top-down notions of sustainability serve to guide them. However, from the perspective of transformative consumer research, these top-down approaches beg a number of questions such as the following: what does sustainability means from the perspective of those living in subsistence and how does it translate to enhanced well-being from the perspective of those living in subsistence.

Whereas there are a number of approaches to poverty and well-being, our approach is consistent with the sustainable livelihoods approach to poverty, sustainable development (see Chambers and Conway 1992), and a bottom-up community level approach to poverty and sustainable development (see Chambers1997 and Pound et al., 2003). Criticisms of narrow indicators of poverty that are confined to income and consumption led to interest in asset/vulnerability approaches to understanding wellbeing and poverty that focus on sustainable local-level poverty reduction strategies which strengthen people's own inventive solutions. "A livelihood comprises the capabilities, assets (including both material and social resources) and activities required for a means of living. A livelihood is sustainable when it can cope with and recover from stresses and shocks and maintain or enhance its capabilities and assets both now and in the future, while not undermining the natural resource base." (Chambers and Conway 1992). The livelihoods approach begins with a need to understand the livelihoods of individuals living in subsistence and the constraints that inhibit a realization of rights improvement of livelihoods on a sustainable basis. This framework identifies different forms of capital/resources–human, social, cultural, and economic capital (Bourdieu 1986; Cohen 1999; Coleman 1988; Putnam 1993) that enhanced well-being.

We draw from research on subsistence marketplaces and a related social initiative on providing marketplace literacy education in South India (Viswanathan, Gajendiran, and Venkatesan, 2008) with implications for well-being in the economic realm. Specifically, our research program has provided a range of insights on well-being as it relates to marketplace activities. Our educational program and its assessment in terms of actual impact on subsistence individuals provide a platform to understand well-being and its relationship with skills, confidence, and awareness and exercise of rights. In turn, our focus has also been on sustainable consumption and production.

Our ongoing research examines sustainability and well-being from the perspective of those living at the lowest strata of society through qualitative research in South India. Subsistence marketplaces with severe resource constraints represent an ideal context in which to study sustainability and well-being. In subsistence marketplaces, severe resource constraints make for a natural sense to conserve and to do more with less. Also subsistence is intertwined with under-consumption and a natural tendency to conserve precious basic necessities by strategic reusing, exchanging, sharing, and saving and reinvesting in future well-being, such as through education. However, the need to use available resources in unsustainable ways to survive the short-term is also crucial; for example, the use of firewood for cooking adding to pollution and causing respiratory illnesses. Conservation may be economically beneficial for well-being (short-term) as well as be socio-culturally beneficial for well-being (long-term; e.g., building trust in communities and tightening community network and solidarity). However, social costs from unsustainable consumptions may degrade and dismantle physical ecology and a sense of community, and hence decrease well-being of both individuals and communities. Our research examines the tension that exists between conserving and consuming from the perspective of customers and entrepreneurs.

Our research is examining the spheres of life where subsistence individuals view conflicts between social, ecological and economic realms and, as a consequence, decreased well-being. Some areas of concern include the local physical environment (e.g., pollution, garbage disposal, plastic use and burning, deforestation, overuse of chemicals such as pesticide in agriculture), basic physical needs (e.g., scarcity and contamination of drinking water, lack of nutritious food), the socio-cultural environment (e.g., weakening of human relationship as well as changes in culture and tradition), and the local economy. In each of these areas with the lack of action among powerful interests as well as the lack of infrastructure and resources that characterize subsistence contexts, individuals adjust to makeshift solutions and try to conserve resources (e.g., reusing plastic containers for storage, using clothes to screen against pollution at home or during travel, using public transportation, shopping and purchasing as a group, making rather than buying to save money and enhance nutrition, harvesting rainwater, locally producing products, using both innovative and traditional cooking methods to retain nutritive ingredients). Our research findings suggest notions of sustainability and well-being which are holistic-an interconnected web of issues ranging from struggles from the deterioration of the physical environment, the lack of civic values (especially trust) and social networks, and the erosion of local culture and human relationships to efforts for overcoming the struggles and moving forward.

References

Bourdieu, P. (1986), "The Forms of Capital," in *Handbook for Theory and Research for the Sociology of Education*, ed. J.G Richardson, 241–258.

Chambers, R. (1997), *Whose Reality Counts? Putting the First Last*, London: Intermediate Technology Publications.

______ and Conway, G. (1992), "Sustainable Rural Livelihoods: Practical Concepts for the 21st Century," *IDS Discussion Paper 296*, Institute of Development Studies, Brighton.

Cohen, J. (1999), "Trust, Voluntary Association and Workable Democracy," in Mark E. Warren (ed.) *Democracy and Trust*, Cambridge: Cambridge University Press, 208-48.

Coleman, J. S. (1988), "Social Capital in the Creation of Human Capital," *American Journal of Sociology*, 94, Supplement, 95-120.

Elkington, J. (1997), *Cannibals with Forks: The Triple Bottom Line of 21st Century Business*, Oxford: Capstone.

Pound, B., S. Snapp, C. McDougall, A. Braun, (2003), *Managing Natural Resources for Sustainable Livelihoods: Uniting Science and Participation,* London: Earthscan.

Putnam, R. D. (1995), "Bowling Alone: America's Declining Social Capital," *Journal of Democracy*, 6(1), 65–78.

Putnam, R. D. (1993), *Making Democracy Work. Civic Traditions in Modern Italy*, Princeton: Princeton University Press.

Viswanathan, M, S. Gajendiran, and R. Venkatesan (2008), "Understanding and Enabling Marketplace Literacy in Subsistence Contexts: The Development of a Consumer and Entrepreneurial Literacy Educational Program in South India," *International Journal of Educational Development*, 28 (3), 300-19.

SPECIAL SESSION SUMMARY

Looking on the Bright Side: The Effects of Optimism on Goals and Behavior

Elaine Chan, Hong Kong University of Science and Technology, Hong Kong

EXTENDED ABSTRACTS:

"The Counteractive Optimism in Goal Pursuit"

Ying Zhang, University of Texas at Austin, USA
Ayelet Fishbach, University of Chicago, USA

The current research proposes counteractive optimism as a self-regulatory process in consumer goal pursuit. Because the presence of obstacles to the attainment of important long-term goals triggers people's internal self-control efforts, and because an optimistic prediction, compared with a more conservative one, can be a more challenging and thus more motivating performance standard, we propose that individuals who are concerned about their performance in goal pursuit will generate an optimistic prediction of their future goal pursuit when anticipating obstacles and use these predictions to direct their subsequent effort. This is called counteractive optimism. For example, a dieter who is concerned about being fit will predict increased ability to resist when shown promotional ads for tempting food items, so as to actually increase the effort to resist the temptation and maintain goal pursuit.

While counteractive optimism increases a person's motivation to invest efforts in pursuing an important goal, this comes at the cost of being less accurate in predictions. Because an obstacle objectively increases the difficulty in attaining a goal, achieving accuracy in prediction requires a more conservative prediction to account for this negative impact. Therefore, we expect individuals to stop using expectation as self-control mechanism and reverse the counteractive optimism whenever the incentive for providing an accurate prediction outweighs that for securing higher performance. In these cases, anticipation of obstacles should result in a more conservative prediction, compared with no obstacles. Because less optimistic predictions set lower standards and are less motivating, individuals will accordingly invest less effort in actually pursuing the goal.

Three studies were conducted to test these hypotheses. Study 1 demonstrated the impact of counteractive optimistic predictions. Participants were asked to perform certain tasks and were offered incentives to perform well. Half of the participants were told the task would be difficult, and the other half were told it would be easy. Before commencing the task, participants were either asked to predict their performance in the task, or not. We found that for participants who were asked to predict their performance, those who expected the task to be difficult (vs. easy) predicted a better performance, a pattern that is consistent with counteractive optimism, and in the end showed higher motivation (i.e., persistence) in completing the task; in contrast, participants who did not predict their performance before commencing the task did not show any difference in task motivation regardless of whether they believed the task was difficult or easy.

Study 2 demonstrated the mediating role of an optimistic prediction. In this study, participants needed to complete a take-home exam and were asked to either give an accurate prediction or a rough one before leaving the lab with the exams. Before they made their predictions, half of them were told the exam would be difficult, while the other half were told that it would be easy. We found that participants who were told to give a rough prediction expected to complete the exam sooner if they believed it would be difficult (vs. easy); however, for participants who were told to be accurate, these results reversed. Participants' actual completion times were highly consistent with the predictions, and were mediated by the predicted times.

Study 3 demonstrated an important moderator for counteractive optimism: the controllability of the obstacle. This study showed that when the obstacles were believed to be beyond one's control, the counteractive optimism effect does not obtain. Specifically, participants in this study were asked to predict their susceptibility to certain health risks. We found that if this risk was believed to be acquired and correctable through behaviors, people predicted themselves to be less susceptible to it when they were told that they were among the high (vs. low) risk group, and they adjusted their subsequent health behaviors accordingly to ensure that their predictions were fulfilled. This pattern, however, went away if the risk was believed to be inherited and no actions can alter one's susceptibility to the risk. In this case, people predicted themselves to be more susceptible when they were told that they belonged to the high (vs. low) risk group, and made no behavioral changes.

Taken together, in this research we identified counteractive optimism as a self-control mechanism that helps people overcome obstacles. Whenever the performance in goal pursuit is critical, anticipated obstacles elicited a counteractive optimistic prediction, which in turn increased people's effort to meet these standards. This self-control mechanism, however, disappears when individuals are concerned about the accuracy of their predictions. In these cases people generate more conservative predictions when anticipating obstacles in goal pursuit, and as a result, their effort drops accordingly.

"Enhancing Self-Control through Future Consequence Elaboration"

Kelly Haws, Texas A&M University, USA
Gergana Nenkov, Boston College, USA

Consumers draw upon a variety of strategies when attempting to exercise self-control (Hoch and Loewenstein 1991), many of which are directly related to the time inconsistent preferences underlying most self-control dilemmas. Self-control strategies specifically bringing attention to future periods of time should allow individuals to consider consequences consistent with their higher-order goals (Fujita et al. 2006). Indeed, many self-help books and old sayings advise people to think before they act, look before they leap, and measure twice before cutting once. Academic research has also established the beneficial effects of considering the outcomes that might occur in the future for the effective control of one's behavior in the present (e.g., Baumeister and Heatherton 1996, Nenkov et al. 2008). However, the question arises: is future outcome consideration always beneficial for people's effective self-control or is it possible that some types of outcome elaboration (e.g., positively biased) might actually hinder it?

In Study 1 we examine the role of providing outcome cues in enhancing self-control effectiveness. Participants (n=137) were asked to indicate how much they would pay on a credit card account. We provided participants with either just basic account information (account balance, minimum payment due, APR, balance due date) or basic information plus future outcome cues (length of time to pay-off and total finance charges, given minimum payments). After filler tasks, we measured consumer spending self-control (Haws and Bearden 2009). A significant interaction between participants' spending self-control and condition ($p<.01$) indicated that the nature of information provided did not affect payment amounts for high self-control consumers, while future outcomes cues significantly increased the intended payments of low self-control consumers.

In our second study, we investigated whether providing outcome cues aided consumers' self-control by focusing them on the potential outcomes of their behavior. Participants (n=142) were asked to imagine that they encountered a desirable product at an electronics store, but that purchasing the item would cause them to reach their credit limit. In the no outcome cues condition, no further information was given, but in the outcome cues present condition, specific potential negative consequences were provided (e.g., unable to repay, credit rating implications). Participants were then asked to decide whether they would buy the item or not and to indicate the extent to which they thought about future outcomes when making the decision. Providing negative outcome cues enhanced self-control for consumers not inherently inclined to exercise it, whereas consumers inherently high in self-control did not differ significantly in the amount of self-control exercised based on the presence or absence of outcome cues in their environment. Furthermore, based on differences in consumer self-control, we found a significant interaction in the extent to which the presence of the cues caused participants to think about the future consequences of their decision. Specifically, those participants high in self-control reported that they thought about future consequences quite a bit in both conditions, while for those consumers low in self-control, the cues significantly increased their focus on future consequences. As such, this study indicates that part of the reason that consumers who are high in self-control might be more successful in exerting self-control is because they naturally elaborate on the potential consequences of their actions more, regardless of environmental cues.

In Study 3 (n=97) we examine the effects of focusing consumers differentially on the positive vs. negative future outcomes on their subsequent self-control. In this study we also extend our effects to different consumer domains and assure personal relevance of the issue to each participant by allowing them to choose one of four self-control issues (i.e., weight management, budgeting, time management, or exercising). Furthermore, we use another related individual difference variable–proclivity to elaborate on potential outcomes (EPO) (Nenkov et al. 2008), which should be relevant to all four contexts. We employ a 2 (outcome elaboration priming: positively biased vs. negatively biased) x 2 (elaboration task framing: self-control success vs. failure—yielding to temptation) between subject design. After engaging in a condition-specific elaboration task in which they listed potential outcomes (e.g. positive outcomes for exerting self-control), participants were asked to respond to a scenario representing a temptation in their chosen domain. Using EPO as a third factor, a three-way interaction emerged suggesting the circumstances under which high EPO consumers might be harmed and low EPO consumers might be helped. Specifically, while consumers high in EPO were generally more effective in exercising self-control, elaborating on the positive outcomes of yielding to temptation (e.g., enhanced life enjoyment) actually decreased their self-control. Low EPO consumers, on the other hand, enhanced their self-control when asked to elaborate on the positive consequences of yielding to temptation or the negative consequences of exerting self-control, both of which serve to draw attention to the fact that the long-term consequences of present indulgence may not be that significant.

Overall, our research has provided new insights into an important strategy that can be utilized by consumers when trying to make decisions. Both our findings from studies 1 and 2 and past research (Nenkov et al. 2008) have found that high EPO consumers are generally more likely to engage in effective self-control. Our study 3 results suggest that different approaches need to be employed to motivate consumers to engage in effective self-control based on their level of EPO. Interestingly, focusing on positive outcomes tended to backfire and decrease self-control for high EPO consumers. On the contrary, improvements in self-control for consumers with low outcome elaboration came from both external negative outcome cues and a "forced" focus on the consequences of indulgence.

References

Baumeister, Roy F. and Todd F. Heatherton (1996), "Self-Regulation Failure: An Overview," *Psychological Inquiry*, 7 (1), 1-15.

Fujita, Kentaro, Yaacov Trope, Nira Liberman, and Maya Levin-Sagi (2006), "Construal Levels and Self-Control," *Journal of Personality and Social Psychology*, 90 (3), 351-367.

Haws, Kelly and William O. Bearden (2009), "The Impact of Consumer Spending Self-Control," working paper, Texas A&M University, College Station, TX.

Hoch, Stephen J. and George F. Loewenstein (1991), "Time-Inconsistent Preferences and Consumer Self-Control," *Journal of Consumer Research*, 17 (March), 492-506.

Nenkov, Gergana Y., J. Jeffrey Inman, and John Hulland (2008) "Considering the Future: The Conceptualization and Measurement of Elaboration on Potential Outcomes," *Journal of Consumer Research*, 35 (1), 126-141.

"Understanding Optimism: Buying What You Can't Use Today but Hope to Use Tomorrow"

Elaine Chan, Hong Kong University of Science and Technology, Hong Kong
Anirban Mukhopadhyay, Hong Kong University of Science and Technology, Hong Kong
Jaideep Sengupta, Hong Kong University of Science and Technology, Hong Kong

Consumers often purchase products that they are unable to use at the time of purchase, in anticipation that they may be able to do so in the future. For instance, why might people buy (as they often do) clothing that is one size too small for them? One possibility is that such purchase decisions are driven by expectations of being able to realize the consumption at some future time. As optimists hold more favorable expectations of the future than pessimists, optimists should be more likely to engage in such behaviors. In this research, we present a more nuanced view of when and why optimism might have such an effect, and in so doing, provide new insights into the different mechanisms underlying optimism.

Optimism, as a positive illusion of the future, is often considered to be a result of mental imagery (Taylor and Brown 1988). Such imagery-based processing, as opposed to more data-driven analytical processing, is marked by increased consideration of self-related expectations. Accordingly, we propose that under imagery processing, the more favorable expectation held by optimists should make them more inclined to engage in anticipatory purchasing than pessimists, but the effect should be diluted under analytical processing. Further, this effect of imagery can be driven by two possible routes: optimists may either imagine the outcome of the purchase as being positive, or the process required to realize the benefits of the purchase as being easy. We propose that either route prevails depending on the depth of processing. Anticipatory purchase typically involves some uncertainty as to whether one can take the steps needed to use the product. When processing is unconstrained, the required confidence level is higher (Eagly and Chaiken 1993), and therefore, focusing the imagination on the process required gives optimists the confidence that they can easily accomplish those steps. This leads them to be more likely to make anticipatory purchases than pessimists. This effect should decrease when focusing on the outcome, because optimists have to think directly about the end result without deliberating on the intervening steps, which reduces their confidence and therefore purchase likelihood. The situation is different when cognitive capacity is constrained, as decisions are now based on a heuristic of whether the final outcome is favorable or not. As optimists think of the outcome as being more positive than pessimists, focusing their attention on the outcome should make them more likely to make anticipatory purchases than pessimists. On the other hand, as their ability to generate steps is constrained by the limited cognitive resources, the effect should be dampened when they are required to think about the intervening process. In sum, we hypothesize that the outcome-focus route to optimism operates under constrained capacity, while the process-focus route operates under unconstrained capacity.

Four experiments tested these hypotheses. Experiment 1 used a 2 (method of processing: analytical vs. imagery) x 2 (optimism: optimists vs. pessimists) between-subjects design to test whether the effect of optimism is obtained under imagery processing, but not under analytical processing. Participants first took part in a survey, which included a question about the size of jeans that they could just fit in. After a filler task, they took part in a different survey about buying jeans. We manipulated method of processing by asking participants either to rely on their imaginations or be careful and well-reasoned while making their decisions. Next, they read the description of the jeans under purchase consideration, which were always one size smaller than their current sizes (as recorded in the earlier survey). They then reported their likelihood to purchase these jeans. Lastly, participants filled out a standard optimism scale (Scheier and Carver 1985). As hypothesized, the imagery instruction induced a higher purchase intention for optimists than pessimists, but there was no such effect under analytical processing.

Experiment 2 used a 2 (focus: outcome vs. process) x 2 (manipulated optimism: optimists vs. pessimists) between-subjects design to look more specifically at the mental simulations leading to the effect of optimism under unconstrained processing. The procedure was similar to that of Experiment 1, except for two changes. First, before the jeans purchase scenario, we manipulated optimism by asking participants to list either 2 vs. 8 examples of optimistic thinking. In accordance with the ease of retrieval effect (Schwarz et al. 1991), participants should find it difficult (vs. easy) to generate 8 (vs. 2) instances, and hence should conclude that they were pessimistic (vs. optimistic). Second, this experiment manipulated thought focus by asking participants to make their decisions by visualizing either the end benefits of wearing the jeans or the process they would go through in order to be able to wear the jeans. In support of our hypothesis, results revealed that optimists were more likely to make anticipatory purchases than pessimists under process-focus, but this difference disappeared under outcome-focus. This pattern of results was replicated in another study (Experiment 2B) using a different product category (musical instruments).

Experiment 3 rounded out the picture by testing the prediction that optimism exerts its effect through an outcome or a process route depending upon the availability of cognitive resources. This experiment used a 2 (cognitive load: high vs. low) x 2 (focus: outcome vs. process) x 2 (optimism: optimists vs. pessimists) between-subjects design. The procedure was similar to that of Experiment 2, except for two changes. First, we measured optimism as in Experiment 1. Second, before the jeans purchase scenario, we manipulated cognitive load by asking participants to memorize either a 2-digit (low load) or an 8-digit number (high-load). Replicating previous findings, results showed that under low cognitive load, optimism enhanced the purchase likelihood under process-focus, but not outcome-focus. Of interest, under high cognitive load, optimists were more likely to purchase than pessimists under outcome-focus, but not process-focus. In effect, Experiment 3 showed that optimism can operate through either process- or outcome-focus, depending on the depth of processing.

Taken together, results from four studies, which included both chronic and situational inductions of optimism, as well as different purchase contexts, provide a theoretically-supported pattern that explains both when and how optimism might have an effect on anticipatory purchase. In doing so, this research both offers new insights into the substantive domain of anticipatory purchasing, and builds theoretical knowledge about optimism.

References

Eagly, Ann H. and Shelly Chaiken (1993), *The Psychology of Attitudes*, Fort Worth, TX: Harcourt.

Scheier, Michael F. and Charles S. Carver (1985), "Optimism, Coping and Health: Assessment and Implications of Generalized Outcome Expectancies," *Health Psychology*, 4 (3), 219-47.

Schwarz, Norbert, Herbert Bless, Fritz Strack, Gisela Klumpp, Helga Rittenauer-Schatka, and Annette Simons (1991), "Ease of Retrieval as Information: Another Look at the Availability Heuristic," *Journal of Personality and Social Psychology*, 61 (2), 195-202.

Taylor, Shelley E. and Jonathon D. Brown (1988), "Illusion and Well-Being: A Social-Psychological Perspective on Mental Health," *Psychological Bulletin*, 103 (2), 193-210.

SPECIAL SESSION SUMMARY

Multidisciplinary Approaches to Communicating Health Risks

Adriana Samper, Duke University, USA

SESSION OVERVIEW

The importance of improving the communication of health risks and prescriptive actions is clear, yet there are many stumbling blocks associated with translating health risk information into consumer action. Questions emerge regarding how accurately individuals may interpret risk information, how they may respond to this risk information (engagement vs. denial or avoidance) and how health risk communications designed in the lab can be effectively presented in the field and scaled up to produce broad impact. This session brings together papers across the spectrum, from micro (e.g., perceptual and emotional) to macro (societal) approaches to understanding consumer reactions to risk. By bringing together papers that take perceptual, emotional, behavioral and societal views of health risk communication, this session will help move consumer research towards integrative solutions for motivating beneficial action.

First, Raghubir models, and empirically documents, fundamental (hard-wired) perceptual bias in risk assessment. Next, Samper, Luce and Purohit suggest emotion-based communication interventions to circumvent consumer bias in risk estimation, revealing that these types of communications can help or hurt depending on the degree of threat present. Keller and Lehmann demonstrate how to integrate across perceptual, emotional and other variables of these kinds to design effective interventions. Finally, Bloom, Block and Trabold address the need to integrate insights from individual studies and "scale up" to improve societal actions. This fourth paper facilitates discussion and integration of all of the papers in the session.

EXTENDED ABSTRACTS

"The Psychophysics of Estimated Risk"

Priya Raghubir, New York University, USA

This paper proposes a psychophysical function that translates raw base-rate information about health risk into perceptions of risk for the average person and one's self. Unlike the standard power functions, in our formulation the exponent of the power function is endogenously determined as a function of the size of the base rate denominator, and varies as a function of base-rates. The value of the exponent is also modeled to be the parameter used to adjust risk estimates for oneself from the starting anchor of estimates of an average person. The model is parsimonious, requires no exogenous assumptions, is based on the psychology of how people process denominator information and an anchor-adjust model of risk estimation, and fits the data from two studies across 13 different causes of death, well.

A base rate is the likelihood of occurrence of an event (n=1), in terms of the size of the population from which it is drawn ("N"):

$$Base\ Rate=1\ /\ N$$

Psychophysical models of estimation have shown that people's estimates may be biased and follow a power law with an exponent<1 (Chandon and Wansink, 2007; Krider et al., 2001; Krishna, 2007), leading to smaller numbers being overestimated relative to larger numbers. In a risk perception context, we propose that the denominator, N, is the focal property being estimated. Therefore, rather than the exponent, α, being applied to the numerator (as is common in other psychophysical representations), it is applied to the denominator, or:

$$Perceived\ Risk=1/\ N^{\alpha},\ where\ 0<\alpha<1,$$

When $\alpha \rightarrow 1$, perceptions are more accurate, and as $\alpha \rightarrow 0$, base rates are overestimated. The size of α has been typically modeled to be a constant, independent of the base estimate to which it is applied. We suggest that α is endogenously determined with its size contingent on the estimation quantity (or base rate) itself, or:

$$\alpha = f(N)$$

This is because the larger the population (denominator N), the more difficult it is to identify with (Raghubir, 2008), leading to a smaller exponent, $\alpha \rightarrow 0$. The larger the overall number of people who are at risk, or the incidence of an event ($n \rightarrow N$), the easier it is to imagine oneself being a part of this group, and the larger the exponent, α, or the closer it is to 1. One representation of this model that satisfies the above conditions is:

$$\alpha = K\ (log\ N)\chi\ ,$$

where K is a scaling constant, and χ is a fraction between 0 and -1. This representation allows the rescaling of large numbers through the use of Log (N) versus N (e.g., 5 and 340,733 are scaled down to 0.70 and 5.53). The fractional exponent, χ, further rescales large differences closer to 1 (e.g., χ=1/8, transforms Log (5) from .70 to .9562, and Log (340,733) from 5.53 to 1.2384). This representation implies the following psychophysical function:

$$Perceived\ Risk=1/\ N\ K\ (log\ N)exp(\chi).$$

The prevalent belief in health risk is that self-perceptions are related to the perception of risk of others with the latter used as a starting anchor (Lin et al. 2003, Raghubir and Menon, 1998). We model self-estimate of risk as a function of the actual estimated risk of the average person (AP):

$$Self\ Perception=K\ (log\ N)\chi * AP\ [AP/\ Perceived\ Risk]$$

This formulation recognizes that the AP in the numerator serves as a starting anchor against which self perceptions of risk are formulated. The AP/ Perceived Risk ratio captures differences in risk perception due to other causes such as the perceived controllability of a cause of death (Lin et al. 2003). The closer the ratio is to 1, the better the fit of the psychophysical function, and the lower the effect of causes external to the actual base-rate itself (e.g., controllability). The constant, α, is a scaling parameter that is itself contingent on the base-rate and is the level of adjustment that people make after they anchor on the risk of the average person. The closer $\alpha \rightarrow 1$, the lower self-other biases in risk estimates, and the closer both perceptions are to actual base-rates.

Two studies were designed to test these two representations. In Study 1, we examine risk perceptions for 13 different causes of death varying odds. Study participants (n=100) were asked to estimate how likely a cause of death was for both themselves and the average person. A 13 (causes of death) x 2 (targets) ANOVA on risk estimates revealed that estimates of risk of the average person are higher than estimates of risk for one's self: the self-positivity bias. There was also main effect of cause reflecting different perceptions of risk for the various causes of death. A significant interaction revealed that the self-positivity bias was absent for three of the causes of death: MVAs, pedestrian accidents, and earthquakes.

We then fitted the psychophysical function to the mean estimate of risk for the average person. The function is characterized by an exponent that ranges from .7843 (for cancer) to .6056 (for fireworks discharge). The scaling constant, k, is .75, and the exponent for log(N) is 1/8. The fit follows actual estimates well. Study 2 examines the moderating role of manner of presentation of risk estimates as numeric versus graphic on risk perceptions.

"Imagine Yourself in This Patient's Shoes: The "Identifiable Patient" and Health Threat"

Adriana Samper, Duke University, USA
Mary Frances Luce, Duke University, USA
Devavrat Purohit, Duke University, USA

Identifiability—the presentation or description of a single, often named, individual as the subject of a message—has been shown to be a powerful instigator of emotion and affective processing (e.g.,Small, Loewenstein, and Slovic, 2007). Most of this work has focused on the domains of altruism and helping behaviors. Researchers have coined the "identifiable victim effect" (Small and Loewenstein, 2003), pointing out that "society is willing to spend far more money to save the lives of identifiable victims than to save statistical victims" (Jenni and Loewenstein, 1997, p. 236). Affective processing has been shown to underlie these differences in giving (Small et al., 2007).

The effect of identifiability on health risk perceptions and behaviors has yet to be addressed. This is a critical gap because health communications aim to motivate recipients to take actions to benefit themselves, whereas prior work on identifiable victims aims to motivate actions to benefit others. Moreover, effective health messages are increasingly "self-relevant," targeting information toward specific demographic groups. To date, research has yet to examine how the self-relevance of a communication might moderate the benefits of specifying an affect-inducing identifiable individual to motivate action.

We address the important questions of whether and how the presentation of an identifiable patient can motivate desired behavior in a health communication context. This research examines the conditions under which identifiability does, and does not, have beneficial effects. In Study 1, college undergraduates were instructed to read a pamphlet about the threat of genital herpes among college students vs. middle-aged adults. This pamphlet was accompanied by a picture of an individual college student (middle-aged adult) said to have genital herpes or a picture of a group of college students (middle-aged adults) with a statistical risk for genital herpes. The identifiable pictures were matched on sex. Underneath all pictures was a caption describing the statistical risk of genital herpes. We find that identifiability increases perceived vulnerability to disease, but only for those individuals presented with the identifiable college student. Thus, self-relevance is necessary for identifiable presentation to increase perceived threat.

Given that a great deal of health information is presented in situations of higher stress (e.g., physician's office, hospital or clinic), in Study 2 we examine the effect of ambient stress on identifiable patient presentations, examining perceived vulnerability to herpes, concern about contracting herpes and intent to be tested for the disease. Participants were presented with herpes information depicting only college students, either identifiable or in a group. Next, we manipulated stress levels by asking participants to complete an easy (difficult) timed anagram task. We find that following the easy task, at low stress levels, identifiable patient presentation increases perceived vulnerability to herpes. However, following the difficult (high stress) anagram task, participants reported significantly reduced perceived vulnerability, suggesting a denial of risk under high stress, identifiable conditions.

Study 2 also revealed that group presentation may be better for promoting concern and screening in high-stress conditions. An interaction of stress by group presentation on concern and intent to be tested indicated that high-stress group presentation leads to both increased concern about contracting herpes as well as increased intent to be tested for herpes relative to low-stress group conditions. Finally, a moderated mediation analysis examining the effect of stress at identifiable and group presentation levels revealed that whereas there are significant positive relationships between stress and concern and stress and intent to be tested (and indirectly, concern and intent to be tested) in the group conditions, in the identifiable conditions, the effect of stress is actually no longer significant and is in fact negative. This supports the notion of a denial response under identifiable patient presentation, whereby increased stress leads to reduced concern and intent to be tested.

This research has important implications for the communication of health messages. While we find that identifiability increases susceptibility under low stress conditions, this effect is no longer present under high stress conditions. In addition, we find that group (non-identifiable) presentation may be optimal for generating behavioral intentions and appraisals of concern under high stress conditions. These findings support the notion that both avoidant and action-oriented responses arise from high threat, and examines how identifiability may activate these mechanisms. Given that identifiable patient advertisements are ubiquitous in the public health space, it is important to understand the boundary conditions that moderate their intended response.

"Promoting Health-Related Consumer Research: ARC Model Application to CDC's Health Campaign"

Punam Anand Keller, Dartmouth College, USA
Donald R. Lehmann, Columbia University, USA

The massive costs of health care ($1.7 trillion and counting) and the problems posed by various diseases (e.g., AIDS, obesity, diabetes, cancer, heart disease, mental illness) are well known and documented. People worry more about their personal health care costs than losing their jobs, being a victim of a violent crime, or terrorist attacks. As a consequence, massive efforts to improve knowledge about detection, prevention, and treatment have been undertaken. Despite growing realization that health communication strategies need to be improved possibly by tailoring them to audience segments, there is no model that guides the design of health communications.

Currently, four barriers prevent the application of consumer research studies to improve the effectiveness of public service health campaigns. First, the focus on one or two message tactics makes it difficult to generalize the results to situations where the audience is faced with a wide variety of message tactics in the same or different health campaigns (cf. Raghubir and Menon, 1996). Second, most consumer research studies do not provide guidelines for tailoring since they do not examine how message formats interact with measurable individual differences such as demographics. Third, small cell sizes in most lab studies raise concerns about whether lab findings can be replicated in the field. Finally, there is no evidence that message formats determine health intentions when other factors such as peer influence are accounted for.

We developed a model, Advisor for Risk Communication (ARC) to overcome these barriers. ARC examines the effects of 22 message tactics and 6 individual differences on intentions to comply with health recommendations. ARC is based on a meta-analysis of 60 studies, 584 different experimental conditions and 22,000 participants

Our results can be viewed as making two key contributions to consumer research: 1) our results indicate which of twenty-two message variables remain significant when the effect of other message variables have been accounted for, 2) our model can be used to predict the effectiveness of health messages for audiences that vary in age, race, gender, regulatory focus, and involvement.

We propose the following model application steps:

1) Code the health communication message to reflect the levels of multiple message formats. What is the social effect? Does it contain pictures? Does it tell a story? Are there a lot of dry numbers? Is the communicator male or female?

2) Use ARC to predict the effectiveness of the health message.

3) Improve the effectiveness of the health message by changing it according to the recommendations in ARC.

The ARC model supports the use of several message tactics: case information (e.g., a story about a real or hypothetical person rather than numbers or percentages), social consequences (e.g., embarrassment works better than physical pain), other-referencing (e.g., focus on people around you rather than yourself), female communicators (are better than male communicators), a message that arouses emotions other than fear, and messages on detection behaviors (rather than prevention or remedial behaviors) to enhance health intentions.

ARC also recommends focusing on discouraging unhealthful behavior rather than promoting healthful behaviors and de-emphasizing source credibility and vividness (e.g., pictures, cf. Keller and Block, 1997). The results of our meta-analysis also indicate that communication dollars may be saved by not spending money on message factors that don't enhance intentions unless they are matched with audience characteristics. For example, contrary to popular use, framed health messages (loss or gain frames) are not advisable without knowledge of target audience goals (promotion vs. prevention, cf. Lee and Aaker, 2004).

The ARC model also identifies effective matches between message tactics and audience characteristics. For example, ARC indicates that low-involvement audiences are more persuaded by moderately fearful gain frames, other-referencing, vivid messages, and strong source credibility, whereas highly involved audiences prefer base information and strong messages that are also moderately fearful, but they do not distinguish between levels of vividness, source credibility, and referencing. Younger audiences prefer social consequences over multiple exposures, whereas older audiences are more influenced by physical consequences regardless of the number of message exposures.

We demonstrate how ARC may be used for improving the effectiveness of public service campaigns by testing its ability to predict health intentions for CDC's VERB campaign to encourage youth to exercise more in their free time. We find the ARC predictions and stated intentions are in close correspondence to each other. ARC predictions are significant predictors for stated intentions and behavior when socio-economic, social influence, beliefs and attitudes, number of ads, and exposure frequency are accounted for. Intention and behavior predictions are approximately equally sensitive to family and social influence, parent education, and recall of message exposures, and in general have less impact than the child beliefs/self-view and ARC predictions. Finally, ARC health intention predictions are significant predictors of self-reported exercise behavior. Taken together, these findings offer many opportunities to use consumer research to tailor health communications for different target audiences.

"Communication Strategies for Scaling Health-Focused Social Entrepreneurial Organizations"

Paul N. Bloom, Duke University, USA
Lauren G. Block, Baruch College, USA
Lauren Trabold, Baruch College, USA

The term "social entrepreneur" is typically used to describe individuals who start up and lead new organizations or programs that are dedicated to mitigating or eliminating a social problem, deploying change strategies that differ from those that have been used to address the problem in the past. Notable social entrepreneurs include (a) Wendy Kopp, founder of Teach for America, which places recent college graduates as teachers in inner-city schools for a two-year stint, and (b) Paul Farmer, founder of Partners In Health, which has provided low-cost treatment for AIDS, TB, and other diseases throughout the developing world. These innovators–and their social entrepreneurial organizations–pursue scaling because they want to have as big an impact as possible on social problems and because their donors and supporters are hungry to achieve high "social" returns on their investments.

The social entrepreneurial organizations that focus on health problems tend to emphasize Prevention, Treatment, or Advocacy, or some combination of the three. Figure 1 presents a way of categorizing these organizations, based primarily on their "change strategy," or on what some would call their "Theories of Change." They have a causal model in mind that links their programs or interventions to a series of outcomes that eventually will help resolve a social problem (Colby, Stone, and Carttar, 2004). We suggest that the "Theories of Change" of health-focused social entrepreneurial organizations tend to fall in one of seven different categories:

•"Promoting Healthier Lifestyles" (a purely prevention approach).

•"Developing/Distributing Medications/Equipment" (a purely treatment approach).

•"Creating Healthier Environments" (a combination prevention and treatment approach).

•"Providing Patient Care/Therapy" (a combination prevention and treatment approach).

•"Training Health Workers" (a combination prevention, treatment, and advocacy approach).

•"Supporting/Assisting Patients" (a combination prevention, treatment, and advocacy approach).

•"Advocating for Better Health Policies" (a purely advocacy approach).

Bloom and Chatterji (2009) propose that successful scaling of social impact by a social entrepreneurial organization will require the possession of some combination of seven organizational capabilities, identified using the acronym SCALERS. This stands for: Staffing, Communicating, Alliance-building, Lobbying, Earnings-generation, Replicating, and Stimulating market forces. They also propose that the extent to which an individual SCALER (i.e., driver or capability) will influence scaling success will depend on certain situational contingencies. Each social entrepreneurial organization may find itself facing rather unique situational contingencies, indicating that the most important capabilities for effective scaling of better health outcomes will vary across organizations.

It is extremely common for health-focused social entrepreneurial organizations to face a situational contingency of having weak public acceptance or support for the behaviors they would like their beneficiaries to engage in. They often have had only limited success in persuading individuals to (a) take preventive actions like wearing sunscreens, using condoms, eating healthier or obtaining inoculations, (b) obtain screening tests for HIV/AIDS, cancer, or other diseases where early-detection can save lives, or (c) comply with therapy and drug regimens. Communicating persuasively about the value of engaging in healthier behaviors has become a critical scaling challenge for many organizations.

In this paper, we offer propositions about communications strategies that have a higher likelihood of changing the behavior of beneficiaries. Based on the literature in consumer behavior, social marketing, and health communications, we identify several communication strategies that can help guide a health-focused social entrepreneurship organization to scale its impact. We provide additional support to the propositions by analyzing several case studies of organizations that seem to have had scaling success, in part, by using some of the identified communications strategies.

As just one example, we illustrate our proposition "When targeting younger audiences, messages that emphasize social consequences are more effective than those that emphasize physical consequences" with the communications experiences of the organization Girls on the Run (Bloom, 2007). This self-esteem enhancement program for pre-teen girls uses games involving running to teach lessons about topics like healthy eating, peer pressure, bullying, and community service, and has grown from serving 13 girls in 1996 to serving over 40,000 per year by 2008. One of the keys to their scaling success appears to be the emphasis they have in their communications and lessons about the value for girls to be themselves. By stressing the social benefits of "being yourself," in part by providing social support for this from the coaches and other girls in the 12-student classes, the program has achieved more success in enhancing self-esteem–and also encouraging healthier eating and exercise behaviors–than if they had stressed the physical consequences associated with diet and exercise.

REFERENCES

Bloom, Paul N. (2007), "A Lot More than a Running Program," *Girls on the Run International*, CASE SE-04, Durham, SC: Fuqua School of Business.

Bloom, Paul N. and Aaron K. Chatterji (2009), "Scaling Social Entrepreneurial Impact," *California Management Review*, 51 (3), Spring 2009, pp. 114-133.

Colby, Susan, Nan Stone, and Paul Carttar (2004), "Zeroing in on Impact," *Stanford Social Innovation Review*, 2 (Fall), 24-33.

Chandon, Pierre, and Brain Wansink (2007), "Is Obesity Caused by Calorie Underestimation? A Psychophysical Model of Meal Size Estimation," *Journal of Marketing Research*, 44 (1), February, 84-99.

Lee, Angela Y. and Jennifer L. Aaker (2004), "Bringing the Frame Into Focus: The Influence of Regulatory Fit on Processing Fluency and Persuasion," *Journal of Personality and Social Psychology*, 86 (2), 205-18.

Lin, Ying Ching, Chien-Huang Lin, and Priya Raghubir (2003), "Avoiding Anxiety, Being in Denial or Simply Stroking Self-Esteem: Why Self-Positivity?" *Journal of Consumer Psychology*, 13 (4), 464-477.

Jenni, K. E., and George Loewenstein (1997), "Explaining the 'identifiable victim effect,'" *Journal of Risk and Uncertainty*, 14 (3), 235-257.

Keller, Punam A. and Lauren G. Block (1997), "Vividness Effects: A Resource Matching Perspective," *Journal of Consumer Research*, 24 (December), 295-304.

Krider, Robert E., Priya Raghubir, and Aradhna Krishna (2001), "Pizzas: π or Square? Psychophysical Biases in Area Comparisons," *Marketing Science*, 20 (4), Fall, 405-425.

Krishna, Aradhna (2007), "Spatial Perception Research: An Integrative Review of Length, Area, Volume, and Number Perception," in *Visual Marketing*, editors Michel Wedel and Rik Pieters, Lawrence Erlbaum Associates.

Raghubir, Priya and Geeta Menon (1996), "Asking Sensitive Questions: The Effects of Type of Referent and Frequency Wording in Counterbiasing Methods," *Psychology and Marketing*, 13 (7), 633-52.

Raghubir, Priya, and Geeta Menon (1998), "AIDS and Me, Never the Twain Shall Meet: Factors Affecting Judgments of Risk," *Journal of Consumer Research*, 25 (1), June, 52-63.

Raghubir, Priya (2008), "Is 1/10>10/100? The Effect of Denominator Salience on Perceptions of Base Rates of Health Risk," *International Journal of Research in Marketing* (Special Issue on Marketing and Health), 25 (4), December, 327-334.

Small, Deborah A. and George Loewenstein (2003), Helping a victim or helping the victim: Altruism and identifiability. *Journal of Risk and Uncertainty*, 26 (1), 5-16.

Small, Deborah A., George Loewenstein and Paul Slovic (2007), "Sympathy and Callousness: The Impact of Deliberative Thought on Donations to Identifiable and Statistical Victims," *Organizational Behavior and Human Decision Processes*, 102 (2), 143-153.

Special Session Summary

Deviating From or Resetting Consumers Ethical Standards

Shahar Ayal, Duke University, USA
Francesca Gino, University of North Carolina, USA

SESSION OVERVIEW

Recent studies in the marketing literature have started exploring how consumers face purchase decision that entail tension between behaving honestly or ethically and maximizing one's own self-interests. This research has shown that consumers often resolve this tension through a creative interpretation of ambiguity around dishonest behaviors. Specifically, they behave dishonestly enough to profit from their unethicality but honestly enough to maintain a positive self-concept and balance their own ethical scale (for example, Mazar, Amir & Ariely, 2008). Building on this prior work, the papers in the current symposium will address two main questions (1) how do people evaluate products that are ethically tainted and how does using such products affect their behavior? and (2) what mechanisms help consumers maintain a balance between their moral self and their use of unethically made products and unethical actions? That is, how might consumers go about cleansing themselves from the guilt of their previous immoral behaviors?

The first two papers explore factors impacting the likelihood that ethically questionable behavior will occur during consumption or during purchase decisions. Gino and Norton examine the influence of wearing and using counterfeit products on both one's own dishonest behavior and on one's perceptions of others' dishonest behavior. Cavanaugh and Fitzsimons' work, instead, explores how people choose products when information about the unethical manufacturing practices of such products is available to them. In the third paper, Ayal and Ariely examine the effects of confession and forgiveness on one's dishonesty acts and its role as a mechanism for turning over a new leaf. Finally, Inbar, Pizarro and Gilovich report findings showing that individuals with feelings of guilt seek to metaphorically "balance the scales" through self-induced physical punishment.

We believe the session will draw the attention of a diverse audience, including scholars interested in deceptive advertising, corporate social responsibility, and dark side marketing behaviors, as well as scholars interested more generally in the influence of emotions on consumer behavior. In addition, this symposium will make an important contribution to consumer research by highlighting when and why consumers might regularly cross ethical boundaries, even without being aware of it.

EXTENDED ABSTRACTS

"The Counterfeit Self: The Deceptive Costs of Faking It"

Francesca Gino, University of North Carolina at Chapel Hill, USA
Michael Norton, Harvard Business School, USA

As with their other consumption decisions–the products people buy to adorn themselves or decorate their homes and offices (Belk, 1988; Gosling, Ko, Mannarelli, & Morris, 2002)–people buy counterfeit products to signal positive traits, to themselves and others (Bodner & Prelec, 2002). Counterfeits, however, have an additional property, in that they signal an aspiration to be something one is not–for example, to feel wealthier than one's income allows. We contend that counterfeit products do cause people to be something they are not, but in ways they do not expect: Counterfeit products cause people to be not admirable but unethical, generating in them a feeling of a "counterfeit self" that leads them to behave unethically.

As with other research exploring signaling conflicts, such as between public and private signals (Goffman, 1956; Kuran, 1995), counterfeits serve as an interesting case in which desired signals (I am an admirable person) may conflict with actual signals (I am a fake). We suggest that counterfeit products create a particular kind of conflict: Though the wearer intends them to signal positive traits, wearing counterfeits can in fact send a negative signal to the self. Indeed, given the well-documented effects of primes on behavior, such that the mere presence of objects can influence behavior (Berger & Fitzsimons, 2008; Berkowitz & LePage, 1967), we suggest that the negative impact of wearing counterfeit products is likely to occur despite their owners' desire to use them for positive signaling.

If wearing counterfeits can influence the signals one sends to oneself, what are the likely consequences? We hypothesize a link between wearing counterfeits, feeling "fake" or inauthentic, and behaving unethically: We suggest that a product's lack of authenticity may cause their owners to feel less authentic themselves–despite their belief that the product will actually have positive benefits–and that these feelings then cause them to behave dishonestly and to view others' behavior as more dishonest as well. In short, we suspect that feeling like a fraud makes people more likely to commit fraud.

We tested these predictions in four experiments. We first show that wearing purportedly counterfeit sunglasses causes people to cheat more on tests when given the opportunity–both when they believe they have an inherent preference for counterfeit products (Experiment 1A) and when they were randomly assigned to wear counterfeits (Experiment 1B). Indeed, the impact of counterfeits extends even beyond the individual, causing individuals not just to behave unethically but also to see the behavior of others as more unethical as well (Experiment 2). Finally, we investigate the mechanism underlying these effects, showing that wearing counterfeits causes people to feel inauthentic, and these feelings of inauthenticity–their counterfeit self–drive unethical behavior (Experiment 3).

While people adopt counterfeit products because they are trying to improve their self-image, our studies show that counterfeits have the ironic consequence of harming self-image via inauthenticity, inducing a "counterfeit self." Why then do people buy counterfeit products? One view, of course, is that the benefits of counterfeits simply outweigh these costs, and that people are making a calculated tradeoff between the two. We suspected that people may not be making this tradeoff, however, but rather may simply overlook the possible negative consequences of adopting counterfeits. Indeed, when we asked a separate set of students ($N=86$; $M_{age}=22$, $SD=2.20$) to predict the impact of counterfeits, they were unaware of the consequences for ethical behavior. We gave these students the average performance on the matrix task of our study participants, and asked them to predict the self-reported performance in three experimental conditions: Counterfeit sunglasses, authentic sunglasses, and a control condition. The students correctly predicted that, overall, participants across conditions would cheat ($M_{real}=9.62$, $M_{fake}=9.59$, $M_{control}=9.34$; $F[3,255]=43.67$, $p_{rep}>.99$). However, they did not anticipate that cheating would vary across the three described conditions (F[2,170]<1, p_{rep}=.56; p_{rep}<.72 across all comparisons). This difference between people's predictions about the impact of counterfeits and their actual behavior in our experiments suggests that the influence of wearing counterfeits is deceptive, in that they have an unexpected influence on individuals' ethicality.

The obvious differences between laboratory settings and real-world contexts aside, our results have worrisome implications for the many consumers who buy counterfeit goods. Given the economic and social relevance of the counterfeiting epidemic, future research on the psychology of counterfeits and their potential moral costs seems warranted. Indeed, given that cost savings is a primary motivation for the purchase of counterfeits (Eisend & Schuchert-Guler, 2006), individuals who buy counterfeits for themselves or gift them to others may believe that they are simply getting similar products for less money, but in fact may be paying a price in terms of their long-term morality. Perhaps most troublingly, our results from Experiment 2 demonstrate that the negative impact of counterfeits accrue not just to the buyer, but extend more broadly to the social environment, suggesting that overlooking the negative impact of counterfeits may have far-reaching negative consequences.

"'Mirror... Mirror on the Wall, Whose the Greenest Giver of Them All?': Understanding When and Why Men and Women Gift Ethically-Made Products"

Lisa Cavanaugh, University of Southern California, USA
Gavan Fitzsimons, Duke University, USA

While most people claim they care about ethical issues and view themselves as honest individuals, it is likely that, in the past, they have chosen to purchase unethically produced products (e.g., products produced through child labor, unsafe working conditions, or environmental degradation). Companies making these products are often the subject of scrutiny as suggested by the large literature on corporate social responsibility (CSR). To date, very little is known about the role that consumers play in propagating a system that implicates harm (Devinney et al., 2007), and, more specifically, little is known about what drives consumers' demand for products that are produced in less socially responsible ways.

The present research addresses this gap and asks the following questions: 1) when and why do consumers buy unethically made products for themselves or for others? and 2) how do their choices for unethically vs. ethically made products vary based on the relationship they have with the person they are buying the product for?

In our first study we were interested in understanding how people choose products that will be gifted to a romantic partner when price and ethicality in the way the product was produced are in conflict with each other or not. The study employs a 2 (media exposure: yes vs. no) x 2 (respondent's gender: male vs. female) x 2 (pair type: conflict vs. no conflict) between-subject factorial design. Our media exposure manipulation consisted of participants watching a 4-minute video clip from NBC's Today Show about opportunities to buy ethically responsible products for Valentine's Day prior to making their choices (media exposure condition) or not watching such a clip (no media condition).

Our pair type manipulation consisted of participants choosing between different pairs of products whose features varied on two different desirable attributes. As a gift giver, we argue, people are likely to be motivated to choose a product that looks expensive so that they can signal they really care about the other person (gift recipient). Indeed, prior research has demonstrated that people commonly associate price with product quality–i.e., they often infer quality from price based on the belief that the two factors are positively correlated (Monroe, 1973; Monroe & Petroshius, 1981; Ordonez, 1998). Thus, we assume product quality (as signaled by product cost) is a desirable attribute of products that gift givers take into account when making their purchase decisions. A second attribute we are interested in is whether the product is ethically produced or not. We assume that, as a gift giver, people consider products that are ethically produced as more desirable than products that are unethically produced (e.g., products manufactured using child labor). This assumption is supported by survey evidence showing that a large number of consumers incorporate ethical considerations into their product purchase decisions (e.g., Cone 2009; Crane, 2001; Strong, 1996; Rogers, 1998). We manipulated whether there was conflict between these two desirable product attributes (price and ethicality) or no conflict when participants selected one of the two products included in each pair.

We used two pairs of products, which varied on the same dimensions of price and ethicality for both women and men. The first pair consisted of an inexpensive product which was ethically produced, and an expensive product which was unethically produced (pair involving conflict between two desirable product dimensions, namely price and ethicality). The second pair consisted of an expensive product which was ethically produced, and an inexpensive product which was unethically produced (pair not involving conflict). We used chocolate as a product category for men (gifting their chocolate to their partner), and greeting cards as a product category for women (gifting the card to their partner). We chose these products (chocolates and cards) because these are the types of products that are regularly purchased for romantic partners by these two genders around Valentine's Day.

In the study, participants were asked to choose one of the two products in their assigned pair as a Valentine Day gift for their romantic partner. Only participants who were currently in a relationship could participate in the study. The study was conducted during the week prior to Valentine's Day, and 5% of the participants (randomly chosen) received the actual product of their choice during the study to give as a gift to their partner.

Studies 2-5 push these findings to demonstrate when and how consumers' decisions change based on the venue in which the gift is given (e.g., public vs. private), the type of product (e.g., durable vs. non-durable), and the type of relationship with the recipient (e.g., romantic partner, friend, colleague. Together the study results suggest that there are important differences in the way men and women weigh ethical considerations in their product purchase decisions and use products to signal their commitment to relationships in different ways. The results also demonstrate that, under certain circumstances, making an ethical standard salient can reduce the desire to buy attractive products that have been unethically produced (e.g., produced through the use of child labor).

We argue and find that asymmetries exist between the genders in their motivations to buy green gifts for different significant others in their lives. Compared to men, women are more likely to choose the unethical / cheap option as a gift for their romantic partner. However, they are willing to choose the ethical/expensive option for a female friend when the ethical cue is durable or explicit. Specifically, the probability of choosing a green gift depends largely on the giver's perception of its signal value to the recipient (i.e., it is more about what the green gift signals about the giver than the receiver). We find that women derive more meaning when choosing green gifts for other women than when choosing green gifts for men.

"Finding Balance on The Moral Scale: The Effect of Forgiveness on Dishonest Behavior"

Shahar Ayal, Duke University, USA
Dan Ariely, Fuqua School of Business, Duke University, USA

Consumers face ethical choices on a daily basis. In some cases, they know that if they succumb to dishonest behavior, forgiveness may be available to them. Do the expectation of being forgiven and forgiveness itself influence an individual's likelihood to engage in unethical behavior? The current paper aims to test the psychological mechanisms underlying forgiveness and their implications to dishonest behavior of consumers. In particular, three studies explore whether the likelihood of dishonest behavior varied before and after simulation of confession, and if so, how the effect of this confession is influenced by temporal distance.

Generally, expectations of receiving forgiveness might influence the likelihood that consumers will engage in dishonest behavior in two main ways. The first concerns the saliency of ethicality at the moment a particular behavior is considered. Previous research has found that drawing consumers' attention to moral standards could reduce dishonest behavior (Mazar, Amir & Ariely, 2008). These results suggest that when unethical behavior is made salient, consumers may pay greater attention to the importance of ethical behavior and moral standards. Thus, the saliency account predicts that consumers will avoid dishonest behavior after receiving forgiveness. Furthermore, it suggest that any type of self reflection on one own sins should decrease the level of dishonesty.

The second way in which forgiveness might influence dishonesty is captured by consumers' reactions to their current self-moral image, or their concerns- for- moral- balancing. According to this explanation, consumers resolve the tension between honesty and economic interests through a creative interpretation of ambiguous dishonest behaviors: they behave dishonestly enough to profit, but honestly enough to maintain a positive self-concept (Baumeister 1998; Gino, Ayal & Ariely, 2009; Mazar & Ariely, 2006). Thus, this account predicts that expected forgiveness allows consumers to protect their moral self-image from damage, so that they can maximize their profits by increasing the level of dishonest behavior.

The predictions of these two mechanisms were tested in three studies. The first two studies use hypothetical scenarios to examine individuals' intuitive beliefs about the effects of both expected and received forgiveness. In Study 1, we used a scenario describing a woman (Laura) who faced a strong temptation to engage in unethical behavior either before or after an important event. We manipulated two independent variables: The first manipulation concerned the nature of the event that Laura is scheduled to attend (confession vs. control). The second manipulation concerned the timing of the potential dishonest behavior in regard to the event.

The results show that participants' sensitivity to the timing manipulation was obtained only in the confession condition but not in the control condition. In particular, people expect dishonest behaviors to be more likely before rather than after confession. These results are consistent with the predictions of the concerns-for-moral-balancing account. Study 2 used the same Laura's scenario to examine if this effect can be replicated within participants and test the influence of time distance. Similarly to the results of Study 1, the lowest likelihood to act in a dishonest manner was obtained a short time after the confession. In addition, in line with the saliency account this positive effect of confession was eliminated and even reversed with time distance.

Finally, a third study tested for the effect of confession on one own sins in a laboratory setting where we could directly measure dishonest behavior. The study employed a computerized perceptual task, in which participants placed in situations that induced conflict between honesty and maximizing one's self-interests and we observed their number of dishonest responses. The perceptual task was divided into two phases, and we introduced our manipulation (i.e., different types of introspective writing tasks) between these phases. Half of the participants who were assigned to the confession condition, were asked to describe one bad thing that they have done, and then to close their eyes and ask "God" or any other entity for forgiveness about that event. The other half who were assigned to the control condition, were asked to describe typical evening activities such as how they make dinner.

As expected, the two groups did not differ in their behavior in phase 1, and both groups exhibited very similar level of dishonesty behavior with moderate increase within that phase. However, the main difference between the two groups occurred after our manipulation. The level of dishonesty behaviors in phase 2 was significantly lower in the confession condition than in the control condition. That is, participants in the confession condition reduced their level of dishonest behavior as a result of the writing task, but participants in the control condition continued in their tendency to cheat more as a function of time. Taken together, our findings suggest that reflection on one's own sins might produce beneficial effects on honest behavior (at least for a certain extent of time) only when consumers do not expect to receive forgiveness. Thus, it appears that societies should be open to granting sequential forgiveness, while remaining silent about their capacity to do so.

References

Baumeister, R. F. (1998), "The Self," in D. T. Gilbert, S. T. Fiske, and G. Lindzey (Eds.), *Handbook of Social Psychology* (4th ed.), 680-740.

Gino, F., S. Ayal, and D. Ariely (2009), "Contagion and Differentiation in Unethical Behavior: The Effect of One Bad Apple on the Barrel." *Psychological Science*, 20(3), 393-398.

Mazar, N. and D. Ariely (2006), "Dishonesty in Everyday Life and Its Policy Implications," *Journal of Public Policy and Marketing*, 25(1), 117-126.

Mazar, N., O. Amir, and D. Ariely (2008), "The Dishonesty of Honest People: A Theory of Self-concept Maintenance," *Journal of Marketing Research*, 45, 633-644.

"Morality and Masochism: Feeling Guilt Leads to Physical Self-Punishment"

Yoel Inbar, Harvard University, USA
David Pizarro, Cornell University, USA
Tom Gilovich, Cornell University, USA

Past research has demonstrated that people deal with feelings of guilt and immorality in numerous ways: For example, studies have shown that guilt and immoral thoughts can motivate subsequent prosocial behavior and lead people to make amends in order to repair a relationship (Baumeister, Stillwell, and Heatherton, 1994). Another important way in which people seem to deal with feeling guilty is through metaphorical actions, such as physical cleansing in order to "wash away" misdeeds (Zhong & Liljenquist, 2006). In the current research, we investigated whether individuals with feelings of guilt seek to metaphorically "balance the scales" through self-inflicted physical punishment. Physical self-punishment has been a common theme in purification rituals (e.g. self-flagellation) across many religious traditions throughout history, so we predicted that participants who felt guilty would be more likely to desire to purify themselves by engaging in self-punishment.

Study 1

Forty-six participants (25 female) wrote about a time that they felt guilty or sad, or about a neutral event. They then took part in an ostensibly unrelated task in which they administered electric shocks to themselves. The task was comprised of six trials; shocks always started at 30 volts, and on subsequent trials participants decided whether to increase or decrease the voltage up to a maximum of 80 volts.

Five participants expressed suspicion of our hypotheses and were removed from the analysis. Shock voltages from the remaining participants were subjected to a repeated-measures analysis of variance with condition as a between-subjects factor, and gender as a covariate. This analysis revealed the expected main effect of condition, $F(3, 37)=3.29$, $p<.05$: participants in the guilt condition gave themselves more powerful shocks (M=53.5V) than did those in the sadness condition (M=43.7V) or the neutral condition (M=43.1V). Follow-up contrasts showed that the guilt condition differed significantly from the neutral condition, $F(1, 37)=5.81$, $p=.02$; and from the sadness condition, $F(1, 37)=3.29$, $p=.05$. The latter conditions did not differ significantly from each other, $F(1, 37)=.20$, ns.

Study 2

Study 2 was intended primarily as a replication of Study 1. Twenty-seven undergraduates (19 male) wrote about a time that they did something unethical, or, in the control condition, wrote about the last time they went grocery shopping. They then followed the same six-trial shock procedure used in Study 1. We predicted that participants in the unethical condition would choose to increase the shock level more rapidly than participants in the control condition, leading to a condition x trial interaction for voltage level.

Three participants expressed suspicion of our hypotheses and were removed from the analysis. Shock voltages from the remaining participants were subjected to a repeated-measures analysis of variance with condition as a between-subjects factor, and gender as a covariate. This analysis showed the expected condition x trial interaction, $F(4, 18)=2.93$, $p=.05$: Shock voltages were nearly identical between conditions on Trial 2 ($M_{unethical}=38.2$, $M_{control}=35.4$) but participants in the unethical condition increased the voltage more quickly, leading to a 10-point difference between conditions on the last trial ($M_{unethical}=63.5$, $M_{control}=53.5$).

We also assessed the effect of shock voltage on participants' feelings of guilt. At the end of the study, participants were asked how much they felt guilt, regret, and shame ($\alpha=.90$). Participants in the shock condition scored marginally higher on this guilt index ($M_{shock}=1.70$, $M_{control}= .38$, $t(22)=1.31$, $p=.06$), but the more shock participants in the guilt condition administered, the less guilty they felt at the end of the study, $r(11)=-.66$, $p=.03$. There was no relationship between shock voltage and guilt in the control condition, $r(13)=-.15$, ns.

Discussion

Participants who wrote about a time that they felt guilty (Study 1) or about a time that they did something unethical (Study 2) administered more intense shocks to themselves, and increased the level of shock more quickly, than did participants who wrote about a time that they felt sad or about a neutral event. This study adds to the extant research concerning the ways in which people deal with guilt by showing that people react to guilty feelings by engaging in symbolic atonement through physical self-punishment.

This suggests that under some circumstances (i.e. when they are feeling guilty), consumers might show a preference for physically unpleasant or uncomfortable experiences.

References

Baumeister, R. F., A. M. Stillwell, and T. F. Heatherton (1994), "Guilt: An interpersonal Approach," *Psychological Bulletin*, 115, 243-267.

Zhong, C. B. and K. Liljenquist (2006), "Washing Away Your Sins: Threatened Morality and Physical Cleansing," *Science*, 313, 1451-1452.

SPECIAL SESSION SUMMARY

Assimilation and Contrast: Comparison Processes in Judgments and Evaluations

Xianchi Dai, University of Chicago, USA

SESSION OVERVIEW

How happy are you with a $5 prize? How much do you like the dinner you are having now? How big is the cake on the plate? Answers to such kind of questions are usually affected by comparison standards people have in mind. This session investigates factors that affect the selection of comparison standards and their effects on judgments and evaluations.

Research in marketing and social psychology has shown that human judgments are comparative in nature (Kahneman and Tversky 1979; Mussweiler 2003; Gilbert, Giesler, and Morris 1995), that the comparison processes systematically affect consumer preference and decision making (Dhar and Simonson 1992; Dhar, Nowlis, and Sherman 1999; Hsee 1996), and that characteristics of evaluation targets and comparison standards determine whether assimilation or contrast will result (Herr 1986; Herr, Sherman, and Fazio 1983; Brewer and Weber 1994; Mussweiler and Bodenhausen 2002).

Despite the extensive research done in this field over the years, this session demonstrates that it remains a fertile area for continued research. The session presents three papers, each focusing on different aspects of comparison processes. In particular, they demonstrate that 1) need states and ownership status systematically affect the construction and the use of comparison standards. 2) Selection of comparison standards is determined by consumers' motivation as well as their cognitive capacity to compare. 3) Forward looking comparison standards are more impactful than backward looking ones, and their impact on evaluations of current experiences depends on characteristics of the current experience.

The first paper by Dai and Hsee demonstrates in three studies that motivational states induce expectation, which in turn serves as a reference point for evaluations. Furthermore, these evaluations can be contrasted against or assimilated toward the expectation, depending on ownership status. Specifically, when a person owns an object (e.g., a piece of cake), evaluation of a target contrasted against expectation; whereas when he or she does not own the object, evaluation of a target is assimilates toward expectation.

Kassam, Morewedge, and Gilbert show that the selection of comparison standards is determined by both motivation and cognitive capacity to compare. They distinguish between present standard, those that are physically present at the time the comparison, and absent standard, those that are physically absent at the time the comparison is made and must therefore be retrieved from memory or generated by imagination. In two studies they demonstrate that people automatically compare their own gains with present standard, whereas they compare with absent standard only when they are motivated and have cognitive capacity to compare.

Finally, Meyvis and Nelson examine the effect of anticipated experience on the enjoyment of current experience. Across 7 studies they find that, while people do not compare current experience with proceeding experience (Novemsky and Ratner 2003), they do compare it with anticipated experience. However, this contrast effect is not always present. When the valence of the current experience is ambiguous, evaluation of current experience actually assimilates toward the anticipated experience.

Overall, the three papers were chosen for this session because (1) they center on the same topic of comparison processes and examine intriguing new directions in reference point construction and selection, (2) they all demonstrate contrast and/or assimilation effect in evaluations of products, experiences, or feelings, and (3) in terms of methodology, the session represents experimental work from both behavioral decision making and social psychology perspectives. Different approaches complement each other and can potentially inspire new insights for future research. Together, the three papers form a cohesive set of explorations into some fundamental issues of judgment and evaluation processes that is central for understanding consumer decision making.

EXTENDED ABSTRACTS

"How Does Motivation Affect Evaluations?"

Xianchi Dai, University of Chicago, USA
Christopher Hsee, University of Chicago, USA

Does a hungry person perceive a piece of cake bigger or smaller in size than a person who is not so hungry? Does a consumer who cares about quality very much perceive the quality of a product higher or lower than a consumer who cares less about quality? These kinds of questions are ubiquitous in our daily life and are very important antecedents of consumer decision making. They concern the effect of motivation (e.g., need states) on evaluations (i.e., quantity, quality, probability, or other judgments).

Two lines of literature provide opposite predictions for these questions. On the one hand, new look psychology (e.g., Bruner and Goodman 1947) and its recent development (Balcetis & Dunning, 2006; Brendl, Markman and Messner 2003; Kunda, 1990) found that consumers usually see what they want to see. That is, a hungry person would perceive the same cake to be bigger than a less hungry person would, and a consumer who cares about quality a lot would perceive the quality of a specific product to be higher than a consumer who cares little about the quality. On the other hand, Dai and colleagues (Dai, Wertenbroch and Brendl 2008; Dai, Brendl and Wertenbroch 2009) demonstrated that the more people value a product, the more scarce they perceive it to be. In other words, consumers high in need would perceive a piece of cake smaller, the quality of a specific product lower, than their counterparts who are low in need.

In the current paper, we propose a model that reconciles these opposite predictions and systematically explains the effect of motivation on evaluations. Specifically, we propose that when a person owns an object (e.g., a piece of cake), the more the person wants it, the smaller (or worse) she perceives it to be; whereas when she does not own the object, the more she wants it, the bigger (or better) she perceives it to be. We argue that this is because motivation (e.g., need states) automatically activates expectation, which serves as a reference for judgments. This reference can lead to either contrast or assimilation effect, depending on ownership status. For what people own and value (e.g., they have high level of need for it), they want the object to be as big (or good) as possible. They automatically compare what they have with what they ideally want to have (expectation), and thus feel that the reality is not as big (or good)–perceived reality is contrasted away from the expectation. Whereas for what people do not own, the more they want it, the bigger they perceive it to be because of wishful thinking- perceived reality is assimilated to the expectation.

We tested the predictions and the underlying processes of our model in three studies. Study 1 tested our model in quantity estimations. Participants were first induced high or low levels of thirst and were then asked to estimate the volume of a cup of water.

Consistent with our prediction, when participants were told that the cup of water was for them to consume, those who were thirsty estimated the volume to be smaller than those who were not thirsty. Conversely, when they were told that the cup of water was not for them to consume, the reverse was true. In study 2, participants were first asked to imagine and elaborate on either an experience of cliff climbing (with a rope) or an experience of jump roping. Then they were asked to evaluate the thickness of a rope. When the rope was described to be the one that they were using in the imagined experience, those who imagined a cliff climbing experience (and thus wanted to have a thick rope) estimated the rope to be thinner than those who imagined a rope-jumping experience. However, when the rope was described to be one that is irrelevant to the imagined experience, those who imagined a cliff climbing experience estimated the rope to be thicker than those who imagined a rope-jumping experience. Furthermore, the correlation between measured expectation (expected thickness of the rope they were using in the imagined experience) and rope thickness judgment was negative when the rope was described to be the one that they used, and was positive when the rope was described to be irrelevant. These results suggest that expectation leads to contrast when the object is "mine" and assimilation when the object is not "mine". Finally, study 3 replicated the same pattern of results in product quality judgment. Specifically, consumers who cared about product quality a lot perceived a specific product to be lower in quality when the product was the one they used for a specific experience, and higher in quality when the product was one that was irrelevant to their experience, than consumers who cared less about product quality.

Overall, these studies provide strong support for our model, confirming that motivational state induces expectation, which in turn serves as a reference point for evaluations. Furthermore, these evaluations can be contrasted to or assimilated toward the expectation, depending on ownership status.

"Motivation and Capacity in the Selection of Comparison Standards"

Karim Kassam, Harvard University, USA
Carey Morewedge, Carnegie Mellon University, USA
Daniel Gilbert, Harvard University, USA

Gains may be valued by comparing them with alternatives that are present at the time the comparison is made or with alternatives that are absent at the time the comparison is made. We offer a two-stage model in which people (a) initially make "present comparisons," and (b) subsequently make "absent comparisons" when they have the cognitive resources and motivation to do so. This model predicts that when a present comparison is favorable ("What I got is better than what I didn't get") people will be unmotivated to make a subsequent absent comparison; but when a present comparison is unfavorable ("What I got is worse than what I didn't get") people will be motivated to make a subsequent absent comparison ("But at least what I got is better than what I had").

People's affective responses to outcomes are influenced by the standards with which they compare them, and one factor that determines the selection of a standard is the person's motivation. People may compare their outcomes with a wide variety of standards including previous outcomes, alternative outcomes, and other people's outcomes, and research suggests that people tend to select those standards that produce the most favorable comparison. For example, people tend to compare with those who are less fortunate than themselves, to avoid comparing with those who are more fortunate than themselves, to compare on those dimensions on which they are more fortunate than others, to perpetuate misfortune for those with whom they compare, to exaggerate how unfortunate they once were, and so on.

But in addition to motivation there is a second factor that determines the selection of standards and that is a person's cognitive capacity. Some comparisons require conscious deliberation and others arise spontaneously and are made with little effort. Morewedge, Gilbert, Myrseth, Kassam and Wilson (2009) distinguished between (a) present standards (those that are physically present at the time the comparison is made and can thus be perceived through the senses) and (b) absent standards (those that are physically absent at the time the comparison is made and must therefore be retrieved from memory or generated by imagination). They argued that it is typically more effortful to imagine or remember "that which isn't" than to perceive "that which is," and thus, all else being equal, people are more likely to compare with present standards than with absent standards.

Our two-stage model therefore suggests that people spontaneously and effortlessly compared their prizes to present standards because it's easy to do so. Those for whom that comparison is favorable are not motivated to generate or remember an absent standard. Those for whom present comparison is unfavorable, on the other hand, will be motivated to generate or remember absent standards that would produce more favorable comparisons, if they have sufficient cognitive capacity.

We tested several basic predictions of this model in two studies in which participants learned that they had won one of two cash prizes. We defined "winners" as participants who had won the superior prize and "losers" as participants who had won the inferior prize. We also varied the face value of the prize won ($7, $5, $3, or $1). In Experiment 1, we expected that winners would naturally compare their superior prize to the inferior prize, feel good, and stop comparing. Because the difference between the superior and inferior prizes was the same in the large and small conditions, winners' feelings were uninfluenced by the face value ($7, $5 or $3) of their superior prizes. On the other hand, we expected losers to naturally compare their inferior prize to the superior prize and feel bad, motivating them to make absent comparisons and resulting in sensitivity to face value. This is in fact what we found, losers' reported happiness depended on the value of the prize won ($5, $3 or $1). In Experiment 2, we put some participants under cognitive load, which we expected would impair their ability to compare their current and previous states of wealth. We found winners' feelings to be uninfluenced by the face value ($5 or $3) of their prizes whether they were or were not under load. Losers' feelings were influenced by the face value ($5 or $3) of their prizes when they were not under load, but were not influenced by face value when they were under load.

In summary, we present data supporting a two-stage model which suggests that people initially compare with present standards and subsequently compare with absent standards if they have both the motivation and capacity to do so.

"Contrast Against the Future: The Unexpected Effect of Expectation"

Tom Meyvis, New York University, USA
Leif Nelson, University of California at Berkeley, USA

We do not just derive utility from our current experience, but also from the anticipation of future experiences (Loewenstein 1987): we dread a visit to the dentist and we savor an upcoming trip to a tropical island. Yet, aside from this direct effect on our current happiness, the anticipation of future events can also change our enjoyment of a specific current experience. For instance, knowing that we are about to embark on a vacation may change how we experience our time at the dentist. Or, similarly, knowing that we are about to visit the dentist may change how much we enjoy our time at the beach.

One possibility is that the anticipatory dread or savoring contaminates our current experience. Or, stated differently, the current experience may be assimilated towards the upcoming experience: the visit to the dentist becomes less painful when anticipating the vacation, while the time at the beach becomes less enjoyable when anticipating the visit to the dentist. This contamination effect has some intuitive appeal: anticipating the vacation makes the visit to the dentist more tolerable, while thought of the dentist office makes it harder to enjoy the beach.

However, a second possibility is that we contrast the enjoyment of our current experience against the enjoyment of the anticipated experience: the visit to the dentist becomes even more painful when anticipating the vacation, while the time at the beach becomes even more enjoyable when anticipating the visit to the dentist. Yet, although perceptual contrast is a very robust phenomenon, and although people routinely believe in hedonic contrast, there is little evidence that it actually occurs (Novemsky and Ratner 2003). Then again, past research has exclusively focused on comparisons with preceding experiences rather than anticipated experiences. Although the current dinner may not taste worse when the previous dinner was fabulous, it may actually taste worse when the next dinner is expected to be fabulous. Indeed, consistent with the forward-looking view of emotion (Frijda 1988), previous research has shown that the anticipation of future experiences is more intense than the reflection on past experiences (Van Boven and Ashworth 2007). If this generalizes to hedonic comparisons, then a visit to the dentist may be more painful when anticipating a vacation, even though it is not more painful following a vacation.

Before testing between these two possible effects (hedonic assimilation versus hedonic contrast), we assessed people's intuitions about the effect of hedonic comparisons. We simply asked participants how their experience of a pleasant (unpleasant) experience would change if it preceded (followed) an unpleasant (pleasant) experience. Consistent with prior research, a clear majority believed in retrospective hedonic contrast effects: 84% believed that being preceded by an unpleasant experience would make a pleasant experience even more pleasant, while 74% believed that being preceded by a pleasant experience would make an unpleasant experience even worse. Interestingly, they had the opposite intuition for comparisons with upcoming events: 92% believed that the anticipation of an unpleasant event would make a pleasant event less pleasant, while 84% believed that the anticipation of a pleasant event would make an unpleasant event less aversive. In other words, participants' intuition suggested forward-looking hedonic assimilation, rather than forward-looking hedonic contrast. We next tested whether these intuitions corresponded to people's actual experiences.

In a first study, all participants listened to pleasant piano music and were asked to indicate how much they enjoyed this music. People in the control condition only listened to the music, while people in the retrospective comparison condition first listened to an annoying sound (noise + music). Finally, people in the prospective comparison condition also first listened to the annoying sound, but in addition anticipated that the sound would return after the pleasant music (noise + music + noise). The results were the exact opposite of the intuitions from the pilot study: Whereas the music did not become more enjoyable when people first listened to the annoying sound, it did become more enjoyable when participants anticipated that the annoying sound would return after the music—consistent with forward-looking hedonic contrast.

We replicated this forward-looking hedonic contrast in a series of subsequent studies. In study 2, we asked participants to listen to a vacuum noise and found that their irritation with this noise did not change as a function of the sound they heard earlier (pleasant piano music or an even more irritating drilling sound), but did depend on the sound they were anticipating to hear afterwards. The vacuum noise became more irritating when people anticipated pleasant music than when they anticipated the drilling noise. In study 3, we demonstrated that this effect was not purely driven by the comparison with the even more irritating drilling noise: 50 secs of vacuum noise was experienced as more irritating when participants anticipated 10 secs of pleasant music than when they anticipated 10 more secs of vacuum noise. In study 4, we found that the comparison was not just sensitive to changes in valence, but also to changes in the magnitude of (dis)pleasure: An annoying sound became more annoying when people anticipated listening to a moderately enjoyable pop song, but even more so when they anticipated listening their favorite pop song.

If people engage in forward-looking hedonic contrast (rather than the hedonic assimilation they intuit), then their preference for improving sequences may sometimes be misguided. Indeed, in study 5, we find that people who taste improving sequences of jellybeans enjoy these jellybeans less than those who taste declining sequences of jellybeans—even though people in both groups strongly prefer the improving sequence. Finally, we conducted two studies to examine the boundary conditions of this hedonic contrast effect. In study 6, we replicate the contrast effect with an unambiguously valenced target experience (a looped vacuum noise), but we observe an assimilation effect with an ambiguously valenced target experience (looped new age music); and in study 7, we replicate the comparison effect when the anticipated experience is expected to immediately follow the target experience, but not when participants first expect more of the target experience.

REFERENCES

Balcetis, Emily and David Dunning (2006), "See What You Want to See: Motivational Influences on Visual Perception," *Journal of Personality and Social Psychology*, 91, 612-625.

Brewer, M. B. and J. G. Weber (1994), "Self-Evaluation Effects of Interpersonal versus Intergroup Social Comparison," *Journal of Personality and Social Psychology*, 66, 268-275.

Brendl, C. Miguel, Arthur B. Markman, and Claude Messner (2003), "The Devaluation Effect: Activating a Need Devalues Unrelated Choice Options," *Journal of Consumer Research*, 29, 463-473.

Bruner, J. S. and C. C. Goodman (1947), "Value and Need as Organizing Factors in Perception," *Journal of Abnormal Social Psychology*, 42, 33-44.

Dai, Xianchi, Klaus Wertenbroch, and C. Miguel Brendl (2008), "The Value Heuristic in Judgments of Relative Frequency," *Psychological Science*, 19, 18-19.

Dai, Xianchi, C. Miguel Brendl, and Klaus Wertenbroch (2009), "Value, Scarcity, and Preference Polarization," Working Paper.

Dhar, Ravi and Itamar Simonson (1992), "The Effect of the Focus of Comparison on Consumer Preferences," *Journal of Marketing Research*, 29 (4), 430-40.

Dhar, Ravi, Stephen M. Nowlis, and Steven J. Sherman (1999), "Comparison Effects On Preference Construction," *Journal of Consumer Research*, 26 (December), 293-306.

Frijda, Nico H. (1988), "The Laws of Emotion," *American Psychologist*, 43, 349-58.

Gilbert, Daniel T., Brian Giesler, and Kathryn A. Morris (1995), "When Comparisons Arise," *Journal of Personality and Social Psychology*, 69, 227-236.

Herr, Paul M. (1986), "Consequences of Priming: Judgment and Behavior," Journal of Personality and Social Psychology, 51, 1106-1115.

Herr, Paul M., Steve J. Sherman, and Russell H. Fazio (1983), "On the Consequences of Priming: Assimilation and Contrast Effects," *Journal of Experimental Social Psychology*, 19, 323-340.

Hsee, Christopher K. (1996), "The Evaluability Hypothesis: An Explanation for Preference Reversals between Joint and Separate Evaluations of Alternatives," *Organizational Behavior and Human Decision Processes*, 67, 247-257.

Kahneman, Daniel and Amos Tversky (1979), "Prospect Theory: An Analysis of Decisions under Risk," *Econometrica*, 47, 313-327.

Kunda, Ziva. (1990), "The Case for Motivated Reasoning," *Psychological Bulletin*, 108, 480-498.

Loewenstein, George (1987), "Anticipation and the Valuation of Delayed Consumption," *The Economic Journal*, 97(387), 666-684.

Morewedge, Carey K., Daniel T. Gilbert, Kristian O. R. Myrseth, Karim Kassam and Timothy D. Wilson (2009), "Consuming Experiences: Why We Don't Make the Comparisons We Anticipate," Working Paper, Carnegie Mellon University.

Mussweiler, Thomas (2003), "Comparison Processes in Social Judgment: Mechanisms and Consequences," *Psychological Review*, 110, 472-489.

Mussweiler, Thomas and Galen Bodenhausen (2002), "I Know You Are but What Am I? Self-Evaluative Consequences of Judging In-group and Out-group Members," *Journal of Personality and Social Psychology*, 82, 19–32.

Novemsky, Nathan and Rebecca Ratner (2003), "The Time Course and Impact of Consumer's Erroneous Lay Beliefs about Hedonic Contrast Effects," *Journal of Consumer Research*, 29, 507-516.

Van Boven, Leaf and Laurence Ashworth (2007), "Looking Forward, Looking Back: Anticipation Is More Evocative than Retrospection," *Journal of Experimental Psychology: General*, 136 (2), 289-300.

SPECIAL SESSION SUMMARY

Cue Substitution: Inferential Processes in Judgements and Experiences of Time

David Faro, London Business School, UK
Claire Tsai, University of Toronto, Canada

SESSION OVERVIEW

Many consumption settings involve time as an important evaluation variable. For example, assessing how long a drug typically takes to show its effect can affect its evaluation and the timing of its future consumption. Assessing how time seems to pass ("flying" or "dragging") during a song or a movie may affect people's evaluation of how enjoyable that experience was. Similarly, deciding how much time to allocate to leisure activities or unpleasant chores can affect people's plans and decisions for other activities. The judgment of time and the evaluation of experiences that take place over time is a complex task subject to various influences and judgment strategies (see McGrath & Tschan, 2003 for a recent collection of work in this literature). This session focuses on one such judgment strategy, bi-directional use of correlated cues (cue substitution), as a way to judge time and evaluate experiences over time.

Cue substitution is a common judgment strategy in many consumption settings (Frederick & Kahneman, 2002; Kardes et al., 2004). When people are uncertain about one variable but have access to a correlated variable, they tend to use the latter variable to infer the level of the first. Researchers have examined different instances of this process in several domains, including price-quality inferences (Cronley et al., 2005; Rao & Monroe, 1988) and familiarity-liking judgments (Zajonc, 1968; Monin, 2003). The papers in this session show three examples of this judgment strategy, each with time as either the substituted or substituting cue. Further, we discuss the implications for the accuracy and consistency of consumer time judgments and the consequences of biased retrospective hedonic evaluations. The three papers also elucidate the underlying mechanisms of the cue-substitution judgment strategy by identifying some of its moderators and mediators.

The first paper (Faro) shows that when consumers are uncertain about how long products have taken to show their effects, they rely on their causal beliefs to judge elapsed time. The second paper (Tsai et al.) shows that when consumers are uncertain about the duration of future activities but have access to information about the component parts of the experience and their valence, they use that information to estimate future duration. And the third paper (Sackett et al.) shows that when consumers are uncertain about how much they enjoyed an experience but have access to the perceived speed at which time passed, they use that apparent time distortion to retrospectively infer the level of hedonic experience.

Faro demonstrates that people's recollection of the time elapsed before they experienced an effect of a product is influenced by the degree to which they believe the product was responsible for that effect. The current research extends previous research in this area (Faro et al., 2005; Haggard et al., 2002) by focusing on the influence that biased time estimates of a previous experience have on future consumption. In one study, for instance, participants estimated that chewing a piece of gum took less time to improve their performance on a concentration task when they focused on the gum as the sole cause of improvement than when they considered it along with another possible cause. On a later consumption occasion, because they held shorter perceptions of time-to-onset, these participants decided to use the gum closer in time to a similar concentration task, started working on a similar task earlier upon use of the gum, experienced its effect on their performance earlier, and were less inclined to try competing products.

Whereas the first paper shows cue substitution of causal beliefs for product onset time, the second paper (Tsai et al.) shows the substitution of anticipated affective aspects of activities for predicted time allocation. Tsai et al. find that time estimates of a target event are systematically influenced by the valence and by the representation of that event (unpacking an event into several of its constituent activities or packing the constituent activities into one single event). For example, thinking of visiting a museum as visiting exhibits X, Y, and Z, rather than just the museum, increases the time estimates for the museum visit, whereas thinking about visiting mind-numbing exhibits X, Y, and Z for a school assignment, rather than just the museum, decreases the time estimates for the museum visit. Using a series of lab and field experiments in the context of discrete and continuous events—social and leisure activities and watching video clips—Tsai et al. demonstrate that unpacking an event into its constituent activities increases the time estimate for pleasant events but decreases the time estimate for unpleasant events. As an underlying mechanism for this effect, we hypothesize and show that unpacking increases the extremity of the predicted enjoyment/pain of the target event, which in turn mediates this pattern of the results. The studies also address issues including task-related knowledge, task complexity, mood, and mental accounting.

Faro and Tsai et al. show that when time is the uncertain variable to be judged, people base their judgments on a correlated semantic or affective cue. This is indeed often necessary because the mind is not equipped with a reliable time organ (Tourangeau et al. 2003). However, objective temporal information sometimes becomes available and contradicts subjectively experienced duration. In such cases, that discrepancy can act as the cue that people rely on to judge experiences. Through a series of five studies, Sackett et al. show that people do indeed use perceived time distortion as a cue to judge consumption experiences. Specifically, when time seems to "fly by" (because more time passes than one realizes), tasks retrospectively seem more engaging, noises less irritating, and songs more enjoyable. People conceptualize apparent time distortion as a metacognitive cue and in fact relying on, the naïve theory that "time flies when you're having fun." Understanding the role of experienced duration as a variable that affects the evaluation of experiences suggests, for example, ways for service providers to improve consumers' subjective evaluations without changing the core features of the experience.

This special-topic session features three recent papers that connect research on time judgments and the evaluation of experiences over time with issues important to marketers. Specifically, this session will bring to light how time durations can be inferred and estimated from consumption cues (Faro; Tsai et al.), as well as how its perceived passage can be used as a cue to evaluate consumption experiences (Sackett et al.). Session participants should come away with an increased understanding of the bi-directional relationships of time and causal beliefs (Faro) and time and affect (Tsai et al.; Sackett et al.). Participants will also discover how these temporal relationships affect variables directly important to marketers, such as preferences, repeat purchases, and inferences about future consumption.

EXTENDED ABSTRACTS

"Changing the Future by Reshaping the Past: The Influence of Causal Beliefs on Recollections of Time-to-Onset"

David Faro, London Business School, UK

Consumers' assessments of the time-to-onset of an effect refer to the amount of time they believe it takes for a product to show its effect after consumption. These assessments play an important role in many consumption settings. For some products, such as pharmaceuticals sold by prescription and over-the-counter medications, consumers care not only about whether the product has an effect, but also how quickly it begins. Furthermore, time-to-onset must often be assessed by consumers to plan future consumption. In particular, they may need to experience the effect of a product before starting another activity. Examples include caffeine before an exam, digestion aids before food consumption, relaxation drugs before a flight, and erectile dysfunction drugs before a sexual encounter. In such cases, assessments of time-to-onset can affect the timing of consumption, the timing of subsequent activity, and, consequently, both the perceived and real effectiveness of the product.

Two studies show that people's recollection of the time elapsed before they experienced an effect of a product is influenced by the degree to which they believe the product was responsible for that effect. Specifically, the studies show that a) stronger causal beliefs shorten time-to-onset estimates for past consumption and b) these shortened estimates later have an independent effect on future consumption and experience. Therefore, people appear to substitute their causal impressions about products to judge time-to-onset, and their altered estimates later affect future consumption decisions and experience

In the first study participants chewed a chewing gum in one part of the study and then took part in an attention task. Later in the study they were told that chewing a gum increases attention, and were asked some questions about its effect on their performance. Some participants considered only the effect of chewing the gum, while other participants considered an additional factor, the effect of practice with the task. All participants later estimated how much time elapsed until chewing the gum had an effect on their performance in the task (if it did). After some filler studies, participants consumed a second chewing gum and took part in a second task. They indicated the moment at which the second gum had an effect on their performance, and indicated whether they wanted to try a competing product (energy bar).

Results showed that participants who considered only the gum (and hence believed more strongly in its causal role) gave shorter estimates of time-to-onset for the gum than participants who also considered practice with the task. On a later consumption occasion, these participants reported to experience the gum's effect earlier, and were less interested in trying a competing product. Estimates of time-to-onset mediated the effect of causal beliefs on future consumption.

The second study showed two additional consequences of the effect and examined the underlying process. Participants chewed a chewing gum in one part of the study and later took part in an attention/memory task. They were then told that the chewing gum contained an ingredient which could (or was unlikely) to improve their performance. All participants estimated how much time elapsed until chewing the gum had an effect on their performance. After a filler study, participants were presented with a second gum, followed by a similar task. They indicated the latest time they would like to have the second piece of gum before beginning the next task, and once they consumed it, indicated when they wanted to begin the task. A manipulation of cognitive load took place prior to making time estimates for the first gum and was completed prior to making decisions about the second gum.

Results showed that participants who believed more strongly that the ingredient could improve attention/memory gave shorter estimates of time-to-onset for the gum. These participants were comfortable using the second gum closer to the task, and began working on the task earlier than their counterparts. There was an interaction effect of cognitive load and causality on time-to-onset estimates, as well as on future consumption decisions. The time shortening effect was strongest under cognitive load. This suggests that the effect of causal beliefs on time estimates reflects a low-effort, default, possibly unconscious use of causality as a cue to temporally bind causes and effects. Further, because the cognitive load manipulation was completed prior to making any decisions about the second gum, the interaction suggests that time-to-onset estimates for the first consumption drove future decisions.

Overall the two studies show that causal beliefs about products can shape consumers' perceptions of time-to-onset for past consumption, and these perceptions can have an independent effect on future consumption. The first study suggests that shortened perceptions of time-to-onset may give the target product an added advantage. Participants who held shorter perceptions of time experienced the gum's effect earlier on a future consumption occasion, and were less interested in trying other products. The second study suggests some possibly negative consequences for the product and for consumers. Participants who held shorter perceptions of time were more likely to use the product too late, and more likely to begin an activity which depends on the effect of the product too early. The paper concludes with a discussion of the implications of the findings for consumers and marketers.

"The Effect of Unpacking and Valence on Future Time Estimates"

Claire Tsai, University of Toronto, Canada
Min Zhao, University of Toronto, Canada
Jing Wan, University of Toronto, Canada

The present research examines how subdividing a multifaceted event with different valences will influence time estimates of those events. Drawing on findings regarding probability judgments in support theory (Rottenstreich and Tversky 1997; Tversky and Koehler 1994) and hedonic editing (Thaler 1985), we propose that unpacking systematically influences time judgments. Specifically, we propose an interactive effect of unpacking and the valence of the target event on its time judgment.

Using a series of two field and three lab experiments, we demonstrated that unpacking a pleasant, multifaceted event into several pleasant sub-activities increases the time estimated to spend on the event; whereas unpacking an unpleasant, multifaceted event into several unpleasant sub-activities decreases the time estimated to spend on the event. In addition, we found that predicted enjoyment/pain mediates the interaction between the representation and valence of the target event on the time estimation.

In the first field experiment, we borrowed the research paradigm from the support theory literature (Tverskey and Koehler 1994). We varied the representation of a museum visit by unpacking it into the experience of several exhibits and asked visitors to estimate the time they expected to spend (unpacked condition) or simply asked visitors to predict how long they would stay in the museum without mentioning the specific exhibits (packed condition). As predicted, time estimates were greater in the unpacked condition than that in the packed condition, replicating the support theory effect on time judgments.

However, the effects can be attributed to the knowledge that visitors had about the exhibits at the museum. That is, when making the time estimate, participants in the packed condition were not aware of all the exhibits in the museum or not considering as many exhibits as participants in the unpacked condition did. To control for the knowledge about the target events in experiments 2-4, we provided all participants with identical information about the target activities and only varying the representation of the events. This method provides direct assessments of the extent to which representation of a target event influences time estimates.

In experiment 2, participants were asked to estimate the time they would spend on two social activities: meeting a blind date and attending a birthday party. In the pleasant conditions, the date was attractive and the birthday party was something they were looking forward. In the unpleasant condition, the date was unattractive and the party was something they wanted to avoid. The results showed that for pleasant activities, the derived sum of the time estimates in the unpacked condition was greater than the single time estimate in the packed condition, whereas the pattern of the results was reversed for unpleasant activities.

One possible explanation for experiment 2 is the similarity of the sub-activities. It is possible that the effect of unpacking only occurs for activities similar in nature because it is easier to consider them as one multifaceted activity. Thus, we tested this account in experiment 3 by replacing the social activities with two dissimilar leisure activities: reading for leisure in either a quiet or noisy coffee shop, and chatting with either a good friend or a dislikeable acquaintance over the phone. The results fully replicated the findings of experiment 2.

Another potential account for the results of experiments 1-3 is the amount of attention that participants paid to the task. Perhaps the more finely the event is unpacked, the more attention will be paid to the prediction task and thus time estimates will increase regardless of the valence of the event. We addressed this issue in experiment 4 by providing participants with three activities (date, birthday party, and phone conversation). In addition, we asked participants to predict the pleasantness of each individual activity. Again, we replicated the pattern of results of experiments 2-3 even with increased number of sub-activities. Also, as expected, we found that predicted levels of enjoyment/pain mediated this interactive pattern.

How does unpacking affect the accuracy of time judgments? In another field experiment we asked participants to self-generate either pleasant or unpleasant activities. We have preliminary evidence to show that unpacking led to more accurate prediction for pleasant activities but had an opposite effect for unpleasant activities.

In conclusion, our research showed that unpacking can influence the time estimates for that event but the direction of that change depends on the valence of the event. Our research adds to the time judgment literature by identifying an important mechanism that influences time perception or estimation, namely, the interaction of event presentation (packed vs. unpacked) and event valence. At the same time, we contribute to the support theory literature by extending its findings to time estimation and attesting to its robustness in different domains.

"You're Having Fun When Time Flies: The Hedonic Consequences of Subjective Time Progression"

Aaron Sackett, University of Chicago, USA
Benjamin Converse, University of Chicago, USA
Tom Meyvis, New York University, USA
Leif Nelson, University of California at Berkeley, USA
Anna L. Sackett, University at Albany, SUNY, USA

People walking out of dark theaters, finishing transactions after waiting in long lines, or driving home from a day on the town may catch a glimpse of a clock and find themselves surprised at how much (or how little) time has passed. Duration estimates are influenced by many factors, including attentional engagement (Chaston and Kingstone 2004), arousal (Gruber and Block 2003), and motivation (Conti 2001). Thus, subjective duration often diverges from objective duration. When this occurs, time feels distorted: When more time passed than one realized, it feels like time flew by; when less time passed than one thought, it feels like time dragged on.

The feeling of time distortion may prompt people to seek an explanation, and a ready answer may come from overgeneralization of the common naïve theory that "time flies when you're having fun." Given that attentional demands shorten duration estimates (Block and Zakay 1997; Chaston and Kingstone 2004) and that highly enjoyable activities can monopolize attention (Csikszentmihalyi 1975, 1990), time and enjoyment may come to share an intuitive link in people's perceptions of experience. The current work is concerned with how, in the face of otherwise inexplicable time distortions, this presumed relationship may be overgeneralized, leading to causal inferences. We predict that people's sense that time "flew" will enhance their evaluations of experiences, whereas their sense that time "dragged" will worsen their evaluations.

In the first experiment, we created the illusion of fast or slow time progression by misleading participants about how much time had actually passed. In experiment 1a, students completed a mundane word-underlining task in the absence of external time cues. All participants learned that the task would last for precisely 10 minutes. The task actually lasted for 5 minutes in the time-flies condition, and 20 minutes in the time-drags condition. As expected, participants in the time-flies (vs. time-drags) condition rated the task as more enjoyable. To ensure that the observed effect could not be explained merely by differences in actual duration (i.e., underlining words for only 5 minutes might be better than underlining words for 20 minutes), we replicated experiment 1a, but held actual time constant while manipulating perceived duration. In experiment 1b, all participants actually did the task for 10 minutes but they were either told that it lasted for 20 minutes (time flies) or 5 minutes (time drags). Again, participants rated the task as more enjoyable in the time-flies than in the time-drags condition. Experiments 2 and 3 replicated this basic effect for a more positive experience (listening to popular songs), a more negative experience (listening to synchronized dot matrix printers), with a different manipulation of time distortion (accelerated vs. decelerated timers), and compared to a normal-time control condition.

In experiments 4a and 4b we tested the proposed role of the "time flies" naïve theory more directly. In 4a, participants solved anagram tasks for exactly 7.5 minutes. The task was either described as a 10-minute task (time flies) or a 5-minute task (time drags). Participants rated their enjoyment and, after some filler items, indicated the extent to which they endorse the saying "time flies when you're having fun." Once again, those in the time-flies (vs. time-drags) condition reported greater enjoyment of the task.

More importantly, this effect was significantly more pronounced among participants who more strongly endorsed the "time flies" naïve theory.

In experiment 4b we manipulated endorsement of the naïve theory. Participants read fabricated news stories, ostensibly as part of a memory test, that either supported or refuted the "time flies" belief based on scientific evidence. Then they completed a word-underlining task with timing procedures identical to experiment 1a. Among those who read an article supporting the time-flies theory, the word task was rated more positively in the time-flies (vs. time-drags) condition. Among those who read the article refuting this theory, there was no significant difference in enjoyment across the two time conditions.

Experiment 5 followed the procedures of 1a, with two important differences. First, all participants wore foam earplugs during the task. Second, after completing the task, but prior to evaluating it, half of the participants read a survey item suggesting that wearing earplugs may distort their sense of time (in the direction of the current time condition) because of differences in sensory input. As predicted, participants reported greater enjoyment of the task in the time-flies (vs. time-drags) condition only when they did not receive the alternative attribution. Among those who read the survey item saying that time may have flown (dragged) because of the earplugs, there was no difference in reported enjoyment across the two time conditions. When time distortion could be explained by some external cause, there was no need to invoke the enjoyment explanation, thus eliminating the time-flies effect.

Taken together, these findings have important implications for understanding and influencing hedonic experience. There can be value in improving subjective experience without changing core features of the task at hand, and influencing subjective time perception may provide such an opportunity. The current research thus provides insight into new ways to improve people's subjective enjoyment of a wide range of consumption experiences.

REFERENCES

Block, Richard A. and Dan Zakay (1997), "Prospective and Retrospective Duration Judgments: A Meta-Analytic Review," *Psychonomic Bulletin and Review*, 4 (2), 184-97.

Chaston, Anthony and Alan Kingstone (2004), "Time Estimation: The Effect of Cortically Mediated Attention," *Brain and Cognition*, 55 (2), 286-89.

Conti, Regina (2001), "Time Flies: Investigating the Connection between Intrinsic Motivation and the Experience of Time," *Journal of Personality*, 69 (1), 1-26.

Cronley, Maria L., Steven S. Posavac, Tracy Meyer, Frank R. Kardes, and James J. Kellaris (2005), "A Selective Hypothesis Testing Perspective on Price-Quality Inference and Inference-Based Choice," *Journal of Consumer Psychology*, 15 (2), 159-169.

Csikszentmihalyi, Mihaly (1975), *Beyond Boredom and Anxiety: The Experience of Flow in Work and Games*, San Francisco, CA: Jossey-Bass.

______ (1990), *Flow: The Psychology of Optimal Experience*, New York: Harper Collins.

Faro, David, France Leclerc, and Reid Hastie (2005), "Perceived Causality as a Cue to Temporal Distance," *Psychological Science*, 16 (9), 673-77.

Gruber, Ronal P. and Richard A. Block (2003), "Effect of Caffeine on Prospective and Retrospective Duration Judgments," *Human Psychopharmacology*, 20 (4), 275-86.

Haggard, Patrick, Sam Clark, and Jeri Kalogeras (2002), "Voluntary Action and Conscious Awareness," *Nature Neuroscience*, 5 (4), 382-85.

Kahneman, D. and Shane Frederick (2002), "Representativeness Revisited: Attribute Substitution in Intuitive Judgment," in Tom Gilovich, Dale Griffin, and Daniel Kahneman (Eds.), *Heuristics & Biases: The Psychology of Intuitive Judgment,* New York. Cambridge University Press.

Kardes, Frank R., Maria L. Cronley, J. Kellaris James, and Steven S. Posavac (2004), "The Role of Selective Information Processing in Price-Quality Inference," *Journal of Consumer Research*, 31 (2), 368-374.

Monin, Benoît (2003), "The warm glow heuristic: When liking leads to familiarity," *Journal of Personality and Social Psychology*, 85(6), 1035-1048.

Rao, Akshay R. and Kent B. Monroe (1988). "The Moderating Effect of Prior Knowledge on Cue Utilization in Product Evaluations," *Journal of Consumer Research*, 15(2), 253-265.

Rottenstreich, Yuval and Amos Tversky (1997), "Unpacking, Repacking, and Anchoring: Advances in Support Theory," *Psychological Review*, 104, 406–415.

Thaler, Richard H. (1985), "Mental accounting and consumer choice," *Marketing Science*, 4, 199-214.

Tourangeau, Roger, Lance J. Rips, and Kenneth Rasinski (2000), *The Psychology of Survey Response,* New York, NY, US: Cambridge University Press.

Tversky, Amos and Derek J. Koehler (1994), "Support Theory: A Nonextensional Representation of Subjective Probability," *Psychological Review*, 101, 547–567.

Special Session Summary

Effects of Minor Language Variations on Consumer Persuasion

Aner Sela, Stanford University, USA

SESSION OVERVIEW

A great deal of research on consumer persuasion has focused on explicit factors such as the quality of arguments, the characteristics of the message source, or the perceiver's motivation to process information, and the effects of these types of variables are well understood. However, little attention has been devoted to the effects of much more subtle features of marketing communications, such as minor language variations in the message, on persuasion. What effect, if any, do these more subtle factors have on consumer persuasion?

The present session seeks to provide an in-depth look at the significant effects of seemingly inconsequential wording variations on preferences, brand perceptions, and attitude change. For example, what are the mechanisms by which specific word use can influence the construction of preferences? Might different consumers respond to the same wording in different ways? The session will address these and other related questions as it works to deepen our understanding of the role of language in persuasion.

One of the interesting conclusions that emerge from the present session is that subtle language variations can influence consumers' actual experiences when consuming products. Jongmin Kim, Jing Wang, Nathan Novemsky, and Ravi Dhar (paper 1) reveal in their research that asking product evaluation questions using fancy words (e.g., "velvety wine") can increase actual liking for the product, as compared to logically equivalent but less fancy words (e.g. "smooth wine"). The research suggests that the use of fancy words activates associated knowledge in memory nonconsciously, which in turn biases the processing of ambiguous experiences in a confirmatory manner. In contrast, when fancy language is perceived as unambiguously inconsistent with the evaluation target, it can actually decrease liking for the product.

Another surprising finding is that minor wording variations can influence perceptions of real-life brands with which consumers have had long-lasting working relationships. Aner Sela and Christian Wheeler (paper 2) demonstrate how subtle changes in the use of relationship-implying terms (e.g., "you and Wells Fargo" vs. "we") can affect perceptions of brand attributes and, consequently, attitudes toward the brand among its customers. They find that subtle linguistic changes have different effects among current customers and non-customers of the brand, because these groups have different perceptions of the ongoing relationship with the brand. These effects depend further on the brand category and its associated relationship norms.

Finally, Nicole Mayer and Zakary Tormala (paper 3) examine the effect of minor language variations, such as saying "I feel" versus "I think", on persuasion among people whose attitudes are either affectively or cognitively oriented. They find that when a persuasive message appears to reflect the source's feelings versus thoughts, it will be more persuasive to recipients whose attitudes or general orientations are primarily affective versus cognitive, respectively.

Marketers carefully manage their communications with consumers in order to shape beliefs, attitudes, and behavior. The three papers in this session extend and deepen our understanding of the impact of seemingly inconsequential language variations and how they interact with concrete features of the target (e.g., product quality), perceptions of consumer-brand relationships, and consumers' affective vs. cognitive orientations. Thus, the session speaks to the importance of tailoring the exact message wording to the situation. It would be of interest to researchers and marketers interested in consumer persuasion and implicit social cognition.

EXTENDED ABSTRACTS

"Persuasion under the Radar: Effects of Question Wording on Product Evaluation"

Jong Min Kim, , Yale University, USA
Jing Wang, Singapore Management University, Singapore
Nathan Novemsky, Yale University, USA
Ravi Dhar, Yale University, USA

Consumers' preferences are often constructed and largely determined by the task characteristics, the choice context, and the description of options (e.g. Simonson, 2008). Some research suggests that if the task or context is perceived as being manipulated by a marketer and having persuasive intent, consumers are likely to protect themselves from the marketing actions (Friestad and Wright, 1984). The present research reveals that asking evaluation questions on scales that are associated with high quality (e.g. velvety) vs. regular quality products (e.g. smooth) can influence preferences for the product in a nonconscious manner. Specifically, consumers who rated a product on dimensions described using fancy words (e.g., How velvety would you say the texture of the wine is?) make more positive evaluations than those who rated the same product on dimensions described using typical words (e.g., How smooth would you say the texture of the wine is?). We posit that the effects occur because answering the rating questions evokes a mental representation of the product without any suspicion. By answering the rating questions people engage in positive hypothesis testing (e.g. Klayman and Ha, 1987) and test the possibility that the product has the provided set of attributes. This increases the accessibility of the fancy/non-fancy attributes of the product and this accessible knowledge is used in overall evaluations of the product (Strack and Mussweiler, 1997). We demonstrate these language effects across a series of studies.

In Study 1, participants were shown pictures of chocolates and asked to rate the product on five dimensions described using either fancy or non-fancy words (e.g. how velvety/smooth would the texture of the chocolates be?). Participants who rate the chocolates on fancy attributes indicate that they would like the chocolate more and that they are more likely to purchase the chocolates. In study 2, we find that the effects persist even after direct experience with a product. Participants in this study were members of a Wine Club and were given a wine sample. They were randomly assigned to evaluate it on either the fancy or the non-fancy rating scales. Participants who evaluated the wine on fancy attributes (e.g. velvety, harmonious, lingering, etc) liked the wine more and were more likely to purchase the wine compared to those who rated it on non-fancy attributes (e.g. smooth, balanced, long-lasting, etc).

Study 3 and Study 4 replicate and extend these findings, identifying boundary conditions for the language effects. Study 3 shows that the language effect occurs only when the target product is ambiguous. This study manipulates ambiguity by presenting either agreeing or disagreeing expert opinions (Hoch and Ha, 1986). This information about the wine was provided to participants before a wine sample was given to them. In the ambiguous condition, participants read a set of scores varying widely across experts, while participants in the unambiguous condition saw scores that were quite consistent across experts. The results show that only when the product is ambiguous, do we observe any effect of the language used in rating scales. When participants have information that is diagnostic of the product, the scales (fancy vs. non-fancy) have no effect on overall evaluation.

Study 4 examines another moderator for the language effect: fit between fancy scales and the product. Using fancy words that do not seem to fit the target product category may not result in a positive evaluation of the product. In this case, it is possible that the fancy rating scales can result in lower evaluations than a rating task involving less fancy words. To examine this moderating role of fit, we choose wine as a fancy product and Soju, a Korean lowbrow alcoholic beverage, as a non-fancy product (Study 4 was conducted in Korea). Participants were given a sample of either wine or Soju and asked to rate the product on either fancy or non-fancy scales. Replicating our previous results, participants are willing to pay more for wine when they answer the questions asking about fancy attributes. They even consumed more wine in the fancy scale condition. However, the effect of language on evaluation reversed for Soju. Participants were willing to pay less for Soju when they rated it on scales anchored by fancy words compared to those rating it on non-fancy scales. They also consumed less Soju in the fancy scale condition.

In summary, we posit that different language embedded in a ratings scale can influence preference for a product. These effects arise without any explicit claim about any aspect of the product. This is precisely why consumers keep their defenses down and do not consider the rating task a persuasion attempt (Williams et al, 2004). As result they may be more persuaded than if an explicit claim had been made.

For further information contact: Jongmin Kim, Yale School of Management, Yale University, 135 Prospect Street, New Haven, CT 06511, E-mail: jongmin.kim@yale.edu

References

Friestad, M. and P. Wright (1994), "The Persuasion Knowledge Model: How People Cope with Persuasion Attempts," *Journal of Consumer Research*, 21, 1-31.

Hoch, S. J. and Y. W. Ha (1986), "Consumer Learning: Advertising and the Ambiguity of Product Experience," *Journal of Consumer Research*, 13, 221–33.

Klayman, J. and Y. W. Ha (1987), "Confirmation, Disconfirmation, and Information in Hypothesis Testing," *Psychological Review*, 94, 211-228.

Simonson, I. (2008), "Will I Like a 'Medium' Pillow? Another Look at Constructed and Inherent Preferences," *Journal of Consumer Psychology*, 18, 155-169.

Strack, F. and T. Mussweiler (1997), "Explaining the Enigmatic Anchoring Effect: Mechanisms of Selective Accessibility," *Journal of Personality and Social Psychology*, 73, 437-446.

Williams, P., G. J. Fitzsimons, and L. G. Block (2004), "When Consumers Do Not Recognize 'Benign' Intention Questions as Persuasion Attempts," *Journal of Consumer Research*, 31, 540–550.

"You and We: Causal Effects of Minor Language Variations on Brand Perceptions"

Aner Sela, Stanford, University, USA

S. Christian Wheeler, Stanford University, USA

Marketers often desire to promote consumers' feelings of being in a close relationship with the brands they market. Accordingly, they frequently portray brands as intimate partners with consumers, believing that this should lead to more favorable attitudes. This belief has intuitive appeal, but does it actually foster favorable brand perceptions? The present research examines this issue by studying whether subtle differences in marketing communications, such as using the terms "we" versus "you and us," can affect attitudes and perceptions toward the brand. Although these types of terms are linguistically equivalent, we suggest that they can subtly convey information about a consumer's relationship with the brand that can have either positive or negative effects.

Research on consumer-brand relationships has suggested that consumers often relate to brands in ways that correspond to different relationship profiles, each entailing different relational scripts and norms (Fournier 1998). This literature suggests that people may respond positively to brand actions that are perceived as consistent with the believed consumer-brand relationship, but might respond negatively when these actions are inconsistent with the relationship (Aggarwal 2004).

Consistent with earlier research (e.g., Brown and Gilman 1960), we expect more intimate and informal language use (e.g., "we") to be perceived as consistent with consumer-brand relationships that are believed to be closer and based on shared goals. In contrast, we expect language that emphasizes the separateness of relationship partners (e.g., "you and I") to be perceived as consistent with consumer-brand relationships that are more distant. We predict that language consistent with the believed consumer-brand relationship norms will lead to more favorable attitudes.

Several factors can affect the perceived closeness between consumers and brands. Specifically, consumers may associate some product categories with a relationship based on closeness, cooperation, and shared goals. Other product categories, however, may be associated with a more distant relationship, one that is based less on mutual goals and more on "zero-sum" behavior. Another important dimension concerns whether one is a customer of the brand or not. Whereas existing brand customers may have specific expectations of their relationship with the brand and corresponding communication norms, non-customers may have different expectations.

In sum, we examine the following questions. First, can subtle changes in the use of relationship-implying terms (e.g., "you and [the brand]" vs. "we") affect perceptions of brand attributes and, consequently, attitudes toward the brand? Second, do these subtle changes have different effects among current customers and non-customers of the brand? Third, do these effects depend further on the brand category and its associated relationship norms?

We test two mediation hypotheses for these effects. First, the effect of language on attitudes could be mediated by perceptions of brand honesty. Specifically, when the intimacy implied by language is in harmony with consumers' perception of their ongoing relationship with the brand, the brand may be perceived as more trustworthy and consequently more favorable overall. However, when the language is inconsistent with the relationship, the brand might be perceived as less trustworthy, leading to less favorable attitudes. Alternatively, people could respond more favorably to relationship-congruent language simply because it is easier to process (i.e., fluent), being consistent with their expectation (Lee and Labroo 2004; Schwarz 2004).

To test our hypotheses, we first conducted a pretest, which suggested that people tend to perceive their working relationships with their bank as relatively close and intimate, but perceive their relationships with a health insurance provider as more distant.

Consequently, in experiment 1, we predicted that existing customers, but not non-customers, of a prominent banking brand would have more favorable attitudes toward the brand when a message referred to the brand and the consumer as "we" than when it referred to the brand and the consumer as "you and [the brand]".

Participants read a short message about a prominent banking brand, allegedly taken from an advertisement. Some participants read a message that used the phrase "you and [the brand]," whereas others read a message in which "you and [the brand]" was replaced with "we". Then, they were asked to rate their attitudes toward the brand. At the end of the experiment, participants were asked whether they were actually banking with the brand.

As hypothesized, consumers with an ongoing working relationship with the banking brand reported more favorable attitudes when the message used the pronoun "we". Conversely, non-customers had somewhat more positive attitudes toward the brand when the message used the term "you and Wells Fargo".

Experiment 2 replicated the results of experiment 1, using the same procedure with additional banking brands, and tested our two mediation hypotheses. Mediated moderation analyses suggested that the moderated effect of language and customer status on attitudes was fully mediated by perceived brand honesty. In contrast, although the interaction of language and customer status predicted fluency, fluency was not a significant predictor of attitudes.

Experiment 3 used a banking brand and a health insurance brand as our stimuli. We predicted that referring to the brand and the consumer as "we"–rather than "you and [the brand]"–would lead to more favorable attitudes among existing customers when the brand is a bank. In contrast, we predicted that using "we" would lead to less favorable attitudes when the brand is a health insurance provider, because our pretest indicated that these brands are perceived as partners in a distant relationship. We also predicted that non-customers in both categories would prefer less intimate language. The results of this experiment support our hypotheses, suggesting opposite effects of language on attitudes toward the bank vs. health insurance brands. Furthermore, these effects were mediated by perceived brand honesty in both cases.

The present research contributes to the literature on language in interpersonal cognition by suggesting that language conveys meaning and influences attitudes not just directly, in an assimilative manner (e.g., Fitzsimons and Kay 2004), but also through implicit assessments of the congruity between the language and prior beliefs about the relationship. From a practical viewpoint, these findings promote the idea that marketers should not only think of their consumers as relationship partners in general, but also mind the differences in how specific types of consumers relate to their brands in the context of its product category.

References

Aggarwal, Pankaj (2004), "The Effects of Brand Relationship Norms on Consumer Attitudes and Behavior," *Journal of Consumer Research*, 31 (June), 87–101.

Brown, Roger and Albert Gilman (1960), "The Pronouns of Power and Solidarity," in *Style in Language*, ed. Thomas A. Sebeok, Cambridge, MA: MIT Press, 253-76.

Fitzsimons, Gráinne M. and Aaron C. Kay (2004), "Language and Interpersonal Cognition: Causal Effects of Variations in Pronoun Usage on Perceptions of Closeness," *Personality and Social Psychology Bulletin*, 30 (5), 547–57.

Fournier, Susan (1998), "Consumers and Their Brands: Developing Relationship Theory in Consumer Research," *Journal of Consumer Research*, 24 (March), 343-73.

Lee, Angela Y. and Aparna A. Labroo (2004), "The Effect of Conceptual and Perceptual Fluency on Brand Evaluation," *Journal of Marketing Research*, 41 (2), 151-65.

Schwarz, Norbert (2004), "Metacognitive Experiences in Consumer Judgment and Decision Making," *Journal of Consumer Psychology*, 14 (4), 332-48.

"'Think' Versus 'Feel' Framing Effects in Persuasion"

Nicole Mayer, Stanford University, USA

Zakary L. Tormala, Stanford University, USA

When people express opinions or share ideas, they often do so by referencing their thoughts or feelings. When attempting to persuade someone to adopt a new product, for example, one might frame the exact same substantive argument in terms of thoughts (e.g., "I think this camera is the best on the market") or feelings (e.g., "I feel that this camera is the best on the market") without changing the essence of the appeal. Whether one says "I think" or "I feel," or even "my thought is" or "my feeling is," the common assumption is that one is introducing a statement that reflects one's subjective impression of an object or issue. The current research explores the possibility that although think and feel message frames are used interchangeably, their effects might not be interchangeable at all. In particular, we investigate whether think and feel message frames might be differentially persuasive, even when the substantive content of the message itself is held constant.

Over the years, considerable research attention has been paid to the notion that attitudes can vary in their underlying cognitive or affective bases. Moreover, this distinction has important implications for persuasion. In general, affective attitudes are more susceptible to persuasion by affective messages, whereas cognitive attitudes are more susceptible to persuasion by cognitive messages (e.g., Drolet and Aaker 2002; Edell and Burke 1987; Edwards 1990; Fabrigar and Petty 1999; Haddock et al., 2008). In the current research, we propose that even when one receives the exact same arguments from a persuasive message, believing those arguments reflect their source's thoughts or feelings can interact with one's own cognitive/affective orientation to determine persuasion. Our primary hypothesis is that messages that appear to reflect their source's feelings (thoughts) will be more persuasive when the target attitude or message recipient is primarily affective (cognitive) in orientation. Furthermore, building on past research linking matching, or fit, effects with processing fluency (e.g., Lee and Aaker 2004), we propose that this effect will be mediated by ease of processing. That is, matched messages will be experienced as easier to process than mismatched messages, and this ease will translate into greater persuasion.

In Study 1, we introduced participants to the topic of blood donation and assessed their initial cognitive versus affective orientations toward the issue. Following this assessment, we presented both cognitive and affective individuals with a persuasive message advocating frequent blood donation. This message contained numerous arguments in favor of blood donation, and these arguments were framed in terms of their source's thoughts or feelings. For instance, in the "feel" condition, the message opened with the line: "I feel that donating blood is one of the most important contributions I can make to society." By contrast, in the "think" condition, the opening line was: "I think that donating blood is one of the most important contributions I can make to society." Aside from the use of the word "think" or "feel" throughout the message, the content of the arguments was identical. Immediately following the message, participants reported their intentions to donate blood in the future. As hypothesized, we obtained a significant interaction between initial orientation and message frame. Cognitively oriented individuals reported greater intention to donate blood following the "think" message, whereas affectively oriented individuals reported greater intention to donate blood following the "feel" message.

Study 2 had several aims: to manipulate affective versus cognitive orientation, to directly measure attitudes following the persuasive message, and to test the processing fluency mechanism. This study essentially replicated Study 1, but we primed affective versus cognitive orientation by giving participants an initial message, negative toward blood donation, that was affective (e.g., "The nurse gripped my arm with one hand and slid the large spike of the needle into my skin.") or cognitive (e.g., "I learned some surprising facts about human biology that make me think blood donation would be unwise.") in tone. Following this prime, participants received the "think" or "feel" advocacy from Study 1, reported attitudes, and indicated how easy it was to process and comprehend the second (positive) message. Results indicated a significant interaction on both attitudes and ease of processing. When participants received the affective prime, they reported more favorable attitudes toward blood donation, and greater processing ease, in response to the "feel" rather than "think" message. When participants received the cognitive prime, these effects were reversed. Furthermore, perceived ease of processing mediated the attitude effect.

Finally, Study 3 tested a practical application of these findings by presenting male and female consumers with an advertisement containing think- or feel-framed arguments. Past research suggests that women self-identify as experiencing and expressing more intense emotions than do men and that women are more attuned than men to the emotions of others (for a review see Hall and Schmid Mast 2008). In a pilot study, we confirmed that women self-reported being more emotionally oriented than did men. Consistent with this notion, Study 3 revealed that female participants were more persuaded by the feel-framed advertisement, whereas male participants were more persuaded by the think-framed advertisement.

In summary, using both measured and manipulated approaches, we found that attitudes and message recipients with cognitive (affective) orientations were more susceptible to persuasion by arguments framed in terms of their source's thoughts (feelings). This effect was particularly striking given that the substantive content of the arguments was exactly the same across conditions. Moreover, the persuasion outcome was mediated by processing fluency. Participants found it easier to process the matched rather than mismatched message, and they attributed this feeling of ease to the message's persuasiveness. Implications for attitude structure and consumer behavior are discussed.

References

Drolet, Aimee and Jennifer Aaker (2002), "Off-Target? Changing Cognitive-Based Attitudes," *Journal of Consumer Psychology*, 12 (1), 59-68.

Edell, Julie A. and Marian C. Burke (1987), "The Power of Feelings in Understanding Advertising Effects," *Journal of Consumer Research*, 14 (December), 421-33.

Edwards, Kari (1990), "The Interplay of Affect and Cognition in Attitude Formation and Change," *Journal of Personality and Social Psychology*, 59, 202-16.

Fabrigar, Leandre R. and Richard E. Petty (1999), "The Role of the Affective and Cognitive Bases of Attitudes in Susceptibility to Affectively and Cognitively Based Persuasion," *Personality and Social Psychology Bulletin*, 25 (3), 363-81.

Haddock, Geoffrey, Gregory R. Maio, Karin Arnold, and Thomas Huskinson (2008), "Should Persuasion be Affective or Cognitive? The Moderating Effects of Need for Affect and Need for Cognition," *Personality and Social Psychology Bulletin*, 34 (6), 769-78.

Hall, Judith A., and Marianne Schmid Mast (2008), "Are Women Always More Interpersonally Sensitive than Men? Impact of Goals and Content Domain," *Personality and Social Psychology Bulletin*, 34 (1), 144-55.

Lee, Angela Y. and Jennifer L. Aaker (2004), "Bringing the Frame into Focus: The Influence of Regulatory Fit on Processing Fluency and Persuasion," *Journal of Personality and Social Psychology*, 86 (2), 205-18.

Special Session Summary

Psychological Distance and Metacognitive Experience

Claire Tsai, University of Toronto, Canada
Manoj Thomas, Cornell University, USA

SESSION OVERVIEW

There is a growing interest among consumer researchers to understand the antecedents and consequences of psychological distance. Psychological distance is a fundamental construct in human cognition and it can manifest itself in the perceived geographical distance (close vs. remote), temporal distance (recent vs. distant), or construal level (concrete vs. abstract; how vs. why mindset). Psychological distance can have a direct effect on consumer behavior by changing the perceived distance to stores and cities (e.g., Raghubir and Krishna 1996) and thus influence preferences, choices, and willingness to pay (WTP). It can also have an indirect effect by changing how consumers construe the available information (e.g., Liberman, Trope, and Wakslak 2007). In this special session, we address an issue that has received limited attention in the extant literature: the role of metacognitive experiences in perceived psychological distance. We bring together four papers that examine the interplay of metacognitive experience and psychological distance in judgments and decisions. The first two papers in the proposed session investigate how metacognitive experience influences perceived distance and its consequences. The third and fourth papers examine how psychological distance moderates the effect of metacognitive experience on judgments. Together, these four papers offer new insights into how metacognitive experience and psychological distance interactively influence judgments and decisions.

Using a series of seven experiments, Alter, Oppenheimer, and Shah manipulate metacognitive experiences arising from different sources of processing fluency–font, conceptual priming, and linguistic structure–to investigate its influence on perceived geographical distance, construal levels, and its consequences. Thomas, Lindsey and Lakshmanan extend this work to show that metacognitive experience induced by familiarity has a similar effect on perceived geographical distance. They test the origins of this effect, ascribing it to misattribution for expectancy disconfirmation.

Tsai and McGill further investigate metacognitive experiences by uncovering conditions in which consumers may reverse the cue relationship between judgments and fluency. Using a series of three experiments, Tsai and McGill demonstrate that choice confidence is systematically influenced by fluency but that these effects are moderated by levels of construal (how vs. why mindset), which evoke different theories to interpret the subjective experiences of ease. At lower construal levels, fluency informs the feasibility of achieving the outcome but at higher construal levels fluency signals low investment in decision and thus lack of confirmation for outcome desirability.

Similarly, Smith and Schwarz show that when consumers make inferences based on the reported experiences of others, such inferences are moderated by temporal distance from the event and the vividness of this report. Specifically, experiences closer in time should be more relevant to predictions of enjoyment than experiences that occurred long time ago, a concept consumers understand in the abstract but which they may reverse when the experience is highly vivid (and so seemingly better remembered) due to the metacognitive belief that more extreme events are better remembered (i.e., more vivid).

These four papers feature on-going work that connects research on psychological distance with issues important to marketers. Session participants should come away with increased understanding of the influence of met cognition on variables directly important to marketers such as shopping distance, confidence in choice, inferences of future quality based on word of mouth reports. These papers also explore seemingly incongruent findings to help map the interactive effect of fluency and psychological distance on judgments and decisions.

EXTENDED ABSTRACT

"Fluency and Psychological Distance: Consequences for Construal and Discounting"

Adam L. Alter, New York University, USA
Daniel M. Oppenheimer, Princeton University, USA
Anuj K. Shah, Princeton University, USA

Psychological distance—the subjective experience of distance from a target stimulus—influences many important judgments and decisions, including how objects in the environment are represented mentally, and which of two future monetary rewards people prefer. Researchers typically show these effects by manipulating how far the target stimuli are from the perceiver. In contrast, we suggest that people make such distance calculations spontaneously, even without explicit instruction. In particular, we argue that a stimulus feels psychologically close to the extent that it is easy to process. In Studies 1 and 2, we began by showing that people use processing fluency—the ease with which they process a stimulus—as a cue to determine the psychological distance of a stimulus (for related research, see: Alter and Oppenheimer, 2006, 2008, 2009; Alter, Oppenheimer, Epley and Eyre 2007).

In Study 1, participants believed that cities printed in a disfluent font were farther away than cities printed in a fluent font. Replicating this effect using a different instantiation of fluency, participants in Study 2 estimated the distance of cities whose names they either had or had not read in an earlier, ostensibly unrelated phase of the study. As expected, participants rated the cities as nearer when their names had been primed, and were therefore more fluent.

Having shown that fluency influences distance estimates, we examined the effects of fluency on mental construal, and future reward preferences. According to Construal Theory (Trope and Liberman 2003), the nearer we are to a stimulus, the more likely we are to focus on its concrete, specific details. As we move further away, we focus on its abstract, global properties. Participants in Study 3 were asked to write a one-sentence description of New York city. The request was printed in either an easy to read or a difficult to read font. As expected, participants generated more abstract descriptions of New York when the request was printed in the difficult to read font.

Study 4 replicate this effect using the conceptual fluency priming paradigm described in Study 2. Participants in Study 4 preferred concrete descriptions of Los Angeles when they had earlier been primed with the name of the city, but relatively preferred abstract descriptions when they were not earlier primed.

In Study 5, we showed that this effect also holds in a naturalistic environment, using a third instantiation of fluency: linguistic fluency. We collected archival data from a web-based community of Balderdash contestants. In the game of Balderdash, players attempt to generate plausible definitions for obscure English words. Consistent with Studies 3 and 4, participants generated more abstract definitions for words that were difficult to pronounce.

Psychological distance has similarly profound effects on intertemporal choice. When making intertemporal choices, people often discount the value of delayed rewards. This discounting is best modeled by hyperbolic or hyperbola-like functions (Green and Myerson 2004). These models of choice predict that adding a constant delay in front of two rewards might lead to preference reversals. For example, a person choosing between $10 immediately versus $15 in one week might prefer the immediate reward. However, when choosing between $10 in ten weeks versus $15 in 11 weeks this person might prefer the later reward, even though the absolute time difference between the two rewards is still one week.

Consistent with these findings, in Study 6, we found that participants were more likely to choose a larger, later reward (LL) than a shorter, sooner reward (SS) when the questionnaire was printed in a disfluent font rather than a fluent font. Since disfluency made both rewards seem more psychologically remote, the displeasure of waiting for the larger reward figured less prominently in participants' choices.

In contrast to this result, for immediate vs. delayed reward choices, we might expect disfluency to lead to diminishing preferences for the LL reward, because it would be perceived as farther away while the perception of the immediate reward would not change.

To test this prediction, participants in Study 7 imagined receiving a $75 Visa gift card that had no expiration date. Half of the participants were told that the gift card could be used immediately, half were told that the card could only be used after waiting for one year. They were then asked to imagine having to wait an additional two months before using the gift card and asked how much more they would need to be paid in order to wait. Half of the participants received questionnaires printed in a fluent font, whereas the other half received questionnaires printed in a disfluent font. As expected, when considering the immediately available gift card, participants in the disfluent condition asked for more money to wait than did participants in the fluent condition, whereas, when considering the delayed gift card, participants in the disfluent condition asked for less money to wait than did participants in the fluent condition.

This research therefore suggests that processing fluency is one plausible mechanism behind several fundamental processes in human cognition. Since fluency is cheap and easy to manipulate, these studies have useful implications for marketing researchers and practitioners who seek to shape how people construe goods and services.

References

Alter, Adam L. and Daniel M. Oppenheimer (2006), "Predicting Short-Term Stock Fluctuations by Using Processing Fluency," *Proceedings of the National Academy of Sciences*, 103 (June 13th), 9369-72.

Alter, Adam L. and Daniel M. Oppenheimer (2008), "Easy On The Mind, Easy on the Wallet: The Roles of Familiarity and Processing Fluency in Valuation Judgments," *Psychonomic Bulletin and Review*, 15 (October), 985-90.

Alter, Adam L. and Daniel M. Oppenheimer (2009), "Uniting the Tribes of Fluency to Form a Metacognitive Nation," *Personality and Social Psychology Review*, 13 (August), 219-35.

Alter, Adam L., Daniel M. Oppenheimer, Nicholas Epley, and Rebecca N. Eyre (2007), "Overcoming Intuition: Metacognitive Difficulty Activates Analytic Reasoning," *Journal of Experimental Psychology: General*, 136 (November), 569-76.

Green, Leonard and Joel Myerson (2004), "A Discounting Framework for Choice with Delayed and Probabilistic Rewards," *Psychological Bulletin*, 130 (September), 769-92.

Trope, Yaacov and Nira Liberman (2003), "Temporal Construal," *Psychological Review*, 110 (July), 401-21.

"Why Does Familiarity Affect Distance Judgments? The Discrepancy Attribution Hypothesis"

Manoj Thomas, Cornell University, USA
Charles Lindsey, State University of New York, USA
Arun Lakshmanan, University at Buffalo, State University of New York, USA

The burgeoning literature on the role of psychological distance in everyday decisions has prompted researchers to examine factors that influence distance judgments. In this research we focus on the role of metacognitive experience in distance judgments. Recent work by Alter and Oppenheimer (2008) has shown that distance judgments are influenced not only by the available cognitive information but also by the metacognitive experience evoked by the information. We extend this research by addressing two important questions about the role of fluency in distance judgments. First, we examine the generalizability of this effect by testing whether the metacognitive experience induced by familiarity has the same effect as that caused by manipulations of font, conceptual priming, or linguistic structure. While the latter manipulations are very useful tools to delineate the role of processing fluency in judgments in laboratory settings, familiarity is a more ubiquitous antecedent of metacognitive experience in everyday judgments. Some cities are more familiar than other ones. So distance judgments will feel easier for the familiar than for the unfamiliar cities. Will the metacognitive experience induced by familiarity with cities affect peoples' judgments of distance from the city? The first two experiments (Experiments 1A and 1B) reported in this research were designed to address this question. Our hypothesis is that people will judge familiar cities to be more proximal than unfamiliar cities and further, the familiarity effect in distance judgments will affect their economic decisions.

Second, we examine when and why familiarity affects distance judgments. Several researchers have suggested that familiarity is hedonically marked and that it elicits a positive affective response (e.g., Alter and Oppenheimer, 2008; Garcia-Marques and Mackie, 2000; Winkielman and Cacioppo, 2001; Winkielman, Schwarz, and Nowak 2002). For example, Winkielman & Cacioppo (2001) showed that familiarity affects physiological measures of positive affect. They found that familiar stimuli generated an incipient smile that manifested as higher activity over the zygomaticus major region of the face (cheek muscle). It has also been suggested that the relationship between familiarity and positive affect is bidirectional: illusions of familiarity can be produced through unobtrusive inductions of positive affect (Garcia-Marques & Mackie, 2000). However, all researchers do not agree with this perspective. Some have suggested that familiarity is affectively neutral and is subjectively interpreted based on contextual factors

(Mandler et al., 1987; Whittlesea and Williams 2001a; 2001b). Proponents of such familiarity-attribution models suggest that familiarity influences judgments only when it is perceived as surprising or discrepant. Experiments 2 and 3 were designed to test this discrepancy misattribution hypothesis.

Experiment 1A: Distance Judgments. The purpose of this study was to test the hypothesis that familiarity of a city can bias participants' distance judgments. In this experiment participants were asked to judge the distance between a famous US city (New York) and a relatively less known city (Ithaca). The same question was asked to resident of Ithaca as well as to residents of New York City. Participants were students recruited from university campuses in Ithaca and New York City were paid $5 for completing a short questionnaire. As predicted participants in NYC judged the distance between the two cities to be longer (M=5.92) than those in Ithaca did (M=5.18; F(1, 57)=4.07, p=.048). Experiment 1B demonstrates that such familiarity-induced bias could also affect participants WTP for products.

Experiment 2 & 3: Hedonic Familiarity or Discrepancy Attribution? These experiments were designed to investigate whether the familiarity effect in distance judgments is better characterized by the hedonic familiarity account or by the discrepancy misattribution account. Participants were asked to judge the relative distance to 24 US cities. We selected 12 pairs of US cities such that each pair was equidistant from the experimental location, but one city was relatively better known than the other (e.g., Los Angeles, CA and Hemet, CA are equidistant from the experimental location but the latter is unfamiliar). Some of these pairs were in the same state as the experimental location, while the other pairs were in far-flung states. If familiarity is hedonically marked, then we would expect the familiarity effect for all pairs irrespective of their actual distance from the experimental location. In contrast, the discrepancy misattribution hypothesis suggests that people expect themselves to be familiar with proximal but not distant cities. Therefore, they will find unfamiliarity to be discrepant only for the proximal cities. Results support the discrepancy misattribution hypothesis. The familiarity effect manifested only for proximal cities. Further, in Experiment 3, we identified the locus of the bias and found that the bias in distant judgments is caused by unfamiliarity and not by familiarity. These results do not support the hedonic familiarity hypothesis.

References

Alter, A. and D. Oppenheimer (2008), "Easy on the Mind, Easy on the Wallet: The Roles of Familiarity and Processing Fluency in Valuation Judgments," *Psychonomic Bulletin & Review*, 15(5), 985-990.

Alter, A. and D. Oppenheimer (2008), "Effects Of Fluency on Psychological Distance and Mental Construal (Or Why New York is a Large City, but New York is a Civilized Jungle)," *Psychological Science*, 19(2), 161-167.

Garcia-Marques, L. and D. Mackie (1999), "The Impact of Stereotype-Incongruent Information on Perceived Group Variability and Stereotype Change," *Journal of Personality and Social Psychology*, 78(4), 736-748.

Mandler, G., Y. Nakamura, and B. Van Zandt (1987), "Nonspecific Effects of Exposure on Stimuli that Cannot be Recognized. *Journal of Experimental Psychology: Learning, Memory, and Cognition*, 13(4), 646-648.

Whittlesea, B. (1993), "Illusions of Familiarity," *Journal of Experimental Psychology: Learning, Memory, and Cognition*, 19(6), 1235-1253.

Winkielman, P., N. Schwarz, and A. Nowak (2002), "Affect and Processing Dynamics: Perceptual Fluency Enhances Evaluations," in S. Moore and M. Oaksford (Eds.), *Emotional Cognition: From Brain to Behaviour,* Amsterdam, NL: John Benjamins, 111-136.

Winkielman, P. and J. Cacioppo (2001), "Mind at Ease Puts a Smile on the Face: Psychophysiological Evidence that Processing Facilitation Elicits Positive Affect," *Journal of Personality and Social Psychology*, 81(6), 989-1000.

"On the Psychology of Confidence-The Effects of Fluency and Construal Level on Confidence Judgments"

Claire Tsai, University of Toronto, Canada
Ann McGill, University of Chicago, USA

The present research explores the influence of the meta-cognitive cues on consumers' confidence judgments and proposes an important moderator for the fluency effect on confidence judgments, specifically, construal level (Trope & Lieberman, 2003). We find that when consumers adopt a low construal level, which highlights the feasibility of an outcome, fluency increases confidence. However, when consumers adopt a high construal level, which highlights the desirability of an outcome, fluency decreases confidence. We trace this latter effect, a reversal of prior findings regarding the role of fluency, to lay theories regarding the relationship between outcome desirability and effort.

Recent research has shown that fluency may not always have a positive effect on the underlying judgment, depending on the extent to which meta-cognitive experiences are judged to be diagnostic, the judgmental heuristics or theories used to interpret the subjective experiences of ease, and processing motivation. The present research adds to this emerging literature by positing that people interpret feelings of ease differently depending on construal level.

We hypothesize that when people think about feasibility, that is, at a low construal level, feelings of subjective ease should bolster confidence. Greater ease logically signals greater likelihood of achievement. By contrast, when thinking about desirability, that is, at a high construal level, people will reverse the effect. When people are confident that an outcome is desirable, they are willing to allocate more resources to achieving that outcome (Simmons & Nelson, 2006; Tsai et al., 2008) and would probably put forth greater effort. Hence, they may reverse this association and interpret greater effort to reflect greater confidence in the outcome. These hypotheses imply an interaction of fluency and construal level on confidence. This prediction distinguishes our work from two alternative explanations, sunk cost fallacy and cognitive dissonance. Both of these accounts predict a main effect, that is, greater effort leads to greater confidence in choice, but not an interaction effect.

We tested our proposition in two ways. In studies 1 and 3, we manipulated retrieval fluency by asking participants to think either of a few (easy) or many (difficult) reasons for their choice. In study 2, we manipulated processing fluency and presented a choice set using either an easy or a difficult to read typeface. Across all studies, we manipulated people's construal levels by using a priming task that appears to be irrelevant to the choice task.

In studies 1 and 2, we demonstrated the interactive effect of fluency and construal level on confidence judgments. In study 1, participants finished the priming task first and then proceeded to the main choice task where they were presented descriptions of two digital cameras and they generated either two or ten reasons for preferring one camera to the other. They were then asked to choose a product and indicate their confidence in their choice. As predicted, participants at lower construal levels exhibited the retrieval fluency effect and reported greater confidence when thought listing was easy (two reasons) than when it was difficult (ten reasons). On the contrary, participants at higher construal levels reversed the fluency effect and reported greater confidence when processing was difficult than when processing was hard. Study 2 replicated the results of study 1 with the typeface manipulation.

Study 3 was designed to obtain direct evidence for the role of retrieval fluency and construal level. We used a misattribution paradigm and showed that when participants attributed processing difficulty to the background music rather than the decision, the effects of retrieval fluency on confidence were eliminated. Study 3 not only generalized the findings of study 1 in a different product category (movie) but also showed that the effects of retrieval fluency and construal level on confidence were moderated by the interpretation of that feeling.

These findings provide a clearer picture of how fluency affects confidence judgments and identify construal level as an important moderator. To the extent that choices vary in their mode of presentation and that consumers vary in their internal states, the fluency experienced during choice and levels of construal will also vary. This variation will induce changes in confidence in choice and thus affect actual purchase decisions and the amount that consumers are willing to pay for an item.

References

Simmons, Joseph P. and Leif D. Nelson (2006), "Intuitive Confidence: Choosing Between Intuitive and Nonintuitive Alternatives," *Journal of Experimental Psychology: General*, 135 (August), 409–28.

Trope, Yaacov and Nira Liberman (2003), "Temporal construal," *Psychological Review*, 110 (July), 403-21.

Tsai, Claire I., Joshua Klayman, and Reid Hastie (2008), "Effects of Amount of Information on Judgment Accuracy and Confidence," *Organizational Behavior and Human Decision Processes*, 107 (November), 97-105.

"When it Happened Tells Us What Happened: The Effects of Temporal Distance and Metacognitive Inference on Word-Of-Mouth"

Robert Smith, University of Michigan, USA
Norbert Schwarz, University of Michigan, USA

A growing body of research shows that consumers draw inferences from their own metacognitive experiences (Lee 2004; Schwarz 2004), such as their subjective ease or difficulty of recall (Schwarz et al. 1991). What consumers conclude from these experiences depends on their naïve theories of mental processes. Most people assume, for example, that recent or important events are easier to remember than distant and unimportant ones. Hence, they conclude from ease of recall that the event was recent or important (Schwarz 2004). We extend this research by showing that consumers also draw inferences from the memory performance of others, an observation that is particularly important for the impact of word-of-mouth (WOM) information. Moreover, we document use of a naïve theory that has not been addressed in earlier research, namely that extreme events are better remembered than less extreme ones. Applying this theory to WOM reports, consumers are likely to infer from otherwise identical WOM information that a described service episode was more extreme, the more distant it is in time.

As a first test of these assumptions, participants in experiment 1 imagined that a friend was telling them about his experience at a restaurant. They then read a vivid, highly detailed paragraph about an enjoyable or unenjoyable restaurant visit that happened one week or one year ago and answered questions about how their friend felt about his restaurant experience. This 2 (valence) x 2(temporal distance)-factorial experiment revealed an interaction of both factors: when the event was negative, participants inferred that the experience was worse when it occurred one year rather than one week ago; the influence of temporal distance was less pronounced, and not significant, when the event was positive.

Follow-up experiments tested whether these inferences influence consumers' own behavioral intentions. On the one hand, the inferences observed in experiment 1 suggest that consumers may express less interest in going to the restaurant after receiving negative WOM information about a temporally distant rather than recent service experience. On the other hand, WOM accounts of distant service events are less diagnostic of the likely current service quality than accounts of recent service events–the unfriendly staff from last year may long have left, but the staff from last weekend will probably still be there. Hence, consumers may infer that the distant event was very bad, given that it is still remembered in detail, but may discount it as irrelevant when deciding whether they want to visit the restaurant themselves.

To assess whether consumers realize that distant service events are less predictive of what they might expect if they went to the restaurant now, experiment 2 asked participants to imagine that they are considering a restaurant visit. They then reported whether they would prefer to talk to someone who went to the restaurant a week ago or to someone who went there a year ago. Participants nearly unanimously preferred talking with someone who visited the restaurant a week ago, indicating that they clearly understand that recent service experiences are more diagnostic than distant ones. However, does this insight imply that they discount vivid reports of distant service events once they receive them? Or is the inferred extremity of the event so compelling that WOM information is nevertheless more influential when it pertains to distant rather than recent service events?

Experiment 3 addressed this question. Participants again read about a friend's positive or negative restaurant experience that happened one week or one year ago, resulting in a 2 (valence) x 2 (temporal distance)-factorial between-participants design. Replicating experiment 1, they inferred that their friend's negative experience was more extreme when his otherwise identical report pertained to last year rather than last week. However, the influence of temporal distance on inferences from positive events was small and nonsignificant. Paralleling this pattern, participants reported less interest in going to the restaurant if the recounted negative event occurred one year rather than one week ago; their intention to visit the restaurant was unaffected by temporal distance when the described event was positive. Thus, consumers' own intentions were influenced by their metacognitive inferences from the observation that a friend still remembered a negative service experience one year later, despite their general insight that distant service events are less diagnostic than recent ones.

On the theoretical side, these findings extend the analysis of metacognitive inferences in several ways. First, they provide first evidence that metacognitive inferences are not limited to inferences from one's own memory performance; instead, people also attend to others' memory performance as a source of information. However, second, they may only engage in this additional inferential work when the declarative information signals a problem that warrants extensive thought, that is, when the information is negative. This adds to the growing body of research showing a negativity effect in WOM (e.g., Ahluwalia 2002). Third, our findings also add to the growing list of naïve theories people use in drawing metacognitive inferences (Schwarz 2004): extreme events are better remembered than less extreme events. Hence, detailed memory of a distant event implies extremity; we term this the Distance-Extremity Bias. Finally, it is worth noting that this bias influenced consumers own intentions (experiment 3) despite the fact that they generally understand that distant events are less predictive of future service experiences than recent ones (experiment 2). On the managerial side, our findings highlight the importance of service recoveries, stressing the counterintuitive notion that service errors that occurred long ago may actually do more damage through WOM than recent service errors.

References

Ahluwalia, Rohini (2002), "How Prevalent is the Negativity Effect in Consumer Environments?" *Journal of Consumer Research*, 29 (September), 270-279.

Lee, Angela (2004), "The Prevalence of Meta-Cognitive Routes to Judgment," *Journal of Consumer Psychology*, 14(4), 349-355.

Schwarz, Norbert, Herbert Bless, Fritz Strack, Gisela Klumpp, Helga Rittenauer–Schatka, and Annette Simons (1991), "Ease of Retrieval as Information: Another Look at the Availability Heuristic," *Journal of Personality and Social Psychology*, 61 (August), 195–202.

Schwarz, Norbert (2004), "Metacognitive Experiences in Consumer Judgment and Decision Making," *Journal of Consumer Psychology*, 14 (4), 332-348.

SPECIAL SESSION SUMMARY

New Insights into Consumers' Inherent Preferences

Itamar Simonson, Stanford University, USA

SESSION OVERVIEW

"Inherent preferences" (Simonson 2008a, 2008b) refer to preferences that are established prior to a decision context and are thus distinguished from "constructed preferences" (e.g., Bettman et al. 1998). Following a lively debate on the subject in the JCP Dialogue (Summer 2008) as well as a lively ACR session in October 2007, the next challenge is to start an empirical research program on the determinants of inherent preferences. The objective is to gain a better understanding of often dormant inherent preferences (e.g., the preference for the experience involved in using a motion-sensitive remote that existed before Nintendo introduced the Wii videogame system) and the manner in which they may be revealed. That is the overarching goal of the proposed session.

There are different types of inherent preferences, ranging from previously constructed preferences to "hard-wired," inherited preferences. Regardless of the specific type, it has been proposed that dormant (i.e., yet to be uncovered) inherent preferences are most likely to be revealed through product experience, rather than during the decision process. The first paper in the session, by Chris Hsee and Adelle Yang, examines alternative sources of information regarding future experiences and corresponding inherent preferences. In particular, Hsee and Yang show (in a series of already completed studies) that other consumers' subjective experience evaluations with an object, especially if those were elicited in separate (rather than joint) option evaluations, are better predictors of a target consumer's inherent preference for the object than if the consumer him/herself tries to assess the object based on its objective attribute values.

The two other papers in the session use different methodologies to examine specific inherent preferences that can be described as hard-wired or even genetically-based. Shane Frederick examines the impact of inherent sex differences on time preferences and risk attitudes. Using his "Cognitive Reflection Test" or CRT (Frederick, 2005), he disentangles inherent vs. acquired origins of such fundamental differences. He also shows that, after controlling for CRT, the female "advantage" in time preference widens, and the female "deficit" in risk tolerance diminishes. The data further yield the surprising result that in the domain of losses, women are more risk-seeking than men. These studies have been completed.

Itamar Simonson, Aner Sela, and Gary Swann examine genetic influences on consumers' inherent preferences. Contrasting the preference similarity between identical twins and nonidentical twins, they identify the types of consumer preferences for which genetics appears to be a significant determinant and those that are not inherited. In particular, according to the data already available (at this point, about 70 pairs of each twin type), the tendency to not/compromise appears to have a significant genetic origin, whereas the tendency to not/seek asymmetrically dominating options does not differentiate identical and nonidentical twins. This finding is consistent with the notion that the reasoning function (involved in the decision whether to compromise) evolved more recently than the perceptual system (involved in the perception of relative attractiveness), which is more universal and less dependent on individual genes.

We believe that the session will be of much interest to attendees of the ACR conference regardless of their particular area of research (i.e., not just BDT types). It explores a new domain, which has not previously received much attention, and the various studies and sources of data are rather novel to our field and may lead to further research.

Our discussant will be Drazen Prelec of MIT, who will present his insights on the subject and the papers and moderate what is likely to be a lively discussion.

All participants have agreed to their role in the session.

EXTENDED ABSTRACT

"The Supremacy of Subjective Evaluations as Indicators of Inherent Preferences"

Christopher Hsee, University of Chicago, USA
Adelle Yang, University of Chicago, USA

Prior research suggests that inherent preferences are most likely to be revealed through experience. This project examines alternative predictors of experience. Suppose that you are shopping for a stereo system and have narrowed your options to two models. The two models are identical, except for the following: Model A can be remotely controlled and Model B cannot, whereas Model B delivers more output power than Model A. Since you are shopping online, you cannot hear their sound and therefore cannot tell how much more powerful Model B is relative to Model A. However, you could obtain one of the following three types of information regarding their sound powerfulness: (a) *Objective specifications*, that is, objectively measured output wattages (e.g., Model A is 100 watts and Model B is 200 watts); (b) *Subjective ratings elicited in comparison*, as obtained using the following procedure by an impartial research firm: A group of consumers similar to you were asked to audition and to compare the two models and then rate their sound powerfulness. You are then given the mean ratings of the two models; (c) *Subjective ratings elicited without comparison*, as obtained using the following procedure by an impartial research firm: Two groups of consumers similar to you were each asked to audition one of the two models without comparison. Each group then rated the sound powerfulness of the model they had auditioned on the 10-point scale. You are then given the mean ratings of the two groups/two models.

Suppose that you can receive only one of these three types of information, which one do you prefer, and which type of information will enable you to choose the model that best matches your inherent preferences and maximizes your overall satisfaction? The present research seeks to answer questions like the above. Through a large-scale experiment involving stimuli analogous to those described in the example above, we find, among others, the following two results. First, most consumers prefer objective specifications to subjective ratings elicited in comparison, and most consumers prefer subjective ratings elicited in comparison to subjective ratings elicited without comparison. Second, in contrast to their lay preferences, our study shows that consumers who receive the subjective ratings without comparison are most likely to choose the option that renders the best consumption satisfaction, and those who receive the objective specifications are least likely to do so. The reason is: subjective ratings without comparison best match consumers' inherent preference during consumption. Consumption is a matter of subjective experience rather than objective specifications, and consumption usually takes place in the non-comparative mode rather than in the comparative mode.

As will be discussed in presentation, this research both advances theory and yields significant practical implications. Theoretically, the present research extends three previous lines of research, relating not only to inherent preferences, but also to "lay rationalism" (Hsee et al. 2003), specification seeking (Hsee et al. 2009), and distinction bias (Hsee and Zhang 2004). In particular, the research shows that non-comparative subjective information provided by others can be better than objective specifications, because such subjective information best matches consumers' inherent preference during consumption. Practically, the present research suggests a new way of conveying information to potential buyers, especially online buyers. Currently, most online stores do provide objective specifications of their products, but do not often provide other consumers' (subjective) evaluations. Even if other consumers' evaluations are provided, they are not elicited systematically. Our research suggests a need for independent research firms to elicit non-comparative subjective ratings of the relevant attributes of target products, and for marketers to provide potential buyers such subjective information rather than objective specifications.

"Antecedents of Inherent Preferences: Cognitive Reflection and Other Sex Differences"

Shane Frederick, Yale University, USA

For most decision theorists, inherent dispositions (to avoid risk, maximize payoffs, seek variety, live close to campus, and minimize rent, ...) are taken as a given, and analyses revolve around the contextual features that highlight or suppress varied considerations which alter the weight that competing motives receive. By contrast, evolutionary biologists who study decisions usually focus on explaining the origins of the motives themselves in terms of historical selective pressures which may apply differently to different groups (e.g., women vs. men). In a distinction championed by Simonson (2008), decision theorists usually focus on "constructed preferences," in which choices are seen to shape preferences, whereas biologists focus on "inherent preferences," which choices merely reveal. Inherent preferences can accommodate constructed preferences provided the observed behavior is not so inconsistent as to invalidate the putative existence of the construct being assessed. Moreover, both approaches can coexist. For example, there may be evolutionary reasons why individuals are more risk seeking in losses than gains, but you can also "create" or accentuate this preference by focusing respondents attention on losses rather than on, say, probability or expected value.

In work which falls within the "inherent preferences" paradigm, Frederick (2005) found: (1) that scores on a "Cognitive Reflection Test" predict fundamental decision making characteristics, such as time preferences and risk attitudes, and (2) that males score much higher on this test. Those two facts jointly imply a third result which that paper did not discuss: (3) that controlling for CRT scores may modify conclusions about sex differences. For example, since lower scoring people are less patient, and since women score lower than men, the finding that men and women were equally patient suggests that sex would emerge as a significant predictor of time preferences if CRT scores were controlled for.

To test this logical implication, a composite patience index was formed for each respondent according to the proportion of times they chose a later, larger reward over a smaller, sooner reward (in choices such as $3,400 this month vs. $3,800 next month, $100 now vs. $140 next year). Although this index showed no significant sex differences, sex emerged as a significant predictor of time preferences after CRT scores were controlled. Indeed, for any given CRT score, females were significantly more patient than males. Thus, sex differences in CRT act to mask other (perhaps more essential) sex differences that affect time preference. These results suggest a rethinking of claims that sex plays a small role in determining time preferences, such the conclusion from Silverman's meta-analysis (2003, p. 459) that "gender accounts for only a small proportion of the variance in the ability to delay gratification."

In the domain of risky choice, including CRT as a covariate also has opposite implications for conclusions about sex differences. Specifically, since women score lower than men, and since lower scoring respondents are more risk averse, the marked sex differences in risk preferences is due partly to CRT differences (that is, to the cognitive variables that mediate performance on the CRT). Thus, though controlling for CRT does not affect the qualitative generalization that women are more risk averse than men (Byrnes, Miller, & Schafer, 1999), it does suggest that sex, per se, becomes a less potent predictor of risk preferences once CRT scores are controlled. Risk attitudes were assessed in terms of the proportion of times each respondent chose a gamble over a sure reward with smaller expected value (in choices such as $100 for sure vs. a 75% chance of $200, $100 for sure vs. a 3% chance of $7000, and so on). Men chose the gambles significantly more often than women (43% vs. 30%; $p<0.0001$), but these differences were smaller after CRT was controlled for.

A final analysis examined the effects of CRT and sex on risk seeking in the domain of losses. Surprisingly, there is next to no research on this topic. Even more surprisingly, the general finding that women are more risk averse than men is reversed in this domain. When faced with hypothetical choices between a sure loss and a gamble with a more negative EV (e.g., between losing $100 for sure or taking a 3% chance to lose $7,000), women chose the riskier gamble significantly more often than men (54% vs. 45%; $p<0.0001$). A control for CRT did not affect the average size of this effect, but did reveal that the sex difference increased with CRT score: among men and women who scored a "0" (out of 3), women chose the gambles only slightly more often than men (53% vs. 49%), but among those scoring a 3, the difference was considerable (55% vs. 42%; $p<0.05$).

Evolutionary or "socio-biological" accounts can accommodate some of the presented findings. For example, Baumeister (2008) conjectures that men's greater appetite for risk may reflect their historically larger reproductive upside of big payoffs. For example, a man might rationally prefer a 3% chance of 70 over 1 for sure if those reward units translate into offspring (since a man could father 70 children). However the upside of the great payoff is much smaller for women, who cannot birth more than a dozen or so children. Moreover, as a consequence of their rationally greater appetite for risks, males may expect to die sooner, which could help explain why males discount the future more than women (holding cognitive ability constant).

However, much more investigation is needed to separate the truthful components of these reasonable, but ad hoc conjectures. First, the evolutionary story does not account for the large effects of cognitive ability on such preferences. Second, sex differences in risk taking may be explained in terms of differences in probability weighting (see Fehr-Duda, De Gennaro, & Schubert, 2006), not differences in the curvature of the underlying value function. Third, the finding here that women are more risk-seeking in the domain of financial losses is not readily fitted into the customary evolutionary accounts.

"On the Heritability of Choice, Judgment, and "Irrationality": Are People Born To Live On the Edge or in the Mainstream?"

Itamar Simonson, Stanford University, USA
Aner Sela, Stanford University, USA

Most consumer preferences may appear too specific and context-driven in nature to be determined (in part) by genes. We were probably not born with any microwave oven gene, a Coke versus Pepsi gene, or even a peach ice cream gene. One does not need to be a strong (preference) "constructionist" (e.g., Bettman et al. 1998; Simonson 1993; Lichtenstein and Slovic 2006; Tversky et al. 1988) to know that most such product preferences are acquired, based largely on things such as experience, adaptation, social influence, and information. However, recent research does suggest the possibility that genetics plays a role in certain preferences and choices, such as jazz music (Tesser 1993), alcohol (e.g., Prescott and Kendler 1999), and voting behavior (Fowler et al. 2008). Moreover, there is robust evidence that intelligence (Bouchard 1996) and personality, especially the extroversion and neuroticism factors (e.g., Pedersen et al. 1988), are largely (~50%) genetically determined. The genetic origins of personality, in turn, lead to other predictable differences, including people's well-being (Weiss et al. 2008).

In the current project, we identify types or categories of preferences that might be, in part, genetically determined. Although we cannot have a strong theoretical basis for predicting that one particular preference will have a genetic component and another will not, we seek types of preferences for which we could develop reasonable hypotheses regarding genetic influence, because they appear to represent potentially inherent differences. To clarify, consider, for example, the difference between the tendency to compromise (versus selecting an "extreme" option from a given set) and the tendency to perceive an asymmetrically superior or dominating option as attractive (Huber et al. 1982; Simonson and Tversky 1992). Prior research has shown that the decision whether to compromise is conscious and "cognitive" whereas perceptions of (and preferences for) asymmetrically dominating options are "perceptual" and mostly unconscious (Dhar and Simonson 2003; Simonson 1989). Considering that the perceptual apparatus has evolved much earlier than the reasoning system, the latter is likely to be associated with greater variance across different pools of genes (e.g., families).

Accordingly, we expect to observe a stronger genetic effect on the tendency to not/compromise than on the tendency to select dominating options. Similarly, we selected several other preference types for which we believe that genetic influences could emerge and be explained based on general principles. These preference types include: (a) the tendency to select a variety of options across consumption occasions (e.g., Simonson 1990); (b) the tendency to balance rather than highlight/"go all the way" (Dhar and Simonson 1999); (c) consumer experiences that involve exhilaration/stimulation, such as riding motorcycles, roller coasters, and extreme sports, (d) artistic preferences, and (e) unique flavors (e.g., licorice, cilantro, and dark chocolate). In addition, we test whether certain judgment biases (e.g., representativeness, anchoring) have a genetic component.

Alternative methodologies for measuring the relative influence of genetics and the environment, and their respective shortcomings, have been discussed and debated extensively (e.g., Billings et al. 1992; Borkenau et al. 2001). The most commonly used method involves contrasting identical (or monozygotic) twins with nonidentical (dizygotic) twins (e.g., Fowler 2008; Weis et al. 2008). If identical twins (with 100% identical chromosomes) tend to be more similar than nonidentical twins on a certain dependent variable, controlling for shared environmental factors, then one can conclude that that DV has a genetic component. It is noteworthy that this methodology is not flawless, for example, because identical twins have been shown to meet (later in life) more often, and they might be treated differently by others (including their parents). We will use suitable covariates to try to control for these potential confounds.

We rely on this methodology in the current ongoing project, using the SRI International Twins Registry. Participants (N=140 pairs; expected final N=200 pairs) complete a 30-minute questionnaire online, which includes a broad range of previously pretested tasks from the decision making literature. Our data analysis has focused initially on the contrast between preferences for compromises and perceptually dominating options. The results so far appear to support the proposition that compromising, but not dominance, have a significant genetic component. More generally, this project has the potential to provide "deep" insights into the determinants of inherent preferences and enhance our understanding of the drivers of consumer decision making.

Special Session Summary

Where's My Bailout? A New Look at Factors Affecting Consumer Fairness Perceptions in the Age of Vengeful Populism

John Pracejus, University of Alberta, Canada

SESSION OVERVIEW

Populist outrage has arisen over a wide variety of behaviors in the wake of the financial crisis. Perceived unfairness seems to be a key driver of this outrage. Consumer research is uniquely situated to understand the factors that impact perceived unfairness, as we have been investigating it (in the context of prices) for over 20 years. The present special session proposal, therefore, brings together researchers who are exploring important factors affecting fairness perceptions of consumers. The session looks at how cultural, psychological and situational factors impact perceptions of fairness. Specifically, Bolton, Keh and Alba provide evidence that consumers in collectivist cultures are more influenced by group membership in their appraisal of fairness than are consumers in more individualist cultures. Furthermore, within a given culture, Popa and Pracejus demonstrate that a consumer's social value orientation can impact the degree to which they perceive it to be fair to pay more for something. Finally, Gneezy and Epley show that the perceived fairness of breaking (or exceeding) promises seems critically dependent upon whether the consumer is the maker or receiver of the promise. Taken together, these research streams converge to reveal that fairness assessments are far from universal, both across individuals and across situations. Given the particular importance of understanding how people assess fairness at this point in history, we believe that this session will not only be of interest to fairness researchers, but to a wider ACR audience who are certainly considering the new importance of such constructs in many consumer domains. The format of the session will be three presentations, no discussant. The session chair will briefly outline the idea of the session and the relationship between the presentations (2 minutes) followed by each presentation (18-20 minutes) and questions about individual presentations (4-5 minutes). After questions about the third presentation, if time allows, the session chair will encourage a general discussion about our evolving understanding of consumer fairness perceptions.

EXTENDED ABSTRACTS

"How Do Price Fairness Perceptions Differ Across Culture?"

Lisa E. Bolton, Penn State University, USA
Hean Tat Keh , Penn State University, USA
Joseph W. Alba, University of Florida, USA

A developing stream of research on consumer price perceptions has examined perceived fairness, including how reference points affect perceptions (Bolton, Warlop, and Alba 2003; for a review, see Xia, Monroe, and Cox 2004). More recently, Haws and Bearden (2006) found that price differences across customers (i.e., paying a higher price than another customer for the same product from the same vendor at the same time) led to particularly strong unfairness perceptions relative to price differences across products, vendors, or time. Following Haws and Bearden, we examine how dynamic pricing affects price fairness perceptions; however, we do so from a cross-cultural perspective. Previous research has examined the influence of culture on various aspects of consumer behavior, but cross-cultural research is scant with regard to price fairness. The present research addresses this issue by contrasting price fairness perceptions in two dominant economies: China and the United States.

China serves as a compelling contrast to the United States for several reasons. First, Chinese culture is commonly characterized as higher in collectivism and lower in individualism than American culture. Whereas Western cultures tend to define the self in terms of individual autonomy (i.e., that individuals are independent of one another), Eastern cultures define the self in terms of social connectedness (e.g., Markus and Kitayama 1991). The latter orients the Chinese toward in-groups and away from out-groups, given the in-group's greater self-relevance (Oyserman 1993; Oyserman, Coon, and Kemmelmeier 2002). Second, collectivist cultures are more concerned with face (i.e., status earned in a social network; cf. Ho 1976), scoring higher on measures of face concern (Zane and Yeh 2002; Oetzel and Ting-Toomey 2003) or face consciousness (Bao, Zhou, and Su 2003). In addition, Chinese language has more words for concepts related to face (such as losing face, and emotions related to loss of face) than does the English language (Ho, Fu, and Ng 2004; Bedford 2004; Hu 1994).

In a price-fairness setting, it seems reasonable to expect differences in price fairness perceptions arising from these cultural factors. We argue that paying a different price from others summons concern about face such that consumers gain (lose) face when paying a lower (higher) price than another consumer. In a collectivist (Chinese) culture, consumers are oriented toward the in-group, and therefore face concerns are stronger for in-group than out-group comparisons. Put simply, the gain (loss) in face of paying less (more) than another consumer is greater for in-group than out-group comparisons. Thus, collectivist (Chinese) consumers should experience a greater loss of face when a friend pays a lower price than when a stranger pays a lower price. (Similarly, collectivist/Chinese consumers should experience a greater loss of face when paying a higher price to a vendor with whom they have a long-term relationship than to a newly encountered vendor.) In contrast, face concerns among individualist (American) consumers are not expected to differ between in-group and out-group comparisons.

In a series of studies we investigate how cultural differences affect price fairness reactions to across-customer price differences. Study 1 provides an initial test by examining price fairness judgments by individualist (American) and collectivist (Chinese) consumers who pay a higher or lower price than an in-group or out-group member. Studies 2-4 provide evidence for psychological process. Special effort is made to determine the causal role of cultural differences through a manipulation of self-construal (study 2), measurement of the emotional role of shame evoked by face concerns (study 3), and analysis of the moderating role of public/private price comparisons (study 4). Finally, studies 5 and 6 test the robustness of the phenomena, utilizing an alternative operationalization of the in-group/out-group construct to extend our findings from customer-only relationships to customer-firm relationships (study 5) and to establish boundary conditions arising from other transaction factors (study 6).

The present research makes several contributions to the price fairness literature. First, we illuminate the role of culture (individualism/collectivism) in determining fairness reactions to across-customer price comparisons. Second, we provide evidence for multiple moderators in determining fairness response to across-customer price comparisons, including the type of referent (in-group/out-group and loyal/first-time buyer) and the public/private nature of the comparison. Third, we provide evidence for psychological process through causal evidence for the role of culture (via manipulations of independent/interdependent self-construal) and the role of face (via the face-related emotional responses of shame and anger across culture). Finally, we discuss the implications of our results for dynamic pricing and relationship marketing. To our knowledge, past research has not investigated price fairness reactions from a cross-cultural perspective nor, naturally, factors that would contribute to cross-cultural differences.

From a theoretical standpoint, we suggest that future cross-national research on price fairness should consider two fundamental dimensions: cultural differences and marketplace differences. We agree with other researchers who call for a more expansive consideration of cross-cultural variation beyond individualism/ collectivism and believe that face merits particular attention. Moreover, we suggest that the cultural environment "on the ground" also merits further attention—in this case, the characteristics of the marketplace (such as social norms, traditional practices, and socio-economic history) experienced by consumers that likely shape their attitudes, expectations, beliefs and behaviors. Further research on fairness and culture would contribute to a greater understanding of marketplace metacognition (Wright 2002)—how consumers think the marketplace does and should work—and how it is shaped by culture and developed through experience.

References

Bao, Yeqing, Kevin Zheng Zhou, and Chenting Su (2003), "Face Consciousness and Risk Aversion: Do They Affect Consumer Decision-Making," *Psychology & Marketing*, 20 (8), 733-755.

Bedford, Olwen A. (2004), "The Individual Experience of Guilt and Shame in Chinese Culture," *Culture & Psychology*, 10 (1), 29-52.

Bolton, Lisa E., Luk Warlop, and Joseph W. Alba (2003), "Consumer Perceptions of Price (Un)Fairness," *Journal of Consumer Research*, 29 (March), 474-91.

Haws, Kelly L., and William O. Bearden (2006), "Dynamic Pricing and Consumer Fairness Perceptions," *Journal of Consumer Research*, 33 (December), 304-311.

Ho, David Yau-fai (1976), "On the Concept of Face," *American Journal of Sociology*, 81 (Jan), 867-884.

Ho, David Yau-Fai, Wai Fu, and S.M. Ng (2004), "Guilt, Shame and Embarrassment: Revelations of Face and Self," *Culture & Psychology*, 10 (1), 64-84.

Hu, Hsien Chin (1944), "The Chinese Concepts of 'Face,'" *American Anthropologist*, 46 (1), 45-64.

Markus, Hazel Rose, and Shinobu Kitayama (1991), "Culture and the Self: Implications for Cognition, Emotion, and Motivation," *Psychological Review*, 98 (2), 224-253.

Oetzel, John G., and Stella Ting-Toomey (2003), "Face Concerns in Interpersonal Conflict," *Communication Research*, 30 (Dec), 599-624.

Oyserman, Daphna (1993), "The Lens of Personhood: Viewing the Self, Others, and Conflict in a Multicultural Society," *Journal of Personality and Social Psychology*, 65 (5), 993-1009.

Oyserman, Daphna, Heather M. Coon, and Markus Kemmelmeier (2002), "Rethinking Individualism and Collectivism: Evaluation of Theoretical Assumptions and Meta-Analyses," *Psychological Bulletin*, 128 (1), 3-72.

Wright, Peter (2002), "Marketplace Metacognition and Social Intelligence," *Journal of Consumer Research*, 28 (March), 677-682.

Xia, Lan, Kent B. Monroe, and Jennifer L. Cox (2004), "The Price is Unfair! A Conceptual Framework of Price Fairness Perceptions," *Journal of Marketing*, 68 (Oct), 1-15.

Zane, Nolan, and May Yeh (2002), "The Use of Culturally-Based Variables in Assessment: Studies on Loss of Face," in *Asian American Mental Health: Assessment Theories and Methods*, ed. K.S. Kurasaki, S. Okazaki and S. Sue, New York: Kluwer Academic/Plenum Publishers, 123-138.

Zhou, Kevin Zheng, Chenting Su, and Yeqing Bao (2002), "A Paradox of Price-Quality and Market Efficiency: A Comparative Study of the US and China Markets," *International Journal of Research in Marketing*, 19 (4), 349-365.

"Not Just Fairness: Understanding Consumers' Intentions to Buy FairTrade Products"

Monica Popa, University of Alberta, Canada
John Pracejus, Universtiy of Alberta, Canada

As disparities between developed and developing countries became more apparent, the recognition that different nations do not benefit to the same extent from growth of trade gave rise to the phenomenon of FairTrade. The principle of FairTrade advocates the sale of products at greater than free trade prices based on the premise that producers in developing countries have the right to a living wage, safe working conditions and human dignity. In practice, FairTrade allows consumers to help disadvantaged producers by paying higher prices for agricultural products, textiles and handcrafts. The process is overseen by the Fair Trade Labeling Organization, an international certification body that works with producers in over 55 countries.

Although the notion of fairness plays a crucial role in the FairTrade ideology, research has yet to establish whether consumers are indeed driven by fairness concerns when purchasing FairTrade products. The present paper examines this issue building on the marketing literature that studied perceived fairness (e.g. Bolton and Alba, 2006; Campbell, 1999; Haws and Bearden, 2006; Xia, Monroe, and Cox 2004) from the standpoint of equity and distributive justice. Equity theory (Adams, 1965) posits that individuals gauge the fairness of an exchange by comparing the ratios of their contributions versus the resulting outcomes. An exchange is perceived as fair if all parties receive the same outcome or ratio, whereas disparate ratios result in perceived unfairness. However, consumers often accept to pay higher prices to support a charitable cause, because this act is seen as a good deed and is encouraged by society norms. Importantly, research has pointed out that charitably paying a higher price is perceived as fair only for basic products, but not for luxury items such as chocolate truffles (Martins and Monroe, 1994).

Extending these ideas to the FairTrade domain, it is expected that consumers will be willing to pay the premium for FairTrade if they believe that it is equitable, and furthermore, this premium will be perceived as fair only in the case of basic products. Luxury items are, almost by definition, more expensive than basic products. Because a luxury-items-producer is typically able to command high prices, consumers will not find necessary to help it by paying an extra premium for FairTrade. In contrast, because a producer of basic commodities is less able to reap decent compensation, consumers will perceive a FairTrade premium for such products as being justified/ equitable. Thus, we hypothesize based on equity theory that consumers will be more willing to pay the FairTrade premium if the product is basic rather than a luxury.

An opposite prediction can be forwarded based on the charitable donations literature. Strahilevitz and Myers (1998) used the notion of affect-based-complementarity to show that donations are more likely to occur when bundled with hedonic/frivolous products (as opposed to utilitarian/practical products), because the monetary contribution alleviates the guilt associated with purchasing hedonic items such as chocolate truffles. Thus, affect-based-complementarity suggests that consumers will be more likely to contribute to FairTrade if the products offered are hedonic (rather than utilitarian). To the extent that luxury products can be equated with hedonic/frivolous products, and basic products can be approximated with utilitarian/practical products, equity theory and affect-based-complementarity generate contradictory predictions regarding the role of product type in consumers' willingness to buy FairTrade. These conflicting perspectives were experimentally tested in our research.

A pretest involving thirty-nine undergraduate students from a large North-American university identified rice and chocolate as appropriate utilitarian/hedonic stimuli. Respondents classified rice as primarily utilitarian and basic necessity, and chocolate as a primarily hedonic, luxury item.

In experiment 1, ninety-three participants who were prescreened to have no prior experiences with FairTrade products were randomly assigned to the utilitarian or the hedonic condition. Participants were presented with general information about FairTrade, followed by the dependent variable-likelihood to pay the FairTrade premium. Specifically, participants were asked to indicate if a FairTrade product costs 10% more than a regular product, how likely they would be to choose the FairTrade one (1= very unlikely; 7= very likely). The price premium of 10% was controlled based on prior research guidelines (e.g. Maietta, 2003). The results produced no main effect of product type, suggesting that neither equity theory nor affect-based-complementarity can be used as stand-alone frameworks for explaining consumers' likelihood to pay the FairTrade premiums. However, to investigate the possibility that both frameworks might be applicable, albeit for different consumer segments, individual differences were taken into account. Participants' social value orientation (SOV; a stable dispositional variable that reflects an individual's concern with equity) was measured following Kuhlman and Marshello (1975). Participants were classified as either prosocial or proself based on their SOV. Because prosocials are sensitive to fairness, whereas proself individuals do not have such concerns, we assumed that prosocials' behavior would be predicted by equity theory, and hypothesized that prosocial (but not proself) individuals would be more likely to pay the FairTrade premium if the product is utilitarian rather hedonic. Results supported this prediction, as a significant two-way interaction between product type and SOV was obtained. The mean difference between likelihood to pay the FairTrade premium when the product was utilitarian as compared to hedonic was significant and positive for prosocials, and insignificant for proself individuals.

In study 2, the influence of product type on consumers' likelihood to pay the Fair Trade premium was again assessed using a sample of seventy-eight North American undergraduates with no prior FairTrade product experiences. As in study 1, no main effect of product type was found. Fairness concerns were gauged using a priming procedure (e.g. Aart et al. 2005). Specifically, it was assumed that situational cues may impact individuals' concern with equity. As such, priming consumers with the concept of fairness should make them more likely to pay the FairTrade premium if the product is utilitarian. Participants in the equity-prime condition received a scrambled sentence task containing the words "equitable", "fair", "even", and "just", while those in the neutral-prime condition received words unrelated to any particular motivation. As expected, a significant two-way interaction between product type and priming was found. Participants primed with equity were more likely to pay the FairTrade premium if the product was utilitarian (vs. hedonic), whereas participants in the neutral prime condition were not significantly influenced by product type.

References

Adams, J. Stacey (1965), "Inequity in Social Exchange," in *Advances in Experimental Social Psychology*, Vol. 2, Berkowitz, Leonard (Ed), Academic Press, New York, 267-299.

Bolton, Lisa E., and Joseph Alba (2006), "Price Fairness: Good and Service Differences and the Role of Vendor Costs," *Journal of Consumer Research*, 33, 258-265.

Campbell, Margaret C. (1999), "Perception of Price Unfairness: Antecedents and Consequences of Satisfaction," *Journal of Marketing Research*, 36 (May), 187–199.

Chowdhury, Rafi M. M. I., G. Douglas Olsen, and John W. Pracejus (2008) "Affective Responses to Images in Print Advertising: Affect Integration in a Simultaneous Presentation Context," *Journal of Advertising*, 37, 3 7-18

De Pelsmacker, Patrick, Liesbeth Driesen, and Glenn Rayp (2005), "Do Consumers Care about Ethics? Willingness to Pay for Fair-Trade Coffee," *Journal of Consumer Affairs*, 39 (2), 363-385.

Haws, Kelly L. and William O. Bearden (2006), "Dynamic Pricing and Consumer Fairness Perceptions," *Journal of Consumer Research*, 33, 304-311.

Kuhlman, D. Michael, and Alfred F. Marshello (1975), "Individual Differences in Game Motivation as Moderators of Preprogrammed Strategy Effects in Prisoner's Dilemma," *Journal of Personality and Social Psychology*, 32, 922-931.

Martins, Marielza and Kent B. Monroe (1994), "Perceived Price Fairness: a New Look at an Old Construct," in *Advances in Consumer Research*, Vol. 21, Allen, Chris and John, Deborah R. (Eds), Association for Consumer Research, Provo, UT, 75-78.

Pham, Michel Tuan, Joel B. Cohen, John W. Pracejus, and G. David Hughes (2001) "Affect-Monitoring and the Primacy of Feelings in Judgment," *The Journal of Consumer Research*, 28, 2, 167-188

Pracejus, John W., G. Douglas Olsen and Norman R. Brown (2004) "On the Prevalence and Impact of Vague Quantifiers in Cause Related Marketing," *The Journal of Advertising*, 32, 4, 19-28.

Pracejus, John W. and G. Douglas Olsen (2004) "The Role of Brand/Cause Fit in the Effectiveness of Cause-Related Marketing Campaigns," *The Journal of Business Research*, 57, 6, 635-640.

Olsen, G. Douglas, John W. Pracejus, and Norman R. Brown (2003) "When Profit Equals Price: Consumer Confusion about Donation Amounts in Cause-Related Marketing," *The Journal of Public Policy and Marketing*, 22, 2, 170-180.

Strahilevitz; Michal and John G. Myers (1998), "Donations to Charity as Purchase Incentives: How Well They Work May Depend on What You Are Trying to Sell," *Journal of Consumer Research*, 24 (4), 434-446.

Xia, Lan, Kent B. Monroe, and Jennifer L. Cox (2004), "The Price Is Unfair! A Conceptual Framework of Price Fairness Perceptions," *Journal of Marketing*, 68 (October), 1-15.

"Doing More, Doing Less: Consequences of Exceeding vs. Falling Short of Promises"

Ayelet Gneezy, University of California—San Diego, USA
Nick Epley, University of Chicago, USA

Promises are a part of our daily lives; everyone makes promises, some of which are kept and others that are not. People make and receive promises from friends, family members, and colleagues. Children my promise their parents things they do not intend to deliver, and parents sometimes make promises they cannot keep.

Despite the prevalence of promises in social interactions, relatively little research investigates the consequences of making and keeping promises. This research takes a first step in understanding how promise makers and receivers account for promise keeping, and in particular examines how their judgments vary as a function of delivery level—whether the promise maker delivers more, less, or exactly as promised. We further look at the effect that one's role (promise maker or receiver) has on the way people account for promise keeping.

Based on past research that looked at how people integrate fairness considerations when evaluating others (Folger & Cropanzano, 1998; Tyler & Smith, 1998), supplemented by the pervasive dominance of negativity bias (Amabile, T. M., & Glazebrook, A. H., 1982; Cacioppo & Berntson, 1994), we predict that people's judgments of promise keeping will be systematically asymmetric, and specifically that relative to keeping a promise, falling short of one's promise will result in extremely negative responses, whereas exceeding a promise would have no effect. This prediction is further supported by the fact that people's fairness judgments tend to follow a binary scale where a behavior is either fair or unfair. We predict that keeping and exceeding promises would both be labeled as fair whereas falling short of a promise would be labeled as unfair.

Our second hypothesis stipulates that promise makers will consistently mispredict the effect that their behavior has on recipients, and in particular will tend to underestimate these effects. We expect promise makers to predict that recipients will be less appreciative of promises that are kept or exceeded, and more forgiving toward unfulfilled promises, than they actually are. Factors that contribute to this effect include egocentrism (Gilovich, Savitsky, & Medvec, 1998; Kruger, Epley, Parker, & Ng, 2005), the use of private information (Van Boven, Dunning, & Loewenstein, 2000), motivated reasoning (Kunda, 1990), and Social Contract Theory (Cosmides, 1989).

The first three experiments use hypothetical scenarios to test our hypotheses by manipulating participants' role and the extent to which the promise was kept (less, exactly, or more than promised). After reading the scenario participants reported happiness with the outcome, likelihood to trust the promise maker in the future, and interest in helping them in the future. The results provide an initial support for both the asymmetry, and misprediction hypotheses.

Experiment 1b used the same scenario to elicit responses, only this time we asked participants to characterize promise makers and in particular rate the extent to which they are selfish, fair and generous under each of the six scenarios. Consistent with our predictions, participants rated promise makers that delivered more than promised to be as generous and fair as promise makers that merely kept a promise. However, falling short of a promise resulted in significantly less favorable ratings. The results further support the misprediction hypothesis, indicating a significant difference between predicted and actual ratings of individuals' fairness and selfishness. The difference in generosity rating was non-significant. In Experiment 1c we explore whether, as would be predicted by Social Contract Theory, promise makers and recipients differ in the way they perceive promises, and consequently in their perceptions of individuals that fall short of promises. This was achieved by asking participants to rate the extent to which various personality traits (e.g., reliability, trustworthiness) describe promise makers. As predicted, promise makers failed to predict the extent to which recipients would perceive them as untrustworthy when falling short of a promise. Role had not effect on participants' ratings when promises were kept and exceeded. An additional scenario-based experiment provides support to our postulation that recipients' judgments of outcomes that follow promises are different than their judgment of outcomes that follow 'simple' reference points (Kahneman & Tversky, 1979).

The next experiment uses a more ecologically validated manipulation to test the asymmetry and misprediction hypotheses. Specifically, we asked participants to recall past experiences that involved promise making and keeping, and use those to elicit happiness ratings. This experiment used a 2(role: promise maker, promise recipient) X3(delivery level: less, exact, before) experimental design. Results support the asymmetry and misprediction hypotheses. Additionally, the results suggest that exceeding promises does not increase happiness because keeping a promise is highly regarded, not leaving space for improved evaluation of exceeded promises. A mediation analysis suggest that recipients are using actual delivery level to infer how much effort their counterparts expended in the attempt to keep their promises, which in turn influences their evaluations.

The final experiment utilized a natural setting that required students to complete an assignment for their class in pairs. In this experiment, we instructed one student in each pair to promise the other student that he will send his part of the assignment after 3 days. We instructed these students on what promise to make (complete 3/6 questions) and to what extent to keep their promise (complete either, 2, 3 or 4 questions). In addition to further supporting the two main hypotheses, the results of this experiment suggests that in addition to effort, recipients use promise makers' actual behavior (the extent to which they keep their promise) to infer their sincerity in making the promise. These inferences mediated recipients' overall attitude towards, and judgments of, promise makers.

To sum, it seems that contrary to lay belief, doing more than one promised has the exact same effect as merely keeping a promise. Falling short of one's promise, however, produces extremely negative evaluations. Interestingly, our results suggest that recipients' judgments of promise makers are guided by fairness judgments, perceived sincerity and inferred effort. Due to asymmetric information and motivated reasoning, promise makers consistently fail to predict the effect that their behavior has on recipients.

References

Alicke, M. D. (1985), "Global Self-Evaluations as Determined by the Desirability and Controllability of Trait Adjectives," *Journal of Personality and Social Psychology*, 49, 1621-1630.

Amabile, T. M. and A. H. Glazebrook (1982), "A Negativity Bias in Interpersonal Evaluation," *Journal of Experimental Social Psychology*, 18, 1-22.

Ames, D., F. J. Flynn, and E. U. Weber (2004), "It's the Thought That Counts: On Perceiving How Helpers Decide to Lend a Hand," *Personality and Social Psychology Bulletin*, 30, 461-474.

Anderson, N. H. (1965), "Averaging Versus Adding as a Stimulus-Combination Rule in Impression Formation," *Journal of Personality and Social Psychology*, 2, 1-9.

Andreoni, J. (1990), "Impure Altruism and Donations to Public Goods: A Theory of Warm-Glow Giving," *Economic Journal*, 100, 464-477.

Axelrod, R. (1984), *The Evolution of Cooperation*, New York: Basic Books.

Bazerman, M. H. (1985), "Integrative Bargaining in a Competitive Market," *Organizational Behavior and Human Decision Processes*, 35, 294.

Bem, D. J. (1967), "Self-perception: An Alternative Interpretation of the Cognitive Dissonance Phenomena," *Psychological Review*, 74, 183-200.

Blount, S. (1996), "The Price is or is it? A Reference Point Model of Two-Party Price Negotiations," *Organizational Behavior and Human Decision Processes*, 68, 1.

Berg J., J. Dickhaut, and K. McCabe (1995), "Trust, Reciprocity and Social History," *Games and Economic Behavior*, 10, 122-142.

Blau, P. M. (1964), *Exchange and Power in Social Life*, New York: John Wiley.

Brown, J. D. (1986), "Evaluations of Self and Others: Self-Enhancement Biases in Social Judgments," *Social Cognition*, 4, 353-376.

Brown, J. D. (1990), "Evaluating One's Abilities: Shortcuts and Stumbling Blocks on the Road to Self-Knowledge," *Journal of Experimental Social Psychology*, 26, 149-167.

Brown, J. D. and K. A. Dutton (1995), "Truth and Consequences: The Costs and Benefits of Accurate Self-Knowledge," *Personality and Social Psychology Bulletin*, 21, 1288-1296.

Cacioppo, J. T. and G. G. Berntson (1994), "Relationship Between Attitudes and Evaluative Space: A Critical Review, with Emphasis on the Separability of Positive aAnd Negative Substrates," *Psychological Bulletin*, 115, 401-423.

Cacioppo, J. T., W. L. Gardner, and G. G. Bemtson (1997), "Beyond Bipolar Conceptualizations and Measures: The Case of Attitudes and Evaluative Space," *Personality and Social Psychology Review*, 1, 3-25.

Campbell, J. D. (1986), "Similarity and Uniqueness: The Effects of Attribute Type, Relevance, and Individual Differences in Self-Esteem and Depression," *Journal of Personality and Social Psychology*, 50, 281- 294.

Campbell, W. K. and C. Sedikides (1999), "Self-Threat Magnifies the Self-Serving Bias: A Meta-Analytic Integration," *Review of General Psychology*, 3(1), 23-4

Charness, R. and M. Rabin (2000), "Social Preferences: Some Simple Tests and a New Model," *Mimeo*.

Clark, M. S. (1986), "Evidence for the Effectiveness of Manipulation of Communal and Exchange Relationships," *Personality and Social Psychology Bulletin*, 12 (4), 414-425

Clark, M. S., and J. Mills (1993), "The Difference Between Communal and Exchange Relationships: What it Is and Is Not," *Personality and Social Psychology Bulletin*, 19, 684-691.

Cosmides, L. (1989), "The Logic of Social Exchange: Has Natural Selection Shaped How Humans Reason? Studies with the Wason Selection Task," *Cognition*, 31, 187-276

De Cremer, D. and C. Sedikides (2005), "Self-Uncertainty and Responsiveness to Procedural Justice," *Journal of Experimental Social Psychology*, 41(2), 157-173.

Dholakia, U. M. and I. Simonson (2005), "The Effect of Explicit Reference Points on Consumer Choice and Online Bidding Behavior," *Marketing Science*, 24(2), 206-217.

Dunning, D. (1993), "Words to Live By: The Self and Definitions of Social Concepts and Categories," in J. Suls (Ed.), *Psychological Perspectives on the Self,* Vol. 4, Hillsdale, NJ: Erlbaum, 99-126.

Dunning, D., A. Leuenberger, and D. A. Sherman (1995), A New Look at Motivated Inference: Are Self-Serving Theories of Success a Product of Motivational Forces? *Journal of Personality & Social Psychology*, 69, 58-68.

Eibach, R. P. and J. Ehrlinger (2006), "Keep Your Eyes on the Prize: Reference Points and Racial Differences in Assessing Progress Toward Equality," *Personality and Social Psychology Bulletin*, 32(1), 66-77.

Emerson, R. (1976), "Social Exchange Theory," *Annual Review of Sociology*, 2, 335-362.

Epley, N., B. Keysar, L. Van Boven, T. Gilovich (2004), "Perspective Taking as Egocentric Anchoring and Adjustment," *Journal of Personality and Social Psychology*, 87, 327-339.

Fishbach, A. and Y. Trope (2005), "The Substitutability of External Control and Internal Control in Overcoming Temptation," *Journal of Experimental Social Psychology*, 41, 256-270.

Fiske, A. P. (1992), "The Four Elementary Forms of Sociality: Framework for a Unified Theory of Social Relations," *Psychological Review*, 99 (4), 689-723.

Folger, R. and R. Cropanzano (I998), *Organizational Justice and Human Resource Management*, Thousand Oaks, CA: Sage.

Gilovich, T., V. H. Medvec, and K. Savitsky (2000), "The Spotlight Effect in Social Judgment: An Egocentric Bias in Estimates of the Salience of One's Own Actions and Appearance," *Journal of Personality and Social Psychology*, 78, 211-222.

Gilovich, T., K. Savitsky, and V. H. Medvec (1998), "The Illusion of Transparency: Biased Assessments of Others' Ability to Read Our Emotional States," *Journal of Personality and Social Psychology*, 75, 332-346.

Gilly, M. C. and B. D. Gelb (1982), "Post-purchase Consumer Processes and the Complaining Consumer," *Journal of Consumer Research*, 9, 323-328.

Greenberg, J. (1991), "Motivation to Inflate Performance Ratings: Perceptual Bias or Response Bias? *Motivation and Emotion*, 15, 81-97.

Greenberg, J., T. A. Pyszczynski, and S. Solomon (1982), "The Self-serving Attributional Bias: Beyond Self-Presentation. *Journal of Experimental Social Psychology*, 18, 56-67.

Greenwald, A. G. (1980), "The Totalitarian Ego: Fabrication and Revision of Personal History," *American Psychologist*, 35, 603-618.

Guth, W., R. Schmittberger, and B. Schwartze (1982), "An Experimental Analysis of Ultimatum Bargaining," *Journal of Economic Behavior and Organization*, 3, 367-388.

Heath, C., Larrick, R. and G. Wu (1999), "Goals as Reference Points,“ *Cognitive Psychology*, 38, 79-109.

Heider, F. (1958), *The Psychology of Interpersonal Relations*, New York: Wiley.

Hirschman, A. O. (1970), "Exit, Voice, and Loyalty: Responses to Decline in Firms," *Organizations And States,* Cambridge, MA: Harvard University Press.

Hobbes, T. (1651), *Leviathan, or The Matter, Form and Power of a Commonwealth Ecclesiastical and Civil.*

Holyoak, K. J. and P. C. Gordon (1983), "Social Reference Points," *Journal of Personality and Social Psychology*, 44(5), 881-887.

Ito, T. A, J. T. Larsen, N. K. Smith, and J. T. Cacioppo (1998), "Negative Information Weighs More Heavily on the Brain: The Negativity Bias in Evaluative Categorizations," *Journal of Personality and Social Psychology*, 75, 887-900.

James, W. (1890), *The Principles of Psychology*, (Vol. 1), New York: Holt.

Jones, E. E. and R. E. Nisbett (1971), "The Actor and the Observer: Divergent Perceptions of the Causes of Behavior," in E. E. Jones, D. Kanouse, H. H. Kelley, R. E. Nisbett, S. Valins, & B.Weiner (Eds.), *Attribution: Perceiving the Causes of Behavior,* New York: General Learning Press, 79-94.

Kahneman, D. and A. Tversky (1979), "Prospect Theory: An Analysis of Decisions Under Risk," *Econometrica*, 47, 313-327.

Kelly, H. (1967), "Attribution Theory in Social Psychology," in D. Levine (Ed.), *Nebraska Symposium on Motivation*, Vol. 15, Lincoln, NE: University of Nebraska Press, 192-238.

Keysar, B. (1994), "The Illusory Transparency of Intention: Linguistic Perspective Taking in Text," *Cognitive Psychology*, 26, 165-208.

Kirmani, A. (1997), "Advertising Repetition as a Signal of Quality: If It's Advertised So Much, Something Must Be Wrong. *Journal of Advertising*, 26, 77-86.

Kruger, J., N. Epley, J. Parker, and Z. Ng (2005), "Egocentrism Over Email: Can We Communicate as Well as We Think? *Journal of Personality and Social Psychology*, 89, 925-936.

Kruger, J. and T. Gilovich (2004), "Actions, Intentions, and Trait Assessment: The Road to Self-Enhancement Is Paved With Good Intentions," *Personality and Social Psychology Bulletin*, 30, 328-339.

Kunda, Z. (1990), "The Case Formotivated Reasoning," *Psychological Bulletin*, 108, 480-498.

Lind, E. A. and T. R. Tyler (1988), *The social Psychology of Procedural Justice*, New York: Plenum.

Locke, J. (1689), *Two Treatises on Government.*

Mittal, V. and W. A. Kamakura (2001), "Satisfaction, Repurchase Intent, and Repurchase Behavior: Investigating the Moderating Effect of Customer Characteristics," *Journal of Marketing Research*, 38, 131-142.

Nickerson, R. S. (1999), "How We Know—and Sometimes Misjudge—What Others Know: Imputing One's Own Knowledge to Others," *Psychological Bulletin*, 125, 737-759.

Offerman, T. (1998), "Hurting Hurts More Than Helping Helps: The Role of the Self-Serving Bias," *Mimeo.*

Rabin, M. (1993), "Incorporating Fairness Into Game Theory and Economics," *American Economic Review*, 83, 1281-1302.

Richins, M. (1983), "Negative Word-of-mouth By Dissatisfied Consumers: A Pilot Study. *Journal of Marketing*, 47, 68-78.

Richins, M. (1987), "A Multivariate Analysis of Responses to Dissatisfaction," *Academy of Marketing Science*, 15, 24-31.

Ritov, I. (2000), "The Role Of Expectations in Comparisons," *Psychological Review*, 107, 345-357.

Robinson, R. J., D. Keltner, A. Ward, and L. Ross (1995), "Actual Versus Assumed Differences in Construal: 'Naive Realism' in Intergroup Perception and Conflict," *Journal of Personality and Social Psychology*, 68, 404-417.

Ross, L. and A. Ward (1996), "Naive Realism in Everyday Life: Implications for Social Conflict and Misunderstanding," in T. Brown, E. Reed, and E. Turiel (Eds.), *Values and Knowledge,* Hillsdale, NJ: Lawrence Erlbaum Associates, 103-135.

Rozin, P. and E. B. Royzman (2001), "Negativity Bias, Negativity Dominance, and Contagion," *Personality and Social Psychology Review*, 5, 296-320.

Rousseau, J. (1762), *The Social Contract, or Principles of Political Right.*

Savitsky, K., N. Epley, and T. Gilovich (2001), "Do Others Judge Us As Harshly as We Think? Overestimating the Impact of Our Failures, Shortcomings, and Mishaps," *Journal of Personality and Social Psychology*, 81, 44-56

Sedikides, C. and A. P. Gregg (2003), "Portraits of the Self," in M. A. Hogg and J. Cooper (Eds.), *Sage Handbook of Social Psychology*, London: Sage, 110–138.

Sedikides, C. and M. Strube (1995), "The Multiply Motivated Self," *Personality and Social Psychology Bulletin*, 21, 1330-1335

Sedikides, C. and M. J. Strube (1997), "Self-evaluation: To Thine Own Self Be Good, to Thine Own Self Be Sure, to Thine Own Self Be True, and to Thine Own Self Be Better," in M. P. Zanna (Ed.), Advances in Experimental Social Psychology, Vol. 29, New York: Academic Press, 209–269.

Simmel, G. (1950), *The Sociology of George Simmel*, New York: The Free Press.

Singh, J. (1990a), "A Typology of Consumer Dissatisfaction Response Styles," *Journal of Retailing*, 66, 57-99.

Singh, J. (1990b), "Voice, Exit, and Negative Word-of-mouth Behaviors: An Investigation Across Three Service Categories," *Journal of the Academy of Marketing Science*, 18, 1-15.

Sobel, M. E. (1982), "Asymptotic Confidence Intervals for Indirect Effects in Structural Models," in S. Leinhardt (Ed.), *Sociological Methodology*, San Francisco: Jossey-Bass, 290–312.

Straughan R. D. and M. W. Lynn (2002), "The Effects of Salesperson Compensation on Perceptions of Salesperson Honesty," *Journal of Applied Social Psychology*, 4, 719-731.

Szykman, L. R, P. N. Bloom, and J. Blazing (2004), "Does Corporate Sponsorship of a Socially-Oriented Message Make a Difference? An Investigation of the Effects of Sponsorship Identity on Responses to an Anti-Drinking and Driving Message," *Journal of Consumer Psychology*, 14, 13-20.

Taylor, S. E. and J. D. Brown (1988), "Illusion and Well-Being: A Social Psychological Perspective on Mental Health," *Psychological Bulletin*, 103, 193-210

Thaler, R.H. (1980), "Towards a Positive Theory of Consumer Choice," *Journal of Economic Behavior and Organization*, 1, 39-60.

Tooby, J. and L. Cosmides (1996), "Friendship and the Banker's Paradox: Other Pathways to the Evolution of Adaptation for Altruism," in W. Runciman, J. Maynard Smith, and R. Dunbar (Eds.), *Evolution of Social Behavior Patterns in Primates and Man.* Proceedings of the Boritish Academy, 88, 119-143.

Trivers, R. (1971), "The Evolution of Reciprocal Altruism," *Quarterly Review of Biology*, 46, 35-57

Tversky, A. and D. Kahneman (1991), "Loss Aversion in Riskless Choice: A Reference-Dependent Model," *Quarterly Journal of Economics*, (106), 1039-1061.

Tyler, T. R. and E. A. Lind (1992), "A Relational Model of Authority in Groups," in M. Zanna (E,d.), *Advances in Experimental social psychology*, Vol. 25, San Diego, CA: Academic Press, 115-191.

Tyler, T. R. and H. J. Smith (1998), "Social Justice and Social Movements," in D. Gilbert, S. T. Fiske, and G. Lindzey (Eds.), *Handbook of Social Psychology*, Vol. 4, Boston: McGraw-Hill, 595-629.

Van Boven L., D. Dunning, and G. Loewenstein (2000), Egocentric Empathy Gaps Between Owners and Buyers: Misperceptions of the Endowment Effect," *Journal of Personality and Social Psychology*, 79, 66-76.

Special Session Summary

A Voter Among Voters: Political Decisions in the Social Context

Yesim Orhun, University of Chicago, USA

SESSION OVERVIEW

There has been a resurgence of interest recently in looking at politics and voting as a context in which to investigate broader issues in consumer decision making (e.g. Bechwati and Morrin 2007; Goldstein, Imai and Gollwitzer 2009, Hedgcock, Rao, and Chen 2009; Kim, Rao, and Lee 2009, Phillips, Urbany and Reynolds 2008, Zemborian and Johar 2007).

This session takes the point of view that political contexts are often an ideal environment in which to investigate the role of social influences on choice, judgment and evaluation, and the resulting consequences. For example, in an election, voters are largely responding to the same events as other voters as the campaign proceeds, and are simultaneously affected by pivotal events in a campaign, such as a debate or a high-profile negative advertisement. Furthermore, voters encounter information about how others are reacting to the campaigns and often spontaneously form inferences about the attitudes and intentions of other voters. The combination of information and inferences that voters have are then an important driver of the choices they make, and of the actions taken by campaigns.

In the first paper, Orhun and Urminsky study the inferences voters made about the electorate in the 2008 presidential election. They extend the intuition of false consensus to projection of evaluations underlying choice, providing evidence that it is this projection of candidate evaluations that underlies projection of candidate choice. They further demonstrate that voters project the way in which own evaluations led to choice, rather than evaluations themselves, onto both like-minded voters and supporters of the opposing candidate, contrary to the literature.

In the second paper, Ramanathan, McGill, Phillips, Schill and Kirk study the effect of social influences on undecided voters watching the general election debates. They find that evaluations made by people attitudinally distant from each other to begin with tended to co-vary to a greater extent with each other when such individuals sat next to each other as opposed to separately, while those who were attitudinally close to each other to begin with were not affected by seating arrangement. In particular, sitting next to someone with very different views led to greater polarization in post-debate attitudes.

In the third paper, Lovett and Shachar use a detailed secondary dataset on recent US congressional and presidential races to investigate the impact of voters' knowledge on campaigns decision to "go negative" in their advertising. They present an econometric model in which ads inform voters on the good traits of the candidate or the bad traits of his opponent. They find that, consistent with the model, the proportion of negative ads increases with voters' knowledge and candidate budget, helping to explain why negative ads are more prevalent in close races.

This special session is aimed at furthering current interest in the area and will help identify promising directions for future research. Akshay Rao, who has himself conducted influential research in this area, will serve as discussant, encouraging an audience discussion of the papers as well as a more general discussion of the role of social influences on political behavior and the implications of these findings for understanding social influences on consumer behavior.

EXTENDED ABSTRACTS

"Choosing Differently But in the Same Way: How Self Impacts Beliefs About Other Voters"

Yesim Orhun, University of Chicago Booth School, USA
Oleg Urminsky, University of Chicago Booth School, USA

Political decision-making fundamentally involves strategic behavior, such that decisions about who to vote for, how much resources to devote to a candidate and whether to vote involve beliefs about what others are likely to do. Traditional economic approaches assume that beliefs about others are not systematically biased. In contrast, psychological research has provided evidence for systematic biases, with own choices impacting inferences about others' choices, such as false consensus (Ross, Greene and House 1977) and other projective biases (e.g. Monin and Norton 2003).

The literature on social projection has generally demonstrated that endorsement of an attitude leads to higher estimation of the degree of endorsement in a population, and that this effect will be moderated by perceived similarity to the reference population (e.g. Ames 2004). We argue that, beyond simple endorsement, the intensity of attitudes and preferences plays a key role in social projection onto beliefs about the attitudes and preferences of others, which has not been systematically investigated in the literature. Furthermore, the literature has largely concluded that there is little or no projection of own attitudes when making estimates for an out-group population (e.g. meta-analysis by Robbins and Krueger 2005). In contrast, we argue that while voters do not directly project their own evaluations onto out-groups (i.e. supporters of the opposing candidate) they do in fact utilize their own preferences in making these evaluations. Specifically, voters will recognize the difference in candidate preferences between themselves and the out-group, and will instead project the way their own views gave rise to their own choice in estimating the views in the out-group. This notion of conditional preference projection implies that the more strongly a voter supports their own candidate, the more they will infer that supporters of the opposing candidate strongly support their own candidate as well.

We present data from three studies conducted during the 2008 presidential election, as well as a reanalysis of historical data from the 2000 and 2004 elections. These include a national poll of voters making inferences about other national voters conducted shortly before the general election, a two-wave national poll conducted directly before and after the first presidential debate and an incentive-compatible lab study in which participants were compensated based on the accuracy of their inferences. Across the studies, we also addressed some methodological limitation in the literature, which generally involves estimating binary responses or typical responses on a continuous scale, which confounds inferences about summarizing the population as a whole with inferences about a single exemplar. In our studies participants estimated the entire distribution of responses for the reference population. Furthermore, our data enables us to account for the distinction between the effects of actual similarity and perceived similarity, to both in-group (like-minded voters) and out-group (supporters of the opposing candidate).

Across the studies, we replicate the false consensus effect for estimates of choices among all voters, and demonstrate that this choice projection is driven by the projection of underlying candidate evaluations. Furthermore, for the in-group of voters supporting one's own candidate, we find that projection of evaluations explains differences in beliefs across voters making the same choice. Inferences about the candidate ratings of other like-minded voters are systematically biased towards one's own candidate evaluations. Thus, we demonstrate that the projection of attitudes extends beyond mere endorsement to intensity of attitudes and preferences.

For the out-group of voters supporting the opposing candidate, our studies demonstrate a novel effect of projecting the way one's evaluations lead to choice onto others with opposing views. Our findings are consistent with our proposed framework of conditional preference projection, but are inconsistent with the processes proposed to account for social projection, particularly the anchoring hypothesis, which assumes that projection does not extend to the out-group. Specifically, we find that the higher voters rated their preferred candidate, the more they believed that supporters of the opposing candidate would rate that opposing candidate highly. Importantly, we find no effect on same-candidate evaluations: the degree of liking of own candidate (e.g. Obama among Obama-voters) did not affect the estimated liking of that candidate in the out-group (e.g. Obama among McCain-voters). This supports our argument that the inference that occurs is a higher-level projection of a rule of liking (e.g. they support their candidate in the same way I support mine), and helps rule out alternative explanations such as scale bias, motivated responding or simple assimilation-contrast effects.

These effects are found to be highly robust across populations and elicitation methods and are demonstrated both across individuals as well as within respondents who have changed their views over time. We will also discuss the impact of these findings on inferences for related actions (such as donating and volunteering) as well as the implications of our findings for strategic behavior in general.

"Are Political Opinions Contagious? An Investigation on the Effects of Seating Position and Prior Attitudes on Moment-to-Moment Evaluations During the Presidential Debates"

Suresh Ramanathan, University of Chicago Booth School, USA
Ann McGill, University of Chicago Booth School, USA
Joan Phillips, Loyola University, USA
Daniel Schill, Southern Methodist University, USA
Rita Kirk, Southern Methodist University, USA

Political opinions evolve as a result of a variety of factors including information gathered from news sources and opinion leaders, and interactions with friends, family and neighbors. Casual remarks made by a friend or discussions with neighbors across the backyard fence may guide people's attitudes towards a candidate. Individuals are thus embedded in a larger social network that may determine the degree of exchange of information (Eulau 1986, Huckfeldt and Sprague 1987). However, most prior research has focused on tangible exchange of information in well-formed social networks. In this paper, we show that social influence may color political views despite no obvious or tangible communication among individuals brought together in an ad hoc social group of undecided voters. Specifically, we show that people who are more distant from each other in their attitudes towards candidates are more sensitive to social influences, but in a direction leading to greater polarization of attitudes. We contrast our findings to Ramanathan and McGill (2007), who showed that greater synchrony among strangers sharing an experience led to more positive evaluations of the experience.

The data for this study were the responses of 30 undecided voters on a CNN rating panel during the third Presidential debate in 2008. Respondents (12 Democrats, 11 Independents and 7 Republicans) provided their political identification, degree of liberal or conservative values and initial attitudes towards Obama and McCain, both as a summary judgment on a 100 point scale as well as in the form of evaluations on a 12-item scale (qualified, sophisticated, honest, believable, successful, attractive, friendly, sincere, calm, aggressive, strong, active). They then evaluated the candidates' performance on the debate via a rating dial anchored on 0=Not at all positive and 100=Very positive. The debate lasted approximately 90 minutes and data were collected every second. Following the debate, respondents were again asked to provide their attitudes towards each candidate on both the summary scale and the 12-item scale. They were also asked to indicate whom they would be voting for. A seating map indicated the position of each respondent in the room.

After mean-centering the time-series data, we applied a band-pass filter to remove high frequency noise. Our interest was in a band of frequencies ranging from every minute to every 15 minutes. Given that each candidate spoke for at least one minute at any time, and the length of the longest segment in the debate was about 15 minutes, this band of frequencies seems reasonable. We wished to see if there was any influence of the two people to the immediate left and right of a focal respondent. A cross-spectral analysis of each pair of participants was used to determine the "coherence" in the two time series (see Ramanathan and McGill 2007). A high coherence at a given frequency indicates that one person's evaluations predict the other's evaluations very well at that frequency. For each triad, we computed a measure called multiple coherence, which represents the coherence between one person's evaluations and an optimal linear combination of the evaluations of the persons to the left and right (Jenkins and Watts 1968). For each triad, we also computed the attitudinal distance among the respondents. This was done by treating the attitudes of the neighbors as forces of influence along two dimensions–support for Obama and support for McCain. The magnitude of the resultant vector is computed as the square root of the sum of the squares of the net pull towards Obama and the net pull towards McCain. For a statistical control, we constructed arbitrary triads of participants from the same data, using people not sitting next to each other, but sharing the same political leanings and opinions as the ones actually sitting next to each other. Thus, we created false triads with the same political characteristics as the true triads.

A regression on the multiple coherence for each triad was run with seating arrangement (true versus false neighbors), mean-centered attitudinal distance and the interaction term as predictors. Results showed a significant main effect of seating arrangement with a greater coherence among true versus false neighbors. This was qualified by a significant interaction between seating and attitudinal distance. Attitudinally distant participants had a greater coherence when they sat next to each other compared to the false neighbor condition; people who were attitudinally close to each other did not experience any greater coherence due to seating. Importantly, the greater coherence among attitudinally distant people sitting close to each other was not due to agreement but rather more predictable disagreement–the evaluations of these participants were always out of phase by between 90-180 degrees in the spectral analysis, suggesting lack of synchrony.

Further, we found that the increased coherence in evaluations led to more sharply polarized attitudes post-debate. This effect was particularly pronounced among McCain supporters, suggesting that social signals emitted by Obama supporters during the debate may have been particularly impactful on McCain supporters, leading them to polarize in their attitudes. The effect of initial attitudinal distance on final distance was mediated by coherence, but only for those seated next to each other.

Our findings suggest that political opinions can indeed leak via subtle social influence and cause people to alter their own opinions. We are presently analyzing the data from the second debate and will be able to present findings from both debates at the conference.

"The Seeds of Negativity: Knowledge and Money"

Mitchell J. Lovett, University of Rochester, USA
Ron Shachar, Duke University, USA

In commercial environments firms can improve their standing (profits, stock value, etc.) either by becoming more attractive to their audience (i.e., positive appeals) or by making their competitors less appealing (i.e., negative appeals). While some combative acts, such as sabotaging competitors' products, are forbidden by law, comparative (which implicitly includes negative appeals) advertising is not only allowed, but even encouraged by the Federal Trade Commission. Furthermore, the portion of comparative advertisements out of all advertisements has been approximated as close to one out of three (Niemann 1987), representing a substantial advertising volume. Further, recent media claims even suggest that negative advertising in commercial settings is on the rise (York 2008).

This study presents a model of negative advertising and examines it empirically. In order to learn the most about negative advertising, we focus on an application in which negativity is frequent and exhibits high variation—political campaigns. In their own right, political campaigns represent an important advertising market with over $2.5 billion in ad spending in 2008 (Atkinson, Dec. 2008) and, of course, important consequences. Further, political campaigns present an understudied, interesting empirical regularity about negativity—that is, the greater tendency to go negative in competitive elections. For example, in the 2000 Senate elections the portion of all ads that were negative was 33% in noncompetitive races but 65% in competitive races (Goldstein and Freedman 2002a). This empirical regularity is important both because it is a central feature of the application studied here (i.e., political campaigns) and because, more generally, it is an intriguing relationship between competition and advertising tone. Thus, we believe that a model that can explain this regularity is likely to be insightful about the strategic forces behind negative advertising. Thus, we model candidates' decisions to go negative in political advertising and aim to explain this regularity.

We present a model of electoral competition with two candidates—a Republican and a Democrat. Each candidate has good traits (e.g., effective manager) and bad traits (e.g., performs badly under pressure). Of course, voters' utility increases in the candidate's good traits and decreases in the bad traits, but not all of the traits are known to the public. Each candidate faces a limited budget and tries to maximize total votes by allocating his budget between ads that present his good traits (i.e., positive advertising) and ads that present his opponent's bad traits (i.e., negative advertising). Voters combine this information from ads with other sources of information to form impressions of candidates. As a point of departure from existing studies, we incorporate recent psychological evidence that supports nonlinear asymmetric responses of overall attitudes to positive and negative beliefs (Holbrook et al. 2001). We find that in equilibrium the proportion of negative ads increases with voters' knowledge and the candidate's budget. Interestingly, close races are not only characterized by high negativity, but also by (a) high media coverage (West 1994) which can lead to high knowledge and (b) large marketing spending (i.e., large budgets) by the candidates (Goldstein and Freedman 2002a). In this sense, our model can tie together these three empirical regularities.

In order to examine the model and its implications, we collect data on the elections for the US House of Representative in 2000, 2002 and 2004 and for US president in 2000 and 2004. Our key theoretical variables of interest are the portion of all ads that are negative, the total budget of ads, the closeness of the race, and voter knowledge. There are various challenges in the data collection. The most dramatic of which is getting information on voters' knowledge, particularly measures that distinguish the positive and negative aspects of knowledge about a particular candidate. Furthermore, this task is especially difficult for the congressional elections, where very little candidate specific information is available through surveys. Still, the evidence is supportive for our theory. Our results suggest that our theoretical variables contribute significantly to the explanation of candidate negativity. As expected by our model, as budget increases negativity increases and as both positive knowledge about a candidate increases and the negative about the opponent increases, the candidate goes more negative. Further, once accounting for knowledge and budget, the effect of closeness is significantly attenuated. Thus, the data is quite supportive for the effects of knowledge and budget on negativity and the theory helps to explain why close political races are more negative.

We finish with a discussion of the implications of this study. We discuss future directions for research in political advertising including extending this research to a dynamic context. Finally, we discuss the potential for transfer of the ideas to commercial settings.

REFERENCES

Ames, D. R. (2004), "Strategies for Social Inference: A Similarity Contingency Model of Projection and Stereotyping," *Journal of Personality and Social Psychology*, 87 (5).

Atkinson, Claire (2008), "2008 Political Ads Worth $2.5 Billion to $2.7 Billion," *Broadcasting & Cable*, 12/1/2008 11:00PM MT (retrieved online).

Bechwati, Nada Nasr and Maureen Morrin (2007), "Understanding Voter Vengeance," *Journal of Consumer Psychology*, 17 (4), (Oct), 277-291.

Eulau, Heinz (1986), *Politics, Self, and Society*, Cambridge, MA: Harvard University Press.

Goldstein, D. G., K. Imai, A. S. Göritz, and P. M. Gollwitzer (2009), "Nudging Turnout: Mere Measurement and Implementation Planning of Intentions to Vote," Working Paper.

Goldstein, Ken and Paul Freedman (2002a), "Lessons Learned: Campaign Advertising in the 2000 Elections," *Political Communication*, 19, 5-28.

Jenkins, Gwilym M. and Donald G. Watts (1968), *Spectral Analysis and Its Applications*, San Francisco, CA: Holden-Day.

Hedgcock, William, Akshay Rao, and Haipeng Chen (2009), "Could Ralph Nader's Entrance and Exit Have Helped Al Gore? The Impact of Decoy Dynamics on Consumer Choice," *Journal of Marketing Research*, forthcoming.

Holbrook, Allyson L., Jon A. Krosnick, Penny S. Visser, Wendi L. Gardner, and John T. Cacioppo (2001), "Attitudes Toward Presidential Candidates and Political Parties: Initial Optimism, Inertial First Impressions, and a Focus on Flaws," *American Journal of Political Science*, 45 (4), 930-950.

Huckfeldt, Robert and John Sprague (1987), "Networks in Context: The Social Flow of Political Information," *The American Political Science Review*, 81 (4), 1197-1216

Kim, Hakkyun, Akshay Rao, and Angela Lee (2009) "It's Time to Vote: The Effect of Matching Message Orientation and Temporal Frame on Political Persuasion," *Journal of Consumer Research*, 35 (6) (Apr), 877-889.

Monin, B. and M. Norton (2003), "Perceptions of a Fluid Consensus: Uniqueness Bias, False Consensus, False Polarization, and Pluralistic Ignorance in a Water Conservation Crisis," *Personality and Social Psychology Bulletin*, 29, 559.

Niemann, Janet (1987), "The Trouble With Comparative Ads," *Ad Week*, 12, BR4-5.

Phillips, Joan M., Joel E. Urbany, and Thomas J. Reynolds (2008), "Confirmation and the Effects of Valenced Political Advertising: A Field Experiment," *Journal of Consumer Research*, 34 (6), (Apr), 794-806.

Ramanathan, Suresh and Ann McGill (2007), "Consuming with Others: Social Influences on Moment-to-Moment and Retrospective Evaluations of an Experience," *Journal of Consumer Research*, 34 (December), 506-524.

Robbins, Jordan and Joachim Krueger (2005), "Social Projection to Ingroups and Outgroups: A Review and Meta-Analysis," *Personality and Social Psychology Review*, 9 (1), 32-47.

York, Emily Bryson (2008), "Brand vs. Brand: Attack Ads on the Rise," *Advertising Age*, Oct. 27.

West, Darrell M. (1994), "Political Advertising and News Coverage in the 1992 California U.S. Senate Campaigns," *Journal of Politics*, 56 (4), 1053-1075.

Zemborain, Martin R. and Gita V. Johar (2007) "Attitudinal Ambivalence and Openness to Persuasion: A Framework for Interpersonal Influence," *Journal of Consumer Research*, 33 (4), 506-514.

SPECIAL SESSION SUMMARY

Long-term Decisions and Focusing on the Future

Daniel M. Bartels, University of Chicago, USA

SESSION OVERVIEW

How people think about and choose between immediate outcomes and those in the more distant future has been one of the central issues in consumer behavior, and behavioral science more generally (Loewenstein, Read, and Baumeister 2003). Building on the existing diverse literatures on time discounting (Frederick, Loewenstein, and O'Donoghue 2002), construal level theory (Trope and Liberman 2003) and the philosophy of personal identity (Martin and Barresi 2002) , the proposed session will contribute to a better understanding of how evaluations and decisions are driven by perceptions of how our future-self will experience potential long-term outcomes. The papers investigate how the degree to which we both attend to the future and feel connection to that future self affect the pursuit of gains over concern for losses, the exertion of self-control in the face of depletion and the willingness to defer compensation in favor of longer-term gains. This session will unify the findings of the individual papers into a broader framework for investigating the impact on consumer choice of how we think about the self in the context of the future.

Given the relevance of the proposed topic to central issues in consumer research, this session is likely to have a significant effect on future research in a number of areas and contribute to a cross-pollination of approaches to studying long-term outcomes. The papers employ a variety of approaches (lab and field experiments, as well as neuro-imaging), and the session will offer a broad perspective on the ways in which the degree of goal proximity plays a role in consumer behavior.

In the first paper, Shu provides evidence that while individuals focus on losses in immediate choices (per prospect theory), they instead focus on gains when thinking about themselves in the more distant future. This long-run focus on gains leads to a systematic difference in outcome valuations and choice in gambles and political choices for the long vs. short-term.

Both the Bartels, Urminsky, and Rips and the Ersner-Hershfield, Wimmer, and Knutson papers examine the influence of perceived psychological connectedness (i.e. continuity with future selves) on intertemporal choice. Bartels, Urminsky and Rips demonstrate that to the degree people anticipate changes in identity, they are less willing to defer benefits. They show that when people's own sense of continuity with the future self is reduced, they accept smaller, sooner monetary rewards, become less willing to wait to buy a computer in order to save money, and demand a larger delay premium to receive a gift card. Neuro-imaging research by Ersner-Hershfield, Wimmer and Knutson provides further evidence for the link between perceiving discontinuities and greater discounting of long-term outcomes. They ask participants to make judgments about the current and future self, and other people and compare levels of activation in areas of the brain associated with thinking about the self to those associated with thinking about social targets. They find that those people for whom thinking about the future self resembles thinking about other people (in terms of the neural activation elicited) had a stronger tendency to devalue delayed monetary rewards.

Lastly, research by Agrawal and Wan examines how drawing attention to the future vs. the present (construal level) influences the performance of consecutive self-control which requires sustained effort and is vulnerable to self-control resource depletion effects. When thinking about the future, individuals focus on goals relevant to the future self (e.g., health goals) and exert self-control depending on the importance of the task to their long-term goal. In contrast, when focused on the present, individuals attend to the resource accessibility experienced by the current self and will exert self-control depending on their perceived fatigue.

Given the centrality of long-term outcomes in this session, we anticipate that it will build toward an integrated intuition that contrasts a short-term decision maker, disconnected from the future self, who is impatient, loss-averse and impacted by depletion with a long-term decision maker, connected to the future self, who is more patient, gains-seeking and focused on goals. The session chair will facilitate audience discussion that explores relationships between the papers.

EXTENDED ABSTRACTS

"The Role of Self-Connectedness in Short Run Losses and Long Run Gains"

Suzanne Shu, UCLA, USA

Research on optimistic predictions finds that thinking about positive outcomes can affect judgment. For instance, as individuals think about a desirable focal outcome, they often put undue weight on that outcome relative to other possibilities; this has effects on probability estimates, affective forecasting, and other judgment tasks (Koehler 1994; Wilson et al. 2000; Rottenstreich and Kivetz 2006). Additional work has looked at how these optimistic predictions vary over time. Individuals are typically more optimistic the farther they are from the point at which the outcome will become known (Gilovich, Kerr and Medvec 1993), while work on resource slack, temporal construal, and regulatory focus also offers evidence that individuals see far-off things more holistically and positively than immediate events (Trope and Liberman 2003; Zauberman and Lynch 2005; Pennington and Roese 2003; Eyal et al 2004).

While much of the prior research has focused on outcome predictions or reasons for or against an option, less has been done to explore how optimistic predictions influence valuation and choice for future risky outcomes. For example, we know that for immediate gambles, individuals are loss averse (Kahneman and Tversky 1979). But for far-off gambles, is it possible that some form of optimism bias or wishful thinking causes the individual to focus on the gain outcome rather than the loss outcome? And what might this imply for valuation of those future outcomes within a Prospect Theory framework?

The research presented here suggests that individuals put more focal attention on gambles' gains for long-run outcomes, but shift attention toward losses in the short run. This occurs both for scenarios when the loss is incurred immediately (lottery ticket purchase) or expected to occur in the future (casino gamble). This overall pattern suggests that losses dominate in the short-run but that gains become the focal outcome as distance from the loss increases. Stronger focal attention on gains relative to losses for long-run outcomes has implications for how choices are evaluated, with the result that gains are more heavily weighted for a far-off outcome. This differential attention to gains and losses for temporally removed risky outcomes applies to many decision-making domains; for example, a study of two messages, matched for overall content, finds that participants prefer a hope message focused on future gains over a "reverse losses" message when the choice is for a future term, but they prefer a "reverse losses" message when the choice is for the present term.

These findings suggest that curvature of the Prospect Theory value function may change once time is incorporated. Prior research on loss aversion has suggested that loss aversion has a basis in emotional reactions to the outcomes –specifically, a more emotionally charged reaction to negative outcomes, consistent with work on visceral effects and empathy gaps. Solicitation of individual Prospect Theory value functions once temporal distance has been manipulated shows that loss aversion diminishes as individuals feel themselves to be farther in time from the gamble they are considering.

The final study examines whether the differential focus on losses and gains is a function of how connected the individual feels to their future self. A test of Prospect Theory style gambles for individuals considering themselves at future times shows that gamble choices shift according to the degree of connectedness participants feel with that future self, based on a connectedness measure from Parfit (1984) and used by Bartels, Urminsky, and Rips (2009), suggesting that high connectedness is an important aspect of short-run loss aversion. Thus, it is actually degree of connectedness, rather than absolute temporal distance, which affects valuation.

Together, these studies provide evidence that individuals focus on loss outcomes in the short run but gain outcomes in the long run, that this long-run focus on gains has measurable impact on choices and valuations, and that this focus is moderated by individuals' feelings of connectedness to their future selves. A better understanding of how individuals evaluate short run losses and long run gains may provide useful insight into human capital investment, risk taking, and other long run behaviors.

"How the Perceived (Dis)Continuity of Identity Affects Intertemporal Choice"

Daniel M. Bartels, University of Chicago, USA
Oleg Urminsky, University of Chicago, USA
Lance J. Rips, Northwestern University, USA

The literature on time preference has documented extremely high implicit discount rates in both hypothetical choices and observed behavior as well as inconsistency in the discount rate over time (Ainslie 1975; Thaler 1981; Frederick, Loewenstein, and O'Donoghue 2002). Economists offer several reasons why a rational actor might choose to consume a smaller amount of some good now, rather than a larger amount later—most of which concern the way that time affects the magnitude (or probability) of utility conferred by a delayed consumption experience. Most of these accounts of rational choice assume, however, that the preference for sooner-smaller options is due to the need to be compensated for the delay of benefit being received only by the future self, who is otherwise undistinguished from the current self. In this view, rationality demands acting in a manner consistent with maximizing some function of self-interest over time, and that the implied discount rate should relate to the cost of capital, and perhaps a risk premium relating to illiquidity or loss of the delayed outcome (Samuelson 1937); deviation from this rule has been characterized as myopia (e.g. Strotz 1955).

One account that differs radically from standard economic views is offered by Parfit (1984), who maintains that rationality does not require you to treat all parts of your life equally: He argues that personal identity consists of a series of partially-overlapping persons extending over time. One implication is not all descendant future selves are equally "you". Thus, just as you are not rationally required to care as much about others' welfare as your own, so too, if your descendent future self is sufficiently different in terms of personality, beliefs, and desires from your current self, you are not rationally required to care as much about your future self's welfare. Impatience can thereby be justified, distinct from normative discounting, by anticipated changes in connectedness over time.

In the current studies, we test the influence of people's intuitions about the (in)stability of personal identity over time on (im)patience for future utility. Study 1 investigated the relation between elicited patience and perceptions of psychological connectedness in people's judgments about their own future selves. Participants in this study rated the connectedness between their present state and their likely state at different times in the future and made judgments about the equivalence of present and future goods. We observe greater impatience in time periods with larger decreases in connectedness, consistent with connectedness explaining non-constant discounting.

In Study 2, we rule out a time perception explanation, using a projective method, in which participants read about fictional characters experiencing symbolically life-changing events (such as a religious conversion) that would normally decrease psychological connectedness but not impact monetary outcomes. We balanced the life-changing events so that they happen to different characters at different points in the future. Participants made timing decisions for annuity payouts on behalf of these characters. In time intervals perceived to represent large changes in psychological connectedness, participants made relatively impatient decisions—choosing to cash in annuities more quickly than for those intervals where they perceive smaller changes in connectedness.

In Study 3, we presented underclassmen with hypothetical choices between sooner, smaller valued gift cards versus gift cards plus a delay premium after reading either that identity changes radically in early adulthood (especially during the college years) or that the core features of one's identity are fixed in early childhood (and stable during college). Participants demanded a greater delay premium after reading about how they would change than after reading stability of identity.

In Study 4, we manipulate people's certitude in the stability of their identity indirectly, by asking them to judge how difficult it would be to generate either 2 or 10 reasons why their identity will remain very stable over the next 12 months. Participants in the 2 reasons condition reported less difficulty with the reason-generation task, and subsequently exhibited greater patience about when to buy a computer expected to decline in price over the next 12 months.

In Study 5, we conducted a field study using similar methods as Study 3. College seniors who were about to graduate read a passage that described graduation as either a major life-changing experience or one not impacting self-identity and chose between lotteries for delayed gift cards of increasing value over time. When participants were told their impending graduation presaged a major (vs. trivial) change in self-connectedness, they exhibited more impatience and were more likely to choose the smaller-sooner gift card. The effect was robust controlling for their individual beliefs about future availability of money and time after graduation.

In all five studies, we find evidence that when large changes in psychological connectedness are anticipated, people behave relatively impatiently—choosing to speed up the consumption of utility. Conversely, when anticipating small changes, people appear more patient. Our findings have the potential to shed light on the long-standing issues of "excessively" high discount rates as well as nonconstant discount rates.

"Saving for the Future Self: Neural Measures of Future Self-Continuity Predict Temporal Discounting"

Hal Ersner-Hershfield, Stanford University, USA
G. Elliott Wimmer, Stanford University, USA
Brian Knutson, Stanford University, USA

Why do some people fail to save for the future? Theorists from economics, philosophy, and psychology have characterized saving as an "intertemporal choice" problem involving a decision between benefits that occur now versus in the future (Frederick, Loewenstein, and O'Donoghue 2003). Research shows that people often care less about future outcomes than they do about present ones, a phenomenon known as temporal discounting (Frederick 2003). According to an early model of temporal discounting, while people devalue future gains as a function of temporal distance from the present, individuals vary in the degree to which they devalue future gains. This tradeoff between time and magnitude was originally described with an exponential function (Samuelson 1937), but is better fit by a hyperbolic or quasi-hyperbolic function (Laibson 1997).

Theorists have argued that temporal discounting might emerge from conflicts of interest between temporally different selves (Parfit 1971; Schelling 1984). According to this view, psychological connectedness of the present to the future self varies as a function of time, such that people feel more connected to their potential self of five years than their potential self of fifty years. Thus, people might care less about more temporally distant future selves to the point at which an extremely distant future self may seem like a different person altogether (Parfit 1971; Pronin and Ross 2006). This "multiple selves" view has implications for financial saving. If people consider the future self as a stranger, then they may rationally have no more reason to save money for themselves than to give the money to a stranger. Critically, this account predicts that the degree to which an individual feels disconnected from his or her future self should correlate with the degree to which that individual discounts future rewards (i.e. the "future self-continuity hypothesis.")

Neuroimaging methods allow for a novel way of testing this hypothesis. Previous neuroimaging research suggests that people show decreased activation in cortical midline structures when considering information about others versus the self (Kelley et al. 2002), and increased activation when engaging in self-reflection or introspection (Raichle et al. 2001). If people effectively consider their future selves as others, judgments about the future versus current self should elicit reduced activation in cortical midline structures. Further, individuals with greater decreases in activation for the future vs. current self should more steeply discount future rewards.

The goal of this experiment was to determine whether neural indices of future self-continuity could predict temporal discounting. To test these hypotheses, subjects were scanned with event-related fMRI while making judgments about the extent to which trait adjectives applied to their current self, a future self, a current other, or a future other. A week later, subjects completed a temporal discounting task that yielded an estimate of the degree to which each individual discounted future rewards. Analyses focused on changes in activation in the MPFC and rACC during current vs. future self-ratings. First, we predicted that rating the self versus another person would increase activation in the MPFC and rACC (Kelley et al. 2002), consistent with previous findings. Second, we predicted that rating the current versus future self would increase MPFC and rACC activation. Finally, based on the future self-continuity hypothesis, we predicted that individual differences in current versus future self rating elicited MPFC and rACC activation would predict individual differences in temporal discounting, tested behaviorally at least a week later. This represents the first attempt to link a neural index of future self-continuity to temporal discounting.

Results indicated that there was a neural difference between thoughts about the current self versus thoughts about the future self: there was greater activation in a portion of the anterior cingulate cortex for current self compared to future self judgments. Importantly, lending support to the future self-continuity hypothesis, individual differences in the magnitude of this effect predicted the tendency to devalue future rewards. That is, the greater the difference in neural activation between current self and future self judgments, the more a given individual discounted future rewards. If individual differences in savings partially depend upon future self-continuity, then savings behavior might be modified either by altering perceptions of the future self or by projecting the current self into the future. The findings thus may hold implications both for understanding and encouraging saving for the future self.

"Goals or Means: How Psychological Distance Influences Depletion Effects"

Kellogg Nidhi Agrawal, University of Hong Kong, China
Echo Wen Wan, University of Hong Kong, China

Consumers often need to exert self-control in multiple activities in succession. Previous research has suggested that self-control relies on self-control resources (Muraven and Baumeister 2000). Performing consecutive self-control is particularly vulnerable to suffer the depletion effect: individuals reduce control on a self-control task after having exerted great self-control on a preceding task (Baumeister et al. 1998). This research examines how temporal perspective affects consecutive self-control (depletion effects) by systematically highlighting either goals or resources.

In the current research we employed the goal-means approach to examine how construal influences depletion effects. Construal level theory (Trope and Liberman 2003) posits that the same event or object can be represented at multiple levels. Higher-level construals (e.g. associated with long-term outcomes) highlight central goals associated with an event, while lower-level construals (e.g associated with near-term outcomes) highlight means and resources (Liberman and Trope 1998). At higher-level construals, individuals focus on self-relevant goals. Thus, they should show more self-control on the second task when they view this task as important (vs. unimportant) to their goals, regardless of their depletion state. In contrast, at lower-level construals, individuals will focus on resources accessible to the self (e.g., their fatigue) rather than on goals. Thus they will perform poorer on the second task when they are in a depletion (vs. non-depletion) state.

Three experiments examine our proposition in a consumer health context. In all experiments participants performed two consecutive self-control tasks. The first task manipulated initial depletion by having participants process messages about Hepatitis that communicated a high or low self-risk perception. Prior research has suggested that processing high-risk health messages presents a trade-off between long-term benefits and short-term interests (e.g., Agrawal, Menon, and Aaker 2007; Menon et al. 2007) and thus requires self-control. The second task involved processing health messages about a different disease that also require self-control. Construal levels were manipulated between the two tasks.

In Experiment 1 participants first read a Hepatitis message and then worked on a mindset task that manipulated construal levels by thinking about near future versus distant future in a writing task (Fujita et al. 2006; Liberman and Trope 1998). Then participants read an article about dental health describing symptoms, prevention, and treatment of dental diseases. Time spent reading this article served as the measure of self-control. The results show that for participants primed with lower-level construals, those who read a high-risk message spent less time reading about dental health than those who read a low-risk message. For participants primed with higher construal levels, because dental health is highly relevant to their health goal, participants spent substantial time on reading the dental health article whether they processed a high or low-risk Hepatitis message. The same results pattern emerged on an additional behavior measure of self-control-flossing.

Experiment 2 followed a similar procedure as used in Experiment 1, using a different type of disease in the second task. The importance of this disease to participants' own health goal was manipulated. The results are that participants at lower-level construals exhibited a depletion effect whether the unfamiliar disease was described as important or unimportant. Focus on fatigue mediated this effect. Participants at higher-level construals spent more time reading the disease article when the disease was described as highly relevant to themselves (and thus to their health goal) than when it was described as irrelevant to them, regardless of initial depletion. Participants' perceived higher-level benefit of reading this article mediated this effect.

Experiment 3 employed a similar procedure to that used in Experiment 1, with an additional independent variable: Participants were told that the Hepatitis task was effortful or non-effortful when they finished this task. The results suggest that individuals at higher- versus lower-level construals systematically differ in their reliance on this effort information. While lower level construal use this information to assess their ability, higher level construal interpret the same effort cue in terms of their own goals.

These findings suggest that differences in construal level, due to taking either a short-term or long-term perspective, influence self-control due to inducing assessment of either the self's current resources or the self's longer-term goals.

REFERENCES

Agrawal, N., G. Menon, and J. L. Aaker (2007), "Getting Emotional About Health," *Journal of Marketing Research*, 44, 100-113.

Ainslie, G. (1975), "Specious Reward: A Behavioral Theory of Impulsiveness and Impulse Control," *Psychological Bulletin*, 82, 463–496

Baumeister, R. F., E. Bratslavsky, M. Muraven, and D. M. Tice (1998), "Ego Depletion: Is the Active Self a Limited Resource?" *Journal of Personality and Social Psychology*, 74, 1252-1265.

Frederick, S. (2003), "Time Preference and Personal Identity," in G. Loewenstein, D. Read, and R. Baumeister (Eds.), *Time and Decision,* New York: Sage, 89-113.

Frederick, S., G. Loewenstein, and T. O'Donoghue (2002), "Time Discounting and Time Preference: A Critical Review," *Journal of Economic Literature*, 40, 351–401.

Fujita, K., Y. Trope, N. Liberman, and M. Levin-Sagi (2006), "Construal Levels and Self-Control," *Journal of Personality and Social Psychology*, 90, 351-367.

Gilovich, T., M. Kerr, and V. H. Medvec (1993), "The Effect of Temporal Perspective on Subjective Confidence," *Journal of Personality and Social Psychology*, 64, 552-560.

Kelley, W. M., C. N. Macrae, C. L. Wyland, S. Caglar, S. Inati, and T. F. Heatherton (2002), "Finding the Self? An Event-related fMRI Study," *Journal of Cognitive Neuroscience*, 14, 785-794.

Koehler, D. J. (1994), "Hypothesis Generation and Confidence in Judgment," *Journal of Experimental Psychology: Learning, Memory, and Cognition*, 20, 461-469.

Laibson, D. (1997), "Golden Eggs and Hyperbolic Discounting," *Quarterly Journal of Economics*, 112, 443-477.

Liberman, N. and Y. Trope (1998), "The Role of Feasibility and Desirability Considerations in Near and Distant Future Decisions: A Test of Temporal Construal Theory," *Journal of Personality and Social Psychology*, 75, 5-18.

Loewenstein, G., D. Read, and R .F. Baumeister (Eds.) (2003), *Time and Decision,* New York: Sage.

Martin, R. and J. Barresi (Eds.) (2002), *Personal Identity,* Oxford: Blackwell.

Menon, G., L. Block, and S. Ramanathan (2002), "We're at as Much Risk as We're Led to Believe: Effects of Message Cues on Judgments of Health Risk," *Journal of Consumer Research*, 28, 533-549.

Muraven, M. and R. F. Baumeister (2000), "Self-Regulation and Depletion of Limited Resources: Does Self-Control Resemble a Muscle?" *Psychological Bulletin*, 126, 247-259.

Parfit, D. (1971), "Personal Identity," *Philosophical Review*, 80, 3-27.

Parfit, D. (1984), *Reasons and Persons*, Oxford, UK: Oxford University Press.

Pennington, G. L. and N. J. Roese (2003), "Regulatory Focus and Temporal Distance," *Journal of Experimental Social Psychology*, 39, 563-576.

Pronin, E., L. Ross (2006), "Temporal Differences in Trait Self-Ascription: When the Self is Seen as an Other," *Journal of Personality and Social Psychology*, 90, 197-209.

Raichle, M. E., A. M. MacLeod, A. Z. Snyder, W. J. Powers, D. A. Gusnard, and G. L. Shulman (2001), "A Default Mode of Brain Function," *Proceedings of the National Academy of Sciences*, 98, 676-682.

Rottenstreich, Y. and R. Kivetz (2006), "On Decision Making without Likelihood Judgment," *Organizational Behavior and Human Decision Processes*, 101, 74-88.

Samuelson, P. (1937), "A Note on Measurement," *The Review of Economic Studies*, 4, 155-161.

Schelling, T. C. (1984), "Self-command in Practice, in Policy, and in a Theory of Rational Choice," *The American Economic Review*, 74, 1-11.

Strotz, R. H. (1955), "Myopia and Inconsistency in Dynamic Utility Maximization," *Review of Economic Studies*, 23, 165-80.

Thaler, Richard (1981), "Some Empirical Evidence on Dynamic Inconsistency," *Economic Letters*, 8.

Trope, Y. and N. Liberman (2003), "Temporal Construal," *Psychological Review*, 110, 403-421.

Vohs, K. and B. Schmeichel (2003), "Self-regulation and the Extended Now: Controlling the Self Alters the Subjective Experience of Time," *Journal of Personality and Social Psychology*, 85, 217-230.

Wan, E. W. and B. Sternthal (2008), "Regulating the Effects of Depletion through Monitoring," *Personality and Social Psychology Bulletin*, 34, 47-60.

Zauberman, G. and J. G. Lynch (2005), "Resource Slack and Propensity to Discount Delayed Investments of Time versus Money," *Journal of Experimental Psychology: General*, 134, 23-37.

Special Session Summary

The Influence of Lay Beliefs on Consumers' Food Consumption Decisions

Rajagopal Raghunathan, University of Texas at Austin, USA

SESSION OVERVIEW

The purpose of this proposed special session is to explore the impact that lay beliefs have on consumers' food consumption decisions. The obesity epidemic has emerged as one of the most challenging problems of our time (Flegal et al. 2000; Mokdad et al. 2000; Ogden et al. 2006), and its prevalence and links to numerous health problems (Manson and Bassuk 2003) underscore the importance of understanding why people make poor food choices. The four papers in this session (all of which contain at least two completed studies) propose previously unexplored psychological factors that can explain why consumers choose unhealthy foods.

The first paper (by Raghunathan et al.) explores whether a specific lay belief, namely, that the healthiness of food is negatively correlated with its tastiness (i.e., the "unhealthy=tasty" intuition in Raghunathan et al. 2006), leads those who believe in this intuition to make unhealthy food choices. The second paper (by Bhattacharjee et al.) demonstrates that erroneous consumer beliefs about drugs and supplements underlie a boomerang effect of weight management drug marketing, resulting in unhealthy consumption. The third paper (by Deng et al.) shows that consumers infer the perceived weight of a food product based on the location of the product imagery featured on the packaging, with images located on the top of packaging leading consumers to believe that the product is less filling, encouraging them to eat more. The fourth paper (by McFerran et al.) examines the impact of consumers' views of others on food consumption decisions, exploring the implications that body type of serving personnel may have for restaurateurs and consumers.

The session's focus on the influence of lay beliefs on food consumption decisions will hopefully contribute not only to the literature on obesity and food choices, but will also appeal to a diverse range of conference attendees, including researchers with an interest in decision making, lay beliefs, and self-control. Lastly, the session theme is consistent with ACR's support of transformative consumer research. Identifying the type of psychological causes for unhealthy food consumption discussed in this session (vs. physiological or genetic causes) is crucial, since such causes are more amenable to control through policy interventions (Loewenstein, Brennan, and Volpp 2007; Ratner et al. 2008; Vandeveer 2008).

EXTENDED ABSTRACTS

"Evil Intuitions: Why Belief in the "Unhealthy=Tasty" Intuition Leads to Unhealthy Food Choices"

Rajagopal Raghunathan, The University of Texas at Austin, USA
Rebecca Walker Naylor, The Ohio State University, USA
Kalpesh Kaushik Desai, The State University of New York at Binghamton, USA
Kelly L. Haws, Texas A&M University, USA
Karthik Sridhar, The State University of New York at Buffalo, USA

The purpose of this research is to document the role that the "unhealthy=tasty" intuition—which refers to the belief that the healthiness of food is negatively correlated with its tastiness (Raghunathan, Naylor, and Hoyer 2006)—plays in steering people's preferences toward more (vs. less) healthy foods. There are at least three reasons why the intuition steers preferences towards unhealthy (vs. healthy) options. First, assuming that people develop their (lay) theories about the relationship between healthiness and tastiness by observing the correlation between these two dimensions in the items they typically consume, it follows that, while those with strong belief in the intuition are likely to choose among items that are healthy or tasty, those with weaker belief in it are more likely to choose among items that are healthy and tasty. This leads to a greater proportion of less healthy items in the consideration (and consumption) sets of those with stronger (vs. weaker) belief in the unhealthy=tasty intuition. Second, we propose that consumers with stronger (vs. weaker) belief in the unhealthy=tasty intuition derive greater utility from unhealthy (vs. healthy) food options since: (1) they expect the unhealthy (vs. healthy) items to taste better—in accordance with the hypothesis confirmation bias—and (2) they attach greater relative importance to tastiness (vs. healthiness) in deciding what to consume. Finally, because consumers with stronger (vs. weaker) belief in the intuition encounter more frequent and more emotionally draining tradeoffs between tastiness and healthiness, the self-regulatory resources of those with stronger belief in the intuition are more likely to be depleted when making food consumption decisions (Vohs et al. 2008), resulting in more self-control failures (i.e., consumption of unhealthy food).

We conducted four studies to test these predictions. The first study used a combination of two data sources: (1) scanner panel choice data from a grocery chain and (2) data gathered from a survey that was mailed to a subset of the panelists. Results showed that, as belief in the intuition increased, the proportion of unhealthy (vs. healthy) purchases in two popular categories—ice cream and beer—increased, $?_{Ice\ cream}=.06$; $t(2, 88)=2.03$; $p<.04$ and $?_{Beer}=.09$; $t(2, 95)=2.69$; $p<.001$. Thus, consumers with stronger belief in the unhealthy=tasty intuition exhibited a higher propensity to purchase less (vs. more) healthy food—a finding that is consistent with the idea that those with stronger (vs. weaker) belief in the intuition are less likely to consider (and hence consume) more (vs. less) healthy food. Results from the second study showed that the same snack—M&Ms—are: (1) enjoyed more and (2) consumed in larger quantities by participants with stronger (vs. weaker) belief in the unhealthy=tasty intuition when the snack is perceived to be more (vs. less) unhealthy (through labels identifying the candy as either regular plain M&Ms or new, "low fat" M&Ms). This finding indicates that those with stronger (vs. weaker) belief in the intuition derive greater utility from less (vs. more) healthy options.

Study 3 was designed to assess whether the self-control resources of those with stronger (vs. weaker) belief in the unhealthy=tasty intuition are depleted to a greater extent when contemplating the consumption of healthy food, leading, thereby, to a greater propensity to consume less (vs. more) healthy food on a future consumption occasion. Participants were first asked to imagine consuming a certain set of healthy dinners over the course of the next five evenings. Then, participants indicated the extent to which the consumption of the healthy meals would deplete their self-control resources and how likely they would be to consume, for the next day, each of a set of unhealthy and healthy options (e.g., pizza, broccoli, etc.). Finally, participants indicated the extent of their belief in the unhealthy=tasty intuition. Consistent with our expectations, participants who more strongly believed in the unhealthy=tasty intuition reported a greater preference for the less healthy food, $?=.31$, $t(129)=2.31$, $p<.05$. Further, participants who expressed greater belief in the intuition reported greater depletion of self-control, $?=.11$, $t(1, 129)=2.46$, $p<.05$. Finally, consistent with our expectation that depletion of self-control resources enhances preference for unhealthy food, we found that the more depleted one's self-control resources, the higher the preference for less healthy options, ?=.73, t(1, 129)=3.51, p<.01. When both belief in the unhealthy=tasty intuition and depletion of self-control were jointly used as predictors of preference for the unhealthy food, only the latter was significant, ?=.76, t(1, 129)=2.68, p<.01, and the effect of belief in the intuition was reduced to non-significance, t<1, indicating that the depletion of self-control resources fully mediates the relationship between belief in the intuition and the propensity to consume unhealthy food. Finally, results from Study 4—a real-world survey in which participants reported the extent of their belief in the unhealthy=tasty intuition and also provided their heights and weights—indicated that belief in the intuition was positively related to BMI, ?=.33, F(1, 382)=3.09, p=.08.

"License to Lapse: The Effects of Weight Management Product Marketing on a Healthy Lifestyle"

Amit Bhattacharjee, University of Pennsylvania, USA
Lisa E. Bolton, Pennsylvania State University, USA
Americus Reed II, University of Pennsylvania, USA

Even as obesity rates have risen dramatically in recent years (Ogden et al. 2006), consumers have been trying increasingly harder to maintain a healthy lifestyle; the coincidence of these trends has been dubbed the "American obesity paradox" (Heini and Weinsier 1997). Given these developments, the demand for safe and effective weight management solutions has intensified, and an assortment of weight management and fat-fighting products has proliferated. Though such weight management solutions appeal to many consumers, recent research suggests that there may be unintended consequences of the marketing of these products that actually undermine consumers' intentions to engage in a healthy lifestyle. Hence, marketing of such products may unwittingly exacerbate risky decision making and reduce, rather than improve, consumer welfare.

Consistent with the notion that consumers adaptively cope with perceived risk in the environment (e.g., Floyd, Prentice-Dunn, and Rogers 2000), recent research suggests that remedy messages undermine risk avoidance and increase risky behavioral intentions, particularly for those consumers most at risk. Specifically, problem status (or the relative attractiveness of the problem domain) moderates the effects of remedy marketing messages (Bolton, Cohen, and Bloom 2006). Recent evidence suggests that two psychological mechanisms drive this boomerang effect. First, drug marketing reduces consumer perceptions of health risk and lessens the perceived importance of complementary health-protective behaviors, so consumers are less motivated to engage in these healthy behaviors. Second, drugs are associated with poor health, reducing consumers' perceptions of their own health and their self-efficacy, and thereby diminishing their perceived ability to engage in complementary behaviors (Bolton, Reed, Volpp, and Armstrong 2008). Lacking both motivation and perceived ability to undertake health-supportive behaviors, consumers are unlikely to do so, leading to less healthy lifestyle intentions and a reduction in consumer welfare. Interestingly, this pattern does not hold for supplements: unlike drugs, supplements are not associated with poor health and are perceived as just one aspect of an overall health-protective regimen.

Building on prior research, we present a series of five studies conducted across samples of university students and field samples of adults from a daycare center and members of a fitness club. To examine the role of weight management product marketing, we focus on consumer beliefs that guide the processing of such messages and underlie corresponding behavior (c.f. Chandon and Wansink 2007; Raghunathan, Naylor, and Hoyer 2006). Results can be summarized as follows: (1) Actual consumption of high-fat foods increases with a single exposure to weight management drug versus supplement marketing messages, particularly for those participants who are hungriest, and thus most attracted to the problem domain; (2) Healthy behavioral intentions decrease when participants imagine taking a weight management drug versus supplement, particularly for those participants who suffer from body image issues and have a problematic relationship with this domain of unhealthy behaviors; (3) As theorized, the boomerang effect of weight management drug marketing on healthy behavioral intentions is mediated by decreased motivation and a perceived decrease in ability to engage in health protective behaviors; (4) Evidence from two field samples of real consumers with a range of knowledge levels suggests that erroneous consumer beliefs about drugs and supplements underlie the boomerang effect of weight management drug marketing. While the boomerang is partially mitigated by more accurate knowledge, only the highest levels of knowledge (reflecting specialized medical training or expertise) are sufficient to eliminate it completely.

Our findings make several notable contributions. To our knowledge, the present research is the first to demonstrate the boomerang effect of drug marketing on actual behavior and the first to demonstrate a boomerang arising from a single exposure to a drug marketing message. Our research also indicates that the boomerang effect can be influenced by both transient visceral factors (e.g., hunger) and relatively stable individual differences (e.g., body image), suggesting that it is not just certain "types" of consumers that are susceptible. Together, these results provide initial evidence that while drug marketing can influence mindful, intentional consumer behavior, it can also impact consumer behavior in relatively mindless eating contexts, highlighting the power and robustness of the boomerang phenomenon. Moreover, the present research provides evidence for the underlying role of erroneous consumer beliefs, suggesting that lay theories regarding weight management products lead consumers to reduce healthy lifestyle behaviors in response to weight management marketing. Finally, the present research investigates the role of consumer knowledge across a range of consumer samples. Only highly specialized medical training appears to mitigate the erroneous beliefs underlying the boomerang, suggesting that the beliefs held by most consumers are not "normative." Even otherwise well-educated consumers are susceptible, supporting the robustness of the phenomenon.

"Using the Product Image "Location Effect" to Help Consumers Control Eating Patterns"

Xiaoyan Deng, University of Pennsylvania, USA
Barbara E. Kahn, University of Miami, USA
Sara Michalski, University of Miami, USA

Recently, consumer researchers have shown that marketing attempts designed to help consumers control their eating habits can cause boomerang effects. For example Mandel et. al (2008) showed that consumers who were self-identified as "restrained eaters" tended to eat more from smaller, portion controlled packages than from larger packages because consumers experienced a lapse in judgment due to the conflict inherent in experiencing high caloric food packaged as diet food. Pieters et.al (2008) found similar behavior, although they hypothesized that the problem was due to a lack of self-regulation on the part of the consumers because of the perceived regulation the packaging provided. This latter explanation mirrors the "Subway effect" identified by Chandon and Wansink

(2007) where it was shown that people tended to eat more side dishes and desserts when the restaurant claims to be healthy as opposed to when it does not.

Consistent with these previous findings, we hypothesize that consumers who eat by cognitive "rules," as opposed to consumers who eat as a function of hunger desires, are more likely to overeat when they believe that their responsibility for watching calories has been deliberately taken care of by the marketer, for example through portion controlled sizes, "100 calorie bags," or healthy eating claims. However, if the marketer can cue the desirability of smaller portions through a perceptual, automatic route rather than through a deliberate claim, the marketer may be more successful at controlling overeating.

Deng and Kahn (2009) showed that when product images are placed at the top of a package, the product seems lighter than when product images are placed at the bottom of a package. In this research, we extend this result to show that the perceived weight of the product as a function of image location on the package can extend to consumers' perceptions of how filling and satisfying in terms of taste that the food product will seem. Further we show that this perceptual conclusion is an intuitive process, as opposed to a rule-based analytic process. Thus, we hypothesize that although deliberate, highly cognitive marketing tactics to help consumers control eating may backfire, that boomerang effect will be mitigated if the product imagery can be used to automatically cue that the product is more filling and more tasty, and hence eating less will be satisfactory.

We have conducted several experiments to test this theory. In one computer-based experiment, we show participants large bags of cookies or smaller, portion controlled size bags of cookies labeled "100 calorie" portions. We also vary whether the image of the product is at the top of the package (the light location) or at the bottom of the package (the heavy location), and we tell the participants to indicate how filling the cookies look and how many they want to eat. We also measure whether the participants use cognitive rules to control eating or not. We find that all of the consumers think that cookies in "100 calorie" packs will be less filling than those in unmarked packs ($p<.001$), supporting past results. However, for restricted eaters this effect of "100 calorie" packaging making cookies appear less filling goes away when the product image is in the heavy location, whereas non-restricted eaters continue to see the "100 calorie" packages as less filling when the product image is in the heavy location or light location (interaction $p<.05$). When asked how many cookies they would like to eat, none of the packaging effects affected the quantity of cookies chosen for unrestricted eaters, but the restricted eaters indicated wanting a cookie and a half more when the product image was in the light location as opposed to the heavy location ($p<.05$).

In another experiment we asked participants to look at cookie packages and to taste the cookies from that package where we had manipulated whether the cookie image was on the top or bottom of the package. We further manipulated load to test whether the product image effect was automatic or cognitive. The interaction between cognitive resource and product image location was significant ($p<.05$). When participants did not have the cognitive resources to process the cue, the location effect occurred. Cookies from the package using the heavy location tasted more satisfying than did cookies from the package using the light location. However, when participants had sufficient cognitive resources, this effect disappeared. These results show that when participants are processing the packaging automatically they are likely to eat less when the product is in the heavy location than when in the light location. We are in the process of running several other experiments to further test and replicate these findings.

"Might a Heavier Waitress Make You Eat More, Less, or Differently?"

Brent McFerran, University of British Columbia, Canada
Darren W. Dahl, University of British Columbia, Canada
Gavan J. Fitzsimons, Duke University, USA
Andrea C. Morales, Arizona State University, USA

Consumers make over 200 food choices per day (Wansink 2006), and thus it is important to understand the antecedents to unhealthy food choices. However, little research in marketing has examined context effects influencing how consumers make the food choices they do. For instance, what if a heavy waitress recommended an indulgent choice or something very healthy? Would her weight influence your choice? Might her weight cause you to eat more food or less than if she was thin? Past research has shown that consumption decisions are influenced by those who are physically present. In a food context, studies have found that social influence can have either a facilitating or attenuating effect on consumption, depending on the context (see Herman, Roth, and Polivy 2003 for an excellent review). They argue that food choice is influenced by a desire to convey a certain impression or adhere to social norms (Leary and Kowalski 1990; Roth et al. 2001). Although, Herman et al. (2003) argue that making a good impression usually means eating less, other research has found that people may eat more, rather than less in the presence of another person (e.g. Conger, Conger, Costanzo, Wright and Matter 1990). Another line of research has examined the impact of obesity on consumption. Priming people with overweight images has been shown to lead to an increase in quantity consumed (Campbell and Mohr 2008).

The above lines of research have focused either on how much others eat or on the social influence of obesity, but little research has examined the influence of the two jointly. In social influence work more generally, the effects of the social "other" have been shown to be moderated by whether the person is a member of an aspirational or dissociative group (Escalas and Bettman 2005; White and Dahl 2005, 2008). Since thin models are seen as an ideal standard in North American society (Durkin and Paxton 2002) and obesity is a stigma that most wish to avoid (Johnson 2002), the body type of others should interact with their food choice (indulgent vs. moderate) in forming evaluations of them. Specifically, Campbell and Mohr (2008) found that overweight (vs. thinner) images led consumers to believe they would eat less food, and thus it would be reasonable to predict that a thinner server would lead to greater consumption and be a more persuasive recommender of a food choice. However, we also argue that there may be another factor at play in determining how social others impact food consumption. Research has shown that dieters often do not make the same food choices as non-dieters (Federoff, Herman, and Polivy 1997; Polivy and Herman 2002). Specifically, studies have shown that dieters sometimes exhibit a backfire effect, eating more when small food is placed in small packages (Scott, Nowlis, Mandel, and Morales 2008) or eating more (rather than less) following a "preload" of calories (e.g. Knight and Boland 1989; Polivy 1976). We propose, based on recent research on reference groups (Berger and Heath 2007; 2008; Berger and Rand 2008; White and Dahl, 2008) and dieting (Scott, Nowlis, Mandel, and Morales 2008), that consumers should react differently in a food choice context to obese versus thin servers.

Using a professionally-constructed obesity prosthesis, an identical confederate portrayed both a thin and a heavy experimenter in identical clothes. Study 1 was a one factor design (obese vs. thin experimenter) plus a measured variable capturing participants' dieting orientation and was conducted as a taste test. The experimenter (wearing the prosthesis or not) told participants they must choose only one of two sweet snacks (bite size cookies or glazed rice cakes) to evaluate, but that they could eat as much of their choice as they wished. She then recommended the chocolate cookies to participants. Results showed that while participants' snack choice did not vary as a function of the confederate's body type, their consumption quantity did. An interaction effect (treating dieting orientation as a continuous variable) showed dieters ate more snacks when the recommender was heavy, but non-dieters ate more when she was thin.

Study 2 used a sample consisting only of dieters, and the procedures were the same as Study 1, but we directly manipulated the snack the experimenter recommended by including a healthy choice in a 2(obese vs. thin experimenter) x 2(recommends cookies or carrot sticks) between subjects design. Results of a logistic regression showed a significant interaction effect: when cookies were recommended, dieters chose cookies more often when the experimenter was heavy (vs. thin), but when carrots were recommended, they selected cookies with a greater frequency when she was thin (vs. heavy). Dieters followed the recommendation of the heavy server more, choosing both the healthy and the unhealthy snack more often when it was recommended to them by a heavy (vs. a thin) experimenter. These two studies point to the implications that body type of serving personnel may have for restaurateurs and consumers.

Special Session Summary

Consuming in Self-Defense: Consumer Responses to Self Threat

Eugenia Wu, Duke University, USA

SESSION OVERVIEW

"Self-defence is nature's eldest law."
—John Dryden, poet and playwright

As living beings, we have a fundamental need to protect ourselves when we come under threat. Thus, we bristle with indignation when someone insults us, we come out with fists flying when someone physically attacks us and we invest in insurance policies to guard against unpredictable events that may threaten our wellbeing. This need for self-protection underlies each human existence and influences every aspect of human behavior, including consumption behaviors. The three papers in this session all focus on how the need to defend against threats to the self influence the way consumers think, feel and make decisions. More specifically, each of the three papers examines how a threat to the self may cause consumers to engage in very different consumption behavior than they might otherwise have. Broadly construed, this symposium aims to examine how consumer behavior is affected when consumers are focusing on self-protective needs.

The self is a multi-faceted entity where each facet may become threatened and in need of protection at one point or another. The papers in this session examine threat to two particular aspects of self: threat to the self's sense of its place in the world and threat to the self's very existence. To offer a fuller understanding of how self threats may impact consumption behavior, each paper examines a distinct type of behavior that is affected by self threat and provides a unique perspective. First, Cutright, Wu, Kay and Fitzsimons (2009) examine the extent to which product choices and ad attitudes change when consumers' sense of the self as part of a legitimate and just external system (e.g., government organizations, etc.) is threatened. Second, Schmid and Argo (2009) explore how self threat in the form of mortality salience causes individuals to adopt previously extraneous possessions to form a new self identity. Finally, Fernandes, Mandel and Smeesters (2009) focus on how existential self threat can lead individuals to engage in increased variety seeking behavior as a way to experience unrestrained freedom. Together, these papers suggest that when a given aspect of the self is threatened, consumers will alter their consumption patterns in order to cope with and defend against that threat. Importantly, each of these papers also suggests important boundary conditions for the role of threat on consumption, particularly with respect to individual differences.

Though consumer behavior clearly takes place within the context of self-threat, consumer research has generally treated such threats as unacknowledged background factors rather than as interesting topics in their own right. In the increasingly competitive and rapidly changing environment that we live in today however, aspects of the self may be frequently threatened, leading to significant changes in the way individuals feel, think and behave. This symposium aims to contribute to consumer research by bridging the gap between research on consumer behavior and on protecting against self-threats.

We hope that this symposium will attract a wide ACR audience, from researchers interested in self-threat specifically to the broad range of researchers who examine the role of situational influence in consumer psychology. This symposium is also relevant for marketers interested in identity and emotional coping. Of note, these papers are all in advanced stages of completion.

EXTENDED ABSTRACTS

"When Your World Must Be Defended: Consuming to Justify the System"

Keisha Cutright, Duke University, USA
Eugenia Wu, Duke University, USA
Aaron Kay, University of Waterloo, Canada
Gavan Fitzsimons, Duke University, USA

In this age of unceasing social, political and economic turmoil, individuals are increasingly likely to be faced with threatening information about the legitimacy of their socio-political systems. How do they deal with such information? System justification theory (Jost and Banaji, 1994) suggests that individuals are generally motivated to maintain the view that the external system that they interact with (i.e. overarching institutions, organizations and social norms) is fair, legitimate, and justifiable (Kay & Zanna, in press). This tendency has been shown to have a variety of important consequences including support for inequality (Laurin & Kay 2008) and decreased interest in social change (Kay et al. 2008). The present research is designed to explore how this tendency to defend the status quo against threat might also have important consequences for consumption-related behavior. Additionally, this research aims to further enhance system justification theory by introducing important individual difference moderators.

The system justification motive is assumed to help people avoid the psychological threat of perceiving that the system in which they live is illegitimate, unfair, and undesirable (Jost & Hunyady 2002). Consequently, the system justification motive is especially active in contexts which exacerbate this threat (Kay & Zanna, in press). Such contexts include situations where one feels that the legitimacy of the system is being directly attacked ("system threat"; Jost & Hunyady 2002; Kay, Jost & Young 2005), when one feels a high sense of dependence on the system ("system dependence"; Laurin & Kay 2008) and when one seeks a sense of control in the system to compensate for a lack of personal control ("personal control"; Kay et al. 2008).

We leverage these three contexts across a series of four studies to demonstrate the effects of the system justification motive on consumption-related choices. We predict that the enhanced need for system justification will lead participants to prefer consumption alternatives that represent traditional and well-accepted norms in society over those that do not. Importantly, we also suggest that there are key individual difference factors that will more precisely determine when the system justification motive will have the greatest impact on consumption preferences. We propose that one's chronic level of confidence in the legitimacy of the system will be especially important. Perhaps counterintuitively, we expect to see the greatest effects of threat on people who have low levels of confidence in the system ("low system endorsers"). We reason that low system endorsers experience a significant gap between their current state and the need for system justification that is aroused as a result of certain threatening contexts. In other words, their fragile sense of confidence in the justness of the system is highly salient and threatening when the system justification motive is activated.

Thus, in line with classic principles of motivation, they are especially motivated to justify the system, and do so through means that provide immediate and concrete symbols of system endorsement such as consumption. By contrast, consumers that are highly confident in the system ("high system endorsers") maintain a strong sense that the system is just, regardless of threat, and therefore have no need to rely on consumption for justification.

In the first study, we examine the impact of system threat and chronic levels of system endorsement (as measured by Kay & Jost's 2003 System Justification Scale) on preferences among pairs of national versus international brands. Participants are asked to read an article which describes a writer's negative opinion of America or a neutral article. We find that low system endorsers prefer fewer international brands when threatened than when not threatened, while high system endorsers do not differ in their choices across conditions.

In study 2, we use a system dependence manipulation and examine its effects on attitudes towards sales people who represent traditional vs. nontraditional values. Participants are asked to read about the U.S. government having a significant impact on their future outcomes in life vs. a neutral paragraph. They are then asked to rate a series of print ads. Half of the ads reflect traditional American values, while the others reflect nontraditional values. We find that low system endorsers rate the nontraditional salespersons as significantly lower in attractiveness and likeability when threatened than when not threatened. As predicted, high system endorsers do not differ in their ratings across conditions.

In study 3, we again use a system dependence manipulation. Participants are then asked to rate a series of ads which we predicted would be more threatening and salient to men than women. Thus, we expected to see a pattern similar to studies 1 and 2, but only among men. Indeed, among men, we find that low system endorsers rate nontraditional ads lower in the high system dependence condition than the control. High system endorsers show no differences across conditions.

In study 4, we activate the system justification motive by manipulating participants' sense of personal control, thereby generalizing our findings beyond contexts that involve direct threats to one's system. Participants are asked to write about something positive that happened to them that was out of their control (threatening condition) versus something positive that happened which was in their control (neutral condition). After the writing exercise, participants are asked to review a list of movies and choose 10 that they would like to watch. Our results indicate that low system endorsers choose fewer movies with a negative tone towards the United States when their sense of personal control is threatened versus the control condition.

In sum, we find that when the threatening consequences of living in an unjust system are made salient, individuals who are generally the least confident in the legitimacy of the system are the most likely to justify it through consumption (by embracing traditional versus nontraditional consumption options). Conversely, individuals who are highly confident in the system are able to withstand threats and do not turn to consumption to justify the system.

References

Jost, John T. and Mahzarin R. Banaji (1994), "The Role of Stereotyping in System-Justification and the Production of False Consciousness," *British Journal of Social Psychology, Special Issue: Stereotypes: Structure, Function and Process*, 33(1), 1-27.

Kay, Aaron C., Danielle Gaucher, Jamie. L. Napier, Mitchell J. Callan, and Kristin Laurin (2008), "God and the Government: Testing a Compensatory Control Mechanism for the Support of External Systems of Control," *Journal of Personality and Social Psychology*, 95, 18-35.

Kay, Aaron C. and Mark P. Zanna (2008), "A Contextual Analysis of the System Justification Motive and its Societal Consequences," in *Social and Psychological Bases of Ideology and System Justification*, ed. John T. Jost, Aaron C. Kay, and Hulda Thorisdottir, Oxford University Press, forthcoming.

Laurin, Kristin and Aaron C. Kay (2008), Unpublished Data.

Jost, John T. and Hunyady (2002), *The Psychology of System Justification and the Palliative Function of Ideology*, Hove, England: Psychology Press/Taylor and Francis (UK).

Kay, Aaron C., John T. Jost, and Sean Young (2005), "Victim-Derogation and Victim-Enhancement as Alternate Routes to System-Justification," *Psychological Science*, 16, 240-246.

Kay, Aaron C. and John T. Jost (2003), "Complementary Justice: Effects of "Poor but Happy" and "Poor but Honest" Stereotypes on System Justification and Implicit Activation of the Justice Motive," *Journal of Personality and Social Psychology*, 85, 823-837.

"The Morphing Self: Changing Self-Concept as a Response to Threats"

Christian Schmid, University of Alberta, Canada
Jennifer J. Argo, University of Alberta, Canada

Consumers are ever increasingly exposed to news coverage about topics of crime, murder, and terrorism. During the period from 1990-1998 alone, while the total number of murders in the US decreased by 20 percent, media coverage on network newscasts about stories on the topic increased by an astonishing 600 percent (Glassner 2004). To date, the limited research that has studied the impact of fear has investigated the impact of reminders of mortality on consumers' acquisition decisions (Ferraro, Shiv, and Bettman 2005, Mandel and Heine 1999, Mandel and Smeesters 2008). However, this is only one side of the consumption equation as according to Holbrook (1987) consumption entails more than just acquisition but also disposition. Given this in the present research, we seek to build on this initial work by investigating the influence of mortality salience on product disposition and do so using a new conceptual framework guided by research on the self and in particular self-affirmation theory (Aronson et al. 1999; Sherman and Cohen 2002, 2006; Steele 1988).

The basic premise of self-affirmation theory is that individuals are motivated to protect the perceived integrity and worth of the self (Steele 1988). One way people may cope with a threat to the self is to implement indirect psychological adaptations by affirming other elements of the self not threatened. In the present research we propose a novel mechanism through which one can self-affirm when faced with a threat: morphing the self through the possession with which one identifies. Given that possessions can serve as an extension of the self (Belk, 1988) it seems reasonable to conclude that consumers may use possessions within their extended self to protect the self through self-affirmation in the face of a threat. More specifically, similar to the notion that the acquisition of new products can signify a change in consumers' extended self-concept when the self is threatened, we argue that the disposal of older possessions can complete this transition into a new self (i.e., morph) as such possessions are constant reminders of the old identity and until they are let go one cannot move on. Support for the expectation that once important possessions will decrease in importance when faced with a mortality reminder is found in qualitative consumer research (e.g., Pavia and Mason 2004).

Our unification of previous work that has been conducted on acquisition in the time of threat with insights into disposal behaviors presents a more complete picture of consumers' relationships with products. In addition, we qualify our findings by reporting materialism as a boundary condition. Indeed, the findings are especially likely to occur for those consumers who are highly invested with material objects but are attenuated for those lower in materialism. Three studies are reported that support the notion of a morphing self.

The first study examined the likelihood of consumers distancing themselves from possessions after they encounter a threat. We used a 2 (mortality salience threat: present vs. absent) x 2 (possession importance: important vs. unimportant) x (materialism) mixed design. We find that when mortality is salient, as consumers' material values increase, they tend to be more likely to distance themselves from possessions as compared to consumers in the control condition who are less likely to distance themselves from material objects as material values increase. This is especially the case for possessions with lower importance to consumers' self.

The second study had two primary objectives. First, the study sought to determine whether the type of threat to the self is critical to consumers' disposition tendencies of possessions once included as a part of the extended self. Second, the study explored if a threat is powerful enough for consumers to actually separate the self completely from a once previously important possession when mortality is made salient. To achieve this second objective, participants completed a baseline assessment of their identity as defined by the possession they associated with in the absence of a threat and a second assessment of their identity after facing a threat, one week apart. We used a 2 (type of threat: mortality salience threat vs. social threat) x (possession importance) x (materialism) mixed design to examine whether the type of threat affects which possessions consumers include into their selves. We find in the mortality salience condition that the more materialistic consumers are the less likely they are to identify important possessions as part of their selves during both time periods. We find the opposite pattern in the social threat condition as participants who were more materialistic were increasingly more likely to identify important possessions at both points in time.

In study 3 we explored what happens within consumers' selves for those possessions that are retained after consumers encounter a mortality salience threat (vs. no threat). If our main premises are correct, mortality salience should disrupt the self and as a result possessions that were formerly an important aspect of the self should become less important. At the same time, possessions that were an extraneous part of the immediate self should gain in importance. We used a 2 (mortality salience threat: present vs. absent) x (possession importance) x (materialism) mixed experimental design. Results reveal that in the presence of a high mortality salience threat participants distanced themselves from possessions that in the control condition they had considered closely related to their selves while possession deemed unrelated to the immediate self in the control condition became more strongly associated with the self in the face of a threat. This effect was qualified by material values. Participants who had high material values used possessions to a significantly greater extent to redefine their self-concept when MS was present (versus absent).

In three studies, we demonstrate that mortality salience threats have important effects on consumers' selves. When a mortality salience threat is present, self-concept consistency is disrupted and a change in consumers' extended self-concept as defined by the possessions that are part of their identity can be observed. The notion that reminders of mortality can disrupt the stability of the self-concept has important implications for consumers' well-being.

References

Aronson, Joshua, Geoffrey L. Cohen, and Nail, P. R. (1999), "Self-Affirmation Theory: An Update and Appraisal," in E. Harmon-Jones and J. Mills (Eds.), *Cognitive Dissonance Theory: Revival with Revisions and Controversies*, Washington, DC: American Psychological Association, 127-147.

Belk, Russell W. (1988), "Possessions and the Extended Self," *Journal of Consumer Research*, 15 (September), 139-68.

Ferraro, Rosellina, Baba Shiv, and James R. Bettman (2005), "Let Us Eat and Drink, for Tomorrow We Shall Die: Effects of Mortality Salience and Self-Esteem on Self-Regulation in Consumer Choice," *Journal of Consumer Research*, 32(June), 65-75.

Glassner, Barry (2004), "Narrative Techniques of Fear Mongering," *Social Research*, 71 (Winter), 819-826.

Holbrook, Morris B. (1987), "What is Consumer Research?" *Journal of Consumer Research,* 14 (June), 128-132.

Mandel, Naomi and Steven J. Heine (1999), "Terror Management and Marketing: He Who Dies with the Most Toys Wins," *Advances in Consumer Research*, 26, 527-32.

Mandel, Naomi and Dirk Smeesters (2008), "The Sweet Escape: Effects of Mortality Salience on Consumption Quantities for High- and Low-Self-Esteem Consumers," *Journal of Consumer Research*, 35 (August), 309-323.

Pavia, Teresa M. and Marlys J. Mason (2004), "The Reflexive Relationship between Consumer Behavior and Adaptive Coping," *Journal of Consumer Research*, 31 (September), 441-54.

David K. Sherman and Geoffrey L. Cohen (2002), "Accepting Threatening Information: Self-Affirmation and the Reduction of Defensive Biases," *Current Directions in Psychological Science*, 11 (August), 119-123.

Steele Claude M. (1988), "The Psychology of Self-Affirmation: Sustaining the Integrity of the Self," in L. Berkowitz (Ed.), *Advances in Experimental Social Psychology*, Vol. 21, New York: Academic Press, 261-302.

"The Spice of Life: Effects of Mortality Anxiety on Preference for Variety"

Daniel Fernandes, Erasmus University, The Netherlands
Naomi Mandel, Arizona State University
Dirk Smeesters, Erasmus University, The Netherlands

Terror management theory (Greenberg, Solomon, and Pyszczynski 1986) posits that people's survival instincts, coupled with their knowledge of inevitable death, can trigger high levels of internal conflict and anxiety. When reminded of their mortality, people can mitigate this conflict by defending their cultural worldviews, bolstering their self-esteem, or both. Recently, several studies have shown the effects of mortality salience (MS) on consumer behavior. Priming death thoughts can lead consumers to choose products that bolster their self-esteem (Ferraro, Shiv, and Bettman 2005), overconsume to escape self-awareness (Mandel and Smeesters 2008), or prefer domestic over foreign products (Liu and Smeesters in press).

Although research has shown how MS affects product preference and the quantities one wants to purchase, it is unclear how MS affects the variety in one's choices (i.e., the number of switches between products or brands over a series of choices; Kahn and Isen 1993). Prior research suggests that MS might lead to either more variety-seeking or less variety-seeking. For example, variety seeking increases with mild positive mood, because novelty gained from experiencing nonthreatening stimuli provides pleasant stimulation and because positive mood heightens a person's desire for such stimulation (Menon and Kahn 1995). This suggests that threatening stimuli, such as death thoughts, might decrease variety seeking. Furthermore, research by Rindfleisch, Burroughs, and Wong (in press) has shown that individuals form stronger connections with brands when death anxiety is high, because they perceive their brands as an important source of meaning in their lives. Again, this finding suggests that consumers might search for less variety when they are reminded of the inevitability of their death, due to stronger loyalty to their favorite brands.

On the other hand, there is reason to believe that MS may lead to increased variety-seeking behavior. Koole, Greenberg, and Pyszczynski (2006) argued that unrestrained freedom might be a way to buffer against death-thoughts. When mortality is salient, individuals might want to experience the feeling of freedom by seeking for excitement and novelty. Hence, consumers might be more willing to try other alternatives to experience unrestrained freedom when death-thoughts are accessible. Individuals in a liberal mindset should be particularly more open to new experiences than conservatives (Jost et al. 2003). Moreover, prior research on left-right wing differences related conservatism to mental rigidity, stimulus aversion, and close-mindedness (Wilson, 1973). Therefore, we hypothesize that the increasing effect of MS on variety-seeking should only occur for individuals with a liberal mindset, but not for those with a conservative mindset.

We conducted three experiments to examine the effects of MS on variety seeking behavior. In study 1, we examined the effect of MS on exploratory behavior. First, participants completed either the Fear of Death scale (Boyar 1964) in the mortality salient condition or the Depression scale (Zung 1965) in the control condition. Next, all participants completed Raju's (1980) Exploratory Behavior Scale (a=.77; 7-point scale). Participants primed to think about their own eventual deaths exhibited a higher level of exploratory behavior (M=4.33) than did control participants (M=4.07; $F(1, 301)=5.92$, $p<.01$). This finding provides preliminary evidence that MS increases variety seeking.

Study 2 extended study 1 by testing the effect of mortality salience on actual behavior, rather than on responses on a scale. Participants were randomly assigned to either the MS or control condition. Next, participants chose ten jellybeans to eat while completing a presumably unrelated questionnaire. The number of flavors they chose served as the dependent measure of variety seeking. Mortality salient participants chose significantly more flavors than did control participants ($M_{MS}=7.49$ vs. $M_{control}$ 6.81 out of 10 possible flavors; $F(1, 227)=4.11$, $p<.05$).

Study 3 extended the earlier studies by testing the effect of MS on the choices made in a sequential variety-seeking paradigm (whereas study 2 used a simultaneous variety-seeking paradigm). In addition, we also primed a liberal versus conservative mindset in participants, by using a scrambled sentences test. Hence, we used a 2 (mortality salience vs. control) x 2 (liberal vs. conservative) between-participants design. After the manipulations, participants were asked to imagine that they were doing their weekly grocery shopping at the nearby grocery store (cf. Menon and Kahn 1995, experiment 2). On each of four sequential shopping occasions, participants chose the brand of snack (among four brands) that they wanted to purchase. Variety seeking was coded in three ways (Mitchell, Kahn, and Knasko 1995): (1) the number of different choices participants made, ranging from 1 (same choice made across all weeks) to 5 (each week a different choice), (2) the number of switches in the choice history, ranging from zero (no switches) to six (no repetition), and (3) the number of switches between successive choices. The interaction effect of MS and primed mindset on the number of different choices made was significant ($F(1, 64)=5.84$, $p=.01$). Planned contrasts showed that MS led to more variety seeking behavior among those primed with a liberal mindset ($M_{MS}=2.76$ vs. $M_{control}=1.58$; $F(1, 64)=2.51$, $p=.01$) and not among those primed with a conservative mindset ($M_{MS}=2.52$ vs. $M_{control}=2.15$; $F(1, 64)=0.85$, $p=.40$). Similar effects were found for the two other measures of variety seeking.

Overall, in three studies, we show that mortality salience leads to enhanced variety seeking. Further, we demonstrated that the effect mainly occurs among those having a liberal mindset, but not among those with a conservative mindset. Future studies will explore the underlying process by which MS increases variety seeking behavior. Specifically, we will examine whether individuals (and especially those with a liberal mindset) have a higher need to experience freedom following a MS manipulation, and whether this mediates the MS effect on variety seeking. Furthermore, we will also examine whether MS leads consumers to make more unique choices, which is also a way to self-express and assert freedom (Kim and Drolet 2003).

References

Rindfleisch, Aric, James E. Burroughs, and Nancy Wong (in press), "The Safety of Objects: Materialism, Existential Insecurity, and Brand Connection," *Journal of Consumer Research.*

Boyar, Jerome I. (1964), "The Construction and Partial Validation of a Scale for the Measurement of Fear of Death," *Dissertation Abstracts*, 25, 20-21.

Ferraro, Rosellina, Baba Shiv, and Jim R. Bettman (2005), "Let Us Eat and Drink, For Tomorrow We Shall Die: Effects of Mortality Salience and Self-Esteem on Self-Regulation in Consumer Choice," *Journal of Consumer Research*, 32, 65-75.

Greenberg, Jeff, Tom Pyszczynski, and Sheldon Solomon (1986), "The Causes and Consequences of a Need for Self-Esteem: A Terror Management Theory," in *Public Self and Private Self*, ed. R. F. Baumeister, New York: Springer, 189-192.

Greenberg, Jeff, Tom Pyszczynski, Sheldon Solomon, Abram Rosenblatt, Mitchell Veeder, Shari Kirkland, and Deborah Lyon (1990), "Evidence for Terror Management Theory II: The Effects of Mortality Salience on Reactions to Those Who Threaten or Bolster the Cultural Worldview," *Journal of Personality and Social Psychology*, 58, 308–18.

Higgins, E. Tory (1997), "Beyond Pleasure and Pain," *American Psychologist*, 52, 1280–1300.

Jost, John T., Jack Glaser, Ari W. Kruglanski, and Frank Sulloway (2003), "Political Conservatism as Motivated Social Cognition," *Psychological Bulletin, 129,* 339-75.

Kahn, Barbara E. and Alice M. Isen (1993)," The Influence of Positive Affect on Variety Seeking among Safe, Enjoyable Products," *Journal of Consumer Research*, 20, 257-70.

Kim, Heejung S. and Aimee Drolet (2003), "Choice and Self-Expression: A Cultural Analysis of Variety Seeking," *Journal of Personality and Social Psychology*, 85, 373-82.

Koole, Sander L., Jeff Greenberg, and Tom Pyszczynski (2006), "Introducing Science to the Psychology of the Soul: Experimental Existential Psychology," *Current Directions in Psychological Science*, 15, 212-16.

Liu, Jia and Dirk Smeesters (in press), "Have You Seen the News Today? The Effect of Death-Related Media Contexts on Brand Preferences," *Journal of Marketing Research.*

Mandel, Naomi and Dirk Smeesters (2008), "The Sweet Escape: Effects of Mortality Salience on Consumption Quantities for High- and Low Self-Esteem Consumers," *Journal of Consumer Research*, 35, 309-23.

Menon, Satya and Barbara E. Kahn (1995), "The Impact of Context on Variety Seeking in Product Choices," *Journal of Consumer Research*, 22, 275-95.

Mitchell, Deborah J., Barbara E. Kahn, and Susan C. Knasko (1995), "There's Something in the Air: Effects of Congruent and Incongruent Ambient Odor on Consumer Decision Making," *Journal of Consumer Research*, 22, 229-38.

Raju, Puthankurissi S. (1980), "Optimum Stimulation Level: Its Relationship to Personality, Demographics and Exploratory Behavior," *Journal of Consumer Research*, 7, 272-82.

Wilson, Glenn D. (1973), *The Psychology of Conservatism*, London: Academic Press.

Zung, William W. K. (1965), "A Self-Rating Depression Scale," *Archives of General Psychiatry*, 12, 63-70.

Special Session Summary

In Pursuit of the Prime Suspects: Insights from Second Generation Research on Nonconscious Influences of Consumer Behavior

Robin J.Tanner, UW Madison, USA

SESSION OVERVIEW

The last two decades of research in social cognition have produced many findings indicating that much of human behavior is driven by factors and processes that operate outside of immediate conscious awareness. For consumer behavior researchers in particular, demonstrations that environmental cues can nonconsciously influence consumer behavior (Chartrand et al. 2008) are both challenging and exciting. Challenging because a world where consumers are exposed to an ever increasing onslaught of marketing cues and primes raises the stakes for researchers trying to understand the processes by which such cues may combine and interact to influence choice and consumption. Exciting because the very idea of a parallel nonconscious goal system opens the door to new directions for research. Previously unexplained behaviors may now find resolution in the context of richer theories of consumer behavior, which recognize and integrate both conscious and nonconscious elements. In this session three papers present insights from second generation research into nonconscious influences of consumer behavior with a particular focus on improving our understanding of the mechanisms by which environmental cues can influence consumers. The papers in the session demonstrate several unexpected ways in which specific marketing-relevant primes influence behavior and explore a method for measuring/diagnosing the relevant goal activations that these primes invoke.

All three papers in this session share a common focus on deepening our theoretical understanding of how marketing-relevant primes can influence downstream consumer behaviors. The first paper, by Laran, Dalton and Andrade, demonstrates unexpected differences between the priming efficacy of sentences, brands, and slogans. In particular, the authors find that slogans, by virtue of their overt persuasive intent, invoke a form of nonconscious reactance that can actually prime behaviors opposite to those intended by the slogan writers. Fascinatingly, this negative priming effect transfers to sentences presented simultaneously with subliminal exposure of the word "slogan". This result not only reinforces the nonconscious nature of the core effect, but also constitutes initial evidence of the capability of subliminal cues to hijack and modify the meaning of consciously perceived stimuli.

The second paper, by Goldsmith and Dhar, demonstrates an entirely different mechanism by which environmental cues can ironically influence consumer behavior. The authors show that when choosing between two goal congruent options, incidental activation of a conflicting goal actually increases choice of the option which most conflicts with the new goal. Thus Goldsmith and Dhar identify circumstances where goal activation can actually invoke behavior that is entirely inconsistent with the goal, a result which they demonstrate is driven by consumers' desire to justify their choices.

One implication of these first two papers is to provide a salient reminder of the variety of (often unexpected) ways in which peripheral cues can conspire to automatically influence consumer behavior. This presents considerable challenges both to researchers concerned with identifying possible priming effects in their stimuli and for practitioners desirous of fully understanding the totality of possible effects caused by their marketing efforts. The final paper, by Carlson et al., speaks directly to this issue by presenting evidence that goals automatically invoked by peripheral cues, and which operate outside of conscious awareness, can actually be measured. By interrupting choice tasks before they are complete (where goal activation levels should be maximal), and using sensitive measures, these authors demonstrate the important finding that it is actually possible to measure the activation of goals invoked by supraliminal primes, subliminal primes, or the choice context itself. The methodological ability to measure online goal activation opens the possibility of testing a range of theories that hypothesize the role of specific goals, like Goldsmith and Dhar's goal of justifying choices.

These three papers all feature research that makes substantial theoretical contributions to contemporary research in psychology while also being grounded in consumption phenomenon that are relevant to many consumer researchers. Taken together, these three papers substantively deepen our understanding of the psychological processes underlying automatic effects on behavior caused by peripheral environmental cues.

EXTENDED ABSTRACTS

"The Curious Case of Behavioral Backlash: Nonconscious Reactance to Marketing Slogans"

Juliano Laran, University of Miami
Amy Dalton, Hong Kong University of Science and Technology
Eduardo B. Andrade, University of California, Berkeley

Marketing practitioners rely on an impressive arsenal of persuasion tools, including brands, salespeople, prices, and slogans, in their attempt to influence consumer spending. A solid foundation of research in psychology and marketing would suggest that these tools can "persuade" consumers under the radar of consciousness. This research would further suggest a process whereby marketing tools have a positive impact on consumers' responses, with incidental exposure to, say, a brand or slogan triggering behaviors that are consistent with that brand or slogan. However, while this priming process may occur in most environments, it may not generalize to marketing environments. Marketing environments have idiosyncrasies that could dampen or even reverse the intended effects of marketers' tools.

One idiosyncrasy of marketing stimuli is that, unlike other environmental stimuli, people believe marketing stimuli exist to persuade them. That being said, this belief exists to varying degrees as a function of the marketing stimuli themselves. For instance, while people may relate to brands as innocuous relationship partners, the persuasive intent of slogans is much clearer. To address this issue empirically, we conducted a pretest examining consumers' perceptions about the persuasive intent of two common persuasion tools: marketing slogans and brands. For this pretest, 50 participants were shown a series of five slogans, brands, or sentences, and asked to rate on a 7-point scale the extent to which they perceived each stimulus as an attempt to persuade them. The purpose of asking about the persuasive intent of sentences was simply to establish a baseline. Results showed that participants perceived the persuasive intent of brands (M=3.20) to be only trivially higher than that of sentences (M=3.00), while the persuasive intent of slogans was perceived to be quite high (M=5.13), and significantly higher than that of brands ($F(2, 44)=3.47$, $p<.05$).

Thus, while brands were perceived to be innocuous (no different than common sentences in their persuasive intent), slogans were perceived more clearly as persuasive appeals.

The perception that marketing tools are persuasive appeals sets these stimuli apart from other environmental stimuli. However, it is unclear how consumers respond to persuasive tools on a nonconscious level. One might argue that because the impact of priming on behavior is nonconscious (or, at least, people are not sufficiently aware to verbalize it), any defense mechanism against persuasion tools should not work. On the other hand, perhaps people can react against a persuasion tool without awareness of its presence or potential influence. This response could develop in the same way that other processes become automatic. That is, if people repeatedly and consistently responded to a persuasion tool with conscious reactance, over time they should come to nonconsciously react against it. In the context of the current research, we would therefore predict nonconscious reactance against slogans because consumers consciously perceive that slogans are persuasion tools. We would not, however, predict nonconscious reactance against brands because consumers lack the perception that brands are persuasion tools. These predictions were tested in study 1.

Study 1 used a 3 X 3 design (N=435), with prime tool (brand, slogan, or sentence) and prime message (save, spend, or neutral) manipulated between-subjects. Participants' first task was a bogus memorization task in which we presented sentences, brands, or slogans that were related to either saving money (e.g., "He wore cheap attire", "Dollar Store", "The Best Deals Are Always Here!"), spending money (e.g., "He wore high-end attire", "Tiffany", "Luxury, you deserve it"), or were neutral (e.g., "He wore blue pants", "Barnes and Noble", "Time is what you make of it"). In a supposedly unrelated second experiment on shopping tendencies, we asked participants to imagine that they went shopping with $500, and indicate how much of the $500 they would like to spend. Their response was our dependent variable.

We included the sentences as a control condition and predicted that participants who were exposed to sentences would show prime-consistent behavior. This is precisely what we found. Relative to neutral sentences (M=$145.93), sentences with a message to save decreased spending (M=$105.91) and sentences with a message to spend increased spending (M=$185.18). As predicted, the same pattern of results was obtained among participants primed with brands. Willingness to spend in the neutral brands condition (M=$150.70) fell in between the savings brands condition (M=$94.29) and the spending brands condition (M=$189.27). Importantly, however, this pattern of results failed to hold among participants primed with slogans, who actually showed the exact opposite pattern of spending. Relative to slogans with a neutral message (M=$142.93), slogans with messages to save increased spending (M=$184.58) and slogans with messages to spend decreased spending (M=$105.23), all p's<.05. Thus, while priming with brands (and sentences) produced prime-consistent behavior, priming with slogans produced prime-inconsistent behavior–a behavioral backlash.

We propose that consumers need not be consciously aware of a marketing tool's persuasive intent for this behavioral backlash to occur. However, because participants in study 1 were exposed to prime tools supraliminally, conscious responses could have influenced consumer spending. Extensive debriefing suggested this was unlikely; nevertheless, in study 2, we used a more conservative, subliminal priming procedure to minimize conscious mediation, demand effects or hypothesis guessing. In addition, we dropped the brand condition and controlled for the stimuli presented by using the exact same phrases in both the sentence and slogan conditions. Therefore, the only difference between the conditions was subliminal priming of the word "sentence" or "slogan".

Study 2 used a 2 X 3 design, with prime tool (slogan or sentence) and prime message (save, spend, or neutral) manipulated between-subjects (N=229). Participants were instructed to memorize the same sentences used in study 1's bogus memorization task. However, while the sentences were presented in the center of the screen, the word "sentence" or "slogan" was presented for 60 ms in alternating, randomly-determined quadrants. Participants indicated whether each "flash" appeared on the left or right. Results revealed that among participants subliminally primed with the word "sentence", messages to save reduced spending (M=$115.94) and messages to spend increased spending (M=$211.68) relative to neutral messages (M=$156.82). Conversely, among participants subliminally primed with the word "slogan", messages to save increased spending (M=$197.22) and messages to spend decreased spending (M=$106.68) relative to neutral messages (M=$151.06), all p's<.05. Thus, while activating the concept "sentence" produced prime-consistent behavior, "slogan" produced prime-inconsistent behavior.

In summary, certain persuasion tools may backfire and generate effects opposite to those intended by marketers. Our results provide an initial demonstration of this phenomenon by showing that stimuli structured as slogans (study 1) or represented as slogans (study 2) can incite a nonconscious behavioral backlash. Our findings suggest that this behavioral backlash is rooted in consumers' conscious beliefs about the persuasive intent of marketing tools. These results underscore the necessity of understanding marketing's idiosyncrasies before we can fully understanding priming effects in marketing environments.

"Ironic Effects of Goal Activation on Choice"

Kelly Goldsmith, Northwestern University
Ravi Dhar, Yale University

Consider a consumer who is choosing between two indulgent desserts. Further imagine that prior to choosing a dessert she notices a health magazine on a nearby table. How would exposure to the health magazine affect her choice? While it is now well established that consumer choice is goal driven, relatively little is known about how the incidental activation of a goal that conflicts with the goal associated with a choice task (hereafter referred to as the "choice goal") will affect the choices that people make. For example, would this person be more or less likely to choose a more indulgent and less healthy dessert in comparison to a person for whom the health goal was not activated?

This paper explores how choice between two options is impacted when these alternatives pose a violation to another goal that has been activated prior to the choice. We draw from research on goal systems theory and behavioral decision theory to propose that when an incidental goal (e.g., health) that conflicts with the choice goal (e.g., to enjoy an indulgent treat) becomes activated prior to the choice, all available choice options will present a violation of the incidental goal. Thus when making their choice, consumers will experience the need to justify their incidental goal violation. As a consequence, consumers will be more likely to choose the option in the set that offers maximum attainment of the choice goal (e.g., a more indulgent special treat) than when the conflicting goal is not activated. Options providing maximum goal attainment may be easier to justify, when they offer the consumer a special or unique experience. Thus we predict an ironic effect of goal activation on choice: Goal activation can increase choice of the option that conflicts most with that goal.

Our predictions are tested in a series of six studies. Study 1 demonstrates the proposed effect. Using non-conscious goal priming, we manipulate if a conflicting goal (e.g., savings) is incidentally activated prior to choice (e.g., a choice between two expensive, luxury rental cars). The results demonstrate that the activation of a conflicting goal can ironically increase choice of the option the presents a greater conflict to that goal (e.g., the more expensive, luxury rental car). Study 2 demonstrates an important boundary condition. By manipulating both incidental goal activation (health goal vs. control) and goal conflict (a choice between two high calorie options that conflict with a health goal vs. a choice between two low calorie options that do not conflict), we show that goal activation leads to ironic effects only when none of the options in the choice set allow for pursuit of the incidentally activated goal. Study 3 rules out an alternate account for the pattern of results, replicating the choice effect and demonstrating that the incidental goal prime increases the accessibility of that goal, as intended. Testing for the mechanism behind this effect, Study 4 replicates these ironic effects with real choices (e.g., a choice between two unhealthy donuts for consumption), and assesses how goal conflict affects consumers' interests in special or unique options. The results demonstrate that goal conflict increases interest in special or unique options, and further that this increase in interest in special or unique options mediates the effect of goal conflict on choice. Study 5 further examines the underlying process and rules out a second alternate account for the pattern of results by showing that these results cannot be explained by goal conflict increasing interest in options that offer "maximum violations". Finally, in Study 6, we test if external prompts to justify a choice result in similar effects, by manipulating both goal conflict and an additional need for justification. The results show that goal conflict and the additional need for justification have an analogous effect on choice.

As the need for justification can affect consumer decisions and shift preference towards options that are supported by the best reasons, this research has clear implications for marketers seeking to maximize their understanding of consumer decision processes at the point of choice. For example, in an additional study we manipulated if a savings goal was incidentally activated (vs. a control), then gave participants a choice between two expensive, luxury suitcases that were priced equally ($695), one of which was labeled "only two left." The results of this study showed that participants experiencing goal conflict (savings goal prime) were significantly more likely to choose whichever option was labeled as "only two left." Building on the current set of studies, these results suggest that goal conflict and the need for justification may increase interest in products supported by many different reasons (e.g., limited availability). We hope that the current research will prompt future inquiry into this area.

"Catching Goals in the Act of Decision Making"

Kurt Carlson, Georgetown University
Robin J. Tanner, University of Wisconsin, Madison
Margaret G. Meloy, Pennsylvania State University
J. Edward Russo, Cornell University

Although consumers may prefer to think that their decisions are guided by conscious thought, accumulating evidence suggests that many choices are influenced by subtle and unrecognized environmental cues. Perhaps nowhere is the relevance for understanding consumer behavior more profound than in the advances that have been made in the area of nonconscious goal pursuit (Chartrand and Bargh 1996). Though the very idea of a parallel nonconscious goal system opens the door to new directions for research, many of these directions are challenged by the complexities of studying goals of which consumers are not aware. This paper introduces and validates a method for measuring goal activation levels during the consumer choice process. Rather than using free-form responses, or all-or-none measures of goal activation, we use a goal log that requires participants to assess the activation of a set of goals on an 11-point scale. Assessment happens midway through the decision to align assessment with the period of maximal goal activation. The method is tested across three studies.

In study 1, two goal primes, Memorize or Form an Impression, and the priming task (sentence completion) were borrowed from Chartrand and Bargh (1996). After the priming task, participants (N=51) made a choice between two scholarship applicants. Midway through the choice process, participants were interrupted and reported how active nine different goals were at that moment. Goal activation levels were recorded on an 11-point scale (0 =not at all active; 10=maximally active). Participants then resumed reading the remaining information about the candidates, and selected the one they preferred. After their choice they reported whether the focal goals had been active (yes/no) during the choice process. If participants were aware of their goal activation levels, the difference in goal activation (Form an Impression–Memorize) should have been greater when the Form an Impression goal was primed than when Memorize was primed. This comparison revealed a greater difference when the Form an Impression goal was primed (M=5.08) than when the Memorize goal was primed (M=2.71, p<.05). However, post-choice measures revealed such no difference—the same proportion of Ps indicated that the Memorize goal was active (68%) in both conditions, and slightly more indicated the Form an Impression goal was active in the Memorize condition (91%) than in the Form an Impression condition (88%). Whereas the mid-choice continuous assessment revealed prime consistent differences in goal activation, the post-choice measure produced the null result found repeatedly in prior research (e.g., Chartrand and Bargh 1996).

Other research has established that the consistency goal can be activated subliminally and that its activation influences consumer choice processes (Russo, Carlson, Meloy and Yong 2008). In study 2, we follow Russo et al. (2008) by activating the Consistency goal via parafoveal priming. We then measure goal activation levels for several goals, including the Consistency goal. We do so twice, once midway through and once just before the end of the choice. After the choice, participants (N=110) were debriefed for awareness (Chartrand and Bargh 1996).

Similar to study 1, activation of the consistency goal measured midway through the choice was greater for participants who had been subliminally primed with consistency words (M=7.27) than it was for participants who were exposed to goal-neutral words (M=6.58; p<.05). The same was true for the measure of consistency taken after participants had seen all six of the attributes ($M_{consistency}$=7.58; $M_{neutral}$=6.89; p<.05). Importantly, the activation levels of the other goals did not differ across condition for the early assessment (all p>.38) or the late assessment (all p>.24).

To deal with difficult tradeoffs, consumers often seek out choice alternatives that allow them to avoid making those painful tradeoffs (Luce 1998). When no such alternatives are available, the desire to avoid negative emotions "in-process" can become active (p. 21, Luce, Bettman, and Payne 2001). That is, difficult tradeoffs can activate the goal to avoid negative emotions. Following this logic, we reasoned that making tradeoffs salient would cause the Avoid Negative Feelings goal to increase in activation. We posited that having participants engage in attribute-based processing of non-alignable information for three appealing alternatives (hotels), would make the difficulty of the tradeoffs salient, which would lead to substantial activation of the Avoid Negative Emotions goal. In contrast presenting the alternatives serially (thereby requiring alternative-based processing), would not highlight tradeoffs across the alternatives, which would keep the Avoid Negative Emotions goal relatively inactive (i.e., at something like its chronic or background level of activation during a typical choice).

In Study 3, participants (N=50) decided between three hotels described by three attributes (Location, Pool, Services) in one of two information conditions, attribute-based or alternative-based processing. After reading all of the information, but before selecting their preferred hotel, participants reported the activation levels for 11 processing goals, including Avoid Negative Emotions.

As expected, participants in the attribute-based processing condition reported higher activation of the Avoid Negative Emotion goal (M=6.96 on the 0-to-10 scale) than participants in the alternative-based processing condition (M=2.92, p<.01). This result shows that the choice architecture, with no change in information content, can influence the activation of processing goals.

In conclusion, this research explores whether consumers can report goals that have been activated outside of their awareness. Perhaps the key takeaway is that even though consumers are typically unaware of what factor(s) in the environment caused a goal to become active, they can report if that goal is active when a sensitive assessment method is used. Our hope is that this method for catching goals in the act of decision making will help researchers identify goals that (a) underlie important consumer behaviors, (b) are activated by common contextual factors, and (c) are related to each other either through causal activation or through simple relatedness to a higher order goal.

REFERENCES

Chartrand, Tanya L. and John A. Bargh (1996), "Automatic Activation of Impression Formation and Memorization Goals: Nonconscious Goal Priming Reproduces Effects of Explicit Task Instructions," *Journal of Personality and Social Psychology*, 71 (September), 464-478.

Russo, J. Edward, Kurt A. Carlson, Margaret G. Meloy and Kevyn Yong (2008), "The Goal of Consistency as a Cause of Information Distortion," *Journal of Experimental Psychology: General*, 137 (3), 456-70.

Special Session Summary

The Rosy Side of Negative Emotions

Uzma Khan, Stanford University, USA

SESSION OVERVIEW

Recent decades have witnessed a burgeoning interest in the role of emotions in decision-making across several different fields including, marketing, psychology and economics (Pham 2007, Schwartz 2000; Vohs and Baumeister 2007). Conventional wisdom and most of past research suggests that emotions, especially negative ones, can adversely affect decision-making and can have both short and long-term consequences. For example, a study by Shiv, Loewenstein and Bechara (2005) showed that people who do not experience negative emotions after losses (due to brain damage) end-up making more money than those who do. The idea being that experiencing of negative emotions can guide bad decisions. Similarly, Tiedens and Linton (2001) showed that negative affect (e.g., anger) leads to impulsiveness and shallow-processing of information. Others have similarly documented detrimental effects of negative affect on performance (Zeelenberg and Beattie 1997), product evaluation and brand attitude (De Houwer, Thomas, and Baeyens 2001). Hence a picture that emerges from the above literature consistently portrays that negative emotions generally impair judgment and decision-making.

Papers in the present session take another in-depth look at the functioning of commonly experienced negative emotions and uncover how negative affect, despite its reputation, can help improve decision-making and wellbeing in certain contexts. The session includes three papers, which are all in advance stages of completion. Contrary to the established findings, the papers show positive effects of everyday negative emotions, such as anger, regret and sadness in several different domains including, product evaluations and choice satisfaction, self-control, learning, and judgment-biases.

In the first paper, Nelson, Malkoc and Shiv examine the upside of regret. They argue that, unlike past literature which has mainly focused on negative impact of regret, regret can play a functional role in learning from past mistakes. They show that manipulation of only the emotional component of experienced regret leads to better performance on decisions within the domain where regret is experienced, but not in dissimilar domains.

In the second paper, Khan, Maimaran and Dhar show positive influence of anger-an emotion generally perceived to have adverse effects-on choice behavior and satisfaction. For example, they find that angry people are less likely to defer choice and end up being more satisfied with their chosen options. They also demonstrate that anger decreases a bias to choose the compromise option and can induce more goal-consistent actions.

Finally, the third paper by Zemack-Rugar shows how negative emotions can improve self-control. She shows that sad individuals increase self-control as compared to a neutral baseline. These findings are contrary to existing research which argues that negative emotions are detrimental to self-control (Tice et al., 2001) and are explained by accounting for emotion-regulation goals and a new variable–emotion regulation cognitions.

Taken together, the papers in this session shed a new light on the functioning of common negative emotions and deepen our understanding of their role in judgment and decision-making with particular implications for choice satisfaction, learning, brand evaluations and self-control. Given the prevalence of negative emotions in everyday life, it is important to not only understand their detrimental effects but also to appreciate how they can improve decision-making.

EXTENDED ABSTRACTS

"Functional Regret: The Positive Effects of Regret on Learning from Negative Experiences"

Noelle Nelson, University of Minnesota, USA
Selin A. Malkoc, Washington University in St. Louis, USA
Baba Shiv, Stanford University, USA

Popular wisdom encourages people to "learn from experiences", but not regret past actions, implying that people can gain all necessary information from their mistakes without enduring the pain. Academic literature can also view regret and negative emotion as somewhat detrimental. For example, participants who lost money in a negotiation task lose even more money on a subsequent negotiation task when they anticipate regret (Zeelenberg and Beattie 1997). Also, Shiv, Loewenstein and Bechara (2005) showed that brain damaged patients who do not suffer negative emotional feedback after a financial loss end up making "better" decisions (i.e., stick to high-risk, high-return investments)..

Regret has both cognitive and emotional components (Zeelenberg 1999). Most work on regret deals with the cognitive feedback (i.e. correctness of decision) and finds that regret hurts later decisions or induces switching from a regretted choice (whether appropriate or not). To our knowledge, no research has examined the role of the emotional component. We attempt to fill this gap by taking the evolutionary perspective that regret is functional and necessary for learning from negative experience and that regret is useful beyond simply inducing switching behavior; it affects effort.

First, our research argues that feeling the negative emotion associated with an experience leads to learning in a subsequent situation. Second, regret will not always have a positive effect on learning. Some stimulus in the new environment must trigger the emotion associated with the initial event (Baumeister et. al. 2007) for it to be functional. The stronger the trigger (i.e. initial emotion) the more effective regret is for learning.

H1: Experiencing more emotional regret will demonstrate more learning in subsequent similar decisions.

H2: Experiencing more emotional regret will demonstrate no learning in subsequent dissimilar decisions.

To test our hypotheses, study 1 examined field data from the 2008 Olympics. We analyze swimmers who swim multiple final races of the same (similar domain) and different (dissimilar domain) strokes. The change in time from one race to another is our dependent variable. We operationalized regret based on prior research indicating that athletes who win silver medals (second place) experience greater negative emotion than people who win bronze medals (even though they perform objectively better; Medvec, Madey and Gilovich 1995). Therefore, swimmers who placed second (third) in their first race serve as our high (low) regret condition. We find that swimmers who come in second (third) in a previous race perform relatively better (worse) in a subsequent similar race. There is no effect for swimmers who competed in two dissimilar races. Because second place swimmers feel more regret, their performance is enhanced in a subsequent similar trial.

Study 2 tested whether the negative emotion experienced in an earlier web search task would carry over to affect subsequent search behavior. Participants searched the internet for the lowest price they could find for a blender (which they thought would win them a cash prize). All participants "missed" the prize by a small amount. Regret was manipulated with the size of the prize ($5 vs. $50). After a filler task, participants searched for a knife set they would give as a gift. As expected, participants who missed $50 ($5) and felt high (low) regret put more (less) effort (i.e. time) into searching a gift.

Our third study manipulated the intensity of emotional regret felt, while keeping the experience (and cognitive feedback) constant. Sawyer et al (1992) demonstrated that caffeine heightens emotion. Accordingly, we manipulated regret with caffeinated or decaf coffee. After drinking coffee, subjects completed a yoked buying task where they were given 5 tokens. Participants were told that they would see a random number of products in a random order and that they should indicate whether or not they wanted to buy each product. The rigged task resulted in everyone buying the U of Minnesota decal for 2 tokens and ending up 1 token short when the more desirable electronic game was presented. Therefore, all subjects felt regret. Lastly, participants indicated their willingness to pay for a related item (U of M keychain; triggering the initial experience) and an unrelated item (notebook).

We analyzed only the infrequent coffee drinkers, as these participants were expected to display sensitivity to the manipulation. A significant interaction emerged between the product type and caffeine level. Participants who consumed caffeine (high regret) were willing to pay less for the U of M keychain than those drank the decaf (low regret). However, there was no effect of caffeine on WTP of the dissimilar product (notebook).

Study 4 was similar to study 3, but regret level was manipulated by the attractiveness of the product the participant "missed". Participants went through the rigged buying task, bought the car decal and were unable to buy either an electronic game (low regret) or an iPod (high regret). The resulting design was a 2 (felt-regret: high vs. low) x 2 (decision domain: similar vs. dissimilar). Participants then indicated WTP for the similar (U of M keychain) and dissimilar (Eiffel tower keychain) products. We found a significant interaction such that participants who had felt high (low) regret over buying the U of M decal were willing to pay significantly less (more) for the U of M keychain, but there were no differences in WTP for the Eiffel tower keychain.

Overall, we propose and demonstrate that regret is necessary for learning from mistakes and can be functional. Unlike previous literature, we examine experienced emotional regret and find that in domains they have failed before, regret actually helps consumers' make higher quality decisions.

References

Baumeister, Roy F., Kathleen D. Vohs, C. Nathan DeWall, and L.Q. Zhang (2007), "How Emotion Shapes Behavior: Feedback, Anticipation, and Reflection, Rather Than Direct Causation," *Personality and Social Psychology Review*, 11, 167-203.

Medvec, Victoria H., Scott F. Madey, and Thomas Gilovich, T. (1995), "When Less is More: Counterfactual Thinking and Satisfaction Among Olympic Athletes," *Journal of Personality and Social Psychology*, 69, 603-610.

Sawyer Deborah A., Harry L. Julia, and Alan C. Turin (1982), "Caffeine and Human Behavior: Arousal, Anxiety, and Performance Effects," *Journal of Behavioral Medicine*, 5, 415-39.

Shiv, Baba, George Loewenstein, and Antoine Bechara (2005), "The Dark side of Emotion in Decision-Making: When Individuals with Decreased Emotional Reactions Make More advantageous Decisions," *Cognitive Brain Research*, 23 (1), 83-92.

Zeelenberg, Marcel (1999), "Anticipated Regret, Expected Feedback and Behavioral Decision-making," *Journal of Behavioral Decision Making*, 12, 93-106.

Zeelenberg, Marcel and Jane Beattie (1997), "Consequences of Regret Aversion: Additional Evidence for Effects of Feedback on Decision Making," *Organizational Behavior and Human Decision Processes*, 72, 63-78.

"Positive Upshots of Anger in Decision-Making"

Uzma Khan, Stanford University, USA
Michal Maimaran, Kellogg–Northwestern University, USA
Ravi Dhar, Yale University, USA

The role of emotions in decision-making is gaining increased attention (Schwartz 2000). Generally, emotions have been shown to have negative effects on decision quality (Shiv et al. 2005). For example, one of the most frequently encountered emotions, anger, is perceived as a negative affect that leads to impulsiveness and shallow-processing (Tiedens and Linton 2001), higher action tendencies against others (Frijda, Kuipers and Schure 1989), careless thought and increased risk-seeking (Lerner and Tiedens 2006). Hence, the conventional wisdom is that anger leads to hasty and inferior decisions. In the current research, we argue that negative emotions like anger can have positive effects on decision-making. Specifically, we suggest that in certain decision contexts anger can lead to better outcomes due to a less careful processing of local tradeoffs.

We examine this proposition for two well-established context effects—choice-deferral and compromise-effect. Tradeoff difficulty, resulting from effortful processing of available options and greater focus on local comparisons, has been implicated in both choice-deferral (e.g., when all options are highly attractive; Dhar 1997) and a tendency to choose the middle option (e.g., to avoid loss on either dimension; Simonson 1989). To the extent that angry individuals engage in less careful processing of local tradeoffs, we predict that they will be less susceptible to choice-deferral as well as a compromise-effect as both these biases arise due to in-depth processing of difficult tradeoffs. In summary, we predict that angry individuals are less likely to base their choice on in-depth processing of the local characteristics of the decision context. This in-turn reduces decision biases that results from a focus on the local context of the decision and hence increase long-term decision satisfaction. We tested these propositions in five studies.

In Study 1 participants were induced with anger or neutral emotion and asked to choose between two flight-tickets or defer the decision. Past research has shown that people often defer a choice when provided several attractive options even though each option by itself is seen as sufficiently attractive (Iyengar and Lepper 2000). We hypothesize that angry individuals are less likely to suffer from such decision-inertia. Consistent with our prediction significantly fewer participants deferred the decision to purchase the flight ticket in the anger condition as compared to the neutral-condition (17% vs. 42%).

In Study 2 we examined the effect of anger on choice of the compromised option. Participants chose from either a 2- or 3-options choice-sets in four product categories (laptops, binoculars, restaurants and flashlights). Collapsing across the categories we found the expected compromise effect among neutral-mood participants i.e., a 28% increase for neutral participants in the share when an alternative became a middle-option compared to only a 9% increase in its share among angry participants. We explain that since anger leads to shallower processing and lower risk-aversion, angry people are less likely to go for the middle option which is generally the result of trade-off difficulty and need-for-justification

We tested our prediction regarding reduced reliance on local tradeoffs in Studies 3 and 4 and found that 1) angry people reported fewer attribute-level tradeoffs in the explanations of their choice and 2) the decreased tendency to choose the compromise option observed among angry participants was mediated by the level of attribute-level tradeoffs.

Finally, Study 5 used real choices between two different packs of cookies and showed that angry participants were 1) more likely to choose a pack as opposed to taking the no-choice option and 2) reported greater satisfaction with their choice a week later than sad or neutral-mood participants. Besides illustrating the positive affect of anger on choice-satisfaction, the study also demonstrates that the affect of anger are unique and different from other negative emotions such as sadness.

These findings suggest that anger plays an important role in determining individuals' tendency to make a decision, the type of decisions they make, and how satisfied they are with their decisions in the long-run.

References

Dhar, Ravi (1997), "Consumer Preference for a No-choice Option," *Journal of Consumer Research*, 24, 215-231.

Frijda, Nico H., Peter Kuipers, and Elisabeth Schure (1989), "Relations Among Emotion, Appraisal, and Emotional Action Readiness," *Journal of Personality and Social Psychology*, 57, 212-228.

Iyengar, Sheena S. and Mark R. Lepper (2000), "When Choice is Demotivating: Can One Desire Too Much of a Good Thing?" *Journal of Personality and Social Psychology*, 79, 995-1006.

Lerner, Jennifer S. and Larissa Z. Tiedens (2006), "Portrait of the Angry Decision Maker: How Appraisal Tendencies Shape Anger's Influence on Cognition," *Journal of Behavioral Decision Making*, 19, 115-137.

Shiv, Baba, George Loewenstein, and Antoine Bechara (2005), "The Dark Side of Emotion in Decision-making: When Individuals with Decreased Emotional Reactions Make More Advantageous Decisions," *Cognitive Brain Research*, 23 (April), 85-92.

Schwarz, Norbert (2000), "Emotion, Cognition, and Decision-Making," *Cognition and Emotion*, 14, 433-440.

Simonson, Itamar (1989), "Choice Based on Reasons: The Case of Attraction and Compromise Effects," *Journal of Consumer Research*, 16 (September), 158-174.

Tiedens, Larissa Z. and S. Linton (2001), "Judgment Under Emotional Certainty and Uncertainty: The Effects of Specific Emotions and Their Associated Certainty Appraisals on Cognitive Processing," *Journal of Personality and Social Psychology,* 81, 973-988.

"Negative Emotions Can Lead to Increases in Self Control: The Mediating Role of Emotion-Regulation Cognitions"

Yael Zemack-Rugar, Virginia Tech, USA

Negative emotions and self control are considered antithetical. Contrary to this view, this research shows that under certain conditions negative emotions can increase self-control.

Previous theory on an emotion-as-motivation framework. It argues that the goal to emotion-regulate (i.e., feel better in a negative emotion) is contrary to self control. We extend this theory by accounting for a heretofore unaccounted for variable–emotion-regulation cognitions. These cognitions refer to thoughts individuals have regarding what (self-control) behaviors they believe would make them feel better. We draw a more nuanced theoretical and empirical mapping of the relationship between negative emotions and self control.

We applying the two basic premises of goal theory: (1) that emotion-regulation cognitions (i.e., thoughts individuals have about what behaviors are useful for goal attainment) should affect emotion-regulation goal-related behavior, and (2) that these cognitions should only affect behavior when the goal is active. In three studies we demonstrate the centrality of emotion-regulation cognitions in predicting behavior and rule out alternative explanations.

In study 1 we manipulate emotion-regulation cognitions (ERC henceforth), making participants believe that reducing self-control will make them feel either better/worse. We expected an interaction of emotion by ERCs such that in a sad (negative) emotion condition, where the emotion-regulation goal (to feel better) is active, participants will increase/reduce self control in accordance with ERCs. We expected that in a neutral condition, where the emotion-regulation goal is inactive, ERCs will not affect behavior. These predictions were confirmed. Additionally, sad participants whose ERCs suggested reducing self-control was harmful for emotion-regulation showed an absolute increase self control.

These results are contrary to resource-depletion theory. Equally depleted (sad) individuals show different self-control levels; these levels occur despite equal activation of the emotion-regulation goal. Further, these differences emerge due to differences in ERCs and disappear when the emotion-regulation goal is inactive (neutral), lending initial support for our theory.

In study 2 we measure ERCs across two different negative emotions (sadness and guilt) in a pretest. The data shows that guilty individuals' ERCs indicate self-control is less useful for emotion regulation than sad individuals' ERCs. Given the hypothesized importance of ERCs, we predicted that guilty participants would show higher self control than sad participants.

Consistent with goal theory, this effect should disappear when the emotion-regulation goal is inactive. We deactivate this goal for half of our participants; when the emotion-regulation goal was inactive, no differences were expected. We also include a neutral condition as a baseline.

Our predictions were confirmed showing (a) guilty participants showed higher self control than sad and neutral ones, and (b) these effects disappeared when the emotion-regulation goal was deactivated. These findings show the importance of ERCs in predicting behavior and provide a second demonstration of absolute increases in self control in a negative emotion, even when the emotion-regulation goal is active.

In study 3 we seek to demonstrate the mediating role of ERCs and to rule out an alternative explanation based on appraisal theory. We also identify a moderator that helps in the prediction of ERCs.

We conducted a three-phase study (same participants in all phases) inducing sadness/guilt/neutral in each phase, and measuring ERCs, self-control behavior, and cognitive and appraisals and EPO. First, this design allows us to test the mediating role of ERCs in determining self-control behavior.

Second, this design allowed us to examine an alternative explanation based on cognitive appraisals. One might argue that the appraisal of control/responsibility (which differs between sad/guilty) leads to differences in self-control behavior. We argue that appraisals and ERCs are distinct theoretically; the former has to do with how we came to feel the way we do, and the latter has to do with how we can stop feeling the way we do. There is also empirical evidence for this distinction. In our study 1 appraisals were identical for all sad participants, but self-control behavior differed; this difference was based on ERCs. Given these empirical and theoretical points, we predicted appraisals would not predict behavior or ERCs.

Third, we examine in study three the actual relationship between ERCs and appraisals. We predicted this relationship was moderated by a third variable—EPO. EPO is a measure of the degree to which consumers focus more on the negative vs. positive outcomes of self control. Those high in EPO, tend to focus more on the negative outcomes of reducing self control.

We predicted when control appraisal was low, consumers would feel that no effort would affect their emotional outcome. Thus, their ERCs would suggest that exerting self-control effort is useless for emotion-regulation. However, if control appraisal was high, consumers would consider whether exerting self-control effort was worthwhile based on whether they thought the outcome of that effort would be positive/negative; this is measured with EPO. Those consumers high on EPO (think the outcome of reducing self-control is relatively negative) would have ERCs suggesting reducing self control is hurtful for emotion-regulation; the opposite would be true of those low in EPO.

All of the predictions for study three were confirmed. Consistent with study 2, guilty participants' ERCs showed reducing self control was less useful for emotion regulation than sad and neutral ones; they, therefore showed higher levels of self control in choice. Importantly, ERCs mediated the effects of emotions on self-control behavior.

Appraisals did not predict ERCs directly, nor did they predict behavior. Instead, the predicted interaction of appraisals by EPO predicted ERCs. This interaction did not predict behavior. In models including all variables, ERCs was consistently the only significant predictor.

These findings together suggest the important role that ERCs play in the relationship between negative emotions and self control. They demonstrate that we should account for ERCs in order to create a more nuanced view of this relationship.

SPECIAL SESSION SUMMARY

Morality, Suspicion, and Modification: New Directions After 15 Years' Persuasion Knowledge Research

Guang-Xin Xie, University of Massachusetts Boston, USA
Tracy Rank, DePaul University, USA

SESSION OVERVIEW

Although marketing is essentially used by companies to communicate with consumers, sometimes, marketers use tricky, devious, and even immoral persuasion tactics. Due to the constant exposure to marketers' tactics consumers may then become habitually suspicious about marketplace persuasion. Over time, routine suspicion can turn into more schematic knowledge about the tactics that marketers use in persuasion attempts (Friestad and Wright 1994). During the past fifteen years, researchers have examined how the persuasion knowledge (PK) can change the perceived meaning of a persuasion attempt in ways that were not originally intended by marketers. This special session provides a new direction that extends the current persuasion knowledge research.

Existing literature has documented that PK-induced judgments of an influence agent tend to be negative due to the general defensive mechanism of suspicion (Campbell and Kirmani 2000; Darke and Ritchie 2007). The consequential responses can be either relatively automatic leading to bias (Darke, Ashworth, and Ritchie 2008); or more deliberate and modified by consumers' goals, experiences, and preferences (Kirmani and Cambpell 2004). This special session further explores these intriguing and sometimes contradictory issues regarding the potential boundary conditions for suspicion and inference. More specifically, the four papers proposed for this session investigate consumer perceptions of the morality of marketers' persuasion tactics, the effects of suspicion, and motivational and situational cues that modify the initial PK-induced judgments and reactions. Under what conditions are marketing tactics viewed as being more (or less) morally acceptable to consumers, and under what conditions are consumers more (or less) suspicious about these tactics? The findings throughout this session shed further light on how consumers cope with persuasion attempts.

Paper 1 (Kirmani et al.) examines how consumers make tradeoffs between an influence agent's competency (an intrinsic utilitarian judgment) and morality (an extrinsic moral judgment) when suspicion is activated. A "sinful success" vs. "virtuous failure" dilemma appears salient. This dilemma, however, can be accounted for by the immediacy of the decision and the consumer's relationship with the influence agent. Paper 2 (Grayson and Rank) further demonstrates that consumers differ in their intuitive theories about the extent to which a persuasion tactic is socially appropriate. Consumers with more advanced persuasion knowledge tend to view tactics normatively appropriate, but morally inappropriate. Paper 3 (Darke) describes strategies for combating the persistent negative bias induced by the defensive suspicion. Multiple trust cues, knowledge of government regulation, and the use of aschematic tactics are all effective in buffering against the otherwise persistent effects of defensive suspicion. Finally, paper 4 (Xie et al.) identifies situations when proactive or reactive responses occur as a result of suspicion, depending upon consumers' regulatory focus and persuasion knowledge to manage interactions with an influence agent.

Combined, these four papers examine how consumers react against marketers' potentially immoral persuasion tactics and how their suspicions about these tactics can be enhanced or attenuated. These papers advance the literature in three ways. First, these studies provide insights about a number of factors that either strengthen or weaken consumers' suspicion. Second, the results suggest that consumers do not view persuasion tactics used by marketers as simply black and white, wrong or right; instead consumers rely on both utility value and moral value to judge the appropriateness of a persuasion tactic. Third, the studies extend previous research on persuasion knowledge by specifying situations when consumers can pragmatically adjust the PK-induced negative judgments of the influence agents. After fifteen years of persuasion knowledge research, scholars continue to ask new thought-provoking questions. This session captures cutting edge research that contributes to the theoretical advancement of consumer behavior in response to marketplace persuasion.

EXTENDED ABSTRACTS

"Which Agent Do You Prefer: A Sinful Succeeder or a Virtuous Failure?"

Amna Kirmani, University of Maryland, USA
Rebecca W. Hamilton, University of Maryland, USA
Debora V. Thompson, Georgetown University, USA

We examine how consumers' trade off competence and morality when evaluating marketing agents. Although the general information formation literature predicts that individuals place greater weight on morality than competence, we predict that in marketing contexts, consumers may value an agent's competence more than morality. We investigate three factors that might affect how consumers weigh competence and morality: 1) the immediacy of the decision making horizon; 2) self vs. other perspective; and 3) the target-agent relationship. Three studies find support for the predictions.

Competence and morality are two fundamental dimensions in social perception (Rosenburg, Nelson, and Vivekananthan 1968). Morality encompasses traits such as honesty and caring, while competence includes traits such as cleverness and skill. An interesting question that has not been addressed in prior research is how consumers trade off morality and competence when choosing a marketing agent.

The literature on general impression formation predicts that morality-related traits are more important than competence-related traits. For example, Wojciszke (1994) finds that evaluation of individuals is more favorable under *virtuous failure* (the behavior is moral, but incompetent) than under *sinful success* (the behavior is competent, but immoral). In contrast, we propose that in marketing contexts, consumers may place greater weight on competence than morality. Particularly in short-term transactions, the consumer's objective is likely to be to achieve his/her purchase goals (Kirmani and Campbell 2004). If the consumer is focusing on the agent's ability to help achieve purchase goals, competence-related traits should be salient.

We examine several conditions under which sinful success may be preferred to virtuous failure: 1) the immediacy of the decision making horizon; 2) self vs. other perspective; and 3) the target-agent relationship.

The immediacy of the decision making horizon refers to how quickly the consumer must accomplish his/her marketing goals. We predict that immediacy will encourage a consumer to prefer a sinful success over a virtuous failure. This was tested in a 2 (Type of Agent: virtuous failure vs. sinful success) X 2 (Immediacy of Decision making: high vs. low) between-subjects design. Participants were asked to imagine that they were looking for a real estate agent to sell their house. The agent was described as moral but less successful (virtuous failure) or as deceptive but successful (sinful success). Immediacy was manipulated by informing participants that they needed to sell their house in three months (high immediacy) or without mentioning a time horizon (low immediacy). Consistent with our prediction, participants in the low immediacy condition were significantly more likely to hire the moral, less successful agent, while those in the high immediacy condition were marginally more inclined to hire the deceptive but successful agent.

In the second study, we predicted that, consistent with the fundamental attribution error, participants would believe these factors would influence others' decisions more than their own. This study was a 2 (Type of Agent: virtuous failure vs. sinful success) X 2 (Perspective: self vs. other) between-subjects design. The agent factor was manipulated through the real estate scenario described earlier. Perspective was manipulated by asking participants to imagine that they (or their neighbor) were looking for a real estate agent to sell their house. An ANOVA revealed a significant interaction effect, indicating that, for themselves, participants were more likely to hire the virtuous failure than the sinful success agent, but thought others would be marginally more likely to hire the sinful success agent.

In the third study, we used a within subjects manipulation of type of agent in order to highlight the trade-off between competence and morality. The study was a 2 (Type of agent: virtuous failure vs. sinful success) X 2 (Target-Agent relationship: short vs. long term) X 2 (Tactic: harmful vs. not harmful) mixed design. Participants read about two sales agents, Dave and Eric, who work in a sporting goods store. Dave's description will with sinful success, while Eric was described as a virtuous failure. The target-agent relationship was manipulated through specifying the purchase situation as one-time or as an ongoing relationship. Tactic was manipulated by whether the sinful behavior directly affected the consumer or not. We predicted that in short-term relationships, sinful success will be preferred to virtuous failure, but that this preference was reversed in long-term relationships. When the tactic could hurt the consumer, however, the morality effect prevailed in the short run.

"Persuasion Knowledge and Moral Judgment"

Kent Grayson, Northwestern University, USA
Tracy Rank, DePaul University, USA

Previously, persuasion knowledge (PK) research has focused primarily on how consumers' beliefs about motives and tactics help them to cope with persuasion attempts. Friestad and Wright (1994) also propose that PK will influence consumers' perceptions of the appropriateness of marketing tactics. However, they make no specific suggestions about the nature of these judgments. *Do consumers with high levels of PK tend to judge persuasion tactics to be more appropriate—or less?*

The answer to this question is not immediately obvious. Those with higher levels of PK could be more sensitive to the manipulativeness of persuasive tactics and therefore tend to view them as being *less* appropriate. Alternatively, those with higher levels of PK might be more comfortable with the "rules of the game" of persuasion and therefore judge persuasion tactics as being *more* appropriate.

Exploratory Study. Independent Variables: We asked respondents (N=63) to rate Campbell and Kirmani's (2000) scenario in which a salesperson flatters a customer either before the sale or after, and then asked them to respond to the Bearden et al. (2001) PK scale. *Dependent Variables*: Appropriateness was defined and operationalized as "normatively acceptable" (Friestad and Wright 1994, p. 10). *Results*: Although level of PK predicted differences in perceived honesty of the salesperson, it did not predict significant differences in perceived appropriateness.

Study One. Based on the results of Campbell and Kirmani's (2000) study three, we hypothesized that priming respondents with PK might prompt perceived differences in appropriateness. Study one was the same as our exploratory study, with the exception that half of our respondents (N=228) were asked to complete the PK scale before evaluating the sales scenario, and half after. *Results*: Unprimed respondents mirrored the null results of our exploratory study. However, when primed, those with low PK significantly lowered their perceptions of overall appropriateness. Therefore, Study One suggests that (when primed) those with low PK view sales scenarios as being less appropriate than those with high PK.

Study Two. Will those low in PK always rate a sales scenario as being less appropriate than those high in PK? We hypothesized that when the salesperson is also a friend, this may create a conflict in normative expectations: is it more appropriate for the person to act like a friend or like a persuasion agent? Results (N= 268) show that those with high PK rated the salesperson's flattery as being more appropriate when it occurred after the sale (as opposed to before), whereas those with low PK rated the salesperson's flattery as being more appropriate when it occurred before (as opposed to after). These results add evidence to the proposition that those with high PK differ from the expectations of those with low PK.

Study Three. Appropriateness has two dimensions—whether the behavior is appropriate to the situation and whether the behavior is ethically or morally appropriate (Friestad and Wright 1994, p. 5, 10). We hypothesized that while those with high PK may believe that persuasive behavior is more normatively appropriate in sales situations, their high level of knowledge in such situations makes them more sensitive (than those low in PK) to the moral implications of persuasive tactics.

The protocol for this study drew from Cohen and colleagues' (1991, 1993, 2001) moral judgment research. One of Cohen's test scenarios describes a store salesperson who behaves in a morally questionable way, while other scenarios focus on morally questionable behavior in other business situations. Results (N=123) show that those with high PK rated the salesperson scenario as being less morally acceptable than those with low PK. However, regarding two other scenarios, there were no differences in the ratings of those with high (versus low) PK.

Combined, the results of our three studies suggest that PK does influence perceptions of tactic acceptability. However, our studies also find that the direction of the link between level of knowledge and acceptability depends on how "acceptability" is defined. When defined as normatively appropriate, those with higher PK view tactics as being more appropriate. When defined as morally acceptable, those with higher PK view tactics as being less appropriate.

"Shedding the Veil of Suspicion: Avoiding the Effects of Defensive Suspicion"

Peter R. Darke, York University, Canada

The defensive suspicion model (DSM; Darke and Ritchie 2007) recognizes that judgments of suspicion involve both deliberative and automatic information processing. Moreover, while accuracy goals may drive judgment, suspicion often involves more defensive, self-protective goals. The latter involve ego-threat, and lead to persistent biases in judgment aimed at reducing such threat. Like the PKM, the DSM is essentially a dual process model.

However, the PKM focuses more on deliberative forms of information processing and accuracy goals whereas the DSM is more focused on automatic processing and defense goals.

The DSM model was tested in series of experiments (Darke and Ritchie 2007; Darke et al. 2008). Consistent with predictions, consumers deceived by an initial advertisement were less trusting and had more negative attitudes towards second-party advertisements. This generalized suspicion effect operated through defensive stereotyping (Sinclair and Kunda 1999), where deception evoked the broad stereotype that no advertising could be trusted. Ego threat was a necessary condition for generalized suspicion to occur. Generalized suspicion also proved difficult to counteract. For instance, strong arguments were no more effective in combating generalized suspicion than weak arguments, and the existing reputation of the second advertiser did little to protect it from generalized suspicion. This talk presents new research identifying factors that moderate the otherwise robust effects of defensive suspicion.

Study one examined whether *multiple trust cues* would provide greater evidence a firm can be trusted through cross-validation. To test this idea, deception was manipulated in an initial advertising study (Darke et al. 2008) and the effects of generalized suspicion were examined in a "different study" concerning the purchase of a used book from a second-party retailer. The brand name (trusted vs. unknown) and the consensus of customer satisfaction ratings (high, average, low) for the retailer were varied in a between subjects design. The results showed that while brand name and high satisfaction ratings alone were ineffective, their combination successfully buffered against generalized suspicion.

Monitoring by regulators is known to be important in maintaining trust in economic exchanges (Pavlou and Gefen 2005). Study two tested whether *regulation* would thwart generalized suspicion in an investment context. Subjects read financial statements from the CEO of an initial firm and half of them were informed these statements were false. Subjects then completed a purportedly unrelated investment game, where they were given financial information from an unrelated firm and could purchase the company's stock using real money. This financial information was either reported in accordance with Sarbanes-Oxley (SOX), or no mention of SOX was made. Consistent with predictions, fraud induced generalized suspicion and lowered investment when SOX was absent, whereas SOX fully neutralized generalized suspicion.

Study three examined sales promotions. The question was whether an EDLP claim would be less vulnerable to generalized suspicion than a discount claim. Consumers are often highly suspicious of discounts (Fry and McDougall 1974), whereas EDLPs provide a relatively straightforward means of providing good value (Darke and Chung 2005). If so, EDLPs should fit less with stereotypes for deceptive advertising practices, and suspicions should generalize less readily to EDLP versus discount offers. Subjects were exposed to either a discount or EDLP offer on flooring materials and a fake debriefing informed deception subjects the level of savings was overstated. Subjects then completed a filler task, followed by a final study where they indicated the deal value for either an EDLP or discount offer for a television from a second firm. Regardless of its origin (discount or EDLP), deception induced greater suspicious towards the second-party discount offer, whereas it actually led to an increase in the perceived value of the subsequent EDLP offer. That is, advertising deception led to suspicion of discounts in particular, whereas consumers actually became more positive towards the aschematic, no-nonsense of an EDLP.

"A Tale of Two Modes: When Do Consumers Approach or Avoid Persuasion Attempts?"

Guang-Xin Xie, University of Massachusetts Boston, USA
David M. Boush, University of Oregon, USA
Lynn R. Kahle, University of Oregon, USA
Peter L. Wright, University of Oregon, USA

Persuasion knowledge does not only consist of schema about an influence agent's motives and tactics, but also how to respond effectively (Friestad and Wright 1994). In some situations consumers actively approach the salesperson to achieve their goals while others avoid, resist, or withdraw (Kirmani and Campbell 2004). The current study extends previous research by further examining the role of persuasion knowledge and regulatory focus. We predict that consumers are more likely to approach an influence agent when they are promotion-focused to achieve positive outcomes, and more likely to avoid when they are prevention-focused to prevent negative outcomes. Persuasion knowledge moderates the effect of the regulatory fit between consumers' goals and persuasion situations on coping tendencies.

Study One: We used a 2 (Suspicion: high vs. low) X 2 (Regulatory Focus: prevention vs. promotion) X 2 (Persuasion Knowledge: high vs. low) between-subject design. Participants read a shopping scenario in which a salesperson made positive remarks on his/her choice of a more expensive jacket. Suspicion was manipulated by the timing of positive remarks before or after the purchase decision (Campbell and Kirmani 2000). Regulatory focus was manipulated by priming goals to achieve a positive outcome or avoid a negative outcome (Lockwood, Jordan, and Kunda 2002). Persuasion knowledge was measured independently (Bearden et al. 2001) and tested using a median split. Two dependent measures (approach/avoid tendencies) were adapted from the "sentry vs. seeker" framework (Kirmani and Campbell 2004) based on a factor analysis of eighteen behaviors. The results show that promotion (prevention) focus predicts approach (avoid) tendencies. Also, participants high in persuasion knowledge were less likely to avoid interacting with the salesperson than those low in persuasion knowledge, while persuasion knowledge was not found to regulate approach tendency.

Study Two: We used a 2 (Regulatory Focus: prevention vs. promotion) X 2 (Purchase Relevance: high vs. low) X 2 (Persuasion Knowledge: high vs. low) between-subject design to control for personal relevance in making a purchase. Only the high suspicion condition was retained. Relevance was manipulated by the purpose of the purchase: *"…for an important interview"* or *"…for those just in case times."* The results show that promotion/prevention-focused participants in the high relevance conditions were equally suspicious about the salesperson's ulterior sales motive. In the low relevance conditions, however, promotion-focused participants were more suspicious than prevention-focused participants. Further, a three-way interaction was evident with regard to the avoidance tendency. For those low in persuasion knowledge, prevention-focused participants were more vigilant when relevance was low. When relevance was high, promotion/prevention focus did not make a significant difference. In comparison, for those high in persuasion knowledge, when relevance was high, prevention-focused participants were more likely to avoid a persuasion attempt. However, when relevance was low, promotion-focused participants were more inclined to act defensively.

Study Three: We used a 2 (Regulatory Focus: prevention vs. promotion) X 2 (Message Framing: positive vs. negative) X 2 (Persuasion Knowledge: high vs. low) between-subject design to further examine the regulatory fit between goals and messages. Only the high suspicion/high relevance conditions were retained.

The salesperson's remarks were framed as positive *("...that's a great jacket. I think it looks very professional, and it will be a good choice for an interview")* or negative *("...that's a nice jacket. But I think it looks too casual, and it will not be a good choice for an interview")*. In both conditions, the salesperson recommended the more expensive jacket as a better choice. This experiment replicated the findings regarding regulatory focus effect on avoidance tendency. However, no support was found regarding the effect of regulatory fit on suspicion or coping tendencies.

In three experiments, we demonstrated that persuasion knowledge, regulatory focus, and purchase relevance can influence approach/avoid coping tendencies in response to interpersonal marketing persuasion. In particular, promotion-focused consumers can be more vigilant than prevention-focused consumers when the purchase relevance is low. Also, high persuasion knowledge consumers must be motivated enough to simply react against a persuasion attempt.

REFERENCES

Bearden, William O., David M. Hardesty, and Randall L. Rose (2001), "Consumer Self-Confidence: Refinements in Conceptualization and Measurement," *Journal of Consumer Research,* 28 (June), 121-33.

Campbell, Margaret C. and Amna Kirmani (2000), "Consumers' Use of Persuasion Knowledge: The Effects of Accessibility and Cognitive Capacity on Perceptions of an Influence Agent," *Journal of Consumer Research*, 27 (June), 69-83.

Cohen, Jeffrey and Laurie W. Pant (1991), "Beyond Bean Counting: Establishing High Ethical Standards in the Public Accounting Profession," *Journal of Business Ethics*, 10 (January), 45-56.

Cohen, Jeffrey, Laurie W. Pant, and David Sharp (1993), "A Validation and Extension of a Multidimensional Ethics Scale," *Journal of Business Ethics*, 12 (January), 13-26.

Cohen, Jeffrey and Louise E. Single (2001), "An Examination of the Perceived Impact of Flexible Work Arrangements on Professional Opportunities in Public Accounting," *Journal of Business Ethics*, 32 (August), 317-28.

Darke, Peter R., Laurence T.A. Ashworth and Robin B. Ritchie (2008), "Damage From Corrective Advertising: Causes and Cures," *Journal of Marketing*, 72 (November), 81-97.

Darke, Peter R. and Cindy M.Y. Chung (2005), "Effects of Pricing and Promotion on Consumer Perceptions: It Depends on How You Frame It," *Journal of Retailing*, 81 (1), 35-47.

Darke, Peter R. and Robin J. B. Ritchie (2007), "The Defensive Consumer: Advertising Deception, Defensive Processing, and Distrust," *Journal of Marketing Research*, 44 (February), 114-27.

Friestad, Marian and Peter Wright (1994), "The Persuasion Knowledge Model: How People Cope with Persuasion Attempts," *Journal of Consumer Research*, 21 (June), 1-31.

Fry, Joseph N. and Gordon H. McDougall (1974), "Consumer Appraisal of Retail Price Advertisements," *Journal of Marketing*, 38 (July), 64-74.

Kirmani, Amna and Margaret C. Campbell (2004), "Goal Seeker and Persuasion Sentry: How Consumer Targets Respond to Interpersonal Marketing Persuasion," *Journal of Consumer Research,* 31 (December), 573-82.

Kirmani, Amna and Rui (Juliet) Zhu (2007), "Vigilant Against Manipulation: The Effect of Regulatory Focus on the Use of Persuasion Knowledge," *Journal of Marketing Research*, 44 (November), 688-701.

Kramer, Roderick M. (1998), "Paranoid Cognition in Social Systems: Thinking and Acting in the Shadow of Doubt," *Personality and Social Psychology Review*, 2 (4), 251-75.

Lockwood, Penelope, Christian H. Jordan, and Ziva Kunda (2002), "Motivation by Positive or Negative Role Models: Regulatory Focus Determines Who Will Best Inspire Us," *Journal of Personality and Social Psychology*, 83 (October), 854-864.

Pavlou, Paul A. and David Gefen (2005), "Psychological Contract Violation in Online Marketplaces: Antecedents. Consequences, and Moderating Role," *Information Systems Research*, 16 (December), 372-99.

Rosenberg, Seymour V., Carnot Nelsonand, P. S. Vivekananthan (1968), "A Multidimensional Approach to the Structure of Personality Impressions," *Journal of Personality and Social Psychology,* 9 (August), 283-94.

Sinclair, Lisa and Ziva Kunda (1999), "Reactions to a Black Professional: Motivated Inhibition and Activation of Conflicting Stereotypes," *Journal of Personality and Social Psychology*, 77 (November), 885-904.

Wojciszke, Bogdan (1994), "Multiple Meanings of Behavior: Construing Actions in Terms of Competence or Morality," *Journal of Personality and Social Psychology*, 67 (August), 222-32.

Special Session Summary

The Distinct Effects of Hope in Consumption

Karen Winterich, Texas A&M University, USA

SESSION OVERVIEW

Whether yearning to achieve your goals or rewarding yourself for a job well-done, feelings of hope and feelings of pride are regularly regarded as important emotional triggers of consumption behavior. Hope is pervasive in marketing and consumer acquisition in numerous industries such as diet and exercise, medicine, and finance (MacInnis 2005). In addition, consumers often take pride in the products they purchase or avoid, making hope and pride two prevalent positive emotions in consumption. Previous research on hope (e.g., de Mello et al. 2007; MacInnis and de Mello 2005) and pride (e.g., Tracy and Robins 2007; Williams and DeSteno 2009) has shown that these two positive emotions are important motivators of behavior; however, it is unclear whether these distinct positive emotions influence different consumption behaviors in a similar way. Do hope and pride influence behavior similarly across different consumption contexts (e.g., purchasing novel products, eating behavior, and investment decisions)? Moreover, do hope and hopefulness have distinct effects on consumption decisions? This session highlights important differences in the behaviors motivated by hope in contrast to other positive emotions such as pride and hopefulness across distinct consumption contexts.

Hope is a positive emotion, which represents the degree to which one yearns for a good outcome that seems possible even if it might not be likely (MacInnis and Chun 2007). In the first paper, Cavanaugh et al. explore how two specific positive emotions–hope and pride–influence cognitive processing and purchase behavior. They find that hope causes consumers to be willing to pay more for novel products than does pride when resources are constrained (i.e., non-optimal time of day). Further, hope improves performance relative to pride on tasks requiring fluid intelligence. These findings suggest an interesting interaction between experienced emotion and consumption context and raise an important question—when might hope and hopefulness help (versus potentially harm) consumers?

While some previous research demonstrates that positive affect may lead individuals to control their impulses, other research suggest positive affect leads to indulgence. In the second paper, Winterich and Haws try to reconcile these findings through considering the differential effects of hope in contrast to pride and happiness on eating and spending self-control. In a series of four studies, they find that hope may increase self-control relative to neutral, proud, or happy emotional states.

The third paper by Nenkov, MacInnis, and Morrin, distinguishes hope from hopefulness, demonstrating the distinct effects of these two emotions on retirement investment decisions. Defining hope as the extent of yearning for and hopefulness as the perceived likelihood of a goal-congruent outcome, their work finds that consumers' levels of hope and hopefulness are differentially associated with personality traits such as optimism and risk aversion. Furthermore, hopefulness influences 401(k) participation rates whereas hope influences information search and risky decision making.

Addressing the effects of positive emotions which are pervasive in consumption, this symposium presents findings suggesting that hope may differentially impact processing, self-control, and decision making. In contrast to traditional research on positive affect, the three papers in this session demonstrate that positive emotions can have vastly different and even opposing consequences. Theoretically, the set of papers clarify the characteristics of hope, pride, and hopefulness that are influential in consumption. As such, specific positive emotions such as hope, pride, and hopefulness can be used by marketers as strategic tools. Moreover, consumers and public policy makers need to consider the extent to which positive emotions may unknowingly influence consumers' decisions, resulting in poorer health or financial security (Baumeister et al. 2007).

EXTENDED ABSTRACTS

"Hope, Pride, and Processing During Optimal and Nonoptimal Times of Day"

Lisa A. Cavanaugh, University of Southern California, USA
Keisha M. Cutright, Duke University, USA
Mary Frances Luce, Duke University, USA
James R. Bettman, Duke University, USA

Most research involving positive affect and emotion argues that various positive emotional states have similar effects on behavior (Fredrickson 1998, 2001; Isen 2001), such as problem-solving and cognitive flexibility. In this research, we show that specific positive emotions can differentially influence cognitive flexibility and consumption behavior, particularly when inhibitory resources are low.

Work on mood freezing and cognitive load suggests that the magnitude of emotion's effect can be increased or decreased based on the availability or perceived availability of an individual's resources (e.g., Shiv and Fedorikhin 2002). One naturally occurring factor that influences the availability of cognitive resources is an individual's circadian rhythm (Kruglanski and Pierro 2008; Yoon, May, and Hasher 2000). During different times of day (i.e. morning vs. evening), individuals have been found to feel and operate at their personal best or not (i.e. optimally or nonoptimally) based on their personal circadian rhythms. Thus, one important factor that may amplify or lessen the effects of emotion is time of day. Specifically, during nonoptimal times of day resources are less readily available, and therefore automatic, association-based processing (Kahneman and Frederick 2005; Stanovich and West 2002) is more likely (Bodenhausen 1990; May et al. 2005). We contend that association-based emotion mechanisms are likely to be more prevalent during nonoptimal times of day when processing resources are reduced and inhibitory control is lower (Hasher et al. 1999).

Based on reasoning about distinct emotion associations, we contrast the emotions hope and pride. The unique associations with hope suggest that a valued goal is possible, while associations with pride suggest a valued goal has already been achieved. Hope is differentially associated with concepts such as striving, possibility, effort, or the future, whereas pride is associated with concepts such as achievement, fulfillment, or the past. We believe that the distinct set of associations for each emotion can have important processing implications, particularly for fluid processing tasks requiring mental exploration or cognitive flexibility.

We hypothesize that during nonoptimal times of day hope will promote more fluid processing, i.e., more mental exploration and generation of possibilities, than pride. In Experiment 1 we use a preference valuation task where fluid processing seems likely to facilitate generation of possible or potential uses for considered items; in experiment 2 we use an intelligence task where fluid processing appears to facilitate generation of possible solutions and ultimately performance. As a result, we expect hope, but not pride, to increase valuation of items in assessing preferences in real-time, i.e. constructive preferences (experiment 1), and performance on measures of fluid problem-solving (experiment 2) during nonoptimal times of day.

Experiment 1. Experiment 1 consisted of a 2 (time of day: optimal vs. nonoptimal) x 3 (emotion induction: hope, pride, neutral) between subjects factorial design. Approximately one week before participating in the main experiment, participants completed the Horne and Ostberg (1976) Morningness-Eveningness Questionnaire (MEQ), a validated individual measure of when people reach their functional peak during the day (i.e. "optimal time of day"). Participants were categorized as morning-types or evening-types based on established scoring procedures and then randomly assigned to take the main experiment in the morning or the evening. Thus, participants were randomly assigned to take the study at their "optimal" time of day or "nonoptimal" time of day. Upon arrival for the main experiment, participants were randomly assigned to an emotion induction condition (hope, pride, neutral) following Lerner and Keltner's (2001) procedure. Participants were then asked to indicate how much they would be willing to pay for a variety of items for which they had little repeat- purchasing experience (Vohs and Faber 2007) and thus little crystallized knowledge to draw from in constructing their willingness to pay estimates.

We found a 2-way interaction of emotion condition and time of day for the total amount of money that a participant was willing to pay for the collection of items. Hope lead to greater valuation of items than pride or neutral in the nonoptimal time of day condition. No difference was found between neutral and pride, although pride was directionally lower. For the pride condition, participants in the nonoptimal condition were willing to pay significantly less than their counterparts in the optimal condition. Further, the emotion inductions did not significantly impact performance at optimal times of day.

Experiment 2. The purpose of experiment 2 was to better understand the process underlying our experiment 1 findings using a measure of fluid processing performance. Experiment 2 consisted of a 2 time of day (optimal vs. nonoptimal) x 3 emotion induction (hope, pride, neutral) between subjects factorial design. The time of day and incidental emotion manipulations were accomplished as in Experiment 1. Participants were then asked to complete two well-established measures of intelligence. The first task was a measure of fluid intelligence called "matrix reasoning." The second task required participants to complete a test of crystallized intelligence consisting of vocabulary related questions (see Goldstein et al. 2007) using analogies and sentence completion.

Analyses replicated the established time of day findings that participants in a neutral emotional state perform better on fluid, but not crystallized, intelligence measures at optimal times (Goldstein, Hahn, Hasher, Wiprzycka, and Zelazo 2007). There was no effect of time of day on crystallized intelligence. We found the expected 2-way interaction of emotion condition and time of day for fluid intelligence performance. As predicted, hope led to better performance than pride or neutral at nonoptimal times of day. No difference was found between neutral and pride. As predicted, the difference between emotions did not impact performance at optimal times of day. Interestingly, within the hope condition, participants at their nonoptimal time of day actually performed better than their optimal counterparts.

Thus, the results of two experiments demonstrate that two different positive emotions, hope and pride, affect processing differentially at nonoptimal times of day. Specifically, hope increases individuals' willingness to pay for items with which they have little prior knowledge or experience compared to pride and a neutral condition. Moreover, hope improves objective performance on tasks requiring fluid processing compared to pride and a neutral emotional state.

"Helpful Hopefulness: The Positive Impact of Hope on Self-Control"

Karen P. Winterich, Texas A&M University, USA
Kelly L. Haws, Texas A&M University, USA

If you receive an "A" on an exam and feel hopeful about your future class performance will your self-control differ than if you experience happiness from receiving this "A"? We propose that the characteristics of specific positive emotions influence whether positive affect increases or decreases self-control. For some time researchers utilized a global category of "happiness" to cover all positive emotions, but recent research has differentiated positive emotions, finding critical differences (Siemer et al. 2007). Some research finds that positive mood can stimulate eating (Macht et al. 2002) and lead individuals to feel both unconstrained and deserving (Rook and Fisher 1995). However, research also suggests that positive affect may enhance self-control (Raghunathan and Trope 2002), particularly when no mood maintenance goal is accessible (Fishbach and Labroo 2007). Given these divergent findings, we focus our investigation on impact of incidental hope in contrast to other incidental positive emotions on self-control.

Hope is a positively-valenced emotion evoked in response to an uncertain but possible goal-congruent outcome, which results in a determination to find pathways to achieve goals (Lazarus 1991; Snyder et al. 1991). The goal-driven characteristics of hope (de Mello et al. 2007), in combination with the desire to expend effort (Ellsworth and Smith 1988), allow hopeful individuals to overcome obstacles and achieve objectives, which should positively influence self-regulation in that present decisions will be more consistent with the achievement of long-term goals (MacInnis and de Mello 2005). Therefore, we argue that hopeful individuals will demonstrate greater self-control than those in a neutral state.

In our first two studies, we used a two-factor between subjects design with either hopeful or neutral emotion manipulations, in which participants wrote about something that makes them most hopeful or their typical evening (neutral condition). In study 1, participants were given a bowl containing 50 grams of pretzels (2.5 servings) at the start of the emotion induction which was said to be a thank you for completing the studies. Pretests suggested the pretzels were perceived as hedonic enough to enact self-control mechanisms. Remaining grams of pretzels were measured at the end of the study. An ANCOVA including the emotion condition with time of day and gender as covariates indicated that those in the hopeful condition ate significantly fewer pretzels than those in the neutral condition.

In study 2, participants indicated their willingness to pay for a movie pass and a restaurant gift card at the present time and six months in the future with the order of both products and timeframe counterbalanced. The premium was the dependent measure, previously used as a proxy for self-control (Fujita et al. 2006). ANCOVA analyses revealed that the premiums participants were willing to pay to speed up consumption differed by emotion condition, such that those who were hopeful demonstrated enhanced self-control as expressed by a smaller premium to speed up consumption than their neutral counterparts. Across domains of eating and spending, hope appears to increase self-control. How is this effect related to other distinct positive emotions, as research has suggested positive affect can decrease self-control?

Pride is a positively-valenced self-conscious emotion, derived from known accomplishments, and as such is more present and inward focused than hope (Ellsworth and Smith 1988). This focus on one's achievements may lead one to feel worthy or deserving of present indulgence, resulting in decreased self-control in unrelated domains (Baumeister and Exline 1999; Giner-Sorolla 2001). As such, when individuals feel they have accomplished a goal, pride may provide a license to indulge in other areas. Overall, we anticipate that pride will decrease self-control relative to hope.

In study 3, participants were randomly assigned to one of three emotion inductions: hope, pride, and neutral. Procedures were the same as Study 1 with pretzel consumption as the dependent variable. An ANCOVA including time of day and gender as covariates revealed a significant effect of emotion on pretzel consumption. Follow-up contrasts revealed that hope resulted in less pretzel consumption than either pride or neutral.

Finally, in study 4 we examined product type as a potential boundary condition. We chose two products that clearly differed in hedonicness (raisins and M&Ms) and allowed participants the opportunity to consume either or both of these snack foods. We anticipated that emotion would impact the consumption of the hedonic M&M option but not raisins. We focused our investigation on hope in contrast to another positive emotion, happiness. The effect of emotion condition was moderated by product type such that participants in a happy state consumed a larger portion of the hedonic food than those in a hopeful state but there was no difference in consumption of the less hedonic food between emotion states.

Together our experiments demonstrate that specific positive emotions can differentially impact a consumer's ability to exercise self-control. Hope tends to increase self-control relative to other positive emotions such as pride and happiness. Replicating the effect both with eating and spending enhances our confidence in the generalizability of these findings. The uncertain, future outcome associated with the emotion of hope along with a focus on more situational factors contrasts with the certain, self-focused, and past-oriented outcome that engenders feelings of pride and happiness. These differential effects of positive emotions on goal-relevant behaviors are important given the current lack of control individuals' exhibit (Baumeister et al. 2007).

"Differentiating the Psychological Impact of Threats to Hope and Hopefulness"

Gergana Y. Nenkov, Boston College, USA
Deborah MacInnis, University of Southern California, USA
Maureen Morrin, Rutgers University, USA

Recent work identifies hope (the degree to which one yearns for a good outcome that seems possible even if it might not be likely) as an under-explored and potentially important emotion (e.g., MacInnis and Chun 2007). That same work suggests that hope can be differentiated from an often confused emotion–hopefulness (the extent to which one believes that a positive outcome is actually likely), as these two emotions are not necessarily related and can operate differently. Previous research has not made a distinction between hope and hopefulness, nor has it examined their separate behavioral effects.

In this paper we investigate the effects of both hope and hopefulness on consumers' decisions and actions related to retirement investing. For this purpose we ran a field experiment where 272 real world consumers had to decide 1) whether to invest in a 401(k) retirement plan offered by their employer and 2) how to allocate their money across eight available mutual funds. We first measured participants' current levels of hope and hopefulness for having enough money to retire. Hope was measured by asking respondents about their desire to retire with enough money, the importance of having a financially secure retirement for their psychological well-being, and the pleasure that this outcome would give them. Hopefulness was measured by asking participants to assess the likelihood of having enough money to retire using a scale of 0% to 100%.

Participants were then randomly assigned to one of two experimental conditions: a control condition, in which current levels of hope and hopefulness were not manipulated but only measured and a condition, in which hope and hopefulness were threatened. Specifically, in the threat condition, respondents read a document indicating that recent reports have revealed that the likelihood of attaining a secure retirement is worse than they thought since many experts now agree that Americans are doing an even worse job of saving for retirement than the industry typically proclaims. In the control condition they read a similar document, but it presented neutral information that stated that the likelihood of attainting a secure retirement is unchanged and that prior projections about Americans' retirement saving are correct and consistent with their likely need.

After reading this information, participants had to decide whether to invest in a hypothetical 401(k) plan offered by their employer. Respondents were shown detailed descriptions of eight mutual funds with various levels of risk and return. They were then asked to indicate what portion of the $15,500 they are allowed they would actually invest, and how they would allocate the money across the eight funds. After they made their allocations, participants' information search patterns were measured by asking them to check all the funds they had considered investing in, whether or not they actually invested in them.[1]

Influence of prior levels of hope and hopefulness. First, the correlations of participants' hope and hopefulness with their psychological traits and investment decisions were examined. Analysis, performed in the control condition of the experiment, where prior levels of hope and hopefulness were not manipulated, revealed that strong hope and strong hopefulness for retiring securely tend to be related to different consumer traits and characteristics.

Overall, stronger hope seems to be related to less rational behavior. Results revealed that participants with higher hope seem to have more anxiety about investing and search for more information before making a decision–perhaps because they are less experienced with investment decisions. They think about the consequences of their decisions to a greater extent and seem to be slightly more risk averse in general. Paradoxically, they tend to expect a higher return from their investments, but tend to invest more conservatively. Stronger hopefulness, on the other hand, seems to be related to more rational behavior. Participants with higher hopefulness are more knowledgeable about investments, less risk averse, and more optimistic. They find the investment decision less difficult and are more satisfied with it once they have made it. In sum, these individuals seem to have more peace of mind with their decisions–yet they take more risks.

Influence of threats to hope and hopefulness. Results revealed that threats to hope and threats to hopefulness have different effects on consumer's responses to the investment scenario. Specifically, threats to hopefulness were found to affect 401(k) participation rates. Compared to the control condition, threatening hopefulness increased the likelihood of joining a 401(k) plan for those with high

[1]Next, we administered manipulation and confound checks, measured several individual traits (optimism, consideration of future consequences, risk aversion, and knowledge about investing), and collected demographic information.

initial levels of hopefulness. However, people with low initial levels of hopefulness, who were slightly less likely to enroll in the control condition, reduced their participation rates even further as a result of the threat. It seems that threatening individuals' high hopefulness motivates them to constructive action, such as enrolling in the proposed plan, while this threat backfires for people who are less hopeful. This result is consistent with past research, which has suggested that hopefulness is a major condition for motivation and action (MacInnis and Chun 2007).

Threats to hope impacted different aspects of the investment decision process by affecting the extent of information search and risky decision making. First, when people's strong hope was threatened they searched for more information regarding investment choices by considering more mutual funds and more asset classes, compared to participants in the control condition. It seems that when the hoped for outcome is seen as less likely, people increase their efforts to find information confirming the possibility of the outcome. These findings are consistent with past research that argued that the amount of information search is affected by the extent to which information supports the possibility of achieving the goal (de Mello, MacInnis, and Stewart 2007).

Threats to hope were also found to affect the level of risk participants were willing to take. Even though people with stronger hope were more risk averse in the control condition, when their hope for a secure retirement was threatened, they allocated more money to the riskier stock funds and less to the risk-free money market fund. These findings are consistent with a previously untested hypothesis that strong yearning for an outcome makes people willing to bear more risk in order to achieve this outcome (MacInnis and de Mello 2005).

These results underscore the value of differentiating the construct of hope from the construct of hopefulness and also reveal the differing psychological impact of threats to each of these constructs. Findings from this project are likely to have important implications for the design, presentation, and communication of defined-contribution retirement plans and financial products in general, and for the growing practice of developing investor education programs and campaigns targeted at improving investment practices and boosting retirement savings.

REFERENCES

Baumeister, Roy F. and Julie Juola Exline (1999), "Virtue, Personality, and Social Relations: Self-Control as the Moral Muscle," *Journal of Personality*, 67 (6), 1165-1194.

Baumeister, Roy F., Kathleen D. Vohs, and Dianne M. Tice (2007), "The Strength Model of Self-Control," *Current Directions in Psychological Science*," 16 (6), 351-355.

Bodenhausen, Galen V. (1990), "Stereotypes as Judgmental Heuristics: Evidence of Circadian Variations in Discrimination," *Psychological Science*, 1(5), 319-322.

de Mello, Gustavo, Deborah J. MacInnis and David W. Stewart (2007), "Threats to Hope: Effects on Reasoning about Product Information," *Journal of Consumer Research*, 34 (August), 153-161.

Ellsworth, Phoebe C. and Craig A. Smith (1988), "Shades of Joy: Patterns of Appraisal Differentiating Pleasant Emotions," *Cognition and Emotion*, 2 (4), 301-331.

Fishbach, Ayelet and Aparna Labroo (2007), "Be Better or Be Merry: How Mood Affects Self-Control," *Journal of Personality and Social Psychology*, 93 (August), 158-173.

Fredrickson, Barbara L. (1998), "What Good are Positive Emotions?" *Review of General Psychology*, 2(3), 300-319.

Fredrickson, Barbara L. (2001), "The Role of Positive Emotions in Positive Psychology: The Broaden-and-Build Theory of Positive Emotions," *American Psychologist*, 56(3), 218-226.

Fujita, Kentaro, Yaacov Trope, Nira Liberman, and Maya Levin-Sagi (2006), "Construal Levels and Self-Control," *Journal of Personality and Social Psychology*, 90 (March), 351-367.

Giner-Sorolla, R. (2001), "Guilty Pleasures and Grim Necessities: Affective Attitudes in Dilemmas of Self-control," *Journal of Personality and Social Psychology*, 80 (2).

Goldstein, David, Constanze S. Hahn, Lynn Hasher, Ursula J. Wiprzycka, and Philip David Zelazo (2007), "Time of Day, Intellectual Performance, and Behavioral Problems in Morning versus Evening Type Adolescents: Is there a Synchrony Effect?" *Personality and Individual Differences*, 42(3), 431-440.

Hasher, Lynn, Rose T. Zacks, Cynthia P. May, Daniel Gopher, and Asher Koriat (1999), "Inhibitory Control, Circadian Arousal, and Age," in *Attention and Performance XVII: Cognitive Regulation of Performance: Interaction of Theory and Application*, Cambridge, MA, US: The MIT Press, 653-675.

Horne, James A. and Olov Ostberg (1976), "A Self-assessment Questionnaire to Determine Morningness-Eveningness in Human Circadian Rhythms," *International Journal of Chronobiology*, 4, 97-110.

Isen, Alice M. (2001), "An Influence of Positive Affect on Decision Making in Complex Situations: Theoretical Issues with Practical Implications," *Journal of Consumer Psychology*, 11(2), 75-85.

Kahneman, Daniel and Shane Frederick (2005), "A Model of Heuristic Judgment," In K. J. Holyoak & R. G. Morrison (Eds.), *The Cambridge Handbook of Thinking and Reasoning*, New York, NY, US: Cambridge University Press, 267-293.

Kruglanski, Arie W. and Antonio Pierro (2008), "Night and Day, You are the One: On Circadian Mismatches and the Transference Effect in Social Perception," *Psychological Science*, 19(3), 296-301.

Lazarus, Richard S. (1991), *Emotion and Adaptation,* New York: Oxford University Press.

Lerner, Jennifer S. and Dacher Keltner (2001), "Fear, Anger, and Risk," *Journal of Personality and Social Psychology*, 81(1), 146-159.

Macht, Michael, S. Roth, and Heinrich Ellgring (2002), "Chocolate Eating in Healthy Men During Experimentally Induced Sadness and Joy," *Appetite*, 39, 147-158.

MacInnis, Deborah J. (2005), "Presidential Address: Finding Legs: Generativity and the Everyday Language of the Consumer," Vol. 32, Association for Consumer Research, 1-5.

MacInnis, Deborah J. and Hae Eun Chun (2007), "Understanding Hope and Its Implications for Consumer Behavior: I Hope, Therefore I Consume," *Foundations and Trends® in Marketing*, 1(2), 97-189.

MacInnis, Deborah J. and Gustavo E. de Mello (2005), "The Concept of Hope and Its Relevance to Product Evaluation and Choice," *Journal of Marketing*, 69 (January), 1-14.

May, Cynthia P., Lynn Hasher, and Natalie Foong (2005), "Implicit Memory, Age, and Time of Day: Paradoxical Priming Effects," *Psychological Science*, 16(2), 96-100.

Raghunathan, Rajagopal and Yaacov Trope (2002), "Mood-as-a-Resource in Processing Persuasive Messages," *Journal of Personality and Social Psychology*, 83 (September), 510-25.

Rook, Dennis W. and Robert J. Fisher (1995), "Normative Influences on Impulsive Buying Behavior," *Journal of Consumer Research*, 22 (December), 305-13.

Shiv, Baba and Alexander Fedorikhin (2002), "Spontaneous Versus Controlled Influences of Stimulus-based Affect on Choice Behavior," *Organizational Behavior and Human Decision Processes*, 87(2), 342-370.

Siemer, Matthias, Iris Mauss, and James J. Gross (2007), "Same Situation-Different Emotions: How Appraisals Shape Our Emotions," *Emotion*, 7 (3), 592-600.

Snyder, C. R., Cheri Harris, John R. Anderson, Sharon A. Holleran, Lori M. Irving, Sandra X. Sigmon, Lauren Ybshinobu, June Gibb, Charyle Langelle, and Pat Harney (1991), "The Will and the Ways: Development and Validation of an Individual-Difference Measure of Hope," *Journal of Personality and Social Psychology*, 60 (April), 570-85.

Stanovich, Keith E., and Richard F. West (2002), "Individual Differences in Reasoning: Implications for the Rationality Debate?" in T. Gilovich, D. Griffin & D. Kahneman (Eds.), *Heuristics and Biases: The Psychology of Intuitive Judgment*, New York, NY, US: Cambridge University Press, 421-440.

Tracy, Jessica L. and Richard W. Robins (2007), "The Psychological Structure of Pride: A Tale of Two Facets," *Journal of Personality and Social Psychology*, 92 (2), 506-525.

Vohs, Kathleen D. and Ronald J. Faber (2007), "Spent Resources: Self?Regulatory Resource Availability Affects Impulse Buying," *Journal of Consumer Research*, 33 (March), 537-547.

Williams, Lisa A., and David DeSteno (2009), "Pride: Adaptive Social Emotion of Seventh Sin?" *Psychological Science*, 20 (3), 284-288.

Yoon, Caroline, Cynthia P. May, and Lynn Hasher (2000), "Aging, Circadian Arousal Patterns, and Cognition," in D. C. Park & N. Schwarz (Eds.), *Cognitive Aging: A Primer,* New York, NY, US: Psychology Press, 151-171.

SPECIAL SESSION SUMMARY

Why Reproduction Involves More Than Sex: The Diverse Effects of Mating Motivation on Consumer Behavior

Vladas Griskevicius, University of Minnesota, USA

SESSION OVERVIEW

Consumer behavior is often thought to have little to do with evolution or biology. After all, our ancestors did not shop at Wal-Mart, we do not have genes for preferring Coke over Pepsi, and consumers rarely consider how a purchase helps propagate their genes. Emerging research at the intersection of evolutionary biology and cognitive science, however, shows that our evolved social motivation systems have important implications for modern consumption and decision-making. The papers in this session examine how activation of the most evolutionary-critical social motivation system—the mating system—influences consumer behavior.

From an evolutionary perspective, social motivation systems have been shaped by natural selection to produce behaviors to increase reproductive fitness. For any social animal, including Homo sapiens, reproduction involves a great deal more than sex. Because successful reproduction is influenced by a wide variety of behaviors (many of which are not overt acts of sexual reproduction), recent research demonstrates that mating motives operate across a remarkably diverse range of behavioral outcomes, including conspicuous consumption, aggression, altruism, conformity, and creativity. The first two papers in this special session investigate how sexual cues influence risky financial decisions and the desire for distinctiveness. The last paper presents a field study that examines how mating motives vary as a function of the ovulatory cycle, showing how women's hormonal changes across the cycle influence tipping.

Van den Bergh, Millet, and Griskevicius examine how mating motivation influences financial risk-taking and intertemporal choice. They find that exposure to sexual cues leads to a preference for smaller but certain monetary rewards, over larger but uncertain monetary rewards. Berger and Shiv examine how the mating motivation system shares features with other evolved systems such as hunger. They find that exposure to sexual images or activation of hunger has similar effects, such as increasing desire for distinctive goods and choices. Miller examines how mating motivation varies as a function of the female ovulatory cycle. In a unique field study conducted in gentlemen's clubs, he finds that lap dancers earn significantly more money in tips specifically when they are most fertile in their ovulatory cycle.

After the three papers, Griskevicius will lead a 20-minute discussion. The first part of the discussion will integrate the three talks. The second part will be a broader audience-involved discussion of the strengths and weakness of evolutionary approaches to studying behavior. For this broader discussion, Griskevicius will be joined by Dr. Miller (the third presenter). Miller is a renowned world expert on evolution and consumer behavior. He has written a best-selling book on evolution (The Mating Mind, 2000) and has a forthcoming book on evolution and consumer behavior (Spent: Sex, Evolution, and Consumer Behavior, May 2009). The proposed session would be of interest to a breadth of consumer researchers, and of special interest to those interested in field experiments, motivation, nonconscious processes, mating and sex, evolutionary theory, and hormonal influences on consumption. We hope that this session will spur discussion, debate, and ideas for further research.

EXTENDED ABSTRACT

"Sex, Certainty, and Financial Risk: Why Bikinis Lead People to Want a Sure Thing"

Bram Van den Bergh, K.U. Leuven, Belgium
Kobe Millet, K.U. Leuven, Belgium; Free University Amsterdam, the Netherlands
Vladas Griskevicius, University of Minnesota, USA

After touching lingerie, rather than a T-shirt, men have a heightened preference for immediate, but small monetary rewards rather than delayed, but large monetary rewards (Van den Bergh, Dewitte, and Warlop 2008). Temporal discounting might arise because with longer delays, there is a greater risk that the expected or promised reward will not be received. Delayed benefits may be lost during waiting time and less likely to be realized. In this research, we propose that the tendency to devalue temporally distant outcomes ('temporal discounting') is driven by the tendency to devalue improbable outcomes ('probability discounting'). Indeed, the distinction between the present and the future can be conceptualized as the certainty of the former and the inherent uncertainty associated with the latter. We hypothesize that exposure to sexual cues should lead to a disproportionate increase in the desire for sure gains.

Researchers have suggested that the discounting of subjective value produced by delay and by probability are fundamentally the same process (e.g., Halevy 2008). Indeed, individuals who value immediacy (e.g., "I'd rather get \$1 immediately than \$2 tomorrow") tend to value certainty (e.g., "I'd rather get \$1 for sure than \$2 with 50% probability") (Frederick 2005). If discounting of value produced by delay and probability are fundamentally the same process, exposure to sexual cues should not only lead to a preference for immediacy (Van den Bergh et al. 2008) but also to a preference for certainty. In three experiments, we obtained evidence for the hypothesis that activating mating motivation produces risk aversion in the presence of sure gains.

In the first experiment, we hypothesized that mating motivation would instigate a preference for a smaller, more certain reward over a larger, more risky reward. After exposure to sexual cues, proposers in an ultimatum game should be more likely to make higher, more fair offers to responders, as fair offers are less likely to be rejected. Consistent with our hypothesis, we found that proposers made significantly higher offers after exposure to pictures featuring sexy women dressed in a bikini (rather than pictures featuring women in casual clothes). Upon sex cue exposure, proposers in an ultimatum game maximized the likelihood of a reward rather than the size of the reward.

In the second experiment, we predicted that individuals would prefer a smaller, certain reward (\$1 for the self, \$1 for the anonymous other) rather than trusting an anonymous individual who could increase the size of the reward (\$2 for the self, \$2 for the anonymous other), but who could also take away the reward (\$0 for the self, \$3 for the anonymous other) (i.e., trust game). The results confirmed the hypothesis that sexual cues instigate risk aversion: After exposure to pictures featuring sexy women (rather than pictures featuring women in casual clothes), individuals preferred a smaller, certain monetary reward over trusting an anonymous individual, thereby giving up the chance of a larger, but more uncertain reward.

In the third experiment, we tested our hypothesis more directly by using an ecologically valid manipulation. We offered individuals several choices between a smaller, certain reward and a larger, uncertain reward (e.g., receive $1000 for sure versus flip a coin and receive $2000 if heads or $0 if tails). After exposure to a female experimenter in sexy attire, individuals were more likely to choose the smaller, certain reward.

These experimental studies suggest that mating motivation leads to a disproportionate increase in the desire for sure gains, so that seeking risky alternatives is decreased. These findings are consistent with the Somatic Marker Model (Bechara and Damasio 2005), which predicts that when one is in a positive state (i.e., after exposure to sexual cues), risk aversion in the face of sure gains is enhanced. Neuroscientific observations are also consistent with our results: Increased activation of the amygdala, a brain structure highly responsive to sexual cues, is associated with the tendency to be risk-averse for sure rewards (De Martino et al. 2006). These findings potentially explain why men devalue delayed monetary rewards after touching lingerie (Van den Bergh, Dewitte, and Warlop 2008): Because there is a greater risk that the delayed reward will not be received, men prefer immediate, certain rewards upon sex cue exposure.

References

Bechara, Antoine and Antonio R. Damasio (2005), "The Somatic Marker Hypothesis: A Neural Theory of Economic Decision," *Games and Economic Behavior*, 52 (2), 336-72.

De Martino, Benedetto, Dharshan Kumaran, Ben Seymour, and Raymond J. Dolan (2006), "Frames, Biases, and Rational Decision-Making in the Human Brain," *Science*, 313 (5787), 684-87.

Frederick, Shane (2005), "Cognitive Reflection and Decision Making," Journal of Economic Perspectives, 19 (4), 25-42.

Halevy, Yoram (2008), "Strotz Meets Allais: Diminishing Impatience and the Certainty Effect," *American Economic Review*, 98 (3), 1145-62.

Van den Bergh, Bram, Siegfried Dewitte, and Luk Warlop (2008), "Bikinis Instigate Generalized Impatience in Intertemporal Choice," *Journal of Consumer Research*, 35 (1), 85-97.

"Sex, Food, and the Hunger for Distinction"

Jonah Berger, University of Pennsylvania, USA
Baba Shiv, Stanford University, USA

Similarity and distinction play an important role in identity processes, decision making, and motivation more broadly. People avoid giving their children names that are too popular and buy clothes that let them fit in, while also feeling unique. Indeed, researchers have long noted that while the strength of these motives varies across individuals and cultural-contexts, people have a need for distinction (Brewer, 1991; Snyder and Fromkin, 1980).

The exact nature of this "need," however, is less clear (Vignoles et al. 2000). Most existing research has treated distinction as a secondary motive, valued only as it enhances self-image and contributes to self-enhancement (Lynn and Snyder, 2002; Tian, Bearden, and Hunter 2001). Another perspective, however, argues for the intriguing possibility that distinctiveness may be a fundamental human need (Brewer, 1991; Vignoles et al. 2000). This debate has important implications for understanding the role of distinctiveness in identity processes, but lack of empirical tests has made it hard to reach any conclusions.

We examine the nature of distinctiveness by testing whether it shares kinship with other basic rewards arising from physiological needs such mating motives. To do so, we turn to recent work on motivation. Physiological drives (e.g., sex) can increase the desirability of relevant reward stimuli, but this link can also work in the opposite direction, such that reward stimuli can themselves strengthen relevant drive states. Further, by activating dopaminergic reward systems, such stimuli can increase reward responsiveness more generally (Van den Bergh, Dewitte, and Warlop, 2008; Wadhwa, Shiv and Nowlis 2008).

If similarity and distinction share kinship with basic physiological drive states such as mating, then they should have similar motivational properties. To the extent that distinctiveness is rewarding, exposure to basic reward cues should influence the desirability of distinction. Sexually arousing images, for example, ought to influence preferences for distinctive goods. Conversely, manipulations that activate distinctiveness should have corresponding effects on the desirability of basic physiological rewards. Priming distinctiveness, for example, should influence people's desire for romantic partners.

Five experiments test these possibilities. First, we examine whether exposure to sexual cues or a strong desire for food influences the desirability of distinctive products. In Study 1, participants were approached either right after they had eaten dinner or right before (when they were hungry). In Study 2, we built on prior work in indicating that sexual images activate reward circuitry (Aharon et al. 2001) and exposed participants either swimsuit model or control pictures. We then asked participants in each study to choose amongst options that varied in their distinctiveness (i.e., some had been selected by prior participants, or were preferred by a greater percentage of others). As predicted, differences in basic physiological needs influenced preferences for distinction. Study 1 found that hungry participants (those approached before dinner) were more likely to avoid options selected by another participant ($M=4.12$ vs. 3.35; $F(1, 36)=6.25$, $p=.02$). Study 2 found that participants exposed to sexual images preferred more distinctive options (2.20 vs. 1.88; $F(1, 58)=11.34$, $p<.001$).

The first two studies illustrate that activation of basic physiological drives such as mating can influence preferences for distinction, but if distinctiveness is truly a basic human need, the effects should work in the opposite direction as well. Distinctiveness itself should influence the desirability of other reward stimuli. The next two studies tested this possibility by priming half the subjects with distinctiveness and then measuring the desirability of other rewarding stimuli. As predicted, (Study 3) priming participants with distinctiveness increased the desirability of other rewards such a romantic encounters and led participants to reporting willingness to walk more blocks to get their favorite food ($M=12.28$ vs. 7.82; $F(82)=4.56$, $p=.04$).

The last study provides further evidence for our conceptualization by examining whether the observed effects would reverse for cultural groups (East Asians) who find assimilation (rather than distinctiveness) rewarding. Using a similar set-up to Study 2, participants were exposed to either swimsuit models or control images and we measured their preference for distinctive products while also recording their cultural background. As expected, exposure to other reward cues had opposite effects on European Americans and East Asians participants, ($F(1,73)=13.33$, $p<.001$). Compared to the control condition, a general appetitive state increased the choice of distinctive products among European Americans ($F(1, 73)=12.12$, $p<.001$) but it decreased the choice of distinctive products for East Asians ($F(1,73)=5.37, p<.05$). Taken together, these results suggest that distinction has similar motivational properties to other basic needs such as mating. The findings provide insight into the nature of distinctiveness and its motivational effects more generally.

References

Brewer, M. B. (1991), "The Social Self: On Being the Same and Different at the Same Time," *Personality and Social Psychology Bulletin*, 17 (5), 475-82.

Snyder, C. R. and H. L. Fromkin (1977), "Abnormality as a Positive Characteristic: The Development and Validation of a Scale Measuring Need for Uniqueness," *Journal of Abnormal Psychology*, 86 (October), 518-527.

Tian, K. T., W. O. Bearden, and G. L Hunter (2001), "Consumers' Need for Uniqueness: Scale Development and Validation," *Journal of Consumer Research*, 28 (June), 50-66.

Van den Bergh, B., S. DeWitte, and L. Warlop (2008), "Bikinis Instigate Generalized Impatience in Intertemporal Choice," *Journal of Consumer Research*, 35, 85-97.

Vignoles, V. L., X. Chryssochoou, and G. M. Breakwell (2000), "The Distinctiveness Principle: Identity, Meaning, and the Bounds of Cultural Relativity," *Personality and Social Psychology Review*, 4 (4), 337-354.

"What Marketers Can Learn From Lap-Dancers: A Field Study of Ovulatory Cycle Effects on Consumer Behavior"

Geoffrey Miller, University of New Mexico, USA; Queensland Institute of Medical Research, Australia

Evolutionary psychology has revolutionized our understanding of human female sexuality in the last 15 years. This new research has profound implications for understanding women's consumption patterns and preferences, but it remains almost unknown to the consumer research community.

In particular, dozens of papers have found that women of reproductive age (c.15 to 40) think, feel, and behave quite differently depending on whether they are in the menstrual, follicular, estrus, or luteal phases of their monthly cycle. This work has overturned the century-long assumption that human females uniquely had 'lost' estrus. Estrus is the phase around ovulation (maximum fertility) of increased sexual receptivity, increased sexual attractiveness to males, and increased sexual attraction to males who show signs of high genetic quality. Female estrus now appears to be universal across all vertebrate species such as the 10,000 birds and 5,400 mammals, including all 394 primates such as humans (Gangestad & Thornhill, 2008).

This talk reviews the evolutionary logic of estrus and previous research on ovulatory cycle effects in women, presents some striking new example of cycle effects on cash earnings by lap-dancers working in gentlemen's clubs, and discusses implications of this research program for understanding women's behavior as both consumers and marketers.

The evolutionary benefits of estrus arise from sex itself. In sexually reproducing species, two individuals combine their genes to produce offspring, so the genetic quality of one's mate determines half the genetic quality of one's offspring–and thus their likelihood of surviving and reproducing in turn. Thus, in the 530 million years that nervous systems have been evolving, one of their key jobs has been to prefer good mates with good genes–the oldest version of a consumer preference for a luxury good. The stakes are especially high for female mammals, who invest more energy in parental care throughout pregnancy and breast-feeding, and who therefore cannot produce as many offspring per lifetime as a highly promiscuous male. So, females evolved to be choosier about their sexual partners, and to be especially choosy when they might actually get pregnant from a sexual encounter–i.e. just before ovulation, during estrus. Previous research has now shown that women during estrus compared to other phases of the cycle do show stronger preferences for males who are healthier, taller, more athletic, more muscular, more masculine-looking, more socially dominant, and more creative, whether painting works of art or launching start-up companies (Haselton & Miller, 2006).

Ovulatory cycle effects are not limited to women's preferences; they also affect women's sexual attractiveness. Given that fertile females had to compete against each other for the attentions of the few highest-quality male sires (whose own long-term partners resented infidelity), women evolved to be maximally attractive during estrus, when it was most important to 'poach' the good genes. Previous lab and questionnaire research has shown that women during estrus compared to other cycle phases are indeed more attractive to men with regard to body scent, voice quality, facial appearance, breast symmetry, waist-to-hip ratio, verbal fluency, self-confidence, mental health, and overall mood. Also, women in estrus dress in more stylish and revealing clothing, travel more miles per day, go out more often at night to crowded night-spots, have more sexual fantasies about men other than their current boyfriends or husbands, receive more cell phone calls from jealous boyfriends, and have more actual one-night stands and affairs.

Use of hormonal contraception such as the Pill (which eliminates ovulation) eliminates all of these cycle effects on women's mate preferences, sexual attractiveness, mate search effort, and short-term mating. Conversely, dissatisfaction with a current long-term mate (boyfriend or husband) seems to amplify all of these effects.

However, it was not clear whether women's estrus shifts in attractiveness cashed out in the real world of women's work as marketers and service providers. To investigate the economic effects of estrus, my colleagues and I examined ovulatory cycle effects on earnings by professional lap dancers working in Albuquerque gentlemen's clubs. Eighteen dancers recorded their menstrual periods, work shifts, and cash earnings for 60 days each on a study web site. Hierarchical linear modeling of the data (representing earnings from about 5,300 lap dances) showed main effects of cycle phase [$F(2, 236)=27.46, p<.001$] and Pill use [$F(1, 17)=6.76, p<.05$], plus the expected interaction between cycle phase and pill use [$F(2, 236)=5.32, p<.01$]. Normally cycling dancers (those who did not use the Pill, and thus had an estrus phase) earned about $335 per 5-hour shift during estrus, $260 per shift during the luteal phase (after ovulation) or the early follicular phase (before ovulution), and $185 per shift during menstruation. By contrast, dancers using the Pill showed no estrus earnings peak, but did show the menstrual-period drop. Also, Pill use reduced earnings by an average of more than $80 per shift–more than $10,000 per year in lost earnings. This is the first economic evidence for the importance of estrus in a real-world work setting.

Taken together, these findings have many implications for consumer behavior research. Since so much of consumer behavior is driven by unconscious mating effort, especially among young single adults (Griskevicius et al., 2007; Miller, 2009), cycle effects may profoundly influence women's consumer behavior. If estrus affects women's mate preferences regarding male height, facial features, body types, social dominance, and creativity, it may also shift their consumer preferences regarding the appearance and behavior of male service providers, entertainers, spokesmen, and sales staff. If estrus affects women's scent, voice, appearance, self-image, and mood, it may also affect their consumer preferences regarding cosmetics, clothing, fitness products, self-help books, and mood-altering products such as chocolate, alcohol, tobacco, and romance novels. Finally, if estrus provokes more travel, going out in the evenings, and sexual affairs, it may affect women's consumer preferences and consumption patterns regarding cars, restaurants, night clubs, movies, hotels, cell phones, and social internet sites. Thus, consumer behavior researchers and marketers could better understand female consumers by routinely measuring their current cycle phase and Pill use, which can be done reliably with a one-page questionnaire.

References

Gangestad, S.W., and R. Thornhill (2008), "Human Oestrus," *Proceedings of the Royal Society B*, 275, 991-1000.

Griskevicius, V., J. M. Tybur, J. M. Sundie, R. B. Cialdini, G. F. Miller, and D. T. Kenrick (2007), "Blatant Benevolence and Conspicuous Consumption: When Romantic Motives Elicit Costly Displays," *Journal of Personality and Social Psychology*.

Haselton, M. and G. F. Miller (2006), "Women's Fertility Across the Cycle Increases the Short-Term Attractiveness of Creative Intelligence," *Human Nature*, 17 (1), 50-73.

Miller, G. F. (2009), *Spent: Sex, Evolution, and Consumer Behavior*, Viking Press.

Special Session Summary

Effects of Social Influence on Consumer Spending Decisions

Didem Kurt, University of Pittsburgh, USA

SESSION OVERVIEW

The majority of research on the effects of social influence in the marketplace has documented the impact of the simple presence or absence of others in a given consumer choice situation (e.g., choice under public versus private settings). Less is known about the impact of the source of the influence and the process of transmission of the influence from the source to the receiver. Although the importance of some sources of influence is readily apparent (e.g., salespersons), consumers may be subject to the social influence stemming from more subtle, unexpected sources as well. This session focuses on these subtle, but powerful, sources of social influence on consumer decisions. For instance, how does the presence of an accompanying friend influence the amount spent? What happens when the influencer is not physically present at the time purchase, but is instead physically associate with the object of purchase (e.g., deciding on how much to pay for objects that were once owned by well-liked or despised individuals)? And finally, how does subtle physical contact by another person influence the type of decisions that a consumer makes? The goal of this session is to present papers that address these subtle, incidental sources of social influence on consumer decision-making.

The three presentations also look at different degrees of connectedness between the consumers and the influencer. The first paper (by Kurt, Inman, and Argo) examines whether the presence of a friend can create an unintentional financial cost to the consumer when in the marketplace. They show that consumers spend more when they shop with a friend compared to when they shop alone and that individual differences in consumers' agency-communion orientation and self-monitoring moderate the relation between an accompanying friend and consumers' spending. The second paper (by Argo and Levav) examines how a gentle, open-palmed touch affects individuals' feeling of security and financial risk-taking propensity. They find that such a touch on the shoulder generate higher risk-seeking. Finally, the third paper (by Newman, Diesendruck, and Bloom) focuses on the case where the influence is transmitted through the object considered to be purchased by the consumer rather than a direct connection between the influencer and the consumer. Specifically, they examine why celebrity objects are valued and whether consumers value the items once owned by disliked figures for the same reasons that they value those previously owned by liked figures. They find that a contagion model can better explain the valuation of objects previously owned by liked people, whereas presumed marketability of items previously owned by disliked people is the sole driver of their valuation.

Collectively, the three papers in this session will provide new insights regarding psychological mechanisms underlying the process of social influence shaping consumers' decision making. The set of papers should lead to an interesting discussion regarding subtle and unexpected social influence in the market place (e.g., negative and unintended consequences of shopping with a friend). In addition, we believe that the variation in the degree of connection between the influencer and the consumer examined in the papers will lead to a lively session. We expect this session to generate considerable interest among ACR members because the papers draw upon a variety of theoretical perspectives (agency-communion theory, law of contagion) and the studies range from lab experiments (Newman et al., Argo and Levav) to field studies (Kurt et al.) to analysis of secondary data sets (Kurt et al.).

EXTENDED ABSTRACTS

"How Friends Promote Consumer Spending"

Didem Kurt, University of Pittsburgh, USA
J. Jeffrey Inman, University of Pittsburgh, USA
Jennifer Argo, University of Alberta, Canada

It is well-established in the literature that social influences play a pervasive role in shaping consumers' affect and behaviors (e.g., Argo, Dahl, and Manchanda 2005; Dahl, Manchanda, and Argo 2001). For instance, while high levels of attractiveness and persuasiveness of a salesperson have been shown to enhance the effectiveness of an influence attempt (e.g., Argo, Dahl, and Morales 2008; Doney and Cannon 1997), high levels of persuasion knowledge and cognitive capacity of consumers have been shown to inoculate them from such an influence (e.g., Campbell and Kirmani 2000). However, not all occurrences of influence may be intentionally inflicted, and as such, it seems likely that consumers may not always be prepared to draw from their repertoire of protective strategies to shield themselves from the influence. An example of such an occurrence may be when the social influence arises from an unexpected source such as the presence of individuals for whom the consumer cares about (i.e., our friends). The goal of this research is to examine whether an accompanying friend in the marketplace can create an unintentional cost to the consumer.

Previous research has shown that friends can be influential, serving as not only sources of product information (e.g., Urbany, Dickson, and Wilkie 1989) but also through their activation of impression management concerns on the part of the consumers (e.g., Childers and Rao 1992). For instance, Ratner and Kahn (2002) demonstrate that consumers seek more variety in public (versus private) contexts as they expect others to evaluate a varied set as more interesting. Thus, we predict that consumers spend more when they shop with a friend as compared to when they shop alone.

Furthermore, we argue that the direction of consumer spending is moderated by consumers' agency-communion orientation (i.e., the tendency to focus on the self or others; Bakan 1966). Specifically, we predict that agentic consumers (i.e., males) spend more when they shop with a friend than when they shop alone, whereas communion consumers (i.e., females) are more likely to control their shopping in the presence of a friend. This prediction is consistent with "feminine modesty effect" (e.g., Heatherington et al. 1993) suggesting that in response to normative pressures, females are more likely to be modest in public versus private contexts. In contrast, society deems it acceptable for males to engage in self-promotion (Griskevicius et al. 2007). Finally, given that consumers differ in their responsiveness to interpersonal cues of situationally appropriate behavior (Gangestad and Snyder 2000), we argue that this interactive effect is moderated by self-monitoring such that friends are especially influential for consumers who are high in self-monitoring despite their orientation, albeit the effects occur in opposite directions (i.e., agentic (communion) consumers spend more (less) in the presence of a friend).

In Study 1, we use the data provided by the Point of Purchase Advertising Institute (POPAI). In-store intercept interviews were conducted at 14 mass merchandise stores. Consumers were intercepted randomly as they entered the store and were asked several questions, including how much they planned to spend in the store. After respondents finished shopping, they returned for the exit interview. Agency-communion orientation was operationalized as gender (78% of 1,208 respondents were female). We estimated a model with OLS regression where the dependent variable was the amount spent and the main independent variables were the amount planned to be spent, social influence categories (indicator variables for being accompanied by friend, spouse, etc.), gender and social influence*gender interactions. We found a significant main effect for friend (β_2=0.12, p<.05) and a significant friend x gender interaction (β_{18}=0.15, p<.01). Specifically, male (i.e., agentic) consumers spend 56% more when they shop with a friend than when they shop alone, while female (i.e., communion) consumers spend 4% less when they shop with a friend than when they shop alone, albeit this latter difference is not statistically significant.

Study 2 employs a 2 (orientation: agency vs. communion) x 2 (social presence: alone vs. accompanying friend) between-subjects design. 87 students (51% female) completed the study. Orientation was operationalized as gender. We manipulated the friend's presence via a trained confederate assuming the role of a friend that is present during the shopping trip. Participants were given $5.00 and asked to purchase a package of four AA batteries at the bookstore. After categorizing the brands into three groups based on price level, we ran an ordered logistic regression with price level as the dependent variable. We found a significant main effect for friend (β =0.81, χ^2=11.64, p<.01). Importantly, the analysis revealed a significant friend x gender interaction (β =0.65, χ^2= 7.58, p<.01), suggesting that the probability of a male (female) consumer choosing a more expensive brand is greater (attenuated) when a friend is present as compared to when the consumer is alone.

Finally, in Study 3, we conducted a field study where customers were intercepted as they entered a shopping mall in Turkey. Only customers who were either shopping alone or accompanied by a single friend were invited to participate in the study (52% of 126 respondents were female). In this study, the exit survey also included scales measuring agency/communion and self-monitoring individual differences. By conducting OLS regression where the dependent variable was the amount spent, we found a significant main effect for friend (δ_2=0.14, p<.05). The interaction between friend and ACDIF (difference between a respondent's agency and communion scores) was also significant (δ_{13}=0.27, p<.05). Furthermore, there was a significant three-way interaction between friend, ACDIF, and self-monitoring (δ_{16}=0.30, p<.05). The results support our prediction that agentic (communion) consumers who are high in self-monitoring spend significantly more (less) in the presence of a friend.

Our findings suggest that the friend effect has the greatest implications for agentic consumers (i.e., males) because shopping with a friend is likely to have negative ramifications for their pocketbook–they spend more and tend to buy the most expensive brand with an accompanying friend. However, this caveat does not appear to hold for communion consumers (i.e., females). In fact, communion consumers who are high in self-monitoring spend significantly less when they shop with a friend than when they shop alone.

"Once More, With Feeling: The Effect of Touch on Risk-Taking"

Jennifer Argo, University of Alberta, Canada
Jonathan Levav, Columbia University, USA

Physical contact is a fundamental aspect of both the human and other mammalian experience. It is the cornerstone of the connection between mother and infant, and is the most primitive form of interpersonal expression. Among its many effects, touch can increase people's likelihood of accepting requests (Kleinke 1977) and can be used to communicate status (Mehrabian 1970). In this paper we focus on an aspect of touch whose effect originates in the earliest moments of life: touch as a source of security.

In his classic experiments on the nature of love, Harlow (1958) shows that infant monkeys can become attached to a "mother" made of soft cloth that the infant monkey likes to touch, but not to a "mother" made of wire that he does not. According to Harlow, infant monkeys placed in a room with the soft mother use "her" as a base of operations and source a source of security, and are more likely to explore stimuli around the room. This is not the case for the untouched, wire mother. The connection between touch and security at infancy and exploratory behavior is even more apparent in Ainsworth's (1978) strange situation paradigm, wherein young children are placed in a room with strange stimuli and are left to explore on their own. Children with stronger attachment patterns—physical and otherwise—are more likely to engage in exploratory behavior.

In this paper we argue that certain forms of touch can similarly increase consumers' sense of security and in turn lead them to engage in similar form of exploratory behavior. Specifically, we study how touch affects financial risk tasking. Our prediction is partially drawn from work by Hsee and Weber (1999) that shows that Chinese are more willing to take financial risks because of their strongly interdependent culture provides a measure of security should their risk fail. Hsee and Weber call this "the cushion hypothesis," as the potential fall is cushioned by the tight social network that is characteristic of Eastern cultures. Although in the Hsee and Weber studies the sense of security experienced by Chinese participants is real, in our study the sense of security is perceived, rather than actual (more below).

The touch that we focus on in our studies is an open-palmed, comforting light pat on the shoulder. We present three experiments with both hypothetical as well as real payoffs.

In our first study participants are greeted by an experimenter and are either verbally ushered to a table where the experimental task awaits or are verbally ushered and touched lightly (not pushed!) on the shoulder. The experiment was run individually for each participant; this was the case for the next two studies as well. The experimenter was a mildly attractive female. The experimental task was taken directly from Hsee and Weber (1999) and consisted of a series of choices between sure, low payoffs and risky, higher payoff gambles. We find that participants in the touch condition were significantly more likely to accept the riskier gambles (i.e., they showed greater risk tolerance). We find no interaction with gender; both male and female participants were equally influenced by the experimenter's touch (this was a consistent finding in all three studies and will not be discussed further).

In our second study we contrasted different security-evoking and non-security-evoking forms of touch and tested whether a measure of sense of security could mediate our effect. To this end, in addition to our no touch and shoulder touch conditions, we also added a handshake condition wherein the experimenter greeted the participants with a handshake also prior to presenting the experimental task. Based on previous research, we reasoned that a handshake would not provide the same perceived sense of security as a touch on the shoulder, and that as a result we would not see elevated levels of risk taking in the handshake condition. The task this time was an investment decision wherein participants were given $10 in cash and received financial data about an unnamed publicly-traded company. They were then given a choice between investing all or some of the $10 in the company's stock (to make matters more realistic, each $1 in cash was made equivalent to $100) and investing the money in a government bond with a fixed payoff. The payoff for the stock investment was probabilistic and was based on the company's financial performance. Participants kept their winnings. Having completed the investment task, participants then completed a battery of measures to assess their mood and feelings of security. We find that participants were significantly more likely to invest their money in the riskier equity in the shoulder touch condition than in either the no touch or handshake conditions. There were no differences in mood between conditions, suggesting that affect does not drive our effect. Importantly, however, we do find that feelings of security mediate people's propensity to take risk and invest in the risk equity.

Finally, in the third study we further probed the role of perceived security using a manipulation approach. Participants were either asked to write about a situation in their past where they felt insecure or a situation where they felt secure. They were then sent to a different room, where a mildly attractive female experimenter either touched them on the shoulder or not as in the previous two studies. The task was the same investment decision as in study, again with a real monetary payoff. We find that participants in the insecure essay conditions made riskier choices if they were touched versus not touched. The levels of risk taking in the insecure essay/touch condition were equally high to those in either of the secure essay conditions. The interaction is significant. In other words, touching participants in the insecure essay condition reversed the effect of insecurity on people's risky choices, making them more risk-seeking.

"Celebrity Contagion and the Value of Objects"

George Newman, Yale University, USA
Gil Diesendruck, Bar-Ilan University, Israel
Paul Bloom, Yale University, USA

Artifacts are usually valued because of their utility—a watch tells time, a coat provides warmth, and so on. But, in some cases, they also get value by dint of their histories. People have paid large sums of money for a tape measure owned by President Kennedy, an autograph by astronaut Neil Armstrong, and the pop star Britney Spears' chewed-up bubble gum (see Bloom and Gelman 2008; Hood and Bloom 2007). Curiously, there is also a substantial market for items once belonging to despised individuals, such as Charles Manson's hair, a painting by John Wayne Gacy, and the personal effects of Saddam Hussein (Stone 2007). Why are these celebrity objects valued? And, do people value 'negative' celebrity items for the same reasons that they value 'positive' ones?

One explanation is that these objects are valued because of their associations. Objects that were owned or touched by specific people remind us of those people. This captures the fact that objects associated with admired individuals are positively valued, however it predicts as well that objects belonging to individuals that are explicitly disliked should carry no value at all.

A second account has to do with intuitions about how these objects are valued by others. For instance, we might value objects that belonged to celebrities because we believe that there are other people who would later purchase them from us at higher prices, or because others would be impressed that we own such things.

A third account is rooted in "the law of contagion" (Frazer 1959; Mauss 1972; Rozin et al. 1986). This is the belief that through physical contact, a person's immaterial qualities or 'essence' can be transferred to an object. For example, people are reluctant to purchase a t-shirt if it was just tried on by someone else (Argo, Dahl, and Morales 2006), but they are more likely to purchase a product if it came into contact with someone attractive (Argo, Dahl, and Morales 2008). This provides a potential explanation for why people value objects that have been touched by admired people, though it fails to explain the appeal of objects that have been in contact with despised individuals.

The goal of the present studies was to explore these alternative accounts. Experiment 1 recruited 219 adult participants (M_{age}=35). Using a method similar to Nemeroff and Rozin (1994), participants first were asked to list the name of either a person that they deeply admired or a person that they despised. Participants were then asked report the maximum amount of money they would be willing to bid on an item that belonged to the person they had just listed. After reporting this initial amount, participants in both conditions were asked on subsequent pages to imagine that the object was "transformed" in several different ways. The transformations included sterilizing the object such that no physical traces of the previous owner remained, purchasing the object with the stipulation that they could never resell it, purchasing the object with the stipulation that they could never tell anyone that they owned it, and increasing the number of such objects in existence. Participants again reported their willingness-to-pay for the item in light of each transformation, which was repeated for all four transformations.

Experiment 1 revealed an interaction between the valence of an object, and the effectiveness of a transformation in changing its perceived value ($p<.01$). For items owned by a positive target, sterilizing the object was the only transformation that significantly impacted judgments value (M=-29.5%), $p<.001$. The effects of "can't resell", "can't tell others" and "increase number" were comparatively minimal (Ms=+10.4%, +0.7%, and -9.8%, respectively, all ps>.2, except for a marginal effect of "increase number," which was p=.064). In contrast, only the "can't resell" transformation had a significant impact on the negative items (M=-31.5%), $p<.001$, while the effects of "sterilization", "can't tell others", and "increase number" were comparatively minimal (-10.1%, -16.0%, and +6.3%, respectively, all ps>.2). This result suggests a contagion account best explains the value of positive objects, while a market account best explains the value of negative objects. The effect of sterilization, as well as the fact that at least some participants said they would pay money for negative objects, rules out a strict version of the association account.

In Experiment 2 we assessed the interaction between object valence and transformation type more directly by making two changes in the design. First, we included only the two transformations that proved most effective in Experiment 1: sterilization and can't resell. Second, we manipulated these transformations between-, rather than within- subjects. We also included an additional measure regarding participants' willingness to have contact with the object.

Results from 310 new participants (M_{age}=33.4) indicated a significant interaction between valence (positive vs. negative) and transformation type (sterilization vs. can't resell), $p<.001$. Consistent with the results of the previous experiment, sterilizing the "positive" object decreased its value, significantly more than did limiting the ability to resell it ($p<.05$). Conversely, limiting the ability to resell the negative object decreased its value significantly more than did sterilizing it ($p<.05$).

Analysis of willingness-to-wear, however, revealed a different pattern. Sterilizing the 'positive' sweater made participants want to wear it significantly less than did limiting the ability to resell it ($p<.05$). However, sterilizing the 'negative' sweater made participants want to wear it significantly more than did limiting the ability to resell it ($p<.01$).

These experiments suggest that people value objects that have come into contact with famous vs. infamous individuals for different reasons. Valuation of positive objects is best accounted for by a contagion model—these objects are believed to hold some physical remnant of their previous owner, and people are willing to pay money for the possibility to have contact with such remnants. Objects previously owned by negative figures, in contrast, were valued for their presumed marketability. In cases where negative objects were valued, prohibiting participants from reselling the object significantly decreased the amount of money they were willing to pay for it. Interestingly, while sterilization did not affect participants' willingness to pay, it did affect their willingness to wear a negative object. This finding suggests that while people seem to believe that negative objects contain possibly contagious remnants of their previous owners, these beliefs do not affect people's monetary valuation of objects (also see Rozin et al. 2007).

Previous work on contagion has demonstrated that the belief in a physical transmission of 'essence' is arguably pervasive across cultures (Frazer 1959; Mauss 1972). The present studies offer a new perspective on this phenomenon as they illustrate the ways in which contagion and monetary valuations of objects may either converge, or diverge, depending on the valence of the individual who touched them and the market demands surrounding them.

REFERENCES

Ainsworth, Mary D. S., Mary C. Blehar, Everett Waters, and Sally Wall (1978), *Patterns of Attachment: A Psychological Study of the Strange Situation*, Hillsdale, New Jersey: Erlbaum.

Argo, Jennifer J., Darren W. Dahl, and Rajesh V. Manchanda (2005), "The Influence of a Mere Social Presence in a Retail Context," *Journal of Consumer Research*, 32 (September), 207-212.

Argo, Jennifer J., Darren W. Dahl, and Andrea C. Morales (2006), "Consumer Contamination: How Consumers React to Products Touched by Others," *Journal of Marketing*, 70 (April), 81-94.

______ (2008), "Positive Consumer Contagion: Responses to Attractive Others in Retail Contexts," *Journal of Marketing Research*, 45 (December), 690-701.

Bakan, David (1966), *The Duality of Human Existence*, Chicago: Rand McNally & Company.

Bloom, Paul and Susan A. Gelman (2008), "Psychological Essentialism in Selecting the 14th Dalai Lama," *Trends in Cognitive Science*, 12, 243.

Campbell, Margaret and Amna Kirmani (2000), "Consumers' Use of Persuasion Knowledge: The Effects of Accessibility and Cognitive Capacity on Perceptions of an Influence Agent," *Journal of Consumer Research*, 27 (June), 69-83.

Childers, Terry L. and Akshay R. Rao (1992), "The Influence of Familial and Peer-based Reference Groups on Consumer Decisions," *Journal of Consumer Research*, 19 (September), 198-211.

Dahl, Darren W., Rajesh V. Manchanda and Jennifer J. Argo (2001), "Embarrassment in Consumer Purchase: The Roles of Social Presence and Purchase Familiarity," *Journal of Consumer Research*, 28 (December), 473-481.

Doney, Patricia M. and Joseph P. Cannon (1997), "An Examination of the Nature of Trust in Buyer-Seller Relationships," *Journal of Marketing*, 61(2), 35-51.

Frazer, James G. (1959), *The New Golden Bough: A Study in Magic and Religion* (abridged), New York: Macmillan (Edited by T. H. Gaster, 1922; Original work published 1890).

Gangestad, Steven W. and Mark Snyder (2000), "Self-Monitoring: Appraisal and Reappraisal," *Psychological Bulletin*, 126 (4), 530-555.

Griskevicius, Vladas, Joshua M. Tybur, Jill M. Sundie, Robert B. Cialdini, Geoffrey F. Miller, and Douglas T. Kenrick (2007), "Blatant Benevolence and Conspicuous Consumption: When Romantic Motives Elicit Strategic Costly Signals," *Journal of Personality and Social Psychology*, 93 (1), 85-102.

Harlow, Harry F. (1958), "The Nature of Love," *American Psychologist*, 13, 673-685.

Heatherington, Laurie, Kimberly A. Daubman, Cynthia Bates, Alicia Ahn, Heather Brown, and Camille Preston (1993), "Two Investigations of "Female Modesty" Effect in Achievement Situations," *Sex Roles*, 29, 739-754.

Hsee, Christopher K. and Elke U. Weber (1999), "Cross-National Differences in Risk Preference and Lay Predictions," *Journal of Behavioral Decision Making*, 12, 165-179.

Hood, Bruce M. and Paul Bloom (2008), "Children Prefer Certain Individuals over Perfect Duplicates," *Cognition*, 106, 455-462.

Kleinke, Chris L. (1977), "Compliance to Requests Made by Gazing and Touching Experimenters in Field Settings," *Journal of Experimental Social Psychology*, 13 (3), 218-223.

Mauss, Marcel (1972), *A General Theory of Magic*, R. Brain, trans. New York: W. W. Norton.

Mehrabian, A. (1970), *Tactics of Social Influence*, Englewood Cliffs, New Jersey: Prentice-Hall.

Nemeroff, Carol and Paul Rozin (1994), "The Contagion Concept in Adult Thinking in the United States: Transmission of Germs and of Interpersonal Influence," *Ethos*, 22, 158-186.

Ratner, Rebecca K. and Barbara E. Kahn (2002), "The Impact of Private versus Public Consumption on Variety-Seeking Behavior," *Journal of Consumer Research*, 29 (September), 246-257.

Rozin, Paul, Linda Millman, and Carol Nemeroff (1986), "Operation of the Laws of Sympathetic Magic in Disgust and Other Domains," *Journal of Personality and Social Psychology*, 40, 703-712.

Rozin, Paul, Heidi Grant, Stephanie Weinberg, and Scott Parker (2007), "Head versus Heart: Effect of Monetary Frames on Expression of Sympathetic Magical Concerns," *Judgment and Decision Making*, 2, 217-224.

Urbany, Joel E., Peter R. Dickson, and William L. Wilkie (1989), "Buyer Uncertainty and Information Search," *Journal of Consumer Research*, 16 (September), 208-215.

Stone, Gigi (2007), "'Murderabilia' Sales Distress Victims' Families", *ABC News Online*, (April 15), [available at http://abcnews.go.com/WNT/US/Story?id=2999398&page=1]

Special Session Summary

Consumer-Generated Advertising: Creators and Spectators

Burçak Ertimur, Fairleigh Dickinson University, USA

EXTENDED ABSTRACTS

"Consumer-Generated Advertising: Creators and Spectators"

Burçak Ertimur, Fairleigh Dickinson University, USA
Mary C. Gilly, University of California, Irvine, USA

The emergence of consumer-generated advertising (CGA) has greatly affected the advertising landscape by eroding the separation between the producer and the consumer and challenging the traditional view of advertising as non-personal, unidirectional, and paid-for communication (Berthon, Pitt, Campbell 2008). Many companies jumped on the CGA bandwagon; however, the results have been inconsistent (Petrecca 2007), leaving the question of whether the hype of CGA can live up to the standards of traditional advertising unanswered. There has been very limited research on the new concerns brought up by CGA, hindering our understanding of consumers' capabilities in crafting CGAs as well as their perceptions and interpretations of these new types of ads. This symposium explores the phenomenon of CGA from the perspective of both the creators and the spectators through the presentation of three completed empirical studies. The objective of this session is to provide a better understanding of CGA's effectiveness, specifically in terms of its content and communication value, and to stimulate further research exploring the realm of CGA.

The first paper by Schau, Thompson, and Muniz focuses on the creators of CGAs, and examines the collaborative and prolonged process through which the Twilight brand community members collectively create, disseminate, and distill content. Research by Brunel, Lawrence and Fournier shifts the focus towards consumers' reactions to CGA. Based on a lab experiment and a phenomenological inquiry, the authors discuss the potential of CGAs in facilitating consumer engagement and provide insights into the key facets of engagement, the underlying processes, and the conditions under which different patterns of engagement may emerge. In the third paper, Ertimur and Gilly augment our understanding of consumers' reactions to CGA by scrutinizing the communication value of CGAs as evidenced in consumers' evaluations of credibility. Using netnographic and interview data, the authors assess the appeal of CGAs vis-à-vis traditional advertising and highlight the impact of consumers' evaluations on brand associations. Following the presentations, our discussant, Robert Kozinets, offers his insights and comments on the three studies and closes the session with suggestions for future research directions. We hope that these three presentations along with our discussant's integrative comments provide the grounds for building theory regarding this new phenomenon and offer novel insights for consumer researchers interested in advertising theory and practice.

"Fanning the Flames of Consumer Engagement: Inspiring and Nurturing Communally-embedded Consumer Generated Content"

Hope Jensen Schau, University of Arizona, USA
Kate Thompson, University of Arizona, USA
Albert Muniz, De Paul University, USA

Many studies have demonstrated that members of brand communities are capable of extensive creation of brand content (Brown, Kozinets and Sherry 2003; Muniz and Schau 2007; Schau and Muniz 2006; Schau, Muniz and Arnould 2009). Indeed, the ascendancy of communally-embedded, empowered consumers is now a marketplace reality (Flight 2005; Ives 2004; Morrissey 2005). Such customer evangelism goes by many names, including "homebrew ads" (Kahney 2004), "folk ads" (O'Guinn 2003), "open source" branding (Garfield 2005) and "vigilante marketing" (Ives 2004; Muniz and Schau 2007). While several marketers have begun to actively solicit Consumer Generated Content (CGC) for occasional, ad hoc use in advertising campaigns (e.g. Doritos Super Bowl 2009), little if any research has addressed collaborative CGC, nor the role of the firm in encouraging prolonged CGC endeavors that require relinquishing considerable control of the brand meaning and messages. Moreover, the research on CGC thus far has focused primarily on male consumers with advanced technical skills who work independently or with a discrete set of known partners on a single CGC project for which they most often get explicit credit and even monetary rewards. Currently missing are studies that examine prolonged collaborative CGC among relatively unknown partners where the creative impetus lies in complex and nuanced narrative and character analysis, rather than technological mastery.

Stephenie Meyer, author of the Twilight saga, inspires passion and devotion in individual readers, but importantly she also incites and nurtures widespread collective engagement with the brand in the form of a brand community demonstrating the markers identified in Muñiz and O'Guinn (2001): consciousness of kind, rites and rituals, and moral responsibility. Twilight fans read the books and discuss them in online and offline book clubs and events. Often these fans are brought together by their mutual interest in, and admiration for, the brand and little else (scant contact beyond brand-based experiences). Yet, Twilight fans collectively create CGC and influence brand production.

Our data consist of: the Twilight saga (including an unauthorized draft novel), a feature film, literary and film criticism of the Twilight media products, naturalistic and participant observation in three online fan forums and two offline events, collectively created CGC (videos, images and texts), as well as, email and face-to-face interviews with brand fans inside and outside the brand community and CGC creators. Our data were iteratively collected and thematically coded and recoded following the hermeneutic tradition.

Like American Girl (Diamond, Sherry, Muniz, McGrath, Kozinets and Borghini, 2009), we find the Twilight brand community members are primarily female (currently underrepresented in brand community research), and generally range from 12-65. The older women in the brand community are often the mothers of daughters who were first Twilight fans and "turned them on" to the books. We find that the community contains factions based on age, life stage, character affiliation, plot interpretations, and broad ideological identification.

Through the Twilight brand community we demonstrate the strategic use of open text branding to invite collective action, the deliberate encouragement of vigilante marketing to promote the brand, and the interplay of contrived heterogeneity within the brand community as an impetus for prolonged brand community engagement and collaborative CGC. We find at the center of the phenomenon is the perpetual melodrama emanating from an inability to achieve closure and a desire to close narrative loops. These vampires are immortal, but suspended in adolescence, perpetually coming of age; this means their conflicts cannot be entirely resolved. Fans universally find the vampires and werewolves sympathetic and their efforts to exist without harming humans to be noble. The vampire quest for legitimacy and acceptance and the werewolf desire to peacefully co-exist within human society is intriguing and fan discourse compares these to race, ethnicity and class struggles in contemporary society. Collaboratively created CGC employs direct references to larger macro-social plights such as the Civil Rights Movement in the US and abroad, US and global feminist issues and peace activists in their CGC. These macro issues play out against the backdrop of a popular melodramatic media brand with full-approval of the producer. Twilight is a platform for fans to engage in these larger social issues; for many Twilight is the first impetus to consider these topics and the first time that these people have engaged in collective debate of the issues.

Our data demonstrate effective CGC that is collectively created, disseminated and distilled within a strong consumer controlled and producer nurtured brand community. The Twilight collectively created CGC is predominately antithetical to previous studies where CGC is assumed to be inspired by personal brand attachment and/or the desire to see discrete-authored CGC disseminated, or even motivated by monetary reward. Authorship of collaboratively produced CGC is virtually untraceable, unknown and monetarily uncompensated (much like Wikipedia). The true reward is the process and the outcome is not reliant on technical prowess but rather semiotic manipulation, narrative manipulation and complex character development. Like previous studies (Muniz and Schau 2007), we find consumers quite adept at appropriating and mimicking the styles, tropes, logic and grammar of advertising and film trailers. More significantly, Twilight consumers demonstrate mastery of intertextuality (O'Donohoe 1997) by utilizing the permeable boundaries between marketing communications and other socio-cultural texts via appropriation. They demonstrate mastery of polysemy (Kates and Goh 2003; Ritson and Elliott 1999), creating artifacts with different meanings for different groups.

"Towards A Contingency Theory of Consumers' Engagement with CGAs"

Frédéric Brunel, Boston University, USA
Benjamin Lawrence, Boston University, USA
Susan Fournier, Boston University, USA

With the proliferation of personal digital media technology, today's consumers have the toolbox to cheaply and quickly produce, distribute and engage in sophisticated marketing content (Muñiz and Schau 2007). Though past studies have looked at the effects of interactive versus traditional advertising (Bezjian-Avery, Calder, and Iacobucci 1998), there has been limited research (Berthon, Pitt, and Campbell 2008; Muñiz and Schau 2007) on CGAs. CGA needs to be better understood with respect to its effectiveness relative to traditional advertising and to the processes that consumers use to interpret and react to these new ads.

Many companies such as Jones Soda have embraced consumer co-creation and CGA as part of their core marketing strategies while others have confined it to specific promotions or competitions (e.g., Frito-Lay, Unilever, Chevrolet, and Heinz). Yet, one thing appears common to all who include CGA in their communication strategies: a belief that CGA engages consumers more deeply with the brand.

Consumer engagement is a central preoccupation in the advertising community, with industry groups such as the Advertising Research Council, the Association of National Advertisers, and the American Association of Advertising Agencies creating specific Engagement Councils "to provide an industry-leading peer discussion forum, for the continuous refinement and application of the Engagement construct" (thearf.org). One ultimate question remains: does CGA actually facilitate consumer engagement? More specifically, do CGAs engage consumers in the same way as traditional company-generated ads? If not, how are they different? What are the key drivers of CGA effectiveness?

We designed a multi-method program of study to answer these questions. First, in a lab experiment, we compared advertising responses when the same advertisements were either identified as having been created by consumers or no source information was provided. This study explored whether CGAs present communication advantages and investigates processing factors that drive CGA responses. We chose Toyota Yaris as the focal brand for this study for two reasons: 1) it is targeted to a young driver audience similar to our pool of student respondents, and 2) consumers have created ads for this brand. Four judges selected four (out of thirty) 30-second Yaris CGAs with varying levels along two dimensions known to affect advertising response: execution quality and product information content (Mitchell 1986). Based on a random assignment, 196 student respondents were assigned to view one of the ads, and were instructed either that the ad had been created by a consumer or were not told anything about the creator.

Confirming our hypothesis there was a significant main effect of ad creator source on various ad response measures. Respondents who were told the ad was a CGA reported higher attitudes toward the ad ($p<.05$) and higher evaluations of the executional quality ($p<.05$). They also reported that the ad was more engaging ($p<.05$) and they were more likely to seek information about the Yaris brand and consider the Yaris as a potential future car (also $p<.05$). Further, additional path analyses suggested the advertising response pattern in the CGA condition was akin to a high involvement/central processing response pattern, whereas the response pattern in the no-source condition was consistent with low involvement processing. These results confirm that consumers appear to react more favorably to CGAs and CGAs can increase engagement.

Our second study was a phenomenological inquiry of responses to CGA in a natural viewing environment that provides a holistic understanding of consumers' engagement with different types of CGAs. We content analyzed responses (i.e., verbatim transcripts of 671 YouTube posts) to eight CGAs: six contest-driven CGAs (Dove, Doritos, and Chevy HRR) and two organically-created CGAs (Firefox, and Wii). Focal ads spanned multiple product categories, brands, and advertising strategies (i.e., product information, humor, consumer values).

Our findings provide both support for –and challenge of—the contention that CGAs present systematic advantages in terms of consumer engagement. All Dove CGA ads, as well as the Wii and Firefox CGA ads, exhibited high levels of consumer engagement, as defined in terms of personal involvement, cognitive elaboration, and ad elaboration. However, two additional and dominant facets of engagement were uncovered. For the Dove ads, engagement centered on community- and relationship-building dialogues. In particular, the comments evidenced protracted viewer-viewer and viewer-creator conversations involving the ads and the brand, and professed support for and interdependency between viewers. On the other hand, engagement for the Firefox and Wii ads involved brand evangelism, brand advocacy, and the characteristic in-group/out-group brand debates defining community brands. Postings originated from focal brand supporters and also from opposing brand loyalists, spurring heated emotional debate and confrontations. Inducting from our findings, one key difference driving these engagement patterns is the participation and involvement (or absence) of the oppositional community group (i.e., Microsoft Xbox and Sony PS2 against Wii, and Internet Explorer versus Firefox): a key tenet defining community status for a brand (per Muniz and O'Guinn 2001).

Interestingly, two of the CGAs under study—Chevy HHR and Doritos—did not evidence any of the engagement facets uncovered above. Responses for these ads concerned entertainment value and not much more. In this sense, the humor advertising strategies used in these ads swamped any potential deeper engagement. Based on our findings it seems that depending on the ad strategy, CGA ads may in fact provide no observable engagement benefit.

In summary, across the two studies we found evidence that CGA can influence viewer's engagement and ad response, yet there does not appear to be a "wholesale" CGA effect. CGA effects are complex and must be viewed in the context of the brand type and the ad strategy in which they are embedded. In our lab study, limited to one brand and one product category, we were able to show that CGA can improve consumer reactions and engagement with the ad and brand. However, in a natural environment, different patterns of consumer engagement with CGAs emerged and were manifest only under specific conditions. Together our findings provide the foundation for a contingency-based understanding of the effects of CGA, though a complete contingency theory is yet to be defined.

"The Impact of Consumer-Generated Advertising on Brand Associations"

Burçak Ertimur, Fairleigh Dickinson University, USA
Mary C. Gilly, University of California, Irvine, USA

A common way for organizations to evoke favorable associations is through advertising (Dowling 2001). Yet the effectiveness of such efforts is often questionable because consumers tend to be skeptical about advertising messages and distrust the media as well as corporate advertising (Elliott, Eccles, and Hodgson 1993; Mohr, Webb, and Harris 2001). With the emergence of consumer-generated advertising (CGA), however, advertising is no longer a company-controlled form of communication. CGA also provides a direct avenue for consumers to participate in creating brand images. An emerging stream of research examines what drives consumers to generate ads and whether they are successful in their advertising creation endeavors (e.g., Muniz and Schau 2007). CGAs also reach other current and potential customers of the companies featured in CGA (McConnell and Huba 2007). Little is known, however, about such consumers' perceptions and reactions towards CGA.

In this study, we examine consumers' reactions towards two types of CGAs. The first type is solicited CGA, initiated by companies designing contests and inviting consumers to create ads for their products (e.g., Doritos). The second type is unsolicited CGA, meaning that consumers create an ad on their own without any support from the company (e.g., George Masters' ad for Apple iPod). To assess how different types of CGAs contribute to brand associations, we study consumers' responses to and interpretations of CGAs vis-à-vis traditional ads. We also seek to understand communication value of CGAs, and specifically, how consumers evaluate them in terms of credibility. On the one hand, both types of CGAs may be seen as similar to conventional ads in that they are intended to be persuasive and they look as well as feel like ads. On the other hand, CGAs may be viewed as word-of mouth (WOM) communications given that they are created by consumers, not marketers, and are not commercially motivated. Subsequently, CGAs may provide benefits such as increased credibility in comparison to traditional ads as is the case in WOM communications.

To address these issues, we investigate and compare consumer responses to both types of CGAs as well as a company ad in contexts where the ad source is known versus unknown. We gathered three different types of ads that feature an instant stain remover produced by Procter and Gamble (P&G) called Tide-to-Go. P&G ran a Tide-to-Go ad during the Super Bowl in 2008 and followed it up with a CGA contest that asked consumers to create their own version of this ad. In addition to the solicited CGAs and the company ad, there were already CGA for Tide-to-Go that were uploaded on YouTube prior to P&G's announcement of their contest. We use a combination of in-depth interviews (McCracken 1988) and netnography (Kozinets 2002) to collect data from consumers and consumer sites online. We conducted fourteen interviews with target consumers of Tide-to-Go to understand how consumers make sense of the different types of Tide-To-Go ads. The netnographic data consist of consumer comments generated in response to the three types as they appeared on YouTube and the company website as well as company and brand mentions online. While consumers in the face-to-face interviews did not know the source of the ads, the online commentators in the netnographic study knew them. The netnographic data on the company and brand mentions create the background against which consumers' responses to the ads are analyzed. Data collection and analysis followed an iterative process (Spiggle 1994) and the analytic techniques offered by Strauss and Corbin (1998) were used to arrive at themes.

The analysis of online comments shows that consumers recognize CGAs as ads and they understand the underlying effort to sell. However, in contrast to previous work on consumer skepticism toward advertising (e.g., Scott 1994), consumers do not resist being influenced by these ads. Rather they adopt a marketer's frame and critique these ads' effectiveness. They do so by relying on their persuasion knowledge (Friestad and Wright 1994) at the expense of their brand knowledge. This is evident in their evaluations that draw largely on their beliefs about the role played by psychological events evoked by the ad and ad creators' persuasion goals as well as their ideas about the effectiveness and appropriateness of marketers' tactics in general. These responses lack thoughts and beliefs about the brand, accounts of prior experiences with the brand, and the brand message conveyed by the ad. Our face-to-face interviews also substantiate the idea that CGAs are perceived as persuasion attempts and reveal that consumers are capable of differentiating amongst the different types. Consumers recognize the dual source of CGAs, and interactions between the perceptions of these sources determine these ads' credibility. In particular, they perceive the creator component of CGAs' source as unfamiliar, which in turn, makes CGAs' credibility doubtful. Consumers believe that anyone could have created these ads regardless of belonging to the target market or having any experience with the brand. They appreciate other consumers' perspectives on Tide-to-Go conveyed though CGAs; nevertheless they question these creators' expertise and authority. The findings further suggest that this detraction from the credibility of CGAs due to the unfamiliarity with the creator component of the source may somewhat be compensated through knowledge about the sponsor and/or the brand.

In conclusion, we find that consumers evaluate CGAs in their own right, independent of the product they feature, by drawing on their persuasion knowledge as a resource. Although the development of persuasion knowledge is historically contingent (Friestad and Wright 1994), consumers use their existing persuasion knowledge about company ads to make sense of these new forms of ads (i.e., solicited and unsolicited CGAs). Our study also demonstrates that CGAs cannot be merely viewed as word of mouth communications and stresses the complexity of consumers' perceptions of CGA. This new hybrid persuasion device, CGA, is viewed as neither company propaganda nor simple consumer recommendations. Our findings contribute to building theory regarding source credibility in this new medium.

REFERENCES

Berthon, Pierre, Leyland Pitt, and Colin Campbell (2008), "Ad Lib: When Customers Create the Ad," *California Management Review*, 50 (4), 6-30.

Bezjian-Avery, A., B. Calder, and D. Iacobucci (1998), "New Media Interactive Advertising Vs. Traditional Advertising," *Journal of Advertising Research*, 38, 23-32.

Brown, Stephen, Robert V. Kozinets and John F. Sherry, Jr. (2003), "Teaching Old Brands New Tricks: Retro Branding and the Revival of Brand Meaning," *Journal of Marketing*, 67 (July), 19-33.

Diamond, Nina, John F. Sherry Jr., Albert M. Muniz, Jr., Mary Ann McGrath, Robert V. Kozinets, and Stefania Borghini (2009), "American Girl and the Brand Gestalt: Closing the Loop on Sociological Branding Research," *Journal of Marketing*, 73 (May), 118-134.

Dowling, G. R. (2001), *Creating Corporate Reputations,* New York: Oxford Universitiy Press.

Elliott, Richard, Susan Eccles, and Michelle Hodgson (1993), "Re-Coding Gender Representations: Women, Cleaning Products, and Advertising's 'New Man,'" *International Journal of Research in Marketing*, 10 (3), 311-324.

Ferriss, Paul (2002), "Jeep Rides with New Logo, Old Tag," *Marketing Magazine*, 10/14/2002, Vol. 107, Issue 41.

Flight, Georgia (2005), "Companies Tap Into Consumer Passion," *Business 2.0*, October 2005.

Friestad, M. and P. Wright (1994), "The Persuasion Knowledge Model: How People Cope with Persuasion Attempts," *Journal of Consumer Research*, 21, 1–31.

Garfield, Bob (2005), "Listenomics," *Advertising Age*, Vol. 76, Issue 41, p.1.

Ives, Nat (2004), "Unauthorized Campaigns Used By Unauthorized Creators To Show Their Creativity Become A Trend," *New York Times*, December 23, section C, 3.

Kahney, Leander (2004), "Home-Brew IPod Ad Opens Eyes" Wired News, December 13, http://wired.com/news/mac/0,2125,66001,00.html

Kates, Steven M. and Charlene Goh (2003), "Brand Morphing: Implications for Advertising Theory and Practice," *Journal of Advertising*, 32 (Spring), 59-68.

Kozinets, Robert V. (2002), "The Field Behind the Screen: Using Netnography for Marketing Research in Online Communities," *Journal of Marketing Research*, 39 (February), 61-73.

McConnell, Ben and Jackie Huba (2007), *Citizen Marketers,* Chicago: Kaplan Publishing.

McCracken, Grant (1988), *The Long Interview,* Beverly Hills, CA: Sage.

Mitchell, Andrew A. (1986), "The Effect of Verbal and Visual Components of Advertisements on Brand Attitudes and Attitude toward the Advertisement," *Journal of Consumer Research*, 13 (1), 12-24.

Mohr, Lois A., Deborah J. Webb, and Katherine E. Harris (2001), "Do Consumers Expect Companies to be Socially Responsible? The Impact of Corporate Social Responsibility on Buying Behavior," *Journal of Consumer Affairs*, 35 (1), 45-71.

Morrissey, Brian (2005), "Crowd Control: Handing Creative to the Masses," *AdWeek*, September 26.

Muñiz, Albert M. and Hope J. Schau (2007), "Vigilante Marketing and Consumer-Created Communications," *Journal of Advertising*, 36 (3), 35-50.

Muñiz, Albert M. Jr. and Lawrence O. Hamer (2001), "Us Versus Them: Oppositional Brand Loyalty and the Cola Wars," in *Advances in Consumer Research*, Provo, Utah: Association for Consumer Research, Vol. 28, 355-361.

Muñiz, Albert M.and Thomas C. O'Guinn (2001), "Brand Community," *Journal of Consumer Research*, 27(4), 412-432.

O'Guinn, Thomas C. (2003), "(Brand) Community Support for the (Brand) Orchestra," presentation to Marketing Science Institute Conference on Brands, Orlando, Florida.

O'Donohoe, Stephanie (1997), "Intertextuality and Young Adult Experiences of Advertising," *in Buy This Book: Studies in Advertising and Consumption*, London: Routledge, 257-275.

Petrecca, Laura (2007), "At Cannes: Madison Avenue Wants You!" USA Today Available at: http://www.usatoday.com/money/advertising/2007-06-20-cannes-cover-usat_N.htm.

Ritson, Mark and Richard Elliott (1995), "Advertising Literacy and the Social Signification Of Cultural Meaning," *European Advances in Consumer Research*, Vol. 2, 113-117.

Schau, Hope Jensen and Albert M. Muniz, Jr. (2006), "A Tale of Tales: Narratives of the Apple Newton Brand Community," *Journal of Strategic Marketing*, 14 (1/2).

Schau, Hope Jensen and Albert M. Muniz, Jr., and Eric J. Arnould (forthcoming 2009), "How Brand Community Practices CreateValue," *Journal of Marketing*.

Scott, Linda M. (1994), "The Bridge from Text to Mind: Adapting Reader-Response Theory to Consumer Research," *Journal of Consumer Research*, 21 (December), 461-479.

Spiggle, Susan (1994), "Analysis and Interpretation of Qualitative Data in Consumer Research," *Journal of Consumer Research*, 21 (December), 491-503.

Strauss, A. and J. Corbin (1998), *Basics of Qualitative Research: Techniques and Procedures for Developing Grounded Theory,* Second ed. Thousand Oaks, CA: Sage Publications.

Special Session Summary

Emotional and Motivational Drivers of Our "Want" and "Should" Desires

Cynthia Cryder, Carnegie Mellon University, USA

EXTENDED ABSTRACTS

"Wanting Versus Choosing: A Disconnect between What Moves Us and What We Prefer"

Cynthia E. Cryder, Washington University in St. Louis, USA
Elizabeth, E. Mullen, Carnegie Mellon University, USA
George Loewenstein, Carnegie Mellon University, USA

A growing body of research finds that decisions that we make when considering multiple options yield different preferences than those that we make when considering options one at a time (e.g., Hsee et al. 1999). For example, when considering options one at a time, people prefer options with high relative payoffs to themselves versus an opponent, but when considering multiple options at once, people prefer options with high absolute payoffs to themselves, and relative payoffs become less important (Bazerman et al. 1992).

This preference reversal between separate versus joint evaluation (considering one option at a time versus considering multiple options at a time) prompts a question about how decisions made about motivation, which are typically made in separate evaluation (Will I do a task for Incentive X?), and decisions made about preference, which are typically made in joint evaluation (Do I prefer Incentive X or Incentive Y?), may differ. The current paper seeks to investigate the motivational consequences of joint versus separate preference patterns, and in the process, contribute insights that inform the design of effective incentive and promotion schemes.

Drawing on prior research by Bazerman and colleagues (e.g., Bazerman et al. 1998; 1999), we predicted a discrepancy between rewards that people choose and rewards that most strongly motivate people to act. Across three experiments, when incentives were offered individually, hedonically appealing want incentives like lotteries and chocolate were equally or more motivating than practical should incentives like sure cash payments. In choices between incentives, however, should options were more popular.

In Experiments 1 and 2, in exchange for completing a survey, participants were offered an emotionally evocative want incentive (Experiment 1: a Toblerone candy bar, Experiment 2: a Lottery), a practical should incentive (both experiments: a sure $3 payment), or a choice between the two incentives. When incentives were offered individually in Experiment 1, participants were equally motivated by want and should incentives; however, when participants decided directly between the two options, they chose the should incentive ($3) significantly more often. Experiment 2 produced a full preference reversal in which participants were more motivated by the want incentive (a lottery) when the incentives were offered individually, but chose the should incentive (a sure $3) more often when asked to choose between the two options.

Experiment 3 tested whether an opportunity for comparison was sufficient to make decisions made in separate evaluation to resemble those made using joint evaluation. In a new condition, participants were offered only one incentive in exchange for effort (the Toblerone bar or the sure $3), but they were informed that the other incentive existed. Consistent with the idea that comparison of multiple options triggers a preference for more practical alternatives, participants in the new condition who had an opportunity to compare were more motivated by the should incentive (the sure $3) than by the want incentive (the Toblerone bar). These results suggest that, the pattern of preference for should incentives in matters of choice and want incentives in matters of motivation is primarily due to the structure of the decision task (in joint versus separate evaluation) instead of due to a fundamental difference in the types of incentives that are preferred in motivation versus choice contexts. When participants could compare options as in joint evaluation, preferences in separate evaluation (motivation) contexts resembled those in the joint evaluation (choice) contexts. In fact, simply mentioning the existence of a should incentive was sufficient to change decisions about motivation (made in separate evaluation) to emulate decisions made in joint evaluation.

The findings question a common belief among both behavioral researchers and practicing marketers that individuals' choices among options signal what motivates them or makes them happy. The common practice of asking focus group members to pick between promotional items may not reveal which incentive will be successful in motivating people. Although people may strongly prefer one item over another when both items are presented side-by-side, the favored item may flop as a motivational tool. In sum, this work adds new information about a discrepancy between choice and motivation to a host of research on preference reversals (Grether and Plott 1979; Lichtenstein and Slovic 1973; Slovic and Lichtenstein 1968), all of which underscores the necessity to carefully match the mode of an inquiry to the context in which the results will be applied.

References

Bazerman, Max H., George F. Loewenstein, and Sally B. White (1992), "Reversals of Preference in Allocation Decisions: Judging an Alternative Versus Choosing Among Alternatives," *Administrative Science Quarterly*, 37 (2), 220-40.

Bazerman, Max H., Don A. Moore, Anne E. Tenbrunsel, and Kimberly A. Wade-Benzoni (1999), "Explaining How Preferences Change across Joint Versus Separate Evaluations," *Journal of Economic Behavior and Organization*, 39 (1), 41-58.

Bazerman, Max H., Anne E. Tenbrunsel, and Kimberly A. Wade-Benzoni (1998), "Negotiating with Yourself and Losing: Understanding and Managing Conflicting Internal Preferences," *The Academy of Management Review*, 23, 225-41.

Grether, David M. and Charles R. Plott (1979), "Economic Theory of Choice and the Preference Reversal Phenomenon," *American Economic Review*, 69 (September), 623-38.

Hsee, Christopher K., George Loewenstein, Sally Blount, and Max H. Bazerman (1999), "Preference Reversals between Joint and Separate Evaluations of Options: A Theoretical Analysis," *Psychological Bulletin*, 125 (5), 576-90.

Lichtenstein, Sarah, and Paul Slovic (1973), "Response-induced Reversals of Preference in Gambling: An Extended Replication in Las Vegas," *Journal of Experimental Psychology*, 101 (1), 16-20.

Slovic, Paul, and Sarah Lichtenstein (1968), "The Relative Importance of Probabilities and Payoffs in Risk Taking," *Journal of Experimental Psychology Monographs*, 78 (November), 1-18.

"Reinforcing 'Shoulds': The Effect of Mindsets on Sequential Choices"

Kelly Goldsmith, Northwestern University, USA
Uzma Khan, Stanford University, USA
Ravi Dhar, Yale University, USA

Imagine a consumer who is going through his day making a series of choices. Earlier in the day he decides to go to the gym and exercise. Later, as he is walking out of the gym, he is approached by a representative from a local charity with a request for donation. Would choosing to exercise make him more or less likely to donate? Recent research has observed two distinct patterns in sequential choices: reinforcement and balancing (Dhar et al. 2007; Dhar and Simonson 1999; Huber et al. 2007; Khan and Dhar 2006). Reinforcement occurs when an initial choice strengthens commitment to the related goal, leading to a similar subsequent choice. Conversely, balancing occurs when an initial choice satisfies and hence inhibits the related goal, allowing for the pursuit of an alternate goal on a subsequent choice. The present research proposes that reinforcement or balancing in sequential decisions can depend on how the choices are interpreted. Specifically, we posit that an initial choice will lead to reinforcement when the choices are interpreted at a higher level of abstraction. On the other hand, when choices are interpreted more concretely, an initial choice leads to balancing in subsequent decisions. We build on the notion that seemingly different choices (e.g., exercising and charitable giving) may be viewed as more related when interpreted at a higher level, as both indicate relative virtues (or shoulds as opposed to wants, Bazerman et al. 1998). Since choices interpreted at a higher level are also more likely to be seen in terms of their relationship to higher order goals that define one's self-concept (Trope and Liberman 2003), inconsistent choices would have the negative effect of highlighting a conflicting self image; thus we expect higher level processing to facilitate reinforcement across choices. By the same token, as lower level processing allows the choices to be viewed as unrelated, we predict lower level processing will facilitate balancing across decisions even when the choices are seen as relevant for self-image.

To test our propositions, we turn to abstract vs. concrete consumer mindsets, which have been shown to affect cognitive processes and systematically influence consumers' interpretation of their choices. For example, prior research on sub-goals has demonstrated that in an abstract mindset actions are seen as indicating goal commitment whereas in concrete mindset actions are seen as indicating goal progress (Fishbach et al. 2006). Specific to the current research, an abstract mindset focuses attention on central, holistic features and higher-order goals whereas a concrete mindset facilitates lower-level representations and goals enriched with details (Trope and Liberman 2003). Building on this, we predict that an initial should choice will beget subsequent unrelated should choices when a consumer is in an abstract mindset. Conversely, an initial should choice will facilitate subsequently unrelated want choices when a consumer is in a concrete mindset. We explore this effect and its underlying mechanism in four experiments. For example, in Experiment 1 participants completed a mindset manipulation and subsequently we manipulated if an initial should choice was made (e.g., a choice between cardiovascular activity vs. weight training at the gym) or not. Finally, all participants were given a choice between working on an assignment (a should) or watching a favorite television show (a want). In line with our predictions, we find that initially choosing a should option in an abstract mindset increases the likelihood of subsequently choosing a should option (i.e., working on an assignment); whereas the opposite pattern holds in a concrete mindset. That is, participants in a concrete mindset were more likely to choose a want option (i.e., watching a favorite television show) after an initial should choice. We replicate this pattern of results across different sets of initial should choices and should vs. want dependent measures, and the results consistently support the predicted interaction between mindsets and an initial want choice. Further, in support of our predicted process, we demonstrate that participants in an abstract mindset rated seemingly unrelated choices as more related compared to those in a concrete mindset. Lastly, we show that relating the initial choice to the self-concept is a key driver of reinforcement in the abstract mindset.

We believe this research has important implications for accomplishing long term, self-improvement goals. Our work goes beyond research on sub-goals (e.g., Fishbach et al. 2006) as we focus on choices that are not directly related and hence provide insight into goals that require persistence on several dimensions that may not be seen in conflict when viewed at a lower level (e.g., maintaining good health and success in exams).

References

Bazerman, M. H., A. E. Tenbrunsel, K. A. Wade-Benzoni (1998), "Negotiating with Yourself and Losing: Making Decisions with Competing Internal Preferences," *Academy of Management Review*, 23(2) 225-241.

Dhar, R., J. Huber, and U. Khan (2007), "The Shopping Momentum Effect," *Journal of Marketing Research*, 64 (August), 370-378.

Dhar, R. and I. Simonson (1999), "Making Complementary Choices in Consumption Episodes: Highlighting versus Balancing," *Journal of Marketing Research.*

Fishbach, A., R. Dhar, and Y. Zhang (2006), "Subgoals as Substitutes or Complements: The Role of Goal Accessibility. *Journal of Personality and Social Psychology*, 91,232-242.

Huber, Joel; Kelly Goldsmith, and Cassie Mogilner (2008), "Reinforcement versus Balance Response in Sequential Choice," *Marketing Letters*, 19 (December) 229-239.

Khan, U. and R. Dhar (2006), "Licensing Effect in Consumer Choice," *Journal of Marketing Research*, 43 (2), 259-266.

Trope, Y., and N. Liberman (2003), "Temporal Construal," *Psychological Review*, 110, 403-421.

"Guilt as Motivation: Strategic Self-Management of Motivation in Consumer Self-Control"

Xianchi Dai, INSEAD, France
Klaus Wertenbroch, INSEAD, France
Miguel Brendl, INSEAD, France

We propose a novel consumer self-control strategy, the self-imposition of moral liability. Consumers purposely engage in tempting hedonic activities to increase their motivation to perform subsequent tasks that require self-control. For example, students might prefer to attend a party the night before starting to study for an important exam. Or, consider people's indulgences during Carnival, which immediately precedes Lent. Building on a mental accounting framework, we show that consumers choose the hedonic behavior to self-impose a moral liability that can be canceled by persisting in the self-control task. For example, farsighted (sophisticated) consumers strategically self-impose guilt when facing self-control problems. Guilt is a self-conscious emotion that induces a desire to repair or undo what we have done to ourselves or to others (Elster 1999; Tangney and Fischer 1995), which yields extra motivation to complete subsequent self-control tasks.

Five studies provide support for our propositions and rule out alternative explanations based on theories of licensing (e.g., Khan and Dhar 2006), balancing (e.g., Dhar and Simonson 1999), self-handicapping (e.g., Berglas and Jones 1978), and ego depletion (e.g., Muraven et al. 1998). Experiment 1 examined consumers' intuitions about the motivating effects of self-imposed moral liability. Participants predicted the motivational intensity they would experience after resting at home or after going to a party before studying for an exam. For an unimportant task (studying for unimportant exam), resting led to greater predicted motivation and effort, whereas for an important task (studying for an important exam), attending the party led to greater predicted motivation and effort input. These effects on predicted motivation levels were mediated by experienced guilt.

Studies 2 and 3 showed that self-imposed moral liability affects consumer preferences and choices. In study 2, participants who faced a subsequent self-control task, in which they freely chose their effort level (from 1-3 days of volunteer work), were more likely than participants who faced a task with fixed effort levels (3 days of volunteer work) to attend a party in order to motivate themselves to work longer. Individual-level analyses provided further support for our proposition: when the future task effort was fixed, preferences did not differ, whereas when the future task effort was variable (and thus required greater self-control), those low in (self-rated) self-control were more likely to party than stay at home. In study 3, consumers with a variable-effort future self-control task (hiking to 1, 2, or 3 sites) were more likely to buy more luxurious hiking boots than those facing a fixed task (hiking to 3 sites).

Study 4 showed that those who were less confident in their ability to finish an important future task that were more likely to reward themselves before the task (rather than after the task) than those who were more confident. In contrast, when the future self-control task was not important, there was no such difference between those who were more and less confident, again consistent with our proposition that consumers self-impose moral liability to build up their motivation for a future task.

Finally, we examined the dynamics of motivation before and after a decision. We hypothesized that high planners (those who chronically think from a long term perspective) are more likely to self-impose moral liability as a self-control strategy than low planners. Results confirmed our proposition: high planners were more likely to indulge when facing a challenging future task. More importantly, for high planners, those who indulged predicted higher self-efficacy for their future task completion than a control group (high planners who didn't make a choice at all) and those who chose not to indulge. In contrast, low planners showed no difference among these three conditions, suggesting that the low planners' choice of indulgence was not driven by the strategic self-imposition of moral liability.

These results provide converging evidence for our hypothesis of self-imposing moral liability as a self-control strategy. They contribute to the growing literature on consumer self-control by demonstrating a new type of self-control strategy, in addition to the well-known strategies of exercising willpower (e.g., Hoch and Loewenstein 1991; Baumeister 2002) and precommitment (e.g., Ariely and Wertenbroch 2002; Wertenbroch 1998). They also add to the extant literature on emotions, which suggests that people avoid negative emotions. In contrast, our results suggest that consumers strategically self-impose moral liability, a specific type of aversive negative emotion.

References

Ariely, Dan and Klaus Wertenbroch (2002), "Procrastination, Deadlines, and Performance: Self-Control by Precommitment," *Psychological Science*, 13 (May), 219-224.

Baumeister, Roy F. (2002), "Yielding to Temptation: Self-Control Failure, Impulsive Purchasing, and Consumer Behavior," *Journal of Consumer Research*, 28 (March), 670-676.

Berglas, Steven, and Edward E. Jones (1978), "Drug Choice as Self-Handicapping Strategy in Response to Success," *Journal of Personality and Social Psychology*, 36, 405-417.

Dhar, Ravi and Itamar Simonson (1999), "Making Complementary Choices in Consumption Episodes: Highlighting Versus Balancing," *Journal of Marketing Research*, 36 (February), 29-44.

Elster, Jon (1999), *Alchemies of the Mind*, Cambridge, UK: Cambridge University Press.

Hoch, Stephen J. and George F. Loewenstein (1991), "Time-inconsistent Preferences and Consumer Self-Control," *Journal of Consumer Research*, 17 (March), 492-507.

Khan, Uzma and Ravi Dhar (2006), "Licensing Effect in Consumer Choice," *Journal of Marketing Research*, 43(2), 259-266.

Muraven, Mark, Dianne M. Tice, Roy F. Baumeister (1998), "Self-control as Limited Resource: Regulatory Depletion Patterns," *Journal of Personality and Social Psychology*, 74, 774-789.

Tangney JP, Fischer KW (1995), *Self-Conscious Emotions: Shame, Guilt, Embarrassment*, and Pride," New York: Guilford.

Wertenbroch, Klaus (1998), "Consumption Self-Control by Rationing Purchase Quantities of Virtue and Vice," *Marketing Science*, 17 (4), 317-337.

"Wanting What I Shouldn't Have and Finding a Way to Get It: When Guilt Increases Hedonic Consumption"

Yael Zemack-Rugar, Virginia Tech, USA
Lisa A. Cavanaugh, University of Southern California, USA
Gavan J. Fitzsimons, Duke University, USA

Consumer researchers have been interested in guilt because it affects hedonic consumption. Specifically, guilty individuals tend to self-deprive and self-punish (Bybee 1998). As a result, guilt has been shown to be incompatible with hedonic want consumption. This is particularly true for consumers high in an individual measure called guilt-proneness (GP henceforth; Tangney et al. 1992). These guilty, high GP consumers have been shown to consistently reduce consumption of hedonic products (Zemack-Rugar 2009, Zemack-Rugar et al. 2007).

In the present research, we reverse these findings. We provide evidence that guilty participants high in GP sometimes indulge more than both neutral and other guilty (low GP) participants. We examine a situation in which the hedonic product is attached to a charitable cause. We demonstrate several unique effects. We show that attaching a social cause to a hedonic product (1) leads to a larger increase in consumption for guilty, high GP, than for neutral (or guilty, low GP) participants, (2) leads to an increase in consumption even when the charity is disliked or distrusted, and (3) leads to an increase in consumption even when a non-hedonic option associated with charity is available.

In five studies we demonstrate these effects and argue for an underlying process of emotion-regulation. Specifically, we argue that since hedonic consumption is pleasant, it offers the opportunity to feel better. Guilty participants want this opportunity. However, selecting this want product can feel like a should not for guilty, high GP participants who find self-reward inappropriate. Attaching a helping opportunity (e.g., charity) to the product turns the should not into a should allowing guilty, high GP consumers to enjoy what they truly want!

In studies 1a and 1b, we demonstrate our basic effects. We place participants in a neutral/guilty emotion and offer a choice between a utilitarian product and a hedonic want product with/without charity. We also measure GP. We find a three-way interaction of emotion by charity presence by guilt proneness. Participants who are guilty and high in GP indulge more than guilty, low GP and neutral participants. Thus we show that attaching a charity does not simply "rebound" guilty, high GP participants to the level of hedonic consumption typical of their neutral (and low GP) counterparts, but rather catapults them to a hedonic consumption level higher than both.

To further examine this theory, we create a situation in which the charity attached to the hedonic product is disliked. According to existing theories, liking of the charity is critically important (Bhattacharya and Sen 1993). However, we argue that for guilty, high GP individuals, it is not critical. Specifically, if helping is what it takes to allow a guilty, high GP consumer to enjoy the emotional benefits of what they want, then the guilty, high GP consumer will be motivated to interpret any helping as sufficient justification for hedonic consumption.

In study 2 we provided neutral/guilty participants with a hedonic product associated with either a liked/disliked charity and measured GP. We predicted that guilty participants high in GP would be most likely to increase consumption of the "wanted" hedonic product even when the charity was disliked. This was confirmed.

In study 3 we examine this tendency of guilty, high GP consumers to turn want into should through meager excuses, by associating the hedonic product with either a trustworthy/non trustworthy charity. As in study 2, we find that guilty, high GP participants increased consumption of the hedonic product associated with the non-trusted charity compared to both neutral and guilt, low GP participants and compared to when the charity was trusted.

A study in progress examines whether these effects occur simply because guilty, high GP individuals are most likely to help or because they seek an excuse to consume the want item. We provided guilty participants with a pleasant (chocolate for charity) and an unpleasant (cold water dunk for charity) helping option. If guilty, high GP participants just want to help, they should choose the unpleasant charity. However, if they want the dual benefits of helping and indulging, they should choose the pleasant charity. Initial (directional) data shows that guilty, high GP participants chose the pleasant charity more often than the unpleasant one.

These findings together suggest that due to the need to feel better, guilty consumers want to indulge in pleasant and fun hedonic products, but feel they should not. Attaching any charity cause to these products, no matter how meager, gives these consumers a way to do so!

References

Bhattacharya, C.B. and Sankar Sen (2003), "Consumer-Company Identification: A Framework for Understanding Consumers' Relationships with Companies," *Journal of Marketing*, 67 (2), 76-88.

Bybee, Jane (1998), *Guilt and Children*, San Diego, CA: Academic Press.

Tangney, June P., Patricia Wagner, and Richard Gramzow (1992), "Proneness to Shame Proneness to Guilt and Psychopathology," *Journal of Abnormal Psychology*, 101 (3), 469-478.

Zemack-Rugar, Yael, James R. Bettman, and Gavan J. Fitzsimons (2007), "The Effects of Nonconsciously Priming Emotion Concepts on Behavior," *Journal of Personality and Social Psychology*, 93 (6), 927-939.

Zemack-Rugar, Yael (2009), "Negative Emotions and Self Control Behavior: The Mediating Role of Emotion-Regulation Cognitions," working paper.

Antecedents and Consequences of Consumer Confusion: Analysis of the Financial Services Industry

Paurav Shukla, University of Brighton, UK
Madhumita Banerjee, The University of Warwick, UK
Phani Tej Adidam, University of Nebraska at Omaha, USA

ABSTRACT

Our study is an empirical test of the antecedents and consequences of consumer confusion in the context of the financial services industry. Using quantitative analysis the findings reveal that expectations, attribute and information confusion significantly affect overall confusion. Moreover, expectations and attribute confusion do not affect satisfaction while information confusion has a significant impact on information satisfaction. Furthermore, we find significant impact of overall confusion, attribute satisfaction and information satisfaction on purchase decision. In comparison with earlier studies the findings also suggest that confusion is an industry specific construct and highlights the need for further research in this area.

INTRODUCTION

In the latter part of the 20th century financial services institutions (FSI) changed their role from consumer banking to multiple financial services providers (Harrison 1994; Brooks 1997). This has altered the structure and function of FSIs and has led to the proliferation of choice in the market for consumers (Henson and Wilson 2002). Consequently, consumers are now subjected to a combination of plentiful and conflicting information, an excessive number of brands, and product replications. For example, most banks today provide multiple types of current accounts, savings accounts, insurance, loans, mortgages, credit cards, capital and bond market investment services and so on. While this one-stop service philosophy brought about ease in transactions, it also created false confidence within the consumers regarding their financial judgment leading to the present day credit crisis (Greenyer 2008). For example, the latest figures reveal that the total outstanding consumer debt has increased by 7.3 per cent to in the UK (Butterworth 2008). Similarly, in the US the Federal Reserve in 2008 announced the total US consumer debt for credit cards alone had reached USD 2.55 trillion at the end of 2007.

Researchers in the field of consumer research have hypothesized that product variety can have a positive effect on consumer decision making (Kahn and Sarin 1998). However, results from empirical studies found that over-choice and overload of information deters customers from engaging with a service provider due to confusion over a product's value (Dhar & Simonson 2003; Herbig & Kramer 1994). The present era of over-choice and information overload, especially in financial services (Turnbull et al. 2000), creates increasing amounts of consumer confusion. While the role of consumer confusion has been recognised within the service industry, earlier studies have focused mostly on products such as telecommunications products (Turnbull et al. 2000), personal computers (Leek and Kun 2006), mobile phones (Leek and Chansawatkit 2006), watches (Mitchell and Papavassiliou 1997), fashion (Cheary 1997), and own-label brands (Balabanis and Craven 1997; Murphy 1997). Despite its importance, no consistent approach has been taken to defining and measuring antecedents and consequences of consumer confusion (Walsh, Hennig -Thurau and Mitchell 2007).

Furthermore, it has been proposed by researchers (Shukla et al. 2008) that confusion has a direct impact on satisfaction and final purchase decision; however limited attention has been paid to the same phenomenon in prior research (Cohen 1999). While consequences of confusion have been mentioned to be elevated amounts of dissatisfaction (Foxman et al. 1990) and decreased tendency to purchase (Mitchell and Papavassiliou 1999), empirical testing of such constructs demands further attention (Walsh et al. 2007). It is also believed that the concept of consumer confusion is highly relevant for managers because confused consumers are less likely to make rational buying decisions and consequently may not choose the optimal offer or best value for money (Huffman and Kahn 1998; Mitchell and Papavassilliou 1999) which may create dissatisfaction later on.

This study builds on previous work in the area of consumer confusion (Cohen 1999; Mitchell & Papavassiliou 1999) and satisfaction (Spreng et al. 1996; Oliver 1997). Furthermore, we extend the model into the area of purchase decision by looking at the impact of satisfaction on purchase decision with regard to consumer confusion. In our paper, we address two specific research questions namely: *(1) what are the causes of consumer confusion?* and *(2) what is the impact of confusion on behavioural constructs such as satisfaction and purchase decision?* We propose and empirically test a model which focuses on the antecedents and consequences of consumer confusion within the FSI sector. Our paper is structured as follows. The next section provides a brief literature review leading to hypotheses development and a model followed by the methodology and results. The final section discusses the research findings and then draws conclusions based on the findings.

LITERATURE REVIEW

Consumer confusion is a mental state characterised by a lack of clear and orderly thought and behaviour (Leek & Kun 2006). Confused consumers find it difficult to select, interpret and evaluate stimuli (Mitchell et al. 2005). With the greater volume of information, excessive amounts of brands and product replications it is easy for a consumer to become confused with FSI services. Prior studies reveal that overall confusion is caused by information overload (Huffman & Kahn, 1998); over choice (Mitchell & Papavassiliou 1999; Drummond 2004); ambiguous and misleading information (Keiser and Krum 1976; Golodner 1993); similarity of characteristics (Loken et al. 1986; Mitchell et al. 2005); and expectations fuelled by various communication avenues (Leek & Kun 2006). The review of previous studies assisted in conceptualizing antecedents of consumer confusion. Our view is that confusion is fuelled by consumers' general expectations, attribute similarity between products or services (i.e. attribute confusion), and overload, conflict or ambiguity of information (i.e. information confusion). This, we believe affects consumers' information processing and decision-making abilities and therefore has a direct effect on satisfaction and purchase decision. With a plethora of me-too products and communication messages (Devlin & Gerrard 2004), FSIs provide an engaging environment to study the above stated phenomenon.

Antecedents of consumer confusion

Expectations have been viewed as the standard against which consequent performance is judged (Westbrook 1987). Most researchers share a similar opinion that consumer expectations, prior to a service encounter, impact on customers' evaluation of service performance (Cronin et al. 2000; Parasuraman *et al.* 1985). In the service literature the expectations construct has been divided into two parts namely, predictive expectations (Tam, 2007) and evaluative expectations (Spreng et al., 1996). The predictive expectations construct is associated with the level of performance and evaluative expectations construct is associated with an estimation of performance. For example, a consumer holding all his financial transactions including banking, mortgage, credit cards, and personal loans among others with a single FSI (approximately 40.5% of all FSI customers in the UK belong to this category) as suggested by Gower (2008) calls the customer services department for an emergency situation such as stolen cards or identity fraud. At this juncture, the consumer expects the call to be answered in reasonable time (predictive expectations) and also expects that whoever answers the call is in the right frame of mind and possesses knowledge related to the problem (evaluative expectations). In most of the FSIs, all the service departments operate separately and therefore the consumers will be asked to call each of them separately leaving the consumer angry, anxious and confused (Patricio et al. 2008) as to is he dealing with a single FSI or multiple FSIs? Therefore, we believe that expectations have a direct relation with overall consumer confusion. In line with the above discussion, we hypothesise that:

H1: *Expectations have a significant impact on overall consumer confusion.*

Several researchers suggest that tangible attributes of products or services such as the similarity of the offer, lead to consumer confusion (Turnbull et al. 2000; Leek and Chansawakit 2006). Furthermore, Wakefield and Blodgett (1999) argue that intangible features also have a major role in consumer evaluations. For example brand image influences the manner in which consumers perceive a product (Mitchell et al. 2005). Similarity in available tangible and intangible features of products, services and brands in the FSI sector creates the likelihood of consumer confusion (Loken et al. 1986; Mitchell & Papavassiliou 1999). Thus we hypothesise that:

H2: *Attribute confusion (tangible and intangible attributes) has a significant impact on overall consumer confusion.*

Information relating to a product or service aims not only at informing but also persuading consumers to make a specific choice (Cohen 1999). Consumers have limitations in their capacity to assimilate and process large amounts of information (Dhar & Simonson 2003), which leads to information confusion, described as 'Unclarity Confusion' by Mitchell et al. (2005). Keller and Staelin (1987) suggest that information confusion influences the effectiveness of consumer decision making. This impact can be attributed to two phenomena namely; (a) consumers' inability to locate the relevant information due to the sheer volume of information (overload); (b) oversight in identifying critical insights out of the information presented (ambiguity) and (c) variety of information provided through various information sources (conflict). Therefore, we propose the following hypothesis:

H3: *Information confusion (information overload, ambiguous information and conflicting information) has a significant impact on overall consumer confusion.*

2.2 Consequences of consumer confusion

In recent decades, customer satisfaction has been seen as a pivotal factor through which managers and firms have tried to maintain a positive relationship between their products and consumers (Chitturi, Raghunathan and Mahajan 2008). According to Oliver (1997), the issue of satisfaction is present in any transaction undertaken by consumers. Almost every model of satisfaction formation posits that feelings of satisfaction occur when consumers compare their perceptions with expectations. Many researchers view expectations as primarily perceptions of the likelihood of some event (Westbrook 1987; Westbrook and Reilly 1983). While others argue that expectations consist of an estimate of the likelihood of an event plus an evaluation of the goodness of the event (Churchill and Surprenant 1982; Oliver 1980). Satisfaction literature has focused on expectation disconfirmation as one of the key determinant of satisfaction (Oliver 1997). Spreng et al. (1996) described overall satisfaction as a function of attribute satisfaction and information satisfaction. Attribute satisfaction relates to the satisfaction with product performance when compared to consumers' initial expectations (Spreng et al. 1996). Information satisfaction relates to the evaluation of information about particular products and services, defined as a subjective satisfaction judgment of the information used in the decision making process (Westbrook 1987). With the increasing similarities of the features and brands in the FSI sector as well as the abundance of information available, we believe that expectations, attribute confusion and information confusion will have a significant impact on product satisfaction and information satisfaction respectively.

Repeat purchase is an essential ingredient for a successful long-term relationship which in turn provides a strong measure of loyalty. It depicts the tendency of a customer to choose one business or product over another for a particular need (Oliver 1997). Loyalty has been defined by Dick and Basu (1994) as repeat purchase behaviour led by favourable attitudes or as a consistent purchase behaviour resulting from the psychological decision-making and evaluative process. Previous research depicts a positive effect of cumulative satisfaction on repeat purchase and this is strongly supported across industries (Fornell et al. 1996). Furthermore, researchers suggest that when the decision situation offers many equally acceptable alternatives and none can be easily verified as best, it may create feelings of confusion which leads to a reluctance to commit an action (Dhar 1997). This non-commitment will have a direct effect on consumer purchase decision. However, prior studies have not examined the impact of attribute and information confusion as well as attribute and information satisfaction on purchase decision separately. Therefore, we hypothesise:

H4: *Expectations have a significant impact on (a) attribute satisfaction and (b) information satisfaction.*

H5: *Attribute confusion has a significant impact on (a) attribute satisfaction and (b) information satisfaction.*

H6: *Information confusion has a significant impact on (a) attribute satisfaction and (b) information satisfaction.*

H7: *Overall consumer confusion has a significant impact on purchase decision.*

H8: *Attribute satisfaction has a significant impact on purchase decision.*

H9: *Information satisfaction has a significant impact on purchase decision.*

The model depicted in Figure 1 represents the hypothesized relationships.

RESEARCH METHODOLOGY

Guided by our aim to measure and validate the antecedents and consequences of consumer confusion, we adopted a quantitative methodology employing a structured questionnaire. The questionnaire was developed modifying various existing scales. Predictive

FIGURE 1
Model overview

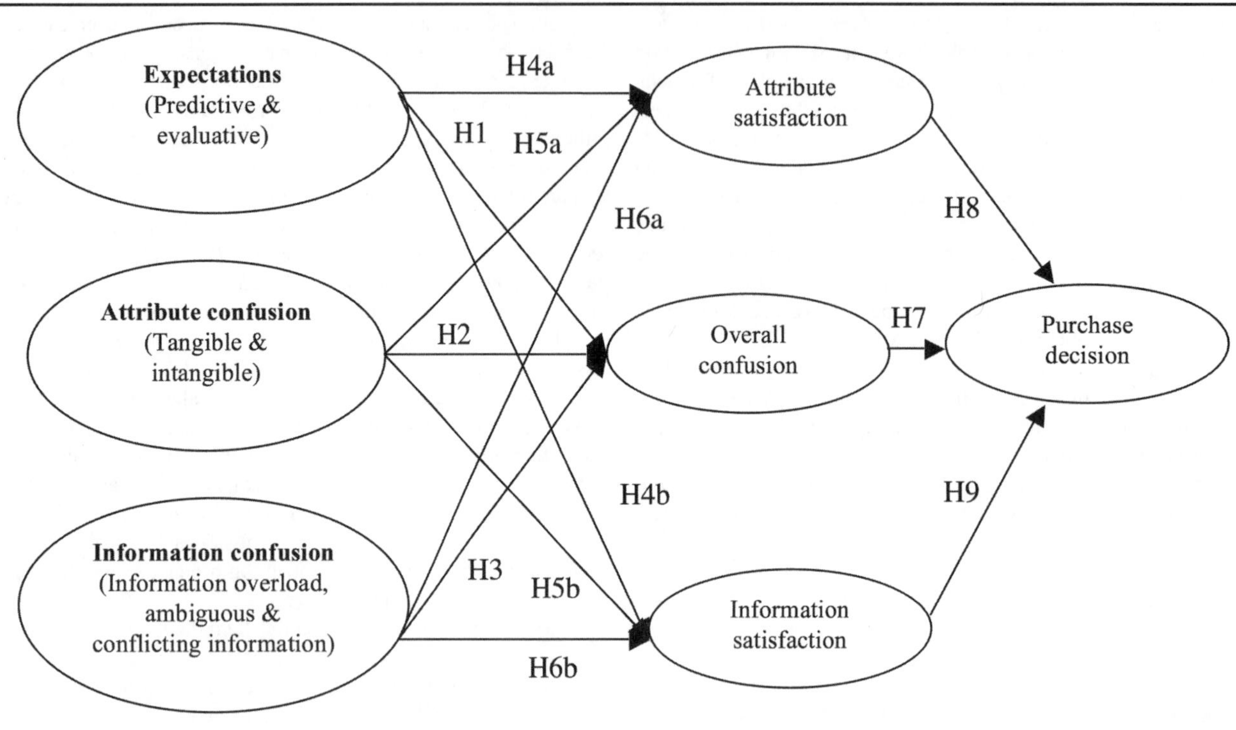

and evaluative expectations were measured using the 13 item scale developed by Burgers et al. (2000). The attribute and information confusion scales involved 6 and 4 items respectively which were developed using the study of Leek and Kun (2006), Leek and Chansawatkit (2006) and Turnbull et al. (2000). Overall confusion was measured using 3 items. The attribute and information satisfaction scales included 19 and 7 items respectively and were developed from studies by Spreng et al. (1996) and Hallowell (1996). The purchase decision construct was adopted from McMullan (2005) consisting of 11 items.

The questionnaire was tested for content validity as suggested by Zaichkowsky (1985). The resulting questionnaire was then pretested in a small survey of respondents (n=12) adding to the content validity. The questionnaire consisted of three sections. The first section included the classification information focusing on demographics and engagement with FSIs. The second section included the antecedent's related scales and the third section included the consequences scale items.

The questionnaire was administered to more than 900 randomly selected consumers on the high streets of two cities in the UK, of which 460 participated in the study. After coding and editing, 325 (response rate 36.11%) usable questionnaires formed the final sample. All variables in the second and third sections were measured with multiple-item scales. All the items were closed-ended along with a five-point bipolar scale with "strongly agree" to "strongly disagree" as anchors.

RESULTS

Our model was analysed through the maximum likelihood estimator of LISREL8.70 by using the covariance matrix of the measured variables as an input. A two stage approach (Anderson and Gerbing 1988) was adopted–firstly, estimating the measurement model and obtaining the standardised regression coefficients, and secondly, estimating the structural model. Confirmatory factor analysis (CFA) was used for establishing the validity of the constructs. Unidimensionality is a necessary condition for reliability and construct validation (Mak & Sockel 2001). The unidimensionality of the constructs was analysed by specifying a measurement model for each construct. According to Joreskog (1993), a goodness of fit index (GFI) of 0.90 or above suggests that each of the constructs is unidimensional. The GFI value of all constructs is above the recommended level. Convergent validity was examined using the Normed fit index (NFI) (Bentler and Bonett 1980). All of the constructs have NFI values above the recommended level of 0.90. Therefore, convergent validity was achieved for all the constructs in the study. For reliability, the items were subjected to reliability analysis via Cronbach's alpha. The reliability values of all the factors ranged from 0.71–0.92, satisfying the threshold of 0.70 recommended by Nunnally (1978). The average variance extracted for the measures was found to be 0.50 and above for all constructs, which is greater than the recommended level by Dillon and Goldstein (1984). Discriminant validity was assessed using the test suggested by Fornell and Larcker (1981). This test suggests that a scale possesses discriminant validity if the average variance extracted by the underlying latent variable is greater than the shared variance (i.e. the squared correlation) of a latent variable with other latent variable.

As shown in table 1, this criterion was met by all of the variables in the study as no correlation exceeds the square root of the average variance extracted. Furthermore, the composite reliability was found to be above 0.7 across the constructs, exceeding the recommended threshold value, which also provides strong evi-

TABLE 1
Correlation matrix between latent variables

	Exp	AC	IC	OC	AS	IS	PD
Exp	0.88						
AC	0.54	*0.83*					
IC	0.35	0.63	*0.93*				
OC	0.39	0.17	0.12	*0.94*			
AS	0.21	0.05	0.26	0.29	*0.90*		
IS	0.20	0.04	0.29	0.42	0.73	*0.83*	
PD	0.10	0.27	0.43	0.21	0.68	0.70	*0.89*

Note: Exp=expectations; AC=Attribute confusion; IC=Information confusion; OC=Overall confusion; AS=Attribute satisfaction; IS=Information satisfaction; PD=Purchase decision.
Values in italics in the main diagonal are square root of Average Variance Extracted (AVE).

TABLE 2
Summary of results

Path	Path coefficient	T-value
Expectations → Overall confusion (H1)	0.41	6.32*
Attribute confusion → Overall confusion (H2)	0.19	2.53*
Information confusion → Overall confusion (H3)	0.16	2.60*
Expectations → Attribute satisfaction (H4a)	0.07	1.47
Expectations → Information satisfaction (H4b)	0.04	0.71
Attribute confusion → Attribute satisfaction (H5a)	0.13	1.77**
Attribute confusion → Information satisfaction (H5b)	0.13	1.74**
Information confusion → Attribute satisfaction (H6a)	0.04	0.67
Information confusion → Information satisfaction (H6b)	0.29	4.63*
Overall confusion → Purchase decision (H7)	0.21	3.37*
Attribute satisfaction → Purchase decision (H8)	0.64	10.91*
Information satisfaction → Purchase decision (H9)	0.62	10.46*

Chi square=3972.35 (1770); RMSEA=0.06; NFI=0.94; CFI=0.96; GFI=0.94

Note: * relationship significant at p <0.01; ** relationship significant at p <0.001

dence of discriminant validity. Table 2 presents the summary of results and reports goodness of fit indices, standardised parameter estimates and their t-values for the structural model.

The results clearly show that the model fits the data well on all fit measures, except the chi-square statistics. Fornell and Larcker (1981) expressed doubts over using the chi-square statistics in isolation, as it is considered to be an excessively stringent test of model fit. Its use is generally recommended only in comparative model testing (Joerskog 1993). Overall, the model identification was achieved, and the global fit indices suggested that the model adequately represented the input data, with GFI being 0.94, RMSEA being 0.06, NFI being 0.94 and CFI being 0.96. From table 2, it can be observed that hypotheses H1, H2, H3, H7 and H8 are accepted while H4, H5 and H6 are partially accepted. The impact of expectations on overall confusion was found to be significant supporting H1 (p<0.01). Furthermore, attribute confusion (H2) and information confusion (H3) significantly impacted overall confusion (p<0.01). Contrary to prior research (Spreng et al. 1996), expectations did not significantly affect attribute (H4a) or information satisfaction (H4b). However, in the case of attribute confusion significant impact on attribute (H5a) and information satisfaction (H5b) was observed (p<0.001). Information confusion was found to be having significant impact on information satisfaction (H6b) while was not associated with attribute satisfaction (H6a). Overall confusion (H7) had a significant impact on purchase decision ($p<0.01$). Attribute satisfaction (H8) and information satisfaction (H9) had by far the strongest influence on purchase decision among all parts in the model ($p<0.01$).

CONCLUSIONS AND IMPLICATIONS

Our study focuses on conceptualizing and empirically testing antecedents and consequences of consumer confusion in the FSI sector. Using quantitative methodology and established scales in the fields of psychology and consumer behaviour, we empirically tested the antecedents and consequences of consumer confusion. The findings suggest that expectations, attribute confusion and information confusion significantly affect overall confusion. Furthermore, we also found that attribute confusion significantly affects attribute and information satisfaction however expectations do not. Furthermore, it was observed that information confusion significantly affected information satisfaction but did not affect attribute satisfaction. We also found the significant impact of overall confusion; attribute satisfaction and information satisfaction on purchase decision. Our results concur with the conceptualization by Mitchell et al. (2005) that consumer confusion is a multi-dimensional phenomenon with significant impact on behavioural intentions. There are several theoretical and managerial implications from the above findings.

Increasing understanding of consumers and decreasing confusion is one of the major aims of any organization. Moreover, in markets like financial services, where many similarities of expectations, attributes and information exist within consumer minds (Patricio et al. 2008), reduction in consumer confusion can become a source of competitive advantage (Walsh et al. 2007). The framework for this study provides managers with a first hand idea of where and how consumer confusion is caused. This will assist managers in optimizing their organizational resources to manage the multi-faceted phenomenon of consumer confusion. Managers treating consumer confusion as a single tier construct may receive undesirable results. For example, just improving the product or service feature may reduce attribute confusion. However, poor communication and highly raised expectations may still elevate the overall confusion. Similarly, a good communication campaign with a less differentiated product or service may also elevate confusion in consumers' minds. Further, the findings indicate that information confusion has an impact on information satisfaction and which in turn, has a strong influence on purchase decision. In the context of financial services industry, this issue merits consideration particularly where consumers are faced with wide ranging technical and complex information on the financial products which can create implications for purchase decision.

Managers can also use the study instrument in developing competitive intelligence by comparing the confusion caused by theirs as well as competitors' products or services. This, we believe will yield rich managerial insights for firms and develop a better and unique campaign in comparison to competitors. The findings highlight the importance of prior expectations in causing confusion. This means that if the company communicates itself via advertisements and other means as a single entity and does not act like one in real-life, there are increased chances that it will make the consumers feel confused. The companies will have to simplify their offer to attract consumers. This is also reflected in the phenomena of attribute and information confusion. To avoid attribute and information confusion, managers will have to differentiate their product and simplify their communication to the consumers. While this might not be easy especially because of the legal requirements associated with FSI products, it is highly desirable.

The impact of confusion on satisfaction and purchase decision also needs further attention. It was observed that expectations did not affect the attribute or information satisfaction. This suggests that consumers do not see their expectations to be affecting their satisfaction, which is contradictory to earlier research in the area (for further information see, Spreng et al. 1996). Furthermore, the significant impact of attribute confusion on attribute and information satisfaction indicates that the tangible and intangible aspects associated with the service have significant impact on consumer engagement with the service. This requires much close scrutiny by managers there is little differentiation observed in FSIs with regard to attribute differentiation. If in further studies, this is found to be the case, then managers need serious reconsideration with regards to their branding, positioning and differentiation efforts. The significant impact of attribute confusion on attribute and information satisfaction concurs with earlier studies which focused on technology products (Leek & Kun 2006; Leek & Chansawatkit 2006). This suggests that the impact of confusion on satisfaction is not just industry specific. Therefore, managers could use our study dimensions to check the impact of confusion within other industries.

The findings also reveal the significant impact of information confusion on information satisfaction. However the impact is non-significant in the case of attribute satisfaction. Therefore, we suggest the use of attribute and information satisfaction as separate constructs in future studies rather than using overall satisfaction as a single construct. Furthermore, the study findings also highlight the complexity of relationship between the constructs. Managers should ensure that they treat these constructs as stand-alone rather than assuming a causal relationship.

LIMITATIONS AND FUTURE DIRECTIONS

Several limitations associated with this study provide opportunity for future research. First of all, consumer confusion as a construct needs much further consumer research as most prior studies have focused on either trademark infringement issues (Miaoulis and D'Amato 1978) or brand confusion issues (Balabanis and Craven 1997; Foxman, Muehling, and Berger 1990). Our study focused on three confusion constructs and we did not focus on the impact of socio-demographics on consumer confusion. Future research can take into account the impact of socio-demographic matters as well as study the impact of contextual factors on consumer confusion. An investigation of these issues is likely to enrich the construct further. In addition, the level of product and related information complexity and its impact on consumer confusion can be investigated. For example, products such as mortgages, insurance and credit card interest rates are more complex compared to current and savings accounts. Our research has also revealed attribute confusion having a significant impact on attribute satisfaction in the context of financial services. Future research can investigate the same issue in the context of other industries such as retail and airlines for example to test the results presented in this study and uncover other facets. Furthermore, we found the sector specificity of consumer confusion construct and therefore would also suggest looking into cross-national and cross-cultural impact of this construct.

REFERENCES

Anderson, James C. and David W. Gerbing (1988), "Structural equation modelling in practice: A review and recommended two-step approach," *Psychological Bulletin*, 103 (3), 411-23.

Balabanis, George and Samantha Craven (1997), "Consumer confusion from own brand lookalikes: an exploratory investigation," *Journal of Marketing Management*, 13 (4), 299-313.

Bentler, P. M. and Douglas G. Bonett (1980), "Significance tests and goodness of fit in the analysis of covariance structures," *Psychological Bulletin*, 88, 588-606.

Brooks, Nigel A. L. (1997), "Strategic issues for financial services marketing," *Journal of Services Marketing*, 1 (1), 57-66.

Burgers, Arjan, Ko de Ruyter, Cherie Keen, and Sandra Streukens (2000), "Customer expectation dimensions of voice-to-voice service encounters: a scale-development study," *International Journal of Service Industry Management*, 11 (2), 142-61.

Butterworth, Myra (2008), "Bankruptcy fears for families as average debt hits £60,000," Vol. 2008. London: The Daily Telegraph.

Cheary, Natalie (1997), "Fashion Victim," *Marketing Week*, 20 (October), 36-39.

Chitturi, Ravindra, Rajagopal Raghunathan, and Vijay Mahajan (2008), "Delight by Design: The Role of Hedonic Versus Utilitarian Benefits," *Journal of Marketing*, 72 (3), 48-63.

Churchill, Gilbert A. and Carol Surprenant (1982), "An Investigation into the Determinants of Customer Satisfaction," *Journal of Marketing Research*, 19 (4), 491-504.

Cohen, Marcel (1999), "Insights into Consumer Confusion," *Consumer Policy Review*, 9 (6), 210-13.

Cronin, Joseph J., Michael K. Brady, and G. Thomas M. Hult (2000), "Assessing the effects of quality, value, and customer satisfaction on consumer behavioral intentions in service environments," *Journal of Retailing*, 76 (2), 193-218.

Devlin, James F. and Philip Gerrard (2004), "Choice Criteria in Retail Banking: An Analysis of Trends," *Journal of Strategic Marketing*, 12 (1), 13-27.

Dhar, Ravi (1997), "Consumer Preference for a No-Choice Option," *Journal of Consumer Research*, 24 (2), 215-31.

Dhar, Ravi and Itanmar Simonson (2003), "The Effect of Forced Choice on Choice," *Journal of Marketing Research*, 40 (2), 146-60.

Dick, Alan S. and Kunal Basu (1994), "Customer Loyalty: Toward an Integrated Conceptual Framework," *Journal of the Academy of Marketing Science*, 22 (2), 99.

Dillon, William R. and Matthew Goldstein (1984), *Multivariate analysis: Methods & Applications*: Wiley New York.

Drummond, Graeme (2004), "Consumer confusion: reduction strategies in higher education," *The International Journal of Educational Management*, 18 (5), 317-23.

Fornell, Claes, Michael D. Johnson, Eugene. W. Anderson, Jaesung Cha, and Barbara E. Bryant (1996), "The American Customer Satisfaction Index: Nature, Purpose, and Findings," *Journal of Marketing*, 60 (4), 7-18.

Fornell, Claes and David F. Larcker (1981), "Evaluating Structural Equation Models with Unobservable Variables and Measurement Error," *Journal of Marketing Research*, 18 (1), 39-50.

Foxman, Ellen R., Darrel D. Muehling, and Phil W. Berger (1990), "An Investigation of Factors Contributing to Consumer Brand Confusion," *Journal of Consumer Affairs*, 24 (1), 170-89.

Golodner, Linda F. (1993), "Healthy Confusion for Consumers," *Journal of Public Policy & Marketing*, 12 (Spring), 130-32.

Gower, Isla (2008), "Top Markets: Financial Services," London: KeyNote, 146.

Greenyer, Andrew (2008), "Are we paying attention?," *International Journal of Bank Marketing*, 26 (3), 200-07.

Hallowell, Roger (1996), "The relationships of customer satisfaction, customer loyalty, and profitability: an empirical study," *International Journal of Service Industry Management*, 7 (4), 27-42.

Harrison, Tina S. (1994), "Mapping Customer Segments for Personal Financial Services," *International Journal of Bank Marketing*, 12 (8), 17-25.

Henson, Steve W. and Joey C. Wilson (2002), "Case study: Strategic challenges in the financial services industry," *Journal of Business and Industrial Marketing*, 17 (5), 407-18.

Herbig, Paul A. and Hugh Kramer (1994), "The Effect of Information Overload on the Innovation Choice Process Innovation Overload," *Journal of Consumer Marketing*, 11 (2), 45-54.

Huffman, Cynthia and Barbara E. Kahn (1998), "Variety for sale: Mass customization or mass confusion?," *Journal of Retailing*, 74 (4), 491-513.

Joreskog, Karl (1993), "Testing Structural Equation Models," in *Testing Structural Equation Models*, Kenneth A. Bollen and J. Scott Long, Eds. Newbury Park CA: Sage.

Kahn, Barbara E. and Rakesh K. Sarin (1988), "Modeling Ambiguity in Decisions Under Uncertainty," *The Journal of Consumer Research*, 15 (2), 265-72.

Keiser, Stephen K. and James R. Krum (1976), "Consumer Perceptions of Retail Advertising with Overstated Price Savings," *Journal of Retailing*, 52 (3), 27-36.

Keller, Kevin L. and Richard Staelin (1987), "Effects of Quality and Quantity of Information on Decision Effectiveness," *Journal of Consumer Research*, 14 (2), 200-13.

Leek, Sheena and Suchart Chansawatkit (2006), "Consumer confusion in the Thai mobile phone market," *Journal of Consumer Behaviour*, 5 (6), 518-32.

Leek, Sheena and Dai Kun (2006), "Consumer confusion in the Chinese personal computer market," *Journal of Product and Brand Management*, 15 (3), 184-93.

Loken, Barbara, Ivan Ross, and Ronald L. Hinkle (1986), "Consumer confusion of origin and brand similarity perceptions," *Journal of Public Policy and Marketing*, 5 (2), 195-211.

Mak, Brenda L. and Hy Sockel (2001), "A confirmatory factor analysis of IS employee motivation and retention," *Information & Management*, 38 (5), 265-76.

McMullan, Rosalind (2005), "A multiple-item scale for measuring customer loyalty development," *Journal of Service Marketing*, 19 (7), 470.

Miaoulis, George and Nancy D'Amato (1978), "Consumer confusion and trademark infringement," *Journal of Marketing*, 42 (2), 48-55.

Mitchell, Vincent-Wayne and Vassilios Papavassiliou (1999), "Marketing causes and implications of consumer confusion," *Journal of Product & Brand Management*, 8 (4), 319-39.

______, and ______ (1997), "Exploring the concept of consumer confusion," *Market Intelligence & Planning*, 15, 164-9. Gianfranco Walsh, and Mo Yamin (2005), "Toward a conceptual model of consumer confusion," *ACR Conference, Portland, OR*, 32 (1), 143-50.

Murphy, Charles (1997), "17% of shoppers take own-label brands in error," in Marketing Vol. March 6. London.

Nunnally, Jum C. (1978), *Psychometric theory*: McGraw-Hill New York.

Oliver, Richard L. (1997), *Satisfaction: A Behavioral Perspective on the Consumer*: McGraw Hill.

______ (1980), "A Cognitive Model of the Antecedents and Consequences of Satisfaction Decisions," *Journal of Marketing Research*, 17 (4), 460-69.

Parasuraman, A., Valarie A. Zeithaml, and Leonard L. Berry (1985), "A Conceptual Model of Service Quality and Its Implications for Future Research," *Journal of Marketing*, 49 (4), 41-50.

Patricio, Lia, Ray. P. Fisk, and J. Falcao e Cunha (2008), "Designing Multi-Interface Service Experiences: The Service Experience Blueprint," *Journal of Service Research*, 10 (4), 318-334.

Shukla, Paurav, Keith Perks, and Noviano Achakobe (2008), "A study measuring the impact of integrated technologies on consumer confusion in the mobile phone market," in Academy of Marketing Conference, Bill Donaldson and Andrew Turnbull (Eds.). Aberdeen, UK: Academy of Marketing.

Spreng, Richard A., Scoff B. MacKenzie, and Richard W. Olshavsky (1996), "A Reexamination of the Determinants of Consumer Satisfaction," *Journal of Marketing*, 60 (3), 15-32.

Tam, Jackie L. M. (2007), "Managing customer expectations in financial services: Opportunities and challenges," *Journal of Financial Services Marketing*, 11 (4), 281-89.

Turnbull, Peter, Sheena Leek, and Grace Ying (2000), "Customer confusion: The mobile phone market," *Journal of Marketing Management*, 16, 143-63.

Wakefield, Kirk L. and Jeffrey G. Blodgett (1999), "Customer response to intangible and tangible service factors," *Psychology and Marketing*, 16 (1), 51-68.

Walsh, Gianfranco, Thorsten Hennig-Thurau, and Vincent-Wayne Mitchell (2007), "Consumer confusion proneness: scale development, validation, and application," *Journal of Marketing Management*, 23 (7-8), 697-721.

Westbrook, R. A. (1987), "Product/Consumption-Based Affective Responses and Postpurchase Processes," *Journal of Marketing Research*, 24 (3), 258-70.

Westbrook, Robert A. and Michel D. Reilly (1983), "Value-percept disparity: an alternative to the disconfirmation of expectations theory of consumer satisfaction," *Advances in Consumer Research*, 10 (1), 256-62.

Zaichkowsky, Judith L. (1985), "Measuring the involvement construct," *Journal of Consumer Research*, 12 (3), 341-52.

The Influence of Attachment Anxiety on Attitudes for Ads Related to Interpersonal Goals

Hyewook Genevieve Jeong, UCLA, USA
Aimee Drolet, UCLA, USA

ABSTRACT

Researchers have theorized that people with different attachment styles think, feel, and behave differently in a variety of domains. The present research investigated how attachment anxiety influences how consumers process different types of ads, in particular ads that focus on interpersonal versus self goals. Results from a study showed that consumers with higher chronic attachment anxiety had more favorable attitudes towards couple-focused versus self-focused ads. This research provides initial empirical evidence as to the effects of attachment style on persuasion outcomes.

Throughout their lives, people desire to grow closer to and gain approval from their relationship partners, including friends, family members, and romantic partners. Indeed, relationship partners can be strong elicitors of influential motivations that shape our perceptions, attitudes, and behaviors (Fitzsimons and Bargh 2003; Gillath et al. 2006). Recent studies have shown that just thinking about one's significant others can automatically and unconsciously activate goals associated with significant others. For example, when college students are asked to think about their mother, they show higher achievement motivation and better performance on an achievement test (e.g., Shah 2003). Individuals who are motivated in certain respects (e.g., due to high self-monitoring or a need to belong) try to achieve goals that their significant others set for them, even if these goals do not match their own self goals (Morrison, Wheeler, and Smeesters 2007).

Given the importance of relationship partners in daily life, it is not surprising that advertising messages often emphasize how the use of certain products can advance consumers' interpersonal goals. Thus, it is important for researchers to understand how different groups of consumers are influenced by ads that highlight interpersonal goals to different degrees. So far, little research has examined how consumers process and in turn are influenced by persuasive appeals that highlight interpersonal goals versus other goals, in particular self goals.

The present research examined how attachment style influences consumers' responses to ads related to the advancement of interpersonal goals versus personal goals. Past studies have not attempted to link attachment style to persuasion. Our study provides initial empirical evidence as to the effects of attachment style on ad attitudes.

ATTACHMENT THEORY AND RESEARCH

During the first few years of life, infants become emotionally attached to their primary caregiver, the caregiver with whom they interact with the most often. Originally, attachment theory was developed to explain the nature of the infant-caregiver relationship. Later, attachment researchers, notably Bowlby (e.g., 1980, 1982), argued that the core function of the attachment system continues through life. This is the basic assumption of the "internal working model" (Bowlby 1969). Internal working models of attachment are thought to be cognitive-affective motivational schemas. Whereas traditional approaches to schemas have tended to focus on semantic knowledge, internal working models of attachment emphasize the representation of motivational elements, such as needs or goals (Shaver, Collins, and Clark 1996).

Internal working models play an important role in shaping how individuals interpret their interpersonal relationships and the social world in which they reside. Main, Kaplan, and Cassidy (1985) proposed that an internal working model during childhood is composed of specific experiences of one's self and others. Over time, these specific experiences become more generalized beliefs and expectations about the warmth and responsiveness of others, worthiness of the self, and the level of security in the world. Thus, internal working models are expected to become solidified through repeated experience and increasingly generalized. Although the presentation of self and others changes and evolves over people's lifetimes as they form new relationships with others, research suggests that internal working models remain strongly influential (Collins and Read 1994). Once developed, people's histories of interpersonal experiences and their unique sets of memories, beliefs, and expectations shape how they think and feel about relationships with others and how they behave in relationships. Moreover, these internal working models of attachment function are largely automatic (Bowlby 1979; Collins and Allard 2001). Below, we review research on adult attachment style, which is believed to be rooted in chronic differences in internal working models of the self and others developed in infanthood. We then review how these systematic differences would be expected to influence how certain types of ads, those that emphasize interpersonal goals versus self goals, are processed.

Attachment Style and Pursuit of Interpersonal goals

Attachment style refers to an individual's habitual pattern of relational perceptions, emotions, and behaviors in interpersonal relationships (Collins and Read 1990). Researchers have theorized that there are three prototypical attachment styles that develop based on infants' reactions to separation and reunion with a primary caregiver: 1) secure; 2) anxious; and 3) avoidant (Ainsworth, Salter, Blehar, and Wall 1978). Here, we focus on relationships between attachment style and interpersonal goals. People with different attachment styles differ in the extent to which they are motivated to seek closeness, avoid rejection, and maintain autonomy.

Adults with a secure attachment style tend to be more comfortable with closeness, intimacy, and interdependence in their interpersonal relationships. They are generally willing to rely on others when necessary and are confident that they are worthy of the love of others. They tend to have a favorable self view, and this makes securely-attached adults less dependent on receiving other people's validation or support (Collins and Read 1994). Securely-attached people have a more balanced preference for between autonomy versus closeness. Getting close to others does not threaten securely-attached people's sense of autonomy. And, maintaining autonomy does not provoke worries about being abandoned or rejected by others.

On the contrary, insecurely-attached people (both avoidantly-attached and anxiously-attached) are less able to balance closeness and autonomy desires. Because individuals with an avoidant attachment style have a largely negative view of human nature, they tend to distrust trust other people, maintain emotional distance from them, and show less interest in forming close relationships (Bowlby 1982; Shaver and Hazan 1988). Although individuals with an avoidant attachment style have negative views about others, they generally have a favorable self view. Avoidant people tend to believe that independence and self-reliance are more important than the support or positive views of other people. They desire distance from others and self-control.

Whereas avoidantly-attached people prefer not to depend on others, anxiously-attached people are highly dependent on others' reactions and behaviors. Anxiously-attached people are relatively insecure about their partner's feelings and doubt their partner's love (Hazan and Shaver 1987). They habitually worry about being rejected or abandoned. This anxiety produces a strong desire for closeness, proximity seeking, and dependence on others. Anxiously-attached people tend to pursue interpersonal goals accorded with their strong needs for closeness which causes them to behave in a dependent manner. They tend to think that they are unlovable unless they are able to meet others' expectations (Collins and Read 1990; Mikulincer 1998). Anxiously-attached people are motivated to meet certain standards of worth in order to get approval from others and satisfy others. Indeed, their level of personal happiness and well-being is directly related to the amount of approval they receive from others and to the amount of satisfaction they produce in others (Bartholomew 1990). For example, Collins and colleagues (2004) found that, compared with securely-attached people, the anxiously-attached tend to overemphasize the importance of their partner's love and support. Accordingly, anxiously-attached people are likely to focus their attention on others.

This is in contrast to the tendencies of securely-attached people, who feel confident about the love and availability of their attachment figures, or to tendencies of avoidantly-attached people, who are relatively indifferent to what others think of them (Bartholomew and Horowitz 1991; Davis, Shaver, and Vernon 2004). For these two groups, attentional focus is not on others. For example, because the motivation of the avoidantly-attached is to minimize attachment concerns, they tend to direct attention away from information that makes others' needs salient (Fraley, Davis, and Shaver 1998).

There has not been much empirical work that has directly assessed the information processing goals of individuals with different attachment styles. However, a few studies provide some evidence. Mikulincer (1997) provided indirect evidence that attachment-related goals influence information processing. In his study, participants were asked to evaluate a product and select how much information they wanted to hear about the product. In addition, they were told that the time spent listening to the information would affect how much time they had left for a second task. Half of the participants were told that the second task was related to a social interaction. The rest of participants were told that it was not related to a social interaction. The study showed that participants with an anxious attachment style chose to spend less time during the first task when the second task was social versus nonsocial. In contrast, participants with an avoidant attachment style preferred to spend more time during the first section when the second task was social versus nonsocial. Participants with a secure attachment style did not show any difference in terms of the amount of time selected during the first section, regardless of whether the second task was social or nonsocial. These results indicate that participants allocated their attention in ways that served their chronically-active goals due to attachment style.

Attachment Style and Persuasion

As discussed above, past research has demonstrated ways in which attachment style affects how people think, feel, and behave in situations such as romantic relationships (Hazan and Shaver 1994) and friendships (Trinke and Bartholomew 1997). Some research has attempted to incorporate attachment theory into the consumer domain. A recent study showed that consumers with different attachment styles are respond differently to types of brand personalities. Specifically, whereas consumers who are both anxiously- and avoidantly-attached prefer exciting brands, consumers who are anxiously-attached but not avoidantly-attached prefer sincere brands (Swaminathan, Stilley, and Ahluwalia 2009). Thomson and Johnson (2001) showed that knowledge of different attachment styles can be used to predict satisfaction in consumer-brand relationships. They found that consumers with either higher or lower scores on *both* avoidance and anxiety measures reported greater satisfaction in consumer-brand relationships. Consumers who were higher on one dimension but not the other were likely to report lower satisfaction in consumer-brand relationships. According to Nguyen and Munch (2006), consumers with different attachment styles exhibit different gift-giving behaviors. Anxiously-attached consumers view giving a gift to their romantic partners as an obligation. After giving gifts to their romantic partners, they expect to receive appreciation in return. Alternatively, consumers with high avoidance attachment who give gifts to their romantic partners do not expect gratitude. Another study demonstrated that avoidantly-attached consumers are generally less attached to possessions after a loss than are securely-attached consumers (Ferraro, Escalas, and Bettman 2006).

Overview

As of yet, there have been no studies directly examining the association between attachment style and persuasion. The premise of the present research is that understanding structures and functions of internal working models can provide insight into this issue. In our study, we investigated whether different types of ad appeals, those that focus on the fulfillment of interpersonal goals versus self goals, produce different persuasion effects among anxiously-attached consumers. In the present research, we view an interpersonal ad as an ad that emphasizes how a product can increase social interaction with and the satisfaction of a romantic partner through the use of the advertised product. We view a self ad as an ad that emphasizes the satisfaction the individual consumer can gain through use of the advertised product outside of any interpersonal context. In view of the above, we predicted that consumers with high (vs. low) attachment anxiety would have relatively more favorable attitudes towards an ad highlighting the emotional value a romantic couple (vs. an individual) would receive from buying and using the advertised product.

STUDY

Pretest

In order to create ads that emphasized the fulfillment of interpersonal goals versus personal goals, we conducted a pretest (n=102; 56 % female; M_{age}= 21). Participants viewed an ad that depicted either a single individual (self-focused ad condition) or a couple (couple-focused ad condition) enjoying and benefiting emotionally from a product. The product we selected was a digital camera because consumers can enjoy taking pictures for their own pleasure and/or for the pleasure of others. We used a fictitious brand name for the digital camera so participants could not rely on potentially preexisting brand attitudes. Each of the two ads we created had 11-12 lines of ad copy. The ads differed in that the couple-focused ad showed a romantic couple benefiting from the use of the product whereas the self-focused ad showed an individual benefiting from the use of the product. Each ad included 3-4 clip-art pictures that showed either a happy couple or a happy individual.

All participants read:

"Picture your life with a Pentex digital camera. Pentex digital cameras offer superb image quality with vibrant colors, detail and performance. Equipped with the latest technology, Pentex digital cameras have all the features you want, and their intuitive design makes using these features easy."

Participants in the self-focused ad condition then read the following ad copy:

"Taking a photograph is more than just documenting your experience. It's a way to capture and hold onto the feelings you felt during those singular moments in your life. These photos will reflect those moments that make up the store of your life. Pentex Digital Cameras will make you happy."

The copy for the couple-focused ad stated:

"Taking a photograph is more than just documenting your experience. It's a way to capture and hold onto the feelings you shared during those special moments spent with your special someone. These photos will reflect the joy and love that make up the story of your life. Pentex Digital Cameras will make your special someone happy."

After reading the ad, all participants reported the degree to which the ad made them focus on people with whom they have an interpersonal relationship (1=Not much at all, 7=Very much). As expected, we found that participants in couple-focused ad condition focused more their interpersonal relationships compared to participants in self-focused ad condition ($M_{couple=}$4.42 vs. M_{self}=3.20; $t(101)=3.22$, $p<.01$).

Method

The study was a 2 (ad type: self-focused vs. couple-focused) X 3 (attachment style: secure vs. anxious vs. avoidant). These factors were not fully crossed as was possible that participants could score high or low along more than one attachment style (see below). Three hundred and two college-age students (58% female; M_{age}= 21) at a West Coast University were paid $5 to participate in an advertising study. Participants were randomly assigned to one of one of the ad conditions. After reading the ad, they rated their attitude toward it (Aad). Participants then completed demographic questions. After several filler items (from unrelated studies), participants completed the Collins and Read (1990)'s adult attachment scale measure. This 18-item scale includes three subscales based on Hazan and Shaver's (1987) three category measure of adult attachment scale: (a) comfort with closeness (attachment security), (b) comfort depending on others (attachment avoidance), and (c) anxiety in relationships (attachment anxiety). Example items include: "I find it difficult to allow myself to depend on others" (attachment avoidance); "I often worry my partner will not want to stay with me" (attachment anxiety); and "I find it relatively easy to get close to others" (attachment security). Each item was rated on a seven-point Likert scale, from "not at all like me" (1) to "very much like me" (7).

Past studies have used either a categorical measure of the three types of adult attachment style or a two-dimension continuous measure of attachment avoidance and attachment anxiety. Neither of these measures fully captures adult attachment. That is, individuals cannot be cleanly divided into one category of attachment style. Individuals can score high or low on more than one attachment style measure. The two dimensional measure focuses only on attachment avoidance and anxiety ignores attachment security; low attachment avoidance and anxiety are presumed to be high in attachment security. However, some individuals score highly on both attachment anxiety and attachment security, thereby qualifying for both attachment dimensions. In our research, we used three different continuous attachment measures (secure, anxious, and avoidance) and analyzed each separately. Thus, we do examine potential interactions among different attachment styles, although one might find them. As we discuss below, this may be viewed as a limitation of the present research.

Results

We tested our predictions using three separate ANOVAs. The three attachment styles were analyzed separately. The continuous measure for each attachment style was used in all analyses.

Participants completed 3 items that measured their ad attitudes (bad-good, dislike-like, and unfavorable-favorable, 1-7 scale). We averaged these items (α=.92). ANOVA revealed a significant interaction between the anxious attachment measure and ad condition ($F(1, 298)=6.95, p<.01$). Follow-up analysis showed that there was no effect of anxious attachment style in the self-focused ad condition ($F(1, 147)=1.86, p=.17$) whereas there was a significant positive effect of anxious attachment style in the couple-focused ad condition ($F(1, 151)=5.62$, $p<.02$). A median split (Med.=3.44) illustrates that anxiously-attached participants had more favorable ad attitudes in the couple-focused ad condition compared to participants not anxiously attached (M_{High}=4.97 vs. $M_{Low=}$4.40). There were no significant interaction effects on ad attitudes among securely-attached participants ($F(1,298)=.10, p=.75$) or avoidantly-attached ($F(1, 298)=.30$, $p=.58$).

Discussion

These results show that consumers with different attachment styles respond differently to the two ad types. As predicted, anxiously-attached participants had more favorable attitudes toward the couple-focused ad. These results are consistent with the view that anxiously-attached people are more dependent on others and that the couple-focused ad is preferred because it shows how product purchase can fulfill their (chronic) goal of positive interpersonal interaction.

GENERAL DISCUSSION

Summary

Consumer researchers have not paid much attention to the role of attachment style in persuasion. This research investigated the influence of consumers' attachment styles on ad attitudes. Our study sheds light on the link between attachment style and persuasion outcome. Due to positive and warm interactions with their primary caregivers, people with a secure attachment style seek to balance autonomy and interdependence goals. Due to inconsistent care-giving from their primary caregivers, people with an anxious attachment style doubt their own lovability and depend on others for approval (Mikulincer 1998). Results from our study showed that anxiously-attached versus securely-attached consumers had more favorable attitudes towards a couple-focused ad versus a self-focused ad.

Taken together, this research provides the first empirical evidence that attachment styles are related to responses to ads having to do with interpersonal goals. However, this research should be viewed only as an initial step in the exploration of the complex association between consumers' attachment style and persuasion process.

Limitations and Follow-up Study

There are several limitations to this research that need to be examined in future research. One limitation of the study was that it used fictional ads and did not have a no-people control condition (i.e., an ad that shows a picture of an individual or a couple with the product). While this enabled us to control for potential pre-existing brand attitudes, our results might not generalize. We ran a follow-up study (n=100; 64% female; M_{age}=20) which used real ads and had a no-people control ad condition. The study was a 3 (appeal type: self-focused vs. couple-focused vs. control) X 3 (attachment style: secure vs. anxious vs. avoidant) within subject design. Participants read three ads (randomly ordered). They then completed the attachment measures.

Participants in the self-focused ad condition read:

"Some of the greatest fights don't involve an opponent. Everlast. Greatness is within." The ad shows a single person punching a sandbag. In the couple-focused ad condition, participants read:
"Reveal your natural tone and reveal the real you. New NIVEA natural tone moisturizer with even tone complex helps fight the discoloration caused by aging, dryness and too much sun. So you have beautifully even-toned skin in all over. And the confidence to get as close as you want. NIVEA. Touch and be touched."

The ad shows a couple (two individuals looking at each other. In the control condition, participants read:

"Do you really have to spend "60,000 to get a $60,000 car? Building an exceptional $60,000 luxury sedan is an amazing accomplishment. Designing it to cost less than $40,000, however, is nothing short of a miracle. Which brings us to the remarkable new 2009 Genesis. With rear-wheel drive and a 4.6 L, 375-horsepower V8, it's more powerful than the far pricier BMW 550i, yet as spacious as a 760Li or Mercedes-Benz S-Class."

The ad shows only the product (a car) without a person or couple. A manipulation check confirmed that participants viewed the couple-focused ad as more couple-focused compared to the self-focused ad (M_{couple}=3.79 vs. M_{self}=2.26; t(182)=5.60, p<.001). ANOVA found a significant interaction effect on ad attitudes between ad condition and attachment anxiety (F(2, 276)=3.33, p<.04). There was no significant effect of attachment anxiety in the self-focused ad and control ad conditions but there was a significant effect in the couple-focused ad condition (F(1, 80)=13.90, p<.001). A median split along the attachment anxiety measure (Med.=3.63) showed that anxiously-attached participants (vs. not) had more favorable attitudes towards the couple-focused ad (M_{High}=4.82 vs. $M_{Low=}$3.92). As in the main study, there was no significant effect of ad type on the ad attitudes of avoidantly-attached or securely-attached participants. Thus, the results of the follow-up study are consistent with the results of the main study. They confirm that attachment anxiety influences responses to ads related to interpersonal versus self goals. Attachment anxiety did not influence attitudes towards the self-focused or control ads. These results notwithstanding, a clear limitation of the follow-up study is that it does not control for product type across ad conditions.

Another limitation of the main study is that it did not examine interactions among different attachment styles. The three attachment styles were studied separately. Yet, there may be interactions among attachment styles. A further limitation of the present research is that it relies on chronic attachment style to effect variation in attachment style strength. Research has demonstrated that attachment (in)security can be induced by priming techniques (e.g., Swaminathan et al. 2009). Given that, in many cases, marketers may not know their customers' attachment styles, it would be extremely useful to confirm our results in a future study that primes attachment style.

Conclusion

Attachment researchers have long theorized that people with different attachment styles think, feel, and behave differently in a variety of domains. Despite the potential importance of attachment style to consumer behavior, attachment style has not been extensively studied by consumer researchers. This research provides initial evidence that consumers with different attachment styles respond differently to ads related to self versus interpersonal goals. Indeed, we believe that attachment theory provides a useful framework for understanding a wide variety of persuasion issues. Our results have implications for marketers who may find it very useful and productive to target different kinds of ads to segments of consumers with different attachment styles.

REFERENCES

Ainsworth, Mary D., Mary C Salter, Everett W. Blehar, and Sally Wall (1978), *Patterns of Attachment*, Hillsdale, NJ: Lawrence Erlbaum.

Bargh, John A. (1984), "Automatic and Conscious Processing of Social Information," in *Handbook of Social Cognition,* Vol. 3, ed. Robert S. Wyer, Jr. and Thomas K. Srull, Hillsdale, NJ: Lawrence Erlbaum, 1-43.

Bartholomew, Kim (1990), "Avoidance of Intimacy: An Attachment Perspective," *Journal of Social and Personal Relationships, 7*, 147-178.

Bartholomew, Kim and Leonardo M. Horowitz (1991), "Attachment Styles among Young Adults: A Test of a Four-Category Model," *Journal of Personality and Social Psychology*, *61*, 226-244.

Bowlby, John (1969), *Attachment and Loss: Vol 1. Attachment,* Hogarth Press, NY: Basic Books.

Bowlby, John (1979), "Psychoanalysis as Art and Science," *International Review of Psychoanalysis,* 6, 3-14.

Bowlby, John (1980), *Attachment and Loss: Vol 3. Sadness and Depression*, Hogarth Press, NY: Basic Books.

Bowlby, John (1982), *Attachment and Loss. Vol 1. Attachment* (2nd Ed.), Hogarth Press, NY: Basic Books.

Brennan, Kelly A. and Jennifer K. Bosson (1998), "Attachment-Style Differences in Attitudes toward and Reactions to Feedback from Romantic Partners: An Exploration of the Relational Bases of Self-Esteem," *Personality and Social Psychology Bulletin*, *24* (7), 699-714.

Collins, Nancy. L. and Stephen J. Read (1990), "Adult Attachment, Working Models, and Relationship Quality in Dating Couples," *Journal of Personality and Social Psychology*, *58*, 644-663.

______ (1994), "Cognitive Representations of Attachment: The Structure and Function of Working Models," in *Advances in Personal Relationships*, Vol. 5, ed. Daniel Perlman and Kim Bartholomew, London: Jessica Kingsley, 53-90.

Collins, Nancy. L., and Lisa M. Allard (2001), "Cognitive Representations of Attachment: the Content and Function of Working Models," in *Handbook of Social Psychology*: Vol. 2, ed. Garth. J. O. Fletcher and Margaret. S. Clark, United Kingdom: Blackwell Publishers, 60-85.

Davis, Deborah, Philip R. Shaver and Michael L. Vernon (2004), "Attachment Style and Subjective Motivation for Sex," *Personality and Social Psychology Bulletin*, *8*, 1076-1090.

Ferraro, Rosellina, Jennifer Escalas, and James R. Bettman (2006), "Attachment style, Psychological Security, and Consumer Response to Special Possession Loss," *Advances in Consumer Research*, Vol 33.

Fitzsimons, Grainne M. and John A. Bargh (2003), "Thinking of You: Nonconscious Pursuit of Interpersonal Goals Associated with Relationship Partners," *Journal of Personality and Social Psychology, 84*, 148-164.

Fraley, R. Chris, Keith E. Davis and Philip R. Shaver (1998), "Dismissing-Avoidance and the Defensive Organization of Emotion, Cognition, and Behavior," In *Attachment Theory and Close Relationships*, ed. Jeffry A Simpson, William Steven Rholes, New York: Guilford Press, 249-279.

Gillath, Omri, Mario Mikulincer, Grainne M. Fitzsimons, Phillip R. Shaver, Dory A. Schachner and John A. Bargh (2006), "Automatic Activation of Attachment-RelatedGoals," *Personality and Social Psychology Bulletin*, 32(10), 1375-1388.

Hazan, Cindy and Philip R. Shaver (1987), "Romantic Love Conceptualized as an Attachment Process," *Journal of Personality and Social Psychology*, 52, 511-524.

______ (1994), "Attachment as an Organizational Framework for Research on Close Relationships," *Psychological Inquiry, 5*, 1-22.

Main, Mary, Nancy Kaplan, and Jude Cassidy (1985), "Security in Infancy, Childhood and Adulthood: A Move to the Level of Representation," *Monographs of the Society for Research in Child Development, 50*,1-2.

Mikulincer, Mario (1995), "Attachment Style and the Mental Representation of the Self," *Journal of Personality and Social Psychology, 69*, 1203–1215.

Mikulincer, Mario (1997), "Adult Attachment Style and Information Processing: Individual Differences in Curiosity and Cognitive Closure," *Journal of Personality and Social Psychology, 72*, 1217-1230.

Mikulincer, Mario (1998), "Adult Attachment Style and Affect Regulation: Strategic Variations in Self-Appraisals," *Journal of Personality and Social Psychology, 75*, 420-435.

Mikulincer, Mario and Philip R. Shaver (2001), "Attachment Theory and Intergroup Bias: Evidence that Priming the Secure Base Schema Attenuates Negative Reactions to Out-groups," *Journal of Personality and Social Psychology, 81*, 97-115.

______ (2003), "The Attachment Behavioral System in Adulthood: Activation, Psychodynamics, and Interpersonal Processes," in *Advances in Experimental Social Psychology,* Vol 35, ed. Mark P. Zanna, NY: Academic Press, 53-152.

Morrison, Kimberly R., S. Christian Wheeler, and Dirk Smeesters (2007), "Significant Other Primes and Behavior: Motivation to Respond to Social Cues Moderates Pursuit of Prime-Induced Goals," *Personality and Social Psychology Bulletin, 33*, 1661-1674.

Nguyen, Hieu P. and James M. Munch (2007), "Gift-Giving Behaviors: Views from an Attachment Perspective," *Advances in Consumer Research*, Vol 33, 16-17.

Shah, James Y. (2003), "Automatic for the People: How Representations of Significant Others Implicitly Affect Goal Pursuit," *Journal of Personality and Social Psychology, 84*, 661-681.

Shaver, Philip R, Nancy Collins and Katherine L. Clark (1996), "Attachment Styles and Internal Working Models of Self and Relationship Partners," in *Knowledge Structures in Close Relationships: A Social Psychological Approach*, ed. Garth. J. O. Fletcher and Julie Fitness, Mahwah, NJ: Lawrence Erlbaum, 25-61.

Shaver, Philip R. and Cindy Hazan (1988), "A Biased Overview of a Study of Love," *Journal of Social and Personal Relationships, 5*, 473-501.

Shaver, Philip R. and Mario Mikulincer (2002), "Attachment-Related Psychodynamics," *Attachment and Human Development, 4*, 133-161.

Simpson, Jeffry A. (1990), "Influence of Attachment Styles on Romantic Relationships," *Journal of Personality and Social Psychology, 39*, 971-980.

Swaminathan, Vanitha, Karen M. Stilley, and Rohini Ahluwalia (forthcoming), "When Brand Personality Matters: The Moderating Role of Attachment Styles," *Journal of Consumer Research, 35* (April).

Thomson, Matthew and Allison R. Johnson (2001), "Investigating the Role of Attachment Dimensions as Predictors of Satisfaction in Consumer-Brand Relationships," *Advances in Consumer Research*, Vol 28.

Trinke, Shanna J. and Kim Bartholomew (1997), "Attachment Hierarchies in Young Adults," *Journal of Social and Personal Relationships*, 14, 603-625.

Consumer Response to Service Failures: The Role of Emotional Intelligence and Coping

Yuliya Strizhakova, Rutgers University, USA
Yelena Tsarenko, Monash University, Australia

ABSTRACT

The goal of the study was to understand how consumers use their intrinsic resources in situations of service failures. Specifically, we examined how consumers applied their Emotional Intelligence (EI) to deal with negative emotions when facing service failures with varying degrees of recovery, to implement their copying strategies and to engage in negative word-of-mouth. We also assessed idiosyncratic effects of the four EI dimensions. Overall, consumer EI played a critical role in managing negative emotions and activating relevant coping strategies but EI dimensions exhibited some antagonistic effects. Recovery efforts by a service provider moderated some EI effects.

INTRODUCTION

Research has established importance of emotions in marketing and consumer decision making (Luce 1998, Nyer 1997, Pham 1998, Ruth 2001); however, the question of how consumers manage and use their emotional capabilities in their everyday consumption remains unanswered. The notion that customers are able to harness and draw on emotions as a resource is based on the assumption that emotions can be understood and managed. Emotions are merely one element of an individual's psychological resources that are instrumentally applied in a range of circumstances (Averill et al. 1994). Mayer and Salovey (1997) refer to this ability as emotional intelligence (EI), i.e., one's ability to skillfully use emotional information to solve problems and reach desired outcomes.

What makes EI of a particular importance to consumer behavior is that it corresponds to a mental process involved in the recognition, use, understanding and management of one's emotional states to solve problems and regulate behaviors (Mayer and Salovey 1997). Understanding consumer employment of emotional resources can assist marketers in better serving customers and in predicting their consumption choices and behaviors. Even though this construct has been widely applied in interpersonal conflict situations (e.g. work productivity, intimate relationships, education and health), only a few studies of buyer-seller interactions that focus solely on customer-oriented selling (Manna and Smith 2004, Rozell et al. 2004) and service provider competency (Bardzil and Slaski 2003, Kernbach and Schutte 2005) have examined it; however, none of these takes the perspective of customers. A recent study by Kidwell, Hardesty and Childers (2008) applies the construct of EI to consumer decision making and calls for more extensive research on EI across multiple consumption contexts, including coping with negative emotions.

The goal of the present study is to examine the role of consumer EI in situations of service failures where negative emotions are inevitably evoked and consumers are forced to cope with them. Several factors make service failures an attractive context for the study. First, service failure is an unavoidable occurrence in service encounters. Second, in an attempt to gain a deeper understanding of the service failure process the emphasis of research has been recently directed toward examining the role of customers in unfavorable service incidents. The way customers manage and express their emotions, cope with stress and evaluate recovery outcomes requires researchers to develop a richer, more fine-grained understanding of the role of consumer personality in the service encounter. Third, understanding the role of consumer EI in service failures can help providers mitigate negative consequences of such failures and potentially re-establish positive relationships with customers.

Our second goal is to understand consumer processes of coping with event-induced stress, a realm that has largely been neglected in consumer research. Recent research in this area has focused on development of coping scales (Duhachek 2005) and conceptual framework (Moschis 2007); however little research has empirically tested antecedents or outcomes of the coping process. In this paper, we investigate effects of consumer EI on coping and negative word-of-mouth. Our third goal is to explore individual effects of EI dimensions in service failures. Although these dimensions typically form a composite EI construct, their individual effects on consumer behavior in certain contexts may diverge and therefore it is crucial to understand how they impact the overall consumption process (Kidwell, Hardesty and Childers, 2008). We address a gap in consumer research by devising and empirically testing a framework that captures consumers' emotional states under stressful conditions of various degrees.

THEORETICAL PERSPECTIVES

Emotional Intelligence and Negative Emotions

Emotional intelligence has evoked a great deal of interest with its further theoretical and empirical developments in psychology, education, clinical settings (Petrides et al. 2007), and management (Jordan et al. 2002). Although the concept is not new, it has gained popular interest with the release of Goleman's bestseller (1996) in which he argues that emotions and intelligence do not belong to separate domains and that any fundamental distinction between the two is arbitrary. The intersection of emotional and cognitive processes implies that people posses "the ability to perceive accurately, appraise and express emotion; the ability to access and/or generate feelings when they facilitate thought; the ability to understand emotion and emotional knowledge; and the ability to regulate emotions to promote emotional and intellectual growth" (Mayer and Salovey 1997, 35). This mental ability is captured by the EI concept, which differentiates it from other so-called mixed models of EI (e.g., Bar-On 1997, Cooper and Sawaf 1997, Goleman 1996) that combine mental abilities with a variety of characteristics, such as motivation, states of consciousness and social activity (Mayer et al. 2000).

Ability models of EI claim that four distinct processes define the construct: perceiving, facilitating, understanding and managing emotions (Salovey et al. 1999). The first three processes are quite abstract (Kidwell et al. 2008). Perceiving refers to consumer emotional appraisal and expression; facilitating refers to consumer ability to access, generate and use emotions to facilitate problem solving and thinking; and understanding involves consumer ability to analyze and comprehend emotions. Managing is the least abstract dimension that refers to consumer emotional regulation to achieve desired outcomes. Because of varying degrees of abstractness, these individual dimensions are likely to exhibit differentiating effects on consumption and its outcomes across specific contexts.

Even though service recovery efforts have been shown to impact customer behavioral responses to a service failure (Wirtz and Mattila 2004), the role of EI in managing service failures remains unexplored. In circumstances of a service failure, the disparity between customer expectations and perceived delivery of service inevitably creates negative emotions (Kelley and Davis 1994, Smith and Bolton 2002). Consumers EI is likely to minimize this negativity. Salovey et al. (1999) suggest that EI is used to rebound from negative feelings and to repair damage created by negative moods. Those with high levels of EI are not only attentive to their emotions but have the ability to gain emotional clarity; hence, demonstrate better coping with negative events and are less likely to engage in a prolonged ruminative process. When service providers minimize emotional damage of a service failure by engaging in recovery efforts with a maximum of excellence, effects of EI are likely to be stronger. We predict:

H1a: Consumer EI decreases negative emotions elicited by a service failure.

H1b: Effects of consumer EI on negative emotions are moderated by service recovery efforts: negative effects of EI are stronger when excellent recovery efforts are made.

Because of limited research on individual EI dimensions, we ask:

RQ1: Which EI dimensions decrease negative emotions elicited by a service failure?

Emotional Intelligence and Coping

Coping in the psychological literature is defined as an individual response mechanism that involves "the constant changing of cognitive and behavioral efforts to manage specific external and/or internal demands that are appraised as taxing or exceeding the resources of the person" (Lazarus and Folkman 1984, 141). This suggests that, when faced with negative consumption-related tensions, customers respond by engaging in coping strategies to regulate their emotions and adjust their cognitive and behavioral dispositions in order to better cope with the stressful environment (Nyer 1997, Luce 1998, Yi and Baumgartner 2004).

Coping encompasses a myriad of thoughts, emotions and behaviors that present a challenge to capture and classify in a meaningful typology (Folkman and Moskowitz 2004). The manner of coping is situation-specific and multidimensional. One of the main approaches to coping stems from earlier work by Folkman and Lazarus (1980), which distinguishes problem-focused (managing the problem) and emotion-focused (managing elicited emotions) coping. In the consumption context, Yi and Baumgartner (2004) developed a typology of eight coping strategies and mapped them against these two strategies. Although the two coping strategies are commonly conceptualized at opposite ends of a spectrum, researchers have argued that they should be treated as complementary rather than contrasting (Lazarus 1996).

In contrast, Duhachek (2005) proposed a more universal scale of coping, which can be used in a range of stressful consumption episodes. This scale consists of three dimensions: active coping, expressive coping and avoidance/denial that, in turn, capture eight constructs of coping. The "active" dimension resembles the problem-focused coping and captures the idea of consumer employment of resources to deal with the problem at hand. The "expressive" dimension resembles the emotion-focused coping but captures the idea of consumers' support seeking behaviors to deal with negative emotions and stress. The "avoidance/denial" dimension reflects an alternative way of coping that is more related to problem dismissal rather than problem solving.

Research that examines the impact of EI on coping is not particularly advanced (Zeidner et al. 2006). Rozell et al. (2004) highlight the fact that emotionally intelligent individuals are more aware of their own feelings as well as the feelings of others, better able to identify emotions and communicate emotions when appropriate. Salovey and Mayer (1990) also suggest that through EI customers can regulate their own emotions by maintaining positive moods and relieving negative affective states. As Zeidner and Roberts (2002) note, an emotionally intelligent person is not just successfully adapted but adaptable, in the sense of being competent to deal with new challenges (p. 26). Given this adaptability, we expect consumer EI to increase consumer engagement in more approach-oriented coping styles (active and expressive coping) but do not relate to more passive avoidance/denial coping. We hypothesize and posit:

H2: Consumer EI has a positive effect on consumer engagement in "active" and "expressive" coping but is not associated with "avoidance/denial" coping.

RQ2: Which EI dimensions impact a) "active", b) "expressive" and c) "avoidance/denial" coping?

Emotional Intelligence and Word-of-Mouth

Word-of- mouth is a complex outcome of a service encounter. On the one hand, a positive word-of-mouth is a desired outcome for any service provider as it ameliorates efforts of an organization in promoting its service or products. On the other hand, word-of-mouth is to some degree an extension of the coping process, particularly in negative incidents. Engaging in repeated conversations about one's own experience with a service provider helps consumers organize and better understand their own thoughts and emotions. By using language to disclose their inner psychological state, customers who experience a service failure are likely to see a negative experience in a more coherent way, i.e., to position it more meaningfully in their world (Salovey et al. 1999). Furthermore, the theory of stress and coping states that successful coping assumes that individuals are open to their emotional experiences and EI plays a central role in how these emotional experiences are framed. Specifically, individuals who use "balance in emotion words (moderate amount of negative words accompanied by a greater amount of positive emotion words)" (Salovey et al. 1999, 155) when disclosing their negative incidents exhibit less distress and cope more effectively overall.

Past consumer research found consumption emotions to be significant predictors of complaining and both positive and negative word-of-mouth (Nyer 1997, Westbrook 1987). Although it can be speculated that the majority of consumers recognize that service failures are inevitable, we expect that customers with higher EI are more likely to arrive at this reasoning due to higher emotional control and more successful coping; thus, they are less likely to engage in negative word-of mouth as compared to those with lower EI. Given that consumer EI is a personality variable that impacts both emotional reactions to a service failure and coping strategies, its effects on the service outcome (word-of-mouth) are likely to be mediated by the salience of emotional reactions and customer engagement in coping. We predict and posit:

H3a: Consumer EI decreases negative word-of-month in circumstances of service failure.

H3b: Effects of EI on negative word-of-mouth are mediated by negative emotions elicited by a service failure and consumer active and expressive coping.

RQ3: Which EI dimensions impact consumer negative word-of-mouth?

TABLE 1
Means and ANOVA F-test by Recovery Conditions

	Poor Recovery	Weak Recovery	Excellent Recovery	F-test
Negative Emotions	4.78	3.85	3.03	89.69***
Active Coping	5.10[a]	5.19[a]	5.40	6.16**
Expressive Coping	4.13	4.41	4.66	16.27***
Denial Coping	2.30[b]	2.43[b]	2.78	7.76***
Negative WOM	6.15	5.43	3.14	218.52***
Composite EI	4.36	4.35	4.42	.56 n.s.
EI: Perceiving	5.21	5.24	5.35	1.35 n.s.
EI: Managing	2.80	2.77	2.76	.15 n.s.
EI: Understanding	4.36	4.39	4.47	.46 n.s.
EI: Facilitating	5.07	4.99	5.08	.83 n.s.

Note: identical letter superscripts indicate no significant differences in the means on a given variable. ** differences are significant at p<.01, *** differences are significant at p<.001.

METHOD

Design

To ensure variability of negative emotional reactions to a service failure, we manipulated recovery efforts expressed by service providers to a service failure in our scenario-based design. The use of scenarios avoids the expense and ethical consideration associated with observing or enacting an actual service failure while avoiding the response bias due to memory lapses and rationalization likely to be present in recall-based surveys (McCollough et al. 2000) and is frequently employed in service failure studies (Bitner 1990). The service failure context was a hotel reservation for a summer vacation trip to a foreign country. In all scenarios, participants experienced a double booking on their reservation. Next, participants either did not receive any room from the hotel staff (poor recovery), received the only vacant room available of smaller size and lower price (weak recovery) or got an upgrade to a suite at the initial price (excellent recovery). After reading the scenario, participants reported their levels of emotional responses to the service failure. Next, they completed questions regarding their coping styles and word-of-mouth. Participants were also asked basic demographic and EI questions.

Sample

Our sample was recruited by a marketing research firm from their existing customer database. Within a week, we collected 655 responses (poor recovery: n=251; weak recovery: n=251; excellent recovery n=153). The sample of respondents was composed of 327 (50%) men and 328 (50%) women, ranging in age from 18 to 79 (M=48.77, SD= 14.46). In terms of education, 50.8% of respondents had a college degree or higher, while 49.2% had a high school diploma or less. ANOVA tests did not indicate any significant differences among participants in relation to their gender ($F(2;653)=1.52, p>.05$), age ($F(2;653)=1.48, p>.05$), and education ($F(2;653)=1.94, p>.05$) composition across the three conditions.

Measures

All measures employed seven-point scales. Based on past research (Jordan et al. 2002, Mayer et al. 2003, Kidwell et al. 2008, Schutte et al. 1998), we adapted 16 items of CEIS to the context of service failures that tapped into four distinct dimensions of EI: perceiving (3 items, $\alpha=.76$, M=5.26, SD=.84), facilitating (5 items, $\alpha=.81$, M=5.04, SD=.84), understanding (3 items, $\alpha=.80$, M=4.40, SD=1.08) and managing (5 items, $\alpha=.82$, M=2.78, SD= .69). Pearson correlation coefficients between dimensions were in the .29-.51 range. We also averaged all items to derive a composite measure of EI ($\alpha=.88$, M=4.37, SD= .64). To measure consumer coping, we adapted Duhachek's (2005) three-dimensional eight-factor coping style scale comprised of 32 items. The three coping styles in our study were "active" coping (16 items, $\alpha=.93$, M=5.20, SD=.87), "expressive" coping (13 items, $\alpha=.88$, M=4.44, SD=.94) and "denial" (3 items, $\alpha=.86$, M=2.46, SD= 1.21). To measure consumer negative emotional reactions to a service failure, we asked participants how strongly they felt six emotions: anger, frustration, anxiety, threat, fear and worry after their exposure to a given scenario. EFA resulted in a uni-dimensional resolution explaining 69% of variance ($\alpha=.91$, M=4.01, SD= 1.47). We asked two questions (reverse-coded from Maxham and Netemeyer 2002) to measure negative word-of-mouth ($\alpha=.96$, M=2.83, SD= 1.84). We coded manipulation of recovery efforts as 1=poor, 2=weak and 3=excellent.

RESULTS

Manipulation Check

To assess effectiveness of our manipulation of recovery efforts, we used ANOVA to compare participants' means across recovery conditions. Consistent with our manipulation, participants experienced the weakest negative emotional response when facing excellent recovery efforts and the highest negative emotional response when facing poor recovery efforts. Participants also expressed highest levels of all types of coping (active, expressive and denial) and lowest negative WOM when facing excellent recovery efforts. ANOVA did not reveal any significant differences among participants on their composite EI or any of its dimensions across the three conditions (see Table 1 for means and F-tests).

Analyses

To test our hypotheses and answer research questions, we used simultaneous and hierarchical multiple regression analyses. Our first set of hypotheses and a research question related to effects of EI on the negative emotional response elicited by a service failure (see Tables 2 and 3). As predicted in H1a, consumer EI decreased consumer negative emotional response ($\beta= -.12$). As predicted in

TABLE 2
Regression Analysis on Negative Emotional Response with Composite EI

Variable	Model 1		Model 2	
	β	*t-value*	*β*	*t-value*
Recovery Efforts	-.46	-13.37***	-.07	-.69
Composite EI	-.12	-3.65**	-.10	-3.65**
Recovery Efforts x EI			-.32	2.62**
R^2	.22		.23	
F	93.99***		63.22***	

TABLE 3
Regression Analysis on Negative Emotional Response with EI Dimensions

Variable	Model 1		Model 2	
	β	*t-value*	*β*	*t-value*
Recovery Efforts	-.47	-13.68***	-.47	-13.68***
EI: Perceiving	.01	.31	.01	.31
EI: Managing	-.18	-4.63***	-.18	-4.63***
EI: Understanding	.01	.29	.01	.29
EI: Facilitating	.01	.21	.01	.21
Recovery Efforts x Perceiving			.01	.03
Recovery Efforts x Managing			-.28	-1.99*
Recovery Efforts x Understanding			-.12	-.71
Recovery Efforts x Facilitating			-.17	-1.62
R^2	.24		.25	
F	41.83***		23.95***	

H1b, the interaction term of EI with recovery efforts was also significant (β=-.32). Specifically, EI had a strong negative effect on consumer emotional reaction when recovery efforts were excellent (β= -.21, p <.01); but this effect was only marginally significant in the weak and poor recovery conditions (β= -.08 and β= -.10, p <.10). In response to our RQ1, regression analysis indicated that only the managing dimension of EI had a significant negative effect on consumer emotional response (β= -.18). Similarly, the interaction between recovery efforts and the managing dimension was significant (β= -.28). The managing dimension of EI had the strongest negative effect when excellent recovery efforts were made (β= -.30, p <.001), followed by weak (β= -.20, p <.001), and poor (β= -.12, p <.10) recovery.

Our H2 and RQ2 discussed effects of EI on consumer coping. We used hierarchical regression analysis where consumer emotional response and recovery efforts were entered at step 1 as controls and consumer EI (model 2a) or its dimensions (model 2b) were entered at step 2. As predicted, consumer EI significantly increased "active" coping (β=.43) and "expressive" coping (β=.19) but had no significant effect on "denial" (β= -.02). Interestingly, consumer negative emotional response had a significant negative effect (β= -.18) on "active" coping but a positive effect (β=.49) on "expressive" coping. Excellence in recovery efforts had a significant positive effect on "denial" (β=.11). Effects of all interactions were not significant (p>.10) and were consequently omitted (see Table 4, model 2a). Next, we examined effects of the four EI dimensions on consumer coping. Three EI dimensions had significant positive effects on "active" coping: facilitating (β=.30), perceiving (β=.21), and managing (β=.10). Two dimensions had significant positive effects on "expressive" coping: facilitating (β=.14) and understanding (β=.10). In relation to "denial" coping, we found antagonistic effects of the two EI dimensions. On the one hand, perceiving emotions had a significant negative effect on "denial" (β= -.24). On the other hand, managing emotions had a significant positive effect on "denial" (β=.12). Understanding emotions also increased denial coping (β=.09). All interaction effects were not significant (p>.05) (see Table 4, model 2b).

Finally, we examined effects of EI on consumer negative word-of-mouth. Consistent with H3a, the effect of EI was negative and significant in a bivariate regression (F(1;654)=10.56, p<.01, β= -.13). However, this effect became non-significant when consumer coping, emotional response and recovery efforts were entered into the hierarchical regression model. Both "active" coping (β= -.12) and "denial" (β= -.20) decreased negative WOM, whereas "expressive" coping increased it (β= .08). Excellence in recovery efforts had a negative effect (β= -.46) and negative emotional response had a positive effect (β=.18) on the word-of-mouth (see Table 5, model 2a). Interaction effects were non-significant (p >.05). Consistent with Baron and Kenny's (1986) mediation steps, 1) EI had significant effects on the negative emotional response, active and expressive coping 2) consumer emotional response, active and expressive coping had significant effects on the word-of-mouth, and 3) the effect of EI on the word-of-mouth became non-significant with the three mediators in the regression. Thus, effects of EI on consumer

TABLE 4

Regression Analyses on Consumer Coping

Active Coping						
Variable	Model 1		Model 2a		Model 2b	
	β	*t-value*	*β*	*t-value*	*β*	*t-value*
Step 1						
Recovery Efforts	.05	1.08	.06	1.48	.06	1.60
Emotional Response	-.18	-4.25***	-.13	-3.42**	-.13	-3.48**
Step 2a						
Composite EI			.43	12.39***		
Step 2b						
EI: Perceiving					.21	4.99***
EI: Managing					.10	2.30***
EI: Understanding					-.03	-.64
EI: Facilitating					.30	7.40***
R^2	.04		.23		.27	
F	14.96***		63.45***		40.54***	

Expressive Coping						
Variable	Model 1		Model 2a		Model 2b	
	β	t-value	*β*	t-value	*β*	t-value
Step 1						
Recovery Efforts	-.01	.23	.01	.36	.00	.07
Emotional Response	.49	12.64***	.51	13.42***	.49	12.64***
Step 2a						
Composite EI			.19	5.52***		
Step 2b						
EI: Perceiving					.08	1.87
EI: Managing					-.06	-1.56
EI: Understanding					.10	1.99*
EI: Facilitating					.14	3.51***
R^2	.24		.27		.28	
F	100.05***		79.88***		42.21***	

Denial Coping						
Variable	Model 1		Model 2a		Model 2b	
	β	t-value	*β*	t-value	*β*	t-value
Step 1						
Recovery Efforts	.11	2.55*	.11	2.54*	.13	3.05***
Emotional Response	-.07	-1.68	-.08	-1.72	-.06	-1.51
Step 2a						
Composite EI			-.02	-.46		
Step 2b						
EI: Perceiving					-.24	-5.04***
EI: Managing					.12	2.78***
EI: Understanding					.09	2.00*
EI: Facilitating					.03	.63
R^2	.03		.03		.07	
F	8.49***		5.73**		7.90***	

TABLE 5
Regression Analysis on Negative Word-of-Mouth

Variable	Model 1		Model 2a		Model 2b	
	β	t-value	β	t-value	β	t-value
Step 1						
Active Coping	-.13	-4.44***	-.12	-3.41**	-.13	-3.41**
Expressive Coping	.06	1.87*	.08	1.93*	.08	1.93*
Denial	-.20	-6.87***	-.20	-6.84***	-.20	-6.84***
Emotional Response	.18	4.72***	.18	4.59***	.18	4.59***
Recovery Effort	-.46	-13.87***	-.46	-13.95***	-.47	-13.95***
Step 2a						
Composite EI			-.05	-1.65		
Step 2b						
EI: Perceiving					.07	1.81
EI: Managing					-.05	-1.58
EI: Understanding					-.06	-1.46
EI: Facilitating					-.04	-1.18
R^2	.46		.46		.48	
F	109.98***		92.35***		63.83***	

negative word-of-mouth were fully mediated by consumer "active" and "expressive" coping and their negative emotional responses to a service failure. Hypothesis 3b was supported. A similar pattern of results was observed for the two EI dimensions: managing and understanding emotions. Although initially they had significant negative effects on the word-of-mouth (β= -.10 and β= -.12 correspondingly, p <.05), these effects became fully-mediated in a hierarchical model (see Table 5, model 2b). Interaction effects were non-significant (p >.05).

DISCUSSION

Research in services marketing has traditionally conceptualized behavioral and emotional responses of the service provider as the main drivers of the service encounter. The customer's role in service encounters has often been simplified to be that of a passive appraiser that matches pre-established expectations and perceived delivery of the service to evaluate the encounter. This research not only answers the call for a greater understanding of the role of emotions in service encounters and consumption experiences (Bardzil and Slaski 2003, Kernbach and Schutte 2005) but most importantly accounts for the consumer as a co-producer of the unfolding consumption experience. Specifically, we investigate the role of emotional intelligence as an antecedent to customer negative emotional responses, coping, and subsequent word-of-mouth in situations of service failure. Although EI has been extensively applied in psychological and managerial studies (e.g., Jordan et al. 2002, Mayer et al. 2003), examination of consumer EI is a relatively novel topic. A recent study by Kidwell et al. (2008) developed and applied a measure of consumer EI and its individual dimensions to consumer decision making. Our work extends their research on EI to the context of negative service encounters. Additionally, we evaluated effects of individual EI dimensions that in some contexts differed from those of a composite EI measure (consistent with Kidwell et al. 2008). Understanding effects of these dimensions is crucial to better serving customers and their needs. Finally, we gained a deeper understanding of consumer coping with the event-induced stress and the role of EI in consumer coping.

The first finding of our study confirms that consumer EI plays a significant role in consumption contexts that elicit strong negative emotions. Consumers with high EI are able to control and minimize negative emotions across various levels of service recovery. However, when service providers undertake a maximum of efforts to fix a failure, consumer EI has the strongest effect on the negative emotional response. Thus, appropriate service provider measures at the point of failure corroborated by consumer EI can ultimately minimize induced stress and restore broken customer relationships. Next, we found that EI showed strong positive effects on active and expressive coping. Thus, in stressful consumption contexts, EI helps consumers actively seek issue-resolution and alleviate emotional stress by engaging in expressive behaviors. As a composite trait, EI did not yield any significant effects on denial coping. A stronger negative emotional response to a service incident decreased consumer ability to seek problem resolution but increased expressive coping. In addition, appropriate recovery efforts increase likelihood of consumers denying the failure in the first place. The latter finding is consistent with earlier work on adaptive coping that suggests denial may be an opted choice for consumers who are offered an appropriate and satisfying solution to a stressful event by service providers (Pavia and Mason 2004). Effects of EI on consumer word-of-mouth were fully mediated by emotional response, active and expressive coping. Overall, then, when providers ensure a maximum of recovery efforts, consumers with high EI are able to experience lower levels of induced stress and actively seek resolutions to a failure, which, in its turn, is more likely to result in a positive outcome for the provider.

In addition to analyzing effects of the composite EI measure, we evaluated potential contextual differences across its individual dimensions. In general, consumers were likely to express higher levels of perceiving emotions and facilitating thinking to resolve the problem rather than managing their emotions. Consistent with Kidwell et al.'s (2008) proposition, perceiving, facilitating and understanding are much more abstract in their nature than the managing dimension. Our results showed that different dimensions were responsible for different effects in situations of service failure. Specifically, managing emotions had a vital role in lowering negative emotions and for consumer active coping and denial. Possibly, then, those who are capable of managing emotions are more likely to either actively solve the issue at hand or deny it depending on its complexity, relevance or importance. In contrast, the most abstract dimension of perceiving decreased consumer denial but increased active coping. Neither the most abstract dimension-perceiving-nor the least abstract dimension-managing-had any effects on expressive coping. Thus, we confirm that different EI dimensions have unique and even antagonistic effects on consumption outcomes and should probably be examined along the composite EI trait.

Our findings suggest that consumer EI should receive attention across multiple aspects of the service process and delivery and not be limited to a service failure alone. More significantly, integration of EI into a service setting reveals that consumer EI influences both a coping response as well as evaluation of the service experience. Future consumer research is warranted that would assess effects of EI on other stressful consumption experiences, purchasing choices and decisions, product failures, and dyadic and group conflicts in consumption situations. Examination of both the composite measure of EI and its individual dimensions can provide valuable insights for both consumer researchers and marketers.

This study is an early step toward integrating the theory of EI in consumption experience, thus several caveats need to be raised. First, the measurement of EI is based on a self-administered questionnaire (for discussion see Dulewicz and Higgs 2000, Davies et al. 1998). It would be of interest to conduct complementary studies that assess customers' level of EI by means of more objective measures (Davies et al. 1998). Second, we relied on a scenario-based methodology that minimizes biases due to memory and recall limitations present in survey research (McCollough et al. 2000). Future observational and experimental studies that observe or manipulate the experience of a service failure are warranted to increase external validity of current findings. We examined only one failure outcome-negative word-of-mouth. Future work should examine additional measures, such as consumer complaining behaviors, re-purchasing behaviors, or actual customer patronage. Finally, the scope of the study does not include illegitimate complaint behavior and dysfunctional customer behavior described by Harris and Ogbonna (2002). But it is acknowledged that the execution of a coping response can be based on deviant intentions facilitated by customers' level of EI.

REFERENCES

Averill, James R., LeDoux, Joseph E., Levenson, Robert W., Ekman, Paul and Davidson, Richard J. (1994) Can We Control Our Emotions? In Ekman, P. & Davidson, R. J. (Eds.) *The Nature Of Emotion: Fundamental Questions*. London: Oxford University Press.

Bar-On, Reuven (1997) Bar-On Emotional Quotient Inventory: A Measure of Emotional Intelligence, *Technical Manual*, Toronto: Multi-Health Systems.

Bardzil, Philip and Slaski, Mark (2003) Emotional Intelligence: Fundamental Competencies for Enhanced Service Provision. *Managing Service Quality*, 13(2003), 97-104.

Baron, Reuben M. and Kenny, David A. (1986) The Moderator-Mediator Variable Distinction in Social Psychological Research: Conceptual, Strategic, and Statistical Considerations. *Journal of Personality and Social Psychology*, 51(6), 1173-1182.

Bitner, Mary Jo (1990) Evaluating Service Encounters: The Effects of Physical Surroundings and Employee Responses. *Journal of Marketing*, 54(April), 69-82.

Cooper, Robert K. and Sawaf, A. (1997) *Executive EQ: Emotional Intelligence in Leadership and Organizations*, New York: Grossett/ Putnam.

Davies, Michaela, Stankov, Lazar and Roberts, Richard D. (1998) Emotional Intelligence: In Search of an Elusive Construct. *Journal of Personality & Social Psychology*, 75(4), 989-1015.

Duhachek, Adam (2005) Coping: A multidimensional, Hierarchical Framework of Responses to Stressful consumption Episodes *Journal of Consumer Research*, 32(June), 41-53.

Dulewicz, Victor and Higgs, Malcolm (2000) Emotional Intelligence-A Review and Evaluation Study. *Journal of Managerial Psychology*, 15(4), 341-372.

Folkman, Susan and Lazarus, Richard S. (1980) An analysis of coping in a middle-aged community sample. *Journal of Health and Social Behavior*, 21(September), 219-239.

Goleman, Daniel (1996) *Emotional intelligence: why it can matter more than IQ*, London: Bloomsbury.

Harris, Lloyd C. and Ogbonna, Emmanuel (2002) Exploring Service Sabotage: The Antecedents, Types and Consequences of Frontline, Deviant, Antiservice Behaviors. *Journal of Service Research*, 4(Feb), 163-183.

Jordan, P.J., Ashkanasy, N.M. and Hartel, C. (2002) Emotional Intelligence As a Moderator of Emotional and Behavioral Reactions to Job Insecurity. *Academy of management review*, 27(3), 361-372.

Kelley, S. W. and Davis, Mark A. (1994) Antecedents to Customer Expectations for Service Recovery. *Journal of the Academy of Marketing Science*, 22(Winter), 52-61.

Kernbach, Sally and Schutte, Nicola S. (2005) The Impact of Service Provider Emotional Intelligence on Customer Satisfaction. *The Journal of Services Marketing*, 19(2005), 438-444.

Kidwell, Blair, Hardesty, David M and Childers, Terry L (2008) Consumer Emotional Intelligence: Conceptualization, Measurement, and the Prediction of Consumer Decision Making. *Journal of Consumer Research*, 35(1), 154-166.

Lazarus, Richard S. (1996) The Role of Coping in the Emotions and How Coping Changes Over the Life Course. In Magai, C. & McFadden, S. H. (Eds.) *Handbook of Emotions, Adult Development, and Aging*. San Diego, CA: Academic.

Lazarus, Richard S. and Folkman, Susan (1984) *Stress, appraisal, and coping*, New York, Springer Pub. Co.

Luce, Mary Frances (1998) Choosing to Avoid: Coping with Negatively Emotion-Laden Consumer Decisions. *Journal of Consumer Research*, 24(March), 409-433.

Manna, Dean R. and Smith, Alan D. (2004) Exploring the Need for Emotional Intelligence and Awareness Among Sales Representatives. *Marketing Intelligence & Planning*, 22(1), 66-83.

Maxham, James G. and Netemeyer, Richard G. (2002) A longitudinal study of complaining customers' evaluations of multiple service failures and recovery efforts. *Journal of Marketing*, 66(October), 57-71.

Mayer, John D. and Salovey, Peter (1997) What is emotional intelligence? In Salovey, P. & Sluyter, D. J. (Eds.) *Emotional development and emotional intelligence : educational implications*. BasicBooks.

Mayer, John D., Salovey, Peter and Caruso, David (2000) Models of Emotional Intelligence. In Sternberg, R. J. (Ed.) *Handbook of intelligence*. Cambridge, New York: Cambridge University Press.

Mayer, John D., Salovey, Peter, Caruso, David and Sitarenios, Gill (2003) Measuring Emotional Intelligence with the MSCEIT V2.0. *Emotion*, 3(1), 97-105.

McCollough, Michael A, Berry, Leonard L and Yadav, Manjit S (2000) An empirical investigation of customer satisfaction after service failure and recovery. *Journal of Service Research*, 3(2), 121-137.

Moschis, George P. (2007) Stress and consumer behavior. *Journal of the Academy of Marketing Science*, 35(3), 430-444

Nyer, Prashanth U (1997) A study of the relationships between cognitive appraisals and consumption emotions. *Academy of Marketing Science. Journal*, 25(Fall), 296-304.

Pavia, Teresa M. and Mason, Marlys J. (2004) The Reflexive Relationship between Consumer Behavior and Adaptive Coping. *Journal of Consumer Research*, 31(2), 441.

Petrides, K. V., Pita, Ria and Kokkinaki, Flora (2007) The location of trait emotional intelligence in personality factor space. *British Journal of Psychology*, 98(2), 273-289.

Pham, Michael Tuan (1998) Representativeness, Relevance, and the Use of Feelings in Decision Making. *Journal of Consumer Research*, 25(September), 144-159.

Rozell, Elizabeth J., Pettijohn, Charles E. and Parker, R. Stephen (2004) Customer-Oriented Selling: Exploring the Roles of Emotional Intelligence and Organizational Commitment. *Psychology & Marketing*, 21(June), 405-424.

Ruth, Julie (2001) Promoting a Brand's Emotion Benefits: The Influence of Emotion Categorization Processes on Consumer Evaluations. *Journal of Consumer Psychology*, 11(2), 99-113.

Salovey, Peter, Bedell, Brian T., Detweiler, Jorusha B. and Mayer, John D. (1999) Coping Intelligently: Emotional intelligence and the coping process. In Snyder, C. R. (Ed.) *Coping: the psychology of what work*. New York: Oxford University Press.

Salovey, Peter and Mayer, John D. (1990) *Emotional Intelligence. Imagination, cognition and personality*, 9(3), 185-211.

Schutte, Nicola S., Malouff, John M., Hall, Lena E., Haggerty, Donald J., Cooper, Joan T., Golden, Charles J. and Dornheim, Liane (1998) Development and Validation of a Measure of Emotional Intelligence. *Personality and Individual Differences*, 25(2), 167-177.

Smith, Amy K and Bolton, Ruth N (2002) The effect of customers' emotional responses to service failures on their recovery effort evaluations and satisfaction judgments. *Academy of Marketing Science. Journal*, 30(Winter), 5-23.

Westbrook, Robert A. (1987) Product/Consumption-Based Affective Responses. *Journal of Marketing Research*, 24(August), 258-270.

Wirtz, Jochen and Mattila, Anna. S. (2004) Consumer Responses to Compensation, Speed of Recovery and Apology After a Service Failure. International *Journal of Service Industry Management*, 15(2), 150-166.

Yi, Sunghwan and Baumgartner, Hans (2004) Coping with Negative Emotions in Purchase-Related Situations. *Journal of Consumer Psychology*, 14(3), 303-316.

Zeidner, Moshe, Matthews, Gerald and Roberts, Richard D. (2006) Emotional Intelligence, coping with stress, and adaptation. In Ciarrochi, J., Forgas, J. P. & Mayer, J. D. (Eds.) *Emotional intelligence in everyday life*. Publisher: New York : Psychology Press.

Zeidner, Moshe and Roberts, Richard D. (2002) *Emotional intelligence: science and myth*, Cambridge, Mass.: MIT Press.

Lighting and Perceived Temperature: Energy-Saving Levers to Improve Store Evaluations?

Gwenaëlle Briand, University of Paris Dauphine, France
Bernard Pras, University of Paris Dauphine and ESSEC Business School, France[1]

ABSTRACT

Light intensity and thermal conditions have energy savings implications. Based on environmental psychology, ergonomics and in-store environment research, this study analyzes the direct and interaction effects of lighting and perceived temperature on store evaluations. Three evaluative dimensions emerged from the factor analysis: stimulation, upmarket positioning and relaxation. A 2 x 2 x 3 experiment (lighting x perceived temperature x retail outlet) shows that lighting and its interaction with perceived temperature influence stimulation and upmarket positioning. Perceived temperature has a direct impact on stimulation. The type of retail outlet (jeans, books, and furniture) affects stimulation, upmarket positioning and relaxation.

Most marketing research studying store environment has focused on variables, such as music, color or scent (e.g., Crowley 1993; Spangenberg, Crowley, and Henderson 1996; Yalch and Spangenberg 2000). Lighting and temperature are said to have a major impact on energy savings and are important variables in this respect.[2] They also affect the individual's emotions and behaviors (Anderson 1989; Lam 1998; Rosenthal 2005) and are considered essential by retailers and experts in sensometry (Petit, Siekierski, and Lageat 2003; Roullet 2006). Yet they are understudied aspects of store environment. The influence of in-store lighting has never been studied in a controlled environment. A few researchers have studied the effect of display lighting (Areni and Kim 1994; Summers and Hebert 2001) and of additional lighting in a specific shelf (Bakini Driss, Ben Lallouna Hafsia, and Zghal 2008) on shopping behavior and the effect of pleasant or unpleasant lighting on shoppers' affective reactions (Lemoine 2002). However, a systematic and controlled analysis of the effect of in-store lighting on consumers' evaluation has not yet been done. Furthermore, no marketing research specialized in atmospheric factors has ever been conducted on either actual or perceived temperature.

Assessing the impact of lighting and temperature stimuli on consumers' store evaluations therefore sounds extremely useful. Stramler, Kleiss and Howell (1983) have shown a significant effect of purported temperature increase on perceived comfort, even when the actual temperature is not changed. This means that non-physical factors can play a role in the perception of thermal comfort. Implications for energy savings and in-store atmosphere perception are real. Perceived temperature may affect consumer's sensation of comfort while shopping as well as the actual temperature. According to specialists, an actual 1.8°F decrease, from 68°F (20°C) to 66.2°F (19°C) results in energy savings of 7%. Experts[3] in lighting and temperature also suggest that lighting can enhance a store image while temperature can affect consumer's sensation of comfort while shopping. The aim of our research is to highlight the direct and interaction effects of perceived temperature and lighting on consumers' store evaluations. It focuses on the following questions: To what extent do lighting and perceived temperature affect individuals' evaluations and behavior, considering prior ergonomic or psychological results? To what extent can these results be extended to consumers' perception of store environment and store positioning? Consequently, we introduce some propositions and study the influence of two lighting and two perceived temperature levels in three types of retail outlets (clothing, books, furniture) on the individual's evaluations of store environment and store positioning.

CONCEPTUAL FRAMEWORK

First of all, this research is based on environmental psychology applied to a retail store context (Donovan and Rossiter 1982; Spangenberg et al. 1996). Stimuli (S) influence the internal evaluations of the environment (O) which in turn influence the consumer in-store behavior. The internal evaluations of the environment can have affective or stimulating dimensions as well as a positioning dimension (for example perceived quality of the goods, upmarket store). The consumer behavioral responses (R) can be approach or avoidance responses. Many articles in marketing have focused on the behavioral responses (R) consecutive to various stimuli such as color or music (S) (Bitner 1992; Yalch and Spangenberg 1990). We study here less or never studied relevant stimuli, that are lighting and temperature such as suggested by Bitner (1992), and their potential influence on store evaluation (affective, stimulative or positioning perceptions). The positioning relates to perceptions, and the beliefs one has of a product or a store environment, and of a categorization of the store mentally (Bitner 1992). It should also be mentioned that Spangenberg et al. (1996) or Bitner (1992) propositions are an adaptation of Mehrabian and Russell's model (1974) to the store atmosphere context. Among PAD (Pleasure, Arousal and Dominance) dimensions of Mehrabian and Russell's model, Bitner (1992) as well as Spangenberg et al. (1996) do not retain the dominance dimension[4] in a store context. This is consistent with Donovan and Rossiter (1982) research findings and Russell and Pratt (1980) recommendations.

Second of all, this research is also grounded in the lighting and temperature literature in environmental and applied psychology, and ergonomics. This leads to some propositions in a store evaluation context, further analyzed through an experiment.

---

[1]The authors thank Priya Raghubir for her helpful comments and suggestions.

[2]Retail buildings account for the largest energy costs (over $20 billion each year-Source, EIA, CBECS 2003) of commercial buildings in the US, and management's desire to save energy and reduce energy expenses is more and more frequent. Energy efficiency measures are adopted with the help of the Environmental Protection Agency. Moreover, the Energy Independence and Security Act of 2007 focused on energy savings implications of compact fluorescent lights and, actually, will ban the sales of most current incandescent light bulbs by 2014. Assessing the impact of lighting and temperature on store perceptions is of paramount importance.

[3]Working group: "Lighting and energy saving", Popai France, Paris, October 2008 and Conference: "Light and health", EDF (Electricité de France) and AFE (Lighting French Association), Paris, January 2009.

[4]Dominance "is based on the extent to which he (an individual) feels unrestricted or free to act in a variety of ways" (Russell and Mehrabian, 1974: 19).

Lighting[5]

Research in different scientific fields has revealed the various effects of light on individuals. Psychiatric and medical research have demonstrated that light illuminance modulates circadian rhythm (and specifically hormonal cycles) leading to a succession of stimulating (arousal and activation) and relaxing (detente and sleepy) periods (Lam 1998; Rosenthal 2005). Clinical psychology has suggested an increasing cardiovascular activity and a stimulation of physiological arousal (Kumari and Venkatramaiah 1974). Research in marketing has also demonstrated an effect of light on in-store behavior. Supplemental lighting or bright light influences the number of items examined and handled and the time spent in stores or display (Areni and Kim 1994; Summers and Hebert 2001). Therefore, bright light can be expected to positively affect the stimulative dimension[6] of store perception.

P. 1: Within normal levels, increasing the lighting's brightness has a positive influence on the stimulative perception of a store environment.

Biological effects of lighting on humans (Lam 1998; Rosenthal 2005) induce psychological responses (cognitive, aesthetic and emotional). According to ergonomic studies, a bright light and a cool light color temperature are more associated with comfort and spaciousness (Manav 2007). In addition, order perception is also achieved with bright light in conditions of wall washing (Durak et al. 2007), the wall washing being a diffuse lighting on the wall. Comfort, spaciousness, and order perceptions will be called here upmarket store perceptions.

P. 2: Within normal levels, increasing the lighting's brightness has a positive influence on upmarket store perception.

However, brightness by itself does not seem to have an influence on relaxation. Subjects have reported more positive affect (Baron 1990), feelings of relaxation and intimacy (Carr and Dabbs 1974; Durak et al. 2007) in conditions of low lighting. Manav (2007) has pointed out that a warm light (2700 K) leads to the impression of a relaxing atmosphere. But a feeling of relaxation can also be reported in conditions of wall-washing (Manav and Yener 1999), uplighting (Manav and Yener 1999: 43–47) and cove lighting (Durak et al. 2007), under different lightings' brightness conditions.

P. 3: Within normal levels, decreasing the lighting's brightness has a positive influence on intimacy, but not necessarily on relaxation.

Finally, the preferred lighting level has been associated with the social situation and the type of activities (Biner et al. 1989). Moreover, Summers and Hebert (2001) have demonstrated an interaction effect between lighting and display. According to the retail merchandising perspective, it seems to be necessary to match the lighting to the retail objectives and characteristics.

P. 4: There is an interaction effect of lighting conditions x types of retail outlets upon the evaluations of the stores.

Temperature

A social psychology research has reported an affective impact of temperature on individuals. Aggressive behavior and riots, negative affects and antisocial behavior in a crowded situation (Anderson 1989; Griffitt and Veitch 1971) increase as the temperature increases. The negative affect also grows as temperature dips (< 62°F: Bell and Baron 1977). This suggests that a "range of comfort" exists and that a negative affective state could be attributed to hot or cold temperatures (Baker and Cameron 1996). "Range of comfort" can be assimilated to "thermal comfort" that is the "condition of mind which expresses satisfaction with the thermal environment and is assessed by subjective evaluation" (Rohles 2007, 14). It seems to be impossible to define an optimal temperature level for all individuals, but Fanger (1970) has developed the Predicted Mean Vote (PMV) model with the Predicted Percentage Dissatisfied, used to predict the thermal sensations of a large group of people. The thermal comfort and PMV depend on the activity level and clothing worn by individuals, along with thermal conditions. Indoor thermal comfort perception ranges from 68°F to 74°F, extended to 66°F with warm clothing and 78°F with light clothing, for a low activity level. Stramler et al. (1983) have shown that individuals responded comparably, in terms of perceived comfort shifts, to actual and purported rises of temperature. This is consistent with Rohles and Kerulis' technical report[7] in which subjects had similar distributions of comfort and thermal sensation votes when they were shown a specific temperature reading (74°F), whether the actual temperature was actually 74°F or in a "68°F-72°F" range. The perceived temperature can therefore be manipulated.

A research in the United Kingdom (Humphreys and Hancock 2007) has used ASHRAE Scale, based on Fanger research (1970). It has demonstrated that most individuals (for a low activity) preferred to experience a "slightly warm" or "warm" rather than "neutral" or "cool" sensation, whatever the seasonal period.[8] This suggests that for a low level of shopping activity in a store environment, and within the "comfort range", the store evaluation is positively correlated to a moderately high perceived level of temperature rather than to a moderately low perceived level of temperature.

P. 5: Within the comfort range, a high perceived temperature is preferred by consumers and associated to better store evaluations than a relatively low perceived temperature.

Finally, Rohles' ergonomic research (1980) has suggested that temperature is perceived as warmer in decorated and very furnished room than in an empty space, while both spaces are at the same temperature level.

P. 6: The perceived temperature will be lower in a relatively empty space than in a more furnished space.

---

[5]Low level of lighting is associated to soft lighting and high level of lighting to bright light. For color temperature, a warm light is associated to red light and cool light is associated to white or blue light.

[6]The stimulative dimension corresponds to "excitement" such as defined by Russell and Pratt's (1980), as meaning the combination of arousing and pleasant.

[7]Technical report, reported by Stramler, Kleiss and Howell (1983:187).

[8]ASHRAE Scale measures the subjective thermal sensation, that is to say the subjective point of view about the personal thermal sensation instead of the temperature of the atmosphere.

P. 7: There is an interaction effect of perceived temperature x type of retail outlet (more or less furnished) upon store evaluations.

Main effects of lighting versus temperature and interaction effects

Baker and Cameron's (1996) conceptual framework suggests the possibility to study a wide range of environmental factors (such as temperature and lighting) and their influence on affect and the perception of waiting time. Analyzing main and interaction effects of temperature and lighting does seem necessary to explore and understand a "polysensory person".

Indeed, perception will give priority to the "best" sensory modality for the task at hand (Guttman 2005, 228). Perception gives precedence to vision for spatial judgments (Welch 1999). In case of divided attention with various sensory modalities, Schifferstein and Desmet (2007) suggest that, under conditions of normal vision, the information provided by vision attracts the majority of attention, which is in line with claims from previous research. It can be inferred from these findings that, within normal conditions, lighting will take precedence over temperature in store evaluation.

P. 8: The positioning evaluation of a store will be more influenced by lighting than by perceived temperature.

P. 9: There is an interaction effect of "lighting x perceived temperature" upon store evaluations.

METHOD

We used a 2 (lighting) X 2 (perceived temperature) X 3 (types of retail outlets) factorial design experiment, based on digitally manipulated pictures in order to create the desired lighting and perceived temperature conditions. The lighting conditions (bright vs. soft), the perceived temperature (low vs. high within the comfort range) and the types of retail outlets (jeans, books and furniture) are presented below as well as the experiment.

Lighting Conditions

Actually, in physics, light is a form of energy known as electromagnetic radiation that may be perceived by the normal unaided human eyes. Light illuminance level (brightness vs. softness) can be associated to a CCT (Correlated Color Temperature that is a cool or a warm color temperature).[9] CCT describes the ambiance that a lamp provides, i.e. how "warm" or "cool" the light makes a room be perceived.[10] According to experts and following the famous Kruithof (1941) curve.[11] the preferred combination of illuminance level (Bright vs. soft) and correlated color temperature (CCT: Cool vs. warm) are "bright and cool lighting" on the one hand and the "soft and warm lighting" on the other hand. On the contrary, two combinations are considered to be unpleasant: "Bright and warm lighting" has been claimed to create a colorful and artificial environment, while "Soft and cool lighting" has been considered to create a drab and cold environment. Therefore, from a managerial point of view, this research focuses on pleasing perceptions of lighting that could entail a positive evaluation of an environment and in turn entail an approach behavior: "bright and cool lighting" for bright light and "soft and warm lighting" for soft light.[12]

Perceived Temperature and Types of Retail Outlets

As underlined above, we focus on the range of comfort for light and perceived temperature. The critical point is to present visual clues corresponding to different perceived temperature levels. As already indicated, previous research has shown that actual temperature changes within the range of comfort had an impact upon thermal sensations similar to that of identical purported temperature changes (Stramler et al. 1983). Temperature changes of 4-5°F (2.3°C-3.3°C) represent a substantial change in the comfort-response distribution according to well-established norms.

As the comfort level depends on the activity level and the clothing, we used pictures representing a female teenager standing in front of the display, therefore with a low activity. On these pictures, we implemented two temperature levels by changing teenager's clothes: light clothing for warm conditions and a coat for cool conditions. A manipulation check over 180 individuals reveals significant differences in perceived temperature changes, going from 4°F (2.3°C) for furniture store to 6°F (3.3°C) for jeans and bookstore. The average perceived temperatures range from 66°F in the cool conditions to 72.5°F in the warm conditions.[13]

The shopping behavior was perfectly similar in the two lighting conditions ("bright and cool light" and "soft and warm" light) and the three different stores. Pictures got retouched by a professional photographer using Photoshop to create the two lighting conditions. In each store represented on pictures, no brand or no corporate name appeared. Three types of retail outlet were selected according to literature and experts' advice. Besides, each type of retail outlet is expected to allow a homogeneous store environment from one display to another inside the specific store, as compared to supermarkets which are composed of heterogeneous store environments.

Experiment Implementation, Subjects and Questionnaire

Experiment and Subjects. The sample consisted of 115 French "MS in Management" students in Paris, France. A within-subjects experiment was conducted in June and resulted in 12 combinations of temperature, lighting and store. The same room, with the same temperature level and the same light illuminance level, was used during the whole experiment, and the weather remained constant. We constructed four sets of three combinations with three retail outlets[14] that we replicated in order to have eight sets (twice the same four sets x three combinations). The experiment was administered by the same researcher to groups of eight subjects at a time. In each group, subjects were randomly assigned to one of the eight sets. Each respondent had to figure himself in the shopping situa-

[9]Light illuminance is expressed in lux and color temperature is measured in Kelvin.

[10]www.osram.com

[11]Kruithof curve (1941) relates the illuminance and color temperature of visually pleasing light sources.

[12]Ambient fluorescent tubes lighting in retail stores is commonly Bright cool lighting. The Energy Bill (2007) bans the incandescent light bulbs by 2014, which are to be replaced by energy savings bulbs. These bulbs can be used for accent light in retail stores, and can possibly be bright or soft, and warm or cool.

[13]A manipulation check was necessary since we used pictures (visual stimuli) to simulate temperature levels.

[14]Mixing the modalities and the order (with Jeans (S1), Books (S2), Furniture (S3), Bright light (L1), Soft light (L2), Cool temperature (T1), Warm temperature (T2)), the 4 basic sets were: Set 1 (S1L1T1/S2L1T2/S3L2T2); Set 2 (S2L2T2/S3L1T1/S1L2T1); Set 3 (S3L2T1/S1L1T2/S2L1T1); Set 4 (S2L2T1/S1L2T2/S3L1T2).

TABLE 1
FACTORS OF STORE EVALUATIONS
(LOADINGS, COMMUNALITY AND ALPHA-VARIMAX ROTATION)

Items	Stimulation	Upmarket Positioning	Relaxation	Communality
Cheerful	.791	.170	.143	.674
Stimulating	.772	.157	.132	.638
Attractive	.771	.273	.328	.777
Positive	.732	.237	.298	.681
Lively	.714	-.004	.095	.519
Motivating	.698	.183	.119	.535
Colorful*	.661	.026	.225	.488
Upmarket	.257	.805	.063	.718
Modern	.378	.740	-.035	.692
Spaciousness	.190	.708	.175	.568
Well ordered*	-.180	.609	.256	.470
Relaxed	.224	.266	.777	.725
Unstressful	.296	.075	.753	.661
Intimate*	.154	.068	.656	.459
Cronbach's alpha (factor)	$\alpha 1$=.886	$\alpha 2$=.747	$\alpha 3$=.659	
Cronbach's alpha (scale)	α=.880			

*We have decided to keep: colorful, well ordered and intimate (communality>.45) according to their conceptual interest (Rossiter 2002) in reference with previous research (Spangenberg et al. 1996; Carr and Dabbs 1974; Durak et al. 2007).

tion. For each photograph, that is each retail outlet with a light/temperature combination, we submitted a questionnaire about the store environment evaluation, the store positioning and the product quality perceptions. The final sample was composed of 110 subjects: 63 females and 47 males. 330 questionnaires were validated, which made 27 or 28 subjects for each combination.

Questionnaire Construction. The questionnaire construction was based on Fisher's scale (1974) and Spangenberg et al. (1996) research. The first list was supplemented with items suggested by 12 individuals from the same population as the respondents. They were asked to write a list of items describing a store environment to guarantee the semantic saturation. Then, one expert in lighting, one expert in thermal comfort and one expert in marketing were also asked to complete and to validate this list and avoid redundant items. The final list was composed of 21 non-redundant items. Evaluation of store environment was measured using the seven-point "Judgments of Environmental Quality Scale" (Stimulating-boring; motivating-unmotivating; comfortable-uncomfortable; cheerful-depressing; positive-negative; attractive-unattractive; lively-unlively; good-bad; bright-dull; pleasant-unpleasant; relaxed-tense; colorful-drab) (Fisher 1974). Four seven-point items have completed the Fisher's (1974) scale according to their relevance to our stimuli (cold welcome-warm welcome; friendly-unfriendly; unstressful-stressful, intimate-impersonal), following interviews with experts. Evaluation of store positioning was measured using four seven-point scales (Spacious-cramped (Durak et al. 2007; Manav 2007); well ordered-unordered (Expert); upmarket-downmarket (Expert); outdated-modern (Bellizzi, Crowley and Hasty 1983). Product evaluation was assessed using a seven-point scale (Low/High Quality) (Spangenberg et al. 1996).

DATA ANALYSIS AND RESULTS

Store Evaluations

To examine the existence of distinct components within the subject's responses to the stimuli, a principal component analysis using Varimax rotation was conducted (table 1).

Three main factors of store evaluation emerged from the analysis: an "activation or stimulative" dimension, in the sense of a lively environment (Russell and Pratt 1980), which combines arousal (stimulating, motivating, lively and colorful) and pleasure (attractive, positive and cheerful) evaluations; an "upmarket positioning" dimension and a "relaxation" dimension (Russell and Pratt 1980) of store evaluation which is composed of relaxed, unstressful and intimate items. The three factors explain 61.5% of the total variance in 14 variables. The eliminated variables loaded poorly on the retained factors, and no additional factor emerged by including these variables.

Effects of Light Illuminance, Perceived Temperature and Type of retail outlet

The effects of light, perceived temperature and type of retail outlet on "stimulation", "upmarket positioning" and "relaxation" are tested (table 2), using MANOVA; the Levene's test for equality of variances is not significant (p>.05 for each factor).

A "bright and cool" light influences the "stimulative" evaluation (F=48.50; p<.001) of a store environment. This result strongly supports Proposition 1 and confirms the stimulation dimension of a store environment in conditions of bright light, consistent with Areni and Kim (1994), Kumari and Venkatramaiah (1974), Mehrabian (1976), and Summers and Hebert (2001) suggestions,

TABLE 2
EFFECTS OF LIGHT AND TEMPERATURE ON STORE EVALUATIONS: STIMULATIVE, UPMARKET POSITIONING AND RELAXATION DIMENSIONS

Stimuli	Factors	*F*	*p*
Light	Stimulation	48.50	.000
	Upmarket positioning	5.31	.002
	Relaxation	0.78	.379
Temperature	Stimulation	8.06	.005
	Upmarket positioning	0.20	.658
	Relaxation	0.97	.326
Type of retail outlet	Stimulation	20.87	.000
	Upmarket positioning	88.80	.000
	Relaxation	13.55	.000
Temperature * Light	Stimulation	4.86	.028
	Upmarket positioning	7.77	.006
	Relaxation	0.56	.453
Temperature * Type of retail outlet	Stimulation	0.75	.474
	Upmarket positioning	3.75	.025
	Relaxation	2.08	.127
Light * Type of retail outlet	Stimulation	18.23	.000
	Upmarket positioning	2.05	.130
	Relaxation	0.11	.897
Temperature * Light * Type of retail outlet	Stimulation	0.48	.619
	Upmarket positioning	0.459	.632
	Relaxation	0.547	.579

and with the founding research on internal responses (Mehrabian and Russell 1974). A "soft and warm" light has a significant effect on the "upmarket positioning" dimension (F=5.31; p<.05) and seems inconsistent with Proposition 2. Actually, a "soft and warm" light has a significant positive impact on the upmarket item but no effect on the modern, spacious and well-ordered items. Further research is needed about these sub-dimensions. As expected, there is no significant effect of the light level upon the "relaxation" dimension perceived by subjects and a "soft and warm" light is positively related to the intimacy item. This indicates that Proposition 3 makes sense. There is a significant interaction effect of "lighting x type of retail outlet" on evaluation of the "stimulative" dimension of store environment such as suggested in Proposition 4 (figure 1). A "bright and cool" light in stores with no product physical involvement such as furniture and bookstores enhances a stimulative evaluation of store environment (F=18.23; p<.001). Our research has focused on the range of thermal comfort, such as determined by previous research. A perceived warm temperature within this range has a positive effect on the "stimulation" factor (F=8.06; p<.05), which supports Proposition 5.[15] It has no influence on the "relaxation" dimension but on the intimate item. There is a type of retail outlet effect. The furniture store, which is the most spacious, is perceived as less warm than the others, according to the manipulation check. This result supports Proposition 6. The interaction effect (temperature x type of retail outlet) has a significant impact on the upmarket factor (F=3.75; p<.05), consistently with Proposition 7 (figure 1). We can also point out that lighting has a significant effect on "upmarket positioning" while temperature has not, consistently with Proposition 8 which suggested that cognitive evaluation of a store would be more influenced by lighting than by temperature. And the "temperature x light" interaction has a significant effect on the evaluation of the "stimulative" factor (F=4.86; p<.05) and the upmarket positioning (F=7.77; p<.05) (figure 1). This interaction effect provides evidence supporting Proposition 9. Finally, the type of retail outlet influences the three dimensions (p<.001) emerged from the factor analysis. Consumers perceive the store atmosphere as more relaxing and more stimulating in furniture and bookstores (vs clothing). This could be explained by the "low physical involvement" of furniture and books. Moreover, subjects have considered furniture and clothing stores more upmarket positioned than the bookstore, probably because furniture and clothes are more expensive and show more space than does the bookstore.

DISCUSSION AND CONCLUDING REMARKS

The systematic impact of light intensity, perceived temperature level, type of retail outlet, and lighting x temperature upon the store evaluation on the "stimulative" factor is one of the main

[15]Univariate analysis of variance also shows that "warm temperature" has a nearly significant positive impact (p=0.058) on perception of a good environment. No other significant result appears with other eliminated items.

FIGURE 1

INTERACTION EFFECTS OF LIGHT, TEMPERATURE AND TYPE OF RETAIL OUTLET ON STIMULATIVE AND UPMARKET POSITIONING DIMENSIONS

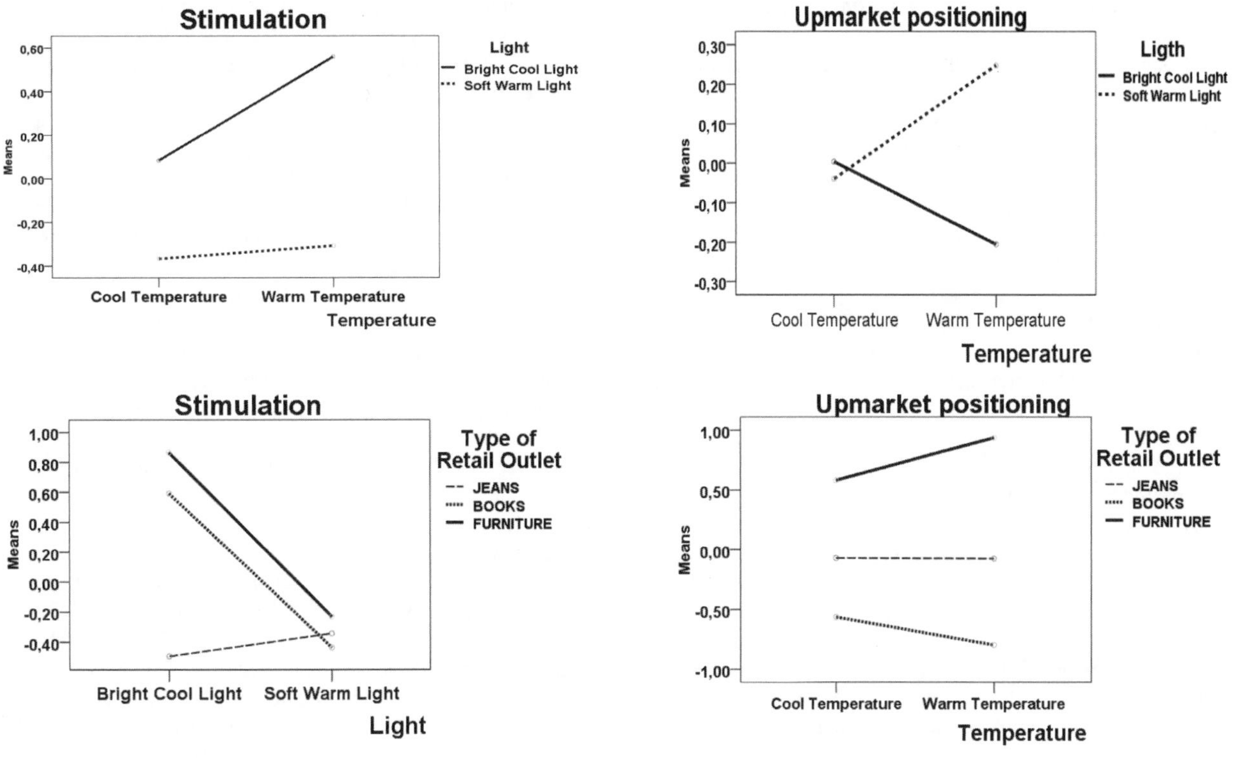

results of this exploratory study. In addition, almost all propositions based on ergonomics and environmental psychology prove well-founded in a store evaluation context. Interestingly enough, even if the upmarket positioning results did not match the propositions exactly, it clearly appears that upmarket positioning is influenced by light intensity, type of retail outlet and temperature x light and temperature x type of retail outlet interactions. As for relaxation, light intensity has an impact upon intimacy perception but not on relaxation. Experiments with wall washing effects would seem useful, following Manav suggestions in ergonomics (2007).

An important element in this exploratory research is the relevance of experiments with simulated temperature levels via pictures, with controlled indicators: winter or summer clothes at a given activity level like recommended by Fanger (1970). Perceived temperature becomes a controllable variable, which has been shown to influence store perceptions. A perceived temperature higher than an actual temperature has high energy savings implications. Another contribution of this research is the range of modalities studied. Even though previous marketing research has focused on illumination or supplemental lighting, practitioners have pointed out the role of Correlated Color Temperature of lighting on the individual's perception. We therefore focused on pleasing modalities of illuminance level, which had not been done before. We also concentrated on the range of comfort. A warmer perceived temperature within comfort range is preferred by respondents. This is consistent with prior studies. Perceived warmness influences the stimulation dimension and the intimacy item of the relaxation factor.

This is the first research on lighting and perceived temperature effects on evaluations of store environment and positioning conducted under controlled conditions. It provides strong enough evidence supporting ergonomic and environmental psychology research to pursue further research in real and controlled settings. This should be done with actual and purported (or perceived) temperature levels.

A limit of this research, as is true of most of the environmental psychology studies, is that we test for effects under a limited set of conditions. Changing the level of any one of the factors (lighting or temperature) is likely to alter the effects of the others. Replicating this research with other levels, and in particular in unpleasant conditions, would be useful in terms of external validity and theory development. Extending the work to look at avoidance behavior rather than simply pleasing perceptions would also respond to managers' concerns when they do not want consumers to linger in some environments.

REFERENCES

Anderson, Craig A. (1989), "Temperature and Aggression: Ubiquitous Effects of Heat on Occurrence of Human Violence," *Psychological Bulletin*, 106 (July), 74-96.

Areni, Charles S. and David Kim (1994), "The Influence of In-Store Lighting on Consumers' Examination of Merchandise in a Wine Store," *International Journal of Research in Marketing*, 11 (March), 117-25.

Baker, Julie and Michaelle Cameron (1996), "The Effects of the Service Environment on Affect and Consumer Perception of Waiting Time: An Integrative Review and Research Propositions," *Journal of the Academy of Marketing Science*, 24 (September), 338-49.

Bakini Driss, Fatma E., Hajer Ben Lallouna Hafsia, and Mustapha Zghal (2008), "L'Impact d'un Eclairage Additionnel dans un Point de Vente sur les Réactions Comportementales des Consommateurs," *La Revue des Sciences de Gestion, Direction et Gestion*, 229 (Janvier-Février), 41-9.

Baron, Robert A. (1990), "Lighting as a Source of Positive Affect," *Progressive Architecture*, 71 (November), 123-24.

Bell, Paul A. and Robert A. Baron (1977), "Aggression and Ambient Temperature: The Facilitating and Inhibiting Effects of Hot and Cold Environments," *Bulletin of the Psychonomic Society*, 9 (6), 443-45.

Bellizzi, Joseph A., Ayn E. Crowley, and Ronald W. Hasty (1983), "The Effects of Color in Store Design," *Journal of Retailing*, 59 (Spring), 23-45.

Biner, Paul M., Darrell L. Butler, Ann R. Fisher, and Amy J. Westergren (1989), "An Arousal Optimization Model of Lighting Level Preferences: An Interaction of Social Situation and Task Demands," *Environment and Behavior*, 21 (January), 3-16.

Bitner, Mary Jo (1992), "Servicescapes: The Impact of Physical Surroundings on Customers and Employees," *Journal of Marketing*, 56 (April), 57-71.

Carr, Suzanne J. and James M. Dabbs Jr. (1974), "The Effects of Lighting, Distance and Intimacy of Topic on Verbal and Visual Behavior," *Sociometry*, 37 (December), 592-600.

Crowley, Ayn E. (1993), "The Two-Dimensional Impact of Color on Shopping," *Marketing Letters*, 4 (January), 59-69.

Donovan, Robert J. and John R. Rossiter (1982), "Store Atmosphere: an Environmental Psychology Approach," *Journal of Retailing*, 58 (Spring), 34-57.

Durak, Ayse, Nilgün C. Olguntürk, Cengiz Yener, Dilek Güvenç, and Yusuf Gürçiunar (2007), "Impact of Lighting Arrangements and Illuminances on Different Impressions of a Room, "*Building and Environment*, 42 (October), 3476-482.

Fanger, Ole (1970), *Thermal Comfort Analysis and Applications in Environmental Engineering*, Copenhagen, Danish Technical Press.

Fisher, Jeffrey D. (1974), "Situation-Specific Variables as Determinants of Perceived Environmental Aesthetic Quality and Perceived Crowdedness," *Journal of Research in Personality*, 8 (August), 177-88.

Griffitt, William and Russell Veitch (1971), "Hot and Crowded: Influences of Population Density and Temperature on Interpersonal Affective Behaviour," *Journal of Personality and Social Psychology*, 17 (January), 92-8.

Guttman Sharon E., Lee A. Gilroy, and Randolph Blake (2005), "Hearing What the Eyes See: Auditory Encoding of Visual Temporal Sequences," *Psychological Science*, 16 (March), 228-35.

Humphreys, Michael A. and Mary Hancock (2007), "Do People Like to Feel 'Neutral'? Exploring the Variation of the Desired Thermal Sensation on the ASHRAE Scale," *Energy and Building*, 39 (July), 867-74.

Kruithof, Arie A. (1941), "Tubular Luminescence Lamps for General Illumination," *Philips Technical Review*, 6, 65-96.

Kumari, Bharathi K. and S.R. Venkatramaiah (1974), "Effects of Anxiety on Closure Effect Disappearance Threshold (Brain Blood Shift Gradient)," *Indian Journal of Clinical Psychology*, 1, 114-20.

Lam, Raymond W. (1998), *Seasonal Affective Disorder and Beyond: Light Treatment for SAD and non SAD Conditions*, Washington D.C, American Psychiatric Press.

Lemoine, Jean-François (2002), "Perception de l'Atmosphère du Point de Vente et Réactions Comportementales et Emotionnelles du Consommateur," *Actes du 5ème Colloque Etienne Thil*, Université de La Rochelle, CD-ROM.

Manav, Banu (2007), "An Experimental Study on the Appraisal of the Visual Environment at Offices in Relation to Colour Temperature and Illuminance," *Building and environment*, 42 (February), 979-83.

Manav, Banu and Cengis Yener (1999), "Effects of Different Lighting Arrangements on Space Perception," *Architectural Science Review*, 42 (March), 43-8.

Mehrabian, Albert (1976), *Public Spaces and Private Spaces: The Psychology of Work, Play, and Living Environments*, New York: Basic Books.

Mehrabian, Albert and James A. Russell (1974), *An Approach to Environmental Psychology*, Cambridge MA: MIT Press.

Petit, Cécile, Edouard Siekierski, and Thierry Lageat (2003), "Du Confort Thermique à la Caractérisation Sensorielle des Ambiances," *Revue Française du Marketing*, 194, 29-47.

Rohles, Frederick H. Jr (2007), "Temperature and Temperament: A Psychologist Looks at Comfort," *ASHRAE Journal*, 49 (February), 14-22.

Rosenthal, Norman E. (2005), *Winter Blues*, New York, Guilford Press.

Rossiter, John R. (2002), "The C-OAR-SE Procedure for Scale Development in Marketing," *International Journal of Research in Marketing*, 19 (December), 305-35.

Roullet, Bernard (2006), "Comment Gérer les Couleurs et les Lumières ?," in *Le Marketing Sensoriel du Point de Vente*, ed. Sophie Rieunier, Paris, Dunod, 133-68.

Russell, James A. and Geraldine Pratt (1980), "A Description of the Affective Quality Attributed to Environments," *Journal of Personality and Social Psychology*, 38 (February), 311-22.

Schifferstein, Hendrik N.J. and Pieter M.A. Desmet (2007), "The Effects of Sensory Impairments on Product Experience and Personal Well-Being," *Ergonomics*, 50 (December), 2026-48.

Spangenberg, Eric R., Ayn E. Crowley, and Pamela W. Henderson (1996), "Improving the Store Environment: Do Olfactory Cues Affect Evaluations and Behaviors?," *Journal of Marketing*, 60 (April), 67-80.

Stramler Carla S., James A. Kleiss, and William C. Howell (1983), "Thermal Sensation Shifts Induced by Physical and Psychological Means," *Journal of Applied Psychology*, 68 (February), 187-93.

Summers, Teresa A. and Paulette R. Hebert (2001), "Shedding Some Light on Store Atmospherics Influence of Illumination on Consumer Behavior," *Journal of Business Research*, 54 (November), 145-50.

Welch, Robert B. (1999), "Meaning, Attention, and the ''Unity Assumption'' in the Intersensory Bias of Spatial and Temporal Perceptions," in *Cognitive contributions to the perception of spatial and temporal events*, ed. Gisa Aschersleben, Talis Bachmann and Jochen Musseler, Amsterdam: Elsevier, 371–87.

Yalch, Richard F. and Eric R. Spangenberg (1990), "Effects of Store Music on Shopping Behavior," *Journal of Consumer Marketing*, 7 (2), 55-63.

______ (2000), "The Effects of Music in a Retail Setting on Real and Perceived Shopping Times," *Journal of Business Research*, 49 (August), 139-47.

Tobacco Consumption in the Home: Impact on Social Relationships and Marking Territory

Kathy Hamilton, University of Strathclyde, UK
Louise Hassan, University of St Andrews, UK

ABSTRACT

In this paper we move beyond viewing the home as a mere context for consumer decision-making to explore consumption practices and socio-spatial relationships within the home in relation to tobacco consumption. Based on focus groups conducted across ten European countries, our findings suggest that smokers view the home as a safe haven where they are sheltered from the outside regulatory environment. However, tension between smokers and nonsmokers demonstrates that consumption practices within the home may become a process of negotiation, resulting in smokers marking territory in efforts to avoid conflict.

INTRODUCTION

The home represents the single most expensive purchase that a person is likely to make and as a research setting offers rich possibilities for exploring cultural symbolism and personal meaning (Claiborne and Ozanne 1990). The meaning of home has been a prominent theme within the disciplines of sociology, human geography, architecture, psychology, philosophy and anthropology. However, consumer research on the home is limited and has been studied mainly as a context for consumer decision-making (Bardhi 2006), neglecting the consumption practices that take place within and transform a dwelling unit into a home (Despres 1991). Rose (1999, 248) suggests that physical space needs to be seen as "practised, a matrix of play, dynamic and iterative, its forms and shapes produced through the citational performance of self-other relations". Thus, in order to gain a deeper understanding of the home, research must focus on the consumption practices and interpersonal relationships that are played out within the home. In this paper, we explore these issues in the context of tobacco consumption.

Nearly one fifth of all deaths in the United States each year are attributed to tobacco, representing almost 440,000 US citizens with 4.8 million smoking related deaths annually worldwide (Centers for Disease Control and Prevention (CDC) 2002). It is therefore unsurprising to find that a significant portion (6-8%) of annual personal health expenditure in the US is directly related to treating tobacco related diseases, namely, lung cancer, heart disease and chronic obstructive pulmonary disease (Warner 2000). Beyond the personal harm caused by tobacco, the Surgeon General's report on secondhand smoke in 2006 states that "there is no risk-free level of exposure to secondhand smoke" (CDC 2006). To address the dangers of secondhand tobacco smoke many states and countries have enacted comprehensive smoke-free laws in public places. Evaluations have shown support for such legislation and high levels of compliance (Fong et al. 2006, Biener et al. 2007). Recent efforts in tobacco control have moved to restricting smoking in the home within multi-unit dwellings. California is the first state to implement such smoking bans in two cities (Semrad 2007). With continued pressures to legislate in this area it is important to understand the meaning and importance of the home in relation to tobacco consumption. As previous research has predominantly considered smoking in public places and evaluations of smoke-free laws (Fong et al. 2006, Biener et al. 2007), research exploring tobacco consumption in the home is limited. We therefore address this significant and important research gap. In particular, we examine the following research questions: (1) When and where is tobacco consumed in the home? (2) How does tobacco consumption in the home impact on social relations? (3) In what ways do smokers and non-smokers negotiate consumption of tobacco in the home? Answers to these three research questions will allow us to gain a better understanding of how power is regained by the smoker when the home is free from external legislative constraints, yet within the home such power is subject to negotiations and conferment with inevitable compromises in the attempt at harmony with significant others. Our contribution is twofold; first we offer theoretical contributions in relation to negotiated consumption and assigned consumption space in the home. Second, in light of the increasing acknowledgement of the dangers of secondhand smoke we offer public policy makers insight on issues pertaining to the home.

THE HOME

Meaning of the Home

The home has an increasingly central role in everyday life, with many layers of meaning and a rich social, cultural and historical significance (Moore 2000). Place attachment is a central theme in relation to the home, used to explain the "positively experienced bonds, sometimes occurring without awareness, that are developed over time from the behavioural, affective, and cognitive ties between individuals and/or groups and their socio-physical environment" (Brown and Perkins 1992, 284). Such interactional processes between people and places contribute to identity definition (Kleine and Baker 2004) and in this way, home becomes an important extension of the self (Belk 1988). As Czikszenthmihalyi and Rochberg-Halton (1981, 123) suggest "a home is much more than a shelter; it is a world in which a person can create a material environment that embodies what he or she considers significant. In this sense the home becomes the most powerful sign of the self of the inhabitant who dwells within". The home as self-definition may involve territorial behavior in terms of the personalization of and communication that a place is "owned" by a person or group (Altman 1975). This may include the way in which consumers incorporate aesthetics into their everyday consumption experiences in the home (Venkatesh and Meamber 2008), emphasizing the link between place and possession attachment (Kleine and Baker 2004).

The significance and centrality of the home as having symbolic meaning has been highlighted by consumer researchers considering the loss of the home (Gross 2007, Hill 1991, Sayre 1994). For example, one of Gross' (2007) informants at the beginning of the foreclosure process lamented "It's like if you lost a child or something" while one of Sayre's (1994) informants who lost her home as the result of fire suggested, "What's missing is my territory, my space. I am still me, but many of the things that identify my purpose and creativity are not there. My territory had my markings, my routines, my responsibilities, my purpose clearly defined." This issue of territory is further discussed in the following section.

Personal Space and Dominion within the Home

Claiborne and Ozanne (1990) found that consumers often have a need for personal space within the home, a special space which is their own over which they have dominion and control. Place attachment to the home is stronger when a person is able to regulate his or her privacy which in turn provides a basis for a sense of autonomy, self worth and self identity (Harris, Brown and Werner 1996). While the home is a confined space, the outside is perceived as imposing and demanding different rules of engagement with people, places and things (Mallet 2004). As such, home as privacy represents a freedom from surveillance; a back region where the need to maintain role performance is relaxed and where one can be oneself (Goffman 1971, Saunders and Williams 1988).

This also corresponds to the notion of the home as "safe haven," a sacred space that has the potential to offer self-transcendence (Belk, Wallendorf and Sherry 1989). As McCracken (2005, 32) suggests, the homey space can be "embracing" in terms of a "descending pattern of enclosure" where the occupant is "protected from the outside world by an intricate series of baffles and mediants". In this way, McCracken (2005) argues that the homey space has the same symbolic and psychological value as a parental embrace, offering protection from both real and imagined dangers. However, some critics argue that this perspective of the home as safe haven is an idealized notion that neglects to recognize the tensions surrounding the use of domestic space that are characteristic of the lived experience of home. Indeed, the home can be seen as a "major political battleground; feminists see it in terms of gender domination and liberals in terms of personal autonomy and a challenge to state power " (Saunders and Williams 1988, 91).

Socio-spatial relations are central to the construction of home. Drawing on Giddens' (1984) concept of the locale, Saunders and Williams (1988) suggest that the home is a crucial locale where forms of social relations and social institutions are composed, accomplished and contextualized. Similarly, Valentine (1999, 57) argues that the negotiation of space requires that we position ourselves "physically, socially, morally, politically and metaphorically in relation to others". Familial relations are particularly central with McCracken (2005, 38) suggesting that homeyness for many people becomes an "adhesive" that attaches them to family.

The concept of the home is important in the context of tobacco consumption for several reasons; firstly, with few exceptions, the home is an unregulated space and governments and the media have raised concerns about how smoke-free legislation in public places may increase consumption of tobacco in the home through displacement, which might be detrimental for other residents, particularly children. However such harmful displacement has yet to be evidenced (Biener et al. 2007). Secondly, anti-smoking adverts such as the European Union "HELP–for a life without tobacco" campaign have used the potential dangers of smoking in the home as a key campaign message. Further insight into this consumption space may benefit the development of future anti-smoking campaigns in the home context. Finally, given that smoking is an emotive issue generating strong opinions, potential for conflict amongst family or household members may be increased.

METHODOLOGY

Findings are based on thirty focus groups conducted across ten European Union member states (three focus groups in each country, see Table 1 for focus group composition). The ten countries were chosen on the basis of geographic spread across Europe, the amount of tobacco control legislation in each country as well as cultural variables and scores. In line with the need for compatible participants in focus groups (Morgan 1998), participants in each country were allocated to focus groups based on their age (15-17, 18-25 and 26-35), smoking status (heavy smoker, light smoker and non-smoker), and social class (working class, middle class). Focus groups were mixed in terms of gender. The research is part of the 'HELP–for a life without tobacco' European Union anti-smoking campaign and as a result, the age range of participants was guided by the target age group of the campaign.

A leading market research agency (IPSOS) was employed to recruit respondents, co-ordinate data collection and ensure consistency in practices. The agency employs recruiters who live in each of the countries, resulting in access to information-rich respondents. Additionally, working with a professional recruitment firm lowered the no-show rate (Morgan 1998). Each focus group consisted of between 6 and 8 participants and lasted between 2 and 2 1/2 hours. National representatives from the European Network for Smoking Prevention were also invited to attend the focus groups as observers to increase the likelihood of practical benefits arising from the research and advance the transformative consumer research agenda.

A topic guide was developed to ensure key research areas were covered whilst also encouraging free discussion and the expression of respondents' ideas in their own terms. The topic guide centered on three areas; general smoking awareness, attitudes and behavior; anti-smoking campaigns and the HELP campaign generally; and pre-testing of specific anti-smoking advertisements. In this paper we draw predominantly on discussions from the first topic area.

With respondent's consent, all focus groups were recorded and transcribed from the native language into English. Transcripts formed the basis of data analysis, which was carried out using the techniques proposed by Spiggle (1994). This involves categorizing data, completed in an inductive manner as categories emerged from the data rather than identified a priori to the research. Abstraction then grouped categories into more general conceptual classes and comparison allowed the exploration of differences and similarities across incidents within the data and the identification of any patterns. We present our findings in relation to places of tobacco consumption and issues of (dis)empowerment, marking territory in the home and social relations in the home.

ANALYSIS AND DISCUSSION

Places of Tobacco Consumption and Issues of (Dis)empowerment

Many smokers in the study admitted that they feel uncomfortable and experience embarrassment when smoking in public places.[1] This is partly attributable to their belief that others make negative judgments of their decision to smoke, echoing Goffman's (1963, 18) suggestion that shame can be a central possibility arising from the individual's perception of falling short of "what he really ought to be." For example:

> *"If you are on the street and you are walking along the street there are just people who just grimace at you because they don't like you smoking."* (Italy, 26-35, Heavy Smokers)

> *"if I sit with somebody who doesn't smoke then I feel strange."* (Czech Republic, 18-25, Light Smokers)

For some respondents the negative connotations stem from feelings of exclusion created by regulations that prevent smoking in public places.

> *"I feel it's a bit shameful, I have to go outside the restaurant and smoke, banned from coming in, that's where you can stand and stink up."* (Sweden, 18-25, Light Smokers)

---

[1]It must be noted that this is not generalizable to all smokers; indeed findings suggest that some consumers engage in cigarette consumption primarily to gain social acceptance amongst peer groups and as a route to inclusion in certain social situations.

TABLE 1
Focus Group Composition

Region	Country	Tobacco Policy	Age (Years)	Smoking Status	Social Class
West	UK	High	15-17	Non	Working
West	UK	High	18-25	Heavy	Middle
West	UK	High	26-35	Non	Working
West	Sweden	High	15-17	Non	Middle
West	Sweden	High	18-25	Light	Working
West	Sweden	High	26-35	Non	Middle
South	Italy	High	15-17	Light	Working
South	Italy	High	18-25	Non	Middle
South	Italy	High	26-35	Heavy	Working
West	France	Medium	15-17	Non	Working
West	France	Medium	18-25	Non	Middle
West	France	Medium	26-35	Heavy	Working
East	Czech Republic	Medium	15-17	Heavy	Middle
East	Czech Republic	Medium	18-25	Light	Working
East	Czech Republic	Medium	26-35	Non	Middle
East	Hungary	Medium	15-17	Non	Working
East	Hungary	Medium	18-25	Non	Middle
East	Hungary	Medium	26-35	Heavy	Working
West	Germany	Low	15-17	Non	Working
West	Germany	Low	18-25	Heavy	Middle
West	Germany	Low	26-35	Light	Working
North	Netherlands	Low	15-17	Heavy	Middle
North	Netherlands	Low	18-25	Light	Working
North	Netherlands	Low	26-35	Non	Middle
South	Portugal	Low	15-17	Non	Working
South	Portugal	Low	18-25	Heavy	Middle
South	Portugal	Low	26-35	Light	Working
East	Slovenia	Low	15-17	Light	Middle
East	Slovenia	Low	18-25	Heavy	Working
East	Slovenia	Low	26-35	Light	Middle

NOTE.— The classification of the countries as low, medium and high was based on the WHO country profiles; social class was derived from the occupation of the head of the household, local definitions were used to categorise respondents into working and middle class categories.

> *"I feel excluded. More and more, and angrier because over some years they've created a national level policy that the people that smoke are stupid and disturb everyone because they smoke."* (Portugal, 18-25, Heavy Smokers)

Due to an ever-tightening policy environment, smokers experience physical separation from others in certain public settings. As a result, findings indicate that, even those living in countries with low levels of tobacco restrictions experience a sense of exclusion. Such exclusion goes hand in hand with disempowerment as smokers are restricted and at times prevented from engaging in a consumption practice that they feel is important.

In comparison, the home is seen as personal space and thus an escape where smokers can enjoy smoking outside the gaze of a perceived "disapproving" general public. For some the home has always been a place where smoking has been present:

> *"If I hadn't seen it from my very young age at home I would not smoke, but I do because I have seen it since I remember"* (Czech Republic, 15-17, Heavy Smokers).

> *"In the presence of other people sometimes I can be tolerant and other times I can be very intolerant…. if I am at my home and somebody comes to see me then I wouldn't be considerate either because it is my home but when I am somewhere else I have to follow rules and it is alright and then I tolerate it"* (Germany, 26-35, Light Smokers).

> *"I also smoke in my room, my own room so that is my private sphere"* (Germany, 26-35, Light Smokers).

The home thus becomes a "back region" (Goffman 1971), a place where smokers do not feel vulnerable to undesirable stereotypes. In this way, the home is established as a safe haven where individuals live by their own rules and are free to regulate their activities and practices, in turn creating empowerment and self worth.

> *"I think when I smoke it just enables me to be by myself, it's my cigarette and I. I mean it enabled me to just go away and isolate myself, just by myself, you know… It's not to share, it's*

just to be by myself, to isolate myself. Cut myself off from the others" (France, 26-35, Heavy Smokers)

The home is then placed in opposition to the world outside (Mallet 2004). In contrast to the regulated outside environment that imposes constraints on smoking behavior, consumers are afforded more freedom in terms of their behavior "behind closed doors" (Miller 2001). As Miller (2001, 1) suggests, "it is the material culture within our home that appears as both our appropriation of the larger world and often as the representation of the world within our private domain". Indeed, cigarette consumption becomes a central ingredient to other activities that occur within the privacy of the home. Respondents smoke "after dinner," "in front of the TV," "in bed," "first thing in the morning" and when drinking coffee– "the two go together virtually all the time." Indeed, some respondents freely admitted that smoking is a "ritual," "a force of habit" and even an "addiction" that leaves them "hooked" and "dependent." Given the centrality of cigarette consumption to smokers' daily lives, it is perhaps unsurprising that for many respondents smoking forms part of a normal ritual in the home where they regain their displaced power. We now move on to consider how this could change when smokers and non-smokers live together.

Social Relations in the Home

Findings suggest that a divergence of attitudes towards smoking can provoke a degree of conflict between smokers and non-smokers as each party competes to have their preferences met, creating a "tricky" and "difficult" relationship. Both smokers and non-smokers discussed the tension that this could create:

> *"My mate's girlfriend smokes and while we were still in the flat together he initially let her smoke in the flat. I came back in and I smelled it and I said get her out. That started tension between us because of the smoking"* (UK, 26-35, Non-smokers).

> *"I don't live with my parents but they still don't tolerate my smoking. I took up smoking in high school because everybody was smoking but my parents never accepted it and there was constant quarrelling and fighting and when I lived at home I got used to having to go outside to smoke"* (Hungary, 26-35, Heavy Smokers).

> *"I go home and my partner doesn't smoke and she is annoyed by the smoke and sometimes after work I go to the pub with my mates and have a few beers and of course we smoke and then it is the line 'Oh you have been to the pub again'"* (Germany, 18-25, Heavy Smokers).

Within the household, conflict has been an elusive concept, particularly within the family context (Commuri and Gentry 2000). However intra-familial and intra-household decisions are more complex than a simple aggregation of individual behaviors (Hall et al. 1995). Rather, within the household, there can be contradictory consumption practices and values that are difficult to reconcile. Such a combination of individual preferences may make conflict probable (Lee and Collins 2000). Within our context, potential for conflict is enhanced because what is essentially a private consumption practice has an impact on other members of the home due to the effects of secondhand tobacco smoke. As such, "where the desire for a purified environment is not shared by all members of a household, the house becomes a place of conflict" (Sibley 1995, 91).

The presence of children within the home adds another dimension to the issue of social relations. Many smokers prefer to avoid smoking in front of young people with one Czech smoker suggesting, *"When young people can see me I feel like I'm spoiling them."* Many smokers in the study demonstrated awareness that the family context of interpersonal communication has the greatest influence on consumer socialization (Ward 1974) and consequently made efforts to avoid "setting a bad example".

> *"I've got a baby cousin and I go outside if she's in my house and so does my mum, we don't smoke. Before I even touch her I wash my hands"* (UK, 18-25, Heavy Smokers).

> *"It's also a pretty bad role model for kids to smoking in the future... I do, yes I think about that a lot.... I don't smoke in front of my boyfriends younger sister who is 10/12 or something because she knows I smoke but I won't smoke in front of her because she gets that image"* (Sweden, 18-25, Light Smokers)

This reinforces the indirect and emotional power of children to shape consumption practices in the home and encourages smokers to regulate their smoking behavior if young people are present. However, for some smokers, the grip of their addiction is too strong to resist. As one of our Portuguese informants commented, *"I know that I am prejudicing my son. I shouldn't smoke at home, but I can't stop."* Again, this highlights the additive nature of tobacco that leads some smokers to possess a negative self-view and reduce self esteem. Therefore although smoking in the home can afford an escape from the regulated 'outside' thus releasing feelings of empowerment, the presence of significant others can result in a loss of power in the home and feelings of discomfort. We now move on to consider how this tension is negotiated.

Marking Territory in the Home

In some of the focus groups with non-smokers the issue of smoking in the home provoked strong emotional responses. In the Netherlands focus group of 26-35 year old non-smokers, several respondents agreed that *"in my house there's absolutely no smoking. If someone comes, then they go out, but not in my house."* Two main reasons emerged for this reaction to smoking. First, in relation to decor, respondents wanted to avoid *"nicotine yellow on the walls"* and second, those who had children didn't want any cigarette smoke in the environment where children are present. Other non-smoking focus groups shared these strong opinions:

> *"My dad, he smokes but he is only allowed to smoke in the basement and also outside but not in the house"* (Germany, 15-17, Non-smokers).

> *"In my family, my mum used to be a strong smoker. We literally chase her out of the house, even if it's minus 20 degrees, she has to be outside. My father said that he won't tolerate smoking inside the house"* (Hungary, 18-25, Non-smokers).

In response to this tension, the issue of marking territory comes to the forefront when smokers and non-smokers share the same living space. The result is the division of space within the home with certain spaces deemed more acceptable for tobacco consumption than others:

> *"I lived with a non smoker for a while and we marked our territory. I was allowed to smoke in the kitchen, at the window.*

Never in the bedroom, not in the dining room or on the balcony" (France, 26-35, Heavy Smokers).

Within the home the negotiation of "acceptable" behavior then becomes central as consumers need to be aware of not only their own but also other people's norms and values. Findings suggest that this is also true for other shared spaces such as cars

"I smoke in the car, it is my car and I can do it but when somebody is with me who doesn't smoke then I open a window" (Germany, 26–35, Light Smokers).

Marking territory can be viewed as a way of "regulating" social interactions for as Altman (1975, 140) suggests, "With everyone having "places," there is no need to continually negotiate who belongs where or who has rights to what, so that day-to-day life smoothes out by virtue of territorial assignments or ownership". In many cases, this "smoothing out" is aided by smokers adopting territories where the smell of tobacco smoke can be easily dispersed or masked, such as "near the chimney" or "at the window." Or as another smoker suggested:

"I light up a candle so I can put out the candle and there's no smell. And I sit on the floor and throw the cigarette to the fire. My husband doesn't smoke so he keeps pestering me. So I don't feel okay sitting on our sofa and smoking" (Portugal, 26-35, Light Smokers).

Some smokers adhered to the viewpoint that smoking could damage the ambience, recognizing that "*in the house it's much better to feel the smell of cleanness than to get into a house that smells like a cigarette*". Here we witness a contradiction in the relationship between smokers and their homes. Despite the desire to smoke, smokers can be aware that cigarette odors can damage the atmosphere in their homes. The challenge then becomes for smokers to create their own private space where they can smoke without disturbing the wider ambiance of the home and without complaints from others. Territories are marked for such consumption in areas where the effects of tobacco smoke are minimal thus restoring a safe haven for their "sacred" ritual. So although the home may be free from formal regulations preventing smoking, it can be subject to more informal yet strict regulations that are initiated and negotiated among household members.

CONCLUSIONS

Research interest on spatiality of consumption tends to relate to visible and spectacular sites of consumption such as flagship stores (Peñaloza 1998) and festival shopping malls (Maclaran and Brown 2005), neglecting more private and mundane consumption spaces. In the paper we raise the profile of the home as an important consumption site. We advance current theory that tends to examine the home as a context for consumer decision-making by exploring consumption practices and consumer interpersonal relationships in the home. We suggest first, the home offers an empowering space for consumption practices, second, consumers strive to maintain the home as a sacred space and third, contradictory consumption values incite the negotiation of space and consumer relations within the home.

Our analysis reveals that the home offers a space where consumers have power and dominion, a space where they are separated and sheltered from the outside world and a space where they have greater agency in their consumption practices. The home becomes an escape, a refuge where consumers are freed from the anxieties and intrusions associated with public scrutiny. It becomes a place for the expression of self-identity and a site of stability in comparison to the ever-changing and restrictive regulation in the external environment. It is a site of emotional attachment, providing "a sense of daily and ongoing security and stimulation, with places and objects offering predictable facilities, opportunities to relax from formal roles, the chance to be creative and control aspects of one's life" (Low and Altman 1992, 10).

In this sense, the home is "a church in that it is the place where ultimate goals can be cultivated" (Csikszentmihalyi and Rochberg-Halton 1981, 123). This religious metaphor parallels research on sacred consumption (Belk, Wallendorf and Sherry 1989) as the home demands reverence and respect and consumers strive to avoid or limit any practices which may taint or contaminate the environment. In this regard, we start to glimpse something of a paradox. On the one hand, the home is a space where consumers have free reign over their consumption activities and on the other hand, the desire to maintain a purified environment may constrain certain consumption activities that threaten such an environment. In this way, cigarette consumption and other consumption practices which may potentially damage the sacred quality of the home demand careful management and negotiation. Given the significance of smoking for some respondents, the fact that consumers are willing to sacrifice and reduce their cigarette consumption provides further evidence of the sacredness of the home.

Our analysis also clearly establishes the link between space and social relations in that consumption practices within the home may become a process of negotiation, reaffirming the home as a site of both individual and collective consumption. As Csikszentmihalyi and Rochberg-Halton (1981) suggest, different people in the home can be seen as inhabiting different symbolic environments even though they are in the same household. Given that prior research has found minimal evidence of conflict in the home (Commuri and Gentry 2000), we argue that tension and conflict is most likely to emerge in relation to risky and emotive consumption practices such as tobacco consumption.

The public policy issues raised by this research are complex. On the one hand, the impact of passive smoking is the home is serious, particularly for children, and policy makers have a responsibility to protect people from these dangers. On the over hand, despite the clear and demonstrable harm caused by tobacco, it is still a legitimate choice for consumers to smoke and smokers' needs must also be considered. Given strong tobacco control policies regarding public space, smokers need private space to exercise dominion to realize the 'benefits' of their consumption. Thus legislators implementing smoke-free laws, and particularly restrictions in personal spaces like the home, need to fully assess the impact of such legislation on not only physical health but also on psychological health and well-being.

The research also questions the effectiveness of anti-smoking adverts concerning smoking in the home as findings indicate that smokers can be resistant to attempts to control their behavior. Although some authors (van den Putte et al. 2005) argue that smokers and non-smokers need to start a dialogue about smoking, this may result in negative consequences if arguments and tensions arise. This power struggle between members of the household will only be a valid target and effective campaign advertising message if cessation is shown and believed to be an effective strategy to reduce this tension. However, if this message is not effectively conveyed, using the home as a campaign setting might evoke negative reactions and resentment if smokers are coerced into facing the home as a battle ground.

REFERENCES

Altman, Irwin (1975), *The Environment and Social Behavior: Privacy, Personal Space, Territory, Crowding*, Monterey, CA: Brooks/Cole.

Bardhi, Fleura (2006), "An Examination of the Concept of Postmodern Home and the Role of Consumption in Home-making Practices," in *Advances in Consumer Research*, Vol. 33, ed. Connie Pechmann and Linda Price, Duluth, MN : Association for Consumer Research, 651-658.

Belk, Russell. W. (1988), "Possessions and the Extended Self," *Journal of Consumer Research*, 15 (2), 139-168.

Belk, Russell, Melanie Wallendorf, and John Sherry (1989), "The Sacred and the Profane in Consumer Behavior: Theodicy on the Odyssey," *Journal of Consumer Research*, 16 (June), 1-38.

Biener, Lois, Catherine A. Garrett, Margie Skeer, Michael Siegel, and Gregory Connolly (2007), "The Effects on Smokers of Boston's Smoke-free Bar Ordinance: A Longitudinal Analysis of Changes in Compliance, Patronage, Policy Support, and Smoking at Home," *Journal of Public Health Management and Practice*, 13 (6), 630-636.

Brown, Barbara and D. Perkins (1992), "Disruptions in Place Attachment," in *Place Attachment: Human Behavior and Environment (vol. 12)*, ed. I. Altman and S. Low, New York: Plenum, 279-304.

Centers for Disease Control and Prevention (2002), "Cigarette Smoking Among Adults–United States–2000," *Morbidity and Mortality Weekly Report*, 51 (29), 642-45.

Centers for Disease Control and Prevention (2006), *The Health Consequences of Involuntary Exposure to Tobacco Smoke: A Report of the Surgeon General*, Office on Smoking and Health, Atlanta.

Claiborne, C.B. and Julie L. Ozanne (1990), "The Meaning of Custom-Made Homes: Home as a Metaphor for Living," in *Advances in Consumer Research*, Vol. 17, ed. Marvin E. Goldberg, Gerald Gorn and Richard W. Pollay, Provo, UT : Association for Consumer Research, 367-374.

Commuri, Suraj and James W. Gentry (2000), "Opportunities for Family Research In Marketing," *Academy of Marketing Science Review*, http://www.amsreview.org/articles/commuri08-2000.pdf

Csikszentmihalyi, Mihaly and Eugene Rochberg-Halton (1981), *The Meaning of Things: Domestic Symbols and the Self*, Cambridge: Cambridge University Press.

Despres, C. (1991), "The Meaning of Home: Literature Review and Directions for Future Research and Theoretical Development," *Journal of Architectural and Planning Research*, 8 (2), 96-115.

Fong, Geoffrey T., Andrew Hyland, Ron Borland et al. (2006), "Reductions in Tobacco Smoke Pollution and Increases in Support for Smoke-free Public Places following the Implementation of Comprehensive Smoke-free Workplace Legislation in the Republic of Ireland: Findings from the ITC Ireland/UK Survey," *Tobacco Control*, 15 (suppl III), 51–58.

Giddens, Anthony (1984), *The Constitution of Society: Outline of the Theory of Structuration*. Cambridge: Polity.

Goffman, Erving (1963), *Stigma: Notes on the Management of Spoiled Identity*, London: Penguin Books.

Goffman, Erving (1971), *Relations in Public*. Middlesex: Penguin.

Gross, Barbara (2007), "The Experience of Home Foreclosure: Coping with Involuntary Loss of Home and Transition of Identity," in *European Advances in Consumer Research* Vol. 8, ed. Stefania Borghini, Mary Ann McGrath and Cele Otnes, Duluth, MN : Association for Consumer Research, 87-93.

Hall, John, Mike Shaw, Melissa Johnson, and Peter Oppenheim (1995) "Influence of Children on Family Consumer Decision Making," in *European Advances in Consumer Research*, Vol. 2, ed. Flemming Hansen, Provo, UT: Association for Consumer Research, 45-53.

Harris, Paul B., Barbara B. Brown and Carol M. Werner (1996), "Privacy Regulations and Place Attachment: Predicting Attachments to a Student Family Housing Facility," *Journal of Environmental Psychology*, 16 (4), 287-301.

Hill, Ronald Paul (1991), "Homeless Women, Special Possessions, and the Meaning of "Home": An Ethnographic Case Study," *Journal of Consumer Research*, 18 (December), 298-310.

Kleine, Susan Schultz and Stacey Menzel Baker (2004), "An Integrative Review of Material Possession Attachment," *Academy of Marketing Science Review*, http://www.amsreview.org/articles/kleine01-2004.pdf

Lee, Christina Kwai-Choi and Brett Collins (2000), "Family Decision Making and Coalition Patterns", *European Journal of Marketing*, 34 (9/10), 1181-1198.

Low, Setha and Irwin Altman (1992), "Place Attachment: A Conceptual Inquiry", *Place Attachment: Human Behavior and Environment (vol. 12)*, ed. I. Altman and S. Low, New York: Plenum, 1-12.

Maclaran, Pauline and Steven Brown (2005), "The Center Cannot Hold: Consuming the Utopian Marketplace," *Journal of Consumer Research*, 32 (September), 311-323.

McCracken, Grant (2005), *Culture and Consumption II*, Indiana: Indiana University Press.

Mallet, Shelley (2004), "Understanding Home: A Critical Review of the Literature," *The Sociological Review*, 62-89.

Miller, Daniel (2001), *Home Possessions*, London: Berg Publishers.

Moore, Jeanne (2000), "Placing Home in Context," *Journal of Environmental Psychology*, 20, 207-217.

Morgan, D. (1998), *Planning Focus Groups*, Thousand Oaks: CA, Sage.

Peñaloza, Lisa (1998), "Just Doing It: A Visual Ethnographic Study of Spectacular Consumption Behavior at Nike Town," *Consumption, Markets and Culture*, 2 (4), 337-465.

Rose, Gillian (1999), "Performing Space," in *Human Geography Today*, eds. Doreen Massey, John Allen and Philip Sarre, Malden: Polity Press, 247-259.

Saunders, Peter and Peter Williams (1988), "The Constitution of the Home: Towards a Research Agenda," *Housing Studies*, 3 (2), 81-93.

Sayre, Shay (1994), "Possessions and Identity in Crisis: Meaning and Change for Victims of the Oakland Firestorm," in *Advances in Consumer Research*, Vol. 21, ed. Chris T. Allen and Deborah Roedder John, Provo, UT: Association for Consumer Research, 109-114.

Semrad, Staci (2007), "A New Arena in the Fight Over Smoking: The Home," *The New York Times*, (November 5), (accessed January 7, 2009),

Sibley, David (1995), *Geographies of Exclusion: Society and Difference in the West*, London, Routledge.

Spiggle, S. (1994), "Analysis and Interpretation of Qualitative Data in Consumer Research", *Journal of Consumer Research*, 21 (Dec), 491-503.

Valentine, Gill (1999), "Imagined Geographies," in *Human Geography Today*, ed. Doreen Massey, John Allen and Philip Sarre, Malden: Polity Press, 47-61.

van den Putte, Bas, Marco C. Yzer, and Suzanne Brunsting (2005), "Social Influences on Smoking Cessation: A Comparison of the Effect of Six Social Influence Variables," *Preventive Medicine*, 41, 185-193.

Ventakesh, Alladi and Laurie A. Meamber (2008), "The aesthetics of consumption and the consumer as an aesthetic subject," *Consumption Markets and Culture,* 11 (1), 45-70.

Ward, Scott (1974), "Consumer Socialisation," *Journal of Consumer Research*, 1(September), 1-14.

Warner, Kenneth E. (2000), "The Economies of Tobacco: Myths and Realities," *Tobacco Control*, 9, 78-89.

Early Adopters in the Diffusion of an HIV/AIDS Public Health Innovation in a Developing Country

Marylouise Caldwell, Norwegian School of Economics and Business Administration, Norway
Ingeborg Astrid Kleppe, Norwegian School of Economics and Business Administration, Norway

ABSTRACT

Public demonstration by early adopters of innovation benefits tends to reduce consumer resistance to HIV/AIDS public health innovations. However, elevated stigmatization, bifurcated culture, gender power relations and poverty make such public displays hard to enact in developing countries. To learn more about this difficult context for diffusion of a public health innovation, we investigate early adopters who act as public spokes-models of HIV/AIDS Positive Living in Botswana. With limited institutional support these consumers create and enact multiple roles, such as buddy, lay educator, support group member/leader and social entrepreneur. Analysis of these highly committed courageous individuals expands our understanding of the requisite personal qualities, capacities and roles of early adopters of HIV/AIDS public health innovations in developing countries.

INTRODUCTION

Early adoption is central to diffusion of innovations theory. Yet the consumer literature is remarkably silent regarding early adoption of HIV/AIDS public health innovations (PHIs) (for an exception see Rothschild 1999). We address this theoretical lacuna by investigating early adopters of HIV/AIDS Positive Living, a public health innovation in Botswana. HIV/AIDS Positive Living comprises a set of interrelated behaviours such as knowing and accepting one's HIV status, disease management including adherence to medication regimes, caring for people living with HIV/AIDS (PLWHAs), supporting the PLWHA community and engaging in social and political outreach. Our research draws upon an ethnographic study of The 2005 Miss HIV/AIDS Stigma Free beauty pageant, The 2006 Mister HIV/AIDS Positive Living contest in Botswana and follow-up interviews in the period 2006-2009. Competitors are some of the very few people living with HIV/AIDS (PLWHAs) in Botswana to go public with their HIV+ status and to advocate positive living. We observe that these consumers attempts to influence potential adopters are severely impacted by: (1) the stigma associated with a potentially deadly sexually transmitted disease, (2) resistance to an obviously Western styled bio-medical model that fails to address negative attitudes to external intervention in post colonial countries (Swidler 2006); and (3) denial of the disease's existence stemming from cultural beliefs about the origins illness, gender relations, fertility and sexual practices (Liddell, Barrett, and Bydawell 2004).

This paper comprises a short literature review of the diffusion of PHIs and early adopter roles in diffusion of HIV/AIDS PHIs. Findings are presented in two sections as follows: (1) the different pathways to the adoption of HIV testing, (2) the adoption of Greater Participation of PLWHAS Principles (GIPA). The discussion highlights implications for HIV/AIDS PHIs. We conclude with contributions and future directions for research.

EARLY ADOPTION OF HIV/AIDS PUBLIC HEALTH INNOVATIONS

Rothschild (1999) explains that consumers typically resist public health innovations (PHIs) for distinctive reasons. When confronted by PHIs, consumers tend to act in a self-centred manner adopting a short term perspective. They refuse to acknowledge that their individual failure to adopt could result in negative consequences for themselves and broader society. The benefits of non adoption are often immediate; while the benefits of innovation adoption are delayed and appear vague. Goldberg (1995) points out that upstream factors, such as economic, political, cultural, technological, and public sector infrastructure factors, can increase consumer resistance to PHIs (Goldberg 1995). For example, PLWHAs who are poor and have poor food security can stop taking their antiretrovirals (ARVs) because the medication increases their appetite and prevents them from experiencing a restful night's sleep.

Who are the most effective endorsers of HIV/AIDS innovations? An extensive review of spokespersons in HIV/AIDS PHIs finds that experts, rather than HIV+ educators are most influential when they demographically and behaviourally match their target audience (Durantini, Albarracín, Mitchell, Earl, and Gilette 2006). Elaborating upon this idea, Watts and Dodds' (2007) propose that a critical mass of "moderately influential" early adopters (the common man) are the ones who propagate widespread diffusion of innovations generally. Rossiter and Bellman (2005) suggest that the common man is well suited to public health announcements as targets typically seek to identify with the spokespersons in such messages. These ideas suggest that one way to optimize the advantage of expert credibility and consumer matching is to sufficiently increase common-man consumer expertise.

Consumers are likely to face numerous barriers when considering testing to know one's HIV status, the essential first step in Positive Living. The primary barrier to HIV testing is the fear of learning one's status (Valdiserri et al. 1999). High risk persons may be more worried about the result and tend to postpone HIV testing. Most HIV-infected persons remain undiagnosed until the onset of AIDS (Valdiserri et al. 1999). For consumers in developing nations such as Botswana, social stigma, lack of perceived HIV risk, and fear of having to change sexual practices also hinder testing (Weiser et al. 2006b). In developing countries with limited social security and employee rights protection, a sero-positive HIV- test tends to change a person's one's life radically. PLWHAs often lose most sources of emotional and economic support, namely their jobs, partners and friends.

Informed by this short review, this paper focuses on two broad research questions: (1) what propels consumers in developing nations to adopt bio-medical HIV-testing and how do they adapt to their sero-positive status?; and (2) what roles do early adopters who go public with their positive status take in the early diffusion of knowledge about living positively with HIV/AIDS? In Botswana, as in many other countries, very few PLWHAs talk about their status. Hence the testimonies of PLWHA informants who want to play a public role in diffusion of HIV/AIDS PHIs are very unique.

RESEARCH CONTEXT AND METHOD

Botswana, an economic and socially stable postcolonial African democracy, has one if the highest HIV/AIDS prevalence rates in the world (NACA 2009). Despite substantial government health campaigns since 1989 (Avert 2009), by the end of 2004, only 11.4% of Botswana's population of 1.7 million had ever tested to know their HIV status (NACA 2009). Estimates around this time placed Botswana's infection rate as 24% of adults (Stover et al., 2008). In 2002, Botswana was the first African country to provide free antiretroviral treatment countrywide. In 2004 Botswana introduced routine testing public health facilities (NACA 2009) to reduce the stigma linked to seeking testing at designated HIV/AIDSs testing centres.

Data sources: Data comprises multiple types and sources. Field notes and conducted interviews were conducted at the Global Health Conference and Gender Office in November 2005 in Gaborone, Botswana. This data collection was followed by extensive video-taping of interviews in March-April 2006 in Botswana of two participants from The 2005 Miss HIV Stigma Free Beauty Contest, six participants in 2006 Mr Positive Living Contests, five HIV/AIDS experts working in the public health sector, a national leader of a PLWHA support group, a Pentecostal pastor and a volunteer youth leader. Thereafter follow-up interviews via email, phone and face were conducted in the period 2006-2009. See Appendix 1 for Informant Details.

We shot video-tape of The Mr Positive Living Contest, related workshops and events. Subsequently we regularly collected data via email, telephone conversations and follow-up interviews over a period of three years. We collected over fifty related press articles. We transcribed videos produced by the BBC, Botswana TV and home videos made by informant's families. All interviews and footage were transcribed and described in full. Materials in Setswana[1] were translated into English by a native Setswana speaker. The two authors individually and together watched all the video footage and read the transcripts. Throughout this interactive process we structured and coded the data/quotes guided by theory. A research assistant from Botswana with over eight years experience in medicine, public health and HIV/AIDS in Botswana reviewed our findings for factual reliability and face validity.

FINDINGS

Informants' reports indicate that early adoption of HIV/AIDS Positive Living involves two adoption processes: 1) initial HIV/AIDS testing, and 2) adoption of The Greater Participation of People Living with HIV (GIPA) Principles. HIV/AIDS testing involves two sub-pathways: The normative and delayed testing pathways. Figure 2 presents these early adoption pathways as flow charts. We discuss these pathways below.

1. HIV/AIDS Testing Adoption Pathways

1.1 The Normative Testing Pathway (NTP): The normative testing pathway is the mode of early adoption to HIV testing typically underlying PHI design. This pathway assumes a proactive consumer who is educated about the disease and on his/her own accord seeks testing. Three of our informants fit the definition of NTP as they clearly recall exposure to the HIV/AIDS PHI messages in the media and/or at public health facilities, which makes them aware of their high risk lifestyles. Subsequently they attend health facilities and request testing. "I just took the initiative to do such, urged by what I regularly heard on the radio, TV…So considering my life style… recollecting all that I had done…is what made me plunge the courage to go testing. I wasn't exactly an innocent and careful boy, you know" (Otsile–smiles). Amogelang, also admitting to multiple sex partners, initially tests because she wants a baby. After testing negative, she has unprotected sex with males who reassure her of their negative status. Retesting reveals she has subsequently become infected with the virus. To outsiders, her behaviour might seem reckless, yet it is more understandable when one appreciates that in Botswana infertile individuals are socially invisible (Upton 2001). Joseph and Bontle do not openly admit to a sense of risk but test anyway: "We heard on the radio…When we went for testing, we did not suspect we were HIV+. We just went to know our status" (Bontle). Perhaps Joseph's period in the army, in which he spent many months away from his wife, and his discharge from the army for drunkenness, is an unspoken reason for testing between husband and wife.

1.2 The Delayed Testing Pathway (DTP): This pathway suggests that consumers are in heavy denial of their HIV/AIDS risk and hence resist testing, despite suffering chronic illnesses. They provide not any, or only vague reports of exposure to HIV/AIDS PHI messages. Arguably high risk consumers attend poorly to such messages because they do not regard themselves as part of high risk groups (Raghubir and Menon 1998; Valdiserri et al. 1999). Precious, a technical college educated ex-legal secretary, with a school teacher mother, admits her to promiscuous ways. She believed that she was immune from the disease; perceiving she was not from the social-class linked to the disease, that is, poor, rural, and uneducated. She elaborates that the family of her HIV+ boyfriend's upper middle-class family does not openly acknowledge his HIV+ status, despite the death of his previous girlfriend and their baby (a grandchild) from HIV/AIDS. After testing positive, Precious becomes very suspicious that not one of the upper level Batswana[2] officials that test publicly, tests positive. These accounts add weight to the idea that Batswana, like many people worldwide, regard HIV/AIDS as the disease of a heavily stigmatised other.

DTP informants acknowledge the contribution of excess alcohol to unsafe sex. Joseph, an ex-soldier, explains that drunken men don't take no for an answer. "When he is drunk, there is no control. If a girl says: "No, no I don't like it."… He will force the lady to make love, or to have sex with him. "After learning of their HIV+ status, some DTP informants experience prolonged self-stigma, anger, denial, and desire to escape, including contemplating or attempting suicide. Precious explains: "Then they told me 'Woman, you're HIV positive.' Then I just took off ….I had anger, denial, blame to an extent that I even started saying I had been bewitched by my family… I thought I was a black sheep in the family (Precious)." Precious suffers many serious illnesses before a doctor persuades her to test in 2000. Critical to her test decision, is the influence of an international PLWHA celebrity role model, and the knowledge that treatment is available. "Then they showed me these tablets–'Combivir' and said 'these days it's unlike before, when you are positive–you can be given antiretroviral medication to help you. So if they detect the virus in you, then you can take these tablets and you'll be just like Magic Johnson.' Because I used to be a sports lady playing table tennis …because I had heard about Magic Johnson, I wanted to be just like Magic Johnson! Then I said 'Okay. Well let me go have the test.' (Precious)." In 2000 only .02% of Batswana had ever tested (NACA 2009) and Precious's bravery cannot be overstated.

A comparison of the normative and delayed testing pathways points to aspects of theory. Testing by our informants suggests that they have a greater preparedness to take risks compared to the rest of the population. As stated earlier only 11.4% of Batswana had ever tested by December 2004 (NACA 2009), a time point at which all informants had tested. This finding validates the diffusion of innovation literature, which suggests that early adopters (typically first 16% of the population to adopt) are more risk-prone (Watts and Dodds 2007). However deviating from the diffusion of innovation literature, most of our informants do not have higher incomes, formal education or greater social participation compared to others. Rather they tend to come from poor backgrounds, have little formal education and confine themselves to village life.

Informants' behaviour suggests that the degree to which a person experiences feelings of self efficacy after learning of a HIV+

[1] Setswana is the national and majority language of Botswana.

[2] Batswana are members of a Bantu people living chiefly in Botswana and western South Africa.

FIGURE 2
EARLY ADOPTION PATHWAYS FOR POSITIVE LIVING

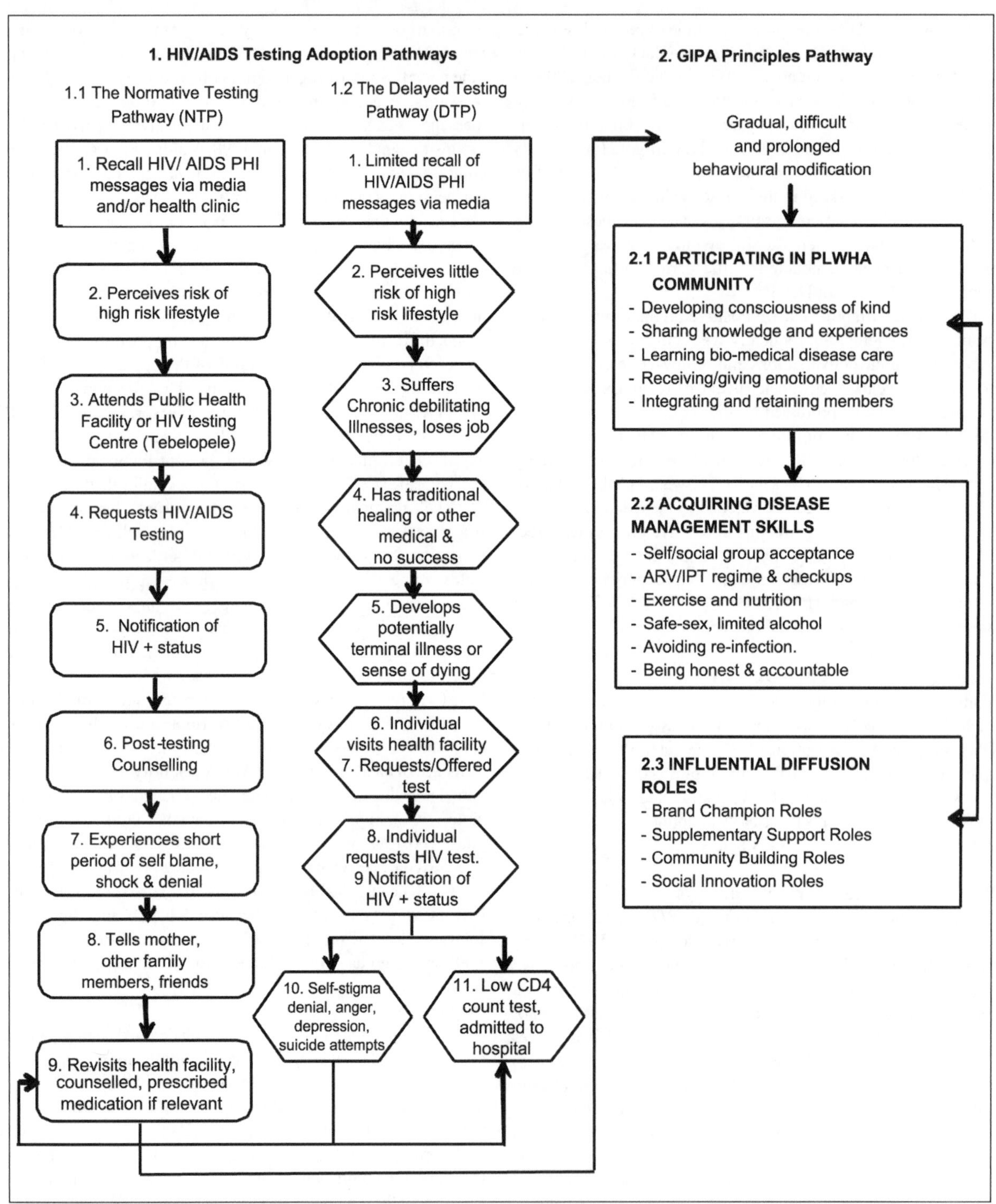

result influences their ability to manage the disease. Schwarzer and Renner (2000) find that a person with high self efficacy is likely to take positive steps to address HIV+ status, whereas a person with low self efficacy is likely to experience feelings of hopelessness. Contrasting Paul and Precious's cases illustrates this point. Paul refuses to stigmatize himself and takes a matter of fact attitude towards his medication. "I sat down, and re-evaluated myself. And then came up with a thought of say 'What is this?' 'This is just a condition I acquired'. And I couldn't do anything because I never made an application to it…I have to accept. Because I don't want to die–I don't want to kill myself… So I must accept…I'm taking the ARVs, it's more like food…you are eating food in order to live...it doesn't bother me (Paul)."

At the other extreme are Precious's mixed reactions. After testing positive, Precious falls into despair, despite strong family support. She does not take her ARVs regularly and becomes resistant to the drugs. She attempts suicide. Upon recovering, she resolves no longer to play the AIDS victim. She strictly adheres to a drug of last resort. She becomes an active member of the PLWHA community and goes onto become a celebrity spokes model for positive living. Despite her efforts, Precious develops a severe form of uterine cancer and receives radiation therapy to eliminate the tumour. So weakened is her health by the radiation, that she develops a deadly strain tuberculosis during a trip to a HIV/AIDS conference in Canada. After six months hospitalisation, she is flown home. Tragically Precious dies a few days later, six years after testing positive. Precious's plight underscores the importance of testing to know one's status. Drug therapies don't work so well for those who have been infected for a long time (Brashers, Neidig, Cardillo, Dobbs, Russell and Hass 1999).

Implicit to the normative and delayed testing pathways are very different assumptions about the tactics that induce early adoption of HIV testing. The normative testing pathway assumes that few factors impede the motivation, opportunity and ability to test (Rothschild 1999). Consumers are motivated to test by self interest, because free life-saving ARVs are available (NACA 2009). Consumers have the opportunity to test because testing sites are conveniently located in Botswana (Steen et al. 2007). Finally, partners or family do not reduce consumer's ability to test through social disapproval. The delayed testing pathway wrongly assumes that education is enough to motivate testing and hence fails. Unless consumers truly believe that effective and manageable treatment is available and that they are at risk, the extreme stigma associated with a deadly contagious sexually transmitted disease such as HIV/AIDS will largely prevent testing.

2. Adopting Greater Participation of PLWHAs' (GIPA) Pathway

Informants report that adopting GIPA principles is a gradual, difficult and prolonged process. "It is not an overnight thing you can achieve" (Paul). Essential to this adoption process is participation in the PLWHA community, by initially becoming a member of a local support group.

2.1 Participating in PLWHA Community. All informants report substantial benefits from attending local support groups. First and foremost, meeting regularly with other PLWHAs and sharing stories, makes them feel less isolated, less ashamed and better able to manage their disease. "After meeting with the leader of the support group, she... told me that she herself is HIV positive, that she has been living positively with HIV for many years. That she is public and open about her positive living with HIV... Therefore, that encouraged me to be open and tell my friends about my HIV positive status (Otsile)." These sentiments contrast markedly with Otsile's previous stigmatisation of PLWHAS. "Before I knew my status, I didn't want anything to do with an individual living with HIV...I hated them (Otsile)." For Precious, meeting with other PLWHAs changes her life. "That was a turning point...I saw an advert written 'Coping Centre for People Living with HIV and AIDS-COCEPWA', saying they were looking for a secretary–someone living with the virus...but I thought 'let me just go to COCEPWA and hear–maybe I will have more information about HIV/AIDS'." At COCEPWA Precious learns about the HIV virus and AIDS and trains in counselling and public speaking. She goes public about living with HIV. Her opening line in public settings becomes "My name is Precious and I am a lady living with HIV/AIDS." Such a bold statement is very unique for a PLWHA anywhere, and should be considered a peak moment for expressed consumer voice in a developing nation.

Informants realise that going public about their sero-positive status contributes to building a consciousness of kind amongst PLWHAs in Botswana. "If I become Mr Positive Living, HIV Positive Living...I want to see the people taking action identifying themselves with me-to create or establish a common front or the onslaught of this virus (Paul)." They also realise that PLWHA community building is a means of gaining empowerment and achieving better treatment from civil society and the government. "The leaders think that as PLWHAS... we are powerless and worthless. So there is no one advocating for us, (so we do) (Precious)."

2.2 Acquiring Disease Management Skills. Being accepted by others as well as self is important for PLWHAS. Public disclosure reduces the high stress of living secretly with the disease that can erode the immune system (Holt, Court, Verdhara, Nott, Homes and Snow 1998). Some asymptomatic informants report that achieving social acceptance within their immediate social groups is difficult. People don't believe they are infected. "After I went public about my status, some people accused me of lying... I mean even when I show them my hospital records; some of them disregard them and insist on wanting to have unprotected sex" (Amogelang). PLWHAs need to have safe sex if they wish to reduce HIV infection rates. They also need to publicly show that they are being socially responsible otherwise they will be further stigmatised. Precious states: "It's my virus. I do not share it with no one." PLWHAs should also seek to avoid re-infection; unprotected sex can result in cumulative re-infection as well as infection by new strains of HIV/AIDS. PLWHA couples can find conversion to safe sex difficult. "It was hard for us to change our behaviour. Especially using condoms...In the beginning I was worried she is falling in love with someone but in the end I heard what the counsellors said (Joseph)." In strongly patriarchal societies, such as Botswana, condom adherence may be especially difficult. A widespread saying in Botswana, derides use of male condoms: "A sweet is never eaten with the wrapper-you have to uncover the sweet and then it becomes–sweet" (Helle-Valle 1999). Informants often emphasised the importance of eating nutritious meals to stave off disease progression. However observation suggests that on a daily basis PLWHA informants often had little idea of where their next meal would be coming from.

2.3 Influential Diffusion Roles. An emic account of the data suggests that early adopters who are public spokes models can adopt at least twelve roles that potentially influence adoption of Positive Living. The capacity of informants to enact such roles is a function of i) individual commitment and goals and ii) role related competencies. The latter are in part developed through participation in support group workshops in which PLWHAS are trained in lay counselling, public speaking, speaking to journalists and advocating change to politicians. We present details of these roles, in the context of four broad categories likely to associate with the diffusion of GIPA: 1) Brand Champion Roles, 2) Supplementary Service Roles, 3) Community Building Roles and 4) Social Innovation Roles.

1. Brand Champion Roles: These roles associate with being the first people to promote positive living and provide "social proof" that the disease exists through public disclosure.

(i) Pioneers: are amongst the very first people to test and to publicly admit nationally their HIV+ status. Pioneers need to be courageous, determined and visionary. As Donald explains: "Discrimination and isolation was very rife at the time... [A study in Kasane, Botswana] revealed that the majority of people said all people living with HIV/AIDS should be castrated, ostracised and quarantined. It became even more scary. The AIDS/STD Unit of Ministry of Health and Red Cross continued to give me all the necessary support and counselling...24th of November, 1993 I declared my status in public through the radio and television" (Donald).

(ii) Local Initiators: are the first to admit within a social group to having tested HIV+. Local initiators need to be open, autonomous and qualified risk-takers. Despite the fear of stigma, they share their experiences with family and friends, admitting that the burden of their sero-positive status is too hard to bear alone. They are often very aware that the news of their positive status will spread to other locals. "I knew that telling one individual will automatically lead to a chain reaction because they would not be able to keep it between us (Otsile)."

(iii) Public Spokes Models: act as role models and public speakers about effectively living with HIV/AIDS for PLWHAS nationally. Public spokes-models need to be accountable, high self-monitors, articulate and be well versed in effective disease management. "My transformation…I used to change partners...I drank every day and big time. So by the time I went public with my status I was like I have to practice what I preach… I can't just go to a bar and sit down with people drinking…because maybe I will get tempted and start drinking again. And what will people start thinking of me (Precious)." Public spokes-models are typically competitors from The Miss HIV Stigma Free or Mr Positive Living contests.

2. Supplementary Service Roles: These roles complement the inadequate government services needed to maintain widespread PLWHA adherence to Positive Living. Failure to achieve this goal is loaded with huge social and political significance. "The need for treatment outstrips our ability to deliver it. There is a lot of pressure on us, because if we fail people will say: 'Botswana had everything going for it and it failed, so why should we help anyone in Africa?' (Dr Moffat, superintendent Princess Marina clinic)"(Avert 2009).

(iv) Lay Counsellors: regularly encourage others within their social networks to test and give homespun advice about disease and lifestyle management. Lay counsellors need to be friendly, patient, giving and available to others. "You can't go to the men and say he must go ….and check their status. No. First of all you must be friendly to a person. Start to be friendly to a person be patient. Come to a person. Visit a person. If he needs your help, then help him. Until you see that your friendship gets close. That's the time you can start to [talk to him] (Joseph)."

(v) Volunteer Carers: look after PLWHAS who are suffering from the chronic illnesses that typify HIV, often because they cannot be cared for by the public health system. Volunteer carers need to be in good health, compassionate and realise that their behaviour likely fortify norms of reciprocity amongst PLWHAs. "I go there–changing their nappies, feeding them. Because I know how it is living with HIV and AIDS. I have experience of it. Maybe one day it will be me. And somebody else will come and help me. So that's what I am doing at the moment" (Precious).

(vi) Buddies: are experienced with ARVs and acts as guides to PLWHAs beginning the drug regime. Buddies need to be experienced and reliable. "Ah, a buddy operation is whereby you give the sick I would say…love, care, and support...to get for the medication or the doctor…medical services, health services...because when you get onto the services you get confused a bit then. Which are the better ones [What are the challenges to working on the buddy program?]... First of all you give yourself time to remind, to always frequent, visit the client. To check how on well he or she is keeping up…any side effects, and nutrition" (Paul).

3. Community Building Roles: These roles reflect the need to access the financial, personnel, and socio-political resources needed to consolidate and grow the PLWHA community nationally/internationally.

(vii) Support Group Members: As earlier discussed, support group members are essential to sharing information about disease management, providing emotional support and completing projects intended to enhance government PHIs. Support group members need to sharing, co-operative and committed to support group goals.

(viii) PLWHA Support Group Leaders: ensure that local support group members are motivated to complete group projects. Support group leaders need to be consumer oriented, accountable, resourceful, respected and have organisational ability. "It's good to prioritise , even if you are busy at home with your own projects…be involved and available, for patients and people in your support group. As a chairperson, you need to lead by example, be disciplined with whatever financial support of funding you get not to abuse it. Serve the purpose of... the agreed agenda or people will lose hope, alienate and abandon the project (Joseph)."

(ix) National PLWHA Community Leaders: inspire broader society to acceptance PLWHAS by acting as a community spokesperson and advocate. They forge useful connections between PLWHAs and non-PWHAS leaders. They need to be articulate, confident, open to change and aware of the general populations attitudes to PLWHAS. Kagiso warns: "They know to be careful not to bite the hand that feeds them!"

4. Social Innovation Roles: These roles underpin the modification or creation of HIV/AIDS PHIs by PLWHAS and hence tend to reflect an improved and much needed consumer orientation.

(x) Social Entrepreneurs: initiate support groups or other community organisations likely to enhance PLWHAS physical, emotional and material wellbeing. Social entrepreneurs need to be innovative, highly passionate, determined and connected. Donald, as indicated is a pioneer. He now heads up a major national PLWHA support group founded by him. He is also a frequent critic of the Botswana governments' inadequate support of PLWHAs. Another example is Precious's care and counselling centre for HIV affected youth in her home village, set up posthumously by her family according to her wishes.

(xi) Advocates: fight for better treatment of infected and affected individuals of HIV/AIDS who are neglected by the government or NGOS. Advocates need to be exceedingly resourceful, independent, passionate and long term oriented. "These kids really need help…I'm advocating for them because there's no one to advocate for them. I'm a person living with HIV and AIDS, I'm not working but I'm able. How 'bout these kids? They don't have anything… It's only from my heart…It's a long process…The government I can say…are not giving us support" (Precious).

(xii) The Politician: wants the power to create change. Not one informant was a politician but at least two of them aspired to the position: "You see I'm more politically inclined really. My challenge is to see visible changes in our country, changes for the better….I want everyone employed (Amogelang)."

Summary: An overview of the twelve roles suggests two underlying dimensions: 1) The Capacity for Positive Deviance and 2) The Capacity for Social Outreach. The former dimension associates with the capacity of everyday people to create beneficial solutions for themselves to social, economic and/or health problems that differ from the mainstream (Sternin et al; 1998). The latter dimension includes social domains ranging from self/family/social group, to local and national PLWHA community to broader society, nationally and internationally

DISCUSSION AND CONCLUSIONS

This study is an early attempt to unpack the different early adopter roles to which consumers adapt in the extremely challenging context of HIV/AIDS in a developing nation. More research on this topic is needed to further theorize the roles PLWHAs can play in HIV/AIDS PHIs and their effectiveness. However our informants are living proof that PLWHAs can have strong motivation and resources to play public roles in disseminating HIV/AIDS message, educating other PLWHAs, and in modifying and expanding existing HIV/AIDS PHIs. They have negotiated and made their own way from private despair to a position where they can help others. They are the "moderately influential" early adopters who can propagate the diffusion process because they give the disease a face with which other PLWHAs easily can identify (Watts and Dodds 2007). However, PLWHAs are heavily stigmatized and are hence are a deviant minority. They lack power, status, and often competence to instigate validation processes and to exert influence. They badly need more public support, especially from powerful politicians who support the views and activities of PLWHA spokespersons.

REFERENCES

Avert (2009), *HIV & AIDS in Botswana*, last updated 23/2.2009.

Brashers, D.E., J.L. Neidig, L.W. Cardillo, L.K. Dobbs, J.A. Russell and S.M. Hass (1999), "In an important way I did die: uncertainty and revival in persons living with HIV or AIDS," *AIDS Care*, 11, 2, 201-219.

Deroïan, Frédéric (2002), "Formation of social networks and diffusion of innovations," *Research Policy*, 31, 5, July, 835-846.

Durantini Marta R., Dolores Albarracin, Amy L. Mitchell, Allison N. Earl and Jeffrey C. Gillette (2006), "Conceptualising the Influence of Social Agents on Behaviour Change: A Meta-Analysis of the effectiveness of HIV-Prevention Interventionists for Different Groups," *Psychological Bulletin*, 132, 2, 212-248.

Goldberg, Marvin E. (1995), "Social Marketing: Are We Fiddling While Rome Burns," *Journal of Consumer Psychology*, 4, 4, 347-370.

Helle-Valle, Jo (1999), "Sexual Mores and Promiscuity in Botswana," *Ethnos*, 64, 3, 372-96.

Holt, R, P. Court, K.Verdhara, K.H. Nott, J. Homes and M.H. Snow (1998), "The role of disclosure in coming to terms with HIV infection," *AIDS Care*, 10, 49-60.

Liddell, Christine, Louise Barrett, and Moya Bydawell (2005), "Indigenous Representations of Illness and AIDS in Sub-Saharan Africa," *Social Science & Medicine*, 60, 691-700.

Moscovici, Serge (1980), "Toward a Theory of Conversion Behavior," *Advances in Experimental Social Psychology*, 13, 209-37.

NACA (2009), "October to December 2008 Quarterly Report," Botswana

Public Opinion Formation," *Journal of Consumer Research*, 34 (Dec), 441-458.

Raghubir, Priya and Geeta Menon (1998), "AIDS and Me, Never the Twain Shall Meet: The Effects on Information Accessibility on Judgments of Risk and Advertising Effectiveness," *Journal of Consumer Research*, 25 (June), 52-62.

Rogers, Everett (2003), *Diffusion of Innovations*, 5th ed., New York, Free Press.

Rossiter, John and Stephen Bellman (2005), *Marketing Communications: Theory and Applications*, Pearson: Prentice-Hall.

Rothschild, Michael L. (1999), "Carrots, Sticks, and promises: A Conceptual Framework for the Management of Public Health and Social Issue Behaviors," *Journal of Marketing*, 63, Oct, 24-37.

SADC?" Development Update, Dec, 5, 3, 225-244.

Schwarzer, Ralf and Britta Renner (2000), "Social-cognitive predictors of health behavior: action self efficacy and coping self-efficacy," *Health Psychology*, September, 19, 5, 487-95.

Steen, Tore W., Khumo Seipone, Florindo de la Hoz Gomez, Marina G. Anderson, Marble Kejelepula, Koona Keapoletswe, and Howard J. Moffat (2007), " Two and a half year of Routine Testing in Botswana," *Journal of Acquired Immune Deficiency Syndromes*, 44, 4, April, 484-88.

Sternin, Monique, Jerry Sternin David Marsh (1998), "Designing a Community-Based …the Positive Deviance Approach," positivedeviance.org

Stover, John, Boga Fidzani, Batho Chris Molomo, Themba Moeti and Godfrey Musuka (2008), "Estimated HIV Trends and Effects in Botswana,"" *PLoS ONE*, November, 3, 11, 1-4

Swidler, Ann (2006), "Syncretism and subversion in AIDS governance: how locals cope with global demands," *International affairs*, 82, 2, 269-284.

Upton, Ruth (2001) 'Infertility Makes You Invisible': Gender, Health and the Negotiation of Fertility in Northern Botswana," *Journal of Southern African Studies*, 27, 2, 349-362.

Valdiserri, Ronald O, David R. Holtgrave, and Gary R.West (1999), "Promoting Early HIV Diagnosis and Entry into Care," *AIDS*, 3: 2317-30.

Watts, Duncan J. and Peter Sheridan Dodds (2007), "Influentials, Networks, and

Weiser et al (2003)[3] "Barriers to Antiretroviral Adherence for Patients Living with HIV Infection and AIDS in Botswana," *JAIDS*, 34, 281-88.

Weiser et al (2006),[4] "Routine HIV Testing in Botswana: A Population-Based Study on Attitudes, Practices, and Human Rights Concerns," *PLoS*, 3, 7 (July), 1013-10-22.

---

[3]Over 8 authors so due to space restrictions not stated.

[4]Over 8 authors so due to space restrictions not stated.

APPENDIX

Informant Details (all names are pseudonyms)

Informant Demographic Details	Year of diagnosis	Disease orientation
PLWHAS		
Amogelang • 29 years old, female, single • Unemployed • Runner-up Miss HIV Stigma Free Beauty Pageant • Aspiring politician	• 2003 • Early presenter as no illness apparent	• Currently on ARVs • Tested negative 1996, then tried to become pregnant through unprotected sex with males who stated they were HIV negative. • 2005-one of less than 20 people to go public with HIV+ status
Andrew • In 30' s, male, defacto relationship with 3 children • Unemployed (former building contractor)	• 2004 • Late presenter (very sick at diagnosis)	• Currently on ARVs • Sexually active, uses condoms • 2006-went public nationally.
Bontle • 30 years old, female, Wife of Joseph, 2 children, younger child HIV+ • Housewife	• 2004 • Early presenter as no illness apparent	• Currently on ARVs • Sexually active, uses condoms • 2006-went public in local community
Donald • 56 years old, male, married at least twice, three children and two grandchildren • Founder/Director National PLWHA Support Group – membership of 4000 (former truck driver and farmer)	• 1993 • Late presenter (very sick at diagnosis)	• Currently on ARVs • Sexually active, uses condoms • First person in Botswana to go public with HIV+ status.
Joseph 37 years old, male, Married with 2 children, younger child HIV+ Commercial Artist (former soldier)	• 2004 • Early presenter as no illness apparent	• Currently on ARVs • Sexually active, uses condoms 2006-went public nationally
Otsile 27 years old, male, single, lives with parents, at least one child Un-employed, recreational football player in HIV+ team and bodybuilder.	• 2004 • Early presenter as no illness apparent	Not on ARVs but on IPT (TB prevention medication) Not sexually active 2006 went public nationally
Paul 40 years old, male, single, 6 children Volunteer (Local home-based-care society) and Buddy	• 2004 Late presenter, very sick at diagnosis	Currently on ARVs Not sexually active 2006 went public nationally
Precious • 37 years old, female, single, • Part-time receptionist, volunteer advocate, spokesperson, public role model (former legal secretary) • Winner Miss HIV Stigma Free Beauty Pageant	• 2000 • Late presenter, very sick at diagnosis	• Currently on last ARV combination possible. • Not sexually active • 2005-one of less than 20 people to go public with HIV+ status.
Robert • 37 years old, male, has a girlfriend. • Volunteer carer, former insurance consultant/ driving school instructor, HIV/AIDS Volunteer • Runner Up Mr Positive Living	• 2002 • Late presenter (very sick at diagnosis)	• Currently on ARVs • Sexually active • 2006 went public nationally
Non PLWHA Consumers		
Ruth	• Volunteer community organiser, local rural youth community organisation	
Morapedi	• Pastor, Penta-costal Holiness Church.	
Experts		
Bolokang	• Programme assistant, National Coordinating Body, Botswana	
Brian	• Project manager, National PLWHA Support Group, Botswana	
Kagiso	• Masters Student of Public Health in a Western Nation, 8 yrs experience studying/working on HIV/AIDS in Botswana	
Itumeleng	• Consultant to Ministry of Health, Botswana	
Kefilwe	• Officer, Gender Affairs, Botswana	

Does a Marketer's Responsibility for a Surcharge Moderate Price Partitioning Effects?

Silke Bambauer-Sachse, University of Fribourg, Switzerland
Sabrina Mangold, University of Fribourg, Switzerland

ABSTRACT

In this paper we build on an established model that contains basic effects of price partitioning and introduce a new variable which has not been considered in previous studies yet. Based on the so-developed theoretical framework, we conduct a new empirical study. The results of our empirical study show that the marketer's responsibility for a surcharge on the base price plays an important role in the context of effects of partitioned versus total prices.

INTRODUCTION

Some products and services are divided into several (often two) components which are charged single prices but can only be bought in combination (Bertini and Wathieu 2005; Lee and Han 2002). An examples is a fitness club membership and the joining fee. Morwitz, Greenleaf, and Johnson (1998) call this strategy partitioned pricing and refer to the larger price component as the base price and to the smaller component as the surcharge. Surcharges are most often monetary surcharges, but in some cases the surcharge is a percentage of the base price.

Although some authors dealt with basic effects of price partitioning and found either positive (Chakravarti et al. 2002; Morwitz et al. 1998; Xia and Monroe 2004) or negative effects (Bambauer-Sachse and Gierl 2008; Gierl and Bambauer-Sachse 2007; Lee and Han 2002), the body of research on conditions under which price partitioning is rather advantageous or disadvantageous is limited. Therefore, we build on an established model that contains basic effects of price partitioning and introduce and examine a new variable that might be relevant in the context of price partitioning effects but that has not been considered in previous studies. The variable we look at in this paper is the marketer's responsibility for the surcharge. Examples from marketing practice show that in some cases in which partitioned prices are used, the marketer is responsible for a surcharge on a base price. For example, charging a fee for the parking lot in addition to the price for a hotel room is at the marketer's own discretion. However, there are other cases in which the marketer is not responsible for the surcharge. For example, an airline has to charge an airport tax in addition to the price of the airline ticket itself or hotel managers have to charge a visitor tax in addition to the room price.

As attribution theory suggests that people think about the reasons other people have for a certain behavior (Kelley and Michela 1980), we think that it could be interesting to examine whether this reasoning also applies to the context of price partitioning effects and whether effects of partitioned versus total prices differ depending on the marketer's responsibility for a surcharge on a base price.

By deriving possible effects of a new moderator variable from existing theory and testing the assumed effects in an empirical study, which means looking in detail at conditions under which price partioning effects might differ, our paper extends the existing body of research. Therefore, the approach presented here offers new insights in the mechanisms that underlie the effects of partitioned versus total prices.

In addition to addressing researchers, our paper addresses marketers who need to know under which conditions it might be beneficial to use partitioned prices instead of total prices. By explaining under which conditions price partitioning is rather advantageous or rather disadvantageous, our research enables marketers to plan their pricing strategies more carefully when deciding whether to indicate total or partitioned prices.

THEORETICAL AND EMPIRICAL BACKGROUND

Previous Research on Effects of Price Partitioning

In a first step, we shortly summarize major findings of previous studies on price partitioning effects. Morwitz et al. (1998) found that price partitioning increases consumer demand compared to all-inclusive prices. Lee and Han (2002) report from their findings that using partitioned prices can cause negative consumer reactions, which leads to a negative change of brand attitude. Chakravarti et al. (2002) found that a product with a partitioned price for its components was evaluated more favorably and chosen more frequently than the same product with a total price. Xia and Monroe (2004) report that price partitioning has positive effects on consumers' price satisfaction and their purchase intentions. Burman and Biswas (2007) found support for their assumption that price presentation (partitioned price vs. total price) only has effects on consumers with a high need for cognition. Their findings show that these consumers interpret partitioned prices as comparatively fair prices. Sheng, Bao, and Pan (2007) derive from their results that price partitioning (using total prices) is more advantageous with regard to purchase intention if the surcharge is only a small (a comparatively large) fraction of the base price. Moreover, they found that in the case of an unfair (fair) surcharge, consumers have lower (higher) purchase intentions when exposed to partitioned prices than when exposed to total prices. A study conducted by Carlson and Weathers (2008) shows that partitioning prices into a large number of price components negatively affects perceived fairness and purchase intentions when the total price is not presented. Clark and Ward (2008) found in their study on price partitioning effects in online auctions where bidders had to pay their bid plus shipping costs that many bidders appear to be subject to an anchoring and adjustment bias or even to ignore the shipping costs completely. Thus, their findings suggest a positive effect of price partitioning. In a recent study, Hamilton and Srivastava (2008) focused on effects of different partitions of the same total price. The results of their four studies show that consumers prefer partitions in which they pay a lower amount for the low-perceived benefit component and a higher amount for the high-perceived benefit component. Bertini and Wathieu (2008) conducted four studies to examine attention arousal through price partitioning and found that total prices distract consumers from a thorough evaluation of the offer while partitioned prices draw consumers' attention to secondary product attributes.

Two studies that are most appropriate to build the basis of our new empirical study are the studies conducted by Bambauer-Sachse and Gierl (2008) and Gierl and Bambauer-Sachse (2007). In one of their papers, they developed and tested a basic model that is able to reflect both positive and negative effects of price partitioning (vs. using total prices) on product evaluation. In a consecutive study, they extended this model by including the cognitive effort spent on processing price information as a moderator variable. The major finding of this study was that using partitioned prices can only be recommended if consumers spend little cognitive effort in the situation of processing price information and if low surcharges are used. We will integrate the moderator variable we are interested in here in the basic model presented in the two studies of Bambauer-Sachse and Gierl (2008) and Gierl and Bambauer-Sachse (2007) because this model is the only model that can be found in the existing literature that explicitly captures both positive and negative effects of price partitioning.

In the next section we will shortly summarize the theoretical background that led to the model that we will use as a theoretical basis of our new study.

Theoretical Background of Basic Price Partitioning Effects

In the context of explaining price partitioning effects, three variables proved to be relevant mediators in the relation between price presentation (partitioned prices vs. total price) and product evaluation (Bambauer-Sachse and Gierl 2008; Gierl and Bambauer-Sachse 2007). These variables are perceived price attractiveness, clarity versus complexity of the price structure (Xia and Monroe 2004) and consumers' feeling of being manipulated by the marketer.

Price Attractiveness. The concept of price attractiveness has often been analyzed in studies on pricing effects (Danziger and Segev 2006; Janiszewski and Lichtenstein 1999) and refers to the idea that consumers have beliefs about normal prices for certain product categories and that they judge prices on this basis. Xia and Monroe (2004) referred to a similar concept as "satisfaction with the price". Lichtenstein, Bloch, and Black (1988) used the term "price acceptance" for a similar phenomenon. Some theoretical approaches that are appropriate to explain the effect of price partitioning on perceived price attractiveness let assume a positive effect whereas others suggest a negative effect. As previous studies found this effect to be predominantly positive (Bambauer-Sachse and Gierl 2008; Gierl and Bambauer-Sachse 2007), we only summarize theoretical approaches that provide arguments for a positive effect.

When being faced with partitioned prices consumers can either ignore the surcharge which is the smaller price component (Morwitz et al. 1998) or try to calculate the total price. In the first case, perceived price attractiveness is believed to be comparatively high because one price component is not at all processed. In the second case, most of the consumers are believed to apply simplifying heuristics (Tversky and Kahneman 1974) to estimate the total price because they might find it too difficult to exactly calculate the total price (Biswas and Burton 1993). One such heuristic that lets assume positive effects on perceived price attractiveness is the so-called anchoring and adjustment heuristic (Block and Harper 1991; Carlson and Weathers 2008; Chapman and Johnson 1994; Davis, Hoch, and Ragsdale 1986; Jacowitz and Kahneman 1995; Northcraft and Neale 1987). Applying the anchoring and adjustment argument to the processing of partitioned prices leads to the assumption that consumers anchor on the base price, the larger price component. Estimating the total price by starting from this anchor is likely to lead to an estimate that is biased toward the base price (Morwitz et al. 1998). Consequently, price attractiveness is believed to be comparatively high.

Consumers' Feeling of Being Manipulated by the Marketer. The fact that consumers might feel manipulated by the marketer can be based on the following arguments. Research on consumer persuasion knowledge provides the notion that consumers develop beliefs about the objectives marketers pursue with certain persuasion strategies (Friestad and Wright 1994; Hardesty, Bearden, and Carlson 2007). Research on pricing strategies has shown that consumers sometimes speculate on the marketer's motives for applying certain strategies (Hamilton and Koukova 2008; Homburg, Hoyer, and Koschate 2005). This phenomenon occurs when prices are unusual, for example, in the case of an unexpected price increase (Campbell 1995; Maxwell 1995). As price partitioning might come across unexpectedly and surprisingly in some situations, consumers might speculate on the marketer's motives for using this pricing technique. Thus, a plausible explanation from the consumer point of view might be that the marketer tries to mask a possibly excessive total price and to mislead the consumer by indicating a partitioned price, which serves to increase his profit. When being faced with partitioned prices consumers are believed to ascribe a higher manipulative intent to the marketer than when being faced with total prices because they might assume that the marketer tries to mislead them by using several price components. This assumption is likely to lead to a comparatively unfavorable product evaluation.

Perceived Complexity of the Price Structure. The concept of perceived complexity of the price structure mirrors the fact that consumers have more or less difficulties in determining the correct total price when being faced with a partitioned price. As consumers expect marketers to use transparent prices, they might be dissatisfied when the price structure is more complex (less transparent) than they have expected (Lee and Han 2002). Presumably the price structure of a partitioned price is more complex than the one of a total price because in the first case there are at least two components which have to be processed. The dissatisfaction resulting from the unexpectedly high complexity is believed to be transferred to the product and thus to lead to a negative attitude toward the product.

In the next section we present theoretical arguments that can be applied to explain effects of the marketer's responsibility for the surcharge.

Theoretical Background of Effects of the Marketer's Responsibility

In this section, we argue that the marketer's responsibility for a surcharge has a moderating effect on the three basic effects of price partitioning versus using total prices discussed above.

Before presenting a theoretical background of effects of the marketer's responsibility, we have to differentiate the concept of responsibility considered here from another concept which might appear as a similar concept but which is different in fact. Sheng et al. (2007) examined effects of perceived fairness in the context of consumers' processing of partitioned prices. This latter concept is broader than the marketer's responsibility because the surcharge can be perceived as being unfair for other reasons than for the reason that the marketer is responsible for this surcharge.

In order to explain the role of the marketer's responsibility for the surcharge in the context of price partitioning effects, we draw on attribution theory which has already been applied to other contexts where people try to explain the behavior of other people they are in any relationship with. Such contexts were for example employees who tried to understand the rationale behind certain management practices of their employer (Nishii, Lepak, and Schneider 2008), consumers' coping strategies with regard to disasters related to companies they were customers of (Jorgensen 1994), customers' reactions to negative publicity for a company (Dean 2004; Griffin, Babin, and Attaway 1991), consumers' responses to negative word of mouth communication (Laczniak, DeCarlo, and Ramaswami 2001), and consumers' reactions to product failure (Folkes 1984).

Attribution theory in general deals with causal principles that people use to explain other people's behavior. According to this theoretical approach, people have a basic need to predict and control the environment. Understanding the causes of behaviors or events enables them to do so (Heider 1958). Moreover, people's interpretations of causes of behavior have effects on their attitudes and their own behavior (Kelley and Michela 1980). Furthermore,

FIGURE 1
RESEARCH MODEL

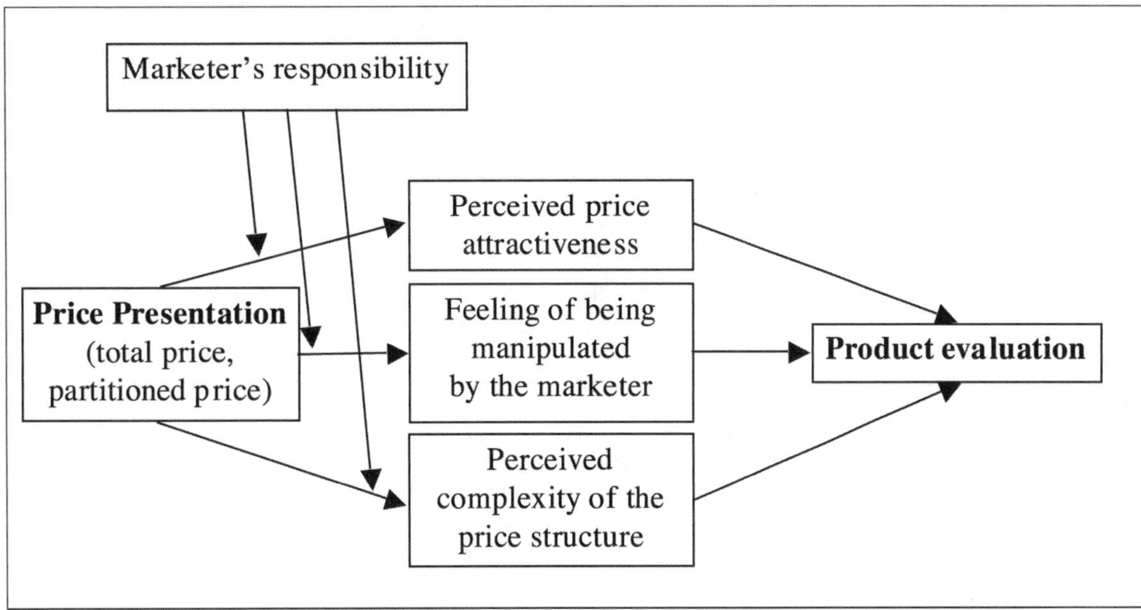

when people try to find reasons for a certain behavior of other people, they think about whether the locus of causality is internal (dispositional) or external (environmental) to the person of interest (Kelley and Michela 1980). Internal attributions are more strongly related with cognitions, feelings, and behavior (Weiner et al. 1972) than external attributions which reveal less about the underlying motivation of the behavior of the person of interest (Jones, Davis, and Gergen 1961; Jones and McGillis 1976; Kelley and Michela 1980). Following these arguments, we assume that consumers try to elaborate whether the marketer is responsible for charging a surcharge on a base price. Moreover, attribution research provides the notion that the more a person judges another person to be responsible for his or her behavior, the stronger is the effect of this behavior from the first person's point of view (Weiner 1979). Thus, transferred to the case considered here, we argue that if consumers have the impression that the marketer is responsible for charging the surcharge, the effect of charging the surcharge is comparatively strong. Combining this assumption with the notion that price partitioning (vs. using total prices) has positive effects on price attractiveness leads to our first hypothesis:

H1: If the marketer is responsible (not responsible) for the surcharge, price attractiveness is higher in the total price (partitioned price) condition.

Furthermore, attribution literature provides the argument that frustrating actions that are internally attributed have even more intensive and more negative effects (Kelley and Michela 1980) than externally attributed actions. Transferred to the case considered here, we argue that the fact of being confronted with such a negative add-on as a surcharge on a base price is somehow frustrating to consumers. Consequently, we argue that consumers' belief that a marketer is responsible for the surcharge has comparatively negative effects and thus worsens negative effects of using partitioned prices. Based on these arguments, we assume with respect to the two mediator variables that mirror negative effects of price partitioning:

H2a: The feeling of being manipulated by the marketer is stronger in the case of partitioned than in the case of total prices.

H2b: In the partitioned price condition, the feeling of being manipulated is even stronger if the marketer is responsible for the surcharge.

H3a: Perceived complexity of the price structure is stronger in the case of partitioned than in the case of total prices.

H3b: In the partitioned price condition, perceived complexity of the price structure is even higher if the marketer is responsible for the surcharge.

The theoretical considerations presented above lead to the research model shown in Figure 1.

Research Model

In order to analyze moderator effects of the marketer's responsibility for the surcharge in the context of price partitioning effects, we integrate the new variable into the basic model of price partitioning effects described by Bambauer-Sachse and Gierl (2008). The resulting model is shown in Figure 1.

EMPIRICAL STUDY

Experimental Design

In our empirical study we used partitioned prices that consisted of two components and total prices. We chose test stimuli that were familiar to the respondents. Furthermore, the examples were chosen in compliance with the condition that both total and partitioned prices were realistic for these products. We only used a low monetary surcharge because high and percentage surcharges have been shown to have negative effects in previous studies (Bambauer-Sachse and Gierl 2008; Gierl and Bambauer-Sachse 2007; Sheng et al. 2007). The selected surcharge amount was 3.5 percent of the base price. With regard to many real surcharges in marketing practice, this amount is a realistic value. In addition, this amount falls into the range of low surcharges proposed by Sheng et al.

TABLE 1
Experimental Design

Product example (base price)	Total price condition	Partitioned price condition
City hotel (room price per night)	€ 60	€ 58 + € 2
Airline ticket (flight price)	€ 90	€ 87 + € 3

TABLE 2
Manipulation Check

	Respondents' perception of marketer's responsibility*					
Manipulated responsibility	Pooled data (n=320)		Hotel data (n=160)		Airline data (n=160)	
Marketer is not responsible	2.49	t=29.83	2.53	t=21.49	2.45	t=20.70
Marketer is responsible	5.69	(p<.001)	5.80	(p<.001)	5.59	(p<.001)

*measured on a 7-point rating scale ranging from 1=rather not responsible to 7=rather responsible

(2007). We chose two examples for each experimental condition (city hotel, airline ticket). Table 1 gives an overview of the chosen product examples and their prices. The total product prices are equal across conditions.

Responsibility was manipulated by selecting different types of surcharges a marketer typically is responsible (is not responsible) for. In the "marketer is responsible" condition, we used parking and fuel fees as surcharges. In the "marketer is not responsible" condition, we used a visitor and an airport tax as surcharges. Regarding the responsibility manipulation we did a manipulation check with two objectives. First, we intended to prove that the responsibility manipulation has been generally successful. Second, we wanted to show that the manipulations are comparably successful for the two different products. The results (mean values, t-test statistics) of the manipulation check are summarized in Table 2.

The findings in Table 1 show that the responsibility manipulation has been successful and that the manipulations are comparable across product examples. However, one might criticize that the responsibility for the surcharge is confounded with product attributes because different product attributes were chosen to represent the responsibility conditions (e.g., surcharge for parking vs. surcharge for visitor tax). However, we think that choosing two different product attributes that realistically represent responsibility is more credible than using only one attribute for the surcharge and manipulating responsibility by indicating in one condition that the marketer is responsible for the surcharge and indicating in the other condition that the marketer is not responsible for the same surcharge.

Scenarios and Measures

We created short scenarios containing product and price information to put the respondents in purchase situations which were as realistic as possible. The basic scenarios for both product examples were as follows: "Please imagine you are planning a weekend in Paris, you are planning to get there by car, and you are looking for a nice hotel" (city hotel) and "Please imagine you are planning to visit a good friend in Berlin over the weekend and you decide to go there by plane because doing so saves lots of time" (airline ticket). The varying scenario descriptions that followed these basic scenarios are shown in Table 3.

The model variables were measured by using several items. Price attractiveness was measured by using three items such as "well-priced" (Alpha=.91). The feeling of being manipulated and perceived complexity of the price structure were operationalized through two items each. The items used to measure the feeling of being manipulated were "supplier demands an unfair price" and "my friends would judge this price as being unfair" (correlation: .53). Perceived complexity of the price structure was measured by using the items "price presentation is unclear" and "cannot notice this price at a glance" (correlation: .62). Product evaluation was operationalized through four items such as "this offer is convincing" (Alpha=.93). We used seven-point scales to measure the model constructs. High/low scale values represent a positive/negative product evaluation, high/low price attractiveness, high/low perceived complexity of the price structure, and a strong/weak feeling of being manipulated by the marketer. The sufficiently high Alpha values and correlations allow for calculating the overall construct values as arithmetical means of the single indicators for each construct. These arithmetical means are used in the analyses presented subsequently.

The constructs perceived complexity of the price structure and feeling of being manipulated might be considered as being related. However, the correlation between both variables is comparatively low (.204). Consequently, both constructs can be clearly separated from each other.

Procedure

160 respondents (75 men, 85 women) participated in our study in 2008 in Germany (80 participants per experimental group). Each respondent evaluated the two product examples shown in Table 2 in the same experimental condition. Having each participant evaluating two examples served as a sample multiplier. The respondents read the first scenario, evaluated the first product, and indicated their perception of price attractiveness, of complexity of the price structure and their feeling of being manipulated by the marketer (statements on 7-point scales). They then read the second scenario

TABLE 3
Scenarios

Product example (base price)	Marketer *is* responsible: Total price condition	Marketer *is* responsible: Partitioned price condition	Marketer *is not* responsible: Total price condition	Marketer *is not* responsible: Partitioned price condition
City hotel (room price per night)	The hotel that meets your expectations best, offers you a room at ¤ 60 per night including parking lot.	The hotel that meets your expectations best, offers you a room at ¤ 58 per night plus ¤ 2 for the parking lot.	The hotel that meets your expectations best, offers you a room at ¤ 60 per night including visitor tax.	The hotel that meets your expectations best, offers you a room at ¤ 58 per night plus a ¤ 2 visitor tax.
Airline ticket (flight price)	The flight that fits best into your schedule is offered at ¤ 90 including fuel charges.	The flight that fits best into your schedule is offered at ¤ 87 plus ¤ 3 fuel charge.	The flight that fits best into your schedule is offered at ¤ 90 including airport tax.	The flight that fits best into your schedule is offered at ¤ 87 plus ¤ 3 airport tax.

TABLE 4
Effects on the Mediator Variables

Mediator variable	Interaction effect of price presentation and marketer's responsibility				
	Marketer *is not* responsible for the surcharge		Marketer *is* responsible for the surcharge		F_{price} presentation x responsibility (*p* value)
	Total price	Partitioned price	Total price	Partitioned price	
Perceived price attractiveness[1]	4.49	4.90	4.89	4.87	F=2.17 (p>.10)
Feeling of being manipulated[3]	2.86	4.70	4.80	5.11	F=19.07 (p<.001)
Perceived complexity of the price structure[2]	2.58	3.04	3.18	4.94	F=12.51 (p<.001)
N	80	80	80	80	

[1]: 1=very low price attractiveness, …, 7=very high price attractiveness
[2]: 1=low complexity, …, 7=high complexity
[3]: 1=weak feeling of being manipulated, …, 7=strong feeling of being manipulated by the marketer

and completed the corresponding scales. The order of the scenarios varied from person to person to counterbalance order effects. Finally, the respondents provided demographic information. Both groups are structurally equal with regard to age (t=1.04, p>.10) and gender (X^2=1.26, p>.20).

Data Analysis and Results

The paths of the basic model have already been tested in previous studies (e.g., Bambauer-Sachse and Gierl 2008; Gierl and Bambauer-Sachse 2007), but for reasons of completeness, we show that the data collected for this study are able to reproduce the assumed effects. In a first step we prove the existence of the right part of our research model (effects of the mediator variables on product evaluation). The results of a regression analysis (R^2=.71) show that perceived price attractiveness (β=.65, t=15.10, p<.001) has a significantly positive effect on product evaluation, whereas perceived complexity of the price structure (β=-.10, t=-3.48, p<.01) and the feeling of being manipulated (β=-.23, t=-4.71, p<.001) have significantly negative effects on product evaluation.

In the second step, we focus on the left part of the research model that consists of the effects of price partitioning versus using total prices on the mediator variables as well as of the moderator effect of the marketer's responsibility. The effects assumed with regard to this part of the model are examined by using an ANOVA with interaction effects. The results are summarized in Table 4.

With regard to the effect of price presentation on perceived price attractiveness, the results show that if the marketer is not responsible for the surcharge, perceived price attractiveness is higher in the partitioned price condition than in the total price condition (M=4.90 vs. 4.49, t=1.68, p<.05). However, contrarily to the initial assumption we found that if the marketer is responsible for the surcharge, perceived price attractiveness is not significantly higher in the total price condition than in the partitioned price condition (M=4.89 vs. 4.87, t=0.09, p>.10). Thus, the data indicate that the positive sign of the effect of price partitioning on perceived price attractiveness does not turn negative if the marketer is responsible for the surcharge. However, the positive effect is neutralized if the marketer is responsible for the surcharge. Consequently, hypothesis 1 is only partly supported.

With regard to the effect of price presentation on consumers' feeling of being manipulated, the results show that the feeling of being manipulated is significantly higher in the partitioned price condition than in the total price condition (marketer is not responsible: M=4.70 vs. 2.86, t=7.49, p<.001; marketer is responsible: M=5.11 vs. 4.80, t=1.39, p<.10). Moreover, in the partitioned price condition, consumers' feeling of being manipulated is even stronger if the marketer is responsible for the surcharge (M=5.11 vs. 4.70, t=2.04, p<.05). Thus, hypotheses 2a and 2b are supported.

The findings for the effect of price presentation on perceived complexity of the price structure show that price structure is perceived as being more complex in the partitioned price condition than in the total price condition (marketer is not responsible: M=3.04 vs. 2.58, t=1.79, p<.05; marketer is responsible: M=4.94 vs. 3.18, t=2.52, p<.01). In addition, the results indicate that in the partitioned price condition, perceived complexity is significantly higher if the marketer is responsible for the surcharge (M=4.94 vs. 3.04, t=7.71, p<.001). Thus, hypotheses 3a and 3b are supported.

CONCLUSION

The goal of the present paper was to draw on previous research on price partitioning effects and to extend the existing body of research by examining moderator effects of a new variable that might play a role in the context of price partitioning effects.

First of all, our data confirmed the paths assumed in the basic models by Bambauer-Sachse and Gierl (2008) and Gierl and Bambauer-Sachse (2007). Moreover, the results of our study show that the marketer's responsibility indeed plays an important role in the context of effects of partitioned versus total prices. In more detail, we found that, when processing partitioned prices, consumers consider whether the marketer is responsible for the surcharge on the base price or not. Based on our finding that negative effects of price partitioning are less strong if the marketer does not account for the surcharge, we recommend using partitioned prices only under this condition. In cases where the marketer is responsible for the surcharge, the negative effects of using partitioned instead of total prices are even stronger.

A first starting point for further studies might be to analyze circumstances that drive consumers to ascribe responsibility for a surcharge to a marketer. In addition, we suggest analyzing price partitioning effects in field experiments in retail stores because up to now, such effects have only been analyzed in simulated experiments. Moreover, it might be interesting to examine price partitioning effects for very low or very high priced products because the products considered in the study here are medium-priced. Finally, consumers' knowledge about the marketer's objectives that are pursued with a specific pricing strategy might also play a role in the context of effects of partitioned prices and thus might be an interesting variable to be examined in further studies.

REFERENCES

Bambauer-Sachse, Silke and Heribert Gierl (2008), "Should Marketers Use Price Partitioning or Total Prices?" in *Advances in Consumer Research,* Vol. 35., ed. Angela Y. Lee and Dilip Soman, Duluth, MN: Association for Consumer Research, 262-268.

Bertini, Marco and Luc Wathieu (2005), "Price Format and the Evaluation of Multicomponent Goods," *Working Paper* #05-087, Harvard Business School: http://www.hbs.edu/research/pdf/05-087.pdf.

Bertini, Marco and Luc Wathieu (2008), "Attention Arousal Through Price Partitioning," *Marketing Science*, 27 (2), 236-246.

Biswas, Abhijit and Scot Burton (1993), "Consumer Perceptions of Tensile Price Claims in Advertisements: An Assessment of Claim Types Across Different Discount Levels," *Journal of the Academy of Marketing Science,* 21 (3), 217-229.

Burman, Bidisha and Abhijit Biswas (2007), "Partitioned Pricing: Can We Always Divide and Prosper?" *Journal of Retailing,* 83 (4), 423-436.

Block, Richard A. and David R. Harper (1991), "Overconfidence in Estimation: Testing the Anchoring-and-Adjustment Hypothesis," *Organizational Behavior and Human Decision Processes,* 49 (2), 188-207.

Campbell, Margaret C. (1995), "Perceptions of Price Unfairness: Antecedents and Consequences," *Journal of Marketing Research*, 36 (2), 187-199.

Carlson, Jay P. and Danny Weathers (2008), "Examining Differences in Consumer Reactions to Partitioned Prices With a Variable Number of Price Components," *Journal of Business Research,* 61 (7), 724-731.

Chakravarti, Dipankar, Rajan Krish, Paul Pallab, and Joydeep Srivastava (2002), "Partitioned Presentation of Multicomponent Bundle Prices: Evaluation, Choice, and Underlying Processing Effects," *Journal of Consumer Psychology*, 12 (3), 215-229.

Chapman, Gretchen B. and Eric J. Johnson (1994), "The Limits of Anchoring," *Journal of Behavioral Decision Making,* 7 (4), 223-242.

Clark, John M. and Sidne G. Ward (2008), "Consumer Behavior in Online Auctions: An Examination of Partitioned Prices on Ebay," *Journal of Marketing Theory and Practice*, 16 (1), 57-66.

Danziger, Shai and Ruthie Segev (2006), "The Effects of Informative and Non-Informative Price Patterns on Consumer Price Judgments," *Psychology and Marketing,* 23 (6), 535-553.

Davis, Harry L., Stephen J. Hoch, and Easton E.K. Ragsdale (1986), "An Anchoring and Adjustment Model of Spousal Predictions," *Journal of Consumer Research,* 13 (1), 25-37.

Dean, Dwane Hal (2004), "Consumers Reaction to Negative Publicity: Effects of Corporate Reputation, Response, and Responsibility for a Crisis Event," *Journal of Business Communication*, 41 (2), 192-211.

Folkes, Valerie S. (1984), "Consumer Reactions to Product Failure: An Attributional Approach," *Journal of Consumer Research*, 10 (4), 398-409.

Friestad, Marian and Peter Wright (1994), "The Persuasion Knowledge Model: How People Cope with Persuasion Attempts," *Journal of Consumer Research*, 21 (1), 1-31.

Gierl, Heribert and Silke Bambauer-Sachse (2007), "Effects of Price Partitioning on Product Evaluation," *Marketing–Journal of Research and Management,* 3 (2), 61-74.

Griffin, Mitch, Barry J. Babin, and Jill S. Attaway (1991), "An Empirical Investigation of the Impact of Negative Public Publicity on Consumer Attitudes and Intentions," *Advances in Consumer Research*, 18 (1), 334-341.

Hamilton, Rebecca W. and Joydeep Srivastava (2008), "When 2+2 Is Not the Same as 1+3: Variations in Price Sensitivity Across Components of Partitioned Prices," *Journal of Marketing Research*, 45 (4), 450-461.

Hamilton, Rebecca W. and Nevena T. Koukova (2008), "Choosing Options for Products: The Effects of Mixed Bundling on Consumers' Inferences and Choices," *Journal of the Academy of Marketing Science,* 36 (3), 423-433.

Hardesty, David M., William O. Bearden, and Jay P. Carlson (2007), "Persuasion Knowledge and Consumer Reactions to Pricing Tactics," *Journal of Retailing*, 83 (2), 199-210.

Heider, Fritz (1958), *The Psychology of Interpersonal Relations*, New York: Wiley.

Homburg, Christian, Wayne D. Hoyer, and Nicole Koschate (2005), "Customers' Reactions to Price Increases: Do Customer Satisfaction and Perceived Motive Fairness Matter?" *Journal of the Academy of Marketing Science,* 33 (1), 36-49.

Jacowitz, Karen E. and Daniel Kahneman (1995), "Measures of Anchoring in Estimation Tasks," *Personality and Social Psychology Bulletin,* 21 (11), 1161-1166.

Janiszewski, Chris and Donald R. Lichtenstein (1999), "A Range Theory Account of Price Perception," *Journal of Consumer Research,* 25 (4), 353-368.

Jones, Edward E., Keith E. Davis, and Kenneth J. Gergen (1961), "Role Playing Variations and Their Informational Value for Person Perception," *Journal of Abnormal Social Psychology*, 63 (2), 302-310.

Jones, Edward E. and Daniel McGillis (1976), "Correspondent Inferences and the Attribution Cube: A Comparative Reappraisal," in *New Directions in Attribution Research*, ed. John H. Harvey, William J. Ickes, and Robert F. Kidd, Hillsdale, NJ: Erlbaum, 389-420..

Jorgensen, Brian K. (1994), "Consumer Reaction to Company-Related Disasters: The Effect of Multiple Versus Single Explanations," *Advances in Consumer Research*, 21 (4), 348-352.

Kelley, Harold H. and John L. Michela (1980), "Attribution Theory and Research," *Annual Review of Psychology*, 31, 457-501.

Laczniak, Russel N., Thomas E. DeCarlo, and Sridhar N. Ramaswami (2001), "Consumers' Responses to Negative Word-of-Mouth Communication: An Attribution Theory Perspective," *Journal of Consumer Psychology*, 11 (1), 57-73.

Lee, Yih Hwai and Cheng Yuen Han (2002), "Partitioned Pricing in Advertising: Effects on Brand and Retailer Attitudes," *Marketing Letters*, 13 (1), 27-40.

Lichtenstein, Donald R., Peter H. Bloch, and William C. Black (1988), "Correlates of Price Acceptability," *Journal of Consumer Research,* 15 (2), 243-252.

Maxwell, Sarah (1995), "What Makes a Price Increase Seem "Fair"?" *Pricing and Practice,* 3 (4), 21-27.

Morwitz, Vicki G., Eric A. Greenleaf, and Eric J. Johnson (1998) "Divide and Prosper: Consumers' Reactions to Partitioned Prices," *Journal of Marketing Research,* 35 (4), 453-463.

Nishii, Lisa H., David P. Lepak, and Benjamin Schneider (2008), "Employee Attributions of the "Why" of HR Practices: Their Effects on Employee Attitudes and Behaviors, and Customer Satisfaction," *Personnel Psychology*, 61 (3), 503-545.

Northcraft, Gregory B. and Margaret A. Neale (1987), "Experts, Amateurs, and Real Estate: An Anchoring-and-Adjustment Perspective on Property Pricing Decisions," *Organizational Behavior and Human Decision Processes,* 39 (1), 84-97.

Sheng, Shibin, Yeqing Bao, and Yue Pan (2007), "Partitioning or Bundling? Perceived Fairness of the Surcharge Makes a Difference," *Psychology & Marketing*, 24 (12), 1025-1041.

Tversky, Amos and Daniel Kahneman (1974), "Judgment under Uncertainty: Heuristics and Biases," *Science*, 185 (4157), 1124-1131.

Weiner, Bernard (1979), "A Theory of Motivation for Some Classroom Experiences," *Journal of Educational Psychology*, 71 (1), 3-25.

Weiner, Bernard, Irene Frieze, Andy Kukla, Linda Reed, Stanley Rest, and Robert M. Rosenbaum (1972), "Perceiving the Causes of Success and Failure," in *Attribution: Perceiving the Causes of Behavior*, ed. Edward E. Jones, David E. Kanouse, Harold H. Kelley, Richard E. Nisbett, Stuart Valin, and Bernard Weiner, New York: General Learning Press, 95-120.

Xia, Lan and Kent B. Monroe (2004), "Price Partitioning on the Internet," *Journal of Interactive Marketing*, 18 (4), 63-73.

Word-of-Mouth: Are We Hearing What the Consumer is Saying?

Martin A. Pyle, Queen's University, Canada

On a given night, if you look at the moon through a telescope you will see peaks and valleys, craters and crevices. From this perspective, you can make numerous assumptions and study individual elements which combine to make the whole. However, what you see is only half of a sphere; the other half is shrouded in darkness. This is akin to taking a singular perspective for examining word-of-mouth (WOM), which raises the question: what are we missing? The motivation behind WOM research over the past fifty years has been primarily managerial, seeking to understand and harness word-of-mouth's persuasive power. Generally approaching the phenomenon of WOM from a positivist perspective, marketing researchers have sought an understanding of the causal link between company actions and consumer WOM responses. Two underlying assumptions guide most of the work in this area: (1) consumers are information-seeking cognitive processors seeking to maximize their utility and (2) the sole purpose of word-of-mouth is to spread an evaluation of the product or service between fellow consumers. These assumptions are deeply rooted in the origins of WOM research and manifest themselves in how researchers commonly define WOM: an informal communication of information about, and evaluations of, a company or brand between two individuals (Brown, Barry, Dacin and Gunst 2005; Chung and Darke 2006; Dichter 1966). However, by relaxing the assumption that consumers are only spreading information about products or services to make rational decisions, and examining word-of-mouth through a lens of consumer culture theory (which adopts different philosophical assumptions), we can explore WOM from a new perspective and reveal what is hidden about WOM.

Extant research examining word-of-mouth (WOM) can be broadly subdivided into three streams of research. In the mid 1960s WOM researchers began examining the network aspect of WOM in an attempt to understand how the information moved from consumer to consumer (e.g., Arndt 1967, Sheth 1971) and the role of individuals as marketplace influencers (e.g., opinion leaders) and information seekers (e.g., Reynolds and Darden 1971; Stafford 1966). In the 1980s two other WOM streams emerged: an examination of negative WOM (e.g., Richins 1983) and individual constructs which influence the persuasiveness of WOM (e.g., Bearden and Etzen 1982). When combined, all three streams of research have produced a large, rich body of literature expanding our understanding of WOM. However, the underlying assumptions and motivations have left certain unexplained gaps and have not captured important factors required for a better understanding of WOM phenomena. Adopting a different perspective would allow us to apply different assumptions and address the unexplored aspects of the WOM phenomenon.

This conceptual paper begins with the dominant perspective of the consumer in the existing WOM research and subsequently demonstrates how early development in the area has led to the three major streams of WOM research. Next, I highlight the limitations of the extant WOM research and suggest that the consumer culture theory (CCT) literature offers a unique perspective that can compliment and extend our understanding of the phenomenon. I conclude the paper by proposing three new WOM research domains derived from integrating the CCT identity literature with the extant WOM research.

WOM: PERCEPTIONS OF THE CONSUMER

The roots of the marketing discipline itself have influenced the direction taken by many WOM researchers. Marketing research flowed out of economics, resulting in many early marketing researchers also adopting the *economic man* view of the consumer. The *economic man* framework depicts the consumer as someone who is motivated by the desire to maximize the economic utility of his decisions. To accomplish this goal, the individual seeks as much information as possible about the available alternatives in his consideration set, and with this information, the person is able to make the most rational and value-maximizing decision (e.g., Whyte 1954). While this perspective has been overtly dropped from the literature, many of the assumptions from this view continue to permeate WOM research.

THE DIFFUSION LITERATURE

Social Networks

Although researchers and practitioners have long been aware of the existence of WOM as a persuasive influence, very little was known about WOM's underlying mechanisms early on. As Arndt (1967) described, "[w]ord-of-mouth advertising [had] been thought to be an almost mysterious force, with its effects taken for granted" (Arndt 1967, 291). This gap in understanding led to the emergence of the WOM diffusion literature, which focused on social networks and the role of marketplace influencers.

Whyte (1954) provided one of the first examinations of the makeup of a social network. During a walk through Philadelphia, Whyte (1954) observed a striking phenomenon. By marking homes that displayed air conditioners in the window on a diagram of the neighborhood, it was possible to discern a pattern of ownership. He followed up these findings by conducting interviews with family members from a portion of these households and found that many of the decisions to buy the air conditioners could be linked to the influence of neighbors. The diffusion research continued through the 1980s, examining the relationships within the social networks and seeking to understand their inner workings (e.g.,Reingen, Brown, Foster and Seidman 1984; Reingen and Kernan 1986). In general, this stream of research suggested that strong social ties were not required for passing along opinions. Weak ties could provide the bridge from one social group to the next, allowing word-of-mouth to spread a great distance (Brown and Reingen, 1987).

More recently, the diffusion literature has examined social networks in the context of the Internet. As consumers began to embrace online word-of-mouth, it became apparent that this technology provided an unprecedented increase in the size of social networks (Dellarocas 2003) and the amount of information available to consumers (Chatterjee 2001) far exceeded traditional word-of-mouth. However, increasing the scope and scale of word-of-mouth has not generated many unique or significant insights about how information travels within and between social networks. In short, as a body of research, the diffusion literature has contributed to our understanding of how information travels through social networks, however this research stream would benefit from an infusion of new perspectives that can generate new research questions, rather than applying existing knowledge to new contexts.

Marketplace Influencers

During this same period of network examination, another group of researchers was concurrently seeking to identify and understand the originators of the networks. Marketing literature has defined three distinct categories of marketplace influencers: opinion leaders, innovators and 'market mavens'. Opinion leaders tend to have influence within a specific domain or product category (Reynolds and Darden 1971; Stafford 1966;). Innovators are early product adopters who spread the word to others about the benefits (or faults) of the product or service (Clark and Goldsmith 2005; Leonard-Barton 1985). Marketing mavens tend to be the most sought-after supporters by retailers as they influence the decisions of other consumers in multiple product domains (Feick and Price 1987).

Marketing researchers have extensively sought an understanding of the marketplace influencers' motivation for disseminating product information. Swan and Combs (1976) believed a logical motivating factor for spreading WOM was product satisfaction. An early definition of satisfaction reflects the perception of the consumer as a logical, information seeker: consumers gathered information about products, made predictions about performance of a product leading to expectations, consumed the product, and then compared the actual and predicted performance on relevant attributes (Swan and Combs 1976). In this bi-modal view, if the comparison was favorable, the consumer was satisfied; otherwise he was dissatisfied. Tying together satisfaction with identification, some research has shown that one's level of commitment has a moderating influence on the link between satisfaction and positive word-of-mouth (Brown, Barry, Dacin and Gunst 2005). However, the extant literature is somewhat equivocal in linking positive WOM to satisfaction with a product or service. While Brown et al. (2005) were able to demonstrate this link, other researchers have offered evidence that satisfaction cannot be related to WOM dissemination (e.g., Arnett, German and Hunt 2003; Bettencourt 1997).

THE RELEVANCE OF VALENCE

Emerging out of the satisfaction and opinion leader literature, the second stream of WOM research examines the effects of valence on the persuasiveness of WOM. In particular, marketing researchers examining negative WOM have focused on the cognitive reasons why negative information is more persuasive than positive WOM and the underlying motivations behind disseminating negative feedback. Arndt's (1967) study indicated that while favorable product experiences were more numerous, unfavorable word-of-mouth was far more effective at deterring new product adoption. Examining this differential influence, Mizerski (1982) suggested an attribution-based explanation for why negative information appeared to be more persuasive (i.e., the negativity effect). Specifically, while the motivation behind positive WOM could be attributed to a variety of reasons (e.g., social norms, message source), negative WOM tended to be attributed solely to the product itself (Mizerski 1982). Just as the extant WOM diffusion literature assumes that satisfaction stemming from direct contact with the product or service drives positive WOM, much of the negative WOM literature is based on the assumption that disseminators of negative WOM have experienced dissatisfaction with the product or service (e.g., Richins 1983).

The product-centric assumptions from the initial research examining WOM are also prevalent in the WOM valence literature. This literature suggests that the consumer spreading negative information to his fellow information seekers does so based on a poor experience with a product and is seeking justice for this wrongdoing (e.g., Blodgett, Granbois and Walters 1993). Furthermore, the valence literature tends to focus on the dissuasion of consumers by this negative information. These assumptions bias the research questions being examined, and yield gaps that remain unexplained. For example, Liu (2006) examined the relationship between WOM and movie success using a data set from a popular online message board. In summary, Liu found that the volume of WOM (*regardless* of valence) acted as a good predictor for box-office revenue, suggesting that negative feedback did not have the predicted effect of dissuading others from purchasing the product. The proscribed relationship between product experience, dissatisfaction and negative WOM also does not explain anecdotal evidence whereby consumers spread negative WOM based on a company's policies, without having direct experience with that company (e.g., negative WOM regarding Wal-Mart's anti-union position). Researchers have also spent considerable time examining which factors, beyond valence, impact the persuasiveness of WOM communications.

CHARACTERISTICS AFFECTING PERSUASIVENESS

The third stream of WOM research adopts a reductionist perspective on the topic, identifying specific characteristics which impact the persuasiveness of WOM and testing them in an experiment. For example, researchers have demonstrated an effect on the persuasiveness of interpersonal influence by source credibility (Dichter 1966), the type of product (i.e., luxury or necessity), private versus public consumption (Bearden and Etzel 1982), as well as the similarity of the referent and his/her perceived expertise (Price, Feick and Higie 1989). Bone (1995) examined the effects of WOM on short- and long-term judgments and found effects for both, particularly when the information was contrary to previous experience. Another factor found to be influential in the level of persuasion was vividness of the positive word-of-mouth description (Herr, Kardes and Kim 1991). The authors found that participants retrieved vividly presented information more easily from memory, and this information had a positive influence on subsequent judgments.

Although researchers have examined the effect of many characteristics on WOM, the researchers have tended towards a positivist approach using experimental methodologies. This methodological approach removes the contextual impact from WOM, attempts to determine causal relationships and thus, may miss certain relevant factors. For example, information received from an acquaintance at a party may be interpreted differently than when that same person provides information in a workplace.

LIMITATIONS IN CURRENT WOM RESEARCH

An analysis of the extant WOM research highlights the dominance of the positivist approach to examining the WOM phenomenon. This, in turn, has resulted in a singular method of examination (primarily experimental) as well as certain deep-seated assumptions. Cumulatively, this approach has impacted the nature of the questions researchers in the area have sought to answer. The majority of WOM research has typically adopted a view of the consumer as an information-seeking and information-processing individual. This perspective of the consumer has tended to result in a product-centric approach to WOM content, whereby the focus of the communication is strictly on the brand. This focus on the consumer as a product-information-seeker led to the assumption of a sole motivation for generating WOM: a reaction to a direct experience with a product or service.

I suggest that WOM research would benefit from an integration of the philosophical perspectives and research stemming from the CCT paradigm, and the methodological approaches typically adopted within this research stream. This perspective brings with it a different set of assumptions (e.g., different views of the consumer and the impact of context) and thus seeks to address different research questions. Positivism and interpretivism differ at an epistemological level, and though it can be (and has been) argued that the two are therefore incommensurable, I propose that the research deriving from these philosophical positions is complementary and serves to enhance our understanding of various phenomena. In the context of WOM, the existing and future positivist research exposes one view of WOM, while an interpretivist approach to future research in the area, drawing on a different body of literature and methodologies, would serve to illuminate additional elements of WOM which currently remain unexplored (Figure 1).

CONSUMER CULTURE THEORY: AN OVERVIEW

Consumer culture theory is not one specific theory, but rather a theoretical perspective that views consumer actions, the market and cultural meanings as interconnected (Arnould and Thompson 2005). At a broad level, CCT research focuses on "…how consumers actively rework and transform symbolic meanings encoded in advertisements, brands, retail settings, or material goods to manifest their particular personal and social circumstances and further their identity and lifestyle goals" (Arnould and Thompson 2005, 871). Work in the identity subsection of CCT research conceives of the consumer as an identity seeker and maker. CCT researchers seek to investigate the consumption experience within the sociocultural context because "…an understanding of consumer symbolism and lifestyle orientations is essential to successful marketing strategies" (Arnould and Thompson 2005, 871).

WOM AND CCT: SHARED VIEWS

Integrating the CCT identity stream of literature into WOM research is not an unreasonable task. The two bodies of research share several similar conceptual frameworks based on networks, particularly in the WOM diffusion area of research. Arnould and Thompson (2005) describe consumer culture itself as "…a densely woven network of global connections and extensions through which local cultures are increasingly interpenetrated by the forces of transnational capital and the global mediascape" (Arnould and Thompson 2005, 869), a description similar to how researchers envision WOM networks.

The WOM research on marketplace influencers also provides a good example how WOM and the CCT identity literature relate at the construct level. Taking a reductionist approach, some WOM researchers have examined opinion leaders and marketing mavens to determine if they share particular traits or motivations for engaging in WOM communication (e.g., Feick and Price 1987). The extant research in the area suggests that a common motivation is the desire to be perceived as an 'expert' by others (Walsh, Gwinner and Swanson 2004). The CCT identity literature expands on this social motivation by suggesting that consumers classify themselves through specific action-related consumptive experiences such as rituals or traditions (Holt 1995). For example, Holt (1995) refers to "mentoring" as being an action which contributes to an individual's authority and legitimacy, strengthening the individual's socially visible bond to the brand. As Holt (1995) describes it, mentoring is akin to a demonstration of one's expertise on a particular topic.

CCT: PERCEPTIONS OF THE CONSUMER AND CONSUMPTION

Arnould and Thompson (2005) suggest that the consumer is a social being and part of a community. This cultural view conceptualizes the consumer as someone who engages in an ongoing personal narrative and creates personal meaning through consumption experiences (Thompson and Troester 2002). Whereas the traditional marketing view suggests that brand meanings emanate from the company, the CCT perspective tends to conceptualize meaning as being co-created with the consumer drawing together various cultural meanings in a form of bricolage to create a personally relevant meaning. Furthermore, these symbolic meanings are not static, but instead "[i]n narrative, people continually make sense of their world 'on the fly' … the flow of events is given an articulate form, made into a kind of model" (Shore 1996, as cited in Thompson and Troester 2002, p. 553). Thus, these consumer narratives are fluid and contextually dependent, drawing on salient elements from the given situation (Thompson 1997).

Holt and Thompson (2004) explore the idea of internal conflict resolution as it applies to this notion of a personal narrative. The authors suggest that consumers often address internal tension caused by perceptions of conflicting social norms by drawing on cultural artifacts and meanings in a playful manner to create a personal space where there is no conflict. The concept of play is related to how we draw from the varying cultural artifacts and put them together in new and varied combinations. At times these combinations can serve a social purpose, as with the consumer-created Doppelganger brands attacking Starbucks (Thompson, Rindfleisch and Arsel 2006), while in other contexts this playfulness is related to consumer fantasy (e.g., Kozinets et al. 2004).

From this perspective, we can suggest that WOM is part of the ongoing consumer narrative, but it is a distinguishable subsection in that while the storytelling aspect described by CCT authors refers to all consumption experiences, WOM in particular assumes an evaluative position for or against a brand. The concept of play suggests that consumers can create these ongoing narratives by drawing from a variety of cultural and personal meanings and combining them in ways that suit the context. Using this alternative view of consumers, we can shift from viewing WOM as product-centric and instead consider a consumer-centric perspective where WOM becomes a particular form of narrative for other uses.

IMPLICATIONS: IDENTITY CONSTRUCTION

The CCT identity literature can contribute to WOM research by supporting the notion that WOM provides consumers with a means for constructing their identities. Holt (1995) argues that consumers sometimes use consumption as a means of classifying themselves for others, that "[c]onsuming not only involves directly engaging consumption objects but also includes using consumption objects as resources to interact with fellow consumers" (Holt 1995, 9). In a social situation, discussing a common brand association can serve "… to construct and sustain meaningful ties between otherwise heterogeneous consumers" (Holt 1995, 10). In this sense, adopting an evaluative position about a brand can act as a heuristic or short-hand for signaling to others a particular aspect of one's identity. The specific meanings associated with this position are derived both through the cultural meanings available at the time, and the personal meanings created by the individual.

Using an experimental approach, Chung and Darke (2006) demonstrate that people are more likely to engage in WOM with others when the product is personally relevant as compared to products which they perceive as utilitarian. In their theoretical development, Chung and Darke (2006) suggest that people may use WOM as a means of self-presentation, and that impression management goals may, in fact, cause consumers to adjust the views which they choose to reveal. In short, the authors demonstrate a link between WOM volume and the self-relevance of the brand in question, but they do not examine how the participants integrate

FIGURE 1

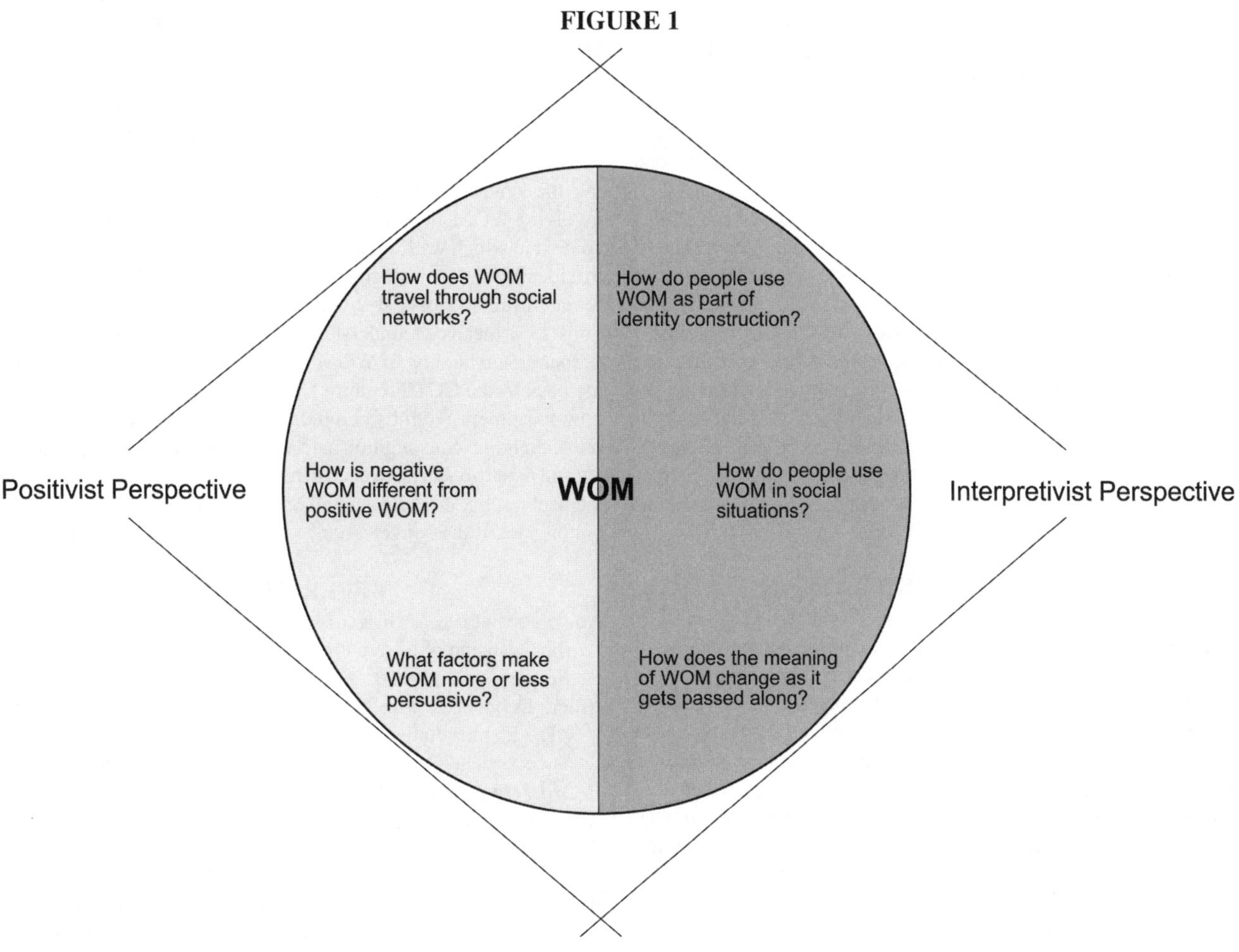

aspects of self-presentation into their comments. The experimental nature of this research demonstrates that identity construction can be a motivation but does not capture *how* we discuss and use brands to create these identities. To gather this richness of understanding we turn to the interpretivist methodologies and theories.

Drawing on self-presentation theory, but from an interpretivist perspective, Schau and Gilly (2003) suggest that consumers use a personal Web space as a means of broadcasting constructed identities to the masses, demonstrating that it "…is a consumer narrative where multiple selves are made comprehensible" (Schau and Gilly 2003, 400). The authors found evidence that their participants were reflective about the content and construction of these Web sites, planning and integrating aspects of their identities through discourse and brand images, extending the physical self into the digital context. Some participants maintained multiple Web sites with different themes representing differing aspects of their lives (e.g., a site for promoting professional qualifications and a second fan site for music tastes).

While maintaining a personal Web space is similar to engaging in interpersonal WOM in many ways, it also differs in meaningful aspects. Incorporating brand logos and discussing favored or disliked brands on a Web space is akin to making recommendations during a social interaction. However, whereas a broad audience may read the recommendations on a Web space, when engaging in interpersonal WOM we may customize what we say based on our specific audience and the responses we may have gotten from previous discussions. Schau and Gilly (2003) found that their participants spent time consciously deciding how to construct their digital identity, and while the authors found that the digital self was not vastly different from the real-life self, the specific fragments of participants' identities were purposefully chosen and comparatively static. Because many consumer narratives, interpersonal WOM in particular, occur in 'real-time', such conversations are much more fluid and dynamic, resulting in both conscious and unconscious influences which affect both the content and the framing of the message. In describing the personal Web space, Schau and Gilly (2003) treat it as a digitally created identity, something linked to the creator's identity but also separate from the person in that it exists without the creator's presence. Interpersonal WOM, on the other hand, is far more ephemeral, integrated with the speaker as part of a conversation, and ceases to exist in any tangible way once spoken. Considering WOM in this way, one can see how consumers might use their evaluations to construct and communicate a particular identity to another person. This also leads one to consider other ways in which consumers integrate WOM into their narratives during social interactions.

IMPLICATIONS: SOCIAL INTERACTION

Much of the existing WOM research assumes that a person who disseminates information is doing so from a direct relationship with the product or service. Thompson, Rindfleish and Arsel, however, demonstrate the power and influence of social perceptions with respect to WOM. As the authors suggest, "…brand image is much more a matter of perceived meaning and cultural mythology … than an aggregation of verified evidence" (Thompson, Rindfleish and Arsel 2006, 55). In social situations, consumers may alter their personal narrative as a means of fitting-in with others, adopting a particular position on a brand to solidify in-group membership without necessarily having had that direct experience. In other words, at a social gathering a person may define himself as anti-Starbucks without ever having been into one of the coffee shops, simply because the cultural meaning of such a position can be used to enhance and clarify his identity.

Adopting this CCT perspective about consumers and WOM allows for the pursuit of another interesting stream of research: examining how consumers adjust identity-relevant WOM based on the social context. Because such a stream of research would focus on subtle changes to content and 'real-world' social contexts, a phenomenological or ethnographical method would be well suited to gaining this understanding. This approach would provide insights into how consumers play with the fusion of social context, larger cultural meanings and microcultural specific meanings to adapt and adopt specific positions about brands. This adjustment of WOM meaning could also lead to questions regarding how meaning changes as people pass along WOM.

IMPLICATIONS: MEANING TRANSFORMATION

Children will sometimes engage in a form of play called "The Telephone Game". The children sit in a circle and one child will whisper a phrase into his neighbor's ear. The children pass along the phrase until it returns back to the original speaker, at which point the message typically has been garbled significantly, resulting in laughter by all involved. Adopting the views of personal narratives and play, researchers can examine how WOM moves between speakers and how the meaning of the message changes as it moves through a social network. Assuming that consumers integrate elements of their own identities when sharing information, and that they playfully draw from multiple cultural resources when engaging in narratives, much like the Telephone Game, the nature and meaning of the information being passed along will quickly cease to resemble the original message. Consumers will likely not simply pass along the message verbatim as they hear it, but rather integrate related meanings into their narrative.

Such a research stream might have larger implications for understanding the formation of cultural myths and misconceptions. Often times, these myths can transform into perceived fact by consumers, as more and more 'credible' sources provide the same or supporting evidence. For example, despite being influential in the significant rise in the overall number of coffee shops, a common consumer perception is that Starbucks is responsible for crushing the local entrepreneur (Thompson, Rindfleish and Arsel 2006). While a positivist approach could provide insight into how information travels through social networks and perhaps make predictions as to which factors might increase the likelihood of passing along WOM, the standard tools and methodologies used are ill-equipped to examine the subtle transformations of meaning during this journey. Conversely, interpretivist approaches, drawing on methodologies such as netnographies and hermeneutics are particularly adept for capturing and interpreting the necessary data, drawing theoretical support from the CCT body of literature. Together, these approaches could provide researchers in both domains with a more thorough understanding of the phenomenon.

SUMMARY

The goal of this paper has been to examine the development of WOM literature in order to appreciate the current state of thought and research in the area. As part of this analysis, I have identified limitations and assumptions which result in gaps in our understanding of WOM. By relaxing these assumptions and infusing this research with insights from the CCT perspective, this paper demonstrates how these limitations may be addressed and our knowledge of WOM broadened.

By integrating the work from the CCT literature, I am able to suggest how a consumer's identity narrative may impact WOM and how engaging in WOM can be perceived as a form of identity construction. The CCT perspective also offers a means for examining the simultaneous shaping which occurs in social situations involving WOM, how we might adopt positions based on the social context in which we find ourselves. Working from the assumption that identity and social factors impact the content of WOM, a further research stream can be developed to examine WOM communications as a means of understanding consumer-created myths. A deeper understanding of WOM communications can also contribute back to the CCT literature by yielding additional insight into how consumers playfully combine and integrate cultural meanings into their larger consumption narrative. For over 50 years, researchers and practitioners have been listening to consumers talk amongst themselves, but until we expand our views of WOM, we will miss out on a lot of the conversation.

REFERENCES

Arndt, Johan (1967), "Role of Product-Related Conversations in the Diffusion of a New Product," *Journal of Marketing Research*, 4 (August), 291-295.

Arnett, Dennis B., Steve D. German and Shelby D. Hunt (2003), "The Identity Salience Model of Relationship Marketing Success: The Case of Nonprofit Marketing," *Journal of Marketing*, 67 (April), 89-105.

Arnould, Eric J. and Craig J. Thompson (2005), "Consumer Culture Theory (CCT): Twenty Years of Research," *Journal of Consumer Research*, 31 (4), 868-882.

Bearden, William O. and Michael J. Etzel (1982), "Reference Group Influence on Product and Brand Purchase Decisions," *Journal of Consumer Research*, 9 (September), 183-194.

Bettencourt, Lance A. (1997), "Customer Voluntary Performance: Customers As Partners In Service Delivery," *Journal of Retailing*, 73 (3), 383-406.

Blodgett, Jeffrey G., Donald H. Granbois and Rockney G. Walters (1993), "The Effects of Perceived Justice on Complainants' Negative Word-of-Mouth Behavior and Repatronage Intentions," *Journal of Retailing*, 69 (4), 399-428.

Bone, Paula Fitzgerald (1995), "Word-of-Mouth Effects on Short-term and Long-term Product Judgments," *Journal of Business Research*, 32, 213-223.

Brown, Jacqueline Johnson and Peter H. Reingen (1987), "Social Ties and Word-of-Mouth Referral Behavior," *Journal of Consumer Research*, 14 (3), 350-362.

Brown, Tom J., Thomas E. Barry, Peter A. Dacin and Richard F. Gunst (2005), "Spreading the Word: Investigating Antecedents of Consumers' Positive Word-of-Mouth Intentions and Behaviors in a Retailing Context," *Journal of the Academy of Marketing Science*, 33 (2), 123-138.

Chatterjee, Patrali (2001), "Online Reviews: Do Customers Use Them?," *Advances in Consumer Research*, 28, 129-133.

Chung, Cindy M. Y. and Peter R. Darke (2006), "The consumer as advocate: Self-relevance, culture and word-of-mouth," *Marketing Letters*, 17, 269-279.

Clark, Ronald A. and Ronald E. Goldsmith (2005), "Market Mavens: Psychological Influences," *Psychology and Marketing*, 22 (4), 289-312.

Dellarocas, Chrysanthos (2003), "The Digitization of Word of Mouth: Promise and Challenges of Online Feedback Mechanisms," *Management Science*, 49 (10), 1407-1424.

Dichter, Ernest (1966) "How Word-of-Mouth Advertising Works," *Harvard Business Review*, 44 (November-December), 147-166.

Feick, Lawrence F. and Linda L. Price (1987), "The Market Maven: A Diffuser of Marketplace Information," *Journal of Marketing*, 51 (January), 83-97.

Herr, Paul M., Frank R. Kardes and John Kim (1991), "Effects of Word-of-Mouth and Product-Attribute Information on Persuasion: An Accessibility-Diagnosticity Perspective," *Journal of Consumer Research,* 17 (March), 454-462.

Holt, Douglas B. (1995), "How Consumers Consume: A Typology of Consumption Practices," *Journal of Consumer Research*, 22 (June), 1-16.

Holt, Douglas B. and Craig J. Thompson (2004), "Man-of-Action Heroes: The Pursuit of Heroic Masculinity in Everyday Consumption," *Journal of Consumer Research*, 31, 425-440.

Kozinets, Robert V. (2001), "Utopian Enterprise: Articulating the Meaning of *Star Trek*'s Culture of Consumption," *Journal of Consumer Research*, 28 (June), 67-88.

Kozinets, Robert V., John F. Sherry, Jr., Diana Storm, Adam Duhachek, Krittinee Nuttavthisit and Benet Deberry-Spence (2004), "Ludic Agency and Retail Spectacle," *Journal of Consumer Research*, 31, 658-672.

Leonard-Barton, Dorothy (1985), "Experts as Negative Opinion Leaders in the Diffusion of a Technological Innovation," *Journal of Consumer Research*, 11 (March), 914-926.

Liu, Yong (2006), "Word of Mouth for Movies: Its Dynamics and Impact on Box Office Revenue," *Journal of Marketing*, 70 (July), 74-89.

Mizerski, Richard W. (1982), "An Attribution Explanation of the Disproportionate Influence of Unfavorable Information," *Journal of Consumer Research*, 9 (December), 301-310.

Price, Linda L., Lawrence F. Feick, and Robin A. Higie (1989), "Preference Heterogeneity and Coorientation as Determinants of Perceived Informational Influence," *Journal of Business Research*, 19 (November), 227-242.

Reingen, Peter H., Brian L. Foster, Jacqueline Johnson Brown and Stephen B. Siedman (1984), "Brand Congruence in Interpersonal Relations: A Social Network Analysis," *Journal of Consumer Research*, 1984 (December), 771-783.

Reingen, Peter H. and Jerome B. Kernan (1986), "Analysis of Referral Networks in Marketing Methods and Illustration," *Journal of Marketing Research*, 23 (November), 370-378.

Reynolds, Fred D. and William R. Darden (1971), "Mutually Adaptive Effects of Interpersonal Communication," *Journal of Marketing Research*, 8 (November), 449-454.

Richins, Marsha L. (1983), "Negative Word-of-Mouth by Dissatisfied Consumers: A Pilot Study," *Journal of Marketing*, 47 (1), 68-78.

Schau, Hope Jensen and Mary C. Gilly (2003), "We Are What We Post? Self-Presentation in Personal Web Space," *Journal of Consumer Research*, 30 (3), 385-404.

Sheth, Jagdish N. (1971), "Word-of-Mouth in Low-Risk Innovations," *Journal of Advertising Research*, 11 (June), 15-18.

Stafford, James E. (1966), "Effects of Group Influences on Consumer Brand Preferences," *Journal of Marketing Research*, 3 (February), 68-75.

Swan, John E. and Linda Jones Combs (1976), "Product Performance and Consumer Satisfaction: A New Concept," *Journal of Marketing*, 40 (April), 25-33.

Thompson, Craig J. (1997), "Interpreting Consumers: A Hermeneutical Framework for Deriving Marketing Insights from the Texts of Consumers' Consumption Stories," *Journal of Marketing Research*, 34 (4), 438-455.

Thompson, Craig J., Aric Rindfleisch and Zynep Arsel (2006), "Emotional Branding and the Strategic Value of the Doppelgänger Brand Image," *Journal of Marketing*, 70 (January), 50-64.

Thompson, Craig J. and Maura Troester (2002), "Consumer Value Systems in the Age of Postmodern Fragmentation: The Case of the Natural Health Microculture," *Journal of Consumer Research*, 28 (4), 550-571.

Walsh, Gianfranco, Kevin P. Gwinner and Scott R. Swanson (2004), "What makes mavens tick? Exploring the motives of market mavens' initiation of information diffusion," *Journal of Consumer Marketing*, 21 (2), 109-122.

Whyte, William H. Jr. (1954), "The Web of Word of Mouth," *Fortune*, 50 (November), 140-143.

Threshold Lives: Exploring the Liminal Consumption of Tweens

Kevina Cody, Dublin Institute of Technology, Ireland, UK
Katrina Lawlor, Dublin Institute of Technology, Ireland, UK
Pauline Maclaran, Royal Holloway, University of London, UK

"It is in this gap between ordered worlds that almost anything can happen" (Turner, 1974: 13)

INTRODUCTION

The intervening spaces of socio-cultural organisation have proved sources of fascination and powerful theory development in the fields of sociology, psychology and anthropology (e.g. Douglas, 1966; Van Gennep, 1961; Freud, 1950, Foucault, 1977). Consumer culture research has hitherto acknowledged the potency of studying transitional phenomena, spaces and places and the interactions of varied ontologies with the consumption experiences of the individuals or group in flux and evolution (e.g. Davies and Fitchett, 2004; Maldonado and Tansuhaj, 1999; Gentry, 1997; Schouten, 1991). But what of those whose reality is the threshold between two ordered and defined worlds, the centre of nowhere?

This research focuses on the premise that for those whose sense of self is vague or blurred by the experience of existing midway between two distinct social spheres, belonging to neither, but embedded in both, consumption practices take on a divergent focus. Centring specifically on the pre-adolescent or tween, who has come to embody conceptualisations of a categorical anomaly (James, Jenks and Prout, 1998; Cook, 2004), a socio-cultural miasma (Jenks, 2005), the lived experience of a tween is explored using personal diaries, in-depth interviews and accompanied shopping trips. Thus we set out to explore the dynamics of consumer culture most recently articulated as 'a social arrangement in which the relations between lived culture and social resources, and between meaningful ways of life and the symbolic and material resources on which they depend, are mediated through markets' (Arnould & Thompson, 2005: 869), specifically amongst those who exist on the threshold of sociocultural organisation. This paper presents one of the theoretical conclusions of this longitudinal research project–the theory of metaconsumption–which explores consumption within their liminal shadow of activity and regeneration readying these social neophytes for the biggest performance of their lives.

EVERYTHING AND NOTHING–THE THEORETICAL FRAMEWORK OF LIMINALITY

Defined by Turner & Turner (1978: p.249) as 'the state and process of mid-transition in a rite of passage', a 'moment in and out of time' (Turner, 1969: p.96), the liminal phase of a transition, represents an instance of incompleteness, when the liminars (the ritual subjects in this phase) 'elude or slip through the network of classifications that normally locate states and positions in cultural space' (Turner, 1969: p.95). Understanding the attributes of liminal entities also serves to illustrate the core ideologies of the theory. One such attribute is structural and social invisibility, seclusion from the spheres of everyday life (Turner, 1967). In addition, ideologies of liminal theory espouse characteristics such as tabula rasa, symbolisation of concurrent degeneration and gestation or parturition (Turner, 1967), heteronomy, silence, equality and obscurity.

Turner's (1967, 110) 'invitation to investigators of culture to focus their attention on the phenomena and processes of mid-transition' has resulted in contrasting disciplines welcoming liminality and its constituent dimensions into their midst to enrich an understanding and analysis of many phases of cultural change. Several bodies of literature forming a hybridism of theoretical perspectives with liminality unite around a core trope of illness and loss (e.g. Little et al, 1998; Gough, 2005, Jones et al, 2007). Anderson (2003), Campbell et al (2005), Landzelius (2001) and Waskul (2005) have engaged with contextual specificities such as implantable cardioverter defibrillators (ICDs), advertising, incubated pre-term babies and internet personas respectively in their integration of this anthropological theory of structural anomalies.

Contexts as disparate as place and space (Pritchard & Morgan, 2006; Matthews et al, 2000), performance (Dunne, 2002; Rill, 2006; Brown, 2007; Hooker, 2007), and Postmodernity (Bhabha, 2004; Zukin, 1991; Bettis, 1996) highlight the infusion and contribution of many areas of socio-cultural research with ideologies of the liminal, adding vividness and analytical depth to contemporary lived experiences of socio-cultural evolvement and disruption.

LIMINAL CONSUMPTION

But what of liminal consumption? Have the ideologies of interim states been used as a lens of analysis for consumption practices and behaviours? Schouten (1991) represents the inaugural integration of this anthropological perspective on mid-transition with individual consumption practices. Despite introducing a link between liminality and consumption, the overall emphasis of Schouten's (1991) research is divided between self-concept theories, role transitions, rites of passage and liminal ideologies. This multi-theoretical focus implies that less in-depth insights of specifically liminal consumption behaviours are garnished. Schouten (1991, 422) himself concludes that 'little is yet known about the consumption behaviours of liminal people'.

Despite focusing on a proposed relationship between liminal transitions, symbolic consumption and the extended self, the work of Noble & Walker (1997) gravitates around the notion of transitions as opposed to the state of liminality itself and additionally utilises a positivist framework and quantitative methodology to align with its dissemination in predominantly psychologically oriented fields of inquiry.

Several other studies have approached the phenomenon of consumption in a liminal state (Hogg et al, 2004; Landzelius, 2001; Pavia & Mason, 2004). Although generating fascinating insights in their own right, these studies commonly relegate the liminal to a constituent dimension of a wider terrain of focus. It appeared that Schouten's (1991) cry to rally the troops towards explorations of this potential reservoir of symbolic meaning and consumer experiences had been relegated to the margins of interpretivist consumer research. Thus this research aimed to explore the interweaving of consumption and identity amongst those whose sense of self is as much about past as future; selves that are embedded in what was but gravitating towards what is to come.

METHODS

In order to explore the interaction of liminal lived experiences and tween consumption practices, there were several methodological considerations and implications. Firstly, cognisant of the inherent ideologies of liminality, an instance of time deemed fundamentally disruptive or ambiguous in the life of a pre-adolescent was selected so as to capture lived experience of 'betwixt and between' at its most lucid. Therefore, a longitudinal study of a year was undertaken spanning the participants' final months of primary school and early months of secondary education.[1] Three main sites of access were utilised; drama schools, personal contacts and primary schools.

Second, in line with Richardson's (1994) conceptualisation of multiple methods within the interpretivist domain as 'crystallisation', this year-long exploratory research project was interjected at various points by a constellation of data collection techniques. A focal point of Richardson's (1994) theorisation is the premise that 'what we see depends on the angle of our repose' (p.523). Five data collection methods were employed; namely in-depth interviews (which were conducted at two separate intervals), personal diaries, accompanied shopping trips, e-collages and researcher diaries. Each method was chosen so as to reflect a divergent angle of repose on the lived experience and consumption practices of a liminar. However, due to space constraints, only interview data will be integrated into this paper.

Analysis of such a myriad set of data collection techniques required a specific combination of rigour and creativity. In line with the work of Strauss and Corbin (1998), a grounded theory process of analysis was used which proved 'mechanistic and indeterminate in roughly equal portions' (McCracken, 1988: p.41). Following this process of analysis which inherently involves stages of memo writing, axial coding and selective coding, core categories were developed around which the other categories and constructs revolved and offered explanatory power (Spiggle, 1994). This process of data analysis culminated in a stage of data interpretation in the manner of 'a hermeneutic circle' (Arnold and Fischer, 1994: p.63).

RESEARCH FINDINGS AND INTERPRETATION

The following section details one of the central findings of the first phase of data collection–during the last months of primary school–the theory of metaconsumption. Although the main focus of this paper is the metaconsumption theorised as reflective of the consumption practices engaged with by the liminal tweens, it is necessary to briefly ground this theory in the context in which it emerged. This contextual grounding lays the foundation for the emergence of the metaconsumption theory.

The Liminal Tween

As discussed throughout the literature review, the theoretical framework of liminality (Turner, 1967; 1969; 1974) was utilised as a prism for interpreting the cultural and social categorisation of these ambiguously located beings. Due to space constraints there will be a brief delineation of one of the component concepts of the notion of the liminal tween. This and many other instances of liminality that emerged throughout the data add empirical credence to the social invisibility experienced by these 'betwixt and between' girls. This sense of being socially imperceptible would emerge as a focal point for the metaconsumption strategies engaged with by these interstital consumers.

Legal Vs Social Age

One of the most overtly liminal components of the tween identity was the tension experienced between their legal and social age. Testament to the conceptualisation that these girls are no longer; but not yet, their social and legal categorisations were often at odds with one another, resulting in an acute sense of social invisibility for the girls. Elaine informs me that although she is given the responsibility of caring for her own brother and sister, many people outside of her family would consider her 12 years of age, too young to be held responsible for young children. However she is keen to point out that she does not hold the same view:

E: *'but I am far more mature than a lot of 13 year olds I know. I think it is more to do with the fact that people hear 12 years old and they think oh that's too young to babysit children..'*
K: *'and when do you think they would be okay with it....other people?'*
E: *'I think at about 14 or 15 it is more acceptable, by other people, to be babysitting for children'.*

Here Elaine finds herself grappling with her own sense of social development and the views of those who ascribe to the legal indications of age-aligned development. She exists uncomfortably at the threshold of what is deemed acceptable legally and how she considers herself socially. This incongruence between legal and social age is manifest also in the social invisibility that seems to pervade their existence. Angela points out that their ambiguous social categorisation, their alignment with the interstices of culture means that an outlet for them in the community is often lacking or intangible.

K: *'what is it like being 12...?'*
A: *'I don't know...it's not deadly anyway...coz you can't do much'*
K: *'what do you mean....what can't you do?'*
A: *'there's nothing to do in Kilkenny and there's nothing to do around here really'*
K: *'and what kind of stuff do you want to do that maybe you can't'*
A: *'well you can't really go to the cinema much at my age coz you're always too young to see them.....like something could look really good but it's probably like 15s or something'.*

The Egocentric Tween

The incorporation of a theoretical perspective from the field of psychology was an emergent development following initial data analysis. Elkind's (1967) notion of egocentrism is considered by those specialising in the field of adolescent psychology, to be an under-researched idea, with constructive potential for anyone attempting to theorise on the lived experiences of young adolescents (Elliot & Feldman, 1990). In essence, Elkind's theory centres on the advanced cognitive capabilities of those approaching adolescence status in particular their increased ability to incorporate the perspectives of others into their own way of thinking and understanding themselves and the world around them. What differentiates adolescents however, and perhaps most pertinent to this research, is the tendency of this group to overgeneralise and believe themselves to be the focus of most other people's attention all of the time akin to an 'imaginary audience' (Elkind, 1967).

Amanda's interview illustrates vividly her tendency to incorporate an imagined audience into her developing self-system. She explains that the impending move to secondary school has meant divesting herself of any stationary that would be considered young or child like, in the hope of avoiding what she imagines would be certain disdain and ridicule from her new class mates.

K: *'what else did you have to buy for secondary school?'*
A: *'yea like I used to have all these little parers and little fancy girly parers but then I was like I'd probably get into*

[1]These stages of education correspond to junior and senior high school in the United States

trouble....people would be like 'why do you have that'...so I went for a plain pencil parer'...

K: *'what would people think if you have a plain pencil parer?'*

A: *'if you had a big girl sittin up on the table they might be like hmmmmm...baby....*

Here Amanda is using the imagined reactions of her peers to alter her consumption repertoire and future buying habits. It is almost like how she envisages her class-mates reacting to her display of consumption objects, is harnessed and utilised as a gauge for what will be suitable to bring along to secondary school. At this point in time, Amanda has not yet experienced the social environs of secondary school at first hand. However her advancing cognitive abilities have allowed her to consider the perspective of those girls she has yet to meet, albeit to an exaggerated degree. Even something as seemingly unrelated to social judgements and ridicule as the theft of her MP3 player is reflective of the egocentric nature of Amanda's developing self.

A: *'I nearly made myself sick thinking about it....i dunno why I got so upset about it....'*

K: *'was it to do with losing your zen...or that it was robbed by someone....'*

A: *'I dunno...I guess it was a bit of both....i just dunno....i just cracked....i imagined everyone will think I can't look after stuff...'*

In this example it appears that what had unsettled Amanda so much following the theft of her MP3 player was less to do with the physical void of the item but more with what she imagined the incident conveyed to others about her ability to be responsible for her possessions. Egocentrically, she believes this mishap to be the sole focus of others' attentions.

Metaconsumption

As outlined above, the liminars' lived experiences are characterised by social ambiguity, categorical invisibility and an overt preoccupation with how they appear in the eyes of those around them. It emerged throughout the data analysis that despite their conveyed annoyance at their status as social non-descripts, their shadowed realities were a vital resource.

As evidenced in the data, various consumption strategies were being utilised by the tweens in order to paradoxically evade definite categorisation via consumption owing to their egocentric tendencies and fear of social reprisal, prior to a more assured and competent entry into teenager-hood. But concurrently these strategies enable the tweens to tentatively participate in the consumer culture towards which they know their imperatives must be oriented if they are to be accepted by friends and envisaged onlookers.

A relatively recent consideration within the domain of cognitive analysis is that of second order thinking; or 'thinking about thinking' (Keating, 1990). Metacognition is frequently studied within the realm of psychology as 'the ability to monitor one's own cognitive abilities and activity for consistency, for gaps in information that need to be filled' (Keating, 1990: p75). This theory appeared to have potential for application within the domain of this instance of consumer research. When re-appropriated to analyse the emergent consumption practices of these liminal tweens, the theory of metaconsumption emerged as a viable theoretical process.

Fundamentally metaconsumption was envisaged as involving consumption about consumption. During this liminal existence, metaconsumption strategies served to realise the main preoccupation of a tween; remaining covertly active. It appears to be one of the primary preoccupations of the liminal experience, the main product of this ambiguous, obscure interval. Eluding definite categorisation as either child or teen, the tweens channel this cultural anonymity into preparing for one of the most socially pertinent roles of their lives thus far; becoming a teenager. These metaconsumption strategies, as will be delineated, allow the girls to paradoxically both evade definite categorisation via consumption prior to a more assured and competent entry into teenager-hood but also enables them to tentatively participate in the consumer culture towards which their imperatives must be oriented.

Brand Apathy

The nexus of the metaconsumption strategy is thus the maintenance of an unobtrusive, yet concurrently burgeoning site of consumption, which the liminal period appears to represent for these girls. Several strategies had at their core the notion that any activity, which wrenched the girls from the comfort of their categorical ambiguity and assign them to either a child or teen status before they feel prepared, is detrimental. One concept reflective of the tweens' striving towards consumption practices that facilitate preservation of their social anonymity, for fear of premature emergence before their imagined audience, is brand apathy. Pervasive throughout the first interview data is a definite reluctance by the girls to express an alignment with or affinity to branded products for fear of making an error conducive to social exclusion and ridicule. Contrary to the abundant secondary research in this area (e.g. Siegal et al, 2004; Lindstrom, 2003b; McNeal, 1992), the girls displayed a noticeable reticence when a discussion of brands and their importance to them arose.

In this example Nicola dismisses the notion that brands are important to her, but acknowledges that 'some people' like to revolve their consumption patterns around them.

K: *'so do you think brands matter to people your age?'*

N: *'well some people do...like they have to get all the brand....it doesn't matter to me'*

K: *'does it not...so what's important to you'*

N: *'just kind of if I like the top or not.'*

At this stage, she is still a novice when it comes to buying her way into the teen/consumption dialectic. By refusing to commit to an engagement with brand labels, she is not expected to know anything about them and thus cannot err in her discourse around brands and consumption. Her social status cannot be allocated and she can remain in the interstices of categorisation until such a time when she is equipped with enough social-kudos oriented information to emerge.

Another metaconsumption strategy seemingly utilized in order to convey a purposeful apathy about branded items is price preoccupation. There are numerous examples throughout the first interview data, which suggest that reverting to the reliable utilitarian justification of 'because non-branded things are cheaper', allays the possibility that their incompetence with consumer culture will be brought to notice.

Two excerpts from Rachel's interview add credence to the notion that apathy or resistance toward acknowledging the centrality of brands to their lived experiences is a strategic defence mechanism often couched in a fixation on value for money, designed to protect the shadow side of their being, their liminal regeneration.

K: *'and do you think brands matter to people in your class....well not just your class...but your friends....do ye talk about brands at all?'*

R: *'amm....not really....the main place that we go is penneys[2]....coz its so cheap and it actually does have some nice clothes and stuff…and they just have everything at a really cheap price… and say if you went into somewhere else…like where would you go…am…really expensive like Pauls or somewhere….and you'd see the same string top or the same jumper for like fifty euro and like the one you could get in penneys would be like fifteen or twenty…'*

In this first passage, Rachel's attitude is analogous to the other tweens, in that she justifies her supposed detachment from branded goods by referral to the value for money at non-branded stores. However just minutes later, Rachel recalls the experience of buying a new outfit for her confirmation a couple of months previously.

K: *'and what other shops would you go to….say if you went in with your mum?'*
R: *'well radical[3] I bought my confirmation outfit in.*
K: *'what kind of outfit did you get?'*
R: *'well I got these grey bench combats….they're really nice and I got this tee-shirt and I love it I wear it all the time…and I got a bench hoody….and am its really cool you can put on the sleeve you can put your thumb through a little hole in it…its really cool…and I got my runners[4] there aswell….they're van.'*

It is clear therefore that Rachel's earlier expressed indifference to brands is not consistent with her behaviour. In this instance, when her mother's financial agency enters the equation, and Rachel has had a tangible experience with a brand, Rachel's priorities change and the non-branded shop doesn't get a mention. Rather she manages to list two big brands in her purchases. Surely if the non-branded store is such good value, her mother's financial resources would have gone a long way further? Clearly Rachel's interview, visible in part through this inconsistency, suggests that indifference is a defence mechanism. Expressing a detachment from the world of labels, logos and symbolism is less important a goal when resources not available to the neophyte materialise.

Parody

Cognisant of the fact that the core of the metaconsumption strategy is its focus on existing without exhibiting, I was made aware of yet another component of this strategy during the accompanied shopping trips. This strategy centred on the agentive dimension of this liminal shadow in which the tweens exist; consumption strategies that evinced monitoring and acquiring of information and competencies needed when the time came to lead their liminal cocoon and embrace young teen identity.

During these shopping trips, the ambiguity and ensuing tension that the girls experienced in many of the shops seemed to stem from their recurring mislocation as a group or social category. At times the shops we visited were so beyond the realm of possibility for these girls on every level, while concurrently other stores evinced notions of a former childhood self that they were eager to forsake. In other words, it was palpable throughout these trips, that expressing interest in particular items was a risky, value-laden endeavour. Signalling interest in an item deemed 'inappropriate' in any dimension appeared to represent social suicide. I soon realised that these weren't just shopping trips, but opportunities to manage, protect and accumulate the knowledge that was expected of them as young, female consumers.

---

[2]Penney's is a discount clothing and accessories store in Ireland

[3]Radical is a store in Ireland which stocks branded clothing and footware

[4]Runners is Irish slang for trainers/sneakers

The concept of parody emerged as a means through which the girls could openly experiment with possible signifiers and configurations of consumption, but maintain a distance from any personal reflections ensuing because of these experiments at the same time. It allowed them to exist without exhibiting. During the shopping trip with three tweens for example, I witnessed first hand the use of this strategy. On entering one particular store, the girls picked up random tops and skirts claiming 'this is so you' or 'this is my dream outfit'. I only realised after chatting to the girls later on, that this was a statement of sarcasm meant to denote that something was not to their taste and they weren't at all genuine in their sentiments. However although it was not genuine admiration they espoused, expressing opinions or preferences couched in parody or mockery, protects the girls' vulnerability at a time when their level of consumer experience is limited.

The Fake Facilitators

This concept refers to the conclusion that many of the girls chose to forsake a preoccupation with having the genuine brand and instead focused on manipulating and utilising the sign value even associated with counterfeit versions to assert a provisional foot into the world of teen consumption. Therefore although many of the 'brands' they possess are in fact fakes, these products nonetheless facilitate a participation in a version of consumer culture, however diluted. This strategy allows for an engagement with the imperatives that dominate teen consumption but concurrently does not demand the resources only attributed to those of a more defined societal categorisation such as finances, life experience or definite market place allocation. In this example, Katie is taking me through some of the possession in her room, including a fake Von-Dutch cap. Interestingly she herself points out that it is a fake.

K: *'What other brands do you use?'*
KL: *'von dutch…I got those in Majorca…they have lasted me two years now'*
K: *'wow…and do you have any other von dutch stuff….do you know much about the brand?'*
Katie roots underneath her bed
K: *'ooh a cap…do you wear that much'*
KL: *'yeah…its fake von dutch…but it's still von dutch'*

What Katie seems to mean here is that to others, it still appears to be Von Dutch, or at the very least she is appearing to others to be engaging with the brands that form the appropriate staple diet of any normative teen. The important thing for Katie then is appearances rather than authenticity. Appearances maintain the shadow side of their being so that they can incur as little anticipated social ridicule as possible while they experiment with the intricacies of the teen persona/consumption dialectic.

Rachel also displayed an affinity for the non-authentic version of some well-known brands.

K: *(reading diary)…Louis Vitton is one of my favourite designers. I love his bags….so which one is yours?'*
R: *'well I got the both of them off my next door neighbour (laughs), she got them…*
K: *'what do you like about those bags'*
R: *'I think they look really cool…and I don't mind of they're fake…because no-one really knows'*

Rachel here articulates the key element of the fake facilitator concept, as a metaconsumption strategy. Counterfeit products allow the liminal tweens, despite their lack of agency as a socially ambiguous category, to engage with a desirable facet of consumer culture; the repository of symbolic meaning and social implications behind the Louis Vitton logo. Although the use of fake brands is not a consumption practice limited to this age group, the role that these brands play in the lived experience of a liminal tween is significant towards understanding how consumption is enacted during a time of social invisibility.

DISCUSSION

This paper has described some of the constituent parts of metaconsumption; the theorisation of the liminars' consumption practices. Being neither a child consumer nor a teen purchaser implies that there exists a gap between the self they were and the self they long to be and the liminal status that ensues. In addition, advancing cognitive capacities instil the tweens with a flagrant sense of trepidation regarding their neophyte-like social standing and potential public transgressions. Consequently they long to reside in the shadowed side of being, attempting to learn, monitor and accumulate socially oriented consumer knowledge, but all the while protect and maintain the anonymity that shields them from social scrutiny and insinuations. This intense period of 'consumption focused on consumption' aligning oneself with the nuances and mores of the social sphere which will help sculpt their entry into teenager-hood, provides examples of a myriad consumption strategies and practices which further a theorisation of liminal beings and their consumption practices.

Thus this desire to exist without exhibiting is the core characteristic of the liminal existence and subsequently the theory of metaconsumption has an integral role in its manifestation. For example, the visible propensity of the tweens to convey decided apathy and even resistance towards branded consumption with the variant but related strategy of price preoccupation, was reflective of an effort to preserve the unspecific nature of their social categorisation. Not committing to a brand meant not committing to an (unfinished) teen identity. This theoretical conclusion stands in stark contrast to the prevalent literature on branded consumption, whether conceptually, theoretically or managerially oriented (Lindstrom, 2003; McDougall & Chantrey, 2004; Elliot & Leonard, 2004) that convey brand-oriented consumption as a transparently positive and desired facet of tween consumer culture.

However it is equally as intrinsic to the liminal existence that this period of time is not entirely static. As theorised by Douglas (1966, p.137) in relation to interstitial existences ' there is energy in the margins and unstructured areas'. A degree of agency must become part of the metaconsumptive practices of the tween if they are to progress towards the essence of their teen identity (Jenks, 2003). Thus the concepts of the fake facilitators and parody encapsulate the covert but fervent accumulation of consumer-oriented knowledge and experience that concurrently embodies the liminar's 'betwixt and between' existence. For example, parody, akin to the foundational premise of the other metaconsumption strategies is both an enabling and a protective mechanism in that it facilitates the tweens' engagement with the appearance of teen consumerism but yet safeguards the anonymity necessary to prevent premature alignment with a teen identity that are ill prepared for.

Cognisant of the tweens' concurrent engagement with and detachment from consumption practices, the liminal period is proposed to represent a fruitful darkness (Turner, 1967, p110). Akin to understudies waiting in the wings anxiously ingesting as much information as possible in order to better prepare themselves for the biggest performative role of their lives to date–which as of yet is just out of sight–the fructile chaos of the fruitful darkness facilitates a private rehearsal for what will eventually be a very public performance. The metaphor of the fruitful darkness embodies the concurrent darkness and energy, the restorative obscurity that epitomises the liminars' experiences with consumer culture within the interstices of socio-cultural categorisation. Although at times the tweens appear passive or nonchalant about many of the signifiers of teen culture, this passivity appears to belie a fervent task. Turner (1967, p.102) similarly theorised when he claimed that during the liminal period 'his apparent passivity is revealed as an absorption of powers which will become active after his social status has been redefined…'

CONCLUSION

Fundamentally the theory of metaconsumption engages with the work of those who revel in exploring the myriad ways in which socio-cultural contexts and identity interact with and are mediated by market forces. This theory reflecting on the tendency of those who exist in an ambiguously defined social category to engage with 'consumption about consumption' also resonates with the 'consumer as identity seeker' conceptualisation pursued by those within the field of interpretive research. As argued by Arnould & Thompson (2005), what is most integral to the strength of consumer culture theory is its ability to transcend context and generate theoretical insight. In the case of this research, although the tween is an integral component of this work, the theory of metaconsumption has the potential to surpass its genesis within the micro-level of the lived experience of young adolescents and become an effective theoretical lens at a meso-level for exploring consumption practices throughout many other liminal experiences.

REFERENCES

Anderson, C. C. (2003), Phenomology of Implantation: The Liminal Body and the Implantable Cardioverter Defibrillator, Unpublished Doctoral Dissertation, Griffith University.

Arnold, S. J. and Fischer, E. (1994), 'Hermeneutics and Consumer Research,' *Journal of Consumer Research*, 21 (1), 55-70.

Arnould, E. J. and Thompson, C. J. (2005), 'Consumer Culture Theory (CCT): Twenty Years of Research, *Journal of Consumer Research*, 31 (4), 868-882.

Bettis, P. J. (1996), 'Urban Students, Liminality and the postindustrial context,' *Sociology of Education*, 69 (2), 105-125.

Bhabha, H. K. (2004), *The Location of Culture*, New York: Routledge.

Brown, K. B. (2007), 'Introduction: Liminality and the Social Location of Musicians,' *Twentieth Century Music*, 3 (1), 5-12.

Campbell, N., O' Driscoll, A. & Saren, M. (2005), 'Cyborg Consciousness: A Visual Culture Approach to the Technologised Body', In: Ekstrom, K. M. & Brembeck, H. (Eds). *Proceedings of the European Advances in Consumer Research Conference*, Gothenburg, Duluth, MN: Association for Consumer Research.

Cook, D. T. (2004), 'Beyond Either/Or,' *Journal of Consumer Culture*, 4 (2), 147-153.

Davies. A. & Fitchett, J. A. (2004), 'Crossing Culture: A Multi-Method Enquiry into Consumer Behaviour and the Experience of Cultural Transition', *Journal of Consumer Behaviour*, 3 (4), 315-330.

Douglas, M. (1966), *Purity and Danger: An Analysis of the Concepts of Pollution and Taboo*, London: Allen Lane.

Dunne, M. (2002), 'Resolving a Paradox Through Liminality,' *Journal of Popular Film and Television*, 29 (4), 182-189.

Elkind, D. (1967), 'Egocentrism in Adolescence,' *Child Development*, 38 (4), 1025-1034.

Elliot, G. R. and Feldman, S. S. (1990), 'Capturing the Adolescent Experience,' in Elliot, G. R. and Feldman, S. S, eds. *At the Threshold: The Developing Adolescent*, US: Harvard University Press.

Elliot, R. and Leonard, C. (2004), 'Peer Pressure and Poverty: Exploring Fashion Brands and Consumption Symbolism among Children of the British Poor,' *Journal of Consumer Behaviour*, 3 (4), 347-359.

Foucault, M. (1977), *Language, Counter-Memory, Practice (contains the 1963 essay 'Preface to Transgression')*, New York: Cornell University Press.

Freud, S. (1950), *Totem and Taboo*, New York: Routledge & Kegan Paul Ltd.

Gentry, J. W. (1997), 'Life-Event Transitions and Consumer Vulnerability,' *Advances in Consumer Research*, 24 (1), 29-31.

Gough, A. (2005), 'Body/Mine: A Chaos Narrative of Cyborg Subjectivities and Liminal Experiences,' *Women's Studies*, 34 (3-4), 249-264.

Hogg, M. K., Curasi, C. F. & Maclaran, P. (2004), 'The (Re-) Configuration of Production and Consumption in Empty Nest Households/Families,' *Consumption, Markets and Culture*, 7 (3), 239-259.

Hooker, L. (2007), 'Controlling the Liminal Power of Performance: Hungarian Scholars and Romani Musicians in the Hungarian Folk Festival,' *Twentieth-Century Music*, 3 (1), 51-72.

James, A. Jenks, C. & Prout, A. (1998), *Theorizing Childhood*, Cambridge: Polity Press.

Jenks, C. (2003), *Transgression*, London: Routledge.

Jenks, C. (2005), *Childhood*, New York: Routledge.

Jones, K. T., Zagacki, K. S. and Lewis, T. V. (2007), 'Communication, Liminality and Hope: The September 11th Missing Person Posters,' *Communication Studies*, 58 (1), 105-121.

Keating, D. P. (1990), 'Adolescent Thinking'. In Elliot, G. R. and Feldman, S. S, eds. *At the Threshold: The Developing Adolescent*, US: Harvard University Press.

Landzelius, K. M. (2001), 'Charged Artifacts and the Detonation of Liminality: Teddy-Bear Diplomacy in the Newborn Incubator Machine,' *Journal of Material Culture*, 6 (3), 323-344.

Lindstrom, M. (2003), *Brand Child*, London: Kogan Page Limited.

Little, M., Jordens, C. F., Paul, K., Montgomery, K. and Philipson, B. (1998), 'Liminality: A Major Category of the Experience of Cancer Illness,' *Social Science & Medicine*, 47 (10), 1485-1494.

Maldonado, R. & Tansuhaj, P. (1999), 'Transition Challenges in Consumer Acculturation: Role Destabilization and Changes in Symbolic Consumption, *Advances in Consumer Research*, 26 (1), 134-140.

Matthews, H., Taylor, M., Percy-Smith, B. and Limb, M. (2000), 'The Unacceptable Flaneur: The Shopping Mall as a Teenage Hangout,' *Childhood*, 7 (3), 279-294.

McCracken, G. (1988), *Culture and Consumption*, Bloomington: Indiana University Press.

McDougall, J. and Chantrey, D. (2004), 'The Making of Tomorrow's Consumer,' *Young Consumers*, 5 (4), 8-18.

McNeal, J. U. (1992), *Kids as Customers: a Handbook of Marketing to Children*, New York: Lexington Books.

Noble, C. H. and Walker, B. A. (1997), 'Exploring the Relationships among Liminal Transitions, Symbolic Consumption and the Extended Self,' *Psychology & Marketing*, 14 (1), 29-47.

Pavia, T. M. and Mason, M. J. (2004), 'The Reflexive Relationship between Consumer Behaviour and Adaptive Coping,' *Journal of Consumer Research*, 31 (2), 441-454.

Pritchard, A. and Morgan, N. (2006), 'Hotel Babylon? Exploring Hotels as Liminal Sites of Transition and Transgression,' *Tourism Management*, 27 (5), 762-772.

Richardson, L. (1994), 'Writing: A Method of Inquiry,' In Denzin, N. K. and Lincoln, Y. S, eds. *Handbook of Qualitative Research*, Thousand Oaks, CA: Sage.

Rill, B. (2006), 'Rave, Communitas and Embodied Idealism,' *Music Therapy Today*, 7 (3), 648-661.

Schouten, J. W. (1991), 'Selves in Transition: Symbolic Consumption in Personal Rites of Passage and Identity Reconstruction,' *Journal of Consumer Research*, 17 (4), 412-425.

Siegal, D. L., Coffey, T. J. and Livingston, G. (2004), *The Great Tween Buying Machine: Capturing your Share of the Multibillion Dollar Tween Market*, US: Dearborn Trade Publishing.

Slater, D. (1997), *Consumer Culture and Modernity*, Oxford, UK: Polity Press.

Spiggle, S. (1994), 'Analysis and Interpretation of Qualitative Data in Consumer Research, *Journal of Consumer Research*, 21 (3), 491-503.

Strauss, A. and Corbin, J. (1998), *Basics of Qualitative Research*, California: Sage.

Turner, V. W. & Turner, E. (1978), *Image and Pilgrimage in Christian Culture: Anthropological Perspectives*, New York: Columbia University Press.

Turner, V. W. (1967), *The Forest of Symbols: Aspects of Ndembu Ritual*, Ithaca: Cornell University Press.

Turner, V. W. (1969), *The Ritual Process: Structure and Anti-Structure*, Ithaca: Cornell University Press.

Turner, V. W. (1974), *Dramas, fields and metaphors: symbolic action in human society*, Ithaca: Cornell University Press.

Van Gennep, A. (1961), *The Rites of Passage*, US: Chicago University Press.

Waskul, D. D. (2005), 'Ekstasis and the Internet: Liminality and Computer-mediated Communication,' *New Media & Society*, 7 (1), 47-63.

Zukin, S. (1991), *Landscapes of Power: From Detroit to Disneyworld*, London: University of California Press Ltd.

Causes Customers Ascribe to Low Prices in Discount Stores

Stephan Zielke, University of Göttingen, Germany

ABSTRACT

This paper identifies and analyzes the causes customers ascribe to low prices in discount stores. Such causes are inferior product quality, unfair relations to employees and suppliers, fair relations to customers (profit waive), an efficient business model, and psychological tricks in price communication. The paper demonstrates how these attributions impact perceptions, emotions and behavioral intentions to buy in discount stores. The results underline that each attribution type has specific effects on certain dependent variables. The study has important implications, as it shows that companies can influence customer perceptions, emotions and shopping intentions by changing specific attributions to low prices.

INTRODUCTION

Grocery discounters have experienced rising market shares in many European countries (Colla 2003; Delleersnyder et al. 2007), and they are also successful in the US (Brown and Bury 2008; Springer 2008). Discounters offer continuously low prices and many products are cheaper than in stores from other formats (Rondán Cataluña et al. 2005; Wood and Pearson 2006).

Although discounters have this price advantage, they attract certain customers while others avoid these stores. Attribution theory (Heider 1958; Kelley 1973; Kelley and Michela 1980) offers an explanation for this observation, as customers can ascribe different causes to low prices in discount stores. Customers might, for example, believe that discount stores offer lower prices than supermarkets because they compromise product quality. Other causes might be unfair relations to employees and suppliers, fair relations to customers (profit waive), an efficient business model, and psychological tricks in price communication.

Even though attribution theory is used in many different marketing contexts (Folkes 1988; Mizerski et al. 1979), attributions to low prices are not analyzed systematically. This paper closes this gap by analyzing attributions to low prices in grocery retailing. It identifies the positive and negative causes customers ascribe to low prices in discount stores and demonstrates how the diverse attributions impact perceptions, emotions and behavioral intentions to buy in discount stores. The results underline that each attribution type has *specific* effects on certain dependent variables. The study has important implications, as it shows that companies can influence customer perceptions, emotions and shopping intentions by changing specific attributions to low prices.

THEORETICAL FRAMEWORK AND LITERATURE ANALYSIS

Attribution theory constitutes the theoretical framework of this study (Heider 1958; Kelley 1973; Kelley and Michela 1980). This theory concerns the way in which individuals assign causes to observed actions or events. According to Folkes (1988), "attribution is concerned with all aspects of inference: how people arrive at causal inferences, what sort of inferences they make, and what the consequences of these inferences are". In marketing and consumer behavior literature, many applications of this theory exist (Folkes 1988; Mizerski et al. 1979).

However, the literature does not provide many applications of attribution theory in price-related contexts. One research stream investigates attributions regarding price promotions with discount claims. Lichtenstein et al. (1989) found that attributions concerning the advertiser's motives for a price discount offer have a significant effect on the consumers' evaluations of the offer. Burton et al. (1994) observed that the extent of retailer and product attributions regarding a discount claim depends on the price positioning of the retailer. They also demonstrated that attributions to the retailer have a positive effect on different psychological and behavioral variables (perceived value, attitude toward the ad, shopping intentions) while product attributions have a negative effect. Other researchers investigated internal (customer) or external attributions with regard to price deals and satisfaction with rebate shopping experiences (Hunt et al. 1995; Schindler 1989, 1998).

A second research stream analyzes attributions to price increases. Several researchers argue that the inferred motives for a price increase have an impact on the perceived price fairness (Campbell 1999; Kahneman et al. 1986). Vaidyanathan and Aggarwal (2003) apply attribution theory to investigate the conditions under which even cost-justified price increases are perceived as unfair. They demonstrate that a cost-justified price increase is perceived as less fair when the locus of causality is internal to the seller and/or when the price increase is within the volitional control of the respective company.

The literature analysis illustrates that most applications of attribution theory are related to person (retailer) vs. stimulus (product) and circumstance (situational) or internal (customer) vs. external (other causes) attributions. In contrast to these studies, the present research analyzes attributions on a less abstract level. The aim of this study is to identify concrete causes to which customers attribute low prices in discount stores, and to analyze their impact on store perceptions, emotions and shopping intentions. It is noteworthy that the present paper also differs from previous studies in that it focuses on attributions regarding the price level of a store instead of a single product, promotion or price increase.

ATTRIBUTIONS TO LOW PRICES IN DISCOUNT STORES

Before developing hypotheses about the impact of attributions to low prices in discount stores, the nature of such attributions should be discussed.

Product-related attributions exist if customers attribute a discount store's low prices to the *inferior quality* of the assortment. These attributions might be the consequence of price-quality inferences, where customers associate higher prices with better quality. Many empirical studies have identified such inferences (Völckner and Hofmann 2007). The inferior quality attribution is not necessarily limited to search and experience qualities, such as color or taste. Especially concerns about credence qualities might prove relevant in price-quality inferences for food products. Credence qualities include food safety, origin of products, environmental compatibility and animal welfare (Becker 2000; Brunsø et al. 2002; Grunert 2005; Northen 2000). To sum up, the inferior quality attribution is a product-related attribution with a negative character.

In contrast, retailer-related attributions for low prices are often described as positive attributions. Burton et al. (1994) give examples of such positive attributions, e. g. "meeting competitors' prices" or "passing on savings from bulk purchases from manufacturers". Generally, discount retailers can meet their competitors' prices by smaller margins or lower costs. Smaller margins can be interpreted as *fair relations to customers*, as managers or owners waive a part of their profit. A *more efficient business model* is a positive cause for lower cost. It costs far less to operate a discount store than a mainstream supermarket (Kaas 1994). Furthermore, discount retailers buy large quantities of exclusive private label products, resulting in lower purchase costs and a more efficient supply chain management (Colla 2003). Customers might believe that discount stores are low-priced because they pass on these savings.

However, negative retailer attributions also exist. Customers might infer that discount stores have lower prices than other stores because they *behave unethically towards different stakeholders*, for example employees and suppliers. These attributions are supported by press reports on aggressive purchasing policies (e. g. McGreevy 2008) and the exploitation of employees (e. g. Boyes 2008). Even if some discount retailers actually pay higher wages than some of their supermarket competitors (Springer 2008), their customers might believe the contrary.

Finally, customers can ascribe the competitive price image of discount stores to *psychological tricks in price communication*. Customers might be aware of pricing tactics retailers use to improve their price perception (Hardesty et al. 2007) and they might be skeptical towards price claims in advertisements (Obermiller and Spangenberg 2000).

To recapitulate, customers can ascribe five types of causes to low prices in discount stores. These are inferior quality, unfair relations to suppliers and employees, fair relations to customers (profit waive), the efficiency of the business model and psychological tricks in price communication.

HYPOTHESES

The following section derives hypotheses about the impact of the five types of attributions on different dependent variables, such as perceptions, emotions and shopping intentions.

Perceptions

Firstly, it is assumed that customer attributions have an impact on several perceptions, such as price level perception, quality perception, perceived value for money, price fairness and ease of price evaluation. With the exception of product quality, these constructs are all dimensions of a retailer's price image (Zielke 2006, 2009a).

Price level perception refers to the amount of money customers have to pay for a selected basket of goods without taking quality differences compared to other stores into account. The efficiency and the tricks attribution should especially have an impact on price level perception. If customers believe that discount stores operate more efficiently than other stores, they should perceive discount store prices as more competitive. However, if they suppose that the discount stores' price image results from psychological tricks, they will rate the prices as more expensive.

H1: The stronger (a) the efficiency and the weaker (b) the tricks attribution, the better (lower) the perceived price level.

The inferior quality attribution should especially determine the quality perception of the store. This results from the nature of both constructs.

H2: The weaker (a) the inferior quality attribution, the better the perceived quality.

Value for money is defined as the result of matching price and performance evaluations (Dodds and Monroe 1985; Zeithaml 1988). Hence, the attributions influencing price level and quality perception should also influence perceived value.

H3: The weaker (a) the inferior quality and (b) the tricks attribution, and the stronger (c) the efficiency attribution, the better the perceived value for money.

Price fairness is defined as a judgment if prices are reasonable, acceptable or just (Xia et al. 2004). Some studies in the literature explain the perceived fairness of a price increase based on customer attributions related to the cause of the increase (Campbell 1999; Kahnemann et al. 1986; Vaidyanathan and Aggarwal 2003). Furthermore, previous research found strong relations between value and fairness and some authors even operationalize price fairness very similarly to value for money (Bei and Chiao 2001). Hence, the attributions influencing value perception should also influence price fairness. In addition, the fair relations to customers and the unfair relations to stakeholders attributions should influence this construct.

H4: The weaker (a) the inferior quality, (b) the unfairness and (c) the tricks attribution, and the stronger (d) the fairness and (e) the efficiency attribution, the better the perceived price fairness.

Ease of price evaluation is related to price uncertainty (Mazumdar and Jun 1992) and describes how easily customers perceive the evaluation of a store's prices (Zielke 2006, 2009a). The psychological tricks attribution should especially influence this price image dimension, as the prices might seem to be more competitive than they really are.

H5: The weaker the (a) psychological tricks attribution, the better the ease of price evaluation.

Emotions

Secondly, attributions to low prices should influence several emotions which are related to price and quality perception. The role of attributions as antecedents of emotions is extensively discussed in the literature, such as in Weiner's attributional theory of emotions (Weiner 1985, 1986). The emotional consequences of attributions to low prices may be manifold; however, the present study concentrates on the negative emotions of shame and guilt, which might be especially relevant and interesting in discount shopping contexts.

Shame and guilt are both self-related emotions. Guilt results when customers believe that their actions violate societal or internal standards (Dahl et al. 2003), while shame or embarrassment result when actions violating moral or societal standards are observable for others (Izard 1977). Customers might believe that buying low quality food for the sake of saving money violates standards of good nutrition. Similarly, buying in a store that exploits farmers and employees to offer low prices might be perceived as a violation of standards regarding fairness in business relationships. Hence, the inferior quality and the unfair relations to stakeholders attribution should increase shame and guilt.

H6: The stronger (a) the inferior quality attribution and (b) the unfairness attribution, the greater the shame.

H7: The stronger (a) the inferior quality attribution and (b) the unfairness attribution, the greater the guilt.

Shopping intentions

Finally, it is assumed that all attributions influence intentions to buy in discount stores. This hypothesis is supported by previous studies, where price-related attributions influenced shopping intentions and behavior (e. g. Burton et al. 1994; Schindler 1998).

H8: The weaker (a) the inferior quality, (b) the unfairness and (c) the tricks attribution, and the stronger (d) the fairness and (e) the efficiency attribution, the stronger the intentions to buy in discount stores.

RESEARCH DESIGN AND SAMPLE

A paper-and-pencil questionnaire was designed to test the hypotheses. The item-scale for the attributions was developed based on a discussion with students from a Master's course in retail pricing at a large European University. The question "why are prices in discount stores so low?" was discussed with the students, their arguments were collected and then translated into an item-scale. A pre-test proved that the wording of the items was clear and understandable. The twenty items cover aspects of product quality, fair relations to customers, the efficiency of the business model, relations to employees and suppliers, and psychological tricks in price communication. A large scale pilot study with 597 respondents confirmed the hypothesized factor structure of the attributions (Zielke 2007). However, as the factor loadings and alpha values were not completely satisfactory, the item-scale was refined to a shorter and more manageable scale of 13 items. In this scale, each attribution is measured by not more than three items. Perceptions, emotions and behavioral intentions were measured with three to five items each. Scales for all these dependent variables are based on prior research (Zielke 2009a, 2009b) and presented in the appendix. All items were measured on 7-point scales ranging from 1 (strongly disagree) to 7 (strongly agree).

The respondents were asked to evaluate one particular discount store. Similar to Zielke (2009a, 2009b), they selected the store from a list of different grocery discounters. This was necessary to guarantee that the respondents have at least a rudimental impression of the store they evaluate. The questionnaires were distributed to people of different levels of age, gender, household size and income buying groceries at least once a week. The respondents usually completed the questionnaires at home and then returned them to the research team personally or by post. This procedure resulted in 402 usable questionnaires. The mean age of the respondents was 35 years, 57.8 percent of the respondents were female and the median net income ranged between 1,501 and 2,000 euros per month.

ANALYSIS AND RESULTS

The first part of the results section analyzes the factor structure of the attributions to low prices in discount stores. The second part investigates the hypothesized effects of these attributions on perceptions, emotions and shopping intentions.

The factor structure of attributions

Firstly, the factor structure of the attribution scale was analyzed with exploratory and confirmatory factor analyses. The exploratory analysis was conducted to replicate the results from the pilot study. The principal component analysis of the 13 attribution items yielded five factors with eigenvalues greater than one, explaining 74.1 percent of the item variance (table 1). The factors are identical to those found in the pilot study and clearly interpretable as inferior quality (F1), unfair relations to stakeholders (F2), profit waive or fair relations to customers (F3), the efficiency of the business model (F4) and psychological tricks in price communication (F5). Alpha values indicate an acceptable amount of convergent validity. Only the alpha value for fairness to customers is slightly below the level of .70.

In addition to the principal component analysis, a confirmatory factor analysis tested the convergent and discriminant validity. Table 2 presents the results from a confirmatory analysis conducted in Mplus using the MLR estimator (Muthén and Muthén 2007). The fit indexes are acceptable (CFI: .955, RMSEA: .048, SRMR: .055, $\chi 2$/df: 122/55). For each attribution type, the variance explained is larger than any squared correlation with another attribution. Hence, the discriminant validity is given according to Fornell and Larcker's criterion. Furthermore, the average variance explained for each attribution is close to or above 50 percent.

The impact of attributions on perceptions, emotions and shopping intentions

Before testing the hypotheses, alpha values for the dependent variables were calculated. Only the coefficient for ease of price evaluation was below .70, but still acceptable (.61). Furthermore, discriminant validity between attributions and all dependent variables was sufficient according to Fornell and Larcker's criterion. The only exception was the inferior quality attribution, which correlates strongly with quality perception. After testing convergent and discriminant validity, a separate structural equation model was calculated for each dependent variable. Again, all fit-indexes are acceptable, CFI is between .940 and .964 and SRMR is between .044 and .050 (table 3).

H1 assumed that the stronger the efficiency and weaker the tricks attribution, the better the perceived price level. The results support this hypothesis with a positive coefficient for efficiency (.50) and a negative coefficient for the tricks attribution (-.26). Furthermore, H2 is supported by a negative impact of the inferior quality attribution on quality perception (-.82). In addition, there are small effects from the fairness (.16) and efficiency attribution (.14), which were not hypothesized. Supporting H3, the inferior quality (-.30), the efficiency (.37) and the tricks (-.23) attribution influence value in the hypothesized direction. H4 is only partly supported. The inferior quality (-.32), the unfairness (-.23) and the psychological tricks attribution (-.22) have a negative impact on price fairness. The coefficient for efficiency (.12) is only significant for a ten percent level of significance. Surprisingly, the fairness to customers attribution has no impact on price fairness. Supporting H5, psychological tricks have a negative effect on the ease of price evaluation (-.27). In addition, the efficiency attribution has a positive effect on the ease of price evaluation, which was not hypothesized (.24).

H6 is supported by the positive impact of the inferior quality attribution on shame (.32). Interestingly, the effect of the unfairness attribution on shame is small and not significant. H7, in contrast, is completely supported. The inferior quality (.34) and the unfairness attribution (.31) both have a significant impact on guilt.

According to H8, the inferior quality, the unfairness to stakeholders and the psychological tricks attribution should have a negative impact on shopping intentions, while the fairness to customers and the efficient business model attribution should have a positive impact. However, the results only support H8 for the inferior quality (-.36), the unfairness to stakeholders (-.20) and the efficiency of the business model attributions (.23).

GENERAL DISCUSSION

The results support most of the hypothesized effects. Beyond the (intuitive) finding that positive attributions have positive effects while negative attributions have a negative impact, the results illustrate that specific attributions influence different dependent variables and that some attributions have stronger effects than others. The inferior quality attribution is the strongest predictor of perceived quality, price fairness, shame, guilt and shopping inten-

TABLE 1
Factor structure of attributions

Prices in discount stores are so low ...	Factor 1	Factor 2	Factor 3	Factor 4	Factor 5
because they do not attach great importance to quality management	.81				
because they compromise product quality	.84				
because their products contain more artificial ingredients	.74				
because discount stores exploit their employees		.82			
because discount stores exploit their suppliers		.84			
because discount stores behave unethically towards suppliers and farmers		.84			
because management salaries are smaller than in other companies			.85		
because owners and managers are more modest than in other companies			.86		
because these companies buy larger quantities				.81	
because the business model is more efficient				.77	
because they purchase products at lower prices				.79	
however, prices in these stores are not as low as many people believe					.87
however, these stores are only perceived as low-priced because they use psychological tricks					.86
Cronbach's alpha	.77	.84	.65	.72	.82

Factor loadings smaller than .40 are suppressed

TABLE 2
Discriminant validity (variance explained and squared correlations)

Attribution		QUAL	UNF	FAIR	EFF	TRICK
Inferior quality	QUAL	.54				
Unfair relations	UNF	.27	.64			
Fair relations	FAIR	.01	.00	.56		
Efficient business model	EFF	.06	.01	.03	.46	
Psychological tricks	TRICK	.22	.18	.02	.14	.70

CFI: .955; RMSEA: .048; SRMR: .055; χ^2/df: 122/55

tions. The efficiency attribution influences price level perception and value for money most strongly. The psychological tricks attribution is the strongest predictor of the ease of price evaluation. Unfairness to stakeholders is also an important attribution, which influences price fairness, guilt and shopping intentions. Fairness to customers (profit waive) seems the least important as this attribution only has a small impact on the quality perception.

The study has several theoretical implications. It extends the previous research by providing a typology of attributions to low prices. In addition, the empirical results underline that these attributions explain differences in customers' perceptions of discount stores, emotions related to these stores and their shopping intentions. Therefore, the results contribute to the understanding of discount buying.

Some effects are especially interesting from a theoretical perspective. The results contribute to price fairness research as they show that unfairness to employees and suppliers has a strong impact on general price fairness. Therefore, unfair relations to stakeholders

TABLE 3
Results of hypotheses tests

Dependent Variable	QUAL Beta (sig.)	UNF Beta (sig.)	FAIR Beta (sig.)	EFF Beta (sig.)	TRICK Beta (sig.)	Latent Var. R-Square	CFI SRMR
Price level perception	.08 (.358)	-.13 (.088)	.12 (.171)	**.50** (.000)	**-.26** (.003)	.454	.954 .047
Quality perception	**-.82** (.000)	.06 (.350)	**.16** (.025)	**.14** (.024)	.07 (.308)	.722	.953 .048
Value for money	**-.30** (.001)	-.07 (.264)	.12 (.151)	**.37** (.000)	**-.23** (.020)	.544	.940 .050
Price fairness	**-.32** (.000)	**-.23** (.005)	.07 (.350)	.12 (.089)	**-.22** (.009)	.445	.960 .048
Ease of price evaluation	-.20 (.069)	-.04 (.677)	-.04 (.849)	**.24** (.016)	**-.27** (.013)	.304	.955 .047
Shame	**.32** (.008)	.03 (.694)	-.06 (.631)	-.03 (.818)	.13 (.123)	.182	.964 .044
Guilt	**.34** (.000)	**.31** (.000)	-.04 (.488)	-.09 (.253)	-.07 (.376)	.302	.958 .046
Shopping intentions	**-.36** (.000)	**-.20** (.003)	.02 (.676)	**.23** (.008)	.00 (.986)	.329	.954 .048

should be integrated in price fairness research. Also, the effects on shame and guilt are remarkable. While guilt has different attributional antecedents (inferior quality and unfair relations), only the inferior quality attribution influences shame. Customers do not feel ashamed when they attribute low prices to the exploitation of employees and suppliers. Hence, although shame and guilt are similar constructs, they depend on different antecedents. The findings for the tricks attribution are also remarkable. This attribution has a negative impact on a number of perceptions, while the effects on emotions and shopping intentions are not significant. Hence, customers are aware of such tricks, but they do not change their behavior. This explains why some stores which are known for using such tricks are still very successful.

The results also have important managerial implications. They show that retailers can influence store perceptions, emotions and shopping intentions by influencing customers' attributions to low prices. If discount retailers want to improve shopping intentions, they should especially communicate the existence of quality management systems and results from independent product tests to their customers, but also the efficiency of their business model. While communicating results from product tests is a matter of course, communicating the business model's efficiency is not common practice. This is problematic as the results show that the efficiency attribution significantly influences price and quality perceptions.

Moreover, discount retailers should attach greater importance to establishing and communicating fair relations to their employees and suppliers. Reducing the unfairness to stakeholders attribution is important as this attribution has a negative impact on perceived price fairness and increases guilt. In practice, some discount retailers pay their cashiers higher wages than their supermarket competitors, although this is often unknown to the public (Springer 2008).

If discounters want to improve price and quality perception, they should also try to reduce the psychological tricks attribution by conducting and communicating objective price comparisons with their competitors. However, whether this also increases customer shopping intentions is questionable.

Finally, some limitations and implications for future research should be discussed. Firstly, this study analyzed the impact of attributions on a number of different dependent variables with separate structural equation models. This allowed a clean analysis of the hypothesized effects. However, as there might be relationships between emotions, perceptions and shopping intentions, attributions can influence shopping intentions via a number of indirect effects. Hence, future research should develop an integrated model of attributions, emotions and perceptions to explain discount buying more holistically. Another limitation refers to individual differences in the strength and impact of attributions. Future research should investigate whether customer segments with different attributions to low prices exist. Furthermore, customers selected the evaluated store from a list of different grocery discounters. This procedure guaranteed that the respondents have at a least a rudimental impression of the store, but store selection can also bias the results. Finally, the fair relations to customers scale seems somewhat problematic as the items are only indirectly related to concerns about customer welfare. This might explain why this factor had so little impact on the dependent variables.

REFERENCES

Becker, Tilman (2000), "Consumer Perception of Fresh Meat Quality: A Framework for Analysis," *British Food Journal*, 102(3), 158-176.

Bei, Lien-Ti and Yu-Ching Chiao (2001), "An Integrated Model for the Effects of Perceived Product, Perceived Service Quality, and Perceived Price Fairness on Consumer Satisfaction and Loyalty," *Journal of Consumer Satisfaction, Dissatisfaction and Complaining Behavior*, 14, 125-140.

Boyes, Roger (2008), "Lidl, the Big Brother Supermarket, is Watching You," *The Times*, 27. March 2008 (http://www.timesonline.co.uk).

Brunsø, Karen, Thomas Ahle Fjord, and Klaus G. Grunert (2002), *Consumers' Food Choice and Quality Perception*, Working Paper No. 77, Aarhus, Danmark: Aarhus School of Business.

Burton, Scot, Donald R. Lichtenstein, Abhijit Biswas, and Katherine Fraccastoro (1994), "The Role of Attributions in Customer Perceptions of Retail Advertisements Promoting Price Discounts," *Marketing Letters*, 5(2), 131-140.

Brown, Ely and Chris Bury (2008), "Grocery Shopping for the Cost-Conscious: Chain Store Aldi Offers Deep Discounts on Food Staples," *ABC News*, 24. November 2008 (http://abcnews.go.com).

Campbell, Margaret C. (1999), "Perceptions of Price Unfairness: Antecedents and Consequences," *Journal of Marketing Research*, 36(2), 187-199.

Colla, Enrico (2003), "International Expansion and Strategies of Discount Grocery Retailers: The Winning Models," *International Journal of Retail & Distribution Management*, 31(1), 55-66.

Dahl, Darren W., Heather Honea, and Rajesh V. Manchanda (2003), "The Nature of Self-Reported Guilt in Consumption Contexts," *Marketing Letters*, 14(3), 159-171.

Deleersynder, Barbara, Marnik G. Dekimpe, Jan-Benedict E. M. Steenkamp, and Oliver Koll (2007), "Win-Win Strategies at Discount Stores," *Journal of Retailing and Consumer Services*, 14(5), 309-318.

Dodds, William B. and Kent B. Monroe (1985), "The Effect of Brand and Price Information on Subjective Product Evaluations," *Advances in Consumer Research*, 12, 85-90.

Folkes, Valerie S. (1988), "Recent Attribution Research in Consumer Behavior: A Review and New Directions," *Journal of Consumer Research*, 14(4), 548-565.

Grunert, Klaus G. (2005), "Food Quality and Safety: Consumer Perception and Demand," *European Review of Agricultural Economics*, 32(3), 369-391.

Hardesty, David M., William O. Bearden, and Jay P. Carlson (2007), "Persuasion Knowledge and Consumer Reactions to Pricing Tactics," *Journal of Retailing*, 83(2), 199-210.

Heider, Fritz (1958), *The Psychology of Interpersonal Relations*, New York, NJ: Wiley.

Hunt, Keneth A., Susan M. Keaveney, and Moonkyu Lee (1995), "Involvement, Attributions and Consumer Responses to Rebates," *Journal of Business and Psychology*, 9(3), 273-297.

Izard, Caroll E. (1977), *Human Emotions*, New York, NY: Plenum Press.

Kahneman, Daniel, Jack L. Knetsch, and Richard Thaler (1986), "Fairness as a Constraint on Profit Seeking: Entitlements in the Market," *The American Economic Review*, 76(4), 728-741.

Kaas, Philippe (1994), "The Rise of Discount: How to Survive the Profit Squeeze," *British Food Journal*, 96(2), 18-23.

Kelley, Harold H. (1973), "The Process of Causal Attribution," *American Psychologist*, 28(2), 107-128.

______ and John L. Michela (1980), "Attribution Theory and Research," *Annual Review of Psychology*, 31, 457-501.

Lichtenstein, Donald R., Scot Burton, and Bradley S. O'Hara (1989), "Marketplace Attributions and Consumer Evaluations of Discount Claims," *Psychology & Marketing*, 6(3), 163-180.

Mazumdar, Tridib and Sung Youl Jun (1992), "Effects of Price Uncertainty on Consumer Purchase Budget and Price Thresholds," *Marketing Letters*, 3(4), 323-329.

McGreevy, Ronan (2008), "Anger over Margins Paid to Supermarket Suppliers," *Irish Times*, 1. August 2008 (http://www.timesonline.co.uk).

Mizerski, Richard W., Linda L. Golden, and Jerome B. Kernan (1979), "The Attribution Process in Consumer Decision Making," *Journal of Consumer Research*, 6(2), 123-140.

Muthén, Linda K. and Bengt O. Muthén (2007), *Mplus User's Guide* (4th ed.), Los Angeles, CA: Muthén & Muthén.

Northen, James R. (2000), "Quality Attributes and Quality Cues: Effective Communication in the Meat Supply Chain," *British Food Journal*, 102(3), 230-245.

Obermiller, Carl and Eric R. Spangenberg (2000), "On the Origin and Distinctness of Skepticism toward Advertising," *Marketing Letters*, 11(4), 311-322.

Rondán Cataluña, Francisco Javier, Manuel J. Sánchez Franco, and Angel Francisco Villarejo Ramos (2005), "Are Hypermarket Prices Different from Discount Store Prices?," *Journal of Product & Brand Management*, 14(5), 330-337.

Schindler, Robert M. (1989), "The Excitement of Getting a Bargain: Some Hypotheses Concerning the Origins and Effects of Smart-Shopper Feelings," *Advances in Consumer Research*, 16, 447-453.

______ (1998), "Consequences of Perceiving Oneself as Responsible for Obtaining a Discount," *Journal of Consumer Psychology*, 7(4), 371-392.

Springer, Jon (2008), "The Secret's OUT: Discounter Aldi is Well-Positioned and Growing , and Doesn't Mind Telling You So," *Supermarket News*, 25. August 2008 (http://supermarketnews.com).

Vaidyanathan, Rajiv and Praveen Aggarwal (2003), "Who is the Fairest of Them All? An Attributional Approach to Price Fairness Perceptions," *Journal of Business Research*, 56(6), 453-463.

Völckner, Franziska and Julian Hoffman (2007), "The Price-Perceived Quality Relationship: A Meta-Analytic Review and Assessment of its Determinants," *Marketing Letters*, 18(3), 181-196.

Weiner, Bernard (1985), *An Attributional Theory of Motivation and Emotion*, New York, NY: Springer.

______, "An Attributional Theory of Achievement Motivation and Emotion," *Psychological Review*, 92(4), 548-573.

Wood, Lisa M. and Barry J. Pierson (2006), "The Brand Description of Sainsbury's and Aldi: Price and Quality Positioning," *International Journal of Retail & Distribution Management*, 34(12), 904-917.

Xia, Lan, Kent B. Monroe, and Jennifer L. Cox (2004), "The Price is Unfair! A Conceptual Framework of Price Fairness Perceptions," *Journal of Marketing*, 68(4), 1-15.

Zeithaml, Valarie (1988), "Consumer Perceptions of Price, Quality, and Value: A Means-End Model and Synthesis of Evidence," *Journal of Marketing*, 52(3), 2-22.

Zielke, Stephan (2006), "Measurement of Retailers' Price Images with a Multiple-Item Scale," *The International Review of Retail, Distribution and Consumer Research*, 16(3), 297-316.

APPENDIX
Item-scale

Price level perception	The prices are more competitive than in other stores. The prices are generally very low here. You can buy cheap groceries here.
Quality Perception	You can buy good quality products in this store. In this store, the product quality is only moderate.* The product quality is perfectly alright. The product quality is considerably better compared to other stores. The product quality is here worse than in other stores.*
Value for money	The prices here are appropriate in relation to what I get for my money. The prices here are excessive in relation to what I get for my money.* I get good value for money here. Compared to other stores, the price-performance ratio is very good here. The ratio between price and performance is considerably worse here than in other stores.*
Price fairness	This store sometimes behaves unfairly regarding the prices.* This store sometimes behaves dubiously regarding the prices.* This store always behaves very correctly regarding prices.
Ease of price evaluation	I can assess this store very well regarding the prices. I cannot assess this store at all regarding the prices.* I find it difficult to assess the prices in this shopping establishment.*
Shame	I feel embarrassed buying food in this shop. I feel a bit embarrassed when I have to shop here. I feel awkward offering guests food from this shop.
Guilt	I have a bad conscience when I buy groceries here. It is not correct to buy food from this shop. I feel irresponsible when I buy groceries here.
Shopping intentions	I should shop at this store as often as possible. I should shop at this store as seldom as possible.* I should consider this store for my shopping. I should disregard this store for my shopping.*

* reverse coded

______ (2007), "Why are Discount Stores so Cheap?," in *Proceedings of the 34th International La Londe Research Conference in Marketing*, ed. Søren Askegaard, Dwight Merunka, and Joseph M. Sirgy, La Londe les Maures, France, 132-139.

______ (2009a), "How Price Image Dimensions Influence Shopping Intentions for Different Store Formats," *European Journal of Marketing*, forthcoming.

______ (2009b), "Exploring How Perceived Store Price-Level and Customer Characteristics Influence Price-Related Emotions," *Advances in Consumer Research*, 36, 325-331.

Promoting Health: Producing Moralisms?

Dorthe Brogård Kristensen, University of Southern Denmark, Odense, Denmark
Søren Askegaard, University of Southern Denmark, Odense, Denmark
Lene Hauge Jeppesen, University of Southern Denmark, Odense, Denmark
Thomas Boysen Anker, University of Copenhagen, Denmark[1]

INTRODUCTION

"Consumers don't eat as healthily as they should". This is a claim that a vast amount of people all over the world now accepts as a truth. Due to the individual and socio-economic costs of the current obesity-epidemic, there is great public concern about healthy living. This is underlined by various reports from transnational health agencies as well as national agencies in America and Europe but increasingly also the Asian region and was mentioned as one of the most important issues to be dealt with by transformative consumer research in the introduction to a recent special issue of the Journal of Consumer Research (Mick 2008).

The traditional way of dealing with public health promotion has been trough promotional campaigns that provide consumers with information on healthy eating: education on healthy diet, nutrition labels on food products, campaigns trying to promote healthy product categories like fruits and vegetables, etc. This reflects a nutrition policy that typically focuses on individual food choices and how they can be best informed (Holm 2003: 534). However, nutritional information and education is not sufficient to change consumer behavior. One major review of 58 European studies and reports concluded that there is a widespread interest in nutritional information on labels, that there is a positive attitude towards simplified information on the front of the packaging, but also that there is little knowledge about how nutritional information and labeling is used in real-life shopping situations (Grunert & Wills 2007).

The work of Wansink and Chandon (2007, 2006) has tried to sophisticate the "nutritional labeling approach" and thereby overcoming some of its limitations by addressing the lure of "health halos"–health claims from suppliers that are thought to provide relatively healthy food–which make consumers underestimate the caloric content of the food consumed. Furthermore, Wansink and van Ittersum (2007) and Wansink, Painter and North (2005) investigated the effects of visual cues such as the impact of portion sizes on quantities consumed. Considering the widespread affirmative signs that we are in the middle of an obesity-epidemic, it is not surprising that 6 out of 13 contributions to the abovementioned recent special issue of Journal of Consumer Research dealt with health, and four of those more specifically with eating patterns and obesity issues. Three of these contributions are more or less direct extensions and qualifications of Wansink's research on visual cues, this time focusing on packaging size and investigate for example avoidance of extreme package size (leading to industry motivations to "upsize" standards) (Sharpe, Staelin & Huber 2008), and perverse effects of package size leading consumers to consume more when packages are smaller, contrary to what was found by Wansink in his studies (Coelho do Vale, Pieters and Zeelenberg 2008). Finally, in the third of the three articles, similar results were reported by Scott, Nowlis, Mandel and Morales (2008) with the significant addition that the "perverse effect" (consuming more when packages are smaller) was found to be dependent on whether the consumer could be classified as so-called "restrained eater" or not. These studies highlights the relationship between package size and inclination to consume as well as the importance of distinguishing between different types of consumers and their personal life worlds when it comes to health-related eating behavior. Most notably, the study of Scott et al. (2008) points towards the relevance of such issues.

Consumer researchers may look towards CCT related research (Arnould & Thompson 2005) in order to better grasp the social context of eating and health-oriented behaviour. It is therefore interesting to note that health-oriented behavior is relatively absent from the tradition of CCT. Closest to establishing such a tradition is the work of Craig Thompson with its focus in the socialized body (Thompson & Hirschman 1995), the consumption of natural health and the mythologies attached to it (Thompson and Troester 2002; Thompson 2004), and the risk perception linked to "natural birth practices" (Thompson 2005). Beyond this stream of research, there is relatively little coverage of health-oriented consumption in the CCT literature. Within the consumer research tradition pertaining to the general issues of relations between eating behavior and health policies there exist only a few studies (Holm 2008, Järvelä et al. 2006)

Mick (2008) calls for a more contextually embedded insight into consumer behaviour in the daily shopping and cooking practices, and how the contemporary discourses about health influence (or fail to influence) this behavior. He notes that "the problems and challenges related to consumer behaviours today include, but are not restricted to, unhealthy eating… (p. 377)". Such a broadening of the scope on consumer behaviour related to health and eating reflects the call for new approaches in relation to improve strategies for health promotion (World Health Organization 2003; 2007) following the prevalence of changing life styles and dietary related diseases. The Danish government and its agencies for public health and nutritional information have decades of experience concerning informational campaigns about relations between food consumption and health. However, these campaigns have almost exclusively been based on providing information to consumers, thus tacitly adopting the picture of the consumer as an information-processing agent, who will change evaluation of food alternatives based on information about their potential impact on personal health. .

As a consequence of this search, and in order to test new strategies for changing consumers' eating behaviours, The Danish Strategic Research Council has sponsored a large, cross-disciplinary research project in order to investigate the usefulness of branding techniques as a supplement to or a replacement for the traditional information based approach. The study, which is cross-disciplinary in character, includes an ethnographic study of consumer discourses relevant in the social construction of health, a major study evaluating various ways in which branding techniques can be applied for the promotion of healthier eating behaviour and a philosophical study of the ethical issues permeating publicly sponsored health branding efforts.

THE STUDY

In this paper, we present initial results from the part of the general health branding project that investigates the social con-

[1]Acknowledgements: This study presents results from the project "Health Branding" funded by the Danish Strategic Research Council.

struction of "health" in consumers' everyday lives and their construction of consumption practices based on contemporary ideas about health as well as inherited and/or adopted food cultural patterns. This project, then, aims at obtaining a deeper understanding of symbols and meanings that consumers relate to in response to health. An interdisciplinary group of researchers, including an anthropologist, two consumer researchers, and a philosopher specializing in ethics, conducted the study. The primary data consists of in depth interviews with 34 consumers (25 women and 9 men) between 20 and 60 years of age. In some cases also family members were included in the data collection. The study includes in depth interviews about food culture and eating behaviour, observational studies in shopping and cooking contexts and a follow-up interview on health and brand symbolism. Within the limits of the study, we have tried to get a rich picture of the consumers´ life styles. The focus of the analysis has been on moral values and perceptions of healthy food/unhealthy food (Warde 1997), brands & health claims (e.g., Evans 2008), dietary recommendations, notions of performance and body image (Thompson & Hirschman 1995; Turner 1997).

Approximately half of the interviews were conducted in the capital city of Denmark, and half were conducted in a major provincial city. Due to space limits, we will not go any further into demographic and geographical differences here. A preliminary coding and analysis of the interviews demonstrated that the post-structuralist life style dimensions (Holt 1997) used as a frame of analysis of American and Danish women's relation to the use of cooking fat and their culinary life styles (Askegaard, Jensen & Holt 1999) were prevalent also in the current material. Thus, these dimensions have been applied in order to analyze similarities and differences among our informants and the discourses concerning health and eating. Furthermore, the application of this framework of analysis has permitted the updating and qualification of a two-by-two matrix reflecting fundamental variations in social meanings concerning health and eating behaviour. As a consequence, it can be used to distinguish different kinds of discourses in relation to health and eating.

THE PUBLIC HEALTH DISCOURSE IN A DANISH CONTEXT

Contemporary commercial marketers and public health campaigns in Northern European countries perceive health as a notion associated with personal responsibility, informed choice and the availability of healthy food products (Vallgårda 2001, 2007a, 2007b; Yoder 2002). Thus, both public health promotion and commercial health branding[2] is based on the notion, that citizens and consumers make voluntary, responsible and healthy choices, if proper information and healthy food products are available. Another underlying link and a powerful incitement for improving the health condition of the citizens is the association between health and economy. As stated in a recent article "If consumers are unable to process and comprehend the needed information, they will be unable to make the healthiest and most financially prudent decision. The result is increased cost to society" (Levy & Royne 2009: 368). The moral and social implications of this viewpoint have been pointed out by several scholars, among these Scott Yoder, who argues that a discourse based on personal responsibility and autonomy often leads to a victim-blaming "We are told how to improve our health or reduce our risk of illness by eating properly, exercising regularly, or taking a aspirin daily. While this information empowers us, it also burdens us. If we can control our health, we can be blamed for being ill" (Yoder 2002: 23).

Turning to the Danish context similar ideas emerge. According to the historian Signild Vallgårda Denmark, Norway and Sweden share the same major health problems, that is, cancer, heart disease, diabetes, musculoskeletan diseases, and mental illness (Vallgårda 2007: 205). The political strategy to deal with health problems, however, varies to a high degree. By comparing public health white papers from Denmark, Norway and Sweden, Vallgårda argues that the Danish programme differs from its Norwegian and Swedish counterparts with regard to explanations and suggested solutions to the problems. Whereas the Danish programme stresses the importance of individual behaviour, personal responsibility and autonomy, the Norwegian and Swedish counterparts stress social relations, living conditions as well as political responsibility. Furthermore, the Danish programme focuses almost exclusively on lifestyles and risk factors associated with certain forms of behaviour (Vallgårda 2007: 208). In Denmark all age groups are hit by the obesity-epidemic. From 1985-1994 massive national public campaigns were conducted to reduce the fat intake in the Danish population (Astrup 1998: 573).

Key areas in current health promotion include; tobacco, alcohol, diet and exercise. The public authorities have the obligation to inform the population about risky and unhealthy behaviours as well as to deliver messages and provide solutions (Vallgårda 2001: 390). Thus, in the public health discourse in Denmark unhealthy behaviour is primarily regarded as the major cause of disease and behaviour that is dependent on the individuals' free choice. Therefore, the individual is assumed to be responsible for his/her health condition (Ibid). In the Danish white paper it is phrased in the following way: "Individuals are responsible for their own lives. Everyone has the right to live their lives as they wish: to make their own choices". "Respecting individual autonomy is decisive. The public sector should not control our lives" (cited in Vallgårda 2007a: 208). The health improvement strategy is to help citizens make their own informed choices. As a consequence poor health is overall depicted as the result of individuals inappropriate behaviour (Vallgårda 2007b: 45). However, and very importantly, the role of the state is much more active with regard to "vulnerable" and "disadvantaged"[3] adults, who should be introduced to health programmes in order to change their behaviour. This intervention normally takes place through public health professionals. Respecting the autonomy of these groups seem to be less of an issue (Vallgårda 2007a: 209)

The Danish public discourse on health leads us to hypothesize that, in the consumers' life worlds, the notions of the individual responsibility and autonomy is strongly present. In fact, it was crucial for the people in this study to show that they were capable of controlling their food consumption acting as responsible and morally respectable citizens. However, this focus on individual control, discipline and principles, also creates various moral dilemmas, especially in the relation to the notion of health risk and the consumers' capabilities to respond to this. Further the public discourse of health apparently produces different health discourses

---

[2]Commercial marketers use branding to build strong relationships (positive associations, identification, and loyalty) between consumer and healthy products/ brands (Evans 2008), and thereby encourage the individual consumer to make 'the right' choices.

[3]The disadvantaged groups were by the social democratic minister of health Birte Weiss in 1998 described as "people who belong to a high-risk social group and who also suffer from bad health and may therefore require help from social agencies as well as health services, are often found among long-term recipients of disability benefits and dole money, as well as among people with frequent contacts with social services department, doctors and hospitals" (Weiss 1998, cited in Vallgårda 2007b: 50)

FIGURE 1
A typology* of four different approaches to food and health

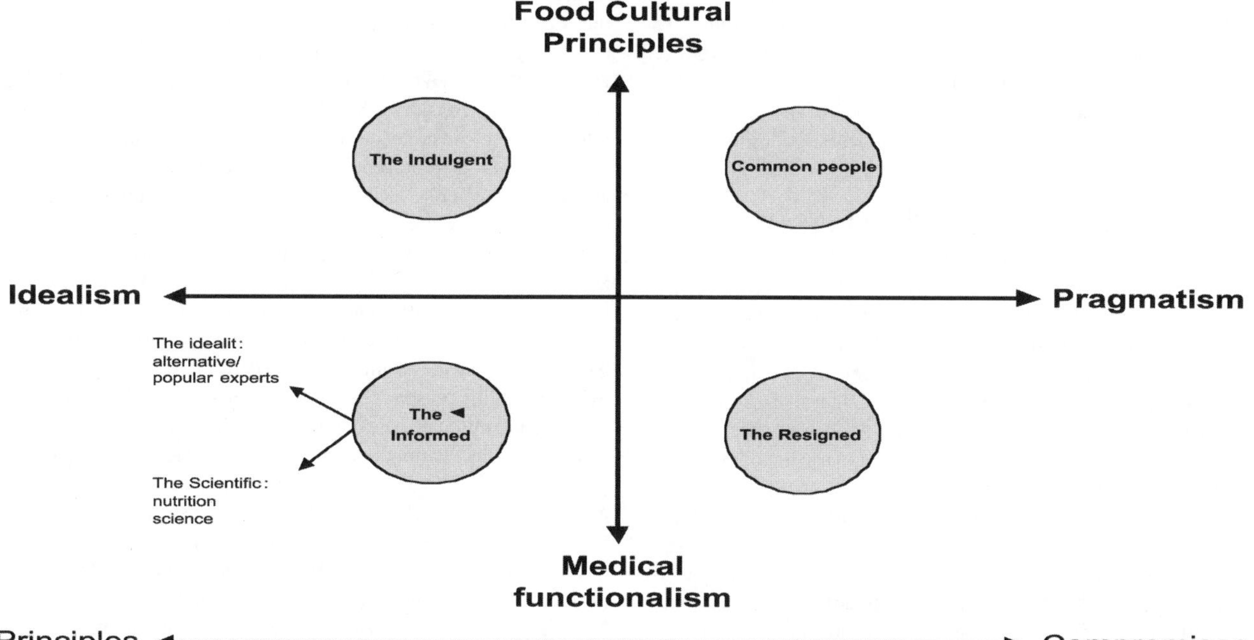

*We are currently validating the consumer discourses through a quantitative survey of 400 Danish respondents, thereby also turning the mapping of discourses into a potential tool for distinguishing between different consumer "health segments". However, as of this writing, the survey is still in the data collection phase, and we are not able to discuss the more specific character of each of the potential segments, nor are we able to generate reliable estimates of the relative size of different segments. Due to the recurring structure distinguishing principle versus pragmatic orientations and gastronomical versus medical-functional orientations as found also by Askegaard et al. (1999), we are confident, however, that the structuring principles will not be or only be slightly modified by the survey results, since a pilot study has already been carried out in order to eliminate the variables of insufficient reliability with satisfying results.

and classifications of people in the consumers' life-world. By presenting social meanings and moralisms, which Danish consumers attach to health and eating, we would like to question to the idea of the consumer as an independent and rational agent who makes rational choices if properly informed. It is important to show that consumers' health behaviour is emotional and embedded in a social context rather than rational, because the notion of the consumer as a rational decision maker is still a prevalent assumption in public health promotion in Scandinavia The findings are supported by Bourdieu (1992), Lindbladh & Lyttkens (1992), Thomson & Hirchman (1995), and Rose (1998), who all underline that a strictly individualistic and rational-agent approach is insufficient to account for health-related behaviour. This is because such an approach it fails to consider the social order and political agenda and its emergent discourses and its impact on consumers' discourses.

TOWARDS A SOCIAL UNIVERSE OF HEALTH DISCOURSES

Our findings show that the informants respond very differently to the notions of health, risk and morality. On this backdrop, we suggest a typology of four different types of consumer discourses; "common people's discourse", "informed discourse" "resigned discourse" and "the indulgent discourse". Figure 1 illustrates the relationship between these four discourses. One of the oppositions, on which this approach is based, relates to a medical and functionalistic approach to food based on a perception of health risk (medical functionalism axis) as opposed to an approach of gastronomical and a notion of "the good life" (food cultural principles). The main principle behind medical functionalism is that consumers are more interested in the functional content of food and health risk thus sacrificing taste or quality (i.e. a "gastronomically" good life). This means that this type of consumers are willing to compromise on taste or quality (i.e. a "gastronomically" good life) to reduce risk and/or optimise nutritional content. On the other opposition, food cultural principles are associated with culinary pleasure; as a consequence these consumers are willing to sacrifice healthy eating for the sake of a culinary pleasure. The other opposition is between an idealistic approach to the structuration of eating behaviour (idealism axis) and a pragmatic approach (pragmatism axis). In terms of healthy eating, the idealistic approach is related to firm principles towards a healthy diet as a response to health risk. On the other hand, the pragmatic approach is regarded as an aversion towards firm principles in relation to healthy diet and a movement towards compromises.

The discourse of what we dub common people is the most dominant one. Its main characteristic is a balanced and relaxed attitude towards health claims and health in general. These consumers are concerned with food cultural principles, living a good life and not being too extreme towards healthy eating. In contrast, indulgent consumers are closely aligned to a discourse that put strong emphasis on food cultural principles and the "good life" and who are not much concerned about health risk. To them taste and quality are the most important product characteristics. Informed consumers–as opposed "common people" – stress strict discipline and firm principles and are very conscious of health risks and healthy eating. To some extent resigned consumers resemble "common people" due to their pragmatic attitude towards healthy eating. However, resigned consumers have to a certain degree adopted the discourse of the informed with its emphasis on health risk, but apparently lack the balance between indulgence and discipline. The resigned tend to think that an unbalanced lifestyle is partly produced by external conditions and constraints, and partly caused by a morally weak character. In the next section we will exemplify the theoretical model through a presentation and discussion of major findings from our qualitative study.

COMMON PEOPLE: THE SIGNS OF AN UNHEALTHY BODY

> "Cola makes you fat and unhealthy. You do not see fat people on the street without a cola in their hand. They always come strolling down the streets with this 1/2 litre bottle of cola in their hand...people seem addicted to that stuff...and again, those fat people, I cannot stand the thought of it...drinking cola is one of the great sins for the real overweight people...it makes me...uhh...cola is being gulped down in huge amounts. Maybe we should ration the purchase of cola. Then each family could buy no more than one litre of cola a week...that would be a great idea...*of course it is up to people themselves if they want to be fat...but some just need help...*when I look at all the teenagers and grown ups who are getting fat I feel really sorry for them. No one feels good about looking fat...I feel so sorry for them"

The quote is from Rikke, a middle-aged woman living in a major Danish city, who in recent years has gained an increased interest in healthy living due to her daughter's diagnosis of rheumatism. Rikke leads a healthy life style as this is crucial to both her own and her family's well being. She is very concerned about family-life and traditions, loves cooking and thinks she has always been aware of eating quite healthy in the sense that vegetables have always been a part of her daily food intake. She is trying to reduce high fat and sometimes buy organic vegetables, and does not consider highly processed food as healthy.

Even though Rikke has become increasingly health conscious during the last year, she can still be characterized as belonging to the discourse of the common people, because she is primarily concerned with living a good life and does not adhere to strict discipline and principles towards healthy eating. She aims at what she considers a sound balance between indulgence and principles towards healthy eating. There should be a space for sinning and for both healthy and unhealthy eating, but in a regulated and controlled way. Rikke herself has a love for cakes, and feels a bit guilty, but also manages to control her desire. Though in no way fanatic, many people as Rikke associate fat intake with morality. If you eat too much fat food or consume too much coca cola, you feel "guilty", while exercise and eating vegetables makes you feel good "in the soul". As indicated in the quote from Rikke common people seem very judgemental towards people who do not control their intake of unhealthy food. And the bodyweight seems to be the indicator for whether you lead a problematic life in the sense of being socially incapable of controlling your own life.

In other words common people are not too concerned about health on a daily basis, but do connect health risk with lack of control of food consumption. In the quote from Rikke cola stands as the direct cause of obesity and an unhealthy body condition, and the consumption of cola is considered a sign of an unhealthy body. Moreover the quote illustrates the perception among common people that health is first and foremost an individual responsibility; the consequence is that obesity is perceived as a consequence of lack of discipline and therefore connected to moral meanings and judgements. Those who fail to make healthy choices, are the ones to pity as well as the ones who are exposed to a moral judgement that questions their capacity to live a good life and to make healthy choices. In the quote it is suggested that the state should interfere. Here we clearly see the parallel to the public discourse on health, which exactly considers that the state should take a more active intervening role in connection with "vulnerable" groups. To Rikke such a group is represented as "fat people with uncontrolled consumption of cola". Rikke as many other consumers attributes positive characteristics as the ability to self-manage and control impulses to people who have the right body size. Furthermore many associate healthiness with a hard-working character. Hardly surprising many of the common consumers describe unhealthy people as "people without character" as "lazy" and "people who do not work". A 42-year-old woman described this the following way: "To me an unhealthy person is one who is overweight and who neglects himself, and might also be unemployed". The physical appearance is here taken as the major sign of a person's moral character.

Gudrun is 59-year-old woman, who is very concerned with good quality in food. This contributes to an increased life quality in her family life. She is a mother of two, and together with her husband she used to run a clothes shop. However due to her husband's health problem (heart condition) they have both retired. Now they are very occupied with enjoying the last part of their life. Gudrun likes food and cooking and always goes for the best quality, which to her is associated with good vegetables, fruit, and low fat meat. She prefers well-known and Danish brands and likes to shop in local shops, for instance the local butcher. The bread is always homemade. She avoids fat and sugar, and exercises regularly to keep fit and slim. To her health is very much about the display of personal responsibility of being healthy, which she associates with discipline and good manners. Gudrun associates discipline, health, moral character and physical appearance in this way:

> "A healthy person is someone who takes responsibility for his own life. *You yourself have to do something, this also concerns health.* I know that there are people who become sick, who cannot do much about it, you can still become sick even though you live healthy. But if you smoke 40 cigarettes a day then you have NOT taken the responsibility of being healthy.
> I: How would you describe a healthy person to me?
> B: A healthy person is one who is not too blurred. I am here referring to physical appearance, but also to good behaviour. It makes me totally insane when you go to Copenhagen and you see people in a café with their legs on the chairs. I simply cannot tolerate that. Then you don´t respect people around you".

As in the quote from Rikke, we see how health is closely intertwined with a notion of self-control and to the idea that the state of one's body is a material sign of a moral character (Thompson & Hirschman 1995). To many consumers who can be said to represent the discourse of common people, health is connected to moral discourse that echoes Christian notions of morality, where unhealthy eating and drinking (mostly of fat food and alcohol) is considered "a sin" that makes you feel guilty, while healthy living makes you feel "good in the soul". Gudrun seems to be rather influenced by recent health campaigns; she mentions a campaign of eating fish twice a week that sat a standard for consumption of fish. She has consumed lots of fruits for many years, but after the launch of campaign "6 a day" (which aimed at increasing the average intake of fruit and vegetables to six a day), she reports her intake of fruits and vegetables to have increased. Each morning she eats what she estimates as "400 gram of fruits". That means that she is close to the target of eating 600 grams or 6 a day already from the beginning of the day. But eating healthily is not considered the main factor in securing a good quality in life.

> "What is healthiness? It is not just a matter of what you eat, but it also has to do with your life quality. I consider it of vital importance that you are happy and satisfied with your life, that you are not stressed that you are content with husband and kid. Frankly speaking that is more important than what you eat".

However, Gudrun feels there is too much focus on health today, and that there are to many conflicting messages "one day they tell you that red wine is healthy, and the next day they forbid it". There also has to be room for the "sinning", which in Gudrun's case means having a glass of good quality beer or wine and some sweets or good chips. As she says: "When I sin I do it properly". She opposes herself strongly to people, who adapt to strict rules and regimes in eating and to all fanatism.

> "If young ladies think it is necessary to get up early and make fibre rolls in order for you kids to survive, then things have gone completely wrong. It must be difficult to be young today and live with all those rules. When I was young and had small kids, we used to slaughter pigs, and of course we ate all of it. Of course we also ate all the bacon. And my kids became competitive swimmer and they are both healthy and big. They did not suffer any injuries. In that sense I believe it is all very exaggerated".

In this way the discourse of the common people both put moral judgements on those failing to control and discipline their food consumption, as those too concerned about health risk with very strict principles in regard to eating.

THE INDULGENT: LIVING THE GOOD LIFE

The discourse of the indulgent evolves around the desire of living a "good life". For the consumers aligned with the indulgent discourse taste and quality are more important product characteristics than healthiness. Hence they are willing to spend more money to get the best quality. The discourse represented by the indulgent is autonomy in the sense that most recommendations from neither the food industry nor the public health authorities taken into account. This does not mean that the indulgent is leading an unhealthy lifestyle, but he feels comfortable judging for himself what is "good or bad".

Per represents a typical consumer living through the discourse of the indulgent. Per seems very relaxed concerning all aspects in life, and to him living the good and pleasant life is highly prevalent. He is of course concerned about societal affairs such as for example animal welfare and environmental aspects, but nothing seems to bother him to such an extent that it would interfere with his food preferences. To him the good life is pretty much about one of the big qualities in life is being able to enjoying the best of food. Eating tasty and good food is important not only as an individual pleasure, but also as a social act. Per is quite suspicious and sceptical towards commercials and advertisements promoting healthy food, and when choosing food he feels better off judging from own experience and common sense. The indulgent is convinced that the producers do only have a commercial interest in selling their products and are not very concerned with moral aspects towards the consumers as such. When it comes to food the general perception is that when you buy food of good quality it is also healthy–or at least not that unhealthy. Consequently the principles of eating for this kind of consumer is associated with high quality food which equals good taste. Fast food is only an option in very few occasions if you are really busy. That is enjoying life and life quality plays a dominant role, while healthiness plays a minor role in their everyday life and food choices.

THE INFORMED; KNOWLEDGE, DISCIPLINE AND THE SEARCH FOR THE UNSPOILED

Another consumer discourse is represented by the informed, who is characterized by having firm principles and a strict discipline with respect to healthy eating. Consumers aligned with this discourse are very concerned about both healthy eating and nutritional knowledge, and are constantly seeking information on how to find healthy food. Generally food they refer to health food as "natural" and "pure". The informed does not seem to trust experts, authorities and food claims from the food industry. He is skeptical and therefore filters and evaluates any type of information he receives. The informed considers health as a more important characteristic of his diet than quality and taste and any advice to healthy eating should resonance with either scientific proof or/and his inner feelings.

Lars is a medical doctor of 38, married with three children, and lives in major city in Denmark; he describes himself as very health-conscious. As a consumer he is of course also confused by divergent health messages, but never gives up trying to navigate through the health jungle, and his medical training here provides him with certain skills. He is aware of the premises or conditions for scientific knowledge, and the fact that it is sometimes difficult to live in accordance with this knowledge, as it changes and brings up divergent messages. But he will, unlike the more pragmatic types, never give up trying to evaluate what is healthy or unhealthy. He is kind of calculating with a certain margin for being mistaken once in a while.

> "Even though it is annoying never really feeling secure that you do the right thing, I never give up. I remember when my girl was a baby; I loved her so much and only wanted to do the best for her. So I bought this cold-pressed organic thistle oil for her, and later on it was taken off the marked because it turned out to be bad to your health."

So the informed are characterized by being very resolute in the search for the right things to do, as the alternative to sometimes being mistaken, is to give up and become resigned. As he says: "what is the alternative, should I just accept to eat something bad and mass produced food…oh I can't even think of it, so I just have to accept the conditions…"

Lars is a consumer, who is often referring to scientific statements, numbers and specific claims, and is typically reflecting upon the messages trying to evaluate possible risks and benefits of food. The primary motivation for eating healthy is as Lars claims: "if you eat unhealthy, there will be a bill to pay later on". In this way Lars is quite judgemental against people–as the common people–who fail to reflect on health risk and to adopt a strict dietary regime based on nutritional knowledge. Here most informed perceive natural and organic as nutritional, while anything artificial and ready-made food is considered as unhealthy and potentially risky to eat, therefore one should keep one's intake of additional and e.g. artificial sugar at a minimum. And of course this kind of consumer knows the scientific words for different ingredients. The informative label is of interest to this consumer, and different labelling systems are referred to and are well known. Lars is almost reflecting, counting and evaluating everything his children eat, and he is very worried if they will not eat the amount of fruit and vegetables he has planned for them to eat. Then he starts compensating. And he is quite upset because most of what they want to eat is from the bottom of the food pyramid. He then starts to calculate what they actually eat during the day, and feels a little relieved when he concludes that maybe they do not get that many vegetables but on the other hand they eat a lot of fruit. He spends quite some time considering how he makes them eat "the right things".

Other informed are less concerned with scientific proof and calculation and prefer to depend on what they coin "their own inner feelings". Their notion of health is based on holism that is a equilibrium between body, mind, and spirit. An example is the 41-year-old Birgit, who considers healthy eating as absolutely crucial for feeling good about one-self. She is characterized by a profound scepticism against authorities and marketers, whom she accuses for not being "truly" concerned about the health of the people. Hardly surprising she is often criticising information from the health authorities for being too simple and sometimes even misleading, even though she is sympathetic to some campaigns, for instance the advice of eating "6 a day"[4] and a campaign for eating fish twice a week. But she feels that she lacks clear guidance of how actually to eat healthy. She has also a pronounced scepticism towards the food industry, which she blames for not being responsible towards people's health but only interested in financial profit. This is shown in the way they add unhealthy ingredients to many food products.

Birgit: *"I really find it grotesque that it is so difficult to find a pure product. Apparently they put all sorts of things into it such as colouring, food additives, and apparently also sugar. And I ask myself, why has it developed in this way, why hasn't the industry been more concerned about healthy food, I find it really strange, is it because it is much cheaper adding all these things than doing it in a healthy way?"*

Hardly surprising, the scepticism towards commercials is also very profound. Christine a 28-year old tension educator says:

Christine: *"There is so much seduction in commercials. They just want to tempt you to buy something that will not make you any happier. Ideally people should not need commercials to find out what they need to put in their shopping basket. The horse knows by itself that grass it what it needs. We should feel inside ourselves, what we really need".*

She believes that common peoples' belief that fat is the main risk for a good health, is far too simplified and even misleading and they accuse them of ignorance and lack of principles in health matters. To her health is strongly associated with clear principles and ethics, and she finds really no excuse for not eating healthy, if you want to feel good about yourself. By putting emphasis on priorities and principles, the informed somehow escapes the oscillation between healthy/ unhealthy eating, and its associated characteristics of sin/ guilt. The informed in a way admits to feel superior to people who fail to prioritize and find no valid excuses. As Christine says:

"It is really a question of priorities. I buy a lot of fruit and vegetables that are sometimes a bit costly, but then I would never consider buying a Coca Cola or a pizza. I don't have a television, I don't smoke, I never go out to have an expensive drink (laughs) when I am in town. It is really a question of priorities".

Healthy eating is a top priority, and for this reason Christine uses quite a lot of energy in seeking information about healthy food products through social circles, books, public debate, and the Internet. She also prefers shops with clear ethical, humanitarian and environmental principles, and doesn't mind to pay extra for a product. In sum the informed are characterized by a strong awareness of health risk; this creates various moral dilemmas, firstly their own quest for finding "really" healthy and "pure" products that fulfil their criteria, secondly their demand for full control of both their body and the marketplace is very ambitious. Here knowledge–based on science or their own inner feelings–is the most important tool. However this very occupation with knowledge and principles often make them appear too fanatic and hysterical in the eyes of other segments, as the example with Gudrun shows. Furthermore it may go to such an extreme that the informed become obsessed with healthy food, the so-called ortorexia nerviosa, a term proposed by the American doctor Steven Bratman. Most informed, hardly surprising, however, are quite upset about this term, and do find their own interest in health as sound and necessary.

THE RESIGNED: THE BURDEN OF THOSE FAILING TO LIVE HEALTHILY

The last type of discourse that we will present in this paper is presented by consumers being judged as "unhealthy" by others. In this context we prefer to use the denominator the resigned. To a certain degree these consumers have adopted the discourse of the common people with their pragmatic alternation between principles/ discipline on the one hand and indulgence on the other, however with one crucial difference. That is they themselves have not managed to balance indulgence and discipline, which they themselves explain as a result of a lack of time due to long working hours (working for a "living") or more often through the lack of personal discipline and moral character ("the guilty ones"). The resigned do have knowledge about health risk, which they mostly associate with uncontrolled intake of fat, sugar and additives. To some extent they have adopted the ideology of self-control and discipline as the way to a healthy and morally correct life. In this way their self-perception is informed by the discourses that surround them, of which health risk plays a crucial part.

Mogens is a 41-year-old factory worker, who has moved from a smaller city to the capital Copenhagen. He is single and hard-working man, and finds it difficult to find time and resources to live and eat healthy: "A lot of us eat the wrong things. I eat too much of that (points to a cake) and many are eating at McDonalds far to often ...I have considered going on a diet. But I need to be stronger first". Mogens is quite health conscious, but lacks clear principles and the discipline to follow them, as he often feels overruled by his desire for the "forbidden". Mogens has given up on actively searching for health information but remains a passive receiver of any health information that may come up. In this case, however, this leads to a moral judgement–both by consumers aligned with the other discourses–and by himself. He claims that he fails to live up to a healthy live style as he gives into temptation far too often.

Sara is a 20-year-old girl in high school. She is the daughter of Yugoslavian immigrants, but is born and raised in Denmark. As most high school girls she seems very occupied with her look: She

[4] 6 is to be understood as recommendations to eat 600 grams of fruit/ vegetables a day

is smartly dressed wearing a lot of jewellery along with a perfect make-up and seems very well-articulated. Apparently she is also very concerned about eating the "right and healthy food" and gave us a long lecture on tasty and healthy eating at the first interview in the supermarket. Getting a closer glance of her world, one realizes that she lives in a world full of rules that she can not herself live up to, as well as a constant anxiety caused by her failure to keep a strict diet. She really likes vegetables and fruits and does normally go for low fat and light products in order to keep fit and healthy. However, she complains about her failures in keeping slim. She has tried what she refers to as a "tons of diets", and does regularly have periods where she exercises very intensively. However, she lacks perseverance, and also suffers from "attacks, where she indulges in sweets and cakes. She regards her overweight as the main indicator of her "failure" to keep a strict discipline, a fact that she constantly returns to in conversation. Another theme both she and her mother–a cleaning assistant – bring up, is the social isolation and lack of resources they felt as belonging to people with another ethnic background. However, as in the discourse of common people, Sara is sure that obesity is a clear sign of the unhealthy body, and that the main sinners here are fat and sugar. Nevertheless even though she considers fat as unhealthy, she herself believe she has a weak character, in this way she also connects obesity with morality, but claims to have given up. Even though she in no way considers herself as "healthy" she is actually quite occupied with health risk, at the point of having monthly tests taken at the medical doctor.

Sara: *"It is not like that I eat a kilo of bread and potatoes. I don´t-I also do eat healthy food, but sometimes I just have days, where I just need to have something sweet.*

Interviewer: *"Is it some special days?"*

Sara: *It happens mostly during weekends. Then we relax and eat sweets. But when I have a bad day, then I have to find something sweet in the house, and if I don´t find any then everything just goes wrong. I get tired, but I still try to fight, because I have health problems. I go to see a medical doctor each month, to have my blood tested and everything, and luckily everything is fine. That is I don´t have problems with increased blood pressure. But I do have a little overweight, but I have heard that it is not that unhealthy.*

As this last quote illustrates, the eating habits of Sara–a resigned-may resemble the eating habits of the common people. What marks the difference, however, is the picture of herself as belonging to the category of the "uncontrolled" and therefore "morally weak". Even though she apparently does not lack nutritional information and to some degree is concerned about health risk and susceptible to health messages and health claims, healthiness is a topic that brings up emotions and frustrations. In the following quote from Sara it is illustrated that the focus on control and individual responsibility for making the "right" food choices, apparently increases a sense of anxiety.

Sara: *I just think, there are these days where there is so much focus on what is healthy and what is unhealthy, who is fat and who is slim. In a way I don´t care, I don´t care because I know how I want to live, I just don´t think the society should decide how we should live. If they were really concerned about our health they would raise the prices of the unhealthy and reduce the prices of the healthy.*

Interviewer: *Are you saying that in a way society does not help people to become healthy and at the same time they point fingers at you?*

Sara: *Yes, then they complain that overweight cost billions and billions each year. There is just too much focus on that part. I know it by own experience, I have tried a ton of diets, I have tried everything, pills, powder, and with what gain? I am still the way I am. I am overweight, but I am not going to feel ashamed about my body. If people cannot accept the way I look I don't really care.*

Interviewer: *And have you experienced that some people could not accept the way you look?*

Sara: *Yes, bloody hell. One day a guy said that fat people would be prohibited to go to McDonalds. I felt like hitting him. Why on earth should he decide whether I could go to McDonalds?*

We here see a link between the public health discourse in Denmark and Sara's self-perception. As a person who consumes "unhealthy" food products (cake, sweets, coca-cola) and who is also overweight, she is not adhering to the picture of the responsible and autonomous consumer who takes informed and healthy choices. In the consumers' discourses this is expressed as an association between physical appearance, principles and morality. The fat person is a person who lacks discipline and principles and consumes the "wrong" food in an uncontrolled way; this is taken as a threat to public morality. To avoid this threat that the fat body presents, it is proposed that society regulates the food consumption of these morally weak persons. As the suggestion of prohibition of going to McDonalds, and as Rikke suggests; if people are not capable of being responsible in their own lives, society should take over the regulation. Hence we have a public discourse that regards health as first and foremost an individual responsibility and ascribes autonomy and personal responsibility to the capable citizens, furthermore it proposes intervention in the case of the more "vulnerable" group. It is interesting seeing how this discourse is echoed in the consumers' discourses, but in a somehow distorted version. In Sara's case, being fat is not explained with reference to any genetic disposition, nor is it seen in the light of her social and economic background. Rather the overweight is the display of a public failure to take control of ones life: to this reason she is considered an "economic burden". No wonder Sara responds to the "pointed fingers" in a quite aggressive way. Furthermore, hardly surprisingly, she is also overtly self-defensive and argues in the following way "I actually think it is possible to have 40 kilos overweight and still be a good person".

CONCLUSION

In this paper we have presented preliminary data from a qualitative study of consumers' perception of healthy food. Food represents part of our identity construction, and as Fischler (1988) puts it: "Food makes the eater". Hence food defines and communicates who you are, and within this construction a dilemma arises: the balance between desire and control. A negotiation between health risk, the good life and control (personal restraints that comes from body images, public health claims etc); this is mirrored in life style and identity (who am I, what do I want to signalize to myself and the surroundings). Since nobody (or very few) seem to escape the oscillation between the pleasures of eating and the potential health consequences that are often associated with eating and food choice, we concur with Wilk (2001) that the sin/guilt cycle provides a basic rhythm of consumer culture. The food market definitely constitutes a domain of "moral conflicts over consumption", as Wilk calls it. Additionally, the current discourse of obesity epidemics allegedly drabbing many parts of the world adds new, ironic and for some tragic meaning to the moral discourse of (and against) overconsumption.

We have described the public health discourse in Denmark and its focus on individual responsibility and autonomy. We have presented how this discourse has penetrated consumers´ notion of health as closely connected to notions of personal responsibility, discipline and control, as well as moral meanings and judgements. We have proposed that the public discourse has produced four main discourses among consumers that both serves to classify people and as displaying a guiding principle in eating behaviour. In the paper we have described four types of consumer discourses, which we have labelled discourses of the common people, the informed, the indulgent and the resigned. Lastly we have suggested that by individualizing health factors and by failing to take into consideration genetic, structural and social determinants of health, the dominant discourse of health among Danish consumer poses a risk of stigmatizing people suffering from especially life style diseases (Ogden 2003). Furthermore by attributing responsibility to individuals for their own health you risk blaming people for being ill and for taking "unhealthy" choices, as in the case of Sara. The consequence is that overweight and obese persons come to present a failure to respond to health risk though discipline and control, despite the fact that the correlation between what is taken as "signs of an unhealthy body" and actual medical risk is, however, far from straightforward (Gard & Wright 2005). We thus conclude, that under the pretext of promoting health the dominant public discourse contributes to creation of new moralities in consumers' discourses that implicates a construction of social stigma and lower life quality in certain parts of the population.

REFERENCES

Arnould, Eric J. & Craig J. Thompson (2005) "Consumer Culture Theory (CCT): Twenty Years of Research", *Journal of Consumer Research*, vol. 31 (March), 868-882.

Askegaard, Søren, Anne Jensen & Douglas Holt (1999), "Lipophobia: A Translantic Concept?", E.J. Arnould & L.M. Scott, eds., *Advances in Consumer Research*, vol. XVI, Ann Arbor, MI: Association for Consumer Research, 331-336.

Astrup, Arne (1998), "The American Paradox: The Role of Energy-dense Fat-Reduced Food in the Increasing Prevelance of Obesity", *Current Opinion in Clinical Nutrition & Metabolic Care* 1 (6), 573-577.

Chandon, Pierre & Brian Wansink (2007), "The Biasing Health Halos of Fast Food Restaurant Health Claims: Lower Calorie Estimates and Higher Side-Dish Consumption Intentions", *Journal of Consumer Research*, vol. 34 (October), 301-314.

Coelho do Vale, Rita, Rik Pieters & Marcel Zeelenberg (2008), "Flying under the Radar: Perverse Package Size Effects on Consumption Self-Regulation, *Journal of Consumer Research*, vol. 35 (October), 380-390.

Evans, Douglas (2008) *Public Health Branding Applying Marketing for Social Change*. Oxford: Oxford University Press.

Fischler, Claude (1980) Food Habits, Social Change and the Nature/Culture Dilemma. *Social Science Information*, 19, 937-53.

Fischler, Claude (1988) Food, self and identity. *Social Science Information*, 27, 275-292.

Gard, Michael & Jan Wright (2005), *The Obesity Epidemic. Science, Morality and Ideology*, London: Routledge.

Grunert, Klaus G. & Josephine M. Wills (2007), "A Review of European Research on Consumer Response to Nutrition Information on Food Labels", *Journal of Public Health*, vol. 15 (5), 385-99.

Holm, Lotte (2003), "Food Health Policies and Ethics: Lay Perspectives on Functional Foods", *Journal of Agricultural and Environmental Ethics* 16: 531-544.

Järvelä, Katja, Johanne Mäkelä and Sanna Piiroinen (2006) "Consumers' everyday food choice in Finland", *International Journal of Consumer Studies*, 30: 309-317.

Levy, Marian & Marla Royne (2009) "The Impacts of Consumers' Health Literacy on Public Health", *Journal of Consumers Affairs*, vol. 43: 367-372.

Lindbladh, Eva & Carl Hampus Lyttkens (2002) Habit versus choice: the process of decision-making in health-related behavoir, *Social Science & medicine* 55: 451-465.

Mick, David Glen (2008), "Introduction: The Moment and Place for a Special Issue", *Journal of Consumer Research*, vol. 35 (October), 377-79.

Ogden, Jane (2003) *The Psychology of Eating. From Healthy to Disordered Behavior*, Oxford: Blackwell Publishing.

Rose, Nicolas (1998) *Inventing Ourselves. Psychology, Power and Personhood.* Cambridge: Cambridge University Press.

Scott, Maura L., Stephen M. Nowlis, Naomi Wandel & Andrea C. Morales (2008), "The Effects of Reduced Food Size and Package Size on the Consumption Behavior of Restrained and Unrestrained Eaters", *Journal of Consumer Research*, vol. 35 (October), 391-405.

Sharpe, Kathryn M., Richard Staelin & Joel Huber (2008), "Using Extremeness Aversion to Fight Obesity: Policy Implications of Context Dependent Demand", *Journal of Consumer Research*, vol. 35 (October), 406-422.

Slater, Michael D. (1996) "Theory and Method in Health Audience Segmentation", *Journal of Health Communication*, vol. 1, 267-283.

Thompson, Craig (2004), "Marketplace Mythology and Discourses of Power", *Journal of Consumer Research*, vol. 31 (June), 162-180.

Thompson, Craig (2005), "Consumer Risk Perceptions in a Community of Reflexive Doubt", *Journal of Consumer Research*, vol. 32 (September), 235-248.

Thompson, Craig & Elisabeth Hirschman (1995), "Understanding the Socialized Body: A Poststructuralist Analysis of Consumer's Self-conceptions, Body Images, and Self Care Practices", *Journal of Consumer Research*, vol. 22 (September), 139-153.

Thompson, Craig J. & Maura Troester (2002), "Consumer Value Systems in the Age of Postmodern Fragmentation: The Case of the Natural Health Microculture", *Journal of Consumer Research*, vol. 28 (March), 550-571.

Vallgårda, Signe (2001), "Governing People's Lives. Strategies for Improving the Health of the Nation in England, Denmark, Norway and Sweden". *European Journal of Public Health* 11: 386-392.

Vallgårda, Signe (2007a), "Public Health Policies: A Scandinavian Model?" *Scandinavian Journal of Public Health* 35: 205-211.

Vallgårda, Signe (2007b), "Health Inequalities: Political Problematizations in Denmark and Sweden" *Critical Public Health* 17 (1): 45-56.

Wansink, Brian & Pierre Chandon (2006), "Can 'Low-Fat' Nutrition Labels Lead to Obesity?", *Journal of Marketing Research*, vol. 43 (4), 605-17.

Wansink, Brian James E. Painter & Jill North (2005), "Bottomless Bowls: Why Visual Cues of Portion Size May Influence Intake", *Obesity Research*, vol. 13 (1), 93-100.

Wansink, Brian & Koert van Ittersum (2007), "Portion Size Me: Downsizing Our Consumption Norms", *Journal of the American Dietetic Association*, 107 (July), 1103-06.

Wilk, Richard (2001), "Consuming Morality", *Journal of Consumer Culture*, vol. 1 (2), 245-260.

Yoder, Scott (2002), "Individual Responsibility for Health. Decision, not Discovery". *Hastings Center Report* 32, no. 2: 22-31.

The Impact of Un/ethical Corporate Conduct on Consumers' Ethical Perceptions-A Multidimensional Framework

Katja H. Brunk, Université Libre de Bruxelles, Belgium
Christian Bluemelhuber, Université Libre de Bruxelles, Belgium

INTRODUCTION

In the context of globalization, large-scale industrial changes have taken place, which have been brought about through mergers, takeovers, or bankruptcies of many businesses in the marketplace. This consolidation has led to the creation of large multi-national corporations and conglomerates that have altered the social, political, cultural, and physical environment in which they operate. Gradually, the influence of corporations reached far beyond the normal business context and into politics and policymaking and, in line with their size, grew their overall societal impact. Numerous well-known, high-profile scandals (i.e., Nike, GAP, Shell, Nestlé) illustrate how corporations abused their increasingly powerful positions. The subsequent public outrage and gradual loss of trust in the business community resulted in the emergence of discourses centering on the power and legitimization of the corporation, the morality of corporate behavior and the overall societal impact of business. Anti-globalization and anti-corporate movements fuelled the debate, focusing on the notion of corporate greed and encouraging consumer boycotts that not only caused a decrease in sales revenues but also sustainably damaged brand image and the reputation of the affected corporations.

Grounded in the socio-historical debate on globalization, issues of business ethics and Corporate Social Responsibility (CSR) have increasingly taken centre stage in public discourse leaving companies concerned about their ethical image. Today, most corporations designate resources (i.e., CSR managers–a job profile largely unknown 10 years ago) at the highest seniority level to audit internal and external activities of the company, negotiate among constituents and, most importantly, portray the company and its brands as ethical players. Altruistic behaviors, such as cultural sponsoring, community involvement or charitable giving are among the types of activities companies openly engage in in order to showcase their commitment to being a good citizen–to be perceived as ethical.

In spite of ample evidence confirming the impact of unethical perceptions on consumer attitudes and purchasing behavior, to this day, little is known about how an un/ethical image of a company emerges in the consumer's mind. This article conceptualizes the way in which business practices may influence consumer perceived ethicality (CPE), understood as the consumer's aggregate perception of a subject's (i.e., a company, brand, product or service) ethicality. An improved understanding of CPE formation will facilitate a deeper insight into ethical consumerism and provide an essential extension to existing work.

BACKGROUND

A plethora of diverse issues relating to the broad subject of ethical consumerism have recently been investigated. The book The Ethical Consumer (Harrison, Newholm, and Shaw 2005) and the October 2007 special edition of the "Journal of Consumer Behaviour" which studied ethical consumption (Newholm and Shaw 2007) reflect expanding interest in this important area of research. Acknowledging that the subject is barely in its adolescence and that many questions remain open, various scholars emphasize the need for further in-depth exploration of the consumer (versus corporate) perspective of business ethics and CSR (Mohr, Webb, and Harris 2001; Newholm and Shaw 2007; Sen and Bhattacharya 2001).

Recent research establishes a link between a company's CSR or business ethics and consumer responses (Berens, Van Riel, and Van Bruggen 2005; Biehal and Sheinin 2007; Creyer and Ross 1996 1997; De Pelsmacker, Driesen, and Rayp 2005; Folkes and Kamins 1999; Gürhan-Canli and Batra 2004; Lichtenstein, Drumwright, and Braig 2004; Luo and Bhattacharya 2006; Madrigal and Boush 2008; Sen and Bhattacharya 2001). Favorable or unfavorable perceptions about a company's ethics impact consumer evaluation of that business, their attitude towards and relationship with its brands, and may consequently steer purchase behavior. Yet, the question of how such a positive or negative ethical image of a brand or company evolves in consumers' minds has not been investigated.

The majority of existing studies focusing on consumer reactions to corporate ethics and CSR consists of experiments that induce CPE with the help of various hypothetical examples of un/ethical company behavior. Commonly the choice of manipulation scenario relates to prototypical ethical issues such as employment practices like sweatshop conditions, child labor and suppressed wages (Sen and Bhattacharya 2001; Carrigan and Attala 2001; Folkes and Kamins 1999; Lichtenstein et al. 2004); deceiving the consumer about product benefits (Creyer and Ross 1996); environmental records; and philanthropy such as charitable giving (Berens et al. 2005; Brown and Dacin 1997; Creyer and Ross 1996; Lichtenstein et al. 2004; Madrigal and Boush 2008; Mohr and Webb 2005). In most cases, the selection of the type of corporate behavior intended to manipulate CPE appears arbitrary and authors refrain from reasoning about their choice of scenario. In other studies, consumers are subjected to a company characterized as unethical, without reference to the origin of this negative connotation (Creyer and Ross 1997).

While the creation of scenarios referring to child labor and environmental pollution will almost guarantee negative perceptions, it may not be the case that all un/ethical behaviors have the same impact on CPE, a conjecture nourished by findings from an experiment conducted by Mohr and Webb (2005). The authors induce levels of CSR with the help of environment- and philanthropy-related scenarios and observe that "CSR had a stronger effect on evaluation of the company when it was in the environmental than in the philanthropic domain" (141-2). Bearing in mind both this finding and the multiplicity of activities capable of evoking ethical connotations (Brunk forthcoming), attention must be directed towards the intriguing question of how ethical perceptions are shaped by various kinds of corporate behavior. Conceptualizing these dynamics will facilitate an improved understanding of CPE formation and fill a research gap in the existing corporate ethics and ethical consumerism literature. Results should not only prove valuable for future explorations but may have implications for interpreting existing research findings.

METHOD

The lack of earlier research in the area called for an explorative approach aimed at seeking a grounded understanding of consumers' ethical perception formation process. The objective of exploration (versus quantification) naturally pointed towards qualitative research. As part of a larger study face-to-face consumer interviews were conducted and serve as the main source of data collection.

Sample

Typically, qualitative research focuses on an in-depth exploration of a small and diverse sample. McCracken (1988, 17) considers eight respondents sufficient for most research purposes. For this research, 20 long interviews (ibid.) were conducted with general consumers. Creating contrast in respondent selection is of utmost importance in order to "manufacture distance" (ibid., 37) and to enable as broad a review as possible (Stake 1995; Strauss and Corbin 1990)–a prerequisite for capturing the variety of prevailing attitudes, evaluations and perceptions. To achieve such a diverse respondent pool, a theoretical sampling procedure was followed, guided by its characteristic ongoing comparison process (ibid.). Contrary to existing, US-dominated research on CSR and business ethics, the focus is on European consumers, with Germany and the UK as the countries of research. Interviewees were recruited via convenience and multiplicity (snowball) sampling. The resulting pool of participants offers diversity in terms of age (17-83 years old), gender, marital status, education, and employment status to include students, retirees, self-employed, unemployed, as well as employees at various seniority levels (management versus non-management). A full list of all interviewees' demographic profiles is available upon request.

Data Collection

Taking into account that consumers' evaluation of ethics or morality is an inherently personal, subjective and sensitive topic and therefore, as previous research points out, prone to social desirability effects (Mohr et al. 2001; Vantomme et al. 2006; Vermeir and Verbeke 2006; Worcester and Dawkins 2005), face-to-face interviews were considered the most appropriate method of data collection and preferred over focus groups in order to minimize self-presentational concerns (Wooten and Reed 2000) and circumvent the danger of participants complying with the opinion of dominant members (Bristol and Fern 2003).

Interviews were conducted at the respondents' home. A semi-structured interview format provided a focused, yet open form of dialog and encouraged discussion. The more informal interview style combined with the familiar and comfortable surroundings of their home created a relaxed atmosphere and consequently participants were very willing to engage and answer openly. This was crucial given the sensitivity of the subject and the objective of minimizing social desirability bias.

The interview guide was developed following four expert interviews and a review of analytical and cultural categories to facilitate a process of familiarization and defamiliarization (McCracken 1988). Subject to minor refinements after pilot testing, the guide continually evolved in line with emerging concepts and patterns (Strauss and Corbin 1990). The question format was open and all respondents covered the same topics, starting with more general grand-tour questions referring to responsibilities of businesses today, and then becoming increasingly specific, concluding with examples of various types of perceived un/ethical behavior and a discussion of company/brand-specific cases. The data-collection phase concluded after 20 interviews, when the last three interviews failed to reveal any new concepts and dynamics, suggesting theoretical saturation. Depending on the level of active participation and interaction, interviews lasted between 45 and 120 minutes.

Data Analysis

With the permission of participants, all but one interview–with an 83-year-old female feeling intimidated by the presence of the tape recorder–were recorded and transcribed at full length, yielding a total of 308 pages of verbatim transcripts and 47 pages of field notes for analysis.

Data analysis was on-going and gradually evolved throughout the data-collection process (Strauss and Corbin 1990). The constant comparison and subsequent refinement allowed both processes to intermingle, a strategy particularly useful for exploratory research purposes (McCracken 1988).

To extract meaning, transcripts were re-read repeatedly and analyzed in search of recurring patterns, themes and relationships between them. In line with Spiggle (1994), analysis proceeded by employing the recommended procedures of categorization (coding deductively and inductively), abstraction, comparison, dimensionalization, integration, iteration, and refutation. Following these analytical operations and the subsequent integration of the data, a dialog and review process was initiated in order to strengthen the validity of the findings (Kvale 1996). This confirmation phase included sharing results with six of the interviewees and two experts. Reviewers were requested to provide feedback on the interpretations and to debate any issues in question.

No significant differences between emerging categories were detected when the data from the UK and Germany was compared. As the types of corporate actions that participants perceive as ethical/unethical are close to identical in both countries, the findings presented hereafter reflect the views of the combined sample from the UK and Germany.

FINDINGS

Identifying CPE Impact Dimensions

The analysis of the consumer data results in the finding that the impact of un/ethical business transactions on consumers' ethical perception is asymmetric. Consumer narratives suggest varying degrees of impact on CPE, meaning that not all types of business conduct commonly regarded as ethical or unethical resonate with the same intensity. The notion is in line with findings from the previously mentioned experiment by Mohr and Webb (2005). Three categories of corporate behavior that differ in direction and magnitude of impact on consumers ethical perceptions emerge from the data as follows:

1) Positive/Negative: Activities that can have either a positive or negative effect and proportionally in/decrease CPE depending on the company's commitment.
2) Negative: Corporate behavior that has a detrimental effect when consumer expectations are not met but does not generate a positive impact when exceeded.
3) Positive: Transactions that have the ability to positively enhance CPE, yet their omission does not cause unethical connotations.

The dynamics, nature and dimensionality of the identified categories bear resemblance with existing quality or satisfaction models (Cadotte and Turgeon 1988; Herzberg, Mausner, and Snyderman 1959; Kano 1984; Oliver 1995, 1997; Swan and Combs 1976), which broadly summarize antecedents into: satisfiers, dissatisfiers, criticals and neutrals, based on their influence on (product-, customer-, and employee-) satisfaction (Vargo et al. 2007). These satisfaction models' main contribution lies in the discovery of the

FIGURES 1A)–C)

The Three Dimensions of CPE Impact

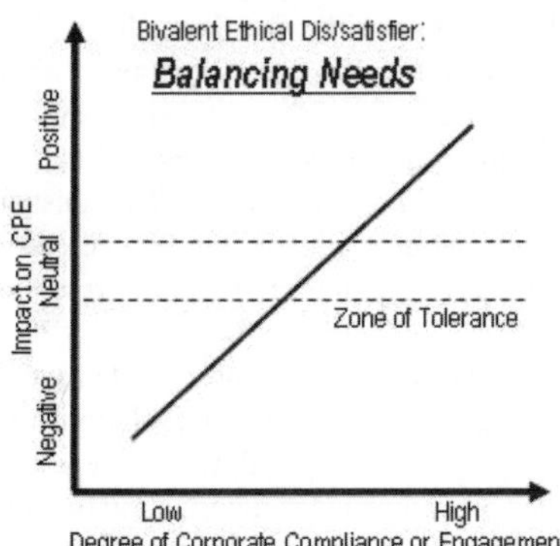

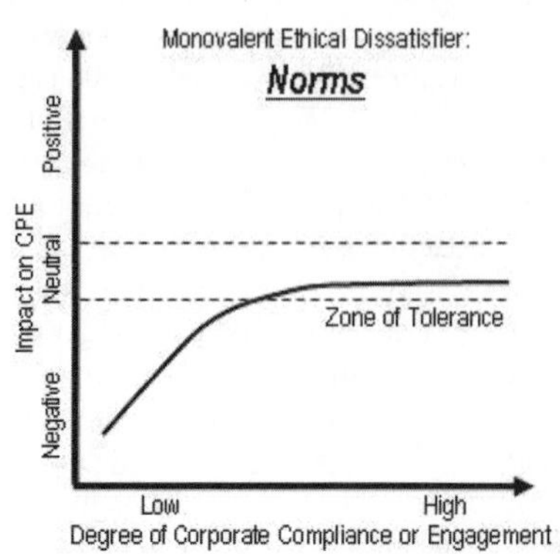

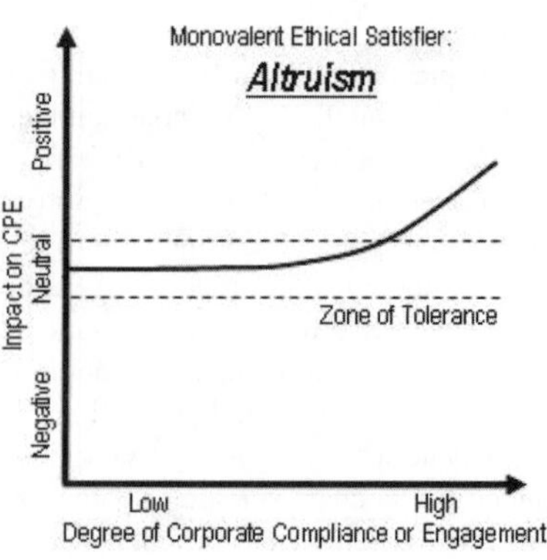

existence of varying impact dimensions. The identification of features that may be attributed to each dimension is highly case-specific, hence in order to understand which feature acts as a dis/satisfier individual, product-specific tests are required. Reflecting the close resemblance between the identified CPE and satisfaction model impact dimensions, the above CPE impact dimensions were named bivalent ethical dis/satisfiers, monovalent ethical dissatisfiers, and monovalent ethical satisfiers respectively.

Linking Types of Un/Ethical Corporate Behavior with CPE Impact Dimensions

While existing dis/satisfaction models are unable to reach beyond the broader categorization into satisfier, dissatisfier, critical, and neutral dimensions, the data generated throughout this research not only reveals the existence of various impact dimensions but furthermore allows for a conceptualization of the types of behavior comprising each dimension. Therefore, the resulting CPE impact taxonomy presented here extends beyond a general classification by linking types of business behavior with each impact dimension and by distinguishing the nature of corporate activities that can act as either monovalent or bivalent ethical dis/satisfiers.

Figures 1a-1c depict the emerging conceptualization after communalities and differences across categories with varying dynamics had been identified. The framework presents each CPE impact dimension by relating the nature of business activities to one of the following principles:

- Norms (Monovalent ethical dissatisfier),
- Balancing needs (Bivalent ethical dis/satisfier) or
- Altruism (Monovalent ethical satisfier).

Furthermore a zone of tolerance depicts an area within which corporate efforts are likely to remain without consequences on consumers' ethical perceptions.

Norms (Monovalent ethical dissatisfier). Monovalent ethical dissatisfiers are transactions that relate to the principle of fulfilling norms. The most basic and fundamental of the three CPE impact dimensions comprises the kind of behavior consumers take for granted and resembles the must-be dimension of the Kano model (Kano 1984; Walden 1993). In line with Joyner and Payne (2002) who state that insufficient compliance with legal regulation may be deadly, participants expect companies to fully comply with legal standards and act in accordance with basic moral norms. Failing to adhere to laws and norms violates these "minimum requirements", leading to a detrimental effect on CPE, as highlighted by Maria, one of the participants, who refers to the moral principle of honesty: "The thing that happened with the meat. When they repacked it and resold it despite the sell-by date was expired. Being so dishonest is the worst for me, without a doubt. That's not just unethical, it's close to criminal even."

Compliance on the other hand simply meets these basic consumer expectations and consequently causes a neutral–but not a positive–reaction, as James underlines: "They (companies) have to abide by the laws, the financial laws of the state or the country, on top of that, environmental, they need to adhere to the environmental rules and laws of the country, and last, the labor laws of the country. It doesn't mean I'd consider them particularly ethical because that's like the absolute minimum I would expect, just fulfilling their obligation."

Balancing Needs (Bivalent ethical dis/satisfier). This impact dimension refers to activities that can have both a favorable and unfavorable effect on CPE. The core evaluation principle is to strike the optimal balance between harm and welfare for all affected by the business activity or transaction in question. Balancing needs calls for corporate decision making processes that involve careful weighing of positive or negative consequences on any of the company's stakeholders. Fiona stresses the importance of this principle by describing her perceptions of a company that disregards potential harm to the environment: "Knowingly damaging the environment if [emphasized] you can do something about it is very unethical… I think if you are doing everything you can to reduce it, then it's not unethical but if people just don't worry about it at all then it's highly unethical." Or take Peter, whose narrative connects to the ongoing socio-cultural discourses on the morality of outsourcing production abroad and increasing unemployment in the home country. His quote highlights that the (perceived) motivation of the company's action is a key component of his judgment: "If suddenly they close a factory in Wales that's got no chance of other employment, then I guess it becomes really unethical! If they are just doing it to make more profit and more, you know, damage the community and damage a lot of people. But if it's just a natural sort of process that it slowly moves into, then it's ok, it really depends how it's done."

The expected impact is commensurate with a company's efforts. Therefore, the more a company appears to act righteously and balances its business needs versus the interests of others, the more favorable the effect on CPE. Referring to the car manufacturer Volkswagen, Sandra offers one such positive example: "For me that's ethical: For instance, when firstly you communicate you have such and such problem, so everyone can comprehend the situation. OK. The normal consequence would be that we would have to let a certain number of employees go. But then, it is about looking for solutions in collaboration with the employees, for instance to say: OK, you won't get a 13th month salary and won't get a raise for a while and maybe some of you have to work part-time, but in return, we will guarantee your job until 2010, despite our financial challenges. That for me, this is really ethical… But to just throw people out on the street without actively looking for a suitable solution for everyone, that is just unacceptable!"

Conversely, the same participant goes on to demonstrate how acting purely out of self-interest and therefore harming others will generate a detrimental impact, citing a case of self-righteous management behavior: "I have to spontaneously think about Deutsche Telekom because I found this truly absurd. They laid-off so many people, at the same time the compensation of the Board of Directors was considerably increased. And now, here it comes, they can still afford to have Robbie Williams sing at their Christmas party. Something like that, it really makes me sick… If they hadn't got Robbie Williams, maybe they could have kept some of their people employed."

It has to be acknowledged that, due to the subjective nature of perceptions, a company's well-intended efforts and motivations to balance the interests of all stakeholders may not be recognized as such by the public. For instance, a decision to outsource production to a low-wage country may genuinely be the optimal solution for all constituents involved (i.e., as a measure of securing the company's survival), yet consumers could simply fail to perceive the decision as balanced. Shaped by the prevailing public discourse on corporate greed, the act of outsourcing could instead be interpreted as self-righteously motivated to increase profits while creating unemployment at home, in which case the impact on CPE would be a negative one. The subjectivity of perceptions highlights the fact that effective communication is critical and that–particularly with highly debated, contentious matters central to public discourse, such as outsourcing–well-intended efforts must be clearly conveyed and openly publicized in order to avert misperceptions and counteract prevailing truths, such as 'all corporations are greedy'.

Altruism (Monovalent ethical satisfier). Monovalent ethical satisfiers are corporate transactions of altruistic character, such as philanthropy, or activities going well above and beyond the company's core business responsibilities. In fact, many of these acts are not directly linked to its day-to-day business. By nature the altruism dimension mirrors the delighter category in the Kano (1984) taxonomy, characterized as nice-to-see but not expected. Hence, in comparison with the other two dimensions, these activities do not share the same level of importance with consumers. Frank supports this notion with his remark about firms that actively engage in social activities and charitable giving: "In principle I think it's really good that it exists and that many companies do these kind of things, and I think it's a pity that some don't engage in these kind of things… But, it's not criteria number one for me, very clearly. But in principle I think it's good and important." Others, like John, expect altruistic actions only from companies that make sufficient profit: "…a company can give money to charity as well as a good cause. What's the word–philanthropy–for the companies with a lot of spare money around."

Not only philanthropic engagement, such as charitable giving, but also other altruistically motivated acts pertain to this dimension, such as employee benefits extending far beyond the normal scope of duty as suggested by Emily: "You know the other thing that would be nice to see, if they (companies) could make sure their employees have adequate homes, or adequate facilities to get a mortgage."

While engaging in altruistic behavior may enhance CPE, its omission will not cause a detrimental effect. Hence, refraining from engaging in philanthropy or other pro-social corporate activities remains without consequences. Yet a company's association with altruistic behavior can delight consumers and result in positive ethical connotations.

In reality however, such noticeable positive impact on CPE rarely occurs. Very few interviewees were able to cite a company or brand they perceived as ethical, an observation Worchester and Dawkins (2005) and Folkes and Kamins (1999) share. According to the data, altruistic efforts can only enhance ethical perceptions under the condition that consumer expectations on the other two dimensions are met. This suggests that a vital prerequisite for a positive ethical loading to occur is to refrain from vice, as Frank illustrates: "… behind our backs they lead their waste into the river but then they say, yes, but here we made a big donation, making a big fuss and that way just diverting attention away from the things where they do not behave correctly… and when I read things like that, I really don't want anything to do with them (company) anymore." Frank's quote furthermore underlines the non-compensatory nature of the altruism dimension, meaning that the display of virtuous qualities, such as philanthropy, cannot offset other transgressions. Skowronski and Carlston (1987) provide a possible explanation with their cue diagnosticity framework of impression formation by suggesting a negativity bias with morality based judgments. It builds on the assumption that bad people do not consistently display negative behavior but sometimes act in a virtuous way, while good people almost exclusively act in a positive way. For a company to be considered ethical, behavior must be consistently virtuous, whereas a single transgression is sufficient to establish a negative perception. Therefore, it is crucial a company avoids and refrains from activities known to generate unethical perceptions.

The lesser likelihood of positive ethical association is also connected to the type of information on which consumers base their judgment. In line with Berry and McEachern (2005) and Mohr and Webb (2005), participants inherently mistrust corporate communication that openly demonstrates virtuous behavior. Thus they prefer to rely on independent media as their primary source of information. However, media reporting skews towards highlighting misconduct and prevailing sensationalism fosters predominantly negative reporting.

Discussions with consumers convey the impression that graphically the slope of the altruism dimension runs less steeply when compared to the norms dimension, implying that marginal impacts differ across dimensions. Given a similar variation in absolute company performance, the magnitude of negative impact on CPE, when violating norms, is larger than the positive impact of altruistic behavior. The finding is in accordance with prospect theory (Kahneman and Tversky 1979; Tversky and Kahneman 1992) which posits that people are risk-averse. They care more about negative than positive outcomes, hence perceived losses have a bigger impact than gains. However, providing empirical evidence in support of this hypothesis is beyond the scope of this exploration.

Zone of Tolerance. Consumer narratives point to the existence of a zone of tolerance. Corporate activities within this zone are unlikely to generate any effect on ethical perceptions, hence a zone of tolerance exhibits consumers' threshold of acceptability before negative or positive loading occurs. Talking about his negative ethical perceptions of the company Müller, Frank implies the presence of an impact threshold: "Well with Müller, it really made an impression on me, with other companies I might not be aware of it, but when something becomes so severe then I really pay attention... almost like when a certain acceptance limit has been reached."

The present study only detects such a threshold in conjunction with negative examples (i.e., in the context of unethical behavior) which is not surprising given that the majority of consumer comments are negative. However, despite the lack of grounded evidence substantiating the presence of a positively valenced zone of tolerance, its existence is probable, and also likely to be somewhat larger than its negative counterpart, due to differences in the dimensions' slopes.

CONCLUSIONS AND IMPLICATIONS

This research contributes to the existing literature on ethical consumerism by investigating the impact strength and dimensionality of un/ethical business practices on consumers' ethical perceptions. Grounded in data, the study reveals the novel finding that the effect of im/moral corporate behavior is multi-dimensional. The resulting taxonomy not only establishes the existence of three distinctive CPE impact dimensions, but additionally identifies the nature of business practices pertaining to each dimension: (1) Monovalent ethical dissatisfiers are corporate acts that can have a negative impact on CPE and refer to adhering to norms; (2) Bivalent ethical dis/satisfiers are business activities that relate to the principle of balancing the needs of the company versus others and, commensurate with a company's efforts, can positively or negatively influence global CPE; and (3) Monovalent ethical satisfiers may have a positive impact on CPE and include all company transactions relating to altruism, such as philanthropy or other activities going well beyond the scope of standard business responsibilities. A crucial prerequisite for the ethical satisfiers' ability to favorably influence ethical perceptions is that consumers' expectations on the norms and balancing needs dimension are met.

The presented findings have important implications for the academic community investigating ethical consumption and the business community, specifically CSR and general management as well as marketing professionals. The fact that altruistic engagement may only enhance ethical perceptions when all other basic moral expectations are met, presents an essential lesson for managers. A company's first priority should therefore be to get their house in order (so to speak) and prevent any type of behavior known to negatively affect CPE, such as disrespecting laws and moral norms as well as insufficiently balanced decision making. For some companies this may call for strategic re-prioritization of CSR activities, particularly in the common case where a companies' CSR focus is predominantly on philanthropy. Such altruistic efforts must be backed-up by a scrutinizing audit of operational procedures, processes and standards of business conduct encompassing all business units and suppliers for any potential sources of perceived misconduct, which need to be addressed in turn.

In terms of academic implications, the results of this study provide a useful perspective for interpreting previously cited experimental research that focuses on consumer reactions to un/ethical corporate behavior or CSR initiatives. The fact that not all business transactions have the same degree of impact on CPE requires consideration when interpreting and generalizing findings. Furthermore, considering the prerequisites for a positive ethical loading to occur, employing philanthropy-related stimuli (as in many of the above studies) may lead to an overestimation of CPE enhancement.

REFERENCES

Berens, Guido, Cees B.M Van Riel, and Gerrit H. Van Bruggen (2005), "Corporate Associations and Consumer Product Responses: The Moderating Role of Corporate Brand Dominance", *Journal of Marketing*, 69 (3), 35-48.

Berry, Hannah and Morven McEachern (2005), "Informing Ethical Consumers", in *The Ethical Consumer*, eds. Rob Harrison, Terry Newholm, and Deirdre Shaw, London: Sage, 69-87.

Biehal, Gabriel J and Daniel A. Sheinin (2007), "The Influence of Corporate Messages on the Product Portfolio", *Journal of Marketing*, 71 (2), 12-25.

Bristol, Terry and Edward F. Fern (2003), "The Effects of Interaction on Consumers' Attitudes in Focus Groups", *Psychology and Marketing*, 20 (5), 433-54.

Brown, Tom J. and Peter A. Dacin (1997), "The Company and the Product: Corporate Associations and Consumer Product Responses", *Journal of Marketing*, 61 (1), 68-84.

Brunk, Katja H. (forthcoming), "Exploring origins of ethical company/brand perceptions–A consumer perspective of corporate ethics", *Journal of Business Research*.

Cadotte, Ernest R. and Normand Turgeon (1988), "Dissatisfiers and Satisfiers: Suggestions from Consumer Complaints and Compliments", *Journal of Consumer Satisfaction, Dissatisfaction, and Complaining Behavior*, 1, 74-9.

Carrigan, Marylyn and Ahmad Attalla (2001), "The myth of the ethical consumer–do ethics matter in purchase behavior?", *Journal of Consumer Marketing*, 18 (7), 560-77.

Creyer, Elizabeth H. and William T. Ross, Jnr (1996), "The impact of Corporate Behavior on Perceived Product Value", *Marketing Letters*, 7 (2), 173-85.

______ (1997), "The influence of firm behavior on purchase intention: do consumers really care about business ethics?", *Journal of Consumer Marketing*, 14 (6), 421-32.

De Pelsmacker, Patrick, Liesbeth Driesen, and Glenn Rayp (2005), "Do consumers care about ethics? Willingness to pay for fair-traded coffee", *Journal of Consumer Affairs*, 39, 363-87.

Folkes, Valerie S. and Michael A. Kamins (1999), "Effects of information about firms' ethical and unethical actions on consumer attitudes", *Journal of Consumer Psychology*, 8 (3), 243-59.

Gürhan-Canli, Zeynep and Rajeev Batra (2004), "When Corporate Image Affects Product Evaluations: The Moderating Role of Perceived Risk", *Journal of Marketing Research*, 41 (2), 197-205.

Harrison, Rob, Terry Newholm, and Deirdre Shaw (2005), *The Ethical Consumer*, London: Sage.

Herzberg, Frederick B, Bernard Mausner, and Barbara B. Snyderman (1959), *The Motivation to Work*, New York, NY: Wiley.

Joyner, Brenda E. and Dinah Payne (2002), "Evolution and Implementation: A Study of Values, Business Ethics and Corporate Social Responsibility", *Journal of Business Ethics*, 41, 297-311.

Kahneman, Daniel and Amos Tversky (1979), "Prospect Theory: An Analysis of Decision under Risk", Econometrica, 47 (2), 263-91.

Kano, Noriaki (1984), "Attractive Quality and Must-be Quality", *Hinshitsu: The Journal of the Japanese Society for Quality Control*, 14 (2), 39-48.

Kvale, Steinar (1996), *Interviews: An Introduction to Qualitative Research Interviewing*, Thousand Oaks, CA: Sage.

Lichtenstein, Donald R., Minette E. Drumwright, and Bridgette M. Braig (2004), "The Effect of Corporate Social Responsibility on Customer Donations to Corporate-Supported Nonprofits", *Journal of Marketing*, 68 (3), 16-32.

Luo, Xueming and C.B. Bhattacharya (2006), "Corporate Social Responsibility, Customer Satisfaction, and Market Value", *Journal of Marketing*, 70 (3), 1-18.

Madrigal, Robert and David M. Boush (2008), "Social responsibility as a unique dimension of brand personality and consumers' willingness to reward", *Psychology and Marketing*, 25 (6), 538-64.

McCracken, Grant (1988), *The Long Interview*, Newbury Park, CA: Sage.

Mohr, Lois A. and Deborah J. Webb (2005), "The Effects of Corporate Social Responsibility and Price on Consumer Responses", *The Journal of Consumer Affairs*, 39 (1), 121-47.

Mohr, Lois A., Deborah J. Webb, and Katherine E. Harris (2001), "Do Consumers Expect Companies to be Socially Responsible? The Impact of Corporate Social Responsibility on Buying Behavior", *The Journal of Consumer Affairs*, 35 (1), 45-72.

Newholm, Terry and Deirdre Shaw (2007), Editorial: "Studying the ethical consumer: A review of research", *Journal of Consumer Behavior*, 6 (5), 253-70.

Oliver, Richard L. (1995), "Attribute Need Fulfillment in Product Usage Satisfaction", *Psychology and Marketing*, 12, 1-17.

______ (1997), *Satisfaction: A Behavioral Perspective of the Consumer*, New York, NY: McGraw Hill.

Sen, Sankar and C.B. Bhattacharya (2001), "Does Doing Good Always Lead to Doing Better? Consumer Reactions to Corporate Social Responsibility", *Journal of Marketing Research*, 38 (2), 225-43.

Skowronski, John J. and Donal E. Carlston (1987), "Social judgment and social memory: the role of cue diagnosticity in negativity, positivity and extremity ", *Journal of Personality and Social Psychology*, 52, 689-99.

Spiggle, Susan (1994), "Analysis and Interpretation of Qualitative Data in Consumer Research", *Journal of Consumer Research*, 21 (3), 491-503.

Stake, Robert Earl (1995), *The Art of Case Study*, Thousand Oaks, CA: Sage.

Strauss, Anselm and Juliet Corbin (1990), *Basics of Qualitative Research: Grounded Theory Procedures and Techniques*, Newbury Park, CA: Sage.

Swan, John E. and Linda J. Combs (1976), "Product Performance and Consumer Satisfaction: A New Concept", *Journal of Marketing*, 40, 25-33.

Tversky, Amos and Daniel Kahneman (1992), "Advances in Prospect Theory: Cumulative Representation of Uncertainty", *Journal of Risk and Uncertainty*, 5: 297-323.

Vantomme, Delphine, Maggie Geuens, Jan De Houwer, and Patrick De Pelsmacker (2006), "Explicit and Implicit Determinants of Ethical Consumerism", *Advances in Consumer Research*, 33, 699-703.

Vargo, Stephen L., Kaori Nagao, Yi He, and Fred W. Morgan (2007), "Satisfiers, Dissatisfiers, Criticals, and Neutrals: A Review of Their Relative Effects on Customer (Dis)Satisfaction", *Academy of Marketing Science Review*, 11 (2), 1-19.

Vermeir, Iris and Wim Verbeke (2006), "Sustainable food consumption: Exploring the consumer attitude-behaviour gap", *Journal of Agricultural and Environmental Ethics*, 19 (2), 169-94.

Walden, David (1993), "Kano's Methods for Understanding Customer-defined Quality:Introduction to Kano's Methods", *Center for Quality of Management Journal, 2 (4), 2-37.*

Worcester, Robert and Jenny Dawkins (2005), "Surveying Ethical and Environmental Attitudes", in *The Ethical Consumer*, eds. Rob Harrison, Terry Newholm, and Deirdre Shaw, London: Sage, 189-203.

Wooten, David B. and Americus II Reed (2000), "A Conceptual Overview of the Self-Presentational Concerns and Response Tendencies of Focus Group Participants", *Journal of Consumer Psychology*, 9 (3). 141-53.

Consumer Cognitive Perspectives of Web Ads: Country Comparisons, Analysis, and Implications

Chin-Feng Lin, National Pingtung Institute of Commerce, Taiwan

ABSTRACT

This study based the means-end chain methodology aims to understand consumer cognition of mutual fund advertisements on the Internet. Through constructing the hierarchical value maps, this study focuses mainly on elucidating consumer cognition of mutual funds, revealing cross-country website cognitive structures of mutual funds, comparing the differences in cognitive structures between consumers and cross-country websites and, finally, understanding important mutual fund attributes for both consumers and website designs in terms of values. The analytical results can not only provide marketers with valuable information for designing web ad content, but also be used to develop effective marketing strategies on the Internet.

INTRODUCTION

The commercial opportunities associated with the accelerated growth the Internet have brought business into the battle for Internet advertising. According to a NetValue survey (http://tw.netvalue.com), approximately one-fifth of Taiwanese Internet users habitually browse financial or securities websites and complete financial transactions on the Internet. Hence, financial institutions and companies have responded to new Internet business opportunities by exploring the feasibility of web applications for further development of their businesses.

Since 1991, the National Science Foundation in the United States has encouraged the opening of the Internet for commercial use. The trade patterns of e-commerce have gradually replaced traditional one-way marketing with interactive web marketing. Internet advertising campaigns are now an inevitable trend. Thus, some business strategies have been forced to change in order to meet new web applications and developments. Through advanced Internet technologies, businesses can not only introduce or promote their products by placing text, graphics, images, animation and sound on the web, but can also process customer orders and requests immediately.

Given increasingly shorter product life cycles, business product design has focused on product development and miscellaneous product mixes, explaining the increasing diversity of investment products. Hence, satisfying target customer demands and developing effective interactive marketing strategies are the keys to business survival in this environment. In the marketing field, means-end chain (MEC) methodology proposed by Gutman (1982) is the predominant approach for analyzing the relationship between consumer product preference and value satisfaction. Such a relation enables marketers to design their products to comply with consumer preferences.

The research objects in this study are mutual fund websites. Analyzing product characteristics of mutual fund websites by applying the MEC methodology reveals consumer cognitive structures associated with these websites. Such cognitive structures demonstrate the product attributes preferred by consumers, the perceived benefits or consequences upon product consumption and how consumer value demands can be achieved in terms of attribute-consequence-value (A-C-V) chains. Understanding consumer A-C-V chains enables marketers to design effective advertisements on their mutual fund web pages. This study analyzes the survey results to understand consumer preferences for various mutual fund attributes; the web ad contents of different sales agencies (investment trust, investment adviser, securities dealers, and banks) were compared regions, i.e. China, Hong Kong, Taiwan and the United States, to reveal differences in Internet marketing. This study focuses mainly on elucidating consumer cognition of mutual funds, revealing cross-country website cognitive structures of mutual funds, comparing the differences in cognitive structures between consumers and cross-country websites and, finally, understanding important mutual fund attributes for both consumers and mutual fund website designs in terms of values.

LITERATURE REVIEW

Origin and Development of Mutual Funds

Mutual fund investing originated in Europe, and the first pooled fund in the United States was formed for the staff and faculty of Harvard University in 1893. In 1924, the first publicly listed mutual fund was created: the Massachusetts Investors Trust. The individual retirement account introduced in 1981 contributed to the rapid development of the mutual fund since it created a new mutual fund type for employers and employees. Owing to its liquidity and easy-to-operate characters, such mutual funds are still very popular today.

According to investorwords.com (2008), a mutual fund is "an open-ended fund operated by an investment company which raises money from shareholders and invests in a group of assets, in accordance with a stated set of objectives. Mutual funds raise money by selling shares of the fund to the public and then take the money they receive from the sale of their shares to purchase various investment vehicles, such as equity, bonds and money market instruments." Mutual funds based on specific investment vehicles include money market funds, bond/income funds, balanced funds, equity funds, global/international funds, specialty funds and index funds (Levinthal & Myatt, 1994; Chordia, 1996).

Means-End Chains (MECs)

Means-end chain (MEC) methodology is a laddering approach for linking product attribute (A), consequence (C) and value (V) in a hierarchical cognition structure for consumers (Gutman, 1982). Peter and Olson (1993) indicated that product attributes are conferred by the benefit or value cognitions of consumers upon product consumption. Restated, such attributes are means of achieving consumer desires in terms of product benefits or values.

The knowledge structure of means-end chain broadly includes personal cognitions of a particular product or brand. Different consumers may have different perspectives, prefer different product attributes, perceive different consequences or perceive different benefits upon product consumption, and all of which may result in different value satisfaction (Lin, 2003; Reynolds and Olson, 2001). Reynolds and Gutman (1988) proposed the MEC methodology for constructing consumer attribute-consequence-value (A-C-V) hierarchies. In consumer self-construction, product attribute preferences, consequence upon product consumption and value satisfaction do not link to each other; restated, there is no concrete A-C-V existing in the consumer minds. Consequently, how to elicit ab-

TABLE 1
Product attribute and attribute level

Item	Attribute (A)	Attribute level (A_L)
1	Fund numbers	Fund count
2	Fund type	• Investment targets: Equity fund, Bond fund, Balanced fund, and Currency fund. • Investment regions: Global fund, Regional fund, and a Single National fund
3	Fund manager	Gender, Years of service, Qualification, Experience, and Investment ideas
4	Time of return	One month, Three months, Six months, One year, Three years, Five years and Ten years.
5	Related fees	Processing fee, Management fee, and the Percentage of Custodial fee
6	Minimum purchase amount	Single and periodic investment amount
7	Fund size	Currency base: NT$ 10 million
8	Currency	NT$, US$, HK$, RMB$, British Pound, and the Euro
9	Founding date	Years of founding date to present
10	Sales agency	Investment trust, Investment adviser, Securities dealers, Banks, Fund management company, Asset management company and etc.
11	Custody bank	Public sector bank, Private bank and Foreign bank

stract thoughts of consumers through in-depth interviews and transform them into concrete means-end hierarchies has become important for understanding the psychological cognitions of consumers.

Classifications of Value

The customer orientation advocates that establishing the constructs of consumer consumption processes and experiences provides information regarding consumer cognitions of product position, which can be used by marketers to formulate effective product strategies (Day *et al.*, 1979; Gutman, 1981). Practically, the cognitive structures of consumers are related to their value systems (Rokeach, 1968; Vinson *et al.*, 1977). Several researchers (Reynolds & Gutman, 1988; Gutman, 1982) have emphasized that consumer value systems can be evaluated by micro or macro perspectives. Micro perspectives focus on the connections between product attributes and consequences whereas macro perspectives focus on classifications using consumer value systems such as VALS2 (value and lifestyles 2) of SRI company (Kotler, 1997), LOV (List of Values) (Kahle & Kennedy, 1989) and RVS (Rokeach Value Survey) (Rokeach, 1968).

METHODOLOGY

Variables

Kotler (1994) asserted that a product attribute is composed of several attribute levels. Thus, this study adopted attribute level (A_L), attribute (A), benefit (B) and value (V) as the research variables to construct consumer cognitive structures.

1). Attribute level (A_L) and attribute (A): Based on investment manuals (*e.g.,* enterprise brochure, mutual fund DM, *etc.*) of mutual fund companies, this study summarized eleven characteristics (attributes). Table 1 describes the elements (attribute level) of each characteristic.

2). Consequence (benefit): According to the web ads of mutual fund sales agencies, this study summarized fourteen benefits perceived by consumers: "profession", "tax saver", "low investment cost", "good performance", "portfolio variety", "spreading risk", "transnational investment", "investment assistance", "liquidity", "well known", "good reputation", "large scale", "convenience" and "safe".

3). Value: This study directly adopted the LOV inventory developed by Kahle and Kennedy?1989?which includes the following measures: "sense of belonging", "excitement", "warm relationships with others", "self-fulfillment", "being well respected", "fun and enjoyment of life", "security", "self-respect" and "sense of accomplishment".

Questionnaire and Data Collection

Separate questionnaires were developed for individual investors and the companies with mutual fund web ads; each included three categories: A-C-V linkages of mutual funds; mutual fund attribute levels; personal or company information.

Based on the information provided by the official finance websites of China, Hong Kong, Taiwan and the United States, this study gathered data from the websites of mutual fund sales agencies and from interviews with mutual fund investors. Table 2 lists the official finance websites of the four countries.

To understand the cognitive structures of individual investors or customers, this study interviewed mutual fund investors in banks, investment trusts, securities dealers and others. Two hundred thirteen valid samples were gathered. For analysis of web ads of mutual funds, this study examined whether the sales agency has a web address, whether it sells mutual funds and whether its website provides mutual fund information to gather data from its web ads. The 145 analyzed companies or institutions included ninety companies in Taiwan, eleven in China, thirty-four in Hong Kong and ten in the United States. Each company or institution selected ten mutual funds. If the company offered more than ten mutual funds, then ten funds were randomly selected for analysis; otherwise, all company funds were analyzed. Thus, 1242 mutual funds were selected for analysis.

Analytical Method

Means-end methodology was applied by surveying consumer perspectives of a given mutual fund by in-depth interviews. Through a laddering technique, all interview data were tabulated and transformed to construct a hierarchical value map. Content analysis of the web ads was performed to reveal mutual fund attribute levels,

TABLE 2
Financial institutions of four countries

Country	Institution	Number	No. of websites	Source
China	Fund management company	18	11	China Securities Regulatory Commission (www.csrc.gov.cn)
Hong Kong	Fund management company	44	34	Hong Kong Investment Fund Association (www.hkifa.org.hk)
Taiwan	• Investment trust	41	38	Ministry of Finance, Securities and Futures Bureau (www.sfb.gov.tw)
	• Investment adviser company	219	6	Ministry of Finance, Securities and Futures Bureau (www.sfb.gov.tw)
	• Securities dealers	214	11	Ministry of Finance, Securities and Futures Bureau (www.sfb.gov.tw)
	• Banks	55	35	Ministry of Finance (www.mof.gov.tw)
USA	Standard and Poor's	228	10	Standard and Poor's (www2.standardandpoors.com)

TABLE 3
Consumer demographics

Variable	Classification	Number	Percentage	Variable	Classification	Number	Percentage
Gender	Female	130	61.3%	Family monthly income	$50000 or less	81	38.2%
	Male	82	38.7%		$50001-100000	80	37.7%
Age	20 years old or younger	1	0.5%		$100001-200000	27	12.7%
	21-25 years old	45	21.1%		$200001-400000	6	2.8%
	26-30 years old	48	22.5%		$400001-600000	2	0.9%
	31-35 years old	47	22.1%		$600001-800000	1	0.5%
	36-40 years old	35	16.4%		$800001-1000000	5	2.4%
	41-45 years old	26	12.2%		$1000001 or more	10	4.7%
	46-50 years old	6	2.8%	Average hours of using internet per week	None	17	8.0%
	51 years old or older	5	2.3%		Less than 1 hour	25	11.7%
Educational level	High school or less	19	9.0%		1-3 hours	48	22.5%
	College/University	180	84.9%		3.1-5 hours	34	16.0%
	Master degree or higher	13	6.1%		5.1-7 hours	29	13.6%
Position	Student	31	15.0%		7.1-9 hours	21	9.9%
	Staff	82	39.8%		9.1-11 hours	10	4.7%
	Technician	4	1.9%		More than 11 hours	29	13.6%
	Sales	36	17.5%	Period of investing funds	6months or shorter	33	15.6%
	Specialist	24	11.7%		6.1 months-1year	29	13.7%
	Managerial people	17	8.3%		1.1-2 years	50	23.6%
	Top executive	6	2.9%		2.1-3 years	40	18.9%
	Boss	1	0.5%		3.1 years or longer	60	28.3%
	Others	5	2.4%	Risk tolerance	$9.5-$10.5	14	6.6%
Investment amount per year (NT$	$100000 or less	135	63.7%		$8.5-$11.5	64	30.2%
	$100001-$500000	60	28.3%		$7.5-$12.5	86	40.6%
	$500001-$1000000	11	5.2%		$6.5-$13.5	27	12.7%
	$1000001-$3000000	6	2.8%		$5.5-$14.5	21	9.9%

attributes, and the contents of benefits and values for attracting investors.

1). Category and analytical unit: In this study, the first questionnaire category was related to the A-C-V linkages of mutual funds; the benefits upon mutual fund investment were classified by fourteen items, and the nine values were directly adopted from LOV (Kahle & Kennedy, 1989).

2). Coding and reliability: Based on the 1242 web pages (web ads) for 145 sales agencies in four different regions, this study analyzed the contents of web ads by the word stems in the text of the web ads. Through content analysis, four coders examined the web ad content and classified the word stems. The mean intercoder agreement benefit and value variables were 0.868 and 0.804, respectively. The reliabilities were 0.96 and 0.94 for benefits and values, respectively, which meet the acceptable criteria proposed by Kassarjian (1977).

DISCUSSION

Data Description

Table 3 lists consumer demographics. Risk tolerance represents the acceptable net volatility of $10 investment and the minimum annual return acceptable to an investor. Table 4 summa-

TABLE 4

Attribute levels of mutual funds and preference percentages

Product characters	Factor	Number	Percentage
Fund numbers	5 or less	68	33.3%
	6-15	49	24.0%
	14-25	40	19.6%
	26-30	18	8.8%
	31-45	21	10.3%
	46 and above	10	4.9%
Fund type I (Investment target)	Equity funds	133	63.3%
	Bond funds	51	24.3%
	Balanced funds	70	33.3%
Fund type II (Investment regions)	Global fund	136	64.8%
	Regional fund	73	34.8%
	A Single National fund	34	16.2%
Fund manager	Gender	5	2.4%
	Years of service	58	27.5%
	Qualification	33	15.6%
	Experience	133	63.0%
	Investment ideas	148	70.1%
	Others	5	2.4%
Time of return	One month	20	9.7%
	Three months	21	10.1%
	Six months	38	18.4%
	One year	66	31.9%
	Three years	50	24.2%
	Five years	34	16.4%
	Ten years.	13	6.3%
Minimum purchase amount I: Single investment amount (NT$)	$10000 or less	81	38.2%
	$10001-30000	50	23.6%
	$30001-50000	53	25.0%
	$50001 and above	31	14.6%
Minimum purchase amount II: Periodic investment amount (NT$)	$3000	114	53.8%
	$4000	9	4.2%
	$5000	60	28.3%
	$5001 and above	33	15.6%

Product characters	Factor	Number	Percentage
Related fees (the highest acceptable rate)	1% or less	65	30.5%
	1.1% - 3%	124	58.2%
	3.1% -5%	24	11.3%
	5.1% -7%	4	1.9%
	7.1%and above	1	0.5%
Fund size (NT$)	$1 billion or less	26	12.8%
	$1(excluded) -2 billion	49	24.1%
	$2(excluded) -3 billion	42	20.7%
	$3(excluded) -4 billion	22	10.8%
	$4(excluded) -5 billion	30	14.8%
	$5 billion and above	37	18.2%
Currency	NT$	92	43.2%
	US$	143	67.1%
	HK$	1	0.5%
	Yen	10	4.7%
	British Pound	3	1.4%
	The Euro	54	25.4%
	Others	2	0.9%
Founding date	5 years or less	49	23.0%
	5.1-10 years	95	44.6%
	10.1-15 years	27	12.7%
	15.1-20 years	16	7.5%
	20.1-25 years	7	3.3%
	25.1-30syears	14	6.8%
	30.1 and above	10	4.8%
Sales agency	Investment trust	68	31.9%
	Investment adviser	40	18.8%
	Banks	134	62.9%
	Securities dealers	30	14.1%
	Others	4	1.9%
Custody bank	Public sector bank	118	55.4%
	Private bank	50	24.0%
	Foreign bank	69	33.2%
	Others	7	3.4%

TABLE 5

The analysis results of mutual fund web pages

Characteristics	Category	Number	Percentage
Country	Taiwan	90	62.07%
	Hong Kong	34	23.45%
	Mainland China	11	7.59%
	USA	10	6.90%
Company type	Investment trust	38	26.21%
	Investment adviser	6	4.14%
	Banks	37	25.52%
	Securities dealers	11	7.59%
	Asset management company	12	8.28%
	Fund management company	19	13.10%
	Investment management company	14	9.66%
	Financial services company	6	4.14%
	Others	2	1.38%
Years of services	1-5 years	36	27.07%
	6-10 years	29	21.80%
	11-15 years	14	10.53%
	16-20 years	10	7.52%
	21-40 years	18	13.53%
	41-60 years	11	8.27%
	61 years and above	15	11.28%
Cross-country number	0 country	32	33.33%
	1 countries	5	5.21%
	2 countries	7	7.29%
	3 countries	4	4.17%
	4 countries	4	4.17%
	5 countries or more	44	45.83%

Characteristics	Category	Number	Percentage
On-line transaction	Yes	65	45.14%
	No	79	54.86%
Sales office	1	10	20.83%
	2-10	10	20.83%
	11-40	14	29.17%
	41 or more	14	29.17%
Origin	Taiwan	66	46.81%
	Hong Kong	11	7.8%
	Mainland China	13	9.22%
	USA	26	18.44%
	Canada	5	3.55%
	Europe	13	9.22%
	Others	7	4.96%
Business projects	1 item	42	36.52%
	2-3 items	20	17.39%
	4-5 items	21	18.26%
	6 items	32	27.83%
Capital (NT$)	$1 billion or less	14	25.93%
	$1-10 billions	9	16.67%
	$10.1-20 billions	12	22.22%
	$20.1 billions and above	19	35.19%
Managing fund asset (NT$)	$30 billions or less	13	22.81%
	$30.1-100 billions	15	26.32%
	$100.1-5000 billions	18	31.58%
	$5000.1 billions and above	11	19.30%

TABLE 6

Attribute levels of mutual fund web sites

Product characters	Levels	Number	Percentage
Related fees (the highest acceptable rate)	1_or less	73	9.80%
	1.1_-3_	250	33.56%
	3.1_-5_	274	36.78%
	5.1_-7_	119	15.97%
	7.1_and above	29	3.89%
Fund size (NT$)	$1 billion or less	280	39.22%
	$1(excluded) -2 billion	108	15.13%
	$2(excluded) -3 billion	60	8.40%
	$3(excluded) -4 billion	35	4.90%
	$4(excluded) -5 billion	25	3.50%
	$5 billion and above	206	28.85%
Currency	NT$	294	38.2%
	US$	315	43%
	HK$	13	1.8%
	Japanese Yen	22	3.1%
	British Pound	32	4.5%
	The Euro	103	14.3%
	Others	38	5.3%
Founding date	5 years or less	481	52.80%
	5.1-10 years	227	24.92%
	10.1-15 years	138	15.15%
	15.1-20 years	26	2.85%
	20.1-25 years	16	1.76%
	25.1-30syears	5	0.55%
	30.1 and above	18	1.98%
Sales agency	Investment trust	198	30.9%
	Investment adviser	11	1.7%
	Banks	346	54.0%
	Securities dealers	146	22.8%
	Others	243	37.9%
Custody bank	Public sector bank	65	15.8%
	Private bank	242	58.9%
	Foreign bank	58	14.1%
	Others	49	11.9%

Product characters	Levels	Number	Percentage
Fund numbers	5 or less	23	15.86%
	6-15	38	26.21%
	14-25	10	6.90%
	26-30	6	4.14%
	31-45	4	2.76%
	46 and above	64	44.14%
Fund type I (Investment target)	Equity funds	606	70.7%
	Bond funds	169	19.7%
	Balanced funds	63	7.4%
	Currency funds	19	2.2%
Fund type II (Investment region)	Global fund	145	17.3%
	Regional fund	148	17.7%
	A Single National fund	544	65%
Fund manager	Gender	78	12.9%
	Years of service	309	51.6%
	Qualification	506	78%
	Experience	514	79.2%
	Investment ideas	249	40.4%
	Others	85	14.1%
Time of return	One month	514	68.9%
	Three months	533	70.6%
	Six months	468	61.6%
	One year	670	89.5%
	Three years	479	66.1%
	Five years	317	44.8%
	Ten years.	94	13.3%
	Others	614	84.8%
Minimum purchase amount I: Single investment amount (NT$)	$10000 or less	280	50.63%
	$10001-30000	38	6.87%
	$30001-50000	83	15.01%
	$50001 and above	152	27.49%
Minimum purchase amount II: Periodic investment amount (NT$)	$3000	212	84.46%
	$4000	1	0.40%
	$5000	16	6.37%
	$5001 and above	22	8.76%

rizes the attribute levels preferred by investors. Such attribute levels can help mutual fund managers design their portfolios.

Table 5 lists the analytical results for the mutual fund institution web pages. Table 6 lists the attribute levels of individual mutual funds available on web sites and the preference percentages of investors.

Mutual Fund Cognitive Structure of Consumers and Web Pages

Based on the interview data and web ad messages, all data were entered into the summary implication matrix to construct mutual fund cognitive ladders (Attribute-Benefit-Value; A-B-V). Using the 93rd percentile as a cutoff point, the valid A-B-V linkages were used to construct a hierarchical value map (HVM) for mutual fund investors. In the HVM, the deciles 3 of these valid A-B-V linkages defined as strong, medium and weak linkages are illustrated by thick, middle and thin lines.

According to Figure 1, investors indicated that "fund type", "fund manager", "custody bank" and "related fee" attributes (strong linkages) were quite important investing considerations. These salient attributes may yield different perceived benefits to investors and further satisfy different value demands. For example, a given "fund type" attribute (A) can provide investors with "good performance" benefits (B) and yield "security" (V) value satisfaction. Further, a "fund manager" (A) is also important to investors for his "professionalism" (B) , which increases investor "security" (V) value.

This study also examined the A-B-V linkages of mutual fund web ads across four regions (China, Hong Kong, Taiwan and the United States). The 93rd percentile was used as a cutoff point. The three deciles of these valid A-B-V linkages were also defined as strong, medium and weak linkages. In Taiwan, the web ads emphasized the importance of "fund type" and "time of return" due to considerations of "portfolio variety" and "investment assistance" benefits yielding "self-fulfillment" and "security" values (Figure 2).

Figures 3, 4 and 5 illustrate the web ads HVM for Hong Kong, Mainland China and USA, respectively. Different regions may have different emphases in their mutual fund web ads due to different investor desires of value satisfactions.

Comparisons of Investor Cognitions and Web Ads Offering

In Taiwan, both investors and mutual fund web pages emphasized the importance of "security" and "sense of belonging" value achievement (Table 7). For investors, "fund type", "fund number", "fund scale", "time of return", "fund manager" and "custody bank" attributes may yield "portfolio variety", "spreading risk", "profession", "good performance", "well known", "good reputation", and "large scale" benefits satisfying their "security" value demand. However, for the web ads to achieve investor "security" value satisfaction, "fund type", "time of return", "currency", "fund manager", and "sales agency" are more important attributes to help investors obtain "portfolio variety", "spreading risk", "transnational investment", and "investment assistance" benefits were considered

FIGURE 1
Investor hierarchical value map of mutual funds

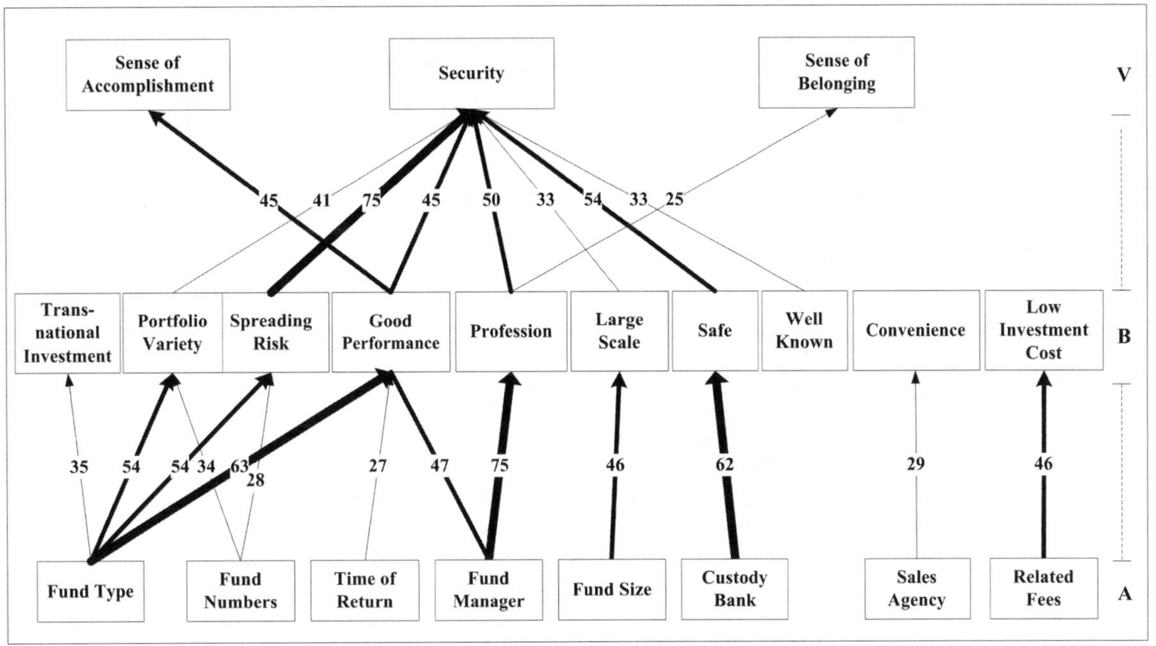

FIGURE 2
The HVM of Taiwan web pages

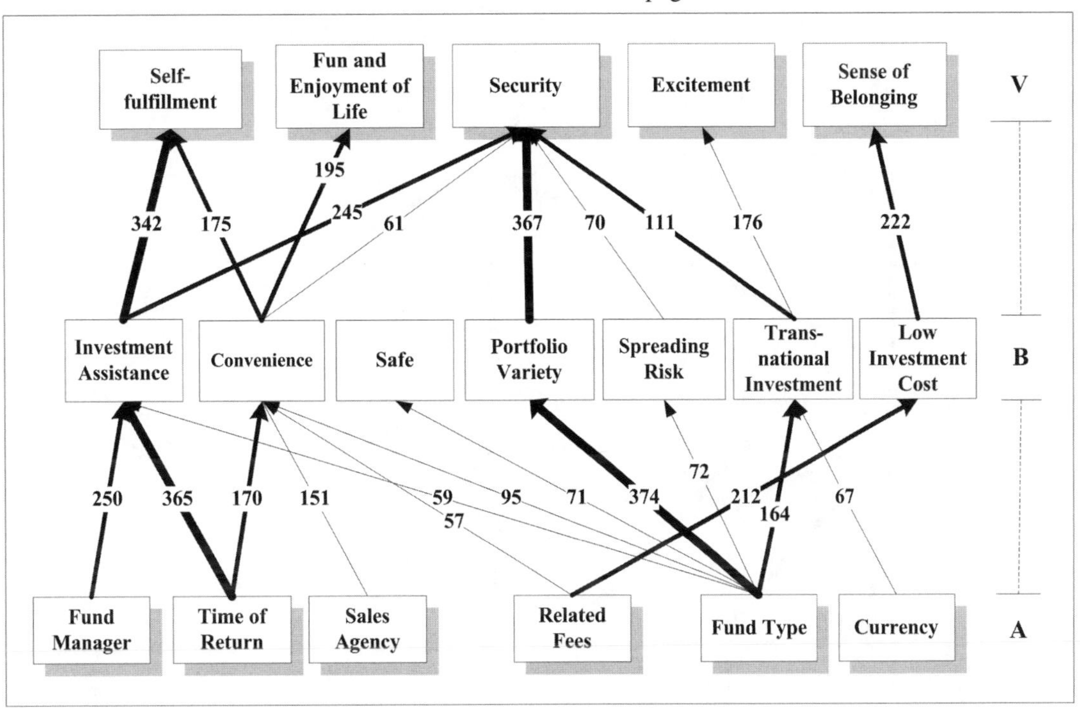

FIGURE 3
The HVM of Hong Kong web pages

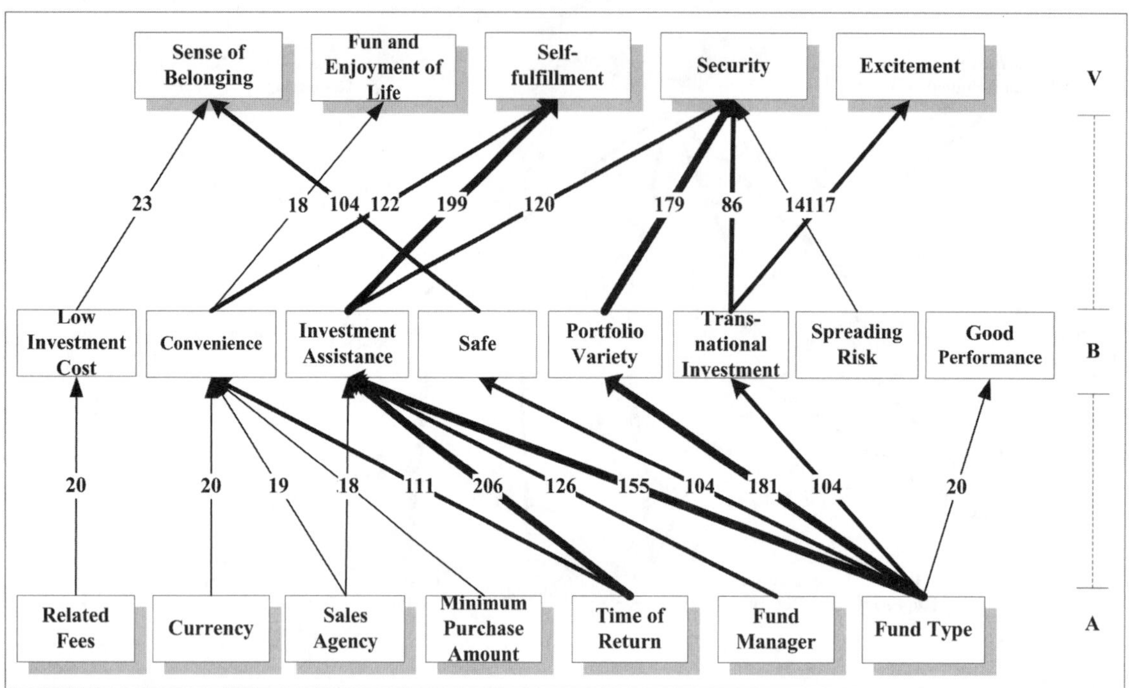

FIGURE 4
The HVM of Mainland China web pages

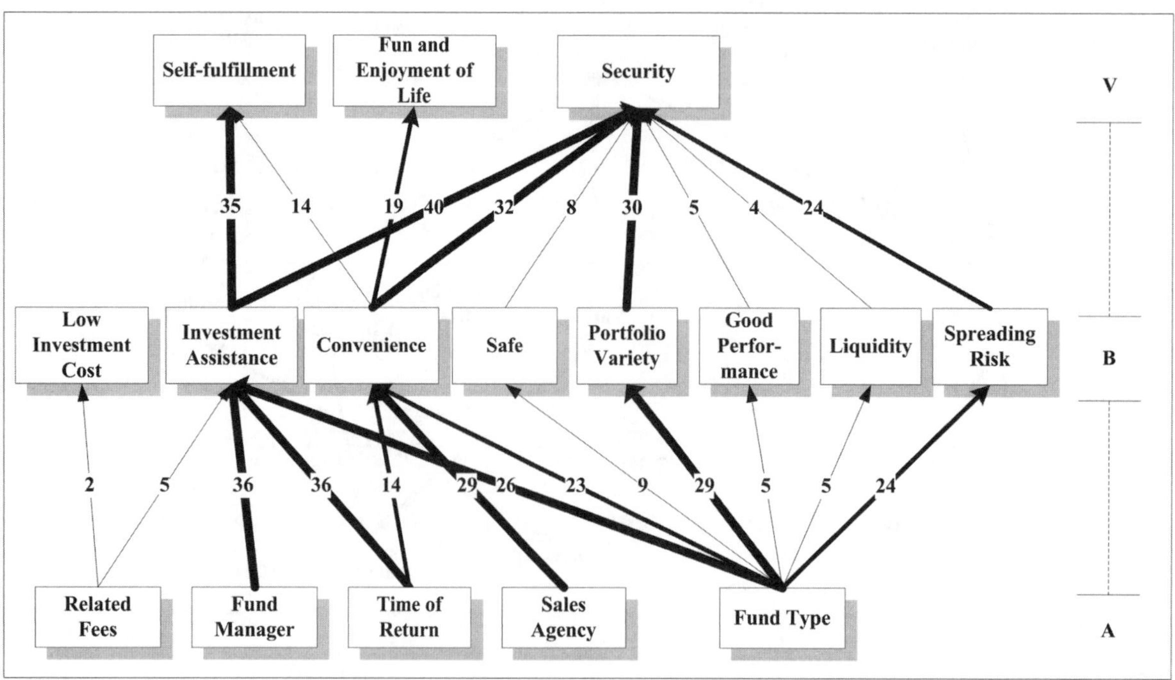

FIGURE 5
The HVM of USA web pages

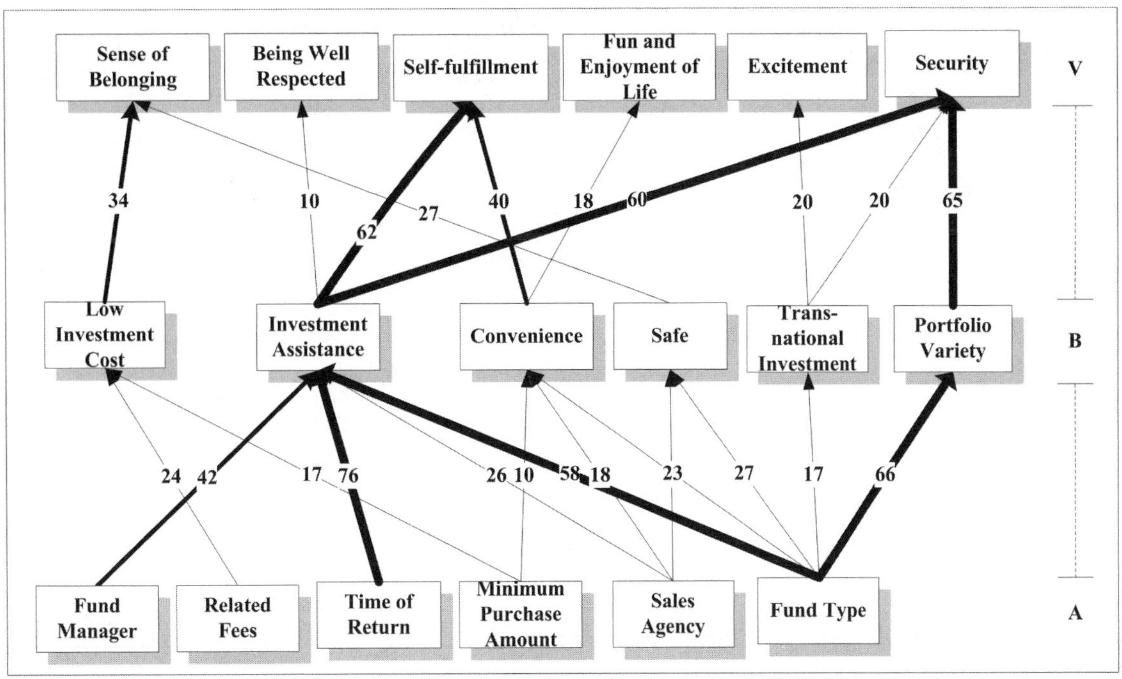

FIGURE 6
The HVM of web pages in four regions

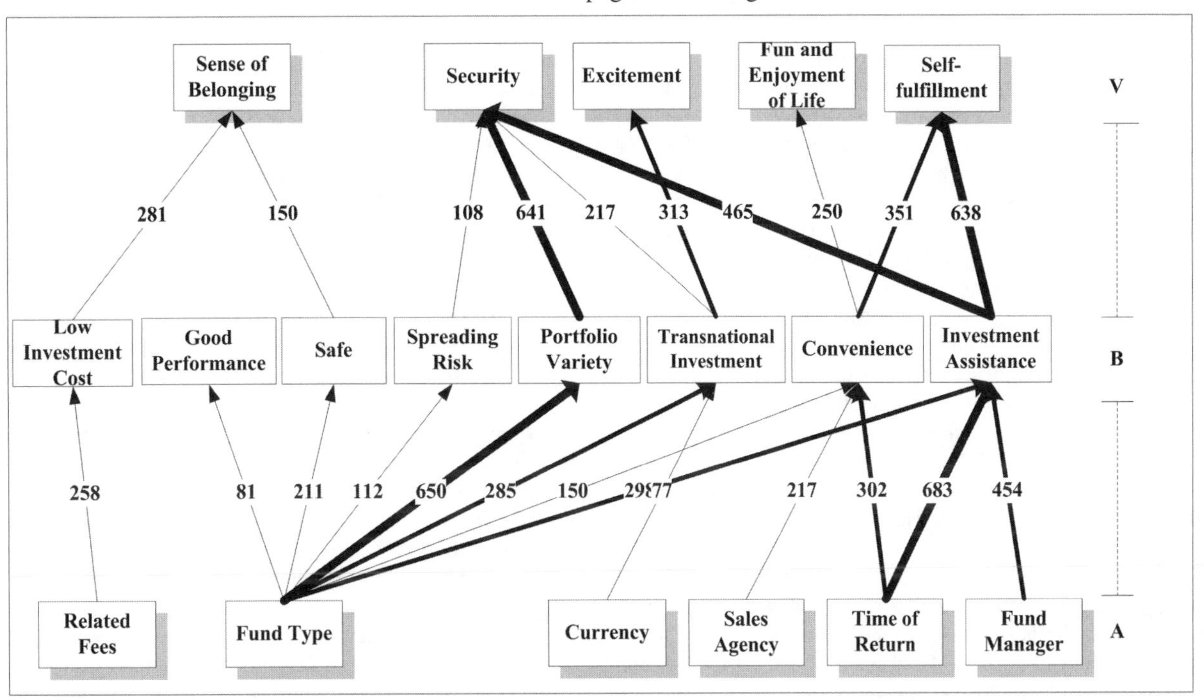

TABLE 7

Cognitive comparisons of investors and web pages in Taiwan

Object	Product attribute (A)	Benefit (B)	Value (V)
Web pages	Related fees	Low investment cost	Sense of Belonging
Consumers	Fund manager	Profession	
Web pages	Fund type、Currency	Transnational investment	Excitement
Consumers	-	-	
Web pages	Fund manager、Time of return、Fund type	Investment assistance	Self-Fulfillment
	Sales agency、Time of return、Related fees、Fund type	Convenience	
Consumers	-	-	
Web pages	Sales agency、Time of return、Related fees、Fund type	Convenience	Fun and Enjoyment of Life
Consumers	-	-	
Web pages	Fund manager、Time of return、Fund type	Investment assistance	Security
	Sales agency、Time of return、Related fees、Fund type	Convenience	
	Fund type	Portfolio variety	
	Fund type	Spreading risk	
	Fund type、Currency	Transnational investment	
Consumers	Fund type; Fund numbers	Portfolio variety	
	Fund type; Fund numbers	Spreading risk	
	Fund type、Time of return、Fund manager	Good performance	
	Fund manager	Profession	
	Fund size	Large scale	
	Custody bank	Safe	
	-	Well known	
Consumers	Fund type、Time of return、Fund manager	Good performance	Sense of Accomplishment

most important. Further, to achieve "sense of belonging" value, investors who perceived the "related fee" attribute as offering a "low investment cost" benefit. Web ads, conversely, expected that "fund manager" attributes provide a "professional" image for investors. Additionally, from the investor perspective, "fund type", "time of return" and "fund manager" are means of achieving their "sense of accomplishment" value desire whereas web ads are expected to provide investors with "excitement" and "fun and enjoyment of life" value satisfaction.

Comparing the web ads of China, Hong Kong, Taiwan and the United States revealed that "sense of accomplishment", "fun and enjoyment of life" and "security" messages were the ultimate values that businesses try to deliver to their investors (see Table 8). In the "sense of accomplishment" message delivery, web ads use "fund manager", "sales agency", "time of return", "related fee" and "fund type" attributes offer "convenience" and "investment assistance" benefits to attract investors. Moreover, web ads in four regions emphasize the importance of "sales agency" to obtain the "convenience" benefit, which yields "fun and enjoyment of life" value. Notably, the U.S. web ads were the only ads that attempted to deliver "being well respected" value to the public investors.

Based on the previous analytical results, this study further used the fund attributes investors and web ads preferred the most to construct an extended HVM. The extended HVM can not only demonstrate the most important A-B-V linkages but also shows more detailed attribute characteristics referred to here as "attribute levels."

Figure 7 illustrates that "fund type", "fund manager" and "custody bank" were the most important fund attributes for both investors and web ads designs. To examine further, the author found that "equity funds (A_L)" and "global funds (A_L)" were the two "fund types (A)"most preferred by investors because of their "good performance (B)" leading to investors' "sense of accomplishment (V)" value satisfaction. Investors also care about the "investment idea (A_L)" and "qualification (A_L)" of "fund manager (A)", because these two attribute levels can show the "profession" of fund managers and then attain "sense of belonging" and security" values of investors. Moreover, investors believed that the "public sector bank (A_L)" is more trustworthy than "custody bank (A)" for investment. It provides "safety (B)" and "security (V)" to investors. Thus, the extended HVM provides marketers with more precise data regarding the product characteristics preferred by investors than the original HVM does.

For the mutual fund web pages across the four regions in Figure 8, "equity funds (A_L)" and "a single national fund (A_L)" are the emphasis of "fund type (A)", because of the "investment assistance (B)" benefit and "security (V)" value achievement. On the web pages, the "time of return (A)" includes "one month (A_L)", "three months (A_L)", "six months (A_L)", "one year (A_L)" and "three years (A_L)". These fund-attribute levels yield "portfolio variety (B)" benefit and lead to "security (V)" and "sense of accomplishment (V)" value satisfaction.

CONCLUSION, LIMITATION, AND FUTURE RESEARCH

The Internet pervades daily life. On-line transactions are now common for purchasing products and services. On-line transactions involve no real shops-entities. Hence, web ads are important for attracting customers or investors. Whether the ads can communicate with target investors and whether such ads can effectively adhere to investor needs is now an important issue in web page design. Based on the analytical results, the suggestions for web designers of mutual fund are shown as followings:

1). Investors: Most fund attributes, benefits and values preferred by investors are exactly as shown on fund web pages. However, the interviews revealed that many investors were disappointed by the low rates of return on their fund investments. Consequently, they felt that their fund investments had accomplished little. Thus, mutual fund managers may con-

TABLE 8
Cognitive comparisons of web ads cross four regions

Region	Attribute（A）	Benefit（B）	Value（V）
Taiwan	Related fees	Low investment cost	Sense of Belonging
Hong Kong	Related fees	Low investment cost	
	Fund type	Safe	
Mainland China	-	-	
USA	Related fees、Minimum purchase amount	Low investment cost	
	Sales agency、Fund type	Safe	
Taiwan	Fund type、Currency	Transnational investment	Excitement
Hong Kong	Fund type	Transnational investment	
Mainland China	-	-	
USA	Fund type	Transnational investment	
Taiwan	Fund manager、Time of return、Fund type	Investment assistance	Self-Fulfillment
	Sales agency、Time of return、Related fees、Fund type	Convenience	
Hong Kong	Currency、Sales agency、Minimum purchase amount、Time of return	Convenience	
	Sales agency、Time of return、Fund manager、Fund type	Investment assistance	
Mainland China	Related fees、Fund manager、Time of return、Fund type	Investment assistance	
	Time of return、Sales agency、Fund type	Convenience	
USA	Fund manager、Time of return、Sales agency、Fund type	Investment assistance	
	Minimum purchase amount、Sales agency、Fund type	Convenience	
Taiwan	-	-	Being Well Respected
Hong Kong	-	-	
Mainland China	-	-	
USA	Fund manager、Time of return、Sales agency、Fund type	Investment assistance	
Taiwan	Sales agency、Time of return、Related fees、Fund type	Convenience	Fun and Enjoyment of Life
Hong Kong	Currency、Sales agency、Minimum purchase amount、Time of return	Convenience	
Mainland China	Time of return、Sales agency、Fund type	Convenience	
USA	Minimum purchase amount、Sales agency、Fund type	Convenience	
Taiwan	Fund manager、Time of return、Fund type	Investment assistance	Security
	Sales agency、Time of return、Related fees、Fund type	Convenience	
	Fund type	Portfolio variety	
	Fund type	Spreading risk	
	Fund type、Currency	Transnational investment	
Hong Kong	Sales agency、Time of return、Fund manager、Fund type	Investment assistance	
	Fund type	Portfolio variety	
	Fund type	Transnational investment	
	-	Spreading risk	
Mainland China	Related fees、Fund manager、Time of return、Fund type	Investment assistance	
	Time of return、Sales agency、Fund type	Convenience	
	Fund type	Safe	
	Fund type	Portfolio variety	
	Fund type	Good performance	
	Fund type	Liquidity	
	Fund type	Spreading risk	
USA	Fund manager、Time of return、Sales agency、Fund type	Investment assistance	
	Fund type	Transnational investment	
	Fund type	Portfolio variety	

FIGURE 7
The extended HVM of investors

Sense of Accomplish
Sense of Belonging
Security
V
45
45
25
50
54
Good Performance
Profession
Safe
B
63
75
62
Fund Type
Fund Manager
Custody Bank
A
Equity Fund 63.3%
Global Fund 64.8%
Qualification 63%
Investment Ideas 70.1%
Public Sector Bank 56.7%
AL

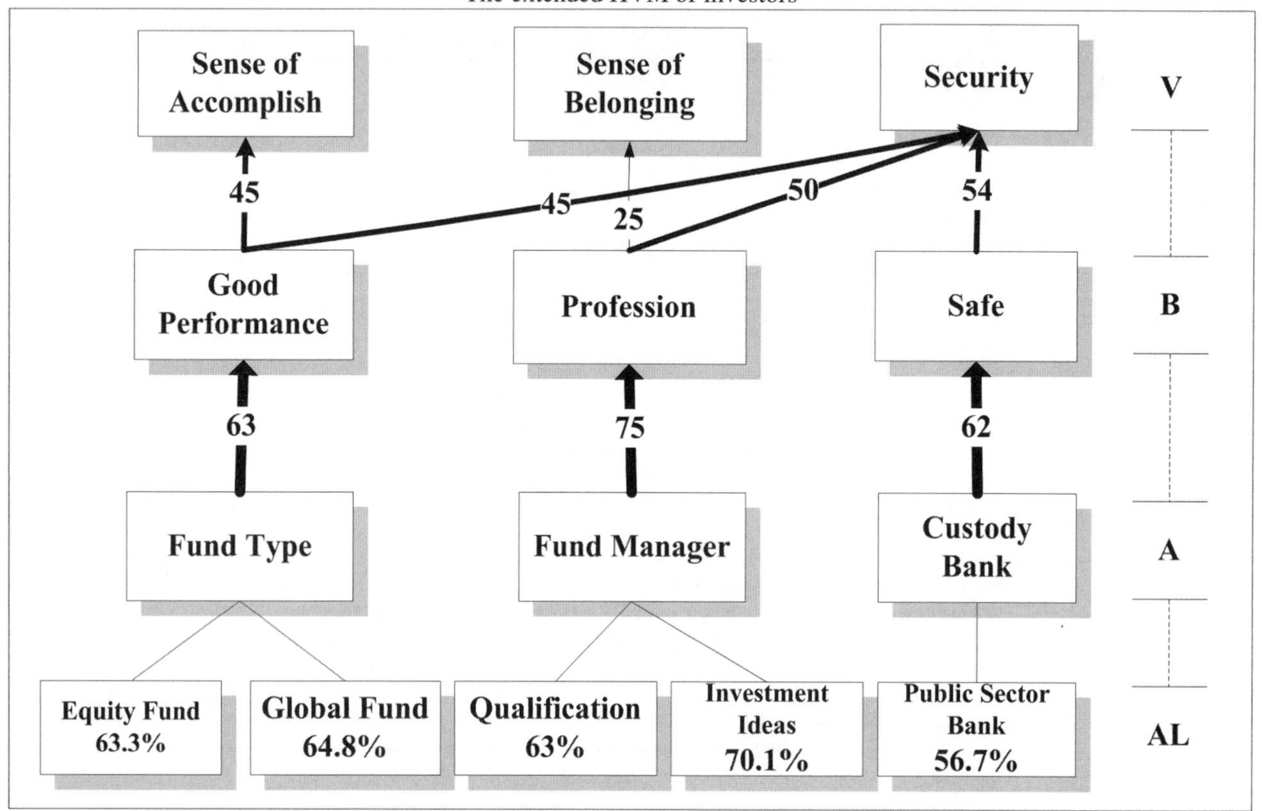

FIGURE 8
The extended HVM of fund web pages across four regions

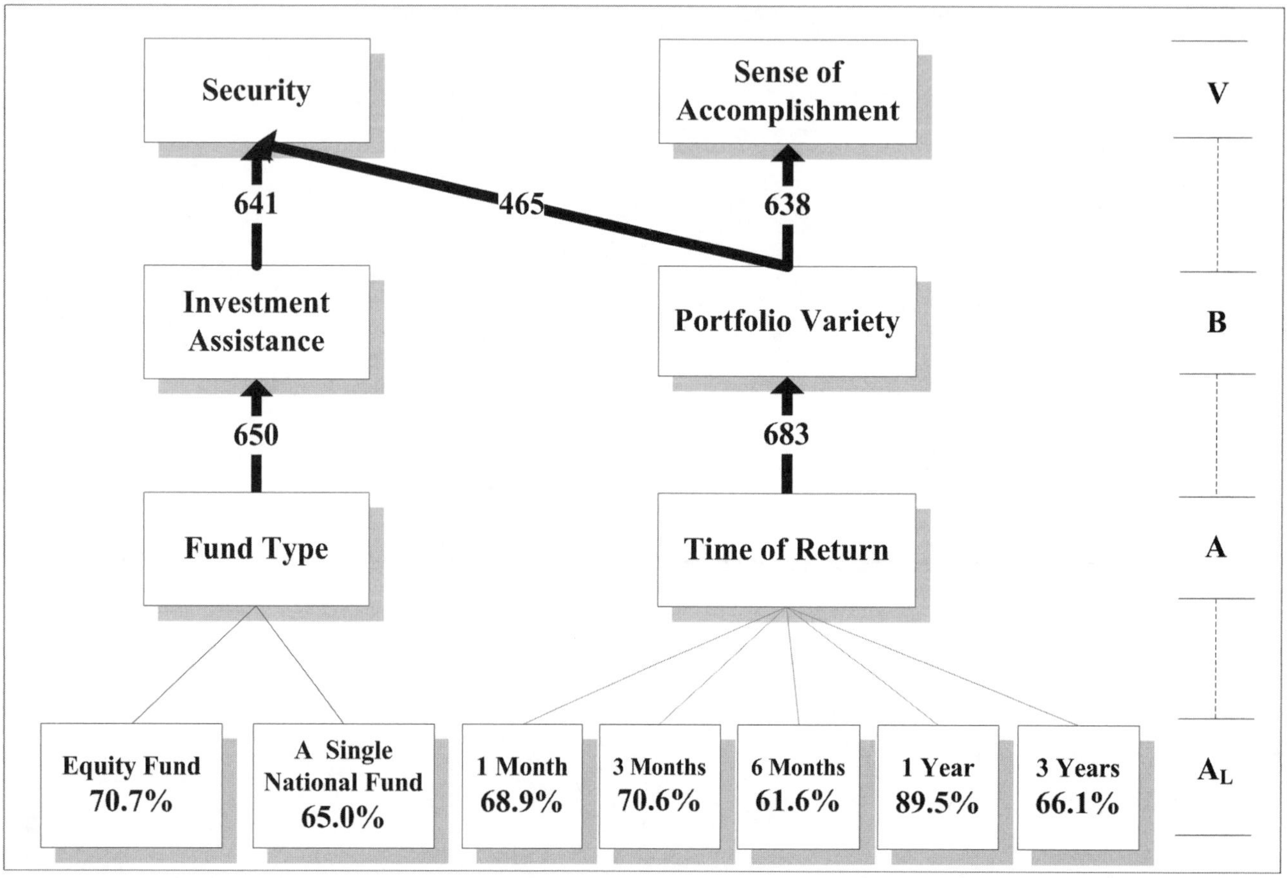

Security
Sense of Accomplishment
V
641
465
638
Investment Assistance
Portfolio Variety
B
650
683
Fund Type
Time of Return
A
Equity Fund 70.7%
A Single National Fund 65.0%
1 Month 68.9%
3 Months 70.6%
6 Months 61.6%
1 Year 89.5%
3 Years 66.1%
AL

sider providing investors with more positive and persuasive news to encourage them in the dynamic environment.

2). China: Chinese websites lacked key information. The web designers may consider adding more fund-attribute information such as "currency" and "minimum purchase amount" and content which provides investors with value satisfaction such as "excitement" and "sense of belonging".

3). Hong Kong: In this study, Hong Kong was the only region that provided complete fund attributes on the web pages. The web designers may need to enhance their web pages by delivering "sense of accomplishment" and "being well respected" messages to their target investors.

4). Taiwan: Web designers can refer to USA web ads for adding the element of "being well respected" to investors. Also, designers may consider including messages regarding "minimum purchase amount" and "good performance" in their web ad designs.

5). United States: The USA web pages provided investors with the most information in achieving investors' value satisfaction. The web page designs may require more information about the benefits of investing in funds such as "spreading risk" and "good performance" of certain funds.

This study compared the web ads of only four regions. Therefore, the analytical results cannot be generalized to global web ad design. Future researchers may consider increasing the number of research objects in various countries or adopting an individual country as a research object to make a cross-national comparison. Furthermore, investment products are significantly influenced by dynamic economy. Hence, comparing the contents of cross-nation HVM toward a give investment instrument in different stage of economic dynamics can help business understand the timing for developing effective promotion or advertising strategies. Additionally, fund investments are only one investment instrument. Other financial products require further comparisons in order to provide investors with valuable information for investment.

ACKNOWLEDGEMENTS

The author wishes to acknowledge the financial support of this paper by the National Science Council, Taiwan. No.: NSC 98-2410-H-251 -001.

REFERENCES

Chordia, Tarun (1996), "The Structure of Mutual Fund Charges," *Journal of Financial Economics, 41 (1), 3-39.*

Day, George S., Shocker, Allan S., and Rajendra K. Srivastava (1979), "Consumer-Oriented Approaches to Identifying Product-Markets," *Journal of Marketing*, 43(Fall), 8-19.

Gutman, Jonathan (1981), "A Means-End Model for Facilitating Analyses of Product Markets Based on Consumer Judgment," *Advances in Consumer Research*, 8, 116-121.

Gutman, Jonathan (1982), "A Means-End Chain Model Based on Consumer Categorization Processes," *Journal of Marketing*, 46(Spring), 60-72.

InvestorWords.com (2008). Mutual fund definition. http://www.investorwords.com/3173/mutual_fund.html, retrieval date: 10/31/2008.

Kahle, Lynn R. and Patricia Kennedy (1989), "Using the List of Values (LOV) to Understand Consumers," *Journal of Consumer Marketing*, 6(Summer), 5-12.

Kassarjian, Harold H. (1977), "Content Analysis in Consumer Research", *Journal of Consumer Research*, 4(June), 8-18.

Kotler, Philip (1994), *Marketing Management, Analysis, Planning, Implementation and Control*, New Yersey: Prentice-Hall International Editions.

Kotler, Philip (1997), *Marketing Management, Analysis, Planning, Implementation, and Control*, Prentice-Hall Inc., NJ. USA., 10, 173, 313-314, 731.

Levinthal, Daniel A., and Jennifer Myatt (1994) *"Co-Evolution of Capabilities and Industry: The Evolution of Mutual Fund Processing,"* Strategic Management Journal, *15(1), 45-62.*

Lin, Chin-Feng (2003), "Quality-delivery System: A Conceptual Framework of Attribute Level-Value Linkages," *Total Quality Management & Business Excellence*, 14(10), 1079-1092.

Peter, J. Paul and Jerry C. Olson (1993), *Consumer Behavior and Marketing Strategy*, Richard D. Irwin, Inc., 85-109.

Reynolds, Thomas. J. and Jonathan Gutman (1988), "Laddering Theory, Method, Analysis, and Interpretation," *Journal of Advertising Research*, 28(1), 11-29.

Reynolds, Thomas J. and Jerry C. Olson (2001). *Understanding Consumer Decision Making: The Means-end Approach to Marketing and Advertising Strategy*. Lawrence Erlbaum Associates, Publishers, Mahwah, New Jersey.

Rokeach, Milton (1968), *Beliefs, Attitudes and Values*, San Francisco: Jossey Bass.

Vinson, Donald E., Scott, Jerome E., and, Lawrence H. Lamont (1977), "The Role of Personal Values in Marketing and Consumer Behavior," *Journal of Marketing*, 41(April), 44-50.

Status within a Consumption-Oriented Counterculture: An Ethnographic Investigation of the Australian Hip Hop Culture

Damien Arthur, University of Adelaide, Australia
Claire Sherman, University of Adelaide, Australia

ABSTRACT

This study identifies the determinants of status within a consumption-oriented counterculture. The results of an ethnographic study of the Australian Hip Hop culture suggest that embodied subcultural capital and subculture-specific social capital confer status on countercultural members. In contrast to previous findings, these two forms of capital were found to more consistently confer status than a member's commitment to the culture's consumption values or their commitment of time and resources. This distinction is most prevalent amongst hard-core members who vary in both levels of commitment and their objectification of subcultural capital. Theoretical and managerial implications are discussed.

The purpose of this study is to explore the nature of status within a consumption-oriented counterculture. The paper begins with a review of the literature, specifically that which deals with the nature and structure of consumption-oriented countercultures and their relationship with subcultural capital. An overview of the methodology, a four-year ethnographic study of the Australian Hip Hop culture, is then provided. An analysis of the findings which identify the determinants of status within a consumption-oriented counterculture follows, and a discussion of the theoretical and managerial implications concludes the paper.

LITERATURE REVIEW

Consumption-Oriented Countercultures

Consumption-oriented countercultures are entities that provide space for members to develop and express their self-concepts alongside other members with similar interests, while at the same time allowing them to position their unique values, attitudes and opinions against the dominant and mass culture. Consumption-oriented countercultural theory emerged in the 1970's, largely from researchers at the Birmingham Centre for Contemporary Cultural Studies who investigated the punk (Hebdige 1979), mod (Hebdige 1975), motorbike boy (Willis 1978), ted (Jefferson 1975), skinhead (Clarke 1975a), and hippy (Willis 1975, 1978) cultures.

These studies found that members of countercultures consumed distinctive, yet uniform styles opposing the dominant and mass cultures which they found to be politically manipulated and undifferentiated (e.g. Clarke 1975a; Hebdige 1979; Willis 1978). In doing so, counterculture members consumed in a manner which strictly adhered to their counterculture's rules and expressed their allegiance to the counterculture's values and attitudes (Clarke 1975b). The expression of a culture's values through the consumption of a style that closely parallels the culture's ideology has been termed 'homology' and was the focus of many of the early counterculture studies (Willis 1978). For example, Willis (1978) found that 'the motor-bike boys' did not dress with the functional requirements of riding a motor cycle in mind, instead their dress was found to be a formidable expression of identity which was powerfully developed around many of the culture's central values. Similarly, homologous relationships were also found between the values of the hippy, ted, punk, skinhead and mod cultures and their members' consumption habits (Clarke 1975a; Hebdige 1975, 1979; Jefferson 1975; Willis 1978).

While more recent studies of consumption-oriented countercultures have not focused specifically on their homologous nature, their results tend to support the earlier findings and describe a homologous relationship between the consumption of the subculture's members and the values of the group (Arthur 2006a; Kozinets 2001; Schouten and McAlexander 1995). For example, Schouten and McAlexander's (1995) ethnography of the new bikers found that the core values of the counterculture were based around personal freedom, patriotism and machismo, and were visually expressed though the consumption of long hair, bushy beards, loud powerful bikes, the American flag, the bald eagle, tattoos and black leather. One exception, a study by Kates (2002), found that no single homologous style existed in the gay community. Instead, Kates found consumption to be characterized by a multitude of shifting, malleable meanings open to multiple interpretations and considerable debate. Hence, unlike the consumers presented in previously mentioned studies, these subcultural members did not sacrifice creative self-expression in order to communicate their belonging to a group, they accomplished both simultaneously.

The Structure of a Consumption-Oriented Counterculture

Consumption-oriented countercultures have been found to be comprised of individuals who vary in their level of identification and commitment, with some members being very closely tied to the group and others being only peripherally related (Fox 1987; Hebdige 1979; Kates 2002; Schouten and McAlexander 1995). Fox (1987) first described the structure as a series of three concentric circles based on one's level of commitment to the subcultures ideology. Those participants most heavily committed to the counterculture were located within the most inner-concentric circle and hence became known as the hard-core members.

Hard-core members devotion and commitment to their counterculture's values has been found to be a full time and enduring process, and can represent a major dimension in their lives and conceptualization of self (Fox 1987; Hebdige 1979; Schouten and McAlexander 1995). As such, previous studies suggest that hard-core members must be relatively uncommitted to other cultural groups, and have the freedom and spare time to devote themselves wholly to the counterculture's cause (Irwin 1973). In contrast, the next concentric circle consists of 'soft-core' members whose commitment to the subculture is less complete and whose roles are subordinate to, and dictated by, the hard-core members. While these individuals are less dedicated to the subculture, their degree of involvement with the subculture is still high, though not necessarily enduring. As such, while they outnumber the hard-core members, they are less respected and do not occupy the same social status or demand the same level of influence (Fox 1987). Furthermore, soft-core members tend to be more interested in the symbolic qualities of the products, brands and activities consumed than their functional attributes, as they rely on such consumption to communicate their self and group identity to others.

In her study of the punk counterculture, Fox (1987) described the outer circle of peripheral members as 'preppie punks'. While these individuals frequent the countercultural site and consume in a homologous fashion, the hard and soft-core members do not necessarily see them as part of the subculture as they lack the ideological commitment. These individuals are often only interested in the counterculture for the novelty it provides and because, at a particular point in time, it is deemed fashionable. As such, for many it is seen as a passing fad, or a bit of light relief from the monotonous but none the less paramount realities of school, home and work (Hebdige 1979). Hence, these members treat such subcultural experiences as identity play and are able to quickly abandon their associations in situations that would sanction them negatively.

Whilst the framework for viewing the structure of a consumption-oriented counterculture as three distinct categories has received much academic support (e.g. Fox 1987; Schouten and McAlexander 1995), Kates (2002) suggests that such a categorisation imposes a fixed, rigid structure that does not resemble the reality of the neo-tribal consumer (Maffesoli 1996). In contrast, Kates found an individual's position in the gay community to be based on a fluid, contested and negotiated assessment of the individual's accumulated subcultural capital.

Subcultural Capital

In her study of club cultures, Thornton (1995) coined the term subcultural capital to describe the knowledge, experience and skills that bestow status within a subculture. Her work is guided by that of Pierre Bourdieu, and specifically his book 'Distinction' (1984), in which he used the term 'cultural capital' to describe the knowledge that is acquired through our upbringing and education and which confers status and enhances one's standing within society. Bourdieu conceptualized the structure of society as being dictated by the consumption of markers of distinction which affirm one's taste. While Thornton has been credited for taking the concept out of the realm of 'high class' consumption via her definition (Bennett 1999; Kates 2002), a closer reading of Bourdieu (1984) reveals that he did not mean for the term to be so confined. In fact, throughout his work he argues that in all fields, including subcultures, a system of differences exists where expressive consumption and social differences are made explicit.

Expanding on the concept in a later article, Bourdieu (1986) argues that capital can present itself in three fundamental forms: as cultural capital, economic capital and social capital. Cultural capital, being the knowledge one has acquired that is expressed through one's taste, can be found in three states: embodied, objectified, and institutionalized. Embodied cultural capital is the knowledge, skills and expertise that exist within an individual that is acquired through the process of education, both formal and informal. This may be expressed through an understanding of a culture's values, rituals and traditions. For example, within high class culture good manners and an appreciation and understanding of fine art and wine are examples of embodied cultural capital (Bourdieu 1984). In contrast, amongst Thornton's (1995) ravers, subcultural capital was embodied in the form of being 'in the know,' understanding and using current slang and performing the latest dance styles. The accumulation of such embodied cultural capital presupposes a personal cost of time and other sacrifices and cannot be transmitted easily or instantaneously (Bourdieu 1986). It can however be acquired over time, and the accumulation can be hastened if one has freedom from other commitments.

Once one has acquired embodied cultural capital, it may be objectified through the consumption of symbolic goods that infer such knowledge. For example, in the high class culture the display of books and paintings in the family home constitute objectified cultural capital. Alternately, in Thornton's (1995) rave culture, subcultural capital was objectified in the form of fashionable haircuts and carefully assembled record collections. Hence, knowledge of the symbolic properties of goods and consumption styles is an example of embodied cultural capital, whereas the consumption of these symbolic goods is an example of objectified cultural capital. Economic capital will facilitate this process, however, knowing what products to consume and the manner in which to consume them to enhance one's standing in society requires the accumulation of embodied cultural capital (Bourdieu 1986). Lastly, institutionalized cultural capital is expressed in the form of qualifications which are presumed to guarantee cultural capital, such as formally recognized education (Bourdieu 1986).

In addition to cultural capital, Bourdieu (1986) describes social capital as the value that is created through the use and influence of social networks. The value created is dependent on how much cultural and economic capital is created upon mobilizing one's social network. Hence, those with many and/or powerful connections have an abundance of social capital and an elevated status within society.

As explained, each of these forms of capital may be used to enhance status; yet, the majority of research investigating the structure of consumption-oriented countercultures has overlooked this finding and assumes commitment to be the primary determinant of one's position in the status hierarchy. The findings presented in this study address this gap. The Australian Hip Hop culture was selected as it is a counterculture firmly rooted in the consumer based objects of music, clothes and symbols. Furthermore, previous research has shown it to be excellent site for gaining insights into the symbolic consumption practices of countercultural members (Arthur 2006a, b; Chalmers and Arthur 2008; Maxwell 2003).

METHODOLOGY

Status within the Australian Hip Hop culture was investigated using five methods of ethnographic research: prolonged participant observation, researcher introspection, semi-structured in-depth interviews, non-participant netnography, and an ongoing review of the literature. Ethnography was chosen as this approach has been found to be particularly effective when little is known about a targeted group (Mariampolski 2006). A grounded approach to theory generation was utilised as it is the standard approach adopted by ethnographers and has been acknowledged to have considerable potential within the field of consumer behaviour (Goulding 1998).

The first author undertook the ethnographic research between June 2002 and June 2006. Extended presence and participation in the field allowed the researcher to 'learn the language' of those under investigation, and to experience life as one of the subjects (Elliott and Jankel-Elliott 2003). The Hip Hop culture revolves around four key activities: rapping, graffiti art, breakdancing and DJing. An Adelaide Hip Hop DJ who was an acquaintance of the researcher facilitated initial entry into the Hip Hop culture in Australia and the researcher accompanied the gatekeeper and a number of his friends to around 150 Hip Hop nights held across Adelaide, and around Australia. In addition, the researcher accompanied the gatekeeper through a wide variety of contexts that Agar (1996) would describe as 'hanging out' such as playing records, playing basketball, watching television, shopping, socialising, drinking and partying.

Becoming a member of a counterculture meant entering as an aspiring member and undergoing a process of socialisation whereby status was obtained. Hence, the nature of the ethnographic process was evolving, which allowed the researcher to interact with different elements of the counterculture and to experience the signifying practices of Hip Hop consumption as an insider. During this period, the researcher kept field notes of his observations and informal conversations, which were then written up as soon as possible after the event. Furthermore, the researcher kept a personal diary of the process, which was a useful record of his cognitive and emotional

FIGURE 1
Status Within A Consumption-Oriented Counterculture

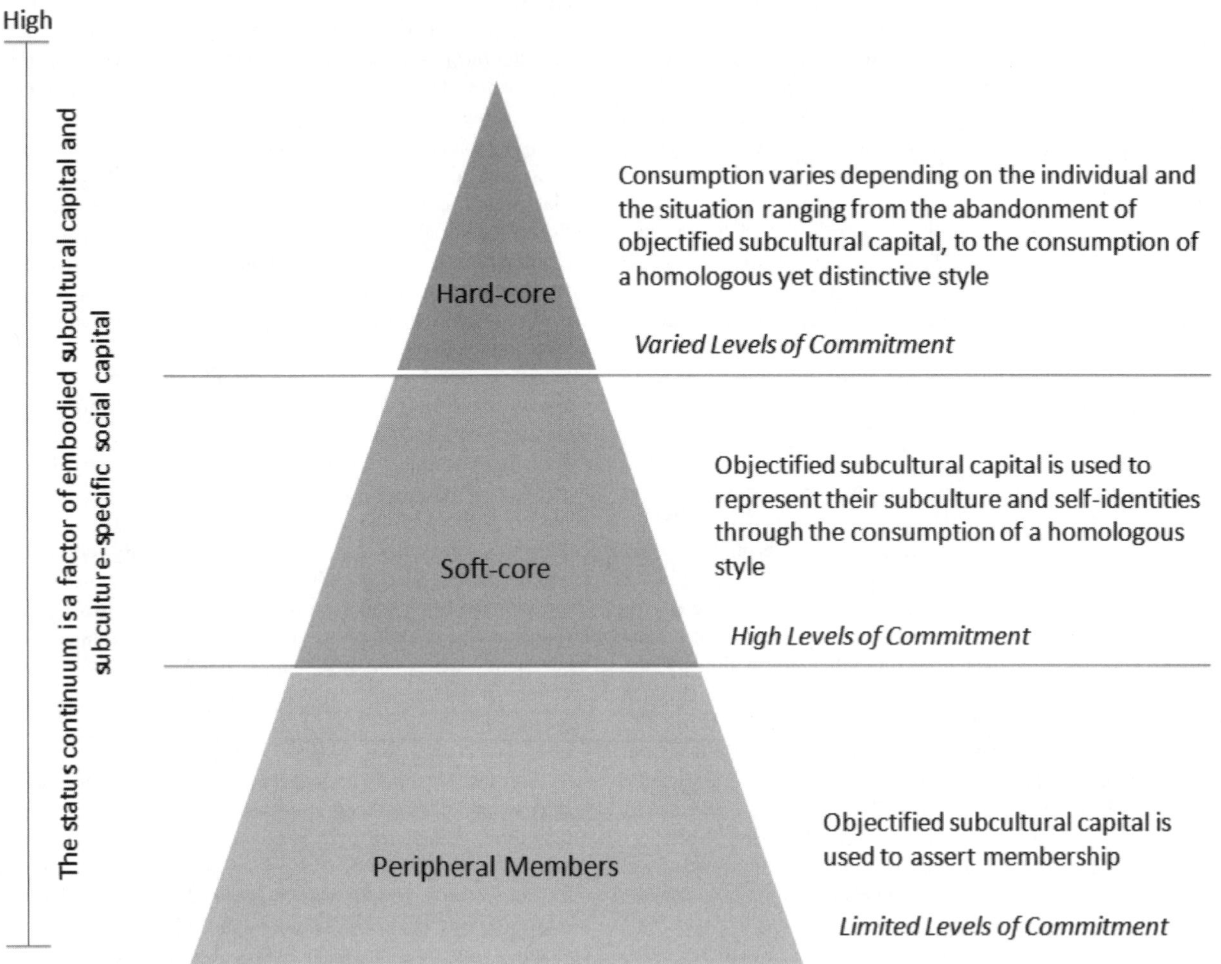

experience, and allowed him to conduct personal introspection (Elliott and Jankel-Elliott 2003; Shankar 2000).

During the course of the study, 30 semi-structured in-depth interviews with peripheral, soft-core and hard-core members of the Australian Hip Hop culture were undertaken. The researcher utilised guided introspection to obtain the necessary data: as he had obtained membership status himself, a good rapport with the interviewees was established, and hence the information was of quality (Elliott and Jankel-Elliott 2003; Shankar 2000). This technique was chosen as it has been found to be particularly useful when cultural categories are under investigation (McCracken 1988; Wells 1993). Furthermore, netnographic research of a web forum regularly visited by members of the Australian Hip Hop culture www.ozhiphop.com was conducted using the methods prescribed by Kozinets (2002b).

The researcher's field notes, personal diary, interview transcripts and netnographic threads were imported into QSR N6 for coding. Selective coding was used to synthesise and relate data to conceptual topics of interest, such as subcultural commitment and symbolic consumption. This process ensured that the resulting interpretation reflected persistent themes, and enhanced the researcher's familiarity with the data, thus facilitating the derivation of meaning (Pettigrew 2002). Finally, every effort has been made to conduct the ethnographic investigation into the Australian Hip Hop culture in an ethical manner and as such the names of all the participants have been changed.

FINDINGS

The subculture investigated was inherently countercultural in nature. It provided members with the opportunity to develop and express their unique and local identities alongside likeminded individuals and to position their values, attitudes and opinions against the dominant and mass culture. In addition, the Australian Hip Hop culture was found to be a gender salient, neo-tribal, male enclave where the rebel model of masculinity was enacted (Arthur 2006c; Holt and Thompson 2004). Furthermore, it should be noted that the predominantly white members of the Australian Hip Hop culture overcome their race and claimed Hip Hop authenticity via proficient knowledge of and respect toward the culture, and truthful representation of their identity (Arthur 2006a).

The overall findings of the ethnographic research have been summarised and presented in Figure 1. The analysis revealed that one's position within the counterculture's status hierarchy was a factor of one's embodied subcultural capital and subculture-specific social capital. Hence, over time, as individuals advanced their Hip Hop skills and acquired further Hip Hop and specifically Australian Hip Hop knowledge, their status within the Australian Hip Hop community was enhanced. This discovery supports previous findings which suggest that subcultural capital confers within-group status amongst countercultural participants (Kates 2002; Thornton 1995b). However, the results of this study further our understanding of the nature of status within consumption-oriented countercultures through the inclusion of subculture-specific social capital as a determinant of status. That is, the findings revealed that the standing of an individual's social connections and the individual's ability to influence them also had an impact on their position in the status hierarchy. For example, personally knowing a well-respected DJ enhanced one's standing in the status hierarchy, and securing his services for a party advanced one's standing further.

In addition, the results of this study further our understanding of the phenomenon by revealing that the objectification of subcultural capital through consumption was not necessarily more common as one's status advanced. That is, while Thornton's findings were mirrored in that both embodied and objectified subcultural capital conferred status, only embodied subcultural capital was found to be consistently associated with one's position within the status hierarchy. In contrast, the use of objectified subcultural capital as a marker of distinction varied as individuals evolved through the status hierarchy. Peripheral members used objectified subcultural capital to assert their membership, whereas soft-core members were found to use objectified subcultural capital to represent their culture through homology. In contrast, the consumption of objectified subcultural capital for hard-core members was found to vary depending on the individual, as illustrated in the following quote by hard-core member Kab:

> Kab: People who get involved in something, anything they feel passionate about, once they get to a point of being sort of accepted, say socially in those kind of groups, and they're doing something of a quality level, there's no need for any kind of identity clothes-wise... Some of the best dudes that do graffiti, you could not pick them out in the crowd man. They just wear nothing that's related to Hip Hop. Usually the better ones go into other areas as well because they don't feel confined by subculture. That's basically what happens, as people get older and better they tend to sort of move into other areas as well. And then there's guys who are into Hip Hop one hundred per cent, four element theory, all that stuff, dress that way and they're wild writers as well.

It should be noted that whilst Figure 1 presents the findings as if an individual progresses through a structured transformation commencing as a non-member and culminating with hard-core membership, the researcher rarely found himself or others being placed in such distinct, fixed and rigid categories by the countercultural participants. Rather, as individuals furthered their Hip Hop skills and knowledge, and advanced social relationships with Hip Hop members, their status within the Australian Hip Hop culture was enhanced. Henceforth, status within the Australian Hip Hop culture was viewed as a continuum ranging from those individuals with no embodied subcultural capital or subculture-specific social capital to those with an abundance of it. Furthermore, an individual's position in the status hierarchy was found to be fluid, contested, frequently negotiated and dependent on the individual making the evaluation. That is, gauging one's status was in effect an approximation of one's accumulated skills and knowledge and the value of one's social network. These approximations were often revised as new information came to hand that provided a more accurate indication. In addition, evaluations of both subcultural capital and subculture-specific social capital varied considerably depending on the subcultural capital of the individual making the assessment. Hence, while an individual's subcultural capital and the extent and influence of their social network may have remained constant, perceptions of their position in the status hierarchy differed depending on the Hip Hop knowledge of the individual making the evaluation. As such, an individual's position within the status hierarchy frequently moves up and down as different members make and revise assessments of their capital, however, over time, as they expand their network, advance their relationships, and further their Hip Hop knowledge and skills, they generally advance up the hierarchy. While the structure encountered was more fluid and negotiated than the three distinct groups reported by Fox (1987) and Schouten and McAlexander (1995), these broad categories did exist, and as such, as displayed in Figure 1, have been transposed upon the status continuum to enhance the analysis of consumption as an individual evolves through the status hierarchy, and to enable the comparison of findings with previous studies.

The results presented in this study, specifically that one's position within a consumption-oriented counterculture was dependent on one's embodied subcultural capital and subculture-specific social capital, is in contrast to previous research findings by Fox (1987) and Schouten and McAlexander (1995). As previously discussed, their findings suggest that one's position in the status hierarchy is dependent on one's commitment to the ideology and consumption values of the counterculture. As such, these studies found that for hard-core punks and bikers, participation was a full-time commitment that was displayed conspicuously in a homologous style, such as through the consumption of amphetamines and mohawks, or a Harley Davidson and associated garb. While these studies should be commended for drawing our attention to the evolution of a subcultural self, their theory could not be applied to the current case for two reasons. First, within the neo-tribal Australian Hip Hop culture a full-time commitment was not a necessary requirement of hard-core membership. Whereas the hard-core punks and bikers were found to have looked down upon those with a less than full-time commitment (Fox 1987, Schouten and McAlexander 1995), part-time participation was accepted within the Australian Hip Hop culture, as it was for Goulding, Shankar and Elliot's (2002) ravers. While the results show that a full-time commitment to the culture's ideology was the norm for soft-core members, and this commitment increased steadily as they had progressed through the status hierarchy, hard-core members were found to be more likely and capable of compartmentalising their work, family and leisure. As a number of the hard-core members had aged beyond their teens and early twenties, the responsibilities of work and family had, for many, encroached on their countercultural lifestyles. Furthermore, the leisure pursuits of hard-core members had often broadened beyond Hip Hop. These hard-core members were still admired and respected for their embodied subcultural capital and subculture-specific social capital, despite their current lack of full-time commitment. Hence, the results suggest that a near full-time commitment was necessary for members as they climbed the countercultural hierarchy as much time and effort was required to enhance their subcultural skills and knowledge, and to develop and nurture social relationships with other Hip Hop members. In contrast, hard-core members had already obtained much embodied subcultural capital and the amount of time required to keep these skills and knowledge up-to-date was less substantial. Similarly, their social networks were well established and their maintenance required a less significant time contribution by comparison. Hence, hard-core members' abundance of embodied subcultural capital and subculture specific-social capital exonerated them from the full-time subcultural commitment required for gaining Hip Hop knowledge and skills, and developing social relationships.

In addition, the results of this study show that in the case of the Australian Hip Hop culture one's commitment to the subculture's consumption values did not necessarily increase as one advanced up the status hierarchy. Once again, this contradicts the previous findings by Fox (1987), and Schouten and McAlexander (1995), where hard-core members were found to display their extreme commitment to the subculture's values through the consumption of a homologous style. In the current study, commitment to the subculture's consumption values heightened as members advanced through the peripheral and soft-core membership stages, but varied considerably once an individual had achieved hard-core membership. As indicated in Figure 1, due to their abundance of embodied subcultural capital and subculture-specific social capital, it was not necessary for hard-core members to display extreme levels of commitment to the subculture's consumptions values. Rather, commitment to the subculture's consumption values was found to vary depending on the individual.

The results of the analysis were consistent with the views of the countercultural participants who flatly rejected the assertion that one's position in the status hierarchy was in part determined by one's commitment to the culture's consumption values. Members perceived Australian Hip Hop to be a masculine and esoteric counterculture and members remarked that status based on one's consumption habits implied shallow, weak, conformist and feminine qualities. In contrast, the assertion that a subcultural hierarchy was based on one's Hip Hop knowledge and skill was met with strong support. In fact, on occasions, members of the Australian Hip Hop culture referred to 'Hip Hop knowledge' as being the fifth element of Hip Hop culture (in addition to DJing, MCing, graffiti, and break-dancing), an interpretation that was promoted by Hip Hop DJ and Pioneer Afrika Bambaataa (2008). As such, obtaining a basic understanding of Hip Hop's history was viewed as an essential criterion for Hip Hop membership and having an advanced knowledge of Hip Hop history enhanced one's position in the hierarchy. Take the following extract from an interview with OB MC for example:

> OB MC: It's poisoned man… You've got kids coming out of school that are listening to all that poof, that real faggot shit… It's really destroying our culture, because music like that has got no culture. I want to see 50 Cent here in front of me, I'll give him a spray can and tell him to do me a piece or I'll put him on a deck and say scratch to this beat, he wouldn't know what's going on, and I think that's wrong. To get into Hip Hop, the real Hip Hop, you've got to know the elements, you've got to know who started it, you've got to know who Grandmaster Flash is, who Africa Bambaataa is. You've got to appreciate the thing you're in not just because it's great to be in, but you've got to pay homage, you've got to pay respect to the people that invented it, you've got your KRS-Ones, you know people like that, there should be temples man where people can go and pray to these fucking people, you know what I mean? I think you're missing the point if you don't know who these people are and who's done this, or who was the first person to scratch, or who was the first person to do a blockbuster piece, you know? Who the first person was to ever do a train, who was the first person was to do a tag in New York, or in the Bronx, the first break dancing crews, you know what I mean?

Throughout the interview OB MC reveals that he treats seminal people, places and events in Hip Hop history with what Belk, Wallendorf, and Sherry (1989) would describe as sacred reverence. Such an admiration was common amongst hard-core Hip Hop members. Participation in the culture with ignorance of such valued knowledge, or a lack of Hip Hop skill, was perceived as inauthentic and profane as it failed to differentiate the Australian Hip Hop culture from the mass culture (personified by artists such as 50 Cent) which members positioned themselves against. Hence, OB MC perceives individuals who partake in Hip Hop with a lack of Hip Hop skills and understanding of the culture's history and values as non-members who are 'missing the point' and threatening the subculture's legitimacy. As such, esteem was placed upon members based on the assessor's perception of the individuals Hip Hop knowledge and skills. Hence, in the above example embodied subcultural capital explained one's standing within the community rather than one's commitment to culture's ideology and consumption values. While this may not have been the case in previous studies that link one's commitment to the counterculture's consumption values to one's position in the status hierarchy (Fox 1987; Schouten and McAlexander 1995), it is possible that the researchers have misinterpreted their findings and confused simultaneity between the two constructs with causation, particularly as one evolves through peripheral and soft-core membership stages. For example, Schouten and McAlexander's (1995) reading of the seniority, participation, leadership in group activities, and riding experience as commitment, could have just as easily been interpreted as the informal education necessary to have acquired much embodied subcultural capital. Similarly, the visible indicators of commitment described in the study (tattoos, motorcycle customisation, club-specific clothing, and sew-on patches), could easily have been interpreted as the objectification of subcultural capital by soft-core members and a limited number of hard-core members. In fact, Schouten and McAlexander (1995) even provide some indication that a small number of the hard-core bikers had abandoned the use of objectified subcultural capital or were consuming in a homologous yet distinctive style of consumption as they were 'at liberty to deviate from established custumery and create individual styles' (p.56).

DISCUSSION

The findings from this study make several important contributions to consumer research. The identification of embodied subcultural capital and subculture-specific social capital as determinants of status enhances our understanding of status conferral within consumption-oriented countercultures. That is, in addition to one's knowledge and skills, the value of one's social network will enhance one's position in the status hierarchy. Hence, a well-connected and influential countercultural member is capable of playing a pertinent role in shaping the consumption values of the counterculture. Also, hard-core members have been found to be opinion leaders (Donnelly 1981), and are often identified and targeted by marketers due to their influence, thus practitioners would also be advised to look for more than the skills, knowledge and expertise that a member possesses and also consider the breadth and power of their connections within a counterculture. Furthermore, researchers should theorize status within consumption-oriented countercultures in light of this new status continuum. In addition, future studies should verify whether a similar status continuum exists in brand-focused and non-brand focused consumption-oriented subcultures that are not countercultural in nature.

The findings outlined here differ from previous studies as they have identified embodied subcultural capital and subculture-specific social capital as the determinants of status within consumption-oriented countercultures rather than a member's commitment of time, effort and resources, or their commitment to the culture's consumption values. In a practical sense, this theorization is not necessarily problematic as a commitment of time, effort and resources will often facilitate the achievement of the relevant knowledge, skills and expertise. Thus the two processes are often paralleled. However, it should be noted that both the input and outcome are not the same. Much like economic capital, commitment of time and effort may help to achieve embodied subcultural capital, but alone does not necessarily generate the skills, knowledge and expertise that are valued. Thus, a highly committed member does not necessarily have the most embodied subcultural capital and members with an abundance of embodied subcultural capital are not always the most committed. This is an important theoretical distinction and contributes to a more accurate definition of the hard-core member. In addition to time and effort, the findings suggest that a commitment to the consumption values of the culture is not a necessary requirement for hard-core members. This finding has implications for consumer research as it refocuses the importance of consumption values to the earlier stages of subcultural membership.

The results also suggest that a distinction between embodied and objectified subcultural capital is important as both forms have different effects on status as the individual moves along the status continuum. Where embodied subcultural capital maintains a positive relationship with status, the objectification of subcultural capital does so only at the peripheral and soft-core membership stages. Moreover, hard-core members' objectification of subcultural capital varied considerably ranging from an abandonment of symbolic consumption through to the consumption of a homologous yet distinctive style. As hard-core members are most influential in disseminating countercultural styles, marketing practitioners should engage hard-core members who continue to consume the homologous style to endorse their Hip Hop brands. Furthermore, as hard-core members who continued to consume the homologous style did so in a way that differentiates them from the group, new lines of Hip Hop brands will have great appeal to these hard-core members as they provide a means for consumption that is simultaneously expressive of the subculture, yet distinguishes them as unique.

In conclusion, the purpose of this study was to explore the nature of status within a consumption-oriented counterculture. Our ethnographic investigation of the Australian Hip Hop culture identified embodied subcultural capital and subcultural-specific social capital as the determinants. How embodied subcultural capital was attained influenced its ability to act as a differentiating symbol. In addition, this study found that an individual's commitment and use of objectified subcultural capital did not necessarily enhance as one's position in the status hierarchy advanced. Theoretical and practitioner implications were discussed.

REFERENCES

Agar, Michael (1996), *The Professional Stranger: An Informal Introduction to Ethnography*, London: Academic Press.

Arthur, Damien (2006a), "Authenticity and Consumption in the Australian Hip Hop Culture," *Qualitative Market Research: An International Journal*, 9 (2), 140-56.

______ (2006b), "Glocalisation, Authenticity, and Consumption: A Qualitative Investigation of the Australian Hip Hop Culture," in *European Advances in Consumer Research*, Vol. 7, ed. Karin M. Ekstrom and Helene Brembeck, Goteborg, Sweden.

______ (2006c), "Hip Hop Consumption and Masculinity," in *8th ACR Conference on Gender, Identity and Consumption*, Edinburgh, Scotland.

Bambaataa, Afrika (2008), "Hip Hop History Month," http://www.zulunation.com/hip_hop_history_2.htm.

Belk, Russell W., Melanie Wallendorf, and John F. Sherry (1989), "The Sacred and the Profane in Consumer Behavior: Theodicy on the Odyssey," *Journal of Consumer Research*, 16 (June), 1-38.

Bennett, Andy (1999), "Subcultures or Neo-Tribes? Rethinking the Relationships between Youth, Style and Musical Taste," *Sociology*, 33 (3), 599-617.

Bourdieu, Pierre (1984), *Distinction: A Social Critique of the Judgment of Taste*, Cambridge, MA: Harvard University Press.

______ (1986), "The Forms of Capital," in *Handbook of Theory and Research for the Sociology of Education*, ed. John G. Richardson, New York: Greenwood Press.

Chalmers, Tandy and Damien Arthur (2008), "Hard-Core Members' of Consumption-Oriented Subcultures Enactment of Identity: The Sacred Consumption of Two Subcultures," in *Advances in Consumer Research*, Vol. 35, ed. Angela Y. Lee and Dilip Soman, Duluth: ACR, 570-75.

Clarke, John (1975a), "The Skinheads and the Magical Recovery of Community," in *Resistance through Rituals*, ed. Stuart Hall, London: Hutchinson.

______ (1975b), "Style," in *Resistance through Rituals*, ed. Stuart Hall, London: Hutchinson.

Donnelly, Peter (1981), "Toward a Definition of Sport Subcultures," in *Sport in the Sociocultural Process*, ed. M. Hart and S. Birrell, Iowa WC: Brown, 565-87.

Elliott, Richard and Nick Jankel-Elliott (2003), "Using Ethnography in Strategic Consumer Research," *Qualitative Market Research: An International Journal*, 6 (4), 215-23.

Fox, Kathryn Joan (1987), "Real Punks and Pretenders," *Journal of Contemporary Ethnography*, 16 (3), 344-70.

Goulding, Christina (1998), "Grounded Theory: The Missing Methodology on the Interpretivist Agenda," *Qualitative Market Research: An International Journal*, 1 (1), 50-57.

Goulding, Christina, Avi Shankar, and Richard Elliott (2002), "Working Weeks, Rave Weekends: Identity Fragmentation and the Emergence of New Communities," *Consumption Markets and Culture*, 5 (4), 261-184.

Hebdige, Dick (1975), "The Meaning of Mod," in *Resistance through Rituals*, ed. Stuart Hall, London: Hutchinson.

______ (1979), Subculture: The Meaning of Style, London: Routledge.

Holt, Douglas B. and Craig J. Thompson (2004), "Man-of-Action Heroes: The Pursuit of Heroic Masculinity in Everyday Consumption," *Journal of Consumer Research*, 31 (September), 425-40.

Irwin, John (1973), "The Natural History of an Urban Scene," *Urban Life and Culture*, 2 (2), 131-60.

Jefferson, Tony (1975), "Cultural Responses of the Teds," in *Resistance through Rituals*, ed. Stuart Hall, London: Hutchinson.

Kates, Steven M. (2002), "The Protean Quality of Subcultural Consumption: An Ethnographic Account of Gay Consumers," *Journal of Consumer Research*, 29 (December), 383-99.

Kozinets, Robert V. (2001), "Utopian Enterprise: Articulating the Meanings of Star Trek's Culture of Consumption," *Journal of Consumer Research*, 28 (June), 67-88.

______ (2002b), "The Field Behind the Screen: Using Netnography for Marketing Research in Online Communities," *Journal of Marketing Research*, 39 (February), 61-72.

Maffesoli, Michel (1996), *Time of the Tribes: The Decline of Individualism in Mass Society*, London: Thousand Oaks.

Mariampolski, Hy (2006), *Ethnography for Marketers: A Guide to Consumer Immersion*, Thousand Oaks, California: Sage Publications.

Maxwell, Ian (2003), *Phat Beats, Dope Rhymes: Hip Hop Down under Comin' Up*, New Hampshire: Wesleyan University Press.

McCracken, Grant (1988), *The Long Interview*, Vol. 13, Newbury Park: Sage Publications.

Pettigrew, Simone (2002), "A Grounded Theory of Beer Consumption in Australia," *Qualitative Market Research: An International Journal*, 5 (2), 112-22.

Schouten, John W. and James H. McAlexander (1995), "Subcultures of Consumption: An Ethnography of the New Bikers," *Journal of Consumer Research*, 22 (June), 43-61.

Shankar, Avi (2000), "Lost in Music? Subjective Personal Introspection and Popular Music," *Qualitative Market Research: An International Journal*, 3 (1), 27-37.

Thornton, Sarah (1995a), *Club Cultures: Music, Media, and Subcultural Capital*, Cambridge: Polity.

______ (1995b), "The Social Logic of Subcultural Capital," in *The Subcultures Reader*, ed. Ken Gelder and Sarah Thornton, London: Routledge, 200-09.

Wells, William (1993), "Discovery-Oriented Consumer Research," *Journal of Consumer Research*, 19 (March), 489-504.

Willis, Paul E. (1975), "The Cultural Meaning of Drug Use," in *Resistance through Rituals*, ed. Stuart Hall, London: Hutchinson.

______ (1978), *Profane Culture*, London: Routledge.

"Pixelize Me!": A Semiotic Approach of Self-digitalization in Fashion Blogs

Gachoucha Kretz, HEC School of Management, France

ABSTRACT

Drawing on Jensen Schau and Gilly's findings (2003) on self-presentation on personal webspaces, the purpose of this research is to get a better description of how consumers self digitalize on personal webspaces using specific digital stimuli. Using a semiotic approach on fashion blogs, we demonstrate that consumers self-digitalize to generate authenticity, caricature, fiction or artefact. Strategies employed pertain to exemplarity, "mise-en-scène", "digital likeness" or "brand overwhelming". Possible impacts on brand relationship management are further developed, for example, brand-consumer association through self-stereotypes.

INTRODUCTION

Consumption markets have become a place where consumers serve identity projects (Belk 1988; Holt 2002; Levy 1981) through the consumption of "mythic and symbolic resources" (Arnould and Thompson 2005). Favourite possessions help consumers self-present. Self-presentation may be defined as the performance of actions that "symbolically communicate information about the self to others" (Schlenker 2003) and therefore, as a meaning making process about the self. Accumulating specific possessions may thus carry symbolic meanings that influence the responses of others to self and help self-presentation goals. Literature building on the relationship between possessions and self-construal has mainly considered material possessions (Belk 1988).

However, Jensen Schau and Gilly (2003) have demonstrated that possessions need not be physically material to digitally present the self. Indeed, whereas possessions need to exist physically in the Real Life, constructing a "telepresence" to readers on personal webspaces only requires digital elements consumers do not necessarily possess in the Real Life. Consequently, carefully selected digital items help consumers present a desired "digital self" (Jensen Schau and Gilly 2003) on personal websites. However, even if the authors mention the digital elements used as usually taking the shape of "digital stimuli", hyperlinks, products and brands, they do not provide further detail on their nature, form, presentation or combination on personal webspaces, and even more important, on their possible meaning.

Personal web sites appear as a "playground for postmodern personalities" and thus appeal to the consumers whose aim is to "invest time to create and maintain identities" (Marcus, Machilek, and Schutz 2006). And yet, consumer research (as opposed to communication research) has hardly addressed self-presentation on personal websites, nor the digital processes through which desired identities are translated from the real life to the personal webspaces. Jensen Schau and Gilly (2003) have reported that consumers usually enact specific and self-valuable real-life selves with which they choose to communicate with other Web participants. The authors have also shown how consumers select digital stimuli, links, products and brands to present themselves on their personal webspaces. That symbolic use of digital possessions reveals highly semiotic in nature, in that digital objects and possessions used as a means for self-presentation may serve as "digital collages" (Jensen Schau and Gilly 2003), hence as "signifiers" for a deeper and more intangible "signified" identity or self-concept. Consequently, semiotics may prove useful to disentangle such a meaning-making process as digital self-presentation and to point out some possible exemplars of selves thus created in a sample of personal websites. Substantial conceptual issues related to the study of identity and self-concept may occur, making the "core" or "real" self hardly tangible for researchers. Therefore, limiting investigation to the level of self-presentation, that is, where identity meaning is made thanks to a combination of digital "signifiers", may alleviate such conceptual issues while making it possible to focus on the meaning-making processes that lead to generate "exemplars" of identities on those websites.

Personal webspaces and more precisely Web logs (or "blogs") offer consumers an almost unlimited space for self-expression on the Internet (Kozinets 2006). Blogs are personal websites, "usually maintained by an individual with regular entries of commentary, descriptions of events, or other material such as graphics or video, where entries are commonly displayed in reverse-chronological order" (Wikipedia 2009). Some popular bloggers attract a large audience (346 million readers worldwide and 78 million unique visitors in the United States according to Wikipedia) and are considered by brands a new kind of journalists, or at least influencers who may turn into brands' advocates thanks to VIP treatments.

Popular bloggers thus reveal a relevant sample for the study of digital self-presentation, especially when it comes, first to defining self-digitalization, second to understanding the role of brands in such processes, where "individualized brand meanings and brand practices is accessible" (Kozinets 2006). The present research focused on popular fashion blogs held by so-called "Fashionistas" for several reasons. First, because popular fashion bloggers highly maintain and improve their personal pages, and particularly through the insertion of digital stimuli, links, products and brands; second, because they ensure daily ongoing and rich nurturance of their webspace; last, because daily visitors are numerous.

The purpose of this research is to get a better description of how consumers organize and process their digital self-presentation (or "self-digitalization"), using specific digital stimuli, hyperlinks, products and brands and therefore to better understand the consumer-brand association processes and their possible impacts on the consumer-brand relationships (Fournier 1998).

CONCEPTUAL FRAMEWORK

Consumers who hold personal weblogs and particularly "fashionistas" usually make use of the Internet to self-present, particularly through their consumption habits of fashion and luxury brands, Literature on self-presentation therefore proves relevant to analyse the "self-digitalization" process.

Self-Presentation in the "Real Life"

Self-presentation in the Real Life is described as a means for an individual to control impressions of themselves towards an audience (Schlenker 2003). In sociology, self-presentation has been popularized by Ervin Goffman. For Goffman (1959), people behave as actors, creating identities by playing different roles on different stages and to different audiences. People thus modify their behavior to influence the impressions other people form about them, and perform self-presentation by doing so. Self-presentation in the Real Life has been much tackled by different research disciplines. In his review of self-presentation literature in the Real Life, Schlenker (2003) reports the major themes and directions that have generated much of the research. They mainly pertain to authenticity and deceptiveness in self-presentation, the automatic versus controlled processes in self-presentation, configuring of self-presentations and the influence and role of others in self-presentation. How self-presentations are configured and constructed may reveal of high interest for the present study and will therefore be addressed subsequently.

Self-Presentation in virtual spaces or "self-digitalization"

Self-presentation in virtual spaces (or "self-digitalization"), has mostly been studied by communication research that either focused on the mere description of personal pages thanks to socio-demographical and psychographic elements (Magnuson and Dundes 2008; Marcus et al. 2006; Schutz and Machilek 2003), or more deeply analyzed the self-presentation strategies developed by personal webpages owners (Gibbs, Ellison, and Heino 2006; Taejin, Hyunsook, and McClung 2007). Descriptive studies thus report the websites' content such as pictures, links, textual contents, style, self and personality cues or insights on the gender, age and personality traits of the informants selected (Marcus et al. 2006; Schutz and Machilek 2003) , or study gender differences in self-presentation in personal webspaces (Magnuson and Dundes 2008). However, they do not mention self-presentation strategies. Gibbs et al. (2006) have addressed self-presentation in the context of online dating and anticipated future offline relationships but only through a successful expected outcome. Indeed, self-presenters were considered to self-disclose in a way that would lead to self-presentation success defined as "the degree to which users feel they are able to make a good impression on others and achieve favorable self-presentation through online dating". However, self-presenters may also not want to practice such a "selective self- presentation" (Walther and Burgoon 1992) but instead genuinely and authentically self-present, should they make a "not-so-good" impression on others. Taejin et al. (2007) have addressed that issue by making account of the five self-presentation strategies used in the Real Life and developed by Jones (1990), including unfavorable "intimidation" ("I want you to think I am dangerous") and "supplication" ("I want you to think I am weak and powerless") that rely on negative self-disclosure to create potentially negatively perceived self-presentation. The authors finally found that bloggers use self-presentation strategies and are motivated in ways identical to those described by Jones (1990). In consumer research, Jensen Schau and Gilly (2003) have made a great contribution to the theory of self-presentation on virtual spaces, bringing valuable insights on the rationale driving consumers to self-present on personal webspaces and describing their self-presentation strategies. However, the authors conclude that individuals seem to always practice favorable self-presentation through "selective self-presentation", which seems to contradict previous findings. In addition, how the digital self, likeness and associations are constructed thanks to digital stimuli, links, brands and products (or self-presentation configuration), has been partially mentioned. Literature drawing upon configuring self-presentation in the Real Life may serve as a helpful theoretical framework for translating self-presentation configuration in the Real Life to self-presentation configuration in virtual spaces (or "self-digitalization").

Configuring Self-Presentation and Self-Digitalization

"Self-presentations incorporate features of the actor's self-concept, personality style, salient social roles, and beliefs about their audience's preferences" (Schlenker 2003). On personal webspaces self-digitalization may then go through the digital actualization or enactment of those features thanks to the combination of digital stimuli (images, pictures, colours, fonts, page organization …), links, brands and products, to generate meaning about the self. Jensen Schau and Gilly's findings (2003) about how consumers create a digital self and especially what real features are enacted to become digital ones are consistent with existing research on self-presentation configuration in the real life.

Exemplar-Based Self-Presentation. Consumers may construct a digital self relating to "one or more roles played by an informant" (Jensen Schau and Gilly 2003). Indeed, social psychology reports that individuals have a good knowledge of a vast array of exemplars of identity types ("Clint Eastwood, the tough" for example), social roles (the banker or the hairdresser), or personality traits (introversion versus extraversion). When "self-digitalizing", informants may thus create "self exemplars" designed to produce exemplar-based inferences within the audience. There has been so far no insight on how those self-exemplars have been created. Hypothesis could be made that consumers exaggerate carefully selected salient features and therefore digitally distort self-presentation to some salient features' benefit (as would a favorable caricature do). Drawing on that premise, chances are that consumers use "selective self-presentation" (Walther and Burgoon, 1992) by selecting digital features, links, products and brands that help magnify the selected self-exemplar(s). By carefully selecting self-exemplars to manage self-presentation and impressions on others, the consumers might present a self on a continuum starting from a balance between favorable and less positive exemplars describing the self in the Real Life, to an end where selected exemplars are overwhelmingly favorable. Since the literature provides a strong support for the general principle that people search for beneficial self-presentations (Schlenker 2003), the possibility of an existing wholly negative end to that continuum has been ruled out. The balanced end of the continuum may pertain to some caricatured presentation of the self, whereas the positive end of that continuum may relate to some "self-myth creation", see some self-glorification. In their findings, Jensen Schau and Gilly (2003) do not mention the possibility for a "balanced" self-presentation, where favorable and less favorable salient self-attributes are presented on personal websites.

Presenting a desired self: a transactional view. In the Real Life, research shows that individuals present a desired (and therefore favorable) self according to motivational goals (Baumeister 1982; Schlenker 2003). The strategies developed differ in their goals and audiences. For Schlenker (2003), any self-presentation integrates the audience's beliefs of preferences or feedbacks. According to that transactional view, it is important to understand how individuals create a desirable self in the Real Life and why others find those self-presenters desirable or not, so as to understand how to "digitalize" such desirability. Research on self-presentation strategies (ingratiation and self-construction) and self-presentation criteria for desirability (beneficial and desirable) in the Real Life may prove transferable to online spaces.

"Ingratiation" consists in "pleasing the audience" to gain potential reward (Baumeister 1982) such as self-esteem enhancement (Leary and Baumeister 2000; Schlenker 2003), by presenting oneself "favorably" according to an audience's values and expectations. Alternatively, "self-construction" (Baumeister 1982) or "self-consistency" (Schlenker 2003) consists in both attaining a self fitting one's ideals and values and impressing others, by making one's public image congruent with one's ideal self (Baumeister 1982). Such self-presenters show "good qualities" to others that are equivalent to their own values and ideals.

Two features help define the desirability of self-presentations: is self-presentation beneficial to the individual? Is it believable? Beneficial self-presentations will help the individual reach his or her goals, values and ideals. Literature review on that issue, however, shows that self-presentation need not be favorable or socially desirable. That contradicts Jensen Schau and Gilly's (2003) conclusion that individuals seem to always want to present a favorable and desirable self on digital spaces. Further investigation should therefore analyse whether personal websites may present unfavorable self-features. In addition, people create desirable self-image directly, by communicating self qualities and accomplishments, and indirectly, by linking with associates or enemies whose qualities and glory may reflect on them (Cialdini, Finch, and De Nicholas 1990): inference of qualities is made between the concepts that have been linked in the minds of the perceivers. By linking themselves to successful and admirable others, individuals look better to others and feel better about themselves. Jensen Schau and Gilly (2003) have shown that consumers use links as a self-presentation device. Therefore, drawing on the literature about indirect desirable self-presentation, investigation on what links are selected, how, by whom and on what association is made by the self-presenter between him- or herself and the objects linked (people, brands or products for example) may generate further knowledge on consumer-brand association and consumer-brand relationships. Believable self-presentations need to be accurate and honest enough to be perceived as credible. Social norms prescribe that people be reliable and trustworthy and produce obligations for individuals who self-present to be what they say they are, with the risk of personal and interpersonal sanctions (Goffman 1959). Further investigation is needed to understand how trustworthiness and credibility are created, probably through "authenticity-generating devices".

METHODOLOGY

The objective of the present study was to gain specific insight about a bloggers' community of female fashion and luxury brands' addicts ("Fashionistas"). Since understanding "consumers in the online communal and cultural context" (Kozinets 2006) of fashion bloggers was of main interest, Netnography (Kozinets 2002) has been selected as the methodology most capable of building "Grounded Knowledge" (Kozinets 2002) on Fashionistas and particularly on how such consumers self-digitalize in the blogs they maintain. Observational netnography (Brown, Kozinets, and Sherry 2003; Langer and Beckman 2005) was carried out since mere unobtrusive research was intentionally sought for. Because a forthcoming research plans to interview Fashionistas and thus needs "unbiasing" and unobtrusive observation, the selected bloggers did not know they were monitored and no member checks were made. Therefore, only "entrée" and "data collection and analysis" procedures (Kozinets 2002) were followed. Finally, choice was made, for the present study, to focus on visual digital stimuli used for self-presentation. Further analysis focusing on textual elements (usually self narratives) will be presented in a forthcoming research.

Entrée

Why select fashion blogs? Fashion and luxury brands' addicts were hypothesized to put more effort into self-digitalizing on their blogs than any other kind of bloggers, since fashion addicts carefully self-present in the Real Life. In addition, whereas most bloggers usually do not spend much of their expression space to describe particular consumption habits and brands' stories (Kozinets 2006), self-brand stories, fashion and luxury products or brands' consumption habits, brand practices and meanings seem to be more central to Fashionistas in their blogs. A fashion bloggers' community thus revealed highly relevant for the research question aiming at studying self-digitalization, specifically through digital stimuli, links, products and brands.

Constitution of the corpus. A first corpus of blogs was built up by typing in "fashion blogs" into Google.fr. Results lead to a very active fashion bloggers' community at that time (www.hautetfort.com in June 2006). As time has passed by, many influential bloggers of that community migrated to more efficient blogging platforms in terms of storage and maintenance facilities. However, records and archives where also transferred and such a migration had no impact for the present study. Criteria retained to select bloggers among that community followed those prescribed by Kozinets (2006): high traffic, high number of posts, high level of social interactions (comments and links) and rich self-presentation data (particularly visual material such as pictures, logos and drawings) combined with detailed description of self-brand stories and brand practices. The majority of the blogs selected were linked one to another. The sample turned out to consist of too homogeneous and similar blogs, especially because of imitation behaviors occurred among the fashion bloggers. Since the collected data was to be studied through a visual semiotic analysis, the constituted corpus needed to reach saturation to ensure representativeness. Greimas and Courtés (1979) define saturation as "the model, constructed on the basis of a segment chosen intuitively, is later on applied for confirmation, complement, or rejection to other segments until all the data are used". The next blogs were thus selected either randomly or because they were frequently quoted in fashion magazines. The variety of the corpus dramatically increased and saturation occurred pretty fast. The sample finally consists in 60 fashion blogs held by Fashionistas.

Data collection and analysis

Netnographic data collection. Direct data collected pertains to the blogs' content, that is, very diverse visual and textual elements, such as pictures, drawings, logos, wallpapers, texts, colors, videos ... Observation data relates to the researcher's inscribing of the observations about the fashion bloggers' community. Since self-digitalization through visual digital stimuli was the focus of the study, observation data consists in a synchronic report of how pages are visually configured (combining different visual parts such as banners, wallpapers, pictures, links ...) and what similarities and differences appear throughout blogs. Pointing out differences and similarities is required as a first step for any semiotic analysis and shows that structural invariant visual features stand across blogs: for example, personal banners, introducing the blog on the top of the welcome page, wallpapers, side-column tags, links, archives, categories and miscellaneous. A central text body supports written posts, illustrative drawings, pictures or even videos and varies with each post. Reversely, differences may embody for example in the presence or absence of a self-disclosure page and/or picture, of a contact e-mail address, of advertisements' inserts and commercial links, or of a personal signature (a small sentence describing the content of the blog and sometimes explaining the name of the blog).

Semiotic visual data analysis. Semiotics provides powerful techniques and rich theories to explore consumption behaviors and communication (Mick 1986; Mick and Oswald 2006). "Semiotics analyses the structures of meaning-producing events, both verbal and non-verbal [...] investigate[s] the sign systems or codes [...] with a more intense focus on meaning" (Mick 1986). Semiotics thus proves highly relevant when it comes to studying self-digitalization in fashion blogs thanks to visual codes fostering symbolic meanings and practices. Semiotics has been used for some time in consumer research (Floch 2003; Holbrook and Hirschmann 1993; Mick and Oswald 2006; Zhao and Belk 2008). However, the existing research most of the time addresses textual or verbal elements, exploiting semiotic techniques derived from linguists' work like Saussure (1968) or Barthes, but scarcely studies visual-only elements (Floch 2003). And yet, Courtés (1995), building upon Saussure's paradigmatic and syntagmatic relations between words (Saussure 1968), offers insight on how to analyse visual systems. The first step, or paradigmatic analysis (Courtés 1995; Saussure 1968), consists in drawing out similarities and differences across the corpus to designate invariants and more episodic visual stimuli already mentioned as "blog content". The second step, or syntagmatic analysis (Courtés

FIGURE 1

Semiotic square of self-digitalization (credibility semantic plane)

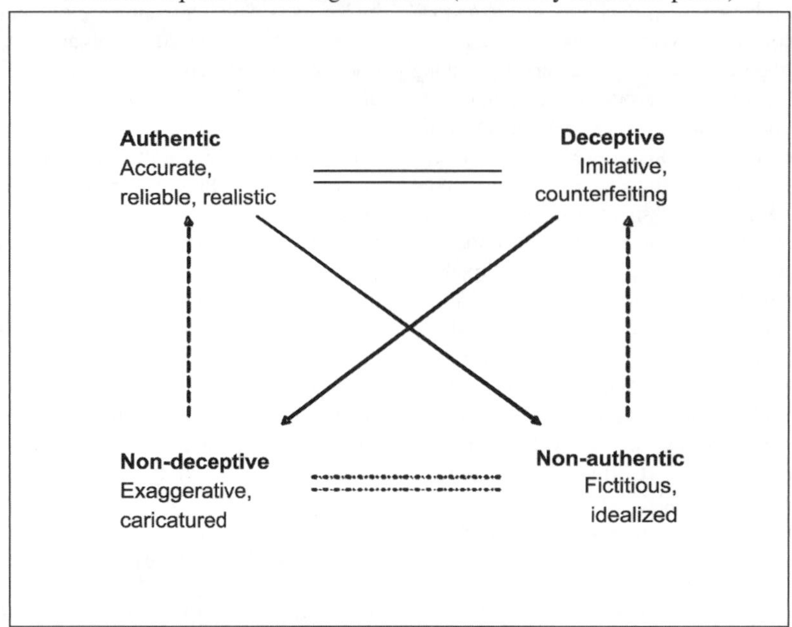

1995; Saussure 1968), shows how visual signs combine to provide meanings and values about self-digitalization. Finally, results about visual self-digitalization are presented in a "semiotic square" (Greimas and Rastier 1968), building on the latent values and ideals revealed by the semiotic visual analysis.

FINDINGS

Effects of self-digitalization on audience's perceptions

How the audience perceives of the bloggers will depend on the self-digitalization process and effects, specifically concerning credibility. The semiotic square presented in figure 1 helps structuring the audience's different possible perceptions of self-digitalization processed on fashion blogs.

Literature review on self-presentation has shown that credibility (as opposed to desirability) is always required. Consequently, credibility was selected as a semantic plane for self-digitalization. Since it may be attained by presenting a realistic, sincere and reliable self (Schlenker 2003), thus requiring accuracy, the semantic axis opposed "authenticity" to "deceptiveness", which proved relevant with existing literature on self-digitalization (Walker 2000). "Deceptiveness" describes counterfeiting, imitative and labored self-digitalization processes, or presentations that are not what they seem, introducing the notion of dishonesty. "Non-authenticity" relies on fictitiousness but dishonest intentions are not taken into account. "Non-deceptiveness" is not dishonest and aims at some accuracy but is not necessarily identical to reality, exaggerating salient more or less favorable "Real Life features" translated to the online space.

The semiotic square elaborated on the credibility plane presents how readers may perceive fashion bloggers when self-digitalizing. Self-digitalization may thus be perceived as reliable and realistic, imitative and counterfeiting, fictitious or exaggerative and caricatured by the audience.

How do consumers self-digitalize?

Figure 2 details how fashion bloggers self-digitalize. Drawing upon the credibility semantic plane and semiotic square, digital stimuli combinations were studied, in order to describe self-digitalization methods used by fashion bloggers. Bloggers aiming at authenticity use high digital likeness (Jensen Schau and Gilly 2003), that is translate as many Real Life stimuli as possible to the digital world. Self-disclosure, accuracy and transparency are the blogs' guidelines. Bloggers are really committed into their blogs and use them almost as a business card. Self-digitalization thus follows the rules of a facsimile. Bloggers who target idealized and fictitious presentation use a mise-en-scène of the self. They try to create evocative settings, personal self-fantasies, private universes. Their blog is a place where they can play with themselves and others, and use their imagination. Self-digitalization here follows the rules of a fiction. Bloggers who are searching for non-deceptiveness and exaggeration carefully select all the Real Life stimuli they chose to translate to their virtual spaces. By being that selective, bloggers self-stereotype through a systematic search for exemplarity. Stress is put on specificities, details and identification to reach typicality and exemplarity of the Fashion addict. Careful selection of brands and links is thus here crucial. Self-digitalization, in that case, follows the rules of caricature. Finally, some bloggers hold personal pages mainly for commercial or business purposes. Of course, they do not so to say pursue deceptiveness but readers do perceive their blogs as such and "flame" those bloggers in the spaces left for comments (when comments are not closed). Those blogs borrow all the codes and stimuli used by the other bloggers. However, cues such as a felt distance, too many commercial links, an overwhelming mentioning of brands and/or events, no clear self-disclosure, mentions that the author is not paid for advertising or comments closed are quite accurate warnings for a deceptive fashion personal blog. Here, self-digitalization follows the rules of artefacts.

DISCUSSION

Authentic blogs in the corpus are mainly composed of fashion experts' and professionals. "CaféMode" started her blog when she attended Paris fashion school "Institut Français de la Mode" four years ago. She has progressively made herself known as a fashion specialist: she now uses her blog as a window-dressing for her

FIGURE 2
Self-digitalization options

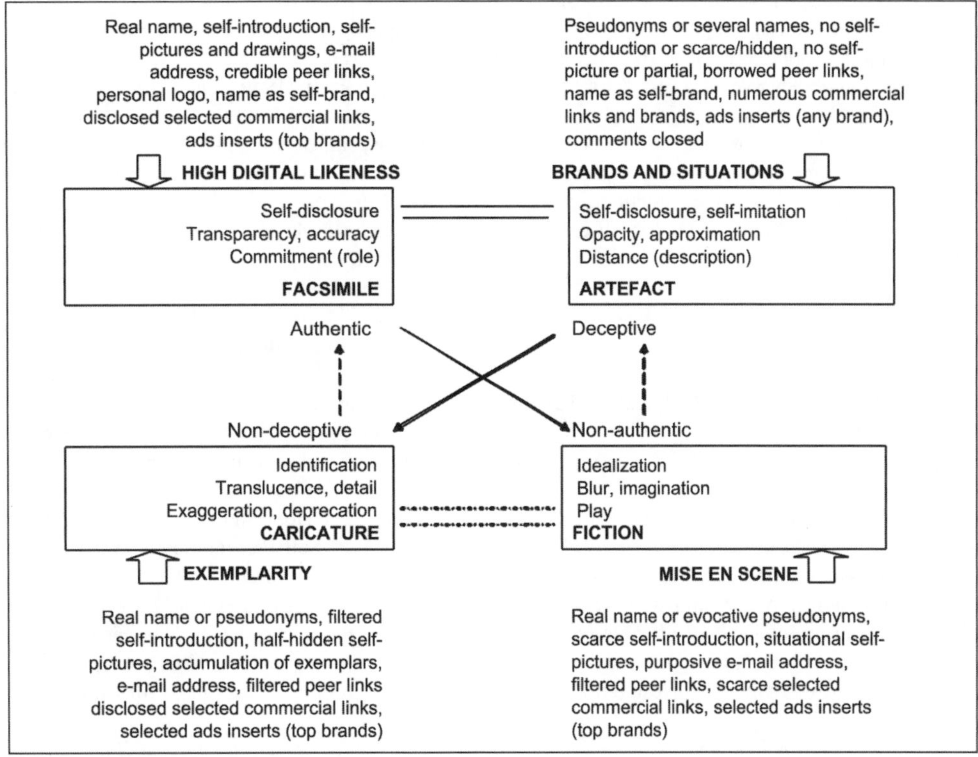

consulting and journalist's activities, and thus for self-consistency. Fictitious blogs comprise blogs where individuals present an idealized self, which makes up for the majority of the fashion blogs we monitored. They set up a mise-en-scène of themselves as would do a fashion magazine with models or celebrities. Those bloggers really love fashion, work in the industry or usually occupy jobs close to arts, marketing or communication. For example, "Pandora" studies the Fine Arts in Paris but want to present as a sharp fashion expert with her own universe and fashion fantasies. Usually, bloggers who managed to present a successful "fictitious" blog quickly gain rewards such as integrating brands' databases as "influencers" and trendsetters which gives access to prestigious parties, complimentary luxury week-ends, high value gifts or are proposed thrilling positions in the fashion industry. Fictitious blogs therefore seem first, to digitalize self-presenters who pursue ingratiation in order to gain rewards, confirming that ingratiation may be translated to personal webspaces, second, to be the step preceding a "professionalization" of the blog and blogger. They gain credibility because their self-digitalization usually "fits" fashion brands or fashion magazines. Deceptive or counterfeiting blogs are fashion blogs that look like personal ones, but serve the blogger's or one or several brands' commercial purposes. For example, "Be fashion" presents and praises pretended loved new products or brands. However, she is also brand strategy consultant and works for many of the praised brands and thus might be prone to interest conflicts. Such blogs are scarce because their strategies backfire on themselves: readers usually violently criticize such hidden commercial purposes and launch "flaming" campaigns in the comments to destroy the blog's reputation on the Web. Audience reaction to deceptive blogs is consistent with Schlenker's claim that self-presentation must be credible and trustworthy and confirms that self-digitalization needs credibility and particularly honesty. Caricatured blogs present fashion bloggers both in favorable and less favorable situations. Self-presenters exaggerate their existing "Real Life" features, whether positive or not, to generate either humorous or caricatured self-presentation. For example, "Galliane" presents herself in funny and often ridiculous situations or outfits. This finding somewhat contradicts Jensen Schau and Gilly (2003) in that self-digitalization is not always aiming at favorable self-presentation, at least, at first intent. However, caricatured blogs may use self-deprecation or exaggerated honesty either to attract the readers' sympathy through humour or to enhance credibility, that explanation being consistent with communication research's findings on source credibility. Those bloggers are often fashion-addicts who also end up in the fashion industry or in close job positions. They made end up as professionals because they set up credibility on honesty or self-deprecation.

CONCLUSION

The present research builds on Jensen Schau and Gilly's (2003) previous research. Consistent with their findings, we concluded that "digital likeness" does occur. However, further investigation on that self-digitalization strategy shows that, consumers use full "digital likeness" only when they want or need to stress a specific role or expertise, particularly because they "professionalized" thanks to their blogs. Thus, "digital likeness" may turn to "exemplarity" when bloggers want to self-digitalize as stereotypes such as "fashion-addicts", or to "mise-en-scène" when they want to self-digitalize as an ideal character they would like to embody on their virtual space. As for personal fashion blogs that end up showing commercial intentions, overwhelming brands, products, situations, and commercial links appear. Such blogs are usually deceptive. In addition, full detail of the digital stimuli combined to self-digitalize depending on the self-digitalization option has been presented. Important conclusions concerning brand-consumers relationship on the Net appear. Indeed, expert bloggers are more likely not to accept sponsors, or very few, for the sake of credibility and honesty. Caricatured bloggers may accept sponsors who perfectly fit with their self-stereotypes, and not only fashion or luxury brands since incongruency may be a source for self-deprecation or humour. Idealized bloggers may accept only fashion and luxury brands fully congruent with their imagined universe and digital self. Finally, since deceptive sites are subject to flaming and brand cluttering, brands should avoid them systematically.

The "Real Life" self-presentational goals (self-consistency and ingratiation) seem to translate perfectly to virtual webspaces. Particularly, self-consistency may be pursued in authentic, professional and expert blogs, whereas ingratiation may be looked for by bloggers who want to create some idealized character. Results also show that bloggers not always target desirable self presentation on blogs, which contradicts Jensen Schau and Gilly (2003). This might be explained by the fact that individuals may use honesty see self-deprecation to appear more credible. Credibility is indeed a crucial criterion in self-digitalization and relies either on the fit between the self-digitalized and the fashion brands and magazines praised, either on honesty or humorous self-deprecation.

Finally, consumers seem to first self-digitalize either as fictitious fashion characters or as fashion caricatures before entering the small world of experts and professionals if their blogs encounter large audience and success. Self-digitalization may thus imply evolution throughout time needing further investigation.

LIMITATIONS

How readers may perceive of the different self-digitalization options need cross validation through interviews with the readers. In addition, further investigation should be carried out to better understand the brand-consumer association depending on the self-digitalization option. Finally, conclusions show that further longitudinal analysis of self-digitalization is needed.

REFERENCES

Arnould, Eric J. and Craig J. Thompson (2005), "Consumer Culture Theory (CCT): Twenty Years of Research," *Journal of Consumer Research*, 31 (March), 868-82.

Baumeister, Roy F. (1982), "A Self-Presentational View of Social Phenomena," *Psychological Bulletin*, 91 (January), 3-26.

Belk, Russell W. (1988), "Possessions and the Extended Self," *Journal of Consumer Research*, 15 (September), 139-68.

Brown, Stephen, Robert V. Kozinets, and John F. Sherry (2003), "Teaching Old Brands New Tricks: Retro Branding and the Revival of Brand Meaning," *Journal of Marketing*, 67 (July), 19-33.

Cialdini, Robert B., John F. Finch, and Maralou E. De Nicholas (1990), "Strategic Self-Presentation: the Indirect Route," in *The Psychology of Tactical Communication*, ed. Michael J. Cody and Margaret L. McLaughlin, Philadelphia, PA: Multilingual Matters Ltd, 194-206.

Courtés, Joseph (1995), *Du Lisible au Visible: Initiation à la Sémiotique du Texte et de l'Image*, Bruxelles: De Boeck Université.

Floch, Jean Marie (2003), *Sémiotique, Marketing et Communication : Sous les Signes, les Stratégies*, Paris: Presses Universitaires de France.

Fournier, Susan (1998), "Consumers and Their Brands: Developing Relationship Theory in Consumer Research," *Journal of Consumer Research*, 24 (March), 343-53.

Gibbs, Jennifer L., Nicole B. Ellison, and Rebecca D. Heino (2006), "Self-Presentation in Online Personals The Role of Anticipated Future Interaction, Self-Disclosure, and Perceived Success in Internet Dating," *Communication Research*, 33 (2), 152-77.

Goffman, Ervin (1959), *The Presentation of Self in Everyday Life*, London: Penguin Books.

Greimas, Algirdas J. and François Rastier (1968), "The Interaction of Semiotic Constraints," *Yale French Studies*, 41, 86-105.

Greimas, Algirdas Julien and Joseph Courtés (1979), *Semiotics and Language: An Analytical Dictionary*, Bloomington, IN: Indiana University Press.

Holbrook, Morris B. and Elizabeth C. Hirschmann (1993), *The Semiotics of Consumption: Interpreting Symbolic Consumer Behavior in Popular Culture and Works of Art*, New York, NY: Mouton de Gruyter

Holt, Douglas B. (2002), "Why do brands cause trouble? A dialectical theory of consumer culture and branding," *Journal of Consumer Research*, 29 (June), 70-90.

Jensen Schau, Hope and Mary C. Gilly (2003), "We Are What We Post? Self-Presentation in Personal Web Space," *Journal of Consumer Research*, 30 (December), 385-404.

Jones, E (1990), *Interpersonal Perception*, New York: Freeman.

Kozinets, Robert V. (2002), "The Field Behind the Screen: Using Netnography for Marketing Research in Online Communities," *Journal of Marketing Research* (February), 61-72.

______ (2006), "Netnography 2.0," in *Handbook of Qualitative Research Methods in Marketing*, ed. Russell W. Belk, Northampton, MA: Edward Elgar Publishing Inc, 129-55.

Langer, Roy and Suzanne C. Beckman (2005), "Sensitive Research Topics: Netnography Revisited," *Qualitative Market Research*, 8 (2), 189-203.

Leary, Mark R. and Roy F. Baumeister (2000), "The Nature and Function of Self-Esteem: Sociometer Theory," *Advances in Experimental Social Psychology*, 32, 2-51.

Levy, Sidney J. (1981), "Intepreting Consumer Mythology: A Structural Approach to Consumer Behavior," *The Journal of Marketing* (Summer), 49-61.

Magnuson, Melissa Joy and Lauren Dundes (2008), "Gender Differences in "Social Portraits" Reflected in MySpace Profiles," *CyberPsychology & Behavior*, 11 (2), 239-41.

Marcus, Bernd, Franz Machilek, and Astrid Schutz (2006), "Personality in Cyberspace: Personal Web Sites as Media for Personality Expressions and Impressions," *Journal of Personality and Social Psychology*, 90 (June), 1014-31.

Mick, David Glen (1986), "Consumer Research and Semiotics: Exploring the Morphology of Signs, Symbols, and Significance," *Journal of Consumer Research*, 13 (September), 196-213.

Mick, David Glen and Laura R. Oswald (2006), "The Semiotic Paradigm on Meaning in the Marketplace," in *Handbook of Qualitative Research in Marketing*, ed. Russell W. Belk, Northampton, MA: Edward Elgar Publishing Inc, 31 -45.

Saussure, Ferdinand de (1968), *Cours de Linguistique Générale* Paris: Payot.

Schlenker, Barry R. (2003), "Self-Presentation," in *The Handbook of Self and Identity*, ed. Mark R. Leary and June P. Tangney, New York, NY: The Guilford Press 492–518.

Schutz, Astrid and Franz Machilek (2003), "Who Owns a Personal Home Page? A Discussion of Sampling Problems and a Strategy Based on a Search Engine," *Swiss Journal of Psychology*, 62 (June), 121-30.

Taejin, Jung, Youn Hyunsook, and Steven McClung (2007), "Motivations and Self-Presentation Strategies on Korean-Based "Cyworld" Weblog Format Personal Homepages," *CyberPsychology & Behavior*, 10 (1), 24-31.

Walker, Katherine (2000), ""It's Difficult to Hide It": The Presentation of Self on Internet Home Pages," *Qualitative Sociology*, 23 (March), 99-120.

Walther, Joseph B. and Jundee K. Burgoon (1992), "Relational Communication in Computer-Mediated Interaction," *Human Communication Research*, 19, 50-88.

Wikipedia (2009), "Blog " http://en.wikipedia.org/wiki/Blog.

Zhao, Xin and Russell W. Belk (2008), "Politicizing Consumer Culture: Advertising's Appropriation of Political Ideology in China's Social Transition," *Journal of Consumer Research*, 35 (August), 231-44.

Context as a Source of Clarity: The Effects of Ad Context and Gender on Consumers' Processing of Product Incongruity

Theodore J. Noseworthy, University of Western Ontario, Canada
Seung Hwan (Mark) Lee, University of Western Ontario, Canada
June Cotte, University of Western Ontario, Canada

ABSTRACT

In two studies, the authors provide evidence that ad context can be used to alter the elaboration threshold for both males and females. The findings suggest that in a competing ad context (a series of ads for similar goods), females were better able to resolve an extremely incongruent product (an extremely odd-looking camera), and males, counter to their natural predisposition for item-specific elaboration, processed information in a relational manner. In both instances, their extremity of evaluation was enhanced. However, in the unrelated ad context (a series of ads for disparate goods), all gender differences in elaboration were extinguished.

Marketers of an extremely novel product face a challenge when deciding how best to promote their new offering. One key question is whether they want consumers to compare the new product to others of its ilk (that camera is different!), or to allow the new product to stand on its own (is that a camera?). We argue that a competing ad context (several ads for similar goods) will cue relational elaboration and facilitate the processing of an extremely incongruent product. Conversely, an unrelated ad context (several ads for disparate goods) will cue item-specific elaboration, making it difficult to process extreme incongruity. Furthermore, we believe these effects will vary by gender. As researchers have argued that females are more amenable to relational elaboration, we predict that they will have little difficulty resolving extreme incongruity in a competing ad context. Males, on the other hand, due to a natural predisposition for item-specific elaboration, should find the task decidedly more difficult.

CONCEPTUAL BACKGROUND

Consistent with previous research, we define product incongruity as the degree of fit (or lack thereof) between a product and its respective product category (Campbell and Goodstein 2001; Meyers-Levy and Tybout 1989; Peracchio and Tybout 1996). An example might be a circular (rather than square) laptop computer. Research has shown that the act of resolving product incongruity can enhance consumers' extremity of evaluation (Aggarwal and McGill 2007; Campbell and Goodstein 2001; Meyers-Levy and Tybout 1989; Peracchio and Tybout 1995; Stayman, Alden, and Smith 1992). This phenomenon has been coined the schema congruity effect (Meyers-Levy and Tybout 1989).

Mandler (1982) cautioned that enhanced evaluations only occur when consumers can successfully discern the incongruent object and fit it into an existing schema. When incongruity levels rise past a certain threshold, the ability to elaborate diminishes exponentially (Meyers-Levy and Tybout 1989). The task is then often too taxing, resulting in negative evaluation ("I can't understand it, so I don't like it"). This nonmonotonic effect has proven to be very robust (Campbell and Goodstein 2001; Mandler 1982; Meyers-Levy and Tybout 1989; Peracchio and Tybout 1996; Stayman et al. 1992).

While the schema congruity effect has been extended to predict consumers' processing of anthropomorphized products (Aggarwal and McGill 2007), brand extensions (Meyers-Levy, Louie, and Curren 1994), taste (Stayman et al. 1992), and new product attributes (Meyers-Levy and Tybout 1989), research has yet to explore whether the advertisement context itself can affect the robust nature of the phenomenon. Moreover, literature has yet to examine how incongruity is actually processed when accommodation occurs. Thus, we turn to Einstein and Hunt's work (1980) for some insights into the cognitive underpinnings of the different types of processing.

Research on elaboration suggests that there are at least two types of cognitive processing: item-specific and relational (Einstein and Hunt 1980; Hunt and Einstein 1981; Klein, Loftus, and Shell, 1994; Malaviya, Meyers-Levy, and Sternthal 1999). (Please note that the prior work has used elaboration and processing as synonyms. Perhaps the term should be elaborative processing, but for simplicity, we follow the prior linguistic convention.) Item-specific processing emphasizes attribute information that is distinct to a particular claim (Meyers-Levy 1991). This involves the generation of precise associations to a particular product, in isolation of other products (Malaviya, Kisielius, and Sternthal 1996; Malaviya et al. 1999). In contrast, relational processing emphasizes shared themes among disparate goods (Meyers-Levy 1991) and focuses the consumer on the category in which the target product holds membership (Malaviya et al. 1999; Malaviya et al. 1996).

Although the literature has yet to explore the two types of elaboration in terms of the schema congruity effect, there is research that suggests that product evaluations can be enhanced when the ad context evokes both item-specific and relational processing, as opposed to when one of these is dominant (Malaviya et al. 1996; Malaviya 2007). Because item-specific processing enables consumers to focus on the particular features and attributes of the product, and relational processing enables consumers to access the product category, together they increase the persuasive impact of the ad. Malaviya (2007) coined this phenomenon the dual elaboration hypothesis. It seems plausible that the dual elaboration hypothesis could help explain the processing of incongruent product information.

If we are to test our idea that consumers' processing influences the resolution of extreme incongruity, we must also explore whether specific circumstances encourage one type of processing over another. We will further explore one of the more obvious and well-defined dichotomies that has been shown to be associated with different modes of processing: gender (Meyers-Levy and Maheswaran 1991; Meyers-Levy and Sternthal 1991).

Researchers have demonstrated that men and women process information differently (Kempf, Laczniak, and Smith 2006; Meyers-Levy and Maheswaran 1991; Meyers-Levy and Sternthal 1991). McGuiness and Pribram (1979) found, for example, that males processed objects in terms of physical attributes, whereas females processed objects in terms of interpretive concepts. This distinction became the catalyst for the selectivity hypothesis (Meyers-Levy 1989; Meyers-Levy and Maheswaran 1991; Meyers-Levy and Sternthal 1991), which proposed that women engage in more elaborative processing, unless extrinsic motivational factors prompt men to do so as well. Putrevu (2001) also argued that men are more likely to perform item-specific processing, focusing on attributes, and refraining from drawing relationships among message cues. In contrast, women are more likely to relationally process, actively exploring interrelationships among message cues (Kempf et al. 2006; Putrevu 2001).

Meyers-Levy and Sternthal (1991) found that when cued to elaborate on an incongruent event, woman were more deliberate and attentive in their processing than men. They concluded that women tend to elaborate on incongruity, and thus facilitate similarity judgments, whereas men were less responsive to such subtle cues. Similarly, Meyers-Levy and Maheswaran (1991) found that females were indeed more likely to elaborate than males, however, when the task became taxing these differences were eliminated. These studies did not examine the schema congruity effect, nor was that their intent. Moreover, neither study explored the ability of advertising context to enhance a gender-related predisposition in elaboration. This is the goal of our research.

As discussed, a key tenet of the dual elaboration hypothesis is that when both forms of elaboration cue simultaneously, the process should enhance consumers' extremity of evaluation (Malaviya 2007; Malaviya et al. 1996). Accordingly, if males are naturally predisposed to item-specific elaboration, and an ad context is introduced that facilitates relational elaboration, males will engage in both types of processing; this will increase evaluation extremity. We predict, however, that this phenomenon will only manifest for males. If females have a natural predisposition for relational elaboration, an ad context featuring competing products would only serve to augment their dominant processing style (relational).

H1: Males will view a competing ad context more favorably than an unrelated ad context. Females will not differ in evaluations, regardless of ad context.

Item-specific elaboration is more likely to happen when a target ad is presented with ads that belong to unrelated categories, whereas relational elaboration is more likely to happen when a target ad is presented alongside competing ads that make the product category more salient (Malaviya 2007). In part, we propose to replicate Malaviya's findings. However, we posit an underlying gender difference he did not examine. Specifically, we predict that males will engage in more item-specific elaboration when the target ad is positioned with unrelated goods, but not when the ad is positioned with competing goods. Conversely, because females are already oriented towards relational elaboration, we predict this will hold across both conditions.

H2: Males will demonstrate a greater propensity for item-specific elaboration when the ad is viewed within an unrelated context than a competing context. Female will use relational elaboration, regardless of ad context.

STUDY 1: GENDER DIFFERENCES IN CONTEXTUALLY DERIVED PROCESSING

Method

Design. A total of 125 university students (51% females) were recruited to participate in the study for course credit. Participants were assigned to one of four experimental conditions in a 2 (advertising context: unrelated vs. competing) x 2 (gender) between-subject factorial design.

Stimuli. The manipulation of advertising context followed prior procedures (Malaviya 2007). In the unrelated condition, the target advertisement (Minox camera) was placed with three unrelated ads from disparate product categories (Hawth Beer, Nexus Bags, and ProPal Calculators). In the competing condition, the target advertisement was placed with three competing ads from the same product category (Nexus, ProPal, and Hawth cameras). Both ad context manipulations had identical copy and consistent visuals in terms of size, spacing and positioning within the ads. The ad placements were counterbalanced to control for order effects, and the color schema and fonts were counterbalanced to control for preference. A pre-test (n=43) confirmed that there were no discrepancies in comprehensiveness, informativeness, and familiarity among the ads (Fs<1). Moreover, post-test analyses verified the absence of order effects (F<1).

Procedure. Participants were provided with a booklet that consisted of a series of the four fictitious ads and a questionnaire. After examining the ads, participants evaluated the target camera (Minox) on five seven-point evaluation items (bad/good, likeable/unlikeable, few/many unique features, low/high performance product, lacks/offers important benefits).

Next, in accordance with the procedures outlined by Malaviya et al. (1996), participants were asked to list as many thoughts as they could about the target ad. A two-minute time limit was imposed during the thought-listing task to increase the likelihood of capturing only the most accessible thoughts (Cacioppo and Petty 1981). The thoughts were coded by two unaffiliated judges, both of whom were unaware of the research hypotheses. The judges were instructed to rate any thought that relates to the target ad as item specific (e.g., "I like the flash on the Minox"), and any thought that relates to the product category (e.g., "digital cameras are more stylish that other cameras") or usage (e.g., "it's good to take on vacation") as relational. The two coders' results were consistent (r=.87). All outstanding disagreements were resolved through discussion.

Participants also responded to demographic questions, including measures of their knowledge and expertise with cameras, as well as their familiarity with the (fictitious) brands. Post-test analyses confirmed that these variables had no influence (Fs<1).

Results

ANOVAs were conducted on a 2 (context) x 2 (gender) between-subject factorial design. Table 1 reports all treatment means and standard deviations for experiment 1.

Product Evaluation. A factor analysis confirmed that all evaluation items loaded on one factor. Thus, the items were averaged to form an internally consistent measure (α=.91). A two-way ANOVA indicated the presence of a main effect of advertisement context; participants rated the target product more favorably in the competing ad context (M=4.33) than in the unrelated ad context (M=3.63), (F(1, 121)=10.41, p<.005, ω^2=.07). As predicted (hypothesis 1), a planned comparison revealed that male participants viewed the target ad in the competing context more favorably (M=4.21) than in the unrelated context (M=3.53), (F(1, 121)=8.83, p<.005, ω^2=.06), whereas females did not significantly differ in their evaluations across ad context conditions (F<1).

Elaboration Index. Consistent with prior research, an elaboration index was constructed by taking the difference between the number of item-specific thoughts and the number of relational thoughts, divided by the total number of thoughts (Malaviya 2007; Malaviya et al. 1996). Zero indicates an equal number of item-specific and relational thoughts, a positive number indicates more item-specific thoughts, and a negative number more relational thoughts.

A main effect of ad context was observed; participants scored the unrelated context as more item-specific (M=.09) and the competing context as more relational (M=-.04), (F(1, 121)=3.86, p=.05, ω^2=.02). A main effect of gender was also observed; males pro-

TABLE 1

Treatment Means and Cell Counts for Experiment 1

	Unrelated		Competing	
	Male	Female	Male	Female
Evaluation	3.53 (.85)	3.80 (1.09)	4.21 (.78)	4.13 (.79)
Elaboration Index	.23 (.35)	-.06 (.40)	-.03 (.34)	-.05 (.37)
Number of Thoughts	4.40 (2.13)	4.55 (1.63)	5.00 (1.50)	4.44 (1.16)
Relational Thoughts	.53 (.86)	1.32 (1.33)	1.31 (1.33)	1.47 (1.29)
Item-Specific Thoughts	1.70 (1.49)	1.10 (1.04)	1.16 (1.29)	1.19 (1.15)
Cell Size	30	32	31	32

Note: Standard deviations are reported in parentheses

cessed more in an item-specific manner (M=.10), females in a relational manner (M=-.06), ($F(1, 121)=5.75$, $p<.05$, $\omega^2=.04$). As predicted (hypothesis 2), these main effects were qualified by an interaction between gender and context ($F(1, 121)=4.07$, $p<.05$, $\omega^2=.02$). Simple effects tests revealed males processed the unrelated ad context as more item-specific (M=.23) and the competing ad context as more relational (M=-.03), ($F(1, 121)=7.87$, $p<.01$, $\omega^2=.05$). Females processed both contexts in a relational manner ($M_{\text{Unrelated}}=-.06$ vs. $M_{\text{Competing}}=-.05$), ($F<1$).

Discussion

In this study, we offer additional support for claims that advertising context can alter consumers' elaboration (Malaviya 2007; Malaviya et al. 1996). An unrelated context can cue more item-specific than relational processing, whereas a competing context can cue more relational than item-specific processing. We also support existing theory on gender differences in processing (Meyers-Levy 1989; Putrevu 2001). Males were more likely to engage in item-specific processing, whereas females were more likely to engage in relational processing. The contribution of this study, however, is in the interaction between the two. Processing predispositions were moderated by advertisement context; males tended to process in an item-specific manner when the ads were presented within an unrelated ad context, but not within a competing ad context. Females tended to process in a relational manner regardless of the context.

On the surface, it may seem that males and females respond differently in a competing ad context. There is, however, an alternate explanation. The competing context might have equally contributed to relational processing for both genders, but because females are oriented that way (Meyers-Levy 1989), the impact of ad context could have been far more obvious for males (sort of like a ceiling effect). This is supported by our finding that males viewed the competing context more favorably than the unrelated context, whereas females did not differ in their evaluations. Consistent with the dual elaboration hypothesis (Malaviya 2007; Malaviya et al. 1996), male evaluations may have increased because of their natural predisposition for item-specific processing in conjunction with a competing ad context that encouraged them to engage in relational processing. This line of reasoning would also explain why evaluations did not change for females (both their predisposition and the ad context reinforced only relational processing). Thus, female evaluations did not benefit from aggregating two styles.

What is perhaps more interesting than individual differences, is the suggestion that ad context may enhance a predisposed processing style. In particular, evidence from study 1 alludes to the possibility that females may be able to extend their elaboration thresholds given the proper contextual stimulus. This brings us back to our initial research question: What happens when the advertising context incorporates inconsistent or incongruent information? Could a context help give an object membership? Researchers have yet to test product incongruity across varying ad contexts. Perhaps individuals use context to enhance their cognitive elaboration when accommodating incongruity. This would suggest that the ad context might raise a consumer's elaboration threshold to accommodate a level of incongruity that might be otherwise too taxing to resolve (extreme incongruity).

It has been argued that extreme incongruity results in negative evaluations due to one's inability to accommodate an object at the superordinate level (Meyers-Levy and Tybout 1989). Given that females have an elaboration threshold that can tease out fine distinctions (Meyers-Levy 1989), they should be better equipped to utilize the ad context to handle extreme product variations. We predict that if assisted through a competing ad context, females will be able to process levels of incongruity that males cannot distinguish.

> *H3*: Females will view an extremely incongruent product more favorably in a competing ad context than in an unrelated ad context. Males will not differ in their evaluations of an extremely incongruent product, regardless of ad context.

If females are better equipped to use a competing ad context, they should demonstrate a greater propensity for relational processing when appraising an extremely incongruent product. In contrast, if male elaboration thresholds are such that they are unable to process extreme incongruity regardless of the context, then males should revert to item-specific processing.

> *H4*: When an extremely incongruent product is positioned within a competing context, females will engage in more relational (vs. item-specific) processing, whereas males will engage in more item-specific (vs. relational) processing. When an extremely incongruent product is positioned within an unrelated context, there will be no difference in processing between males and females.

STUDY 2: THE EFFECTS OF CONTEXT AND GENDER ON THE ACCOMODATION OF INCONGRUENT GOODS

Method

Design. In total, 286 students (49.7% females) participated in the study for course credit. Each participant was randomly assigned to one of 12 experimental conditions, creating a 2 (advertising context: unrelated vs. competing) x 2 (gender) x 3 (product congruity: congruent vs. moderately incongruent vs. extremely incongruent) between-subject factorial design.

Stimuli. We used the same ad context manipulation as described in study 1. Given the nature of the manipulation (unrelated vs. competing), two pre-tests were conducted to secure the product congruity manipulation within-subjects (n=40; 50% females) as well as between-subjects (n_130; 44% females). Using real digital cameras that were newly introduced to the market, a preliminary examination (n=52) reduced the initial selection (five cameras) to three by excluding any camera that did not significantly vary in perceived typicality (three 7-point scales anchored by not at all unique/very unique, very unlikely/very likely, and (matches) not at all well/very well). Similar to previous work (Campbell and Goodstein 2001), the pre-test items loaded on one factor and were averaged to form an internally consistent measure (?=.67).

The between-subjects pre-test confirmed a main effect of camera type on perceived typicality (F(2, 124)=37.43, p<.001). The within-subjects pre-test replicated the effect (F(1.93, 73.17)=263.46, p<.001). Planned/repeated comparisons verified that camera #1 (standard) was viewed as more typical ($M_{Between}$=5.30 and M_{Within}=6.15) than camera #2 (ultra thin) ($M_{Between}$=4.55; F(1, 124)=7.31, p<.01 and M_{Within}=5.85; F(1, 38)=5.22, p<.05), which in turn was rated far more typical than camera #3 (round) ($M_{Between}$=2.97; F(1, 124)=37.22, p<.001 and M_{Within}=2.63; F(1, 38)=257.22, p<.001). There was no effect of camera order in the within-subjects pre-test (Fs<1). More importantly, there was no effect of gender on measures of evaluation, price perception or perceived typicality in either pre-test (Fs<1). Both pre-tests confirmed that the standard camera was seen as congruent, the ultra-thin camera as moderately incongruent, and the round camera as extremely incongruent.

Procedure. Participants were instructed that the purpose of the study is to learn their opinions about different advertisements. Each research participant was asked to review a seven-page booklet (visual and editorial content) at his or her own pace and to complete the accompanying tasks. In line with experiment 1, the booklets consisted of either four camera ads (competing) or four disparate ads (unrelated), with the target camera ad being the incongruity manipulation in both contexts. On average, it took respondents 10-minutes to complete the task.

Participants first evaluated the target camera (Minox) on 10 seven-point items (bad/good, dislike/like, few/many unique features, low/high performance product, poor/good picture quality, lacks/offers important benefits, not useful/useful, not superior/superior, difficult/easy to use, and poor/good lens quality). Embedded with these items were three seven-point typicality items (listed previously). Lastly, participants were asked to complete the same thought task listed in study 1. In addition to the procedures described in the first experiment, the two unaffiliated judges were required to further record whether respondents—if prone to engage in relational processing—were dissimilarity-focused ("this camera looks easier to use than other cameras") or similarity-focused ("digital cameras are easy to use"; Kim and Meyers-Levy 2008). The judges' results were indexed and any outstanding disagreements were resolved through discussion.

Once again, as possible covariates, participants responded to a set of demographic questions, including measures pertaining to expertise with cameras, how attentive they were during the task, as well as their familiarity with the (fictitious) brands used in the study. None of these factors contributed to the treatment effects (Fs<1).

Results

ANOVAs were conducted on a 2 (context) x 2 (gender) x 3 (product congruity) between-subject factorial design. Table 2 reports all treatment means for experiment 2.

Perceived Typicality. In line with our pre-test results, the three typicality items loaded on one factor and were averaged to form an internally consistent measure (α=.71). A planned comparison using a Bonferroni adjusted alpha level of .017 per test (.05/3) indicated that the congruent product was perceived to be far more typical (M=5.43) than the moderately incongruent product (M=3.82), (F(1, 274)=123.52, p<.001, ω^2=.18), which was in turn seen as far more typical than the extremely incongruent product (M=2.62), (F(1, 274)=68.4, p<.001, ω^2=.10). The average typicality of the two incongruity conditions combined (M=3.21) was significantly lower than that of the congruent condition (M=5.43), (F(1, 274)=322.01, p<.001, ω^2=.47). Thus, the congruity manipulation was perceived as intended.

Product Evaluation. Consistent with prior research (Malaviya 2007), the 10 evaluation items loaded on one factor and thus were averaged (α=.85). An ANOVA revealed a three-way interaction of advertising context, product congruity, and gender on product evaluation (F(2, 274)=3.74, p<.05, ω^2=.02). Simple effects tests revealed that product evaluations varied by gender. Specifically, when the target ad was evaluated by male participants, a significant main effect of product congruity emerged (F(2, 274)=10.88, p<.001, ω^2=.06). Consistent with the schema congruity effect (Meyers-Levy and Tybout 1989), planned contrasts revealed that males perceived the moderately incongruent product more favorably (M=4.51) than both the congruent product (M=4.03), (F(1, 274)=6.25, p<.05, ω^2=.02), and the extremely incongruent product (M=3.63), (F(1, 274)=21.32, p<.001, ω^2=.07).

In contrast, when the target ad was evaluated by female participants, a significant interaction between product congruity and ad context emerged (F(2, 274)=3.25, p<.05, ω^2=.01). Simple effects revealed that the nature of the interaction was such that the schema congruity effect manifested for females only in the unrelated ad context (F(1, 274)=7.30, p<.005, ω^2=.04); females evaluated the moderately incongruent product ($M_{Unrelated}$=4.67) more favorably than both the congruent product ($M_{Unrelated}$=4.10), (F(1, 274)=4.43, p<.05, ω^2=.01) and the extremely incongruent product ($M_{Unrelated}$=3.63), (F(1, 274)=14.55, p<.001, ω^2=.04). There were no differences in female evaluations across the product congruity conditions in the competing ad context (Fs<1). As predicted (hypothesis 3), a planned comparison confirmed that females viewed the extremely incongruent product more favorably in the competing ad context (M=4.23) than in the unrelated ad context (M=3.63), (F(1, 274)=4.97, p<.05, ω^2=.01). Thus, the absence of the schema congruity effect in the competing ad context was due to female participants evaluating the extremely incongruent product on par with the moderately incongruent and congruent products.

Elaboration Index. Following the same procedures outlined in study 1, participants' thoughts were catalogued by two unaffiliated coders (r=.91) and an index was calculated. Consistent with the first experiment, a main effect of advertising context emerged; partici-

TABLE 2
Treatment Means and Cell Counts for Experiment 2

	Congruent		Moderately Incongruent		Extremely Incongruent	
	Male	Female	Male	Female	Male	Female
Unrelated:						
Evaluation	3.82 (.64)	4.10 (.76)	4.49 (1.03)	4.67 (.86)	3.79 (.97)	3.63 (.97)
Typicality	5.60 (.95)	5.38 (.93)	3.81 (1.20)	4.30 (.99)	3.03 (1.05)	2.49 (.91)
Elaboration	.12 (.37)	-.06 (.23)	-.03 (.30)	.03 (.19)	.06 (.18)	.02 (.15)
Cell Size	24	24	24	23	24	23
Competing:						
Evaluation	4.25 (.83)	4.23 (.92)	4.53 (.93)	4.30 (1.18)	3.48 (1.05)	4.23 (.77)
Typicality	5.39 (1.00)	5.36 (1.04)	3.69 (.90)	3.49 (1.00)	2.18 (.88)	2.75 (.94)
Elaboration	-.09 (.35)	-.02 (.35)	.02 (.26)	-.11 (.24)	.06 (.24)	-.14 (.29)
Cell Size	24	24	24	24	24	24

Note: Standard deviations are reported in parentheses; Elaboration = elaboration index

pants processed the unrelated context as more item-specific (M=.02) and the competing context as more relational (M=-.05), (F(1, 274)=5.10, p<.05, ω^2=.01). Similarly, there was a main effect of gender; males processed more in an item-specific manner (M=.02), females in a relational manner (M=-.05), (F(1, 274)=4.58, p<.05, ω^2=.01). The effects were qualified by a three-way interaction of advertising context, product congruity and gender (F(2, 274)=4.96, p<.05, ω^2=.03). Closer examination revealed that the nature of the interaction varied by the level of product congruity. Specifically when respondents evaluated the congruent target product, a significant interaction between gender and ad context emerged (F(1, 274)=4.90, p<.05, ω^2=.01). In line with study 1, simple effects tests revealed that males processed the unrelated ad context as more item-specific (M=.12) and the competing ad context as more relational (M=-.09), (F(1, 274)=7.06, p<.01, ω^2=.02). In contrast, females processed both the unrelated and competing congruent ad context in a relational manner ($M_{Unrelated}$=-.06 vs. $M_{Competing}$=-.02), (F<1).

As predicted, the pattern of effects were reversed when participants evaluated the extremely incongruent product; females processed the unrelated ad context as more item-specific (M=.02) and the competing ad context as more relational (M=-.14), (F(1, 274)=4.46, p<.05, ω^2=.01). In contrast, males processed both the unrelated and competing extremely incongruent ad contexts in an item-specific manner ($M_{Unrelated}$=.06 vs. $M_{Competing}$=.06), (F<1). Males and females did not significantly differ in their elaborations between the unrelated or competing moderately incongruent ad contexts (p>.05).

Discussion

In this experiment, we not only replicate effects from study 1, but we also offer additional support for the nonmonotonic relationship between product congruity and product evaluation (vis. the schema congruity effect; Meyers-Levy and Tybout 1989). The contribution of this study, however, lies in the interaction between context, gender and incongruity. Consistent with past examinations (viewing a product in isolation from comparable goods), the schema congruity effect was robust in the unrelated ad context. In the competing ad context, however, the phenomenon only manifested for males. The lack of effect for females, coupled with the increase in relational elaboration as the product increased in perceived typicality, supports our core proposition: using the competing ad context, females were able to extend their processing to accommodate an extremely incongruent product. They properly understood it within its product category and evaluated it more positively.

GENERAL DISCUSSION

The two experiments here provide strong evidence that advertising context can be used to facilitate consumers' ability to accommodate incongruent goods. Malaviya (2007) illustrated the merits of the dual elaboration hypothesis. We were able to replicate and extend his framework to provide evidence that ad context can be used to alter the elaboration threshold of both males (experiment 1) and females (experiment 2), and do so in different ways. Furthermore, the two experiments not only replicated the schema congruity effect (Meyers-Levy and Tybout 1989), but they also lent support to the notion that males and females differ in their elaboration strategies. Our findings suggest that given a context that facilitates a means of comparison, women can resolve what would otherwise be too difficult (an extremely odd-looking camera). Additionally, given that same contextual cue, males will adopt a processing strategy that is antithetical to a natural predisposition (they will begin to relationally process information, instead of processing in an item-specific manner).

In line with the selectivity hypothesis (Meyers-Levy and Maheswaran 1991), when the task alone was too difficult (unrelated), all gender differences in elaboration were extinguished. However, when the task was accompanied by a context that facilitated a means of comparison (competing), the differences re-emerged and were even more dramatic. These findings have important implications for marketing practice. Both males and females seemed to enjoy the product the most when it was at least moderately incongruent, and when the product was in a context of similar goods that helped to classify it. Indeed, such a technique could be used in product placement on retail shelves, end of aisle displays, and special features in magazines and newspapers. What is perhaps more interesting, however, is the idea that a competing context could be used to facilitate the introduction of an extremely incongruent good. In such a scenario, the results of this study would caution that marketers be sensitive to gender variations in elaboration, which seem to gain in severity as the product becomes increasingly novel. Future research will have to explore limits of this phenomenon.

REFERENCES

Aggarwal, Pankaj and Ann L. McGill (2007), "Is That Car Smiling at Me? Schema Congruity as a Basis for Evaluating Anthropomorphized Products," *Journal of Consumer Research*, 34 (December), 468-79.

Cacioppo, John. T. and Richard E. Petty (1981), "Social Psychological Procedures for the Cognitive Response Assessment: The Thought Listing Technique," in *Cognitive Assessment*, ed. Thomas V. Merluzzi, Carol R. Glass and Myles Genest, New York: Guilford Press, 309-42.

Campbell, Margaret C. and Ronald C. Goodstein (2001), "The Moderating Effect of Perceived Risk on Consumers' Evaluations of Product Incongruity: Preference for the Norm," *Journal of Consumer Research*, 28 (December), 439-49.

Cohen, Joel B. and Kunal Basu (1987), "Alternative Models of Categorization: Toward a Contingent Processing Framework," *Journal of Consumer Research*, 13 (March), 455-72.

Einstein, Gilles O. and R. Reed Hunt (1980), "Levels of Processing and Organization: Additive Effects of Individual-Item and Relational Processing," *Journal of Experimental Psychology: Human learning and memory*, 6 (September), 588-98.

Hunt, R. Reed and Giles O. Einstein (1981), "Relational and Item-Specific Information in Memory," *Journal of Verbal Learning and Verbal Behavior*, 20 (October), 497–514.

Kempf, DeAnna S., Russell N. Laczniak, and Robert E. Smith (2006), "The Effects of Gender on Processing Advertising and Product Trial Information," *Marketing Letters*, 17 (January), 5-16.

Klein, Stanley B., Judith Loftus, and Terry Shell (1994), "Repeated Testing: A Technique for Assessing the Roles of Elaborative and Organizational Processing in the Representation of Social Knowledge," *Journal of Personality and Social Psychology*, 66 (May), 830-39.

Malaviya, Prashant (2007), "The Moderating Influence of Advertising Context on Ad Repetition Effects: The Role of Amount and Type of Elaboration," *Journal of Consumer Research*, 34 (June), 32-40.

Malaviya, Prashant, Jolita Kisielius, and Brian Sternthal (1996), "The Effect of Type of Elaboration on Advertisement Processing and Judgment," *Journal of Marketing Research*, 33 (November), 410–21.

Malaviya, Prashant, Joan Meyers-Levy, and Brian Sternthal (1999), "Ad Repetition in a Cluttered Environment: The Influence of Type of Processing," *Psychology and Marketing*, 16 (March), 99-118.

Mandler, George (1982), "The Structure of Value: Accounting for Taste," in *Affect and Cognition: The Seventeenth Annual Carnegie Symposium on Cognition*, ed. Margaret S. Clarke, and Susan T. Fiske, Hillsdale NJ: Erlbaum, 3-36.

McGuiness, Dianne and Karl H. Pribram (1979), "The Origins of Sensory Bias in the Development of Gender Differences in Perception and Cognition," in *Cognitive Growth and Development*, ed. Morton Bortner, New York: Bruner/Mazel Publishers, 3-56.

Meyers-Levy, Joan (1989), "Gender Differences in Information Processing: A Selectivity Interpretation," in *Cognitive and Affective Responses to Advertising*, ed. Patricia Cafferata and Alice Tybout, Lexington, MA: Lexington.

______ (1991), "Elaborating on Elaboration: The Distinction between Relational and Item-Specific Elaboration," *Journal of Consumer Research*, 18 (December), 358–67.

Meyers-Levy, Joan, Therese A. Louie, and Mary T. Curren (1994), "How Does the Congruity of Brand Names Affect Evaluations of Brand Name Extensions?" *Journal of Applied Psychology*, 79 (February), 46-53.

Meyers-Levy, Joan and Durairaj Maheswaran (1991), "Exploring Differences in Males' and Females' Processing Strategies," *Journal of Consumer Research*, 18 (June), 63-70.

Meyers-Levy, Joan and Brian Sternthal (1991), "Gender Differences in the Use of Message Cues and Judgments," *Journal of Marketing Research*, 28 (February), 84-96.

Meyers-Levy, Joan and Alice M. Tybout (1989), "Schema Congruity as a Basis for Product Evaluation," *Journal of Consumer Research*, 16 (June), 39-55.

Peracchio, Laura A. and Alice M. Tybout (1996), "The Moderating Role of Prior Knowledge in Schema-Based Product Evaluation," *Journal of Consumer Research*, 23 (December), 177-92.

Putrevu, Sanjay (2001), "Exploring the Origins and Information Processing Differences between Men and Women: Implications for Advertisers." *Academy of Marketing Science Review*, 10, 1-15.

Stayman, Douglas. M., Dana L. Alden, and Karen M. Smith (1992), "Some Effects on Schematic Processing on Consumer Expectations and Disconfirmation Judgments," *Journal of Consumer Research*, 14 (September), 240-55.

To Be or not to Be? Virtual Experience and Immersion on a 3D Commercial Web Site

Marion Garnier, SKEMA, LSMRC, Univ. Nord de France, France
Ingrid Poncin, SKEMA, LSMRC, Univ. Nord de France, France

INTRODUCTION

The rapid growth of multimedia technologies and the Internet in its various forms is changing the way of doing e-commerce. The success of virtual universes such as Second Life (SL), or games such as World of Warcraft (WOW) has now opened new opportunities for the development of online shopping experience. Major technological developments in advanced interactive techniques drawn from MMORPG[1] and virtual universes now sustain and allow fully 3D shopping malls, showrooms or shopping websites. In the realm of current technological development, the practice is ahead of theory in some instances, mainly due to the rapid pace of emerging new technologies, thus leaving academic researchers a little behind in their efforts to make sense of their impact. At the same time, as underlined by Venkatesh (1998), the pioneers in the world of practice need guidance from academic researchers to provide conceptual schemes that can sharpen their practices in hypercompetitive environments.

Despite the huge potential, we know little about the way to use adequately these new technologies to improve consumers experience on a commercial website. There is a big gap in management's understanding of what constitutes a shopping experience on 3D commercial website for a consumer. This issue, until recently, was a black box to academic scholars as well. The situation is now changing, since the seminal work of Hoffman and Novak (1996), literature has highlighted flow, immersion and social and spatial presences as important antecedents of Internet behaviour. If some researchers have studied these concepts in virtual reality (Tomaseti, Ruiz and Reynolds, 2009), only few have focused on the context of a 3D commercial website, if we except precursory and visionary reflexion of Burke (1996) on virtual shopping. Hence, most of the academic literature has been devoted to demonstrate that using an interactive animated 'avatar' on computer screens could provide a source of social presence and trust building capabilities (Wood, Solomon and Englis, 2005; Holzwarth, Janiszewski and Neumann, 2006; Keeling and McGoldrick ,2008). But, to our knowledge, if many researches were interested in avatars in universes such as SL, only one published research has dealt with the representation of the consumer by an avatar on a commercial website (Crete, Saint-Onge, Merle, Arsenault and Nantel, 2008).

Therefore, our research aims at understanding what could be the influence of the 3D technology on the shopping experience on a 3D commercial website. More especially, this research contributes to explain how the consumer-avatar is a key issue in the virtual experience on a 3D merchant website, through its links with embodiment, realism and presence. To begin with, the concept of virtual experience will be briefly introduced. The second part of the paper will present our research methodology and analyses: an interpretative and understanding qualitative research process was adopted, that leads the researcher to a theoretical elaboration building on the collected verbatims. The third part will then deal with results of the research, on the basis of constant comparison with theory. Conclusion will highlight main contributions, limits and research perspectives.

[1]*Massively Multiplayer Online Role Playing Games*

VIRTUAL EXPERIENCE AT THE AGE OF 3D

Improving the virtual experience has become a major issue for e-marketers. As stated by Childers, Carr and Peck (2001) or Mathwick, Malhotra and Rigdon (2001), developing the hedonic value of websites and improving the virtual shopping experience on Internet should lead to a better conversion rate, more satisfaction, stickiness and loyalty. Visiting a website can be considered as a consumption activity through the interaction with the consumption object (Holt, 1995). This activity can also be considered as an experience beyond a potential utilitarian value (acquisition of information or material goods...), and covers symbolic and hedonic dimensions (spending an enjoyable time shopping on an online shop for example). Since Hirschman and Holbrook (1982)'s seminal work on consumption experience, high attention has been paid to the way consumption can lead individuals to satisfy hedonic and experiential needs beyond functional needs (Csikszentmihalyi, 2000). And even if the Internet offers wide utilitarian opportunities, some authors stated that the more immersive, hedonic aspects of Internet could play at least an equal role in predicting online attitudes and behaviours (Childers et al., 2001; Mathwick et al., 2001). In this perspective, 3D websites seem particularly adapted to generate diversified sensorial stimulations, immersion and experience in consequence.

Immersion in computer-mediated environment is defined as "the extent to which the computer displays are capable of delivering an illusion of reality to the senses of the human participant" (Slater and Wilbur, 1997). On a broader scope, immersion appears in any case in which an individual is plunged, involved or absorbed in a totally different world (Fornerino, Helme-Guizon and Gotteland, 2006). This immersion-that can be partial or total, durable or temporary, wanted or undergone–or "feeling of" immersion of an individual in a physical or virtual universe consists in entering the universe and absorb / be absorbed by its atmosphere. In computer-mediated environments, immersion is often considered through the concept of flow (Hoffman and Novak, 1996; Csikszentmihalyi, 1990; Novak, Hoffman and Yung, 2000). Flow is defined as "the state occurring during network navigation which is characterized by a seamless sequence of responses facilitated by machine interactivity, intrinsically enjoyable, accompanied by a loss of self-consciousness and self-reinforcing" (Novak et al. 2000). If immersion and flow share concentration and focus on the consumption object, flow also implies a high control of actions, due to a confrontation between high stakes and high skills (Fornerino et al., 2006) while this is not a basic condition for immersion to develop.

Rich media technologies and web 2.0 concepts have considerably broadened the extent to which websites can be used in an experiential and entertaining way (Helme-Guizon, 2001; Jeandrain and Limbourg, 2002) and possibly generate immersion by going beyond the flat "inhuman" screen and display of traditional websites. Those techniques, such as high quality sound, video/audio streaming or 3D object manipulation can lead to a decrease in the perception of the computer mediation. Jeandrain and Diesbach (2008) noticed that those technologies all follow the same pattern: reach media transparency and generate immersion, or so called feeling of "presence", the perceptual illusion of non-mediation (Lombard and Ditton, 1997). In consequence, our research aims at understanding to what extent and how a commercial 3D website can generate experiential value to its users and contributions will

TABLE 1
Samples descriptions

	Focus Groups	Individual interviews
Number	8	35
Total nb of respondents	58	35
Age of respondents	From 20 to 22 years old	From 22 to 59 years olds:
Men/women repartition	Men: 33% Women: 66%	Men: 45% Women: 55%
Sample characteristics	Exclusively students. Variety in Internet expertise and Internet usage habits.	Variety in professional categories, education levels, Internet expertise and Internet usage habits
Time length	1h per focus group	40 to 90 mns per interview

demonstate how and why the representation of the consumer as an avatar is a key issue.

METHODOLOGY

3D Website Application Case: Victoria Couture

Access to Victoria Couture 3D website can be found on the brand 2D website. Direct access to the 3D shop is available on http://www.victoriacouture.com/boutique3d-e-6-g-3d.html. This is the first integrally 3D e-shop on which it is possible to buy products: if other 3D commercial malls or e-shops exist, they do not allow online purchase-for which consumers are then connected to traditional 2D websites. In Victoria Couture 3D Shop, The user enters a fully 3D shop (environment, structures and shelves, product display) and is represented by an avatar he can personalize and uses it to navigate. He can also visualize (picture or 3D display) products and try them on, chat online with avatars of other consumers, and possibly ends his visit by purchasing.

Sample And Data Collection

Two qualitative data collections were conducted: semi-directive individual interviews and focus groups. Both are relevant qualitative methods for an exploratory study aiming at a deep understanding of consumption situations and new or unknown phenomenons (Morgan, 1998; Malhotra, 1999; Evrard et al., 2003). A description of samples is provided in Table 1.

Each data collection followed the same process: (1) display and effective visit of the website (manipulation of the website, navigation and test of the functionalities–avatar personalization, online chat, 3D product display, trial of the clothes, etc.); and (2) semi-directive discussion during and after the visit. They were conducted on the basis of a guide, as recommended in qualitative research (for a summary: see Jolibert and Jourdan, 2006). The interview guide was only composed of a restricted number of themes: interviewer's function was to deepen each important element in the respondents' speeches and to remain flexible on the progress of the discussion, while encouraging respondent's freedom of expression. As each focus group was supposed to last only one hour, one theme was assigned to and deepened in each session (avatar, virtual experience, shopping in 2D vs 3D, shopping online vs shopping in real shops–2 focus groups per theme were realized), so to complete and saturate data from individual interviews dealing with all issues. Each interview and focus group was fully retranscribed in order to preserve the accurateness of recorded speeches. The data corpus is finally composed of 510 pages and around 265 000 words (interventions of interviewers included).

Data Analysis

Data analysis was conducted according to an interpretative process and double coding, using the content analysis software Weft QDA: textual data were analyzed by two independent coders, on the basis of the interview guide and same coding units (groups of words). Flexibility was preserved through an open coding process, to identify and integrate new themes that could emerge from data. Codings were then compared and discussed so to reach consensus. Semantical saturation was reached with the 25th individual interview[2]. Focus groups and additional interviews comforted categories stability and reinforced semantical saturation. In the second step of the analysis, theory emerged on the principle of constant comparison that is to say by systematically confronting open coding results to literature.

RESULTS AND DISCUSSION

Corpus analysis highlights various aspects of the experience related to immersion and experience in the 3D environment that justify the identified categories (Figure 1). As a matter of fact, the consumer-avatar (an avatar representing the consumer in the virtual shop) emerges as a central issue in the understanding of the virtual experience on the website.

In a computer-mediated environment, an avatar is defined as "a pictorial representation of a human in a chat environment" (Bahorsky, Jeffrey and Mason, 1998), "a representation of the user as an animated character in virtual worlds" (Loos, 2003), or "graphic personifications of computers or processes that run on computers" (Halfhill, 1996). Many researches have dealt with Embodied Virtual Agents (EVA) and their impact on consumer behaviour and consumption experience (Cassell et al. 2000; Holzwarth et al. 2006; Wang et al., 2007; Jeandrain and Diesbach

[2]Beyond themes and categories that are dealt with in this paper, more larger and/or peripheric themes were evoked and discussed by respondents (perspectives and attitudes towards utilitarian vs hedonic features and use of the website, comparison of 3D shopping with real-life and 2D shopping, virtual experience on a whole, brand-related features, etc.). All those themes help reaching saturation but couldn't be explored in this paper, focused on the key issue of the avatar.

FIGURE 1
Categories

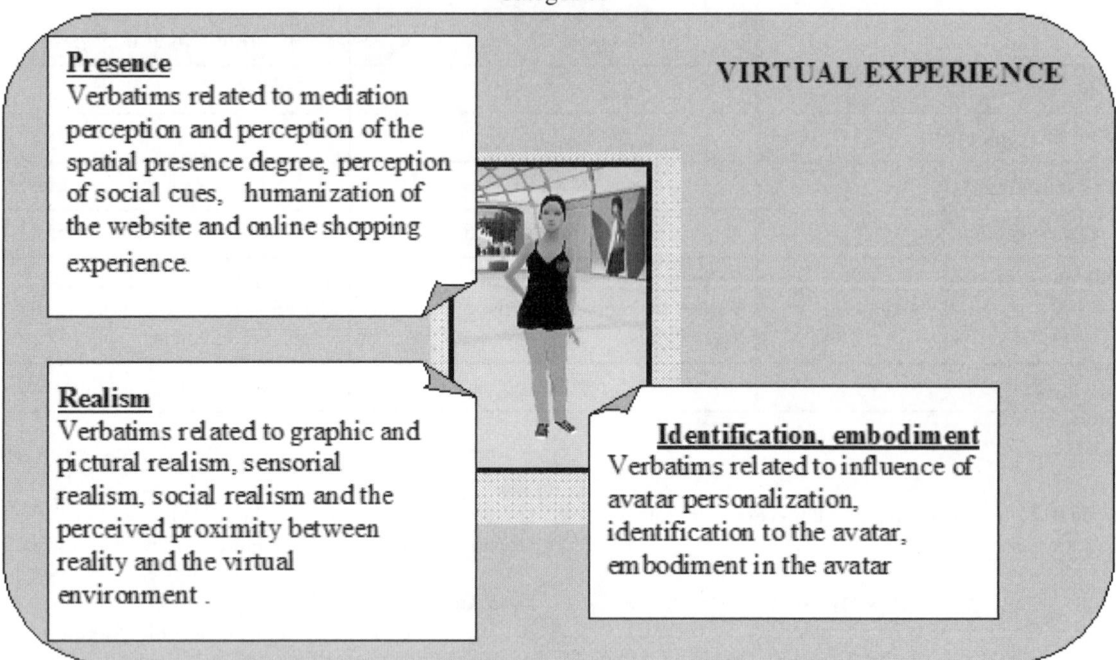

2008) or with avatars in other settings (for example Wood, Solomon and Allan, 2008 in Second Life; Yong, Baker and Song, 2007 in virtual communities). But, to our knowledge, only one research (Crete et al., 2008) deals with the influence of consumer-avatar, that is to say an avatar representing the consumer on a shopping website.

Identification to The Avatar and Embodiment. As a majority, respondents spontaneously attempted to create an avatar that looked like them, so to be represented and embodied on the website: "What I am interested in is to create a character like me. To know how I will be" (Monique, female, 58). Nevertheless, respondents then express a general lack of identification to and embodiment the avatar. A great majority of respondents refer to the avatar using words such as "person", "model", "fellow", "character" controlled through technology. "That sort of statue with that kind of bunches, it is far from being sufficiently human... It is difficult to identify with. (…) Yes, it a model but also someone in reality. It is not sufficiently human." (Barbara, female, 33). Such metaphors serve as "moving less-than-conscious thought into the realm of consciousness" (Joy and Sherry, 2003): through the language participants used, embodiment, or here lack of embodiment and identification, is expressed.

Indeed, identification to an avatar refers to the imaginary process invoked in response to a character represented in the mediated environment (Peng, 2008): narration is absorbed and the virtual identity can take place of the real-life identity. Thanks to embodiment in the avatar, users can play an active role, providing himself a nearly direct experience (enactive experience), more powerful than mere observation. Though, in our case, the weak identification seems highly related to a strong detachment from the avatar that is no more referred to as an embodied representation of the user, but as an other artificial being. Indeed, the pronoun "I" is not used to refer to avatar's actions-referred as "he" or "she"-but to individual's actions in the real world. The avatar is perceived as a puppet controlled through the computer (arrows, mouse): respondents clearly mention they are on a computer, manipulating the avatar and not "shopping for real": "You go for a walk like you could go for a walk on Saturday in the malls... You go for a walk but "it is not for real" like we said when we were younger" (Franck, male, 40) "Unfortunately, there is always this space between me and the computer" (Emilie, female, 23). Acting on the 3D shopping website appears as a metaphor of the real, with distinct spaces and bodies (the real-life environment and body vs the online world and character controlled via the real world).

So, while theories on immersion in computer-mediated environments suggest an illusion of non-mediation by the human-machine interface (Lombard and Ditton, 1997), with embodiment in the avatar facilitating this illusion, the perception of this mediation is particularly prominent in speeches, especially through references made by participants to their own avatar. The perceived outstanding mediation implies respondents don't seem to feel immerged in the virtual environment thanks to the avatar, and despite resemblance between them and their avatar, they don't feel embodied on the virtual universe: "Honestly, for me, it is a character, it is not me" (Dominique, female, 48). Though, the perception of one's own physical body related to self-construction and projection in a virtual body has been showed to be an important issue in virtual environments (Ulusoy and Vicdan, 2009) as embodiment plays an essential role in human experience (Joy and Sherry, 2003), even in virtual universes experiences. Three main related explanations can be suggested to understand why participants expressed such as frontier and detachment between them and the avatar.

First, the 3rd-person view seems to decrease the possible embodiment by creating strong detachment and weak appropriation of the space (Carù and Cova, 2003). In online gaming, 3rd-person view is giving the gamer a direct observation angle on his character, usually from behind. This view is usually opposed to the 1st-person or subjective view, in which the gamer is taking the character's place, seeing the word through its eyes, as he sees the real world through his own eyes (Computer Gaming Lexicon, available at http://www.jeuxvideopc.com/lexique/). One specificity of 3D universes is to allow a subjective vision through the eyes of the avatar, with regard to an external vision of the scene. Tisseron (2008, p.178) presents the specificities and consequences of those different points of view: "In each of his moves, my avatar allows me to see the world with "his eyes"–through subjective view–or to see it detached from myself, as in a dream. Either I live inside of him or outside of him. In the first case, I only see of him what I can see of my own body: my arms, my legs, ... In the second case, I'm free to observe all parts of my anatomy that are usually invisible to me, such as my back or the top of my head. I can even stare at a point where I'm not and see myself in middle of the environment."

Moreover, Tisseron (2008) suggested that manipulating an avatar necessarily implies detachment: the individual need to think about moves to make, and how to make them. Behavior of any organism (human or else) is not a series of discrete actions but a continuous flow of activity: the flow of unconscious low-level or automatic moves (for example, folding knees and pelvis) turns into high-level behaviours (sitting down on a chair) (Whalen, Petriu, Petriu and Cordea, 2003). Technology for controlling the avatar allows executing a restricted set of atomic moves through keyboards and mousing in order to accomplish high-level behaviors. On a shopping website, it more specifically implies to be aware of automatic everyday high-level behavior such walking, turning left or right, taking a cloth on a shelf, so to execute appropriate atomic moves with the help of technology (click in the appropriate way so that the avatar moves his arm and hand toward the shelf). This is at the opposite of fantasy and unusual acting in MMORPG-where high immersion can be found -, in which high-level behaviours, as they are unusual (for example throwing a fireball), have to be consciously learned: in turn, atomic moves more rapidly become automatisms, thus reducing detachment with the avatar. So, in some cases, the ability to act does not necessarily require detachment: one can be taken in the process of flow and simply perform what has to be done (Joy and Sherry, 2003): when the body performs an activity unconsciously, individuals tend to experience flow (Csikszentmihalyi and Robinson 1990), the body simply takes over because of competence and experience (Joy and Sherry, 2003). So self-projection and embodiment in the avatar, as in virtual universes (Tisseron, 2008) and its impact on immersion could be questioned and deepened on merchant 3D websites as a key issue of the virtual experience.

Finally, lack of self-projection and embodiment in the virtual universe can be related, as expressed by respondents, to poor realism of the experience.

Realism on 3D The Commercial Website. As stated by Rosenblom (2003), some virtual universes can be very affective at creating the illusion of reality: the more they immerse users in stimuli corresponding to their expectations of the virtual world, the more compelling is their experience. This is especially relevant for a realistic virtual universe such as a 3D merchant website.

Three kinds of realism have been identified in participants' speeches: graphic (or pictural) realism, sensory realism and social realism. Analysis clearly points out the lack of realism of the avatar and the 3D environment on those three facets.

Graphic Realism And Sight Sense Mobilization. Participants explicitly verbalize their difficulties with the visual characteristics and atmosphere of the website: "That is to say that the shop looks like a fake. It really looks like cubes and rods; while clothes should have looked as real as possible. (...) One doesn't know if it's real or not real" (Emilie H., female, 23) "Whatever improvements that could be done, it's not the same sight as with our eyes. (...) It's flat. (...) There is no relief" (Marc, male, 59). This feeling is enhanced by the low perceived realism of the avatar, considered as "cartoon-like" and too much virtual and imprecise to convey visual aspects of a real human body. "It is like Albator. It is like cartoons. What a pity!" (Barbara, female, 33) "I have the feeling to be in a game, to be a Sims... in the Sims game" (Damien A., male, 29)

As stated by Tisseron (2008, p.170), "In virtual worlds, there is no way to touch. Everything is deliciously or desperately visual, according to your ability to be satisfied with it."

Sight sense, although it is supposed to be highly stimulated by 3D display, is not enough to mobilize senses in a sufficiently comprehensive and satisfying way to favour experience. As stated by Joy and Sherry (2003), the experience is tightly linked to the ability to sense accurately: "If you use only one of the senses, you acquire only one-fifth of the aesthetic experience. In synesthesia, however, several of the senses are included, and, hence, a more holistic appreciation is possible." This issue is particularly prevalent and relevant in a computer-mediated environment.

Sensory realism. In the unavoidable absence of touch sense on the Internet, a great majority of respondents highlight a further sensory isolation due to the absence of noise or music. "I don't like that too virtual aspect. There is even no music. (She looks for something to turn sound on the computer). (…) I find it so weird there is no music. When you go in a shop, there is music!" (Marion, female, 26). « Well… everything happens with our eyes, you can't touch, you can't… well… You can't hear noise coming from other persons… We are completely cut off the world… This is slightly limiting the shopping feeling we can have, compared to classical shopping" (Emilie H. female, 23)

Ambient music, voice noises (discussions) or step noises play a fundamental role in sales point atmosphere. But this sense is not really mobilized on Internet in general and particularly on the website, though it has been shown for example that subjects can 'lose' themselves when immersed in sound, (Dyson 1996; Schafer 1977 in Joy and Sherry, 2003). Moreover, beyond creating realism compared to a traditional sales point, using music and noise on websites can contribute to improve website visit experience (Galan and Helme-Guizon, 2003). According to Volle (2000), virtual atmosphere distinguishes from real atmosphere through the weak number of stimulated senses, as well as through a supposed higher degree of interactivity, which in inherent to Internet (Ghose et Dhou, 1998). As any website can be highly interactive, virtual atmosphere has a crucial differentiating role to play, by counterbalancing the freedom of quitting and finding another interactive website. A 3D website should beneficiate from this advantage on more classical configurations, through its capacity to associate product and service to an universe that can be sensory immersive and stimulate mental imagery in a more persuasive way.

Social realism. "You are rarely alone when you go for shopping on a Saturday at 5.00pm in a supermarket. So, I expected to meet other people there. But there, there is no salesman, a person you can click (...) I expected also to be with more clients to see which articles are the most attractive for people… see what they think about these articles there. Try to make a kind of small discussion group (chat) on the site, discuss with the avatar of someone else who is in Paris or Marseille…(…), but there is nobody in there!" as states Damien A (male, 25). Neither consumer-avatar in 3D nor the online chat tool seem to be able to compensate for the lack of humanity and the impersonality people usually blame websites for. But paradoxically, if some respondents blame the website for its social emptiness and seem to be longing for communication with others, many respondents also blame that social aspect of meeting and chatting with other people, because it could turn them away from their purchase goal, as if online shopping was considered as mainly utilitarian: "We turn away from the goal, we forget the purchase and we focus on the avatar. It becomes like a game in which we are walking... one meeting other avatars" (Nacera, female, 22).

Crete et al. (2008), in the only research dealing with consumer-avatar, studied its impact on a merchant website, through the use of a personalized avatar specific tool on a traditional 2D fictitious website, and demonstrated its positive influence on website perceived quality, attitude and stickiness. In that case, the consumer-avatar was mainly utilitarian: it was not used to wander in a fully 3D shop, and, as a consequence, was not considered as a potentially immersive and experiential cue, while in our case, consumer-avatar can be considered as a socializing asset of the website, enhancing perceived humanity as the consumer is represented in the e-shop and can socialize with other clients represented by their own avatars. Indeed, the physical sense of interacting with others should contributes to the experience of embodied perception (Joy and Sherry, 2003). Though, the question can be asked to what extent this is possible in a virtual worlds of avatars, as individuals can be embodied in multiple identities (real-life individual or multiple identities and roles, virtual identity(ies)). The lack of social realism encountered could also be related to the perception of a potentially blurred "social game" due to those identities issues.

With regards to those findings on identification, embodiment, self-projection and sensory realism on one hand and social realism on the other hand related to virtual experience and immersion on the 3D website, the proxy of the concept of presence, usually considered when dealing with immersion in a computer-mediated environment, emerges as the more relevant way to characterize the virtual experience and immersion through the eyes of an avatar.

Avatar and Presence. Presence refers to "a psychological state in which even though part or all of an individual's current experience is generated by/or filtered through human-made technology, part or all of the individual perception fails to accurately acknowledge the role of the technology in the experience" (ISPR, 2003): the individual has the perceptual illusion of non-mediation by technology (Lombard and Ditton, 1997) and feels deeply immerged in the experience. The feeling of presence (or telepresence, Steuer, 1992) is then seen as a basic condition for immersion or flow to develop. As stated by Van Schaik et al. (2004), realism associated with presence leads to immersion. Immersion can then be seen as a direct consequence of being present in the virtual world.

Lombard and Ditton (1997) distinguish two kinds of presence : (1) spatial presence, defined as "the extent to which a person feels his/her existence as rather located in the mediated space than in the real environment": the higher spatial presence is, the more the individual feels transported in the mediated place, the more he/she is attentive to stimuli from the mediated environment and less to those from the real environment (Csikszentmihalyi 1990); and (2) social presence, that refers to the sense of "being together with another", inducing perceptual awareness of other entities, access to their cognitive and affective states and a shared sense of intersubjective interaction (Bickmore and Picard, 2003): social presence can lead to "as if" para-social relationships (Lombard and Ditton, 1997).

On the one hand, with high spatial presence, an individual is supposed to behave as an actor and adopt behaviors as in the real world (Lombard and Ditton, 1997). In our case, as previously stated on embodiment, respondents seem to feel spectators of their avatar, experiencing a lack of coherence between their real actions (click to move) and what happens (hitting a shelf). They clearly don't perceive their existence in the virtual worl

d and express that their experience is an "as if" experience. "Precisely, the fact that we have an avatar, so as to take a walk in a store, make window-shopping, perhaps behave as a real client in real life" (Ouardia, female, 28). So, as in Jeandrain and Diesbach (2008), respondents reject the idea of full spatial presence.

On the other hand, as all consumers are humanly represented in the 3D shop, social presence should be enhanced. Indeed, avatars are implemented in order to humanize e-shopping and create a feeling of social interactions. But due to the lack of spatial presence, and despite the presence of a chat module, consumer-avatar doesn't seem to be an outstanding enough social cue, as it has been demonstrated for virtual communities (Yong et al., 2007): "The avatar will never replace someone, the opinion of a person or a friend" (Agathe, female, 22)

Nevertheless, a special interest emerged for EVA: all our respondents mentioned they were expecting or looking for a salesperson as the main social cue of the website. "Can I sit down here and wait for a saleswoman?" (Damien M., male, 29) "There are no saleswomen (...) A presence is missing." (Françoise, female, 54).

Those results are related to findings on the influence of EVA (Cassell et al., 2000; Holzwarth et al., 2006), especially on presence and immersion (Jeandrain et Diesbach, 2008). Though, results are contrasted: Jeandrain and Diesbach (2008) highlighted the negative impact of the EVA on social presence, while Wang et al. (2007) concluded on the positive impact of an EVA as a social cue on a shopping website.

CONCLUSION

Although we live in a three-dimensional world, nowadays most of the commercial websites are primarily in two dimensions. However, improving the virtual experience has become a major issue for e-marketers. As already stated, developing the hedonic value of websites and improving the virtual shopping experience on Internet should lead to a better conversion rate, more satisfaction, stickiness and loyalty (Childers et al., 2001). In this perspective, our findings are quite telling. In line with Malter, Antonio and Garbarino (2008) pointing the importance of the online avatar's realism and authentic representation of the real world, our work highlights the key role of the avatar and the concepts of presence (Steuer, 1992; Lombard and Ditton, 1997) and realism as basic conditions for immersion in the context of a 3D commercial website. Specifically, we bring to the light the importance of the avatar embodiment for consumer in merchant 3D environments and its influence on immersion as well as the importance of social presence. The context of interviews does not favour a natural situation of immersion and might explain why most respondents seem to feel spectators of their avatar and don't express the illusion of non-mediation that should make them actors. However, we observe interestingly that four of our respondents (Jean-Marc (male, 59), Emilie (female, 23), Medhi (male, 23) and Romain (male, 25) experienced a kind of immersion since they have interrupted the interviewer in order to further explore the website.

Perceived value is one of the essential outcomes of the marketing activity (Holbrook 1999). In this perspective, the retail experience,-in this case the commercial website visit, must deliver value so to turn a one-time visitor into a repeat customer. Both practitioners and researchers believe that the best way to gain customer loyalty is to ensure that customers have an "emotional" experience with products or service or in the retailing environment (Holbrook, 1999, Filser, 2002). Building on the work of Holt (1995), the 3D commercial website visit might be considered as a consumption activity in the sense of interaction with the consumption's object. Holt (1995, p.2) considers two dimensions of the consumption, structure and purpose: "In terms of structure, consuming consists both of actions in which consumers directly engage: consumption objects (object actions) and interactions with other people, in which consumption objects serve as focal resources (interpersonal actions). In terms of purpose, consumers' actions can be both ends in themselves (autotelic actions) and means to some further ends (instrumental actions)". In this two-by-two matrix, the value of the

3D commercial website might appear more as autotelic, consuming as a play (social presence, hedonic value of the experience) or as experience than instrumental. In this line, Jeandrain and Limbourg (2002) observed that experiential shoppers seem to prefer 3D online environments, whereas the instrumental shopper is less impressed by it. Therefore, the adding value seems to lay more in experiential retailing than in merchandise itself. As consumers are living more and more of their lives online, the possibility to interact with other consumers, to share experience of shopping represent an avenue of possible researches in order to understand how shared experiences on the web contribute to the perceived value of a commercial website as well as to consumer social relationships both online and offline.

Managerial consequences are multiples. The impact of the 3D commercial website has to be considered both directly in terms of direct sales but mainly indirectly in terms of consumers' community, image of the company and potential vector of transchannel behaviour of consumers. In the perspective of virtual malls, these two points appear as particularly prevalent. From a theoretical point of view, this research contributes to a better understanding of the virtual experience in a 3D commercial website context, pointing out the key role of the avatar. While technological development are outpacing consumers' ability to cope with developments, researchers are struggling to develop and apply appropriate models of consumer behaviour that would potentially enrich consumers participation in those new shopping environments. Research and managerial perspectives can be suggested, especially website configuration and display, above all concerning the view, and presence of an EVA and interactions with consumer-avatars.

Some limits can be highlighted. The study was realized mainly on one website, related to a specific product category. Victoria Couture is a high-range brand, with few physical shops, and this could have been a reason why few people were connected on the website, inducing a possible bias on social presence perception. The website is mainly designed for women, and though precautions have been taken with male respondents (they were asked to imagine they were buying something for a female friend/girlfriend/wife), this could have caused a bias in the perception and evaluation of the avatar. Our research qualitative method by interviews is not the most favourable for immersion, as respondents are forced to detachment and "go back to reality" to express their feelings and discuss with the interviewer. Finally, this paper, as stated previously, focuses on key issues around the role of avatar in the embodied experience and immersion. Other themes such as utilitarian vs hedonic aspects of shopping in this settings, identity role-playing in a social presence context, will have to be analyzed.

Research perspectives cover a wide area of confirmatory researches, both qualitative (deeper analyses to highlight specific patterns through speeches, new interviews with actual users, expert or future users such as teenagers who are used to 3D virtual universes ans games) and quantitative, through experiments, related to the consumer-avatar and its impact on presence and immersion, the influence of sensory (sight, hearing) display of the 3D environment on virtual experience. Perspectives in line with actual Human-Computer Interfaces research issues can also be considered: aesthetics in designing those 3D shopping interfaces and the link of aesthetics with experience, anthropomorphism (or fantasy) in avatar design, emotions and affect in 3D retailing-as an embodied experience can generate highly intense feelings. In fact, the present investigation has obviously just scratched the surface of an enormous iceberg.

REFERENCES

Bahorsky, Russ, Graber Jeffrey and Steve Mason (1998), *Official Internet Dictionary: A Comprehensive Reference for Professionals Reviews*. Portland: ABS Consulting.

Bickmore, Timothy W. and Rosalind W. Picard (2003), "Subtle Expressivity by Relational Agents", *Proceedings CHI 2003 Workshop on Subtle Expressivity for Characters and Robot*, April, Fort Lauderdale, USA, 15-18.

Burke, Raymond (1996), "Virtual Shopping: Breakthrough in Marketing Research", *Harvard Business Review*, March-April, 120-131.

Carù, Antonella and Bernard Cova (2003), "Approche Empirique de l'Immersion dans l'Experience de Consommation: Les Operations d'Appropriation", *Recherche et Applications en Marketing*, 18(2), 47-65.

Cassell, Justine, Timothy W. Bickmore, Lee Campbell, Hannes Vilhjalmsson and Hao Yan (2000), "More Than Just a Pretty Face: Affordances of Embodiment", *Proceedings of 2000 International Conference on Intelligent User Interfaces*, New Orleans, USA (online).

Childers, Terry, Chris Carr and Joan C. Peck (2001), "Hedonic and Utilitarian Motivations for Online Retail Shopping Behaviour", *Journal of Retailing*, 77(4), 511-35.

Crete, David, Anick Saint-Onge, Aurélie Merle, Nicolas Arsenault and Jacques Nantel (2008), "Personalized Avatar, a New Way to Improve Communication and E-Services", *Proceedings of the 37th EMAC Conference*, Brighton, UK (CD-Rom).

Csikszentmihalyi, Mihaly (1990), *Flow: The Psychology of Optimal Experience*, New York : H & Row.

Evrard, Yves, Eliette Roux and Bernard Pras (2003), *Market : Etudes et Recherches en Marketing, 3rd ed.*, Paris: Nathan.

Filser Marc (2002), "Le Marketing de la production d'expérience: Statut théorique et implications managériales", *Décisions Marketing*, 28, 13-23.

Fornerino, Marianela, Agnès Helme-Guizon and David Gotteland (2006), "Mesurer L'immersion dans Une Expérience De Consommation : Premiers Développements", *Proceeding of the 22nd Conference of French Marketing Association*, Nantes (online).

Galan, Jean-Philippe and Agnès Helme-Guizon (2003), "L'utilisation de La Musique Comme Elément De l'Atmosphere Des Sites Web: Considérations Techniques Et Théoriques", *6ème Colloque Etienne Thil sur la Distribution*, La Rochelle, France (CD-Rom).

Ghose, Sanjoy and Wenyou Dhou (1998), "Interactive Functions and Their Impacts on the Appeal of Internet Presence Sites", *Journal of Advertising Research*, 38(2), 29-43.

Halfhill, Tom R. (1996), "Agents and Avatars", *Byte*, 21 (February), 69–72.

Helme-Guizon, Agnès (2001), "Le Comportement Du Consommateur Sur Un Site Marchand Est-Il Fondamentalement Différent De Son Comportement En Magasin? ", *Recherche et Applications en Marketing*, 16(3), 25-37.

Hirschman, Elizabeth C. and Morris B. Holbrook (1982), "Hedonic Consumption: Emerging Concepts, Methods and Propositions", *Journal of Marketing*, 46(3), 92-101.

Hoffman, Donna L. and Thomas P. Novak (1996), "Marketing in Hypermedia Computer-Mediated Environments: Conceptual Foundations", *Journal of Marketing Research*, 60(July), 50-68.

Holbrook Morris B. (1999), Consumer Value. A framework for Analysis and Research, Londres and New York, NY, Routledge.

Holt, Douglas B. (1995), "How Consumers Consume: A Typology Of Consumption Practices", *Journal of Consumer Research*, 22(1), 1-16.

Holzwarth, Martin, Chris Janiszewski and Marcus M. Neumann (2006), "The Influence of Avatar on Online Consumer Shopping Behavior", *Journal of Marketing*, 70(October), 19-36.

International Society for Presence Research (2003). The Concept of Presence: Explication Statement. Available at http://ispr.info [Date accessed: 04.12.08]

Jeandrain, Anne-Cécile and Brice-Pablo Diesbach (2008), "Immersion In An Online Merchant Environment: Are Consumers Ready To Feel Their Presence In Such Environment?", *Proceedings of the 37th EMAC Conference*, Brighton, UK (CD-Rom).

Jeandrain, Anne-Cécile and Quentin Limbourg (2002), "On Application Of Virtual Environments To Marketing", *Proceedings of Virtual Reality Concept 2003 Symposium*, November, Biarritz, France, 325-32.

Jolibert, Alain and Philippe Jourdan (2006), *Marketing Research*, Paris: Dunod

Joy, Annama and John F. Sherry Jr (2003), "Speaking of Art as Embodied Imagination: A Multisensory Approach to Understanding Aesthetic Experience", *Journal of Consumer Research*, 30, 2, 259-82.

Keeling Kathleen and Peter J. McGoldrick (2008), "Relationship with a Byte ? Attractions, Interaction and Intention for Avatar use a retail website", in *Advances in Consumer Research Volume 35*, eds. Angela Y. Lee and Dilip Soman, Duluth, MN : Association for Consumer Research, Pages: 84-89.

Lombard, Matthew and Theresa B. Ditton (1997), "At The Heart Of It All: The Concept Of Presence", *Journal of Computer-Mediated Communication*, 3(2), (online).

Loos, Peter (2003), "Avatar", in *Lexicon Electronic Business*, ed. Thomas Schildhauer, Munich: Oldenbourg, 16-19.

Malhotra, Naresh (1999), *Marketing Research, an applied orientation*, 3rd ed., NJ: Prentice Hall

Malter Alan J., Rosa José Antonio, Ellen C. Garbarino (2008), « Using Virtual Models to Evaluate Real Products for Real Bodies », in *Advances in Consumer Research Volume 35*, eds. Angela Y. Lee and Dilip Soman, Duluth, MN: Association for Consumer Research, Pages 87-88.

Mathwick, Charla, Naresh Malhotra and Edward Rigdon (2001), "Experiential Value: Conceptualization, Measurement And Application In The Catalog And Internet Shopping Environment", *Journal of Retailing*, 77(1), 511-35.

Merleau-Ponty, Maurice (1962), Phenomenology of Perception, trans. Colin Smith. London: Kegan Paul.

Morgan, DL (1998), *The Focus Group Guidebook*, Thousand Oaks, CA : Sage Publications

Novak, Thomas P., Donna L. Hoffman and Yiu-Fai Yung (2000), "Measuring the Flow Construct in Online Environment: A Structural Modeling Approach", *Marketing Science*, 19(1), 22-44.

Peng, Wei (2008), "The Mediational Role of Identification in the Relationship between Experience Mode and Self-Efficacy: Enactive Role-Playing versus Passive Observation," *CyberPsychology & Behavior*, 11(6), 649-52.

Rosenblom, Andrew (2003), "A Game Experience in Every Application", *Communications of the ACM*, 46(7), 28-31.

Shang, Ron-An, Yu-Chen Chen and Lysander Shen (2005), "Extrinsic versus intrinsic motivations for consumers to shop on-line", *Information and Management*, 42(3), 401-13.

Slater, Mel and Sylvia Wilbur (1997), "A Framework for Immersive Virtual Environments (FIVE): Speculations on the Role of Presence in Virtual Environments", *Presence: Teleoperators and Virtual Environments*, 8, 560-65.

Steuer, Jonathan (1992), "Defining Virtual Reality: Dimensions Determining Telepresence", *Journal of Communication*, 42(4), 73-93.

Tisseron, Serge (2008), *Virtuel Mon Amour: Penser, Aimer, Souffrir, A l'Ere Des Nouvelles Technologies*, Paris : Albin Michel.

Tomaseti, Eva, Salvador Ruiz and Nina Reynolds (2009), "Flow and Attitude toward the website on the evaluation of products present by means of virtual reality: a conceptual model" in *Advances in Consumer Research, Volume 36*, eds. Ann L. McGill and Sharon Shavitt, Duluth, MN : Association for Consumer Research

Ulusoy, Ebru and Handan Vicdan (2009), "Bodily Experiences of Second Life Consumers (37:04)", in *Advances in Consumer Research, Vol. 36*, eds Ann L. McGill and Sharon Shavitt, MN: Association for Consumer Research.

Van Schaik, Paul, Triece Turnbull, Anna Van Wersch and Sarah Drummond (2004), "Presence Within a Mixed Reality Environment", *CyberPsychology & Behavior*, 7(5), 540-52.

Venkatesh Alladi (1998), "Special Session Summary virtual spaces as consumer environments: theoretical and applied issues", in *Advances in Consumer Research Volume 25*, eds. Joseph W. Alba & J. Wesley Hutchinson, Provo, UT : Association for Consumer Research, Pages 60-61

Volle, Pierre (2000). "Du Marketing Des Points De Vente à Celui Des Sites Marchands : Spécificités, Opportunités et Questions de Recherche", *Revue Française du Marketing*, 177/178, 83-100.

Yong, Jin Kim, Jeff Baker and Jaeki Song (2007), "An Exploratory Study Of Social Factors Influencing Virtual Community Members' Satisfaction With Avatars", *Communications of the Association for Information Systems*, 20, 567-93.

Wang, Liz C., Julie Baker, Judy A. Wagner and Kirk Wakefield (2007), "Can a Retail Website be Social?", *Journal of Marketing*, 71(July), 143-57.

Whalen, Thomas E., Dorina C. Petriu, Lucy Yang, Emil E. Petriu and Marius D. Cordea (2003), "Capturing Behaviour for the Use of Avatars in Virtual Environments", *CyberPsychology & Behavior*, 6(3), 537-44.

Wood, Nathalie T., Michael R. Solomon and Basil G. Englis (2005), "Personalization of Online Avatars: Is the Messenger as Important as the Message?", *International Journal of Internet Marketing and Advertising*, 2(1/2), 143-61.

Wood, Nathalie T., Michael R. Solomon and David Allan (2008), "Welcome to The Matrix: E-Learning Gets a Second Life", *Marketing Education Review*, 20, 2, 47-53.

Developing Brand Literacy among Affluent Chinese Consumers
A Semiotic Perspective

Laura R. Oswald, University of Illinois, USA

ABSTRACT

In this paper, I focus on a form of consumer acculturation I call "brand literacy," e.g. the ability of consumers in emerging markets to acquire and manipulate the codes structuring brand meaning as it is communicated in advertising signs and symbols, retail spaces, and packaging. I base this theoretical inquiry on early stage findings from an ethnography of affluent consumers in Shanghai (2007-2008). Findings suggest that Chinese consumers purchase luxury goods such as watches, bags, and cosmetics, without tapping into the deep, emotional, and imaginary worlds that create value for European luxury brands. Respondents in Shanghai tended to collapse brand distinctions into a somewhat generic association of all luxury brands with high price, status, and distinction. They claimed that luxury purchases did not express their own personalities, and that luxury advertising fell short of helping them personalize their brands. I contend that acquiring the rather sophisticated codes necessary to read and integrate brand discourses resembles language learning, because brand literacy, like language acquisition, is structured by cultural codes and follows specific stages of acquisition. I develop a structural semiotics approach to brand "literacy," and suggest ways that advertising may contribute to this type of acculturation process.

INTRODUCTION

In this paper I develop a theory of brand literacy that accounts for the stages involved in the acquisition of fluency in reading and internalizing brand meanings. This research has particular resonance for consumers in developing markets, such as the People's Republic of China, who may be the first or second generation of consumers to purchase branded products instead of trading vouchers for commodities. Findings have implications for consumer acculturation theory, advertising research, and brand management.

Drawing upon structural semiotics, I approach brands as discourses that are structured by codes. Since semiotic codes are rooted in cultural conventions similar to language, they offer a window onto the mechanisms involved in meaning exchange across cultural borders. In this paper I examine early stage findings from in-depth consumer research with 16 affluent consumers in Shanghai between 2007 and 2008, on the topic of luxury brand consumption. The study was limited to research on European fashion categories, from leather goods to couture, watches, and cosmetics. Consumers discussed their own experiences of luxury, their understanding of Chinese luxury traditions, their perception of European brands, and their interpretation of brand communication in magazine advertisements for global brands such as Louis Vuitton, Dior, and Patek Philippe.

Early stage findings suggest that Chinese consumers stop short of identifying the emotional associations that distinguish luxury brands from each other and as a result, often lack a visceral, personal connection to the brands they purchase. Since brand value on the marketplace is founded on nothing less than the personal and emotional associations consumers associate with brands, these findings have serious implications for the growth of the European luxury sector and also raise important questions about brands in translation, consumer cultures in contact, and the limits of consumer assimilation to global consumer culture.

Findings Summary

The next generation of the new rich in China expect more of luxury brands than to display their money and success. They expect luxury brands to both express and inform their savoir faire, personality, and taste. They also expect advertising to assist them in learning how to "read" and appreciate brand meanings. Respondents moving up the economic ladder with their new MBA's and rich husbands consistently expressed disappointment with their expensive purchases because they did not identify with the persona of the brand or the emotional dimensions of luxury that were suggested in luxury advertising. They had trouble making qualitative distinctions between luxury brands and failed to connect with brands in a "visceral" way (Wetlaufer 2001). Though they sought brands that would reflect their personalities, the brands they bought did not satisfy this need. Their luxury bags and shoes did not extend their personal identities much beyond the meanings of 'status' and *savoir faire*. Several respondents reported losing interest in their LV bags once they got them home, leaving them in the closet with indifference. As the goods piled up in their closets, these same consumers expressed strong interest in finding a "match" with a brand that satisfied their need for self-expression and met their expectations, fueled by advertising, that luxury consumption would enrich their fantasy life.

Consumers struggled to move beyond the somewhat generic interpretation of luxury brands as "expensive" and "high quality." They also interpreted luxury through the lens of Confucian values, associating luxury consumption with a noble character and, ironically, the simple life.

THE HISTORICAL CONTEXT

Specific historical and ideological conditions in China have interfered with local traditions of luxury, not only since the victory of Communism in 1949, but as one author suggests (Xiou 2008), for the past 150 years, as the result of colonial invasions, wars, and the frugal ideology of Confucianism. Most recently, luxury traditions and values were repressed by Mao Tse Dong, who tortured rich property owners, destroyed or stole their luxury possessions, and banished them to the countryside during the Cultural Revolution.

This may explain why respondents did not draw upon local traditions and values related to luxury as means of interpreting and assessing the meaning and value of European luxury brands. The signs and symbols of luxury represented in European ads were thus meanings that lacked a referent in a deep, context-rich experience of luxury. As a result, consumer responses to European luxury focused on the most general meanings of luxury, such as price. In linguistic terms, their responses betrayed tensions between the meaning and reference of brand symbolism. The CG logo may signify success, because they are so well known, etc. But these brands do not conjure up any emotional experience, fantasy, or image that the consumer can relate to. Consumers struggle to find a brand that links brand symbolism to their personal values, lifestyles, and fantasies.

Barriers to identification

The same respondents seemed to have less difficulty assimilating the meaning of goods in other product categories, such as household goods. I discuss further on the case of one respondent who had adopted lock, stock, and barrel what I call the "Good Housekeeping" consumer culture of the West, including Kohler kitchens and baths, a child centric household, and a self-effacing yet stylish demeanor. Other researchers also report that in categories such as spirits and tourism, managers have been able to forge transnational brand identities by means of advertising that plays with contrasts and similarities among national identities and values (see Cayla and Eckhardt 2008).

Thus history and ideology have diminished the meaning and value of luxury in the popular consciousness. As a result, consumers grasped the general meanings of luxury, such as "expensive," "successful," and "royal" ("like the British royal family"). They also interpreted luxury through the lens of Confucianism, a philosophy that values personal virtues and filial piety over materialism. Several respondents actually stated that people who purchased luxury fashion brands were probably "took care of their parents." Luxury brands can also make other people happy.

BRAND LITERACY

In semiotic perspective, I claim that the acquisition of brand literacy follows a course similar to the acquisition and of language and is regulated by semiotic codes. I focus in particular on the work of Russian linguist Roman Jakobson. I then extrapolate the theories of language acquisition and cognition to the realm of social semiotics and the acquisition of the cultural codes that enable consumers to understand what each luxury brand "means." Moreover, rather than simply take the European meaning of luxury at face value, the brand literate consumer would be able to manipulate the luxury codes in ways that would enable them to transform brand meanings from a foreign culture into their own personal brand experiences. The purpose of this investigation is to find out what stands in the way of brand literacy for Chinese affluents in this sector, and to suggest ways that marketers could improve this process through changes in current marketing strategy.

Barriers to Acceptance

To summarize, research findings suggest that several factors inhibit Chinese consumers' ability to make qualitative distinctions between brands and to use luxury brands to express their personal tastes or "extend" their personas (Belk 1988). They include:

- Misleading assumptions about the meaning and function of luxury for Chinese consumers. Bourke (1996) and Calya & Eckardt (2008) show that the acculturation of consumers in emerging markets depends upon a two-way understanding and appreciation of the complex cultural systems of the brand culture on the one hand, and the local consumer culture on the other, for successful brand adoption.
- Over-reliance on the single-image luxury magazine ad by marketers. As Bourke (1996) demonstrates in his analysis of consumer acculturation in Zimbabwe, an array of marketing events, including in-home demonstrations and personal selling, contribute to the acculturation process.
- Insufficient contextualization of the brand–not to mention the luxury category in general-in the culture of consumers.
- Lack of an account of cultural differences in the way Asians, as opposed to Westerners, interpret the world of meaning in general.

LITERATURE REVIEW

The current paper fills a gap in the literature on consumer acculturation, brand meaning, and advertising by proposing a theoretical account of the ways consumers learn how to read brands and acquire "brand literacy" over time. (Otnes and Scott 1996, Hirschman et al 1998, McCracken 1986, Sherry and Camargo 1987; McQuarrie and Mick 1999; Mick 1986, Mick and Buhl 1992; Stern 2007, Fournier 1998, Grayson and Schulman 2000, Cook 2004, Douglas and Isherwood 1996/1976, Belk 1988, Hirschman et al 1989, Sherry and Camargo 1987). The question of brand literacy may seem moot in developed markets such as North America, even though it applies to advanced consumer cultures as well. Brand literacy has obvious consequences in developing economies, where individuals may still be learning to become consumers, relate to advertising, and make brand choices based on the strengths of advertising to communicate the benefits of one brand over another.

Sherry (1987, p.456) first referenced the idea of brand literacy in an essay in *Marketing and Semiotics*, using the term 'illiterati' to reference consumers in developing consumer societies targeted by advertising. Sherry emphasizes the role of advertising in the dialectical process of consumer acculturation, as advertising forms a site for communicating messages and also for consumers to project their own meanings into the advertisement. Sherry anticipated the cultural tensions that globalization would foster as consumer culture expanded beyond its western borders, encountering deeply entrenched indigenous cultures in its wake.

The issue of brand literacy might suggest to some that consumers in the developing world should "learn the dominant language," and assimilate into global consumer culture. To the contrary, I contend that developing markets are more likely to resist cultural hegemony by becoming brand literate, inasmuch as brand literacy does not stop at teaching consumers how to 'read' western culture, but enables consumers to manipulate cultural codes along the lines of local values, meanings, and priorities.

The researcher seeking to understand *how* brands mean must consider advertising as a medium for moderating the intersection of cultures in contact and for potentially providing a guidebook for translating brand meanings from one cultural system to another. As findings from the current ethnography suggest, translating brands is a dialectical process moderated by the intersection of the marketing message and the perceptions of consumers. Our research suggests that consumers in developing markets are not likely to be assimilated easily or completely into a monolithic global consumer culture, because they either fail to link the signs in the ads with anything beyond the literal meaning, or filter these messages through the lens of local values and ideology and misconstrue the brand meaning altogether.

Becoming a Consumer in China. The current study stands out from the current literature on consumer acculturation in Asia, by deriving insights from speaking directly with consumers about their brand perceptions. Extant research relies primarily on inferences from advertising analysis (Zhou and Belk 2004). Notable and worthy examples include Zhao and Belk (2008a, 2008b), who analyze communication strategies for resolving tensions between the Communist egalitarian ideology and consumer spending in Chinese advertising; Cayla and Eckhardt (2008), who examine advertising strategies that leverage common goals and cultural distinctions among regional Asian cultures to create a pan-Asian consumer culture; and Tse et al (1989) who infer cultural and ideological differences among consumers in the PRC, Taiwan, and Hong Kong, by means of a content analysis of advertisements in those locations. Such studies are based on the assumption that advertising is a "cultural system" that reflects the needs and wants of consumers in the marketplace (see Sherry 1987). However, such studies do not account for the complexity of the cognitive and cultural processes involved in reading and internalizing brands.

Consumer Acculturation. The current study advances the literature on consumer acculturation in several ways. It extends Cook's (2004) work on the acculturation of children into consumer culture by breaking down the consumer acculturation process into stages of acquisition, internalization, and implementation of brand awareness and identity. By drawing parallels between brand literacy and language acquisition, I show how brand literacy develops in stages and is influenced by social, educational, and marketing variables. I extend Schroeder's work on visual culture by foregrounding the role of cultural codes to structure the way consumers unite in a kind of collective imagination around the brand. I even place in question the tendency of marketers in the West, most notably in the luxury sector, to privilege vision over the other senses, which may form a barrier to acceptance among consumers of other cultures.

Advertising Research. My approach also advances extant research on advertising communication. First, I approach brands as discourses structured, like language, by codes and modeled after structural semiotics. These semiotic codes account for the ability of consumers to share meanings communicated in advertising. Second, I focus on consumers in emerging markets who do not automatically "speak the language: of Western consumer culture. Third, I study the acquisition of brand literacy in diachronic perspective, highlighting the stages consumers must pass through in order to understand the depth and breadth of meanings associated with brands.

1. *Brands as discourses.* The advertising research literature abounds with theories of the ways consumers interpret meanings, from content analysis to reader response theory and semiotics. However, most studies make inferences about the question of advertising as a language based on the effects of advertising on consumers, rather than on analysis of the codes structuring meaning production in the brand discourse (Mick and Buhl 1992; Scott 1994; Hirschman et al 1998; Scott and Vargas 2008). The argument goes something like this: if consumers all agree on the meaning of an ad, or change their behavior because of a marketing campaign, then, by a logic of cause and effect, the advertisement must be structured like a language.

2. *Multi-Cultural Research.* The extant research has been conducted mainly with mainstream American consumers who have high fluency in reading brand discourses because American culture is inseparable from consumer culture. In emerging markets, consumers must translate Western brands into terms that have meaning and relevance for their values, ideology, and history. Research that is limited to consumers in developed markets take for granted that we all speak the same "language" when it comes to understanding the codes shaping symbolic consumption. Symbolic consumption is structured by sophisticated, culture-specific rules that transform commodities into meaning-systems that consumers learn to love. Cross-cultural advertising research sheds light on meaning exchange between cultures in contact and draws attention to semiotic and cognitive processes that transform goods into meanings in any social context.

3. *Brand Literacy in Diachronic Perspective.* Previous approaches to the question of how consumers make meanings of advertising have focused on the synchronic structure of individual ads and consumers' readings of them. Findings from an ethnographic study of affluent consumers in Shanghai suggest that consumers in emerging markets pass through various stages of brand literacy in order to identify and identify with the precise meanings and worlds associated with brands. I therefore approach brand literacy from a diachronic perspective, in order to account for specific stages of literacy acquisition.

Stages of Brand Literacy

During the fieldwork I identified three consumer segments based on their readiness to interpret brand meanings represented in western ads for luxury brands. The stages in this process include: 1. a literal reading of the message, e.g. Louis Vuitton is a famous luxury brand from France, 2. a nuanced reading of connotations associated with the message by reference to a context e.g. wearing Louis Vuitton communicates that I have *savoir faire* and participate in the global luxury culture), and 3. internalization of the brand message and wearing the brand to express or extend one's self-construction and culture. Each stage of this literacy acquisition process involves distinct semiotic operations. They include deciphering the literal meaning of a brand message; reading the nuances and connotations of the message; and relating the message to the context, including the mindsets of consumers.

The Role of Advertising. Degree of brand literacy was associated with several social factors, including 1) travel to advanced consumer societies, including Hong Kong, 2) the kind of work one did (the housewife was more knowledgeable about household brands, 3) a passion for design and luxury, which prompted respondents to find out more about the luxury category and culture. However, I am more interested in the ways western luxury advertising may create barriers to brand literacy by failing to relate brand meanings in a single ad to a cultural context that has relevance for affluent consumers in developing consumer markets. For example, while marketers might use personal selling, shopping mall tutorials, and other non-traditional media to educate consumers about a category or brand, luxury marketers rely to a great extent on the single magazine photograph. Luxury advertising isolates the brand from the lived context and experience of consumers and privileges visual culture over other forms of communication. Both of these factors present barriers to acceptance for Chinese consumers.

A Semiotic Perspective

The very notion of brand literacy is grounded in the assumption that non-linguistic sign systems such as advertising are structured like language, by means of codes or conventions that are embedded in the culture of consumers. Structural semiotics, like linguistics, offers a rigorous, repeatable methodology for analyzing the codes underlying the structure of meaning and reference to the cultural context in discourses such as advertising and consumer behavior. Semiotics has the advantage over content analysis by identifying objective criteria such as codes, rhetorical operations, and other formal dimensions, that transcend the content of the message itself and point to structural systems, patterns, and rules that bring order and meaning to phenomena under the rubric of culture,

Structural semiotics transcends its origins in Russian Formalism (Lemon and Reis 1965) by moving beyond the simple formal analysis of texts and taking account of the implication of form and meaning in a given cultural context, such as the family meal. Though meals have a beginning, middle, and end, the meal preparation, the disposition of the family members around the table, and the foods brought to the table are inseparable from the cultural values, priorities, and traditions of the family.

The notion that discourses are structured both by the internal organization of signs and external references to the context of the communication originates with the linguistic theories of Swiss linguist Ferdinand de Saussure ((1983/1971/1913) in the 19th century. It has been refined and expanded over the years by experts in the areas of semantics and culture theory. They emphasize the importance not only of the structure of discourse but the reference of discourse to the context of the communication.

Brand literacy operates both on the level of the *structural* meaning of signs–their literal, "dictionary meaning," and the *semantic* meaning of signs formed by the relation of the dictionary meaning to the context of discourse. Writers such as Eco (1979), Greimas (1983/1966), and Benveniste 1971) extend structural semiotics by emphasizing that discourses are not only meaningful because of the codes structuring the coherence of the sign system itself, but the semantic codes that embed discourses in the context of the communication event. Irony is a good example of the importance of context. The utterance, "What a beautiful day!" taken at face value, signifies meanings associated with good weather. When someone utters this same statement in order to remark on yet another cold and rainy day in Detroit, the meaning becomes an ironic comment on the bad weather. In other words, two distinct levels of semiotic organization–the internal structure of signs and the reference to a semantic context, drive meaning production.

The distinction between the meaning and reference of discourse, we shall see, has great importance for understanding the dynamics of brand literacy. Though I will elaborate in more detail on this dynamic further on, suffice it to say that consumers must be able to not only understand the meaning of brand signifiers (e.g. "This is an expensive brand.")-but relate them to the semantic context of the brand world, the product category, and their own lifestyles (e.g. "This brand expresses my desire to be youthful, reckless, and sexy."). It is precisely the inability of consumers in this study to relate luxury European brands to their own lifestyles that forms a barrier to differentiating, personalizing, and choosing one brand over another.

Levels of Meaning

Brand literacy affects various levels of brand semiotics, from the logo to the broad system of associations brands communicate over time. These levels include

- Denotation, or the literal association of a signifier with a signified, the way logos stand for the company. The CC logo references the Coco Chanel brand.
- Connotation, the association of a signifier with an esthetic signified, such as the association of the logo with the brand's quality, positioning, and benefits for consumers. The sign /CC/ stands for exclusivity, high status, and classic beauty;
- Symbolism, the association of brand signifiers, from the logo to celebrity endorsers, with the brand culture and identity. The Chanel woman is classic, intelligent, assertive, and sophisticated.

THE SEMIOTICS OF LUXURY ADVERTISING

In this section I reproduce an exercise I use in the classroom to initiate students into the practice of semiotic analysis. It involves sorting, classifying, and analyzing brand distinctions in a set of advertisements for luxury perfume. The exercise displays the complexity of the semiotic systems at work in advertising that contribute to brand distinctiveness, appeal, and cultural relevance, all of which contribute to the value of brands. It also defines the parameters of the kinds of meanings that consumers, with some prodding, can identify in advertisements. Students in the West are able rather quickly to enter into the analysis of the ads, highlighting a range of semiotic operations and levels of meaning that structure differences and similarities between major brands and contributed to consumer distinctions between brands as personalities. However, most respondents in Shanghai produced a limited repertoire of emotional associations with the advertisements, which led to their difficulty differentiating one brand from the other on the basis of qualitative values.

Luxury perfume advertisements are distinct from everyday brands inasmuch as they reinforce the fantasy of the woman set apart from the mundane details associated with shopping and saving money. A quick binary sort of the ads produced a binary set of images: one set used only black and white, the other stack only used color photography. The black and white ads employed metonymy to engage the spectator in the narrative depicted in the image — we see a part of a story and must fill in the details; the color ads employed metaphor to make comparisons between the perfume and the feminine icon in the image. Further analysis revealed a paradigmatic set of of oppositions beginning with rhetorical style and extending to the kinds of characters, their points of view in the image, the camera angles, and cultural cues. (Figure 1)

Branding Cultural Myths

Like works of art, luxury brands tap into the myths and icons of culture, and promise the consumer access to transcendent experiences such as beauty, limitless wealth, and immortality. Since perfume itself is ephemeral and impermanent, the brand benefits of the luxury perfume category are entirely based on the delivery of intangible esthetic associations of the brands with idealized representations of women at personal, social, and existential levels of discourse. The strategic question, then, was how different luxury brands were positioned with reference to the question, "What is Woman?"

Though a longer account would draw attention to the broad and complex range of meanings communicated in the ads in this exercise, this limited discussion highlights how, with some probing, consumers make sense of advertising, reference advertising to build an image or personality for specific brands, and acquire preferences and emotional attachments to some brands rather than others.

This cursory analysis nonetheless highlights the difficulties consumers in non-Western markets might have to enter into this semiotic game, missing the nuances and emotional meanings that define brand equity and identity. Though even undergraduate students in the United States are able to identify the semiotic dimensions of these ads to some extent, respondents in Shanghai displayed, to varying degrees, limited abilities to elaborate upon the distinctions among brands or the cultures represented by these brands. Such consumer responses to advertising are symptomatic of a deep divide between the culture of the target market and the culture of the brand, and threaten the perceived value of the brand for these consumers.

The Structure of Literacy

Russian linguist and semiotician Roman Jakobson (1956/1990) discovered that language literacy occurred in stages and that not all people followed these stages in the same way. By studying the stages of language loss experienced by aphasics and comparing findings with the stages children pass through to in language acquisition, Jakobson developed a binary schema for mapping the literacy process in terms of a double axis formed by associations by similarity (the paradigm or set of all possible replacements) and associations by contiguity (the syntagm or concatenation of all terms in a given message). These semiotic structures, in Jakobson's schema, parallel cognitive operations of substitution and alignment in the mind.

Jakobson also identified two distinct types of aphasia, distinguished by the relative emphasis on the ability to create associations by similarity and the ability to create associations by contiguity. He

FIGURE 1
Positioning the Feminine

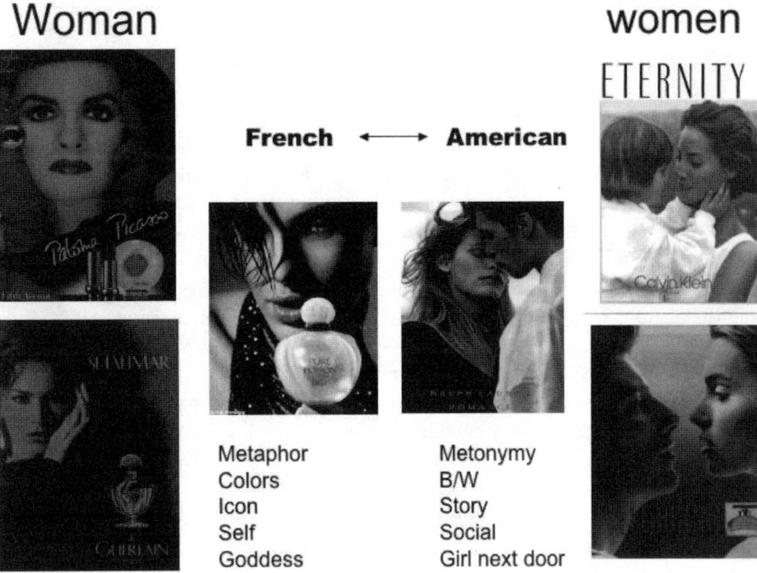

finds that one set of aphasics gradually loses the ability to combine signs on the basis of their similarity–they can define a word, for instance, but they cannot replace it with something like it, as in the paradigmatic association of a knife with similar tools using a blade. The other set of aphasics gradually loses the ability to combine signs on the basis of their contiguity–their logical or physical association with each other, as in the linear or syntagmatic association of the table knife with all other utensils in a serving set.

In typical Structuralist fashion, Jakobson extrapolates these findings about two types of aphasic disturbances to a general theory of "two aspects of language" that account for non-linguistic forms of literacy associated with cultural systems other than language, such as prose and poetry.

Jakobson's schema has important implications for consumer acculturation and brand literacy because it enables the researcher to separate the broad associations consumers make between a brands in the paradigmatic set defined by a product category, such as all luxury brands, and the unique associations they make between the brand and other meanings, rituals, and symbols on the syntagmatic axis, associations that distinguish it from other brands in the category. By mapping consumer responses to brands on these two axes, we are able to identify sites of semiotic productivity and resistance in relation to the luxury category.

In the present, Chinese context, we could say that affluent consumers seem better able to associate one brand with others in the paradigmatic set of all luxury brands, but have limited ability to find syntagmatic associations between a single brand and the meanings, rituals, and personal identities that contribute to the brand's positioning in the marketplace. The inhibition of consumers' ability to generate rich associations with the brand on the syntagmatic axis is symptomatic of low brand performance in this market, due perhaps to cultural barriers between the way Western luxury is communicated in advertising and the way Chinese consumers experience these messages.

The Limits of Structural Semiotics

Though it is important to know that there are broad mental operations governing the association of semiotic units in discourses, there are limitations to Jakobson's structural system. Though he defines the structural parameters shaping the acquisition of language (semiotic) literacy, his approach does not account for the role of the cultural context in this process. This criticism forms a dividing line between structuralism and post-structuralism in semiotic theory, because as it stands Jakobson's approach defines an ideal world of language, rather than language exposed to the instability and play of speakers/consumers as they navigate cross-cultural contexts.

I propose to extend Jakobson's binary system of discourse by including a third term, the relationship of the isolated meaning of a statement and references to the cultural context of the communication event. For it is at this juncture that advertising in the European luxury sector falls short. It takes for granted the unity of luxury signifier and signified in a single vision of luxury culture, fails to establish the cultural parameters which provide depth and breadth of associations between the brand and the world of luxury, and fails in its larger purpose of negotiating differences between the codes of western luxury and the values, beliefs, ideology and history of luxury consumers in emerging economies.

Implications for Advertising Strategy

The brand literacy of consumers in these growth economies has important economic implications, not only for particular companies but for the global economy, inasmuch as brands grow in value to the extent that consumers understand brand messages about the perception of quality, develop loyal relationships with brands, and expand the meanings of brands into personal associations (Aaker 1991, Fournier 1996, Yankelovich1964).

Economic Implications

Luxury manufacturers in the West rely on the double-digit growth in emerging markets such as China. Revenues for LVMH have declined steadily since 2006, reflecting not only the global economic downturn, but declining brand value in this sector. While the first generation new rich in China may have been content to show off famous, expensive brand names even if they did not connect with them on emotional levels, the newer generation of affluent consumers may seek other outlets for their luxury purchases because the current brands do not satisfy their needs for brand relationship and self-expression. Perhaps the models do not communicate the values and distinctions Chinese consumers expect of luxury goods. Advertising plays a role here, since advertising has the ability to link brand identity with the culture of consumers by means of multi-cultural signs and symbols (Sherry 1989; Cayla and Eckhardt 2008). Perhaps luxury advertisers should follow the lead of marketers in other categories, abandoning the assumption that luxury transcends time and culture (Wetlaufer 2001) and finding ways of weaving their brands into the lives of Chinese consumers. Perhaps they should follow the lead of the Louis Vuitton "Journey" campaign and feature notable celebrities in advertising that speak to the moral values and beliefs the Chinese associate with luxury, not just their fashion appeal. (On the role of celebrity endorsers and consumer morality, see Wicks et al. 2007).

Advertisers may err in assuming that Chinese consumers already know the 'rules of the road' relating to luxury goods, rituals, and culture. With the market opening in China in the 1980's, global advertising has the potential to exceed its marketing function and serve as a moderator for consumer acculturation in relation to western representations of luxury. Moderating consumer acculturation means strengthening the relevance and intensity of the emotional and cultural connections Chinese consumers make with Western brands and consumer rituals, thereby growing loyalty and future growth in the European luxury sector.

REFERENCES

Aaker, David A. (1991), *Managing Brand Equity*, New York, Free Press.

Belk, Russell (1988), "Possessions and the Extended Self," *Journal of Consumer Research*, Vol. 15, pp. 139-168.

Benveniste, Emile (1971/1966), *Problems in General Linguistics,* translated from French by Mary Elizabeth Meek Coral Gables, FL: University of Miami Press.

Burke, Timothy (1996), *Lifebuoy Men, Lux Women: Commodification, Consumption and Cleanliness in Modern Zimbabwe*, Durham and London: Duke University Press.

Cayla, Julien and Giana M. Eckhardt (2008), "Asian Brands and the Shaping of a Transnational Imagined Community," *Journal of Consumer Research*, 35, pp. 216-230.

Cook, Daniel Thomas (2003); Spatial Biographies of Children's Consumption: Market Places and Spaces of Childhood in the 1930s and Beyond, *Journal of Consumer Culture*, Vol, 3; 147–169.

Douglas, Mary and Baron Isherwood (1996), *The World of Goods*, New York: Routledge.

Eco, Umberto (1979), *Theory of Semiotics*, Bloomington: Indiana University Press.

Fournier, Susan (1996), "Consumers and their Brands: Developing Relationship Theory in Consumer Research," *Journal of Consumer Research*, Vol. 24, March, 343-373.

Goffman, Erving (1956) *The Presentation of Self in Everyday Life*, New York: Anchor Press.

Grayson, Kent and David Shulman (2000), "Indexicality and the verification function of irreplaceable possessions: A semiotic analysis," *Journal of Consumer Research* 27 (June), 17-30.

Greimas, Algirdas Julien (1983/1966), *Structural Semantics: An Attempt at a Method*, translated by Ronald Schleifer, Daniele McDowell, and Alan Velie.

Harvey, Michael and Malcolm Evans (2001), "Decoding competitive Propositions: a Semiotic Alternative to Traditional Advertising Research," *International Journal of Market Research*, Vol 43, pp. 171-187.

Hirschman, Barbara, Linda Scott, and William B. Wells (1998), "A Model of Product Discourse: Linking Consumer Practice to Cultural Texts, *Journal of Advertising*, Vol. 27, no. 1, Spring, pp. 33-49

Holt, Douglas (2004), *How Brands Become Icons: The Principles of Cultural Branding*, Cambridge: Harvard University Press.

Jakobson, Roman (1956/1990), "Two Aspects of Language Two Types of Aphasic Disturbances," in *On Language*, edited by Linda R. Waugh and Monique Monville-Burston, Cambridge: Harvard University Press, pp. 115-133.

Lemon, Lee T. and Marion J. Reis (1965), *Russian Formalist Criticism: Four Essays*, Omaha, Nebraska, University of Nebraska Press.

Lu, Pierre Xiao (2008), *Elite China: Luxury Consumer Behavior in China*, New York City, N.Y.: John Wiley & Sons.

McCracken, Grant (1986), "Culture and Consumption: A Theoretical Account of the Structure and Movement of the Cultural Meanng of Consumer Goods," *Journal of Consumer Research*, Vol. 13, June, pp. 71-84.

McQuarrie, Edward F. and David Glen Mick (1999),"Visual rhetoric in advertising: Text-interpretive, experimental, and reader-response analyses," *Journal of Consumer Research* 26 (June), 37-54.

Mick, David Glen (1986), "Consumer research and semiotics: Exploring the morphology of signs, symbols, and significance," *Journal of Consumer Research*, 13 (2), 196-213.

______ and Claus Buhl (1992), "A Meaning Based Model of Advertising Experiences," *Journal of Consumer Research*, 19, (December), pp. 317-338.

Oswald, Laura (1999) Culture Swapping: Consumption and the Ethnogenesis of Middle-Class Haitian Immigrants," *Journal of Consumer Research*, Vol. 25, March.

Otnes, Cele and Linda Scott (1996), "Something Old, Something New: Exploring the Interaction between Ritual and Advertising," the *Journal of Advertising*, Vol. XXV, No. 1, Spring, pp. 33-50.

Peñaloza, Lisa (1994) 'Atravesando Fronteras/Border Crossings: A Critical Ethnographic Exploration of Consumer Acculturation of Mexican Immigrants, *The Journal of Consumer Research*, Vol. 21, No. 1 (June), pp. 32-54.

Saussure, Ferdinand de (1983/1971/1913), *Course in General Linguistics*, a translation of *Cours de linguistique générale*, Paris: Payot. Translated by Roy Harris, London: G. Duckworth Publishers.

Schroeder, Jonathan E. (2002), *Visual Consumption*, London: Routledge.

Scott, Linda M. and Patrick Vargas (2007), "Writing With Pictures, Toward a Unifying Theory of Consumer Response to Images," *Journal of Consumer Research, Vol. 34, October, pp. 341-356.*

______ (1994), "Images in Advertising: The Need for a Theory of Visual Rhetoric," *Journal of Consumer Research*," 21 (September), pp. 252–273.

______ (1990), "The Bridge from Text to Mind, Adapting Consumer Response Theory to Consumer Research," *Journal of Consumer Research*,

Sherry, John (1987), "Advertising as a Cultural System," in *Marketing and Semiotics*, edited by Jean Umiker-Sebeok, New York: Mouton de Gruyter Press, pp. 441-461.

Sherry, John and Eduardo Camargo (1987), "May Your Life Be Beautiful," *Journal of Consumer Research*, Vol. 14, pp. 174-188).

Tse, David K, Russell W. Belk, and Nan Zhou (1989), "Becoming a Consumer Society: A Longitudinal and Cross-Cultural Content Analysis of Print Ads from Hong Kong, the People's Republic of China, and Taiwan, *Journal of Consumer Research*, Vol 15, March, pp. 457-472.

Üstüner, Tuba, and Douglas B. Holt (2007), "Dominated Consumer Acculturation: The Social Construction of Poor Migrant Women's Consumer Identity Projects in a Turkish Squatter," *Journal of Consumer Research*, Vol. 34, June.

Wetlaufer, Suzy (2001), "The Perfect Paradox of Star Brands: An Interview with Bernard Arnault of LVMH," in *Harvard Business Review*, October, pp. 117-123.

Gaya Wicks, Agnes Nairn and Christine Griffin (2007). *"The Role of Consumption Culture in Children's Moral Development: the Case of David Beckham." Consumption, Markets and Culture*, Vol. 10 No. 4, December.

Yankelovich, Daniel (1964), "New Criteria for Market Segmentation," *Harvard Business Review*, March-April, pp. 83-90.

Zhang, Zi and Bernt Schmitt (2001), "Creating Local Brands in Multilingual International Markets," *Journal of Marketing Research*, August, pp. 313-325,

Zhao, Xin and Russell W. Belk (2008a) "Patriotic Shoppers and Treasonous Merchants: Advertising Nationalism in 1930s' Shanghai," *Journal of Advertising*.

______ (2008b)"Politicizing Consumer Culture: Advertising's Appropriation of Political Ideology in China's Social Transition," *Journal of Consumer Research*, 35 (August), 231-45.

Zhou Nan and Russell W. Belk (2004), "Chinese Consumer Readings of Global and Local Advertising Appeals," *Journal of Advertising*, Fall, No. 33, 3, pp. 63-76.

Galloping through the Global Brandscape: Consumers in a Branded Reality

Kaleel Rahman, American University in Dubai, United Arab Emirates
Helene Cherrier, American University in Dubai, United Arab Emirates

ABSTRACT

The idea that endless numbers of brands shape people's day-to-day life is known as "brandscape" (Biel, 1993; Sherry, 1998; Soloman, 2003). When consumers live in another country for an extended period of time not only it is necessary to engage in various consumer behaviors in order to conduct everyday life but also brandscape becomes part of their life. The aim of this study was to explore consumer acculturation to an unfamiliar brandscape. A grounded theory analysis of case study type interviews resulted in three broader domains with seven themes: "sentiments" with *experiential tension, nostalgia and patriotism*; "brandscape" with *global brands, missing brands, ethno-brands and beloved brands*; and "consumer acculturation". The paper discusses the findings of the study and the implications of the emergent themes.

INTRODUCTION

Jordan, a 34 year old Aussie bloke! Jordan woke up this morning at 6.40, jumped out of his *Ikea* bed, put on his weird *Dunlop* slippers, rushed into the bathroom, brushed his teeth using his *Colgate* toothpaste, had a clean shave with his *Gillette Sensor* razor and *Old Spice* shaving cream, and had a warm shower scented with his *Herbal Essence*. Having had a quick breakfast and a quick spray of *Obsession by Calvin Klein*, he jumped into his *Toyota Camry*, switched on to *2DayFM* radio. On the way, he filled up at the *Mobil* petrol station next to the *Microsoft* head office. Jordan arrived at work, approached his hot desk, said 'good morning' to his colleague who had her aromatic *Starbucks* coffee cup, and he sat on his chair and switched on the *Dell* desktop.

Although I have not described even two hours of Jordan's life, you may have gained a reasonably good picture about what kind of a person he is. Flavoured by his likes and dislikes, the brands I have mentioned define who he is. The idea that endless numbers of brands shape people's day-to-day life is known as "brandscape" (Biel, 1993; Sherry, 1998; Soloman, 2003). As you may notice, Jordan merely know some of these brands, others he uses frequently; He has strong feelings towards some but not towards some others.

Assume that suddenly you go to a new country to spend about three years. Would you take all of "your" brands with you? Would you expect your brands to be available in that country? Would you miss the brands that you leave at home? How would you react to the new brands that you encounter in the new country? What are some of the feelings, emotions and thoughts, both positive and negative, that you would experience with regard to brands when you are in the new country? As a consumer, how would you acculturate to your new brand-related environment? These questions motivate this research.

The study of global brands has become an important area of research in marketing. The special issue devoted to "branding in the global marketplace" in the *Journal of International Marketing* in 2008 with notable contributions from consumer researchers (Cayla and Arnould, 2008) who critique the currently prevalent technique-oriented scholarship in global branding , and practitioner-related books like "The Global Brand: How to Create and Develop Lasting Brand Value in the World Market" (Hollis, 2008), are some examples reflecting this importance. Although there is substantial research relating to consumers' reactions to the globalization of brands, almost all this research generally focuses on consumers in the home country. For instance, Echhardt and Houston (2002) studied how McDonald's is perceived by people in Shanghai, and Dimofte and his colleagues (2008) recently studied reactions of U.S. consumers to global brands. In a search of the existing literature the author found no research on how consumers react to their familiar and new brands when they are in a foreign land.

Understanding how consumers react to their brands in a foreign country is important for several reasons. When living in another country for an extended period of time it is necessary to engage in various consumer behaviors in order to conduct everyday life. Often, the marketplace brandscape is very different from that which was left behind, both in terms of the brands available and the way of conducting transactions. In addition, when consumers leave their country of birth their meaning of brands and possessions may change because most of their own possessions and brands are left behind (Belk, 1992). From a practical point of view, one aspect of globalization of brands is known as "glocalization" where certain product features, brand elements, and distribution systems of a brand are customized to local consumer tastes (Svensson, 2001). For example, Nestle has a very strong emphasis on meeting local tastes while preserving its global orientation. As consumers move across the nations, encountering their brands being glocalized may evoke certain feelings, and it is important to understand how they react to such glocalization of their brands. Next, there are large numbers of students who move to foreign countries for their higher education. For example, in the US alone there were 454,000 international students enrolled in colleges (Field, 1999), and in the UK overseas students made up 12.7% of the higher education population (*Students in Higher Education Institutions*, 2003), while in Australia 18.8% of all commencing tertiary students in 2000 were international fee-paying students (Michael et al., 2003) and the income from overseas students has become "bigger than wool, nearly as big as wheat" (King, 2002). In addition, developments in information technology and increases in the service-based economy have all resulted in a situation where a large number of short-term immigrants are moving across countries as expatriates (Thompson and Tambyah, 1999). How do these people who move to a new country react to the unfamiliar brandscape in general?

The aim of this study was to explore consumers' reactions to their brandscape in the context of consumer acculturation. To address this question, a phenomenological in-depth interview approach was undertaken. Interviews were analysed using "grounded theory" and "associative group analysis" approaches. The theoretical background of the study is presented here along with the research questions, followed by the findings of the study and a discussion of implications for researchers and practitioners.

CONCEPTUAL BACKGROUND AND RESEARCH QUESTIONS

Since branding has become an effective tool for marketers to package a whole range of meanings (Kapferer, 2008), consumers today are faced with a proliferation of brands in their daily life–a branded reality. The idea of branded reality has been advanced by several authors, with terms including Sherry's "brandscape" (1998), Biel's "brandspace" (1993), and Soloman's "consumerspace" (2003). A brandscape is a "material and symbolic environment that consumers build with marketplace products, images, and messages, that they invest with local meaning, and whose totemic significance largely shapes the adaptation consumers make to the modern world" (Sherry, 1998, p. 112). As Soloman (2003) suggests, people tend to rely upon brands to define their identities and make sense of the world around themselves. Thus, what a brand means is largely derived from associations emanating from the *contexts* where the brand is consumed (Biel, 1993). As McCracken's meaning transfer model (1986) posits, meaning moves from aspects of the cultural world such as fashion, class systems and advertising to the brands, and then from these brands to the individual consumer. However, as Penaloza (1989) posits, a consumer enters the new culture with an abundance of consumption knowledge previously acquired in the consumer's culture of origin. What would happen to the consumer (who has already been defined by his own consumption context) if he or she moves to a different culture where the fashions, social classes and advertising all are different? According to McCracken, the consumers must redefine themselves; as changes happen, they would be constantly constructing and reconstructing themselves by a way of new meaning or new ways of defining themselves as they react to the brands in a new cultural context.

This new way of defining themselves in a new culture may be understood by consumer acculturation (Penaloza, 1994; Askagaard et al., 2005; Ustuner and Holt, 2007) which refers to "the acquisition of skills and knowledge relevant to engaging in consumer behavior in one culture by *members* of another culture" (Penaloza, 1989, p. 110). Aacculturation is a term typically used in reference to immigrants planning to stay permanently in their host country (Penaloza, 1994). Yet, it can also apply to other forms of movement (e.g., peasants into cities) even within the same country (Ustuner and Holt, 2007). Since the goal of this paper is to understand how consumers "feel" in response to their brandscape as part of their acculturation, a brief review of feelings warrants attention.

Prior research contends that certain feelings can be "evoked" in response to brands (Keller, 2001). Kahle and his colleagues (1998) point out six types of feelings that may be evoked in response to a brand: warmth, fun, excitement, security, social approval and self-respect. According to the notion of "brand relationships", consumers not only have feelings toward brands but also consider brands as relationship partners (Fournier, 1998). She posits that consumers have feelings and possible forms of relationships with their brands, akin to arranged marriages, casual friendships, committed partnerships, enmities, and secret affairs. As the former CEO of Saatchi and Saatchi posits, future success of brands largely depends on their ability to evoke emotional responses such as joy, surprise, pride and love (Roberts, 2004).

The present paper, specifically in the context of the consumers being in a new country, examines the emerging concepts relating to the emotions they feel towards the brands they had back home and the brands they encounter in the host country. Keeping the background of brandscape, consumer acculturation, brand feelings and brand relationships in mind, the following research question is put forward: How do consumers coming into a new country acculturate to an unfamiliar brandscape?

METHODOLOGY

In keeping with the exploratory and theory-developing objectives of the study, in-depth interviews were used to reveal consumers' reaction to a new brandscape, permitting an understanding of the subjective meaning of consumers' experiences with brands in a new country. This method also provides a deep understanding of a phenomenon from the consumer's perspective (Hudson and Ozanne, 1988).

Because of the small sample size permitted by the context of the study, purposive sampling was employed. Participants were selected on the basis of specific criteria so that they shared broad similarities (Lincoln and Guba, 1985). While maintaining these similarities, participants from different parts of the world were recruited. Thus in-depth case study interviews were conducted in Australia with seven selected participants: (1) Zhao, a 24-year-old doctoral student in Finance coming from Vietnam (Ms V); (2) Shelly, a 23-year-old Masters student in Marketing coming from England (Ms E); (3) Gordon, a 26-year-old Masters student in Sociology coming from Canada (Mr C); (4) Heidi, a 25-year-old doctoral student in Sociology coming from France (Ms F); (5) Shaima, a 32-year-old doctoral student in Economics coming from Bangladesh (Ms. B); (6) Rachel, a 24 year old Masters student in Public Health coming from Canada (Ms. C); (7) Ali, 41 year old doctoral student in Organizational Behavior coming from Saudi Arabia (Mr. S).

These participants had been in Australia for an average of six months and each had a student visa. They were recruited through collegial networks and no compensation was provided for their participation. The interviews lasted an average of 65 minutes (range 40–85 minutes). Each interview was conducted on a one-to-one basis, with the participant being assured of anonymity and the freedom to withdraw at any stage. An interview guide which consisted of direct questions in terms of his/her interactions with brands was used. Although an interview guide was used, the questions were adapted in the course of the interview and the flow was largely determined by the informants. In order to maintain a holistic perspective, as employed by Fournier (1998), all interviews and analyses were conducted by the author. The interviews were audio-taped and transcribed verbatim into pages of text. In addition, the interviewer noted comments relating to each participant's behaviour, verbal expression, and other nonverbal circumstances.

Furthermore, a member check phase (Wallendorf and Belk, 1989) was conducted whereby participants were each given a draft report of their case study and asked to critique it, comment on it, or request amendments. The purpose of this process was to confirm that the report had captured the information as delivered by the participants or, if not, for them to correct, amend or extend it. As a result of this procedure, some minor modifications were made to the transcripts.

The transcripts were coded based on Straus and Corbin's (1998) grounded theory method, including open, axial and selective coding, and theoretical sampling techniques. Accordingly, the first interview was coded and analysed before conducting the second interview. Based on this approach, an attempt was made to identify emerging themes, and to map relationships between these themes from the interviews. The data collection process was extended until no new themes emerged from the interview data (Lincoln and Guba, 1985; Straus and Corbin, 1998). Grounded theory method was supplemented by associative group analysis (Szalay and Bryson, 1974) in which any particular "domain" consists of several "themes" and a theme consists of several individual concepts. For example, in a study by Szalay and Deese (1978), the *domain* of "education" consisted of the *themes* politeness, school features, knowledge, educated, and educators. The *theme* "politeness" in turn consisted of a range of concepts including polite, decent, respect, manners, social, good, and agreeable. In addition to transcripts, the data examined in the analysis also included details observed (e.g., facial expression) during the interviews.

FINDINGS

In this section, an overview of findings is presented along with an emerging conceptual framework followed by details of emergent themes. The grounded theory analysis of the interviews based

FIGURE I

A Framework of the host country brandscape

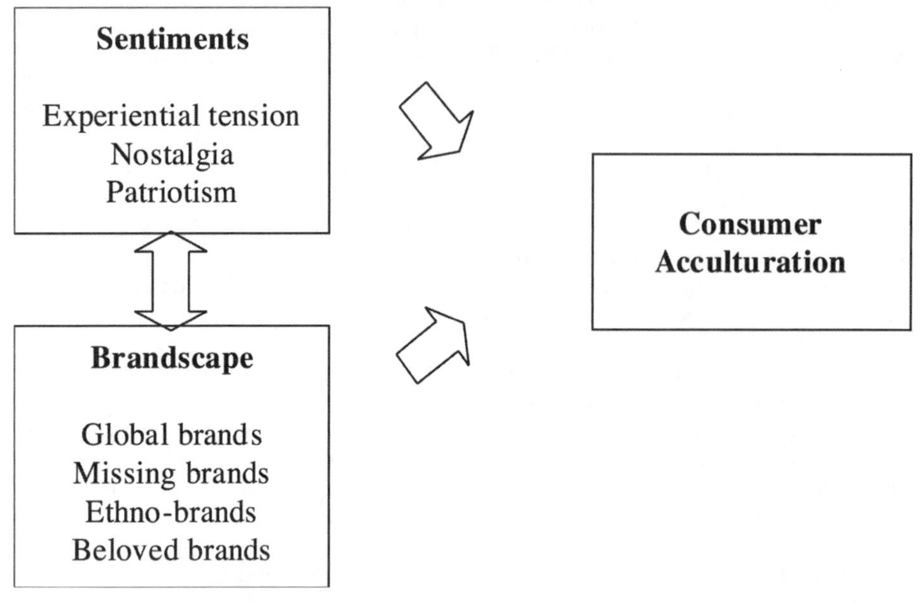

on concepts, properties and dimensions (Straus and Corbin, 1998) along with themes and domains of associative group analysis (Szalay and Bryson, 1974) can be postulated in a meaningful framework as presented in Figure I. The framework comprises three broader domains of themes. The "sentiments" domain emerged as participants expressed their emotions in terms of experiential tension of being in a new culture, feelings of patriotism and nostalgic reactions. The "brandscape" domain emerged as they narrated their brand stories referring to global brands, brands with which they had had close relationships, brands available and unavailable in the host country, and brands that they were unable to find in the host country. The "consumer acculturation" domain emerged as they reported the way they adjusted to their new environment, in terms both of their life in general and of brands in particular. Despite the presence of arrows leading to subsequent domains in Figure I, there was no attempt in this study to establish causal relations between these domains, since its purpose was exploratory in nature. In the following section the emergent themes are discussed in detail.

Sentiments domain

Experiential tension. The first theme that emerged was consumer experiential tension. Experiential tension is a milder form of cultural shock, usually resulting from differences in culture, consumption situation and product unavailability. Experiential tension is characterized by feelings of conflict and ambivalence, such as "emotional work involved in establishing new social networks, the stresses of learning how to be a consumer in the new locale, and small pleasures of established routines as well as familiar surrounding and products" (Thompson and Thambyah, 1999 p. 221). All seven participants expressed some form of experiential tension relating to their own experiences. One aspect of this tension is very similar to cultural shock (Winkelman, 1994):

> *"I think there is too much emphasis here on independence… like people respect privacy too much–it makes you isolated–when I came here first there was a neighbour next room and that person did not want to know about me! That upset me" (Ms V).*
>
> *"I lived all my life in Saudi, I was born there, all my friends are there, my social network is there, by coming here I lose all of that, I lose the social network, I come into a place where I know no one, I have no friends, I have no family!" (Mr. S).*

Another aspect of experiential tension was directly related to the consumption of goods and services. Some of the concepts emerged where the participants found that the same brands were offered but had a different taste, an identification of some glocalization (Svensson, 2001): "cheese is another category I miss, they have the same brands here but taste different" (Mr C); "Cadbury's dairy milk, but we got them here in Australia but the ones from the UK taste completely different–that's the ones I am used to. Australian ones are sweeter." (Ms E).

The participants also complained that package sizes or quantities were also different from their previous experience: "Every product is bigger here… I was really surprised to see when people buy huge popcorn in the cinemas! None will buy that in France!" (Ms F); "Everything you can buy in bulk in Canada. I remember some girls complaining in my class about when they buy razor blades in the US they buy a big bag of razors but here they buy 2 or 3, very expensive" (Mr. C).

Although complaints regarding smaller packaging are related to the cost factor, participants also made direct comments about prices and charges where products and services in Australia were perceived as being relatively more expensive than in their home country: "The (bank) charges are terrible, like the amounts they charge for using an ATM is absolutely terrible. They charge you for everything. Every little thing you can think of they charge you." (Ms E).

Nostalgia. As one would expect, the next emergent theme was nostalgic in nature. Nostalgia is usually characterized by "things used to be better in the good old days" (Rindfleisch and Sprott,

2000). Research in consumer behaviour suggests that products and brands are likely to evoke memories of past times and to inspire nostalgic reflection (Holbrook, 1993). Nostalgic reflection was strongly evident amongst most of the participants regarding to brands that they used back home:

"Not the shampoo, not the toothpaste, but the bags (Mountain Equipment) yes. Every time I go out I carry the bag, and it reminds me of my old bags" (Mr. C).
"We got Foxtel recently and we got UK TV, that reminds me of back home, all UK programs, you watch it just for nostalgia you watch it and I go you know, oh God, that's England, that noise, that sound the look of drizzle, rain, and the settings!" (Ms E).
"Recently, a friend of mine took me to Home Bush Bay outlet mall and I found a D&G t-shirt there. You know what? I got the same thing, same color! That day I was thinking about my bedroom, my friends and smoking shisha with them" (Mr. S).

Patriotism. The third theme emerging in the "sentiments" domain was patriotic sentiment in general. Three of the participants specifically commented on various aspects of patriotic sentiment. At times, their body language was also obvious in such reactions. The first aspect of patriotic feeling identified was directly expressed patriotism (Gelb, 2002) towards the home country.

"Out here we are English, that link.. England is doing really well. I really wanted to buy an England t- shirt, I probably wouldn't have done if I were in England, because I am here I wanted to identify with my country" (Ms E).

However, much of the patriotic feeling was expressed through "ethnocentrism" (Shimp and Sharma, 1987) and "country of origin effect" led by emotions (Maheswaran and Chen, 2006). From an ethnocentric point of view, the respondent from England made reference to Richard Branson as a successful Englishman and took pride in expressing her "Englishness". This sentiment was also evident in her reference to the Mini Cooper as a "very British" car. On the contrary, from a country-of-origin point of view, the respondent from Vietnam was delighted to see some global brands that were made in Vietnam, as the following quote illustrates:

"When I bought Nescafe I found that was made in Vietnam. You know I use Colgate toothpaste, my favourite one, once I found that was made in Vietnam too. See, I am in Australia and they are selling these products from my country! These brands go with my feelings, but not Visa or Coke since I cannot really relate them to my country" (Ms V).

Similarly, the participants also commented about patriotic activities in Australia. Specifically, all of the participants' comments indicated that they had noticed the "Buy Australian Made" campaign (Acharya and Elliott, 2003), and surprisingly it annoyed them in some cases. For example, the informant from England sarcastically hinted "obviously the big thing they have over here is Australian Holden!" The informant from Canada was annoyed about the strong emphasis on domestic goods:

"I find that there is more emphasis on domestic goods here.... even though GM is American, the Aussies think it (Holden) as an Australian icon. Australians are proud of that–Canadians don't have that.... Here on TV, they go–here the three reasons to buy this products, reason 1, reason 2, reason 3, buy Australian!" (Mr C).

Brandscape domain

Global brands. In terms of the brandscape domain, one of the most obvious themes was centered around some references and reactions to global brands (Holt, 2002). With their multinational presence, global brands are usually quite familiar to the global audience. Accordingly, the participants were very familiar with the global brands.

One obvious comment about global brands were related to 'convenience' which means saving time and effort. Although convenience generally refers to certain convenient product categories such as 'fast food' or 'frozen vegetables', the importance of convenience as a construct applicable to brands in general has been noted (Berry et. al., 2002). The participant from Bangladesh said encountering Western global brands did not evoke any feelings but they were still "convenient" as she knew these brands would be available in a "Western country". She further commented "I used Dove soap in Bangladesh and I use it here too, I didn't have to look for any other brand… no I didn't bother if it would be available in Australia, it is just a soap you know". When asked her reaction to specific global brand like Coca Cola, Kodak, and Pantene, the participant from Vietnam said "these brands make my life easier since I already know these brands".

A somewhat related to convenience was 'global brands as objects'. That is, encountering objects such as pencil, a toothbrush or shoes should evoke no surprise from anyone from any part of the globe as people generally expect them to be present everywhere. Similarly, as the participants hinted, encountering brands such as Visa, Coca Cola and McDonald's in a new country should surprise none. The following quotes illustrate this premise:

"These brands you pretty much expect anywhere you go in the world. It's not something that you are surprised about" (Ms E).
"Because everyone has Coke, it may be a bit insulting to ask this question" (Ms F).
"They are everywhere! I saw Kodak store, …Coca Cola signs and all that around me in Vancouver in the downtown area–all those signs. So used to having them everywhere" (Mr C).

Although global brands in general do not surprise anyone, it seems to come as a surprise when consumers find such brands positioned differently, again some reference to 'glocalization' (Svensson, 2001). To illustrate, the participants from Vietnam and Bangladesh reported that McDonald's is a prestige and upper class brand in their countries but they find that McDonald's is the cheapest food in Australia. They also reported that ANZ Bank and Pizza Hut seem to have a similar gap in brand image between the countries. Although one might attribute this phenomenon to the level of development of the countries involved, the brand image disparity was evident in other respondents' comments as well:

"Esprit, a French one originally, I thought it's too expensive and upper class, never went even inside in the UK. For some reason it seems to be a lower class here in Australian and I actually go into Esprit here" (Ms E).
"A car like Honda Civic is very common, very average in Saudi, but here in Australia it seems like a cool car" (Mr S).

Missing (absent) brands. The next emergent theme was "missing brands", which involves (non-global) brands one normally used at home but is unable to find in the host country. Although they do not seem to have strong feelings towards these brands, they still had trusted these brands from their prior experience with them, and in someway expected them to be present in a host country. As is evident, missing brands often result in some form of experiential tension. For example, one respondent tried to apply for a Visa Debit card:

"In the UK you can use your debit card like a credit card (Barklay Visa debit), like you can buy things online, they don't do that over here, it's very annoying when you can't buy things online even though you got money" (Ms E).

Although consumers may not have strong feelings toward certain brands and may use them only occasionally, the brands may still be important, as the following quote indicates:

"There is this eye-drop I used in Vancouver called Gentel, very common in Canada, my optometrist had recommended that too, and I went into a chemist shop and asked for a Gentel eye drop, and they go "what?" they don't have that here. Okay, "can I buy something similar to that?" and then, "well, what's in it?" then I said, "I don't know what's in it, I buy it all the time", now I have to find what I usually use and find what is the ingredient it's got. But I don't know what's in it–how do I find what's in it? I was really surprised about that" (Mr C).

Beloved brands. Beloved brands refer to brands towards which consumers have developed strong feelings, but which are not usually found in the host country. 'Beloved brands' theme is different from 'missing brands' theme because beloved brand theme is associated to strong feelings. Since these brands were not accessible to the participants in Australia, the brand stories of the informants generally resulted in nostalgic reactions, as the following quotes illustrate:

"My school bag, the best backpack in Canada is Mountain Equipment Corp. Very well known very high quality back packs. I have three bags and they are Mountain Equipments. The reason that the Mountain Equipment is hanging around with me is because I really like the brand, it's really good quality, it's not cheap. The first bag I got was when I was 13, so I still have that bag, but I tried other brands in the meantime, but they are bad" (Mr C).
"I miss Marks and Spencers sooo much and their sandwiches are absolutely amazing, they are the number one sandwich maker, it's got such good choice, I miss that a lot" (Ms E).
"I miss my Ispahani tea brand a lot, we wanted to bring some when went last time but unfortunately forgot, so we got some from our friend's" (Ms B).

At times, consumers can develop strong feelings towards certain brands even though they are not the leading brands in a category. Despite its being a low profile brand, the Canadian informant had strong feelings toward Washburn guitars, as the following quote illustrates:

"This means lot to me because that's the first guitar I ever bought–it is called Washburn, never forgot the name. It's not available in Australia. ... It was the first thing I bought from my own money. Very memorable ... Over a year of savings, $60-70 a month work." (Mr C).

Ethno-brands. Another emergent theme regarding brandscape was "ethno brands". Ethno brands refer to brands for which consumers have strongly developed feelings from their home country, and the brand is also available in the host country. The participants expressed their strong feelings towards such brands both verbally and nonverbally while narrating their stories. There were some cases where the participants expressed strong feelings when they found brands which were unique to their home country. For example:

"I also found L'ccitante from my country, it's like the Body Shop, I was really surprised to see that in Queen Victoria Building, I bought a lot of things there. (Ms F)
"We have a very popular noodle called PhuQuoc and I found that even in Australian supermarkets ..." (Ms V).
"Marmite, yes, I found it in British Lolly Shop, I was happy to see it here. Otherwise I have to get my friends to bring it here" (Ms E).

Participants also reported that they found their favourite brands, not necessarily unique to their home country, in Australia. They become close to these brands from their home country:

"My Fender Strata Castor, the electric one. It's considered to be the best guitar in the world, it's available in Australia. I love to play guitar in my room on my own. It's the same guitar Jimmy Henry used, top guitar in the world. I would have been surprised if I didn't find that in Australia" (Mr C).
"I actually use the same shampoo Herbal Essence I used back home. Don't know if it's made in France, but I love it" (Ms F).
"I use Finesse typically. I tried other ones, I tried Head and Shoulders, and others, say 5 or 6, I didn't like them, but when I tried this I liked it" (Mr S).

Consumer Acculturation domain

The last theme (and domain) that emerged was consumer acculturation. The present study found evidence of consumer acculturation where participants found ways to adjust their feelings regarding their life in general and brands in particular. While finding alternative brands in place of their regular brands, the participants eventually fell in love with some Australian brands. The participant from Canada, extremely conscious of his spending, reported that he was addicted to a new apple juice called "Australian Fresh" although it was almost double the price of other brands of fresh apple juice. The participants from France and England were delighted to report not only that they regularly bought Australian Tim Tam biscuits but also that they would take a lot of them home. Coming from a very basic consumption culture where most of the grocery purchases are made by counter-feeding, the participant from Bangladesh had to adjust to her new consumption context: She was surprised to see that Nivea moisturizer was available in different flavours and versions while she had known only a single Nivea Moisturiser back home; she found her new Nivea Moisturiser by experimenting a few of them. She had never tasted a pizza but she got almost addicted to Dominos in Sydney. She was surprised to see the number of Kellogg's cereal options available to her and she noted "sometime I spend even half an hour browsing and choosing the right cereal!" On the other hand, the participant from Saudi Arabia, coming from a very upscale family brought up in an ultra luxury setting changed his style in a dramatic way: he learned to mingle with everyone in the hostel "because I had no choice", he said, "I ate what they ate, I bought what they bought" and "this was the first time I ever travelled in a Hyundai car, and I liked it".

The following quote captures this theme succinctly:

"It kind of gets confused because I have now become familiar with Australian brands and I will miss some of these when I go to the UK. Sometimes you actually forget what was available

back home, what wasn't available here, and vice versa, and you go, "you sure we have that in England or Australia?" My boyfriend's the same. You know he says something and goes, "we could get that in England" and I go, "no you couldn't". We sort of forget what was available in the UK and you become familiar with Australian ones. I found that funny when I went to the UK I actually missed some of the things from Australia. Some of the silly things like Twisties, Tim Tams. They have Vegemite there, I don't know why they don't sell Marmite here. Boundaries between countries have become a lot less. Brands should become available in all the different countries" (Ms E).

DISCUSSION AND CONCLUSION

This paper has presented the findings of a study of consumer acculturation to an unfamiliar brandscape. The study illustrates the way consumers feel about their brands when they move to a new country for an extended but limited period of time. While living in the new country for some time they go through a range of sentiments including experiential tension, patriotic reactions and nostalgic excitement. They also manifest none to very close feelings towards their brandscape, some of which relate to brands not available to them in the host country. Their brandscapes were identified as comprising global brands, missing brands, ethno brands and beloved brands. Finally, largely influenced by the presence of alternative and new brands in the host country, their brandscape becomes acculturated to the point where they adjust their life both in terms of their brands and their sentiments.

This study provides strong support for the notion of brandscape (Biel, 1993; Sherry, 1988; Soloman, 2003), where consumers are bombarded with a large number of brands that shape their identity both knowingly and unknowingly. The following quote illustrates this notion: "brands not only furnish the environment in which I live, but they also enrobe me, and by doing so, help define who I am" (Biel, 1993, p. 68). This study showed that consumers continue to engage with their brand environment–they comment on the global brands, the brands unique to their home country, the brands with which they have strong feelings towards, the brands they wanted to use but unable find, the brands they used in the past and left at home. More specifically, the study showed that consumers are well aware of the image differences of brands, which implies that they use them to express their identity. The participants easily recognized some differently positioned brands in different countries. Thus, the present study extends the notion of brandscape to a context in which consumers face a challenging situation where they have, in many cases, no access to the brands they used back home, are presented with alternative brands for their routine consumption, and are faced with new brands they never heard of. Consequently, as McCracken's (1986) meaning transfer model hinted, the participants voluntarily adjusted their brand usage by becoming accultured to the new environment. For example, Shaima, the participant from Bangladesh was redefined to some extent by her new usage of Domino's Pizza, new Nivea Moisturiser, and the effort spent browsing a large number Kellogg's cereal varieties available to her. The participant from England, by acculturated to her new brandscape, eventually got confused whether some brands belonged to Australia or England.

Several researchers have pointed out the importance of emotions in understanding consumer behaviour (Richins, 1997). This study supports the premise that consumers have emotional relationships with (Fournier, 1998) or feelings towards (Keller, 2001) brands and circumstances involving brands can evoke different types of feelings (Kahle, 1998). According to Roberts (2004), there are two types of emotions: people feel primary emotions such as joy and surprise when they are alone; they feel secondary emotions such as love and pride when they relate to someone else. This study found that consumers exhibit a range of primary and secondary emotions when they interact with brands when they are in new country. Experiential tension was related to irritation and uneasy feelings, nostalgia was like pleasant excitement, and patriotic sentiments were related to joy, excitement and happy. Missing brands evoked some frustration, beloved brands evoked some sadness, and ethno-brands evoked some excitement. This observation is also consistent with much previous research where brands are anthropomorphized, consumers are reported to accord even sacred status to brands (Belk et al., 1989), and brands are perceived as having personalities (Aaker, 1997).

Several implications can also be drawn from the findings. As a larger number of people than ever before travel to other countries to study and work, it is important to understand how these people feel about their brands in the new country. The findings of this study suggest that, if marketed successfully across countries, brands can offer convenience as a "time and effort-saving heuristic" (Berry et.al., 2002 p.9). The findings also suggest that brands can achieve the status of objects where they may become some standard of international comparison. For example, the presence or absence of McDonald's in a country may provide two different images of that country. When asked about Coca Cola, it was warned that it may be a bit insulting to ask if they have Coke in their country since brands like that considered as objects or even symbols. This is in line with the contention that buying global brands make consumers feel like the citizens of the world (Strizkova, Coulter and Price, 2008). The study also suggests that consumers take special pride in identifying with brands specific to their own country or brands made in their country, and brands serve as a form of national pride. The respondent from England was excited to refer to Richard Branson as a successful "Englishman" and Mini Cooper as a "very British" brand. These findings are consistent with brand as "citizen-artists", contributing as a cultural resource (Holt, 2002) and global brands as a cultural form (Cayla and Arnould, 2008) such as folk tales. The study also implies that relationships with and feelings towards brands left at home become even stronger and enduring as consumers recollect such brands with nostalgia.

Another important implication refers to glocalization–adapting features and branding to local tastes. Accordingly, certain brands are forced to be positioned differently in different countries. This difference seemed to cause some surprise to the participants as the brands they had known had changed in some ways. For example, the respondent from England found Espirit to be somewhat lower class leading her to feel more comfortable in shopping at Espirit in Australia. However, because her Dairy Milk chocolates in Australia tasted sweeter, she had to order her originals from England. The Canadian participant was annoyed as he could not buy his shampoo in bigger bottles.

In sum, this paper contributes to the literature concerning brands by (a) showing how consumers feel about "their" brands in a new country; (b) providing a framework of domains of themes incorporating sentiments, brandscape and consumer acculturation in terms of possible antecedents and consequences of brandscape in a host country; and (c) describing and interpreting the specific themes that emerged.

Ultimately, although the study provides grounded empirical evidence of the way some individuals feel about their brands in a foreign country, further research would enrich the findings and would reveal whether the themes uncovered in this study have relevance and potential application. Future research efforts could be directed towards increasing the sample size in order to strengthen the generalizability of findings. Furthermore, quantitative research also needs to be undertaken to test the frameworks that emerged in this research. Finally, the study should be replicated in different geographical locations employing informants from other parts of the world.

REFERENCES

Aaker, J. (1997), "Dimensions of Brand Personality," *Journal of Marketing Research*, 34 (August), 347-357.

Acharya, C. and Elliott, G. (2003) "Consumer ethnocentrism, perceived product quality and choice–an empirical investigation", *Journal of International Consumer Marketing*, Vol. 15, No. 4, pp. 87-115.

Belk, R. (1992). Moving Possessions: An Analysis Based on Personal Documents from the 1847—1869 Mormon Migration. *Journal of Consumer Research*, *19*(3), 339-361.

Belk, R., Wallendorf, M. and Sherry, J. (1989) "The sacred and profane in consumer research", *Journal of Consumer Research*, Vol. 25, December, pp. 218-240.

Berry, L. L., Seiders, K. and Grewal, D. (2002) "Understanding service convenience", *Journal of Marketing*, Vol. 66, July, pp. 1-17.

Biel, A. (1993) "Converting image into equity" in *Brand Equity & Advertising: Advertising's Role in Building Strong Brands*, Eds. Aaker, D. and Biel, A., Lawrence Erlbaum Associates: New Jersey, pp. 67-81

Cayla, J., & Arnould, E. (2008). A Cultural Approach to Branding in the Global Marketplace. *Journal of International Marketing*, *16*(4), 86-112.

Dimofte, C., Johansson, J., & Ronkainen, I. (2008). Cognitive and Affective Reactions of U.S. Consumers to Global Brands. *Journal of International Marketing*, *16*(4), 113-135.

Eckhardt, G. and Houston, M. (2002) "Cultural paradoxes reflected in brand meaning: McDonald's in Shanghai, China", *Journal of International Marketing*, Vol. 10, No. 2, pp. 68-82.

Field, A. (1999) "The college student market segment: a comparative study of travel behaviours of international and domestic students at a Southeastern university", *Journal of Travel Research*, Vol. 37, No. 4, pp. 375-382.

Fournier, S. (1998) "Consumers and their brands: Developing relationship theory in consumer research", *Journal of Consumer Research*, Vol. 24, March, pp. 343-373.

Gelb, Betsy D. (2002) "Market patriotism: Advertising dilemma", *Journal of Advertising Research,* Vol. 42, No. 1, pp. 67-69.

Holbrook, M. B. (1993) "Nostalgia and consumption preferences: Some emerging patterns of consumer tastes", *Journal of Consumer Research*, Vol. 20, No. 2, pp. 245-257.

Hollis, Nigel (2008) The Global Brand: How to Create and Develop Lasting Brand Value in the World Market, Palgrave Macmillan: NY

Holt, D. (2002). Why Do Brands Cause Trouble? A Dialectical Theory of Consumer Culture and Branding. *Journal of Consumer Research*, *29*(1), 70-90.

Hudson, L. and Ozanne, J. (1988) "Alternative ways of seeking knowledge in consumer research", *Journal of Consumer Research*, Vol. 14, March, pp. 508-521.

Kapferer, Jean-Noel (2008) The New Strategic Brand Management: Creating and Sustaining Brand Equity Long Term 4th edition, Kogan Page: NY

Kahle, L., Poulos, B., and Sukhdial, A. (1998) "Changes in social values in the United States during the past decade", *Journal of Advertising Research*, February/March, pp. 35-41.

Keller, K. L. (2001) "Building customer-based brand equity", *Marketing Management*, Vol. 10, No.2, pp. 14-19.

King, T. (2002) "Unis fleece wool", *Waverly Leader*, July, p. 21.

Lincoln, Y. and Guba, R. (1985) *Naturalistic Inquiry*, Beverly Hills, CA: Sage.

Maheswaran, D., & Chen, C. (2006). Nation Equity: Incidental Emotions in Country-of-Origin Effects. *Journal of Consumer Research*, *33*(3), 370-376.

McCracken, G. (1986) "Culture and consumption: A theoretical account of the structure and movement of the cultural meaning of consumer goods", *Journal of Consumer Research*, Vol. 13, June, pp. 71-84.

Michael, I., Armstrong, A. and King, B. (2003) "The travel behaviour of international students: The relationship between studying abroad and tourist destinations", *Journal of Vacation Marketing*, Vol. 10, No. 1, pp. 57-66.

Peñaloza, Lisa (1989) "Immigrant consumer culture", Advances in Consumer Research, Vol. 16, pp. 110-118

Peñaloza, Lisa (1994), "Atravesando fronteras/Border Crossings: A Critical Ethnographic Exploration of the Consumer Acculturation of Mexican Immigrants," *Journal of Consumer Research*, 21 (June), 32–54.

Richins, M. (1997). Measuring emotions in the consumption experience. *Journal of Consumer Research*, *24*(2), 127-146.

Rindfleisch, A. and Sprott, D. (2000) "Moving forward on looking backward: Advancing theory and practice in nostalgia", *Advances in Consumer Research*, Vol. 27, pp. 34-35.

Roberts, K. (2004) *Lovemarks: The Future Beyond Brands*, Powerhouse Books: NY.

Sherry, J. (1998) "The Soul of the Company Store: Nike Town Chicago and the Emplaced Brandscape" in *Servicescapes: The Concept of Place in Contemporary Markets*, Eds by John F. Sherry Jr., McGraw-Hill : New York, pp. 109-146

Shimp, T. and Sharma, S. (1987) "Consumer Ethnocentrism: Construction and Validation of the CETSCALE", *Journal of Marketing Research*, Vol. 24, No. 3, pp. 280-290.

Soloman, M. (2003) *Conquering Consumerspace: Marketing Strategies for a Branded World*, American Management Association: New York

Strauss, A. and Corbin, J. (1998) *Basics of Qualitative Research: Techniques and Procedures for Developing Grounded Theory* 2nd Ed, SAGE Publications:Thousand Oaks.

Students in Higher Education Institutions (2003) *The Higher Education Statistics Agency*, 1996/97–2002/2003.

Strizhakova, Y., Coulter, R., & Price, L. (2008). Branded Products as a Passport to Global Citizenship: Perspectives from Developed and Developing Countries. *Journal of International Marketing*, *16*(4), 57-85

Svensson, G. (2001) "Glocalization of business activities: a glocal strategy approach", *Management Decision*, Vol. 39, No. 1, pp. 6-19

Szalay, L. B., & Bryson, J. A. (1974). Psychological meaning: Comparative analyses and theoretical implications, *Journal of Personality and Social Psychology*, 30 (6), 860-70.

Szalay, L. B., & Deese, J. (1978). *Subjective Meaning and Culture: An Assessment Through Word Association*. Hillsdale, NJ: Lawrence Erlbaum Associates.

Thompson, C. and Tambyah, S. (1999) "Trying to be cosmopolitan", *Journal of Consumer Research*, Vol. 26, December, pp. 214-241.

Üstüner, Tuba and Douglas B. Holt (2007), "Dominated Consumer Acculturation: The Social Construction of Poor Migrant Women's Consumer Identity Projects in a Turkish Squatter," *Journal of Consumer Research,* 34 (1), 41-55.

Wallendorf, M. and Belk, R. (1989) "Assessing trustworthiness in naturalistic consumer research", *Interpretive Consumer Research*, pp. 69-83.

Winkelman, M. (1994) "Cultural shock and adaptation", *Journal of Counseling and Development*, Vol., 73, No. 2, pp. 121-127.

Consumers' Attitude Towards Applying fMRI in Marketing Research

Monika Koller, Vienna University of Economics and Business (WU Wien), Austria

INTRODUCTION

Observational research techniques have had a long history in marketing research in general and consumer behavior research in particular (Lee and Broderick 2007). Regarding contemporary marketing research, sophisticated technological innovations such as internet-based innovations like Web 2.0 but also technologies adopted from other disciplines such as neuroscience allow for new insight into consumer behavior from another angle and on a higher level of precision and accuracy. Whereas Web 2.0 provides new possibilities regarding some parts of the research process, such as, data collection and recruitment of participants (see, e.g., Kozinets 2002), methods from neuroscience revolutionize the whole research process. The predominantly employed research tools can be roughly grouped into two main categories according to the underlying mechanisms measured, electroencephalography (EEG) and magnetoencephalography (MEG) measuring electrical brain activity versus positron-emission-tomography (PET) and functional magnetic resonance imaging (fMRI) measuring metabolic activity (for a more detailed discussion of these methods see, e.g., Cacioppo et al. 2003; Houser and McCabe 2009; Kenning et al. 2007a; Schilke and Reimann 2007; Willingham and Dunn 2003). Among those four techniques, EEG, MEG and fMRI have proven to serve particularly well regarding experimental procedures in marketing research (see, e.g., Ambler et al. 2004; Kenning et al. 2007a; Lee et al. 2007; Schilke and Reimann 2007; Senior et al. 2007). As PET uses radioactive tracers, the application to a wider population in marketing research is limited. Compared to EEG, MEG has a better spatial resolution but incurs relatively high costs of measurement. The complex data analysis further limits its practical applicability (Kenning et al. 2007a). EEG provides a good temporal resolution, implies relatively moderate equipment costs and a straightforward data analysis. Moreover, it has had a long tradition in marketing research and related disciplines such as psychology (Murphy et al. 2008; Rothschild et al. 1988). For instance, well-established latent constructs like cognitive dissonance, in which both psychology and marketing have always been interested, was investigated in an EEG-study (Harmon-Jones et al. 2008). Recently, there have been several methodological publications on the combined application of fMRI and EEG to obtain both spatial and temporal resolution (Herrmann and Debener 2008; Moosmann et al. 2008), but this technique is not well established yet (Willingham and Dunn 2003), especially in marketing research. In a marketing research context, fMRI is currently the most frequently used brain imaging technique, as it has a very good spatial resolution (Kenning et al. 2007a) and therefore serves best for mapping brain activities providing neural correlates of, e.g., decision-making, brand perception and, most important, unconscious emotional processes accompanying and/or influencing conscious decision-processes (Hubert and Kenning 2008). Explaining individual purchase decision-making has always been of high interest in consumer behavior. Over the past 50 years, various models have been established incorporating underlying cognitive and emotional phenomena (for an overview see, e.g., Hansen 1972; Hansen 2005). Since the technological innovation of fMRI in the early 1990s, a new era of explaining human behavior has started (Bandettini 2007; Senior et al. 2007). "Neuromarketing" (see Wilson et al. 2008 for a detailed description on the emergence of this term) is by no means a step towards mind-reading (Grimes 2006), however, the understanding of brain functions substantially contributes to fundamental knowledge and perfectly complements contemporary consumer behavior research.

As the application of fMRI has been constantly increasing in consumer behavior research, it is essential to have a closer look at the consumers' evaluation of this development. It is the consumer who serves as a test subject in empirical marketing research studies and it is finally also the consumer who is wanted to buy the products or services created and advertised by industry based on the data gained from market research. Apart from the leading work by Albaum, Evangelista and Medina (1998) and Evangelista, Albaum and Poon (1999) on theoretical explanations of survey response behavior (Albaum et al. 1998; Evangelista et al. 1999), to the best of my knowledge, little is known about how people feel about various methods and research techniques applied for marketing research purposes, neither regarding traditional behavioral methods nor alternative neuroscientific ones. This is a major shortcoming, because more detailed knowledge would provide guidance to researchers in terms of enhancing respondent cooperation and therewith accurate and truthful reporting of data. Scholarly publications are dealing with issues such as how to increase response rates and the usage of incentives (Cobanoglu and Cobanoglu 2003; Deutskens et al. 2004) but empirical studies on psychological constructs and personality traits explaining the willingness to participate as test subjects are scarce. This is unfortunate as an over- or underrepresentation of test subjects regarding certain parameter values can lead to problems regarding the generalizability of results. In the present study it is hypothesized that people scoring higher on psychological constructs such as perceived risk or technology anxiety are less willing to take part in an fMRI-experiment and may therefore be underrepresented. While the interest in "neuromarketing" started in marketing research more than a decade ago, the "neuromarketing"-approach has become quite popular nowadays in the industry as well and attracts public interest. Following Wilson, Gaines and Hill (2008), today there are more than 90 consulting agencies who specialized in "neuromarketing" (Wilson et al. 2008). "Googling" the term "neuromarketing" currently yields more than 800 000 hits" (Hubert and Kenning 2008, p. 274) and even newspapers have started to report about this emerging issue. Esch (2008) notes that besides the groundbreaking findings in research there are also various questionable publications and objectives (Esch 2008). Consequently, all the information on "what neuromarketing can or cannot do" can be quite confusing for the consumer. Concerns and ethical reservations about "neuromarketing" as both method of data collection and marketing and communication approach applied by the industry, are more likely to arise compared to traditional questionnaire-based and self-report methods. Based on these issues, the present paper is about consumers' attitude towards the application of fMRI in marketing research. An online-questionnaire with a final sample of n=901 was administered, investigating psychological constructs explaining the acceptance of this alternative approach in consumer behavior. Based on these quantitative findings, a mixed-methods-design was followed by subsequently addressing selected important topical areas such as "ethics in neuromarketing" in a first focus group discussion as basis for further research.

THEORETICAL BACKGROUND

Neuroscientific Methods in Marketing Research–Promises and Limitations

Whereas the main advantages of applying neuroimaging techniques within the field of marketing research are quite evident from a scientific point of view–alternative possibility of investigating unconscious phenomena and emotions, better handling of response bias or measurement effects occuring in traditional self-report-studies-this is not necessarily the case from the perspective of the consumer who in the end is asked to participate as a test subject. Regarding the future application of neuroscientific methods in marketing research, among neuroimaging techniques, EEG and fMRI applied in combination with traditional quantitative and qualitative methods are thought to have the greatest potential (Page 2008). For pragmatic reasons, EEG is likely to see wider use than fMRI, but its application to everyday marketing field research is also limited. Moreover, another possible big winner is eye-tracking (see, e.g., Lorigo et al. 2008), as the technology has advanced to be essentially robust and also cost-efficient (Page 2008). Regarding future fundamental research in consumer behavior, fMRI-studies are the most promising for which the present study exclusively addresses the application of fMRI in marketing research. Neural information complements traditional methods of investigating human behavior and especially human decision-making. This is analogous to what Harmon-Jones and Devine (2003) cite about the application of neuroscientific methods in social psychology: "[…] to understand mechanisms underlying mind and behavior, both biological and social approaches are needed." (Cacioppo and Berntson 2002, in Harmon-Jones and Devine 2003, p. 590). Neuroimaging techniques can contribute to fundamental research in terms of a better conceptual understanding of latent constructs in consumer behavior. Measuring neural correlates within an fMRI-experiment allows not only for challenging but also adding new facets and providing a better explanation of already well-established models of decision-making, processing of information or the perception of brand and advertisements. For instance, Yoon et al. (2006) added new information regarding the brand personality concept based on fMRI data (Yoon et al. 2006). Regarding the measurement of latent constructs, these techniques explore neural correlates and thereby contribute to content and construct validity of traditional measures. As these concepts have been developed within traditional experimental settings and/or qualitative and quantitative field studies, additional information from neuroscience is appreciated. This knowledge will contribute to overcoming the obstacles traditional quantitative marketing research has always had to deal with and will help to establish sound and valid measures to capture, e.g., cognitions, emotions or attitudes. All in all, the author supports the view that it is the combination of traditional and technology-based new and mutlidisciplinary methods that will significantly frame the future of consumer behavior research. Besides these advantages of fMRI in marketing research, there are still some major limitations. An fMRI-study is very cost-intensive, regarding both the need for an experienced and skilled multidisciplinary research team and financially (Ambler 2008). Furthermore, there are issues of internal as well as external validity that have to be taken into account. Being in an fMRI-scanner during a laboratory experiment is not really comparable to a real consumption situation. Taking part in an fMRI-experiment can be stressful for the test subjects. The operating expense of the whole experiment is high. Regarding the status quo and the possible future development of fMRI in marketing and consumer behavior research, Ambler (2008) maintains that: "The tools have not advanced to the point where researchers can offer practitioners significant paybacks with any certainty. No doubt this will happen just as X rays moved from Marie Curie's laboratory to every dentist's surgery but that took 70 years." (Ambler 2008, p. 9).

Consumers' evaluation of research methods in marketing research

To be able to conduct more neuroimaging studies in the near future, people willing to participate in these studies are needed. The quality of results heavily depends, among other factors, on the participants' compliance with the tasks they have to perform. There are special requirements regarding the person itself as well as the data collection procedure that have to be granted. For instance, the whole experiment is very time consuming (the average scanning procedure for one participant takes between 60 and 90 minutes (Schilke and Reimann 2007). There is a considerable space restriction within the scanner and there is the necessity of non-metallic clothing and removal of any (body) jewellery because of the strong magnetic field. Respondents' attitudes towards different research methods can significantly influence the whole data collection process, if, e.g., the test person doesn't want to properly accomplish the tasks required. Roe et al. (2009) found out that recruits with more conservative general risk attitudes and higher measures of harm avoidance are less likely to agree to participate in biomedical experiments involving a fMRI session or a blood sample obtained via phlebotomy. These results indicate a major threat to the generalizability of economic studies applying biomedical techniques to the general population due to a possible sampling bias. In order to enhance the quality of the results as well as to avoid loss of resources, those possible threats should be taken into account when designing fMRI experiments. Even with traditional marketing research techniques, there is still known little about, e.g., motives or personality traits influencing the willingness to participate. Ognibene's results suggesting that questionnaire response is affected by leadership traits and ambitious reading habits date back to the 1970s (Ognibene 1970). Regarding the quality of marketing research in terms of representative samples, more in-depth and up-to-date knowledge about these issues is important. As new technologies have found their way into marketing research, a better understanding of peoples attitudes towards current methods and techniques is vital. This knowledge can help to establish a meaningful database (e.g., online-panels) for conducting offline- and/or online-surveys. In the case of neuroscientific methods, the issue is even more challenging. The application of neuroimaging methods is often quite new to researchers and even more unfamiliar to test subjects involved in empirical studies. Taking part in an EEG, MEG or fMRI-study is not an everyday experience for the average consumer. Still a small number of publications have dealt with participants' needs and requirements when taking part in neuroscientific studies. Roe et al. (2009) discussed the issue of a possible selection bias in test subject pools for experiments involving neuroimaging and blood samples (Roe et al. 2009). Cooke et al. (2007) and Senior et al. (2007) addressed the participants' experiences of taking part in research involving fMRI or MEG procedures by applying a mix of quantitative and qualitative methods. As they interviewed people right after their participation in an fMRI or MEG experiment, the sample size was rather small (n=21 for fMRI and n=23 for MEG) (Cooke et al. 2007; Senior et al. 2007).

EMPIRICAL DEMONSTRATION

Quantitative Study–Conceptual Research Model and Empirical Design

As consumer behavior research is interested in the consumer in order to derive knowledge about real-life purchasing, the author

FIGURE 1
Conceptual Research Model

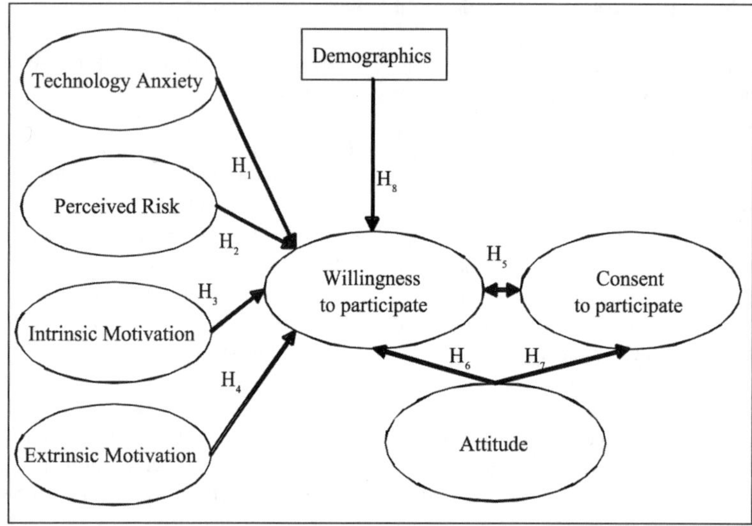

wanted to gain information on what the average consumer thinks about the usage of fMRI for marketing research purposes, under which conditions people would be willing to participate, whether there is a need for providing (financial) incentives or whether they have any concerns, e.g., health-related or ethical reservations. Getting information on participants' needs and requirements will help designing future projects and evading any interferences due to non-compliance of the participants during data collection. As fMRI-studies are very cost-intensive (Ambler 2008), the researcher is advised to have comprehensive knowledge not only about the whole experimental procedure but also about the participant's needs and requirements in order to be able to prevent any disturbances during the experiment. The present study covers both exploratory questions to gain first descriptive insight into how consumers feel about the topic in general and an effort to reveal (causal) relations between explanatory psychological phenomena and the willingness to participate as a test subject in an fMRI-study. In the questionnaire, after the exploratory questions, there was a detailed description of applying fMRI in marketing research in order to guarantee that all participants in the survey had sufficient knowledge about what they would have to expect as test subjects in an fMRI-experiment. Literature-based information on the application of fMRI in marketing research in general and on the possible experimental setting in particular was given. A picture of a person lying in an fMRI-scanner complemented the explanation. The conceptual research model was based on the key findings of Cooke, Peel, Shaw and Senior (2007) and Senior, Smyth, Cooke, Shaw and Peel (2007) as well as on general literature regarding psychological constructs involved in explaining attitude and behavioral intention. Regarding the latter, literature on (technology) acceptance models applied in a marketing context (James et al. 2006; Kulviwat et al. 2007; Meuter et al. 2005; Meuter et al. 2000; Suh and Han 2002; Yoon and Kim 2007; Yu et al. 2005) caught the author's attention. Some explanatory variables for the willingness (intention) to participate in a highly technology-driven experimental setting lend themselves to being applied. The validated measurement scales for perceived risk, intrinsic and extrinsic motivation, technology anxiety and attitude were adopted to the present research context. The dependent variable, i.e., the expressed willingness to participate, is complemented by another behavioral control variable named "consent to participate". Whereas the "willingness to participate" doesn't involve a concrete action, in answering the variable of "consent to participate" respondents had to act on their intention. This control variable allows for a more accurate estimation of how the respondents really feel. While agreeing to the question whether one would be willing to participate (willingness to participate) expresses some commitment, filling in ones contact details in a binding list of participants (consent to participate, for more details on the operationalization of the main constructs see table 1) represents a particularly high degree of commitment. Figure 1 shows the conceptual research model.

The hypothesized relationships incorporated are as follows:

- $H_{1\text{-}4}$: Perceived risk, technology anxiety, intrinsic and extrinsic motivation are assumed to explain the willingness to participate in a causal way. Following the findings of Evangelista, Albaum and Poon (1999) on the relevance of exchange theory, intrinsic and extrinsic motivation are assumed to explain the willingness to participate as a test subject. As fMRI is a quite unfamiliar new technology for most of the participants, perceived risk and technology anxiety are assumed to be negatively related to the willingness to participate.
- H_5: The articulated willingness to participate and the consent to participate are assumed to have a high positive correlation.
- $H_{6\text{-}7}$: Attitude and both willingness to participate and consent to participate are assumed to be positively correlated.
- H_8: Demographic variables (gender, age, income, blood donation behavior and previous medical MRI-experience) are assumed to explain the willingness to participate. Age is expected to be negatively correlated with the willingness to participate as older people tend to be more averse to accept new technologies.

Demographics and Selected Descriptive Results

The final sample consists of 901 respondents with 38.4% males and 61.6% females. The average age is 25.26 with the youngest participant being male and 15 years of age and the oldest being 61 and also male. In terms of education, 1.6% have basic education, 1.2% attended high school, 77.8% completed college level, and 19.4% obtained a university degree. The relatively young age and high level of education go along with the job categories mentioned; 74.7% are students, 19.9% employees, 3.1% entrepreneurs, 0.6% unemployed and 1.8% have another sort of occupation. Regarding monthly income, 79.9% earn up to $2.325, 12.8% between $2.325 and $4.651 and 7.4% more than $4.651. As it is to a large extent a student sample, the comparability with and the evaluation of previous fMRI-studies, which were often based on student samples as well, is granted. Nevertheless, regarding the literature on the problematic issue of using mainly student subjects in marketing research (Burnett and Dunne 1986), this limitation of the present study has to be taken into account when interpreting the findings. Furthermore, information on health-related behavioral tendencies was collected. For instance, the respondents were asked whether they donate blood or plasma on a regular basis. 11.2% do so in case of blood donation but only 1% regularly donate plasma. 93.3% have already heard about magnetic resonance imaging, and 29.1% indicate that they already collected some more information on the technology. 22.9% have already had a medical examination involving magnetic resonance imaging, 25.2% had already undergone a computed tomography (CT). Those people who indicated that they had already a medical MRI-examination were asked additional questions on how they experienced the whole process in the scanner. Items worded like 'How did you experience the noise' were offered with a rating-scale ranging from 1=very pleasant to 5=very unpleasant. The majority of respondents experienced the whole setting rather negatively, especially regarding the disturbing noise (M=3.43, 83.9% of the respondents were scoring between 3 and 5, therefore assumed to have had a rather negative experience), the confined space in the scanner (M=3.07, 69.1% scoring between 3 and 5), the length of the procedure (M=2.99, 68.6% scoring between 3 and 5), the ban on moving (M=2.97, 63.4% scoring between 3 and 5) and the examination in general (M=2.76, 58.6% scoring between 3 and 5). These findings confirm the results found by Cooke, Peel, Shaw and Senior (2007) where 43% indicated the confined space being "a bit upsetting". On the other hand, regarding the percentages stated above, there were also a number of respondents in the present study who remember the medical MRI-examination as a rather positive experience, respectively. Nevertheless, when being asked in an open-ended question what they remember most, the disturbing noise, the ban on moving and the confined space are mentioned most frequently. Importantly, 46.4% have considerable ethical concerns regarding the application of fMRI for marketing research purposes. This is a very interesting finding that needs to be investigated further. By now, there are still few publications dealing with the ethical issue in neuromarketing (see, e.g., Murphy et al. 2008; Wilson et al. 2008). Therefore, as a second empirical step, a focus group discussion (seven students aged between 22 and 28 years) on "ethics in neuromarketing" was conducted. Preliminary results indicate, that people are ambivalent regarding ethical issues in the "neuromarketing"-context. The focus group participants were very excited about fMRI-studies, very interested in the whole topic and also willing to participate as test subjects in the future. However, the fact that results of fMRI-experiments in marketing research can in the end be the basis for tailored marketing activities by a company raised some discomfort among the participants. More focus groups are already scheduled in order to recheck the initial findings.

Furthermore, the removal of any metallic material is inevitable for a participation due to the strong magnetic field. When participating in an fMRI-study, almost 95% (n=901) would be willing to remove all metallic parts of clothing (scoring between 1 and 2 on a 5-point rating scale, end-points verbalized as 1=fully agree, 5=fully disagree), and 94.1% would remove any piercings jewellery or hair styling gel. These results indicate that the rest is unwilling to participate by not fulfilling the requirements properly. Surprisingly, only 88.9% indicate that they would fully comply with the instructions given by the research team. Only 61.7% would fully trust in the expertise of the research team. 92.8% want to get detailed information about the whole experimental procedure before giving their consent to participate. These results indicate that people are slightly skeptical about the whole procedure. For instance, 10.8% even think that MRT-examinations are a health hazard. At least 25.1% think that fMRI should not be applied in marketing research (item: "I am against the application of fMRI in marketing research", scoring 1 and 2 on a 5-point rating scale, end-points verbalized as 1=fully agree, 5=fully disagree).

Constructs and Scale Assessment

Each item measuring the latent independent constructs in the questionnaire was offered with a 5-point rating scale with end points verbalized as 1="fully agree" and 5="fully disagree". Items taken from existing scales were adapted to the present application of attitude towards fMRI in marketing research. Additionally, some new items were generated based on qualitative pre-studies. The present paper can be classified as first empirical large sample sized insight into the topic. Due to this reason, next to the above stated framework of hypothesized causal relationships between attitudinal and behavioral constructs, there was a set of descriptive questions helping to gain first ideas about the overall topic. Therefore, confirmatory factor analysis or structural equation modelling was not applied at this stage of the project. Scale purification was based on exploratory factor analysis and Cronbach's alpha using SPSS 15.0.

Regarding validity of the central constructs, exploratory factor analyses indicated stable unidimensional results. In the case of perceived risk, 2 items had to be eliminated due to low factor loadings. As shown in table 1, alpha coefficients are on a satisfactory level. The dependent variable "willingness to participate" was measured by two items.

FINDINGS

H_{1-4} assume a causal relationship between perceived risk, technology anxiety, intrinsic motivation, and extrinsic motivation as the independent variables and the willingness to participate as the dependent variable. The results of the multiple regression analysis only partly support this assumption. While technology anxiety had no significant impact on the willingness to participate in an fMRI-study (p=.725), perceived risk, intrinsic and extrinsic motivation explain almost 73% of the variance of the willingness to participate (r^2= .725, p<.001, n=901). Standardized beta-coefficients indicate intrinsic motivation (.79) to have by far the strongest influence on the willingness to participate, followed by perceived risk (-.13) and extrinsic motivation (.11). The existence of intrinsic motivation is therefore the most important precondition. More than two-thirds of the respondents are motivated by the prospect of watching their brains work ('I love the idea of watching my brain work', scoring 1 or 2). Extrinsic motivators such as monetary incentives or vouchers have a minor impact. People are either willing to participate because they are personally driven or nothing, not even monetary incentives, can persuade them. In case of incentives for participation being offered, 90.1% would prefer to get paid. When being asked in an open-ended question, more than 63% mention amounts between $7 to $80 as an appropriate compensation. Extreme responses range from $0 to $100.000. Some said 'this amount is not quantifiable', 'inestimable'. Asked about participation for about

TABLE 1

Central Constructs of the Study

Construct	# of items		Reliability	Wording of items
	Initially[a]	After FA[b]	Alpha	(Examples partly abbreviated)
Perceived Risk	11	9 (47.89)	.885	"I think the magnetic field is a health risk" "Thinking about being in the scanner makes me feel uncomfortable"
Technology Anxiety	4	4 (45.59)	.745	"I have avoided technology because it is unfamiliar to me"
Intrinsic Motivation	4	4 (55.16)	.820	"I like the idea of watching my brain work" "I would like to participate for serving science"
Extrinsic Motivation	operationalized by two items, score (mean) for further analysis			"Monetary incentives would motivate me to participate" "I would not participate without being paid"
Attitude	9	9 (43.60)	.848	"I feel positive about fMRI-studies" "fMRI should not be applied in marketing research"
Willingness to Participate	operationalized by two items, score (mean) for further analysis			"I basically feel up to participating in an fMRI-study" "I would love to take part in an fMRI-study"
Consent to Participate	operationalized by the item: "I want to participate in an fMRI-study and will therefore fill in my contact data in ..." - response categories offered: a) "a binding list of participants", b) "a non-binding list of participants", c) "I am not interested at all".			

[a] Items administered in the questionnaire; [b] Items in the final scale after scale evaluation applying Exploratory Factor Analysis (total variance explained in % in brackets) and Reliability Analysis

$45, which reflects the average actual amount paid reported in literature, 59% agreed and 41% disagreed respectively.

H_5 postulates the intention to participate to be positively related to the expressed consent to participate. The non-parametric correlation amounts to Spearman rho=.64 (n=901, p<.001) affirming H_5. The relatively low correlation coefficient again underlines the discrepancy that non-binding expression of intention is not necessarily equivalent to actual behavior.

$H_{6\text{-}7}$ postulate attitude towards fMRI in marketing research to be positively related to the intention to participate. The same relationship should hold for the expressed consent of participation. The correlation amounts to r=.79 (n=901, p<.001) for attitude and intention and to Spearmans rho=.54 (n=901, p<.001) for attitude and consent to participate affirming $H_{6\text{-}7}$.

H_8 assumes demographics and health related personal tendencies to explain the variance of the willingness to participate. The ANOVA showed no significant influence of gender, income, blood donation behavior and previous medical MRI experience (p=.283). There was only found a significant but very low correlation between age and the willingness to participate (r=.14, p<.001). Younger people are more willing to serve as test subjects. Regarding this finding, recruiting among students is appropriate. New technological advances such as Web 2.0 offer new possibilities of recruitment. As the younger age group is also more affine to these innovations, recruiting in, e.g., online communities is promising. Surprisingly, except age, all other demographic variables have no influence on the willingness to participate in fMRI-studies. Most astonishing, previous experience gained by medical MRI-examinations has also no influence on the expressed willingness to participate.

Qualitative analysis of additional individual statements indicate, that for respondents who are basically positive about brain research but rather negative about market research, it is not easy to state their attitude and opinion on the application of fMRI in marketing. To test whether the general attitude towards marketing research has an impact on the willingness to participate in fMRI-studies, 5 items measuring the construct of "attitude towards marketing research" (EFA: 54.25% of variance explained, Cronbach's alpha= .853) were administered. The correlation between this construct and the willingness to participate amounts to r=.33, p<.001 (n=901). Respondents who are basically positive about marketing research have a higher intention to participate also in neuroscientific marketing studies.

As the variable "consent to participate" reflects actual behavior it is of particular interest. If respondents had chosen the answers a) or b) (see table 1), they were asked to fill in their contact details in a registration form subsequently. 21 out of 22 respondents indicating response a="binding list of participants" filled in the binding registration form. Only 246 out of 308 respondents indicating b="non-binding list of participants" effectively stated their contact information. The majority of respondents, 63.4% (n=571), indicated not being interested in actually participating. These results clearly reflect the discrepancy between indicated intention and actual behavior. This finding has to be considered when interpreting (technology) acceptance studies where intentional behavior is modeled as the dependent variable. Another explanation of the discrepancy could lie in the fact that it was an online questionnaire. A lack of trust in secure data processing via the internet could have kept some people from filling in their contact details.

DISCUSSION AND FURTHER RESEARCH

The number of marketing-related studies applying neuroscientific methods has been constantly increasing over the past decade (Ambler et al. 2004; Chamberlain and Broderick 2007; Kenning et al. 2007b; Lee et al. 2007; Plassmann et al. 2007; Schilke and Reimann 2007; Weber et al. 2007). The results of the present study show, that the application of fMRI in marketing is not universally embraced by the respondents. There are, e.g., some ethical reservations. Overall, the attitude towards the application of fMRI in marketing research is ambivalent, albeit slightly positive (M=2.88, n=901). In any case, there is potential for enhancement in order to boost the willingness to participate as a test subject. Detailed information prior to the experiment is inevitable to enhance trust in the expertise of the research team and the technology. If the actual experience during the experiment does not match prior expectations, proper data collection is at risk for the test subject does not comply with the specific requirements associated with fMRI. Providing more information about the strengths and advantages of the method to a broader population can also enhance trust in and attitude towards its application in marketing research. Intrinsic motivation turned out to have the highest impact on the willingness to participate. This is an interesting finding easing the argumentation in the recruiting process. On the other side, results of fMRI-studies are at risk to be blurred by a sampling bias, if only people scoring high on intrinsic motivation take part in fMRI-experiments as they may also be different from the general population regarding other personality trait variables.

Furthermore, the present study revealed that some negatively toned phenomena are relevant as well. As the whole scanning process can be experienced as rather unsettling, it turned out to be very important to actively enhance the scanning experience. In order to lower any perceived risk involved, detailed information on the whole experimental setting, the scanning procedure, the technology itself, the role of the participant her/himself should be given even prior to the participant's final consent to participate. It is important that the research team is sensitive to any discomfort experienced by the participant during each single experimental run. These observations should be included in the development of future experimental designs being more "participant friendly". The comfort of the participant is certainly a major concern when measuring neural correlates as it can easily bias the affective state. Only satisfied and fully cooperative participants provide high quality data without any disturbances due to moving artefacts. Further research is needed regarding participants' preferences for different marketing research methods in general and regarding different experimental, physiological and neuroscientific procedures in particular. By now, theoretical explanations on why people prefer, e.g., quantitative methods over qualitative ones or vice versa are still scarce. As consumer behavior research has always been interested in the motives and underlying psychological phenomena of why people show a certain behavior, it is necessary to also pay more attention and get more comprehensive knowledge about the empirical methods it is applying.

REFERENCES

Albaum, Gerald S., Felicitas Evangelista, and Nila Medina (1998), "Role of Response Behavior Theory in Survey Research: A Cross-National Study," *Journal of Business Research*, 42 (2), 115-25.

Ambler, Tim (2008), "Getting the Mind around Neuroscience," Department of Marketing, Center for Marketing Communication, *Proceedings of the ConNEcs, Conference on Neuroeconomics*, Copenhagen Business School, Denmark, 1-13.

Ambler, Tim, Sven Braeutigam, John Stins, Steven Rose, and Stephen Swithenby (2004), "Salience and Choice: Neural Correlates of Shopping Decisions," *Psychology and Marketing*, 21 (4), 247-61.

Bandettini, Peter (2007), "Functional MRI today," *International Journal of Psychophysiology*, 63, 138-45.

Burnett, John J. and Patrick M. Dunne (1986), "An Appraisal of the Use of Student Subjects in Marketing Research," *Journal of Business Research*, 14 (4), 329-43.

Cacioppo, John T., Gary G. Berntson, Tyler S. Lorig, Catherine J. Norris, Edith Rickett, and Howard Nusbaum (2003), "Just Because You're Imaging the Brain Doesn't Mean You Can Stop Using Your Head: A Primer and Set of First Principles," *Journal of Personality and Social Psychology*, 85 (4), 650-61.

Chamberlain, Laura and Amanda J. Broderick (2007), "The application of physiological observation methods to emotion research," *Qualitative Market Research: An International Journal*, 10 (2), 199-216.

Cobanoglu, Cihan and Nesrin Cobanoglu (2003), "The effect of incentives in web surveys: application and ethical considerations," *International Journal of Market Research*, 45 (4), 475-88.

Cooke, Richard, Elizabeth Peel, Rachel L. Shaw, and Carl Senior (2007), "The neuroimaging research process from the participants' perspective," *International Journal of Psychophysiology*, 63 (2), 152-58.

Deutskens, Elisabeth, Ko De Ruyter, Martin Wetzels, and Paul Oosterveld (2004), "Response Rate and Response Quality of Internet-Based Surveys: An Experimental Study," *Marketing Letters*, 15 (1), 21-36.

Esch, Franz-Rudolf (2008), *Strategie und Technik der Markenführung*. München: Vahlen.

Evangelista, Felicitas, Gerald Albaum, and Patrick Poon (1999), "An empirical test of alternative theories of survey response behaviour," *Journal of the Market Research Society*, 41 (2), 227-44.

Grimes, Anthony (2006), "Are we listening and learning? Understanding the nature of hemispherical lateralisation and its application to marketing," *International Journal of Market Research*, 48 (4), 439-58.

Hansen, Flemming (1972), *Consumer Choice Behavior. A Cognitive Theory*. New York: The Free Press.

Hansen, Torben (2005), "Perspectives on consumer decision making: An integrated approach," *Journal of Consumer Behaviour*, 4 (6), 420-37.

Harmon-Jones, Eddie and Patricia G. Devine (2003), "Introduction to the Special Section on Social Neuroscience: Promise and Caveats," *Journal of Personality and Social Psychology*, 85 (4), 589-93.

Harmon-Jones, Eddie, Cindy Harmon-Jones, Meghan Fearn, Jonathan D. Sigelman, and Peter Johnson (2008), "Left Frontal Cortical Activation and Spreading of Alternatives: Tests of the Action-Based Model of Dissonance," *Journal of Personality and Social Psychology*, 94 (1), 1-15.

Herrmann, Christoph S. and Stefan Debener (2008), "Simultaneous recording of EEG and BOLD responses: A historical perspective," *International Journal of Psychophysiology*, 67 (3), 161-68.

Houser, Daniel and Kevin McCabe (2009), "Experimental Neuroeconomics and Non-cooperative Games," in *Neuroeconomics. Decision Making and the Brain*, Paul W. Glimcher and Colin F. Camerer and Ernst Fehr and Russell A. Poldrack, Eds. London: Elsevier, 47-62.

Hubert, Mirja and Peter Kenning (2008), "A current overview of consumer neuroscience," *Journal of Consumer Behaviour*, 7 (July-October), 272-92.

James, Tabitha, Taner Pirim, Katherine Boswell, Brian Reithel, and Reza Barkhi (2006), "Determining the Intention to Use Biometric Devices: An Application and Extension of the Technology Acceptance Model," *Journal of Organizational & End User Computing*, 18 (3), 1-24.

Kenning, Peter, Hilke Plassmann, and Dieter Ahlert (2007a), "Applications of functional magnetic resonance imaging for market research," *Qualitative Market Research: An International Journal*, 10 (2), 135-52.

______ (2007b), "Consumer Neuroscience. Implikationen neurowissenschaftlicher Forschung für das Marketing," *Marketing ZFP*, 29 (1), 55-66.

Kozinets, Robert V. (2002), "The Field Behind the Screen: Using Netnography for Marketing Research in Online Communities," *Journal of Marketing Research*, 39 (1), 61-72.

Kulviwat, Songpol, Gordon C. Bruner II, Anand Kumar, Suzanne A. Nasco, and Terry Clark (2007), "Toward a Unified Theory of Consumer Acceptance Technology," *Psychology & Marketing*, 24 (12), 1059-84.

Lee, Nick and Amanda J. Broderick (2007), "The past, present and future of observational research in marketing," *Qualitative Market Research: An International Journal*, 10 (2), 121-29.

Lee, Nick, Amanda J. Broderick, and Laura Chamberlain (2007), "What is 'neuromarketing'? A discussion and agenda for future research," *International Journal of Psychophysiology*, 63 (2), 199-204.

Lorigo, Lori, Maya Haridasan, Hrönn Brynjarsdóttir, Ling Xia, Thorsten Joachims, Geri Gay, Laura Granka, Fabio Pellacini, and Bing Pan (2008), "Eye Tracking and Online Search: Lessons Learned and Challenges Ahead," *Journal of the American Society for Information Science and Technology*, 59 (7), 1041-52.

Meuter, Matthew L., Mary J. Bitner, Amy L. Ostrom, and Stephen W. Brown (2005), "Choosing Among Alternative Delivery Modes: An Investigation of Customer Trial of Self-Service Technologies," *Journal of Marketing*, 69 (April), 61-83.

Meuter, Matthew L., Amy L. Ostrom, Robert I. Roundtree, and Mary J. Bitner (2000), "Self-Service Technologies: Understanding Customer Satisfaction with Technology-Based Service Encounters," *Journal of Marketing*, 64 (July), 50-64.

Moosmann, Matthias, Tom Eichele, Helge Nordby, Kenneth Hugdahl, and Vince D. Calhoun (2008), "Joint independent component analysis for simultaneous EEG-fMRI: Principle and simulation," *International Journal of Psychophysiology*, 67 (3), 212-21.

Murphy, Emily R., Judy Illes, and Peter B. Reiner (2008), "Neuroethics of neuromarketing," *Journal of Consumer Behaviour*, 7 (July-October), 293-302.

Ognibene, Peter (1970), "Traits Affecting Questionnaire Response," *Journal of Advertising Research*, 10 (3), 18-20.

Page, Graham (2008), "Beyond The Pretty Pictures-The Future For Neuroeconomics In Marketing Research," Department of Marketing, Center for Marketing Communication, *Proceedings of the ConNEcs, Conference on Neuroeconomics*, Copenhagen Business School, Denmark, 1-24.

Plassmann, Hilke, Tim Ambler, Sven Braeutigam, and Peter Kenning (2007), "What can advertisers learn from neuroscience?," *International Journal of Advertising*, 26 (2), 151-75.

Roe, Brian E., Timothy C. Haab, David Q. Beversdorf, Howard H. Gu, and Michael R. Tilley (2009), "Risk-attitude selection bias in subject pools for experiments involving neuroimaging and blood samples," *Journal of Economic Psychology*, 30 (2), 187-89.

Rothschild, Michael L., Yong J. Hyun, Byron Reeves, Esther Thorson, and Robert Goldstein (1988), "Hemispherically Lateralized EEG as a Response to Television Commercials," *Journal of Consumer Research*, 15 (September), 185-98.

Schilke, Oliver and Martin Reimann (2007), "Neuroökonomie: Grundverständnis, Methoden und betriebswirtschaftliche Anwendungsfelder," *Journal für Betriebswirtschaft*, 57, 247-62.

Senior, Carl, Hannah Smyth, Richard Cooke, Rachel L. Shaw, and Elizabeth Peel (2007), "Mapping the mind for the modern market researcher," *Qualitative Market Research: An International Journal*, 10 (2), 153-67.

Suh, Bomil and Ingoo Han (2002), "Effect of trust on customer acceptance of Internet banking," *Electronic Commerce Research and Applications*, 1 (3-4), 247-63.

Weber, Bernd, Andreas Aholt, Carolin Neuhaus, Peter Trautner, Christian E. Elger, and Thorsten Teichert (2007), "Neural evidence for Reference-dependence in real-market-transactions," *NeuroImage*, 35 (1), 441-47.

Willingham, Daniel T. and Elizabeth W. Dunn (2003), "What Neuroimaging and Brain Localization Can Do, Cannot Do, and Should Not Do for Social Psychology," *Journal of Personality and Social Psychology*, 85 (4), 662-71.

Wilson, R. Mark, Jeannie Gaines, and Ronald Paul Hill (2008), "Neuromarketing and Consumer Free Will," *The Journal of Consumer Affairs*, 42 (3), 389-410.

Yoon, Carolyn, Angela H. Gutchess, Fred Feinberg, and Thad A. Polk (2006), "A Functional Magnetic Resonance Imaging Study of Neural Dissociations between Brand and Person Judgments," *Journal of Consumer Research*, 33 (June), 31-40.

Yoon, Cheolho and Sanghoon Kim (2007), "Convenience and TAM in a ubiquitous computing environment: The case of wireless LAN," *Electronic Commerce Research and Applications*, 6 (7), 102-12.

Yu, Jieun, Imsook Ha, Munkee Choi, and Jaejeung Rho (2005), "Extending the TAM for a t-commerce," *Information & Management*, 42 (7), 965-76.

The Ritualization of Cultural, Social, and Economic Capital in Establishing In-Group Acceptance

Lee McGinnis, Stonehill College, USA
James Gentry, University of Nebraska-Lincoln, USA

ABSTRACT

Using Bourdieu's three forms of capital (economic, social, and cultural), we demonstrate how in a short period of time these forms become part of the ritual of inclusion and exclusion in golf. Because golf on its face is not a highly masculine activity (i.e., lacking physicality, machismo, and endurance), more benign methods are used to include or exclude same gender players. The transformation of power happens quickly through four stages: the greeting, the feeling out, the chest pounding, and acceptance/ rejection. It is through these stages that one either becomes part of the capital elite or excluded.

INTRODUCTION

In this study, we formulate an understanding of how three forms of capital (Bordieu 1986) become ritualized in a round of golf, which is considered a ritual performance in and of itself (McGinnis, Gentry, and Gao 2008). Through observations with male golfers, we show how cultural, social, and economic capital weave their way through golf's ritual stages in establishing either inclusion or exclusion. In-group inclusion is evident in several consumption subcultures. Knowing the group's norms, understanding how to conduct oneself intellectually, and having appropriate economic resources and proper social connections all interact to create a hierarchy of inclusion or exclusion within the in-group.

LITERATURE REVIEW

Bourdieu (1986) provides three types of capital: economic, social and cultural. Economic capital is maintained through domination of cash, assets, property, and other forms of currency that give certain individuals power. Those with high economic capital but not necessarily high cultural capital tend to have consumption patterns that are reflective of middlebrow tastes (Trigg 2001).

Social capital is using the influence of friends and social networks to maintain or establish power and significance. Having such capital is important not only for achieving social status, but can also have an impact on earnings (Kim 2009). Furthermore, Bourdieu (1986) indicates that such capital is linked to the possession of a durable network of institutionalized relationships with mutual acquaintances. In this case then, social capital acts upon those social relationships that are perceived as prestigious and commonly known throughout a given social sphere or community. It can also be imparted through membership in a group, whether it is a common last name, a class, or school. Social capital gains its strength through shared understandings and limits of relationships, which are reproduced through unceasing efforts of sociability (Bourdieu 1986). It follows from this account that those are who well known are worthy of being known due to more widespread capital.

Cultural capital presents itself in terms of the skills, knowledge, and attitude that parents or other significant influences pass onto their children or others. Cultural capital in the United States creates a divide in terms of taste, with those having high cultural capital enjoying a privileged life in terms of occupations, the arts, and cosmopolitan consumption, while those with low cultural capital consume objects that have more mass appeal and therefore are considered less cultured (Holt 1998). The power of cultural capital in terms of acquiring such things as extreme success (Gladwell 2008) and scholarly advantage (Sacks 2007) has been well advanced in popular literature.

Bourdieu (1986) speaks of three types or states of cultural capital: embodied, objectified, and institutionalized. The embodied is so called because of its direct link to the body, which often implies a sacrifice of the body itself in terms of physical exertion, mental labor (e.g., an education) time, and money. In the objectified state, capital can be transmitted in terms of ownership, such as when one takes over ownership of artwork or some other cultural artifact. The institutionalized state infers that a standard can be made with capital thus allowing for shared meanings of its value.

Rituals are symbolic behaviors or performances that tend to be repeated over time, which include as well as exclude participants (Rothenbuhler 1998). Rituals provide social order, transformation, and community (Driver 1991), all of which can be advantages or disadvantages to participants and non-participants alike. Rook (1985) suggests that there are four components of ritual: artifacts, a script, performance roles, and an audience, all of which can be present in a round of golf (McGinnis 2002).

The role of rituals and ritual behavior in marketing has been explored in advertising (Otnes and Scott 1996), college-aged drinking (Treise, Wolburg, and Otnes 1999), hair grooming (Rook 1985), baseball viewing (Holt 1992, 1995), Thanksgiving (Wallendorf and Arnould 1991), and sacred consumption (Belk, Wallendorf, and Sherry 1989). Ritual use has also been noted in skydiving (Celsi, Rose, and Leigh 1993) and whitewater rafting (Arnould and Price 1993). Gainer (1995) showed how consumers use rituals in performing arts to construct themselves socially.

In this study we use golf as our context because it has been noted to involve rituals capable of producing communitas, to have symbolic behaviors and artifacts, and to have explicit and implicit rules for behavior (McGinnis 2002). Golf, too, has been referred to as an activity that is not necessarily replete with masculine markers (McGinnis, McQuillan, and Chapple 2005). We contend that male golfers must find ways to make their domain more rugged in a world and atmosphere that Holt and Thompson (2004) argue has become emasculated. Confusion as to what it means to be a man in Western society has increased greatly in past decades (Garcia 2008; Lemon 1995; Pleck 1981; Salzman, Mathathia, and O'Reilly 2005; Seidler 2006; Thompson and Fletcher 2006).

METHOD

Observations for this study were conducted over the spring and summer of 2008. We chose golf because of its public accessibility, ritual enactments, and elitist perceptions. The primary author, who himself has 30 years of avid golf experience, observed approximately 25 rounds of golf (either 9 or 18 holes) to determine the ritual activity that might be occurring in exclusive domains, and from there developed preliminary working categories from the etic perspective (see Holt 1995). The primary author played golf primarily with foursomes, where he was often the fourth person added or the "outsider," which provided him with firsthand experience of the different ways in which in-group participation is formed. He also played with some groups and single golfers multiple times in which singles or twosomes were added. In these latter cases, the primary author was able to see in-group movement from the "insider"

TABLE 1

Capital Usages Displayed During Ritual Formalization in Golf

Ritual stage	Capital displays
Stage I: The Greeting	Dominated by cultural capital displays of handshakes, introductions, etiquette, and rules of golf.
Stage II: The Feeling Out	Dominated by social capital displays of social networks, knowing prominent golfers, and banter.
Stage III: The Chest Pounding	Dominated by economic displays of courses played, equipment, and careers.
Stage IV: Acceptance/Rejection	Dominated by social capital exchanges if relationship is accepting and economic and cultural capital displays if relationship is being rejected.

perspective. Management would often place a single or twosome in the group in order to improve time efficiencies and profitability.

We used a grounded theory method (Glaser and Strauss 1967) to establish the major themes involved in the ritualization of in-group formation. Specifically, we started with open coding to gain an idea of how the concepts fit the data (Strauss 1987). For example, examination of our early notes indicated that in the beginning of each round, participants would often demonstrate their intricate knowledge of the game by showing a sound pre-shot routine. Conceptually stepping back from the data, a common practice in open coding when one may know too much experientially about the phenomenon of interest (Strauss 1987), and reading the literature indicated that this might be considered an element of the cultural capital. At this point, we became aware of other forms of capital that might be present and observed them more acutely in our data in the different stages of in-group inclusion. We then used an axial coding process once we discovered that elements of capital were prevalent in establishing in-group acceptance. Axial coding can be used to show the conditions around which a process occurs (Strauss 1987). In doing so, we noticed that exchanges of cultural, social, and economic capital were prevalent in forming relationships, and that the usage of these different forms was considered the major constraints in establishing these barriers.

FINDINGS

Stage I: The Greeting

Our results indicated that cultural capital is used primarily in the beginning stage of the ritual to demonstrate one's knowledge of proper manners and the intricate knowledge and formalities of golf (see table 1). Demonstrations not necessarily unique to golf include the handshake, eye contact, and forms of salutation. This is where the "sizing up" of the fellow golfer or competitor was initialized. A failure in this impression management exercise (Goffman 1967) could negatively set the tone for the rest of the round, where if an unfamiliar player did not extend his hand in the round or failed to introduce himself properly to others he would be treated somewhat coldly. Greetings (i.e., handshakes) are considered serious forms of ritual (Rook 1985).

Context specific forms of the greeting (i.e., those that are unique to golf) included establishing order of play, partners, and in some cases betting games. The cultural capital being displayed here was that of insider knowledge, which is gained through years of playing golf. As Allen and Anderson (1994) argued and found in our data as well, the cultural capital earned here is achieved through a "comfortable familiarity" with the game and not some special knowledge that is naturally bestowed upon the cultural elite. It takes on the embodied form because the owner through years of time investment earns it. It is used in the same vein one might be weeded out in other consumption groups for being pretenders or wannabes (Fox 1987; Schouten and McAlexander 1995). Establishing order of play among strangers was often done through the tossing of a golf tee, whereupon the sharp end of the tee indicated first to play. It was in this stage, too, that participants commonly gained knowledge of others' capital by throwing out such betting terms as "skins," "presses," and "two-two-two." Failure to understand or use these terms correctly could create barriers to ritual inclusion. Not understanding bets or formats of play could also indicate low cultural capital, such as when one would call a game a "best ball" (when each player plays his own ball and best score net handicap is posted for the pair or group) when it was actually a "scramble" (when all players hit from the spot of the most optimal shot in the group). Insider knowledge of the more obscure games indicated knowledge that Bourdieu might term as ideationally difficult to obtain (Holt 1998) and would therefore signify in this realm high cultural capital. Lack of rules knowledge could doom the new player, especially when violations occurred in league play or times when competition was more serious. Golf rules are quite rigid and are generally followed, though many foursomes will bend them to some extent. Determining the magnitude of that extent can create awkwardness when the members of the foursome do not know each other well.

Although participants in golf used the greeting as a way to determine unknown or relatively unknown participants' worthiness, the next aspect of this stage determined whether one could "walk the walk." The first shot on the tee signified one's savvy in terms of play, where those who demonstrated knowledge of the game had to match their game with a sound pre-shot routine (i.e., perfected practice swing and alignment). Players of all levels when matched with unfamiliar others could be seen as nervous.

Etiquette and rules of the game were vital on the first tee. Taking a prolonged period of time in the pre-shot routine (e.g., excessive practice swings and standing too long over the ball) could set a negative tone, with the other participants giving each other incredulous looks behind the primary actor's back. Lacking cultural capital in this case meant the existence either of self-awareness of one's wrongdoings or of inconsideration by not helping others establish a rhythm and flow. This would be akin to a person talking excessively about oneself in a social setting or simply being unaware.

The greeting stage, too, was when players would first discover the extent to which they could get away with informal play, such as using "mulligans" (an extra tee shot, usually on the first tee), "winter rules" (i.e., preferred lies), and "gimmes" (putts given within a certain distance). Each of these forms of cultural capital represents violations of the rules of golf, but were often altered when poor conditions warranted such actions, when players had marginal skill, when it took a while to "warm up," or, and perhaps more importantly, when one was trying to gauge latitude. Each form also represented a way to establish rapport, as if the reaction to the violation was a way to test the waters of serious play, and because the one asking usually presented the requests in a half-joking manner, it allowed him to "save face" (Goffman 1967) if the other person were more serious.

Betting seemed to be a harbinger as to what other activities one might expect (e.g., drinking, risqué jokes, derogatory conversation, etc.). If a bet were on, or if play occurred during serious competition, liberal bending of the rules could dampen future relations. Usually, however, newcomers to the group would know from the first tee the expectations of serious play. Liberal gimmes were used during league play, even though play was serious, as the format (i.e., match play) usually permitted such action under the rules. However, length of the gimmes seemed to vary with the seriousness of the competition, with friendlier pairings giving longer putts. Wagering appeared to be hugely symbolic of the relationship. Though many bets were extremely nominal, where the loser might end up paying $10 at the most, the act itself signified the nature of the competition and relationship. How one responded to such an act was clearly a difference maker in the first step toward invitation to join the in-group.

Stage II: The Feeling Out

Social and economic capital displays were dominant in the feeling out stage. Using social capital as a basis for ritualization, participants in this study used name-dropping, banter, and nostalgic ties as ways to either include or exclude, the tone of which was determined by felt commonality with the new golfer. It was incumbent among groups where members were new to each other to show their cards in terms of common acquaintances. In some cases, the common people were used to further connections within the group with benign intent while other times it was used to demonstrate superiority. The ritual would usually begin with a question of what do you do for a living or where do you normally play golf. Narratives of power connections took place when the participants connected themselves to head golf professionals, tour players, and other superior players. At this stage, participants were feeling the others out in mostly a socially compliant way in order to establish influence parameters, pecking orders, and willingness to reciprocate. The name-dropping displays indicated a sense of network vitality and to determine whether the person with whom the exchange was taking place was worthy of being known (see Bourdieu 1986). Many of the informants demonstrated their knowledge of other golfers both at the club to which they belonged or in the larger golfer community in the city or region. This showed currency in the field, much like an academician citing notable authors and scholars. Social capital was also exchanged when participants would gain knowledge of where one went to college or high school, or membership in civic organizations or church affiliations.

Banter also provided a means toward acceptance. Usage of profanity was common, as was making light of one's masculinity or lack thereof. Not going for long shots or being too tentative was often an invitation for giving one the "business" for lacking manhood or masculinity. Indicating that one must have suffered a castration or lacking testicles was a common expression. Retorting with customary f-bombs was also common. These forms of banter showed a willingness to participate and thus encouraged further engagement, indicating his belonging to the group (Lennox Terrion and Ashforth 2002).

Social capital would often be displayed in terms of nostalgia as well, especially when the players wanted to demonstrate to the outsider in the group how long they had known one another. Oftentimes, golfers could alienate younger newcomers by discussing items that were unique to their age cohort, thus creating a barrier to entry for the younger golfer by demonstrating "membership" in an age group. If the younger golfer tried to relate, the conversation could end abruptly, could result in the older golfers laughing off the younger golfer's act of entry, or "code switching" (Goffman 1981) could occur where the older golfers altered their language to references hard for the younger golfer to understand. This act of having "been-there" represented a pilgrimage of sorts in which those with common experiences could only relate, such as that found after white water rafting (Arnould and Price 1993) or in skydiving (Celsi et al. 1993).

Stage III: The Chest Pounding Stage

Displays of economic capital usually prevailed after social capital or in conjunction with it in the "chest pounding stage." At this stage, the participants would often brag of equipment, courses played, and sometimes careers and cars. These occurrences seemed to increase when play was more serious or when a player was not performing well. They would also become more prevalent if the relationship had taken a turn for the worse, or if disparities occurred between levels of either cultural or social capital. For example, if one player displayed cultural capital that was superior to his new acquaintance in terms of knowledge, skill level, or etiquette, the deficit holder (in terms of the form of equipment and/or places played) would often seek redemption. In this sense, the deficit holder would often attempt to "buy his game," an expression commonly known in golf for those who are unskilled, lazy, or too time-deprived to develop a game "legitimately." Oftentimes, in order to thwart this perception, golfers with high cultural capital (Holt 1998) carry in their bags old, unique, or special clubs, clubs that had been "around the block" and had unique stories attached to them. Buying a game among lesser players is often seen as uncultured, thereby an expression of low cultural capital (Holt 1998).

Several of the respondents donned hats, clothing, and equipment that provided lead-ins to "been-there" type stories. The stories began with a logo on a hat, a bag badge, or club that had a long history of either great performances or experiences. The golfers would normally wait for some other golfer to respond to the display in a "funny-you-should-ask" humility, which would then lead to a series of questions and answers that allowed the holder of the item to demonstrate his cultural capital.

Stage IV: Acceptance/Rejection

The next stage of the capital establishment is the make it or break it stage of in-group inclusion, or the stage in which exclusionary practices were either heightened and players just tolerated one another or when players welcomed each other and developed closer ties. If players welcomed the outsider, friendly banter increased and displays of economic capital seemed to lessen. For example, in-group participants would often give the outsider golf tips, make fun of poor shots, make noise during shots, or include him in jokes or some other form of banter to indicate group inclusion. If, however, the relationship worsened, capital displays often increased. If an outsider was obviously left out of the in-group, any misstep with cultural capital could be heightened. Being overly sensitive to etiquette infractions was common, such as being ridiculed for standing in a golfer's line of site during a putt, talking during a pre-shot routine, or casting a shadow in a golfer's peripheral vision.

Inclusion into the in-group would often result in discussion of drinking or getting drinks at the 19th hole (i.e., the clubhouse), from the beverage cart, or at the turn (i.e., between the ninth and tenth holes). Outsiders given the green light would often be included in this ritual by being offered a drink. Though most of the drinking commenced after the round was completed, a few of the participants engaged in moderate to heavy drinking at the midway point or during the round when the beverage service arrived. Drinking was given the same latitude on the course as it is in bars, where excessive consumption was allowed. Some respondents tied golf and the ritual of drinking so closely that disposing of or changing the nature of this ritual artifact (see Rook 1985) would be nearly impossible, similar to the rite of passage of binge drinking among college students when they turn the age of 21 (Treise et al. 1999). Lack of drinking in golf appeared to be more mocked than drinking itself.

DISCUSSION

The findings in this study can be applied to many consumer-to-consumer contexts where initiation into the in-group happens in a short period of time and where different forms of capital are present in making an impression. For example, the same process might be found in hunting trips, girls' nights out, white-water rafting, group aerobic exercises, and even motorcycle clubs. This process may be present anytime entry into a consumption subculture is marked by superior knowledge of the activity's rituals, where above average financial resources is needed, and where peers value such activities. Service providers need to be more sensitive to exclusionary processes involved in customer-to-customer interactions, as their own efforts to attract customers may be undermined by those C2C exchanges.

We find that the Bourdieu forms of capital appear to happen primarily in sequence and are used to establish worthiness of peers in a very systematic way. If one happens before the other (e.g., enactments of economic capital before cultural capital), the actor doing so may either be stigmatized (Goffman 1963) and be forced to redeem himself or save face (Goffman 1959). Early faux pas in the cultural capital stage can render subsequent displays of social and economic capital useless.

Economic capital enactments are often seen as displays of desperation and can be perceived as boorish or uncultured, preserved for those lacking in the other two forms of capital. Future studies may determine that those resorting to economic superiority displays tend to be the least satisfied with their golfing lives (i.e., or general lives, for that matter), and turn to economic displays when dissonance occurs in other capital areas. Burroughs and Rindfleisch (2002) have found similar relationships between materialism and general well being.

We contend that the cultural capital stage is the most important step in this ritual sequence because of first impression management (Goffman 1959) and that it should be the focus among managers seeking to reduce churns or retain customers, thereby helping to establish community and perhaps communitas, which may ultimately lead to enduring involvement (McGinnis et al. 2008). Knowledge of game rules, local rules, etiquette, and other subtle nuisances establish confidence and open the doors for cultural and social capital to be honed, developed, and demonstrated. Managers should take an active role in creating better customer-to-customer relationships.

REFERENCES

Allen, Douglas E. and Paul F. Anderson (1994), "Consumption and Social Stratification: Bourdieu's Distinction," *Advances in Consumer Research*, 21, 70-74.

Arnould, Eric J. and Linda L. Price (1993), "River Magic: Extraordinary Experience and the Extended Service Encounter," *Journal of Consumer Research*, 20 (June), 24-45.

Belk, Russell W., Melanie Wallendorf, and John F. Sherry, Jr. (1989), "The Sacred and the Profane in Consumer Behavior: Theodicy on the Odyssey," *Journal of Consumer Research*, 16 (June), 1-38.

Burroughs, James E. and Aric Rindfleisch (2002), "Materialism and Well-Being: A Conflicting Values Perspective," *Journal of Consumer Research*, 29 (December), 348-370.

Bourdieu, Pierre (1986), "The Forms of Capital," in *J.G. Richardson's Handbook for Theory and Research for the Sociology of Education*, pp. 241–258.

Celsi, Richard L., Randall L. Rose, and Thomas W. Leigh (1993), "An Exploration of High-Risk Leisure Consumption Through Skydiving," *Journal of Consumer Research*, 20 (June), 1-23.

Driver, Tom (1991), *The Magic of Ritual*, New York: Harper Collins.

Fox, Kathryn J. (1987), "Real Punks and Pretenders: The Social Organization of a Counterculture," *Journal of Contemporary Ethnography*, 16 (3), 344-70.

Gainer, Brenda (1995), "Ritual and Relationships: Interpersonal Influences on Shared Consumption," *Journal of Business Research*, 32 (March), 253-260.

Garcia, Guy (2008), *The Decline of Men*, New York: Harper Collins.

Gladwell, Malcolm (2008), *Outliers: The Story of Success*, New York, NY: Little Brown.

Glaser, Barney G. and Anselm L. Strauss (1967), *The Discovery of Grounded Theory*, Chicago: Aldine.

Goffman, Erving (1959), *The Presentation of Self in Everyday Life*, New York, NY: Doubleday.

______ (1963), *Stigma: Notes on the Management of Spoiled Identity*, Englewood Cliffs, NJ: Prentice-Hall.

______ (1967), *Interaction Ritual*, New York: Doubleday.

______ (1981), *Forms of Talk*, Philadelphia: University of Pennsylvania Press.

Holt, Douglas B. (1992), "Examining the Descriptive Value of 'Ritual' in Consumer Behavior: A View from the Field," *Advances in Consumer Research*, 19, 213-218.

______ (1995), "How Consumers Consume: A Typology of Consumption Practices," *Journal of Consumer Research*, 22 (June), 1-16.

______ (1998), "Does Cultural Capital Structure American Consumption?" *Journal of Consumer Research*, 25 (June) 1-25.

______ and Craig J. Thompson (2004), "Man-of-Action Heroes: The Pursuit of Heroic Masculinity in Everyday Consumption," *Journal of Consumer Research*, 31 (September), 425-440.

Kim, Harris H. (2009), "Networks, Information Transfer, and Status Conferral: The Role of Social Capital in Income Stratification among Lawyers," *The Sociological Quarterly*, 50, 61–87.

Lemon, Jennifer (1995), "Masculinity in Crisis?" *Agenda*, 25, 61-71.

Lennox Terrion, Jennepher and Blake E. Ashforth (2002), "From 'I' to 'We': The Role of Putdown Humor and Identity in the Development of a Temporary Group," *Human Relations*, 55 (1), 55-88.

McGinnis, Lee P. (2002), "Examining the Gender Gap in Participatory Golf Using a Ritual Dramaturgical Framework and Gender Perspective," doctoral dissertation, University of Nebraska-Lincoln, Lincoln, Nebraska.

______, James W. Gentry, and Tao Gao (2008), "The Impact of Flow and Communitas on Enduring Involvement in Extended Service Encounters," *Journal of Service Research*, 11 (August) 74-90.

______, Julia A. McQuillan, and Constance L. Chapple (2005), "I Just Want to Play: Women, Sexism and Persistence in Golf," *Journal of Sport and Social Issue*, 29 (August), 313-337.

Otnes, Cele and Linda M. Scott (1996), "Something Old, Something New: Exploring the Interaction Between Ritual and Advertising," *The Journal of Advertising*, 25 (Spring), 33-50.

Pleck, Joseph H. (1981), *The Myth of Masculinity*, London: Massachusetts Institute of Technology.

Rook, Dennis W. (1985), "The Ritual Dimension of Consumer Behavior," *Journal of Consumer Research*, 12 (December), 251-264.

Rothenbuhler, Eric W. (1998), *Ritual Communication: From Everyday Conversation to Mediate Ceremony*, Thousand Oaks, CA: Sage Publications.

Sacks, Peter (2007), *Tearing Down the Gates: Confronting the Class Divide in American Education*, Berkeley and Los Angeles, CA: University of California Press.

Salzman, Marian, Ira Matathia, and Ann O'Reilly (2005), *The Future of Men*, New York: Palgrave MacMillan.

Schouten, John W. and James H. McAlexander (1995), "Subcultures of Consumption: An Ethnography of the New Bikers," *Journal of Consumer Research*, 22 (June), 43-61.

Seidler, Victor J. (2006), *Young Men and Masculinities: Global Cultures and Intimate Lives*, New York: Zed Books.

Strauss, Anslem L. (1987), *Qualitative Analysis for Social Scientists*, San Francisco: Cambridge University Press.

Thompson, Julie and Kristin Fletcher (2005), "Leo Burnett Sheds Light on Global Male Identity Crisis with New Man Study," www.leoburnett.com/manstudy/contact/htm

Treise, Debbie, Joyce M Wolburg, and Cele C. Otnes (1999), "Understanding the "Social Gifts" of Drinking Rituals: An Alternative Framework for PSA Developers," *Journal of Advertising*, 28 (Summer), 17-31.

Trigg, Andrew B. (2001), "Veblen, Bourdieu and Conspicuous Consumption," *Journal of Economic Issues*, 35 (1), pp. 99–115.

Wallendorf, Melanie and Eric J. Arnould (1991), "We Gather Together: Consumption Rituals of Thanksgiving Day," *Journal of Consumer Research*, 17 (June), 13-31.

An Exploratory Study into the Disposition Behaviour of Poor Bottom-of-the-Pyramid Urban Consumers

Stephen G. Saunders, Monash University, Australia

ABSTRACT

This study explores the critical events, decisions and emotions associated with the disposition of basic household items of poor urban consumers. The method chosen to describe the poor consumers experience in the disposition of possessions was that of existential-phenomenology. Open-ended in-depth interviews were conducted with 10 poor urban consumers. The results showed that the disposition behaviour of these poor consumers, while significantly influenced by their religious beliefs, occupied the same psychological stages of disposition as observed by Roster (1989). However, while the psychological stages of disposition were very similar, the behavioural outcomes were quite different to that experienced in wealthier communities. These differences were presented before discussing the implications of these differences. In particular, the decisive role that religion played in influencing disposal behaviour of these poor consumers was discussed before suggesting areas of further research.

INTRODUCTION

Consumer behaviour is defined by Schiffman, et al. (2005:6) as the behaviour that consumers display in "seeking, purchasing, using, evaluating and disposing of products and services". While the academic marketing literature publishes any abundance of theories and empirical studies on seeking, purchasing, using and evaluating behaviour, there are very few studies on the disposition of products and services. Some notable exceptions include a taxonomy for describing consumer disposition behaviour (Jacoby, Berning and Dietvorst, 1977; Hanson, 1980), a conceptual model of consumer disposition of possessions (Young and Wallendorf, 1989), two empirical studies into the disposition of special possessions by older consumers and disposition possessions among families of people living with AIDS (Price, Arnould and Curasi, 2000; Kates, 2001), and a theoretical model on the disposition of meaningful possessions to strangers (Lastovicka and Fernandez, 2005).

It is surprising that the disposition facet of consumer behaviour is so under researched given that the study of disposition is highly relevant to a number of contemporary marketing problems. First, disposition behaviour is an integral component of the consumption cycle and potentially an important antecedent of future consumer buying behaviour. As consumption behaviour is cyclical in nature, an understanding of the disposition of "old" goods and services prior to "new" purchases would underscore a diversity of marketing implications (Jacoby et al., 1977). In fact, early pioneers of consumer theory such as Belk (1988) encouraged research into the experiential facets of consumption that included disposition processes; recommending that the disposition phenomena should be analysed from a macro-, meso- and micro-theoretical perspective (Arnould and Thompson, 2005).

Second, there is some evidence that an understanding of consumer disposition could provide a new perspective on consumer attitudes and expectations. For example, the current cultural trends towards anti-consumerism could be aided by an understanding of consumer voluntary disposition (Cherrier and Murray, 2007).

Third, understanding consumer disposition of products especially environmentally unsafe products and services (i.e. medical products, batteries, computers and other potentially harmful products) is a necessary element to an effective environmentalist marketing strategy. Marketers are increasingly interested in the impact that marketing has on the environment and the need to market products that are easier to recover, reuse and recycle (Hart, 1997).

Last, marketing has begun to acknowledge that poor (the so called "bottom of the pyramid") consumers are a significant untapped marketing opportunity (Prahalad, 2004). As possessions of the poor consumer are relatively scarce, an understanding of disposition decisions and behaviour is perhaps a logical precondition to understanding the poor consumers' behaviour. In other words, to gain a comprehensive view of the poor consumer, the analysis of disposition is as important as acquisition and consumption behaviour. Successfully building markets at the "bottom-of-the-pyramid" will require marketers to understand poor consumers seeking, purchasing, using and evaluating behaviour but also understanding poor consumer's disposition behaviour.

This article explores the preceding events, emotions and decisions associated with the disposition of possessions by poor consumers. The research examines the disposition of basic goods that are seen as indispensable to poor consumers. These potentially include stoves, pots, bed, shoes, clothing, mattresses and basic hygiene items. For poor consumers possessions are scarce (Mehta and Belk, 1991) and disposition of these scarce, often "irreplaceable" or "special" possessions requires the researcher to focus on the preceding events, emotions and decisions associated with disposition, providing valuable insight in the behaviour of poor consumers (Grayson and Shulman, 2000; Price et al., 2000).

The theoretical foundations of consumer disposition are presented, before describing the empirical methods. A thematic description of the consumers lived experience is presented. Finally conclusions and directions for future research are provided.

DISPOSITION

Research into consumer behaviour over the past 20 years has tended to focus on developing and refining theories on consumer acquisition and consumption as these processes were perceived to affect shopping behaviour and that could be induced by the power of marketing (Arnould and Thompson, 2005). Research into disposition behaviour (i.e. the act of getting rid of something), on the other hand, has received comparatively little attention, despite early consumer theorists such as Jacoby et al (1977) and Hanson (1980) insight that disposition behaviour could affect subsequent acquisition and consumption intentions.

Jacoby et al (1977) called attention to disposition decisions by describing the taxonomy of consumer disposition behaviour. The three general choices available to consumer when contemplating disposition of a product and the related consumer decisions are presented in Figure 1.

Jacoby et al (1977) found that the decisions of consumers when contemplating disposition is based on psychological decisions of the consumer (e.g. personality, attitudes, emotions, perceptions, peer pressure, social conscience), factors intrinsic to the product (condition, size, style, value, technological innovation, adaptability, reliability, durability, initial cost, replacement cost), and situational factors extrinsic to the product (e.g. finances, storage space, urgency, fashion changes, circumstances of acquisition, functional use, economics, legal considerations). Hanson (1980) extended the work of Jacoby et al (1977) by offering a framework of consumer product disposition processes. According to Hanson (1980) the disposition process consists of four stages: problem recognition

FIGURE 1

Taxonomy for Describing Consumer Disposition Behaviour

Keep the product	-Continue to use it for its origin purpose -Convert it to serve another purpose -Store it, perhaps for later use
Permanently dispose of the product	-Throw it away or abandon it -Give it away -Sell it -Trade it
Temporarily dispose of the product	-Loan it -Rent it to someone else

Adapted from Jacoby et al (1977:22)

(i.e. a cue that triggers a need to dispose), search and evaluation (i.e. information sources are utilised which have a varying influence on disposition behaviour), disposition decision, and post disposition outcomes (i.e. disposition decisions influence attitudes toward subsequent disposition and acquisition intentions). Continuing the research stream initiated by Jacoby et al (1977) and Hanson (1980), Harrell and McConocha (1992) investigated the rationale consumers' use when choosing disposal options, including redistribution options (such as charities, donations and waste management) which were not previously considered.

Young and Wallendorf (1989: 34) concluded that "disposition is a process rather than a discrete event" where it is "impossible to pinpoint the moment when emotional or physical detachment occurs". Supporting these conclusions, Roster (2001) found that disposition involves a psychological process from initial detachment (distancing behaviour, critical events, and ongoing value and performance assessments) to physical severance, outcome assessment and finally psychological and emotional severance.

The subsequent research into disposition of products dealt largely with the symbolic and emotional meaning of disposition and the significance of disposition on a consumer's self concept (Price, et al., 2000; Kates, 2001; Lastovicka and Fernandez, 2005; Shelton and Okleshen Peters, 2006; Cherrier and Murray, 2007). While this research contributed to a better understanding of the preceding events, emotions and decisions associated with disposition, they tended to focus on exceptional dispositional events rather than dispositional events experienced by a wide range of consumers. For example, Price et al. (2000) and Kates (2001) explore the disposition of special possessions by old consumers and the disposition of possessions among families of people living with AIDS. Similarly, Shelton and Okleshen Peters (2006) investigates the disposition of tattoos (i.e. tattoo removal), Lastovicka and Fernandez (2005) examined garage sales and on-line auctions, while Cherrier and Murray (2007) explores the disposition of possessions of individual who have radically changed their consumption lifestyle by consuming less (i.e. downshifting). This contemporary research into disposition made a meaningful contribution to the disposition literature and the understanding of consumer behaviour; however, the research was focused on exceptional dispositional behaviour that most consumers do not experience in everyday life. Inglis (2005) argues that the great majority of consumer behavioural activities occur-not during exceptional experiences-but during the "banality" (i.e. unexceptional, mundane routine) of everyday life. Rather than focusing on exceptional dispositional events, this research focuses on the disposition of common household possessions by poor consumers as part of everyday life experiences.

METHOD

The method chosen to describe the poor consumers experience in the disposition of possessions is that of existential-phenomenology (Thompson, Locander and Pollio, 1989). Existential-phenomenological description provides a basis for exploring consumer experience in non-dualistic terms which allows for a first-person description of lived experiences. While the emphasis is on the experience of the first-person, the first-person is influenced by the social and cultural beliefs of the lived experience. Infusing the consumer experience, with a description of the lived meaning, can significantly benefit the understanding of the behaviour of poor consumers. The research goal is to provide a thematic description of the experience of the disposition of possessions by poor consumers.

The data collection process began by placing an advertisement in the community centre of a very poor informal (shack) settlement north of Johannesburg, South Africa. The advert invited residents to participate in a market research project. A toll-free number was provided to avoid any expense for the potential participants. Each potential participant who contacted the researcher was screened to ensure that they were a resident of the informal settlement. In total 10 participants were chosen to participate.

Given that the goal of the research was to provide a thematic description of the experience of the disposition of possessions by poor consumers, the researchers conducted open-ended in-depth interviews on the disposition experiences relating to common household possessions that were seen as indispensable to poor consumers. The format resembled the methodology of existential-phenomenological interviewing (Thompson, Locander and Pollio, 1989). The interviewer began by asking if the participant owns any of the following possessions: stove, pots, bed, shoes, clothing, mobile phone and a toothbrush. The interviewer then systematically asked if the participant had disposed of any of these possessions or similar possessions in the past. If the participate did dispose of any of these possessions, the participant would be asked for details regarding the preceding events, emotions and decisions associated with the disposition of that possession. The dialogue with the participant was conversational and allowed to emerge on the basis of the participant's story. When conducting the interviews, every effort was be made to keep the participants on track by prompting the participant for details regarding the disposition experience (without being directive).

Consistent with existential-phenomenological interpretation (Thompson, Locander and Pollio, 1989), the transcribed interviews were interpreted by means of an iterative back-and-forth process of relating individual parts of the verbatim text to the whole text, so making it possible to form interpretations in the context of the lived

FIGURE 2
The Process of Disposition Model

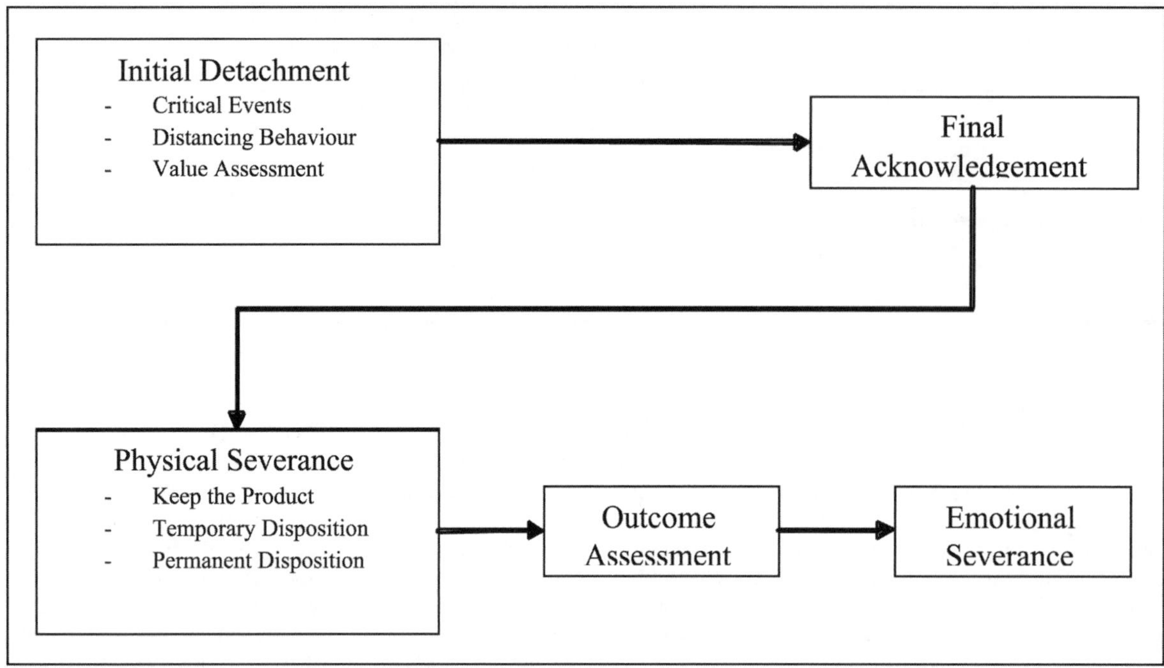

Adapted from Jacoby et al (1977) and Roster (2001)

meaning. After each interview was interpreted, the researcher widened the interpretive context to identify common patterns across interview transcripts. These common patterns were labelled under various 'themes'. The "themes" were then interpreted in terms of Roster's (2001) psychological process of disposition and Jacoby et al (1977) taxonomy for describing consumer disposition behaviour. The process of disposition model is presented in Figure 2.

RESULTS AND INTERPRETATIONS

All the participants were very poor unemployed urban consumers that could be classified as "bottom-of-the-pyramid" consumers. While the ages of the participants varied from 25-56 years (six females and four males), the experiences and emotions conveyed during the interviews were all very similar, resulting in data saturation after the 10 interviews. In the interviews all the participants expressed the hardships experienced of coming to Johannesburg with absolutely no possessions other than the clothes on their back and the constant daily struggle to feed themselves and their families. The participants also expressed a sense of absolute desperation when first arriving in Johannesburg as there was little hope of employment or any source of income.

The average day, in the informal settlement, was spent fetching water, cooking, praying, sleeping and talking to fellow community members. Sundays morning were spent attending church. From time-to-time the participants did engage in casual employment, (averaging no more than two to three days work per month) which was largely arranged by the local church.

After analysis and interpretation of the text, three broad conceptual categories or themes emerged. These were very similar to Roster's (2001) themes for the psychological process of disposition. As the themes were very similar, it was decide to use Roster's categories for the analysis of the themes, namely: initial detachment, physical severance, outcome assessment and psychological and emotional severance.

Initial Detachment

When participates were asked if they owned any basic possessions, all of the participants commented that all the possessions that they owned (other than some high value items) were given to them by a nearby Christian church.

> "Many things I wear today, it comes from the church; the father gives me blankets, duvets, clothes, shoes" (BF 41).

For all the participants the initial detachment for items was always preceded by some "critical event". The overriding "critical event" mentioned by all the participants was the initial meeting with the Pastor of the nearby Christian church. The participants recounted the "critical event" of meeting the pastor of the nearby Christian church on the first day or two of arriving in Johannesburg. The pastor would offer food to the participants and invite them to the church.

> "Now I give you this bread and I think you can go to the church and pray to God, God can give you bread everyday until you die and after that I go with Pastor and see that Pastor give me a big, big, big night for the god. I am with Pastor and I see that I am not suffering because the days before I was suffering but now I am not suffering...I said I got no food, I see that Pastor can come to give me food, if got no clothes, Pastor can give me clothes" (BF 43).

"He is working by the squatter camp and give the people food and tell the people about God and tell the people that food come from God, because me I got food because I know God, and I think if you go to the church you can know of God" (BF 44).

All the participants were invited to join the church and were all (except one person) baptised by the Pastor.

"And then all of the sudden I get Pastor under Father's [Gods] ministry and I was baptised and then all my life get changed..." (BF 56).

"I am with Pastor and I see that I am suffering because the days before [baptism] I was suffering but now I am not suffering" (BF 43).

After joining the church the participants were not only provided food but clothes, shoes, blankets, and basic toiletries (such as soap, Vaseline and toothbrushes). In fact, the participants provided the church with their clothing and shoe sizes so that the church could source the correct size of clothing or shoes. These items were given to the church by the church members.

At times, when the participants were able to gain casual employment (normally organised by the church), the participants would buy a 10kg bag of maize meal and often more basic toiletries. This food and basic toiletries would be made to last until the participants received another source of income.

Some of the participants owned "high value" possessions such as mattresses, furniture, paraffin stoves, mobile phones and car batteries (to power radios or lights). These possessions (other than the mattresses and furniture) were also acquired after earning some money through casual employment.

"When that people give me money, I put the money away. I put the money away because I get the food from Pastor, and the clothes from Pastor, and when it was enough I buy the phone. I buy Motorola for R279" (BF 44).

The mattresses and furniture were either given to them from a family member, found at the local rubbish dump, or borrowed from a friend.

"I was suffering. I was staying with my cousins. She get married now and now she give me old mattress" (BM 43)

Physical Severance

Using Jacoby's (1977) taxonomy to group the general choices available to the participants when contemplating physical severance from a product, it was found that all three choices were displayed. Each choice is discussed in turn.

Keep the Product. A number of participates expressed the desire to store items that did not work. For example, a number of participates had found non-working televisions and radios at the local rubbish dump and even though they never anticipated that they would be fixed, they continued to store these items indefinitely. For example, a TV was often displayed in a prominent place in the shack, with the participant proudly remarking that they owned a television, even though they admitted it did not work and probably would never be fixed.

Temporarily dispose of the product. Temporary disposition of items was largely restricted to furniture or mattresses that were lent to family members or friends. These items were never loaned for monetary gain but temporary lent until they were needed again.

"I am sleeping on the bed, but it is not mine. It's for another somebody, who is staying here...I don't know when he will take it [back] but maybe in two months...Before I was using a sponge to sleep on. I give [loan] it to somebody who's like me, before I was sleeping up there [on the bed]" (BF 25).

The death of a family member who was using the mattress or chair was often cited as a reason for loaning the item. The participants remarked that the item would be recalled if an additional member of their family came to live with them in Johannesburg. There seemed to be a strong sense of sharing "high value" possessions in the community. As Belk (2007) comments sharing is another form of distribution that is distinct from market exchange and gift-giving, that fosters a community spirit, saves resources and creates certain synergies. Belk (2000) established that African cultures have a strong tradition of sharing their wealth with extend family and the community.

Permanently dispose of the product. The permanent disposition of items showed some similarities in disposition patterns as observed by Hibbert, Horne and Tagg (2003). Some of the similar patterns that emerged were the trading-in of old batteries and the selling of stove burners for scrap metal.

"I take it to the Battery Bay, I sell it back again, so when I sell it, they sell a battery for R250 that is new...so when you sell that old battery is not working you have to add R150 on that battery so you must get the other new battery" (BF 41).

"[When the stove burner] is broken we sell it to some other old man who take the stove to scrap yard and there he sells it for scrap" (BF 20).

However for other items a very different pattern of disposition emerged. For items that the participant considered "beyond repair", "broken" "too old" or "of no use", the participant would throw the item in a fire so that the item would be destroyed. These items included old clothing, shoes, furniture and mattresses. Two participants reasoned that it was better to burn these items than throw them away so as to "not to destroy the environment" or the physical surroundings. This behaviour is rather surprising as the participants acknowledged that these items, if not burnt, would be found in the streets or municipal rubbish bins and subsequently used by fellow residents.

"When they are torn, eh, I am going to burn them [so] there is no way out...they are still over, they are torn, they are teared all over, there's no way out" (BM 25).

These participants expressed that it would be undignified for a member of the community to give away clothing or shoes that they have deemed "beyond repair", "broken" "too old" or "of no use". It was seen that the appropriate behaviour was to avoid giving other members of the community the choice to decide if the pair of clothing is wearable or an item is usable.

Old toothbrushes and other personal hygiene items were also destroyed. However, this was done for very different reasons to the above. All the participants that have disposed of these items cited hygiene reasons for destroying their toothbrush or other basic hygiene items.

"When [it] is old, not right to use it, I can put, eh, make a fire and put by the fire and light the fire and toothbrush can burn, because I don't want somebody to use my toothbrush...because I know the toothbrush got a disease, I can't give somebody toothbrush I am using" (BF 43).

"If don't want to give the people if I got something...like a nail cutter [clipper] if is broken, I put it by the toilet, because I don't want somebody to use because of disease (BM 42).

Items that were deemed "useable" by participants were never sold but given away to other members of the community, (even if these items had a relatively high emotional connection or monetary value to the participant).

"I sell nothing because I see that nobody sell something to me, but I get everything from the church and by the church I can't pay a cent to take the clothes, new shoes, blankets to sleep and now I don't like to sell something to somebody if I see I got enough I take it and I give to somebody" (BF 25).

What was interesting was that these acts of disposition are all associated with the participant's religious identity and the Christian practice of giving to the poor as a means of further identifying with the suffering of Jesus Christ (Shelton and Okleshen, 2006). These disposed items are seen as religiously "sacred" (Belk, Wallendorf and Sherry, 1989) and the act of disposition served as a means of expressing the social role of the "Good Christian Samaritan".

Outcome Assessment and Psychological Severance

According to Roster's (1998) Psychological Process of Dispossession, participants often reflect on their decisions to dispose of certain items, and the impact this may have on the participant's relationship with the severed item. For all the participants, the reflection elicited positive emotions, and never feelings of relief that they were free from the obligations of the item (as found by Pavia, 1993). The participants express the joy of being able to demonstrate the same sense of generosity that was previously shown to them. Furthermore, the outcome assessment was largely verbalised through "storytelling" (Roster, 1998). Participants would relay the story of first meeting the Pastor and how their religious conversion ensured a better life.

"I tell how Pastor find the people to go to church to know God, how God helps you...how the church gives us things to wear and to eat" (BF 42).

Unlike Belk's et al (1989) view that "sacred" items are never sold or disposed, the participants expressed a sense of "community relationships" involving meeting other people's needs without regard for reciprocity (Clark and Mills, 1979).

"You just give, because even Pastor don't want money from me, just to give, because he teach us if you give somebody, God can give you" (BF 43).

Similarly, unlike Young and Wallendorf's (1989) view that disposition is a painful process "in which consumers experience the death of the piece of their lives with each possession lost" (Lastovicka and Fernandez, 2005:814), participants expressed a sense of religious elucidation with the disposition of items.

"If I see the people haven't got that thing, I give it. I feel much better it I can share because Pastor give me and that one [person] is not going to church and [they] know nothing about the church. I sit down and tell them that Pastor give me shoes because I am going to the church. Because you know, when we go to church we make prayer, and you can see everything can come to you. Now I give to that lady or child who haven't got" (BF 37).

This disposition behaviour is very similar to the disposition of special possessions of older consumers. Price et al. (2000) found that older consumers disposing of cherished possessions tried to ensure a good home for the items and/or influence the future lives of the recipients. In fact, the participants through their disposition behaviour seemed to play an important role in poverty relief for other poor consumers. While there is no clear consensus on the role that religion plays in prompting relief for the poor (Regnerus, Smith and Sikkink, 1998), the participant's disposal of items to other poor consumers had a clear intent of religious conversion. Bem (1967) presents a theory of self perception where disposition provides the consumer with a means to incorporate a new role in society into their existing self-concept. The new role of also giving to the poor provides additional evidence of their existing self-concept of being the "Good Samaritan".

"If I see I can be nice to somebody, I can give it to somebody...I never sell" (BM 34).

While disposition is typically seen as a means of separating an undesirable feature of a person's self-concept through the disposal of an item that is no longer compatible with the self (Belk, 1988; Young, 1991) or as a means of emptying the meaning of an item before passing it along (McCracken, 1986), the participants rather saw disposition as a means of passing on religious symbolism which was consistent with the persons religious identity or self-concept. Recently, Lastovicka and Fernandez (2005: 821) demonstrates how a shared self leads a "consumer to believe that the stranger–who may become the new owner of a meaningful possession–would perpetuate the meaningful possession's legacy". In the case of the participants, it would be the legacy of the "Good Samaritan".

According to Roster (2001) critical events (such as changes in employment status, health and size of family) can alter the relationship between owner and item by heightening a sense that the product no longer represents relevant aspects of the self. However, the critical event of religious conversion of the participants created a heightened sense that the product was a more relevant aspect of the self and that emotional and psychological ties associated with the item were strengthened. Severance from the item was not a matter of empting the meaning and symbolic properties of the item, but rather ensuring, the "safe passage" of the item (Richins, 1994).

CONCLUSIONS AND DIRECTIONS FOR FUTURE RESEARCH

To gain a better understanding of the four billion poor consumers worldwide, it is not only important to understand their consumption behaviour, but also their disposition behaviour. As first it would seem contradictory that poor consumers would want to voluntarily dispose of items that are not only treated as "special" (in the words of Price et al, 2000), but that are so scarce in poor communities. Furthermore, it would also seem contradictory that such poor consumers would voluntarily give away (i.e. "never sell") these disposed items or to take it upon themselves to decide if an item is useful for other members of the community, (often burning the item rather than letting somebody else decide the usefulness, value or worth of the item).

In this study poor consumer occupied the same psychological stages of disposition as observed by Roster (1989); however the behavioural outcomes were quite different to that experienced in wealthier communities. Firstly the results clearly showed that disposition plays an important role in the consumption cycle but may not necessarily be the antecedent to future purchasing behaviour. In fact, participants often acquired "new" items before making a decision about disposing of any "old" items. This suggests that the consumption cycle does not necessarily progress in a uni-directional fashion but may in fact be multi-directional.

Second poor consumers provided a new perspective on consumer attitudes and expectations. For example, poor consumers seem to want to keep items of high social value (e.g. televisions), even though these items never work and in all probability would never be fixed. In this case the television may reflect a symbolic connection to a better life or as Campbell (1987) argues, the poor emulate the wealthier communities for purposes of identity enhancement.

The temporary disposition behaviour of poor consumers also provided a new perspective on consumer attitudes. Contrary to the notion of Western materialism and possessive individualism (Belk, 2007), these very poor African consumers demonstrated a true sense of sharing with the extended community. It was found that the temporary disposition behaviour extended beyond immediate family and friends (as is typical Western culture) to all members of the community and that it was mainly "high value" possessions that were shared. Loaning items was never done for monetary gain and always fostered a sense of community spirit. This type of consideration for compassion and communality displayed by African cultures through their disposition behaviour is often referred to as the African concept of "ubuntu" or humaneness. According to Mangaliso, (2001) Christianity is becoming more prevalent within the belief system of Ubuntu, as found in this study.

Thirdly, poor consumers made the decision to permanently dispose of certain items that were deemed "beyond repair", "broken" "too old" or "of no use" even though other poor consumers, in all probability, would value these items. Two explanations emerged from the findings. The first explanation is that consumers expressed that if an item is of no worth to them, it would be demeaning to allow a fellow member of the community the undignified option of using or wearing the item. In Ubuntu, fellow members of the community are always treated as ones own family. If the item is of no use to the family it cannot be of use to others. The second explanation is the misplaced belief that items that deal with personal hygiene cannot be "sterilised" and then used by another person. The simple act of boiling a toothbrush to "sterilise" the item was either not known or considered. This further provides a unique perspective on the disposition of "unsafe" items where the consumer wrongly believes that the item to be "unsafe" so not allowing the item to be recovered, reused or recycled. This then raises the point (that environmentalist marketing strategies need to take into consideration), that consumers may have the wrong beliefs about what can and cannot be recovered, reused and recycled.

Finally, there are a number of limitations that need to be considered when interpreting the findings from this study. First, the collected data was restricted to one small informal (shack) settlement in Johannesburg. While the socio-economic status of this settlement is largely representative of urban informal settlements in Southern Africa, the economic survival of the members of the community were largely dependent on a single Christian organisation in the area. Furthermore, the findings may not elucidate the differences in disposal behaviour in other poor communities were other religious, governmental, non-governmental and charity groups are the major economic contributor to the poor consumer. The study also recounts the participants reported behaviour rather than actual disposal behaviour. The level of actual disposal of items to other members of the community may be less than reported due to a social desirability of altruistic behaviour (Hibbert et al, 2005).

In order to build on this study, attention needs to be placed on the influence that religion plays in influencing disposal behaviour amongst vulnerable communities (in particular the poor). This study has shown that religion plays a decisive role in influencing the disposal behaviour of poor consumers and needs to be investigated further.

REFERENCES

Arnould, Eric J. and Craig J. Thompson (2005), "Consumer Culture Theory (CCT): Twenty Years of Research," *Journal of Consumer Research*, 31(March), 868-882.

Belk, Russell W. (1988), "Possessions and the Extended Self," *Journal of Consumer Research*, 15(September), 139-168.

______ (2000), "Consumption Patterns of the New Elite in Zimbabwe," *Journal of Macromarketing*, 20, 204-205.

______ (2007), "Why Not Share Rather Than Own?," *The ANNALS of the American Academy of Political and Social Science*, 611, 126-140.

Belk, Russell W., Melanie Wallendorf and John F. Sherry Jr. (1989), "The Sacred and the Profane in Consumer Behavior: Theodicy on the Odyssey," *The Journal of Consumer Research*, 16(1), 1-38.

Bem, Daryl (1967), "Self-perception: An Alternative Interpretation of Cognitive Dissonance Phenomena," *Psychological Review*, 74, 183-200.

Campbell, Colin (1987), *The Romantic Ethic and the Spirit of Modern Consumerism*, Oxford: Blackwell.

Cherrier, Hélène and Jeff B. Murray, (2007), "Reflexive Dispossession and the Self: Constructing a Processual Theory of Identity," *Consumption, Markets and Culture*, 10(1), 1-29.

Clark, Margaret S. and Judson Mills (1979), "Interpersonal Attraction in Exchange and Communal Relationships," *Journal of Personality and Social Psychology*, 37, 12-24.

Grayson, Kent and David Shulman (2000), "Indexicality and the Verification Function of Irreplaceable Possessions: A Semiotic Analysis," *Journal of Consumer Research*, 27(June), 17-30.

Hanson, James W. (1980), "A Proposed Paradigm for Consumer Product Disposition Processes," *The Journal of Consumer Affairs*, 14(1), 49-67.

Harrell, Gilbert D. and Diane M. McConocha (1992), "Personal Factors Related to Consumer Product Disposal Tendencies," *The Journal of Consumer Affairs*. 26(2), 397-408.

Hart, Stuart L. (1997), "Beyond Greening: Strategies for a Sustainable World," *Harvard Business Review*, Jan-Feb, 66-76.

Inglis, David (2005), *Culture and Everyday Life*, London: Routledge.

Jacoby, Jacob, Carol K. Berning and Thomas F. Dietvorst (1977), "What about Disposition?" *Journal of Marketing*, (April), 22-28.

Kates, Steven M. (2001), "Disposition of Possessions Among Families of People Living With Aids," *Psychology and Marketing*. 18(4), 365-387.

Lastovicka, John L. and Fernandez, Karen V. (2005), "Three Paths to Disposition: The Movement of Meaningful Possessions to Strangers," *Journal of Consumer Research*, 31(March), 813-823.

Mangaliso, Mzamo P. (2001), "Building Competitive Advantage from Ubuntu: Management Lessons from South Africa," *Academy of Management Executive*, 15(3), 23-33.

McCracken, Grant. (2001), "Culture and Consumption: A Theoretical Account of the Structure and Movement of the Cultural Meaning of Consumer Goods," *Journal of Consumer Research*, 13(1), 71-84.

Mehta, Raj and Russell W. Belk (1991), "Artifacts, Identity, and Transition: Favorite Possessions of Indians and Indian Immigrants to the United States," *Journal of Consumer Research*, 17(March), 398-411.

Pavia, Teresa. (1993), "Dispossession and Perceptions of Self in Late Stage HIV Infection," in *Advances in Consumer Research*, Vol. 20, eds. Leigh McAllister and Michael Rothschild, Provo, UT: Association for Consumer Research, 425-428.

Prahalad, Coimbatore K. (2004), *The Fortune at the Bottom of the Pyramid: Eradicating Poverty Through Profits*, Upper Saddle. River, NJ: Wharton School Publishing.

Price, Linda L., Eric J. Arnould, and Caroline F. Curasi, (2000), "Older Consumers' Disposition of Special Possessions," *Journal of Consumer Research*, 27(September), 179-201.

Regnerus, Mark D., Christian Smith and David Sikkink (1998), "Who Gives to the Poor? The Influence of Religious Tradition and Political Location on the Personal Generosity of Americans towards the Poor," *Journal of the Scientific Study of Religion*, 37(3), 481-493.

Richins, Marsha, L. (1994), "Valuing Things: The Public and Private Meaning of Possessions," *Journal of Consumer Research*, 21(December), 504-521.

Roster, Catherine A. (2001), "Letting Go: The Process and Meaning of Dispossession in the Lives of Consumers," in *Advances in Consumer Research*, Vol. 28, eds. Mary Gilly and Joan Meyers-Levy, Provo, UT: Association for Consumer Research, 425-430.

Schiffman, Leon, David Bednall, Aron O'Cass, Angela Paladino and Leslie Kanuk (2005), *Consumer Behaviour*, Third Edition, Frenchs Forest, NSW: Pearson Education.

Shelton, Jeremy A. and Cara L. Okleshen Peters (2006), "Actions Speak as Loud as Products: Disposition as a Self-Perspective Method of Identity Incorporation. *Consumption," Markets and Culture*, 9(3), 207-233.

Thompson, Craig J., William, B. Locander and Howard R. Pollio (1989), "Putting Consumer Experience Back into Consumer Research: The Philosophy and Method of Existential-Phenomenology," *Journal of Consumer Research*, 16(September), 133-146.

Young, Melissa M (1991), "Disposition of Possessions During Role Transitions," in *Advances in Consumer Research*, Vol. 18, eds. Rebecca H. Holman and Michael R. Solomon, Provo, UT: Association for Consumer Research, 33-39.

Young, Melissa M. and Melanie Wallendorf (1989), "Ashes to Ashes, Dust to Dust: Conceptualizing Consumer Disposition of Possessions," *American Marketing Association Winter Educators' Conference Proceedings*. Chicago: American Marketing Association.

The More the Merrier: Imagined Social Presence and Service Failure

Yi He, California State University, East Bay, USA
Qimei Chen, University of Hawai'I, USA
Dana L. Alden, University of Hawai'I, USA

EXTENDED ABSTRACT

Most customers can recall a service failure, in which he/she experiences problems in a service delivery process (Lewis and Spyrakopoulos 2001). Usually, during such a service failure, the customer may find him/herself become the focus of other customers' attention as a result of a heated conversation. This phenomenon begs answer to an interesting question: what is the effect of social presence on an individual's reactions to a service failure? Does it exaggerate the negative outcome of a service failure? Or more interestingly, does it alleviate such negative outcome? And how? The answers to all these questions lie in the premise that social presence may dramatically shift a customer's service failure experience.

Despite the topic's clear importance, social presence effects on consumption remain understudied (for a few exceptions, see Dahl, Manchanda and Argo 2001; Argo, Dahl and Manchanda 2005; Zhou and Soman 2003; Mangleburg, Doney and Bristol 2004). In particular, researchers have not integrated this social factor into the service literature. In addition, the underlying mechanism of social presence effects has yet to be uncovered. Seeking to bridge these gaps, we have conducted an experiment to: 1) evaluate the impact of social presence during a service failure, 2) examine the processing mechanism under which social presence impacts service evaluation, and 3) build a nomological net that features social presence and outcome attribution.

Investigations concerning the effects of social presence have thus far based upon two major theories: the Evaluation-Apprehension theory and the Distraction-Conflict theory. The first one is linked to seeking and maintaining positive public image (e.g., Bone 1982; Seta et al. 1989; Baumeister 1982), and the latter is associated with attention conflict and cognitive overload (Baron 1986; Baron, Moor and Sanders 1978). The Evaluation-Apprehension theory (Cottrell 1972; Bond 1982; Berger et al. 1981; Baumeister 1982) suggests that with the presence of a social audience, individuals tends to inspect themselves from an observer's perspective (Duval and Wicklund 1972; Wicklund and Duval 1971). In so doing, the difference between the current self and the ideal self becomes salient and produces an aversive state, which alters emotional response. Following the Evaluation-Apprehension theory, the direct consequence of social presence is altered emotional experience. In other words, the underlying processing mechanism of social presence effects may be affective in nature. For example, the negative emotions (e.g., embarrassment) elicited by a service failure may become more salient due to social presence. The intensified negative emotions may consequently affect evaluation.

A rival theory of social presence, the Distraction-Conflict theory, asserts that social presence creates attention conflict and leads to cognitive overload (Baron 1986; Baron, Moor and Sanders 1978). Following the Distraction-Conflict theory, the social presence effect may be explained based upon a cognitive processing mechanism. For example, it can be argued that as a result of reduced cognitive resources caused by a public audience, customers may have difficulty forming a negative evaluation for a service failure.

The two rival theories propose competing explanations for social presence effects. To date, attempts to pinpoint a superior theory have yet to reach any conclusive results (e.g., Feinberg and Aiello 2006). Most recently, researchers interested in this line of research have argued for an integrative model, which posits that an individual may have multiple reactions to social presence that are co-occurring (Uziel 2007). This research applies this integrated model and posits that each different reaction to social presence can be made salient at a given moment due to a situational factor, outcome attribution. We argue that the Evaluation-Apprehension theory explains social presence effects when the service failure is externally-attributed, whereas the Distraction-Conflict theory accounts for social presence effects when the service failure is internally-attributed.

The experiment examined the impact of social presence on service evaluation during a service failure and tested the two rival theories that explain social presence effects. A total of 121 college students participated in the experiment. Participants were asked to read a cartoon scenario depicting a disagreement between a customer and a bookstore cashier. Internally- versus externally-attributed service failure were manipulated by scenarios in which either the bookstore employees or the customer was clearly responsible for the problem leading to the disagreement. This treatment was pretested to ensure that it induced the intended emotions. The second factor, social presence, was manipulated by depicting other customers (versus no customers) in the vicinity of the checkout counter and cashier. As such, the experiment featured a 2 social presence (no social presence versus social presence) X 2 outcome attribution (external-attribution versus internal-attribution) between-subject factorial design.

The planned contrast results indicated that compared with no social presence condition, social presence was associated with higher service evaluation pertaining to the service failure regardless of outcome attribution [M's=3.31 *versus* 4.25, $t(106)=3.09$, $p<.01$]. Further mediating analyses, however, uncovered the complexity of the above findings. In particular, the results demonstrated that anger fully mediated the relationship between social presence and service evaluation when a service failure was externally-attributed. When the service failure was internally-attributed, number of negative thoughts fully mediated the relationship between social presence and service evaluation. This indicated that when the service failure was externally-attributed, the affective process proposed by the Distraction-Conflict theory accounted for the social presence effects. When the service failure was internally-attributed, the cognitive process suggested by the Evaluation-Apprehension theory droved the social presence effects.

To conclude, this research holds theoretical significance in that investigating social presence as a moderating factor related to consumer reactions to a service failure helps enrich the traditional service evaluation paradigm. This research also holds managerial significance as understanding the crucial role of social presence in service encounter may help service providers to be more conscientious about the social environment, which consequently leads to improved service evaluation.

REFERENCES

Argo, Jennifer J, Darren W. Dahl and Rajesh V. Manchanda (2005), "The Influence of a Mere Social Presence in a Retail Context," *Journal of Consumer Research*, 32(3), 207-212.

Baker, Thomas L.Tracy Meyer, and James Johnson (2008), "Individual differences in perceptions of service failure and recovery: the role of race and discriminatory bias," *Journal of the Academy of Marketing Science*, 36(4), 552-564.

Bonifield, Carolyn and Catherine A Cole, (2008), "Better him than me: social comparison theory and service recovery," *Journal of the Academy of Marketing Science,* 36(4), 565-577.

Costa, Marco, Wies Dinsbach, Antony S. R. Manstead, and Pio Enrico Ricci Bitti (2001), "Social Presence, Embarrassment, and Nonverbal Behavior," *Journal of Nonverbal Behavior*, 25(4), 225-240.

Dahl, Darren W., Rajesh V. Manchanda and Jennifer J. Argo, (2001), "Embarrassment in Consumer Purchase: The Roles of Social Presence and Purchase Familiarity," *Journal of Consumer Research*, 28(3), 473-481.

Dong, Beibei, Kenneth R. Evans, Shaoming Zou (2008), "The effects of customer participation in co-created service recovery," *Journal of the Academy of Marketing Science*, 36(1), 123-137.

Goffman, Erving (1967), *InteractionRitual: Essays on Face-to-Face Behavior*. Garden City: Anchor.

Izard, Carroll E. (1977), *Human Emotions*, New York: Plenum.

Mangleburg, Tamara F., Patricia M. Doney and Terry Bristol (2004), "Shopping with Friends and Teens' Susceptibility to Peer Influence," *Journal of Retailing,* 80(2), 101-116.

Menon, Kalyani and Laurette Dube (2000), "Ensuring Greater Satisfaction by Engineering Salesperson Response to Customer Emotions," *Journal of Retailing, 76* (3), 285-307.

Oliver, Richard L. (1997). *Satisfaction: A Behavioral Perspective on the Consumer*. New York: McGraw-Hill.

Ratner, Rebecca K. and Barbara E. Kahn (2002), "The Impact of Private versus Public Consumption on Variety-Seeking Behavior," *Journal of Consumer Research*, 29 (September), 246-257.

Rook, Dennis W. and Robert J. Fisher (1995), "Normative influences on impulsive buying behavior," *Journal of Consumer Research*, 22(3), 305-313.

Schlenker, Barry R., and Mark R. Leary (1982), "Social Anxiety and Self-Presentation-A Conceptualization and Model," *Psychological Bulletin, 92*(3), 641-669.

Uziel, Liad (2007), "Individual differences in the social facilitation effect: A review and meta-analysis," *Journal of Research in Personality*, 41, 579–601.

Zhou, Rongrong and Dilip Soman (2003), "Looking Back: Exploring the Psychology of Queuing and the Effect of the Number of People Behind," *Journal of Consumer Research*, 29(4), 517-530.

Zhuang, Guijun, Alex S.L. Tsang, Nan Zhou, Fuan Li and J.A.F. Nicholls (2006), "Impacts of situational factors on buying decisions in shopping malls An empirical study with multinational data," *European Journal of Marketing*, 40(1/2), 17-43.

Ambivalence in Consumption: The Case of Anticipatory Emotions

Colleen Bee, Oregon State University, USA
Robert Madrigal, University of Oregon, USA

EXTENDED ABSTRACT

Emotion plays an important role in marketing, particularly in understanding consumer behavior. In fact, it may be difficult to identify a purchase situation where multiple emotional elements are not present. This research examines factors that affect emotional ambivalence in the consumption experience. Appraisal theory is used as a theoretical foundation in the current research. Cognitive appraisal theorists believe that emotions are elicited from an appraisal of a situation or event and it is not the specific event that produces the emotion, but the appraisal of the event (Roseman and Smith 2001; Smith and Ellsworth 1985). Key appraisals considered in this research are congruence, which determines valence based on goal desirability, and outcome probability, which identifies the specific emotion within a congruence appraisal. Two categories of emotions studied in this research are anticipatory emotions (optimism and worry) and outcome-based emotions (joy and anger). In the only research that explicitly examines anticipatory emotions, Baumgartner, Pieters, and Bagozzi (2008) differentiated between anticipatory and anticipated emotions and related both to behavioral intentions. However, optimism and worry have not been explicitly examined in marketing and consumer behavior research, yet these emotions seem particularly relevant in purchase and consumption decisions as many consumption situations involve elements of uncertainty and differing levels of desirability.

The purpose of study 1 is to consider information congruency appraisals and examine the relevance of anticipatory emotions in consumption. The first hypothesis proposes that conflicting information (i.e., congruent and incongruent) will lead to higher levels of emotional ambivalence. Second, we propose that the anticipatory emotions of optimism and worry will be experienced more strongly than the outcome-based emotions of joy and anger emotions, as discrete emotions and as emotional ambivalence. Finally, we expect that optimism-worry objective ambivalence will be a better predictor of subjective ambivalence than discrete emotions or joy-anger objective ambivalence.

The results in study 1 indicate that information congruency significantly affects the valence of emotions and that conflicting information significantly increases the experience of emotional ambivalence. Anticipatory emotions were experienced more strongly than outcome-based emotions. Although multiple emotions are experienced, the anticipatory set of mixed emotions was a better predictor of subjective ambivalence.

In study two we consider how congruency appraisals affect ambivalence and confidence at different points in time in the consumption process. Additionally, the mediating role of subjective ambivalence is considered. Although the experience of conflict is similar among dissonance, attitude ambivalence, and emotional ambivalence, a key differentiating factor is that dissonance typically occurs after a commitment has been made, whereas emotional ambivalence can occur prior to making a commitment or decision (van Harreveld et al., 2009). In fact, van Harreveld et al. propose that level of commitment to an available alternative is the primary distinction between ambivalence and dissonance. In this case, feelings of conflict and discomfort related to ambivalence will be most pronounced when a choice needs to be made. When a situation does not involve choice, there is not as much reason for ambivalence and subsequent discomfort. Ambivalence should therefore be enhanced with the prospect of a decision.

The consumption process is dynamic and changing, where consumers receive multiple pieces of information at different stages of the process. As a result, not only is it expected that ambivalence will be affected by the information presented but also by the timing of this information. van Harreveld et al. (2009) suggest that when people are forced to make a discrete choice that they anticipate possible negative and positive outcomes associated with each alternative. This indicates that perhaps a choice situation can lead to modest levels of ambivalence even in the absence of conflicting information. Ambivalence and confidence levels are expected to fluctuate based on the information presented and the timing of this information.

In the second study, information congruency and time of information were found to interact in their influence on ambivalence and confidence. Specifically, prior to a favorable purchase, ambivalence is higher than prior to consumption as consumers anticipate positives and negatives. In contrast, ambivalence is lessened prior to an undesirable purchase when compared to consumption as there are few positives. With conflicting information it is difficult to integrate contradictory evaluations and ambivalence persists throughout a consumption experience. Confidence was found to have an inverse relationship with ambivalence. Finally, the discomfort that consumers feel in the form of subjective ambivalence mediates the effect of optimism-worry emotional ambivalence on confidence.

Optimism and worry are two categories of emotion likely to be elicited during purchase and consumption experiences. However, these two emotions have not been explicitly examined in previous consumer behavior research. In the current research, optimism and worry are future-directed emotions that were found to be important in influencing feelings of ambivalence, discomfort and confidence in decision making. Additionally, extending appraisal theory, consumers presented with conflicting information experienced more emotional ambivalence than those presented with consistent information. Consumption is dynamic and, in addition to information congruency, the stage of the purchase process is important in determining the level of ambivalence experienced. Finally, the experience of emotional ambivalence is associated with feelings of conflict and uncertainty. These feelings of conflict were found to mediate the effect of emotional ambivalence on confidence.

REFERENCES

Bagozzi, Richard P., Hans Baumgartner, and Rik Pieters (1998), "Goal-directed emotions," *Cognition & Emotion*, 12 (January), 1-26.

Bagozzi, Richard P., Mahesh Gopinath, and Prashanth U. Nyer (1999), "The Role of Emotions in Marketing," *Journal of the Academy of Marketing Science*, 27 (Spring), 184-206.

Baumgartner, Hans, Rik Pieters, and Richard P. Bagozzi (2008), "Future-oriented Emotions: Conceptualization and Behavioral Effects," *European Journal of Social Psychology*, 38, 685-696.

Baron, Reuben M and David A. Kenny (1986), "The Moderator-Mediator Variable Distinction in Social Psychological Research: Conceptual, Strategic, and Statistical Considerations," *Journal of Personality and Social Psychology*, 51(6), 1173-1182.

Festinger, Leon (1957). *A Theory of Cognitive Dissonance.* Stanford, CA: Stanford University.

Frijda, Nico H. and Marcel Zeelenberg (2001), "Appraisal: What Is Dependent?" in *Appraisal Processes in Emotion: Theory, Methods, and Research*, ed. Klaus R. Scherer Angela Schorr, and Tom Johnstone, New York, NY: Oxford University Press, 141-156.

Larsen, Jeff T. (2001), "Emotions in Evaluative Space: Can Pleasure and Displeasure Co Occur?" *Dissertation Abstracts International*, 62(08B).

Lazarus, R. (1991). *Emotion and adaptation.* New York, NY: Oxford University Press.

McGregor, Ian, Ian R. Newby-Clark, and Mark P. Zanna (1999), ""Remembering" Dissonance: Simultaneous Accessibility of Inconsistent Cognitive Elements Moderates Epistemic Discomfort," in *Cognitive Dissonance: Progress on a Pivotal Theory in Social Psychology*, ed. Eddie Harmon-Jones and Judson Mills, Washington, DC: American Psychological Association, 325-353.

Nyer, Prashanth U. (1997), "A Study of the Relationship Between Cognitive Appraisals and Consumption Emotion," *Journal of the Academy of Marketing Science*, 25(4), 296-304.

Ortony, A., Clore, G.L., & Collins, A. (1988). *The cognitive structure of emotions.* Cambridge, UK: Cambridge University Press.

Priester, Joseph R. and Richard E. Petty (1996), "The Gradual Threshold Model of Ambivalence: Relating the Positive and Negative Bases of Attitudes to Subjective Ambivalence," *Journal of Personality and Social Psychology*, 71(3), 431-449.

Richins, Marsha L. (1997), "Measuring Emotion in the Consumption Experience," *Journal of Consumer Research*, 24(September), 127-146.

Roseman, Ira J. (1991), "Appraisal Determinants of Discrete Emotions," *Cognition and Emotion*, 5, 161-200.

Roseman, Ira J. and Andreas Evdokas (2004), "Appraisals Cause Experienced Emotions: Experimental Evidence," *Cognition and Emotion*, 18(1), 1-28.

Roseman, Ira J. and Craig A. Smith (2001), "Appraisal Theory: Overview, Assumptions, Varietie Controversies," in *Appraisal Processes in Emotion: Theory, Methods, Research*, Klaus R. Scherer and Angela Schorr and Tom Johnstone, eds. New York, NY: Oxford University Press.

Russell, James A., and James M. Carroll (1999), "On the Bipolarity of Positive and Negative Affect," *Psychological Bulletin*, 125(1), 3-30.

Smith, Craig A., and Phoebe C. Ellsworth (1985), "Patterns of Cognitive Appraisals in Emotion," *Journal of Personality and Social Psychology*, 48, 813-838.

Soscia, Isabella (2007). "Gratitude, delight, or guilt: The role of consumers' emotions in predicting postconsumption behaviors," *Psychology & Marketing*, 24(10), 871-894.

Thompson, Megan M., Mark P. Zanna, and Dale W. Griffin (1995), "Let's Not Be Indifferent About (Attitudinal) Ambivalence," in *Attitude Strength: Antecedents and Consequences*, ed. Richard E. Petty and Jon A. Krosnick, Mahwah, NJ: Lawrence Erlbaum Associates, 361-386.

van Harreveld, Frenk, Joop van der Plight, and Yael N. de Liver (2009). "The agony of ambivalence and ways to resolve it: Introducing the MAID model," *Personality and Social Psychology Review*, 13(1), 45-61.

Williams, Patti and Jennifer L. Aaker (2002), "Can Mixed Emotions Peacefully Coexist?," *Journal of Consumer Research*, 28(March), 636-649.

Be Tolerable or Be Angry? A Situation of Relationship Norm Conflict in Failure

Lisa C. Wan, Lingnan University, Hong Kong, China
Michael K. Hui, Chinese University of Hong Kong, Hong Kong, China

EXTENDED ABSTRACT

Prior research has generally agreed that establishing friendships with consumers work well in mitigating consumer dissatisfaction in failures. However, this paper argues that a friendship may not always work and sometimes it may even magnify consumer dissatisfaction in failures. Drawing from the communal-exchange relationship framework (Clark and Mills 1979), this paper proposes two conflicting norms may have been activated simultaneously in communal relationships when a failure happens. The first norm focuses on self-obligation, that is, because s/he is my good friend, I have to tolerate his/her mistakes. The second norm focuses on other-obligation, that is, because s/he is my good friend, s/he has to provide me with good services. The relative salience of these two conflicting norms may influence communal consumers' dissatisfaction level to be different from exchange consumers. Building on the psychological contract theory (Rousseau 1989), it is suggested that promise breach type is a moderator that influences the relative salience of the two norms in governing communal consumer responses. Specifically, communal (vs. exchange) consumers would be less dissatisfied in an implicit promise breach, but the reverse pattern would occur in an explicit promise breach.

In addition, this paper demonstrates that self-construal further moderate the interactive effect of relationship type and promise breach type on consumer dissatisfaction. Note that people reactions to social norms and obligations have been demonstrated to vary significantly according to their independent and interdependent self-construals (Markus and Kitayama 1991; Singelis 1994). Given that relationship norms are the key in driving the different dissatisfaction levels across communal and exchange relationships in failures, it is possible that the interactive relationship between relationship type and promise breach type on consumer dissatisfaction would also differ across independent and interdependent self-construals. Two experiments with different consumption contexts provide convergent evidence of the proposed hypotheses.

Research Hypotheses

- H1: When there is an implicit promise breach in a failure, communal consumers will be less dissatisfied than exchange consumers.
- H2: When there is an explicit promise breach in a failure, communal consumers will be more dissatisfied than exchange consumers.
- H3: When there is an implicit promise breach in a failure: (a) The pattern of communal consumers are less dissatisfied than exchange consumers would be more pronounced for interdependents than for independents, and (b) this pattern is mediated by the tendency of self-obligation thought.
- H4: When there is an explicit promise breach in a failure: (a) The pattern of communal consumers are more dissatisfied than exchange consumers would be more pronounced for interdependents than for independents, and (b) this pattern is mediated by betrayal feeling.

Method and Results

In experiment 1, a 2 (relationship type: communal vs. exchange) x 3 (promise breach: no promise vs. implicit promise vs. explicit promise) between-subjects design was used. Results confirm that the impact of relationship type on consumer dissatisfaction is contingent on promise breach type. Specifically, communal (vs. exchange) consumers are less dissatisfied in an implicit promise breach, but the reverse pattern occurs in an explicit promise breach. In addition, self-obligation thought is the mediator of an implicit promise breach and betrayal feeling is the mediator of an explicit promise breach.

In experiment 2, a 2 (self-construal prime: independent versus interdependent) × 2 (relationship type: communal versus exchange) × 2 (promise breach type: implicit promise breach versus explicit promise breach) between subject design was used. It demonstrates that self-construal moderates the interactive effect of relationship type and promise breach type on consumer dissatisfaction. More specifically, communal participants were less dissatisfied than exchange participants in an implicit promise breach, and this pattern was more pronounced in the interdependent self-construal condition than in the independent self-construal condition. In contrast, communal participants were more dissatisfied than exchange participants in an explicit promise breach, and this pattern, again, was more pronounced for participants who primed with an interdependent (vs. independent) self-construal. In addition, convergent evidences were found for the underlying mechanism between an implicit and an explicit promise breach. In brief, the self-obligation thought (betrayal feeling) tendency mediates the interactive effect of relationship type and promise breach type on consumer dissatisfaction in an implicit (explicit) promise breach.

References

Clark, Margaret S. and Judson Mills (1979), "Interpersonal Attraction in Exchange and Communal Relationships," *Journal of Personality and Social Psychology*, 37 (1), 12-24.

Markus, Hazel R. and Shinobu Kitayama (1991), "Culture and the Self: Implications for Cognition, Emotion, and Motivation," *Psychological Review*, 98 (2), 224-53.

Rousseau, Denise M. (1989), "Psychological and Implied Contracts in Organizations," *Employee Responsibilities and Rights Journal*, 2 (2), 121-39.

Singelis, Theodore M. (1994), "The Measurement of Independent and Interdependent Self-Construals," *Personality and Social Psychology Bulletin*, 20 (5), 580-91.

Consumer Response to Firm Crisis Information: The Moderating Role of Regulatory Focus on Selective Exposure

Sunghun Chung, KAIST Business School, Korea
Yeosun Yoon, KAIST Business School, Korea
Ingoo Han, KAIST Business School, Korea

EXTENDED ABSTRACT

Firms frequently must deal with anomalous events, referred to as firm crisis, that induce high levels of uncertainty and are potential crucial factors to viability (Pearson and Clair 1998). Consumers today have access to a wide variety of firm crisis-relevant information, including traditional media and new media, such as online news forums, webcasts, and personal home pages. Batteries in electronic products spark fires, and negative publicity in case of the Enron incident are recognized as examples of firm crisis. Despite the potential impact of firm crisis in the market, there are few studies dealing with how consumers process such information and how firms can make strategies to overcome its effects. In addition, crisis research that addresses marketing issues is scant, and little is known about the effects of different response strategies resulting from critical motivation variables such as the regulatory focus.

In this research, we lay the foundation for a theoretical framework of firm crisis information processing by focusing on consumers' motivational orientation: self-regulation. The objective of our research is to provide an understanding of how consumers react to firm crisis information, and we argue that motivational orientation factor-namely, regulatory focus-moderate the processing and impact of firm crisis information. Also, we expect that increasing firm crisis-relevant information leads the firm in an opposite attitudinal direction, depending on the regulatory focus of the consumers.

According to regulatory focus theory (Higgins 1997), promotion-focused people emphasize aspirations and achievements and focus on the presence and absence of positive outcomes. However, prevention-focused people are concerned with responsibilities and safety and focus on the presence and absence of negative outcomes (Idson et al. 2000; Shah et al. 1998). In this regard, in the context of firm crisis, promotion-focused consumers display greater eagerness in striving toward a positive-framed outcome (inconsistent with firm crisis facts) than moving away from its absence (consistent with firm crisis facts). In contrast, prevention-focused consumers are concerned about a negative-framed outcome (consistent with firm crisis facts) more intensely than a positive framed outcome. Through experiment, we tested the differential responses to firm crisis by consumers who are either prevention or promotion orientated in self-regulation, and the psychological processes as firm crisis-relevant information increases.

Fischer and his colleagues (2008) make clear psychological processes that underlie the moderating role of information quantity on selective exposure. According to their study, when confronted with 10 pieces of information, consumers systematically preferred information that is consistent with their prior evaluation, whereas when confronted with only 2 pieces of information, they strongly preferred inconsistent information. Building upon Fischer's work (2008), we tested how consumers' regulatory focus moderates the effect of information quantity on selective exposure. We contend that whether firm crisis-relevant information will be discounted in a biased manner or will be weighted heavily depends on the consumer's self-regulation (promotion-focused or prevention-focused), and the quantity of firm crisis-relevant information will moderate these outcomes.

Finally, we confirmed the moderating role of consumers' regulatory focus to the effect of information quantity on selective exposure in the context of firm crisis. According to mediational analysis, prevention-focused consumers exhibited a lower evaluation in response to increasing the quantity of firm crisis-relevant information because they support-argued it solidly, whereas the promotion-focused consumers resisted information quantity because they effectively counterargued it. Further, the underlying response strategies of both prevention-focused consumers and promotion-focused consumers (support argument vs. counterargument) trigger negatively in the case that they are faced with the restricted quantity of firm crisis-relevant information. Theoretically, we added consumers' regulatory focus as an important moderator to previous crisis literatures dealing with factors such as commitment (Ahluwalia et al. 2000), consumer expectations (Dawar and Pillutla 2000), cognitive style (Monga and John 2008), and even the face of company (Gorn et al. 2008).

From a managerial perspective, in new media such as online news, consumers' opinions dealing with firm crisis facts (online commentaries) can influence others' evaluations on the firm, and be a fitting instrument for the context of selective exposure. The results of the study indicate that a firm has little to lose by taking an affirmative public atmosphere through media. Inconsistent information on firm crisis in market is likely to redress consumers' lowering attitude, but consistent information on firm crisis is likely to cause consumers' disappointment and suspicion. Marketers may have help by considering different filtering responses of firm crisis including consistent or inconsistent with crisis facts depending on consumers' regulatory focus.

Collectively, current findings provide an impetus for further investigations of each of the firm crises characterizing either corporate ability or corporate social responsibility. Further understanding of the psychological processes that underlie consumers' reactions to real companies should help companies to manage their crisis more efficiently and effectively to achieve both goals.

REFERENCES

Ahluwalia, Rohini, Robert E. Burnkrant, and H. Rao Unnava (2000), "Consumer Response to Negative Publicity: The Moderating Role of Commitment," *Journal of Marketing Research*, 37 (2), 203-214.

Dawar, Niraj and Madan M. Pillutla (2000), "Impact of Product-Harm Crises on Brand Equity: The Moderating Role of Consumer Expectations," *Journal of Marketing Research*, 37 (2), 215-226.

Fischer, Peter, Dieter Frey, and Stefan Schulz-Hardt (2008), "Selective Exposure and Information Quantity: How Different Information Quantities Moderate Decision Makers' Preference for Consistent and Inconsistent Information," *Journal of Personality and Social Psychology*, 94 (2), 231-244.

Gorn, Gerald J., Yuwei Jiang, and Gita Venkataramani Johar (2008), "Babyfaces, Trait Inferences, and Company Evaluations in a Public Relations Crisis," *Journal of Consumer Research*, 35 (1), 36-49.

Higgins, E. Tory (1997), "Beyond Pleasure and Pain," *American Psychologist*, 52 (12), 1280-300.

Idson, Lorraine Chen, Nira Liberman, and E. Tory Higgins (2000), "Distinguishing Gains from Nonlosses and Losses from Nongains: A Regulatory Focus Perspective on Hedonic Intensity," *Journal of Experimental Social Psychology*, 36 (3), 252-274.

Monga, Alokparna Basu and Deborah Roedder John (2008), "When does negative brand publicity hurt? The moderating influence of analytic versus holistic thinking," *Journal of Consumer Psychology*, 18 (4), 320-332.

Pearson, Christine M. and Judith A. Clair (1998), "Reframing Crisis Management," *Academy of Management Review*, 23 (1), 59-76.

Shah, James, E. Tory Higgins, and Ronald S. Friedman (1998), "Performance Incentives and Means: How Regulatory Focus Influences Goal Attainment," *Journal of Personality and Social Psychology*, 74 (2), 285-293.

Fantasies Come True, and Soon: Mental Construal as a Function of Regulatory State and Time Horizon

Yael Steinhart, University of Haifa, Israel
David Mazursky, The Hebrew University of Jerusalem, Israel
Michael A. Kamins, Stony Brook University, USA

EXTENDED ABSTRACT

Part of our indulgence in desired experiences to come, may involve thinking in detail about just how our experience may be. We savor with anticipation and cloak ourselves with exciting expectations about those wonderful moments to come. Essentially we borrow the expected feeling from the future and place it in the here and now, so as to brighten up our present. Conversely, if that future event is undesired, we may try to shun it, and avoid thinking about it in detail, giving way to what we current experience, for whatever it is worth.

The current research examines the nature of the mental construal process as a function of the consumer's regulatory focus state and time horizon. It proposes that when individuals are in a promotion state, such as being offered an attractive job when graduating, they savor the experience through anticipation and therefore are expected to consider a more detailed shopping list for the graduation party in the distant as opposed to near future. Alternatively, when individuals are in a prevention state, such as graduating with no job offer, they are expected to shun the experience and avoid thinking about it in details in the distance future more so than in the near future when they ultimately have to "face the music".

Recent research has directly focused on the form of mental construal as a function of the time horizon. In addition, there is ample evidence about the relationship between regulatory focus and the abstractness of mental construal. However, the role of temporal perspective in mediating the relationship between the type of regulatory state and the type of mental construal process has not been examined until now.

The research consists of four studies which demonstrate the "savor or shun" effect and its underlying mechanism in varying consumer contexts. The first study is designed to measure the anticipated breadth of categories formed in a decision task as a function of regulatory state and events that take place either in the near or distant future. It explores the research hypotheses under a realistic scenario of facing either an economic recession or prosperity, today or in the distant future, and asks participants to prepare a shopping list for each of the conditions. Its findings demonstrate that participants generated more categories in the distant future than in the near future when expecting prosperity; whereas the number of categories was higher in the near future than the distant future when expecting an economic recession. The second study extends the first by keeping the event constant (family weekend) and manipulating the regulatory state in an unrelated manner to the event. It further provides the participants with the list of items (rather than coming up with list by themselves) in order to better control the categorization process. Its findings replicate the ones of the first study both in terms of the number of categories and in terms of their content. The third study examines the "savor or shun" effect on actual decision choice, contingent with the item's level of abstractness. Results indicate that when exposed to both abstract and concrete items within a shopping list, individuals under a promotion focus selected relatively more abstract than concrete items in the near future than in the distant future. Alternatively, individuals under a prevention focus selected relatively more abstract over concrete items in the distant future than in the near one. Finally, the fourth study demonstrates the underlying mechanism of the "savor or shun" effect through mediation by scales relating to shunning and savoring.

From a practical perspective, the "savor or shun" effect has significant managerial implications by highlighting how marketers should frame the product (i.e. elaborate about the process of reaching the decision or about its post-usage benefits) and the amount of details they should provide given the state the consumer is in. In terms of positioning, the current research proposes that under a promotion state, consumers would prefer to get more information about the process of reaching a decision over the consequence of their decision. Therefore, when promoting promotional products, marketers should communicate about the process of attaining the product more than about the benefits of having the product. On the other hand, under a prevention state, consumers would prefer to get more information about the consequences of completing their decision than about the process of reaching it. In terms of how to describe the process or the outcomes; the proposed research implies that the degree of abstractness of the product description, should be as a function of the consumer's level of anticipation toward the product, and/or the time frame of the impending decision, because such factors affect the way information is categorized. Consider consumers anticipating the new model year of their desired car or a couple planning their wedding. In these cases, as the time frame approaches for the launching of the new model or for the wedding, our research suggests that consumers favor a broader description. This is especially true for events that are fixed at a given point in time and hence occur at the same time for everyone (e.g. Valentine's Day).

The Persuasive Power of Regulatory Nonfit

Lora Harding, Northwestern University, USA
Monika Lisjak, Northwestern University, USA
Angela Y. Lee, Northwestern University, USA

EXTENDED ABSTRACT

Past research has shown that persuasive appeals that fit (vs. conflict) with a person's regulatory focus tend to be more persuasive (Lee and Higgins 2009). Because regulatory fit information is consistent with people's current motivational orientation or way of thinking, it is easier to process and understand than information that is inconsistent with their regulatory orientation and thus tends to be processed more deeply (Lee and Aaker 2004). Recent research suggests that fit information is most persuasive when people allocate few cognitive resources to process information. For example, Wang and Lee (2006) reported that participants were more persuaded by information that fit their regulatory focus, but only under low-involvement conditions.

An important question is: What happens when people are motivated to process persuasive appeals? To the extent that elaboration leads to greater persuasion, our view is that people will be more persuaded by information that mismatches their regulatory focus. To fully comprehend regulatory nonfit information, we expect that highly involved people will engage in more extensive processing due to the fact that nonfit information is inconsistent with their current way of thinking. As a result of more elaborative processing of regulatory nonfit information, highly involved people will be more persuaded by regulatory nonfit appeals. In contrast, people who are less motivated to process information will selectively attend to regulatory fit information because it is easier to process, and thus will be more persuaded by regulatory fit appeals.

We tested this hypothesis in experiment 1, manipulating level of involvement (high vs. low), regulatory focus (promotion vs. prevention), and appeal type (promotion vs. prevention) in a between-subjects design, collapsing regulatory focus and appeal type conditions into fit and nonfit cells for analysis. Participants in the promotion-prime condition were asked to list five current hopes or aspirations as well as three attributes they would ideally like to possess, whereas those in the prevention-prime condition were asked to list five current duties and obligations as well as three attributes they ought to possess (Higgins et al. 1994; Higgins, Shah, and Friedman 1997). Next, they were exposed to a high- or low-involvement manipulation (Briley and Aaker 2006). Participants then read one of two advertisements for Welch's grape juice, one emphasizing its promotion benefits and the other emphasizing its prevention benefits (Aaker and Lee 2001). Finally, they evaluated the target product. As expected, a two-way interaction between involvement and regulatory fit emerged, whereby nonfit (fit) appeals were more persuasive under high- (low-) involvement conditions. These results provide the first evidence that regulatory nonfit appeals may indeed be more persuasive then fit appeals, but only when people are motivated and able to process nonfit information.

Experiment 2 was designed to test the robustness of the nonfit effect under high involvement as well as to provide insight into the underlying process. Specifically, we predicted that nonfit appeals would prompt greater processing engagement, resulting in greater persuasion. In order to test this prediction, all participants were first told that the study was very important and instructed to pay close attention. They were then given a promotion or prevention prime (see experiment 1) and asked to read a promotion- or prevention-oriented Welch's appeal. Participants then evaluated the product and reported their processing engagement (i.e., how involved and interested they were while processing the appeal). The results revealed a main effect of regulatory fit on persuasion, such that nonfit (vs. fit) appeals elicited more favorable brand attitudes under high-involvement conditions. The results also revealed the predicted main effect of regulatory fit on processing engagement, such that participants were more engaged while reviewing the nonfit (vs. fit) appeal. Finally, we found that heightened processing engagement mediated the positive relationship between nonfit appeals and brand attitudes, thus providing support for the processing engagement mechanism.

Experiment 3 was designed to provide further evidence of the mechanism underlying the regulatory nonfit effect. We reasoned that if highly involved people were more engaged while processing nonfit (vs. fit) information, then those exposed to nonfit (vs. fit) appeals should be more sensitive to differences in argument strength. Therefore, in addition to priming regulatory focus (asked to write an essay about their hopes and aspirations or duties and obligations; Higgins et al. 1994) and giving all participants a high-involvement manipulation (told that the advertised sun protection product, SunSkin, was targeted exclusively to college students and would be launched locally in just a few months; Wang and Lee 2006), we also manipulated the strength of the message arguments. Specifically, participants were exposed to one of four appeals—strong promotion, weak promotion, strong prevention, or weak prevention—followed by a request to evaluate the product. Aside from a main effect of argument strength, whereby strong appeals elicited more favorable attitudes, the results also revealed the expected two-way interaction between argument strength and regulatory fit, such that participants exposed to nonfit appeals were more discerning between strong and weak arguments than those exposed to fit appeals. Thus, these results provide further evidence of the process underlying the regulatory nonfit effect on persuasion by conforming to the premise that if people exposed to nonfit (vs. fit) appeals are indeed more engaged, they should be more sensitive to differences in argument strength.

In summary, the results across the three experiments provide convergent evidence for the hypothesized moderating role of involvement in regulatory focus-based persuasion. Whereas fit appeals are more persuasive under low-involvement conditions, nonfit appeals are more persuasive under high-involvement conditions. Furthermore, we find that the nonfit effect on persuasion is the result of heightened processing engagement, whereby people are more discerning of argument strength. These results provide the first evidence that regulatory nonfit appeals may be more persuasive than fit appeals, but only when people are motivated and able to process nonfit information.

REFERENCES

Aaker, Jennifer. L. and Angela Y. Lee (2001), "'I' Seek Pleasures and 'We' Avoid Pains: The Role of Self Regulatory Goals in Information Processing and Persuasion," *Journal of Consumer Research*, 28 (June), 33–49.

Briley, Donnel A. and Jennifer L. Aaker (2006). "When Does Culture Matter? Effects of Personal Knowledge on the Correction of Culture-Based Judgments," *Journal of Marketing Research*, 43 (August), 395–408.

Higgins, E. Tory, Christopher J.R. Roney, Ellen Crowe, and Charles Hymes (1994), "Ideal Versus Ought Predilections for Approach and Avoidance: Distinct Self-Regulatory Systems," *Journal of Personality and Social Psychology*, 66 (February), 276–86.

Higgins, E. Tory, James Shah, and Ronald Friedman (1997), "Emotional Responses to Goal Attainment: Strength of Regulatory Focus as Moderator," *Journal of Personality and Social Psychology*, 72 (March), 515–25.

Lee, Angela Y. and Jennifer Aaker L. (2004), "Bringing the Frame Into Focus: The Influence of Regulatory Fit on Processing Fluency and Persuasion," *Journal of Personality and Social Psychology*, 86 (February), 205–18.

Lee, Angela Y. and E. Tory Higgins (2009), "The Persuasive Power of Regulatory Fit," in *Frontiers in Social Psychology: Social Psychology of Consumer Behavior*, ed. Michaela Wänke, New York: Psychology Press, 319–33.

Wang, Jing, and Angela Y. Lee (2006), "The Role of Regulatory Focus in Preference Construction," *Journal of Marketing Research*, 43 (February), 28–38.

The Role of Regulatory Focus in the Endorsement of Material Values

Inge Lens, K.U. Leuven, Belgium
Mario Pandelaere, Ghent University, Belgium
L. J. Shrum, University of Texas at San Antonio, USA
Jaehoon Lee, University of Texas at San Antonio, USA

EXTENDED ABSTRACT

Materialism reflects the belief that wealth is an essential determinant of a successful, happy life (Richins and Dawson 1992). Apart from the influence of materialism, consumers' goal-striving is driven by their regulatory focus (cf. Higgins 1997). A promotion focus directs consumers' attention to their aspirations and hopes (ideals), whereas a prevention focus directs their attention to duties and responsibilities (oughts). Three studies are presented to test the proposition that both promotion and prevention are related to materialism, but through different mechanisms.

Research has shown that prevention is negatively related to self-esteem, whereas promotion is positively related to self-esteem (McGregor et al. 2007; Moss 2009). Because materialism is associated with uncertainty feelings (e.g. Chang and Arkin 2002; Christopher et al. 2006) that may stem from an unfulfilled need for self-esteem (Chaplin and John 2007; Kasser 2002), we propose that promotion and prevention foci may have opposite effects on materialism, given their opposite effects on self-esteem. In addition to differences in self-esteem, differences in extrinsic goal pursuit between prevention- and promotion-focused consumers may also lead to differences in materialism. In many capitalist societies, wealth is considered the key to a successful life (cf. Ger and Belk 1996). Correspondingly, striving for money and status (extrinsic goals; Deci and Ryan 2000; Kasser and Ryan 1993, 1996) is related to materialism (Kasser 2002). Given their concern with success, achievement (Higgins 1997), and realizing their ideal self (Lockwood, Jordan, and Kunda 2002), promotion-focused individuals may be more likely to adopt culturally promoted, extrinsic goals than prevention focused consumers. This is to some extent evidenced in their preference for luxury and hedonic consumption (Higgins 2002; Wang and Lee 2006; Werth and Föster 2007).

In sum, we hypothesize that promotion will be related to materialism through two routes, a positive one (mediated by extrinsic goal pursuit) and a negative one (mediated by self-esteem). In contrast, prevention will be negatively related to self-esteem, which in turn will be negatively related to materialism (net positive relation between prevention and materialism). In addition to the general materialism effects, we expect promotion and prevention focus to relate differentially to specific dimensions of materialism. It would be consistent with striving for achievement and success (cf. Higgins 1997) that promotion-focused consumers in particular believe that wealth communicates success. Thus, promotion may be particularly highly correlated with the success subscale of materialism (Richins and Dawson 1992). If prevention is related to materialism, and if low self-esteem accounts for this relation, it is plausible that prevention-focused consumers think that money would buy them happiness. Thus, prevention focus may be particularly highly correlated with Richins and Dawson's (1992) happiness subscale.

Study 1 used European students to test the hypothesis that regulatory focus is related to materialism. Regulatory focus was assessed with the Regulatory Focus Questionnaire (Lockwood et al. 2002). Materialism was measured with the Material Values Scale (Richins and Dawson 1992). Overall, our hypotheses were supported. Prevention significantly predicts overall materialism, but promotion does not, consistent with our reasoning that promotion influences materialism both positively and negatively through different mechanisms, thus suppressing the effect. In addition, prevention, not promotion, significantly predicts scores on the happiness dimension of materialism. Promotion positively predicts scores on the success dimension, but prevention does not.

Study 1 confirmed that prevention is positively related to materialism, but this study did not allow testing both predicted paths between promotion and materialism. If our assumptions hold, materialism should decrease in consumers who are in an induced promotion focus who experience a self-esteem boost, compared to promotion focused individuals whose self-esteem is not boosted. In study 2, 38 participants were randomly assigned to either think about achieved goals (past promotion), or about future aspirations (future promotion). Considering achieved and future aspirations induces promotion focus (cf. Lockwood et al. 2002; Pham and Avnet 2004; Zhu and Meyers-Levy 2007), and thinking of past successes was expected to enhance self-esteem (cf. Leonardelli et al. 2007). Next, participants indicated selling prices for five products. Selling price has been shown to be a reliable measure of (temporal) materialism (Lens and Pandelaere 2009). As predicted, participants in the past promotion condition demanded lower prices than participants in the future promotion condition, suggesting that enhanced self-esteem due to promotion success decreases materialistic pursuits.

In study 3, we replicated the findings of studies 1 and 2 in an American, non-student sample. This study extends the previous studies by explicitly measuring self-esteem (Rosenberg 1965) and extrinsic goal pursuit (Aspiration Index; Kasser and Ryan 1993, 1996). Regulatory focus and materialism were measured as in study 1. To assess the predicted relations between overall materialism, prevention, and promotion, we estimated a path model. The model adequately fits the data. In a second model, happiness and success were regressed separately on self-esteem and extrinsic goal pursuit. The model is improved significantly if we allow for a direct relation between prevention and happiness (not mediated by self-esteem). As expected, prevention was positively related to materialism, and this effect was mediated by self-esteem. Promotion was positively related to materialism via the mediating role of extrinsic goal pursuit, but negatively related to materialism through self-esteem. In addition, as hypothesized, the effects for prevention on materialism were driven by the happiness dimension, whereas the effects for promotion were driven by the success factor.

These findings show that consumers may adopt different "types" of materialism, and through different mechanisms, as suggested by the fact that promotion- and prevention-focused consumers tend to value different aspects of materialism congruent with their goal orientation.

REFERENCES

Chang, LinChiat and Arkin Robert M. (2002), "Materialism as an Attempt to Cope With Uncertainty," *Psychology & Marketing*, 19 (5), 389-406.

Chaplin, Lan Nguyen and Deborah Roedder John (2007), "Growing up in a Material World: Age Differences in Materialism in Children and Adolescents," *Journal of Consumer Research*, 34 (December), 480-493.

Christopher, Andrew N., Kansie Drummond, Jason R. Jones, Pam Marek, and Kelli M. Therriault (2006), "Beliefs About One's Own Death, Personal Insecurity, and Materialism," *Personality and Individual Differences*, 40, 441-51.

Deci, Edward L. and Richard M. Ryan (2000), "The "What" and "Why" of Goal Pursuits: Human Needs and the Self-Determination of Behavior," *Psychological Inquiry*, 11 (4), 227-68.

Ger Güliz and Russell W. Belk (1996), "Cross-Cultural Differences in Materialism", *Journal of Economic Psychology*, 17, 55-77.

Higgins, E. Tory (1997), "Beyond Pleasure and Pain," *American Psychologist*, 52 (12), 1280-300.

______ (2002), "How Self-regulation Creates Distinct Values: The Case of Promotion and Prevention Decision Making," *Journal of Consumer Psychology*, 12 (3), 177-91.

Kasser, Tim (2002), *The High Price of Materialism*, Cambridge: MIT Press.

Kasser, Tim and Richard M. Ryan (1993), "A Dark Side of The American Dream: Correlates of Financial Success as a Central Life Aspiration," *Journal of Personality and Social Psychology*, 65 (2), 410-22.

______ (1996), "Further Examining the American Dream: Differential Correlates of Intrinsic and Extrinsic Goals," *Personality and Social Psychology Bulletin*, 22 (March), 280-87.

Lens, Inge and Mario Pandelaere (2009), "Understanding the Role of Materialism in the Endowment Effect," in *Advances of Consumer Research*, 36, ed. Ann L. McGill and Sharon Shavitt, Duluth, MN: Association for Consumer Research, 658-9.

Leonardelli, Geoffrey, Jessica L. Lakin, and Robert M. Arkin (2007), "A Regulatory Focus Model of Self-Evaluation," *Journal of Experimental Social Psychology*, 43, 1002-9.

Lockwood, Penelope, Christian H. Jordan, and Ziva Kunda (2002), "Motivation by Positive or Negative Role Models: Regulatory Focus determines Who Will Best Inspire Us," *Journal of Personality and Social Psychology*, 83 (4), 854-64.

McGregor, Ian, Matthew T. Gailliot, Noelia A. Vasquez, and Kyle A. Nash (2007), "Ideological and Personal Zeal Reactions to Threat Among People With High Self-Esteem: Motivated Promotion Focus," *Personality and Social Psychology Bulletin*, 33 (11), 1587-99.

Moss, Simon (2009), "Cultivating the Regulatory Focus of Follower to Amplify Their Sensitivity to Transformational Leadership," *Journal of Leadership and Organizational Studies*, 15 (3), 241-59.

Pham, Michel Tuan and Tamar Avnet (2004), "Ideals and Oughts and the Reliance on Affect Versus Substance in Persuasion," *Journal of Consumer Research*, 30 (March), 503-18.

Richins, Marsha L. and Scott Dawson (1992), "Materialism as a Consumer Value: Measure Development and Validation," *Journal of Consumer Research*, 19 (December), 303-16.

Rosenberg, Morris (1965), Society and the Adolescent Self-image, Princeton, NJ: Princeton University Press.

Wang, Jing and Angela Y. Lee (2006), "The Role of Regulatory Focus in Preference Construction," *Journal of Marketing Research*, 43 (1), 28-38.

Werth, Lioba and Jens Förster (2007), "How Regulatory Focus Influences Consumer Behavior," *European Journal of Social Psychology*, 37, 33-51.

Zhu Rui and Joan Meyers-Levy (2007), "Exploring the Cognitive Mechanism that Underlies Regulatory Focus Effects," *Journal of Consumer Research*, 34 (June), 89-96.

Decision Making on the Small Screen: Adaptive Behavior in Constrained Information Environments

Nicholas H. Lurie, Georgia Institute of Technology, USA
Doe-Hyun Song, Digital Solutions Inc., USA
Sridhar Narasimhan, Georgia Institute of Technology, USA[1]

EXTENDED ABSTRACT

More and more, consumers are accessing large amounts of information through small screen devices. For consumers in many countries, the mobile phone is the primary portal to the Internet (Wright 2008). High-speed wireless networks and the growing distribution of ever more powerful cell phones and wireless devices mean that even consumers with access to traditional desktop displays are increasingly using mobile devices to gather product information and make purchases (Alam Khan 2008). Despite a dramatic increase in the usage of mobile devices, little is known about how such devices affect consumer behavior.

Examining how decisions are made in environments that substantially constrain the decision maker's visual field raises a number of interesting issues not addressed in prior research. For example, most research on decision processes is conducted in environments in which decision makers can view all available information simultaneously (e.g., Bettman et al. 1993; Payne, Bettman, and Johnson 1988) but users of small screen devices can often only see a small portion of the information that desktop users see (Chae and Kim 2004). Prior research on decision making has also focused almost exclusively on how informational characteristics affect the *cognitive* processes associated with different decision strategies (e.g., Bettman et al. 1993; Jarvenpaa 1989; Lurie 2004; Payne et al. 1988), but small screens also require substantial *physical* effort (e.g., Albers and Kim 2000; Chae and Kim 2004). Finally, previous research has assumed that the way in which information is displayed to the consumer is under the control of the marketer (Diehl 2005; Häubl and Trifts 2000); yet mobile users view and access information on devices that vary in the amount of information displayed and whether more information is displayed on the vertical versus horizontal axis. These device-specific differences in the visual representation of information likely change the way in which information is used to make decisions (Lurie and Mason 2007; Wedel and Pieters 2007).

This article argues that, when using small screen devices to make decisions, consumers will adapt their decision processes in two important ways: 1) Consumers will account for physical as well as cognitive effort in their information acquisition and decision strategies; and (2) They will adapt their information acquisition and decision strategies to reflect the amount of information that can be accessed simultaneously (i.e., that portion of the underlying information that can be seen without scrolling). If consumers are able to employ decision strategies that minimize effort while maintaining fairly high levels of accuracy (Payne et al. 1988), declines in decision quality when using small screens should be small. If the accuracy of decision strategies depends on whether decision makers process by alternative or by attribute (Bettman et al. 1993), decision quality should be influenced by screen orientation as well as size.

These ideas are tested in two process-tracing experiments and a Monte-Carlo simulation. Results from the first experiment support the idea that the increased physical effort of making decision on small screen devices leads to reductions in cognitive effort. In particular, a reduction in screen size leads consumers to acquire less information, spend less time per acquisition, spend less time on information acquisition, and be more likely to process by attribute than by alternative. This leads to significant declines in decision quality but these declines are not as large as might be expected given large differences in the amount of information displayed. Experiment results also support the proposal that the constraints of the small screen lead consumers to focus on information that is currently shown, reducing the information reacquisition and decreasing selectivity. Importantly, Experiment 1 also shows that what information is shown is as important as how much information is shown. In particular, screens that show more attributes than alternatives lead to by-alternative processing and higher quality decisions. The second experiment shows that the results found in Study 1 hold regardless of whether attributes are displayed in rows or in columns.

To help explain the experimental results, a Monte-Carlo simulation examined how screen characteristics affect the effort and accuracy of five idealized decision strategies (Johnson and Payne 1985; Payne et al. 1988), that account for physical as well as cognitive processes. Results from the simulation show that screen size has a much smaller effect on decision effort for non-compensatory than compensatory decision strategies. Although effort increases substantially when compensatory decision strategies are employed, increases in effort are minimal for non-compensatory strategies. The Monte-Carlo simulation also explicitly shows how screen orientation changes the effort involved with employing by-attribute or by-alternative strategies and helps explain why changing screen orientation leads to shifts in decision strategies that affect decision quality.

Beyond these substantive implications for decision making on mobile devices in particular, this article contributes to decision-making research more generally. First, the perspective taken here integrates the physical costs of searching for information with the cognitive costs of processing it; suggesting that consumers make tradeoffs between physical and cognitive costs when making decisions. In this way, this article bridges research on information search (Moorthy, Ratchford, and Talukdar 1997; Ratchford, Lee, and Talukdar 2003) and research on how characteristics of information affect decision making (Bettman et al. 1993; Lurie 2004). Second, this article suggests that the visual representation of information; more specifically, depth of field (Lurie and Mason 2007), affects decision strategies. Finally, this article builds on prior research on the use of simulations of human decision making (Bettman et al. 1993; Hastie and Stasser 2000; Johnson and Payne 1985; Payne et al. 1988) to show that simulations can be used to explicitly account for environmental as well as cognitive characteristics when modeling decision processes. This approach can be generalized to assess a wide variety of decision environments in which device characteristics are likely to affect the way in which decisions are made.

REFERENCES

Alam Khan, Mickey (2008), "Nielsen Mobile Sees Uptick in Mobile Commerce," in *Mobile Marketer*, http://mobilemarketer.com/cms/news/research/1148.html.

[1]The authors thank Zoey Chen and Charlotte Mason for their helpful comments.

Albers, Michael J. and Loel Kim (2000), "User Web Browsing Characteristics Using Palm Handhelds for Information Retrieval," in *Proceedings of the 18th Annual ACM International Conference on Computer Documentation: Technology & Teamwork*, ed. Susan B. Jones and Beth Weise Moeller, Cambridge, Massachusetts: ACM, 125-35.

Bettman, James R., Eric J. Johnson, Mary Frances Luce, and John W. Payne (1993), "Correlation, Conflict and Choice," *Journal of Experimental Psychology: Learning, Memory, and Cognition*, 19 (4), 931-51.

Chae, Minhee and Jinwoo Kim (2004), "Do Size and Structure Matter to Mobile Users? An Empirical Study of the Effects of Screen Size, Information Structure, and Task Complexity on User Activities with Standard Web Phones," *Behaviour & Information Technology*, 23 (3), 165-81.

Diehl, Kristin (2005), "When Two Rights Make a Wrong: Searching Too Much in Ordered Environments," *Journal of Marketing Research*, 42 (August), 313-22.

Hastie, Reid and Garold Stasser (2000), "Computer Simulation Methods for Social Psychology," in *Handbook of Research Methods in Social and Personality Psychology*, ed. Harry T. Reis and Charles M. Judd, New York: Cambridge, 85-114.

Häubl, Gerald and Valerie Trifts (2000), "Consumer Decision Making in Online Shopping Environments: The Effects of Interactive Decision Aids," *Marketing Science*, 19 (1), 4-21.

Jarvenpaa, Sirkka L. (1989), "The Effect of Task Demands and Graphical Format on Information Processing Strategies," *Management Science*, 35 (3), 285-303.

Johnson, Eric J. and John W. Payne (1985), "Effort and Accuracy in Choice," *Management Science*, 31 (4), 395-414.

Lurie, Nicholas H. (2004), "Decision Making in Information-Rich Environments: The Role of Information Structure," *Journal of Consumer Research*, 30 (March), 473-86.

Lurie, Nicholas H. and Charlotte H. Mason (2007), "Visual Representation: Implications for Decision Making," *Journal of Marketing*, 71 (January), 160-77.

Moorthy, Sridhar, Brian T. Ratchford, and Debabrata Talukdar (1997), "Consumer Information Search Revisited: Theory and Empirical Analysis," *Journal of Consumer Research*, 23, (March), 263-77.

Payne, John W., James R. Bettman, and Eric J. Johnson (1988), "Adaptive Strategy Selection in Decision Making," *Journal of Experimental Psychology: Learning, Memory & Cognition*, 14 (3), 534-52.

Ratchford, Brian T., Myung-Soo Lee, and Debabrata Talukdar (2003), "The Impact of the Internet on Information Search for Automobiles," *Journal of Marketing Research*, 40 (2), 193-209.

Wedel, Michel and Rik Pieters (2007), *Visual Marketing: From Attention to Action*, Mahwah, NJ: Lawrence Erlbaum.

Wright, Tom (2008), "Poorer Nations Go Online on Cellphones," *The Wall Street Journal*, December 5, 2008, B4.

The Effect of Customization Strategy and Recommendations on Consumer Decision-Making

Brent Coker, University of Melbourne, Australia
Anish Nagpal, University of Melbourne, Australia
Partha Krishnamurthy, University of Houston at Texas, USA

EXTENDED ABSTRACT

As a result of recent advances in production and selling technologies, firms are increasingly offering their customers a degree of customization in their product offerings. Although offering customized products benefits the firm as well as customers (Dellaert and Stremersch 2005; Dewan et al. 2003; Syam and Kumar 2006), the degree of mental effort required to make a purchase is considerably more than when decisions on attribute inclusion or exclusion are not required (Bettman et al. 1990; Dellaert and Stremersch 2005; Payne et al. 1993; Shugan 1980). To ease this effort, firms such as Dell offer a recommendation of which attribute to choose. For example Dell, in addition to offering several sizes of hard drive to the consumer, will also recommend one of the options (say, 240 GB hard drive). Little is known about how recommendations such as these offered during a product customization task influence decision making. In this research, we studied the impact recommendations have on customized choices.

We evaluated the effect of recommendation in two types of customization strategy. In the first type, participants were given a base model notebook computer (default model) and invited to increase attribute level options to their desired configuration (more hard drive space, more memory, faster CPU etc.). In the second customization strategy, participants were given a fully featured notebook computer (default model), and invited to remove attribute option levels they did not need. When no recommendations are offered by the vendor, the default configuration provides a point of reference from which decisions to add or remove options are made. However, when a recommendation is offered, there exists two points of reference, one is the default configuration, and the other is the recommended configuration. Based on prior research, we suggest that consumers will be influenced by one of the reference points more than the other, depending on the relative salience of the reference point (Crum et al. 1981; Kahneman and Tversky 1979; Kristensen and Garling 1997; March and Shapira 1987; March and Shapira 1992; White et al. 1994)). The salience of the reference point is a function of feature specification, with higher feature specifications having more salience than lower feature specifications.

We hypothesized that 1). When adding options, the price of the final configured product for those given a recommendation will be significantly higher than those not given a recommendation; 2) When removing options, the price of the final configured product for those given a recommendation will not be significantly different from those not given a recommendation, and; 3) People will have more recommendation-based thoughts when adding options than when removing options.

Our hypotheses were tested in three experiments. Study 1 was a 2 (Customization Strategy: Building-up/Paring-down) x 2 (Recommendation: Yes/No) between-subjects design conducted online. Participants were given the chance to customize a computer online, either by adding or removing attributes, in a similar fashion to the Dell.com website. For those in the paring down condition, the highest level of each attribute was pre-selected (default option). For those in the building up condition, the lowest level of each attribute was pre-selected (default option). Recommendation was also manipulated between subjects, and operationalized as a suggestion to choose the mid range option level of each attribute. Final configured price was the dependent variable. Hypotheses 1 and 2 were tested and supported.

In study two, the design was the same, but with a bigger range of attribute levels given for each attribute, and two extra conditions of a higher level recommendation (two-thirds of the way up the range of level options), and a lower recommendation (one-third of the way up). Although we again found support for the hypotheses 1 and 2, the results suggested that when the price of the recommended option is too high, people will not respond to the recommendation as they would when the recommendation was at the middle option level.

In study 3, the design was similar to studies 1 and 2, but the recommendation was manipulated within subjects to evaluate the robustness of the effects. Also included in study 3 were open ended and scale questions to compare the number of recommendation-based thoughts in each condition to test hypothesis 3. We found that participants had more number of recommendation-based thoughts when building-up than when paring-down, indicating the greater influence of the recommendation when building-up. Second, consumers using a building-up customization strategy had equal number of feature-based and price-based thoughts, indicative of the recommendation becoming more salient, leading to reference point shifting from the base model to the recommended level. Third, consumers in the paring-down customization strategy had a greater number of feature-based thoughts than price-based thoughts, indicative of the recommendation not becoming salient, leading to the reference point not shifting to the recommended option. Taken together, the open-ended responses provide evidence that the reference-point may shift in the building-up strategy but not in the paring-down strategy.

Overall, our results suggest that recommendations influence decisions adding options, but are ignored when removing options. These findings have implications for marketers offering customized product options, and shed light onto conditions of reference point shift when decision making.

REFERENCES

Bettman, Jamer R., Eric J. Johnson, and W. John Pawyne (1990), "A Componential Analysis of Cognitive Effort in Choice," *Organizational Behavior & Human Decision Processes*, 45 (1), 111-40.

Crum, Roy L., Dan J. Laughhunn, and John W. Payne (1981), "Risk-Seeking Behavior and Its Implications for Financial Models," *Financial Management* (1972), 10 (5), 20-27.

Dellaert, G. C. Benedict and Stefan Stremersch (2005), "Marketing Mass-Customized Products: Striking a Balance Between Utility and Complexity," *Journal of Marketing Research*, 42 (May), 219-27.

Dewan, Rajiv, Bing Jing, and Abraham Seidmann (2003), "Product Customization and Price Competition on the Internet," *Management Science*, 49 (8), 1055-70.

Kahneman, Daniel and Amos Tversky (1979), "Prospect Theory: An Analysis of Decision under Risk," *Econometrica*, 47, 263-91.

Kristensen, H. and T Garling (1997), "Adoption of Cognitive Reference Points in Negotiations," *Acta Psychologica*, 97 (3), 277-88.

March, James G and Zur Shapira (1992), "Variable Risk Preferences and the Focus of Attention," *Psychological Review*, 99 (1), 172-83.

March, James G. and Zur Shapira (1987), "Managerial Perspectives on Risk and Risk Taking," *Management Science*, 33 (11), 1404-18.

Payne, John W., Jamer R. Bettman, and Eric J. Johnson (1993), *The Adaptive Decision Maker*. New York: Cambridge University Press.

Simonson, Itamar and Amos Tversky (1992), "Choice in Context: Tradeoff Contrast and Extremeness Aversion," *Journal of Marketing Research*, 29 (3), 281-95.

Syam, N. B. and N. Kumar (2006), "On Customized Goods, Standard Goods, and Competition," *Marketing Science*, 25 (5), 525-37.

White, Sally Blount, Kathleen L. Valley, Max H. Bazerman, Margaret A. Neale, and Sharon R. Peck (1994), "Alternative Models of Price Behavior in Dyadic Negotiations: Market Prices, Reservation Prices and Negotiator Aspirations," *Organizational Behavior & Human Decision Processes*, 57 (3), 430-47.

The Influence of Social Norms in Consumer Behavior: A Meta-Analysis

Vladimir Melnyk, Wageningen University, The Netherlands
Erica van Herpen, Wageningen University, The Netherlands
Hans C. M. van Trijp, Wageningen University, The Netherlands

EXTENDED ABSTRACT

Social norms are major drivers of human behavior and crucial in consumer decision making. Consumers often take expectations and behavior of others into consideration when they decide what is appropriate and social norms thus profoundly influence their preferences and behavior (Cialdini, Reno, and Kallgren 1990). How much to drink at a party, whether to subscribe to a fitness club and how much to eat are all decisions that are at least partly guided by social norms. Although social norms can substantially influence consumer decision making, understanding of how the specification of the norm determines its effect is limited. Despite a large body of research on social norms, empirical findings about their effect in consumer decision making are not consistent (Schultz et al. 2007). For example, Sheeran, Abraham, and Orbell (1999), in their meta-analysis of the willingness to use condoms (121 studies out of which 21 include social norms) find that subjective norms are weak predictors of intentions (r=.26), whereas Rivis and Sheeran (2003) in their meta-analysis of the theory of planned behavior (21 studies) find a more substantial correlation between norms and intentions (r=.44).

This meta-analysis examines the association between social norms on the one hand and consumer's attitudes, behavioral intentions, and behavior on the other hand, while accounting for study characteristics (study domain, gender and age of participants, type of culture) and methodological factors. We expect that several aspects of norm specification will influence the strength of these associations. First, norms can be specified in a descriptive or prescriptive (i.e., injunctive) way, a distinction which has previously been shown to determine their influence on consumer decision making (Cialdini et al. 1990). Injunctive norms focus consumers on what is approved and may activate the typical attitudes associated with the group, whereas descriptive norms specify the behavior of others, and consumers may follow such norms without giving it much thought. Thus we expect descriptive norms have a larger effect on behavior but a smaller effect on attitudes than an injunctive norms. Second, the influence of social norms may depend on the concreteness with which the required behavior, the consequences of following or deviating from the norm, and the target person are specified (Shaffer 1983). Concrete information is generally more engaging and memorable than abstract information, and could therefore be more persuasive. Third, norms may be more relevant, and hence more influential, when these come from persons with whom the consumer can easily identify. Fourth, because public behavior is noticed and corrected by others, norms relating to public behavior should have more influence than norms relating to private behavior.

The sample consisted of 200 studies, producing 659 effect sizes. As a measure for effect sizes, we chose the Pearson correlation coefficient, converted to the normally distributed Fisher's z scores. Because attitudes are both strongly correlated with norms and have a strong influence on intentions (behavior), the total correlation between norms and intentions (behavior) may contain some of the effect of attitudes and thus overestimate the effect of social norms. To account for this, we also examined partial correlations between norms and intentions (behavior), controlling for attitudes.

Results showed that effect sizes obtained from partial correlations were significantly lower than effect sizes obtained from total correlations for both behavioral intentions and behavior. This implies that indeed a substantial part of the effect of social norms on intentions and behavior can be accounted for by the covariation between attitudes and social norms. Descriptive norms were shown to have a larger effect on behavior than injunctive norms, whereas injunctive norms have a larger effect on attitudes than descriptive norms. Hence, for changing attitudes, injunctive norms may be more effective, whereas for changing behavior, descriptive norms are more appropriate. Effects on behavior are also stronger when norms come from close and concrete sources (vs. authority figures or abstract others) and when the behavior is public (vs. private). No effects were found for specifications of the expected behavior, the consequences, or the target person. In addition, we examined interaction effects between independent variables and no significant effects were found.

The study also demonstrated that the effect of social norms differed across domains. Compared with decisions related to healthy lifestyle, social responsibility, or sex, everyday consumption decisions such as choices between food, drinks, and leisure time activities showed a high consistency between social norms and attitudes. Interestingly, social norms had a relatively large effect on social responsible behaviors. These are behaviors where societal benefits are involved, and where social norms should drive human behavior to prevent free-riding problems. Our study showed that social norms indeed are relatively influential for consumer behavior in this domain.

Our study has several implications. The meta-analysis reveals a high association between social norms and attitudes, and one possible extension to theoretical models that include normative components is to examine this relationship. It has recently been posited that social norms influence attitudes (Terry et al. 2000), and our study shows that the strength of this influence depends on the specification of norm aspects.

Additionally, consumers respond differently to injunctive versus descriptive norms, and, more importantly, an injunctive specification of a norm leads to stronger effects on attitudes but weaker effects on behavior than a descriptive formulation. This implies that an investigation of the effect of social norms which examines only attitudes or only behavior does not provide a complete picture of the effect of social norms. To truly understand the effect of social norms, attitudes, behavioral intentions, and behavior need all be examined. In addition, further research could examine other aspects of social norms, such as group size, or uncertainty, which could influence their effectiveness. This meta-analysis is obviously bound to prior research that has been conducted, but more aspects remain to be investigated. We hope that our study presents a stepping stone towards a deeper understanding of when and how social norms drive consumer attitudes, intentions, and behavior.

REFERENCES

Albarracín, Dolores, Blair T. Johnson, Martin Fishbein, and Paige A. Muellerleile (2001), "Theories of Reasoned Action and Planned Behavior as Models of Condom Use: A Meta-Analysis," *Psychological Bulletin*, 127 (1), 142-61.

Armitage, Christopher J. and Mark Connor (2001), "Efficacy of the Theory of Planned Behaviour: A Meta-Analytic Review," British *Journal of Social Psychology*, 40, 471-99.

Bijmolt, Tammo H. A. and Rik G. M. Pieters (2001), "Meta-Analysis in Marketing When Studies Contain Multiple Measurements," *Marketing Letters*, 12 (2), 157-69.

Cialdini, Robert B., Raymond. R. Reno, and Carl A. Kallgren (1990), "A Focus Theory of Normative Conduct: Recycling the Concept of Norms to Reduce Littering in Public Places," *Journal of Personality and Social Psychology*, 58 (6), 1015-26.

Reno, Raymond R., Robert B. Cialdini, and Carl A. Kallgren (1993), "The Transsituational Influence of Social Norms," *Journal of Personality and Social Psychology*, 64 (1), 104-12.

Rivis, Armanda and Paschal Sheeran (2003), "Descriptive Norms as an Additional Predictor in the Theory of Planned Behaviour: A Meta-Analysis," *Current Psychology*, 22 (3), 218-33.

Schultz, P. Wesley, Jessica M. Nolan, Robert B. Cialdini, Noah J. Goldstein, and Vlades Griskevicius (2007), "The Constructive, Destructive and Reconstructive Power of Social Norms," *Psychological Science*, 18 (5), 429-34.

Shaffer, Leigh S. (1983), "Toward Pepitone's Vision of a Normative Social Psychology: What Is a Social Norm?," *Journal of Mind and Behavior*, 4 (2), 275-93.

Sheeran, Paschal, Charles Abraham, and Sheina Orbell (1999), "Psychosocial Correlates of Heterosexual Condom Use: A Meta-Analysis," *Psychological Bulletin*, 125 (1), 90-132.

Terry, Deborah J., Michael A. Hogg, and Katherine M. White (2000b), "Attitude-Behavior Relations: Social Identity and Group Membership " in *Attitudes, Behavior, and Social Context: The Role of Norms and Group Membership*, ed. Deborah J. Terry and Michael A. Hogg, London: Lawrence Erlbaum 67-94.

Feeling, Thinking, and Differential Decision Making Under Risk

Steven J. Andrews, University of Oregon, USA
Joan L. Giese, University of Oregon, USA
David M. Boush, University of Oregon, USA

EXTENDED ABSTRACT

Prospect theory is one of the most influential theories that deal with how people make decisions under risk and uncertainty. A key tenet of prospect theory is that the same person might be more risk averse in some contexts than in others. The original proponents of prospect theory acknowledged that there were still unexplained inconsistencies in their own observations of decision making that need to be addressed. To date, the reasons for nonconformity have never been thoroughly examined. The research question this study explored involves whether individual differences in preferences for using affective or cognitive decision making processes might systematically lead some people to exhibit differential decision making behavior under risk than what would be predicted by prospect theory.

Modern decision theory formally acknowledges the importance and centrality of affect in decision making. There is abundant evidence that affect plays a primary role in decision making because affective information includes information about the subjective value of the environmental cues being responded to in the decision process. More recent theories demonstrate both the centrality of affect in the decision making process and the potential for integration of affective and cognitive information in decision making. The theory of affect-as-information plausibly asserts that emotions are not merely byproducts or after-effects of a decision, but that emotional content deemed relevant to a decision is used in real-time during the decision making process. Furthermore, the risk-as-feelings hypothesis, in conjunction with theories of the affect heuristic in risky decision making, assert that affective and cognitive decision making systems are separate but potentially integrated systems. When the two systems diverge, however, it is actually the affective system that most prominently drives the decision making process.

The degree to which affect is utilized as information translates into meaningful difference in judgment and behavior. Based on the call to study individual difference phenomena in specific domains and in the context of theoretical frameworks, the present research builds on the affect-as-information and the risk-as-feelings frameworks to examine more closely differential decision making behavior under risk that is not accounted for by prospect theory. Specifically, this research categorizes people according to whether their decisions tend to involve a lot of thought (high cognition), a lot of feeling (high affect) or both (high cognition/affect) in the context of decision making under risk. This research sought to establish that such differential decision making tendencies are meaningful and that they influence the underlying mechanisms involved in making risky decisions.

The first study explored the extent to which information processing tendencies might influence differential decision making behavior within the original prospect theory risky decision making contexts. There is evidence that high affect/high cognition people seem to be amenable to making risky choices. Also, people who are high in affect but low in cognition might be most likely to succumb too heavily to highly aversive emotional influences in a risky decision context and would seek the least risky option, regardless of whether the decision is framed as a gain or a loss. Using an individual difference measure derived from the Need for Cognition scale and an internally developed scale measuring the tendency to use affect as information, participants were categorized into four information processing groups based on median splits in the two scales. Next, participants examined four risky decision scenarios, two framed as a potential loss and two framed as a potential gain, taken from the work of Kahneman and Tversky (1982) and Tversky and Kahneman (1981). Choice probabilities were such that prospect theory predicted the risky choice in all four scenarios. Results showed that high affect/high cognition took significant risk when the decision was framed as a potential loss of $750, whereas high affect only subjects avoided risk when the decision was framed as a potential $240 gain. Looking at high affect and low affect participants only, those high in affect were considerably less likely to take a risk even when expected to do so by prospect theory.

The second study explored more directly the extent to which people with different information processing tendencies anticipate negative consequences associated with risk in everyday situations. This study also examined differential anticipation of well-documented psychological factors, specifically regret, inherent in making decisions under risk. Participants were categorized into information processing groups as in study 1. Next, participants identified three common decisions they make every day that contains an element of risk and they identified the risky element. These answers will be used in future studies to create more content-appropriate decision tasks for studying college students. Participants then rated on a scale from 1 to 7 the expected severity of the consequences of the risky outcome if it were to happen. Finally, participants rated from 1 to 7 the extent to which they anticipated feeling regret if the risky outcome were to happen. Results showed that people high in affective processing and low in cognitive processing were much more likely to rate the consequences of the risky outcome as severe, and these same people were much more likely to anticipate feeling regret if the risky outcome were to happen.

In summary, this research showed that differential tendencies in affective and cognitive information processing provided some explanation as to why some people fail to conform to prospect theory under some decision contexts. This research also shed some light on the differential influence that key psychological mechanisms involved in risky decision making have on people who process information in different ways. Regret as a component of decision making under risk was originally established as a justification for prospect theory's predictions that people do not always make the rational choice. Regret is a complex emotion with a cognitive component consisting of counterfactual thinking and a particularly aversive emotional component centered on self-accountability. Future studies should probe more deeply into the differential effects that negative anticipation of the consequences of risk and the anticipation of regret had on decision making in relation to information processing tendencies.

REFERENCES

Bell, David E. (1982), "Regret in Decision Making under Uncertainty." *Operations Research*, 30, 961-999.

Cacioppo, J.T., R.E. Petty and C.F. Kao. (1984), "The efficient assessment of need for cognition." *Journal of Personality Assessment*, 48, 306-307.

Connolly, T. and M. Zeelenberg. (2002), "Regret in Decision Making." *Current Directions in Psychological Science*, 11, 212-216.

Coricelli, Giorgio, Hugo D. Critchley, Mateus Joffily, John P. O'Doherty, Angela Sirigu and Raymond J. Dolan. (2005), "Regret and its avoidance: a neuroimaging study of choice behavior." *Nature Neuroscience*, 8, 1255-1262.

Damasio, Anton. (1994), Descartes' Error: Emotion, Reason and the Human Brain. New York:Avon.

DeBruin, Wandi Bruine, Andrew M. Parker and Baruch Fischhoff. (2007), "Individual Differences in Adult Decision-Making Competence." *Journal of Personality and Social Psychology*, 92 (5), 938-956.

Finucane, Melissa L., Ali Alhakami, Paul Slovic and Stephen M. Johnson. (2000), "The Affect Heuristic in Judgments of Risk and Benefits." *Journal of Behavioral Decision Making*, 13, 1-17.

Giese, Joan L. and Jane Z. Sojka. (1998), "The Relationship Between Processing Styles and Self-Control Behavioral Characteristics." *Marketing Letters*, 9 (4), 371-382.

Gohm, Carol L. and Gerald L. Clore. (2002), "Affect as Information: An Individual Differences Approach." in *The Wisdom of Feeling: Psychological Process in Emotional Intelligence*, Lisa Feldman Barrett and Peter Salovey, ed(s), New York:The Guilford Press, 89-113.

Kahneman, D. and A. Tversky. (1982). "The Psychology of Preferences." *Scientific American* 246, 160-173.

Kahneman, Daniel. (2003), "Maps of Bounded Rationality: Psychology for Behavioral Economics." The American Economic Review, 93 (5), 1449-1475.

Kahneman, Daniel and Amos Tversky. (1979), "Prospect Theory: An Analysis of Decision Under Risk." *Econometrica*, 47, 263-292.

Kahneman, Daniel and Dale T. Miller. (1986), "Norm Theory: Comparing Reality to Its Alternatives." *Psychological Review*, 93 (2), 136-153.

Kahneman, Daniel and Carol A. Varey. (1986), "Propensities and Counterfactuals: The Loser That Almost Won." *Journal of Personality and Social Psychology*, 59 (6), 1101-1110.

Kidwell, Blair, David M. Hardesty and Terry L. Childers. (2008), "Consumer Emotional Intelligence: Conceptualization, Measurement, and the Prediction of Consumer Decision Making." *Journal of Consumer Research*, 35 (1) (June), 154-166.

Loewenstein, George. (2001), "The Creative Destruction of Decision Research." Journal of Consumer Research, 28, 499-505.

Loewenstein, Goerge, Elke U. Weber, Christopher K. Hsee and Ned Welch. (2001), "Risk as Feelings." *Psychological Bulletin*, 127 (2), 267-286.

Loomes, Graham and Robert Sugden. (1982), "Regret Theory: An Alternative Theory of Rational Choice Under Uncertainty." *Economic Journal*, 92, 805-824.

Meyvis, Tom and Alan D.J. Cooke. (2007), "Learning from Mixed Feedback: Anticipation of the Future Reduces Appreciation of the Present." *Journal of Consumer Research*, 34 (August 2007), 200-211.

Pham, Michel Tuan. (2004), "The Logic of Feeling." *Journal of Consumer Psychology*, 14, 360-369.

Pham, Michel Tuan, Joel B. Cohen, John W. Pracejus and G. David Hughes. (2001), "Affect Monitoring and the Primacy of Feelings in Judgment." *Journal of Consumer Research*, 28, 167-188.

Schwarz, Norbert and Gerald L. Clore. (2006), "Feelings and Phenomenal Experiences." in *Social Psychology. Handbood of Basic Principles* (2nd edition), A. Kruglanski and E.T. Higgens, ed(s), New York:Guilford, 1-30.

Slovic, Paul, Ellen Peters, Melissa L. Finucane and Donald G. MacGregor. (2005), "Affect, Risk, and Decision Making." *Health Psychology*, 24 (4 (suppl)), S35-S40.

Taylor, Steven A. (2007), "The addition of anticipated regret to attitudinally based, goal-directed models of information search behaviors under conditions of uncertainty and risk." *British Journal of Social Psychology*, 46, 739-768.

Thaler, Richard. (1985), "Mental Accounting and Consumer Choice." *Marketing Science*, 4, 199-214.

Tsiros, Michael. (1998), "Effect of Regret on Post-choice Valuation: The Case of More Than Two Alternatives." *Organizational Behavior and Human Decision Processes*, 76 (1), 48-69.

Tsiros, Michael and Vikas Mittal. (2000), "Regret: A Model of Its Antecedents and Consequences in Consumer Decision Making." *Journal of Consumer Research*, 26, 401-417.

Tversky, Amos and Daniel Kahneman. (1981), "The Framing of Decisions and the Psychology of Choice." *Science*, 211 (4481), 453-458.

Tversky, Amos and Daniel Kahneman. (1986), "Rational Choice and the Framing of Decisions." *The Journal of Business*, 59 (4, pt. 2), S251-S278.

Tversky, Amos and Daniel Kahneman. (1992), "Advances in Prospect Theory: Cumulative Representation of Uncertainty." *Journal of Risk and Uncertainty*, 5 (1992), 297-323.

Zeelenberg, Marcel and Rik Pieters. (2007), "A Theory of Regret Regulation." *Journal of Consumer Psychology*, 17 (1), 3-18.

Schadenfreude and the Self: The Effect of Self-Construal on Malicious Delight at Others' Unfortunate Decisions

Thomas Kramer, Baruch College, CUNY, USA
Ozge Yucel Aybat, Baruch College, CUNY, USA

EXTENDED ABSTRACT

"Mr. Borovina is indulging in what seems to be the summer's favorite guilty pleasure–delighting in others' misfortune, or schadenfreude. Between Martha Stewart, Michael Ovitz, L. Dennis Kozlowski, Kenneth Lay and Jeffrey Skilling, and Samuel D. Waksal, there is plenty of misfortune going around, and, as it turns out, plenty of delight."
St. John (2002)

Usually, we feel happy when good things happen to others, and sad when misfortunes befall them. However, at times it is others' bad luck that makes us happy and induces schadenfreude–pleasure in their misfortunes (Heider 1958). Referred to as a socially reprehensible emotion that is elicited through social comparison in response to others' failure (Feather and Sherman 2002; Foster 1972), schadenfreude is certainly not a new phenomenon. Socrates ruminated on a trigger for malicious pleasure over 2,500 years ago: "Did we not say that pleasure in the misfortunes of friends was caused by envy?" (cited by Smith et al. 1996). In another recent instance of malicious joy, or schadenfreude, coffee drinkers rejoiced at Starbucks' financial woes and its subsequent decision to close down 600 stores: "I'm so happy; I'm so not a Starbucks person," says one aficionado of small independent cafes (Wulfhorst 2008). Finally, persuasive messages often seek to elicit schadenfreude. For example, the recent "more bars in more places" AT&T advertising campaign featured comical situations in which misfortunes (such as a house destroyed by an exploding deep-fried frozen turkey) befall cell phone owners because they had made the wrong choice of cell phone service and could hence not be reached in time to avert the calamity.

Yet, even though schadenfreude is often discussed in the popular press and may indeed arise in many situations, it has received surprisingly little attention in the psychology and marketing literatures. Recent research has started to examine empirically the antecedents of schadenfreude, including envy (Smith et al. 1996), liking (Hareli and Weiner 2002), resentment (Feather and Nairn 2005; Feather and Sherman 2002), and deservingness (Brighman et al. 1997; van Dijk et al. 2005). For example, Smith et al. (1996) found that student subjects felt significantly more schadenfreude when an academically superior versus average student was caught stealing amphetamines, even when controlling for subjects' level of self esteem and liking for the target student.

Furthermore, the degree to which everyday choices can elicit schadenfreude has not been explored. For example, do individuals find delight in others' decisions that turn out badly, such as their choice of a risky over a safe option and losing, and if so, under which conditions? Clearly, others' unfortunate choices will not elicit the same level of schadenfreude in all individuals alike. We propose that self-construal is one important variable likely to impact schadenfreude in decision-making that has not received any attention, even though a great deal of literature suggests that differences in self-construal have robust effects on everyday experiences, including on cognition, affect, and motivation (e.g., Aaker and Williams 1998; Markus and Kitayama 1991; Mesquita and Frijda 1992). Self-construal describes how individuals construe the self, others, and the interdependence between the two (Markus and Kitayama 1991). An independent self-construal is associated with an emphasis on separateness, individuals' internal attributes, and the importance of uniqueness. Conversely, individuals with an interdependent self tend to be more relationship-driven and stress relationships with others, connectedness, and the social context. We expect that those individuals who are relatively close to others, care for others, or in general feel more interdependent with them, will get less pleasure out of others' unfortunate choices. Although many people may feel happy when a competitor's choices turn out badly, one would hardly expect the same kind of response following the unfortunate choices of close others, like family or friends. Further, individuals with interdependent selves, for whom maintaining connectedness and harmony with others is important, tend to be more sensitive to others. For these individuals, feelings of schadenfreude would be detrimental to their focus on maintaining close social relationships.

The purpose of the current research is therefore to explore the effect of self-construal on schadenfreude in decision-making to start filling this gap in the literature. In particular, we seek to examine if, or more specifically, under which conditions others' choices of options that turn out badly elicit schadenfreude. Study 1 shows that schadenfreude in response to others' unfortunate choices of a granola bar is greater for individuals with a predominant independent (vs. interdependent) self-construal. Next, study 2 replicates this finding for others' unfortunate choices of a bet option and also demonstrates that the differential levels of schadenfreude are driven by differences in competitive tendencies associated with an independent versus interdependent self-construal. Based on our proposition that others' choices that go against the norm may be perceived as more deserving of misfortune, study 3 finds that self-construal has a greater impact on schadenfreude when others' choices of an unconventional (i.e., a hedonic option: a foot massage), as compared to a conventional (i.e., a utilitarian option: school supplies) option turns out badly. Finally, our last study demonstrates the impact of schadenfreude on decision-making of individuals who differ in their self-construal, and differentiates it from that of happiness. In particular, we show that the experience of schadenfreude, as compared to happiness, increased the choice share of a conventional (i.e., compromise) option for individuals with a predominant independent self. Presumably, once schadenfreude is accessible, individuals with an independent self seek to avoid a misfortune similar to the one they feel happy about, and become more risk-averse by choosing a compromise option. In contrast, self-construal has no effect on choice share of the compromise option for those who had been primed with happiness. Overall, these results suggest that schadenfreude as happiness in response to others' misfortunes has a unique impact on choice for individuals differing in their self-construal; an impact distinct from that of happiness in response to others' fortunes.

REFERENCES

Aaker, Jennifer L. and Patti Williams (1998), "Empathy versus Pride: The Influence of Emotional Appeals across Cultures," *Journal of Consumer Research*, 25 (3), 241-61.

Brigham, Nancy L., Kimberly A. Kelso, Mark A. Jackson, and Richard H. Smith (1997), "The Roles of Invidious Comparisons and Deservingness in Sympathy and Schadenfreude," *Basic and Applied Social Psychology*, 19 (3), 363-80.

Feather, N. T. and Katherine Nairn (2005), "Resentment, Envy, Schadenfreude, and Sympathy: Effects of Own and Other's Deserved and Undeserved Status," *Australian Journal of Psychology*, 57 (2), 87-102.

Feather, N. T. and Rebecca Sherman (2002), "Envy, Resentment, Schadenfreude, and Sympathy: Reactions to Deserved and Undeserved Achievement and Subsequent Failure," *Personality and Social Psychology Bulletin*, 28 (7), 953-61.

Foster, George M. (1972), "The Anatomy of Envy: A Study in Symbolic Behavior," *Current Anthropology*, 13 (2), 165-202.

Hareli, Shlomo and Bernard Weiner (2002), "Dislike and Envy as Antecedents of Pleasure at Another's Misfortune," *Motivation and Emotion*, 26 (4), 257–77.

Heider, Fritz (1958), *The Psychology of Interpersonal Relations*, New York: Wiley.

Markus, Hazel R. and Shinobu Kitayama (1991), "Culture and the Self: Implications for Cognition, Emotion, and Motivation," *Psychological Review*, 98 (2), 224-53.

Mesquita, Batja and Nico H. Frijda (1992), "Cultural Variations in Emotions: A Review," *Psychological Bulletin*, 112, 179-204.

Smith, Richard H., Terence J. Turner, Ron Garonzik, Colin W. Leach, Vanessa Urch-Druskat, and Christine M. Weston (1996), "Envy and Schadenfreude," *Personality and Social Psychology Bulletin*, 22(2), 158–168.

St. John, W. (2002) "Sorrow so Sweet: A Guilty Pleasure in Another's Misfortune," *New York Times*, August 24, B7.

van Dijk, Wilco W., Jaap W. Ouwerkerk, Sjoerd Goslinga, and Myrke Nieweg (2005), "Deservingness and Schadenfreude," *Cognition and Emotion*, 19 (6), 933-39.

Wulfhorst, Ellen (2008), "Some Coffee Fans Get Grim Delight in Starbucks Woes," *http://www.reuters.com/article/domesticNews/idUSN0437926720080706?sp=true*.

Effect of Self-Construal on New Product Adoption Decisions: Role of Innovation Newness and Risk Type

Zhenfeng Ma, University of Ontario Institute of Technology, Canada
Zhiyong Yang, University of Texas at Arlington, USA

EXTENDED ABSTRACT

The self-construal theory recognizes two distinct self-views, that is, the independent versus interdependent self-views. The two self-views are associated with different social orientation and regulatory focus. Individuals with predominantly independent self-views (the 'independents') view themselves as different from others and are motivated to seek autonomy, achievements, and success relative to others (Trafimow et al. 1991). People with predominantly interdependent self-views define themselves as part of a group and are motivated to seek social harmony, affiliation with others, and avoidance of risks (Aaker and Lee 2001). Although the existing literature has examined the effect of self-construal on various marketing outcomes such as persuasion, risk-taking, and impulsive consumption, there is little research into the effect of self-construal on new product adoption decisions. We posit that situationally primed self-views have systematic effect on consumers' new product adoption decisions, and that such effects are dependent on both the innovation newness of the products and on the salience of different risks associated with the products (e.g. performance vs. social risks).

Research on innovation distinguishes between incrementally new products (INPs) and really new products (RNPs) (Hoeffler 2003). RNPs offer newer and more unique benefits but also pose higher risks than INPs (Ram and Sheth 1989). Given the independents' and interdependents' different proclivity to risks and benefits, it can be expected that consumers primed with different self-views may react differently to products that vary in innovation newness. Prior research also shows that situational contexts can make certain types of risks salient to consumers. We posit that the independents' and interdependents' purchase intentions towards RNPs and INPs may vary according to whether the risks associated with the products are salient, and if they are salient, the types of risks that are made salient (e.g. social vs. performance risks).

When the risks associated with the products are implicit, the interdependents would give more weight to the unique benefits of RNPs than to the potential risks of such products, given their orientation towards achievements and self-enhancement. On the contrary, the interdependents may attend more to the potential risks of RNPs than their benefits, owing to their general inclination to avoid risks. However, when the product is an INP, the independents may not be more likely to adopt the product than the interdependents, because the limited incremental benefits offered by INPs are not sufficient to satisfy the independents' promotion-oriented goals.

> *H1*: When the product innovation newness is high, consumers primed with independent self-views state higher purchase intention than those primed with interdependent self-views. When the product innovation newness is low, consumers primed with independent versus interdependent self-views do not differ in stated purchase intention.

When social risks about the new products are made salient, the independents may be either more or less willing to adopt the product than the interdependents, depending on the innovation newness of the product. When the product is an RNP, social risks information may have minimal impact on the independents' adoption intentions, because the unique benefits offered by RNPs in terms of self-expression and self-enhancements are weighed more heavily by the independents than the risks of social disapproval. Thus, when social risks are salient, the independents may still be more willing to adopt RNPs than the interdependents. However, when the product is an INP, the independents are not motivated to adopt the products in the first place, due to limited incremental benefits of such products. Moreover, in the absence of strong motivation to adopt, the salience of social risks may further dampen the independents' adoption intention towards the INP. This is because the independents would expect to gain little from such products in terms of intrinsic benefits or differentiation from others. Thus, the independents may exhibit lower purchase intentions toward the INP than the interdependents when social risks are salient.

> *H2*: When a product's social risks are made salient, consumers primed with independent self-views are more willing to adopt a really new product, but less willing to adopt an incrementally new product than consumers primed with interdependent self-views.

When the performance risks about the products are made explicit, the independents and interdependents may be equally unlikely to adopt the product. Performance risks associated with a product not only have the potential to render the product incapable of delivering the intended benefits, but may also cause safety hazards to the users. When the products' safety or reliability is called into question, the independents will be as unlikely as the interdependents to adopt the products, regardless of their innovation newness.

> *H3*: When performance risks are salient, the independents and interdependents do not differ in their product adoption decisions, regardless of innovation newness of the product.

We tested the research hypotheses using two experimental studies. The purpose of Experiment 1 is to test the effect of self-construal on new product adoption decisions when risks are not salient (H1). Ninety-eight undergraduate students participated in Experiment 1, which featured a 2 (independent vs. interdependent self views) x 2 (INPs vs. RNPs) design. Participants first read a scenario about a tennis match that was pretested to elicit different self-views, and were then prompted to imagine a scenario about a new car, which were pretested to differ in terms of innovation newness. ANOVA of stated purchase intention (PI) showed that, consistent with H1, the independents reported higher PI than the interdependents when the product was an RNP, but their PI did not differ when the products are INPs. Mediation analysis suggests that the effect of self-construal and innovation newness was mediated by perceived product benefits.

The purpose of Experiment 2 is to test the effect of self-construal on new product adoption decisions when different types of risks (social vs. performance risks) are made salient. Two hundred and ninety two undergraduate students participated in this experiment, which featured a 2 (self construal) x2 (newness) x 2 (risk types: social vs. performance risks) designs. Both self-construal and innovation newness were manipulated in the same way as in Experiment 1. Social risks about the products were made salient by highlighting the negative feedback from other consumers to the car in a purported news report. Performance risks were made salient by highlighting the fact that the car's safety and reliability has not been fully proven. An ANOVA of stated PI showed a three-way interaction among self-construal, newness and risk types. Separate ANOVA of PI within the social risk context shows that consumers primed with independent self-views are more willing to adopt a really new product, but less willing to adopt an incrementally new product than consumers primed with interdependent self-views. Thus, H2 was supported. Moreover, mediation analysis shows that observed effect between self-construal and innovation newness was mediated by perceived product benefits. The ANOVA of PI within the performance risks context shows that the independents and interdependents did not differ in their product adoption decisions, regardless of innovation newness of the product. Thus, H3 was also supported.

REFERENCES

Aaker, Jennifer L. Angela Y. Lee (2001), "'I' Seek pleasures and 'We' Avoid Pains: The Role of Self-Regulatory Goals in Information Processing and Persuasion," *Journal of Consumer Research*, 28 (June), 33-49.

Hoeffler, Steve (2003), "Measuring Preferences for Really New Products," *Journal of Marketing Research*, 40(4), 406-420.

Ram, Sundaresan and Jagdish N. Sheth (1989), "Consumer Resistance to Innovations: The Marketing Problem and Its Solutions," *Journal of Consumer Marketing*, 6(Spring), 5-14.

Trafimow, David, Harry C. Triandis, and Sharon G. Goto (1991), "Some Tests of the Distinction Between the Private Self and the Collective Self," *Journal of Personality and Social Psychology*, 60 (5), 649-655.

Adoption of Network Externality Products: The Interactive Influence of Self-construal, Branding Strategy, and Source of Information

Napatsorn Jiraporn, Binghamton University, SUNY
Kalpesh Kaushik Desai, Binghamton University, SUNY

EXTENDED ABSTRACT

Given the increasing importance of technological products in the current economy, this research examined the consumer, brand, and product factors on the adoption of network externality products. 'Network effect' or 'network externality' refers to a phenomenon where the utility of a product increases as the number of its adopters increases (Shapiro & Varian 1999). Standard competition is commonly present in the market with network effects (Chakravarti & Xie 2006). Some examples of such products and their competing standards are computer operating system (Windows vs. Mac OS) and DVD formats (Blue-ray vs. HD). In this market condition, consumers encounter a tradeoff between the differentiation of product features and the compatibility with current technology of other products in the market. We later showed that differentiation and compatibility are orthogonal constructs.

Using conceptual underpinnings from literatures in network externality, self-construal, and branding, this research proposes and finds that consumers exhibit different attitude and behavior towards non-network vs. network products. We first hypothesize that when facing non-network products, independent-self consumers, motivated by utility maximization (Aaker & Lee 2001), will prefer highly differentiated but incompatible products whereas interdependent-self consumers, motivated by preference for status quo (Chernev 2004), will prefer less differentiated but compatible products. Conversely, when facing network products, independent-self consumers, who define themselves as more separated from other consumers (Markus & Kitayama 1991), will be less confident in predicting adoption decision of other consumers. Hence, relative to interdependent-self consumers, independent-self consumers will seek compatibility in network products and will show greater preference for less differentiated but compatible network products. On the other hand, interdependent-self consumers who tend to define themselves in relation to others may feel more comfortable to predict behavior of other consumers. They are more experienced in adapting themselves to fit in a larger societal group, thus, should be more capable of coping with the issue of incompatibility. Therefore, interdependent-self consumers will show greater preference for highly differentiated but incompatible network products.

The second study is to further investigate the adoption decision of the highly differentiated but incompatible network products due to greater challenges it faces in the market. We hypothesize that when brand and information from trial users are simultaneously available; consumers consider information from trial users as more influential than brand information (Sheth & Venkatesan 1968). In contrast to the extant literature (Brown & Reingen 1987), the information provided by dissimilar (vs. similar) trial users may be more diagnostic for network product categories because it provides prediction about adoptions of other consumers whose opinions are less predictable. Hence, we anticipate that when consumers receive information from dissimilar trial users, consumers will be motivated to process more information and include brand in their decisions. In such cases, building on the prior literature in branding (Ng & Houston 2006), we hypothesize that independent-self consumers will prefer a brand with existence in multiple product categories (broad brand) whereas interdependent-self consumers will prefer a brand with existence in limited product categories (narrow brand). In contrast, when similar trial users provide information, which is less diagnostic, consumers will be less likely to incorporate brand in their decision process. Therefore, the two selves will not differ in their preference between a broad vs. a narrow brand.

Two experiments tested these hypotheses. ANOVAs and planned comparisons were used when appropriate. Study 1 aims to establish evidence that consumers varying in self-construal differ in their responses to a network vs. non-network product. In exchange for extra credit, 122 students from a northeastern university participated in a 2 (self-construal: independent vs. interdependent) x 2 (product type: network vs. non-network) x 2 (product strategy: revolution vs. evolution) between-subject experiment. Note that a revolutionary product is highly differentiated but incompatible with current technology while an evolutionary product is less differentiated but compatible with current technology in the market. First, participants were primed into either an independent or an interdependent self. Participants were asked to read information about a new microwave oven vs. a new cell phone in the non-network vs. network condition, respectively. Then, participants rated their attitude towards the focal product. Results showed no difference in attitude scores between the two selves in the non-network condition for both product strategies (p>.1). However, consistent with the prediction, independent-self participants, relative to their interdependent-self counterpart, reported more positive attitude towards the less differentiated but compatible network product and reported less positive attitude towards the highly differentiated but incompatible network product (p <.1).

Study 2 aims to examine how consumers varying in self-construal rely on brand and information from trial users when encountering a revolutionary network product. 145 students from the same university with those in study 1 were randomly assigned into a 2 (self-construal: independent vs. interdependent) x 2 (brand breadth: broad vs. narrow) x 2 (trial users: similar vs. dissimilar) between-subject experiment. Participants, primed into either an independent or an interdependent self, were asked to read information about a new cell phone in the market with a highly differentiated feature but incompatible technology with other cell phone technologies in the market. Participants in the broad (*narrow*) brand condition read that this new cell phone was offered by Samsung (*Motorola*). Participants in the similar condition were shown feedback from trial users who are college students in New York, where the experiment was conducted. Those in the dissimilar condition were shown feedback from trial users who are college students in California. Then, participants rated their attitude, buying likelihood and willing-to-pay amount for the product. Results were significant and consistent across three dependent variables. When the similar trial users presented information about the new product, the two selves showed no difference in preference between a broad and a narrow brand (p>.1). When the dissimilar trial users presented the same information, independent-self participants showed greater preference for the new cell phone from a broad brand whereas interdependent-self participants showed greater preference for the new cell phone from a narrow brand (p<.05).

Along with managerial implications, this research has important theoretical contributions both to the self-construal literature and to the network externality literature by providing evidence that independent-self consumers may avoid innovation when the incompatibility is a concern. The research contributes to the branding literature by identifying the boundary condition for the brand breadth effect—independent-self consumers prefer a broad brand while interdependent-self consumers prefer a narrow brand, only when the information is sufficiently diagnostic to reduce risk. Managerially, the research suggests that, under the influence of network effects, trial feedback from users who are dissimilar to the target consumers should be used for broad brands in the markets dominated by an independent culture and for narrow brands in the markets dominated by an interdependent culture.

REFERENCES

Aaker, Jennifer L. and Angela Y. Lee (2001), "I Seek Pleasures and We Avoid Pains: The Role of Self-Regulatory Goals in Information Processing and Persuasion," *Journal of Consumer Research*, 28 (1), 33-49.

Brown, Jacqueline J. and Reingen (1987), "Social Ties and Word-of-Mouth Referral Behavior,' *Journal of Consumer Research*, 14(3), 350-62

Chakravarti, A. (2006), "The Impact of Standards Competition on Consumers: Effectiveness of Product Information and Advertising Formats," *JMR, Journal of marketing research*, 43 (2), 224.

Chernev, Alexander (2004), "Goal Orientation and Consumer Preference for the Status Quo," *Journal of Consumer Research*, 31 (3), 557-65.

Markus, H. R. and Kitayama S. (1991), "Culture and the Self: Implications for Cognition, Emotion, and Motivation," *Psychological review*, 98 (2), 224.

Ng, Sharon and Michael, J Houston (2006), "Exemplars or Beliefs? The Impact of Self-View on the Nature and Relative Influence of Brand Associations," *Journal of Consumer Research*, 32 (4), 519-29.

Shapiro, C. and Varian (1999), *Information Rules a Strategic Guide to the Network Economy,* Harvard Business School Press

Sheth, Jagdish N. and M. Venkatesan (1968), "Risk-Reduction Processes in Repetitive Consumer Behavior," *Journal of Marketing Research*, 5 (3), 307-10.

Overlap and Dissociation of Mental Representations of Self and Brand

Rebecca Trump, University of Arizona, USA
Merrie Brucks, University of Arizona, USA

EXTENDED ABSTRACT

The pioneering psychologist William James posited that the self is comprised of many things including one's body, family, material possessions, and social relationships (James 1890). The present research investigates whether brands may also be a part of the self. Specifically, we propose that consumers go beyond connecting with brands (e.g., Escalas and Bettman 2003): Consumers may actually include loved brands into their psychological selves (self-brand overlap). Complementary to James' notion that the self is comprised of many things, people also define themselves in terms of what they are not (e.g., Tajfel and Turner 1979). It follows that people avoid brands with which they do not want to be identified (e.g., Escalas and Bettman 2005). Therefore, we further propose that disliked brands will be excluded from the psychological self (self-brand dissociation).

Brands are important to consumers' self-concepts (e.g., Escalas and Bettman 2003). If a brand is loved by consumers, it has been suggested that it may actually become integrated into their identities (Carroll and Ahuvia 2006; Oliver 1999). Complementarily, beginning with Fournier's seminal paper in 1998, a growing stream of research views human relationships as a fruitful metaphor for consumer-brand relationships. This may be a result of consumers thinking of brands in human-like terms, attributing personality traits to them (Aaker 1997) and applying norms of social interactions to their relationships with brands (Aaker, Fournier, and Brasel 2004; Aggarwal 2004). At the same time, some argue that the personification of brands, and especially the notion of human-like relationships, stretches the anthropomorphic metaphor too far (Bengtsson 2003; Breivik and Thorbjørnsen 2008). By adapting theory and measurement techniques from interpersonal relationship research, the present research has the opportunity to provide credence to, or rebuff, the metaphor of consumer-brand relationships.

In addition to loved brands being important to consumers, disliked brands may have an impact on the consumer self. In fact, the noted anthropologist Richard Wilk has argued that what consumers choose not to consume is often more socially and personally significant to them than what they choose to consume (Wilk 1997). Empirical evidence documents that consumers may avoid brands that represent something with which they do not want to be associated, such as outgroups (Escalas and Bettman 2005; White and Dahl 2007). Here we examine the impact of disliked brands on consumers' psychological selves.

The present research applies social cognitive measurement techniques to examine the inclusion of the mental representations of loved brands into the psychological self and the exclusion of disliked brands from the psychological self. To do so, we utilize a response time methodology introduced in interpersonal relationship research, which demonstrates that people's mental representations of self overlap with their representations of close relationship partners (Aron et al. 1991; Aron and Fraley 1999; Smith, Coats, and Walling 1999). Applying this methodology to the study of consumer-brand bonds is appropriate since brands that are loved by consumers may be viewed as relationship partners and brands are inextricably linked to consumers' self-concepts. Therefore, the mental representations of brands may impact the mental representations of self, similarly to the impact close relationship partners have on the psychological self.

Aron et al. (1991) pioneered the testing of the inclusion of others in the self by finding that personality characteristics of close others impact the self. Specifically, they find that characteristics that are shared by the self and other are more accessible than characteristics that distinguish the self from the other. In two studies, we mirror that finding for loved brands. Specifically, in an initial study, we replicated the methodology used in the interpersonal relationship domain and find that, just like close relationship partners, the mental representations of loved brands overlap the psychological self (as evidenced by the greater accessibility of shared characteristics, compared to distinguishing characteristics). In a second study, we adapted the methodology to apply more directly to brand personality characteristics (Aaker 1997) and, again, find support for self-brand overlap.

Conversely, in both studies, we find that characteristics that are shared with disliked brands are less accessible than characteristics that distinguish the self from the disliked brand, providing support for self-brand dissociation. In sum, through two studies we find support for both the notion of self-brand overlap and self-brand dissociation. This adds to the accumulating body of evidence that consumers view brands similarly as they do other individuals and provides an implicit measure of the psychological relationship between consumers and both their loved and disliked brands.

Further, our finding of self-brand dissociation is the first evidence that we are aware of that the psychological self is dissociated from the mental representation of another entity. It is worth noting that this research investigated the extreme case of dissociation of the self and a disliked brand. It is possible that the psychological self may be dissociated from brands that are not disliked. For example, a woman may desire to dissociate from masculine brands, not because she dislikes the brand but, because it does not represent her feminine self. Future research should seek to determine the boundary conditions of both self-brand overlap and dissociation.

REFERENCES

Aaker, Jennifer L. (1997), "Dimensions of Brand Personality," *Journal of Marketing Research*, 34 (3), 347-56.

Aaker, Jennifer L., Susan Fournier, and S. A. Brasel (2004), "When Good Brands Do Bad," *Journal of Consumer Research*, 31 (1), 1-16.

Aggarwal, Pankaj (2004), "The Effects of Brand Relationship Norms on Consumer Attitudes and Behavior," *Journal of Consumer Research*, 31 (1), 87-101.

Aron, Arthur, Elaine N. Aron, Michael Tudor, and Greg Nelson (1991), "Close Relationships as Including Other in the Self," *Journal of Personality and Social Psychology*, 60 (2), 241-53.

Aron, Arthur, and Barbara Fraley (1999), "Relationship Closeness as Including Other in the Self: Cognitive Underpinnings and Measures," *Social Cognition*, 17 (2), 140-60.

Bengtsson, Anders (2003), "Towards a Critique of Brand Relationships," in Advances in Consumer Research, Volume 30, eds. Punam Anand Keller and Dennis W. Rook, Valdosta, GA: Association for Consumer Research, 154-158.

Breivik, Einar, and Helge Thorbjørnsen (2008), "Consumer Brand Relationships: An Investigation of Two Alternative Models," *Journal of the Academy of Marketing Science*, 36 (4), 443-472.

Carroll, Barbara A., and Aaron C. Ahuvia (2006), "Some Antecedents and Outcomes of Brand Love," *Marketing Letters*, 17 (2), 79-89.

Escalas, Jennifer E., and James R. Bettman (2003), "You are What They Eat: The Influence of Reference Groups on Consumers' Connections to Brands," *Journal of Consumer Psychology*, 13 (3), 339-48.

______ (2005), "Self-construal, Reference Groups, and Brand Meaning," *Journal of Consumer Research*, 32 (3), 378-89.

Fournier, Susan (1998), "Consumers and their Brands: Developing Relationship Theory in Consumer Research," *Journal of Consumer Research*, 24 (4), 343-373.

James, William (1890), *Principles of psychology*. New York: Holt.

Oliver, Richard L. (1999), "Whence Consumer Loyalty?" *Journal of Marketing*, 63 (Special Issue), 33-44.

Smith, Eliot R., Susan Coats, and Dustin Walling (1999), "Overlapping Mental Representations of Self, In-group, and Partner: Further Response Time Evidence and a Connectionist Model," *Personality and Social Psychology Bulletin*, 25 (7), 873-882.

Tajfel, Henri and John C. Turner (1979), "An Integrative Theory of Intergroup Conflict," in *The Social Psychology of Intergroup Relations*, eds. William G. Austin and Stephen Worchel. Monterey: CA: Brooks-Cole, 33-47.

White, Katherine, and Darren W. Dahl (2007), "Are All Out-groups Created Equal? Consumer Identity and Dissociative Influence," *Journal of Consumer Research*, 34 (4), 525-36.

Wilk, Richard R. (1997), "A Critique of Desire: Distaste and Dislike in Consumer Behavior," *Consumption, Markets and Culture*, 1 (2), 175-196.

We are What We Drive: A SRM Analysis of Human-Brand Personality Associations

Maxim Polonsky, University of Connecticut, USA
Robin Coulter, University of Connecticut, USA

EXTENDED ABSTRACT

We draw upon self-congruity, symbolic interactionism, and interpersonal perception theories to model brand/human personality interdependence. We identified ten automobile brands for which consumers have some shared agreement about brand personality, and conducted a round-robin experiment with twenty three/four person limited acquaintance groups. Group members rated themselves and each other on seven personality characteristics, and answered: "How likely do you see yourself driving [brand]?" "How likely do you see [group member] driving [brand]?" and "How likely do you think that [group member] sees you driving [brand]" Using the Social Relations Model, we assess the extent to which consumers perceive brands and consumers as sharing personality characteristics.

Nearly a half-century ago, Levy (1959) advanced the idea that brands are reflective symbols of the self. More recent work has considered how consumers use brands to create and communicate identity (Belk 1988; Escalas and Bettman 2005; Kleine, Kleine and Kernan 1993; Kleine, Kleine, and Allen 1995; Sirgy 1982; Solomon 1983), as well as to reinforce attitudes toward self (Escalas and Bettman 2003; McCracken 1988). Aaker's seminal work (1997) on the association of human personality characteristics to brands has been extremely influential in spurring the dialogue about how companies and customers anthropomorphize their brands. In the ensuing years, marketers and consumer researchers have focused on leveraging and understanding brand personality, that is, the set of human characteristics associated with a brand (Aaker 1999; Aaker, Benet-Martinez, and Garolera 2001; Johar, Sengupta, Aaker 2005). As a consequence, we are lead to contemplate questions about consumers' brands and their personality characteristics, such as: "Do you infer an individual's personality based on his/her ownership of specific brands? Similarly, when you observe an individual's personality, do you associate that individual with a specific brand? Finally, are your opinions unique, or are they shared by others?

Several theories of the self, individually and in a social context, are important to contemplate in the context of human-brand personality work. Briefly, self-congruity theory argues that consumers prefer brands with a symbolic function that is congruous with their self-identity (Sirgy 1982; Swann et al. 1992); symbolic interaction theory focuses on an individual's beliefs about how he is perceived by others (Cooley 1902, Mead, 1934; Solomon 1983); and interpersonal perception theory suggests that person perception consists of interdependent levels, but can be decomposed to understand an individual's perceptions of self, of another individual, and perceptions of how others see him (Malloy and Kenny 1986; Kenny 1994). In this paper, we draw upon these three theoretical perspectives, as well as the Social Relations Model (SRM; Kenny 1993, 1994; Kenny and Albright 1987; Kenny, Kashy, and Cook 2006) to further explicate and model brand and human personality interdependence. The SRM approach, using dyadic data, enables us to address questions such as: If Jane is seen to be extraverted, is she also associated with an extraverted brand? If Jane sees herself as being extraverted and prefers extraverted brands, do others also see her as extraverted and preferring those brands? If Jane sees herself using extraverted brands, does she see others using those brands?

Our research involved three data collections. As a basis for our experiment which focuses on the intersection of human and brand personalities, we engaged in two preliminary studies to understand consumers' associations with automobile brands and personality characteristics. Our work focuses on the automobile product category because research in marketing and consumer behavior has documented that this product category includes brands that are associated with personality characteristics by groups of consumers (Bagozzi and Dholakia 2006; Muniz and O'Guinn 2001). We identified 23 brands and had 70 undergraduate students evaluate the brands on 34 semantic differential items with regard to the Big Five personality characteristics–Agreeableness, Extraversion, Conscientiousness, Emotional Stability, and Openness (Goldberg 1990) and two additional brand personality characteristics, Sophistication and Ruggedness (Aaker 1997). Additionally, we provided 40 MBA students with a definition of the seven personality characteristics and via a free association task asked participants to name one automobile brand that they associated with each personality characteristic. Based on these data collections, we identified ten brands (Jeep, Volvo, Toyota, Hummer, Jaguar, Mercedes, BMW, Audi, Honda, and VW) which had shared meaning for our main experiment.

Our focal study employs a round-robin experiment using 20 three or four person limited acquaintance groups, that is, groups in which the members were unfamiliar with one another. After a short (seven minute) introduction period, group members rated themselves and each group member on seven human-brand personality characteristics, including conscientiousness, extraversion, agreeableness, emotional stability, openness to experience, sophistication, and ruggedness (Aaker 1997). Then, participants answered the following brand use questions: 1) "How likely do you see yourself using brand X?" 2) "How likely do you see [group member] using the brand X?" and 3) "How likely do you think that [group member] sees you using brand X?" These data were analyzed using the Social Relations Model (Kenny 1988; Kenny et al. 2006) to assess the extent to which consumers perceive individual brands and consumers as sharing personality characteristics, and to determine if the Devil really wears Prada.

Our work demonstrates that even short interaction encounters enable participants to come to consensual conclusions regarding individual traits associated with specific brands. Moreover, for some brands we found perceiver-target accuracy so the ratings of participants correlated with target self-ratings. Both, consensus and accuracy speak to the existence of the socially shared meanings among individuals, as well as between personality traits and brands. Meta-accuracy further validates the symbolic-interactionism perspective: an individual thinking that others see her driving a Jaguar and being accurate in her perceptions indicates that a person is capable of understanding how others perceive her (table 3). The symbolic-interactionism perspective posits that people perceive and internalize others' attitudes to form the concept of self (Depaulo et al. 1987). Solomon (1983, 320) argued that people define themselves and social reality via product symbolism, relying "upon the social information inherent in products to shape self-image and to maximize the quality of role performance."

Our research on brands and their personalities provides evidence of symbolic interactionism in the context of consumption. We illustrate how the Social Relations Model decomposes the multiple levels of social interaction as related to brands, their users, and observers. In conclusion, our work demonstrates that consumer and brand personalities are interdependent and points to a shared meaning system that is used to make inferences about individuals and products. Shared assumptions about physical appearance and shared interpretations of behaviors enable perceivers to come to consensual judgments about targets' personalities and brand use after seven-minute interaction periods. Moreover, such judgments can be accurate, reflecting targets' self-views.

KEY REFERENCES

Aaker, Jennifer (1997), "Dimensions of Brand Personality," *Journal of Marketing Research*, 34 (8), 347–56.

Ambady, Nalini, and Rosenthal, Robert (1992), "Thin Slices of Expressive Behavior as Predictors of Interpersonal Consequences: A Meta-Analysis," *Psychological Bulletin*, 111, 256–74.

Escalas, Jennifer Edson and James R. Bettman (23), "You Are What They Eat: The Influence of Reference Groups on Consumer Connections to Brands," *Journal of Consumer Psychology*, 13 (3), 339-48.

Fournier, Susan (1998), "Consumers and Their Brands: Developing Relationship Theory in Consumer Research," *Journal of Consumer Research*, 4 (March), 343–73.

Keller, Kevin L. (1993), "Conceptualizing, Measuring, and Managing Customer-Based Brand Equity," *Journal of Marketing*, 57 (1), 1–22.

Kenny, David A. (1993), "A Coming-of-Age for Research on Interpersonal Perception," *Journal of Personality*, *61*, 789-87.

Kenny, David A., Linda Albright, Thomas E. Malloy, and Deborah A. Kashy, (1994), "Consensus in Interpersonal Perception: Acquaintance and the Big Five," *Psychological Bulletin*, 116 (2), 245–58.

Kenny, David A., Cynthia D. Mohr, and Maurice J. Levesque (21), "A Social Relations Variance Partitioning of Dyadic Behavior," *Psychological Bulletin*, 127(1), 128–41.

Kleine, Robert E. III, Susan Schultz-Kleine, and Jerome B. Kernan (1992), "Mundane Everyday Consumption and the Self: A Conceptual Orientation and Prospects for Consumer Research," *Advances in Consumer Research*, 19 (1), 411–15.

McCracken, Grant (1988), *Culture and Consumption: New Approaches to the Symbolic Character of Consumer Goods and Activities*, Bloomington, IN: Indiana University Press.

Sirgy, Joseph M. (1982), "Self-Concept in Consumer Behavior: A Critical Review," *Journal of Consumer Research*, 9 (December), 287–3.

Solomon, Michael R. (1983), "The Role of Products as Social Stimuli: A Symbolic Interactionism Perspective," *The Journal of Consumer Research*, 1 (December), 319-29.

Walker, Rob (28), *Buying In: The Secret Dialogue between What We Buy and Who We Are*. Random House.

Leader-focused Search: The Influence of an Emerging Preference on Information Selection

Kurt Carlson, Georgetown University, USA
Abhijit Guha, Wayne State University, USA

EXTENDED ABSTRACT

It is important to understand how consumers search for information in choices involving unfamiliar options, because search has the greatest impact on choice when consumers know very little about the options. In choices involving unfamiliar options, consumers develop an emerging preference for one of the options early in the choice process. Then, consumers support this leading option (or leader) throughout the remainder of the choice process by biasing new information to support the leader (Meloy and Russo 2004). Though Brownstein (2003) suggests that consumers may also seek information that supports their leader, the question of how exactly the leader influences information search remains unexplored.

This research considers two possibilities. The first possibility, leader-supporting search, involves the preference for information that is expected to support the leader over the trailer. The second possibility, leader-focused search, involves the preference for information that is expected to be about the leader, irrespective of whether such information is expected to support or denigrate the leader. By conditioning information search preferences on the leader, we examine the relative incidence of leader-supporting search versus leader-focused search.

Two elements are needed for this examination: (1) identification of each participant's leader, and (2) a choice that distinguishes between leader-supporting search and leader-focused search. To identify the leader, we use a horse race metaphor and ask each participant to reveal the current leader in the choice process (see Meloy and Russo 2004). With respect to information choice, we rely on the negative information choice condition, which requires a choice between two information sources, each of which is expected to provide negative information about one of the options. In this condition, leader-supporting search predicts that consumers prefer information about the trailer, because such information should help support the leader over the trailer. In contrast, leader-focused search predicts the exact opposite (i.e. that consumers prefer information about the leader, because such information allows consumers to focus on the leader). This distinction is not evident in positive information choice conditions, because then the two types of search make the same prediction, i.e. consumers prefer (positive) information about the leader over (positive) information about the trailer.

Across six studies, we examine the relative incidence of leader-supporting search versus leader-focused search. Studies 1 and 2 find that consumers are three times as likely to engage in leader-focused search (as leader-supporting search). Study 3 finds that consumers sacrifice source credibility to obtain information about their leader, suggesting that leader-focused search may undermine choice quality. Study 4 reveals finds that, all else equal, consumers prefer negative information about their leader from more credible sources–this suggests that consumers are not looking for information that they can conveniently counter argue. Studies 5 and 6 provide evidence of leader-focused search using methods that do not require informing consumers about the expected valence of the information. Also, Study 5 finds that consumers forgo learning about the trailer on a relatively important attribute, to learn about the leader on a less important attribute. And Study 6 finds that consumers prefer reading information about the leader before reading information about the trailer.

In sum, this research introduces a new information search phenomenon, leader-focused search. Ongoing research looks at when exactly does leader-focused search give way to leader-supporting search, and also looks at how to make use of the propensity for leader-focused search to help predict consumers' hidden preferences.

REFERENCES

Meloy, Meg and Jay Russo (2004), "Binary choice under instructions to select versus reject," *Organizational Behavior and Human Decision Processes*, 93(2), 114-128.

Brownstein, Aaron (2003), "Biased predecision processing," *Psychological Bulletin*, 129, 545-568

Impression Evolution During Ad Exposure: Typicality Effects from 100 ms Onwards

Millie Elsen, Tilburg University, The Netherlands
Rik Pieters, Tilburg University, The Netherlands
Michel Wedel, University of Maryland, USA

EXTENDED ABSTRACT

In advertising theory and practice, atypicality is considered to be an effective creative strategy to break through the clutter, and to boost ad evaluations and memory for the ad and brand (Heckler and Childers 1992; Smith and Yang 2004). However, research on this issue is limited (Smith and Yang 2004). Moreover, most advertising research used long and forced ad exposures of up to thirty seconds or longer to investigate advertising processing and effectiveness (reviewed by Meyers-Levy and Malaviya 1999), whereas attention to ads is much shorter in practice, typically a few seconds or less (Pieters and Wedel 2004). It remains unclear whether the positive effects of atypicality carry over to these much shorter durations. In fact, considering people's basic need for certainty (Loewenstein 1994), there is reason to believe that the effects of atypicality may be different at shorter exposures.

The present research focuses on information processing within the first exposure to the ad, from 100 ms onwards. Motivated to identify the stimuli they are exposed to, people attempt to identify the ads that they encounter, i.e., what they are for. In three experiments, we show that, depending on the typicality of the ad, this identification process can take different forms over the course of a single exposure, which in turn influences how evaluations develop over time (experiment 1 and 2), the attention devoted to the ad (experiment 3), and subsequent memory (experiment 2).

Typical ads display objects and scenes that are expected for the advertised category (Mervis and Rosch 1981), such as a car in a car ad. The product category of these ads is rapidly identified and with certainty in 100 ms or even less ("Ha, it's a car ad"; Pieters and Wedel 2009), and this identification certainty contributes to an immediately positive ad evaluation (Loken and Ward 1990). Additional information that becomes available after the first glance confirms the immediate identification, leaving the ad evaluation at relatively high levels of positivity, until boredom eventually befalls these ads. We distinguish two types of atypical ads, hereafter referred to as "atypical" and "typical-other" ads. Atypical ads display objects and scenes that do not immediately bring up a product category, leading to identification uncertainty ("What is that ad for?"). This negatively affects the initial ad evaluation. When exposure to the ad continues, additional information and cognitive integration contribute to ad comprehension reducing identification uncertainty ("Aha, it's a car ad"). This increased certainty is appreciated, leading to a positive updating of the evaluation. Finally, typical-other ads display objects and scenes that are typical for another category, such as a lady misting her face in a car ad. These ads are initially identified with certainty ("Ha, it's a fragrance ad"), which is liked. However, new information that becomes available during exposure disconfirms the initial identification, which needs to be revised ("Oh no, it is a car ad"). This need to revise one's initial identification may lead to confusion and requires more cognitive effort, which is disliked and leads to a downward adjustment of the initially positive evaluation.

Thus, typicality determines the identification process—identification confirmation (typical), identification disconfirmation (typical-other) or uncertainty reduction (atypical)—which has predictable effects on how ad evaluations are updated within a single exposure. In addition, it influences attention and memory, and we predict different effects depending on whether recall or recognition performance is assessed. Typical ads do not retain attention well, since they are immediately identified and additional processing does not provide much "new" information. However, because a connection between the ad and the advertised category is immediately established upon exposure, and the ad category serves as a useful retrieval cue (Goodman 1980), they are recalled well, even after brief exposures. Recall performance of atypical ads, in contrast, is relatively poor after brief exposures, but strongly improves when additional processing leads to ad comprehension (Bransford and Johnson 1982). Because atypical ads cannot be immediately identified, they retain attention longer, such that memory should be good. In case of typical-other ads, rapidly identified inconsistencies between the initial identification and newly processed information motivate people to prolong attention to the ad. However, recall performance remains relatively poor for these ads despite additional time attending, because of source-confusion (Roediger and McDermott 2000). Recognition performance, in contrast, is poor after very brief exposures for all three ad types, but strongly improves with additional time attending (Loftus and Bell 1975), except for typical ads, that remain relatively difficult to discriminate from other ads. Due to their typicality, these ads appear familiar regardless of whether they were presented or not, increasing false recognition (Silva, Groeger, and Bradshaw 2006).

We tested and found support for our predictions about the dynamic identification, evaluation and memory processes within a single exposure in experiments 1 and 2, where we systematically varied the exposure duration of ads between-conditions from 100 ms (which is less than a single eye fixation) up to 10 seconds (cf. Donders 1868). Finally, support for the prediction that atypical and typical-other ads retain attention longer than typical ads was provided in experiment 3, where participants freely viewed a large set of ads. These findings are the first to provide insights into the rapid advertising processes from 100 ms onwards. They reveal that the effects of typicality critically depend on the exposure duration, and require revision of the idea of atypicality as a universal creative strategy to improve advertising effectiveness. Although we observe the benefits of atypical ads, we also find that their effectiveness crucially depends on their ability to retain the consumer's attention. Typical ads, in contrast, do not require such sustained attention in order to develop positive ad evaluations and memory traces for the ad and brand. Moreover, we argue for careful consideration of the type of atypicality, since typical-other ads failed on almost all accounts in the present research. We believe that the proposed theory and methodology are applicable to other situations where initial feelings may be rapidly updated, and point to repeated ad exposures as a relevant area of future research.

REFERENCES

Bransford, John D. and Marcia K. Johnson (1972), "Contextual Prerequisites for Understanding: Some Investigations of Comprehension and Recall," *Journal of Verbal Learning and Verbal Beha*vior, 11, 717-726.

Donders, F.C. (1868), "On the Speed of Mental Processes," *Acta Psychologica: Attention and Performance*, 30, 412-431.

Goodman, Gail S. (1980), "Picture Memory: How the Action Schema Affects Retention," *Cognitive Psychology*, 12, 473-495.

Heckler, Susan E. and Terry L. Childers (1992), "The Role of Expectancy and Relevancy in Memory for Verbal and Visual Information: What is Incongruency?" *Journal of Consumer Research*, 18 (March), 475-92.

Loewenstein, George (1994), "The Psychology of Curiosity: A Review and Reinterpretation," *Psychological Bulletin*, 116 (1), 75-98.

Loftus, Geoffrey R. and Susan M. Bell (1975), "Two Types of Information in Picture Memory," *Journal of Experimental Psychology: Human Learning and Memory*, 104 (2), 103-113.

Loken, Barbara and James Ward (1990), "Alternative Approaches to Understanding the Determinants of Typicality," *Journal of Consumer Research*, 17, 111-26.

Mervis, Carolyn B. and Eleanor Rosch (1981), "Categorization of Natural Objects," *Annual Review of Psychology*, 32, 89-115.

Meyers-Levy, Joan and Prashant Malaviya (1999), "Consumers' Processing of Persuasive Advertisements: An Integrative Framework of Persuasion Theories," *Journal of Marketing*, 63 (Special Issue), 45-60.

Pieters, Rik and Michel Wedel (2004), "Attention Capture and Transfer in Advertising: Brand, Pictorial, and Text-Size Effects," *Journal of Marketing*, 68, 36-50.

______ (2009), "Gist in a Glance: Determinants of Immediate Advertising Identification," Unpublished manuscript, Tilburg University.

Roediger, Henry L. and Kathleen B. McDermott (2000), "Distortions of Memory," in Endel Tulving and Fergus I.M. Craik (eds.), *The Oxford Handbook of Memory*, Oxford, UK: Oxford University Press, 149-62.

Silva, Mariana M., John A. Groeger, and Mark F. Bradshaw, "Attention-Memory Interactions in Scene Perception," *Spatial Vision, 19 (1)*, 9-19.

Smith, Robert E. and Xiaojing Yang (2004), "Toward a General Theory of Creativity in Advertising: Examining the Role of Divergence," *Marketing Theory*, 4 (1/2), 31-58.

Consumer Processing of Irrelevant Brand Associations

Claudiu V. Dimofte, Georgetown University, USA
Richard F. Yalch, University of Washington, USA

EXTENDED ABSTRACT

Researchers agree that environmental stimuli (e.g., words processed via the auditory route, objects perceived visually, and olfactory excitants) stimulate multiple thoughts, which often have only one thing in common. However, when the common element is activated, there might be confusion as to which of the many possible associations are relevant. When presented with ambiguous information in the form of concepts that share some associations, individuals may initially think about (retrieve) many possible references and rely on contextual cues to narrow their thoughts to the intended one. However, thought suppression is often difficult and frequently even counterproductive (Wenzlaff and Wegner 2000). Neuroimaging studies confirm that individuals frequently find themselves dealing with task-unrelated thoughts (Binder et al. 1999). Although these thoughts may not seem logically meaningful in context, they are generally linked to the target stimuli either semantically or perceptually.

Inspired by Bargh's (2002) review of automatic influences on consumer judgments, we focus on identifying conditions when simultaneous exposure to objects having minimal attributes in common leads to an illogical transfer of associations between them because of suppression failures. We show that such thoughts may be implicit but still have an effect on consumers' brand associations and evaluations of at least one of the objects. Borrowing from the extensive research on the mere exposure effect, we label the implicit transfer of meanings or affect from logically unrelated stimuli as the mere association effect (cf. Walther 2002) and propose that its underlying process is a failure to suppress unintended automatic associations.

Previous research has shown that mere or incidental exposure is sufficient to activate implicit associations of logically unrelated concepts (labeled a cognitive transfer), but mainly for those individuals familiar with the respective concepts. Among individuals familiar with the concepts involved, incidental priming with a common-node concept should activate nodes that result in the mere association of two concepts indirectly linked via the common-node concept (e.g., exposure to a John Deere lawn mower might create an implicit association between John and nature as well as strengthen the implicit association of deer and grass for outdoor enthusiasts). The presence and influence of these mere associations is captured via participants' explicit and implicit responses. In addition to the simple semantic linking of two concepts via a third concept to which both are related (i.e., cognitive transfer), it is proposed in a second case that the valence associated with these concepts can also be transferred via an indirect path (labeled an affective transfer). For example, exposure to Goodwill charity brochures might positively alter the implicit evaluation of one's last will and testament (and simultaneously make the inclusion of charitable donations in it more likely). Again, the effect is expected for those familiar enough with the concepts involved to be likely to activate these valenced associations.

Study 1 provides an illustration of the mere association effect based on cognitive transfer. Priming consumers with the slow terrapin concept was sufficient to influence participants in making an unconscious association between slowness and the track-and-field team of a university whose mascot is the terrapin. In study 2a, participants made more familiar with the Mayo clinic expressed less favorable attitudes toward a prefix-sharing product (mayonnaise), without any explicit mention of the health concerns some consumers associate with eating mayo.

The mere association effects described above are not universal. As demonstrated in study 1 by group assignment based on measured familiarity and in studies 2a and 2b by direct manipulation, the mere association effect requires well-established associations between the concepts being incidentally linked. In studies 2a and 2b, only individuals exposed to information familiarizing them with the history and operations of the Mayo Clinic showed evidence of a transfer (explicit and implicit) of the less desirable aspects of health clinics to a food product. Apparently, individuals for whom the alternative conceptual meanings are likely to be easily accessed make the conceptual meaning transfer. Low familiarity individuals are less likely to activate associated meanings when exposed to the prime, limiting the meaning transfer.

Study 3 focused on the affective transfer base of the mere association effect. A wine bottle featuring a frog was chosen more often when participants were primed with frog or a proper name, Kermit, often positively associated with frogs but less often when primed with a negative associate–warts. This study extends previous literature findings by Labroo, Dhar, and Schwarz (2008) on conceptual and perceptual fluency by demonstrating how an implicit transitive association transfer related to a phonetical association (i.e., the valence of associated words) may counter any fluency effect attributable to prior exposures.

Finally, study 4 illustrates selectivity in the transfer of associations. When the two to-be-associated nodes belongs to the same semantic category, inhibition from one to the other occurs and the mere association effect is suppressed. Thus, a soft drinks brand explicitly associated with cold ice did not produce perceptions of a physically colder product, but did elicit colder emotional feelings toward the brand.

This investigation supports the increasing amount of consumer research looking at attitude formation as the result of consumers' own mental associations to specific brands or companies. Zaltman's Metaphor Elicitation Technique (Zaltman 1997) and Roedder et al.'s (2006) Brand Concept Mapping method are examples of this innovative work. Our results contribute by suggesting that qualitative research findings that discover linkages between brands and consumer thoughts that seem far removed from the product category (e.g., colors, shapes, flavors, animals) may reflect networks of mere associations that can influence product beliefs, attitudes and choices. On the other hand, it suggests that the associations activated in a particular context may vary from the usual ones because of the presence of entities not consciously recognized as being associated with the focal brand or product.

REFERENCES

Bargh, John (2002), "Losing Consciousness: Automatic Influences on Consumer Judgment, Behavior, and Motivation," *Journal of Consumer Research*, 29 (2), 280-85.

Binder, Jeffrey R., Julia A. Frost, Thomas A. Hammeke, Patrick S. Bellgowan, Stephen M. Rao, and Robert W. Cox (1999), "Conceptual Processing during the Conscious Resting State: A Functional MRI Study," *Journal of Cognitive Neuroscience*, 11 (1), 80-93.

Labroo, Aparna A., Ravi Dhar, and Norbert Schwarz (2008), "Of Frog Wines and Frowning Watches: Semantic Priming of Perceptual Features and Brand Evaluation," *Journal of Consumer Research*, 34 (6), 819-31.

Roedder John, Deborah, Barbara Loken, Kyeongheui Kim, and Alokparna B. Monga (2006): "Brand Concept Maps: A Methodology for Identifying Brand Association Networks," *Journal of Marketing Research*, 43 (4), 549-63.

Walther, Eva (2002), "Guilty by Mere Association: Evaluative Conditioning and the Spreading Attitude Effect," *Journal of Personality and Social Psychology*, 82 (6), 919-34.

Wenzlaff, Richard M. and Daniel M. Wegner (2000), "Thought Suppression," *Annual Review of Psychology*, 51, 59-91.

Zaltman, Gerald (1997), "Rethinking Marketing Research: Putting People Back In," *Journal of Marketing Research*, 34 (4), 424-37.

Doing a Good Thing or Just Doing It: The Effects of Attitude Priming and Procedural Priming on Consumer Behavior

Hao Shen, Chinese University of Hong Kong, Hong Kong
Fengyan Cai, Chinese University of Hong Kong, Hong Kong
Robert S. Wyer, Jr., University of Illinois at Urbana-Champaign, USA

EXTENDED ABSTRACT

Individuals form behavior-related concepts at different levels of generality. Thus, several different behaviors (walking slowly, eating slowly, etc.) may become associated with a more general concept (i.e., doing things slowly). Based on research on knowledge accessibility (Wyer 2008), it seems reasonable to suppose that performing a situation-specific behavior may activate a more general concept that it exemplifies. Furthermore, once this concept becomes accessible in memory, it may increase the likelihood that other exemplars of the concept are activated and employed under conditions in which they are applicable.

However, at least two quite different conceptualizations have implications for the above effect. One, Fishbein and Ajzen's (1976) theory of reasoned action, assumes that behavioral decisions are based on a conscious evaluation of the behavior's consequences or, alternatively, on the intrinsic pleasure that one expects to derive from performing it. The second conceptualization is based on Anderson's (1982, 1983) formulation of procedural knowledge, which assumes that previously acquired concepts and knowledge, along with features of the immediate stimulus situation, can elicit a behavior spontaneously with a minimum of cognitive mediation. In previous research, these two conceptualizations have normally been examined independently and the conditions in which process is likely to predominate in any given situation are unclear. In this paper, we are interested in the conditions that determine the relative impact of attitude-based and procedure-based processing on consumer behavior.

In experiment 1, participants were asked to shadow a speech that was either conveyed at a fast or slow speed. After that, they were asked to finish an unrelated marketing survey. We found that participants finished more questions in the survey if they had been induced to speak fast than slowly in the previous situation.

The objective of experiment 2 was to identify attitude-based and procedure-based processing on consumer behavior. Participants were again asked to shadow a speech that was delivered at either given at a fast or slow speed and then were asked to complete the marketing survey administered in experiment 1. Before doing so, however, they were asked to write down either positive or negative thoughts they had about shadowing a speech at the speed to which they were exposed. Furthermore, some participants were forewarned that they might not be able to finish all the questions within the time allotted, thus inducing them to think about the speed of answering the survey items. But this procedure was omitted for other participants.

We assumed that writing down positive or negative thoughts about the speed of speaking during the shadowing task would have implications for the desirability of doing tings quickly or slowly in general. Therefore, these thoughts would provide the basis for the strategy they decided to employ in completing the survey when they were likely to make a conscious decision about how quickly they should complete it. When participants' attention was not called to their speed of completing the questionnaire, we expected that the speed of performing the first task would influence their speed of working on the marketing survey independently of their attitude toward working quickly or slowly. The results of experiment 2 supported these assumptions.

In experiment 2, participants were unaware of how quickly or slowly they completed the marketing survey unless it was called to their attention, and so their attitude toward this behavior had little effect. However, participants are typically conscious of *which* behavior they choose to perform and are more likely to use their attitude toward the behavior as a basis for their decision. In this case, increasing their cognitive load when making this decision should decrease the impact of attitude-based considerations, leading the effects of procedural knowledge to be evident.

Experiment 3 examined this possibility. Participants first completed a questionnaire in which they were asked to indicate whether or not they would participate in a number of activities. In one questionnaire form, the activities had socially desirable implications (e.g., supporting human rights, protecting the environment, etc.). In a second form, they had undesirable implications (harming the country, breaking the law, etc.). In responding to each question, however, some participants were asked to circle the option they favored ("join" vs. "not join") whereas others were asked to circle the option they opposed.

Participants were expected to have a positive attitude toward participating in socially desirable activities and a negative attitude toward participating in undesirable ones, and these attitudes were expected to be reflected in their responses. That is, if the activities in the questionnaire were desirable, they were expected to choose the "join" option when they are asked which option they favored and to choose the "not join" option when they are asked which option they oppose. When the activities were undesirable, they were expected to choose the "not join" opinion in the first case and the "join" option in the second. Thus, participants' responses to the opinion items ("join" or "not join") were manipulated independently of the attitude conveyed by these responses.

Participants after completing this survey were asked to decide whether to participate in an unrelated promotion for a soft drink being offered by a foreign country. While making this decision, however, they were either asked to remember a 12-digit number or 2-digit number.

The effects of completing the opinion questionnaire on participants' reactions to the promotion were expected to depend on their ability to think carefully about these reactions when making a decision. That is, priming a motor procedure of circling "join" or "not join" affected participants' decision to join a marketing promotion. This influence depended on their attitude toward this procedure when they had sufficient cognitive resources to compute this attitude. When participants were put under cognitive load, however, they were more likely to join a promotion if they had repeatedly circled "join" rather than "not join" in the priming task, independently of their attitude toward this behavior.

To summarize, our research is the first to demonstrate that performing a behavior can activate both attitude-based and procedure-based processing strategies, and to identify conditions that influence thee relative impact of these strategies on behavior.

REFERENCES

Anderson, John R. (1982), "Acquisition of Cognitive Skill," *Psychological Review*, 89(4), 369-406.

______ (1983), *The Architecture of Cognition*. Cambridge, MA: Harvard University Press.

Fishbein, Martin and Icek Ajzen (1975), *Belief, Attitude, Intention, and Behavior: An Introduction to Theory and Research,* MA: Addison-Wesley.

Wyer, Robert S. (2008), "The Role of Knowledge Accessibility in Cognition and Behavior: Implications for Consumer Information Processing," in *Handbook of Consumer Research*, ed. Curtis Haugtvedt, Frank Kardes, and Paul Herr, Mahwah, NJ: Erlbaum, 31–75.

When Products Are Valued More but Sold for Less: The Impact of Waste Aversion on Disposal Behavior

Aaron R. Brough, Northwestern University, USA
Mathew S. Isaac, Northwestern University, USA

EXTENDED ABSTRACT

While purchasing, using, or disposing of products, consumers often judge a product's value. For example, when disposing of an unneeded product, consumers may consider the extent to which the product is still usable and estimate its worth. Products with greater residual value (e.g., newer products) generally command higher prices in the marketplace. Therefore, sellers with profit-maximization goals should be motivated to overestimate a product's value in order to increase its selling price.

In this research, however, we document the counterintuitive effects of a competing motivation—waste aversion—that decreases selling prices despite inflated value judgments. We characterize waste aversion as the desire to ensure that a product's residual value is fully exhausted before it is discarded, regardless of who benefits from the product's utilization. Because high selling prices can decrease the purchase likelihood of a used product, waste aversion should cause sellers to under-price a product to avoid the possibility that it will be discarded and its residual utility wasted. Prior research has examined consumers' aversion to purchase duplicate goods (Bolton & Alba, 2008) or to dispose of products without fully utilizing their value (Arkes 1996). We extend this work by examining how waste aversion influences value judgments, which provides additional insight into the processes that underlie disposal decisions. In particular, we argue that value judgments made by waste-averse consumers highlight a product's attractiveness even if such judgments result in financial loss.

Three empirical studies provide converging evidence that waste aversion, by shifting consumers from a profit-maximization to a product-utilization orientation, can bias value judgments.

Study 1. Study 1 shows that despite perceiving an owned product as newer, consumers primed with waste decrease its acceptable selling price. Online participants imagined either throwing away (waste condition) or moving (control condition) their favorite pair of shoes. Following this manipulation, participants indicated the minimum amount that they would be willing to accept in exchange for their shoes as well as the length of time they had owned the shoes. As predicted, participants in the waste (versus control) condition were willing to accept significantly less money as compensation for their shoes. However, this effect does not appear to be caused by devaluation; participants in the waste condition estimated their favorite shoes to be newer than participants in the control condition.

The results of study 1 are consistent with the notion that waste-aversion shifts sellers from a profit-maximization to a product-utilization orientation and influences value judgments. When primed with wasteful disposal, product owners appear motivated to make judgments about a product that increase its attractiveness to potential buyers and thereby diminish the possibility of needless waste. Offering a relatively new product at a relatively low price increases the likelihood that a product will be sold to an interested buyer and used rather than discarded and wasted. Given that consumers typically dispose of things that are no longer needed, asking people to imagine throwing away their favorite pair of shoes is admittedly unrealistic. In Study 2, we use a more realistic scenario and operationalize the wastefulness of disposal in a different way.

Study 2. The objective of study 2 was to manipulate wasteful disposal more realistically and examine its impact on value judgments. Online participants were assigned to either a wasteful or non-wasteful disposal condition. In the wasteful disposal condition, participants read the following scenario:

> "John enjoys listening to music on his iPod each day as he exercises. Yesterday, John received a new iPod as a birthday present and is now trying to decide whether to *KEEP* or *THROW AWAY* his old iPod. John finally decided to keep his old iPod rather than throwing it away. Yesterday, someone offered to buy John's old iPod from him. What is the minimum amount you think the buyer would have to offer John to persuade him to sell his old iPod?"

In the non-wasteful disposal condition, participants read an identical scenario with one exception: the word "THROW" was replaced by "GIVE." Giving is a disposal method that provides an opportunity for residual value to be consumed by someone else rather than wasted. As predicted, participants in the wasteful disposal condition provided a lower acceptable selling price than participants in the non-wasteful disposal condition. Although waste aversion can explain these results, it is possible that participants in the wasteful disposal method inferred that the iPod had low residual utility since John was considering throwing it in the trash. To address this concern, a follow-up experiment was conducted in which participants who read the first two sentences from the above stimuli and then estimated the number of times that John would use the old iPod over the next year if he decided to keep it as well as the likelihood that he would in fact keep it. Results indicated that participants who considered the wasteful disposal method estimated that John would use the old iPod more and be more likely to retain it. Thus, participants who considered a wasteful disposal method did not infer a lower product value, but in fact reacted by inflating the perceived value of the product.

Study 3. If waste aversion shifts sellers from a profit-maximization to a product-utilization orientation, the effect should not be observed when participants take the role of a buyer rather than a seller. Therefore, study 3 used a 2 (role: buyer vs. seller) x 2 (disposal: wasteful vs. non-wasteful) between-subjects design in which participants were assigned to take the role of either a buyer or a seller and respond to scenarios that involved wasteful or non-wasteful disposal. Consistent with the results of studies 1 and 2, results from study 3 indicate that sellers who consider wasteful (vs. non-wasteful) disposal judge products to be more valuable but are willing to accept a lower price for them. On the other hand, buyers who consider wasteful (vs. non-wasteful) disposal show a decrease in both perceived value and willingness to pay.

Across three studies, we show that the wastefulness of a disposal option influences value judgments. Economic theory assumes that sellers are motivated to maximize profit and are indifferent regarding the state of a sold product after the transaction has been completed. However, in this research we find that sellers primed with the notion of wastefulness perceive greater value in used products (as measured by newness, future usage, and retention likelihood) while simultaneously agreeing to sell them for less money. These findings are consistent with our explanation that waste aversion causes sellers to be more concerned with product utilization than with financial gain.

REFERENCES

Arkes, Hal R. (1996), "The Psychology of Waste," *Journal of Behavioral Decision Making*, 9(3), 213-224.

Bolton, Lisa E. and Joseph W. Alba (2008), "When Less is More: Consumer Aversion to Waste," Working Paper: The Wharton School, University of Pennsylvania.

Accounting for the Role of Habit in Regular Saving

Caezilia Loibl, Ohio State University, USA
David S. Kraybill, Ohio State University, USA
Sara W. DeMay, Ohio State University, USA

EXTENDED ABSTRACT

Conceptualization

What is the relationship between habit and saving? The many public calls for consumers to establishing a habit of saving indicate that it is a desired behavior, but, obviously, a difficult one to achieve. Savings habits are frequently practiced behaviors, done without a particular sense of awareness, with the goal of freeing up funds for saving or debt reduction. Automatically packing lunch for work, browsing supermarket shelves for discounted products, calling friends after 9 p.m. and on weekends when the phone rates are low are thrifty behaviors that appear to be habitual for many. Using the self-report habit index (Verplanken and Orbell 2003) and applying it to saving for the first time, survey data were collected to (1) validate the role of habits in regular savings; (2) test whether participation in a savings program aids in the formation of savings habits; and (3) examine the role of habits in the perception of financial strain.

Method

The treatment group included participants in a federally funded, multi-year savings program that provides incentives for low-income individuals to save toward purchasing a home, financing higher education, or capitalizing a small business. American Dream Demonstrations have documented the exceptional effectiveness of the program, based on mandatory deposits, matched savings, intensive financial education, and regular one-on-one counseling. In spring 2008, a paper survey was distributed to participants in this savings program who had enrolled with a program network in the U.S. Midwest; the response rate was 52% (n=94). The comparison group consisted of low-income individuals in the general population who lived in counties served by the network but who were not savings program participants. Addresses of 2,200 individuals were purchased to collect data by mail survey; the response rate was 15% (n=291). Nearest-neighbor matching without replacement was used to pair comparison group with treatment group observations to account for demographic differences (N=128).

Saving habits were measured with the Self-Report Habit Index (Verplanken and Orbell 2003), which was developed to reflect the different facets of habit, including the frequency, lack of awareness and control, and mental efficiency of behavior (Honkanen, Olsen, and Verplanken 2005). It compared well to other published measures of habit (Verplanken, Myrbakk, and Rudi 2004) and has been proved useful for a diverse number of common behaviors. The present study contributes to this literature by measuring habit formation during a behavioral intervention and applied to financial behaviors.

Major Findings

To validate the discriminant validity of the habit concept, the individual volume of savings deposits was regressed on attitude, subjective norm, perceived control and intention, past deposit frequency, and habit. Habit emerged as a significant predictor of savings deposits, confirming its role as an independent factor in explaining saving.

To examine the influence of program participation on habit formation, the length of participation was divided into six-month intervals. Compared to non-participants, the savings habit of program participants increased over time, peaked at 19-24 months, and then flattened. There was no difference in savings habit between non-participants and new enrollees, thus supporting successful habit formation during savings program participation.

While habit tends to be associated with overt behavior, the habit literature notes its influence on mental processes (Verplanken 2006; Verplanken et al. 2007). Results of hierarchical regression analysis support the independent role of habit for reducing the perception of financial strain above the influence of household income and savings. This analysis parallels findings on the influence of mental habits on self-esteem (Hilton and Devall 1997).

Study findings document the role of habit for regular saving and the success of targeted educational and behavioral interventions on developing savings habits.

REFERENCES

Hilton, Jeanne M., and Esther L. Devall (1997), "The Family Economic Strain Scale: Development and evaluation of the instrument with single- and two-parent families," *Journal of Family and Economic Issues*, 18 (fall), 247-271.

Honkanen, Pirjo , Svein Ottar Olsen, and Bas Verplanken (2005), "Intention to consume seafood—the importance of habit," *Appetite*, 45 (2), 161-168.

Verplanken, Bas (2006), "Beyond frequency: Habit as a mental construct," *British Journal of Social Psychology*, 45, 639-656.

Verplanken, Bas, Oddgeir Friborg, Catharina E. Wang, David Trafimow, and Kristin Woolf (2007), "Mental habits: Metacognitive reflection on negative self-thinking," *Journal of Personality and Social Psychology*, 92 (3), 526-541.

Verplanken, Bas, Vemund Myrbakk, and Erik Rudi (2004), "The measurement of habit," In *Routines of decision making*, edited by T. Betsch. Mahwah: Lawrence Erlbaum.

Verplanken, Bas, and Sheina Orbell (2003), "Reflections on past behavior: A self-report index of habit strength," *Journal of Applied Social Psychology*, 33 (6), 1313-1330.

Choosing Your Future: Temporal Distance and the Balance Between Self-Control and Indulgence

Juliano Laran, University of Miami, USA

EXTENDED ABSTRACT

This project investigates how temporal distance influences consumers' self-control. We find evidence that self-control is dependent on the content of currently active information in decisions for the future. When indulgence information is currently active, decisions for the future tend to be oriented toward self-control. When self-control information is currently active, decisions for the future tend to be oriented toward indulgence. In a series of studies investigating two self-control domains (healthy eating and saving money), we find evidence for an information activation/inhibition account of the influence of temporal distance on self-control decisions.

Temporal distance has a wide array of implications (see Trope, Liberman, and Wakslak 2007). According to construal level theory (Trope and Liberman 2003), the greater the temporal distance the more likely it is that events will be represented in abstract terms (high-level construal) as opposed to concrete terms (low-level construal). Thinking about eating right now may be represented as preparing the food and eating it, while thinking about eating a year from now may be represented as trying to feel good and be healthy. According to time discounting theories (Frederick, Loewenstein, and O'Donoghue 2002 for a review), the greater the temporal distance to an outcome the smaller the perceived value of this outcome. A tasty, rewarding meal may not be perceived to be so rewarding if it will happen in the distant future. This paper proposes an additional way in which temporal distance can influence preferences in decisions requiring self-control. Based on research on the role of activation and inhibition processes in the representation of knowledge structures (Kruglanski et al. 2002), we propose that an increase in temporal distance may lead to inhibition of currently active information. Inhibition of currently active information may result in activation of competing information, which will in turn influence the value of objects. Therefore, when information about indulgence (regulation) is currently activated, people will make indulgent (regulatory) choices for the present, but regulatory (indulgent) choices for the future.

In study 1, we used a scrambled sentence task to prime information about indulgence, self-control, and neutral. Then, we asked participants to choose a snack for their participation in the study. They either chose a snack that they would receive at the end of the experimental session or at the end of the semester for their participation in the semester studies, manipulated between-subjects. A binary logistic regression indicated an interaction between the information prime and time frame factors (*Wald* $\chi^2(2)=18.83$, $p<.01$). In the indulgence information prime condition, participants were less likely to choose a healthy snack in the present time frame (22.8%) than in the future time frame condition (62.5%), ($\chi^2(1)=13.84$, $p<.01$). In the self-control information prime condition, participants were more likely to choose a healthy snack in the present time frame (58.9%) than in the future time frame condition (30.0%), ($\chi^2(1)=6.54$, $p=.01$). In the neutral information prime condition, participants were as likely to choose a healthy snack in the present time frame (50.0%) as they were in the future time frame condition (48.8%), ($\chi^2<1$).

In study 2, the same procedure was used with the exception that we measured implicit goal accessibility (i.e., latency of word recognition) after participants thought about snacks they would like to get in the present vs. in the future. A positive score indicates activation of the self-control concept (i.e., faster reaction times for self-control-related words than for neutral words), while a negative score indicates inhibition of the self-control concept (i.e., slower reaction times for self-control-related words than for neutral words). There was again an interaction ($F(1, 209)=17.12$, $p<.01$). In the indulgence information prime condition, participants showed inhibition of the self-control concept in the present time frame condition ($M_{Present}$=-75 ms), but activation of the self-control concept in the future time frame condition (M_{Future}=80 ms; $F(1, 209)=9.22$, $p<.01$). In the self-control information prime condition, participants showed activation of the self-control concept in the present time frame condition ($M_{Present}$=59 ms), but inhibition of the self-control concept in the future time frame condition (M_{Future}=-73 ms; $F(1, 209)=7.90$, $p<.01$).

Study 3 asked participants how much money they were interested in donating to some local charities after information about saving or spending money was primed. We told participants that they could either spend money on shopping or save their money and donate it to charity (the more money they were willing to donate to charity, the more money they were willing to save). There was again an interaction ($F(2, 247)=4.44$, $p<.05$). There was an effect of time frame in the spending money information prime condition. Participants were willing to donate less money in the present than in the future ($M_{Present}$=\$41.09, M_{Future}=\$81.98; $F(1,247)=4.45$, $p<.05$). There was an effect of time frame in the saving money information prime condition. Participants were willing to donate more money in the present than in the future ($M_{Present}$=\$78.55, M_{Future}=\$34.24; $F(1,247)=4.41$, $p<.05$). There was not an effect of time frame in the neutral information prime condition. Participants were willing to donate the same amount of money in the present and in the future ($M_{Present}$=\$63.50, M_{Future}=\$60.75; $F<1$).

These results show that the content of currently active information can influence the construal of a situation in decisions for the future. In decisions involving a conflict between indulgence and regulation, information that is currently active tends to be inhibited as temporal distance increases. As a consequence of inhibition, this information content decreases in importance for the decision in hand. Marketers may be able to use the operations of these processes to their advantage. A retailer may use the store environment to make information about saving money currently active, but then motivate people to make purchases for a certain occasion (e.g., anniversary, child's birthday) in advance. A store environment that has information about saving money may attract more customers, but these customers may end up spending a lot of money rather than saving money when making purchases for the distant future.

REFERENCES

Frederick, Shane, George Loewenstein, and Ted O'Donoghue (2002), "Time Discounting and Time Preference: A Critical Review," *Journal of Economic Literature*, 40 (June), 350-401.

Trope, Yaacov and Nira Liberman (2003), "Temporal Construal," *Psychological Review*, 110 (July), 403-21.

Trope, Yaacov, Nira Liberman, and Cheryl Wakslak (2007), "Construal Levels and Psychological Distance: Effects on Representation, Prediction, Evaluation, and Behavior," *Journal of Consumer Psychology*, 17 (2) 83-95.

Kruglanski, Arie W., James Y. Shah, Ayelet Fishbach, Ron Friedman, Woo Young Chen, and David Sleeth-Keppler (2002), "A Theory of Goal Systems," in *Advances in Experimental Social Psychology*, Vol. 34, ed. Mark P. Zanna, San Diego, CA: Academic Press, 331-78.

Debiasing and Rebiasing the Illusion of Delayed Incentives

Dilip Soman, University of Toronto, Canada
Maggie Wenjing Liu, University of Toronto, Canada

EXTENDED ABSTRACT

Individuals often need to choose between options that trade off money with effort. For instance, a student could choose from two summer jobs, one which pays more but involves a lot of effort, and another which pays less but is relatively easy. A shopper could buy a do-it-yourself piece of furniture and assemble it at home, or purchase a fully assembled piece. Choices like these can be modeled in a multi-attribute context as a simple tradeoff between the extra effort required for one option and the additional cost of the other option (Payne, 1982).This trade-off approach not only applies to situations in which the choice and subsequent purchase are relatively concurrent, but also those purchase with a temporal delay after choice.

Past research shows that the evaluation of Effort–Money transactions (e.g.., working in exchange for money) depends on whether the transaction is immediate or delayed (Lynch and Zauberman, 2005, Soman, 1998, 2004). Soman (2004) showed that receiving monetary reward conditioning on performing efforts might appear attractive when both the effort and money are in the future, but unattractive when both are imminent. Soman (1998) refers to the perceived attractiveness of the delayed transaction as an ''illusion,'' suggesting that it is a bias. He proposes that when the transaction is in the future, effort gets discounted to a greater degree than the monetary reward. Consequently, transactions that appear attractive from a temporal distance start appearing increasingly unattractive as the temporal distance decreases. Following Soman (1998), we refer to this phenomenon as the "illusion of delayed incentives." Soman (2004) studied the problem in a multi-attribute product context and further suggested that the degree of discounting is the highest for the effort attribute, and lower for the quality and price attributes. He found preference reversals between such pairs of products as a function of the temporal perspective of the decision-maker.

Given the illusion of delayed rewards, what can individuals do to minimize this bias? In this research, we ask two questions: (1) How can the illusion of delayed incentives be corrected? (2) What debiasing and rebiasing mechanisms are involved in these corrections.

The extent to which cognitive strategies can improve reasoning and correct biases is a source of debate (Larrick, 2004). Although people recognize and correct their bias, some raise questions about whether people can truly debias themselves (Kahneman, 2003). One goal of studying biases is not only to demonstrate irrationality, but to help people make better decisions (Larrick, 2004). This paper offers a first step of corrective strategies for intertemporal preference reversals arising out of different discounting of effort and money.

The present research shows not only that people discount different attributes separately, but also that discounting of one attribute could be corrected singly. We show preference reversals using correcting strategies and proposed four potential reasons of such debiasing or rebiasing effects. Besides common debiasing and rebiasing strategies, we further suggest unbiasing strategies (changing an external factor which eliminates the bias) as an alternative correcting method applicable for bias intervention.

REFERENCES

Ainslie, G. & Haslam, N. (1992). Hyperbolic discounting. In G. Loewenstein & J. Elster (Eds.), *Choice over time*. New York, NY: Russell Sage Foundation.

Akerlof, G. A. (1991). Procrastination and obedience. *American Economic Review*, 81(2), 1-19.

Bouchard, C., Shephard, R.J., & Thomas, S. (1993). *Physical activity, fitness and health consensus statement*. Human Kinetics Publishers, England.

Dodge, R. (1917). The law of relative fatigue. *Psychological Review*, 14, 89-113.

Gandevia, S.C. (2001). Spinal and supraspinal factors in human muscle fatigue. *Physiology Review*, 81, 1725-1789.

Hogarth, R. (1987). *Judgment and choice*. New York: John Wiley and Sons.

Huey, B.M., & Wilson G.F. (1993). *Workload transition: Implication for individual and team performance*. Washington, D.C.: National Academy Press.

Kahneman, D. (2003). Representation revisited: Attribute substitution in intuitive judgment. In T. Gilovich, D. Griffin & D. Kahneman (eds.), *Heuristics and Biases*. New work: Cambridge University Press.

Larrick, R. P. (2004). Debiasing. In *Handbook of Experimental Psychology* (ed.) Derek Koehler and Nigel Harvey. Blackwell Publishing.

Mazur, J. (1987). An adjustment procedure for studying delayed reinforcement. In M. Commons, J. Mazur, J. Nevin, & H. Rachlin (Eds.), *Quantitative analysis of behavior: The effects of delay and interventing events on reinforcement value*. Hillsdale, NJ: Erlbaum.

Mischel, W., & Staub, E. (1965). Effects of expectancy on working and waiting for longer rewards. *Journal of Personality and Social Psychology*, 2, 625-633.

Prelec, D. (1989). *Decreasing impatience: Definitions and consequences*. New York: Russell Sage Foundation.

Rachlin, H., & Raineri, A. (1992). Discount reversal effects. In G. Loewenstein & J. Elster (Eds.), *Choice over time*. New York: Russell Sage Foundation.

Reichenbach, H. (1924). *Axiomatik der relativistischen Raum-Zeit-Lehre* (English translation *Axiomatization of the theory of relativity*, Berkeley: University of California Press, 1969)

Simonson, I. (1989). Choice based on reasons: The case of attraction and compromise effects. *Journal of Consumer Research*, 16 (September), 158-174.

Smit, A.S., Eling, P.A., Hopman, M.T. & Coenen, A.M. (2005). Mental and physical efforts affect vigilance differently. *International Journal of Psychophysiology*, 57, 211-217.

Soman, D. (1998). The illusion of delayed incentives: Evaluating future money–effort transactions. *Journal of Marketing Research*, 34, 427-437.

______ (2004). The effect of time delay on multi-attribute choice. *Journal of Economic Psychology*, 25, 153-173.

Trope, Y., & Liberman, N. (2003). Temporal construal. *Psychological Review*, 110(3), 403-421.

Weinger, M.B, Vredenburgh, A.G., Schumann, C.M., Marcario, A., Kalsher, M.J., Smith, B, Truong, P.C., and Kim, A.(2005). Quantitative description of the workload associated with airway management procedures, *Journal of Clinical Anesthesia*, 12, 273-282.

Zauberman, G. & Lynch, J. G. (2005). Resource slack and propensity to discount delayed investments of time versus money. *Journal of Experimental Psychology*, 134 (1), 23.

The More is Less Effect: How Adding Positive Arguments Can Undermine Attitude toward an Object

Kurt Carlson, Georgetown University, USA
Suzanne Shu, University of California at Los Angeles, USA

EXTENDED ABSTRACT

The number three is an important number in human learning (Tenenbaum and Xu, 2000), perception of streaks (Carlson and Shu 2007), and advertising (Belch and Belch 2001). In this article we posit and test a new role for the number three as the optimal number of arguments for message design. Thus, three positive claims should produce a more positive impression than one, two, or four positive claims. The surprising aspect of this prediction is that four positive claims should be less persuasive than three. We refer to this as the more is less (persuasive) effect. We draw from work on social intelligence, marketplace metacognition, and persuasion knowledge to propose that the more is less effect occurs because consumers, upon seeing a fourth positive claim, infer that something is amiss and that the set of claims is too good to be true, thus producing a lesser overall impression than would have occurred had the message contained just three positive claims. This article presents results from four studies that test for and explore this effect.

The first study used a 3 (target object: cereal, restaurant, friend's new partner) by 3 (number of arguments: 2, 3, 4) design, with target object as a within-participant factor and number of arguments a between-participant factor. Each participant read a description of the current target object with two, three, or four positive adjectives to operationalize the two, three, and four argument conditions. These adjectives were designed and pretested for importance and positivity. Participants then indicated their agreement with four statements about the object on a 7-point Likert scale to give an overall attitude toward the object. Higher average responses reflect a more positive attitude toward the object.

We analyzed overall attitudes toward the objects across all three domains simultaneously using a repeated measures ANOVA, with subject as a random factor and target object and number of arguments as fixed effects. The model revealed a significant effect of number of arguments ($F(2, 295)=3.33$, $p<.05$), as expected. Three arguments made for a slightly more positive attitude than did two, and four arguments produced a significantly less positive ($M=3.24$) attitude than did three arguments ($M=3.53$; $t(335)=2.78$, $p<.01$). In other words, these data reflect the more is less effect.

The second study explored if the more is less effect would be reduced or even eliminated if product improvement claims on a box of cereal were verified by a credible neutral party (e.g. Consumer Reports). Participants were assigned to one of four conditions created by crossing number of arguments (three versus four) with verification of the arguments (verified by Consumer Reports versus no mention of any attempt to verify the arguments). We find a significant interaction ($F(1, 218)=7.08$, $p<.01$). Planned contrasts revealed that attitude toward the cereal was more positive under four claims than it was under three claims when claims were verified ($t(53)=1.96$, $p=.055$), but it was less positive under four claims than it was under three claims when claims were unverified ($t(165)=2.13$, $p=.035$). In sum, the more is less effect replicated when the claims were not verified.

The third study tested if participants under cognitive load would exhibit the more is less effect. If inferences about the marketer's motives are at the heart of the more is less effect, then cognitive load should reduce and possibly even reverse the effect. We used the three argument and four argument cereal conditions from Study 2, crossed with a cognitive load manipulation. Low cognitive load participants were required to remember a two-digit number, while those in the high load condition were required to remember a seven-digit number.

We find a significant interaction ($F(1, 124)=10.73$, $p<.001$); decomposition of this interaction revealed that the more is less effect occurred under low load ($t(57)=3.05$, $p< .01$) but did not occur under high cognitive load. Those under high load who received four positive descriptors of the cereal had a slightly more positive (though not statistically significant) attitude toward the cereal ($M=4.58$) than those who received three positive descriptors ($M=4.31$; $t(67)=1.32$, $p=.19$).

The final study was designed to determine if marketers could do anything to avoid the more is less effect. To this end, we examined whether admitting a weakness at the outset would insulate against the effect. The design was a 2 (number of positive arguments: three versus four) x 2 (negative argument added: yes versus no) between-participants design. Participants read a short description of a political candidate and answered three questions that were used to form a measure of overall attitude toward the politician.

An ANOVA with main effects for number of arguments and negative argument added and an interaction term revealed a significant interaction ($F(1, 129)=4.85$, $p<.05$). Decomposition of this interaction revealed that the more is less effect occurred in the condition where the unrelated negative feature was not mentioned. The politician was viewed marginally more positively after three positive claims ($M=3.70$) than after four positive claims ($M=3.23$; $t(64)=1.73$, $p=.08$) by participants in this condition. The effect was reversed directionally (i.e., four claims were more effective than three) when a negative feature was acknowledged at the outset ($t(65)=1.35$, $p=.18$).

Four studies found the more is less effect across a wide range of domains. It is eliminated when the claims are verified by a neutral party, when consumers are under cognitive load, and when the target revealed a single negative claim. Taken together these data suggest that the effect stems from an inference, due to use of persuasion knowledge, that the target is trying too hard to make the positive claims. Given its generality, we believe the more is less effect has important implications for nearly every aspect of marketing that is related to persuasion.

REFERENCES

Belch, G. E., & Belch, M. A. (2001). *Advertising and Promotion: An integrated marketing communications perspective.* New York: McGraw-Hill.

Carlson, K., and Shu, S. (2007), "The Rule of Three: How the Third Event Signals the Emergence of a Streak," *Organizational Behavior and Human Decision Processes*, 104 (1), 113-121.

Tenenbaum, J.B., & Xu, F. (2000). "Word learning as Bayesian inference," *Proceedings of the 22nd Annual Conference of the Cognitive Science Society.*

How Multiple Anchors Affect Judgment: Evidence from the Lab and eBay

Yan Zhang, National University of Singapore, Singapore
Ye Li, Columbia University, USA
Ting Zhu, University of Chicago, USA

EXTENDED ABSTRACT

People's estimates of uncertain quantities are systematically influenced by externally-provided or self-generated numbers, or "anchors" (Englich and Mussweiler 2005; Epley and Gilovich 2001; Tversky and Kahneman 1974). The anchoring effect is robust to many domains (Simonson and Drolet 2004; Wansink, Kent, and Hoch 1998). However, most of the research has focused on the case where only one anchor is provided. Less is known about how people make estimates when they encounter more than one anchor. In this research, we examined how multiple anchors affect estimates.

When there is only one anchor, research shows a positive correlation between anchor values and estimates: single extremely low anchors lead to lower estimates relative to less extreme ones (Chapman and Johnson 1994; Strack and Mussweiler 1997). We predict, however, that this effect can be reversed by adding a second, plausible anchor that is higher than the original first anchors: extremely low anchors paired with a plausible high anchor should instead lead to higher estimates. We suggest that this occurs because presenting multiple anchors together highlights the plausibility of each anchor and makes it easier to evaluate their plausibilities than when there is only one anchor present (Hsee 1996). As a result, when paired with a moderate anchor, extremely low anchors are judged as implausible and thus exert less influence on final estimates. The second, moderate anchor now has bigger influence on final estimates. Therefore, when paired with a moderate anchor, an extremely low anchor leads to a higher estimate than a less extremely low anchor.

We first demonstrate the basic effect in a laboratory experiment. As expected, across four different trivia questions, participants generated lower estimates for extremely low anchors than for less extremely low anchors. However, when the anchors were paired with a second, moderately high anchor, the pattern was reversed: extremely low anchors led to higher estimates than less extremely low anchors.

We tested the proposed mechanism in a second lab experiment. In this experiment, we held the anchor values constant but manipulated the contrast between the two anchors by changing the colors in which they were displayed. Using a manipulation adopted from Cheema and Soman (2008), we expected participants to pay more attention to the difference between the two anchors if they were presented in different colors. Consequently, participants should rely more on the more plausible anchor in making their estimates than when the two anchors were presented in the same color. As predicted, we found that participants who saw an extremely low anchor paired with a more plausible anchor in different colors rated the plausibility of the extremely low anchor even lower than those who saw the anchors in the same colors, and consequently gave higher final estimates. The opposite was true for extremely high anchors paired with a more plausible anchor: participants who saw the anchors in different colors generated lower final estimates.

We corroborated these experimental results with analysis using archival data from Buy-It-Now auctions on eBay. In Buy-It-Now auctions, bidders can either buy at the "Buy-It-Now" price or participate in the bidding process in order to try to pay less for the same item. Because the buy-it-now price disappears once anyone places a bid higher than the hidden reserve price set by the seller, subsequent bidders in Buy-It-Now auctions in the United States only observe the starting bid price but not the Buy-It-Now price. However, this policy of removing the Buy-It-Now price is not implemented in China, so bidders there can observe both the starting bid price and the Buy-It-Now price throughout the auction. This difference between the two markets constitutes a natural experiment where bidders are affected by a single anchor (starting bid price) for transactions in the United States but are affected by two anchors (starting bid price and Buy-It-Now price) for transactions in China. After controlling for other variables known to affect final price such as number of bidders, number of bids, and buyer and seller ratings, etc, we found a pattern of results consistent with those found in the two laboratory experiments. In the United States, extremely low starting bid prices resulted in lower final prices than less extremely low starting bid prices. The reverse was true in China: extremely low starting bid prices resulted in higher final prices than less extremely low starting bid prices. In order to control for other between-country differences, we also examined pure auctions (with no Buy-It-Now option) in the two markets. In pure auctions, bidders only observe the starting bid price in both countries. The analysis shows no between-country difference in the effect of starting bid price on final prices for pure auctions, which suggests that the difference for Buy-It-Now auctions is due to the difference in number of anchors but not other between-country differences.

This research has important implications for pricing strategies. For instance, an extremely low historical sale price might lead to a higher willingness-to-pay when it is paired with the current market price, as consumers may infer that the low historical price is not relevant to the price that a buyer can possibly get in the present. In contrast, although providing a high "manufacturer suggested retail price" (MSRP) usually increases consumers' willingness-to-pay, this strategy may backfire when consumers compare the MSRP to the sale price (a plausible anchor since it is actually available at this price). If the MSRP is too high to be plausible, consumers may have a lower willingness to pay than if the MSRP is more reasonable.

REFERENCES

Chapman, Gretchen B. and Johnson, Eric J. (1999), "Anchoring, activation, and the construction of values," *Organizational Behavior and Human Decision Processes*, 79(2), 115-153.

Cheema, Amar and Dilip Soman (2008), "The effect of partitions on controlling consumption," Journal of Marketing Research, 45(6), 665-675.

Englich, Birteand and Mussweiler, Thomas (2001), "Sentencing under uncertainty: Anchoring effects in the courtroom," *Journal of Applied Social Psychology*, 31, 1535-1551.

Epley, Nicholas and Thomas Gilovich (2001), "Putting adjustment back in the anchoring and adjustment heuristic: Differential processing of self-generated and experimenter-provided anchors," *Psychological Science*, 12, 391-396.

Hsee, Christopher K. (1996), "The evaluability hypothesis: An explanation for preference reversals between joint and separate evaluations of alternatives," *Organizational Behavior and Human Decision Processes*, 67, 247-257.

Simonson, Itamar and Aimee Drolet (2004), "Anchoring Effects on Consumers' Willingness-to-Pay and Willingness-to-Accept," *Journal of Consumer Research*, 31, 681-690.

Strack, Fritz and Thomas Mussweiler (1997). "Explaning the enigmatic anchoring effect: Mechanisms of selective accessibility," *Journal of Personality and Social Psychology*, 73, 437-446.

Tversky, Amos and Daniel Kahneman (1974), "Judgment under uncertainty: Heuristics and biases," *Science*, 185, 1124-1131.

Wansink, Brian, Robert J. Kent, and Stephen J. Hoch (1998), "An anchoring and adjustment model of purchase quantity decisions," *Journal of Marketing Research*, 35(1), 71-81.

When is Life Like a Box of Chocolates?: Providing Multiple Units of a Good Attenuates the Endowment Effect

Katherine Burson, University of Michigan, USA
David Faro, London Business School, UK
Yuval Rottenstreich, Stern School of Business, New York University, USA

EXTENDED ABSTRACT

The endowment effect is the well-known demonstration of loss aversion in which those endowed with an item value it more than a non-endowed group. Kahneman et al. (1990) demonstrated the robustness of the endowment effect in a series of studies in which half of participants were given an item that they might sell for some price (their willingness to accept, WTA) and the other half of participants were given the option to purchase the item for some price (their willingness to pay, WTP). Sellers and buyers rarely agreed in their offers. Another classic demonstration of the effect is with reluctance to trade (Knetsch 1989). Here, people are randomly endowed with one of two goods and are given the trade to trade their endowment for the other good. Trading proportions in these studies are typically much lower than would be predicted by distribution of preferences for the two goods.

The WTA-WTP gap and reluctance to trade follow from two fundamental findings of Tversky and Kahneman (1981; 1986): (i) reference-dependent preferences that (ii) reveal loss aversion, a heightened sensitivity to losses relative to gains. Thus, sellers feel greater pain of loss when they sell their endowed object than buyers feel giving up their money. Similarly, the pain of loss when an endowed object is traded for alternative object is greater than the joy of gaining that alternative.

Recent research has shown that patterns of attention and memory co-vary with the magnitude of the endowment effect (Carmon and Ariely 2000; Johnson, Haubl, and Keinan 2007). Specifically, the endowment effect is at least in part driven by asymmetric queries. Participants focus on the change that selling or trading would be from their reference point. A typical query for a chocolate owner might be: "should I give up a chocolate to get money?" Participants who are encouraged to think in a more symmetric way (e.g. "which do I prefer, chocolates or money?") show less of an endowment effect (Johnson, Haubl, and Keinan 2007).

We hypothesize that similar attenuation can be achieved by endowing participants with multiple units of a good. We suspect that multiple unit settings promote symmetric thinking: Rather than considering a query that focuses on entailed changes, a participant endowed with many chocolates may be prone to consider final outcomes. Intuitively, the offering of multiple units makes highly salient the issue of exchange rates. Thus, many participants, their attention drawn to exchange rates, might focus or dwell on this issue, essentially considering something akin to the symmetric question "is five dollars worth nine chocolates?" In essence, when attention is drawn to quantities and exchange rates, it might be drawn away from gains and losses, thereby blocking the operation of loss aversion and eliminating any chance of an endowment effect.

We test the attenuation of endowment effects for multiple units in two studies. One study examines endowment effects in a trading paradigm and the other in a pricing paradigm. We endow participants with either one unit of a good (e.g., one chocolate, one pen), several units of a good (e.g., nine chocolates, eleven pens), or nothing. Participants are given the opportunity to either sell (or trade) their entire endowment, or keep it. Note that no partial deals were allowed. We then observe a three-fold pattern. First, when participants are given one unit of a good, we replicate the classic endowment effect in both pricing and trading contexts. Second, when participants are given several units of a good, we observe no endowment effect. Third, and finally, an endowment effect occurs whenever participants are presented with a single, well-defined unit, no matter how large or inclusive the unit. For instance, participants given one chocolate show an endowment effect, but so do participants given one box of chocolates. This is so, despite the fact that the box of chocolates we use packs together individual pieces, and that participants given the same number of individual pieces unboxed show no endowment effect.

These results not only suggest a straightforward solution to endowment-effect driven inefficiencies in the market (have marketers and consumers deal in multiple units), they shed light on the process underlying the effect, complementing a great deal of work that identifies factors that may attenuate or prevent the endowment effect.

REFERENCES

Carmon, Ziv, and Dan Ariely (2000), "Focusing on the Forgone: How Value Can Appear So Different to Buyers and Sellers," *Journal of Consumer Research*, 27, 360-370.

Johnson, Eric J., Gerald Häubl, and Anat Keinan (2007), "Aspects of Endowment: A Query Theory of Value Construction," *Journal of Experimental Psychology: Learning, Memory and Cognition*, 33, 461-474.

Kahneman, Daniel, Jack L. Knetsch, and Richard Thaler (1990), "Experimental Tests of the Endowment Effect and the Coase Theorem," *Journal of Political Economy*, 98, 1325-1348.

Tversky, Amos, and Daniel Kahneman (1986), "Rational Choice and the Framing of Decisions," *Journal of Business*, 59, S251-S278.

______ (1981), "The Framing of Decisions and the Psychology of Choice," *Science*, 211, 453-458.

Don't I Owe You? The Discrepancy Between Expected and Experienced Gratitude

Benjamin A. Converse, University of Chicago, USA
Ayelet Fishbach, University of Chicago, USA

EXTENDED ABSTRACT

Philosophers, religious leaders, and parents scolding young children have long extolled the virtues of gratitude. Psychologists point to intrapersonal benefits of gratitude such as improved well-being (Emmons and McCullough 2003) and to interpersonal benefits such as prosocial action and reciprocation (McCullough et al. 2001), and savvy marketing campaigns use rewards or free gifts to induce gratitude, thus generating loyalty and reciprocation (Cialdini 2001).

In this research we ask, when, over the course of a helpful encounter, do beneficiaries feel the strongest gratitude toward their helpers and when do the helpers expect the most gratitude in return? Specifically, we explore whether gratitude increases or decreases after help is provided.

We assume a motivational perspective to address this question. Helpers provide assistance to people in the midst of goal pursuit, and in doing so initiate helping goals of their own. From this perspective, gratitude may serve a functional role: to keep people on track while pursuing goals and to help them disengage from completed goals. The specific dynamics likely depend on one's role in the helping interaction.

We propose that receivers of help (beneficiaries) experience gratitude more strongly toward a person who is currently instrumental (i.e., when the beneficiaries have an active goal for which the other person is a viable means). This suggests that experienced gratitude will be higher before help is provided than after.

This dynamic of experienced gratitude would reflect a functional use of resources from the beneficiary's perspective. Gratitude is an interpersonal cost because it comes with aversive feelings of indebtedness and dependence (Greenberg and Westcott 1983). Recipients are therefore motivated to invest in helpers only as long as they are instrumental to current goals. Our proposal that gratitude fluctuates with goal activation is based on decades of work demonstrating that active goals increase the accessibility and evaluation of goal-related constructs, relative to goal-irrelevant constructs (for reviews, Fishbach and Ferguson 2007; Kruglanski 1996).

In contrast, we propose that helpers will expect more gratitude after providing help than before. For helpers, gratitude is the benefit they receive from pursuing a helping goal. By conditioning expected gratitude on task completion, helpers motivate themselves to continue helping. This analysis thus makes opposite predictions about the effects of goal pursuit on experienced versus expected gratitude. Whereas experienced gratitude should be strongest before help is finished, expected gratitude should be strongest afterwards.

Experiment 1 examined students' gratitude for academic help, using a 2(goal: active vs. completed) x 2(gratitude judgment: experienced vs. expected) mixed design. We approached undergraduates during the last week of the autumn academic term. They reflected on their experience working with a particular student in one of their current classes. We manipulated their perceived role in this instrumental relationship, casting them as beneficiaries by asking about help received, or as helpers by asking about help provided. Beneficiaries indicated experienced gratitude and helpers indicated expected gratitude. They repeated these evaluations at the beginning of the following academic term.

An ANOVA of gratitude ratings yielded the expected goal x judgment interaction. As expected, beneficiaries felt more gratitude in the autumn (for help in a class with a rapidly approaching exam) than in the winter (for help in a class finished last term). Although we predicted that helpers' ratings of expected gratitude would be higher in the winter than in the fall, we found no difference. Nonetheless, the predicted mismatch between experienced and expected gratitude emerged.

Experiment 2 examined gratitude in an economic-exchange game that modeled a business partnership. The experiment used a 2(instrumental: yes vs. no) x 2(gratitude judgment: experienced vs. expected) between-participants design. We endowed one participant, the investor, with $1. He "invested" by sending it to the other player, the dictator, who "produced a return" of $5. The dictator then faced a profit-sharing decision. She could keep as much as she wanted and give the rest. Thus, the dictator was instrumental to the investor's money-making goal. Both participants made gratitude judgments either immediately before the dictator's decision (instrumental condition) or immediately after (but before the decision was revealed; non-instrumental condition).

An ANOVA yielded the expected instrumentality x judgment interaction. Although dictators expected to be appreciated more after their decision than before, investors actually appreciated them more before than after the decision. Consistent with the proposed motivational account, we thus found support for the prediction that people would appreciate another person less right after (rather than before) that person decided to share some money with them.

In experiment 3, pairs of participants worked on an administrative task. We used a 2(goal: active vs. completed) x 2(gratitude judgment: experienced vs. expected) mixed design. A captain (beneficiary) and an assistant (helper) worked toward a monetary performance bonus in a task requiring joint contributions. Captains and assistants first made gratitude judgments during a break in the team task (active goal condition) and then again a few minutes later, after the task (completed goal condition).

An ANOVA revealed the expected goal x judgment interaction. Captains said they owed their assistants more during the administrative task than after. Assistants felt they were owed more after they finished helping than before.

Across three experiments, we find mismatches in expected and experienced gratitude. Beneficiaries felt more gratitude before rather than after help was delivered, but helpers expected more gratitude after rather than before they delivered that help. We believe this is consistent with a motivational account of gratitude whereby beneficiaries invest in their helpers more strongly when they are instrumental to current goals and helpers use expected gratitude as motivation to complete the task.

Marketers should take these goal-based evaluations into account when analyzing consumer feedback on goods and services. Our results suggest, for example, that consumers' purchasing intentions might be higher in response to an awaited-reward than to a delivered-reward. We believe these results also have important implications for potential conflict in social interactions. Without understanding the divergent role of motivation in "I owe you" versus "you owe me," people may exhibit inopportune timing when asking for favors or counting on grateful good-will.

REFERENCES

Cialdini, Robert B. (2001), *Influence: Science and Practice* (4th edition), Boston: Allyn & Bacon.

Emmons, Robert A. and Michael E. McCullough (2003), "Counting Blessings Versus Burdens: An Experimental Investigation of Gratitude and Subjective Well-Being in Daily Life," *Journal of Personality and Social Psychology*, 84 (2), 377-89.

Fishbach, Ayelet and Melissa J. Ferguson (2007), "The Goal Construct in Social Psychology," in *Social Psychology: Handbook of Basic Principles*, ed. Arie W. Kruglanski and E. Tory Higgins, New York: Guildford, 281-94.

Kruglanski, Arie W. (1996), "Goals as Knowledge Structures," in *The Psychology of Action: Linking Cognition and Motivation to Behavior*, ed. Peter M. Gollwitzer and John A. Bargh, New York: Guilford, 599-618.

Martin S. Greenberg and David R. Westcott (1983), "Indebtedness as a Mediator of Reactions to Aid," in *New Directions in Helping*, Vol 1: Recipient Reactions to Aid, ed. Jeffrey D. Fisher, Arie Nadler, and Bella DePaulo, New York: Academic Press, 85-112.

McCullough, Michael E., Shelley D. Kilpatrick, Robert A. Emmons, and David B. Larson (2001), "Is Gratitude a Moral Affect?" *Psychological Bulletin*, 127 (2), 249-66.

Measurement of Emotions Elicited by Advertising

Andrea Groeppel-Klein, Saarland University, Germany
Oliver Hupp, GfK, Germany
Philipp Broeckelmann, Saarland University, Germany
Anja Dieckmann, GfK, Germany

EXTENDED ABSTRACT

Emotional experiences shape people's attitudes towards brands and products (Bagozzi et al., 1999) and also emotions elicited by advertising affect the advertising's success (Keller, 2008a, 2008b; McEwen, 2004; Percy & Rossiter, 2001). Thus, it is highly important to gain insights into consumers' emotional reactions to advertising and to measure them in a valid way. Until now, there has been no uniform, broadly accepted definition of emotions. Rather, most current definitions are confined to a list of characteristics (Scherer, 2005; Plutchik, 1991), according to which emotions are complex reactions to events that are relevant to a person's subjective wellbeing. They involve changes in physiology, behaviour (including facial expressions), and subjective experience. Emotions depend on the conscious or unconscious appraisal of the triggering event and are associated with certain behavioural responses, which are partly formed by evolution. They can be distinguished from other affective phenomena by their relatively fast onset, short duration and high intensity.

Basically, one can distinguish two different traditions in emotion theories: Appraisal theorists propose that emotions result from the comparison between a desirable or undesirable goal and the degree of goal attainment. Lazarus (e.g., 1982) considers cognitive activity a necessary precondition for emotions. According to his theory, emotional experience requires the understanding that an event can have positive or negative consequences for subjective wellbeing (Bagozzi, Baumgartner & Pieters, 1998). Also, people can anticipate and revive emotions by pure mental activity, which in turn can lead to physical reactions (Pham, 1998). According to biologically oriented emotion theorists, emotions are genetically programmed (e.g., Zajonc, 1980). They can be triggered automatically and without higher cognitive processing by innate or learned stimuli, even before one becomes conscious of these stimuli (e.g., LeDoux, 1996). With the help of modern brain-imaging technologies, neuroscientists have in recent years done impressive work in shedding light upon such automatic emotional processes. A series of studies now demonstrates that emotions can bias decisions in a certain direction before any conscious thought process occurs (Bechara et al., 2005; Damasio, 1996). Today, most current emotion researchers regard both theoretical accounts as legitimate. Emotions can occur automatically and unconsciously, facilitating fast reactions (e.g., "freezing", LeDoux, 1996). But they can also result from conscious assessments in cortical areas.

If emotions can be both, biologically pre-wired and arising from higher cognitive activity, their measurement in marketing and advertising effectiveness research becomes even more challenging (Scherer, 2005). Can emotions simply be captured by self-report or standardized verbal scales? Biologically oriented emotion researchers often apply neuroscientific methods to measure physiological indicators of emotions such as heart rate, electrodermal reaction, or regional brain responses. Observational methods for capturing emotional facial expressions are also popular, such as the Facial Action Coding System (FACS; Ekman & Friesen, 1975). These approaches have obvious advantages. They are highly objective and can capture emotions while they are occurring. But there are also disadvantages, especially when it comes to their application in marketing. For instance, not all emotions have a unique physiological or mimic pattern. Especially secondary emotions can hardly be deduced in an unambiguous way. Additionally, application of these methods requires much time, effort and high levels of expertise, making them almost impracticable for large sample research.

Appraisal theorists mainly concentrate on capturing the conscious emotional experience by verbal methods, such as thinking-aloud techniques or questionnaires. Indeed, self-reports provide the only access to the subjective experience level of emotions, despite all the progress in the neurosciences. The variety of more complex secondary emotions cannot be revealed in any other way. Additionally, questionnaires are easy to apply and cost-effective, both in data-collection and in analysis (e.g. Pleasure/Arousal/Dominance-Scale (PAD) by Russell and Mehrabian (1977), Differential Emotional Scale (DES) by Izard (1977), Emotions Profile Index (EPI) by Plutchik (2003), Consumption Emotion Set (CES) by Richins (1997) or Watson and Tellegen's (1985) Two-Factor Structure of Affect). But they can lead to problems as well. Verbal methods are often criticised for inducing rationalizations in respondents and preventing intuitive responses. This raises serious concerns: Do respondents have sufficient insight into their emotions to be able to answer questions truthfully? Does the interview situation induce cognitive filtering of emotional experiences, thereby increasing the tendency to give socially desirable answers? Which unconscious or automatic components of the emotional reactions are missed by verbal measurement approaches?

Picture-based approaches (e.g. Desmet's (2003) PrEmo-Scale), unlike purely verbal questionnaires, are expected to facilitate intuitive access to emotions that are difficult to verbalize or which respondents are reluctant to talk about. At the same time, picture-based scales can give a fresh impetus to the interview and increase interest, motivation, and, ultimately, response rates. However, selection and validation of the pictures for such scales requires special care. It is very difficult to find truly unambiguous pictures that represent the same emotion for most people, especially if the scale is to be extended beyond the basic emotions. For instance, misinterpretations can result when the depicted emotional scene is not taken as metaphor for an emotion.

The number of emotions whose marketing relevance has been demonstrated in numerous studies extends far beyond the basic emotions (Bagozzi, Gopinath & Nyer, 1999). As mentioned above, both verbal and picture-based methodologies have pros and cons. The final decision for one approach–verbal or pictorial or a combination of both formats–will thus be based on an empirical comparison. To allow for a fair comparison, special attention needs to be paid to the selection of appropriate, unambiguous pictures. The development of the scale for capturing emotions can therefore be divided into different steps (identification of emotions, search for pictures and validation of pictures). This article summarizes the development of a picture-based scale and its validation in different steps. Finally, different scale variants (verbal, pictorial, and combinations of them) are used to capture emotional responses to TV ads and then evaluated on different performance criteria (scale validity, scale handling, ease of use, enjoyment of the survey and expert judgments). To sum up, the scale formats with "pictures/collages + labels" outperform the purely pictorial formats (pictures, collages) and "word only" on almost all comparison criteria. Assignments that are solely due to similar motifs of pictures and TV-ads can thus be avoided. The comparison between the two labeled pictorial formats and the purely verbal format reveals several advantages of presenting a picture in addition to a verbal label. Labeled pictures lead to more pronounced differentiation across both emotions and TV spots. Socially desirable answers can be reduced, as indicated by higher selection rates for the negative emotions that a spot is expected to elicit in terms of the expert judgments. In general, labeled pictures produce higher levels of agreement with expert judgments and the scale handling gets better ratings compared to the other formats. Regarding the comparison between labeled single pictures and labeled collages no conclusive recommendation can be derived. In conclusion, we recommend using our labeled picture-scale for testing TV-ads for their emotional content.

REFERENCES

Bagozzi, R.P., Baumgartner, H. & Pieters, R. (1998). *Goal-Directed Emotions. Cognition and Emotion*, 12 (1), 1-26.

Bagozzi, R.P., Gopinath, M. & Nyer, P.U. (1999). The Role of Emotions in Marketing. Journal of the Academy of Marketing *Science*, 27 (2), 184-206.

Bechara, A., Damasio, H., Tranel, D. & Damasio, A.R. (2005). The Iowa Gambling Task and the Somatic Marker Hypothesis: Some Questions and Answers. *Trends in Cognitive Sciences*, 9 (4), 159-62.

Damasio, A.R. (1996). The Somatic Marker Hypothesis and the Possible Functions of the Prefrontal Cortex. *Philosophical Transactions of the Royal Society of London–Series B*, 351, 1413-1420.

Desmet, P. (2003). Measuring Emotions. Development and Application of an Instrument to Measure Emotional Responses to Products. In: M.A. Blythe, A.F. Monk, K. Overbeeke, & P.C. Wright (Eds.), *Funology: From Usability to Enjoyment*, 111-123.

Ekman, P. & Friesen, W.V. (1975). *Unmasking the Face: A Guide to Recognizing Emotions from Facial Clues*, Englewood Cliffs, NJ.

Izard, C.E. (1977). *Human Emotions*, New York.

Lazarus, R.S. (1982). Thoughts on the Relations between Emotion and Cognition. *American Psychologist*, 37 (9), 1019-1024.

LeDoux, J.E. (1996). *The Emotional Brain*, New York.

McEwen, W.J. (2004). Getting Emotional about Brands. *Gallup Management Journal Online*, 9.9.2004, 1-4.

Percy, L. & Rossiter, J.R. (2001). *Strategic Advertising Management*, Oxford.

Pham, M.T. (1998). Representativeness, Relevance, and the Use of Feelings in Decision Making. *Journal of Consumer Research*, 25 (2), 144-159.

Plutchik, R. (1991). *The Emotions*, Lanham, MD.

Plutchik, R.E. (2003). *Emotions and Life–Perspectives from Psychology, Biology and Evolution*, Washington, D.C.

Richins, M.L. (1997). Measuring Emotions in the Consumption Experience. *Journal of Consumer Research*, 24 (2), 127-146.

Russell, J.A. & Mehrabian, A. (1977). Evidence for a Three-Factor Theory of Emotions. *Journal of Research in Personality*, 11, 273-294.

Scherer, K.R. (2005). What are Emotions? And How Can They Be Measured? *Social Science Information*, 44, 693-727.

Watson, D. & Tellegen, A. (1985). Toward a Consensual Structure of Mood. *Psychological Bulletin*, 98 (2), 219-235.

Zajonc, R.B. (1980). Feeling and Thinking. Preferences Need No Inferences. *American Psychologist*, 35 (2), 151-175.

(When) Does Choice Overload Occur? A Meta-Analysis

Benjamin Scheibehenne, Indiana University, USA
Rainer Greifeneder, University of Mannheim, Germany
Peter M. Todd, Indiana University, USA

EXTENDED ABSTRACT

In today's market democracies, people face an ever-increasing number of options to choose from. While individuals may often be attracted by this variety, some scholars argue that an overabundance of choice might eventually lead to a decrease in the motivation to choose and/ or in a decrease of satisfaction with the finally chosen option. The possibility of a negative effect of large assortment sizes has important practical and theoretical implications. From a theoretical perspective, it challenges most choice models in marketing, psychology, and economics according to which expanding a choice set cannot make decision makers worse off, and it violates the regularity axiom, a cornerstone of classical choice theory (Savage 1954; Benartzi and Thaler 2001; Rieskamp, Busemeyer, and Mellers 2006). From an applied perspective, marketers and public policy makers would need to re-think their practice of providing ever-increasing assortments to choose from, since they could possibly boost their success by offering less variety.

Given these implications, it is important to learn how robust choice overload is, and to what extent it occurs in different situations. Therefore, in this paper we aim to thoroughly re-examine the too-much-choice effect by means of a meta-analysis across all experiments that we are aware of that investigated the influence of number of options on choice and satisfaction.

Data for the meta-analysis was collected via an extensive literature search, personal communication with scholars in the field, and a call for relevant studies (published or unpublished) that went out to several internet newsgroups covering the areas of consumer behavior, marketing, decision making, and social psychology. The meta-analytical integration of different studies requires that designs and research questions are comparable. Therefore, we only included data from randomized experiments in which participants were given a real or a hypothetical choice from an assortment of options, with the number of options being subject to experimental manipulation in a between- or a within-subject design. The dependent variable was either a continuous measure of self-reported satisfaction based on a Likert scale (usually requiring a forced-choice paradigm), or a measure of propensity to make an active choice. To enable meta-analytical integration across the dataset, we transformed the difference in the dependent variable between the small and the large assortment of each experiment into a Cohen's *d* effect size measure that expresses the difference between the experimental conditions in terms of the pooled standard deviations (Cohen 1977).

The total dataset consisted of 50 experiments, 26 of which stem from 12 published or in-press journal articles, 11 from 3 Master's or PhD theses, and 13 from 8 conference contributions or unpublished working papers which were made available by their respective authors. The dataset embraces a total of 5,036 participants. We integrated the results of all experiments by calculating a random effects model in which the effect sizes for each study are assumed to be randomly distributed around a grand mean effect size *D*.

The mean effect of size of choice overload across all 50 experiments was D=0 (CI_{95} -0.13 to 0.13). The between-study variance equaled τ^2= 0.14 (CI_{95} 0.089 to 0.317). The I^2 statistic that quantifies the proportion of variance due to non-random heterogeneity equaled 71% which indicates high heterogeneity. When the dataset was trimmed by 20% by excluding the 5 studies with the highest effect sizes and the 5 studies with the lowest, the mean effect size was unaffected ($D_{trimmed=}$-.02) but the unexplained variance fell to I^2=28%. This indicates that most of the heterogeneity in the dataset is due to a few studies reporting large effect sizes.

To further explore how much of the variance can be explained by potential moderator variables, we extended the random effects model by a meta-regression in which the mean effect size D is predicted by a linear combination of a set of predictor variables. This analysis showed that a "more choice is better" effect is to be expected for studies that use consumption quantity as a dependent measure. Also, published articles are somewhat more likely to report an effect of choice overload as compared to unpublished manuscripts, which indicates a slight publication bias in favor of "positive" results. The degree of choice overload apparently does not depend on whether the dependent variable is satisfaction or choice. The data further indicates no difference in choice overload whether the choice task in the experiment is hypothetical or real. Likewise, there seems to be no difference between experiments conducted in Europe and the US, which questions cultural differences as an explanation for the effect, at least on this broad level. Within the tested range, the effect also does not depend on the difference in size between the small set and the large set. Likewise, we found no curvilinear relationship between assortment size and choice overload. With all moderators included, the unexplained variance drops to I^2=60%, indicating that the identified moderators still leave some variance unexplained.

Together, our results indicate that the negative effect of choice overload is not as robust or widespread as previously thought. Still, our findings do not rule out the possibility that the too-much-choice effect can be reliably elicited with the presence of particular moderator variables, and a growing number of studies aim to identify such moderators. Towards this goal, it is essential to develop a more theory-driven understanding of the too-much-choice effect based on the interaction between the structure of assortments–beyond the mere number of options available–and the decision processes that people adopt.

REFERENCES

Savage, L. J. (1954). *The foundations of statistics*. New York: Wiley.

Benartzi, S., and Thaler, R. H. (2001). Naïve diversification strategies in defined contribution saving plans. *The American Economic Review*, 91, 79-98.

Rieskamp, J., Busemeyer, J. R., and Mellers, B. A. (2006). Extending the Bounds of Rationality: Evidence and Theories of Preferential Choice. *Journal of Economic Literature*, 44, 631-661.

Cohen, J. (1977). *Statistical power analysis for the behavioral sciences*. Hillsdale, NJ: Lawrence Erlbaum Associates.

Impact of Missed Opportunities on Subsequent Action Opportunities: A Functional Counterfactual Perspective

Partha Krishnamurthy, University of Houston at Texas, USA
Demetra Andrews, University of Houston, USA
Anu Sivaraman, University of Delaware, USA

ABSTRACT

According to the inaction inertia literature, the discrepancy between the missed and current opportunity induces counterfactual thinking which produces regret. As the attractiveness of the missed opportunity increases, the level of regret increases, thus reducing the likelihood of accepting the inferior opportunity. In this research we argue that this conclusion may be misleading because counterfactual thinking not only induces regret, it also helps prepare for future behavior. This suggests that as the attractiveness of the missed opportunity increases, the impetus to change course increases resulting in action rather than continued inaction. In two studies, we find that inaction leads to hyper-action when the decision-makers' past choices are facilitative of corrective functional counterfactuals.

Moderating Role of Parental Responsiveness in the Impact of Psychological Control on Youth Smoking: A Longitudinal Perspective

Zhiyong Yang, University of Texas at Arlington, USA
Charles M. Schaninger, University at Albany, USA

EXTENDED ABSTRACT

In public policy and marketing research, two parenting strategies—namely parental responsiveness and behavioral control—have long been regarded as two important inhibitors of consumer misbehavior among children and adolescents, such as credit card abuse (Palmer, Pinto, and Parente 2001), and risky sexual behavior (Tanner et al. 2008). Similarly, in the psychology and public health literatures, parental responsiveness and behavioral control are viewed as two important predictors of undesirable adolescent behaviors such as smoking cigarettes (Simons-Morton 2002; Tucker et al. 2003). These studies have yielded intriguing findings, but the impact of another key parenting strategy—psychological control—on child smoking initiation or progression is largely ignored. In addition, most studies on parenting-smoking linkages have mainly focused on the direct effect of parenting strategies on child smoking, ignoring their indirect effect through self-esteem. Exploring the role of self-esteem as the underlying mechanism through which parenting strategies affect child smoking may yield important new counter-marketing insights on how changing parenting strategies might be useful in avoiding or curbing youthful tobacco use.

This research intends to fill the gaps in the literature by developing an integrative model specifying that psychological control, and its interactions with parental responsiveness and behavioral control, drives self-esteem trajectories, which in turn drive smoking trajectories (initial level and slope). Self-esteem is the key focal mechanism because it is the single most important indicator of an individual's social well-being. Kaplan's (1982) self-derogation theory holds that adolescents low in self-esteem defend their egos by alienating themselves from conventional role models and rebelling against their standards. This leads to involvement with deviant peers and engaging in such delinquent behaviors as smoking, drinking, or taking illegal drugs. Because child self-esteem is influenced by extended interaction with parents (Hoelter and Harper 1987), we argue that psychological control influences child smoking development both directly and indirectly via influencing the changing pattern of child self-esteem.

We develop a series of latent growth modeling (LGM) analyses to examine the interactive impact of psychological control and other parenting strategies on self-esteem and smoking trajectories, using longitudinal data from ages 10 to 17. This coincides with transition to high school, puberty, and the development of an independent mature self-identity and ego. During this significant developmental period, self-esteem deteriorates over time and clearly has a negative slope (Blyth, Simmons and Carlton-Ford 1983; Simmons, Carlton-Ford, and Blyth 1987) through at least age 15. Correspondingly, smoking demonstrates a parallel but positive progression in frequency (Audrain-McGovern et al. 2004; Mayhew, Flay and Mott 2000).

To our knowledge, this research represents the first effort to examine the extent to which children's smoking initiation and progression is influenced by psychological control, or the extent to which the impact of psychological control is moderated by the other two parenting factors. In addition, we are among the first to examine trajectory-to-trajectory influences of self-esteem on smoking, and show that the indirect effects of parenting, through self-esteem, are stronger and more insightful than the direct effects. From a public policy perspective, our findings suggest ways to improve the effectiveness of parent-oriented anti-smoking campaigns. Recent campaigns such as Tobacco Free Kids have recognized the importance of parenting by educating parents about conduct that is most likely to curtail teen smoking. Our findings suggest that the existing parent oriented anti-smoking campaigns have one major shortcoming. These campaigns have mainly focused on two parenting strategies—namely parental responsiveness and behavioral control—by emphasizing the importance of parental monitoring and open communication and problem solving discussions between parents and teenagers. In contrast, based on our findings, educating parents about the harmful effects of psychological control is even more important because psychologically controlling parenting can directly increase children's adoption of smoking and indirectly increase their adoption and progression of smoking through influencing their self-esteem.

REFERENCES

Audrain-McGovern, Janet, Daniel Rodriguez, Kenneth P. Tercyak, Jocelyn Cuevas, Kelli Rodgers, and Freda Patterson (2004), "Identifying and Characterizing Adolescent Smoking Trajectories," *Cancer Epidemiology, Biomarkers, and Prevention*, 13 (December), 2023-2034.

Blyth, Dale A., Roberta G. Simmons, and Steven Carlton-Ford (1983), "The Adjustment of Early Adolescents to School Transitions," *The Journal of Early Adolescence*, 3 (Spring), 105-120.

Kaplan, Howard B. (1982), "Self-Attitudes and Deviant Behavior: New Directions for Theory and Research," *Youth & Society*, 14 (December),185-211.

Mayhew, Kathryn P., Brian R. Flay, and Joshua A. Mott (2000), "Stages in the Development of Adolescent Smoking," *Drug and Alcohol Dependency*, 59 (May), 561-81.

Palmer, Todd Starr, Mary Beth Pinto, Diane H. Parente (2001), "College Students' Credit Card Debt and the Role of Parental Involvement: Implications for Public Policy," *Journal of Public Policy & Marketing*, 20 (1), 105-113.

Simmons, Richard Burgeson, Steven Carlton-Ford, and Dale A. Blyth (1987), "The Impact of Cumulative Change in Early Adolescence," Child Development, *Special Issue on Schools and Development*, 58 (October), 1220-1234.

Simons-Morton, Bruce G. (2002), "Prospective Analysis of Peer and Parent Influences on Smoking Initiation among Early Adolescents," Prevention Science, 3, 275–283.

Tanner, John F., Les A. Carlson, Mary Anne Raymond; Christopher D. Hopkins (2008), "Reaching Parents to Prevent Adolescent Risky Behavior: Examining the Effects of Threat Portrayal and Parenting Orientation on Parental Participation Perceptions," *Journal of Public Policy & Marketing*, 27 (2), 149-155.

Tucker, Joan S., Phyllis L. Ellickson, and David J. Klein (2003), "Predictors of the Transition to Regular Smoking during Adolescence and Young Adulthood," *Journal of Adolescent Health*, 32, 314–324.

Dealing with Anxiety: How Effective Health Messages Undermine Self-Control

Nidhi Agrawal, Northwestern University, USA
Echo Wen Wan, University of Hong Kong, Hong Kong, China

EXTENDED ABSTRACT

Health messages often attract consumers' attention by highlighting the high risk of their contracting a disease. Past research in marketing and health psychology has found that communicating health risk perceptions of a disease increases awareness and interest in that disease, and encourages preventative and healthy behaviors (Raghubir and Menon 1998; Raghunathan and Trope 2002). However, other research has also found that creating high perceptions of vulnerability to a disease might have negative repercussions such as leading consumers to avoid processing the health message or to counter-argue it (Block and Williams 2002; Keller, Lipkus, and Rimer 2003). The existing literature, however, has mainly focused on examining the effect of health risk perception about one disease (e.g., hepatitis) on behaviors related to this disease (e.g., getting tested for hepatitis virus). In this paper we go beyond previous research and examine the impact of processing high-risk health message on self-control behavior in general.

Recent research on health communication has suggested that the negative repercussion of processing high-risk health messages might be related to individuals' emotional deterioration in such contexts (Agrawal, Menon, and Aaker 2007; Raghunathan and Trope 2002). Reading messages describing symptoms and severe disease consequences will make individuals feel disturbed and uncomfortable (Agrawal et al. 2007). Moreover, the perception of high self-risk will challenge individuals' unrealistic optimism regarding their health (Menon and Raghubir 1998; Taylor et al. 2000), which will induce the feeling of uncertainty. Negative emotions with an uncertainty component are typically associated with anxiety (Tiedens and Linton 2001). Kahn and Luce (2003) found that participants who received false positive test results (perceiving at high risk) in the context of breast cancer, as compared with participants who did not receive such a false alarm, felt more stressful and consequently had lower intentions to comply with testing procedures.

Literature on emotion specificity and emotion regulation has suggested that coping with anxiety may consume self-regulation resources–resources involved in the deliberate regulation of responses (Muraven and Baumeister 2000). Anxiety signals to individuals that the situation is uncertain, which will make them feel lack of confidence about the situation and therefore prompt them to engage in effortful cognitive processes to change the state (Pelham and Wachsmuth 1995; Tiedens and Linton 2001). Previous studies have provided evidences that coping with anxiety requires regulatory resources. For example, Richeson and Trawalter (2005) argued that interacting with people of different race will cause anxiety that makes such interactions depleting in regulatory resources. Supporting this view, they found that 1) interracial interaction (vs. same-race interaction) led to poorer performance on Stroop task-an inhibitory task requires regulatory resources (Gailliot et al. 2007); and 2) the negative impact of interracial interaction on the Stroop performance was eliminated when participants' needs to regulate anxiety in their interracial interaction were reduced.

Research on regulatory depletion posits that self-regulation resources are limited in amount, and predicts a *depletion effect*: using regulatory resources in one task reduces the amount of resource available and thus will undermine performance on an immediate subsequent self-regulation task (Muraven and Baumeister 2000). Depletion effects have been documented to affect a wide range of consumer behaviors involving self-regulation such as impulse purchase (Vohs and Faber 2007) and alcohol drinking (Muraven, Collins, and Nienhaus 2002).

By integrating research on health risk, emotion regulation, and regulatory depletion, we propose that processing high-risk health messages consumes self-regulatory resources and will impair subsequent self-control, whether such self-control is concerned with health or behaviors in general domains. Moreover, this detrimental effect on self-control occurs because of a depletion of resources in coping with anxiety resulting from high self-risk perceptions.

One laboratory experiment and two field studies examine the predicted effect, the underlying mechanism, and the boundary condition. In all studies the first task manipulates self-risk perception in health messages and the second task assessed subsequent self-control.

In Study 1 participants first read a message communicating a perception of being at high or low risk of getting Hepatitis C, a health risk manipulation adapted from past research (Menon, Block, and Ramanathan 2002). Next, participants were provided the opportunity to eat chocolate chip cookies. We found that participants who read the high-risk message ate more cookies than those who read the low-risk message.

Study 2 replicates the finding of Study 1 in a field study where participants firstly viewed advertisements about the consequence of second-hand smoking and then were provided the opportunity to eat cheese sticks. We found that second-hand smokers, perceived at higher self-risks of getting smoking-related diseases, ate more cheese sticks than non second-hand smokers. Moreover, we demonstrated that this effect was mediated by participants' anxiety after viewing the second-hand smoking ads.

Finally, Study 3 identifies the boundary condition for when anxiety from processing health risks has helpful versus harmful effects. We proposed that when individuals take a cognitive perspective to reduce the uncertainty, they will be more likely to engage in health practice because doing so will help them diminish their uncertainty about their health conditions. A typical context where individuals are likely to take a cognitive stance is when the subsequent behavior is obviously related to the focal disease causing the risk perception and anxiety. Supporting this view, Study 3 shows that participants who perceived at high (vs. low) self-risk of contracting Avian flu had greater intention to get tested for the avian flu virus but lower intention to do a check-up in a different health domain-dental health. Anxiety mediated the disease relevance x health risk interaction.

Our research enriches literature on health communication by documenting an unknown repercussion of using high-risk messages–processing high-risk messages impair performances on general self-control beyond health behavior related to the focal risky disease. It also adds to the literature on emotion and self-regulation by showing that coping with a specific emotion–anxiety involves depletion of regulatory resources and that taking a cognitive stance of coping with anxiety will overcome the depletion effect. Our findings also provide implication for marketing practice of health information communication.

REFERENCES

Agrawal, Nidhi, Geeta Menon, and Jennifer L. Aaker (2007), "Getting Emotional about Health," *Journal of Marketing Research*, 44 (February), 100-13.

Baron, Reuben. M. and David A. Kenny (1986), "The Moderator-Mediator Variable Distinction in Social Psychological Research: Conceptual, Strategic, and Statistical Considerations," *Journal of Personality and Social Psychology*, 51 (December), 1173-182.

Baumeister, Roy F., Ellen Bratslavsky, Mark Muraven, and Dianne M. Tice (1998), "Ego Depletion: Is the Active Self a Limited Resource?" *Journal of Personality and Social Psychology,* 74 (5), 1252-265.

Baumeister, Roy F., Todd F. Heatherton, and Dianne. M. Tice (1994), *Losing control: How and why people fail at self-regulation.* San Diego: Academic Press, Inc.

Becker, Marshall H. (1974), "The Health Belief Model and Personal Health Behavior," *Health Education Monographs,* 2 (4), 409-19.

Block, Lauren G. and Patti Williams (2002), "Undoing the Effects of Seizing and Freezing: Decreasing Defensive Processing of Personally Relevant Messages," *Journal of Applied Social Psychology*, 32 (4), 803-33.

Chaiken, Shelly and Durairaj Maheswaran (1994), "Heuristic Processing can Bias Systematic Processing: The Effects of Task Importance, Argument Ambiguity and Source Credibility on Persuasion," *Journal of Personality and Social Psychology*, 66 (March), 460-73.

Gailliot, Matthew T., Brandon J. Schmeichel, and Roy F. Baumeister (2006), "Self-Regulatory Processes Defend Against the Threat of Death: Effects of Self-Control Depletion and Trait Self-Control on Thoughts and Fears of Dying," *Journal of Personality and Social Psychology*, 91 (1), 49-62.

Gross, James J. (1998), "Antecedent- and Response-Focused Emotion Regulation: Divergent Consequences for Experience, Expression, and Physiology," *Journal of Personality and Social Psychology*, 74 (1), 224-37.

Kahn, Barbara E. and Mary Frances Luce (2003), "Understanding High-Stakes Consumer Decisions: Mammography Adherence Following False Alarm Test Results," *Marketing Science*, 22 (3), 393-410.

Keller, Punam Anand, Isaac M. Lipkus, and Barbara K. Rimer (2003), "Affect, Framing, and Persuasion," *Journal of Marketing Research*, 40 (February), 54-65.

Menon, Geeta, Lauren G. Block, and Suresh Ramanathan (2002), "We're At as Much Risk as We're Led to Believe: Effects of Message Cues on Judgments of Health Risk," *Journal of Consumer Research*, 28 (March), 533-49.

Muraven, Mark and Roy F. Baumeister (2000), "Self-Regulation and Depletion of Limited Resources: Does Self-Control Resemble a Muscle?" *Psychological Bulletin*, 126 (March), 247-59.

Muraven, Mark, R. Lorraine Collins and Kristen Nienhaus (2002), "Self-control and Alcohol Restraint: A Test of the Self-control Strength Model," *Psychology of Addictive Behaviors,* 16 (2), 113-20.

Pelham Brett W. and Jeff Orson Wachsmuth (1995), "The waxing and waning of the social self: assimilation and contrast in social comparison," *Journal of Personality and Social Psychology,* 69 (5), 825-38.

Raghubir, Priya and Geeta Menon (1998), "AIDS and Me, Never the Twain Shall Meet: The Effects of Information Accessibility on Judgments of Risk and Advertising Effectiveness," *Journal of Consumer Research*, 25 (June), 52-63.

Raghunathan, Rajagopal and Yaacov Trope (2002), "Walking the Tightrope Between Feeling Good and Being Accurate: Mood as a Resource in Processing Persuasive Messages," *Journal of Personality and Social Psychology*, 83 (September), 510-25.

Richeson Jennifer A. and Spphie Trawalter (2005), "Why Do Interracial Interactions Impair Executive Function? A Resource Depletion Account," *Journal of Personality and Social Psychology,* 88 (6), 934–47.

Taylor, Shelley E., Margaret E. Kemeny, Julienne E. Bower, Tara L. Gruenewald, and Geoffrey M. Reed (2000), "Psychological Resources, Positive Illusions, and Health," *American Psychologist*, 55 (January), 99-109.

Vohs, Kathleen D. and Ronald J. Faber (2007), "Spent Resources: Self-Regulatory Resource Availability Affects Impulse Buying," *Journal of Consumer Research*, 33 (March), 537-47.

Vohs, Kathleen D, Roy F. Baumeister, Brandon J. Schmeichel, Jean M. Twenge, Noelle M, Nelson, and Dianne M. Tice (2008), "Making Choices Impairs Subsequent Self-control: A Limited-Resource Account of Decision Making, Self-regulation, and Active Initiative," *Journal of Personality and Social Psychology*, 94 (5), 883–98.

Weinstein, Neil D. (1980), "Unrealistic Optimism about Future Life Events," *Journal of Personality and Social Psychology*, 39 (October), 806–20.

Time-Inconsistent Preferences vs. Price Discrimination: How do Firms Increase Profits via Mail-in Rebate Promotions?

Beom Joon Choi, California State University, Sacramento, USA
Joseph Kissan, University of Kansas, USA
James Lemieux, University of Kansas, USA

EXTENDED ABSTRACT

Mail-in rebates are widely believed to be employed as a marketing tool because they motivate purchase, yet result in consumers failing to redeem the rebate offer (Bulkeley 1998). By some estimates, nearly 40 percent of all rebates never get redeemed because of such "breakage" (Grow 2005). Two streams of literature offer an explanation for this phenomenon. The first literature stream implies that consumer valuation of the costs and benefits of rebates changes over the time between purchase and redemption. Accordingly, a rebate that may initially appear worthwhile is perceived to be excessively costly to redeem after the purchase. Such time-inconsistent preferences are exemplified by several theories including: hyperbolic discounting (cf. O'Donoghue and Rabin 1999; Hoch and Loewenstein 1991; Soman 1998), time-construal theory (Trope and Liberman 2003), resource slack theory (Zauberman and Lynch 2005), procrastination (Silk 2005) and future optimism (Mowen and Mowen 1991). In contrast, the second literature stream implies that consumers self-select into groups characterized by their intention to redeem. Hence, rebates act as a price discrimination tool that attracts certain types of people who intend to redeem, but yet ensure that those who have no intention to redeem pay full price (Chen, Moorthy, and Zhang 2005; Lu and Moorth 2007). Thus, the appearance of 'breakage' may simply reflect the group of high-valuation consumers who never intended to redeem in the first place.

In light of these two explanations for breakage, the efficacy of time-inconsistent preferences and price discrimination to explain rebate profitability is tested using an actual rebate program with university students. In the experimental setting, subjects were given the choice of obtaining an immediate cash reward or the possibility of a greater cash reward upon completion of rebate offer. This is analogous to the situation where consumers choose between two products in the market place: one with a low price and another with a higher initial price but with a lower final price obtained via a mail-in rebate offer.

Since the greater cash reward was contingent upon completing the redemption requirements in the future, this choice represents the same type of forward decision making required in an actual rebate program. Since no accompanying product was offered for sale, this study design focuses exclusively on the rebate decision process.

A pretest determined the amount of cash reward and rebate effort that yielded a statistically significant number of redeemers. In the main experiment, the cash reward and rebate effort were manipulated at levels close to those used in the pre-test to ensure similar response rates. A follow-up questionnaire was conducted to measure subjects' individual characteristics relevant to the study. In addition, rebate profitability was assessed by testing whether the observed redemption rate significantly exceeded the requisite 'threshold' for profitability. Finally, for those who accepted the rebate offer, an additional rebate offer was made to assess whether the subjects "learned" from their previous redemption experience.

This manuscript experimentally demonstrates that although both time-inconsistent preferences and the price discrimination mechanisms are present in a rebate program, the conditions which increase the occurrence of time-inconsistent preferences decreases the size of the intended redeemer segment and thereby limits rebate profits. In addition, the ability of sellers to profit via this route is further limited to the extent that consumers have many opportunities to learn about their rebating propensity across many product categories (Hoch and Deighton 1989). In the follow-up study of those who participated in the experiment, subjects who had accepted the rebate offer were given the opportunity to make an additional choice between accepting an immediate cash reward and the possibility of greater reward in the future through a second rebate offer. In comparing the choice of the subsequent rebate offer between subjects who redeemed the first offer and those who did not redeem the first offer, it was found that prior success with rebates significantly increased the likelihood of choosing the subsequent rebate offer. Specifically, nearly 82% of those who had redeemed the first offer choose to accept the second rebate offer. In comparison, only 15% percent of those who failed at rebate redemption chose to accept the second rebate offer. This suggests that the subjects had learned substantially from their prior (failed) experiences in accepting a rebate. This finding further supports the main results that marketers are limited in their long-term ability to take advantage of time-inconsistent preferences to improve rebate profitability.

This study also finds substantial evidence for the premise that rebates serve as a price discrimination mechanism. Specifically, the construct of rebate involvement had a significant impact on rebate choice even after controlling for face value and redemption effort. Moreover, this trait is positively correlated with price consciousness and deal proneness, thereby providing evidence for the basic preference structure implicit in the price discrimination mechanism. The results here suggest that marketers may wish to employ rebates in markets characterized by heterogeneity in price elasticity. Furthermore, it may be premature to invoke regulation to curb the use of rebates if rebates simply act as another price discrimination tool.

The current experimental design did not allow us to consider the case where the rebate offers bring new low valuation customers into the market. If these customers are induced to purchase a product in the expectation of receiving rebates but fail to redeem, rebate profitability may indeed increase. However, given the situation where the low-valuation customers typically tend to claim rebates, the incremental sales may not guarantee higher profits. Nonetheless, we admit this is one of the limitations of the present study and leave this issue to future research.

REFERENCES

Bulkeley, Williams M. (1998), "Rebates' secret appeal to manufacturers: Few consumers actually redeem them," *Wall Street Journal*, (February 10) B1.

Chen, Yuxin, Sridhar Moorthy, and Z. John Zhang (2005), "Research note—price discrimination after the purchase: rebates as state-dependent discounts," *Management Science*, 51 (7), 1131(10).

Grow, Brian (2005), "The Great Rebate Runaround," *Business Week*.

Hoch, Stephen J. and John Deighton (1989), "Managing What Consumers Learn from Experience," *Journal of Marketing*, 53 (April), 1-20.

______ and George F. Loewenstein (1991), "Time-Inconsistent Preferences and Consumer Self-Control," *Journal of Consumer Research,* 17 (4), 492-507.

Lu, Qiang and Sridhar Moorthy(2007), "Coupons versus Rebates," *Marketing Science*, 26 (January-February), 67-82.

Mowen, John and Maryanne Mowen (1991), "Time and Outcome Valuation: Implication for Marketing Decision Making," *Journal of Marketing*, 55 (October), 54-62.

O'Donoghue, Ted and Matthew Rabin (1999), "Doing It Now or Later," *The American Economic Review*, 89 (1), 103-24.

Silk, Tim (2005), "The Influence of Deadline Length on the Purchase and Redemption of Mail-in Rebates," *working paper*, Moore school of Business, University of South Carolina.

Soman, Dilip (1998), "The Illusion of Delayed Incentives: Evaluating Future Effort-Money Transactions," *Journal of Marketing Research*, 35 (4), 427-37.

Trope, Yaacov and Nira Liberman (2003), "Temporal Construal," *Psychological Review*, 110(3), 403-421.

Zauberman, Gal and Gerald Lynch (2005), "Resource Slack and Propensity to Discount Delayed Investments of Time Versus Money," *Journal of Experimental Psychology: General*, 134 (1), 23-37.

Paying More but Choosing Less: How Input Factors Drive Preference Reversals in Consumer Decisions

Ritesh Saini, University of Texas at Arlington, USA
Fiona Sussan, George Mason University, USA
Anupam Jaju, George Mason University, USA

EXTENDED ABSTRACT

Previously it has been observed that input factors (like the amount of effort put in, direct costs, etc) which are likely to be non-diagnostic about the true utility derived from an item, significantly influence the preference for an item. In this paper we demonstrate that such non-diagnostic input factors have a greater influence on preference when consumers are asked to *price* items than when they are asked to *choose* from the same items. This leads to an input factors driven preference-reversal for consumer products. We demonstrate that this effect persists even when input factors are not monetary or quantifiable. In this manner we rule out scale compatibility hypothesis as a key driver for our results and instead propose a transaction fairness hypothesis.

Economics views individual decision makers as outcome-maximizers. This implies that all consumer decisions will be driven by the personal utility that an item provides to the consumer. However, consumer research has repeatedly shown that consumers invoke a variety of guiding principles and behavioral rules. Such rules can often undermine utility maximization. In this paper, we look at one such rule–consideration of input factors/ costs, and not just outcome utility, in constructing preferences for a consumption item.

In our first study, we asked respondents to express their preference for two paintings–one which was visually more appealing, while the other which had taken a longer time to finish. Participants who were asked to choose amidst the two chose the former more frequently. However, participants who were asked to price the paintings were willing to pay a higher price for the former.

In our second study we compared the pricing of the two products with the choice share of these two products. Products differ in terms of input factors. There were several pricing and choice conditions in the experiment. In some conditions, the products were priced separately (i.e. respondents who priced product A did not price product B and vice versa). This was done to more accurately reflect the reality in markets where consumers often focus on a singular item while pricing it, like bidding on eBay. In other conditions, products were priced jointly. In addition, in some conditions target products were chosen or priced when they were tied-in with other products. Our main hypothesis is that input factors influence pricing more than choice. Specifically, conditions 1-5 were pricing conditions while Conditions 6 & 7 were choice conditions. In the pricing conditions, participants were asked to state the maximum amount of money they are willing to pay to purchase a high (hardware) or low (software) input factor product with or without bundled (free) goods. In the choice condition, participants were asked to choose between high or low input factor product with or without bundled goods. The key findings of this experiment were that participants priced the high input factor more than the low input factor in the pricing condition. However this preference order was reversed when participants were asked to choose amidst these two options. Our main hypothesis was supported. We also found that input factors influence pricing more than choice for tie-in products, and even when prices are elicited in a joint-evaluation mode. Significantly, our choice and description of experimental stimuli was such that we rule out scale compatibility hypothesis as the key driver of our results.

The third experiment manipulated input costs within the same product category thereby controlling for any confounds. Again, in the pricing condition, participants valued the high input factors option (Restaurant B) more than the alternative; however in the choice condition participants chose the low input factors option more.

One of the most basic assumptions of the rational theory of preferences is the principle of extensionality (Arrow 1982) or invariance (Tversky & Kahneman1986). This states that the preference ordering should not depend on the description of the options (description invariance) or on the method of elicitation (elicitation invariance). The present studies add to the evidence of elicitation invariance driven by a consumer's perception of the input costs and efforts involved in making a good. In this paper we have demonstrated that input bias significantly influences preferences, more in a pricing task than in a choice. This effect is not solely driven by scale compatibility, but continues to influence pricing even when input factors are not easily quantifiable. Also, we demonstrate that the pricing task primes the goal of transaction fairness which leads to higher pricing of the high input factors option. This hints at the possibility of such pricing-choice differences for all situations where non-diagnostic factors have been shown to influence preferences.

REFERENCES

Amir, O., Ariely, D., & Carmon Z. (2008). The dissociation between monetary assessments and predicted utility. Marketing Science *(forthcoming)*.

Arrow, K. J. (1982). Risk perception in psychology and economics. *Economic Inquiry*, *20*(1), 1-9.

Baron, J. (1988, 1994, 2000, 2008). *Thinking and Deciding*. New York: Cambridge University Press.

Baron, J., & Maxwell, N. P. (1996). Cost of public goods affects willingness to pay for them. *Journal of Behavioral Decision Making*, *9*, 173-183.

Berg, J. E., Dickhaut, J.W., & O'Brien, J. R. (1985). Preference reversal and arbitrage. *Research in Experimental Economics*, *3*, 31-72.

Bettman, J.R., Luce, M.F., & Payne, J.W. (1998). Constructive consumer choice processes. *Journal of Consumer Research*, *25*(3), 187-217.

Bohm, P. (1994). Time preference and preference reversal among experienced subjects: The effects of real payments. *Economic Journal*, *104*, 1370-1378.

Bolton, L. E., Warlop, L., & Alba, J.W. (2003). Consumer perceptions of price (un)fairness. *Journal of Consumer Research*, *29*(March), 474-91

Bolton, L. E., & Alba J.W. (2006). Price fairness: good and service differences and the role of vendor costs. *Journal of Consumer Research*, *33*(September), 258-265.

Boothe, J., Schwartz, J. A., & Chapman, G. B. (2007). Preference reversals resulting from a market value heuristic. *Marketing Theory*, *7*(1), 27–38.

Campbell, M. C. (1999). Perceptions of price unfairness: antecedents and consequences. *Journal of Marketing Research*, *36*(May), 187-99.

Chinander, K., & Schweitzer, M. (2003). The input bias: The misuse of input information in judgments of outcomes. *Organizational Behavior and Human Decision Processes, 91*(2), 243-253.

Cho, H. & Schwarz, N. (2008). Of great art and untalented artists: Effort information and the flexible construction of judgmental heuristics, *Journal of Consumer Psychology, 18,* 205-211.

Desvousages, W.H., Johnson, F.R., Dunford, R.W., Hudson, S.P., Wilson, K.N., & Boyle, K.J. (1993). Measuring natural resource damages with contingent valuation: Test of validity and reliability (pp.91-164). In J.A. Housman (ed.) *Contingent Valuation ?A Critical Assessment*, Amsterdam: HorthHolland.

Eyal, T., Sagristano, M., Trope, Y., Liberman, N., Chaiken, S. (2008) When values matter: Expressing values in behavioral intentions for the near vs. distant future. *Journal of Experimental Social Psychology,* In Press.

Fiedler, K. (2007). Construal level theory as an integrative framework for behavioral decision making. *Journal of Consumer Psychology, 17* (April), 101–106.

Fischer, G. W., & Hawkins, S. A. (1993). Strategy compatibility, scale compatibility, and the prominence effect. *Journal of Experimental Psychology: Human Perception and Performance, 19*, 580-597.

Folkes, V.S., & Kamins, M.A. (1999). Effect of information about firms' ethical and unethical actions on consumers' attitudes. *Journal of Consumer Psychology, 8*(3), 243-259.

Frederick S., & Fischoff, B. (1998). Scope (in)sensitivity in elicited valuations. *Risk Decision and Policy 3*(2), 109–123.

Grether, D., & Plott, C. R. (1979). Economic theory of choice and the preference reversal phenomenon. *American Economic Review, 69*, 623-638.

Gouldner, A. W. (1960). The norm of reciprocity: A preliminary statement. *American Sociological Review*, *25*, 161–178.

Hsee, C. K. (1996). The evaluability hypothesis: An explanation for preference-reversal between joint and separate evaluations of alternatives. *Organizational Behavior and Human Decision Processes, 67*, 247-257.

Hsee, C. K. (1999). Value seeking and prediction– Decision inconsistency: Why don't people take what they predict they'll like the most? *Psychonomic Bulletin and Review, 6*(4), 555-561.

Huber, J., Payne, J.W., & Puto, C. (1982). Adding asymmetrically dominated alternatives: Violations of regularity and the similarity hypothesis. *Journal of Consumer Research, 9*, 90-98.

Irwin, J. R., & Baron, J. (2001). Response mode effects and moral values. *Organizational Behavior and Human Decision Processes, 84*, 177-197.

Janis, I. L., & Mann, L. (1977). *Decision Making: A Psychological Analysis of Conflict, Choice and Commitment.* New York: Free Press.

Kahneman, D. (1994). New challenges to the rationality assumption. *Journal of Institutional and Theoretical Economics, 150*, 18-36.

Kahneman, D., Knetsch, J., & Thaler, R.H. (1986). Fairness as a constraint on profit seeking: Entitlements in the market. *The American Economic Review, 76*, 728-741.

Knez, M., and Smith, V. (1987). Hypothetical valuations and preference reversals in the context of asset trading. In A. Roth, (ed.), *Laboratory Experimentation in Economics: Six Points of View*, Cambridge: Cambridge University Press.

Kruger, J., Wirtz, D., Van Boven, L., & Altermatt, W. (2004). The effort heuristic. *Journal of Experimental Social Psychology, 40*, 91–98.

LeBoeuf, R. A., & Shafir, E. (2003). Deep thoughts and shallow frames: Effortful thinking and susceptibility to framing effects. *Journal of Behavioral Decision Making, 16*(2), 77-92.

Lee Y. H., & Malmendier, U. (2007). The bidder's curse. *NBER Working Paper* No. W13699.

Lichtenstein, S., & Slovic, P. (1971). Reversals of preference between bids and choices in gambling decisions. *Journal of Experimental Psychology, 89*, 46-55.

Liberman, N., Sagristano, M. and Trope, Y. (2002). The effect of temporal distance on level of mental construal, *Journal of Experimental Social Psychology,* 38, 523–534.

Liberman, N. and Trope, Y. (1998). The role of feasibility and desirability considerations in near and distant future decisions: A test of temporal construal theory, *Journal of Personality and Social Psychology, 75,* 5–18.

McFarland, S. G. 1981. Effects of question order on survey responses. *Public Opinion Quarterly, 45*,208-215.

Morales, Andrea C. (2005). Giving firms an "E" for effort: Consumer responses to high-effort firms. *Journal of Consumer Research, 31*(March), 806-812.

Nagel, T.T., & Holden, R.K. (2002). The strategy and tactics of pricing: A guide to profitable decision making. *Journal of Revenue & Pricing Management, 1*, 286–287.

Nisbett, R. E., Zukier, H., & Lemley, R.E. (1981). The dilution effect: Nondiagnostic information weakens the implication of diagnostic information. *Cognitive Psychology, 13*, 248-277.

Nowlis, S.M., & Simonson, I. (1997). Attribute-task compatibility as a determinant of consumer preference reversals, *Journal of Marketing Research, 34* (May), 205-218.

Nunes, J., Hsee, C. K. & Weber, E. U. (2004). Why are people so prone to steal software? The effect of products' cost structure on payment and purchase intentions. *Journal of Public Policy and Marketing, 23*, 43-53.Onay, S., & Onculer,A. (2007). Intertemporal choice under timing risk: An experimental approach. *Journal of Risk Uncertainty, 34*, 99-121.

Payne, J. W., Bettman, J. R. & Johnson, E. J. (1993). *The Adaptive Decision-Maker.* Cambridge University Press.

Raghunathan, R., Naylor, R.W., & Hoyer, W.D. (2006). The 'unhealthy=tasty' intuition and its effects on taste inferences, enjoyment, and choice of food products. *Journal of Marketing, 70*(October), 170-184.

Russo, J. E., & Schoemaker, P.J.H. (1988). *Decision traps: The ten barriers to brilliant decision-making and how to overcome them.* New York: Simon & Schuster.

Schwarz, N. (1999). Self-reports: How the questions shape the answers. *American Psychologist, 54*, 93-105.

Schkade, D. & Johnson, E. (1989). Cognitive processes in preference reversals. *Organizational Behavior and Human Decision Processes, 44*, 203-231.

Shafir, E. (1993). Choosing versus rejecting: Why some options are both better and worse than others. *Memory & Cognition, 21*(4), 546-556.

Shafir, E., Diamond, P., & Tversky A. (1997). Money illusion. *Quarterly Journal of Economics, 112*(May), 341-374.

Simonson, I. (1989). Choice based on reasons: the case of attraction and compromise effects. *Journal of Consumer Research, 16* (September), 158-174.

Slovic, P. (1975). Choice between equally valued alternatives. *Journal of Experimental Psychology: Human Perception and Performance*, *1*, 280-287.

Slovic, P., & Lichtenstein, S. (1968). The importance of variance preferences in gambling decisions. *Journal of Experimental Psychology*, *78*, 646-654.

Slovic, P., Griffin, D., & Tversky, A. (1990). Compatibility effects in judgment and choice. In T.Gilovich, D. Griffin, & D. Kahneman (Eds.) *Heuristics and Biases: The Psychology of Intuitive Judgment* (pp. 217-229). New York: Cambridge University Press.

Tetlock, P., & Boettger, P. (1989). Accountability: A social magnifier of the dilution effect. *Journal of Personality and Social Psychology*,*57*(3), 388-398.

Thaler, R. H. (1985). Mental accounting and consumer choice. *Marketing Science*, *4*, 199-214.

Tversky, A., & Kahneman, D. (1981). The framing of decisions and the psychology of choice. *Science*, *211*, 453–458.

Tversky, A., & Kahneman, D. (1986). Rational choice and the framing of decisions. *The Journal of Business*, *59*(4), S251-S278.

Tversky, A., Sattath, S., & Slovic, P. (1988). Contingent weighting in judgment and choice. *Psychological Review*, *95*, 371-384.

Tversky, A., Slovic, P., & Kahneman, D. (1990). The causes of preference reversal. *American Economic Review*, *80*, 204-217.

Xia, L., Monroe, K.B., & Cox J.L. (2004). The price is unfair! A conceptual framework of price fairness perceptions. *Journal of Marketing*, *68*(October), 1-15.

Yeung, C., & Soman, D. (2007). The duration heuristic. *Journal of Consumer Research*, *34* (October), 315-326.

An Integrated Model of Reference Prices and their Impact on Satisfaction

Felix Tang, Hang Seng School of Commerce, Hong Kong
Jianmin Jia, The Chinese University of Hong Kong, Hong Kong

EXTENDED ABSTRACT

The Motivation

This article develops a satisfaction model that incorporates the concepts of the types of reference prices, perceived fairness, retrospective regret, and disappointment. Previous studies have examined *whether* reference prices lead to consumer satisfaction (e.g., Bolton and Lemon 1999; Fornell et al. 1996; Mittal, Ross, and Baldasare 1998; Varki and Colgate 2001; Voss et al. 1998); however, *how* reference prices lead to satisfaction remains unclear for two reasons. First, except for Voss et al. (1998), causality cannot be established when prices are not manipulated directly in the study. Second, except for Bolton and Lemon (1999), the underlying mechanism driving the relationship has not been examined.

The exploration of *how* reference prices influence satisfaction leads to two research questions. The first question concerns the relationships between different types of reference prices on the antecedent of satisfaction (i.e., fairness, regret, and disappointment). Inman, Dyer, and Jia (1997) define regret and disappointment according to the type of comparison. Their findings suggest that each antecedent is influenced by a specific type of reference prices. However, Bolton, Warlop, and Alba (2003) find that perceived fairness can be influenced by different types of reference prices, such as prices comparing across consumers and prices comparing across time. Their findings suggest that each antecedent may be influenced by multiple types of reference prices. Clarifying these contradicting predictions allows a better understanding of reference prices and satisfaction. The second question concerns the explanatory power of fairness, regret, and disappointment, and the robustness of existing model without one or more of these antecedents. Whether satisfaction can be adequately explained by one, two, or all of the antecedents is both theoretically and practically important.

The objective of this article is to develop an integrated model to capture the influence of how different types of reference prices influence consumer satisfaction. This article adopts Bolton et al.'s (2003) transaction space framework and proposes that the influence of reference prices on satisfaction can be separated into three types: across-time reference price, across-consumer reference price, and across-firm reference price. The levels of reference price are manipulated to draw causal inference. Furthermore, disappointment, fairness, and regret are included in the model to examine if they can moderate the effect of reference price on satisfaction.

The Conceptual Framework

An integrated model must be able to encompass the influence of different types of reference prices on satisfaction. This article transforms Bolton et al.'s (2003) transaction-space framework into a new reference price typology. Our model adopts the consumer (across-consumer reference price), firm (across-firm reference price), and time (across-time reference price) dimensions and relates them to fairness, regret, and disappointment.

Disappointment is a cognition-laden and psychological reaction to an outcome that falls below one's expectation (Bell 1985). Perceived fairness is a judgment that the distribution of resources is based on the principle of equity, equality, and needs according to the distributive justice theory (Deutsch 1975). Regret is an unpleasant, cognitively determined, backward-looking emotion experienced when realizing or imagining that the present situation would have been better if actions had been done differently (Zeelenberg and Pieters 2007). The effects of disappointment, perceived fairness, and retrospective regret on consumer satisfaction have been independently demonstrated in previous studies (Bolton and Lemon 1999; Darke and Dahl 2003; Taylor 1997).

The relationship between fairness and regret and the relationship between fairness and disappointment were freed in the model estimation. The fairness-regret relationship was suggested by Tang and Jia (2007) that consumers are motivated to accept responsibility and such cognitive appraisal leads to the experience of regret. The fairness-disappointment relationship was hinted by Bell (1985) that one may feel disappointed at receiving such an unexpected, unfair outcome.

The Experiment

An experiment with a 3 (across-consumer reference price: favorable, same, unfavorable) x 3 (across-firm reference price: favorable, same, unfavorable) x 3 (across-time reference price: favorable, same, unfavorable) between-subjects factorial design was conducted to generate the price variations along different dimensions of reference price. The experiment was scenario-based, describing an Internet shopping experience of a DVD movie. Six-hundred-seventy undergraduate students participated in this study. All dependent variables were measured on a multi-item, seven-point Likert scale. The manipulations were successful.

The Findings

The proposed model is examined using structural equation modeling. Confirmatory factor analysis indicated excellent fit of the measurement model (χ^2=87.25, df=47, CFI=.99, RMSEA=.038, SRMR=.020). Reliability of and discriminant validity among the constructs were also established. The proposed model fit the data well (χ^2=112.62, df=51, CFI=.97, RMSEA=.045, SRMR=.025). The structural model suggests that perceived fairness, retrospective regret, and disappointment mediate the effect of reference price on satisfaction. Several nested models were also examined for model comparison. The findings in model comparison suggest that the impact of reference prices on satisfaction is type-dependent. That is, the influence of across-consumer reference price on customer satisfaction is larger than that of across-time or across-firm reference price. Our findings support Inman et al. (1997)'s conceptualization of regret and disappointment; however, the findings do not support their one-to-one mapping assumption from the types of reference prices to the antecedents of satisfaction.

The findings in the model comparison suggest that the model with all three antecedents of satisfaction, as well as the model with fairness and regret and the model with disappointment and regret, provide a good fit for the data. The other seven alternative models fit the data significantly worse and the estimators are directionally larger than the corresponding estimators in the proposed model. This observation hints that models ignoring one or more antecedents of satisfaction may have inflated the predictive power of other antecedents on satisfaction. Specifically, satisfaction models that ignore regret (e.g., Feinberg et al. 2002) and models that only measure regret (e.g., Tsiros and Mittal 2000) may have inflated estimators. The paths from regret or fairness to satisfaction in these models should be interpreted with caution.

REFERENCES

Bell, David E. (1985), "Disappointment in Decision Making under Uncertainty," *Operations Research*, 33 (1), 1-27.

Bolton, Lisa, E., Luk Warlop, and Joseph W. Alba (2003), "Consumer Perceptions of Price (Un)Fairness," *Journal of Consumer Research*, 29 (4), 474-491.

Bolton, Ruth N. and Katherine N. Lemon (1999), "A Dynamic Model of Customers' Usage of Services: Usage as an Antecedent and Consequence of Satisfaction," *Journal of Marketing Research*, 36 (2), 171-186.

Darke, Peter R. and Darren W. Dahl (2003), "Fairness and Discounts: The Subjective Value of a Bargain", *Journal of Consumer Psychology*, 13 (3), 328-338.

Deutsch, Morton (1975), "Equity, Equality, and Need: What Determines which Value will be Used as the Basis for Distributive Justice?" *Journal of Social Issues*, 31 (3), 137-150.

Feinberg, Fred M., Aradhna Krishna, and Z. John Zhang (2002), "Do We Care What Others Get? A Behaviorist Approach to Targeted Promotions," *Journal of Marketing Research*, 39 (3), 277-291.

Fornell, Claes and David F. Larcker (1981), "Evaluating Structural Equation Models with Unobservable Variables and Measurement Error," *Journal of Marketing Research*, 18 (1), 39-50.

Inman, J. Jeffrey, James S. Dyer, and Jianmin Jia (1997), "A Generalized Utility Model of Disappointment and Regret Effects on Post-choice Valuation," *Marketing Science*, 16 (2), 97-111.

Mittal, Vikas, William T. Ross, Jr., and Patrick M. Baldasare (1998), "The Asymmetric Impact of Negative and Positive Attribute-Level Performance on Overall Satisfaction and Repurchase Intentions", *Journal of Marketing*, 62 (1), 33-47.

Tang, Felix and Jian-min Jia (2007), "Would Perceived Unfairness Lead to Regret?" *Advances in Consumer Research* (35), 350.

Taylor, Kimberly A. (1997), "A Regret Theory Approach to Assessing Consumer Satisfaction," *Marketing Letters*, 8 (2), 229-238.

Tsiros, Michael and Vikas Mittal (2000), "Regret: A Model of Its Antecedents and Consequences in Consumer Decision Making," *Journal of Consumer Research*, 26 (4), 401-417.

Varki, Sajeev and Mark Colgate (2001), "The Role of Price Perceptions in an Integrated Model of Behavioral Intentions," *Journal of Service Research*, 3 (3), 232-240.

Voss, Glenn B., A. Parasuraman, and Dhruv Grewal (1998), "The Roles of Price, Performance, and Expectations in Determining Satisfaction in Service Exchanges," *Journal of Marketing*, 62 (4), 46-61.

Zeelenberg, Marcel and Rik Pieters (2007), "A Theory of Regret Regulation 1.0," *Journal of Consumer Psychology*, 17 (1), 3-18.

Others Matter: The Effect of Peer Connectedness to Television Series on Product Placement Effectiveness

Valeria Noguti, University of Technology Sydney, Australia
Cristel A. Russell, University of Auckland, New Zealand

EXTENDED ABSTRACT

There is a growing body of research focusing on the impact on consumers of products and brands placed in the content of entertainment media such as movies, television series, and talk shows, a practice referred to as product placement (Auty and Lewis 2004; Babin and Carder 1996; d'Astous and Seguin 1999; Russell 2002; Russell and Stern 2006). Yet, surprisingly little research has addressed how the social environment affects product placement effectiveness. Drawing a parallel with research on self-connectedness, defined as the referential relationships that people develop with television series (Russell, Norman and Heckler, 2004), we introduce the construct of peer connectedness. We define peer connectedness to television series as the perceived referential influence of television series on others. In other words, peer connectedness reflects the degree to which others are perceived as having developed referential relationships with the series and its characters, and therefore as being influenced by its content, including the products placed in the series.

Consistent with the extant literature on interpersonal influences in many realms of behavior, we theoretically propose and demonstrate that peer connectedness contributes significant explanatory power to predictions of purchase intentions for placed products. As peer connectedness involves one's perceptions of what others think and do themselves, the construct of peer connectedness is akin to Cialdini and colleagues' notion of descriptive social norms, defined as individuals' perceptions of others' behaviors (Cialdini, Kallgren, and Reno 1991).

As peer connectedness effects on behavior inherently depend on the degree to which people care about others' opinions, we further propose that the effect of peer connectedness on behavior should be greater when the consumer is more concerned about the social environment. As such, we demonstrate that the effect of peer connectedness on purchase intentions is moderated by susceptibility to normative interpersonal influence.

One field study was conducted with consumers of a leather goods brand often placed in Brazilian soap operas. Participants responded to a two-page questionnaire involving brand attitudes, purchase intentions, perceived peer connectedness and self-connectedness to the series, susceptibility to normative influences, and demographics. We proposed that peer connectedness affects purchase intentions by moderating consumers' willingness to act upon their attitudes through their concerns with group norms. Indeed, the regression of consumers' purchase intentions (PI) on brand attitude, peer connectedness, susceptibility to normative influence (SNI), and the two-way and three-way interaction terms reveal the predicted three-way interaction. On the one hand, consumers who held strongly positive brand attitudes but were low in SNI still report considerably high PI, regardless of perceived peer connectedness. On the other hand, for consumers who had positive brand attitudes but were high in SNI, PI is affected by peer connectedness (i.e., higher when peer connectedness is high).

A follow-up experiment conducted with US college students investigated how the perception of peer connectedness is affected by self-connectedness, and ultimately, how the resulting perceived peer connectedness affects consumers' intentions to purchase brands placed in television series. Viewers of a popular television series participated in an experiment presented as a set of four separate studies. Attitudes toward a series of brands, including brands placed in the series, were collected in the first section. After an unrelated study presented in the second section, the third section focused on participants' viewing history with the selected TV series and included a measure of self-connectedness. Participants were then randomly assigned to a majority or minority peer connectedness condition: explicit information was provided by stating that either a minority or a majority of other viewers are connected to that series. The participants' resulting perception of peer connectedness was then measured. In the final section, intentions to purchase a series of brands were collected, and SNI was measured. Regression results showed that, as predicted, the peer connectedness manipulation affected perceived peer connectedness. In turn, perceived peer connectedness mediated the effect of the peer connectedness manipulation on purchase intentions when SNI is low. When SNI is high, consumers have stronger pre-existing perceptions of peer connectedness and are less influenced by external peer connectedness information.

These two studies provide support for the proposition that peer connectedness to television series is an important factor in predicting consumers' intentions to purchase products placed in these series. The field study demonstrates that high perceived peer connectedness relates to higher purchase intentions for consumers who are more susceptible to normative influences. The laboratory experiment, in which peer connectedness was manipulated, demonstrates its causal effects on purchase intentions. Explicit information about peer connectedness creates a perception of peer connectedness that significantly predicts consumers' intentions to buy brands placed in the series. The resulting perceived peer connectedness mediates the effect when susceptibility to normative influences is low but not when high. Taken together, our results demonstrate the importance of incorporating peer connectedness when testing the effects on audiences of product placements in television series.

REFERENCES

Auty, Susan and Charlie Lewis (2004), "Exploring Children's Choice: The Reminder Effect of Product Placement," *Psychology & Marketing*, 21 (9), 697-713.

Babin, Laurie A. and Sheri Thompson Carder (1996), "Viewers' Recognition of Brands Placed within a Film," *International Journal of Advertising*, 15 (2), 140-51.

Bearden, William O., Richard G. Netemeyer, and Jesse E. Teel (1989), "Measurement of Consumer Susceptibility to Interpersonal Influence," *Journal of Consumer Research*, 15 (4), 9p.

Brewer, Marilynn B., ed. (2003), *Optimal Distinctiveness, Social Identity, and the Self*, New York, NY,US: Guilford Press.

Cialdini, Robert B., Carl A. Kallgren, and Raymond R. Reno (1991), "A Focus Theory of Normative Conduct: A Theoretical Refinement and Reevaluation of the Role of Norms in Human Behavior," in *Advances in experimental social psychology*, Vol. 24, ed. Leonard Berkowitz, San Diego: Academic Press, 201-34.

Cohen, Geoffrey L. (2003), "Party over Policy: The Dominating Impact of Group Influence on Political Beliefs," *Journal of Personality and Social Psychology*, 85 (5), 808-22.

d'Astous, Alain and Nathalie Seguin (1999), "Consumer Reactions to Product Placement Strategies in Television Sponsorship," *European Journal of Marketing*, 33 (9/10), 896-910.

Deutsch, Morton and Harold B. Gerard (1955), "A Study of Normative and Informational Social Influences Upon Individual Judgment," *Journal of Abnormal and Social Psychology*, (51), 629-36.

Goldstein, Noah J., Robert B. Cialdini, and Vladas Griskevicius (2008), "A Room with a Viewpoint: Using Social Norms to Motivate Environmental Conservation in Hotels," *Journal of Consumer Research*, 35 (3), 472-82.

Johnston, Kim L., Katherine M. White, and Paul Norman (2004), "An Examination of the Individual-Difference Approach to the Role of Norms in the Theory of Reasoned Action," *Journal of Applied Social Psychology*, 34 (12), 2524-49.

Kenrick, Douglas T., Jon K. Maner, Jon Butner, Norman P. Li, D. Vaughn Becker, and Mark Schaller (2002), "Dynamical Evolutionary Psychology: Mapping the Domains of the New Interactionist Paradigm," *Personality & Social Psychology Review* (Lawrence Erlbaum Associates), 6 (4), 347-56.

Krendl, Kathy A. and Ron Warren (2004), "Communication Effects of Noninteractive Media: Learning in out-of-School Contexts," in *Handbook of Research for Educational Communications and Technology*, Vol. 1, ed. D. H. Jonassen, Mahweh, NJ: Lawrence Erlbaum Associates, 59-78.

La Pastina, Antonio (2001), "Product Placement in Brazilian Prime Time Television: The Case of the Reception of a Telenovela," *Journal of Broadcasting & Electronic Media*, 45 (4), 541-57.

Nolan, Jessica M. , P. Wesley Schultz, Robert B. Cialdini, Noah J. Goldstein, and Vladas Griskevicius (2008), "Normative Social Influence Is Underdetected," *Personality and Social Psychology Bulletin*, 34 (7), 913.

Preacher, Kristopher J., Derek D. Rucker, and Andrew F. Hayes (2007), "Addressing Moderated Mediation Hypotheses: Theory, Methods, and Prescriptions," *Multivariate Behavioral Research*, 42 (1), 185-227.

Russell, Cristel Antonia (2002), "Investigating the Effectiveness of Product Placements in Television Shows: The Role of Modality and Plot Connection Congruence on Brand Memory and Attitude," *Journal of Consumer Research*, 29 (3), 306-18.

Russell, Cristel Antonia, Andrew T. Norman, and Susan E. Heckler (2004), "The Consumption of Television Programming: Development and Validation of the Connectedness Scale," *Journal of Consumer Research*, 31 (1), 150-61.

Russell, Cristel Antonia and Barbara B. Stern (2006), "Consumers, Characters, and Products: A Balance Model of Sitcom Product Placement Effects," *Journal of Advertising*, 35 (1), 7-21.

Sherif, Muzafer (1937), "An Experimental Approach to the Study of Attitudes," *Sociometry*, I, 90-98.

Smith, Ted, James R. Coyle, Elizabeth Lightfoot, and Amy Scott (2007), "Reconsidering Models of Influence: The Relationship between Consumer Social Networks and Word-of-Mouth Effectiveness," *Journal of Advertising Research*, 47 (4), 387-97.

Thompson, Leigh and Gary Alan Fine (1999), "Socially Shared Cognition, Affect, and Behavior: A Review and Integration," *Personality & Social Psychology Review* (Lawrence Erlbaum Associates), 3 (4), 278.

Stimulating Referral Behavior May Backfire: The Effect of Referral Failure on Susceptibility to Persuasion

Bart Claus, K. U. Leuven, Belgium
Kelly Geyskens, University of Maastricht, The Netherlands
Kobe Millet, K. U. Leuven, Belgium; Free University Amsterdam, The Netherlands
Siegfried Dewitte, K. U. Leuven, Belgium

EXTENDED ABSTRACT

Consumers often rely on vicarious experience information when deciding about a product or service (Herr, Kardes, and Kim 1991). The effects of WOM behavior on the receiver of the information conveyed have extensively been investigated. Amazingly, the field knows virtually nothing about the effect of WOM on the sender, although senders are crucial agents in the WOM process (Goldenberg et al. 2009), and may very well react differently depending on whether or not their recommendations are followed. We distinguish the situation in which the sender's recommendations were followed (what we call referral success), or ignored (what we call referral failure) and look at the sender's subsequent openness to new information.

A literature review suggests that referral failure may be more informative than referral success. People tend to overweigh negative information. This greater sensitivity of individuals to negative than to positive information has been called the negativity bias (Cacioppo and Berntson 1994). This allows us to predict that referral failure will have a more pronounced effect than referral success.

The act of subjecting oneself to the scrutiny of a receiver of information, allowing that receiver to evaluate the sender's information, is something that goes far beyond that information itself. To some extent, not following advice signals that the receiver may not value the sender's judgment or even doubt his or her expertise. Earlier research found that the mere act of exposing oneself to public evaluation boosts self-image as a way to compensate for the threat of failure (compensatory self-inflation) (Greenberg and Pyszczynski 1985). Additionally, Sherman, Presson, and Chassin (1984) state that when the self is threatened, perceptions of consensus may be increased by a motivation to seek normalization and support for one's own behavior. This latter might lead to an exaggerated belief in support for one's own opinions, leading to choices that might diverge from choices that were hinted at by an advising party. Steele (1988) stated that when the self is threatened in one domain, a normal coping mechanism is to boost the ego in a general way, a thesis denoted as the "fluid compensation" principle. Finally, Rudman, Dohn, and Fairchild (2007) show self-worth compensation in response to threats to the self involving identity and social rejection as subtle as losing as small football knowledge quiz, something quite comparable to being questioned about e.g. product knowledge through referral failure.

Earlier we predicted that the effects of referral outcome would be more pronounced when the outcome is negative. The literature about ego threat further develops this stance, and ads to it the notion that if referral failure indeed poses a threat to the ego, people will react with a boost in self-worth to compensate for this pending blow to their ego. Furthermore, any effects of referral failure will be moderated by the extent to which this ego boost adequately covers for the ego threat at hand. We tested the proposed effects of referral failure and self activation on subsequent susceptibility to persuasion in four studies.

In study 1 we tested the effect of referral outcome on subsequent susceptibility to advice originating from a third person. In this first assessment of the effects of referral outcome on subsequent susceptibility to persuasion, we wanted to avoid effects of interaction between different genders. Therefore, we used only men for this study. The participants in this study were told they were testing a communication setup for online interactions between two consumer labs over the internet. The actual task involved recommending products to a person in the other lab, of whom they saw a photograph. This (preprogrammed) interaction partner then chose products from sets based on these recommendations. The preprogrammed interaction partner was set to follow the subject's recommendation either five out of six, or one out of six times, which comprises the manipulation of referral outcome. Subsequently the roles were reversed, but the participant was teamed up with another partner. The dependent measure was the number of times the subject followed the interaction partner's advice. The results were in line with our expectations, yielding less susceptibility to follow advice after referral failure in the first phase.

Study 2 was a replication of the first, but with minor adjustments to streamline the procedure. Also, this time, the sample included women. We replicated the results of study 1, generalizing the effect towards women.

Study 3 used a scenario to induce a feeling of referral failure, where participants were asked to imagine them being the child of a movie theater owner and their friends either always or seldom following up on their recommendations of movies. This study also included a baseline measure, where no recommendations had to be made. The dependent measure was ostensibly unrelated to this manipulation, as it consisted of reading an expert's report in a magazine, and then choosing combinations of products of which some were, and some were not, recommended in the report. Also in this study, participants were assessed for differences in activation of the self. Results were in line with studies 1 and 2. Additionally, we found that differences in activation of the self moderated the effect of referral outcome. By comparing the results within conditions with those in the baseline condition, we could establish that it is indeed referral failure that causes these effects, and that referral success corresponds to the baseline situation.

In a fourth study, participants had to choose their favorite movie poster and motivate their choice to another–preprogrammed–participant. This preprogrammed participant then either indicated that he or she would be unlikely or likely to switch his or her own choice towards that of the participant. The dependent measure was the same as in study 3, but used absolute measures. A measure of activation of the self was again included. The results replicated those of the previous studies.

Overall, these studies establish the referral backfire effect and show that this effect is moderated by differences in activation of the ego. Implications and recommendations for future research are discussed.

REFERENCES

Goldenberg, Jacob, Sangman Han, Donald R. Lehmann, and Jae W. Hong (2009), "The Role of Hubs in the Adoption Process," *Journal of Marketing*, 73 (2), 1-13.

Greenberg, Jeff and Tom Pyszczynski (1985), "Compensatory Self-Inflation: A Response to the Threat to Self-Regard of Public Failure," *Journal of Personality & Social Psychology*, 49 (1), 273-80.

Herr, Paul M., Frank R. Kardes, and John Kim (1991), "Effects of Word-of-Mouth and Product-Attribute Information on Persuasion-an Accessibility-Diagnosticity Perspective," *Journal of Consumer Research*, 17 (4), 454-62.

Rudman, Laurie A., Matthew C. Dohn, and Kimberly Fairchild (2007), "Implicit Self-Esteem Compensation: Automatic Threat Defense," *Journal of Personality & Social Psychology*, 93 (5), 798-813.

Sherman, Steven J., Clark C. Presson, and Laurie Chassin (1984), "Mechanisms Underlying the False Consensus Effect: The Special Role of Threats to the Self," *Pers Soc Psychol Bull*, 10 (1), 127-38.

Steele, Claude M. (1988), "The Psychology of Self-Affirmation: Sustaining the Integrity of the Self.," in *Advances in Experimental Social Psychology*, Vol. 21, ed. Berkowitz Leonard, New York: Academic Park, 261-302.

When Do Entertaining Promotions Trigger Caution?

Donnel A. Briley, University of Sydney, Australia
Shai Danziger, Ben-Gurion University, Israel

EXTENDED ABSTRACT

We propose that promotional efforts that attempt to entertain shoppers (e.g., "instant-win" games) can make deals less attractive for some consumers. In particular, such promotions can activate persuasion knowledge, triggering a cautious outlook and skepticism about the accompanying deal—but only for consumers who have a strong need to preserve their sense of self determination. Consistent with this persuasion knowledge conceptualization, we find in three studies that consumers who do not have strong needs for self determination find entertaining promotions more attractive than those who have strong needs, and that this difference disappears when all are prompted to adopt a cautious mindset.

Marketers use a variety of promotional vehicles to entice point of sale purchases, and sometimes these vehicles endeavor to entertain consumers. An example is the lottery-like *scratch-and-win* card that consumers must actively scratch to reveal possible deals. Presumably, the entertaining gaming experience increases the chances that shoppers will take advantage of the offered deal. In this research we test this assertion, suggesting that the effects can sometimes be negative. We propose that the attractiveness of deals delivered via a gaming experience is moderated by consumers' self determination beliefs.

Lay theory suggests that infusing entertainment into purchase situations could be an effective tool in driving sales. The entertainment benefit, which applies to promotional games, giveaways and other events, encompasses the "active play" and "reactive aesthetic" values identified by Holbrook (1994). This benefit is yielded when shoppers have fun either engaging in promotional games or watching events and outcomes related to these promotions. Positive hedonic responses prompted by these entertaining experiences translate into more positive associations for the associated brand (Ward, Hill and Gardner 1987) and, consequently, increase purchase likelihood.

Other evidence indicates that games can be effective in improving deal sales. For example, coupons that shoppers unexpectedly receive in the store are 35% more effective in compelling purchases than off-the-shelf price discounts that offer the same monetary incentive (Dhar and Hoch, 1996). One might expect, then, that games could be similarly effective in converting deal purchase. Darke and Freedman (1995) suggest that promotional games might be particularly appealing because they "give each customer a chance to win a discount rather than giving everyone the same standard sale price". The appeal of this approach, they suggest, could come from people's desires to feel that they are lucky in obtaining the deal opportunity.

On the other hand, a case can be made that adding an entertaining aspect to promotions can hurt deal purchase rates. When consumers experience an entertaining event that is tied to a promotional deal, these relatively novel events might trigger a more cautious outlook in which the consumer becomes skeptical of the accompanying deal opportunity. More specifically, encountering the entertaining activity could activate consumers' knowledge and beliefs regarding persuasion (Friestad and Wright, 1994), as they become sensitive to the fact that they are in the midst of a persuasive episode. This caution could lead to reactance (Brehm, 1966) and in so doing, increase the chances of deal rejection.

We propose that promotions that make a special attempt to entertain are more likely than more typical promotions to trigger caution. Games are a relatively elaborate medium for offering deals, and this rather complex framing could sensitize consumers to the underlying purpose of the effort—influencing their selections.

When is Entertainment Effective?

Some people believe that they determine their own destinies, perceiving a strong degree of contingency between their own actions and the outcomes of events they encounter; though others perceive a lesser degree of influence, viewing forces outside of their control as principal determinants (Rotter, 1966). We suggest that deals offered through an entertaining promotional vehicle are more likely to be chosen by the latter type of people than the former. People who have strong beliefs in self determination should give high priority to protecting themselves against events and people who impede their autonomy, and people who do not have such beliefs should give lower priority to these protections. Each of these belief system types spawns knowledge structures that support and maintain the system: Different goals, motives and attitudes are likely to develop. In particular, differences in self determination priorities should be accompanied by difference in the accessibility of knowledge structures that pertain to sensing and fending off efforts to sway one's attitudes and choices. People who believe strongly versus weakly in self determination are likely to access such knowledge more frequently. As a result, those strong rather than weak in self determination should have this knowledge more accessible in memory.

This difference in accessibility of persuasion-related knowledge might not influence decisions when the promotion of interest is typical, but could be important when a promotion involving features that could signal the efforts intention to influence consumers. We suggest that promotions that include entertainment, specifically games, should receive different responses depending on the self determination beliefs of the consumer. For those strong in self determination, entertaining promotions are expected to trigger persuasion knowledge, because this knowledge is relatively accessible. A more cautious outlook is likely to follow, leading to skepticism about the deal. But, people with relatively weak beliefs regarding self determination, because persuasion knowledge is less accessible, are not likely to have the same response. Persuasion knowledge is less likely to become salient in the mind, and the positive effects of entertaining promotions, discussed above, are possible in this case.

Overview of Studies

A pre-test confirmed that people infer greater influence intent from game-based promotions than more typical in-store promotions. In studies 1 and 2 we included Chinese, who tend to be low on self determination, and Americans, who tend to be high. We expected that differences in self determination needs across the two cultures would moderate choices of a promoted item delivered via "scratch and win" card. In study 1, Chinese participants were more likely to select a two-for-one tissue deal when it was offered via a "scratch-and-win" card than when offered as a regular store promotion. In contrast, the game based deal eroded selection among American participants. This pattern was replicated in study 2 for a golf umbrella deal. Again, the scratch-and-win delivery improved deal attractiveness among Chinese participants, but hurt it among American participants. Additionally, self-reported externality tendencies mediated the effects of culture on deal selection when promotions were entertainment focused. Last, study 3 garnered evidence for our persuasion knowledge conceptualization whereby the attractiveness of an entertaining promotion delivery vehicle is moderated by whether it alerts shoppers to these promotions' intent to influence. Activating a "cautious" mindset by means of a priming manipulation, the study found that those low on self determination no longer found the entertaining promotion attractive. As predicted, the priming manipulation did not influence selection when the promotion was offered at an end of aisle display.

REFERENCES

Brehm, Jack W. (1966), *A Theory of Psychological Reactance*, New York: Academic Press.

Chandon, Pierre, Brian, Wansink, and Gilles Laurent (2000), "A Benefit Congruency Framework of Sales Promotion Effectiveness," *Journal of Marketing*, 64 (October), 65-81.

Clee, Mona A. and Robert A. Wicklund (1980), "Consumer Behavior and Psychological Reactance," Journal of Consumer Research, 6 (4), 389-405.

Darke, Peter R. and Jonathan L. Freedman (1995), "Nonfinancial Motives and Bargain Hunting," *Journal of Applied Social Psychology, 25 (18),* 1597–610.

Dhar, Sanjay K. and Stephen J. Hoch (1996), "Price Discrimination Using In-Store Merchandising," Journal of Marketing, 60 (1), 17-30.

Fitzsimons, Gavan J. and Donald R. Lehmann (2004), "Reactance to Recommendations: When Unsolicited Advice Yields Contrary Responses," *Marketing Science*, 23 (1), 82-94.

Friestad, Marian and Peter Wright (1994), "The Persuasion Knowledge Model-How People Cope With Persuasion Attempts," *Journal of Consumer Research*, 21 (1), 1-31.

Holbrook, Morris (1994), "The Nature of Customer Value," in *Service Quality: New Directions in Theory and Practice*, R. T. Rust and R. L. Oliver, eds. Thousand Oaks, CA: Sage Publications, 21-71.

Kivetz, Ran (2005), " Promotion Reactance: The Role of Effort-Reward Congruity," *Journal of Consumer Research*, 31 (March), 725-36.

Morris, Michael W., Tanya Menon and Daniel Ames (2001), "Culturally Conferred Conceptions of Agency: A Key to Social Perception of Persons, Groups, and Other Actors," *Personality and Social Psychology Review*, 5 (2), 169-82.

Robertson, Thomas S. and John R. Rossiter (1974), "Children and Commercial Persuasion: An Attribution Theory Analysis," *Journal of Consumer Research*, 1 (1), 13–20.

Rothbaum, Fred, John Wolfer and Madelon Visintainer (1979), "Coping Behavior and Locus of Control in Children," *Journal of Personality,* 47 (1), 118–35.

Rotter, Julian B. (1966), "Generalized Expectancies for Internal Versus External Control of Reinforcement," *Psychological Monographs*, 80 (1), 1-28.

Simonson, Itamar, Ziv Carmon and Suzanne O'Curry (1994), "Experimental Evidence on the Negative Effect of Product Features and Sales Promotions on Brand Choice," *Marketing Science*, 13 (1), 23-40.

Ward, James .C, Ronal P. Hill and Meryl P. Gardner (1987), "The Effects of Promotional Games on Participants' Moods and Resulting Information Processing Behavior," in *Advances in Consumer Research*, Michael J. Houston, ed. Boston, MA: Association for Consumer Research, 135-140.

Roles of Food Consumption in the Experience of Homesickness among College Students

Elizabeth Crosby, University of Illinois at Urbana-Champaign, USA
Cele C. Otnes, University of Illinois at Urbana-Champaign, USA

EXTENDED ABSTRACT

Homesickness is described as a "complex cognitive-motivational-emotional state ...associated with ruminations about home, an intense desire to return home, depressed mood and somatic symptoms" (Fisher and Hood 1987, 426). This study explores how college students, a population that is specifically vulnerable to homesickness, experience this condition. In particular, we explore the ways food consumption shapes students' experiences of homesickness, by examining how consumption both specifically triggers homesickness and enables students to cope with it. Focusing on food consumption within this cohort is important, both because of the increase in obesity among young people and because diet quality, eating habits, and weight control often are adversely affected in college (Conklin and Lambert 2005).

As part of a larger study on how homesickness influences consumption, we collected 209 narratives. We eliminated 12 of these due to poor quality, leaving us 197 narratives that yielded over 700 pages of data. Although we did not anticipate an overwhelming discussion of food consumption, 164 of 197 narratives mentioned food consumption as either a trigger and/or coping mechanism for homesickness.

In analyzing the text, we sought out emergent themes while engaging in dialectical tacking (Strauss and Corbin 1998), immersing ourselves in the interdisciplinary literature on homesickness, food consumption, and product symbolism to help illuminate our informants' experiences. We read all narratives multiple times to identify salient and emergent themes (McCracken 1988). Although we did not initially intend to focus on how consumers use food consumption as a coping strategy for homesickness, the quantity of food discussions prompted us to concentrate on the construct.

In the consumer narratives, we find informants use food consumption in multiple ways to try to alleviate homesickness. Specifically, we describe six different food consumption patterns: (1) quintessential food consumption, (2) substitution, (3) channeling, (4) nationalistic or regional food consumption, (5) food ritual recreation, (6) binge or recreational eating.

Quintessential Food Consumption. Belk, Wallendorf, and Sherry (1989) describe quintessential goods as those that represent the ultimate in a product category. With quintessential food consumption, informants consume food to alleviate homesickness that they believe best represents the food they ate at home. Informants do so to immediately reconnect to their home of origin, and lessen their feelings of separation.

Substitution. Informants use substitution when they find they are unable to consume the quintessential food that would remind them of home. In substitution the informants replace the quintessential food item with something that is as similar as possible. Even if our informants cannot duplicate the exact types of foods that they would have consumed at home, substitute products allow them to transcend the limitations of space and reduce the sense of being separated from their homes (Otnes and Ruth 2008).

Channeling. With channeling, informants consume foods that are favorites of the people they have left behind at their home of origin. Interestingly, however, they themselves did not typically eat those foods. This strategy therefore reflects our informants' use of food as a conduit to reconnect them to a particular person from their home.

Nationalistic or Regional Food Consumption. Many informants cope with their homesickness by consuming foods that they associate with their home country or region. Informants consume these types of foods even if they had never or rarely used these brands when they were at home.

Food Ritual Re-creation. Informants also may cope by attempting to recreate food rituals to preserve a connection to their home to decrease homesickness. Many informants discuss recreating special family dinner nights, such as Wednesday night barbeque or Friday night pizza. Reliving these family dinner nights help informants feel connected to their families and homes even though they cannot be with the people who originated these traditions.

Binge or Recreational Eating. Many of the informants engage in binging or recreational eating to try to alleviate their homesickness. In this case, they do not eat to establish a connection to home, but rather to take their minds off of their feelings of homesickness and to make themselves feel better. Although these foods do not remind our informants of some aspect of their home, they do help in terms of providing a short-term mood boost.

We also find three ways food consumption causes or increases homesickness. First, many informants report that the foods that reconnect them with home also increase their homesickness simply because they are such powerful reminders of home. In consuming these foods, informants often continue to dwell on their absence from these places, reinforcing the separation in their own minds. Second, food consumption can trigger homesickness even if our informants were not experiencing this condition prior to consuming these foods. In these cases, the food consumption provokes thoughts of home. Third, eating food that is not prepared in the same manner as food at home can also trigger or exacerbate homesickness. Many informants complain that the substandard quality of dining commons food serve to remind them of their home. The substandard food acts as a trigger because of the immediate comparison informants make the superior food that was prepared at home.

The relationship between homesickness and food consumption can have both physical and emotional negative consequences on consumer welfare. Using food consumption as a coping mechanism for homesickness can be counterproductive, as it can increase homesickness and along with it the feelings of loneliness, stress, anxiety, and depression. Furthermore, several informants report that they gained weight from using food as a coping mechanism which significantly affects their overall health. Others report a lack of energy and increased feelings of sluggishness.

The negative ramifications of using food consumption to cope with homesickness make it extremely important to assist college students in coping with this condition. By educating students about the psychological effects of homesickness, they will be better prepared to cope with it. Furthermore, we believe that public policy makers could use the findings in this study to help develop nutritional information and messages that are aimed at helping college students realize the deleterious effects of using food consumption as a coping strategy for homesickness.

References available from the authors.

Becoming a Mother: Negotiating Discourses Within the Life-Framing Identity Project of Motherhood

Emma N. Banister, Lancaster University, UK
Margaret K. Hogg, Lancaster Unversity, UK
Mandy Dixon, Lancaster University, UK

EXTENDED ABSTRACT

Introduction

We explore women's experiences of identity conflicts and contradictions (Arnould and Thompson 2005) within the context of the consumption of discourses around motherhood. We particularly examine the intersection between the culturally pervasive discourse of self-management (Fischer et al. 2007) and more locally-bound discourses around women's identity framing projects as new mothers. We focus on the strategies women devise to allow them to negotiate the transition into new motherhood and integrate a variety of potentially conflicting possible selves in order to become relative experts. Drawing on three women's cases we identify how women variously reconcile themselves to discourses around good mothering, or resist or disengage from these discourses while developing viable mothering identities.

Identity projects, identity transitions and discourses

Motherhood requires the integration of different possible mothering selves which are informed by discourses that frame understandings of what it means to be a mother and reflect the conflicts, contradictions and ambivalence encountered. Discourses have been classified into two types: life-project framing and culturally pervasive (Fischer et al. 2007). "Life-project framing discourses are those that animate goals in a particular context" (Fischer et al. 2007:426). Miller (2007) argues that life-project framing discourses can leave women with unrealistic expectations of motherhood, partly through emphasizing mothers as natural and instinctive but also through failing to take account of women's diverse experiences and the relevance of individual differences. Culturally pervasive discourses are "those that are less germane to particular goals in a given context but that nonetheless inform consumers' thoughts and actions in particular contexts" (Fischer et al. 2007:426). The main culturally pervasive discourse that affects women's identity projects as new mothers relates to self-management (Fischer et al. 2007:433) and encourages individuals to develop their own understandings and knowledge in response to the diversity of expert (e.g. medical) discourses. Negotiating their way between culturally pervasive and life-framing discourses means new mothers have to reconcile their personal experiences and values with broader discourses. We examine identity work undertaken at the intersection between discourses by exploring the transition women make from pregnancy to new motherhood and the development of relative expertise. We therefore seek to understand how women respond to commonly held expectations of motherhood, which Miller (2007) argues are socially embedded and emphasized via prevailing discourses.

Research design

Our study focuses on three stories from a sample of first time mothers. Our depth interviews were loosely structured and informed by themes around mothering from earlier studies. We began with an over arching question: "tell me about your experiences of motherhood so far". Data analysis was ongoing throughout the data collection.

Findings

Drawing on three women's cases we identify how women respond to the discourses around mothering using three self management strategies: resisting the discourses; reconciling the discourses; or disengaging from the discourses. These strategies are used by women to make sense of their early mothering experiences and ultimately allow them to define their own version of the 'ideal' mothering self as they become more experienced and confident mothers. We reveal how women adopt these strategies within the context of prevailing (and often localized) discourses of ideal motherhood, to redefine their expectations of motherhood and to emerge in various ways, as becoming relative experts or 'good enough' mothers.

First, Olga's story revolves around resisting discourses of ideal motherhood. Olga's story reveals how some women resist what they perceive as normative discourses associated with mothering, such as the expectation to breastfeed, to have a particular physical appearance, and to purchase particular branded goods. Although at first women may struggle with resistance, over time expectations are reframed in the light of early mothering experiences, and women become more confident in their resistance and develop reframed expectations of the 'good enough' mothering self.

Second, Grace's story tells how she sought to reconcile potentially conflicting discourses. In her transition to motherhood, Grace struggles with, but eventually manages to reconcile, her initial expectations of her new mothering self versus the reality of her lived experience of new motherhood. Reconciliation involves a re-evaluation of initial possible selves and recognition of (prioritizing) what is important and feasible within the new mothering context.

Third, Nina's story exemplifies disengagement from ideal motherhood discourses. Nina chooses to ignore the discourses associated with 'pregnancy as (identity) project' (Brewis and Warren, 2001), which involves the assumption that women will inform themselves, attend classes, and make particular consumption decisions as part of the motherhood project. Although aware of these 'expert' discourses, some women prefer to ignore them, instead preferring to find their own way, through trial and error, developing an emerging confidence, expertise and belief in themselves as 'good enough mothers.'

Discussion

Arnould and Thompson argue that the marketplace provides a structuring influence and "produces certain kinds of consumer positions that consumers can choose to inhabit" (2005:871). However, consumers are faced with conflicts, contradictions and ambivalence which "frequently engender the use of myriad coping strategies, compensatory mechanisms, and juxtapositions of seemingly antithetical meanings and ideals" (2005:871). Our findings suggest that while these cultural scripts are prevalent and influential, some women do not feel able to align their identities with particular positions and others will consciously and purposefully resist elements that do not fit with their own understanding and experiences.

In addition to identifying the self management strategies that women adopt in response to discourses about motherhood, our research also reveals that the process of transition involved in becoming a (good) mother is somewhat more prolonged than might first be assumed. By interviewing women at different stages of new motherhood we have explored some of the ways in which women gradually accumulate the experience necessary to become a relative expert (Miller 2007). Despite pregnancy in itself representing a period of liminality, our findings suggest liminality continues after birth, as women develop "their own ways of knowing" (Miller 2007:351), which involves negotiating their path through a variety of life project framing discourses and the development of effective self-management strategies (Fischer et al. 2007) in order to cope with the often "seemingly antithetical meanings and ideals" (Arnould and Thompson 2005:871).

References

Arnould, E. and C.J. Thompson (2005), "Consumer Culture Theory (CCT): Twenty Years of Research," *Journal of Consumer Research*, 31 (March) 868-882.

Brewis, Joanna and Samantha Warren (2001), "Pregnancy as project: organizing reproduction," *Administrative Theory and Praxis*, 23 (3) 383-406.

Bristor, Julia and Eileen Fischer (1993), "Feminist Theory and Consumer Research," *Journal of Consumer Research*, 19 (March), 518–36.

Fischer, Eileen, Cele C. Otnes and Linda Tuncay (2007), "Pursuing Parenthood: Integrating Cultural and Cognitive Perspectives on Persistent Goal Striving," *Journal of Consumer Research*, 34 (Dec) 425-440.

Miller, Tina (2007), "Is This What Motherhood is All About?: Weaving Experiences and Discourses through Transition to First-Time Motherhood," *Gender and Society*, 21: 337-358.

Catch Me If You Can: Rethinking the Relationship of Body and Self through Pregnancy

Hyun Jeong Min, University of Utah, USA
Lisa Peñaloza, EDHEC Business School, France

EXTENDED ABSTRACT

The present study examines the relationship between body and self through the experiences of pregnancy and childbirth. Experiences related to pregnancy were considered an appropriate area to study due to four reasons. First, pregnancy is an epiphanic experience (Denzin 1989) that ruptures routines and lives, and provokes radical redefinitions of the self (Strauss 1959). Second, women tend to become more reflexive about their body when they are pregnant because they want to keep their body safe and healthy. In addition, they feel tension between their new self as a mother and the individual who is struggling to get a particular body and self back, and this makes them more reflexive about their body. Third, it should be noted that body changes accompanying pregnancy are not imposed by one's own self concept but are naturally occurring. Finally, pregnancy usually leads to changes in consumption behaviors.

Several researchers were interested in body related consumer practices such as plastic surgery (Schouten 1991; Sayre 1999; Askegaard, Gertsen, and Langer 2002), tattooing (Watson 1998; Kjeldgaard and Bengtsson 2005) and consumers' self-care practices (Thompson and Hirschman 1995). These studies have shed light on the dynamic relationship between body and self and showed the malleability of bodies to construct consumers' self-identity. What is common in these studies is that the researchers chose body modification practices as their empirical setting. Body modifications are usually based on a consumer's idea about ideal self. In other words, the consumer's mind is the starting point of the bodily changes, and this choice of research settings tends to leave out naturally occurring body changes (e.g., changes caused by pregnancy, childbirth, and aging) in the discussion. Unlike in body modification, consumers don't have a clear idea about what happens to their body during naturally occurring body changes. For instance, pregnant women expect that they will experience a certain amount of weight increase. However, they cannot know how much weight they will gain. Sometimes, unexpected changes happen in their body such as prenatal diabetes, which one of my informants had experienced during her pregnancy. So it would be natural to assume that naturally occurring body changes would evoke very different dynamics between body and self from those discovered in body modification practices.

Data was collected using in-depth ethnographic interviews (Spradley 1979) with six Korean women who experienced pregnancy in the U.S.. Analysis was based on extensive coding and memo writing (Lofland, Snow, Anderson, & Lofland 2006). For a guideline, the coding procedures of grounded theory (Glaser and Strauss 1967; Corbin and Strauss 1998) were used.

Through the analysis, three themes emerged: 1) Disavowal of changed body from self making effort; 2) A paired identity and body project; and 3) Korean women situated in the American culture. The most notable thing in the informants' experience of pregnancy was their refusal to accept their changed body into their self concept. They tended to think that their changed body was just temporary and could be restored to its condition before pregnancy. For this reason, most of them excluded their changed body from self construction efforts.

Second, the informants started to accept their changed body as inevitable emphasizing the importance of their baby and their identity as a mother. Their identity as an individual woman gave way to the identity as a mother, which cannot exist without being a pair with a child. They showed many behaviors of self sacrifice for their children. When they were confronted with the conflict between their personal desires and maternal duties, they almost always chose the maternal duties over their own desires even if there was an alternate option for them to use.

Third, the importance of social context in body project and self making discovered again as seen in previous research of body modification. Informants said that they might have behaved differently in terms of their bodily consumption if they were situated in a different social context.

By examining women's pregnancy and childbirth experiences, this study complemented the research findings from body modification research. As consumers experience disturbing body changes, they did not accept these changes into their self concept due to their hope of getting back the body they had before changes. This disavowal of changed body led to delaying and degrading consumption showing the gap between ontological self and epistemological self. In addition, this study also illuminated the importance of relational self identity. Recognizing a new identity as a mother helped informants accept the body changes. Moreover, they sacrificed their desires and needs giving priorities to their child's needs and wants. The role of a situated context of consumers also shed light on the relational aspects of bodily consumption.

REFERENCES

Ahuvia, Aaron C. (2005), "Beyond the Extended Self: Loved Objects and Consumers' Identity Narratives," *Journal of Consumer Research*, 32 (June), 171-184.

Bailey, Lucy (1999), "Refracted Selves? A Study of Changes in Self-identity in the Transition to Motherhood," *Sociology*, 33 (2), 335-352.

Baudrillard, Jean (1998), *The Consumer Society: Myths and Structures*, London; Thousand Oaks, CA: Sage.

Beauvoir, Simone de (1990), *She Came to Stay*, London: Norton.

Belk, Russell. W. (1988), "Possessions and Extended Self," *Journal of Consumer Research*, 15(September), 139-168.

Charmaz, Kathy (1995), "The Body, Identity, and Self: Adapting to Impairment," *The Sociological Quarterly*, 36(4), 657-80.

______ (2006), *Constructing Grounded Theory: A Practical Guide through Qualitative Analysis*, London: Sage.

Clarke, C.J.S. (1996), *Reality Through the Looking Glass*, Edinburgh: Floris Books.

Corbin, Juliet M. (2003), "The Body in Health and Illness," *Qualitative Health Research*, 13(2), 256-267.

Denzin, Norman K. (1989), *Symbolic Interactionism and Cultural Studies: The Politics of Interpretation*, Cambridge, MA: Blackwell Publishers

Domzal, Teresa. and Jerome B. Kernan (1993), "Mirror, mirror: Some postmodern reflections on global advertising," *Journal of Advertising*, 22(4), 1-20.

Epp, Amber M. and Linda L. Price (2008), "Family Identity: A Framework of Identity Interplay in Consumption Practices," *Journal of Consumer Research*, 35 (1), 50-70.

Foucault, Michel (1978), *The History of Sexuality*, New York: Pantheon Books.

______ (1979), *Discipline and Punish: The Birth of the Prison*, New York: Vintage Books.

Giddens, Anthony (1991), *Modernity and Self-Identity: Self and Society in the Late Modern Age*, Cambridge, MA: Polity

Glaser, Barney G. and Anselm Strauss (1967), *The Discovery of Grounded Theory: Strategies for Qualitative Research*, New Brunswick, NJ: Aldine Transaction

Hesse-Biber, Sharlene (1996), *Am I Thin Enough Yet?: The Cult of Thinness and the Commercialization of Identity*, NY: Oxford University Press.

Joy, Annamma and Alladi Venkatesh (1994), "Postmodernism, Feminism, and the Body: The Visible and the Invisible in Consumer Research," *International Journal of Research in Marketing*, 11 (4), 333-57.

Kjeldgaard, Dannie and Anders Bengtsson (2005), "Consuming the Fashion Tattoo," *Advances in Consumer Research*, 32 (1), 172-7.

Lee, Dong Hwan (1990), "Symbolic Interactionism: Some Implications for Consumer Self-Concept and Product Symbolism Research," *Advances in Consumer Research*, 17, 386-393.

Leifer, Myra (1980), "Pregnancy," *Signs: Journal of Women in Culture and Society*, 5 (4), 754-765.

Levy, S. J. (1959), "Symbols for Sale," *Harvard Business Review*, 37 (July-August), 117-24.

Lofland, John, David A. Snow, Leon Anderson and Lyn Lofland (2005), *Analyzing Social Settings: A Guide to Qualitative Observation and Analysis*, Belmont, CA: Wadsworth Publishing

Lowenstein, E. A. (1994), "Dissolving the myth of the unified self: The Fate of the Subject in Freudian Analysis," *Psychoanalytic Quarterly*, 63, 715-732.

Merleau-Ponty, Maurice (1962), *The Phenomenology of Perception*, London: Routledge & Kegan Paul.

Merleau-Ponty, Maurice (1968), *The Visible and the Invisible : Followed by Working Notes*, Evanston [Ill.]: Northwestern University Press.

Miller, Michele and John Ford (2005), "Sexism in Advertising and Marketing to Women," *International Journal of Advertising*, 24 (1), 113-115.

Murphy, Robert F. (1987), *The Body Silent*, New York: Norton

Shilling, Chris (1993), *The Body and Social Theory*, London: Sage.

Schott, G. R. (2001), "The Relational Self-Concept Scale: A Context-Specific Self-Report Measure for Adolescents," *Adolescence*, 36(Spring), 85-103.

Schouten, John (1991), "Selves in Transition: Symbolic Consumption in Personal rites of Passage and Identity Reconstruction," *Journal of Consumer Research*, 17(March), 412-425.

______ and James H. McAlexander (1995), "Subcultures of Consumption: An Ethnography of the New Bikers," *Journal of Consumer Research*, 22 (June), 43-61.

Schroeder, Jonathan E. and Detlev Zwick (2004), "Mirrors of Masculinity: Representation and Identity in Advertising Images," *Consumption, Markets, & Culture*, 7(1), 21-52.

Sirgy, M. (1982), "Self-Concept in Consumer Behavior: A Critical Review," *Journal of Consumer Research*, 9 (December), 287-300

Spradley, James P.(1979), *The Ethnographic Interview*, New York: Holt, Rinehart & Winston.

Strauss, Anselm L. and Juliet Corbin (1998), Basics of Qualitative Research: Grounded Theory Procedures and Techniques, Thousand Oaks, CA: Sage.

Svendsen, Lars (2006), *Fashion : A Philosophy*, London: Reaktion.

Thompson, Craig and Elizabeth Hirschman (1995), "Understanding Socialized Body: A post structuralist analysis of consumers' self-conception, body images, and self-care practices," *Journal of Consumer Research*, 22 (September), 139-153.

Tucker, W.T. (1957), Foundations for a Theory of Consumer Behavior, eds. Ickes and E. Knowles, New York: Springer-Verlag.

Upton, Rebecca L. and Sallie S. Han (2003), "Maternity and its Discontents: "Getting the Body Back" after Pregnancy," *Journal of Contemporary Ethnography*, 32 (6), 670-692

Watson, J. (1998), "'Why Did You Put That There?': Gender, Materialism and Tattoo Consumption," *Advances in Consumer Research*, 25 (1), 453-460.

Wattanasuwan, K (2005), "The Self and Symbolic Consumption," *The Journal of the American Academy of Business*, 6 (1), 179-184.

Wong, N. Y. and Ahuvia, A. C. (1998), "Personal Taste and Family Face: Luxury Consumption in Confucian and Western Societies," *Psychology & Marketing*, 15(5), 423-441.

Guilt Appeals in Cause-Related Advertising: When Does a Guilt Appeal Backfire?

Chun-Tuan Chang, National Sun Yat-sen University, Taiwan
Ting-Ting Chen, National Sun Yat-sen University, Taiwan

EXTENDED ABSTRACT

Corporate social responsibility (CSR) has been prompted by companies because a good business should be perceived as socially responsible. Sharing the business ethics and value of "paying back to society", CSR has become popularly recognized by industries or companies. One way to fulfill CSR is to partner a product with a cause, referred to strategically as cause-related marketing (CRM), where money is donated to a charity each time a consumer makes a purchase. Recent studies have begun to examine potential factors that might affect CRM effectiveness and how consumers respond to CRM initiatives (e.g., Strahilevitz, 1999; Strahilevitz and Myers, 1998; Subrahmanyan, 2004; Webb and Mohr, 1998). One influential variable that has been identified to determine the success of CRM is its advertising (Chang, 2008). A variety of advertising techniques are adopted to persuade consumers to buy products and services. Emotional appeals are widely used to "cut through the clutter" and arouse persuasive communication. Among them, guilt appeals are identified as popular, especially in contexts related to charitable donation (Hibbert et al., 2007).

Complementing previous research on the effects of guilt appeals in charitable giving contexts (Basil et al., 2006 and 2008; Bennett, 1998; Hibbert, Smith, and Ireland, 2007), this research shows how the guilt appeal can be relevant to CRM. This article contributes to this evolving stream of research by applying guilt appeals in CRM campaigns to demonstrate that guilt appeals might not be equally persuasive in all conditions, and could be moderated by product type and donation magnitude. This research also incorporates a product type combining both practical functions and hedonic rewards to examine how consumers perceive different product types and how these perceptions interact with CRM effects in a systematic way. The moderating roles of product type and donation magnitude on guilt appeals in CRM advertising effectiveness were explored in a 2 (guilt appeals: guilt vs. non-guilt) X 3 (product type: hedonic vs. practical vs. both) X 2 (donation magnitude: low vs. high) factorial design. In order to eliminate the effects of product-selection bias, two products were chosen for each product type based on a pre-test. Therefore, 24 experimental versions were produced. The experiment was conducted through the Internet. Participants were randomly assigned to one of the 24 conditions above. After successful manipulation checks, a series of analysis of variance controlling gender were conducted to examine proposed hypotheses.

The results support the general proposal that CRM effectiveness depends on complicated interrelationships among guilt appeal, product type, and donation magnitude. After the applying of guilt appeals in the CRM promotion business, the results show that a guilt appeal leads to higher persuasiveness than a non-guilt appeal. This confirms that guilt appeals can be an effective tool for influencing consumer behavior, notably in product purchase behaviors. From a practical point of view, the findings here should be considered encouraging companies who wish to employ guilt appeals in initiating CRM ads. The other goal of the present study was to extended earlier work on guilt appeals by identifying boundary conditions associated with the role of guilt appeals in consumer evaluations of CRM ads. In doing so, the study is capable of providing insight into the important, but previously unanswered question of "When does a guilt appeal backfire?" The results indicate that focusing on a comparison between guilt and non-guilt appeals may be overly simplistic. Indeed, the findings presented here establish that the influence of guilt appeals on consumer response is relatively complex and contingent on product type and donation magnitude. Four observations are noteworthy.

First, in terms of the relative effects of different product types, this study shows systematic effects on consumer responses by comparing hedonic products, practical products, and those containing both values. When a non-guilt appeal is used to frame CRM promotion, the main effect of product type is observed. The advantage of perceived product hedonism resides in its ability to elicit more favorable consumer attitudes toward the company and toward the sponsoring firm. Products linked to the cause are most likely to be preferred when they are hedonic, followed by those products containing both hedonic and practical value. The results demonstrate the previously observed effects of product type on CRM by comparing practical and hedonic products (Chang, 2008; Strahilevitz, 1999; Strahilevitz and Myers, 1998). The current investigation provides guidance for practitioners to frame the nature of the product in CRM campaigns. Perceived product hedonism is an important element in CRM. Transforming a product with perceived practical value into one with clear hedonic value can be an important re-positioning strategy for a company using CRM to successfully promote the product.

Second, a boomerang effect of perceived product hedonism is found when the CRM message is framed with a guilt appeal. To be specific, when a guilt appeal is employed, a practical product or a product containing both practical and hedonic value is more effective than a hedonic product for promoting CRM. Experiencing guilt from hedonic product purchases can affect an individual's willingness to contribute to charity. When consumers face a hedonic product with a guilt appeal, the guilt-appeal ad appears to be a deliberate attempt to seduce consumers into buying and makes consumers feel manipulated. The differences in participants' maladaptive responses from the experimental results validate this argument. This study here echoes the idea that guilt can generate negative responses and disrupt the advertiser's intended objectives as well (Cotte et al., 2005). Therefore, when consumers face a hedonic product, the CRM message in the guilt appeal reduces advertising effectiveness. These findings should be helpful to those seeking to use guilt appeals.

Third, a high donation magnitude presented in an ad would eliminate the CRM effectiveness of the guilt appeal. High donation magnitude could mean a large sacrifice for consumers since it involves a higher cost passed on to them. Consumers tend to become skeptical toward the CRM promotion and the company's inferred motives. These unfavorable evaluations have been identified in previous research (Barone et al., 2007; Berglind and Nakata, 2005; Gupta and Pirsch, 2006; Smith and Stodgill, 1994; Webb and Mohr, 1998). The current study empirically indicates that, with the guilt appeal, the participants who viewed the CRM message with a high donation magnitude generated more maladaptive responses than those who viewed one with a low donation magnitude. On the contrary, when a donation magnitude is perceived as low, the guilt appeal can become an effective peripheral cue in CRM advertising allowing consumers to process favorably the promotion message.

Fourth, the interaction between guilt appeal and donation magnitude is significant when promoting hedonic products with CRM. When the donation magnitude is low, a non-guilt appeal is more influential than a guilt appeal due to the boomerang effects of a product's hedonic nature. The results of the experiment indicated that when participants faced a guilt-appeal ad, they were likely to generate more maladaptive responses. Marketers need to use caution when employing a guilt appeal due to the negative effects of the donation magnitude on consumer responses, especially when promoting hedonic products.

Findings from this investigation are informative both theoretically and pragmatically. This study contributes to the academic literature and industry by increasing our understanding of guilt appeals in a CRM context by proposing product type and donation magnitude as factors that moderate the relationships between guilt appeals and consumer responses toward the promoted product and the sponsored company. Furthermore, maladaptive responses as the process measure are incorporated into the current study to provide evidence about potential drives behind how consumers process CRM messages. The findings underscore the importance for marketers to learn more about whether guilt appeals work, and in turn describe how practitioners can avoid negatively toward guilt appeals. The present research should serve a starting point for entry into this under-researched area.

REFERENCES

Barone, M. J., Norman, A. T., and Miyazaki, A. D. (2007), "Consumer Responses to Retailer Use of Cause-Related Marketing: Is More Fit Better?" *Journal of Retailing*, 83(4), 437-445.

Basil, D. Z., Ridgway, N. M., and Basil, M. (2006), "Guilt Appeals: The Mediating Effect of Responsibility," *Psychology and Marketing*, 23, 1035-1054.

Basil, D. Z., Ridgway, N. M., and Basil, M. (2008), "Guilt and Giving: A Process Model of Empathy and Efficacy," *Psychology and Marketing*, 25, 1-23.

Bennett, R. (1998), "Shame, Guilt and Responses to Non-Profit and Public Sector Ads," *International Journal of Advertising*, 17(4), 483-499.

Berglind, M., and Nakata, C. (2005), "Cause-Related Marketing: More Buck Than Bang?" *Business Horizons*, 48(5), 443-453.

Chang, C. (2008), "To Donate or Not to Donate? Product Characteristics and Framing Effects of Cause-Related Marketing on Consumer Purchase Behavior," *Psychology and Marketing*, 25(12), 1089-1110.

Cotte, J., Coulter, R., and Moore, M. (2005), "Enhancing or Disrupting Guilt: The Role of Credibility and Perceived Manipulative Intent," *Journal of Business Research*, 58(3), 361-368.

Gupta, S., and Pirsch, J. (2006), "A Taxonomy of Cause-Related Marketing Research: Current Findings and Future Research Directions," *Journal of Nonprofit and Public Sector Marketing*, 15(1), 25-43.

Hibbert, S., Smith, A. D., and Ireland, F. (2007), "Guilt Appeals: Persuasion Knowledge and Charitable Giving," *Psychology and Marketing*, 24(8),723-742.

Smith, G., and Stodghill, R. (1994), "Are Good Causes Good Marketing?" *Business Week*, 3363, 64-66.

Strahilevitz, M. (1999), "The Effects of Product Type and Donation Magnitude on Willingness to Pay More for a Charity-Linked Brand," *Journal of Consumer Psychology*, 8(3), 215-241.

Strahilevitz, M., and Myers, J. G. (1998), "Donations to Charity as Purchase Incentives: How Well They Work May Depend on What You Are Trying to Sell," *Journal of Consumer Research*, 24(4), 434-446.

Subrahmanyan, S. (2004), "Effects of Price Premium and Product Type on the Choice of Cause-Related Brands: A Singapore Perspective," *Journal of Product and Brand Management*, 13(2), 116-124.

Webb, D. J., and Mohr, L (1998), "A Typology of Consumer Responses to Cause-Related Marketing: From Skeptics to Socially Concerned," *Journal of Public Policy and Marketing*, 17(2), 226-238.

The Impact of Anchors on Donors' Behavior: A Field Experiment

Sonja Prokopec, ESSEC Business School, France
Arnaud De Bruyn, ESSEC Business School, France

EXTENDED ABSTRACT

A recurring and important challenge facing managers working in the fundraising sector is how much they should ask for when soliciting donations. The effectiveness of any campaign to solicit donations depends upon compliance rates as well as the magnitude of the help. A standard practice in donation requests is to present a set of suggested amounts, hereafter referred to as a donation grid. As we will show in this paper, designing the appropriate donation grid requires strategic trade offs as the donation amounts that are too high might lead to relatively low compliance rates whereas those that are too low might negatively impact the average amount donated.

Anchoring is an extremely robust phenomenon that appears in many contexts, even among experts as well as with important decisions (cf. Wansink, Kent, and Hoch, 1998). Donation grids have been shown to act as de facto frames of reference, directly altering judgment (Schwarz et al. 1991). Fundraising organizations use donation grids to artificially influence donation amounts. When faced with a request for donation, one must decide whether to respond at all, followed by the decision about the amount to be donated. How a consumer makes a decision about the donation is affected partly by the way in which information is presented and partly by his/her own internal characteristics (Lynch, Chakravarti and Anuaree, 1991; Tversky and Kahneman, 1981). While several mechanisms have been identified to positively influence likelihood of donation as well as amounts donated, there is little research that has shown that some anchoring mechanisms might have adverse consequences on consumers' donation decisions.

The purpose of this study is to explore how different designs of donation grids affect the likelihood to donate and the magnitude of donations. In addition, we also explore how donors' individual characteristics impact their compliance with the donation grids. This study makes several contributions to the literature: we identify different donation grid designs that positively as well as negatively impact donation behavior, we show that donors with strong internal reference points are less influenced by the donation grids per se, and finally, our results have both internal and external validity by use of a controlled field experiment.

We ran a large field experiment in which a charity solicited 50,000 of its donors, and tailored suggested donation amounts based on their past behavior. The nonprofit organization and the research team manipulated donation grids to study their impact on actual donation behavior. The manipulations were twofold. First, we manipulated how the donor's internal reference point (i.e., her last donation amount) was embedded in the donation grid. The reference point (the first amount, or left end of the grid) was manipulated as follow:

- Lower — the first suggested amount (the left end of the grid) is actually lower than the donor's last gift;
- Equal — the first suggested donation amount is equal to the donor's last gift;
- Higher — the first suggested donation amount is higher than the donor's last gift.

Second, further suggested amounts were proportionally increased (influencing the right end of the grid), and the steepness of this increase was manipulated, as follow:

- Low — suggested donation amounts were increasing at a 20% rate;
- Medium — suggested donation amounts were increasing at a 50% rate;
- High — amounts were increasing at an 80% rate.

Our final sample consisted of 50,208 donors. The summary of results is as follows: Increasing the left end of the donation grid seems to discourage donations, consistent with out theoretical development. Manipulating the steepness of the donation grid, however, does not affect the likelihood of donation, and none of the differences across conditions achieve statistical significance, consistent with our hypothesizing.

Of the 50,208 solicited donors, 4,539 (9.0%) made a donation. As expected, both anchoring mechanisms affect donation amounts, although changing the reference point (the left end of the grid) has the greatest effect.

Regarding the proposed moderating effects, we suggested that donors who have made in the past numerous donations to the charity might have developed a strong internal reference point, and that this reference point might counterbalance the influence of anchoring mechanisms, hence reducing their amplitude. Data confirm this hypothesis. Furthermore, it was hypothesized that for recent donors, the donation behavior would be more vivid in the memory, and would serve as a strong internal reference point which anchoring mechanisms might not be able to influence. This hypothesis is confirmed when it comes to likelihood of donation but not donation amounts. Finally, we found that the less generous donors were much more influenced by anchoring mechanisms, whether the manipulation was the reference point or the steepness of the donation grid than more generous donors.

While our results confirm that both anchors (manipulating the left end and the right end of the donation grid) increase donation amount, we showed that manipulating the left end of the donation grid also decreased the likelihood of donation, hence adversely affecting overall donations. We also showed that the amplitude of these effects predictably varied based on donors' characteristics. Donors who have strong internal reference points, either due to frequent donations or to large amounts donated, were not influenced by the donation grids. What our study results suggest is that fundraising managers should not only use donation grids to facilitate donations, but as an active tool to optimize them. For example, frequent and/or generous donors could be contacted with a donation grid that includes amounts at high as their previous donation amounts or higher. This paper is important both for academics and practitioners, demonstrating for the first time in a large-scale experiment the potentially adverse consequences of anchoring mechanisms on donation likelihood, and the need for future research in this area.

REFERENCES

Abraham, M., and Bell, R. (1994), "Encouraging charitable contributions–an examination of three models of door-in-the-face compliance," *Communication Research*, 21(2), 131–153.

Cialdini, R. B., Kallgren, C. A., and Reno, R. R. (1991), "A focus theory of normative conduct: A theoretical refinement and reevaluation of the role of norms in human behavior," *Advances in Experimental Social Psychology*, 24, 201-234.

Davison, A.C. and Hinkley D.V. (1997). *Bootstrap Methods and Their Application. Cambridge Series in Statistical and Probabilistic Mathematics,* Cambridge University Press.

Desmet, Pierre and Fred M. Feinberg (2003), "Ask and Ye Shall Receive: The Effects of the Appeals Scale on Consumers' Donation Behavior," *Journal of Economic Psychology*, Vol. 24 (3), 349-376.

Doob, A., and McLaughlin, D. (1989), "Request size and donations to a good cause," *Journal of Applied Social Psychology*, 19(12), 1049–1056.

Fraser, C., Hite R.E., and Sauer P.L. (1988), "Increasing contributions in solicitation campaigns: The use of large and small anchor points," *Journal of Consumer Research*, 15 (September), 284 -287.

Heiser, Robert (2006), "Normative Influences in Donation Decisions," *Journal of Nonprofit and Public Sector Marketing*, 15(1/2), 127–149.

Helson, H. (1964), *Adaptation-level theory: An experimental and systematic approach to behavior*, New York: Harper & Row.

Jiobu, R. M. and Knowles, E. S. (1974), "Norm strength and alms giving: An observational study," *The Journal of Social Psychology*, 94, 205-211.

Lynch, J.G., Chakravarti, D.,and Mitra Anuaree (1991), "Contrast effects in consumer judgments: Changes in mental states or rating scales?" *Journal of Consumer Research*, 18, 284-297.

Monroe, K.B. and Petroshius S.M. (1981), "Buyers' Perceptions of price: An update of the evidence," in *Perspectives in Consumer Behavior*, eds. Harold H. Kassarjian and Thomas S. Roberston, Glenview, IL: Scott, Foresman, 43-55.

Schwarz, N., Bless, H., Bohner, G., Harlacher, U., and Kellenbenz, M. (1991), "Response scales as frames of reference–the impact of frequency-range on diagnostic judgments," *Applied Cognitive Psychology*, 5(1), 37–49.

Schwarzwald, J., Bizman, A., and Raz, M. (1983), „The foot-in-the-door paradigm: Effects of second request size on donation probability and donor generosity," *Personality and Social Psychology Bulletin*, 9 (September), 443-450.

Sherif, M., Taub, D., and Hivland, C. (1958), "Assimilation and contrast effects of anchoring stimuli on judgments," *Journal of Experimental Psychology*, 55 (2), 150-156.

Simonson, I. and Tversky, A. (1992), "Choice in context: Tradeoff contrast and extremeness Aversion," *Journal of Marketing Research*, 29 (August), 281-295.

Tversky, A. and Kahneman, D. (1974), "Judgment under uncertainty: Heuristics and biases," *Science*, 185, 453-458.

Tversky, A. and Kahneman, D. (1981), "The framing of decisions and the psychology of choice," *Science*, 211, 1124-1131.

Urbany, J.E., Bearden, W.O., and Weilbaker, D.C. (1988), "The effect of plausible and exaggerated reference prices on consumer perceptions and price search," *Journal of Consumer Research*, 15, 95 -110.

Wansink, B., Kent R.J., and Hoch R.J. (1998), "An anchoring and adjustment model of purchase quantity decision," *Journal of Marketing Research*, 35(1), 71-81.

Causes at the Checkout: The Role of Temporal Construal in Consumer Reactions to Corporate Social Responsibility

Reetika Gupta, Lehigh University, USA
Sankar Sen, Baruch College, CUNY, USA

EXTENDED ABSTRACT

Marketplace polls today point to large and growing swaths of consumers who want to buy products and services that not only are good but also do good. For instance, according to a recent marketplace poll (Cone 2007), 87% consumers said that they are likely to switch from one brand to another (price and quality being about equal) if the other brand is associated with a good cause. At the same time, however, the advantage of CSR products at the checkout remains unsubstantiated.

We draw on temporal construal theory to examine why consumers express strong purchase intentions for brands associated with a cause in polls but balk at acting on their intentions at the point of purchase. According to the temporal construal theory, distant future events are represented in more abstract terms where desirability concerns guide preferences, whereas near future events are represented in more concrete terms, with preferences being guided largely by feasibility concerns (e.g., Liberman and Trope 1998). We predict that in a poll setting, the purchase intent expressed by consumers for the distant unspecified future is influenced significantly by the desirability aspect of the brand (i.e., a strong CSR record signaling a responsible company). In contrast, the CSR record has a more muted impact on imminent consumer purchase decisions (e.g., at the point of purchase); in these situations, the consumer is influenced more by the nitty-gritties (feasibility concerns), such as affordability of brand or the presence of functional attributes.

Moreover, we suggest that this interplay between effects of CSR actions and the time horizon for consumer purchases is likely to vary across consumer groups who differ on the extent to which they believe that a firm's CSR efforts, in general, detract (in terms of available resources) from, rather than reinforce, the companies' resources. Sen and Bhattacharya (2001) have shown that consumers' general beliefs about the trade-offs companies make to support CSR activities do influence consumer perceptions of CSR actions. Specifically, we demonstrate that the contribution of CSR to consumers' purchase intentions will be more susceptible to temporal construal among consumers who think CSR efforts detract from company resources; consumers who perceive that CSR efforts reinforce company resources will display their loyalty to CSR-based products, regardless of the purchase timeframe.

Three studies were conducted to test our research propositions. Study 1 had a between-subjects design with subjects asked to imagine a supermarket visit in one of the two purchase timeframes (near, far). As expected, subjects were more likely to buy products that were associated with a cause when their purchases were in the distant, rather than in the near, future. In Study 2, using a conjoint design where consumers had an opportunity to compare the ethical attributes with other functional attributes (price, style) across the two purchase timeframes (near, far), we provide evidence that the focus on ethical attributes do get heightened in the distant future, while it has a muted impact in the near future. In Study 3, we examined if the beliefs related to the trade-offs companies make to engage in CSR activities influence the pattern of relationships between CSR actions, timeframe and purchase intent. Study 3 had a between-subjects design with three factors: 2 (purchase timeframe: near future or distant future) X 2 (attribute: CSR record or DVD-RW drive) X 2 (trade-off CSR beliefs: CSR activities detract, CSR activities reinforce). Participants were primed with a near or distant laptop purchase scenario. Half of the participants in each condition responded to a series of purchase decision questions about a brand that engaged in CSR activities and the other half responded to a series of purchase decision questions about a brand possessing a DVD-RW drive. To measure consumers' trade-off CSR beliefs, participants responded to a set of items that captured their beliefs about whether CSR activities detract or reinforce company resources (e.g., companies that engage in socially responsible behavior produce worse products than firms that do not worry about social responsibility). As expected, in the CSR condition, participants indicated a stronger intention to purchase the product if it is associated with a cause, when the purchase is in the distant future than in the near future. We found a moderating effect of trade-off CSR beliefs such that the temporal construal-based difference in the effects of CSR actions on purchase intent exist for those who, in general, believe that CSR activities detract from company resources but these differences are not observed among those who believe that CSR activities reinforce company resources. These results did not play out in the baseline DVD-RW drive condition, indicating the absence of temporal construal-based effects among functional attributes.

From a theoretical standpoint, the findings advance research in both CSR and temporal construal theory by demonstrating that consumers lay more emphasis on abstract aspirational features such as CSR records in the distant future than in the near future. In addition, this research reveals that these temporal construal-based effects are limited by the extent to which consumers think CSR actions detract from company resources.

REFERENCES

Cone Inc. (2007), "Cone Cause Evolution and Environmental Survey," [available at http://www.coneinc.com/files/2007Cone SurveyReport.pdf].

Liberman, Nira and Yaacov Trope (1998), "The Role of Feasibility and Desirability Considerations in Near and Distant Future Decisions: A Test of Temporal Construal Theory," *Journal of Personality and Social Psychology*, 75 (July), 5-18.

Sen, Sankar and C. B. Bhattacharya (2001), "Does Doing Good Always Lead to Doing Better? Consumer Reactions to Corporate Social Responsibility," *Journal of Marketing Research*, 38 (May), 225-243.

The Reparation Effect: Indulgent Consumption Increases Donation Behavior

Promothesh Chatterjee, University of South Carolina, USA
Arul Mishra, University of Utah, USA
Himanshu Mishra, University of Utah, USA

EXTENDED ABSTRACT

Donations from the public constitute more than 75% of charitable contributions and thus are a major source of funds for charitable organizations (Giving USA 2007). Several ways have been researched to encourage charitable donations (Aunel and Basil 1994; Cialdini and Ascani 1976; Reingen 1978; Weyant and Smith 1987). This article proposes an unlikely prior act—food consumption—that could influence people's donation behavior. Specifically, we propose and find evidence that people who consumed an indulgent food (e.g., ice cream or chocolates, which are often considered vices) donate more money to charitable causes than those who consumed a non-indulgent food (e.g., sandwiches).

In this research, we posit that the guilt originating from indulgent consumption increases subsequent acts of donation. Contributing to a charitable cause provides people a means to alleviate their guilt. Therefore, people are likely to donate more money after consuming an indulgent food option than after consuming a non-indulgent food option. We call the phenomenon the "reparation effect", in which prior consumption of an indulgent option produces guilt, and as reparation for the act of consumption, people engage in charitable activities to alleviate their guilt.

In the first study, we approached people exiting eateries which specialized in either chicken sandwiches or ice creams at a large public university campus for filling up questionnaires in lieu of a chance to win a coupon for free ice cream or chicken sandwich depending on the location of the encounter. After several filler questions, we informed the participant about the activities of Red Cross and asked them to indicate the amount of money they would be willing to donate. In a subsequent unrelated questionnaire, participants were asked questions intended to measure consumption guilt. The results of study 1 demonstrated that participants were willing to donate more money after indulgent consumption than after non-indulgent consumption, thereby demonstrating the reparation effect. Also, it generated support for our claim that guilt mediated this willingness to donate.

Study 2 had two objectives. The first was to use a choice versus no-choice task to provide further support for the proposed guilt-based mechanism underlying the reparation effect. The second objective was to rule out a demand artifact explanation (i.e., the possibility that the results of the previous studies may be explained by a self-selection procedure). A poster was put up which described that participation in a research study would enable the participants to get a meal coupon. One hundred and nineteen participants approached the table where one of the authors and two research assistants sat. The participants were told that they had to participate in a short survey and as a token of appreciation they would get a meal coupon. This survey took place in two stages; one part of the questionnaire was completed before consuming food and the other part after consuming. The participants were informed that there were two conditions in the survey, one where the participant gets to choose what to eat and the other where the experimenter decides what they should eat. If allocated the choice condition the participants will have to choose between an ice-cream coupon and a chicken sandwich coupon, otherwise the experimenter would determine whether participant receives an ice-cream or a sandwich coupon. The logic behind such a procedure was that participants who were in the experimenter allocated ice-cream condition could have a justifiable reason for external attribution of indulgent consumption. We then randomly divided the participants into two groups. The participants in one group (choice group) were allowed to choose between two coupons entitling them to either a chicken sandwich or an ice-cream. The participants in the other group (no-choice group) were randomly allotted either the chicken sandwich or the ice-cream coupons. The participants then filled up the first part of the questionnaire which contained the demographic details and a question to assess their hunger state. The participants were then handed the coupons and proceeded with the research assistant to redeem their coupons. Once the participants had redeemed their coupons and consumed the product, immediately the research assistant then asked them to fill up the final part of the questionnaire which contained questions previously described in study 1. The results of study 2 replicate the findings of the reparation effect and also rule out self-selection bias as an alternate account since we randomly allocated participants to the ice-cream and chicken sandwich conditions. The results also find support for the proposed guilt-based mechanism.

In study 3, we wanted to lessen the impact of extraneous influences prevalent in field studies 1 and 2 by examining the reparation effect in a lab setting. Another objective was to investigate the influence of the quantity consumed on the reparation effect. If our conceptualization is true, then greater consumption of the indulgent food option should result in greater guilt and hence higher donation amounts. A final objective was to ensure that there were no differential influences due to the food items. It could be argued that ice cream and chicken sandwiches have different qualities (e.g., sugar vs. no sugar) and may be more or less filling. In order to address this concern we used the same chocolates for participant consumption but defined them as indulgent or non-indulgent. Participants were then asked to indicate the amount of money they would be willing to donate to such charitable institutions. The results of this study replicated the reparation effect and provided further evidence for our suggested account. We found an increased engagement in charity for those in the indulgent description condition compared to those in the non-indulgent description condition. Moreover, the effect was pronounced for those who consumed a higher number of indulgent chocolates.

The charity market is intensely competitive and guilt-appeals for donations are ubiquitous. Our findings suggest that charitable organizations will have a higher efficacy with donation appeals if they target post-indulgent behavior. Thus, the place at which an appeal is made is equally as important as when it is made.

REFERENCES

Amodio, David M., Patricia G. Devine and Eddie Harmon-Jones(2007), "A Dynamic Model of Guilt: Implications for Motivation and Self-Regulation in the Context of Prejudice," *Psychological Science*, 18(6), 524-530.

Aunel, R. Kelly and Michael D. Basil (1994), "A Relational Obligations Approach to the Foot-In-The-Mouth Effect," *Journal of Applied Social Psychology*, 24(6), 546-556.

Baron, Reuben M. and David A. Kenny (1986), "The Moderator-Mediator Variable Distinction in Social-Psychological Research," *Journal of Personality and Social Psychology*, 51, 1173-1182.

Baumeister, Roy F., Arlene M. Stillwell and Todd F. Heatherton (1994), "Guilt: An Interpersonal Approach," *Psychological Bulletin*, 115, 243–267.

Bloom, Paul N. and William D. Novelli (1981), "Problems and Challenges in Social Marketing," *Journal of Marketing*, Spring, 79-88.

Burnett, Melissa S. and Dale A. Lunsford (1994), "Conceptualizing Guilt in the Consumer Decision Making Process," *Journal of Consumer Marketing*, 11, 33–43.

Bybee, J. A., and Zigler, E. (1991), "Self-image and Guilt: A Further Test of the Cognitive-Developmental Formulation," *Journal of Personality*, 59(4), 733-745.

Carlson, Michael, Ventura Charlin and Norman Miller (1988), "Positive Mood and Helping Behavior: A Test of Six Hypotheses," *Journal of Personality and Social Psychology*, 55, 211–229.

Cialdini, Robert B. and K. Ascani (1976), "Test of a Concession Procedure for Inducing Verbal, Behavioral, and Further Compliance with a Request to Give Blood," *Journal of Applied Psychology*, 61(3), 295-300.

Coulter, Robin H. and Mary B. Pinto (1995), "Guilt Appeal in Advertising: What are Their Effects?" *Journal of Applied Psychology*, 80, 697–705.

Fabrikant, Geraldine (2008), "Economy Expected to Take a Toll on Charitable Giving," *New York Times*, September 30, C1.

Giving USA (2007), Annual Report of Philanthropy for the Year 2007. Glenview, IL: Giving USA Foundation.

Hoch, Steve and George Loewenstein (1991), "Time-Inconsistent Preferences and Consumer Self-Control," *Journal of Consumer Research*, 17 (March), 492–507.

Hyman, Michael R. and Richard Tansey (1990), "The Ethics of Psychoactive Ads," *Journal of Business Ethics*, 9, 105–114.

Kivetz, Ran and Itamar Simonson (2002), "Earning the Right to Indulge: Effort as a Determinant of Customer Preferences towards Frequency Program Rewards," *Journal of Marketing Research*, 39 (May), 155–170.

Maitner, Angela T., Diane M. Mackie and Eliot R. Smith (2006), "Evidence for The Regulatory Function of Intergroup Emotion: Emotional Consequences of Implemented or Impeded Intergroup Action Tendencies," *Journal of Experimental Social Psychology*, 42, 720–728.

Novemsky, Nathan and Ravi Dhar (2005), "Goal Fulfillment and Goal Targets in Sequential Choice," *Journal of Consumer Research*, 32(3), 396-404.

Okada, Erica M. (2005), "Justification Effects on Consumer Choice of Hedonic and Utilitarian Goods," *Journal of Marketing Research*, 42 (February), 43-53.

Prelec, Drazen and Richard J. Herrnstein (1991), "Preferences or Principles: Alternative Guidelines for Choice," in *Strategy and Choice*, ed. Richard J. Zeckenhauser, Cambridge, MA: MIT Press, 319–340.

Prelec, Drazen and George Loewenstein (1998), "The Red and the Black: Mental Accounting of Savings and Debt," *Marketing Science*, 17 (1), 4–28.

Reingen, Peter H. (1978), "On Inducing Compliance with Requests," *Journal of Consumer Research*, 5(2), 96.

Shafir, Eldar, Itamar Simonson and Amos Tversky (1993), "Reason-Based Choice," *Cognition*, 49, 11-36.

Tangney, June P. (1991), "Moral Affect: The Good, The Bad, and The Ugly," *Journal of Personality and Social Psychology*, 61, 598–607.

Thaler, Richard H. (1980), "Toward a Positive Theory of Consumer Choice," *Journal of Economic Behavior and Organization*, 1, 39–60.

Weyant, James M. and Stephen L. Smith (1987), "Getting More by Asking for Less: The Effects of Request Size on Donations of Charity," *Journal of Applied Social Psychology*, 17(4), 392-400.

It Takes the Chronic to Know the Prime: Understanding the True Benefits and Costs of Priming

Monika Lisjak, Northwestern University, USA
Daniel C. Molden, Northwestern University, USA
Angela Y. Lee, Northwestern University, USA

EXTENDED ABSTRACT

Priming is widely used in consumer research to systematically investigate how increased accessibility of cognitions and goals influence information processing and decision making (Higgins, Rholes and Jones 1977; Bargh, Lombardi and Higgins 1988). Researchers sometimes rely on priming and other times use chronic measures to provide convergent evidence for their hypotheses and ensure construct validity (e.g., Gardner, Gabriel and Lee 1999; Higgins, Shah and Friedman 1997). For example, Ramanathan and Menon (2006) either measured participants' chronic hedonic goals or primed them with hedonic goals to investigate impulsive behaviors. In this research, we argue that there are costs to priming. Across three studies, we show that priming individuals with a regulatory goal that is inconsistent with their chronic orientation creates a disruptive experience that is cognitively depleting.

The literature is replete with evidence showing that goals can be primed (Kruglanski et al. 2002; Fishbach and Ferguson 2007). Although there are individual differences in how people represent goals in memory, research shows that it is possible to override these chronic dispositions through priming. In fact, the current perspective is that priming a regulatory goal orientation has the same effects on people's judgments and behavior as having that orientation chronically accessible (see Shah and Higgins 1997; Shah, Higgins and Friedman 1998; Förster, Higgins and Bianco 2003).

In the current work, we examine the effects of priming a regulatory goal orientation on self-regulation. Regulatory focus theory suggests that people have two motivational systems: a promotion system that involves a concern for advancement and growth needs, and a prevention system that involves a concern for security and safety needs (Higgins 2000). When people pursue goals with strategies that fit their motivational orientation they experience regulatory fit, which leads to increased engagement and feelings of rightness (Hong and Lee 2008). We draw on and extend regulatory fit theory by hypothesizing that priming a regulatory goal orientation that is inconsistent with the chronic disposition disrupts people's chronic state; and this shift in regulatory goal orientation is cognitively depleting and impairs people' ability to self-regulate. We tested our hypothesis in three experiments.

In experiment 1, participants completed the regulatory focus questionnaire (RFQ) that measures chronic regulatory orientation. Then, participants were randomly assigned to describe their hopes and aspirations (promotion prime condition) or their duties and obligations (prevention prime condition) (Higgins, Roney, Crowe and Hymes 1994). Finally, participants were administered the color-naming Stroop task to assess their ability to resolve attentional conflict. Participants were asked to name the colors in which color words were printed. For example, the word "blue" may be presented in red, and the task is to identify the color red. On congruent trials, the color of the word matches the semantic meaning of the word, and hence, there is no conflict with the correct response. On incongruent trials, the color of the word mismatches its semantic meaning, creating a conflict with the correct response. Thus, participants have to inhibit their natural impulse to read the word, and focus instead on the color in which the word is printed (Kane and Engle 2003). The results showed that participants who were primed with a regulatory goal orientation that was inconsistent with their chronic orientation were slower at identifying the color in the incongruent (vs. congruent) word trials as compared to participants who were primed with a consistent regulatory orientation.

In experiment 2, we demonstrated that inconsistent priming influences people's ability to exert attention. Participants first completed the RFQ and then went through the same priming manipulation as in experiment 1. Next, participants completed a lexical decision task. They were presented with a series of letter strings and had to decide as quickly as possible whether each letter string was a word or a non-word. The word stimuli were either neutral (e.g., table), promotion related (e.g., grow) or prevention related (e.g., guard) words. By design, non-words differed from actual words only by one letter (e.g., scangal instead of scandal), and hence required more cognitive resource to identify. Our results showed that participants were faster at recognizing words consistent with the primed regulatory orientation; whereas the chronic orientation did not matter. However, the chronic and the primed orientation interacted to influence the speed with which participants discriminated non-words. Participants primed with an inconsistent regulatory orientation were slower at discriminating non-words compared to participants primed with a consistent orientation.

In our final experiment, we explored whether inconsistent priming undermines people's ability to engage in logical reasoning. A different priming manipulation was used to provide convergent evidence for our results. Participants first completed the RFQ and then engaged in an ostensibly unrelated memory task that included a framing manipulation. We framed the contingency of the memory task to emphasize the objective of gaining points (promotion prime condition) or of not losing points (prevention prime condition) (adapted from Förster et al. 2003). Later, participants engaged in an ostensibly unrelated study in which they were asked to solve problems from the Analytical section of the GRE for seven minutes (adapted from Schmeichel, Vohs and Baumeister 2003). In line with our hypothesis, participants primed with an inconsistent regulatory orientation solved fewer problems than participants primed with a consistent orientation. To uncover the underlying process at work, we asked a separate group of participants to report the extent to which they felt motivated after the priming manipulation. Participants primed with an inconsistent regulatory orientation reported lower levels of motivation compared to participants primed with a consistent orientation.

These studies advance our understanding on priming. Extant literature suggests that it is the accessibility of people's regulatory goals that matter when it comes to people's attitudes and behavior; whether the goal is temporarily made salient or chronically accessible does not make a difference. This research shows that it may be important to distinguish between the two types of accessibility—chronic and temporarily enhanced—given the influence of their interplay on people's ability to self-regulate.

REFERENCES

Bargh, John A., Wendy Lombardi, and E. Tory Higgins (1988), "Automaticity of Chronically Accessible Constructs in Person x Situation Effects on Person Perception: It's Just a Matter of Time," *Journal of Personality and Social Psychology*, 55 (October), 599–605.

Fishbach, Ayelet, and Melissa Ferguson (2007), "The Goal Construct in Social Psychology," in *Social Psychology: A Handbook of Basic Principles*, ed. Arie W. Kruglanski and E. Tory Higgins, New York: Guilford, 490–515.

Förster, Jens, E. Tory Higgins, and Amy Taylor Bianco (2003), "Speed/Accuracy Decisions in Task Performance: Built-in Trade-off or Separate Strategic Concerns?" *Organization Behavior and Human Decision Processes*, 90 (January), 148–164.

Gardner, Wendi L., Shira Gabriel, and Angela Y. Lee (1999), "I Value Freedom, But We Value Relationships: Self-Construal Priming Mirrors Cultural Differences in Judgment," *Psychological Science*, 10 (July), 321–326.

Higgins, E. Tory (2000), "Making a Good Decision: Value from Fit," *American Psychologist*, 55 (November), 1217–1230.

Higgins, E. Tory, William S. Rholes, and Carl R. Jones (1977), "Category Accessibility and Impression Formation," *Journal of Experimental Social Psychology*, 13 (2), 141–154.

Higgins, E. Tory, Christopher J.R. Roney, Ellen Crowe, and Charles Hymes (1994), "Ideal Versus Ought Predilections for Approach and Avoidance: Distinct Self-Regulatory Systems," *Journal of Personality and Social Psychology*, 66 (February), 276–286.

Higgins, E. Tory, James Shah, and Ronald Friedman (1997), "Emotional Responses to Goal Attainment: Strength of Regulatory Focus as Moderator," *Journal of Personality and Social Psychology*, 72 (March), 515–525.

Hong, Jiewen and Angela Y. Lee (2008), "Be Fit and Be Strong: Mastering Self-Regulation Through Regulatory Fit," *Journal of Consumer Research*, 34 (February), 682–695.

Kane, Michael J. and Randall W. Engle (2003), "Working-Memory Capacity and the Control of Attention: The Contributions of Goal Neglect, Response Competition, and Task Set to Stroop Interference," *Journal of Experimental Psychology*, 132 (March), 47–70.

Kruglanski, Arie W., James Y. Shah, Ayelet Fishbach, Ron Friedman, Woo Young Chun, and David Sleeth-Keppler (2002), "A Theory of Goal Systems," in *Advances in Experimental Social Psychology*, Vol. 34, ed. Mark P. Zanna, San Diego: Academic Press, 331–378.

Ramanathan, Suresh and Geeta Menon (2006), "Time-Varying Effects of Chronic Hedonic Goals on Impulsive Behavior," *Journal of Marketing Research*, 43 (November), 628–641.

Schmeichel, Brandon J., Kathleen D. Vohs, and Roy F. Baumeister (2003), "Intellectual Performance of Ego Depletion: Role of the Self in Logical Reasoning and Other Information Processing," *Journal of Personality and Social Psychology*, 85 (July), 33–46.

Shah, James and E. Tory Higgins (1997), "Expectancy x Value Effects: Regulatory Focus as Determinant of Magnitude and Direction," *Journal of Personality and Social Psychology*, 73 (September), 447–458.

Shah, James Y., E. Tory Higgins, and Ronald S. Friedman (1998), "Performance Incentives and Means: How Regulatory Focus Influences Goal Attainment," *Journal of Personality and Social Psychology*, 74 (February), 285–293.

The Effect of Quasi Social Cue on Web Site Evaluation: Social Presence and Social Support Approach

Eun-Jung Lee, Kent State University, USA

EXTENDED ABSTRACT

Introduction

Store atmospheric qualities of online retailing are distinctive from those in offline retailing, often negatively affecting customer's shopping experiences within the context. In particular, as a fundamental characteristic of computer-mediated experience (Hoffman & Novak, 1996), the lack of social appeals in a cyber shopping space is often blamed as a main reason for low-level involvement and satisfaction of online customers (McCabe & Nowlis, 2003; Hoffman & Novak, 1996), as it generates psychological distance (Sproull & Kiesler, 1986). Given the combination of increasing attention to the importance of store environment in online customers' shopping experience (e.g., Eroglu, Machleit, & Davis, 2003) and the crucial role of positive social influence in retail contexts (e.g., Argo, Dahl, & Manchanda, 2005), more academic efforts should be made with regard to the dynamics of social factors in the online retail environment. Therefore, building on the social presence and the social support theories, this study investigates the viable impacts of quasi social cue on online customers' Web site evaluation, and the psychological dynamics underlying the impacts.

Conceptualization

Social presence and quasi social cue. Communication psychologists believe that the sense of other people's being is not solely based on physical presence ("to be together") but also on social presence ("the sense of others"). Social presence refers to "the degree of salience of the other person in the interaction and the consequent salience of an interpersonal relationship (Short, Williams, & Christie, 1976, p.65)," which is a subjective perception determined by the amount of (verbal and nonverbal) social cues available within the medium (Sproull & Kiesler, 1986). More recently, communication psychologists indicate that social presence does occur in computer mediated communication contexts (e.g., online learning, email or web survey) with no physical interpersonal presence, and this also determines effectiveness of the medium (e.g., Biocca et al., 2003). Extending this view into the electronic commerce contexts, it can be argued that intrinsic deputy of social interaction in a cyber store-as well as its negative consequences like low interest in products and low attachment to the Web store-could be alleviated by managing the amount and quality of available social cues within the contexts, and in overall, this would ultimately enhance the quality of shopping experiences that online customers have in their shopping. In the Internet retail environment there exist various types of quasi social cue that resemble in part the role of employee or other shoppers' presence within a traditional retail store. Increasing the amount of such quasi social cue would raise the perception of social presence, and in turn, heightens positive influences of social presence in the online retailing. Two fundamental types of quasi social cue in online retailing (i.e., seller's information, customer review) are tested in the current study.

Online social support. Social support theory is adapted in this study to gain an understanding of mediating psychological dynamics underlying the quasi social presence effects. In general, positive social interaction generates positive psychological consequences like social support, which in the social psychology discipline refers to the psychological benefits that people receive from interpersonal contacts (Cohen & Wills, 1985). Applied to the context of retail surroundings, the study of social support focuses more on weak social ties occurring in a store setting (e.g., interaction with a salesperson) while the theory originally focuses on strong social ties in social interaction (e.g., Adelman, Ahuvia, & Goodwin, 1994; Rosenbaum, 2006; Rosenbaum & Massiah, 2007). Online social support refers to the psychological benefits that people gain from social presence in the Internet circumstances. Although no study has adapted social support theory into store environments of online retailing, it could be intuitively assumed that if a web store generates some positive social interaction during its transaction with shoppers, there could evoke social support which accordingly leads to positive shopping experiences of online customers. Building on the social presence and social support theories, it could be argued that if quasi social cue in an online store could be perceived as positive social interaction by customers, it would influence their evaluation on the Web store, with the mediation of their perception of online social support. Therefore, hypotheses are developed as follows:

- H1. Customers who shop at a Web site providing quasi social cue will perceive higher level of online social support than those who don't.
- H2. Customers who shop at a Web site providing quasi social cue will give higher Web site evaluation than those who don't.
- H3. Customers who perceive higher level of online social support will give higher Web site evaluation than those who perceive lower level of online social support.
- H4. The level of perceived online social support will mediate the positive influence of quasi social cue on Web site evaluation.

Method

A 2 (information vs. no information) x 2 (review vs. no review) experimental study was performed with one hundred and eighty four undergraduates. Independent variables were two common types of quasi social presence (i.e., service provider information and customer review) selected from the pre-test results, and determinant variables were i) Web site attitude, ii) overall service quality, and iii) loyalty intention. A fictitious, Web-based wine shop (Goodwine.com) was designed and used as the stimulus of this research, in order to control any past experience that participants may have. Subjects were randomly assigned to one of the four conditions and with two quasi social cues manipulated within the Web site: those for the information condition were exposed to a written company information, CEO greetings with a picture, and sommerlier's recommendation on each wine (seller's information manipulation) and participants for the review condition are given customer reviews in addition to the basic wine information (customer review manipulation). After viewing all the contents of the Web site, participants were led to a Web-based survey, which involved measurements of online social support, Web site evaluations, basic demographics, and items for manipulation checks. A three-factor (i.e., emotional support, companionship, information support/affiliation) online social support measurement was used, referring to the social support scales in the psychology and consumer literature (e.g., Chronister et al., 2006; Rosenbaum, 2006).

Scales for Web site evaluation used the measurements suggested by prior work (Coyle & Thorson, 2001; Wolfinbarger & Gilly, 2003; Zeithaml et al., 1996).

Findings and Conclusion

MANOVAs were performed to test hypothesis 1 and 2. As hypothesized, results show significant main effect of providing service provider's information and customer review on the three dimensions of online social support (H1). The three variables of Web site evaluation were significantly different across the conditions with two types of quasi social cue, indicating significant main effects of service provider's information and customer reviews (H2). Also, results from a regression analysis revealed that perceived high level of online social support predicts higher Web site evaluation, supporting hypothesis 3. Finally, results of MANCOVA showed the mediating effect of perceived online social support in the social cues–Web site evaluation mechanism, supporting hypothesis 4.

This study examines the impact of quasi social cue in the context of online retailing and its underlying psychological dynamics. The results provide empirical supports to the hypothesized positive link between two common types of quasi social cue and Web site evaluations. In addition, positive mediating effects of online social support are empirically identified, providing a theoretical explanation of online customers' psychological reasons lying underneath the impact. This research contributes to a growing research stream on online retail store environments, by providing empirical supports on the effect of social factors online and new psychological explanations. Findings of the study indicate that social factors are crucial in the context of online retailing as they are in the traditional store atmosphere. Furthermore, findings of this study may present some useful empirical suggestions to managers, regarding how to implement quasi social cue in their Web site environments to provide richer shopping experiences to customers.

References

Adelman, M. B. and Aaron. C. Ahuvia (1995), "Social support in the service sector," *Journal of Business Research*, 32 (March), 273-282.

Adelman, M. B., Ahuvia, A. and Goodwin, C. (1994), Beyond smiling: Social support and service quality, In R. T. Rust & R. L. Oliver (Eds.), *Service quality: New directions in theory and practice*, (pp.139–171), London: Sage Publications.

Argo, J.J., Dahl, D. W. and Manchanda, R. V. (2005), "The Influence of a Mere Social Presence in a Retail Context," *Journal of Consumer Research*, 32 (Sep.), 207-212.

Baker, J., Grewal, D. and Parasuraman, A. (1994), "The influence of store environment on quality inference and store image," *Journal of the Academy of Marketing Science*, 22 (4), 328-339.

Baker, J., Levy, M. and Grewal, D. (1992), "An experimental approach to marketing retail store environmental decisions," *Journal of Retailing*, 68 (Winter), 445-460.

Barker, R. G. (1968), *Ecological Psychology: Concepts and Methods for Studying the Environment and Human Behavior*, Stanford, CA: Stanford University Press.

Baron, R. M. and Kenny, D. A. (1986), "The moderator-mediator variable distinction in social psychological research: Conceptual, strategic, and statistical considerations," *Journal of Personality and Social Psychology*, 52, 1173-1182.

Biocca, F., Harms, C. and Burgoon, J. K. (2003), "Toward a More Robust Theory and Measure of Social Presence: Review and Suggested Criteria," *Presence: Teleoperators & Virtual Environments*. 12(5), 456-480.

Bitner, M. J. (1992), "Servicescapes: The Impact of Physical Surroundings on Customers and Employees," *Journal of Marketing*, 56 (April), 57–71.

Bolger, N., Zuckerman, A. and Kessler, R. C. (2000), "Invisible support and adjustment to stress," *Journal of Personality and Social Psychology*, 79, 953-961.

Boneva, B., Kraut, R. and Frohlich, D. (2001), "Using E-mail for Personal Relationships," *American Behavioral Scientists*, 45 (3), 530-549.

Carver, C. S., Scheier, M. F. and Weintraub, J. K. (1989), "Assessing coping strategies: A theoretically based approach," *Journal of Personality and Social Psychology*, 56, 267-283.

Chronister, J. A., Johnson, E. K. and Berven, N. L. (2006), "Measuring social support in rehabilitation," *Disability and Rehabilitation*, 28 (2), 75–84.

Cohen, S. (2004), "Social relationships and health," *American Psychologist*, 59 (November), 676-84.

Cohen, S. and Wills, T. A. (1985), Stress, social support, and the buffering hypothesis: A theoretical analysis. In A. Baum, S. E. Taylor, & J. Singer (Eds.), *Handbook of psychology and health*, (Vol. 4, pp. 253-268). Hillsdale, NJ: Erlbaum.

Coyle, J.R. and Thorson, E. (2001), "The Effects of Progressive Levels of Interactivity and Vividness in Web Marketing Sites," *Journal of Advertising*, 30 (3), 65-77.

Crosby, L. A., Evans, K. R. and Cowles, D. (1990), "Relationship Quality in Services Selling: An Interpersonal Influence Perspective," *Journal of Marketing*, 54 (3), 68-81.

Donovan, R. J. and Rossiter, J. R. (1982), "Store atmosphere: An environmental psychology approach," *Journal of Retailing*, 58 (Spring), 34- 57.

Eroglu, S. A., K. A. Machleit and L. M. Davis (2001), "Atmospheric qualities of online retailing: A conceptual model and implications," *Journal of Business Research*, 54 (2), 177-1784.

Eroglu, S. A., K. A. Machleit and L. M. Davis (2005), "Empirical testing of a model of online store atmospherics and shopper responses," *Psychology & Marketing*, 20 (2), 139-150.

Gefen, D. and Straub, D. W. (2004), "Consumer trust in B2C e-Commerce and the importance of social presence: experiments in e-Products and e-Services," *Omega*, 32 (6), 407-424.

Griffitt, W. and Russell Veitch (1971), "Hot and Crowded: Influences of Population Density and Temperature on Interpersonal Affective Behavior," *Journal of Personality and Social Psychology*, 17 (1), 92–98.

Haytko, D. L. and Baker, J. (2004), "It's all at the mall: Exploring adolescent girl's experiences," *Journal of Retailing*, 80 (1), 67-83.

Hoffman, D. L. and Novak, T. P. (1996), "Marketing in hypermedia computer-mediated environments: conceptual foundations," *Journal of Marketing*, 60, 50-68.

Horton, D. R. and Wohl, R. (1956), "Mass communication and para-social interaction: Observations on intimacy at a distance," Psychiatry, 19 (3), 215–229

Kotler, P. (1973/1974), "Atmospherics as a Marketing Tool," *Journal of Retailing*, 49 (Winter), 48- 64.

Kraut, R. E. (1982), "Social Presence, Facial Feedback, and Emotion," *Journal of Personality and Social Psychology*, 42 (5), 853–863.

Kreijns, K., Paul A. Kirschner, P. A., & Jochems, W. (2003), "Identifying the pitfalls for social interaction in computer-supported collaborative learning environments: a review of the research," *Computers in Human Behavior*, 19 (3), 335-353.

McCabe, D. B. and Nowlis, S. M. (2003), "The effect of examining actual products or product descriptions on consumer preference," *Journal of Consumer Psychology*, 13 (4), 431-439.

Mehrabian, A. and Russell, J. (1974), An approach to environmental psychology, Cambridge, MA: MIT Press.

Oakes, S. (2000), "The influence of the musicscape within service environments," *Journal of Services Marketing*, 14 (7), 539–56.

Rosenbaum, M. S. and Massiah, C. A. (2007), "When customers receive support from other customers: Exploring the influence of intercustomer social support on customer voluntary performance," *Journal of Service Research*, 9 (3), 257–270.

Rosenbaum, M. S. (2006), "Exploring the social supportive role of third places in consumers' lives," *Journal of Service Research*, 9 (1), 59–72.

Russell, J. A. and Ward, L. M. (1982), "Environmental psychology," *Annual Review of Psychology,* 33. 259–288.

Short, J. A., Williams, E. and Christie, B. (1976), *The social psychology of telecommunications*, New York: John Wiley & Sons.

Sproull, L. and Kiesler, S. (1986), "Reducing social context cues: Electronic mail in organizational communication," *Management Science*, 32, 1492-1512.

Suurmeijer, T. P. B. M., Doeglas, D. M., Briancon, S., Krijnen, W. P., Krol, B., Sanderman, R., et al. (1995), "The measurement of social support in the European research on incapacitating disease and social support: The development of the social support questionnaire for transactions (SSQT)," *Social Science & Medicine*, 40 (9), 1221-1229

Thoits, P. A. (1995), "Stress, coping and social support processes: Where are we? What next?" *Journal of Health and Social Behavior*, 35, 53-79.

Wellman, B., Salaff, J., Dimitrova, D., Garton, L., Gulia, M. and Haythornthwaite, C. (1996), "Computer Networks as Social Networks: Collaborative Work, Telework, and Virtual Community," *Annual Review of Sociology*, 22, 213-238.

Wills, T. A. and Shinar, O. (2000), Measuring perceived and received social support, In Sheldon Cohen, Lynn G. Underwood, and Benjamin H. Gottlieb (Eds.), *Social Support Measurement and Intervention* (pp. 86-135), New York: Oxford University Press.

Wills, T. A. (1991), Social support and interpersonal relationships. In M. S. Clark (Ed.), *Prosocial behavior* (pp.265-289), Newbury Park, CA: Sage.

Wolfinbarger, M. and Gilly, M. C. (2003), "eTailQ: Dimensionalizing, measuring and predicting etail quality," *Journal of Retailing*, 79, 183–198.

Zeithaml, V. A., Berry, L. L. and Parasuraman, A. (1996), "The Behavioral Consequences of Service Quality," *Journal of Marketing*, 60, 31-46.

Zhou, R. and Soman, D. (2003), "Looking Back: Exploring the Psychology of Queuing and the Effect of the Number of People Behind," *Journal of Consumer Research*, 29 (4), 517–30.

Mortality Salience and Brand Attitudes: The Moderating Role of Social Presence

Marieke L. Fransen, University of Amsterdam, The Netherlands
Dirk Smeesters, Erasmus University Rotterdam, The Netherlands
Bob M. Fennis, Utrecht University, The Netherlands

EXTENDED ABSTRACT

The fear of death is so fundamental to human beings that it pervades all aspects of life. People tend to cope with the aversive thought of one's own death in various ways. Several coping strategies have been identified and investigated, including self-esteem striving, in-group affiliations, and self-serving biases (see Pyszczynski et al. 2004 for a review). More recently another domain of human behavior has been added to this list, that of consumer behavior. Several studies have already provided empirical evidence for a relationship between mortality salience and consumer behavior. For example, it has been shown that individuals are more attracted to high status products (Heine, Harihara, and Niiya 2002; Mandel and Heine 1999), show a preference for domestic over foreign products (Fransen, Pruyn, Fennis, and Das 2008; Liu & Smeesters in press), evaluate their financial future more positive (Kasser and Sheldon 2000), intend to purchase and actually eat higher quantities of food products (Mandel and Smeesters 2008), and become more materialistic (Arndt et al. 2004) when they are reminded of their mortality.

The explanation for the relationship between mortality salience and various forms of consumer behavior has mainly been sought in 'distal' defense mechanisms (Terror Management Theory -TMT-; Greenberg, Pyszczynski, and Solomon 1986). These defense mechanisms are aimed at increasing self-esteem levels. Self-esteem is subsequently expected to serve as a buffer against mortality-related anxiety. It has been argued that consumerism and materialism are important values intrinsic to our contemporary western worldview (Arndt et al. 2004). Our current society turned into a consumer society in which the defining activity of individuals is consuming; money and possessions can therefore be seen as measures of self-worth (Bauman 1995). It is argued therefore that people can derive self-esteem by living up to these 'new' culturally valued norms of being wealthy, spending loads of money and live exorbitantly. Living up to these norms provides people with high levels of self-esteem functioning as a buffer against existential threat.

But are these coping strategies invariant across different consumption situations? We argue that they are not. Rather, the present paper will present evidence showing that consumption related terror management strategies are especially likely to unfold when consumption is public, and can be witnessed by others, rather than when consumption is private. More specifically, the present paper investigates the role of social presence in consumer-related mortality salience effects. As mentioned before, TMT states that individuals derive self-esteem from living up to culturally prescribed values and norms because meeting these norms allows people to feel like valuable persons in a valuable society. However, it remains unclear whether one directly derives self-esteem from looking at oneself and knowing that one behaves according to valued norms or that self-esteem is derived more indirectly from the fact that other society members witness how 'correctly' one behaves?

From research on Social Impact Theory (Latané 1981) we know that individuals desire to be viewed in a positive light by others (Baumeister 1982; Frey 1978; Leary and Kowalski 1990; Riordan, James, and Dunaway 2001), and therefore have the tendency to engage in impression management strategies when other persons are present or only imagined to be present. For instance, consumers are more likely to purchase expensive luxury brands when others are present in a retail environment whereas consumers who are alone in a store opt more often for a cheaper brand (Argo et al. 2005). Consumers seem to be motivated to gain the approval of others, which can be achieved by behaving in ways that are approved within a situation or cultural worldview (Kallgren, Reno, and Cialdini 2000). But why do individuals need social approval? Research on Sociometer theory (e.g., Leary 2003; Leary, Baumeister, and Zanna 2000; Leary, Downs, and Kernis 1995; Leary, Haupt, Strausser, and Chokel 1998) demonstrated that social approval positively affects self-esteem, which according to TMT is essential for dealing with mortality-related thoughts. Therefore, we argue that not only behaving according to cultural norms but also the knowledge that others see and witness one's culturally approved behavior is essential in dealing with existential anxiety. Hence, social presence might be an important factor in explaining mortality salience effects. In accordance with TMT, we propose that individuals derive self-esteem from living up to cultural norms which makes them valuable persons in their society. In extension, we proffer that self-esteem will receive an even greater boost when others (can) witness their socially approved behavior. Hence, based on the notion that social approval leads to enhanced levels of self-esteem (e.g., Leary 2003; Leary, Downs, and Kernis 1995), we expect that people are especially prone to show culturally prescribed behavior (i.e., expressing favorable attitudes towards luxury brands and less favorable attitudes towards non-luxury brands) when other members of their cultural worldview can witness their behavior but less so when others are not present.

The results of Studies 1 and 2 indeed showed that the (imagined) presence of others increased the effects of mortality salience on brand evaluations. Individuals who were reminded of their mortality evaluated luxury brands more positive (Studies 1 and 2) and non-luxury brand more negative (Study 2) under conditions of social approval. This implies that self-esteem receives an extra boost when one knows that others are aware of one's culturally prescribed behavior.

In sum, the present research reveals that mortality salience effects are moderated by social presence in such way that these effects become stronger when people are pointed to the notion that others will observe their behavior. This implies that people experience an extra self-esteem boost when they know that others observe (and approve) their culturally prescribed behavior.

REFERENCES

Argo, Jennifer J., Darren W. Dahl, and Rajesh V. Manchanda (2005), "The Influence of a Mere Social Presence in a Retail Context," *Journal of Consumer Research*, 32(2), 207-12.

Arndt, Jamie, Sheldon Solomon, Tim Kasser, and Kennon M. Sheldon (2004), "The urge to splurge: A terror management account of materialism and consumer behaviour," *Journal of Consumer Psychology*, 14(3), 198-212.

Bauman, Zigmund (1995), Life in Fragments: Essays in Postmodern Morality, Oxford: Blackwell.

Baumeister, Roy F. (1982), "Self-esteem, self-presentation, and future interaction: A dilemma of reputation," *Journal of Personality*, 50(1), 29-45.

Fransen, Marieke L., Bob M. Fennis, Ad Th. H. Pruyn, and Enny Das (2008), "Rest in Peace? Brand-induced mortality salience and consumer behaviour," *Journal of Business Research*, 60, 1053-61.

Frey, Dieter (1978), "Reactions to success and failure in public and in private conditions," *Journal of Experimental Social Psychology*, 14(2), 172-79.

Greenberg, Jeff, Tom Pyszczynski, Sheldon Solomon (1986), "The Causes and Consequences of a Need for Self-esteem: A Terror Management Theory," in *Public Self and Private Self*, Ed. Roy F. Baumeister, New York/Berlin: Springer-Verlag, 189-92.

Heine, Steven J, Motoke Harihara, and Yu Niiya (2002), "Terror management in Japan," *Asian Journal of Social Psychology*, 5(3), 187-96.

Kallgren, Carl A., Raymond R. Reno, and Robert Cialdini (2000), "A focus theory of normative conduct: When norms do and do not affect behaviour," *Personality and Social Psychology Bulletin*, 26 (8), 1002-12.

Kasser, Tim, and Kennon M. Sheldon (2000), "Of wealth and death: Materialism, mortality salience, and consumption behaviour," *Psychological Science*, 11(4), 348-51.

Latané, Bibb (1981), "The psychology of social impact," *American Psychologist*, 36(4), 343-56.

Leary, Mark R. (2003), "Interpersonal Aspects of Optimal Self-Esteem and the Authentic Self: Comment," *Psychological Inquiry*, 14(1), 52-54.

Leary, Mark R., Roy F. Baumeister, and Mark P. Zanna (2000), "The nature and function of self-esteem: Sociometer theory," In *Advances in experimental social psychology*, Vol. 32. (pp. 1-62). San Diego, CA, US: Academic Press.

Leary, Mark R., Diane L. Downs, and Michael H. (1995), "Interpersonal functions of the self-esteem motive: The self-esteem system as a sociometer," in *Efficacy, agency, and self-esteem*, (pp. 123-44). New York, NY, US: Plenum Press.

Leary, Mark R., Alison L. Haupt, Kristine S. Strausser, and Jason T. Chokel (1998), "Calibrating the sociometer: The relationship between interpersonal appraisals and the state self-esteem," *Journal of Personality and Social Psychology*, 74(5), 1290-99.

Leary, Mark R. and Robin M. Kowalski (1990), "Impression management: A literature review and two-component model," *Psychological Bulletin*, 107(1), 34-47.

Liu, Jia and Dirk Smeesters (in press), "Have You Seen the News Today? The Effect of Death-Related Media Contexts on Brand Preferences," *Journal of Marketing Research*.

Mandel, Naomi, and Steven J. Heine (1999), "Terror management and marketing: He who dies with the most toys wins," *Advances in Consumer Research*, 26(1), 527-32.

Mandel, Naomi and Dirk Smeesters (2008), "The Sweet Escape: Effect of Mortality Salience on Consumption Quantities for High and Low Self-Esteem Consumers," *Journal of Consumer Research*, 35 (August), 309-23.

Pyszczynski, Tom, Jeff Greenberg, Sheldon Solomon, Jamie Arndt, and Jeff Schimel (2004), "Why do people need self-esteem? A theoretical and empirical review," *Psychological Bulletin*, 130(3), 435-68.

Riordan, C. A., M. K. James, and F. A. Dunaway (2001), "Interpersonal determinants of helping and the transgression-compliance relationship," *The Journal of Social Psychology*, 125 (3), 365-72.

Consumer and Product Face-to-Face: Antecedents and Consequences of Spontaneous Face-Schema Activation

Linda Miesler, University of St. Gallen, Switzerland
Jan R. Landwehr, University of St. Gallen, Switzerland
Andreas Herrmann, University of St. Gallen, Switzerland
Ann L. McGill, University of Chicago, USA

EXTENDED ABSTRACT

The concept of anthropomorphism is gaining in popularity in marketing and product design. Particularly in automotive design, the trend to develop cars whose fronts look like the human face is increasing (e.g., VW Beetle, Mini). But, in striving for product success, whether the mere morphological shape of a product's design is sufficient to activate a human schema is, as yet, an unanswered question. In the context of marketing-mix activities, what specific contribution can anthropomorphic product design make to developing a product's personality? To answer these questions, evidence on the psychological process which underlies anthropomorphizing is needed. Aggarwal and McGill (2007) recently proposed the schema-congruity theory to explain how anthropomorphism works, but their experimental approach left it open if consumers anthropomorphize products spontaneously when they see a human-like product (i.e., according to an automatic bottom-up process) or whether it has to be triggered externally.

In our project, we were particularly interested in the tendency to anthropomorphize products due to their similarity to a human face. We chose real cars as objects of investigation and compared car fronts with car sides, since we assumed that the design of car fronts should resemble a human face, whereas the design of car sides should obviously not. To gain deeper insights into the cognitive mechanisms, we investigated in study 1 whether the activation of a face-schema in memory is an automatic, feature-driven process leading to anthropomorphizing car fronts but not car sides and, in study 2, we examined the effects of anthropomorphizing on explicit product evaluations.

Study 1: To investigate whether a car might be associated spontaneously with a human face solely due to its design features we settled on a lexical decision task (LDT) which was performed by 165 native German speakers. The participants' task was to categorize a target stimulus as a word versus a non-word ignoring a preceding picture prime. For all participants, words stemmed from two categories (face-words vs. car-words). With regard to the preceding picture primes, participants were randomly assigned to one of three priming conditions, so that they were primed either with pictures of cars presented in front view, cars presented in side view, or faces. Latency for participants' lexical decisions was recorded in milliseconds for each trial.

If the mere product design really accounts for the activation of a human schema, different response latencies to face- and car-words between the three priming conditions should occur. We hypothesized that average response patterns in the face condition should be similar to response patterns in the car front condition, but different from response patterns in the car side condition.

As expected, the priming condition (car front, car side, face) interacted significantly with the word target's category (face vs. car) ($F(2,162)=3.28$, $p=.040$). More precisely, participants who were primed with car fronts responded significantly faster to face-words than to car-words ($t(52)=1.69$, $p=.050$), whereas participants who were primed with car sides responded significantly faster to car-words than to face-words ($t(46)=-1.87$, $p=.030$). Further between-group comparisons showed that latency patterns did not differ between the car front and face condition ($t(116)=0.44$, $p=.660$), but both were significantly different from the car side condition (face vs. side: $t(110)=-0.20$, $p=.044$; front vs. side: $t(98)=2.52$, $p=.013$) which was also congruent with our expectations.

Study 2: The same participants who performed the LDT were asked to rate pictures of cars on different scales (the pictures were identical to the pictures which were used in the LDT as primes). One group of participants rated cars shown in front view, the other group rated cars shown in side view. The scales assessed general marketing variables (e.g., liking, willingness to pay) and specific evaluative tendencies which should go together with anthropomorphizing (e.g., attribution of a human personality to the car). Furthermore, we also assessed the participants' personal disposition to anthropomorphize cars.

We assumed as explicit evaluative consequences of automatic face-schema activation and, therefore, anthropomorphizing that participants should rate car fronts higher than car sides on the anthropomorphism scales and, therefore, car fronts are maybe also evaluated better than car sides with regard to the marketing variables. As ratings on the anthropomorphism-related scales were highly correlated ($r=.74$, $p<.001$), we created a composite variable, named the anthropomorphism score. Overall, to our surprise, participants did not rate car fronts significantly higher on the anthropomorphism score than car sides ($F(1, 82)=2.45$, $p=.122$). However, when controlling for a participant's personal disposition to anthropomorphize, we found the expected main effect of the car view on the anthropomorphism score with fronts being more anthropomorphized than sides ($F(5, 71)=8.54$, $p=.005$). Likewise, participants were willing to pay more for cars seen in front vs. side views ($F(1, 71)=4.55$, $p=.036$) and general positive affect elicited by cars was higher for front than side views ($F(1, 71)=10.65$, $p=.002$), when controlling for personal disposition in both analyses.

General discussion: Our results support the assumption that consumers anthropomorphize products spontaneously solely due to anthropomorphic design features and provide insights into the relative priority of anthropomorphic thoughts. Specifically, findings show that car fronts not only bring to mind the human schema more so than car sides bring forth this schema, they bring to mind the human schema more than the actual product category schema. This remarkable, but maybe also non-intuitive effect could be explained by the growing evidence from neuropsychological studies indicating that face-selective responses have very short latencies what makes the processing of faces special compared to the processing of non-face objects (e.g., Farah et al. 1998; Seeck and Grüsser 1992). Furthermore, spontaneous anthropomorphizing also seems to affect explicit product evaluations positively under certain conditions, for example, depending on personal variables. Our pattern of results suggests that future research is needed to examine the interplay and relative influence of implicit and explicit anthropomorphic thoughts on consumer behavior.

REFERENCES

Aaker, Jennifer (1997), "Dimensions of Brand Personality," *Journal of Marketing Research*, 34 (August), 347–57.

Aaker, Jennifer, Susan Fournier, and S. Adam Brasel (2004), "When Good Brands Do Bad," *Journal of Consumer Research*, 31 (June), 1–16.

Aggarwal, Pankaj (*2004*), "The Effects of *Brand Relationship* Norms on Consumer Attitudes and Behavior," *Journal of Consumer Research*, 31 (June), 87–101.

Aggarwal, Pankaj and Ann L. McGill (2007), "Is That Car Smiling at Me: Schema Congruity as a Basis for the Evaluation for Anthropomorphized Products," *Journal of Consumer Research*, 34 (December), 468–79.

Anderson, John R. (1983), *The Architecture of Cognition*, Cambridge, MA: Harvard Press.

Bajo, M. Teresa and José J. Canas (1989), "Phonetic and Semantic Activation During Picture and Word Naming," *Acta Psychologica*, 72 (2), 105–15.

Bargh, John A. and Tanya L. Chartrand (2000), "The Mind in the Middle: A Practical Guide to Priming and Automaticity Research," in *Handbook of Research Methods in Social and Personality Psychology*, ed. Harry T. Reis and Charles M. Judd, New York: Cambridge, 253–85.

Benfield, Jacob A., William S. Szlemko, and Paul A. Bell (2006), "Driver Personality and Anthropomorphic Attributions of Vehicle Personality Relate to Reported Aggressive Driving Tendencies," *Personality and Individual Differences*, 42 (2), 247–58.

Bloch, Peter H. (*1995*), "Seeking the Ideal Form–Product Design and Consumer Response," *Journal of Marketing*, 59 (3), 16–29.

Bush, Donald J. (*1990*), "Body Icons and Product Semantics," in *Semantic: Visions in Design*, ed. Susann Vihma, Helsinki: UIAH, C1-C14.

Callcott, Margaret F. and Barbara J. Phillips (1996), "Observations: Elves Make Good Cookies: Creating Likeable Spokes-Character Advertising," *Journal of Advertising Research*, 36 (5), 73–78.

Caporael, Linnda R. (1986), "Anthropomorphism and Mechanomorphism: Two Faces of the Human Machine," *Computers in Human Behavior*, 2 (3), 215–34.

Chartrand, Tanya L., Gráinne M. Fitzsimons, and Gavan J. Fitzsimons (2008), "Automatic Effects of Anthropomorphized Objects on Behavior," *Social Cognition*, 26 (2), 198–209.

Chaudhuri, Arjun and Morris B. Holbrook (2001), "The Chain of Effects from Brand Trust and Brand Affect to Brand Performance: The Role of Brand Loyalty," *Journal of Marketing*, 65 (2), 81–93.

Collins, Allan M. and Elizabeth F. Loftus (1975), "A Spreading-Activation Theory of Semantic Processing," *Psychological Review*, 82 (6), 407–28.

DiSalvo, Carl and Francine Gemperle (2003), "From Seduction to Fulfillment: The Use of Anthropomorphic Form in Design," in *Proceedings of the 2003 International Conference on Designing Pleasurable Products and Interfaces*, 67–72.

Epley, Nicolas, Adam Waytz, and John T. Cacioppo (2007), "On Seeing Human: A Three-Factor Theory of Anthropomorphism," *Psychological Review*, 114 (4), 864–86.

Farah, Martha J., Kevin D. Wilson, Maxwell Drain, and James N. Tanaka (1998), "What Is 'Special' about Face Perception?" *Psychology Review*, 105 (3), 482–98.

Fournier, Susan (1998), "Consumers and Their Brands: Developing Relationship Theory in Consumer Research," *Journal of Consumer Research*, 24 (March), 343–73.

Gauthier, Isabel, Pawel Skudlarski, John C. Gore, and Adam W. Anderson (2000), "Expertise for Cars and Birds Recruits Brain Areas Involved in Face Recognition," *Nature Neuroscience*, 3 (2), 191–97.

Guthrie, Steward E. (1993), *Faces in the Clouds: A New Theory of Religion*, New York: Oxford.

Ingram, Jack and Louise Annable (2004), "'I See You Baby, Shakin' That Ass': User Perceptions of Unintentional Anthropomorphism and Zoomorphism in Consumer Products," *Proceedings of the 4th Design and Emotion Conference*, Ankara, Turkey.

Irvin, Deborah J. and Stephen J. Lupker (1983), "Semantic Priming of Pictures and Words: A Levels of Processing Approach," *Journal of Verbal Learning and Verbal Behavior*, 22 (1), 45–60.

Kiesler, Sara, Aaron Powers, Susan R. Fussell, and Christen Torrey (2008), "Anthropomorphic Interactions with a Robot and a Robot-Like Agent," *Social Cognition*, 26 (2), 169–81.

Kroll, Judith F. and Mary C. Potter (1984), "Recognizing Words, Pictures, and Concepts: A Comparison of Lexical, Object, and Reality Decisions," *Journal of Verbal Learning and Verbal Behavior*, 23 (February), 39–66.

Kwan, Virginia S. Y., Samual D. Gosling, and Oliver P. John (2008), "Anthropomorphism as a Special Case of Social Perception: A Cross-Species Social Relations Model Analysis of Humans and Dogs," *Social Cognition*, 26 (2), 129–42.

Mandler, George (1982), "The Structure of Value: Accounting for Taste," in *Affect and Cognition: The 17th Annual Carnegie Symposium*, ed. Margaret S. Clark and Susan T. Fiske, Hillsdale, NJ: Erlbaum, 3–36.

McNamara, Timothy P. (1994), "Theories of Priming II: Types of Primes," *Journal of Experimental Psychology: Learning, Memory, and Cognition*, 20 (3), 507–20.

Meyers-Levy, Joan and Alice M. Tybout (1989), "Schema Congruity as a Basis for Product Evaluation," *Journal of Consumer Research*, 16 (June), 39–54.

Mondloch, Catherine, J., Terri L. Lewis, D. Robert Budreau, Daphne Maurer, James L. Dannemiller, Benjamin R. Stephens, and Kathleen A. Kleiner-Gathercoal (1999), "Face Perception during Early Infancy," *Psychological Science*, 10 (September), 419–22.

Seeck, Margitta and Otto-Joachim Grüsser (1992), "Category-related Components in Visual Evoked Potentials: Photographs of Faces, Persons, Flowers, and Tools as Stimuli," *Experimental Brain Research*, 92 (2), 338–49.

Theios, John and Paul C. Amrhein (1989), "Theoretical Analysis of the Cognitive Processing of Lexical and Pictorial Stimuli: Reading, Naming, and Visual and Conceptual Comparisons," *Psychological Review*, 96 (1), 5–24.

Vanderwart, Mary (1984), "Priming by Pictures in Lexical Decision," *Journal of Verbal Learning and Verbal Behavior*, 23 (1), 67–83.

Welsh, Jonathan (2006), "Why Cars Got Angry," *Wall Street Journal*, March 10, W1.

Windhager, Sonja, Dennis E. Slice, Katrin Schaefer, Elisabeth Oberzaucher, Truls Thorstensen, and Karl Grammer (2008), "Face to Face: The Perception of Automotive Designs," *Human Nature*, 19 (December), 331–46.

The Effect of Shipping Fee Structures on Consumer Evaluations of Online Offers

Nevena Koukova, Lehigh University, USA
Joydeep Srivastava, R. H. Smith School of Business, University of Maryland, USA
Martina Steul-Fischer, University of Erlangen-Nuremberg, Germany

EXTENDED ABSTRACT

According to Forrester Research, Inc. the online spending in US was $141 billion in 2008 and is expected to reach $156 billion in 2009 (Ranasinghe and Yee 2009). Given the large number of products ordered online, an important decision related to online and catalogue retailing is how to design and communicate shipping fees to potential customers. Shipping fees not only significantly influence order incidence rates and average expenditures (Lewis 2006), but are also considered a major reason for consumers to abandon their shopping cards and discontinue the purchase process (Schindler, Morrin and Bechwati 2005). The purpose of this research is to understand how consumers evaluate and respond to different shipping fee structures.

Online and catalogue retailers have a variety of options with regard to shipping fees. A common practice is to waive shipping fees for orders that reach a specific dollar amount threshold (Lewis, Singh and Fay 2006). For example, Staples and Office Depot offer free delivery for orders above $50, and The Vitamin Shoppe offers free shipping for orders above $99. Another commonly used policy is to charge a flat shipping fee independent of order value similar to what Swanson Health Products ($4.99 for any size order) and Ann Taylor Loft ($6.00 standard shipping for all orders) are doing. The flat shipping fee could also increase according to a step function as order size increases, for instance $5.99 for orders below $25, $6.99 for orders $25.01 to $35.00 and so on. Given the variety of shipping practices in the marketplace and the level of experimentation occurring online (e.g., Amazon.com decreased its free shipping threshold from $99 to $25 in 2003, Lewis et al. 2006), there is a need to better understand consumers responses to different shipping fee structures, and provide guidelines to companies on how to communicate them to consumers.

In this paper we systematically investigate how consumers perceive and respond to two common shipping fee structures–flat fee shipping and free shipping threshold. We argue that the flat fee shipping and the free shipping threshold policies differ in the frame of reference from which evaluations and choices are made. Specifically, consumers being charged a flat shipping fee use as a reference point the expected shipping charge, whereas consumers facing a free shipping threshold policy use as a reference point the free shipping offered for orders exceeding the threshold. The flat shipping fee consumers are likely to consider the fee as a transaction cost that every consumer is incurring and evaluate it based on prior experiences and/or knowledge. The free shipping threshold consumers, however, are likely to think of the charge for offers below the threshold as a penalty or loss, and of the (lack of) charge for offers above the threshold as a bonus or quantity discount. Therefore, the two shipping fee structures are predicted to influence offer evaluations differentially based on whether the offer value exceeds the free shipping threshold or not. In addition, we propose that shopping goal concreteness and alternative reference price act as moderators of the effect of shipping fee structure on evaluations and choice.

We test our predictions in a series of thee studies. Study 1a demonstrates that consumers evaluate the offer more negatively and are more likely to abort their purchase when a free shipping threshold is provided and they do not cross the threshold compared to a flat shipping fee. For order values above the free shipping threshold, consumers evaluate the offer more positively and are less likely to abort the purchase when a free shipping threshold is provided compared to a flat shipping fee. Study 1b shows that when the shopping goals are less concrete, consumers evaluate the free shipping threshold offer more positively as compared to a flat shipping rate regardless of offer value. The free shipping threshold also acts as a goal for consumers, motivating them to buy additional product(s) to reach the threshold. Finally, study 2 suggests that the free shipping threshold serves as a reference point, and consumers evaluate the offer relative to this reference point. Importantly, when an alternative reference point is provided, the free shipping threshold does not play a role anymore.

Our results have important implications for the marketing theory and practice. From a theoretical point of view our study provides evidence about the differential effect of flat fee and free shipping threshold policies on evaluations and behavioral intentions, and clarifies the process driving the results. Regarding insights for practitioners, our results suggest that managers may provide alternative reference points to consumers to make free shipping thresholds (and the shipping charges in general) less salient. This motivates consumers to move to higher order values and evaluate the overall offer in a more positive way. When the average order value is below the optimal free shipping threshold, firms are better off by employing a flat fee shipping policy than a free shipping threshold policy.

REFERENCES

Bolton, Lisa, Luk Warlop, and Joseph W. Alba (2003), "Consumer Perceptions of Price (Un)Fairness," *Journal of Consumer Research*, 29 (March), 471-94.

Campbell, Margaret C. (1999), "Perceptions of Price Unfairness: Antecedents and Consequences," *Journal of Marketing Research*, 36 (May), 187-99.

Chakravarti, Dipankar, Rajan Krish, Pallab Paul, and Joydeep Srivastava (2002), "Partitioned Presentation of Multi-Component Bundle Prices: Evaluation, Choice, and Underlying Processing Effects," *Journal of Consumer Psychology*, 12 (3), 215-29.

Chandran, Sucharita and Vicki G. Morwitz (2006), "The Price of "Free"-dom: Consumer Sensitivity to Promotions with Negative Contextual Influences," *Journal of Consumer Research*, 33 (December), 384-92.

Dholakia, Utpal M. and Itamar Simonson (2005), "The Effect of Explicit Reference Points on Consumer Choice and Online Bidding Behavior," *Marketing Science*, 24 (2), 206-17.

Hamilton, Rebecca W. and Joydeep Srivastava (2008), "When 2+2 Is Not the Same as 1+3: Variations in Price Sensitivity Across Components of Partitioned Prices," *Journal of Marketing Research*, 45 (4), 450-61.

Haws, Kelly L. and William O. Bearden (2006), "Dynamic Pricing and Consumer Fairness Perceptions," *Journal of Consumer Research*, 33, 304-10.

Heath, Chip, Richard P. Larrick, and George Wu (1999), "Goals as Reference Points," *Cognitive Psychology*, 38, 79-109.

Heyman, James E. and Barbara A. Mellers (2008), "Perceptions of Fair Pricing," in *Handbook of Consumer Psychology*, eds. Curtis P. Haugtvedt, Paul M. Herr and Frank R. Kardes, Mahwah, NJ: Lawrence Earlbaum Associates Publishers, 683-98.

Kahneman, Daniel, Jack L. Knetsch, and Richard Thaler (1986), "Fairness as a Constraint on Profit Seeking: Entitlements in the Market," *The American Economic Review*, 76 (4), 728-41.

Kahneman, Daniel and Amos Tversky (1979), "Prospect Theory: An Analysis of Decision under Risk," *Econometrica*, 47 (March), 163-91.

Lee, Leonard and Dan Ariely (2006), "Shopping Goals, Goal Concreteness, and Conditional Promotions," *Journal of Consumer Research*, 33 (1), 60-70.

Lewis, Michael (2006), "The Effect of Shipping Fees on Customer Acquisition, Customer Retention, and Purchase Quantities," *Journal of Retailing*, 82, 13-23.

Lewis, Michael, Vishal Singh, and Scott Fay (2006), "An Empirical Study of the Impact of Nonlinear Shipping and Handling Fees on Purchase Incidence and Expenditure Decisions," *Marketing Science*, 25, 51-64.

Mazumdar, Tridib, S. P. Raj, and Indrajit Sinha (2005), "Reference Price Research," *Journal of Marketing*, 69 (October), 84-102.

Morwitz, Vicki G., Eric A. Greenleaf, and Eric J. Johnson (1998), "Divide and Prosper: Consumers' Reactions to Partitioned Prices," *Journal of Marketing Research*, 35 (November), 453-63.

Ranasinghe, Dhara and Lee Cyen Yee (2009), "As Access Improves, Online Shopping Takes off in Asia," *International Herald Tribune*, Feb. 18.

Schindler, Robert M., Maureen Morrin, and Nada Nasr Bechwati (2005), "Shipping Charges and Shipping Charge Skepticism: Implications for Direct Marketers' Pricing Formats," *Journal of Interactive Marketing*, 9, 41-53.

Xia, Lan, Kent B. Monroe, and Jennifer L. Cox (2004), "The Price is Unfair! A Conceptual Framework of Price Fairness Perceptions," *Journal of Marketing*, 68 (October), 1-15.

Adding Promotions to Online Services: How Goal Relevance Ambiguity Shapes Consumer Response

S. Adam Brasel, Boston College, USA

EXTENDED ABSTRACT

Consumer services, from utility bill payments to concert ticket purchases, have increasingly moved online. While online consumer services offer increased convenience for many, there is also increased potential for confusion and service errors in an automated online environment where the traditional face-to-face rules of service do not necessarily apply. In fact, more than 9 out of 10 consumers have experienced online service failure (Deutschkron 2008), and over 80% of consumers are routinely frustrated by their online service experiences. Even given this consumer confusion, online services have begun to explore ways to increase revenue by embedding promotional elements into the service process. For example, concert ticket sites may offer free mp3s, while an address change service may offer moving-related coupons.

This research explores how adding promotional elements to online service transactions creates behavioral and affective responses in consumers, and how the goal-driven nature of online services and the goal-relevance ambiguity of service-embedded promotions drives these consumer reactions. The study shows that promotions within online services achieve higher response rates than identical promotions on other websites, but do so at the cost of consumer confusion, frustration, and anger.

One key difference between traditional web browsing and online service transactions are that service transactions are explicitly goal-driven in nature. Consumers using online services have a clear end-goal in mind for the web interaction, which makes online service transactions a more linear process than more free-form and exploratory traditional web browsing. Goal-directed online behavior appears different from exploratory web behavior (Sánchez-Franco & Roldan 2005), and goals create both cognitive and attentional pressures to focus on goal-relevant information and marginalize goal-irrelevant information (Desimone & Duncan 1995, Allport 1993). Goals also have a powerful impact on felt affect, and goal relevance can guide affect above and beyond contextual, interpersonal, and temporal cues (Fleeson & Cantor 1995).

Individuals use routinized heuristics or schema for navigating the web, generating personal scripts for online behavior. (Calisir & Karaali 2008, Wirth et al 2007) Service transactions also follow generalized scripts, and experienced consumers know the order in which various steps in service transactions will take place (Jenkins, Corritore & Weidenbeck 2003). Disrupting the consumer's script in a goal-directed service transaction by promotion insertions is a more serious issue in comparison to inserting promotions into more free-form web-browsing. In browsing, there is little penalty for delay or changing course through the website. But in a linear service transaction, unexpected elements can cause a consumer's script to 'derail' leading to confusion and frustration (Bessiere et al 2004). Even if the promotional element does not derail the service, it still represents a goal-delaying impediment, and goal-impeding stimuli are a key source of frustration (Lazarus 1991).

This suggests a system of four hypotheses:

1. Promotional messages in online services generate stronger negative affect than promotional messages in other forms of websites.

2. Consumers have difficulty determining the goal-relevance of promotional messages in goal-driven websites.

3. Participation rates will be higher for promotions embedded into online service transactions compared to promotions in other forms of websites.

4. Increased levels of goal-direction in the website create increased levels of negative affect towards promotional messages.

To explore whether consumers comprehend the goal-relevance of online service-embedded promotions and their potential negative affective consequences, an online study examined the insertion of promotions into linear service websites and freeform exploratory websites. The study design compared the effects of promotions in an online service environment (linear transactional) with three other common website styles; storefront (exploratory transactional), local blog (linear informational), and headline news page (exploratory informational). The linear sites contained 6 sequential pages of content, while the exploratory site contained a master page and 18 smaller sub-pages of content. Two versions of each site were created, one with two promotional pages included and one without promotions. 147 participants were randomly assigned to a website and explored it according to instructions. After using the website, a survey was collected where their perceived goal-direction, goal-relevance of the promotions, and negative affect (confusion, frustration, anger, annoyance, and distraction) was measured using various scales.

An ANOVA analysis revealed linear websites and transactional websites generated more goal-direction than exploratory and informational websites, and a significant interaction showed that linear transactional websites, the type of site exemplified by online services, experienced the strongest goal-direction overall. Not surprisingly, sites with promotions present generated more negative affect than sites without promotions, with the strongest negative affect created in the linear transactional service website. Promotions were also seen as highly goal-uncertain, with goal-uncertainty the highest in the service-style linear transactional website condition.

With respect to promotion compliance, linear and transactional sites significantly outperformed exploratory and informational sites. There was also a significant interaction, where the linear transactional service had the highest promotional compliance, over 15% higher than any other condition. This increased compliance comes at an affective cost, however. Interactions reveal that sites with increased goal-direction generate more negative affect when a promotion is inserted; and the highly goal-directed linear transactional service website with promotions generates considerably more confusion, frustration, and anger than its promotion-free counterpart.

In conclusion, online service transactions are linear and goal-directed tasks, and consumers have goal-relevance in mind as they move through the service process. As companies insert promotional elements into online services, there is a large risk of consumer confusion, frustration, and anger. Inserting promotions into online services does generate increased levels of consumer response, but also generates strong negative affect due to consumers having a difficult time discerning the goal-relevance of the promotional stimuli. While initial compliance with service-embedded promotions appears high, this compliance is inflated by consumers agreeing to participate for fear of non-compliance generating a service failure. This pattern of results suggests that companies need to be more active in declaring the goal-relevance of their promotions, and should explore new ways to ensure that promotions do not interfere with the service scripts that consumers use to navigate the online service process.

REFERENCES

Allport, Alan (1993), "Attention and Control: Have We Been Asking the Wrong Questions? A Critical Review of Twenty-Five Years, In D.E. Meyer & S. Kornblum (Eds.), *Attention and Performance* XIV (pp. 183-218). Cambridge: MIT Press.

Bessiere, Katie, John E. Newhagen, John P. Robinson, and Ben Shneiderman (2004), "A Model for Computer Frustration: the Role of Instrumental and Dispositional Factors on Incident, Session, and Post-Session Frustration and Mood," *Computers in Human Behavior*, 22, 941-961

Calisir, Fethi and Demet Karaali (2008). "The Impacts of Banner Location, Banner Content, and Navigation Style on Banner Recognition," *Computers in Human Behavior*, 24(2), 535-543.

Deutschkron, Shoshana (2008), "2008 Online Transactions Report. Research Report," *TeaLeaf Technology & Harris Interactive*.

Desimone, Robert and John Duncan (1995), "Neural Mechanisms of Selective Visual Attention," *Annual Review of Neuroscience*, 18, 193-222.

Fleeson, William and Nancy Cantor (1995), "Goal Relevance and the Affective experience of daily life: ruling out situational explanations," *Motivation and Emotion*, 19(1), 25-57.

Jenkins Christine, Cynthia Corritore and Susan Wiedenbeck, (2003), "Patterns of Information Seeking on the Web: a Qualitative Study of Domain Expertise and Web Expertise," *IT & Society*, 1, 64–89.

Lazarus, Richard S. (1991), *Emotion and adaptation,* New York: Oxford University Press.

Sánchez-Franco, Manuel J., and Jose L. Roldan (2005), "Web Acceptance and Usage Model: A Comparison Between Goal-directed and Experiential Web users," *Internet Research*, 15, 21–48.

Wirth, Werner, Tabea Bocking, Veronika Karnowski, V. and Thilo von Pape (2007), "Heuristic and Systematic Use of Search Engines," *Journal of Computer-Mediated Communication*, 12(3), 778-800.

Promotional Bundles and Consumers' Price Judgments: When the Best Things in Life Aren't Free

Michael Kamins, Stony Brook University, USA
Valerie Folkes, University of Southern California, USA
Alexander (Sasha) Fedorikhin, Indiana University, USA

EXTENDED ABSTRACT.

The literature on pricing and promotions suggests that when a "free" product is bundled together with another product and offered for one price, consumers are willing to pay less for the "free" product when it is sold alone (Raghubir 2004). Our research shows that freebie also devalues the focal more expensive product in the bundle. With respect to the bundle as a whole, we show that the freebie devaluation effect does not occur unless the consumer is prompted to think about why a company would offer a product for free or the task is simplified by providing a bundle comprised of two identical items.

Because valuation of a bundle of two disparate products demands cognitive resources and consumers tend to conserve those resources, valuations of bundles with freebies can be similar to valuations of bundles that lack the "freebie" designation.

Our conceptual framework expands on previous pricing research by integrating recent insights about knowledge systems with the principles that the nature of the task and the consumers' cognitive resources influence judgments, and that shifts between knowledge systems are effortful. The valuation task can involve at least two systems of knowledge, a numerical system and an inferential system. Shifts from one system to another are effortful, which favors the numerical system since consumers focus on the numerical system when they need to generate a price. When the judgment task is difficult, consumers tend to conserve mental resources through information selectivity. The valuation of a bundle is more difficult than the valuation for each of the disparate individual products comprising the bundle. Hence, freebies can lower the amount a consumer is willing to pay (WTP) for the individual products comprising the bundle without lowering WTP for the overall bundle price.

Three experiments examined consumers' judgments about WTP for the focal product and for the overall bundle when the bundle included a freebie. The first study was conducted in the field with online auction bidders on eBay. The second and third studies were laboratory experiments that offered a more controlled setting in which to test effects of the free designation when the difficulty in arriving at a WTP judgment varies.

Study 1 conducted in the field showed that the final auction price for the focal product differed depending on the type of bundle sold concurrently. The focal product (the moderately expensive Indian penny coin) sold alone concurrently with a *free* bundle realized a lower price than when sold concurrently with a *non-free* bundle (M_{free}=\$3.77, SD=1.49, n=25, vs. $M_{non\text{-}free}$=\$4.67, SD=1.54, n=25), ($t_{(48)}$= 2.09, p<.05). Consistent with our theorizing, there was no difference between the final price realized at the end of the auction in the free versus non-free condition for the mixed bundle ($M_{non\text{-}free}$=\$4.47; SD=1.34; n=45, vs. M_{free}=\$4.25, SD=1.73, n=45, NS).

Study 2 conducted in the lab with shampoo and conditioner used as parts of a mixed bundle manipulated whether or not the supplemental item (conditioner) was free (free vs. no mention of free) and the type of judgment required (price for the focal product from the mixed bundle, price for the mixed bundle, and price for the homogeneous bundle consisting of two bottles of shampoo). The results show freebie devaluation effect for the focal product and the homogeneous bundle, but not for the mixed bundle, suggesting that WTP for a bundle varies depending on the resources available for making inferences about the free offer. The lack of difference between the mixed bundle prices is consistent with our notion that the cognitive demands of the task deter respondents from taking into account negative inferences when arriving at the total bundle price. When the WTP task itself required fewer resources (e.g., as in a homogeneous bundle), describing one item as free reduced the price respondents were willing to pay for the bundle as a whole.

We conducted Study 3 in the lab with the same stimuli, manipulating motive salience for offering a free product (salience present vs. salience absent), the availability of resources for making judgments (time pressure vs. no time pressure), and the type of judgment required (focal product vs. overall bundle). Only freebie bundles were used in study 3. Consistent with our theorizing, making motives salient had no effect on focal product WTP when time was unlimited ($M_{salience\ present}$=\$2.95 vs. $M_{salience\ absent}$=\$3.03), but resulted in lower WTP when time was limited ($M_{salience\ present}$=\$3.30 vs. $M_{salience\ absent}$=\$4.16). Focal product valuation is a fairly simple task that does not require a lot of cognitive resources. Hence, consumers make inferences about company's motives for the freebie promotion, even when the motive is not made salient. Under time pressure, making the motive salient helps them incorporate it in their WTP.

Unlike focal product conditions, making motives salient lead to lower overall bundle WTP when time was unlimited ($M_{salience\ present}$=\$3.79 vs. $M_{salience\ absent}$=\$4.92). Salience had no effect on WTP when time was limited ($M_{salience\ present}$=\$5.03 vs. $M_{salience\ absent}$=\$4.87). Mixed bundle valuation is a relatively more difficult task, which means that making the motive salient only helps consumer incorporate this knowledge into their WTP if there is no time pressure. Under time pressure, the task becomes simply too difficult, and even making motive for the promotion salient is not sufficient to help consumers incorporate it into their judgments.

Consistent with our reasoning, the number of negative thoughts about the product mediated the effect of the three-way interaction on WTP.

REFERENCES

Raghubir, Priya (2004), "Free Gift with Purchase: Promoting or Discounting the Brand," Journal of Consumer Psychology, 14 (1-2), 181-86.

Effects of Confusion on Resistance to Persuasion

Hélène Deval, University of Cincinnati, USA
Bruce E. Pfeiffer, University of New Hampshire, USA
Frank R. Kardes, University of Cincinnati, USA
Edward R. Hirt, Indiana University, Bloomington, USA
Samuel C. Karpen, Indiana University, Bloomington, USA
Bob M. Fennis, Utrecht University, The Netherlands

EXTENDED ABSTRACT

Most theories of persuasion focus on strategies that rely on clear, unambiguous reasoning to achieve compliance (e.g., Cialdini 2001). Hence, the idea of using confusing or negative information to enhance persuasion might seem counterintuitive. Yet, in some circumstances, the use of confusing information (Davis and Knowles 1999; Fennis, Das, and Pruyn 2004; Kardes et al. 2007) or acknowledging negatives (Ward and Brenner 2006) can be effective.

Instead of relying on strong reasoning to encourage compliance, these strategies operate by reducing resistance to persuasion (Knowles and Lin 2004). The Disrupt-Then-Reframe (DTR) technique (Davis and Knowles 1999) demonstrates how introducing a subtle disruption followed by an immediate reframing can increase compliance. Further, Ward and Brenner (2006) found that acknowledging a negative quality led perceivers to evaluate this quality less negatively than if no acknowledgement was provided. In two experiments, we investigate possible extensions and boundary conditions related to resistance to persuasion.

Although the DTR technique has been shown to be quite robust, all prior studies rely on a similar monetary manipulation to enhance persuasion. It still needs to be established if this technique is effective beyond this common manipulation. Experiment 1 used a personal sales simulation to investigate the generalizability of the DTR technique. Video recordings of a sales person describing the superior features of a plasma TV over an LCD TV were used in the simulation.

Participants were asked to imagine that they had planned to buy a new TV and were randomly assigned to one of three conditions: disrupt-then-reframe (DTR), disrupt only, or reframe only. In the DTR condition, participants were presented with technical information about a plasma TV (the disruption) followed by an explanation of the concrete benefits of the TV for the user (the reframe). The disrupt only condition consisted of only the first part of the sales presentation (the technical jargon). The reframe only condition consisted of only the second half of the presentation (the concrete benefits for the user).

Overall, the results replicate previous findings (Davis and Knowles 1999, Kardes et al., 2007) while successfully extending the DTR technique beyond the common monetary manipulation. Participants expressed greater preference for the Plasma TV in the DTR condition than they did in the two other conditions.

Experiment 2 used a technical manual to investigate the effectiveness of negative acknowledgement (Ward and Brenner 2006) while examining individual differences in the Need for Structure (NFS) (Neuberg, Judice, and West 1997) dimension of the Need for Cognitive Closure (NFCC) scale (Webster and Kruglanski 1994) as a potential boundary condition. It was predicted that the effects of negative acknowledgement may involve epistemic freezing on the acknowledgement.

Participants were asked to examine a technical manual about the features and installation of a digital sound system projector. The negative acknowledgement condition included a comment acknowledging some negative qualities of the manual (technical and confusing). In the control condition, participants only received a small set of instructions describing the task. In addition to these two conditions, a mumble condition, that was not present in Ward and Brenner (2006), was included. It was adapted from Erikson (1964) and was designed to confuse the participants (similar to the disrupt only condition of experiment 1).

As expected, while the negative acknowledgement condition resulted in the highest product evaluations, the mumble condition behaved similarly to the disrupt only condition in experiment 1. It led to increased confusion resulting in the poorest product evaluations. Further, only individuals high in NFS were sensitive to the use of negative acknowledgement. This seems to indicate that negative acknowledgement works as a heuristic and that careful processing limits its effectiveness.

Again, although much of the research on persuasion focuses on strategies that rely on clear, unambiguous reasoning to achieve compliance, other methods focusing on reducing resistance to persuasion are also effective. Both of these experiments illustrate how the use of confusing information can be beneficial to persuasion. The DTR technique and negative acknowledgment leverage the persuasive power of what would usually be considered detrimental information.

REFERENCES

Cialdini, Robert B. (2001), *Influence: Science and Practice*, 4th ed., Boston: Allyn & Bacon.

Davis, Barbara Price and Eric S. Knowles (1999), "A Disrupt-then-Reframe Technique of Social Influence," *Journal of Personality and Social Psychology*, 76 (2), 192-99.

Eagly, Alice H. (1974), "Comprehensibility of Persuasive Arguments as a Determinant of Opinion Change," *Journal of Personality and Social Psychology*, 29 (6), 758-73.

Erickson, Milton H. (1964), "The Confusion Technique in Hypnosis," *American Journal of Clinical Hypnosis*, 6, 183-207.

Fennis, Bob M., Enny H. H. J. Das, and Ad Th. H. Pruyn (2004), "'If You Can't Dazzle Them with Brilliance, Baffle Them with Nonsense': Extending the Impact of the Disrupt-Then-Reframe Technique of Social Influence," *Journal of Consumer Psychology*, 14 (3), 280-90.

Fennis, Bob M., Enny Das, and Ad Th H. Pruyn (2006), "Interpersonal Communication and Compliance: The Disrupt-Then-Reframe Technique in Dyadic Influence Settings," *Communication Research*, 33 (2), 136-51.

Hirt, Edward R., Frank R. Kardes, and Keith D. Markman (2004), "Activating a Mental Simulation Mind-set Through Generation of Alternatives: Implications for Debiasing in Related and Unrelated Domains," *Journal of Experimental Social Psychology*, 40 (3), 374-83.

Kardes, Frank R., Bob M. Fennis, Edward R. Hirt, Zakary L. Tormala, and Brian Bullington (2007), "The Role of the Need for Cognitive Closure in the Effectiveness of the Disrupt-then-Reframe Influence Technique," *Journal of Consumer Research*, 34 (3), 377-85.

Knowles, Eric S. and Jay A. Linn (2004), "Approach-Avoidance Model of Persuasion: Alpha and Omega Strategies for Change," in *Resistance and Persuasion*, ed. Eric S. Knowles and Jay A. Linn, Mahwah, NJ: Erlbaum, 117–48.

Kruglanski, Arie W. and Donna M. Webster (1996), "Motivated Closing of the Mind: 'Seizing' and 'Freezing,'" *Psychological Review*, 103 (2), 263-83.

Neuberg, Steven L., T. Nicole Judice, and Stephen G. West (1997), "What the Need for Closure Scale Measures and What It Does Not: Toward Differentiating among Related Epistemic Motives," *Journal of Personality and Social Psychology*, 72 (6), 1396-412.

Ward, Andrew and Lyle Brenner (2006), "Accentuate the Negative: The Positive Effects of Negative Acknowledgment," *Psychological Science*, 17 (11), 959-62.

Webster, Donna M. and Arie W. Kruglanski (1994), "Individual Differences in Need for Cognitive Closure," *Journal of Personality and Social Psychology*, 67 (6), 1049-62.

Negative Effects of Event Sponsoring and Ambushing: The Case of Consumer Confusion

Manuela Sachse, Chemnitz University of Technology, Germany
Jan Drengner, Chemnitz University of Technology, Germany
Steffen Jahn, Chemnitz University of Technology, Germany

EXTENDED ABSTRACT

Event sponsorship is one important marketing tool for companies to favorably influence brand awareness, attitudes or purchase intention. Since numerous sponsors use different leveraging techniques to promote their event engagement, these companies create a cluttered environment (Cornwell et al. 2000; Séguin and O'Reilly 2008). In the case of major events, this effect will be increased by several ambushers that actively try to confuse people about who is official sponsor of an event and who is not (Dalakas, Madrigal, and Burton 2004). As a result, memory for sponsors might be reduced, diminishing the goal of awareness enhancement (Cornwell et al. 2006; Johar and Pham 1999). Such a consumer failure to develop a correct interpretation of various facets of a stimulus during the information processing procedure has been described as consumer confusion (Turnbull, Leek, and Ying 2000). The aim of the present study is to develop a theoretically sound conceptualization of consumer confusion and relate it to dark-side effects of sponsorship.

Drawing on Turnbull et al. (2000), we define consumer confusion as interfered information processing which impedes consumers' ability to select and interpret relevant stimuli. We argue that this 'core' of the construct should be separated from the following antecedents (Mitchell and Papavassiliou 1999; Mitchell, Walsh and Yamin 2005):

- Perceived stimuli overload, resulting from the accumulated effects of many messages by a large number of sponsors and ambushers during an event.
- Perceived stimuli similarity, evolving from sponsors' and ambushers' similar communication content and formal similarity (e.g., slogan, pictures), especially in situations of high similarity of the advertised products.
- Perceived stimuli ambiguity as ambiguous, misleading, inadequate, and conflicting information, reflecting a typical side effect in information-rich environments (e.g., different sponsor categories during mega sports events).

Consequently, we derive a first set of hypotheses to test this conceptualization.

H1a: The higher the stimuli ambiguity, the higher the consumer confusion.
H1b: The higher the stimuli similarity, the higher the consumer confusion.
H1c: The higher the stimuli overload, the higher the consumer confusion.

According to Bijmolt et al. (1998), we argue that the quantitative overload is upstream of the antecedents that refer to qualitative stimuli (i.e., ambiguity, similarity).

H2a: The higher the stimuli overload, the higher the stimuli ambiguity.
H2b: The higher the stimuli overload, the higher the stimuli similarity.

Since sponsorship aims at influencing brand awareness (Johar and Pham 1999), the following hypotheses link consumer confusion with this outcome (Mitchell and Papavassiliou 1999).

H3a: The higher the consumer confusion, the less the correct classification (recall) of sponsoring brands as sponsors.
H3b: The higher the consumer confusion, the higher the misclassification of ambushing brands as sponsors.

Besides multiple sponsorships and ambusher activities, danger of mix-ups exists with regard to brands that have been sponsors of similar events. In such situations, retrieval of the correct sponsor is more difficult (Cornwell et al. 2006). We suppose that due to carryover effects the 'other-event sponsors' are perceived as being official sponsors.

H3c: The higher the consumer confusion, the higher the misclassification of other-event sponsors as sponsors.

In addition to memory interference, research shows that consumers feel annoyed by confusion (Dalakas et al. 2004). Annoyance, in turn, is likely to influence the attitude toward the company's sponsorship activities.

H4: The higher the consumer confusion, the more negative the attitude toward the sponsorship.

A further reaction could be opposite buying behavior to punish companies using the event for their communication (Séguin and O'Reilly 2008). Such opposite behavior might be expressed by so-called reactant behavioral intentions (Brehm and Brehm 1981).

H5: The higher the consumer confusion, the stronger the reactant behavioral intention.

Furthermore, research indicates that attitude toward sponsorship positively affects the purchase of sponsors' products (Madrigal 2001). Hence, negative attitudes should lead to reactant intentions.

H6: The more negative the attitude toward the sponsorship, the stronger the reactant behavioral intentions.

To test the new conceptualization, 465 German participants completed an online survey during UEFA EURO 2008 (M=25.4 years, 44.3% female). We measured confusion, overload, ambiguity, and similarity with items generated by two focus group discussions and two quantitative pretests. Measuring attitude toward the sponsorship and reactant intentions, we modified existing scales (Hong and Page 1989; MacKenzie and Lutz 1989). Awareness was measured by aided recall. The list for this task included 11 main sponsors (42.45% correctly identified as sponsors), 11 ambushers (93.0% correctly rejected as sponsors), 4 brands that were sponsors of the FIFA Soccer World Cup 2006 (89.5% rejected), and 5 foils (96.4% rejected). That the five foils were detected as non-sponsors by almost all respondents implies that respondents were not lead astray.

Using structural equation modeling (LISREL 8) to test the hypotheses, the measurement models exhibit high reliability, convergent and discriminant validity (Fornell and Larcker 1981). Fit indexes ($\chi^2(181)=457.74$, $p<.01$; *RMSEA*=.057; *CFI*=.97, and *NNFI*=.96) suggest that the hypothesized model fits the data well.

All but two hypotheses are supported. Consumer confusion is influenced by ambiguity (H1a; .56), but not similarity (H1b; .05) and overload (H1c; .08). Perceived stimuli overload impacts on both ambiguity (H2a; .38) and similarity (H2b; .68). Consumer confusion reduces memory for sponsors (H3a; -.41) and increases the likelihood that ambushers (H3b; .10) and other-event sponsors (H3c; .11) are perceived as official sponsors. Furthermore, confused consumers have a worse attitude toward the sponsorship engagement (H4; -.13) and show reactant intentions (H5; .15). Reactant intentions are higher the more negative the attitude toward the sponsorship (H6; -.43).

Concluding, we show that confused consumers have less memory of sponsors and are more likely to perceive ambushers and sponsors of other events as official sponsors. The most influential antecedent of consumer confusion is perceived stimuli ambiguity, which in turn is influenced by perceived stimuli overload. Thus, it is the combination of multiple sponsorships and ambusher activities that confuses consumers. Furthermore, we provide evidence that high levels of confusion negatively impact on the attitude toward the sponsorship and evoke reactant intentions. Ironically, this effect particularly impacts both sponsors and ambushers which were successful in linking their companies or brands to the event.

REFERENCES

Bijmolt, Tammo H. A., Michel Wedel, Rik G. M. Pieters, and Wayne S. DeSarbo (1998), "Judgments of Brand Similarity," *International Journal of Research in Marketing,* 15 (3), 249–68.

Brehm, Sharon S. and Jack W. Brehm (1981), *Psychological Reactance: A Theory of Freedom and Control*, New York, NY: Academic Press.

Cornwell, T. Bettina, Michael S. Humphreys, Angela M. Maguire, Clinton S. Weeks, and Cassandra L. Tellegen (2006), "Sponsorship-Linked Marketing: The Role of Articulation in Memory," *Journal of Consumer Research,* 33 (December), 312–21.

______, George E. Relyea, Richard L. Irwin, and Isabelle Maignan (2000), "Understanding Long-Term Effects of Sports Sponsorship: Role of Experience, Involvement, Enthusiasm and Clutter," *International Journal of Sports Marketing & Sponsorship*, 2 (2), 127–44.

Dalakas, Vassilis, Robert Madrigal, and Rick Burton (2004), "Understanding Ambush Marketing: Implications of Information Processing," in *Sports Marketing and the Psychology of Marketing Communication*, eds. Lynn R. Kahle and Chris Riley, Mahwah, NJ: Lawrence Erlbaum Associates, 293–304.

Fornell, Claes and David F. Larcker (1981), "Evaluating Structural Equation Models with Unobservable Variables and Measurement Error," *Journal of Marketing Research*, 18 (February), 39–50.

Hong, Sung-mook and Sandra Page (1989), "A Psychological Reactance Scale: Development, Factor Structure and Reliability," *Psychological Reports*, 64 (2), 1323–26.

Johar, Gita V. and Michel T. Pham (1999), "Relatedness, Prominence, and Constructive Sponsor Identification," *Journal of Marketing Research*, 36 (August), 299–312.

MacKenzie, Scott B. and Richard J. Lutz (1989), "An Empirical Examination of the Structural Antecedents of Attitude toward the Ad in an Advertising Pretesting Context," *Journal of Marketing*, 53 (April), 48–65.

Madrigal, Robert (2001), "Social Identity Effects in a Belief-Attitude-Intentions Hierarchy: Implications for Corporate Sponsorship," *Psychology & Marketing*, 18 (2), 145–65.

Mitchell, Vincent-Wayne and Vassilios Papavassiliou (1999), "Marketing Causes and Implications of Consumer Confusion," *Journal of Product & Brand Management*, 8 (4), 319–39.

______, Gianfranco Walsh, and Mo Yamin (2005), "Toward a Conceptual Model of Consumer Confusion," in *Advances in Consumer Research*, Vol. 32, eds. Geeta Menon and Akshay R. Rao, Duluth, MN: Association for Consumer Research, 143–50.

Séguin, Benoit and Norm O'Reilly (2008), "The Olympic Brand, Ambush Marketing and Clutter," *International Journal of Sport Management and Marketing*, 4 (1), 62–84.

Turnbull, Peter W., Sheena Leek, and Grace Ying (2000), "Customer Confusion: The Mobile Phone Market," *Journal of Marketing Management*, 16 (1–3), 143–63.

Determinants of Sponsorship Fit: A Multilevel Analysis

David M. Woisetschläger, TU Dortmund University, Germany
Christof Backhaus, TU Dortmund University, Germany
Heiner Evanschitzky, Strathclyde University, Scotland, UK
Manuel Michaelis, TU Dortmund University, Germany

EXTENDED ABSTRACT

Sponsorship fit is frequently mentioned and empirically examined as a success factor of sponsorship (e.g. Becker-Olsen and Hill 2006; Cornwell, Weeks, and Roy 2005; Simmons and Becker-Olsen 2006; Speed and Thompson 2000). Sponsors that are perceived as congruent with the sponsored object have been found to benefit more from their sponsorship engagements in terms of increasing brand equity (Becker-Olsen and Hill 2006; Gwinner and Eaton 1999; Simmons and Becker-Olsen 2006) and purchase intentions (Speed and Thompson 2000) than incongruent sponsors. From a theoretical point of view, a low sponsorship fit is equivalent to incongruence between sponsor and sponsored object. Such incongruence causes psychological tensions in the consumer's mind and forces to reestablish congruence (Festinger 1957). Hence, a perceived miss-fit is often related to a negative evaluation of the sponsor, and, therefore causes lower brand equity and purchase intentions.

While sponsorship fit has been considered as a determinant of sponsorship success, little knowledge exists about the antecedents of sponsorship fit. Commonly, sponsorship fit is conceptualized as "fit in a general sense" (e.g., Speed and Thompson 2000). From a managerial point of view and especially for sponsors that are in a particular situation of low fit, identifying antecedents of (in)congruence is highly relevant for improving the effectiveness of sponsorships. On the one hand, sponsorship fit can be seen as a result of a cognitive process including different antecedents which is different for each individual. On the other hand, sponsorship fit is likely to be different between brands, i.e. the group level as a result of different sponsorship policies and other influencing factors. While previous research provides insights on individual drivers of sponsorship fit, explaining differences resulting from varying sponsorship policies (i.e., sponsorship deal characteristics) is mentioned as a noteworthy area of research (Cornwell 2008).

Hence, the present paper contributes to the literature by examining the individual and sponsor-level antecedents of sponsorship fit. To test our hypotheses, we draw on (1) a sample of 1,579 soccer fans from 18 clubs of the first German league to obtain individual drivers of sponsorship fit and (2) objective characteristics of the shirt sponsorship deals of these clubs to explain between-group differences. Given the hierarchical structure of the data, hierarchical linear modelling (HLM) is an adequate method for analysis and hence applied in this study.

Individual Fan Perceptions as Determinants of Sponsorship Fit

Several factors have been mentioned in previous studies that are proposed to contribute positively to sponsorship fit or sponsorship related outcomes. Functional similarity (Gwinner and Eaton 1999), relatedness to the sponsored activity, perceived benefits of the partnership (Woisetschläger and Haselhoff 2009), regional identification of the sponsor (Woisetschläger and Haselhoff 2009), the sponsors sincerity (Speed and Thompson 2000), dominance in the partnership, and the ubiquity of the sponsorship (Speed and Thompson 2000) are potential determinants of sponsorship fit.

Sponsorship Characteristics as Determinants of Sponsorship Fit

Besides determinants of sponsorship fit that are perceived differently by individual fans, characteristics of the sponsorship partnership are proposed to affect sponsorship fit. Typically, sponsorship contracts can be characterized by the contract value (i.e., the amount paid by the sponsor per year), and the duration of the contract. These objective measures indicate the firm's commitment (Farrelly and Quester 2005) in terms of budget and timeline. Differences in contract value and contract length are expected to partially explain differences of the level of sponsorship fit over different sponsor-partnerships.

Methodology

Sample. To test the hypotheses, consumer-level data was collected via an internet survey among fans of the 18 clubs of the first German soccer league. A total of 1,579 respondents participated in the survey and fully answered all questions.

Measures. Our study comprises two levels of analysis: the individual fan-level and the sponsor-level. All measures are adapted from the literature. Sponsorship fit is measured with seven items using the scale employed by Simmons and Becker-Olsen (2006). Items to measure functional similarity are taken from Gwinner and Eaton (1999). Relatedness to the sponsored activity is operationalized using items by Speed and Thompson (2000). Scales to measure perceived benefits and regional identification of the sponsor are adopted from Woisetschläger and Haselhoff (2009). Sincerity and ubiquity of the sponsor are measured with items from Speed and Thompson (2000). Situation specific reactance (Wendlandt and Schrader 2007) is adopted to measure the degree of sponsor dominance.

On the second level (sponsor-level), we measure key characteristics of the sponsor partnerships from secondary sources. More specifically, contract value is measured by the total yearly amount spent by a particular firm for the actual sponsorship contract. Past contract length is measured by the number of years that a particular firm has been a sponsor of the particular club. Future contract length is the contract duration in number of years starting from today.

Results, Implications, and Future Research

Our findings reveal that, on the individual fan level, perceived benefits are the strongest determinant of sponsorship fit. Sponsors should therefore actively communicate the benefits of their engagement. Regional identification is also an important antecedent of sponsorship fit. Firms that show their belongingness to the region of the club are perceived as in-group members, and therefore as congruent to the club. Perceived sincerity of the sponsor is also a positive determinant of sponsorship fit. Therefore, firms should communicate that they are reliable partners of the particular club but should avoid to be perceived as a dominator of the club. Relatedness to other sports activities is also positively contributing to sponsorship fit. Contrary to our propositions, functional similarity and perceived ubiquity are not significantly related to sponsorship fit. The individual-level determinants explain about 45 % of the variance in sponsorship fit.

On a sponsor-level, results show that past and future contract lengths contribute positively to sponsorship fit and explain 41 % of the variance between the 18 groups. Sponsors that strive for short-term impact are evaluated less favorable. Contrary to our expectations, contract value is not significantly related to sponsorship fit. Hence, firms should invest in long-term sponsorship relations instead of spending more of their budget over a shorter time period.

The model is limited to a few–yet central–proxy variables to characterize sponsorship deals. Results show that a good part of the variance of sponsorship fit between the 18 sponsor partnerships is explained by these variables. The remaining part could be explained by including additional variables that characterize sponsorship deals and the nature of the sponsoring brand.

REFERENCES

Becker-Olsen, Karen L. and Ronald P. Hill (2006), "The Impact of Sponsor Fit on Brand Equity-The Case of Nonprofit Service Providers," *Journal of Service Research*, 9 (1), 73-83.

Cornwell, T. Bettina (2008), "State of the Art and Science in Sponsorship-Linked Marketing," *Journal of Advertising*, 37 (3), 41-55.

______, Clinton S. Weeks, and Donald P. Roy (2005), "Sponsorship-linked marketing: Opening the black box," *Journal of Advertising*, 34 (2), 21-42.

Farrelly, Francis J. and Pascale G. Quester (2005), "Examining important relationship quality constructs of the focal sponsorship exchange," *Industrial Marketing Management*, 34 (3), 211-219.

Festinger, Leon (1957), *A Theory of Cognitive Dissonance*, Stanford: Stanford University Press.

Gwinner, Kevin P. and John Eaton (1999), "Building Brand Image Through Event Sponsorship: The Role of Image Transfer," *Journal of Advertising*, 28 (4), 47-57.

Simmons, Carolyn J. and Karen L. Becker-Olsen (2006), "Achieving Marketing Objectives Through Social Sponsorships," *Journal of Marketing*, 70 (4), 154-69.

Speed Richard and Peter Thompson (2000), "Determinants of Sports Sponsorship Response," *Journal of the Academy of Marketing Science*, 28 (2), 226-38.

Wendlandt, Mark and Ulf Schrader (2007), "Consumer Reactance Against Loyalty Programs," *Journal of Consumer Marketing*, 24 (5), 293-304.

Woisetschläger, David M. and Vanessa J. Haselhoff (2009), "The Name Remains the Same for Fans–Why Fans Oppose Naming Right Sponsorships," *Advances in Consumer Research*, 36, 775-776.

Sport Sponsorship Effects on Spectators' Consideration Sets: Impact With and Without Brand-event Link Recognition

Jean-Luc Herrmann, Paul Verlaine Metz University CEREFIGE, France
Björn Walliser, Nancy University CEREFIGE, France
Mathieu Kacha, Paul Verlaine Metz University CEREFIGE, France

EXTENDED ABSTRACT

Sponsorship effectiveness' evaluation relies heavily and mainly on recall and recognition tests (Cornwell, Weeks, and Roy 2005; Walliser, 2003). The legitimacy of these tests lies in the assumption that brand-event recognition is a necessary condition for sponsorship success (Sandler and Shani 1989). Such an assumption can however be challenged on at least two points. First, sponsorship messages can be considered peripheral elements (Ydewalle and Tasmin 1993) for the spectator and may not be retrievable during a direct memory search (Shapiro, MacInnis, and Heckler 1997). Second, recall and recognition tests focus more on the control of the brand-event association, than on the perception of the sponsor brand per se (Holden and Vanhuele 1999).

Authors investigating incidental exposure effects in marketing (Acar 2007; Holden and Vanhuele 1999; Janiszewski 1988) postulate that the effect of exposure without memory of the exposure itself operates through familiarity or perceptual fluency. Among the effects that appear to be mediated by perceptual fluency or familiarity, the mere exposure effect indicates that repeated exposure to a stimulus increases stimulus' likability even in the absence of stimulus' recognition (Zajonc 1968). Fang, Singh, and Ahluwalia (2007) consider affect as a key process underlying the mere exposure effect and deduct a strengthening of these effects under resource-constrained decision-making situations characterizing many marketplace environments. It is thus expected that spectator exposure to a sponsor brand during an event increases the likelihood of the brand to be included in the spectator's stimulus-based consideration set, even if the spectator does not recognize the brand as sponsor (H1).

Stipulating a non-conscious sponsor effect does not exclude the existence of a conscious sponsorship effect which may become manifest in the spectator's ability to recognize the sponsor brand. Most major concepts and mechanisms identified in the literature to explain sponsorship effects (Cornwell et al., 2005)–such as for example perceived congruency and its articulation to "create fit" (Becker-Olsen and Simmons 2002), Heider's balance theory (1958), meaning transfer (McCracken 1989), social identification (Gwinners and Swanson 2003), and attribution theory (Dean 2002; Rifon, Choi, and Trimble 2004)-rely on the consciousness of the brand-event link. Even if sponsorship is characterized by numerous incidental exposure occasions, there are moments when the spectator is less absorbed by the "primary task". An arrival on site before the (sport) action starts as well as interruptions at halftime are examples of occasions favouring the consciousness and a semantic processing of the brand-event link. It is thus expected that spectator exposure to a sponsor brand during an event increases the likelihood of the brand to be included in the spectator's stimulus-based consideration set, through the recognition of the brand as sponsor (H2).

Data collection took place over four days of a one-week international tennis tournament. Face-to-face interviews were conducted before the spectators entered the stadium (control group) as well as inside the arena after spectators had assisted to one or several matches (experimental group). No significant differences between both groups are observed.

In order to determine the stimulus-based consideration set, respondents were given a list of 16 brand/company names within the target product category, including the sponsor name (Shapiro et al. 1997), and were asked which of these brands/companies they would consider for personal use or recommend to a friend. Subsequently, sponsor recognition was tested on a list of 16 brands including four "dummy" brands.

Following a series of successive (logistic) regressions analyses recommended to test for the existence of mediating effects (Baron and Kenny 1986), a significant positive effect of exposure (Expo) on the target brand's likelihood (Cset) to be included in the consideration set (p=.02, odds ratio Exp(β)=3.6), as well as on the presumed mediator process (p=.002) are observed. Exposure simultaneously multiplies the likelihood of the target brand to be included in the stimulus-based consideration set by a factor close to 3.5 and the chances to recognize the sponsor brand by a factor greater than five.

The presumed mediating variable Reco (recognition) is found to have a significant influence (p<.001, odds ratio Exp(β)=6.4) on the variable Cset when controlling for the influence of exposure. Thus, the target brand's recognition appears to mediate the influence of exposure on the target brand's likelihood to be included in the stimulus-based consideration set, supporting H2. Concerning the partial vs. complete mediation test, a significant positive effect (p=.029) of brand exposure on the likelihood of the sponsor brand to be included in the consideration set is observed if the sponsor brand is not recognized. Compared to the control group, the likelihood for the sponsor brand to be part of the consideration set under conditions of exposure without recognition is multiplied by a factor greater than four, supporting H1.

A dual route of sponsorship impact seems to exist. Sponsorship increases the chances of a brand to be part of the stimulus-based consideration set of spectators, both for persons conscious and unconscious about the brand-event link. Since most previous studies on sponsorship effectiveness concentrated on conscious effects only, sponsorship impact may have been underestimated in the past. In advertising, improved perceptual fluidity of brands as a consequence of increased (unconscious) exposure is found to positively influence stimulus-based brand choice (Lee 2002). If the same was true for sponsorship, sponsors whose products or services are typically chosen based on cues available in the physical purchase environment (Reilly and Parkinson 1985) would greatly benefit from their sponsorship investment. Furthermore, the results of this study call for a change of sponsorship measurement approaches. If conscious and unconscious sponsorship effects occur simultaneously, both have to be taken into account.

REFERENCES

Acar, Adam (2007), "Testing the effects of incidental advertising exposure in online gaming environments," *Journal of Interactive Advertising*, 8 (1), 1-36.

Baron, R. M. and D.A. Kenny (1986), "The moderator-mediator variable distinction in social psychological research: conceptual, strategic and statistical considerations," *Journal of Personality and Social Psychology*, 51 (6), 1173-82.

Becker-Olsen, Karen and Carolyn J. Simmons (2002), "When Do Social Sponsorships Enhance or Dilute Equity? Fit, Message Source, and the Persistence of effects," *Advances in Consumer Research*, 29, 287-289.

Bornstein, R.F. and P.R. D'Agostino (1992), "Stimulus recognition and the mere exposure effect," *Journal of Personality and Social Psychology*, 63 (4), 545-552.

______ (1994), "The Attribution and Discounting of Perceptual Fluency: Preliminary Tests of a Perceptual Fluency/ Attributional Model of the Mere Exposure Effect," *Social Cognition*, 12 (2), 103-128.

Cornwell, Bettina T. (2008), "State of the art and science in sponsorship-linked marketing," *Journal of Advertising*, 37 (3), 41-55.

Cornwell, Bettina T., Clinton S. Weeks, and Donald P. Roy (2005), "Sponsorship-linked marketing: opening the black box," *Journal of Advertising*, 34 (2), 21-42.

Dean, Dwane Hal (2002), "Associating the Corporation with a Charitable Event Though Sponsorship: Measuring the Effects on Corporate Community Relations," *Journal of Advertising*, 31 (4), 77-87.

Fang, Xiang, Surendra Singh, and Rohini Ahluwalia (2007), "An examination of different Explanations for the mere exposure effect," *Journal of Consumer Research*, 34, 97-103.

Greenwald, A.G. and C. Leavitt (1984), "Audience Involvement in Advertising: four Levels," *Journal of Consumer Research*, 11 (1), 581-593.

Gwinner, Kevin and John Eaton (1999), "Building Brand Image Through Event Sponsorship: The Role of Image Transfer," *Journal of Advertising*, 28 (4), 47-57.

Gwinners, Kevin and Scott R. Swanson (2003), "A Model of Fan Identification: Antecedents and Sponsorship Outcomes," *Journal of Services Marketing*, 17 (3), 275-294.

Hannah, D. B. and B. Sternthal (1984), "Detecting and Explaining the Sleeper Effect," *Journal of Consumer Research*, 11, 632-642.

Hawkins, S. and S.J. Hoch (1992), "Low-Involvement learning: Memory without evaluation," *Journal of Consumer Research*, 19, 212-225.

Heider, Fritz (1958), *The Psychology of Interpersonal Relations*, New York: John Wiley.

Holden, Stephen J.S. and Marc Vanhuele (1999), "Know the Name, Forget the Exposure: Brand Familiarity versus Memory of Exposure Context," *Psychology & Marketing*, 16 (6), 479-496.

Humphreys, Michael S., T. Bettina Cornwell, Clinton S. Weeks, and Anna R. McAlister (2007), "An Examination of Recall Measures of Sponsorship Awareness," *Advances in Consumer Research*, 34, 383.

Irwin, J.R. and G.H. McClelland (2001), "Misleading heuristics and moderated multiple regressions models," *Journal of Marketing Research*, 38 (1), 100-109.

Jacoby, L.L., C. Kelley, J. Brown, and J. Jasenchko (1989), "Becoming famous overnight: Limits on the Ability to Avoid Unconscious Influences of the Past," *Journal of Personality and Social Psychology*, 56 (3), 326-338.

Janiszewski, Chris (1988), "Preconscious processing effects: the independence of attitude formation and conscious thought," *Journal of Consumer Research*, 15 (2), 199-209.

______ (1993), "Preattentive Mere Exposure Effect," *Journal of Consumer Research*, 20, 376-392.

Johar, Gita V. and Michel T. Pham (1999), "Relatedness, prominence, and constructive sponsor identification," *Journal of Marketing Research*, 36 (3), 299-312.

Johar, Gita V., Michel T. Pham, and Kirk L. Wakefield (2006), "How Event Sponsors Are Really Identified: A (Baseball) Field Analysis," *Journal of Advertising Research*, June, 183-198.

Lee, A.Y. (2002), "Effect of implicit memory on memory based versus stimulus-based brand choice," *Journal of Marketing Research*, 39 (4), 440-454.

McCracken, Grant (1989), "Who Is the Celebrity Endorser? Cultural Foundations of the Endorsement Process," *Journal of Consumer Research*, 16 (3), 310-321.

MacInnis, Deborah J. and Bernard J. Jaworski (1989), "Information processing from Advertisements: toward an Integrative Framework," *Journal of Marketing*, 53 (4), 1-23.

Mandler, George (1980), "Recognizing : The judgment of previous occurrence," *Psychological Review*, 87 (3), 257-271.

Mandler, George, Yoshio Nakamura, and Billie J. Van Zandt (1987), "Nonspecific Effects of Exposure on Stimuli that cannot be Recognized," *Journal of Experimental Psychology: Learning, Memory and Cognition*, 13 (4), 646-648.

Pham, Michel T. and Gita V. Johar (1997), "Contingent Processes of Source Identification," *Journal of Consumer Research*, 24 (3), 249-265.

Pham, Michel T. and Marc Vanhuele (1997), "Analyzing the Memory Impact of Advertising Fragments," *Marketing Letters*, 8 (4), 407-417.

Reilly, Michael and Thomas Parkinson (1985), "Individual and Product Correlates of Evoked Set Size for Consumer Package Goods," *Advances in Consumer Research*, 12, 492-497.

Rifon, Nora J., Sejung Marina Choi, Carrie S. Trimble (2004), "Congruence Effects in Sponsorship: The Mediating Role of Sponsor Credibility and Consumer Attribution of Sponsor Motive," *Journal of Advertising*, 33 (1), 29-42.

Sandler, Dennis M. and David Shani (1989), "Olympic Sponsorship vs. 'Ambush' Marketing: Who Gets The Gold?" *Journal of Advertising Research*, 29 (4), 9-14.

Shapiro, Stewart (1999), "When an ad's influence is beyond our conscious control: perceptual and conceptual fluency effects caused by incidental ad exposure," *Journal of Consumer Research*, 26 (1), 16-36.

Shapiro, Stewart, Deborah J. MacInnis, and Susan E. Heckler (1997), "The effects of incidental ad exposure on the formation of consideration sets," *Journal of Consumer Research*, 24 (1), 94-104.

Trendel, Olivier and Luk Warlop (2007), "Positive Implicit Memory Effects For Event Incongruent Sponsorship," *Advances in Consumer Research*, 34, 102-103.

Walliser, Björn (2003), "An international review of sponsorship research: extension and update," *International Journal of Advertising*, 22 (1), 5-40.

Winkielman, Piotr and John T. Cacioppo (2001), "Mind at Ease Puts a Smile on the Face: Psychophysiological Evidence That Processing Facilitation Increases Positive Affect," *Journal of Personality and Social Psychology*, 81 (6), 989-1000.

Winkielman, Piotr, Norbert Schwartz, Tedra A. Fazendeiro, and Rolf Reber (2003), "The Hedonic Marking of Processing Fluency: Implications for Evaluative Judgment," in *The Psychology of Evaluation: Affective Processes in Cognition and Emotion*, ed. Jochen Musch and Karl C. Klauer, Mahwah, NJ: Erlbaum, 189-217.

Ydewalle, G. and F. Tamsin (1993), "On the visual processing and memory of incidental information: advertising panel in soccer games," *Visual Search*, 2, 401-408.

Zajonc, Robert B. (1968), "Attitudinal effects of mere exposure," *Journal of Personality and Social Psychology*, Monograph Supplement, 9 (2), 1-27.

Affect-Gating

Dan King, University of Florida, USA
Chris Janiszewski, University of Florida, USA

EXTENDED ABSTRACT

Extant theories of affective networks (e.g., Bower 1981) assume that affect is a unitary construct. This article integrates emerging findings in the neuroscience literature to show that there are, in fact, two major types of affect: *state* affect and *hedonic* affect (Barbano and Cador 2007), and that state affect can influence the experience of hedonic affect in surprising ways. First, positive affect can come in the form of positive *state* affect and positive *hedonic* affect. Positive *state* affect is mediated by dopaminergic activation and generates a light, airy feeling that makes people feel upbeat (Sacks et al. 1972). In contrast, positive *hedonic* affect is mediated by opioidergic activation and generates a pleasurable feeling that causes people to like a specific stimulus (Pecina, Smith, and Berridge 2006). Similarly, negative affect can come in the form of negative state affect and negative hedonic affect. Negative state affect is mediated by corticotrophin-releasing factor (CRF), and generates a heavy feeling that makes people feel downcast (Panksepp 1998). In contrast, negative hedonic affect is mediated by inhibition of orbitofrontal cortex firing, and generates a feeling of satiation or even aversion for the stimulus (Rolls 2004, 2005). Because there is significant pathway interaction in the affective circuits for both types of affect, state affect can influence the experience of hedonic affect in surprising ways. Negative state affect, for example, can lead to more intense positive hedonic affect, leading to a result that is surprising from the standpoint of mood-congruent models of affective influence on perception (e.g., Bower 1981; Isen 1989). Likewise, positive state affect can lead to less intense positive hedonic affect.

Animal research in mammals (who share a similar neural architecture with humans in terms of affective circuits) suggests how state affect can influence hedonic affect. Neurological research demonstrates that organisms are more attuned to different sensory channels during different affective states (Martel et al. 1993). In the process of natural selection (Darwin 1859), the relative value of information in different sensory channels changes as a function of the affective state. For example, mammals under negative affect are more attuned to tactile stimulation, because negative affect indicates separation from the mother, and tactile stimulation indicates reunion with the mother (Keverne, Martensz, and Tuite 1989). In contrast, mammals under positive affect are more attuned to visual stimulation, because positive affect indicates self-sufficiency and the organism's ability to search for rewards (Panksepp 1998). Affective states thus perform a gating function for the sensory-perceptual system (hence "Affect Gating"), in which information from different sensory channels are overweighted or underweighted as a function of the affective state. Marketers who understand the affective gating process will thus benefit from knowing which attributes to focus on for particular product categories and segments. Consumers who are using a product to comfort themselves (e.g., lotions, comfort food) will be more sensitive to tactile information, whereas consumers who are using a product to celebrate will be more sensitive to visual information.

Experiment 1 suggests that consumers are more attuned to tactile attributes of a product during a negative affective state. Consumers under negative affect generated more perceptions of the lotion's tactile qualities, such as its creaminess and moisturizing properties. In contrast, consumers under positive affect generated more perceptions of the lotion's visual qualities, such as its blue color. Experiment 2 suggests that consumers under negative affect were more attuned to the product's tactile qualities, and experienced more hedonic pleasure, than consumers under positive and neutral affect. Mediation analyses suggest that greater attunement to tactile qualities led to hypervaluation of the product (greater willingness-to-pay). Experiment 3 suggests that consumers under negative affect were more sensitive to changes in the veridical tactile quality of the product, whereas consumers under positive and neutral affect could not perceive changes in tactile quality. Experiment 4 aims to show that blocking the visual channel amplifies the information coursing through the tactile channel, hence amplifying the hedonic experience for consumers in negative affect. This may explain the phenomenon of why people close their eyes when they receive a massage. Experiment 5 shows that negative affect induces a physiological response of coldness (to induce organisms to seek social support under negative states), and experiment 6 shows that adding warming agents to lotions amplifies the tactile experience, hence improving the hedonic experience of consumers under negative affect. The article discusses conceptual implications of the "two affects" view and the gating process.

REFERENCES

Barbano, Flavia and Martine Cador (2007), "Opioids for Hedonic Experience and Dopamine to get Ready for it," *Psychopharmacology,* 191 (April), 497-506.

Bower, Gordon (1981), "Mood and Memory," *American Psychologist*, 36 (February), 129-48.

Darwin, Charles (1859), *The Origin of Species: By Means of Natural Selection or The Preservation of Favoured Races in the Struggle for Life,* Murray (United Kingdom).

Isen, Alice (1989), "Some Ways in Which Affect Influences Cognitive Processes: Implications for Advertising and Consumer Behavior, in *Cognitive and Affective Responses to Advertising*, ed. Alice M. Tybout and Patricia Cafferata, Lexington, MA: Lexington Books, 3–37.

Keverne, Eric, Nicholas Martensz, and Bernadette Tuite (1989), "Beta-endorphin Concentrations in Cerebrospinal Fluid of Monkeys Are Influenced By Grooming Relationships," *Psychoneuroendocrinology*, 14, 155-61.

Martel, Frances M., Claire M. Nevison, David F. Rayment, Michael J.A. Simpson, and Eric B. Keverne (1993), "Opioid Receptor Blockade Reduces Maternal Affect and Social Grooming in Rhesus Monkeys," *Psychoneuroendocrinology*, 18 (March), 307-321.

Panksepp, Jaak (1998), *Affective Neuroscience: The Foundations of Human and Animal Emotions,* New York, NY: Oxford University Press.

Rolls, Edmund (2004), "The Functions of the Orbitofrontal Cortex," *Brain and Cognition*, 55 (June), 11-29.

Rolls, Edmund (2005), *Emotions Explained*, Oxford: Oxford University Press.

Sacks, Oliver W.; Kohl, Marjorie S.; Messeloff, Charles R.; and Schwartz, Walter F. (1972), "Effects of Levodopa in Parkinsonian Patients with Dementia," *Neurology*, 22 (May) 516-519.

Differential Reliance on Feelings in the Present vs. the Future (or Past): Affect as a Decision Making System of the Present

Hannah H. Chang, Singapore Management University, Singapore
Michel Tuan Pham, Columbia University, USA

EXTENDED ABSTRACT

Consumer judgments and decisions can be made either in a more cognitive, reason-based manner (by assessing, weighing, and combining attribute information into an overall evaluative judgment) or in a more affective, feeling-based manner (by inspecting one's momentary feelings toward the options). An emerging body of evidence suggests that the two modes of judgment and decision may tap into two separate systems: a reason-based, analytical system and a feeling-based affective system. However, the conditions under which either system dominates are still unclear.

The present research suggests that, everything else equal, the affective, feeling-based system is more likely to be engaged in judgments and decisions that are set in the present than in similar judgments and decisions that are set in the future or in the past. This broad proposition generalizes the established finding that compared to reason-based decisions, affect-based decisions tend to be more myopic (Loewenstein 1996; Metcalfe and Mischel 1999; Ariely and Loewenstein 2006). Previous explanations of this myopia have focused on the differential accessibility of affective feelings across time perspectives. Because the immediate feelings that one experiences in relation to a present stimulus are more accessible than those that one can only imagine in relation to a future state of the world, the reliance on feelings in judgments and decisions steers preferences toward myopic options that are immediately rewarding compared to farsighted options that are superior in the long-run (e.g., Mischel et al. 1989; Loewenstein 1996; Metcalfe and Mischel 1999; Shiv and Fedorikhin 1999; Loewenstein et al. 2001).

We agree that the differential accessibility of feelings is a major contributor to the myopic tendencies of affect-based decisions. However, we suggest that this phenomenon is only one facet of a more general property of the affective system. We propose that the affective system is inherently a decision-making system of the present (Pham 2004; 2007). We derive this proposition from the rationale that, as a remnant of our distant evolutionary past (Epstein 1994; Lieberman et al. 2002), the affective system was originally meant to guide behavioral choices that our ancestors faced in their immediate (i.e., present) environment (see Cosmides and Tooby 2000, Pham 2007). Because of its original emphasis on immediate behavioral choices, the affective system has retained a distinctive orientation toward the present. Our general thesis is thus that the entire affective system of decision-making is more likely to be engaged in judgments and decisions that are set in the present than in similar judgments and decisions that are set in a more distant time, whether in the future or in the past.

As an initial test of this general proposition, the present set of studies tests the more specific hypothesis that, holding accessibility of feelings constant, affective feelings are weighted more heavily in consumers' judgments and decisions that are set in the present than in equivalent judgments and decisions that are set in the future or in the past. The effect of time perspectives on consumers' reliance on the feeling-based vs. reason-based system in judgment and decision making was tested in three separate marketing contexts, including apartment choices, video game evaluations, and evaluations of past vacations. In the first experiment, we demonstrate that—when given a choice between two apartments, one that is superior on the affective dimensions (e.g., breathtaking views) and one that is superior on the cognitive dimensions (e.g., bigger rooms) —consumers deciding for the immediate future tend to choose the apartment that is superior on the affective characteristics, whereas consumers deciding for the distant future tend to choose the apartment that is superior on the cognitive characteristics. To further demonstrate that consumers are more likely to use their feelings as inputs in deciding about present events rather than about distant events, we show in Experiment 2 that consumers' incidental moods (positive vs. negative) are more likely to influence their decisions to rent a particular apartment when these decisions are imminent than when the same decisions are remote. Hence, even though their incidental feelings were equally accessible, consumers are more likely to use their feelings as information under a present orientation than a future orientation.

Providing more process-related evidence, Experiment 3 shows that consumers find the reliance on feelings (as opposed to reasons) more "natural" in decisions set in a near future than in decisions set in a more distant future. These three experiments thus far have focused on contrasting the influence of feelings on decisions for the present vs. for the future. In the fourth and fifth studies, we also demonstrate that consumers are more likely to rely on their feelings in their evaluation for video games and their evaluation of past vacation when prompted to think about the recent past than about the distant past. Specifically, in Experiment 4, we conceptually replicated Experiment 2 using past perspectives—we show that consumers' incidental moods (positive vs. negative) are more likely to influence their evaluations of video games when these games were produced recently than when the same games were produced in the distant past. In Experiment 5, we found that students' incidental moods were also more likely to influence their evaluations of a recent spring break (recent past) than evaluations of spring break two years ago (distant past). Importantly, results from these studies emerge holding the affective experience constant and outside of the delay of gratification and self-control domains.

These findings suggest that—given two systems available for decision making—consumers seem to shift the relative weights they place on their affective vs. cognitive systems in assessing value in judgments and decisions, using their feelings selectively depending on the time perspectives. In another related work, we examine indirectly the relative engagement of the affective system under present orientation through a well-known characteristic of the affective system in valuation—the scope-insensitivity bias—in the context of charitable donation, willingness-to-pay for music CDs, and evaluations of past video games. This finding is further evidence that affect is inherently a decision-making system of the present.

REFERENCES

Ariely, Dan and George Loewenstein (2006), "The Heat of the Moment: The Effect of Sexual Arousal on Sexual Decision Making," *Journal of Behavioral Decision Making*, 19, 87-98.

Cosmides, Leda and John Tooby (2000), "Evolutionary Psychology and the Emotions," *Handbook of Emotions*.

Epstein, Seymour (1994), "Integration of the Cognitive and the Psychodynamic Unconscious," *American Psychologist*, 49 (8), 709-24.

Lieberman, Matthew D., Ruth Gaunt, Daniel T. Gilbert, and Yaacov Trope (2002), "Reflexion and Reflection: A Social Cognitive Neuroscience Approach to Attributional Inference," *Advances in Experimental Social Psychology*, 34, 199-249.

Loewenstein, George (1996), "Out of Control: Visceral Influences on Behavior," *Organizational Behavior and Human Decision Processes*, 65 (3), 272-92.

Loewenstein, George, Elke U. Weber, Christopher K. Hsee, and Ned Welch (2001), "Risk as Feelings," *Psychological Bulletin*, 127 (2), 267-86.

Metcalfe, Janet and Walter Mischel (1999), "A Hot/Cool-System Analysis of Delay of Gratification: Dynamics of Willpower," *Psychological Review*, 106 (1), 3-19.

Mischel, Walter, Yuichi Shoda, and Monica I. Rodriguez (1989), "Delay of Gratification in Children," *Science*, 244 (4907), 933-38.

Pham, Michel Tuan (2004), "The Logic of Feeling," *Journal of Consumer Psychology*, 14 (4).

Pham, Michel Tuan (2007), "Emotion and Rationality: A Critical Review and Interpretation of Empirical Evidence," *Review of General Psychology*, 11 (2), 155-78.

Shiv, Baba and Alexander Fedorikhin (1999), "Heart and Mind in Conflict: The Interplay of Affect and Cognition in Consumer Decision Making," *Journal of Consumer Research*, 26 (3), 278-92.

Negative Affect and Choice: The Moderating Effect of Procedural and Outcome Accountability

Nitika Garg, University of Mississippi, USA
Vikas Mittal, Rice University, USA
J. Jeffrey Inman, University of Pittsburgh, USA

EXTENDED ABSTRACT

Negative affect in decision making has captured the interest of researchers for quite some time in both psychology and marketing. Incidental affect, also known as ambient affect, is affect that a consumer may imbue from her environment in isolation to the decision on hand. More recently, the focus has shifted away from simple emotion valence (positive, negative) to more specific, discrete affective states such as sadness, anger and fear (Desteno et al. 2000; Lerner and Keltner 2000, 2001; Tiedens and Linton 2001; Raghunathan and Pham 1999). Researchers have found differences not only between negative and positive affect but also between different discrete emotions having the same valence (e.g., anger/ sadness, pride/happiness). Lerner and Keltner (2000, 2001) proposed the 'appraisal-tendency' approach, which hypothesizes that 'each emotion activates a predisposition to appraise future events in line with the central appraisal dimension that triggers the emotion'. For example, they find that fearful people make pessimistic risk assessments and future events judgments whereas angry people make optimistic assessments in the same scenarios.

Research has also shown that while incidental affect influences many aspects of judgment and decision making, there are moderating factors that successfully attenuate the effect of emotions. For example, Desteno et al. (2000) find that making subjects aware of the source of their affect wipes out the influence of affect. Another factor that has been consistently shown to moderate the effect of emotions is accountability. Accountability refers to the implicit or explicit expectation that one may be called on to justify one's beliefs, feelings and/or actions to others (Lerner and Tetlock 1999). Past research has shown that increasing the level of accountability makes the decision process more elaborate and effortful (Chaiken 1980; Thompson et al. 1994). It has also been found to lead to attenuation of the effect of incidental emotions on unrelated judgments (Bodenhausen, Kramer and Susser 1994; Lerner, Goldberg and Tetlock 1998). Lerner et al. (1998) found that the tendency of anger to elicit punitive attributions of responsibility was reduced when subjects were accountable. However, more recent research in accountability has revealed that there are two forms of accountability–process and outcome based–that can have differential influence on decision making (Simonson and Staw 1992; Zhang and Mittal 2005). Under process accountability (PA) decision makers are accountable for the procedure used to arrive at a decision whereas under outcome accountability (OA) they are accountable only for the quality of the outcome, with no evaluation of their decision process (Escalas and Luce 2004). This research also shows that PA and OA differentially influence the perceived difficulty of a decision and that decision biases are relatively lower under PA than under OA. However, the few empirical studies comparing PA and OA have not examined how the influence of a contextual factor such as incidental affect on consumer choice is moderated by these two types of accountability.

The objective of this research then, is to examine the interactive effect of incidental negative affect with the accountability degree (low vs. high) and type (PA vs. OA). Specifically, we examine the differential impact of two discrete, negative emotions–anger and fear–on consumer choice with accountability degree (study 1) and type (study 2) as the moderating factors. We hypothesize that consumers experiencing different negative emotions will display differential reliance on the avoidance choice strategies such as delaying the decision, and that this effect will be moderated by accountability. Our reasoning for the above hypothesis is that anger versus fear differentially impacts subject's degree of certainty. Previous research has shown anger to have a higher degree of certainty associated with it as compared to fear (Smith and Ellsworth 1985). Garg, Inman and Mittal (2005) have further, shown that this difference in certainty can lead to angry individuals choosing the avoidance option more than sad (fear is close to sad in terms of 'certainty') individuals when faced with a difficult decision. On the other hand, we predict that fearful individuals should exhibit similar choice patterns under both types of accountability and under low versus high accountability as their lack of certainty should lead them to make the decision more deliberately, irrespective of the accountability degree and type.

Study 1 finds that making people accountable for their decision (i.e., manipulating degree) actually amplifies the decision bias in angry condition which results in angry individuals choosing to defer choice, an avoidance response. As expected, fearful individuals do not exhibit any difference in avoidance choice across the two accountability conditions. Study 2 manipulates accountability type. We expect that under OA which has higher perceived difficulty (Zhang and Mittal 2005), angry individuals will choose the avoidance option more than fearful or neutral individuals will and also, more than angry individuals will under PA. Thus, we predict that unlike OA, PA will negate the influence of incidental affect on choice and lead to more balanced choice process, highlighting the differences across the two types of accountability.

Study 2 supports these predictions. The two studies together, highlight an interesting insight into the nature of accountability–accountability degree implicitly manipulates outcome accountability. That is, when no accountability type is specified, accountable people assume outcome accountability. This is evident when we compare results for high accountability and those for OA across Study 1 and 2. The final study (study 3) seeks to not only replicate the results from Study 2 but also, examine the role of optimism in so far, as emotions with varying levels of certainty are linked to differential levels of optimism (Lerner and Keltner 2001). Examining optimism should provide a greater understanding of the underlying mechanisms that might be implicated in this phenomenon. The implications of the findings for academics as well as managers, are discussed.

REFERENCES

Bodenhausen, Galen V., Geoffrey P. Kramer, and Karin Susser (1994), "Happiness and Stereotypic Thinking in Social Judgment," *Journal of Personality and Social Psychology, 66 (April)*, 621-632.

Brown, Christina L. (1999), "Do the Right Thing: Diverging Effects of Accountability in A Managerial Context," *Marketing Science*, 18 (3), 230-246.

Chaiken, Shelly (1980), "Heuristic versus Systematic Information Processing and the Use of Source versus Message Cues in Persuasion," *Journal of Personality and Social Psychology*, 39 (April), 752-766.

Chatterjee, Subimal and Timothy B. Heath (1996), "Conflict and Loss Aversion in Multiattribute Choice: The Effects of Trade-Off Size and Reference Dependence on Decision Difficulty," *Organizational Behavior and Human Decision Processes*, 67 (August), 144-55.

DeSteno, David, Richard E. Petty, Duane T. Wegner and Derek D. Rucker (2000), "Beyond Valence in the perception of likelihood: The role of emotion specificity," *Journal of Personality and Social Psychology*, 78 (March), 397-416.

Escalas, Jennifer Edson and Mary Frances Luce (2004), "Understanding the Effects of Process-Focused versus Outcome-Focused Thought in Response to Advertising," *Journal of Consumer Research*, 31 (September), 274-85.

Garg, Nitika, J. Jeffrey Inman and Vikas Mittal (2005), "Incidental and Task-Related Affect: A Re-Inquiry and Extension of the Influence of Affect on Choice," *Journal of Consumer Research*, 32 (June), 154-159.

Johnson, Eric J. and Amos Tversky (1983), "Affect, generalization and the perception of risk," *Journal of Personality and Social Psychology*, 45 (July), 20-31.

Lerner, Jennifer S., Julie H. Goldberg and Philip E. Tetlock (1998), "Sober Second Thought: The Effects of Accountability, Anger and Authoritarianism on Attributions of Responsibility," *Personality and Social Psychology Bulletin, 24 (June)*, 563-574.

______ and Dacher Keltner (2001), "Fear, Anger and Risk," *Journal of Personality and Social Psychology*, 81 (July), 146-159.

______ and Philip E. Tetlock (1999), "Accounting for the Effects of Accountability," *Psychological Bulletin*, 125 (March), 255-275.

Raghunathan, Rajagopal and Michel T. Pham (1999), "All Negative Moods Are Not Equal: Motivational Influences of Anxiety and Sadness on Decision Making," *Organizational Behavior and Human Decision Processes*, 79 (July), 56-77.

Sengupta, Jaideep and Gita Venkataraman Johar (2002), "Effects of Inconsistent Attribute Information on the Predictive Value of Product Attitudes: Toward a Resolution of Opposing Perspectives," *Journal of Consumer Research*, 29 (June), 39-56.

Siegel-Jacobs, Karen and J. Frank Yates (1996), "Effects of Procedural and Outcome Accountability on Judgment Quality," *Organizational Behavior and Human Decision Processes*, 65 (January), 1-17.

Simonson, Itamar and Barry M. Staw (1992), "Deescalation Strategies: A Comparison of Techniques for Reducing Commitment to a Losing Courses of Action," *Journal of Applied Psychology*, 77(4), 419-26.

Tetlock, Philip E. (1983), "Accountability and Complexity of Thought," *Journal of Personality and Social Psychology*, 45 (January), 74-83.

Tiedens, Larissa Z. and Susan Linton (2001), "Judgment under Emotional Uncertainty: The Effects of Specific Emotions on Information Processing," *Journal of Personality and Social Psychology*, 81 (December), 973-988.

Thompson, Erik P., Robert J. Roman, Gordon B. Moskowitz, Shelly Chaiken and John A. Bargh (1994), "Accuracy Motivation Attenuates Covert Priming: The Systematic Reprocessing of Social Information," *Journal of Personality and Social Psychology*, 66 (March), 474-489.

Zhang, Y. and Mittal, V. (2005), "Effects of Procedural and Outcome Accountability," *Journal of Consumer Research*, 32(3), 465-472.

Pride: A License to Indulge or a Cue for Greater Self-Control?

Keith Wilcox, Babson College, USA
Thomas Kramer, Baruch College, CUNY, USA
Sankar Sen, Baruch College, CUNY, USA

EXTENDED ABSTRACT

Consumers frequently face choices in which personal goals of long-term importance conflict with indulgent pursuits that are inconsistent with their long-term objectives. When faced with such decisions, most consumers try to exercise self-control, but they often fail and make indulgent choices that undermine their long-term goals. Recent research has linked emotions to indulgence. However, much of this research has focused on the effect of incidental happiness (versus sadness) on consumption (Garg et al. 2007). Thus, we know very little about how other incidental positive emotions, such as pride, affect consumers' long-term goal pursuit and their preference for indulgent options that undermine such goals.

When consumers face indulgent decisions, self-regulatory processes facilitate their ability to act in accordance with their long-term goals (Baumeister 2002). A central component of successful self-regulation is that the person must have the capacity to monitor her behavior to ensure that it is consistent with her goal. Carver and Scheier (1998) propose that when people are consciously monitoring their behavior relative to a goal, negative emotions signal goal failure, which leads them to try harder to reach their goal. Positive emotions, however, signal goal attainment, which licenses them to reduce subsequent effort in the domain.

Interestingly, this suggests that positive emotions may reduce a person's effort toward a long-term goal, which, in turn, should increase his or her preference for indulgent options that undermine such goals. Yet, this appears counter to what we already know about the motivational properties of emotions since happiness has been shown to reduce indulgent behavior compared to sadness (Garg et al. 2007). We suggest, however, that because pride is experienced in response to the successful pursuit of long-term goals, upon experiencing pride, consumers are likely to infer that they have achieved or have made satisfactory progress toward a long-term goal. Consequently, when consumers face an indulgent choice and they begin to monitor their behavior relative to a long-term goal, they should misattribute the experience of pride as having temporarily satisfied the goal, which, in turn, should license indulgence.

Recent evidence suggests that specific emotions may also influence goal pursuit beyond that of the information providing during the monitoring process. When individuals experience an emotion or are primed with an emotion, it activates cognitions and action tendencies that are linked to that emotion in memory (Lang et al. 1998). These concepts can lead individuals to perform emotion appropriate behavior (Zemack-Rugar et al. 2006). Because pride is experienced in response to the achievement of long-term goals, it is linked in memory to cognitions associated with the successful pursuit of long-term goals (Eyal and Fishbach 2009). Thus, the experience of pride should activate these concepts, which, in turn, should serve as salient cues to guide behavior. Consequently, pride may decrease consumers' preference for indulgent options by serving as a behavioral cue through an automatic process.

In sum, we argue that the experience of pride influences consumers' pursuit of long-term goals through dual pathways that predict different outcomes in terms of their preference for indulgent products. When consumers are consciously monitoring their behavior, pride serves as a source of information that licenses indulgence. Otherwise, the experience of pride will decrease consumers' preference for indulgent products through an automatic process by cueing behaviors consistent with the successful pursuit of long-term goals. We demonstrate the dual pathways in two studies. First, we show that pride licenses indulgence, unless a) individuals are unable to monitor their behavior or b) the experience of pride is discredited as a source of information. Second, we demonstrate that another positive emotion (i.e., happiness) does not have a similar influence on behavior.

In study 1, we presented respondents with an indulgent decision in the health domain that involved a choice between french fries or salad as a side dish with their lunch entrée. Prior to making their decision, respondents were primed to experience pride, happiness or no emotion (control group). The extent to which individuals were able to monitor their behavior was manipulated using a cognitive load manipulation. Consistent with our prediction, when respondents were able to monitor their behavior (high cognitive load), those that were primed with pride were more likely to make an indulgent choice compared to the control group. When individuals were unable to monitor their behavior (low cognitive load), those that were primed with pride were less likely to make and indulgent choice compared to the control group. Additionally, no difference was observed between the happiness and control conditions at high and low levels of cognitive load.

In the second study, respondents were given an indulgence decision in the money domain that involved a choice between two $25 gift certificates where one could be used for entertainment products (indulgent option) and the other could be used for school supplies. Prior to making their decision, respondents were primed to experience pride or no emotion (control group). For half of the respondents, the experience of pride was discredited by having them focus on the source of their feelings prior to making their decision. As expected, when the source of their feeling was not discredited, respondents that experienced pride were more likely to make an indulgent choice compared to the control group. However, when the experience of pride was discredited, respondents were less likely to make an indulgent choice compared to the control group. Thus, the results of the second study demonstrate the dual pathways even where individuals have the capacity to monitor their behavior.

This research makes an important contribution to the literature on the motivational properties of emotions by a) identifying the process through which pride affects goal pursuit and b) demonstrating the effect of its experience on consumer preference. Our findings also contribute to the decision-making literature, which has focused primarily on discrete negative emotions (Raghunathan, Pham and Corfman 2006), by demonstrating that distinct positive emotions (pride versus happiness) can have unique effects on consumer choice.

REFERENCES

Baumeister, Roy F. (2002), "Yielding to Temptation: Self-Control Failure, Impulsive Purchasing, and Consumer Behavior," *Journal of Consumer Research*, 28 (4), 670-76.

Carver, Charles S., and Michael F. Scheier (1998), *On The Self-Regulation of Behavior*, New York: Cambridge University Press.

Eyal, Tal and Ayelet Fishbach (2009), "Two Affective Systems in Self-Control Conflicts," Working Paper, Ben Gurion University.

Garg, Nitika, Brian Wansink and Jeffrey J. Inman (2007), "The Influence of Incidental Affect on Consumers' Food Intake," *Journal of Marketing*, 71 (1), 194-206.

Lang, Peter J., Margaret M. Bradley and Bruce N. Cuthbert (1998), "Emotion, Motivation, and Anxiety: Brain Mechanisms and Psychophysiology," *Biological Psychiatry*, 44 (12), 1248–263.

Ramanathan, Suresh, Pham, Michel T. and Corfman Kim P. (2006), "Informational Properties of Anxiety and Sadness, and Displaced Coping," *Journal of Consumer Research*, 32 (4), 596-601.

Zemack-Rugar, Yael, James R. Bettman and Gavan J. Fitzsimons (2007), "The Effects of Nonconsciously Priming Emotion Concepts on Behavior," *Journal of Personality and Social Psychology*, 93 (6), 927-39.

Impact of Age on Repeat Choice and Attitude Certainty

Raphaëlle Lambert-Pandraud, ESCP-Europe, France
Gilles Laurent, HEC Paris, France
David Dubois, Northwestern University, USA
Derek Rucker, Northwestern University, USA
Etienne Mullet, Ecole pratique des Hautes Etudes, France

EXTENDED ABSTRACT

We investigate the impact of age on repeat choice and attitude certainty. This research is motivated by the apparent contradiction between two series of previous results on the impact of age: impact on attitude strength, impact on repeat purchase.

Visser and Krosnick (1998) study attitude strength in the context of a new topic (e.g., a fictitious foreign conflict), for which respondents, by definition, have to develop online, during the interview, a new attitude (for or against a US intervention in the conflict), and to take a position on the spot. Researchers then supply additional "information:" Each respondent is told that the United Nations have a position opposite to the one s/he has just taken, and asked whether s/he holds to her/his first attitude or changes it. Visser and Krosnick find an inverted U-shape impact of age on attitude strength. Attitude stability is at its maximum for mature persons (between 40 and 60), while both younger and older respondents are more likely to change their position.

This seems to contradict results on age-related differences in brand choice. For example, Lambert-Pandraud, Laurent, and Lapersonne (2005) find that choice stability increases mononically across age ranges: Older car buyers are more likely to consider and repeat purchase the previous car brand, and less likely to explore alternative choices.

Could this apparent contradiction be due to the type of attitude under investigation? Visser and Krosnick investigate, after a few minutes, the stability of a rootless attitude: Since the foreign conflict is fictitious, the respondent does not bring a previous attitude, let alone a network of related attitudes, to the survey. In contrast, Lambert-Pandraud et al. investigate stability towards the previous car brand, for which consumers have likely developed a rooted attitude, based on daily usage over several years, and on their lifelong experience with cars.

Besides, are attitude stability and attitude certainty correlated?

Study One

In contrast with Visser and Krosnick, we therefore analyze a domain in which respondents have had lifetime opportunities to develop rooted attitudes: A presidential election. We perform a secondary analysis of survey data collected in the two months preceding the French 2007 presidential election (n=17,622). We analyze respondents' certainty about their planned vote (a binary answer to "Is you choice final or can it still change?") in relationship with choice stability (whether the planned 2007 vote is the same as at the previous [2002] presidential election, coded by the authors on the basis of separate questions on the planned 2007 vote and on the previous 2002 vote).

Age has a very significant positive impact on choice stability. The probability of a repeat vote increases linearly across age ranges.

Attitude stability and certainty are correlated. At any age, respondents who plan to vote in 2007 as they voted in 2002 are more likely to be certain about their future vote ("My choice is final") than respondents who plan to change their vote.

However, we find contrasted age-related patterns: There is indeed a monotonic growth in certainty among respondents who plan to vote in 2007 as they voted in 2002, but an inverted U-shape relationship for respondents who plan to change their vote.

This suggests a possible avenue to reconcile the apparent contradiction described above. One may distinguish the impact of age on attitude certainty, depending on whether the current attitude remains consistent with the attitude held in the past (in our case, with the 2002 vote), or the current attitude is new, in the sense of either differing from the attitude held in the past (in our case, changing the vote) or being formed online, in answer to a new topic (as in Visser and Krosnick).

Study Two

Study One and the Visser and Krosnick study (1998) are not comparable: different subjects in different countries, under different circumstances, using different questions to measure attitude certainty. In Study Two, we therefore obtain more comparable data on rootless and rooted attitudes by comparing answers provided by the same respondents in the same study, using the same questions to measure certainty.

We interview US respondents (n=245 respondents in an Internet survey) about one week before the 2008 presidential election. For the rooted attitude, we replicate Study One by asking their voting intentions. For the rootless attitudes, we ask for their online attitudes towards two minor fictitious stimuli (a healthcare program about a benign Mediterranean skin disease, and a program by Volkswagen to develop an environment-friendly car in France). On each of the three attitudes, we measure respondent confidence with the same question.

As in Study One, older respondents have a higher likelihood of planning to vote for the same party at the 2008 presidential election as at the 2004 presidential election. Also, older respondents have a higher confidence in their planned vote, and the increase is monotonic. However, we find no significant correlation of confidence with the intention to vote for the same party as in 2004.

In contrast, in agreement with Visser and Krosnick, we observe, for each of the two online attitudes, an inverted U-shaped impact of age on confidence. The highest average confidence in their attitude is obtained among mature respondents (between 55 and 60 years of age). Older respondents display a lower average confidence.

Discussion

Combining both studies, we find that respondent age has a significant impact on consumer confidence, but that the shape of the relationship differs, depending on the attitude under study. For voting intentions, which are rooted in the respondents' political attitudes developed over their lifetime, we find that average consumer confidence (measured on a confidence scale, or by the likelihood of stating "My choice is final") increases monotonically across older age ranges. For online attitudes, in contrast, we replicate Visser and Krosnick (1998) finding that, for respondent confidence in an online attitude just developed about a previously unknown topic, the impact of age on confidence follows an inverted U-shaped relationship.

Further research could replicate these findings for other consumer decision domains, and investigate mediating variables between age and observed results.

REFERENCES

Lambert-Pandraud, Raphaëlle, Gilles Laurent, and Eric Lapersonne (2005), "Repeat Purchasing of New Automobiles by Older Consumers: Empirical Evidence and Interpretations," *Journal of Marketing*, 69 (2), 97-113.

Visser, Penny S., Krosnick, Jon A. (1998), "Development of Attitude Strength over the Life Cycle: Surge and Decline," *Journal of Personality and Social Psychology*, Vol 75(6), Dec 1998. pp. 1389-1410.

The Effect of Referent Age on Interpersonal Influence in Domains Related to Factual Information, Values, and Style

Todd Pezzuti, University of California, Irvine, USA
Cornelia Pechmann, University of California, Irvine, USA
Dante Pirouz, University of California, Irvine, USA
Adilson Borges, Reims Management School, France
Carolina Werle, Grenoble Ecole de Management, France

EXTENDED ABSTRACT

The effect of referent age on interpersonal influence is explored in a series of studies. Researchers commonly assume that individuals are more influenced by someone who is of the same gender, race, and age than by those who are different on these dimensions (Chang 2008; Tajfel and Turner 1986). However, a critical evaluation of age as a construct reveals that in some situations this characteristic may have a unique effect on influence that is not well understood. Chronological age may be especially relevant when assessing persuasive messages since this characteristic is easily inferred and age-related features likely act as environmental cues that guide socially and biologically functional behavior (Montepare and Zebrowitz 1998).

Despite the logical connection between referent age and influence, very little is known about this subject beyond the work on similarity. One study that explored this topic found that advertisements featuring elderly models negatively affected retail patronage intentions for young adults for conspicuous services, but not inconspicuous services (Day and Stafford 1998). Though these findings are informative, much more research is needed in order to develop a deep and insightful understanding of how an important and pervasive social cue such as age affects interpersonal influence.

Although the effect of age on interpersonal influence has been largely neglected, some insight is offered by research that focuses on how trait inferences that are indirectly linked to age affect judgments and decisions. Research on inferences of competence stands out as particularly relevant to how people may respond when faced with messages that pertain to factual information or values since inferences of competence emerges as a universal dimension of social cognition that influences important decisions and social judgments (Fiske, Cuddy, and Glick 2007). Importantly, researchers draw a connection between inferences of competence and facial maturity (Zebrowitz and Montepare 2005) and the positive consequences of facial maturity and competence have been observed in numerous contexts including the public image of chief executive officers (Gorn et al. 2008).

A connection between chronological age and judgments of competence and facial maturity exists because older individuals are generally perceived as more competent with more mature features than younger individuals; however older individuals can possess more babyish features and be perceived as less competent as well. Nevertheless, differences in these trait inferences are likely to be ascribed to different age groups which should affect how people respond to messages pertaining to factual information and values. Influence in matters pertaining to factual information was first assessed in Study 1 by asking participants to rate whether they would consider the opinions of referents in regards to facts and statistics (referents varied on age; children of 10 years, teen-ages of 17 years, young adults of 25, and mid-aged adults of 45 years). Study 2 evaluated the effect of referent age on messages related to values and ethics in a consumer context. In this study participants selected a brand based on value-related recommendations. The effect of referent age on messages related to factual information was also assessed in a consumer context. In study 3 participants evaluated brands of enhanced bottled water based on referent claims related to technical aspects of the water (e.g., antioxidants). In each study, the older referents were more influential than younger referents and this effect was mediated by judgments related to competence and facial maturity.

When messages relate to style, characteristics other than competence and facial maturity are likely to be relevant since style is about appearance and looks. In this domain, creating an appearance that is highly valued in society is socially and biologically functional and according to sexual selection theory and empirical evidence, society values physical attributes that signal high reproductive value (Jones 1996). Importantly, reproductive health and fertility largely depend on age and the key features of physical attractiveness reflect fertility which peaks in young adulthood around 25 years of age (e.g., ideal waist-to-hip ratios and facial proportions) (Jones 1996). The reproductive status of this age group is also connected to their heightened concern over appearance and fashion, and, as a result, young adults may make good sources for determining what is stylish and fashionable (Berger 2008; Biddle and Mutrie 2001). With this in mind, people should be more open to messages related to style and taste when the source is a young adult since creating an image and appearance like these individuals is functional. This reasoning extends to teens as well since the teen years are also marked by high levels of reproductive value, albeit to a lesser extent than young adults (Jones 1996). To test the assumption that age and sexual appeal relate to style-related influence, participants were asked to choose a brand based on referent recommendations in terms of what is stylish and unique (Study 2). As hypothesized, young adults were most influential, followed by teens, then middle age adults and children and this effect was mediated by sexual appeal.

These results indicate that individuals use the perceived age of a referent as a proxy for expertise when evaluating information even in situations in which there is no direct connection between a referent's age and actual expertise and all referents state precisely the same product claim. The findings are substantively useful as marketing practitioners can use this information to choose a spokesperson or model that best fits the desired message. The findings are also theoretically important as they illustrate how fundamental environmental cues influence judgments and decisions.

REFERENCES

Berger, Kathleen S. (2008), *The Developing Person: Through the Lifespan*, New York: Worth.

Biddle, Stuart and Nanette Mutrie (2001), *Psychology of Physical Activity: Determinants, Well-Being, and Interventions*. London: Routledge.

Chang, Chingching (2008), "Chronological Age Versus Cognitive Age for Younger Consumers," Journal of Advertising, 37 (Fall), 19-32

Day, Ellen and Marla R. Stafford (1997), "Age-Relate Cues in Retailing-Services Advertising: Their Effect on Younger Consumers," *Journal of Retailing*, 73 (Summer), 211-33.

Fiske, Susan T., Amy J. Cuddy, and Peter Glick (2007), "Universal Dimension of Social Cognition: Warmth and Competence," Trends in Cognitive Science, 11 (February), 77-83

Gorn, Gerald J., Yuwei Jiang, and Gita V. Johar (2008),"Babyfaces, Trait Inferences, and Company Evaluations in a Public Relations Crisis," *Journal of Consumer Research*, (June), 36-49.

Jones, Doug (1996), *Physical Attractiveness and the Theory of Sexual Selection*, Ann Harbor, MI: University of Michigan. Museum of Anthropology.

Montepare, Joann M. and Leslie A. Zebrowitz (1998), Person Perception Comes of Age: The Salience and Significance of Age in Social Judgments," *Advances in Experimental Social Psychology*, 30, 93-153.

Tajfel, Henri and John Turner (1986), "The Social Identity Theory of Inter-group Behavior," in *Psychology of Inter-group Relations*, ed. Steven Worchel and William Austin, Chicago: Nelson-Hall.

Zebrowitz McArthur, Leslie A. and Reuben M. Baron (1983), "Towards an Ecological Perspective of Social Perception," *Psychological Review,* 90 (July), 215-38.

Trust, Commitment, and the Elderly: Exploring Age Differences in Consumer-Brand Relationships

Steffen Jahn, Chemnitz University of Technology, Germany
Hansjoerg Gaus, Saarland University, Germany
Tina Kiessling, Chemnitz University of Technology, Germany

EXTENDED ABSTRACT

In industrialized Western countries, the population is rapidly aging. Companies took a long time to realize that this fact is relevant for their businesses and often responded with inappropriate marketing activities (Moschis 2003, Weijters and Geuens 2006). Thus, in order to improve strategies aimed at mature consumers, we have to understand their behavior, investigate their consumption needs, and identify whether the older consumer market should be treated as homogeneous or further subdivided (Moschis, Lee, and Mathur 1997). Psychological and consumer research indicates that there are indeed differences within the segment of consumers older than 50 years (e.g., Carstensen, Isaacowitz, and Charles 1999; Helson and Soto 2005) and that consumers boycott brands that mistakenly treat the elderly as being all equal (Tepper 1994; Weijters and Geuens 2006). In this vein, changes in emotion regulation that come along with aging (Carstensen, Isaacowitz, and Charles 1999) might influence consumer behavior through differences in brand attachment. Thus, we argue that there are differences in consumer-brand relationships (Fournier 1998) across age segments. Despite the widely accepted importance of a brand relationship perspective and the need for research incorporating older consumers, we are aware of only one study that connects these perspectives (Olsen 1999). However, in this qualitative research the five women all were around the age of fifty and no age-specific differences could be analyzed.

So far, extant age-related research mainly focused on declining cognitive abilities of older people (Yoon 1997; Yoon, Cole, and Lee 2009). There is growing evidence, however, that not all older adults exhibit marked declines in performance of executive function tasks (Yoon and Cole 2008). More important for changing behavior might be changes in motivation across the life span (Carstensen, Fung, and Charles 2003). Thus, we draw on socioemotional selectivity theory which suggests changes in emotion regulation due to perception of time as limited (Carstensen, Isaacowitz, and Charles 1999). Supporting this view, Williams and Drolet (2005) show that consumers older than 65 years have higher liking and recall of emotional appeals in advertisements. In contrast, young adults have higher liking and recall of rational appeals. While, on average, people older than 50 years give more importance to emotional goals than younger adults, research suggests a further increase around the age of 65 (Carstensen, Fung, and Charles 2003; Carstensen, Isaacowitz, and Charles 1999; Williams and Drolet 2005). Thus, consumers' emotional attachment to brands is likely to differ between groups of 50-65 year olds and older people. More precisely, relationships among important marketing variables like self-concept connection, partner quality, brand trust, and affective commitment are assumed to differ across what we call "younger elderly" and "older elderly" consumers.

Following prior studies, trust was considered to be a determinant of relationship commitment (Chaudhuri and Holbrook 2001; Morgan and Hunt 1994). In addition, self-concept connection and partner quality were seen as determinants of trust and commitment (Breivik and Thorbjørnsen 2008; Escalas 2004; Kressmann et al. 2006; Laurenceau, Barrett, and Pietromonaco 1998). Regarding differences between both age groups, the effect of trust on commitment is assumed to be higher for the younger elderly, relative to the older ones (Charles, Mather, and Carstensen 2003; Williams and Drolet 2005). In contrast, the effects of partner quality on commitment and trust are expected to be higher for the older elderly (Carstensen, Fung, and Charles 2003; Carstensen, Isaacowitz, and Charles 1999; Helson and Soto 2005; Williams and Drolet 2005). In addition, self-concept connection is supposed to impact on commitment to a higher extent within the group of older elderly consumers (Carstensen, Fung, and Charles 2003; Carstensen, Isaacowitz, and Charles 1999). Due to common heuristics in the identification-trust link (Butler 1991; Dunn and Schweitzer 2005), we expect only low if any age-group differences in the effect of self-concept connection on trust (Yoon and Cole 2008).

We empirically tested the hypotheses in a survey among 341 women over the age of 50. Coffee as a frequently purchased packaged good was chosen because here strong brand relationships may continue to impact on buying behavior even into old age. Moderator analyses with LISREL reveal significant path differences between the younger elderly and the older elderly groups for the influences of partner quality on commitment and trust. In addition, the path from trust on commitment is higher for the younger elderly. However, two results are counter-intuitive. The path from self-concept connection on commitment did not differ across groups. Its influence on trust differed, being stronger within the younger elderly group. A reason might be that this link is more cognitively driven than expected. Hence, the younger elderly process the information more deeply and form their trust judgments on the basis of identification. While trust represents the major determinant of commitment for the younger elderly, commitment is not affected by trust within the older senior segment. For the latter, commitment heavily depends on perceived partner quality. Self-concept connection has little impact on commitment in the entire sample with no difference across both age groups. Older elderly's trust process is determined by partner quality, while both partner quality and self-concept connection affect trust judgments within the group of younger elderly.

Overall, the findings support the theoretically derived assumption of shifts in brand relationships with respect to consumers' life cycle. Socioemotional selectivity theory (Carstensen et al. 1999) has been successfully used to describe these shifts. In general, for younger elderly it seems to be important how the brand is, expressed by the links between self-concept connection, trust, and commitment. For the older elderly it appears to be more relevant what the brand does. Consequently, a high partner quality drives their brand trust and affective commitment. "What a brand does" seems to fit older people's needs and generate positive emotions. In line with socioemotional selectivity theory, this affects motivation and behavior. Younger elderly appear to be more able or willing to put cognitive effort in the brand relationship process. Concluding, this study contributes to the understanding of the 50+ market by analyzing differences in consumer-brand relationships between two groups of elderly consumers, namely those between 50 and 65 and those above 65 years of age. In addition, we demonstrate that chronological age is a valuable segmentation criterion for both consumer researchers and marketing managers. The findings challenge prior research that generally devaluated chronological age in favor for other measures such as cognitive age.

REFERENCES

Breivik, Einar and Helge Thorbjørnsen (2008), "Consumer Brand Relationships: An Investigation of Two Alternative Models," *Journal of the Academy of Marketing Science*, 36, 443-472.

Butler, John K., Jr. (1991), "Toward Understanding and Measuring Conditions of Trust: Evolution of a Conditions of Trust Inventory," *Journal of Management*, 17, 643-663.

Carstensen, Laura L., Helene H. Fung, and Susan Turk Charles (2003), "Socioemotional Selectivity Theory and the Regulation of Emotion in the Second Half of Life," *Motivation and Emotion*, 27 (June), 103-123.

______ , Derek M. Isaacowitz, and Susan Turk-Charles (1999), "Taking Time Seriously: A Theory of Socioemotional Selectivity," *American Psychologist*, 54 (March), 165-81.

Charles, Susan Turk, Mara Mather, and Laura L. Carstensen (2003), "Aging and Emotional Memory: The Forgettable Nature of Negative Images for Older Adults," *Journal of Experimental Psychology: General*, 132 (2)310-324.

Dunn, Jennifer R. and Maurice E. Schweitzer (2005), "Feeling and Believing: The Influence of Emotion on Trust," *Journal of Personality and Social Psychology*, 88 (5), 736-48.

Escalas, Jennifer Edson (2004), "Narrative Processing: Building Consumer Connections to Brands," *Journal of Consumer Psychology*, 14 (1&2), 168-80.

Fournier, Susan (1998), "Consumers and Their Brands: Developing Relationship Research in Consumer Research," *Journal of Consumer Research*, 24 (4), 343-73.

Helson, Ravenna and Christopher J. Soto (2005), "Up and Down in Middle Age: Monotonic and Nonmonotonic Changes in Roles, Status, and Personality," *Journal of Personality and Social Psychology*, 89 (2), 194-204.

Kressmann, Frank, Joseph M. Sirgy, Andreas Herrmann, Frank Huber, Stephanie Huber, and Dong-Jin Lee (2006), "Direct and Indirect Effects of Self-Image Congruence on Brand Loyalty," *Journal of Business Research*, 59 (9), 955-64.

Laurenceau, Jean-Philippe, Lisa Feldmann Barrett, and Paula R. Pietromonaco (1998), "Intimacy as an Interpersonal Process: The Importance of Self-disclosure, Partner-disclosure, and Perceived Partner Responsiveness in Interpersonal Exchanges," *Journal of Personality and Social Psychology*, 74 (5), 1238–1251.

Morgan, Robert M. and Shelby D. Hunt (1994), "The Commitment-Trust Theory of Relationship Marketing," *Journal of Marketing*, 58 (3), 20-38.

Moschis, Georg P. (2003), "Marketing to Older Adults: An Updated Overview of Present Knowledge and Practice," *Journal of Consumer Marketing*, 20 (6), 516-25.

Moschis, Georg P., Euehun Lee, and Anil Mathur (1997), "Targeting the Mature Market: Opportunities and Challenges," *Journal of Consumer Marketing*, 14 (4/5), 282-93.

Olsen, Barbara (1999), "Exploring Women's Brand Relationships and Enduring Themes at Mid-Life," in *Advances in Consumer Research*, Volume 26, eds. Eric J. Arnould and Linda M. Scott, Provo, UT: Association for Consumer Research, 615-20.

Tepper, Kelly (1994), "The Role of Labeling Processes in Elderly Consumers' Responses to Age Segmentation Cues," *Journal of Consumer Research*, 20 (4), 503-519.

Weijters, Bert and Maggie Geuens (2006), "Evaluations of Age-Related Labels by Senior Citizens," *Psychology & Marketing*, 23 (9), 783-98.

Williams, Patti and Aimee Drolet (2005), "Age-Related Differences in Responses to Emotional Advertisements," *Journal of Consumer Research*, 32 (3), 343-354.

Yoon, Carolyn (1997), "Age Differences in Consumers' Processing Strategies: An Investigation of Moderating Influences," *Journal of Consumer Research*, 24 (3), 329-42.

______ and Catherine A. Cole (2008), "Aging and Consumer Behavior," in *Handbook of Consumer Psychology*, eds. Curtis P. Haugtvedt, Paul M. Herr, and Frank R. Kardes, New York, NY: Taylor & Francis, 247-270.

______,______, and Michelle P. Lee (2009), "Consumer Decision Making and Aging: Current Knowledge and Future Directions," *Journal of Consumer Psychology*, 19, 2-16.

Threat Perception in Product Harm Crises: Do Older Consumers Feel More Vulnerable?

David H. Silvera, University of Texas at San Antonio, USA
Tracy Meyer, University of North Carolina at Wilmington, USA
Daniel Laufer, Yeshiva University, USA
R. Justin Goss, University of Texas at San Antonio, USA
Ashley Rae Arsena, University of Texas at San Antonio, USA

EXTENDED ABSTRACT

Age-related declines in physical and cognitive abilities are well-documented (Schneider and Rowe 1991). These declines result in older adults having a reduced ability to actively cope with problems and being more susceptible to potential threats than younger consumers (Heckhausen 1997). Although there is ample evidence that older adults experience an increase in real susceptibility to threat, there is relatively little evidence indicating whether perceptions of susceptibility to threat increase similarly with age. The present research attempts to examine this question within a marketing context by (a) examining how older consumers evaluate potential threats in relation to negative marketing events in the form of product harm crises, and (b) studying how threat perceptions influence marketing outcomes for involved companies.

The existing literature provides two competing predictions regarding how age will relate to perceived threat. The most straightforward prediction is that real increases in susceptibility to threat in older adults should be paralleled by increases in perceived susceptibility to threat. There is substantial research indicating not only that older adults experience real decline in many domains, but also that people of all ages are aware that mental, physiological, and psychological decline is associated with old age. Furthermore, these declines are most prominent in the physical domain, which has been the focus of most research on product harm crises.

However, more recent research suggests that this common sense hypothesis might not be correct and that instead older adults might view themselves as less susceptible to threat than younger adults. This alternative hypothesis is based on Heckhausen and Schulz' (1995) proposition that there are age-related differences in primary versus secondary control processes. Primary control processes are typically active and outwardly directed, and represent an effort to change the present or future environment to fit one's needs or desires (e.g., by avoiding threatening circumstances, for example by not purchasing a dangerous product); secondary control processes are primarily cognitive and inwardly directed and involve psychological adjustment to accept existing circumstances as they are (e.g., altering perceptions to perceive a situation as less threatening, for example by viewing the danger associated with a product harm crisis as being exaggerated by the media). Research suggests that, whereas the ability to engage in primary control declines across the adult lifespan, secondary control becomes more prevalent with age. Secondary control involves altering one's own perceptions so that a problem (which typically can't be resolved via primary control processes) is viewed as less threatening and thus more acceptable to the individual. Protection Motivation Theory (Rogers 1975) describes threat perception as being derived from the perceived severity of a negative event and perceptions of personal vulnerability to negative outcomes associated with that event. Thus, reductions in perceptions of severity and personal vulnerability would be evidence for a stronger impact of secondary control processes on judgments related to a product harm crisis.

Based on the proposition that older adults have a reduced ability to engage in threat protection via primary control and thus compensate with increased secondary control, our hypotheses are that, compared to younger adults: (1) Older adults will engage in less primary control, meaning that they will have stronger intentions to purchase or recommend a product associated with a product harm crisis; (2) older adults will engage in more secondary control, meaning that they will perceive themselves as less personally vulnerable and a product harm crisis as less severe; and (3) older adults will place less blame on the company involved in a product harm crisis due to lower threat perceptions based on the defensive attribution hypothesis (Robbennolt 2000). A theoretical model is also proposed in which age predicts secondary control (perceived severity and vulnerability), secondary control predicts blame to the company, and blame to the company predicts purchase and recommendation intentions toward the company's products.

Two studies were conducted to test these hypotheses. In each study, older versus younger consumers were presented with a scenario describing a product harm crisis (involving televisions in study 1 and coffee in study 2). After reading the scenario, participants completed measures of their perceptions of the severity of the product harm crisis, their perceptions of their own vulnerability in relation to the crisis, the degree to which they blamed the company for the crisis, and their intentions to purchase and recommend the involved company's products in the future.

In both studies, the hypotheses were fully supported: Compared to younger adults, older adults had lower perceptions of severity and vulnerability in association with the product harm crisis, blamed the company less, and had stronger intentions to purchase and recommend the company's products. The theoretical model was also supported in both studies, with one exception: For the television crisis (study 1), blame to the company was predicted by perceived severity but not by perceived personal vulnerability. For the coffee crisis (study 2), however, perceived personal vulnerability was a stronger predictor of company blame than perceived severity. Thus, although older participants exhibited stronger secondary control processes with regard to both aspects of threat perception in both studies, this result suggests that different aspects of secondary control might be more relevant under different circumstances.

In conclusion, we find evidence that, contrary to the perceptions of many in the general public regarding the elderly, real increases in susceptibility to a threat due to aging are not associated with increases in consumers' perceptions of the danger posed by that threat. In fact, the present results suggest that perceptions of threat related to a product harm crisis actually decrease with age. Older adults appear to focus less on the negative information associated with a crisis, and are thus less likely to incorporate this negative information into their attitudes and preferences. This research provides unique insights to marketers relative to a growing and under-researched segment of the world population.

REFERENCES

Arbuckle, James L. (2006), *Amos 7.0 User's Guide*, Spring House, PA: Amos Development Corporation.

Dalbert, Claudia (1999), "The World is More Just for Me than Generally: About the Personal Belief in a Just World Scale's Validity," *Social Justice Research*, 12 (2), 79-98.

Dawar, Niraj and Madan M. Pillutla (2000), "Impact of Product-harm Crises on Brand Equity: The Moderating Role of Consumer Expectations," *Journal of Marketing Research*, 37 (2), 215-26.

Folkes, Valerie S. (1988), "Recent Attribution Research in Consumer Behavior: A Review and New Directions," *Journal of Consumer Research*, 14 (4), 548-65.

Heckhausen, Jutta (1997), "Developmental Regulation across Adulthood: Primary and Secondary Control of Age-related Challenges," *Developmental Psychology*, 33 (1), 176-87.

Heckhausen, Jutta and Paul B. Baltes (1991), "Perceived Controllability of Expected Psychological Change across Adulthood and Old Age," *Journal of Gerontology: Psychological Sciences*, 46 (4), 165-73.

Heckhausen, Jutta and Richard Schulz (1995), "A Life-span Theory of Control," *Psychological Review*, 102 (2), 284-304.

Hu, Li-tze and Peter M. Bentler (1999), "Cutoff Criteria for Fit Indexes in Covariance Structure Analysis: Conventional Criteria versus New Alternatives," *Structural Equation Modeling*, 6 (1), 1-55.

John, Deborah R. and Catherine A. Cole (1986), "Age Differences in Information Processing: Understanding Deficits in Young and Elderly Consumers," *Journal of Consumer Research*, 13 (3), 297-315.

Jones, Jeri and Karen Middleton (2007), "Ethical Decision-making by Consumers: The Roles of Product Harm and Consumer Vulnerability," *Journal of Business Ethics*, 70 (3), 247-64.

Kohn, Donald L. (2007), "Testimony of Vice Chairman Donald L. Kohn on The Aging Workforce before the Special Committee on Aging, U. S. Senate, February 28, 2007," http://www.federalreserve.gov/newsevents/testimony/kohn20070228a.htm.

Laufer Daniel and Kate Gillespie (2004), "Who's to Blame? Differences in Consumer Attributions of Blame between Men and Women: The Role of Perceived Vulnerability and Empathic Concern," *Psychology and Marketing*, 21 (2), 209-22.

Laufer, Daniel, Kate Gillespie, Brad McBride, and Silvia Gonzalez (2005), "The Role of Severity in Consumer Attributions of Blame: Defensive Attributions in Product Harm Crises in Mexico," *Journal of International Consumer Marketing*, 17 (2/3), 33-50.

Laufer, Daniel, David H. Silvera, and Tracy Meyer (2005), "Exploring Differences between Older and Younger Consumers in Attributions of Blame for Product Harm Crises," *Academy of Marketing Science Review* [online], 2005 (7), http://www.amsreview.org/articles/laufer07-2005.pdf.

Moschis, George, Carolyn Curasi, and Danny Bellenger (2004), "Patronage Motives of Mature Consumers in the Selection of Food and Grocery Stores," *Journal of Consumer Marketing*, 21 (2), 123-33.

Otte Christian, Stacey Hart, Thomas C. Neylan, Charles R. Marmar, Kristine Yaffe, and David C. Mohr (2005), "A Meta-analysis of Cortisol Response to Challenge in Human Aging: Importance of Gender," Psychoneuroendocrinology, 30 (1), 80-91.

Robbennolt, Jennifer K. (2000), "Outcome Severity and Judgments of Responsibility: A Meta-analytic Review," Journal of Applied Psychology, 30 (12), 2575-2609.

Rogers, Ronald W. (1975), "A Protection Motivation Theory of Fear Appeals and Attitude Change," *Journal of Psychology: Interdisciplinary and Applied*, 91 (1), 93-114.

Rosengren, Annika, Lars Wallentin, Maarten Simoons, Anselm K. Gitt, Solomon Behar, Alexander Battler, and David Hasdai (2006), "Age, Clinical Presentation, and Outcome of Acute Coronary Syndromes in the Euroheart Acute Coronary Syndrome Survey," *European Heart Journal*, 27 (April), 789-95.

Schneider, Edward L. and John W. Rowe (1991), *Handbook of the Biology of Aging* (3rd edition), San Diego, CA: Academic Press.

Silvera David H. and Daniel Laufer (2005), "Recent Developments in Attribution Research and their Implications for Consumer Judgments and Behaviour," in *Applying Social Cognition to Consumer-Focused Strategy*, ed. Frank R. Kardes, Paul M. Herr, and Jacques Nantel, Mahwah, NJ: Erlbaum, 53-77.

Siomkos, George J. and Gary Kurzbard (1994), "The Hidden Crisis in Product-harm Crisis Management," *European Journal of Marketing*, 28 (2), 30-41.

Williams Patti and Aimee Drolet (2005), "Age-related Differences in Responses to Emotional Advertisements," *Journal of Consumer Research*, 32 (3), 343-54.

Yoon, Carolyn (1997), "Age Differences in Consumers' Processing Strategies: An Investigation of Moderating Influences," *Journal of Consumer Research*, 24 (3), 329-42.

Examining Structural Relationships among Environmental, Behavioral Factors, and Childhood Obesity

Myoung Kim, University of Wisconsin-Madison, USA
Nancy Wong, University of Wisconsin-Madison, USA

EXTENDED ABSTRACT

The startling growth in the obesity epidemic facing American children has been a leading public health concern over the past several decades. It is becoming clear that the consequences of this dramatic growth in childhood obesity are severe. The childhood obesity epidemic results in not only severe health consequences, but also the attendant medical, psychological, and social costs (Allison, Fontaine, and Naraya 1999; Rippe and Aronne 1998). A considerable body of research has focused on understanding various factors associated with childhood obesity. Past research has identified two main factors associated with childhood obesity: behavioral and environmental factors. Behavioral factors include a sedentary lifestyle and consumption of excess calories, which lead to low energy expenditure and high energy intake, while environmental factors consist of (1) family factors, (2) school factors, (3) community factors, and (4) media factors.

However, these relationships have often been examined individually without consideration for how these factors could jointly contribute or mitigate the effects of each other. Furthermore, due to the limitations of past study samples, it was often not possible to account for the child's psychological traits in these studies. In order to develop more effective intervention programs, we must consider these factors jointly (Davison and Birch 2001) and also test for possible moderating effects of certain key psychological factors. With that in mind, the goal of this study is to develop and test a comprehensive model on factors influencing childhood obesity. By applying the theory of consumer socialization (Moschis and Churchill 1978), we postulate that children's behaviors related to obesity-prevention such as (un)healthy eating patterns and physical activities are (1) learned "consumer skills" through the socialization process and are (2) influenced by social agents (i.e., family, school, community, and media). We further examine the potential moderating role of the child's psychological traits, such as self-control and internalizing problems, in the relationship among environmental, behavioral factors and children's weight status.

We analyze data on fifth graders from the Early Childhood Longitudinal Study (ECLS-K) conducted by the National Center for Educational Statistics. The longitudinal survey was performed in the fall and the spring of kindergarten (1998-99), the fall and spring of 1st grade (1999-2000), the spring of 3rd grade (2002), 5th grade (2004), and 8th (2007) grade. The ECLS-K used the nationally representative sample of a cohort of children who entered kindergarten in the fall of 1998 from approximately 1000 schools. A multistage probability sample design was employed to select the ECLS-K sample. Information about children was obtained from parents (through CATI interview), teachers (through paper survey) and students (through in-person interview and paper survey). However, we focused on the 5th grade data (2004) because the ECLS-K started to include information on children's food consumption since 5th grade; furthermore, the 7th grade data are not yet available to the public. Among a total of 11,820 students from the 5th grade data, our sample was limited to 9,019 students who attended public schools and provided information on BMI.

For the purpose of testing the proposed model by incorporating multiple factors simultaneously, we use the structural equation modeling (SEM) approach. We first tested the measurement model to examine whether the measurement items have the appropriate properties to represent each construct included in the model. We then evaluated the structural model by examining overall model fit and structural relationships specified in the model. LISREL 8 (Joreskog and Sorbom 1993) was used for evaluating both the measurement and structural models.

The results from this study provide empirical support of identifying relative importance among multiple factors contributing to childhood obesity. The major findings from our study are: (1) When family, school, community, and media factors are considered jointly, the family factors appear to be the most significant determinants of a child's involvement with (un)healthy eating patterns and physical activities, (2) especially, mothers' working hours more than 35 hours and children's TV viewing time have a significant and direct impact on children's weight status, (3) while the school factors and community factors have relatively less significant impact on children's behaviors related to obesity-prevention, and (4) children's psychological traits such as self-control and internalizing problems moderate the relationships among environmental, behavioral factors and children's weight status.

The findings from our study are important in several ways. First, it might be the one of the first studies to look at the relationship between childhood obesity and multiple factors including both environmental and behavioral factors simultaneously. In so doing, we overcome conflicting past findings based on largely bivariate relationships. Second, the relative importance of family or parental factors contributing to childhood obesity leads to a re-examination of the current intervention programs. More effective education materials and health communication tools targeting parents are critical in improving children's healthy eating and increased physical activities. Third, the moderating effect of children's self-control confirms that school records regarding children's test scores for psychological traits can be used as a tool to evaluate children at being risk of obesity. Political support that aids systematic intervention programs is needed.

While findings from this study may offer vital implications on the prevention of childhood obesity, we acknowledge several limitations of this study and offer possible directions for future research: (1) perform a longitudinal analysis of the models developed in this study, (2) include other potential environmental variables from the comprehensive model, (3) improve the measurements used in our study, and (4) incorporate qualitative insights from parents and children.

REFERENCES

Allison, D., K. Fontaine, and K. Naraya (1999), "The Direct Health Care Costs of Obesity in the United States," *American Journal of Public Health*, 89 (8), 1194-1199.

Davison, K. K. and L. L. Birch (2001), "Childhood Overweight: A Contextual Model and Recommendations for Future Research," *Obesity Review*, 2 (3), 159-171.

Joreskog, Karl and Dag Sorbom (1993), *LISREL 8 User's Reference Guide*, Chicago: Scientific Software International.

Moschis, George P. and Gilbert A. Churchill, Jr. (1978), "Consumer Socialization: A Theoretical and Empirical Analysis," *Journal of Marketing Research*, 15 (November): 599-609.

Rippe, J. and L. Aronne (1998), "Public Policy Statement on Obesity and Health from the Interdisciplinary Council on Lifestyle and Obesity Management," *Nutrition in Clinical Care*, 1, 34-37.

Empty Pockets Full Stomachs: How Monetary Scarcity and Monetary Primes Lead to Caloric Desire

Barbara Briers, Tilburg University, The Netherlands
Sandra Laporte, HEC Paris, France

EXTENDED ABSTRACT

Briers et al. (2006) showed that desire for monetary resources motivates people to acquire or maintain resources in the food domain. Their study demonstrates that people eat more candy in a taste test when they desire money than when their desire for money is lower. In this research, we set out to investigate how monetary scarcity might lead to higher food intake. We identify and test two ways in which money, a commodity that has no biological significance in itself, can become a strong motivator for gathering food. Specifically, we test whether the effect of monetary scarcity on food consumption results from the instrumental, secondary reinforcer value of money rather than its primary rewarding qualities. In line with the value heuristic (Dai, Wertenbroch, and Brendl 2008), we also assume that monetarily deprived people perceive food items as less caloric because they value calories more. Accordingly, this perception can lead to a preference for more caloric food and/or bigger portions.

Money represents an instrument to obtain natural incentives (e.g., food) but is not directly consumable. According to operant psychology, money therefore is a conditioned (or secondary) reinforcer that gains its motivational property only because of its repetitive pairing with unconditioned (or primary) reinforcers (Skinner 1953). Similarly, standard economic theory posits that money is an instrument or tool for obtaining biologically relevant incentives (Lea and Webley 2005). Once a Pavlovian association exists, the conditioned stimulus (e.g., money) can trigger a motivation (desire) for an unconditioned reward (e.g., food) (Berridge and Robinson 2003). Because of its instrumental quality, money might be conditioned to different types of primary incentives. According to Skinner (1953), if a single kind of conditioned reinforcer gets paired with many different kinds of unconditioned reinforcers, the reinforcing effect will become independent of the deprivation of any of them. Thus, money would have the same motivational properties as natural incentives or primary rewards.

Recent consumer research offers evidence that induced appetites can instigate a greater urgency to consume anything rewarding (Li 2008; Van den Bergh, Dewitte, and Warlop 2008; Wadhwa, Shiv, and Nowlis 2008). Appetitive stimuli (e.g., rich desserts, sex cues, food samples) can prompt people to seek anything that offers a high incentive value (e.g., money, candy bars, a massage) and thus affect subsequent consumption across domains. Both Van den Bergh and colleagues (2008) and Wadhwa and colleagues (2008) suggest that a general reward system gives rise to this effect. That is, if money alone can instigate an increase in appetitive motivation, just as a primary reward does, it also may induce people to desire more food, as well as other kinds of reward. The effect of monetary scarcity on caloric intake thus may be driven by the activation of a general reward system.

As far as we know, money cues have not been used as the independent variable in this stream of research. Moreover, recent advances in parsing rewards into specific psychological components might challenge a view of money as a primary reward. Berridge and Robinson (2003) distinguish between "liking" and "wanting," though both are necessary for rewards to occur in the fullest sense. Yet wanting may occur without liking: Drug addicts crave drugs, such as nicotine, even when they do not derive much pleasure from them. It is the attribution of wanting that makes a conditioned stimulus an object of desire. As an instrument, money may be conditioned on food rewards but is not directly consumable; money is "wanted" but not "liked," in which case it may not be a reward with appetitive properties. Building on the distinction between wanting and liking, we posit that the association between money and food may be driven by the instrumental, secondary reinforcer value of money rather than by its primary rewarding qualities.

In four experiments, we consider both explanations and thereby obtain more evidence that suggests the effect derives from the instrumental value of money, that is, money as a conditioned stimulus of food. In study 1, we show that that the effect of monetary scarcity differs for food versus nonfood rewards. The results also suggest that participants' sensitivity to rewards does not moderate the effect of monetary scarcity on subsequent food choices. In study 2, we pit the two possible explanations against each other by investigating the role of symbolic meanings of money (Rose and Orr 2007). Specifically, in study 2a, we find that the effect of monetary scarcity on caloric desire is greater for persons who view money as an instrument, and in study 2b, we establish a link between desire for calories and money as an instrument more directly by manipulating, instead of measuring, the meaning of money. To follow up on the idea of money as a conditioned stimulus strongly associated with food, in study 3, we investigate whether priming people with money (i.e., priming as an unconscious reminder of the concept of money) produces the same results. In a 2 (money vs. fish screensavers; Vohs et al. 2006) X 2 (monetary satiation vs. control) between subjects design, participants primed with money on average choose a larger brownie, but only when money is scarce. Furthermore, study 2 and 3 also imply that calorie (under)estimation is mediating the effect of monetary scarcity and money primes on subsequent food choices.

In sum, this research illustrates how money scarcity, as well as money primes, can induce people to consume more (caloric) food. We also demonstrate that money can lead people to underestimate the caloric content of food, which prompts them to choose larger food portions or more caloric dishes. This effect of money (scarcity and primes) on food consumption stems from the Pavlovian association that results from a pairing of money and food, in which money represents a secondary reinforcer or instrument to acquire food. Although this series of experiments contributes to a growing body of research that shows out-of-domain effects of appetitive stimuli (Li 2008; Van den Bergh et al. 2008; Wadhwa et al. 2008), we do not believe a general reward system gives rise to this effect.

Investigating the money–food association further might help explain why poor people appear especially vulnerable to overeating and its poor health effects (Drewnowski and Specter 2004). Although reduced physical activity and specific food manufacturing and marketing practices might be (partly) responsible for the societal correlation between obesity and poverty, no research attempts to understand why, for example, food manufacturing and marketing practices have a stronger impact on poor people than on rich people. Perhaps in modern societies, the attraction to money is so powerful that (all-pervading) monetary cues can tempt money-deprived people easily to eat more (caloric) food. That is, this series of experiments might render a proximal account for the well-documented societal link between obesity and poverty, based on individual experiences of money deprivation.

REFERENCES

Berridge, Kent C. and Terry E. Robinson (2003), "Parsing Reward," *Trends in Neurosciences,* 26 (9), 507-13.

Briers, Barbara, Mario Pandelaere, Siegfried Dewitte, and Luk Warlop (2006),"Hungry for Money: The Desire for Caloric Resources Increases the Desire for Financial Resources and Vice Versa," *Psychological Science,* 17 (11), 939-43.

Dai, Xianchi, Klaus Wertenbroch, and Miguel C. Brendl (2008), "The Value Heuristic in Judgments of Relative Frequency, " *Psychological Science,* 19 (1), 18-19.

Drewnowski, Adam and S.E. Specter (2004), "Poverty and Obesity: The Role of Energy Density and Energy Costs," *American Journal of Clinical Nutrition*, 79, 6–16.

Lea, Stephen E.G. and Paul Webley (2006), "Money as Tool, Money as Drug: The Biological Psychology of a Strong Incentive," *Behavioral and Brain Sciences*, 29 (2), 161–209.

Li, Xiuping (2008), "The Effects of Appetitive Stimuli on Out-of-Domain Consumption Impatience," *Journal of Consumer Behavior*, 34 (5), 649-56.

Rose, Gregory M. and Linda M. Orr (2007), "Symbolic Money Meanings: Refinements in Conceptualization and Measurement," *Psychology and Marketing*, 24 (9), 743-61.

Skinner, Burrhus F. (1953), *Science and Human Behavior*, New York: Macmillan.

Van den Bergh, Bram, Siegfried Dewitte, and Luk Warlop (2008), "Bikinis Instigate Generalized Impatience in Intertemporal Choice," *Journal of Consumer Research,* 35 (1), 85-97.

Vohs, Kathleen D., Nicole L. Mead, and Miranda R. Goode (2006), "The Psychological Consequences of Money," *Science,* 314, 1154-6.

Wadhwa, Monica, Baba Shiv, and Stephen M. Nowlis (2008), "A Bite to Whet the Reward Appetite: The Influence of Sampling on Reward-Seeking Behaviors," *Journal of Marketing Research,* 45 (4), 403-13.

Place, Prosocial Activity, and Unhealthy Consumption

Brennan Davis, Baylor University, USA
Connie Pechmann, University of California at Irvine, USA

EXTENDED ABSTRACT

The academic literature increasingly recognizes a relationship between retail placement and unhealthy consumption in adolescents (Lu et al. 2007; Patel et al. 2007; Powell et al. 2006; Novak et al. 2006; Weitzman et al. 2003; Scribner, Cohen and Fisher 2000). At the same time, there is an emerging literature showing that youth prosocial activity is associated with unhealthy consumption (Xue, Zimmerman and Caldwell 2007; Eitle, Turner and Eitle 2003; Elder et al. 2000; Cooley et al. 1995). Prosocial activity means involvement in group functions liked sports teams, religious groups and clubs (Duncan et al. 2002). It is surprising that these streams have not been brought into consumer research, given the wealth of studies on retail placement as a marketing strategy (Fox and Hoch 2005; Mittal, Kamakura and Govind 2004) in marketing and on prosocial behavior (Small and Simonsohn 2008; Bagozzi and Moore 1994) in consumer research. We study unhealthy consumption as a function of both place and prosocial activity.

Our study offers an empirical examination of hypotheses related to Third Place Theory (Oldenburg 1983), which says that people frequent public places outside of home and work to gather for prosocial activity. Past work on Third Place Theory has been primarily theoretical and qualitative (Rosenbaum 2006; Cheang 2002; Oldenburg 1982), leaving a gap for quantitative tests. We examine hypotheses supporting Third Place Theory on a large sample of students with varying levels of prosocial activity.

We consider rival hypotheses to the traditional ones about place and prosocial activity. The traditional hypothesis about place says that nearby fast food is associated with unhealthy consumption and obesity. The traditional hypothesis about prosocial activity says that prosocial activity is negatively related to unhealthy consumption and obesity. Third Place Theory says that people frequent public places outside home and work for the purpose of prosocial activity and consumption. They are both geographically accessible to consumers and spatially commodious for social activity. Hence, Third Place Theory describes an interaction of place and prosocial activity.

In our study, we expect fast-food restaurants around schools to serve as Third Places for students seeking social interaction with other students. Research has shown that fast-food venues are places for social gathering, leading to unhealthy consumption for those who are socializing there (Cheang 2002; Rosenbaum 2006). If fast food serves as a Third Place for youth with greater prosocial activity, then access to nearby fast food may lead to an increase in unhealthy consumption and obesity among those with greater prosocial activity. Our study offers the first empirical tests of Third Place Theory to our knowledge. Past work on Third Place Theory has been theoretical or qualitative, leaving a gap for quantitative tests (Cheang 2002; Oldenburg 1982; Rosenbaum 2006).

Specifically, we posit that prosocial activity moderates the effect of place on unhealthy consumption and obesity. We predict that students with greater prosocial activity will be affected by their exposure to fast-food placement around schools. Students with lesser prosocial activity will not be affected by nearby fast food. Because fast-food restaurants host prosocial activity, we predict that the nearby fast food will be associated with unhealthy consumption and obesity for students with greater prosocial activity.

Some may argue that prosocial activity is a moderator merely because of the activity rather than prosocial nature of prosocial activity. Activities are time consuming, increasing the need for convenient food options that nearby fast food provides. If this were true, then for students with greater participation in activities that are not prosocial, nearby fast food should also be associated with unhealthy consumption. However, in support of Third Place as the main theory behind place effects in fast food, we predict that non-social activity will fail to moderate the role of place on unhealthy consumption because fast food is acting as a third place for prosocial gathering. For increasing non-social activity, nearby fast food will not increase its association with unhealthy consumption and obesity.

Our methodological approach uses geographic information systems (GIS) data, which are site addresses linked spatially to the earth's latitude and longitude coordinates. We link GIS data with survey results from individual consumers. First, we collect GIS data on a student's school and on the fast-food sites around a student's school. Then, we link the GIS data with survey data on a student's prosocial activity, consumption habits and body weight. Last, we compare the unhealthy consumption and obesity of students whose schools are near versus not near fast food. We make this comparison across two student segments: those with greater versus lesser prosocial activity.

We use GIS data and survey results on almost 500,000 youths from 2002-2005 with multivariate regression models to estimate associations among fast food around schools; student measures of prosocial activity; consumption of soda and fried potato foods; and youth obesity. The measures of fast-food placement around schools come from Microsoft Streets and Trips, the California Department of Education, and Technomic, a food industry consultant. The measures of prosocial activity, consumption and obesity come from the California Healthy Kids Survey. We control for individual, school, and environment variables like grade, race/ethnicity, school enrollment, county, and urbanicity.

Our results demonstrate that, for students with greater prosocial activity, those exposed to nearby fast food around their schools: 1) consume more servings of soda and fried potato foods; and 2) are more likely to be obese relative to similarly situated youths whose schools are not near fast food. However, the presence of fast food does not affect students with lesser prosocial activity. We also find that, for students with greater non-social activity, nearby fast food does not increase its association with unhealthy consumption and obesity, as hypothesized. The results provide evidence for fast food as third places that attract youths looking for prosocial activity. Our results bridge the research on place and prosocial activity, empirically test formal hypotheses about Third Place Theory, and inform public policy.

REFERENCES

Bagozzi, Richard P, and David Moore (1994), "Public Service Advertisements: Emotions and Empathy Guide Prosocial Behavior," *Journal of Marketing*, 58 (January), 56-71.

Cheang, Michael (2002), "Older Adults' Frequent Visits to a Fast-Food Restaurant-Nonobligatory Social Interaction and the Significance of Play in a 'Third Place'," *Journal of Aging Studies*, 16 (August), 303-321.

Cooley, Van E., L.W. Henderson, C. Van Nelson and Jay C. Thompson, Jr. (1995), "A Study to Determine the Effect of Extracurricular Participation on Student Alcohol and Drug Use in Secondary Schools," *Journal of Alcohol and Drug Education*, 40 (Winter), 71-87.

Duncan, Susan C., Terry E. Duncan, Lisa A. Strycker, and Nigel R. Chaumeton (2002), "Relations between Youth Antisocial and Prosocial Activities," *Journal of Behavioral Medicine*, 25 (March), 425-438.

Eitle, David, R. Jay Turner, and Tamela McNutty Eitle (2003), "The Detterence Hypothesis Reexamined: Sports Participation and Substance Use among Young Adults," *Journal of Drug Issues*, 33 (January), 193-222.

Elder, Craig, Deirdre Leaver-Dunn, Min Qi Wang, Steven Nagy, and Lee Green (2000), "Organized Group Activity as a Protective Factor against Adolescent Substance Use," *American Journal of Health Behavior*, 24 (March/April), 108-114.

Fox, Edward J. and Stephen J. Hoch (2005), "Cherry-Picking," *Journal of Marketing*, 69 (January), 46-62.

Lu, Yao, Minal Patel, William J. McCarthy, and Ritesh Mistry (2007), "Teen Student Smoking and School-adjacent Tobacco Retailer Density in California: A GIS Analysis," working paper, University of California Los Angeles.

Mittal, Vikas, Wagner Kamakura, and Rahul Govind (2004), "Geographic Patterns in Customer Service and Satisfaction: An Empirical Investigation," *Journal of Marketing*, 68 (July) 48-62.

Patel, Minal, William J. McCarthy, Ritesh Mistry, Yao Lu, Stanislav Parfenov, and David Cowling (2007), "Tobacco Retailer Proximity to Schools & Teen Smoking: A Geospatial Analysis," working paper, University of California Los Angeles.

Powell, Lisa, M. Christopher Auld, Frank J. Chaloupka, Patrick J. O'Malley, and Lloyd D. Johnston (2006). "Access to Fast Food and Food Prices: Relationship with Fruit and Vegetable Consumption and Overweight among Adolescents," in *Advances in Health Economics and Health Services Research.*

Novak, Scott P., Sean F. Reardon, Stephen W. Raudenbush, and Stephen L. Buka (2006), "Retail Tobacco Outlet Density and Youth Cigarette Smoking: A Propensity-Modeling Approach," *American Journal of Public Health*, 96 (April), 670-676.

Oldenburg, Ray and Dennis Brisset (1983), "The Third Place," Qualitative Sociology, 5(Autumn), 265-284.

Rosenbaum, Mark S. (2006), "Exploring the Social Supportive Role of Third Places in Consumers' Lives," *Journal of Service Research*, 9 (August), 59-72.

Scribner, Richard, Deborah Cohen, and William Fisher (2000), "Evidence of a Structural Effect for Alcohol Outlet Density: A Multilevel Analysis," *Alchoholism: Clinical and Experimental Research*, 24 (February), 188-195.

Small, Deboreh A., and Uri Simonsohn (2008), "Friend of Victims: Personal Experience and Prosocial Behavior," *Journal of Consumer Research*, 35(October), 532-542.

Weitzman, Elissa, Alison Folkman, Kerry Lemieux Folkman, and Henry Wechsler (2003), "The Relationship of Alcohol Outlet Density to Heavy and Frequent Drinking and Drinking-Related Problems among College Students at Eight Universities," *Health and Place*, 9 (March), 1-6.

Xue, Zimmerman and Caldwell (2007), "Neighborhood Residence and Cigarette Smoking among Urban Youths: The Protective Role of Prosocial Activities," *American Journal of Public Health*, 97 (October), 1865-1872.

When Flippers Flop: Goal Reversion in Consumer Choice

Kurt Carlson, Georgetown University, USA
Meg Meloy, Penn State Univeristy, USA
Liz Miller, Boston College, USA

EXTENDED ABSTRACT

Imagine choosing between two restaurants (A and B), one which has tastier food and one which has healthier food. Suppose you first learn that Restaurant A has very decadent food, which is good because it fits one of your goals–to have a delicious meal. Next, you learn that Restaurant B uses fresh, local ingredients, which fits another of your goals–to eat healthfully. Though you were leaning towards Restaurant A originally, this new information causes you to switch your preference to Restaurant B (i.e. you flip from A to B). Suppose you then encounter additional neutral information about the two restaurants. How does your prior decision process, particularly the inhibition of the initial goal, influence your final restaurant choice?

We argue that because the two choice options align with different goals (to eat tasty food and to eat healthy), a consumer's restaurant preference at any point during the choice process can be used to infer which goal is more active at that point. Further, when a consumer switches preference from one option to another (as in the example above), he must inhibit one goal to pursue the other. This inhibition of the original goal should cause it to increase in activation (Atkinson and Birch 1970; Bargh et al. 2001). Therefore, we predict that when a consumer inhibits one goal to pursue another (by switching his preference from A to B), the original goal should increase in activation, leading the individual to be more likely to switch back to the original option when given the opportunity (i.e., upon encountering additional information). We refer to this as the *goal reversion hypothesis*. In this paper we report findings from three experiments designed to test this hypothesis.

Participants in experiment 1 chose between two unfamiliar restaurants based on four attributes that they read in sequence. The initial two attributes revealed that one of the restaurants had food that was more decadent and tasty. The third attribute revealed that the other restaurant had food that was healthier. We expected that this ordering of the information would establish the more decadent restaurant as preferred after the first two attributes, and that many participants would switch to the healthier restaurant after reading the third attribute (to pursue the competing goal). This subset of participants constitutes our focal sample, because these participants have inhibited one goal in pursuit of another. Our main interest is what happens to preferences of participants in the focal sample upon reading an additional attribute that is uncorrelated with tastiness or healthiness of the food. The goal reversion hypothesis predicts that a greater proportion of subjects should be expected to flop back to the more decadent option than would be normatively expected. Our results support this hypothesis. Forty-six percent of participants in the focal sample reverted back to the initial choice option after viewing the final attribute. This proportion was significantly greater than predicted by normative standards (χ^2=6.47, p<.01).

Experiment 2 attempts to replicate the findings from experiment 1, and to examine whether those for whom the goal to eat tasty is most important are most likely to revert. Goal reversion is also observed in this experiment, and reversion is most prevalent among those who place the greatest importance on the goal to eat tasty food. As expected, this indicates that self impeding an important goal causes greater activation than self impeding a less important goal.

The third and final experiment examines whether goal reversion is symmetric for different goal types. In addition, the experiment examines Need for Decisiveness as a possible moderator of the effect. Participants again read four attributes about two restaurants. Based on the ordering of the information, half the participants were led to favor the healthy option first, while the other half were led to favor the tasty option. Reversion rates for both groups were significantly higher than that predicted by normative standards (both ps<.01). In addition, participants who started with a taste goal were marginally more likely to revert to the original goal than those who started with a health goal. This result fits with the idea that the goal to eat tasty is more desirable and so is more goal-like than the goal to eat healthy. An examination of various individual difference measures revealed that reversion is not a function of self-control or preference for consistency, but is related to an individual's Need for Decisiveness. Specifically, those high in Need for Decisiveness are less likely to exhibit goal reversion.

These findings provide support for the goal reversion hypothesis, and increase our understanding of the role goals play in the earliest stages of preference construction. In addition, our methodology illustrates a new technique for tracking which goal is most active at any point of a choice process. Specifically, we examine which option is leading in a choice process with competing goals and use these preferences to infer which goal is active at a particular time. The advantage of this procedure is that it can be used to study the effects of self-inhibition of goals and how consumers switch between goals during a choice process with minimal interference of the choice process itself. Our findings highlight the importance of understanding order effects and preference reversals during choice processes and suggest that managers may want to consider the timing of information that could help an initial goal re-emerge.

REFERENCES

Atkinson, John W. and David Birch (1970), *The Dynamics of Action,* Oxford England: John Wiley.

Bargh, John A., Peter M. Gollwitzer, Annette Lee-Chai, Kimberly Barndollar, and Roman Trötschel (2001), "The Automated Will: Nonconscious Activation and Pursuit of Behavioral Goals," *Journal of Personality and Social Psychology*, 81 (December), 1014-1027.

Contextual Cues and Descriptive Norms: Do People Stick to Context When They Know What Others Choose?

Alessandra Zammit, University of Bologna, Italy
Elisa Montaguti, University of Bologna, Italy

EXTENDED ABSTRACT

Retailers are likely to influence consumers' shopping behavior though featuring, display and other marketing instruments. Increasingly this implies providing information on the behavior of other customers. Companies like Amazon.com and Barnes and Nobles regularly provide customers with a list of items previously selected by consumers similar to the prospects. Their behavior is driven by the belief that consumers are influenced by those around them (Asch 1955; Burnkrant and Cousineau 1975). Additionally, the same companies often manipulate their assortment to favor one or another product alternative. They can use specific comparison among products to influence potential buyers as the selection of an alternative is influenced by the other alternatives included in the same choice set (Hamilton 2003; Shocker et al. 1991). Increasingly, companies both in online and offline contexts try to jointly generate these effects by simultaneously presenting socially relevant information and constructing assortments that favor a specific alternative.

Literature in marketing and consumer behavior document that the choice set composition can favor the selection of the intermediate option in a ternary choice set (Simonson 1989; Simonson and Tversky 1992), because most consumers are extreme averse. The compromise alternative is often selected because individuals compare themselves with the information on the products presented and they chose the alternative that best matches their own preferences and the context-based information (Burson 2007; Prelec, Wernerfelt, and Zettelmeyer 1997).

There is ample evidence that individuals' both judgments and choices can be shifted when the judgment and the choices of others are known (Ariely and Levav 2000; Nemeth and Markowski 1972). When consumers observe or learn that others have opted for a specific alternative they are getting information on descriptive norms (how most people have acted in a specific circumstance). This suggests that norms alter consumers' assessment of the context-based information as knowledge on the most popular alternative modifies their inferences on the underlying distribution of other consumers' preferences and choices.

Our work posits that the effectiveness of strategies based on social norms (Cialdini and Goldstein 2004; Griskevicious et al. 2009) varies with the nature of the popularity they choose to emphasize. In particular, the gain associated to the intermediate position is modified by the likelihood of the extreme alternative to be the most frequently purchased in a overall market or in a smaller group of consumers who share some basis for social identification (Shang, Reed, and Cronson 2008). These kinds of norms could influence the ability of the compromise heuristic to identify the safe and easy to justify alternative in two ways. First, consumers may engage in an identification process with an extreme-positioned alternative that is popular with their reference group and move away from the compromise alternative which is considered more suitable for the majority of the consumers. Second, when an extreme-positioned alternative is popular among the majority of the consumers, both the extreme popular and the compromise alternatives appear safe and easy to justify. This will diminish the share of the compromise alternative, but not vanish the compromise effect as two options can now match the needs of the average customer: the most popular-extreme option and the compromise option.

To test our predictions we run five studies. Study 1 analyzes the role played by social information in moderating the compromise effect. Our results show that social norms can diminish the total share of the middle option but cannot vanish the compromise effect itself. Study 2 aims at ruling out the possibility that social information, acting upon the attribute-importance balance, might change the structure of the choice context needed to identify an option as extreme and/or compromise. Our results are consistent with the findings of Study 1. Studies 3A and 3B further investigate the influence exerted by social information on compromise effect while examining how differences in the degree of social identification can lead to different context-based inferences and perception of self-extremeness. Our results show that that social norms shift people preferences away from compromise alternatives, but this happens only when the social norm is held by a reference group. In particular, in Study 3A we find that consumers update the information embedded in the context with the social information cue and this leads to a shift in the match between the inferred product ranking and their own relative rank. Interestingly, this process does not mitigate the compromise effect per se, but determines a reduction in the absolute share of the intermediate alternative. This process also increases the level of uncertainty associated with the choice and modifies the perceived extremeness of the extreme alternative. By contrast, Study 3B shows that social information related to a reference group can vanish the compromise effect, but does not affect the structure of the contest (the perception of extremeness).

Finally, in Study 4 we show that the reduction on the compromise effect due to the social cue is attenuated when context is more uncertain. When the presented products outline a market characterized by a large dispersion in the product array, consumers rely on the context to make inferences about their position in the market. As a consequences, social information does not influences preferences and compromise effect is still present.

This article contributes to extant literature in several ways. First, we provide evidence as to how the advantage related to the compromise position can be overcome by extreme alternatives in a choice set. Second, drawing on research on the informational content of context (Prelec et al. 1997) we show that social norms can act on both the shape of the market distribution of preferences (when social information refers to market behavior) or on the matching consumers make between themselves and the best product choice in the context (when social information refers to reference group behavior). Finally, this article documents how and when social norms interact with context-generated inferences in modifying either consumers' perception of the self without altering the structure of choice context or in changing consumers' perception of preferences of others without affecting the perception of the self.

REFERENCES

Ariely, Dan and Jonathan Levav (2000), "Sequential Choice in Group Settings: Taking the Road Less Traveled and Less Enjoyed," *Journal of Consumer Research*, December, 27.

Asch, Solomon E. (1955), "Opinions and Social Pressure," *Scientific American*, 193, 31-35.

Burson, Katerine A. (2007), "Interpersonal miscalibration and its impact on product choice," *Journal of Consumer Research*, 34 (June), 104-110.

Burnkrant, Robert E. and Alain Cuosineau (1975), "Informational and Normative Social Influence in Buyer Behavior," *Journal of Consumer Research*, Vol. 2 January.

Cialdini, Robert B., and Noah J. Goldstein (2004), "Social Influence: Compliance and Conformity," *Annual Review of Psychology*, 55, 591-621.

Griskevicius, Vladas, Noah.J. Goldstein, Chard R. Mortenson, J. M Sundie, Robert B. Cialdini, and Douglas T. Kenrick, (2009), "Fear and Loving in Las Vegas: Evolution, Emotion, and Persuasion," *Journal of Marketing Research*, Vol 46 June.

Hamilton Rebecca W. (2003), "Why Do People Suggest What They Do Not Want? Using Context Effects to Influence Others' Choices," *Journal of Consumer Research*, March, 29.

Nemeth, Charlan, Jack Markowski (1972), "Conformity and Discrepancy of Position," *Sociometry*, Vol. 35, N. 4, 562-575.

Prelec, Drazen, Birger Wernerfelt, and Florian Zettelmeyer (1997), "The role of inference in context effects: inferring what you want from what is available," *Journal of Consumer Research*, 24, 1 June.

Shang Jen, Americus Reed II, and Rachel Cronson (2008), "Identity Congruency Effects on Donations," *Journal of Marketing Research*, Vol. 45 June, 351-361.

Shocker, Allan D., Moshe Ben-Akiva, Bruno Boccara, and Prakash Nedungadi (1991), "Consideration set influences on consumer decision-making and choice: issues, models, and suggestions," *Marketing Letters*, 2, 181-197.

Simonson, Itamar (1989), "Choice Based on Reasons: the Case of Attraction and Compromise Effect," *Journal of consumer research*, 16 September, 158-174.

Simonson, Itamar, and Amos Tversky (1992), "Choice in Context: Tradeoff Contrast and Extremeness Aversion," *Journal of Marketing Research*, n°29, pp. 281-295.

Fair is Fair: Consumer Just World Beliefs and Intentions and Behaviors Towards Fair Trade Products

Katherine White, University of Calgary, Canada
Rhiannon MacDonnell, University of Calgary, Canada
Leslie Lamont, University of Calgary, Canada
Ellard John, University of Calgary, Canada

EXTENDED ABSTRACT

While a large body of research has examined consumers' perceptions of fairness as they pertain to their own experiences and outcomes (e.g., Smith, Bolton, and Wagner 1999), research has not examined consumers' fairness beliefs as they relate to concerns for justice for others. We examine consumers' perceptions of fairness for others in the context of fair trade. Fair trade refers to a social movement that encourages the payment of a fair price for products, while aiming to alleviate poverty, promote sustainable development, and assist producers marginalized by the traditional economic model (De Pelsmacker and Janssens 2007). Researchers have recently lamented the fact that it is often difficult to encourage consumers to actually choose and purchase products that are fair trade (Chatzidakis, Andreas, and Smith 2007). We utilize a just world framework (Lerner 1970) to investigate what factors make consumers more likely to support and choose fair trade products when they learn about marginalized coffee and tea producers.

Just World Theory proposes that people are motivated to construe the world as a just place in which individuals get what they deserve and deserve what they get. Further, when evidence is provided that the world is not fair (e.g., learning of an innocent victim's suffering), this threatens just world beliefs. To reconcile evidence that the world is not just, people demonstrate varied reactions, which can range from rationalizing the victim's situation, to engaging in helping behaviors (Hafer and Begue 2005; Lerner and Simmons 1966). We show that the tendency to assist others in need through supporting and choosing fair trade coffees (pilot study, study 1, and study 2) and teas (study 3) can be decreased (increased) by varying factors that heighten (reduce) defensive reactions to just world threat.

One commonly held view among marketing practitioners and researchers is that, when appealing to consumers to engage in prosocial behaviors, highlighting a high degree of perceived need should enhance helping (Bendapudi, et al. 1996; Fisher and Ackerman 1998). However, a just world framework predicts that, in the absence of alternative avenues for ameliorating just world threat, a high degree of need may decrease willingness to engage in prosocial behaviors (Hafer 2000). We tested for this possibility in a pilot study. Participants read about a situation for coffee producers in Malawi that either depicted a high or moderate degree of need. Participants then reported their behavioral intentions towards purchasing a fair trade product—Karma Coffee, which was described as a fair trade coffee that would support coffee producers in Malawi. Consistent with predictions, participants were significantly more inclined to help by purchasing fair trade products when perceived severity of need was moderate versus high ($p<01$). Following from this study, we set out to test for a series of moderating and mediating variables to elucidate the role that justice concerns play in determining the consumption of fair trade products.

In Study 1, we examined the role of duration of suffering. We predicted that if the situation for marginalized coffee producers is described as being a long-term, chronic issue this should increase just world threat (particularly under high need), whereas if it is more acute in nature this will be less threatening. Participants took part in a 2(Severity of Need: moderate vs. high) x 2(Duration of Suffering: short-term vs. long-term) design. As anticipated, under conditions long-term suffering, participants reported a lesser willingness to purchase fair trade products when perceived need was high rather than moderate ($p<.001$). These effects were mediated by beliefs about victim deservingness.

In Study 2, we examine a condition under which helping will be more likely when need is high versus moderate—ability to impact justice is high (vs. low). When helping has a larger impact on the ability to restore justice for coffee producers (i.e., a high percentage of the fair trade purchase goes to producers), defensive reactions under conditions of high need should be mitigated. Participants took part in a 2(Degree of Need: moderate need vs. high need) x 2(Ability to Impact Justice: low vs. high) design. Among those who believed that ability to impact justice was low, people were less inclined to purchase fair trade products when need was high versus moderate ($p<.05$). However, when the ability to impact justice was high the reverse effect was found, whereby those in the high need condition were more likely to help than were those in the moderate need condition ($p<.01$). These effects were mediated by justice restoration beliefs.

In study 3, we examine actual choices of fair trade (vs. non-fair trade) teas. In addition, we elucidate the underlying role of justice concerns by directly manipulating whether or not the purchase of fair trade leads to positive justice outcomes (restored justice vs. unrestored justice vs. control) and by examining the moderating role of BJW. A just world framework would predict that when the notion that justice can be restored via choosing fair trade is highlighted, those high in BJW (who are particularly sensitive to fairness information) should be more likely to choose fair trade products (Hafer and Begue 2005). Those high in BJW were more likely to select fair trade teas when justice was restored versus unrestored, or in the control condition ($p<.01$), but no significant differences emerged for those low in BJW.

This research demonstrates that novel factors such as the duration of suffering, ability to restore justice, and justice outcomes predict inclinations towards purchasing fair trade and actually choosing fair trade products. We find that factors that heighten (reduce) defensive reactions to just world threat can decrease (increase) helping responses. This research also has practical implications for marketers. Although a common assumption is that increasing perceived need should enhance helping, the current work suggests that, under certain conditions, highlighting a high degree o severity of need or injustice for others can be detrimental. Further, highlighting severity of need works best when accompanied with information that efficacy of helping is high and that justice can be restored.

REFERENCES

Bendapudi, Neeli, Surendra N. Singh, and Venkat Bendapudi (1996), "Enhancing Helping Behavior: An Integrative Framework for Promotion Planning," *Journal of Marketing*, 60 (3), 33-49.

Chatzidakis, Andreas, Sally Hibbert, and Andrew P. Smith (2007), "Why People Don't Take Their Concerns about Fair Trade to the Supermarket: The Role of Neutralisation," *Journal of Business Ethics*, 74, 89-100.

De Pelsmacker, Patrick, Liesbeth Driesen, Glen Rayp (2005), "Do Consumers Care about Ethics? Willingness to Pay for Fair-Trade Coffee," *Journal of Consumer Affairs*, 39 (2), 363-85.

De Pelsmacker, Patrick and Wim Janssens (2007), "A Model for Fair Trade Buying Behavior: The Role of Perceived Quantity and Quality of Information and Product-Specific Attitudes," *Journal of Business Ethics*, 75, 361-80.

Fisher, Robert J. and David Ackerman (1998), "The Effects of Recognition and Group Need on Volunteerism: A Social Norm Perspective," *Journal of Consumer Research*, 25 (3), 262-75.

Hafer, Carolyn L. (2000), "Do Innocent Victims Threaten the Belief in a Just World? Evidence from a Modified Stroop Task," *Journal of Personality and Social Psychology*, 79 (August), 165-73.

Hafer, Carolyn. L. and Laurent Begue (2005), "Experimental Research on Just-World Theory: Problems, Developments, and Future Challenges," *Psychological Bulletin*, 131 (1), 128-67.

Lerner, Melvin. J. (1980), The Belief in a Just World: A Fundamental Delusion, New York: Plenium Press.

Lerner, Melvin J. and Carolyn H. Simmons (1966), "Observer's Reaction to the 'Innocent Victim:' Compassion or Rejection?" *Journal of Personality*, 4 (2), 203-210.

Smith, Amy K., Ruth N. Bolton, and Janet Wagner (1999), "A Model of Customer Satisfaction with Service Encounters Involving Failure and Recovery," *Journal of Marketing Research*, 36 (August), 356-72.

When Knowledge is De-motivating: Consumer Knowledge and Assortment Size

Hadar Liat, IDC Herzliya, Israel
Sanjay Sood, UCLA Anderson School of Management, USA

EXTENDED ABSTRACT

Marketers have long been trying to determine how much choice to offer consumers. Evidence from consumer research as well as psychological research has shown that consumers prefer choice over no choice: when offered choice participants are more motivated to make a good decision and are more satisfied with the product. However, recent studies have indicated that too much choice can be motivating. In particular, it was shown that consumers who were offering over 20 options were less likely to purchase the product than consumers who were offered about 6 options (Iyengar and Lepper 2000). We suggest that the impact of choice set size on choice is mediated by consumer knowledge. We rely on previous findings, showing that knowledgeable consumers limit the amount of information search and the number of options considered, whereas less knowledgeable search for more information and consider more options (Johnson and Russo 1981; 1984). We hypothesize that knowledgeable consumers are more likely to purchase a product with small choice sets because they are not interested in considering many options; however, we conjecture that ignorant consumers are more likely to purchase a product with large choice sets because large assortments offer more options and afford more learning opportunities about the product category. Our hypothesis was supported in three studies.

In the first study participants were presented with a list of 5 or 25 red wines. They were asked to choose their favorite bottle and to indicate whether they would prefer receiving the chosen bottle or an equivalent amount of $20. Half of the participants were presented with a list of Chilean wines (ignorance group) and half were presented with a mixed list of wines (control group). A manipulation check verified that participants knew less about Chilean wines than about the mixed list of wines. Replicating previous results, we found that in the control group, the proportion of participants who preferred the wine over the $ amount was higher among those who were presented with a small choice set (5 wines) than a large choice set (25 wines). An opposite pattern emerged among participants who were presented with Chilean wines: the proportion of participants who preferred the wine over the $ amount was lower among those who were presented with a small choice set (5 wines) than a large choice set (25 wines). The results of study 1 thus supported our hypothesis, showing that assortment size can have both negative and positive impact on choice, depending on whether consumers are knowledgeable about the product category or not.

The knowledge manipulation employed in study 1 was based on familiarity with the product, and thus different experimental groups were presented with different stimuli (different wine lists). Study 2 was designed to replicate the results using a comparative knowledge manipulation, in which all participants were presented with the same stimuli, and knowledge was manipulated by presenting comparison groups that are more/less knowledgeable than the participant pool. Participants were asked to choose a video game from a list o five or 25 games, and to indicate whether they would prefer $5 or the chosen video game. They were informed of the general participant population, which was either similar to them in terms of knowledge about video games (undergraduate students—control condition) or more knowledgeable (undergraduate students and professional video game programmers—comparative ignorance condition). The results indicated that participants in the control were more likely to prefer the video game over the cash when presented with five games than 25 games, but that participants in the comparative ignorance condition revealed the reversed pattern. In addition, we found that the interactive impact of comparative knowledge and assortment size on choice was mediated by the degree of self-reported knowledge of video games.

A third study examined the impact of comparative ignorance as well as comparative competence on consumer choice. Participants were asked to choose their favorite body lotion from a list of five or 25 lotions. Then, they were asked to indicate whether they would prefer $5 or the chosen body lotion. Participants were informed of the general participant population, which was either similar to them in terms of knowledge about video games (undergraduate students—control condition), more knowledgeable (undergraduate students and dermatologists—comparative ignorance condition), or less knowledgeable (undergraduate students and elementary school students—comparative competence condition). The results showed that participants in the control group were more likely to prefer the body lotion over the cash when presented with five rather than 25 games; participants in the comparative competence condition revealed a similar yet stronger pattern; participants in the comparative ignorance condition revealed the reversed pattern: they were more likely to prefer the video game over the cash when presented with 25 games. Moreover, as in study 2, this choice pattern was mediated by self-reported knowledge.

The results presented in this paper reconcile two different, well established, schools of thought in consumer research–one suggesting that marketers should offer consumes as much choice as possible, and the other suggesting that limited assortments are preferred because excessive choice may be de-motivating, by showing that choice set size should depend on consumer knowledge. We conclude that marketers should consider an estimate of consumer knowledge about the product category when deciding how much choice to offer. Extensive choice may increase sales when consumers are believed to have limited knowledge about the product category, whereas limited choice may increase sales when consumers are believed to be knowledgeable about the product category.

REFERENCES:

Iyengar, Sheena, S. and Mark R. Lepper (2000), "When Choice is Demotivating: Can One Desire Too Much of a Good Thing?" *Journal of Personality and Social Psychology*, 79(6), 995-1006.

Can Buy Me Love: How Mating Cues Influence Single Men's Interest in High-Status Consumer Goods

Kim Janssens, K.U. Leuven, Belgium
Mario Pandelaere, Ghent University, Belgium
Bram Van den Bergh, Erasmus University, The Netherlands
Kobe Millet, K.U. Leuven, Belgium; Free University Amsterdam, The Netherlands
Inge Lens, K.U. Leuven, Belgium
Keith Roe, K.U. Leuven, Belgium; Free University Amsterdam, The Netherlands

EXTENDED ABSTRACT

With the purpose of catching and holding consumers' attention advertisers often make use of sexually provocative images (Dahl, Sengupta, and Vohs 2009). Given that provocative images often are of no or little relevance to the advertised product (Reichert and Lambiase 2003) advertisers thus seem to assume that consumers can be influenced by sexual cues. This assumption is based on the well-known male preference for young, attractive mates (Maner et al. 2003). It appears that this insight is extensively applied in advertising practices (Colarelli and Dettmann 2003) in order to draw consumers' attention and to increase sales.

The current research examines how variation in goal motivation affects men's interest in high-status products in a mating environment. The two studies presented in this paper demonstrate that exposing men to cues of women in sexy attire leads the single- but not the committed-men to automatically pay attention to and to long for high-status products. In Study 1, single men (N=24) and men in committed relationships (N=39) were exposed to 15 pictures of women. In the mating cue condition, the models were dressed in a sexually appealing manner (e.g. wearing lingerie or a bikini). In the control condition, the models wore unrevealing clothing. After exposure, participants filled in the prestige sensitivity scale (Lichtenstein, Ridgway, and Netemeyer 1993). Participants indicated higher interest in high-status goods in the mating cue condition (M =-.68, SD=1.02) than in the control condition (M =-.98, SD=.64). Single men indicated higher interest in high-status goods in the mating cue condition (M =-.33, SD=1.08) than in the control condition (M =-1.20, SD=.68), (t(59)=2.52, p=.01). For committed men, no differences were obtained between the mating cue condition (M =-.95, SD=.91) and the control condition (M =-.88, SD=.61), (t(59)=.25, NS). Study 1 suggests that exposure to mating cues increases men's interest in high-status products. Based on Markman and Brendl (2000), we predicted and demonstrated that the value of high-status products increases because these products may enhance and facilitate reaching the mate attraction goal.

In Study 2, single men (N=72) and men in committed relationships (N=61) were shown ten visual displays on a computer screen. Each display consisted of the pictures of six different products: five functional products (e.g. a desk lamp) and one high-status product (e.g. a Breitling watch). Each display remained on screen for one second. After a display disappeared, participants had 20 seconds to write down as many products as they had seen on the screen. Before engaging in this visual display task, we exposed the participants to a female experimenter who either wore sexy clothing (mating cue condition) or plain clothing (control condition). Sexy clothing should temporarily trigger the goal of displaying social status. In turn, this heightened goal of displaying social status should render high-status goods in the visual display more salient than functional products (Moskowitz 2002). We therefore hypothesized that men in the mating cue condition would notice the high-status goods more than men in the control condition. In addition, we expected this difference to be obtained for single men only.

Overall, a higher proportion of high-status goods (M=.36, SD=.16) than of functional products (M=.32, SD=.05), (F(1, 129)=6.91, p=.01) was remembered. However, participants in the mating cue condition (M=.38, SD=.15) recalled a higher proportion, but not significantly so, of the high-status products than participants in the control condition (M=.34, SD=.16), (t(131)= -1.60, NS). The pattern for functional products was reversed ($M_{mating\,cue}$=.31, SD=.06 vs. $M_{control}$=.33, SD=.05), (t(131)=2.34, p=.02). The elevated attention for high-status products was obtained for single men only (F(1, 129)=4.42, p=.04). Single men recalled a higher proportion of the high-status products in the mating cue condition (M=.43, SD=.17) than in the control condition (M=.33, SD=.15), (t(129)=-2.80, p<.01). In contrast, committed participants recalled almost the same proportion of high-status products in both conditions ($M_{mating\ cue}$=.33, SD=.13 vs. $M_{control}$=.35, SD=.17), (t(129)=.43, NS). Conversely, single men recalled more of the functional products when exposed to the control condition (M=.34, SD=.06) than to the mating cue condition (M=.31, SD=.06), (t(129)=1.92, p=.06). Participants with committed relationships recalled not significantly more of the functional products in the control condition (M=.33, SD=.04) than in the mating cue condition (M=.31, SD=.05), (t(129)=-1.31, NS). Study 2 suggests that exposure to mating cues may automatically increase interest in conspicuous consumption. Exposure to mating cues increased men's attention to high-status products in a task where this was irrelevant. Apparently, the presence of a sexily dressed female set off a process of heightened automatic attention for luxury and status-evoking products in single men.

A host of studies already suggest that images of attractive models in advertising may elicit positive feelings that are transferred to the advertised brand (Kim, Allen, and Kardes 1996). Moreover, when endorsing high-status products targeted at men, attractive models may not only function as a heuristic cue, influencing brand attitudes through affect transfer, but also as a central argument: "This is the brand that may increase your mating chances!" (Kang and Herr 2006). Presumably, mate attraction cues in the shopping environment may lure men into purchasing a more expensive brand than they had planned. So, the mere presence of a sexy woman may suffice to increase sales of high-ticket items. These effects, however, may be limited to single men.

REFERENCES

Colarelli, Steve M. and Joseph R. Dettmann (2003), "Intuitive Evolutionary Perspectives in Marketing Practices," *Psychology and Marketing*, 20 (September), 837-65.

Dahl, Darren W., Jaideep Sengupta, and Kathleen D. Vohs (2009), "Sex in Advertising: Gender Differences and the Role of Relationship Commitment," *Journal of Consumer Research*, 36 (August), 215-31.

Kang, Yong-Soon and Paul M. Herr (2006), "Beauty and the Beholder: Toward an Integrative Model of Communication Source Effects," *Journal of Consumer Research*, 33 (June), 123-30.

Kim, John, Chris T. Allen, and Frank R. Kardes (1996), "An Investigation of the Mediational Mechanisms Underlying Attitudinal Conditioning," *Journal of Marketing Research*, 33 (August), 318-28.

Lichtenstein, Donald R., Nancy M. Ridgway and Richard G. Netemeyer (1993), "Price Perceptions and Consumer Shopping Behavior: A Field Study," *Journal of Marketing Research*, 30 (May), 234-45.

Maner, Jon K, Douglas T. Kenrick, D. Vaughn Becker, Andrew W. Delton, Brian Hofer, Christopher J. Wilbur and Steven L. Neubur (2003), "Sexually Selective Cognition: Beauty Captures the Mind of the Beholder," *Journal of Personality and Social Psychology*, 85 (6), 1107-20.

Markman, Arthur B. and C. Miguel Brendl (2000), "The Influence of Goals on Value and Choice," *Psychology of Learning and Motivation: Advances in Research and Theory*, 39, 97-128.

Moskowitz, Gordon B. (2002), "Preconscious Effects of Temporary Goals on Attention," *Journal of Experimental Social Psychology*, 38, 397-404.

Reichert, Tom and Jacqueline Lambiase (2003), "One Phenomenon, Multiple Lenses: Bridging Perspectives to Examine Sex in Advertising," in *Sex in Advertising. Perspectives on the Erotic Appeal,* Ed. Tom Reichert, Jacqueline Lambiase, NJ: Erlbaum, 1-8.

To Defend or To Improve, That Is a Question: Self Views and Evaluations of Self Improvement Products

Fang Wan, University of Manitoba, Canada
Pingping Qiu, University of Manitoba, Canada
Darren Dahl, University of British Columbia, Canada

EXTENDED ABSTRACT

Body aesthetics industry is one of the major subcomponents of the Self-Improvement Product (SIP) industry, promoting hope of personal betterment or promise improvement in various domains of a person's life: appearance, body shape, relationship satisfaction, career achievement and self-esteem (MacInnis & De Mello 2005). One of the advertising strategies for body aesthetics SIPs is to employ super-slim and super-fit models, with the intended outcome to induce consumers' want (vs. need) of the product to minimize the discrepancy between the real and an ideal state (MacInnis & De Mello 2005). However, whether these idealized images facilitate or obstruct the effectiveness of SIP advertisements has rarely been studied. Moreover, previous research has dealt with the impact of idealized images on female consumers' self-evaluations and psychological health (e.g., Richins 1991; Stice & Shaw 1994; Smeesters & Mandel 2006), but little has been done to further investigate whether and how consumers' attitude toward and choice of SIPs are affected by the self-image goals activated in the viewing contexts.

In the present research, we put forth a conceptual framework for studying the impact of self-image goals activated by contextual information (e.g., idealized images presented within advertisement viewing context or in focal SIP advertisements) on consumers' evaluation of SIPs and the effectiveness of SIP advertisements. Drawing research from social and cognitive psychology (Bargh 1982; Bargh 2002; Vohs & Heatherton 2001), consumer research and advertising studies (e.g., Dunning 2007; Richins 1991; MacInnis & De Mello 2005; Escalas & Luce 2004), we propose that consumers' attitude toward SIPs is influenced by self-image goals—the goals of presenting and maintaining positive self beliefs (Dunning 2007), which can be triggered in the advertisement viewing process or by other contextual information. How consumers cope with the self-deficiency may determine what self-image goal (whether a self-defending or a self-improvement goal) is activated. If consumers cope with self-deficiency in a defensive manner, they will adopt strategies such as reappraisal (e.g., Gross 2002) to restore a positive self belief, as well as counter-arguing and dismissal of product or endorser credibility (Duke 2002). As a result, SIPs will be evaluated negatively. However, if self-deficiency is moderately triggered, or the focal advertisement invites consumers to contemplate on the possibility of enhancing the current state and reaching an ideal state, a self-improvement goal will be activated. In this case, SIPs will be viewed as a means to reach the ideal state. As a result, SIPs will be evaluated positively. We report three experiments conducted to examine the major propositions.

Study 1 intended to investigate the working of self defending goal in SIP evaluations. Specifically, we explored consumers' evaluations of a dietary supplement product after a prior exposure to idealized images in a preceding and seemingly unrelated advertisement evaluation task. We expected to find that subjects whose self-deficiency is activated by the exposure to idealized images are more likely to evaluate the product less favorably and demonstrate lower purchase intention. As the negative effect of idealized images in media is mostly observed among female consumers (Rodin, Silberstein & Striegel-Moore 1985), we expected to observe the effects to emerge among females but not males. Results of a 2 (self-deficiency activation) x 2 (gender) between-subjects experiment supported our hypotheses. A follow-up Study 1b further evidenced the defensive mechanism among males when threatening information came from a domain (intelligence) which is more crucial for men's self-esteem.

In Study 2 we tried to uncover whether the negative SIP evaluations in Study 1 were the results of the activation of a self-defending goal among the female subjects. Adopting research from self-affirmation (Spencer et al. 1998; Schwinghammer, Stapel & Blanto 2006), we inferred that dismissing the value of SIPs or denying a need to improve is indicative of a self-defending goal, which can be directly tested by adding a self-affirmation task between the priming task and the SIP evaluation task. We hypothesize that if a self-defending goal is activated, self-affirmation task (receiving bogus positive feedbacks) can deactivate the goal. In addition, we intend to study the moderating effect of self esteem on the relationship between self-affirmation and product evaluation. Research on threats to self-esteem has demonstrated that individuals with different trait self-esteem (high vs. low) respond differently in information seeking once being threatened. After receiving an ego threat, high self-esteem (HSE) individuals, compared to the low self-esteem (LSE) individuals, tend to be more sensitive to competency feedback (Vohs & Heatherton 2001). In our research context, we expected that the self-affirmation task will be more effective at deactivating self-defending goal, i.e., enhancing evaluations of self improvement products, for HSE individuals than for low LSE individuals. Hypotheses were supported by results of Study 2.

The first two studies demonstrated that self-deficiency activated by the idealized images lowered consumers' intention to purchase SIPs. This effect was however alleviated by a self-affirmation task among HSE individuals. This research finding seems to run contradictory to the intended outcome of most SIP advertisements. The intention of Study 3 was to explore how to activate a self-improvement goal. Based on limited research in this area, we argue that advertisements focusing on inspiration and hope, rather than self-deficiency (which triggers self defense, as what was studied in Study 1 and 2), are the keys to activate people's desire to improve (MacInnis & De Mello 2005). We manipulated the hope appeal by different headlines of the advertisements as well as different instructions for viewing the ads (Escalas & Luce 2004). Results of Study 3 evidenced that SIP can be evaluated positively if the SIP advertisement emphasizes the possibilities of attaining an ideal state, instead of making the gap between ideal and current state more salient (as what was implicitly done in our previous studies).

Put together, we discovered from Study 1 and 2 the negative impact of idealized image priming on SIP evaluations could be due to the activation of a self-defending goal. Consumers are motivated to restore a self worth once their self image is threatened and they tend to penalize the SIP made available to them right after the ego threat. Findings in Study 3 provided some hope for SIP advertisements. In spite of self-deficiency activated by exposure to idealized images, consumers can evaluate SIPs positively and consider purchasing them if the SIP advertisements contain messages of hope and inspiration.

REFERENCES

Bargh, J. A. (1982), "Attention and automaticity in the processing of self-relevant information," *Journal of Personality and Social Psychology*, 43, 425-436.

Bargh, J. A. (2002), "Losing consciousness: Automatic influences on consumer judgment, behavior and motivation," *Journal of Consumer Research*, 29, 280-285.

Duke, L (2002), "Get real!: Cultural relevance and resistance to the mediated feminine ideal," *Psychology & Marketing*, 19, 211-233.

Dunning, D. (2007), "Self-image motives and consumer behavior: How sacrosanct self-beliefs sway preferences in the marketplace," *Journal of Consumer Psychology*, 17, 237–249.

Escalas, J. E. & Luce, M. F. (2004), "Understanding the effects of process-focused versus outcome-focused thought in response to advertising," *Journal of Consumer Research*, 34, 274-285.

Gross, James (2002), "Emotion Regulation: Affective, Cognitive and Social Consequences," *Psychophysiolog*, 39, 281-291.

MacInnis, D. J. & de Mello G. E. (2005), "The concept of hope and its relevance to product evaluation and choice," *Journal of Consumer Research*, 69, 1-14.

Richins, M. L. (1991), "Social Comparison and the Idealized Images of Advertising," *Journal of Consumer Research*, 19, 71-83.

Rodin, J., Silberstein, L., & Striegel-Moore, R. (1985), "Women and weight: A normative discontent," In T. B. Sonderegger (Ed.), *Psychology and gender: Nebraska Symposium on Motivation* (pp. 267-307), Lincoln, NE: University of Nebraska Press.

Schwinghammer, S. A., Stapel, D. A., & Blanton, H. (2006), "Different Selves Have Different Effects: Self-Activation and Defensive Social Comparison," *Personality and Social Psychology Bulletin*, 32(1), 27-39.

Smeesters, D. & Mandel, N. (2006), "Positive and Negative Media Image Effects on the Self," *Journal of Consumer Research*, 32(4), 576-582.

Spencer, Steven, Steven Fein, Connie T. Wolfe, Christina Fong and Meghan A. Dunn (1998), "Automatic Activation of Stereotypes; The Role of Self-Image Threat," *Personality and Social Psychology Bulletin*, 24, 1139-1152.

Stice, E. & Shaw, H. E. (1994), "Adverse effects of the media portrayed thin-ideal on women and linkages to bulimic symptomatology," *Journal of Social and Clinical Psychology*, 13 (3), 288-308.

Vohs, K. D. & Heatherton, T. F. (2001), "Self-esteem and threats to self: Implications for self-construals and interpersonal perceptions," *Journal of Personality and Social Psychology*, 81, 1103-1118.

Disposable People: Commoditization and Redefinition of Self as Rubbish

Angela Hausman, Howard University, USA
Chris Manolis, Xavier University, USA

EXTENDED ABSTRACT

We investigate disposable people thrown away as a consequence of extensive abuse of alcohol and/or drugs. Building on theories of commoditization, disposal, and rubbish, we pose the following questions: Can people become rubbish, and, if so, how does this process work? How does addiction affect users' relationships with self and others and their tendencies to treat others as rubbish? What happens when an individual internalizes the rubbish label and redefines self as such? Finally, we propose means by which such understanding might be used in rehabilitating users.

According to a recent report, 8.3 % of the US population reported illicit drug use within the last month (Office of Applied Statistics 2007). Alcohol abuse is nearly as high and has increased over 53 % between 1992 and 2002. The individual and societal consequences of this abuse are dire (National Institute on Drug Abuse 2006). Of those who get treatment, between 27 and 82 % fail to finish rehab programs (**Wickizer 1994), and, of those who do finish, less than 20 % are addiction-free four years later (Simpson and Sells 1982).** Unfortunately, drug and alcohol abuse is far from victimless and it may be the involvement of innocent bystanders that contributes to society's desire to discard abusers.

There are various theoretical perspectives that contribute to the concept of disposable people. These include human commoditization and consumer disposition, which have been used extensively in consumer behavior, as well as rubbish theory, which has yet to be systematically incorporated. Human commoditization begins with the eroding of consumer choice, which transforms decisions that were once considered trivial into life and death situations. It is this absence of meaningful choice that eliminates personal identity and makes maintenance of self difficult (Hirschman and Hill 2000). Next, people are stripped of clothing, material artifacts, and even personal identifiers, such as hair, becoming non-differentiated units (Hirschman and Hill 2000). The final stage of the process enforces invariant patterns of behavior so that commoditized individuals not only look the same, but act the same. Decent into rubbish involves commoditization and subsequent negative attitudes toward the object (person in this case) and its means of disposition. Dispossessed rubbish is temporally linked with a lack of desire for the object (Lucas 2002).

In order to begin understanding the construction of people as rubbish, we interviewed individuals addicted to drugs and/or alcohol. Informants came from three sources: a residential treatment facility, a detox center, and a non-residential treatment facility. These facilities were not the spa-type rehab centers frequented by celebrities or even more modest, insurance-supported treatment facilities, but public and charity supported facilities that serve vast numbers of low income and indigent abusers who are often sent by court order or as a condition of parole. Residents of the various facilities shared, among other things, diminished consumer choice and behavioral control, as well as a devalued sense of self.

Within the theme of disposable people, several sub-themes were detected: 1) the process of commoditization and decent into rubbish; 2) how relationships with others were constructed and contributed to definitions of self; 3) dispossession; and, 4) events leading to internalization and maintenance of self as rubbish. Through the voices of these informants, we see the progression from having control (as a non-commoditized person) to being out-of-control. Consistent with commoditized persons, informants often found themselves living on the streets, being cast out or disposed of by family and friends, and possessing few of the niceties, if not necessities of life, such as nutritious food and clean clothing. Not only do we find an absence of consumer choice, but evidence of a break with conventions of behavior (stealing and cheating) that reflects the final step toward communization. They also begin to sell their bodies, perhaps the last vestige of self, to become truly commoditized.

We also see evidence of the weakening relationship between the commoditized individual and his/her friends and family who normally form an important support system for the non-commoditized individual. Substance abuse becomes a driving force, reducing or eliminating the addicts' engagement with society and its norms, as well as free will and choice. The defining characteristic that moves commoditized people into the category of rubbish is their diminished level of societal value, a strong theme reflected by our informants (Thompson 1979). Through abusers' stories, we see the de-evolution from commoditization to rubbish is complete when the individual is living surrounded by other rubbish (trash, etc.), including other de-valued people who often engaged in non-constructive activities, such as stealing.

The preceding discussion suggests that people do, in fact, transition to commodities then rubbish as they increasingly lose value through their substance abuse. They also commoditize those around them, both other addicts and family and friends. Rubbish people have also lost everything of value in their lives; material possessions, close relationships, and, possibly most important, their sense of self. This suggests that transforming the rubbish person back into something durable, something society recognizes for its inherent value, may be an important part of the recovery process.

Unfortunately, our informants reflected on the difficulties encountered in regaining this value. For instance, one informant talked about the near impossibility of finding a job with a drug conviction on his record. Therefore, in his mid-twenties, he had already given up trying to find a job. Reconnecting with family and friends is also difficult, as some of the informants implied. One male resident lamented he had never met his grandchildren because of his addiction. Others have been abandoned by family who are disillusioned after being treated badly by the addict. The rubbish person seems to develop a certain inertia, potentially remaining rubbish for an extended period of time, which makes recovery problematic.

Preference Reversal in Risky Choices under Time Pressure

Najam Saqib, Ryerson University, Canada
Eugene Chan, University of Toronto, Canada

EXTENDED ABSTRACT

One pervasive aspect of decision-making under time pressure is the salience of negative information. Research has repeatedly concluded that "the harassed decision maker" tends to weigh the possible negative consequences of his or her action heavily to the relative disregard of the possible positive rewards of those same actions. In this paper, we propose that the salience of negative information under time pressure not merely leads to risk-aversion, but that it may reverse an individual's usual preferences.

Individuals are typically either risk-seeking or risk-averse. Research outside the time pressure domain has shown that, when negative information becomes salient, risk-seeking individuals perceive little room for further gains but large likelihood of accruing losses, causing them to adopt risk-averse behaviours. In a choice between a modest-but-certain and greater-but-uncertain gamble, risk-seeking individuals tend to adopt risk-averse behaviours whereas risk-averse individuals tend to adopt risk-seeking ones. Meanwhile, for risk-averse individuals, the salience of negative information only adds to the extant negativity, causing them to adopt risk-seeking behaviours with the hopes of removing the negative state. We extend these findings to the time pressure domain and suspect that time pressure would likewise be one instance where individuals would reverse their usual risk preferences to adapt to the salience of negative information. We examine this possibility in three studies.

In Study 1, participants with positive (negative) affect chose a riskier (certain) lottery to a NHL hockey game when there was no time pressure, but adopted the certain (riskier) approach under time pressure. We thus demonstrated the basic outline of our hypothesis.

In Study 2, we used a gambling task in which participants stated their willingness to gamble for specific dollar amounts. We also added a thought protocol to assess the participants' emphases on positive versus negative outcomes during the gambling process. Under no time pressure, risk-seeking (risk-averse) individuals focused more on positive (negative) outcomes than negative (positive) ones. Under time pressure, however, risk-seeking (risk-averse) individuals focused more on negative (positive) outcomes than positive (negative) ones. The focus on positive versus negative information for risk-seeking and risk-averse individuals reversed under time pressure. These differences in foci on positive versus negative outcomes mediated the preference reversal.

In Study 3, we explored a similar preference reversal in regulatory orientation using a consumer choice task involving toothpaste and grape juice brands as well as investment choices. Under no time pressure, promotion- (prevention-) focused individuals preferred promotion- (prevention-) framed and risk-seeking (risk-averse) brands and choices. Under time pressure, however, promotion- (prevention-) focused individuals preferred prevention- (promotion-) framed and risk-averse (risk-seeking) brands and choices.

Taken together, the three studies suggest that individuals tend to reverse their preference for risky choices under time pressure compared to situations under no such constraint. It is important to note, however, that preference reversals in risky choices do not occur because risk-seeking individuals want to avoid risks or that risk-averse individuals want to take risks, but that they need to. Risk-seeking individuals adopt risk-averse behaviours when negative information becomes salient because such an approach can secure gains, in line with the goals of risk-seeking. Conversely, risk-averse individuals adopt risk-seeking behaviours when negative information becomes salient because such an approach can avoid further losses, in line with the goals of risk-aversion. Thus, preference reversals are not in innate risk preferences, but in the perception and adoption of the behaviours that best serve their objectives given the circumstance. Our findings have important marketing implications since consumers often face decision-making tasks under time pressure in everyday life.

REFERENCES

Arkes, Hal R., Lisa T. Herren, and Alice M. Isen (1988), "The Role of Potential Loss in the Influence of Affect on Risk-Taking Behavior," *Organizational Behavior and Human Decision Processes*, 42 (October), 181-93.

Baron, Reuben M. and David A. Kenny (1986), "The Moderator-Mediator Variable Distinction in Social Psychological Research: Conceptual, Strategic, and Statistical Considerations," *Journal of Personality and Social Psychology*, 51 (December), 1173-82.

Ben Zur, Hasida and Shlomo J. Breznitz (1981), "The Effect of Time Pressure on Risky Choice Behavior," *Acta Psychologica*, 47 (February), 89-104.

Crowe, Ellen and E. Tory Higgins (1997), "Regulatory Focus and Strategic Inclinations: Promotion and Prevention in Decision-Making," *Organizational Behavior and Human Decision Processes*, 69 (February), 117-32.

Higgins, E. Tory (1997), "Beyond Pleasure and Pain," *American Psychologist*, 52 (December), 1280-1300.

______ (1998), "Promotion and Prevention: Regulatory Focus as a Motivational Principle," in *Advances in Experimental Social Psychology*, Vol. 30, ed. Leonard Berkowitz and Mark P. Zanna, New York: Academic Press, 1-46.

Isen, Alice M. and Nehemia Geva (1987), "The Influence of Positive Affect on Acceptable Levels of Risk: The Person with a Large Canoe Has a Large Worry," *Organizational Behavior and Human Decision Processes*, 39 (April), 145-54.

Johnson, Eric J. and Amos Tversky (1983), "Affect, Generalization, and the Perception of Risk," *Journal of Personality and Social Psychology*, 45 (July) 20-31.

Kahneman, Daniel and Amos Tversky (1979), "Prospect Theory: An Analysis of Decision Under Risk," *Econometrica*, 47 (March), 263-91.

Lee, Angela Y. and Jennifer L. Aaker (2004), "Bringing the Frame into Focus: The Influence of Regulatory Fit on Processing Fluency and Persuasion," *Journal of Personality and Social Psychology*, 86 (February) 205-18.

Lerner, Jennifer S., Deborah A. Small, and George Loewenstein (2004), "Heart Strings and Purse Strings: Carryover Effects of Emotions on Economic Decisions," *Psychological Science*, 15 (May), 337-41.

Lockwood, Penelope, Christian H. Jordan, and Ziva Kunda (2002), "Motivation by Positive or Negative Role Models: Regulatory Focus Determines Who Will Best Inspire Us," *Journal of Personality and Social Psychology*, 83 (October), 854-64.

Novemsky, Nathan and Daniel Kahneman (2005), "The Boundaries of Loss Aversion," *Journal of Marketing Research*, 42 (May), 119-28.

Nowlis, Stephen M. (1996), "The Effect of Time Pressure on the Choice between Brands that Differ in Quality, Price, and Product Features," *Marketing Letters*, 6 (October), 287-95.

Payne, John W., James R. Bettman, and Eric J. Johnson (1988), "Adaptive Strategy Selection in Decision Making," *Journal of Experimental Psychology: Learning, Memory, and Cognition*, 14 (July), 534-552.

Pham, Michel T. (1998), "Representativeness, Relevance, and the Use of Feelings in Decision Making," *Journal of Consumer Research*, 25 (September), 144-59.

Pham, Michel T. and E. Tory Higgins (2005), "Promotion and Prevention in Consumer Decision Making: The State of the Art and Theoretical Predictions," in *Inside Consumption: Consumer Motives, Goals and Desires*, ed. S. Ratneshwar and David G. Mick, London: Routledge, 8-43.

Prelec, Drazen and George Loewenstein (1991), "Decision Making Over Time and Under Uncertainty: A Common Approach," *Management Science*, 37 (July), 770-86.

Scholer, Abigail A. and E. Tory Higgins (2008), "Distinguishing Levels of Approach and Avoidance: An Exploration Using Regulatory Focus Theory," in *Handbook of Approach and Avoidance Motivation*, ed. Andrew J. Eliot, Hillsdale, NJ: Erlbaum, 489-504.

Scholer, Abigail A., Steven J. Stroessner, and E. Tory Higgins (2008), "Responding to Negativity: How a Risky Tactic Can Serve a Vigilant Strategy," *Journal of Experimental Social Psychology*, 44 (May), 767-74.

Schwarz, Norbert and Gerald L. Clore (1983), "Mood, Misattribution, and Judgments of Well-Being: Informative and Direct Functions of Affective States," *Journal of Personality and Social Psychology*, 45 (September), 513-23.

Sitkin, Sim B. and Amy L. Pablo (1992), "Reconceptualizing the Determinants of Risk Behavior," *The Academy of Management Review*, 17 (January), 9-38.

Svenson, Ola and Anne Edland (1987), "Change of Preferences under Time Pressure: Choices and Judgments," *Scandinavian Journal of Psychology*, 28 (4), 322-330.

Tversky, Amos and Daniel Kahneman (1981), "The Framing of Decisions and the Psychology of Choice," *Science*, 211 (January), 453-8.

Watson, David, Lee A. Clark, and Auke Tellegen (1988), "Development and Validation of Brief Measures of Positive and Negative Affect: The PANAS Scales," *Journal of Personality and Social Psychology*, 54 (June), 1063-70.

Wright, Peter (1974), "The Harassed Decision Maker: Time Pressures, Distractions, and the Use of Evidence," *Journal of Applied Psychology*, 59 (October), 555-61.

Zhou, Rongrong and Michel T. Pham (2004), "Promotion and Prevention across Mental Accounts: When Financial Products Dictate Consumers' Investment Goals," *Journal of Consumer Research*, 31 (December), 125-35.

Examining the Paradoxical Effects of Counterfactual Generation in Negative Consumption

Candy K. Y. Ho, Hong Kong Baptist University, Hong Kong
Jessica Y. Y. Kwong, The Chinese University of Hong Kong, Hong Kong

EXTENDED ABSTRACT

After a negative consumption experience (e.g., missed a flight), consumers often muse about how their consumption might have turned out better (e.g., "If I had taken another transport to the airport, I might have caught the flight," or "I would have been enjoying my vacation if I had caught the flight.") The generation of these imaginations, called counterfactual thoughts, has been viewed to pose paradoxical effects on people's responses to these experiences. On one hand, counterfactual thoughts are functional because they provide corrective information that helps solve problems associated with the consumption (Epstude and Roese 2008; Markman et al. 1993; Roese 1994). On the other hand, they are painful to consumers because they accentuate negative feelings about the consumption (Gleicher et al. 1990; Markman et al. 1993). In this research, we attempt to tease out these paradoxical effects and argue that a counterfactual thought is not likely to exert both problem-solving and affect accentuation effects. Rather, these effects are more likely to be independently induced by counterfactual thoughts that have different structural contents.

In this research, we first propose two new types of counterfactuals, namely, process- and outcome-focused counterfactuals. Then, this classification becomes the means to tease out the two effects of counterfactual generation. We argue that while process-focused (vs. outcome-focused) counterfactuals pose a stronger problem-solving effect; outcome-focused (vs. process-focused) counterfactuals exert stronger affect accentuation effect. This implies that consumers may enjoy the problem-solving function of counterfactual generation without hurting their feelings.

To start with, this research proposes thought focus as a new dimension to classify counterfactuals into process- and outcome-focused counterfactuals. Process-focused counterfactuals focus on the process of how an imagined outcome might have been brought about (e.g., If I had taken another transport to the airport, I might have caught the flight). They mentally construct the actions (e.g., taking another transport) that, had they been taken, might have led people to the imagined outcome (e.g., had caught the flight). Outcome-focused counterfactuals, however, focus on the benefits the imagined outcome, had it been obtained, would have provided (e.g., I would have been enjoying the vacation if I had caught the flight).

We further argue that process- and outcome-focused counterfactuals have differential consequences to consumers who experienced negative consumption. First, process-focused (vs. outcome-focused) counterfactuals are more effective in promoting corrective actions for better consumption outcomes. This is because process-focused counterfactuals highlight the most promising actions (e.g., taking another transport to the airport) that, had they been taken, might have improved the consumption outcome (e.g., had caught the flight). Outcome-focused counterfactuals, however, elaborate only on how much better off consumers would have been (e.g., enjoying vacation) had they received a better-off outcome. They give no information on *how* this better-off outcome might have been obtained. Hence, consumers who generated process-focused (vs. outcome-focused) counterfactuals are more likely to identify the appropriate corrective actions that solve problems associated with the consumption, such that they will have an increased chance of yielding better consumption outcomes in subsequent encounters.

Second, it is argued that outcome-focused (vs. process-focused) counterfactuals are more likely to accentuate consumers' negative feelings (e.g., disappointment and sorrow) about a negative consumption outcome. Outcome-focused counterfactuals highlight the benefits brought by the better-off imagined outcome, which contrast with the reality and induce consumers to feel worse about the factual outcome than when these benefits are not highlighted (Schwarz and Bless 1992).

We tested our contentions in a scenario-based experiment. The scenario described a situation where the participants went through some job assessments. To begin with, the participants were provided two computer programs, which were superior in different aspects, to work on in an assessment task. They were told they selected either one of the two programs and completed the task. Regardless of their program choice, however, they failed in the assessment. At this point, the participants were prompted to generate different types of counterfactuals in relations to their assessment result. The participants were then told that they were now given a second chance to complete another similar assessment using either one of the two different programs. They reported their intention to switch to another program in the second assessment and their negative feelings about their first assessment result.

We predicted that the process-focused (vs. outcome-focused) participants would have a lower switching intention, because the process-focused counterfactuals they generated helped them identify how they might have made use of the computer program they used in the first assessment to increase their chance of success. They should therefore have increased confidence in using the program again in the second assessment and hence reduced switching intention. We also predicted that outcome-focused (vs. process-focused) participants would report more negative feelings about their first assessment result.

Supporting the idea that process- and outcome-focused counterfactuals are distinct, analysis on the participants' open-end thoughts indicated that (1) the classification on what types of counterfactuals these thoughts were had a high inter-rater agreement (.97); and (2) the two types of counterfactuals were independently manipulated. In addition, the process-focused participants, who imagined what actions, had they been taken, might have made them pass the assessment, were found to have a lower switching intention than the control and the outcome-focused participants. The outcome-focused participants, who imagined how much better off they would have been had they passed the assessment, felt more negatively about their first assessment result than did the control and the process-focused participants.

To conclude, this research not only contributes to the existing literature by showing that process- and outcome-focused counterfactuals are distinct, but it also advances our understanding on the paradoxical effects of counterfactual generation in negative consumption. It teases out these effects and demonstrates that they are independently induced by these two types of counterfactuals. The findings suggest that consumers who experienced negative consumption should (1) focus their attention on the *process* leading to a better-off imagined outcome, and (2) draw their attention away from how better off their consumption might have been. This will increase their chance of having better future consumption outcomes at no incremental psychological cost.

REFERENCES

Epstude, Kai and Neal J. Roese (2008), "The Functional Theory of Counterfactual Thinking," *Personality and Social Psychology Review*, 12 (2), 168-192.

Gleicher, Faith, Kathryn A. Kost, Sara M. Baker, Alan J. Strathman, Steven A. Richman, and Steven J. Sherman (1990), "The Role of Counterfactual Thinking in Judgments of Affect," *Personality and Social Psychology Bulletin*, 16 (June), 284-95.

Markman, Keith D., Igor Gavanski, Steven J. Sherman, and Matthew N. McMullen (1993), "The Mental Simulation of Better and Worse Possible Worlds," *Journal of Experimental Social Psychology*, 29, 87-109.

Roese, Neal J. (1994), "The Functional Basis of Counterfactual Thinking," *Journal of Personality and Social Psychology*, 66 (5), 805-18.

Schwarz, Norbert and Herbert Bless (1992), "Constructing Reality and Its Alternatives: An Inclusion/Exclusion Model of Assimilation and Contrast in Social Judgment," in *The Construction of Social Judgments*, ed. Leonard L. Martin and Abraham Tesser, Hillsdale, NJ: Erlbaum, 217-45.

Does Thinking Make It So? The Effect of Counterfactual Thinking on Product Evaluations

Kai-Yu Wang, Brock University, Canada
Minli Liang, University of Wisconsin-Milwaukee, USA
Laura Peracchio, University of Wisconsin-Milwaukee, USA

EXTENDED ABSTRACT

Counterfactual thinking (CFT) refers to the process of reflecting on past events and simulating alternative possible outcomes. People engage in CFT in their everyday life at home, school, work, and shopping. Consumer researchers have explored related issues, such as how anticipation of counterfactual regret influences decision-making and behavior (Hetts, Boninger, Armor, Gleicher, and Nathanson 2000) as well as how CFT affects information processing (Krishnamurthy and Sivaraman 2002). Previous studies provide evidence that CFT may be the cognitive mechanism underlying the generation of regret (Tsiros and Mittal 2000). Unlike previous research on CFT, the present research focuses on the impact of counterfactual thinking on product evaluations and uses the direction of counterfactual thinking, upward or downward, to explain the process underlying such evaluations. This research also explores a factor that seems likely to qualify the impact of counterfactual thinking on product evaluations, namely, the level of consumers' processing extensiveness.

We present three studies demonstrating the impact of counterfactual thinking on product evaluations. In study one, we explore the effect of counterfactual thinking on product evaluations after people experience either a positive or a negative purchase outcome. Experiment 2 provides an extension of experiment 1 and establishes the robustness of the documented findings. In study 2, a follow-up customer survey, instead of a counterfactual thinking instruction, was used to induce participants to engage in CFT. Experiment 3 examines how such post-purchase marketing efforts, customer surveys, may influence the direction of CFT and product evaluations.

Recent research by Roese, Sanna, and Galinsky (2005) has explored the relationship between CFT and outcome valence. In response to a positive outcome, people generate more downward than upward counterfactual thoughts, simulating more outcomes that are worse than actuality. By contrast, in response to a negative outcome, people generate more upward than downward counterfactuals, producing a greater number of outcomes that are better than actuality. Previous studies (e.g., Schwarz and Bless, 1992) indicate that downward counterfactuals induce positive affect while upward counterfactuals induce negative affect. Further, Markman et al. (1993) finds that the direction of counterfactual thought also influences satisfaction. That is, a positive outcome induces not only relatively more downward counterfactuals but also greater feelings of satisfaction, whereas a negative outcome evokes not only relatively more upward counterfactuals but also greater feelings of dissatisfaction.

According to this view, satisfied consumers engaging in downward counterfactual thinking may become more satisfied. By contrast, dissatisfied consumers engaging in upward counterfactual thinking may become more dissatisfied. The latter situation, in particular, is thought to create a reciprocal cycle (Sanna, Turley-Ames, and Meier 1999). In this research, we investigate the possibility that consumers can break the cycle of dissatisfaction and upward CFT and instead enhance their product evaluations via counterfactual thinking.

We propose that the extensiveness of information processing, whether such cognitive resources are ample or in short supply, may provide a potential boundary condition for the reciprocal cycle of upward counterfactual thinking.

In experiment 1, as anticipated, after experiencing a negative purchase outcome, higher Need for Cognition individuals generated more favorable product evaluations than lower Need for Cognition individuals when given a counterfactual thinking instruction. By contrast, absent instructions to think counterfactually, lower NFC individuals generated more favorable product evaluations than higher NFC individuals after experiencing a negative purchase outcome. In the positive purchase outcome condition, there were no effects of either counterfactual thinking instructions or individuals' level of Need for Cognition.

The protocols reinforce our theorizing that, in a negative outcome condition, if a CFT instruction is provided, higher NFC individuals generate fewer upward counterfactual thoughts than lower NFC individuals. By contrast, in a negative outcome condition, when offered instructions to think counterfactually, higher NFC individuals generate a greater proportion of downward counterfactuals than lower NFC individuals. If instruction to think counterfactually is not provided, higher NFC individuals, as compared to lower NFC individuals, produce more thoughts focused on comparing the two possible alternatives. Such thoughts appear to result in less positive product evaluations.

Experiment 2 successfully replicated experiment 1's findings with a different manipulation of counterfactual thinking and an alternative procedure for varying information processing extensity. The results from experiment 2 are important in advancing our understanding of the effects that underlie respondents' processing in negative purchase outcome conditions. The findings from experiment 2 demonstrated that after experiencing a negative purchase outcome and receiving a follow-up customer survey, higher motivation respondents generated more downward counterfactuals and fewer upward counterfactuals than lower motivation respondents. And, the respondents in the higher motivation condition evaluated the product more favorably than those respondents in the less processing extensiveness condition. When they do not receive a follow-up survey, respondents with higher motivation produced more comparison thoughts and evaluated the product less favorably than respondents in the lower motivation condition.

The purpose of experiment 3 was to examine whether the direction of CFT could be influenced by post-purchase marketing efforts via customer surveys. In experiment 3, we added two additional surveys with directional questions, asking customers to comment on satisfying or dissatisfying aspects of the purchased product. As expected, we found that the former design (satisfying) induced respondents to engage in more downward CFT whereas the latter design (dissatisfying) generated greater upward CFT.

Together, the three studies support our proposed theorizing regarding how counterfactual thinking can affect people's product evaluations after a positive or a negative purchase experience. The studies reveal that when instructions to think counterfactually are given following a negative product outcome, individuals engaging in more extensive processing generate higher product evaluations and more downward than upward counterfactual thoughts as compared to when instructions to think counterfactually are not available. This conclusion does not hold true for individuals engaging in less extensive processing whose product evaluations were equivalent across conditions.

REFERENCES

Hetts, John J., David S. Boninger, David A. Armor, Faith Gleicher, and Ariel Nathanson (2000), "The Influence of Anticipated Counterfactual Regret on Behavior," *Psychology & Marketing*, 17 (April), 345-68.

Krishnamurthy, Parthasarathy and Anuradha Sivaraman (2002), "Counterfactual Thinking and Advertising Responses," *Journal of Consumer Research*, 28 (March), 650-58.

Markman, Keith D., Igor Gavanski, Steven J. Sherman, and Matthew N. McMullen (1993), "The Mental Simulation of Better and Worse Possible Worlds," *Journal of Experimental Social Psychology*, 29 (January), 87-109.

Roese, Neal J., Lawrence J. Sanna, and Adam D. Galinsky (2005), "The Mechanics of Imagination: Automaticity and Control in Counterfactual Thinking," in *The New Unconscious*, ed. Ran R Hassin, James S. Uleman, and John A. Bargh, New York, NY: Oxford University Press, 138-70.

Sanna, L. J., Turley-Ames, K. J., & Meier, S. (1999), "Mood, self-esteem, and simulated alternatives: Thought-provoking affective influences on counterfactual direction," *Journal of Personality and Social Psychology*, 76, 543-558.

Schwarz, Nobert and Herbert Bless (1992), "Constructing Reality and Its Alternatives: Assimilation and Contrast Effects in Social Judgment," in *The Construction of Social Judgment*, ed. Leonard L. Martin and Abraham Tesser, Hillsdale, NJ: Erlbaum, 217-45.

Tsiros, Michael and Vikas Mittal (2000), "Regret: A Model of Its Antecedents and Consequences in Consumer Decision Making," *Journal of Consumer Research*, 26 (March), 401-17.

Order In Choice: Effects of Serial Position on Preferences

Antonia Mantonakis, Brock University, Canada
Pauline Rodero, Brock University, Canada
Isabelle Lesschaeve, Vineland Research and Innovation Centre, Canada
Reid Hastie, University of Chicago, USA

EXTENDED ABSTRACT

Our primary interest is to determine if there are biases in a final choice simply as a function of the location of each option in the temporal sequence–what we call order effects on choice. Notice that we are assuming that on-line evaluation is taking place (Hastie and Park 1986) and that the chooser has a goal of making a relative assessment of personal preferences for the options throughout the task.

We distinguish this task from closely related tasks that are associated with some well-known serial position or sequence effects. Although there are several prior studies of the effects of location in a sequence on end-of-sequence choices, there is still no clear answer to the question: Which location in a sequence is most advantageous? Several researchers have concluded that there are "primacy effects": (Carney and Banaji 2008) and many descriptive studies of consumer choice find primacy (Berg et al. 1955). But, some researchers predict and observe "recency effects" (de Bruin 2005). We conjecture that there are both primacy and recency effects under certain conditions.

We propose that when participants sample the options, knowing they will be asked to make a choice, they repeatedly compare each new option with their current favorite. Such a pair-wise competitive evaluation strategy will produce an advantage for later items, especially in longer sequences, where an early option has to beat more options to become the overall favorite. Also, we expect a primacy advantage for early options driven by high levels of attention, lower levels of proactive interference, and the common habit of satisficing (Simon 1955). Thus, our basic hypothesis is that we will observe primacy effects, especially pronounced for short sequences, and recency effects as well in longer sequences. We speculate that this pattern may be moderated by participants' sophistication about the options. Since the pair-wise comparison strategy is demanding of cognitive resources, we predict that participants who are more interested and knowledgeable about the choice options will be more persistent in making pair-wise comparisons and hence are likelier to show recency effects. We report an experimental study of serial position effects on choice and then return to a discussion of the serial evaluation process.

Participants were instructed that they would taste several samples of locally produced wines and then were randomly assigned to taste one sequence with a length of two, three, four, or five samples. At the end of the tasting sequence each participant was asked, "Which ONE of ALL the wines that you have tasted today is your favorite?" Finally, participants completed various questions including a test of wine expertise (Hughson and Boakes 2001).

Each preference serial position curve shows a primacy effect with the first wine preferred more than the second and third in every sequence length. Longer sequences also show a recency effect with the last wine preferred more than the previous two or three wines. When examining high-knowledge versus low-knowledge participants, it is apparent that a simple primacy effect pattern best describes the low-knowledge participants' choices in only the five-wine condition; while the primacy plus recency pattern in the combined data set is only clearly apparent for the high-knowledge participants.

Taken together, globally we have a primacy advantage for all conditions; and a recency effect for four-option and five-option choice sets. Second, the global pattern is qualified by the expertise moderator: There is a primacy advantage for all sets for both low- and high-knowledge participants, and there is also a recency effect for the high-knowledge participants (only for four-option and five-option choice sets). Finally, the primacy effect is larger for the high-knowledge participants in the two-option and three-option choice sets.

Participants expected to be asked for evaluations. This means they were evaluating each wine as they tasted it. Also, all the wines tasted "good" and would get positive evaluations if sampled by themselves. Finally, the wines were difficult to discriminate between for our participants. Thus, our first assumption is that the participants were engaged in a "competitive" evaluation process for each pair of wines sampled. When they sampled the first wine, it became their favorite. When they sampled the second wine they compared their memory of the first wine's goodness to the second wine and concluded with a current favorite; and so on.

We propose that two biases operated within that sequential competitive evaluation process. First, there is a first-is-best bias that accounts for our consistent primacy advantage. Second, we propose that the high-knowledge participants tried harder (than the low-knowledge participants) to discern differences between the wines. Compared to low-knowledge participants, high-knowledge participants were more persistently looking for a better wine, later in the sequence, if there was one.

This means, for high-knowledge participants there is a substantial chance that the new wine in each competition might surpass the current favorite and this habit produces the pronounced recency effect in longer sequences for high-knowledge participants. For example, suppose each new wine has a .30 chance of beating the "current favorite" and the "current favorite" remains favorite with a .70 probability. The pair-wise model provides an almost perfect fit to the data if we add one more assumption about the comparison process. In the original model, we assume that all current favorites have a .70 versus .30 advantage in all pair-wise comparisons. If we suppose that the "current favorite advantage" increases for later favorites (e.g., if the third option wins its pair-wise competition its advantage increases .75 versus .25), then the model almost perfectly fits the data.

The pair-wise comparison process model is a hybrid of the two major psychological explanations for sequence effects in the extant literature. The primary contribution of this research is a clear answer to the question of which serial position locations in a sequentially-presented choice set have an advantage in the final choice of a single option. The answer is that primacy is always an advantage and that recency has an advantage in longer sequences and especially when the choosers are knowledgeable about the choice options.

REFERENCES

Berg, H. W., Ferer E. Filipello, Elly Hinreiner, and F. M Sawyer (1955), "Consumer wine-preference methodology studies at California Fairs," *Food Technology*, 9, 90-93.

Carney, Dana R., and Mahzarin R Banaji. (2008), "First is best in rapid social judgment and consumer decision," Harvard University, Unpublished Manuscript.

de Bruin, Wändi B. (2005), "Save the last dance for me: Unwanted serial position effects in jury evaluations," *Acta Psychologica*, 118, 245-260.

Hastie, Reid, and Bernadette Park (1986), "The relationship between memory and judgment depends on whether the judgment is memory-based or on-line," *Psychological Review*, 93, 258-268.

Hughson, Angus L., and Robert A. Boakes (2001), "Perceptual and cognitive aspects of wine expertise," *Australian Journal of Psychology*, 53, 103-108.

Simon, Herbert A. (1955), "A behavioral model of rational choice," *Quarterly Journal of Economics*, 69, 99-118.

Restrained Pursuit of Luxury: Wealthy Shanghainese Attitudes towards Upscale Consumption

Junko Kimura, Hosei University, Japan
Hiroshi Tanaka, Chuo University, Japan

EXTENDED ABSTRACT

Although Chinese economy is in full bloom, at this point we cannot necessarily claim that we know sufficiently about Chinese consumers. Our knowledge on the Chinese consumer is often limited just like a patchwork of fragmented images. We were interested in their perception towards consumption, as it may be an only recently formed concept among newly rich Chinese consumers. More specifically, our research agenda was the following: How do the Chinese consumers perceive the concept of consumption? How is their notion of upscale consumption similar or dissimilar to that of US or Japan?

This time our research focus was wealthy Chinese' perception of luxury, as they may hold distinctive notions of luxury with their unique background of society and culture, and at the same time they are nouveau riche in the uprising Chinese economy. Our previous studies about luxury revealed that four different types of values are included in the notion of luxury among Japan and US female consumers: Distinctive, Relevant, Conspicuous, and Superfluous. We expected Chinese consumers may have different ideas on luxury or on upscale consumption.

Four Shanghainese female homemakers with annual income of more than 100,000 US dollars were recruited for video interview. All of the interviewees lived in Shanghai City area and owners of their own apartments. These female informants lived with her family with three members of their core family; husband, wife, and a child.

Before we actually visited these families, we had imagined their apartments must be splendid condominiums: What we saw, however, were unexpectedly modest apartments. Four informants expressed their perceptions of luxury during the interview. Their perceptions were categorized as follows:

1. Spiritual luxury: pursuant of luxury of attaining the spiritual satisfaction instead of materialistic satisfaction.

This notion was brought to us by an informant woman who was a devout Buddhist, and she is engaged in the marketing of mandala drawings.

2. Socially acceptable luxury: Setting one's level of luxury according to the standard of the society.

This idea of luxury was from an internationalized woman who had an experience of attending a hotel management school in Switzerland. She is currently in charge of sales in a manufacturer, and is an independent person who is willing to earn her own money.

3. Socially balanced luxury: Enjoying the luxury that does not deviate from the social norm and that is, therefore, socially tolerable.

The informant was an ambitious housewife who launched her own trading company in Shanghai, taking advantage of human networks that she had cultivated during her study in Japan, and she became quite successful within a few years.

4. Disciplined luxury: Enjoying the luxury within a boundary of certain standard shared by the peer.

The informant who gave us this notion of luxury was the most rich among the four informants. Her husband, a successful realtor, was born in Taiwan and he holds the U.S. citizenship. Her family hires a maid who, among others, goes to the grocery shopping for the family. The entire family goes out for shopping and entertainment every week.

What these four types commonly seem to reveal is that luxury in modern Shanghai is not at all uninhibited; Shanghainese luxury is firstly restricted by the traditional Confucian values. It also has to be within the boundary of socially acceptable norm. Furthermore, Shanghainese housewives in their 30s and 40s are still under the strong influence of consumption ethics of their parents' generation which had undergone the atrocious hardship during the Great Cultural Revolution. Observing the rapid growth of the Chinese economy, it appears that, deep down, these Chinese homemakers might well have been convinced that they should prepare for the ever-changing society. It might be concluded that the the modern wealthy Shanghainese' perception towards upscale consumption can be characterized as "restrained luxury". This notion may have been generated in a country in transition from a developing economy to a more advanced economy.

Doing the Right Things and Doing the Things Right-Endorsers in Retail Store Flyer Advertising

Bernhard Swoboda, University of Trier, Germany
Stefan Elsner, University of Trier, Germany
Thomas Foscht, University of Graz, Austria
Hanna Schramm-Klein, University of Siegen, Germany

EXTENDED ABSTRACT

Store flyer advertising is a medium that is well accepted by consumers and also popular among retailers. Nevertheless, the body of research available on the effectiveness of store flyer advertising is very small (Arnold, Kozinets and Handelman 2001, 245). Of course, findings on print advertising could be transferred to store flyer advertising in some cases, but there are some distinct differences such as available advertising space. Unlike printed ads, for example, store flyers usually consist of more than four pages. Thus, retailers are able to promote more products or can use the advertising space available for other design elements, such as endorsers. Some retailers, for example Wal-Mart, use photos of the entrepreneurs with their associates as endorsers to build up a retail image on the basis of trustworthiness and honesty (Arnold et al. 2001). Other retailers, particularly large retail chains, use physically attractive endorsers on the basis of the "What-is-beautiful-is-good" hypothesis to apply persuasiveness in advertising (DeShields, Kara, and Kaynak 1996). Indeed, the extensive use of endorsers in advertising is not a recent phenomenon, as the vast endorser literature indicates. However, the impact of depicting entrepreneurs with their associates on advertising effectiveness has been less analyzed (Reidenbach and Pitts 1986).

Against this background, our study has two objectives. Firstly, we propose to investigate for the first time in a field setting the efficiency of showing entrepreneurs with their associates and of using physically attractive models in terms of consumer perception and purchasing behavior, i.e. which endorser type is better. Furthermore, in order to assess whether the use of endorsers is generally justified, we propose investigating the effectiveness of endorsers, i.e. is it better to depict entrepreneurs with their associates or physically attractive models rather than no endorsers at all?

We have, therefore, developed a conceptual framework based on the dual mediation hypothesis. In order to test these hypotheses, we conducted our survey in a field setting. For this purpose we printed three original store flyers, differing only in the endorser groups and one flyer without any endorser, in cooperation with a local medium-sized retailer and a professional advertising agency. The impact of the endorsers on consumer perceptions was then evaluated in 300 face-to-face interviews using a standardized questionnaire. We measured attitude toward the ad (A_{AD}), perceived corporate credibility, store image perceptions, and visit intention on established, seven-point semantic differential scales. Subsequently, we analyzed the impact of different endorser types on purchasing behavior. We divided the trading area of the retailer advertised into three regions with the same statistical distribution of the corresponding population in terms of age, gender and number of households. Then 90,000 store flyers (30,000 of each type of flyer) were disseminated evenly throughout the regions on a Sunday by a local newspaper. A baseline approach was employed to measure the purchasing behavior for each region. Thus, we recorded the number of customers making a purchase of the advertised product category two weeks before (control weeks) and two weeks after distribution (experimental weeks) and aligned them to the region of origin.

In the analysis of consumer perceptions, our conceptual framework indicates partial mediation and provides strong support for the dual mediation hypothesis. We conclude that the A_{AD} mediates the store image perceptions directly as well as indirectly by means of the perceived corporate credibility, whereas the indirect effect is even stronger, meaning that the perceived corporate credibility strengthens the impact. Hence, our findings underline the notion that the perceived corporate credibility plays an important role in advertising persuasiveness.

In order to investigate the moderating effect, the results of the mean value comparison and the path strength comparison show ambiguous results. The mean value comparisons indicate that depicting of entrepreneurs with their associates leads to a more positive effect in terms of A_{AD}, perceived corporate credibility, and store image perceptions compared to use of physically attractive models. This result is in accordance with Goldsmith et al. (2000), who also identified highly credible endorsers as an efficient advertising instrument. Moreover, our results demonstrate that depicting of entrepreneurs with their associates also outperforms the store flyer with no endorsers at all in terms of perceived corporate credibility and store image perceptions. On the other hand, the flyer using physically attractive models is ranked even lower in terms of corporate credibility than the control flyer with no endorsers. In summary, we conclude that depicting of entrepreneurs with their associates is more efficient than depicting physically attractive models and also more effective than no endorser at all for non-attraction-related products in store flyer advertising, while depicting of physically attractive models is even detrimental. However, the results of the path analysis demonstrate no significant differences. Thus, we conclude according to MacKenzie and Spreng (1992) that the moderating effect of different endorser types influences the extent, but not the nature of information processing.

The analysis of purchasing behavior does not show the same results. This can be explained by several factors. Firstly, we can assume that there is an attitudinal behavior gap. Chandon, Morwitz, and Reinartz (2005) stated that attitude could be overestimated in such a way that behavior could not be measured. Secondly, by analyzing purchasing behavior shortly after flyer distribution we only take the direct effect into consideration. However, in order to improve store image perception in particular, a certain time period must be allowed to elapse. Nevertheless, the analysis of purchasing behavior reveals interesting findings for retailers. Firstly, according to Burton, Lichtenstein, and Netemeyer (1999), we identified a strong direct effect by store flyer advertising on sales, with an increase of nearly 19%. This underlines the considerable importance of this advertising medium. Secondly, the baseline approach applied offers retailers an easy-to-handle means of measuring the performance of their store flyer advertising.

As with all empirical studies, this study has limitations. A major limitation is the single product setting of our study, which limits the extent to which our findings can be generalized. Thus, additional multi-product studies are needed to establish whether the effects are also stable for attraction-related products.

REFERENCES

Arnold, Stephen J., Robert V. Kozinets, and Jay M. Handelman (2001), "Hometown Ideology and Retailer Legitimation: The Institutional Semiotics of Wal-Mart Flyers," *Journal of Retailing*, 77 (Summer), 243-71.

Burton, Scot, Donald R. Lichtenstein, and Richard G. Netemeyer (1999), "Exposure to Sales Flyers and Increased Purchases in Retail Supermarkets," *Journal of Advertising Research*, 39 (September/October), 7-14.

Chandon, Pierre, Vicki G. Morwitz, and Werner J. Reinartz (2005), "Do Intentions Really Predict Behavior? Self-Generated Validity Effects in Survey Research," *Journal of Marketing*, 69 (April), 1-14.

DeShields, Oscar W., Ali Kara, and Erdener Kaynak (1996), "Source effects in purchase decisions: The impact of physical attractiveness and accent of salesperson," *International Journal of Research in Marketing*, 13 (February), 89-101.

Goldsmith, Ronald E., Barbara A. Lafferty, and Stephen J. Newell (2000), "The Impact of Corporate Credibility and Celebrity Credibility on Consumer Reaction to Advertisements and Brands," *Journal of Advertising*, 26 (Fall), 43-54.

MacKenzie, Scott B. and Richard A. Spreng (1992), "How Does Motivation Moderate the Impact of Central and Peripheral Processing on Brand Attitudes and Intentions?" *Journal of Consumer Research*, 18 (March), 519-29.

Reidenbach, Eric H. and Robert E. Pitts (1986), "Not all CEOs are created equal as advertising spokespersons: Evaluating the effective CEO Spokesperson," *Journal of Advertising*, 15 (March), 30-46.

Positive Affect, Intertemporal Choice, and Levels of Thinking: Increasing Consumers' Willingness to Wait

Jin Seok Pyone, Cornell University, USA
Alice M. Isen, Cornell University, USA

EXTENDED ABSTRACT

Individuals frequently make choices requiring self-control, some of which involve a trade-off between taking an immediate small gain, versus taking a delayed larger gain. Although the basic principles that may underlie the effect that we study apply to many kinds of self-control, in this article we address the phenomenon of intertemporal choice–perceived differences in the value of rewards over time.

How to reduce impulsivity and increase self-control has been of interest to researchers in several fields. The literature shows that self-control can be enhanced through cognitive processes that relate to ways of thinking about situations and options. For example, thinking about one's action at a higher level, in terms of its consequences and implications, can enhance self-control (Fujita et al. 2006; Vallacher and Wegner 1989). Also, research has shown that focusing on other, non-consumatory, aspects of tempting stimuli can increase delay-of-gratification in children (e.g., Mischel, Shoda, and Rodriguez 1989).

Interestingly, the affect literature suggests that positive affect has an influence on thinking that is compatible with what has just been described as conducive to improved self-control–increased cognitive flexibility, resulting multiple ways of thinking about stimuli and situations, and broadened scope of cognition (e.g., Fredrickson and Branigan 2005; Isen and Daubman 1984; Kahn and Isen 1993; Staw and Barsade 1993; Isen 2007 for discussion). For example, a series of studies shows that positive affect leads to more flexible categorization–multiple aspects of situations and ways of categorizing considered–but at the same time with more typical ways of categorizing not lost. In addition, research has shown that positive affect improves problem solving, including medical decision making (e.g., Estrada, Isen, and Young 1997), by facilitating flexible and integrative thinking. Additionally, positive affect has been shown to influence the way people construe present and future rewards. For example, individuals in a positive state are able to see how present situations are linked to possible future outcomes, and to their own effort (Erez and Isen 2002). Thus, when there is a trade-off between short-term rewards and long-term gains, they are willing to forgo present enjoyment in favor of long-term gains (e.g., Isen and Reeve 2005; Gervey, Igou, and Trope 2005).

Concerning intertemporal choices, researchers interpret a person's loss of self-control or impulsive behavior as based on a human tendency to value immediate rewards over delayed future rewards (i.e., "present-biased preferences" or "hyperbolic discounting"). That is, people discount the value of rewards set to take place in the future, and the discounting rate is greater for shorter time horizons than for longer time horizons (e.g., Frederick, Loewenstein, and O'Donoghue 2002). Recent research suggests that an individual's mindset or level of construal influences these present-biased preferences, such that construing a situation at a high level (or an abstract mindset) leads to long-term thinking and greater self-control, and thus to a decreased level of present bias (Fujita et al. 2006; Malkoc, Zauberman, and Bettman 2007).

Because positive affect has been shown to facilitate flexible thinking and the ability to conceptualize situations in such high-level ways, and thus to facilitate self-control, we propose that positive affect will influence self-control in the specific domain of intertemporal choices. We test this idea using a delay-of-gratification paradigm suited to adult consumers, and temporal-discounting paradigms that assess change in value with delay, and willingness-to-pay to expedite delivery. Specifically, we propose that people in positive affect will be more likely than those in neutral affect to think of the intertemporal choice situation with a long-term perspective, and thus to be more willing to wait for more desirable later outcomes that are at least moderately better than the available immediate outcome, and to show decreased present bias. In addition, we examine some possible underlying mechanisms by which positive affect influences consumers' self-control in such intertemporal choices.

Studies 1 and 2 investigated the impact of positive affect, induced in two different ways, on participants' choices between an instant rebate returning a smaller amount of money and a mail-in rebate returning a larger amount of money. The results revealed that individuals in the positive-affect conditions were more likely than those in the neutral-affect conditions to choose the mail-in rebate, especially when the difference between the instant and mail-in rebates was moderately large (but not when the difference was small). In addition, for people in whom positive affect had been induced, compared to controls, the rebates appeared to be cognitively represented in a less vivid ("cooler") way.

Studies 3 and 4 tested whether positive affect leads to decreased present-biased preference, by examining participants' willingness to pay. In Study 3, participants indicated how much they would pay for a product if they received it immediately versus one month later. Overall, participants were willing to pay less for the delayed product than for the product immediately (i.e., present bias), but the willingness-to-pay decreased less in the positive-affect condition than in the neutral. In Study 4, participants were asked how much they would pay for expediting delivery of their product by 3 or 10 days. Again, overall, participants were willing to pay more per day to expedite the delivery over a shorter delay than over a longer delay, showing present bias, but the decrease in daily premiums was less in the positive-affect condition.

Studies 5 and 6 investigated some possible cognitive processes involved in this effect. Study 5, using the Behavior Identification Form developed by Vallacher and Wegner (1989), to examine whether induced positive affect can foster a higher level of thinking, found that individuals in positive affect, compared to control-affect participants, were more likely to think of behaviors at a high level. Study 6 investigated the level of thinking in terms of time perspective orientation. Past research suggests that a future-oriented time perspective is related to pursuing future, long-term, rather than short-term, present-oriented, goals. Time orientation, as reflected by the Future-Time-Perspective scale (Carstensen and Lang 1996), was more future-oriented among people in the positive-affect condition than among people in neutral affect.

REFERENCES

Carstensen, Laura L. and Frieder R. Lang (1996), "Future Time Perspective scale," unpublished manuscript, Stanford University, CA 94305.

Erez, Amir and Alice M. Isen (2002), "The Influence of Positive Affect on the Components of Expectancy Motivation," *Journal of Applied Psychology*, 87 (6), 1055-67.

Estrada, Carlos A., Alice M. Isen, and Mark J. Young (1997), "Positive Affect Facilitates Integration of Information and Decreases Anchoring in Reasoning among Physicians," *Organizational Behavior and Human Decision Processes*, 72 (1), 117-35.

Frederick, Shane, George F. Loewenstein, and Ted O'Donoghue (2002), "Time Discounting and Time Preference: A Critical Review," *Journal of Economic Literature*, 40 (2), 351-401.

Fredrickson, Barbara L. and Christine Branigan (2005), "Positive emotions broaden the scope of attention and thought-action repertoires," *Cognition and Emotion*, 19 (3), 313-32.

Fujita, Kentaro, Yaacov Trope, Nira Liberman and Maya Levin-Sagi (2006), "Construal Levels and Self Control," *Journal of Personality and Social Psychology*, 90 (3), 351-67.

Gervey, Ben, Eric R. Igou, and Yaacov Trope (2005), "The role of positive mood in pursuing primary self-evaluation goals," *Motivation and Emotion*, 29 (4), 269-96.

Isen, Alice M. (2007), "Positive affect, cognitive flexibility, and self-control," in *Persons in Context: Building a Science of the Individual*, eds.Yuichi Shoda, Daniel Cervone, and Geraldine Downey, New York: Guilford Press, 130-47.

______ and Kimberly A. Daubman (1984), "The Influence of Affect on Categorization," *Journal of Personality and Social Psychology*, 47 (December), 1206-17.

______ and Johnmarshall Reeve (2005), "The Influence of positive affect on intrinsic and extrinsic motivation: Facilitating enjoyment of play, responsible work behavior, and self-control," *Motivation and Emotion*, 29 (4), 297-325.

Kahn, Barbara E. and Alice M. Isen (1993), "The Influence of Positive Affect on Variety Seeking among Safe, Enjoyable Products," *Journal of Consumer Research*, 20 (2), 257-70.

Malkoc, Selin A., Gal Zauberman, and James R. Bettman (2007), "Impatience is In the Mindset: Carryover Effects of Processing Abstractness in Sequential Tasks," in *Advances in Consumer Research*, Vol. 9, eds. Gavan Fitzsimons and Vicki Morwitz, Duluth, MN : Association for Consumer Research, 654-60.

Mischel, Walter, Yuichi Shoda, and Monica L. Rodriguez (1989), "Delay of Gratification in Children," *Science*, 244 (4907), 933-38.

Staw, Barry M. and Sigal G. Barsade (1993), "Affect and Managerial Performance: A Test of the Sadder-but-Wiser vs. Happier-and-Smarter Hypotheses," *Administrative Science Quarterly*, 38 (2), 304-31.

Vallacher, Robin R. and Daniel M. Wegner (1989), "Levels of Personal Agency: Individual Variation in Action Identification," *Journal of Personality and Social Psychology*, 57 (4), 660-71.

The Inhibition Effects of Repetition on Non-target Ad Recall: The Role of Affect Valence

Hieu P. Nguyen, California State University–Long Beach, USA
James M. Munch, Wright State University, USA
Meryl P. Gardner, University of Delaware, USA

EXTENDED ABSTRACT

Repeat advertising exposure is often used to strengthen top-of-mind awareness and recall. The effects of ad repetition on attitude and recall in cluttered and uncluttered/isolated contexts have been researched extensively (e.g., Burke and Srull 1988, Campbell and Keller 2003, D'Souza and Rao 1995, Kirmani 1997, Lane 2000, Malaviya, Meyers-Levy, and Sternthal 1999, Malaviya 2007). However, little is known about how repetition of some ads may affect consumers' memory for the *remaining* ads in the exposure set. Specifically, we have three main research questions: (1) Does exposure to a subset of previously viewed print advertisements strengthen or inhibit recall of the remaining ads? (2) Are the effects specific to a particular affective valence? Does exposure to positive ad cues inhibit only recall of positive ads and not negative ads? Does exposure to negative ad cues inhibit only recall of negative ads and not positive ads? (3) What are the boundary conditions of any observed effects? Does exposure to neutrally valenced ads inhibit recall of only neutrally valenced ads and not emotionally valenced ads? Does exposure to emotionally valenced ads inhibit recall of only emotionally valenced ads and not neutrally valenced ads?

We draw on findings in the psychology literature on part-list cuing inhibition effects to construct our theoretical foundation. Part-list cuing inhibition refers to the observation that the presentation of a subset of previously learned items as retrieval cues often inhibits recall of the remaining noncue items (Aslan, Bauml, and Grundgeiger 2007). The earliest and most predominant theoretical account is the retrieval competition hypothesis (Rundus 1973). It suggests that exposure to cue words strengthen their memory traces compared to those of noncue words. When individuals attempt to recall noncue items at test, the higher retrievability of the cue items decreases the probability of accessing noncue items directly (Bauml 2007, Nickerson 1984). Based on the retrieval competition hypothesis, we predict that compared to uncued participants, cued participants will show poorer recall of ads (H1). However, this effect is also affect-specific. Bower's associative network theory (1981) suggests that the affect node is connected by associative pointers to other aspects of the emotion. Activation of a node is accomplished either by presentation of the corresponding stimulus pattern or by prior activation of an associated thought. Bower also suggests that "each emotion may reciprocally inhibit an emotion of opposing quality, as fear inhibits joy and sexual arousal." (p. 135). We follow Bower's theory and argue that exposure to positive ad cues should activate the positively valenced node, which can transmit excitation to other positive nodes but not negative nodes, eventually helping retrieval of positive ads. Therefore, when participants see positive ad cues, they should be able to recall other positive ads. However, the covert retrieval of the positive *ad cues* at recall inhibits the retrieval of *uncued* positive ads. Compared to uncued participants, positive cue participants will show poorer recall of the remaining positive ads while recall of negative ads will not differ (H2). Similarly, compared to uncued participants, negative cue participants will show poorer recall of the remaining negative ads while recall of positive ads will not differ (H3). For neutral ads, emotion is not a salient aspect. Exposure to emotional ad cues should only result in inhibition for emotional ads but not neutral ads, because these ads are not associatively linked to emotional ads in memory structure. Neutral ad recall will not differ significantly between uncued and emotionally cued participants (H4). Neutral valence is not a salient aspect of one's experience. Ads which are not emotional are unlikely to be remembered for their neutral moods, and are not expected to be organized by emotional valence. Drawing from Bower's associative network theory, exposure to neutral cues should not inhibit recall of neutral ads only (because neutral ads are not an affective category in memory, therefore neutral nodes are not linked to other neutral nodes in the same fashion that positive and negative nodes are linked to positive and negative nodes, respectively). In line with the retrieval competition hypothesis, we predict that exposure to neutral ads as cues will inhibit recall of positive, negative, and neutral ads alike (H5).

One hundred forty seven undergraduate students participated in the experiment for partial course credit. Participants were randomly assigned to one of four cue conditions (no cue, positive cue, negative cue, neutral cue). Each participant viewed 26 ads (eight per affective valence type plus two buffer ads). After that, those in the experimental conditions were shown four randomly selected and ordered ads from the slideshow they had just seen. These four cue ads matched the valence type of the participants' assigned condition. Participants in the control condition solved some simple reasoning tasks. We found support for all hypotheses. Our findings indicate that exposure to ad cues inhibits recall of uncued ads, and more importantly, this inhibition effect if affect-specific. Our research makes an important contribution to the ad repetition literature because it sheds light on the effect of repetition of target ads on non-target ads. For advertisers, using the same affective valence in all of their ads might result in situations where some of the ads will be forgotten because of exposure to other ads of the same affective tone.

REFERENCES

Aslan, Alp, Karl-Heinz Bauml, and Tobias Grundgeiger (2007), "The Role of Inhibitory Processes in Part-List Cuing," *Journal of Experimental Psychology, 33*(2), 335-341.

Bauml, Karl-Heinz (2007), "Making Memories Unavailable: The Inhibitory Power of Retrieval," *Journal of Psychology, 215*(1), 4-11.

Bower, Gordon H. (1981), "Mood and Memory," *American Psychologist, 36*, 129-48.

Burke, Raymond R. and Thomas K. Srull (1988), "Competitive Interference and Consumer Memory for Advertising," *Journal of Consumer Research, 15*, 55-68.

Campbell, Margaret and Kevin L. Keller (2003), "Brand Familiarity and Advertising Repetition Effects," *Journal of Consumer Research, 30*, 292-304.

D'Souza, Giles and Ram C. Rao (1995), "Can Repeating an Advertisement More Frequently Than the Competition Affect Brand Preference in a Mature Market?" *Journal of Marketing, 59*, 32-42.

Kirmani, Amna (1997), "Advertising Repetition as a Signal of Quality: If It's Advertised So Much, Something Must Be Wrong," *Journal of Advertising, 26(3)*, 77-86.

Lane, Vicki R. (2000), "The Impact of Ad Repetition and Ad Content on Consumer Perceptions on Incongruent Extensions," *Journal of Marketing, 64(2)*, 80-91.

Malaviya, Prashant, Joan Meyers-Levy, and Brian Strenthal (1999), "Ad Repetition in a Cluttered Environment: The Influence of Type of Processing," *Psychology & Marketing, 16(2)*, 99-118.

Malaviya, Prashant (2007), "The Moderating Influence of Advertising Context on Ad Repetition Effects: The Role of Amount and Type of Elaboration," *Journal of Consumer Research, 34*, 32-40.

Nickerson, Raymond S. (1984), "Retrieval Inhibition from Part-Set Cuing: A Persisting Enigma in Memory Research," *Memory & Cognition, 12*, 531-52.

Rundus, Dewey (1973), "Negative Effects of Using List Items as Recall Cues," *Journal of Verbal Learning and Verbal Behavior, 12*, 43-50.

Shaver, Philip, Judith Schwartz, Donald Kirson, and Cary O'Connor (1987), "Emotional Knowledge: Further Explanation of a Prototype Approach," *Journal of Personality and Social Psychology, 52*, 1061-86.

Tulving, Endel and Zena Pearlstone (1966), "Availability Versus Accessibility of Information in Memory for Words," *Journal of Verbal Learning and Verbal Behavior, 14*, 294-303.

Not All Products are Placed Equal: A Quasi-Experimental Approach to the Integration Effects of Conspicuous Product Placement on Affective Brand Attitude

Sukki Yoon, Bryant University, USA
Yung Kyun Choi, Dongguk University, South Korea
Sujin Song, University of Rhode Island, USA

EXTENDED ABSTRACT

Imagine two consumers, Jason and Sarah, watching movies on TV. Jason, viewing a scene from Runaway Bride, sees Julia Roberts jump on a truck that conspicuously displays the FedEx logo. Sarah, watching The Thomas Crown Affair, sees Rene Russo march to a vending machine, pull out a can of Pepsi, with its logo prominent, and guzzle it down. In both scenes the brands are noticeably displayed; the actors touch or consume the products. Jason and Sarah instantly recognize that the products have been placed with obvious, persuasive intent. Who will feel more positively toward the product featured? Jason or Sarah? Will they feel differently if they are cognitively busy while viewing these scenes, if they are, say, speaking on the phone or browsing the Internet? And will their feelings toward brands that are not shown–UPS and Coke–be influenced as well? How Jason and Sarah respond may vary, depending on, among other things, how well the product has been integrated into the storyline.

As the practice of product placement is becoming more overt and blatant, marketers and consumers alike are increasingly accepting this "in-your-face" practice. Because costs associated with the placement and the centrality (e.g., close-ups) of the placement are directly linked, marketing practitioners have a heightened need to understand how and when such conspicuously placed placements help or damage the brand. Previous research has compared prominent placement and subtle placement as a primary construct responsible for effects on cognitive variables. However, few studies have yet to focus on how conspicuous placements in themselves–arguably the most common form of product placements in today's media–can differently affect consumers' feelings toward the brand. The present research aims to fill this gap.

Today's discerning consumers seem to see both gratifying and disturbing aspects of product placement. They acknowledge that a well-placed product enriches the plot, heightens realism, and adds enjoyment to their entertainment experience, but when the product placement is poorly done, they see it as an intrusive and unwelcome distraction. According to one survey, 80 percent of American consumers have positive views toward conspicuous product placements, but 46 percent agree that it "depends on how it's done". Academics share this view. Some researchers have argued that well-integrated placement increases persuasion, but poorly integrated placement has the opposite effect. Using real movie scenes as stimuli, this paper focuses therefore on the factor that makes the difference between persuasion and dissuasion—integration.

The objectives of this research are to (1) identify exemplar scenes of conspicuous placement, well-integrated and poorly integrated, from current films (Pretests 1-4), (2) test whether a well-integrated placement indeed enhances a brand's image, whereas a poorly integrated placement damages a brand's image (Study 1), (3) examine how consumers' cognitive busyness moderates the placement integration effects (Study 2), and (4) explore whether a consumer's exposure to a conspicuous brand placement (e.g., Pepsi) influences the consumer's evaluation of the apparent competitor that is not shown (e.g., Coke; Study 2).

First, through a series of extensive pretests we selected two real movie scenes with conspicuous product placements that represent contrasting sides of placement-plot integration: well integrated product placement and poorly integrated product placement. These two scenes were further validated for conspicuousness, integratedeness, and relevancy. In addition, we quasi-experimentally controlled for program length, brand-exposure duration, and program liking.

Second, in Study 1, we tested a rather straightforward but yet-to-be-experimentally tested effect: A well-integrated conspicuous brand placement will evoke a higher affective evaluation than will a poorly integrated conspicuous placement (H1).

Third, in Study 2, we tested the following hypothesis: For a well-integrated conspicuous placement, cognitively busy participants will have lower affective evaluation of the placed brand than will cognitively non-busy participants, but for a poorly integrated conspicuous placement, cognitively busy participants will have higher affective evaluation of the placed brand than will cognitively non-busy participants (H2).

Fourth, in Study 2, we tested two additional hypotheses: 1) For the poorly integrated conspicuous placement, cognitively non-busy participants will have a lower affective evaluation of the placed brand than of the not-shown competing brand (boomerang effect), but cognitively busy participants will have a higher affective evaluation of the placed brand than of the not-shown competing brand (H3.1). 2) However, for the well-integrated product placement, the two-way interaction effect specified in H3.1 will be absent (H3.2).

In sum, using real movie scenes as stimuli, this paper demonstrates that consumer feelings toward the placed brand improve when the product is seamlessly integrated, but deteriorate when the product is intrusively integrated. We also identified the boundary condition under which such integration effects are altered: that is, poor integration's brand-damaging effect can be reversed to a brand-enhancing effect if viewers are cognitively preoccupied with another task. In addition, the results suggest that poor integration's reactance-induced boomerang effect might not only decrease the affective evaluation of the placed brand, but might also increase the affective evaluation of the not-shown competitor.

Power and Choice: Do Powerful Consumers Prefer Bold Options?

Mehdi Mourali, University of Calgary, Canada
Frank Pons, Laval University, Canada

EXTENDED ABSTRACT

Power is a basic feature of social life (Russell 1938). Most societies are organized in a hierarchical fashion, with some members enjoying more power than others. Even so, people regularly experience feelings of being both powerful and powerless, regardless of where they stand in the social hierarchy. Being asked for one's expert advice, for example, may induce a psychological state of feeling powerful, whereas being evaluated by one's peers may evoke a sense of powerlessness. The evident ubiquity of power in our everyday life prompts a critical question: Do people make different consumption decisions when feeling powerful versus powerless? Although the role of power in consumer behavior has received relatively little attention (Rucker and Galinsky 2008; Dwyer 1984), recent developments in psychological research suggest that possessing versus lacking power can have a significant influence on how people think, feel, and act in a variety of social situations (Fiske 1993; Guinote 2007; Keltner, Gruenfeld, and Anderson 2003; Overbeck and Park 2001; Smith and Trope 2006).

The approach/inhibition theory of power (Keltner et al. 2003) posits that power influences the relative activation of the behavioral approach and inhibition systems–the two fundamental action tendencies that regulate behavior associated with rewards and threats respectively. The theory holds that elevated power activates the behavioral approach system, whereas reduced power activates the behavioral inhibition system. Building on the approach/inhibition theory of power, this paper proposes that power significantly and predictably influences consumer preferences in a number of decision contexts. In particular, we focus on decision contexts in which consumers choose between extreme versus compromise options (Simonson 1989), hedonic versus utilitarian options (Dhar and Wertenbroch 2000), enriched versus impoverished options (Shafir 1993), and unique versus standard options (Maimaran and Wheeler, forthcoming). These four types of decisions share a common characteristic: they all involve a choice between bold and timid options (Maimaran and Simonson 2008). Bold options (i.e., extreme, hedonic, enriched, and unique options) are defined as less conventional, more distinctive, and more self expressive, whereas timid options (i.e., compromise, utilitarian, impoverished, and standard options) are more conventional and less self-expressive. We propose that a heightened sense of power increases consumers' tendency to make bold choices. Furthermore, power often comes with a sense of responsibility (Overbeck and Park 2001). This sense of responsibility can raise the perceived constraints that a powerful individual feels (Smith and Bargh 2008), and lead to reduced approach-related tendencies. Thus, we expect that the effect of power on choice of bold versus timid options would disappear under conditions of high responsibility.

Studies 1 and 2 tested the main effect of power on choice of bold versus timid options. Power was manipulated using a scrambled sentence task (Smith and Trope 2006) in study 1 and a writing task (Galinsky et al. 2003) in study 2. Using different types of choice problems, these studies offered converging evidence that when consumers' sense of power is elevated, they are more likely to choose bold options over timid ones. However, reducing consumer's sense of power did not increase their preference for timid options. Moreover, the observed effects were not mediated by consumers' mood.

Study 3 tested the moderating role of responsibility. Power was manipulated using a role-based procedure adapted from (Galinsky et al. 2003), and responsibility was manipulated by telling a group of respondents that they were highly responsible for the outcome of the project and the wellbeing of others. As expected, power had a significant effect on choice of bold versus timid options in the low responsibility condition but not in the high responsibility condition.

REFERENCES

Dhar, Ravi, and Klaus Wertenbroch (2000), "Consumer Choice between Hedonic and Utilitarian Goods," *Journal of Marketing Research*, 37 (1), 60-71.

Dwyer, F. Robert (1984). Are two better than one? Bargaining behavior and outcomes in an asymmetrical power relationship. *Journal of Consumer Research*, 11, 680-683.

Fiske, Susan T. (1993), "Controlling Other People: The Impact of Power on Stereotyping," *American Psychologist*, 48(June), 621-28.

Galinsky, Adam D., Deborah H. Gruenfeld, and Joe C. Magee (2003), "From Power to Action," *Journal of Personality and Social Psychology*, 85(September), 453-66.

Guinote, Ana (2007), "Power Affects Basic Cognition: Increased Attentional Inhibition and Flexibility," *Journal of Experimental Social Psychology*, 43 (July), 685-97.

Keltner, Dacher, Deborah H. Gruenfeld, and Cameron Anderson (2003), "Power, Approach, and Inhibition," *Psychological Review*, 110 (April), 265-84.

Maimaran, Michal, and S. Christian Wheeler (forthcoming), Circles, Squares, and Choice: The Effect of Shapes Arrays on Uniqueness and Variety Seeking," *Journal of Marketing Research.*

Maimaran, Michal, and Itamar Simonson (2008), "The Bold-Timid Divide in Consumer Choice," Working paper: Stanford University.

Overbeck, Jennifer R., and Bernadette Park (2001), "When Power Does Not Corrupt: Superior Individuation Processes among Powerful Perceivers," *Journal of Personality and Social*

Rucker, Derek D., and Adam D. Galinsky (2008), "Desire to Acquire: Powerlessness and Compensatory Consumption," *Journal of Consumer Research*, 35 (August), 257-67.

Russell, Bertrand (1938), *Power: A New Social Analysis*, New York: Norton.

Shafir, Eldar (1993), "Choosing versus Rejecting: Why Some Options are both Better and Worse than Others," *Memory and Cognition*, 21 (4), 546-56.

Simonson, Itamar (1989), "Choice Based on Reasons: The Case of Attraction and Compromise Effects," *Journal of Consumer Research*, 16 (September), 158-74.

Smith, Pamela K., and John A. Bargh (2008), "Nonconscious Effects of Power on Basic Approach ad Avoidance Tendencies," *Social Cognition*, 26 (1), 1-24.

Smith, Pamela K. and Yaacov Trope (2006), "You Focus on the Forest When You're in Charge of the Trees: Power Priming and Abstract Information Processing," *Journal of Personality and Social Psychology*, 90(April), 578-96.

Choice Facilitating Effects of Online Shopping Agents in the Face of Missed Opportunities

Demetra Andrews, University of Houston, USA

EXTENDED ABSTRACT

To date, research on the influence of missed opportunities has largely focused on "offline" purchases in which a decision-maker evaluates the available alternatives without external assistance or information (see Kumar (2004) for an exception in which the purchase behavior of a referent other is available to the decision maker). However, consumer use of the Internet to facilitate purchase decisions is rapidly increasing (Haubl and Trifts 2000). In a recent study by comScore, Inc. (Fuglioni and Abraham 2008), nearly three-fourths of respondents stated that the Internet affords them better pricing information and almost 25% indicated its particular value in identifying sales and special offers. Of specific relevance to the current research, the comScore report indicated that, from 2007 to 2008, the number of unique users of online search and comparison tools increased by 7% to 67MM, providing vivid evidence of consumers' increasing reliance on these tools.

The purpose of the current research is to enhance our understanding of the influence that one type of Internet-based interactive decision aid, online shopping agents (OSAs), exerts on two consequential reactions to missed opportunities that have been noted in the literature, increased likelihood of choice deferral (Arkes, Kung and Hutzel 2002; Tykocinski and Pittman 1998; Tykocinski, Pittman and Tuttle 1995) and brand switching (Zeelenberg and van Putten 2005). Findings from three studies demonstrate the efficacy of OSAs in reducing the likelihood of both choice deferral and brand switching and offer ideas regarding possible drivers of this positive influence. Thus, the current research extends the current literature by addressing the question of whether the influence of OSAs can dissipate the shadows of missed opportunities.

Popular examples of such OSAs include MySimon.com, pricegrabber.com, and shopping.com. OSAs scour the Internet to identify alternatives that match consumer-input preference information. At the conclusion of their search and filtering activity, they return a list of available alternatives ranked according to those preferences. Prior research has shown that OSAs exert a strong influence on consumer behavior. Among the noted effects are changes in price sensitivity (Diehl, Kornish, and Lynch 2003), reduced search effort (Haubl and Trifts 2000; Ratchford, Talukdar, and Lee 2007), and improved decision quality (Haubl and Trifts 2000).

One of the core behaviors observed in prior research on missed opportunities is an increased incidence of choice deferral such that missing out on a good opportunity reduces the likelihood that a lesser opportunity will be accepted, even if it is better than the standard offer (Tykocinski et al. 1995). This finding has been consistent in multiple studies and proposes an unattractive prospect for marketers that employ hi-lo pricing strategies or promotional offers. However, the question of whether this pattern would hold in the presence of online shopping agent influences is yet unanswered. Thus, the current body of research was undertaken.

In Study 1, I manipulated whether the missed opportunity was caused by an OSA or the decision-maker and whether the information on the currently-available offer was discovered by the OSA or the decision-maker. Findings showed that use of an OSA significantly reduced the likelihood of choice deferral over conditions where no OSA was employed. Moreover, when the information on the currently-available offer came from an OSA, the deferral rate held constant (at approximately 30%), but when the decision-maker was the source of the new information the likelihood of choice deferral varied as a function of the cause of the missed opportunity (Self or OSA).

Choice deferral is but one troublesome response to a missed opportunity. Research by Zeelenberg and van Putten (2005) and Tsiros (2009) suggests that, rather than go without a desired item, people may switch to another brand to avoid purchasing an item on which a special offer was missed. Such a negative influence on brand loyalty is unattractive to marketers, thus I undertook studies 2 and 3 in order to evaluate the efficacy of OSAs in mitigating brand switching. Studies 2 and 3 followed a design similar to that of Study 1, but rather than evaluate whether a choice was made or not, the key dependent variable was whether the originally desired brand was selected vs. another available brand.

In Study 2, the "currently-available" choice set included a brand that was identical to the one for which a sale was missed. The results showed the lowest likelihood of brand-switching when an OSA was both the cause of the initial missed opportunity and the source of information on the current offer. In Study 3, the currently-available choice set included a brand that was highly similar to the one for which a sale was missed, rather than identical to it. Thus, the study was likely more reflective of real life choices. Under this condition, the results showed that an OSA-caused missed opportunity generated less brand-switching behavior than did a self-caused miss. In particular, the lowest likelihood of brand-switching was observed when an OSA caused the initial miss but the decision-maker discovered the information about the current offer. When this finding is compared to that observed in Study 2, the difference suggests that the use of OSA to aid choice may be beneficial to brand loyalty even if the decision-maker decides not to use a faulty OSA in the second stage of the choice process.

Taken together, findings from these three studies suggest that the increasing usage of online shopping agents in consumer choice may bode well for marketers in that OSA usage may reduce the likelihood of both choice deferral and brand-switching in response to missed opportunities.

REFERENCES

Arkes, Hal R., Yi-Han Kung and Laura Hutzel (2002), "Regret, Valuation, and Inaction Inertia," *Organizational Behavior and Human Decision Processes*, 87 (March), 371-385.

Fuglioni, Gain and Madrid Abraham, (2008, August 6), "State of the U.S. Online Retail Economy," *comScore, Inc*.

Diehl, Kristin, Laura J. Kornish and John G. Lynch, Jr. (2003), "Smart Agents: When Lower Search Costs for Quality Information Increase Price Sensitivity," *Journal of Consumer Research*, 30 (June), 56-71.

Haubl, Gerald and Valerie Trifts (2000), "Consumer Decision Making in Online Shopping Environments: The Effects of Interactive Decision Aids," *Marketing Science*, 19 (Winter), 4-21.

Kumar, Piyush (2004), "The Effects of Social Comparison on Inaction Inertia," *Organizational Behavior and Human Decision Processes*, 95 (November), 175-185

Ratchford, Brian T., Debabrata Talukdar, Myung-Soo Lee (2007), "The Impact of the Internet on Consumers' Use of Information Sources for Automobiles: A Re-Inquiry," *Journal of Consumer Research*, 34 (June), 111-119.

Tsiros, Michael (2009), "Releasing the Regret Lock: Consumer Response to New Alternatives after a Sale," *Journal of Consumer Research*, 35 (April), 1039-1059.

Tykocinski, Orit E., Thane S. Pittman and Erin E. Tuttle (1995), "Inaction Inertia: Foregoing Future Benefits as a result of an Initial Failure to Act," *Journal of Personality and Social Psychology*, 68 (November), 793-803.

Tykocinski, Orit E. and Thane S. Pittman (1998), "The Consequences of Doing Nothing: Inaction Inertia as Avoidance of Anticipated Counterfactual Regret," *Journal of Personality and Social Psychology*, 75 (September), 607-616.

Zeelenberg, Marcel and Marijke van Putten (2005), "The Dark Side of Discounts: An Inaction Inertia Perspective on the Post-Promotion Dip," *Psychology & Marketing*, 22 (August), 611-622.

Effects of Resource Availability on Consumer Decisions on Counterfeit Products: Role of Justification

Jungkeun Kim, Auckland University of Technology, New Zealand
Jae-Eun Kim, Auckland University of Technology, New Zealand
Jongwon Park, Korea University, Korea

EXTENDED ABSTRACT

People consider counterfeit products to be unethical, yet sometimes engage in counterfeit purchases. Previous research has identified various determinants of counterfeit purchases, including price benefits, perceived risks, demographic factors, and personality variables. For example, it has been shown that the most important motive for purchasing counterfeit products over genuine ones is their functional quality and physical appearance comparable to that of originals (Wee, Tan, and Check, 1995). It has also been shown that consumers' risk perceptions about counterfeits and their moral beliefs against them decrease purchases for counterfeit products (Logsdon, Thompson, and Reid, 1994; Moores and Chang 2006). However, most of these findings are generally descriptive and based on correlational analyses. In addition, situational influences and cognitive processes underlying these influences have rarely been investigated.

The present research investigated the effect of resource availability on the consumption of counterfeit products. We contend that to the extent that counterfeit purchases being considered as unethical behavior, people need to be able to justify their decisions in order to engage in counterfeit purchases. However, the justification process requires considerable amount of cognitive resources. Consequently, people are more likely to consider purchasing counterfeits when they have cognitive resources than when they do not. This effect is more likely to occur among people who have strong moral beliefs against unethical consumption behaviors in general. If people do not consider the counterfeit purchase as unethical, however, they may feel no need to justify their purchases, thus are likely to consider purchasing counterfeit products regardless of whether their cognitive resource is non-limited or limited. On the other hand, if people are required to explain and justify their purchase decisions to others, they may not be able to generate sufficient justification for counterfeit purchase, thus unlikely to consider counterfeit purchase regardless of resource availability.

These possibilities were examined in four studies. In experiment 1, participants were asked to perform either a resource-depleting task or a control task, which was to manipulate the amount of cognitive resources available for a subsequent task (limited resource vs. non-limited resource). Then, participants were introduced to a purchase situation for knit sweaters and were asked to decide whether they would like to buy counterfeits over genuine products. As expected, participants reported a higher level of purchase intentions for counterfeits when their cognitive resource was non-limited rather than limited. In addition, this effect was mediated by the effect of resource availability on participants' perceptions of justifiability about the counterfeit purchase. Finally, a follow-up study replicated these results in a different product category and in addition, eliminated a mood-based alternative explanation for the effect.

Experiment 2 replicated results from experiment 1 in another different product category and in addition, identified consumers' moral beliefs against unethical consumptions as a moderator for the effect. To do so, participants' moral beliefs were assessed. In addition, resource availability was manipulated by a distraction task during the counterfeit purchase situation rather than by a depletion task prior to the purchase situation for generalizability of results. As expected and consistent with experiment 1, resource availability increased counterfeit purchase intentions. As also expected, however, this effect was restricted to individuals who have high moral beliefs, whereas participants with low moral beliefs exhibited high purchase intentions for counterfeits regardless of resource availability conditions. This difference was evidenced by a significant interaction of moral beliefs and resource availability, and was mediated by participants' justification perceptions about the counterfeit purchase.

Experiment 3 identified accountability of decisions as another moderator for the effect. When participants were required to account for their decisions to others and thus found it difficult to fully justify their decisions, their purchase intentions for counterfeits was low, regardless of people's resource availability.

In sum, these and other results suggest that people intend to purchase counterfeits if they can justify their decision, but that such justification requires cognitive resources. Theoretical and managerial implications are discussed.

When Unique (Nonalignable) Differences Acquire Greater Importance than Shared (Alignable) Ones: The Role of Noncomparison-Based Choice Processes

Amitav Chakravarti, New York University, USA
Suzanne A. Nasco, Southern Illinois University, USA

EXTENDED ABSTRACT

Choices are often a function of the shared (i.e., alignable) and the unique (i.e., nonalignable) attributes of the options under consideration. Past research in a variety of areas has shown that alignable attributes tend to have a greater impact on choice than nonalignable attributes. This is marked by a well-documented tendency for decision makers to choose options that are superior on the alignable attributes (i.e., the alignable-better brand) over options that are superior on the nonalignable attributes (i.e., the nonalignable-better brand). We refer to this robust and well-documented phenomenon as the alignable superiority effect (ASE).

In this paper, across five studies, we show that several individual-level, contextual, and situational factors are capable of either attenuating or enhancing this effect. More importantly, the studies presented collectively provide strong evidence that the degree of noncomparison-based processing is a critical factor in determining the relative influence of alignable and nonalignable attributes in choice tasks. Alignables dominate in decisions involving extensive comparisons; however, nonalignables loom larger when decision makers are encouraged to engage in non-comparison based processing. This conceptual rubric not only explains the moderators we present in this paper, but it might also explain moderators that have been documented in the past. In fact, we believe that the dominance of alignability found in consumer behavior studies so far, is in part due to the fact that most of the experimental tasks encouraged extensive, attribute-by-attribute, comparison-based processing of choice alternatives. In fact, as we later demonstrate, small changes to these often-used experiment features can have important consequences for the alignable superiority effect.

The preceding discussion naturally begets the question, what is noncomparison based processing? The details regarding the theoretical underpinnings of our argument regarding the impact of noncomparison-based processing on the ASE are provided in the main body of the paper. However, to provide a nutshell summary, we essentially propose that anything that dampens the comparison processes that are usually ubiquitous in choice decisions, either directly (e.g., by reducing the number of attribute-by-attribute comparisons), or indirectly (e.g., by increasing holistic, alternative-based processing), should significantly weaken the ASE. We conducted five studies to investigate this basic proposition. Studies 1-4 were designed to investigate the impact of reduced comparisons on the ASE, and study 5 was designed to look at the joint effects of reduced comparisons and increased holistic processing on the ASE.

We first show that individual-level predispositions to not engage in comparisons mitigate the ASE (study 1). More specifically, we showed that the ASE is prominent among individuals predisposed to engage in comparative behavior (e.g., those who score high on the Comparison Orientation scale), but that the ASE is significantly attenuated among individuals predisposed to not engage in such comparisons (e.g., those who score low on the Comparison Orientation scale).

We then manipulate the contextual descriptions of product features and show that if contextual characteristics discourage extensive comparison of the choice options, then reliance on the nonalignable attributes increases significantly and the ASE is eliminated (study 2). We find that a relatively simple manipulation of the information presentation format suffices in reducing the ASE, in keeping with past research (e.g., Bettman and Kakkar 1977, and Painton and Gentry 1985) that has shown that relative to a tabular format, a paragraph presentation format tends to inhibit a decision maker's ability to make comparisons. Thus, study 2 showed that a paragraph (tabular) information presentation format inhibited (facilitated) comparisons and attenuated (bolstered) the ASE.

In study 3 we extended the generalizability of our research by replicating our findings in three different product replicates, each with a varied set of attributes. We also varied the kind of attribute descriptions that were used as alignable or nonalignable attributes by "rotating" the attributes that were used as alignables with the ones that were used as nonalignables.

As a more complete test of our proposed relationship between the ASE and comparisons, we not only show that discouraging comparisons weakens the ASE (like in studies 1-3), but also demonstrate that encouraging comparison-based processing actually strengthens the ASE (study 4). To situationally induce a more comparative mindset we used Mussweiler's (2003) procedural priming method, that has been successfully used in a wide variety of domains, from classic anchoring-adjustment tasks (Keil, Mussweiler, and Epstude 2006) to financial decisions regarding stocks (Mussweiler and Schneller 2003). To induce a less comparative mindset we used Shiv and Huber's (2000) intervention, in which participants are asked to anticipate satisfaction with the options prior to making a choice. Thus, by simultaneously showing both that noncomparison-based processing favors the nonalignable-better brand, and that encouraging comparison-based processing has an effect that is opposite to that of noncomparison-based processing, these results provide stronger support for the central claims of our research. In addition, given the description of the manipulations above, this study also showed that unrelated situational factors, like the comparative mindset induced in an independent and unrelated preceding task, could also significantly affect the ASE.

Finally, study 5 addresses one missing piece of the puzzle. We had claimed that there were two possible routes to dampening the ASE. So far, in looking at personality (study 1), contextual (studies 2-3), and situational (study 4) factors that dampen or augment the ASE, we have always implicated either a reduction, or an increase, in comparative processing as the key driving force behind our results. Study 5 provides strong support for the second route, and shows that greater holistic processing can, independently, dampen the primacy of the alignables that has been observed in the past.

The issue of comparability is central to structural alignment theory, since it is only through comparisons that alignment is established. Logically, therefore, comparisons should play a big role in the dominance of alignable attributes that has been observed in past work. Up to now, however, this comparison process that should be so central to the dominance of alignables over nonalignables, has gone relatively unexamined. We try to address this gap through this research.

REFERENCES

Bettman, James R. and Pradeep Kakkar (1977), "Effects of Information Presentation Format on Consumer Information Acquisition Strategies," *Journal of Consumer Research*, 3 (March), 233-240.

Keil, Andreas, Mussweiler, Thomas, and Kai Epstude (2006), "Alpha-Band Activity Reflects Reduction of Mental Effort in a Comparison Task: A Source Space Analysis," *Brain Research*, 1121,117-127.

Mussweiler, Thomas (2003), "Comparison Processes in Social Judgment: Mechanisms and Consequences," *Psychological Review*, 110 (3), 472-489.

Mussweiler, Thomas and Karl Schneller (2003), "What Goes Up Must Come Down–How Charts Influence Decisions to Buy and Sell Stocks," *Journal of Behavioral Finance*, 4 (3), 121-130.

Painton, Scott and James W. Gentry (1985), "Another Look at the Impact of Information Presentation Format," *Journal of Consumer Research*, 12 (September), 240-244.

Shiv, Baba and Joel Huber (2000), "The Impact of Anticipating Satisfaction on Consumer Choice," *Journal of Consumer Research*, 27 (September), 202-216.

Does Cultural Orientation Influence Consumers' Propensity to Trust?

Yinlong Zhang, University of Texas at San Antonio, USA

EXTENDED ABSTRACT

Consumer trust is essential to all kinds of modern exchanges; the very concept of marketing (Bagozzi 1975), from buying a used car, purchasing on-line, deciding on a relationship partner, to choosing among different careers. The importance of consumer trust has been further enhanced by the development of E-commerce and globalization (Doney, Cannon, and Mullen 1998), as more and more transactions and marketing operations take place in a global scale. With the increasing pace of globalization, it is important to understand the role of cultural orientation on consumer trust, for example, what is the role of individualism/collectivism orientation on consumer trust?

Empirical findings on the relationship between cultural orientation and trust are very inconsistent in the literature. For example, through surveys, Yamagishi and his colleagues (1994) found that U.S. participants showed higher level of trust than their Japanese counterparts. Through a 20-year analysis of economic development, Putnam (1993) found the similar pattern of results that U.S. participants showed higher level of trusting tendency than those from Asia such as Korea, China and Japan. More recently, while comparing seven-markets (China, Hong Kong, Japan, Korea, Malaysia, Taiwan and U.S. Hawaii and Illinois), Huff and Kelley (2003) found extremely strong evidence showing that individualistic American show much higher trusting tendency than collectivistic Asians. In the contrast, using an investment game, Buchan and her colleagues (Buchan, Croson and Dawes 2002; Buchan and Croson 2004) found that collectivistic Chinese showed higher trusting tendency than individualistic Americans. This pattern of results has been obtained by other researchers. For example, in the World Values Survey, Inglehart, Basanez, and Moreno (1998) found participants from Asian countries such as China, Japan and South Korea showed higher level of trusting tendency than those from U.S. (see Buchan et al. 2002 for a detailed review).

As Oyserman, Coon, and Kemmelmeier (2002) have noted, countries differ on many cultural dimensions other than individualism. Because many studies have divided countries into groups based on only one variable (individualism) and assumed that differences in the dependent variable are caused by individualism, researchers actually have no way of knowing whether it is that predictor variable, or perhaps some other cultural variables, that influences the correlation between individualism and trust. As discussed by Camerer (2003), cross-cultural comparisons are interesting but need to address the potential confound such as income differences. Additionally, most of the existing studies have not even measured the construct of individualism/collectivism in their cross-country comparisons. This further compounded the problem in the cross-country comparison. The current research aims to address these concerns.

Four studies are reported to investigate the impact of cultural orientation on consumers' propensity to trust. A cross-country comparison of trust tendency across 59 countries from World Value Surveys (study 1) indicated that an individualism orientation is associated with greater trust tendency than a collectivism orientation. An individual level of survey confirmed this country-level relationship. One additional experiment that manipulated self-construal provided causal evidence on this relationship. In the fourth study, we used investment game to test our hypothesis. We found that the self-construal effect on consumer trust held for the friend not for stranger condition. Divergent operationalization of cultural orientation and measurement of trust indicates this relationship is robust.

REFERENCES

Aaker, Jennifer L. and Angela Y. Lee (2001), "'I' Seek Pleasures and 'We' Avoid Pains: The Role of Self-Regulatory Goals in Information Processing and Persuasion," *Journal of Consumer Research*, 28 (June), 33-49.

Arnett, Jeffrey J. (2002), "The Psychology of Globalization," *American Psychologist*, 57 (10), 774-83.

Bagozzi, Richard P. (1975), "Marketing as Exchange," *Journal of Marketing*, 39 (4), 32-9.

Berg, Joyce, John Dickhaut, and Kevin McCable (1995), "Trust, Reciprocity, and Social History," *Games and Economic Behavior*, 10, 122-142.

Briley, Donnel A., Michael W. Morris, and Itamar Simonson (2000), "Reasons as Carriers of Culture: Dynamic Versus Dispositional Models of Cultural Influence on Decision Making," *Journal of Consumer Research*, 27 (September), 157-178.

Buchan, Nancy R., Rachel T.A. Croson, and Robyn Dawes (2002), "Swift Neighbors and Persistent Strangers: A Cross-Cultural Investigation of Trust and Reciprocity in Social Exchanges," *American Journal of Sociology*, 108 (July), 168-206.

Buchan, Nancy R., and Rachel T.A. Croson (2004), "The Boundaries of Trust: Own and Others' Actions in the US and China," *Journal of Economic Behavior and Organization*, 55, 485-504.

Cadsby, C. Bram, Yasuyo Hamaguchi, Toshiji Kawagoe, Elizabeth Maynes, and Fei Song (2007), "Cross-National gender differences in behavior in a threshold public goods game: Japan versus Canada," *Journal of Economic Psychology*, 28, 242-260.

Colquitt, Jason A., Brent A. Scott, and Jeffery A. Lepine (2007), "Trust, Trustworthiness, and Trust Propensity: A Meta-Analytic Test of their Unique Relationships with Risk Taking and Job Performance," *Journal of Applied Psychology*, 92 (4), 909-927.

Camerer, Colin F., (2003), *Behavioral Game Theory*, Russell Sage Princeton.

Doney, Patricia M., Joseph P. Cannon, and Michael R. Mullen (1998), "Understanding the Influence of National Culture on the Development of Trust," *Academy of Management Review*, 23 (3), 601-620.

Gardner, Wendi L., Shira Gabriel, and Angela Y. Lee (1999), "'I' Value Freedom, But 'We' Value Relationships: Self-Construal Priming Mirrors Cultural Differences in Judgment," *Psychological Science*, 10 (July), 321-26.

Hamilton, Rebecca W. and Gabriel J. Biehal (2005), "Achieving Your Goals or Protecting Their Future? The Effect of Self-View on Goals and Choices," *Journal of Consumer Research*, 32 (September), 277-283.

Hofstede, Geert (2001), *Culture's Consequences: Comparing Values, Behaviors, Institutions, and Organizations Across Nations*, 2nd ed., London: Sage Publications.

______ (2005), "Geert Hofstede's Cultural Dimensions," http://www.geert-hofstede.com/hofstede_dimensions.php.

Hong, Ying-yi, Michael W. Morris, Chi-yue Chiu, and Veronica Benet-Martinez (2000), "Multicultural Minds: A Dynamic Constructivist Approach to Culture and Cognition," *American Psychologist*, 55 (July), 709-20.

Huff, Lanard, and Lane Kelley (2003), "Levels of Organizational Trust in Individualist Versus Collectivist Societies: A Seven-Nation Study," *Organization Science*, 14 (1), 81-90.

Inglehart, Ronald, Miguel Basanez, and Alejandro Moreno (1998), *Human Values and Beliefs: A cross Cultural Sourcebook*. Ann Arbor: University of Michigan Press.

Knack, Stephen, and Philip Keefer (1997), "Does Social Capital Have an Economic Payoff? A Cross-Country Investigation," *The Quarterly Journal of Economics,* 112 (November), 1251-1288.

Markus, Hazel R. and Shinobu Kitayama (1991), "Culture and the Self: Implications for Cognition, Emotion and Motivation," *Psychological Review*, 98 (April), 224-53.

Moorman, Christine, Gerald Zaltman and Rohit Deshpande (1992), "Relationships Between Providers and Users of Market Research: The Dynamics of Trust Within and Between Organizations," *Journal of Marketing Research,* 26 (August), 314-328.

Moorman, Christine, Rohit Deshpande, and Gerald Zaltman (1993), "Factors Affecting Trust in Market Research Relationships," *Journal of Marketing,* 57 (January), 81-101.

Nisbett, Richard E. (2003). *The geography of thought: How asians and westerners think differently… and why.* New York: Free Press.

Oyserman, Daphna, Heather M. Coon, and Markus Kemmelmeier (2002), "Rethinking Individualism and Collectivism: Evaluation of Theoretical Assumptions and Meta-Analyses," *Psychological Bulletin,* 128 (January), 3-72.

Oyserman, Daphna and Spike W. S. Lee (2008), "Does Culture Influence What and How We Think?" *Psychological Bulletin,*134 (March), 311-42.

Parker, Philip M. (1997), *National Cultures of the World: A Statistical Reference*, Westport, CT: Greenwood Press.

Putnam, Robert D. (1993), *Making Democracy Work: Civic Traditions in Modern Italy*. Princeton, N.J.: Princeton University.

Rotter, Julian B. (1980), "Gneralized Extectancies For Interpersonal trust," *American Psychologist*, 1, 1-7.

Rousseau, Denise M., Sim B. Sitkin, Ronald S. Burt, and Colin Camerer (1998), "Not So Different After All: A Cross-Discipline View of Trust," *Academy of Management Review,* 23 (3), 393-404.

Russell Sage Foundation News (2000), "Examining the Role of Trust in Society," 6.

Shankar, Ganesan (1994),"Determinants of Long-Term Orientation in Buyer-Seller Relationships," *Journal of Marketing*, 58 (April), 1-19.

Singelis, Theodore M. (1994), "The Measurement of Independent and Interdependent Self-Construals," *Personality and Social Psychology Bulletin*, 20 (October), 580-591.

Sirdeshmukh, Deepak, Jagdip Singh, and Barry Sabol (2002), "Consumer Trust, Value, and Loyalty in Relational Exchanges," *Journal of Marketing*, 66 (January), 15-37.

Sobel, M. E. (1982), "Asymptotic Intervals for Indirect Effects in Structural Equations Models," In S. Leinhart (Ed.), *Sociological Methodology*, 290-312. San Francisco: Jossey-Bass.

Trafimow, David, Triandis, Harry C., & Goto, Sharon G. (1991), "Some Tests of the Distinction between the Private Self and the Collective Self," *Journal of Personality and Social Psychology,* 60, 649-655.

White, Tiffany Barnett (2005), "Consumer Trust and Advice Acceptance: The Moderating Roles of Benevolence, Expertise, and Negative Emotions," *Journal of Consumer Psychology,* 15 (2), 141-148.

World Values Study Group (1994), *World Values Survey, 1981-1984 and 1990-1993*, Inter-University Consortium for Political and Social Research (ICPSR) version (computer file), Ann Arbor: Institute for Social Research, University of Michigan.

Yamagishi, Toshio, and Midori Yamagishi (1994), "Trust and Commitment in the United States and Japan," *Motivation and Emotion,* 18 (2), 129-166.

Zak, Paul J., and Stephen Knack, "Trust and Growth," *The Economic Journal*, 111 (April), 295-321.

Social Inertia: Ignoring my Benefits for the Community

Dominic Thomas, Monash University, Australia
Adam Finn, University of Alberta, Canada

EXTENDED ABSTRACT

Social change drives social marketing practice (Andreasen, 2002). Whether a campaign discourages smoking or promotes vaccination against the HPV virus, the marketer's goal is to discern societal perceptions of desirable behavior and then persuade consumers to act in certain ways. However, the consumer may experience *social inertia*—the tendency to maintain current patterns of behavior—possibly resulting from the perception of community consensus regarding that product or service. In certain contexts, the consumer's perception of community attitudes may strongly influence the evaluation and subsequent acceptance or rejection of a product or service. To date, no research has examined how an individual's perception of the community's tendency to sustain current patterns of behavior in relation to particular products or services affects evaluation of the product or service in question. Such research is necessary if we are to expand our understanding of social exchange (Blau, 1964).

The existing literature focuses primarily on acceptance of a good or service as influenced by the physical presence of the group. A two-fold rationale supports the need for research directed at acceptance as influenced by the imagined or implied presence of the community. First, when people experience conflict with their social group, they are as likely to comply with the group's attitudes and practices as to act upon their own felt needs and desires. Second, when individuals feel that they are functioning as representatives of a community, their perception of the community's general acceptance and continued use of the product and/or service will determine their evaluation of it.

We propose that this effect of the group will be greater for individuals with higher collectivistic orientation. A defining attribute for collectivism states that collectivists will give priority to the group goals, and a complementary defining attribute for individualism states that individualists will give priority to the personal goals (Triandis, 1995). We extend the discussion of collectivist and individualist priorities to the evaluation of new products and services. We contend that individual participants who regard themselves as functioning in a representative capacity will be more influenced by perceived community wants than by their own personal wants. The individual's social identity as a member of the group supersedes the sense of unique identity, so that a perception of community consensus becomes salient. Given their importance in shaping individual choice, perceived community desires are quite likely to become deeply ingrained in the individual psyche, making the individual subject to them not only when the group is physically present but also when it is absent.

Using two experimental studies, we demonstrate that consumers with higher collectivistic orientation are more likely to be influenced by the salience of their social identity so as to lower their willingness to pay for new electronic services when they perceive their community wants to continue with the existing services. We demonstrate the underlying role of the dynamic nature of self in explaining this effect. Unlike individualist consumers, collectivist consumers are influenced when social identity is made salient, and lower their willingness to pay for new electronic services if they perceive that their community prefers the existing service. In addition, this effect is dominant in case of social goods in comparison to private goods.

Our research makes three important contributions to the theoretical literature. First, this study enlarges the literature on the dynamic nature of self. Self-categorization theory (Oakes, Haslam & Turner 1994) proposes that the salience of social identity is context-dependent. We provide evidence to support our prediction: when the context makes social identity salient, the SCT fails to hold true for people low on collectivism, although it does hold true for people high on collectivism. Second, we demonstrate the influence of an individual's perception of the community's reluctance to accept a product on his/her own evaluation of a new service, that is, the concept of social inertia. Social inertia occurs even without the direct, physical presence of community members. Finally, we also show the influence of the salience of social identity on the evaluation of new services. This finding is relevant to the literature on valuation of public goods. In this stream of literature, researchers have the tough task of associating a monetary value to public goods. Public policy makers, environmentalists, and others use methods such as contingent valuation and choice experiment to associate a monetary value with a particular public good. Our research could prompt questions concerning their valuation process. Researchers generally describe a public good (either real or hypothetical) and then ask respondents to value these services based on the description. Our paper raises the question of how the particular ways in which these descriptions are construed might influence the participants' responses. It becomes important whether these descriptions have been stated so as to make personal identity salient or social identity salient, or to leave the situation neutral.

REFERENCES

Andreasen, Alan R. (2002), "Marketing Social Marketing in the Social Change Marketplace," *Journal of Public Policy & Marketing*, 21(Spring), 3-13.

Blau, M. Peter (1964), *Exchange and Power in Social Life*, New York: John Wiley.

Oakes, Penelope J., S. Alexander Haslam, & John C. Turner (1994), *Stereotyping and social reality*, Oxford: Blackwell.

Triandis, Harry C. (1995), *Individualism and Collectivism, New Directions in Social Pshycology,* Richard E Nisbett eds., Boulder: West View Press.

Forewarned is Forearmed: Conserving Self-Control Strength to Resist Social Influence

Loes Janssen, Tilburg University, The Netherlands
Bob M. Fennis, Utrecht University, The Netherlands
Ad Th. H. Pruyn, University of Twente, The Netherlands

EXTENDED ABSTRACT

As consumers, it is often difficult to resist (unsolicited) influence attempts of advertisers, fundraisers, and other compliance professionals. As recent research has shown, resisting persuasion is frequently a costly process involving active self-regulation. Resisting an influence attempt consumes self-regulatory resources, with the inevitable consequence that when these resources are low, one's attempts at resistance are more likely to fail (Burkley 2008; Fennis, Janssen, and Vohs 2009; Janssen et al. 2008; Wheeler, Briñol, and Hermann 2007). Hence, resisting (unwanted) influence is more successful when self-regulatory resources are high rather than low, but the present research demonstrates that all is not lost for consumers in a state of self-regulatory resource depletion.

According to the limited-resource model of self-control (for a review, Baumeister, Vohs, and Tice 2007) any act of deliberate and regulated responding by the self draws on a limited intrapsychic resource which, akin to strength or energy, becomes depleted with use. Recently, research started to test the notion that resisting persuasion is an activity which also draws on this resource. Indeed, a state of self-regulatory resource depletion weakens resistance to temptations and (unwanted) influence attempts (Baumeister 2002; Burkley 2008; Vohs and Faber 2007; Wheeler et al. 2007). More specifically, Fennis et al. (2009) and Janssen et al. (2008) forwarded resource depletion as an important underlying factor mediating the effectiveness of sequential request social influence techniques, such as a foot-in-the-door (Freedman and Fraser 1966). They showed that actively responding to the initial request of such a technique depleted self-control resources, resulting in increased compliance with a subsequent (charitable) target request, such as freely donating time, effort or money. Importantly, depleted participants were not susceptible to influence by default, but rather because they relied more on compliance-promoting heuristics that were present in the persuasion context, such as authority, reciprocity, or likeability (cf. Cialdini's [1993] principles of influence).

In sum, and in line with dual-process models of persuasion (Petty and Wegener 1999), a state of self-regulatory resource depletion appears to reduce systematic or central-route processing, and enhances the weight on heuristic processing in consumer judgment and decision making. A key means to encourage more systematic processing could be to increase consumers' awareness of an upcoming influence attempt in advance. Multiple studies have suggested that forewarning people of an upcoming persuasive communication motivates them to counterargue the message in order to reassert their attitudinal freedom, and thereby inhibit subsequent persuasion (see Wood and Quinn 2003 for a review).

But what if the motivation to counterargue is present, but the ability to engage in counterargumentation is lacking because of previous depletion of regulatory resources? We argue that in these conditions, forewarning motivates people to conserve their remaining resources and mobilize them in the service of this counterargumentation. This presupposes that a depleted state does not reflect a complete exhaustion of resources but merely a temporary deficit, a notion that was recently supported by Muraven, Shmueli, and Burkley (2006). They suggested that individuals are (at either a conscious or an unconscious level) motivated and able to conserve their current regulatory energy when the benefits of using the resource in the future apparently outweigh the benefits of using it right now. We expect that forewarning consumers of an upcoming influence attempt will motivate them to conserve self-control strength in the service of resisting the impending influence attempt. We expect this especially to be the case when there is a clear rationale for doing so, that is when they previously suffered a loss of self-control resources.

A first experiment tested whether forewarning increases resistance to persuasion among depleted individuals, using a 2 (self-regulatory resource depletion condition: depletion vs. no depletion) x 2 (forewarning: forewarning of an influence attempt vs. no forewarning) between-subjects design. Resource depletion was induced with a self-control task adopted from Muraven et al. (2006). Participants retyped a paragraph as quickly as they could, yet participants in the resource depletion condition were instructed to retype the paragraph without using the letter "e" or the space bar. Next, half the participants were forewarned about an upcoming encounter with a representative of the 'Campus Clean' student project, who was actively looking for volunteers to clean-up the lecture halls of the campus buildings. After performing a filler task, all participants were asked to indicate how much time they would be willing to volunteer for 'Campus Clean'. Results indeed show that when initially depleted, forewarned participants complied far less with the request (they were willing to volunteer less time) to clean-up their lecture halls as compared to their not forewarned counterparts, and resisted as much as non-depleted participants.

A second study was performed to uncover the assumed underlying psychological process: is it indeed a matter of conserving self-control strength that drives this effect? To test this notion, we included a validated measure of self-control performance after the depletion and forewarning manipulations, before compliance was measured. For most part, the design and procedure parallel that of study 1. As expected, results show that a forewarning of an impending influence attempt motivates depleted people to conserve their resources; they performed worse than participants in any other condition on the intermediate measure of self-control performance. Conserving resources appeared to be beneficial: as in study 1, when subsequently confronted with a request, initially depleted participants resisted as much as non-depleted participants.

Although the forewarning itself may or may not accompany an influence attempt in commercial settings, advanced *awareness* of the upcoming persuasion attempt may well be a default mode for consumers when they enter marketing spheres, such as shopping malls, or commercial websites. Indeed, work on the persuasion knowledge model (Friestad and Wright 1994) supports the notion that consumers are typically prone to infer the (self-serving) motives of marketers and advertisers, and this knowledge could function as a source of self-generated forewarnings. Hence, as consumers, we should be comforted by the present results which imply that we are still proficient in defending ourselves despite a general increase in susceptibility to influence. Even in these instances we will not always end up with products and services that we do not want or need.

REFERENCES

Baumeister, Roy F. (2002), "Yielding to Temptation: Self-Control Failure, Impulsive Purchasing, and Consumer Behaviour," *Journal of Consumer Research*, 28 (March), 670-76.

Baumeister, Roy F., Kathleen D. Vohs, and Dianne M. Tice (2007), "The Strength Model of Self-Control," *Current Directions in Psychological Science*, 16 (December), 351-55.

Burkley, Edward (2008), "The Role of Self-Control in Resistance to Persuasion," *Personality and Social Psychology Bulletin*, 34 (March), 419-31.

Cialdini, Robert B. (1993), *Influence: Science and Practice* (3rd ed.). New York, NY: Harper Collins.

Fennis, Bob M., Loes Janssen, and Kathleen D. Vohs (2009), "Acts of Benevolence: A Limited-Resource Account of Compliance with Charitable Requests," *Journal of Consumer Research*, 35 (April), 906-24.

Freedman, Jonathan L. and Scott C. Fraser (1966), "Compliance without Pressure: The Foot-in-the-Door Technique," *Journal of Personality and Social Psychology*, 4 (August), 195-202.

Friestad, Marian and Peter Wright (1994), "The Persuasion Knowledge Model: How People Cope with Persuasion Attempts," *Journal of Consumer Research*, 21 (June), 1-31.

Janssen, Loes, Bob M. Fennis, Ad Th. H. Pruyn, and Kathleen D. Vohs (2008), "The Path of Least Resistance: Regulatory Resource Depletion and the Effectiveness of Social Influence Techniques," *Journal of Business Research*, 61 (October), 1041-45.

Muraven, Mark, Dikla Shmueli, and Edward Burkley (2006), "Conserving Self-Control Strength," *Journal of Personality and Social Psychology*, 91 (September), 524-37.

Petty, Richard E. and Duane T. Wegener (1999), "The Elaboration Likelihood Model: Current Status and Controversies," in *Dual-Process Theories in Social Psychology*, ed. Shelly Chaiken, Yaacov Trope, New York, NY: Guilford, 37-72.

Vohs, Kathleen D. and Ronald J. Faber (2007), "Spent Resources: Self-Regulatory Resource Availability Affects Impulse Buying," *Journal of Consumer Research*, 33 (March), 537-47.

Wheeler, S. Christian, Pablo Briñol, and Anthony D. Hermann (2007), "Resistance to Persuasion as Self-Regulation: Ego-Depletion and Its Effects on Attitude Change Processes," *Journal of Experimental Social Psychology*, 43 (January), 150-56.

Wood, Wendy and Jeffrey M. Quinn (2003), "Forewarned and Forearmed? Two Meta-Analytic Syntheses of Forewarnings of Influence Appeals," *Psychological Bulletin*, 129 (January), 119-38.

Cognitive Structure Complexity in Social Cognition and Its Effect on Interpersonal Preference Prediction

Yu Hu, Salem State College, USA

EXTENDED ABSTRACT

Consumers frequently purchase products or services that are intended to be consumed by their social partners. Decisions like buying birthday gifts or Christmas presents often involve predictions of other people's preferences, a task that most consumers are not very good at, as suggested by academic researchers (e.g., Davis, Hoch, and Ragsdale 1986; Lerouge and Warlop 2006). What makes it so difficult for us to correctly predict our partners' preferences? Past research has identified important antecedents (e.g., Kenny and Acitelli 2001; Swann and Gill 1997) but paid little attention to the cognitive mechanisms that could explain the effects of social relation on judgment and decision-making.

The present paper intends to close this empirical gap: borrowing the social cognitive view of the seminal Construal Level Theory (CLT, Trope and Liberman 2003), I propose that a mediating role played social relations is that it affects the cognitive structures that people use to process social information. Specifically, as I contend, the complexity level of cognitive structures that individuals employ to process and store their partners' information, such as product preferences, is a function of the social distances between them and their partners: people are more likely to use an complex, detailed category structure, as manifested as of greater number and/or narrower breadth of categories, to process information that pertains to their close social partners (e.g., spouses or best friends); whereas people are more likely to use a simple, abstract category structure, as manifested as of fewer number and/or wider breath of categories, to process information that pertains to distant social partners (e.g., co-workers or casual acquaintances). Furthermore, a diluting effect of this structure complexity in close relation is that it might lead people to spend unnecessary efforts on and assign unnecessary weights to evaluatively non-diagnostic, secondary (vs. primary) information, which could affect people's memory and subsequent judgments of their partners.

Two experiments were conducted to test these propositions. Study 1 examined the category structures used to process information related to other people. Participants were first primed with a target person of different social relationship (best friend vs. stranger) and then acted on behalf of that person to sort objects into groups (i.e., categories). As predicted, greater number of groups and smaller group size were used to categorize objects that were allegedly to be used by their best friends (vs. strangers). Study 2 examined how category structure affects information processing and its evaluative consequences. After the relationship priming used in Study 1, participants were given the opportunity to request job information that might assist them to better predict the target person's job preference. Both evaluatively diagnostic (i.e., primary attributes) and non-diagnostic (i.e., secondary attributes) job information were available to be requested. As expected, participants requested more non-diagnostic job information for best friends than for strangers, whereas no difference was found in the amount of diagnostic information requested. Two days later, the same participants reviewed a similar job position that contained positive secondary attributes but ambiguous primary attributes. They were instructed either to predict the target person's preference for the job or express their own attitudes toward the job. Results showed that while participants' own judgment of the job did not differ between the two experimental groups, those in the best friend group gave significantly higher preference ratings to the job when judging on behalf of the target person than for their own. This result not only provided direct evidence of the effect of categorization on the delayed prediction accuracy of other people's preference, it also interestingly revealed individuals' strategic, selective use of category knowledge in forming preferences for the self and for others.

To conclude, this paper examined the effect of social relation on people's processing of information pertaining to their partners and the subsequent memory-based judgment about their partners. Past research has already shown that non-diagnostic, secondary information could impair prediction accuracy in close relations (e.g., Kenny and Acitelli 2001). The current study demonstrated the potential cause of the accumulation of secondary information: individuals tend to use more complex cognitive structures to process their partners' information as the relationship becomes closer and the expanded category structure not only enables the accumulation of less-important information, it also consequently affects how individuals search, categorize, and remember that information, and how they use the information to make subsequent decisions or judgments about their partners.

From a managerial perspective and for future research, notice that this paper mainly focuses on the negative effects of category structure on judgments and evaluations in close relationship. However, perhaps a more important role of the expanded category structures is to assist individuals to accommodate complex social information generated from long, intimate interactions with their close relationship partners. The resultant greater number of, and narrower breadth of categories used by people to classify partner-related information might affect the formation of a consideration set when making a surrogate purchase and it might also give marketers a chance to fine-tune their segmentation strategies when there is a product offering targeted at consumers' gift-buying needs. A great deal of research is needed in this area.

REFERENCE

Alba, Joseph W. and J. Wesley Hutchinson (2000), "Knowledge Calibration: What Consumers Know and What They Think They Know," *Journal of Consumer Research*, 27 (2), 123–56.

Davis, Harry L., Stephen J. Hoch, and E. K. Easton Ragsdale (1986), "An Anchoring and Adjustment Model of Spousal Predictions," *Journal of Consumer Research*, 13 (1), 25-37.

Fitzsimons, Gráinne M. and John A. Bargh (2003), "Thinking of You: Nonconscious Pursuit of Interpersonal Goals Associated with Relationship Partners", *Journal of Personality and Social Psychology*, 84 (January), 148-63.

Kenny, David A. and Linda K. Acitelli (2001), "Accuracy and Bias in the Perception of the Partner in a Close Relationship," *Journal of Personality and Social Psychology*, 80 (3), 439-48.

Kim, Kyeongheui, Meng Zhang, and Xiuping Li (2008), "Effects of Temporal and Social Distance on Consumer Evaluations," *Journal of Consumer Research*, 35 (4), 709-713.

Liberman, Nira, Michael D. Sagristano, and Yaacov Trope (2002), "The Effect of Temporal Distance on Level of Mental Construal," *Journal of Experimental Social Psychology*, 38 (6), 523-534.

Liberman, Nira, Yaacov Trope, and Elena Stephan (2007), "Psychological Distance," in *Social Psychology: Handbook of Basic Principles*, Vol. 2, ed. Arie W. Kruglanski and E. Tory Higgins, New York: Guilford, 353–83.

Lerouge, Davy and Luk Warlop (2006), "Why It Is So Hard to Predict Our Partner's Product Preferences: The Effect of Target Familiarity on Prediction Accuracy," *Journal of Consumer Research*, 33 (3), 393-402.

Liviatana, Ido, Yaacov Trope, and Nira Liberman (2008), "Interpersonal Similarity as a Social Distance Dimension: Implications for Perception of Others' Actions," *Journal of Experimental Social Psychology*, 44 (5), 1256-1269.

Pronin, Emily; Justin Kruger, Kenneth Savtisky, and Lee Ross (2001), "You Don't Know Me, But I Know You: The Illusion of Asymmetric Insight," *Journal of Personality and Social Psychology*, 81 (4), 639-656.

Smith, Pamela K. and Yaacov Trope (2006), "You Focus on the Forest When You're in Charge of the Trees: Power Priming and Abstract Information Processing," *Journal of Personality and Social Psychology*, 90 (April), 578-96.

Trope, Yaacov and Nira Liberman (2003), "Temporal Construal," *Psychological Review*, 110 (July), 403-21.

Trope, Yaacov, Nira Liberman, and Cheryl Wakslak (2007), "Construal Levels and Psychological Distance: Effects on Representation, Prediction, Evaluation, and Behavior," *Journal of Consumer Psychology*, 17 (2), 83–95.

Swann, William B. and Michael J. Gill (1997), "Confidence and Accuracy in Person Perception: Do We Know What We Think We Know about Our Relationship Partners?" *Journal of Personality and Social Psychology*, 73 (4), 747–57.

Wyer, Robert S. and Thomas K. Srull (1986), "Human Cognition in Its Social Context," *Psychological Review*, 93, 322-59.

Motivated Valuation: A Motivational Perspective on the Disparity between Willingness-to-Accepted and Willingness-to-Pay

Francine Espinoza, ESMT Berlin, Germany
Joydeep Srivastava, University of Maryland, USA

EXTENDED ABSTRACT

The disparity between willingness-to-accepted (WTA) and willingness-to-pay (WTP) refers to the finding that individuals tend to ask for a higher price when they are giving up an item as opposed to when they are acquiring it (Thaler 1980). Descriptive economic explanations derived from prospect theory (Kahneman and Tversky 1979) state that this disparity rests largely on notions of reference dependence and loss aversion. Thereby sellers, when they become endowed with an object, experience loss aversion, and because losses loom larger than gains, the discrepancy in valuation of the object emerges (Kahneman, Knetsch, and Thaler 1990). Loss aversion is perhaps the most accepted explanation for the effect (Brenner et al. 2007). Current interpretations of loss aversion in the WTA/WTP disparity build on the notion that it is sellers' concern with losing an object and buyers' concern with losing their money that are equally responsible for the effect (Zhang and Fishbach 2005). Despite the enlightening conceptualizations (e.g., Carmon and Ariely 2000, Nayakankuppam and Mishra 2005), it appears that explanations solely based on loss aversion fail to capture some aspects of the valuation process (Brenner et al. 2007; Horowitz and McConnell 2003; Novemsky and Kahneman 2005; Sayman and Öncüler 2005), perhaps because of its primary focus on what is being foregone or given up while what one is getting is relatively ignored.

This research proposes an alternative explanation for the disparity between WTA and WTP. We argue that a seller and a buyer differ primarily in their intrinsic motivational orientation, and the different motivations underlying the valuation process lead to the disparity between WTA and WTP. Our basic premise is that the role of a seller and a buyer activates different intrinsic motivations predisposing individuals in each role to behave accordingly (Buss 1995). Giving up a good is an intrinsic part of being a seller as is acquiring a good an intrinsic part of being a buyer. Given that in most transactions, the good being exchanged is identical and constant for both parties, the motivational orientation of both the seller and the buyer is likely to center on the mutable aspects of the transaction (e.g., monetary valuation of the non-mutable good). Because of the different motivational orientations, sellers and buyers differ in terms of the aspects of the transaction that they primarily attend to in the valuation process. Specifically, when individuals adopt the role of a seller or a buyer, the intrinsic motivations and cognitions associated with each role are activated (Ferguson, Hassin, and Bargh 2008) such that sellers are primarily concerned with what they are getting and are motivated to maximize that, and buyers are primarily concerned with they are giving up and are motivated to minimize that. The conflicting motivational orientation of the seller and the buyer leads to the disparity between WTA and WTP. Note that loss aversion would account only for buyers' motivation of minimizing what they are giving up, but not sellers' motivation of maximizing what they are getting.

We adopt a motivation-as-cognition approach (e.g., Kruglanski et al. 2002), which treats motivation as a dynamic construct and allows us to investigate goal pursuit of buyers and sellers in five studies. Studies 1-3 test the prediction that the role of a seller is associated with the goal of maximizing what they are getting whereas the role of a buyer is associated with the goal of minimizing what they are giving up. Study 1 suggests that sellers approach transactions with a "make money" mindset and buyers approach transactions with a "save money" mindset. Study 2 examines participants' reaction time to words related to the proposed goals of sellers and buyers and show that sellers respond faster to words related to maximization (e.g., maximize, high, increase) and buyers respond faster to words related to minimization (e.g., minimize, low, reduce). Study 3 shows that priming the goal of selling or buying to neutral traders produces the same disparity between WTA and WTP. Studies 4 and 5 investigate conditions under which goal pursuit of buyers and sellers might change and, consequently, buyers may be willing to pay more for a product, and sellers may be willing to accept less for the same product. We manipulate two factors that are expected to moderate goal pursuit in a systematic way, namely the pursuit of multiple goals (Shah, Friedman, Kruglanski 2002; Shah and Kruglanski 2008) and goal fluency (Avnet and Higgins 2006; Labroo and Lee 2006). Study 4 primes the alternative goals of competition or cooperation and shows that when participants are primed with a competition goal, the price disparity effect is observed, and when participants are primed with a cooperation goal, buyers are willing to pay more and sellers are willing to accept less. Study 5 shows that goal fluency moderates the effect such that the disparity between WTA and WTP was eliminated in the low goal fluency (versus the high goal fluency) condition.

Taken together, the five studies build on goal theory to provide support for the motivated valuation explanation. The basic premise is that sellers' primary motivation is to maximize what they are getting whereas buyers' primary motivation is to minimize what they are foregoing or giving up. Understanding of the motivations that underlie the valuation process provides deeper insights into the factors that affect the valuation process and the conditions under which the WTA-WTP disparity exists.

REFERENCES

Avnet, Tamar and E. Tory Higgins (2006), "How Regulatory Fit Affects Value in Consumer Choices and Opinions," *Journal of Marketing Research*, 43 (1), 1-10.

Brenner, Lyle, Yuval Rottenstreich, Sanjay Sood, and Baler Bilgin (2007), "On the Psychology of Loss Aversion: Possession, Valence, and Reversals of the Endowment Effect," *Journal of Consumer Research*, 34 (3), 369-76.

Buss, David M. (1995), "Evolutionary Psychology: A New Paradigm for Psychological Science," *Psychological Inquiry*, 6 (1), 1-30.

Carmon, Ziv and Dan Ariely (2000), "Focusing on the Forgone: How Value Can Appear So Different to Buyers and Sellers," *Journal of Consumer Research*, 27 (3), 360-70.

Ferguson, Melissa, Ran Hassin, and John Bargh (2008), "Implicit Motivation: Past, Present, and Future," in *Handbook of Motivation Science*, ed. Shah, James and Wendi Gardner, New York: Guilford, 150-68.

Horowitz, John and Kenneth E. McConnell (2003), "Willingness to Accept, Willingness to Pay, and the Income Effect," *Journal of Economic Behavior and Organization*, 51 (4), 537-46.

Kahneman, Daniel and Amos Tversky (1979), "Prospect Theory: An Analysis of Decision Under Risk," *Econometrica*, 47 (2), 263-91.

Kahneman, Daniel, Jack Knetsch, and Richard H. Thaler (1990), "Experimental Tests of the Endowment Effect and the Coase Theorem," *Journal of Political Economy*, 98 (6), 1325-48.

Kruglanski, Arie, James Shah, Ayelet Fishbach, Ron Friedman, Woo Young Chun, and David Sleeth-Keppler (2002), "A Theory of Goal-Systems," in *Advances in Experimental Social Psychology*, Vol. 34, ed. Mark P. Zanna, San Diego, CA: Academic Press, 331-78.

Labroo, Aparna and Angela Lee (2006), "Between Two Brands: A Goal Fluency Account of Brand Evaluation," *Journal of Marketing Research*, 43 (3), 374-85.

Nayakankuppam, Dhananjay and Himanshu Mishra (2005.), "The Endowment Effect: Rose-Tinted and Dark-Tinted Glasses," *Journal of Consumer Research*, 32 (3), 390-95.

Novemsky, Nathan and Daniel Kahneman (2005), "The Boundaries of Loss Aversion," *Journal of Marketing Research*, 42 (2), 119-28.

Sayman, Serdar and Ayse Öncüler (2005), "Effects of Study Design Characteristics on the WTA-WTP Disparity: A Meta Analytical Framework," *Journal of Economic Psychology*, 26 (2), 289-312.

Shah, James, Ron Friedman, and Arie Kruglanski (2002), "Forgetting All Else: On the Antecedents and Consequences of Goal Shielding," *Journal of Personality and Social Psychology*, 83 (6), 1261-80.

Shah, James and Arie Kruglanski (2008), "Structural Dynamics: The Challenge of Change in Goal Systems," in *Handbook of Motivation Science*, ed. Shah, James and Wendi Gardner, New York: Guilford, 434-47.

Thaler, Richard H. (1980), "Toward a Positive Theory of Consumer Choice," *Journal of Economic Behaviour and Organization*, 1(1), 39-60.

Zhang, Ying and Ayelet Fishbach (2005), "The Role of Anticipated Emotions in the Endowment Effect," *Journal of Consumer Psychology*, 15 (4), 316-324.

Scope Neglect in Spending Time

Ritesh Saini, University of Texas at Arlington, USA

EXTENDED ABSTRACT

People are quite rationally willing to pay more money for obtaining more quantities of a desirable good or outcome. However this relationship is not always linear and usually the monetary willingness to pay exhibits a concave relationship with increasing quantity. In this paper we explore what kind of a relationship exists when people have to pay in time, instead of money, for increasing quantities of a desirable outcome.

Scope (or magnitude) neglect is the tendency to ignore higher utility derived by higher amounts of a desired good or outcome. An expected value-maximizing individual should display a linear relationship between utility and an economically desirable resource. However descriptive models have proposed that for virtually any resource, we have marginally diminishing utility. Psychology and economics have explained this phenomenon using the concepts of satiation, diminishing sensitivity, and affect. While these factors have been known to enhance scope neglect, we investigate whether the currency of payment itself can influence this effect. In most studies showing scope neglect, the willingness-to-pay has always been elicited using monetary currency. What will happen to the evinced nonlinear relationship between stimulus scope and willingness to pay when the method of payment is something other than money? This is the primary research question of our paper.

People often spend time, instead of money, to acquire desirable outcomes. The default economic assumption is that spending time is similar to spending money (Becker 1965, Graham 1981) and therefore both are mutually tradable using a linear economic exchange rate. However, recent research has demonstrated several ways in which consumer's monetary decisions are different from their temporal spending decisions (Okada and Hoch 2004, Leclerc, Schmitt, and Dube 1995, Soman 2001, Zauberman and Lynch 2005, Saini and Monga 2008). Specifically, Saini & Monga (2008) have demonstrated greater susceptibility to heuristic people when spend time. This is primarily because time is more ambiguous, and less fungible, than money and therefore temporal (vs. monetary) information is more difficult to process. In such situations, instead of continuing efforts to utilize this relevant information, people make a qualitative shift to a different form of decision making in which they rely on heuristics (Payne, Bettman, and Johnson 1993). From engaging in more reasoned, deliberative processing, people regress to a more heuristic-based processing mode where they make judgments based on simple, accessible cues, oftentimes ignoring other relevant information. Previously Hsee and Rottenstreich (2004) have explained the concavity of the value function using very similar information processing mechanisms. Simply put, we propose that temporal decisions cause greater heuristic-use thereby leading to diminished scope sensitivity.

In the first experiment, we demonstrate that consumers' willingness to pay is more sensitive to changes in the magnitude of the outcome when they are paying in money than in time. In a between-subjects setting consumers have to pay in time/money for 2/10 music CDs. In both time and money conditions, participants were willing to pay more for 10 CDs (vs. 2 CDs). However the difference was much larger in the case of money ($49.7 vs. $ 14.5, i.e. 242% increase), than time (55.2 min. vs. 48.8 min., i.e. 13% increase). In support of our underlying psychological mechanism, we also demonstrate that consumers found temporal decisions to be more difficult than monetary spending decisions. In the second experiment, we again test this time-money difference in both between- and within-subject settings and find that scope neglect breaks down for both time and money in the latter settings. In the third experiment, we extend this phenomenon to the domain of qualitatively different outcomes and demonstrate that when paying in time, consumers ignore not just the (quantitative) magnitude of the stimulus but also the qualitative variation between one stimulus versus another. Instead of changing the number of items at stake, we had two qualitatively different items as stimuli–an indoor grill & a digital tire gauge. In both time and money conditions, participants were willing to pay more for the indoor grill. However the difference was much larger in the case of money ($48.27 vs. $ 17.42, i.e. 177% increase), than time (28.70 min. vs. 19.56 min., i.e. 47% increase). In the fourth experiment we find that, when asked to put a monetary value to an item before deciding how much time to spend to procure it, some of the scope neglect diminishes. The final experiment investigates scope neglect for non-market outcomes, and finds a similar time-money difference, thereby also ruling out any congruency effects. When asked to donate time/money for helping save one/four panda bears, participants were more sensitive to scope when donating in money.

REFERENCES

Ariely, Dan and George Loewenstein (2000), "The importance of duration in ratings of, and choices between, sequences of outcomes," *Journal of Experimental Psychology: General*, 129 (4), 508-523.

Ariely, Dan, George Loewenstein, and Drazen Prelec (2006), "Tom Sawyerand the Construction of Value," *Journal of Economic Behavior and Organization*. (60), 1-10.

Baron, Jonathan, and Joshua Greene (1996), "Determinants of insensitivity to quantity in valuation of public goods: Contribution, warm glow, budget constraints, availability, and prominence," *Journal of Experimental Psychology: Applied*, 2, 107–125.

Becker, Gary S. (1965), "A Theory of the Allocation of Time," *Economic Journal*, 75 (September), 493-517.

Bernoulli, Daniel (1738/1954), "Exposition of a new theory on the measurement of risk," *Econometrica* Vol 22: 23–36 (Translation of Bernoulli D 1738 Specimen theoriae novae de mensura sortis;Papers Imp. Acad. Sci. St. Petersburg), (5): 175–192).

Camerer, Colin, Linda Babcock, George Loewenstein, and Richard Thaler (1997), "Labor Supply of New York City Cab Drivers: One Day at a Time," *Quarterly Journal of Economics*, May, 1997, 109-126.

Chatterjee, Subimal and Timothy B. Heath (1996), "Conflict and Loss Aversion in Multi-attribute Choice: The Effects of Trade-Off Size and Reference Dependence on Decision Difficulty," *Organizational Behavior and Human Decision Processes*, 67(2), 144–55.

Csikszentmihalyi, Mihaly (1993), *The Evolving Self–A Psychology for the Third Millennium*, Harper Perennial.

DeVoe, Sanford E. and Jeffrey Pfeffer (2007), "When Time is Money: The Effect of Hourly Payment on the Evaluation of Time," *Organizational Behavior and Human Decision Processes*, 104 (September), 1-13.

Desvousges, William. H., F. Reed Johnson, Richard W. Dunford, Sara P. Hudson, K. Nicole Wilson, and Kevin J. Boyle (1993), "Measuring resource damages with contingent valuation: Tests of validity and reliability," In J. Hausman (Ed.), *Contingent valuation: A critical assessment* (pp. 91–164). Amsterdam: North-Holland.

Ditto, Peter H., David A. Pizarro, Eden B. Epstein, Jill A. Jacobson, and Tara K. MacDonald (2006), "Motivational myopia: Visceral influences on risk taking behavior," *Journal of Behavioral Decision Making*, 19(2), 99-113.

Dunn, Elizabeth W., Lara B. Aknin, and Michael I. Norton (2008), "Spending money on others promotes happiness," *Science,* 319, 1687-1688.

Elster. Jon and George Loewenstein (1992), "Utility from Memory and Anticipation," in George Loewenstein and J. Elster (Eds.), *Choice over Time*, NY: Russell Sage.

Fetherstonhaugh, David, Paul Slovic, Stephen Johnson, and James Friedrich (1997), "Insensitivity to the value of human life: A study of psychophysical numbing," *Journal of Risk and Uncertainty, 14,* 283-300.

Frederick, Shane, and Baruch Fischhoff (1998), "Scope (in)sensitivity in elicited valuations," *Risk, Decision, and Policy,* 3, 109–123.

Fredrickson Barbara L. and Daniel Kahneman (1993), "Duration Neglect in Retrospective Evaluations of Affective Episodes," *Journal of Personality and Social Psychology*, 65 (1), 45-55.

Graham, Robert J (1981), "The Role of Perception of Time in Consumer Research," *Journal of Consumer Research*, 7 (4), 335-342.

Hsee, Chris K., and Yuval Rottenstreich (2004), "Music, Pandas and Muggers: On the Affective Psychology of Value," *Journal of Experimental Psychology: General*, 133(1), 23-30

Kahneman, Daniel (1986), "Comments," In: Cummings, R.G., Brookshire, D.S., Schulze, W.D. (Eds), *Valuing Environmental Goods: An Assessment of the Contingent Valuation Method*, Rowman and Allanheld, Totowa, NJ.

Kahneman, Daniel, and Shane Frederick (2002), "Representativeness revisited: Attribute substitution in intuitive judgment," In T. Gilovich, D. Griffin, and D. Kahneman (Eds.), *Heuristics of intuitive judgment: Extensions and applications* (pp. 49–81). New York: Cambridge University Press.

Kahneman, Daniel and Amos Tversky (1979), "Prospect Theory: An Analysis of Decision Under Risk," *Econometrica*, 47(March), 263-92.

Kahneman, Daniel, Ilana Ritov, and David Schkade (2000), "Economic preferences or attitude expressions? An analysis of dollar responses to public issues," In D. Kahneman and A. Tversky (Eds.), *Choices, values, and frames* (pp. 642–672). New York: Cambridge University Press.

Kogut, Tehila, and Ilana Ritov (2005), "The ''identified victim'' effect: an identified group, or just a single individual?" *Journal of Behavioral Decision Making*, 18, 157–167.

Leclerc, France, Bernd H. Schmitt, and Laurette Dube (1995), "Waiting Time and Decision Making: Is Time like Money?" *Journal of Consumer Research,* 22 (June), 110-19.

McFadden, Daniel and Gregory K. Leonard (1995), "Issues in the contingent valuation of environmental goods: methodologies for data collection and analysis," In *Contingent valuation: a critical assessment*, ed. J. A. Hausman. Amsterdam: North Holland.

Mogilner, Cassie & Aaker, Jennifer (2009), "The Time Vs. Money Effect: Shifting Product Attitudes through Personal Connection," *Journal of Consumer Research* (forthcoming).

Monga, Ashwani and Saini, Ritesh (2008), "Currency of Search: How Spending Time of Search is Not the Same as Spending Money," *Journal of Retailing* (forthcoming).

Okada, Erica M. and Stephen J. Hoch (2004), "Spending Time versus Spending Money," *Journal of Consumer Research,* 31 (September), 313-23.

Payne, John, James Bettman, and Eric Johnson (1993), *The Adaptive Decision Maker,* New York, NY: Cambridge University Press.

Reed, Americus II, Karl Aquino and Eric Levy (2007), "Moral Identity and Judgments of Charitable Behaviors," *Journal of Marketing,* 71 (January), 178-93.

Saini, Ritesh and Ashwani Monga (2008), "How I Decide Depends on What I Spend: Use of Heuristics is Greater for Time than for Money," *Journal of Consumer Research*, 34 (6), 914-922.

Sloman, Steven A. (1996), "The empirical case for two systems of reasoning," *Psychological Bulletin, 119,* 3–22.

Simonson, Itamar (1989), "Choice Based on Reasons: The Case of Attraction and Compromise Effects," *Journal of Consumer Research,* 16 (September), 158-74.

Small, Deborah A., and George Loewenstein (2003), "Helping the victim or helping a victim: Altruism and identifiability," *Journal of Risk and Uncertainty*, 26(1), 5–16.

Soman, Dilip (1998), "The Illusion of Delayed Incentives: Evaluating Future Effort-Money Transactions," *Journal of Marketing Research,* 35 (November), 427-37.

Soman, Dilip (2001), "The Mental Accounting of Sunk Time Costs: Why Time is not Like Money," *Journal of Behavioral Decision Making,* 14 (July), 169-85.

Thaler, Richard (1980), "Toward a Positive Theory of Consumer Choice," *Journal of Economic Behavior and Organization*, 1 (1), 39-60.

Tukey, John W. (1977), *Exploratory data analysis*, AddisonWesley; Reading (MA).

Tversky, Amos and Daniel Kahneman (1974), "Judgment under Uncertainty: Heuristics and Biases," *Science,* 27, 185 (September), 1124-131.

Tversky, Amos and Daniel Kahneman (1981), "The Framing of Decisions and the Psychology of Choice," *Science* 211: 453-458.

Varey, Carol and Daniel Kahneman (1992), "Experiences Extended Across Time: Evaluations of Moments and Episodes," *Journal of Behavioral Decision Making*, 5, 169-185.

Zauberman, Gal and John G. Lynch, Jr. (2005), "Resource Slack and Propensity to Discount Delayed Investments of Time versus Money," *Journal of Experimental Psychology: General,* 134 (February), 23-37.

A Meta-Analytic Review of Just Below Pricing Effects

Traci Freling, University of Texas at Arlington, USA
Leslie Vincent, University of Kentucky, USA
Robert Schindler, Rutgers University-Camden, USA
David Hardesty, University of Kentucky, USA
Jason Rowe, University of Kentucky, USA

EXTENDED ABSTRACT

Just-below prices–prices that are expressed so their endings fall just below a round number–have been a prominent feature of the retailing landscape for decades (Gabor and Granger 1964; Knauth 1949). However, research on just-below pricing dating back to the 1930s (Bader and Weinland 1932; Ginzberg 1936) offers disparate viewpoints and ambiguous empirical results. While some published studies show just-below pricing can significantly improve sales (Anderson and Simester 2003; Kalyanam and Shively 1998), others demonstrate that such effects are product-specific or situational (Blattberg and Wisniewski 1987; Schindler and Kibarian 1996). Still other researchers report finding *no* just-below pricing-related effects (Dodds and Monroe 1985; Holdershaw 1995). Despite marketplace endorsement of just-below pricing and 70 years of research investigating the efficacy of this tactic, the body of work examining just-below pricing effects seems to yield inconclusive findings.

In addition to the equivocal nature of the empirical research findings regarding just-below pricing, *how* just-below pricing may operate is not well understood. The *association hypothesis* suggests consumers construe meaning from price endings through incidental or low involvement learning (Postman 1964; Hawkins and Hoch 1992), which may lead to: (1) a *low-price image effect*, wherein the consumer comes to associate a just-below price with a low, decreased, or discount price, which generally leads to higher sales for products carrying a just-below price because the consumer is likely to see the product as being a bargain or perceive it as being on sale; or, (2) a *low-quality image effect*, which results from an association of a just-below price with inferior product quality and encourages consumers to regard just-below-priced products less favorably because they are viewed as possessing lower quality. The *underestimation hypothesis* suggests consumers routinely distort their perceptions of just-below prices, mentally transforming them into perceptually lower prices than their actual value and thus interpreting them more favorably than round-number prices (Lambert 1975; Nagle and Holden 1995). This is believed to occur due to: *rounding down* of just-below prices, since rounding up to a whole number requires more cognitive effort (Gabor and Granger 1964; Schindler and Kirby 1997); *left-to-right processing* of pricing information and relative inattention to a price's rightmost digits (which causes consumers to perceive just-below prices as lower than they actually are) (Poltrock and Schwartz 1984; Thomas and Morwitz 2005); or, humans' innately limited *memory capacity* (Schindler and Kibarian 1993; Schindler and Wiman 1989).

Pricing theorists have failed to converge on a unifying theoretical framework that cogently and comprehensively explains just-below pricing effects. Extant explanations are not mutually exclusive (Coulter 2001), and evidence for both the association and underestimation hypotheses has been found across and within research studies (Stiving and Winer 1997).

Methodology

We followed the procedures for conducting a meta-analysis described by Hunter and Schmidt (2004). We identified 25 papers containing 106 independent samples that reported both the Pearson correlation between just-below-ending prices and other constructs and the sample size (Janiszewski, Noel, and Sawyer 2003). The sample size for the meta-analysis across all retained samples was 130,139 observations. The average and median sample sizes were 1228 and 202 observations, respectively.

In addition to investigating six depending variables (i.e., *choice*, *sales*, *recall*, *low-price image*, *low-quality image*, and *value*), we also examined the impact of the following variables identified in the literature that have theoretical justification as potential moderating factors and could be coded from the extant studies and analyzed using a generalized least squares regression (GLS) approach (Geyskens, Steenkamp, and Kumar 1998): *price-ending manipulation* ; *price magnitude* ; *nature of the product* ; *product durability* ; *product realism*; *research design*; *research setting*; and *sample characteristics*.

Major Findings

The results of this meta-analysis suggest that, on average, products bearing a just-below price are associated with (1) more frequent product choice, (2) higher sales levels, (3) less attention to the rightmost digits of prices in recall tasks (and greater accuracy in recalling the leftmost pricing digits), (4) perceptions of a more discounted price, (5) a lower quality image, and (6) more favorable perceptions of value. So, just-below pricing does appear to consumers in a variety of ways.

However, our results indicate that the impact of just-below pricing on choice, sales, underestimation due to inaccurate recall of just-below prices, and low-price image perceptions is contingent upon important price- and product-related contextual variables. We found no significant differences in the size of just-below pricing effects for 5-ending just-below prices versus 9-ending just-below prices on any of the outcome variables. This result suggests that retailers who use just-below pricing should choose prices with *9* instead of *5* as the rightmost digit, and benefit from the extra four cents revenue on each sale. Results relating to price magnitude imply that just-below pricing will be most effective for high-priced products when the objective is to stimulate demand, impair memory of pricing information for more expensive products, or communicate favorable low-price-image perceptions.

We found just-below pricing to be more effective for actual brands in terms of low-price image and recall, suggesting it may be used to communicate a discount or bargain image for well-established brands in the marketplace. Conversely, because consumer choice is more favorably influenced by just-below pricing for unknown or hypothetical brands, it may also be used to induce trial and purchase of new or less dominant brands. Other interesting product related findings relate to the nature of the good and durability of products that have been investigated in just-below pricing research. While just-below pricing is likely to stimulate choice and communicate favorable price image associations for services, just-below pricing appears to favorably impact choice, price image, and recall of pricing information for durable goods.

Finally, this meta-analysis uncovers some discrepancies across empirical efforts and highlights methodological issues relating to research design, setting, and subjects that qualify just-below pricing effects. This indicates a need for programmatic research in this area, that seeks to reproduce results obtained in diverse settings with different methodologies, stimulus products, and pricing manipulations, and a variety of samples.

References

Anderson, Eric T. and Duncan I. Simester (2003), "Effects of $9 Price Endings on Retail Sales: Evidence from Field Experiments," *Quantitative Marketing and Economics*, 1 (March), 93-110.

Assmus, Gert, John U. Farley, and Donald R. Lehmann (1984), "How Advertising Affects Sales: Meta-Analysis of Econometric Results," *Journal of Marketing Research*, 21 (February), 65-74.

Bader, Louis and James D. Weinland (1932), "Do Odd Prices Earn Money?" *Journal of Retailing*, 8 (January), 102-04.

Bettman, James R. and C.Whan Park (1980), "Effects of Prior Knowledge, Experience, and Phase of the Choice Process on Consumer Decision Processes: A Protocol Analysis," *Journal of Consumer Research*, 7 (December), 234-48.

Bizer, George Y. and Robert M. Schindler (2005), "Direct Evidence of Ending-Digit Drop-Off in Price Information Processing," *Psychology & Marketing*, 22 (October), 771-83.

Blattberg, Robert C. and Kenneth J. Wisniewski (1987), "How Retail Price Promotions Work: Empirical Results," Working Paper No. 42, Chicago, IL: Graduate School of Business, University of Chicago.

Brenner, Gabrielle A. and Reuven Brenner (1982), "Memory and Markets, or Why are you Paying $2.99 for a Widget?" *Journal of Business*, 55 (January), 147-58.

Burnkrant, Robert E. and Alan G. Sawyer (1983), "Effects of Involvement and Message Content on Information Processing Intensity," in *Information Processing Research in Advertising*, ed. R. Harris, Hillsdale, NJ: Lawrence Erlbaum, 498-549.

Daily Mail (2000), "Asda Axes the 99p Price Ploy," *London*, May 22, 15.

Dalrymple, Douglas J. and George H. Haines, Jr. (1970), "A Study of the Predictive Ability of Market Period Demand-Supply Relations for a Firm Selling Fashion Products," *Applied Economics*, 1 (January), 277-85.

Dhar, Ravi and Klaus Wertenbroch (2000), "Consumer Choice between Hedonic and Utilitarian Goods," *Journal of Marketing Research*, 37 (February), 60-71.

Dodds, William B. and Kent B. Monroe (1985), "The Effect of Brand and Price Information on Subjective Product Evaluation," in *Advances for Consumer Research*, Vol.12, ed. Elizabeth C. Hirschman and Morris B. Holbrook, Provo, UT: Association for Consumer Research, 85-90.

Dubin, R. (1978), *Theory Building*, New York, NY: Free Press.

Estelami, Hooman (1999), "The Computational Effect of Price Endings in Multi-Dimensional Price Advertising," *Journal of Product & Brand Management*, 8 (3), 244-56.

Friedman, Lawrence (1967), "Psychogical Pricing in the Food Industry," in *Prices: Issues in Theory, Practice, and Public Policy*, ed. Almarin Phillips and Oliver E. Williamson, Philadelphia: University of Pennsylvania Press, 187-201.

Gabor, Andre and Clive W.J. Granger (1964), "Price Sensitivity of the Consumer," *Journal of Advertising Research*, 4 (December), 40-44.

Gendall, Phillip, Judith Holdershaw, and Ron Garland (1997), "The Effect of Odd Pricing on Demand," *European Journal of Marketing*, 31 (11/12), 799-813.

Georgoff, David M. (1972), *Odd-Even Retail Price Endings: Their Effects on Value Determination, Product Perception, and Buying Propensities*, East Lansing, MI: Michigan State University.

Geyskens, Inge, Jan-Benedict E.M. Steenkamp, and Nirmalya Kumar (1998), "Generalizations About Trust in Marketing Channel Relationships Using Meta-Analysis," *International Journal of Research in Marketing*, 15 (3), 223-48.

Ginzberg, Eli (1936), "Customary Prices," *The American Economic Review*, 26 (June), 296.

Hawkins, Scott A. and Stephen J. Hoch (1992), "Low-Involvement Learning: Memory without Evaluation," *Journal of Consumer Research*, 19 (September), 212-25.

Hedges, Larry V. and Ingram Olkin (1985), *Statistical Methods for Meta-Analysis*, Orlando, FL: Academic Press.

Holdershaw, Judith L. (1995), "The Validity of Odd pricing," Unpublished MBS Thesis, Palmerston North: Massey University.

Huffcutt, Allen I. and Winfred Arthur, Jr. (1995), "Development of a New Outlier Statistic for Meta-Analytic Data," *Journal of Applied Psychology*, 80 (2), 327-34.

Hunter, John E. and Frank L. Schmidt (2004), *Methods of Meta-Analysis: Correcting Error and Bias in Research Findings*, Thousand Oaks, CA: Sage Publications.

Huston, John and Nipoli Kamdar (1996), "$9.99: Can 'Just-Below' Pricing Be Reconciled with Rationality," *Eastern Economic Journal*, 22 (Spring), 137-45.

Janiszewski, Chris, Hayden Noel, and Alan G. Sawyer (2003), "A Meta-Analysis of the Spacing Effect in Verbal Learning: Implications for Research on Advertising Repetition and Consumer Memory," *Journal of Consumer Research*, 30 (June), 138-49.

Johnson, Eric J. and J. Edward Russo (1984), "Product Familiarity and Learning New Information," *Journal of Consumer Research*, 11 (June), 324-33.

Kalyanam, Kirthi and Thomas S. Shively (1998), "Estimating Irregular Pricing Effects: A Stochastic Spline Regression Approach," *Journal of Marketing Research*, 35 (February), 16-29.

Knauth, Oswald (1949), "Considerations in Setting Retail Prices," *Journal of Marketing*, 14 (July), 1-12.

Kreul, Lee M. (1982), "Magic Numbers: Psychological Aspects of Menu Pricing," *Cornell Hotel and Restaurant Administration Quarterly*, 23 (August), 70-75.

Lambert, Zarrel V. (1975), "Perceived Prices as Related to Odd and Even Price Endings," *Journal of Retailing*, 51 (Fall), 13-22, 78.

Liang, Jianping and Vinay Kanetkar (2006), "Price Endings: Magic and Math," *Journal of Product and Brand Management*, 15 (6), 377-85.

Nagle, Thomas T. and Reed R. Holden (1995), *The Strategy and Tactics of Pricing: A Guide for Profitable Decision Making*, Englewood Cliffs, NJ: Prentice-Hall.

Naipaul, Sandra A. and H.G. Parsa (2001), "Menu Price Endings that Communicate Value and Quality," *Cornell Hotel and Restaurant Administration Quarterly*, 42 (February), 26-37.

Peterson, Robert A. (2001), "On the Use of College Students in Social Science Research: Insights from a Second-Order Meta-Analysis," *Journal of Consumer Research*, 28 (December), 450-61.

Poltrock, Steven E. and David R. Schwartz (1984), "Comparative Judgements of Multidigit Numbers," *Journal of Experimental Psychology: Learning, Memory, and Cognition*, 10 (January), 32-45.

Postman, Leo (1964), "Short-term Memory and Incidental Learning," Pp 145-201 in *Categories of Human Learning*, Arthur W. Milton (ed). New York, NY: Academic Press.

Rosenberg, M.S., D.C. Adams, and J. Gurevitch (2000), *MetaWin: A Statistical Software for Meta-Analysis*, Sunderland, MA: Sinauer Associates.

Rosenthal, Robert (1979), "The 'File Drawer Problem' and Tolerance for Null Results," *Psychological Bulletin*, 86 (May), 638-41.

Rosenthal, Robert and Ralph L. Rosnow (2008), *Essentials of Behavioral Research: Methods and Data Analysis*, Boston, MA: McGraw Hill.

Rudolph, H.J. (1954), "Pricing for Today's Market," *Printers Ink*, May 28, 22-24.

Schindler, Robert M. (1984), "Consumer Recognition of Increases in Odd and Even Prices," *Advances for Consumer Research*, 11 (1), Thomas C. Kinnear (ed). Provo, UT: Association for Consumer Research, 459-62.

Schindler, Robert M. (2006), "The 99 Price Ending as a Signal of a Low-Price Appeal," *Journal of Retailing*, 82 (March), 71-77.

Schindler, Robert M. and Thomas Kibarian (1993), "Testing for Perceptual Underestimation of 9-Ending Prices," *Advances in Consumer Research*, 20 (1), Provo, UT: Association for Consumer Research, 580-85.

Schindler, Robert M. and Thomas M. Kibarian (1996), "Increased Consumer Sales Response Though Use of 99-Ending Prices," *Journal of Retailing*, 72 (Summer), 187-99.

Schindler, Robert M. and Thomas M. Kibarian (2001), "Image Communicated by the Use of 99 Endings in Advertised Prices," *Journal of Advertising*, 30 (Winter), 95-99.

Schindler, Robert M. and Patrick N. Kirby (1997), "Patterns of Rightmost Digits Used in Advertised Prices: Implications for Nine-Ending Effects," *Journal of Consumer Research*, 24 (September), 192-201.

Schindler, Robert M. and Lori S. Warren (1988), "Effect of Odd Pricing on Choice of Items from a Menu," in *Advances in Consumer Research*, 15, ed. Michael J. Houston, Provo, UT: Association for Consumer Research, 348-53.

Schindler, Robert M. and Alan R. Wiman (1989), "Effect of Odd Pricing on Price Recall," *Journal of Business Research*, 19 (November), 165-77.

Stiving, Mark and Russell S. Winer (1997), "An Empirical Analysis of Price Endings with Scanner Data," *Journal of Consumer Research*, 24 (June), 57-67.

Sultan, Fareena, John U. Farley, and Donald R. Lehmann (1990), "A Meta-Analysis of Applications of Diffusion Models," *Journal of Marketing Research*, 27 (February), 70-77.

Thomas, Manoj and Vicki Morwitz (2005), "Penny Wise and Pound Foolish: The Left-Digit Effect in Price Cognition," *Journal of Consumer Research*, 32 (June), 54-64.

Multi-Unit Discounting and Discount Size: Getting More Out of Less

Devon DelVecchio, Miami University, USA
Timothy Heath, Miami University of Ohio, USA

EXTENDED ABSTRACT

Despite their widespread use, only three published studies have investigated the effects of multi-unit discounts (Blattberg and Neslin 1990; Manning and Sprott 2007; Wansink, Kent, and Hoch 1998). These studies indicate that multi-unit discounts stimulate higher purchase quantities; an effect that appears to arise from anchoring processes. However, three important issues remain unresolved. First, whereas Manning and Sprott (2007) find that "2 for" deals do not result in greater unit sales than a single-unit discount, Wansink et al. (1998) report a significant increase in purchase quantities most "two for" deals. Thus, the first issue we consider is the effectiveness of small unit quantity deals. Second, although the size of multi-unit discounts has not been studied systematically, prior results suggest that discount size may matter. Our second focus, therefore, is the possibility that discount size moderates the effectiveness of multi-unit discounts. Third, Manning and Sprott (2007) speculate that high-quantity anchors "may generate negative deal perceptions" (p. 420). This implies that a mechanism other than anchoring and adjustment may affect the efficacy of multi-unit discounts. Together, these issues lead to our research question: How does the value of a multi-unit discount affect consumer deal evaluations and resulting choice quantities?

First, we assessed 2,383 discounted purchases in a store located in a Midwestern city. ANCOVA results indicate that, consistent with expectations, increasing the number of units associated with the discount increased purchase quantities (F(2, 2382)=46.90, p<.001). Mean purchase quantities were greater when discounts were offered as "2 for" (M=1.70; F(2, 2382)=65.76, p<.001) or "3 or more for" (M=1.78; F(2, 2382)=45.74, p<.001) deals than when offered as a single-unit deal (M=1.23). In addition, the number-of-units in the deal moderated the effect of discount size (F(2, 2382)=3.75, p<.05). Larger discounts increased purchase quantities in the context of single-item deals (F(1, 2382)=3.57, p<.05) and for the two-for deals (F(1, 2382)=4.17, p<.05), but had no effect in the context of 3+-for deals (F(1, 2382)=1.05, ns).

Next, student participants (n=243) completed a simulated shopping experiment in which they selected between brands including a brand offering the focal promotion. The base design was a 3 (promotional units: 1, 2, 6) x 2 (discount size: 15%, 33%) between-subjects factorial. Participants also indicated the reason they would purchase the indicated quantity, responded to three positive affect and three negative affect items from the positive and negative affect schedule (PANAS, Watson, Clark, and Tellegen 1988) to identify deal-derived affect, and completed a five-item scale of deal value (e.g., Lichtenstein, Burton, and Karson 1991).

ANCOVA results indicate that purchase quantity intentions increased as deal units increased (F(2, 242)=6.41, p<.01). Mean purchase quantity intentions were greater for the "6 for" deals (M=2.22) than for the "2 for" deals (M=1.51, F(2, 242)=4.53, p<.05) and the single-item deals (M=1.08, F(2, 242)=12.55, p<.001). Purchase quantities did not differ for "2 for" and single-item deals (F(2, 242)=2.08, p=.15).

Number-of-units in the deal also interacts with the value of the discount (F(2, 242=3.25, p<.05) such that discount size affects purchase quantity intentions to a lesser extent as the number of units in the promotion increases. Purchase quantities are significantly greater for the 33% discount (M=1.64) than the 15% discount (M=0.51) in the single-item condition (F(1, 242)=6.40, p<.05). The 33% discount performs marginally better in terms of purchase quantity intentions (M=1.86) than the 15% discount (M=1.11) in the "2 for" condition (F(1,242)=2.66, p=.10). Purchase quantity intentions did not differ across the 33% (M=2.22) and 15% (M=2.25) discount values in the "6 for" conditions (F(1,242)=0.81, ns).

Regarding the process variables, perceived deal value exhibited a main effect of discount size (F(1, 242=11.99, p=.001) and a main effect of deal units (F(2, 242)=3.30, p<.05). However, controlling for perceived deal value does not eliminate the interactive effect of deal units and deal value on purchase quantity intentions (F(2, 242)=3.22, p<.05).

Consistent with an anchoring explanation of multi-unit deal effects, the number of usage-related thoughts indicated in the open-ended question regarding purchase quantity rationale was positively related to the number of items in the deal (F(2, 242)=2.98, p=.05). However, usage thoughts were not a function of the deal unit by deal value interaction (F(2, 2423)=0.53, ns) and controlling for usage thoughts had little mediating effect on the deal unit by deal value interaction on purchase quantity intentions (F(2, 242)=2.94, p=.055).

Finally, net affect (positive affect minus negative affect) exhibited was (at least marginally) a function of deal units (F(2, 242)=7.21, p<.01), discount value (F(1, 242)=3.41, p=.07), and the deal unit by discount value interaction (F(2, 242)=2.51, p=.08). Furthermore, controlling for net affect eliminated the deal unit by discount value interaction on purchase quantity intentions (F(2, 242)=2.14, p>.10).

The results indicate that multi-unit discounts lead to greater purchase quantities than single unit discounts of equivalent value. In both studies there were instances (statistically in Study 1, directionally in Study 2) in which multi-unit discounts led to greater purchase quantities than did single unit discounts of greater value. Thus, retailers may be able to get greater sales at higher margins by employing multi-unit discounts. The results of Study 2 indicate that, consistent with an anchoring process, multi-unit discounting does lead to greater usage-related thoughts but this outcome, and the resulting purchase quantity, is tempered by the less positive affect stemming from larger unit deals.

REFERENCES

Blattberg, Robert C. and Scott A. Neslin (1990), *Sales Promotion: Concepts, Methods, and Strategies*, Englewood Cliffs, NJ: Prentice-Hall.

Lichtenstein, Donald R., Scott Burton, and Eric J. Karson (1991), "The Effect of Semantic Cues on Consumer Perceptions of Reference Price Ads," *Journal of Consumer Research*, 18 (December), 380-391.

Manning, Kenneth C. and David E. Sprott (2007), "Multiple Unit Price Promotions and Their Effects on Quantity Purchase Intentions," *Journal of Retailing*, 83 (December), 411-421.

Wansink, Brian, Robert J. Kent, and Stephen J. Hoch (1998), "An Anchoring and Adjustment Model of Purchase Quantity Decisions," *Journal of Marketing Research*, 35 (February), 71-81.

Watson, David, Anna Lee Clark, and Auke Tellegen (1988), " Development and Validation of Brief Measures of Positive and Negative Affect: The PANAS Scales," *Journal of Personality and Social Psychology*, 54 (June), 1063-1070.

Breaking through Complexity: How the Interplay between Visual and Conceptual Complexity Affects Logo Evaluation across Repeated Exposures

Irene Scopelliti, Bocconi University, Italy
Gaetano 'Nino' Miceli, University of Calabria, Italy
Maria Antonietta Raimondo, University of Calabria, Italy

EXTENDED ABSTRACT

According to experimental aesthetics (e.g., Berlyne 1971) and consumer research (e.g., Janiszewski and Meyvis 2001), the level of complexity of a visual stimulus has steady effects on consumer evaluations. Complexity, however, appears to be a multi-faceted construct that concerns both perceptual and conceptual aspects whose joint effect on consumer reactions is not yet clear.

In this paper, we analyze the effects of both visual complexity (VC-the amount and variety of visual information inherent in a stimulus) and conceptual complexity (CC-the number of different meanings associated with a stimulus), in the context of brand logos, using single and repeated exposures. Specifically, we propose arguments and hypotheses on how the main and interaction effects of visual and conceptual complexity depend on the number of previous exposures to the logo.

Based on experimental aesthetics (Berlyne 1971), we hypothesize that, at a single exposure, logo VC has an inverted U-shaped effect on attitude (H1). Based on studies on conceptual fluency, which propose that the ease with which the meaning of a stimulus comes to mind (Hamann 1990; Lee 2002) positively influences stimulus evaluations, we expect that, at a single exposure, high levels of CC lower attitude toward the logo (H2).

Crossing VC and CC, we define four basic types of logos. One might expect that high-VC/low-CC logos (do induce arousal and learning, and are clear in their meaning hence easily interpretable) will show the most favorable evaluations; low-VC/high-CC logos (do not induce arousal and learning, and are vague and unclear in their meaning) will show the lowest evaluations; low-VC/low-CC, and high-VC/high-CC logos will show intermediate evaluations. These expected results suggest the absence of interaction between VC and CC at a single exposure.

This pattern, however, may change over multiple exposures. Although it is difficult to formulate predictions for all the four of VC/CC combinations, we expect that evaluations of high-VC/low-CC logos will suffer a decline as the number of exposures increases. Such a prediction lies in the idea that perceptual elements are quickly elaborated and exhausted in terms of arousal potential. Moreover, high VC is likely to be related to multiple perceptual dimensions thus being unlikely to generate fluency (Janiszewski and Meyvis 2001), while low CC implies quick habituation and boredom. Based on similar arguments, one may expect that evaluations of low-VC/high-CC logos will increase across exposures due to the generation of perceptual fluency (low VC is more likely related to a uniform perceptual dimension), as well as to the relevant potential for elaboration and learning. Conceptual fluency is, indeed, sensitive to time and to opportunity for elaboration. Eventually, evaluations of low-VC/high-CC logos may decline as additional increases in the number of exposures make the source of fluency too salient to be misattributed to the stimulus. Low-VC/low-CC and high-VC/high-CC logos stimulate similar mechanisms but in opposite directions. It is therefore difficult to predict a specific pattern for these types of logos. Overall, expected changes in evaluations of high-VC/low-CC and low-VC/high-CC logos across number of exposures suggest the hypothesis of a three-way interaction between VC, CC, and number of exposures (H3).

Our conceptual analysis also suggests that the independent two-way interactions of VC and CC with the number of exposures qualify this three-way interaction. We expect that low-VC logos will initially show low evaluations (see H1). An increase the number of exposures might instill perceptual fluency, as low-VC logos tend to manifest a uniform perceptual dimension. Therefore, we predict that, across exposures, evaluations of these logos will increase, but only up to a certain threshold, when boredom intervenes causing the logo wear-out (H4a). A high-VC logo starts with an average or high evaluation depending on the inflection point of the quadratic effect (see H1). Apparently, the arousal and learning potential of such a logo should cause an improvement in the evaluations over repeated exposures. However, we also expect absence of or little perceptual fluency, as high-VC logos tend to refer to multiple perceptual dimensions. Moreover, perceptual information is elaborated very quickly, particularly in stimuli as small as logos, therefore dampening any arousal and learning potential. Hence, we expect a slight fall in high-VC logos evaluations over repeated exposures (H4b).

We expect that low-CC logos initially show high evaluations due to stimulus-driven conceptual fluency (see H2). However, one might expect a decrease in evaluations over repeated exposures due to quick habituation (H5a). High-CC logos will initially show low evaluations (see H2). Since conceptual fluency is sensitive to the opportunity to elaborate the stimulus, we expect that increasing the number of exposures will boost evaluations of high-CC logos. Further increases in the number of exposures may eventually dampen the learning potential. These arguments suggest a reverse U-shaped pattern of attitude toward high-CC logos (H5b).

Results of a survey (Study 1) with multiple respondents (cf. Henderson and Cote 1998) support H1 and H2, and also show that VC and CC do not interact with each other in shaping attitude at one exposure. Findings from an experiment (Study 2) offer general support to H3, H4a, H4b, H5a, and H5b.

From a theoretical perspective, we integrate within a unified conceptual framework the effects of two forms of complexity across repeated exposures on attitude toward a logo. Our analysis allows understanding the processes that co-occur to explain consumer preference for hybrid logos, such as those high in VC and low in CC, which may reflect the concept of "simplicity in complexity" proposed by Reber et al. (2004). Furthermore, our findings propose that VC and CC affect attitude following different patterns across the multiple exposures. Finally, our research suggests, therefore, that ignoring either VC or CC in the analysis of consumers' reactions to the complexity of visual stimuli may hide relevant mechanisms and processes.

REFERENCES

Berlyne, Daniel E. (1971), *Aesthetics and Psychobiology*, New York: Appleton-Century-Crofts.

Hamann, Stephan B. (1990), "Level-of Processing Effects in Conceptually Driven Implicit Tasks," *Journal of Experimental Psychology: Learning, Memory, and Cognition*, 16 (November), 970-977.

Janiszewski, Chris and Tom Meyvis (2001), "Effects of Brand Logo Complexity, Repetition, and Spacing on processing Fluency and Judgment," *Journal of Consumer Research*, 28(June), 18-32.

Lee, Angela Y. (2002), "Effects of Implicit Memory on Memory-Based Versus Stimulus-Based Brand Choice," *Journal of Marketing Research*, 39(November), 440-454.

Reber, Rolf, Norbert Schwarz and Piotr Winkielman (2004), "Processing Fluency and Aesthetic Pleasure: Is Beauty in the Perceiver's Processing Experience?" *Personality and Social Psychology Review*, 8(4), 364-82.

Consumer Responses to the Mass Customization of Product Aesthetics

Ruth Mugge, Delft University of Technology, The Netherlands
Frédéric Brunel, Boston University, USA
Jan Schoormans, Delft University of Technology, The Netherlands

EXTENDED ABSTRACT

Mass-customization strategies allow consumers to create individualized products that match their personal needs. Although mass-customization can appeal to broad audiences and is becoming more available in the marketplace, research on this topic has been somewhat limited (Hauser, Tellis, and Griffin 2006). Specifically, we have an emerging body of evidence on the processes that determine consumers' evaluation of the mass-customization of functional elements (e.g., Dellaert and Stremersch 2005), but lack a complementary understanding regarding the mass-customization of product aesthetics. Although there are some similarities between mass-customization of functional features and aesthetics, we believe that there are unique aspects to aesthetic mass-customization as well. An important difference is that aesthetic mass-customization has a strong affective and symbolic nature. Hence, different constructs might drive consumers' reactions to these mass-customization configurators. This paper explores the value of aesthetic mass-customization for self-expression and identity management. Specifically, we investigate the importance of the extent of mass-customization and the public consumption of the mass-customized product for realizing the full potential of aesthetic mass-customization.

Mass-customization configurators differ in the extent of customization that is offered. In some configurators, the extent of mass-customization is narrow, because consumers are only offered a small number of choices, whereas in others they can make selections amongst an immense number of options. Research on functional mass-customization demonstrated that increasing the extent of functional mass-customization allows consumers to achieve greater functional value, because the product can be better customized to fit one's technical requirements (Dellaert and Stremersch 2005). Similarly, to match consumers' individual aesthetic preferences, consumers should be offered a great extent of aesthetic mass-customization. Then, the product can be aesthetically customized to fit one's unique taste and reflect one's identity. In contrast, the importance of functional mass-customization for self-expression will be limited, because functional components are often internal, and therefore, less visible than aesthetic elements. Furthermore, consumers' aesthetic preferences are heterogeneous, whereas functional preferences are often uniformed within consumer segments, and thus, less effective in supporting one's unique identity. Accordingly, we hypothesize that the extent of aesthetic mass-customization positively impacts the mass-customized product's self-expressive value (H_{1a}), whereas the extent of functional mass-customization positively affects its functional value (H_{2a}).

Increasing the extent of functional and/or aesthetic mass-customization may also have a negative effect on consumer responses. Consumers may become overwhelmed by the great number of possibilities at their disposal (Huffman and Kahn 1998). Accordingly, we hypothesize that the perceived complexity of the mass-customization process is positively affected by the extent of aesthetic (H_{1b}) and functional (H_{2b}) mass-customization.

Based on the former, two opposing effects are expected for consumers' purchase intention of mass-customized products. Whereas the mass-customized product's functional (H_{3a}) and self-expressive value (H_{3b}) will enhance purchase intentions, perceived complexity (H_4) will reduce these.

Nevertheless, we expect that consumers' perceptions of the self-expressive value of mass-customized products are impacted by more than just the extent of aesthetic mass-customization. People derive their identity more from social interactions with others than from internal, psychological forces (Kleine, Kleine, and Kernan 1993). Consequently, a product's self-expressive value depends on its visibility to others. Accordingly, we propose that for aesthetic mass-customization the benefit of self-expressiveness is enhanced if the mass-customized product is publicly consumed (H_5). Because the value of functional mass-customization for self-expression is limited, public consumption will not affect this type of mass-customization.

In Study 1, 364 undergraduate students were presented with one of the eight generated mass-customization configurators for a laptop. For the manipulation of functional mass-customization, the breadth (4 vs. 8 technical aspects) and depth (2 vs. 4-6 options for each aspect) of functional mass-customization choices was varied. Extent of aesthetic mass-customization was manipulated by offering a choice among four colors or the possibility to personally create the motif for the laptop's appearance. For the manipulation of public/private consumption, we primed the respondents by telling them that they are interested in purchasing a new laptop to replace their current desktop, because it is portable and allows the user to work anywhere they want (public) or because it takes less space in their bedroom (private). Each condition was explained in text and by showing pictures of the mass-customization configurator. Next, responses to several multi-item measures were obtained.

To test our hypotheses, we performed a structural equation model with latent variables in LISREL. The fit statistics for the model indicated a good fit and only the hypothesized relationships were significant. These results confirmed past findings on functional mass-customization and supported our hypotheses on the different processes that are involved with aesthetic mass-customization.

In Study 2, we investigated the robustness and generalizability of our findings. Specifically, we stepped outside the laboratory setting and tested our theory amongst a heterogeneous group of consumers, using a home cordless telephone as a product category, and a different manipulation of public/private consumption. Public/private consumption was manipulated by varying the customized elements of the telephone. The configurator allowed the consumers to customize an aspect of the telephone that would be more (shell) or less (display) visible to others. By varying the number of aesthetic options, three conditions were generated to manipulate the extent of aesthetic mass-customization. Members of a consumer panel (n=218) were asked to evaluate one of the six different configurators. After conducting several steps in the data analysis, this model resulted in a good fit and replicated all effects regarding aesthetic mass-customization as found in Study 1.

In conclusion, our research shows that aesthetic mass-customization is different from functional mass-customization, because it provides symbolic value through the product's ability for self-expression. In contrast, functional mass-customization is valued because it provides a better fit to individual technical requirements. Consequently, different antecedents may drive the two types of mass-customization, which is supported by the effect of public/private consumption on the evaluation of aesthetic mass-customization. Finally, our findings show that increasing the extent of aesthetic mass-customization has a positive (through the self-expressive value) as well as a negative (through perceived complexity) effect on the intention to purchase the mass-customized product. These opposing effects have to be carefully managed when offering mass-customization configurators.

REFERENCES

Bardakci, Ahmet and Jeryl Whitelock (2004), "How 'Ready' Are Customers for Mass Customisation? An Exploratory Study," *European Journal of Marketing*, 38 (11/12), 1396-1416.

Bearden, William O. and Michael J. Etzel (1982), "Reference Group Influence on Product and Brand Purchase Decision," *Journal of Consumer Research*, 9 (September), 183-194.

Belk, Russell W. (1988), "Possessions and the Extended Self," *Journal of Consumer Research*, 15 (September), 139-168.

Bettman, James R., Eric J. Johnson, and John W. Payne (1990), "A Componential Analysis of Cognitive Effort in Choice," *Organizational Behavior and Human Decision Processes*, 45 (1), 111-139.

Blom, Jan O. and Andrew F. Monk (2003), "Theory of Personalization of Appearance: Why Users Personalize Their PCs and Mobile Phones," *Human-Computer Interaction*, 18, 193-228.

Burroughs, W. Jeffrey (1991), "Predicting Personality from Personal Possessions: A Self-Presentational Analysis," *Journal of Social Behavior and Personality*, 6 (6), 147-163.

Dellaert, Benedict G. C. and Stefan Stremersch (2005), "Marketing Mass-Customized Products: Striking Balance between Utility and Complexity," *Journal of Marketing Research*, 42 (May), 219-227.

Dodds, William B., Kent B. Monroe, and Dhruv Grewal (1991), "Effects of Price, Brand, and Store Information on Buyers' Product Evaluations," *Journal of Marketing Research*, 28 (August), 307-319.

Fiore, Ann Marie, Seung-Eun Lee, and Grace Kunz (2004), "Individual Differences, Motivations, and Willingness to Use a Mass-Customization Option for Fashion Products," *European Journal of Marketing*, 38 (7), 835-849.

Franke, Nikolaus and Frank T. Piller (2003), "Key Research Issues in User Interaction with User Toolkits in a Mass Customisation System," *International Journal of Technology Management*, 26 (5/6), 578-599.

______ (2004), "Value Creation by Toolkits for User Innovation and Design: The Case of the Watch Market," *Journal of Product Innovation Management*, 21 (6), 401-415.

Gosling, Samuel D., Sei Jin Ko, Thomas Mannarelli, and Margaret E. Morris (2002), "A Room with a Cue: Personality Judgments Based on Offices and Bedrooms," *Journal of Personality and Social Psychology*, 82 (3), 379-398.

Hauser, John, Gerard J. Tellis, and Abbie Griffin (2006), "Research on Innovation; a Review and Agenda for Marketing Science," *Marketing Science*, 25 (6), 687-717.

Huffman, Cynthia and Barbara E. Kahn (1998), "Variety for Sale: Mass-customization or Mass Confusion," *Journal of Retailing*, 74 (4), 491-513.

Kiesler, Tina and Sara Kiesler (2005), "My Pet Rock and Me: An Experimental Exploration of the Self Extension Concept," in *Advances in Consumer Research*, Vol. 32, Eds. Gita Menon and Akshay Rao, Provo, UT: Association for Consumer Research, 365-370.

Kleine, Robert E., Susan Schultz Kleine, and Jerome B. Kernan (1993), "Mundane Consumption and the Self: A Social-Identity Perspective," *Journal of Consumer Psychology*, 2 (3), 209-235.

Kleiser, Susan B. and Susan Powell Mantel (1994), "The Dimensions of Consumer Expertise: A Scale Development," *AMA Summer Educators' Proceedings*, 5, 20-26.

Mugge, Ruth, Jan P. L. Schoormans, and Hendrik N. J. Schifferstein (2009), "Emotional Bonding with Personalized Products," *Journal of Engineering Design*, 20 (5), 467-476.

Piller, Frank and Melanie Müller (2004), "A New Marketing Approach to Mass Customisation," *International Journal of Computer Integrated Manufacturing*, 17 (7), 583-593.

Piller, Frank, P. Schubert, Michael Koch, and Kathrin Möslein (2004), "From Mass-customization to Collaborative Customer Co-Design," in *European Conference on Information Systems*.

Pine, Buddy J. (1993), *Mass-customization*, Boston, MA: Harvard Business School Press.

Randall, Taylor, Christian Terwiesch, and Karl Ulrich (2007), "User Design of Customized Products," *Marketing Science*, 26 (2), 268-280.

Schreier, Martin (2006), "The Value Increment of Mass-Customized Products: An Empirical Assessment and Conceptual Analysis of Its Explanation," *Journal of Consumer Behaviour*, 5 (July-August), 317-327.

Solomon, Michael R. (1983), "The Role of Products as Social Stimuli: A Symbolic Interactionism Perspective," *Journal of Consumer Research*, 10 (December), 319-329.

Townsend, Claudia and Sanjay Sood (2009), "Self-Affirmation through the Choice of Good Design," *Working paper*.

White, Katherine and Darren W. Dahl (2006), "To Be or Not Be? The Influence of Dissociative Reference Groups on Consumer Preferences," *Journal of Consumer Psychology*, 16 (4), 404-414.

Zipkin, Paul (2001), "The Limits of Mass-customization," *Sloan Management Review*, 42 (3), 81-87.

Effects of Exaggerated Priming and Fluent Processing on the Evaluation of Design

Irene Scopelliti, Bocconi University, Italy
Paola Cillo, Bocconi University, Italy
David Mazursky, The Hebrew University of Jerusalem, Israel

EXTENDED ABSTRACT

In several industries competition is based on the continuous proposal of new styles, in a sort of dynamic innovation process based mostly, if not exclusively, on product design and on a planned obsolescence of that design. This process is called stylistic innovation, and refers to all changes in design that are not purely the results of engineering advances (Robinson 1958; Cappetta et al. 2006). Apparel, cars, furniture and home appliances are just some instances of industries featuring competition based on stylistic innovation, for which success is strictly dependent on consumers' fast and rapid adoption of the new design.

In some design-based industries, the launch of a new design is realized by mean of showpieces featuring in an exaggerated way, i.e., by emphasizing the central features of the design up to the point of appearing wacky, the same design that will be then delivered to the market in a more moderate form. This launch strategy is widely adopted in the apparel industry, but also elsewhere (e.g., new car models are often presented as concept cars during trade shows). Exposure to exaggerated showpieces might shock consumers since such exemplars are typically disruptive, and they are often perceived as bizarre or extravagant. However, exposure to showpieces could help improving consumers' attitude toward a moderate form of the new design: the visual exaggeration of the distinctive features of a design may enable a more fluent processing of the same features in subsequent encounters with other exemplars of the same design (Reber et al. 2004), by leaving a deeper trace in consumers' implicit memory than a moderate form of the design would do.

This article examines whether the strategy of introduction of novel designs used in some fashion-based industries (i.e., introduction with exposure to an exaggerated showpiece) is more effective in terms of favorability than a standard launch strategy in which consumers are exposed directly to a moderate marketable form of the design. Differences in the effectiveness of such a strategy of introduction between consumers holding different levels of prior knowledge of the product category, and between showpieces with different levels of structural redundancy with respect to the target design, are also examined.

Experiment 1 shows that initial exposure to exaggerated showpieces generates a more favorable evaluation of a moderate target design than initial exposure to moderate exemplars or no initial exposure, with this effect being driven by the evaluations of experts (measured expertise). We argue that experts' advantage is the outcome of highly effective encoding of the visual information contained in the exaggerated showpiece, and of a more fluent processing of the target design favored by the trace left by the showpiece in subjects' implicit memory. Experiment 2 adds external validity to Experiment 1, and replicates the results of the previous experiment by making use of a group of real experts (fashion design students and young fashion professionals) compared to a group of non-experts (management students). This effect could be explained by the fact that experts, compared to non-experts, are able to process and to learn the structure of the design in a more effective way upon exposure to exaggerated exemplars, and are able to elaborate more fluently the same structural elements of the showpiece featured in the target design. The greater shifts in the evaluation of the target design on behalf of experts should signal such higher fluency, because of the positive valence associated to processing fluency–the so called hedonic marking of fluency (Winkielman et al. 2003) that is misattributed to the target stimulus. This idea is explored in Experiment 3, where we test the hypothesis that experts' stronger shift in the evaluation of the target design is not a function of expertise per se, but of higher processing fluency, by manipulating a visual feature of the design able to make processing more fluent, i.e., the redundancy (Reber et al. 2004; Garner 1974) between the exemplars shown in initial exposures and the target design. Redundancy is a variable that makes the structural alignment between the two stimuli (exaggerate showpiece and moderate target design) more salient, and therefore improves the processing of the visual information contained in the target design (Markman and Gentner 1997). Experiment 3 indicates that experts' advantage is eliminated when redundancy increases, resulting in comparable evaluations of the target design by experts and non-experts in the case of high redundancy: all subjects evaluate the target more favorably when exposed to exaggerated and highly redundant exemplars, whereas experts evaluate the target significantly more favorably than non-experts when exposed to exaggerated but low-redundancy exemplars.

Results generally support the idea that exposure to exaggerated showpieces is able to improve the evaluation of a moderate target design, shedding light on the effects of exaggeration in the domain of visual information. Exaggerated stimuli, despite less attractive than prototypical stimuli (Rhodes and Tremewan 1996), have a great potential in terms of emphasis on the most relevant elements of a message, and of impact on the encoding of information. Our findings suggest that exaggeration is a visual feature able to affect the ease of processing visual information, i.e., perceptual fluency, as hypothesized by Reber et al. (2004). We also find that greater structural alignment, as favored by visual redundancy within the set of stimuli, is able to affect evaluation of the target design upon exposure to an exaggerated exemplar, by again improving the fluency experienced in the elaboration of visual information.

Some relevant implications for managerial practice can be drawn from our results. Firms competing in design-based industries engage in a process of dynamically continuous innovation that sees each new design competing with others to overcome the previous design in consumers' preferences. The comparison of alternative strategies that could be easily managed by firms when presenting a new design in terms of impact on consumers' evaluation might help them to launch their new designs in the most effective way.

REFERENCES

Cappetta, Rossella, Paola Cillo, and Anna Ponti (2006), "Convergent Designs in Fine Fashion: An Evolutionary Model for Stylistic Innovation," *Research Policy*, 35 (9), 1273-90.

Garner, Wendell R. (1974), *The Processing of Information and Structure*, New York: Lawrence Erlbaum Associates.

Markman Arthur B, and Dedre Gentner (1997), "The Effects of Alignability on Memory," *Psychological Science*, 8, 363-67.

Reber, Rolf, Norbert Schwarz, and Piotr Winkielman (2004), "Processing Fluency and Aesthetic Pleasure: Is Beauty in the Perceiver's Processing Experience?" *Personality and Social Psychology Review*, 8 (4), 364-82.

Rhodes, Gillian, and Tanya Tremewan (1996), "Averageness, Exaggeration, and Facial Attractiveness," *Psychological Science*, 7, 105-10.

Robinson, Dwight E. (1958), "Fashion Theory and Product Design," *Harvard Business Review*, 36 (November/December), 126-38.

Winkielman, Piotr, Norbert Schwarz, Tedra Fazendeiro, and Rolf Reber (2003), "The Hedonic Marking of Processing Fluency: Implications for Evaluative Judgment," in J. Musch & K. C. Klauer, eds., *The Psychology of Evaluation: Affective Processes in Cognition and Emotion*, 189-217, Mahwah, NJ: Erlbaum.

The Interpersonal Hot Hand Fallacy: How Similarity with Previous Winners Increases Subjective Probability of Winning

Sandra Laporte, HEC Paris, France
Gilles Laurent, HEC Paris, France

EXTENDED ABSTRACT

This paper tries to explain a prevailing advertising practice for promotional and state lotteries. Organizers often showcase a photograph of a recent winner together with some personal information (e.g. name, age, place of living, occupation). Further, the profile of the featured winner is similar to the typical profile of potential participants. The repeated use of this technique by multiple lotteries in different countries suggests it must be an efficient tool to increase participation in the next drawing. We propose that the underlying mechanism is based on what we call the "interpersonal hot hand" fallacy. In the hot hand fallacy, basketball fans believe (contrary to objective evidence) that a specific player has a higher chance to hit the basket if he was successful in his previous attempt (Gilovich et al. 1985). In the Interpersonal Hot Hand Fallacy, consumers believe that they have higher odds of winning the next drawing if they are similar to the previous winner than if they are dissimilar. This effect induces a greater participation intention.

The entry decision is made under uncertainty since most of the real-life advertisements for these lotteries do not state explicitly the probability of winning. Moreover, the entry decision is likely to be low-involving because of the minimal costs at stake. As a consequence, consumers may rely on heuristics to estimate their probability of winning. A highly accessible heuristic attribute appears in the similarity information that the advertisement implicitly offers by providing very basic, general demographic information about previous winners. Regarding the direction of the similarity effect, we propose that advertisements, by showcasing "lucky" previous winners, focus on a potential human cause, while they overlook the inanimate random character of the lottery by not mentioning the probability of winning. According to the literature about the antecedents of the hot hand and the gambler's fallacies (Ayton and Fischer 2004, Burn and Corpus 2004, Sundali and Croson 2006), we hypothesize that this focus leads potential participants to attribute the outcome of the drawing to the previous winners' luck and, in the absence of objective information about their chances to win, estimate they have higher chances if they feel similar to these "lucky" previous winners.

Study 1 aims at testing the impact of the similarity with previous winners on the intention to participate in a sweepstake, and at contrasting it with the effect of the number of prizes to win. We manipulate both factors in a 2x2 between-subject design. In the similar condition, the advertisement for the sweepstake shows the picture of a couple of previous winners with about the same age as the respondents (college students), while in the dissimilar condition, featured previous winners are much older. In the 'high number of prizes' condition, ten week-ends are offered as prizes, while there is only one week-end to win in the 'small number of prizes' condition. Age similarity has a significant positive effect on how much time respondents are willing to spend to enter the sweepstake measured by a 7-point scale ($F(1,113)=5.02$, $p<.03$), while multiplying the number of prizes by ten has no significant impact.

In Study 2, we test directly the interpersonal hot hand fallacy by manipulating interpersonal similarity using gender to rule out an attractiveness alternative explanation. The scenario indicates that a social network website for students regularly organizes a random drawing among its members, and features two previous winners with their photographs and verbal legends. Respondents estimate their probability to win the impending drawing (open-ended answer) to be higher when the last two winners have the same gender as them rather than the opposite gender ($t(48)=1.817$, p(one-tailed)$<.05$). We also rule out the simulation heuristic (Kahneman and Tversky 1982) as an alternative explanation.

Study 3 replicates this result with educational background as a new similarity manipulation: participants evaluate their chances of winning to be higher when the two previous winners pursue the same kind of academic studies as they do ($t(60)=2.643$; p(one-tailed)$<.05$).

In Study 4, we show that featuring a similar winner is particularly effective for people who are not particularly attracted by promotional games. Respondents with a high sweepstakes proneness (Lichtenstein et al. 1995) have the same high probability to participate whatever their similarity with previous winners ($\beta=-.557$; $t=-1.265$; p(one-tailed)$>.10$), while respondents with a low sweepstakes proneness will be more likely to participate if they are similar to previous winners ($\beta =.861$; $t=1.934$; p(one-tailed)$<.05$). Most importantly, the estimated probability of winning mediates the impact of similarity on participation likelihood, while the similarity has no impact on the attitude towards the organizing brand ruling out another alternative possible mechanism.

If the impact of similarity with the previous winner on the respondent's intention to participate is mediated by the respondent's estimated probability to win, the effect of similarity should disappear if respondents benefit from objective information on their probability to win. In Study 5, we compare two conditions: One in which respondents are only given (as in real life) indications on the number of prizes to be won, and one in which they are also given indications on the number of participants, allowing them to do an objective estimation of the probability to win. Indeed, in the first condition, we replicate the preceding results on the impact of similarity on participation intention ($F(1,52)=8.227$; $p<.01$), while, in the second condition, there is no impact of similarity on intention to participate.

The main contribution of this research is to show a new kind of hot hand fallacy caused by a similarity judgment. This explains why the widespread technique consisting in presenting a recent winner may boost the participation of similar consumers. It also adds a new result to the vast literature on interpersonal similarity that has already emphasized how similarity with others can affect our attitudes, beliefs and behaviours. This paper shows that, when making judgments under uncertainty, what just happened to similar others can impact our estimated probability of benefiting from the same random positive outcome.

REFERENCES

Ayton, Peter, and Ilan Fischer (2004), "The Hot Hand Fallacy and the Gambler's Fallacy: Two Faces of Subjective Randomness?" *Memory and Cognition*, 32 (8), 1369-78.

Burns, Bruce D. and Bryan Corpus (2004), "Randomness and Inductions from Streaks: 'Gambler's Fallacy' versus 'Hot Hand,'" *Psychonomic Bulletin & Review*, 11 (1), 179-84.

Gilovich, Thomas, Robert Vallone, and Amos Tversky (1985), "The Hot Hand in Basketball: on the Misperception of Random Sequences," *Cognitive Psychology*, 17, 295-314.

Kahneman, Daniel, and Amos Tversky (1982), "The Simulation Heuristic," in *Judgment Under Uncertainty: Heuristics and Biases*, D. Kahneman, P. Slovic and A. Tversky, eds. New York: Cambridge University Press, 201-208.

Lichtenstein, Donald R., Richard G. Netemeyer, and Scott Burton (1995), "Assessing the Domain Specificity of Deal Proneness: A Field Study," *Journal of Consumer Research*, 22 (December), 314-26.

Sundali, James and Rachel Croson (2006), "Biases in Casino Gambling: The Hot Hand and the Gambler's Fallacy," *Judgment and Decision Making*, 1 (1), 1-12.

The Role of Seed Money and Threshold Size in Optimizing Fundraising Campaigns: Past Behavior Matters!

Griet Verhaert, Ghent University, Belgium
Dirk Van den Poel, Ghent University, Belgium

EXTENDED ABSTRACT

Fundraising appeals often announce seed money by showing the audience that some funds have already been raised in order to reach the threshold. The technique is based on the theory of charitable fundraising proposed by Andreoni (1998). His theory predicts that publicly announced seed contributions will increase charitable donations. Seeking to contribute to the existing debate on the use of seed money, we investigated the role of seed money in combination with the threshold size and de type of the audience.

Academics attach more and more importance to the investigation of charitable behavior outside the laboratory because of the benefit of measuring real donation behavior instead of intentions. Recently, two studies on the use of seed money in direct-mail campaigns were examined in the field. First, List and Lucking-Reily (2002) tested three different levels of seed money based on a cold list of prospects. They found that 67% seed is the optimal level considering a threshold of $3,000. On the other hand, Rondeau and List (2008) found a 50% seed level as optimal with a threshold of $5,000 soliciting from a relatively warm list of contributors. The role of the threshold size in combination with the seed percentage however, is never examined. Therefore, based on a field experiment, we test both optimal seed levels in combination with different threshold sizes for a cold list as well as a warm list of contributors.

Moreover, various authors indentified moderating effects of past behavior on the effectiveness of different types of direct-mail campaigns (e.g., Rust and Verhoef 2005). Therefore, we do not only distinguish between prospects and past contributors but we also want to separate the more loyal donors from the less loyal ones based on transactional data. Knowing that past behavior could play a crucial role in the effectiveness of direct-mail campaigns, we would like to investigate the use of seed money in combination with the threshold size across real donor segments.

Taking the previous into account, we set up a 2x3x3 between-subjects design in a real charity context. Our design manipulates the level of the threshold (low versus high) and the percentage of seed money (no seed, 50% and 67%). Based on previous research, we expect differences between donors depending on their past behavior. Therefore, based on the charity database, we include three groups in the experiment. The first segment consists of prospects (i.e., the cold list), whereas the second group incorporates current donors with a lower loyalty score, and the last considers existing donors with a higher loyalty score. We calculated this score based on historical giving behavior. Starting from the original campaign, we created several smaller campaigns, each representing one of the six versions. The final campaign was send to 25,617 households.

For each donor segment, we examined the persuasiveness of the different appeals on participation rate, gift size and overall revenue. In general we only found effects on the response of the campaigns and no effects on the size of individual contributions. Consequently the overall revenue was driven by the participation rate. We found that the use of seed money, regardless of the size of the threshold, is a good strategy in direct-mail appeals targeted at prospects and donors with a lower loyalty score. These results are in agreement with those reported by List and Lucking-Reily (2002) and Rondeau and List (2008). Moreover, we can conclude that the proposed optimal level in both studies, respectively 50% and 67%, are equally successful.

By contrast, when analyzing the most behaviorally loyal contributors, we neither found a main effect of seed money nor a main effect of the size of the threshold. Interestingly, we revealed a predominating interaction effect between the use of seed money and the size of the threshold. More specifically, when announcing a relatively low threshold, it is pernicious to announce seed contributions. On the other hand, seed money remains a good technique when the threshold is rather high. This finding appears to be somewhat in contrast with previous authors who consistently found that seed money is generally a valuable strategy. However, we want to remark that previous studies reached response rates much lower (i.e., below 5%) than we obtained in our loyal segment (i.e., around 15%) which suggests that this type of loyal segment is never studied before. Our finding suggests that the still required residual money should be set high enough to encourage the best donors. At the same time, we showed the need for incorporating past behavior as input for a differentiated communication approach across donor segments.

Our study has important implications on the academic literature of seed money in charity appeals. Especially when focusing on loyal contributors of the charity, we recommend considering the size of the threshold when investigating the role of seed contributions. Moreover, research on the effectiveness of fundraising campaigns should take into account past behavior of the target audience. The findings also have many practical implications. We demonstrate different effects according to the donor segment indicating a need for differentiation in the communication strategy as well as the importance of using the database. In general, announcing seed money is always a valuable strategy except when raising funds for a relatively low threshold. In this latter situation, it is more efficient not to announce seed money in appeals towards the best donors because of its detrimental effect.

Exploring other distinctions between donor segments (e.g., previous donation size and frequency) on the warm list would undoubtedly be a fruitful area for further research as would be to incorporate reactivation campaigns. Finally, it would be worthwhile to further explore additional levels of seed money and threshold sizes. In conclusion, this research is the first to demonstrate the effect of both seed money and size of the threshold on charitable contributions across donor segments. It reveals an important restriction of the announcement of seed contributions. Finally, it clearly shows the necessity of a differentiation in direct-mail appeals by considering past behavior of the contributors.

REFERENCES

Andreoni, James (1998), "Toward a Theory of Charitable Fund-Raising," *Journal of Political Economy*, 106(6), 1186–1213.

List, John A. and David Lucking-Reiley (2002), "The Effects of Seed Money and Refunds on Charitable Giving: Experimental Evidence from a University Capital Campaign," *Journal of Political Economy*, 110(1), 215–33.

Rondeau, Daniel and John A. List (2008), "Matching and Challenge Gifts to Charity: Evidence from Laboratory and Natural Field Experiments," *Experimental Economics*, 11(3), 253-367.

Rust, Roland T. and Peter C. Verhoef. (2005), "Optimizing the Marketing Interventions Mix in Intermediate-Term CRM," *Marketing Science*, 24(3) 477–89.

The Role of Activation in Advertising

Yael Steinhart, University of Haifa, Israel

EXTENDED ABSTRACT

The current research explores the relationships between action, advertisement evaluation, and attitudes toward the product presented in the advertisement.

Actions in the context of advertising can be considered a "foot in the door" technique, in which the advertiser initially promotes the viewer to attend to the advertisement, although the advertiser's ultimate goal is to generate a favorable attitude toward the product. Therefore, the present research examines direct and indirect effects of actions on attitudes toward the product via the mediating variable of advertisement evaluation.

The proposed research examines physical activities that are strongly associated with the advertisement message. This type of action is labeled as the Activation technique. The activation technique includes a physical action, which can be executed immediately upon viewing the ad, and the action's results highlight the message conveyed in the advertisement.

The effect of activation on advertisement and product evaluations is proposed to be based on the extent of compatibility between the type of action and the content of the message conveyed in the advertisement. When the physical action is congruent with the content message, activation is proposed to enhance not only the evaluation of the advertisement but also generate a favorable attitude toward the product. On the other hand, when the physical action is not congruent with the content of the message, activation is anticipated to indirectly elicit a negative attitude toward the advertised product.

The underling mechanism for the activation effect is proposed to rely on the advertisement processing fluency. That is, ease of processing contributes to the formation of an overall impression of an advertisement. In the case of compatible activation, the action is expected to facilitate advertisement processing since the performance of the action bolsters the punch-line of the advertisement. In this situation, it is proposed, activation will increase the overall advertisement evaluation. On the other hand, in the case of a less compatible action, the action is expected to increase processing difficulty. That is, it will be harder to form an impression of the advertisement, leading to lower advertisement evaluations compared to a condition in which the same ad does not instigate an action.

The research comprises three studies all of which focus on a single physical action (i.e. turning a page upside-down) that was related either to a call to reverse the situation of the needy by donating the cost of meals, or a call to reverse the viewer's situation by purchasing a dinner card that constitutes a routine breaker.

The first study examines the compatibility between the action and the advertisement message. Its results support the fluency of processing mechanism, which either facilitates or inhibits advertisement comprehension and consequently influences overall advertisement evaluation. The second study explores the direct effect of activation on advertisement evaluation as a function of action compatibility. The final study investigates the direct and indirect effects of action compatibility on the attitude toward the advertised product via the mediating variable of advertisement evaluation. Its findings pointed out the direct effect on attitude formation in the case of action and message compatibility. When activation was less compatible with the message, activation influenced the attitude toward the advertised product indirectly via the advertisement evaluation.

To sum, this research highlights the possible "cost" of implementing the activation technique in advertising as a function of its compatibility to the messages conveyed in the advertisement. Specifically, the effect of activation on both advertisement evaluation and attitude formation was found to be contingent upon the messages of the advertisement.

Future research may examine the compatibility between different types of actions (such as scratching or folding a page) and different types of messages. This would enable to further generalize the phenomenon.

The Experiential Information Exchange in Electronic Word-of-Mouth Communications

Lei Huang, Dalhousie University, Canada

EXTENDED ABSTRACT

Word-of-mouth (WOM) is usually viewed as a credible and objective diffusion mechanism for information (e.g., Gilly et al. 1998). While WOM has been traditionally spread among acquaintances through personal "contagions" (Barlas and Huang 2009), the Internet has dramatically increased the scale of WOM communication (Dellarocas 2003). Examples of such electronic word-of-mouth (e-WOM) communications include online product review forums, internet discussion groups, instant messaging, chat rooms, mailing lists and Web logs. As an important format of e-WOM, Bulletin Board Systems (BBS) can easily facilitate individuals in their communication with people who have similar interests, experiences, or attitudes, regardless of differences in location, socioeconomic background, or personal relationships (e.g., friends, acquaintances). One major purpose of this paper is to investigate participants' information exchange behavior that has no basis in an existing (or trusted) relationship.

A very large percentage of the consumers who post their consumption experiences on BBS do so with little deliberate intention of "evangelizing" or "persuading" others. These consumer-generated-messages (CGMs) may or may not have an intended "target" within his or her trusted social network, yet his or her archived opinions may have a lasting impact on the awareness, trial, and purchase behavior of other consumers. Some of the CGMs can be very insightful and initiate a passionate response to the focus topic. Therefore, BBS are much more than just the buzzword-of-the-week sites, because they cannot be forced and are often a natural process. Furthermore, evidence from both marketing and social psychology has supported the role of experiential processing in decision-making and behavior. According to the cognitive-experiential self-theory (CEST) (Epstein et al. 1996), people process information by two parallel but interactive systems: one operates by context-specific, heuristic rules; whereas, the other operates by abstract, general rules guided by analysis and logic. The former deals with information that is affective in nature, and is associated with crude and emotional aspects; the latter processes information that is cognitive in nature, and is associated with refined and rational aspects. WOM is usually generated by cues that serve both systems. In accordance with CEST, this paper defines experiential information as imprecise emotional or sensual reactions to subjective characteristics drawn from the consumption of products or services. Cognitive information, however, concerns the objective features, utilitarian functions and economic values of the product or service.

Specifically, this paper argues that the experiential versus cognitive aspects of the information communicated are similar to some extent to the characteristics of goods in consumption. It crystallizes as "goods" entities, the meaning of which crucially depends on the context and on irreducibly subjective elements, such as a pleasant message, a joke that makes everyone laugh, or a story centered around the course of consuming a product or service. The idea of social exchange in WOM (and e-WOM) depicts communicators entering an interaction as having an endowment of resources that are, subsequently, transferred to the other parties. This obscures the fact that WOM communication generates something that did not exist before, and that communicators act as co-producers of this something–*recreational consumption information*. The normative significance of the correspondence of experiential information may help to explain why recreational consumption information is important for our sense of well-being (Barlas and Huang 2009; Huang and Barlas 2009).

In addition, the advent of the Internet has made it possible to increase the experiential processes with browsers, including viral marketing, online advergames, and interactive advertising (Fong and Burton 2006; Porter and Golan 2006; Winkler and Buckner 2006). Indeed, the information contained in CGMs on BBS underlies both experiential and cognitive processes. By using the social relationship matrix and multilevel modeling methods to study individuals' CGMs on an online travel forum, this paper aims to answer the question of how the experiential versus cognitive CGM influences online information exchange behavior. Different from previous research on the topic of information search and Internet that mostly used "review" websites (e.g., the review section of Amazon, Rotten Tomato, etc.), the context of BBS adopted in this paper appears to be less structured than "review" websites, which creates a different information exchange dynamic. Also, BBS is more prone to an actual discussion than "review" websites (though people sometimes reply to each other in a review section of a website), which creates a more natural setting.

This study employed publicly available data from a major online travel forum for independent travelers, Travelblog.org. The data downloaded in this research were from the "Oceania Travel Forum" that contained 205 threads and 497 posts. There were 119 participants involved in discussions during the period of 2004-11-26 to 2007-11-19. Results from aggregated analysis suggest that, compared with cognitive posts, experiential posts generally had a higher proportion at the beginning of the discussion (M_{t1}=.54), and this advantage enjoyed a systematic increase as time went by (M_{t2}=.63, χ^2=9.48, p<.002). In other words, the more experiential posts a thread had, the more discussion on the topic under this thread occurred. Further analysis from the multilevel model illustrates that the more positive posts a thread contained, the more likely this thread had higher ratings on the experiential contents of its posts (t=2.21, p<.05). Interestingly, opinion leaders' participation led to a significant increase of experiential information in discussions, especially among those positive posts (t=3.08, p<.01).

One major contribution of this research is to demonstrate that people exchange experiential more than cognitive information on BBS. Jointly, according to experiential information transmission characteristics and the incidental variances in the BBS, marketers can make use of this "recreational consumption information" to create favorable e-WOM communication for both customer acquisition and retention. Moreover, aspects of the Internet also lend themselves well to e-WOM communication. We may not know that person, but we relate to–and often trust–posts originated from their *experiences*, especially for those virtual participants viewed as opinion leaders or "mavens." Consequently, an extensive implication of this paper is to help marketers generate proactive WOM contents in order to unleash advocacy among enthusiasts (or opinion leaders) who will exercise influence or social-currency among certain networks and communities.

REFERENCES

Barlas, Sema. and Lei Huang (2009), "What Do People Talk about in Word-of-mouth Communication?" *Advances in Consumer Research*, 36, 763-764.

Dellarocas, Chrysanthos N. (2003), "Strategic Manipulation of Internet Opinion Forums: Implications for Consumers and Firms," *Management Science*, 52(10), 1577-1593.

Epstein, Seymour, Rosemary Pacini, Veronika Denes-Raj, and Harriet Heier (1996), "Individual Differences in Intuitive-Experiential and Analytical-Rational Thinking Styles," *Journal of Personality and Social Psychology*, 71(2), 390-405.

Fong, John and Suzan Burton (2006), "Electronic Word-of-Mouth: A Comparison of Stated and Revealed Behavior on Electronic Discussion Boards," *Journal of Interactive Advertising*, 6(2), 61-70.

Gilly, Mary C., John L. Graham, Mary F. Wolfinbarger, and Laura L. Yale (1998), "A Dyadic Study of Interpersonal Information Search," *Journal of the Academy of Marketing Science*, 26(2), 83-100.

Huang, Lei and Sema Barlas (2009), "When Will People Tell You Something You Do Not Know?" *Advances in Consumer Research*, 36, 761-762.

Porter, Lance and Guy J. Golan (2006), "From Subservient Chickens to Brawny Men: A Comparison of Viral Advertising to Television Advertising," *Journal of Interactive Advertising*, 6(2), 30-38.

Winkler, Tina and Kathy Buckner (2006), "Receptiveness of Gamers Embedded Brand Messages in Advergames: Attitudes towards Product Placement," *Journal of Interactive Advertising*, 7(1), 37-46.

The "Name-Ease" Effect and its Dual Impact on Importance Judgments

Aparna Labroo, University of Chicago, USA
Soraya Lambotte, University of Chicago, USA
Yan Zhang, University of Chicago, USA

EXPANDED ABSTRACT

Existing research has established that subjective feelings of ease can arise while processing a target stimulus. For instance, prior exposures to a target stimulus or improved clarity of visual features of the stimulus can result in the perceptual features of the stimulus being processed more easily, and increased expectancy of seeing the stimulus can make processing of its meaning feel easy (Lee and Labroo 2004; Reber et al. 1998; Zajonc 1980). It has further been argued that because things that are personally relevant and important are processed more easily, once feelings of ease arise people mistakenly make a reverse inference that ease must equal personal relevance and importance. Thus, feelings of ease can increase perceived importance of a target stimulus, its perceived relevance, and liking towards the stimulus.

In the current research we argue that merely naming (vs. not naming) a finding also elicits subjective feelings of ease. But in contrast to existing studies, we further show that the impact of ease on perceived importance of the finding can depend on whether people are making inferences about how understandable or how memorable the finding is. In particular we suggest that feelings of ease that arise from merely naming a finding, might be associated with how memorable or how understandable the presented information is. If people associate ease with how memorable the information is, the finding appears more important. This is because things that are important are usually recalled more easily, but people also mistakenly reverse this inference. Thus, information that feels easy-to-recall is also judged more important. However, if alternatively, ease is associated with understanding the information, the finding appears unduly simplistic, less novel, and unimportant. This is because usually people exert more effort to understand information they think is important, and they thus equate importance with effort-to-understand. But when trying to understand information, people also invert this relationship and infer that feelings-of-effort imply importance. In this case, feelings of subjective difficulty, not ease, increases the perceived importance, and naming a finding makes it feel easy-to-understand and trivial. We test these effects across five experiments.

Across five experiments, participants evaluate a popular research finding: a psychological effect, an economic principle, a jury decision, or a medical condition. In experiment 1, we established people's natural inference in evaluating a finding's importance. Participants evaluated a psychological effect or an economic theorem that was named or not named, and endorsed which strategy they had used in evaluating importance afterwards. We found that naming a finding always increased feelings of ease, but its effects on importance were driven by the extent to which participants reported having judged the finding for memory or understanding.

In the subsequent experiments, we manipulated ease of processing by either associating a name with the finding or not, and attributed those feelings of ease either to recalling or understanding the information. Specifically, experiments 2a-b examined the presence of a name (vs. no name) atop the descriptions of a jury decision or a psychological effect, and resulted in participants finding the information more important when making a memory-based evaluation in which participants were primed to focus on recall but less important when making a stimulus-based one in which they were primed to focus on understanding. A post-test revealed that including the name increased the perceived ease-of-processing. However, depending on whether ease was associated with recalling or understanding the information, ease increased or decreased, respectively, the perceived importance of the findings. In experiment 2b, we further explored this interaction and found that ease of processing mediated the effect such that ease-of-recall was positively correlated with importance, while ease-of-understanding was negatively correlated with importance.

Finally, in experiments 3a-3b we extended these findings to judgments pertaining to the importance of funding research for a medical condition. We additionally investigated who is more likely to fall prey to such reverse inference rules: people who pay more or less attention to information. We predicted that although low attention people usually fall prey to heuristics, in the case of these particular inference rules it is people high in attention who will more likely fall prey to such rules. This is because people who pay more (vs. less) attention to information are also those people who are more likely to put effort to understand information that is important. Thus, they will be more likely to associate effort-to-understand with importance. Also, ironically, it is these high attention people who will be more likely to recall important information more easily, because they probably attended to the important information more carefully when they came across it. Thus, for them, ease of recall is also more likely to be associated with perceived importance of information. We found that this is indeed the case.

As a set, these studies thus demonstrate that merely naming a finding always increases ease of processing the information, but ease can increase or decrease perceived importance of that finding depending on whether decision makers associate ease with memory or with understanding. Thus, the direction of impact of naming a finding on its perceived importance is moderated by the inference rule people use (memorable or understandable) and the extent of influence of naming a finding on its perceived importance is mediated by the feelings of ease that result from naming the finding.

Buyer Beware of Your Shadow: A Dual Process Explanation of Name Letter Branding and Avoidance

Luke Kachersky, Fordham University, USA
Sankar Sen, Baruch College/CUNY, USA

EXPANDED ABSTRACT

According to the work on implicit egotism (Pelham, Carvallo and Jones 2005) and name letter branding, people subconsciously gravitate toward others, professions, and brands (Brendl et al. 2005) with names that ever so slightly resemble their own. For example, *D*enise has a propensity to fall in love with *D*ennis, become a *D*entist, and prefer *D*ove chocolate. These tendencies are in line with many other effects in which people prefer things associated with the self (e.g., mere ownership; Beggan 1992). What is counter-intuitive is that these tendencies extend to negative performance outcomes (Nelson and Simmons 2007). In other words, *D*enise is also likely to earn more *D* grades. It has been proposed that this paradox arises because preference for name letter objects is an automatic effect. Can consumers defend against their own vanity?

As with other automatic effects, we suggest there are boundaries to name letter branding and implicit egotism. Building on the idea that these effects are automatic, we propose that a reversal is possible when people are motivated to protect their feelings about themselves. Specifically, people should be motivated to protect their self-concepts from associations that reflect poorly on the self (Snyder, Lassegard and Ford 1986). When an association with a negative product is established via a shared name letter, people should be motivated to distance themselves from that association. But, self-protective action requires cognitive resources even if the contents of the process are not consciously accessible (Murray et al. 2008). We propose that when Denise's cognitive resources are being utilized on academic exams, for instance, it depletes the resources required for self-protective activity (i.e., distancing from D grades). But if those resources were available, we predict that people would prefer name letter objects *less* when it comes to negative stimuli. This effect, called *name letter avoidance*, fits with name letter branding within the context of the heuristic-systematic model (Chaiken 1980). In name letter branding, name letters are processed heuristically and consumers automatically prefer the brand to identical, non-name letter brands. In name letter avoidance, the inconsistency between one's positive self-beliefs and the presence of one's name letters on a negative product results in systematic but still subconscious processing that enables distancing (Giner-Sorolla and Chaiken 1997; Murray et al. 2008).

We first tested these ideas in an experiment with a 2 (product valence: positive, negative) x 2 (cognitive load: high, low) mixed design, in which participants assigned brand names to a series of products. Participants first received a cognitive load manipulation in which they were asked to hold either a one-digit (low load condition) or an eight-digit (high load condition) number in memory (Gilbert and Osborne 1989). They then assigned one of two brand name choices to several products. Included were one product that was pre-tested to be positively valenced (flat screen television) and one product that was pre-tested to be negatively valenced (rifle). The television names were constructed as *XXX*yvia, where *XXX* represents the first three letters of the participant's own name for the name letter (NL) choice, but represents the first three letters of a fellow participant's name for the non-name letter (NNL) choice. Similarly, the rifle brand name choices were constructed as *XXX*ylok. Results showed that under high cognitive load, people chose the NL name at a rate greater than chance for both the television (N_{NL}=59, N_{NNL}=39; $\chi^2(1, n=98)=4.08$, $p<.05$) and the rifle (N_{NL}=59, N_{NNL}=39; $\chi^2(1, n=98)=4.08$, $p<.05$). However, under low cognitive load, people chose the NL name at a rate less than chance for the rifle (N_{NL}=38, N_{NNL}=58; $\chi^2(1, n=96)=4.17$, $p<.05$), but still chose the NL name at a rate greater than chance for the television (N_{NL}=61, N_{NNL}=35; $\chi^2(1, n=96)=7.04$, $p<.01$).

To identify the scope of name letter avoidance and test the affective underpinnings of the distancing mechanism, we also tested our framework using risk in lieu of product valence, as risk has been linked to self-protective behavior (Josephs et al. 1992). This study employed an Internet auction scenario and used a 2 (cognitive load: high, low) x 2 (risk: high, low) x 2 (seller name: name-lettered (NL), non-name-lettered (NNL)) between subjects design. Participants first read a passage stating that either 80% (high risk condition) or 5% (low-risk condition) of Internet auction participants encountered fraud. Following the passage, cognitive load was manipulated as in the first study. Participants then evaluated an Internet auction listing for a calculator. The seller's name was constructed as *XX*_Math, where *XX* represents the first two letters of the participant's own name in the NL condition or the first two letters of a fellow participant's name in the NNL condition. They then rated their purchase intent, attitude toward the seller, and perceived risk. Under high cognitive load, participants demonstrated greater purchase intent for the NL seller in both the high-risk (M_{NL}=2.97 vs. M_{NNL}=2.08, $p<.05$) and low-risk conditions (M_{NL}=2.70 vs. M_{NNL}=2.03, $p<.05$). Under low load, participants had *lower* purchase intent for the NL seller under high risk (M_{NL}=1.79 vs. M_{NNL}=2.60, $p<.05$), but still had *higher* purchase intentions for the NL seller under low risk (M_{NL}=3.05 vs. M_{NNL}=2.06, $p<.05$). Under high risk the influence of name letters on purchase intent was mediated by attitude toward the seller, suggesting that derogation is the mechanism for distancing in name letter avoidance.

Name letter avoidance is different from name letter branding in that it has a motivated component in the form of self-protection. In turn, the self-protection system requires some degree of mental resources to enable distancing. The framework tested here demonstrates that name letter branding can be automatic, but that people are capable of correcting its maladaptive effects and distancing themselves from potentially damaging associations.

REFERENCES

Baron, Reuben M. and David A. Kenny (1986), "The Moderator-Mediator Variable Distinction in Social Psychological Research: Conceptual, Strategic and Statistical Considerations," *Journal of Personality and Social Psychology*, 51(6), 1173-82.

Beggan, James K. (1992), "On the Social Nature of Nonsocial Perception: The Mere Ownership Effect," *Journal of Personality and Social Psychology*, 62(2), 229-37.

Blaine, Bruce and Jennifer Crocker (1993), "Self-Eteem and Self-Serving Biases in Reactions to Positive and Negative Events: An Integrative Review," in *Self-Esteem: The Puzzle of Low Self-Regard*, ed. Roy F. Baumeister, New York: Plenum, 55-85.

Brendl, C. Miguel, Amitava Chattopadhyay, Brett W. Pelham, and Mauricio Carvallo (2005), "Name Letter Branding: Valence Transfers When Product Specific Neeeds Are Active," *Journal of Consumer Research* , 32(3), 405-15.

Chaiken, Shelly (1980), "Heuristic Versus Systematic Information Processing and the Use of Source Versus Message Cues in Persuasion," *Journal of Personality and Social Psychology*, 39(5), 752-66.

Devine, Patricia G. (1989), "Stereotypes and Prejudice: Their Automatic and Controlled Components," *Journal of Personality and Social Psychology*, 56(1), 5-18.

Eidelman, Scott and Monica Biernat (2003), "Derogating Black Sheep: Individual or Group Protection," *Journal of Experimental Social Psychology*, 39(6), 602-09.

Förster, Jens (2004), "How Body Feedback Influences Consumers' Evaluation of Products," *Journal of Consumer Psychology*, 14(4), 416-26.

Garner, Randy (2005), "What's in a Name? Persuasion Perhaps," *Journal of Consumer Psychology* , 12(2), 108-16.

Gilbert, Dan T. and Randall E. Osborne (1989), "Thinking Backward: Some Curable and Incurable Consequences of Cognitive Busyness," *Journal of Personality and Social Psychology*, 57(6), 940-9.

Giner-Sorolla, Roger and Shelly Chaiken (1997), "Selective Use of Heuristic and Systematic Processing Under Defense Motivation," *Personality and Social Psychology Bulletin*, 23(1), 84-97

Gürhan-Canli, Zeynep and Rajeev Batra (2004), "When Corporate Image Affects Product Evaluations," *Journal of Marketing Research*, 41(2), 197-205.

Jones, John T., Brett W. Pelham, Mauricio Carvallo, and Matthew C. Mirenberg (2004), "How Do I Love Thee? Let Me Count the J's: Implicit Egotism in Interpersonal Attraction," *Journal of Personality and Social Psychology*, 87(5), 665-83.

Josephs, Robert A., Larrick, Richard P., Steele, Claude M., Nisbett, Richard E. (1992), "Protecting the Self from the Negative Consequences of Risky Decisions," *Journal of Personality and Social Psychology*, 62(1), 26-37.

Koole, Sander L., Ap Dijksterhius, and Ad van Knippenberg (2001), "What's in a Name: Implicit Self-Esteem and the Automatic Self," *Journal of Personality and Social Psychology*, 80(4), 669-85.

Larrick, Richard P. (1993), "Motivational Factors in Decision Theories: The Role of Self Protection," *Psychological Bulletin*, 113(3), 440-50.

McCusker, Leo X., Michael L. Hillinger, and Randolph G. Bias (1981), "Phonological Recoding and Reading," *Psychological Bulletin*, 89(2), 217-45.

Murray, Sandra L., Jaye L. Derrick, Sadie Leder, and John G. Holmes (2008), "Balancing Connectedness and Self-Protection Goals in Close Relationships: A Levels-of-Processing Perspective on Risk Regulation," *Journal of Personality and Social Psychology*, 94(3), 429-59.

Nelson, Leif D. and Joseph P. Simmons (2007), "Moniker Maladies: When Names Sabatoge Success," *Psychological Science*, 18(12), 1106-12.

Nuttin, Jozef M. (1985), "Narcissism Beyond Gestalt and Awareness: The Name Letter Effect," *European Journal of Social Psychology* , 15(3), 353-61.

Pelham, Brett W., Mauricio Carvallo, and John T. Jones (2005), "Implicit Egotism," *Current Directions in Psychological Science*, 14(2), 106-10.

Schimel, Jeff, Jeff Greenberg, Tom Pysczynski, Heather O'Mahen, and Jamie Arndt (2000), "Running from the Shadow: Psychological Distancing from Others to Deny Characteristics People Fear in Themselves," *Journal of Personality & Social Psychology*, 78(3), 446-62.

Snyder, C. R., MaryAnne Lassegard, and Carol E. Ford (1986), "Distancing after Group Success and Failure: Basking in Reflected Glory and Cutting off Reflected Failure," *Journal of Personality and Social Psychology*, 51(2), 382-8.

Sommer, Kristin L. (2001), "Coping with Rejection: Ego Defensive Strategies, Self-Esteem, and Interpersonal Relationships," in *Interpersonal Rejection*, ed. Mark R. Leary, New York: Oxford University Press, 167-88.

Spinks, John A., Ying Liu, Charles A. Perfetti, and Li Hai Tan (2000), "Reading Chinese Characters for Meaning: The Role of Phonological Information," *Cognition*, 76(1), 1-11.

Illusionary Progress in Loyalty Programs: Moderating Role of Perceived Ease of Estimation and Medium's Magnitude on Consumer Perceptions

Rajesh Bagchi, Virginia Tech, USA
Xingbo Li, Virginia Tech, USA

EXPANDED ABSTRACT

Compare the following promotions–"Earn a free lunch after accumulating 10,000 points. Get 1,000 points with every lunch purchase." versus "Earn a free lunch after accumulating 100 points. Get 10 points with every lunch purchase." In both cases (10,000-high magnitude and 100-low magnitude), consumers need to purchase 10 lunches to avail the 11th lunch for free. Thus, perceptions of the promotion (e.g., attractiveness, ease of attainability) and progress (e.g., time and money needed to redeem the reward) should not be differentially influenced. However, we believe that the magnitude of the medium in which the judgment is elicited will influence consumers' perceptions, even when the effort and expense incurred in earning these rewards remain the same. Specifically, we posit that the perceived ease with which consumers think they can estimate redemption costs (hard vs. easy) will influence how the medium's magnitude affects perceptions and study these contingent on consumers' distance from the reward (far vs. near).

When costs associated with points accruals are made more ambiguous (e.g., "Get 100 points with every lunch purchase that costs $5 or more"), the true costs are harder to discern (a lunch could cost $5 or $10). In such instances, consumers may use the only other cue available to them, that is, the medium's magnitude, to make inferences about the program. However, when costs are made more obvious (e.g., "Get 100 points with every $1 spent"), consumers may believe that the redemption costs will be easier to estimate and may make an attempt to infer them. To do so, however, consumers will first need to attend to the rate of return in the medium (i.e., number of points earned per dollar) and then divide the number of required points by this rate. Given the complexity involved in the second step, we do not expect consumers to follow through with the computation and instead (fallibly) use the rate of return as a proxy for making program inferences. Thus, participants may overweigh the rate of return and adjust insufficiently for the influence of the number of points. We draw from research in marketing and psychology to develop our hypotheses and report findings from four scenario-based studies.

In study 1A we only focus on the hard to estimate costs condition. We manipulate magnitude (high vs. low) and reward-distance (far, near) and study contingent effects on program attractiveness and progress. In this study participants learn that they can earn a free lunch after accumulating a certain number of points in a restaurant. Every lunch costing $5 or more will result in a fixed number of redeemable points, for example, 150 points in the high magnitude condition and 7.5 points in the low magnitude condition. Participants need to earn 1,500 points and 75 points respectively in the high- and the low- magnitude conditions to redeem the reward. We manipulate reward-distance by informing participants how many points they have already earned. Because the real rate of return is unclear ($5 or more per lunch), the true redemption costs are harder to discern. In such a situation, we expect consumers to use the medium's magnitude and reward-distance to make inferences. In the high magnitude conditions the distances appear larger. Thus, consumers in the far condition feel that they have to travel a much larger distance to earn the reward relative to those in the near condition. In contrast, in the low magnitude condition, where distances appear much smaller, consumers' perceptions of progress are not influenced by reward-distance. Correspondingly, judgments of program attractiveness and attainability are influenced by reward-distance in the high magnitude condition but not so in the low magnitude condition. We also find that attainability perceptions mediate the relationship between magnitude and reward-distance on program attractiveness. Study 1B replicates the results of Study 1A.

In study 2A we focus on the easy to estimate costs condition in a credit card context where points could be redeemed for an $8 gas card. As in the earlier studies, we also manipulate magnitude (high vs. low) and reward-distance (far, near) and study contingent effects on program attractiveness and progress. However, in this study we make the rate of return more explicit. Participants learn that every dollar that they spent would fetch a certain number of redeemable points. In the high magnitude condition the rate of return is higher relative to the low magnitude condition, but participants need to accumulate more points to earn the reward. We manipulate reward-distance by informing participants the number of points that they have already earned. Because the rate of return is specified clearly, participants feel that they will be able to easily estimate the redemption costs and pay attention to the rate of return. However, in reality, the cost computations are harder than they appear. Consequently, instead of using this rate to compute redemption costs, participants use this rate as a cue to make program inferences. In the high magnitude condition, the rate of return is higher and so consumers are not influenced by reward-distance. In contrast, in the low magnitude condition, the rate of return is significantly lower and participants who have to traverse a longer distance to earn the reward may feel that they have made less progress relative to those who are closer to earning the reward.

Therefore, in direct contrast to the findings of studies 1A and 1B, program attractiveness and attainability perceptions are influenced by reward-distance only in the low magnitude condition, but not in the high magnitude condition. Consistent with findings from study 1A, we also find that attainability perceptions mediate the relationship between magnitude and reward-distance on program attractiveness. In study 2B, we use the same procedures as in study 2A, but ask participants to calculate redemption costs before responding to all the other measures. Calculating redemption costs requires paying attention to both the rate of return as well the points required and as expected, this attenuates the influence of magnitude and reward-distance on attractiveness and attainability. These findings suggest that individuals may not have calculated redemption costs in study 2A, or for that matter in studies 1A and 1B, and may have anchored on other factors (e.g., rate of return in study 2A), which led to perceptions of illusionary progress. We discuss theoretical and managerial implications and suggest avenues for future research.

The Simple (and Complex) Effects of Scent on Retail Shoppers: Processing Fluency and Ambient Olfactory Stimuli

Friederike Haberland, University of St. Gallen, Switzerland
David Sprott, Washington State University, USA
Jan R. Landwehr, University of St. Gallen, Switzerland
Andreas Herrmann, University of St. Gallen, Switzerland
Eric R. Spangenberg, Washington State University, USA

EXTENDED ABSTRACT

Research in marketing suggests that customers within a retail store can be influenced by ambient scents. Unfortunately, there have been few theoretical explanations offered for observed effects. The major goal of this paper is to explore how ambient scent impacts expenditures and the extent to which specific characteristics of the olfactory cue itself plays a role. In particular, we propose that the ease with which olfactory cues are processed (i.e., processing fluency) will affect how such cues influence customer behavior. According to processing fluency, stimuli that are easier processing will trigger positive affect, which in turn will result in greater liking of a stimulus and other positive outcomes (e.g., increased spending in the presence of such a cue). In this research, we examine the perceived ease of processing of a simple versus complex olfactory cue, such that ease of processing effects are significantly stronger for simple, rather than for complex, scents (stimulus complexity is a traditional manipulation of processing fluency).. To provide insights in the underlying process and support a processing fluency explanation, we explore the mediating role of affective responses on the observed effects.

In this research, two pretests were conducted for stimuli selection, followed by two experiments designed to explore the major issues of interest. In pretest 1 (N=208), we tested different scents varying in terms of complexity (or processing fluency), but that did not differ along other theoretically relevant dimensions. In cooperation with a commercial scent supplier, experimental stimuli contained only one a single scent for the simple scent condition or multiple scents for the complex condition. Participants rated scents (provided in an opaque vial) regarding stimuli complexity, pleasantness and congruency with the retail store. A significant complexity by scent interaction emerged for the selected scents but, as intended, no interactions emerged with regard to perceived congruency or pleasantness of the scent. In pretest 2 (N=156), the complexity of scents selected from the first pretest were examined in a real-world setting by diffusing the scents in a retail store. Shoppers were stopped randomly and asked to fill out a questionnaire. Using the same measures as first pretest, we obtained a significant effect on perceived complexity as expected.

In study 1 (N=186), customers were exposed to simple and complex ambient scents diffused within a retail store, or to no scent at all (in the control condition). After passing the cash register, customers were asked to indicate their spending and complete a short survey. As expected, results indicated a significant impact of ambient scent on sales, but only for simple scents. In particular, shoppers spent more money when exposed to a simple ambient scent, as compared to a complex ambient scent or no scent at all. Sales between the complex and no scent conditions did not differ. To understand the postulated underlying processes of fluency, we explore in study 2 the psychological process underlying observed effects.

In study 2 (N=220), customers were exposed to simple or complex scents, or no scent at all, within a retail store. Additionally, we assessed customers' affective response. Results of this experiment were nearly identical to those of study 1. Given the similar result, the mediating role of affective reactions was tested via OLS regression. These results showed that the direct effect of the simple ambient scent on spending was significantly mediated by consumers affective responses, such that when consumers' affective reactions are included in the model, the relationship weakens to non significance.

Nearly all prior research on scent has applied the S-O-R model to explain the effects of scent on customers. In our research, we demonstrate the theoretical importance of processing fluency by demonstrating stronger effects for simple (versus complex) ambient scents on sales. One of the most intriguing findings of the current research concerns our demonstration that processing fluency can be applied to olfactory stimuli, something that has yet to be shown in the fluency literature.The results of the current research are not only of theoretical interest to those in marketing and psychology, but also have important managerial implications by indicating the nature of scents that should be employed by firms and marketing managers. In particular, firms would be well served to consider the actual nature of scents and to consider employing scents that are simpler and therefore easier to process by consumers.

REFERENCES

Bone, Paula Fitzgerald and Pam Scholder Ellen (1999), "Scents in the Marketplace: Explaining a Fraction of Olfaction," *Journal of Retailing*, 75 (Summer), 243-62.

Bornstein, Robert F. (1989), "Exposure and Affect: Overview and Meta-Analysis of Research, 1968-1987," *Psychological Bulleting*, 106 (September), 265-89.

Bosmans, Anick (2006), "Scents and Sensibility: When do (In)congruent Ambient Scents Influence Product Evaluations," *Journal of Marketing*, 70 (July), 32-43.

Chebat, Jean-Charles and Richard Michon (2003), "Impact of Ambient Odors on Mall Shoppers' Emotions, Cognition, and Spending: A Test of Competitive Causal Theories," *Journal of Business Research*, 56 (July), 529-39.

Cohen, Joel B. and Charles S. Areni (1991), "Affect and Consumer Behavior," in *Handbook of Consumer Behavior*, Thomas S. Robertson and Harold H. Kassarjian, eds. Englewood Cliffs, NJ: Prentice Hall, 188-240.

Fox, John (2008), *Applied Regression Analysis and Generalized Linear Models*. Thousand Oaks, CA: Sage Publications.

Goldstein, E. Bruce (1996), *Sensation and Perception*, 4th ed. Pacific Grove, CA: Brooks/Cole Publishing.

Halberstadt, Jamin B. and Gillian Rhodes (2003), "It's Not Just Average Faces That Are Attractive: Computer-Manipulated Averageness Makes Birds, Fish, and Automobiles Attractive," *Psychonomic Bulletin and Review*, 10 (March), 149-56.

Hirsch, Alan (1995), "Effects of Ambient Odors on Slot Machine Usage in a Las Vegas Casino," *Psychology & Marketing*, 12 (October), 585-94.

Advances in Consumer Research
Volume 37, © 2010

Labroo, Aparna A. and Angela Y. Lee (2006), "Between Two Brands: A Goal Fluency Account of Brand Evaluation," *Journal of Marketing Research*, 43 (August), 374–85.

Lee, Angela Y. and Aparna A. Labroo (2004), "The Effect of Conceptual and Perceptual Fluency on Brand Evaluation," *Journal of Marketing Research*, 49 (May), 151-65.

Lévy, C. M., A. MacRae, and E. P. Köster (2006), "Perceived Stimulus Complexity and Food Preference Development," *Acta Psychologica*, 123 (November), 394-413.

Milliman, Ronald E. (1982), "Using Background Music to Affect the Behavior of Supermarket Shoppers," *Journal of Marketing*, 46 (April), 86-91.

Mitchell, Deborah J., Barbara E. Kahn, and Susan Knasko (1995), "There's Something in the Air: Effects of Congruent or Incongruent Ambient Odor on Consumer Decision Making," *Journal of Consumer Research*, 22 (September), 229-38.

Morrin, Maureen and S. Ratneshwar (2003), "Does It Make Sense to Use Scents to Enhance Brand Memory?" *Journal of Marketing Research*, 40 (1/ February), 10-25.

Reber, Rolf and Norbert Schwarz (2006), "Perceptual Fluency, Preference, and Evolution," *Polish Psychological Bulletin*, 37 (1), 16-22.

Reber, Rolf, Piotr Winkielman, and Norbert Schwarz (1998), "Effects of Perceptual Fluency on Affective Judgments," *Psychological Science*, 9 (January), 45-48.

Schwarz, Norbert (2004), "Metacognitive Experiences in Consumer Judgment and Decision Making," *Journal of Consumer Psychology*, 14 (4), 332-48.

Spangenberg, Eric R., Ayn E. Crowley, and Pamela W. Henderson (1996). "Improving the Store Environment: Do Olfactory Cues Affect Evaluations and Behaviors?" *Journal of Marketing*, 60 (April), 67-80.

Spangenberg, Eric R., David E. Sprott, Bianca Grohmann, and Daniel L. Tracy (2006), "Gender-Congruent Ambient Scent Influences on Approach and Avoidance Behaviors in a Retail Store," *Journal of Business Research*, 59 (November), 1281-87.

Zajonc, Robert B. (1968), "Attitudinal Effects of Mere Exposure," *Journal of Personality and Social Psychology Monographs*, 9 (2, Pt. 2), 1-27.

Verbalizing or Visualizing Metaphors? The Moderating Effects of Processing Mode and Temporal Orientation

Yi He, California State University–East Bay, USA
Qimei Chen, University of Hawaii, USA
Dana L. Alden, University of Hawaii, USA

EXTENDED ABSTRACT

The Internet, with its "seemingly endless opportunities to inform, teach, and connect" (Silberg et al. 1997, p. 1244), has become one of the most important channels for pro-healthful persuasive communications. Central to many of these communications is the use of metaphor. Despite this, understanding of metaphor processing mechanisms remains limited. For example, theory has yet to incorporate mental imaging as mediator of metaphor's enhanced persuasiveness. This is the case despite the centrality of imagery processes to metaphor comprehension (Marschark, Katz, and Paivio 1983; Gibbs and Bogdonovich 1999). The extent to which processing mechanisms differ by type of metaphor also remains unknown. To address these gaps, the first objective of this research is to identify underlying processing mechanisms for alternative metaphor formats (i.e., abstract versus concrete metaphors).

A second objective is to extend current theory regarding relationships between metaphor message strategies and "processing fluency." Processing fluency refers to the ease with which message content is evaluated and understood (Petrova and Cialdini 2005; Thompson and Hamilton 2006; Lee and Aaker 2004). Enhanced processing fluency has been associated with the use of imagery appeals (Petrova and Cialdini 2005), comparative advertising (Thompson and Hamilton 2006), and certain message frames (Lee and Aaker 2004). However, researchers have yet to test the impact of metaphor (e.g., abstract versus concrete metaphors) in conjunction with other communication tactics (e.g., processing goals or temporal orientation priming) on processing fluency as a mediator of message effectiveness. Closing these theoretical gaps, this research further examines ways that congruency between metaphor format (i.e., abstract versus concrete metaphors) and processing instructions (i.e., low- versus high-imagery instructions) impacts persuasion by enhancing processing fluency. Similar congruency effects between metaphor format (i.e., abstract versus concrete metaphors) and temporal orientation priming (i.e., long-term versus short-term priming) are also investigated.

Experiment 1 examines the processing mechanism of abstract versus concrete metaphor. Although imagery has yet to be incorporated into the metaphor processing mechanism, prior research has consistently underscored the role of imagery in comprehending metaphoric messages (Bottini et al. 1994; Burgess and Chiarello 1996). In addition, the level of mental imagery may vary by type of metaphor. For example, Gibbs and Bogdonovich (1999) demonstrated that concrete metaphors were usually processed through higher imagery mode than abstract metaphors. In addition, as imagery processing is believed to have superiority over discursive processing, concrete metaphors may be expected to be more persuasive than abstract metaphors. Experiment 1 tested the information processing mode of abstract versus concrete metaphors and the effect of metaphor format on message persuasion. Experiment 1 features a 2 metaphor format (abstract metaphor versus concrete metaphor) one-factor between-subject experimental design. Experiment 1 reveals that concrete (versus abstract) metaphors activate higher levels of imagery processing, and increase message effectiveness.

Experiment 2 investigates the effect of congruency between metaphor format and processing mode on persuasion. Congruency between message format and processing mode is believed to positively affect persuasion. Such effect is expected based on processing fluency theory (Winkielman and Cacioppo 2001). Processing fluency is defined as the experienced ease or fluency of ongoing processing (Unkelbach 2007). Processing fluency may also result from congruency between 1) the information and organization of information, and 2) the type of processing being done (Bettman et al. 1986). As found in Experiment 1, abstract (concrete) metaphors are more compatible with lower (higher) imagery processing. Then it can be predicted that compared with concrete (abstract) metaphors, abstract (concrete) metaphors lead to greater persuasion when low-imagery (high-imagery) processing was made salient. To test these hypotheses, Experiment 2 features a 2 metaphor format (abstract metaphor versus concrete metaphor) X 2 processing instructions (low- versus high-imagery instructions) factorial design. Experiment 2 shows that congruency between metaphor format and processing goals facilitates processing fluency, and thereafter enhances message effectiveness.

Experiment 3 extends the same analogy and tested similar congruency effects between metaphor format (i.e., abstract versus concrete metaphor) and temporal orientation priming (i.e., long- versus short-term priming). Temporal orientation priming was selected due to its close associations with health related behaviors (Orbell and Hagger 2006). Prior research revealed that an individual can be primed to either focused on the long-term, the pursuit of distant rewards and achievement, or alternatively focused on the short-term, the pursuit of immediate gains and returns (Liu and Aaker 2007). According to the Temporal Construal Theory (Trope and Liberman 2003), abstract (concrete) metaphors are congruent with long-term (short-term) temporal orientation. Following the regulatory fit hypothesis (e.g., Lee and Aaker 2004; Aaker and Lee 2006), one may expect that when there is congruency between an individual's regulatory orientation (e.g., long- versus short-term) and communication message (e.g., abstract versus concrete metaphor), the ideas conveyed in the message are conceptually more fluent, and hence are more effective. To test these hypotheses, Experiment 3 features a 2 metaphor format (abstract metaphor versus concrete metaphor) X 2 temporal orientation priming (long- versus short-term priming) factorial design. Experiment 3 reveals the positive effects of congruency between metaphor format (i.e., abstract versus concrete metaphors) and temporal orientation priming (i.e., long-term versus short-term priming) on message effectiveness due to increased processing fluency.

This research contributes to the collective knowledge of marketing in the following aspects. First, by developing a more precise model of the processing mechanism related to metaphors, this research advances the collective knowledge concerning how to effectively deliver metaphoric marketing appeals. Second, by examining the match or mismatch of different kinds of metaphors to other communication tactics (e.g., processing goals or temporal orientation priming), the present research may help identify ways to optimize the blending of linguistic and non-linguistic advertising elements. These analyses should assist marketers in answering important strategic questions in today's highly competitive global marketplace.

REFERENCES

Aaker, Jennifer L. and Angela Y. Lee (2006), "Understanding Regulatory Fit," *Journal of Marketing Research*, 43 (1), 15-19.

Baron, Reuben M. and David A. Kenny (1986), "The Moderator-Mediator Variable Distinction in Social Psychological Research: Conceptual, Strategic, and Statistical Considerations," *Journal of Personality & Social Psychology*, 51 (6), 1173-82.

Bergadaa, Michelle M. (1990), "The Role of Time in the Action of the Consumer," *Journal of Consumer Research*, 17 (4), 289-302.

Bettman, James R., John W. Payne, and Richard Staelin (1986), "Cognitive Considerations in Designing Effective Labels for Presenting Risk Information," *Journal of Public Policy & Marketing*, 5 (1), 1-28.

Bone, Paula F. and Pam S. Ellen (1992), "The Generation and Consequences of Communication-Evoked Images," *Journal of Consumer Research*, 19 (2), 93-104.

Burgess, Curt and Christine Chiarello (1996), "Neurocognitive Mechanisms underlying Metaphor Comprehension and Other Figurative Language," *Metaphor and Symbolic Activity*, 11 (1), 67-84.

Escalas, Jennifer E. (2004), "Imagine Yourself in the Product," *Journal of Advertising*, 33 (2), 37-48.

Gibbs, Raymond W. and Jody Bogdonovich (1999), "Mental Imagery in Interpreting Poetic Metaphor," *Metaphor and Symbol*, 14 (1), 37-44.

Grossman, Randi Priluck and Brian D. Till (1998), "The Persistence of Classically Conditioned Brand Attitudes," *Journal of Advertising*, 27 (1), 23-31.

Hoffman, Donna L. and Thomas P. Novak (1996), "Marketing in Hypermedia Computer-Mediated Environments: Conceptual Foundations," *Journal of Marketing*, 60 (3), 50-68.

Hunt, Shelby D. and Anil Menon (1995), "Metaphors and Competitive Advantage: Evaluating the Use of Metaphors in Theories of Competitive Strategy," *Journal of Business Research*, 33 (2), 81-90.

Janiszewski, Chris and Elise Chandon (2007), "Transfer-Appropriate Processing, Response Fluency, and the Mere Measurement Effect," *Journal of Marketing Research*, 44 (2), 309-23.

Keller, Punam Anand and Lauren Goldberg Block (1996), "Increasing the Persuasiveness of Fear Appeals: The Effect of Arousal and Elaboration," *Journal of Consumer Research*, 22 (4), 448-59.

Lee, Angela Y. and Jennifer L. Aaker (2004), "Bringing the Frame into Focus: The Influence of Regulatory Fit on Processing fluency and Persuasion," *Journal of Personality & Social Psychology*, 86 (2), 205-18.

Liu, Wendy and Jennifer Aaker (2007), "Do You Look to the Future or Focus on Today? The Impact of Life Experience on Intertemporal Decisions," *Organizational Behavior and Human Decision Processes*, 102 (2), 212-25.

MacInnis, Deborah J. and Linda L. Price (1987), "The Role of Imagery in Information Processing: Review and Extensions," *Journal of Consumer Research*, 13 (4), 473-91.

Marschark, Marc, Albert N. Karz, and Allan Paivio (1983), "Dimensions of Metaphor," *Journal of Psychological Research*, 12 (1), 17-39.

McCabe, Allyssa (1988), "Effect of Different Contexts on Memory for Metaphor," *Metaphor and Symbolic Activity*, 3 (2), 105-32.

McQuarrie, Edward F. and Barbara J. Phillips (2005), "Indirect Persuasion in Advertising," *Journal of Advertising*, 34 (2), 7-20.

Menon, Geeta, Lauren G. Block, and Suresh Ramanathan (2002), "We're at as Much Risk as We Are Led to Believe: Effects of Message Cues on Judgments of Health Risk," *Journal of Consumer Research*, 28 (4), 533-49.

Morgan, Susan E. and Tom Reichert (1999), "The Message is in the Metaphor: Assessing the Comprehension of Metaphors in Advertisements," *Journal of Advertising*, 28 (4), 1-12.

Orbell, Sheina and Martin Hagger (2006), "Temporal Framing and the Decision to Take Part in Type 2 Diabetes Screening: Effects of Individual Differences in Consideration of Future Consequences on Persuasion," *Health Psychology*, 25 (4), 537-48.

Petrova, Petia K. and Robert B. Cialdini (2005), "Fluency of Consumption Imagery and the Backfire Effects of Imagery Appeals," *Journal of Consumer Research*, 32 (3), 442-52.

Schlosser, Ann E., David Glen Mick, and John Deighton (2003), "Experiencing Products in the Virtual World: The Role of Goal and Imagery in Influencing Attitudes versus Purchase Intentions," *Journal of Consumer Research*, 30 (2), 184-98.

Shen, Fuyuan and Qimei Chen (2007), "Contextual Priming and Applicability," *Journal of Advertising*, 36 (1), 69-80.

Sherman, Steven J., Robert B. Cialdini, Donna F. Schwartzman, and Kim D. Reynolds (1985), "Imagining can Heighten or Lower the Perceived Likelihood of Contracting a Disease: The Mediating Effect of Ease of Imagery," *Personality and Social Psychology Bulletin*, 11 (1), 118-27.

Silberg, W. M., G. D. Lundberg, and R. A. Musaccio (1997), "Assessing, Controlling, and Assuring the Quality of Medical Information on the Internet: Caveat Lector et Viewor-Let the Reader and Viewer Beware," *Journal of the American Medical Association*, 277, 1244-45.

Thompson, Debora Viana and Rebecca W. Hamilton (2006), "The Effects of Information Processing Mode on Consumers' Responses to Comparative Advertising," *Journal of Consumer Research*, 32 (4), 530-40.

Trope, Yaacov and Nira Liberman (2003), "Temporal Construal," *Psychological Review*, 110 (3), 403-21.

Unkelbach, Christian (2007), "Reversing the Truth Effect: Learning the Interpretation of Processing Fluency in Judgments of Truth," *Journal of Experimental Psychology: Learning, Memory, and Cognition*, 33 (1), 219-30.

Unleashing the Imagination through Priming: Prompting and Facilitating Effects of the Imagery Mindset

Massimiliano Ostinelli, University of Wisconsin-Milwaukee, USA
Ulf Bockenholt, McGill University, Canada

EXPANDED ABSTRACT

Imagery-evoking advertisements (i.e., ads that prompt and/or facilitate the generation of mental images) are often used to promote products and services. The widespread use of these advertisements is justified by empirical evidence suggesting that imagining consumption-related behaviors can lead to favorable product evaluations (e.g., MacInnis & Price, 1987; Petrova & Cialdini, 2005, 2007; Thompson & Hamilton, 2006) and increase purchase behavior (Gregory, Cialdini, & Carpenter, 1982).

Imagery-evoking ads, however, are not always effective. Their persuasiveness depends on both a consumer's propensity to imagine and ability to generate vivid mental images (e.g., Keller & McGill, 1994; Petrova & Cialdini, 2005; Thompson & Hamilton, 2006). Propensity to imagine can be increased through imagery instructions (Keller & McGill, 1994; Thompson & Hamilton, 2006), whereas one's ability to imagine is influenced by individual differences and, in particular, by one's dispositional imagery vividness (Petrova & Cialdini, 2005). Since the persuasiveness of imagery-evoking advertisements is ultimately determined by the information processing mode used by consumers and their dispositional imagery vividness, these types of ads may be a risky option from an advertiser's point of view: Asking to imagine the content of an imagery-evoking ad may be an effective means of persuasion when dispositional imagery vividness is high, but it may backfire when dispositional imagery vividness is low (Petrova and Cialdini 2005).

We propose that the persuasiveness of an imagery-evoking ad also depends on the tasks a consumer performs before encountering the ad and, in particular, on the amount of mental imagery these tasks elicit. We draw on the literature on procedural priming (e.g., Kolers & Perkins, 1975; Kolers & Roediger III, 1984; Shen & Wyer, 2007; Xu & Wyer, 2008) to suggest that tasks evoking mental imagery (e.g., reading a narrative) may prime an imagery mindset—defined as a state of enhanced accessibility of an imagery processing mode—which affects the evaluation of advertisements subsequently presented.[1] More specifically, we suggest that priming an imagery mindset may simultaneously prompt a consumer to imagine—we call this effect prompting effect—and facilitate imagery processing—we call this effect facilitating effect. The prompting effect activates an imagery processing mode, as imagery instructions do, whereas the facilitating effect increases the ease of imagery processing, as dispositional imagery vividness does. Thus, the combined effect of the prompting effect and the facilitating effect may increase the persuasiveness of imagery-evoking advertisements.

The first two studies supported this proposition by showing that performing a task that elicits mental imagery can increase the persuasiveness of imagery-evoking advertisements subsequently presented. In Study 1, participants who read imagery-evoking, as opposed to abstract, descriptions of an apartment and a restaurant had higher (lower) purchase intentions toward a tropical resort whose description was imagery-evoking (abstract). In Study 2, participants who made 20 size judgments (e.g., select the item that is larger in real life: Camel/Cow)—a task that evokes mental imagery (Paivio, 1975)—as opposed to 20 vowel judgments (e.g., select the word with more vowels: Camel/Cow)—a task that does not elicit mental imagery—, had more favorable evaluations of a tropical resort described in an imagery-evoking way.

We also propose that the impact of an imagery mindset on persuasion may be moderated by both the presence of imagery instructions and a person's dispositional imagery vividness. In the absence of imagery instructions, the prompting effect activates an imagery processing mode that may increase the persuasiveness of imagery-evoking ads for individuals high in dispositional imagery vividness—who can easily generate mental images—, but it may decrease the persuasiveness of imagery-evoking ads for individuals low in dispositional imagery vividness (Petrova & Cialdini, 2005)—who cannot easily generate mental images. The facilitating effect, on the other hand, may have a null impact for individuals high in dispositional imagery vividness—who can easily generate mental images regardless of the activation of an imagery mindset—and a positive impact for individuals low in dispositional imagery vividness—who otherwise would not easily generate mental images. Thus, in the absence of imagery instructions, priming an imagery mindset may have a positive net effect on the persuasiveness of imagery-evoking messages for individuals high in dispositional imagery vividness and a null effect for individuals low in dispositional imagery vividness (since the positive facilitating effect may neutralize the negative prompting effect). Study 3 supported this prediction by showing that, in the absence of imagery instructions, priming an imagery mindset through size judgments increased preferences toward a cell phone with positive vivid attributes (i.e., imagery-evoking product option), as opposed to positive abstract attributes, but only for participants high in dispositional imagery vividness. As expected, priming an imagery mindset had no significant effect on preferences when participants were low in dispositional imagery vividness.

In the presence of imagery instructions, consumers' propensity to imagine is high regardless of the activation of an imagery mindset. Therefore, the prompting effect may be influential. The facilitating effect, however, may increase the ease of imagination for individuals low in dispositional imagery vividness and, in turn, the persuasiveness of imagery-evoking messages. On the other hand, the facilitating effect may have a null effect for individuals high in dispositional imagery vividness—who can easily generate mental images regardless of the activation of an imagery mindset. Thus, in the presence of imagery instructions, priming an imagery mindset may have a positive net effect on the persuasiveness of imagery-evoking messages for individuals low in dispositional imagery and a null effect for individuals high in dispositional

[1]Preliminary evidence in favor of the existence of an imagery mindset has been provided by Adavel and Wyer (1998) who, unexpectedly, found that evaluating an imagery-evoking (i.e., a narrative), as opposed to an abstract (i.e., a bullet-style description), brochure of a vacation destination led to more favorable evaluations of a second vacation destination described in an imagery-evoking format. In a post-hoc explanation of these findings, the authors suggested that evaluating an imagery-evoking message might activate an information processing mode that affects the evaluation of successive messages. Despite this evidence and the compelling explanation, no formal account of the notion of an imagery mindset has been provided yet.

imagery. Study 4 supported this prediction by showing that activating an imagery mindset by memorizing and retrieving a series of pictures, as opposed to performing a numerical task, increased attitudes toward an imagery-evoking restaurant review preceded by imagery instructions for individuals low in depositional imagery vividness, but it had no significant effect on individuals high in dispositional imagery vividness.

From a managerial point of view, this work suggests implications of interest for the placement of print advertisements. For example, an advertisement that asks consumers to imagine enjoying a Caribbean vacation may be more persuasive when presented after an imagery-evoking narrative than after, for example, a Sudoku puzzle (a low imagery-evoking task).

REFERENCES

Adaval, R., & Wyer, R. S. (1998) "The Role of Narratives in Consumer Information Processing," *Journal of Consumer Psychology*, 7(3), 207-245.

Gregory, W. L., Cialdini, R. B., & Carpenter, K. M. (1982), "Self-Relevant Scenarios as Mediators of Likelihood Estimates and Compliance: Does Imagining Make It So?" *Journal of Personality and Social Psychology*, 43(1), 89-99.

Keller, P. A., & McGill, A. L. (1994) "Relative Influence of Product Attributes Under Alternative Processing Conditions: Attribute Importance Versus Attribute Ease of Imagability," *Journal of Consumer Psychology*, 3(1), 29-49.

Kolers, P. A., & Perkins, D. N. (1975) "Spatial and Ordinal Components of Form Perception and Literacy," *Cognitive Psychology*, 7(2), 228-267.

Kolers, P. A., & Roediger III, H. L. (1984) "Procedures of Mind," *Journal of Verbal Learning and Verbal Behavior*, 23(4), 425-449.

MacInnis, D. J., & Price, L. L. (1987), "The Role of Imagery in Information Processing: Review and Extensions," *Journal of Consumer Research*, 13(4), 473-491.

Paivio, A. (1975), "Perceptual Comparisons Through the Mind's Eye," *Memory and Cognition*, 3(6), 635-647.

Petrova, P. K., & Cialdini, R. B. (2005), "Fluency of Consumption Imagery and the Backfire Effects of Imagery Appeals," *Journal of Consumer Research*, 32(3), 442.

Petrova, P. K., & Cialdini, R. B. (2007), "Evoking the Imagination as a Strategy of Influence," In C. P. Haugtvedt, P. M. Herr & F. R. Kardes (Eds.), *Handbook of Consumer Psychology*, (pp. 505-523). New York: Psychology Press.

Shen, H., & Wyer, R. S. (2007), "Procedural Priming and Consumer Judgments: Effects on the Impact of Positively and Negatively Valenced Information," *Journal of Consumer Research*, 34(5), 727.

Thompson, D. V., & Hamilton, R. W. (2006), "The Effects of Information Processing Mode on Consumers' Responses to Comparative Advertising," *Journal of Consumer Research*, 32(4), 530-540.

Xu, A. J., & Wyer, R. S. (2008), "The Comparative Mind-Set: From Animal Comparisons to Increased Purchase Intentions," *Psychological Science*, 19(9), 859-864.

Uncovering the Coexistence of Assimilation and Contrast Effects in Hedonic Sequences

Tanuka Ghoshal, Carnegie Mellon University, USA
Eric Yorkston, Texas Christian University, USA
Joseph C. Nunes, University of Southern California, USA
Peter Boatwright, Carnegie Mellon University, USA

EXTENDED ABSTRACT

Most judgments that consumers make everyday are part of sequences and hence unlikely to be context-free. Whether test driving cars, evaluating courses of a menu, dating (in particular, speed-dating), tasting wines or completing a customer satisfaction survey, it is difficult to imagine how the results from one evaluation would not affect the next. The literature in marketing is replete with examples of how the context in which a stimulus is embedded can have a significant impact on people's judgment of that stimulus. The two context effects that have been most reliably demonstrated in psychology and marketing are assimilation and contrast. Assimilation refers to a positive relationship between the value people place on the contextual stimuli surrounding a target and the value they place on that target itself. Contrast refers to a negative relationship between these two values (Martin, Seta, and Crelia 1990).

What has been consistent across previous research on assimilation and contrast across sequences of experiences is that these are two opposing and mutually exclusive effects. It is assumed that one or the other takes place and that characteristics of the context, such as domain match (Meyers-Levy and Sternthal 1993, Raghunathan and Irwin 2001), product knowledge (Bickart 1993), availability of cognitive resources (Meyers-Levy and Tybout 1997), or context set range (Lynch, Chakravarti, and Mitra 1991) dictate which one occurs. We propose that within a sequence of comparative evaluations, both assimilation and contrast can co-occur and that previous analyses focusing and thus testing for one or the other exclusively may have failed to pick up one or the other. More specifically, if these effects coexist, controlling for one (e.g. assimilation) may reveal the other (contrast) where it was not observed before, which is the main contribution of this work.

A relatively recent stream of research in this domain focuses on characterizing context effects in sequences of hedonic experiences (i.e., incidents of pleasure or pain). The findings have been mixed. For example, Raghunathan and Irwin (2001) document contrast effects in respondents' prospective evaluations of descriptions of vacation spots and cars when there is a domain match but assimilation effects in cases of a domain mismatch. Novemsky and Ratner (2003) find that although individuals expect and predict contrast effects, evaluations provided at the time of the actual experience of consuming jellybeans provide no evidence of contrast effects. Even today researchers (Morewedge et al 2009) are searching for empirical evidence for contrast effects in actual experience, which is another important contribution of this work.

We obtained eight years of judging data from a national beer brewing competition. All entries are grouped into sequences or "flights" ranging from five to 13 beers. All beers within a flight belong to the same broad category (example: Pilsner), but could belong to different subcategories (example: American or German Pilsner). Each flight is rated by two independent certified (expert) judges who sample all the beers within the flight in the same order. Each beer is scored out of 50 points, and each score is recorded while tasting the specific beer and written down prior to moving on to the next beer in the flight, ensuring that the evaluations in our sample are actual real-time experience data and not recalled experience or retrospective evaluation data.

For our hypotheses we draw on literature in order effects and sequential evaluation, and context effects. We propose the following hypotheses regarding context effects in sequential evaluation:

- H_1: Ratings of the stimulus in the first position will be higher on average than ratings of subsequent stimuli.
- H_2: Across a sequence of trials, ratings assimilate to one another.
- H_3: Ratings within a sequence contrast to extreme stimuli.
- H_{4a}: Ratings will contrast more strongly with stimuli within the same subcategory.
- H_{4b}: Ratings of the stimulus in the first position of a new subcategory will be higher on average compared to the ratings of subsequent stimuli.

Unlike previous work in this area that has documented these effects utilizing separate tests, we test for these effects simultaneously using a multilevel modeling approach. Our first estimation establishes significant assimilation effects at the level of the flight. Scores of the focal beer assimilate to the score of the beer immediately preceding it, and to the running maximum and minimum scores (extremes) of the flight. However, we are unable to detect contrast effects in this model. In the second stage, we "adjust" for the variation in scores across flights by incorporating individual flight dummies. We now find contrast effects against extreme scores as hypothesized. Statistical testing reveals that the flight coefficients are significantly different from each other, indicating that assimilation effects at the level of the flight cause beers to anchor to one other, and influence between-flight variation. Once flight differences are accounted for, the effects of beers within a flight being pitted (directly compared to) against each other are visible and hence contrast effects emerge. In terms of the other results, we find that stimuli in the first position of the flight and sub-flight score higher on average compared to the rest of the stimuli, however, subcategories within a flight do not impact (either enhance or attenuate) contrast effects. In summary, we find support for hypotheses 1, 2, 3 and 4b, but not for hypothesis 4a.

In conclusion, with our multilevel estimation approach, we were able to control for assimilation and simultaneously isolate contrast effects that had previously been masked by assimilation. We posit that assimilation drives the overall evaluation or impression of a sequence or group, while contrast effects influences within-group evaluations. Thus the two effects occur simultaneously, but they operate at different levels within the same sequence of hedonic experiences. Contrary to other researchers (Novemsky and Ratner 2003), we are also able to document contrast effects in real-time sequential hedonic evaluations. By documenting how two seemingly opposing effects such as assimilation and contrast effects can coexist, and how controlling for one reveals the other, our work contributes to numerous research streams including work on sequential evaluation, taste, and the evaluation of hedonic experiences.

REFERENCES

Bickart, Barbara A. (1993), "Carryover and Backfire Effects in Marketing Research," *Journal of Marketing Research*, 30 (February), 52-62.

Lynch, John G., Jr., Dipankar Chakravarti, and Anusree Mitra (1991), "Contrast Effects in Consumer Judgments: Changes in Mental Representations or in the Anchoring of Rating Scales," *Journal of Consumer Research*, 18 (December), 284-297.

Martin, Leonard L., John J. Seta, and Rick A. Crelia (1990), "Assimilation and Contrast as a Function of People's Willingness and Ability to Expend Effort in Forming an Impression," *Journal of Personality and Social Psychology*, 59 (July), 27-37.

Morewedge, Carey K., Daniel T. Gilbert, Kristian O. R. Myrseth, and Timothy Wilson (2009), "Consuming Experiences: The Problem of Shifting Standards in Affective Forecasting," Working Paper.

Meyers-Levy, Joan, and Brian Sternthal (1993), "A Two-Factor Explanation of Assimilation and Contrast Effects," *Journal of Marketing Research*, 30 (August), 359-368.

Meyers-Levy, Joan, and Alice M. Tybout (1997), "Context Effects at Encoding and Judgment in Consumption Settings: The Role of Cognitive Resources," *Journal of Consumer Research*, 24 (June), 1-14.

Novemsky, Nathan, and Rebecca K. Ratner (2003), "The Time Course and Impact of Consumers' Erroneous Beliefs about Hedonic Contrast Effects," *Journal of Consumer Research*, 29 (March), 507-516.

Raghunathan, Rajagopal, and Julie R. Irwin (2001), "Walking the Hedonic Product Treadmill: Default Contrast and Mood-Based Assimilation in Judgments of Predicted Happiness with a Target Product," *Journal of Consumer Research*, 28 (December), 355:368.

Haptic Product Information and Consumers' Recall of Haptic Imagery Information

Shannon B. Rinaldo, Texas Tech University, USA
Terry L. Childers, Iowa State University, USA

EXPANDED ABSTRACT

Although the role of haptic processing within marketing has been increasingly studied, haptic imagery use has not received the same level of attention. Imagery is a mental representation similar to the initial phases of perception but occurs without actual perception of a stimulus (Kosslyn, Thompson, and Ganis 2006). The nature of imagery consists of an experience to the individual that may appear as real as perception, where no perception is taking place.

Imagery is said to be functionally equivalent to perception in that similar behavioral and physiological responses have been observed during imagery as are observed during perception within a perceptual modality (Finke 1989). This phenomenon was first published in the marketing literature by Unnava, Agarwal, and Haugtvedt (1996), who studied the effects of perceptual modality on participants' ability to recall imagery information from an advertisement. Auditory signals were detected more slowly when participants were holding auditory images in their minds than when they were holding visual images. Similar interference for detection of visual signals was shown when visual images were being held. Other studies investigating perception and imagery interaction have found imagery to facilitate perception in that imagery appears to improve a person's ability to perceive stimuli (Finke 1989). This is the first study to investigate the interaction of haptic imagery and haptic perception in this way. Following the path laid by the two literatures, shape perception should differentially interfere with or facilitate the ability to recall shape imagery information, while texture perception should differentially interfere with or facilitate the recall of texture imagery information.

Evidence in the behavioral and neurological literatures indicates that the visually impaired have unique abilities in the haptic modality (Davidson 1976). Not only is this population well practiced in both haptic perception and imagery, but evidence is growing that shows that their brains react differently to haptic stimuli and memories than do the brains of their sighted counterparts (Röder et al. 1997; Sadato et al. 2002). These facts allow for a unique comparison for the study of haptic imagery's use in consumer product evaluation. The researchers predicted, therefore, that blind consumers would differ in their results.

Sixty-two sighted and sixty-four blind consumers were recruited to participate in an experiment. Participants listened to auditory advertisements that were embedded with texture and shape salient imagery. Participants then evaluated textured or shape salient products while recalling information from the advertisement. Additional variables were collected via self report questionnaire: extent and type of imagery evoked by the advertisement; attitude toward the advertisement; attitude toward the product; frustration with the task; and confidence with the task. The Communication Evoked Imagery Scale was also used to measure the nature and extent of mental imagery evoked (Babin and Burns 1998).

A general linear model revealed that visual status (i.e., sighted versus blind) was significant ($F=2.218$, $p<.05$), supporting the prediction that blind and sighted participants would differ in their results. Visual status was significantly related to the number of non-imagery statements ($M_{sighted}=1.98$ vs. $M_{blind}=2.48$), ($F=4.0$, $p<.05$), quantity of imagery evoked by the target ad ($M_{sighted}=3.28$ vs. $M_{blind}=3.93$), ($F=3.202$, $p=.076$), attitude toward the target ad ($M_{sighted}=4.4$ vs. $M_{blind}=5.1$), ($F=6.610$, $p<.05$), confidence in recall ($M_{sighted}=3.52$ vs. $M_{blind}=4.52$), ($F=14.847$, $p<.0001$), overall rating of the ad ($M_{sighted}=3.51$ vs. $M_{blind}=4.37$), ($F=12.83$, $p<.001$), overall rating of the product ($M_{sighted}=3.85$ vs. $M_{blind}=4.73$), ($F=8.778$, $p<.01$), and haptic imagery evoked by the ad ($M_{sighted}=4.63$ vs. $M_{blind}=5.36$), ($F=4.342$, $p<.05$).

The research question stated that when participants were evaluating stimuli while recalling imagery elements from an advertisement, properties of the stimulus touched would interact with the nature of the imagery advertisement content recalled. Because visual status was significant in the overall GLM, the data were split by visual status and an overall test of effect was conducted. In line with Unnava et al. (1996), a t-test was performed to test the overall effects of match/mismatch of stimulus evaluated with imagery statements. This is essentially a contrast of recall means when stimulus quality matched the recall statement modality (Texture/Texture or Shape/Shape) versus when modalities did not match (Texture/Shape or Shape/Texture). Results indicated that there was a significant difference in both groups. The sighted participants recalled significantly more imagery statements when there was a modality match ($M=1.57$ vs. $M=1.04$), ($t=11.306$, $p<.0001$). Blind participants results followed the same trend where a modality match resulted in more imagery recall statements ($M=1.55$ vs. $M=.88$), ($t=8.826$, $p<.0001$). These results indicate that in this case modality match resulted in the facilitation of matched imagery recall.

Participants who reported having both visual imagery and haptic imagery from the target ad had significantly better overall attitudes toward the ad itself ($F=25.595$, $p<.0001$, $SS=64.307$). A hierarchical regression removed variance attributable to the visual imagery item in the haptic imagery item (Cohen and Cohen 1983). The residual variance of the haptic imagery item was regressed on attitude toward the ad and the relationship was significant apart from the portion attributable to the visual imagery question ($F=8.847$, $p<.01$, $SS=206.608$). The same was true for likelihood of purchase ($F=6.82$, $p=.01$, $SS=401.869$) and for attitude toward the product ($F=7.409$, $p<.01$, $SS=315.077$).

The utility of non-visual imagery use in advertising and other consumer marketing has yet to be fully realized (Unnava et al. 1996). This study is the first to offer evidence that the use of haptic imagery in advertising is likely to be effective. Participants in this study who reported experiencing haptic imagery while listening to the advertisement also indicated a more positive attitude toward the advertisement, more positive attitude toward the product, and higher likelihood of purchase. This study is also the first to show how product properties can affect recall of imagery statements from an advertisement upon product evaluation. The study specifically showed that when evaluating a shape salient product, participants were more likely to recall shape imagery and when evaluating a texture salient product, participants were more likely to recall texture imagery statements.

REFERENCES

Aleman, André, Laura van Lee, Mariska H. M. Mantione, Ilse G. Verkoijen, and Edward H. F. de Haan (2001), "Visual Imagery without Visual Experience: Evidence from Congenitally Totally Blind People," *Neuroreport: For Rapid Communication of Neuroscience Research*, 12 (11), 2601-04.

Amedi, Amir, Lotfi B. Merabet, Felix Bermpohl, and Alvaro Pascual-Leone (2005), "The Occipital Cortex in the Blind: Lessons About Plasticity and Vision," *Current Directions in Psychological Science*, 14 (6), 306-11.

Argo, Jennifer J., Darren W. Dahl, and Andrea C. Morales (2006), "Consumer Contamination: How Consumers React to Products Touched by Others," *Journal of Marketing*, 70 (April), 81-94.

Babin, L. A. and A. C. Burns (1998), "A Modified Scale for the Measurement of Communication-Evoked Mental Imagery," *Psychology & Marketing*, 15 (3), 261-78.

Bailes, Sally M. and Robert M. Lambert (1986), "Cognitive Aspects of Haptic Form Recognition by Blind and Sighted Subjects," *British Journal of Psychology*, 77 (4), 451-58.

Betts, G.H. (1909), *The Distribution and Functions of Mental Imagery*, New York: Columbia University Teacher's College.

Blanco, Florentino and David Travieso (2003), "Haptic Exploration and Mental Estimation of Distances on a Fictitious Island: From Mind's Eye to Mind's Hand," *Journal of Visual Impairment and Blindness*, 97 (5), 298-300.

Carpenter, Patricia A. and Peter Eisenberg (1978), "Mental Rotation and the Frame of Reference in Blind and Sighted Individuals," *Perception and Psychophysics*, 23 (2), 117-24.

Childers, Terry L. and Michael J. Houston (1983), "Imagery Paradigms for Consumer Research: Alternative Perspectives from Cognitive Psychology," *Advances in Consumer Research*, 10 (1), 59-64.

Cohen, Jacob and Patricia Cohen (1983), *Applied Multiple Regression/Correlation Analysis for the Behavioral Sciences*, Hillsdale, NJ: Lawrence Erlbaum Associates.

D'Esposito, M., J. A. Detre, G. K. Aguirre, M. Stallcup, D. C. Alsop, L. J. Tippet, and M. J. Farah (1997), "A Functional Mri Study of Mental Image Generation," *Neuropsychologia*, 35 (5), 725-30.

Davidson, Philip W. (1976), "Haptic Perception and Blindness: An Overview," *Journal of Pediatric Psychology*, 1 (3), 21-25.

Djordjevic, J., R. J. Zatorre, M. Petrides, and M. Jones-Gotman (2004), "The Mind's Nose: Effects of Odor and Visual Imagery on Odor Detection.," *Psychological Science*, 15 (3), 143-48.

Farah, M. (1985), "Psychophysical Evidence for a Shared Representational Medium for Mental Images and Percepts.," Journal of Experimental *Psychology: General*, 114, 91-103.

Farah, M. J., L. L. Weisberg, M. Monheit, and F. Peronnet (1989), "Brain Activity Underlying Mental Imagery: Event Related Potentials During Mental Image Generation," *Journal of Cognitive Neuroscience*, 1, 302-16.

Farah, M. and A. F. Smith (1983), "Perceptual Interference and Facilitation with Auditory Imagery," *Perception & Psychophysics*, 33, 475-78.

Finke, R. A. (1980), "Levels of Equivalence in Imagery and Perception," *Psychological Review*, 87, 113-32.

______ (1986), "Some Consequences of Visualization in Pattern Identification and Detection.," *American Journal of Psychology*, 99, 257-74.

______ (1989), *Principles of Mental Imagery*, Cambridge, MA: MIT Press.

Grohmann, Bianca, Eric R. Spangenberg, and David E. Sprott (2007), "The Influence of Tactile Input on the Evaluation of Retail Product Offerings," *Journal of Retailing*, 83 (2), 237-45.

Herman, James F., Therese G. Herman, and Steven P. Chatman (1983), "Constructing Cognitive Maps from Partial Information: A Demonstration Study with Congenitally Blind Subjects," *Journal of Visual Impairment and Blindness*, 77 (5), 195-98.

Hollins, Mark (1985), "Styles of Mental Imagery in Blind Adults," Neuropsychologia, 23 (4), 561-66.

______ (1986), "Haptic Mental Rotation: More Consistent in Blind Subjects?," Journal of Visual Impairment and Blindness, 80 (9), 950-52.

Kaski, D. (2002), "Revision: Is Visual Perception a Requisite for Visual Imagery?" *Perception*, 31 (6), 717-31.

Klatzky, Roberta L., Susan J. Lederman, and Dana E. Matula (1991), "Imagined Haptic Exploration in Judgments of Object Properties," *Journal of Experimental Psychology: Learning, Memory, and Cognition*, 17 (2), 314-22.

Klatzky, Roberta L., Susan J. Lederman, and Catherine L. Reed (1987), "There's More to Touch Than Meets the Eye: The Salience of Object Attributes for Haptics with and without Vision," *Journal of Experimental Psychology: General*, 116 (4), 356-69.

Kosslyn, S. M., Giorgio Ganis, and William L. Thompson (2001), "Neural Foundations of Imagery," *Nature Reviews*, 2, 635-42.

Kosslyn, Stephen M., William L. Thompson, and Giorgio Ganis (2006), *The Case for Mental Imagery*, New York: Oxford University Press.

Kosslyn, Stephen Michael (1994), *Image and Brain*, Cambridge, MA: MIT Press.

Kosslyn, Stephen Michael, A. Pascual-Leone, O. Felician, S. Camposano, J. P. Keenan, W. L. Thompson, G. Ganis, K. E. Sukel, and N. M. Alpert (1999), "The Role of Area 17 in Visual Imagery: Convergent Evidence from Pet and Rtms," *Science*, 2, 167-70.

Kosslyn, Stephen Michael, W. L. Thompson, and N. M. Alpert (1997), "Neural Systems Shared by Visual Imagery and Visual Perception: A Positron Emission Tomography Study," *NeuroImage*, 6 (4), 320-34.

Krech, D., M. Rosenzweig, and E. Bennett (1963), "Effects of Complex Environment and Blindness on Rat Brain," *Archives of Neurology*, 8, 403-12.

Kroll, Neal E. A. and Theodore E. Parks (1978), "Interference with Short-Term Visual Memory Produced by Concurrent Central Processing," *Journal of Experimental Psychology: Human Learning and Memory*, 4 (2), 111-20.

Lederman, Susan J. and Roberta L. Klatzky (1998), "The Hand as a Perceptual System," in *The Psychobiology of the Hand*, ed. Kevin J. Connolly, Cambridge: Cambridge University Press, 16-35.

Lederman, Susan J., Roberta L. Klatzky, and Paul O. Barber (1985), "Spatial and Movement-Based Heuristics for Encoding Pattern Information through Touch," *Journal of Experimental Psychology: General*, 114 (1), 33-49.

Lyman, Brian J. and Mark A. McDaniel (1990), "Memory for Odors and Odor Names: Modalities of Elaboration and Imagery," *Journal of Experimental Psychology: Learning, Memory, and Cognition*, 16 (4), 656-64.

Mertz, S., S. Belkhenchir, and J. C. Lepecq (2000), "Evidence of Imagined Passive Self-Motion through Imagery-Perception Interaction," *Acta Psychologica*, 105 (1), 57-78.

Okada, H. and K. Matsuoka (1992), "Effects of Auditory Imagery on the Detection of a Pure Tone in White Noise: Experimental Evidence of the Auditory Perky Effect," *Perceptual & Motor Skills*, 74 (2), 443-48.

Peck, Joann and Terry L. Childers (2003a), "Individual Differences in Haptic Information Processing: The 'Need for Touch' Scale," *Journal of Consumer Research*, 30 (December), 13.

______ (2003b), "To Have and to Hold: The Influence of Haptic Information on Product Judgments," Journal of Marketing, 14.

Peck, Joann and Jennifer Wiggins (2006), "It Just Feels Good: Customers' Affective Response to Touch and Its Influence on Persuasion," *Journal of Marketing*, 70 (4), 56-69.

Perky, C. W. (1910), "An Experimental Study of Imagination," *American Journal of Psychology*, 21, 422-52.

Posner, Michael I. and Steven W. Keele (1967), "Decay of Visual Information from a Single Letter," *Science*, 158, 137-39.

Reed, Catherine L., Shy Shoham, and Eric Halgren (2004), "Neural Substrates of Tactile Object Recognition: An Fmri Study," *Human Brain Mapping*, 21, 236-46.

Richardson, Alan (1983), "Imagery: Definition and Types," in *Imagery: Current Theory, Research, and Application*, ed. Anees A. Sheikh, New York: John Wiley & Sons, 3-42.

Röder, Brigitte, Frank Rösler, and Erwin Hennighausen (1997), "Different Cortical Activation Patterns in Blind and Sighted Humans During Encoding and Transformation of Haptic Images," *Psychophysiology*, 16.

Sadato, Norihiro, Tomohisa Okada, Manabu Honda, and Yoshiharu Yonekura (2002), "Critical Period for Cross-Modal Plasticity in Blind Humans: A Functional MRI Study," *NeuroImage*, 16, 398-400.

Segal, S. J. and V. Fusella (1970), "Influence of Imaged Pictures and Sounds on Detection of Visual and Auditory Signals," *Journal of Experimental Psychology*, 83, 458-64.

Servos, P., Susan J. Lederman, D. Wilson, and J. Gati (2001), "Fmri Derived Cortical Maps for Haptic Shape, Texture, and Hardness," *Cognitive Brain Research*, 12, 307-13.

Shrout, P.E. and J.L. Fleiss (1979), "Intraclass Correlations: Uses in Assessing Rater Reliability," *Psychological Bulletin*, 2, 420-28.

Uhl, F., T. Kretschmer, G. Lindinger, and G. Goldenberg (1994), "Tactile Mental Imagery in Sighted Persons and in Patients Suffering from Peripheral Blindness Early in Life," *Electroencephalography & Clinical Neurophysiology*, 91 (4), 249-55.

Unnava, H. Rao, Sanjeev Agarwal, and Curtis P. Haugtvedt (1996), "Interactive Effects of Presentation Modality and Message-Generated Imagery on Recall of Advertising Information," *Journal of Consumer Research*, 23, 81-88.

Unnava, H. Rao and Robert E. Burnkrant (1991), "An Imagery-Processing View of the Role of Pictures in Print Advertisements," *Journal of Marketing Research*, 28, 226-31.

Yoo, Seung-Schik, Daniel K. Freeman, James J. McCarthy, III, and Ferenc A. Jolesz (2003), "Neural Substrates of Tactile Imagery: A Functional Mri Study," *Neuroreport: For Rapid Communication of Neuroscience Research*, 14 (4), 581-85.

Yoo, Seung-Schik, Chang Lee, and Byung Gil Choi (2001), "Human Brain Mapping of Auditory Imagery: Event-Related Functional Mri Study," *NeuroReport*, 12 (14), 3045-49.

Zhang, Minming, Valerie D. Weisser, Randall Stilla, S. C. Prather, and K. Sathian (2004), "Multisensory Cortical Processing of Object Shape and Its Relation to Mental Imagery," *Cognitive, Affective and Behavioral Neuroscience*, 4 (2), 251-59

Sizing Up Package Size Effects

Natalina Zlatevska, Bond University, Australia
Marilyn Y. Jones, Bond University, Australia

EXPANDED ABSTRACT

Repackaging food into smaller servings has become a popular strategy among food marketers but recent research surprisingly suggests that smaller packs may lead to more food consumed (Coelho de vale et al. 2008). Studies have found that, when comparing dieters with non-dieters, dieters were more likely to over-consume from smaller packs (Scott et al. 2008). These results are unexpected as smaller sized potions are typically used as a dietary aid (Wansink et al 2005). The aim of the present research is to explore the usefulness of using smaller package sizes as a tool for monitoring consumption. In particular, we explore this in situations where distractions are present.

The main prediction of the present study is that small package sizes are beneficial for dieters, though usage needs to be in circumstances where no distractions are present. It is expected that restrained eaters (dieters) will consume more from smaller package sizes when distracted than when not distracted. This is because dieting individuals will be unable to monitor the visual consumption cues or benchmarks offered by a smaller package and will therefore believe that they have consumed less, because the portions are smaller, than what they actually have. Moreover, because consumption volume is proportionate to package and serving size, the more that is placed in front of a distracted dieter, the more they will eat, it is expected that dieters will consume more from larger packages when distracted than when not distracted.

The design of the study was a 2x2x2 mixed design with one measured variable, dietary restraint (restrained, unrestrained) and two manipulated variables, serving size (small, large), and distraction (TV on, TV off). The main dependent variable of the study was the amount of candy consumed during the experiment. Depending on the condition, participants were either given a number of small packs (5 x 20g) or one large pack (1 x100g) of chocolate rocks confectionary. Participants in the distraction condition were shown an episode of a popular television show during the study. The amount of candy consumed during the experiment was weighed once participants completed a final, short questionnaire.

The results reveal that as expected, restrained eaters consume more from smaller packages when distracted than when not distracted. This is because for restrained eaters, the visual cues of package size are used as a consumption monitoring device. Distracting environments distort a dieter's ability to accurately monitor consumption. The findings illustrate this point further, with respondents stating that when distracted they found it much more difficult to regulate consumption behaviour than when not distracted.

Somewhat surprisingly, although distraction has a negative effect on consumption for restrained eaters consuming from smaller packages, distraction has an overall positive effect on consumption from larger packages and on the consumption patterns of unrestrained eaters. The results reveal that, restrained eaters consume more from large packets when not distracted than when distracted. They also consume more from large packets when not distracted than they do from small packets when distracted. A possible explanation for the unexpected results is that, although visual contact with food and close attention to consumption cues is extremely important in providing dietary benchmarks when monitoring intake of smaller sized portions, visual contact and attention also creates increased tension and exposes dieters to greater temptation when faced with larger sized servings. Because restrained eaters rely heavily on consumption cues and norms, when not distracted and focused solely on the large serving of food placed in front of them, they are more likely to consume more.

In summation, repackaging bulk snack food into smaller sized servings is beneficial for individuals, though only when the repackaged food is consumed in environments where distractions are not present. Distractions distort an individual's impression of dietary intake. Conversely, larger serving sizes under conditions of no distraction may create increased cognitive tension and temptation. When distracted some of the internal conflict and stress, of being faced with a large serving size is removed. This finding is consistent with popular dieting wisdom suggesting that those who absorb themselves in activities that do not relate to food are more successful at keeping temptations at bay.

Although smaller package sizes are beneficial for dieters, consumption needs to be in situations where distractions are not present, a scenario that is quite difficult to replicate in everyday circumstances. Rarely does an individual consume food in situations where no children, television, radio, co-workers or friends are present. Consistent with the conclusions drawn by Scott et al (2008) and Coelho de vale et al. (2008), dieters should opt for traditional larger package sizes over smaller package sizes in circumstances where they might lose track of the number of smaller packets consumed.

REFERENCES

Bell, Rick and Patricia L. Pliner (2003), "Time to Eat: The Relationship between the Number of People Eating and Meal Duration in Three Lunch Settings," *Appetite*, 41 (2), 215-18.

Berry, Leonard L., Kathleen Seiders Albert C. Hergenroeder (2006), "What business can do about obesity," *Organizational Dynamics*, 35(4), 341–356

Boden, Joseph M. and Roy F. Baumeister (1997), "Repressive Coping: Distraction Using Pleasant Thoughts and Memories," *Journal of Personality and Social Psychology*, 73 (1), 45-62.

Brownell, Kelly D. (1991), "Dieting and the search for the perfect body: Where physiology and culture collide," *Behavior Therapy*, *22*, 1-12.

Butler, Lisa D. and Susan Nolen-Hoeksema (1994), "Gender Differences in Responses to Depressed Mood in a College Sample," *Sex Roles*, 30 (5-6), 331-46.

Cheema, Amar and Dilip Soman (2008), "The Effect of Partitions on Controlling Consumption," *Journal of Marketing Research (JMR)*, 45 (6), 665-75.

Coelho do Vale, Rita, Rik Pieters, and Marcel Zeelenberg (2008), "Flying under the Radar: Perverse Package Size Effects on Consumption Self Regulation," *Journal of Consumer Research*, 35 (3), 380-90.

Csikszentmihalyi, Mihalyi (2008), *Flow: The Psychology of Optimal Experience*, New York: Harper Collins.

Fishbach, Ayelet and Yaacov Trope (2005), "The Substitutability of External Control and Self-Control," *Journal of Experimental Social Psychology*, 41 (3), 256-70.

Herman, C. Peter, Nicola E. Fitzgerald, and Janet Polivy (2003), "The Influence of Social Norms on Hunger Ratings and Eating," *Appetite*, 41 (1), 15-20.

Herman, C. Peter and Janet Polivy (1975), "Anxiety, Restraint, and Eating Behavior," *Journal of Abnormal Psychology*, 84 (6), 66-72.

______ (1993), "Mental Control of Eating: Excitatory and Inhibitory Food Thoughts," *Handbook of mental control*, 491-505.

Kahn, Barbara E. and Brian Wansink (2004), "The Influence of Assortment Structure on Perceived Variety and Consumption Quantities," *Journal of Consumer Research*, 30 (4), 519-33.

Kenneth E. Hart, Patricia Chiovari (1998), "Inhibition of Eating Behavior: Negative Cognitive Effects of Dieting," *Journal of Clinical Psychology*, 54 (4), 427-30.

Larsen, Randy J. and Zvjezdana Prizmic (2004), "Affect Regulation," in *Handbook of Self Regulation Research Theory and Applications*, ed. Roy F. Baumeister and Kathleen D. Vohs, New York: Guilford, 40-61.

Martin, Leonard L. and Abraham Tesser (1995), *Striving and Feeling: Interactions among Goals, Affect and Self Regulation*, Mahwah NJ: Lawrence Erlbaum.

Nolen-Hoeksema, Susan (1991), "Responses to Depression and Their Effects on the Duration of Depressive Episodes," *Journal of Abnormal Psychology*, 100 (3), 569–82.

Nolen-Hoeksema, Susan (1998), "The Other End of the Continuum: The Costs of Rumination," *Psychological Inquiry*, 9 (3), 216-19.

Rosenbaum, Michael (1980), "Individual Differences in Self-Control Behaviours and Tolerance of Painful Stimulation," *Journal of Abnormal Psychology*, 89 (4), 581-90.

Schmeichel, Brandon J and Roy F. Baumeister (2004), "Self-Regulatory Strength," in *Handbook of Self-Regulation*, ed. Roy F. Baumeister and Kathleen D. Vohs, New York: Guilford Press., 84-98.

Scott, Maura L., Stephen M. Nowlis, Naomi Mandel, and Andrea C. Morales (2008), "The Effects of Reduced Food Size and Package Size on the Consumption Behavior of Restrained and Unrestrained Eaters," *Journal of Consumer Research*, 35 (3), 391-405.

State-Specific prevalence of obesity among adults — United States. In Morbidity and Mortality Weekly Report, July 18, 2008. Retrieved January 19, 2008 from http://www.cdc.gov/mmwr/preview/mmwrhtml/mm5728a1.htm, July 18, 2008 / 57(28);765-768.

Stroebele, Nanette and John M. De Castro (2004), "Effect of Ambience on Food Intake and Food Choice," *Nutrition*, 20 (9), 821-38.

Wansink, Brian (1996), "Can Package Size Accelerate Usage Volume?," *The Journal of Marketing*, 60 (July), 1-14.

______ (2004), "Environmental Factors That Unknowingly Increase a Consumer's Food Intake and Consumption Volume," *Annual Review of Nutrition*, 27, 455-79

Wansink, Brian and Pierre Chandon (2006), "Can Low Fat Nutrition Labels Lead to

Wansink, Brian, James E. Painter, and Jill North (2005), "Bottomless Bowls: Why Visual Cues of Portion Size May Influence Intake," *Obesity Research*, 13 (1), 93-100.

Is What You See What You Get? Consumer Responses to Product Packaging Transparency

Rishtee Batra, Indian School of Business, India
Benjamin Lawrence, Boston University, USA
Sucharita Chandran, Boston University, USA

EXTENDED ABSTRACT

As much as 73% of all purchases are made at the point of sale, with packaging heavily influencing not only what products are included in consumers' consideration sets but also which of those are ultimately selected (Rettie and Brewer 2000). While product packaging encompasses several different dimensions, research in visual aesthetics has focused most prominently on package shapes, colors, and proportions (Orth and Malkewitz 2008; Raghubir and Greenleaf 2006) while largely neglecting other characteristics of packaging such as its transparency. This finding is curious, given a recent trend in the marketplace toward using packaging transparency as a means of innovation and differentiation. While intuitively this seems to be a good way to differentiate products in a cluttered market, we currently lack a theoretical understanding of the impact of transparency in consumers' judgments of product packaging.

In this research we examine the relationship between the transparency of packaging and consumers' product evaluations for a variety of product categories that vary in levels of sensory attributes. Using a series of three experiments we propose and test three hypotheses that predict transparency preference and find that both product specific factors and product packaging cues can moderate the relationship between transparency and perceptions of performance.

We find that for those products that are high on sensory attributes such as turkey and cotton tips, participants show a clear preference for transparent packaging while they are indifferent to packaging for those products low on sensory attributes (DVDs, highlighters; Study 1). However it is possible to mitigate this transparency advantage, through the provision of other relevant market information which can be visual (picture of cotton tips) or verbal (claim that opaque packaging prevents freezer burn of Turkey; Study 2). Finally there are instances where this transparency advantage not only does not manifest but that there is in fact an opacity advantage–i.e. opaque packaging is preferred (nausea medicine; study 3). Such contexts represent boundary conditions to the transparency advantage and are likely to manifest when transparency of packaging may instantiate negative emotional reactions (such as disgust, fear, embarrassment) to the problems that the product serve as solutions for.

We support the notion here that given the primacy of firsthand experience in product evaluation, marketers have the ability to shape this firsthand experience through the transparency of packaging. To a great degree, allowing visual inspection of contents of the package through transparent packaging provides sensory information not only related to sight but may also serve as a proxy for other sensory information such as taste, touch and smell. In absence of the ability to provide such a direct visual inspection it is possible through other means to mitigate the opacity disadvantage. Marketers can transform the way an indirect, secondhand experience occurs by changing the way in which the sensory attribute is framed. This can occur through some kind of a proxy of firsthand sensory experience by the use of market information such as a salient product image on the package and/or a relevant product claim.

In this research we have focused solely on the impact of visual inspection through transparent packaging. However we still lack an understanding of how such a visual examination helps or falls short of serving other sensory evaluations–such as smell, touch, taste. Also, it would be interesting to examine how opaque packaging with some other sensory dimension, such as scent, may serve as an indirect diagnostic visual experience. An orange scented opaque package for orange juice may invoke visual images of fresh oranges and may perform adequately or even better than a transparent package. Our findings also suggest that other relevant cues may provide diagnostic information that acts as a proxy to mitigate the absence of visual information in evaluation. Such a transformation may change either the relative weights attached to the associated sensory and cognitive attributes or may in fact change their relative value. The precise mechanism of the transformation between the impact of sensory and cognitive cues in determining the effect of transparency of packaging is also an interesting question for future investigation.

More generally, this is an area of substantive interest because of the important implications of packaging in marketing strategy. Not only does packaging have the ability to influence purchase decisions (Creusen and Schoormans 2005), it also holds the power to damage consumer relationships if not thought out carefully, as in the recent case of Pepsico's redesign of Tropicana Orange Juice. The packaging of a product can be thought to "do the talking" for its contents and therefore it is necessary to ensure that the packaging is communicating the right message. It is therefore important to understand how consumers react to and process package-related information so that marketers might align their packaging's message to consumer needs.

REFERENCES

Creusen, M. E. H. and J. P. L. Schoormans (2005), "The Different Roles of Product Appearance in Consumer Choice," *Journal of Product Innovation Management*, 22 (1), 63-81.

Orth, Ulrich R. and Keven Malkewitz (2008), "Holistic Package Design and Consumer Brand Impressions," *Journal of Marketing*, 72 (3), 64-81.

Raghubir, Priya and Eric A. Greenleaf (2006), "Ratios in Proportion: What Should the Shape of the Package Be?" *Journal of Marketing*, 70, 95-107.

Rettie, R. and C. Brewer (2000), "The Verbal and Visual Components of Package Design," *Journal of Product and Brand Management*, 9 (1), 56-70.

Not as Big as it Looks: Attribution Errors in the Perceptual Domain

Zachariah Sharek, Carnegie Mellon University, USA
Sam Swift, Carnegie Mellon University, USA
Francesca Gino, University of North Carolina at Chapel Hill, USA
Don Moore, Carnegie Mellon University, USA

EXTENDED ABSTRACT

People routinely assume correspondence between acts and dispositions, a systematic error prior research has labeled "correspondence bias." Three laboratory studies investigate the robustness and generality of this tendency, and suggest that it may be even more fundamental than prior theories have supposed. Most of the research documenting the correspondence bias uses paradigms in which the behavior is more salient and easier to assess than is the situation. Our studies employ a new paradigm in which people have perfect information about both the situation and the behavior. Using this paradigm across different settings, we find that the correspondence bias generalizes to inanimate objects.

Participants in our first study evaluated the height of ten target individuals, some of whom happened to be standing on cinderblocks. The height of the cinderblock was common knowledge. Using this setting, we were interested in testing whether people made correspondent inferences and reported believing that those standing on cinderblocks were taller than those who did not. Such an effect could not easily be explained by the theories offered previously to explain the correspondence bias.

Consistent with the correspondence bias, participants were more likely to select candidates on blocks as among the five tallest candidates. Had participants always chosen the five tallest candidates, then, on average, 2.5 of the five candidates they chose would have been standing on cinderblocks. In fact, 2.8 of those chosen were standing on cinderblocks, a significant difference, $t(78)=3.37$, $p=.001$.

To examine the effect of the cinderblock on each candidate's rated height, we conducted a mixed model analysis of the ten repeated measures from each participant, including the candidate's actual height and the presence of a cinderblock as covariates. The results reveal that each inch of actual height increased a candidate's rated height by .26 units ($t\,[652]=25.02$, $p<.001$) and that the eight inches contributed by the cinderblock contributed an additional .15 units ($t\,[90]=2.3$, $p=.02$).

In this study, both the outcome of interest (height) and the situational effect (standing on a cinderblock) were obvious and quantifiable. Unlike so many prior studies of the correspondence bias, the situational was visible. Nevertheless, the correspondence bias persists. Its effect is modest in size but still robust. We wondered, however, whether the effect we obtained in Study 1 was somehow due to the fact that we had used a subjective response scale, and whether people might be able to arrive at more accurate numerical judgments when forced to estimate the exact height in feet and inches. Study 2 replicates Study 1 and varies the response scale participants used. Given our interest in the quantifiability of judgments, we also wanted to know how important the presence of the ruler was in the pictures participants saw in Study 1.

Like most research on the correspondence bias, our focus thus far has been on attributions about people. But we wonder whether the correspondence bias might be more basic and more general than these explanations suggest. This experiment put participants in the role of a shopper who has to choose from a selection of products that vary in both packaging weight and net weight of the product. Complicating the judgment was a significant variance in the weight of the product packaging. This is a task which should put participants on guard against the ulterior motives and potential manipulation of vendors for whom it is less costly to provide packaging than product (see Fein, 1996; Fein, Hilton, & Miller, 1990). We used as stimulus materials a set of similarly sized pint glasses of different weights, covered with colored construction paper and lids, and filled with various quantities of M&Ms. The M&Ms were the focal product, while the pint glasses of varying weights provided a situational influence.

Participants each made nine estimates of the net weight of the contents of the nine products they were given. The 60 participants generated a total of 540 estimates, from which we created a repeated measures mixed model with container weight and content weight predicting participants' estimates of content weight with random effects modeled on the participant level. Both container weight and content weight were highly significant. A one gram increase in the weight of the container led to a .206 gram increase in the estimated weight of its contents, $t\,(179)=8.49$, $p<.001$, and a one gram increase in the weight of the cup's contents led to an increase of .467 grams in its estimated weight, $t\,(198)=9.99$, $p<.001$. Recall that an accurate estimate of the contents' weight requires that one completely factor out the weight of the container. The highly significant predictive value of container weight suggests that participants failed to factor out the weight of the container.

Gilbert and Malone's (1995) analysis of the correspondence bias suggested four contributing causes: (a) lack of awareness of the situation, (b) unrealistic expectations for behavior, (c) improper categorizations of behavior, and (d) incomplete corrections. None of the first three offer plausible explanations for the data we present in this paper. While each of these may undoubtedly contribute to the correspondence bias in some contexts, none of them appear to be necessary conditions for the presence of the effect.

It appears that our participants were committing a far more basic and rudimentary error, one that Kahneman and Tversky (1972) attributed to a "representativeness heuristic" in human judgment. The representativeness heuristic leads us to want the cause to look like—to be representative of—the effect. The world is more orderly when smart people perform better on quizzes, when tall people appear tall, and when heavy things feel heavy. Assuming that a smart person will perform well on quizzes is reasonable, but the representativeness bias can lead people to mistakenly assume the converse: that someone who performs well on a quiz is smart. This does not follow, because even unintelligent people can perform well on easy quizzes.

Our results do, however, underscore the robustness and generality of the correspondence bias. We found that the bias generalized to inanimate objects and persisted even in situations where avoiding it amounted to a simple subtraction problem. We are prompted to remember that in 1990, Ned Jones proposed the correspondence bias as "a candidate for the most robust and repeatable finding in social psychology" (p. 138). We would tend to agree.

REFERENCES

Aristotle, (350 B.C.), *Physica.*

Bless, H., Strack, F., & Schwarz, N. (1993), "The informative functions of research procedures: Bias and the logic of conversation," *European Journal of Social Psychology,* 23(2), 149-165.

Block, J., & Funder, D. C. (1986), "Social roles and social perception: Individual differences in attribution and error," *Journal of Personality and Social Psychology*, 51(6), 1200-1207.

Darley, J. M., & Batson, C. D. (1973), "From Jerusalem to Jerricho': A study of situational and dispositional variables in helping behavior," *Journal of Personality and Social Psychology*, 27, 100-108.

Epley, N., Savitsky, K., & Gilovich, T. (2002), "Empathy neglect: Reconciling the spotlight effect and the correspondence bias," *Journal of Personality and Social Psychology*, 83(2), 300-312.

Fein, S. (1996), "Effects of suspicion on attributional thinking and the correspondence bias," *Journal of Personality and Social Psychology*, 70(6), 1164-1184.

Fein, S., Hilton, J. L., & Miller, D. T. (1990), "Suspicion of ulterior motivation and the correspondence bias," *Journal of Personality and Social Psychology*, 58(5), 753-764.

Galilei, G. (1632), *Dialogue concerning the two chief world systems,* Pisa, Italy.

Gawronski, B. (2004), "Theory-based correction in dispositional inference: The fundamental attribution error is dead, long live the correspondence bias," *European Review of Social Psychology*, 15, 183-217.

Gilbert, D. T. (1994), "Attribution and interpersonal perception," in A. Tesser (Ed.), *Advanced Social Psychology*, (pp. 99-147), New York: McGraw-Hill.

Gilbert, D. T. (1998), "Ordinary personology," in D. T. Gilbert, S. T. Fiske & G. Lindzey (Eds.), *The Handbook Of Social Psychology* (4th ed., Vol. 2, pp. 89-150), Boston, MA: McGraw-Hill.

Gilbert, D. T., & Jones, E. E. (1986), "Perceiver-induced constraint: Interpretations of self-generated reality," *Journal of Personality and Social Psychology*, 50(2), 269-280.

Gilbert, D. T., Krull, D. S., & Pelham, B. W. (1988), "Of thoughts unspoken: Social inference and the self-regulation of behavior," *Journal of Personality and Social Psychology*, 55(5), 685-694.

Gilbert, D. T., & Malone, P. S. (1995), "The correspondence bias," *Psychological Bulletin*, 117(1), 21-38.

Jones, E. E. (1990), *Interpersonal Perception*, New York: Freeman.

Jones, E. E., & Harris, V. A. (1967), "The attribution of attitudes," *Journal of Experimental Social Psychology*, 3, 1-24.

Kahneman, D., & Tversky, A. (1972), "Subjective probability: A judgment of representativeness," *Cognitive Psychology*, 3(3), 430-454.

Krull, D. S., Loy, M. H.-M., Lin, J., Wang, C.-F., Chen, S., & Zhao, X. (1999), "The fundamental fundamental attribution error: Correspondence bias in individualist and collectivist cultures," *Personality and Social Psychology Bulletin*, 25(10), 1208-1219.

Lewin, K. (1931), "The conflict between Aristotelian and Galileian modes of thought in contemporary psychology," *Journal of General Psychology*, 5, 141-177.

Lewin, K. (1951), *Field Theory In Social Science*, New York: Harper & Row.

Miyamoto, Y., & Kitayama, S. (2002), "Cultural variation in correspondence bias: The critical role of attitude diagnosticity of socially constrained behavior," *Journal of Personality and Social Psychology*, 83, 1239-1248.

Moore, D. A., & Healy, P. J. (2008), "The trouble with overconfidence," *Psychological Review*, 115(2), 502-517.

Moore, D. A., Swift, S. A., Sharek, Z., & Gino, F. (2007), "Correspondence bias in performance evaluation: Why grade inflation works," Tepper Working Paper 2004-E42, Available at SSRN: http://ssrn.com/abstract=728627

Morris, M. W., Larrick, R. P., & Su, S. K. (1999), "Misperceiving negotiation counterparts: When situationally determined bargaining behaviors are attributed to personality traits," *Journal of Personality and Social Psychology*, 77(1), 52-56.

Morris, M. W., & Peng, K. (1994), "Culture and cause: American and Chinese attributions for social and physical events," *Journal of Personality and Social Psychology*, 67(6), 949-971.

Ross, L. (1977), "The intuitive psychologist and his shortcomings: Distortions in the attribution process," in L. Berkowitz (Ed.), *Advances in Experimental Social Psychology*, (Vol. 10, pp. 173-220). New York: Academic.

Ross, L., Amabile, T. M., & Steinmetz, J. L. (1977), "Social roles, social control, and biases in social-perception processes," *Journal of Personality and Social Psychology*, 35(7), 485-494.

Ross, L., & Nisbett, R. E. (1991), *The Person and the Situation: Perspectives of Social Psychology*, New York: McGraw-Hill.

Schwarz, N. (1996), Cognition and Communication: Judgmental Biases, Research Methods, and the Logic of Conversation, Mahwah, NJ: Erlbaum.

Snyder, M., & Jones, E. E. (1974), "Attitude attribution when behavior is constrained," *Journal of Experimental Social Psychology*, 10(6), 585-600.

Surowiecki, J. (2008, November 3), "Greasing the slide," *New Yorker*.

Tversky, A., & Kahneman, D. (1983), "Extensional versus intuitive reasoning: The conjunction fallacy in probability judgment," *Psychological Review*, 90(4), 293-315.

Van Boven, L., Kamada, A., & Gilovich, T. (1999), "The perceiver as perceived: Everyday intuitions about the correspondence bias," *Journal of Personality and Social Psychology*, 77, 1188-1199.

Not Just Gustation: The Cognitive Effects of Multi-Sensory Advertising on Taste Perceptions

Ryan S. Elder, University of Michigan, USA
Aradhna Krishna, University of Michigan, USA

EXTENDED ABSTRACT

Food advertising is big business. Kraft Foods spent $1.5 billion in 2007 on advertising in the U.S. alone, whereas PepsiCo spent $1.31 billion, and McDonalds spent $1.14 billion (Advertising Age Data Center 2008). Not surprisingly, most of these advertisements focus on increasing awareness, purchase intentions, and overall brand attitudes. However, few ads focus on the actual taste of the product, and those that do fail to incorporate the multi-sensory determinants of taste (i.e., smell, touch, vision, sound). This research utilizes prior literature in consumer behavior and physiology to posit that cognitions directed by ads can have an impact on sensory perceptions, and that taste is affected more positively by multiple-sense ads than ads that focus on taste alone. Across three studies we show that advertisements focusing on multi-sensory components of taste result in higher taste perceptions than ads focusing on taste alone. These effects are mediated by sensory cognitions (study 1), and as such are attenuated when cognitive resources are constrained (study 2). Further, the individual's ability to sensorially imagine consumption experiences interacts with the ad and product familiarity to reverse the effect of multiple-sense ads (study 3).

Despite our seemingly constant exposure to food, we have remarkable difficulty in discerning one taste from another. Part of this ineptitude stems from the limited number of distinct tastes that we can detect. Our taste buds alone (pure gustation) detect only sweet, sour, salty, bitter, and umami tastes. This leads to a general ambiguity in taste experiences that is reduced in large part by our ability to incorporate multiple sensory inputs into our ultimate taste perceptions. The primary accompanying sense for taste is olfaction (how the food smells). Taste is further affected by vision (how the product looks), as well as audition (the sound the item makes when chewed). The convergence of these sensory inputs occurs in the orbitofrontal cortex, labeled as a secondary taste cortex (Rolls 2005) and leads to a complete composition of taste.

In addition to a reliance on other senses, the ambiguity of taste experiences also leads to a reliance on external cues (Hoch and Ha 1986). Within the present context, the ambiguity of a taste experience would then lead to more susceptibility to, and increased utilization of advertising and verbal descriptions. Prior literature in marketing has shown that verbal labels can affect product preferences (Allison and Uhl 1964; Levin and Gaeth 1988, Raghunathan, Naylor, and Hoyer 2006), taste discrimination (Hoegg and Alba 2007), as well as altering the taste experience itself (Lee, Frederick, and Ariely 2006). We build on this literature to show that sensory cognitions created by ads will impact taste perceptions, and thus contribute to both the sensory marketing literature and general perception literature.

In study 1, we test the basic effect of multiple-sense ads on taste perceptions. The ads created were pretested to be equal on informativeness, complexity, and overall attitudes toward the ad. The ads either listed three sensory components aside from taste (e.g., texture, smell) or listed three distinct taste components. Individuals were randomly assigned to either the multiple-sense or single-sense ad conditions and, upon reading the ad, were given a cup of potato chips. Participants then listed their thoughts regarding the consumption experience and rated the taste of the potato chips. Thoughts were coded for valence and sensory nature. The results from study 1 show that the multiple-sense ad leads to significantly higher taste perceptions than the single-sense ad, and that the excess of positive over negative sensory thoughts mediates the effect of ads on taste.

Study 2 was designed to further explore the cognitive process of ads on taste. We used a 2 (cognitive load: yes, no) x 2 (ad: multiple-sense, single-sense) design with the experimental procedure following closely that of study 1. Cognitive load was imposed by having participants memorize a class roster of first and last names. We conducted an ANOVA with taste perception as the dependent variable and ad and cognitive load as independent variables. There was a significant main effect of ad on taste perceptions with the multiple-sense ad leading to higher taste perceptions than the single-sense ad. This main effect was qualified by the hypothesized two-way interaction of load and ad on overall taste perception. Simple effect tests revealed a significant difference between the multiple- and single-sense ads in the no load conditions, with taste perceptions in the multiple-sense ad condition being significantly higher; however, there was no significant difference between the multiple- and single-sense ads in the load condition. Thus, the effects of the multiple-sense ad (vs. single-sense ad) are reduced when participants were restricted in their cognitive ability.

Study 3 explored additional moderators of the ad-taste effect, namely sensory imagery ability and product familiarity, creating a 2 (ad: multiple-, single-sense) x 2 (product: familiar, unfamiliar) design with sensory imagery ability used as a measured third factor. We chose popcorn as the familiar food, with soy popcorn as the unfamiliar food. With an unfamiliar food, we expect individuals who are less able to imagine sensory experiences on their own will rely more heavily on the ad for the image generated. In contrast, those who are high in imagery ability should rely on their own imagination of the experience and less on the ad and its positive direction for sensory thoughts. Indeed, we find that for an unfamiliar food, sensory imagery interacts with the ad so that a multiple-sense (vs. single-sense) ad leads to better taste for low imagers (vs. high imagers). Interestingly, for high imagers taste perceptions are significantly lower in the multiple-sense condition than in the single-sense condition, showing a backfire effect of multiple-sense ads. This may stem from previously reported negative perceptions of soy as an ingredient (Wansink et al. 2000). For a familiar food we replicate our findings from studies 1 and 2, leading to a three way interaction with familiarity, ad, and imagery ability.

Our results across these three studies exhibit the cognitive effects of ads on sensory perceptions and contribute both theoretically and substantively to the perception and marketing literature.

REFERENCES

Advertising Age Data Center (2008): http://adage.com/datacenter/article?article_id=127915&search_phrase=top%20spenders.

Allison, Ralph I. and Kenneth P. Uhl (1964), "Influence of Beer Brand Identification on Taste Perception," *Journal of Marketing Research*, 1 (August), 36-39.

Hoch, Stephen. J. and Young-Won Ha (1986), "Consumer Learning: Advertising and the Ambiguity of Product Experience," *Journal of Consumer Research*, 13 (September), 221-33.

Hoegg, Joandrea and Joseph W. Alba (2007), "Taste Perception: More Than Meets the Tongue," *Journal of Consumer Research*, 33 (March), 490-498.

Lee, Leonard, Shane Frederick, and Dan Ariely (2006), "Try It, You'll Like It: The Influence of Expectation, Consumption, and Revelation on Preferences for Beer," *Psychological Science*, 17 (12), 1054-58.

Levin, Irwin P and Gary J. Gaeth (1988), "How Consumers are Affected by the Framing of Attribute Information Before and After Consuming the Product," *Journal of Consumer Research*, 15 (December), 374-78.

Raghunathan, Rajagopal, Rebecca W. Naylor, and Wayne D. Hoyer (2006), "The Unhealthy = Tasty Intuition and its Effects on Taste Inferences, Enjoyment, and Choice of Food Products," *The Journal of Marketing*, 70 (October), 170-84.

Rolls, Edmund T. (2005), "Taste, Olfactory, and Food Texture Processing in the Brain, and the Control of Food Intake," *Physiology & Behavior*, 85 (May), 45-56.

Wansink, Brian, Se-Bum Park, Steven Sonka and Michelle Morganosky (2000), "How Soy Labeling Influences Preference and Taste," *International Food and Agribusiness Management Review*, 3, 85-94.

The Intersectionality Paradigm and Consumer Culture Theory

Ahir Gopaldas, York University, Canada

EXTENDED ABSTRACT

This article offers a paradigmatic view of intersectionality organized into the following sections: (1) grammatology, (2) ontology, (3) epistemology, (4) methodology, and (5) axiology. Thereafter, to explore the scope of intersectionality's value to consumer culture theory (CCT; for a review, see Arnould and Thompson 2005), the article analyzes exemplars of social taxonomy research in the CCT canon and develops avenues for intersectionality research in marketplace contexts.

Intersectionality as paradigm. Intersectionality is an interdisciplinary field of social studies whose shared objective is to explicate social phenomena in terms of multiple identity systems (e.g., race, class, gender, education, marital status, sexuality, religion, nationality, immigration status, disability, *et cetera*). Intersectionality has been diversely described as an analytical tool (e.g., Collins 1998), buzzword (e.g., Davis 2008), concept (e.g., Crenshaw 1989), perspective (e.g., Shields 2008), paradigm (e.g., Hancock 2007), *et cetera*. Hence, our choice to present intersectionality as a paradigm, which subsumes the other descriptors, warrants explanation.

In knowledge production cycles, a set of ideas often begins as a perspective, gains acceptance, undergoes formalization, and yields a paradigm (Denzin and Lincoln 2005). In this progressive sense, our use of paradigm is meant to signal a maturing set of ideas. However, far from ending scholarly conversation, a paradigm (Kuhn 1962) is a worldview that precedes the empirical research process; in other words, paradigms make theorizing possible. Paradigms stimulate theoretical conversations by proposing (1) a grammatology: propositions on the representation of phenomena using language, (2) an ontology: propositions on the nature of being or the constitution of phenomena, (2) an epistemology: propositions on the legitimation of knowledge, (4) a methodology: propositions on data collection and analysis, and (5) an axiology: propositions on the purpose or value of empirical research and emergent knowledge.

In Kuhn's (1962) sociology of knowledge, science is argued to evolve sporadically on account of 'revolutions'–social competitions between incommensurable emergent and extant paradigms. By contrast, in subsequent assessments (Denzin and Lincoln 2005; Feyerabend 1975; Laudan 1977), science, especially social science, is argued to evolve continually on account of researcher bricolage–creative configurations of paradigms, methods, and theories to solve substantive problems. The latter model better explains the development of intersectionality. In our assessment, the intersectionality literature has assimilated select tenets from constructivism, critical theory, feminism, neo-positivism, post-colonialism, post-modernism, post-structuralism, and structuration to inform research on social taxonomy.

In the intersectionality purview, identity categories (e.g., "black" and "white"; "working class" and "middle class"; "man" and "woman") are not mere verbal representations of inevitable distinctions so much as powerful tools that construct social distinctions and economic implications. Intersectionality is "the interaction [among] categories of difference in individual lives, social practices, institutional arrangements, and cultural ideologies and the outcomes of these interactions in terms of power" (Davis 2008: p.68).

Intersectionality and CCT. Three studies published in recent volumes of the Journal of Consumer Research (Crockett and Wallendorf 2004; Henry 2005; Thompson 2004) are among the more intersectional analyses of social taxonomy in the CCT canon. These articles are not directly informed by current intersectionality literature, but are sensitized to some of its logics via precursory and parallel literatures: men's and women's studies, feminist and post-structuralist theories, and Bourdieulian thought. We review aspects of these studies through the lens of intersectionality. Our purpose in doing so is to enliven the logics of intersectional research and highlight best practices among consumer culture theorists. Viewing CCT through the lens of the intersectionality paradigm also illuminates several avenues for future research.

One promising avenue of research is to examine the emerging identity categories and systems in marketscapes. Marketscapes, especially virtual and transnational marketscapes, are marked by a high degree of semantic flux (Kozinets 2008) because such scapes connect people across traditional geopolitical and sociocultural boundaries (Muniz Jr. and O'Guinn 2001), for example, via online networking (e.g., *Facebook*) or matchmaking (e.g., *eHarmony*) services. What novel identity categories and systems do these marketscapes produce and which historical identity systems of (dis)advantage do they reproduce? In marketscapes, where a temporary emancipation from identity categorization (a.k.a. anonymity) is technologically feasible, how do consumers' and producers' interventions thwart such emancipation? Which identity markers are prerequisites for participation and which are optional?

Another promising avenue of research is to compare and contrast historical and emerging identity categories. An example of a market-mediated context where both types of categories predominate is the transnational news media (e.g., *CNN International*), wherein news anchors, celebrities, and experts reproduce historical identity categories and reify emerging ones simply by repeated invocation of them. Such comparative studies might confirm whether emerging categories are indeed more fluid than historical ones (Firat and Venkatesh 1995) and, if so, whether encouraging continual re-categorization of identities might be one strategy for weakening social structures and strengthening individual agency. After all, intersectionality research is undertaken not merely to identify structural (dis)advantages, but primarily to alleviate them.

REFERENCES

Arnould, Eric J. and Craig J. Thompson (2005), "Consumer Culture Theory (CCT): Twenty Years of Research," *Journal of Consumer Research*, 31 (4), 868-82.

Collins, Patricia H. (1998), *Fighting Words: Black Women and the Search for Justice*, Minneapolis: University of Minnesota Press.

Crenshaw, Kimberlé (1989), "Demarginalizing the Intersection of Race and Sex: A Black Feminist Critique of Antidiscrimination Doctrine, Feminist Theory and Antiracist Politics," *University of Chicago Legal Forum*, 1989, 139-67.

Crockett, David and Melanie Wallendorf (2004), "The Role of Normative Political Ideology in Consumer Behavior," *Journal of Consumer Research*, 31 (3), 511-28.

Davis, Kathy (2008), "Intersectionality as Buzzword: A Sociology of Science Perspective on What Makes a Feminist Theory Successful," *Feminist Theory*, 9 (1), 67-85.

Denzin, Norman K. and Yvonna S. Lincoln (2005), *The Sage Handbook of Qualitative Research*, Thousand Oaks, CA: Sage Publications.

Feyerabend, Paul K. (1975), *Against Method: Outline of an Anarchistic Theory of Knowledge*, London: NLB.

Firat, A. Fuat and Alladi Venkatesh (1995), "Liberatory Postmodernism and the Reenchantment of Consumption," *Journal of Consumer Research*, 22 (3), 239.

Hancock, Ange-Marie (2007), "When Multiplication Doesn't Equal Quick Addition: Examining Intersectionality as a Research Paradigm," *Perspectives on Politics*, 5 (1), 63-79.

Henry, Paul C. (2005), "Social Class, Market Situation, and Consumers' Metaphors of (Dis)Empowerment," *Journal of Consumer Research*, 31 (4), 766-78.

Kozinets, Robert V. (2008), "Technology/Ideology: How Ideological Fields Influence Consumers' Technology Narratives," *Journal of Consumer Research*, 34 (6), 865-81.

Kuhn, Thomas S. (1962), *The Structure of Scientific Revolutions*, Chicago: University of Chicago Press.

Laudan, Larry (1977), *Progress and Its Problems: Toward a Theory of Scientific Growth*, Berkeley, CA: University of California Press.

Muniz Jr., Albert M. and Thomas C. O'Guinn (2001), "Brand Community," *Journal of Consumer Research*, 27 (4), 412-32.

Shields, Stephanie (2008), "Gender: An Intersectionality Perspective," *Sex Roles*, 59 (5/6), 301-11.

Thompson, Craig J. (2004), "Marketplace Mythology and Discourses of Power," *Journal of Consumer Re*search, 31 (1), 162-80.

Consumer Culture Plots in Television Advertising: Consequences of Globalization in Emerging Markets

Adesegun Oyedele, St, Cloud State University, USA

EXTENDED ABSTRACT

In the marketing and advertising literature, researchers have employed several methods including content analysis of commercial ads to explicate the impact of Western cultural values on the promotion of goods and services in the global marketplace (e.g., Lin 1993; Tse, Belk and Zhou 1989; Mueller 1987). However, in recent years, researchers have problematized the use of content analysis technique by suggesting that the outcome of this technique lacks the required rigor for developing theory.

In response to the call by these researchers (e.g., Zhao and Belk 2008; Ger and Belk 1996) for more studies about the cultural complexity of globalization in advertising, the current study employs a semiotic approach in addressing the following research questions: 1) What are the plots used in promoting consumer culture in television advertising from Nigeria? 2) Are there signals of global and local contention in television advertising in Nigeria? 3) Is there any evidence to suggest that the symbolic elements of the local traditional culture are transformed to promote a culture of consumption or global consumer culture?

The development of global consumer culture in Nigeria can be linked to: 1) the colonization activities of the British and other European super powers; 2) the missionary activities of the British and Europeans in Nigeria; 3) the activities of newly emerging Christian evangelist churches in Nigeria and 4) the availability of cable network programs (e.g., CNN, MTV)

The methodology used in this study is based on the theoretical frameworks of semiotics (Mick 1986), visual rhetoric (Barthes 1977; Goldman and Papson 1996; Scott 1994), the theories of dramatic performance in advertising, and motion picture narrative structure (e.g., Boller and Olson 1991; Wright 1975). These techniques are appropriate when the underlying objective is to evaluate the content (e.g., visual, sound imagery, settings, story lines, characters) of the advertisement beyond the obvious message implied by the advertisement (Zhao and Belk 2008).

A non-probability convenience sampling technique was used in collecting the sample advertisements. The advertisements (N=196) were recorded from two popular national channels (National Television Authority Channel 7 and Channel 5). The advertisements included in the final sample were selected based on three criteria. First, the ad must promote a consumer product; all non-consumer product ads were excluded from the final sample. Second, the ads must have human characters must be over 10 seconds long. The final requirement was the conceptual richness of the narrative plot. This form of selective sampling is common in studies using semiotic analysis (e.g., Mick and Oswald 2006). The evaluation and interpretation of the advertisements from Nigeria was conducted by the author and a linguistic graduate who is a native of Nigeria

The initial analysis revealed seven main plots. However, a closer examination of these initial plots and more iteration resulted in the identification of three unique plots: 1) Male breadwinner 2) The Big man plot and 3) Masqueradization of Western Ideals.

Male breadwinner. The Male breadwinner (MBW) plot usually begins in a family house or the breadwinner's place of work. If the setting is a family house, the housewife is usually busy with housekeeping activities such as cooking and bringing food to the family. In this plot, the male breadwinner is either at work, coming home from work, or on his way to work. If his coming back home from work, his arrival at the house tends to coincide with dinner time. For this plot to be complete, the product or service must be useful to the housewife in appeasing the husband.

The big man plot. The protagonist in this plot is the big man (TBM). The big man (TBM) is well informed and eager to provide advice for resolving problems. The big man exhibits contradictory traits; he's endowed with both altruistic and egoistic traits. For example, if someone is ill or distressed, TBM will offer product information that can help cure the illness. In some cases, TBM will offer a free trial of the product, but not without openly rebuking the person needing assistance. TBM ideal in Nigeria, or Oga mentality, is synonymous with hegemonic masculinity (Linsay 2003). TBM is the man who spreads resources to his family members, extended family members and networks outside his family (Linsay 2003). TBM ethos is the most dominant male aspiration in Nigeria (Falola 1999; Linsay 2003). TBM plot also provides some clues about the dynamics of leadership, power relations, and social hierarchy in Nigeria.

Masqueradization of Western Ideals. The general gist of the plot is that people can derive hedonic experiences (happiness, enjoyment, pleasure) by constructing identity that mimics Western ideals. The *masquerading* concept is underscored because the context always involves dancing, festivities, enjoyment and fun. Additionally, the notion of masquerading is an analogy for illustrating the three dominant themes associated with the plot. The dominant themes associated with the masqueradization plot are: 1) masquerading Western aesthetics (e.g., Western bodily beauty, Western music and Western architecture), 2) masquerading classical Western theatrical performance (expressing Western rock star-like personality, mimicking Western romantic motifs) and 3) Appreciating modern products and showcasing traditional fashion.

Overall, the results showed that advertisers in Nigeria highlight the global through the overwhelming display of Western aesthetic attributes (e.g., Western music, Western-style design—furnishing, images of Western cities, architecture). The presentation of the global is not modified or re-signified to fit the local. The local is relegated and suppressed via wholesale presentation of Western aesthetic attributes. Occasionally, the use of traditional-style fashion may be used to legitimize the overwhelming display of Western aesthetic attributes. The findings concerning the interplay between the local and the global suggests that the global is more powerful in transforming the aesthetic of the local but less powerful in transforming social order attributes associated with the local.

REFERENCES

Barber, Benjamin R. (1996), *Jihad Vs. Mcworld: How Globalism and Tribalism Are Reshaping the World*, New York: Times Books.

Barthes, Roland (1977), *Rhetoric of the Image, in Image-Music-Text*, New York: Hill and Wang, 33-51.

Berger, Arthur, A. (1989), Seeing is Believing, Mayfield CA.

Boller Gregory, W. and Jerry Olson (1991), "Experiencing Ad Meanings Crucial Aspects of Narrative/Drama Processing," in *Advance in Consumer Research*, Vol. 18, ed. Rebecca H. Holman and Michael R. Solomon, Provo, UT. Association for Consumer Research.

Blunt, Peter and Merrick L. Jones (1992), *Managing Organizations in Africa*, Berlin: De Gruyter.

Chelariu, Cristian, Abdoulaye Quattarra and Koffi Q. Dadzie (2002), "Market Orientation in Ivory Coast: Measurement Validity and Organizational Antecedents in a Sub-Saharan African Economy," *Journal of Business and Industrial Marketing*, 17 (6), 456-470.

Cleveland, Mark and Michel Laroche (2007) "Acculturation to the Global Consumer Culture: Scale Development and Research Paradigm," *Journal of Business Research*, 60 (3), 249-259

Cooper, Frederick (2002), *CoAfrica Since 1940 The Past of the Present New Approaches to African History*, Cambridge University Press.

Falola, Toyin. (1999), *The History of Nigeria*, Westport, CT: Greenwood Press.

Firat, A. Fuat, and Alladi Venkatesh (1995), "Liberatory Post-modernism and the Reenchantment of Consumption," *Journal of Consumer Research*, 22 (September), 239-267.

Ger, Guliz, and Russell W. Belk (1996), "I'd Like to Buy the World a Coke: Consumptionscapes of the Less Affluent World," *Journal of Consumer Policy*, 19 (September), 271-304

Goldman Robert and Stephen Papson (1996), *Sign Wars: The Cluttered Landscape of Advertising*, New York: Guildford.

______ (1992), *Reading Ads Socially*, London: Routledge.

Hannerz, Ulf (1990), "Cosmopolitans and Locals in World Culture," in *Global Culture: Nationalism, Globalization and Modernity*, Mike Featherstone, ed., London: Sage.

Hofstede, Geert (1997), *Cultures and Organizations: Software of the Mind*, NY: McGraw-Hill.

Hong, Jae W., Aydin, Muderrisoglu and George M. Zinkhan (1987), "Cultural Differences and Advertising Expression: A Comparative Content Analysis of Japanese and U.S. Magazine Advertising," *Journal of Advertising*, 16 (1), 55-62.

Hunt, Nancy Rose. (1990), "Domesticity and Colonialism Belgian Africa: Usumbura's Foyer Social, 1946-1960. Signs," *Journal of Women in Culture and Society*, 15(3), 447-474.

Leeds-Hurwitz (1993), *Semiotics, and Communication: Signs, Codes, Culture*, Lawrence Erlbaum Assoc Inc.

Lin, Carolyn, A. (1993), "Cultural Difference in Message Strategies: A Comparison Between American and Japanese TV Commercials," *Journal of Advertising Research*, 33 (4), 40-48.

Linsay, Lisa (2003) "Working with Gender: The Emergence of the 'Male Breadwinner' in Colonial Southwestern Nigeria," Catherine M. Cole, Takyiwaa Manuh, and Stephan F. Miescher eds., *Africa After Gender?*, Bloomington: Indiana University Press.

Manning, Patrick. (1998), *Francophone sub-Saharan Africa: 1880-1995*, Cambridge University Press.

Mattelart, Armand (1979), *Multinational Corporations and the Control of Culture. Atlantic Highlands*, New Jersey: Humanities Press.

McQuarrie, Edward F. (1989), "Advertising Resonance: A Semiological Perspective," in *Interpretive Consumer Research*, Elizabeth C. Hirschman, ed., Provo, UT: Association for Consumer Research, 97-114.

Meyer, Birgit (1998), "Make a Complete break with the Past: Memory and Postcolonial Modernity in Ghanaian Pentecostal Discourse." in *Memory and the Postcolony: African Anthropology and the Critique of Power*, ed., Steven R. Werbner. New York: Zed Books.

Mick, David Glen (1986), "Consumer Research and Semiotics: Exploring the Morphology of Signs, Symbols and Significance," *Journal of Consumer Research*, 13 (September), 196-213.

______, and Laura R. Oswald (2006), "The Semiotic Paradigm on Meaning in the Marketplace," in *Handbook of Qualitative Research Methods in Marketing*, Russell W. Belk, ed., New York: Edward Elgar, 31-45.

Milner, Laura (2005), "Sex-Role Portrayal in African Television Advertising: A Preliminary Examination with Implications for Use of Hofstede's Research," *Journal of International Consumer Research*, 17(2/3), 73-91.

Mitchell, Ivor.S., and Agenmonmen, Anthony I. (1984), "Marketers' Attitudes Toward theMarketing Concept in Nigerian Business and Non-Business Operations," *Columbia Journal of World Business*, 19 (3), 62-72.

Mueller, B. (1987) "Reflection of Culture: An Analysis of Japanese and American Advertising Appeals," *Journal of Advertising Research*, 27 (June/July), 51-59.

Pels, Peter (1999), *A Politics of Presence: Contacts between Missionaries and Waluguru in Late Colonial Tanganyika*, Amsterdam: Harwood.

Peirce, Charles Sanders (1955), *Philosophical Writings of Peirce, Justus Buchler*, ed., New York: Dover.

Posner, D.N. (2004), "Measuring Ethnic Fractionalization in Africa," *American Journal of Political Science*, 48 (4), 849-863.

Ritzer, George (2004), *The Globalization of Nothing*, Thousand Oaks, CA: Pine Forge Press.

Rodney, Walter (1974), *How Europe Underdeveloped Africa*, Washington, D.C.: Howard University Press.

Rose, Gillian (2001), *Visual Methodologies: An Introduction to the Interpretation of Visual Materials*, London: Sage.

Rupert, James (1998), "Denied Wealth, Nigerian take Dire Steps." *Washington Post: Foreign Service*, 18.

Saussure, Ferdinand de ({1915}) 1983), *Course in General Linguistics*, Charles Bally and Albert Sechahaye, eds., Roy Harris, trans., London: Duckworth.

Scott, Linda M. (1994), "Images in Advertising: The Need for a Theory of Visual Rhetoric," *Journal of Consumer Research*, 21 (September), 252-273.

Spear Thomas (2003), "Neo-traditionalism and the Limits of Invention in British Colonial Africa," *The Journal of African History*, 44 (1), 3-27.

Stern, Barbara (1994) "Classical and Vignette Television Advertising Dramas: Structural Models, Formal Analysis, and Consumer Effects," *Journal of Consumer Research*, 20(March), 601-615.

Taylor, Charles R (2005), "Moving International Advertising Research Forward: A New Agenda," *Journal of Advertising*, 34 (1), 7-16.

Tse, David K, Russell W. Belk and Nan Zhou (1989), "Becoming a Consumer Society: A Longitudinal and Cross-Cultural Content Analysis of Print Ads From Hong Kong, the People's Republic of China and Taiwan," *Journal of Consumer Research*, 15 (March), 457-72.

Wright, Will (1975), *Sixguns & Society: A Structural Study of the Western*, Berkeley CA: University of California Press.

Zhao, Xin and Russell W. Belk (2008), "Advertising Consumer Culture in 1930s SHANGHAI–Globalization and Localization in Yuefenpia," *Journal of Advertising*, 37(2), 45-56.

Consumer Culture Theory: Constitution and Production

Ahir Gopaldas, York University, Canada

EXTENDED ABSTRACT

Consumer culture theory (CCT) is a continually evolving field of social science that extends methods and theories from various disciplines to the domain of consumption and marketing. This essay offers (1) an inventory of the elements that compose the field (major influences, frequently examined phenomena, common contexts of investigation, theoretical foci, data collection and analysis methods, conceptions of the consumer, focal stages of the consumption life cycle, *et cetera*) and (2) a dialectical model of interdisciplinary knowledge production.

Constitution. CCT is an interdisciplinary field of social science that encompasses explanatory, interpretive, critical, and transformative analyses of the experiential, ideological, material, and praxeological dimensions of marketing and consuming in their myriad manifestations since modernity (for a review, see Arnould and Thompson 2005). Several sibling fields examine terrain similar to that of CCT; some of them are: comparative media studies (for a review, see Jenkins, McPherson, and Shattuc 2002); consumption anthropology (for a review, see Miller 1995); consumption sociology (for a review, see Zukin and Maguire 2004); critical marketing studies (for a review, see Saren et al. 2007); cultural studies (for a review, see Grossberg 2006); and interpretive consumer research (for a review, see Cova and Elliott 2008). Though much Western social theory on production and consumption in the 20th century can be traced back to Adam Smith's (1776) *Wealth of Nations*, Karl Marx's (1867) *Capital*, and Thorstein Veblen's (1899) *Theory of the Leisure Class*, more recent theorists such as Bourdieu (e.g., 1984), Foucault (e.g., 1970), and Giddens (e.g., 1984) have had more direct and visible impact on CCT. Furthermore, CCT draws on numerous social science disciplines such as anthropology, cultural studies, media studies, social psychology, and sociology.

Among CCT's most frequently examined phenomena of investigation are consumption-related actants such as consumers, producers, brands, products, and markets; consumption-related discourses such as consumerism (Zhao and Belk 2008) and materialism (Belk 1985); and market-motivated variants of enduring human logics such as (brand) communities (Muniz and O'Guinn 2001) and (marketplace) mythologies (Thompson 2004). Consumer culture theorists often select long-term, high-stakes, interrelated, multi-service, consumption contexts such as healthcare (e.g., Fischer, Otnes, and Tuncay 2007; Wong and King 2008), leisure activities (e.g., Arnould and Price 1993; Celsi, Rose, and Leigh 1993), and technology (e.g., Kozinets 2001; Mick and Fournier 1998). The theoretical goal of many CCT studies is to explain cultural and structural processes and to extrapolate sociological or anthropological models of consumer-consumer relations (e.g., Epp and Price 2008; Mathwick, Wiertz, and de Ruyter 2008; Wooten 2006), consumer-consumable interactions (e.g., Chen 2009; Coupland 2005; Lastovicka and Fernandez 2005), and marketplace reconfigurations (e.g., Giesler 2008; Thompson and Tian 2008; Zhao and Belk 2008). Consumer culture theorists often collect data using observation, participation, interviews, surveys, projection techniques, or historical archives and analyze data using critical discourse analysis, grounded theory, multidimensional scaling, or semiotics. Cova and Elliot (2008) suggest that CCT is the domain of theories while interpretive consumer research (ICR) is the corresponding domain of methods.

No single metaphor encapsulates CCT's conception of the consumer, which is an important point of distinction. The philosophic orientation of consumer information processing (CIP) and consumer decision making (CDM), namely positivism, necessitates a singular and stable metaphor of the consumer to sustain theoretical development in each field. The metaphors (of the consumer as an information processor and consumer as a decision maker) form the foundations (rather than the frontiers) of CIP's and CDM's theoretical programs (Newell and Broder 2008). By contrast, we observe that metaphors of the consumer are plural and evolving in CCT research because they are the frontiers (rather than the foundations) of research attention. CCT's conceptions of the consumer include: meaning-maker (Mick and Buhl 1992; Thompson 1996); (dis)empowered reproducer of class stratification (Allen 2002; Henry 2005); identity bricoleur (Holt 2002; Kates 2002); dynamic self concept extending to possessions (Belk 1988; Tian and Belk 2005); market-incentivized tribesperson (for a review, see Cova, Kozinets, and Shankar 2007); dramatic performer of marketplace scripts (Deighton 1992; Giesler 2008); *et cetera*. Historically, CCT has distinguished itself from other fields of consumer research by focusing on the consumption (i.e., engagement or experience) stage of the consumption life-cycle (e.g., Goulding et al. 2009; Muniz Jr. and Schau 2005; Rose and Wood 2005; Ustuner and Holt 2007), though some studies have also examined the acquisition (e.g., Fischer and Arnold 1990; Sherry 1990) and disposition (e.g., Lastovicka and Fernandez 2005; Price, Arnould, and Curasi 2000) stages.

Production. Arguably, one of the most important transdisciplinary questions in the social sciences is: how does science progress (Feyerabend 1975: anything goes; Kuhn 1962: paradigm shifts/scientific revolutions)? Or more broadly, how does knowledge evolve (Foucault 1970, 1972)? Over the course of the 20th century, these questions provoked numerous debates. While these debates continue among philosophers of science, academic fields often have their preferred philosophic approach to knowledge production. Denzin and Lincoln (2005) have proposed bricolage as a metaphor for interdisciplinary knowledge production in the social sciences. For them, bricolage is the mixing and matching of ontologics, epistemologics, methodologics, axiologics, and theories from multiple disciplines to solve the research problems at hand. Adapting Denzin and Lincoln's metaphor of bricolage, we supplement Kuhn and Feyerabend's canonic models of scientific progress with a recognition that paradigmatic pluralism in an interdisciplinary field of social science, such as CCT, can foster a pair of contrasting ideologies that we term intellectual bureaucracy and bricolage. The ideology of bureaucracy favors tradition, conformity, and essentiality, thrives in authoritarian environs, and permits incremental intra-disciplinary research developments, but hinders breakthrough and inter-disciplinary progress. By contrast, the ideology of bricolage favors novelty, multiplicity, and hybridity, thrives in anarchic environs, and encourages the forging of new theoretical linkages across disciplinary divides, but disregards the origins of ideas and the situated intentions of their creators. Within this dialectical model, exemplary interdisciplinary research is conceived of as reasoned ideological compromise between bureaucracy and bricolage.

REFERENCES

Allen, Douglas E. (2002), "Toward a Theory of Consumer Choice as Sociohistorically Shaped Practical Experience: The Fits-Like-a-Glove (Flag) Framework," *Journal of Consumer Research*, 28 (4), 515-32.

Arnould, Eric J. and Linda L. Price (1993), "River Magic: Extraordinary Experience and the Extended Service Encounter," *Journal of Consumer Research*, 20 (1), 24.

Arnould, Eric J. and Craig J. Thompson (2005), "Consumer Culture Theory (CCT): Twenty Years of Research," *Journal of Consumer Research*, 31 (4), 868-82.

Belk, Russell W. (1985), "Materialism: Trait Aspects of Living in the Material World," *Journal of Consumer Research*, 12 (3), 265.

— (1988), "Possessions and the Extended Self," *Journal of Consumer Research*, 15 (2), 139.

Bourdieu, Pierre (1984), *Distinction: A Social Critique of the Judgement of Taste*, Cambridge, Mass.: Harvard University Press.

Celsi, Richard L., Randall L. Rose, and Thomas W. Leigh (1993), "An Exploration of High-Risk Leisure Consumption through Skydiving," *Journal of Consumer Research*, 20 (1), 1.

Chen, Yu (2009), "Possession and Access: Consumer Desires and Value Perceptions Regarding Contemporary Art Collection and Exhibit Visits," *Journal of Consumer Research*, 35 (6), 925-40.

Coupland, Jennifer Chang (2005), "Invisible Brands: An Ethnography of Households and the Brands in Their Kitchen Pantries," *Journal of Consumer Research*, 32 (1), 106-18.

Cova, Bernard and Richard Elliott (2008), "Everything You Always Wanted to Know About Interpretive Consumer Research but Were Afraid to Ask," *Qualitative Market Research: An International Journal*, 11 (2), 121-29.

Cova, Bernard, Robert Kozinets, and Avi Shankar (2007), *Consumer Tribes*, Oxford, UK: Elsevier.

Deighton, John (1992), "The Consumption of Performance," *Journal of Consumer Research*, 19 (3), 362.

Denzin, Norman K. and Yvonna S. Lincoln (2005), *The Sage Handbook of Qualitative Research*, Thousand Oaks, CA: Sage Publications.

Epp, Amber M. and Linda L. Price (2008), "Family Identity: A Framework of Identity Interplay in Consumption Practices," *Journal of Consumer Research*, 35 (1), 50-70.

Feyerabend, Paul K. (1975), *Against Method: Outline of an Anarchistic Theory of Knowledge*, London: NLB.

Fischer, Eileen and Stephen J. Arnold (1990), "More Than a Labor of Love: Gender Roles and Christmas Gift Shopping," *Journal of Consumer Research*, 17 (3), 333.

Fischer, Eileen, Cele C. Otnes, and Linda Tuncay (2007), "Pursuing Parenthood: Integrating Cultural and Cognitive Perspectives on Persistent Goal Striving," *Journal of Consumer Research*, 34 (4), 425-40.

Foucault, Michel (1970), *The Order of Things: An Archaeology of the Human Sciences*, London: Tavistock Publications.

______ (1972), *The Archaeology of Knowledge*, London: Tavistock Publications.

Giddens, Anthony (1984), *The Constitution of Society: Outline of the Theory of Structuration*, Cambridge, UK: Polity Press.

Giesler, Markus (2008), "Conflict and Compromise: Drama in Marketplace Evolution," *Journal of Consumer Research*, 34 (6), 739-53.

Goulding, Christina, Avi Shankar, Richard Elliott, and Robin Canniford (2009), "The Marketplace Management of Illicit Pleasure," *Journal of Consumer Research*, 35 (5), 759-71.

Grossberg, Larry (2006), "Does Cultural Studies Have Futures? Should It? (or What's the Matter with New York?): Cultural Studies, Contexts, and Conjunctures," *Cultural Studies*, 20 (1), 1-32.

Henry, Paul C. (2005), "Social Class, Market Situation, and Consumers' Metaphors of (Dis)Empowerment," *Journal of Consumer Research*, 31 (4), 766-78.

Holt, Douglas B. (2002), "Why Do Brands Cause Trouble? A Dialectical Theory of Consumer Culture and Branding," *Journal of Consumer Research*, 29 (1), 70-90.

Jenkins, Henry, Tara McPherson, and Jane Shattuc (2002), "The Culture That Sticks to Your Skin: A Manifesto for a New Cultural Studies," in *Hop on Pop: The Politics and Pleasures of Popular Culture*, Durham, NC: Duke University Press, 3-25.

Kates, Steven M. (2002), "The Protean Quality of Subcultural Consumption: An Ethnographic Account of Gay Consumers," *Journal of Consumer Research*, 29 (3), 383-99.

Kozinets, Robert V. (2001), "Utopian Enterprise: Articulating the Meanings of Star Trek's Culture of Consumption," *Journal of Consumer Research*, 28 (1), 67-88.

Kuhn, Thomas S. (1962), *The Structure of Scientific Revolutions*, Chicago: University of Chicago Press.

Lastovicka, John L. and Karen V. Fernandez (2005), "Three Paths to Disposition: The Movement of Meaningful Possessions to Strangers," *Journal of Consumer Research*, 31 (4), 813-23.

Marx, Karl ([1867] 1970), *Capitaal: A Critique of Political Economy*, Vols. 1-3, London, UK: Lawrence and Wishart.

Mathwick, Charla, Caroline Wiertz, and Ko de Ruyter (2008), "Social Capital Production in a Virtual P3 Community," *Journal of Consumer Research*, 34 (6), 832-49.

Mick, David Glen and Claus Buhl (1992), "A Meaning-Based Model of Advertising Experiences," *Journal of Consumer Research*, 19 (3), 317.

Mick, David Glen and Susan Fournier (1998), "Paradoxes of Technology: Consumer Cognizance, Emotions, and Coping Strategies," *Journal of Consumer Research*, 25 (2), 123-43.

Miller, Daniel (1995), "Consumption and Commodities," *Annual Review of Anthropology*, 24, 141-61.

Muniz Jr., Albert M. and Thomas C. O'Guinn (2001), "Brand Community," *Journal of Consumer Research*, 27 (4), 412-32.

Muniz Jr., Albert M. and Hope Jensen Schau (2005), "Religiosity in the Abandoned Apple Newton Brand Community," *Journal of Consumer Research*, 31 (4), 737-47.

Newell, Ben R. and Arndt Broder (2008), "Cognitive Processes, Models and Metaphors in Decision Research," *Judgment and Decision Making*, 3 (3), 195-204.

Price, Linda L., Eric J. Arnould, and Carolyn Folkman Curasi (2000), "Older Consumers' Disposition of Special Possessions," *Journal of Consumer Research*, 27 (2), 179-201.

Rose, Randall L. and Stacy L. Wood (2005), "Paradox and the Consumption of Authenticity through Reality Television," *Journal of Consumer Research*, 32 (2), 284-96.

Saren, Mike, Pauline MacLaran, Christina Goulding, Richard Elliott, Avi Shankar, and Miriam Catterall (2007), *Critical Marketing: Designing the Field*, Oxford: Butterworth-Heinemann.

Sherry Jr., John F. (1990), "A Sociocultural Analysis of a Midwestern American Flea Market," *Journal of Consumer Research*, 17 (1), 13.

Smith, Adam ([1776] 1985), *An Inquiry into the Nature and Causes of the Wealth of Nations*, New York, NY: Modern Library.

Thompson, Craig J. (1996), "Caring Consumers: Gendered Consumption Meanings and the Juggling Lifestyle," *Journal of Consumer Research*, 22 (4), 388.

______ (2004), "Marketplace Mythology and Discourses of Power," Journal of Consumer Research, 31 (1), 162-80.

Thompson, Craig and Kelly Tian (2008), "Reconstructing the South: How Commercial Myths Compete for Identity Value through the Ideological Shaping of Popular Memories and Countermemories," *Journal of Consumer Research*, 34 (5), 595-613.

Tian, Kelly and Russell W. Belk (2005), "Extended Self and Possessions in the Workplace," *Journal of Consumer Research*, 32 (2), 297-310.

Ustuner, Tuba and Douglas B. Holt (2007), "Dominated Consumer Acculturation: The Social Construction of Poor Migrant Women's Consumer Identity Projects in a Turkish Squatter," *Journal of Consumer Research*, 34 (1), 41-56.

Veblen, Thorstein Bunde ([1899] 1970), *The Theory of the Leisure Class*, London, UK: Unwin.

Wong, Nancy and Tracey King (2008), "The Cultural Construction of Risk Understandings through Illness Narratives," *Journal of Consumer Research*, 34 (5), 579-94.

Wooten, David B. (2006), "From Labeling Possessions to Possessing Labels: Ridicule and Socialization among Adolescents," *Journal of Consumer Research*, 33 (2), 188-98.

Zhao, Xin and Russell W. Belk (2008), "Politicizing Consumer Culture: Advertising's Appropriation of Political Ideology in China's Social Transition," *Journal of Consumer Research*, 35 (2), 231-44.

Zukin, Sharon and Jennifer Smith Maguire (2004), "Consumers and Consumption," *Annual Review of Sociology*, 30, 173-97.

Leave Your Mark: Afterlife Belief Strength's Effect on Durability Focus in Creative Consumption

Huimin Xu, SUNY Oneonta, USA
Merrie L. Brucks, University of Arizona, USA

EXTENDED ABSTRACT

Consumers participate in various types of creative consumption. Some types of creative consumption leave long-lasting products (e.g., photography) whereas others do not (e.g., cooking and karaoke improvisation). When do consumers place more emphasis on producing tangible, durable creative outcomes and when are they content with short-lived creative experiences? In this research, we conceptualize creative consumption as a way of coping with threats to the self's very existence and identify afterlife belief strength as a driver of the durability focus placed on creative outcomes.

Terror Management Theory posits that unconscious anxiety over one's mortality is a basic driver of human behavior. To manage such anxiety, humans have developed a number of coping strategies including belief in an afterlife (Dechesne et al. 2003) and engagement in creative pursuits for self-esteem enhancement. Rank (1932) argues that creative pursuit is essentially the externalization and preservation of personality and soul. By lending concrete, presumably indestructible existence to the abstract ideas of the soul, creative work imbues the creator with a sense of immortality. To render the creator's ideas truly immortal, however, the creative product must also be durable. Thus, individuals who are existentially threatened prefer creative activities that leave durable outcomes. To the extent that afterlife belief and creative activities both relieve existential anxiety, they may be negatively related. Rank (1932) states that "Art was at first, and for a long time to come, the handmaid of religion" and observes that art rises in the wane of religious faith.

We explore the link between durability focus in creative consumption and afterlife belief in four experimental studies. We hypothesize that experimentally weakened afterlife belief should increase durability focus in creative consumption while experimentally strengthened afterlife belief should reduce it.

In experiment 1, we induced mortality salience in all respondents. Afterwards respondents read either an article that argued for the validity of afterlife (i.e., the "stronger" condition) or an article that argued against it (i.e., the "weaker" condition). From a list of pre-tested durable creative activities, respondents selected an activity and indicated their current interest in engaging in it. Respondents also rated their interest in participating in a non-durable creative activity: ice sculpting. We found that while weakened afterlife belief increased interest in the chosen durable creative activity, it had no effect on interest in the non-durable creative activity. Using the difference between interest in the durable and non-durable activities as a measure of durability focus, we found a marginally higher level of durability focus in the weakened belief condition. Interestingly, the afterlife belief manipulation had no effect on intention to attend a workshop to improve creative skills for (and presumably the outcome quality of) the chosen creative activity. The effect of mood as an alternative mechanism (as gauged with the PANAS) was ruled out in experiment 1 and the following 3 studies.

Experiment 2 used a 2 (mortality salience vs. control) x 2 (weaker vs. stronger afterlife belief manipulation) between-subjects design. We employed a different measure of durability focus in this study. Prior to the manipulations, respondents selected an activity from each of 3 categories: durable creative activities (e.g., photography), non-durable creative activities (e.g., cooking), and non-creative activities (e.g., watching TV). After the two manipulations, respondents allocated 100 points among the three activities based on their current levels of interest. Durability focus was operationalized as the ratio of points allocated to the durable creative activity relative to the total points allocated to both durable and non-durable creative activities combined. Results showed that strengthened afterlife belief reduced durability focus and that this effect was not moderated by mortality salience–that is, the baseline level of existential anxiety was sufficient for the hypothesized effect to hold. Again, the afterlife belief manipulation had no effect on interest in improving creative skills.

The first two studies were conducted in the U.S. where a large population strongly believes in an afterlife and where an individualistic culture promotes leaving a personal mark. We ran experiment 3 in China to test whether the effects are particular to certain cultures or reflect a more pervasive motive. We chose China because it is a largely secular, collectivist society. The 2 x 2 between-subjects design and dependent measure of experiment 3 are similar to that of experiment 2. Again, our hypothesis was supported and the effect was not moderated by mortality salience. Interestingly, whereas the U.S. respondents in the previous two studies reacted to a weaker afterlife belief by beefing up interest in durable creative consumption, the Chinese respondents coped by curbing interest in non-durable creative consumption.

Research has suggested that individuals in collective cultures tend to be more prevention-focused whereas individuals in more individualistic cultures tend to be more promotion-focused. To explore whether the cross-cultural differences observed in experiment 3 arose from differences in self-regulatory focus, experiment 4, conducted in the U.S., used a 2 (weaker vs. stronger afterlife belief manipulation) x 2 (promotion vs. prevention regulatory focus manipulation) between-subjects design. When prevention focus was primed, we found a greater loss of interest in non-durable creativity as affected by a weaker afterlife belief relative to when promotion focus was primed. As in the previous studies, strengthened afterlife belief again reduced durability focus and the belief manipulation did not have an effect on interest in improving creative skills.

Overall, our research identifies a hydraulic relation between creative consumption and a basic belief system component–afterlife belief–in coping with existential threat. Apart from its business implications, our findings more importantly point out one particular attribute of creative consumption that can render this seemingly ordinary activity more potent at ameliorating a fundamental source of anxiety: a threat to the self's very existence.

REFERENCES

Dechesne, Mark, Tom Pyszczynski, Jamie Arndt, Sean Ransom, Kennon M. Sheldon, Ad van Knippenberg and Jacques Jansen (2003), "Literal and Symbolic Immortality: The Effect of Evidence of Literal Immortality on Self-Esteem Striving in Response to Mortality Salience," *Journal of Personality and Social Psychology*, 84 (4), 722-737.

Rank, Otto (1932), *Art and Artist: Creative Urge and Personality Development*, New York: Knopf.

After The Box Has Been Opened: Goal Orientation as the Driver of New Product Usage and the Moderating Effects of Product Knowledge and Perceived Newness

Qing Wang, University of Warwick, UK
David Alexander, University of St. Thomas, USA
John G. Lynch Jr., University of Colorado at Boulder, USA

EXTENDED ABSTRACT

The success of an innovation ultimately depends on consumers' acceptance and sustained use of that innovation—not necessarily the easiest thing for firms to ensure. Customers who buy a product and use it less than expected will be less inclined to invest further in the technology (Farley et al. 1987). Given the importance of understanding the processes driving consumers' continued product use, it is surprising how little attention the subject has traditionally drawn from researchers (Rogers 2003); Especially for technological products where consumers initial usage experiences are quite complex (Mick and Fournier 1998). Some recent research has, however, begun to examine the effect of usage on successful adoption (e.g., Shih and Venkatesh 2004; Wood and Moreau 2007).

The extant literature has tended to examine product usage in isolation from motivational factors and, in particular, in isolation from consumers' goals, even though goals are central to consumer decision making (Bettman, Luce, and Payne 1998; Higgins 2002). In a three wave, longitudinal field study with real consumers reporting their usage of new communication and entertainment products, we combine goal orientation theory (e.g. Dweck 1986; Nicholls 1984; Elliot and Sheldon 1997) with recent studies of consumer cognitive and emotional responses to new technological products to examine the drivers and consequences of new product usage. We ask why some new product purchases are followed by rapidly increasing use, while others are followed by little or no use. We examine the attainment of long-term product usage as a function of consumers' goal orientation. Goal orientation consists of two dimensions: approach goal orientation and avoidance goal orientation. We find that consumers' goal orientation has a strong self-reinforcing effect throughout the three waves.

Next we are interested to know how the perceived newness of a product will moderate the relationship between goal orientation and usage. Linking perceived newness to goal orientation theory, we reason that, because individuals with approach goal orientation perceive the achievement setting as a challenge, the newer the product is perceived by these individuals, the greater the challenge product use is perceived to be. This construal in turn is likely to generate more excitement, encourage more affective and cognitive investment, and facilitate greater concentration and task absorption. In contrast, people with avoidance goal orientation perceive the achievement setting as a threat; the newer the product is perceived to be, the greater the threat product use is perceived to be. This construal in turn elicits more anxiety and encourages greater self-protective withdrawal of affective and cognitive resources. Additionally, new consumer tech products are characterized by innovative and often complex features (Thompson, Hamilton, and Rust 2005) that deliver superior customer benefits (Zhao, Meyer, and Han 2006). To extract high utility from such products requires consumers' investments in time and money and, more importantly in knowledge acquisition. The empirical results of our fieldwork support our conceptualization that approach goal orientation acts as the key driver for long term usage particularly when combined with perceived product newness and product knowledge. In contrast, avoidance goal orientation has a negative effect on product usage that is resilient; it is unaffected by product knowledge but is reinforced by perceived product newness.

We also reason in our framework that for consumers, new and technologically complex products are characterized by high uncertainty about the value of new benefits and the appropriate cost-benefit trade-offs to use in evaluating the products (Hoeffler 2003; Alexander, Lynch and Wang 2008). Since this uncertainty is particularly high before actual use of the product, consumers likely encounter unexpected joys or frustrations which lead to experienced emotions (i.e., surprises) when they start using the product. We argue that individuals with avoidance goal orientations tend to focus on negative aspects of product relevant information, likely generating negative emotional responses. Individuals with approach goal orientations, on the other hand, focus on positive aspects of product relevant information, likely generating positive emotional responses. Additionally, surprises experienced during the initial period of product use partially mediate the reinforcing effect of initial goal orientation on subsequent goal orientation.

In sum, in a three wave, longitudinal field study we empirically tested our conceptual framework. Using structural equation modeling (i.e. Amos 7.0) to analyze the data, we find support for our hypotheses. Most importantly, we find that the reinforcing effect of goal orientation results in two distinct paths of consumption: consumers either use the new product more and more (i.e. the approach goal orientation path) or less and less (i.e. the avoidance goal orientation path). In addition, we find that consumers on the approach goal orientation path are more likely to spread positive word of mouth than consumers on the avoidance goal oriented path. We discuss the implications of these findings for marketers of technological consumer products and for managing customer relationship and providing service.

REFERENCE

Alexander, David L., John G. Lynch Jr. and Qing Wang (2008), "As Time Goes By: Do Cold Feet Follow Warm Intentions for Really New Versus Incrementally New Products," *Journal of Marketing Research*, Vol. XLV (June), 307–319.

Bettman, James R., Mary F. Luce, and John W. Payne (1998), "Constructive Consumer Choice Processes," *Journal of Consumer Research*, 25 (3), 187-217.

Dweck, C. (1986), "Motivational processes affecting learning," *American Psychologist*, 41, 1040-1048.

Elliot, Andrew J. and Kennon M. Sheldon (1997), "Avoidance Achievement Motivation: A Personal Goal Analysis," *Journal of Personality and Social Psychology*, 73 (1), 171-185.

Farley, John U., Barbara Kahn, Donald R. Lehmann, and William L. Moore (1987), "Modeling the Choice to Automate," *Sloan Management Review*, 28 (2), 5-15.

Higgins, E. Tory (2002), "How Self-Regulation Creates Distinct Values: The Case of Promotion and Prevention Decision Making," *Journal of Consumer Psychology*, 12 (May), 177–91.

Hoeffler, Steve (2003), "Measuring Preferences for Really-New Products," *Journal of Marketing Research*, 40 (November), 406-420.

Mick, David Glen and Susan Fournier (1998), "Paradoxes of Technology: Consumer Cognizance, Emotions, and Coping Strategies," *Journal of Consumer Research*, 25 (September), 123-143.

Nicholls, J. (1984), "Achievement motivation: Conceptions of ability, subjective experience, task choice, and performance," *Psychological Review*, 91, 328-346.

Rogers, Everett M. (2003), *Diffusion of Innovations*, 5th ed. New York: The Free Press.

Shih, Chuan-Fong and Alladi Venkatesh (2004), "Beyond Adoption: Development and Application of a Use-Diffusion Model," *Journal of Marketing*, 68 (January), 59–72.

Thompson, Debora Viana, Rebecca W. Hamilton, and Roland T. Rust (2005), "Feature Fatigue: When Product Capabilities Become Too Much of a Good Thing," *Journal of Marketing Research*, 42 (November), 431–42.

Wood, Stacy L. and C. Page Moreau (2006), "From Fear to Loathing? How Emotion Influences the Evaluation and Early Use of Innovations," *Journal of Marketing*, 70 (July), 44-57.

Zhao, Senghui, Robert J. Meyer, and Jin Han (2006), "A tale of two judgments: Biases in prior valuation and subsequent utilization of novel technological product attributes," Unpublished working paper, The Wharton School, University of Pennsylvania.

First Things First? The Value of Originality

Kobe Millet, K.U. Leuven, Belgium; Free University Amsterdam, The Netherlands
Bram Van den Bergh, K.U. Leuven, Belgium
Mario Pandelaere, Ghent University, Belgium

EXTENDED ABSTRACT

We suggest in a series of studies that subtle indicators pointing to the originality of a product might increase it's attractiveness. This may explain why brands often communicate to consumers when they originated. For example, Heinz states that its tomato ketchup dates back from 1869. Heinz' label "since 1869" might not only indicate that Heinz has been around for a long time, but might also suggest that it was first, and thus original, in the ketchup category. Bolton (2006) proposes that people might have a kind of "folk wisdom" that being first (e.g., in invention, arts) is better and that "folk wisdom" leads to a positive evaluation of pioneers as they are "first" and therefore better. Swinyard, Rinne and Keng Kau (1990) note that Western societies have a preoccupation with the protection of original work which finally led to copyright, patent, and trade-secret legislation. In contrast, copyright and other legislation to protect original work may strongly go against the grain of Asian cultures. In fact, Asian cultures seem to support the concept of sharing of individual creative work, instead of protecting the creator of the original work. In support of this view, software piracy rates appear to be higher in Asian than in Western economies (Ding & Liu 2009), and it turns out that these rates are not only a function of the level of poverty in a given society, but also of the societal degree of collectivism (Moores 2003 and 2008). Summarized the originality of a product may not matter in collectivistic cultures, while it may have a special status in individualistic cultures. We argue in the present manuscript that (1) perceptions of (un)originality are important in consumers' evaluation and (2) that this especially holds for the individualistic consumer.

In study 1 we test the hypothesis that originality indicators have a beneficial effect on preferences, which leads to a preference for the original or "first" object among similar objects (hypothesis 1). In study 1a, we presented abstract paintings in different rotations and found that seemingly original rotations (0° & 360°) were preferred over any other rotation (although 90° was actually the real original orientation). Study 1b shows that participants rate an 'original' picture more favorably than other participants who were led to believe that that same picture was photoshopped This is consistent with the idea that digit alteration harms the perceived originality of a picture. Summarized, study 1 demonstrates that perceived originality affects consumer evaluations.

It is important to note that originality has an all-or-none character (i.e., only one object can be the first and thus original): The presumed effect of originality differs from an effect in which earlier objects are preferred to later objects. In study 2, we test the hypothesis that in a set of similar objects the first, "original" product will be preferred, but not earlier to later objects (hypothesis 2). In study 2a, participants indicated their preference for one of two movies after seeing the two movie trailers. The movie trailers were labeled "Life on Earth I" and "Life on Earth II" ("originality" condition) or "Life on Earth II" and "Life on Earth III" ("earlier" condition). Participants preferred "Life on Earth I" to "Life on Earth II" but did not prefer "Life on Earth II" to "Life on Earth III" (hypothesis 2). We made use of nature documentaries to rule out the alternative explanation that one would need to watch the movies in proper order to understand 'the plot'. Study 2b eliminates an interpretation in terms of preference for earlier stimuli entirely. Participants listened to two alternate versions of the same song, released in 1964 and 1967, but were told that another version existed. In the earlier condition, the third alternate version was presumably released in 1962 whereas in the control condition, this third version was presumably released in 1969. We predicted that the 1964 version would be preferred to the 1967 version in the control condition in which the 1964 version could be perceived as being first, but not in the 'earlier' condition in which the 1964 version was preceded by another (1962) version. This pattern of results was obtained. Perceived originality might explain why "earlier" stimuli–which are not the first–are not preferred to subsequent stimuli: only the very first stimulus may truly be considered original.

Study 3 aims to show that indicators of unoriginality have a strong detrimental impact on evaluations when consumers have an 'individualistic mindset', but not when consumers have a 'collectivistic mindset' (hypothesis 3). To test this hypothesis, Study 3 used the same design as study 1b, with one exception. Before seeing the pictures, participants were primed with individualism, collectivism or received no prime. In the no prime condition, we replicated the effect of study 1b, showing that participants rate an 'original' picture more favorably than other participants who were led to believe that that same picture was photoshopped. We obtained the same effect in the individualism condition. However, an unoriginality indicator did not have any effect in the collectivism condition: Evaluations of photoshopped pictures in this condition were as favorable as 'original' pictures in all conditions.

Our research might have practical implications as it shows that the use of originality indicators might be helpful to enhance consumer attraction. After all, we never observed negative effects of originality indicators, only indicators pointing to unoriginality appear detrimental for consumer evaluations. For several product categories, consumers are not able to identify which one is the 'original' or first brand on the market (Alpert & Kamins, 1995; Golder & Tellis, 1993; Kamins, Alpert & Elliott, 2000). For those categories, the potential power of originality indicators is enormous: Our research shows that any given brand/product may profit from the use of some sort of originality indicator to increase its attractiveness. On the other hand, the effect of originality indicators may be diluted as multiple brands are suggesting they are the one and only original. To address this latter issue, more research is needed.

REFERENCES

Alpert, Frank H., and Michael A. Kamins (1995), "An empirical investigation of consumer memory, attitude and perceptions towards pioneer and follower brands," *Journal of Marketing*, 59, 34-45.

Bolton (2006), "Believing in first mover advantage," Working paper, Marketing Department, The Wharton School, University of Pennsylvania, Philadelphia, PA

Ding, Cnerng G., & Na-Ting Liu (2009), "Productivity changes of Asian economies by taking into account software piracy," *Economic Inquiry*, 47, 135-145.

Golder, Peter N., & Gerard J. Tellis (1993), "Pioneer advantage: marketing logic or marketing legend?" *Journal of Marketing Research*, 30, 158-170.

Kamins, Michael, Frank Alpert and Michael Elliott (2000), "The Independent and Interactive Effects of Exposure Sequence, Labeling and Product Trial on Consumer Evaluation of a Pioneer Brand," *Journal of Consumer Psychology*, 9, 223-229.

Moores (2003), "The effect of national culture and economic wealth on global software piracy rates," *Communications of the ACM*, 46, 207-215.

Moores, Trevor T. (2008), "An analysis of the impact of economic wealth and national culture on the rise and fall of software piracy rates," *Journal of Business Ethics*, 81, 39-51.

Swinyard, William R., Heiki Rinne and Ah Keng Kau (1990), "The morality of software piracy: a cross-cultural analysis," *Journal of Business Ethics*, 9, 655-664.

How Do 'Leading-edge' Opinion Leaders Bridge the Innovation Gap? Advancing a New Adopter Category

Salah S. Hassan, George Washington University, USA
Philippe Duverger, Towson University, USA

EXTENDED ABSTRACT

Empowering users and/or involving them in the new product development (NPD) process defines the customer-centric organization. Some researchers have even argued for involving users with particular characteristics allows the firm to tap into new markets needs, develop radical innovation and move the firm closer to market orientation.

From a diffusion theory perspective, rate of adoption is dependent on the consumer's propensity to accept the new product. The traditional adoption categorization model by Rogers emphasizes the importance of opinion leadership in increasing adoption rates, and a recent study shows that users presenting high leading-edge status also have high opinion leadership qualities. These leading-edge users tend to perceive attributes that are less complex and more innovative when assessing new innovations within their particular domain of user expertise. Hence, firms that are seeking rapid diffusion of their radical innovations should target user segments that possess high levels of both leading-edge status and opinion leadership qualities.

This paper presents empirical research evidence advancing "leading-edge opinion leaders" as a new adopter category. The purpose of this paper is threefold: (1) to evaluate the influence of leading-edge opinion leaders on accelerating the diffusion rate, (2) to measure their propensity to switch brands and pay a price premium, and (3) to offer insights on the characteristics of the proposed new adopter category that will provide directions for future research and immediate application for management.

Adoption By Leading-Edge Users

Rogers observed that potential adopters assess the following attributes of innovations: relative advantage, compatibility, complexity, trialability, and observability. Several researchers have studied the diffusion phenomenon in light of the adopters categories and have explained the rate of diffusion as a function of the characteristics of each category relative to the perceived attractiveness of the innovation based on the set of attributes observed by Rogers. Within the adopters' categories, the innovators and the early adopters share similar characteristics that would allow these two groups to successfully convince the other groups to adopt the innovation at a later point in time. Modelling that phenomenon, Bass demonstrates that the diffusion follows a two-step communication process. Other researchers have challenged the two-step process in light of the level of usability or relative advantage of the innovation as perceived by the innovators and early adopters versus the mass market, while others have expanded the model to show the social networking effect.

Opinion leadership is a defining characteristic of the opinion leader. It is also a strong characteristic of the early adopter. Therefore, it explains the high personal communication effort (WOM and eWOM/ "Word of Mouse") used by the opinion leader to influence the behavior of other people in terms of search, purchasing and usage of new products. Generally, the communication mode of the opinion leaders is informal; however, they play a major role in influencing the consumer decision-making process as they represent a reliable source of information. As a result, marketers work to create communication channels to reach opinion leaders in order to encourage them to spread positive word of mouth.

Accordingly, this research identifies three types of users: 1) Leading-edge users with high levels of opinion leadership, from here on called "leading-edge opinion leaders"; 2) Leading-edge users with low levels of opinion leadership, now referred to as "leading-edge users"; and 3) consumers with low level of leading-edge status and opinion leadership referred to as "the Mass consumers". At the aggregate level, it is proposed that the behavior of a new adopter category possessing lead-user characteristics and opinion leadership attributes will accelerate the rate of innovation diffusion.

Methods and Results

This study evaluated the perception and adoption intentions of leading-edge users when confronted with a choice between a current new product, and a radical new innovation. Our first task was to develop a radical new innovation that would be believable to the participants. In the first stage, we extracted leading-edge users' ideas on innovative laptop features using an electronic ideation process (244 respondents to an electronic survey, from which 58 ideas were extracted from 52 participants). The ideas were then ranked using the Amabile consensus assessment technique (CAT) where higher scores define the most creative ideas as assessed by the expert panel composed of 11 people averaging 9.6 year of experience in the technology field.

Using a stepwise regression with the idea scores as dependant variables and the characteristics of the respondents as independent variables (participants' characteristics construct measures were taken from the existing literature and confirmatory factor analyses led to satisfactory goodness-of-fit measures greater than 0.95 and alpha coefficients greater than 0.70) led to a good fit of the model (Global F p-value<0.0001) and significant parameter estimates for the leading-edge user and opinion leader characteristics (both $p<0.0001$). Out of the 76 ideas extracted from the toolkit participants 34 of the most creative ideas (ideas above the mean of 164.45) were selected for the second stage of our analysis.

The adoption of innovation construct was measured using two manifest variables: the intent to purchase the idea if it was available on the market (a 5 point-likert scale was used) and the intent to speak (WOM) to a friend, family or colleague about the idea. Using a latent score method, an analysis of the interaction effect between the underlying characteristics: leading-edge status and opinion leadership as they relate to the adoption of radical innovation construct was conducted.

This research demonstrates that leading-edge users have a critical role in the diffusion of radical product. Beyond the widely accepted adopter categories, a new hybrid category named: "Leading-edge Opinion Leaders" can be seen as emerging from the known innovators and early adopters categories. They will help diffuse the radical new product by adopting it, propagating it to others, and will pay a price premium to acquire it. Managerial implications of this research relate directly to the possibility of an extension of the traditional adoption categories.

REFERENCES

Amabile, T. M. (1982), "Children's artistic creativity: detrimental effects of competition in a field setting," *Personality and Social Psychology Bulletin*, 8, 573-578.

Amabile, T. M. (1996), *Creativity in Context*, Boulder, Colorado: Westview Press.

Bass, F. M. (1969), "A new product growth for model consumer durables," *Management Science*, 15 (5), 215-227.

Bower, J. L and Christensen, C. M. (1995), "Disruptive Technologies: catching the wave," *Harvard Business Review*, 73, 43-53.

Franke, N. and Piller, F. (2004), "Toolkits for User Innovation and Design: an exploration of user interaction and value creation," *Journal of Product Innovation Management*, 21, 401-415.

Franke, N. and Shah, S. (2003), "How communities Support Innovative Activities: An exploration of assistance and sharing among End-Users," *Research Policy*, 32(1), 157-178.

Franke, N, von Hippel, E., and Schreier, M. (2006), "Finding Commercially Attractive User Innovations: A Test of Lead-User Theory," *Journal of Product Innovation Management*, 23(4), 301-315.

Goldsmith, R. E., and Witt, T. S. (2005), "The Predictive Validity of an Opinion Leadership Scale," *Journal of Marketing Theory and Practice*, (Winter), 28-35.

Gupta, A. K. and Rogers, E. M. (1991), " Internal Marketing: Integrating R&D and Marketing Within the Organization," *The Journal of Service Marketing*, 5(2), 55-68.

Hassan, Salah S. (2008), "Harnessing Lead-User Innovation: From Collaborative User Communities to Mass Market," *HBS-MIT User and Open Innovation Workshop*, Harvard Business School, Boston, Massachusetts, August.

Hauser, J., Tellis, G. J. and Griffin, A. (2006), "Research on Innovation: A Review and Agenda for Marketing Science," *Marketing Science*, 25(6), 687-732.

Keller, K. L. (2003), *Strategic Branding Management: Building, Measuring, and Managing Brand Equity*, NJ: PrenticeHall (2nd Ed.).

Keller, K. L.; and Lehmann, D. R. (2002), "The brand value chain: linking strategic and financial brand performance," Tuck School of Business, Dartmouth College working paper.

Kirca, A. H., Jayachandran, S., and Bearden, W. O. (2005), "Market orientation: A meta-analytic review and assessment of its antecedents and impact on performance," *Journal of Marketing*, 69, 24-41.

Lüthje, C. and Herstatt, C. (2004), "The Lead User Method: An Outline of Empirical Findings and Issues for Future Research," *R&D Management*, 35(5), 553-568.

Lyons, B. and Henderson, K. (2005), "Opinion leadership in a computer-mediated environment," *Journal of Consumer Behaviour*, 4(5), 319-329.

March, A. (1994), "Usability: The New Dimension of Product Design," *Harvard Business Review*, 72(5), 144-149.

Morrison, P. D.; Roberts, J. H.; von Hippel, E. (2000), "Determinants of User Innovation and Innovation Sharing in a Local Market," *Management Science*, 46(12), 1513-1527.

Myers, J. H. and Robertson, T. S. (1972), "Dimensions of Opinion Leadership," *Journal of Marketing Research*, 4 (February), 41-46.

Piller, F. T. and Walcher, D. (2006), "Toolkits for Idea Competitions: A Novel Method to Integrate Users in New Product Development," *R&D Management*, 36(3), 307-318.

Rogers, E.M. (2003), *Diffusion of Innovations*, (5th ed.) New York: The Free Press.

Shah, D., Rust, R. T., Parasuraman, A., Staelin, R., and Day, G. S. (2006), "The path to customer centrality," *Journal of Service Research*, 9(2), 113-124.

Schreier, M.; Oberhauser, S.; and Prügl, R. (2007), "Lead Users and the Adoption and Diffusion of New Products: Insights from Two Extreme Sports Communities," *Marketing Letters*, 18 (1-2), 15-30.

Schumaker, R. E., and Lomax, R. B. (1996), *A Beginner's Guide to Structural Equation Modeling*, Hillsdale, NJ: Erlbaum.

Slater, F. S., and Naver, J. C. (1998), "Customer-led and market-oriented: Let's not confuse the two," *Strategic Management Journal*, 19(10), 1001-1006.

Urban, G. L., and von Hippel, E. (1988), "Lead User Analyses for the Development of New Industrial Products," *Management Science*, 34(5), 569-582.

Van den Bulte, C., and Lilien, G.L. (2001), "Medical Innovation Revisited: Social Contagion versus Marketing Effort," *American Journal of Sociology*, 106(5), 1409-1435.

von Hippel, E. (2005), *Democratizing Innovation,* The MIT Press, USA.

von Hippel, E. (1986), "Lead Users: A Source of Novel Product Concepts," *Management Science*, 32(7), 791-805

Walker, G. (1985), "Network position and cognition in a computer firm," *Administrative Science Quarterly*, 30, 103-130.

Consumer Creativity and Ideological Conflicts: An Investigation of the Free/Open Source Software Community

Tiebing Shi, Queen's School of Business, Queen's University, Canada[1]
Jay M. Handelman, Queen's School of Business, Queen's University, Canada

EXTENDED ABSTRATCT

A turn to consumer creativity is emerging (Prahalad and Ramaswamy 2000). In the literature on consumer creativity, two different streams of studies are located along a continuum anchored by individualistic creativity (IC) on one end and contextualized creativity (CC) on the other (Sawyer 2006). The first stream sees consumer creativity as a largely isolated, individual process (Bagozzi and Foxall 1996; Burroughs and Mick 2004; Dahl and Moreau 2007). The second stream sees consumer creativity as a contextualized process, assuming that a community of individuals collaborates towards a creative project (von Hippel 2005; Kozinets, Hemetsberger, and Schau, 2008). Despite this difference, both streams assume that creativity is an enjoyable, harmonious process free from ideological conflicts.

We use Berman's (1970, 1988) view of creativity as our theoretical lens. For Berman, creativity is a community-based, political-cultural process in which individuals engage in innovative practices in their daily interactions with fellow community members to achieve their ultimate life goals (e.g., self-actualization and self-expression). For Berman, the process of consumer creativity is rich in paradoxes, conflicts, ideological struggles, and political implications concerning the distribution of authority, power, and status in a consumer community and a society.

Specifically, at the individual level, individual members might experience intrapersonal paradoxes (e.g., a member simultaneously holds the values of individualism and collectivism). At the community level, there might be conflicts among collaborating members, ideological conflicts between collaborating subgroups of a community, and conflicts between individual members and the community as a whole (e.g., a consumer contributes an idea to his/her community and this idea could be rejected by authoritative community members as mediocre and/or inappropriate according to certain criteria; this consumer might feel hurt and be motivated to become an authoritative member or to challenge the criteria). At the society level, there might be competition and ideological conflicts between a consumer community and firms as well as ideological conflicts between a consumer community and copyright laws. These three levels of conflicts are intertwined with each other and reflected in the process of consumer creativity. Drawing on Berman's view, we aim to contribute to the literature on consumer creativity by empirically examining the creative process of individual members within the dynamic free/open source software (FOSS) community.

We seek to contextualize consumer creativity by considering the conflicts inherent in the creative process. In doing so, we consider the following questions: (1) How does an individual consumer negotiate the self-expressive aspects of creativity in the face of social judgment within his/her community and society? (2) How do individual consumers interact with each other and with firms to express their identities in the process of creating their common products (e.g., an idea, an experience, or a solution)? (3) What are the political and cultural implications of consumer creativity?

Because the studied interactions, conflicts, and related political and cultural implications are sensitive to situational contexts, we adopt a netnography methodology (Kozinets 2002b). In particular, we seek a community context where members' creative contribution is central to the community. To this end, we choose the FOSS community. In their daily creative activities, FOSS developers (who are both producers and users of FOSS) generate rich ideological discourses, which we examine through a netnographic method.

Data were collected from online archives of consumer discourses of websites of Emacs (a FS project), Go-oo (an OSS project), and OpenOffice (an OSS project), and blogs and online papers and books of FOSS developers. We followed a data-driven procedure to collect data. In particular, based on our integrative analysis of the literature, we arrived at four characteristics of creativity that guided our selection and analysis of discussion threads: self-expressiveness (i.e., one engages in creative activities to actualize and express one's dynamic, multiple selves), social judgment (i.e., an activity and its outcome need to be judged as creative or not by relevant authoritative members in a community or a society), process (i.e., creativity is an ongoing, dynamic process in which an idea is generated, expressed, and socially judged), and novelty (i.e., an idea should be judged by community members as new, fresh, and original). So, we define consumer creativity as a process of self-expression that consumers engage in to individually and/or collectively generate something that is socially judged as innovative and appropriate. Our data analysis and interpretation follows a constant comparative method to seek patterns of meaning and to formulate themes (Spiggle 1994).

Two themes emerge from our data. The first one is "Ideologies and Authority Underlying Creativity." In their creative process, FOSS developers (who hold the ideology of community ownership) engage in an ongoing ideological debate with proprietary software firms (who hold the ideology of private ownership) leading to a power struggle with certain authoritative community members as some developers might not feel fulfilled, but rather, frustrated. Paradoxically, FOSS developers strategically use the ideology of private ownership to promote that of community ownership. The second theme is "Idealism Blended with Rationalism." By strategically blending idealism and rationalism in their creative process, FOSS developers construct their unique ideology—a rationality-based, idealistic, individual freedom-oriented, evolving creative anarchy, which enhances the legitimacy of their creative process and product (i.e., FOSS) and reduces the legitimacy and power of proprietary software firms (who extol their more rational software development process) in the marketplace.

Our paper contributes to the literature on consumer creativity by (1) considering the conflicts inherent in the creative process of consumer communities, (2) revealing that consumers could strategically use conflicting ideologies to fight against perceived constraining dominant forces in the marketplace for freedom of self-actualization and self-realization, and (3) illustrating that the creative process in the context of consumer communities could be full of conflicts (e.g., between individual members and their communities, and between the consumer communities and some dominant firms and copyright laws).

[1]The author thanks the Monieson Centre, Queen's School of Business, Queen's University, for its generous research funding for this study.

REFERENCES

Bagozzi, Richard P. and Gordon R. Foxall (1996), "Construct Validation of a Measure of Adaptive-Innovative Cognitive Styles in Consumption," *International Journal of Research in Marketing*, 13 (July), 201-213.

Berman, Marshall (1970), *The Politics of Authenticity: Radical Individualism and the Emergence of Modern Society*, New York: Atheneum.

______ (1988), *All That Is solid Melts Into Air: The Experience of Modernity*, New York: Penguin Books.

Burroughs, James E. and David Glen Mick (2004), "Exploring Antecedents and Consequences of Consumer Creativity in a Problem-Solving Context," *Journal of Consumer Research*, 31 (September), 402-411.

Csikszentmihalyi, Mihaly (1999), "Implications of A Systems Perspective For the Study of Creativity," in *Handbook of Creativity*, ed. Robert J. Sternberg, Cambridge University Press, 313-335.

Dahl, Darren W. and C. Page Moreau (2007), "Thinking Inside the Box: Why Consumers Enjoy Constrained Creative Experiences," *Journal of Marketing Research*, 44 (August), 357-369.

Firat, A. Fuat and Alladi Venkatesh (1995), "Liberatory Postmodernism and the Reenchantment of Consumption," *Journal of Consumer Research*, 22 (December), 239-267.

Franke, Nikolaus, and Sonali Shah (2003), How Communities Support Innovative Activities: An Exploration of Assistance and Sharing Among End-Users," *Research Policy*, 32 (1), 157-178.

Füller, Johann, Gregor Jawecki, and Hans Mühlbacher (2007), "Innovation Creation by Online Basketball Communities," *Journal of Business Research*, 60 (1), 60-71.

Hemetsberger, Andrea (2005), "When David Becomes Goliath: Ideological Discourse in New Online Consumer Movements," *Advances in Consumer Research*, 33; 494-502.

______ and Christian Reinhardt (2006), "Learning and Knowledge-building in Open-source Communities: A Social-Experiential Perspective," *Management Learning*, 37 (June), 187-214.

Hirschman, Elizabeth C. (1980), "Innovativeness, Novelty Seeking, and Consumer Creativity," *Journal of Consumer Research*, 7 (December), 283-295.

Holt, Douglas B. (2002), "Why Do Brands Cause Trouble? A Dialectical Theory of Consumer Culture and Branding," *Journal of Consumer Research*, 29 (June), 70–90.

Kozinets, Robert V. (2002a), "Can Consumers Escape the Market? Emancipatory Illuminations from Burning Man," *Journal of Consumer Research*, 29 (June), 20–38.

______ (2002b), "The Field Behind the screen: Using Netnography for Marketing Research in Online Communities," Journal of Marketing Research, 39 (February), 61-72.

______ , Andrea Hemetsberger, and Hope Jensen Schau (2008), "The Wisdom of Consumer Crowds: Collective Innovation in the Age of Online Community," *Journal of Macromarketing*, 28 (December), 339-354.

Levi, Daniel (2001), Group Dynamics for Teams, Sage Publications.

Moreau, C. Page and Darren W. Dahl (2005), "Designing the Solution: The Impact of Constraints on Consumers' Creativity," *Journal of Consumer Research*, 32 (June), 13-22.

Prahalad, C.K. and Venkat Ramaswamy (2000), "Co-opting Customer Competence," *Harvard Business Review*, 78 (January-February), 79-87.

Raymond, Eric Steven (1998), "The Halloween Documents," http://www.catb.org/~esr/halloween/.

______ (2006), The Cathedral and the Bazaar, http://www.catb.org/~esr/writings/cathedral-bazaar/.

Sawyer, R. Keith (2006), *Explaining Creativity: The Science of Human Innovation*, Oxford University Press.

Seitz, Jay A. (2003), "The Political Economy of Creativity," *Creativity Research Journal*, 15 (4), 385-392.

Spiggle, Susan (1994), "Analysis and Interpretation of Qualitative Data in Consumer Research," *Journal of Consumer Research*, 21 (December), 491-503.

Thompson, Craig J. (2004), "Marketplace Mythology and Discourses of Power," *Journal of Consumer Research*, 31 (June): 162-180.

von Hippel, Eric (2005), *Democratizing Innovation*, The MIT Press.

"Your Office Suite," http://go-oo.org/, visited on March 1st, 2008.

A Balancing Act: Governance in a Virtual P3 Community

Caroline Wiertz, City University London, UK
Charla Mathwick, Portland State University, USA
Ko de Ruyter, University of Maastricht, The Netherlands
Benedict Dellaert, Erasmus University Rotterdam, The Netherlands

EXTENDED ABSTRACT

Introduction

Since the wide-spread diffusion of networking technologies, consumers convene in various online community contexts to collectively produce and consume content relevant to their needs and interests. As a result, community forms of production and consumption of information, word-of-mouth, advice, entertainment, and even physical products are gaining in importance and have been heralded as ideal forms of collaboration (e.g., Kozinets, Hemetsberger, and Schau 2008). Much of the existing literature paints an almost utopian picture of online community, describing it as an environment characterized by altruism, mutuality, and social capital, in which consumers voluntarily sacrifice time and effort and work together to produce collective outcomes (e.g., Giesler 2006; Kozinets et al. 2008; Mathwick, Wiertz, and de Ruyter 2008). But like most voluntary social collectives that produce a public good, online communities are faced with the collective action problem, since members who free-ride can benefit equally from the public good that the community produces–for example, knowledge–as members who actively contribute to its production (Olson 1965; Wasko and Faraj 2005). Therefore, these communities have a regulatory interest to align potentially self-interested actors into producing a shared good. Yet little is known about how self-organizing online consumer communities govern themselves to encourage collaborative contribution to the shared community resource while discouraging free-riding.

Background

We propose that online communities can rely on two governance mechanisms to enhance collective action: normative governance, and meritocratic governance. Normative governance relies on the regulatory power of the specific social norms that emerge in the community through social interaction, and are enforced through peer pressure (Feldman 1984). Social norms are formed in any social group, and serve as explicit and/or implicit guidelines of appropriate behavior. As such, social norms are thought to be pro-social in nature and to foster social cohesiveness.

Meritocratic governance, in contrast, operates through non-economic incentives that accrue to individuals when they contribute to the collective community resource (Coleman 1990). One of the most powerful incentives for collective action in the community context is the attainment of social status (Lampel and Bhalla 2007), for example as enabled by online feedback systems. Feedback systems not only provide an evaluation of a member's individual contributions, but on an aggregate level, also of the member him/herself. As such, each participant constructs an online identity that is first and foremost characterized by the highly visible cumulative evaluation received through the feedback system. Prior research has consistently found that this not only fosters trust between members and improves the quality of contributions, but also motivates repeated contribution behavior, as participants strive to enhance their social status in the community (Dellarocas 2003; Lampel and Bhalla 2007; Moon and Sproull 2008).

The meritocratic governance approach incorporated through online feedback systems has dramatically risen in importance and is considered the solution to instilling trust and stabilizing virtual communities (Dellarocas 2003). Most online market places (most famously eBay), online review sites (e.g., Tripadvisor), as well as open source communities have implemented online feedback systems. Extensive studies in recent years (e.g., Dellarocas 2003; Moon and Sproull 2008) have succeeded in demonstrating their positive effect on a variety of beneficial member behaviors. However, the potential dark sides of such systems have received much less attention. We speculate that by providing visual means of status distinction, effectively creating status groups, online feedback systems might lead to conflict between those members who are recognized by the system and have achieved status and those who have not. Status is by definition a scarce social resource that introduces competition: if status was easily attainable, its value would diminish (Weber 1978). Hence, status holders should be bent on maintaining their privileged position, while those without status should be bent on improving theirs. A number of key questions arise when considering the effect of status on those who have attained it as compared to those who have not. For example, does the elevated status of some community members facilitate or inhibit community exchange? Do all members, regardless of status, have an equal say in shaping the social norms of their community?

Method

This study was set in the context of a virtual peer-to-peer problem-solving (P3) community (Mathwick et al. 2008), which ais a type of online creative consumer community (Kozinets et al. 2008) that focuses on the exchange of advice and best practice with regards to consumption-related problems (in our case, technical support). Netnography was used to explore governance, meritocracy, social norms, and status groups in this particular context (Kozinets 2002).

Findings

We find that both normative and meritocratic governance mechanisms operate in the community and that meritrocratic governance enabled through online feedback systems indeed has a dark side. The online feedback system provides visual status symbols to members, effectively creating status groups. We find evidence that the high-status group is using its advantageous position to shape the community purely according to its taste and to dominate the low-status members. Our results show a widening disconnect between status groups as low-status members feel intimidated and unwanted and disengage from the community.

References

Coleman, James S. (1990), *Foundations of Social Theory*, Cambridge, MA: Harvard University Press.

Dellarocas, Chrysanthos (2003), "The Digitization of Word of Mouth: Promise and Challenges of Online Feedback Mechanisms," *Management Science*, 49 (10), 1407-1424.

Feldman, Daniel C. (1984), "The Development and Enforcement of Group Norms," *Academy of Management Review*, 9 (1), 47-53.

Giesler, Markus (2006), "Consumer Gift Systems," *Journal of Consumer Research*, 33 (September), 283-290.

Kozinets, Robert V. (2002), "The Field Behind the Screen: Using Netnography for Marketing Research in Online Communities," *Journal of Marketing Research*, 39 (February), 61-72.

______ , Andrea Hemetsberger, and Hope Jensen Schau (2008), "The Wisdom of Consumer Crowds: Collective Innovation in the Age of Networked Marketing, *Journal of Macromarketing*, 28 (4), 339-354.

Lampel, Joseph and Ajay Bhalla (2007), "The Role of Status Seeking in Online Communities: Giving the Gift of Experience," *Journal of Computer-Mediated Communication*, 12 (2), Article 5, http://jcmc.indiana.edu/vol12/issue2/lampel.html.

Mathwick, Charla, Caroline Wiertz, and Ko de Ruyter (2008), "Social Capital Production in a Virtual P3 Community," *Journal of Consumer Research*, 34 (6), 832-849.

Moon, Jae Yun and Lee S. Sproull (2008), "The Role of Feedback in Managing the Internet-Based Vounteer Work Force," *Information Systems Research*, 19 (4), 494-515.

Olson, Mancur (1965), *The Logic of Collective Action*, Cambridge, MA: Harvard University Press.

Wasko, Molly, and Samer Faraj (2005), "Why Should I Share? Examining Social Capital and Knowledge Contribution in Electronic Networks of Practice," *MIS Quarterly*, 29 (1), 35-58.

Weber, Max (1978), *Economy and Society*, Berkeley, CA: University of California Press.

Balancing Intrinsic Motivation and Extrinsic Rewards: An Exploratory Investigation into User Generated Content Production

Charla Mathwick, Portland State University, USA

EXTENDED ABSTRACT

User generated content (UGC) is fast becoming one of the most valuable and influential sources of information in the on-line world, supporting millions of consumers who have come to rely on product and service reviews to support the purchase process. UGC is uncompensated and voluntary, which suggests that the motivation driving this type of consumer behavior is sustained largely by the intrinsic pleasure derived from its production. The purpose of this exploratory study is to examine the underlying intrinsic and extrinsic motives driving UGC production. The research question investigated in this study relates to how the intrinsically motivating character of UGC production is maintained while simultaneously recognizing contribution (Deci and Ryan 1985).

The context for this exploratory study is Amazon's Top Reviewer Community and the automated reward system Amazon administers for that community. Amazon's UGC is created by thousands of volunteers whose book and product reviews have become an influential decision aid for Amazon's customer base and a differentiating advantage for Amazon itself. On October 23, 2008, Amazon announced changes to the algorithm that drives the reviewer automated feedback system used to calculate UGC contributor rank in that community.

Two theoretical perspectives—Cognitive Evaluation Theory (CET; Deci and Ryan 1985) and theories of distributive and procedural justice (Rawls 1971; Rhoades and Eisenberger 2002)—frame the investigation of the impact of Amazon's announced changes to its ranking system. CET offers a framework for interpreting the effect reward systems can have on eliciting or undermining intrinsically motivated behaviors. CET is augmented with insights drawn from the electronic word-of-mouth literature and from theories of justice related to reward distribution in organizations. This theoretical framework is combined with the results of a netnographic analysis to develop propositions to guide future research.

The Motivation to Create UGC

The production of UGC provides an outlet for the autonomous self-expression of opinions and expertise. It not only serves to develop and affirm personally valued skills, it establishes a basis for relationships among the community of contributors as well as the readers who follow a reviewer's work when making purchase decisions. Readership feedback perceived to have no ulterior motive other than to express appreciation or acknowledge reviewer expertise, appears to produce a particularly strong motivation to produce UGC. This direct market feedback, however, appears to also threaten the perceived autonomy of some of the reviewers, particularly when reader feedback was experienced as an attempt to control or coerce rather than inform (Deci and Ryan 1985).

A reviewer's relationship with peers engaged in UGC production, paints a picture of a community that is as supportive as it is antagonistic. Peer interactions reflect a competitive environment, populated by contributors who are pre-occupied with issues of personal recognition, peer performance quality, and identification with the group. UGC which is a manifestation of the 'engage and co-create' economy said to be emerging online (Tapscott and Williams 2008), appears to be a complex combination of competitive, supportive, and antagonistic interactions that mirror traditional work environments.

The reviewer's relationship with Amazon is centered around the automated reward system they administer. As important as recognition appears to be in motivating UGC production, consistency, and predictability in the allocation of rewards and the perceived fairness of the procedures used to administer the reward system is perhaps more important. Reward systems offer a reason to participate for some and are irrelevant or border on insulting to others. Consequently, the procedures underlying automated feedback must strike a balance between these competing interests in ways that deepen engagement rather than alienate.

Conclusion And Discussion

Amazon has engaged their community of volunteers to produce UGC by implementing a reviewer ranking system and by supporting the review experience with a full complement of interactive tools. The intrinsic pleasure of pursuing an 'interesting hobby', the freedom of self-expression, and the social connections created as reviewers develop a loyal readership and relationships with their peers contribute to the motivation to produce UGC. Community ranking operates as a powerful extrinsic influencer of UGC production and appears to be the primary motivator for a substantial portion of the contributing base. For reviewers who are intrinsically motivated to produce UGC, however, Amazon's ranking system and the relationships built around the product review process, can undermine the fragile sense of autonomy so crucial to sustaining these voluntary contributions. The key to establishing stability in the reviewer community seems to be striking a balance between these countervailing forces.

From the perspective of a UGC producer, there are three relevant sources of feedback: the buyers who rely on UGC to support the buying process, fellow reviewers, and the community moderator who maintains the official ranking system. Feedback from buyers tends to offer some of the most important motivation supporting UGC production. For reviewers who attract a following, the social and reputational benefits they experienced appeared to mean more to them than the ranking system devised by Amazon. It appeared that the authenticity of readership comments trumped the economically-tainted feedback attributed to Amazon. Peer-to-peer relationships between reviewers also provides social benefits, however community rank appears to introduce a competitive element to the UGC experience that can be motivating for some while alienating to others.

Marketers interested in leveraging the expertise of their customer base will need to meet the challenge of balancing what are often incompatible forces, in order to encourage their users to contribute to UGC production. This view into the world of UGC production provides insight into the nature of that challenge.

References

Deci, E.L. and R. M. Ryan (1985), *Intrinsic Motivation and Self-Determination in Human Behavior*, New York: Plenum.

Rawls, J. (1971), *A Theory of Justice*, Cambridge, Massachusetts: Belknap Press of Harvard University Press.

Rhoades, L. and R. Eisenberger (2002), "Perceived Organizational Support: A Review of the Literature," *Journal of Applied Psychology*, 87, 698-714.

Tapscott, D. and A. D. Williams (2008), *Wikinomics: How Mass Collaboration Changes Everything*, New York: Portfolio.

The Pursuit of Identity Augmentation: Self-Expansion and Self-Extension as Distinct Strategies

Paul M. Connell, Stony Brook University, USA
Hope Jensen Schau, University of Arizona, USA

EXTENDED ABSTRACT

As consumers are active identity seekers and makers (Arnould and Thompson 2004), they sometimes engage in attempts to grow identity beyond the corporeal self (Aron, Aron, and Smollan 1992; Aron et al 1991; Belk 1988). Scholars in both consumer research (Belk 1988) and in social psychology (Aron et al 1991; Aron et al 1991) have produced impactful frameworks for how individuals engage in identity augmenting behavior. Belk's (1988) framework, originally appearing in the Journal of Consumer Research, was written in the context of possessions, and a large percentage of its many citations are within the realm of business or consumer research. Aron's framework (1991, 1992), originally appearing in the Journal of Personality and Social Psychology, was written in the context of close relationships with other people. Similarly, a very large percentage of the citations for this research are in psychology journals. While these two parallel theories have similarities, there are important differences between them as well.

In Belk's (1988) paper on possessions and the extended self, he asserts that individuals cathect objects with meaning and extend their identities from themselves into objects. Two papers by Aron and his colleagues (1991, 1992) offer a theoretical framework for how individuals envelope aspects of a close other's identity into their own identities and a scale to measure inclusion of other in the self. However, consumer researchers have tended to neglect the Aron framework and psychologists have tended to neglect the Belk framework. This is not entirely surprising, given the focus of the Belk framework on possessions and the Aron framework on relationships. In this research, we argue that neither framework is superior to the other. Rather, we believe that the Belk framework is also useful in the context of human relationships, and the Aron framework is similarly useful in the context of consumer behavior. We parse out the differences between these two theories and suggest that they actually represent two distinct strategies for growing identity beyond the corporeal self, and we offer the term identity augmentation to encompass the two different strategies.

We conducted depth interviews with 36 informants and find them using distinct strategies of self-extension (Belk) and envelopment/self-expansion (Aron) in pursuing their identity projects. Because we were interested in how individuals either seek to extend their relationships with objects of consumption to others or envelope aspects of a close other's consumption relationships into their own identities, we conducted nineteen of our interviews with individuals from nine different families. In these cases, we separately interviewed both parents and children in order to gain emic perspectives of both relationship partners when identity augmentation attempts are made.

We find that individuals indeed engage in attempts to both extend their consumption relationships to close others as well as envelope/expand aspects of consumption relationships from close others. Identity extension (active attempts to instill a consumption behavior in another) was commonly observed among parents when interacting with their children. Behavior ranged from subtle attempts to influence the child's consumption to unapologetic, overt consumption mandates. In contrast, identity expansion (enveloping aspects of another's consumption) was commonly observed among children (minor or adult) toward their parents.

When conducting our interviews, we found several instances where the identity extender's attempt to augment was met either enthusiastically or without resistance from the potential identity expander/enveloper. In this case, both parties were satisfied, as both were able to augment identity simultaneously, and shared consumption was at best extremely satisfying for both parties or at worst uneventful. We also observed instances in which the extender's attempt to augment identity through consumption was rejected. If the object of consumption was not important to the extender's identity, the augmentation attempt was typically abandoned. However, in cases where the object of consumption was indeed very important to the extender's identity, he or she was forced to negotiate with the relationship partner about which aspects of the consumption the other was willing to absorb.

We also found instances in which heavily involved partners in an identity augmentation project left others out. In this case, (1) extension was not attempted and (2) some individuals were not successfully able to self-expand/envelope aspects of identity from close others. In these cases, those left behind often felt resentful or abandoned, while those engrossed in the identity augmentation project tended not notice the feelings of the person left behind, and chalked their lack of involvement in the identity augmentation project as disinterest in it.

In summary, we find evidence that consumers engage in distinct strategies of augmenting identity. We find that neither Belk's nor Aron's framework is superior to the other in describing identity augmenting behavior, bur rather describe two unique strategies of doing so. Further research could possibly reveal other distinct augmentation strategies. Finally, we observe that while successful attempts to augment identity generally yield positive results for all involved, failed attempts can lead to potential damage to close relationships.

REFERENCES

Arnould, Eric J. and Craig J. Thompson (2005), "Consumer Culture Theory: Twenty Years of Research," *Journal of Consumer Research*, 31 (4), 868-82.

Aron, Arthur, Elaine N. Aron, and Danny Smollan (1992), "Inclusion of Other in the Self Scale and the Structure of Interpersonal Closeness," *Journal of Personality and Social Psychology*, 63 (4), 596-612.

Aron, Arthur, Elaine N. Aron, Michael Tudor, and Greg Nelson (1991), "Close Relationships as Including Other in the Self," *Journal of Personality and Social Psychology*, 60, 241-53.

Belk, Russell, "Possessions and the Extended Self," *Journal of Consumer Research*, 15 (2), 139-68.

"My Possessions are Mine and Your Possessions are Mine Too" Using Hong Kong Chinese Consumers' Narratives to Illuminate the Boundaries between Extended Possessions and the Extended Self

Phoebe Wong, Lancaster University, UK
Margaret K. Hogg, Lancaster University, UK

EXTENDED ABSTRACT

Possessions and the extended self (Belk, 1988) have received extensive attention in consumer research. Belk (1984) has suggested that there are different cultural interpretations of the concepts of self and possessions. Western studies have focused on objects that demonstrate consumers' interpersonal ties (Wallendorf and Arnould, 1988, Csikszentmihalyi and Rochberg-Halton, 1981, Dittmar, 1989, Richins, 1994, Schultz et al., 1989). Eastern research, in contrast, has suggested a different set of boundaries between the self and possessions compared with Western findings i.e.: "a little of you in me and a little of me in you" (Yang 1994: 297). In this paper, we aim to address this research gap in our understanding of what constitutes both the extended self and potentially extended possessions in Hong Kong Chinese culture; and investigate the nature of the boundaries between the extended self and possessions for Hong Kong Chinese consumers.

Chinese consumers tend to place more emphasis on the interdependent view of the self-construal that focuses on togetherness and embeddedness with significant others or in-groups (Triandis, 1989, Markus and Kitayama, 1991). The Chinese sense of self is defined mainly by webs of relationships (Morris, 1994) and is constructed by the connectedness to and interpersonal relationships with significant others, family and friends (Aaker and Maheswaran, 1997) so that an individual with the interdependent self-construal becomes "a single thread in a richly textured fabric of relationships" (Kondo 1990:33).

Possessions are artefacts of the self (Kleine et al., 1995). "Self-artefacts help narrate stories of the self and reflect self-developmental tasks similar to those underlying life narratives" (Kleine et al 1995, p. 341). People reveal different aspects of their selves by retelling stories of their possessions. According to Schultz et al (1989) and Kleine et al (1995), possessions involve many aspects of people's self-development tasks, e.g. affiliation, autonomy and temporal orientations. Affiliation possessions are related to the interdependent self where people establish interpersonal connections with others in their culture through shared meanings. Autonomy possessions are often associated with the independent self, where people seek to establish autonomy from others and also to maintain a personal and unique identity. In addition, gift-receipts are often regarded as people important possessions "as a positive extension of self" (Belk 1988: 150). Gift-giving plays a substantial part in Chinese culture in terms of maintaining, harmonizing and enhancing interpersonal relationships in social systems (Wong & Ahuvia 1998, Belk and Coon 1993). As Yang (1994) noted the importance of gift-giving in Chinese society as "primacy and binding power of personal relationships and their importance in meeting the needs and desires of everyday life" (p. 6).

In the present study, informants were asked to share stories about their meaningful and important possessions. Their selves and identities are embedded in their stories as Georgakopoulou (2002) says that "if selves and identities are constituted in discourse, they are necessarily constructed in stories" (p. 428). The snowball technique was used in identifying twenty informants (ten males, ten females). Data analysis yielded a number of themes that revealed how informants interpreted what constituted their important, often extended, possessions and their extended selves.

Our findings showed that informants narrated stories not only about the gifts that they themselves had received as being their important possessions and thus constituting part of their extended self; but they also described objects that they had given as gifts to close others as part of their own possessions and these extended possessions thus constituted part of their own extended selves. Possessions create different layers of symbolic ties to other people. We examine informants' stories about their personal relationships with close others in relation to two dimensions: firstly "Gift-receipts as part of the informant's important possessions"; and secondly "Gifts to close others still regarded as part of the informant's important possessions".

The objective of this research was to explore the boundaries between the extended self and extended possessions i.e. what constituted ownership of what might be called extended possessions among Chinese consumers. Against the backdrop of Chinese interdependent culture, Hong Kong informants narrated stories about their important possessions ranging from objects that they owned to objects that actually belonged to close others, not to the informants themselves. Our research findings reveal that a broader interpretation of possessions and the extended self (as seen from these Hong Kong stories) could contribute to and enhance the existing literature on possessions and the extended self.

REFERENCE

Aaker, J. L. and D. Maheswaran (1997), "The Effect of Cultural Orientation on Persuasion," *Journal of Consumer Research*, 24, 315–328.

Belk, R. W. (1984), "Cultural and Historical Differences in Concepts of Self and their Effects on Attitudes toward Having and Giving," in *Advances in Consumer Research*, 11, eds. Thomas C. Kinnear, Provo: UT: Association for Consumer Research, 754–763.

Belk, R. W. (1988) "Possessions and the Extended Self," *Journal of Consumer Research*, 15, 139–168.

Belk, R. W. and G. S. Coon (1993), "Gift Giving as Agapic Love: An Alternative to the Exchange Paradigm Based on Dating Experiences," *Journal of Consumer Research*, 20, 393–417.

Csikszentmihalyi, M. and E. Rochberg-Halton (1981), *The Meaning of Things: Domestic Symbols and the Self*, Cambridge, Cambridge University Press

Georgakopoulou, A. (2002), "Narrative and Identity management: Discourse and Social identities in a Tale of Tomorrow," *Research on Language and Social Interaction*, 35, 427-451.

Kleine, S. S., R. E. Kleine III and C. T. Allen (1995), "How is a Possession "Me" or "Not Me"? Characterizing Types and an Antecedent of Material Possession Attachment," *Journal of Consumer Research*, 22, 327-343.

Markus, H. R. and S. Kitayama (1991), "Culture and the Self: Implications for Cognition, Emotion, and Motivation," *Psychological Review*, 98, 224-253.

Morris, B. (1994), *Anthropology of the Self: the Individual in Cultural Perspectives*, London, Pluto Press.

Richins, M. L. (1994), "Valuing Things: The Public and Private Meanings of Possessions," *Journal of Consumer Research*, 21, 504-521.

Schultz, S. E., R. E. Kleine and J. B. Kernan (1989), "These Are a Few of My Favourite Things" Toward an Explication of Attachment as a Consumer Behaviour Construct," *Advances in Consumer Research*, 16, eds. Thomas K. Srull, Provo, UT: Association for Consumer Research, 359-366.

Triandis, H. C. (1989), "The Self and Social Behavior in Differing Cultural Contexts," *Psychological Review*, 96, 506-520.

Wallendorf, M and E. J. Arnould (1988), "My Favorite Things: A Cross-Cultural Inquiry into Object Attachment, Possessiveness, and Social Linkage," *Journal of Consumer Research*, 14, 531-547.

Wang, J., F. Piron and M. V. Xuan (2001), "Faring One Thousand Miles to Give Goose Feathers: Gift Giving in the People's Republic of China," *Advances in Consumer Research*, 28, eds. M. C. Gilly and J. Meyers-Levy, Provo, UT: Association for Consumer Research, 58–63.

Wong, N. Y. and A. C. Ahuvia (1998), "Personal Taste and Family Face: Luxury Consumption in Confucian and Western Societies," *Journal of Psychology and Marketing*, 15, 423-441.

Yang, M. H. (1994) *Gifts, Favors and Banquets: The Art of Social Relations in China*, Ithaca, N.Y., Cornell University Press.

Heterotopias of Emerging Same-Sexuality: Spaces and Places of Consumption Among Young Female Consumers "Coming out of the Closet"

Andreas Pantazopolous, Bradford University, UK
Shona Bettany, Bradford University, UK

EXTENDED ABSTRACT

Consumer research has exhibited an interest in non-heterosexual consumers since the early 1990s. Penaloza (1996) suggests that some features of the gay and lesbian market have been presented as more than attractive for marketers, labeling them a "dream market". Gay and lesbian consumers, it is argued, spend in a more symbolic way, perhaps because of a felt need to promote, negotiate or display their sexual identity (Kates 2000) by buying products/brands that communicate to their peers masculinity/femininity (Rudd 1996), exclusiveness (Wardlow 1996), superior status or/and a radical lifestyle (Schouten and McAlexander 1995) and are less price-sensitive and looking for the "intangible" aspect of the goods (Tuten 2005). Although this market was viewed as a relatively new one by consumer researchers, Penaloza (1996) concluded ten years ago that things were rapidly changing and a wide spectrum of businesses started serving the needs of this group; media, vacation companies, legal, medical, financial, communications and community support services. Same-sex union agreements and the constitution of adoption rights to lesbian couples affect these consuming patterns (Borgerson et al 2006 , Johnson and Piore 2004) and offer new opportunities to businesses making an understanding of non-heterosexual consumption important.

Chasin (2000) and Kates (1998) suggest that most consumer research focuses on gay men's consumer behaviour, and lesbian women are somewhat neglected by the literature. This might be due to the perception that gay men have a much higher disposable income than lesbian women and the persistence of the myth of the "gay spender" (Kates 1999). Gay consumption is often stereotypically associated with hedonistic lifestyles and self indulgent conspicuous over-consumption (Hennesey 2000) and there is a proliferation of images in advertising and the media of white, middle class, articulate, attractive "straight looking" gay men who spend a significant amount of their income on non-utility goods (Penaloza 1996, Borgerson et al 2005). Where research has attended to lesbian consumption, this has been usually in the form of presenting lesbian women as an already existing category or segment to be studied (Wilkes and Lavernes 2002). We would argue that there is a need to develop consumer research understanding of female non-heterosexuality and to move beyond notions of viewing this phenomenon as an already existing market segment towards studies that explore the part consumption has to play within the complexities of the negotiation of female sexuality.

Living within the high tension zone of the negotiation of non-traditional identities is to navigate intensely charged flows of power and knowledge in which consumption objects and activities can act as grounding and /or transformatory nodes. It is accepted in consumer research that material objects and consumption activities are enfolded into the construction of narratives of belonging and identity, (Belk 1988, 1995, Bonsu and Belk 2003, Holt 1995, Wallendorf and Arnould 1988) particularly during moments of transition and transformation (Zwick and Dholakhia 2006). It has been noted in addition that this seems particularly prescient in negotiation of non-heterosexual identities (Perriera 2008). The consumption activities and objects enfolded into the "coming out of the closet" process, taken here to mean ontological oscillations both generative and constitutive of the formation of a non-heterosexual identity, have profound parts to play in formations of subjectivity. In this paper we explore how such consumption activities and objects co-emerge with negotiations of sexuality and identity among four young women engaging in same-sex relations for the first time.

This work emerged from an initial phenomenological study that aimed to map consumption activities onto processes of "coming out of the closet" (that is, to "reveal" ones identity as a non-heterosexual) in female university students to explore the consumption activities engaged in during stages of this important identity negotiation (Pantazopoulos 2007). During this study recurring questions about the adequacy of the frameworks of action implied in "coming out of the closet" emerged. We found that many of our participants upon first questioning their sexuality at university were exposed to the dominant Cass process model (Cass 1979) which is employed on many university websites and through university counselling services as an explanatory framework of the processes involved in coming out as gay or lesbian (Fig.1). The Cass model carefully maps out stages in this process, from initial confusion about sexuality, leading to exploration, guilt, disclosure, pride and finally assimilation into a fully exposed gay or lesbian sexuality. Our research found that this model jarred somewhat with actual experiences and accounts of the negotiation of sexuality and the sexuality "play" engaged in by our respondents to the extent that we felt that the model was too simplistic to explain the data. Moreover, the concept of "coming out of the closet" itself seemed ontologically too simplistic to account for the complexity of our research findings, and was incommensurate with contemporary theoretical frameworks around identity negotiation. Furthermore, in our research, the assumptions underpinning the idea of "coming out of the closet" were woven into negotiations of sexuality by our participants such that it became an important actor of normalcy in the cultural terrain. This led to a reappraisal of our initial research which sought to map consumption activities onto process stages, and recognition that an alternative theoretical approach was necessary. In developing our theoretical contribution we instead utilize Persson and Richard's (2008) alternative conceptualisation to "coming out of the closet" based on Foucault's (1986) notion of heterotopias to explore the spaces enacted through our participants consumption activities and suggest this alterative conceptualisation as a way for consumer and marketing researchers to better understand this valuable and interesting sub-cultural group.

We found during out study that respondents produced multiple heterotopias around their emerging sexuality, summarized here as "heterotopias of nowhere", "heterotopias of gay space" and "heterotopias of the body". These heterotopias were imaginatively and creatively deployed and occupied by these women and facilitated sexual identity play, interwoven with consumption activities such as engaging in the consumption of drugs and alcohol, a photography hobby and the purchase and display of particular items of clothing. We suggest that the concept of heterotopias has much to recommend it as a replacement or enhancement to the traditional "coming out of the closet" model that has become habitually invoked as a universal metaphor for revealing a range of identities and conditions that might be viewed as carrying a social stigma. We argue, following Person and Richards (2008), that in the absence of careful analysis, applying this metaphor as conceptual shorthand homogenizes experiences of negotiating "stigmatized" identities, and may hamper our attentiveness to the cultural specificities of lives and stories. Heterotopias, because they do not carry the negative burden of the assumption of gradually coming to terms with a stigmatized identity, can be used to build more sensitive accounts of identity construction among groups traditionally targeted by these models.

REFERENCES

Alsop, Ronald (1999), "In Marketing to Gays, Lesbians are Often Left Out," *Wall Street Journal*, 234, (71), B1.

Borgerson, J., Isla, B., Schroeder, J., Thorssen, E., (2005), "The representations of gay families in advertising: consumer responses to an emergent target group", in *European Advances in Consumer Research*, Volume 7, 143-152.

Butler, J (1990), *Gender Trouble: Feminism and the Subversion of Identity*, Routledge, London.

Cass, V.C. (1979), "Homosexual Identity Formation: A Theoretical Model," *Journal of Homosexuality*, 4 (3), Spring.

Chen, J., M., Aung, Liang, J., and Sha, O., (2004), "The Dream Market: An Exploratory Study of Gay Professional Consumers' Homosexual Identities and Their Fashion Involvement and Buying Behavior," in *Gender and Consumer Behavior*, Volume 7.

Crocco, L., Gutmann, E., Strehlau, V.I., Bacha, M. (2006), "Barbies and Bears: Nightclub Gay Segmentation," in *Gender and Consumer Behavior*, Volume 8, 12.

Foucault, M (1986), "Of other spaces," *Diactritics*, 16 (1), 22-27

Kates, Steven M. (2002), "The Protean Quality of Sub-Cultural Consumption: An Ethnographic Account of Gay Consumers," *Journal of Consumer Research*, 29 (December), 383-399.

Kates, S.M. (2001), "Marketing's interpretive communities: a case study of gay men's responses to advertising," in *European Advances in Consumer Research*, Volume 5, 168.

Kates, M. S. (1998), *Twenty Million New Customers! Understanding Gay Men's Consumer Behavior*, The Harrington Park Press.

Oakenfull, G.K., Greenlee, T.B., (2004), "Using market-specific symbols in advertising to attract gays and lesbians without alienating the mainstream," in *Advances in Consumer Research*, Volume 31, 652-653.

Oakenfull, G.K. (2005), "The effect of gay identity, gender, and gay imagery on gay consumers' attitude towards advertising," in *Advances in Consumer Research*, Volume 32, 641-642.

Penaloza, L. (1996), "We're Here, We're Queer, And We're Going Shopping! A Critical Perspective On The Accommodation of Gays and Lesbians in the US Marketplace," *Journal Of Homosexuality*, 31 (1-2), 9-41.

Persson, A., & Richards, W. (2008), "From closet to heterotopia: A conceptual exploration of disclosure and 'passing' among heterosexuals living with HIV Culture," *Health & Sexuality*, January, 10(1), 73–86.

Pereira, B. & Ayrosa, E. (2008), "A study of the discourse of possessions in coping with the stigmatized gay identity," in *Latin American Advances in Consumer Research*, Volume 2, 207-207.

Ruangwanit, N., and Wattanasuwan, K. (2009), "Living in double world: harmonizing homosexuality and masculinity through symbolic consumptions in private space," in *Asia-Pacific Advances in Consumer Research*, Volume 8, 12-22.

Rust, P. (1992), "The Politics of Sexual Identity: Sexual Attraction And Behavior Among Lesbian And Bisexual Women," *Social Problems*, 39, 366-386.

Wan-Hsiu Sunny Tsai (2004), "Gay Advertising as Negotiations: Representations of Homosexual, Bisexual and Transgender People in Mainstream Commercials," in *Gender and Consumer Behavior*, Volume 7.

Wilkes, R.E. and Laverne, D.A. (2002), "Toward understanding the dynamics of non-traditional consumers: an exploratory consideration of lesbian couples in america," in *Advances in Consumer Research*, Volume 29, 421-427.

Tales of Invisible Cities: Methodological Avenues for Multi-sited Researcher Autoethnography

Yuko Minowa, Long Island University–Brooklyn Campus, USA
Pauline MacLaran, Royal Holloway, University of London, UK
Luca M. Visconti, Università Bocconi, Italy

EXTENDED ABSTRACT

Multi-sited consumer research, in general, and multi-sited ethnography, in particular, have gained attention and popularity in the contemporary consumer research. Belk, Ger, and Askegaard (2003), for instance, conducted a phenomenological study on desire, based on the data collected in the USA, Turkey, and Denmark. Borghini, Visconti, Anderson, and Sherry (2008) studied street arts in urban cities in Italy, the UK, Ireland, and the USA. The multiplication of sites for data collection and interpretation requires collaborating researchers to pay special attention to cultural heterogeneity of their own, as much as their informants, throughout the course of ethnographic study.

While taking advantage of cultural dynamism, the differences may spawn problems at any stage of the study, and the trustworthiness of results may become questionable. According to Hall (1976, 37), "what gives man his identity no matter where he is born–is his culture, the total communication framework." In the communication system, meanings can be read correctly only if one is familiar with the behavior in its historical, social, and cultural context. In this regard, although a researcher's apprehension of his/her own culture, and those of collaborators, is the key for a successful collaborative ethnographic work, there is a paucity of methodological study to address this issue.

This paper aims to propose a new research method, "xenoheteroglossic autoethnography," as a preliminary step to full-scale multi-sited ethnographic study. Combining the Greek word *xenos*, or foreigner, and Bakhtin's first definition of heteroglossia (1934/1981), the term signifies an ethnographically-driven researchers' introspection (autoethnography) generating, within a given account, a multiplicity of voices attributable to the various national and cultural ties of the researchers (xenoheteroglossic).

The choice of focusing our introspection on an ethnographic inquiry of the cities we inhabit has a twofold explanation. First for methodological reasons connected to the aim of the paper, we were looking for a topic that could emphasize the preeminence of the researcher's cultural background, and assumed the way we live our cities largely reflect our idiosyncratic cultural bonds. The second motivation is conceptual. As researchers, we are used to interrogating consumers and companies, and even the market cultures in which their interactions take place. Still, we often avoid interpreting the city context in which such market exchanges and consumption experiences bloom.

We first review literature on introspection in consumer research followed by discussion on autoethnography in social science. Then, we discuss our proposed methodology in terms of making cultural rapport within and beyond the self; gathering and documenting data; analyzing and communicating data; and ensuring trustworthiness.

1. Making Cultural Rapport Within and Beyond the Self

There are two layers of cultural rapport the researcher needs to make: with the self and with collaborators. Initially, the researcher is the sole introspecter and examines him/herself as informant. Being exposed to globalizing media and cultural and social influx, the researcher may be multivalent in value system and ambivalent in his/her cultural identity. Thus, prior to examining cultures external to the self, the very first step is the analysis of the self. On the other hand, learning about the collaborator's cultural background and sharing the information about self examination about cultural polyvalence and ambivalence, which both affect the later polyphonic conversations, seem indispensable as the first stage of xenoheteroglossic autoethnographic study.

2. Gathering and Documenting Data

After research questions are selected, calibrated, and honed, autoethnographic researchers generate either or both generalized and/or particularistic data. Further, the data may be a direct "quotation" of the researcher's inner feelings and thoughts without intentional articulation, or the data may be the researcher's inscription about what he or she observes about the self as the subject of the study. An important procedural guideline while documenting the data is to make sense of cultural and social phenomena and their relation to ourselves by comparing, contrasting, replicating, and classifying the data. This leads to the necessity of constantly contrasting newly emerging interpretations amongst ourselves. This rigorous hermeneutic triad, cyclical process of explicating, explaining and exploring data, may be used in drawing inferences about patterns of co-occurrence, covariation, or mutual shaping (Wallendorf and Brucks 1993), all useful in developing theory in the later stage in multi-sited ethnographic study.

3. Analyzing and Communicating Data

In the xenoheteroglossic autoethnography, analyzing and communicating the result of the introspection is challenging. The difficulties arise as a result of differences in language and their uses in the cultural context. With respect to culture, Hall states (1976, 49), "the paradox of culture is that language, the system most frequently used to describe culture, is by nature poorly adapted to this difficult task." When researchers from high-context cultures and low-context cultures work together, an additional caution should be noted. The implications of these differences is that in analyzing and communicating the autoethnographic data, these researchers must be extremely sensitive to the concealed or unspoken, covert feelings of other collaborators. Another difference was the style of documentation. An autoethnographer may use an essay format while his/her colleagues may use poems and an excerpt from a fiction. Since the ultimate purpose of reportage is communication, taciturn self-reliance and self-complacency should be consciously noted by the self and to the others, and colleagues should feel free to request clarification in the communication process.

4. Ensuring Trustworthy Xenoheteroglossic Autoethnography

Trustworthiness for interpreting the result of autoethnographic study is not easily measurable. Based on the evaluative criteria for ethnographic study and introspection discussed previously (Lincoln and Guba 1985; Wallendorf and Belk 1989; Wallendorf and Brucks 1993), in xenoheteroglossic autoethnography, we consider our cycle of continuous introspecting and ongoing analysis of the results as the primary component in generating trustworthy results. The iteration should be continued until saturation is felt to have been achieved. During the procedural cycle, autoethnographers should discuss the result of introspection, then polarize particular aspects that had been absent in the previous result of the introspection. While iterating this cyclical procedure, the researchers become more sensitized to the cultural nuances. This ensures the trustworthiness in xenoheteroglossic autoethnography, and also contributes to fostering cultural sensitivity that would be integrated into full-blown multi-sited ethnographic study.

REFERENCES

Bakhtin, Mikhail M. (1934/1981), *The Dialogic Imagination: Four Essays*, ed. English translation Michael Holquist, Austin: University of Texas Press.

Belk, Russell W., Güliz Ger, and Søren Askegaard (2003), "The Fire of Desire: A Multisited Inquiry in Consumer Passion," *Journal of Consumer Research*, 30 (3), (December), 5-61.

Borghini, Stefania, Luca M. Visconti, Laurel Anderson, and John F. Sherry (2008), "Use of Public Spaces as Creative Acts. Phenomenology of Street Art in a Cross-Cultural Perspective," *European Advances in Consumer Research*, 8: 362-63.

Hall, Edward (1976), *Beyond Culture*, Garden City, NY: Anchor Press.

Lincoln, Yvonna S. and Egon G. Guba (1985), *Naturalistic Inquiry*, Beverly Hills, CA: Sage Publications.

Wallendorf, Melanie and Russell W. Belk (1989), "Assessing Trustworthiness in Naturalistic Consumer Research," in *Interpretive Consumer Research*, ed., Elizabeth C. Hirschman, Provo, UT: Association for Consumer Research, 69-84.

Wallendorf, Melanie and Merrie Brucks (1993), "Introspection in Consumer Research: Implementation and Implications," *Journal of Consumer Research*, 20 (December), 339-59.

The Influence of Prototypicality and Level of Exposure on Consumers' Responses to Product Designs: Field Evidence from German Car Buyers

Jan R. Landwehr, University of St. Gallen, Switzerland
Daniel Wentzel, University of St. Gallen, Switzerland
Andreas Herrmann, University of St. Gallen, Switzerland

EXTENDED ABSTRACT

In recent years, a growing number of industries have begun to regard product aesthetics as a fundamental part of their competitive strategy (Cox and Cox 2002). Yet, there is surprisingly little research that relates specific components of a product's design to consumers' aesthetic responses (Bloch 1995). Put differently, very few studies have investigated why some product designs are considered to be more aesthetically pleasing than others (for exceptions see, Cox and Cox 2002; Veryzer and Hutchinson 1998). One factor that has been investigated as a potential determinant of consumers' aesthetic responses is a design's prototypicality. That is, product designs that are typical of their general category have been found to elicit more positive evaluations than product designs that are atypical of their category (e.g., Veryzer and Hutchinson 1998).

However, there are numerous examples showing that some products succeed in the marketplace precisely *because* their designs are unique and revolutionary. How can one account for this apparent discrepancy? One explanation may be based on the fact that most studies have only measured participants' reactions to designs varying in prototypicality after a single exposure. However, consumers usually have multiple opportunities to observe a product before making a decision. Considering decision processes of this kind is important since research from other areas demonstrates that the aesthetical appeal of a stimulus is influenced by the level of exposure (Bornstein 1989). Therefore, this research examines if and to what extent the relationship between a design's prototypicality and consumers' preferences is moderated by the extent of exposure.

The most common explanation for the positive effects of prototypicality is based on the concept of fluency, which refers to the cognitive ease that people experience when processing a stimulus. Research in this area has shown that stimuli that are more prototypical can be processed more fluently than stimuli that are less prototypical (Winkielman et al. 2006). Fluency, in turn, may be hedonically marked and may elicit positive affect that is subsequently transferred to the stimulus (Winkielman and Cacioppo 2001). From this perspective, products with prototypical designs should be preferred over products with atypical designs.

Current theorizing, however, also indicates that fluency-based affect emerges at very early stages of information processing (Winkielman et al. 2003). Hence, if consumers only have a single opportunity to observe a product, the fluency signal is a very relevant information for forming a judgment. When, however, consumers have multiple exposures, they may be able to extract additional information from the product, such that the fluency signal is not the only information available (Novemsky et al. 2007). This, in turn, may affect how consumers respond to different designs. Whereas prototypical designs may initially elicit a positive response, they may feel boring once all their features have been extracted. Atypical designs, however, may still feel interesting after multiple exposures. Consequently, we postulate that more prototypical designs will lose in aesthetic appeal after multiple exposures, whereas less prototypical designs will gain in aesthetic appeal. Two studies focusing on German car buyers were conducted to test this prediction.

Study 1 experimentally manipulated the prototypicality of a car's design (prototypical, not prototypical) and the level of exposure (3, 6, 9 exposures). We also examined two different car segments (compact cars and mid-size executive cars) to increase the generalizability of our findings. To create car designs that varied in terms of their prototypicality, we relied on image morphing techniques. To this end, we took standardized pictures of 16 compact cars and 12 mid-size executive cars and created two different morphs out of these images for each segment. One of the morphs was particularly typical of its segment, whereas the other was particularly atypical. Afterwards, we asked a total of 306 German car buyers to evaluate these images and manipulated the level of exposure. The results confirmed our predictions and showed that the relationship between prototypicality and aesthetic liking is moderated by the extent of exposure. Whereas prototypical car designs began to lose in aesthetic appeal after 9 exposures, atypical car designs were considered more attractive with increasing amounts of exposure.

Study 2 sought to enhance the external validity of these findings by examining if the interaction between prototypicality and exposure also affects sales. To this end, we calculated a prototype similarity score for each of the 28 cars in our sample (Winkielman et al. 2006). Furthermore, we assumed that the extent of exposure would be determined by how long a car has been available on the market. Again, the results confirmed our hypothesis. While sales for prototypical cars increase rapidly in the first years, they reach a peak fairly quickly, after which sales drop again at a rapid rate. Atypical cars, however, take a much longer time to reach their peak. At the same time, they also show a slower rate of decline, such that they are sold successfully for longer periods of time than cars that are prototypical.

This research makes several contributions to the literature. Firstly, our studies show that the effect of design prototypicality is moderated by the level of exposure. Assuming that consumers have multiple exposures to a product before making a decision, atypical designs may eventually be more successful than very prototypical designs. Secondly, our studies also contribute to the literature on fluency and consumer choice. Research in this area has typically found that consumers are more likely to choose a product when they experience feelings of fluency (Schwarz 2004). Building on these findings, our studies suggest that fluency effects are more likely to be observed when consumers have limited opportunity to process a product in great depth, but may be less pronounced with increasing amounts of exposure.

REFERENCES

Benson, Philip J. and Daniel I. Perret (1993), "Extracting Prototypical Facial Images from Exemplars," *Perception*, 22 (3), 257-62.

Berlyne, Daniel E. (1970), "Novelty, Complexity, and Hedonic Value," *Perception and Psychophysics*, 8 (November), 279-86.

Bloch, Peter H. (1995), "Seeking the Ideal Form: Product Design and Consumer Response," *Journal of Marketing*, 59 (July), 16-29.

Bornstein, Robert F. (1989), "Exposure and Affect: Overview and Meta-Analysis of Research, 1968-1987," *Psychological Bulleting*, 106 (2), 265-89.

Bornstein, Robert F., Amy R. Kale, and Karen R. Cornell (1990), "Boredom as a Limiting Condition on the Mere Exposure Effect," *Journal of Personality and Social Psychology*, 58 (5), 791-800.

Carbon, Claus-Christian and Helmut Leder (2005), "The Repeated Evaluation Technique (Ret). A Method to Capture Dynamic Effects of Innovativeness and Attractiveness," *Applied Cognitive Psychology*, 19 (5), 587-601.

Cox, Dena and Anthony D. Cox (2002), "Beyond First Impressions: The Effects of Repeated Exposure on Consumer Liking of Visually Complex and Simple Product Designs," *Journal of the Academy of Marketing Science*, 30 (2), 119-30.

Deffenbacher, Kenneth A., Thomas Vetter, John Johanson, and Alice J. O'Toole (1998), "Facial Aging, Attractiveness, and Distinctiveness," *Perception*, 27 (10), 1233-43.

Fitzmaurice, Garrett M., Nan M. Laird, and James H. Ware (2004), *Applied Longitudinal Analysis*, Hoboken, NJ: Wiley.

Golder, Peter N. and Gerard J. Tellis (2004), "Growing, Growing, Gone: Cascades, Diffusion, and Turning Points in the Product Life Cycle " *Marketing Science*, 23 (2), 207-18.

Hekkert, Paul and Piet C. W. van Wieringen (1990), "Complexity and Prototypicality as Determinants of the Appraisal of Cubist Paintings," *British Journal of Psychology*, 81 (4), 483-95.

Kreuzbauer, Robert and Alan J. Malter (2005), "Embodied Cognition and New Product Design: Changing Product Form to Influence Brand Categorization," *Journal of Product Innovation Management*, 22 (2), 165-76.

Langlois, Judith H. and Lori A. Roggman (1990), "Attractive Faces Are Only Average," *Psychological Science*, 1 (2), 115-21.

Martindale, Colin and Kathleen Moore (1988), "Priming, Prototypicality, and Preference," *Journal of Experimental Psychology: Human Perception and Performance*, 14 (November), 661-70.

Mitchell, Russ (1999), "Maximizing Imacs," *U.S. News & World Report*, January 18, 43-45.

Novemsky, Nathan, Ravi Dhar, Norbert Schwarz, and Itamar Simonson (2007), "Preference Fluency in Choice," *Journal of Marketing Research*, 44 (3), 347-56.

Page, Christine and Paul M. Herr (2002), "An Investigation of the Processes by Which Product Design and Brand Strength Interact to Determine Initial Affect and Quality Judgments," *Journal of Consumer Psychology*, 12 (2), 133-47.

Perret, D. I., K. A. May, and S. Yoshikawa (1994), "Facial Shape and Judgments of Female Attractiveness," *Nature*, 368 (6468), 239-42.

Pocheptsova, Anastasiya, Aparna A. Labroo, and Ravi Dhar (2009), "When Products Feel Special: Low Fluency Leads to Enhanced Desirability," *Advances in Consumer Research*, 36.

Reber, Rolf, Norbert Schwarz, and Piotr Winkielman (2004), "Processing Fluency and Aesthetic Pleasure: Is Beauty in the Perceiver's Processing Experience?," *Personality & Social Psychology Review*, 8 (4), 364-82.

Schwarz, Norbert (2004), "Metacognitive Experiences in Consumer Judgment and Decision Making," *Journal of Consumer Pyschology*, 14 (4), 332-48.

Tellis, Gerard J. and Joseph Johnson (2007), "The Value of Quality," *Marketing Science*, 26 (6), 758-73.

Veryzer, Robert W. and J. Wesley Hutchinson (1998), "The Influence of Unity and Prototypicality on Aesthetic Responses to New Product Designs," *Journal of Consumer Research*, 24 (March), 374-94.

Winkielman, Piotr and John T. Cacioppo (2001), "Mind at Ease Puts a Smile on the Face: Psychophysiological Evidence That Processing Facilitation Increases Positive Affect," *Journal of Personality and Social Psychology*, 81 (6), 989-1000.

Winkielman, Piotr, Jamin Halberstadt, Tedra Fazendeiro, and Steve Catty (2006), "Prototypes Are Attractive Because They Are Easy on the Mind," *Psychological Science*, 17 (9), 799-806.

Winkielman, Piotr, Norbert Schwarz, Tedra Fazendeiro, and Rolf Reber (2003), "The Hedonic Marking of Processing Fluency: Implciations for Evaluative Judgment," in *The Psychology of Evaluation: Affective Processes in Cognition and Emotion*, ed. Jochen Musch and Karl Christoph Klauer, Mahwah, NJ: Erlbaum, 189-217.

Blurred Boundaries between Consumers and Producers inside Brand Communities: About Some Negative Outcomes

Bernard Cova, Euromed Management of Marseille, France
Pascale Ezan, Rouen University, France

EXTENDED ABSTRACT

The erasure of boundaries between consumers and producers is a hot topic that recent theories in consumer research (Arnould and Thompson, 2005) and in marketing (Vargo and Lusch, 2004) have helped to popularized. For the CCT, the performance of the consumer turns her/him into a producer (Kozinets et al., 2004). For the SDL, the company's co-creation of value together with the consumer(s) is the key process in this new marketing logic (Lusch and Vargo, 2006). With brand communities (Algesheimer, Dholakia and Hermann, 2005; Muniz and O'Guinn, 2001; Schouten, McAlexander and Koenig, 2007), the concepts of productive consumers and of value co-creation have been pushed to the limit insofar as brands are being transformed into virtual platforms (Arvidsson, 2006) used to stage the aggregation of contact persons and consumers united by the same passion. The advantages derived from these kinds of community strategies for the brands are said to be significant (Atkin, 2004), leading to greater satisfaction and consumer loyalty, more information, an amplified word-of-mouth effect, etc. It remains that several harbingers have raised fears about the possibility that things could go wrong, damaging contact persons firstly but also consumers as illustrated by the Warhammer case. It had been said that employee-fans are also part-time consumers, with consumer-fans becoming part-time producers (Manolis et al., 2001). This is particularly true in the case of Warhammer, where the connection between contact persons and fans in the community derives from their shared passion rather than some commercial relationship. Clearly, the concept has a basis in traditional commercial transactions, but these are masked by a Warhammer universe and collective environment from which the concept of money has been eliminated. Player-consumers mainly view staff members as 'fellow fans'. Thus, through a process that some might define as reciprocal compromise, consumers try to look past the commercial aspects of their representations of contact persons whereas the latter are happy to acknowledge consumers' expertise and competency and recognize the excellence of their output (Kozinets et al., 2004).

Three ethnographic approaches were used during the study of the Warhammer community: quasi-participant observation (participation in community events but not in the games) was undertaken by one of the authors, whose spouse and children have been Warhammer fans for eight years; participant observation with photographs and CD recordings at the annual 'Games Day' event that brought 3,500 fans to *Stade de France* in Paris on 20 April 2008; non-participant observation and non-directive interviews conducted over a period of two years by the other author, working with a group of Warhammer fans who met every Saturday afternoon at the Games Workshop-the company owing Warhammer-store in the author's city in South France.

With the development of brand community approaches, today's contact persons are no longer only being asked to fulfil the role of simple employees but also to act as employee-fans (Rémy and Kopel, 2002). In the case of Warhammer, it is difficult for employees to remain great fans of a brand when they see things from the inside. Over the long run, the Pollyanna vision that permeates the Warhammer community, which consists of believing that employees' participation in Sunday tournaments is a sign of their passion for the brand, is irritating to staff members, who often find it hard to understand consumers' jealousy because they are working in such fun conditions. They cannot say anything in return, however, since they too are part of the tribe. They have no opportunity to openly criticise their working conditions or wages, since this would be assimilated with treachery or a lack of loyalty that other players would likely have problems understanding. With their dual role as staff members and community members, employees put themselves into a schizophrenic situation. They can no longer disagree with the company without giving off the impression that they are betraying the community and its members.

This problem for staff members should not detract from a second problem, relating to the mood of consumer-fans. Games Workshop solicits consumers-construed as fans–in several ways. They are asked, where need be, to offer an opinion, come up with new ideas or criticize rules. Customers' opinions, especially when communicated in online chat rooms, enable Games Workshop to improve its products and bring out new items that will solidify fans' loyalty, especially since the ultimate consumers are the people who actually came up with the idea for the innovations in the first place. However, some consumers harbour serious doubts about Games Workshop's role, accusing it making exorbitant profits from players. This criticism is embodied in many players' joke that Games Workshop's acronym G.W. actually stands for 'Great Weasel'. This theme is particularly prevalent on-line. Companies that rely heavily on a Consumer Generated Content approach such as Warhammer can ultimately exploit consumers in two ways, since the latter are ready to pay for their cult brands' products without receiving anything in return for all of the ideas, stories and connections that they produce to enhance the brand's value (Zwick, Bonsu and Darmody, 2008).

Passion, which is the cornerstone of brand communities, is what brings staff members together with consumers, offering a lever that helps people to get involved and even transcend themselves. This Warhammer case study has stressed how brand communities overcome commercial activities' traditional barrier between contact persons and consumers (Godbout, 2007). In this way, brand communities encourage a perception of brand value that prioritizes extra-commercial aspects rooted in emotional interactions amongst fans. However, thought must also be given to the negative consequences of this confusion of roles between employees and consumers in brand communities. The porosity featured here is not without risks for employees who overwork to respond to requests from consumer-fans. It also creates a situation where consumers, construed as partners of the company, aspire to be heard (and even remunerated) for any ideas they suggest.

REFERENCES

Algesheimer, René, Utpal M. Dholakia and Andreas Hermann (2005), "The Social Influence of Brand Community: Evidence from European Car Clubs," *Journal of Marketing*, 69(3), 19-34.

Arnould, Eric J. and Craig J. Thompson (2005), "Consumer Culture Theory (CCT): Twenty Years of Research," *Journal of Consumer Research*, 31 (March), 868-82.

Arvidsson, Adam (2006), *Brands. Meaning and Value in Media Culture*, Oxon: Routledge.

Atkin, Douglas (2004), *The Culting of Brands: When Customers Become True Believers*, New York: Portfolio.

Caillé, Alain (2007), *La quête de reconnaissance: nouveau phénomène social total*, Paris: La Découverte.

Cova, Bernard, Robert V. and Avi Shankar (eds.) (2007), *Consumer Tribes*, Burlington, MA: Elsevier/Butterworth-Heinemann.

Cova, Bernard, Stefano Pace and David J. Park (2007), "Global Brand Communities across Borders: the Warhammer Case," *International Marketing Review,* 24(3), 313-329.

Dujarier, Marie Anne (2008), *Le travail du consommateur. De McDo à eBay: comment nous coproduisons ce que nous achetons*, Paris: La Découverte.

Firat, A. Fuat and Nikhilesh Dholakia (1998), *Consuming People: From Political Economy to Theaters of Consumption,* London: Routledge.

Godbout, Jacques T. (2007), *Ce qui circule entre nous*, Paris: Seuil.

Kozinets, Robert V., John F. Sherry, Diana Storm, Adam Duhachek, Krittinee Nuttavuthisit and Benet Deberry-Spence (2004), "Ludic Agency and Retail Spectacle," *Journal of Consumer Research*, 31(3), 658-672.

Lusch, Robert F. and Stephen L. Vargo (eds.) (2006), *The Service-Dominant Logic of Marketing: Dialog, Debate, and Directions*, Armonk, New York: M.E. Sharpe.

Lazzarato, Maurizio (1997), *Lavoro Immateriale, Forme di vita e produzione di soggettività*, Verona: Ombre Corte.

Manolis, Chris, Laurie A. Meamber, Robett D. Windsor and Charles D. Brookes, C. (2001), "Partial Employees and Consumers: A Post-Modern, Meta-Theoretical Perspective of Services Marketing," *Marketing Theory*, 1(2), 225-243.

Muniz, Albert M. Jr. and Thomas C. O'Guinn, T.C. (2001), "Brand Community," *Journal of Consumer Research*, 27(March), 412-432.

O'Guinn, Thomas C. and Albert M. Jr. Muniz (2005), "Communal Consumption and the Brand" in Ratneshwar, S. and David Glen Mick (eds.), *Inside Consumption: Frontiers of Research on Consumer Motives*, Routledge: London, 252-272.

Rémy, Eric and Sandrine Kopel (2002), "Social Linking and Human Resources Management in the Service Sector," *The Service Industries Journal*, 22(1), 35-56.

Schouten, John W., James H. McAlexander and Harold F. Koenig (2007), "Transcendent Customer Experience and Brand Community," *Journal of the Academy of Marketing Science,* 35(3), 357-368.

Sunderland, Patricia L. and Rita M. Denny (2007), *Doing Anthropology in Consumer Research*, Walnut Creek, Ca.: Left Coast Press Inc.

Thompson, Scott A. and Rajiv K. Sinha (2008), "Brand Communities and New Product Adoption: The Influence and Limits of Oppositional Loyalty," *Journal of Marketing,* 72(6), 65-80.

Vargo, Stephen L. and Robert F. Lusch (2004), "Evolving to a New Dominant Logic for Marketing", *Journal of Marketing*, 68(1), 1-18.

Wipperfürth, Alex (2005), *Brand Hijack: Marketing without Marketing*, New York: Portfolio.

Zwick, Detlev, Samuel K. Bonsu and Aron Darmody (2008), "Putting Consumers to Work: `Co-creation` and New Marketing Govern-Mentality," *Journal of Consumer Culture*, 8(2), 163-196.

Lifting the Veil on Infidel Brands: Islamist Discourses of Anticonsumerism

Elif Izberk-Bilgin, University of Michigan-Dearborn, USA

EXTENDED ABSTRACT

The rapid rise of Islamism[1] in many developing countries in Asia, North Africa, and Middle East has been interpreted as a critique of modernization, capitalism, and consumerism (Ray 1993, Sklair 1995, Barber 1995). While there is a growing ideological discourse on the threat Islam poses to Western civilization as well as future integration between East and West, little is known about how Islamist sentiments actually materialize in every day life in these transitional economies. Particularly of interest is how global brands as potent symbols of a global consumer culture are interpreted in developing countries in light of growing Islamist[2] sentiments. Uneven economic and cultural globalization has been fostering consumer resentment to the ideals of market society and thereby also mobilizing political Islam as a counter-ideology (Ahmed 2007), which nourishes new meanings of global brands in these locales as 'infidel's and symbols of 'injustice and oppression'. Such interpretations portray a remarkably different kind of consumer resentment towards global brands than the hedonic, aesthetic, and self-expressive consumer activism examined in Western countries (Holt 2002, Kozinets 2002, Thompson and Arsel 2004), urging us to re-examine existing assumptions about anticonsumptionist discourses. As such, this paper explores what renders a global brand an infidel brand and what stimulates consumer rejection of these brands in a developing country, Turkey.

Past research on anticonsumption issues portrays the activist consumer as playfully confronting an unfettered capitalist ideology and unbounded globalization. Despite the significance of these causes, previous research concludes that such a defiant stance is driven by a profound desire to construct an authentic and sovereign self in a mass-manufactured world. Critical consumers strive to distinguish themselves from the stereotypical 'mindlessly consuming' mainstream consumer by leading fringe lives (Holt 2002), temporarily enacting gift-economy at the Burning Man festival (Kozinets 2002), performing esoteric healthcare practices (Thompson 2003), or condemning Starbucks for sanitizing and debasing the coffee experience (Thompson and Arsel 2004, Kozinets 2002b). Evidence of such hedonic, aesthetic, and self-expressive qualms abounds in the literature (exceptions (Dobscha and Ozanne 2001), Kozinets and Handelman 2004), suggesting that the postmodern consumer, liberated from the concerns of satisfying basic needs, engages in anti-materialist, anti-corporate, and environmentally conscious discourses and practices as a therapeutic and socially privileging endeavor. While this portrayal may aptly describe the identity anxieties of consumers in economically advanced countries, it hardly characterizes the lived-experiences of consumers and concomitant attitudes toward consumption in developing countries. Marked by poverty, double digit rates of unemployment and inflation, periodic devaluations of local currency, and lack of democratic institutions, these consumptionscapes clearly bear unique motivations of anticonsumerism than those examined in the U.S. and Western Europe.

One such motivation is provided by the anticonsumptionist stance of political Islam. Amidst the economic, cultural, social, and political turmoil that generally plagues developing countries, Islamism emerges as an antidote to the disenfranchised consumers' quest for an alternative identity. By espousing modesty and promising eternal justice political Islam provides a justifying and soothing existential discourse for many disempowered consumers (Crockett and Wallendorf 2004). Furthermore, the socio-historical conditions such as colonialism, Cold War, the modernization attempts undertaken in several developing countries, the Israel-Palestine conflict, along with the recent Iraq War not only promote Islamism but also energize an anticonsumerist stance vis-à-vis global brands among Muslim consumers.

Through a critical ethnography, this paper examines Islamist anticonsumptionist attitudes in Turkey. Particularly of interest to this study are the Islamist interpretations of global brands as 'infidel's and symbols of 'injustice and oppression'. Turkey as a transitional country with a rising Islamist class presents an excellent opportunity to explore diverse readings of global brands in a non-Western context. The critical ethnography draws from participant observation, in-depth interviews, researcher's field notes, and textual material analysis. Informants include 45 individuals from diverse socio-economic and educational backgrounds, although this paper focuses on 15 informants with Islamist dispositions. The identification of Islamist informants was initially driven by their distinctive physical appearance. For the purposes of this research, I sought Islamist informants primarily among women who wore çarşaf -also known as chador, a full-length black outer garment that covers the whole body except the eyes (Saktanber 1997)-because they are among the most extreme public displays of Islamist ideology in Turkey. These informants were further identified as Islamist consumers based on their ideology and lifestyles as evinced through fieldwork. The data was analyzed following the procedures described in Penaloza (1994) and (Arnould and Wallendorf 1994).

This research identifies three unique Islamist discourses of anticonsumerism: modesty, helal-haram, and zulm (oppression) that construct the meaning of global brands as infidel brands. These discourses are analyzed and introduced in the order in which they appear in informants' emic accounts. In other words, Islamist consumers first and foremost explain their anticonsumerist attitudes through Islamic ideals of modesty and later through the religious criteria of helal-haram; yet a deeper analysis reveals the essence of Islamist resentment toward global brands: the perception of global brands as oppressors of Muslim faith and the greater Islamic community. While the discourse of modesty and helal-haram essentially concern spiritual and bodily refrainment from material world and brands, the discourse of zulm is deeply entwined with socio-historical conditions such as the colonization of Muslim countries and the establishment of an Israeli state in the Middle East as well as the tensions between secularists and Islamists in Turkey. Through the discourses of modesty, helal-haram, and zulm Islamists create the boundaries of infidel brands to include any brand that poses an ideological threat to the much espoused and romanticized Islamic lifestyle.

In addition to examining the notion of infidel brands, this study extends past research by illustrating how Islamist anticonsumerism discourses conceptually differ from the postmodern and

[1]Islamism is a political ideology distinct from Islam as a body of faith and is defined as "a form of instrumentalization of Islam by individuals, groups, and organizations that pursue political objectives" as a reaction to contemporary societal challenges (Denoeux, 61).

[2]*Islamist* refers to those individuals who are not just "much more pious than other Muslims, but also search for an alternative Islamic life politics and new social order" (Saktanber 2002, p. 257).

postmaterialist consumer activism as previously explored in Western contexts. In contrast to the hedonic and therapeutic consumer resistance found in these locales, Islamist anticonsumerism not only embodies a critique of the merits of Western ideals such as modernization, capitalism, and market society, but also a strong desire for a qualitatively different social order than the one modern market society offers.

REFERENCES

Ahmed, Akbar S. (2007), *Journey into Islam : The Crisis of Globalization*, Washington, D.C.: Brookings Institution Press.

Arnould, Eric J. and Melanie Wallendorf (1994), "Market-Oriented Ethnography: Interpretation Building and Marketing Strategy Formulation," *Journal of Marketing Research*, 31 (4), 484-504.

Barber, Benjamin R. (1996), Jihad Vs. Mcworld, New York: Ballantine Books.

Belk, Russell W., Güliz Ger, and Søren Askegaard (2003), "The Fire of Desire: A Multisited Inquiry into Consumer Passion," *Journal of Consumer Research*, 30 (3), 326-51.

Crockett, David and Melanie Wallendorf (2004), "The Role of Normative Political Ideology in Consumer Behavior," *Journal of Consumer Research*, 31 (3), 511-28.

Dawar, Niraj and Philip Parker (1994), "Marketing Universals: Consumers' Use of Brand Name, Price, Physical Appearance, and Retailer Reputation as Signals of Product Quality," *Journal of Marketing*, 58 (2), 81-95.

Denoeux, Guilain (2002), "The Forgotten Swamp: Navigating Political Islam," *Middle East Policy*, 9 (2), 56-81.

Dobscha, Susan and Julie L. Ozanne (2001), "An Ecofeminist Analysis of Environmentally Sensitive Women Using Qualitative Methodology: The Emancipatory Potential of an Ecological Life," *Journal of Public Policy and Marketing*, 20 (2), 201-14.

Hassan, Salah S. and Lea P. Katsanis (1994), "Global Market Segmentation Strategies and Trends," in *Globalization of Consumer Markets: Structures and Strategies*, ed. Salah S. Hassan and Erdener Kaynak, New York: International Business Press, 47-62.

Hirschman, Elizabeth C. (1993), "Ideology in Consumer Research, 1980 and 1990: A Marxist and Feminist Critique," *Journal of Consumer Research*, 19 (4), 537.

Holt, Douglas B. (2002), "Why Do Brands Cause Trouble? A Dialectical Theory of Consumer Culture and Branding," *Journal of Consumer Research*, 29 (1), 70-90.

Holt, Douglas B., John Quelch, and Earl Taylor (2004), "How Global Brands Compete," *Harvard Business Review*, 82 (September), 68-75.

Kozinets, Robert V. (2002a), "Can Consumers Escape the Market? Emancipatory Illuminations from Burning Man," *Journal of Consumer Research*, 29 (1), 20-38.

Kozinets, Robert V. (2002b), "The Field Behind the Screen: Using Netnography for Marketing Research in Online Communities," *Journal of Marketing Research*, 39 (1), 61-72.

Kozinets, Robert V. and John F. Sherry (2004), "Dancing on Common Ground: Exploring the Sacred at Burning Man," in *Rave Culture and Religion*, ed. Graham St. John, London ; New York: Routledge, 287-303.

Kozinets, Robert V. and Jay M. Handelman (2004), "Adversaries of Consumption: Consumer Movements, Activism, and Ideology," *Journal of Consumer Research*, 31 (3), 691-704.

Muñiz Jr., Albert M. and Hope Jensen Schau (2005), "Religiosity in the Abandoned Apple Newton Brand Community," *Journal of Consumer Research*, 31 (4), 737-47.

Öncü, Ay se and Petra Weyland (1997), *Space, Culture and Power : New Identities in Globalizing Cities*, London; Atlantic Highlands, N.J.: Zed Books.

Penaloza, Lisa (1994), "Atravesando Fronteras/Border Crossings: A Critical Ethnographic Exploration of the Consumer Acculturation of Mexican Immigrants," *Journal of Consumer Research*, 21 (1), 32.

Ray, Larry (1993), Rethinking Critical Theory : Emancipation in the Age of Global Social Movements, London ; Newbury Park, CA: Sage Publications.

Saktanber, Ay?e (1997), "Formation of a Middle Class Ethos and its Quotidian: Revitalizing Islam in Urban Turkey," in *Space, Culture, and Power: New Identities in Globalizing Cities*, ed. Ay?e Öncü and Petra Weyland, London: Zed Books, 140-157.

Saktanber, Ay?e (2002), "We Pray Like You Have Fun: New Islamic Youth in Turkey between Intellectualism and Popular Culture," in *Fragments of Culture: The Everyday of Modern Turkey*, ed. Deniz Kandiyoti and Ay?e Saktanber, New Jersey: Rutgers University Press, 254-277.

Sandıkçı, Özlem and Güliz Ger (2005), "Aesthetics, Ethics, and Politics of the Turkish Headscarf," in *Clothing as Material Culture*, ed. Susanne Küchler and Daniel Miller, Oxford, UK ; New York: Berg, 61-83.

Sherry, John F. and Robert V. Kozinets (2007), "Commedy of the Commons: Nomadic Spirituality and the Burning Man Festival," in *Consumer Culture Theory*, ed. Russell W. Belk and John F. Sherry, San Diego: JAI Press, 119-51.

Sklair, Leslie (1995), *Sociology of the Global System*, Baltimore: Johns Hopkins University Press.

Strizhakova, Yuliya, Robin A. Coulter, and Linda L. Price (2008), "The Meanings of Branded Products: A Cross-National Scale Development and Meaning Assessment," *International Journal of Research in Marketing*, 25 (2), 82-93.

Thompson, Craig J. (2003), "Natural Health Discourses and the Therapeutic Production of Consumer Resistance," The Sociological Quarterly, 44 (1), 81-107.

Thompson, Craig J., Aric Rindfleisch, and Zeynep Arsel (2006), "Emotional Branding and the Strategic Value of the Doppelgänger Brand Image," *Journal of Marketing*, 70 (1), 50-64.

Thompson, Craig J. and Zeynep Arsel (2004), "The Starbucks Brandscape and Consumers' (Anticorporate) Experiences of Glocalization," *Journal of Consumer Research*, 31 (3), 631-42.

Üstüner, Tuba and Douglas B. Holt (2007), "Dominated Consumer Acculturation: The Social Construction of Poor Migrant Women's Consumer Identity Projects in a Turkish Squatter," *Journal of Consumer Research*, 34 (1), 41-56.

The Effects of Regulatory Focus on Consumer Judgments Involving Self and Others' Payoffs

Subimal Chatterjee, Binghamton University, USA
Ashwin Vinod Malshe, Binghamton University, USA
Timothy B. Heath, Miami University (Ohio), USA
Glenn Pitman, Binghamton University, USA

EXTENDED ABSTRACT

Many decisions involve choices that affect not only the self or one's organization but also others and other organizations. For example, consumers can factor in both their own position and that of the dealer when negotiating a car's price. Aggressive managers may weight relative performance so heavily that they prefer options that damage their own profitability just because it is slightly more damaging to a competitor (Kalra and Soberman 2008). The current study extends such research by assessing the potential impact of regulatory focus on decisions that determine self and other payoffs.

Consider the following two scenarios. In Scenario 1, a consumer has to select between two options, A and B. Option A consists of the consumer wining $100 for sure, whereas in Option B a chance event decides if the consumer wins either $150 or $80 (e.g., winning the $150 depends on picking a yellow ball from a jar containing 100 yellow and white balls). If asked for the minimum number of yellow balls the jar must contain for the individual to still prefer Option B, consumers focused on avoiding the worst outcome should state a higher minimum acceptable probability (MAP) than those focused on obtaining the best outcome (Bohnet and Zeckhauser 2004). Scenario 2 is identical to Scenario 1 except that consumers now share payoffs with a confederate. Option A splits $200 equally between the two so that each receives $100. However, in Option B, a chance event determines whether the two consumers split $300 equally ($150 each), or whether the consumer receives $80 while the confederate receives $220. Consumers who like sharing money with others or who do not mind receiving less should like Option B more in Scenario 2 than in Scenario 1. However, consumers who do not like sharing money with others or who dislike receiving less than others should like Option B less in Scenario 2. The consumer's self-explicated MAP, now determined by risk for money and aversion to inequality, should reflect this potential change in Option B's attractiveness. If, as we hypothesize, consumers dislike sharing money and/or receiving less than do others, their MAP's should be higher in Scenario 2, an elevation we refer to hereafter as an *inequality premium.*

This study tests for the existence of an inequality premium as well as the possibility that regulatory focus moderates that premium. Consumers typically self regulate by focusing on either acquiring the best outcome (promotion focus) or avoiding the worst outcome (prevention focus; Higgins 1997). However, to the extent that a particular regulatory focus also involves a self-view intent on distinguishing oneself from others or integrating oneself with others (Lee, Aaker, and Gardner 2000), we expect promotion-focused consumers to be more sensitive to coming out ahead and prevention-focused consumers to be more sensitive to fitting in harmoniously. Accordingly, promotion-focused consumers should find Scenario 2's risky Option B to be especially distasteful as they now have to share any larger win with someone else or endure a loss in money not only relative to Option A's sure thing, but relative to what someone else wins as well. On the other hand, prevention-focused consumers should not be so concerned with their payoffs relative to others, such that moving from Scenario 1's non-social situation to Scenario 2's social situation should have relatively little impact on them.

In Study 1, we explore if regulatory focus affects consumers' enjoyment of winning money if they win the money alone, or others win with them. We assigned forty-nine undergraduate students (24 females) to one of two regulatory focus conditions. Following the procedure outlined by Higgins and others (1994), we asked participants in the promotion-focused (prevention-focused) condition to write a brief essay about their hopes and aspirations (duties and obligations) at present as well as five years from now. Following their essay, participants imagined that they would receive a cash prize but how much cash they would receive depended upon a lottery's outcome. We described two lotteries. In Lottery 1, the participants, playing by themselves, could win $150 or $80. In Lottery 2, the participant, paired with a classmate, could win $150 (with the classmate also winning $150), or $80 (with the classmate winning $220). Consistent with our expectations, promotion-focused participants were less happy with the $80/$220 split relative to winning $80 alone ($M$=6.29 on a 9-point scale where 9.0=Less happy, significantly greater than the scale's mid-point of 5.0; $t(23)=4.86, p<.001$). Prevention-focused participants also expressed less happiness if a confederate came out ahead, but on a much smaller magnitude (M=5.68, not significantly different from the scale's mid-point of 5.0; $p>.05$).

In Study 2, we assigned fifty-two undergraduate students (16 females) to one of two regulatory focus conditions using the same priming manipulation as in Study 1. After writing their essay, participants imagined that they had to choose between Options A and B in Scenarios 1 and 2 (described above). After reading each scenario, participants indicated their MAP of selecting Option B to Option A by writing a number between 1 and 100 (smaller numbers mean a stronger preference for the risky Option B). In Scenario 1, the MAP for promotion-focused participants (M=54.19) was smaller than the MAP for prevention-focused participants (M=64.42; $F(1, 49)=4.25, p<.05$). However, as predicted, promotion-focused participants demanded a significant inequality premium when moving from Scenario 1 to Scenario 2 (M's=54.19 vs. 69.00; $F(1, 24)=43.86, p<.0001$), and one that was significantly larger than the premium demanded by prevention-focused participants (M's=64.42 vs. 68.50; $F(1, 24)=2.35$, p>.10).

These findings are important for both theory and practice. Prevailing theory and research suggests that promotion-focused consumers are more risk seeking than prevention-focused consumers. The current study shows, however, that the addition of a social dimension such as payoffs relative to others can eliminate this difference. For practice, marketers hoping to sell risk-reducing products such as established, trusted brands might be able to enhance their chances by invoking social risks. Whereas a fear tactic focusing on the embarrassment of being worse off than others might affect all consumers, it should be especially potent for reining in the risk seeking tendencies of more promotion-focused consumers who might be more inclined to try a new and unproven competitor.

REFERENCE

Bohnet, Iris and Richard Zeckhauser (2004), "Trust, Risk and Betrayal," *Journal of Economic Behavior and Organization*, 55 (4), 467-84.

Florack, Arnd and Juliane Hartmann (2007), "Regulatory Focus and Investment Decisions in Small Groups," *Journal of Experimental Social Psychology*, 43 (4), 626-32.

Friedman, Ronald S. and Jens Forster (2001), "The Effects of Promotion and Prevention Cues on Creativity," *Journal of Personality and Social Psychology*, 81 (6), 1001-13.

Harcar, Talha, John E. Spillan, and Orsay Kucukemiroglu (2005), "A Multi-National Study of Family Decision Making," *Multinational Business Review*, 13 (Summer), 3-21.

Higgins, E. Tory (1997), "Beyond Pleasure and Pain," *American Psychologist*, 52, 1280-300.

Higgins, E. Tory, Christopher J. R. Roney, Ellen Crowe, and Charles Hymes (1994), "Ideal Versus Ought Predilection for Approach and Avoidance: Distinct Self-Regulatory Systems," *Journal of Personality and Social Psychology*, 66 (2), 276-86.

Hong, Kessely and Iris Bohnet (2007), "Status and Distrust: The Relevance of Inequality and Betrayal Aversion," *Journal of Economic Psychology*, 28 (2), 197-213.

Kalra, Ajay and David A. Soberman (2008), "The Curse of Competitiveness: How Advice from Experienced Colleagues and Training Can Hurt Marketing Profitability," *Journal of Marketing*, 72 (May), 32-47.

Keller, Poonam Anand (2006), "Regulatory Focus and Efficacy of Health Messages," *Journal of Consumer Research*, 33 (1), 109-14.

Lee, Angela Y. and Jennifer L. Aaker (2004), "Bringing the Frame into Focus: The Influence of Regulatory Fit on Processing Fluency and Persuasion," *Journal of Personality and Social Psychology*, 86 (2), 205-18.

Lee, Angela Y., Jennifer L. Aaker, and Wendi L. Gardner (2000), "The Pleasures and Pains of Distinct Seif-Construals: The Role of Interdependence in Regulatory Focus," *Journal of Personality and Social Psychology*, 78 (6), 1122-34.

Loewenstein, George F., Leigh Thompson, and Max H. Bazerman (1989), "Social Utility and Decision Making in Interpersonal Contexts," *Journal of Personality and Social Psychology*, 57 (3), 426-41.

Markus, Hazel Rose and Shinobu Kitayama (1991), "Culture and the Self: Implications for Cognitions, Emotion, and Motivation," *Psychological Review*, 98 (2), 224-53.

Triandis, Harry C. and Michele J. Gelfand (1998), "Converging Measurement of Horizontal and Vertical Individualism and Collectivism," *Journal of Personality and Social Psychology*, 74 (1), 118-128

Werth, Lioba, Jennifer Mayer, and Thomas Mussweiler (2006), "The Influence of Regulatory Focus on Integrative Negotiations," *Zeitschrift Fur Sozialpsychologie*, 37 (1), 19-25.

Yeo, Junsang and Jongwon Park (2006), "Effects of Parent-Extension Similarity and Self Regulatory Focus on Evaluations of Brand Extensions," *Journal of Consumer Psychology*, 16 (3), 272-82.

Culture, Regulatory Goals, and Response Styles

Ashok K. Lalwani, University of Texas at San Antonio, USA
L. J. Shrum, University of Texas at San Antonio, USA
Chi-Yue Chiu, Nanyang Technological University, Singapore

EXTENDED ABSTRACT

Whether and how people engage in socially desirable responding–the tendency of people to portray themselves in more favorable light on survey questionnaires than their thoughts or actions may actually warrant—is a topic of considerable interest to scholars of marketing and consumer behavior both from theoretical and methodological standpoints (Fisher 1993; Mick 1996). Recent research suggests that these tendencies span cultures (Lalwani et al. 2006; 2009; Shavitt et al. 2006).

Although research has examined the effects of culture on consumer goals and their tendency to engage in socially desirable responding, the system of relations between culture, goals, and socially desirable responding is not well understood. In fact, although factors that influence responses on surveys have received considerable attention, little research has addressed the underlying processes (see Lalwani 2009, for an exception). The purpose of the current research is to fill this gap by exploring in more detail the possible connections between culture and types of socially desirable responding, the underlying processes, and factors that impact the strength of the relations. We posit that culture would be differentially related to socially desirable responding. Individualists would tend to engage in self-deceptive enhancement, the tendency to report exaggerated beliefs of one's competence, skills, and abilities, but not impression management, the tendency to provide normatively appropriate responses to look good. In contrast, collectivists would tend to engage in impression management, but not self-deceptive enhancement.

Beyond this general set of hypotheses, however, there are still important unanswered questions regarding the processes that may underlie these links. In particular, little is known about the motivational links between cultural values and socially desirable responding. The inconsistent findings on the relation between cultural values and socially desirable responding allude to the existence of variables that may mediate or moderate these relationships. For instance, it is possible that these relationships are stronger for certain kinds of people than for others. Hence, another objective of this paper is to propose and test such mediating and moderating variables. One possibility, which we investigate in the studies to be presented, is that regulatory focus underlies these effects, and that consumers' self-consciousness (public or private) influences the strength of these relationships.

Regulatory focus theory is a theory of self-regulation that proposes two distinct foci: a promotion focus that is primarily concerned with maximizing positive outcomes and a prevention focus that is primarily concerned with minimizing negative outcomes (Aaker and Lee 2001; Higgins 1997). People who are promotion focused eagerly pursue gains or successes. Focusing on accomplishments, achievements, and the pursuit of ideals, they are oriented towards fulfilling their hopes and aspirations and they scrutinize their social world for information that bears on the pursuit of success. In contrast, people with a prevention focus strive to avoid negative outcomes. Driven by the need to feel secure and to meet their obligations, these individuals are primarily concerned with preventing failures or losses, and their information processing and interpersonal tactics are geared towards avoiding undesirable outcomes (Higgins 1997). Lee, Aaker, and Gardner (2000) provided evidence that people with an independent self-construal tend to be promotion focused, whereas people with an interdependent self-construal tend to be prevention focused.

In the following studies, we explore the possible interrelations between culture, regulatory focus, and socially desirable responding. Our overarching hypothesis is that regulatory focus mediates the relation between cultural orientation and socially desirable responding. More specifically, we hypothesize that a promotion focus mediates the relation between individualism and self-deceptive enhancement, and a prevention focus mediates the relation between collectivism and impression management.

To further explicate the mediating role of regulatory focus in the relation between culture and socially desirable responding, we were interested in exploring possible boundary conditions of this pattern of effects. Specifically, we were interested in determining whether the relations just proposed are stronger for some types of people than for others. One possible variable that we investigated is self-consciousness. Research suggests that self-consciousness can be conceived of along two orthogonal dimensions: public and private (Fenigstein, Scheier, and Buss 1975). Those who are high (vs. low) in private self-consciousness are more likely to attend to their own inner thoughts and feelings. As such, their focus is on cognitions that deal primarily with the self, they tend to reflect about themselves, and they are attentive to the workings of their mind. In contrast, those who are high (vs. low) in public self-consciousness are especially attuned to other people's perspectives. They view themselves as social objects, and are sensitive to others' reactions to their behavior. As such, they regulate their conduct by taking into account the desires and expectations of others (Carver and Scheier 1998) and are interested in getting along by going along (Schlenker and Weigold 1990).

Because people who are high (vs. low) in private self-consciousness are attentive to their inner feelings, they may be more realistic about their capabilities and skills, even when they are from individualistic cultures which tend toward self-deceptive enhancement. As a result, they may be less likely to engage in self-deceptive enhancement, a response style in which people hold exaggerated, unrealistic, and glorified notions of their skills and abilities. If so, the mediating relationship between individualism, promotion focus, and self-deceptive enhancement proposed earlier should be weaker for people who are high (vs. low) in private self-consciousness. In other words, private self-consciousness should moderate the mediating relationship between individualism, promotion focus, and self-deceptive enhancement.

In contrast, people high in public self-consciousness are the epitome of the social animal (Schlenker and Weigold 1990). They not only take the role of others to imagine their reactions, but also actively mold their behavior to appeal to others (Buss 1980; Carver and Scheier 1998). Because people who are high (vs. low) in public self-consciousness are more concerned about managing others' impressions of themselves, and are also more affected by possible rejection from others (Fenigstein 1987), they may be highly motivated to engage in impression management, even if they come from collectivistic cultures that already tend toward impression management. If so, then the mediating relationship between collectivism, prevention focus, and impression management should be stronger for people who are high (vs. low) in public self-consciousness. In other words, public self-consciousness should moderate the mediating relationship between collectivism, prevention focus, and impression management.

Four studies provide robust support for the framework we have proposed. Across the four studies, the operationalizations of the major variables (individualism—collectivism, regulatory focus, and socially desirable responding) were varied in order to maximize generalizability. In Study 1, we compared the socially desirable responding and regulatory focus of Hong Kong Chinese and European Americans, and examined whether cultural variations in socially desirable responding were mediated by regulatory focus. In Studies 2-4, we measured participants' chronic individualism and collectivism in a U.S. sample. The research makes a number of theoretical, methodological, and practical contributions.

REFERENCES

Aaker, Jennifer L. and Angela Y. Lee (2001), "'I' Seek Pleasures And 'We' Avoid Pains: The Role of Self-Regulatory Goals in Information Processing and Persuasion," *Journal of Consumer Research*, 28 (June), 33-49.

Buss, Arnold H. (1980), *Self-Consciousness and Social Anxiety*, San Francisco: W. H. Freeman & Co.

Carver, Charles S. and Michael F. Scheier (1998), *On the Self-Regulation of Behavior*, New York: Cambridge University Press.

Fenigstein, Allan (1987), "On the Nature of Public and Private Self-Consciousness," *Journal of Personality*, 55 (3), 543-54.

Fenigstein, Allan, Michael F. Scheier, and Arnold H. Buss (1975), "Public and Private Self-Consciousness: Assessment and Theory," *Journal of Consulting and Clinical Psychology*, 43 (4), 522-27.

Higgins, E. Tory (1997), "Beyond Pleasure and Pain," *American Psychologist*, 52 (12), 1280-300.

Lalwani, Ashok K. (2009), "The Distinct Influence of Cognitive Busyness and Need for Closure on Cultural Differences in Socially Desirable Responding," *Journal of Consumer Research*, 36 (2), 305-16.

Lalwani, Ashok K. and Sharon Shavitt (2009), "The "Me" I Claim to Be: Cultural Self-Construal Elicits Self-Presentational Goal Pursuit," *Journal of Personality and Social Psychology*, 97 (1), 88-102.

Lalwani, Ashok K., Sharon Shavitt, and Timothy Johnson (2006), "What Is the Relation between Cultural Orientation and Socially Desirable Responding?" *Journal of Personality and Social Psychology*, 90 (1), 165-78.

Lee, Angela Y., Jennifer L. Aaker, and Wendi L. Gardner (2000), "The Pleasures and Pains of Distinct Self-Construals: The Role of Interdependence in Regulatory Focus," *Journal of Personality and Social Psychology*, 78 (6), 1122-34.

Mick, David Glen (1996), "Are Studies of Dark Side Variables Confounded by Socially Desirable Responding? The Case of Materialism," *Journal of Consumer Research*, 23 (2), 106-19.

Schlenker, Barry R. and Michael F. Weigold (1990), "Self-Consciousness and Self-Presentation: Being Autonomous Versus Appearing Autonomous," *Journal of Personality and Social Psychology*, 59 (4), 820-28.

Shavitt, Sharon, Ashok K. Lalwani, Jing Zhang, and Carlos Torelli (2006), "The Horizontal/Vertical Distinction in Cross-Cultural Consumer Research," *Journal of Consumer Psychology*, 16 (4), 325-42.

Generic Advertising Campaigns: A Goals-Based Perspective on the Effect of Market Trends and Solicitation Messages on Voluntary Contributions

Shweta Oza, University of Miami, USA
Joydeep Srivastava, University of Maryland, USA

EXTENDED ABSTRACT

Millions of dollars are spent every year on generic advertising campaigns that are designed to promote an entire product category. Generic advertising campaigns are intended to stimulate primary category demand (i.e., increase the size of pie) (Forker and Ward 1993). Some common examples of generic advertising are the "Got Milk?" campaign, "The New Steel" campaign, "Pork: The Other White Meat" campaign, and "Cotton: The Fabric of Our Lives" campaign. Despite the importance and prevalence of generic advertising campaigns, such campaigns have received relatively little attention in the marketing literature.

The few studies that examine generic advertising campaigns have focused either on the effect of such advertising on consumers (Borden 1965; Chakravarti and Janiszewski 2004) or the relationship between generic and brand advertising in identifying conditions under which firms should focus more on generic versus brand advertising (Bass et al. 2005; Krishnamurthy 2000). As such, relatively little is known about the trials and tribulations of organizing and funding generic advertising campaigns (Krishnamurthy, Bottom, and Rao 2003). While many generic advertising campaigns, particularly in the agriculture and commodities market, are funded via mandatory contributions (also called check-offs) of the individual producers (members); several others (like "Cotton: The Fabric of Our Lives") are funded by voluntary contributions from the individual members (Krishnamurthy 2000).

Voluntarily funded generic advertising campaigns benefit all individual members, regardless of whether an individual member contributes towards the campaign (Forker and Ward 1993) and the benefits do not reduce for any member just because another member has benefited from it. Voluntarily funded generic advertising campaigns can thus be conceptualized as a social dilemma or more specifically as a public goods problem (Dawes 1980). First, individual members benefit from generic advertising even if they do not contribute towards the campaign. The dominant strategy for a member is thus not to contribute at all with the hope that other members will contribute. Second, if all members decide not to contribute, no one benefits. The dilemma arises because the dominant strategy based on individual rationality is for an individual member to contribute nothing whereas the optimal strategy based on group rationality is for every member to contribute the maximum (Dawes and Thaler 1988). This research views voluntarily funded generic advertising campaigns from a public goods lens and examines factors that may influence cooperation and thus increase members' voluntary contributions. Specifically, this research examines the influence of situational (or market) factors and solicitation messages on individual members' contribution decisions towards a generic advertising campaign.

Situational factors at the macro level such as market or industry trend, more or less, affect every firm within a specific industry and have the potential to affect the level of competition or cooperation among firms (e.g., Rotemberg and Saloner 1986). However, the findings are conflicting as some studies show that cooperation decreases among firms in periods of increasing market demand (Rotemburg and Saloner 1986) whereas others show that there is less cooperation in periods of declining market demand (Green and Porter 1984; Scherer 1980). In the present context, industry trend provides the milieu in which individual members decide on whether to contribute to a generic advertising campaign, and if so, how much? In other words, contribution decisions may be influenced by whether the individual members face a market with an increasing versus decreasing demand (and profitability). On one hand, facing a declining trend in profitability, resource constrained members may curtail their marketing and advertising budgets. On the other hand, members may feel the need to cooperate and increase their advertising budget in tough market conditions (Krishnamurthy et al. 2003). Given the scant empirical evidence on the effect of market level factors on members' contribution decisions towards a generic advertising campaign (Krishnamurthy et al. 2003) and the conflicting theories regarding its effect on the level of cooperation, this research examines contribution decisions towards a generic advertising campaign when a specific market faces an increasing versus a decreasing profitability trend.

The second factor that we examine is solicitation message. It is common practice for industry-wide consortiums to use solicitation messages to encourage individual members to contribute towards a generic advertising campaign (Forker and Ward 1993). The effectiveness of solicitation messages is likely to vary with the message used and the manner in which the messages are framed (e.g., Maheswaran and Meyers-Levy 1990; Rothman and Salovey 1997). Further, since contribution decisions about generic advertising campaigns are made in the context of situational factors, the effectiveness of different solicitation messages is likely to vary with the prevailing market trend. Although there is considerable research which shows that message effectiveness depends on how it is framed (e.g., Levin, Schneider, and Gaeth 1998), the findings regarding the conditions under which different frames (e.g., positive/negative or gain/loss) are most effective are mixed and inconsistent (e.g., Block and Keller 1995; Lee and Aaker 2004; Maheswaran and Meyers-Levy 1990). Some studies suggest that positively framed messages are more effective (e.g., Maheswaran and Meyers-Levy 1990; Meyers-Levy and Maheswaran 2004) whereas other studies suggest that negatively framed messages are more effective (e.g., Block and Keller 1995). In the present context, the question is how should a message be framed to maximize its effectiveness in different market conditions? This research addresses this question by examining the effectiveness of different message frames in increasing contributions towards a generic advertising campaign when a market faces an increasing as well as a decreasing trend in demand and profitability.

Importantly, we develop a conceptual framework based on goal systems theory (Kruglanski et al. 2002) that allows us to predict the simultaneous effects of market trends and solicitation messages on voluntary contributions. The results of three studies are reported that are consistent with the conceptual framework. Study 1 showed that voluntary contributions towards a generic advertising campaign were higher in the decreasing market trend relative to the increasing market trend and that the market trends induced different goals and these goals mediated the effect of market trends on voluntary contributions. Specifically, an increasing market trend primarily induced the goal of increasing profits whereas a decreasing profit trend induced the goal of preventing a decline in profits.

Study 2 showed that different solicitation messages are effective in the different market trend conditions. When the market trend was positive the solicitation message that was most effective in increasing voluntary contributions towards a generic advertising campaign was positive in action and positive in consequence. In contrast, when the market trend was negative, the most effective solicitation message was positive in action but negative in consequence. The results of Study 2 are consistent with our argument that market trends induce different goals and the solicitation message that is congruent with the mean-goal association is likely to be most effective in increasing voluntary contributions. Recognizing that goals are one of many factors that may be affected by the different market trends, Study 3 was designed to demonstrate that the findings are indeed due to the different goals induced by the different market trends. Instead of manipulating market trends, Study 3 primed the goals of "increase profits" and "prevent a decline in profits" and showed that the results are consistent with the findings of Study 2.

Together, the results point to the importance of goals in decision making. Our findings suggest that situational factors may induce different goals that then lead to different behavioral tendencies (Higgins 2002; Kruglanski et al. 2002). In the generic advertising context, the market situation that an industry confronts provides the milieu within which the voluntary contribution decisions are made. The different market trends induce different goals, which in turn influence the choice and importance of available means to attain the induced goals thereby leading to differences in voluntary contributions.

REFERENCES

Andreoni, James (1995), "Cooperation in Public-Goods Experiments: Kindness or Confusion?" *The American Economic Review*, 85 (4), 891-904.

Bargh, John A., and Kimberly Barndollar (1996), "Automaticity in action: The unconscious as repository of chronic goals and motives," In P. M.Gollwitzer & J. A.Bargh (Eds.), *The Psychology Of Action*, New York: Guilford Press, 457–481.

Baron, R. M., & Kenny, D. A. (1986), "The moderator-mediator variable distinction in social psychological research: Conceptual, strategic, and statistical considerations," *Journal of Personality and Social Psychology*, 51, 1173-1182.

Bass, Frank M., Anand Krishnamoorthy, Ashutosh Prasad, and Suresh P. Sethi (2005), "Generic and Brand Advertising Strategies in a Dynamic Duopoly," *Marketing Science*, 24 (4), 556-568.

Block, Lauren G., and Punam Anand Kellar (1995), "When to Accentuate the Negative: The Effects of Perceived Efficacy and Message Framing on Intentions to Perform Health-Related Behavior," *Journal of Marketing Research*, 32 (2), 192-203.

Borden, Neil H. (1965), "Summary of the Effects of Advertising on Primary and Selective Demand," in *Advertising Management*, ed. Harper W. Boyd and Joseph W. Newman, Homewood, IL: Irwin, 3–16.

Chakravarti, Amitav and Chris Janiszewski (2004), "The Influence of Generic Advertising on Brand Preference," *Journal of Consumer Research*, 30, 487-502.

Dawes, Robyn M. (1980), "Social Dilemmas," *Annual Review of Psychology*, 31, 69-93.

Dawes, Robyn M. and Richard H. Thaler (1988), "Anomalies: Cooperation," *Journal of Economic Perspectives*, 2 (3), 187-197.

Forker O. D., and R. W. Ward (1993), *Commodity Advertising: The Economics and Measurement of Generic Programs*, New York: Lexington Books.

Green, Edward, J., and Robert H. Porter (1984), "Noncooperative Collusion under Imperfect Price Information," *Econometrica*, 52 (1), 87-100.

Higgins, E. Tory (1987), "Self-Discrepancy: A Theory Relating Self and Affect," *Psychological Review*, 94 (3), 319-340.

Higgins, E. Tory (2002), "How Self-Regulation Creates Distinct Values: The Case of Promotion and Prevention Decision Making," *Journal of Consumer Psychology*, 12 (3), 177-191.

Higging, E. Tory (2000), "Making a Good Decision: Value from Fit," *American Psychologist*, 55, 1217–1230.

Iacobucci, Dawn (2001), "Analysis of Variance," *Journal of Consumer Psychology*, 10, 5-35

Krishnamurthy, Parthasarthy, Patrick Carter, and Edward Blair (2001), "Attribute Framing and Goal Framing Effects in Health Decisions," *Organizational Behavior and Human Decision Processes*, 85 (2), 382-399.

Krishnamurthy, Sandeep (2000), "Enlarging the Pie vs. Increasing One's Slice: An Analysis of the Relationship between Product Class and Brand Advertising," *Marketing Letters*, 11 (1), 37-48.

Krishnamurthy, Sandeep, William P. Bottom, and Ambar G. Rao (2003), "Adaptive Aspirations and Contributions to a Public Good: Generic Advertising as a Response to Decline," *Organizational Behavior and Human Decision Processes*, 92, 22-33.

Kruglanski, Arie, James Y. Shah, Ayelet Fishbach, Ron Friedman, Woo Young Chun and David Sleeth-Keppler (2002), "A Theory of Goal Systems," in *Advances in Experimental Social Psychology*, Eds. M. P. Zanna 34, 331-378.

Labroo, Aparna A., and Angela Y. Lee (2006), "Between Two Brands: A Goal Fluency Account of Brand Evaluation," *Journal of Marketing Research*, 43 (3), 374-385.

Lee, Angela Y., and Jennifer L. Aaker (2004), "Bring the Frame Into Focus: The Influence of Regulatory Fit on Processing Fluency and Persuasion," *Journal of Personality and Social Psychology*, 86, 205-218.

Levin, Irwin P., Sandra L. Schneider, and Gary J. Gaeth (1998), "All Frames Are Not Created Equal: A Typology and Critical Analysis of Framing Effects," *Organizational Behavior and Human Development Processes*, 76 (2), 149-188.

Maheswaran, Durairaj and Joan Myers-Levy (1990), "The Influence of Message Framing and Issue Involvement," *Journal of Marketing Research*, 27 (3), 361-367.

Messick, M., and K. Brewer (1983), "Solving Social Dilemmas: A Review," in *Review of Personality and Social Psychology*, ed. L. Wheeler and P. Shaver, Beverly Hills, CA: Sage Publications, Inc.

Myers-Levy Joan, and Durairaj Maheswaran (2004), "Exploring Message Framing Outcomes When Systematic, Heuristic, or Both Types of Processing Occur," *Journal of Consumer Psychology*, 14 (1&2), 159-167.

Rotemberg, Julio, J., and Garth Saloner (1986), "A Supergame-Theoretic Model of Price Wars during Booms," *American Economic Review*, 76 (3), 390-407.

Rothman, A. J., and P. Salovey (1997), "Shaping Perceptions to Motivate Healthy Behavior: The Role of Message Framing," *Psychological Bulletin*, 121, 3-19.

Scherer, Frederic M., (1980), *Industrial Market Structure and Economic Performance*, 2nd ed. Boston: Houghton Mifflin.

An Investigation Into Individual's Repeated Attempts at Behavior Change

Courtney Droms, Valdosta State University, USA

EXTENDED ABSTRACT

Recent research has shown that individuals make repeated attempts at behavior change prior to actually being successful. For example, typically individuals try to change their dieting behaviors on 4 to 5 occasions prior to actually being successful (Polivy and Herman 2002). Many of the dark side of consumer behavior areas identified by Mick (1996), such as smoking, drug use, shopping, and gambling, are behaviors that individuals try to change on a repeated basis. As consumer researchers, however, we do not have a clear understanding of how people interpret behavior change failures and persist in their efforts to change their behaviors after such failures. In an effort to understand these behavior change attempts, this research replicates and extends the Theory of Trying (Bagozzi and Warshaw 1990), to include feedback loops from the outcomes of behavior change attempts to attitudes towards trying to change again.

Theoretical Model

The theoretical model is based on the model developed in the Theory of Trying (Bagozzi and Warshaw 1990). The theory of trying is employed in this context because it includes two variables that seem very relevant to repeated attempts at changing behaviors (i.e. the frequency and recency of prior attempts at changing behaviors). However, the model proposed by Bagozzi and Warshaw (1990) ends at trying to change behaviors. While the author does suggest that the outcomes of these behavior change attempts feedback into attitudes, they do not explore the nature of the feedback. In order to explore the nature of the feedback from outcomes to attitudes, this paper employs three constructs–attributions for outcomes, self-esteem, and hope. Each of these factors will now be briefly discussed.

Weiner's (1974) theory of attributions posits that there are three dimensions to attributions–locus, stability, and controllability–that assist individuals in understanding the causes of their behaviors and behavioral outcomes. In the model, specific hypotheses, consistent with prior literature on attributions and the self-serving bias, have been developed that explicate how outcomes for success and failure are attributed along each dimension. These attributions also act as input to attitudes towards trying again and as such, hypotheses have been developed to examine several combinations of dimensions that will have the most impact on attitudes.

Self-esteem is defined as in individual's subjective appraisal of him or herself (Sedikides and Gregg 2003), which can be influenced by both goal achievement and goal failure (Crocker et al. 2003). As such, individuals in this study are expected to have lower levels of self-esteem post-failure rather than post-success at trying to change behaviors. Hypotheses were also developed and tested to capture the complexity of the interplay between self-esteem and attributions. Finally, an individual's self-esteem is also hypothesized to have a direct effect on that individual's attitudes towards trying to change in the future.

MacInnis and de Mello (2005) define hope as a positive emotion attached to a goal. There are three important dimensions to hope: goal congruency (i.e. the extent to which an environment is conducive to fulfilling a specific goal), certainty (i.e. the level of confidence an individual has in being able to achieve his or her goal), and importance of the goal. All three of these dimensions should be affected by the individual's success or failure at trying to change behaviors, such that failure at trying to change behaviors should lower an individual's level of hope. Hope is also hypothesized to affect the ways in which individuals understand and attribute the causes of their behavior change outcomes. Finally, individuals with high levels of hope should have a more positive outlook on the possibilities present in the future, which should enable them to have more positive attitudes towards changing in the future.

Methodology

An internet survey of 363 people from across the United States who are currently trying to diet was completed. Modifying the procedure employed by Bagozzi and Warshaw (1990), data was collected in two stages, one month apart. Participants were asked to complete a series of measures in the first stage designed to capture their attitudes and intentions to try, the frequency and recency of prior attempts at trying to change behavior, and their current levels of self-esteem and hope. At stage two, one month later, individuals completed a second survey including measures of trying, the outcome of trying, and attitudes towards trying again in the future. Participants will also complete measures capturing their attributions for the outcome of their attempts at behavior change, as well as their updated levels of self-esteem and hope.

Results and Discussion

Overall, this research enlightens the discussion of how people repeatedly change their health behaviors. The results indicate that individuals attribute the cause of their success or failure at their most recent behavior change attempt in such a way that it enables them to have a more positive attitude towards trying to change again in the future. The results from structural equation modeling show that the participants in this study attributed their failure to achieve their behavior change goal to causes that were unstable and controllable which resulted in both the stability and controllability dimensions of attributions having a significant positive effect on their attitudes towards trying again in the future. In addition, the results show that the individual's attributions mediate the effect that hope has on their attitude towards changing in the future. Moreover, I find that attributions moderate the effect that the outcome of their behavior change attempt has on the individual's level of self-esteem. Such that, individuals who makes stable attributions for failure show a substantial decrease in their self-esteem compared to those who make unstable attributions for failure. Finally, the results also indicate that the individual's change in self-esteem from before to after their behavior change attempt has a direct effect on their attitude towards trying again, such that individuals whose self-esteem decreased after their behavior change attempt have a higher attitude towards trying to change again in the future than their counterparts whose self-esteem increased post-behavior change. There are important implications for both marketing and public policy as a result of this study.

References

Bagozzi, Richard P. and Paul R. Warshaw (1990), "Trying to Consume," *Journal of Consumer Research*, 17 (September), 127-140.

Crocker, Jennifer, Andrew Karpinski, Diane M. Quinn, and Sara K. Chase (2003), "When Grades Determine Self-Worth: Consequences of Contingent Self-Worth for Male and Female Engineering and Psychology Majors," *Journal of Personality and Social Psychology*, 85, 507-516.

MacInnis, Deborah J. and Gustavo E. de Mello (2005), "The Concept of Hope and Its Relevance to Product Evaluation and Choice," *Journal of Marketing*, 69 (January), 1-14.

Mick, David Glen (1996), "Are Studies of Dark Side Variables Confounded by Socially Desirable Responding? The Case of Materialism," *Journal of Consumer Research*, 23 (September), 106-121.

Polivy, Janet, and C. Peter Herman (2002), "If at First You Don't Succeed: False Hopes of Self-Change," *American Psychologist*, 57(9), 677-689.

Sedikides, Constantine and Aiden P. Gregg (2003), "Portraits of the self," in M. A. Hogg & J. Cooper (Eds.), *Sage Handbook of Social Psychology*, London: Sage Publications, 110-138.

Weiner, Bernard (1974), *Achievement Motivation and Attribution Theory*, Morristown, NJ: General Learning Press.

Development of a Coding Instrument to Measure Interactivity of Websites

Hilde A. M. Voorveld, University of Amsterdam, The Netherlands
Peter C. Neijens, University of Amsterdam, The Netherlands
Edith G. Smit, University of Amsterdam, The Netherlands

EXTENDED ABSTRACT

Interactivity is often perceived as the most important difference between traditional and new media (Chung and Zhao 2004) and as a key aspect of effective online marketing (Thorbjornson, et al. 2002). Two constructs are central in the theoretical discussion about interactivity: actual (i.e. objectively assessed) interactivity and perceived interactivity (Song and Zinkhan 2008; Liu and Shrum 2002). Although there are numerous instruments to measure the perceived interactivity of a website (e.g., Liu 2003; Song and Zinkhan 2008), instruments to map the actual interactivity of a website are scarce.

In the field of marketing, several studies have investigated the actual interactivity of brand websites because such websites have become an important marketing tool. However, most studies used an outdated coding instrument which is not linked to current theoretical knowledge on interactivity. The aim of the current study is to fill the gap in the literature by developing a new coding instrument to map the interactivity of brand websites. To test the applicability of the new coding instrument, a content analysis of the interactivity of top global brand websites is performed. In addition, we tested whether the instrument was applicable to different contexts. Therefore, websites from two countries (the United States and the Netherlands) and several types of products were coded.

Following Liu and Shrum (2002, 54), in this study we used the following definition of interactivity: "The degree to which two or more communicating parties can act on each other, on the communication medium, and on the messages and the degree to which such influences are synchronized." Liu and Shrum (2002) also specified three interactivity dimensions. The first dimension is two-way communication. "Two-way communication refers to the ability for reciprocal communication between companies and users, and users and users" (Liu and Shrum 2002, 55). The second dimension, synchronicity, refers to "the degree to which users' input into a communication and the response they receive from the communication are simultaneous" or without delay (Liu and Shrum 2002, 55). The third dimension is active control. "Active control is characterized by voluntary and instrumental action that directly influences the controller's experience" (Liu and Shrum 2002, 54).

The coding instrument included 50 interactive functions that were acquired from the literature about interactivity (e.g., Ghose and Dou 1998). The 50 interactive functions were categorized into the three interactivity dimensions: two-way communication, synchronicity, and active control. To validate whether these 50 interactive functions were correctly categorized into the three dimensions, we conducted an expert test to test the face validity and content validity of our categorization. Based on the results of this expert study, three interactive functions were omitted from the instrument.

To test the applicability of the instrument, a content analysis of 66 American and 66 Dutch brand websites was performed. Two bilingual coders coded two parts of the websites: (1) the home pages of each website and (2) all hyperlinked pages from the home page.

Results showed that coders were able to use the instrument, and that reliability levels were good. Moreover, the instrument was internationally applicable and was able to differentiate between websites from the U.S. and the Netherlands. The instrument was also applicable to websites from different product categories and was able to differentiate between product categories.

The results of our content analysis also gave insight in the interactivity of brand websites. In sum, the results showed that interactive functions representing the active control dimension of interactivity were most common. Frequently used functions within this dimension were the presence of hyperlinks, sitemaps, search functions, software downloading, and an option to subscribe to a newsletter. Functions facilitating two-way communication were somewhat scarcer. Commonly used functions within the two-way communication dimension were the presence of multiple modes of contact, online job placement, and online shopping facilities. Interactive functions representing synchronicity were scarce. Only one function was present on a considerable amount of websites: an animation that displays the time it takes for the website to load. The results also showed interesting differences between American and Dutch websites and between websites for durable goods, non-durable goods, and services.

In conclusion, our study has provided a vital step towards developing a coding instrument to measure interactivity of brand websites. The instrument showed high levels of inter-coder reliability. In addition, an initial effort was made to assess face and content validity of the instrument by conducting a test among experts in the field. Furthermore, the instrument can be used in different contexts and it was sensitive enough to differentiate between brands and countries.

Now that we know which interactive functions are present on top global brand websites, future research might investigate the relationship between objectively assessed interactivity and perceived interactivity. Strikingly, little research has examined which interactive functions contribute to the perceived interactivity of a website. The coding instrument that was developed in this study might be a helpful tool for such an effort.

REFERENCES

Chung, Hwiman and Xinshu Zhao (2004), "Effects of Perceived Interactivity on Web Site Preference and Memory: Role of Personal Motivation," *Journal of Computer-Mediated Communication*, 10 (1).

Ghose, Sanjoy and Wenyu Dou (1998), "Interactive Functions and Their Impacts on the appeal of internet presence sites," *Journal of Advertising Research*, 38 (2), 29-44.

Liu, Yuping (2003), "Developing a Scale to Measure the Interactivity of Websites," *Journal of Advertising Research*, 43 (2), 207-16.

Liu, Yuping and L.J. Shrum (2002), "What is Interactivity and is it Always such a Good Thing? Implications of Definition, Person, and Situation for the Influence of Interactivity on Advertising Effectiveness," *Journal of Advertising*, 31 (4), 53-64.

Song, Ji Hee and George M. Zinkhan (2008), "Determinants of Perceived Website Interactivity," *Journal of Marketing*, 72 (2), 99-113.

Thorbjornsen, Helge & Supphellen, Magne & Nysveen, Herbjorn & Pedersen, Per E. (2002), "Building Brand Relationships Online: A Comparison of Two Interactive Applications," *Journal of Interactive Marketing*, 16 (3), 17-34.

How to Measure Brand Values?

Hansjoerg Gaus, Saarland University, Germany
Steffen Jahn, Chemnitz University of Technology, Germany
Tina Kiessling, Chemnitz University of Technology, Germany
Jan Drengner, Chemnitz University of Technology, Germany

EXTENDED ABSTRACT

In the branding literature it has been common for a long time to speak of brand values (Aaker 1996; de Chernatony, Drury, and Segal-Horn 2004; Keller 2008). In the research presented in this paper, brand values refer to human values consumers associate with brands. A number of studies underscore both the relevance and viability of such a concept for consumer behavior (Allen 2002; Allen, Gupta, and Monnier 2008; Alsem, Wieringa, and Hendriks 2007; Lages and Fernandes 2005; Limon, Kahle, and Orth 2009; Quester, Beverland, and Farrelly 2006; Strizhakova, Coulter, and Price 2008). However, this concept is not well developed. Consequently, a sound instrument to measure brand values does not exist.

Only recently, two studies use Schwartz's Value Survey (SVS) scale (Schwartz 1992) to measure brand values (Torelli et al. 2008; Zhang and Bloemer 2008). Even if we acknowledge the strengths of Schwartz's value theory and measurement instrument, we argue that the interpretation of brand perceptions based on the original SVS may be misleading. Not only some of the 10 Schwartz value types but also many indicator items might not be applicable to the brand context (Lages and Fernandes 2005). Moreover, genuine brand value types not covered by the SVS might exist.

In this paper we report the methodology and findings of a multi-method study aimed at developing a theory-driven conceptualization of brand values and a valid and reliable brand values scale. For that, we combined knowledge from psychological values research with results from research on consumer behavior and branding.

Our first empirical step was aimed at clarifying whether it is adequate to work with the original SVS scales. 64 respondents evaluated both the single items' applicability to brands in general and with regard to different categories of products or services. Since nearly 80% of the items were not considered being applicable to specific brands, we concluded that the original SVS scale's practicality to assess a brand's perceived values is not given.

In order to evaluate more deeply the suitability of the Schwartz value types in a branding context, in the next step a focus-group interview with a panel of nine marketing experts was carried out. The experts not only discussed the values' meaning with regard to brands in general but also named brands being strongly related to each value type. Although-with the exception of conformity-all Schwartz value types were accepted as being suitable for brand values, the semantic interpretation of some value types (i.e., achievement, power, security, tradition, and universalism) seems to differ significantly from Schwartz's (1992, 1994) original definitions. Consequently, we reformulated inadequate indicator items. A further review panel consisting of 12 marketing experts tested the reformulated list of items. This led to the elimination of items judged being generally inadequate for describing brands.

In the following step, the resulting preliminary brand values scale with 39 indicators was subjected to a survey. A sample of 99 students from three German universities evaluated to what extent each of the items was descriptive of four brands from different categories. The interpretation combined results from exploratory factor analysis and multidimensional scaling with knowledge about the original content of Schwartz's value types, the empirical findings in the earlier studies and recent values research in psychology and consumer behavior. From the nine brand value types identified, five were consistent with Schwartz's human value types (benevolence, hedonism, self-direction, stimulation, tradition). However, there were also significant particularities. Achievement and power were found being merged into a single brand value type. The most important finding was that there might be three brand value types not present as separate human value types in Schwartz's model (aesthetics, ecology, and health).

Since the preliminary scale had shown some limitations (brand value types with intermixed items, three brand value types measured with only one indicator), in the final research step reported here an improved version of the brand values scale with 31 items was tested. A sample of 339 students from two German universities evaluated to what degree each of the items was descriptive of the same brands as in the previous survey. A series of confirmatory factor analyses supported the proposed conceptualization with nine brand value types (achievement/power, aesthetics, benevolence, ecology, health, hedonism, self-direction, stimulation, tradition). In order to gain insights into our brand values scale's nomological validity, we assessed its explanatory strength with regard to brand emotional appeal measured with items drawn from Fombrun, Gardberg, and Sever (2000) and Keller (2008). 157 respondents from a German university completed the questionnaire for two brands. Regressions run on the brand value types revealed significant effects for almost all brand value types, thus indicating nomological validity.

This research shows that conceptualizations of brand values based solely on Schwartz's work in the field of human values do not perfectly match the brand context. Our empirical findings provide converging evidence for the existence of nine different brand value types and indicate that brands can be meaningfully differentiated on this basis. While some brand value types are consistent with their human counterparts, others have to be adjusted. However, all adjustments can be explained by the characteristics of brands that obviously do not perfectly match human characteristics. In addition, our findings corroborate the existence of three genuine brand value types, aesthetics, ecology, and health, which are not present as separate value types in Schwartz's (1992) original model. Moreover, our newly developed brand values scale measures the nine brand value types in a valid and reliable way and thus is a promising instrument for consumer research.

REFERENCES

Aaker, David A. (1996), *Building Strong Brands*, New York: The Free Press.

Allen, Michael W. (2002), "Human Values and Product Symbolism: Do Consumers Form Product Preferences by Comparing the Human Values Symbolized by a Product to the Human Values That They Endorse?" *Journal of Applied Psychology*, 32 (12), 2475-501.

Allen, Michael. W., Richa Gupta, and Arnaud Monnier (2008), "The Interactive Effect of Cultural Symbols and Human Values on Taste Evaluation," *Journal of Consumer Research*, 35 (August), 294-308.

Alsem, Karel Jan, Jaap Wieringa, and Marielle Hendriks (2007), "The Relation between Values-Based Self Congruity and Brand Loyalty," *Proceedings of the 36th EMAC Conference*, Reykjavik: European Marketing Academy.

de Chernatony, Leslie, Susan Drury, and Susan Segal-Horn (2004), "Identifying and Sustaining Service Brands' Values," *Journal of Marketing Communications*, 10 (June), 73-93.

Fombrun, Charles J., Naomi A. Gardberg, and Joy M. Sever (2000), "The Reputation Quotient: A Multi-Stakeholder Measure of Corporate Reputation," *Journal of Brand Management*, 7 (4), 241-55.

Keller, Kevin Lane (2008), *Strategic Brand Management: Building, Measuring, and Managing Brand Equity*, 3rd ed., Upper Saddle River, NJ: Prentice Hall.

Lages, Luis Filipe and Joana Cosme Fernandes (2005), "The SERPVAL Scale: A Multi-Item Measurement Instrument for Measuring Service Personal Values," *Journal of Business Research*, 58 (11), 1562-72.

Limon, Yonca, Lynn R. Kahle, and Ulrich R. Orth (2009), "Package Design as a Communications Vehicle in Cross-Cultural Values Shopping," *Journal of International Marketing*, 17 (1), 30-57.

Quester, Pascale, Michael Beverland, and Francis Farrelly (2006), "Brand-Personal Values Fit and Brand Meanings: Exploring the Role Individual Values Play in Ongoing Brand Loyalty in Extreme Sports Subcultures," in *Advances in Consumer Research*, Vol. 33, ed. Connie Pechmann and Linda Price, Duluth, MN: Association for Consumer Research, 21-27.

Schwartz, Shalom H. (1992), "Universals in the Content and Structure of Values: Theoretical Advances and Empirical Tests in 20 Countries," in *Advances in Experimental Social Psychology*, Vol. 25, ed. Mark P. Zanna, San Diego, CA: Academic Press, 1-65.

______ (1994), "Are There Universal Aspects in the Structure and Content of Human Values?," *Journal of Social Issues*, 50 (4), 19-45.

Strizhakova, Yuliya, Robin A. Coulter, and Linda L. Price (2008), "The Meanings of Branded Products: A Cross-National Scale Development and Meaning Assessment," *International Journal of Research in Marketing*, 25 (2), 82-93.

Torelli, Carlos J., Aysegul Ozsomer, Sergio W. Carvalho, Hean Tat Keh, and Natalia Maehle (2008), "A Measure of Brand Values: Cross-Cultural Implications for Brand Preferences," paper presented at the Advances in Consumer Research Conference, San Francisco, CA.

Zhang, Jing & Josée M. M. Bloemer (2008), "The Impact of Value Congruence on Consumer-Service Brand Relationships," *Journal of Service Research*, 11 (2), 161-78.

Digit Ratios Predict Risk Aversion for Both Sexes

Ellen Garbarino, University of Sydney, Australia
Robert Slonim, University of Sydney, Australia
Justin Sydnor, Case Western Reserve University, USA

EXTENDED ABSTRACT

Many of our most important consumption decisions, such as buying a home or car, investing for the future and choosing healthcare options involves risk taking. Despite the importance of risk attitudes and the large literature on the subject, relatively little is known about the determinants of risk taking or the sources of heterogeneity in risk attitudes. One of the most consistent findings in the risk taking literature is that women are more risk averse than men. For example, in a meta-analysis of 150 studies of gender differences in risk taking, men were found to be significantly less risk averse than women on 14 out of 16 risk taking categories (Byrnes, Miller & Schafer, 1999). Most of the explanations for this persistent gender difference involve psychological or sociological theories, such as self-regulation models, social-role theories, or power and status differences. In contrast, little research has explored the biological basis for gender difference in risk taking.

To explore a possible of a biological basis for risk taking; we examine whether differential exposure to *prenatal* androgens affects risk taking in a financially motivated decision task. A persistent biological marker of exposure to prenatal androgens exists in the ratio of the length of the index to the length of the ring finger, commonly called the 2D:4D ratio. Within and across gender a lower ratio results in part from greater exposure to testosterone and lesser exposure to estradiol (Lutchmaya et al., 2004), with men on average having a lower ratio than women. The 2D:4D ratio offers an excellent marker of biological effects since it develops in utero (Malas et al., 2006), persist through puberty (Trivers et al., 2006) and into adulthood (Phelps, 1952). The 2D:4D ratio has been correlated with a wide array of biological and psychological characteristics that show strong sex differentiation suggesting that it is an effective predictor of gender differences (e.g., Manning & Taylor, 2001; Kempel et al., 2005; Austin et al., 2002).

To examine the relationship between 2D:4D and risk taking, we ran a study that included 2D:4D measurement and three financially motivated decisions involving varying levels of risk. Sixty-five female and eighty-six male Caucasian participants made three financial decisions. Building on established procedures for measuring risk preferences (Eckel & Grossman, 2008), each decision required selecting one of six options. The expected payoff increased from options 1 to 5 and was the same for options 5 and 6. Financial riskiness (e.g., variance) increased from options 1 to 6; thus choosing higher options indicates acceptance of greater risk. For each participant, one decision was randomly chosen to be played out and paid. Afterwards, participants' hands were scanned. Second and fourth fingers were measured for both hands by three independent coders (interrater reliability 0.86). Since results are similar across measures, the analysis uses the average ratio averaging across coders and hands.

Consistent with the extant literature, we find that women were significantly more risk averse than men across all three decisions (the average female choice was 0.769 options lower than the male average; $p<0.01$; OLS regression controlling for subject and decision effects) and men have the expected lower 2D:4D ratio (male 2D:4D ratios (.959) were lower than female ratios (.969); $p<0.02$, t-stat=2.23).

However, the main and novel results are that the 2D:4D ratio can partially explain risk taking behavior both within and between genders. The 2D:4D ratio can explain risk taking differences *within* gender; for both sexes, people with lower 2D:4D ratios (i.e., higher relative levels of in utero testosterone exposure) take greater risk ($p<0.011$; OLS regression controlling for subject, decision and gender). A one standard-deviation decrease in the ratio increased the choice riskiness by 0.23 options (equivalently, 0.145 standard-deviations). This 2D:4D effect was the same for men and women (coefficient=0.00, $p>0.99$ for 2D:4D-by-gender interaction). The 2D:4D ratio also explains some of the difference *between* genders in risk taking; the average gender gap fell 11% from 0.769 options lower for women without controlling for 2D:4D to 0.685 options lower controlling for 2D:4D ($p<0.045$, $\chi^2=4.02$). A quartile examination of the data reveals that this decrease in gender difference is driven by those at the high and low extremes of the 2D:4D distribution. We also find that the other physical factors we measured (height, BMI and finger length) do not affect choices across the risky decisions, reinforcing that the predictive power of 2D:4D is not spurious, and adding further support for the role of 2D:4D as an indicator of a biological basis for risk taking behavior.

REFERENCES

Austin, E. J., Manning, J. T., McInroy, K. & Mathews, E. (2002), "A preliminary investigation of the association between personality, cognitive ability and digit ratio," *Personality and Individual Differences*, 33, 1115.

Byrnes, J. P., Miller, D. C. & Schafer, W. D. (1999), "Gender difference in risk taking: A meta-analysis," *Psychological Bulletin*, 125:3, 367-383.

Eckel, C. & Grossman, P. (2008), "Men, women and risk aversion: experimental evidence," *Handbook of experimental results*, eds. C. Plott and V. Smith, forthcoming.

Kempel, P., Gohlke, B. & Kelmpau, J. (2005), "Second-to-fourth digit length, testosterone and spatial ability," *Intelligence*, 33, 215.

Lutchmaya, S., Baron-Cohen, S. & Raggett, P. (2004), "2nd to 4th digit ratios, fetal testosterone and estradiol," *Early Human Development*, 77, 23.

Malas, M. A., Dogan, S., Evcil, E.H. & Desdicioglu, K. (2006), "Fetal development of the hand, digits and digit ratio (2D:4D)," *Early Human Development*, 82, 469–475

Manning, J. T. & Taylor, R. P. (2001), "Second to fourth digit ratio and male ability in sport: implications for sexual selection in humans," *Evolution and Human Behavior*, 22, 61–69.

Phelps, V. R. (1952), "Relative index finger length as a sex-influenced trait in man," *American Journal of Human Genetics*, 4:2, 72–89.

Trivers, R., Manning, J. & Jacobson, A. (2006), "A longitudinal study of digit ratio (2D:4D) and other finger ratios in Jamaican children," *Hormones and Behavior*, 49, 150–156.

Relocating Profane Consumption into Sacredness: Consumer Redemption and Resurrection through Practices of Disposal

Helene Cherrier, American University in Dubai, United Arab Emirates
Kaleel Rahman, American University in Dubai, Dubai, United Arab Emirates

EXTENDED ABSTRACT

This study focuses upon the role of disposal in relation to changes in consumption lifestyle. It argues that adopting a voluntary simplicity lifestyle can lead consumers to experience disposal as a sacrificial ritual. Grounded in anthropological studies, sacrifice is conceptualized as both a liberating act and a process of moving toward sacredness.

The data consists of existential phenomenological interviewing with twelve informants who identify themselves as voluntary simplifiers and have, at one point in their lives, voluntarily lowered the amount of their material possessions. The interviews offer descriptive details on their process of disposal and its relation to a change in values and consumption lifestyle. The hermeneutic analysis shows informants' practice of disposal organized around three main themes: redemption, resurrection, and sacredness.

The theme "redemption" describes informants' practice of disposal as a way to redeem themselves from the social norm to own and display countless objects. Similar to a 'sacrificator', each informant was a bearer of pollution and sins. According to the interviews, they had accumulated and owned objects in excess. Disposing of the material surplus provides the means for cleansing the self of material pollution and sins. Under this theme, disposal is described as a purifying act, focusing on the termination of a self that had been polluted by the ideology of consumer culture, with its emphasis on material success, accumulation, holding on and storing goods.

The second theme "resurrection" shows disposal as a necessary ritual for self-transformation. Disposing of material possessions was for the informants a rite of passage from the termination to the recreation of personhood and lifestyle. Like a sacrificial rite, informants found in the practice of disposal a way to repair equilibriums between their self-concept and their environment, which involves both a deliverance from the slavery of material accumulation and a reconciliation with their self-concept. Recreating this equilibrium called for the disposal of material accumulation by giving to others, including friends, charity organizations and strangers.

Finally, "sacredness" notes disposal as a transcendental experience that prefigures the death of profane consumption and the birth of sacred consumption. The act of disposal represents a gift informants made to others, to nature and/or to God. Impetus for the gift is the informants' understanding that their objects are passed on to others and that their meanings are regenerated in the process. The gift and the regeneration of meanings prolong the life of objects and infuse characteristics of eternity and sacredness within the material. Just as a sacrificial rite opens doors to sacredness, disposal provides the means to participate in the circulation of objects and to enact sacred consumption practices.

The three themes support that disposal entails both a process and an act. It is not just an act of letting go of our belongings, but also a process of becoming (Cherrier and Murray 2007; Lastovicka and Fernandez 2005; Ozanne 1992; Price and Arnould 2000; Young 1991; Young and Wallendorf 1986). This study also notes that consumers do not necessarily divest the private meanings attached to particular objects prior to disposing of them. Instead, informants reflected on broad societal and sacred meanings. It is the reflections on interconnectivity between people and the circulation of objects that lead informants to dispose of their possessions and engage in sacred consumption practice. Furthermore, this study on voluntary simplifiers shows relevant similarities between practices of intentional disposal and the concept of sacrifice. The majority of anthropological studies recognize sacrifice as a personal renunciation of a human life, an animal or a material object that nourishes a higher purpose. In this study informants felt being polluted by material surplus and letting go of their possessions offers the means for cleansing and elevating themselves to higher beings. From this perspective, the personal renunciation of objects nourishes a quest for meanings and sacredness. Here, the accent lies no longer on the suffering and the burden of disposal but on the engagement to a meaningful existence through which, similar to a sacrificial ritual, "a man can find himself anew" (Jung, 1969, p. 260).

This study turns on the very question of disposal as a gain rather than a loss for the owner. For the informants, disposal bears an ontologically promise of value, a promise that motivates and underwrites the process of disposal. Disposal redeemed informants from sins of material accumulation and resurrected them into a transformed state of sacred participation. In a more general sense, disposal was for the informants a symbolic instrument for self-realization. From this perspective, we may question whether the practice of disposal is linked to Mauss' concept of societal obligation for which individuals have to give, to receive and to reciprocate (Mauss 1954).

REFERENCES

Belk, R. W. (1988), "Possession and the Extended Self," *Journal of Consumer Research*, 15 (September), 139-68.

Belk, Rusell W., Seo Joon Yong, and Eric Li (2007), "Dirty Little Secret: Home Chaos and Professional Organizers," *Consumption, Markets & Culture*, 10 (2), 133-40.

Belk, Russell. W., Guliz Ger, and Soren Askegaard (2003), "The Fire of Desire: A Multisited Inquiry into Consumer Passion," *Journal of Consumer Research*, 30 (3), 326-42.

Cherrier, Helene and Jeff B. Murray (2007), "Reflexive Dispossession and the Self: Constructing a Processual Theory of Identity," *Consumption, Markets & Culture*, 10 (1), 1-30.

Crossley, Michele L. (2000), *Introducing Narrative Psychology: Self, Trauma, and the Construction of Meaning*, Buckingham: Open University Press.

Csikszentmihalyi, Mihaly and Eugene Rochberg-Halton (1981), *The meaning of things: domestic symbols and the self*, Cambridge [Eng.] ; New York: Cambridge University Press.

Dreifuss, G. (2006), "Sacrifice in Analysis," *Journal of Analytical Psychology*, 22 (3), 258-67.

Gandolfi F. and Cherrier H. (2008), "Downshifting: a Theoretical and Practical Approach to Living a Simplified Life," *Hyderabad*, India: The ICFAI University Press.

Guliz, Ger (2005), "Religion and consumption: the profane sacred," *Advances in Consumer Research*, 32, 79-81.

Holt, Douglas B. (2004), "Man-of-Action Heroes: The Pursuit of Heroic Masculinity in Everyday Consumption," *Journal of Consumer Research*, 31 (2), 425-40.

Hubert, Henri and Marcel Mauss (1964), *Sacrifice: its nature and function*, London: Cohen & West.

Jung, Carl Gustav (1969), "Transformation Symbolism in The Mass," in *Collected works of C. G. Jung*, Vol. 11. New York: Princeton University Press.

Kayes, Steven M. (2004), "The Dynamics of Brand Legitimacy: An Interpretive Study in the Gay Men's Community," *Journal of Consumer Research*, 31 (September), 455-564.

Kleine, Susan S., Robert E Kleine III, and Chris T. Allen (1995), "How is a Possession 'Me' or 'Not Me'? Characterizing Types and Antecedent of Material Possession Attachment," *Journal of Consumer Research*, 22 (December), 327-43.

Kozinets, Robert (2002), "Can Consumers Escape the Market? Emancipatory Illuminations from Burning Man," *Journal of Consumer Research*, 29 (June), 20-38.

Lastovicka, John L. and Karen V. Fernandez (2005), "Three Paths to Disposition: The Movement of Meaningful Possessions to Strangers," *Journal of Consumer Research*, 31 (4), 813-24.

Mauss (1954), *The Gift*.

McAdams, Dan P. (1997), *The Stories We Live By: Personal Myths and the Making of the Self*, New York, London: Guilford Press.

Mehta, Raj and Russel W. Belk (1991), "Artifacts, Identity, and Transition: Favorite Possessions of Indians and Indian Immigrants to the United States," *Journal of Consumer Research*, 17 (March), 398-411.

Miller, Daniel (1998), *Material Cultures : Why Some Things Matter*. Chicago: University of Chicago Press.

Muniz, Jr. Albert M. and Hope Schau (2005), "Religiosity in the Abandoned Apple Newton Brand Community," *Journal of Consumer Research*, 31 (4), 737-47.

Murray, Jeff B. (2002), "The Politics of Consumption: A Re-Inquiry on Thompson and Haytko's (1997) 'Speaking of Fashion'," *Journal of Consumer Research*, 29 (3), 427-41.

Ozanne, Julie L. (1992), "The role of consumption and disposition during classic rites of passage: The journey of birth, initiation, and death," *Advances in Consumer Research*, 19 (1), 396-98.

Price, Linda L. and Eric Arnould (2000), "Older Consumers' Disposition of Special Possessions," *Journal of Consumer Research*, 27 (2), 179-92.

Roster, Catherine (2001), "Letting Go: The Process and Meaning of Dispossession in the Lives of Consumers," *Advances in Consumer Research*, 27 (2).

Schouten, John. W. (1991), "Personal Rites of Passage and the Reconstruction of Self," *Advances in Consumer Research*, 18 (1), 49-52.

Thompson, Craig J., William B. Locander, and Howard R. Pollio (1989b), "Putting Consumer Experience back into Consumer Research: The Philosophy and Method of Existential-Phenomenology," *Journal of Consumer Research*, 16 (September), 133-47.

Tian, Kelly and Russell W Belk (2005), "Extended Self and Possessions in the Workplace," *Journal of Consumer Research*, 32 (September), 297-311.

Young, Melissa (1991), "Disposition of Possessions During Role Transitions," *Advances in Consumer Research*, 18 (1), 33-40.

Religious Artefacts as Consumer Culture Products

Jeaney Yip, University of Sydney, Australia
Susan Ainsworth, University of Melbourne, Australia

EXTENDED ABSTRACT

Religion has not escaped the effects of consumer culture and is increasingly forced to compete in a spiritual marketplace (Roof 1999). This competition has resulted in constructions of new products and reconstructions of current products. Cultural effects on religious products are not well understood as studies on the consumption of these considered 'sacred' products are few. While relations to the sacred have been documented in previous research (Belk, Wallendorf and Sherry 1989; O'Guinn and Belk 1989; Arnould and Price 2004), they have been predominantly studied as a metaphoric stance rather than specifically about the 'Sacred' per se (Iacobucci 2001). As both a religious and cultural product, Christian artefacts are malleable to socio-cultural forces and consumer culture cultural products are also relatively unexplored (Askegaard 2008, Brownlie, Hewer and Horne 2005, Hirschman 1988).

It is not surprising to find the effects of consumer culture on the sacred as 'marketplace theology' is being produced by mega-churches which cater to the needs of its target audiences (Twitchell 2004). Cultural products need to be conditioned for the market (Miller 2003), much the same way as agribusiness comes up with exotic and new breeds of common produce to stimulate sales of what is otherwise 'plain tomatoes'. Featherstone (1991) noted that the locus of the sacred has shifted from traditional religious institutions to consumer culture. In so doing, "consumer culture co-opts religious subcultures and not the other way around" (Romanowski 1992, 47). The purpose of the research is not to ascertain whether contemporary churches and its artefacts is secularised or not, but to explore *how* church identity is constructed using elements of religious traditions and other familiar, appealing discourses to produce artefacts and experiences that resonate with contemporary consumption ideals of individualism, empowerment, prosperity, immediate rewards and interest in the supernatural.

In an attempt to study *how* secularisation and consumer culture inflects a religious product and a church's identity, a cross section of a church-produced contemporary style of Christian worship music dating from 1992–2007 was selected. This music is chosen due to its close relations to a successful Sydney-based mega church which combines Christian theology with business ideals. Textually-oriented discourse analysis (Fairclough 2003) was used to do a reading (Scott 1994; Stern 1989) of lyrics. This reading is accompanied and interpreted through an assortment of other texts that include visual, audio, and textual data at the church level. In the analysis of these texts, artefacts and social practices, we were concerned with identifying not only what discourses were being drawn upon but also how they were combined in order to understand the basis for their contemporary appeal.

The church and its artefacts, constructs an identity that draws upon secular and business discourses which are hybridised with religious theology. This hybridisation is comfortably reconciled through a process of differentiation (Saussure 1966) which strives to project an image and identity that is *not* religion-like and certainly, *not* like a traditional church. This '*not religion*' discourse instead offers wholeness, healing and inner transformation to the individual unencumbered by stereotypes of traditional institutional religions which connotes formal membership and allegiance. Through this discourse, secular structures and habits are reinforced by a host of practices such as using popular music in praise and worship to heighten emotional contagion, placing a monetary value (ie., price) to church services and events, regular selling of merchandise, marketing preachers and using individualist tenets to repackage religion. The familiar structures and habits of consumer culture re-orient legitimate religious desires into the service of furthering the consumption of religion through music, books, tapes and messages which offers individual self-fulfilment.

Like language, identity can be seen as a system of meaningful differences (Saussure 1966), and in the church studied, the strategy of differentiation is particularly central to its identity construction and discourse. This strategy is enacted in different discursive mediums, for example, in songs and written text as well as through building architecture and design. Through a mixture of humanist, motivational and romantic appeals, the message of God and the Gospel exists theologically but culturally is reconstructed and repackaged to convey a dominant discourse of 'ego-centricness' and 'feel-goodness'. In a context of individualism where the erosion of traditional institutionalised religions is evident our findings support the takeover of religion by the popular discourse of 'spirituality' (Carrette and King 2005). Spirituality, as opposed to religion, is a personal quest for meaning. It is a journey of the soul in order to seek what it's searching for, or to satisfy what Roof (1999) calls 'wholeness hunger'. Through this discourse, religion is transformed into a self-centred therapeutic exercise attributable to consumer culture and commercial marketing. The discourses from the songs and church products have this kind of audience in mind. They appeal to the therapeutic and seeker self (Bellah, Madsen, Sullivan, Swidler and Tipton 1985) by offering empowerment and freedom.

While secularisation theory claims differentiation and separation between religion and other spheres of social life (Chaves 1994), the symbols, practices and myths of traditional religion that once influenced people's lives continue to do so in the form of consumer culture. Rather than separation and differentiation, what is evident in the findings of this research is a strategic combining of religious and secular discourses within the context of a 'deregulated' religious market. In so doing, religion is not able to escape ideological influences exerted by the capitalist marketplace (Thompson 2004). Exposed to the market system and dominated by discourses of freedom and individual choice, religious systems have fragmented as religious consumers can pick and choose. However such 'freeing up' of religion has also enabled religious providers to harness the appeal of contemporary discourses in marketing their own brand of religion that resonates with dominant social values of individualism, empowerment and aspiration to affluence.

Cultural secularisation has transformed religious markers and symbols, expressed through music and theology in this study to exhibit patterns of consumer culture. One might argue that this is simply an expression of a religious institution operating under consumer culture, which Slater (1997) defines as a system in which consumption is dominated by the consumption of commodities and in which cultural reproduction is mediated through markets. This is the dominant discourse that actually prevails, is being reproduced and sustained through mega-churches such as Hillsong. Through this dominant discourse, religious beliefs are re-directed into a consumption choice. The economic rhetoric of the 'marketplace' speaks of a free market and a consumer who is free to choose; a stance that most people in developed societies are comfortable and

Advances in Consumer Research
Volume 37, © 2010

familiar with. It is no surprise that branded churches such as Hillsong employ this rhetoric in marketing religion, enacted through the familiar consumption ideologies of choice, freedom and individual empowerment. While this model of mega-church emerged in a landscape of American Christianity (Twitchell 2004) where the consumption discourse is dominant, it is interesting to see its expansion internationally (Australia, Asia, Africa to name a few) as the practices and dispositions associated with the mega-church spread and colonize other dimensions of Christianity.

REFERENCES

Arnould, Eric J. and Linda L.Price (2004), "Beyond the Sacred-Profane Dichotomy in Consumer Research," in Barbara E.Kahn and Mary Frances Luce. Eds, *Advances in Consumer Research*, volume XXXI, 52-53.

Askegaard, Soren (2008), "This Car of Mine: Hedonism, Play and Coolhunting as reflected in Southern California Music Lyrics," *Consumer Culture Theory Conference*, (June), Boston, 19-22.

Belk, Russell W., Melanie Wallendorf, and John F. Sherry, Jr. (1989), "The Sacred and the Profane in Consumer Behavior: Theodicy on the Odyssey," *Journal of Consumer Research*, 16 (June), 1-38.

Bellah, Robert N., Richard Madsen, William M. Sullivan, Ann Swidler and Steven M.Tipton (1995), *Habits of the Heart*. Berkeley: University of California Press.

Brownlie, Douglas, Paul Hewer and Suzanne Horne (2005), "Culinary Tourism: An Exploratory Reading of Contemporary Representations of Cooking," *Consumption, Markets and Culture*, 8 (1), March, 7–26.

Carrette, Jeremy and Richard King (2005), *Selling Spirituality*, London: Routledge.

Chaves, Mark (1994), "Secularization as Declining Religious Authority," *Social Forces*, March, 72(3), 749-774.

Fairclough, Norman (2003), *Analysing Discourse: Textual Analysis for Social Research*, London: Routledge.

Featherstone, Mike (1991), *Consumer Culture and Postmodernism*, London: Sage Publications.

Hirschman, Elizabeth C. (1988), "The Ideology of Consumption: A Structural-Syntactical Analysis of 'Dallas' and 'Dynasty'," *Journal of Consumer Research*, 15 (December), 4-359.

Iacobucci, Dawn (2001), "Commonalities between Research Methods for Consumer Science and Bibilcal Scholarship," *Marketing Theory*, 1(1), 109-133.

Miller, Vincent J. (2003), *Consuming Religion: Christian Faith and Practice in a Consumer Culture*, New York: Continuum.

O'Guinn, Thomas C, & Russell W. Belk (1989), "Heaven on Earth: Consumption at Heritage Village, USA," *Journal of Consumer Research*, 16 (September), 227-239.

Romanowski, William D. (1992), Roll over Beethoven, Tell Martin Luther the News: American Evangelicals and Rock Music, *Journal of American Culture*, 15(September), 79-88.

Roof, Wade C. (1999), *Spiritual Marketplace; Baby Boomers and the Remaking of American Religion*, New Jersey, Princeton University Press.

Saussure, Ferdinand de (1966), *Course in General Linguistics*, Charles Bally and Albert Sechehaye (ed), New York, McGraw-Hill.

Scott, Linda M. (1994), "The Bridge from Text to Mind: Adapting Reader-Response Theory to Consumer Research," *Journal of Consumer Research*, 21(December), 461-480.

Slater, Don (1997), *Consumer Culture & Modernity*, Cambridge: Polity Press.

Stern, Barbara B. (1989), "Literary Criticism and Consumer Research: Overview and Illustrative Analysis," *Journal of Consumer Research*, 16 (December), 322-335.

Thompson, Craig J. (2004), "Marketplace Mythology and Discourses of Power," *Journal of Consumer Research*, 31(June), 162-180.

Twitchell, James B. (2004), *Branded Nation: The Marketing of Megachurch, College Inc., and Museumworld*, New York: Simon & Schuster.

The Moral Discount: Can Being Socially Responsible Hurt Your Brand?

Stefanie Rosen, University of South Carolina, USA
Stacy Wood, University of South Carolina, USA

EXTENDED ABSTRACT

Corporate social responsibility (CSR) can be used as an effective marketing technique and, to media and consumer praise, companies spent $4.4 billion on CSR in 2007 (Lawrence and Mukai 2008). CSR, defined as a "company's status and activities with respect to its perceived societal obligations" (Brown and Dacin 1997, 68), can increase customer satisfaction with the company (Marin and Ruiz 2007), enhance brand evaluations (Brown and Dacin 1997), and increase consumer willingness-to-pay (Creyer and Ross 1997). However, recent research suggests consumers perceive more ethical brands to be less effective (Luchs et al. 2008). Here, we investigate this "moral discount" and find that the impact of CSR on product evaluations depends on two factors: brand strength and the nature of the "ethical element" (type of CSR attribute).

When a brand engages in a typical CSR campaign (e.g. donating money), the CSR attribute becomes an important piece of accessible information for consumers to use when evaluating the brand. According to the accessibility-diagnosticity model, accessible information will be used as input into judgment if the information is perceived to be more diagnostic than other accessible inputs (Feldman and Lynch 1988). When accessible and diagnostic, consumers use memory-based and context-based information (Menon, Raghubir, and Schwarz 1995). Context-based information, information given during the time of the decision, is used when memory-based information is not accessible. When memory-based information is accessible and diagnostic, context-based information is not used. With an unfamiliar brand, consumers can not rely on previous associations of the brand and therefore, the context-based information of the CSR attribute becomes diagnostic. We predict that when context-based information is related to CSR attributes, consumers will fall prey to Luchs et al. (2008) 'ethical equals less effective' lay theory. However, when a familiar brand engages in CSR, memory-based cues become diagnostic when evaluating the brand. Therefore, consumers will use this context-based information in conjunction with the memory-based cues of the brand (Menon et al. 1995). Thus, the CSR attribute will be inferred to be consistent with the memory-based evaluation of the brand (Dick, Chakravarti, and Beihal 1990). We predict that a brand with a CSR attribute will increase (decrease) perceived (1) brand effectiveness and (2) willingness to pay for a familiar (unfamiliar) brand.

In study 1, we test whether the type of brand, familiar versus unfamiliar, is helped or hindered by a typical CSR attribute, donating money to non-profit organization. Participants were exposed to one of four conditions in a 2 (familiar vs. unfamiliar brand) X 2 (CSR attribute vs. non-CSR attribute) between-subjects design. Participants were shown a picture of a candy bar and told that this was a new product on the market and asked questions related to their anticipated taste ratings and willingness to pay for the product. We conducted two, 2 X 2 ANOVAs with the anticipated taste rating and willingness to pay as the dependent variables. For both variables, there is a significant CSR x Brand interaction, (taste=$F(1, 171)=5.538$, $p<.05$) (willingness to pay=$F(1, 171)=3.752$, $p=.05$). These results support our prediction above.

Study 1 addresses a typical CSR attribute, charity donations, that is extrinsically tied to the brand. CSR attributes can also be intrinsically related to the product (e.g., earth-friendly ingredients). Consumers use both extrinsic and intrinsic cues (e.g., attributes) simultaneously when making evaluations of a brand (Jacoby, Olson, and Haddock 1973). For a familiar brand, an intrinsic CSR attribute presents contradictory evidence to the memory-based perceptions of the brand's physical make-up. While the CSR intrinsic attribute is not necessarily negative, it possesses the same characteristics as a negative cue and alters the perceptions of the brand's quality (Ahluwalia 2002). Therefore, one might predict that with a familiar brand, consumers will perceive a CSR intrinsic attribute more negatively than a CSR extrinsic attribute. For an unfamiliar brand, the consumer does not have memory-based information to judge the new CSR attributes and therefore an intrinsic CSR attribute does not provide inconsistent information to the consumer. We propose that an intrinsic CSR attribute therefore helps an unfamiliar brand because the attribute becomes part of the contextual cues used to define the product. However, extrinsic CSR attributes do not provide the same depth of contextual information about the unfamiliar brand and therefore are not strong indicators of the product.

In study 2, we test whether the type of CSR attribute, acting as an extrinsic vs. intrinsic cue, helps or hurts a familiar vs. unfamiliar brand. We conducted 2 (familiar vs. unfamiliar) X 2 (extrinsic CSR attribute vs. intrinsic CSR attribute) between-subjects design. Participants were shown a picture of detergent and rated the effectiveness of the detergent and their willingness to pay. We conducted a 2 X 2 ANOVA with detergent effectiveness as the dependent variable. There is a significant CSR X Brand interaction ($F(1,233)=4.07$, $p<.05$), which shows that with an unfamiliar brand, effectiveness ratings are higher for intrinsic versus extrinsic CSR attributes, however with a familiar brand, effectiveness ratings are equal for extrinsic versus intrinsic CSR attributes. Unlike detergent effectiveness, we do not see a significant interaction for consumers' willingness to pay ($F=.33$). These results show that consumers perceive an unfamiliar brand with an intrinsic CSR attribute as more effective than an unfamiliar brand with an extrinsic attribute. However, for familiar brands, the data show no difference in the efficacy of extrinsic versus intrinsic CSR attributes.

This research demonstrates that, in promoting socially responsible products, managers should carefully consider both their brand's strength and the type of CSR attribute. Familiar brands may be better able to benefit from extrinsic and intrinsic attributes. However, brands new to the marketplace may want to avoid extrinsic CSR attributes, thus avoiding the moral discount bias.

REFERENCES

Ahluwalia, Rohini (2002), "How Prevalent Is the Negativity Effect in Consumer Environments?" *Journal of Consumer Research*, 29 (September), 270-79.

Brown, Tom J. and Peter A. Dacin (1997), "The Company and the Product: Corporate Associations and Consumer Product Responses," *Journal of Marketing*, 61 (January), 68-84.

Creyer, Elizabeth H. and William T. Ross Jr. (1997), "The influence of firm behavior on purchase intention: Do consumers really care about business ethics?" *Journal of Consumer Marketing*, 14(6), 419-32.

Dick, Alan, Dipankar Chakravarti, and Gabriel Beihal (1990), "Memory-based Inferences During Choice," *Journal of Consumer Research*, 17 (June), 82-93.

Feldman, Jack M. and John G. Lynch Jr. (1988), "Self-Generated Validity and Other Effects of Measurement on Belief, Attitude, Intention, and Behavior," *Journal of Applied Psychology*, 73(August), 421-35.

Jacoby, Jacob, Jerry Olson, and Rafael Haddock (1971), "Price, Brand Name and Product Composition Characteristics as Determinants of Perceived Quality," *Journal of Applied Psychology,* 55 (December), 570-79.

Lawrence, Steven and Reina Mukai (2008), "Foundation Growth and Giving Estimates: Current Outlook," http:// foundationcenter.org/ gain knowledge/research/ pdf/ fgge08.pdf.

Luchs, Michael G., Rebecca Walker Naylor, Julie R. Irwin (2008), "The Ethical Penalty: Consumers Believe that Product Ethicality is Negatively Related to Product Effectiveness," (working paper).

Marin, Longinos and Salvador Ruiz (2007), "I Need You Too!" Corporate Identity Attractiveness for Consumers and The Role of Social Responsibility," *Journal of Business Ethics*, 71(3), 245-60.

Menon, Geeta, Priya Raghubir, and Norbert Schwarz (1995), "Behavioral Frequency Judgments: An Accessibility Diagnosticity Framework," *Journal of Consumer Research*, 22(September), 212-28.

When Brands do Right but Decide Wrongly: The Impact of Perceptions of Procedural and Outcome Fairness on Brand Attitudes

Pragya Mathur, Baruch College, CUNY, USA
Neela Saldanha, University of Pennsylvania, USA
Eric A. Greenleaf, New York University, USA

EXTENDED ABSTRACT

Marketers strive to deliver benefits to consumers, such as reducing late fees on DVD rentals, expecting that such benefits will lead to enhanced brand evaluations. We demonstrate that this expectation may not be accurate and suggest that consumer perceptions of procedural unfairness may negatively impact brand evaluation.

Existing literature on perceived fairness in marketing has dealt mainly with unfavorable outcomes to consumers (e.g. price increases: Bolton and Alba 2006; Bolton, Warlop, and Alba 2003; Xia, Monroe, and Cox 2004). In contrast, the organizational justice literature distinguishes between outcome and procedural fairness (Brockner and Wiesenfeld 1996). Outcome fairness refers to the equity of outcomes (Brockner et al. 2003) and has been empirically shown to be closely related to outcome favorability (Brockner and Wiesenfeld 1996; Brockner et al. 2003; Lind and Tyler 1988). Procedural fairness refers to the fairness of the process to obtain the outcome (Lind and Tyler 1988; Thibaut and Walker 1975; Brockner 2002). Perceptions of procedural unfairness can negatively affect evaluations especially when it is made salient (Brockner et al. 2003). Across three studies we show that favorable outcomes may not lead to enhanced brand evaluations and perceptions of procedural fairness are instrumental in this result.

In Study 1, participants read a vignette about two fictitious movie rental firms and completed a baseline evaluation index (α =.93). Respondents were then told about the favorable activity i.e. the target firm had eliminated its late fees policy. Procedural fairness was manipulated by information that highlighted the self-interested motive of the target firm: in the unfair (fair) condition, participants learnt that the competitor had recently dropped its late fees (retained its late fees). Respondents then completed a post-information evaluation index (α=.96) and manipulation checks. As predicted, fairness ratings were higher in the procedurally fair (versus unfair) condition (M_{fair}=6.65 vs. M_{unfair}=5.88, p<.05). Evaluation was significantly enhanced in the procedurally fair condition (M_{pre}=5.02, M_{post}=5.85, p<.05) but was unchanged in the procedurally unfair condition (M_{pre}=4.62, M_{post}=4.95, p >.1),

In Study 2, we examined the impact of the salience of fairness perceptions on brand evaluations in a 2 (procedural fairness: fair/unfair) x 2 (salience: low/high) between-subjects design. Salience was manipulated by the order in which participants were asked to evaluate fairness: before or after evaluating the brand. All other measures were identical to Study 1. Results indicated a significant three-way interaction between procedural fairness, salience, and the time of brand evaluation (F(1, 65)=11.43, p<.001). When the action was procedurally-fair, brand evaluations were enhanced regardless of salience (Salient: M_{pre}=4.49, M_{post}=5.72, F(1, 65)=28.96, p<.001; Not-Salient: M_{pre} 4.38 vs. M_{post}=5.43, F(1, 65)=16.88, p<.001). In the procedurally-unfair condition, however, brand evaluations were diluted (M_{pre}=4.75, M_{post}=4.01, F(1, 65)=8.94, p<.01) in the salient condition and enhanced in the non-salient condition (M_{pre}=4.13, M_{post}=4.88, F(1, 65)=8.61, p<.001).

In Study 3, we provided more insight into the process by specifically measuring both outcome and process fairness. Salience was manipulated by asking respondents to keep "the outcome (process) of the policy change in mind" after reading the manipulation.

Perceptions of procedural, but not outcome, fairness, were affected by manipulations. There was a significant two-way interaction between fairness and salience (F(1, 98)=6.05, p<.05), and main effects for fairness (F(1, 98)=18.95, p<.001), and salience (F(1, 98)=6.21, p<.05). In the procedurally fair condition, perceptions of procedural fairness were unaffected by salience ($M_{fairness\text{-}salient}$=5.42, $M_{fairness\text{-}non\text{-}salient}$=5.42, F<1), but in the unfair condition, perceptions of procedural fairness were significantly lower in the unfairness salient condition ($M_{unfairness\text{-}salient}$=4.06, $M_{unfairness\text{-}non\text{-}salient}$=5.05, F(1, 98)=10.95, p<.01).

Procedural unfairness impacted brand evaluations. A significant three-way interaction between procedural fairness, salience, and the time of measuring brand evaluation (F(1, 98)=4.81, p<.05) was observed. In the procedurally fair condition, evaluations were enhanced in both the salient (M_{pre}=4.67, M_{post}=5.68, F(1, 98)=16.93, p<.001) and non-salient condition (M_{pre} 4.57 vs. M_{post}=5.78, F(1, 98)=21.11, p<.001). In the procedurally unfair condition, however, brand evaluations were diluted (M_{pre}=4.76 vs. M_{post}=4.01, F(1, 98)=5.55, p<.05) in the salient condition and enhanced in the non-salient condition (M_{pre}=4.31 vs. M_{post}=4.96, F(1, 98)=6.44, p<.05). Respondents also reported being more satisfied when the process was fair (M_{Fair}=5.65 vs. M_{Unfair}=5.06, F(1, 98)=4.23, p<.05) and when fairness was not salient ($M_{Salient}$=4.99 vs. $M_{Not\text{-}Salient}$=5.72, F(1, 98)=6.28, p<.05).

To test if perceptions of procedural fairness mediated the effect of fairness and salience on brand evaluation, perceptions of procedural fairness were used as a covariate in a three-way ANOVA with brand evaluation change as the dependent variable (Gorn et al. 2004; Kim and Markman 2006; Posavac et al. 2006). Perceptions of procedural fairness significantly impacted brand evaluation change (F(1, 97)=4.10, p<.05). The previously significant three-way interaction between fairness, salience, and time of brand evaluation became non-significant (F(1, 97)=3.41, p>.05). Finally, procedural fairness significantly predicted brand evaluation change (β=.41, p<.01). An identical analysis on outcome fairness revealed no evidence of mediation.

Our research indicates the importance of both outcome and procedural fairness in predicting consumer response to marketing activities. Theoretically, our work opens up a new area within fairness research–the importance of fairness in the face of favorable outcomes. Practically, our research helps explain why beneficial marketing actions may not have the expected additional long-term lift and may even have a negative return if competitors, news media or others highlight procedural unfairness in a firm's marketing decisions.

REFERENCES

Bolton, Lisa E. and Joseph W. Alba (2006), "Price Fairness: Good and Service Differences and the Role of Vendor Costs," *Journal of Consumer Research*, 33 (September), 258-265.

______ , Luk Warlop, and Joseph W. Alba (2003), "Consumer Perceptions of Price (Un)Fairness," *Journal of Consumer Research*, 29 (March), 474-491.

Brockner, Joel (2002), "Making Sense of Procedural Fairness: How High Procedural Fairness Can Reduce or Heighten the Influence of Outcome Favorability," *Academy of Management Review*, 27 (January), 58-76.

Brockner, Joel and Batia M. Wiesenfeld (1996), "An Integrative Framework for Explaining Reactions to Decisions: Interactive Effect of Outcomes and Procedures," *Psychological Bulletin*, 120 (September), 189-208.

______, Joel, Larry Heuer, Nace Magner, Robert Folger, Elizabeth Umphress, Kees van den Bos, Riel Vermunt, Mary Magner, and Phyllis Siegel (2003), "High Procedural Fairness Heightens the Effect of Outcome Favorability on Self-evaluations: An Attributional Analysis," *Organizational Behavior and Human Decision Processes*, 91(May), 51-68.

Gorn, Gerald J., Amitava Chattopadhyay, Jaideep Sengupta, and Shashank Tripathi (2004), "Waiting for the Web: How Screen Color Affects Time Perception," *Journal of Marketing Research*, 41(2), 215-225.

Kim, Kyungil and Arthur B. Markman (2006), "Differences in Fear of Isolation as an explanation of Cultural Differences: Evidence from memory and reasoning," *Journal of Experimental Social Psychology*, 42(May), 350-364.

Lind, E. Allan and Tom R. Tyler (1988), *The Social Psychology of Procedural Justice*, New York: Plenum Press.

Posavac, Steven S, J. Josko Brakus, Shailendra Pratap Jain, and Maria Cronley (2006), "Selective Assessment and Positivity Bias in Environmental Valuation," *Journal of Experimental Psychology: Applied*, 12(1), 43-49.

Thibaut, John W. and Laurens Walker (1975), *Procedural Justice: A Psychological Analysis*, Hillsdale, NJ: L Erlbaum Associates.

Xia, Lan, Kent B. Monroe, and Jennifer L. Cox (2004), "The Price is Unfair! A Conceptual Framework of Price Fairness Perceptions," *Journal of Marketing*, 68 (October), 1-15.

The Underdog Effect: The Marketing of Disadvantage through Brand Biography

Neeru Paharia, Harvard University, USA
Anat Keinan, Harvard Business School, USA
Jill Avery, Simmons School of Management, USA
Juliet B. Schor, Boston College, USA

EXTENDED ABSTRACT

"We started Nantucket Nectars with only a blender and a dream…" (Nantucket Nectars label)

"Thanks to a never ending campaign by Apple's powerful public relations machine to protect the myths surrounding the company's origin, almost everyone believes Apple was started in a garage…actually the operation began in a bedroom… when the bedroom became too crowded operations did indeed move to the garage." (Linzmayer 1991:1)

"I was never the likeliest candidate for this office. We didn't start with much money or many endorsements. Our campaign was not hatched in the halls of Washington—it began in the backyards of Des Moines and the living rooms of Concord and the front porches of Charleston." (President-Elect Obama's acceptance speech, Nov. 5, 2008)

Despite Americans' infatuation with winners, stories about underdogs are pervasive in sports, politics, religion, literature, and film. Both candidates in the 2008 United States presidential election, Barack Obama and John McCain, positioned themselves as underdogs to gain the support of voters, as did presidential primary candidates Hillary Clinton, John Edwards, Mike Huckabee, and Ron Paul. Underdog author J.K. Rowling, a welfare mother who wrote seven of the best-selling books of all time, created a lovable underdog character, Harry Potter, an inexperienced but passionate orphan who grew up in a closet. Television coverage of the 2008 Olympics highlighted underdog aspects of many athletes' biographies, from swimmer Michael Phelps's single mother to gymnast Shawn Johnson's parents taking out a second mortgage on their home to pay for her gymnastics lessons.

In this research we examine how marketers can use underdog narratives to positively affect consumers' perceptions of brands. Underdog narratives are often delivered to consumers through the rhetorical device of a brand biography, an unfolding story that chronicles the brand's origins, life experiences, and evolution over time in a selectively told narrative. Many contemporary brand biographies contain underdog narratives which highlight the company's humble beginnings, hopes and dreams, and noble struggles against adversaries. Nantucket Nectar's label informs us that they started "with only a blender and a dream," while brands such as Google, Clif Bar, and Apple profile the humble garages in which they started.

We argue that underdog brand biographies are effective because consumers can relate these stories to their own lives. We demonstrate that the positive effect of underdog brand biographies is driven by identity mechanisms. Specifically, we show that the underdog effect is a) mediated by a consumer's identification with the brand, b) greater for consumers who strongly self-identify as underdogs, c) stronger in purchase contexts that are symbolic of identity, and d) stronger in consumers who are from cultures in which underdog narratives are part of the national identity. These findings suggest that the underdog brand biography is powerful, not only because it invokes a sympathetic response or because it triggers attributions of effort or quality, but because it appeals to consumers' identity needs. Consumers react positively when they see the underdog aspects of their own lives reflected in branded products.

This article is organized as follows. First, we introduce the concept of an underdog brand biography and explore the emergence and dissemination of underdog narratives in culture. Next, we present a series of hypotheses which examine and explain positive consumer response to underdog brand biographies. Since underdog narratives are an under-explored topic in consumer research, we then use factor analysis to develop an underdog scale that reveals two main dimensions of an underdog: 1. external disadvantage, and 2. passion and determination. Next, five studies examine the effect of using an underdog brand biography on purchase intentions, real choice, and brand loyalty, and demonstrate that identity mechanisms both mediate and moderate this process. These studies measure and prime consumers' identities as underdogs, and manipulate the identity value of the purchase situation. We also explore how external disadvantage and passion and determination work together by comparing the effectiveness of the underdog biography to three related brand biographies. Finally, we explore the boundary conditions of the underdog effect by manipulating whether the underdog wins, loses, or is in a situation where the outcome remains uncertain. We also explore the cross-cultural boundaries of the underdog effect by testing it in two distinct cultures: American, in which underdog narratives are part of the fabric of the national identity, and Asian, in which they are not. The discussion section provides a more complete and nuanced conceptualization of an underdog brand biography based on our studies. We conclude with a discussion of the theoretical implications of underdog brand biographies and offer insight into implications for brand management.

REFERENCES

Aaker, David A. (1991), *Managing Brand Equity: Capitalizing on the Value of a Brand Name,* New York: The Free Press.

Aaker, Jennifer, Susan Fournier, and S. Adam Brasel (2004), "When Good Brands Do Bad," *Journal of Consumer Research*, 31 (1), 1-16.

Aaker, Jennifer L. (1997), "Dimensions of Brand Personality," *Journal of Marketing Research*, XXXIV, 347-356.

Adams, James Truslow (1931), *The Epic of America*, Blue Ribbon Books.

Belk, Russell W. (1979), "Gift-Giving Behavior," in *Research in Marketing*, J. Sheth, Ed. Greenwich, CT: JAI.

Ceci, S.J. and E.L. Kain (1982), "Jumping on the Bandwagon with the Underdog: The Impact of Attitude Polls on Polling Behavior," *Public Opinion Quarterly*.

Cialdini, Robert B., Richard J. Borden, Avril Thorne, Marcus Randall Walker, Stephen Freeman, and Lloyd Reynolds Sloan (1976), "Basking in Reflected Glory: Three (Football) Field Studies," *Journal of Personality and Social Psychology*, 34 (3), 366-375.

Cialdini, Robert B. and Maralou E. De Nicholas (1989), "Self-Presentation by Association," *Journal of Personality and Social Psychology*, 57 (4), 626-631.

Cialdini, Robert B. and K.D. Richardson (1980), "Two Indirect Tactics of Impression Management: Basking and Blasting," *Journal of Personality and Social Psychology*, 39, 406-415.

Deighton, John (2002), "How Snapple Got Its Juice Back," *Harvard Business Review*, 80 (1), 47-53.

Deighton, John, D. Romer, and J. McQueen (1989), "Using Drama to Persuade," *Journal of Consumer Research*, 16, 335-343.

Dittmar, Helga (1992), *The Social Psychology of Materials Possessions: To Have Is to Be*, New York: St. Martin's Press.

Escalas, Jennifer Edson (2004), "Narrative Processing: Building Consumer Connections to Brands," *Journal of Consumer Psychology*, 14 (1&2), 168-180.

Escalas, Jennifer Edson and James R. Bettman (2003), "You Are What They Eat: The Influence of Reference Groups on Consumers' Connections to Brands," *Journal of Consumer Psychology*, 13 (3), 339-348.

Fournier, Susan (1998), "Consumers and Their Brands: Developing Relationship Theory in Consumer Research," *Journal of Consumer Research*, 24 (March 1988), 343-373.

Frazier, J.A. and E.E. Snyder (1991), "The Underdog Concept in Sport," *Sociology of Sport Journal*.

Gardner, Burleigh B. and Sidney J. Levy (1955), "The Product and the Brand," *Harvard Business Review*, 33, 33-39.

Green, Melanie C. and Timothy C. Brock (2000), "The Role of Transportation in the Persuasiveness of Public Narratives," *Journal of Personality and Social Psychology*, 79 (5), 701-721.

Hoch, Stephen J. and John Deighton (1989), "Managing What Consumers Learn from Experience," *Journal of Marketing*, 53 (April), 1-20.

Kapferer, Jean-Noel (1992), *Strategic Brand Management: New Approaches to Creating and Evaluating Brand Equity*, New York: The Free Press.

Kassarjian, Harold H. (1971), "Personality and Consumer Behavior," *Journal of Marketing Research*, 8, 409-418.

Keller, Kevin Lane (1998), *Strategic Brand Management: Building, Measuring, and Managing Brand Equity*, Upper Saddle River, NJ: Prentice-Hall.

Kleine, Susan Schultz, Robert E. Kleine, and Chris T. Allen (1995), "How Is a Possession "Me" Or "Not Me"? Characterizing Types and an Antecedent of Material Possession Attachment," *Journal of Consumer Research*, 22 (December 1995), 327-343.

Levy, Sidney J. (1959), "Symbols for Sale," *Harvard Business Review*, 37, 117-124.

Linzmayer, O.W. (1999), *Apple Confidential*, San Francisco: No Starch Press.

Mick, David Glen (1987), "Toward a Semiotic of Advertising Story Grammars," in *Marketing and Semiotics: New Directions in the Study of Signs for Sale*, J. Umiker-Sebeok, Ed. Berlin: de Gruyter.

Mick, David Glen and Michelle Demoss (1990), "Self-Gifts: Phenomenological Insights from Four Contexts," *Journal of Consumer Research*, 17, 322-332.

Niditch, Susan (1987), *Underdogs and Tricksters: A Prelude to Biblical Folklore*, New York: Harper and Row.

Puto, C.P. and W.D. Wells (1984), "Informational and Transformational Advertising: The Differential Effects of Time," *Advances in Consumer Research*, 11, 572-576.

Sastry, J. and C.E. Ross (1998), "Asian Ethnicity and the Sense of Personal Control," *Social Psychology Quarterly*, 61, 101-120.

Schuman, H. and J. Harding (1963), "Sympathetic Identification with the Underdog," *Public Opinion Quarterly*, 27, 230.

Sirgy, M. Joseph (1982), "Self Concept in Consumer Behavior: A Critical Review," *Journal of Consumer Research*, 9, 287-300.

Stern, B.B. (1994), "Classical and Vignette Television Advertising Dramas: Structural Models, Formal Analysis, and Consumer Effects," *Journal of Consumer Research*, 20, 601-615.

Vandello, J.A., N.P. Goldschmied, and D.A.R. Richards (2007), "The Appeal of the Underdog," *Personality and Social Psychology Bulletin*, 33 (12), 1603-1616.

The Influence of Romantic Mindsets on Brand Extension Evaluation

Alokparna Basu Monga, University of South Carolina, USA
Zeynep Gürhan-Canli, Koc University, Turkey

EXTENDED ABSTRACT

Prior research on brand extensions has focused on identifying a variety of factors that influence brand extension evaluations among consumers (Broniarczyk and Alba 1994; Loken and John 1993). One key factor is the degree to which consumers are able to see a connection between the parent brand and the extension. When consumers perceive some kind of fit between the parent brand and the extension (e.g., Gillette shampoo), the brand extension is evaluated favorably. However, when consumers perceive less fit (e.g., Gillette floor cleaner), the brand extension is evaluated negatively (Aaker and Keller 1990; Loken and John 1993).

Missing, however, from this research is a consideration of how transient mindsets might influence brand extension evaluations. Recent research in consumer behavior attests to the wide variety of situations in which transient mindsets affect consumer behavior (Chandran and Morwitz 2005; Liu and Aaker 2008; Xu and Wyer, 2007). In our research, we focus on a specific type of mindset—the romantic mindset, which is an emerging area of research in psychology (Griskevicius et al. 2006).

Recent research demonstrates that individuals in a romantic mindset show boosts in creativity (Griskevicius et al. 2006). For instance, male participants when primed with thoughts about short-term romantic relationships (that is, a romantic mindset) generated stories that were more creative, imaginative and original. In contrast, females did not show this effect. Since romantic mindsets increase the ability to find relationships between remote ideas and associations, they are likely to enhance perceptions of brand extension fit for a dissimilar brand extension. We draw upon this research to propose that male consumers in a romantic mindset would be able to find novel ways to connect the brand and the extension leading to more favorable brand extension fit perceptions and evaluations. This effect would not emerge for female consumers.

Study 1 tested our hypothesis in a 2 (mindset: romantic, non-romantic) x 2 (gender: male, female) between subjects design. Seventy-five students at a southern university participated in our study. Our results demonstrate that male consumers in a romantic mindset perceive higher fit and evaluate a dissimilar brand extension more favorably, compared to those in a non-romantic mindset. Female consumers, however, are not affected by thinking about a short-term mate. An analysis of relational thoughts reveals that male consumers in the romantic mindset are able to think more relationally (connecting the parent brand to the extension) than those in a non-romantic mindset, indicating that the accessibility of relational thoughts may be driving the differences in brand extension responses across romantic and non-romantic mindsets. Results of a mediation analysis demonstrate that relational thoughts mediate the effect of mindset on brand extension evaluations for male consumers but not for female consumers. Importantly, our results are not driven by positive mood, positive arousal or negative arousal. Next, we replicated the results of this study using a different parent brand from the one used in study 1.

Now, we focus on providing stronger evidence for the process mechanism. Prior research suggests that finding relations between words requires cognitive resources (Wegner and Erber 1992). We draw upon this research to propose that when cognitive load is low, male consumers would be able to engage in relational thinking and respond more favorably to a dissimilar brand extension under a romantic mindset than under a non-romantic mindset. However, when cognitive load is high, the ability of male consumers to uncover relationships between the brand and the extension will be constrained. Therefore, the effect of a romantic mindset will diminish under these conditions.

We tested this hypothesis in a 2 (mindset: romantic, non-romantic) x 2 (cognitive load: low, high) between subjects design. One hundred and twelve male students at a southern university participated in our study. Specifically, male consumers under low cognitive load perceived higher fit and reported more favorable brand extension evaluation in a romantic mindset than in a non-romantic mindset. In contrast, when cognitive load is high, male consumers in romantic mindset respond similar to those in a non-romantic mindset. An analysis of relational thoughts reveals a similar pattern. Results of a mediation analysis show that relational thoughts mediate the effects of the mindset on brand extension evaluation when cognitive load is low, but not when it is high. Importantly, mood or arousal was not an explanation for our findings.

REFERENCES

Aaker, David A. and Kevin L. Keller (1990), "Consumer Evaluations of Brand Extensions," *Journal of Marketing*, 54 (January), 27-41.

Broniarczyk, Susan and Joseph W. Alba (1994), "The Importance of the Brand in Brand Extension," *Journal of Marketing Research*, 31 (May), 214-228.

Chandran, Sucharita, and Vicki Morwitz (2005), "Effects of Participative Pricing on Consumers' Cognitions and Actions: A Goal Theoretic Perspective," *Journal of Consumer Research*, 32 (2), 249-259.

Griskevicius, Vladas, Robert B. Cialdini, and Douglas T. Kenrick (2006a), "Peacocks, Picasso, and Parental Investment: The Effects of Romantic Motives on Creativity, *Journal of Personality and Social Psychology*, 91 (1), 63-76.

Liu, Wendy and Jennifer Aaker (2008), "The Happiness of Giving: The Time-Ask Effect," *Journal of Consumer Research*, 35 (3), 543-557.

Loken, Barbara and Deborah Roedder John (1993), "Diluting Brand Beliefs: When do Brand Extensions Have a Negative Impact?" *Journal of Marketing*, 57 (July), 71-84.

Wegner, Daniel M. and Ralph Erber (1992), "The Hyperaccessibility of Suppressed Thoughts," *Journal of Personality and Social Psychology*, 63 (6), 903-912.

Xu, Alison Jing and Robert S. Wyer, Jr. (2007), "The Effect of Mindsets on Consumer Decision Strategies." *Journal of Consumer Research*, (December).

Coping with Guilt and Shame in the Impulse Buying Context

Sunghwan Yi, University of Guelph, Canada
Hans Baumgartner, Pennsylvania State University, USA

EXTENDED ABSTRACT

In this study we studied how consumers cope with guilt and shame in the impulse buying context. As with other instances of self-regulation failure, buying on impulse against one's intention to reduce impulse buying brings about aversive self-awareness, which, in turn, is likely to evoke negative self-conscious emotions, namely, guilt and shame. Even though often used interchangeably, guilt and shame are considered distinct emotions with different antecedents and motivational tendencies (Lewis, 1971; Tangney & Dearing, 2002).

Guilt is a feeling of remorse or regret which involves preoccupation with a particular transgression. Guilt arises when people "wish they had behaved differently or could somehow undo the bad deed that was done" (Tangney, Miller, Flicker, & Barlow, 1996). In other words, guilt involves mentally undoing some aspect of the transgression. Unlike guilt, shame is a more intense and enduring experience and is felt when people perceive that their "deep-seated flaws are revealed to oneself and to others" (Miller & Tangney 1994). As such, shame is tied to the attribution of a certain event to perceived deficiencies of one's core self (Klass, 1990). According to Hoblitzelle (1987), shame differs from guilt in that the former is associated with internal, stable, and global attributions, whereas the latter is associated with internal, specific, and temporary attributions.

Further, guilt and shame are associated with distinct action tendencies and motivation. Since the experience of guilt involves a mental undoing of the transgression rather than self, guilt evokes the motivation or desire to confess, apologize, and repair the harm (Tangney & Dearing, 2002). In contrast, as shame arises from global devaluation of the self, it evokes the motivation or desire to hide, escape, and even strike back. Furthermore, people who are prone to shame use tend to act defensively, such as rage, contempt, transfer of blame, and denial (Kaufman, 1996) and engage in dysfunctional behavior, such as withdrawal, avoidance, attacking self and others (Pattison, 2000).

The primary goal of this paper is to investigate restorative coping strategies consumers use in order to cope with discrete self-conscious emotions, specifically, shame and guilt, in the impulse buying context. Based on psychological research on distinction between guilt and shame, we propose a set of four hypotheses:

Hypothesis 1: Compared to ordinary consumers, consumers with strong impulse buying tendency will experience more intense guilt and shame in the wake of impulse buying.

Hypothesis 2: Consumers' impulse buying tendency will be positively associated with the frequency with which they use avoidant coping strategies, such as denial, distraction, non-disclosure and blaming others.

Hypothesis 3: The intensity of shame experienced after impulse buying will be positively associated with avoidant coping strategies, such as denial, distraction, resignation and blaming others.

Hypothesis 4: The intensity of guilt experienced after impulse buying will be positively associated with problem-focused coping and non-avoidant coping strategies.

Survey methodology was used in order to formally test the hypotheses and develop the coping instrument. W conducted a retrospective approach, in which participants recalled a recent impulse buying and reported the emotions and coping strategies they used. Two thousand and one hundred sixteen individuals logged on our on-line survey, but three hundred and ten people qualified for the study. Thirty six participants did not answer a substantial number of questions and had to be removed from analysis; therefore, the remaining 274 participants' data were used in the analysis. Upon completing the consent form, participants were asked to think back to the last time they went shopping and bought something on a sudden rush of desire, without thinking about whether making that purchase fits with their budget, their long term goals or plans. Furthermore, in order to qualify, participants had to spend at least $80 on a single item for themselves within the last two months. We assessed guilt and shame items by adapting State Shame and Guilt Scale (Marschall, Sanftner, & Tangney, 1994). Next, participants' coping efforts were assessed with the 76-item coping scale specifically intended to assess consumers' coping efforts to deal with negative emotions in the impulse buying context. Participants' impulse buying tendency was assessed with Rook and Fisher's (1992) Buying Impulse Scale. We measured chronic shame and guilt disposition with the TOSCA scale (Tangney et al., 2002). Further, the questionnaire included Rosenberg's (1965) self-esteem scale, Ross & Mirowsky's (1984) depression scale (CES-D), and Faber & O'Guinn's (1993) compulsive buying scale. Lastly, participants were asked to indicate their annual income, disposable monthly income, the amount of savings, credit card debt, the balance on their credit cards in the previous month, and the amount they did not pay towards the balance on credit cards last month. Participants exited the survey after providing demographic data (i.e., age and gender).

Our hypotheses were generally consistent with our survey data. First, consistent with Hypothesis 1, participants with strong impulsive tendency reported experiencing more intense guilt and shame in the event of impulse buying. Even though the effect of impulse buying on both guilt and shame was positive, the path coefficient from impulse buying to shame was higher than the coefficient to guilt. Further, consistent with Hypothesis 2, our data showed that the effect of buying impulsiveness on avoidant coping strategies was significantly positive. Specifically, as buying impulsiveness increased, the frequency of using avoidant coping strategies, such as denial/distraction, rationalization, wishful thinking and resignation, significantly increased. In contrast, the relations between buying impulsiveness and non-avoidant coping strategies were either negative or minimal. Moreover, our data provided support for the hypothesis that the intensity of shame would be positively associated with avoidant coping strategies, whereas the intensity of guilt would be positively associated with non-avoidant coping strategies (i.e., Hypotheses 3 and 4). Specifically, our path analysis showed that the intensity of shame positively influenced denial/distraction, resignation and blaming others, whereas the intensity of guilt positively influenced planning to reduce impulse buying and to make up for monetary loss as well as wishful thinking. This structural model showed a very good fit to the model. This finding that guilt and shame are accompanied by unique coping strategies is even more interesting given that the intensity of guilt and shame is highly correlated in our data. This finding suggests that even though guilt and shame are related emotions, the acute experience of shame is more frequently accompanied by maladaptive coping strategies than guilt.

REFERENCES

Hoblitzelle, Wendy (1987), "Attempts to measure and differentiate shame and guilt: The relation between shame and depression," in *The role of shame in symptom formation*, ed. H. B. Lewis, Hillsdale, NJ: Erlbaum, (pp. 207-235).

Kaufman, Gershen (1996), *The Psychology of Shame*, Second Edition. New York: Springer.

Klass, Ellen T. (1990), "Guilt, shame, and embarrassment: Cognitive-behavioral approaches," in *Handbook of Social and Evaluation Anxiety*, ed. H. Leitenberg, New York: Plenum, 385-414.

Lewis , Helen B. (1971), *Shame & Guilt in Neurosis*, New York: International Universities Press.

Miller, Rowland S. and June P. Tangney (1994), "Differentiating embarrassment and shame," *Journal of Social and Clinical Psychology*, 13, 273-287.

Marschall, Donna, Jennifer Sanftner, and June P. Tangney (1994), *The State Shame and Guilt Scale*. George Mason University, Fairfax, VA.

Pattison, Stephen (2000), *Shame: Theory, Therapy, Theology*, New York: Cambridge University Press.

Rook, Dennis W. and Robert J. Fisher (1995), "Normative influences on impulse buying behavior," *Journal of Consumer Research, 22,* 305-313.

Ross, Catherine E. and John Mirowsky (1984), "Components of depressed mood in married men and women. The Center for Epidemiologic Studies' Depression Scale," *American Journal of Epidemiology*, *119,* 997-1004.

Tangney, June P. and Ronda L. Dearing (2002), *Shame & Guilt*, New York: Gilford Press.

Tangney, June P., Rowland S. Miller, Laura Flicker, and Deborah H. Barlow (1996), "Are shame, guilt, and embarrassment distinct emotions?" *Journal of Personality and Social Psychology*, 70, 1256-1269

Merry Impulsivity: Belief Systems about the Dark and Bright Sides of Being Bad Consumers

Rita Coelho do Vale, FCEE-UCP, Catholic University of Portugal, Portugal

EXTENDED ABSTRACT

Impulsivity is typically considered as a negative behaviour that should be avoided at any cost. Despite this common approach to impulsive behaviors as self-control failures that are regretted latter, we propose that impulsivity may have a bright side that may explain why consumers persistently seem to not pay attention to the constant reminders from various governmental and health-care organizations to perform the adequate and right goal-pursuit activities, and to even consciously act on impulse (Baumeister et al. 1994). The present research analyzes this phenomenon, examining consumers' beliefs on the consequences of acting on impulse and its impact on consumers' happiness/well-being.

Most of the research conducted on the self-control topic implicitly assumes that if somehow consumers would be able to increase their self-regulatory ability, many social problems as obesity and impulsive behavior, would be solved, contributing to a "better world" (Baumeister 2002; Faber and Vohs 2004; Sayette 2004). The offer of self-help books, websites and courses, supposedly to help consumers to become better self-regulators, is soaring. And consumers are systematically confronted with numerous "reminders" of their ongoing pursuits. However, to our knowledge, there are no studies focused in analyzing the possible bright side of impulsivity on consumers' happiness. This is relevant if one considers that a significant percentage of consumers' daily decisions appear to comprise impulsive decisions (Rook, 1987; Rook and Fisher, 1995; Hausman 2000) and that impulsive purchases are considered to represent about 70% of the consumer decisions (Bellenger, Robertson and Hirschman 1978). Moreover, since 38 percent of the adults in an annual national survey responded affirmatively to the statement: "I am an impulse buyer" (Rook and Fisher 1995), makes such phenomenon even more interesting.

Although impulsive behaviors may impair the likelihood of long-term conscious goals' attainment, they also contribute to immediate pleasurable experiences that elicit joy and satisfaction, which may fulfill other high-order and less conscious long-term goals (e.g., to be happy), strengthening the belief that impulsive behaviors build consumers' well-being. Therefore, we suggest that one of the reasons why consumers may persistently seem to fall into temptations with disregard for its long-term consequences may be due to the fact that consumers believe they will benefit from desirable short-term and long-term outcomes by doing so.

Our main hypothesis is that impulsive consumers (low self-regulators) will be considered to be happier and will be associated with a set of higher positive personal characteristics, compared with non-impulsive consumers (high self-regulators). This Merry Impulsivity hypothesis is based on three underlying processes. First, we predict that low self-regulators, compared with high self-regulators, are considered to experience higher positive affect and lower negative affect, typically approached as an indication of happiness (Ryan and Deci 2001). Second, we also predict low self-regulators to focus more on the short-term experiences and therefore to be considered to have a more positive attitude towards uncertainty of future events than high self-regulators, indicating a more general positive attitude towards life, positively influencing consumers' subjective well-being/happiness (Diener et al. 1997; Scheier and Carver 1993). Third, we predict that low self-regulators will be considered to better develop social skills than high self-regulators and to more easily create and nurture interpersonal relationships, a basic human need essential for well-being/happiness (Ryan and Deci 2001).

Support to our predictions offer a possible explanation why consumers pervasively tend to engage in impulsive acts. If consumers believe that impulsive acts contribute positively to a set of positive characteristics, they may engage in those acts in an attempt to enhance their well-being.

Our predictions were tested in two studies. Study 1 analyzed to what extent low self-regulators are considered to be happier and to experience more positive affect than high self-regulators. Study 2 included measures for goal-pursuit attainment as achievements in life and hard-working constructs, as also assessed consumers' beliefs in terms of sociability skills, sensation-seeking tendency, desire for control, and attitude towards life. In addition, it examined the influence of consumers' actual impulsivity (self-assessed) on their beliefs about the dark and bright sides of impulsive consumer behavior.

Findings from study 1 (n=44) showed that consumers who frequently engage in impulsive behaviors are indeed considered to be happier and to more likely experience positive affect than consumers that typically try to refrain impulses in order to pursue overarching goals. In addition, findings from study 2, which re-tested our predictions using 438 randomly selected members of a household panel, showed that impulsive behaviors, despite leading to fewer achievements in life, are considered to contribute to a set of personal characteristics that raise consumers' happiness.

This set of studies addressed an understudied aspect of self-regulation failure: the one of consumers willingly failing to exert self-control, amending the so far universal belief that self-control is the ultimate goal to consumers' well-being. Despite this common idea, impulsive behaviors may actually positively influence consumers' well-being, due to consumers' belief systems about the correlates of impulsivity. Our research demonstrates that consumers who tend to engage in immediate pleasurable experiences with disregard for its long-term consequences are generally believed to be happier, more social, with a more positive attitude towards life, and to experience higher positive affect than consumers who have high consumption/behavioral self-regulatory concerns. Therefore, and as outlined by Baumeister and colleagues (1994), the phenomenon of acquiescence with failure may explain a significant portion of self-control failures. To our knowledge, the present research is the first to address empirically this phenomenon, shedding some light on belief systems that are conducive to consumers persistently engaging in non self-regulatory activities.

REFERENCES

Baumeister, Roy (2002), "Yielding to Temptation: Self-Control Failure, Impulsive Purchasing, and Consumer Behavior," *Journal of Consumer Research*, 28 (March), 670-676.

Baumeister, Roy, Todd Heatherton, and Dianne Tice (1994), *Losing Control: How and Why People Fail at Self-Regulation*, San Diego: Academic Press.

Bellenger Danny, Dan Robertson and Elizabeth Hirschman (1978), "Impulse Buying Varies by Product," *Journal of Advertising Research*, 18(6), 15-18.

Diener, Ed, Eunkook Suh and Shigehiro Oishi (1997), "Subjective Well-Being," *Indian Journal of Clinical Psychology*, 24 (March), 25-41.

Faber, Ronald and Kathleen Vohs (2004), "To Buy or Not to Buy?: Self-Control and Self-Regulatory Failure," in *Handbook of Self-Regulation*, eds. Roy Baumeister and Kathleen Vohs, New York: Guilford, 509-524.

Hausman Angela (2000), "A Multi-Method Investigation of Consumer Motivations in Impulse Buying Behaviour," *The Journal of Consumer Marketing*, 17(5), 403-419.

Rook, Dennis (1987), "The Buying Impulse," *Journal of Consumer Research*, 14 (September), 189-99.

Rook, Dennis and Robert Fisher, (1995), "Normative Influences on Impulsive Buying Behaviour," *Journal of Consumer Research*, 22 (December), 305-313.

Ryan, Richard and Edward Deci (2001), "On Happiness and Human Potentials: A Review of Research on Hedonic and Eudaimonic Well-Being," *Annual Review of Psychology*, 52, 141-166.

Sayette, Michael (2004), "Self-Regulatory Failure and Addiction," in *Handbook of Self-Regulation*, eds. Roy Baumeister and Kathleen Vohs, New York: Guilford, 447-465.

Scheier, Michael and Charles Carver (1993), "On the Power of Positive Thinking: The Benefits of Being Optimistic," *Current Directions in Psychological Science*, 2, 26-30.

What is Moral about Moral Emotions? Guilt Elicits Prosocial Behavior as Well as Antisocial Behavior

Ilona De Hooge, Erasmus University, The Netherlands
Rob Nelissen, Tilburg University, The Netherlands
Seger Breugelmans, Tilburg University, The Netherlands
Marcel Zeelenberg, Tilburg University, The Netherlands

EXTENDED ABSTRACT

Moral emotions have been portrayed as the social mortar of human societies because these feelings encourage us to put the concerns of others above our own and to engage in prosocial behavior. The hallmark moral emotion is guilt, which is typically described as an "adaptive emotion, benefiting individuals and their relationships in a variety of ways" (Tangney, Stuewig, & Mashek, 2007, p. 26). However, is it really the case that moral emotions make the interest of others paramount, neglecting our self-interest?

Guilt mostly arises from a moral transgression in which the actor has violated an important norm and has hurt another person. This elicits a preoccupation with the victim and the ensuing reparative action tendencies are aimed at restoring the relationship between transgressor and victim. This victim-oriented focus explains the often-replicated finding that guilty people contribute more of their endowments to others in comparison to non-guilty people. It is clear that in dyadic situations guilt produces behavior that benefits others.

However, we have reason to believe that the very characteristics of guilt that make it beneficial to the victim in dyadic interactions have disadvantageous side effects for others in the social environment. In dyadic interactions the costs of acting prosocially come necessarily at the expense of oneself. But in daily life it is also possible to act prosocially at the cost of others. We think that the generosity towards the victim has disadvantageous consequences for the social environment. Precisely because guilt induces a preoccupation with restoring the harm to the victim, it simultaneously causes a neglect of others. Consequently, a guilty state may not evoke a disregard for personal concerns (as is often assumed) but rather a depreciation of the concerns of non-victimized others. We predict that when taking such a broader, more ecologically valid perspective, it will appear that people experiencing guilt are motivated to benefit the relationship with the victim, but at the best possible outcomes for themselves. Three experiments investigated if the experience of guilt induces prosocial behavior towards the victim at the expense of others rather than the self.

In Experiment 1, participants reported a personal experience of feeling guilty (Guilt condition), or described a regular weekday (Control condition). They were asked to think of the person they felt guilty towards (guilt condition) or of a person they had met during the weekday (control condition). This person was labeled Person A. Participants then divided ¤50 between the birthday of Person A, the fundraising of the victims of a flood, and themselves. We found that Guilt participants offered more money to Person A than Control participants. At the same time, guilt participants offered *less* money to flood victims than Control participants. Guilt and Control participants did not differ in the amount they kept for themselves.

Experiment 2 explored whether guilty people could also act disadvantageously towards known others. Participants were randomly assigned to the Guilt or Control condition and read a scenario. Next, they divided ¤50 between the birthday of the victim of the scenario, the birthday of another friend, and themselves. Results showed that Guilt participants offered more money to the victim than Control participants, and offered less money to the third party. Participants did not differ in the amount they kept for themselves. Thus, even when the social surrounding consists of family and friends, the costs of compensatory behavior befall those other people rather than oneself.

Experiment 3 tested our assumption that the preoccupation with the victim that characterizes guilt causes disadvantageous side effects for the social environment. This entails that no effects should be found in situations where the victim is not present, which was tested by adding a condition where the victim was not present. Participants were randomly assigned to the conditions of a 2 (Emotion condition: Guilt vs. Control) × 2 (Victim Presence: Victim-present vs. Victim-not-present) design. They were told that during the lab-session they could earn lottery tickets for a lottery. The session started with two rounds of a performance task, ostensibly with another participant. In the first round they could earn 8 lottery tickets for themselves, in the second round 8 tickets for the other player. After the first round, all participants received feedback that they earned the bonus. After the second round, the other player in the Guilt condition did not receive the bonus due to the participant's bad performance. In the Control condition, the other player received the bonus. Participants continued with a three person-dictator game, either with the player from the performance task (Victim-present condition) or with a participant who knew nothing about the performance task (Victim-not-present condition). In all conditions the third player was a participant who knew nothing about the letter task. As the dependent variable, the participant divided twelve lottery tickets among the three players.

We found that participants in the Victim-present Guilt condition offered significantly more to the victim than participants in the Victim-present Control condition, and than participants in the Victim-not-present Guilt condition. They also offered significantly less to the third player than participants in the Victim-present Control condition, and than participants in the Victim-not-present Guilt condition. Higher offers to the victim did not come at personal expense: all conditions did not differ in tickets kept for oneself.

In summary, it appears that guilt, the hallmark moral emotion, can motivate behaviors that do not fit the predicate moral. When people experience guilt, they are preoccupied with repairing the harm done to the victim, leading to disadvantageous effects for others in their social environment. This suggests that the view of moral emotions as (unconditionally) beneficial for others should be rephrased. Moral emotions do not make the interest of others in general paramount, but rather motivate a selective focus on the interests of the wronged other while not forgetting self-interest. This indicates that a thorough understanding of functioning of moral emotions is necessary to fully understand their influence on consumer behavior.

Lying Your Way Out of a Bad Situation

Christina I. Anthony, University of Sydney, Australia
Elizabeth Cowley, University of Sydney, Australia

EXTENDED ABSTRACT

Introduction

Research investigating deception in consumer research has focused on transgressions of marketers (Burke et al. 1988; Deighton and Grayson 1995; Gaeth and Heath 1987). However, consumers also are motivated to be deceitful to gain rewards that are otherwise unattainable (Ekman 1997, 2009). If consumers do tell lies in pursuit of better outcomes, the transgression may have consequences for their affective outcome evaluations. In this research, we examine how lying affects the consumer's happiness with a consumption outcome.

Competing Hypotheses

The literature enables us to hypothesize that liars' affective evaluations will depend on the financial or moral outcomes considered while deliberating over their strategy. According to Decision Affect Theory (DAT: Mellers, Schwartz, and Ritov 1999; Mellers et al. 1997), as a decision becomes more deliberative, more counterfactual thinking should occur, resulting in amplified affective responses. We argue that lying is a more deliberative strategy, than truth telling. In particular, a salient source of deliberation for a person contemplating deception as a means of getting out of a bad situation, are the financial gains attainable if they succeed. Accordingly, DAT predicts that that when a lie succeeds, liars will feel happier than truth tellers because they will generate more counterfactuals about how the outcome could have been worse financially had they not lied. If a lie fails, DAT predicts that liars should feel more regretful than truth tellers because they will generate more counterfactuals about how the outcome could have been better financially had they told the truth.

In addition to the financial outcomes associated with lying, there are also moral outcomes that may be deliberated during decision-making; after all, most people consider lying morally questionable. The concept of morality is consistent with Higgins's notion of 'Value From Proper Means' (VFPM: Camacho, Higgins, and Luger 2003; Molden and Higgins 2005). Value from proper means occurs when the way a goal is pursued coincides with socially accepted rules or normative principles of morality (Higgins et al. 2003; Merton 1957; Pennington and Hastie 1988; Tetlock 1991; Tversky and Shafir 1992).This value is then incorporated into the evaluation of the outcome of an experience. Dishonesty may not provide a good source of 'fit'(Camacho et al. 2003; Carver and Scheier 1990). Therefore, the VFPM perspective predicts that liars will feel worse than truth tellers, as they will counterfactually consider that the outcome could have been better, had they used a morally better means. The importance of morality is also incorporated in equity theory which holds that people prefer outcomes that fair and deserved (Adams 1965; Messick and Cook 1983; Walster, Walster, and Bershcheid 1978). Receiving more than one deserves produces guilt, and receiving less than one deserves causes anger and disappointment (Oliver and Swan 1989; Van den Bos et al. 1997; Van den Bos, Peters, and Bobocel 2006; Van den Bos et al. 1998). Accordingly, equity models, predict that liars will feel worse than truth tellers as they will generate more counterfactuals about how a deal could have been better (more deserved) had they acted fairly and truthfully. However, unlike VFPM, equity models predict that liars will feel better than truth tellers encountering an impasse, as they will counterfactually consider that the outcome could have been worse had they attained an undeserved deal.

Study 1

The purpose of study 1 was to test the competing hypotheses (DAT: financial deliberation vs. VFPM/Equity Models: moral deliberation) for differences in the affective reactions of liars compared to truth tellers. In study 1, participants played the role of consumer in a simulated negotiation task. Lying versus truth telling was induced by manipulating the nature of competitor information provided. Participants were told that the salesperson would endeavor to match currently available competitor offers. Therefore, strong-competitor-information encouraged truth telling as favorable deals were currently available. Weak-competitor-information encouraged lying as favorable deals were currently unavailable. Liars lied by claiming that a favorable but expired competitor offer was currently available. Further, the outcome of the negotiation was manipulated such that half the participants received a deal while the other half encountered an impasse. Study 1 results revealed, that given a deal, liars were happier than truth tellers, and in the event of an impasse, liars were more regretful than truth tellers. The results are consistent with DAT.

Study 2

The objective of study 2 was to examine the counterfactual thinking processes underlying the DAT hypotheses. It is our contention that liars amplified affective reactions occur because lying requires more strategic deliberation which entails increased counterfactual thinking. Therefore, in study 2, we introduce a manipulation that is designed to increase deliberation about their strategy for truth tellers (and therefore counterfactual thinking). Following this, the deliberation manipulation was introduced using an operationalization of risk. Participants were informed that there was a good chance of (not) being believed by the salesperson. Finally, the outcome was manipulated to be deal or impasse. Study 2 results revealed, that increasing the risk for truth tellers amplified their counterfactual thinking and thereby eliminated the observed differences in affect across strategy.

Study 3

The objective of study 3 was to demonstrate that liars amplified affective reactions are counterfactually referenced to the financial risks associated with lying. Priming a morality focus should eliminate the amplification effects. Further, study 3 sought to demonstrate that truth telling is a less strategic option. The outcome, a priming manipulation was introduced to encourage either a financial or morality focus. Study 3 results revealed that the financial priming condition replicated the results of earlier studies; liars displayed more amplified affective reactions compared to truth tellers. Importantly, as hypothesized, morality priming eliminated liars' amplification effects. Also, whilst the levels of the priming manipulation had differential effect on liars, truth tellers were not affected, confirming our contention that truth tellers are affected by the outcome, not their moral strategy.

Discussion

An important implication of our findings is that if marketers do not stand to lose too much financially, it may be advisable to exercise more leniency when negotiating with suspects of deception because marketers ultimately run the risk of wrongfully accusing innocent truth tellers.

References

Adams, John Stacy (1965), "Inequity in Social Exchange," in *Advances in Experimental Social Psychology*, Vol. 2, ed. Leonard Berkowitz, San Diego, CA: Academic Press, 335-43.

Burke, Raymond R., Wayne S. DeSarbo, Richard L. Oliver, and Thomas S. Robertson (1988), "Deception by Implication: An Experimental Investigation," *Journal of Consumer Research*, 14 (March), 483-94.

Camacho, Christopher J., E. Tory. Higgins, and Lindsay Luger (2003), " Moral Value Transfer from Regulatory Fit: What Feels Right Is Right and What Feels Wrong Is Wrong," *Journal of Personality and Social Psychology*, 84 (March), 498-510.

Carver, Charles S. and Michael F. Scheier (1990), "Origins and Functions of Positive and Negative Affect: A Control-Process View," *Psychological Review*, 97 (January), 19-35.

Deighton, John and Kent Grayson (1995), "Marketing and Seduction: Building Exchange Relationships by Managing Social Consensus," *Journal of Consumer Research*, 21 (March), 660-76.

Ekman, Paul (1997), "Lying and Deception," in *Memory for Everyday and Emotional Events*, ed. Nancy L. Stein, Peter A. Ornstein, Barbara Tversky and Charles Brainerd, Hillsdale, New Jersey: Lawrence Erlbaum Associates, 333-47.

______ (2009), *Telling Lies: Clues to Deceit in the Marketplace, Politics, and Marriage*, New York, NY: W.W. Norton & Co.

Gaeth, Gary J. and Timothy B. Heath (1987), "The Cognitive Processing of Misleading Advertising in Young and Old Adults: Assessment and Training," *Journal of Consumer Research*, 14 (June), 43-54.

Higgins, E. Tory, Lorraine Chen Idson, Antonio L. Freitas, Scott Spiegel, and Daniel C. Molden (2003), "Transfer of Value from Fit," *Journal of Personality and Social Psychology*, 84 (June), 1140-53.

Mellers, Barbara A., Alan Schwartz, Katty Ho, and Ilana Ritov (1997), "Decision Affect Theory: Emotional Reactions to the Outcomes of Risky Options," *Psychological Science*, 8 (November), 423-29.

Mellers, Barbara, Alan Schwartz, and Ilana Ritov (1999), "Emotion-Based Choice," *Journal of Experimental Psychology: General*, 128 (September), 332-45.

Merton, Robert K. (1957), *Social Theory and Social Structure*, Glencoe, IL: The Free Press.

Messick, David M. and Karen S. Cook (1983), *Equity Theory: Psychological and Sociological Perspectives*, New York, NY: Praeger.

Molden, Daniel C. and E. Tory Higgins (2005), "Motivated Thinking," in *The Cambridge Handbook of Thinking and Reasoning*, ed. Keith J Holyoak and Robert G Morrison, New York: Cambridge University Press, 295-317.

Oliver, Richard L. and John E. Swan (1989), "Equity and Disconfirmation Perceptions as Influences on Merchant and Product Satisfaction," *Journal of Consumer Research*, 16 (December), 372-83.

Pennington, Nancy and Reid Hastie (1988), "Explanation-Based Decision Making: Effects of Memory Structure on Judgment," *Journal of Experiment Psychology: Learning, Memory, and Cognition*, 14 (July), 521-33.

Tetlock, Philip E. (1991), "An Alternative Metaphor in the Study of Judgment and Choice: People as Politicians," *Theory and Psychology*, 1 (November), 451-75.

Tversky, Amos and Eldar Shafir (1992), "The Disjunction Effect in Choice under Uncertainty," *Psychological Science*, 3 (5), 305-09.

Van den Bos, Kees, E. Allan Lind, Riel Vermunt, and Henk A. M. Wilke (1997), "How Do I Judge My Outcome When I Do Not Know the Outcome of Others? The Psychology of the Fair Process Effect," *Journal of Personality and Social Psychology*, 72 (May), 1034-46.

Van den Bos, Kees, Susanne L. Peters, and D. Ramona Bobocel (2006), "On Preferences and Doing the Right Thing: Satisfaction with Advantageous Inequity When Cognitive Processing Is Limited," *Journal of Experimental Social Psychology*, 42 (May), 273-89.

Van den Bos, Kees, Henk A. M. Wilke, E. Allan Lind, and Riel Vermunt (1998), "Evaluating Outcomes by Means of the Fair Process Effect: Evidence for Different Processes in Fairness and Satisfaction Judgments," *Journal of Personality and Social Psychology*, 74 (June), 1493-503.

Walster, Elaine, G.William Walster, and Ellen Bershcheid (1978), *Equity: Theory and Research*, Boston: Allyn and Bacon, Inc

Do Bettors Categorize Bets?

Greg Durham, Montana State University, USA
Mukunthan Santhanakrishnan, Idaho State University, USA

EXTENDED ABSTRACT

In a frictionless market with rational investors, any price changes are due to changes in fundamental values of the assets. On the other hand, if investors group assets into different categories, then change in preference towards a category may cause changes in prices of assets within that group. Thus, when investors categorize assets, asset prices within a group may move together even when the fundamental values of these assets demonstrate no comovement among them. Such categorization by investors could lead to an allocation of capital that is inefficient in terms of risk and return.

Recent articles provide evidence consistent with the notion that investors categorize assets along various dimensions. Pirinsky and Wang (2006) find that stock returns of companies exhibit a strong degree of comovement with returns of other companies headquartered in the same geo-graphical area. They also find, however, that underlying cash flows (measured as earnings) exhibit negative comovement with cash flows of other local companies. Barberis, Shleifer, and Wurgler (2005) focus on stocks that are added to the Standard & Poor's 500 Index and find that the returns on the newly added stocks co-move more with returns on other S&P 500 stocks than with returns on stocks that are not part of the index. Besides geographic location or membership in an index, another dimension by which investors appear to categorize investments is stock-price magnitude (Green and Hwang (2008)).

A limitation of the Pirinsky and Wang (2006) study is that assets under consideration are multi-period assets; these assets' returns may co-move in a given period of time in anticipation of comovement in earnings in any subsequent periods, without any comovement in contemporaneous earnings. Also, studies of comovement around index additions and stock splits must be cautious of changes in underlying fundamentals surrounding the events of interest: while fundamental values should not change surrounding either type of event, some evidence suggests that market participants' perceptions of future cash flows are influenced by these events (Denis et al. (2003), Kalay and Kronlund (2009)).

The market in which we conduct our study is not characterized by these same limitations or precautions. Each asset (i.e., each sports bet) in the college football betting market has a life of only one period, thereby eliminating the possibility that comovement in current prices is caused by comovement in any cash flows other than contemporaneous ones. Another useful feature of this market is that a sports bet's value is unambiguously realized at the instant a game ends–the cash flow associated with that bet is easy to measure. Another advantage of our marketplace is that required rates of return are nearly constant across all wagers in our entire sample, because risk is the same across all wagers. Therefore, fundamental value of a wager–defined as expected future cash flow discounted at an appropriate required rate of return–is likely to change only if the underlying cash flow changes. This unambiguous relationship, together with the fact that we can clearly measure the single relevant cash flow for each wager, make our market an advantageous venue in which to test whether comovement in prices is driven by comovement in fundamental values.

Bettors may very well be constrained by attention scarcity due to the number of games played each week. In addition, the assets' short lifespans of approximately one week require bettors to update their information sets every week, complicating their task of processing information. In order to simplify the task and the choices involved, bettors may categorize games based on teams involved in each game.

We are interested in the possibility that bettors separate games into different categories based upon the types of teams involved in each contest: (1) Games involving two major-conference teams and games involving at least one non-major-conference team and (2) Conference games and non-conference games. We explore whether percent change in point spread for a game (our market's analog to percent change in prices in financial markets) is influenced more by percent changes in point spreads for other same-category games or by percent changes in point spreads for the complement set of games. We also examine whether any relationships exist among underlying cash flows within and/or across different categories of games.

We test for comovement consistent with categorization, using bivariate regressions, and find that point spreads for a particular category of games co-move with point spreads for other similar games. We further find that the underlying cash flows among similar games do not co-move. Traditional finance theory suggests that if we observe comovement in spreads among a set of games, we should expect to see comovement in underlying cash flows for those games. Our findings that spreads co-move (in the same direction) among similar games, while the underlying cash flows appear to co-move in opposite directions, together are consistent with the presence of "style bettors" in the college football wagering market.

REFERENCES

Barberis, N., Shleifer, A. (2003), "Style Investing," *Journal of Financial Economics*, 68, 161-199.

Barberis, N., Shleifer, A., Wurgler, J. (2005), "Comovement," *Journal of Financial Economics*, 75, 283-317.

Bodurtha, J., Kim, D., Lee, C. (1995), "Closed-End Country Funds and US Market Sentiment," *Review of Financial Studies*, 8, 879-918.

Boyer, B. (2007), "Comovement Among Stocks with Similar Book-to-Market Ratios," unpublished working paper, Brigham Young University.

Brown, J., Ivkovic, Z., Smith, P., Weisbenner, S. (2008), "Neighbors Matter: Causal Community Effects and Stock Market Participation," *Journal of Finance*, 63, 1509-1531.

Chan, K., Hameed, A., Lau, S. (2003), "What If Trading Location is Different from Business Location? Evidence from the Jardine Group," *Journal of Finance*, 58, 1221-1246.

Dare, W., Holland, S. (2004), "Efficiency in the NFL Betting Market: Modifying and Consolidating Research Methods," *Applied Economics*, 36, 9-15.

Dare, W., MacDonald, S. (1996), "A Generalized Model for Testing the Home and Favorite Team Advantage in Point Spread Markets," *Journal of Financial Economics*, 40, 295-318.

Denis, D., McConnell, J., Ovtchinnikov, A., Yu, Y. (2003), "S&P 500 Index Additions and Earnings Expectations," *Journal of Finance*, 58, 1821-1840.

Durham, G., Santhanakrishnan, M. (2008), "The Relative Importance of Strength and Weight in Processing New Information in the College Football Betting Market," *Journal of Prediction Markets*, 2, 13-28.

Froot, K., Dabora, E. (1996), "How Are Stock Prices Affected by the Location of Trade?" *Journal of Financial Economics*, 53, 189-216.

Green, C., Hwang, B. (2008), "Price-Based Return Comovement," *Journal of Financial Economics,* forthcoming.

Greenwood, R. (2008), "Excess Comovement of Stock Returns: Evidence from Cross-Sectional Variation in Nikkei 225 Weights," *Review of Financial Studies*, 21, 1153-1186.

Hong, H., Kubik, J., Stein, J. (2004), "Social Interaction and Stock-Market Participation," *Journal of Finance*, 59, 137-163.

Kahneman, D. (1973), *Attention and Effort*, Englewood Cliffs, NJ: Prentice-Hall.

Kalay, A., Kronlund, M. (2009), "Stock Splits–Information or Liquidity," unpublished working paper, University of Chicago.

Kumar, A., Lee, C. (2006), "Retail Investor Sentiment and Return Comovements," *Journal of Finance*, 61, 2451-2486.

Lee, C., Shleifer, A., Thaler, R. (1991), "Investor Sentiment and the Closed-End Fund Puzzle," *Journal of Finance*, 46, 75-109.

Mullainathan, S. (2002), "Thinking Through Categories," unpublished working paper, Massachusetts Institute of Technology.

Peng, L., Xiong, W. (2006), "Investor Attention, Overconfidence, and Category Learning," *Journal of Financial Economics*, 80, 563-602.

Pindyck, R., Rotemberg, J. (1990), "The Excess Co-Movement of Commodity Prices," *The Economic Journal*, 100, 1173-1189.

Pirinsky, C., Wang, Q. (2006), "Does Corporate Headquarters Location Matter for Stock Returns?" *Journal of Finance*, 61, 1991-2015.

Rosch, E., Lloyd, B. (1978), *Cognition and Categorization*, Mahwah, NJ: Lawrence Erlbaum Associates.

Shiller, R. (1999), "Human Behavior and the Efficiency of the Financial System," in J.B. Taylor and M. Woodford, eds., *Handbook of Macroeconomics*, edition 1, volume 1, chapter 20, 1305–1340.

Veldkamp, L. (2006), "Information Markets and the Comovement of Asset Prices," *Review of Economic Studies*, 73, 823-845.

Wilson, R., Keil, F. (1999), *The MIT Encyclopedia of the Cognitive Sciences*, Cambridge, MA: MIT Press.

The Budget Contraction Effect: Cutting Categories to Cope with Shrinking Budgets

Kurt A. Carlson, Georgetown University, USA
Jared Wolfe, Duke University, USA
Dan Ariely, Duke University, USA
Joel Huber, Duke University, USA

EXTENDED ABSTRACT

Economics provides a clear prediction for how consumers adjust spending when income declines. Consumers will move down the utility surface to an allocation that represents the highest utility for the new income level. Ceteris paribus, this allocation should be the same as the allocation when they were previously at this budget level. Put differently, the income contraction and the income expansion paths should be equivalent. As such, a consumer should arrive at the same allocation whether approached from a prior budget that was smaller or larger than the current budget. This paper presents evidence that budget contraction and expansion paths are not equivalent. Rather, consumers who arrive at a budget from a higher initial budget purchase fewer different types of products or services than consumers who arrive at the same budget from an initially lower one.

Participants in Study 1 (N=398) made nine budget allocations—three allocations for three different domains (groceries to buy with $40, $80, or $120; cities to visit in Europe in 7 days, 14 days, or 21 days; lottery tickets to buy with $5, $10, or $20). For each domain, participants made the three sequential budget allocations with the budget either expanding (e.g., $40, $80, $120) or contracting (e.g., $120, $80, $40).

Results reveal that participants in the expanding grocery budget condition spread their $80 budget across more different products (M=4.69) than did participants in the contracting budget condition (M=4.27; $t(396)=2.76$, $p<.01$). Additionally, the difference in number of items purchased (expanding budget minus contracting budget) decreased as the size of the budget increased from $40 (D=.59) to $120 (D=.38). Though each of these differences is statistically significant (all $p<.05$), the pattern is important because it suggests that the contracting budget is the main driver of the effect. To see why, consider that the comparison between $40 budget allocations involves a comparison of participants who faced two budget contractions to those making their first budget allocation without a prior budget change. If the effect is due to contraction of budgets, the difference should be largest here (e.g., larger than the differences between $120 budget allocations), as it is.

Allocations in the travel and lottery ticket domains mirror these findings. Participants with 14 days to travel planned to visit more cities when the travel budget increased to 14 days (M=6.47) than when it contracted to 14 days (M=5.64; $t(396)=2.71$, $p<.01$). And the difference in number of cities visited (increasing budget minus decreasing budget) decreased from 1.34 ($p<.001$) at the smallest budget (7 days) to .32 (p=.33) at the largest budget (21 days). Likewise, participants in the expanding lottery budget condition selected more different types of lottery tickets (M=3.07) with the $10 budget than participants whose budget contracted (M=2.81). And the difference in allocations is largest and significant for the smallest budget level (mean difference=.31; $t(396)=2.32$, $p<.05$), and not significant (mean difference=.27; $t(396)=1.24$, $p>.20$) for the largest budget level.

Study 2 used an investment domain to test whether the budget contraction effect would extend to situations in which there was carryover from one budget allocation to the next. Participants (N=189) made investment allocation decisions for three different budgets under conditions of an expanding budget ($500, $1000, $1500) or a contracting budget ($1500, $1000, $500). The second and third allocations presumed that the results of the prior allocations were still relevant (i.e. participants still had the allocations from those budgets as part of their retirement portfolio).

When allocating $500 to the four investments, participants in the contracting condition invested in fewer different investments than those in the expanding condition (2.55 versus 3.03; $t(187)=2.79$, $p<.01$). Allocations for the $1000 and $1500 budgets did not differ significantly for budget contraction versus budget expansion ($1000 budget: 3.08 versus 2.95; $t(187)=0.83$, $p=0.41$; $1500 budget: 3.21 versus 3.17; $t(187)=.27$, $p=.79$, respectively). These data strongly support the two-path model and confirm that the driver of the effect is the contracting budget.

Study 3 tested whether the effect extends to real choices consisting of a large number of options. Participants (N=129) selected three assortments of mp3s (4 songs, 8 songs, 12 songs) to purchase from over a million songs available at amazon.com. Participants were told that one participant would be selected at random to actually receive one of their selected assortments. Assortments were made under conditions of an expanding budget (4 songs, 8 songs, 12 songs) or a contracting budget (12 songs, 8 songs, 4 songs). Breadth of each assortment was assessed by coding the number of different artists/bands present in each assortment.

For the 4-song budget, participants in the contracting budget condition chose songs by a significantly smaller number of artists/bands (M=3.40) than those in the expanding budget condition (M=3.76; $t(122)=-2.603$, $p<.01$). However, there were no significant differences in the number of different artists/bands selected between the two groups in either the 8-song budget (Contracting M=6.21, Expanding M=6.61, $t(122)=-1.099$, $p=0.27$) or the 12-song budget (Contracting M=9.18, Expanding M=9.11, $t(121)=.129$, $p=.90$).

These studies have demonstrated an asymmetry in budget expansion and contraction paths such that for a given budget, consumers who arrive at a particular budget from a higher initial budget purchase fewer different products or services than a consumer who arrives at that same budget from an initially lower budget. This asymmetry in budget expansion and contraction paths stems mainly from a decrease in variety of the selected assortment under budget contraction rather than from an increase in variety selected under budget expansion.

Trying Harder and Doing Worse: How Grocery Shoppers Track Their In-Store Spending

Koert van Ittersum, Georgia Institute of Technology, USA
Joost M. E. Pennings, Maastricht University, The Netherlands
Brian Wansink, Cornell University, USA

EXTENDED ABSTRACT

Introduction

An estimated one in three American households has to carefully plan their budgets and spend accordingly. Budget-allocation and spending-behavior models often implicitly assume that budget-constrained shoppers are knowledgeable about the total price of their shopping basket as they shop (Bénabou and Tirole 2004). Because shoppers' price estimates of their shopping baskets mediate the relationship between budget allocation and actual in-store spending, it is critical to understand whether and how shoppers determine the total price of their baskets. Inaccuracies in their estimates likely have implications for consumer welfare (Heath and Soll 1996) and retail performance (Gómez, McLaughlin, and Wittink 2004).

Despite the importance of understanding how budget-constrained shoppers estimate the total price of their baskets while shopping, it remains largely unclear whether, when, and how they keep track of their in-store spending.

Pilot Study: Do Grocery Shoppers Track Their In-Store Spending?

To asses whether, when, and how budget-constrained grocery shoppers keep track of how much they are spending while shopping, a field study was conducted that involved 293 shoppers who were intercepted at the end of their shopping trip in one of two supermarkets: one located in a lower ($22,540/yr) and one located in a higher household income area ($46.478/yr). We find that 84.6% of the 293 participants claim to keep track of how much they are spending while shopping for groceries. By far the most dominant reason for tracking their in-store spending is having budget constraints (87.6%). Three distinct tracking strategies are identified: mental computation strategies (57.4%), calculators (26.4%), and shopping lists (14.5%). Of those who rely on mental computation strategies, 92.3% predominantly add prices up on a price-by-price basis: 45.2% round prices up before adding them, 24.0% round prices up and down to $0.00, $0.10, and $0.25, 14.4% add the exact price of each item, and 11.5% focus only on the dollar amount, ignoring the dollar-cents. The results also show that shoppers who have to pay more than expected based on their own estimate attribute this to the retailer, which in turn negatively influences store satisfaction.

While the pilot study established the relevance of in-store tracking and the predominant reliance on mental computation strategies, the results also raise questions. For instance, why is the rounding strategy the seemingly dominant mental computation strategy? To answer this and other questions, we first discuss the relevant literature and then present the results of two lab studies.

Computational Estimation Strategies

To avoid the stress associated with *calculating* the *exact* total basket price, shoppers are proposed to *estimate* the *approximate* total basket price using *computational estimation strategies*–strategies to find an *approximate* answer to arithmetic problems without actually calculating the *exact* answer (Dowker 1992; Reys 1986). The most common computational estimation strategies are: *a) Front-end Estimation Strategy*. A front-end strategy would lead shoppers to estimate the total price of their shopping basket based on the left, front-end dollar digits, ignoring the right-most digits, the dollar-cents (Lemaire et al. 2000). *b) Rounding Estimation Strategy*. The rounding strategy involves rounding numbers up prior to adding them (Lemaire and Lecacheur 2002). *c) Compatible Numbers Estimation Strategy*. The compatible numbers strategy involves organizing numbers into groups of compatible numbers to make the computation easier (Dowker 1992). *d) Special Numbers Estimation Strategy*. The special numbers strategy involves identifying numbers near "special" values that are easy to compute with (Reys 1986), such as those that are powers of ten or common fractions and decimals, including $0.00. *e) Clustering Strategy*. The clustering strategy is a non-additive strategy that estimates the total basket price by multiplying the number of products in the basket by the estimated median price of the items in the basket.

To gain a better understanding about how people estimate the total price of their baskets using mental computation strategies, we explore if shoppers are adaptive estimators who weigh the importance of being accurate against the cognitive effort they can and are willing to invest and select the strategy that is perceived to offer the best combination of accuracy and complexity given the estimation conditions (Johnson and Payne 1985).

Lab Experiments

To examine the adaptivity of estimators, we take an experimental approach to manipulate specific context and task variables of the estimation task: price endings of the basket items, motivation to be accurate, and estimation task experience. We measure 1) which estimation strategies shoppers rely upon under which conditions, 2) their estimation accuracy, and 3) the perceived task complexity.

We demonstrate that short-term memory constraints prevent shoppers to effectively rely on the *calculation strategy* to estimate the *exact* total price of shopping baskets. Reliance on the calculation strategy results in more biased, less accurate estimates than reliance on *computational estimation strategies*. These results explain why estimation performance reduces with shoppers' motivation to be accurate–motivated consumers are willing to incur more cognitive cost to achieve a higher estimation performance by relying on the calculation strategy. Although motivation has a counterproductive effect on the estimation performance among inexperienced consumers, it improves estimation performance among experienced consumers. We further demonstrate that shoppers adapt their strategy to different price-ending conditions based on the perceived cognitive complexity and accuracy, which explains why shoppers in the pilot study predominantly rely on the rounding strategy to estimate the total price of their shopping baskets.

Field Study

To provide evidence for the assumption that shoppers' estimates influence actual in-store spending, another field study was conducted involving 46 grocery shoppers. The results demonstrate that estimation biases relate to spending biases, putting shoppers underestimating the total price of their basket at risk of spending more than they budgeted for.

Conclusion

Because shoppers' price estimates of their shopping baskets mediate the relationship between budget allocation and actual in-store spending, it is critical to understand whether and how shoppers determine the total price of their shopping baskets. Understanding which estimation strategy is most efficient and accurate in which specific context, among others, allows for more effective consumer education, which in turn may help improve consumer welfare as well as retail performance.

References

Bénabou, Roland and Jean Tirole (2004), "Willpower and Personal Rules," *Journal of Political Economy*, 112 (4), 848-86.

Dowker, Ann (1992), "Computational Estimation Strategies of Professional Mathematicians," *Journal for Research in Mathematics Education*, 23 (1), 45-55.

Gómez, Niguel I., Edward W. McLaughlin, and Dick R. Wittink (2004), "Customer Satisfaction and Retail Sales Performance: An Empirical Investigation," *Journal of Retailing*, 80, 265-278.

Heath, Chip and Jack B. Soll (1996), "Mental Budgeting and Consumer Decisions," *Journal of Consumer Research*, 23 (June), 40-52.

Johnson, Eric J. and John W. Payne (1985), "Effort and Accuracy in Choice," *Management Science*, 31 (4), 395-414.

Lemaire, Patrick and Mireille Lecacheur (2002), "Children's Strategies in Computational Estimation," *Journal of Experimental Child Psychology*, 82, 281-304.

Lemaire, Patrick, Mireille Lecacheur, and Fernand Farioli (2000), "Children's Strategy Use in Computational Estimation," *Canadian Journal of Experimental Psychology*, 54 (2) (June), 141-148.

Reys, Barbara (1986), "Teaching Computational Estimation: Concepts and Strategies," in *Estimation and Mental Computation,* H.L. Schoen and M.J. Zweng, eds. . Reston, VA: National Council of Teachers of Mathematics, 31-44.

Tracking Costs of Time and Money

Robin L. Soster, University of South Carolina, USA
Ashwani Monga, University of South Carolina, USA
William O. Bearden, University of South Carolina, USA

EXTENDED ABSTRACT

People often incur costs first, and receive benefits later, but track both via mental accounts (Thaler 1980, 1985, 1999). For instance, the purchase of a basketball-game ticket could initiate a basketball-game account in the consumer's mind, which eventually gets closed as a net gain (i.e., pleasure) or a net loss (i.e., pain). That is, the account is settled in the black if the consumer receives the benefit (i.e., attends the game), but in the red if the consumer forfeits the benefit (i.e., misses the game) (Prelec and Loewenstein 1998). Because of several reasons, such as the desire to avoid waste (Arkes and Blumer 1985) and the need to justify prior choices (Staw 1981), people often refuse to close an account in the red even when closing it makes economic sense. For instance, after people have incurred costs on tickets to a game, they are willing to brave a snowstorm to attend the game, even though they would readily miss it if they had received the tickets for free (Soman 2001; Thaler 1980, 1999). Such a tendency has been termed the sunk-cost fallacy (Arkes and Blumer 1985; Thaler 1980) because, from an economic standpoint, the decision of going to the game should be based on future benefits (attending the game) and future costs (traveling in a snowstorm), but not on prior costs (cost of ticket). However, because of the pervasiveness of mental accounts, prior costs do influence the propensity to seek future benefits.

Soman (2001) discusses how the mental-accounting processes described above apply to costs of money, but not time. He argues that individuals lack the ability to account for time because, unlike doctors and lawyers, most people do not routinely keep track of time the way they keep track of money. Consequently, unless interventions (e.g., education about the value of time) are employed to make time seem like money, mental accounting for time breaks down. That is, future benefits are not linked to prior costs, and the sunk-cost effect does not emerge.

In the current research, we demonstrate that people do engage in mental accounting for time, and via a process that can be seen as more elaborate than that for money. Specifically, accounts for time consider not only costs and benefits, as accounts of money do, but also "accounting periods" (day, vacation, etc.). Consequently, people link temporal costs to benefits when both costs and benefits belong to the same accounting period, but do not link them when they occur in different periods. In the case of monetary costs, this moderating effect of accounting periods is relatively weak.

The current research adds to prior work on mental accounting (Thaler 1980, 1985, 1999) by introducing the concept of accounting period, which aids our understanding of the process by which people track costs and corresponding benefits. It also augments our understanding of time-money differences. For example, Soman (2001) argues that people are not good at keeping track of prior costs of time, because of which the sunk-cost effect (Arkes and Blumer 1985) does not emerge for time as it does for money. We show that, contingent on the accounting period, people do exhibit sensitivity to past costs of time, and the sunk cost effect does emerge. The concept of accounting periods also provides a new perspective of prior findings in time discounting, consumer search, risk preferences, and other areas.

REFERENCES

Areni, Charles (2008), "Salvation of the Second Shift: Are Wives Immune to Monday Blues?" in *Advances in Consumer Research*, Vol. 36, ed. Ann L. McGill and Sharon Shavitt, Duluth, MN : Association for Consumer Research, Page 136.

Arkes, Hal R. and Catherine Blumer (1985), "The Psychology of Sunk Cost," *Organizational Behavior and Human Decision Processes*, 35 (February), 124-40.

Camerer, Colin, Linda Babcock, George Loewenstein, and Richard Thaler (1997), "Labor Supply of New York City Cabdrivers: One Day at a Time," *Quarterly Journal of Economics*, 112, (May), 407-41.

Feldman, Laurence P. and Jacob Hornik (1981), "The Use of Time: An Integrated Conceptual Model," *Journal of Consumer Research*, 7 (March), 407-19.

Gourville, John T. and Dilip Soman (1998), "Payment Depreciation: The Behavioral Effects of Temporally Separating Payments from Consumption," *Journal of Consumer Research*, 25 (September), 160-74.

Graham, Robert J. (1981), "The Role of Perception of Time in Consumer Research," *Journal of Consumer Research*, 7 (March), 335-42.

Gross, Barbara L. (1987), "Time Scarcity: Interdisciplinary Perspectives and Implications for Consumer Behavior," in *Research in Consumer Behavior*, 2, ed. Jagdish N. Sheth and Elizabeth Hirschman, CT: JAI Greenwich, 1-54.

Jarvis, Sarah and Stephen Jenkins (1998), "How Much Income Mobility is there in Britain?" *The Economic Journal*, 108 (March), 428-43.

Kahneman, Daniel and Amos Tversky (1979), "Prospect Theory: An Analysis of Decision Under Risk," *Econometrica*, 47 (March), 263-91.

LeClerc, France, Bernd H. Schmitt, and Laurette Dubé (1995), "Waiting Time and Decision Making: Is Time Like Money?" *Journal of Consumer Research*, 22 (June), 110-19.

Linville, Patricia W. and Gregory W. Fischer (1991), "Preferences for Separating or Combining Events," *Journal of Personality and Social Psychology*, 60 (January), 5-23.

Monga, Ashwani and Ritesh Saini (2009), "Currency of Search: How Spending Time on Search is Not the Same as Spending Money," *Journal of Retailing*, 85 (September), 245-257.

Okada, Erica Mina and Stephen J. Hoch (2004), "Spending Time versus Spending Money," *Journal of Consumer Research*, 31 (September), 313-23.

Prelec, Drazen and George Loewenstein (1998), "The Red and the Black: Mental Accounting of Savings and Debt," *Marketing Science*, 17 (March), 4-28.

Rizzo, John A. and Richard J. Zeckhauser (2003), "Reference Incomes, Loss Aversion, and Physician Behavior," *Review of Economics and Statistics*, 85 (November), 909-22.

Saini, Ritesh and Ashwani Monga (2008), "How I Decide Depends on What I Spend: Use of Heuristics is Greater for Time than for Money," *Journal of Consumer Research*, 34 (April), 914-22.

Soman, Dilip (2001), "The Mental Accounting of Sunk Time Costs: Why Time is not Like Money," *Journal of Behavior Decision Making*, 14 (July), 169-85.

Soman, Dilip and John T. Gourville (2001), "Transaction Decoupling: How Price Bundling Affects the Decision to Consume," *Journal of Marketing Research*, 38 (February), 30-44.

Staw, Barry M. (1981), "The Escalation of Commitment to a Course of Action," *Academy of Management Review*, 6 (October), 577-87.

Thaler, Richard H. (1980), "Toward a Positive Theory of Consumer Choice," *Journal of Economic Behavior and Organization*, 1 (March), 39-60.

Thaler, Richard H. (1985). "Mental Accounting and Consumer Choice," *Marketing Science*, 4 (Summer), 199-214.

Thaler, Richard H. (1999), "Mental Accounting Matters," *Journal of Behavioral Decision Making*, 12 (September), 183-206.

Relative vs. Absolute Comparison of Prices

Keith S. Coulter, Clark University, USA
Pilsik Choi, Clark University, USA

EXTENDED ABSTRACT

The widely used practice of comparative price advertising has been a focal point of consumer and marketing research for decades (e.g., Compeau and Grewal 1998). Marketers may engage in comparative price advertising by: a) contrasting a higher "regular" price with a lower "sale" price, or b) comparing a "competitor's" price to the marketer's own sale price (Compeau, Grewal, and Chandrashekaran 2002). In either case, the higher regular (or competitor's) price serves as an externally supplied frame of reference, which leads consumers to perceive less benefit from continued search (Urbany, Bearden, and Weilbaker 1988), and to associate less sacrifice with the lower sale price (Compeau et al. 2002). Consequently, comparative price advertising tends to engender more favorable consumer value perceptions, and marketers embrace this form of advertising as a means to affect consumers' purchase decisions and stimulate sales.

Comparison of regular-to-sale or competitor-to-marketer (sale) prices may also lead consumers to assess a price discount. That discount could be perceived in relative (i.e., as a percentage) or absolute terms. Absolute discount is defined as higher price minus lower price, whereas relative (percentage) discount is defined as [(higher price–lower price)/higher price]. Although the latter may involve a more complicated computational procedure, research has demonstrated that consumers exposed to comparative price advertisements containing regular and sale prices are able to assess relative price discounts with a fairly high degree of accuracy, even in relatively low involvement settings that evoke minimum cognitive expenditure (e.g., Coulter and Norberg 2009).

A preponderance of studies in the numerical cognition literature has demonstrated that numerical magnitude comparisons typically follow the Weber-Fechner Law. That is, numerical comparisons follow a log-linear function such that the perceived difference between numbers is compressed as the size of those numbers increases (Dehaene et al., 1990). Consequently, when making quantitative comparisons, one's ability to distinguish between two numbers (e.g., determine which is larger or smaller) is directly related to the *relative* difference between them (Deheane, 1992). Studies within the pricing literature confirm that perceived numerical differences may involve relative, rather than absolute, amounts (e.g., Kruger and Vargas 2008; Coulter and Norberg 2009). However, other recent studies suggest that consumers' evaluation of a price discount can be impacted by the *absolute* difference between the two prices (Thomas and Morwitz 2009). Therefore, a primary goal of the present study is to examine the circumstances under which a price difference might be assessed and encoded in relative versus absolute terms.

Understanding such a distinction is important because it allows the marketer to present his/her price comparison in the most favorable possible light. For example, consider two price discounts: \$222/\$211 and \$45/\$40. If consumers were more likely to assess absolute (relative) discounts in the former (latter) instance, then marketers might communicate the \$11 (rather than 5%) difference for the \$222/\$211 discount, but the 11% (rather than \$5) difference for the \$45/\$40 discount. In addition, research has shown that both conscious and non-conscious processes may operate at encoding to impact the perceived magnitude of a price discount. Price discount effects reported in the literature that are theoretically grounded in these processes include the "physical font size effect" (Coulter and Coulter 2005), "discount-distance congruency effect" (Coulter and Norberg 2009), "left digit effect" (Thomas and Morwitz 2005), "right digit effect" (Coulter and Coulter 2007), and "ease-of-computation effect" (Thomas and Morwitz 2009). All of the aforementioned effects depend on the manner in which prices are compared (i.e., in relative versus absolute terms). Thus knowledge of this comparison procedure allows the marketer to understand (and manipulate) the *other* perceptual processes that operate at encoding to impact discount assessments.

In this paper, we suggest that a comparison of sale price to regular price may be more likely to involve a relative (percent) assessment, whereas a comparison of the marketer's own sale price to a competitor' price may be more likely to involve an absolute difference assessment. We further suggest that the physical placement of prices in a comparative price advertisement may impact how those prices are contrasted. Because horizontal (i.e., side-by-side) physical placement hinders digit-by-digit comparison, that type of format may result in more holistic price processing and a greater tendency to estimate discounts in relative terms. Conversely, vertical (i.e., columnar) placement facilitates digit-by-digit comparison, and therefore may result in a greater tendency to calculate the absolute numerical difference.

We examined our hypotheses in the context of two Experiments. In E1 subjects were asked to evaluate the magnitudes of a series of price discounts, which were represented by two prices presented to them on successive computer screens. The instructions did not specify whether the magnitudes were to be assessed in absolute or relative terms, but did specify that the higher prices referred to either a competitor's prices, or the seller's own "regular" prices. We measured the perceived magnitude of the discounts on a 10-point semantic differential scale anchored by "small" (1) and "large" (10). Reaction time (i.e., the 2nd dependent variable) was measured in milliseconds using a commercially available response-time software. A 2 (separation: horizontal, vertical) x 2 (higher price: competitor vs. regular) x 15 (absolute difference: range=1-92) x 27 (relative numerical difference: range=1.10%-50%) mixed between/within-subjects design was employed. Preliminary ANOVA results revealed that when subjects were told that the higher price referred to a competitor's (regular) price, the absolute (relative) difference between prices affected both discount magnitude perceptions and reaction time. Further when prices were viewed in vertical (horizontal) format, the absolute (relative) difference between prices impacted both discount magnitude perceptions as well as reaction time.

In order to assess the degree to which absolute versus relative difference drives consumer purchase in a forced choice scenario, we conducted a second experiment. In E2 eighteen participants are asked to choose between *two* sets of discounts, and choice/ reaction time was assessed using the same response-time software. Logistic regression revealed that participants chose the greater relative discount for 91% of horizontal comparisons, but for only 56% of vertical comparisons; vertical format was 2.13 times more likely to predict choice of the higher absolute difference than was horizontal format. Participants chose the greater relative discount for 78% of regular high price cases but for only 67% of competitor high price cases; the regular high price was .55 times *less* likely to predict choice of greater absolute discount than competitor high price.

Initial results from our two experiments support our contention that serial/columnar price presentation format and regular/competitor reference price designation will impact whether prices are compared in absolute or relative terms. These results have important implications for the marketing practitioner.

REFERENCES

Compeau, Larry D. and Dhruv Grewal (1998), "Comparative Price Advertising: An Integrative Review," *Journal of Public Policy and Marketing*, 17 (Fall), 257-73.

Compeau, Larry D., Dhruv Grewal, and R. Chandrashekaran (2002), "Comparative Price Advertising: Believe It or Not," *Journal of Consumer Affairs*, 36 (2), 284-94.

Coulter, Keith S. and Robin A. Coulter (2005), "Size Does Matter: The Effects of Magnitude Representation Congruency on Price Perceptions and Purchase Likelihood," *Journal of Consumer Psychology,* 15 (1), 64-76.

Coulter, Keith S. and Robin a. Coulter (2007), "Distortion of Price Discount Perceptions: The Right Digit Effect." *Journal of Consumer Research,* 34 (2), 162-73.

Coulter, Keith S. and Patricia A. Norberg (2009), "The Impact of Physical Distance on Price Discount Perceptions," *Journal of Consumer Psychology*, 19 (2), April, 144-57.

Dehaene, Stanislas (1992), "Varieties of Numerical Abilities," *Cognition*, 44 (1-2), 1-42.

Dehaene, Stanislas, Emmanuel Dupoux, and Jacques Muehler (1990), "Is Numerical Comparison Digital? Analogical and Symbolic Effects in Two-Digit Number Comparison," *Journal of Experimental Psychology: Human Perception and Performance*, 16, 626-41.

Kruger, Justin and Vargas, Patrick (2008), "Consumer Confusion of Percent Differences," *Journal of Consumer Psychology*, 18, 49-61.

Thomas, Manoj and Vicki Morwitz (2005), "Penny Wise and Pound Foolish: The Left Digit Effect in Price Cognition," *Journal of Consumer Research*, 32 (June), 54-64.

Thomas, Manoj and Vicki Morwitz (2009), "The Ease-of-Computation Effect: The Interplay of Metacognitive Experiences and Naïve Theories in Judgments of Price Differences," *Journal of Marketing Research,* 46 (1), 81-91.

Urbany, Joel E., William O. Bearden, and Dan Weilbaker (1988), "The Effect of Plausible and Exaggerated Reference Prices on Consumer Perceptions and Price Search," *Journal of Consumer Research*, 15 (June), 95-110.

What Do these Clinical Trial Results Mean for Me? How Personally Relevant Decisions are affected by Data Framing, Partitioning, and Quantification

Dipayan Biswas, Bentley University, USA
Cornelia Pechmann University of California, Irvine, USA

EXTENDED ABSTRACT

If I take a prescription pain reliever such as Maxalt, what is the probability that I will get relief? If I drive a Toyota Prius and I get in a car crash, what is the probability that I will get seriously hurt? Consumers often make judgments about personal well-being while evaluating products, and regulations increasingly require that clinical trial and product test data be provided to consumers (Landro 2004). However, such data can be quite complicated to interpret and how the interpretation is done may depend on many factors. When consumers make a decision about their own personal well-being or behavior, it is called a personally relevant decision (Levin, Schnittjer, and Thee 1988). Research indicates that for personally relevant decisions, consumers want to process any given data in an unbiased way to make the best judgments (Levin, Schneider, and Gaeth 1998; Levin et al. 1988). However, whether consumers are actually able to do so may depend on the data format. The data format may vary in several ways, but we focus primarily on three factors that have theoretical and practical significance: (1) data partitioning–that is, whether product efficacy results from multiple studies or subject groups are reported separately or aggregated (Morwitz, Greenleaf, and Johnson 1998), (2) data quantification–whether the product efficacy results are presented as frequencies or equivalent percentages (Cuite et al. 2008), and (3) attribute framing–whether the product efficacy results are framed in terms of successes or equivalent failures (Levin and Gaeth 1988).

Prior studies have examined the effects of data partitioning versus aggregation (Cheema and Soman 2008; Morwitz, Greenleaf, and Johnson 1998). However, these studies did not examine the interaction effects between data partitioning and data framing or data quantification. Attribute framing refers to describing outcomes "in terms of success versus failure rates" (Levin, Schneider and Gaeth 1998, p. 159). Numerous studies indicate that framing attribute information about products in terms of successes rather than the equivalent failures enhances product evaluations (Levin et al. 1998; Mittal, Ross, and Tsiros 2002; Zhang and Mittal 2005). It is believed that the positive frame or cue (e.g., 75% lean) evokes favorable thoughts whereas the negative frame or cue (e.g., 25% fat) evokes unfavorable thoughts, generally without conscious awareness (Levin et al. 1998). However, researchers have found that when decisions have personal relevance, the frame is rendered inconsequential (see Levin et al. 1998 review; also Janiszewski et al. 2003; Levin et al. 1988; McElroy and Seta 2003). People are motivated to evaluate the alternate frame in addition to the given frame due to their high level of personal interest in the issue. In other words, people are motivated to consider both the probability of success and failure, regardless of how the data is framed. The question we ask is whether the frame might sometimes bias judgments despite personal relevance. In particular, might the frame bias judgments when the data are in a partitioned frequency format and there is low processing ability? Our research is the first to examine this issue. We conducted four experiments to test our hypotheses.

The results of our first experiment (which used sunscreen as a product) replicated the findings of prior literature, whereby personal relevance enhanced processing motivation. Hence, for decisions made under personal relevance, there were no framing effects. However, framing effects emerged when there was no personal relevance.

The results of our second experiment (which used prescription pain reliever Maxalt as a product, and its actual package insert as experimental stimuli material) showed that the combination of partitioned data and frequency data reduces the ability to process, relative to aggregated data or percentage data. Therefore, the combination of partitioned data and frequency data evoked a framing bias despite personal relevance, in that a success versus failure frame favorably biased judgments. Aggregated data or percentage data did not evoke this bias.

The third experiment again used sunscreen as a product, and examined how data variance might influence the effects of partitioning and framing. This experiment also examined actual consumer choice behavior in terms of choosing between a focal versus a control sunscreen. We wanted to examine if when the partitioned data points have high variance or variability, the frame may be invalidated or discredited as a heuristic cue (Schwarz and Clore 1983, 2003). The results of this experiment supported such a hypothesis. That is, under low data variance, framing bias was observed with partitioned frequency data. However, high data variance nullified the framing bias with partitioned frequency data.

Finally, in our fourth experiment, we attempted to empirically verify our assumption that data partitioning is the major cause of the framing bias that is observed with low variance frequency data. We showed participants a single data point and asked for personally relevant judgments. Then we showed participants a second and a third data point, rendering the data partitioned, and asked for their judgments after each subsequent data point. We posited that there would be no framing bias with a single data point, but that the framing bias would emerge with the second data point and especially with the third data point. That is, the framing bias would appear and strengthen as the data became more partitioned and processing became increasingly difficult. The results of this experiment supported our hypothesis.

In conclusion, the results of our experiments would have implications both for marketers as well as for regulators, in terms of designing optimal formats for presenting information from product and/or clinical trials and tests. In terms of academic implications, this research is the first to examine the interaction effects between data framing, partitioning, and quantification; while prior studies found lack of framing effects under personal relevance, our experiments demonstrate that even when there is personal relevance, framing effect biases can emerge for partitioned frequency data.

REFERENCES

Cheema, Amar and Dilip Soman (2008), "The Effect of Partitions on Controlling Consumption," *Journal of Marketing Research*, 45 (6), 665-75.

Cuite, Cara L., Neil D. Weinstein, Karen Emmons, and Graham Colditz (2008), "A Test of Numeric Formats for Communicating Risk Probabilities," *Medical Decision Making*, 28 (3), 377-84.

Janiszewski, Chris, Tim Silk, and Alan D. J. Cooke (2003), "Different Scales for Different Frames: The Role of Subjective Scales and Experience in Explaining Attribute-Framing Effects," *Journal of Consumer Research*, 30 (3), 311-25.

Landro, Laura (2004), "The Informed Patient: How to Find the Latest on Results of Clinical Trials-as Groups Debate Access to Research, Existing Sources of Information Are Growing," *The Wall Street Journal*, June 17, 2004, 1-4.

Levin, Irwin P. and Gary J. Gaeth (1988), "How Consumers Are Affected by the Framing of Attribute Information before and after Consuming the Product," *Journal of Consumer Research*, 15 (3), 374-78.

______, Sandra L. Schneider, and Gary J. Gaeth (1998), "All Frames Are Not Created Equal: A Typology and Critical Analysis of Framing Effects," *Organizational Behavior & Human Decision Processes*, 76 (2), 149-88.

______, Sara K. Schnittjer, and Shannon L. Thee (1988), "Information Framing Effects in Social and Personal Decisions," *Journal of Experimental Social Psychology*, 24 (6), 520-29.

McElroy, Todd and John J. Seta (2003), "Framing Effects: An Analytic-Holistic Perspective," *Journal of Experimental Social Psychology*, 39 (6), 610-17.

Mittal, Vikas, William T. Ross, and Michael Tsiros (2002), "The Role of Issue Valence and Issue Capability in Determining Effort Investment," *Journal of Marketing Research*, 39 (4), 455-68.

Morwitz, Vicki G., Eric A. Greenleaf, and Eric J. Johnson (1998), "Divide and Prosper: Consumers' Reactions to Partitioned Prices," *Journal of Marketing Research*, 35 (4), 453-63.

Schwarz, Norbert, Herbert Bless, Fritz Strack, and Gisela Klumpp (1991), "Ease of Retrieval as Information: Another Look at the Availability Heuristic," *Journal of Personality and Social Psychology*, 61 (2), 195-202.

Schwarz, Norbert and Gerald L. Clore (1983), "Mood, Misattribution, and Judgments of Well-Being: Informative and Directive Functions of Affective States," *Journal of Personality and Social Psychology*, 45 (3), 513-23.

______ (2003), "Mood as Information: 20 Years Later," *Psychological Inquiry*, 14 (3&4), 296-303.

Zhang, Yinlong and Vikas Mittal (2005), "Decision Difficulty: Effects of Procedural and Outcome Accountability," *Journal of Consumer Research*, 32 (3), 465-72.

It's Been My Number One Source of Stress for Months: The Decision to Pay for Care

Aimee Dinnin Huff, University of Western Ontario, Canada
June Cotte, University of Western Ontario, Canada

EXTENDED ABSTRACT

The experience of choosing care for a family member–a young child or an elderly parent–is not unfamiliar to many consumers. Child and elder care represent a significant area of consumer spending: the American adult nursing care and child care industries include nearly 140,000 facilities, which generated revenue in excess of $160 billion in 2008. Although care decisions and outcomes have been explored in other disciplines, including sociology, gerontology, and economics, we are not aware of any consumer research that has addressed care decisions. Therefore, there is an opportunity to explore and understand the experiences of these decision makers as they interact with the market for care services.

Care decisions are also an important area of study because they are typically experienced very differently than decisions for standard consumer products. Prior research in other fields has shown that care decisions are complex and emotionally distressing, and from a consumer research perspective it seems doubtful that choosing care for one's infant is comparable to shopping for an automobile or choosing a vacation. In this research, we take an interpretive approach to understand how care decisions are experienced within the sociological context. Elder and childcare decisions were chosen because they both involve role transitions pertaining to the needs of immediate family members.

We began with the question, "How do everyday consumers experience care decisions for family member?" Related prompts pertained to the types of emotions and reactions experienced during the decision process, the identification of other factors influencing the decision, and reflections on what informants felt was expected of them. We conducted 18 depth interviews with adults who had recently made a care decision for a child or elderly parent, or who were in the process of making that decision. Following the phenomenological interview method, we asked informants to share their stories about making a care decision. Interviews were conducted one-on-one, face-to-face, and typically lasted 75 minutes. Most interviews took place at informants' homes.

In the spirit of rigorous interpretive analysis, we began our data analysis by reviewing and reflecting on the audiotapes, field notes, and transcripts. After thematically coding individual transcripts, we discussed emergent themes and sought to reveal idiosyncratic and shared meanings. The interpretation process involved part-to-whole comparisons and our findings were developed through much iteration.

At a descriptive level, our research uncovers anxious, often naïve decision-makers, unprepared for the situation and experiencing great difficulty negotiating their new role in the family. What resembles a traditional consumer search process is overlaid with nervousness, anxiety, guilt, and exhaustion, forcing consumers to create and adhere to priorities that help them legitimize their ultimate choices. From our data, it is clear that decision-makers are overwhelmed and exhausted by the decision context and the outcomes related to the choice. Other important aspects of the care decision experience include various coping strategies, and reconciling self-conflict through conscious struggles to come to terms with guilt, real and perceived obligation, and the reality of the choice situation. Although commitment and love for the family members requiring care are unmistakable, our informants' experiences with care decisions are charged with negative emotions.

In our interpretation of the data, we relied on literature pertaining to role transitions, family identity, and production and consumption of caring. Choosing care for a family member marks an important role status transition, and prior research has demonstrated that in times of liminality, consumption can both facilitate and complicate role transitions. As consumers become aware of a need to choose a care service, they experience a turning point where they must juggle multiple roles (e.g., care-giver and professional), interact and make decisions with different relational units within the family, and manage the production and consumption of caring for the family member in need. At each stage of the transition, the decision maker must balance his/her own needs with those of the child or elderly parent. Thus, the turning point ultimately creates tension between the desire for self-fulfillment and feelings of obligation to family members.

The concept of ambivalence is useful for understanding the contradictory normative expectations felt by consumers as they interact with the marketplace to choose care services. Ambivalence is not a state of internal conflict, per se; rather, it can be conceptualized as an awareness of irreconcilability, and a link between individual action and social structure. In this way, an understanding of ambivalence–both at the individual level and the social structural level–can facilitate an interpretation of data because it accounts for contradictory emotions and thoughts experienced as consumers attempt to negotiate incompatible expectations imposed by themselves and relevant social structures (e.g., culture, family, gender).

Our interpretation revealed four themes tied to ambivalence: the desire to prioritize one's own needs and wishes when choosing care for a family member; unease tied to the conscious awareness that reality differs from an ideal situation; consciousness of one's role within the family; and guilt that the outcome is somehow less than optimal and real or perceived expectations have not been met.

We focus on individual decision-makers within the family. Recent advances in consumer literature have demonstrated that the family is an important unit of analysis, and future research could explore how selection of care services is accomplished within the family. It would also be useful to examine childcare and eldercare experiences separately, thereby allowing for a richer understanding of the unique complexities and contexts of each phenomenon. Additionally, future research work could productively focus on the lack of coherent public policy and public support for children and elder care, and the cultural role of stay-at-home parental caregivers.

REFERENCES

Auerbach, Jessica (2007), *And Nanny Makes Three*, New York: St. Martens Press.

Belsky, Jay (1988), "The 'Effects' of Infant Day Care Reconsidered," *Early Childhood Research Quarterly*, 3 (3), 235-72.

Brody, Elaine M. (2004), *Women in the Middle: Their Parent Care Years*, New York: Springer Publishing Company.

Cheever, Susan (2002), "The Nanny Dilemma," in *Global Woman: Nannies, Maids and Sex Workers in the New Economy*, ed. Barbara Ehrenreich and Arlie Russell Hochschild, New York: Owl Books/Henry Hold.

Clarke, Edward J., Mar Preston, Jo Raskin, and Vern L. Bengtson (1999), "Types of Conflicts and Tensions between Older Parents and Adult Children," *The Gerontologist*, 39 (3), 261-70.

Clarke-Stewart, Alison and Virginia D. Allhusen (2005), *What We Know About Childcare*, Cambridge, MA: Harvard University Press.

Connelly, Rachel and Jean Kimmel (2003), "Marital Status and Full-Time/Part-Time Work Status in Child Care Choices," *Applied Economics*, 35 (7), 761-77.

Connidis, Ingrid Arnet (2010), *Family Ties & Aging*, Thousand Oaks, CA: Sage Publications.

Connidis, Ingrid Arnet and Julie Ann McMullin (2002), "Sociological Ambivalence and Family Ties: A Critical Perspective," *Journal of Marriage and Family*, 64 (August), 558-67.

Davies, Andrea, Susan Dobscha, Susi Geiger, Stephanie O'Donohoe, Lisa O'Malley, Andrea Prothero, Elin Brandi Sorensen, and Thyra Uth Thomsen (2010), "Buying into Motherhood? Problematic Consumption and Ambivalence in Transitional Phases," *Consumption, Markets and Culture*, forthcoming.

Ehrenreich, Barbara and Arlie Russell Hochschild (2002), "Introduction," in *Global Woman: Nannies, Maids and Sex Workers in the New Economy*, ed. Barbara Ehrenreich and Arlie Russell Hochschild, New York: Owl Books/Henry Hold.

Ekstrom, Karin M. (2004), "Family Consumption," *Consumption, Markets and Culture*, 7 (3), 185-90.

Epp, Amber M. and Linda L. Price (2008), "Family Identity: A Framework of Identity Interplay in Consumption Practices," *Journal of Consumer Research*, 35 (June), 50-70.

Hogg, Margaret K., Carolyn Folkman Curasi, and Pauline Maclaran (2004), "The (Re-) Configuration of Production and Consumption in Empty Nest Households/ Families," *Consumption, Markets and Culture*, 7 (3), 239-59.

Kaylin, Lucy (2007), *The Perfect Stranger: The Truth About Mothers and Nannies*, New York: Bloomsbury.

Leach, Penelope (2009), *Child Care Today*, New York: Random House

Luescher, Kurn and Karl Pillemer (1998), "Intergenerational Ambivalence: A New Approach to the Study of Parent-Child Relations in Later Life," *Journal of Marriage and Family*, 60 (May), 413-25.

Marks, Nadine F. (1998), "Does It Hurt to Care? Caregiving, Work-Family Conflict, and Midlife Well-Being," *Journal of Marriage & The Family*, 60 (4), 951-66.

Merrill, Deborah M. (1997), *Caring for Elderly Parents: Juggling Work, Family, and Caregiving in Middle and Working Class Families*, Westport, CT: Auburn House.

Moustakas, Clark E. (1994), *Phenomenological Research Methods*, Thousand Oaks CA: Sage Publications Inc.

Penrod, Janice and Cheryl Dellasga (1998), "Caregivers' Experiences in Making Placement Decisions," *Western Journal of Nursing Research*, 20 (6), 706-32.

Pugh, Allison J. (2004), "Windfall Child Rearing: Low-Income Care and Consumption," *Journal of Consumer Culture*, 4 (2), 229-49.

Spiggle, Susan (1994), "Analysis and Interpretation of Qualitative Data in Consumer Research," *Journal of Consumer Research*, 21 (December), 491-503.

Thompson, Craig J., William B. Locander, and Howard R. Pollio (1990), "The Lived Meaning of Free Choice: An Existential-Phenomenological Description of Everyday Consumer Experiences of Contemporary Married Women," *Journal of Consumer Research*, 17 (December), 346-61.

Thompson, Craig J., Howard R. Pollio, and William B Locander (1994), "The Spoken and the Unspoken: A Hermeneutic Approach to Understanding the Cultural Viewpoints That Underlie Consumers' Expressed Meanings," *Journal of Consumer Research*, 21 (December), 432-52.

Vincent, Carol and Stephen J. Ball (2006), *Childcare, Choice and Class Practices*, New York: Routledge.

What is the Relation between Cultural Orientation and Regulatory Mode?

David Silvera, University of Texas at San Antonio, USA
Ashok K. Lalwani, University of Texas at San Antonio, USA
Ashley Arsena, University of Texas at San Antonio, USA

EXTENDED ABSTRACT

Research delineates two distinct self-regulatory modes, which have been labeled *assessment* and *locomotion* (Kruglanski et al. 2000). Assessment is the aspect of self-regulation that focuses on comparisons and critical evaluations of entities or states (i.e., goals or means) in relation to different alternatives, whereas locomotion is the aspect of self-regulation that focuses on movement between states and commitment of psychological resources to initiate and maintain goal-related movement. Thus, both assessment and locomotion are important components of any self-regulatory activity. Indeed, regulatory mode has been shown to influence numerous and important marketing phenomena, ranging from product preferences and assessment of value to the relation between product decision strategies and willingness to pay for the selected product (Avnet and Higgins 2003; Higgins et al. 2003). The current article examines the association between cultural orientation and regulatory mode.

A number of findings suggest that collectivists are more likely to engage in detailed processing regarding social relationships, which is consistent with the focus of the assessment regulatory mode (Avnet and Higgins 2003). Within a collectivist culture, it is important for the individual to be sensitive to transgressions from consensual standards (Lalwani et al. 2006; 2009a; 2009b), and information regarding deviations from collectively shared standards is crucial to developing more appropriate behaviors for the future, affirming one's sense of belonging, and promoting harmony within the group (Kitayama et al. 1997). Because an assessment orientation has direct implications for a person's sensitivity to discrepancies from standards (Kruglanski et al. 2000), this suggests that assessment might be associated with a collectivist cultural orientation. Other evidence confirms that collectivists have a greater tendency than individualists to assess the reactions of others to their behavior in order to maintain harmonious relationships with them (Lalwani 2009).

With regard to locomotion, collectivist cultures are often characterized by clear in-group/out-group distinctions and a high degree of rigidity and inflexibility that makes it difficult for individuals to move from one group to another (Triandis 1989). The relative lack of social mobility in collectivist cultures suggests that locomotion goals might be less compatible with a collectivist cultural orientation. Conversely, the relatively high social mobility that characterizes many individualist cultures suggests that locomotion goals might be more compatible with an individualist cultural orientation. Research also suggests that assessment involves making decisions based on careful analysis and rationality (e.g., cost-benefit analysis; Weber, Ames, and Blais 2004), a decision-making style that has also been associated with individualism (Mintzberg 1989). Indeed, the logical thought process has its roots in individualism (Markus and Kitayama 1991; Gelfand and Dyer 2000). Similarly, in the context of negotiations, research indicates that collectivists are less likely to rely on logical analysis than individualists (Gelfand and Dyer 2000; Goldman 1994). This suggests that individualists will emphasize assessment more than collectivists, and preliminary support for this proposition is provided in a study by Weber et al. (2004), who conducted a content analysis of decisions made by characters in 29 bestselling and classic novels in China and the United States. Weber et al. (2004) found that decisions in Chinese novels were less rational and assessment oriented (i.e., less focused on careful evaluation and making the right or ideal choice) than those in American novels.

Several research findings are also consistent with the proposition that collectivists are more locomotion oriented than individualists. For example, research suggests that locomotion involves making decisions on the basis of intuition, set rules (e.g., time spent on a task) or personal roles (Weber, Ames, and Blais 2004). Collectivists have been shown to be more likely to rely on intuition and emotions than individualists (Mintzberg 1989). This suggests that collectivists may emphasize locomotion more than individualists, which is consistent with Weber et al.'s (2004) content analysis of novels in China and the United States which showed that Chinese decisions were more rule/role based and locomotion oriented than American decisions.

Four studies using a variety of operationalizations of culture (both situational and chronic) and regulatory mode suggest that individualists are more likely to emphasize assessment over collectivists, who in turn are more likely to emphasize locomotion. Moreover, we extend the findings to behavioral scenarios that consumers encounter in their day-to-day lives.

The article makes a number of theoretical and substantive contributions. Previous literature makes conflicting predictions regarding the link between cultural orientation and regulatory mode. The current article contributes to theory by delineating the exact relationships between the cultural values of individualism and collectivism and locomotion and assessment. Moreover, the article sheds unique insights into the goals of individualists and collectivists. For instance, because individualists are found to be assessment oriented, they might be relatively more perfectionistic than collectivists, as they attempt to compare all options available to them before arriving at decision, even if this process takes a long time (Kruglanski, Pierro, and Higgins 2007). Conversely, because collectivists are found to focus on locomotion, they might be especially concerned about making discernible progress on tasks and about making headway, even if the process results in suboptimal decisions (Pierro, Kruglanski, and Higgins 2006). Substantively, the differential self-regulatory functions emphasized by individualists and collectivists have potentially interesting implications in a number of domains, including decision making, self-consciousness, discomfort with ambiguity, decisiveness, and openness to change (Higgins et al. 2003). For instance, because a locomotion orientation has been associated with an increased likelihood of following an "elimination by aspects" decision strategy in choosing products (Kruglanski et al. 2007), collectivists might prefer similar decision strategies that enable them to make steady progress toward a goal.

REFERENCES

Avnet, Tamar and E. Tory Higgins (2003), "Locomotion, Assessment, and Regulatory Fit: Value Transfer from "How" to "What"," *Journal of Experimental Social Psychology*, 39 (5), 525-30.

Gelfand, Michele J. and Naomi Dyer (2000), "A Cultural Perspective on Negotiation:Progress, Pitfalls, and Prospects," *Applied Psychology: An International Review*, 49 (1), 62-99.

Goldman, Alan (1994), "The Centrality of ``Ningensei'' to Japanese Negotiations and Interpersonal Relationships: Implications for Us-Japanese Communication," *International Journal of Intercultural Relations*, 18 (1), 29-54.

Higgins, E. Tory, Arie W. Kruglanski, and Antonio Pierro (2003), "Regulatory Mode: Locomotion and Assessment as Distinct Orientations," in *Advances in Experimental Social Psychology*, Vol. 35, ed. Mark P. Zanna, San Diego, CA, US: Elsevier Academic Press, 293-344.

Kitayama, Shinobu, Hazel Rose Markus, Hisaya Matsumoto, and Vinai Norasakkunkit (1997), "Individual and Collective Processes in the Construction of the Self: Self-Enhancement in the United States and Self-Criticism in Japan," *Journal of Personality and Social Psychology*, 72 (6), 1245-67.

Kruglanski, Arie W., E. Tory Higgins, Antonio Pierro, Scott Spiegel, Erik P. Thompson, M. Nadir Atash, and James Y. Shah (2000), "To "Do the Right Thing" Or To "Just Do It": Locomotion and Assessment as Distinct Self-Regulatory Imperatives," *Journal of Personality and Social Psychology*, 79 (5), 793-815.

Kruglanski, Arie W., Antonio Pierro, E. Tory Higgins, and Dora Capozza (2007), "On the Move or Staying Put: Locomotion, Need for Closure, and Reactions to Organizational Change," *Journal of Applied Social Psychology*, 37 (6), 1305-40.

Lalwani, Ashok K. (2009), "The Distinct Influence of Cognitive Busyness and Need for Closure on Cultural Differences in Socially Desirable Responding," *Journal of Consumer Research*, forthcoming.

Lalwani, Ashok K. and Sharon Shavitt (2009), "The "Me" I Claim to Be: Cultural Self-Construal Elicits Self-Presentational Goal Pursuit," *Journal of Personality and Social Psychology*, forthcoming.

Lalwani, Ashok K., L. J. Shrum, and Chi-Yue Chiu (2009), "Motivated Response Styles: The Role of Cultural Values, Regulatory Focus, and Self-Consciousness in Socially Desirable Responding," *Journal of Personality and Social Psychology*, 96 (4), 870–82.

Mintzberg, Henry (1989), *Mintzberg on Management: Inside Our Strange World of Organizations*, New York: The Free Press.

Pierro, Antonio, Arie W. Kruglanski, and E. Tory Higgins (2006), "Progress Takes Work: Effects of the Locomotion Dimension on Job Involvement, Effort Investment, and Task Perormance in Oganizations," *Journal of Applied Social Psychology*, 36 (7), 1723-43.

Triandis, Harry C. (1989), "The Self and Social Behavior in Differing Cultural Contexts," *Psychological Review*, 96 (3), 506-20.

Weber, Elke U., Daniel R. Ames, and Ann-Renée Blais (2004), "'How Do I Choose Thee? Let Me Count the Ways': A Textual Analysis of Similarities and Differences in Modes of Decision-Making in China and the United States," *Management and Organization Review*, 1 (1), 87-118.

Film Festival

Summary

Russell Belk, York University, Canada
Robert Kozinets, York University, Canada

Not only does the filmmaking craft continue to advance, but as seen in this year's Film Festival, so does the technical and artistic merit of the films and their theoretical orientation and sophistication. Because more of the raw footage for these films is being shot in high definition, many of this year's films seemed to leap off the screen in their clarity. And better miking is simultaneously leading to higher sound quality. Such craft considerations are among the criteria used by jurors (the film equivalent of reviewers) in screening and choosing films to accept from among those submitted to the festival. When it came to choosing the two prize-winning films, craft considerations no doubt continued to play a role, but the treatment and interpretation offered in the film were likely of greater importance. Theoretical sophistication was evident in the winning films' attention to prior literature and their concise condensation of their field-based data's contributions to knowledge. It is the combination of all these factors that influence the People's Choice voting, for they all contribute to how the film engages its audience. These audiences vote for their favorite film. The Jurors' Award is based on a narrower audience composed of the jurors and the Film Festival Co-Chairs.

This year's People's Choice Award went to **"Black Friday: A Video-Ethnography of an Experiential Shopping Event"** by Robert Harrison, Timothy Reilly, and James Gentry. Set in the American Midwest, it is a film about the "Black Friday" opening of Christmas shopping on the day following American Thanksgiving. The film analyzes the shopping strategies of families who plan in advance how to get the special bargains offered on this one day of the year when merchants know they can get people up early in the morning or even get them to spend the night in front of their stores in order to take advantage of limited stock price specials. The film follows these families from their home planning sessions through the pre-opening lines, and into the stores. It provides typologies of different specialized shopper roles and strategies. In so doing, it shows how what seems like frenzied swarming can actually be well-coordinated strategic shopping in pursuit of the bargain in a spectacular environment.

The Jurors' Award this year went to **"Brothers in Paint: Practice-Oriented Inquiry into a Tribal Marketplace Culture"** by Joonas Rokka, Joel Heitanen, and Kristine De Valck. The film uses the extreme sport of paint ball to examine consumer neo-tribalism. What was once an inexpensive informal sport played in the woods, has become an organized, sponsored, and expensive sport with standardized man-made barriers, well-trained teams, and prize money for champions. Like the Black Friday shoppers, these teams use carefully planned strategies in their quests to be victorious in the tournaments. Despite sponsorship and prize money, team members may spend $20,000 a year of their own money equipping themselves and travelling to contests. Building on a recent emphasis on community and consumer tribes in the consumer culture theory literature, the film's narrative analysis helps make sense of such expenditures in terms of a consumer tribal culture.

This year's films continue to show geographic diversity with filmmakers and subjects from the US, England, Brazil, Finland, France, Japan, China, Slovenia, Scotland, Ireland, and Canada. It does not exaggerate to say that the Film Festival is a window on the world. There is a rich variety in the topics and approaches of the films as well as can be seen in the abstracts below. At least one of the films shown this year has already been offered to the wider public through YouTube, an act we heartily endorse. Those wishing to view the films are encouraged to contact the filmmakers for further information.

Presentations

"Black Friday: A Video-Ethnography of an Experiential Shopping Event"

Robert Harrison, Western Michigan University, USA
Timothy Reilly, University of Nebraska-Lincoln, USA
James Gentry, University of Nebraska-Lincoln, USA

The day after Thanksgiving, also known as Black Friday, has become a consumption event with more than 130 million people braving the elements, snarled parking lots, hours of waiting, and early morning crowds to shop on a day that has come to signal the beginning of the American Christmas shopping season. This video-ethnography provides an understanding of this consumer culture by examining the most unusual shopping day in U.S. culture. Based on our interpretation, we identify three categories of Black Friday shoppers, each with different roles, rules, and shopping strategies. Our investigation of the motivations of Black Friday shoppers offering insights into understanding shopping as a cultural spectacle and consumer competition, in addition to understanding extended family and organizational rituals.

"Blogs-Consumption, Behaviour, Interaction"

Carlos Rossi, PPGA-EA/UFRGS, Brazil
João Fleck, PPGA-EA/UFRGS, Brazil
Cristine Schweig, PPGA-EA/UFRGS, Brazil
Francini Ledur, PPGA-EA/UFRGS, Brazil
Oscar Evangelista, PPGA-EA/UFRGS, Brazil
Renato Barcelos, PPGA-EA/UFRGS, Brazil
Ricardo Perlin, PPGA-EA/UFRGS, Brazil
Simone Vedana, PPGA-EA/UFRGS, Brazil

What's the best hair moisturizer? Does that base work as well as in the TV commercial? This and other questionings are made by thousands of women in a daily basis. And what do these vain consumers have in common? They search beauty products with the promised benefits. Here come into place the consumption blogs: by testing, using, researching and reviewing these products, the four interviewed bloggers took the role of advisors, personal beauty consultants of their readers. They evaluate, recommend, defend or warn different products and services. Differently from the usual medias, the interaction allowed in blogs is capable of producing an impact in both buying behaviours': not only the readers, but also the bloggers are affected.

"Fashion, Consumption and Identity"

Carlos Rossi, PPGA-EA/UFRGS-Brazil
João Fleck, PPGA-EA/UFRGS-Brazil
Teniza Silveira, PPGA-EA/UFRGS-Brazil
Alejandro Ojeda, PPGA-EA/UFRGS-Brazil
Christian Albrecht, PPGA-EA/UFRGS-Brazil
Cláudia Lanfredi, PPGA-EA/UFRGS-Brazil
Luís Moura, PPGA-EA/UFRGS-Brazil
Martina Basile, PPGA-EA/UFRGS-Brazil
Priscila Esteves, PPGA-EA/UFRGS-Brazil

What makes somebody uncomfortable with her own appearance? Why look like the others bother us so much? Such questionings show us a conflict in the consumer mind in the search for an unique style against the need of group recognition, creating a reflexive thought on the importance of fashion in our society. The consumers on the video value their dressing way and they help us understanding how consumers build and express their identity through fashion.

"VINILEIROS – Those Crazy Guys that Love Their Vinyl Records"

João Fleck, PPGA - EA/UFRGS, Brazil
Carlos Rossi, PPGA - EA/UFRGS, Brazil
Nicolas Tonsho, EA/UFRGS - Brazil

How much is a record collection worth? Is it possible to complete a collection? What makes someone buy a vinyl record today and pay more for this big black vinyl record than for a small silver CD? Or just download for free the same music from the internet and listen to it on an MP3 Player? Until what level is it just consumption and when does it becomes the passion of an aficionado? Find the answers for these and other questions in VINILEIROS.

"Brothers in Paint: Practice-Oriented Inquiry into a Tribal Marketplace Culture"

Joonas Rokka, Helsinki School of Economics, Finland
Joel Hietanen, Helsinki School of Economics, Finland
Kristine De Valck, HEC Paris, France

The objective of this videography is to explore what opportunities and challenges the emerging practice-oriented approach opens up for conceptualizing tribal consumer culture and marketplace dynamics. Drawing on Schatzki's theorization of the 'site of the social', tribal marketplace culture and change are examined based on findings from a multi-sited ethnography of consumer tribes gathered around the extreme sport of paintball. In doing so, the tribal marketplace culture is conceptualized via constantly evolving nexus of practices and material arrangements; a specific context of human and non-human co-existence where, and apart of which, social life and the marketplace inherently transpires.

"Pirates of the Web: The Curse of Anti-piracy Advertising"

Barbara Culiberg, University of Ljubljana, Slovenia
Domen Bajde, University of Ljubljana, Slovenia

This short video unpacks the discursive contours of a prominent anti-piracy ad and the mashups created in response to it. Fairclough's critical discourse analysis and Kress and Leeuwen's guidelines on "reading images" are applied to 58 piracy-related videos uploaded on Youtube in response to MPAA's "Dowloading is stealing" campaign. We seek to actively include the consumers' voices in the piracy debate and provide a snapshot of the struggles for meaning taking place on online platforms. Our study shows how the representations and practices of "piracy" merge in acts of subversive creative consumption as consumer infringe on copyrights to resist and play with corporate representations of piracy.

"Restrained Pursuit of Luxury: Wealthy Shanghainese Attitudes towards Upscale Consumption"

Junko Kimura, Hosei University, Japan
Hiroshi Tanaka, Chuo University, Japan

In order to examine the Chinese perception of luxury, we visited Shanghai in September 2008 and interviewed four families there with annual income of more than 100,000 US Dollars. Our finding was the restrained perception of luxury shared by wealthy Shanghainese. Their perception was restrained compared to their Western counterparts, probably because by the traditional Confucian values. They are still under the influence of their parents' generation which had undergone the atrocious hardship during the Great Cultural Revolution. They also feel luxurious when they are filled with nonmaterial gains.

"POV: Point of View... Consumers and Ethnographers in Perspective... "

Wendy Hein, University of Edinburgh, Scotland, UK
Annmarie Ryan, Lancaster University, UK
Robert Corrigan, Limerick Institute of Technology, Ireland, UK

This film is based on a female ethnographer's research exploring young Scottish men's consumption practices. It shows how applications of mobile phones helped overcome some of the challenges the ethnographer faced in the field to generate data in a less invasive way. It also describes consumers' own use of mobile phones to record their experiences, legitimising and authenticating their masculinity. This emphasised the importance of consumer experiences for constructing gender identities through culturally situated consumption. We suggest that the role of mobile phones advances the researcher's capability for reflexivity and creates a richer understanding of consumers' points of view.

"Does Green? "

Gary J. Bamossy, Georgetown University, USA
Basil G. Englis, Berry College, USA

In recent years the American market place has seen the re-emergence of a vigorous public discourse around the issues of what are variously called "Environmentalism," "Global Warming", "Sustainable Consumption", "The Environment", or in its simplest and most generic term, "Green". National surveys regarding U.S. consumers' *awareness* regarding "things green" consistently report that over 80% of the American population is aware of Green issues (Mintel, 2008; American Environics, 2008; Makower, 2009; Englis and Bamossy, 2009). Levels of consistent commitment in terms of actual green *behaviors*, however, do vary greatly across segments of American consumers, with lifestyle variables tending to be better predictors of green behavior than demographic variables (Makower, 2009; American Environics, 2008; Englis and Bamossy, 2009). In short, American consumers know about Green, but do not always act on that knowledge. Given the tremendous Green push from both the public and private sectors, along with the never ending coverage of *Things Green* from the media, it seems reasonable to predict that while forms of the Green discourse are likely to change over time, they are not likely to wane.

One of the recurring perspectives that characterizes Green and sustainability research from both the academic and commercial research sectors is to begin with descriptive statistics that are meant to shock us by describing our (potentially disastrous) consumption and disposition behaviors, and then use these research findings as a basis for developing communication strategies which are meant to motivate consumers to become more involved. The orientation of the research is to make action seem perfectly rational, in fact so rational, it can NOT be resisted. The inner logic of the argument assumes that once people understand what is happening to the environment, they will act in positive, constructive ways. The assumption is that once people process this information, their best alternative will be Green action. "*Any sane person will adjust their consumption lifestyle once they learn this*," seems to be the rationale underlying Green strategies of persuasion.

The video, "Does Green?" critiques this logic in a very subtle way, and suggests that this approach is not working. "Does Green?" points the viewer in a number of theoretical directions that may lead to new ideas of how to combine green awareness with green *action*. Capturing consumers' reactions to products as diverse as hybrid cars, light bulbs, and tote bags, this video explores the gaps between consumers' attitudes and behaviors, and sheds light on the strong connections between our sense of Green coupled with fashion, and Green coupled with self representation. Currently, the role of cultural discourse and social change around Green is often seen as a countervailing discourse. We need a new paradigm to frame our thinking about how to motivate acts of green and sustainable consumption, and the intent of this video is to help get this dialogue started.

References

"Green Living—U.S.—2008" *MINTeL Report*, accessed from the Lauringer Library, Georgetown University, August, 2008.

"Roadmap for a Progressive Majority", American Environics, November, 2008, accessed at: http://www.americanenvironics.com/PDF/UpdatetoRoadmap2008.pdf

Englis, Basil, and Gary J. Bamossy, (2009) "Courting America's Greens: Addressing the Gaps Between Green Attitudes and Green Behaviors", working paper, available from first author.

Makower, Joel, (2009) *Strategies for the Green Economy*, 2009, McGraw Hill, New York.

"Remade China: The Re-Production of Chineseness in a Multi-Cultural Society"

Eric Ping Hung Li, York University, Canada
Russell W. Belk, York University, Canada

The intensified global interaction and between different ethnic groups creates problems that related to ethnic identification and representation. This video examines the intersection between ethnicity, immigration, food consumption and festival celebrations among overseas Chinese in Toronto, the most ethnically diverse city in the world. By capturing how Chinese immigrants interpret the notion of multicultural and how they mix and match elements from different cultures in their everyday consumption activities, this video aims to provide a better understanding of how members of the Chinese diaspora re-construct and present their cultural identity through the re-production of "Chineseness" in their new "homeland".

Roundtable
Advancing the Production/Consumption Dialectic in Consumer Culture Theory

Chairs:
Ahir Gopaldas, York University, Canada
Sarah J. S. Wilner, York University, Canada

Participants:
Lisa Peñaloza, EDHEC Business School, France
David Crockett, University of South Carolina, USA
Kent Grayson, Northwestern University, USA
Bernard Cova, Euromed Management Marseilles, France
Hope Jensen Schau, University of Arizona, USA
Jean-Sébastian Marcoux, HEC Montréal, Canada
Fuat Firat, University of Texas-Pan American, USA
Julie Ozanne, Virginia Tech, USA
Clinton Lanier, University of St. Thomas, USA
Robert Kozinets, Schulich School of Business, York University, Canada
Richard Kedzior, Hanken School of Economics, Finland
Jill Avery, Simmons School of Management, USA
Aron Darmody, Schulich School of Business, York University, Canada
Gokcen Coskuner-Balli, Chapman University, USA
Ashlee Humphreys, Northwestern University, USA

The purpose of this roundtable is to provide a forum for interdisciplinary researchers to discuss new concepts, frameworks, and theories that can reformulate and advance the study of the production/consumption dialectic in consumer culture theory (CCT). Though the concepts of production and consumption are defined diversely within and across the disciplines of anthropology, consumer research, cultural studies, economics, marketing, sociology, and media studies, they are widely understood in opposition to one another. However, the relative emphasis on production, consumption, or hybrid conceptualizations has always been contingent on sociohistoric conditions. For example, as capitalism and globalization matured through the 20th century, both business practice and social theory gradually de-privileged production and divided their attention between production and consumption in more equal measure. This trend roughly coincided with shifts from modern ideologies and mass production to postmodern ideologies and market segmentation (Cohen 2004; Firat and Venkatesh 1995; Zhao and Belk 2008).

CCT has a long history of considering production, in addition to consumption, in its analyses (for a review, see Arnould and Thompson 2005). Within CCT, it is often argued that the production/consumption dialectic structures intra-person (e.g. Tian and Belk 2005: work self/home self); inter-person (e.g. Thompson and Coskuner-Balli 2007); and inter-group (e.g. Giesler 2008) identities and activities. Long-standing questions about cultural construction, reproduction, opposition, and transformation in the market sphere remain at the heart of contemporary CCT research: How do dominant cultural producers transform the core ideologies of a society (e.g. Zhao and Belk 2008)? How do marketers employ mass-mediated and micro-cultural discourses to craft compelling offerings and reformulate historical discourses in doing so (e.g. Thompson and Tian 2008)? How do producers imagine and interpellate consumers and consumption communities (e.g. Cayla and Eckhardt 2008; Kozinets 2008)? How do producers and consumers negotiate the (dis)junctures of market and social logics (e.g. Giesler 2008; Thompson and Coskuner-Balli 2007; Tian and Belk 2005)? The agenda of this roundtable may be articulated accordingly:

- What underexplored and unexplored concepts, frameworks, and theories can help researchers explicate the myriad intersections of production and consumption in practice?
- Which contexts, informants, and phenomena are appropriate for investigating these intersections?
- What insights can be gleaned from production/consumption research not only for theory, but also for consumer empowerment, political engagement, and social justice?

Exploring new theoretical directions for this domain of research is perennially important for a number of reasons. First, the production/consumption dialectic is at the core of CCT and its sibling fields of interpretive consumer research (for a review, see Cova and Elliott 2008), consumption anthropology (for a review, see Miller 1995), consumption sociology (for a review, see Zukin and Smith Maguire 2004), and critical marketing studies (for a review, see Saren et al. 2007). What all these fields share is an interest in how market logics are produced, reproduced, opposed, and transformed by cultural, economic, political, and social forces, both within and beyond the marketplace. Accordingly, the production/consumption dialectic gives an extensive network of scholars a node to link their sometimes complementary, sometimes contradictory trajectories of scholarship.

Second, the production/consumption dialectic links to numerous other dialectics that shape the agenda of CCT. For example, the dialectic links to the supply/demand dialectic in economic discourse, the management/marketing dialectic in business discourse, and the work/spend (Schor 1991) or work/life (Tian and Belk 2005) dialectics in social discourse. To advance the reach of CCT, it would behoove consumer culture theorists to challenge such discursive divides and forge links with compatible theorists in other areas of the business academy (e.g. critical management studies [Alvesson and Willmott 1992]) with whom we share critical and interpretive research agendas and domain boundaries.

Third, along with structure/agency theoretics and identity politics, the production/consumption dialectic has inspired increasingly sophisticated understandings of production and consumption and their multi-level (institutional and individual) and multi-sphere (cultural and economic) roles in social reproduction and transformation (e.g. Bourdieu 1984; Giddens 1991; Ritzer 1993). These interlinked understandings of production/consumption, structure/agency, and identity politics are not universal but situated resolutions to theoretical debates. For example, while marketing researchers have proposed that the service-dominant logic of co-creation/co-production is a substantive merger of production and consumption logics (Vargo and Lusch 2004), consumer researchers have argued that these concepts are rhetoric bandages over a sustained divide between the production of exchange-value (i.e., production) and the production of use-value (i.e. consumption) (Humphreys and Grayson 2008). It is through cycles of such dialectic discussions, syncretic conceptualizations, and reformulated dialectics that business practice and theory evolves in society and the marketplace (Giesler 2008).

References

Alvesson, Matts, and Hugh Willmott (eds.) (1992), *Critical Management Studies*, London: Sage.

Arnould, Eric J. and Craig J. Thompson (2005), Consumer Culture Theory (CCT): Twenty Years of Research, *Journal of Consumer Research*, 31 (March), 868-882.

Bourdieu, Pierre (1984), *Distinction: A Social Critique of the Judgment of Taste*, Cambridge, MA: Harvard University Press.

Cayla, Julien and Gianna Eckhardt (2008), "Asian Brands and the Shaping of Transnational Imagined Community," *Journal of Consumer Research*, 35 (August), 216-230.

Cohen, Lizabeth (2003), *A Consumers Republic: The Politics of Consumption in Postwar America*, New York: Knopf.

Cova, Bernard and Richard Elliott (2008), "Everything you always wanted to know about interpretive consumer research but were afraid to ask," *Qualitative Market Research: An International Journal*, 11, 121-129.

Firat, Fuat A. and Alladi Venkatesh (1995), "Liberatory Postmodernism and the Reenchantement of Consumption," *Journal of Consumer Res*earch, 22 (December), 239-67.

Giddens, Anthony (1991), *Modernity and Self-Identity: Self and Society in the Late Modern Age*, Stanford, CA: Stanford University Press.

Giesler, Markus (2008), "Conflict and Compromise: Drama in Marketplace Evolution," *Journal of Consumer Research*, 34 (April), 739-53.

Humphreys, Ashlee and Kent Grayson (2008), "The Intersecting Roles of Consumer and Producer: A Critical Perspective on Co-Production, Co-Creation and Prosumption," *Sociology Compass*, 2/3, 963-980.

Kozinets, Robert V. (2008), "Technology/Ideology: How Ideological Fields Influence Consumers' Technology Narratives," *Journal of Consumer Research*, 34 (April), 865-81.

Miller, Daniel (1995), "Consumption and Commodities," *Annual Review of Anthropology*, 24, 141-161.

Ritzer, George (1993), *The McDonaldization of Society*, Thousand Oaks, CA: Pine Forge Press.

Saren, M., MacLaran, P., Goulding, C., Elliott, R., Shankar, A. and Catterall, M. (Eds.) (2007), *Critical Marketing: Designing the Field*, Oxford: Butterworth-Heinemann.

Schor, Juliet (1991), *The Overworked American: The Unexpected Decline of Leisure*, Basic Books: New York, NY.

Thompson, Craig J. and Gokcen Coskuner-Balli (2007), "Countervailing Market Responses to Corporate Co-optation and the Ideological Recruitment of Consumption Communities," *Journal of Consumer Research*, 34 (August), 135–51.

Thompson, Craig J. and Kelly Tian (2008), "Reconstructing the South: How Commercial Myths Compete for Identity Value through the Ideological Shaping of Popular Memories and Counter Memories," *Journal of Consumer Research*, 34 (February), 595–612.

Tian, Kelly and Russell W. Belk (1995), "Extended Self and Possessions in the Workplace," *Journal of Consumer Research*, 32 (September), 297-310.

Vargo, Stephen L., and Robert F. Lusch (2004), "Evolving to a new dominant logic for marketing," *Journal of Marketing*, 68 (January), 1–17.

Zhao and Russell W. Belk (2008), Politicizing Consumer Culture: Advertising's Appropriation of Political Ideology in China's Social Transition, *Journal of Consumer Research*, 35 (August), 231-244.

Zukin, Sharon and Jennifer Smith Maguire (2004), "Consumers and Consumption," *Annual Review of Sociology*, 30, 173-197.

Roundtable
Towards a Theoretical Vocabulary for Consumer Research on Sustainability

Chairs:
Melea Press, University of Wyoming, USA
Eric J. Arnould, University of Wyoming, USA

Participants:
David Crockett, University of South Carolina, USA
Diane Martin, University of Portland, USA
Guliz Ger, Bilkent University, Turkey
Pierre McDonagh, Dublin City University, Ireland, UK
Krittinee Nuttavuthisit, Chulalongkorn University, Thailand
Alice Grønhøj, Aarhus University, Denmark
Robert Fisher, University of Alberta, Canada
Benet DeBerry-Spence, University of Illinois at Chicago, USA
Julie Ozanne, Virginia Tech, USA
John Schouten, University of Portland, USA
Stacey Baker, University of Wyoming, USA
Jenny Mish, University of Notre Dame, USA
Susan Dobscha, Bentley College, USA
Vladas Griskevicius, University of Minnesota, USA
Robert Caruana, University of Manchester, UK
Gokcen Coskuner-Balli, Chapman University, USA

Purpose

The purpose of this session is to bring together individuals who are conducting, or interested in conducting, research in the broad areas of intersection between sustainability, consumer behavior and marketing. Discussion will focus on how to develop a theoretical vocabulary for sustainability research that transcends the specific contexts that we currently associate with "sustainability," such as subsistence consumers, disaster mitigation, quality of life, equitable development, voluntary simplicity, and above all "green marketing."

Rationale

Consumer research is glaringly absent from conversations and writing about sustainability, even though there is a long tradition of interest in the so-called green consumer segment, consumer resistance, and quality of life issues. Research on sustainable business practice in the private sector has been lead by systems engineers, architects, economists, and CEOs. Consumer research scholars can enrich the discussion of consumer issues in all areas of sustainability, including natural resource consumption (energy, water, etc.), purchasing and lifestyle choices, co-creation and assessment of value, and community health and development. Contributions from consumer researchers to the emerging sustainability paradigm would increase the viability of current and future sustainability initiatives.

Approaches to consumer behaviors associated with sustainability tend to focus on change through information processing or social marketing models, and presume that unsustainable consumer behavior may be changed significantly through such approaches. However, these tactics have not been successful, as evidenced by the fact that exactly 40 years since the founding of Earth Day, and 35 years since the first oil shocks, and despite efforts to promote various "green" practices, we live in an economy that is ever more ecologically unsustainable. And the average consumer if s/he thinks of sustainable consumption at all, probably thinks that shopping at Whole Foods is contributing to sustainability. Unfortunately, the normal habitus of consumer culture, that is, the mundane practices of everyday consumption, build in unsustainability. Perhaps we need to think about approaches to changing consumption that despectacularizes sustainable consumption activities, such as engaging in voluntary simplicity, local food systems, off-grid green homes, and "alternative" practices in general. The effort to provide more information, or "educate" has not resulted in behavior changes that lead to or signal a more sustainable society. We need to address our absence in the sustainability conversation and the weaknesses of our current tools to address the sustainability challenge.

What is the emerging sustainability paradigm? From a marketing perspective, sustainable business practice entails developing strategic thinking that positively impacts firms' long-term economic sustainability in an increasingly volatile and resource constrained world; firms' environmental footprint; and the firms' long-term relationships with stakeholder communities. It also requires not only full, but far more efficient use of company resources. It places innovation at the heart of attempts to move toward clean technology, and resource efficient, climate- and ecology-friendly products and services. It strives to balance the need to develop economically with the need to maintain social and environmental consideration.

Sustainable business practice also involves consumer-centered thinking, approaches that view customers as people with needs beyond material consumption and temporary gratifications. It also includes issues that affect customers' fundamental quality of life, access to air, water, health, markets, and so on. It incorporates a long-turn perspective to consider the needs of stakeholders, not just of the present but of future generations. Finally, sustainable business practice also involves the extension of consumer and market-based solutions to under-served local, regional and global populations.

We could look outside consumer research to find research that calls for systems approaches to sustainability problems. Rudolf Steiner's deep belief in the connection between the spiritual and natural world led to a focus on systems, rather than individual parts of people, society, and activities. His lectures and writings influenced medicine (anthroposophical extended medicine), education (Waldorf schools), and agriculture (Biodynamic farming). In each of these areas he proposed that issues be examined from a whole systems perspective. For example, biodynamic agriculture looks at the farm as an organism. The farm is then seen as a complex organism that can nourish itself. Challenges of growing food and treating disease are approached from the systemic level; that is, as an issue of the entire organism, not an individual piece.

Edward Abbey, a nature writer, pushed the preservation of wilderness through his many works of fiction and non-fiction. His meditations on nature, self-hood, and consumer culture provide a moral foundation for rethinking relationships among the person, civilization, and nature. He points to understanding the limits of ecological constraints, which is seen with growing urgency as we move more deeply into the 21st Century.

Elinor Ostrom, a prolific political scientist, calls for intensely interdisciplinary approaches to addressing the ecological and governance issues we face today. She pulls in experience from medicine to illustrate that simple solutions often lead to unanticipated problems, and suggests that a smart approach to a viable solution to our unsustainable economy is to build strong interdisciplinary research that addresses issues at multiple levels, taking into account the social sciences and ecological constraints. She looks at social and scientific solutions to complex problems facing our world.

Each of these three examples highlights the need for systems thinking and interdisciplinary research, pushing the necessity of breaking down silos to accomplish our goal of sustainable lives, societies, and ecosystems.

Some people are recognizing that "sustainability" has become a more complex and comprehensive consumer research topic than is captured in the traditional "green consumer" framing. Linkages between new consumer practices responding to a host of corporate initiatives new and old, such as green marketing, corporate social responsibility, fair trade, and social entrepreneurship, within an environment of perceived global risk and global Commons crises (global warming, environmental strain, global unrest) offer the potential for renewed research trajectories in consumer research.

Preconference discussions will be facilitated by the organizers. It will happen in two parts. First, we will give participants different ideas and statements to respond to, compile the information, and email it back to them. Then, we will bring participants together with postings on the ACR Knowledge Exchange Forum, and through email. Pre-conference idea exchange is very important for the success of this roundtable, because it may be hard to stay on-topic discussing sustainability from a *theoretical* perspective.

Diversity is an important part of discussions about sustainability, and this session brings together new and veteran ACR-goers, as well as people with different methodological orientations. Different points of view are important in working through this topic.

Key questions the roundtable will address include

1. What is sustainability as it pertains to consumer research?
2. What role can consumer researchers play in guiding this conversation?
3. How can we use ecological theories of sustainability to build theory in consumer research?
4. Are we poised to lead interdisciplinary research in this area? What would that look like?

ROUNDTABLE

Navigating the Networked Rivers of the Social Web: Emerging Themes for Consumer Behavior Research on Web 2.X

Chair:
Donna Hoffman, University of California at Riverside, USA

Participants:
Robert Kozinets, Schulich School of Business, York University, Canada
Nicholas Lurie, Georgia Institute of Technology, USA
Wendy Moe, University of Maryland, USA
Albert Muniz, DePaul University, USA
Thomas Novak, University of California at Riverside, USA
Thomas O'Guinn, University of Wisconsin-Madison, USA
Hope Jensen Schau, University of Arizona, USA
Ann Schlosser, University of Washington, USA
Allan Weiss, University of Southern California, USA
Tiffany White, University of Illinois, USA
Jill Avery, Simmons School of Management, USA
Kristine De Valck, HEC Paris, France
Uptal (Paul) Dholakia, Rice University, USA
Markus Geisler, York University, Canada
Andrew Gershoff, University of Michigan, USA
Ashlee Humphreys, Northwestern University, USA
Charla Mathwick, Portland State University, USA
Constance Porter, University of Notre Dame, USA

In a little over a decade and a half, the consumer Internet has evolved from a few directories and online storefronts into a vast, sophisticated network of information stores that millions of people from around the globe interact with on a regular basis. As the Internet matures, it has moved from a static, rigid mechanism for data access into an *operating system* that seamlessly connects applications–and people–across the global network. Increasingly referred to by many as Web 2.0 or the "social Web," this evolving Internet offers online consumers unprecedented opportunities to create and control their online experiences.

More than simply a set of features or applications, new social media forms (such as the social bookmarking site StumbleUpon or the micro blogging application Twitter) are contributing to the evolution of the Web as a social technologies platform that connects consumers in innovative ways with often startling implications for traditional marketing efforts. It is a profound fact that consumers are now both the producers and consumers of their own online content and services. The purpose of this proposed roundtable is to explore the emerging research implications of these social Web consumer behaviors.

The Early Internet–Flat and Static

In the early Web, let's call it "Web 1.0," consumers were required to navigate through relatively inflexible and often rigid online paths. Web 1.0 was a conduit for information, largely consisting of basic text and images. The basic infrastructure for online commerce was built in Web 1.0, in the form of static sites which evolved to include limited dynamic content and interactivity.

Web 2.0–A State of Mind

We are now witnessing Web 2.0, the next logical iteration of the Internet, where the Web is more of an operating system that facilitates sharing and participation. The seamless connection of Web 2.0+ applications and services such as the "mobile+social" dodgeball.com to track one's friends' current geographic locations and Zooomr for photosharing and text messaging in real-time has been referred to as the "mash-up" phase of the Internet with parts that connect (Markoff 2006). Rather than follow relatively inflexible paths and existing navigational structures, Web 2.0 consumers are more in control of their online navigational experiences and are more easily able to engage in only those applications that interest them. Web 2.0 is less about navigating through individual Web sites and more about Web-based applications and environments that can be installed and experienced as the consumer sees fit.

Web 3.0–It Can Think!

If Web 2.0 puts consumers in control, then Web 3.0 will augment that control and give it a brain. Web 3.0, sometimes called the "Semantic Web" (Berners-Lee, Hendler and Lassila 2001), is the next evolution of social networking technologies pioneered in Web 2.0. As the Web begins to "understand itself," it becomes less of a catalog and more of a guide. This phase involves integration of artificial intelligence and the Web and involves human effort integrated across the network. Very early examples are Amazon's Mechanical Turk Web service or Google's Image Labeler game. Virtual Worlds like Second Life, where humans in avatar form serve as guides and mentors and answer questions well beyond the scope of today's search and FAQ technology, provide a glimpse into what information search in the online world of the future may be like.

FIGURE

Emerging Social Web Research Themes Organized According to The "Four C's of Online Consumer Behavior

Create: User Generated Content (individually created content)
- Community identity
- Posters vs. lurkers
- Social dynamics of posting behavior
- Word of mouth models

Create: User Generated Content (collaboratively created content)
- Collective consumer innovation (crowds, hives, mobs and swarms)
- "Community brands"
- Consumer-generated "ad" content in brand communities
- The spatial clickstream

Connect: Social Networks and Online Communities
- Creating value and making meaning in brand communities
- Peer-to-peer problem solving communities
- Social production
- Trust and value in firm-sponsored virtual communities vs organic virtual communities
- Value construction in exchange networks

Consume: Customer Experience
- Brand engagement
- Consumer engagement
- Consumption of performance
- Presence, Telepresence, and Flow

Control: Autonomous User
- Co-creation (brand engagement)
- Participatory advertising
- Personalization and Customization

What is the Social Web?

Some definitions may be useful. We define the social Web as consumers interacting with each other through Web 2.0+ based social media applications. *The currency of interaction is user-generated content.* Social media are Web-based applications that permit creation, sharing, manipulation and consumption of user-generated content. Social networking focuses on the nature of interactions among consumers within a specific category of social media applications–social networking sites.

Roundtable Themes and Objectives

The four C's of online consumer experience (Hoffman and Novak 2009) serve as the organizing framework for the proposed roundtable research themes. As depicted in the Figure, social Web research topics are organized according to consumer creation, connection, consumption and control themes. Key objectives of this proposed roundtable are to: 1) offer a new framework for organizing emerging consumer behavior research on the social Web research frontier, 2) expose interested ACR members to exciting research streams in this emerging area, and 3) generate insights and ideas that can serve as the basis for future collaborations among ACR members.

A total of 19 ACR members, including the organizer, have committed to participate should this roundtable be accepted. These committed participants come from across the globe and run the gamut from assistant professors who have just completed their Ph.D.s on emerging social Web topics to well known academic experts with established reputations in online consumer behavior. As such, ACR attendees, as well as roundtable participants themselves, can expect to participate in a highly engaging roundtable discussion concerning the emerging social Web research themes.

We anticipate that the roundtable is likely to be of interest to a wide variety of consumer behavior researchers, including both "newbies" who are Web 2.X curious and experienced online consumer behavior researchers. *Each roundtable participant has agreed to serve if the proposal is accepted.*

Pre-Conference Interaction Among Participants

Roundtable participants will interact before the roundtable via email exchanges. These exchanges will culminate in a face-to-face dinner in Pittsburgh during the conference in advance of the roundtable, sponsored by the UCR Sloan Center for Internet Retailing.

References

Berners-Lee, Tim, James Hendler and Ora Lassila (2001), "The Semantic Web," *Scientific American*, May.

Hoffman, Donna L. and Thomas P. Novak (2009), "Roles and Goals: Consumer Motivations for Using the Social Web," UCR Sloan Center Working Paper.

Markoff, John (2006), "Entrepreneurs See a Web Guided By Common Sense," *New York Times*, Business Section, November 12.

Recommendation Agents as Consumer Response Heuristic to Information Overload and the Joint Effects on Choice Quality, Choice Confidence, and Website Evaluation

Muhammad Aljukhadar, HEC Montreal, Canada
Sylvain Senecal, HEC Montreal, Canada
Charles-Etienne Daoust, Cossette Communication Group, Canada

The debate on the antecedents and consequences of information overload is ongoing. Given the low online search costs, consumers are particularly exposed to elevated information amounts during product choice. This research integrates the traditional and structural methods in product information measurement to investigate (1) the relationship between information amount (bits) in a product choice set and information overload perceptions, (2) consumers' tendency to employ information processing reduction heuristic (by consulting a recommendation agent) as information bits and overload perceptions increase, and (3) the joint effects on several performance measures.

"In the age of the Internet, developing an understanding of how information-rich environments affect consumer decision making is of crucial importance. Given the disparate ways in which information can be presented to consumers and the high potential for information overload in online environments, it is important to use measures that capture the multiple dimensions of information." (Lurie 2004 p. 484). The literature further indicates that consumer decision support systems (e.g., product recommendation agents) are decision heuristics that alleviate part of processing effort required by consumers while maintaining an acceptable level of choice accuracy (Häubl and Trifts 2000; Todd and Benbasat 1992). Recommendation agents have the potential to reduce consumers' information overload and search complexity while improving decision quality (Haubl and Trifts 2000; Maes 1994).

Researchers studied the consequences of information overload on consumers' choice and purchase of different products, such as laundry detergent (Jacoby, Speller, and Berning 1974a), rice and prepared dinner (Jacoby, Speller, and Berning 1974b), peanut butter (Scammon 1977), houses (Malhotra 1982), calculators (Lurie 2004), and CD players (Lee and Lee 2004). Theory implies that information overload is an expected event because of well-defined limits in humans to assimilate and process information within any timeframe (Jacoby 1977; Jacoby, Speller, and Berning 1974a; Malhotra 1982).

In general, researchers indicate that, faced with large product information amounts (or information bits; the term is adapted and used as in Lee and Lee 2004; Lurie 2004), consumers' limited capacity to process information becomes overloaded, resulting in dysfunctional consequences such as cognitive fatigue and confusion (Hahn, Lawson, and Lee 1992; Keller and Staelin 1987; Malhotra 1984; Scammon 1977; Winzar and Savik 2002). Malhotra (1982 p. 419) concludes that "perhaps the most important generalization that emerges is that an individual is a limited information processing system."

This research contributes to the literature as it (1) simultaneously assesses the traditional and structural methods (see Lee and Lee 2004; Lurie 2004) to measure the information in a product choice set, (2) integrates a perceptual self-reported measure of information overload to show its relationship with information bits as well as performance measures, (3) manipulates three levels of alternatives, three levels of attributes, and two levels of attributes' distribution across alternatives in product choice set conditions to increase the study range and allow for curvilinearity inspection of the relation bits-overload perceptions, (4) includes a robust, observed measure (choice to consult recommendation vs. no consultation) to reflect the occurrence of information overload besides the perceptual measure, (5) inspects the effects on reactance besides the effects on choice quality and consumers' post-choice psychological states (choice confidence and difficulty). Thus the hypotheses developed and supported are:

- H1: Information overload perceptions increase as information bits increase; in addition, the relationship between information bits and overload perceptions is curvilinear.
- H2a: A main effect is expected for information bits on recommendation consultation; that is, the probability of consulting a recommendation agent increases as information bits increase.
- H2b: An interaction is expected so that as information bits increase, consumers low on need for cognition are more probable to consult a recommendation agent than consumers high on need for cognition.
- H3a: A main effect is expected for information overload perceptions on recommendation agent consultation; that is, the probability of consulting a recommendation agent increases as overload perceptions increase.
- H3b: An interaction is expected so that as overload perceptions increase, consumers low on need for cognition are more probable to consult a recommendation agent than consumers high on need for cognition.
- H4: An interaction is expected between information bits and recommendation agent consultation so that as information load or bits increase, consumers who consult a recommendation agent will have higher choice quality than consumers who do not; in addition, an interaction is expected so that recommendation consultation improves choice quality particularly for product choice sets with proportional (vs. disproportional) distribution of attributes' levels across alternatives.
- H5: An interaction is expected between information overload perceptions and recommendation agent consultation so that as overload perceptions increase, consumers who consult a recommendation agent will have higher choice quality than consumers who do not.
- H6: As information overload increases, reactance to recommendation decrease.
- H7: Whereas choice confidence increases as information overload perceptions increase, an interaction is expected so that choice confidence is lower for consumers who consult a recommendation agent and do not choose the recommended product than consumers who consult and choose the recommended product.

A completely randomized experiment (that followed pretests to insure manipulation success and product suitability) with three levels of alternatives, three levels of attributes, and two levels of attributes' distribution across alternatives (proportional vs. disproportional distribution, Lurie 2004) that involved 466 consumers choosing one laptop with the option to consult a recommendation agent prior to final choice was performed. ANOVA and binary logistical regression was used in data analysis (measures adapted scales from the literature).

Results support the hypotheses, show a curvilinear relation between information bits and overload perceptions, and favor the occurrence of information overload because the consumers' tendency to employ a decision heuristic (by consulting the recommendations) increases as information bits and overload perceptions increase. In addition, while recommendation agent consultation upholds choice quality in general as information bits increase, recommendation consultation was particularly salient in enhancing choice quality when product information was less diagnostic (attributes' levels are proportionally distributed across alternatives in the choice set). Recommendation agent consultation further interacted with information overload to improve choice quality, and choice confidence (but mainly for consumers that ended by choosing the recommended product).

References

Hahn, Minhi, Robert Lawson and Young Lee (1992), "The Effects of Time Pressure and Information Load on Decision Quality," *Psychology & Marketing*, 9 (5), 365-79.

Häubl, Gerald and Valerie Trifts (2000), "Consumer Decision Making in Online Shopping Environments: The Effect of Interactive Decision Aids," *Marketing Science*, 19 (1), 4-21.

Jacoby, Jacob, Donald Speller and Carol Berning (1974a), "Brand Choice Behavior as a Function of Information Load," *Journal of Marketing Research*, 11 (1), 63-9.

Jacoby, Jacob, Donald Speller and Carol Berning (1974b), "Brand Choice Behavior as a Function of Information Load: Replication and Extension," *Journal of Consumer Research*, 1 (1), 33-42.

Keller, Kevin L. and Richard Staelin (1987), "Effects of Quality and Quantity of Information on Decision Effectiveness," *Journal of Consumer Research*, 14 (2), 200-13.

Lee, Byung-Kwan and Wei-Na Lee (2004), "The Effect of Information Overload on Consumer Choice Quality in an On-Line Experiment," *Psychology & Marketing*, 21 (3), 159-81.

Lurie, Nicholas H. (2004), "Decision Making in Information-Rich Environments: The Role of Information Structure," *Journal of Consumer Research*, 30 (4), 473-86.

Maes, Pattie (1994), "Agents that reduce work and information overload," *Association for Computing Machinery, Communications of the ACM*, 37 (7), 30-41.

Malhotra, Narish K. (1982), "Information Load and Consumer Decision Making," *Journal of Consumer Research*, 8 (4), 419-430.

Payne, John W., James R. Bettman and Eric J. Johnson (1993), *The Adaptive Decision Maker*. Cambridge: Cambridge University Press.

Scammon, Debra L. (1977), "Information Load and Consumers," *Journal of Consumer Research*, 4 (3), 148-55.

Todd, Peter and Isaac Benbasat (1992), "The Use of Information in Decision Making: An Experimental Investigation of the Impact of Computer-Based Decision Aids," *MIS Quarterly*, 16 (3), 373-93.

Winzar, Hume and Preben Savik (2002), "Measuring Information Overload on the World Wide Web," *AMA Conference Proceedings*, 13, 439-45.

One Without the Other: The Effects of Priming and Perceived Relationships Among Products on Consumer Choice

Jim Alvarez-Mourey, University of Michigan, USA

Daphne Oyserman, University of Michigan, USA

Carolyn Yoon, University of Michigan, USA

Abstract

Relational priming has been shown to influence individuals in the domains of self-construal (i.e., individualism and collectivism), but, to date, the research has been limited to studying self-construal with respect to interpersonal relationships. The current paper extends the theory into the realm of inter-product/service relationships by examining the effect relational priming has on product selection given perceived relationships among products and services. A series of three studies employing priming methodology explore differences in consumption choices based on prime type, perceived product/service relationships, and implied relationships. The results suggest that priming does, in fact, influence consumer choice among related products, elicit reluctance for subjects to break apart items perceived as related, and produce said effects via realistic advertisements beyond traditional laboratory priming techniques. Limitations and future studies are discussed, as are potential managerial implications for the marketing practices of up-selling, cross-selling, and advertising/point-of-purchase displays as priming tools.

Introduction

What is peanut butter without jelly? Barbie without Ken? What is a belt without its buckle or a shirt without pants (aside from slightly risqué)? In a variety of consumption settings, products and services can exist not only as independent items but also as items sharing a relationship or a coexistence with other items. Thus, while a shirt may simply be only a shirt, most clothing retailers take great care in presenting that shirt in the context of an outfit, complete with a matching tie and pants, to illustrate the connection among these items with the hope that consumers will purchase more than just the shirt. Furthermore, consumers may feel a sense of emptiness or incompletion if they only purchase one of a perceived pair or set of products/services, perhaps explaining why consumers so often go into a store with the intent of purchasing only *one* item and return with several.

Research Objective

The research objective of the current paper is to explore the relationship between self-construal (i.e., individualism and collectivism) and product preference/selection, as well as commitment to those preferences/selections, in the consumer context both inter-culturally and intra-culturally. Previous studies have shown that relational priming influences individuals' self-construal, which then affects their behavior, but most of these studies have been with respect to *interpersonal* influence. Thus, making consumers more aware of "relationships" makes them more susceptible to social or peer influence. Unlike the previous research, however, the current paper posits that priming consumers with relational primes will influence their subsequent consumption choices given the perceived relationships *among products*, not people, with respect to being 1) more/less likely to select products that are perceived as related, and 2) more/less likely to select a product if doing so separates that product from related products. In other words, whereas previous studies emphasized the role of self-construal, its effect on interpersonal relationships, and the role of interpersonal relationships on product selection, the current paper investigates the role of self-construal, a heightened awareness of relationships among products/services, and the subsequent preference and selection behaviors of consumers and their commitments to those selections.

Methodology

A series of studies exploring these predictions rely on a priming methodology to influence the self-construal of subjects completing the studies. Previous literature has shown that self-construal can be manipulated via subtle priming techniques, and, as expected, we see differences based on our priming approaches. More specifically, we prime subjects with traditional self-construal primes to activate the notion of relationships and then, following the priming, present subjects with several consumption decisions. In each study we then manipulate the availability of the goods perceived as being related to see how subjects from both conditions respond to the notion of breaking apart related items or the permitted consumption of related items. As expected, we see significant differences between the two groups, their consumption preferences, their satisfaction with the consumption experience, and several other variables including their willingness-to-pay for the products presented. In addition, to show that the effect of priming works regardless of default cultural self-construal, we replicate our findings with East Asian and Hispanic subjects.

Specific Studies & Results

The studies consist of several tests linking self-construal priming with differences in product selection and reluctance to break apart items perceived as being related. In Study 1, the Snack Study, consumers were primed, presented with a beverage, and allowed to select a snack. Somewhat surprisingly, independently-primed subjects were significantly more likely to choose *related* items in their initial selection, whereas collectives were significantly likely to choose *unrelated* items. One potential explanation for this is that collectives "see" more relationships among items, in general, which was supported by thought listing comments. Study 2, the Cute Puppy Study, replicated the findings from Study 1 and found a significant difference between how collective and independents deal with separating related items, with collectives experiencing greater dissonance and opting to consumer entirely different items to prevent separating related products while independents experienced no such dissonance when separating products. Study 3 replicated the results from Studies 1 & 2 in a realistic consumption setting –Amazon.com–while also finding support for *implied* product relationships as operationalized via Amazon's "Better Together" feature. Furthermore, Study 3 showed that priming techniques integrated into realistic advertisements produce the same effects as controlled laboratory priming techniques, which is an important contribution to marketing practitioners.

Theoretical & Managerial Implications

Theoretically, this paper's biggest contribution is the extension of relational priming from basic, interpersonal influence to the influence of perceived relationships among products and services, including the notion of experienced dissonance when such relationships are destroyed or broken. Additionally, the exploration of applied priming methodologies in the laboratory setting, such as advertisements or mock point-of-purchase displays, lends credibility to the external validity of such an approach as opposed to traditional self-construal priming techniques, such as the I/We pronoun-circling task or the Sumerian Warrior task. These contributions, among others, provide great insight to future research in this area.

Another motivation for pursuing this project rests in the significant impact the results of the study have for marketing managers as they develop strategies for marketing their products and services, both domestically and internationally. Implications of the results would be far-reaching, literally impacting each of the core components characterized by the traditional 4 Ps of marketing–product, price, placement, and promotion –in a way that may vary on the international level, culture to culture. To help illustrate the potential impact of the proposed study, let us consider specific examples as they related to these core marketing concepts:

Product: impacting product design decisions emphasizing either a stand-alone product or a product that is considered and included as one part of a related set of products

Price: impacting the ability to charge more for product bundles for collective consumers or taking advantage of up-selling or cross-selling tactics in particular markets

Placement: impacting the decision to sell products individually or as given sets or related items in different markets based on differences in self-construal across cultures

Promotion: impacting the creative design of advertisements emphasizing individualism or collectivism; impacting point-of-purchase displays that influence consumer behavior at the moment of product selection

Given the substantial theoretical and managerial implications presented by this paper's findings, it is the hope of the author that future research exploring the perceived relationships among products/services and measured/manipulated differences in consumers regarding their perception and maintenance of such relationships is pursued.

Selected References

Aaker, Jennifer L., Durairaj Maheswaran. The effect of cultural orientation on persuasion. *Journal of Consumer Research*. Gainesville: Dec 1997. Vol. 24, Iss. 3; p. 315.

Gardner, Wendi L, Gabriel, Shira, Lee, Angela Y. "I" value freedom, but "we" value relationships: Self-construal priming mirrors cultural differences in judgment. *Psychological Science*. New York: Jul 1999. Vol. 10, Iss. 4; pg. 321, 6 pgs.

Monga, Alokparna Basu and Deborah Roedder John (2007), "Cultural Differences in Brand Extension Evaluation: The Influence of Analytic versus Holistic Thinking," *Journal of Consumer Research*, 33 (March), 529-36.

Mourali, Mehdi, Michel Laroche, Frank Pons. Individualistic orientation and consumer susceptibility to interpersonal influence. *The Journal of Services Marketing*. Santa Barbara: 2005. Vol. 19, Iss. 3; pg. 164, 10 pgs.

Oyserman, Daphna, Heather M. Coon, Markus Kemmelmeier. Cultural psychology, a new look: Reply to Bond (2002), Fiske (2002), Kitayama (2002), and Miller (2002) *Psychological Bulletin*. Washington: Jan 2002. Vol. 128, Iss. 1; p. 110.

Singelis, Theodore M. The measurement of independent and interdependent self-construals. *Personality and Social Psychology Bulletin*. Thousand Oaks: Oct 1994. Vol. 20, Iss. 5; pg. 580.

How Does the Unconscious "Think"?

Nelson Amaral, University of Minnesota, USA

Research indicates that when consumers' information processing capacity is limited (e.g., people operate under time pressure), their reliance on normative conscious processing can result in less optimal decisions than if people use a heuristic processing strategy (Payne, Bettman, & Johnson, 1988). This has been attributed to the fact that more elaborate and normative conscious strategies work well only if one is able to take all of the information into account. Extending on this, it also follows that even if external factors do not limit people's processing capacity, individuals' decisions about complex stimuli (e.g., individuals' choice of a vacation destination from a set where all destinations are described on many dimensions) still may not be optimal because of inherent limitations in human's processing capacity. Indeed, it is estimated that the conscious mind can process only about 40-60 bits of information per second (Wilson 2002), whereas the processing capacity of the entire human system (*i.e.* conscious and unconscious processing) is 11,200,000 bits per second (Dijksterhuis, 2004).

Due to people's limited processing capacity, when individuals are presented with a great deal of information in a relatively short period of time, much of the information that is represented in memory is likely to be poorly organized. That is, individual pieces of information are inadequately associated and integrated. Interestingly, recent findings suggest that unconscious thought may circumvent such problems (Dijksterhuis, 2004; Dijksterhuis, Maarten, Nordgren, and Van Baaren, 2006; Payne, Samper, Bettman, and Luce 2008). At present little empirical investigation offers insight into how the unconscious might perform such consolidation. The current research aims to address this question by drawing on recent evidence that potentially sheds some light on the kind of processing that the unconscious employs.

This evidence comes from a recent report, which indicates that when people are in positions of high social power, the decisions they render based on conscious thought are similar to those made under conditions of unconscious thought (Smith, Dijksterhuis and Wigboldus, 2008). In light of research which shows that people in positions of higher power construe information in a more abstract (versus concrete) way (Smith and Trope, 2006), the preceding implies that the unconscious may rely on fairly abstract cognition. To investigate this possibility we sought to replicate the findings of Liberman, Sagristano, and Trope (2002), which found that participants planning a camping trip farther into the future grouped the items they would pack into larger more inclusive groups. The results also indicated that this was a result of thinking more abstractly about far future events than near future events. Our goal was to replicate the results of this grouping task by using the manipulations of the original sets of experiments conducted by Dijksterhuis and his colleagues in which they had participants read information about a set of related products and would subsequently either distract some participants or ask them to deliberate for several minutes before making a judgment or choice about the products they had seen before the period of deliberation (conscious thought) or distraction (unconscious thought). (Dijksterhuis, 2004; Dijksterhuis, Maarten, Nordgren, and Van Baaren, 2006). Our goal was to investigate the following initial hypothesis:

H1: Compared to conscious thought, reliance on unconscious thought will prompt individuals to organize information into broader, more inclusive groups. Thus, individuals who engage in conscious versus unconscious thought will both assign a set of items to a larger number of groups overall and assign fewer items to each group that is formed.

We employed a single factor, between subjects design: thought condition (un/conscious). Participants were undergraduates who entered a lab and were seated in individual cubicles or rooms. Participants were all shown the same list of 37 camping items from Liberman et. al (2002) and asked to study the list for 2 minutes. Participants were told that the information would be used later for an unspecified task. After two minutes passed, all lists were taken away.

Two thought conditions were manipulated in the same manner as employed in studies by Dijksterhuis and his colleagues (Dijksterhuis, 2004; Dijksterhuis et. al 2006). Specifically, in the conscious thought condition, participants were allotted 3 minutes to "think about the list" they had just seen. Alternatively; in the unconscious condition, participants were given 3 minutes to solve a series of anagrams that were unrelated to the listed items. After 3 minutes passed, all participants were provided a blank sheet of paper and asked to write down as many of the items from the list as they could remember. In addition, they were instructed to place the items into groups by drawing circles around similar items. Participants were allowed to take as much or as little time as they needed to perform the tasks.

Supporting our hypothesis, participants in the unconscious versus conscious condition formed larger, more inclusive groups. Specifically, those in the unconscious condition created significantly fewer groups ($p<0.01$), and on average they assigned more items to each group ($p=0.01$). An analysis of variance that included the total number of items recalled as a covariate confirmed that the difference in both the number and size of the groups was not attributable to participants' greater recall of the items in the conscious versus unconscious condition (significance levels remained at p=/<.01). Further, no treatment differences emerged in the number of items that participants accurately recalled, ruling out the possibility that these differences accounted for the outcomes. Finally, neither the number of groups participants formed nor the number of items they assigned to each group differed as a function of the number of anagrams that participants solved in the unconscious condition.

Overall, this study provides some important empirical insight into the "black box" of unconscious thought. Whereas work by Payne et. al (2008) indicates that certain boundary conditions can limit the advantage of unconscious thought when rendering complex decisions, the present research offers clues about why this might be so. Specifically, we found that compared to individuals who engage in conscious thought, those who process information unconsciously construe data at a more abstract (versus concrete) manner. This implies that any advantage offered by unconscious processing should be limited to contexts in which decisions are likely to benefit from abstract as opposed to concrete cognition-an observation that nicely aligns with Payne et al's (2008) findings. Our hope is that by gaining a better understanding of how unconscious thought operates, we can not only better illuminate other boundary conditions that limit the advantage of unconscious thought, but also better anticipate the precise kinds of decision and judgment tasks for which conscious or unconscious processing is best suited.

Bibliography

Dijksterhuis, Ap, Maarten W. Bos, L. F. Nordgren, and Rick B. Van Baaren (2006), "On Making the Right Choice: The Deliberation-Without-Attention Effect," *Science,* 311 Feb., p. 1005-1007

Dijksterhuis, Ap (2004), "Think Different: The Merits of Unconscious Thought in Preference Developent and Decision Making," *Journal of Personality and Social Psychology,* 87 (5) 586-598.)

Kramer, Thomas and Lauren Block (2008), "Conscious and Nonconscious Components of Superstitious Beliefs in Judgments and Decision Making," *Journal of Consumer Research*, 34 (6), 783-93.

Liberman, Nira, Michael D. Sagristano, and Yaacov Trope (2002), "The effect of temporal distance on level of mental construal," *Journal of Experimental Social Psychology*, 38, 523–534

Payne, John W., James R. Bettman and Eric J. Johnson (1988), *The Adaptive Decision Maker,* Cambridge: Cambridge University Press.

Payne, John W., Adriana Samper, James R. Bettman, and Mary Frances Luce (2008), "Boundary Conditions on Unconscious Thought in Complex Decision Making," *Psychological Science*, 19 (11) 1118-1123

Smith, Pamela K. and Yakov Trope (2006), "You Focus on the Forest When You're in Charge of the Trees: Power Priming and Abstract Information Processing," *Journal of Personality and Social Psychology*, 90 (4), 578–596

Exploring the Differential Nature of the Appeal of Visual Advertising to Consumers

Steven Andrews, University of Oregon, USA
Guangxin Xie, University of Massachusetts Boston, USA
David Boush, University of Oregon, USA

Two relatively new streams of research on consumer response to visual advertising, visual fluency and visual rhetoric, suggest that consumers rate visual advertising that is more pleasing to process as more appealing, presumably leading to some advantage in terms of persuasive impact. Both these streams of research adhere to the ideas of Scott's (1994a; 1994b) reader response theory. Reader response theory sought to conceptually link the psychology of the consumer with the attributes of the ad text. Thus, the intention of the author and the response of the reader were connected by shared cultural knowledge, and highly agile, culturally aware, and sophisticated critical readers derived as much (or more) meaning from contextual cues as from the form of the text itself. Thus, aesthetic judgments revolving around the processing of visual information occur primarily through the mental experiences of the person perceiving the visual information.

Visual fluency is defined as the ease or difficulty in which image information can be processed (Winkielman, Schwarz, Reber and Fazendeiro, 2003). Research on visual fluency, derived from research on affect as information (Schwarz and Clore, 2006), suggests that ads which are visually rich yet easy to process cognitively are more appealing to consumers. In contrast, research on visual rhetoric (McQuarrie and Mick, 2003b) in advertising shows that consumers both like and remember ads with rhetorical communication devices such as metaphors and puns to a greater extent. Visual ads containing rhetorical communication devices tend to be simpler visually, e.g. they may contain more white space (Pracejus, Olsen and O'Guinn, 2006) or they may contain two distinct elements juxtaposed together (Phillips and McQuarrie, 2004), yet slightly more complex cognitively. Therefore the point of divergence between these two streams of research seems to lie along the dimensions of visual and cognitive simplicity/complexity. This paper explores this divergence more closely in order to discover some insights into the differing nature of the appeal of visual advertising to consumers.

Approximately 150 participants at a university in the Pacific Northwest examined two pairs of ads which differed from each other in terms of visual and cognitive simplicity/complexity. We attempted as much as possible to control for brand name familiarity, using four fairly popular brands (Guess Jeans, Subaru, Visine, and Columbia Sportswear) that were deemed highly familiar to college students. In each ad pair, one ad was a rich visual ad which contained no rhetorical device while the other ad was visually simple but contained a purely visual rhetorical trope (McQuarrie and Mick, 1999). The non-rhetorical Subaru ad contained vivid colors of blue sky and green country side, while the non-rhetorical Guess Jeans ad contained two highly attractive models, one female and one male. The rhetorical Visine ad contained a very simple visual pun relating to the popular slogan "Visine gets the red out", while the rhetorical Columbia Sportswear Techlite sandals ad contained a visual metaphor linking the sandals to butterflies, for example implying "lightness". After viewing each pair of ads, participants chose which one they liked the most and then expounded on which ad they thought was more memorable and why. After taking a series of filler tests not related to this study, participants were asked to recall as many brand names as possible or if not the name then something about the ad.

Overall 51% of the participants liked the visually rich non-rhetorical ads better while 55% thought the visually simpler rhetorical ad was more memorable. Approximately 6% of the participants thought the ad in the opposite likeability category was more memorable. An overwhelming percentage (81%) of the people changing their answer thought that the rhetorical ad was more memorable despite claiming to like the non-rhetorical ad more. Double blind examination of response patterns suggested that the primary reason for this shift involved either a pleasant or unpleasant reaction to spontaneously trying to interpret the meaning behind the ad. Chi-square analysis showed that unaided recall did not differ significantly across rhetorical vs. non-rhetorical ads.

Response patterns for memorability differed markedly between the two types of advertisements. Collapsing the responses for both non-rhetorical ads together, the reasons for memorability were fairly uniform. About 70% of the subjects listed "rich, appealing visual ad features" as the reason they believed the ad to be more memorable. For the Subaru ad most responses focused on the vivid colors. For the Guess Jeans ad most responses focused on the sexy models. In contrast, collapsing responses across both the rhetorical ads revealed several prominent response categories. The most popular reason participants gave (61%) for rating the rhetorical ads as more memorable was the presence of and/or the interpretation of the meaning behind the rhetorical device. The other popular response patterns included the uniqueness (22%) and simplicity (15%) of the ad.

The patterns of the responses in these findings point to promising avenues for research into individual differences with respect to factors affecting the appeal of processing of visual ads. Specifically, research that suggests inherent tendencies to process information affectively vs. cognitively such as need for cognition (Cacioppo, Petty and Kao, 1984), affect as information (Gohm and Clore, 2002; Schwarz and Clore, 2006) and general information processing individual differences (Giese and Sojka, 1998; Sojka and Giese, 1997) may provide useful insight into psychological mechanisms that influence differential consumer response to visual advertising along the dimensions of visual and cognitive simplicity/complexity.

References

Cacioppo, J.T., R.E. Petty and C.F. Kao. (1984), "The efficient assessment of need for cognition. ." *Journal of Personality Assessment*, 48 306-307.

Giese, Joan L. and Jane Z. Sojka. (1998), "The Relationship Between Processing Styles and Self-Control Behavioral Characteristics." *Marketing Letters*, 9 (4), 371-382.

Gohm, Carol L. and Gerald L. Clore. (2002), "Affect as Information: An Individual Differences Approach." in *The Wisdom of Feeling: Psychological Process in Emotional Intelligence*, Lisa Feldman Barrett and Peter Salovey, ed(s), New York:The Guilford Press, 89-113.

McQuarrie, Edward F. and David Glen Mick. (1999), "Visual Rhetoric in Advertising: Text-Interpretive, Experimental, and Reader-Response Analyses." *Journal of Consumer Research*, 26 (1), 37-54.

McQuarrie, Edward F. and David Glen Mick. (2003b), "The Contribution of Semiotic and Rhetorical Perspectives to the Explanation of Visual Persuasion in Advertising." in *Persuasive Imagery: A Consumer Response Perspective*, LM Scott & Rajeev Batra, ed(s), Mahwah, NJ:Lawrence Earlbaum Associates, Inc, 191-222.

Phillips, Barbara J. and Edward F. McQuarrie. (2004), "Beyond Visual Metaphor: A New Typology of Visual Rhetoric in Advertising." *Marketing Theory*, 4 (1), 113-137.

Pracejus, John W., G. Douglas Olsen and Thomas C. O'Guinn. (2006), "How Nothing Became Something: White Space, Rhetoric, History, and Meaning." *Journal of Consumer Research*, 33 82-90.

Schwarz, Norbert and Gerald L. Clore. (2006), "Feelings and Phenomenal Experiences." in *Social Psychology. Handbood of Basic Principles (2nd edition)*, A. Kruglanski and E.T. Higgens, ed(s), New York:Guilford, 1-30.

Sojka, Jane Z. and Joan L. Giese. (1997), "Thinking and/or Feeling: An Examination of Interaction Between Processing Styles." *Advances in Consumer Research*, 24 (1), 438-442.

Winkielman, Piotr, Norbert Schwarz, Rolf Reber and Tedra A. Fazendeiro. (2003), "Cognitive and Affective Consequences of Visual Fluency: When Seeing is Easy on the Mind." in *Persuasive Imagery: A Consumer Response Perspective*, LM Scott & Rajeev Batra, ed(s), Mahwah, NJ:Lawrence Earlbaum Associates, Inc, 75-90.

Effects of Evaluability on Goal Fulfillment and Satisfaction

Zachary Arens, University of Maryland, USA
Rebecca Hamilton, University of Maryland, USA

Goal theory suggests that goal fulfillment involves evaluating an outcome against the goal's criteria. However, goals differ in their evaluability (Hsee 1996; Hsee et al. 1999). We propose that goals are easy to evaluate when they are specific, defined in terms of product features, or when there is a standard of comparison, but difficult to evaluate when they are vague, defined in terms of benefits or lack standards. These differences in evaluability impact goal fulfillment, product satisfaction and motivation to pursue the goal. Thus, easy-to-evaluate (difficult-to-evaluate) goals create polarized (moderate) levels of satisfaction and motivation, depending on product performance.

Of particular interest to marketing managers, goal evaluability differs for purchase goals depending on whether the goal is defined in terms of product features or benefits (Huffman, Ratneshwar, and Mick 2000). Consider, for example, two consumers who enter a store to buy a set of cookware. The first consumer's goal is to buy a set of cookware that is easy-to-clean; while the second consumer's goal is to buy a set of cookware made of infused anodized aluminum, which creates a nonstick, easy-to-clean surface. Though both may end up buying the same set of cookware, the purchase was motivated by goals that were defined at different levels. The desire for easy-to-clean cookware is a benefit goal, whereas the desire for infused anodized cookware is a feature goal. Although these goals are related, the difference in conceptualization should lead to different motivation to purchase supplementary products. Feature goals are easily evaluated because the evaluation simply requires determining the presence or absence of the desired feature, leading to a high or low degree of goal fulfillment. In contrast, benefit goals lack a natural scale to provide a standard of comparison, making product evaluation difficult. Because benefit goals cannot be definitively achieved, they will lead to a moderate degree of goal fulfillment.

Therefore, if the purchased cookware is infused anodized and easy-to-clean, we expect that the consumer with the feature goal should evaluate the product more positively and be less willing to purchase supplementary products (e.g., brushes that make it easy to clean cookware) than the consumer with the benefit goal. However, when the purchased cookware is not infused anodized and is difficult-to-clean, the consumer with the feature goal should evaluate the product more negatively and be more willing to purchase supplementary products than the consumer with the benefit goal.

To test this, we conducted two studies. In our first study, participants were given a scenario of purchasing a safe car. The goal for a safe car was defined in terms of features (i.e., airbags and anti-lock brakes) or benefits (i.e., feeling safe). The purchased car was described as either having safety characteristics or not. Results suggested that viewing the goal in terms of features or benefits exhibited the predicted moderating effect on participant's evaluations of the product. In other words, participants with a feature goal gave more polarized evaluations of the product than those with a benefit goal.

The second study plans to show that goal evaluability can be impacted by evaluability information and goal specificity. Participants will be given a goal of improving their score on a mental ability test. In order to help them achieve their goal, they will consume a ginseng-based beverage after the first test which they are told can improve mental performance on the next test. Goal specificity will be manipulated by providing participants with a specific goal (i.e., "improve your score by 5 points") or vague goal (i.e., "improve your score substantially") on the mental ability task. Evaluability information will be manipulated by either providing or omitting the average increase in mental ability score (i.e., "the average person's score improves 4 points after consuming ginseng"). Scores will be manipulated such that the ginseng beverage appears to perform well (i.e., score increases 6 by points) or poorly (i.e., score decreases by 6 points). The results are expected to demonstrate that specific goals and evaluability information make the goal easier to evaluate. When the ginseng product performs well (poorly), easy-to-evaluate goals should create high (low) product satisfaction and low (high) motivation to purchase products that enhance mental performance such as omega-3 vitamins, brain teaser exercises and newsmagazines. However when the goal is difficult-to-evaluate, satisfaction and motivation should be moderate regardless of the product's performance.

This research demonstrates that goal evaluability moderates the effect of product characteristics on goal fulfillment, satisfaction and motivation. These results have important implications for managers. Managers of high-performing products that are expected to satisfy consumer's goals can increase customer satisfaction by increasing goal evaluability. For instance, their advertisements should emphasize specific product features or create standards to allow customers to evaluate product benefits. In contrast, managers of poorly-performing products should decrease evaluability by emphasizing product benefits and avoiding comparison standards.

References

Hsee, Christopher K. (1996), "The Evaluability Hypothesis: An Explanation for Preference Reversals between Joint and Separate Evaluations of Alternatives," *Organizational Behavior and Human Decision Processes*, 67 (3), 247-57.

Hsee, Christopher K., George F. Loewenstein, Sally Blount, and Max H. Bazerman (1999), "Preference Reversals between Joint and Separate Evaluations of Options: A Review and Theoretical Analysis," *Psychological Bulletin*, 125 (5), 576-90.

Huffman, Cynthia, S. Ratneshwar, and David Glen Mick (2000), "Consumer Goal Structures and Goal-Determination Processes: An Integrative Framework," in *The Why of Consumption: Contemporary Perspectives on Consumer Motives, Goals and Desires*, ed. S. Ratneshwar, David Glen Mick and Cynthia Huffman, New York: Routledge, 9-35.

Differences in Self-Regulatory Strength as a Function of Self-Construal

Ashley Rae Arsena, University of Texas at San Antonio, USA
Jaehoon Lee, University of Texas at San Antonio, USA
L. J. Shrum, University of Texas at San Antonio, USA
Yinlong Zhang, University of Texas at San Antonio, USA
Joy L. Row, University of Texas at San Antonio, USA

Research examining self-regulation has shown that people possess a limited amount of self-regulatory resources and that an initial act of self-control depletes these resources. Depletion of self-regulatory resources results in poor performance on subsequent tasks of self-regulation. For example, Baumeister et al. (1998) found that when individuals forced themselves to eat radishes instead of more appealing chocolates, they quit sooner on unsolvable puzzles than did individuals who did not engage in this initial act of self-control.

Yet, not all individuals have the same self-regulation abilities. Anecdotal and empirical evidence suggests that differences in self-control exist. For example, research has shown that regular exercises in self-control can increase self-regulation capacity. Muraven, Baumeister, and Tice (1999) found that repeated practice of self-control (i.e., spending weeks monitoring posture) improved self-regulatory ability measured by a handgrip task, much like repeated exercise of a muscle increases its strength (Muraven and Baumeister 2000). Similarly, Gailliot et al. (2007) found that after writing about an obese or homosexual person without using any stereotypes, participants with low motivation to avoid prejudice performed worse on a subsequent self-regulation task than did those with high motivation. Individuals with high motivation to avoid prejudice performed better on subsequent acts of self-regulation presumably because they had engaged in regular exercises of self-control by continually suppressing prejudice thoughts, whereas those who performed poorly on the self-regulation task (low motivation to avoid prejudice) presumably did so because they had little practice at self-control (they rarely engaged in suppression of prejudice thoughts). Thus, not only does motivation increase the likelihood of exercising self-control across situations, but repeated exercise of self-control as a function of this motivation also increases the ability to exercise this self-control.

Another individual difference measure that may be related to both the motivation and ability to exercise self-control is self-construal. Self-construal refers to how people perceive themselves to be linked to others (Markus and Kitayama 1991). People with a predominantly independent self-construal see themselves as independent and autonomous, distinct from the group, and tend to rely more on attitudes than subjective norms when making behavioral decisions (Ybarra and Trafimow 1998). In contrast, interdependents perceive themselves in the context of a larger group, are concerned more with group harmony than individual happiness, rely more on subjective norms than attitudes when making behavioral decisions, and place a high value on conformity and connectedness.

Research shows that interdependents tend to display less impulsive behavior than independents (Kacen and Lee 2002; Zhang and Shrum 2009). However, this does not appear to be the result of naturally occurring desire; independents and interdependents showed no difference on measures of trait buying impulsivity. Rather, the differences appear to be due to greater motivation on the part of interdependent to suppress those buying impulses (Zhang and Shrum 2009). If this is so, then just as with the case of motivation to suppress prejudice, continued exercise of the self-control "muscle" may increase its strength, thereby increasing the ability of interdependents to successfully exercise self-control compared to independents.

To test this hypothesis, the current research investigated whether self-construal influences self-regulation capacity. Specifically, we tested whether interdependents would show more self-control after a self-control depletion task than would independents. Chronic self-construal was measured because repeated practice at self-control is needed to increase self-regulation ability. Self-regulatory resources were depleted using a task adopted from DeWall et al. (2008) in which participants are required to learn a habit, and then are forced to break the habit. Breaking a habit is an act of self-control because it requires one to alter an initial impulse and act in line with a new standard. Participants were given a journal article and instructed to cross out every instance of the letter *e*. In depletion conditions, participants were then required to adhere to new rules (i.e. do not cross out *e*'s if the *e* is followed by a vowel). Participants in no-depletion conditions were asked to continue crossing out the letter *e*, and no other instructions were given. Participants were then asked to indicate the number of chocolates they would want to receive as a reward. The number of chocolates served as the main dependent variable for self-control. As ostensibly part of a second study, participants then completed a 31-item Self-Construal Scale (Aaker 2000; Singelis 1994).

We first classified participants on their level of independence and interdependence separately. We then constructed two groups, one high on interdependence and low on independence (and thus maximally likely to exercise self-control across situations), and the other high on independence and low on interdependence (minimally likely to exercise self-control). The results showed that, consistent with our hypotheses, interdependents took fewer chocolates in the depletion condition than did independents. These results suggest that interdependents perform better on subsequent acts of self-regulation than do independents. This finding supports our reasoning that the self-regulation ability of interdependents is superior to that of independents because interdependents have engaged in regular exercises of self-control (continually suppressing impulsive thoughts or behaviors). In contrast, because independents generally act on their interests and impulses, they have relatively less practice at self-control and thus perform worse on self-regulation tasks. However, contrary to our expectations, there were no differences between self-construal groups in no-depletion conditions. If continual practice at self-control does increase self-regulation ability, then independents should have also taken more chocolates than interdependents in no-depletion conditions. Yet, no differences were found. This may have been because the self-control task (resisting chocolates) was not strong enough to detect initial differences. Nevertheless, the results suggest that differences in self-regulation capacity do exist as a function of self-construal.

References

Aaker, Jennifer L. (2000), "Accessibility or Diagnosticity? "Disentangling the Influence of Culture on Persuasion Processes and Attitudes," *Journal of Consumer Research*, 26 (March), 340-57.

Baumeister, Roy E., Ellen Bratslavsky, Mark Muraven, and Dianne M. Tice (1998), "Ego Depletion: Is the Active Self a Limited Resource?" *Journal of Personality and Social Psychology*, 74 (5), 1252-65.

DeWall, Nathan C., Roy F. Baumeister, Matthew T. Gailliot, and Jon K. Maner (2008), "Depletion Makes the Heart Grow Less Helpful: Helping as a Function of Self-Regulatory Energy and Genetic Relatedness," *Personality and Social Psychology Bulletin*, 34 (12), 1653-62.

Gailliot, Matthew T., E. Ashby Plant, David A. Butz, and Roy F. Baumeister (2007), "Increasing Self-Regulatory Strength Can Reduce the Depleting Effect of Suppressing Stereotypes," *Personality and Social Psychology Bulletin*, 33 (2), 281-94.

Markus, Hazel R. and Shinobu Kitayama (1991), "Culture and the Self: Implications for Cognition, Emotion, and Motivation," *Psychological Review*, 98 (2), 224-53.

Muraven, Mark and Roy F. Baumeister (2000), "Self-Regulation and Depletion of Limited Resources: Does Self-Control Resemble a Muscle?" *Psychological Bulletin,* 126 (2), 247-59.

Muraven, Mark, Roy F. Baumeister, and Dianne M. Tice (1999), "Longitudinal Improvement of Self-Regulation through Practice: Building Self-Control Strength through Repeated Exercise," *Journal of Social Psychology*, 139 (August), 446-57.

Singelis, Ted (1994), "The Measurement of Independent and Interdependent Self Construals," *Personality and Social Psychology Bulletin,* 20 (5), 580–91.

Ybarra, Oscar and David Trafimow (1998), "How Priming the Private Self or Collective Self Affects the Relative Weights of Attitudes and Subjective Norms," *Personality and Social Psychology Bulletin*, 24 (April), 362-70.

Zhang, Yinlong and L. J. Shrum (2009), "The Influence of Self-Construal on Impulsive Consumption," *Journal of Consumer Research*, 35 (February), 838-50.

Imagine Instructions: When Do They Help or Hurt Persuasion?

Ashley Rae Arsena, University of Texas at San Antonio, USA
R. Justin Goss, University of Texas at San Antonio, USA
David H. Silvera, University of Texas at San Antonio, USA
Frank R. Kardes, University of Cincinnati, USA
Bruce Pfeiffer, University of New Hampshire, USA

According to current models of persuasion such as the elaboration likelihood model (Petty and Cacioppo 1983) and the heuristic systematic model (Chaiken 1987), high amounts of thought or elaboration have been found to increase advertising effectiveness and attitude strength. For example, Petty and Cacioppo (1983) found that participants who elaborated on an advertisement message under the central route to persuasion showed a greater increase in attitude strength and persistence of attitudes over time relative to participants who did not engage in extensive elaboration.

Elaboration has been induced in a variety of ways. Pictures, concrete information, and personal relevance have all been found to increase elaboration and, subsequently, increase persuasive impact and attitude strength for the target advertisement message (Haugtvedt and Strathman 1990). Yet, another way to effectively increase elaboration is to instruct consumers to imagine additional information supporting the persuasive message. This imagine technique has been used in many advertisements; for example, consumer protection groups like TheTruth.com have used this technique in a number of anti-tobacco advertisements in which people are presented with an exemplar (e.g., memos indicating that tobacco companies knew smoking increased cancer risk) and then asked to imagine additional related information (e.g., systematic attempts to conceal the association between tobacco and cancer risk).

Research examining the imagine technique has found that instructions to imagine increase elaboration, thus enhancing advertising effectiveness (Kisielius and Sternthal 1984, 1986). However, conditions under which imagine instructions are more or less persuasive have not been identified. The current research aimed to identify conditions under which the imagine technique facilitates greater adherence to the advertisement message.

Several motivational and capacity variables were examined as potential moderators of the tendency to seek out and access unpresented information in a judgmental context. In particular, need for cognitive closure (NFCC) was investigated as a potential moderator of the effectiveness of imagine instructions. Given that individuals with high NFCC have been shown to desire immediate answers over ambiguity (Webster and Kruglanski 1994), high NFCC individuals might fail to elaborate on presented information unless they are specifically instructed to do so. However, because low NFCC individuals are more willing to elaborate, they might imagine additional information and adjust their attitudes to correspond with that information regardless of whether they receive imagine instructions. Thus, imagine instructions should be less influential for low NFCC than for high NFCC individuals.

Construal level was investigated as another potential moderator of the tendency to seek out and access unpresented information in a judgmental context. Construal level theory proposes that high versus low construal level influences peoples' responses by changing the way they mentally represent events (Liberman and Trope 1998). High level construal is associated with abstract and general representation, whereas low level construal is associated with more concrete and detail-oriented representations. Because imagining requires abstraction beyond the provided message, high level construal should facilitate imagination and increase adherence to the target message.

Three studies were conducted to test potential moderators of the imagine technique. All three studies presented participants with a fictitious advertisement and asked them to evaluate the product in the advertisement. In the imagine condition, participants were asked to imagine further information that supported the advertisement's message (e.g., "Imagine what else Special K can do to improve your health"). In the no imagine condition, no further instructions were given.

In the first study, participants viewed an advertisement with a negative message about McDonald's (i.e., McDonald's exploits children). After viewing the advertisement, participants answered questions that assessed attitudes and purchase intentions toward

McDonald's along with the NFCC scale. Participants in the imagine condition expressed more negative attitudes toward McDonald's, which indicates that the imagine technique is an effective persuasion tool because it caused greater adherence to the advertisement message. In addition, high NFCC participants formed more positive attitudes (thus going against the advertisement's negative message) in the no imagine condition relative to the imagine condition. However, low NFCC participants in the no imagine and imagine condition expressed similar negative attitudes toward McDonald's. Thus it appears that the imagine technique is particularly effective for high NFCC individuals but not for low NFCC individuals.

Study 2 investigated whether construal level influenced whether imagine instructions affect attitudes about a positive message about Subway (i.e., Subway can improve your health). Construal level was manipulated via a prime adapted from McCrea et al. (2008) where participants were asked to view a painting by Seurat that drew their attention either to the overall effect of the painting (abstract condition) or to the technique of pointillism (concrete condition). Participants then viewed a positive message and completed an attitude assessment. Participants in the abstract/imagine condition formed more favorable attitudes than participants in the concrete/imagine condition, which indicates that abstract processing facilitates imaginative thinking and increases persuasion.

In the third study, participants viewed an advertisement with a positive message about Special K (i.e., Special K is healthy), with promotion focus measured as a potential moderator of the effectiveness of imagine instructions. Because high promotion focused individuals tend to have strong positive dispositions (Higgins et al. 1994), they might spontaneously imagine additional information to support a positive message; conversely, low promotion focused individuals might generate supporting positive information only when specifically instructed to do so. The results support this proposition; participants in the low promotion focus and no imagine condition rated Special K more negatively than all other groups (thus not supporting the advertisement's message). Thus, presumably because low promotion individuals are predisposed to be less positive, the imagine technique is useful in encouraging attitudes that support a positive message. Consequently, the imagine technique appears to significantly increase adherence to a positive message for low promotion focus individuals but not for high promotion focus individuals.

The present studies expand on previous research examining the effectiveness of the imagine technique by identifying conditions under which imagine instructions are more or less effective. Future studies will continue to examine characteristics of the message, the recipient, and the advertising context that moderate the effectiveness of the imagine technique.

References

Chaiken, Shelly (1980), "Heuristic versus systematic information processing in the use of source versus message quest in persuasion," *Journal of Personality and Social Psychology,* 39 (5), 752–766.

Haugtvedt, Curtis P. and Alan J. Strathman (1990), "Situational personal relevance and attitude Persistence," *Advances in Consumer Research,* 21 (3), 766–769.

Higgins, Tory E., Christopher J. Roney, Ellen Crowe and Charles Hymes (1994), "Ideal versus ought predilections for approach and avoidance: Distinct self-regulatory systems," *Journal of Personality & Social Psychology*, 66 (2), 276-286.

Kisielius, Jolita and Brian Sternthal (1984), "Detecting and Explaining Vividness Effects in Attitudinal Judgments," *Journal of Marketing Research*, 21 (1), 54–64.

______ (1986), "Examining the Vividness Controversy: An Availability- Valence Interpretation," *Journal of Consumer Research,* 12 (4), 418–31.

Liberman, Nira and Yaacov Trope (1998), "The role of feasibility and desirability considerations in near and distant future decisions: A test of temporal construal theory," *Journal of Personality and Social Psychology,* 75 (1), 5–18.

McCrea, Sean, Nira Liberman, Yaacov Trope, and Steven Sherman (2008), "Construal Level and Procrastination," Psychological *Science*, 19 (12), 1308-1313.

Petty, Richard E., John T. Cacioppo, and David Schumann (1983) "Central and peripheral routes to advertising effectiveness: The moderating role of involvement," *Journal of Consumer Research,* 10 (9), 135–146.

Webster, Donna M. and Arie W. Kruglanski (1994), "Individual differences in need for cognitive closure," Journal *of Personality and Social Psychology*, 67 (6), 1049-1062.

Unwanted Objects and Situations: Experiencing Disgust in Consumption Contexts

A. Selin Atalay, HEC Paris, France
Melea Press, University of Wyoming, USA

The goal of this paper is to understand how consumers respond to feelings of disgust. Disgust is experienced in response to unwanted stimuli (Olatunji and Sawchuck 2005). There are two categories of disgust: core and socio-moral disgust. Core disgust refers to physical repulsion (Haidt, Rozin, McCauley and Imada 1997). It is protective of one's body. Socio-moral disgust is elicited by contact with objects that are evil (i.e., a shirt worn by an evil person). It is protective of social order.

In this paper a new elicitor of disgust, *inconvenience*, is discovered. Individuals' responses to disgust in consumption settings are explored.

Study 1

Study 1 was conducted with 107 undergraduates to explore disgust elicitors. Participants were asked to reflect on the last time they felt disgusted, and rate their disgusting experiences.

Results. From 107 participants we collected 101 disgusting experiences. Core and socio-moral elicitors of disgust were prevalent (21% and 41% respectively). Further, the elicitors of disgust have broadened to include a new elicitor; *inconvenience*. *Inconvenience* refers to products, situations or experiences that did not work out as planned, hoped, desired, or imagined and caused discomfort to the person. Thirty-one percent of our respondents stated that they experienced disgust elicited by inconvenience.

Participants rated their experiences on a 0-10 scale where 0 indicated not at all disgusting and 10 indicated extremely disgusting. The elicitors were equally disgusting (F(2,92)= 1.179, p> .3, M= 7.57 (core), M= 8.40 (socio-moral), M= 7.97 (inconvenience)).

Study 2

Study 2 was conducted with 88 undergraduates, to verify the *inconvenience* disgust elicitor. Three scenarios that evoke core, socio-moral, or inconvenience disgust were constructed based on the disgusting incidents reported in study 1. Participants were asked to complete a survey indicating how they expected to feel in response to each scenario. They rated 34 positive and negative emotions on a 0-10 scale.

Results. Participants reported that all three scenarios made them feel equally disgusted F(2, 260)=.683, p>.5; M=7.03 (core), M=7.07(socio-moral); M=6.56 (inconvenience)).

Feelings of being upset, angry, frustrated, annoyed and irritable are associated with disgust (Holbrook and Batra 1987, Nabi 2002). We factor analyzed the emotions that the participants rated and created a composite score. The composite score is a weighted average based on the factor analysis. The elicitors made participants feel different levels of the emotions associated with disgust. F(2,262)=3.657, p<.05: M=5.44 (core), M=5.86 (socio-moral), M=6.22 (inconvenience). The core disgust elicitor did not elicit as much of the disgust related emotions as the socio-moral and inconvenience elicitors did.

Discussion. Study 2 verified that inconvenience elicits disgust as well as the emotions associated with disgust.

Study 3

Study 3 was conducted with 41 undergraduates to explore the action tendencies associated with the inconvenience disgust elicitor.

Two scenarios demonstrating the inconvenience disgust elicitor were created. Participants were asked to indicate how they would feel and what they would do in response to each scenario. Participants also rated how disgusting each scenario is on a 0-10 scale where 0 indicated not at all disgusting and 10 indicated extremely disgusting.

Results. The first scenario involved a frustrating telephone conversation with tech-support. In response participants indicated that they would feel disgusted (M=6.20, t(40)=2.59, p<0.05 two-tailed, test value=5). The second scenario involved encounter with an unhelpful sales associate. In response participants indicated that they would feel disgusted (M=7.00, t(40)=4.88, p<0.0001 two-tailed, test value=5).

Action Tendencies. In response to Scenario 1, 95.1% participants indicated that they would talk about this experience. Sixty-one percent indicated they would leave the disgusting situation. Only 2.4% indicated that they would complain while 19.5% said in the future they would prefer a different company. In response to Scenario 2, 87.8% participants indicated that they would talk about this experience. Sixty-three percent indicated they would leave the disgusting situation. Only 14.6% indicated that they would complain while 39% said in the future they would prefer a different company.

Discussion. Participants indicated, in response to the inconvenience disgust elicitor, they will talk about their experience, but not complain. Talking about disgusting experiences has the potential to create negative word of mouth. Also when customers do not complain the company does not get a chance to rectify the situation.

Study 4

Study 4 explores how a different population responds when they experience disgust. Participants were 28 staff members at a northeastern university. Participants were asked to elaborate on two disgusting consumption experiences that they had. They were asked to explain each experience, and indicate how they responded.

Results. From the 28 participants we collected 45 scenarios. The 45 scenarios were composed of 36% core, 9% socio-moral and 53% inconvenience disgust situations. The socio-moral disgust elicitor was not prevalent in consumption contexts, as such these scenarios were not further analyzed.

Participants rated how disgusting each scenario is on a 0-10 scale. Disgust elicitors are equally disgusting. F(1, 37)=0.56, p >.4: M=6.44 (core), M=6.96 (inconvenience).

In response to the disgusting situations participants reported that they got rid of the product or terminated service (core: 50%; inconvenience: 12.5%); and complained (core: 25%; inconvenience: 54%). Participants also indicated that in the future they are equally likely to complain and talk about their disgusting experiences, measured on a 0-10 likelihood scale where 0 indicated not at all likely and 10 indicated extremely likely (p>.4, p>.9) (Complain: M=6.6 (core), M=7.5 (inconvenience); talk about it: M=7.9 (core), M=7.9 (inconvenience))

Discussion. We replicate the findings with a different population. In consumption contexts core and inconvenience disgust elicitors were mainly reported. This study further demonstrates the prevalence of inconvenience disgust elicitors in consumption contexts.

General Discussion

The definition of disgust is not static (Nabi 2002). It evolves as the society evolves. In the four studies presented here we provide evidence that *inconvenience* a new category of disgust emerges in the consumption context. We showed that individuals feel disgusted by core, socio-moral and inconvenience disgust elicitors, and the action tendencies evoked by the feeling of disgust namely creating word of mouth and not complaining are potentially damaging to businesses.

References

Batra, Rajeev and Morris B. Holbrook (1990), "Developing a Typology of Affective Responses to Advertising," *Psychology and Marketing*, 7 (1), 11-25.

Haidt, Jonathan; Rozin, Paul; McCauley, Clark, and Sumio Imada (1997), "Body, Psyche, and Culture: The Relationship between Disgust and Morality," *Psychology and Developing Societies*, 9 (1), 107-31.

Haidt, Jonathan (2003), "The Moral Emotions," in *Handbook of Affective Sciences. Series in Affective Sciences.* Oxford University Press: New York. Richard J. Davidson, Klaus R. Scherer, H. Hill Goldsmith, eds. p. 852-870.

Holbrook, Morris B. and Rajeev Batra (1987), "Assessing the Role of Emotions as Mediators of Consumer Responses to Advertising," *Journal of Consumer Research*, 14 (3), 404-20.

Nabi, Robin L. (2002), "The Theoretical versus the Lay Meaning of Disgust: Implications for Emotion Research," *Cognition and Emotion*, 16 (5), 695-703.

Olatunji, Bunmi O. and Crag N. Sawchik (2005), "Disgust: Characteristic Features, Social Manifestations, and Clinical Implications," *Journal of Social and Clinical Psychology*, 24(7), p. 932-962.

Rozin, P., Jonathan Haidt, and C.R. McCauley (2000), "Disgust," in *Handbook of Emotions*, M. Lewis and J. M. Haviland-Jones, Eds. 2nd ed. New York: Guilford Press.

Rozin, Paul and April E. Fallon (1987), "A Perspective on Disgust," *Psychological Review*, 94(1), p .23-41.

The Liberating Effect of Guilt-Sharing on Consumers' Preference for Indulgence

Ozge Yucel Aybat, Baruch College, CUNY, USA
Thomas Kramer, Baruch College, CUNY, USA

In choices between indulgent and non-indulgent options, the latter are often preferred because indulgence tends to be associated with guilt. However, we propose that the amount of guilt experienced, and hence preference for indulgence, depends on whether consumers are in a lone versus shared consumption situation. Specifically, relative to choice of fruit salad, we found that respondents were more likely to choose two pieces of chocolate cake to be shared with another consumer than one piece of chocolate cake to be consumed alone. Further analyses support the hypothesis that reductions in feelings of guilt appear to be driving this effect.

Understanding the Situational Appeal of Local Brands in Emerging Economies: The Case of Turkey

Nilufer Z. Aydinoglu, Koc University, Turkey
Rajeev Batra, University of Michigan, USA
Aysegul Ozsomer, Koc University, Turkey

Many multinational companies today are altering their brand portfolios in favor of global brands, out of a belief not only that this will yield various economies of scale but also that consumers around the world prefer such global brands to otherwise equivalent local brands. Previous research has in fact shown that consumers do often prefer such global brands, because of inferred higher quality, perceived prestige, and because owning and consuming such brands offers the consumer a chance to vicariously become a part of global consumer culture (e.g. Batra et al. 2000).

Despite these findings, there is also evidence from other research that in many countries consumers are not rushing headlong into purchases and lifestyles that symbolize global consumer culture, but instead are seeking to blend aspects of local consumer culture with that of incoming global consumer culture. There is by now a significant literature on the phenomenon of consumers "hybridizing" or "creolizing" their lifestyles and consumption patterns, including brand choices (e.g., Sandikci and Ger 2002). This suggests that consumers are pulled in two directions, not only by global cultural flows but also by their local cultures.

While the power and influence of these global cultural forces is understood quite well, that of local cultures is not understood as well. There is indeed work that suggests that local consumers might prefer local to foreign/global brands because of a "home country bias" (Papadoupolos, Heslop and Bemossy 1990) or because of an "ethnocentric" desire to boost local economies (Shimp and Sharma 1987). However, what is less well understood is the ways in which consumers balance and integrate these two forces, such as the situational contingencies that make them weight one over the other, and the reasons why these situational contingencies might occur. Hence, our first objective in this paper is to address this issue by simultaneously exploring the reasons behind local and global brand preference.

The definition of the global brand itself is a controversial issue. Different scholars have provided different definitions and operationalizations as to the degree of globalness a brand holds. However there is no consensus on the degree of standardization required (if any at all) for a brand to qualify as global and also about the extent of availability across different nations. This causes ambiguity in interpreting and comparing the findings of different studies, whose definitions of globalness may be different to start with. In line with this debate, our second objective in this paper is to clarify the distinction between local and global brands. We believe that the degree of brand globalness lies in the perceptions of consumers.

In addressing these objectives, we use two waves of data collection. The first wave consists of focus groups and in-depth interviews to provide insight into consumer perceptions and preferences. We utilize this insight from the qualitative wave to identify the dimensions of (1) consumer perceptions of degree of localness/globalness, (2) perceived benefits of local/global brands and corresponding preferences, and (3) the situational variables affecting consumer preference between local and global brands. This first wave is conducted in two different cities of Turkey, an emerging economy. The second wave, then, tests our proposed model (based on the dimensions we identify) using survey data from Turkey with multivariate analysis.

Based on the insight from our first wave of qualitative data (four focus groups and fifteen in-depth interviews), we identify three dimensions which affect the degree of localness/globalness for a brand as perceived by consumers. The first dimension relates to 'product and company positioning' and measures consumer familiarity with the brand across different countries, and how the product is designed to address the needs and wants of a local versus a global audience. The second dimension relates to 'business behavior' and measures the perceived availability of the brand across countries and the company's ties and relationships with other local and global businesses and institutions, again as perceived by consumers. Finally, the third dimension relates to the brand's 'culture positioning' and investigates how the brand uses associations from the local or the global consumer culture in its promotional activity.

In our proposed model, each brand is measured on the aforementioned three dimensions to arrive at degrees of perceived localness and perceived globalness separately. Next, we investigate how these perceptions translate into consumer benefits under four dimensions of quality, prestige, tradition/values, and price. Finally, perceived benefits feed into determining an overall degree of preference for localness and globalness. We should stress that in all facets of our model, consumers rate both the local and the global dimensions of a brand and report their corresponding preferences. Our simultaneous focus on consumers' global and local brand preferences makes it possible to investigate the situational factors acting on such preferences. We find that the social signaling value of choice and perceived risk of choice are important moderators relating to product category. Furthermore, susceptibility to external influence, cosmopolitanism, and nostalgia proneness come up as individual difference moderators.

Accordingly, we are able to integrate findings from two streams of research discussed earlier, advocating a dominant consumer preference for global brands versus a dominant consumer preference for local brands, by shedding light into some of the situational contingencies determining such preference. While studying consumer preference, our work also contributes to the literature by systematically measuring the degree of globalness and degree of localness as perceived by consumers. Such attempts to identify global versus local brands through direct measurements of consumer perceptions might clarify some of the confusion about the definition of the global brand itself. Further, the dimensions we use to measure perceptions might guide companies trying to move their brand towards a more global (or local) positioning through signaling globalness (or localness).

Selected References

Batra, Rajeev, Venkatram Ramaswamy, Dana L. Alden, Jan-Benedict E. M. Steenkamp, and S. Ramachander (2000), "Effects of Brand Local and Nonlocal Origin on Consumer Attitudes in Developing Countries," *Journal of Consumer Psychology*, 9 (2), 83-95.

Papadopoulos, Nicolas, Louise A. Heslop, and G. Bemossy (1990), "A Comparative Image Analysis of Domestic Versus Imported Products," *International Journal of Research in Marketing*, 7, 283-94.

Sandikci, Ozlem and Guliz Ger (2002), "In-Between Modernities and Postmodernities: Theorizing Turkish Cosumptionscape," *Advances in Consumer Research*, 29 (1), 463-4.

Shimp, Terence A. and Subhash Sharma (1987), "Consumer Ethnocentrism: Construction and Validation of the CETSCALE," *Journal of Marketing Research*, 24 (3), 280-9.

Prototype or Exemplar? Effects of Self Construal on Brand Extension Evaluation in a Multi-Product Brand Context

Pronobesh Banerjee, University of Kansas, USA
Ze Wang, University of Kansas, USA
Sanjay Mishra, University of Kansas, USA
Surendra N. Singh, University of Kansas, USA

Increasing attention has been paid to the stretchability of a brand (Ahluwalia 2008). The traditional view is that consumers will evaluate a brand extension in a favorable manner if the brand extension fits with the parent brand and the parent brand has a positive evaluation. Recent research (Mao and Krishnan 2006) extends this view by specifying two-dimensional fit construct that are often used by consumers to assess an extension—prototype fit (congruency with the beliefs associated with the brand) and exemplar fit (similarity with the existing product of a brand). For example, Nike kneepad, has a prototype fit, which shares the generalized imagery of Nike—"athletic"; Nike car audio, has an exemplar fit, which is analogous to an existing product—"car audio." This research attempts to investigate how consumers with different self-construal (interdependence vs. independence) may vary in their evaluation of different types of brand extensions. Also, this research also examines how consumers' self-construal moderates the dilution effect of extension failure and the enhancement effect on its success.

This research first argues that the evaluation of prototype-based and exemplar-based extensions may be influenced by consumers' self-construal. Recent research in self-construal (e.g., Lee, Aaker and Gardner 2000; Monga and John 2007) provides robust evidence that the nature of self-construal affects the mode of cognition one adopts in their decision making process. Consumers with independent self-construal see themselves as distinct from others and are more likely to involve in a de-contextualized mode of processing. Thus, they focus on the overall brand beliefs derived from the abstraction of behaviors rather than the concrete examples of the brand. In contrast, consumers with interdependent self-construal see themselves as related to others and are more likely to involve in a contextualized mode of processing when evaluating an object. They are then more concerned about the concrete associations or exemplars of the brand. Therefore, the abstract concept of a brand (stylish for Sony) will be more assessable to consumers with independent self-construal compared to a concrete exemplar of a brand (Sony TV). The reverse will hold true for the interdependent.

Based on this idea, this research also proposes how the brand extension success (failure) may enhance (dilute) consumers' evaluation of the parent brand and the flagship product of the same brand. We argue that for individuals with independent self-construal ("independents"), brand extension outcome may impact their attitude at the brand level, but not attitude at the flagship product level. More specifically, the success (failure) of prototype-based extension will enhance (dilute) independents' attitude toward the brand, but not their attitude toward the flagship product. For individuals with interdependent self-construal ("interdependents"), brand extension outcome will impact their attitude at the product level, but not at the brand level. More specifically, the success (failure) of exemplar-based extension will enhance (dilute) interdependents' attitude toward the flagship product, but not their attitude toward the parent brand.

Study 1 tests the hypotheses that consumers' self-construal level will moderate their evaluations of prototype-based and exemplar-based extensions. Based on the pretest results, we designed two fictitious extensions of Johnson & Johnson—hair color (exemplar fit with J&J shampoo) and fabric softener (prototype fit with "softness"). We manipulated the self-construal level using standard procedures (Aluwalia 2008). The hypotheses were supported. Independents evaluated the prototype based extensions more favorably compared to the interdependents, while the interdependents evaluated the exemplar-based extensions more favorably compared to independents.

Study 2 and 3 tested the hypotheses that consumers' self-construal will also impact the dilution/enhance effect based on the failure/success of the extension. We manipulated self-construal using similar methods as in study 1. Two news paper articles were used to manipulate extension failure/success. The pattern of results supported the proposed hypotheses.

In summary, we show that companies should be cautious in designing an extension of a multi product brand for consumers with different self-construal. Findings of this paper show that differential accessibility of the various brand associations across self construal exerts a disproportionate influence in evaluating an extension in the multi product brand context. Therefore, companies should take into consideration the differential accessibility of the various brand associations while launching a multi-product brand extension. We also demonstrate the moderating role of consumers' self-construal in the dilution effect of extension failure and the enhancement effect on its success. Interestingly, we find that a brand's flagship product is not always shielded from the effect of dilution as previously found (e.g., John et al. 1998). Our research shows that consumers with interdependent self-construal will negatively evaluate the flagship product on failure of an exemplar-based extension.

References

Aaker, David A. and Kevin L. Keller (1990), "Consumer Evaluations of Brand Extensions," *Journal of Marketing*, 54 (January), 27–41.

Aaker, Jennifer L. and Durairaj Maheswaran (1997), "The effect of Cultural Orientation on Persuasion," Journal of Consumer Research, 24 (December), 315-28.

Ahluwalia, Rohini. (2008), "How far can a brand stretch? Understanding the Role of Self-Construal," *Journal of Marketing Research*, 45 (June), 337-50.

______ and Zeynep Gurhan-Canli (2000), "The Effects of Extensions on the Family Brand Name: An Accessibility- Diagnosticity Perspective," Journal of Consumer Research, 27 (December), 371-81.

Brewer, Marilynn B. and Wendi Gardener (1996), " Who is this "We"? Levels of Collective Identity and Self Representations," *Journal of Personality and Social Psychology*, 71 (1), 83-93.

Church, Timothy A., Fernando A. Ortiz, Marcia S. Katigbak, Tatyana V. Avdeyeva, Alice M. Emerson, José de Jesús Vargas Flores, and Joselina Ibáñez Reyes (2003), "Measuring Individual and Cultural Differences in Implicit Trait Theories," *Journal of Personality and Social Psychology*, 85 (2), 332–47.

Cousins, Steven D. (1989), "Culture and Self-Perception in Japan and the United States," *Journal of Personality and Social Psychology*, 56, 124–31.

Dacin, Peter A. and Daniel C. Smith (1994), "The Effect of Brand Portfolio Characteristics on Consumer Evaluations of Brand Extensions," *Journal of Marketing Research*, 31 (May), 229-42.

Feldman, Jack M. and John G. Lynch (1998), "Self-Generated Validity and Other Effects of Measurement of Belief, Attitude, Intention, and Behavior," Journal of Applied Psychology, 73 (August), 421-35.

Gardner, Wendi, Shira Gabriel, and Angela Y. Lee (1999), "'I' Value Freedom but 'We' Value Relationships: Self Construal Priming Mirrors Cultural Differences in Judgment," *Psychological Science*, 10 (4) , 321-26.

Gurhan-Canli, Zeynep and Durairaj Maheswaran (1998), "The Effects of Extensions on Brnad Name Dilution and Enhancement," *Journal of Marketing Research*, 35 (November), 337-50.

Heine, Steven J, David R. Lehman, Hazel Rose Markus, and Shinobu Kityama (1999), "Is there a Universal Need for Positive Self-regard," *Psychological Review*, 106 (4), 766-94.

Higgins, E. Tory, Gillian A. King, and Gregory H. Mavin (1982), "Individual Construct Accessibility and Subjective Impressions and Recall," Journal of Personality and Social Psychology, 43 (1), 35-47.

John, Deborah Roedder, Barbara Loken, and Christopher Joiner (1998), "The Negative Impact of Extensions: Can Flagship Products Be Diluted?" *Journal of Marketing*, 62 (January), 19–32.

Keller, Kevin L. and David A. Aaker (1992), "The Effects of Sequential Introduction of Brand Extensions," *Journal of Marketing Research*, 29 (February), 35-50.

______ (1993), "Conceptualizing, Measuring, and Managing Customer- Based Brand Equity,' *Journal of Marketing*, 57 (January), 1-22.

______ (2002), *Branding and Brand Equity*, Cambridge, MA: Marketing Science Institute.

Lane, Vicki and Robert Jacobson (1997), "The Reciprocal Impact of Brand Leveraging: Feedback Effects from Brand Extension Evaluation to Brand Evaluation," Marketing Letters, 8 (3), 261-71

Loken, Barbara and Deborah Roedder John (1993), "Diluting Brand Beliefs: When Do Brand Extensions Have a Negative Impact?" *Journal of Marketing*, 57 (July), 71–84.

Mandel, Naomi (2003), "Shifting selves and Decision Making," *Journal of Consumer Research*, 30 (June), 30-40.

Mao, Huifang and H. Shanker Krishanan (2006), "Effects of Prototype and Exemplar on Brand Extension Evaluations: A Two-Process Contingency Model," *Journal of Consumer Research*, 33 (June), 41-49.

Markus, Hazel and Shinobu Kitayama (1991), "Culture and the Self: Implications for Cognition, Emotion, and Motivation," *Psychological Review*, 98 (April), 224–53.

Monga, Alokparna Basu and Deborah Roedder John (2007), "Cultural Differences in Brand Extension Evaluation: The Influence of Analytic versus Holistic Thinking," *Journal of Consumer Research*, 33 (March), 529-536.

Morrin, Maureen (1999), "The Impact of Brand Extension on Parent Brand Memory Structures and Retrieval Processes," *Journal of Marketing Research*, 36 (November), 517-25.

Ng, Sharon (forthcoming), "Cultural Orientation and Brand Dilution: Impact of Motivation Level and Extension Typicality," *Journal of Marketing Research*, forthcoming.

______ and Michael J.Houston (2006), "Exemplars or Beliefs? The Impact of Self View on the Nature and Relative Influence of Brand Associations," *Journal of Consumer Research*, 32 (March), 519-29.

Nisbett, Richard E., Kaiping Peng, Incheol Choi, and Ara Norenzayan (2001), "Culture and Systems of Thought: Holistic versus Analytic Cognition," *Psychological Review*, 108 (April), 291–310.

Park, C. Whan, Sandra Milberg, and Robert Lawson (1991), "Evaluation of Brand Extensions: The Role of Product Feature Similarity and Brand Concept Consistency," *Journal of Consumer Research*, 18 (September), 185–93.

Tavassoli, Nader T. (1999), "Temporal and Associative Memory in Chinese and English," *Journal of Consumer Research*, 26 (September), 170-81.

Trafimow, D., Harry C. Triandis, and Sharon G. Goto (1991), "Some tests of the Distinction between the Private Self and the Collective Self," *Journal of Personality and Social Psychology*, 60 (5), 649-55.

The Production and Dissemination of Conscious Consumption Discourse in Brazil

Denise Barros, EBAPE/FGV-RJ, Brazil
Alessandra Costa, EBAPE/FGV-RJ, Brazil
Eduardo Ayrosa, EBAPE/FGV-RJ, Brazil
João Felipe Sauerbronn, ECSA-Unigranrio, Brazil

The consumption-driven society holds consumption as central in social life (Kozinets & Handelman, 2004). Consumers live not only for the things, but also through them (Baudrillard, 1995; Belk, 1988). The relationship between consumers and organizations seems to take a central role in consumption studies. However, the study of consumer resistance movements is still a new area (Cova, Kozinets & Shankar, 2007; Hemetsberger, 2006), particularly in Brazil, one of the most important markets for big corporations such as Nestlé, Volkswagen and Coca Cola (O Globo, 2005). This paper aims to suggest a wider discussion on the movements of resistance to consumption in Brazil.

In Brazil, softer forms of resistance predominate: consumers or companies discourses do not emphasize the end of consumption, but rather, more consensual forms of relationship between consumers and markets, based on the concepts of *conscious* and *sustainable consumption* . Brazil's most important voice in this subject is "Akatu Institute for Conscious Consumption", created in 1990 by major Brazilian and global companies to promote responsible consumption. Considering the wide penetration of Akatu's ideas among Brazilian consumers and companies, it would not be an overstatement saying that the discourse of conscious consumption in Brazil has been created by the market itself. So, we ask whether such discourse actually represents a legitimate society claim, or, at the other end, it simply serves to the interest of the big corporations that fund Akatu. By raising such question, we intend to discuss, with a critical approach, the process of social construction of the concept of conscious consumption in Brazil.

An initial discourse analysis of Akatu's website shows that the conscious consumption discourse in Brazil can embed a shift of responsibility from the producer to the individual consumer. Saha & Darnton (2005) point out that 'green' consumption refers to environment, corporate social responsibility, social investment, labor and job conditions, fair trade, responsible communication, transparency and so on. Cohen (2007) posits that more emphasis has been given in the "more efficient consumption", as opposed to "less consumption". It is interesting to notice how the addition of the idea of efficiency can change the direction of the actions. This author says that even if the sustainable development has been described as a "three-party process that gives rise to a careful balance among the social equity, economical and environmental objectives, it has been proven in practice that keeping this multi-objective focus is very difficult" (p. 58).

In Brazil, the discussion seems to be restricted to the so-called sustainable and conscious consumption. Back in the 1970s, several institutions were created in Brazil with the purpose of offering some room for businessmen to discuss and implement projects related to the social, environmental and human rights practices. Such institutions have become experts in the defense and promotion of the collective interests of businessmen, also working as reference models that guided business strategic choices (Cappellin *et al*., 2002). The most successful one, Ethos Institute for Social Responsibility has created Akatu Institute in 1990 with the mission of "mobilizing and making Brazilian citizens aware of their major role, as consumers, in the construction of sustainability of life on the planet" (Akatu, 2008).

Akatu's guiding principles seem to focus solely on individual consumption choices. It assumes that the best way to reach the ideal of a 'cleaner' world is through consumer education. Such principles, stated in Akatu's homepage, are: (1) plan your purchases; (2) evaluate the impact of your consumption; (3) consume only the necessary; (4) reuse products and packages; (5) separate your garbage; (6) use your credit consciously; (7) value company's social responsibility practices; (8) do not buy pirate or smuggled products; (9) contribute with the improvement of products and services; and (10) spread conscious consumption. Note that, as Akatu has been born in the market and is nurtured by corporations, it does not question business' objectives.

The arguments used in the construction of the concept of conscious consumption follow a clear and accurate logic. First, a situation of crisis is presented: "humanity already consumes 25% more natural resources than the capacity of renewal of the Earth (...) if consumption and production standards are kept on current level, in less than 50 years two planets Earth will be necessary to meet our needs of water, energy and food" (Akatu, 2008).

Second, the situation is deemed as unquestionable: "it is needless to say that this situation may make life in the planet difficult, including human life itself" (Akatu, 2008). Also, the solution to the problem seems precise: "the best way of changing this lies in consumption-related choices" (Akatu, 2008).

Within this context, the consumer is the social actor who can–or must–change by being aware of his consuming actions, "maximizing the positive impacts and minimizing the negative ones, therefore contributing with his consumption power for the construction of a better world" (Akatu, 2008). Ironically, the production process and its consequences are not actually challenged. There is a vicious transfer of responsibilities from production to consumption.

Saha and Darnton (2005) noticed that the main motivations for becoming a 'green' company are social pressures, opportunity of businesses, and improvement of corporate image. Therefore, it seems appropriate to suggest that, also in Brazil, companies can benefit from such label without effectively having contributed to the sustainability. Although we can identify a group of companies that seek options of sustainability, alternative consumption behaviors end up being absorbed in the prevailing conscious consumption discourse fostered by companies and used to legitimate social roles and positions. The acknowledgment of environmental and social impact of business activities is dissolved in concepts, such as "conscious consumption", "partnership", "sustainable development ", "social alliances" and "sustainability". The creation of solutions with large impact such as the decrease in the emission of gases in the atmosphere becomes a lesser focus when compared to consumer behavior changes (Getz and Shreck, 2006). The power relations are hidden, and the individual consumer acquires the same status as the businessman/producer, of being *equally responsible* for the future of the planet and for the salvation of life.

References

AKATU (2008). "*Novo Estatuto*". Available at: http://www.akatu.org.br/quem_somos/missao Acesso em: 07 fev. 2008.

BAUDRILLARD, Jean (1995) "*Sociedade de consumo*". Rio de Janeiro: Elfos.

BAZERMAN, M. (2001) "Consumer Research for Consumers", *Journal of Consumer Research*, v. 27, 499-504.

BELK, R. (1988) "Possessions and the extended self", *Journal of Consumer Research*, v. 15, 139-165.

CAPPELLIN, P; GIULIANI, M., MOREL, R; PESSANHA, E. (2002) "As organizações empresariais brasileiras e a responsabilidade social". In: KIRSCHNER, A.; GOMES, E.; CAPPELLIN, P. (Orgs.). *Empresa, Empresários e Globalização*. Rio de Janeiro: Relume Dumará.

COHEN, M.(2007) "Consumer credit, household financial management, and sustainable consumption", *International Journal of Consumer Studies*, v. 31(1), 57-65.

COVA, B.; KOZINETS, R. V.; SHANKAR, A. (2007) "Tribes, Inc." In: COVA, B.; KOZINETS, R. V.; SHANKAR, A. (Eds.) *Consumer Tribes*. Oxford, UK: Elsevier.

ELGIN, B. (2007) "Little Green Lies", *Business Week*, n. 4056.

GETZ, C.; SHRECK, A.(2006) "What organic and Fair Trade labels do not tell us", *International Journal of Consumer Studies*, v. 30(5), 490-501.

O GLOBO (2005). Consumo do Brasil.

HEMETSBERGER, A. (2006) "When David Becomes Goliath", *Advances in Consumer Research*, v. 33, 494-500.

KOZINETS, R.; HANDELMAN, J. (1998) "Ensouling Consumption", *Advances in Consumer Research*, v. 25, 475-480.

SAHA, M.; DARNTON, G. (2005) "Green Companies or green Companies: are companies really green, or are they pretending to be?", *Business and Society Review*, v. 110(2), 117-157.

TWITCHELL, J. (1999) "*Lead us to temptation*". Nova York: Columbia University Press.

Cultivating Hope

Mariam Beruchashvili, California State University, Northridge, USA
Risto Moisio, California State University, Long Beach, USA
James Gentry, University of Nebraska-Lincoln, USA

Hope, the elusive feeling that our lives will somehow be better tomorrow, constitutes an essential aspect of the human experience (Farran, Herth, and Popovich 1995). It represents perhaps "…the very heart and center of a human being" (Lynch 1965, 31) that is crucial to not just our day-to-day existence, but more fundamentally, also to our survival. Our research is positioned in relation to the prevailing cognitive perspective, the view in consumer research that hope is an outcome of an individual's cognitive appraisal of a situation where the possibility of attaining a valued goal gives rise to the experience of hope (de Mello, MacInnis, and Stewart 2007). Such psychological treatises of hope do not illuminate how hope may bind collectivities around the pursuit of common goals, the capacity of hope widely theorized in other scholarship such as history, theology or political science (e.g., Braithwaite 2004a; Braithwaite 2004b; Drahos 2004). Thus, existing perspectives tell us very little about whether and how social settings cultivate hope. Our purpose is to deliver a conceptual insight about how hope is cultivated.

To examine the cultivation of hope, we chose the Weight Watchers as our research context. Our choice is purposive in that prior research leads us to expect that hope permeates the Weight Watchers group meetings, allowing us to extend existing theory on hope (Price, Arnould, and Moisio 2006). Our data collection procedures involved non-participant observation at Weight Watchers' official group meeting sites in three different locations in a midsized Midwestern city over a ten-month period in 2006. Field notes taken during the observation of 100 meetings in the three Weight Watchers weekly group-meeting locations constitute the body of the non-participant observation data. In addition to non-participant observation, we conducted a series of long interviews (McCracken 1988) with 32 Weight

Watchers members who were at varying stages of their weight loss journeys. We followed Burawoy's (1998) suggestion to thematize participation in the social world and use theory to guide our inquiry.

Our findings center on the three processes, hope anchoring, hope reframing, and hope bolstering, grounded in social relationships and interactions that cultivate hope for weight loss through the membership in the Weight Watchers support group. Hope anchoring represents one process through which hope is cultivated. Hope anchoring focuses on connecting members' immediate hope for weight loss through the Weight Watchers–the support group represented by its members and the practices within the group–to a nexus of other mutually reinforcing hopes to uphold the hope for weight loss. Hope reframing, on the other hand, focuses on rendering an individual pursuit for weight loss through the Weight Watchers organization into a more meaningful and broader collective endeavor. Finally, hope bolstering focuses on practices that routinely take place at the Weight Watchers weekly group meetings that strengthen the individual's hope for achieving weight loss through participation in these practices.

Our contributions are the following. First, we advance sociological theorization on the role of emotions in consumption absent from consumer research. Converging on the sociology of emotions tradition (Hochschild 1975; Kemper 1978; Thoits 1989), our findings reveal, in line with Durkheim's (1912/1965) theory of collective sentiments, that hope is a collective product grounded in symbolically charged social interactions and relationships. Second, we also advance a branch of institutional theorizing on emotions in Consumer Culture Theory. Specifically, our findings show that Weight Watchers, as the world's largest support group, specifically focuses on the emotion of hope; it houses, orchestrates, and perhaps even rationalizes the experiences of its members' emotions. The Weight Watchers anchors members' hope to lose weight in the support group and fosters connections to other reinforcing hopes to improve physique, self-esteem, self-control, and health. Third, complementing the psychological theory of goal setting and goal striving (Bagozzi and Dholakia 1999), our research contributes by advancing consumer culture theoretic work on goals. In particular, our research informs understanding of how consumers address their failures to reach goals. Our findings suggest that having failed at a weekly weight loss goal, consumers leverage on fellow members' experiences. Other members' experiences in the perspective of a shared "Weight Watcher" identity offer an additional energy reservoir that boosts Weight Watchers' attempts at losing their own weight. Hearing other members' stories of successes as well as of failures seems to energize members, propelling them to continue on their weight loss journeys despite failures. Our findings contrast directly with the recent psychological research, which suggests that when consumers default on their goals, they are more likely to abandon those goals altogether (Soman and Cheema 2004). Thus, rather than provoking consumers to abandon their goals, our findings indicate that the shared identity and the social interactions within the group may act as antidotes to salient failures to reach goals.

Selected References

Bagozzi, Richard P. and Utpal Dholakia (1999), "Goal Setting and Goal Striving in Consumer Behavior," *Journal of Marketing*, 63 (Special Issue), 19-32.

Braithwaite, John (2004a), "Emancipation and Hope," *Annals of the American Academy of Political and Social Science*, 592 (March), 79-98.

Braithwaite, Valerie (2004b), "The Hope Process and Social Inclusion," *Annals of the American Academy of Political and Social Science*, 592 (March), 128-51.

Burawoy, Michael (1998), "The Extended Case Method," *Sociological Theory*, 16 (March), 4-33.

de Mello, Gustavo, Deborah J. MacInnis, and David W. Stewart (2007), "Threats to Hope: Effects on Reasoning About Product Information," *Journal of Consumer Research*, 34 (August), 153-61.

Drahos, Peter (2004), "Trading in Public Hope," *Annals of the American Academy of Political and Social Science*, 592 (March), 18-38.

Durkheim, Emile (1912/1965), *The Elementary Forms of the Religious Life*, New York: Free Press.

Farran, Carol J., Kaye A. Herth, and Judith M. Popovich (1995), *Hope and Hopelessness: Critical Clinical Constructs*, Thousand Oaks, CA: Sage.

Hochschild, Arlie Russell (1975), "The Sociology of Emotions: Selected Possibilities," in *Another Voice: Feminist Perspectives on Social Life and Social Science*, ed. Marcia Millman and Rosabeth Moss Kanter, Garden City, NY: Anchor Press, 280-307.

Kemper, Theodore D. (1978), *A Social Interactional Theory of Emotions*, New York: Wiley.

Lynch, William F. (1965), *Images of Hope*, Baltiomre, MD: Helicon.

McCracken, Grant (1988), The Long Interview, Newbury Park, CA: Sage

Price, Linda L., Eric J. Arnould, and Risto J. Moisio (2006), "Making Contexts Matter: Selecting Research Contexts for Theoretical Insights," in *Handbook of Qualitative Research Methods in Marketing*, ed. Russell W. Belk, Northampton: Edward Elgar, 106-28.

Soman, Dilip and Amar Cheema (2004), "When Goals Are Counterproductive: The Effects of Violation of a Behavioral Goal on Subsequent Performance," *Journal of Consumer Research*, 31 (June), 52-62.

Thoits, Peggy A. (1989), "The Sociology of Emotions," *Annual Review of Sociology*, 15, 317-42.

The Placement of Code-Switched Ads within a Medium: Investigating Reciprocal Effects of Ad and Media Involvement

Melissa M. Bishop, University of New Hampshire, USA

Code-switching in advertising—the practice of alternating between two or more languages in a single message—is gaining attention among marketing practitioners and academics. However, little is known about how the use of language in general impacts message involvement. Involvement concerns the personal relevance of a stimulus, and is often cited as being composed of two dimensions—the cognitive and the affective. Cognitive involvement addresses informational processing activities whereas affective involvement stresses emotional processing activities (Zaichkowsky 1994). Involvement is important for advertisers because when individuals are more involved in ad content, they are more motivated to process ad information (Swasy and Munch 1985). Thus, the purpose of this study is two-fold: to examine if and how the language of the medium and the main language of a code-switched ad interact to influence cognitive and affective involvement in 1) the ad itself and 2) media content that surrounds the ad. These issues are dealt with from an information processing perspective with testing among Spanish/English bilinguals.

Media Language and Ad Involvement

In terms of language, messages presented in a bilingual's lesser known language are harder to process (Luna and Peracchio 2001). Regarding code-switching, Spivey and Marian (1999) provide evidence that by switching back and forth between two main (or "matrix") languages in a conversation, processing difficulty is increased. They demonstrated through neuroscience that when the matrix language of a conversation changes, a complete deactivation of one language occurs in order to activate another, resulting in increased cognitive processing demands. However, when a second language is alternated to only briefly—as in single word switches rather than entire matrix language switches—the brain does not deactivate one language to process another. In other words, a complete deactivation/activation process does not occur, thus lightening cognitive demands.

In terms of code-switched ad research, when ad information is presented primarily in a language that differs from the medium, it is proposed to be more taxing for the individual to process. This should lower evaluations of cognitive involvement with the ad. Further, Speech Accommodation Theory (Giles, Taylor and Bourhis 1973) states that the more effort the message sender is seen as putting into accommodating the message receiver, the more favorable he will be perceived. Thus, by keeping the main language of a code-switched ad the same as the medium, the advertiser will be perceived as more accommodating, increasing affective ad involvement.

Ad Language and Media Involvement

Although there is considerable debate over how media involvement influences ad involvement (Lloyd and Clancy 1991), how ad involvement affects media involvement is much less in the spotlight. It is examined here whether increasing (decreasing) involvement with an ad, involvement in the medium can also be subsequently increased (decreased). Media content that both precedes and follows exposure to a code-switched ad is addressed to examine this issue.

In the pre-ad exposure stage, the language of the media content (i.e., magazine article) that comes before a code-switched ad sets the stage for language processing as it establishes the original matrix language of the medium. At this stage, the message receiver has only been exposed to content in a single language—which language this is should not make a difference. Therefore, differences in evaluations of cognitive involvement in the media content that precedes ad exposure should not occur in any of the experimental conditions (to be discussed) as the individual has not had to change matrix languages to process information.

However, media content that is viewed *after* exposure to these materials may subject message receivers to increased processing demands in cases where they are required to alternate between matrix languages to process information. For example, if an individual originally reads an article in English, then a code-switched ad that primarily is written in Spanish, and then reads the following article in English, the bilingual has changed matrix languages three times (from English to Spanish to English) in one setting to process the information. In cases such as this, lower cognitive involvement (as processing difficulty is greater) as well as lower affective involvement (as the principle behind Speech Accommodation theory has not been met) should result in media content that follows ad exposure.

Study 1

122 bilingual Hispanics viewed either a code-switched ad composed primarily of English with brief, one-word switches to Spanish or the reverse. The ad was placed between two articles written in either all-English or all-Spanish. Cognitive and affective involvement were measured for both the articles and the ad based on Zaichkowsky (1994). Results showed that cognitive and affective involvement in the ad and in the article that followed the ad were lower when the main language of the ad differed from that of the medium (all p-values$<.05$). No differences were found in involvement in the article that preceded the ad, as predicted. In sum, this study shows that by keeping the main language of a code-switched ad the same as that of its medium, cognitive and affective ad involvement can be increased. Furthermore, involvement in the media following ad exposure can also be increased, pointing towards important implications for media planners.

Study 2

The purpose of this study was to examine lengthier code-switching in advertising to investigate its effects on both ad and surrounding media content involvement. It is proposed that code-switching entire phrases rather than single words (as in Study 1) entails more cognitive effort on the part of the message receiver, thus nullifying the effects based on ease of cognitive processing and speech accommodation. Results from this study nullified most of the effects of Study 1, such that there were no differences in affective ad involvement and affective and cognitive media involvement across conditions. However, cognitive ad involvement was still significantly higher ($p<.05$) when the main language of the ad matched that of the medium despite the lengthier style of code-switching.

Study 3

To extend the results of Study 1, a third study is in progress investigating the effects on involvement when the main language of a *monolingual* ad does not match that of the medium.

References

Giles, Howard, Donald M. Taylor and Richard Y. Bourhis (1973), "Toward a Theory of Interpersonal Accommodation through Speech Accommodation: Some Canadian Data," *Language in Society*, 2 (August), 177-92.

Lloyd, David W. and Kevin J. Clancy (1991), "Television Program Involvement and Advertising Response: Some Unsettling Implications for Copy Research," *Journal of Consumer Marketing*, 8 (4), 61–74.

Luna, David, and Laura A. Peracchio (2001), "Moderators of Language Effects in Advertising to Bilinguals: A Psycholinguistic Approach," *Journal of Consumer Research*, 28 (September), 284-95.
Swasy, John L. and James M. Munch (1985), "Examining the Target of Receiver Elaborations: Rhetorical Question Effects on Source Processing and Persuasion," *Journal of Consumer Research*, 11 (March), Issue 4, 877-886.
Spivey, Michael J. and Viorica Marian (1999), "Cross Talk between Native and Second Languages: Partial Activation of an Irrelevant Lexicon," *Psychological Science*, 10 (May), 281-84.
Zaichkowsky, Judith Lynne *(1994), "The Personal Involvement Inventory: Reduction, Revision, and Application to Advertising," Journal of Advertising*, 23 (December), 59-70.

Thinking Makes Me Hungry: Differences in Restrained and Unrestrained Eating Behaviors in a Rich Food Environment

Melissa Bublitz, University of Wisconsin-Milwaukee, USA
Lauren G. Block, Baruch College, CUNY, USA
Laura Peracchio, University of Wisconsin-Milwaukee, USA

Researchers are concerned with the over-consumption of food and its negative effects on society. This paper synthesizes research from the field of psychology in the area of dietary restraint with research on how marketplace and product cues influence overeating, particularly of unhealthy as compared to healthy foods. Using these two research streams as a platform, we examine the differences between how some consumers, those classified as restrained eaters, respond to consumption cues. Specifically, we propose that the cognitive demands of perpetual restraint may make diet conscious consumers more susceptible to some triggers to overeat and less susceptible to others. Understanding these differences has important public policy implications because food packaging and labeling may not have the intended effect for restrained eaters, resulting in more, rather than less, consumption for this group. In addition, understanding how the behaviors of restrained eaters differ may help nutrition advocates better educate these consumers.

The characteristics and behaviors of restrained and unrestrained eaters have been widely explored in the field of psychology over the past 40 years (Herman and Mack 1975; Herman and Polivy 1980; Heatherton, Striepe, and Wittenberg 1998). Restraint is the perpetual "cognitively mediated effort that an individual makes to combat the urge to eat and restrict food intake to control body weight" (Herman and Mack 1975). Restrained eaters constantly monitor and regulate the food they eat through "self-imposed dietary rules and restrictions" (Ward and Mann 2000, 755). However, this constant focus on food does not result in dietary perfection. In fact, the continuous attention and effort required to restrain ones' eating behavior despite the plethora of temptations faced daily, often results in dietary lapses and overeating by this group (Herman and Mack 1975). By contrast, unrestrained eaters spend less time and cognitive effort focusing on food; they eat when they feel hungry or want the food and generally stop eating when they are full. This important distinction may make restrained eaters more likely to rely on product cues such as package size, specific product claims such as "low-fat" or "high fiber" or their own health beliefs such as the perceived healthfulness of one restaurant as compared to another to determine how much they should eat rather than their own body's signal of satiety.

Research on the role of marketplace and product cues in consumption has increased our understanding of how package size (Scott et al. 2008), serving size (Rolls, Morris, and Roe 2002), serving dishes and utensils (Wansink and Cheney 2005) and product assortment and variety (Kahn and Wansink 2004) influence how much consumers eat. We have also learned more about the underlying factors that prompt eating behaviors. For example, Scott et al. (2008) explore the emotional response of restrained eaters to food. By prompting restrained eaters to consciously think about the food they would consume as nonfood objects, these researchers were able to reverse the consumption differences between restrained and unrestrained eaters (Scott et al. 2008).

Beyond their emotional response to food, restrained eaters are susceptible to dietary lapses whenever outside factors interfere with their ability to devote the cognitive attention required to restrict what they eat. Consumption differences have been attributed to the depleted cognitive (Ward & Mann 2000) or self-control (Baumeister 2002) resources restrained eaters possess due to their continuous efforts to regulate their behavior. One challenge restrained eaters face is the steady stream of daily activities that require their cognitive attention and self-control resources. Recent research shows how the act of continuous decision making during a shopping trip actually reduces both the accuracy and persistence consumers display in subsequent cognitive tasks (Vohs et al. 2008). Similarly, constant pursuit of specific eating goals by restrained eaters may deplete their self-control resources, leading to choices that conflict with their restraint goals.

A wide variety of cues in the marketplace may prompt similar differences in the amount of food restrained and unrestrained eaters consume. This research explores how the variety and assortment of foods may stimulate different consumption patterns. Research by Kahn and Wansink (2004) shows that increasing the variety and assortment increases consumption by enhancing the anticipated pleasure consumers expect to derive from eating more. Similar to the response of restrained versus unrestrained eaters to smaller package sizes (Scott et al. 2008), we expect restrained and unrestrained eaters to respond differently to an increased variety and assortment of food choices. We hypothesize that like the larger package sizes, restrained eaters will anticipate the danger increased variety and assortment present and exercise more vigilance in restraining their consumption. By contrast, we expect unrestrained eaters to follow the pattern Kahn and Wansink (2004) observed, eating more as variety and assortment increase. We also investigate how restrained eaters respond to variety and assortment changes when they are placed in a cognitively taxing situation. Lastly, this research explores how the addition of healthy choices to the variety and assortment of food affects the consumption decisions of restrained eaters. Wilcox and his colleagues (2009) find that the mere presence of healthy choices among less healthy alternatives may actually increase indulgence. We hypothesize that while large assortments of unhealthy foods, such as sweets and snacks, prompt restrained eaters to concentrate on fighting the temptation placed before them, large assortments of foods they view as healthy choices, such as fruits and vegetables, will license restrained eaters to let their guard down resulting in increased consumption of both types of foods.

In this presentation we discuss early findings that explore how restraint behaviors, cognitive processing and a rich food environment interact to affect consumption. This research adds to our understanding of how product and marketplace cues influence consumption for restrained and unrestrained eaters. In addition, we hope our research provides information to empower consumers to use their cognitive and behavioral resources to facilitate healthy food choices. As public policy officials work to combat the obesity epidemic, understanding the influences on food consumption will inform decision-makers as they implement remedies designed to reduce over-consumption and promote healthy lifestyles.

References

Baumeister, Roy F. (2002), "Yielding to Temptation: Self-Control Failure, Impulsive Purchasing, and Consumer Behavior," *Journal of Consumer Research*, 28 (4), 670-676.

Heatherton, Todd F., Meg Striepe, and Lauren Wittenberg (1998), "Emotional Distress and Disinhibited Eating: The Role of Self," *Personality and Social Psychology Bulletin*, 24 (3), 301-313.

Herman, C. Peter and Deborah Mack (1975), "Restrained and Unrestrained Eating," *Journal of Personality*, 43 (4), 647-660.

Herman, C. Peter and Janet Polivy (1980), "Restrained Eating," in *Obesity*, ed. A. J. Stunkard, Philadelphia, PA: W. B. Saunders, 208-225.

Kahn, Barbara E. and Brian Wansink (2004), "The Influence of Assortment Structure on Perceived Variety and Consumption Quantities," *Journal of Consumer Research*, 30 (March), 391-405.

Rolls, Barbara J., Erin L. Morris, and Liane S. Roe (2002), "Portion Size of Food Affects the Energy Intake in Normal-Weight and Overweight Men and Women," *American Journal of Clinical Nutrition*, 76 (6), 1207-1213.

Scott, Maura L., Stephen M. Nowlis, Naomi Mandel, and Andrea C. Morales (2008), "The Effects of Reduced Food Size and Package Size on the Consumption Behavior of Restrained and Unrestrained Eaters," *Journal of Consumer Research*, 35 (Oct), 391-405.

Vohs, Kathleen D., Roy F. Baumeister, Brandon J. Schmeichel, Jean M., Twenge, Noelle M., Nelson, and Dianne M. Tice (2008), "Making Choices Impairs Subsequent Self-Control: A Limited-Resource Account of Decision Making, Self-Regulation, and Active Initiative," *Journal of Personality and Social Psychology,* 94 (5), 883-898.

Wansink, Brian and Mathew M. Cheney (2005), "Super Bowls: Severing Bowl Size and Food Consumption," *Journal of the American Medical Association*, 293 (14), 1727-1728.

Ward, Andrew and Traci Mann (2000), "Don't Mind if I Do: Disinhibited Eating Under Cognitive Load," *Journal of Personality and Social Psychology*, 78 (4), 753-763.

Wilcox, Keith, Beth Vallen, Lauren Block, and Gavan J. Fitzsimons (2009), "Vicarious Goal Fulfillment: When the Mere Presence of a Healthy Option Leads to an Ironically Indulgent Decision," *Journal of Consumer Research,* 36 (3) .

Motivated Bias in Affective Forecasting

Eva Buechel, University of Miami, USA
Carey Morewedge, Carnegie Mellon University, USA
Joachim Vosgerau, Carnegie Mellon University, USA

Affective forecasters exhibit an impact bias, overestimating the intensity and duration of their emotional reaction to future events. We suggest that forecasters make extreme forecasts to motivate themselves to produce desirable outcomes. In two studies, affective forecasts were more extreme when outcomes were more important, and when forecasters could influence an outcome than when it was determined but unknown. Subsequent studies found that the extremity of forecasts determined the amount of mental and physical effort forecasters expended to produce desirable outcomes. Errors in affective forecasting may thus not be solely cognitive in origin, but have a motivated component as well.

To Do with Others or to Have (or To Do Alone)? The Value of Experiences over Material Possessions Depends on the Involvement of Others

Peter Caprariello, University of Rochester, USA
Harry Reis, University of Rochester, USA

How does money promote happiness? Recent studies have addressed this question. People may intentionally buy hedonic goods to increase their happiness (Dhar & Wertenbroch, 2000). Spending money on others makes people happier than spending money on themselves (Dunn, Aknin, & Norton, 2008). Finally, spending money on experiences makes people happier than spending money on material objects (Van Boven & Gilovich, 2003). The present research focuses on the distinction between experiences and material possessions, and their relative effects on happiness.

There are a number of possible reasons why experiential purchases might make people happier than material purchases, but one that has received little attention is the social nature of many experiences. It may be that experiences bring people more happiness than material goods to the extent that others are involved in the activity. Csikszentmihalyi (2000) noted the importance of consumption for satisfying desires for belongingness and connectedness, and recent research has verified that experiential purchases satisfy relatedness needs more than material purchases (Howell & Hill, in press). We take these findings one step further by proposing that an experience by oneself may make people less happy than an experience in which others are included. The current research tests this hypothesis with experimental designs.

In the first study, 89 undergraduates were given a survey in which they were shown pairs of 9 experiences, each framed once as involving others and once as done alone. Participants were asked how happy the purchases would make them and how much money they would spend to acquire each. Results supported the hypothesis that experiential purchases are more valuable when framed as social than as solitary. Participants reported feeling happier with an experience when it involved others than when it was solitary, $t(89)=18.55, p<.001$, and were willing to spend more money to acquire it, $t(87)=13.50, p<.001$. These data suggest that an experience gains value–in terms of willingness to spend money to acquire it and happiness gained upon doing so–when it involves others.

A second study compared the value of social and solitary experiences to material objects. In this study, 84 participants were shown sets of three purchases– material, experiential with others, and the same experience alone–all matched for cost. For each set, participants were asked to indicate which of the three they would choose and which of the three would make them most happy. Partially replicating the results of Van Boven and Gilovich (2003), participants chose the social experience over the other purchases the majority of the time (M=8.75 times per 13 opportunities). Importantly, participants chose material objects significantly more (M=3.47) than solitary experiences (M=0.76). The same pattern was found for happiness ratings. These results suggest that the value of experiential purchases over material objects depends on others being included in the experience. When experiences are solitary, the relative value of material objects increases.

A final study addressed a methodological shortcoming in the second experiment. Namely, when participants pick one purchase from a set of three, the relative value of the two remaining purchases is not clear. Therefore, the final study broke down three purchase options into three between-subjects comparison conditions–material vs. social, material vs. solitary, and solitary vs. social purchases–and asked participants which they would choose and which would make them happier. The final study also included a fourth condition in which material purchases were presented alongside ambiguously social experiences (e.g., "taking a road trip" without specifying whether or not others were involved). Subjects in this condition provided an unprompted, open-ended description of the experience. If participants spontaneously describe the experiences as involving others, this adds support to the overarching hypothesis that the reason experiences promote happiness is because they involve others.

In the final study, 327 participants were randomly assigned to conditions in which they were presented 1 of 4 possible choices–between material objects and social experiences, material objects and solitary experiences, solitary and social experiences, and material objects and ambiguous experiences–and were asked to pick which one they would choose and which would make them happier. Results participants chose social experiences relatively more than material possessions (M=7.63 times per 12 opportunities). Participants chose material possessions relatively more than solitary experiences (M=7.53). Participants chose social experiences relatively more than solitary experiences (M=9.83). Finally, participants were no more likely to choose ambiguous experiences than material objects (M=6.16). However, participants reported that experiences would make them happier than material objects (M=7.20 times) and described the experiences in terms of people involved significantly more than would be expected by chance (63.3% of the time).

The results of three studies suggest that the value of experiential purchases, both in terms of willingness to consume and happiness after consumption, depends on others being involved. Consistent with Van Boven and Gilovich (2003), experiences with others are more desirable and make people happier than material possessions. Experiences without others, though, are less desirable and make people less happy than material possessions. These results are consistent with research by Rosenbaum (2006) suggesting that some consumers consistently patronize establishments that offer feelings of connectedness and social support. In addition, Russell, Norman, & Heckler (2004) demonstrate that television consumption represents an outlet for feeling connected to television characters. Taking into account the relationship context of experiential purchases may be critical to predicting how they best promote happiness.

References

Csikszentmihalyi, M. (2000). The costs and benefits of consuming. *Journal of Consumer Research, 27,* 267-272.

Dhar, R., & Wertenbroch, K. (2000). Consumer choice between hedonic and utilitarian goods. *Journal of Marketing Research, 37,* 60-71.

Dunn, E., Aknin, L., & Norton, M. (2008). Spending money on others promotes happiness. *Science, 319,* 1687-1688.

Rosenbaum, M. (2006). Exploring the social supportive role of third places in consumers' lives. *Journal of Service Research, 9,* 59-72.

Van Boven, L., & Gilovich, T. (2003). To do or to have? That is the question. *Journal of Personality and Social Psychology, 85,* 1193-1202.

Online and Offline Advertising Media: Exploring the Antecedents to Advertising Trust

Jeffrey Carlson, University of Connecticut, USA

Jacqueline Anderson, Forrester Research, USA

Joseph Pancras, University of Connecticut, USA

Abstract

Breaking through the clutter of advertising to reach consumers is no easy feat. Getting consumers to believe and act on the messages delivered is even harder. By understanding which specific media and channels consumers are more trusting of, marketers can more wisely choose where to place their messages for the highest levels of efficiency. This study looks to create a conceptual model outlining the predictors of advertising trust so that marketers can choose an advertising medium based on their target audience. By identifying which sources are most or least trusted by a given type of consumer, marketers will know which channels to choose or avoid when determining their media mix in a campaign.

Introduction and Conceptual Overview

The landscape for advertising is continuously changing with the explosion of new media options. With the options becoming endless, the question turns to the consumer. How do they want to be reached? How will they listen? Specifically, which channel is most trustworthy? Consumers' trust of the messages companies are putting into their advertising has not been increasing. In fact, according to Forrester Research (Kim, 2006), in 2002 only 13% of North American heads of household indicated that they thought companies generally tell the truth in advertisements.

However, the fragmentation of the advertising market into a multitude of marketing channels makes these generalized trust statements hard to subscribe to. Consumers are well aware of the differences in advertising channels and are judging the messages contained in each differently. Recently, Nielsen (2007) surveyed consumers on their attitudes toward thirteen types of advertising, and found vast differences among the types.

Numerous studies have also found that consumers have a higher level of trust for content in traditional media sources (Ganguly, 2007; Parr, 2006; Soh, Reid, and King, 2007). Despite conclusive results indicating that channels differ in trustworthiness, previous research has not reached a consensus on how specific media differ. Flanagin and Metzger (2000), for example, found that beyond newspapers, media trust differed very little. These seemingly contradictory findings reveal that how specific media differ from one another (i.e., TV vs. Internet) should be further explored.

From a marketing perspective, trust of specific channels is essential. Without trust, consumers are less likely to openly receive messages. Furthermore, classic persuasion research shows that trust is an antecedent to attitude and behavioral change. Thus, understanding levels of trust not only across various channels but also between forms on a given channel will help determine the most effective channel and form to use for a given marketing campaign. Although secondary research clearly indicates that consumers do, in fact, trust certain channels more than others, it fails to clearly identify factors that influence consumers' trust perceptions. If one could determine factors (i.e., reliance) that impact trust, a marketing manager could better decide which channel(s) to utilize.

The trust consumers have with various advertisement channels may be impacted by the consumers' experience and reliance with a given channel (e.g., Greer, 2003; Johnson and Kay, 2000; Johnson and Kaye 2004; Nail, 2005). Nail (2005) found that young consumers who were rated as technology optimists (consumers who are comfortable with technology and like to use it) were more likely to notice online ads than technology pessimists. Kim (2006) also suggested reaching out to consumers in the environment that they engage with most. Essentially, people who are trusting of magazine ads are more likely to be trusting of other offline advertising. From this, one could theorize that consumers who spend more time online would be more trusting of online advertising while those who spend more time with any offline channels would be more trusting of offline advertising.

While there have been other analyses undertaken to examine the predictors of consumers' trust levels of web content, there has been little examination of the predictors of consumers' trust levels of online advertising. Shankar, et al (2002) built a model of online trust which helped in predicting consumers' trust of a given online channel. Much of this work centered upon the actual attributes of the website, the consumers' experience with online channels (specifically e-commerce interactions) and security issues. While the study did not speak to trust of online advertising the underlying framework lends itself to further exploration of this specific topic. Thus, we will use this model as a basis from which we will build out a model of online advertising trust predictors. Similarly, the study done by Bart, et al (2005), while focusing on specific determinants of trust in e-commerce experiences across site categories, demonstrates that allowances for differences across types of sites is important. Similarly, we will address differences across types of internet advertisements.

For this particular study we've developed the following preliminary hypotheses:

- Consumers with a higher level of online media usage will be more trusting of online advertising
- Consumers will trust advertising messages more when they are delivered through the medium they spend the most time with
- Demographic factors influencing technology adoption will also influence trust of online advertising

Method

Because of the need for respondents that used both on and offline media we chose to use data collected in a mail survey. The data used was from Forrester Research's 2008 Benchmark mail recontact survey. This survey is part of the Technographics product. The questionnaire was administered by mail to respondents aged eighteen and older from TNS' North American mail survey panel. The survey respondents had also responded to an early Forrester Benchmark survey. Thus, the available sample to pull from was a subset of the original respondents of the Benchmark Survey which had been fielded in January of 2008. The survey respondents were selected to be representative of the North American household and individual population. Targets were used in pulling the sample to match the predicted returns to look like the general US population. Survey respondents were incented with an entry into a sweepstakes to win one of five cash prizes. The total collected sample size was 4,605 respondents.

The survey was fielded in September of 2008. Six weeks were allotted for fielding. The mail based survey was a total of eight legal sized pages with a cover letter asking participants to complete the survey for a chance to win one of five cash prizes. As returns came into TNS they were processed by a DP team at TNS. This team was responsible for reviewing the returned surveys to ensure they were filled out properly and completely. The surveys were then cleaned and coded into a data set.

Preliminary Results

Thus far, we have yielded several general conclusions from preliminary data analyses. The sample consisted of 4,605 adults, ranging from age 18 to 95 (M=48.85). All 50 states were represented in this sample. Of the respondents, 48.7% were male, while 51.3% were female. When analyzing a ranked order of means, respondents indicate that yellow-page advertisements are the most trusted form of advertising (M=3.29) among 24 different types of advertising. Following yellow-page advertisements, the next top 6 forms of advertising are: Online consumer reviews (M=3.18); In-store displays (M=3.16); Newspaper ads (M=3.12); Email ads (M=3.08); Magazine ads (M=3.05); and TV ads (M=2.98). The bottom five types of advertisement (the least trustworthy), are as follows: Celebrity endorsements (M=2.29); Social networking site advertisements (M 2.28); Videogame ads (M=2.25); Blog ads (M=2.24); and Text cell ads (M=2.18).

Multiple regression analyses reveal that both age and gender significantly predict levels of trust in the six ad types (yellow page ads; online customer reviews; in-store displays; videogame ads; blog ads; and cell text ads). The older a respondent is, the more negative reviews will be for both ad types. Furthermore, females rate videogames ads more negatively, but rate online consumer reviews more positively. In addition, preliminary exploratory factor analyses have yielded several technology usage factors (e.g., New Tech Uses such as blogging, wikis, etc.; Online product research and Purchase; Traditional Ad Trust; Newer Tech Ad Trust).

Using AMOS 6.0, a path model also yielded many interesting findings (RMSEA=.024; CFI=.988). First, there were no significant differences among consumers that predicted trust levels in traditional media advertising such as TV, radio, newspapers or magazines. Second, the use of newer Internet technologies (such as blogs and wikis), Internet product use (i.e., the research and purchase of products online), and the overall reliance upon the Internet had a positive impact on trust levels for "controlled" forms of Internet media (e.g., consumer reviews, custom emails, etc).

Other demographic variables were also found to have an impact. Age had a negative impact on trust levels of "controlled" forms (i.e., forms that that consumer typically controls exposure of such as blogs and consumer reviews) of Internet media and for new forms of Internet media. Females had higher trust level ratings for forms of media than males did. And finally, having a college degree negatively impacted a consumer's trust level for most forms of media advertising.

The initial results show that there are differences among individuals who trust offline advertising and those who trust online advertising. The fact that there are no significant differences among consumers that will predict trust levels in traditional media advertising can be attritubted to the established nature of these mediums. This only strengthens the need to further explore the predictors of trust among emerging advertising mediums so that consumers can be properly identified. Similarly, the apparent differences among controlled forms of Internet media versus un-controlled media should be explored as well. This is especially important with the rise of user-generated content on the Internet.

Creating a model of consumer ad trust will greatly empower marketers to make better choices about where to place messages. Further analyses will be connected to more deeply examine the predictors of online advertising trust. The end goal of the analyses will be to not only construct a model to illustrate the predictors of online trust but to create consumer profiles for each type of advertising. These consumer profiles will illustrate to marketers who is and who isn't likely to trust each type of advertising.

References

Bart, Yakov, Shankar, Venkatesh, Sultan, Fareena, and Glen L. Urban (2005), "Are the Drivers and Role of Online Trust the Same for All Web Sites and Consumers?," *Journal of Marketing*, 69, 133-152.

Flanagin, Andrew. J., and Miriam J. Metzger, Miriam (2000), "Perceptions of Internet Information Credibility," *Journalism & Mass Communication Quarterly,* 77(3), 515-540.

Greer, Jennifer. D (2003), "Evaluating the Credibility of Online Information: A Test of Source and Advertising Influence," *Mass Communication & Society,* 6, 11-28.

Johnson, Thomas. J., and Barbara K. Kaye (2000), "Using is Believing: The Influence of Reliance on the Credibility of Online Political Information among Politically Interested Internet Users," *Journalism & Mass Communication Quarterly,* 77, 865-879.

Johnson, Thomas. J. and Barbara K. Kaye (2004), "Wag the Blog: How Reliance on Traditional Media and the Internet Influence Credibility Perceptions of Weblogs among Blog Users," *Journalism & Mass Communication Quarterly,* 81, 622-642.

Kim, Peter (2006), "Consumers Lover to Hate Advertising," Cambridge, MA: Forrester Research.

Kim, Peter (2007), "Advertising Tactics That Win Consumer Trust," Cambridge, MA: Forrester Research.

Nail, Jim (2005), "The Consumer Advertising Backlash Worsens," Cambridge, MA: Forrester Research.

Nail, Jim (2005). "The Truth about Teens and Advertising," Cambridge, MA: Forrester Research.

Neilson (2007), "Trust in advertising: A global Neilson consumer report," The Neilson Company.

Ganguly, Dia (2007), "Technographics Multicountry Analysis: Media Trust in Metropolitan China and the Rest of Asia," Cambridge, MA: Forrester Research.

Parr, Barry (2006), "Trust of Content in Traditional Media Sources Is Higher Than Online," New York, Jupiter Research.

Shankar, Venkatesh, Urban, Glen L., and Fareena Sultan (2002), "Online Trust: A Stakeholder Perspective, Concepts, Implications, and Future Directions," *Journal of Strategic Information Systems,* 11, 325-344.

Shavitt, Sharon., Lowrey, Pamela., and James Haefner (1998), "Public Attitudes toward Advertising: More Favorable Than You Might Think," *Journal of Advertising Research,* 38(4), 7-22.

Soh, Hyeonjin., Reid, Leonard, N., & Karen W. King (2007), "Trust in Different Advertising Media," *Journalism & Mass Communication Quarterly,* 84(3), 455-476.

When Preferences Differ Among Friends: How Positive Affect Influences Choosing to Accommodate Others vs. Choosing to Express Oneself

Cindy Chan, Cornell University, USA

Alice M. Isen, Cornell University, USA

Are people in positive affect more likely to accommodate the preferences expressed by their friend when making consumer choices? Or are they more likely to stay true to their own personal preferences? Indeed, the answer to both questions is yes. Results show people in positive affect are *more likely* than controls to accommodate their friend's preference when their preferences are not extremely different, or when their decision affects both parties. Conversely, they are *less likely* than controls to accommodate their friend when their friend's preference is very different, even when their choice is made in the company of their friend.

Unintended Consequences of Fundraising Tactics

Zoe Chance, Harvard Business School, USA
Michael Norton, Harvard Business School, USA

Prosocial behavior has been correlationally linked to happiness, with individuals who report a greater interest in helping others, an inclination to act in a prosocial manner, or intentions to perform altruistic or courteous behaviors being more likely to rate themselves as dispositionally happy (for a review, see Lyubomirsky, King, & Diener, 2005). Recent studies have shown that prosocial behavior leads to increased happiness (Lyubomirsky, Tkach, and Sheldon, 2004), and, more specifically, that spending money on others may make us even happier than spending the same amount of money on ourselves (Dunn, Aknin & Norton, 2008). Recently, 89% of American households have donated to one or more charitable causes (Independent Sector, 2001), totaling approximately 2% of GDP each year (Andreoni & Petrie 2004). Experimental results from laboratory and field settings finding that incremental giving tends to make people happier (Dunn, Aknin and Norton, 2008), and the uncontroversial assumption that increased funding for charities will have a positive impact on their beneficiaries lead us to believe that the optimal level of national giving has not yet been reached. With that in mind, we are interested in learning how to increase individual charitable donations beyond their current level. In particular, our studies provide warnings to charitable fundraisers that some familiar tactics for increasing donor participation may have the unintended consequences of reducing future contributions.

Charity fundraisers use a variety of methods to increase donations, with three of the most common ones being matching funds, seed money, and thank you gifts. Field experiments have shown that matching funds (Eckel and Grossman, 2008) and seed money (List and Lucking-Reiley, 2002) do, in fact, increase donations during the time of the fund drive. List and Lucking-Reiley, for example, found that increasing seed money from 10 percent to 67 percent of the campaign goal produced a nearly six-fold increase in contributions, with significant effects on both participation rates and average gift size. But few field researchers have examined the long-term results of any fundraising tactics (see Frey and Meier 2004, and Shang and Croson 2006 for exceptions), and we are unaware of any published studies investigating long-term impact of seed money or thank-you gifts.

In our laboratory experiments, we study the impact in future periods of using seed money, matching funds, and thank you gifts to increase giving in the present period, finding that certain levels of all these commonly used "sweeteners" can decrease giving in the long term. In our seed money study, we find that those who donate at the end of a successful capital campaign donate less money in the future–25 percent less than those who donate at the beginning or middle of the campaign, holding initial donation constant. We speculate that perhaps the "warm glow" of altruism (Andreoni 1989, 1990) can at times make us feel as though we have actually done more than we have, decreasing our motivation to give more, since we may feel we have given enough. This hypothesis could help explain our additional finding that high levels of matching funds can decrease future donations–those whose initial contributions were matched at 300 percent subsequently gave 18 percent less than those whose contributions were matched at 100 percent. We found that thank you gifts such as music CDs given away by public radio stations to encourage participation in their fund drives can backfire as well. When donors received a small thank you gift in exchange for their contribution, they gave 20 percent less when solicited again. We propose that the psychological mechanism underlying this behavior may be that structuring the donation event as a trade turns it into an economic rather than a social transaction in the mind of the donor, and this may decrease one's intrinsic motivation to donate. Many studies have shown that extrinsic motivation can undermine intrinsic motivation and impair performance (see Deci, Koestner and Ryan, 1999, for a review), and, in agreement with Gneezy and Rustichini (2000) we suggest this effect extends to charitable giving. We are currently investigating our hypotheses regarding the mechanisms behind the major drops in charitable giving that can result from seed money, matching funds, and thank you gift strategies.

Economists and psychologists have long been investigating the phenomenon of why people give, with crossover between disciplines making this a simultaneously fruitful and challenging line of inquiry. Economists models of giving, such as Andreoni's heavily-cited "warm glow" model of altruism (1989, 1990), typically rely on psychological constructs; and psychologists often turn to evolutionary theories for rational explanations of generosity, such as kin selection and reciprocity (Penner et al, 2005). At the crux of this overlap in disciplines is the issue of motivation. As we explore this area further, we hope to shed some light on how and when using common fundraising strategies can be demotivating despite increasing participation rates. With greater understanding of how their strategies can backfire, charitable organizations may be able to employ similar tactics with less risk.

References

Andreoni, J. & Petrie, R. (2004) Public goods experiments without confidentiality: A glimpse into fund-raising. *Journal of Public Economy,* 88: 1605–1623.

Andreoni, J. (1989) Giving with Impure Altruism: Applications to Charity and Ricardian Equivalence. *Journal of Political Economy*, 97: 1447-58.

Andreoni, J. (1990) Impure Altruism and Donations to Public Goods: A Theory of Warm-Glow Giving. *The Economic Journal*, (100) 401, 464-477

Deci, E., Koestner, R. & Ryan, R. (1999) A meta-analytic review of experiments examining the effects of extrinsic rewards on intrinsic motivation, *Psychological Bulletin,* 125, 627-688.

Dunn, E., Aknin, L. & Norton, M. (2008) Spending money on others promotes happiness. *Science*, 319: 1687–1688.

Eckel, C. & Grossman, P. (2008) Subsidizing charitable contributions: a natural field experiment comparing matching and rebate subsidies. *Journal of Experimental Economics*, 11(3), 234-252.

Frey, B. & Meier, S. (2004) Pro-social behavior in a natural setting, *Journal of Economic Behavior and Organization* 54 (1), 65–88.

Gneezy, U. & Rustichini, A. (2000) Pay Enough or Don't Pay at All, *Quarterly Journal of Economics*, 115 (3), 791-810.

Independent Sector. 2002. *Giving and volunteering in the United States 2001*. Washington, DC: Independent Sector.

List, J. & Lucking-Reiley, D. (2002) The Effects of Seed Money and Refunds on Charitable Giving: Experimental Evidence from a University Capital Campaign. *Journal of Political Economy* 110 (1), 215–33.

Penner, L., Dovidio, J, Piliavin, J. & Schroeder, D. (2005) Prosocial behaviour: multilevel perspectives. *Annual Review of Psychology* 56, 365–392.

Shang, J. & Croson, R. (2005) Field Experiments in Charitable Contribution: The Impact of Social Influence on the Voluntary Provision of Public Goods." http://knowledge.wharton.upenn.edu/paper.cfm?paperID=1313.

Confidence, Mindset, and Self-Efficacy in Goal Pursuit

Chiu-chi Angela Chang, Shippensburg University, USA
Xiaojing Yang, University of Wisconsin-Milwaukee, USA

Consider what is happening at this moment in time: economic downturns make despair palpable to many individuals, who feel unconfident in achieving their retirement or other savings goals. How could these low confidence individuals persevere to save and work toward their goals? The current study is motivated by scenarios like this and examines the possibility of boosting self-efficacy (i.e., a belief in one's ability to achieve something) in view of low confidence.

The marketing literature on hope indicates the effect of strong versus weak hope on product evaluation and choice (e.g., MacInnis and de Mello 2005). In particular, De Mello et al. (2007) find that when consumers have low confidence about achieving their hoped-for goals, they are engaged in motivated reasoning about the effectiveness of products touted as problem solutions. Yet, in an effort to restore hope, besides a biased perception about products, could consumers have biased views about themselves? Indeed, a likely side effect of reduced confidence in a hoped-for goal is low perceived self-efficacy, as both low confidence and low perceived self-efficacy may result from a lack of mastery experience (cf. Bandura 1997). A vicious cycle can occur such that low perceived self-efficacy would, in turn, prevent a consumer from making vigorous, persistent efforts or enhancing the commitment to achieving a goal (Mukhopadhyay and Johar 2005). Therefore, it is relevant to investigate how to boost perceived self-efficacy when consumers have low confidence in reaching their goals.

This study proposes that mindset activated (deliberative vs. implementational) may affect perceived self-efficacy for low confidence consumers. Theoretical support comes from the research on construal levels and self-control (Fujita et al. 2006). Their experiments demonstrate that construing a situation in high-level terms (such as priming a deliberative [vs. implementational] mindset) would promote self-control (such as reduced preferences for immediate over delayed outcomes). To boost self-efficacy in a discouraging, low confidence situation certainly requires self-control, thus it is likely that a deliberative mindset would similarly have a favorable effect on self-efficacy. In addition, it is likely that a deliberative (vs. implementational) mindset would engender a fair and balanced evaluation of the situation (Taylor and Gollwitzer 1995), which may be lacking especially for low confidence consumers. In sum, the prediction is that a deliberative (vs. implementational) mindset would help boost self-efficacy for low (not high) confidence consumers.

To test the aforementioned relation among confidence, mindset, and self-efficacy, a 2 (confidence: low vs. high) x 2 (mindset: deliberative vs. implementation) between-subjects design was employed. Eighty-nine undergraduate respondents were divided into high and low confidence groups based on their answer, on a nine-point scale, to the item: "I am confident that I would get good grades by the end of the semester," which was embedded in a lifestyle survey. They then were primed with either a deliberative or an implementational mindset, following the procedures in Taylor and Gollwitzer (1995). Specifically, respondents in the deliberative mindset condition were asked to consider the immediate and long-term consequences of a personal project, whereas respondents in the implementational mindset condition were asked to write down the implementation steps involved in an intended project. The main dependent measure was perceived self-efficacy. Four domain-specific items of perceived self-efficacy were constructed; for example, "There is a lot that I as a student can do to get the best grades that I can," and "With enough effort I can get very good grades." Questions regarding the extent of studying were also included. Additional measures collected (and later used as covariates) included self-control, self-regulatory focus, mood, involvement, gender, and GPA.

Significant main effects of mindset and of confidence, as well as a moderately significant interaction effect of confidence and mindset on perceived self-efficacy were found ($F(1, 71) = 2.82$, $p = .097$). The interaction pattern was such that high confidence respondents were not influenced by the mindset manipulation, whereas low confidence respondents had higher perceived self-efficacy when they were primed with a deliberative (vs. implementational) mindset, as hypothesized. Another intriguing finding was that prevention-focused low confidence respondents said they would study more in the following week than did promotion-focused low confidence counterparts (no significant effect was found for high confidence respondents).

The finding of the interaction effect of confidence and mindset is consistent with the rationales provided by Fujita et al. (2006) and Taylor and Gollwitzer (1995). That is, a deliberative mindset makes consumers consider both pros and cons (i.e., high-level features), and that helps our low confidence respondents boost perceived self-efficacy because the appraisal of self-efficacy was not colored by low confidence. In other words, a deliberative mindset makes consumers resist the crippling effect of low confidence. On the other hand, it seems that priming an implementational mindset may not be helpful in enhancing perceived self-efficacy for low confidence consumers because these consumers simply lack the confidence about achieving their goals and even taking the necessary steps.

During goal pursuit consumers differ in their confidence about reaching their hoped-for goals (e.g., exercising, dieting, savings). It is important to understand how reduced-confidence consumers can boost their perceived self-efficacy and keep trying persistently. This working paper found that priming a deliberative or an implementational mindset can make a difference in consumers' perceived self-efficacy in a low confidence situation. Follow-up studies are needed to shed more light on our understanding of boosting self-efficacy. Possible directions include: (1) manipulating confidence in reaching a goal; (2) studying the prediction in a different context for generalizability; (3) monitoring, as a dependent measure, real behavior needed for reaching a goal; and (4) exploring additional ways to boost perceived self-efficacy (e.g., inducing a promotion or a prevention self-regulatory focus).

References

Aaker, Jennifer L. and Angela Y. Lee (2006), "Understanding Regulatory Fit," *Journal of Marketing Research*, 43 (February), 15-19.

Bandura, Albert (1997), *Self-Efficacy: The Exercise of Control*, New York: Freeman.

Fujita, Kentaro, Yaacov Trope, Nira Liberman, and Maya Levin-Sagi (2006), "Construal Levels and Self-Control," *Journal of Personality and Social Psychological*, 90 (3), 351-367.

de Mello, Gustavo, Deborah J. MacInnis, and David W. Stewart (2007), "Threats to Hope: Effects on Reasoning about Product Information," *Journal of Consumer Research*, 34 (August), 153-161.

MacInnis, Deborah J. and Gustavo de Mello (2005), "The Concept of Hope and Its Relevance to Product Evaluation and Choice," *Journal of Marketing*, 69 (1), 1-14.

Mukhopadhyay, Anirban and Gita Venkataramani Johar (2005), "Where There Is a Will, Is There a Way? Effects of Lay Theories of Self-Control on Setting and Keeping Resolutions." *Journal of Consumer Research,* 31 (March), 779-786

Taylor, Shelley E. and Peter M. Gollwitzer (1995), "Effects of Mindset on Positive Illusions," *Journal of Personality and Social Psychology*, 69 (2), 213-226.

The Impact of Implicit Theories on Family Brand Evaluations

Joseph Chang, Vancouver Island University, Canada

Introduction

Previous studies examining reciprocal extension effects on family brand evaluations mainly focus on the accessibility and diagnosticity of brand extension information (e.g., Ahluwalia and Gurhan-Canli 2000; Chang 2002, 2007; Chang and Lou 2006), the categorical similarity between brand extensions and their family brands (e.g., Chang 2002; Chang and Lou 2005; Loken and John 2003; Milberg and Sinn 2008; Salinas and Perez 2009), and the nature of family brands, such as varieties and perceived entitativity of family brands (e.g., Chang 2007; Chang and Lou 2005, 2006; Gurhan-Canli, 2003). In social cognition, research on lay theories (entity vs. incremental) indicate that subjects who begin social perception with different initial assumptions follow various cognitive paths and reach various social endpoints of expectations, perceptions, and inferences (Levy, Plaks, Hong, Chiu, and Dweck 2001). As with social cognition, the impact of implicit theorists may also affect reciprocal extension effects on family brand evaluations.

Conceptualization

Entity theorists believe that personal characteristics are fixed or static despite person's efforts or motivation to change them, which means that personal characteristics are beyond personal control. They believe that "everyone is a certain kind of person, and there is not much that can be done to really change that" (measure statement). In contrast, incremental theorists believe that personal characteristics are dynamic or malleable and can be changed over time and with efforts. They believe that "anyone can change even their most basic qualities" (measure statement). Research results indicate that entity theorists are more likely to elicit greater stereotype endorsement, greater perceived outgroup homogeneity effects, more susceptibility to the ultimate attribution error, greater intergroup bias, and more biased behavior toward outgroup members (Levy et al. 2001).

As believing that personality is dynamic or malleable (vs. static or fixed), incremental (vs. entity) theorist are more open to, and lay more weight on, latest relevant information about brand extensions to update their impression about the family brands if they are motivated to process the information on-line. Therefore, it is hypothesized that new brand extension information is more influential or diagnostic on family brand evaluations for incremental (vs. entity) theorists (Study 1). Moreover, as believing that personality is static or fixed (vs. dynamic or malleable), entity (vs. incremental) theorists are more likely to expect the existence of underlying essences of family brands and the congruency of brand extension information. Given the congruency, the processing of integrating the extension information with the family brand is expected to be a relatively easier task for the entity theorists, who subsequently are more highly motivated to spontaneously process new relevant information about the family brands. Therefore, it is hypothesized that, as expecting the existence of underlying essences about family brands, entity theorists tend to perceive the entitativity of family brands higher (Study 2-1). Moreover, as being more highly motivated, entity theorists tend to have spontaneous on-line (vs. memory-based) extension information integration for the impression formation about family brands (Study 2-2). Based on the theory of group level trait transference (GLTT) model (Crawford, Sherman, and Hamilton 2002), the information integration for the impression formation about family brands may involve the three-stage process of attribute abstraction (or inference), stereotyping, and attribute transference. As entity (vs. incremental) theorists are more likely to have spontaneous on-line extension information integration, it is hypothesized that stereotyping and attribute transference within family brands are more likely to occur to entity (vs. incremental) theorists, where as attribute abstraction occurs to both entity and incremental theorists (Study 3-1). Moreover, the processes of stereotyping and attribute transference may amplify the magnitude of extension information and lead to more salient polarization extension effects on consequent family brand evaluations (Chang and Lou 2006; Crawford et al. 2002; Study 3-2).

Methodology

This research consists of three studies. The first study is to verify if new brand extension information is more influential or diagnostic on family brand evaluations for incremental (vs. entity) theorists. The study consists of eight experimental conditions with respondents randomly assigned to groups in a 2 (implicit theorists: static vs. incremental) x 2 (valences of extension information: positive vs. negative) x 2 (categorical similarity: similar vs. dissimilar) between-subjects factorial design; around 200 student participants are expected. The second study is to verify if entity theorists tend to perceive the entitativity of family brands higher and have spontaneous information processing to form on-line (vs. memory-based) impressions about the family brands. The study consists of eight experimental conditions with respondents randomly assigned to groups in a 2 (implicit theorists: static vs. incremental) x 4 (family brand entitativity: high similarity/high goal-derived, high similarity/low goal-derived, low similarity/high goal-derived, low similarity/low goal-derived) between-subjects factorial design; around 200 student participants are expected. The third study is to verify if the stereotyping and attribute transference within family brands, and extension polarization effects on family brand evaluations, are more salient for entity (vs. incremental) theorists. The study consists of a 2 (implicit theorists: entity vs. incremental) x 4 (family brand entitativity: high similarity/high goal-derived, high similarity/low goal-derived, low similarity/high goal-derived, low similarity/low goal-derived) x 6 (attribute counterbalancing) x 2 (trial types: inference vs. transference) mixed-measures design with repeated measures on the fourth factor. The experimental process will follow the procedure of the paradigm of previous research by Crawford et al. (2002); around 180 student participants are anticipated.

Results

The following findings are expected. Firstly, new brand extension information is expected to be more influential or diagnostic on family brand evaluations for incremental (vs. entity) theorists. Secondly, entity (vs. incremental) theorists are expected to perceive the entitativity of family brands higher. Thirdly, entity (vs. incremental) theorists are expected to have spontaneous information processing to form on-line (vs. memory-based) impressions about the family brands. Finally, stereotyping and attribute transference within family brands, and polarization effects on family brand evaluations, are more salient for entity (vs. incremental) theorists.

References

Chang, Joseph W. (2002), "Will A Family Brand Be Diluted by An Unfavorable Brand Extension? A Real Brand Trial-Based Approach," in *Advances in Consumer Research*, Vol. 29, Susan Broniarczyk and Kent Nakamoto eds. Valdosta, GA: Association for Consumer Research, 299-304.

Chang, Joseph W. (2007), "The Diagnosticity of Brand Extension Information for the Judgment of Family Brand Evaluations: A Cue-Diagnosticity Perspective," in *American Marketing Association Summer Educators' Proceedings*, Jakki Mohr and Robert Fisher, eds. Chicago, IL: American Marketing Association, 289.

Chang, Joseph W. and Y. C. Lou (2005), "Perceived Entitativity as A Moderator of Family Brand Evaluations under High Accessibility Situations," in *AMA Winter Proceedings: Marketing Theory and Applications*, Vol. 16, Kathleen Seiders and Glenn B. Voss, eds. Chicago, IL: American Marketing Association, 75-76.

Chang, Joseph W. and Y. C. Lou (2006), "The Polarization Effect of Perceived Entitativity on Family Brand Evaluations," in *SCP Winter Proceedings*, Dan Ariely, Baba Shiv, and Michal Strahilevitz, eds. Washington, DC: Society for Consumer Psychology, American Psychological Association, 132-137 (Sessions II).

Crawford, M. T., S. J. Sherman, and D. L. Hamilton (2002), "Perceived Entitativity, Stereotype Formation, and the Interchangeability of Group Members," *Journal of Personality and Social Psychology*, 83 (5), 1076-1094.

Gurhan-Canli Z. (2003), "The Effect of Expected Variability of Product Quality and Attribute Uniqueness on Family Brand Evaluations," *Journal of Consumer Research*, 30, 105-114.

Levy, Sheri R., Jason E. Plaks, Ying-yi Hong, Chi-yue Chiu, and Carol S. Dweck (2001), "Static Versus Dynamic Theories and the Perception of Groups: Different Routes to Different Destinations," *Personality and Social Psychology Review*, 5 (2), 156-168.

Loken, Barbara and Deborah Roedder John (1993), "Diluting Brand Beliefs: When Do Brand Extensions Have a Negative Impact?" *Journal of Marketing*, Vol. 57 (July), 71-84.

Milberg, S. J. and F. Sinn (2008), "Vulnerability of Global Brands to Negative Feedback Effects," *Journal of Business Research*, 61(June), 684-690.

Salinas, E. M. and J. M. P. Perez (2009), "Modeling the Brand Extensions' Influence on Brand Image," *Journal of Business Research*, 62(January), 50-60.

Varieties of Family Brand Entitativity

Joseph Chang, Vancouver Island University, Canada
Yung-Chien Lou, National Cheng-Chi University, Taiwan

Introduction

Research in social cognition has recently paid a considerable amount of attentions to the influence of perceived entitativity on the impression formation of social groups. Entitativity refers to the wholeness of a group defined as the degree to which a social aggregate is perceived as "having the nature of an entity" (Campbell 1958, p. 17). The concept of perceived entitativity was also just implemented to the research domain in family brand evaluations. Previous research results indicate that high (vs. low) entitative family brands are more favourably evaluated, and perceived entitativity yields asymmetric reciprocal effects on family brand evaluations (Chang and Lou 2005, 2006), which parallel to the results of group perceptions in social cognition (Crawford, Sherman and Hamilton 2002). As categorization is the basis of stereotyping and judgments, as with social groups, family brands with various perceived entitativity are likely to be categorized differently, which leads to different subsequent psychological processes and results in asymmetric reciprocal effects on family brand evaluations. Therefore, this research examines the applicability of the entitativity measures of group perceptions for family brand evaluations.

Conceptualization

The categorization of social groups involves five dimensions with nine entitativity measures, including the global entitativity measure (Lickel, Hamilton, Wieczorkowska, Lewis, Sherman, and Uhles 2000). The first dimension is similarity or homogeneity of group members to each other. The second one is group size. The third dimension is the importance of group membership. The forth one is the interdependence among the members of a group. The interdependence among the members of a group is comprised of the three sub-factors of interaction among group members, common goals among group members, and common outcomes for group members. The last one is inalterability of a group with an essential or basic nature, which is comprised of the two sub-factors of permeability of group boundaries and duration of group.

Groups vary along an entitativity continuum (Hamilton, Sherman, and Lickel 1998). As discussed above, the significance of the eight group properties differs among different social groups, which induces different levels of perceived entitativity. The perceived entitativity of social groups is defined by a pattern of properties, and these patterns differ meaningfully. Perceivers engage in different extents of stereotyping and make different judgments with respect to different degrees of perceived entitativity. Lickel et al. (2000) further identify the importance of the eight antecedents for the social group categorization by rating the perceived entitativity of 40 various social groups. The five properties of interaction, importance, common goals, common outcomes, and similarity are observed to be determinant to the perceptions of entitativity (or groupness), whereas the rest of three factors of size, duration, and permeability are less correlated with the perceived entitativity. Based on the antecedents of eight group properties, social groups are further categorized into four distinct types of groups with different perceived entitativity, which include intimacy groups, task groups, social categories, and loose association groups. Each type of group is comprised of a unique pattern of entitativity-related properties and varies along a considerable range of entitativity continuum. For example, *intimacy* groups are small, significant in interaction, important to their members (significant in the importance of group membership), generally impermeable (or with clear impermeable boundaries), and more durable (or having been in long existence).

Methodology

Following previous research (Lickel et al. 2000), nine measures of perceived entitativity including interaction, importance, outcomes, goals, similarity, duration, size, permeability, and the global measure of perceived entitativity are utilized to cluster 40 prominent family brands (e.g., Coca-Cola, Microsoft, IBM, etc.), which were selected from the Top 100 Global Brands of Businessweek (2008). However, pilot tests showed that respondents were exhausted and bored after spending around 45 minutes in evaluating the 40 brands with the nine entitativity measures (overall 360=9 x 40 evaluative judgments), which may yield respond bias (Aaker 1997, p 349). In order to prevent the respond bias, the research design was further revised to significantly reduce respondents' workload from 40 brands down to 10 brands. By doing like this, the overall evaluative judgments for each respondent are significantly reduced from 360 down to 90. The original 40 brands are firstly reduced down to 37 brands and then divided into four Brand Groups with a common brand, SONY, in each Brand Group. The common brand is included in each Brand Group so that the extent to which the four Brand Groups differs in their brand entitativity measures could be assessed (Aaker 1997).

Overall, two hundred undergraduate participants are expected, in addition to the 70 respondents for the pilot tests. Participants are randomly assigned to one of the four Brand Groups. Each participant evaluates the 10 family brands in the assigned Brand Group with the nine entitativity measures on a 9-point scale ranging from 1 ("Not a brand family at all") to 9 ("Very much a brand family"). A booklet with color brand extension portfolios and brand logos of 10 popular family brands in consumer goods industries (Businessweek 2008) is provided for perceived entitativity evaluations. The family brands are shown to the respondents in random orders to avoid systematic responding biases.

Results

Correlation analysis, factor analyses, regression analysis, cluster analysis, and multidimensional scaling (MDS) are to be performed to select appropriate measures and form dimensions of perceived entitativity for family brand categorization. As with social groups, it is expected that several of these properties, except permeability, are strongly correlated with, and account for a substantial portion of the variation in, the global perceived entitativity (Lickel et al. 2000). Properties of perceived entitativity are effective antecedents that may cluster family brands into groups, which subsequently elaborate different cognitive processes for family brand evaluations.

More reliable results from the revised research design are further expected, while the pilot tests with a sample size of 70 yield some interesting findings. Namely, the five-cluster solution was found to be the relatively stable solution for the interpretation. Cluster 1 family brands (e.g., American Express) are small and have high levels of goals and similarity. Cluster 2 family brands (e.g., GE and Panasonic) are low in similarity, interaction, and outcomes, but of moderate duration and size. Cluster 3 family brands (e.g., Disney) are high in duration and size, but low in outcomes and similarity. Cluster 4 family brands (e.g., AVON) are relatively low in outcomes, size, importance, and interaction. Cluster 5 family brands (e.g., Toyota) are high in duration, goals, and similarity. As expected, results of Correlational analysis indicate that seven properties, except permeability, are positively correlated with entitativity. Further studies are also developed to examine other factors that may affect family brand categorization, such as product ownership with the theory of self-identity (Study 2) and cultural differences with holistic (vs. analytical) thinking (Study 3).

References

Aaker, Jennifer L. (1997), "Dimensions of Brand Personality," *Journal of Marketing Research*, 34 (August), 347-356.

BusinessWeek, "The 100 Top Brands," *BusinessWeek Online*. Available from:<http://bwnt.businessweek.com/brand/2008/> [Accessed March 22, 2008].

Campbell, D. T. (1958), "Common Fate, Similarity, and Other Indices of the Status of Aggregates of Persons as Social Entities," *Behavioral Science*, Vol. 3, 14-25.

Chang, Joseph W. and Y. C. Lou (2005), "Perceived Entitativity as A Moderator of Family Brand Evaluations under High Accessibility Situations," in *AMA Winter Proceedings: Marketing Theory and Applications*, Vol. 16, Kathleen Seiders and Glenn B. Voss, eds. Chicago, IL: American Marketing Association, 75-76.

Chang, Joseph W. and Y. C. Lou (2006), "The Polarization Effect of Perceived Entitativity on Family Brand Evaluations," in *SCP Winter Proceedings*, Dan Ariely, Baba Shiv, and Michal Strahilevitz, eds. Washington, DC: Society for Consumer Psychology, American Psychological Association, 132-137 (Sessions II).

Crawford, M. T., S. J. Sherman, and D. L. Hamilton (2002), "Perceived Entitativity, Stereotype Formation, and the Interchangeability of Group Members," *Journal of Personality and Social Psychology*, 83 (5), 1076-1094.

Hamilton, D. L., S. J. Sherman, and B. Lickel (1998), "Perceiving Social Groups: The Importance of the Entitativity Continuum," in *Intergroup Cognition and Intergroup Behavior*, C. Sedikides, J. Schlpler, and C. A. Insko eds. Mahwah, NJ: Erlbaum.

Lickel, B., D. L. Hamilton, G. Wieczorkowska, A. C. Lewis, S. J. Sherman, and A. N. Uhles (2000), "Varieties of Groups and the Perception of Group Entitativity," *Journal of Personality and Social Psychology*, Vol. 78, 223-246.

Wrath of the Monsoons: Effect of Marketplace Evolution on Acquisition and Storage of Possessions in Recurring Natural Disasters

Sarita Ray Chaudhury, New Mexico State University, USA

Every year, the monsoon season in India occurs approximately from June through September. People await its annual advent with a mix of anticipation and dread. Monsoons provide much needed water resource for the predominantly agricultural country. The rains bring respite from the fierce summer heat simultaneously causing floods and heavy loss of life and property. The United Nations claimed 2007 as "the worst year in living memory" as 2200 lives were lost across South-East Asia, leaving millions homeless and destitute due to Monsoonal floods. In 2008, the Indian government sanctioned approximately $230 Million in aid to victims of Monsoonal floods which claimed 800 lives across the country (The Associated Press 2008).

India's booming economy has led to unexpected windfalls for its middle class. With call centers and retail outlets (such as malls and shopping complexes) mushrooming in small towns, young people are in a position to earn money before finishing college. Therefore, despite living with their parents, adult children manifest their newfound independence in the acquisition of personal possessions. These consumption acts lead to conflicts and tensions in the family due to limited storage space in the house and is further intensified during the monsoon season. This study examines the interplay of family dynamics (between generations such as parents and adult children residing in the same household) and the role of an evolving marketplace in creating such tensions and how family members negotiate to resolve them.

To explore these issues, personal life-history interviews (Mick and Buhl 1992) of eighteen individuals are undertaken in a mid-size city in eastern India. Heads of families, their wives and adult children participated in the interview process which took place during a recent monsoon season. Participants were given a digital camera to take pictures of the storage spaces in their homes. They provided detailed description of the use of the storage spaces during the course of the interview process. All participants are from the lower middle class socio-economic stratum with annual incomes between Rs.25, 000 to Rs.1, 00,000 (approximately $530-$2130 earned by primary household earner). Their homes are located in low-lying areas and are prone to flooding. Almost every year they experience disruption of daily lives, loss of possessions and sometimes even human lives during the monsoon season. In order to understand how evolving marketplace conditions in recent times shape consumption practices, participants were asked to compare the current monsoon season with past experiences. Families with employed adult children living at home experience the most conflict with evolving marketplace conditions. With limited storage space in the house, new acquisitions posit a conflict of interest amongst the different generations of family members living under one roof. Some emergent themes are briefly highlighted and theoretical contributions of this study are discussed.

The EMI factor:

Indian banks experiencing rapid growth in recent years are more moderate in their lending conditions than in the past. With availability of relatively accessible credit, participants acquired televisions, motorbikes and other high-end products that are paid back in EMI-s or equal monthly installments. Fathers wield considerable power in the patriarchal society of India. Consequently, when the head of the household purchased an expensive product, he attributed it towards the benefit of the family. If a son acquired the same product with his own resources, there was conflict in the household as it was then considered an individual and not a family possession. For example, the head of the household purchased a television set which was kept in the family living area for everyone's viewing purposes. However, if the father was present, everyone watched the channel of his choice. The adult son (residing in the household) purchased another television set (with credit) for his own viewing purposes and kept this set in a bedroom shared with other family members. This act of consumption created several sources of conflict amongst family members. Participants worried about keeping these newly acquired possessions safe from flooding during monsoon season. Burdened with paying back loans, participants reported mental stress and strain on finances to safeguard these expensive assets during monsoon season in addition to familial tensions.

Keeping up with the Joneses (or in this case, the Jhas)

Participant's homes are surrounded by newly developed high-rise apartments where only a few short years ago there was nothing. The prosperity of their new neighbors often influenced them to investigate latest marketplace offerings. Participants, specifically young adult children in the family, visited newly built shopping complexes to purchase equivalent or close substitutes of clothing and accessories similar to their more privileged neighbors. Apart from additional drainage of monetary resources which is viewed as wastage (most parents want adult children to save as much of their earnings as possible) by the parents (typically the fathers), storing these possessions during the monsoon season became an issue of discontent in the family as it took up precious space in the house.

Consumer Culture theorists over the last two decades have examined numerous ways in which marketplace resources are used to construct, communicate and legitimize distinctive consumer identities (Arnould and Thompson 2005; Oswald 1999; Penaloza 1994; Schouten and McAlexander 1995). Although India is acknowledged as an emergent market with vast growth potentials, there is little understanding of how consumer identities are shaped and contested in the country's present dynamic marketplace (Varman and Belk 2008). As marketers seek authentic "consumer experience" in consumer research (Richins 2005; Thompson, Locander, and Pollio 1989), this study draws attention to consumers who experience the impact of natural disaster on a recurring basis. It highlights previously unexplored ways in which such consumers; collectively and individually, navigate a radically evolving marketplace to offset challenges such as family role conflicts in storage of possessions during annual monsoon flooding in India.

References

Arnould, Eric J. and Craig J. Thompson (2005), "Consumer Culture Theory (CCT): Twenty Years of Research," *Journal of Consumer Research*, 31 (March), 868–882.

Mick, David Glen and Claus Buhl (1992), "A Meaning-Based Model of Advertising Experiences," *Journal of Consumer Research*, 19 (December), 317-338.

Oswald, Laura (1999), "Culture Swapping: Consumption and the Ethnogenesis of Middle-Class Haitian Immigrants," *Journal of Consumer Research*, 25 (March), 303-318.

Pen˜aloza, Lisa (1994), "Atravesando Fronteras/Border Crossings: A Critical Ethnographic Study of the Consumer Acculturation of Mexican Immigrants," *Journal of Consumer Research*, 21 (June), 32–53.

Richins, Marsha L. (2005), "What Consumers Desire: Goals and Motives in the Consumption Environment," in *Inside Consumption: Frontiers of Research on Consumer Motives, Goals, and Desires*, eds. S. Ratneshwar and David Glen Mick, London: Routledge, 340-347.

Schouten, John W. and James H. McAlexander (1995), "Subcultures of Consumption: An Ethnography of the New Bikers," *Journal of Consumer Research*, 22 (June), 43–61.

The Associated Press (2008), "India Authorizes US$200 Million for Monsoon Floods," http://www.iht.com/articles/ap/2008/08/28/asia/AS-India-Monsoon-Flooding.php

Thompson, Craig J., William B. Locander and Howard R. Pollio (1989), "Putting Consumer Experience Back into Consumer Research: The Philosophy and Method of Existensial-Phenomenology," *Journal of Consumer Research*, 16 (September), 133-146.

Varman, Rohit and Russell W. Belk (2008), "Weaving a Web: Subaltern Consumers, Rising Consumer Culture, and Television," *Marketing Theory*, 8 (September), 227-252.

The Influences of Price Dispersion and the Manufacturer's Suggested Price on Consumers' Boundaries of Acceptable Price: Expected Price as a Mediator

Etta Y. I. Chen, Yuan Ze University, Taiwan
Lien-Ti Bei, National Chengchi University, Taiwan

Price dispersion is defined as the price variability across stores for a specific brand or product (Grewal and Marmorstein 1994; Pan, Ratchford and Shankar, 2004; Stigler 1961; Urbany 1986). The effect of price dispersion on the consumer's internal reference price is most concerned of manufacturers. Therefore, many manufacturers use the suggested price on the package of a product or in advertising to prevent retailers from excessive mark ups or to counteract the negative impact of unexpected retailing prices. The manufacturer's suggested price (MSP) as an anchor may assimilate the expected price under high price dispersion as well as the acceptable price. The boundaries of the expected price and the acceptable price are important for the consumer's price judgment and purchase decision. However, the effect of price dispersion and the MSP on the consumer's expected and acceptable prices are still unknown. Besides, the MSP of a prestige or an inferior brand may have differing impacts. The purpose of this study was to investigate the joint effects of price dispersion, the MSP, and the brand image on the expected price. Furthermore, the research demonstrated how the expected price mediated their effects on the acceptable price.

In this study, high price dispersion was defined as the market price range of a product that exceeded the consumer's acceptable price range of that product category. The manipulation of price range for high price dispersion represented the noticeable price difference for consumers. Also, the highest market price was higher and the lowest market price was lower than those under low price dispersion. Past market prices and contextual factors that consumers encounter in their purchase experiences shape their price expectations (Jacobson and Obermiller 1990; Kalwani et al. 1990; Kopalle and Lindsey-Mullikin, 2003). Therefore, the boundaries of the expected price cannot avoid being influenced by the range effect from price dispersion (as predicted by Range Theory) and the anchoring effect of the MSP. The extreme range of the high price dispersion is expected to enlarge the distance of both boundaries of the expected price, while the MSP is expected to raise both upper and lower boundaries. Based on the assimilation effect (Sherif and Hovland 1961), one can further predict that the upper boundary of the acceptable price will be assimilated toward the anchor value of the MSP, but not the price dispersion. In contrast, the lower boundary of the acceptable price should be assimilated toward the low market prices of high price dispersion. Both effects are expected to work via the boundaries of expected price as mediators.

The expected price corresponds to the cognition of a product's market prices and contributes to the construction of an acceptable price. The expected price is also found to influence the width of the acceptable price (Kalyanaram and Little 1994). Therefore, the mediating effect of the expected price was further hypothesized. This study expected that the lower boundary of the expected price might mediate the effect of price dispersion on the lower boundary of the acceptable price, while the effect of the MSP on the upper boundary of the acceptable price was mediated by the upper boundary of the expected price. In addition, the MSP is closely linked to a manufacturer's reputation and the brand image. Brand image is found to influence the consumer's internal reference price (Grewal et al. 1998). A prestige brand helps to raise the internal reference price more effectively than an inferior brand. The interaction of brand image, the MSP and price dispersion on the range of the acceptable price was included in this research.

The main study employed a 2 (price dispersion: high or low) x 2 (MSP: with MSP or without MSP) x 2 (brand image: prestige or inferior) between-subject experimental design. Three pretests were conducted to decide the focal product category, representative brands, and price range. In pretest 1, 2-liter milk was selected from a list of consumer products. Two real brands, i.e., the representatives of the prestige and inferior brands, were chosen based on respondents' overall impression and quality evaluation. In addition, the operational definition of price dispersion was the difference between the highest and lowest prices across retailers on the market at a given point of time. The levels of the manipulation of price dispersion were decided in Pretest 2 and 3. The ranges of high/low price dispersion were manipulated beyond/within the range of acceptable prices that were acquired from the results of Pretest 2. In the main study, the price stimulus was disguised by a one-page fictitious excerpt from *Consumer Reports* in which the main topic was the quality and price survey of major milk brands on the market. A matrix of seven retailer outlets and five major milk brands (including either the prestige or the inferior brand with four other real median level major brands on the market) was presented. A total of 207 undergraduate students participated in this experiment.

The results indicated a hierarchical relationship between price dispersion, the MSP, the boundaries of the expected, and then the acceptable prices. Price dispersion and MSP influenced both boundaries of the expected price. Price dispersion lowered the lower boundary of the expected price while the MSP raised the upper boundary of the expected price. Also, the lower boundary of the expected price fully mediated the effect of price dispersion on the lower boundary of the acceptable price. In contrast, both boundaries of the expected price fully mediated the effect of the MSP on the upper boundary of the acceptable price. In Litchtenstein and Bearden's (1989) scale of internal price standards, the range of the acceptable price was restricted in that of the expected price and was biased toward the direction of lower prices. The findings of the current study corresponded to their works that the upper boundary of the acceptable price was be mediated by the lower boundary of the expected price. Furthermore, for the prestige brand, the range of an acceptable price was higher than the inferior brand when the price dispersion was high. This study explored the mechanism, during which the boundaries of acceptable prices were influenced by the negative impact of high price dispersion and the counterbalance effect of the MSP. The results of this study also provided manufacturers a strategic perspective of employing MSP to shape consumers' price perceptions.

References

Grewal, Dhruv and H. Marmorstein (1994), "Market Price Variation, Perceived Price Variation, and Consumers' Price Search Decisions for Durable Goods," *Journal of Consumer Research,* 21, (December), 453-60.

Krishnan, R., Julie Baker, and Norm Borin (1998), "The Effect of Store Name, Brand Name and Price Discounts on Consumers' Evaluations and Purchase Intentions," *Journal of Retailing,* 74 (3), 331-52.

Jacobson, Robert and Carl Obermiller (1990), "The Formation of Expected Future Price," *Journal of Consumer Research,* 16 (February), 420-32.

Kalwani, Manohar U., Chi Kin Yim, Heikkj J. Rinne, and Yoshi Sugita (1990), "A Price Expectation Model of Customer Brand Choice," *Journal of Marketing Research,* 27 (August), 251-62.

Kalyanaram, Gurumurthy and John D. C. Little (1994), "An Empirical Analysis of Latitude of Price Acceptance in Consumer Package Goods," *Journal of Consumer Research,* 21 (December), 408-18.

Kopalle, K. Praveen and Joan Lindsey-Mullikin (2003), "The Impact of External Reference Price on Consumer Price Expectations," *Journal of Retailing,* 79, 225-236.

Lichtenstein, Donald. R. and William O. Bearden (1989), "Contextual Influences on Perceptions of Merchant-Supplied Reference Prices," *Journal of Consumer Research,* 16 (June), 55-66.

Pan, Xing, Brian T. Ratchford, and Venkatesh Shankar (2004), "Price Dispersion on the Internet: A Review and Direction for Future Research," *Journal of Interactive Marketing,* 18 (4), 116-135.

Sherif, Muzafer and Carl I. Hovland (1961), *Social Judgment: Assimilation and Contrast Effects in Communication and Attitude Change,* New Haven: Yale University Press.

Stigler, George J. (1961), "The Economics of Information," *The Journal of Political Economy,* 69 (3), 213-25.

Urbany Joel E. (1986), "An Experimental Examination of the Economics of Information," *Journal of Consumer Research,* 13 (September), 257-71

The Influence of Advertising on Decision Strategy

Hui-Yun Chen, Virginia Polytechnic Institute and State University, USA
Jane E Machin, Virginia Polytechnic Institute and State University, USA

Decision strategy is the process used to make a choice: a rejection-based decision strategy occurs when the primary focus of the decision is on rejecting undesired option(s) whereas a selection-based decision strategy occurs when the primary focus of the decision is on selecting the desired option. Prior research suggests that selection and rejection are not complementary strategies and can have different and non-trivial effects on which options are chosen and subsequent satisfaction with those options (e.g. Shafir 1993). Most prior research manipulates decision strategy (e.g. Shafir 1993; Wertenbroch and Dhar 2000). There is currently little understanding therefore of what motivates consumers to *spontaneously* make decisions using either a selection- or rejection-based decision strategy. Our research investigates one potential antecedent: the influence of advertising on decision strategy and, in particular, comparative advertising. In doing so, we improve our understanding of the psychological mechanisms through which comparative advertising works and may help to explain some inconsistencies in research on the effectiveness of comparative advertising.

Comparative advertising is a long-thriving advertising strategy in which comparative evaluations of the advertised brand and the comparison brands on one or more attributes are presented (Goodwin and Etgar 1980). Comparative advertising can be further subdivided into positive and negative comparative advertising. While negative comparative advertising shows how the comparison brands are inferior to the advertised brand, positive comparative advertising claims the advertised brand as superior to the comparison brands (Jain 1993). We hypothesize that negative comparative advertising will direct consumer attention to the undesirable features of the competitor brand, leading them to use a rejection- based decision strategy to avoid those features. In comparison, positive comparative advertising, with its focus on the positive attributes of the advertised brand, will encourage consumers to use a selection-based decision strategy.

Two experiments provide early support for this hypothesis. Study 1 investigated the influence of advertising type on decision strategy and introduced motivation as a potential moderator. Consistent with much prior research on motivation, whereby advertising claims only influence evaluations under conditions of high motivation (Maheswaran and Meyers-Levy 1990; Shiv, Britton, and Payne 2004), we expected that advertising type (positive versus negative versus non-comparative) would only influence decision strategy when consumers were highly motivated to process the claims. As predicted, advertisement type did not influence decision-strategy under conditions of low motivation. However, under conditions of high motivation, negative comparative advertisements led participants to adopt a rejection-based decision strategy relative to positive comparative and non-comparative advertisements.

Study 2 held motivation constant and high for all participants and instead examined the moderating role of brand familiarity on the relationship between advertising type and decision strategy. Prior research has demonstrated that comparative advertising is more effective for new brands compared to established brands (Iyer 1988). Thus, we hypothesized that, for brands that are highly familiar, consumers would rely on their prior knowledge and simply select the brand they normally use, irrespective of advertising type. However for new, unfamiliar brands, consumers should rely more on the advertising claims. In this case, negative comparative advertising should lead to a more rejection-based decision strategy while positive comparative advertising should induce a more selection-based decision strategy. Results support this hypothesis. Across three product categories (toothpaste, fast food restaurants, and canned soup,) when the advertised brands were familiar, there was no difference in decision strategy by advertising type. However, when the brands were unfamiliar, negative comparative advertisements led consumers to use a rejection-based decision strategy relative to positive comparative and non-comparative advertisements. Study 2 also generalized the findings by showing the same pattern of results when both single and multiple comparison brands are used.

These two studies provide early evidence that negative comparative advertisements induce a rejection-based decision strategy relative to positive and non-comparative advertisements. Subsequent studies (data currently being collected) seek to understand how the differential adoption of decision strategy after exposure to a certain advertising type influences attitudes towards the advertisement, attitudes towards the brand and ultimately choice. Prior research on the effectiveness of comparative advertising versus non-comparative advertising and, more specifically, positive versus negative comparative advertising has had mixed results (Block and Keller 1995; Sorescu and Gelb 2000). Furthermore, surprisingly little research has been conducted to investigate the underlying psychological mechanisms through which comparative advertising operates. We believe adding decision strategy to these models may help explain inconsistencies in advertising effectiveness results and also provide insight into the process.

Comparative advertising encourages consumers, explicitly or implicitly, to choose between two or more alternatives. At a general level, therefore, we hypothesize that comparative advertising induces a choice frame, while non-comparative advertising induces a rating frame. Much prior research suggests that the task type (choice or rating) can lead to preference reversal (e.g. Nowlis and Simonson 1997), similar to the kinds seen in studies assessing the effectiveness of comparative versus non-comparative advertising. More specifically, as decision strategy has been shown to influence preferences, we further hypothesize that the effectiveness of positive versus negative comparative advertising will be influenced by the decision strategy used. Specifically, we propose that evaluations of the advertisement and brand will be elevated when advertising type and decision strategy are congruent than when they are incongruent.

To summarize, our initial findings demonstrate that advertising type influences decision strategy, providing one of the first investigations of the antecedents of decision strategy. As decision strategy can influence both the actual choice and subsequent satisfaction with that choice, understanding how consumers spontaneously adopt one strategy over another is important. Our findings also contribute to the literature on comparative advertising by shedding light on the process by which positive, negative and non-comparative advertising works and, with data currently being collected, may ultimately help determine the relative effectiveness of such advertising.

References

Block, Lauren G. and Punam Anand Keller (1995), "When to Accentuate the Negative: The Effects of Perceived Efficancy and Message Framing on Intentions to Perform a Health-Related Behavior," *Journal of Marketing Research*, 32 (2), 192.

Goodwin, Stephen and Michael Etgar (1980), "An Experimental Investigation of Comparative Advertising: Impact of Message Appeal, Information Load, and Utility of Product Class," *Journal of Marketing Research*, 17 (2), 187-202.

Iyer, Easwar S. (1988), "The Influence of Verbal Content and Relative Newness on the Effectiveness of Comparative Advertising," *Journal of Advertising*, 17 (3), 15-21.

Jain, Shailendra Pratap (1993), "Positive Versus Negative Comparative Advertising," *Marketing Letters*, 4 (4), 309-20.

Maheswaran, D. and J. Meyers-Levy (1990), "The Influence of Message Framing and Issue Involvement," *Journal of Marketing Research*, 27 (3), 361-67.

Nowlis, Stephen M. and Itamar Simonson (1997), "Attribute-Task Compatibility as a Determinant of Consumer Preference Reversals," *Journal of Marketing Research*, 34 (2), 205-18.

Shafir, Eldar (1993), "Choosing Versus Rejecting: Why Some Options Are Both Better and Worse Than Others," *Memory & cognition*, 21 (4).

Shafir, Eldar, Itamar Simonson, and Amos Tversky (1993), "Reason-Based Choice," *Cognition*, 49, 11-36.

Shiv, Baba, Julie A. Edell Britton, and John W. Payne (2004), "Does Elaboration Increase or Decrease the Effectiveness of Negatively Versus Positively Framed Messages?," *Journal of Consumer Research*, 31 (1), 199-208.

Sorescu, Alma B. and Betsy D. Gelb (2000), "Negative Comparative Advertising: Evidence Favoring Fine-Tuning," *Journal of Advertising*, 29 (4), 25-40.

Wertenbroch, Klaus and Ravi Dhar (2000), "Consumer Choice between Hedonic and Utilitarian Goods," *Journal of Marketing Research*, 37 (1), 60-71.

Design It, Your Self-Experiences (DIY): Social Creativity and the Social Function of DIY Experiences

Steven Chen, California State University, Fullerton, USA
Jennifer D. Chandler, University of Hawaii, USA

Advancing the creativity literature, this study explores specifically the *social motivations* for consumers to engage in creative DIY experiences. Design-It-Yourself, or Do-it-Yourself (DIY), is a type of creative experience in which consumers create handmade, customized objects for private and commercial consumption (Levine and Heimerl 2008). At the time of writing, DIY has broken out of its origins in home improvement (Davidson and Leather 2000) and underground music cultures (Spencer 2005) to encompass a broad range of craft cultures—scrapbooking, art-making, altered books, knitting, jewelry and apparel—all of which privilege the doctrine of the handmade (Lupton 2006, Wherry 2006).

The primary research question asks: From a social networks perspective, why do consumers engage in DIY experiences? Referring to the appropriation and reconciliation of social bonds through creative experiences and artifacts, a theory of *social creativity* is introduced. Social creativity is seen when designers simultaneously create DIY artforms and their own social networks through the: 1) transformation of intangible, fleeting relations and experiences into representative, tangible, permanent DIY artifacts, 2) inadvertent reconciliation and appropriation of social bonds vis-à-vis the design of DIY artifacts, and 3) departure from ordinary marketscapes through a multi-layered legitimization of social capital. Through a qualitative, grounded theory study that involves long interviews with 14 DIY designers (Strauss and Corbin 1998; Charmaz 2006), the findings reveal that social creativity enables an assertion of self into a world that is wrought with market-centered meanings that claim responsibility and recognition for drawing consumers together (Diamond, Sherry, et al., forthcoming).

DIY industries have witnessed phenomenal growth in recent years, leading experts to refer to this "new wave of craft" (Levine and Heimerl 2008) to include, for example, the home improvement industry with sales almost doubling from approximately $160 billion in 1999 to $290 billion in 2008 (Home Improvement Research Institute 2009) and the scrapbooking industry, rising from a $500 million industry in 2000 (Fram 2005) to a $2.9 billion industry in 2007 (Craft and Hobby Association 2007). Knitting, once an association of elderly women, has become a cool activity for the young, with a resurgence in popularity for women under 30 who embrace the social, meditative, and political aspects of knitting (Gschwandter and Shirobayashi 2007; Stoller 2004; Greer 2008). Finally, DIY-oriented Internet services such as Etsy and Cafepress offer online resources for consumers to design and sell their products. Since Etsy opened in 2005, over 100,000 DIY designers have opened virtual stores on the web portal.

The recent surge in DIY activity and the increasing number of consumers engaging in creative experiences is suggestive of changing socio-cultural trends among consumers. However, previous studies of creativity largely focus on either the individual psychological motivations from a consumer's perspective or the factors that affect industrial design from the firm's perspective. For example, the consumer research literature explores creative experiences as linked to cognitive motivations such as gaining self esteem (Csikszentmihalyi 2000), competence (Watson and Shove 2008) and autonomy (Dahl and Moreau 2007). Meanwhile, the industrial design literature focuses on individual producers' frames of mind, and how various factors and techniques, such as imaginative thinking, analogic thinking, input constraints and empathy, lead to creative results (Dahl, Chattopadyhay and Gorn 1999; Dahl and Moreau 2002; Moreau and Dahl 2005; Dahl and Moreau 2007; Durgee 2004). In short, there is a gap in the consumer creativity literature regarding social motivations of creativity.

The findings begin to address this gap by revealing that the outcomes of DIY as an artform are not limited to the creation of beautiful meaning-laden arts and crafts, but also include the transformation of mundane minutiae of everyday objects into representations of social bonds and experiences. In this way, consumers engage in DIY experiences to mitigate social isolation and the perceived and actual fragmentation of social networks. More specifically, consumers impute meanings that are gleaned from past times, faraway places, and sought after relational spaces into their current lives. DIY designers actively reconcile the lack or conflict of meaning that exists in their current contexts by assembling and integrating banal objects and meanings into DIY artifacts such as scrapbooks, wood sculptures, or quilts that are more representative of their sought after social experiences.

Surprisingly, even though consumers engage in DIY experiences to transform and create artifacts, DIY designers are themselves transformed because the creativity process re-creates the importance they ascribe to their social bonds through an affirmation of social relations, positions and roles imbued into the DIY artifacts. On one level, consumers essentially create storybook social narratives by selectively creating objects that memorialize and legitimize social ideals and happy times, as opposed to lived realities. On the second level, when these artifacts are displayed in their homes or given as gifts, for example, the importance ascribed to their social bonds and social networks is affirmed by others. In this way, consumers bridge their actual lives and their social ideals by transcending and deviating from traditional expectations of social relations. In some situations, social bonds extend beyond nuclear family relations to include friendship relations that are deemed more important than familial relations. In other situations, social bonds that have gone sour are re-created through snapshots of happy times and happy places made permanent because of DIY artifacts.

DIY experiences provide a modern-day 21st century mechanism for consumers to re-establish century-old humanist traditions of group bonding through craft-making and story-telling that takes place outside of markets but is enabled by DIY market processes. Most important, DIY experiences enable consumers to take comfort in social bonds that exist beyond the disintegrating nuclear family (Graham-Niderhaus and Graham 2007) by allowing them to express fondness and confirmation of extended family bonds, non-familial social bonds, and other types of bonds. At a time when fragmentation and uncertainty are at their highest, consumers engage in DIY experiences to reify their experiences of community-building and social bonding to provide evidence–through DIY artifacts–that social bonds still matter.

Select References

Charmaz, Kathy (2006), *Constructing Grounded Theory: A Practical Guide Through Qualitative Analysis*, Newbury Park, London and New Delhi: Sage Publications.

Craft and Hobby Association (2007), www.hobby.org

Csikszentmihalyi, Mihaly (2000), "The Costs and Benefits of Consuming," *Journal of Consumer Research*, 27 (September), 267–72.

Dahl, Darren W., Amitava Chattopadhyay, and Gerald J. Gorn (1999), "The Use of Visual Mental Imagery in New Product Design," *Journal of Marketing Research*, 36 (1), 18-29.

Dahl, Darren W. and Page Moreau (2002), "The Influence and Value of Analogical Thinking during New Product Ideation," *Journal of Marketing Research*, 39 (February), 47-60.

Dahl, Darren W. and Page Moreau (2007), "Thinking Inside the Box: Why Consumers Enjoy Constrained Creative Experiences," Journal of Marketing Research, 44 (August), 357-369.

Davidson, Maggie and Phillip Leather (2000), "Choice or Necessity? A Review of the Role of DIY in Tackling Housing Repair and Maintenance," *Construction Management and Economics*, 18 (7), 747-756.

Diamond, Nina, John F. Sherry, Albert M. Muniz Jr., Mary Ann McGrath, Robert V. Kozinets, and Stefania Borghini (forthcoming), "*American Girl* and the Brand Gestalt: Closing the Loop on Socio-cultural Branding," *Journal of Marketing*

Durgee, Jeffrey F. (2004), "The Co-Creation of Meaning Between Marketers and Consumers; Step 1: How Marketing Creatives Interpret Consumer Motivations," *Advances in Consumer Research*, 32, 162-176.

Fram, Eugene H. (2005), "The Booming Scrapbooking Market in the USA," *International Journal of Retail and Distribution Management*, 33 (3), 215-225.

Graham-Niderhaus, Sharon, and John L. Graham (2007), *Together Again: a Creative Guide to Successful Multigenerational Living*, New York, New York: M. Evans and Company, Inc

Gschwandter, Sabrina and Kiriko Shirobayashi (2007), *Knitknit: Profiles + Projects from Knitting's New Wave*, New York, New York: Stewart, Tabori and Chang STC Craft Melanie Falick Book.

Greer, Betsy (2008), *Knitting for Good: A guide to Creating Personal, Social, and Political Change, Stitch by Stitch*, Boston, MA: Trumpeter.

Home Improvement Research Institute (2009), www.hiri.org

Levine, Faythe and Cortney Heimerl (2008), *Handmade Nation: The Rise of DIY, Art, Craft and Design*, New York, New York: Princeton Architectural Press.

Lupton, Ellen (2006), *D.I.Y.: Design It Yourself*, New York, New York: Princeton Architectural Press.

Moreau, Page and Darren W. Dahl (2005), "Designing the Solution: The Impact of Constraints on Consumers' Creativity," *Journal of Consumer Research*, 32 (June), 13-22.

Spencer, Amy (2005), *DIY: The Rise of Lo-Fi Culture*, London, UK: Marion Boyers.

Stoller, Debbie (2004), *Stitch 'N Bitch: The Knitter's Handbook,* New York, New York: Workman Publishing Company.

Strauss, Anselm and Juliet Corbin (1998), *Basics of Qualitative Research 2nd edition: Techniques and Procedures for Developing Grounded Theory*, Thousand Oaks, London and New Delhi: Sage Publications.

Watson, Matthew and Elizabeth Shove (2008), "Product, Competence, Project and Practice," *Journal of Consumer Culture*, 8 (1), 69-89.

Wherry, Frederick F. (2006), "The Social Sources of Authenticity in Global Handicraft Markets," *Journal of Consumer Culture*, 6 (1), 5-32.

From Why and What to Where I Post: Online Poster Behavior

Yu-Jen Chen, University of Maryland, USA
Amna Kirmani, University of Maryland, USA

Suppose you want to tell others about your recent experience with a new Nikon digital camera. You are a user of the Internet, and you have been on various websites related to digital cameras. Among the numerous websites and online discussion forums that provide digital camera discussion platforms, which type of website might you choose to post your review: a heterogeneous audience, product category website, such as Digital Photography Review, or a more homogeneous audience website that is focused on the Nikon brand, such as Nikonians.com?

There is a large amount of research on word of mouth (WOM) in general (Dichter 1966; Herr, Kardes, and Kim 1991; Ward and Ostrom 2006) and online word of mouth in particular (Godes and Mayzlin 2004). Although research has addressed the importance of online consumer communication, the focus of previous research has been on the effectiveness of online WOM from the information receiver standpoint (Mayzlin 2006; Chevalier and Mayzlin 2006). Some researchers have examined why people might participate in online communication (Ward and Ostrom 2006; Schau and Gilly 2003) or what the content of such communication might be (Schlosser 2005); however, they have not related this to where to post. For instance, Schlosser (2005) finds that online posters tend to provide more negative product reviews than do lurkers (those who only read reviews). However, her research setting is limited to poster behavior on a single website rather than dealing with multiple sites.

In this paper, we examine how consumers' motivation to post (why) as well as the valence of the message (what) affects the decision of where to post. We define posters as people who use the Internet to post public product related information or experience. Such product information could be on a discussion site, a forum, or a bulletin board, but not private communication such as E-mail or personal website. In terms of where to post, we compare two types of online forums: 1) a more heterogeneous audience forum frequented by category users with varying brand preferences (e.g., a product category forum); and 2) a more homogenous forum of consumers who like the specific brand. We examine two motives that might lead consumers to participate in online posting: 1) the motive to influence others' behavior and 2) the motive to affiliate with others. The motive to influence others reflects consumers' desire to persuade others to their own point of view (Engle and Blackwell 1982), to build a reputation as an opinion leader (Robertson, Zielinski, and Ward 1984), or to be seen as knowledgeable. The motive to affiliate with others reflects a desire to associate with others who have similar interests, such as members of relevant reference groups, e.g., brand users.

We predicted that, in general, consumers with an influential motive will be more likely to post on the product category forum because of its heterogeneous audience that provide more potential impact of the post (H1a). In contrast, consumers with an affiliative motive may be more likely to post on a brand forum, since this satisfies their relatedness needs to affiliate others with similar brand interest and attitude (H2a). Moreover, we propose that the relationship between social motives and the choice of where to post is moderated by the valence of the message (e.g., positive or negative). Specifically, H1a and H2a are based on the positive valenced message. However, the salient and diagnostic nature of negativity effect of message could lead to different posting outcomes (Ahluwalia, Burnkrant, and Unnava 2000; Shiv, Britton, and Payne 2004).That is, when the message is negative valenced, posters with influential motive may switch to a brand website either to warn or affect those brand lovers (H1b). Those with affiliative motive might less likely to choose a brand website to avoid weakening relationship with other brand lovers (H2b).

We conducted two studies to test our hypotheses. In Study 1, we manipulate the motivations as well as the message valence by asking participants to imagine the product experience depending randomly assigned conditions. Specifically, the scenario was that participants were instructed to imagine their digital camera (e.g., Nikon D700) experience as either good or bad and were asked to choose a website to post their experience (in the control motive condition) or to make their post have as much impact as possible (in the influential motive condition). Then, participants indicated which website is more appealing to them to post their D700 experience on a seven-point scale (1= definitely Nikonians, a brand website; 7= definitely Digital Photography Review, a product category website). The result of the 2 (motive: influential vs. control) x 2 (valence: positive vs. negative) between-subjects ANCOVA with Nikon familiarity as a covariate supported our predictions. First, as suggested by H1a, when posting positive messages, consumers' where to post decision shows no difference between influential motive and control motive, namely, they are as likely to post on a product category website (Ms=5.9 and 5.4, respectively; $F(1,55)=.89$, $p=.35$). Second, as suggested by H1b, when posting negative messages, posters whose primary motive is influential were more likely to choose a brand site than posters in the control group were (Ms= 4.2 and 5.3, respectively, $F(1,55)=3.62$, $p<.06$).

The proposed Study 2 will include the second posting motive, affiliation motive, and conduct the experiment in the similar manner as we did in the study 1. While the Study 1 focuses on testing only hypothesis 1, the Study 2 attempts to test H1 and H2 simultaneously. We further include two posting options for participants. First, participants will have the alternative to choose not to post to reflect their low involvement in the study or low posting motivation. Second, we provide a new forum option, an anti-brand forum with homogeneous negative brand attitude audience. This allow us to further explore H2b in whether consumers choose not to post negative message on a brand is driven by punishment avoidance (if similar posting preference on a product category forum and on an anti-brand forum) or by affiliation with similar others (if higher posting preference on an anti-brand forum than on a product category forum).

Understanding the Role of Brand Personality Fit and the Moderating Effect of Self-Connection in Brand Extension Evaluations

Zhuohao Chen, University of Warwick, UK
Zhi Lu, Fudan University, China

Brand extension has become an increasingly critical research issue as the scope, stretchability or extension potential determines the boundary of a brand (Ahluwalia 2008; Meyvis and Janiszewski 2004). Prior research asserts that fit or perceived fit between original category and the brand extension serves as an important antecedent of consumer brand extension evaluations (Aaker and Keller 1990; Park et al. 1991). In marketing practice, however, more and more brands extend to apparently unfit or dissimilar categories. Successful examples include Pepsi music, BMW sportswear, and Virgin airlines, media, cola and mobile. We can find that all these brands are embedded with a distinct brand personality. Although they are not necessarily accepted by all the consumers, these brand extensions are favoured by a specific group of consumers, who love and are emotionally connected to the brand. Such brand extensions based on personality are beyond existing understanding of perceived fit. In this research, therefore, it is proposed that brand personality fit, which is supposed to be another dimension of perceived fit and refers to the consistency of consumer brand personality perceptions before and after brand extension, influences consumer brand extension evaluations, and that this brand personality fit is more easily accessible when an individual has self-connection with the brand.

To explore whether a brand with unique brand personality is easier to extend to dissimilar categories, we need to understand the role of brand personality fit. A large amount of literature in brand extension argues that "fit" or "perceived fit" affects consumer brand extension evaluations (e.g., Aaker and Keller 1990; Boush and Loken 1991; Broniarczyk and Alba 1994; Park et al. 1991). In terms of balance theory (Heider 1958), a consumer tends to support a brand extension if he or she has favorable attitude toward the parent brand and perceives fit between core category and the brand extension. Three types of perceived fit can be concluded from prior research. First, category-based fit assumes that feature similarity is the basis of categorization (Tversky 1977) therefore similar category or feature (e.g., white appliance) leads to a favorable brand extension (Boush and Loken 1991). Next, further research finds consumers evaluate fit with a specific benefit or goal (Broniarczyk and Alba 1994; Martin and Stewart 2001). Specifically, similar context of usage aiming at a benefit (e.g. tooth brush and toothpaste for the benefit of dental health) increases perceived fit (Joiner 2006; Ratneshwar and Shocker 1991). Third, brand-based fit theory underlies the fit of brand image or brand concept (Park et al. 1991), which is accessible when consumers evaluate symbolic brand extensions. Here, brand-based fit is a relatively broad concept (Czellar 2003) so that brand personality fit can be viewed as a critical facet of it. Thus, brand personality fit is hypothesized to positively influence consumer brand extension attitude.

However, not all of the consumers achieve the understanding of brand personality fit, which is retrievable when the consumer is emotionally self-connected to the brand. Generally, we can view the process of fit as a cognitive evaluation process, after which brand extension attitude is formed, but some emotional consumers do not evaluate brand extensions step by step. Research finds that consumer brand extension evaluation process can be an affective process, i.e. parent brand attitude can be directly transferred to brand extension attitude without mediation of perceived fit if a consumer has a high brand affect (Yeung and Wyer 2005). Recent research on affective evaluation process (Barone 2005; Barone and Miniard 2002; Barone et al. 2000) also supports that original brand favorability moderates the process of brand extension evaluations. Therefore, it is likely to argue that consumers with various brand relationship will follow different evaluation paths in brand extension attitude formation. Self-connection, which reflects the sense of belonging of a consumer to a brand, is a key dimension of brand relationship (Fournier 1998). In addition, this variable is also influenced by brand personality. If an individual finds his or her personality or expected personality is congruent with the brand personality, he or she will feel more connected to the brand, therefore favors the brand (Aaker 1997; Sirgy 1982). Consider such an extreme situation: a consumer who is firmly connected to a brand will regard himself as a part of the brand, therefore unconditionally favors whatever extensions the brand makes, regardless of perceived fit. In this case, it is congruency between self and brand, rather than fit between original category and brand extension, that determines brand extension attitude. The focus of brand extension evaluation shifts from product to person. So, we hypothesize that self-connection moderates brand extension process. For highly self-connected consumers, core brand attitude directly affects brand extension evaluation without mediation of perceived fit. For low self-connected consumers, core brand attitude affects perceived fit, and perceived fit affects brand extension evaluations.

A main study with three steps of analysis is designed to investigate these effects. Two pretests were conducted to test brand personality (Aaker 1997) and select fictitious brand extensions before the 2 (brands)x2 (category medium fit vs. unfit)x2 (brand personality fit vs. unfit) main study. We collected data in China. Two well-known telecommunication brands under China Mobile were selected: M-zone with unique brand personality of excitement and G-tone with unique brand personality of competence. Digital products (PDA and MP3) represented medium category-fit extensions, while wristwatch represented unfit extensions. G-tone PDA, M-zone MP3, G-tone dress watch, M-zone sports watch represented brand-personality-fit extensions, while G-tone MP3, M-zone PDA, G-tone sports watch and M-zone dress watch were brand-personality-unfit extensions. Respondents were asked to report their attitude and purchase intention toward these extensions. Perceived fit (category-based fit, benefit-based fit and brand personality fit), core brand attitude, self-connection were also measured in the questionnaire. The first step of analysis is aimed to investigate the effect of brand personality fit on brand extension evaluation. Results indicate that personality fit brand extensions have significantly higher evaluations than personality unfit ones, while there is no significant difference between category fit and unfit extensions. In the second step of analysis, we testify a general model, in which perceived fit, including the dimension of brand personality fit, has significant influence on brand extension attitude. In the third step of analysis, we split the samples in terms of self-connection and compare the models by means of grouped structural equation modeling. It is found that the influence of brand personality fit on brand extension attitude differs significantly between the two models. Consumers of highly self-connection yield greater influences than those of low self-connection, which supports the moderating effect of self-connection.

References

Aaker, David A. and Kevin Lane Keller (1990), "Consumer Evaluations of Brand Extensions," *Journal of Marketing*, 54 (1), 27-41.
Aaker, Jennifer L. (1997), "Dimensions of Brand Personality," *Journal of Marketing Research*, 34 (3), 347-56.
Ahluwalia, Rohini (2008), "How Far Can a Brand Stretch? Understanding the Role of Self-Construal," *Journal of Marketing Research*, 45 (3), 337-50.
Barone, Michael J. (2005), "The Interactive Effects of Mood and Involvement on Brand Extension Evaluations," *Journal of Consumer Psychology*, 15 (3), 263-70.
Barone, Michael J. and Paul W. Miniard (2002), "Mood and Brand Extension Judgments: Asymmetric Effects for Desirable versus Undesirable Brands," *Jounal of Consumer Psychology*, 12 (4), 283-90.
Barone, Michael J., Paul W. Miniard, and Jean B. Romeo (2000), "The Influence of Positive Mood on Brand Extension Evaluations," *Journal of Consumer Research*, 26 (4), 386-400.
Boush, David M. and Barbara Loken (1991), "A Process-Tracing Study of Brand Extension Evaluation," *Journal of Marketing Research*, 28 (1), 16-28.
Broniarczyk, Susan M. and Joseph W. Alba (1994), "The Importance of the Brand in Brand Extension," *Journal of Marketing Research*, 31 (2), 214-28.
Czellar, Sandor (2003), "Consumer Attitude toward Brand Extensions: An Integrative Model and Research Propositions," *International Journal of Research in Marketing*, 20 (1), 97-115.
Fournier, Susan (1998), "Consumers and Their Brands: Developing Relationship Theory in Consumer Research," *Journal of Consumer Research*, 24 (4), 343-73.
Heider, Fritz (1958), *The Psychology of Interpersonal Relations*. New York: Wiley.
Joiner, Christopher (2006), "Existing Products and Brand Extension Judgments: Does Brand Category Context Matter?," *Advances in Consumer Research*, 33 (1), 76-81.
Martin, Ingrid M. and David W. Stewart (2001), "The Differential Impact of Goal Congruency on Attitudes, Intentions, and the Transfer of Brand Equity," *Journal of Marketing Research*, 38 (4), 471-84.
Meyvis, Tom and Chris Janiszewski (2004), "When Are Broader Brands Stronger Brands? An Accessibility Perspective on the Success of Brand Extensions," *Journal of Consumer Research*, 31 (2), 346-57.
Park, C. Whan, Sandra Milberg, and Robert Lawson (1991), "Evaluation of Brand Extensions: The Role of Product Feature Similarity and Brand Concept Consistency," *Journal of Consumer Research*, 18 (2), 185-93.
Ratneshwar, Srinivasan and Aallan D. Shocker (1991), "Substitution in Use and the Role of Usage Context in Product Category Structures," *Jounal of Marketing Research*, 28 (3), 281-95.
Sirgy, Joseph (1982), "Self-Concept in Consumer Behavior: A Critical Review," *Jounal of Consumer Research*, 9 (4), 287-300.
Tversky, Amos (1977), "Features of Similarity," *Psychological Review*, 84 (3), 327-52.
Yeung, Catherine W. M. and Robert S. Wyer Jr (2005), "Does Loving a Brand Mean Loving Its Products? The Role of Brand-Elicited Affect in Brand Extension Evaluations," *Journal of Marketing Research*, 42 (4), 495-506.

Once Bitten, Twice Shy: Differences in Social Efficacy Affect the Perceived Efficacy of Anthropomorphizable Products

Bart Claus, K.U. Leuven, Belgium
Luk Warlop, K.U. Leuven, Belgium

Anthropomorphism as a marketing practitioners' technique of imbuing brands and products with human-like qualities such as faces, names, and intentions, has longtime been used, and has proven to be efficient in the development of brand personality (Aaker 1997) and the building of brand relationships (Fournier 1998). Consumer literature has mainly dealt with the effectiveness of anthropomorphism as a practitioners' technique in influencing brand perceptions. The work by Aggarwal and McGill (2007) signals a recent shift in attention from brands towards anthropomorphic products, showing that a fit between the imbued human scheme and the nature of the products helps in anthropomorphizing the product, and that affect towards the evoked human scheme influences the evaluation of the product. A more fundamental shift is that lately, anthropomorphism–the evocation of the human scheme by means of the design or qualities of an object–has been studied from a more phenomenological stance. Instead of studying the anthropomorphic objects, research has turned its attention to the human mind where the anthropomorphization of the product takes place. This shift also comprises interest in the dispositional and situational drivers of anthropomorphization (Epley et al. 2008a; Epley et al. 2008b; Epley, Waytz, and Cacioppo 2007), and ultimately might allow us to understand some human reactions and behavior towards non-human objects in terms of their interpersonal correlates–think of irrational anger towards a failing tool or machine.

Epley and colleagues have conceived a three factor model of anthropomorphization, in which sociality motivations are one of the driving factors (Epley et al. 2007). When people are lonely, they seek human company, and this increases their susceptibility to anthropomorphization of non-human entities, like alarm clocks and pets (Epley et al. 2008a). This might lead to the inference that lonely people are more prone to anthropomorphization in consumer settings, and therefore unambiguously prone to preferring and seeking out products that are easy to anthropomorphize.

However, loneliness can be a result of difficulties in maintaining satisfactory social contact with other humans. Loneliness is usually considered to be co-driven by personal factors and circumstances (Jones, Freemon, and Goswick 1981; Leary 2001). Indeed, loneliness can be the result of social exclusion (Gardner et al. 2005; Leary 1990), rejection (Boivin, Hymel, and Bukowski 1995) and ostracism (Cacioppo and Hawkley 2005; Zadro, Williams, and Richardson 2004). Although people may want to reconnect to others to compensate for the experiences of loneliness, social anxiety and fear of negative outcome might influence their attitude towards new social contacts (Maner et al. 2007). In short, some–not all–loneliness can be a result of poor social efficacy, this latter having profound effects on how people approach subsequent social interactions. With regard to anthropomorphization of products, we expect that lowered social efficacy will translate into lower a priori expectations towards the anthropomorph at hand. We tested this inference in two studies, one gauging for chronic social efficacy, the other using an experimental manipulation.

In the first study we built on Leary et al.'s Sociometer Theory (Leary et al. 1995), in assessing people's chronic efficacy in social interactions. This theory states that self-esteem is a gauge for people's perceived efficacy in their social interactions. We had participants evaluate the expected number of times (out of twenty) that they would indicate the same number (one to five) as a random number generator that was depicted as an ordinary personal computer. In the control condition, we explained that this was in fact a computer that drew random numbers. In the experimental condition, the depicted computer was added with three buttons, of which the configuration resembled that of a human face (one broad button at the bottom resembling a mouth, two at the top left and right corner of the screen to resemble eyes). Also, the description of the computer was altered to a more anthropomorphic one, by giving it a name–"Puck the pc"–and stating that it "has a number in mind". Afterwards, a trait measure of self-esteem (Rosenberg 1965) was administered. Results demonstrate that in the experimental condition, trait self-esteem is positively related to people's estimation of future outcomes the product will deliver–more than in the control condition.

In the second study, we manipulated social efficacy between subjects, using a task that evokes ostracism (Williams, Cheung, and Choi 2000). The product that had to be evaluated was an automatic vacuum cleaner, and we asked participants about their expectations about the efficacy of the product. We manipulated anthropomorphism by describing the product either in terms of its technical characteristics and product code "Samsung VC-RS60H"–in the control condition–or in terms of more human traits ("a helping hand in the household") and the more friendly name "Roomba"–in the experimental condition. A pretest earlier had ruled out differences in liking for the two descriptions. Consistent with study 1, results show that people's estimates of the product's efficacy are lower when they have been ostracized–but only in the experimental condition. A manipulation check confirmed that the manipulation was indeed successful in eliciting human qualities in the product, and that ostracism did not interact with the manipulation of ostracism, ruling out an explanation that would attribute the effects to ostracism leading to a greater susceptibility to anthropomorphize.

In these two studies, different operationalizations–visual and verbal as well as different objects–of anthropomorphism are used, and the anthropomorphization manipulation is checked. We show that differences in social efficacy affect a priori evaluations of the efficacy of products, and we rule out a potential alternative explanation–differences in the degree of anthropomorphization induced by ostracism–of these results. These studies bring anthropomorphization as a phenomenological process into the field of consumer research, relating the effects of anthropomorphization to the anthropomorphizing consumer, and fit the recent shift in attention from anthropomorphism in brands towards anthropomorphism in products. Future studies will further assess the exact nature–trust, anxiety, retreat–of these effects, by including process measures, and establish boundary conditions where the need for humans might overpower these effects.

References

Aaker, J. L. (1997), "Dimensions of Brand Personality," *Journal of Marketing Research*, 34 (3), 347-56.

Aggarwal, Pankaj and Ann L. McGill (2007), "Is That Car Smiling at Me? Schema Congruity as a Basis for Evaluating Anthropomorphized Products," *Journal of Consumer Research*, 34 (4), 468-79.

Boivin, M., S. Hymel, and W. M. Bukowski (1995), "The Roles of Social Withdrawal, Peer Rejection, and Victimization by Peers in Predicting Loneliness and Depressed Mood in Childhood," *Development and Psychopathology*, 7 (4), 765-85.

Cacioppo, John T. and Louise C. . Hawkley (2005), "People Thinking About People: The Vicious Cycle of Being a Social Outcast in One's Own Mind. ," in *The Social Outcast: Ostracism, Social Exclusion, Rejection, and Bullying.*, ed. Kipling D. Williams, Joseph P. Forgas and William von Hippel, New York: Psychology Press, 91-108.

Epley, Nicholas, Scott Akalis, Adam Waytz, and John T. Cacioppo (2008a), "Creating Social Connection through Inferential Reproduction: Loneliness and Perceived Agency in Gadgets, Gods, and Greyhounds," *Psychological Science*, 19 (2), 114-20.

Epley, Nicholas, Adam Waytz, Scott Akalis, and John T. Cacioppo (2008b), "When We Need a Human: Motivational Determinants of Anthropomorphism," *Social Cognition*, 26, 143-55.

Epley, Nicholas, Adam Waytz, and John T. Cacioppo (2007), "On Seeing Human: A Three-Factor Theory of Anthropomorphism," *Psychological Review*, 114 (4), 864-86.

Fournier, Susan (1998), "Consumers and Their Brands: Developing Relationship Theory in Consumer Research," in *Journal of Consumer Research*, Vol. 24: Journal of Consumer Research, Inc., 343-73.

Gardner, Wendi L., Cynthia L. Pickett, Valerie Jefferis, and Megan Knowles (2005), "On the Outside Looking In: Loneliness and Social Monitoring," *Pers Soc Psychol Bull*, 31 (11), 1549-60.

Jones, Warren H., J. E. Freemon, and Ruth Ann Goswick (1981), "The Persistence of Loneliness: Self and Other Determinants," in *Journal of Personality*, Vol. 49: Blackwell Publishing Limited, 27.

Leary, M. R. (1990), "Responses to Social Exclusion-Social Anxiety, Jealousy, Loneliness, Depression, and Low Self-Esteem," *Journal of Social and Clinical Psychology*, 9 (2), 221-29.

Leary, Mark R. (2001), "Toward a Conceptualization of Interpersonal Rejection.," in *Interpersonal Rejection*, ed. Mark R. Leary, New York: Oxford University Press, 3-20.

Leary, Mark R., Ellen S. Tambor, Sonja K. Terdal, and Deborah L. Downs (1995), "Self-Esteem as an Interpersonal Monitor: The Sociometer Hypothesis," *Journal of Personality & Social Psychology*, 68 (3), 518-30.

Maner, Jon K., C. Nathan DeWall, Roy F. Baumeister, and Mark Schaller (2007), "Does Social Exclusion Motivate Interpersonal Reconnection? Resolving The "Porcupine Problem"," *Journal of Personality & Social Psychology*, 92 (1), 42-55.

Rosenberg, Morris (1965), *Society and the Adolescent Self-Image*, Princeton, NJ: Princeton University Press.

Williams, Kipling D., Christopher K. T. Cheung, and Wilma Choi (2000), "Cyberostracism: Effects of Being Ignored over the Internet," *Journal of Personality & Social Psychology*, 79 (5), 748-62.

Zadro, Lisa, Kipling D. Williams, and Rick Richardson (2004), "How Low Can You Go? Ostracism by a Computer Is Sufficient to Lower Self-Reported Levels of Belonging, Control, Self-Esteem, and Meaningful Existence," Journal of Experimental Social Psychology, 40 (4), 560-67.

To Be American Is To Be Rich: Immigrants Use of Possessions Both in the US and in Their Native Countries to Convey Consumer Acculturation

Garrett Coble, Oklahoma State University, USA

Consumer acculturation is a topic that has been investigated in our literature (Oswald 1999; Peñaloza 1994; Thompson and Tambyah 1999). It has been broadly defined as a "general term that encompasses intercultural interaction and adaptation and includes assimilation of a new culture, maintenance of the old culture, and resistance to both new and old cultures" (Peñaloza and Gilly 1999). Scholars have sought to better understand the process immigrants go through in terms of consumption when moving from one culture to another (e.g., Thompson and Tambyah 1999; Ustuner and Holt 2007). The author has looked at the role immigration policy plays on that consumer acculturation process (Coble, Jiménez, and Mason 2008). In the process, a question that has arisen is why some product categories are adopted quicker than others. Another pressing question is how those product categories are consumed when immigrants visit their native countries. Every year, small towns in countries such as Mexico are flooded with immigrants visiting with arms and cars full of possessions from countries such as the US. From the author's experience living in a small Mexican town, he has seen almost an inflated level of consumer acculturation in terms of the possessions returning immigrants have, the language they speak, and the currency they use. This brings to light several questions. If consumer acculturation is inflated, why? What new insight does that give us in terms of acculturation theory? Also, if acculturation is inflated, what is the mechanism behind that?

This paper will contribute to the consumer acculturation literature by examining the role different product categories play in the acculturation process and how that is lived both in the host country and back in the home country. Some questions to be address are "how are products adopted and consumed in the host country?" "when traveling back to their native countries, how do immigrants use possessions?" and "what type of possessions do immigrants value during the transition?" These questions should also address the bigger issue of what role different product categories play in the acculturation process.

Methods

To begin this study, key informants have been questioned regarding their experiences both in the US and back in their native countries. Through those initial interviews, several themes have started to emerge. They are the meaning of the American dream, the expectations of living and working in the US, and the opportunities for conspicuous consumption.

The contexts the author will use to better understand this phenomenon are a large city in the Midwest with a large population of Mexican Americans and a southern state of Mexico where hundreds of Mexicans return every year for the Christmas season. The author has conducted extensive fieldwork and interviews in the US city for other projects regarding immigration and marketing issues. He has worked with the Hispanic chamber of commerce, a local Spanish TV station, and is on the board of directors for the coalition of Hispanic organizations. The town in Mexico where the work will be conducted is small (about 8,000 people), but it was chosen because of the flood of immigrants that return every year for the Christmas season. The author has lived in this small town as an exchange student, but starting in the fall, he will spend extensive time there as a researcher, conduct semi-structured depth interviews, collect artifacts, and use field notes to investigate the consumer acculturation process the returning immigrants are going through as they return to their native country. The entire project will entail training local Mexicans who are returning immigrants to help with the interviews and interpretation of the findings. The work will be conducted both in the US and in Mexico. Interviews and fieldwork in the US will focus on the issues of product categories in the acculturation process. Work conducted in Mexico will center around the issue of the meaning of those products in the transition back home. This work should give us better insight into the acculturation process in terms of product categories and open the door to future work on re-acculturation.

Work Cited

Coble, Garrett, Fernando R. Jiménez, and Marlys Mason (2008), "Environmental Barriers to Consumer Acculturation," *2008 Advances in Consumer Research*, Latin America Conference, Conference Proceedings, Sao Paulo, Brazil.

Oswald, Laura R. (1999), "Culture Swapping: Consumption and the Ethnogenesis of Middle-Class Haitian Immigrants," *Journal of Consumer Research*, 25 (4), 303-18.

Peñaloza, Lisa (1994), "Atravesando Fronteras/Border Crossings: A Critical Ethnographic Exploration of the Consumer Acculturation of Mexican Immigrants," *Journal of Consumer Research*, 21, 32-54.

Peñaloza, Lisa and Mary C. Gilly (1999), "Marketer Acculturation: The Changer and the Changed," *Journal of Marketing*, 63 (3), 84-104.

Thompson, Craig J. and Siok Kuan Tambyah (1999), "Trying to be Cosmopolitan," *Journal of Consumer Research*, 26 (3), 214.

Ustuner, Tuba and Douglas B. Holt (2007), "Dominated Consumer Acculturation: The Social Construction of Poor Migrant Women's Consumer Identity Projects in a Turkish Squatter," *Journal of Consumer Research*, 34 (1), 41-56.

Anchors in Range Pricing: How Do Consumers Choose What to Pay?

Annie Peng Cui, West Virginia University, USA
Jennifer Wiggins Johnson, Kent State University, USA

How do consumers decide what price to pay when they are asked to choose a price within a range of acceptable prices? We suggest that consumers interpret the price range as a range estimate reference price. We show that consumers perceive the endpoints of the range as external anchors and adjust their willingness to pay in the direction of both anchors. In addition, the introduction of a midpoint into the price range increases the likelihood that consumers will choose the midpoint as their price. We further show that different consumers rely more heavily on different anchors in their pricing decision.

The Influence of Regulatory Focus on the Interpretation of Verbal Versus Numerical Probabilistic Information

Ahmad Daryanto, Newcastle Business School, UK

Abstract

This research examines the link between regulatory focus and people's interpretation of verbal versus numerical probabilistic. Our study shows that people's goals associated with regulatory focus influence the interpretation of verbal versus numerical uncertainty information. The findings indicate regulatory fit occurs when prevention focus is matched with numerical information, whereas no fit effect occurs when promotion focus is matched with verbal information. Our study reveals that people in fit effect assign more values to an advocated program and show a higher motivation to engage in the program.

Overview of the Research

In everyday life, people encounter with uncertainty information. The information can be expressed either in words or numbers. For instance, recently, the US presidential candidate, John McCain, commented about current US economic situation: "I would say that it's very likely and more and more economists are saying that, that we are probably in a recession " (CNN Live Feed, Atlanta, GA, 3/7/08). In another occasion, Alan Greenspan, a former US Federal Reserve chairman, preferred to describe the economic situation by using numbers instead of words: "There is more than a 50 percent chance the United States could go into recession" (www.bloomberg.com). Considerable research has examined how people interpret these two modes of information, i.e., verbal versus numerical expression (e.g., Von Winterfeld and Edwards, 1986). However, research findings regarding people preference for these two formats is unequivocal. Some have shown that numerical formats are preferable than verbal formats (e.g., Von Winterfeld and Edwards, 1986), some others demonstrated a greater preference for verbal formats (e.g., Brun and Teigen, 1988), whereas others have documented equal preferences for both formats (e.g., Wallsten, Budescu, and Zwick, 1993; Budescu, Weinberg, and Wallsten, 1988). Although, some research has examined the influence of moderating variables (e.g., perceived risk with respect to the consequences of information; Merz, Druzdzel and Mazur, 1997; availability of specific data in the large amount; Wallsten, Budescu and Zwick, 1993), which may play a role in the preferred mode of information, the potential influence of people's motives in processing of information has received less attention (for an exception Halamish et al., 2008). Therefore, the primary objective of the present research is to examine regulatory focus as another potential moderator. In the present study, we considered the role of regulatory focus (i.e., promotion and prevention focus) on the interpretation of verbal vs. numerical probabilistic information. Our aim is to contribute to the extant literature of probabilistic information processing.

Significance and Implication of the Research

Studies of numerical versus verbal probabilities generally found that verbal information was perceived to be more highly imprecise, vague, and subject to multiple interpretations and was influenced by the severity of the consequences associated with information (e.g., Merz, Druzdzel, and Mazur, 1991). For example, low probability of getting a lower grade was interpreted differently than low chance of passing an exam. Nevertheless, verbal expression was perceived to be more natural than numbers, easier to understand, and better suited to express vagueness (Wallsten, Budescu, and Zwick, 1993). However, Brun and Teigen (1988) found that verbal information is less preferable for patients because they find it difficult to comprehend and imprecise (e.g. "how low is my chance to get the disease?"). Authors who support the preference for verbal over numerical formats argued that verbal probability expression is more consistent with human intuitive thinking than numerical probability expression (e.g., Doupnik and Richter, 2004). Therefore, these calls for a need to gain a deeper understanding how people process probabilistic information.

With respect to processing verbal vs. numerical probabilistic information, we proposed that regulatory fit occurs when promotion focus is matched with verbal formats, whereas when prevention focus is matched with numerical format. In these situations, we expect that promotion-focused people will assign more value to an object and exhibit stronger goal pursuits when they are presented with verbal probability expression rather than numerical probability expression. In contrast, we expect prevention-focused people to assign more value to an object and exhibit stronger goal pursuits when they are presented with numerical probability expression rather than verbal probability expression. To support this prediction, the link between RF and verbal versus numerical processing is established as follows. First, the preference for either a verbal of a numerical format relates to the preference for either abstract of concrete information (Budescu, Weinberg, and Wallsten, 1988, Winschilt and Wells, 1996). In the context of RF, the issue of how people process abstract and concrete information also appears. Semin, Higgins, and Montes (2005) demonstrate that prevention-focused people prefer concrete information because of its relation to a strategic focus on vigilance to maintain security and ought goals (i.e., duty and obligations). In contrast, promotion-focused people prefer abstract information to concrete, because of its relation to a strategic focus on eagerness and ideal goals (i.e., hopes and aspirations). Semin, Higgins, and Montes (2005) also reveal that promotion-focused people indicate greater intentions to exercise when the benefit of that exercise is communicated with abstract terms, such as "exercise can increase endurance levels and energy." In contrast, prevention-focused persons show a higher intention to exercise when its benefits are communicated in more concrete ways, such as "exercise can burn approximately 440 calories per hour."

To test our prediction, we designed a 2x2 between-subjects experiment in which we manipulate regulatory focus (promotion vs. prevention) and the mode of presentation (verbal vs. numeric). We investigate the regulator fit effect in the situation of moderate-to-high probabilities, because under low-to-moderate probabilities (i.e., around 30%), both promotion and prevention-focused respondents have the same subjective interpretation of the likelihood of an event (Kluger et al. 2004). This prediction was tested in a study involving hypothetical scenarios. Participants in the promotion condition read an appeal about the possibility of join unique career training which may help them getting a future job that they really want. Participants in the prevention condition read an appeal about the possibility of joining unique career training which may help them avoiding a future job that they do not want. After reading this text, participants read either verbal (e.g, "it is very likely that you get the job you want") or numerical probabilistic information regarding the benefits of the program (e.g., " an 80% chance of getting the job". After reading the scenario, participants rated their attitudes toward the program (3 items), their intention to join the program (2 items), using 7-point scales, anchored by strongly disagree [1] and strongly agree [7]. We also included items for manipulation checks for the modes of uncertainty information. The scale is adapted from a scale developed by Winschilt and Wells (1996) with the objective of cross checking whether respondents have the same interpretation about the magnitude of verbal and numerical uncertainty information. Participants who viewed the numerical format (i.e., 80% chance) indicated their verbal interpretations of these chances on 11-point scales ranging from impossible to certain. Participants in the verbal format condition (i.e., quite likely) instead indicated their numeric interpretation of this information on 11-point scales ranging from 0% to 100%.

With regard to presentation modes, the results show a non-significant difference between the numerical ($M_{NUMERIC}$=3.2, SD=1.16, i.e., between rather likely–quite likely) and verbal (M_{VERBAL}=3.82, SD=0.81, i.e., 70%-80%, (t(85)=1.35, p>0.05). This result highlights respondents interpret verbal and numerical probability expressions as in the range of moderate-to-high.

To test the regulatory fit effect, the three attitude items (α=0.94) and two intention items are averaged (0.92). As predicted, an analysis of variance yielded a highly significant interaction between regulatory focus and mode of presentation on program attitude F(1,85)=5.43, p<0.05 and intention, F(1,85)=4.33, p<0.05. As predicted, participants who read program benefits framed in prevention had more favourable attitude toward the program when presented with numerical uncertainty information (M =6.21 vs 5.36, t(36)=2.77). Contrary to what we expect, no fit effect was found when participants read program benefits framed in promotion with verbal information.

These finding highlights the importance of fitting regulatory focus with probabilistic information. Additional research is needed to investigate the underlying mechanism of the fit effect (e.g., perceive confidence of the likelihood of event occurrence, the influence of problem context (on-going study)). For instance, the context of our study is promotion. Therefore, this may explain why we did not observe fit effect in the promotion-verbal condition.

References

Budescu, David V., Shalva Weinberg, and Thomas S. Wallsten (1988), "Decisions Based on Numerically and Verbally Expressed Uncertainties," *Journal of Experimental Psychology: Human Perception and Performance*, 14, 281-294.

Brun, W., and Teigen, K.H. (1988), "Verbal Probabilities: Ambiguous, Context-Dependent, or Both?" *Organizational Behavior and Human Decision Processes*, 41, 390-404.

Doupnik, Timothy S., and Martin Richter (2004), "The Impact of Culture on the Interpretation of "In Context" Verbal Probability Expressions" *Journal of International Accounting Research*, 3(1), p1-20.

Merz, F., Marek J. Druzdzel, and Dennis J. Mazur (1991), "*Verbal expressions of probability in Informed Consent Litigation*" *Medical Decision Making,* 11(4), 273-281.

Halamish, Vered, Nira Liberman, Torry E. Higgins, and Lorraine Chen Idson (2008) "Regulatory focus effects on discounting over uncertainty for losses vs. gains." *Journal of Economic Psychology*,29(5), 654-666

Higgins, E. Tory, Lorraine Chen Idson, Antonio L. Freitas, Scott Spiegel and Daniel C. Molden (2003), "Transfer of Value From Fit," Journal of Personality and Social Psychology,.84(6), 1140–1153.

Kluger, Avraharn N., Elena Stephan, Yoah Ganzach, and Meirav Hershkoviz (2004). "The Effect of Regulatory Focus on the Shape of Probability-Weighting Function: Evidence from a Cross-Modality Matching Method". *Organizational Behavior & Human Decision Processes*, 95(1), 20-39.

Perdue, Barbara C. and Summers, John O. (1986), "Checking the Success of Manipulations in Marketing Experiments," *Journal of Marketing Research*, 23 (November), 317-326.

Semin, Gun R., Tory Higgins, and Lorena Gil de Montes (2005), "Linguistic Signatures of Regulatory Focus: How Abstraction Fits Promotion More Than Prevention," *Journal of Personality and Social Psychology*, 89 (1), 36-45.

Weber, E.U., and Hilton, D.J. (1990), "Contextual Effects in the Interpretation of Probability Words: Perceived Base Rate and Severity of Events," *Journal of Experimental Psychology: Human Perception and Performance,* 16, 781-789.

Wallsten, T.S., Budescu, D.V., Rapoport, A., Zwick, R., and Forsyth, B. (1986), "Measuring the Vague Meaning of Probability Terms, *"Journal of Experimental Psychology: General,* 115(4), 348-365.

von Winterfeldt, D. and W. Edwards (1986), *Decision Analysis and Behavioral Research.* Cambridge: Cambridge University Press.

Windschilt, Paul D. and Gary L. Wells (1996), "Measuring Psychological Uncertainty: Verbal versus Numeric Methods," *Journal of Experimental Psychology: Applied*, 2 (4), 343-364.

The Impact of C-executives' Babyfacedness on Purchase Intention

Diana Dávila, Instituto Tecnológico y de Estudios Superiores de Monterrey, Mexico
Olivier Trendel, Grenoble Ecole de Management / Customer Equity Institute, France

Abstract

Business leaders often use their face to strengthen the organizational brand. The objective of this research is to understand the impact of C-executives' facial appearance (babyfacedness vs. maturefacedness) on purchase intention. We show that it is important for a company to match the face of the top executive delivering a message with the topic they articulate. Babyfaced executives should be favored when the topic concerns corporate social responsibility whereas maturefaced executives should be favored when the topic concerns technology or competitor orientation. Perceived benevolence, leadership or competence mediates these effects.

Research Background

Research on appearance-based impressions has demonstrated that people can form strong and reliable impressions about a target's character based on his/her facial appearance (Todorov and Uleman 2002). Babyfaced people who possess round face, large eyes, high eyebrows and small chin are universally attributed child-like characteristics and traits such as trustworthiness, warmth or honesty (Montepare and Zebrowitz 1998; Zebrowitz 1997). On the other side, maturefaced individuals are often attributed traits of leadership and competence (Todorov et al. 2005; Zebrowitz and Montepare 2005).

Perhaps more than at any time, business leaders are putting a public face on their company's brands. Building on the literature on first impressions, we suggest that the facial appearance of top executives can impact consumer purchase intention. Gorn et al. (2008) recently showed that the babyfacedness of a CEO can affect consumer judgments in a public relations crisis. They found that babyfaced CEO were perceived as having a lower intention to deceive than maturefaced CEO. Yet, situational cues, such as the severity of the crisis, can suppress or reverse this effect, thus babyfacedness is not always an advantage (see also Todorov et al. 2005).

Interview is a very common public relation tool for top executives and we suggest that it is important for a company to match the face of the top executive giving the interview with the topic they articulate in the interview. The topics selected in this research are directly linked to the dimensions of market orientation: customer orientation, competitor orientation and technological orientation (Narver and Slater 1990; Gatignon and Xuereb 1997). We also included an interview on corporate social responsibility (CSR) as CSR orientation has been suggested as being part of market orientation (Narver and Slater 1990).

We hypothesized that for an interview concerning customer orientation or CSR, purchase intention will be higher if the top executive has a baby face than if he has a mature face. On the other hand, for an interview concerning competition or technology orientation, purchase intention will be higher if the top executive has a mature face than if he has a baby face. The rational is that customer orientation and CSR require the interviewee to be perceived respectively as warm and benevolent and these traits are associated with babyfaced individuals (Brown et al. 2002; Choi and Wang 2007). Interview on competition and technology require the interviewee to be perceived as competent and leader (Spence and Helmreich 1983). These traits are associated with maturefaced individuals and are contradictory with the perceived submissiveness of babyfaced individuals (Zebrowitz and Mcdonald 1991).

Empirical evidence of the impact of babyfacedness on purchase intention

304 students from a major Mexican business school participated in an experiment using a 2 (face: babyface vs. matureface) x 4 (interview: customer, competitor, technology and CSR) between subject design. Average age of the participants was 20 (62.5% girls). Participants were asked to carefully read a Business Week interview of the CEO of a communication company named Dalmex. The interview featured a photograph of the CEO. Eyes form, eyebrows and chin were manipulated on the photo to make two different versions (baby and mature face) of the same individual. A pretest enabled us to check the successful manipulation of perceived babyfacedness ($p<0.001$). We also checked that perceived age and attractiveness were similar between the 2 pictures. The 4 interviews had the same length and we controlled that readability was the same between interviews. Finally, using the scale developed by Narver and Slater (1990) we used 4 contrasts to check that the manipulation of the topics was successful (all $p<0.001$). Purchase intention was measured on a 1 (definitively would not purchase) to 7 (definitively would purchase) scale.

A 2 (face) x 4 (interview) ANOVA on purchase intention revealed the expected significant interaction effect ($F(3,275)=3.69, p=.012$). As hypothesized, we found a significant main effect of face for the CSR interview($F(1,64)=4.80, p=.032$) such that babyfaced executives lead to higher purchase intention than maturefaced executives. This was however not the case for the customer orientation interview ($F<1$). As hypothesized, we also found a significant main effect of face for the technology interview ($F(1,65)=4.04, p=.048$) as well as for the competitor interview ($F(1, 68)=4.61, p< .035$) such that maturefaced executives lead to higher purchase intention than babyfaced executives.

We used ANCOVAs to test for the meditational role of benevolence for CSR and of competence and leadership for the technology and competitor interviews. The previously significant effects of babyfacedness on purchase intention were no longer significant when the covariates were entered in the analysis (all $p>0.12$) The mean square for the face effect was reduced on average by 55%.

Discussion

This research confirms the effect of top executives' babyfacedness on purchase intention. The topic of the interview given by C-executives moderates this effect such as babyfaced executives should be favored when the topic concerns corporate social responsibility whereas maturefaced executives should be favored when the topic concerns technology or competitor orientation. The facial appearance of C-executives should hence be matched with the topic he or she will articulate. The underlying process was also detailed and it should thus be feasible to extend these finding to other topics (e.g. financial performance). The null effect for customer orientation needs further research.

This research also ads to the body of research studying the role of public relations in shaping brand equity. We provide a case in which corporate associations built through public relations have an impact on purchase intention (a product level outcome) (Brown and Dacin 1997).

References

Brown, Tom and Peter Dacin (1997), "The company and the product: corporate associations and consumer product responses," *Journal of Marketing*, 61 (1), 68-84.

Brown, Tom J., John Mowen, D. Todd Donavan and Jane Licata (2002), "The Customer orientation of service workers: personality trait effects on self and supervisor performance ratings," *Journal of Marketing Research*, 39 (1), 110-119.

Choi, Jaepil and Heli Wang (2007), "The promise of a managerial values approach to corporate Philanthropy," *Journal of Business Ethics*, 75, 345-359.

Gatignon, Hubert, and Xuereb Jean-Marc (1997), "Strategic orientation of the firm and new product performance," *Journal of Marketing Research*, 34 (1), 77-90.

Gorn, J.Gerald, Jiang Yuwei and Venkataramani. J. Gita (2008), "Babyfaces, trait inferences and company evaluations in a public crisis," *Journal of Consumer Research*, 35 (1), 36-49.

Montepare, Jann M. and Leslie Zebrowitz (1998), "Person perception comes of age: The salience and significance of age in social judgments," *Advanced in Experimental Social Psychology*, 30, 93-161.

Narver, John C. and Stanley F. Slatter (1990), "The effect of a market orientation on business profitability," *Journal of Marketing*, 54 (4), 20-35.

Spence, Janet T. and Robert L. Heilmreich (1983), *Achievement Related Motives and Behaviors*, San Francisco: In JT Spence.

Todorov, Alexander and Jim S. Uleman (2002), "Spontaneous trait inferences are bound to actors' faces: Evidence from a false recognition paradigm," *Journal of Personality and Social Psychology*, 83 (5), 1051-1065.

Todorov, Alexander, Anesu N. Mandisodza, Amir Goren and Crystal C Hall (2005), "Inferences of competence from faces predict election outcomes," *Science*, 308 (5728), 1624-1627.

Zebrowitz, Leslie. (Ed.). (1997), *Reading Faces: Window To The Soul?* Boulder, CO: Westview Press.

Zebrowitz, Leslie.A. and McDonald, S (1991). "The impact of litigants' babyfacedness and attractiveness on adjudications in small claims courts," *Law and Human Behavior*, 15, 603-623.

Zebrowitz, Leslie and Joann Montepare (2005). "Appearance DOES matter," *Science,* 308 (5728), 1565-1566.

Mental Rumination: How Unwanted and Recurrent Thoughts Can Perturbate the Purchasing Behavior

Alain Debenedetti, Universite Paris-Est, France
Pierrick Gomez, Reims Management School and Université Paris-Dauphine, France

Rumination is a set of long-lasting, recurrent, unwanted, and counter productive thoughts. In clinical psychology, rumination is often mentioned as a consequence of post-traumatic events (Horowitz, 1976) or as an antecedent of depressive disorders (Nolen-Hoeksema, 1996). Martin and Tesser (1989, 1996, 2006) endorse a general view of rumination, removing it from its clinical context. Whereas individuals have many occasions to ruminate in their consumer's life, especially during their purchase decision process, ruminative thoughts have never been integrated into consumer behavior paradigm. Based on Martin and Tesser's motivational approach, we will first present rumination, then suggest some avenues for future research.

What is rumination?

In Martin and Tesser's model, rumination refers to thoughts '*that recur in the absence of immediate environmental demands requiring the thoughts*' (Martin and Tesser, 1996, p.1). Rumination differs from other thinking processes because:

- It does not only occur once: what is central to rumination is not the content or any other quality of the involved mental activity but the circularity of the process.
- If some situations favor their apparition, ruminative thoughts are unintentional insofar as they revolve in the absence of immediate environmental cueing (Koole *et al.*, 1999).

Put differently, rumination is intrusive, anchored into a temporal dimension, and differs from other thinking processes which often deal with wanted tradeoffs.

Martin and Tesser's theory is based on one core principle: people's thoughts are always goal-directed. People continually compare their desired goal to their current states to regulate their behaviors. When a lack of progress towards the goal is perceived, ruminative thoughts are likely to appear (Martin and Tesser, 1996; Scott and McIntosh, 1999). In theory, each interrupted goal can initiate rumination (e.g. to do well on one's life / to buy a muffin), but the centrality of the goal in the individual's life defines the duration and the frequency of ruminative thoughts. In Martin and Tesser's model, emotions can not be considered as antecedents of rumination but as signals which inform the individuals that a major goal is threatened. The failure in problem solving strategies (instrumental thoughts) initiates ruminative thoughts and the emotions that go with them (affective thoughts).

Rumination is divided into 3 dimensions: the emotional valence of the thoughts (negative vs. positive), their temporal orientation (past, present or future) and the polarisation of thoughts (discrepancy focus vs. attainment focus, i.e., definitively non-attained goal vs. lack of progress towards the goal).

Given the intrusion of these recurrent thoughts into consciousness, rumination leads to an important consumption of cognitive resources (Martin and Tesser, 1989) and more specifically to:

- Increases in the intensity and duration of emotions (Martin and Tesser, 1989 ; Rusting and Nolen-Hoeksema, 1998);
- Lower cognitive performances (Scott and Mc Intosh, 1999): rumination leads to less awareness and less ability to solve problems (Sukhodolsky, Golub and Cromwell, 2001) and is followed by reduced self-confidence;
- Negatively biased judgments which alter individuals' choices and make them a) see problems more threatening than they actually are or b) overemphasize negative information related to their experience (Lyubomirsky *et al.*, 1999);
- A need for more temporal resources in decision making situations (Nolen-Hoeksema, 2000)

Ruminative thoughts in consumer behavior

We believe that rumination theory offers great potential for the study of consumer behavior, and is particularly relevant to better understand perturbations in the decision making process because:

- Consumption is a goal-oriented activity which leads to problem-solving situations (related to information search on products and/or brands, to prices and promotion, *etc.*)
- Rumination may arise at two different stages of the purchasing decision process. At the pre-purchase stage, we suggest that rumination is likely to occur when consumers have difficulties to solve the problem they confront (e.g., being unable to choose an Internet provider, fearing the risk of a wrong choice). At the post-purchase stage, rumination may occur when the decision produces undesirable outcomes (e.g., regretting to have subscribed to a non user-friendly Internet service).

The central role played by goals and the temporal dimension of rumination (e.g., pre-choice, post-choice) presents a significant advantage to understand the perturbations which can occur during consumers' purchase process. In that framework, rumination may play two main roles in the decision making process. Rumination may interact with other variables and moderate some consequences of consumers' decision making process. It could also be a mediator: rumination could have a direct influence on some emotional states or behaviors. This effect however would occur only and to the extent that rumination takes place. Because it considerably affects consumers' cognition and affect, rumination could foster unexpected and/or exacerbeted behaviors (e.g., revenge; systematic choice deferral; systematic removal of brands from the consideration set of alternatives…). It also allows for the adoption of a different point of view on classical relationships between consumer behavior variables (e.g., satisfaction and repurchase, for example when consumers favor simplified choice reasoning).

In previous research on rumination, data are typically based on self reports using questionnaires or on manipulations designed to influence individual's thoughts and/or to put them into situations in which higher order goals could be frustrated. We could devise qualitative works and experiments adapted to the context of consumption behavior that would address the following questions: which (unhappy) consumption episodes instigate rumination? To what extent can marketing actions trigger rumination? Will every frustrated consumption goals initiate rumination or only specific high order consumption goals (related to the self, or high involvement product categories)? What is positive rumination (to date there is no research about positive rumination), when does it occur, does it improve one's image and does it also imply counterintuitive implications (e.g., negative effects, such as choice deferral because consumers do not want the positive thoughts to end…)? At which stage of the purchase process is rumination more likely to occur? How can we prevent consumers from engaging into a rumination process? How can we help companies to reduce the likelihood that their products and/or services (sorting them by categories) will trigger ruminative thoughts? Eventually, are some consumers more likely to ruminate than others?

References

Horowitz, M.J. (1976), *Stress response syndromes*, New York, NY: Jason Aronson.

Koole S.L., Smeets K., Van Knippenberg A., and Dijksterhuis A. (1999), "The Cessation of Rumination Through Self-Affirmation", *Journal of Personality and Social Psychology*, 77, 1, 111-125.

Lyubomirsky S., Tucker K.L, Caldwell N.D and Berg K. (1999), "Why Ruminators Are Poor Problems Solvers : Clues from the Phenomenology of Dysphoric Rumination", *Journal of Personality and Social Psychology*, 77, 5, 1041-1060.

Martin L. and Tesser A. (1989), "Toward a Motivational and Structural Theory of Ruminative Thoughts", in Uleman J. and Bargh J. eds, *Unintended thought*, NY : The Guiliford Press, 306-326.

Martin L. and Tesser A. (1996), "Some Ruminative Thoughts", *in Wyer R. eds, Ruminative* thoughts, *Advances in Social Cognition*, Hillsdale : Erlbaum, 9, 1-47.

Martin L. and Tesser A. (2006), "The Interplay of Thoughts Feelings, and Behaviors", in, Lawrence J. Sanna and Edward C. Chang, (Eds); New York: Oxford University Press, 145-162.

Nolen-Hoeksema S. (1996), "Chewing the Cud and other Ruminations", *in Wyer R. eds, Ruminative thoughts, Advances in Social Cognition*, Hillsdale : Erlbaum, 9, 135-144.

Nolen-Hoeksema S. (2000), "Further Evidence for the Role of Psychosocial Factors in Depression Chronicity", *Clinical Psychology: Science and Practice*, 7, 224-227.

Rusting C. L. and Nolen-Hoeksema S. (1998), "Regulating Responses to Anger: Effects of Rumination and Distraction on Angry Mood", *Journal of Personality and Social Psychology*, *74*, 790-803.

Scott V.B. and McIntosh W.D. (1999). "The Development of a Trait Measure of Ruminative Thought", *Personality and Individual Differences*, 26, 1045-1046.

Sukhodolsky D., Golub A. and Cromwell E. (2001), "Development of the Anger Rumination Scale", *Personality and Individual Differences*, 31, 689-700.

Ad Avoidance and Brand Devaluation: When What They Don't See Can Hurt You

Brittany Duff, University of Illinois at Urbana-Champaign, USA
Ron Faber, University of Minnesota, USA

Every day we see thousands of advertisements, yet consumers actively attend to only a small minority of the ads they are exposed to. Most advertising research looks only at what happens after attention to the ad has occurred. While this is obviously important, it may be equally important to understand what happens to the ads that are not attended to, or purposely ignored.

Several advertising researchers have used the mere exposure effect (MEE) to suggest that avoided ads can have positive outcomes for advertisers (Edwards, Li and Lee 2002; Baker 1999). Zajonc(1968) showed that "unreinforced" exposure to novel stimuli increases liking of that stimuli. This is what has been cited in the many applications of MEE to ignored or passively viewed advertising. Indeed, Bornstein (1989) pointed out that advertising, which may be conceptualized as repeated, unreinforced exposures designed to enhance attitude, represents an important application of MEE. However, "unreinforced" implies that no affective response is attached to the stimuli, something that may not be the case in all instances of ad avoidance.

Distracter Devaluation

In opposition to MEE, recent research has found that non-attended objects (distracters) can lead to negative, rather than positive ratings. Raymond, Fenske and Tavassoli (2003) had participants view stimuli and quickly indicate on which side of the page the target stimulus appeared. Participants later rated their affect toward the attended (target) stimulus, the ignored stimulus, or a previously unseen (novel) stimulus. The ignored stimuli were rated lower than either the novel stimuli or the attended stimuli. This shows that attentional state during initial exposure can influence affective response when the stimulus is encountered again. When the stimulus is actively ignored during exposure it can cause a subsequent negative rating. This is referred to as the distracter devaluation effect.

Further studies demonstrated that overtly knowing what not to look at caused an even stronger negative affective association. This shows that top-down processing may create an emotional response, and that attention and emotion may work together to prioritize the processing of stimuli in order to help people accomplish task related goals (Fenske, Raymond and Kunar 2004). When engaged in visual search, it is inefficient to re-search areas or re-attend to items once it has been determined that they are not what is being sought. Thus we tag items as inhibited or negative so as not to process them again. While this is functional for goal-oriented behaviors, it suggests that ads that interrupt or distract from search efforts may actually harm brand ratings.

Motivational relevance

Object-based inhibition is part of a top-down attentional process and is dependent on limited-capacity resources (Olivers and Humphreys 2002). Top-down processing occurs when there is already a goal in mind (e.g. finding that specific book) versus a bottom-up approach where something may gain attention by catching your eye. We are constantly engaged in some sort of bottom-up processing as we scan our environments, but inhibition primarily occurs in goal-directed searches.

Certain items have been shown to be generally prioritized for processing- such as fearful faces or food. These items can be said to elicit motivated attention (e.g. Schupp et al 2004; Lang, Bradley and Cuthbert 1998). Salience can also be related to physiological drive states with increased attention for items related to eating found for participants who abstain from eating compared to those who didn't (Mogg et al 1998).

Study 1

Study 1 was conducted to determine if a goal-directed (top down) task would create brand devaluation for distracting ads, and if a physiological need state (affecting bottom-up processing) would impact these results. Participants (n=118) viewed 19 webpages that contained food-related news articles and ads (experimenter created). Some ads were repeated while others were included just once. Participants were randomly assigned to one of three conditions. Two groups (Task groups) were asked to find specific information on each page. One of these groups had food related ads on each webpage that were later rated, while the Task-No Ad group had different ads on their webpages that weren't subsequently rated and therefore served as a baseline in ratings. The third group (Non-Task Group) saw pages with the food ads, but were not given any tasks. They were told to look at the pages like they would any webpage that they were seeing for the first time. Each webpage appeared on screen for 15 seconds so that the time exposed to the pages was the same for all groups. Hunger levels were assessed before viewing since this should affect motivational relevance and prioritize the processing of food-related stimuli. This allows for an examination of the impact of both bottom-up and top-down attentional strategies.

Findings supported the hypotheses. A significant difference ($p<.001$) between hungry vs. non-hungry participants emerged. Hungry participants showed no differences between groups on ad liking and trial intent (all p's>.15,n.s.). However, as predicted, non-hungry participants showed significant differences (in the predicted directions, with the AdsTask group showing the lowest means) for ad liking (repeated ads $F(2,57)=3.25, p<.05$; non-repeated $F(2,57)=3.65, p<.05$) and trial intent (repeated $F(2,57)=3.90, p<.05$; non-repeated $F(2,57)=5.97, p<.005$). There were no differences between non-hungry groups on liking or trial for the unseen (novel) ads.

Study 2

Study 2 (n=138) was conducted to clarify and extend study one results. The same stimuli and method were used. Dependent variables focused on mood,[1] self-reported attention to ads (vs. ignoring them), and ad recognition. No mood effects were present for either the hungry (F(2,69)=1.42,p>.2) nor the non-hungry groups (F(2,67)=1.56,p>.2). As expected, for the non-hungry participants there were differences by viewing group with the task groups reporting significantly lower attention to ads (F(2,68)=6.75,p<.005). However, for hungry participants there was no difference in self-reported attention to the ads between groups (F(2,69)=.043,p>.9). This suggests that for hungry participants bottom-up processing may override the top-down goal. Recognition scores also confirm that the devaluation effect most likely occurs without any explicit recognition of ads.

Overall the studies show that the outcome (negative or positive) may depend on goal at time of exposure.

References

Baker, William E. (1999), "When can Affective Conditioning and Mere Exposure Directly Influence Brand Choice?" *Journal of Advertising,* 28(4), 31-46.

Edwards, Steven M., Hairong Li and Jon-Hyun Lee (2002), "Forced Exposure and Psychological Reactance: Antecedents and Consequences of the Perceived Intrusiveness of Pop-Up Ads," *Journal of Advertising*, 31(3), 83-95.

Fenske, Mark J., Jane E. Raymond and Melina A. Kunar (2004), "The affective consequences of visual attention in preview search," *Psychonomic Bulletin and Review*, 11(6), 1055-1061.

Lang, Peter J., Margaret M. Bradley and Bruce N. Cuthbert (1998), "Emotion and Motivation: Measuring Affective Perception," *Journal of Clinical Neurophysiology,* 15(5), 397-408.

Mogg, Karin, Brendan P. Bradley, Harpfreet Hyare and Sui Lee (1998), "Selective Attention to Food-Related Stimuli in Hunger: Are Attentional Biases Specific to Emotional and Psychopathological States, or Are They Also Found in Normal Drive States?" *Behaviour Research and Therapy*, 36(2), 227-237.

Olivers, Christian N.L. and Glyn W. Humphreys (2002), "When Visual Marking Meets the Attentional Blink: More Evidence for Top-Down, Limited Capacity Inhibition," *Journal of Experimental Psychology: Human Perception and Performance*, 28(1) 22-42.

Raymond, Jane E., Mark J. Fenske and Nader T. Tavassoli (2003), "Selective Attention Determines Emotional Responses to Novel Stimuli," *Psychological Science*, 14(6) 537-542.

Schupp, Harold T, Bruce N. Cuthbert, Margaret M. Bradley, Charles H. Hillman, Alfons O. Hamm, and Peter J. Lang (2004), "Brain Processes in Emotional Perception: Motivated Attention," *Cognition and Emotion,* 18(5), 593-611.

Zajonc, Robert B. (1968), "Attitudinal Effects of Mere Exposure," *Journal of Personality and Social Psychology Monograph Supplement*, 9(2), 1-27.

The Sweet Side of Sugar–The Influence of Raised Insulin Levels on Price Fairness and Willingness to Pay

Tim Eberhardt, Zeppelin University, Germany
Thomas Fojcik, Zeppelin University, Germany
Mirja Hubert, Zeppelin University, Germany
Marc Linzmajer, Zeppelin University, Germany
Peter Kenning, Zeppelin University, Germany

Psychologists Daniel Kahneman and Amos Tversky have influenced the research in consumer psychology and behavioral economics over the last thirty years (Tversky and Kahneman 1974). While their findings have been useful in many fields of marketing research, they were particularly useful for research in behavioral pricing (e.g., Conover 1986; Vanhuele and Drèze 2002). Pricing research has traditionally analyzed such concerns as consumer judgment of price fairness in terms of the consumers' relationship to retailers. However, Knutson et al. (2007) moved the research in a new direction when they used event-related fMRI to investigate which distinct brain areas are activated in purchasing decisions dealing with products and prices. They found activity associated with anticipating gains and losses at the nucleus accumbens (NAcc), the insula, and the mesial prefrontal cortex (MPFC). Findings of Knutson et al. (2001) and Kenning and Plassmann (2008) show a specific stimulation of the NAcc in anticipation of a reward, indicating the importance of the NAcc in consumer behavior studies. Further, the role of serotonin, which has long been implicated in social behavior (Kandel et al. 2000) and which is believed to play an important role in activating the NAcc (Purves et al. 2008) can be linked to raised levels of tryptophan in the NAcc (Crockett et al. 2008). If, therefore, raised levels of serotonin are associated with higher levels of tryptophan, and knowing that raised levels of insulin in the blood increase the supply of tryptophan (Daniel et al. 1981), the link between insulin level and social behaviors (particularly those associated with consumer behavior) suggests a valuable area of investigation.

Though the effects of e.g. dopamine levels in humans have increasingly been in the focus of academic scrutiny in the field of economics (Balleine et al. 2009), the effects of serotonin has, to date, received less attention. This investigation is one of the first to explore the biological correlates of raised insulin (and hence serotonin) levels on buying decision behavior in a price fairness task, with the goal of providing new findings for psychologists and marketing researchers.

Our study used a paper-based presentation of 48 convenience goods (24 premium brands, 24 store brands, colored pictures, prices in ¤), intending to activate a low-involvement situation for the participants of the study (Monroe and Lee 1999). Involvement was checked

[1]Diffuse positive affect as shown by mood is posited to be a factor in MEE (Monahan, Murphy and Zajonc, 2000)

using the Purchase Decision Involvement (PDI) scale developed by Mittal (1989), consisting of a four-item measure on seven-point bipolar phrases. Participants had to decide whether or not they considered the given price of a product to be "fair" and, if not, what price they would be willing to pay with the option to adjust prices for each individual product. In the forced-choice-task, each subject had to evaluate six items for one product (288 decisions). A May 2008 pretest containing 10 subjects confirmed validation and distinctiveness of both the stimulus material and the translated items. The pretest also served as a first measure of the effects of different glucose manipulations on the subjects. In February 2009, 37 selected undergraduate students (21 male, 16 female) participated in the main study. We divided the participants into three groups. Subjects of the experimental group (14 subjects) were manipulated using 90 grams (recommended daily allowance for a healthy adult) of pharmaceutical glucose dissolved in 0.3 liter of sparkling water. Control group I (14 subjects) had to drink 0.3 liter sparkling water with no glucose added to the water. Control group II (nine subjects) drank no water and was not manipulated at all. Study design for every participant followed precisely the insulin release curve of a healthy adult metabolic subject (Suckale and Solimena 2008) to match the hypothetical insulin level of the subjects to their respective response behavior.

Statistical analyses were conducted with SPSS. For the analysis of our data we used a simple independent t-test, including "Levene`s Test" to explore equality of means and variances between our study groups. Normal distribution condition was examined with the Shapiro-Wilk-Test, which is generally used for small sample sizes (n<50). The analysis of our data and the identified structures with significant changes between the experimental group and the two control groups revealed very interesting results, confirming our hypothesis that glucose levels change perception of price fairness and willingness to pay.

The experimental group evaluated all prices of our product-portfolio (n=48 products) to be more fair than did their counterparts in both control groups [*product-portfolio*: $M_{experimental\ group}$=69.93; SD=5.98/$M_{control\ group\ I}$=62.30; SD=5.77; 69.93 vs. 62.30; t=3.44, p<.01; $M_{experimental\ group}$/$M_{control\ group\ II}$=63.14; SD=6.00; 69.93 vs. 63.14; t=2.66, p<.05]. Subjects in the experimental group were willing to pay much higher prices for the same products than were subjects in both control groups. This effect was also revealed by testing different prices of store brands (n=24 products, price-range between 0.29-2.55 ?; M=0.79 ?) and premium brands (n=24 products, price-range between 0.55-11.99 ?; M=2.29 ?). Overall, the experimental group accepted higher prices while subjects in both control groups rejected higher price-levels over total response time within the experiment [*store brands*: $M_{experimental\ group}$=20.03; SD=2.21/$M_{control\ group\ I}$=18.69; SD=.73; 20.03 vs. 18.69; t=2.16, p<.05; $M_{experimental\ group}$/$M_{control\ group\ II}$=18.00; SD=0.95; 20.03 vs. 18.00; t=3.03, p<.01; *premium brands*: $M_{experimental\ group}$=49.90; SD=4.36/$M_{control\ group\ I}$=43.61; SD=5.66; 49.90 vs. 43.61, t=3.29; p<.01; $M_{experimental\ group}$/$M_{control\ group\ II}$=45.14; SD=5.68; 49.90 vs. 45.14, t=2.14; p<.05].

Second, we tested differences between two levels of insulin at two intervals (within the first 10 minutes and after 40 minutes), following the insulin release curve of a healthy adult metabolic subject. The above-mentioned effect differential between the experimental group and the two control groups could be confirmed in the first range of our study over all products (within 10 minutes after glucose manipulation; first peak of insulin release curve). [The following figures indicate price variances of the total sum of the product-portfolio: *product-portfolio*: $M_{experimental\ group}$=1.43; SD=2.51/$M_{control\ group\ I}$=5.90; SD=3.93, 1.43 vs. 5.90; t=-3.60, p<.01; $M_{experimental\ group}$/$M_{control\ group\ II}$=5.37; SD=3.47; 1.43 vs. 5.90; t=-2.95; p<.01.] The same effect was identified by testing premium brands with our study groups, but not for store brands. [The following figures indicate price variances of the total sum of the product-portfolio: *premium brands*: $M_{experimental\ group}$=1.43; SD=2.14/$M_{control\ group\ I}$=5.50; SD=3.83; 1.43 vs. 5.50; t=-3.46; p<.01; $M_{experimental\ group}$/$M_{control\ group\ II}$=4.86; SD=3.41; 1.43 vs. 4.86; t=-2.69; p<.05; *store brands*: $M_{experimental\ group}$=-.01; SD= .90/$M_{control\ group\ I}$=.41; SD=.55; -.01 vs. .41; t=-1.48; p>.05; $M_{experimental\ group}$/$M_{control\ group\ II}$=.51; SD=.44; -.01 vs. .44; t=-1.83; p>.05.] In the second range (40 minutes after glucose manipulation; second peak of insulin release curve) the existence of these effects could not be determined significantly.

Our study provided first insights about the biological correlates of raised insulin levels (through oral glucose manipulation) on price fairness perceptions. Statistical analysis showed that higher insulin levels indicate higher price acceptance. The estimated effects could support our assumption that glucose stimulates the monoamine serotonin, which results in neural activation. The effect is likely due to activation in neural areas of emotional regulation. Further research, including the use of fMRI, could determine more reliable insights into the hypothetical "glucose-insulin-tryptophan-serotonin" chain and its effects on distinctive brain areas and, thereby, on consumer behavior.

References

Balleine, Bernhard W., Nathaniel D. Daw and John P. O´Doherty (2009), "Multiple Forms of Value Learning and the Function of Dopamine," in: *Neuroeconomics–Decision Making and the Brain,* ed. Paul W. Glimcher, Colin F. Camerer, Ernst Fehr and Russell A. Poldrack, Oxford (UK): Elsevier, 367-387.

Conover, Jerry N. (1986), "The accuracy of price knowledge: Issues in research methodology," *Advances in Consumer Research,* Vol. 13, 589-593.

Crockett, Molly J., Luke Clark, Golnaz Tabibnia, Matthew D. Lieberman and Trevor W. Robbins (2008), "Serotonin Modulates Behavioral Reactions to Unfairness," *Science,* Vol. 320, 1739.

Daniel, Peter M., E. R. Love, S.R. Moorhouse and Oliver E. Pratt (1981), "The Effect of Insulin upon the influx of tryptophan into the brain of the rabbit," *The Journal of Physiology,* Vol. 312, 551-562.

Ho, Teck H., Noah Lim and Colin F. Camerer (2006), "Modeling the Psychology of Consumer and Firm Behavior with Behavioral Economics," *Journal of Marketing Research*, Vol. 43, Issue 3, pp. 307-331.

Kandel, Eric R., James Schwartz and Thomas M. Jessel (2000), *Principles of Neural Science,* McGraw Hill Medical.

Kenning, Peter and Hilke Plassmann (2008), "How recent neuroscientific research could enhance marketing theory," *IEEE Transactions*, 2008 (14) Suppl. 6: 532-538.

Knutson, Brian, Grace W. Fong, Charles M. Adams, Jerald L. Varner and Daniel Hommer (2001), "Dissociation of reward anticipation and outcome with event-related fMRI," *Neuro Report*, Vol. 12, December, pp. 3683-3687.

Knutson, Brian, Scott Rick, G. Elliott Wimmer, Drazen Prelec and George Loewenstein (2007), „Neural Predictors of Purchase," *Neuron*, Vol. 53, January, 147-156.

Mittal, Banwari (1989), "Measuring Purchase-Decision," *Psychology & Marketing*, Vol. 6., 147-162.

Monroe, Kent B. and Angela Y. Lee (1999), "Remembering versus knowing: Issues in buyers´ processing of price information," *Journal of the Academy of Marketing Science*, Vol. 27, pp. 207-225.

Purves, Dale, George J. Augustine, David Fitzpatrick, William C. Hall, Anthony-Samuel LaMantia, James O. McNamara, S. Mark Williams (2008), *Neuroscience,* New York, Palgrave Macmillan (4th edition).

Suckale, Jakob and Michele Solimena (2008), "Pancreas islets in metabolic signaling–focus on the ß-cell," *Nature Precedings*, hdl:10101/npre.2008.1724.2, posted 2 Jun 2008.

Tversky, Amos and Daniel Kahneman (1974), "Judgment under Uncertainty: Heuristics and Biases," *Science*, Vol. 185, No. 4157, 1124–1131.

Vanhuele, Marc and Xavier Drèze (2002), "Measuring the price knowledge shoppers bring to the store," *Journal of Marketing,* Vol. 66, October, 72-85.

Power Dynamics in Immigrant Families in Britain and Its Effect on Consumption

Onyipreye Worlu, Manchester Business School, UK
Andrew Lindridge, Open University, UK

Research into family networks and how they are constructed and sustained through consumption can be criticised for being inherently western centric and White. Previous studies have tended to focus on key themes such as how individuals influence other family members (Cotte and Wood, 2004), how individuals represent family as aspects of their extended self in terms of consumption (Tian and Belk, 2005), and lastly family member's influence on consumption (Commuri and Gentry, 2005), to name but a few are often lacking in their focus on ethnic minorities. Despite calls for more research on gender differences in immigrant populations, relatively few studies have been conducted and those that have been studied have been product specific or based upon impulse buying behaviour (Mitchell and Walsh, 2004). This research argues that the current research into immigration, family and consumption practices are lacking in their discussion of idealised norms that govern gender relations in particular the construction of consumption behaviour and consequently power dynamics between husband and wife. The research will, therefore, address this research gap by providing an insight into how immigrant women, through consumption, use power dynamics to assert identities.

Inman et al. (2007) argued that women appear to hold the key to the familial structure amongst immigrant families. Cultural inhibitions, such as the belief that a woman's primary role is in the home or that women take second place to men is a widely held belief in most immigrant families (Inman et al., 1999); a belief that may lay in transactional gendered socialisation, and the immigrant and the host society's culture (Jayakar, 1994). However, when migrants' acculturation process is considered, immigrant women may produce a diverse and fluid range of identity (Üstüner and Holt, 2007). This in turn may cause them to begin to challenge their own, ethnic groups, patriarchal cultural values etc. This act of cultural resistance may exist in the miniature of simple, daily activities yet these acts appear to remain relatively unexplored.

One area where cultural resistance may exist is in the cultural inhibition of the woman's role in the family household, i.e. subservience behaviour to her husband. In particular how women, through engaging with the consumption process may have opportunities to express acts of cultural, consumption orientated resistance. It has been well documented that culture and self-identity plays a significant role in consumption; in particular how cultural values manifest through consumption of products (McCracken, 1986; Foxall and Goldsmith, 1994; Lindridge and Dibb, 2003). As a result, for example, cultural resistance may occur in modifying food choices which were once chosen in line of the husband's preference then changed in line of the wife's preference, and so forth. However, research that encompasses acculturation and cultural resistance, within a culturally determined family dynamic are lacking in consumer research.

Methodology

This research will focus on Black Nigerian immigrants living in Britain. The choice of Black Nigerians is partially one of convenience and also because the Black African population, living in the UK, is relatively understudied in comparison with other visible ethnic sub-groups (Daley, 1998).

This research used two sample groups consisting of ten first generation Nigerian couples (husband and wife) living in Britain and ten British White couples. Both the sample groups were matched for construct equivalence (in terms of age, religious background and socio-economic status) and recruited, using the snowball method of sampling, from London and Manchester.

Taking a Black feminist paradigm, the research was qualitative in nature and used semi-structured and in-depth interviews. The first stage of the fieldwork consisted of conducting preliminary interviews followed by further in-depth interviews with the wives of each couple. This two-stage interview process, conducted over a period of three months, aimed to explore the world of our female participants. It also allowed us to juxtapose the narratives shared with their husbands to the narratives of their individual interview, allowing us to highlight the antecedents of various acts of cultural resistance.

Complimenting the interviews, participating couples were asked to keep receipts of items consumed. These receipts provided points of discussions, for example items purchased that may have caused conflict or tension. This allowed us to explore wider aspects of our participants' decision-making and how power dynamics, based on gender roles, were acted out.

Preliminary analysis

Preliminary analysis of the data showed that acts of consumption-orientated resistance were evident for all our participants. British white women and Black Nigerian women tended to show similarity through their career path goals, work/ family conflict, gender based mistreatment, friendship and community. Both groups showed resistance through the purchase of items without approval from their spouse; however they varied by the cost of the product purchased. For example British white women were at times more likely to purchase items that were viewed as capital intensive such as white goods. Whereas Black Nigerian women were more likely to purchase items that were less capital intensive such as food and were highly unlikely to purchase high capital intensive products without consultation with their spouse and their presence in the buying process e.g. the buying of electronics.

However, all our Black Nigerian participants demonstrated varying levels of resistance to what they perceived to be traditional Nigerian, patriarchal values. From a cultural values perspective this manifested through expressing a greater sense of individuality; reflective of their engagements with British White culture. For example, many of the participants exhibited this through personal fashion (e.g. clothes, jewellery, hairstyles and cosmetics) and in some cases spoken language (e.g. the use of British slang). Food purchase and food preparation for the family was also shown to be pivotal in individuality and provided a space in which these immigrant women were also able to exhibit forms of resistance of their traditional cultural and patriarchal values.

Bibliography

Commuri, Suraj and Gentry, James W. (2005), "Resource Allocation in Households with Women as Chief Wage Earners", *Journal of Consumer Research,* 32 (September), 185-95.

Cotte, June and Wood, Stacy L. (2004), "Families and Innovative Consumer Behaviour: A Triadic Analysis of Siblings and Parental Influence", *Journal of Consumer Research,* 31 (June), 78-86.

Daley, Patricia O. (1998), "Black Africans in Great Britain: Spatial Concentration and Segregation", *Urban Studies,* 35 (10), 1703-24.

Foxall, Gordon R. and Goldsmith, Ronald E. (1994), *Consumer Psychology for Marketing*, London: Routledge.

Inman, Arpana G., Constantine, Madonna G., and Ladany, Nicholas (1999), "Cultural Value Conflict: An Examination of Asian Indian Women's Bicultural Experience". In Inman, Arpana G., Howard, Erin E., Beumont, Robin L., and Walker, Jessica A. (2007), "Cultural Transmission: Influence of Contextual Factors in Asian Indian Immigrant Parents' Experiences", *Journal of Counselling Psychology,* 54 (1), 93-100.

Inman, Arpana G., Howard, Erin E., Beumont, Robin L., and Walker, Jessica A. (2007), "Cultural Transmission: Influence of Contextual Factors in Asian Indian Immigrant Parents' Experiences", *Journal of Counselling Psychology,* 54 (1) (January), 93-100.

Jayakar, Kushalata (1994), "Women of the Indian Subcontinent". In Comas-Diaz, Lillian and Greene, Beverly (Eds), *Women of Colour: Integrating Ethnic and Gender Identities in Psychotherapy* (pp. 161-181), New York: Guilford Press.

Lindridge, Andrew M. and Dibb, Sally (2003), "Is Culture a Justifiable Variable for Market Segmentation? A Cross-Cultural Example", *Journal of Consumer Behaviour,* 3 (2), 269-88.

McCracken, Grant (1986), "Culture and Consumption: A Theoretical Account of the Structure and Movement of the Cultural Meaning of Consumer Goods", *The Journal of Consumer Research,* 13 (1) (June), 71-84.

Mitchell, Vincent-Wayne and Walsh, Gianfranco (2004), "Gender Differences in German Consumer Decision-Making Styles", *Journal of Consumer Behaviour*, 3 (4) (June), 331-46.

Tian, Kelly and Belk, Russell W. (2005), "Extended Self and Possessions in the Workplace", *Journal of Consumer Research,* 32 (September), 297-310.

Üstüner, Tuba. and Holt, Douglas (2007), "Dominated Consumer Acculturation: The Social Construction of Poor Migrant Women's Consumer Identity Projects in a Turkish Squatter", *Journal of Consumer Research,* 34 (June), 41-55.

Consumer Response to Stereotype Threat Related to Dissociative Groups

Mohammed El Hazzouri, University of Manitoba, Canada
Sergio W Carvalho, University of Manitoba, Canada
Kelley Main, University of Manitoba, Canada

In everyday life, social identity and stereotypes influence how people behave. The literature on stereotype threat (e.g., Steele, Spencer, and Aronson 2002), for instance, argues that stereotype threat occurs whenever a person who highly identifies with a certain domain but belongs to a group that is stereotyped to be incompetent in that domain, becomes aware that he/she might engage in behavior that would confirm the stereotype. Previous research (e.g., Aronson et al. 1999) has shown that people's academic performance can be significantly impaired by the presence of a stereotype threat. Apparently, the psychological pressure of having to perform well in order to deny the stereotype leads to an opposite outcome–poor performance.

In the consumption setting, it has been found that consumers might be reluctant to use products that send negative cues about themselves (Banister and Hogg 2004) and avoid selecting products that are associated with negative reference groups (White and Dahl 2006). More specifically, recent research suggests that males require an excuse to get involved with female oriented consumption (Argo, Zhu and Dahl 2007).

However, to the best of our knowledge, neither the literature on stereotype threat nor the literature on consumer behaviour has investigated how people react to a stereotype threat when the stereotype domain is related to a dissociative group. The current research that draws on stereotype threat and dissociative groups, examines how consumers respond to situations in which demonstrating competence (ability) in using a product is not desirable since it might associate them with a dissociative group. More specifically, we evaluate how consumers' performance and enjoyment of using products, and their satisfaction with their own performance are affected when consuming products that are associated with a dissociative group.

Consumer response to stereotype threat related to a dissociative group was assessed in a pilot study and an experiment within the context of a gift-wrapping task–a context found to be a gender-related stereotype, which males would like to be dissociated with. Undergraduate business students at a major mid-western university participated in the study for course credit.

The results of a pilot study showed that participants who were told that the task was designed to test the wrapping materials (stereotype threat absent) were more satisfied with their own performance and felt more competent while wrapping the gift box than participants who were told that the gift wrapping task was designed to test their artistic ability (stereotype threat present).

An experiment was then designed to investigate the interactive effects of gender and stereotype threat on consumers' performance and enjoyment, and their satisfaction with their own performance in the gift-wrapping task. Seventy-eight students (50% males) participated in this study. The design was similar to that of the pilot study. With the exception of task performance that was evaluated by independent judges, all of the dependent variables of interest (task enjoyment and satisfaction with own performance) were self-reported measures.

Results revealed a significant two-way interaction of gender and stereotype threat on task performance ($F(1,74)=10.18, p<.01$), task enjoyment ($F(1,74)=6.79, p=.01$), and satisfaction with own performance ($F(1,74)=7.03, p=.01$). Simple effect tests revealed that there was a significant effect of stereotype threat on the performance of male participants ($M_{absent}=5.50$ vs. $M_{present}=4.84$; $F(1,74)=6.03$, $p<.05$), on how much they enjoyed the task ($M_{absent}=4.91$ vs. $M_{present}=4.03$; $F(1,74)=4.58, p<.05$) , and on their satisfaction with their own performance ($M_{absent}=4.24$ vs. $M_{present}=3.24$; $F(1,74)=4.43$, $p<.05$). In addition, within the present stereotype threat condition, compared to female participants, males performed significantly worse ($M_{Males}=4.84$ vs. $M_{females}=6.21$; $F(1,74)=24.48$, $p<.001$), enjoyed the task much less ($M_{Males}=4.03$ vs. $M_{females}=5.75$; $F(1,74)=12.07, p<.001$), and evaluated their own performance much lower ($M_{Males}=3.24$ vs. $M_{females}=5.10$; $F(1,74)=10.21, p<.01$). Male and female participants performed and enjoyed the task equally well when they were told that the gift-wrapping task was designed to evaluate the wrapping materials ($p>.10$).

Conclusion

Overall, results suggest that male participants could perform well but needed an excuse to do so, a finding that is consistent with Argo, Zhu, and Dahl (2007) who demonstrated that males needed an excuse to get involved in an emotional melodramatic story. When we gave males the excuse that the gift-wrapping task was designed to evaluate the wrapping materials, they performed as well as females. Our findings contribute to the literature on stereotype threat by demonstrating that the threat can also take place even when the person is highly disidentified with the stereotype relevant domain. This research also adds to the consumer literature related to dissociative groups by showing that a product perceived to be associated with a dissociative group might not only reduce consumers' preference for that product but also negatively impact consumers' performance and enjoyment in using that product, and personal satisfaction with their performance. From a public policy standpoint, this research can also partly explain the effect of gender stereotypes on females' and males' performance in and enjoyment of domains that are stereotypically gender-related such as arts, and household work.

References

Argo, Jennifer J., Rui (Juliet) Zhu, Darren W. Dahl (2008), "Fact or Fiction: An Investigation of Empathy Differences in Response to Emotional Melodramatic Entertainment," *Journal of Consumer Research*, 34(February), 614-623.

Aronson, Joshua, Michael J. Lustina, Catherine Good, Kelli Keough, Claude M. Steele, and Joseph Brown (1999), "When White Men Can't Do Math: Necessary and Sufficient Factors in Stereotype Threat," *Journal of Experimental and Social Psychology*, 35, 29-46.

Banister, E. N. and M. Hogg, (2004), "Negative Symbolic Consumption and Consumers' Drive for Self-Esteem," *European Journal of Marketing*, 38(7), 850-68.

Steele, Claude M., Steven J. Spencer, and Joshua Aronson (2002), "Contending with Group Image: The Psychology of Stereotype and Social Identity Threat," *Advances in Experimental Social Psychology*, 34, 379-436.

White, Katherine and Darren W. Dahl (2006), "To Be or Not Be: The Influence of Dissociative Reference Groups on Consumer Preferences," *Journal of Consumer Psychology*, 16(4), 404-13.

Transmodern Metaphors and Consumer Spirituality

Esi Abbam Elliot, University of Illinois at Chicago, USA

Benet DeBerry-Spence, University of Illinois at Chicago, USA

This study on transmodern metaphors is positioned at the nexus of consumer spirituality, where *transmodern* is defined as "a way of thinking that combines intuition and spirituality with rational brainwork" (Luyckx, 1999, 971). The term *metaphor* refers to associations that relate abstract concepts to physical things and are used to construct conceptual understandings (Lakoff 1987; Lakoff and Johnson, 1980). Existing consumer research has focused on the cognitive linguistic, psycholinguistic, literary and cultural views of metaphors (Dodd 2002; Lakoff and Johnson 1980; Denny and Sunderland 2005; Coulter and Zaltman 2000; McQuarrie and Mick, 1996; Hirshman 2000; Zaltman and Coulter 1995; Zaltman 1997); yet, limited attention has been given to spirituality and metaphors. This provides the basis for our research, which examines the use of transmodern metaphors associated with consumer spirituality. We contribute to theory by introducing 'meta-connections' as an important metaphorical connectivity relating to consumer spirituality.

Today's global contemporary society finds consumers increasingly interested in and influenced by their own spirituality. Spirituality concerns one's personal quest for understanding answers to ultimate questions about life, meaning, and relationships with the sacred or transcendent (Koenig et al. 2001). Spiritual awareness leads consumers to not only consider secular, rational and scientific approaches to understandings, but to incorporate transmodern considerations. The marketing literature has discussed metaphor and meanings extensively, drawing on two traditions concerning what metaphor represents and how it may be used within a culture (Hirschman 2007). The first tradition is grounded in literary theory and linguistics, while the second draws from symbolic anthropology and is grounded in cultural images (Hirschman 2007). Although anthropological construal of metaphor is grounded in human experience, it is usually meant to reflect phenomena experienced in the natural or social world. The question then becomes, "What about phenomena experienced that fall outside the realm of the natural or social domain, such as the spiritual?" The current study builds on this question and explores metaphorical associations related to consumer spirituality.

To examine consumer use of transmodern metaphors, an initial study was conducted using visuals from advertisements featuring African kente cloth and targeted at African American consumers from the period of 1980 to 2000. The varied properties embedded in a textile (e.g., social, personal, spiritual, cultural, political, historical, etc.) make it potent symbol, enabling it to say things that words often cannot (Schneider and Weiner 1986). Further, the African kente cloth, in addition to being the most well known and commercially successful African fabric (Rabine 2002), often features woven patterns and symbols associated with spirituality (Ross 1998). Advertisements were compiled from a variety of businesses ranging from the food and beverage, fashion, insurance and communication industries. The intent was to incorporate a broad set of kente product and industry usage, thus yielding a diverse set of consumer interpretations.

Initial research indicates consumer interpretations of kente involve metaphorical spiritual associations, which we refer to as meta-connection*s*. The term 'meta' captures those experiences that reflect the metaphysical; that is, those features of reality that exist beyond the physical world and our immediate senses, but nonetheless are part of the consumer's everyday life. In this study, meta-connections are captured in consumer interpretations and spiritual sensing of the vivid colors, geometric symbols and proverbial messages embedded in the advertisement. An example is a Disneyworld advert featuring Mickey Mouse and Miss Collegiate African American 1993, wearing kente textiles with patterns that are interpreted with metaphorical associations of spiritual purity.

The introduction of 'meta-connections' offers a number of advancements. First, it extends the current literature to include metaphorical associations of spirituality that are interpreted and acted on by consumers in their everyday lives. It therefore throws light on transmodern approaches open to consumer spirituality and related belief systems. Second, spiritual aspects of traditional societies continue to be prevalent in many of contemporary ethnic communities. The inclusion of meta-connections as a type of consumer metaphorical association captures the ontological perspectives embedded within many ethnic cultures and acknowledges the importance of these perspectives in understanding consumer behavior.

References

Coulter R. and G. Zaltman (2000), "The Power of Metaphor", In: Ratneshwar S, Mick DJ, Huffman C, Editors. *The Why of Consumption: Contemporary Perspectives on Consumer Motives, Goals, and Desires*. London, Routledge, 259– 81.

Denny, R. M., and P. L. Sunderland (2005), "Researching Cultural Metaphors in Action: Metaphors of Computing Technology in Contemporary U.S. life" *Journal of Business Research* 58 (October), 1456– 1463.

Dodd S.D. (2002), "Metaphors and Meaning— A Grounded Cultural Model of US Entrepreneurship", *Journal of Business Venturing*, 17 (September), 519– 35.

Hirschman E.C. (2007), "Metaphors in the Marketplace" *Marketing Theory*, 7 (March), 227-248.

Koenig, H. G., M. McCullough, and D. B. Larson (2001), *Handbook of Religion and Health: A Century of Research Reviewed*, New York: Oxford University Press.

Lakoff G. (1987), "Women, Fire, and Dangerous Things: What Categories Reveal About The Mind", Chicago, Chicago University Press.

Lakoff, G. and M. Johnson (1980), "Metaphors We Live By", *Chicago University Press*, Chicago.

Luyckx, M. (1999), "The Transmodern Hypothesis: Towards a Dialogue of Cultures", *Futures*, 31 (November), 971-982.

McQuarrie, E., F. and D. G. Mick (1996), "Figures of Rhetoric in Advertising Research", *Journal of Consumer Research*, 22 (March), 424– 38.

Rabine, L. W. (2002), "The Global Circulation of African Fashion", New York: Berg Publishers.

Ross, D. (1998), "Wrapped in Pride: Ghanaian Kente and African American Identity", Hong Kong: Wout Sea International Press.

Schneider, J., and A. B. Weiner (1986), "Cloth and the Organization of Human Experience", *Current Anthropology*, 2 (April), 178 - 184.

Zaltman G. and Coulter R.H. (1995), "Seeing the Voice of the Customer: Metaphor-based Advertising research, *Journal of Advertising Research*, 35 (July), 35 –51.

Zaltman G. (1997), "Rethinking market research: putting people back in", *Journal of Marketing Research*, 34 (November), 424– 37.

Consumer Creativity During Unconstrained Consumption Tasks

Marit Gundersen Engeset, Buskerud University College, Norway
Sigurd V. Troye, Norwegian School of Economics, Norway

Abstract

Interest in consumer creativity reflects an emerging trend in consumer research to understand how consumers themselves construct meaning, create value, and participate actively in every part of the consumption process. Building on creativity theory, consumer researchers have focused on antecedents and consequences of consumer creativity in *constrained* consumption situations. The present research adds to the literature on consumer creativity by demonstrating high variability in creative processing and creative production during a more realistic, *unconstrained* consumption task. The results suggest that creative abilities influence creative processing which in turn influences behavioral intentions towards the solutions.

Background

In marketing and consumer research consumers have traditionally been viewed as destroyers rather than creators of value. Recent research on consumer creativity (Moreau and Dahl 2005, Burroughs and Mick 2004), and on consumers' role as co-creators of value (Xie, Bagozzi and Troye 2008), challenges this view. Empirical and anecdotal evidence suggest that consumers do not always follow the least effortful avenue in their pursuit of goal attainment, but often enjoy exploring alternatives and thinking creatively during consumption tasks (Chernev 2006; Billings and Scherer 1988). The present research adds to the insight of how consumers act creatively in *constrained* consumption tasks (Moreau and Dahl 2005, Burroughs and Mick 2004) by exploring how consumers act creatively in *unconstrained* situations. We will also investigate antecedents and consequences of such creativity.

Creativity research conceptualizes the creative process as a mental process where different categories of knowledge are combined to constructively address an issue (Smith 1995). The process is typically described in terms of phases where the person searches for knowledge to understand and address a given problem (Ward, Smith and Finke 1999). Bottom up thinking, divergent thinking and convergent thinking are indicators of creative processing. Creative production refers to the solution itself. A solution is thought to be creative if it is a novel, appropriate and aesthetic solution to the problem (Burroughs, Moreau, and Mick 2008). Creative abilities are factors that enable the person to think more creatively and produce more creative solutions. Knowledge and motivation are considered critical for creativity (Amabile, 1996). Self efficacy and innovativeness are factors likely to influence creativity in a consumption setting. Consumer creativity has also been found to enhance consumers' positive affect (Burroughs and Mick, 2004); it is therefore likely that satisfaction and purchase intentions will be influenced by consumer creativity.

The Study

273 people participated in the study. A scenario was presented where participants were asked to imagine that they would cook dinner for friends at a dinner party, and write down what they would serve on such an occasion. Since no potential solutions or resources were limited in the scenario, no explicit constraints were imposed on the participants. This was important because the research is concerned with how consumers use creative processing in realistic decision situations. Four judges scored the usefulness of the solutions on a 6 item scale derived from Besemer and O'Quinn's (1986) CPSS scale. Novelty and aesthetics was assessed by measuring uniqueness and richness of the solutions. After creating solutions to the consumption scenarios, subjects were asked to explain in detail how they had been thinking during construction of each of the solutions, what came into mind first, what did they consider during the decision making task, and so on. Those reports were coded by independent judges with regards to three different measures of creative thinking: bottom up thinking, convergent thinking, and divergent thinking. Established scales were used to measure knowledge, motivation, self efficacy, and innovativeness. Three items measured purchase intentions.

Results

A total of 245 usable questionnaires (52% male) were returned. Analysis of creative process suggests that even when little constraints operate, consumers do vary to a great extent in their use of creative processing. Creativity in solutions varied from very low to high. There were significant correlations between creative process and purchase intentions ($r=.286$, $p<.01$), creative abilities and creative process ($r=.211$, $p<.001$), and creative abilities and creative product ($r=.197$, $p<.01$). To test the structural relationships between the constructs in this study, a model where creative abilities influenced creative processing and creative products, creative processing influenced creative production, and both creativity constructs influenced purchase intentions was estimated in LISREL 8.7. The composite reliability of the creative product scale was low (.51). As a result, creative production was removed, and a new model with creative abilities predicting creative processing which in turn predicted purchase intentions was estimated. Fit measures indicated acceptable representation of the data (Kji square=72.52 with 33 df; RMSEA=.070, and AGFI .91). All the paths in the model were significant, and the composite reliability for all constructs was accptable (0,66-0,83).

Discussion

The results presented in this paper suggest high variability in both creative processing and creative production during an unconstrained consumption task. This supports the assumption that creative and noncreative thinking can be conceptualized on a continuum rather than as a dichotomy (Moreau and Dahl 2005; Ward et al 1999). The research contributes with evidence of the existence of creative processes during unconstrained consumption tasks. Creative production correlated with creative abilities, but not with creative processing. This is puzzling, since creativity research typically assumes a strong link between process and production in many domains (Amabile, 1996). The paper discusses how measurement issues regarding creative production may be the reason for this finding, and how this must be addressed to fully understand the relationships tested in this study. Further, although no explicit constraints were imposed on the participants, they may have experienced implicit constraints by imagining a scenario where they would be impression managing (hosting dinner guests). This may have influenced their choices of final solutions more than their creative processing. Despite this weakness, the research reports interesting results regarding creative processing during a consumption task; creative abilities influence creative processing which in turn influence purchase intentions. The practical relevance of focusing on consumer creativity is underscored by the fact that creativity led to higher purchase intentions.

The hope is that this research will contribute to the consumer creativity literature by broadening its scope. By demonstrating that consumers do engage in creative processing and creative production when faced with less constrained consumption problems, new questions rise. What are the factors influencing such creativity? What are the consequences for brand loyalty? Will creative processing influence satisfaction with the product as well as satisfaction with the process and the decision? Some of these questions have been touched upon in this research, but more questions remain unanswered and represent opportunities for future work in this area.

References

Alba, Joseph W. and J. Wesley Hutchinson (1987), "Dimensions of Consumer Expertise," *Journal of Consumer Research,* 13 (March), 411-54

Amabile, Teresa M. (1996), *Creativity in Context,* Boulder, CO: Westview Press Inc.

Bagozzi, Richard P. and Gordon R. Foxall (1996), "Construct Validation of a Measure of Adaptive-Innovative Cognitive Styles in Consumption," International Journal of Research in Marketing, 13 (3), 201-13

Bandura, Albert (1997), *Self-Efficacy. The Exercise of Control,* New York: W.H. Freeman and Company

Besemer, Susan, and Karen O'Quinn (1986), "Analyzing Creative Products: Refinement and Test of a Judging Instrument," *Journal of Creative Behavior,* 20(2), 115-26

Bettman, James R. and C. Whan Park (1980), "Effects of Prior Knowledge and Experience and Phase of the Choice Process on Consumer Decision Processes: A Protocol Analysis," *Journal of Consumer Research,* 7 (December), 234-48

Billings, Robert S. and Stephen A. Marcus (1983), "Measures of Compensatory and Noncompensatory Models of Decision Behavior: Process Tracing versus Policy Capturing," *Organizational Behavior and Human Performance,* 31 (3), 331-52

Billings, Robert S. and Lisa L. Scherer (1988), "The Effects of Response Mode and Importance on Decision-Making Strategies: Judgement versus Choice," *Organizational Behavior & Human Decision Process,* 41, 1-19.

Brucks, Merrie (1985), "The Effects of Product Class Knowledge on Information Search Behavior," *Journal of Consumer Research,* 12 (June), 1-16

Burroughs, James E. and David Glen Mick (2004), "Exploring Antecedents and Consequences of Consumer Creativity in a Problem-Solving Context," *Journal of Consumer Research,* 31 (September), 402-11.

Burroughs, James E., C. Page Moreau, and David Glen Mick (2008), "Toward a Psychology of Consumer Creativity," in *Handbook of Consumer Psychology*, eds. Curtis P. Haugtvedt, Paul M. Herr, and Frank R. Kardes, New York, NY: Psychology Press Taylor & Francis Group, 1011-38.

Byrne, Barbara M (1998), *Structural Equation Modeling with LISREL, PRELIS, and SIMPLIS,* Mahwah, NJ: Lawrence Erlbaum Associates, Inc.

Chernev, Alexander (2006), "Decision Focus and Consumer Choice among Assortments," *Journal of Consumer Research,* 33 (June), 50-59.

Collins, Mary Ann and Teresa M. Amabile (1999), "Motivation and Creativity," in *Handbook of Creativity,* ed. Robert J. Sternberg, Cambridge: Cambridge University Press, 297-312

Diamantopoulos, Admantios and Judy A. Siguaw (2006), *Introducing LISREL,* London: Sage

Guay, Fréderick, Robert J. Vallerand, and Céline Blanchard (2000), "On the Assessment of Situational Intrinsic and Extrinsic Motivation: The Situational Motivation Scale (SIMS)," *Motivation & Emotion*, 24 (3), 175-213

Guilford, Joy Paul (1950), "Creativity," *American Psychologist,* 5, 444-54

Hill, Thomas, Nancy D. Smith, and Millard F. Mann (1987), "Role of Efficacy Expectations in Predicting Decisions to Use Advanced Technologies: The Case of Computers," *Journal of Applied Psychology*, 72 (2), 307-13

Im, Subin, Barry L. Bayus, and Charlotte H. Mason (2003), "An Empirical Study of Innate Consumer Innovativeness, Personal Characteristics, and New-Product Adoption Behavior," *Journal of the Academy of Marketing Science*, 31 (1), 61-73

Johnson, Eric J. and J.Edward Russo (1984), "Product Familiarity and Learning New Information," *Journal of Public Policy and Marketing*, 2, 153-70

Moreau, C. Page and Darren W. Dahl (2005), "Designing the Solution: The Impact of Constraints on Consumer's Creativity," *Journal of Consumer Research,* 32 (June), 13-22.

Park, C.Whan, David L. Mothersbaugh, and Lawrence Feick (1994), "Consumer Knowledge Assessment," *Journal of Consumer Research,* 21 (June), 71-82

Patrick, Catherine (1937), "Creative Thought in Artists," *Journal of Psychology,* 4, 35-73

Runco, Mark A. (1989a), "The Creativity of Children's Art," *Child Study Journal*, 19, 177-89

Runco, Mark A. and Ivonne Chand (1995), "Cognition and Creativity," *Educational Psychological Review,* 7 (3), 243-67

Scwarzer, Ralf (1993), *Measurement of Perceived Self-Efficacy: Psychometric Scales for Cross-Cultural Research,* Berlin: Freie Universität Berlin

Smith, Steven M. (1995), "Fixation, Incubation, and Insight in Memory and Creative Thinking," in *The Creative Cognition Approach,* eds. Steven M. Smith, Thomas B. Ward, and Ronald A. Finke, Cambridge, MA: MIT Press, 135-56.

Sternberg, Robert J. and Todd I. Lubart (1999), "The Concept of Creativity: Prospects and Paradigms" in *Handbook of Creativity,* Ed. Robert J. Sternberg, Cambridge: Cambridge University Press, 3-15

Sternberg, Robert J. and Elena L. Grigorenko (2000-2001), "Guilford's Structure of Intellect Model and Model of Creativity: Contributions and Limitations," *Creativity Research Journal,* 13 (3&4), 309-16

Taylor, W.G.K. (1989), "The Kirton Adaption-Innovation Inventory: A Re-Examination of the Factor Structure," Journal of Organizational Behavior, 10 no 4 (October), 297-303

Ward, Thomas B. (1994), "Structured Imagination: The Role of Category Structure in Exemplar Generation," *Cognitive Psychology,* 27 (1), 1-40

Ward, Thomas B., Steven M. Smith, and Ronald A. Finke (1999), "Creative Cognition" in *Handbook of Creativity,* ed. Robert J. Sternberg, New York, NY: Cambridge University Press, 189-212.

Xie, Chunyan, Richard P. Bagozzi, and Sigurd V. Troye (2008), "Trying to Prosume: Towards a Theory of Consumers as Co-Creators of Value," *Journal of the Academy of Marketing Science,* 36, 109-22.

Examining Immigrant Turkish Household Food Consumption: Consumer Insights for Food Acculturation Models

Elif Akagun Ergin, Cankaya University, Turkey
Carol Kaufman-Scarborough, Rutgers University-Camden, USA

This research examines the food consumption behaviors of Turkish immigrant consumers who migrate to the United States. This population has migrated steadily over many years and establishes stable populations in specific concentrated areas in the Northeastern United States. The families typically establish close relationships within Turkish communities and maintain the food customs of their culture-of-origin throughout numerous years. In the present manuscript, we report on a series of depth interviews with Turkish immigrant consumers regarding their typical food consumption practices and perceptions. This sample is part of a larger study focusing on Turkish immigrant behaviors.

Globalization has given rise to a multicultural society. Researchers have studied the food consumption practices, preferences, and realities of consumers as they emigrate to other cultures. Quite often, unique "hybrids" of their former cultures are created through partial assimilation into the host culture, in this case, the United States. Our study takes the perspective that does not place expectations on the subjects to conform to United States culture, i.e., how much progress they have made in assimilating to U.S. culture. Instead, we are interested in the reality that they have created as members of their own culture while living in the United States. Such realities differ in today's information-rich world since immigrants to the US are likely to have international cell phones, surf the World Wide Web, and watch homeland programming via satellite television.

Researchers have described assimilation as a process in which an immigrant's behavior becomes a mixture or blend of two cultures. The norms of the culture of origin become mixed with the norms of the culture of residence (Wallendorf and Reilly 1983). However, certain product constellations that are strongly linked with the home country culture are thought to be resistant to assimilation, and actually may give rise to a system of protected norms that form generally-accepted standards of consumption. Such is the case of food purchase, preparation, and consumption with Turkish immigrants.

Similar to the dense Mexican population in California, the Turkish immigrants seem to create enclaves that can inhibit the acculturation process as they form a "home away from home" in their local communities (Penaloza and Gilly 1999), with small retail stores and even Turkish elementary schools. Moreover, the longer the immigrants stay in the U.S., they appear to become more proficient at "culture switching." That is, like the Haitian immigrants described in Oswald's study (1999), the Turkish immigrants are adept at switching from Turkish culture to mainstream American culture based on their specific situation. More often than not, however, their food culture appears to be firmly grounded in Turkish customs, values, and practices, while their employment can be well-integrated into the U.S. labor force.

In order to establish a baseline for food behaviors, semi-structured interviews were conducted with seven Turkish immigrants regarding their reasons for immigration, their food-related practices, their shopping and food preparation patterns, and foods that they would like to have but cannot buy in the United States. Six females and one male participated in this phase of the study, with ages ranging from 33 to 50 (average age is 41.5). Participants were recruited and selected in order to include representation from various parts of Turkey: two from Istanbul, Espiye (Black Sea Coast), Bolu, Kayseri (Central Anatolia Region), Edirne, and Samsun (Black Sea Coast).

Like many other cultures, Turkey is rich in cultural variations across regions, with food skills, preferences, and local tastes combining to create a foodways culture that is representative of both regional and country customs. The stories of each person's immigration were similar, although they grew up in different areas of Turkey. Participants were asked to describe how they shopped for food when living in Turkey. The open-ended questions attempted to draw each respondent back into the early formations of their food preferences as well as their present-day practices.

The verbatims were read and re-read to attempt to extract common themes without imposing any anticipated structure to the respondents' comments following Strauss and Corbin (1988) and Miles and Huberman (1994). Interestingly, numerous comments reflected back to each respondent's early childhood days spend with their parents, forming their shopping and food preferences. The data reveal that food consumption choices are more complex than suggested by assimilation models, but instead incorporate childhood sensory experiences, religious practices, taste preferences, the desire to maintain cultural food habits, availability of preferred products, and the desire to retain homeland food practices.

This initial phase of our research provided an insightful view to the complexity of Turkish immigrant food behaviors. It is simply not maintaining past food practices nor learning new ones. For instance, participants spoke to us with concerns regarding "hidden" meat by-products that violate religious customs, such as gelatins that are common ingredients in U.S. foods such as the marshmallows in children's cereals. Additional research is needed to try to unfold how such concerns affect food purchases and practices.

Managerial implications also abound for retailers. Grocery stores, for example, may want to further study whether Turkish customers are able to fulfill their desired purchases within U.S. retail settings. If there is a large enough customer base, it might be in the store's best interest to open an ethnic section for those ethnic groups that provide a large consumer base in the community.

Selected References

Ergin, Elif Akagun and Handan Ozdemir Akbay (2008), "An Empirical Investigation of Turkish Consumers' Online Shopping Patterns," *Journal of Global Business and Technology*, Volume 4, Number 2 (Fall).

Miles, M. B., & Huberman, A. M. (1994). *Qualitative data analysis*. Thousand Oaks, CA: Sage Publications.

Oswald, Laura R. (1999), "Culture Swapping: Consumption and the Ethnogenesis of Middle-class Haitian Immigrants," *Journal of Consumer Research,* March, Vol. 25 Issue 4, 303-319.

Penaloza, Lisa and Mary C. Gilly (1991), "Marketer Acculturation; The Changer and the Changed," *Journal of Marketing,* Vol. 63, No. 3 (July), 84-104.

Strauss, A. and J. Corbin (1988). *Basics of Qualitative Research: Techniques and Procedures for Developing Grounded Theory.* Thousand Oaks, CA: Sage Publications.

Wallendorf, M. and Eric J. Arnould (1991), "We Gather Together: Consumption Rituals of Thanksgiving Day," *Journal of Consumer Research,* 18 (June), 13-31.
Wallendorf, M. and M.D. Reilly (1983). "Ethnic migration, assimilation, and consumption," *Journal of Consumer Research*, 10 (December), 292-302.

It's Fake!? Consumers' Self Creation in a Market with Easy Access to Counterfeit Goods

Marcia Christina Ferreira, EBAPE / FGV, Brazil
Bill Pereira, EBAPE/FGV-RJ. FUCAPE Business School, Brazil

Consumption is a central practice in everyday life supplying meanings and value for the creation and maintenance of the consumer's personal and social world (Wattabasuwan 2005). Symbolic value and meanings are important for consumers not only because they help retain their former sense, but also because they help them to be categorized in society, communicate cultural meanings, traditions and group identity, as well as to shape and communicate their identity through the meanings attributed to their possessions (McCracken 1981; Slater 1997; Belk 1998). Consumption meanings emerge in a dialectical process between its owner and the object as the symbolism assigned to this object reflects both, the image of the subject and the image of the object (Wattabasuwan 2005). An argument well illustrated by Belk (1988: p. 141): "the more we believe we possess or are possessed by an object, the more a part of self it becomes". Therefore, the dialectical process would not be subject-object, but in fact subject-object-subject.

The present research chooses counterfeit consumption as base to explore the dynamic interaction between consumer actions, the marketplace and the cultural meanings (Arnould and Thompson 2005) and aim to better understand consumer's self creations via possessions of counterfeit goods. In a marketplace with abundant supply and easy access to counterfeits consumers can alter their behaviour looking for products "with brand" instead of originals giving uncountable justifications for their actions resulting in a consumption "socially acceptable" (Gentry et al 2001). Therefore a market "plentiful" of counterfeits goods was chosen as context for the present research as it allows exploring the phenomenon as relations between an existent culture and social resources as well as relations between possessions and meanings. A perspective not yet explored in the literature.

The majority of existing literature concentrates in profiling counterfeit consumers as well as investigating their consumptions reasons (Penz and Stöttingner 2008) resulting in studies that search for rational answers driven by utilitarian principles. However, profound explanations need to be done beyond correlations between variables which would be better assessed by qualitative research (Eisend and Schuchert-Güler 2006). Counterfeit consumers present distinctive construction of meanings indicating they consider more personal and subjective value in choosing this product (Gentry, Putrevu and Shultz 2006). Since counterfeits are as closely related to the person's self image and identity as regular products, consumers are capable of transferring part of the meanings from the original to themselves and build their identity, depending on the counterfeit likeness (Hoe, Hogg and Hart 2003).

Looking at the context in question, the literature gives evidence that individuals rate counterfeit consumption as pleasant as regular shopping (Matos Ituassu and Rossi 2007). During their decision making counterfeit consumers might prefer product's meanings instead of quality or price, suggesting a choice based on product's usage (Ferreira, Botelho and Almeida 2008). Moreover counterfeits could contribute for consumer's legitimacy working as symbolic capital and yet becoming socially acceptable (Strehlau, Vasconcelos and Huertas 2006). Finally counterfeit consumer value seems to be ruled by experiences with individuals reacting to meanings existing in original products and then acting through counterfeits as a way to find authentic consumption value, since these goods where mostly consumed playfully and along with non aesthetic value (Ferreira, 2008).

The developing country Brazil was used as research context. In 2008 the turnover of counterfeit goods was between US$ 30 billion and US$ 40 billion, in a country where only 3 in 10 persons do not consume fake products (Bompan 2008). Additionally an anthropologic study shows an abrupt intensification of consumption as a result of economic expansion and political changes. To understand this new reality individuals developed conflicting views putting in one side desires and values and the frustration and political issues on the other (O'Dougherty 2002).

In this marketplace, counterfeit consumers were asked to reflect upon their lifetime experiences while shopping. Fourteen in-depth interviews were conducted using a semi-structured questionnaire with male and females, aged between 20 e 54 years, living in Rio de Janeiro. The sample, selected by convenience, was collected mainly through face-to-face interviews during 45 minutes on average, in locations chosen by the informants (excluding five phone interviews). The data collected were recorded, transcribed and analyzed individually by the researchers (Miles and Huberman 1994). Additionally, the largest trade centre for counterfeits in the country was used for field observations. Researchers talked with dealers and consumers seeking to better understand the consumptions' dynamics in that marketplace. As a working in progress, further investigations will be carried out.

When creating meaning counterfeit consumers appear to arbitrate a dialog between object's representation (counterfeit object) and signification (original object) through rituals of possession determined by distinct levels of self creation. Therefore it's possible to address this phenomenon in the chosen context as a three-way conversation (subject-object-subject) but with the object divided in two: original and counterfeit. Three levels of symbolic action emerge from the analysis of counterfeit consumer's self-extension: (a) controlling level; (b) creative level; (c) fulfilling level. On the first level the counterfeit object was possessed by consumers through strict control over their significance. In this case, such product was consumed mainly by their practical characteristics and justified by their utilitarian trade-off. Therefore, such practice has been allocated on the lowest level of self-extension with fewer presence of symbolic action.

On a second level, the consumers seek for symbolic actions that can be determined by their creativity with an objective to personify such possession. On this level the dialog between representation and significance was permanent and led the consumers to reveal [or remember] incessantly their counterfeit consumption to get closer each time to significance inspired by the original good. Extremely knowledgeable of both objects consumers in the third level of self-extension were capable of divestment of most of the counterfeit representation in search for a fully significance prevailing through the idea of original product. And they did it believing that their personal features (such as beauty, success or wealth) work as a catalyst transferring to the counterfeit object most of the significance from the original item.

References

Arnould, Eric J. and Craig J Thompson (2005), "Consumer Culture Theory (CCT): Twenty Years of Research," *Journal of Consumer Research*, 31, 868-882.

Belk, Russell (1998), "Possession and extended self," *Journal of Consumer Research*, 15, 139-68.

Bompan, Fernanda (2008), "Em 10 meses, Brasil deixa de arrecadar R$ 18 bi com pirataria," [In 10 month Brazil lost R$ 18 billion in tax with piracy] *Gazeta Mercantil,* Rio de Janeiro [Brazil], 11th October.

Eisend, Martin and Pakize Schuchert-Güler (2006), "Explaining Counterfeit purchases: a review and preview," *Academy of Marketing Science Review*, 12, 214-29.

Ferreira, Marcia Christina (2008), "A Falsa Ilusão de Ter: Investigando os Tipos de Valor para o Consumidor de Falsificações," [The false illusion of ownership: Investigating the Counterfeit Consumers Value] *XXXII ANPAD* [National Association of Graduate Studies and Research in Administration] *Meeting*, in digital media.

______, Delane Botelho and Alda Rosana de D. Almeida (2008), "Consumer Decision Making in a Counterfeit-plentiful Market: An Exploratory Study in the Brazilian Context," *Latin American Advances in Consumer Research,* 2, 109-115.

Gentry, James W., Satijav S. Putrevu, Clifford C. Shultz II, and Suraj S. Commuri (2001), "How now Ralph Loren? The separation of brand and product in a counterfeit culture," *Advances in Consumer Research, 28,* 258-265.

______, Satijav S. Putrevu, and Clifford C. Shultz II (2006), "The effects of counterfeiting on consumer search," *Journal of Consumer Behaviour*, 5, 245-56.

Hoe, Lee, Gillian Hogg and Susan Hart (2003), "Fakin'it: Counterfeiting and consumer contradictions," *European Advances in Consumer Research*, 6, 60-67.

McCracken, Grant (1981) ,"Culture and consumption: a theoretical account of the structure and movement of the cultural meaning of consumer goods," *Journal of the Consumer Research*, 13, 71-84.

Matos, Celso A., Cristina T. Ituassu, and Carlos V. Rossi (2007), "Consumer attitudes toward counterfeits: a review and extension," *Journal of Consumer Marketing*, 24,1, 36-47.

Miles, Matthew and Michael A. Huberman (1994), *Qualitative Data Analisys*, 2nd edition, London, UK: Sage.

O'Dougherty, Maurren (2002), *Consumption intensified. The politics of middle-class daily life in Brazil*, US: Duke University Press.

Penz, Elfriede and Barbara Stöttingner (2008), "Original brands and counterfeit brands—do they have anything in common?," *Journal of Consumer Behaviour,7, 146-163.*

Slater, Don (1997), *Consumer culture and modernity*, Cambridge, UK: Polity.

Strehlau, Suzane, Isabella F. G. Vasconcelos, and Malby K. Z. Huertas (2006), "Identidade social e consumo: como se legitimam os consumidores de produtos de luxo falsificado," [Social identity anda consumption: who consumers of luxury fake products legitimize themselves] *X Colóquio Internacional sobre Poder Local* [International Colloquium about Local Power]–*ANPAD* [National Association of Graduate Studies and Research in Administration], in digital media.

Wattanasuwan, Kritsadarat (2005), "The self and symbolic consumption," *The Journal of American Academy of Business,* 6, 179-183.

Doing Qualitative Research with Archival Data: Making Secondary Data a Primary Resource

Eileen Fischer, York University, Canada
Marie-Agnès Parmentier, HEC Montréal, Canada

Since consumer researchers began to publish studies grounded in qualitative data, many have collected archival or secondary data as a matter of course. However archival data has played what can only be regarded as a secondary role in most qualitative consumer research studies. Archival data comprises a wide array of empirical materials created by individuals for their own purposes (e.g. diaries, letters. photographs, weblogs, fan art and discussion list postings) or behalf of organizations (e.g. corporate annual reports, press releases, advertisements, magazine articles, restaurant reviews, ratings websites etcetera). With rare exceptions (notably Belk's (1992) study that relied on personal documents) common methodological practice has been to make use of interview and, less frequently, observational data as the main resource in developing interpretations and analyses of focal phenomena. Archival data has chiefly been used to help develop understandings of the research context, rather than to inform the development of concepts and theories. Evidence supporting this assertion is that virtually every scholar who has collected both interview or observational data *and* archival data offers quotes from interviews or field notes when reporting findings and developing theoretical contributions, but only a tiny minority refer to archival material for the same purposes. And although interviews and observations are fine materials with which to build contributions to consumer research, there are burgeoning opportunities for making greater use of archival data for this purpose. Indeed, in section one of the paper, we argue that there is also an increasing case to be made for the necessity of drawing on archival data as one primary resource.

The claim that archival data is an increasingly viable resource stems from the fact that an ever greater amount of archival verbal and visual material is becoming nearly universally available owing to the internet. Just as the growth of online communities has led to ever growing opportunities for netnography (Kozinets 2002, 2008), so has the proliferation, online, of archives of materials ranging from periodicals to blogs to corporate annual reports to product complaint websites made possible an ever widening scope of systematic, archival research. And as museums and other repositories make portions of their holdings available electronically, this tsunami of available archival data will expand further.

The claim that we should consider archival data as a more primary source of insight stems from the increasingly sophisticated critiques emerging of interview data as a primary resource in qualitative research. Arnould and Wallendorf (1994) have vividly illustrated the disjunctions between what people say and what people do; they make a compelling case that we cannot rely primarily on interviews to provide insights into patterns of and motives for consumers' behaviors. More recently, insightful critiques of neopositivist, romantic and localist views of the qualitative interviews have raised significant challenges to our thinking about which research questions are possible or suitable to address based on interviews alone (Alvesson 2003).

Given this convergence of opportunity and need for greater use of archival data, we must consider how we can best gather and analyze such materials. Existing guidelines for gathering and analyzing "secondary data" are sparse, and typically assume that it will play a secondary role. Moreover, they overlook the fact that qualitative researchers today face challenges not of finding archival data, but rather of deciding how to put limits on what is collected and analyzed systematically. Thus, it is important to develop guidance on tractable and coherent strategies for collecting archival data when it will be used as a primary resource for theory building. And, as its role becomes more central, it is important that we give consideration to appropriate ways of interpreting such data.

The second section of this paper discusses how researchers can decide what archival data to collect when they must determine what to include and what to exclude from a data collection in progress. In initial stages of a research project, researchers benefit from creating an inventory of the sources of archival material they could access, and examining selections of data from each in order to familiarize themselves with their phenomenon of interest and with the contents of each potential archival data source. As the research question(s) of interest are identified it becomes useful for the researchers to consider three factors related to their question(s). The first is the "unit of analysis." While rarely explicitly considered in qualitative research, our paper makes the case that clarity regarding the unit of analysis can help the researcher make defensible decisions to include some archival sources and to exclude others. A second consideration in relation the research question is whether or not it concerns a process that is expected to span some duration. Understanding events in that duration that are of theoretical interest (e.g., emergence, transformation, or termination) can also help to identify which archival sources can be excluded and which are most likely to be usefully included. A third factor related to research question(s) is whether they are concerned with developing hermeneutic understanding of the perspective of some individuals or group of actors. Again, as we elaborate in the paper, clarity on this aspect of the research question can help to identify which sources of archival data are critical to consider as a primary resource and which can be regarded as secondary. Examples are developed to illustrate and elaborate upon these criteria.

In the third section of the paper, we detail a set of questions that researchers can pose about specific sets of archival data that will help them make appropriate choices when analyzing that particular data. Briefly, these questions prompt the researcher to consider the circumstances under which the data was created, the limitations on the perspectives of those who created it, and the possible motivations that shape what is included and omitted, and how the phenomenon of interest is portrayed. Examples are again discussed in this section.

In the concluding section we identify research topics that lend themselves well to investigation using archival data as a primary resource.

Reevaluating Disclaimers and the FTC's Clear and Conspicuous Standards

Kendra Fowler, Kent State University, USA
Veronica Thomas, Kent State University, USA
Richard Kolbe, Kent State University, USA

Disclaimers are "messages intended to fully disclose all information that could affect decision making and elucidate possibly misunderstood statements" (Herbst and Allan 2006, 213). The use of disclaimers in advertising is on the rise and has become almost commonplace in television commercials (Hoy and Andrews 2004; Kolbe and Muehling 1995; Muehling and Kolbe 1997). The Federal Trade Commission in an effort to promote competitive business practices, protect consumers, and regulate advertising (Hoy and Lwin 2007) developed, in 1970, Clear and Conspicuous standards (CCS) for advertising disclosures.

Research shows, however, that consumers are not always able to process the provided information (Morgan and Stoltman 2002). The majority of advertisers, ad agencies, broadcasters and regulatory agencies believe that consumers "do not read, cannot read, and do not attempt to read the fine print" (Muehling and Kolbe 1997, p. 4). Consequently, despite the increase in disclosures, there does not appear to be a corresponding increase in the informational value of the advertisements from the consumers' standpoint. The guidelines set forth to protect consumers from deception need to be revisited. Specifically, the effectiveness of the standards at enhancing consumers' recall of disclosures and the contribution they make to enhance overall understandability of advertising needs to be reanalyzed, a point echoed by the Current FCC Commissioner, Jonathan Edelstein (Eggerton 2006) as well as academics (Hoy and Andrews 2004; Muehling and Kolbe 1997; Stewart and Martin 2004). In an effort to understand the impact of disclosure statements, we analyzed the FTC's current suggested disclosure practices and provide evidence as to the effectiveness of these methods in enhancing disclosure recall and perceptions of understanding.

A total of 327 undergraduate students from a large midwestern university participated in an online survey for extra credit. Sixteen conditions were created to observe how the stylistic elements associated with a disclosure impacts the recall of the disclosed information and perceived understandability of the advertisement. In all of the conditions, participants viewed a stimulus for a well known credit card. Conditions were created to study the effect of modes of delivery, font size, distraction, and technical language. Prevailing industry norms were followed and disclosures were placed at the bottom of the screen near the end of the commercial message and no other sounds aired during the disclosures presentation. The disclaimer in all of the stimuli appeared for only fifteen seconds and consisted of fifty words, requiring the participants to be able to read at a rate of 200 words per minute. This rate was chosen because it was within the range at which an average person could be expected to read (Douglass and Douglass 1993) and was slightly less than the average rate used in most fine print disclosures (Kolbe and Muehling 1997). After viewing the appropriate stimulus for their condition, participants were asked to complete a survey that included measures of disclosure recall and perceived understandability of the advertisement.

In the case of disclosure recall, no significant ($p \leq .05$) interaction effects were found. Looking then at main effects, we find significant results for the effect of distraction ($F(2,255)=5.045$, $p \leq .01$, $\eta^2=.038$) and language ($F(1,255)=10.836$, $p \leq .001$, $\eta^2=.041$) on recall of the disclosure. The effect of audio ($F(1,255)=.588$, $p=.44$, $\eta^2=.002$) and size ($F(1,255)=2.089$, $p=.15$, $\eta^2=.008$), however, failed to reach significance.

As expected, increasing the level of background distraction decreased the recall of the disclosure. Tukey pairwise comparisons indicate no significant differences between conditions of no distraction (M=2.875) and low distraction (M=2.725), but recall under the condition of high distraction (M=2.063) was significantly reduced. Language also impacted recall of the disclosure in the predicted direction. Disclosures written in a nontechnical language scored higher (M=2.992) than did disclosures written in a more technical language (M=2.248).

In the case of perceived understandability of the advertisement, significant ($p \leq .05$) interaction effects were found for the audio x distraction interaction, ($F(2,354)=10.243$, $p \leq .001$, $\eta^2=.055$) and language x distraction interaction ($F(2,354)=3.338$, $p=.04$, $\eta^2=.019$), but all other interactions failed to reach statistical significance. Additionally, the main effect of size failed to meet standard levels of significance ($F(1,354)=3.196$, $p=.08$, $\eta^2=.009$).

Managerially, our results suggest that when recall of the content of the disclosure statement is important, marketers should focus on the background upon which the disclosure appears and the language in which the disclosure is written. However, if the marketer's goal is instead to enhance the overall understandability of the message, simplifying the language in which the disclosure statement is written becomes critical, as in conditions of both no distraction and low distraction, technical language has a significant negative effect on perceived understandability. The effect of the modality of the disclosure should also be considered in light of its effect on perceived understandability. In the case of low distraction, presenting the disclosure in both print and auditory formats has little to no effect on understandability of the advertisement; while in both the moderate and high levels of distraction, dual modality results in lower levels of perceived understandability.

From an academic viewpoint, this study extends previous work in disclosure research by examining the effect of differing conditions under which disclosures appear. We also suggest more concrete alternatives to the FTC's standards for clear and conspicuous disclosure. First, we recommend that visual presentation of the disclosure should have text that is at least 1/25 of the screen and be presented in a color that drastically contrasts with the background. We further propose that the disclosure be presented at a time when there is no music or scene change. Finally, the disclosure should not contain language that the average consumer could not comprehend. It is our belief that these three guidelines, when implemented simultaneously, will ensure that television disclosures are able to meet the challenge of fully divulging "all information that could affect decision making and elucidate possibly misunderstood statements" (Herbst and Allan 2006, p. 213).

References

Douglass, Merrill E. and Donna N. Douglass (1993), *Manage Your Time, Your Work, Yourself.* New York: AMACOM.

Eggerton, John (2006), "Full Disclosure: Adelstein on Ads," *Broadcasting & Cable*, 136(6), 12-14.

Herbst, Kenneth C. and David Allan (2006), "The Effects of Brand Experience and an Advertisement's Disclaimer Speed on Purchase: Speak Slowly or Carry a Big Brand," International Journal of Advertising, *25*, 213-222.

Hoy, Mariea and J. Craig Andrews (2004), "Adherence of Prime-Time Televised Advertising Disclosures to the Clear and Conspicuous Standard: 1990 Versus 2002," *Journal of Public Policy & Marketing,* 23(2), 170-182.

Hoy, Mariea and May O. Lwin (2007), "Disclosures Exposed: Banner Ad Disclosure Adherence to FTC Guidance in the Top 100 U.S. Web Sites," *Journal of Consumer Affairs*, 41(2), 285-325.

Kolbe, Richard H. and Darrel D. Muehling (1995), "An Investigation of the Fine Print in Children's Television Advertising," *Journal of Current Issues & Research in Advertising*, 14(2), 77-95.

Morgan, Fred W. and Jeffrey J. Stoltman (2002), "Television Advertising Disclosures: An Empirical Assessment," *Journal of Business and Psychology*, 16(4), 515-535.

Muehling, Darrel D. and Richard H. Kolbe (1997), "Fine Print in Television Advertising: Views From the Top," *Journal of Advertising*, 26(3), 1-15.

Stewart, David W. and Ingrid M. Martin (2004), "Advertising Disclosures: Clear and Conspicuous or Understood and Used?," *Journal of Public Policy & Marketing*, 23(2), 183-192.

Consumer Transformations: A Hero's Journey

Aubrey Fowler III, Valdosta State University, USA
Courtney Droms, Valdosta State University, USA

Consumers seek to transform themselves, moving from one state of being into another; however, much of the literature that touch upon consumer transformations appears to be concerned with identity projects (i.e., Arnould and Price; Belk and Costa 1998; Kozinets 2001) or with simple modification of the self (i.e., Gimlin 2002; Pitts 2003; Sanders 2008). We take a different approach to understanding consumer transformations by understanding it as something much more than simply modifying the body with a tattoo or plastic surgery or developing an identity that one can carry around like a costume one wears to a party. Instead, we view consumer transformations as a full-body experience where the individual transforms him or herself from one state of being into another. In the case of our research, the consumers we investigate have undergone gastric bypass surgery which allows them to literally as well as figuratively transform themselves from an obese person into a much smaller.

For instance, Peter was, at one time, over three hundred pounds. For most of his life, he had tried, desperately at times, to lose weight using a variety of more traditional means such as dieting and exercise. Furthermore, he had often looked to the marketplace for help, engaging the services of Weight Watchers, doctor-regimented diet plans, and even so-called "diet camps." As failure after failure mounted, Peter became more and more desperate to lose weight. Finally, after much deliberation, he decided to have gastric bypass surgery. Now, a little over a year after the surgery, Peter is over a hundred pounds lighter with more pounds expected to be shed in the coming months. For him, the experience of losing "a whole other person" has been a transformation along the lines of "becoming someone else."

This transformation takes literal form in the shrinking body as well as in his relationships with the world around him. For instance, he has had to relearn how to navigate the world. In his previous life, he had to "squeeze into desk chairs at school or on airplanes in order to fit into a world made for skinny people." Now, he can fit comfortably into desk chairs and no longer feels out of place when he sits them, but he still moves down the airplane aisle in a sideways fashion instead of walking with his body facing straight ahead even though he can do so without bumping passengers that are already seated. Furthermore, he has had to undergo a mental transformation as well, moving from a person who had difficulties with the self-discipline required to maintain various weight-loss programs, to an individual who absolutely needs to maintain self-discipline in order to live. "I slipped one time," he says, "and had too much Gatorade with all that sugar and I was sick for almost a week. I simply can't take in anything like I used to, and I have to be really careful."

Through Peter's story and the narratives of other individuals who have undergone gastric bypass surgery, we find that consumers who transform themselves do so in a pattern that appears to follow the hero's journey as developed by Joseph Campbell (1968). The hero's journey is a mythic structure inherent within the literature and mythologies of many, if not all, cultures where the hero "ventures forth from the world of common day into a region of supernatural wonder" where "fabulous forces are there encountered and a decisive victory won," and then the hero returns to face a new status quo where he (or she) "bestow boons on his fellow man" (Campbell 1968, 30). The three stages of the journey that Campbell identifies are departure, initiation, and return.

Peter's story follows this same series of stages. The separation stage begins with Peter's navigation of the ordinary world of his obesity and ends with his entrance into "the belly of the whale" or the actual surgery itself. His Initiation stage involves the trials and victories that start upon waking up from the surgery and ends with the hero "seizing the sword" (Vogler 1992). In this moment, the hero essentially casts aside the remnants of the old self and takes firm possession of the new self. The return involves the reintegration of the hero into the ordinary world where, in Peter's case, he not only learns to navigate a "new" world in a "new" body, but with a renewed sense of self. Furthermore, he then has the opportunity to provide guidance to others who are seeking to transform themselves.

Our research follows in the tradition of bringing mythological structure to the various activities that consumers engage in. Levy (1981) determined that consumer interviews can be read as mythological narratives much as one might read fairy tales, fables, and other tales. Stern (1995) used Frye's taxonomy in an effort to better understand the various myths contained within both consumer narratives and advertisements dealing with Thanksgiving rituals. Holt and Thompson (2004) examine the various "heroic" myths related to masculinity within Western culture, finding that, in recent years, the "man-of-action" myth has risen as the celebrated cultural model of masculinity. Additional research from the psychology literature has used the hero's journey as a framework for understanding in counseling situations (Lawson 2005) and even spiritual development (Feinstein 1997).

Our research intends to define a framework for understanding consumer transformations that take place in the market. We believe that such a framework will be useful for marketers seeking to understand such transformations as well as though attempting to support those transformations. Ultimately, we believe that the framework that we develop will also move beyond the case presented here and extend into such contexts as helping individuals escape various addictions; deal with the loss of health, property, or loved ones; or even to achieve new states of spirituality, consciousness, or awareness. As such, we believe that our research will contribute to the field of transformative consumer research in addition to our understanding of basic consumer research.

Selected References

Campbell, Joseph (1968), *The Hero with a Thousand Faces*, Princeton NJ: Princeton University Press.

Holt, Douglas B. and Craig J. Thompson (2004), "Man-of-Action Heroes: The Pursuit of Heroic Masculinity in Everyday Consumption," *Journal of Consumer Research*, 31 (September), 425-440.

Levy, Sidney J. (1981), "Interpreting Consumer Mythology: A Structural Approach to Consumer Behavior," *Journal of Marketing*, 45 (Summer), 49-61.

Stern, Barbara B. (1995), "Consumer Myths: Frye's Taxonomy and the Structural Analysis of Consumption Text," *Journal of Consumer Research*, 22 (September), 165-185.

Vogler, Christopher (1992), *The Writer's Journey: Mythic Structure for Storytellers & Screenwriters*, Ann Arbor, Michigan: Braun-Brumfield Inc.

The Effects of Experience-Based Marketing Communication on Brand Relations and Hedonic Brand Attitudes: The Moderating Role of Affective Orientation

Marieke Fransen, University of Amsterdam, the Netherlands

Paulien Lodder, University of Amsterdam, the Netherlands

Introduction

Events such as the "Nike run London", and theme stores such as "M&M's World" and the "New World of Coca Cola" (i.e., experience-based marketing communications) are a growing phenomenon in the area of marketing communication. The emergence of this new form of marketing communication appears to be due to several reasons. First, the overuse of traditional media seems to call for a different strategy to be able to stand out from competitors (e.g., Smit and Neijens 1999). Second, as a result of today's global marketplace where many companies are competing for the same often limited market share, it has become difficult to compete and differentiate on mere product or brand characteristics. Third, consumers are more and more looking for marketing communications that are relevant for them as an individual and recognizes their need for novelty and excitement (Schmitt 1999). Fourth, consumers' growing need for the experiential aspects of consumption (Holbrook 2000; Holbrook and Hirschman 1981) resulting in less rational decision making strategies, calls for a different marketing communication approach.

Despite the continuous attention of marketers to experience-based marketing communication, surprisingly little empirical attention has been paid to this phenomenon. One reason for this could be that there is not one clear term or definition available in the literature. Terms that are proposed include "experiential marketing" (Schmitt 1999), "event marketing" (Wood and Masterman 2008), and "experience marketing" (Pine and Gillmore 1998). Unfortunately, these terms are used interchangeably but do not always apply the same definition. However, there seems to be consensus on several components. First, experience-based marketing communication is initialized by the company. Hence, the event, experience, or theme store is staged by a company distinguishing it from, for example, "event sponsoring" (e.g., Cornwell and Maignan 1998). Moreover, the experience of the consumer, rather than the marketing message (as in traditional forms of marketing communication), is of focal attention in experienced-based marketing communication strategies. Finally, it is generally assumed, but not empirically tested, that experience-based marketing communication enhances brand attitudes and brand relations.

The aim of the present research is to empirically examine the effects of experience-based marketing communication tools on consumer responses. It is hypothesized that a visit to a theme store (i.e., "Heineken the City") or an online co-creation task (designing a label for a Heineken beer bottle) can have a positive influence on brand attitude and brand relation (compared to a control condition). Furthermore, based on the assumption that experience-based marketing tools tap into consumers' emotions (rather than cognitions), it is expected that the effects of experience-based marketing tools on consumer responses is stronger for people with dispositional high (versus low) affective orientation (Booth-Butterfield and Booth-Butterfield 1990).

Method

We used a 3 (experience: visit to Heineken the city vs. designing a label for Heineken beer bottle vs. control) x 2 (affective orientation: high vs. low) between subjects design to test our hypotheses. Consumers (N=101) were randomly assigned to one of the experience conditions. Based on a median split, participants were classified as high or low in affective orientation. One week after visiting the theme store "Heineken the city" or performing the online design task participants received a questionnaire measuring consumer brand attitudes (Voss, Spangenberg, and Grohmann 2003) and brand relation (e.g., Chang and Chieng 2006). Note that participants in the control condition only received this latter questionnaire and were not exposed to any form of marketing communication.

Results and Discussion

A full factorial ANOVA revealed a main effect of experience demonstrating that participants who visited the theme store or designed a label online had a more positive attitude towards the brand (Heineken) and had a stronger brand relation than participants in the control condition. No differences were observed between the two different experience conditions. Moreover, we observed the expected interaction effect between experience and affective orientation showing that particularly participants with high dispositional affective orientation (compared with participants low in affective orientation) are affected by experience-based forms of marketing communications. Again, no differences between the two different forms of experiences (i.e., visit and design condition) were observed.

The present study shows initial evidence for a positive relation between experience-based marketing communication and consumer responses. Moreover, it reveals a boundary condition for these effects to occur, namely, the extent to which people have a dispositional affective orientation. These results provide promising evidence to support the growing field of experience-based marketing communication.

References

Booth-Butterfield, Melanie and Steve Booth-Butterfield (1990), "Conceptualizing affect as information in communication production," *Human Communication Research. 16*, 451-76.

Chang, Pao-Long and Ming-Hua Chieng (2006), "Building consumer-brand relationship: A cross-cultural experiential view," *Psychology & Marketing, 23*(11), 927-59.

Cornwell, T. B. and Maignan, I. (1998), "An international review of sponsorship research," *International Journal of Advertising, 27*(1), 1-22.

Holbrook Morris B. (2000), "The Millennial consumer in the texts of our times: Experience the entertainment," *Journal of Macromarketing, 20*, 178-92.

Holbrook Morris B. and Elizabeth C. Hirschman (1981), "The experiential aspects of consumption: Consumer fantasy, feelings and fun," *Journal of Consumer Research, 9*(2), 132-140.

Pine, B. Joseph and James H. Gilmore (1999), "*The experience economy: Work is theatre and every business is a stage*," Massachusetts, Harvard Business School Press.

Schmitt Bernd H. (1999), "Experiential marketing", *Journal of Marketing Management, 15(1-3)*, 53-57.

Smit Edith G. and Peter C. Neijens, (1999), "Publieksbeinvloeding te midden van overvloed", In: J. J. van Cuilenburg et al, (red). *Media in overvloed.* (pp. 134-149). Amsterdam University press.

Voss, Kevin E., Erik R. Spangenberg, and B. Grohmann (2003), "Measuring the hedonic and utilitarian dimensions of consumer attitude," *Journal of Marketing Research, 40*(3), 310-20.

Wood Emma, H. and Guy Masterman (2008), "Event marketing: Measuring and Experience," *paper presented at the 7th International Marketing Trends Congress, Venice*

Does What Happens in Virtual Worlds Stay in Virtual Worlds? A Theory of Planned Behavior Approach to the Examination of Cognitive Transference in Virtual Marketing Channels

Jason Gabisch, University of Massachusetts, USA

Online virtual environments differ significantly from traditional e-commerce in that virtual worlds move beyond information search by allowing users to simulate behaviors before carrying them out in the traditional channel. Several global companies such as Adidas, BMW, Dell, IBM, Microsoft, Reebok, and Coca-Cola have, or have had, a presence in Second Life. These companies have developed a virtual presence in an attempt to create and increase brand awareness with the hope that these brand experiences will eventually influence real world purchase intentions and behavior (Arakji and Lang 2008). Research has shown that consumers are increasingly employing multiple marketing channels before purchasing products, for instance some consumers search online before making purchases in the store (Kumar and Venkatesan 2005).

The main objective of this paper is to investigate whether brand experiences in the online virtual environment affect purchase intentions and behaviors in the real world. Data is collected specifically from users of the popular 3D virtual world Second Life. A primary gap in the virtual reality literature concerns the lack of empirical data collected from real-time virtual environments. Empirical studies to date have collected data using lab experiments where buyers interact with 3D objects on corporate websites or with computer-operated sales avatars (Li et al 2002; Suh and Lee 2005; Jiang and Benbasat 2005; Wang et al 2007; Holzwarth et al 2006).

The Theory of Planned Behavior (TPB; Ajzen 1991), an established social psychology model for predicting behavior, is employed and extended in this paper in order to improve the model's predictive power for explaining how virtual world brand experience affects real world purchase intentions and behavior. An extended version of the TPB model is presented and tested that includes the additional constructs of virtual world behavior, self-image congruency, and perceived diagnosticity. This paper contributes to the consumer psychology and marketing literature by presenting a conceptual model for understanding the ability of online virtual environments to serve as viable marketing channels for influencing consumer cognitions and behavior, and extends and applies the TPB model across multiple marketing channels.

The literature and concepts reviewed in this article include extant work on extensions to the TPB model, self-image congruency, perceived diagnosticity, and the impact of past behavior on predicting future purchasing behaviors. A conceptual model is developed where virtual world brand experience has a direct effect on purchase intentions and behavior in the TPB. Self-image congruency and perceived diagnosticity are hypothesized to moderate these relationships.

Online virtual environments have been identified in the literature as emerging marketing channels where consumers engage in information search, trial, and purchasing. Behavior in virtual environments may impact real world behavior, and studies have shown that consumer interactions with products in the virtual environment have the potential to increase product knowledge, purchase intentions, and lead to more confident brand attitudes (Li et al. 2002, Suh and Lee 2005). It is hypothesized in this paper that virtual world behavior with the brand will have a significant impact on real world purchasing intentions and behavior.

The self-image congruency construct has been identified in the marketing literature as the degree to which a product or brand matches a consumer' self-concept (Kressmann et al 2006, Sirgy et al 1997). Consumers who perceive brand experiences in the online virtual environment to be consistent with their self-image are more likely to transfer their intentions and behaviors to the real world. Thus, it is hypothesized in this paper that higher self-image congruency strengthens the relationship between virtual world brand behavior and real world purchase intentions and behavior. The perceived diagnosticity construct is a key variable in the product trial and virtual reality literature, and has been defined as "the extent to which a consumer believes that a particular shopping experience was helpful for evaluating the product" (Jiang and Benbasat 2004). It is likely that the more helpful a virtual experience for evaluating a brand, the stronger influence the virtual experience will have on real world purchase intentions and behaviors. It is hypothesized that the higher a consumer's perceived diagnosticity while interacting with brands in the virtual world, the stronger the relationship between virtual world behavior and real world purchase intentions and behavior.

To test the proposed hypotheses, a questionnaire was administered to 209 registered users of the virtual world, Second Life. The survey was made possible by collaborating with a marketing research firm that specializes in data collection within virtual worlds, such as Second Life. A random sample of users was sent online invitations asking them to participate in the survey. Respondents answered questions using memorable experiences with real life brands in Second Life that they could recall from memory. Gender, age, and nationality statistics for the sample were similar to the average reported statistics for the overall population of registered users in Second Life. Multi-item scales were adapted from the literature and used to measure the constructs. All scale reliabilities were above .70. Four hierarchical multiple regression analyses were performed to test the main effects of virtual world behavior on real world purchase intentions and behavior, in addition to exploring the moderation effects of self-image congruency and perceived diagnosticity.

Overall, the findings from this study provide strong support for an extended version of the TPB that includes virtual world behavior, self-image congruency, and perceived diagnosticity. Virtual world behavior is found to explain unique variance in both real world purchase intentions and behavior, thus indicating that brand experiences in the virtual world may have a significant impact on consumer purchasing in the real world. Self-image congruence and perceived diagnosticity are found to moderate the relationship between virtual world behavior and real world purchase intentions. Respondents who perceived their virtual world brand experience as more consistent with their self-concept formed higher purchase intentions, suggesting that consumers may tend to behave in ways that are congruent with their self-image across various marketing channels. Also, the more realistic and helpful brand experiences in the virtual world are perceived to be by consumers, the more influence those virtual world brand experiences have on real world purchasing behavior.

References

Aizen, Icek (1991), "The Theory of Planned Behavior," *Organizational Behavior and Human Decision Processes*, 50 (2), 179-211.

Arakji, Reina Y. and Karl R. Lang (2008), "Avatar Business Value Analysis: A Method for the Evaluation of Business Value Creation in Virtual Commerce," *Journal of Electronic Commerce Research*, 9 (3), 207-218.

Holzwarth, Martin, Chris Janiszewski, and Marcus M. Neumann (2006), "The Influence of Avatars on Online Consumer Shopping Behavior," *Journal of Marketing*, 70 (October), 19-36.

Jiang, Zhenhui, and Izak Benbasat (2004), "Virtual Product Experience: Effects of Visual and Functional Control of Products on Perceived Diagnosticity and Flow in Electronic Shopping," *Journal of Management Information Systems*, 21 (3), 111-147.

Kressmann, Frank, M. Joseph Sirgy, Andreas Herrmann, Frank Huber, Stephanie Huber, and Dong-Jin Lee (2006), "Direct and Indirect Effects of Self-Image Congruence on Brand Loyalty," *Journal of Business Research*, 59 (9), 955-964.

Kumar, V. and Rajkumar Venkatesan (2005), "Who are the multichannel shoppers and how do they perform?: Correlates of multichannel shopping behavior', *Journal of Interactive Marketing*, 19 (2), 44-62.

Li, Hairong, Terry Daugherty, and Frank Biocca (2002), "Impact of 3-D Advertising on Product Knowledge, Brand Attitude, and Purchase Intention: The Mediating Role of Presence," *Journal of Advertising*, 31 (3), 43-57.

Sirgy, M. Joseph, Druv Grewal, Tamara F. Mangleburg, Jae-ok Park, Kye-Sung Chon, C.B. Claiborne, J.S. Johar, and Harold Berkman (1997), "Assessing the Predictive Validity of Two Methods of Measuring Self-Image Congruence," *Journal of the Academy of Marketing Science*, 25 (3), 229-241.

Suh, Kil-Soo, and Young Eun Lee (2005), "The Effects of Virtual Reality on Consumer Learning: An Empirical Investigation," *MIS Quarterly*, 29 (4), 673-697.

Wang, Liz C., Julie Baker, Judy A. Wagner, and Kirk Wakefield, (2007), "Can a Retail Web Site be Social," *Journal of Marketing*, 71 (3), 143-157.

When Avoidable Losses Are Perceived as Gains: Repair Costs and Their Effects in New Product Purchases

Andrew Gershoff, University of Michigan, USA
Beatriz Pereira, University of Michigan, USA

Consumers frequently consider money that they save as a gain, consistent with prospect theory (Kahneman and Tversky 1979). Studies have shown this phenomenon in different purchase situations, such as rebates (Thaler 1985) and trade-ins (Okada 2001). When presented with these savings, consumers show less price sensitivity in new purchases. In particular, saving money can be viewed as a gain by avoiding a loss (i.e. in trade-ins, waste is avoided by attributing a residual value to the used product).

But what about cases where a consumer finds herself facing a payment to repair a broken product or replace a lost item? Does framing the purchase of a better camera as a way to avoid paying to repair the old camera lead to decreased price sensitivity for the new one?

This paper provides evidence that other types of avoidable losses cause a reduction in the price sensitivity of consumers, in particular when a product is in need of repair. Repairing a broken product is painful since the repair cost is perceived as a loss. In order to return to the status quo, the consumer must sacrifice money. This makes a repair quite different from a purchase, where the money is intended to be spent and thus is not viewed as a loss (Novemsky and Kahneman 2005). A similar loss occurs in the case of a consumer losing a possession, and purchasing the same item again. The repurchase only returns the consumer to the status quo.

This research builds on the mental accounting literature (Thaler 1985). If a consumer seriously considers repairing a broken product, the repair cost is likely allocated to its own mental account. Actively searching for repair prices indicates a certain level of commitment to the repair option and also increases the rigor of budgeting (Heath and Soll 1996), as some amount of money is allocated to the repair account.

If the consumer then decides not to repair, the amount allocated to the repair account remains unspent. Hence, we hypothesize that a repair amount that was not spent is likely to be transferred from the repair account to the replacement account. This gain will therefore reduce price sensitivity in the purchase of the replacement. In other words, the higher the repair amount, the less price sensitive the consumer will be in the new purchase. According to prospect theory the perceived gains should increase as the repair costs increase, but at decreasing rates (Kahneman and Tversky 1979; Thaler 1980).

We conducted two experiments to test our hypothesis that repair cost influences repurchase price sensitivity. In the first study, we manipulated repair prices for washing machines and laptop computers, two common household durable goods. Participants were told to imagine that a washing machine they had bought seven years ago for \$500 was in need of repair (or a one year old laptop computer they had bought for \$1,600). The repair price manipulation had levels representing 40%, 80% or 110% of the original price (\$200, \$400 and \$550 for the washer and \$640, \$1,280 and \$1,760 for the laptop). Participants were asked to provide their willingness to pay for a new product using a scale with prices from \$250 to \$750 in \$50 increments for the washer and from \$500 to \$3,000 in \$250 increments for the laptop. As predicted, an ANOVA showed that the mean willingness to pay increased as the repair costs increased (washer: $F(1,81)=12.622, p<.001, M_{40\%}=4.61, M_{80\%}=7.12, M_{110\%}=7.83$; laptop: $F(1,88)=5.590, p<.005, M_{40\%}=4.49, M_{80\%}=5.83, M_{110\%}=6.16$).

In the second study we told participants that they had a 4 megapixels digital camera that recently broke. The choice task was to select a price for a new camera (\$200, \$250 or \$300 for a 4, 5 or 6 megapixels camera, respectively). Half of the participants were asked first whether they would repair the broken camera, and then chose between the three price/feature levels. The others had just one decision task: repair the broken camera or purchase one of the three new alternatives. This manipulation was intended to force participants to broadly or narrowly bracket the decisions (Read, Loewenstein and Rabin 1999), and to support the hypothesis that the repair cost needs to be considered as a separate option to effectively reduce price sensitivity. In this case, setting the decision stages together (broad bracketing) would allow participants to see that the repair was just one of several possibilities, which would not allow them to feel the pain of spending money to return to the status quo. The narrow (sequential) versus broad (one stage) decision making was also included to rule out alternative explanations, such as participants inferring that a higher repair price meant that their original camera was more expensive.

An ANOVA revealed a main effect of repair cost ($F(2,98)=4.546$, $p<.025$) and an interaction between repair cost level and decision format ($F(2,98)=5.267$, $p<.01$). As repair prices increase, participants move from the cheapest camera model to the more expensive ones, but only in the sequential decision condition. The mean willingness to pay for each repair level in the sequential decision was $M_{\$100}=221.88$; $M_{\$150}=255.56$; $M_{\$200}=275$. The willingness to pay means for each repair level in the non-sequential decision was $M_{\$100}=244.12$; $M_{\$150}=235.56$; $M_{\$200}=243.75$. Although we expected that all means in the sequential decision condition would be greater than the means in no non-sequential decision, the mean difference found in the two conditions where the repair price was $100 is not significant. These results support our proposition that the avoided loss–the repair amount–takes the form of a gain by being transferred to the product account.

This research provides support for the hypothesis that repair costs can be perceived as a gain towards the product account when the consumer decides not to do the repair, thus reducing the price sensitivity towards the replacement good. Our findings seem to be relevant both to consumers–that should be aware that money saved is not a gain–and to marketers–that could try to create strategies to sell more expensive products by framing repairs as perceived gains.

References

Heath, Chip, and Jack B. Soll (1996), "Mental Budgeting and Consumer Decisions", *Journal of Consumer Research*, 23 (June), 40-52.

Kahneman, Daniel and Amos Tversky (1979), "Prospect Theory: An Analysis of Decision under Risk", *Econometrica*, 47 (March), 263-291.

Novemsky, Nathan and Daniel Kahneman (2005), "The Boundaries of Loss Aversion", *Journal of Marketing Research,* 42 (May), 119-128.

Okada, Erica Mina (2001), "Trade?ins, Mental Accounting, and Product Replacement Decisions", *Journal of Marketing Research,* 27 (March), 433-446.

Read, Daniel, George Loewenstein and Matthew Rabin (1999), "Choice Bracketing", *Journal of Risk and Uncertainty,* 19 (December), 171-197.

Thaler, Richard (1980), "Toward a Positive Theory of Consumer Choice", *Journal of Economic Behavior and Organization,* 1 (March), 39-60.

Thaler, Richard (1985), "Mental Accounting and Consumer Choice", *Marketing Science,* 4 (summer), 199-214.

Anonymous and Unanimous: The Impact of Anonymity on Judgments of Opinion Representativeness

Dilney Goncalves, INSEAD, France
Amitava Chattopadhyay, INSEAD, Singapore

John is about to write an online review about a digital camera that he just purchased. He wants his opinion to have the greatest impact possible. Should he provide an anonymous opinion or should he identify himself? Common sense and research on communication suggest that identified sources make messages more trustworthy (Rains 2007). The decision to act on an opinion, however, depends not only on its perceived trustworthiness, but also on its perceived *representativeness*: is the opinion representative of the population of customers or just an isolated case? The question we address is: "Are people more likely to infer a more representative (versus more idiosyncratic) opinion when the source is anonymous or identified?" Building on attribution theories, we propose that it is easier to attribute an opinion to idiosyncratic preferences when the opinion is associated with a name than when it is anonymous.

Attribution theories suggest that behaviors result from the summation of dispositions and situational factors (Jones & Davis 1965, Kelley 1967). In our research, the behavior of interest is writing the opinion or review. Thus, a product review reveals the summation of the reviewer's dispositions and situational factors, one of which is the product's actual performance. If a consumer who reads the review wants to infer how good the product is, he or she has to discount the reviewer's dispositions. If the consumer can easily attribute the review to the reviewer's dispositions, he or she will infer that the review does not say much about the product. Consequently, this consumer will think that this is an isolated opinion and not a consensus. When a person expresses an opinion that is known to be a consensus, it is difficult to attribute it to that person's idiosyncratic dispositions. Conversely, if the opinion is known not to be a consensus, it is easy to attribute it to the person who produced it (Jones and Davis 1965).

We hypothesize that people have learned from experience that idiosyncratic opinions are strongly associated to a person's identity whereas consensuses are weakly associated with any one person. Moreover, people use this knowledge to make the reverse causal inferences: if an opinion is difficult to link to one particular person, it is probably a consensus. Thus, we predict that if an opinion is identified (as opposed to anonymous), it is easier to make a dispositional attribution, and therefore the identified opinion is less likely to perceived as representative that the anonymous one.

Study 1

The first study was a 2 (anonymity: anonymous vs. identified) X 2 (opinion valence: positive vs. negative) between-subjects factorial. Participants (n=251) read a scenario where they took the role of a restaurant manager. They were told that they had received some customer feedback. Then they read the feedback which was either positive or negative. In the identified condition, the last line of the feedback form displayed a name–purportedly of the customer who wrote the feedback. Participants in the anonymous condition did not see any name.

Two names were used: one common and one uncommon. After reading the feedback, all participants were asked to estimate the percentage of the restaurant's customers that shared the same opinion as presented in the form.

We obtained a significant interaction between opinion valence and anonymity. People in the negative condition estimated the opinion to be less general in the identified condition (43% of the population of customers) than in the anonymous condition (53%; $F(1,109)=4.16$, $p<0.05$). In the positive condition, there was no significant difference between estimates based on identified and anonymous opinions (55% vs. 53% respectively). The significant difference found in the negative conditions is consistent with more dispositional attributions being made when the name was presented than when it was absent. The lack of a significant difference in the positive conditions might have happened because people did not generate causal attributions. This finding is consistent with research suggesting that negative events generate more spontaneous causal attributions than positive events (Gilbert & Malone 1995). This happens because negative events are usually unexpected, especially given our scenario where participants acted as the restaurant manager. Positive events can lead to spontaneous causal attributions, however, if they are unexpected (Kanazawa 1992). In study 2 we lead participants to engage in causal attributions by using expected versus unexpected reviews. In addition, we measure Need for Cognitive Closure (NFCC), an individual characteristic that should influence the extent to which people make causal attributions (Kruglanski, Webster, & Klem 1993; Webster & Kruglanski 1994).

Study 2

The second study was a 2 (reviews: expected vs. unexpected) x 2 (anonymity: anonymous vs. identified) between-subjects factorial. Participants (n=144) were told they would read a product review purportedly picked at random from Amazon.com. Participants read a review confirming or disconfirming prior–experimentally manipulated–expectations. Anonymity was manipulated just like in study 1. In addition to percentage estimates, we measured the predictability and need for order and structure subscales of the NFCC Scale. We predicted that individuals high in these scales will make more dispositional attributions because dispositional attributions make the world seem more predictable.

We obtained a 3-way interaction between NFCC, expectedness, and anonymity. There was no effect of anonymity among individuals low in NFCC. Among individuals high in NFCC, there was a significant interaction between expectedness and anonymity ($F(1,63)=8.17$, $p=.006$): unexpected anonymous reviews were estimated to represent 59.8% of consumers who had used the product whereas unexpected identified reviews were estimated to represent 43.9% of consumers ($F(1,34)=3.08$, $p=.058$). Expected reviews showed the opposite pattern: identified reviews were estimated to represent 82.5% of consumers whereas anonymous reviews were estimated to represent 64.6% of consumers ($F(1,29)=4.9$, $p=.035$). Whereas the results for unexpected reviews are in accordance with our predictions, those of expected reviews were not predicted.

We showed that anonymity increases perceived representativeness of opinions. Our results suggest that causal attributions underlie the effect. In future studies we will test the process by directly manipulating ease of attribution and how these inferences influence attitudes and choice. This research contributes to the literature in representativeness judgments and word-of-mouth.

Bibliography

Gilbert, D. T., & Malone, P. S. (1995). The correspondence bias. *Psychological Bulletin, 117*(1), 21-38.

Jones, E. E. & Davis, K. E. (1965). From acts to dispositions: The attribution process in person perception.(In L. Berkowitz (Ed.), *Advances in experimental social psychology* (Vol. 2, pp. 219—266). San Diego, CA: Academic Press.)

Kanazawa, S. (1992). Outcome or Expectancy? Antecedent of Spontaneous Causal Attribution. *Personality and Social Psychology Bulletin, 18*(6), 659-668.

Kelley, H. H. (1967). Attribution theory in social psychology.(In D. Levine (Ed.), *Nebraska Symposium on Motivation* (Vol. 15, pp. 192—238). Lincoln: University of Nebraska Press.)

Kruglanski, A. W., Webster, D. M., & Klem, A. (1993). Motivated resistance and openness to persuasion in the presence or absence of prior information. *Journal of Personality and Social Psychology, 65*(5), 861-76.

Rains, S. A. (2007). The Impact of Anonymity on Perceptions of Source Credibility and Influence in Computer-Mediated Group Communication: A Test of Two Competing Hypotheses. *Communication Research, 34*(1), 100-125.

Tversky, A., & Kahneman, D. (1974). Judgment under Uncertainty: Heuristics and Biases. *Science, 185*(4157), 1124-1131.

Webster, D. M., & Kruglanski, A. W. (1994). Individual differences in need for cognitive closure. *Journal of Personality and Social Psychology, 67*(6), 1049-62.

Developing Positive Attitudes and Strong Goals to Purchase Products of Fantasy

R. Justin Goss, University of Texas at San Antonio, USA
Ian M. Handley, Montana State University, USA
Brett M. Runnion, Montana State University, USA

Individuals often fantasize about obtaining better products such as a better car, a new HDTV, or a dream vacation. Yet, as ubiquitous as such fantasies are, they are often times not realized. Oettingen (1996) has suggested that how individuals think about the future may be important in understanding how they come to set, and commit to, goals to achieve fantasies. In her Fantasy Realization Theory (FRT), Oettingen (1996) offers three ways an individual might deal with fantasies about the future, ultimately influencing goal formation and commitment. Two of the possibilities create a readiness to act that is independent of individuals' expectations, whereas the third entails an expectancy-based readiness to act.

First, individuals may largely disregard positive fantasies about the future and instead dwell on a negative reality that blocks a desired future. In this case, individuals experience no need or direction in which to act. Therefore, their expectations about achieving the fantasy do not heavily influence goal formation or strength.

Second, individuals can think about positive fantasies without considering current situations that may impede their fantasy-realization. As a result, they experience no need to act (i.e., overcome impediments), and therefore their expectations about achieving the fantasy do not heavily influence goal formation or strength.

Third, individuals may contrast a positive fantasy with a negative reality that blocks the potential realization of that fantasy. In doing so, the desired future becomes something that is to be attained, and the negative reality becomes something that must be altered. In this case, a necessity to act is produced. If individuals' expectations for attaining the fantasy are high (low), then a goal will (will not) be formed.

Prior FRT research has investigated pre-existing expectations for fantasy realization (Oettingen et al. 2001). In the current research, expectations for fantasy realization were manipulated by presenting participants an advertisement in which strong arguments made electronic products seem easily attainable or weak arguments made electronic products seem less attainable. That is, we took advantage of the idea that strong, persuasive arguments are those that communicate a highly desired (or undesired) outcome is likely (expected) if one adopts what is advocated within the message (Fishbein and Ajzen 1975). Based on FRT, we reasoned that participants who mentally contrast product fantasies and negative realities should consider the expectations within arguments, and form stronger goals to, and more favorable attitudes toward, purchasing an electronics product when doing so is supported by strong versus weak arguments. Further, argument strength will not affect the positive- or negative-only conditions. In the present experiment, goals strength was operationalized as expectations, plans, motivation, and attitudes regarding purchasing a fantasy electronic product.

To test our hypotheses, undergraduate participants were randomly assigned to the conditions of a 3 (Mindset Type: Positive Fantasy vs. Negative Reality vs. Mental Contrast) X 2 (Advertisement Quality: Strong vs. Weak) factorial design. Following Oettingen et al. (2001), participants first listed 4 positive fantasies about owning a desired electronics product and 4 negative realities standing in the way of that fantasy. Participants were then induced to either consider only *positive fantasies* about buying a desired electronics product, dwell on *negative realities* that stand in the way of buying the product, or *mentally contrasting* both. Participants were then presented with an advertisement that offered either excellent incentives (*strong arguments*) or lackluster incentives (*weak arguments*) for buying the electronic product from an advertised store We then administered a questionnaire measuring participants' expectations, plans, motivation, and attitudes regarding purchasing a fantasy electronic product.

For all dependent measures, planned comparison confirmed significant differences between participants who received the strong versus weak advertisement, but only for the mental-contrast conditions. Therefore, for ease of presentation, the fantasy and negative-reality conditions were combined and compared to the mental-contrast condition. As predicted, participants in the mental contrast condition who received a strong versus weak advertisement demonstrated more positive attitudes, higher expectations, and stronger motivation and plans (goals) about buying a fantasy electronics product. Further, participants in the positive-fantasy only and negative-reality only conditions did not differ on these measures, regardless of which persuasive advertisement they received.

These results demonstrate that Fantasy Realization Theory can be used to predict consumer attitudes, expectations, and motivations. Specifically, by prompting consumers to contrast their present reality against a positive consumer fantasy, marketing managers can more successfully create positive consumer attitudes, expectations, and motivations by presenting strong arguments for purchasing a product.

We predict that individuals in the mental-contrast conditions will generate more positive thoughts in response to the strong versus weak advertisement, whereas individuals in the other conditions will not. This idea follows from FRT which suggests that only individuals who mentally contrast reality and fantasy consult their expectations (in this case provided by advertisement arguments) to determine goal commitment. Further, as is commonly observed in persuasion research (Petty and Wegener 1998), these thoughts should mediate the relationship between mental set and ultimate consumer attitudes. We also predict that only individuals in the mental-contrast conditions will indicate in their thought listings more plans and reports of intentions to purchase a fantasy product after reading strong versus weak advertisements. Importantly, this would provide evidence that individuals in this condition spontaneously devise plans and intentions in response to expectations, an effect not yet observed but consistent with FRT.

Selected References

Fishbein, Martin and Icek Ajzen (1975), *Belief, Attitude, Intention, and Behavior: An Introduction to Theory and Research*, Reading, MA: Addison-Wesley.

Oettingen, Gabrielle, Hyeon-ju Pak, and Karoline Schnetter (2001), "Self-Regulation of Goal Setting: Turning Free Fantasies About the Future Into Binding Goals," *Journal of Personality and Social Psychology*, 80 (May), 736-53.

Oettingen, Gabrielle (1996), "Positive Fantasy and Motivation," in *The Psychology of Action: Linking Cognition and Motivation to Behavior*, eds. Peter. M. Gollwitzer and John A. Bargh, New York, NY: Guilford Press, 236-59.

Petty, Richard. E. and Daniel T. Wegener (1998). "Attitude Change: Multiple Roles for Persuasion Variables," in *The Handbook of Social Psychology*, 4th ed., Vol. 1, eds. Daniel Gilbert, Susan T. Fiske, and Gardner Lindzey, New York, NY: McGraw-Hill, 323-90.

Celebrity Endorsements and Advertising Effectiveness: The Importance of Value Congruence

Eda Gurel-Atay, University of Oregon, USA
Lynn Kahle, University of Oregon, USA

A number of companies use celebrities in advertisements to promote different kinds of products. Indeed, millions of dollars are spent on celebrity contracts each year by assuming that the benefits of using celebrities will exceed the costs. Given the popularity and importance of celebrity endorsements, the impact of celebrity endorsements on advertising effectiveness has been studied extensively over the last 30 years. Source variables, i.e., credibility (which includes expertise and trustworthiness) and attractiveness (which includes familiarity, similarity, and likeability), have been used by many researchers to understand the impact of celebrity endorsements. However, the underlying mechanisms used to explain the impact of these source variables on the relationship between celebrity endorsement and advertising effectiveness fail to converge.

One of the theories used frequently by researchers to explain the impact of celebrity endorsements is the match-up hypothesis. It suggests that there should be a good fit between the celebrity and the product; however, it is not clear what constitutes a good fit. Some researchers have focused on the attractiveness dimension and suggested that attractive celebrities will be more effective if they are used to promote attractiveness-related products, such as razors (e.g., Kahle and Homer 1985; Kamins 1990). Other researchers focused on the expertise, or product relatedness, dimension. They claimed that when there is congruency between the product type and the celebrity (as in the case of a sports athlete promoting sports shoes), advertising effectiveness will be enhanced (e.g., Till and Busler 2000). The congruency between celebrities and consumers has also been studied. For instance, Boyd and Shank (2004) showed that when there is a fit between the celebrity and consumer in terms of gender, consumers perceive the celebrity as more trustworthy, regardless of the product type endorsed by the celebrity.

The purpose of this study is to introduce another dimension for the match-up hypothesis: values. Because values are higher-order constructs that can affect other consumer-related constructs, such as consumer attitudes and behaviors, it is important to consider them when examining the impacts of celebrity-product congruence on advertising effectiveness. In other words, the congruency between consumers' perceptions of celebrities' values and product values might play an important role in determining the effectiveness of celebrity endorsements. Specifically, it is posited in this study that when there is a high level of value congruence between celebrities and products, advertisements will be more effective. The fit between celebrities and consumers is also important. As suggested by similarity studies (e.g., Feick and Higie 1992), the values of celebrities should be similar to the values of target consumers for effective celebrity endorsement.

To test the effects of congruency between celebrity's values, product values, and consumer values on advertising effectiveness, an experiment was designed. Several pilot tests were conducted to determine the value that would be used in the experimental ad (an internal value: a sense of accomplishment, cf. Homer and Kahle 1988), select the celebrity that was perceived as endorsing that value (Michael Jordan, M=8.19/9.00), and choose product categories that were perceived as high (congruent: fitness machine, M=5.39/9.00) or low (incongruent: beer, M=2.98/9.00) on that value. In other words, based on pilot tests, it was decided that fitness machine was congruent with Michael Jordan and beer was incongruent with Michael Jordan in terms of "a sense of accomplishment" value.

A 2 (product value: congruent vs. incongruent) X 3 (consumer values: internal vs. external vs. fun/excitement) between-subjects design was used to examine the impact of value congruence on two key dependent variables: attitude toward brand, and purchase intention. Based on Homer and Kahle's suggestion, consumer values were categorized into three dimensions. Internal values reflect the belief that people can fulfill their values by themselves and include self-fulfilling, a sense of accomplishment, and self-respect. External values reflect the belief that people are dependent on others to fulfill their values and include being well-respected, sense of belonging, security, and warm relationships with others. The last dimension includes fun and enjoyment and excitement values and can be fulfilled either internally or externally. Two magazine ads were designed to manipulate the congruence between the celebrity and product categories. In one ad, Michael Jordan was endorsing a treadmill, and in the other ad, he was endorsing beer. Participants first (N=98 college students) were exposed to one of these experimental ads and several real magazine ads. Then, they completed the measures for consumer values (i.e., List of Values, cf. Kahle 1996), attitude toward brand, purchase intention, celebrity characteristics (e.g., likeability, attractiveness, expertise, and familiarity), and manipulation check.

A MANCOVA was conducted on two dependent variables (i.e., attitude toward brand and purchase intention) by using product congruence and consumer values as independent variables, and celebrity characteristics and attitude toward ad as covariates. With the use of Wilks' criterion, the combined DVs were significantly related to one of the covariates, namely attitude toward ad (F (2, 89)=8.815, p<.001). After adjusting for this covariate, product value congruence had a significant main effect on the combined DVs (F (2, 89)=10.05, p<.001), consumer values had a marginal effect on the combined DVs (F (4, 178)=2.152, p<.076), and the interaction between product value congruence and consumer values had a marginal effect on the combined DVs (F (4, 178)=2.053, p<.092). Univariate analysis revealed that product value congruence and consumer values had significant main effects on attitude toward brand but not on purchase intention. Moreover, planned t-tests showed that attitude toward brand was more favorable when participants were exposed to a congruent experimental ad (i.e., when the product value was congruent with the celebrity's value; M=5.69) than when participants were exposed to an incongruent ad (M=4.59; t=4.513, p<.001). Attitude toward brand was also more favorable for participants who endorsed external values (M=5.42) than for participants who endorsed internal values (M=4.69; t=-2.118, p<.038). Univariate analysis also showed that the interaction between product value congruence and consumer values had significant effects on both DVs. Further analyses indicated that when the product value was congruent with the celebrity's value, consumers with external values had more favorable attitudes toward the brand (M=6.41) than consumers with internal values (M=4.93, t=-3.145, p<.005) and consumers with fun/excitement values (M=5.48, t=2.620, p<.015). Similarly, when the product value was congruent with the celebrity's value, consumers with external values had higher intentions to buy the brand (M=4.59) than consumers with internal values (M=2.52, t=-3.288, p<.005) and consumers with fun/excitement values (M=3.34, t=1.767, p<.087).

The present research shows that even a single ad based on value congruence is capable of affecting attitude toward brand and purchase intention. Specifically, this study provides evidence that the congruence between celebrity values and product values has positive impacts on key DVs. Interestingly; more favorable results were obtained when consumers' values were incongruent with the celebrity values and product values. This finding supports the idea that moderate incongruity might be more persuasive through creating some curiosity (e.g., Lee and Thorson 2008).

Overall, this study provide some insights that value congruence adds to the variance explained in advertising effectiveness, beyond and above attractiveness and expertise dimensions of the match-up hypothesis. Moreover, considering consumer values will help researchers and practitioners to measure the effectiveness of celebrity endorsements more reliably.

References

Boyd, Thomas C., and Matthew D. Shank (2004), "Athletes as Product Endorsers: The Effect of Gender and Product Relatedness," *Sport Marketing Quarterly*, 13 (2), 82-93.

Feick, Lawrence, and Robin A. Higie (1992), "The Effects of Preference Heterogeneity and Source Characteristics on Ad Processing and Judgments about Endorsers," *Journal of Advertising*, 21 (2), 9-24.

Homer, P. M. and Kahle, L. R. (1988), "Structural Equation Test of the Value-Attitude-Behavior Hierarchy," *Journal of Personality and Social Psychology*, 54 (4), 638-646.

Kahle, L. R. (1996), "Social Values and Consumer Behavior: Research from the List of Values," in *The Psychology of Values: The Ontario Symposium*, Volume 8, ed. Clive Seligman, James M. Olson, and Mark P. Zanna, Mahwah, NJ: Lawrence Erlbaum Associates, 135-152.

Kahle, Lynn R. and Pamela M. Homer (1985), "Physical Attractiveness of the Celebrity Endorser: A Social Adaptation Perspective," *Journal of Consumer Research*, 11 (March), 954–961.

Kamins, Michael A. (1990), "An Investigation into the Match-Up Hypothesis in Celebrity Advertising: When Beauty May Be Only Skin Deep," *Journal of Advertising*, 19 (1), 4–13.

Lee, Jung-Gyo, and Esther Thorson (2008), "The Impact of Celebrity-Product Incongruence on the Effectiveness of Product Endorsement," *Journal of Advertising Research*, September, 433-449.

Till, Brian D., and Michael Busler (2000), "The Match-Up Hypothesis: Physical Attractiveness, Expertise, and The Role of Fit on Brand Attitude, Purchase Intent, and Brand Beliefs," *Journal of Advertising*, 29 (3), 1-14.

Self-Brand Attraction: An Interpersonal Attraction Approach to Brand Relationships

Lora M. Harding, Northwestern University, USA
Ashlee Humphreys, Northwestern University, USA

Are brand-consumer relationships the same as interpersonal relationships? For almost a decade, brands have been theorized as parasocial entities with which consumers can form personal attachments (Aaker 1997; Fournier 1998). But what is the nature of this relationship? Further, can the interpersonal metaphor truly be extended to the person-brand context? If brands do have personalities, is it enough to simply like the "person"? Or, might a feeling of reciprocated affection from the brand itself also play a role, as human interpersonal attraction theory might predict?

In this research, we build from previous research in marketing that has accounted for brand-consumer connections as relationships (Fournier 1998) and theorized that brands have personalities (Aaker 1997). Specifically, we take both of these ideas seriously by using the interpersonal attraction paradigm from relationship research (Byrne 1961) to better understand brand relationships and to predict self-brand attraction better than competing theorizations (e.g., Keller 1993). Our findings show that felt similarity toward the brand and its associations is necessary, but does not sufficiently account for consumers' opinions toward, connections with, and felt closeness to brands (i.e., the brand relationship). We further specify Fournier's insight by showing that relationships aren't simply about felt kinship with brands; they're dyadic in the sense that one must also consider the reciprocal liking of the brand for the person.

Thus, in accordance with Byrne's theory of interpersonal attraction (Byrne 1971), we predicted participants would convey a closer relationship to the brand the more similar they felt they were to the brand. Also in accordance with Byrne's findings, we predicted the brand's attitude toward the participant would play a role. Specifically, we predicted that the positive relationship between self-brand similarity and brand relationship closeness would only hold when participants felt that the brand did not like them more than they liked the brand. This prediction stems from research in the reciprocity literature, which suggests that excessive liking can convey unselectivity and even desperation (Eastwick, Finkel, Mochon, and Ariely 2007). To test these predictions, we adapted Byrne's interpersonal attraction paradigm to a consumer-brand setting. Whereas Byrne manipulated self-other similarity by varying the extent to which the parties expressed like attitudes toward a variety of topics, we assessed self-brand similarity by measuring these attitudes. Furthermore, whereas Byrne manipulated others' attitudes toward the self by supplying contrived responses to an interpersonal judgment scale, we measured both participants' liking for the target brand and the felt reciprocal liking of the brand for the participant. The details of our survey methodology are described below.

In the first part of the survey, participants were asked to indicate their attitudes toward several topics (e.g., musical tastes; Byrne 1971). After several unrelated filler tasks, participants then took part in the second part of the survey which assessed their relationship with Chevrolet, an automotive brand we anticipated would elicit varied similarity and feeling reciprocation assessments. First, we asked participants to imagine Chevrolet as a person (Aaker 1997) and to write a brief description of that person. Next, they were asked to project the brand's attitudes toward the same topics assessed earlier. Self-brand attitude discrepancies that fell within one standard deviation were considered similar attitudes, the sum of which comprised our self-brand similarity index. We then elicited participants' liking for the brand as a person and the felt reciprocal liking of the brand for the participant (Byrne 1961, 1971). The difference between these ratings was used as our measure of self-brand reciprocation, with higher scores representing over-reciprocation by the participant and lower scores representing over-reciprocation by the brand. Finally, we assessed participants' connection with the brand (Moore and Homer 2008), self-brand overlap (Aron, Aron, and Smollan 1992), and their overall opinion of the brand (four 7-point semantic differentials)—dependent measures selected to capture brand relationship closeness.

Regression analyses were conducted in which each of the dependent measures was regressed on self-brand similarity, self-brand reciprocation, and the product of the two. Results revealed the predicted main effect of similarity. For all three measures of brand relationship closeness, participants expressed a stronger connection to, a greater overlap with, and a more favorable opinion of Chevrolet when they felt they shared attitudes with the brand. Results also revealed the predicted interaction between self-brand similarity and feeling reciprocation for two of the three dependent variables—self-brand overlap and brand attitude. To explore the nature of this interaction, we conducted a 2 x 2 between-participants ANOVA, separating those above and below the median for both independent variables. As predicted, there was a positive relationship between self-brand similarity and brand relationship closeness that held only when the brand is perceived to equally- or under-reciprocate affection.

These findings have several implications for consumer research. First, they prompt a reappraisal of our understanding of brands from a purely cognitive perspective, where brand equity is a product of brand association and valance (Keller 1993). Our findings suggest that brand liking is the product of a complex parasocial interplay that requires both projection of attitudes and reciprocated liking, at least for high-involvement products such as automobiles. Secondly, our work further specifies the nature of the consumer-brand relationship explored in previous research. We find that similarity of attitudes between the consumer and the brand is one important component of the brand relationship. However, we also find that consumers consider the extent to which their feelings toward the brand are reciprocated. In particular, our findings suggest that self-brand similarity exerts a positive influence on brand relationship closeness, but only when consumers feel that the brand does not like them more than they like the brand. In other words, when consumers feel that the brand over-reciprocates their affections, it seems they are "turned off," thereby nullifying the effect of self-brand similarity on relationship closeness. In contrast, when consumers feel that the brand equally or even under-reciprocates their affections, our results suggest they are "turned on," in which case self-brand similarity comes into play. Therefore, when it comes to brand relationships, it is not necessarily the case that consumers and brands of a feather flock together. Consumers must also feel that the brand is a catch, and that a relationship with that brand is not easy to come by.

References

Aaker, Jennifer L. (1997), "Dimensions of Brand Personality," *Journal of Marketing Research,* 24 (August), 347–56.

Aron, Arthur, Elain N. Aron, and Danny Smollan, (1992), "Inclusion of Other in the Self Scale and the Structure of Interpersonal Closeness," *Journal of Personality and Social Psychology,* 63 (4), 596–612.

Byrne, Donn (1961), "Interpersonal Attraction and Attitude Similarity," *Journal of Abnormal and Social Psychology,* 62, 713–15.

Byrne, Donn (1971), *The Attraction Paradigm*, New York: Academic Press.

Eastwick, Paul W., Eli J. Finkel, Daniel Mochon, and Dan Ariely (2007), "Selective versus Unselective Romantic Desire," *Psychological Science,* 18 (4), 317–19.

Fournier, Susan (1998), "Consumers and Their Brands: Developing Relationship Theory in Consumer Research," *Journal of Consumer Research,* 24 (March), 343–73.

Keller, Kevin L. (1993), "Conceptualizing, Measuring, and Managing Customer-Based Brand Equity," *Journal of Marketing,* 57 (January), 1–22.

Moore, David J. and Pamela M. Homer (2008), "Self-Brand Connections: The Role of Attitude Strength and Autobiographical Memory Primes," *Journal of Business Research,* 61, 707–14.

Unconscious Brand Reactions Influence Financial Decision-Making

Philip Harris, University of Melbourne, Australia
Carsten Murawski, University of Melbourne, Australia

Abstract

Recent neuroimaging insights indicate that the reward value associated with brands may impact on affective processes underlying choice. In this research, we explore the possibility that brands with affective value can impact on behaviour by influencing affective systems underlying decision-making. Our results indicate that brand images with affective value can shift decision-making towards affectively-driven choices. Furthermore, these effects occur without conscious awareness of the identity of the brand stimuli. These findings provide initial evidence that brands may impact on behaviour outside of the consumer context by modulating affective systems underlying decision-making.

Introduction

Recent research indicates that exposure to goal-relevant brands automatically primes goal-directed behaviour, even without conscious awareness of the stimulus (Fitzsimons, Chartrand, & Fitzsimons, 2008; Chartrand, Huber, Shiv, and Tanner, 2008). An Apple logo may prime creative behaviour, or a Disney logo may prime honesty. These data indicate that brand exposure can moderate the salience of pre-existing behavioural goals, and may operate via mechanisms that are at least partially inaccessible to conscious introspection.

Increasingly, research drawing on neuroscientific techniques supports the idea that favoured brands may act as reward cues that moderate decision-making. Brand or product preference preferentially engages neural regions associated with reward processing (Plassmann, Kenning, Deppe, Kugel, & Schwindt, 2008; Schaefer & Rotte, 2007); and neural regions that mediate the influence of affect in decision-making (e.g. Deppe et al., 2005; Erk, Spitzer, Wunderlich, Galley, & Walter, 2002; Plassmann et al., 2008; Schaefer, Berens, Heinze, & Rotte, 2006). Further, the reward value associated with stimuli may bias decision-making in the absence of conscious processing (Pessiglioni, Petrovic, Daunizeau et al., 2008). These findings may have important consequences for brand theory. Affective brand responses may impact on behaviour via the modulation of affective processes in parallel with activation of brand-related schema in the absence of conscious processing. In this research we sought to examine these processes. We posed the question: Would unconscious presentation of a brand with affective value impact on decision-making behaviour that is susceptible to the influence of affective motivational states?

Brands and affective bases of decision-making

To consider these effects, we examined a scenario in which an individual is faced with a decision that is susceptible to the influence of affective motivational states-a choice between an immediately available monetary reward and another that is available only after a delay. This scenario pits drive the emotionally-driven drive for impulsive gratification against more reasoned and less impulsive choice behaviour (Hoch and Lowenstein, 1991). Crucially, incidental affective states impact on the extent that delayed rewards are valuable. For example, males devalue delayed financial rewards more heavily after exposure to images of attractive females (Wilson & Daly, 2004). Furthermore, decisions that favour immediate rewards have been shown to engage neural regions linked with affective processing, particularly those associated with reward processing (McClure, Ericson, Laibson, Loewenstein, & Cohen, 2007; McClure, Laibson, & Cohen, 2004).

Hypothesis Development

We believe that favoured brands may act on such decision-making processes. By acting as reward cues, we propose that brands with affective value may directly prime affective processes underlying decision-making mechanisms, and will bias decisions between earlier and later monetary rewards towards earlier reward options. We predict that subliminal presentation of a brand with affective value will prime significant devaluing of delayed financial rewards than other priming stimuli with lesser affective value.

Method

One hundred and thirteen undergraduate college students participated in a computer-based temporal discounting task which offered a series of choices between an immediate reward of $20 and a reward of higher value to be paid at one of six possible delays (1, 10, 21, 55, 90 180 days). Each choice was preceded by the subliminal presentation (16 ms pre- and post-masked) of one of four priming image types: a brand logo (Apple or Windows); a smiling face, or a household object. Participants completed the discounting task four times, once for each of the priming image types. The principal dependent variable was the subjective value assigned to delayed rewards when subliminally primed by each of the four image types. Following the discounting task, participants completed a five-item brand affect scale which incorporated seven-point ratings of brand salience, brand affective value, brand ownership, desire to own brand products, and intention to purchase branded products within the next six months.

Results

Seven participants with discounting rates greater than three standard deviations above the median discounting rate were removed from the data set. Paired t-tests examining brand affect scale ratings indicated that ratings for Apple were significantly higher than for Windows overall, $t(103)=3.40$, $p=.001$, and on individual scale item ratings of affective value, $t(103)=2.20$, $p<.05$, desire to own, $t(103)=5.26$, $p<.001$, and intention to purchase, $t(103)=5.40$, $p<.001$. Responses to the smiles priming condition are not examined in this paper. A repeated measures analysis of variance examined the impact of priming condition (3-Apple, Windows, Neutral) and reward delay time (6) on subjective value of delayed rewards for the remaining 106 participants. Main effects of image priming condition, $F(2,10)=4.10$, $p<.05$, and delay time, $F(5,525)=495.69$, $p<.001$, were observed, whereas an interaction between priming condition and delay time, $F(10,1050)=.41$, p=NS, was not observed. Delayed rewards were significantly less valuable when preceded by an Apple logo than when preceded by a Windows logo, $t(105)=1.92$, $p<.05$, one-tailed, or a neutral image type, $t(105)=2.62$, $p=.005$, one-tailed. Thus, the experimental hypothesis was supported.

Discussion

Our results indicate that the affective value associated with a brand may impact on unrelated decision-making processes. Following presentation of the Apple logo, participants were more likely to choose an immediate reward than when primed by other image types. Further, the impact of this affective value on behaviour occurred without conscious awareness of the priming images. Thus, our findings support a proposal that brand images can impact on behaviour by communicating affective value in the absence of conscious awareness of the stimulus. These findings provide initial evidence that brands may impact on behaviour outside of the consumer context by modulating affective systems underlying decision-making. In addition, an initial analysis indicates that when primed by a favoured brand, preference for immediate rewards is linked with faster response times than preference for delayed rewards, and is insensitive to decision-difficulty. Further analysis of these data will exam the role of heuristic decision-making processes associated with choices for immediate rewards and may provide further support for an affective mechanism evoked by unconscious brand presentation with impact on decision-making processes.

References

Chartrand, T.L., Huber, J., Shiv, B., and Tanner, R.J. (2008). Nonconscious goals and consumer choice. *Journal of Consumer Research*, 35, 189-201.

Deppe, M., Schwindt, W., Kugel, H., Plassman, H., and Kenning, P. (2005). Nonlinear responses within the medial prefrontal cortex reveal when specific implicit information influences economic decision-making. *Journal of Neuroimaging*, 15, 171-182.

Erk, S., Spitzer, M., Wunderlich, A. P., Galley, L., and Walter, H. (2002). Cultural objects modulate reward circuitry. *Neuroreport*, 13(18), 2499-2503.

Fitzsimons, G.M., Chartrand, T.L., and Fitzsimons, G. J. (2008). Automatic Effects of Brand Exposure on Motivated Behavior: How Apple Makes You "Think Different". *Journal of Consumer Research*, 35, 21-35.

Hoch, S.J., and Lowenstein, G.F. (1991). Time-inconsistent preferences and consumer self-control. *Journal of Consumer Research*, 17, 492-507.

McClure, S., Libson, D.I., Loewenstein, G.F., and Cohen, J.D. (2004). Separate neural systems value immediate and delayed monetary rewards. *Science*, 306, 503-506.

McClure, S. M., Ericson, K.M., Laibson, D.I., Loewenstein, G., and Cohen, J.D. (2007). Time discounting for primary rewards. *Journal of Neuroscience*, 27(21), 5796-5804.

Pessiglione, M., Petrovic, P., Daunizeau, J., Palminteri, S., Dolan, R.J., and Frith, C.D. (2008). Subliminal instrumental conditioning demonstrated in the human brain. *Neuron*, 59, 561–567.

Plassmann, H., Kenning, P., Deppe, M., Kugel, H., and Schwindt, W. (2008). How choice ambiguity modulates activity in brain areas representing brand preference: evidence from consumer neuroscience. *Journal of Consumer Behaviour*, 7(4-5), 360-367.

Schaefer, M., Berens, H., Heinze, H.-J., and Rotte, M. (2006). Neural correlates of culturally familiar brands of car manufacturers. *NeuroImage*, 31(2), 861-865.

Schaefer, M., and Rotte, M. (2007). Favorite brands as cultural objects modulate reward circuit. *NeuroReport*, 18(2), 141-145.

Wilson, M., and Daly, M. (2004). Do pretty women inspire men to discount the future? *Proceedings Biological Sciences*, May 7; 271 (Suppl 4), S177-179.

Insights into the Concept of Underconsumption and the Internal and External Mechanisms Consumers Utilize to Underconsume

Jonathan Hasford, University of Kentucky, USA

Abstract

While prior research has used the term underconsumption to characterize certain behavior patterns in consumers (e.g. Heath and Soll 1996), research is currently lacking an understanding of the phenomena of underconsumption. The current research aims to define the construct of underconsumption based on previous consumer research, including research on topics such as frugality (Lastovicka et al. 1999), tightwaddism (Rick, Cryder, and Loewenstein 2007), and hyperopia (Haws and Poynor 2008). Furthermore, this research also provides an understanding of the external and internal mechanisms that consumers utilize to maintain lower amounts of consumption. An exploratory study is conducted to delineate the construct of underconsumption and investigate the mechanisms that consumers utilize.

Prior research has used the term underconsumption to describe patterns in consumer behavior (e.g. Heath and Soll 1996), but an understanding of the concept itself and the mechanisms that consumers utilize to maintain underconsumption behaviors are still unknown (Lee, Fernandez, and Hyman, 2009). In the current research, literature related to frugality (Lastovicka et al., 1999), tightwaddism (Rick, Cryder, and Loewenstein, 2007), and hyperopia (Haws and Poynor, 2008) are used to provide an understanding of underconsumption. Additionally, this research also attempts to understand the mechanisms that consumers utilize in order to underconsume. The ultimate goal of this research is to generate a comprehensive model which explains the antecedents to consumer underconsumption.

Defining Underconsumption

Three related topics of research provide a framework for defining underconsumption. Lastovicka et al. (1999) define frugality as a consumer lifestyle trait in which individuals are restrained in acquiring and resourcefully using economic goods and services to achieve longer-term goals. Tightwads are classified as those whose affective reaction to spending leads to less consumption than the individual's more deliberate self would prefer (Rick et al., 2007). Lastly, hyperopia is defined as the deprivation of hedonic experiences due to excessive overwork and the need for control at one's job (Kivetz and Simonson 2002). While each of these classifications is unique, they all involve lesser amounts of consumption relative to others of similar background and status. Therefore, using these three types of underconsumption, overall underconsumption is defined as consuming fewer goods, services, and experiences than others of similar demographic and socioeconomic status. Since underconsumption consists of frugality, tightwaddism, and hyperopia, these concepts should be empirically related to one another.

Mechanisms that Influence Underconsumption

In addition to developing the concept of underconsumption, the current research also investigates the mechanisms consumers utilize to underconsume. Frugal consumers and tightwads experience affective reactions during consumption decisions, while hyperopic consumers do not. Frugal consumers derive pleasure from saving to meet long-term goals, while tightwads experience anticipatory pain and anxiety toward spending (Rick et al. 2007). Since these forms of underconsumption involve the recognition of future affect, self-control and willpower should help consumers avoid the perceived negative affect that is related to present consumption. Self-control refers to the general strategies that one imposes individually in order to maintain consistency in behavior, while willpower relates to the tactics such as precommitment, economic cost assessment, and regret and guilt that allow people to overcome their desires (Hoch and Loewenstein 1991). A greater presence of these internal mechanisms should lead to increased levels of tightwaddism and frugality as consumers will manage and control their desires in order to meet their affect-laden consumption decisions.

Since individuals are inherently different in their ability to regulate their own consumption levels (Tangney, Baumeister, and Boone 2004), the hyperopic consumer is expected to use different mechanisms. Recall that a hyperopic consumes less due to overwork and the need for control. This very imbalance is the mechanism that the hyperopic consumer utilizes. Desire control, which consists of avoidance, postponement, and distraction, involves the manipulation of one's own reference points in order to reduce the frustration they experience in consumption decisions (Hoch and Loewenstein 1991). Therefore, hyperopic consumers use work and other precommitments as external mechanisms to avoid consumption situations instead of relying on the internal mechanisms of self control and willpower that tightwads and frugal consumers utilize.

Method

Sixty-three undergraduate students completed a questionnaire related to underconsumption and the internal control mechanisms discussed earlier. First, the participants filled out each set of items for frugality (Lastovicka et al. 1999), tightwaddism (Rick et al. 2007), and hyperopia (Haws and Poynor 2008). Then, participants were provided with a scenario in which they were to imagine saving for a spring break trip. The participants were asked to assess their ability to budget themselves and save money for the trip (i.e. willpower). After completing the scenario, participants concluded the study by filling out two self-control scales from Tangney et al. (2004) and Haws and Bearden (2006).

Results

In order to determine whether the concepts of frugality, tightwaddism, and hyperopia fit within the overarching construct of underconsumption, a correlation analysis of the data was conducted. Results showed that hyperopia significantly correlated with frugality ($r=.33$, $p<.01$) and with tightwaddism ($r=.31$, $p=.01$). Frugality was also significantly correlated with tightwaddism ($r=.50$, $p<.01$). Given that all three of these concepts are related to one another, these findings suggest that each classification shares a common underlying concept, in this case underconsumption.

To analyze the concept of self-control and its relationship to the types of underconsumption, a regression analysis was conducted between the total score on the self control items and the total scores of each measure of underconsumption. Findings revealed that increased levels of self control predicted increases in both frugality ($\alpha=.63$, $p<.01$) and tightwaddism ($\alpha=.55$, $p<.01$). Conversely, self control was not predictive of hyperopia ($\alpha=.09$, $p>.47$).

The consumption scenario was also analyzed to provide further insight on the processes that consumers utilize to promote underconsumption. Results demonstrated that greater willpower in the scenario was predictive of increased levels of frugality ($\alpha=.30$, $p<.05$) and tightwaddism ($\alpha=.28$, $p<.05$), and was unrelated to hyperopia ($\alpha=.08$, $p>.53$). The self control and willpower findings together provide support for internal mechanisms of control promoting underconsumption behavior within tightwads and frugal consumers. Furthermore, the lack of self control and willpower in hyperopic consumers suggests that external mechanisms of desire control need to be investigated. A follow-up study will be conducted to determine the influence of avoidance, postponement, and distraction in hyperopic consumers. Ultimately, a comprehensive model of the antecedents to underconsumption will be created.

References

Haws, Kelly L. and Cait Poynor (2008), "Seize the Day! Encouraging Indulgence for the Hyperopic Consumer," *Journal of Consumer Research*, 35 (December), 680-91.

______ and William O. Bearden (2006), "Consumer Spending Self-Control: Conceptual and Measurement Refinements," in Dhruv Grewal, Michael Levy, and R. Krishnan, eds., *Enhancing Knowledge Development in Marketing,* Vol. 17, Chicago, IL: American Marketing Association, 2006 (abstract).

Hoch, Stephen J. and George F. Loewenstein (1991), "Time-inconsistent Preferences and Consumer Self-Control," *Journal of Consumer Research*, 17 (March), 492-507.

Heath, Chip and Jack B. Soll (1996), "Mental Budgeting and Consumer Decisions," *Journal of Consumer Research*, 23 (June), 40-52.

Kivetz, Ran and Itamar Simonson (2002), "Self-Control for the Righteous: Toward a Theory of Precommitment to Indulgence," *Journal of Consumer Research*, 29 (September), 199-217.

Lastovicka, John L., Lance A. Bettencourt, Renee Shaw Hughner, and Ronald J. Kuntze (1999), "Lifestyle of the Tight and Frugal: Theory and Measurement," *Journal of Consumer Research*, 26 (June), 85-98.

Lee, Michael S.W., Karen V. Fernandez, and Michael R. Hyman (2009), "Anti-Consumption: An Overview and Research Agenda," *Journal of Business* Research, 62 (February), 145-7.

Rick, Scott I., Cynthia E. Cryder, and George Loewenstein (2008), "Tightwads and Spendthrifts," *Journal of Consumer Research*, 34 (April), 767-82.

Tangney, June P., Roy F. Baumeister, and Angie Luzio Boone (2004), "High Self-Control Predicts Good Adjustment, Less Pathology, Better Grades, and Interpersonal Success," *Journal of Personality*, 72(2), 271-324.

Conveying an Impression: Effects of the Consumer Review Process on Attitude Communication and Persistence

Stephen Xihao He, Georgia Institute of Technology, USA
Samuel Bond, Georgia Institute of Technology, USA

Abstract

This research examines the long-term impact of review writing on the evaluation of a consumption experience. Relevant theories offer conflicting predictions regarding the extent to which writing a product review will stabilize attitude towards the product. We investigate this question in an experimental setting using short movie clips as target stimuli. Our results indicate that the timing and format of the review task systematically influence attitude persistence over time, as well as readers' inferences regarding that attitude. Implications and extensions of these results are discussed.

Introduction

Increasingly, consumers are involved in reading as well as writing reviews about consumption experiences. Many studies have explored the influence of consumer-created content on attitudes and behaviors of the audience (Chen and Xie 2008; Chevalier and Mayzlin 2006), but research that examines the influence of the creation process on creators themselves has been rare. An exception is recent evidence that writing a product review can change one's attitude toward the product (He and Bond 2009). However, it remains unclear whether any influence of review writing will endure over time. More generally, the intersection of review writing and attitude persistence is a neglected but important topic.

Different research streams imply contradictory predictions for the impact of review writing on attitude persistence. On the one hand, classic models of elaboration such as the ELM and HSM (Chaiken 1980; Petty and Cacioppo 1986) suggest that greater cognitive processing of attitude-relevant information should increase attitude strength and persistence. However, another approach has focused on the effect of reasoning about attitudes on attitude change over time and attitude-behavior consistency (Sengupta and Fitzsimons 2000; Wilson and Schooler 1991). Findings from this stream reveal that analyzing reasons before attitude measurement generally reduces attitude persistence, while analyzing reasons after measurement increases persistence.

In order to reconcile this conflict and make predictions, we consider two cases, in which consumers review a product either *before* or *after* reporting their attitudes. In the first case, we note that review writing is different from typical reasoning manipulations, which force participants to justify their views with reasons and therefore focus on aspects of the experience that are verbalizable and accessible but may not contribute meaningfully to attitudes. Review writers, on the other hand, are instead free to list both positive and negative aspects of their experience without needing to defend or justify their views. Because review writers are not bound to an attitude derived from available reasons, we suggest that their attitudes are likely to cohere with the content of reviews and persist over time (a reinforcement effect). In the case of writing a review after providing one's attitude, both streams of research cited above agree on a reinforcement effect. Therefore, the act of writing about a consumption experience will make initial attitudes more persistent, whether or not the review precedes or follows attitude assessment.

Hypothesis 1: Writing a product review prior to stating one's attitude will increase the stability of that attitude over time.

Hypothesis 2: Writing a product review after stating one's attitude will increase the stability of that attitude over time.

Although some review forums (e.g., *car.com*) request piece-meal, *guided* reviews that discuss specific attributes of the product, others (e.g., *imdb.com*) request open-ended, *unguided* reviews that encompass the whole product experience. We expect that guiding consumers to focus on specific attributes should especially enhance elaboration and encoding of thoughts during the review process, strengthening attitudes and increasing attitude persistence.

Hypothesis 3: The enhancement effect of review writing on attitude persistence will be stronger for reviews that are guided rather than unguided.

Design/Procedure

The study was conducted in a lab with 118 student participants. A mixed design included two between-subjects factors (order: *review-first* vs. *attitude-first*; review type: *guided* vs. *unguided* vs. *filler*) and one within-subjects factor (time: *immediate* vs. *one month later*). At t1, all participants watched the target stimulus, a short animated movie clip portraying an origami artist performing his craft. After viewing the movie, participants were given different instructions according to condition. The *review-first* conditions were asked to generate written reviews: the *guided review* group answered a series of questions focusing on attributes of the clip and the *unguided review* group was instructed to write an integrated, open-ended review. The *filler group* wrote 10-15 sentences summarizing events of the previous day. Next, these participants rated the clip on four 7-point attitude scales; they also answered various follow-up questions and demographic measures. Participants in the *attitude-first* conditions completed the steps above in opposite order. One month later, all participants took part in a second session where identical attitude measures were collected.

Results and Conclusions

Composite attitude measures were formed by averaging the four attitude questions at both t1 and t2. The absolute attitude difference between t1 and t2 was used to represent attitude persistence. For the following analyses, the condition in which attitudes were reported immediately and followed by the filler task serves as an omnibus control.

Data for the control condition showed an average absolute attitude change of .69 over the one-month delay. This change is both surprisingly large and significantly different from zero (t=4.16, p<.001), suggesting participants were generally poor at retrieving their prior attitudes. The main effect of order was marginally significant (F(1, 111)=3.54, p =.06), indicating that whether the attitude was measured before or after review writing influenced the stability of that attitude over time. In support of Hypothesis 1, attitude persistence was increased by the provision of a review before attitude assessment. Planned contrasts revealed that participants who provided guided reviews before reporting their attitudes exhibited marginally less attitude change (M=.42) than those in the control condition (M=.69, F(1, 35)=2.74, p=.11), while participants who provided unguided reviews before reporting their attitudes exhibited attitude change that was directionally less than controls (M=.57, *ns*). The difference between the two review conditions was only directional, lending weak support to Hypothesis 3.

In order to test Hypothesis 2, we compared the attitude change of participants who provided guided reviews after reporting their attitudes (M=.60) to that of participants who provided unguided reviews after reporting their attitudes (M=.71) and the omnibus control condition (M=.69). No reliable differences were observed; therefore, H2 was not supported.

Analysis of within-cell attitude variance at t1 revealed one potential means by which reviews may affect attitude persistence. Specifically, the variance within the rate-first conditions (V=.96) was considerably smaller than that of participants who had written reviews (V=2.19, Leven's test $F(1, 91)=3.53, p=.06$). This suggests that that as a result of cognitive reflection, initial attitudes in the review condition were more well-formed and less subject to fluctuation over time.

Overall, these results provide initial evidence that the act of writing a review can influence consumers' attitude persistence. In subsequent research, we plan to explore the robustness of this finding to consumption experiences that differ in product category, valence, or intensity, and also to analyze the content of reviews themselves for differences that may affect long-term memory and retrieval of the consumption experience.

Selected References

Chaiken, Shelly (1980), "Heuristic Versus Systematic Information Processing and the Use of Source Versus Message Cues in Persuasion," *Journal of Personality and Social Psychology*, 39 (5), 752-66.

Chen, Yubo and Jinhong Xie (2008), "Online Consumer Review: Word-of-Mouth as a New Element of Marketing Communication Mix," *Management Science*, 54 (3), 477-91.

Chevalier, Judith A. and Dina Mayzlin (2006), "The Effect of Word of Mouth on Sales: Online Book Reviews," *Journal of Marketing Research*, 43 (3), 345-54.

He, Stephen Xihao and Samuel Bond (2009), "The Impact of Product Review Writing on Attitude Formation," *Advances in Consumer Research*, 36.

Petty, R. E. and J. T. Cacioppo (1986), *Communication and Persuasion: Central and Peripheral Routes to Attitude Change*: Springer.

Sengupta, Jaideep and Gavan J. Fitzsimons (2000), "The Effects of Analyzing Reasons for Brand Preferences: Disruption or Reinforcement?," *Journal of Marketing Research*, 37 (3), 318-30.

Weiss, Allen M., Nicholas H. Lurie, and Deborah J. MacInnis (2008), "Listening to Strangers: Whose Responses Are Valuable, How Valuable Are They, and Why?," *Journal of Marketing Research*, 45 (4), 425-36.

Wilson, Timothy D. and Jonathan W. Schooler (1991), "Thinking Too Much: Introspection Can Reduce the Quality of Preferences and Decisions," *Journal of Personality and Social Psychology*, 60 (2), 181-92.

Players' Attitudes Toward Preorders and Adoption Intention of New Videogames: A Qualitative Approach

Monica D. Hernandez, Texas A&M University-Corpus Christi, USA
Handan Vicdan, Eastern Kentucky University, USA

Launching of new products connotes high costs and high probability of risk for manufacturers. Marketers of video games, books, music CD, DVD movies, and telecommunication gadgets usually promote new products months ahead of introducing them to the market. Consumers can preorder these products and receive them as soon as they become available. Despite the economic importance of worldwide videogame sales (Magiera 2009), the motives of players relying on preorders have not been explored. Why are consumers willing to pay in advance when they have other readily available alternatives? Why do some consumers buy products when they do not know about their features? How do they choose between a promised superior functionality versus a trialable alternative? We seek to bring insights into these issues. The contribution of this research is threefold: (1) explore the motives of videogame players in preordering, (2) highlight the unique pattern of the phenomenon in the early adoption of new videogames, and (3) adopt a qualitative approach to explore preorder decisions rather than an experimental approach to provide richer and broader coverage of the likely factors associated with the topic of interest.

In the case of videogames, preorders display two patterns: (1) Continuous innovation or an updated and enhanced version of a pre-existing game (e.g. Guitar Hero III, Rock Band), (2) discontinuous innovation or a totally new product including new features and qualities (consider the game Guitar Hero introduced for the very first time). In the former situation, consumers preorder video games when they have had certain experience with an earlier version of the game or at least with the game developer. For instance, players who have been satisfied with the videogame FIFA 2008 are potential buyers of FIFA 2009. We can extend this situation when new video game consoles are introduced. The second situation occurs when some videogames–similar to new telecommunication devices–usually come with totally new features that the consumer has never experienced before.

We conducted focus group interviews with videogame players to obtain insights about preordering behavior. Each session was videotaped and lasted about 70 minutes. We followed a grounded theory approach (Glaser and Strauss 1967) to formulate a theory about the phenomenon of interest. The interviewees were asked to describe their thoughts and experiences regarding the preorder and gaming process. We identified common emerging themes and discussed the implications of these themes on preorder intentions. We classified emerging themes into two groups: purchase and adoption (psychological and product related elements).

Purchase: (1) Securing the purchase: Players expressed their concern about the risk of the unavailability of the videogame. Hui et al. (2008) concluded that the highest point of sales of new products occurs in the preorder stage. After launching the product, sales decline. A plausible explanation is that players rush to preorder a game to secure its acquisition rather than waiting and find it unavailable due to high demand and/or low supply. This situation is akin to Belk et al.'s (2003) description of desire: players' intent on acquiring the symbolic benefits of a desired game rather than the game itself is fulfilled through preordering. True thrill is kept alive through preordering until the actual game is acquired. Once acquired, players undergo exploration of new features stage. Subsequently, players' thrill ends if they no longer have anything to discover or learn about the game, and if perceived challenge or competition is over. *(2) Risk absence:* New technologies derive new tasks for consumers and generate uncertainty (Ziamou 2002). Despite the absence of trialability, consumers expressed no functional (performance) risk involved in the preorder, confirming the claim that a continuous innovation has lower levels of perceived risks. Similarly, they do not perceive any risk of making a poor purchase decision. Players expressed that they never "regretted" a preorder. They also feel confident, as they have the option to opt-out of preorder. *(3) Main sources of information:* For continuous innovations, familiarity with game increases the desire for preordering. For discontinuous innovations, advertising and early reviews increase expectations. High involvement players desire to acquire both discontinuous and continuous innovations.

Adoption: (1) Trialability versus discovery: Rogers (1983) viewed trialability as a dimension of adoption of new products, which relates to the opportunity to be exposed to the innovation. However, this opportunity is inexistent in the case of preorders. Accordingly, lack of trialability may have a negative impact on perceived risk. We found that discovery stage substitutes the lack of trialability. *(2) Desire for status versus desire for process:* High involvement players have a high desire for status ("to win"), focusing on the "outcome." In contrast, low involvement players have a desire for fun and focus on the "process" ("to play"). *(3) Curiosity versus defined expectations:* Players reported their defined expectations from a new videogame to include advanced features that make it more realistic (little discrepancy between the videogame and its actual manifestations in real life) and interactive, and increase sensation. Curiosity or interest in novelty also emerged as a common category. Players perceive new products as providing continuity of a known story, yet with novel features and challenges that create excitement and room for discovery. They seem to be curious about the features to accomplish this goal. Although familiarity with the game increases the desire to preorder, consumers still seek room for discovery (discover added features), which also creates allure and increases the desire to preorder.

References

Belk, Russell W., Guliz Ger and Soren Askegaard (2003), "The Fire of Desire: A Multisited Inquiry into Consumer Passion," *Journal of Consumer Research,* 30 (3), 326-351.

Glaser, Barney G. and Anselm L. Strauss (1967), *The Discovery of Grounded Theory: Strategies for Qualitative Research.* Aldine Publishing Co, Chicago, IL.

Hui, Sam K., Jehoshua Eliashberg and Edward I. George (2008), "Modeling DVD Preorder and Sales: An Optimal Stopping Approach," *Marketing Science,* 27 (6), 1097-1110.

Magiera, Marcy (2009), "Worldwide Game Revenue Passes DVD," *Video Business,* 01/26, 29 (4), 1 and 28.

Robertson, Thomas S. (1971), *Innovative Behavior and Communication.* New York: Holt, Rinehart & Winston.

Rogers, Everett M. (1983), *Diffusion of Innovations.* New York: Free Press.

Ziamou, Paschalina (2002), "Commercializing New Technologies: Consumers' Response to a New Interface," *Journal of Product Innovation Management,* 19 (5), 365-374.

Choice Behavior of Maximizers and Satisficers When Alternatives Are Priced Using Non-monetary Points

Meng-Hua Hsieh, University of Washington, USA
Richard Yalch, University of Washington, USA
Edwin Love, Western Washington University, USA

Abstract

Schwartz et al. (2002) suggested that Herbert Simon's concept of satisficing could be considered an individual difference and developed a scale to measure maximizing-satisficing tendencies. Satisficers settle for non-optimal choices by restricting their information seeking and analysis, whereas maximizers persist and evaluate all or most options. Although clearly relevant to consumer decision-making, little consumer research using this concept has been reported.

A potential application is found in Hsee et al.'s (2003) research demonstrating how making an optimal choice among alternatives varying in effort and reward is complicated when the decision involves a medium such as airline mileage or reward points. Consumers sometimes choose a higher effort alternative to acquire more points even though these points cannot be used to acquire anything of additional value. This phenomenon is explained by the decision being determined by whether the ratio of the relevant medium levels is greater than the ratio of the resultant outcomes. Thus, in their first study, 50% of the subjects selected the option to work for 7 minutes to earn 100 points that could be exchanged for a gallon of pistachio ice cream compared to only 22% when the choice did not involve points (i.e., work for 7 minutes to earn a gallon of pistachio ice cream).

Although many consumers exhibited a myopic reliance on medium differences in making choices, others did not. A possible reason is found in Schwartz et al.'s (2002) suggestion that some individuals accept non-optimal choices rather than exert the extra effort required to identify the best alternative. We propose that Maximizers are more likely than Satisficers to use only the ratios of effort and medium and ignore the exchange rates and the resulting outcome ratios when making their decision.

Research Study

We conducted an experiment based on Hsee et al. (2003) Study 1, with several changes, such as adding a 30/35 minutes effort condition to the original 6/7 minutes effort (equal ratios but increasing the incremental time from 1 to 5 minutes), having individuals rank five ice cream flavors and then presenting them with choices between either their 1st and 2nd most preferred flavors or their 1st and 5th most preferred. Also, to better quantify the effect of the medium on decision making, individuals were asked to state their strength of preference as well as make a discrete choice.

The experimental design was thus a 2 (effort levels: 6/7 or 30/35 minutes) by 2 (outcome equivalence: 1st versus 2nd or 1st versus 5th most preferred flavors) by 2 (medium: no points or 60/100 points) full factorial design. After making a choice (e.g., 6 minutes-60 points-1st preferred or 7 minutes-100 points-2nd most preferred), 203 undergraduate student subjects indicated their strength of preference by dragging a pointer on an on-screen line with end points labeled 1 (strongly preferred Task 1) and 100 (strongly preferred Task 2). Next, subjects responded to an open-ended inquiry about their reasons for making their choice. Response times for the discrete choice and strength-of-preference tasks were recorded. Lastly, subjects responded to the Maximizing-Satisficing scale.

Results

Analysis revealed that we were able to replicate the medium maximization effect in the conditions most similar to Hsee et al.'s Study 1. Forty-two percent of subjects selected the more effortful Task 2 (7 minutes to receive the 2nd flavor) over task 1 (6 minutes to receive the 1st flavor) when points (100 versus 60 points) were involved while only 11% did so when no points were involved. Counter to expectations, the medium maximization effect slightly increased with greater effort time, despite equal ratios, when the flavor choices remained between 1st and 2nd. Forty-six percent of subjects selected Task 2 with points versus only 5% with no points. Although greater outcome disparity did not eliminate the Medium Maximization effect, the effect decreased with more effort despite equal ratios, as predicted. When the effort ratio was 6/7 minutes and the choice was between 1st and 5th most preferred flavors, 35% selected Task 2 with points while no one did so without points. However, when Task 1 was 30 minutes to receive the 1st preferred flavor and Task 2 was 35 minutes to receive the 5th most preferred flavor, no one selected Task 2 when no points were involved and only 22% did so when points were involved.

A logistic regression revealed a significantly positive main effect of including a medium ($p<0.05$) and a significant effect of outcome equivalence ($p<0.05$). The main effect of effort level and all the interactions were not significant. ANOVA analysis using slider preference yielded the same pattern of significance.

Analysis using Maximizing-Satisficing scores found little support for it as a moderator. Further, other analyses (e.g., response time and reasons for choosing Task 2) were not consistent with the notion that Maximizers exert extra effort to optimize their choices. Other researchers (e.g., Diab et al. 2008; Nenkov et al. 2008) have recently questioned the original Maximizing-Satisficing scale's validity while acknowledging the concept's usefulness.

Discussion

This research supports the notion that medium maximization may undermine consumer's ability to select the best alternative in terms of effort and outcome ratios. However, it also demonstrates that medium maximization is less of an issue when outcomes are more easily compared and effort levels differ more at an absolute level. Individual differences in susceptibility to medium maximization could not be clearly predicted from scores on the original Maximizing-Satisficing scale. In order to handle the issues with Schwartz et al.'s scale, a follow-up study was conducted using revised Maximizing-Satisficing scales (e.g., Diab et al. 2008) as well as need for cognition and involvement measures. The results demonstrate that Maximizing-Satisficing is a distinct concept worthy of future research in a consumer context.

References

Diab, Dalia L., Michael A. Gillespie, and Scott Highhouse (2008), "Are Maximizers Really Unhappy? The Measurement of Maximizing Tendency," *Judgment and Decision Making*, 3 (5), 364-70.

Hsee, Christopher K., Fang Yu, Jiao Zhang and Yan Zhang (2003), "Medium Maximization," *Journal of Consumer Research*, 30 (1), 1-14.

Nenkov, Gergana Y., Maureen Morrin, Andrew Ward, Barry Schwartz and John Hulland (2008), "A Sshort Form of the Maximization Scale: Factor Structure, Reliability and Validity Studies", *Judgment and Decision Making*, 3 (5), 371–88.

Schwartz, Barry, Andrew Ward, John Monterosso, Sonja Lyubomirsky, Katherine White and Darrin R. Lehman, (2002), "Maximizing Versus Satisficing: Happiness Is a Matter of Choice," *Journal of Personality and Social Psychology*, 83 (5), 1178-97.

Carrying the Torch: Determinants of Intergeneration Influences as Sources of Brand Loyalty

Kyle Huggins, James Madison University, USA
Kenneth Bates, University of San Diego, USA
Darin White, Samford University, USA

Much of consumer behavior becomes engrained at a very young age. From the time we are born, we consume; and as this process is replicated, we begin to develop preferences for certain products and brands of products. One key relationship that is instrumental in the forming of these preferences is the relationship that a child develops with his or her parents. As a family grows and develops, the purchasing decisions that reflect a family's lifestyle become internalized allowing children to learn to accept them as the norm (Sears 1983). Hence, this socialization process has become an area of particular interest for consumer researchers studying the effect of intergenerational (IG) influences on brand loyalty.

Moore, Wilkie, and Lutz (2002) performed one of the most methodologically challenging studies demonstrating the effects of intergeneration influences on brand equity. They concluded that "intergenerational influences are a real marketplace phenomenon and a factor that merits much closer attention." Even so, little research has since been conducted to provide answers to which specific family factors contribute to this phenomenon. Therefore, this paper seeks to fill that gap by researching the effects of several predictor variables including mother involvement, sibling influence, and family structure on IG influences.

Consistent with Moore et al. (2002), we conducted parallel surveys of 121 mother-daughter dyads. We recruited the daughters from an introductory marketing course from a Southeastern university with the proviso that they must currently live off-campus and shop for groceries. We developed two similar questionnaires where each dyadic member was asked to indicate whether she used each of the twenty-four product categories listed. Respondents then listed their preferred brands as well as listing any additional brands that were "seriously considered." Then we asked participants to report independently their perceived dyadic partner's product usage and brand preference in each category. Students completed their questionnaires first and provided their mother's name and address for the mailing of the parallel survey and cover letter that explained the project. Both dyadic partners were alerted not to communicate about survey responses until all forms were returned.

While data collection was identical, our assessment of the scope of intergeneration influence is different than Moore et al. (2002). The aforementioned authors' measurement of IG brand loyalty consists if, and only if, there is a direct match between the actual choice of the most preferred brand of both mother and daughter. However, exact matches do not take into account the probability of chance or bidirectionality, which the authors admit is a limitation of their research. Therefore, we chose to combine both the dyadic analysis of Moore et al. (2002) with the perceived single-member approach of their earlier predecessors (Childers and Rao 1992; Heckler, Childers, and Arunachalam 1989). Using the exact survey distributed by the Moore et al. (2002), a combination of answers allows for an alternate way to analyze intergenerational brand loyalty. Using a combination of survey items such as acknowledgement of mom's consideration set, whether the daughter chooses from her mom's consideration set, and actual brand preference match, we were able to conceptualize at the individual level different categorizations that account for intentional IG brand loyalty, perceived IG brand loyalty, deliberate avoidance, chance matches, and complete unfamiliarity. These new categorizations of choice data have allowed us to conceptualize IG brand loyalty as the combination of both intentional and perceived IG brand loyalty. Theoretically, we argue that even though the survey data for some mother-daughter dyads do not match in brand preference, there is still an effect of IG influence. For example, we contend that when a daughter knows her mom's consideration set and actually chooses the brand she perceives as her mother's preferred choice, then there is perceived brand loyalty. We contend this data should be considered in the dyadic analysis even though the dyad does not "match" in brand preference. Likewise, these new categorizations allow us to remove matches that are considered to be a product of chance and bidirectionality. We believe the removal of these chance matches along with the addition of perceived IG brand loyalty is one initial contribution to this literature stream as it adds validity to the construct.

Finally, in addition to collecting product and brand preference information, we collected information on a number of independent variables as they relate to predicting IG brand loyalty. We hypothesize that there are direct and interaction effects of the relationships between IG brand loyalty and a number of family related variables such as mother involvement, number of siblings, and household family structure (traditional vs. non-traditional). Here, mother involvement specifically measures post hoc a daughter's perception of actual versus desired level of involvement during the daughters' formative years. The key to this measure is not just the amount of time that daughter and mother spend together, but also the quality of time that will have a profound impact on the nature of the mother-daughter relationship and the daughter's desire to adopt intergenerational brands. Early results indicate that intergenerational influences increase ten percent across all product categories and brands when both intentional and perceived brand matches are included in the analysis. This suggests that IG brand loyalty is even more prevalent than originally expected. Additionally, regression analysis demonstrates that predictor variables are significant and account for a reasonable amount of variance (r-squared=.169). We believe that these results are interesting and adequately respond to the call by Moore et al. (2002) for discovering predictors of intergenerational influence. This is by no means an exhaustive list of determinants, but it is an important step in the understanding of the interactions of the familial socialization process.

References

Childers, Terry L. and Akshay R. Rao (1992), "The Influence of Familial and Peer-Based Reference Groups on Consumer Decisions," *Journal of Consumer Research*, 19 (September), 198-211.

Heckler, Susan E., Terry L. Childers, and Ramesh Arunachalam (1989), "Intergenerational Influences in Adult Buying Behaviors: An Examination of Moderating Factors," in *Advances in Consumer Research*, Vol. 16, Thomas K Srull, ed. Provo, UT: Association for Consumer Research, 276-84.

Moore, Elizabeth S. Moore, William L. Wilkie, & Richard J. Lutz (2002), "Passing the Torch: Intergenerational Influences as a Source of Brand Equity," *Journal of Marketing*, 66 (April), 17-37.

Sears, David O. (1983), "The Persistence of Early Political Predispositions," in *Review of Personality and Social Psychology*, L. Wheeler and P. Shaver, Eds. Beverly Hills, CA: Sage Publications, 79-116.

The Effects of Self-Construal and Moral Identity on Company Evaluations: The Moderating Roles of Social and Personal Relevance of Corporate Social Responsibility Activities

Elif Isikman, University of Southern California, USA
Zeynep Gurhan-Canli, Koc University, Turkey
Vanitha Swaminathan, University of Pittsburgh, USA

In this research, we examine the effects of self-construal and moral identity on company evaluations as a function of social and personal relevance of CSR activities. In a set of two studies, we find that when self construal is independent (vs. interdependent), company evaluations do not vary as a function of social (vs. personal) relevance of the CSR activity. In contrast, when self-construal is independent (vs. interdependent), high personal (vs. social) relevance of CSR activity, leads to more favorable company evaluations. In a third study, we demonstrate that social relevance interacts with symbolization dimension of moral identity to predict company evaluations.

An important objective of corporate social responsibility (CSR) activities is to improve consumers' evaluations of a company or its brands. Extant research examined the effects of CSR activity-company fit (Becker-Olsen, Cudmore and Hill 2006; Lafferty, Goldsmith, and Hult 2004; Simmons and Becker-Olson 2006), fit between CSR efforts and consumer characteristics (Sen and Battacharya 2001), and consumer attributions (Ellen, Webb, and Mohr 2006; Forehand and Grier 2003; Yoon, Gurhan-Canli, and Schwarz 2006) on company evaluations. While previous research (e.g., Sen and Bhattacharya 2001) examined personal relevance of CSR activities on company evaluations, relatively little research investigated the extent to which consumers perceive social benefits from CSR activities and how such perceptions influence company evaluations. In this research, we contribute to this growing body of literature by distinguishing between perceived social and personal relevance of CSR activities and investigating their moderating effects when self-construal and moral identity are present.

Consumers may evaluate CSR activities both from personal and social perspectives. For example, college students may perceive contributions to college (vs. primary school) education personally more relevant although both of these contributions may be evaluated equally high in terms of their social impact. A person may deeply care about arts education but may perceive efforts to address illiteracy more relevant from a social perspective.

Two key concepts that are examined in relation to perceived personal and social relevance are self-construal and moral identity. Self-construal refers to perception of one's self either as an individual entity or in relation to others. Markus and Kitayama (1991) examined individual self-perceptions in relation to cultural identity and divided this construct into two variables, independent and interdependent. Independent individuals see themselves as stable and separate from the interpersonal context and value autonomy and uniqueness. On the other hand, interdependent individuals consider themselves more flexible and interlaced within the social context, and value maintaining group harmony. Arnocky, Stroink, and Decicco (2007) suggested that self-construal has an important role for individuals to determine what types of environmental problems concerns them. Thus, it may also affect the company evaluations based on the adopted CSR activity. We argue that self-construal has different effects on the company evaluations when the level of personal and social relevance to CSR activities changes. Because independent individuals value satisfying their own personal goals and interests, they may respond favorably to CSR activities that match their personal values. Nevertheless, independent individuals may evaluate companies similarly in terms of social relevance of CSR activities as they prioritize the conformity of CSR activities with their self interests. As interdependent individuals value group goals and interests, they may appreciate activities that have high perceived benefits to the society. On the other hand, their company evaluations may not change significantly with respect to the personal relevance of CSR activities as satisfying group interests, as opposed to their own, is more important for them. In sum, we hypothesize that

- $H1_a$: When self-construal is independent (vs. interdependent), high personal (vs. social) relevance of CSR activity, leads to higher company evaluations.
- $H1_b$: When self construal is independent (vs. interdependent), company evaluations should not vary as a function of social (vs. personal) relevance of the CSR activity.

Blasi (1984) and Hart (1998) described moral identity as one kind of self-regulatory mechanism which motivates moral actions. Aquino and Reed (2002) examined moral identity from two different dimensions; internalization and symbolization. Internalization is the long-term process of consolidating and embedding one's private self-concept, one's own beliefs, attitudes, and values. On the other hand, symbolization is the process of reflecting moral values in one's public actions. As moral identity has a role in determining moral actions, individuals with differences in their moral identity may have variances in their company evaluations based on their CSR activities. We propose that moral identity interacts with social and personal relevance of CSR activities in different ways. Internalization represents self-importance of the moral behavior. Therefore, high internalizers may have more favorably attitudes towards companies with CSR activities that match with their personal values. Nevertheless, low internalizers have weaker associations of moral traits with their self-concept. Thus, perceived personal relevance of CSR activities may not alter their company evaluations. Symbolization captures the extent to which individuals are concerned about reflecting their moral values with their actions. As high symbolizers want to convey their moral traits with their behavior, they may have more favorable evaluations towards moral activities that are perceived highly relevant to the society. On the other hand, low symbolizers care less for showing their moral characteristics. Regardless of the social relevance of CSR activities, they may value companies equally. Thus, we hypothesize that

- $H2_a$: When internalization (vs. symbolization) is high, high personal (vs. social) relevance of the CSR activity should lead to more favorable company evaluations.
- $H2_b$: When internalization (vs. symbolization) is low, company evaluations should not vary as a function of personal (vs. social) relevance of the CSR activity.

We ran three experiments among undergraduate students. In these studies, participants read information about the target company and its ongoing CSR activity. In the first study, we measured personal and social relevance; independent and interdependent self-construal. In our second study, we manipulated all our variables and employed a 2 (self construal: independent vs. interdependent) x 2 (social relevance: high vs. low) x 2 (personal relevance: high vs. low) between subjects design. In both studies, findings are consistent with our hypothesis (i.e., $H1_a$ and $H1_b$). In our third study, we measured moral identity, social and personal relevance. Preliminary analyses indicate that our results regarding symbolization dimension are consistent with our predictions. However, we found weak support for the significance of internalization.

References

Aquino, Karl and Americus Reed, II (2002), "The Self-Importance of Moral Identity," *Journal of Personality and Social Psychology*, 83(6), 1423–40.

Arnocky, Steven, Mirella Stroink and Teresa DeCicco (2007), "Self-construal Predicts Environmental Concern, Cooperation, and Conservation," *Journal of Environmental Psychology*, 27, 255-64.

Becker-Olsen, Karen L., B. Andrew Cudmore and Ronald P. Hill (2006), "The Impact of Perceived Corporate Social Responsibility on Consumer Behavior," *Journal of Business Research*, 59 (1), 46-53.

Blasi, Augusto (1984), "Moral identity: Its role in moral functioning," in *Morality, Moral Behavior and Moral Development,* ed. W. Kurtines and J. Gewirtz, NY: Wiley, 128–139.

Ellen, Pam S., Deborah J. Webb, and Lois A. Mohr (2006), "Building Corporate Associations: Consumer Attributions for Corporate Socially Responsible Programs," *Journal of the Academy of Marketing Science*, 34 (2), 147-157.

Forehand, Mark R. and Sonya Grier (2003), "When Is Honesty the Best Policy? The Effect of Stated M Company Intent on Consumer Skepticism," *Journal of Consumer Psychology*, 13(3), 349–56.

Hart, Daniel, Robert Atkins, and Debra Ford (1998), "Urban America as a Context for the Development of Moral Identity in Adolescence" *Journal of Social Issues,* 54, 513–30.

Lafferty, Barbara A., Ronald E. Goldsmith and G. Tomas M. Hult (2004), "The Impact of the Alliance on the Partners: A Look at Cause-brand Alliances," *Psychology and Marketing*, 21 (7), 509-31.

Markus, Hazel R. and Kitayama, Shinobu (1991), "Culture and the Self: Implications for Cognition, Emotion, and Motivation," *Psychological Review*, 98 (2), 224-253.

Sen, Sankar and C. B. Bhattacharya (2001), "Does Doing Good Always Lead to Doing Better? Consumer Reactions to Corporate Social Responsibility," *Journal of Marketing Research*, 38(2), 225-43.

Simmons, Carolyn J. and Karen L. Becker-Olsen (2006), "Achieving Marketing Objectives Through Social Sponsorships," *Journal of Marketing*, 70 (4), 154-69.

Yoon, Yeosun , Zeynep Gurhan-Canli, and Norbert Schwarz (2006), "The Effect of Corporate Social Responsibility (CSR) Activities on Companies with Bad Reputations," *Journal of Consumer Psychology,* 16 (4), 377-90.

Aliterate Consumers in the Marketplace

Haeran Jae, Virginia Commonwealth University, USA
Jodie L. Ferguson, Virginia Commonwealth University, USA

The past few decades have seen "increasing numbers of capable readers who are regularly choosing not to read" (Mikulecky, 1978, p. 3), leading to what has been called an aliteracy phenomenon. Consumers are overloaded with product information in the marketplace. Unfortunately, aliterate consumers avoid much of the available information. Instead of reading the instructions for using products, they rely on trial and error (Wallendorf, 2001).

In this research, the consumer aliteracy construct is developed, including a five-item measure of consumer aliteracy. This research also explores consumer aliteracy relationships with similar consumer behavior constructs. Finally, research questions for examining the effects of consumer aliteracy in the marketplace are offered, including the effects on advertising liking and comprehension.

The Consumer Aliteracy Construct

We define *consumer aliteracy* as the lack of reading habit in a capable reader participating in consumer behavior activities. We conducted a focus group of twelve consumers and we conducted eight in-depth consumer interviews to investigate the domain of the consumer aliteracy construct and to generate an initial pool of 67 scale items. Fifteen expert judges (i.e., marketing faculty and doctoral students at a Midwestern university) were consulted to critique the items. Items were removed that did not demonstrate face or content validity, resulting in a reduced set of 34 scale items. The 34 items were then presented in a survey to 301 consumers, where exploratory factor analysis revealed multiple factors with which the 34 items loaded. More consultations with expert judges resulted in reducing the scale to ten by eliminating items that were context specific or that were not related to consumer behaviors.

One hundred eleven consumers completed a survey that included the ten-item scale. Exploratory factor analysis revealed two factors (Λ_1=4.01 and Λ_2=2.39), however after further consideration, one factor was deemed situation-specific (e.g., reading *nutritional* information on packages, and taking *products* off shelves to read). After the situation-specific items were removed, the remaining five items accounted for 66.36% explained variance, had inter-item correlations ranging from .399-.676, and had Cronbach's alpha of .870. Another survey of 33 consumers confirmed the convergence of the five-items (i.e., Cronbach's alpha=.822). The final five-items to measure consumer aliteracy are: (1) I carefully read a document before I sign it, (2) I read the terms and conditions of a sale before I buy a product, (3) I am the kind of person who reads fine print in shopping, (4) When making a purchase, I read details word for word, and (5) I carefully read all transaction information before purchasing.

The Typical Aliterate Consumer

A survey of 111 respondents (i.e., where 54% were female and 62% were white/Caucasian) at a Southeastern university revealed some insights into the consumer aliteracy construct. Specifically, consumer aliteracy correlations with need for cognition and with consumer assertiveness were examined. Also, reading behaviors were examined to describe differences in aliteracy levels.

Aliterate consumers are not necessarily non-intellectuals, nor are consumer aliteracy synonymic with low need for cognition. In fact, consumer aliteracy did not significantly correlate with need for cognition[2] (i.e., r=-.135, p=.163). Respondents were also measured on consumer assertiveness,[3] the tendency for an individual to request information or assistance (Richins 1983). Consumer aliteracy significantly correlated with assertiveness (i.e., r=.227, p=.017). Consumers who were highly aliterate were also highly assertive, perhaps because they would rather ask for information instead of reading the information for themselves.

---

[2]Need for cognition scale adapted from Wood and Swait (2002)

[3]Assertiveness scale adapted from Richins (1983).

Consumers who had subscriptions to newspapers (i.e., including local or national newspapers such as *USA Today*) or to economic/political/academic periodicals (e.g., Fortune) were lower in consumer aliteracy than those who did not have these types of subscriptions (i.e., $mean_{news}$=2.39, $mean_{no\ news}$=3.10, p=.027, and $mean_{periodical}$=2.53, $mean_{no\ periodical}$=3.18, p=.015). Consumers who admitted to not holding any print subscriptions were more aliterate than those who did have some kind of print subscription (i.e., $mean_{no\ print}$=3.49, $mean_{print}$=2.71, p=.003).

Interestingly, consumers who held subscriptions to either magazines (e.g., *Cosmopolitan* or *Sports Illustrated*) or to hobby periodicals (e.g., *Golf*) did not significantly differ on consumer aliteracy (i.e., p=.181 and p=.236, respectively). Also, consumer aliteracy did not significantly correlate with number of books read in the past 30 days (i.e., r=.158, p=.10), nor did it significantly correlate with print or online newspaper readership (r=-.160, p=.09). This may be evidence that reading strictly for pleasure is not related to consumer aliteracy in the marketplace.

Consumer Aliteracy Research Questions

Additional research is necessary to understand the effects of consumer aliteracy on consumer behaviors. The current research will continue with two additional studies, focusing on the following research questions.

(1) Does consumer aliteracy bring about lower ad comprehension/ad liking? Research on levels of processing effect (e.g., Craik & Lockhart, 1972), holds that there are several factors that affect processing depth. Because they lack the motivation to read, aliterate consumers may not engage in deeper processing levels. In turn, failure to use their processing abilities may cause aliterate consumers to poorly comprehend written materials (Guthrie & Wigfield, 1999).

(2) Does ad complexity moderate the relationship between consumer aliteracy and ad comprehension/ad liking? When message readability gets more complicated, individuals' ability to assess message arguments tends to be reduced because their working memory capacity is reduced (Chebat et al., 2003). Thus, although both literate and aliterate consumers will display a drop in comprehension and subsequent ad liking as text difficulty increases, the drop should be more pronounced among highly aliterate consumers.

(3) Do visual aids in advertisements moderate the relationship between consumer aliteracy and ad comprehension/ad liking? In information processing, aliterate individuals have been shown to rely more on pictorial information than on detailed written information (Kylene, 1996, 110-113). Thus, pictures used as a form of visual aid in product advertisements will benefit aliterate consumers more than such aids will help literate consumers.

Conclusion

The aliteracy social phenomenon is growing but is difficult to detect and thus difficult to counter. An investigation of consumer aliteracy may enable managers to either try to influence the consumer aliteracy tendencies, or use non-word message strategies in order to better communicate with highly aliterate consumers.

References

Chebat, Jean-Charles, Claire Gelinas-Chebat, Sabrina Hombourger, and Arch Woodside (2003), "Testing Consumers' Motivation and Linguistic Ability as Moderators of Advertising Readability," *Psychology and Marketing*, 20(7), 599-624.

Craik, F. I. M., and Lockhart, R. S. (1972), "Levels of Processing: A Framework for Memory Research," *Journal of Verbal Learning and Verbal Behavior*, 11, 671-684.

Guthrie, John T. and Allan Wigfield (1999), "How Motivation Fits Into a Science of Reading," *Scientific Studies of Reading*, 3(3), 199-205.

Kylene, Beers G. (1996), "No time, No Interest, No Way," *School Library Journal*, 42(2), 30-33.

Mikulecky, Larry (1978), "Aliteracy and a Changing View of Reading Goals," Paper Presented at the 23rd Annual Meeting of the International Reading Association, Houston, Texas.

Richins, Marsha L. (1983), "An Analysis of Consumer Interaction Styles in the Marketplace," *Journal of Consumers Research*, 10 (June), 73-82.

Wallendorf, Melanie (2001), "Literally Literacy," *Journal of Consumer Research*, 27 (March), 505-511.

Wood, Stacy L. and Joffre Swait (2002), "Psychological Indicators of Innovation Adoption: Cross-Classification Based on Need for Cognition and Need for Change," *Journal of Consumer Psychology*, 12 (1), 1-13.

Too Many Cooks Spoil the Broth: How Conflicting Nonconscious Goals Influence Consumer Choice

Ji-Hoon Jhang, University of Colorado at Boulder, USA

Consumers are surrounded by a seemingly infinite number of brand images. Since Bargh (1990) proposed powerful effects of environmental cues on behavior, a burgeoning set of research in marketing has demonstrated that 1) environmental cues (e.g., brand images) can activate a consumer goal outside of awareness and 2) consumer choices are affected by this incidentally activated goal (e.g., Chartrand, Huber, Shiv, and Tanner, 2008).

These earlier works, however, leave two important questions unanswered regarding nonconscious goals. First, can various environmental cues encountered in everyday life (e.g., Nordstrom vs. Wal-Mart) activate multiple conflicting goals (e.g., prestige-related vs. thrift-related goals) outside of individuals' awareness? Second, if multiple (conflicting) nonconscious goals can be activated, how can those conflicting nonconscious goals shape consumer behavior? Despite a body of research in which multiple (conscious) goal pursuit has been examined (e.g., Fishbach and Dhar, 2005), no research has yet explored multiple nonconscious goal pursuit (for exception, see Laran and Janiszewski 2009 JCR). This study aims to address these two questions.

The objective of the current study is to examine 1) whether or not conflicting nonconscious goals can be activated and 2) how conflicting nonconscious goals, once activated, influence consumer behavior. I tested three competing hypotheses regarding the pursuit of conflicting nonconscious goals (i.e. inhibition, overriding, and conflicting) using product choice task.

Arguments for each hypothesis

Three competing hypotheses are as follows. The first is *the inhibition hypothesis*; the focal goal pursuit may inhibit the alternative goal pursuit. Both goal shielding theory (Shah et al. 2002) and conflicting goal pursuit literature (Fishbach and Dhar 2005) lend their supports to this hypothesis. The second is *the overriding hypothesis*; the alternative goal pursuit may undermine the focal goal pursuit. This overriding effect is hypothesized by goal pull theory (Shah and Kruglanski 2002) as well as associative network model (Anderson et al. 2004). Finally, the third is *the conflicting hypothesis*; both the focal goal and the alternative goal may be pursued simultaneously so that they compete. Atkinson and Birch (1970)'s *temporal escalation criterion* combined with goal pull theory (Shah and Kruglanski 2002) lends its support to this conflicting hypothesis. In summary, three competing hypotheses will be formally stated as,

H1a (The inhibiting hypothesis): The nonconscious pursuit of the focal goal would inhibit the nonconscious pursuit of the alternative goal.

H1b (The overriding hypothesis): The nonconscious pursuit of the alternative goal would override the nonconscious pursuit of the focal goal.

H1c (The conflicting hypothesis): Both the focal goal and the alternative goal would be nonconsciously pursued simultaneously.

The following experiment was designed to test three competing hypotheses proposed above. By looking at individuals' choice deferral tendencies, I examined which hypothesis is the most viable.

Study

Dhar (1997) showed that people who have to make a choice among equally attractive alternatives often opt not to choose or choose the no-choice option. This no-choice option task provides an experimental circumstance in which proposed three competing hypotheses can be tested.

The experimental design was a 4 (nonconscious goal priming:[4] prestige vs. thrift vs. vs. mingle (prestige-thrift or thrift-prestige) vs. control) between-subjects design. Since the prestige, thrift, and control conditions served as control conditions for each hypothesis, the three competing hypotheses were tested by comparisons between each goal priming condition. For instance, if *the inhibition hypothesis* is correct, the choice pattern between the prestige-thrift condition and the prestige condition would show no difference, and the same result should appear in the comparison between the thrift-prestige condition and the thrift condition. If *the overriding hypothesis* is correct, the choice pattern between the prestige-thrift condition and the thrift condition should be the same, and we should expect no differences between the thrift-prestige condition and the prestige condition as well. If *the conflicting hypothesis* is right, the proportion of the no-choice option should be greater in the mingle conditions than in other conditions.

Method

78 undergraduate students participated in the study for partial course credit. Following the introductory instruction, participants engaged in a scrambled-sentence task. Each participant conducted twenty sets of scrambled-sentence task. For participants in the 'one-goal' conditions (i.e. the prestige goal, the thrift goal), only the first ten sets of words will include goal-relevant words (e.g. "what, did, luxury, want, she") while the goal-relevant words will be replaced with goal-irrelevant words for the following ten sets of words (e.g. "what, did, can, want, she"). For participants in the 'conflicting goals' conditions (i.e., the prestige-thrift goal, the thrift-prestige goal, i.e., the mingle goal), each ten set included either prestige-relevant words or thrift-relevant words. Finally, all twenty sets of words included goal-irrelevant words for the control condition. After completing the sentence-scrambled task, each participant was asked to make a hypothetical choice between two sock options and the no-choice option. The choice task used in Chartrand et al.(2008) was modified and used; a) Nike at $5.25 a pair, b) Hanes at $6 for two pairs, and c) no-choice.

Results

The results supported *the competing hypothesis*. A greater proportion of participants chose the no-choice option in the mingle condition than the other three conditions ($Choice_{mingle}$[5]=42.1%, $Choice_{prestige}$=20% , $Choice_{thrift}$=23.8% , $Choice_{control}$=16.7%, $\chi^2[6]=16.11$, $p=.013$). There was no difference among the prestige, thrift, and control conditions. Also, the other choice proportions reflected the similar pattern found in Chartrand et al. (2008).

Discussion

Above result suggests that participants' choice pattern can be explained by *the competing hypothesis*. Neither the inhibition hypothesis nor the overriding hypothesis explains the choice pattern observed in the above study. Therefore, it is initially demonstrated that conflicting nonconscious goals are pursued simultaneously, rather than being inhibited or overridden. It should be noted, however,

[4]The prestige and thrift goals are chosen because 1) both goals are basic motivations every consumer would already have in their associative networks so that both goals can be activated outside of awareness, 2) both goals are perfectly conflicting and cannot be resolved, and 3) both goals are at similar level of specificity.

[5]There was no differences between the prestige-thrift and thrift-prestige condition, thus two conditions were collapsed and analyzed as the mingle condition.

that these results are just the initial evidence for conflicting nonconscious goal pursuit hypothesis. Thus, further tests should be done to clearly rule out the other two hypotheses.

References

Anderson, John R., Daniel Bothell, Michael D. Byrne, Scott Douglass, Christian Lebiere, and Yulin Qin (2004), "An Integrated Theory of the Mind," *Psychological Review*, 111(October), 1036-1060.

Atkinson, John W. and David Birch (1970), *A Dynamic Theory of Action*, New York: Wiley.

Bargh, John A. (1990), "Auto-motives: Preconscious Determinants of Social Interaction," in *Handbook of Motivation and Cognition*, Vol. 2, ed. E. Tory Higgins and Richard M. Sorrentino, New York: Guilford, 93-130.

Chartrand, Tanya L., Joel Huber, Baba Shive, and Robin J. Tanner (2008), "Nonconscious Goals and Consumer Choice," *Journal of Consumer Research*, 35(August), 189-201.

Dhar, Ravi (1997), "Consumer Preference for a No-Choice Option," *Journal of Consumer Research*, 24(September), 215-231

Fishbach, Ayelet and Ravi Dhar (2005), "Goals as Excuses or Guides: The Liberating Effect of Perceived Goal Progress on Choice," *Journal of Consumer Research*, 32(December), 370-377.

Shah, James Y., Ronald S. Friedman, and Arie W. Kruglanski (2002), "Forgetting All Else: On the Antecedents and Consequences of Goal Shielding," *Journal of Personality and Social Psychology*, 83(December), 1261-1280.

Shah, James Y., Arie W. Kruglanski (2002), "Priming Against Your Will: How Accessible Alternatives Affect Goal Pursuit," *Journal of Experimental Social Psychology*, 38(July), 368-383.

When Does Halo Prevail against Animosity? Country-of-Origin Effects Contingent on Regulatory Focus

He Jia, Nanjing University, China
Yonggui Wang, University of International Business and Economics, China
Yiren Dong, Nanjing University, China
Guocai Wang, Nanjing University, China

Prior research has demonstrated that country-of-origin-related associations with a foreign product play a significant role in consumers' evaluation (Maheswaran and Chen 2006). Two general types of association are indentified as halo and animosity, which influence consumers' product attitude in opposite directions (Hong and Kang 2006). For some foreign products marketed in certain regions, the halo effect and the animosity effect could co-exist when consumers' attention are drawn to the country of origin. Examples abound from Chinese consumers' evaluation of Japanese products to Australian consumers' attitude towards French products (Klein, Ettenson, and Morris 1998).

An important question going unheeded by prior research is: When does the halo dominate over the animosity in determining consumers' evaluation when a product's country of origin could stimulate both the halo effect regarding the association with superior quality and the animosity effect concerned with the persistent or temporary antipathy? This research addresses the aforementioned issue by drawing on regulatory focus theory (Higgins 1997). We propose the dual roles of regulatory focus in influencing consumers' attitude towards foreign products, whose country of origin could make both halo- and animosity-related associations simultaneously accessible to consumers in certain regions (referred to hereinafter as foreign products). Chinese consumers are investigated as a typical group who are susceptible to both the halo effect and the animosity effect when evaluating Japanese products.

Hypothesis Development

Extant country-of-origin literature suggests that consumers are susceptible to halo effect or animosity effect when they rely on the country-of-origin information rather than the attribute information for evaluation. Consumers use the country-of-origin information as a heuristic, whereas they rely on the substantive attribute information when they adopt systematic processing (Gürhan-Canli and Maheswaran 2000). Furthermore, halo and animosity differ in valence. The halo concerning the country-of-origin-related reputation in advanced techniques is positively valenced, whereas the activated animosity toward the country from which the product originates is negatively valenced.

Regulatory focus theory (Higgins 1997) suggests that people can pursue a goal with either a promotion or prevention focus. Promotion focus is oriented at accomplishment, whereas prevention focus is oriented at security. Friedman and Förster (2001) find that promotion-focused people tend to adopt a heuristic style of processing, whereas prevention-focused people are inclined to base their evaluation on a systematic style of processing. Besides, promotion-focused consumers are more sensitive to the presence and absence of positive outcomes, whereas prevention-focused consumers are more sensitive to the presence and absence of negative outcomes (Higgins 1997). As a consequence, the positive component of the focal object is more diagnostic to consumers with a promotion focus than the negative component, whereas the negative component of the focal object is more diagnostic to consumers with a prevention focus than the positive component (Shine, Park, and Wyer 2007).

Based on those findings of country-of-origin research and regulatory focus research, we posit that regulatory focus has dual effects during the process in which consumers evaluate foreign products. In the first stage, a promotion focus should propel consumers to adopt heuristic processing and rely on the country-of-origin information, whereas a prevention focus should propel consumers to adopt systematic processing and rely on the attribute information. In the second stage, a promotion focus makes the positively-valenced country-of-origin-related halo more diagnostic to consumers than the negatively-valenced country-of-origin-related animosity, whereas neither the halo nor the animosity influences prevention-focused consumers' product attitude since their attention are directed to the attribute information instead of the country-of-origin information.

Hence, we hypothesize that for promotion-focused consumers, the country-of-origin-related halo effect on product attitude is greater than the country-of-origin-related animosity effect; for prevention-focused consumers, neither the halo effect nor the animosity effect on product attitude is significant.

Study 1

Ninety-one Chinese students participated in an experiment with a one-factor (regulatory focus: promotion versus prevention) between-subject design. The first part of the study was to prime participants' regulatory focus with the similar tasks employed in Wan, Hong, and Sternthal (2009). In the ostensibly unrelated second part of the study, participants read a description of a LCD flat television. In the description, the television was highlighted as manufactured by a famous Japanese electronic company. Nine attributes were displayed along with a picture. Then, participants completed the measures of product attitude (Russell and Russell 2006), country-of-origin-related halo (Kaynak and Kara 2002), and country-of-origin-related animosity (Russell and Russell 2006).

The influence of regulatory focus on consumers' attitude towards the television (α=0.83) was significant (F (1, 89)=4.67, p<0.05). Participants with a promotion focus (M=5.39) evaluated the television more favorably than those with a prevention focus (M=4.92). Furthermore, product attitude was regressed on halo (α=0.93) and animosity (α=0.75) in the two groups of participants. For promotion-focused participants, the halo effect was significantly positive (β=0.33, p<0.05), whereas the animosity effect was negative but not significant (β=-0.11, *NS*). For prevention-focused participants, neither the halo effect (β=0.22, *NS*) nor the animosity effect (β=0.20, *NS*) was significant. This result provides initial evidence for the hypothesis.

Study 2

Although Study 1 demonstrated that prevention-focused consumers were not subject to country-of-origin-related halo or animosity effect, this study was inadequate to justify that prevention-focused consumers indeed rely on the attribute information for evaluation. Study 2 will solve this limitation. According to our theorizing, promotion-focused consumers' product attitude should remain unchanged no matter whether the attribute strength is strong or weak, for they focus on the country-of-origin information. In contrast, prevention-focused consumers' attitude towards foreign products should vary according to the attribute strength. Therefore, we predict an interaction effect between regulatory focus and attribute strength on consumers' attitude towards foreign products, which will be tested in Study 2.

Discussion

Based on regulatory focus theory, this research is among the initial efforts to investigate when the country-of-origin-related halo dominates over the country-of-origin-related animosity in determining consumers' attitude towards foreign products, which has rarely been explicated in the country-of-origin literature. In addition, the current research synthesizes and examines the dual roles of regulatory focus in shaping consumers' attitude.

Acknowledgment

The authors gratefully acknowledge the financial support of National Natural Science Foundation of China (Grant No. 70672018), the third phase of 211 Project of University of International Business and Economics (Grant No. 73200029), and the Research Center for Economic Transition and Development, Nanjing University, one of the National Key Innovation Centers for Philosophy and Social Science Disciplines of Ministry of Education of China.

References

Friedman, Ronald S. and Jens Förster (2001), "The Effects of Promotion and Prevention Cues on Creativity," *Journal of Personality and Social Psychology*, 81 (6), 1001-1013.

Gürhan-Canli, Zeynep and Durairaj Maheswaran (2000), "Determinants of Country-of-Origin Evaluations," *Journal of Consumer Research*, 27 (June), 96-108.

Higgins, E. Tory (1997), "Beyond Pleasure and Pain," *American Psychologist*, 52 (12), 1280-1300.

Hong, Sung-Tai and Dong K. Kang (2006), "Country-of-Origin Influences on Product Evaluations: The Impact of Animosity and Perceptions of Industriousness Brutality on Judgments of Typical and Atypical Products," *Journal of Consumer Psychology*, 16 (3), 232-239.

Kaynak, Erdener and Ali Kara (2002), "Consumer Perceptions of Foreign Products: An Analysis of Product-Country Images and Ethnocentrism," *European Journal of Marketing*, 36 (7/8), 928-949.

Klein, Jill G., Richard Ettenson, and Marlene D. Morris (1998), "The Animosity Model of Foreign Product Purchase: An Empirical Test in the People's Republic of China," *Journal of Marketing*, 62 (January), 89–100.

Maheswaran, Durairaj and Cathy Y. Chen (2006), "National Equity: Incidental Emotions in Country-of-Origin Effects," *Journal of Consumer Research*, 33 (December), 370-376.

Russell, Dale W. and Cristel Antonia Russell (2006), "Explicit and Implicit Catalysts of Consumer Resistance: The Effects of Animosity, Cultural Salience and Country-of-Origin on Subsequent Choice," *International Journal of Research in Marketing*, 23, 321-331.

Shine, Chul S., Jongwon Park, and Robert S. Wyer Jr. (2007), "Brand Synergy Effects in Multiple Brand Extensions," *Journal of Marketing Research*, 2007, 44 (November), 663-670.

Wan, Echo W., Jiewen Hong, and Brian Sternthal (2009), "The Effect of Regulatory Orientation and Decision Strategy on Brand Judgments," *Journal of Consumer Research*, 35 (April), 1026-1038.

Customization Mode, Decision Outcome, and Task Enjoyment: The Role of Regulatory Focus

He Jia, Nanjing University, China
Yonggui Wang, University of International Business and Economics, China

Mass-customization successfully balances between personalized products demanded by consumers and cost-efficiency pursued by firms (Franke and Schreier 2008). In particular, two customization modes are available for marketers and identified by consumer researchers from a perspective of option screening strategy (Levin et al. 2002; Park, Jun, and Macinnis 2000). Additive customization is to present consumers with a basic product and then invite them to add options to the product, which reflects a screening-in strategy. On the contrary, subtractive customization is to present a fully-loaded product and then invite consumers to delete options from the product, which reflects a screening-out strategy. The purpose of the current research is to investigate how the interplay between customization mode and regulatory focus (Higgins 1997) impacts decision outcome and task enjoyment when consumers participate in customization service.

Conceptual Framework

Customization Decision Outcome. This research examines how customization mode and regulatory focus interactively influence customization decision outcome by drawing on the accessibility-diagnosticity model (Feldman and Lynch 1988), which implies persuasiveness of information is determined by both accessibility and diagnosticity, and accessibility is a precondition for diagnosticity to influence people (Zhao and Pechmann 2007).

Consumers in additive customization regard the basic product as a reference point and perceive the added options as gains in utility, whereas those in subtractive customization take the fully-loaded product as a reference point and perceive the deleted options as losses in utility (Park, Jun, and Macinnis 2000). The loss aversion principle (Tversky and Kahneman 1991) points that a loss is perceived as more intense than a gain of the same objective magnitude (Park, Jun, and Macinnis 2000). This suggests that in subtractive customization the losses of utility due to option deletion are accessible to consumers, whereas in additive customization the gains of utility due to option addition may be not so much accessible to consumers.

Regulatory focus theory distinguishes two motivational orientations during goal pursuit: a promotion focus is oriented at accomplishing aspiration, which makes people assign more value to gains and nongains; a prevention focus is oriented at fulfilling responsibility, which makes people assign more value to losses and nonlosses (Higgins 1997). This implies that potential gains are more diagnostic to consumers with a promotion focus than those with a prevention focus, whereas potential losses are more diagnostic to consumers with a prevention focus than those with a promotion focus.

In subtractive customization, the loss of utility is accessible to both consumers with a prevention focus and those with a promotion focus, but more diagnostic to prevention-focused consumers. In contrast, the gain of utility in additive customization is not so much accessible as the loss in subtractive customization. Consequently, in additive customization the minimal level of accessibility of potential gains inhibits diagnosticity from influencing consumers' choice although potential gains are more diagnostic to promotion-focused consumers. Therefore, we hypothesize that in subtractive customization a prevention focus should propel consumers to delete fewer options and as a result retain more options in the final customized offering than a promotion focus, whereas in additive customization the effect of regulatory focus should disappear.

Customization Task Enjoyment. Based on regulatory fit theory (Higgins 2000), this research also addresses consumers' task enjoyment, another important aspect of customization performance. Regulatory fit is a condition when the strategic means people use to pursue goals fit their regulatory focus (Higgins 2000). An approach strategy (approaching positive outcomes) sustains a promotion focus, whereas an avoidance strategy (avoiding negative outcomes) sustains a prevention focus. When the strategic means for goal pursuit fits one's regulatory focus, people just "feel right" and then unconsciously attribute their feeling to the stimulus they focus on, leading to an even more favorable evaluation (Avent and Higgins 2006).

From a perspective of option screening strategy (Levin et al. 2002), additive customization makes consumers naturally screen in options with desirable attributes, whereas subtractive customization makes consumers naturally screen out options with undesirable attributes. Therefore, additive customization is consistent with an approach strategy, whereas subtractive customization is similar to an avoidance strategy. In correspondence with regulatory fit theory, we hypothesize that promotion-focused consumers should more enjoy additive customization than prevention-focused consumers, whereas prevention-focused consumers should more enjoy subtractive customization than promotion-focused consumers.

Study 1

A group of Chinese students participated in a 2 X 2 between-subject experiment with both regulatory focus and customization mode manipulated, generating 92 valid responses. Participants in the additive customization condition were told that they could add ingredients to a basic pizza, whereas those in the subtractive customization condition were told that they could delete ingredients from a fully-loaded pizza (Levin et al. 2002). The number of options retained in the final customized offering was calculated to measure customization decision outcome. Participants also completed a scale of customization task enjoyment (Park, Jun, and Macinnis 2000).

The interaction effect between regulatory focus and customization mode on decision outcome was found significant (F (1, 88)=4.86, p<0.05) and mainly driven by the effect of regulatory focus in subtractive customization. Moreover, there was a marginally significant interaction effect between those two factors on task enjoyment (F (1, 88)=3.77, p=0.055). Further simple contrasts were also consistent with our predictions (detailed statistics provided upon request).

Study 2

The characteristics of options retained in the final customized offering might influence consumers' task enjoyment. Study 2 will control the quantity and price of options retained in the final product to exclude this possibility and further test the robustness of the findings of Study 1 in another scenario. Besides, the boundary condition for the interaction effect on consumers' customization evaluation will be addressed.

Discussion

Theoretically, this research finds that the effect of regulatory focus on the number of options retained in the final customized offering is contingent on customization mode, which adds knowledge to the multi-option screening literature. Another contribution of the current research is to extend regulatory fit theory into a customization service context. Managerially, this research answers how to match customization mode with regulatory focus in order to accomplish superior customer value in customization service.

Acknowledgment

The authors gratefully acknowledge the financial support of National Natural Science Foundation of China (Grant No. 70672018), the third phase of 211 Project of University of International Business and Economics (Grant No. 73200029), and the Research Center for Economic Transition and Development, Nanjing University, one of the National Key Innovation Centers for Philosophy and Social Science Disciplines of Ministry of Education of China.

References

Avent, Tamar and E. Tory Higgins (2006), "How Regulatory Fit Affects Value in Consumer Choices and Options," *Journal of Marketing Research,* 43 (February), 1-10.

Feldman, Jack M. and John G. Lynch Jr. (1988), "Self-Generated Validity and Other Effects of Measurement on Belief, Attitude, Intention, and Behavior," *Journal of Applied Psychology*, 73 (August), 421–35.

Franke, Nikolaus and Martin Schreier (2008), "Product Uniqueness as A Driver of Customer Utility in Mass Customization," *Marketing Letters*, 19, 93-107.

Higgins, E. Tory (1997), "Beyond Pleasure and Pain," *American Psychologist*, 52 (12), 1280-1300.

Higgins, E. Tory (2000), "Making a Good Decision: Value From Fit," *American Psychologist*, 55 (11), 1217-1230.

Levin, Irwin P., Judy Schreiber, Marco Lauriola, and Gary J. Gaeth (2002), "A Tale of Two Pizzas: Building Up from a Basic Product Versus Scaling Down from a Fully-Loaded Product," *Marketing Letters*, 13 (4), 335-344.

Park, C. Whan, Sung Y. Jun, and Deborah J. Macinnis (2000), "Choosing What I Want Versus Rejecting What I Do Not Want: An Application of Decision Framing to Product Option," *Journal of Marketing Research*, 37 (May), 187-202.

Tversky, Amos and Daniel Kahneman (1991), "Loss Aversion in Riskless Choice: A Reference-Dependent Model," *Quarterly Journal of Economics*, 106 (November), 1039-1061.

Zhao, Guangzhi and Cornelia Pechmann (2007), "The Impact of Regulatory Focus on Adolescents' Response to Antismoking Advertising Campaigns," *Journal of Marketing Research*, 44 (November), 671-687.

Becoming a Responsible Consumer: Using Narratives to Study the Development Paths and Goals

Suvi Joronen, University of Vaasa, Finland

The concept of a new consumer type, an alternative consumer, appeared as far back as the 1970´s so the phenomenon itself is not very new. Characteristics like ethicality, green, fair trade and the concern toward developing countries became to define this new consumer type (Gabriel & Lang, 1995). This paper explores how the responsibility is constructed as a part of a consumer's life.

The theory is drawn here not only trough the attitudinal dimensions, but especially through the personality indicators and the influence of the overall social structure. As Degevos (2005) states, the importance of socio-cultural and socio-psychological determinants should not be underestimated in the consumer studies.

The responsibility can be seen as a consequence led by the particular personality variables and the specific events in the socio-cultural environment. These personality variables include such inner entities as values, motives, moral conceptions and subjective norms. Especially the existence of certain nature related values have been found to have an influence to the responsible consumption behavior (e.g., Grunert & Juhl, 1995). Also, the change in a value system (e.g, anthropocentric values ? ecocentric values) is assumed to precede the behavioral change (see Rokeach, 1973). Besides the normative nature of subjective norms, the social norms often advise consumers to behave in a certain way. It depends on the nature of cultural and political environment how the sustainable consumption is adopted in a certain country. Both the person's subjective development processes as well as the influences outside are here assumed to be the principal factors explaining the process of growing as a responsible consumer.

Qualitative research was conducted to study respondents' subjective experiences about responsible consumption. Written biographies were chosen as a narrative research method (see Riessman, 1993). The written biographies are found to be appropriate in the identity development studies (e.g., Hole, 2007). Therefore, in this study, I used written truth based stories for finding out how responsibility has become an integral part of respondent's self-identity. The study was based on a sample of Finnish and French consumers at the age range from 24 to 63, whit a bias toward the lower ages. There were a total of seventeen informants; four males and fourteen females. Four of the informants were French including two of them living in an autonomic eco-village. The sample choice was a convenience sample followed a snow-ball sampling. It was considered as crucial that the sample members were responsible consumers. In order to assure this, the respondents needed to meet at least one of the following criterions: *1) Buying fair trade and/or organic products regularly 2) Boycotting products found being unethical 3) Collective activity, as a membership in associations.*

A postal questionnaire was developed and which was similar to all informants. In the first part of the questionnaire, the respondents were asked to write a truth based story of a following topic: *"Me as a responsible consumer"*. They were asked to describe the events from childhood until the present day. In the second part of the questionnaire, the respondents were asked about socio-demographic characteristics including age, gender, education and the nature of being a responsible consumer (the frequency of buying fair trade/organic products, participation in associations, boycotts).

The analysis was made at two levels. At the first level, the differences in the thematic structures of stories indicated how the responsible consumption appears mostly as a specific goal for the respondents. Each of these four goals included two main themes which were found through the content analysis. These goals vary particularly according to the motives, the level of commitment and the actualized responsible actions. The goals I nominated as follows: *1) Responsibility as a way to rational consumption 2) Responsibility as a way to healthiness 3) Responsibility as a way to save the nature 4) Being comprehensively responsible*. These goals are not absolute in the sense that the same respondent can have more than just one goal. Moreover, the changes in goals over time became apparent in the stories. For example, the responsibility starts to have more meanings in respondent's life and this lead adopting new goals and perhaps also new behavioral patterns.

At the second level of analysis, the plot structure of stories was used to identify whether there are differences in the developing paths. Through that I noticed that each story can be divided into three life stages: childhood, youth, and maturity. Three distinctive developing paths were nominated as follows: *1) From childhood landscape into eco-consumerism 2) Through teenage rebel into savior of earth 3) Through slowly changing into a critical consumer*. This life stage separation allowed recognizing not the particular stage of life in which the identity as a responsible consumer started to develop but also the possible changes in time concerning the personal commitment and goals. For example, the changes in the subjective values and motives or in social environment seemed to have an influence on the process of growing into a responsible consumer.

The study indicates firstly the different positions of responsible consumption in respondent's life. For example, for one the responsible consumption appears as a goal to be healthy while for another it appears as an intention to change the "bad capitalistic world". For most of the respondents, the commitment appears as daily routines including such actions as recycling, giving donations, buying fair trade/organic products and boycotting unethical business. On the other hand, the goal of being comprehensively responsible indicates more radical form of responsibility (c.f. The Simple Living Movement). Secondly, the life stage division helped to recognize the special events and changes in timeline. This permitted again finding out the specific life period which was significant in terms of growing into a responsible consumer. Worth noting is also the changes in the level of personal commitment and goals which can lead someone to move from modest behavioral patters toward more extreme or vice versa.

References

Degevos, H. (2005), "Consumers as Four-Faced Creatures. Looking at Food Consumption from the Perspective of Contemporary Consumer," *Appetite*, 45(1), 32-39.

Gabriel, Y. and T. Lang (1995), *The Unmanageable Consumer,* London etc.: Sage Publications.

Grunert S. and H.J. Juhl (1995), "Values, Environmental Attitudes, and Buying of Organic Foods," *Journal of Economic Psychology,* 16, 39–62.

Hole, R. (2007), "The Narratives of Identity: A Postructural Analysis of Three Deaf Women´s Life Stories," *Narrative Inquiry*, 17(2), 259-278.

Riessman, M. (1993), *Narrative Analysis*, Newbury Park (Calif.): Sage Publications.

Rokeach, M. (1973), *Nature of Human Values*, New York: The Free Press.

The Role of Quality-of-Experience and Affect in Maladaptive Food Consumption

Luke Kachersky, Fordham University, USA

Sylvia Clark, St. John's University, USA

"Hungry? Why wait," asks a popular advertisement for a candy bar. Perhaps more curious is the inverse, "Waiting? Why hunger?" In a recent survey, 47% of 16-24 year-olds and 40% of 35-44 year-olds reported that they had eaten because they had nothing better to do (BBC News, 2004). This is an important issue since such maladaptive behavior undermines long-term life satisfaction (Kushner and Foster 2000).

The accepted knowledge of consumer behavior posits that consumers exhaust resources in order to satisfy needs. In eating, consumers use up natural resources–animals and plants–to sustain themselves. Yet, as the BBC survey indicates, eating that is not motivated by sustenance is a common occurrence. So which need is satisfied in such consumption? In addition to sustenance needs, people have experiential needs to "keep consciousness in an organized state, focused on some activity that requires attention" (Csikszentmihalyi 2000, p. 270). When people satisfy such needs with high-quality experiences, they also satisfy the ultimate goal of feeling good (Csikszentmihalyi 1993, 1997). The present research proposes that people eat when they are deficient in QOE to improve their experiential and affective states.

There are other options besides eating to satisfy experiential needs; one could engage oneself in work or hobbies, for example. However, humans often use shortcuts to satisfy psychological needs. Eating both immediately engages attention and, as many studies have shown, provides a psychophysical response that improves one's affective state (e.g. Christensen 2001, Van der Does 2001). While this sounds like a promising solution, studies have shown that consumers are happier when they are having high-quality experiences than when they are consuming (Csikszentmihalyi 1997, 1999). As a result, the following relationships among quality-of-experience (QOE), eating, and affect are proposed:

H1: Consumers having high-quality experiences will eat less than those having low-quality experiences.
H2: Consumers having high quality experiences will feel more positive affect than those having low-quality experiences.
H3: Amount of food eaten will be positively correlated to positive affect for consumers having low-quality experiences, but will have no impact on positive affect for those having high-quality experiences.

Our first study was conducted with 34 participants recruited from introductory marketing classes at a large northeastern university. Students were offered extra course credit in exchange for their participation. Participants were first asked to work on a task in which they were given ten minutes to unscramble as many words as possible from a list of 75 scrambled five-letter words. A bag of 60 Skittles candies was placed on each participant's desk, and they were free to partake. At the conclusion of this task, participants were asked to stop working and to place their bag of Skittles underneath their chairs. The number of Skittles eaten served as our measure of food consumption. They then completed a questionnaire measuring positive and negative affect (PANAS; Watson, Clark, and Tellegen 1988); perceived skill and challenge of the word task (Novak 1997; to measure QOE); the last time they ate, and liking for Skittles. Finally, at dismissal participants were told the true purpose of the study and given the option to have their data discarded. No participants chose this option.

Low QOE denotes a person of low-to-moderate skills whose skills are mismatched with the perceived challenge of the experience. High QOE means skills are high and commensurate with the challenge of the experience (Csikszentmihalyi 1990). Participants' responses to the perceived skill and perceived challenge scales were placed on a "map of everyday experience" (Csikszentmihalyi 2003), which is a Cartesian plane with axes defined for challenge and skill. The plane is divided into low-quality experiences (e.g., apathy) and high-quality experiences (e.g., arousal). The resulting classification matched the underlying construct. High QOE participants (N=14) saw themselves as skilled at the word task and perceived the task as offering a similarly high level of challenge (M_{skill}=4.71 vs. $M_{challenge}$=5.11, p=.32). Low QOE participants (N=20) saw themselves as less skilled, and overmatched by the challenge (M_{skill}=2.70 vs. $M_{challenge}$=3.77, p<.01). Across the QOE groups, participants did not differ in their liking for Skittles, the last time they ate, or the number of words they correctly solved (p's>.20).

In keeping with hypothesis 1, high QOE participants ate fewer Skittles than did low QOE participants (M_{high}=7.79 vs. M_{low}=17.65, p<.03). Further, consistent with hypothesis 2, high QOE participants felt more positive affect than low QOE participants (M_{high}=3.44 vs. M_{low}=2.82, p<.03). However, as predicted in hypothesis 3, as low QOE participants ate more Skittles, they also felt more positive affect (r=.55, p<.02), but the same was not true for high QOE participants (r=-.025, p=.93).

Together, these results suggest that a deficiency in QOE can drive people to eat more (hypothesis 1), which improves one's affective state (hypothesis 3), but not to the extent of a high-quality experience (hypothesis 2). This study represents a first step in explaining the causes and consequences of eating to satisfy experiential but not sustenance needs. Follow-up studies will explore ways in which consumers and marketers can cure this maladaptive behavior.

References

BBC News (2004), "Comfort and 'Boredom'-Eating Rife," http://news.bbc.co.uk/go/pr/fr//2/hi/health/3590086.htm.
Christensen, Lawrence (2001), "The Effect of Food Intake on Mood," *Clinical Nutrition*, 20:161-66.
Csikszentmihalyi, Mihaly (1993), *The Evolving Self*, New York: HarperCollins.
______ (1997), *Finding Flow*, New York: Basic.
______ (1999), "If We Are So Rich, Why Aren't We Happy?" *American Psychologist*, 54(10), 821-27.
______ (2000), "The Costs and Benefits of Consuming," *Journal of Consumer Research*, 27(2): 267-72.
______ (2003), *Good Business: Leadership. Flow, and the Making of Meaning*, New York: Penguin Group.
Kushner, Robert and Gary Foster (2000), "Obesity and Quality of Life," *Nutrition*, 16, 947-52.
Novak, Thomas P. and Donna L. Hoffman (1997), "Measuring the Flow Experience Among Web Users," paper presented at the Interval Research Corporation, Palo Alto, CA.
Van der Does, AJ (2001), "The Effects of Tryptophan Depletion on Mood and Psychiatric Symptoms," *Journal of Affective Disorders*, 64, 107-19.
Watson, David, Lee Anna Clark, and Auke Tellegen (1988), "Development and Validation of Brief Measures of Positive and Negative Affect: The PANAS Scales," *Journal of Personality and Social Psychology*, 54(6), 1063-70.

Mine Versus Ours: Does It Matter?

Bernadette Kamleitner, Queen Mary, University of London, UK
Anna Rabinovich, University of Exeter, UK

In particular when it comes to high-involvement acquisitions consumers often jointly buy and own objects such as cars, computers, and houses. Whereas there is extensive literature on how these joint decisions come about (e.g., Davis 1976; Su et al. 2008), there is paucity in research on how joint ownership affects consumer behavior after an acquisition has been made. The question of whether joint ownership leads to differences in consumer behavior has yet to be addressed. Theoretically there are three possibilities. First, there may be no behavioral differences between joint and individual owners as both cases involve factual ownership. For the most part existing consumer literature on ownership effects does not address the issue of different ownership modes (e.g., Beggan 1992; Kahneman, Knetsch, and Thaler 1991); possibly because no differences are to be expected.

Second, joint ownership may have a positive impact on consumer behavior. It has been argued that ownership creates a sense of responsibility for an object (e.g., Furby 1978) which instigates behaviors towards protecting and enhancing the owned object (e.g., Van Dyne and Pierce 2004). Joint ownership signifies that at least two consumers are entitled to use an object and can hence be held responsible to each other. As a consequence joint owners may feel even more responsible towards the owned object than individual owners and may hence take more care of the object.

Third, joint ownership may have a negative impact on consumer behavior. On the one hand joint ownership and the resulting joint responsibility may lead to a decrease in experienced responsibility (Latane 1981) and lead to less behavioral care for the object. On the other hand, there is evidence that effects of ownership are mainly due to the degree to which ownership is perceived as such (e.g., Reb and Connolly 2007). It seems plausible to assume that joint ownership decreases the sense of ownership experienced and hence reduces a consumer's willingness to care for an object.

In two studies we gather initial information on whether joint ownership leads consumers to behave differently towards an object than individual ownership.

Study 1 assessed whether consumers intuitively believe that the mere fact of joint ownership leads to differences in consumer behavior. Participants (53 students) read a scenario about two students who each got a car from their parents. The only difference between the two students is the actual ownership mode. One student is sole owner of the car, one student shares ownership with the mother. Actual usage by other people and expenses are kept constant. After reading the scenario participants indicated which student was more likely to engage in four different acts of caring for the car (e.g., checking it for scratches; alpha=.76), who felt more responsible for the car and who experienced a stronger sense of ownership.

Mean values of all items were compared to the scale midpoint (4=both equally likely). Results show that participants thought that joint ownership decreases the care taken for the car, decreases the responsibility felt for the car, and decreases perceived ownership of the car. In a regression, responsibility and perceived ownership significantly predict the likelihood of caring for the car.

Study 2 assessed whether lay intuitions observed in study 1 are in line with actual consumer behavior. Participants (61 students) were asked to answer questions about the computer or laptop they use most frequently. To assess actual ownership status participants were asked to report the number of regular users as well as the legal ownership situation. In addition, participants were asked to report on perceived ownership, perceived responsibility, and their behavior towards the computer (all alphas >.60). The eight items assessing behavior loaded on two different factors: behavior that prevents the computer from being damaged (e.g., not drinking at the keyboard) and behavior that promotes the computer (e.g., buying add-ons).

In separate regressions, the number of users had no effect on perceived responsibility and prevention behaviors. However, the larger the number of regular users, the less participants engage in behaviors that promote the computer and the lower is their perceived sense of ownership. Perceived sense of ownership predicts promotion behavior. Results were replicated with regard to legal ownership status. Controlling for the time spent with the computer did not alter the results.

To conclude, it seems that compared to individual ownership joint ownership has a detrimental effect on behavior towards an owned object. This effect is reflected in consumers' lay intuition. However, whereas lay intuition seems to relate this finding to both decreased perceived responsibility and decreased perceived ownership, actual behavior was only affected by perceived ownership. In addition, whereas lay intuition seems to assume an effect of joint ownership on all forms of caring behavior, the actual effect was restricted to behaviors that promote the owned object.

Selected References

Beggan, James K. (1992), "On the social nature of nonsocial perception-the mere ownership effect," *Journal of Personality and Social Psychology*, 62 (2), 229-37.

Davis, Harry L. (1976), "Decision making within the household," *Journal of Consumer Research*, 2 (4), 241-60.

Furby, Lita (1978), "Possession in Humans-Exploratory-Study of Its Meaning and Motivation," *Social Behavior and Personality*, 6 (1), 49-65.

Kahneman, Daniel, Jack L. Knetsch, and Richard H. Thaler (1991), "The endowment effect, loss aversion, and status quo bias," *Journal of Economic Perspectives*, 5 (1), 193-206.

Latane, Bibb (1981), "The Psychology of Social Impact," *American Psychologist*, 36 (4), 343-56.

Reb, Jochen and Terry Connolly (2007), "Possessions, feelings of ownership and the endowment effect," *Judgment and Decision Making*, 2 (2), 29-36.

Su, Chenting, Kevin Zheng Zhou, Nan Zhou, and Julie Juan Li (2008), "Harmonizing conflict in husband-wife purchase decision making: perceived fairness and spousal influence dynamics," *Journal of the Academy of Marketing Science*, 36 (3), 378-94.

Van Dyne, Linn and Jon L. Pierce (2004), "Psychological ownership and feelings of possession: three field studies predicting employee attitudes and organizational citizenship behavior," *Journal of Organizational Behavior*, 25 (4), 439-59.

A Meta-Analytic Review of Racial Similarity Effects in Advertising

Ioannis Kareklas, University of Connecticut, USA
Maxim Polonsky, University of Connecticut, USA

The ideological struggle of African Americans during the early 1960s and throughout the 1970s was instrumental in elevating concern for ethnic minorities in American society. Marketing academicians and practitioners alike took note of the social advances which emerged from the civil rights movement. Advertisers started targeting African American consumers more systematically, and begun to feature more African American models in their advertisements (DelVecchio and Goodstein 2004). Academic researchers responded by investigating how majority and minority consumers evaluate racially integrated advertisements.

Underlying this newly found interest in ethnic consumers has been the desire on the part of the advertising community to respond to the moral criticism, which was increasingly directed towards advertisers, summarized by Barban and Cundiff as "You must "integrate" your advertising because it is morally reprehensible to do otherwise" (Barban and Cundiff 1964). Specifically, both the NAACP (National Association for the Advancement of Colored People) and CORE (Congress of Racial Equality) urged national advertisers to feature more African American models in their ads (Block 1972). At least partially in reaction to these pressures, the representation of ethnic minorities in magazine advertisements doubled between 1965 and 1969 (Kassarjian 1969), and there was a proliferation of research examining the effects associated with featuring ethnic minorities in advertisements, with particular attention to assessing reactions by White and Black consumers to ads featuring Black models.

Some studies investigated how White American consumers respond to advertisements featuring minority models (e.g., Bush, Gwinner, and Solomon 1974; Bush, Hair, Jr., and Solomon 1979; Hoon and Ramaprasad 2006; Whittler and DiMeo 1991), whereas others focused on the advertising evaluations of African American consumers in response to ads featuring minority models (e.g., Green 1999; Simpson et al. 2000; Whittler and Spira 2002). Studies also examined the advertising evaluations of both majority and minority consumers in response to advertisements, featuring both White American and African American models in the same ad (e.g., Barban 1969; Cagley and Cardozo 1970; Schmid 2000; Stafford, Birdwell, and Van Tassel 1970). A smaller subset of studies in this domain investigated the advertising evaluations of Asian American consumers (e.g., Brumbaugh and Grier 2006; Forehand and Deshpande 2001; Schumann, Lee, and Watchravesringkan 2004), and Hispanic consumers (e.g., Appiah 2001; Avery, Hernandez, and Hebl 2004; Deshpande and Stayman 1994) in response to ads featuring similar versus different-race models.

As minorities were increasingly being portrayed in media advertisements, a mounting body of research examined the potential for an adverse reaction to this growing practice by White consumers. The basic premise of this argument, which has been termed "White backlash," is that attempts to appear more socially responsible and appeal to minority consumers by featuring Black models in ads may lead to alienating White consumers (Barban 1969; Barban and Cundiff 1964; Block 1972; Stafford, Birdwell, and Van Tassel 1970). Backlash may take the form of a negative attitude towards the ad, the spokesperson, the company, the product, or the brand being advertised (Schmid 2000). If true, this is a justifiable concern given that the purchasing power of White consumers greatly exceeds that of all of the other racial groups in the U.S. (Humphreys 2008). However, early empirical investigations tended to disconfirm the existence of White backlash, finding instead that White consumers did not react adversely to integrated commercials, or commercials featuring all-Black models (e.g., Barban 1969; Barban and Cundiff 1964; Block 1972; Stafford, Birdwell, and Van Tassel 1970).

Some research in this domain has yielded opposite than expected results, with participants preferring racially dissimilar endorsers. For example, David et al. (2002) report that White participants rated Black models as more attractive than White models, and even considered themselves more similar to the Black than the White models. Similarly, a recent study by Wang and Arpan (2008) found that White participants rated Black (as compared to White) spokespersons as more credible, and evaluated Public Service Announcements (PSAs) more favorably when the spokespersons were Black as opposed to when they were White.

The Current Review

The aforementioned studies offer often confounding results. Some researchers suggest that both majority and minority consumers provide favorable advertising evaluations when ads feature similar race (vs. different-race) models (for a review, see Whittler 1991), while others report participants preferring racially dissimilar endorsers (e.g., David et al. 2002; Wang and Arpan 2008). The purpose of this paper is to report the findings of a meta-analysis which was conducted to summarize extant findings related to the effects of racial similarity (vs. dissimilarity) between source and participants on the advertising evaluations of Black, White, Hispanic, and Asian consumers. In total, forty one independent papers spanning forty years of publications (from 1969 to 2009) are included in the meta-analysis, which include responses from a total of 10,056 participants (3,232 Black, 6,263 White, 419 Asian, and 142 Hispanic).

Inclusion Criteria

Studies were deemed eligible for inclusion if they met all of the following criteria: (a) used Black and/or White, and/or Hispanic, and/or Asian participants, (b) exposed participants to advertisements featuring both similar-race and different-race models, (c) provided a measure of participants' advertising evaluations (such as attitude towards the ad, attitude toward the brand, or purchase intention), (d) reported data that came from independent samples, which were not published in any other study already included in the meta-analysis, and (e) provided sufficient quantitative empirical results that allowed calculation of an effect size.

Preliminary Results

A priori moderator analyses revealed that source-participant racial similarity is most important for Hispanic participants (d=.67, 95% CI=.39, .96, p<.001), followed by Black participants (d=.56, 95% CI=.51, .61, p<.001), then by Asian participants (d=.16, 95% CI=.03, .30, p<.05), and finally by White participants (d=.15, 95% CI=.11, .18, p<.001). Additionally, the effect of racial similarity on participants' advertising evaluations for papers published in Psychology journals (d=.57, p<.001) far exceeded effect sizes published in Communication (d=.06, p<.05) and Marketing journals (d=.05, p<.001).

Selected References

(Studies Included in the Meta-Analysis)

Aaker, Jennifer L., Anne M. Brumbaugh, and Sonya A. Grier (2000), "Nontarget Markets and Viewer Distinctiveness: The Impact of Target Marketing on Advertising Attitudes," *Journal of Consumer Psychology*, 9 (3), 127-40.

Appiah, Osei (2001b), "Ethnic Identification on Adolescents' Evaluations of Advertisements," *Journal of Advertising Research*, 41 (5), 7-22.

Avery, Derek R., Morela Hernandez, and Michelle R. Hebl (2004), "Who's Watching the Race? Racial Salience in Recruitment Advertising," *Journal of Applied Social Psychology*, 34 (1), 146-61.

Barban, Arnold M. (1969), "The Dilemma Of" Integrated" Advertising," *The Journal of Business*, 42 (4), 477-97.

Barban, Arnold M. and Edward W. Cundiff (1964), "Negro and White Response to Advertising Stimuli," *Journal of Marketing Research*, 1 (4), 53-56.

Block, Carl E. (1972), "White Backlash to Negro Ads: Fact or Fantasy?," *Journalism Quarterly*, 49 (Summer), 258-62.

Brumbaugh, Anne M. and Sonya A. Grier (2006), "Insights from a 'Failed' Experiment: Directions for Pluralistic, Multiethnic Advertising Research," *Journal of Advertising*, 35 (3), 35-46.

Brunel, Frederic F., Brian C. Tietje, and Anthony G. Greenwald (2004), "Is the Implicit Association Test a Valid and Valuable Measure of Implicit Consumer Social Cognition?," *Journal of Consumer Psychology*, 14 (4), 385-404.

Bush, Ronald F., Joseph F. Hair, and Paul J. Solomon (1979), "Consumers' Level of Prejudice and Response to Black Models in Advertisements," *Journal of Marketing Research*, 16 (3), 341-45.

Cagley, James W. and Richard N. Cardozo (1970), "White Response to Integrated Advertising," *Journal of Advertising Research*, Vol. 10 (2), 35-39.

Choudhury, Pravat K. and Lawrence S. Schmid (1974), "Black Models in Advertising to Blacks," *Journal of Advertising Research*, 14 (3), 19-22.

David, Prabu, Glenda Morrison, Melissa A. Johnson, and Felecia Ross (2002), "Body Image, Race, and Fashion Models: Social Distance and Social Identification in Third-Person Effects," *Communication Research*, 29 (3), 270-94.

DelVecchio, Devon and Ronald C. Goodstein (2004), "Moving Beyond Race: The Role of Ethnic Identity in Evaluating Celebrity Endorsers," in *Diversity in Advertising: Broadening the Scope of Research Directions*, ed. Jerome D. Williams, Wei-Na Lee and Curtis P. Haugtvedt, Mahwah, New Jersey: Lawrence Erlbaum Associates, Publishers.

Deshpande, Rohit and Douglas M. Stayman (1994), "A Tale of Two Cities: Distinctiveness Theory and Advertising Effectiveness," *Journal of Marketing Research*, 31 (1), 57-64.

Forehand, Mark R. and Rohit Deshpande (2001), "What We See Makes Us Who We Are: Priming Ethnic Self-Awareness and Advertising Response," *Journal of Marketing Research*, 38 (3), 336-48.

Fullagar, Clive and Julian Barling (1983), "Social Learning Theory: A Psychological Approach to Advertising Effectiveness?," *South African Journal of Psychology*, 13 (1), 18-22.

Green, Corliss L. (1999), "Ethnic Evaluations of Advertising: Interaction Effects of Strength of Ethnic Identification, Media Placement, and Degree of Racial Composition," *Journal of Advertising*, 28 (1), 49-64.

Guest, Lester (1970), "How Negro Models Affect Company Image," *Journal of Advertising Research*, 10 (2), 29-33.

Hoon, William (2005), "Effects of Model Race/Ethnicity on Responses to Print Advertising: Do Popular Culture Identification and Prejudice Make a Difference?," Ph.D., Southern Illinois University at Carbondale, United States—Illinois.

Hoon, William and Jyotika Ramaprasad (2006), "Effects of Model Race/Ethnicity on Responses to Print Advertising: Do Popular Culture and Prejudice Make a Difference?," in *Conference Papers—International Communication Association*: International Communication Association, 1-25.

Lai, Hsiu-chen Sandra, Zoe Tan, and Marye Tharp (1990), "Receiver Prejudice and Model Ethnicity: Impact on Advertising Effectiveness," *Journalism Quarterly*, 67 (4), 794-803.

Lwin, May O. and Chow-Hou Wee (2000), "The Influence of Spokeperson's Race in Relation to Accents Used in Television Commercials," *Journal of Current Issues & Research in Advertising*, 22 (1), 67-83.

Martin, Brett A. S., Christina Kwai-Choi Lee, and Feng Yang (2004), "The Influence of Ad Model Ethnicity and Self-Referencing on Attitudes: Evidence from New Zealand," *Journal of Advertising*, 33 (4), 27-37.

Muse, William V. (1971), "Product-Related Response to Use of Black Models in Advertising," *Journal of Marketing Research*, 8 (1), 107-09.

Perkins, Lesley A., Kecia M. Thomas, and Gail A. Taylor (2000), "Advertising and Recruitment: Marketing to Minorities," *Psychology & Marketing*, 17 (3), 235.

Qualls, William J. and David J. Moore (1990), "Stereotyping Effects on Consumers' Evaluation of Advertising: Impact of Racial Differences between Actors and Viewers," *Psychology & Marketing*, 7 (2), 135-51.

Raspberry, Patricia Dodson (1997), "Racial Cues, Involvement and Advertising: An Information Processing Perspective," Ph.D., University of Michigan, United States—Michigan.

Schlinger, Mary J. and Joseph T. Plummer (1972), "Advertising in Black and White," *Journal of Marketing Research*, Vol. 9 (2), 149-53.

Schmid, Jill Diane (2000), "White Backlash Revisited: Consumer Response to Model's Race in Print Advertisements," Ph.D., University of Washington, United States—Washington.

Schumann, David W., Jinkook Lee, and Kittichai Watchravesringkan (2004), "The Case for Separation of Asian American Ethnic Groups as We Consider Our Target-Market Strategies," in *Diversity in Advertising: Broadening the Scope of Research Directions.*, Mahwah, NJ: Lawrence Erlbaum Associates Publishers, 341-55.

Simpson, Eithel M., Thelma Snuggs, Tim Christiansen, and Kelli E. Simples (2000), "Race, Homophily, and Purchase Intentions and the Black Consumer," *Psychology & Marketing*, 17 (10), 877-89.

Stafford, James E., Al E. Birdwell, and Charles E. Van Tassel (1970), "Integrated Advertising—White Backlash?," *Journal of Advertising Research*, 10 (2), 15-20.

Sullivan, Ryan Dabo (2004), "A Study Measuring Product-Related Reactions to the Use of Black Models in Advertising," M.S., Oklahoma State University, United States—Oklahoma.

Szybillo, George J. and Jacob Jacoby (1974), "Effects of Different Levels of Integration on Advertising Preference and Intention to Purchase," *Journal of Applied Psychology*, 59 (3), 274-80.

Tolley, B. Stuart and John J. Goett (1971), "Reactions to Blacks in Newspaper Ads," *Journal of Advertising Research*, 11 (2), 11-17.

Wang, Xiao and Laura M. Arpan (2008), "Effects of Race and Ethnic Identity on Audience Evaluation of Hiv Public Service Announcements," *Howard Journal of Communications*, 19 (1), 44-63.

Whittler, Tommy E. (1989), "Viewers' Processing of Actor's Race and Message Claims in Advertising Stimuli," *Psychology & Marketing*, 6 (4), 287-309.

______ (1991), "The Effects of Actors' Race in Commercial Advertising: Review and Extension," *Journal of Advertising*, 20 (1), 54-60.

Whittler, Tommy E. and Joan DiMeo (1991), "Viewers' Reactions to Racial Cues in Advertising Stimuli," *Journal of Advertising Research*, 31 (6), 37-46.

Whittler, Tommy E. and Joan Scattone Spira (2002), "Model's Race: A Peripheral Cue in Advertising Messages?," *Journal of Consumer Psychology*, 12 (4), 291-301.

Williams, Jerome D., William J. Qualls, and Sonya A. Grier (1995), "Racially Exclusive Real Estate Advertising: Public Policy Implications for Fair Housing Practices," *Journal of Public Policy & Marketing*, 14 (2), 225-44.

Why Do We Find It Hard to Choose? Maximizers' Expectations and Their Effect on Choice Strategy

Jonas Kiesekoms, Ghent University, Belgium
Maarten Elen, Ghent University, Belgium
Maggie Geuens, Ghent University, Belgium
Mario Pandelaere, Ghent University, Belgium

Generally, it is assumed that people strive for the best option when confronted with a choice set (i.e. 'maximizing') (Von Neumann & Morgenstern, 1964). However, due to the increased complexity that characterizes our society, maximizing is not always possible. Indeed, people often have a satisficing goal. In other words, people often search for an appropriate choice option which passes a certain acceptance-threshold (i.e. satisficing). (Simon, 1955). Maximizers, on the other hand, spend more effort analyzing each option until they have found the best possible one (Iyengar, Wells & Schwartz 2006). Research links the tendency to maximize with less happiness, less optimism, less confidence and less satisfaction with life. (Schwartz, 2002). Therefore it is important to identify variables that cause people to maximize. The current study examines a possible cause of maximizing, namely impact expectations. It is possible that maximizers strive to optimize choice outcomes, because they have higher expectations concerning the impact of proximate events on their subjective well-being. In other words, maximizers may believe that the choice they make has more impact on their happiness than satisficers do. This might cause maximizers to allocate more effort in choices than satisficers, hence making sure they choose the best.

H1: Maximizers will have higher expectations concerning the impact of proximate events than satisficers.

However, maximizers' impact expectations of delayed events might be lower. Contrary to satisficers, maximizers might take waiting time into account as a cost. Thus, while satisficers might overlook delay costs, maximizers might consider waiting time to be a cost when evaluating the impact of a delayed, (positive) event. In other words, when evaluating the impact of a delayed, (positive) event, maximizers do not simply assess the reward outcome, but evaluate the event-delay outcome.

H2: Maximizers are more sensitive to waiting costs than satisficers.

The current study examines whether maximizers and satisficers differ in intertemporal choices. Such an intertemporal choice implies a choice between an option that is attractive on short term versus an option that is beneficial on long term. A preference for the more immediate reward is called a time-inconsistent choice (Hoch & Loewenstein, 1991). As maximizers might be more sensitive to waiting costs, this may cause them to make more time-inconsistent choices than satisficers.

H3: Maximizers make more time-inconsistent choices than satisficers.

An online survey was set up to provide a first idea of the strength of the hypotheses.

121 subjects participated in an online survey. During the experiment, a control question was asked to determine whether the respondent was sufficiently involved to take part in the experiment. This was the following scale question: "Do not answer this question". Ten respondents who did answer the control question were deleted from the sample. As a result, all analyses were performed on 111 test subjects.

Respondents first answered the maximizing-satisficing scale as taken from Nenkov et al. (2008). This 13 item 7-point likert scale consists of statements of the following type: "Renting videos is really difficult. I'm always struggling to pick the best one". Secondly, *the impact expectations* of "winning 100 euros" and "receiving a favourite cd as a gift" were measured. Each time respondents were asked to indicate how much happier they would be (tomorrow vs today) if this event would occur.

Thirdly, delay discounting was measured. Respondents were given four choices between an immediate, smaller reward or a delayed, larger reward. The four reward pairs were taken from Kirby & Herrnstein (1995): 12¤-16¤, 21¤-25¤, 30¤-34¤, 45¤-52¤. A typical delay discounting question was as follows: "Which reward would you prefer: 12¤ in two days or 16¤ in ten days".

First, a mean split on the scores of the maximizing-satisficing scale was performed to categorize respondents as maximizer (n=46) or satisficer (n=65). Secondly we performed ANOVA tests on the impact expectations. Maximizers had bigger expectations concerning the impact of "winning 100 euros" ($F(1,109)=5.087$, $p<.05$) or "receiving a favourite cd as a gift" ($F(1,109)=6.056$, $p<.05$) on their happiness, thus providing support for the first hypothesis.

Next, Pearson chi-square analyses were performed for each of the four choice pairs. Maximizers and satisficers appeared to differ significantly for two out of the four pairs, namely the 21¤-25¤ and 30¤-34¤ choice pairs. Satisficers chose more than expected the larger, delayed reward than maximizers (respectively $\chi^2(1)=2.729$, p=.099 and $\chi^2(1)=5.447$, p<.05). While results for the other two choice options did not prove to be significant, they showed a similar pattern. This provides partial support for the third hypothesis.

Data concerning the second hypothesis, as well as more support for hypothesis 1 and 3 are being collected. Also, the impact of maximizers' and satisficers' choices on experienced regret is being examined. When 'going for the best' implies 'choosing the immediate', maximizing might be regretful in the long term.

References

Hoch, S.J. & Loewenstein, G.F. (1991). Time-Inconsistent Preferences and Consumer Self-Control. *Journal of Consumer Research*, 17(4), 492-507.

Iyengar, S.S., Wells, R.E., Schwartz, B. (2006). Doing better but feeling worse. Looking for the "best" job undermines satisfaction. *Psychological Science*, 17 (2), pp. 143-150.

Kirby, K.N. & Herrnstein, R.J. (1995). Preference reversals due to myopic discounting of delayed reward. *Psychological Science*, 6 (2), pp. 83-89.

Nenkov, G.Y., Morrin, M., Ward, A., Schwartz, B. & Mulland, J. (2008). A short form of the maximization scale: factor structure, reliability and validity studies. *Judgment and Decision Making*, 3 (5), pp. 371–388.

Schwartz, B., Ward, A., Lyubomirsky, S., Monterosso, J., White, K. & Lehman, D. (2002). Maximizing versus Satisficing: Happiness Is a Matter of Choice. *Journal of Personality and Social Psychology*, 83 (5), pp. 1178-1197.

Simon, H. (1955). A Behavioral Model of rational choice. *Quarterly Journal of Economics*, 59, pp. 99-118.

Von Neumann, J. & Morgenstern, O. (1964). *Theories of Games and Economic Behavior*. New York: Academic Press.

Do Easterners Feel More Discomfort in Response to Positive Information than Westerners?

Chang Soo Kim, McGill University, Canada
Tai Hoon Cha, Hankuk University of Foreign Studies, Korea
Myung-Soo Jo, McGill University, Canada

Do people respond favorably when they perceive positive, favorable information? For example, when frequent consumers of caffe lattes read an article that argues caffe latte is the most delicious form of coffee, they should feel reinforced and comforted, because the information is consistent with their own attitudes and preferences. Yet some people may sense less positive feelings due to their information processing method. In particular, these differences likely are greater across cultures, especially between Eastern and Western cultures. People from Eastern cultures tend to use more situational inferences, experiential knowledge, dialectics, and relationships to process information, whereas Westerners rely more on dispositional inferences, logical thinking, a lack of contradiction, and categorization (Choi, Nisbett, and Norenzayan 1999; Nisbett 2003; Nisbett et al. 2001; Norenzayan, Choi, and Nisbett 2002). Thus, Easterners may respond differently than Westerners to the same favorable product or service information, such that Westerners feel less discomfort when confronted with the same information.

Because they display greater hindsight bias than Westerners, Easterners may be more likely to process positive information as inconsistent (Choi and Nisbett 2000). Hindsight bias involves the tendency to overestimate in hindsight what is known in foresight (Choi and Nisbett 2000; Fischhoff 1975). According to previous research (Choi, Dalai, and Kim-Prieto 1999), Asians engage in more complex information processing than do Americans. If Easterners think more deeply about alternative perceptions of an object (e.g., the dark side), positive information may appear more inconsistent. For example, Easterners reading the positive caffe latte story might ponder it further and realize that caffe latte contains more fat and calories, which may help make it the most delicious coffee. Thus, Easterners would display more discomfort than Westerners when they receive such positive information. In contrast, Westerners likely process the positive information as consistent and focus more specifically on the positive aspects, because they rely on object focusing and categorization processing (Nisbett 2003), which means they do not consider category overlaps (i.e., non-contradiction processing; Nisbett 2003). In turn, Easterners should feel more discomfort than Westerners when they consider the same positive information.

Higher discomfort then may result in greater motivation to reduce the discomfort. That is, Easterners should experience a greater motivation to resolve their discomfort by perhaps ignoring or discarding the information. In contrast, Westerners, with their lower sense of discomfort, likely feel less motivation to resolve what they already perceive as positive and consistent information. Again, Westerners use more focusing and non-contradictory information processing, such that they consider the positive information as nonsituated (Nisbett 2003). Therefore, Easterners should experience more motivation to reduce discomfort than do Westerners for the same positive information.

These varying levels of motivation may in turn affect information processing, especially systematic and counterargument processing. Higher discomfort and motivation should cause Easterners to follow more detailed and counterargument-based processing, because people employ more systematic processing to deal with inconsistent information (Jain and Maheswaran 2000). In contrast, Westerners likely employ less systematic processing and fewer counterarguments to positive information, focusing instead on the presented information (i.e., focal focusing; Nisbett 2003). They believe, "Coffee latte is the best coffee," and thus, they forego systematic or counterargument-based processing. That is, Easterners should display more systematic and counterargument processing than Westerners with regard to the same positive information.

The tests of these hypotheses include both Koreans and Americans who prefer caffe latte over Espresso; that is, only Koreans and Americans who like caffe latte participated in this study. The studies took place in a metropolitan Korean city and a Midwestern U.S. town with subjects from similar demographic backgrounds (i.e., young college students). The same stimuli appear in both the Korean and U.S. studies. The positive information stimulus reads: "The Health & Culture Center (HCC) at Harvard University reports that caffe latte is most preferred coffee by students. HCC also reports that people evaluate caffe latte as the most polished, mildest, and most delicious coffee." Subjects responded to several discomfort and motivation to reduce discomfort items on seven-point scales (discomfort: uneasy, uncomfortable, bothered by the information; motivation: discard, ignore, skip over the information). To measure systematic and counterargument processing, the study used open-ended questions that asked the subjects to describe their thoughts about the presented information.

The findings provide strong support for the hypotheses. Korean subjects exhibited much higher levels of discomfort than did the U.S. subjects in response to the same positive caffe latte information ($p<.01$). Furthermore, the Korean subjects were more motivated to reduce their discomfort than the Americans with the same positive information ($p<.05$). Finally, the subjects' remarks and comments matched the hypotheses: Koreans noted more systematic processing and counterarguments than did the Americans.

Thus, as hypothesized, Easterners experience more discomfort and greater motivation to reduce their discomfort than do Westerners when it comes to positive information. These findings suggest that marketers should employ different methods to present positive information in Eastern countries to elicit the most favorable reactions. For examples, claims that "we are the best" may not be well-received in Eastern cultures, because they would elicit higher levels of discomfort and evoke greater motivation to reject the information and create counterarguments.

References

Choi, I., R. Dalai, and C. Kim-Prieto (1999), "Culture and Judgment of Causal Relevance: Inclusion vs. Exclusion," working paper, University of Illinois, Urbana-Champaign.

Choi, I. and R. E. Nisbett (2000), "Cultural Psychology of Surprise: Holistic Theories and Recognition of Contradiction," *Journal of Personality and Social Psychology*, 79 (6), 890-905.

Choi, I., R. E. Nisbett, and A. Norenzayan (1999), "Causal Attribution Across Cultures: Variation and Universality," *Psychological Bulletin*, 125 (1), 47-63.

Fischhoff, B. (1975), "Hindsight & Foresight: The Effect of Outcome Knowledge on Judgment under Uncertainty," *Journal of Experimental Psychology: Human Perception and Performance*, 1, 288-299.

Jain, S. and D. Maheswaran (2000), "Motivated Reasoning: A Depth-of-Processing Perspective," *Journal of Consumer Research*, 26 (March), 358-371.

Nisbett, R. E. (2003), *The Geography of Thought: How Asians and Westerners Think Differently ... And Why* , New York, The Free Press.

Nisbett, R. E., K. Peng, I. Choi, and A. Norenzayan(2001), "Culture and Systems of Thought: Holistic Versus Analytic Cognition," *Psychological Review*, 108 (2), 292-310.

Norenzayan, A., I. Choi, and R. E. Nisbett(2002), "Cultural Similarities and Differences in Social Inference: Evidence From Behavioral Predictions and Lay Theories of Behavior," *Personality and Social Psychology Bulletin*, 28 (January), 109-120.

The Effects of Corporate Commitment and Cause Commercialization in Cause-Related Marketing

Yoojung Kim, University of Texas at Austin, USA
Jung Lim, University of Texas at Austin, USA
Sejung Marina Choi, University of Texas at Austin, USA

In Cause-Related Marketing (CRM), one of the major Corporate Social Responsibility (CSR) strategies, a participating company makes a donation to a charity or cause each time a consumer purchases an item from that company. According to the IEG Sponsorship Report, U.S. corporate spending on CRM was $1.50 billion in 2008—a dramatic increase from $120 million in 1990. CRM has been widely recognized as an effective marketing strategy that enhances corporate image and boosts sales. As today's consumers become increasingly savvy, consumer responses to CRM may not be uniformly positive, however. Attribution theory suggests that consumers will not evaluate a company's CRM positively if consumers become suspicious of the motives underlying the activity (Webb and Mohr 1998). When consumers become doubtful and attribute the company's motive for CRM efforts mostly to its self-serving benefits, CRM becomes ineffective and may even backfire (Yoon, Gürhan-Canli and Schwarz 2006).

A significant factor leading to positive CRM outcomes is a company's commitment to CSR. Past research suggests that the amount of resources invested by a company in its CRM program, including the duration of the CRM activity, influences consumer perceptions of the company's overall commitment to a social cause. For example, Varadarajan and Menon (1988) proposed that long- versus short-term CRM campaigns have greater potential to enhance a corporate image. Likewise, advertising campaigns with a social dimension are more likely to be successful when accompanied by a long-term commitment (Drumwright 1996). Other investments, such as monetary donations, employee expertise, and volunteer work, also enhance perceived corporate commitment (Brink et al. 2006).

Another factor that may influence the effectiveness of CRM is the cause's level of commercialization. As more and more causes have engaged in CRM, there has been growing concern about cause exploitation and over-commercialization (Varadarajan and Menon 1988). As Gurin (1987) noted, for example, companies generally wish to be associated with popular, risk-free, and highly visible causes to maximize their benefits from CRM programs. As a result, less popular, relatively risky, and less visible causes that are often in greater need of support tend to be neglected and receive little corporate support. Further, over-commercialization of a nonprofit organization could endanger the value of the cause and thus erode its appeal to individual supporters (Gurin 1987). Yet this dimension of CRM has been overlooked in previous research on consumer response to various CRM acts and deserves careful research attention.

Therefore, this study investigated the effects of two variables on CRM effectiveness: a company's commitment to CSR, and the level of commercialization of the cause. As drawn from attribution theory, it was predicted that when a company demonstrates strong commitment to CSR in general by having engaged in various CSR activities over the long term, consumers will infer more altruistic and less self-serving motives from the company's CRM and hold more credible perceptions of and favorable attitudes toward the company than is the case when the company shows little commitment or has no history of CSR activities. Similarly, when the company is aligned with a less commercialized cause that receives little corporate support, consumers will perceive more altruistic and less profit-oriented motives from engaging in CRM and show greater corporate credibility and attitude than would be the case when associated with a more commercialized cause that enjoys a larger roster of corporate sponsors.

To examine how CRM programs with different degrees of corporate commitment to CSR and cause commercialization influence consumers' attribution of corporate motives, credibility, and attitude, this experimental study employed a 2 (CSR commitment: strong vs. weak) X 2 (commercialization of the cause: high vs. low) between-subjects, factorial design. A fictitious beauty care company was used in this study; the subjects were instructed to read the description of the company and its recent activity in supporting a social cause. Specifically, stronger corporate CSR commitment was manipulated by focusing on a long history of corporate involvement in CSR activities and support of various socially worthy causes while weaker corporate commitment was manipulated by stating that the company had no record of CSR engagement until recently. For the commercialization level of the cause, the Susan G. Komen Breast Cancer Foundation (Komen) was chosen as the more commercialized cause based on its popularity and sufficient number of corporate sponsors, while Breast Cancer Action (BCA) was selected for the less commercialized cause that has low visibility and little corporate support. Congruence between cause, company, and cause importance were pretested—no significant differences were found across the four conditions.

As predicted, the results suggest that stronger corporate CSR commitment leads consumers to ascribe more altruistic and less self-serving motives to a company's CRM, and to hold more credible perceptions of and favorable attitudes toward it than does weaker corporate CSR commitment. On the other hand, the level of cause commercialization produced no significant effects on the dependent measures. Study findings expand our theoretical knowledge of the effects of corporate CSR commitment and cause commercialization on consumer attributions of corporate motives in the CRM context that subsequently influence corporate credibility and attitude. This study also has useful implications for managers who seek to optimize the effectiveness of CRM campaigns by indicating the benefits of establishing long-lasting CRM programs and points to the importance of carefully selecting a socially worthy cause.

References

Brink, Douwe van den, Gaby Odekerken-Schroder and Pieter Pauwels (2006), "The Effect of Strategic and Tactical Cause-Related Marketing on Consumers' Brand Loyalty", *Journal of Consumer Marketing*, 23 (1), 15-25.

Drumwright, Minette. E. (1996), "Company Advertising with a Social Dimension: the Role of Noneconomic Criteria", *Journal of Marketing*, 60 (4), 71-87.

Gurin, Maurice G. (1987), "Cause-Related Marketing in Question," *Advertising Age* (July 27), S-16.

Varadarajan, P. Rajan, and Anil Menon (1988), "Cause-Related Marketing: A Coalignment of Marketing Strategy and Corporate Philanthropy," *Journal of Marketing*, 52 (July), 58-74.

Webb, Debora J. and Lois A. Mohr (1998), "A Typology of Consumer Responses to Cause-Related Marketing: from Skeptics to Socially Concerned", *Journal of Public Policy & Marketing*, 17 (2), 226-238.

Yoon, Yeosun, Zeynep Gurhan-Canli and Norbert Schwarz (2006), "The Effect of Corporate Social Responsibility (CSR) Activities on Companies with Bad Reputations," *Journal of Consumer Psychology*, 16 (4), 377-390.

Do Opposites Attract? Understanding How Oppositional Advertisements Work

Anjala Krishen, University of Nevada at Las Vegas, USA
Pamela Miles Homer, California State University, Long Beach, USA

Introduction

In their discussion of advertising language, McQuarrie and Mick (1996) identify schemes and tropes as two key forms of figurative rhetoric. Tropes are theorized to increase destabilization in several forms, one of which is opposition. Recently, scholars distinguish Janusian thinking, a process which involves bringing opposites to mind and creating meaning out of them (Rothenberg 1971; Blasko and Mokwa 1986), as an important form of advertising creativity (Sasser and Koslow 2008; Goldenberg and Mazursky 2008). We hence define opposition in advertising as the practice of pitting two seemingly opposing views in one ad. Oppositional ads can feature either literal or metaphorical opposition, often originating from consumer mythology (Levy 1981). An example of literal binary opposition is one such as inside/outside or weak/strong. On the other hand, a metaphorical opposition may be one such as heart/mind or beauty/power. In this paper, we extend extant research to explore when and why oppositional ads are effective/persuasive. We propose that opposition is a visual tool that simplifies decision-making and perceptual cognition. In a series of two experiments, we demonstrate that the underlying mechanism for opposition is reduction of visual complexity. In our first study that utilizes actual print advertisements, we show that perceived complexity is consistently lower for those ads defined as oppositional. The second experiment connects the lower perceived complexity in an oppositional advertisement to higher ad meaning and ad creativity.

Study 1: Opposition and Perceived Complexity

Due to the sparse academic research on consumer's perceptions of oppositional advertisements, an initial understanding of the role of visual complexity is warranted. The aim of Study 1 (S1) is to determine consumers' perceptions of the complexity level of an oppositional versus a non-oppositional ad across two different product categories (i.e., undergarments and candy). Thus, a 2 (*product category*: undergarments versus candy) x 2 (*ad type*: oppositional versus non-oppositional) mixed-design is used to test the guiding hypotheses: opposition format (*ad type*) serves as the within-subjects factor and *product category* serves as the between-subjects factor (N=60). *Perceived complexity*, the primary dependent variable, is measured with a seven-item (7-point) semantic differential scale (Geissler, Zinkhan, and Watson 2001). Items range as follows: not complex/complex, not dense/dense, not crowded/crowded, no variety/variety, inefficient/efficient, not overwhelming/overwhelming, and simple/complicated.

Results

Analysis of variance (ANOVA) identifies a main effect for *ad type* (F(1, 60)=56.93, p<.01, M=2.84 versus M=4.49) and an *ad type* x *product category* interaction (F(1, 60)=12.85, p<.01) for *perceived complexity*. Planned comparisons reveal that perceived complexity remain relatively constant across the two product categories for oppositional type ads (M=3.03 for the undergarment ads and M=2.54 for the candy ads; t(60)=1.27, *ns*). However, for the non-oppositional advertisements, perceived complexity is greater for the candy ads (M=5.09) compared to the undergarment ads (M=3.89; t(60)=3.0, p<.01).

Discussion

S1 data show that individuals perceive that ads that are oppositional in nature are less complex, and this finding is robust across two different product categories. Next, a second study (S2) connects lower perceived ad complexity, shown in S1, to mechanistic explanations for opposition itself.

Study 2: Oppositional Versus Its Half

To better understand how opposition in advertising works, S2 uses one particular advertisement. The idea is to have one set of respondents view the oppositional advertisement while the others view only the half of the ad that "sells" the product. The complexity level for these two ads is hypothesized to be significantly different, with the oppositional format being perceived as less complex (though it has more physical information). Thus, this experiment (N=54) is a single factor between-subjects design (*ad type*: oppositional versus non-oppositional). *Perceived complexity*, *ad meaning*, and *ad creativity* are the dependent measures of interest. The *ad meaning* construct is the average of three (9-point) scales: meaningless/ meaningful, not believable/very believable, and not credible/very credible (α=.62). Similarly, *ad creativity* averages three 9-point items: not creative /creative, not eye-catching/eye-catching, and not clear /clear (α=.70).

Results

The print advertisement features a popular children's drink and thus, familiarity is treated as a covariate (in all hypothesis tests) to account for prior knowledge and experience with the brand. The two ads are rated as being similar in terms of *uniqueness*, which serves to refute a "novelty" explanation (F(1,53)=2.02, *ns*). For *perceived complexity*, analyses reveal an *ad type* main effect, supporting that the oppositional ad is perceived to be less complex than the non-oppositional ad (F(1,52)=8.84, p<.01, M=3.03 versus M=4.11). In addition, the oppositional advertisement displays higher *ad meaning* than the non-oppositional ad (F(1,51)=4.73, p<.05, M=6.23 versus M=5.52), and is perceived to be more *creative* than the non-oppositional version (F(1,52)=3.86, p=.05, M=6.69 versus M= 5.98).

Discussion

S2 extends the previous study by showing that not only is there lower perceived complexity in the oppositional advertisement (which has physically more information than its non-oppositional counterpart), there are also significant differences in terms of ad meaning and ad creativity. The oppositional ad is perceived to have higher ad meaning and creativity, thus providing an explanation for why individuals prefer opposition.

Concluding Remarks

In summary, these studies extend the concept of opposition in choice sets (Krishen, Nakamoto, and Herr 2008) to advertisements, showing that it is a visual perception phenomenon that cuts across multiple human tasks. As such, we show that opposition not only allows individuals to make easier decisions, but it can also enable more simplistic perceptual processes. Thus, even though opposition does not appear to reduce information load, it is a creative technique that can reduce visual complexity. We plan to share more data at the ACR conference: e.g., a third study is currently underway.

References

Blasko, Vincent J. and Michael P. Mokwa (1986), "Creativity in Advertising: A Janusian Perspective," *Journal of Advertising*, 15 (4), 43-50.

Geissler, Gary, George Zinkhan, and Richard Watson (2001), "Web Homepage Complexity and Communication Effectiveness," *Journal of the Association of Information Systems,* 2 (2), 1-46.

Goldenberg, Jacob and David Mazursky (2008), "When Deep Structures Surface," *Journal of Advertising*, 37 (4), 21-34.

Krishen, Anjala S., Kent Nakamoto, and Paul Herr (2008), *The Dichotomy Heuristic in Choice: How Contrast Makes Decisions Easier*: VDM-Verlag.

Levy, Sidney J. (1981), "Interpreting Consumer Mythology: A Structural Approach to Consumer Behavior," *Journal of Marketing*, 45 (3), 49-61.

McQuarrie, Edward F. and David Glen Mick (1996), "Figures of Rhetoric in Advertising Language," *Journal of Consumer Research*, 22 (4), 424-38.

Sheila, L. Sasser and Koslow Scott (2008), "Desperately Seeking Advertising Creativity," *Journal of Advertising*, 37 (4), 5-19.

US Consumers and Disaster: Observing "Panic Buying" During the Winter Storm and Hurricane Seasons

Owen Kulemeka, University of Illinois at Urbana-Champaign, USA

In the US, consuming is an integral part of preparing for disasters. In Hurricane Katrina's aftermath, government officials have stressed that US residents should not plan on solely relying on charity or government aid after a disaster. Residents are encouraged to purchase emergency supplies prior to a disaster because past disasters have shown that it can take weeks before outside aid arrives (FEMA, 2009).

Despite the emphasis on pre-disaster buying, little academic research has been done on how people purchase emergency supplies. Much of what has been written about purchasing emergency supplies is primarily in the popular press and focuses on what is called "panic buying." Each year before seasonal disasters, government officials and journalists admonish consumers to avoid panic buying. Consumers are criticized for buying supplies too early thus driving prices up or for waiting until the last minute which is seen as neglecting emergency planning (Mitchell, 2008; Perry, 2008).

These criticisms provide little insight into how consumers purchase emergency supplies. Dismissing pre-disaster behavior as "panic buying" provides no answers regarding why some consumers purchase in advance and others wait. To gain insight into consumers' pre-disaster behavior, I am studying how US consumers in areas prone to seasonal disasters make decisions about purchasing emergency supplies.

The study is divided into two parts. In the first part, I have developed a model that describes how consumers make purchasing decisions regarding emergency supplies. To develop this model, I have drawn from research findings regarding the issue of panic in disasters and how people seek information or help on critical needs.

Past research on disasters has shown that contrary to popular views, people rarely panic prior to a disaster or when a disaster is occurring (Drabek, 1986). Helsloot and Ruitenberg's (2004) review of research on panic points out that in a disaster situation (e.g. during an earthquake), the initial fear that occurs due to uncertainty quickly diminishes and people start to look for ways to provide security for themselves and others. Instead of panicking, most people turn to help others and leave an insecure area in an orderly fashion.

When panic does occur, it impacts only a small number of people and lasts a short time (Perry & Lindell, 2003; Quarantelli, 1999; Dynes, 1994). The panic myth has emerged primarily because disaster victims inaccurately describe their response to disasters as panic. Journalists also describe unsuccessful attempts to deal with a disaster (e.g. failing to leave a burning building) as instances of panic. Helsloot and Ruitenberg noted that in many cases, failure to escape a fire is due to disorientation or smoke inhalation rather than panic.

Panic does occur in very limited situations when the following factors are present. First, people perceive an immediate, serious danger. Second, only a few escape routes are present. Third, they feel that escape routes are closing making immediate escape necessary. Fourth, there is a lack of communication about a situation (Helsloot and Ruitenberg, 2004).

In my model, I argue that since panic is rare except in extreme situations when the threat of death is imminent, consumer purchasing before a disaster is rational. In most pre-disaster shopping contexts, people are not facing a life or death situation. Hence, people shop in a manner that is not panicky but instead is aimed at meeting their needs rationally.

The second part of my model focuses on how people seek information and help on critical needs. Research on information seeking has revealed three key findings regarding help and information seeking. First, people (depending on their social status) exist in different levels of information poverty. Individuals who are marginalized (e.g. the poor) often lack information on how to obtain critical help because they cannot easily access information networks (Chatman, 1996).

Second, how people seek information and help is often shaped by the group in which they belong. In a marginalized group (e.g. a minority community), an intense information environment can develop. In these information rounds, individuals share a world view which dictates what outside information and help is accepted (Chatman, 1999). Members of a marginalized round can purposely block out information or help from the outside if it emerges from contexts they cannot control and knowledge could cause distress. Marginalized individuals will seek external information or help when their group agrees that help is needed and life in the round is no longer functioning (Chatman, 1999).

A third finding is that how people act to address critical needs is shaped by the constraints they feel (e.g. How much money do I have?), whether they recognize the situation as a problem (e.g. Is this storm going to be as big as they predict?), and whether they feel personally involved (e.g. Is the storm going to strike my neighborhood?) (Grunig, 1997).

In my model, I argue that consumers' purchasing decisions prior to a disaster are shaped by their level of information poverty (how well connected they are to information networks) and whether their community values preparedness. In addition, how constrained they feel, their level of involvement, and problem recognition influence their decisions.

In the second part of my study, I am observing behavior in supermarkets to see whether it supports my model. In Winter 2009, I travelled to areas under storm watches and observed purchasing behavior. In Fall 2009, I will observe pre-hurricane buying. Preliminary findings from observations reveal that panic, hoarding, and other anti-social behaviors do not characterize pre-disaster shopping. Instead, most pre-disaster shoppers are organized and willing to assist others. Those who delay purchasing cite conflicting information from forecasters and a lack of resources (they fear buying supplies that will be wasted if a storm does not occur) as reasons for waiting until the last minute.

References

Chatman, Elfreda (1996), The Impoverished Life-World of Outsiders. *Journal of the American Society for Information Science*, 47 (3), 193-206.

Chatman, Elfreda (1999), A Theory of Life in the Round. *Journal of the American Society for Information Science*, 50 (3), 207-217.

Drabek, Thomas (1986), *Human System Responses to Disaster: An Inventory of Sociological Findings*. New York: Springer-Verlag.

Dynes, Russell (1994), Community Emergency Planning: False Assumptions and Inappropriate Analogies. *International Journal of Mass Emergencies and Disasters,* 12 (2), 141-158.

FEMA (2009), *Are You Ready?* Retrieved from http://www.fema.gov/areyouready/

Grunig, James (1997), A Situational Theory of Publics: Conceptual History, Recent Challenges and New Research. In D. Moss, T. MacManus, & D. Vercic (Eds.), *Public Relations Research: An International Perspective* (pp. 3-48). London: International Thomson Business Press.

Helsloot, Ira & Ruitenberg, Arnout (2004). Citizen Response to Disasters: A Survey of Literature and Some Practical Implications. *Journal of Contingencies and Crisis Management*, 12, 98-111.

Mitchell, Brian (2008), Hurricane Spurs Gas Rumors and a Buying Spree at Local Pumps. *WDEF TV*. Retrieved fromhttp://www.wdef.com/news/hurricane_spurs_gas_rumors_and_a_buying_spree_at_local_pumps/09/2008

Perry, Charles (2008), AAA: Don't Panic (About Gas Shortage) *Rock Hill Herald*.Retrived from http://www.heraldonline.com/109/story/843618.html

Perry, Ronald & Lindell, Michael (2003), Understanding Citizen Response to Disasters With Implications for Terrorism. *Journal of Contingencies and Crisis Management*, 11 (2), 51–52.

Quarantelli, Enrico (1999), *The Sociology of Panic*. University of Delaware: Disaster Research Center

Effects of Color on Consumers' Perceptions of Package Volumes

Joseph Lajos, HEC Paris, France
Amitava Chattopadhyay, INSEAD, Singapore

A body of research in marketing has examined the effects of visual biases on consumers' judgments of product volumes (see Krishna 2007 and Raghubir 2007 for reviews). Although the potential influences of a package's proportions and shape on consumers' judgments of product volumes have been studied extensively, marketing research has not examined the potential of package color to bias consumers' product volume judgments.

Folkes and Matta (2004) observed that attention and size often covary, and provided evidence that attentional differences contaminate people's judgments of relative size such that objects that attract more attention are judged as larger. Their logic is essentially based on reversing the argument that large sizes attract more attention.

Fashion consultants often suggest that if you want to attract attention, you should wear red (Manji 2009). Research in psychology confirms the common notion that reds (and other high wavelength colors) attract more attention than blues and purples (and other low wavelength colors). Using a variety of methods this research finds that high wavelength colors stand out, "advance," and are more noticeable, whereas low wavelength colors fade away, "retreat," or go unnoticed (e.g., Johns and Sumner 1948; Luckiesh 1918; Pillsbury and Schaefer 1937; Taylor and Sumner 1945).

Combining research suggesting that high wavelength colors attract more attention than low wavelength colors with research suggesting that objects that attract more attention appear larger leads us to hypothesize that consumers judge products to have greater volumes when their packages are colored with a high wavelength hue (e.g., red) versus a low wavelength hue (e.g., purple).

Consistent with our hypothesis, research in psychology that has examined the effect of color on people's size judgments has often found that red objects appear larger than equally-sized purple or blue objects (e.g., Bevan and Dukes 1953; Claessen, Overbeeke, and Smets 1995; Gundlach and Macoubrey 1931; Wallis 1935; Warden and Flynn 1926). It is also notable that differences in the perceived size of the red and blue areas of the French flag (which are actually equally sized) resulted in an official recommendation to reduce the size of the red area compared to that of the blue (Helson 1951).

A weakness of past research on the effect of color on size judgments is that most of this research did not utilize a standardized color system that differentiates between the various shades of colors. Another weakness of past research in this domain is that it is solely empirical, and does not advance a theory to explain the demonstrated results. We report results from three studies that support our hypothesis.

In study 1, we asked 118 participants to view 30 slides, each of which displayed a pair of shapes arranged vertically that differed in color, and to report which of the two shapes appeared larger. On two of the slides, the shapes were actually of an identical size and differed only in color (red vs. purple and green vs. yellow). Consistent with our hypothesis, significantly more participants judged the red shape to be larger than the purple shape (N=55 vs. N=25), (χ^2 (1)=11.25, p<.01). We also obtained this effect with colors that were closer in wavelength, as significantly more participants judged the yellow shape to be larger than the green shape than vice versa (N=58 vs. N=22), (χ^2 (1)=16.20, p<.01).

In study 2, we asked 11 participants to view pictures of 12 product packages, to estimate the volume of each package in fluid ounces, and to answer a series of distracter questions about each product. We photographed the products next to a can of soda that served as a volume reference and used professional software to re-color the products' packages One package, a bucket of fish food, appeared twice in the series, once colored red and once colored purple. Consistent with our hypothesis, a within-subjects ANOVA revealed that participants' estimates of the volume of the fish food bucket were significantly higher in the red condition (M=199.09 fl. oz.) than in the purple condition (M=109.27 fl. oz.), (F(1, 10)=5.21, p<.05).

In study 3, we asked 16 participants to complete the same procedure as in study 2, but with different product packages, and the addition questions about willingness to pay and liking of the package colors. We implemented the red vs. purple color manipulation using a box of detergent. Consistent with our hypothesis a within-subjects ANOVA revealed that participants' estimates of the volume of the detergent box were significantly higher in the red condition (M=3083.33 mL) than in the purple condition (M=2262.67 mL), (F(1, 14)=4.64, p<.05). The color manipulation also affected participants' willingness to pay for the detergent, which was significantly higher in the red condition

(M=\$5.36) than in the purple condition (M=\$3.50), ($F(1, 14)=6.05, p<.05$). Participants reported liking packaging of both colors statistically equally ($M_{red}=-1.87$ vs. $M_{purple}=-.73$), ($F(1, 14)=1.32, p>.2$). Furthermore, the aforementioned effect of color on willingness to pay became non-significant when participants' volume estimates of the red and purple packages were included in the ANOVA as covariates ($F(1, 12)=0.78, p=.4$). In contrast, when participants' liking of the red and purple colors were included in the ANOVA as covariates, the effect of color on willingness to pay strengthened ($F(1, 12)=14.98, p<.005$). Together, these results suggest that color influences willingness to pay via an intermediary influence on volume estimates as opposed to an intermediary influence on attitude toward the packaging.

References

Banks, William P., Robin Mermelstein, and Howard K. Yu (1982), "Discriminations Among Perceptual and Symbolic Stimuli," *Memory & Cognition*, 10 (3), 265-78.

Bevan, William and William F. Dukes (1953), "Color as a Variable in the Judgment of Size," *American Journal of Psychology*, 66, p.283-88.

Chandon, Pierre and Brian Wansink (2007), "Is Obesity Caused by Calorie Underestimation? A Psychophysical Model of Meal Size Estimation," *Journal of Marketing Research*, 44 (1), 84-99.

Claessen, J. P., C. J. Overbeeke, and G. J. F. Smets (1995), "Puzzling Colours," *Color Research and Application*, 20 (6), 388-96.

Ekman, Gosta (1958), "Two Generalized Ratio Scaling Methods," *Journal of Psychology*, 45, 287-95.

Finn, Adam (1988), "Print Ad Recognition Readership Scores: An Information Processing Perspective," *Journal of Marketing Research*, 25 (May), 168-77.

Folkes, Valerie and Shashi Matta (2004), "The Effect of Package Shape on Consumers' Judgments of Product Volume: Attention as a Mental Contaminant," *Journal of Consumer Research*, 31 (2), 390-401.

Frayman, Bruce J. and William E. Dawson (1981), "The Effect of Object Shape and Mode of Presentation on Judgments of Apparent Volume," *Perception and Psychophysics*, 29 (1), 56-62.

Gronhaug, Kjell, Olav Kvitastein, and Sigmund Gronmo (1991), "Factors Moderating Advertising Effectiveness as Reflected in 333 Tested Advertisements," *Journal of Advertising Research*, 31 (5), 42-50.

Gundlach, Carol and Constance Macoubrey (1931), "The Effect of Color on Apparent Size," *American Journal of Psychology*, 43, 109-11.

Helson, Harry (1951), *Theoretical Foundations of Psychology*, 356.

Johns, Eugene H. and F. C. Sumner (1948), "Relation of the Brightness Differences of Colors to Their Apparent Distances," *Journal of Psychology: Interdisciplinary & Applied*, 26, 25-29.

Krider, Robert E., Priya Raghubir, and Aradhna Krishna (2001), "Pizzas: π or Square? Psychophysical Biases in Area Comparisons," *Marketing Science*, 20 (4), 405-25.

Krishna, Aradhna (2007), "Spatial Perception Research: An Integrative Review of Length, Area, Volume, and Number Perception," in *Visual Marketing: From Attention to Action*, ed. Michel Wedel and Rik Pieters, Mahwah, New Jersey: Lawrence Erlbaum Associates, 167-93.

Lennard, Dave, Vincent-Wayne Mitchell, Peter McGoldrick, and Erica Betts (2001), "Why Consumers Under-Use Food Quantity Indicators," *International Review of Retail, Distribution & Consumer Research*, 11 (2), 177-99.

Luckiesh, M. (1918), "Retiring and Advancing Colors," *American Journal of Psychology*, 29, 182.

Manji, Moshin (2009), "What Colors to Wear to a Job Interview," *Ezine @rticles*, accessed on 3 May 2009 at <http://ezinearticles.com/?What-Colors-To-Wear-To-A-Job-Interview&id=1090450>.

Munsell, Alfred H. (1905), *A Color Notation*, Boston.

Pillsbury, W. B. and B. R. Schaefer (1937), "A Note on Advancing and Retreating Colors," *American Journal of Psychology*, 49, 126-30.

Raghubir, Priya (2007), "Are Visual Perception Biases Hard-Wired?," in *Visual Marketing: From Attention to Action*, ed. Michel Wedel and Rik Pieters, Mahwah, New Jersey: Lawrence Erlbaum Associates, 143-67.

Raghubir, Priya and Aradhna Krishna (1999), "Vital Dimensions in Volume Perception: Can the Eye Fool the Stomach?," *Journal of Marketing Research*, 36 (3), 313-26.

Taylor, I.L. and F.C. Sumner (1945), *Journal of Psychology: Interdisciplinary & Applied*, 19, p.79-85.

Teghtsoonian, Martha (1965), "The Judgment of Size," *The American Journal of Psychology*, 78 (3), 392-402.

TripleCode (2009), *Triplecode Munsell Palette*, accessed on 14 April 2009 at <http://www.triplecode.com/munsell/>.

Wallis, W.A. (1935), "The Influence of Color on Apparent Size," *Journal of General Psychology*, 13, p.193-199.

Wansink, Brian and Koert Van Ittersum (2003), "Bottoms Up! The Influence of Elongation on Pouring and Consumption Volume," *Journal of Consumer Research*, 30 (3), 455-63.

Warden, C.J. and E.L. Flynn (1926), "The Effect of Color on Apparent Size and Weight," *American Journal of Psychology*, 37, p.398-401.

Wilson, Timothy and Nancy Brekke (1994), "Mental Contamination and Mental Correction: Unwanted Influences on Judgments and Evaluation," *Psychological Bulletin*, 116 (1), 117-42.

Yang, Sha and Priya Raghubir (2005), "Can Bottles Speak Volumes? The Effect of Package Shape on How Much to Buy," *Journal of Retailing*, 81 (4), 269-81.

Do We Really Want to Keep Up with the Joneses? A Closer Look at Luxury, Concealment, Social Interaction, and Justification

Jannine D Lasaleta, University of Minnesota, USA
Jane Ebert, University of Minnesota, USA
Christine Bennett, University of St. Thomas, USA

Several theories have offered insight as on why people consume luxury items. For example, McCormick (1983) suggests people may "keep up with the Joneses" by buying expensive items to maintain self-esteem. Veblen (1912) proposed that people purchase luxury items to signal wealth and status to others. In contrast to this, recent research (Kivetz and Simonson 2003, Kivetz and Zheng 2006) finds that consumers are often reluctant to purchase luxury items, and they expect to feel guilty if they do. People feel they must earn the right to indulge (e.g., by justifying luxury purchases through effort or good performance) perhaps driven by pervasive cultural norms emphasizing the puritan work ethic. However, a recent intriguing study by Schwarz and Xu (2009) suggests that, while people may expect feelings of guilt for purchasing luxury items, they actually do not feel as guilty as they anticipated.

Building on this research, the current work examines consumers' thoughts and behavior with luxury purchases when interacting with others. Word-of-mouth communication is considered a key channel for luxury marketing, so how people present their luxury purchases to others is likely to be of considerable interest to marketers.

While a consumer's guilt after buying a luxury item may lessen, potentially reducing the consumer's need to justify to one's self, we suspect that the consumer may continue to feel a need to justify purchases to others. Cultural norms or theories that guide a consumer's expectations of own thoughts and feelings following a luxury purchase are likely to guide expectations about others' thoughts and feelings about the purchase. So, just as a consumer expects to feel guilty and judge himself negatively following a luxury purchase, he is likely to expect others will judge him negatively. One way a consumer may deal with this, not previously explored in consumer research, is to *conceal* the luxury purchase from others or to present the purchase in ways that will likely minimize negative judgment by others.

We investigate these ideas in four studies. First, we examine whether people sometimes conceal luxury or indulgent purchases from others (study 1), and whether they prefer to conceal information that might lead to negative judgments by others, in particular information about the cost of the luxury or indulgent item (studies 1 and 2). Next (studies 3 and 4), we examine the effect that describing a past luxury or indulgent purchase to others has on consumers' thoughts and descriptions about the item. Specifically, we propose that when people are asked about their thoughts privately versus when interacting (or expecting interaction) with others, they will naturally present information in ways that are likely to minimize negative judgment by others.

In study 1, participants were asked to think of and describe a situation where they had bought something for themselves and had chosen "to conceal the purchase and/or information about the purchase from someone." They listed the item, its cost, reason for purchase, whom they did and did not tell about the purchase, and why. Participants commonly chose to conceal three types of items: illicit, embarrassing, and (as predicted) luxury or indulgent items. For luxury items, consumers most commonly concealed the item or its cost, and claimed their behavior stemmed from fear of negative judgment by others.

In study 2 we examined what information about a luxury purchase (including cost) people prefer to withhold from friends. Participants imagined they purchased an item from an online luxury retailer, and were asked to give the name and email of a friend who would receive free shipping on his/her next purchase. Participants indicated which of three email options they preferred that varied on information disclosed to their friend about their purchase, and explained why. Option A mentioned the participant's purchase, providing a picture, description, and price; option B mentioned the participant's purchase, providing only the general category of the purchase; option C did not mention the participant's purchase. Participants preferred option B over option A, most commonly explaining their preference as a reluctance to purchase details with their friends. (Option C was disliked for reasons unrelated to the purchase).

In studies 3 and 4, we directly test the effects of presenting luxury purchases to others on what consumers say and think. In study 3, participants brought to mind a luxury item they had bought either in the recent or distant past (manipulated between subjects) and imagined they were using or wearing it. They completed a thought listing about the item or they first imagined a friend complimenting them on the item before completing a thought listing (manipulated between subjects). Finally, they rated their purchased item on scales, including happiness with the item and value for money. Overall, most thoughts consisted of positive descriptors of the item, however when thinking about responding to a friend, participants more frequently also mentioned the cost of the item, presenting this information in ways likely to reduce negative judgment (e.g., emphasizing value for money or low price). This difference was reduced for purchases from the distant past, perhaps reflecting less need for purchase justification. Consistent with this idea, participants rated items purchased in the distant past as better value for money than those bought more recently, even when controlling for item cost.

In study 4, we show that these changes to thoughts only occur with the expectation of interaction with others, not simply when others are present, suggesting that self-presentation concerns drive this effect. Participants were asked to think about a luxury item they had purchased recently and completed a thought listing. Participants did this alone, in the mere presence of others, or in the presence of others with the expectation of discussing their purchases. As in study 3, all participants most commonly listed positive descriptors about the item. However, participants in the expected discussion condition also listed cost related thoughts significantly more often than did participants in the other conditions. As before, they presented this cost information in positive ways likely to minimize negative judgment by others. There were no differences by condition on cost of item.

References

Kivetz, Ran and Itamar Simonson (2003), "Earning the Right to Indulge: Effort as a Determinant of Customer Preferences Toward Frequency Program Rewards," *Journal of Marketing Research,* 39 (May), 155-170.

Kivetz, Ran, and Yuhuang Zheng (2006), "Determinants of Justification and Self-Control," *Journal of Experimental Psychology: General*, 135 (4), 572-587.

McCormick, Ken (1983), "Duesenberry and Veblen: The Demonstration Effect Revisited," *Journal of Economic Issues*, 14 (4), 1125-1129.

Xu, Jing and Norbert Schwarz. (2009), "Do We Really Need a Reason to Indulge?" *Journal of Marketing Research*, 46 (February), 25-36.

Veblen, Thorstein (1912), *The Theory of the Leisure Class*, New York: Macmillan Company.

Instant Wins versus Sweepstakes: Attitudes toward Delayed Promotions

Gilles Laurent, HEC Paris, France
Ayse Onculer, ESSEC Business School, France
Sonja Prokopec, ESSEC Business School, France

Retailers frequently use sales promotion tools as a part of their marketing effort. The market for consumer-oriented activities, such as sweepstakes, discount coupons and free samples, has grown substantially in the last decade, reaching approximately $300 billion in the United States alone (*Promo Trends Report*, 2004). Given this huge volume, it is essential for companies and policy-makers to understand how individuals respond to different types of reward mechanisms.

To our knowledge, experimental studies focusing on consumer response for promotional activities are quite scarce (see Ward and Hill, 1991; Prendergast et al, 2005; Chandran and Morwitz, 2006). The current study investigates the impact of time preferences on attitudes towards sales promotion tools. Our conjecture is that delayed promotions do not always induce the same kind of purchase behavior and that risk attitudes, time preferences and affective responses contribute to differences in consumer reactions.

Sales promotion activities can take various forms with respect to the reward structure. A possible taxonomy is as follows:

1. Risky versus certain: The promotional campaign can offer a risky prize (through a lottery or contest) or a certain one (discount coupons).
2. Immediate versus delayed: The prize can be redeemed immediately (checkout coupons, instant-wins) or in the future (mail-in rebates, sweepstakes).
3. Hedonic versus utilitarian: The prize can be more pleasure-oriented (vacation, perfume, etc) or more functional (monetary reward, gasoline, etc).

Past experimental findings have shown that individuals prefer more hedonic alternatives in a probabilistic setting and hedonic options are more popular as prizes than purchases (O'Curry and Strahilevitz, 2001). There is also evidence that even though individuals are generally risk-averse for immediate lotteries, this aversion decreases over time (Shelley, 1994; Sagristano et al, 2002). Anticipated feelings such as hope and savoring can be one possible reason for this declining risk aversion (Loewenstein 1987, Chew and Ho, 1994). Individuals are also found to be less sensitive to changes in probabilities for affect-rich rewards (Rottenstreich and Hsee, 2001).

Taking these findings as a starting point, we propose that individuals prefer a certain prize to be obtained immediately to an immediate risky prize but this preference for a certain prize over a risky one decreases over time. In addition, the preference for lotteries with hedonic prizes over utilitarian prizes increases with delay.

An experiment is conducted to test these hypotheses. The experiment consists of a ranking task, where subjects (31 MBA students) are asked to rank 8 different promotion packages from the most attractive to the least attractive option. The options are generated in a 2x2x2 design, where we manipulated the type of the reward (perfume or gasoline), the temporal dimension (immediate or in two weeks) and the riskiness (certain or with 10% probability). The preliminary results provide evidence for our hypotheses. On average, the most attractive option was a future hedonic prize: 48% of the subjects ranked "10% chance of winning a ¤100 voucher for a bottle of perfume, to be determined and given in two weeks" as their first option; followed by 32% who ranked "a ¤10 voucher for a bottle of perfume, to be given in two weeks" as their first option (χ^2=33.10, p<.01). The least preferred option was "10 chance of winning a ¤100 voucher for gasoline, to be determined and given immediately", chosen by 45% of the subjects as the least attractive option. Further analysis will examine the interactions between the type of the reward, its temporal distance and its riskiness.

These preliminary results have interesting implications. If a marketer has to choose one single promotional tool, the most attractive option for the average consumer would be a lottery drawing in the future, involving hedonic prizes. In a following experiment, we plan to explore whether preference for promotional tools varies depending on the price of the product. We believe that exploring the behavioral response to different sales promotion activities is a rich vein for future research.

References

Chandran, S. and Morwitz, V. 2006. "The Price of Free-dom: Consumer Sensitivity to Promotions with Negative Contextual Influences". *Journal of Consumer Research*, *33*(3), 384-392.

Chew, S. H., and Joanna L. H. 1994. "Hope: An Empirical Study of Attitude Toward the Timing of Uncertainty Resolution." *Journal of Risk and Uncertainty* 8, no. 3: 267-288.

Loewenstein, G. 1987. "Anticipation and the Valuation of Delayed Consumption" *Economic Journal* 97, no. 387: 666-684.

O'Curry, S. and M. Strahilevitz. 2001. "Probability and Mode of Acquisition Effects on Choices Between Hedonic and Utilitarian Options." *Marketing Letters* 12, no. 1: 37-49.

Prendergast, G., Y. Shi, and K. Cheung. 2005. "Behavioural response to sales promotion tools." *International Journal of Advertising* 24, no. 4: 467-486.

Rottenstreich, Y. and C. K. Hsee. 2001. "Money, Kisses, And Electric Shocks: On the Affective Psychology of Risk." *Psychological Science* 12, no. 3.

Sagristano, M. D., Trope, Y., and Liberman, N. (2002). Time-dependent gambling: Odds now, money later. *Journal of Experimental Psychology: General, 131,* 364-376.

Shelley, M. K. 1994. "Gain/Loss Asymmetry in Risky Intertemporal Choice." *Organizational Behavior & Human Decision Processes* 59, no. 1: 124-159

Ward, J. C., and R. P. Hill. 1991. "Designing Effective Promotional Games: Opportunities and Problems." *Journal of Advertising* 20, no. 3: 69-81.

Transumers: Motivations of Non-ownership Consumption

Stephanie Lawson, Florida State University, USA

Transumers engage in fractional ownership to enjoy products and experiences without the hassles or risks of permanent ownership. The dynamic changes taking place in the global marketplace related to economic, social, and cultural forces have created an environment ripe for fractional ownership. Previous studies forecast the rapid pace of technological innovation will result in a shift toward shared ownership. There is an absence of research on the motivations of fractional ownership. Based on exploratory consumer interviews, a survey instrument was developed and tested. Findings suggest consumers engage in fractional ownership for reasons ranging from environmental consciousness to status seeking.

Imagine having access to the latest luxury handbags or golf clubs whenever you desired or using a car share service and never having to worry about the costs of automobile ownership. This is reality for a growing consumer segment participating in fractional ownership consumption experiences. These individuals, known as Transumers, are defined as, "consumers driven by experience instead of the fixed, by entertainment, by discovery, by fighting boredom, who increasingly live a transient lifestyle, freeing themselves from the hassles of permanent ownership and possessions" (Trendwatching.com 2006). The term Transumer was coined in 2003 by, global design and business consultancy firm, Fitch and originated from the marriage of the words transient and consumer (Trendwatching.com 2006). While the popular press is replete with research related to transumption behaviors, Transumers have not been specifically studied in the consumer behavior literature. Transumers are thought to be motivated by experiences instead of possessions, by entertainment, by discovery, and environmental consciousness. The primary purpose of this research is to understand the motivations and individual difference variables influencing transumption behavior.

The dynamic and unique changes currently taking place in the global marketplace related to economic, social, and cultural forces have created an environment ripe for shared or fractional ownership. According to Zukin and Maguire (2004), consumption is an economic, social, and cultural process of selecting goods reflecting the opportunity and limitations of modern life. As interest in sustainability and green marketing increases, these consumers are of particular interest to businesses seeking to capitalize on the growing interest in protecting the environment by offering alternative consumption experiences. Previous studies have forecasted the increasingly rapid pace of technology change will result in a shift toward shared ownership. By engaging in fractional ownership, consumers have access to the latest and greatest and increased social status with less cost. Nissanoff (2006) believes we will evolve into a society where we view the ownership of most things as temporary–like the perception of leased vehicles. The concept of fractional ownership is not new. For example, car leasing introduced consumers to the idea of temporary ownership of vehicles that were above their ownership threshold (Nissanoff 2006). However, the key characteristic that differentiates Transumers from simply leasing a car or owning a timeshare is their pursuit of experiences *across* consumption categories (Levenson 2007). Consumers do not permanently acquire products, but rather an experience. Bag, Borrow, or Steal; ZipCar; and NetFlix are examples of firms that allow consumers to "own" a product for a flexible amount of time for a usage fee.

A two-part study was conducted to first illuminate common themes among individuals and then to investigate how these individual difference variables influence attitudes and behavioral intentions toward fractional ownership. First, an exploratory qualitative study consisting of semi-structured interviews was conducted with individuals engaging in non-ownership consumption. Coding of interviews revealed five themes which illuminate motivations to participate in non-ownership consumption. Although not exhaustive these themes provide insight into the reasons consumers seek non-ownership consumption opportunities.

Based on the emerging themes and the popular description of Transumers, a survey instrument was developed and tested using PLS. Data were collected with the use of 161 self-report questionnaires from adults in the southeastern United States. The hypothesized model describes the individual difference variables including possessiveness, materialism, variety seeking, status consciousness, frugality, and environmental consciousness and their relationships with attitude toward fractional ownership and behavioral intentions to participate in fractional ownership. The hypothesized model was supported by the data. The findings reveal the strongest motivators of positive attitudes and intentions towards fractional ownership were environmental consciousness and status consciousness.

The primary contribution of this research is the conceptual understanding of a unique and growing consumer segment previously absent from the marketing literature. The purpose of this study was to develop the concept of a consumer that engages in fractional ownership across product categories in an effort to collect new experiences while freeing themselves from the responsibilities of permanent ownership. Findings suggest Transumers are both status seeking and environmentally consciousness which at first appears counterintuitive. However, research suggests that while consumers use luxury goods to symbolize success, their definition of success is changing. Many consumers want the brands they buy to reflect their concern for the environment and social issues. At least 1 in 4 American adults hold environmentalism, global issues, and spiritual searching as personal values (Bendell and Kleanthous 2007).

Further, past research on duration of use and acquisition mode suggests consumers expecting to use a product for a short amount of time, all other variables being equal, would rather rent than own (Moore and Taylor 2008). This counterintuitive finding lends a clue as to why consumers are motivated to participate in a leasing lifestyle. Specifically, the fashion industry is naturally aligned with the trend towards transumption due to the seasonality and temporary nature of style. If consumers are aware that trends change with the seasons, they may expect to use product for a shorter duration resulting in a greater motivation to rent rather than purchase. Luxury consumption has been impacted by a weakening economy; however, several luxury fractional ownership firms have recently experienced an increase in transactions. Michele Krause, the founder of Bling Yourself, an online fractional ownership accessory retailer, says that the economic downturn has not impacted their number of new customers or rentals (Roane 2008). Is fractional ownership not only a way to reduce environmental impact but also the answer to a sustainable economy?

In conclusion, the availability of fractional ownership options means less commitment, enabling consumers to enjoy a product temporarily before moving on to the next experience (Winsper 2007). Future research seeks to create a typology of transuming consumers by conducting interviews across industries and clustering based on theme. Investigating this new consumption trend provides marketers with insight into the motivations of these consumers and further seeks to illuminate the question set forth by Belk (2007), "Why share rather than own?"

References

Belk, Russell W. (2007), "Why Not Share Rather Than Own?," *The ANNALS of the American Academy of Political and Social Science,* 611, 126–140.

Bendell, Jem and Anthony Kleanthous (2007), "Deeper Luxury: Quality and Style When the World Matters," http://www.wwf.org.uk/deeperluxury/_downloads/DeeperluxuryReport.pdf

Levenson, Eugenia (2007), "The Fractional Life: With jewelry, yachts, and vineyards available by the slice, even the superrich are learning to share," http://money.cnn.com/magazines/fortune/fortune_archive/2007/03/05/8401282/index.htm

Moore, Amy and Michael Taylor (2008), "Why buy when you can rent? A brief investigation of difference in acquisition mode based on duration," *Applied Economics Letters*, 1-3.

Nissanoff, Daniel (2006), *FutureShop: How the New Auction Culture Will Revolutionze the Way We Buy, Sell, and Get the Things We Really Want,* Penguin Press.

Roane, Kit R. (2008), "Can't afford bling? Rent it. Some luxury shoppers seek out services that lease jewelry or handbags," http://www.msnbc.msn.com/id/23961430/

Trendwatching.com (2006), "Transumers: Consumers Driven by Experiences," http://www.trendwatching.com/trends/transumers.htm

Winsper, Jeff (2007), "The 6 P's of Luxury Marketing: The Advanced Model for Measuring Consumer's Buying Behavior for Luxury Brands," http://www.winsper.com/6Ps/

Zukin, Sharon and Jennifer Smith Maguire (2004), "Consumers and Consumption," *Annual Review of Sociology,* 30, 173–197.

Is a Gift Always a Gift? An Ethnographic Inquiry into the Diversity of Giving Experiences

Marine Le Gall-Ely, ICI, Université de Bretagne Occidentale, France
Christine Gonzalez, LEMNA, Université de Nantes, France
Caroline Urbain, LEMNA, Université de Nantes, France

In January 2005, after the Asian tsunami, the French Croix-Rouge collected more money in one week than usually collected in an entire year of fundraising (41 millions Euros). Médecins Sans Frontières was approached by 411 volunteers ready to fly to Indonesia, a number usually taking five months to reach. The total amount of giving actually reached far beyond the needs of these associations to face up to this disaster. Why did people give to meet the tsunami disaster ? Maybe because of the situation (Christmas period, death saliency, social influence of children and grand-children…) generating affective reactions (surprise, anxiety, fear...) and resulting in taking giving behaviors in action.

We assume that situations may have a great impact on giving behaviors just as it does on consumption behaviors in general. Situations are defined by Belk (1975) as "momentary encounters with those elements of the total environment which are available to the individual at a particular time". Situational characteristics are physical and social surroundings, temporal perspective, task definition features and antecedent states.

The aim of the present research[6] is to answer the following questions:

Do situations influence giving behaviors?

If they do, how does the situation have an impact on giving?

By focusing on the physical and social surroundings, on the affective and experiential aspects of giving behaviors, we lie within the scope of consumer culture theory (CCT, Arnould and Thompson, 2005). Although givers do not actually consume physical goods or

[6]This research is a part of a larger one, financed by the ANR (the French National Research Agency), aiming at tackling problems encountered by associations by a better understanding of giving behaviors. The research is limited to individual giving behaviors, excluding firms or foundations donations.

services, we believe that they do indeed undergo a consumption experience with persons or associations who benefit from their giving behaviors.

As we cannot assume that the different types of giving behaviors (gifting, donation, volunteering…) are not related, we will study how people imagine and experience giving:

- of money, of time, of gift, but also of blood, of organs,
- to other persons, known (members of the family, friends) or unknown (beggar),
- or to associations (local or international, public or civil, whereas aiming at social tasks, health promotion and risk prevention, education and research, culture, sports and leisure…).

A lot of research in an anthropological (Malinowski, 1922 ; Mauss, 1923-1924 ; Weiner, 1992 ; Godelier, 2002), sociological (Levi-Strauss, 1971 ; Godbout and Caillé, 2001), philosophical (Derrida, 1991) or economical (Cheal, 1988) perspectives pays attention to giving behaviors.

In consumer research, an important research stream has focused on giving since the seminal works of Belk (1979 ; 1993) and Sherry (1983). Most of them have dealt with gift giving (Otnes, Lowrey and Kim, 1993 ; Sherry, McGrath and Levy, 1993 ; McGrath, 1995 ; Otnes, 1996 ; Ruth, Otnes and Brunel, 1999).

When raising the issue of fundraising by associations, the research has concentrated on the influence of socio-demographic and psychological features of givers and volunteers on their behaviors (Guy and Patton, 1988 ; Burnett and Lunsford, 1994 ; Wymer, 1997 ; Wooten, 2000 ; Bennett, 2003 ; Sargeant and Woodliffe, 2007), or less often, on the influence of appeal techniques on giving behaviors (Rothschild, 1979 ; Bendapudi, Singh and Bendapudi, 1996 ; Desmet and Feinberg, 2003 ; Venable *et alii*, 2005 ; Goatman and Lewis, 2007).

Few studies have adressed the question of situational characteristics on giving behaviors, some focusing on social surroundings (Fisher and Ackerman, 1998 ; Bryant and Test, 1967 ; Gillath *et al.*, 2005), on temporal perspective (Fisher, Vandenbosch and Antia, 2008) or on task definition features (Bryant, Slaughter, Kang and Tax, 2003).

To our knowledge, some situational influences, as physical surroundings or antecedent states have not been studied, and, moreover, no comprehensive and integrative study of situational influences on giving behaviors has been conducted, what could be of great interest for associations' marketing.

So, we have designed an ethnographic study aiming at studying behaviors in social and cultural context (Arnould and Wallendorf, 1994 ; Sherry, 1995 ; Sunderland and Denny, 2007). As a first stage, we have conducted depth interviews with 15 persons from January to February 2009. We employed snowball sampling, recruiting informants from among family and acquaintance networks. We have interviewed 8 women and 7 men, from 26 to 65 years-old, living in Paris or west regions of France. They are either workers, retired or housewife, single, married or widow, with or without children in care, with diverse levels of education, of income, practising or not diverse religions (Christianity, Judaism, Muslim religion). We followed Bertaux and Kohli's (2001) and Bertaux (2009) recommendations on life stories questions to elicit holistic descriptions of our informants' representations and experiences of giving. Interviews ranged from 55 to 85 minutes, were audiotaped, transcribed, and yielded to more than 300 pages single-spaced pages of text.

We are in the process of interpreting the text using dialectical tacking (Strauss and Corbin, 1998), immersing ourselves in the interdisciplinary literature on giving behaviors, to seek out consistencies and/or inconsistencies with our text.

Some preliminary results emerge about the situations:

- the existence of different types of experiences (Holbrook and Hirschman, 1982 ; Caru and Cova, 2003) of giving: ordinary as giving a coin to a beggar in the street or old clothes to an association *versus* extraordinary as TV shows or sports events aiming at fundraising, definitions of ordinary and extraordinary experiences being diverse among participants ;
- the physical surroundings, often described as "disappointing", especially in small charity organizations;
- the influence of emotions: for example, the death saliency seems to be important in acting the giving behavior in extraordinary experience, the mood seems to influence more ordinary experiences ; disappointment is also salient in discourse;
- the social aspects of giving: it may be an individual *versus* a social experience.

Life stories also have shed light on the importance of the life path, especially childhood, in framing giving representations and learning to give.

From these preliminary results, we conclude that associations should evolve from a person-association/cause relationship to a person-association/cause-situation relationship as giving decisions are also contingent on situational variables.

Further depth interviews and diaries will be collected and analyzed until the end of 2009. Observations will also be organized.

References

Alvesson, M. and K. Sköldberg (2000), *Reflexive Metholodogy, New Vistas for Qualitative Research*, London: Sage.

Arnould, E. and M. Wallendorf (1994), "Market-Oriented Ethnography: Interpretation Building and Marketing", *Journal of Marketing Research*, 3, 4, 484-505.

Arnould, E.J. and C.J. Thompson (2005), "Consumer Culture Theory (CCT): Twenty Years of Research", *Journal of Consumer Research*, 31, 4, 868-882.

Babin, B.J., C. Gonzalez and C. Watts (2007), "Does Santa Have a Great Job? Gift Shopping Value and Satisfaction", *Psychology and Marketing*, 24, 10, 895-917.

Beckman, S. and R.H. Elliott (eds.) (2000), *Interpretive Consumer Research: Paradigms, Methodologies and Applications*, Copenhagen: CBS Press.

Belk, R.W. (1974), "An Exploratory Assessment of Situational Effects in Buyer Behavior", *Journal of Consumer Research*, 11, 3, 156-163.

Belk, R.W. (1975), "Situational Variables and Consumer Behavior", *Journal of Consumer Research*, 2, 3, 157-163.

Belk, R.W. (1979), "Gift-Giving Behavior", in *Research in Marketing*, JAI Press, 2, 95-126.

Belk, R.W. (1988), "Cultural and Historical Differences in Concepts of Self and their Effects on Attitudes toward Having and Giving", *Advances in Consumer Research*, 753-760.

Belk, R.W. (1996), "The Perfect Gift" in Otnes and Beltramini, *Gift-Giving: An Interdisciplinary Anthology*, Bowling Green: Bowling Green State University Popular Press, 59-84.

Belk, R.W. and G. Coon (1993), "Gift-Giving as Agapic Love: An Alternative to the Exchange Paradigm Based on Dating Experiences", *Journal of Consumer Research*, 20, 3, 393-417.

Bendapudi, N., S.N. Singh and V. Bendapudi (1996), "Enhancing Helping Behavior: An Integrative Framework for Promotion Planning", *Journal of Marketing*, 60, 3, 33-49.

Bennett, R. (2003), "Factors Underlying the Inclination to Donate to Particular Types of Charity", *International Journal of Nonprofit and Voluntary Sector Marketing*, 8, 1, 12-29.

Bergadaà, M. and B. Urien (2006), "Time of Death, Gift Giving and Older Consumers' Disposition of Special Possession", *International Conference, Retroscapes and Futurescapes–Temporal Tensions in Organizations*, Terrasini, Italy.

Bertaux, D. (2009), *Life Stories*, Thousand Oaks: Sage.

Bertaux, D. and M. Kohli (2001), "The Life Story Approach: A Continental View", 142-150 in Denzin N.K. and Y.S. Lincoln (eds), *The American Tradition in Qualitative Research*, Oxford: Sage.

Bryan, J.H. and M.A. Test (1967), "Models and Helping: Naturalistic Studies in Aiding Behavior", *Journal of Personality and Social Psychology*, 6, 4, 400-407.

Bryant, W.K., H.J. Slaughter, H. Kang and A. Tax (2003), "Participating in Philanthropic Activities: Donating Money and Time", *Journal of Consumer Policy*, 26, 1, 43-73.

Burnett, M.S. and D.A. Lunsford (1994), "Conceptualizing Guilt in the Consumer Decision-Making Process", *Journal of Consumer Marketing*, 11, 3, 33-43.

Carù, A. and B. Cova (2003), "Revising Consumption Experience: A More Humble but Complete View of the Concept", *Marketing Theory*, 3, 2, 267-286.

Carù, A. and B. Cova (eds.) (2007), *Consuming Experience*, Oxon: Routledge.

Cheal, D. (1988), *The Gift Economy*, London: Routledge.

Cova, V. and B. Cova (2000), ""Exit, Voice, Loyalty and …Twist": Consumer Research in Search of the Subject", 256-45 in Beckman S. and R.H. Elliott (eds.), *Interpretive Consumer Research: Paradigms, Methodologies and Applications*, Copenhagen: CBS Press.

Cova, V. and E. Remy (2002), "I Feel Good–Who Needs the Market ? Struggling and Having Fun with Consumer-Driven Experiences", 51-64 in Carù A. and B. Cova (eds.) (2007), *Consuming Experience*, Oxon: Routledge.

Derrida, J. (1991), *Donner le temps: la fausse monnaie*, Galilée.

Desmet, P. and F.M. Feinberg. (2003), "Ask and ye Shall Receive: The Effect of the Appeals Scale on Consumers' Donation Behavior", *Journal of Economic Psychology*, 24, 349-376.

Fisher, R. and D. Ackerman (1998), "The Normative Effects of Group Need and Promised Recognition on Volunteer Participation", *Journal of Consumer Research*, 25, 3, 262-275.

Fisher, R.J., M. Vandenbosch and K.D. Antia (2008), "An Empathy-Helping Perspective on Consumers' Responses to Fund-Raising Appeals", *Journal of Consumer Research*, 35, 3, 519-531.

Giesler, M. (2006), "Consumer Gift System", *Journal of Consumer Research*, 33, 2, 283-290

Gillath, O., P.R. Shaver, M. Mikulincer, R.E. Nitzberg, A. Erez and M.H. Van Ijzendoorn (2005), "Attachment, Caregiving, and Volunteering: Placing Volunteerism in an Attachment-Theoretical Framework", *Personal Relationships*, 12, 4, 425-446.

Goatman, A.K. and R.L. Lewis (2007), "Charity E-Volution ? An Evaluation of the Attitudes of UK Charities towards Website Adoption and Use", *International Journal of Nonprofit and Voluntary Sector Marketing*, 12, 33-46.

Godbout, J.T. and A. Caillé (2001), *The World of the Gift*, McGill-Queen's University Press (originally published 1992).

Godelier, M. (2002), *The Enigma of Gift*, Chicago: University of Chicago Press (originally published 1996).

Godelier, M. (2008), *In and out of the West: Reconstructing Anthropology*, Charlottesville: University of Virginia Press.

Guy, B.S. and W.E. Patton (1988), "The Marketing of Altruistic Causes: Understanding why People Help", *Journal of Consumer Marketing*, 6, 1, 5-16.

Holbrook, M.B. and E.C. Hirschman (1982), "The Experiential Aspects of Consumption: Consumer Fantasies, Feelings and Fun", *Journal of Consumer Research*, 9, 2, 132-140.

Komter, A. (2005), *Social Solidarity and the Gift*, Cambridge: Cambridge University Press.

Kozinets, R.V. (2002), "Can Consumers Escape the Market? Emancipatory Illuminations from Burning Man", *Journal of Consumer Research*, 29, 1, 20-38.

Ladwein, R. (2002), "Consumption Experience, Self-Narrative and Self-Identity : The Example of Trekking", 95-108 in Carù A. and B. Cova (eds.) (2007), *Consuming Experience*, Oxon: Routledge.

Lankford, R.H. and J.H. Wyckoff (1991), "Modeling Charitable Giving Using A Box-Cox Standard Tobit Model", *Review of Economics and Statistics*, 73, 3, 460-70.

Levi-Strauss, C. (1971), *The Elementary Structures of Kinship*, Boston: Beacon Press (originally published 1967).

Lieblich, A., R. Tuvak-Mashiach and T. Zilber (1998), *Narrative Research*, Thousand Oaks: Sage.

Malinowski, B. (2008), *Argonauts of the Western Pacific*, Dutton (originally published 1922).

Marcoux, J.-S. (2009), "Escaping the Gift Economy", *Journal of Consumer Research*, to be published in December.

Mauss, M. (2000), *The Gift: The Form and Reason for Exchange in Archaic Societies*, New York : W.W. Norton and Company (original work published in 1922-1923).

McCracken, G. (1986), "Culture and Consumption: A Theoretical Account of the Structure and Movement of the Cultural Meaning of Consumer Goods", *Journal of Consumer Research*, 13, 2, 71-84.

McGrath, MA. (1995), "Gender Differences in Gift Exchanges: New Directions from Projections", *Psychology and Marketing*, 12, 5, 371-393.

Otnes, C. and R.F. Beltramini (1996), *Gift-Giving: An Interdisciplinary Anthology*, Bowling Green: Bowling Green State University Popular Press.

Otnes, C., T.M. Lowrey and Y.C. Kim (1993), "Gift Selection for Easy and Difficult Recipients: A Social Roles Interpretation", *Journal of Consumer Research*, 20, 2, 229-244.

Pine, B.J. and J.H. Gilmore (1999), *The Experience Economy: Work Is Theatre and Every Business a Stage*, Harvard: HBS press.

Rothschild, M.L. (1979), "Marketing Communications in non Business Situations or why it is so Hard to Sell Brotherhood like Soap", *Journal of Marketing*, 43, 2, 11-20.

Ruth, J.A., C. Otnes and F.F. Brunel (1999), "Gift Receipt and the Reformulation of Interpersonnal Relationship", *Journal of Consumer Research*, 25, 4, 385-402.

Sargeant, A. and L. Woodliffe (2007), "Gift Giving: An Interdisciplinary Review", *International Journal of Nonprofit and Public Sector Marketing*, 12, 275-307.

Sherry, J.F. (1983), "Gift Giving in Anthropological Perspective", *Journal of Consumer Research*, 10, 2, 157-168.

Sherry, J.F. (ed.) (1995), *Contemporary Marketing and Consumer Behavior: An Anthropological Sourcebook,* Thousand Oaks: Sage.

Sherry, J.F., M.A. McGrath and S.J. Levy (1993), "The Dark Side of the Gift", *Journal of Business Research*, 28, 3, 225-244.

Strauss, A. and J. Corbin (1998), *Basic Qualitative Research: Techniques and Procedures for Developing Grounded Theory*, 2nd ed., Thousand Oaks: Sage.

Sunderland, P.S. and R.M. Denny (2007), *Doing Anthropology in Consumer Research*, Walnut Creek: Left Coast Press.

Thompson, T.C., B. Stern and E. Arnould (1998), "Writing the Differences: Postmodern Pluralism, Retextualization and the Construction of Reflexive Ethnographic Narratives in Consumer Research", *Consumption, Markets, Culture*, 2, 2, 105-160.

Venable, B.T., G.M. Rose, V.D. Bush and F.W. Gilbert (2005), "The Role of the Brand Personality in Charitable Giving: An Assessment and Validation", *Journal of the Academy of Marketing Science*, 33, 3, 295-312.

Wallendorf, M. and M. Brucks (1993), "Introspection in Consumer Research: Implementation and Implications", *Journal of Consumer Research*, 20, 3, 339-359.

Weiner, A. (1976), *Women of Value, Men of Renown: New Perspectives in Trobriand Exchange*, Austin: University of Texas Press.

Weiner, A. (1992), *Inalienable Possessions: The Paradox of Keeping-While-Giving*, Berkeley: University of California Press.

Wooten, D.B. (2000), "Qualitative Steps toward an Expanded Model of Anxiety in Gift-Giving", *Journal of Consumer Research*, 27, 1, 84-95.

Wymer, W.W. (1997), "Segmenting Volunteers Using Values, Self-esteem, Empathy, and Facilitation as Determinant Variables", *International Journal of Nonprofit and Public Sector Marketing*, 5, 2, 3-28.

The Effect of Emotion on Color Preferences

Chan Jean Lee, University of California at Berkeley, USA
Eduardo Andrade, University of California at Berkeley, USA

Can mood change our color preferences? Would people be attracted to different colors depending on their mood? Even though emotional influence on judgment and decision making has been well established (Schwarz and Clore 1983), little is known how a perceiver's emotion affects his or her aesthetic judgments including color preferences. On the other hand, it is well established that people feel various emotions from colors (Crozier 1996; Guilford and Smith 1959; Ou et al. 2004; Valdez and Mehrabian 1994). For example, people feel calmness or low arousal from short-wavelength colors, such as blue and green. People feel excitement, happiness, or high arousal from long-wavelength colors, such as red and yellow. People feel relaxation and softness from light or pastel tone colors, while tension and hardness from dark colors. Given the strong associations of colors and emotions, we examine if an individual's color preferences are contingent on his emotion.

Specifically, we contrast three potential hypotheses from emotion literature: affective evaluation (Andrade 2005; Schwarz and Clore 1983; Isen et al. 1978), affect regulation (Andrade 2005; Gross 1998), and affective fit. These three hypotheses predict a perceiver's emotional influence on color preference differently.

We used within-subject design to measure color preferences, since individual differences in color preference are rather significant (Schloss and Palmer 2007). Thus, the changes between two color preferences were used as the main dependent variables of the study. We used emotionally laden movies to induce happiness, sadness, and neutral emotion. The movies were edited into black and white films to eliminate color exposure confounding during video watching. We asked participants to evaluate the colors before and after watching emotionally laden movies. As a cover story, participants were told to take part in two unrelated studies, color preference study and video evaluation study. They heard that to avoid their eyes from being tired from evaluating subtly different colors, color preference study would be split into part I and part II and videos study would take tart in between the two parts.

Colors were chosen based on Hue-Saturation-Light (HSL) color scheme, which is widely accepted by color theorists as describing three independent properties of colors (Valdez and Mehrabian 1994). To identify which aspect of colors is influenced by emotions, hue (red, blue, yellow, and green), saturation (saturated vs., muted), and lightness (light, middle, dark) dimensions of colors were fully factorized. Therefore, we used a mixed ANOVA design: 3 emotion (happy, sad, and neutral: between-subjects) x 4 hue x 2 saturation x 3 lightness ANOVA.

One hundred fifty nine undergraduate students from a large western university participated in a study. Emotions were induced successfully as intended. The three hypotheses predicted emotional effect on color preferences in different direction. To test these hypotheses, we conducted a mixed ANOVA examining the effects of a perceiver's emotion (happy, sad, and neutral: between-subjects) on preferences for colors' dimensions (hue x saturation x light). A full factorial ANOVA did not reveal significant effects. However, after grouping hues by wavelength we found a significant interaction among wavelength, lightness, and emotion. In the light and middle lightness levels, the happy group's preferences for long wavelength colors significantly increased. However, the happy group's preferences for dark colors were not different from other groups.

In summary, a perceiver's emotion affects his color preferences. More specifically, when people are happy (vs. neutral), happiness associated colors, that is, highly arousing colors such as light red and yellow, are more preferred.

References

Andrade, E. B. (2005), "Behavioral Consequences of Affect: Combining Evaluative and Regulatory Mechanisms," *Journal of Consumer Research*, 32 (3), 355-62.

Bower, G. H. (1981), "Mood and Memory," *Am Psychol*, 36 (2), 129-48.

Crozier, W. R. (1996), "The Psychology of Colour Preferences," *Review of Progress in Coloration and Related Topics*, 26 (1), 63-72.

Guilford, J. P. and P. C. Smith (1959), "A System of Color-Preferences," *The American Journal of Psychology*, 487-502.

Ou, L. C., M. R. Luo, A. Woodcock, and A. Wright (2004), "A Study of Colour Emotion and Colour Preference. Part I: Colour Emotions for Single Colours," *Color Research & Application*, 29 (3), 232-40.

Schloss, Karen and Stephen Palmer (2007), "Aesthetic Preference for Color Combinations," *http://socrates.berkeley.edu/~plab/pdf/SchlossPalmer.pdf*.

Schwarz, N. and G. L. Clore (1983), "Mood, Misattribution, and Judgments of Well-Being: Informative and Directive Functions of Affective States," *Journal of Personality*, 45 (3), 513-23.

Valdez, P. and A. Mehrabian (1994), "Effects of Color on Emotions," *J Exp Psychol Gen*, 123 (4), 394-409.

Social Attributions of Obesity and Attitudes toward Food Marketing: Implications on Framing Strategy

Jung-Sook Lee, Towson University, USA

Using attribution theory, the study investigates the relationships between social attributions of obesity and consumers' attitudes toward food-marketing policy. Findings from a survey of 316 college students indicate that differences in social attributions, causes of and responsibilities to obesity, are significantly related to consumers' attitudes toward food-marketing policy. Attitudes toward food advertising and beliefs on the importance of obesity are also important in predicting consumers' attitudes toward food-marketing policies, both directly and indirectly through social attributions about obesity. A synergetic framing, instead of a competitive framing, between personal and social attributions is recommended as a message framing strategy to build consumers' support for policies on food marketing.

Antecedents of Attitudes towards Counterfeits of Luxury Brands: A Consumer Misbehavior Model Perspective

Seung-Hee Lee, Ewha Womans University, Seoul, Korea
Boonghee Yoo, Hofstra University, USA

Conceptualization: Counterfeiting is a global phenomenon with a growth rate of 1700% over the past decade (U.S. Department of State, 2006). Estimates of global sales for counterfeit products are about $600 billion per year, accounting for 9% of world trade (Cordeiro 2007). Much research can be found in the literature that deals with anti-counterfeit strategies from the supply side to protect counterfeiting (e.g., Chaudhry et al 2005; Shultz and Nill 2002). However, the counterfeiting problem is not related only to the manufacturers of counterfeit products, but also the demand for these counterfeit products. For better understanding consumer behavior about counterfeit products, the consumer misbehavior model was used for this study. Consumer misbehavior is defined as 'behavioral acts by consumers which violate the generally accepted norms of conduct in consumption situations' (Fullerton & Punj 1997, p.336). This consumer misbehavior has been accepted as a component of consumer experience. More than thirty-five types of consumer misbehavior such as shoplifting, financial fraud, and purchase of counterfeit products have been explained. Based on the literature review, this research involves three elements: 1) product variables such as price and quality, 2) individual variables such as materialism and consumer ethics, and 3) social variables such as subjective norms.

Purpose of this study: Therefore, the purpose of this study was to examine the determinants that influence consumers to purchase counterfeit products, and to propose and test a model that deals with the main antecedents of consumer attitudes toward counterfeits of luxury brands. Six hypotheses were developed. H1: The perceived price-advantage of counterfeits has a positive effect on the attitude toward counterfeit products. H2: The perceived quality of counterfeits has a positive effect on the attitude toward counterfeit products. H3: Materialism has a positive effect on the attitude toward counterfeit products. H4: Consumer ethics has a negative effect on the attitude toward counterfeit products. H5: Subjective norm has a positive effect on the attitude toward counterfeit products. H6: Attitude toward counterfeit products has a positive effect on purchase intention of counterfeits.

Method: Three hundred and sixty-nine undergraduate female students (M=21.4) at a large university in Seoul, Korea took part in this study. Korea is one of the top five biggest manufacturers in counterfeit production worldwide along with China, Taiwan, India and Hong Kong (Casabona 2009). Approximately 70% of the respondents were marketing and fashion majors. Their monthly personal disposable income ranged from $70 to $900 (M=$318). The questionnaire included demographic items and questions as to whether or not participants had purchased counterfeit products. The purchasers of counterfeits 'knowingly' purchased a counterfeit as non-deceptive counterfeits. For measurement, perceived price-advantage, quality of counterfeits, and subjective norms items were adopted from Tom et al (1998)'s scale. Richins and Dawson (1992)'s materialism scale and Muncy and Vitel (1992)'s consumer ethics scale were also used for this study. Each item was accompanied by a 7-point scale (7=strongly agree; 1=strongly disagree). Descriptive statistics and structural equation modeling using AMOS program were conducted for data analyses.

Major Findings: Approximately 67% of respondents had purchased counterfeit fashion products such as clothing, handbags, accessories and shoes. To ensure data validity and reliability in this study, internal consistency, convergent validity, and discriminate validity were examined. As the results, strong evidence demonstrated satisfactory data validity and reliability. As the next step, the subsequent process of identifying the structural model that best fits the data was conducted. The findings indicated the structural model presented in this study showed adequate overall goodness-of-fit with observed data (Chi-square =15.85, d.f. =5, p=.05; GFI=.99; AGFI=.98; CFI=.99; RMSEA=.001, RMR=.028). The results of hypothesis testing showed four hypotheses out of six supported at the significant level of lower than 0.05. That is, the perceived price-advantage of counterfeits (H1: Estimate= .126, p<.05), and perceived quality of counterfeits (H2: Estimate= .373, p<.0001) had a positive effect on the attitude toward counterfeit products. Also materialism (H4: Estimate= -.175, p<.0001) had a negative effect on the attitude toward counterfeit products. Finally, attitude toward counterfeit products (H6: Estimate= .446, p<.0001) had a positive effect on purchase intention of counterfeits. However, H2 and H4 were not supported.

Managerial Implications: Based on these results, consumer's attitudes toward counterfeits is an important predictor of counterfeits of luxury brands. Purchasing counterfeit products is illegal globally and is considered consumer misbehavior. This study will provide practical and useful information for educators, global marketers and policy makers that will be beneficial in the protection of counterfeit misbehavior. Results of this study are only partially conclusive, and further research is necessary to better understand this phenomena.

References

Casabona, Liza (2009), "Seizures of Counterfeit Accessories Increase in 2008, Shoes Lead List," *WWD: Women's Wear Daily*, (January 9). 197(5).

Cordeiro, Anjali (2007), "Trade in Fake Goods Expands," *The Wall Street Journal*. July 11: p. B3A.

Fullerton, Ronald A. and Girish Punj (1997), "Can Consumer Misbehavior Be Controlled? A Critical Analysis of Two Major Control Techniques," *Advances in Consumer Research,* 24: 340-344.

Muncy, James A., and Scott Vitell (1992), "Consumer Ethics: An Investigation of the Ethical Beliefs of the Final Consumer," *Journal of Business Research,* 24(June): 297-311.

Richins, Marsha L. and Scott Dawson (1992), "A Consumer Values Orientation for Materialism and its Measurement: Scale Development and Validation," *Journal of Consumer research*, 19 (December), 303-316.

Shultz II, C., and A., Nill, (2002), "The Societal Conundrum of Intellectual Property rights: A game-theoretical approach to the equitable management and protection of IPR," *European Journal of marketing*, 36(5/6), 667-688.

Tom, Gain, Barbara Garibaldi, Yvette Zeng, and Julie Pilcher (1998), "Consumer Demand for Counterfeit Goods," *Psychology & Marketing*, 15(5), 405-421.

U.S. Department of State (2006), "Focus on Intellectual Property Rights: Fakes Cost more," (accessed July 5) [available at http://usinfo.state.gov/products/pubs/intelprp/chan.htm].

The Effects of Values-Affirmation on Charity Support Behavior: The Mediating Role of Positive Other-Directed Feelings

Yun Lee, University of Iowa, USA
Jing Wang, University of Iowa, USA

Despite charitable organizations' enormous social and economic impacts in our society (Bendapud et al. 1996), charitable giving has stagnated in the U.S over the last 30 years, and philanthropic institutions have found it increasingly difficult to raise needed funds from givers (Merchant and Ford 2008). Given today's daunting situations charities are faced with, in this article, we suggest that affirming important personal values motivate charity support behavior.

This argument follows from self-affirmation theory. Self-affirmation refers to behavioral or cognitive events that bolster the 'perceived integrity of the self" (Steel 1988, p.291). Social psychologists have documented that self-affirmation encourages people to see themselves objectively (Harris and Napper 2005), and helps them buffer against self-threatening information (Armitage et al. 2008; Harris et al. 2007; Koole et al. 1999) and decrease biased information processing of a persuasive message (Cohen et al. 2000; Harris and Napper 2005; Reed et al. 1998). It has also been linked with less motivational processing of dissonance provoking situations (Steele and Liu 1983), increased open-mindedness (Correll et al. 2004; Sherman and Cohen 2006) , and decreased closed-mindedness and inflexibility in negotiation (Cohen et al. 2007). Taken these together, we argue that the process of values-affirmation may increase the persuasiveness of a message about charity support.

H1: Participants in values-affirmation conditions are more likely to support charity than those in control conditions.

Recent studies (Koole et al. 1999; Steele and Liu 1983; Tesser 2000) have argued that values-affirmation increases positive feelings. Along the same line with this argument, Crocker et al. (2008) demonstrated that affirming important personal values induced greater positive other-directed emotions, by enabling people to diminish concern for themselves (Correll et al. 2004) and transcend the self (Crocker et al. 2008). As for the linkage between positive mood and enhanced helping behavior, Weyant (1978) found that when people were on positive mood, they volunteered more than those on neutral mood. This leads us to theorize that values-affirmation increases positive other-directed feelings, and thereby enhance helping behavior.

H2: The enhanced charity support behavior through the process of values-affirmation is mediated by positive other-directed feelings.

In three studies, we investigate whether this is the case. We begin by demonstrating the effects of values-affirmation on donation intent to the Red Cross (Study 1), willingness to help people in crisis (Study2), and willingness to help patients coping with end-stage diseases (Study 3). We then demonstrate that participants in values-affirmation conditions are more likely to help charity on the greater positive other-directed feelings than those in control conditions (Study 2). Finally, we demonstrate that the effect of values-affirmation on willingness to help others is mediated by positive other-directed feelings (Study 3).

Study 1

Method

Participants were asked to rank six values (i.e., business, art-music-theater, social life-relationships, science-pursuit of knowledge, religion-mortality, government-politics) in order of their personal importance (Sherman et al. 2000). Participants were then assigned to either the values-affirmation versus the control condition. In the values affirmation condition, participants were instructed to think about their most important value and write a short essay about why the value was important and meaningful to them. In the control condition, participants were asked to write about their least important value and why it might be important and meaningful to other people (Schmeichel and Vohs 2009). Then participants were presented with the message from the Red Cross and asked whether they would like to make monthly donation to the Red Cross Champions Program (0= do not want to make monthly donation, 1= want to make monthly donation).

Results

Monthly Donation Intention. We measured monthly donation intention as dichotomous and analyzed the data by using Chi-Square test. The results showed that participants (59.4%) in the values-affirmation conditions were more likely to make monthly donation to charity than those (40.6%) in the control conditions ($\chi^2(1)=3.574$, $p=.06$).

Study 2

Method

Participants were asked to rank twelve values (i.e., relations with family and friends, social skills, romantic values, athletics, sense of humor, creativity, managerial skills, spontaneity, neatness or tidiness, aesthetic appreciation, physical attractiveness, and music ability or appreciation) in order of their personal importance (Harris and Napper 2005). As Study 1, participants were then assigned to either the values-affirmation versus the control condition. And we measured their positive other-directed feelings (loving, connected, and grateful; Crocker et al. 2008) using a three-item five-point scale (1= not at all, 5= extremely). Then participants were presented with the message of the Red Cross Champions Program and asked to leave their email addresses, if they were willing to help people in crisis, so that the program coordinator could contact them.

Results

Willingness to help people in crisis. We coded the data of willingness to help as binary (0= did not leave email address, 1=left email address) and analyzed them using Chi-Square test. The results showed that participants (60.4%) in the values-affirmation conditions were more likely to help others in crisis than those (39.6%) in the control conditions ($\chi^2(1)=3.333$, $p=.06$).

Positive Other-directed feelings. The results of a 2 (values-affirmation vs. control) × 2 (email left: yes vs. no) between-subjects ANOVA revealed a significant interaction ($F(1,74)=4.926$, $p=.03$). Participants in the values-affirmation conditions were more likely to help people in crisis on the greater positive other-directed feelings ($\alpha=.79$) than those in the control conditions (Mvalues= 2.86, Mcontrol= 2.17, $t(46)=3.347$, $p=.002$). Furthermore, in the values-affirmation conditions, participants who wanted to help people in crisis showed greater positive other-directed feelings than those who did not want to help (Myes= 2.86, Mno= 2.17, $t(37)=-1.81$, $p=.07$). However participants in the control conditions did not differ on positive other-directed feelings regardless of participants' willingness to help (Mno= 2.35, Myes= 1.93, $t(37)=1.29$, $p>.20$) .

Study 3

Method

As previous studies, participants were asked to work on ranking and writing tasks. Then participants' positive other-directed feelings (loving, connected, and grateful) and positive self-directed feelings (powerful, strong, and admirable) were measured using a six-item five-point scale (1= not at all, 5= extremely; Crocker et al. 2008). Then they were told that a charity organization needed volunteers to help patients coping with end-stage diseases and asked to indicate their willingness to help (1= not at all, 5= very much). They were also asked to leave their email addresses, if they want to help patients, so that the program director could contact them.

Results

Email Left. The results demonstrated that participants (62.3%) in the values-affirmation conditions were more likely to help patients than those (37.7%) in the control conditions ($\chi^2(1)=3.689$, $p=.05$).

Willingness to help. The results of an one-way ANOVA revealed a significant effect for values-affirmation ($F(1, 86)=5.475, p=.02$). Participants in the values-affirmation conditions were more likely to help patients than those in the control conditions (*M*values= 2.9, *M*control= 2.13).

Mediation analyses. The positive other-directed feelings (α= .82) explained the relationship between values-affirmation and willingness to help charity. Values-affirmation significantly enhanced positive other-directed feelings (β= *-.703*, p<.01; most=0, least=1), which in turn predicted an increase in willingness to help (β= *.384*, p<.05). When the positive other-directed feelings was included in the regression analysis predicting willingness to help, however, the effect of values-affirmation on willingness to help (β= *-.768*, p<.05) was no longer significant (β= *-.504*, p>.10, NS), and only the effect of positive other-directed feelings was observed (β= *.353*, p<.05; Sobel z=1.66, p<.10). The positive self-directed feelings (α= .86), however, didn't mediate the effect of values-affirmation on charity support behavior.

Across three studies, we demonstrated that affirming important personal values increased charity support behavior and the effect of values-affirmation on charity support behavior was mediated by positive other-directed feelings. This research suggests that when people are encouraged to affirm important values, they experience greater positive other-directed feelings, and thereby transcend concerns about the self and overcome motivational conflicts between prosocial and selfish impulses.

References

Armitage, Christopher J., Peter R. Harris, Gareth Hepton, and Lucy Napper (2008), "Self-Affirmation Increases Acceptance of Health-Risk Information Among UK Adult Smokers With Low Socioeconomic Status," *Psychology of Addictive Behaviors*, 22 (1), 88-95.

Bendapudi, Neeli, Surendra N. Singh, and Venkat Bendapudi (1996), "Enhancing Helping Behavior: An Integrative Framework for Promotion Planning," *Journal of Marketing*, 60 (July), 33- 49.

Cohen, Geoffrey L., Joshua Aronson and Claude M. Steele (2000), "When Beliefs Yield to Evidence: Reducing Biased Evaluation by Affirming the Self," *Journal of Social Psychology and Bulletin*, 26 (9), 1151- 64.

Correll, Joshua, Steven J. Spencer, and Mark P. Zanna (2004), "An Affirmed Self and An Open Mind: Self-Affirmation and Sensitivity to Argument Strength," *Journal of Experimental Social Psychology*, 40, 350- 56.

Crocker, Jenniffer, Niiya Yu, and Dominik Mischkowski (2008), "Why Does Writing About Important Values Reduce Defensiveness: Self-Affirmation and the Role of Positive Other-Directed Feelings," *Psychological Science*, 19 (7), 740- 47.

Harris, Peter R., Kathryn Mayle, Lucy Mabbott, and Lucy Napper (2007), "Self-Affirmation Reduces Smokers' Defensiveness to Graphic On-Pack Cigarette Warning Labels," *Health Psychology*, 26 (4), 437-46.

Harris, Peter R. and Lucy Napper (2005), "Self-Affirmation and the Biased Processing of Threatening Health-Risk Information," *Personality and Social Psychology Bulletin*, 31 (9), 1250-63.

Koole, Sander L., Karianne Smeets, Ad van Knippenberg, and Ap Dijksterhuis (1999), "The cessation of Rumination Through Self-Affirmation," *Journal of Personality and Social Psychology*, 77, 111-25.

Merchant, Altaf and John Ford (2008), "Nostalgia and Giving to Charity: A Conceptual Framework for Discussion and Research," *International Journal of Nonprofit and Voluntary Sector Marketing*, 13 (February), 13-30.

Reed, Mark B. and Lisa G. Aspinwall (1998), "Self-Affirmation Reduces Biased Processing of Health-Risk Information," *Motivation and Emotion*, 22, 99-132.

Schmeichel, Brandon J., and Kathleen Vohs (2009), "Self-Affirmation and Self-Control: Affirming Core Values Counteracts Ego Depletion," *Journal of Personality and Social Psychology*, 96 (4), 770-82.

Sherman, David K., Leif D. Nelson, and Claude. M. Steele (2000), "Do Messages about Health Risks Threaten the Self? Increasing the Acceptance of Threatening Health Messages via Self-Affirmation," *Personality and Social Psychology Bulletin*, 26, 1046-1058.

Steele, Claude. M. (1988), "The Psychology of Self-Affirmation: Sustaining the Integrity of the Self," *Advances in Experimental Social Psychology*, ed. L. Berkowitz, New York: Academic Press, 21, 261-302.

Steele, Claude M., and Thomas J. Liu (1983), "Dissonance Processes as Self-Affirmation," *Journal of Personality and Social Psychology*, 45, 5-19.

Tesser, Abraham (2000), "On the Confluence of Self-Esteem Maintenance Mechanisms," *Personality and Social Psychology Review*, 4, 290-99.

Weyant, James M. (1978), "Effects of Mood States, Costs, and Benefits on Helping," *Journal of Personality and Social Psychology*, 36 (10), 1169-76.

Effects of Advertising Exposure on Materialism and Self-Esteem: Advertised Luxuries as a Feel-Good Strategy?

Inge Lens, K.U. Leuven, Belgium
Mario Pandelaere, Ghent University, Belgium
Luk Warlop, K.U.Leuven, Belgium

Advertisements communicate that any aspiration can be fulfilled if one possesses the right products and brands (Kasser 2002; Pollay 1986). However, little experimental research has shown this presumed effect of advertising exposure on materialism (e.g., Brand and Greenberg 1994; Han and Shavitt 2005; Zhang and Shavitt 2003). Even less research attempted to disentangle the role of self-esteem in this effect. Given that materialists derive a sense of worth and happiness from the acquisition of possessions (Richins and Dawson 1992), feeling unable to afford advertised products might be problematic for the self-esteem of consumers who repeatedly fail to meet their culturally imposed, materialistic standards (Kasser et al. 2007). In contrast, the pleasant experience of feeling able to afford advertised products may motivate consumers to strive even more for wealth (cf. Vohs and Baumeister 2008). However, this might be less problematic for their self-esteem as these consumers probably feel confident that they will achieve their (material) aspirations (cf. Nickerson et al. 2003). The aim of this research is to investigate these relations between advertising exposure, self-esteem and materialism. We predict that consumers' perceived ability to afford advertised products moderates the effect of advertising exposure on self-esteem and materialism.

In a first experiment, 189 participants were divided over two conditions. Participants in the advertising condition were exposed to five ads for luxurious products. For each ad they indicated to what extent they felt able to afford the product. Participants in the control condition saw no ads. Next, levels of self-esteem (Rosenberg, 1965), chronic materialism (Richins and Dawson, 1992) and momentary importance attached to materialism related goals, e.g., financial success or social status (Aspiration Index, extrinsic subscales; Kasser and Ryan 1993, 1996), were measured. A significant momentary increase in materialism is found in the advertising condition relative to the control condition. Additionally, advertising exposure significantly enhances the self-esteem of consumers who believe they can afford the promoted luxuries, compared to consumers who cannot afford them. However, it is possible that perceived affordability is a consequence rather than an antecedent of self-esteem. Consumers with high self-esteem may be more optimistic about their ability to buy advertised items. In that case, self-esteem measured prior to advertising exposure should predict perceived affordability. To test this hypothesis, participants in the control condition judged the same ads at the end of the study. Their self-esteem scores do not predict affordability, which rules out this alternative interpretation.

Study two aims to replicate these findings and tests whether the effect of affordability concerns is altered if participants are encouraged to imagine themselves owning the advertised products. Forty-seven participants were exposed to six ads for luxury products. After the exposure, 23 participants recalled one ad/product and imagined how they would feel if they would own the product. The other half of the participants did not engage in this mental simulation task. Seventeen participants did not see any ads (control condition). Next, self-esteem (Rosenberg 1965) and temporal materialism (Aspiration Index; Kasser and Ryan 1993, 1996) were measured. Affordability was measured after a number of unrelated tasks to assess whether these concerns affect self-esteem without being actively cued during the advertising exposure (as in study 1). No effect of advertising condition (ad vs. no ads) on materialism is found, yet a significant interaction effect of simulation condition (no imagination vs. imagination) and perceived affordability is found on temporal materialism. In the *no imagination condition,* the regression slope is significant, suggesting that the more one feels able to afford the products, the higher the increase in materialism after the exposure (in comparison to mean materialism in the control condition). In the *imagination condition*, the regression slope is not significant. Also for self-esteem a significant interaction effect of simulation condition and affordability is found. In the *no imagination condition,* the slope is significant, suggesting that the more one feels able to afford the products, the higher the increase in self-esteem after the exposure and vice versa. In the *imagination condition*, the regression slope is not significant.

Both experiments provide preliminary evidence that advertising exposure might induce materialism, most likely in consumers who feel able to afford the advertised products. For consumers who claim being able to buy luxuries, increased levels of materialism after the exposure seem to be less problematic than is usually expected, as they tend to express higher levels of self-esteem. Interestingly, the effects of ad exposure disappear when consumers imagine themselves owning the products. Such outcome-focused thoughts, as opposed to process-focus thoughts, may draw consumers' attention away from actions needed to be taken in order to obtain the product (Escalas and Luce 2004), e.g., being able to buy it. Spending cognitive effort on this imagination process might thus reduce the impact of prior affordability concerns. Interesting would be to assess whether these findings are restricted to luxury advertising or apply to a broader advertising context.

Finally, these results do not necessarily imply that ad exposure is constructive for consumers' self-esteem. Even though the expected inverse relation between materialism and self-esteem (Chaplin and John 2007) was not found, a self-esteem boost resulting from feeling able to afford luxuries seems contingent on social approval. And such extrinsically oriented feelings of self-worth are unlikely to ensure a healthy psychological life in the long run (Kasser, Koestner, and Lekes 2002; Ryan and Deci, 2000).

References

Brand, Jeffrey E. and Bradley S. Greenberg (1994), "Commercials in the Classroom: The Impact of Channel One Advertising," *Journal of Advertising Research, 34* (1), 18-27.

Chaplin, Lan Nguyen and Deborah Roedder John (2007), "Growing up in a Material World: Age Differences in Materialism in Children and Adolescents," *Journal of Consumer Research*, 34 (December), 480-493.

Escalas, Jennifer Edson and Mary Frances Luce (2004), "Understanding the Effects of Process-Focused Versus Outcome-Focused Thought in Response to Advertising," *Journal of Consumer Research, 31*, 274-85.

Han, Sang-pil and Sharon Shavitt (2005), "Westernization of Cultural Values in Korean Advertising: A Longitudinal Content Analysis of Magazine Ads From 1968- 1998," *Advances in Consumer Research, 32*, 249-50.

Kasser, Tim (2002). *The high price of materialism.* Cambridge: MIT Press.

Kasser, Tim and Richard M. Ryan (1993), "A Dark Side of The American Dream-Correlates of Financial Success as a Central Life Aspiration," *Journal of Personality and Social Psychology*, 65 (2), 410-22.

______ (1996), "Further Examining the American Dream: Differential Correlates of Intrinsic and Extrinsic Goals," *Personality and Social Psychology Bulletin,* 22 (March), 280-87.

Kasser, Tim, Richard Koestner, and Natasha Lekes (2002), "Early Family Experiences and Adult Values: A 26-year, Prospective Longitudinal Study," *Personality and Social Psychology Bulletin, 28* (6), 826-35.

Kasser, Tim, Steve Cohn, Allen D. Kanner, and Richard M. Ryan (2007), "Some Costs of American Corporate Capitalism: A Psychological Exploration of Value and Goal Conflicts. *Psychological Inquiry, 18* (1), 1-22.

Nickerson, Carol, Norbert Schwartz, Ed Diener, and Daniel Kahneman (2003), "Zeroing in on the Dark Side of the American Dream: A Close Look at the Negative Consequences of the Goal for Financial Success," *Psychological Science, 14,* 531-36.
Pollay, Richard W. (1986), "The Distorted Mirror: Reflections on the Unintended Consequences of Advertising," *Journal of Marketing, 50* (2), 18-36.
Richins, Marsha L., and Scott Dawson (1992), "Materialism as a Consumer Value: Measure Development and Validation," *Journal of Consumer Research, 19* (December), 303-16.
Rosenberg, Morris (1965), *Society and the Adolescent Self-image*, Princeton, NJ: Princeton University Press.
Ryan, Richard M. and Edward L. Deci (2000), "The Darker and Brighter Sides of Human Existence: Basic Psychological Needs as a Unifying Concept," *Psychological Inquiry, 11* (4), 319-38.
Vohs, Kathleen D. and Roy F. Baumeister (2008), "Can Satisfaction Reinforce Wanting? A New Theory about Long Term Changes in Strength of Motivation," In *Handbook of motivation science,* ed. J. Y. Shah, W. L. Gardner, New York: Guilford Press, 373-92.
Zhang, Jing, and Sharon Shavitt (2003), "Cultural Values in Advertisements to the Chinese X-generation," *Journal of Advertising, 32* (1), 23-33.

The Effect of Physical Enclosing on Negative Emotion Regulation

Xiuping Li, National University of Singapore, Singapore
Liyuan Wei, City University of Hong Kong, Hong Kong, China

In three studies, we had shown that people attained certain closure over negative events by putting materials relating to the event into the envelope. In study 1, we showed that people felt less bad about a decision that they regretted a lot in study 1A (a strong desire that they could not satisfy in study 1B) if they put the recalled event (desire) into an envelope. Experiment 2 found that people felt less negative after reading a sad story print on a paper after putting the paper into the envelope. However enclosing an unrelated task did not soothe emotional reaction.

Despite wishes to feel happy and positive, negative emotions–often triggered by the memory of past experiences–come back to haunt us. How can we stop our mind from being distracted by intrusive memories of negative experiences and get closure?

Memory researchers have discussed the concept of cognitive inhibition and found that an explicit instruction to inhibit an unwanted thought may actually increase the accessibility (and hence recall) of the concept (Wegner et al., 1987). Similarly, literature on emotion regulation has suggested that suppression of negative emotional reactions can backfire (Gross, 1998; Wegner, Erber & Zanakos, 1993). However, other than deliberatively trying hard to forget, lay people do seek remedies by physically locking things up. For instance, a self-help website on how to deal with a broken relationship advises readers to "put everything that reminds you of your ex in a box and seal it..." (Pant, 2007). Do these behavioral strategies to put physical closure on objects work? The premise that physically enclosing and sealing emotion-related items will help people attain psychological closure over emotional experience stems from recent research on embodied cognition and metaphors. We report the results of three experiments which showed that sealing an emotional laden object into an envelope could relieve the related negative emotions people experienced as a result.

In study 1A, eighty students were randomly assigned to the two conditions. In both conditions, participants were first asked to recall a recent decision that they felt greatly regretful. In one condition, after participants recalled the event, they were instructed to put the questionnaire to into an envelope before they handed back the questionnaires; in the other condition, participants were simply asked to hand back the questionnaires. In the second task, participants reported how they felt about the event along four negative emotion scales: regretful, guilty, sad, and worried, all anchored from 1, not at all, to 5 extremely. The four negative emotions were averaged to indicate how negative participants felt about the event at the moment the measurement was taken (cronbach alpha=.79). A simple t test of the treatment factor revealed that participants who put the recalled event into the envelop felt less negatively (M=2. 00) about the event than those who just handed back the recall task without an envelope (M=2.52, t (1, 78)=2.42).

Study 1B was different from 1A along the two aspects. Rather than recalling a regrettable experience, participants were instead asked to report something they wanted to do very badly but could not do it. Second, the study was conducted in the dorms on campus. On specific emotional reactions towards the strong desires, people who were given an envelop to put their questionnaire into felt much less negative on almost all single items that were measured (Sad, disappointed, unsatisfied, anxious $ts(1, 37)>2.33$, $ps<.05$). In addition, in terms of mental disturbance they felt over the their strong desire, those people who experienced the physical closure did felt less distracted or unsettled towards it (t (1, 37) s>2.25, ps<.05).

Study 2 tested whether the difference was driven by the action of putting things into envelope (in the similar fashion as how catharsis works for some negative emotions) or due to the fact that the specific emotion laden material was put to a symbolic closure. The main test had three conditions, and all conditions needed to complete three tasks in the same sequence and at the same pace. In the first task participants were asked to read a recent news report on the death of a baby. The second task, which was totally irrelevant to the news, measured how college students made a few daily hypothetical decisions. In the last task participants were asked to report how they felt at the moment.

In the first condition, every completed questionnaire was collected back by the experimenter before the next questionnaire was handed out (i.e., control condition). In the second condition, after participants completed the first task, they were given a small envelope and instructed to put the task completed into the envelope. After experimenter collected all envelopes, the second questionnaire would be handed out, followed by the third task (i.e., the condition where physical closure was specified at the emotional event). In the third condition, participants they were given a small envelope to put the second task in and handed it back before they were given the last questionnaire (i.e., the condition where physical closure was acted on unrelated task).

The three negative emotions measured have a relatively high correlation (Cronbach's alpha=.90), and were averaged to indicate how negative the sad story made participants felt. Helmert contrasts were conducted first and showed that after participants put the emotional laden materials into the envelope (M=2.90), the negative emotions they felt were significantly less than the rest two conditions ($F(1, 77)=3.89$, $p<.05$). However, the difference between the control condition and the experimental condition where participants were asked to put an unrelated task to the envelope did not differ on the reported emotional states ($M_{control}=4.28$; $M_{unrelated}=4.12$, $F(1, 77)=.32$, $p>.80$).

It is known that the body is closely tied to the processing of emotional information (Niedenthal et al., 2009). Therefore, it is reasonable to expect that bodily experience may also be pivotal in the regulation of emotions. While supporting theories on embodied cognition and embodied emotion, our results took one step further to show that people's emotion regulation process can indeed be facilitated by taking a physical action on the emotional laden materials. The experiments demonstrated that the abstract mental state such as psychological closure over an event appeared to rely on the sensory-motor experiences brought by the simple act of enclosing.

Influence of Self-Relevant Base-Rate Information on Risk Perception of Getting Depression

Ying-Ching Lin, National Dong Hwa University, Taiwan

The aim of this current research is to examine the influence of base-rate information on risk perception in the context of depression. The issue of depression has gained the attention of social marketers and researchers all over the world (*e.g.*, Fontaine & Jones, 1997, Nelson & Craighead, 1977, Tennen & Herzberger, 1987), and has a high incidence in the population studied. The question is whether or not providing this population with the base-rate information on the incidence of depression will be effective to get them to seek help. Therefore, this question is the focus of this paper.

The theoretical framework of this study is based on the impersonal impact hypothesis, which proposes that people's general risk perception may be heightened by the relative information provided, but their personal risk judgments are not(Weinstein, 1989; Tyler & Cook, 1984). Therefore, the purpose of study 1 is to demonstrate that offering social level information such as base-rate information doesn't influence an individual's risk perception, but the personal level information such as the level of depression can indeed influence the risk perception of getting depression and decrease the level of self-positivity bias. Study 2 will examine the individual's perception of the relevance of the base-rate information to see if different levels of self-relevant perception affect their estimations of own risk and other risk of getting depression. While study 2 examines the perception of the relevance to the base-rate information, Study 3 directly manipulates the level of base-rate relevance to see if more self-relevant base-rate information draws the attention of participants to their risk of getting depression and so decrease the difference between their own risk and other's risk of getting depression.

Method

Study 1 examined the effect of social level risk information and personal level risk information on self-risk perception, the updating of self-risk estimates and on the level of self-positivity bias for getting depression. We predict that base-rate information serves as social level risk information and will not change self-risk perception of getting depression, and will remain at the same level of self-positivity bias. However, the result of self-diagnosis inventory serves as a personal level risk judgment and will increase an individual's risk perceptions, and will help to reduce the level of self-positivity bias. At the same time, Study 1 also examines the effect of social level risk information and personnel level risk information on an individual's willingness to update his/her self-risk estimates. A 3 (estimate: self initial / other/ self updated) x 2 (social level risk information—base-rate: present vs. absent) x 2 (personal level risk information—level of depression from self- diagnosis inventory: low vs. high) mixed design was used in this study. Seventy-eight undergraduate students participated in this study.

Study 2 proposes that self-relevant perception of the base-rate information will affect people's risk perception and the updating of their self-risk as well as the level of self-positivity bias. We predict that if people think that base-rate information is not relevant to them, they will continue to hold their self-positivity bias, and they will not update their self-risk estimation after they know the BR information for depression. On the other hand, if they think that the base-rate is related to them, then they will pay more attention to this information and will be prepared to update their self-risk estimation and their self-positivity bias will decrease as well. Study 1 showed that the level of depression plays an important role in risk perception and self-positivity bias. Therefore, study 2 will examine the effect of self-relevant perception of the base-rate information on the risk estimations between depressed and non-depressed groups. A 3(estimate: self initial / other/ self updated) x 2 (self-relevant perception: low vs. high) x 2 (level of depression: high vs. low) mixed design was used in study 2, with the estimating factor manipulated within-subjects, and the remaining factors measured between subjects. One hundred and seventeen undergraduate university students participated in study 2.

Study 3 examines the robustness of these results by directly manipulating the level of base-rate relevance. A 3 (estimate: self initial / other/ self updated) x 2 (self-relevance to base-rate information: low / high) x 2 (level of depression: high / low) mixed design was used in this study, with the estimating factor manipulated within-subjects, base-rate relevant manipulated and level of depression measured between subjects. One hundred and seven undergraduate students participated study 3.

Conclusion

The present study examined the effect of base-rate information on risk judgments about depression. In practice, social marketers provide different risk information to influence the risk perception of their target audiences. However, recent studies on information processing show a different view of the effects of base-rate information on self-positivity bias(e.g. Lin, et al., 2003; Lin & Raghubir, 2005). The present research echoes the findings of previous researches. Study 1 showed that since base-rate information serves as a social level risk information, providing this base-rate information does not change self-risk perception of getting depression, nor the level of self-positivity bias. However, more personal information such as the result of self-diagnosis inventory increased individuals' risk perceptions and helped to reduce the self-positivity bias. That is to say, non-depressed individuals showed self-positivity but depressed individuals showed realism on the risk perception of getting depression(*i.e.,"depressive realism,"* Tennen & Herzberger, 1987). Built on the findings of study 1 and the impersonal impact hypothesis(Tyler & Cook, 1984), study 2 and study 3 showed that if people believe that the base-rate information is highly relevant to them, then this more self-relevant base-rate information can work the same as personal level information. For depressed individuals, providing higher relevant base-rate information increased their risk estimations for getting depression and they showed realism regarding their own chances and those of others of getting depression. For non-depressed individuals, even when they did not show a significant difference for their self-risk between low and high base-rate relevant conditions, they did lower their self-positivity bias when they thought that the base-rate information was more relevant to them. At the same time, the results also showed that relevant perception of base-rate information served as a mediator between base-rate information and risk perception, especially for non-depressed individuals, which provides further evidence that more relevant base-rate information affects an individual's risk perception.

The results of our study also showed that base-rate information affects an individual's self-risk updating. Depressives, who typically have a pessimistic outlook on life, have been shown to be realistic about accepting their likelihood of risk ("depressive realism"; *cf.* Alloy & Abramson, 1979; see Ackermann & DeRubeis, 1991 for a review). They view their life and future in negative terms (Beck, 1967, 1976). Their absolute estimates reflect pessimism, and their relative estimates reflect self-negativity or realism rather than self-positivity (Keller, Lipkus & Rimer, 2002). The results of the present research reflect this pattern. Depressed individuals were realistic once they knew their chances of getting depression, therefore they did not update their risk perception according to the base-rate information (study 3). Even if they did update, their self-risk estimations would be based on their judgments of the base-rate. With other words, if they thought that the base-rate information was not relevant to them, then they decreased their self-risk estimations, but they increased their self-risk estimation if they thought that the base-rate information was more relevant to them(study 2).

Non-depressed individuals, on the other hand, are defined as those whose estimates reflect an absolute level of positivity (*i.e.*, they believe that they are less at risk for a negative event and are more likely to experience a positive event, than they actually are). In the meantime, they tend to have a high self-esteem (Lin et al., 2003; Lin & Raghubir, 2005). Therefore, when they were told the base-rate information, they tended to lower their risk estimations (study 3). More specifically, when they thought that the base-rate information was related to them, they tended to lower their self-risk estimation of getting depression(study 2) in order to maintain their self-esteem(Lin et al., 2003; Lin et al., 2004; Lin & Raghubir, 2005). Although, they would not admit that their risk of getting depression would be higher than they expected once they were given the base-rate information, they tended to lower their self-positivity bias. The base-rate information made the non-depressed individuals notice their risk of getting depression in relative level.

References

Alloy, Lauren B. and Lyn Y. Abramson (1979), "Judgments of Contingency in Depressed and Non-depressed Students: Sadder but Wiser?" *Journal of Experimental Psychology: General,* 108 (December), 441-485.

Beck: Aaron T. (1967). *Depression: Clinical, Experimental, and Theoretical Aspects,* New York: Harper and Row.

Beck: Aaron T. (1976). *Cognitive Therapy and Emotional Disorders,* New York: International Universities Press.

Fontaine, Kevin R. and Lindsay C. Jones (1997), "Self-esteem, Optimism, and Postpartum Depression," *Journal of Clinical Psychology*, 53(January), 59-63.

Keller, Punam A., Isaac M. Lipkus, and Barbara K. Rimer, (2002), "Depressive Realism and Health Risk Accuracy: The Negative Consequences of Positive Mood," *Journal of Consumer Research*, 29(Spring), 57-69.

Lin, Chien-Huang, Ying-Ching Lin and Priya Raghubir(2004), "The Interaction between Order Effects and Perceived Controllability on the Self-positivity Bias," *Advances in Consumer Research*, 31, 23-529.

Lin, Ying-Ching and Priya Raghubir (2005), "Gender Differences in Unrealistic Optimism about Marriage and Divorce: Are Men more Optimistic and Women more Realistic?" *Personality and Social Psychology Bulletin,* 31(February), 198-207.

Lin, Ying-Ching, Chien-Huang Lin, and Priya Raghubir (2003). "Avoiding Anxiety, being in Denial or Simply Stroking Self-esteem: Why Self-positivity?" *Journal of Consumer Psychology,* 13(October), 464-477.

Nelson, R. Eric and Craighead, Edward W. (1977), "Selective Recall of Positive and Negative Feedback, Self-control Behaviors, and Depression." *Journal of Abnormal Psychology*, 86(November), 379-388.

Tennen, Howard A. and Sharon D. Herzberger (1987), "Depression, Self-esteem, and the Absence of Self-protective Attributional Biases," *Journal of Personality and Social Psychology*, 52(August), 72-80.

Weinstein, Neil D. (1989). Effects of personal experience on self-protective behavior. *Psychlogical Bulletin*, 15(January), 31-50.

What You Buy Affects How Old You Feel

Yu-Tse Lin, Fu Jen Catholic University, Taiwan
Kang-Ning Xia, Yuan Ze University, Taiwan

Fashion consumption is a means for consumers to express and display themselves. Personal possession of fashion clothes or accessories could be considered as an extension of the self (Belk 1988). Therefore, fashion consumption is closely related to a consumer's self concept, and many researches have discussed this issue (e.g., Banister and Hogg 2004; Grant and Stephen 2005; Phau and Lo 2004). However, in the past, the researches regarding to self concept and fashion consumption were seldom involved with cognitive age. Actually, the perception of one's age is indeed part of self image (Guptill 1969). Consumer will behave based on their cognitive ages (Kastenbaum, Derbin, Sabatini, and Artt 1972; Stephens 1991; Wilkes 1992), and accordingly, they have their thoughts about what fashion is and what suitable to them is. Correspondingly, although not all of the fashion brands are positioned completely according to age, their positions still are related to age. Hence, for consumers, they will choose the brands or products that they thought are suitable to their age, and what really determinant in their consumption is their cognitive age rather than the chronological age.

Literature

Cognitive age is defined as the age one perceives one's self to be (Barak and Schiffman 1980; Blau 1956; Guptill 1969) and often expressed in terms of how old one feels, thinks, and looks, as well as the things one does (Kastenbaum, Derbin, Sabatini, and Artt 1972; Stephens 1991). Most researches about cognitive age were focused on the relationship between cognitive age and demographic variables with aged people (e.g., Stephens 1991; Markides and Boldt 1983; Bultena and Powers 1978; George, Mutran, and Pennybacker 1980), and seldom researches concerned the effect of cognitive age on general consumer behaviors, such as fashion consumption. Therefore, this study is aimed to probe the relationship between cognitive age and fashion consumption.

Most of the previous researches indicated that fashion attitudes influence fashion consumption behaviors (e.g., Grant and Stephen 2005; Joergens 2006; Park and Burns 2005; Park, Kim, and Forney 2006; Workman and Studak 2006). When further discussing the above relationship, it may be inferred that cognitive age could be the mediator of the fashion attitudes and fashion consumption behaviors. The related evidence is that previous researches showed that fashion attitudes influence the consumer's cognitive age (Barak 1998; Fenigstein, Scheier, and Buss 1975); in other words, when people are more willing toward fashion, more glad to try the new, and more ready to not rely on safe and well-established routines, they will perceived themselves to be younger, and vice versa.

Methods

This study used the two-step structural equations modeling (SEM) to explore the relationship. First, the confirmatory factor analysis (CFA) was performed to evaluate the construct validity. Then a structural analysis was performed to test whether the structural coefficients were significant. In addition, in order to further demonstrate the full or partial mediatory role of cognitive age in each antecedent, three nested competing models were compared with the base model to determine which the better one is. The data come from the 2006 Eastern Integrated Consumer Profile (E-ICP) database, which is a powerful survey of consumers in Taiwan. A self-report questionnaire was completed by 1344 persons aged 13-64 in Taiwan.

In this study, the construct of fashion behavior had three variables: fashion information seeking behavior, purchasing a fashion product, and the new fashion product trial (Raju 1980; Stephens 1991). The fashion attitude also had three variables: high vogue, mature taste, and utilitarian orientation.

The models

The base model is described that the cognitive age plays a mediatory role between fashion attitude and fashion behavior. It fully mediates between high vogue and fashion behaviors. Similarly, it fully mediates between utilitarian orientation and fashion behaviors. However, mature taste has a direct effect on fashion behaviors. In other words, there is only partial mediation between individual taste and fashion behaviors.

Competing model 1 indicates that the cognitive age mediates the impact of fashion attitude on fashion behavior. Especially, that each antecedent is fully mediated, not partially mediated. Competing model 2 indicates that the cognitive age fully mediates between utilitarian orientation and fashion behaviors. However, for the relationship between the mature taste and fashion behaviors, and high vogue and fashion behaviors, the mediation is partial. Competing model 3 indicates that the cognitive age is fully mediated between high vogue and the fashion behaviors. However, it is partially mediated between mature taste and fashion behaviors; it is also partially mediated between utilitarian orientation and fashion behaviors. In addition, some researches indicated that cognitive age may have a direct impact on fashion attitude, rather than the mediatory role between fashion attitude and fashion behaviors (Lumpkin 1985; Tongren 1988). Thus the non-nested competing model 4 was compared with the base model.

Results

The results showed the base model is better than other competing models. First, the chi-square difference between the base model and the competing model 1 is significant ($\Delta\chi^2$=-288.82, d.f.=3, p<.05). This finding indicates the failure of competing model 1 to reduce three paths from the mature taste to fashion behaviors. Second, the chi-square difference between the base model and the competing model 2 is not significant ($\Delta\chi^2$=4.03, d.f.=3, p>.05). This finding indicates the failure of competing model 2 to increase three paths from high vogue to fashion behaviors. Third, the chi-square differences between the base model and the competing model 3 is not significant ($\Delta\chi^2$=4.2, d.f.=3, p>.05). This result indicates the failure of the competing model 3 to increase three paths from the utilitarian orientation to fashion behaviors. The results also showed a good model fit of the base model: the goodness of fit index (GFI) was 0.96; the adjusted goodness-of-fit index (AGFI) was 0.94; the comparative fit index (CFI) was 0.97.

Conclusion

In summary, the results of this study added to the body of knowledge regarding the fashion consumption. This study indicated that cognitive age plays a mediatory role between the fashion attitudes and fashion consumption behaviors. While previous researches ignored the effect of cognitive age, the present study delineated the influence of cognitive age. In addition, this study enriched the researches regarding self-concept and consumption behaviors; this study indicates that cognitive age is also a significant self related factor that can predict the consumption behaviors. Finally, for marketers, as to fashion behavior and its causes, cognitive age is a simple concept that can be easily used to understand and segment consumers, and for the marketing practice, it is believed that cognitive age is more applicable than chronological age.

References

Barak B, Gould S. Alternative age measures: A research agenda. In: Hirschman E, Holbrook M, editor. *Advances in consumer research*, vol. 12. Ann Arbor, MI: Association for Consumer Research, 1985. pp. 53-58.

Barak B, Rahtz DR. Cognitive age: Demographic and psychographic dimensions. *Journal of Ambulatory Care Marketing* 1990; 3(2): 51-65.

Barak B, Schiffman LG.. Cognitive age: A nonchronological age variable. In: Olson J, editor. *Advances in consumer research* vol. 7. Ann Arbor, MI: Association for Consumer Research, 1980. pp. 602-06.

Barak B. Cognitive age: A new multidimensional approach to measuring age identity. International *Journal of Aging and Human Development* 1987; 25(2): 109-28.

Barak B. Inner-ages of middle-aged prime-lifers. *The International Journal of Aging and Human Development* 1998; 46(3): 189-228.

Barak B, Gould, S. Male and female fashion innovativeness and opinion leadership: A research note. In: Hawes JM, Glisan G.B, editor. *Developments in Marketing Science*, vol. 10. Akron, OH: Academy of Marketing Science 1987. pp. 110-14.

Blau ZS. Changes in status and age identification. *American Sociological Review* 1956; 21(April): 198-203.

Blau ZS. Old age in a changing society. NY: Franklin Watts, 1973.

Bultena GL, Powers EA. Denial of aging: Age identification and reference group. *Journal of Gerontology* 1978; 33(October): 748-54.

Carrigan M, Szmigin I. The representation of older people in advertisements. *Journal of the Market Research Society* 1999; 41(July):311-26.

Chua C, Cote JA, Leong SM. The antecedents of cognitive age. In: Goldberg ME, Corn G, Pollay R, editor. *Advances in Consumer Research* vol. 17. Ann Arbor, MI: Association for Consumer Research, 1990. pp. 880-85.

Fenigstein A, Scheier MF, Buss AH. Public and private self-consciousness: Assessment and theory. *Journal of Consulting and Clinical Psychology* 1975; 43(August): 522-27.

Gatignon H, Robertson TS. A propositional inventory for new diffusion research. *Journal of Consumer Research* 1985; 11(March): 849-67.

Gentry JW, Mildred D. Masculinity-femininity related to consumer choice. *Proceedings of the American Marketing Association Educator's Conference* 1977; 10, 423-27.

George LK, Mutran EJ, Pennybacker MR. The meaning and measurement of age identity. *Experimental Aging Research* 1980; 6(June): 283-98.

Guptill, CS. A measure of age identification. *The Gerontologist* 1969; 9(Summer): 96-102.

Guttman J. Self-concepts and television viewing among women. *Public Opinion Quarterly* 1973; 34(Fall): 388-97.

Joreskog KG, Sorbom D. *Lisrel 8: A Guide to the Program and Applications*. Chicago: SPSS, 1993.

Kastenbaum R, Derbin V, Sabatini P, Artt S. The ages of me: Toward personal and interpersonal definitions of functional aging. *Aging and Human Development* 1972; 3(2), 197-211.

Lumpkin JR. Shopping orientation segmentation of the elderly consumer. *Journal of the Academy of Marketing Science* 1985; 13(Winter), 271-89.

Markides KS, Boldt JS. Change in subjective age among the elderly: A longitudinal analysis. *The Gerontologist* 1983; 23(August): 422-27.

Morgan RM, Hunt SD. The commitment-trust theory of relationship marketing. *Journal of Marketing* 1994; 58(July), 20-38.

Morris GP, Edward WC. Acceptance by males of feminine products. *Journal of Marketing Research* 1971; 8(April): 372-74.

Moschis GP. Marketing to older consumers. Westport, CT: Quorum Books, 1992.

Raju PS. Optimum stimulation level: Its relationship to personality, demographics, and exploratory behavior. *Journal of Consumer Research* 1980; 7(December): 272-81.

Reynolds FD, Darden WD. Mutually Adaptive Effects of Interpersonal Communication, *Journal of Marketing Research* 1971; 8(November), 449-454.

Schiffman LG, Sherman E. Value orientations of new-age elderly: The coming of an ageless market. *Journal of Business Research* 1991; 22(March): 187-94.

Stephens N. Cognitive age: A useful concept for advertising? *Journal of Advertising* 1991; 20(December): 37-48.

Tongren HN. Determinant behavior characteristics of older consumers. *Journal of Consumer Affairs* 1988; 22(Summer), 136-157.

Tuckman J, Lavell M. Self-classification as old or not old. *Geriatrics* 1957; 12(November): 666-71.

Van Auken S, Barry TE. An assessment of the trait validity of cognitive age measures. *Journal of Consumer Psychology* 1995; 4(2): 107-32.

Wells WD, Tigert DJ. Activities, interests, and opinions. *Journal of Advertising Research* 1971; 11(August): 27-35.

Wylie RC. *The self concept: A Review of Methodological Considerations and Measuring Instruments*. Lincoln, NE: University of Nebraska Press, 1974.

The Evil Eye on Mimicry: The Influence of Money Primes on Mimicry

Jia (Elke) Liu, University of Groningen, the Netherlands
Dirk Smeesters, Erasmus University Rotterdam, the Netherlands

Social interactions are a central aspect of human existence. Individuals have a constant drive to get along with others. One of the forces that help us connect to others is nonconscious mimicry, the tendency to mimic other individuals' behavior without awareness or intention

(Chartrand and van Baaren, forthcoming). Mimicry serves as a social glue to bond people together (Chartrand and Bargh 1999), and it can even influence consumers' product preference (Tanner et al. 2008). Being mimicked by others makes individuals feel close to these others and more likely to offer them help (van Baaren et al. 2004). However, there are also counter forces in humans' lives that may lead to opposite effects. Money is one of them. Thoughts of money drive people to keep distance from others and offer less help to people in need (Vohs, Mead and Goode 2006, 2008). Which of these forces is stronger in regulating social orientations and shaping consumers' product preference? We will address this question in this paper.

Thoughts of money can influence interpersonal behavior. Vohs et al. (2006) demonstrated that participants who were subtly reminded of money were less likely to offer help and sat further away from a confederate compared to control participants. Furthermore, other literature suggests that the concept of money can induce a business norm (Heyman and Ariely 2004), which might activate a competition orientation and avoidance reaction to interaction others (Kay et al. 2004; Orbell and Dawes 1993). Hence, participants who are reminded of money are expected to mimic another person less compared to control participants.

Mimicry is also a tool to create interpersonal rapport (Lakin et al. 2003). Chartrand and Bargh (1999) found that participants who were mimicked reported liking the other more compared to those who were not mimicked. Then, the question is whether this powerful effect of being mimicked on the creation of liking will still hold when individuals are reminded of money. We think not. We rather expect that when the concept of money is primed, being mimicked will *reduce* the liking of the mimicking other. As people primed with the construct of money strive to avoid connectedness and affiliation with others, they might resist the affiliation attempt executed by the mimicking other. Hence, they might like the other who tried to affiliate even less than when the other did not intend to affiliate.

Experiment 1

Forty-one undergraduates were randomly assigned to either the money or control prime condition. First, participants filled out a battery of questionnaires on a computer. The screen background of the questions was either Euro currency (money condition) or coral (control condition). The money manipulation did not elicit different affect states than the control condition ($ts<1$, *ns*) (also in Experiment 2). Then, participants were left alone in the room and taped for one minute. The number of times participants rubbed their face or shook their foot was measured as a baseline, which did not differ between the money and control conditions ($t<1$, *ns*). Participants were then asked to discuss four advertisements together with the confederate. For each of the four ad discussions, we taped the first minute of the interaction. During this minute, the confederate was instructed to shake his foot twice and to rub his face twice.

Two judges blind to the experimental conditions coded the videotapes. The mimicry scores were subject to a 2 (prime: money vs. control) × 4 (measure: measure 1 vs. measure 2. vs. measure 3. vs. measure 4) mixed ANOVA with prime as a between-participants variable and measure as a repeated-measures factor. This analysis only revealed a main effect of prime ($F(1, 39)=6.77$, $p<.02$). Participants mimicked the confederate less when they were primed with money ($M=0.61$) compared to the control condition ($M=0.93$).

Experiment 2

Fifty-seven undergraduates were randomly assigned to the conditions of a 2 (prime: money vs. control) × 2 (behavior: mimicry vs. non-mimicry) between-participants design. The prime manipulation was the same as in Experiment 1. Then, participants were asked to discuss a set of four ads with a confederate. The confederate was trained to mimic only those behaviors that people do nonconsciously, such as foot shaking and leg crossing. In the non-mimicry condition, the confederate was trained to refrain actively from mimicking any of the participants' gestures and postures. After the discussion, participants received a short questionnaire to evaluate the discussion they just had. Measures of liking for the confederate were also included.

A 2 (prime: money vs. control) × 2 (behavior: mimicry vs. non-mimicry) between-participants ANOVA was conducted on the composite index of participants' liking of the confederate. There was a significant main effect of money ($F(1, 57)=19.09$, $p<.001$), which was qualified by a significant interaction between the prime and mimicry behavior ($F(1, 57)=8.23$, $p<.01$). In the control condition, participants liked the other more when being mimicked by the other ($M=5.33$) compared to not being mimicked by the other ($M=4.35$, $F(1, 57)=4.08$, $p<.05$). However, in the money prime condition, participants liked the other less when being mimicked by the other ($M=2.86$) compared to not being mimicked by the other ($M=3.83$, $F(1, 57)=4.15$, $p<.05$).

General Discussion

Two experiments demonstrated that thoughts of money inhibited the tendency to mimic. Further, the effectiveness of mimicry as a social glue was also impaired by the concept of money. Specifically, instead of liking the interaction partner more, participants primed with money liked the interaction partner less after being mimicked compared to not being mimicked. These results may have implications for consumer behavior. Specifically, the concept of money may inhibit consumers from mimicking the consumption behaviors of other people. Further, whereas being mimicked by another consumer leads to more liking of a product that is introduced in a dyad (Tanner et al. 2008), priming money may actually reverse that effect.

References

Chartrand, Tanya L. and John A. Bargh (1999), "The Chameleon Effect: The Perception?Behavior Link and Social Interaction," *Journal of Personality and Social Psychology,* 76, 893–910.

Chartrand, Tanya L. and Rick B. van Baaren (forthcoming)," Human Mimicry," *Advances in Experimental Social Psychology.*

Heyman, James and Dan Ariely (2004)," Effort For Payment," A Tale of Two Markets," *Psychological Science*, 15, 787-93.

Kay, Aaron C., S. Christian Wheeler, John A. Bargh, and Lee Ross (2004)," Material Priming: The Influence of Mundane Physical Objects on Situational Construal and Competitive Behavioral Choice," *Organizational Behavior & Human Decision Processes,* 95, 83–96.

Lakin, Jessica L., Valerie E. Jefferis, Clara M. Cheng, and Tanya L. Chartrand (2003)," The Chameleon Effect as Social Glue: Evidence For the Evolutionary Significance of Nonconscious Mimicry," *Journal of Nonverbal Behavior,* 27, 145–62.

Orbell, John M. and Robyn M. Dawes (1993)," Social Welfare, Cooperators' Advantage, and the Option Not to Play," *American Sociological Review*,58, 515-29.

van Baaren, Rick B., Rob W. Holland, Kerry Kawakami, and Ad van Knippenberg (2004)," Mimicry and Pro-Social Behavior," *Psychological Science*, 15, 71-74.

Tanner, R. J., Rosellina Ferraro, Tanya L. Chartrand, James R. Bettman, and Rick van Baaren (2008), "On Chameleons and Consumption: The Impact of Mimicry and Choices and Preferences," *Journal of Consumer Research*, 34, 754-66.

Vohs, Kathleen D., Nicole L. Mead, and Miranda R. Goode (2006)," The Psychological Consequences of Money," *Science*, 314, 1154–56.

Vohs, Kathleen D., Nicole L. Mead, and Miranda R. Goode (2008)," Merely Activating the Concept of Money Changes Personal and Interpersonal Behavior," *Current Directions in Psychological Science*, 17, 208–12

The Effect of General Action Goals on Evaluations of Innovative Products

Xuefeng Liu, University of Illinois at Urbana-Champaign, USA
Dolores Albarracin, University of Illinois at Urbana-Champaign, USA

As goal systems are hierarchical in nature, some goals are more general than others. But so far no work has investigated the effects of general goals on product evaluations. General action goals are among the broadest possible goals and can direct amount of cognitive and motor output resulting in a variety of behaviors such as learning and eating. In the present study, participants evaluated an incrementally new product more favorably when they were primed with general action than inaction goals. In contrast, participants evaluated a radically new product similarly whether they were primed with general action or inaction goals.

According to Kruglanski et al (2002) and Bandura (1989), goal systems are hierarchical networks wherein some goals are more general than others. A general goal may connect with many sub-goals and means of attainment. Up to now, the most general set of identified goals concern general action and inaction, which are both ends of a continuum of cognitive and motor output (Albarracín et al. 2008). General action goals produce behavior with high cognitive and/or motor output (such as learning or eating), whereas general inaction goals produce behavior with low cognitive and/or motor output (such as low learning or resting).

Previous studies found that specific goals can significantly influence product evaluations. That is, products are perceived as positive or negative to the extent that they support or hinder the specific goals that individuals happen to be considering at the time (Brendl and Higgins 1996; Markman and Brendl 2000; Brendl, Markman, and Messner 2003). Thus, for example, calling people's attention to the goal of losing weight may lead them to evaluate ice creams less favorably than they otherwise would. However, few studies have been conducted to investigate the effect of general goals on product evaluations. And more importantly, the effect of general goals on product evaluations cannot be easily inferred from the effects of specific goals. The reason is that when a general goal is activated, their sub-goals are probably activated as well. Under this situation, a product (e.g., an ice cream) satisfying one specific goal (e.g., being hedonic) may at the same time hinder the satisfaction of another specific goal (e.g., being healthy) which belongs to the same general goal (e.g., being happy) as the former does. Thus, the effect of general goals should be studied separately.

The purpose of the present study was to investigate the effect of general action goals on evaluations of new products. In prior studies, Albarracín and Handley (2009) found that action goals increase the accessibility and hence resistance of prior attitudes to persuasive message. Correspondingly, inaction goals decrease the accessibility of prior attitudes and the need to adhere to known routines or objects. In other words, relative to inaction goals, action goals make people more likely to resort to their prior attitudes in processing subsequent information and thus to evaluate products basing on their prior attitudes. From this point of view, given consumers generally have a positive attitude towards incrementally new products which are usually new versions of existing products, action goals may facilitate liking of this type of products. Therefore, after reading an ad about the focal incrementally new product, consumers with activated action goals will evaluate it more favorably than those with activated inaction goals. However, if no prior attitude towards an object exists, action goals and inaction goals would not make a difference in terms of subsequent information processing. As a result, action goals and inaction goals may not influence consumers' evaluation towards radically new products which are not strongly associated with any prior attitudes. To sum up, general action goals may produce liking for the incrementally new products whereas it may not influence produce liking for radically new products.

We conducted an experiment with 109 participants randomly assigned to one of the four conditions of a 2 (general goals: action vs. inaction) x 2 (product type: incrementally new product vs. radically new product) between-subject factorial design. The action and inaction goals were primed in a word completion task. Specifically, participants in the action condition were asked to complete 23 incomplete words, 8 of which were action–related such as "go" and "active". Participants in the inaction condition were asked to complete 23 incomplete words, 8 of which were inaction- related such as "relax" and "rest". Upon completion of this task, participants read information about a radically new product (a nap alarm which keeps drivers from falling in sleep when driving) or an incrementally new product (a computer mouse). Both products were described by attribute information and a picture. After reading the product information, participants responded to three product evaluation measures such as "The nap alarm (mouse) in the ad is" ("-5"="very bad" and "5"="very good"), "The nap alarm (mouse) in the ad is" ("-5"="very undesirable" and "5"="very desirable"), and "The nap alarm (mouse) in the ad is something I" ("-5"="dislike very much" and "5"="like very much"). As a manipulation check, all participants reported their attitude towards the statement that "The nap alarm (mouse) in the ad is innovative" ("0"="not at all" and "10"="extremely").

Participants rated the nap alarm (M=4.97) as being more innovative than the computer mouse (M=3.84), $t(107)=2.25, p<.03$, which indicated that our product-type manipulation was successful. Responses to three product evaluation questions were averaged to form a single measure (Cronbach's α= .90). The interactive effect of prime and product type on product evaluation was significant,

$F(1,105)=4.60$, $p=.03$. As predicted, the computer mouse was liked better when action goals were primed than when inaction goals were primed ($M=.29$ vs. $M=-.90$, $F(1,105)=3.89$, $p=.05$). However the nap alarm was evaluated similarly in each of the goal priming conditions ($M=-.40$ vs. $M=-.99$), $F(1,105)=1.10$, $p>.10$.

To verify our assumption that consumers generally have a positive attitude towards incrementally new products but do not have clear attitudes towards radically new products, 21 participants who did not take part in the main study were asked to rate "what is your general attitude towards radically new products" ("-5"="very negative" and "5"="very positive") and "what is your general attitude towards incrementally new products" ("-5"="very negative" and "5"="very positive"). The results supported our assumptions that consumers have a positive attitude towards incrementally new products ($M=2.62$, $t(20)=8.60$, $p<.001$) and a slightly but non-significantly positive attitude towards radically new products ($M=.81$, $t(20)=1.72$, $p>.10$).

Marketers spend a large amount of money on advertising their new products. Our findings suggested that adding action-related words and images into the ads of incrementally new products may activate general action goals in consumers' mind, and thus increase their liking for incrementally new products. In future research, we will use different manipulations of general action and inaction goals and test their influence on consumer judgments in various consumption contexts.

References

Albarracín, Dolores, Ian M. Handley, Kenji Noguchi, Kathleen C. McCulloch, Hong Li, Joshua Leeper, Rick D. Brown, Allison Earl, and William P. Hart, (2008), "Increasing and Decreasing Motor and Cognitive Output: A Model of General Action and Inaction Goals," *Journal of Personality and Social Psychology*, 95 (3), 510-523.

Albarracín, Dolores and Ian M. Handley (2009), "The Time for Active Doing is Not the Time for Change: Effects of General Action and Inaction Goals on Attitude Accessibility and Attitude Change", *Unpublished manuscript*, University of Illinois at Urbana-Champaign.

Bandura, Albert (1989), "Self-regulation of Motivation and Action through Internal Standards and Goal Systems," in *Goal Concepts in Personality and Social Psychology*, ed. Pervin Lawrence A., Hillsdale, NJ: Erlbaum, 19-86.

Brendl, C. Miguel and E. Tory Higgins (1996), "Principles of Judging Valence: What Makes Events Positive or Negative?" *Advances in Experimental Social Psychology*, 28, 95-160.

Brendl, C. Miguel, Arthur B. Markman, and Claude Messner (2003), "The Devaluation Effect: Activating a Need Devalues Unrelated Objects," *Journal of Consumer Research*, 29 (4), 463-473.

Kruglanski, Arie W., James Y. Shah, Ayelet Fishbach, Ron Friedman, Woo Young Chun, and David Sleeth-Keppler (2002), "A theory of Goal Systems," *In Advances in Experimental Social Psychology*, vol. 43, ed. Zanna, Mark P., San Diego: Academy Press, 331-378.

Markman, Arthur B. and C. Miguel Brendl (2000), "The Influence of Goals on Value and Choice," *Psychology of Learning and Motivation*, 39, 97-128.

Brand Dilution: The Impact of the User of Counterfeits on Original Brand Perception

Barbara Loken, University of Minnesota, USA
Nelson Amaral, University of Minnesota, USA

The costs associated with counterfeit goods world-wide has been estimated at about $550 billion, or 5-7% of world trade (Underwriters Laboratories, 2007). However, these costs do not begin to account for the reduction in perceived quality, prestige, and other core brand associations that may result and are difficult to account for on a balance sheet. Despite the magnitude of the problem very little attention has been given to the issue of counterfeits in the marketing literature. Specifically, research on the effects of counterfeit goods on dilution of the brands they imitate is lacking (Loken and John, 2009). Our research addresses this gap directly while also looking at the impact that the user of the counterfeit products might have on the original parent brand.

We suggest that counterfeit products of high-prestige brands dilute the original brands through a weakening of the symbolism of those brands to specific (*i.e.* target) social groups. Research on dissociative reference groups suggests that people avoid brands that are associated with disliked groups (White and Dahl 2006). Furthermore, consumers may abandon brands when out-groups adopt them and the brands stop being distinctive (Berger and Heath 2007). With respect to prestigious brands in particular, there is evidence that an individual's consumption pattern could symbolize his or her social class position (Martineau, 1968). As a result, the consumer's use of a counterfeit product, such as a counterfeit "Louis Vuitton" bag, could have specific effects on the symbolism of that brand for other consumers, depending on the social class of the counterfeit user. We investigate this proposition directly by manipulating the social class of the user of both real and counterfeit products.

The extant literature above results in two hypotheses that are tested by our research:

H1: For participants who are exposed to counterfeit products, the overall beliefs about the prestige of the real brand will be lower than the comparable beliefs of participants exposed to the real brand.

H2: For prestige brands, the impact of counterfeit brands on the original brand will be moderated by the social class of the user of the product such that a user from a lower social class will have a greater effect on the symbolism and therefore ratings of the prestige of the real brand.

Our design results in two between subject factors: product (real vs. counterfeit) and social class of the user ("low" class vs. "high" class). Undergraduates entered the lab and were seated at individual cubicles or rooms. Participants were shown a photograph of a young woman (for females) or a young man (for males) using a prestigious product (males=Rolex watch; females=Prada handbag) and were told that the product in the picture was either a real product or a counterfeit product. A brief description of the individual was used to convey the user's social class. For example, for female participants, the higher class user was described as a 25-year-old recent MBA graduate who bought the product while on a trip to Milan. The lower class user was described as a 25-year-old Applebee's waitress who bought the bag online.

After looking at the picture and reading the description of the user, participants (drawn from a relatively high class pool of subjects–undergraduate students at a large mid-western university) answered a series of questions that were analyzed as manipulation checks and measures of the dependent variables. The key measures were participants' beliefs about (a) the prestige of the original brand and (b) whether the brand was a high class brand, each assessed, on 7-point agree-disagree and likely-unlikely scales (the two scales for each, prestige belief and high-class belief, were highly correlated (both r=0.78) and were averaged as a measure of each). We also measured overall attitudes toward the brand on four 7-point rating scales, with end points: *excellent-poor*, *better-worse than other brands*, a *good-bad value*, *extremely favorable-unfavorable (*these latter four scales were averaged (α=0.83)). Manipulation checks about the product and "user" (the person depicted in the photo and descriptive stimuli) were also collected as well as a few covariates (*e.g.* the number of designer products and counterfeit products the individual owns).

Consistent with our expectations, a simple comparison of means provided strong evidence for the first hypothesis. Specifically, participants who were exposed to counterfeit goods provided lower ratings on both the prestige and high-class beliefs about the brand. We also found lower overall attitudes toward the brand (4-item index) for the original product. More interestingly, an analysis of variance with covariates provided evidence for a significant two way interaction between the two factors in the study such that the social class of the user had a significant impact on the participants' evaluations of the original brand. Specifically, the social class of the user had a significant effect on both the belief (prestige and high-class) and attitude ratings when the user in the photo was seen using a *counterfeit* prestige product, but the same effect did not occur when the user was seen using a real product. When a lower-class individual was seen using a counterfeit product it resulted in significantly lower evaluations than when the same counterfeit product was seen being used by a high-class individual.

Overall, our findings indicate that, for prestige products, the use of counterfeit products can dilute people's perceptions of the original brand. These are the first findings that document these dilution effects on beliefs about the original brand's prestige, beliefs about whether the original brand is high-class, and overall attitudes toward the original brand. These effects of brand dilution of counterfeits on the original brands are not the same for all users. Because of the symbolism of prestige brands for different social classes, the social class of the users of these counterfeits plays an important role in understanding the effects of these counterfeit products on the original products. The contribution of this research to the literature is twofold. First, we demonstrate through experimental evidence the problem posed by counterfeits on beliefs about the original brands and attitudes toward the original brand. Counterfeiting is a costly problem for brands, not only in terms of the reduced sales of the original brands, but dilution to the original brand beliefs and attitudes. Second, we use a social psychological theoretical framework to provide evidence for the importance of understanding how specific consumer groups differ in their response to counterfeit use and how this factor impacts consumer perceptions and attitudes of the original prestige brands.

Bibliography

Berger, Jonah and Chip Heath (2007), "Where Consumers Diverge from Others: Identity Signaling and Product Domains," *Journal of Consumer Research*, 34 (2), 121-34.

Grossman, Gene M. and Carl Shapiro (1988b), "Counterfeit-product trade", *The American Economic Review*, Vol. 78, March, pp. 59-75.

Loken, Barbara and Deborah Roedder-John. (2009, forthcoming), "When Do Bad Things Happen to Good Brands? Understanding Internal and External Sources of Brand Dilution", *Brands and Brand Management: Contemporary Perspectives in Branding Research,* Loken, B., Ahluwalia, R. & Houston, M. (Eds.), Psychology Press.

Martineau, Pierre (1968), "Social class and spending behavior", *Journal of Marketing*, Vol. 23, pp.274-8.

Till, Brian D., and Terence A. Shimp, (1998). Endorsers in advertising: The case of negative celebrity information. *Journal of Advertising*, 27, 67-82.

Underwriters Laboratories (2007) www.ul.com/ace/counterfeiting.html

White, Katherine and Darren W. Dahl (2006), "To Be or Not Be? The Influence of Dissociative Reference Groups on Consumer Preferences," *Journal of Consumer Psychology*, 16 (4), 404-14.

Google or Googol? How Meanings of Sound and Spelling Processes Influence Evaluations for Brand Names

David Luna, Baruch College, CUNY, USA

Marina Carnevale, Baruch College, CUNY, USA

Dawn Lerman, Fordham University, USA

Despite the heavy reliance of consumers on brand names they are exposed to auditorily (i.e., via word of mouth; Hein, 2007), the majority of studies on brand naming typically examine consumers' responses to names they are exposed to visually. Consequently, little is known about how consumers process and later use sounds.

In two studies we explore how brand names are auditorily processed and how transcribing the auditory stimuli affects brand evaluations, given the associations that sounds solicit. Accurate spelling of a brand name presented auditorily is relevant because of the potential influence of correct spelling on the ability to find the brand (e.g., online).

The spelling of a word (e.g., *c-l-o-c-k)* is stored in a sort of mental dictionary that individuals possess and fed by phonetically associated words (i.e., with a similar spelling pattern, such as *lock*) and/or semantically related ones (i.e., associated to the meaning of the word, e.g., *time*). Research suggests that frequency of exposure to a stimuli increases the number of semantic associations solicited (Chaffin, 1997). However, the way sounds are translated into writing might reverse these effects.

Over 72% of the sounds in English can be written in more that one way (Ziegler, Stone, and Jacobs 1997). The brand name "Google", for example, originated from a common misspelling by one of its co-founders of the word "googol". In this case the sound \gól\ can be transcribed into a variety of strings of letters, such as -gol, -gle. The two spelling alternatives, however, differ with respect to their frequency of occurrence within the English lexical system (frequent and non frequent, respectively). This is important because it affects the spelling process of unfamiliar words, such as brand names. When attempting to spell a brand name that contains a frequent sound-to-spelling pattern, individuals will translate each sound into a string of letters by recurring to words that are phonetically associated. The same will happen when a word that sounds like the non-word is presented before the non-word (i.e., lexical priming; Seymour and Dargie 1990). In the case of non-frequent spelling patterns, however, individuals will recur to words that are semantically related (Houghton and Zorzi, 2003). We thus expect brand names with non-frequent spelling patterns to be processed semantically (rather than phonetically). Increased semantic elaboration should lead to greater spelling accuracy and influence brand evaluations.

One way to classify the effects of meanings conveyed by sounds is based on distinctions within vowel (i.e., front vs. back). Brand names containing front (back) vowels may solicit perceptions such as smallness (largeness), lightness (heaviness; Klink, 2000). Lowrey and Shrum (2007) show that the congruency between the meanings conveyed by the sound and the attributes positively valenced for the product category may positively influence brand evaluations. However, such effects should only happen for those brand names that are semantically processed (i.e., with non frequent spelling patterns).

In this research, we examine how increased semantic elaboration can lead to greater spelling accuracy and higher evaluations. We expect that semantic elaboration will enhance brand evaluations only when spelling accuracy is facilitated by spelling prime (Study 1). In Study 2 we explore whether different spelling patterns of brand names may solicit semantically versus phonetically related words and how this affects evaluations.

Study 1

Method. Seventy-five undergraduate students participated in a 2 (Semantic elaboration) x 2 (spelling prime) between-subjects experiment. Each participant was exposed to eight audio clips, and, after each of them, had up to three trials to spell the brand name correctly. The sum of the number of trials left unused by each participant was utilized to assess one of the dependent variables: accuracy of spelling. Following the spelling task, brand evaluation was measured through a seven-item scale.

Each audio clip provided information about: product category, last words in the ad, and brand name. The priming condition consisted of having the last word in the ad either prime (e.g., thinking of the st*aff*) or not prime (e.g., thinking of notes) the intended spelling for the target brand name that immediately followed (e.g., P*aff*.com). Semantic elaboration was operationalized by changing the word used in the priming sentence to be congruent (e.g., fuel) or incongruent (e.g., staff) with the product category (e.g., cars).

Results. Results showed that elaboration and spelling prime each had a significant main effect on spelling accuracy (F (1, 74)=4.54, *p*<0.05 and F(1, 74)=18.45, *p*<.01, respectively). Those effects were qualified by a significant interaction of priming and elaboration on brand evaluations (F(1, 74)=5.75, *p*<0.05). As expected, when primed, participants in the elaboration condition had higher brand evaluations than those in the no-elaboration condition (F(1, 74)=4.10, *p*<.05). In the no-prime condition, however, there was no effect of elaboration on brand evaluations (F(1, 74)=1.816, *p*=.18). Finally, spelling accuracy proved to be a significant predictor of brand evaluations (F (1, 74)=5.99, *p*<0.05).

Study 2

Method. Eighty-nine undergraduate business students participated in a 2 (Phonetic symbolism: congruent or incongruent) x 2 (Frequency: frequent or non frequent) between-subjects experiment. The procedure and measures were the same as in study 1 except for the association task. For the latter, we adapted Chaffin's (1997) procedure. To manipulate frequency, while hearing the audio clip, subjects could read the ad phrase that contained a word with the same frequent (vs. non frequent) spelling pattern of the target name. We referred to the frequency norms provided by Ziegler et al.'s (1997). Following Lowrey and Shrum (2007), we manipulated congruency by varying front versus back vowel to convey meanings that had a positive valence (or not) for the product category in the congruent (or incongruent) condition. The frequency manipulation only changed the target spelling pattern (not the sound).

Results. Results showed a main effect of frequency on semantic associations (F(1, 85)=5.06, p<.05); as expected, brand names with non frequent spelling patterns tended to be semantically rather than phonetically processed Analysis of variance revealed no significant interaction for the factors (congruency/frequency) on brand evaluations. However, semantic associations had a significant impact on evaluations (F(2,85)=3.29, p <.05).

Conclusion

Our results support a greater understanding of how consumers process brand names auditorily and of the effects of phonetic symbolism on brand evaluations.

References

Chaffin, Roger (1997), "Associations to unfamiliar words: Learning the meaning of new words," *Memory and Cognition*, 25 (2), 203–226.

Hein, Kenneth (2007). *Freshen It Up To Keep Sales Hot*. Brand Week, January(22).

Houghton, George, and Marco Zorzi (2003), "Normal and Impaired Spelling in a Connectionist Dual-Route Architecture," *Cognitive Neuropsychology*, 20 (2), 115-62.

Klink, Richard R. (2000), "Creating brand names with meaning: the use of sound symbolism," *Marketing Letters*, 11, 5–20.

Lowrey, Tina M. and Larry L. J. Shrum (2007), "Phonetic Symbolism and Brand Name Preference," *Journal of Consumer Research*, 34 (October), 406-14.

Seymour, Philip H.K., and Alison Dargie (1990), "Associative Priming and Orthographic Choice in Nonword Spelling," *The European Journal of Cognitive Psychology*, 2 (4), 395-480.

Ziegler, Johannes, Gregory O. Stone, and Arthur M. Jacobs (1997), "What is the pronunciation for *-ough* and the spelling for /u/? A database for computing feedforward and feedback consistency in English," *Behavior Research Methods, Instruments & Computers*, 29 (4), 600-18.

Product Placement Effects over Time: The Effects of Brand and Design Attributes in a Dynamic On-Line Choice Task

Ah-reum Maeng, University of Wisconsin-Madison, USA
David Schweidel, University of Wisconsin-Madison, USA
Thomas C. O'Guinn, University of Wisconsin-Madison, USA

Product placement, including branded entertainment continues to gain in popularity as a way of reaching consumers. As television viewers are better able to skip traditional commercials, branded entertainment provides advertisers with a way to reach consumers with their brands in a constructed setting. They can do this whether they are watching television online or engaging in time-shifted viewing. In 2007, among just 10 broadcast television programs, there were more than 25,000 product placements; on cable programs, there were more than 150,000 product placements (Kang, 2009).

Two reasons cited for the increased use of product placement is that it can result in a "stronger emotional connection" with viewers, and allow marketers to target specific groups (Eggerton, 2006). There has also been the widespread belief that branded entertainment benefits from what it is not: highly involving advertising.

Belch (2005) provides a review of the product placement literature. Belch notes that much of the research has focused on the impact of product placement on respondents' memory, attitudes, and occasionally behavior: the usual suspects. In examining the role that product placement plays in consumers' actions, Auty and Lewis (2004) find that exposure to product placement can increase the choice of the featured product among children, with previous exposure to the product placement (such as repeatedly watching the same movie) affecting the choice. Russell and Puto (1999) discuss how product placement may affect viewers based on their connectedness to a program. In sum, these theoretical assertions are diverse and could be said to be "all over the map." No single strong theoretical basis for branded entertainment has yet emerged and been recognized as such by the field.

We contribute to the growing body of research into the impact of product placement by studying how it affects the actual dynamic choice process. While previous studies have supported the notion that product placement can influence choice, it has not considered how consumers who are exposed to product placement may differ in how they progress through a choice task compared to those who have not been exposed to product placement, and certainly not dynamically.

Data were collected from 170 respondents who were told that they were watching a rough cut of a television program and we were interested in their perception of the program and characters. The research was conducted at a large university in the Midwest with a Canadian television program to minimize respondents' familiarity. A professional video editor inserted a featured product (an LG cell phone with a slide design) at three occasions in the episode. The cell phone was originally depicted in a cutaway shot. The control condition featured no product placement, and three other conditions were tested in which the length of cut-away shots were manipulated. After watching the episode, respondents were asked to complete a survey about how much they liked the program and characters in the program. Upon completing this task, they were told that they were also going to participate in a brief study to understand students' preferences for different consumer products. This study contained three different product categories: cell phones and two categories for distraction (coffee machines and computers). In each product category, respondents were first asked how they would like to arrange the choice alternatives, whether by brand or by design. We felt this was a useful choice in its correspondence to how actual on-line shoppers are asked to structure their choice task. They then chose the first choice alternative that they were interested in viewing, based on its attributes. Respondents could then end the choice task by selecting the current product, or view another choice alternative. The sequence of decisions made by the respondent was recorded, as well as the amount of time spent viewing each page.

The data were analyzed using a path model (e.g., Hui, Bradlow and Fader, 2009) that allowed respondents' utilities for each of the alternatives to be updated based on the sequence of choices that were viewed and the duration for which each was viewed. Two different updating processes were considered: one in which only the utility of the current product may be updated, and one in which the utility of all choice-alternatives may be updated based on the attributes that they have in common with the product being viewed currently. For example, if a respondent was viewing an LG flip phone, the utility associated with the LG brand and the utility associated with flip phones may be updated. Thus, in addition to updating the utility of the LG flip phone, the utility of the LG slide phone would be updated (the same brand), as well the utility of the Samsung flip phone (the same design but a competing brand).

Our data show that respondents update the utilities based on the attributes of the product that they are viewing. Though we do not find support for exposure to product placement affecting the preference for the featured design, our results indicate that there are two distinct ways in which exposure to product placement affects preference for the featured brand. First, it increases the initial preference for the brand, resulting in respondents being more likely to choose one of the featured brand's choice alternatives initially. As respondents continued through the choice task, however, they were expected to revise their utility for the featured brand's products downward by a greater magnitude compared to those respondents who were not exposed to product placement. This is what occurred.

Thus, though product placement may spark initial interest in the featured product, suggesting a probably accessibility effect. However, one a realistic on-line choice task is commenced, with different ways of sorting, accessibility is swamped by much more involved on-line (in the cognitive sensed) choice. Simply put, branded entertainment or placement yields a first preference, but is a weak and ephemeral effect once actual choice comes into play. This suggests that product placement is best for low-involvement products for which accessibility and quick decisions are the norm.

Selected References

Auty, Susan and Charlie Lewis (2004), "Exploring Children's Choice: The Reminder Effect of Product Placement" *Psychology & Marketing, 21*(9), 697-713.

Eggerton, John (2006), "More Spot Bucks Board Bandwagon", *Broadcasting and Cable.*

Hui, Sam, Eric Bradlow, and Peter Fader (2009), "Testing Behavioral Hypotheses using an Integrated Model of Grocery Store Shopping Paths and Shopping Behavior", Journal of Consumer Research, 36(3), forthcoming.

Kang, Cecilia (2008), "Product Placement on TV Targeted", *The Washington Post* .

Russell, Cristel Antonia and Christopher P. Puto (1999), "Rethinking Television Audience Measures: An Exploration into the Construct of Audience Connectedness", *Marketing Letter,* 10(4), p 393-107.

Russell, Cristel Antonia and Michael Belch (2005), "A Managerial Investigation into the Product Placement Industry", *Journal of Advertising Research, 45*(1), 73-92.

The Role of Consumers' Attributions during Price Promotions

Igor Makienko, University of Nevada at Reno, USA

Prior research provided strong evidence that attributions play an important role in the price-promotion context (c.f. Kardes, Posavac, and Cronley, 2004). Consumers, however, are not likely to engage in attributional thinking unless they are motivated to expend their effort to process incoming information systematically (Maheswaran and Chaiken, 1991).

Typical price promotions offering typical benefits may not raise any questions. When incoming information is in line with individual's established beliefs, its cognition may proceed almost automatically–through activation of well-developed schemata (Olson, 1977). On the other hand, when observed retailer's behavior deviates from regular business practice it can 'create enough cognitive unrest' (Lichtenstein and Bearden, 1986, p.295) to motivate consumers to find plausible explanation behind such behavior (Brown and Krishna, 2004; Main, Dahl and Darke, 2007).

In price promotion context offering excessive value may be perceived as a violation of the common sense of selling. Consumers know that marketers cannot cross the point after which they will experience losses (Raghubir, 2004). Therefore, they will try to find alternative explanation for such generosity. Prior research shows that bigger discounts may not always be associated with greater value because they may signal low quality (Bagwell and Riordan, 1991; Friestad and Wright, 1994). Consumers' attributions about inferior product quality in such situations will 'restore' the common sense of selling.

Discount is not the only element of price promotion that may be questioned by consumers. Reference price shows original 'pre-sale' price of a product and may also be manipulated by a retailer. Urbany et al. (1988) found that exaggerated reference prices increased consumers' deal evaluations, estimates of regular product price and decreased search intentions. The authors concluded that consumers may be skeptical of reference prices and at the same time be influenced by them.

In our research we develop a model of consumers' attributions during price promotions offering excessive value and suggest that the type of attributions depends on a reference price level. When suspiciously high discount is presented along with a plausible reference price consumers are likely to generate attributions about inferior product quality. Alternatively, when identical discount is presented along with implausibly high reference price consumers are likely to generate attributions about the manipulative intent to enhance perceived value of the deal (by first inflating regular price and then offering an attractive discount). In the latter situation product quality will not be a concern because high discount will push sales price down into the expected sales price range. At the same time, in both situations consumers will generate negative attributions about retailer's manipulative tactics.

Methodology

A 2 (implausibly high discount vs. typical discount) by 2 (implausibly high reference price vs. plausible reference price) incomplete factorial design was employed to investigate the effects of discount and the reference price on consumers' perceptions of price promotions. Implausibly high reference price in the context of regular discount was excluded from the experiment because it did not reflect price promotion practice. Eighty four respondents were exposed to mock print advertising of a digital camera with a blocked out brand name and were asked to answer questions that followed. Combinations of discount and reference price used in the experiment were as follows: \$150/30% off regular price, \$150/80% off regular price and \$600/80% off regular price.

Preliminary Data Analysis

Manipulation check showed that respondents perceived 30% discount as significantly lower than 80% discount regardless of the level of reference price. "\$150/30%" price promotion was evaluated as significantly more believable than two other conditions that were not perceived as significantly different. However, the mean in the 'least believable" conditions were still higher than 3.6 points on a 7 point scale. Means of respondents' product knowledge, usage level and their involvement with a stimulus were higher than 4 points on a 7 point scale and were not significantly different across all three conditions. Additionally, respondents did not question the typicality of the advertised digital camera. Overall, preliminary findings indicate that respondents perceived stimuli as intended, were familiar with digital cameras and exhibited higher than average level of involvement during evaluation process.

Major Findings

Results of a one-way ANOVA showed significant differences among groups in terms of retailer credibility (F=4.14, p=0.019), brand attitude (F=4.70, p=0.012), product quality (F=5.6, p=0.005) and deal evaluations (F=4.55, p=0.013). At the same time respondents' purchase intentions were not different across the three conditions (p=0.301).

Our results provide additional support to findings by Urbany et al. (1988). When exposed to exaggerated reference price respondents did not believe that the amount of advertised price reduction was a truthful claim. However, their deal evaluations were significantly higher than those in a typical "$150/30%" price promotion condition.

In line with our hypotheses respondents' quality perceptions in a "$150/80%" condition were significantly lower than those in two other conditions. However, neutral assessment of product quality in a "$600/80%" condition did not improve respondents' perceptions of retailer credibility. Retailer credibility in this condition was not significantly different from that in a "$150/80%" condition and both were significantly lower than retailer credibility in a typical price promotion condition ($150/30%).

Additionally, brand evaluations in both atypical price promotion conditions were significantly lower than those in a typical price promotion condition.

Overall, our results support our suggestion that consumers will generate different attributions during price promotions offering excessive value. The type of attributions depends on a reference price level. Price promotions with plausible reference prices will be attributed to inferior product quality, while price promotions with implausibly high reference prices will be attributed to the desire of a retailer to enhance perceived value of the deal. Despite respondents' high evaluations of the monetary value of a deal in atypical price promotion conditions, consumers' attributions about retailer's motives adversely affected consumers' brand perceptions in both atypical price promotion conditions. Absence of significant differences in purchase intentions may be explained by the fact that almost 97% of respondents already owned digital cameras and were not going to purchase it in the next six months.

References

Bagwell, Kyle and Michael H.Riordan (1991) "High and declining prices signal product quality," *American Economic Review*, Vol. 81 (1), 224-239.

Brown, Christina L and Aradhna Krishna (2004) "The Skeptical Shopper: A Metacognitive Account for the Effects of Default Options on Choice," *Journal of Consumer Research*, Vol. 31 (3), 529-539.

Friestad, Marian and Peter Wright (1994) "The Persuasion Knowledge Model: How People Cope with Persuasion Attempts," *Journal of Consumer Research*, Vol. 21 (1), 1-31.

Kardes, Frank R., Steven S. Posavac and Maria L. Cronley (2004) "Consumer Inference: A Review of Processes, Bases, and Judgment Contexts," *Journal of Consumer Psychology*, Vol. 14 (3), 230-256.

Lichtenstein, Donald R. and William O. Bearden (1986) "Measurement and Structure of Kelley's Covariance Theory," *Journal of Consumer Research*, Vol. 13 (2), 290-296.

Maheswaran, Durairaj and Shelly Chaiken (1991) "Promoting Systematic Processing in Low-Motivation Settings: Effect of Incongruent Information on Processing and Judgment," *Journal of Personality and Social Psychology*, Vol. 61 (1), 13-25.

Main, Kelley J., Darren W. Dahl and Peter R. Darke (2007) "Deliberative and Automatic Bases of Suspicion: Empirical Evidence of the Sinister Attribution Error," *Journal of Consumer Psychology*, Vol. 17 (1), 59-69.

Olson, Jerry C. (1977) "Price as an Information Cue: Effects on Product Evaluations," in *Consumer and Industrial Buying Behavior*, eds. Arch G. Woodside, Jagdish N. Sheth and Peter D. Bennet. New York: American Elsevier, 267-286.

Raghubir, Priya (2004) "Free Gift with Purchase: Promoting or Discounting the Brand?" *Journal of Consumer Psychology*, Vol. 14 (1/2), 181-186.

Urbany, Joel E., William O. Bearden and Dan C. Weilbaker (1988) "The Effect of Plausible and Exaggerated Reference Prices on Consumer Perceptions and Price Search," *Journal of Consumer Research*, Vol. 15 (1), 95-110.

Artisan Cheese: Pursuing Authentic Consumables in a Mass-Production World

Kathleen Micken, Roger Williams University, USA
Scott Roberts, St Edwards University, USA
W. Brett McKenzie, Roger Williams University, USA

Writers have recently focused on consumers seeking authenticity in their choices. Specific to the consumables area, some have studied tea (Gould 1998) and high-end wine (Beverland 2006). To better understand the complex concept of authenticity, we surveyed knowledgeable consumers about the characteristics of artisan cheese using Beverland's authenticity attributes as a framework. Statistical analysis of our highly involved consumers' responses revealed two overarching dimensions: seeking an authentic product (e.g., inputs are hormone and cruelty free) and preferring an authentic production process (e.g., made by hand, with passion and expertise).

Conceptualization

Recently, many writers (c.f., Chalmers and Price 2009) have focused on consumers seeking authenticity in their choices. Researchers have examined authenticity in a diversity of areas, such as promotion and branding (Gustafsson 2006; Kozinets, et al. 2008), tourism and place consumption (Costa and Bamossey 2001), music (Arthur 2006; Peterson 2005), antiques (Ger and Csaba 2000; Parsons 2008), and the performing arts (Derbaix and Decrop 2007). Specific to the consumables area, some have studied tea (Gould 1998), beer (Beverland, Lindgreen and Vink, 2008), and high-end wine (Beverland 2006).

Beverland proposed six dimensions of authenticity related to wines: heritage and pedigree; stylistic consistency; quality commitment; relationship to place; method of production; and, downplaying commercial motives. While his work is qualitative, its promise encouraged us to develop quantitative measures along similar dimensions. This type of exercise is potentially fraught with imprecision and the possibility of only further muddying an already opaque concept (Grayson 2002) particularly as our reading suggests that authenticity is negotiated between audience and creator (c.f., Peterson 1997). Furthermore, Leigh, et al. (2006), address the challenge even more strongly by noting, "few consumer researchers have explicitly defined *authenticity*" (p. 482).

Both wine and beer have been studied; yet, to our knowledge, the authenticity of artisan cheese has not been addressed. Accordingly, we first read widely and deeply about artisan cheese, understanding what others have said about its defining characteristics. We also interviewed cheese experts, cheese makers, cheese retailers and cheese consumers. We subsequently designed a survey, informed by Beverland's authenticity attributes, for attendees at the Second Annual California's Artisan Cheese Festival. This venue was selected because it provided entree to consumers interested in artisan cheese.

Method

Developing the survey instrument was challenging. Beverland's conceptual work has established guidelines for thinking about the attributes of authenticity. Additionally, while there is some agreement among researchers about what comprises authenticity, no specific measures have been developed. As Chronis and Hampton (2006) explain, "Academic work ... remains vague both in terms of its definition and in its marketing relevance" (p. 367). We therefore considered the characteristics of artisan cheese derived from our readings and our informants in comparison with Beverland's six attributes. We then created statements about cheese to reflect each attribute. The initial effort resulted in 49 items. For the final survey, we reduced the list to twenty, each with a rating scale. Some items directly asked about characteristics of cheese and its making that would reflect the Beverland authenticity attributes. Others focused on the respondents' relationships to food, experiences, and a self-evaluation on their level of expertise with cheese.

Findings

The findings from this study contribute to our understanding of authenticity by considering the consumer's perspective. Data were initially analyzed by factor analysis, to determine if the responses could be explained by the six underlying authenticity attributes. After applying both orthogonal and oblique rotations, the result was that four factors best describe the data. Items from several of the six Beverland authenticity attributes loaded (at more than .3) on each factor. Nevertheless, the factor structure was quite interpretable. Responses seem to focus in two areas: seeking an authentic product (what it is made of, with milk from what animals, how the milk is or is not processed, how the animals are treated, who makes the cheese, and where) and seeking an authentic process (made with passion and skill, by hand, by a cheesemaker who raises his/her own animals).

Interestingly, attributes (from Beverland) of stylistic consistency, heritage and pedigree, and downplaying of commercialization were not important elements of the factor structure (low factor loadings). All three are explained to some extent by recognizing that artisan cheese is a relatively new development in the United States. The stylistic consistency results are reinforced by knowing that artisan cheese inherently varies from season to season and from animal to animal–an attribute more recognized by cheese experts than cheese novices in this study. There is no long history of craft cheese production nor established brand appellation (DOC or AOC designation) to provide heritage and pedigree. And while our participants may not like industrialization, the artisan cheese market is currently highly individualized and has yet to confront consolidation or cooption by conglomerates.

We also analyzed the data with multidimensional scaling (Prefscal) to develop a perceptual map of the authenticity attributes. These results yielded a plot with two dimensions that can be interpreted as "Authentic Product"—"Authentic Process" and as "Maker"—"Cheese." Two clusters, suggested by the factor analysis comprised the Product?Process dimension, again indicating that our respondents focused on the product and process as carriers of authenticity. The contribution of the multidimensional scaling is the attribute clustering in the second dimension (which combines product and process attributes together). This dimension appears to discriminate between the maker–combining "product" attributes of who and where with "process" attributes of skill and passion, of dedication, and of using one's own animals–and the cheese–combining "product" attributes of type of animal and milk, type of milk processing, with "process" attributes of production by hand. External factors, such as awards, pairing with other artisan products (such as bread), purchases at farmer's markets, and the evaluation of the marketing, were of less importance.

Conclusion

As noted in the introduction, authenticity is a complex and problematic concept. The referenced articles base their conclusions primarily on qualitative, ethnographic, historical, and observational analyses. This study broached a more quantitative examination of authenticity from the consumer perspective. Artisan cheese is an especially complex good because the origins of its raw materials (type of milk, season of milking, local of livestock), production (inherited recipe, adapted recipe, new recipe), and regulation (food product safety, processing, labeling) all affect its final form. Our consumers' responses are similarly complex. The responses to the self-evaluation questions show consumers are in some ways self-reflective, in that being able to discern authentic products accrues to their own status as authentic. Examining this confounding may be the key to a clearer definition of authenticity.

Consumer Strategies for Regaining Optimal Distinctiveness

Melissa Minor, University of Florida, USA

Optimal Distinctiveness Theory (ODT) posits that assimilation and differentiation are opposing forces whose equilibrium is optimal distinctiveness (Brewer 1991). The need for assimilation refers to an individual's desire for group membership and inclusion. Differentiation, on the other hand, refers to the need to feel distinct (Pickett & Brewer 2001). When an individual feels that these forces are in balance, the individual is said to have reached optimal distinctiveness, and deviations from optimal distinctiveness should motivate individuals to assimilate or differentiate themselves to regain equilibrium. Research on ODT has found a myriad of effects of heightening either the need for differentiation or assimilation. Individuals primed to feel overly different from (similar to) their peers overestimate (underestimate) the social consensus of their attitudes (Simon et al. 1990) and exaggerate (minimize) perceptions of in-group homogeneity (Pickett & Brewer 2001), importance, and size (Pickett, Silver & Brewer 2002).

The implications of ODT for consumer behavior have not been extensively researched. Because consuming a product places the individual into a group consisting of users of that product or products like it, two differentiation strategies seem particularly applicable to consumerism: identifying with numerically distinct in-groups and identifying with a group that positions itself against the mainstream (Hornsey & Jetten 2004). Indeed, recent work by Timmor and Katz-Navon (2008) suggests that individuals with a heightened need for differentiation will identify with a numerically distinct in-group in a consumption setting: Individuals predisposed to a high need for differentiation (assimilation) were more likely to adopt a new product when they perceived the current group of adopters to be small (large).

However, estimating the size of the in-group associated with a product may not always be easy. Some brands carry with them a cult-like group of consumers (e.g., Apple, Harley Davidson), easily defining the in-group and out-groups for the consumer. However, in other cases, consumption groups are less well-defined. In those situations, consumers' needs for assimilation and differentiation may be more easily met by selecting seemingly "typical" and "atypical" offerings.

Because atypical products or product styles are less frequently instantiated and generally less popular than more typical products or product styles (Loken & Ward 1990), I hypothesize that they will be chosen more often by individuals with a heightened need for differentiation because consumers assume that doing so places the consumer into a numerically distinct in-group and/or a group that positions itself against the mainstream. Alternatively, I hypothesize that individuals with a heightened need for assimilation will select more typical products or product styles because they assume that doing so places them into a numerically larger and/or more mainstream consumption group.

These hypotheses were tested in two studies that investigated consumer choices after their optimal distinctiveness levels were threatened. In both studies, the needs for assimilation and differentiation were manipulated by informing consumers that they were similar to or dissimilar to a large majority of their peers. This information came in the form of feedback from a task where consumers were asked to provide their attitudes toward a variety of well-known brands: After providing their attitudes, consumers either learned that they were similar to 20% of their peers (heightened-need-for-assimilation condition) or 80% of their peers (heightened-need-for-differentiation condition).

In Study 1, after receiving this feedback, consumers were asked to choose between 13 University of Florida t-shirts differing in how typical they were (i.e., in how commonly they were worn by members of the student body). As predicted, individuals who were told that their tastes were very similar to their peers chose less typical t-shirt styles than individuals who were told that their tastes were very different from their peers, $F(1,135)=4.893$, $p<.05$. Open-ended responses also supported the hypotheses: Some consumers explained their atypical choices by saying that the t-shirt was not worn by thousands of students on campus. Alternatively, other consumers explained their typical choice by saying it was the t-shirt they felt best represented the University.

In Study 1, choices among t-shirts apparently allowed consumers to regain optimal distinctiveness, but are all products equally suited to help consumers regain their optimal distinctiveness? Past research suggests that consumers express themselves through classically "symbolic" goods such as cars and clothing (Belk 1988), whereas recent research suggests that consumers express themselves through personally important products such as music preferences or hairstyles (Berger and Heath 2007). Study 2 examined two dimensions: product symbolism and consumption conspicuousness. Specifically, this study explored whether threatening optimal distinctiveness would affect product choices for all product types, or whether only choices among highly conspicuous or symbolic products would be affected by such a threat. Thus, the study featured a 2(feedback: similar to or different from peers) X 2(target product consumed conspicuously or inconspicuously) X 2(target product symbolic or unsymbolic) between-subjects design.

After receiving feedback about their similarity to their peers (as in Study 1), consumers chose between browsing two special collections on two mock websites: "unique, one-of-a-kind offerings" and products with "more mass appeal". Product conspicuousness and symbolism were manipulated by changing the website's name (e.g., www.tshirts.com vs. www.movies.com).

When choosing among products consumed conspicuously, consumers who were told that they were very similar (very different) from their peers chose to browse the "unique" ("mass appeal") offerings ($p <. 05$), as in Study 1. However, when choosing among less conspicuously consumed products, there was no effect of similarity/distinctiveness feedback ($p>.15$). Thus, consumers seem to perceive conspicuously consumed products to be more useful for regaining optimal distinctiveness than inconspicuously consumed products [Feedback X Conspicuous Interaction: $F(1,99)=4.29$, $p<.05$].

The results of these two studies suggest that consumption-based coping strategies exist for helping consumers regain their threatened optimal distinctiveness. Further, Study 2 suggests threatened optimal distinctiveness is best regained publicly. Future studies will examine whether a non-consumption-based affirmation of optimal distinctiveness eliminates this effect, and, if so, whether this affirmation must be made publicly.

References

Belk, Russell W. (1988). "Possessions and the Extended Self," *Journal of Consumer Research*, University of Chicago Press, vol. 15 (2)

Berger, Jonah and Chip Heath (2007), "Where Consumers Diverge from Others: Identity Signaling and Product Domains," *Journal of Consumer Research*, vol. 34, No. 2 (August): 121-134.

Brewer, Marilynn (1991), "The Social Self: On Being the Same and Different at the Same Time," *Personality and Social Psychology Bulletin*, 17, 475-482.

Hornsey, Matthew J. & Jolanda Jetten (2004), "The Individual Within the Group: Balancing the Need to Belong with the Need to be Different," *Personality and Social Psychology Review*, 8(3), 248-264.

Loken, Barbara & James Ward (1990), "Alternative Approaches to Understanding the Determinants of Typicality," *The Journal of Consumer Research*, Vol. 17, No. 2 (Sept): 111-126.

Pickett, C.L. & M.B. Brewer (2001), "Assimilation and Differentiation Needs as Motivational Determinants of Perceived In-Group and Out-Group Homogeneity," *Journal of Experimental Social Psychology*, 37, 341-348.

Pickett, C.L., M.D. Silver & M.B. Brewer (2002), "The Impact of Assimilation and Differentiation Needs on Perceived Group Importance and Judgments of In-Group Size," *Personality and Social Psychology Bulletin*, 28, 546-588.

Simon, L., J. Greenberg, T. Pyszczynski, R. Clement & S. Solomon (1997), "Perceived Consensus, Uniqueness, and Terror Management: Compensatory Responses to Threats to Inclusion and Distinctiveness Following Mortality Salience," *Personality and Social Psychology Bulletin*, 23, 1055-1065.

Timmor, Yaron and Tal Katz-Navon (2008), "Being the Same and Different: A Model Explaining New Product Adoption," *Journal of Consumer Behaviour*, 7 (3), 249-262.

Jack of all Trades, Master of None: The Impact of Assortment Inferences on Choice

Chrissy Mitakakis, Baruch College, CUNY, USA
Thomas Kramer, Baruch College, CUNY, USA

Imagine that Sue and Bob would like to purchase a notebook for school. Sue is shopping for the notebook in a store that has a great assortment variety (i.e., in addition to paper products it also sells household cleaners, fruits, among many others). Bob is shopping in an equally well-known store, which sells only a few different types of items besides notebooks (i.e., only paper products, household cleaners, and fruits). Would the size of the assortment available at the store, which is de facto irrelevant to the choice of the notebook, nonetheless differentially impact Sue and Bob? The current research examines this question. We propose that the number of noncomparable items in an assortment can indeed affect consumers' perceptions and choice of a target product. Although prior studies have investigated the impact of the number of options under consideration (i.e., Chernev 2001, 2003; Lancaster 1990; Broniarczyk, Hoyer, and McAlister 1998; Chernev 2003; Greenleaf and Lehmann 1995; Huffman and Kahn 1998; Kahn and Wansink 2004; Lin and Wu 2006; Menon and Kahn 1995), such research was focused on the number of alternatives from the same product category. However, the literature is lacking an investigation into the effect of assortment size of unrelated options on consumer responses to a particular product. This lack is even more surprising considering the growth of retailing formats such as supercenters or hypermarkets, which sell a seemingly endless variety of products.

In particular, we argue that consumer responses to a product will be less favorable when it is sold in a store with a greater assortment of unrelated products. We further posit that these effects are driven by a lay theory that consumers hold about the marketplace, such that stores that offer products in too many categories cannot offer quality products in all ("jack-of-all-trades-master-of-none"). Thus, we propose that consumers perceive a product that is found in a large assortment of noncomparable products as worse in quality than one that is found in a small assortment of noncomparable products. We define noncomparable products as "those that have few attributes in common" (Bettman and Sujan 1987, p.142), and are generally considered to come from different product categories (Johnson 1984). According to our proposed theory, a large number of noncomparable products can signal the notion that the store's attempt to carry many different types of products detracts from its knowledge about any one product. Consequently, the product will be perceived as having lower quality, compared to the identical one found in an assortment consisting of only a few noncomparable products. Additionally, since these judgments involve conscious, cognitive components, it is also argued that the proposed effects will occur only under full cognitive capacity.

In this research, we propose a new lay theory that consumers hold during the decision making process. Consistent with previous research that has found that people act as intuitive scientists and develop naïve theories about the world around them (Hong, Levy, and Chiu 2001; Kruglanski 1990), research in consumer behavior has been able to identify several different beliefs that consumers may have about the marketplace (Pratap, Mathur, and Maheswaran 2009). For example, consumers have been found to hold lay theories about the relationship between price and quality (Cronley et al. 2005; Kardes, Posavac, and Cronley 2004), ease of accessibility of information (Menon and Raghubir 2005; Schwarz 2004), and hedonic contrast effects (Novemsky and Ratner 2003). Our research proposes that consumers hold a lay theory based on the lack of comparability of surrounding products that are found in an assortment, and thus use this information in making judgments about a single product.

To examine the proposed lay theory consumers have regarding the presence of noncomparable products, we investigated the effects of the size of the assortment of noncomparable products in the purchase environment on consumers' evaluations of a target product (a notebook). In order to assess consumers' utilization of the proposed lay theory, we told participants that the notebook was found in an assortment with either three or twenty noncomparable products (such as household cleaners, food items, etc.), as well varied some participants' cognitive resources with a cognitive load task. After the presentation of the hypothetical shopping scenario, we assessed participants' attitudes toward the product as well as their likelihood of purchasing that product. Our results support the hypothesis that consumers perceive a target product to be of significantly lower quality, and are significantly less likely to purchase it, when it is found in an assortment with several noncomparable products, as opposed to when it is found in an assortment with only a few other noncomparable products. However, as hypothesized, this effect occurs only with participants who have the cognitive resources available for the "jack-of-all-trades-master-of-none" inference.

We contribute to the literature by proposing a new type of lay theory that consumers use when perceiving product assortments containing different, noncomparable products. This paper demonstrates that consumers use a specific lay theory based on the context of the product assortment to render judgments about a target product. In addition to our theoretical contribution, our findings can also help contribute important managerial implications about retailers' assortments. Thus, we offer new insight about consumers' perceptions about a product when the variety of noncomparable products in an assortment increases. Based on our findings, our second study (currently in progress) examines the moderating role of the extent of comparability of other products in an assortment. Future research might also examine whether consumers use this lay theory for all types of products, or whether the product type (i.e., necessity versus luxury) would make a difference.

References

Bettman, James R. and Mita Sujan (1987), "Effects of Framing on Evaluation of Comparable and Noncomparable Alternatives by Expert and Novice Consumers," *Journal of Consumer Research*, 14(September), 141-54.

Broniarczyk, Susan M., Wayne D. Hoyer, and Leigh McAlister (1998), "Consumers' Perceptions of the Assortment Offered in a Grocery Category: The Impact of Item Reduction," *Journal of Marketing Research*, 35(2), 166-76.

Chernev, Alexander (2001), "The Impact of Common Features on Consumer Preferences: A Case of Confirmatory Reasoning," *Journal of Consumer Research*, 27(4), 475-88.

Chernev, Alexander (2003), "Product Assortment and Individual Decision Processes," *Journal of Personality and Social Psychology*," 85(1), 151-62.

Cronley, Maria L., Steven S. Posavac, Tracy Meyer, Frank R. Kardes, and James J. Kellaris (2005), "A Selective Hypothesis Testing Perspective on Price-Quality Inference and Inference-Based Choice," *Journal of Consumer Psychology*, 15(2), 159-69.

Greenleaf, Eric A. and Donald R. Lehmann (1995), "Reasons for Substantial Delay in Consumer Decision Making," *Journal of Consumer Research*, 22(September), 186-99.

Hong, Ying-yi, Sheri R. Levy, and Chi-yue Chiu (2001), "The Contribution of Lay Theories Approach to the Study of Groups," *Personality and Social Psychology Review*, 5(2), 98-106.

Huffman, Cynthia and Barbara E. Kahn (1998), "Variety for Sale: Mass Customization or Mass Confusion?," *Journal of Retailing*, 74(4), 491-513.

Johnson, Michael (1984), "Consumer Choice Strategies for Comparing Noncomparable Alternative," *Journal of Consumer Research*, 11(December), 741-53.

Kahn, Barbara E. and Brian Wansink (2004), "The Influence of Assortment Structure on Perceived Variety and Consumption Quantities," *Journal of Consumer Research*, 30(4), 519-33.

Kardes, Frank R., Steven S. Posavac, and Maria L. Cronley (2004), "Consumer Inferences: A Review of Processes, Bases, and Judgment Contexts," *Journal of Consumer Psychology*, 14(3), 230-56.

Kruglanski, Arie W. (1990), "Lay Epistemic Theory in Social-Cognitive Psychology," *Psychological Inquiry*, 1(3), 181-97.

Lancaster, Kevin (1990), "The Economics of Product Variety: A Survey," *Marketing Science*, 9(3), 189-206.

Lin, Chien-Huang and Pei-Hsun Wu (2006), "The Effect of Variety on Consumer Preferences: The role of Need for Cognition and Recommended Alternatives," *Social Behavior and Personality*, 34(7), 865-76.

Menon, Satya and Barbara E. Kahn (1995), "The Impact of Context on Variety Seeking in Product Choices," *Journal of Consumer Research*, 22(3), 285-95.

Menon, Geeta and Priya Raghubir (2005), "Ease of Retrieval as an Automatic Input in Judgments: A Mere Accessibility Framework?," *Journal of Consumer Research*, 30(September), 230-43.

Novemsky, Nathan and Rebecca K. Ratner (2003), "The Time Course and Impact of Consumers' Erroneous Beliefs about Hedonic Contrast Effects," *Journal of Consumer Research*, 29(March), 507-16.

Pratap, Shailendra, Pragya Mathur, and Durairaj Maheswaran (2009), "The Influence of Consumers' Lay Theories on Approach/Avoidance Motivation," *Journal of Marketing Research*, 46(2), 56-65.

Schwarz, Norbert (2004), "Metacognitive Experiences in Consumer Judgment and Decision Making," *Journal of Consumer Psychology*, 14(4), 332-48.

Ethnic Chinese Representations in Indonesian Advertising

Angeline Nariswari, University of Hawaii at Manoa, USA
Xin Zhao, University of Hawaii at Manoa, USA

This paper moves beyond the primary discourse of advertising as a promotional tool and views advertising as a cultural system (Lears 1994; Leiss 2006; Sherry 1987) that distortedly reflects the social aspirations of consumers, the ideals of its creators (Marchand 1986) and the views of the power dominant (Hall 1997). We take advertising as a cultural text to examine how particular social groups and ethnic minorities are represented.

Existing research shows that images created during slavery period emphasized the subordinate status of black people, deducing them to particular physical characteristics and portraying them as inherently lazy and uncultured (Hall 1997). More recent portrayals present African Americans among others in lower-status roles, perpetuating class distinctions with the White majority (Bristor, Lee and Hunt 1995). On the other hand, Asian Americans are persistently represented as the "model minority," and are strongly associated with technology related products. They are commonly portrayed in business settings but less in social or family settings and relationships (Taylor, Landreth, and Bang 2005; Taylor and Lee 1994; Taylor and Stern 1997). This stream of research is constrained within Western societies and it is unclear how ethnic minorities are represented in other countries.

We focus on the portrayals of ethnic Chinese in Indonesian advertising. Much of the local resentment against the Chinese minority stems from the fact that despite comprising of only 1.45% to 2.04% of the population (Suryadinata, Arifin, and Ananta, 2003), they are perceived to play a dominant role in the Indonesian economy (Tan 2008). Historically, tension between the ethnic Chinese and indigenous Indonesians can be traced back to the time of Dutch colonization. The Dutch "divide and rule" policy positioned the Chinese as being a class higher than indigenous Indonesians (Nanjing 2006). Ethnic Chinese were provided with separate schools (Suryadinata 2005; Tan 2008) but were restricted in access to land ownership and the areas in which they are allowed to reside (Nanjing 2006). These policies contribute to Chinese expertise in trade but also separate them from indigenous Indonesians.

Recent changes towards democracy have introduced Indonesian people to values of freedom, democracy, and tolerance towards diversity. Nevertheless, as prejudice, resentment, and suspicion against the Chinese have never been fully resolved, such sentiments may still loom below the surface. The Indonesian setting provides us with a rich historical context to explore the boundaries of foreignness and localness through texts of consumer culture. We aim to examine how advertising appropriates existing social tensions to promote consumption.

Public display of Chinese tradition and culture is a recent phenomenon that was only reinstated by President Abdurrahman Wahid in 2000. Before the reform era, under Suharto's rule, the three pillars of Chinese culture: language and schooling, press, as well as organizations were banned as part of an assimilation policy (Suryadinata 2005). Expression of Chinese culture and belief, including public celebrations of Chinese holidays, were not permitted (Fang and Wendyartaka 2008). Citizens of Chinese descent were encouraged to forgo their Chinese names and take up Indonesian sounding names (Suryadinata 2004). The government utilized media to demonize the Chinese as being "unpatriotic, exclusive, speculative, pro-China (or Taiwan), indifferent to society, greedy, filthy (eating pork), pertinent to bribery, and controlling Indonesian economy." (Nanjing 2006, 199). Over the course of the reform era, a series of new policies encourage a move towards a more democratic and tolerant society. This study explores whether or not and how such changes in values are reflected and appropriated in advertising.

While most studies explore representations of ethnic minorities through content analysis, this study employs a semiotic approach (Barthes, 1972; Mick, 1986; Rose 2006) to identify the strategies used to represent ethnic Chinese. We gathered advertisements in *Kompas* newspaper and *Femina* magazine during the Chinese New Year season from 2000-2009. These media were chosen for their leading national circulation. While *Kompas* targets a general audience, *Femina* targets the middle-upper female class. Chinese New Year was selected to gain efficient access to commercial texts concentrated around and targeted towards Chinese culture and consumers. The advertisements were chosen based on how conceptually significant each text is in representing ethnic Chinese in Indonesia (Mick 1986; Rose 2006; Zhao and Belk 2008). Interpretations are made based on a semiotics approach, in which denotative as well as connotative meanings of images are explored (Leeuwen 2008).

Our initial exploration generates a number of findings: appearance of stereotypical characters, gender reversal, and arbitrary reinterpretation of Chinese culture. Among the stereotypical characters found are those of the chubby Chinese male or children and the loony elderly figure. Chubbiness becomes a symbol of greed, ugliness, and inability to control one's appetite. It represents excessive wealth and insensitivity towards people in a poor society. An advertisement for a real estate developer depicts an elderly man in traditional Chinese clothing holding an *angpao* (red envelope containing money, normally given out to children during Chinese New Year) with uncontrollable glee. His expression of overwhelming joy represents an obsession with money and a childlike inability to control emotions.

Another theme found is of gender reversals, where men are "demasculanized" and women take leading roles commonly portrayed by males. An ad for a national bank presents a chubby male comically attempting to make kung fu moves. He wears flower-patterned shorts indicative of feminine taste. His lack of kung fu skills and manliness allows him to be laughed at. In contrast, an advertisement for a brand of high-calcium milk presents two women performing the *barongsai* (dragon) dance. One woman stands firmly on the shoulders of the other, while three men play music in the background. Considering that the *barongsai* dance is traditionally performed by males, this ad presents an opposite picture of females taking over a male-dominant role.

One final example reflects how arbitrary interpretation of Chinese culture is made. An advertisement for a telecommunications service provider shows a man holding burning incense in front of a Chinese temple. The incense smoke forms the image of a goat; in line with the celebration of the Year of the Goat. However, such image presents the idea that the Chinese worship the goat rather than their Gods, reflecting a backward pagan culture that lag behind the Muslim majority who worship one God.

While in reality it is the male Chinese businessmen who play the dominant role in the society, they appear to be the dominant target of ridicule or the ones to take on background roles. Interestingly, some of the brands who present such roles are Chinese owned. Putting the ethnic Chinese in such vulnerable roles allows them to appear in a less-threatening and humbling manner. We find Indonesian ads to acknowledge and make use of existing stereotypes to present a safe opportunity for laughter as well as self-humiliation as a temporary mechanism to release tension. As such, we conclude that advertising not only provides a distorted mirror of society (Pollay 1986), but can also function to hide and reverse reality.

References

Barthes, Roland (1972), *Mythologies*, New York: Hill and Wang.

Bristor, Julia M., Renee G. Lee, and Michelle R. Hunt (1995), "Race and Ideology: African-American Images in Television Advertising," *Journal of Public Policy & Marketing*, 14 (1), 48-59.

Fang, Lan and Anung Wendyartaka (2008), "Bangkit Dari Mati Suri," *Kompas*, June 2.

Hall, Stuart (1997), *Representation: Cultural Representations and Signifying Practices*, Thousand Oaks: Sage.

Leeuwen, Theo van (2008), "Semiotics and Iconography," in *Handbook of Visual Analysis*, ed. Theo and Carey Jewitt van Leeuwen, Thousand Oaks: Sage.

Marchand, Roland (1986), *Advertising the American Dream: Making Way for Modernity, 1920-1940* CA: University of California Press.

Mick, David G. (1986), "Consumer Research and Semiotics: Exploring the Morphology of Signs, Symbols, and Significance " *Journal of Consumer Research*, 13 (2), 196-213.

Nanjing, Zhou (2006), "Racial Relations and Nation-Building, a Case Study of the Indonesian Chinese," in *Demarcating Ethnicity in New Nations : Cases of the Chinese in Singapore, Malaysia, and Indonesia* ed. Lee Guan Kin, Singapore: Konrad Adenauer Stiftung and Singapore Society of Asian Studies.

Pollay, Richard W. (1986), "The Distorted Mirror: Reflections on the Unintended Consequences of Advertising," *Journal of Marketing*, 50 (April), 18-36.

Rose, Gillian (2006), *Visual Methodologies: An Introduction to the Interpretation of Visual Methods*, Thousand Oaks: Sage Publications

Suryadinata, Leo (2004), *Chinese and Nation-Building in Southeast Asia*, Singapore: Marshall Cavendish Academic.

______ (2005), *Pribumi Indonesians, the Chinese Minority and China : A Study of Perceptions and Policies*, Singapore: Marshall Cavendish.

Suryadinata, Leo, Evi N. Arifin, and Aris Ananta (2003), *Indonesia's Population: Ethnicity and Religion in a Changing Political Landscape*, Singapore: Institute of Southeast Asian Studies.

Tan, Mely G. (2008), "Ethnic Chinese in Indonesia," in *Etnis Tionghoa Di Indonesia*, Jakarta: Yayasan Obor Indonesia, 1-32.

Taylor, Charles R., Stacy Landreth, and Hae-Kyong Bang (2005), "Asian Americans in Magazine Advertising: Portrayals of The "Model Minority"," *Journal of Macromarketing*, 25 (2), 163-74.

Taylor, Charles R. and Ju Y. Lee (1994), "Not in Vogue-Portrayals of Asian Americans in Magazine Advertising," *Journal of Public Policy & Marketing*, 13 (2), 239-45.

Taylor, Charles R. and Barbara B. Stern (1997), "Asian-Americans: Television Advertising and the ''Model Minority'' Stereotype," *Journal of Advertising*, 26 (2), 47-61.

Zhao, X. and R. W. Belk (2008), "Advertising Consumer Culture in 1930s Shanghai–Globalization and Localization in Yuefenpai," *Journal of Advertising*, 37 (2), 45-56.

Is a "Premium" Private Label Brand for a Marketer Seen as a "Premium" By a Consumer? The Perceptual Categorization of Private Labels Tiers

Magda Nenycz-Thiel, Ehrenberg-Bass Institute for Marketing Science, Australia
Jenni Romaniuk, University of South Australia, Australia

Private labels are now a permanent feature of competitive retail landscapes all around the world. The category is strongest in the UK and Western Europe, where its market share accounts for 20-40% of grocery sales (De Wulf et al. 2005). Although, private label share in the US lags behind the UK and other Western Europeans countries, it is growing at a rate far outpacing the growth of manufacturers' brands (Baltas and Argouslidis 2007). In 2002, US sales of private labels exceeded 50 billion dollars and their share in grocery retailing reached 15% (Sprott and Shimp 2004). Given the current economic conditions it is likely that this growth trend will continue.

Traditionally, private labels have been positioned as low price / good value for money offerings. Their major selling point has been their price advantage and as such private labels themselves can act as a cue to trigger a perception of value (Zeithaml 1988).

However, the rationale for introducing premium private labels is not under the guise of offering something that is cheaper than manufacturer brands, but to create a point of differentiation from other retailers (Corstjens and Lal 2000). In order to achieve this premium positioning the retailers invest in attractive packaging and include words that imply premium, such as *Finest*, in the brands names. Many premium private labels lines are now advertised and have samples inserted into food magazines and distributed in retailing outlets (Lincoln and Thomassen 2008).

Nevertheless, those positioning strategies can only be considered successful if consumers notice them. Drawing from categorization research, consumers' knowledge forms schema-like structures in memory, which enhances information processing efficiency (e.g. Cohen and Basu 1987). If two brands possess similar specifications that differ from other brands, they will be grouped together in consumers' memory, forming a sub-category. The categories or schemas are described by Bettman (1979 pp. 455) as 'cognitive structures representing one's expectations about a domain'. Those expectations may be about typical values on some attributes, importance of those attributes, and finally about how the value of an attribute varies across brands in the category (Sujan and Bettman 1989). If those expectations are strong and well anchored it is difficult to exert any influence on them. Since the schemas reflecting the traditional positioning of private labels have not changed for years, the question arises whether consumers perceive differences between different tiers of private labels? In this paper, we build on categorization theory and examine whether, and based on which cues, such categorization happens for different tiers of private labels.

Research Method

We draw on data from three food categories in the United Kingdom, including tea (N=2,000), instant coffee (N=2,000) and roast coffee (N=2,000). Different respondents were interviewed for each category. The respondent pool was drawn from the Tesco Club Card panel data and past panel buying behaviour was used to confirm that each respondent had bought from the category they were questioned about in the last six months. Each category includes one value and one premium private label, for the purpose of comparison. National brands were also included in the study, but are not the focus of the first stage of analysis.

The data was collected via phone using a free choice, pick-any approach (Barnard and Ehrenberg 1990). Respondents were given a list of brands and then a list of attributes. They were asked which, if any, brands they linked to each attribute. Marketers and researchers who are experts within the industry developed the attribute list. The attributes were chosen based on them being important to consumers when buying from the category. Although the attribute lists varied across categories, there was some overlap. Attributes relating to *value*, *trust*, *good quality* were common across categories, with the remainder reflecting the category specific core performance and benefit attributes, such as *when I want to relax* and *is natural* for the tea category, and *smooth*, *strong flavour* and *to indulge myself* in the coffee categories.

Analysis approach

Based on the actual status of the brand, we coded value private labels as 0 and premium private labels as 1 to create the dependent variable. The independent variables for each category were the attribute responses (also coded as 1: linked the brand to the attribute and 0: did not link the brand to the attribute).

We used binary logistic regression to examine how people categorize private label brands and what (if any) informational cues they use to discriminate between premium and value private labels.

Results

We find that consumers do differ in the attributes they link to premium private labels compared to the more traditional value private labels. The logistic regression models are statistically significant in each category and explain high levels of variance, Nagelkerke R^2's ranging from 36% in the instant coffee category to 43% in the roast coffee category. Consistent across all categories, link to attributes *high quality ingredients*, *would taste good* and *to indulge* increase the probability that a brand was a premium private label. This suggests that enhancement of the extrinsic product cues, such as improved packaging or a distinctive brand name can influence consumers' quality perceptions. Conversely, associations with *good value* and *down to earth* decrease the probability of a private label brand being a premium brand.

After this, there was a succession of category specific attributes that contributed positively or negatively to the categorization into premium private labels. In both coffee categories, associations with *smooth*, *after dinner* and *full bodied* increased the probability that the brand was the premium brand. In the tea category the attribute *has a strong flavour*, also featured significantly in the same way. Conversely, the attributes *mild taste* in the roast coffee category, *when I want to relax* and *natural* in the tea category and a group of attributes in the instant coffee category (*traditional*, *when I want to relax* and *mild taste*) featured as the negative drivers of categorization.

We find that consumers do see premium private labels as a different group of brands compared to the value private labels. Our findings suggest that although the perceptual schemas reflecting traditional positioning of private labels have been reinforced over many years, marketing activities that improve the extrinsic product cues are able to influence consumers' perceptions. Therefore, the consumer perceptions of what a premium private label represents can, by investment in marketing support, be matched with marketers' perceptions. The next step of this research is to see whether the same categorization into premium and non-premium brands is evident for national brands and if the same informational cues are utilized to differentiate between national brands.

References

Baltas, George and Paraskevas C Argouslidis (2007), "Consumer characteristics and demand for store brands," *International Journal of Retail & Distribution Management*, 35 (5), 328-41.

Barnard, Neil R. and Andrew S.C. Ehrenberg (1990), "Robust measures of consumer brand beliefs," *Journal of Marketing Research*, 27 (November), 477-84.

Bettman, James R. (1979), *An Information Processing Theory of Consumer Choice*, Reading, Massachusetts: Addison-Wesley Publishing Company.

Cohen, Joel B. and Kunal Basu (1987), "Alternative Models of Categorisation: Towards a Contingent Processing Framework," *Journal of Consumer Research*, 13 (March), 455-72.

Corstjens, Marcel and Rajiv Lal (2000), "Building Store Loyalty Through Store Brands," *Journal of Marketing Research*, 37 (3), 281-91.

De Wulf, Kristof, Gaby Odekerken-Schröder, Frank Goedertier, and Gino Van Ossel (2005), "Consumer perceptions of store brands versus national brands," *Journal of Consumer Marketing*, 22 (4), 223-32.

Lincoln, Keith and Lars Thomassen (2008), *Private label: turning the retail brand threat into your biggest opportunity*: Kogan Page Publishers.

Sprott, David E. and Terence A. Shimp (2004), "Using product sampling to augment the perceived quality of store brands," *Journal of Retailing*, 80, 305-15.

Sujan, Mita and James R. Bettman (1989), "The Effects of Brand Positioning Strategies on Consumers' Brand and Category Perceptions: Some Insights From Schema Research," *Journal of Marketing Research*, 26 (4), 454-67.

Zeithaml, Valarie A. (1988), "Consumer Perceptions of Price, Quality and Value: A Means-End Model and Synthesis of Evidence," *Journal of Marketing*, 52 (July), 2-22.

Finger Length Ratio and Attitudes toward Several Product Categories

Marcelo V. Nepomuceno, John Molson School of Business, Canada
Gad Saad, John Molson School of Business, Canada
Eric Stenstrom, John Molson School of Business, Canada
Zack Mendenhall, John Molson School of Business, Canada

Recent studies have highlighted the relevance of physiology in understanding human behavior. For instance, Coates and Herbert (2008) have shown that higher levels of testosterone are correlated to male traders' profitability. Similarly, Saad and Vongas (2009) showed that men's testosterone levels increased while driving a luxurious sports car, suggesting a relationship between hormones and conspicuous consumption. Finger length ratio, a sexually dimorphic trait, is a marker of prenatal testosterone (Manning et al. 1998). The second-to-fourth finger length ratio (2D:4D) has been consistently correlated to a wide range of sexually differentiated phenomena, such as athletic ability (Manning and Taylor 2001), spatial ability (Loehlin, Medland, and Martin 2009), risk-taking behavior (Coates and Page 2009), sexual orientation (Manning, Churchill and Peters 2007) and aggression (McIntyre et al. 2007). Yet, little is known about the relationship between 2D:4D and consumption phenomena possessing a strong sex-specificity. One exception is the research conducted by Millet, Kobe (2007) wherein males with low 2D:4D placed in a subordinate condition exhibited greater future discounting rates than high 2D:4D individuals put in the same condition. Moreover, he found that 2D:4D moderates one's susceptibility to media violence. Specifically, individuals with lower digit ratios responded more aggressively and less cooperatively to aggressive music video than those with higher ratios. In the current research, we focus on the relationship between digit ratio and the attitudes that individuals hold toward specific products.

Using a sample of 240 university students, we tested the hypothesis that lower finger length ratio would correlate with attitudes towards product categories that have a strong male penchant. In addition, given that rel2, the length of the index finger relative to the sum of the lengths of all four fingers, has recently been shown to be more accurate than 2D:4D in discriminating between males and females (Loehlin, Medland, and Martin 2009), we propose that rel2 will be more strongly correlated to individuals' product attitudes than will 2D:4D. Trained experimenters measured the lengths of right-hand fingers using digital callipers. Participants responded to several items, which assessed their attitude towards several product categories, namely cosmetics, electronics, pornography, clothing, movies genres (drama, action, science fiction, romance, animation and war), sports (hockey, boxing, synchronized swimming and gymnastics), and video-games genres (First-person Shooter, Real-time Strategy, Party-game, Platformer, and Life Simulator). Each product category possessed a valenced sex-specificity, namely male, female, or neutral. One-way ANOVAs revealed that nine product categories were significantly preferred by males (hockey, boxing, electronics, pornography, action movies, science fiction movies, war movies, First-person Shooter games and Real-time Strategy games), eight by females (drama movies, romance movies, party games, life simulator games, synchronized swimming, gymnastics, cosmetics, and clothing), and two were neutral (animation movies and platformer games). For example, pornography was deemed a male product category given that men held a more positive attitude toward it than did women ($F=54.07$, $p<.001$). All attitudinal items possessed reliability alphas above .80.

Regression analyses were conducted on both ethnically homogeneous (Caucasians only, n=132) and heterogeneous samples (all ethnicities, n=133). Two major findings were obtained. First, rel2 was generally a better predictor of the collected product attitudes than 2D:4D. Second, we found significant ($p<.05$) or marginally significant ($p<.10$) correlations between rel2 and product attitudes held by Caucasians for four out of the nine product categories preferred by males. For example, low rel2 (i.e., indicative of higher exposure in uterus to testosterone) was associated with more positive attitudes towards electronics in the Caucasian sample ($p=.006$, Adjusted $R^2= .055$). Similarly, low rel2 was negatively correlated with attitudes towards pornography in Caucasians ($p=.064$, Adjusted $R^2= .02$). Given that the relations were stronger with an ethnically homogeneous sample (Caucasians only), our results are in accordance with previous finger length ratio studies (Manning, Churchill, and Peters 2007), and reinforce the importance of controlling for ethnicity in future research on digit ratio. Moreover, this study suggests that finger length ratios may be predictive of attitudes toward products possessing a strong sex-specificity.

References

Coates, John M. and Joe Herbert (2008), "Endogenous Stereoids and Financial Risk Taking on a London Trading Floor," *Proceedings of the National Academy of Sciences of the United States of* America, 105 (16), 6167-72.

Coates, John M. and Lionel Page (2009), "A Note on Trader Sharpe Ratios," *PLOS One*, 4 (11), e8036.

Loehlin, John C., Sarah E. Medland, and Nicholas G. Martin (2009), "Relative Finger Lengths, Sex Differences, and Psychological Traits," *Archives of Sexual Behavior*, 38 (2), 298-305.

Manning, John T. and Rogan P. Taylor (2001), "Second to Fourth Digit Ratio and Male Ability in Sport: Implications for Sexual Selection in Humans," *Evolution and Human Behavior*, 22 (1), 61-69.

Manning, John T., Andrew J. Churchill, and Michael Peters (2007), "The Effects of Sex, Ethnicity, and Sexual Orientation on Self-Measured Digit Ratio," *Archives of Sexual Behavior*, 36 (2), 223-33.

Manning, John T., Diane Scutt, J. Wilson, and David I. Lewis-Jones (1998), "The Ratio of 2nd to 4th Digit Length: A Predictor of Sperm Numbers and Concentration to Testosterone, Luteinizing Hormone and Estrogen," *Human Reproduction*, 13 (11), 3000-04.

McIntyre, Matthew H., Emily S. Barrett, Rose McDermott, Dominic D.P. Johnson, Jonathan Cowden, and Stephen P. Rosen (2007), "Finger Length Ratio (2D:4D) and Sex Differences in Aggression during a Simulated War Game," *Personality and Individual Differences*, 42, 755-64.

Millet, Kobe (2007), "Prenatal Testosterone, Personality, and Economic Behavior," doctoral dissertation, Faculty of Business and Economics, Catholic University of Leuven, Naamsestraat 69 bus 3500, B 3000, Leuven, Belgium, 2007.

Saad, Gad and John G. Vongas (2009), "The Effect of Conspicuous Consumption on Men's Testosterone Levels," *Organizational Behavior and Human Decision Processes*, 110 (2), 80-92.

Online Consumer Privacy 2.0

Thuc-Doan Nguyen, California State University, Long Beach, USA
Eric P. H. Li, York University, Canada

The surge of social networking sites (e.g., *Facebook*) and video/photo sharing sites (e.g. *Youtube/Flickr*) generates new issues on consumer privacy in the Web 2.0 era. Moving beyond the concern about the disclosure of personal data such as real name, home address, social security number, credit number, and phone number to advertising agencies or marketers, the current research demonstrates the need for re-visiting the content and concept of "privacy." The study highlights the urgency to develop new policies to mitigate uprising issues related to the disclosure of personal stories and images.

Recently, consumer researchers are interested in understanding the relationship between consumer social interactions and community building in online world from a socio-cultural perspective (e.g., Kozinets 1999; Schau and Gilly 2003). With the improvement and popularization of Internet technology, consumers are actively engaging in different creative activities such as developing personal Web sites (Schau and Gilly 2003) and consumer-created advertisements (Muniz and Schau 2007), and forming different virtual communities (Muniz and Schau 2005).Those research has enriched our knowledge of consumer online behavior. However, an important aspect of virtual world, the concern of privacy, is under-researched in this paradigm. This study is designed to bridge the gap to enhance our understanding of the experience of consumers with web services such as *Facebook*, *MySpace*, *Youtube*, and *Flickr*. Consumers, on one hand, feel empowered in posting and sharing the moments and images of their lives in cyberspace. On the other hand, they feel uncertain about potential misuses of their personal images and stories by unknown audiences. They have limited knowledge on privacy-related issue and under-estimated the impact and potential risk of sharing personal images and stories. With the advancement of online searching technology it is not difficult for Internet users to trace someone's Internet footprint with simple information such as an email address. This challenges the notion of privacy protection in the virtual world as consumers are vulnerable in controlling the dissemination of information they posted on web sites.

Prior research on consumer privacy and Internet security are predominantly focused on the protection of consumers' personal information and the development of a safe environment for online shopping and transactions as well as the use of information/cookies gathered from the websites (Caudill and Murphy 2000; Sheehan and Hoy 2000; Milne and Culnan 2002; Miyazaki 2008). Edwards (2004) argues that the existing protection law did not provide enough protection for consumers in cyberspace, especially issues that related to disclosure and invasion. Recently, marketer researchers considered privacy as one of the key drivers of online trust (Hoffman, Novak, and Peralta 1999; Bart et al. 2005; Baker, Tedesco, and Baker 2006; Miyazaki 2008). However, the increasing popularity of social networking sites and video/photo sharing web sites shifted the context of online privacy from transaction-oriented activities to social-oriented interactions. Consumers' engaging in social networking activities is based on the desire for group belongingness and the emphasis of self-existence. The more they contribute to the social networking sites or video/photo sharing sites, the more social capital they possessed within their social group(s). The more mundane events or activities they posted, the more they affirm their existence. These initial impetus and evolving motivations often force consumers play down their privacy concern. Furthermore, what consumers perceive as privacy concerns in transactions with marketers might not be applicable to their interactions with relatives and friends in the social networking sites. Moreover, consumers sometimes seem to be lack of knowledge about newly developed technologies that challenge to the existing concept of privacy.

In the current study we adopt a phenomenological approach to explore how consumers construct and interpret the concept of privacy in their everyday interaction in the virtual world. We seek to understand how consumers determine which items or information to share (and not to share) and with whom they want to share (or not to share). Our preliminary findings are organized around a series of themes emerging in the data including: the role of social networking activities in consumers' life, the dilemmas that the digitalization of everyday life, including its most private moments, pose for consumers, the personal responsibility and morality of users when they post things on social networking sites, and personal experience related to privacy. Finally, we also trace the development of consumers' idea about online privacy overtime. Our findings note that consumer learning about online privacy varies widely. The meanings consumers ascribed to online privacy reflect the role of virtual world to them and their experience with social networks.

In conclusion, our research aims to contribute to the existing consumer privacy literature by highlighting the multi-dimensionality of the concept of privacy in the new context. Our preliminary findings demonstrate the vulnerability of consumers in latest social networking activities and the challenges to privacy protection in cyberspace. Finally, we emphasize the urgency of renewing policy on consumer privacy and consumer education in the Web 2.0 era.

References

Baker, Emiley M., John C. Tedesco, and Wade H. Baker (2006), "Consumer Privacy and Trust Online: An Experimental Analysis of Anti-Phishing Promotional Effects," *Journal of Website Promotional*, 2 (1/2), 89-113.

Bart, Yakov, Venkatesh Shankar, Fareena Sultan, and Glen L. Urban (2005), "Are the Drivers and Role of Online Trust the Same for All Web Sites and Consumers? A Large-Scale Exploratory Empirical Study," *Journal of Marketing*, 69 (October), 133-52.

Caudill, Eve M. and Patrick E. Murphy (2000), "Consumer Online Privacy: Legal and Ethical Issues," *Journal of Public Policy and Marketing*, 19 (Spring), 7-19.

Edwards, Lilian (2004), "Reconstructing Consumer Privacy Protection On-line: A Modest Proposal," *International Review of Law Computers and Technology*, 18 (November), 313-44.

Hoffman, Donna L., Tom P. Novak, and M. Peralta (1999), "Building Consumer Trust Online," *Communications of the ACM*, 42 (4), 50-68.

Kozinets, Robert V. (1999), "E-Tribalized Marketing? The Strategic Implications of Virtual Communities of Consumption," *European Management Journal*, 17 (3), 252-264.

Milne, George R. and Mary J. Culnan (2002), "Using the Content of Online Privacy Notices to Inform Public Policy: A Longitudinal Analysis of the 1998-2001 U.S. Web Surveys," *The Information Society*, 18, 345-59.

Miyazaki, Anthony D. (2008), "Online Privacy and the Disclosure of Cookie Use: Effects on Consumer Trust and Anticipated Patronage," *Journal of Public Policy and Marketing*, 27 (Spring), 19-33.

Muniz, Albert and Hope Jensen Schau (2005), "Religiosity in the Abandoned Apple Newton Brand Community," *Journal of Consumer Research*, 31 (March), 737-47.

__________ (2007), "Vigilante Marketing and Consumer-Created Communications," *Journal of Advertising*, 36 (Fall), 187-202.

Schau, Hope Jensen and Mary C. Gilly (2003), "We Are What We Post? Self-Presentation in Personal Web Space," *Journal of Consumer Research*, 30 (December), 385-404.

Sheehan, Kim Bartel and Mariea Grubbs Hoy (2000), "Dimensions of Privacy Concern Among Online Consumers," *Journal of Public Policy and Marketing*, 19 (Spring), 62-73.

Thompson, Craig J. and Zeynep Arsel (2004), "The Starbucks Brandscape and Consumers' (Anticorporate) Experiences of Glocalization," *Journal of Consumer Research*, 31 (December), 631-642.

Fighting with Feathers and Bubbles: Consumer Resistance and the Urban Playground Movement

Yesim Ozalp, York University, Canada
Daiane Scaraboto, York University, Canada
Mei-Ling Wei, Saint Mary's University, Canada

Current perspectives on consumer movements define them as ideologically laden, organization-centered and well structured actions focused on fighting particular market and industry practices. However, as markets become increasingly politicized and public spaces increasingly commercialized, less structured forms of consumer resistance emerge. By looking at a series of diverse, fluid and sporadic actions undertaken by consumers in metropolitan cities, we attempt to enrich our understanding of political consumerism. Through an ethnographic investigation of the urban playground movement, we examine how consumers engage in playful interventions while subverting the norms and rules that structure public and market spaces.

A Brand in Hand: Symbolic Props in Self-Presentation

Grant Packard, University of Michigan, USA
Andrew Gershoff, University of Michigan, USA

Considerable evidence exists that people tactically manage verbal communication and bodily expressions to convey a desired impression of the self— and sometimes deceive others in the process (e.g. Argo, White and Dahl 2006; Feldman, Forrest and Happ 2002; Jones and Pittman 1982). Research building on symbolic self-completion (Wicklund and Gollwitzer 1981) finds that individuals who feel under-endowed in signals of a salient self-concept strive to find alternative means to influence others' opinions of them in subsequent verbal interactions.

This paper contributes evidence supporting the use of brands as "props" (Goffman 1959) in such acts. We expect that individuals who feel situationally under-endowed on a desirable personality trait will be more likely than well-endowed individuals to socially display (obscure) a brand that is congruent (incongruent) with positive identity on that trait. This prediction is consistent with recent findings that a "shaken self" motivates choice preference for products that possess self-enhancing trait symbolism (Gao, Wheeler and Shiv 2009). Interaction of trait features with the situation may play a role in moderating the actual use of such products in self-presentation. For example, when one's real abilities are perceived to be difficult to defend in verbal presentation, people may prefer to "tell the truth" or be protective in signaling traits with a brand possession rather than risk being caught in an act of acquisitive or self-enhancing impression management (Arkin 1981; DePaulo 1992; Swann, Pelham and Krull 1989).

Study 1

The first study entailed a 2 (*Brand*: high vs. low symbolic meaning on a specific personality trait) x 2 (*Self*: high vs. low self-evaluation on the same trait) design. Pretests identified brand pairs for which differences existed in selected personality traits for individuals possessing the brands and for the brands themselves. Two magazine brands were selected that measured high vs. low in the trait of "amiability" (*In Touch Weekly* and *The Economist*, respectively), similar in selected other traits, and not different on measures supporting posited alternatives (e.g. awareness, likeability, purchase intent).

A cover story delivered a branded object into participants' possession in a manner meeting Schlenker and Weigold's (1992) criteria for actor, audience and situational factors in self-presentation. Participants were individually told that they would be entering a room to be judged in an interview. Through a ruse regarding "additional studies" to take home with them, participants found themselves in possession of two file folders (delivery order was counterbalanced). One folder had a blank cover. The second had one of the two target brands printed prominently on the cover. Participants completed a bogus test and self-evaluation of their own amiability and then entered the interview room carrying the folders with them. The observed dependent variable was whether the brand printed on one of the folders was displayed or obscured (for example, by placing it beneath the blank folder) by the "interviewee" when it was set down on a table in front of the "interviewer". The observer of the DV was blind to condition and specific hypotheses.

We found the predicted interaction of amiability self-evaluation and brand (β=.06, Wald(138)=6.00, p=.01) and a main effect for brand (β=-.90, Wald(138)=6.19, p=.01) driven by differences within the low amiability condition only. Spotlight analysis (Aiken and West 1991) produces comparable results (+1SD amiability: β=.009, t=.145, p=.89; -1SD amiability: β=-.411, t=-3.51, p<.001). To enhance interpretability, we report the rate of display behavior by amiability self-evaluation median split versus a mean chance expectation ((MCE) 50% display / 50% obscure as "chance") as a conservative test for the behavior. Individuals with low amiability self-evaluations displayed the high amiability brand (*In Touch Weekly*) (72.2% vs MCE; $\chi^2(1,36)=13.69$, p<.001) and obscured the low amiability brand (*The Economist*) (28.1% vs MCE; $\chi^2(1,32)=8.92$, p<.001) from social view. In summary, the brand was displayed (obscured) when it enhanced (detracted from) a desirable self-presentation for those under-endowed in the salient trait. In contrast, individuals with high amiability self-evaluations did not display or obscure either brand at a rate different from chance ($M_{\text{Low Amiability Brand}}$=59.5%, $M_{\text{High Amiability Brand}}$=58.8%, p's>.25). This pattern is consistent with a symbolic self-completion account of brands as alternative symbols for their possessor's traits or abilities.

Study 2

We subsequently sought a preliminary moderator test regarding enhanced social risk of being "caught in a lie" of acquisitive or self-enhancing impression management. A pretest identified intelligence as a socially desirable trait for which a person's ability to verbally convince others of high ability in the interview situation was more difficult than amiability, and highly difficult overall. The design of Study 2 was similar to Study 1 except participants were assigned to either hard or easy intelligence test manipulations, and were told they would be judged by a group rather than a single interviewer.

We again found a significant interaction between the trait manipulation conditions and brand on the rate of display/obscure behavior observed (β=-2.20, Wald(120)=8.36, p<.01), but in the opposite direction. As predicted and in contrast with Study 1, participants in the low intelligence condition were now more likely to display the low vs. high intelligence brand (66.7% vs. 33.3%; $\chi^2(1,60)=6.67$, p<.01). Again, individuals with high self-evaluations on the salient trait did not display or obscure either brand at a rate greater than chance ($M_{\text{Low Intelligence Brand}}$=36.7%, $M_{\text{High Intelligence Brand}}$=56.7%, p's >. 10). The second study's findings provide preliminary support for the argument that contextual perceptions of risk in delivering a believable impression may moderate acquisitive self-presentation using symbolic props (such as brands), motivating more protective and/or self-concept congruent impression management behavior. We are currently planning a third study to better isolate this moderator between subjects within a single experiment and to replicate current findings with different brands.

Preliminary Conclusions

These studies provide evidence that individuals with low self-evaluations on situationally salient trait dimensions may tactically manage the social visibility of brands in their possession. We find that people display (obscure) a brand possessing positive symbolic trait meaning when they feel relatively under-endowed in that trait, but only when abilities on that trait are perceived to be relatively easy to support in verbal self-presentation. To our knowledge, this paper provides the first direct experimental support regarding the use of objects in self-presentation.

References

Aiken, Leona S. and Stephen G. West (1991), *Multiple Regression: Testing and Interpreting Interactions*, Newbury Park, CA: Sage.

Argo, Jennifer J., Katherine White and Darren W. Dahl (2006), "Social Comparison Theory and Deception in the Interpersonal Exchange of Consumption Information", *Journal of Consumer Research*, 33 (June), 99-108.

Arkin, Robert M. (1981), "Self-Presentation Styles," in *Impression Management Theory and Social Psychological Research*, ed. James T. Tedeschi, New York: Academic Press, 311-333.

DePaulo, Bella M. (1992), "Nonverbal Behavior and Self-Presentation", *Psychological Bulletin*, 111 (2), 203-43.

Feldman, Robert S., Forrest, James A. & Happ, Benjamin R. (2002). "Self-presentation and verbal deception: Do self-presenters lie more?", *Basic and Applied Social Psychology*, 24, 163-70.

Gao, Leilei, S. Christian Wheeler and Baba Shiv (2009), "The "Shaken Self": Product Choices as a Means of Restoring Self-View Confidence", *Journal of Consumer Research*, 36 (June), 29-38.

Goffman, Erving (1959), *The presentation of self in everyday life*, New York: Doubleday.

Jones, Edward E. & Pittman, Thane S. (1982), "Toward a general theory of strategic self-presentation" *Psychological perspectives on the self*, Vol. 1, Jerry Suls (ed.), Hillsdale, NF: Erlbaum, 231-62.

Schlenker, Barry and Michael F. Weigold (1992), "Interpersonal Processes Involving Impression Regulation and Management", *Annual Review of Psychology*, 443, 133-68.

Swann, William B. Jr., Brett W. Pelham and Douglas S. Krull, "Agreeable Fancy or Disagreeable Truth? Reconciling Self-Enhancement and Self-Verification", *Journal of Personality and Social Psychology*, 57 (5), 782-91.

Wicklund, Robert A. and Peter M. Gollwitzer (1981), "Symbolic Self-Completion, Attempted Influence, and Self-Deprecation", *Basic and Applied Social Psychology*, 2 (2), 89-114.

Between Two Worlds: The World of Goods and the Management of Gay Identity

Bill Pereira, EBAPE/FGV-RJ. FUCAPE Business School, Brazil
Eduardo Ayrosa, EBAPE/FGV–RJ, Brazil[7]

Brazilian culture is often described by sociologists as full of contrasts and dualisms, where opposites concepts cohabitate in soft and constant struggle (Da Matta, 1991, Barbosa 2006, Fry 1982). Despite cultivating symbols and behavior related to freedom and sensuality, Brazilians still hold some strict and conservatory standards of morality. An instance where such dispositions arise is on attitudes towards homosexuality and gays. In a recent survey from the Brazilian Institute of Social Social Research, results from interviews with 2.014 citizens from 150 Brazilian cities show a high level of rejection of homosexuality. On this survey, informants said that they would not feel at ease with public displays of affection between homosexual couples (INSTITUTO BRASILEIRO DE PESQUISA SOCIAL, 2008). Therefore, homosexuality still seems to be a stigmatized behavior in Brazil.

On the other hand, goods, services and marketing activities directed to the gay public-or, using the words of Peñaloza (1996), the *dream market*-have seen a steep growth in Brazil. Gay pride parades in Brazil have attracted more than three million people, and the São Paulo parade is deemed as the world's largest (Silva 2006). Such duality, peculiar to the Brazilian culture, is present even inside the gay culture of Rio de Janeiro, where homosexuals describe their reality as built upon two opposite but complimentary worlds: the gay and the heterosexual.

The present work aims to explore how gay men use consumption to build and manage symbolic barriers and bridges between the gay and the heterosexual worlds they live in. We seek not only to observe the way the informants manage to cross the boundaries between these two worlds, but also, and more important, how these two worlds are described in their life history, and how social interactions with goods and consumption environments help to build the barriers and bridges between the two worlds.

This work in based on data from ethnographic observation that has been taking place in the city of Rio de Janeiro since 2005. Data collection is based on field notes prepared by one of the authors, as well as long in-depth interviews with 19 gay men that currently live in this city. Informants are openly gay men, with gender identity fully established, that frequently go to gay venues, shops, bars, nightclubs, and all sorts of and consumption environments. Interviews were transcribed and analyzed along with ethnographic field notes. Data analysis involved careful reading and codification of all data, in a process that has been repeated several times upon the same set of data in order to have a full grasp of the narratives. As suggested by Belk *et alii* (1988), we adopted techniques for interpretive studies that included member checks, use of photographs, and analysis of secondary data such as magazines and advertising directed to the gay public (Kates 2002, Belk *et alii* 1988).

Stigma is related to a mark of social inferiority that, apparently or not, a dominant group imposes another. Goffman's (1986) approach about stigma is strongly related to the question concerning identity. According to him, the stigmatized person carries a "spoiled identity", since such identity is seen by the dominant group as shameful and depreciative to its bearer (Crocker at. Al., 1998; Hogg, Hilbbert e Piancentini, 2008). It is important to stress that the stigmatized attributes are culture- and context-dependent. What is seen as a stigma in one culture or context may not be seen the same way in another situation. After all, what is stigmatized is, in fact, not the stigma attribute, but what it represents. For instance, markings of the homosexual condition may be seen as a stigma in smaller cities, where social control over the conduct of the citizen is stronger, than on great metropolitan areas, where the social grids are looser (see Douglas & Isherwood , 1979).

Homosexuality, the homosexual subject, and the "gay man", are inventions dated on the 19th century. Since the second half of the 19th century, the homosexual practice became to define a special kind of person, and consequently, a new social category, namely the homosexual, which came to be marked as a deviant. Persons who, voluntarily or not, were framed in this category, began to live a secret life, marked by segregation (Kates, 1998, Silva, 2006, Trevissan, 2002; Foucault, 1988). Such a "secret life" provided the fertile ground for the development of a whole subculture, the gay culture, with its own behavioral codes, discourse, norms, values, and its own set of social identities. When forming a gay identity, during the process of "getting out of the closet", individuals in this condition use profusely the social meanings attached to goods and services in order to reach the new homosexual identity (Kates, 1998 , 2002).

First conclusions of this study show that gay men's culture actually involve an active symbolic construction of both a gay and a straight world. What seems to be a simplistic division is, in fact, the representation of two separate and complimentary symbolic domains in which gay men live and, depending on the context, manage their social identities. The division of these two worlds lies not only in gay men's imagination, but also in their choices of clothing, accessories, and places like clubs, restaurants, or the beach. Nevertheless, it is through ritualistic activities that the gay men symbolically incorporate these goods, services and places in their culture (McCracken, 2002). This way, through consumption, they attribute meaning to the world. Consumption goods and rituals, then, become instruments of the gay culture to build and manage the gay identity throughout the gay and straight worlds.

References

Barbosa, Lívia and CAMPELL, Collin.. O consumo nas ciências sociais (2006), *Cultura, Consumo e Identidade*. Rio de Janeiro: Editora da Fundação Getulio Vargas.

DaMatta, Roberto e Drury, John (1991), *Carnivals, Rogues, and Heroes: An Interpretation of the Brazilian Dilemma*, Virginia: Notre Tame Press.

Belk, Russell W., John F. Sherry, Jr., and Melanie Wallendorf (1988), "A Naturalistic Inquiry into Buyer and Seller Behavior at a Swap Meet," *Journal of Consumer Research*, 14 (March) 449-470.

Croker, J. e cols. .(1998) Social StigmaIn: Gilbert, D.; FISKE, S. *The Handbook of Social Psychology*, v. 02, p. 504-553, McGraw Hill.

Douglas, M. e B. Isherwood (1979), *The World of Goods: Towards an Anthropology of Consumption*. London: Routledge.

[7]The author would like to thanks the support from Conselho Nacional de Pesquisa Cientifica (CNPq)

Foucault, Michael (1988). *História da Sexualidade I: A Vontade do Saber*. Rio de Janeiro: Edições Graal.
Goffman, Erving. (1986) *Stigma: Notes on the Management of Spoiled Identity,* New York: Touchstone Book.
Hogg, margareth; Hibbert, sally and Piacentini, Maria (2008), Consumption and social stigma in identity projects: stories from fostered children, In Consumer Culture Conference, (July), Boston.
Instituto Brasileiro de Pesquisa Social (2008). *Pesquisa Nacional sobre cidadania e sexualidade*. São Paulo: Editora de Pesquisa Social.
Kates, Steven M. *Twenty Million New Customers! Understanding Gay Men's Consumer Behavior* (1998). New York: Harrigton Park Press.
______, The Protean Quality of Subcultural Consumption: An Ethnographic Account of *Gay* Consumers (2002). *Journal of Consumer Research*. v. 29, p. 383-399.
McCracken, Grant. *Cultura e Consumo: novas abordagens ao caráter simbólico dos bens e das atividades de consumo* (2003). Rio de Janeiro: MAUAD.
Peñaloza, Lisa (1996), We're Here, We're Queer, and We're Going Shopping! A Critical Perspective on the Accommodation of *Gays* and Lesbians in the U.S. Marketplace. *Journal of Homosexuality*, v. 31, n. 1/2, p. 9-41.
Silva, Alessandro S. *Marchando pelo Arco-Íris da Política: A Parada Orgulho LGBT na Construção da Consciência Coletiva dos Movimentos LGBT no Brasil, Espanha e Portugal* (2006). Tese de doutorado do Programa de Estudos Pós-Graduados em Psicologia Social -Pontifícia Universidade Católica de São Paulo, São Paulo.
Trevisan, J.S. *Devassos no Paraíso: a homossexualidade no Brasil, da colônia à atualidade* (2000). 5ª edição, Rio de Janeiro: Record.

Emotional Intelligence, Impulse Buying and Self-Esteem: The Predictive Validity of Two Ability Measures of Emotional Intelligence

Paula Peter, San Diego State University, USA
Sukumarakurup Krishnakumar, North Dakota State University, USA

Abstract

The present study tests for reliable measurement and criterion validity of two ability measures of emotional intelligence: the Consumer Emotional Intelligence Scale (CEIS, 2008) and the Mayer Salovey Caruso Emotional Intelligence Test (MSCEIT, 2002). In specific, we examine EI's influence on impulse buying and self-esteem and how different functional areas of EI uniquely affect these two constructs. The results provide new empirical insights regarding the criterion validity of different measures of EI in the context of consumer research.

Emotional Intelligence (EI) is a set of four broad categories of abilities that together enable individuals to perceive, use, understand, and manage emotions in themselves and others to achieve productive and/or positive ends (Mayer, Roberts, & Barsade, 2008; Mayer and Salovey 1997).

Kidwell, Hardesty, and Childers (2008) have developed the Consumer Emotional Intelligence Scale (CEIS) based on the classic measure of emotional intelligence, the Mayer, Salovey, Caruso Emotional Intelligence Test (MSCEIT; Mayer, Salovey, and Caruso, 2002). The CEIS differs from MSCEIT, in that it is shorter (18 items) and domain specific (marketing), whereas the MSCEIT is longer (141 items) and domain-generic.

Kidwell, Hardesty and Childers (2008) empirically showed that the CEIS is a better predictor of consumer decision making than MSCEIT. The present study aims to provide new and additional empirical insights regarding the criterion and predictive validity of CEIS vs. MSCEIT. We select impulsive buying and self-esteem as important consumer behavior constructs in which the ability to reason about emotions could impact decision quality. Additionally, we also included personality to test incremental predictive validity of EI.

Impulse buying and EI

Impulse buying could be described as unplanned and often uncontrolled urge to buy products. Recent research on impulse buying (e.g. Verplanken et al 2005) suggests that people engage in quick buying mostly due to affective reasons. Therefore, it is important to understand the ability of a consumer to: (a) differentiate between emotions; (b) use emotions to guide thoughts and behavior.

The perceiving emotions branch helps individuals to accurately identify the different emotions that could be elicited as a result of a purchase decision. The cognitive facilitation branch helps individuals to prioritize, think, and act in judiciously based on how they feel.

Because impulsive purchases are made quickly and often driven by hedonic or emotional considerations, we hypothesize that each of these branches and the overall EI will negatively influence impulsive buying behavior.

Self-Esteem and EI

Self-esteem is defined as "how much value people place on themselves" (Baumeister et al. 2003). The interaction between the cognitive and affective components that underlines the construct highlights the fact that affective information is being used to form attitudes of oneself over the long term. Therefore, an individual with higher levels of EI-abilities should be able to reason with and modify emotional information so that over the long term, a positive overall self-evaluation is formed.

The understanding emotions-branch helps individuals to understand the complexities of emotions that are felt. The management branch helps individuals modify the possible negative emotions in frustration into positive emotions, thereby potentially producing a positive self-evaluation or higher self-esteem. Therefore, we hypothesize that each of these branches and the overall EI will positively influence self-esteem.

Method

A total of 152 students (68 females and 79 males) from a southwestern university completed an online study in a controlled environment (lab) for extra credit. The online study included ability measures of EI (MSCEIT 2003 and CEIS 2008), impulse buying (Rook and Fisher 1995), self-esteem (Rosenberg 1965), personality (TIPI) and general demographics. The subjects had 50 minutes to complete the survey and the order of the questions was randomized.

Results and Analysis

To compare the CEIS's and MSCEIT's effects on impulse buying and self-esteem, we compared bivariate correlations between EI scores computed by each of those scales, impulse buying and self-esteem. Both EI scales significantly predicted impulse buying and self-esteem and the correlations weren't statistically different. We also used separate hierarchical regression analyses with personality added at step 1 and CEIS (regression 1) or MSCEIT (regression 2) in step 2. When this was used to predict impulse buying, CEIS significantly added variance over and above personality (β=-.18, ΔR^2=.03, both p<.05), whereas MSCEIT did not. Both CEIS and MSCEIT added significant variance over personality when used to predict self-esteem.

In order to look at the relationship between impulse buying and EI, and self-esteem and EI, we created a combined EI-index created by the mean of normal scores from CEIS and MSCEIT. A hierarchical regression analysis was done with impulse buying or self-esteem as the dependent variable. EI negatively and significantly predicted impulse buying behavior (β=-.21, ΔR^2=.04, both p<.05) and self-esteem (β=.25, ΔR^2=.06, both p<.01) over and above the influence of personality variables.

To test our hypotheses related to the branches of EI, experience and reasoning area-scores obtained from MSCEIT and CEIS were normalized and averaged to form a combined index. Then, those experiential and reasoning area scores were used as independent variables in the regression equation to predict the impulse buying and self-esteem. The experiential area predicted impulse buying (β=-.21, p<.05), whereas the reasoning area did not (β=-.08, ns). The reasoning area predicted self-esteem (β=.27, p<.01), whereas the experiential area did not (β=.09, ns). The results support our hypotheses.

Conclusion

This study was the first attempt to examine incremental, measurement and criterion validity for emotional intelligence in consumer research. Our results suggest that CEIS predicted impulse buying slightly better than MSCEIT over and above the effects of personality.

EI, as a construct, significantly and incrementally predicted both impulse buying (negatively) and self-esteem (positively) over personality. At the branch level, the experiential area of EI was significant in predicting impulse buying and the reasoning area of EI was significant in predicting self-esteem. Our results suggest that consumers might activate different functional areas of emotional intelligence while engaging in consumer behaviors or decisions particularly those in which emotions play an important role.

References

Baumeister, Roy F., Jennifer D. Campbell, Joachim I. Krueger, and Kathleen D.

Vohs (2003), "Does High Self-esteem Cause Better Performance, Interpersonal Success, Happiness, or Healthier Lifestyles ?," *Psychological Science in the Public Interest,* 4 (May), 1-44.

Kidwell, B., Hardesty D. M., & Childers, T. (2008), "Consumer emotional intelligence: Conceptualization, measurement and the prediction of consumer decision making,"*Journal of Consumer Research, 35*(1), 154-166.

Mayer, J., Roberts R. & Barsade, S.G. (2008), "Human Abilities: Emotional Intelligence," *Annual Review of Psychology, 59,* 507-536.

Mayer, J. D., & Salovey, P. (1997), "What is emotional intelligence," in J. D. Mayer & D.J. Sluyter (Eds.), *Emotional development and emotional intelligence: Educational implications* (pp. 3-34), New York: Basicbooks, Inc.

Mayer, J. D., Salovey, P., & Caruso D. (2002), *Mayer-Salovey-Caruso Emotional Intelligence Test (MSCEIT)*, Toronto, Ontario: Multi-Health Systems, Inc

Rook, D. W., & Fisher, R. J. (1995), "Normative influences on impulsive buying behavior," *Journal of Consumer Research*, 22(3), 305-313.

Rosenberg, M. (1965). *Society and the adolescent self-image.* Princeton, NJ: Princeton University Press.

Salovey, Peter and Mayer, John D. (1990), "Emotional Intelligence," *Imagination, Cognition and Personality, 9* (3), 185-211.

Verplanken, B., Herabadi, A.G., Perry, J.A. and Silvera, D.H. (2005), "Consumer style and health: the role of impulsive buying in unhealthy eating," *Psychology and Health*, Vol. 20, pp. 429-41.

The Role of Innovativeness in Environmentally Conscious Consumer Behavior

Diane M. Phillips, Saint Joseph's University, USA
Basil G. Englis, Berry College, USA
Michael R. Solomon, Saint Joseph's University, USA

Abstract

This study seeks to improve the predictive utility of the attitude-behavior link within the realm of environmentally responsible consumption. Using a sample of over 1400 American consumers, we collected data on attitudes about the environment, proclivity for new and innovative ideas, and a wide variety of behaviors with respect to the environment. We find ample evidence to suggest that consumer innovativeness may help bridge the attitude-behavior disconnect by providing an important mediating effect between environmentally conscious attitudes and behaviors.

Why is Predicting Behavior so Difficult?

There is currently a disconnect between consumers' environmental attitudes and behaviors. Marketing decision-makers need evidence that a distinct segment of consumers, making up a substantial number of individuals, will act on their pro-environmental attitudes. Executives understand that it's not enough for customers to say they want green products; they need to "walk the walk" and actually choose these options over other alternatives. The primary purpose of this study is to take a step toward closing this disconnect; we find that innovativeness may be the vehicle by which we can do this.

Why does this disconnect occur at all? Perhaps we should not be surprised. Years of attitude research demonstrate that attitudes don't necessarily align with behavior. With regard to the environmental attitude-behavior link, there are a few additional barriers to behavior. One impediment is of our own making. Consumers may counterargue against green claims because of reports of widespread green-washing. Almost one-fourth of American consumers say they have "no way of knowing" if a product is green or actually does what it claims (Center for Media Research 2009). Because of this, some consumers rely increasingly on third party certifications to determine if a company actually lives up to its green claims (Zmuda and Parekh 2008).

If we assume that green-washing is not the sole culprit, what other impediments make it sometimes difficult for consumers to translate their pro-environmental attitudes into action? Some consumers cite factors in the immediate purchase environment, such as cost and availability (Mintel 2006). Consumer researchers have found a myriad of other constructs that have impacted pro-environmental behavior, such as feelings of empathy (Lee and Holden 1999), perceptions of morality (Borgmann 2000; Caruana 2007), lifestyles (Gilg, Barr, and Ford 2005), gender identity (Dobscha and Ozanne 2001), perceptions of risk (Böhm and Pfister 2008; Lee and Holden 1999), social connectedness (Dolan 2002), demographics (Im, et al. 2003, Hough 2007) and, not surprisingly, price (cf., Anonymous 2008).

Why Innovativeness?

While the issue of environmentalism is not new, for many consumers the specific actions available to them should they wish to ameliorate ecological problems are. Thus, we believe a focus on how consumers come to terms with new and innovative ideas and behaviors will provide greater predictive utility, above and beyond attitudes alone, to our model. Generally speaking, consumer innovativeness is a consumer's predisposition to seek out and be accepting of "new products and brands rather than remain with previous choices and consumption patterns" (Steenkamp, Hofstede, and Wedel 1999). Innovativeness is derived from a consumer's own personality and cognitive style (cf., Goldsmith and Hoffacker 1991, Midgley and Dowling 1993). Researchers propose that we can best describe innovativeness as a generalized predisposition to try new products (Im, Bayus, and Mason 2003). These researchers suggest that innovative consumers are generally more accepting of risk, are eager to try new things, and like to share their discoveries with others (Im, et al. 2003). For most consumers, environmentally responsible behaviors and green products are new. Therefore, within this scope, a willingness to enact these new behaviors and try these new products are innovative actions for these consumers.

Consumers can express their concern for the environment with a wide variety of different behaviors, from recycling their newspapers to riding a bike to work. We also believe that a more generalized characteristic of acceptance of risk and willingness to try new things is in sync with a broad inventory of pro-environmental behaviors. Therefore, when we provide consumers with a variety of behavioral choices (rather than a fixed set of choices), we believe that global consumer innovativeness will provide a useful vehicle by which we can better understand how consumers might proceed through the process of turning their pro-environmental attitudes into pro-environmental behaviors.

In brief:

H1: environmentally relevant attitudes will positively impact environmentally relevant behaviors

H2: global consumer innovativeness will positively impact environmentally relevant behaviors

H3: environmentally relevant attitudes will positively impact global consumer innovativeness

Taken together, we predict that environmentally relevant attitudes will impact global innovativeness which will in turn impact environmentally relevant behaviors. This suggests a meditational impact of global innovativeness on environmentally relevant behaviors.

Method

1443 adult consumers from an online consumer panel filled out a series of measures, including environmental attitudes (Dunlap, et al. 2000), global innovativeness (Tellis, et al. 2003), and behaviors (MacDonald and Oates 2006). All measures achieved high levels of reliability.

Results

Attitudes Impact Behaviors(H1). The attitudes measure that we used had three primary dimensions: Affinity for New Ideas, Nature Rules, and Humans Rule. We regressed environmentally relevant behaviors on the three environmental attitudes. The overall model was significant ($F_{(3, 1439)}$=53.933, p<.0001) as was the effect of Nature Rules (t=6.732, p<.0001) and Humans Rule (t=-5.555, p<.0001). H1 largely supported.

Global Innovativeness Impacts Behaviors (H2). The innovativeness measure we used also had three primary dimensions: Affinity for New Ideas, Early Adopter, and Distrust of New Products. We regressed environmental behaviors on global consumer innovativeness and found that the overall model was significant ($F_{(3,1439)}$=73.071, p<.0001) as were two of the three innovation dimensions. Affinity for New Ideas was strong and positive (t=13.843, p<.0001) and Early Adopter was significant and negative (t=-3.268, p<.001). Further analyses revealed a strong correlation between these two constructs and that most of the impact was due to Affinity for New Ideas. H2 partially supported.

Attitudes Impact Innovativeness(H3). We regressed Affinity for New Ideas dimension on the three dimensions of the NEP scale. The overall model was significant ($F_{(3,1439)}$=77.937, p<.0001) and each of the dimensions was significant. Specifically, Nature Rules was significant and positive (t=15.060, p<.0001), Humans Rule was significant and positive (t=8.326, p<.000), and Growth Limits was significant and negative (t=-4.661, p<.0001). H3 largely supported.

Innovativeness Plays a Mediational Role. We performed a 3-part test of mediation (Baron & Kenney 1986). The first two steps are described above. In the third step, we regressed pro-environmental behaviors on Nature Rules, Humans Rule, Growth Limits, and Affinity for New Ideas. In order for mediation to occur, the effects of the other variables must be significantly reduced and the effect of Affinity for New Ideas has to be strong. This is exactly what occurred. Specifically, the overall model was strong and significant ($F_{(4,1438)}$=96.697, p<.0001), the only significant effect of attitudes was Humans Rule (t=-8.843, p<.0001), and importantly, the strength of Affinity for New Ideas increased (t=14.225, p<.0001).

Conclusion

Innovativeness plays an important role in helping to bridge the divide between environmental attitudes and environmental behaviors. Indeed, the primary driver of the process is the concept of Affinity for New Ideas. This indicates that it is this consumer who is most open to and accepting of new ideas that will be at the forefront of this new consumer movement.

Abbreviated References

Baron, Reuben M. and David A. Kenny (1986), "The Moderator-Mediator Variable Distinction in Social Psychological Research: Conceptual, Strategic, and Statistical Considerations," *Journal of Personality and Social Psychology*, 51 (6), 1173-1182.

Dunlap, R. E. V. L., Kent D.; Mertig, Angela G.; Jones, Robert Emmet (2000). "Measuring Endorsement of the New Ecological Paradigm: A Revised NEP Scale." *Journal of Social Issues* 56(3): 425-442.

Goldsmith, Ronald E. and Charles F. Hofacker (1991), "Measuring Consumer Innovativeness," *Journal of the Academy of Marketing Science*, 19 (3), 209-221.

Im, Subin, Barry L. Bayus, and Charlotte H. Mason (2003), "An Empirical Study of Innate Consumer Innovativeness, Personal Characteristics, and New-Product Adoption Behavior," *Journal of the Academy of Marketing Science*, Winter 31 (1), 61-73.

Lee, Julie Anne and Stephen J.S. Holden (1999), "Understanding the Determinants of Environmentally Conscious Behavior," *Psychology & Marketing*, Vol. 16(5), 373-392.

McDonald, S. and Oates, C.J. (2006). "Sustainability: consumer perceptions and marketing strategies." *Business Strategy and the Environment* 15 (3) 157-70.

Midgley, F. David and Grahame R. Dowling (1993), "A Longitudinal Study of Product Form Innovation: The Interaction Between Predispositions and Social Messages," *Journal of Consumer Research*, Vol. 19 (March), 611-625.

Mintel Group, The (2006), "Green Living-US," *Mintel International Group Limited*, September.

Steenkamp, Jan-Benedict E.M, Frenkel ter Hofstede, and Michel Wedel (1999), "A Cross-National Investigation into the Individual and National Cultural Antecedents of Consumer Innovativeness," *Journal of Marketing*, Vol. 63, April, 55-69.

Tellis, Gerard J., Stephan Stremersh, Eden Yin (2003), "The International Takeoff of New Products: The Role of Economics, Culture, and Country Innovativeness," *Marketing Science*, Vol. 22, No. 2, 188-208.

Effects of Model Body Size and Product Price on Advertising Effectiveness, Purchase Intention, and Body-Related Behaviors

Maxim Polonsky, University of Connecticut, USA
Ioannis Kareklas, University of Connecticut, USA

Marketers claim that thin models are very efficient in selling products (Gillian 2000). Although women generally feel thin fashion models are more elegant and interesting (Martin et al., 2007), research findings on exposure to thin models and advertising effectiveness are mixed. Dittmar and Howard (2004) have shown that while the exposure to thin ideals in ads may harm an individual's body esteem, there is no difference between thin and average-size models in terms of advertising effectiveness (i.e. product and ad evaluation, and purchase intention). On the other hand, it can be argued that after exposure to ads featuring thin models, women may feel worse about themselves, while actually feeling better about the brands and products advertised. In addition, research findings show that consumers generally associate thin with happiness, desirability, and status (Tiggermann 2003).

When asked about the most important aspects in women's life, approximately fifty percent of American females indicate their shape and weight (The Downing Street Group, LLC 2007). Especially for young women, pressures to be thin contribute to lower self-esteem, body image disturbances, and eating disorders, with as many as fifty percent of undergraduate females expressing body dissatisfaction (Bearman et al., 2006). Media exposure has been shown to affect womens'' body esteem by a vast variation of a "thin is in" message.

Research shows that between 1970–1990, the emphasis on fitness increased, and the body shape of models tended to become thinner (Guillen and Barr 1994). A content analysis of popular fashion magazines from 1959 to 1999 found a significant decrease in models' body sizes during the 80s and 90s (Sypeck et al., 2004). For example, Botta (1999), found that exposure to thin body sizes had an influence on young female's endorsement of the ideal thin body and the likelihood to use media models to define what their own bodies should look like. The relationship between exposure to thin-ideal and body image disturbances was also demonstrated in experimental research (Bessenoff 2006; Dittmar and Howard 2004) and supported by two meta-analytic reviews (Grabe et al., 2008; Groesz et al., 2002).

Two important moderators of the relationship between exposure to thin ideals in the media and body-related disturbances are social comparison tendency and thin-ideal internalization. Internalization of a thin-ideal has been viewed as an important risk factor that contributes to the development of eating disorders. Thin-ideal internalization refers to the extent to which an individual accepts the thin-ideal standard of beauty and attractiveness as her own and engages in behaviors that purportedly help to approximate these standards (Thompson et al., 1999).

As a theory, social comparison posits that individuals compare themselves to others to determine their own relative levels of abilities (Festinger 1954). There are two directions for social comparison: an upward comparison that is made when comparison others are perceived to be more fortunate; and a downward comparison that refers to less fortunate comparison others.

Research suggests that when discrepancies between the self and the comparison standard arise, people are motivated to change the self to be more like the comparison standard. Upward comparisons in particular lead to negative moods and lower self-esteem (Gibbons and Gerard, 1989). Social comparison processes may be unintentional, environmentally imposed, and even unwanted (Lyubomirsky and Ross, 1997). Richins (1991) pointed out that that social comparison with media models has unfavorable consequences for female body esteem, since the media body ideal is unattainable. That is why women who are more likely to compare their body to media models have higher levels of body dissatisfaction and lower levels of self-esteem (Stormer and Thompson 1996).

The aforementioned literature illustrates a potential marketing dilemma: images that are most effective in selling products may also harm consumers the most. In our experiment we employ a between-subject 3 x 2 factorial design, investigating the effect of exposure condition (ads featuring thin models, plus-size models, and average models) and price (low and high) on the following outcome variables: 1) advertising effectiveness (attitude toward the ad, purchase intention); 2) body-related behavioral intentions (to get cosmetic surgery, to exercise or diet excessively); and 3) willingness to eat an offered cookie. We introduce a price variable because, as mentioned above, a thin ideal is associated with status. We manipulate price and attempt to investigate whether price interacts with model body size to create the perception of quality and to elicit generally more favorable attitudes toward advertisements.

The location for the online experiment was a computer lab with a sitting capacity of 20 people. Participants had to come to the lab because we were interested in observing direct behavior of taking an offered cookie. Upon login onto the website, participants were randomized into one of the five conditions and told that that they are participating in a marketing research study that explores different communication and appeal strategies (print vs. video, reading detailed information versus watching a short ad, sex appeal vs. humor, etc.) for two product categories–computers and women shoes. After completing a pre-test, participants in each condition were referred to CNET.com page "Best 5 desktops" (http://reviews.cnet.com/best-desktops/?tag=leftColumnArea1.0) or a similar updated page, and asked to read a short one-paragraph review for each of the five computers. Next, participants were asked to answer filler questions about their liking, preference, and purchase intention for any of the reviewed computers. Upon completion, study participants were exposed to the experimental ad and filled out a post-test questionnaire that consisted of: a) questions about advertising effectiveness (e.g. ad evaluation, purchase intention), and b) questions about attitudes toward and behavioral intentions to engage in such behaviors as cosmetic surgery, excessive exercise, and dieting. Participants were deceived that the later part of the post-test was an unrelated small scale survey study that was to be used in designing health interventions.

Our preliminary results suggest that thin body size paired with high price effectively signaled product quality and generated more favorable attitudes toward the ad among study participants. The same experimental condition however, had a positive effect on body-related disturbances. We focus our discussion on these controversial findings as well as on the influence of individual difference moderators.

Key References

Bearman, Sarah, Katherine Presnell, Erin Martinez, and Eric Stice (2006), "The Skinny on Body Dissatisfaction: A Longitudinal Study of Adolescent Girls and Boys," *Journal of Youth and Adolescence, 35,* 229–241.

Bessenoff, Gayle R. (2006), "Can the Media Affect Us? Social Comparison, Self-discrepancy, and the Thin Ideal," *Psychology of Women Quarterly, 30*, 239-259.

Botta, Ranee A. (1999), "Television Images and Adolescent Girls' Body Image Disturbance," *Journal of Communication, 49*(2), 22-42.

Dittmar, Helga and Sarah Howard (2004), "Thin-ideal Internalization and Social Comparison Tendency as Moderators of Media Models' Impact on Women's Body-focused Anxiety," *Journal of Social and Clinical Psychology, 23*, 747-770.

Festinger, Leon (1954), "A Theory of Social Comparison Processes," *Human Relations, 7,* 117–140.

Gibbons, Frederick X. and Meg Gerard (1989), "Effects of Upward and Downward Social Comparison on Mood States," *Journal of Social and Clinical Psychology, 1,* 14–31.

Gillian, A. (2000, may 31). Skinny models 'send unhealthy message'. The Guardian, p. 7.

Grabe, Shelly, Monique L. Ward, and Janet S. Hyde (2008), "The Role of the Media in Body Image Concerns Among Women: A Meta-analysis of Experimental and Correlational Studies," *Psychological Bulletin, 134 (3),* 460-476.

Groesz, Lisa M., Michael P. Levine, and Sarah Murnen (2002), "The Effect of Experimental Presentation of Thin Media Images on Body Satisfaction: A Meta-analytic review," *International Journal of Eating Disorders, 31(1),* 1–16

Guillen, E., and Barr, S. (1994), "Nutrition, Dieting, and Fitness Messages in a Magazine for Adolescent Women, 1970-1990," *Journal of Adolescent Health, 15 (6),* 464-472.

Lyubomirsky, Sonja and Lee Ross (1997), "Hedonic Consequences of Social Comparison: A Contrast of Happy and Unhappy People," *Journal of Personality and Social Psychology, 73,* 1141-1157.

Martin, Brett, Ekant Veer, and Simon Pervan (2007), "Self-referencing and Consumer Evaluations of Larger-sized Female Models: A Weight Locus of Control Perspective," Marketing Letters, *18 (3),* 197-209.

Richins, Marsha L. (1991), "Social Comparisons and Idealized Images of Advertising," *Journal of Consumer Research, 18(1),* 71-83.
Stormer, Susan M. and Kevin J. Thompson (1996), "Explanations of Body Image Disturbance: A Test of Maturational Status, Negative Verbal Commentary, Social Comparison, and Sociocultural Hypotheses," *International Journal of Eating Disorders, 19,* 193-202.
Sypeck, Mia F., James J. Gray, and Anthony Ahrens (2004), "No Longer Just a Pretty Face: Fashion Magazines' Depictions of Ideal Female Beauty From 1959 to 1999," *International Journal of Eating Disorders* **36**, 342–347.
Tiggemann, Marika (2003), "Media Exposure, Body Dissatisfaction and Disordered Eating: Television and Magazines Are Not the Same!" *European Eating Disorders Review, 11,* 418-430.
The Downing Street Group, LLC (2007). The Dove report: Challenging beauty. Available at < www.campaignforrealbeauty.com/uploadedFiles/challenging_beauty.pdf>.
Thompson, Kevin, Leslie J. Heinberg, Madeline N. Altabe, and Stacey Tantleff-Dunn, S. (1999), *Exacting Beauty: Theory, Assessment, and Treatment of Body Image Disturbance*, Washington, DC: APA.

"Please Drink Responsibly!" The Effectiveness of Responsibility Messages in Alcohol Product Advertising

Maxim Polonsky, University of Connecticut, USA
Ioannis Kareklas, University of Connecticut, USA

Among important factors influencing national alcohol consumption is alcohol advertising. Longitudinal studies have shown that exposure to alcohol advertising leads to drinking initiation, and to an increase in drinking rates (Snyder et al., 2006). Alcohol advertising on television keeps growing, especially alcohol advertising toward American youth (Center on Alcohol Marketing and Youth (CAMY) 2007), while alcohol responsibility advertising remains low.

CAMY defines responsibility advertising as alcohol industry-sponsored ads (corporate PSAs) in which responsibility (drinking responsibly, avoiding drunk driving, and addressing underage drinking) is the primary focus of the message. Content analysis using Nielsen data found that corporate PSAs make up less than three percent of the nearly 1.5 million alcohol televised advertising from 2001 to 2005 (CAMY 2007).

CAMY report (2007) dismisses brief warning messages within product ads as "ineffective" and cites Fox et al.'s (1998) study as the evidence. Such dismissal however is puzzling and unfortunate because: a) Fox's study actually concluded that responsibility messages had warning value, albeit a limited one (p. 57), and b) the investigated warnings were all print-based and thusly differed from video messages that last several seconds. The aim of the current study is to address the shortcomings in the literature and to investigate the effectiveness of brief warning messages as it relates to presentation modality.

There is no general consensus on the effectiveness of responsibility messages in alcohol advertisements. Snyder and Blood (1992) as well as Ringold (2002) found support for a boomerang effect under which the exposure to alcohol warnings actually created more favorable attitudes toward alcohol among viewers; however, MacKinnon and Lapin (1998) were not able to find a similar effect in two replication experiments. Just as Fox et al. (1998), these studies investigated print ads. Studies investigating TV ads specifically focused on the effectiveness of corporate PSAs. These studies concluded that responsibility messages sponsored by alcohol companies are ambiguous, and are never dissociated from the actual alcohol consumption and product promotion (Agostinelli and Grube, 2002; CAMY, 2007; Dejong et al., 1992).

The Wine Institute and the Distilled Spirits Council of the United States self-regulate their advertising practices using self-initiated marketing and advertising guidelines. Interestingly, the guidelines do not address either corporate PSA or on responsibility messages within the product ads (ICAP, 2001).

In study 1, we content analyzed brief responsibility messages within the product ads (N=596) of companies promoting alcohol in 2007 on national network and cable television. We found that the most common channel for the responsibility message was through text on the screen (93% of the total advertisements); a small percentage used a voice over only (5%); and 16% used both text and voice messages. Responsibility messages lasted 3 seconds on average for 15 and 30 second spots, and appeared closer to the end of a spot. In addition, 58% of text messages were combined with other textual information in a way that was very difficult to read.

Such numbers are in conflict with existing evidence that: a) messages using both video and textual information are more likely to be remembered compared to one channel alone (Krugman et al., 1994), b) when video and text are shown simultaneously, individuals pay more attention to video (Kallenbach et al., 2007), c) verbal information leads to greater learning relative to textual information (Mcneil, 2005), and d) primacy effect elicits higher recall and elaboration relative to recency placement (Brunel and Nelson 2003; Haugtvedt and Wegener 1994). In other words, if there was a formula on how to strategically place a warning message within an ad it would have to be a complete opposite of what was found. This is ironic, because effective placement and modality of responsibility messages may actually be more important and beneficial to manufacturers and not consumers. Arguably, consumers' attention during and recall after the message presentation may lead to positive evaluations of a product manufacturer as socially responsible. It is relevant to mention that the portrayal of responsibility by alcohol companies was found to be directly correlated to increases in market share, which is a major goal for the industry (Dejong et al., 1992).

The arguments presented above indicate that research on modality of responsibility messages in advertising is long overdue How long should the warnings last in order to be noticed? How should the warning messages be presented? Our second study employs a 4 x 2 between-subjects factorial design, investigating the effect of responsibility message presentation mode (no message, text only, voice only, text + voice) and advertising length (15-second ads and 30-second ads) on the dependent variables of effectiveness: attention and recall, short-term drinking intention, attitudes toward manufacturer. Current drinking behaviors and tendency to enjoy advertising will be tested as moderators. We use industry-manufactured ads as our stimuli. Following our review, we first propose the following hypotheses and research questions regarding message presentation.

H1: Combined text and voice message presentation mode will be more effective than text or voice only.
H2: Voice only message presentation will be more effective than text only message presentation.
RQ1: Is text only presentation mode more effective than no presentation mode?

Because it is not clear whether responsibility messages in 15-second ads will differ in effectiveness from those in 30-second ads, we ask the following:

RQ2: Is there a difference in message effectiveness between 30-second ads and 15-second ads?

Responsibility messages last for approximately three seconds for both length formats, and make up 10 percent and 20 percent of the total length respectively for 30 and 15-second ads. It is possible that higher percentage of the total length will be more effective.

It is important to note that in the current experiment, message effectiveness will be measured in more than one way (i.e. message recall as well as drinking intentions). Hence it is possible that even coherently and effectively presented message might actually not have any impact on individual's responsible drinking behavior. Quite the contrary, exposure to alcohol advertising may overweight the warning message and lead to higher degrees of drinking intentions.

Since there is a potential for responsibility message effectiveness to have a positive effect on manufacturer's perceived social responsibility and good will, we ask:

RQ3: Is there a relationship between message effectiveness and perceived corporate responsibility?

The follow-up experiments will use similar 4 x 2 designs to specifically investigate the effectiveness of primacy and recency placement strategies.

Key References

Agostinelli, Gina and Joel W. Grube (2002), "Alcohol Counter-Advertising and The Media: A Review of Recent Research," *Alcohol Research & Health, 26,* 15-21.

Brunel, Frederic F. and Michelle R. Nelson (2003), "Message Order Effects and Gender Differences in Advertising Persuasion," *Journal of Advertising Research, 43 (3),* 330-341.

Center on Alcohol Marketing and Youth (2007), "Youth Exposure to Alcohol Advertising on Television, 2001 to 2007," http://camy.org/research/tv0608/

DeJong, William, Charles K. Atkin, and Lawrence Wallack (1992), "A Critical Analysis of "Moderation" Advertising Sponsored by the Beer Industry," *The Milbank Quarterly. 70,* 661-678.

Fox, R., Krugman, D., Fletcher, J., and Fischer, P. (1998), "Adolescents' Attention to Beer and Cigarette Print Ads and Associated Product Warnings," *Journal of Advertisting, 27 (3),* 57-68

Haugtvedt, Curtis P. and Duane T. Wegener (1994), "Message Order Effects in Persuasion: An Attitude Strength Perspective," *Journal of Consumer Research, 21,* 205-218.

Kallenbach, Jan, Silja Narhi, and Pirkko Oittinen (2007), "Effects of Extra Information on TV Viewers' Visual Attention, Message Processing Ability, and Cognitive Workload," *Computers in Entertainment, 5 (2),* 1-13.

Krugman, D., Fox, R., Fletcher, J., Fischer, P., and Rojas, T. (1994), "Do Adolescents Attend to Warnings in Cigarette Advertising? An Eye-tracking Approach," *Journal of Advertising Research, 34 (6),* 39-52.

Mackinnon, David P. and Angela Lapin (1998), "Effects of Alcohol Warnings and Advertisements: A Test of the Boomerang Hypothesis," *Psychology and Marketing, 15(7),* 707–726.

Mcneill, Andrea (2005), "The Effects of Training, Modality, and Redundancy on the Development of a Historical Inquiry Strategy in a Multimedia Learning Environment," *Dissertation Abstracts International Section A: Humanities and Social Sciences, 65(7-A),* 2478.

Ringold, Debra (2002), "Boomerang Effects in Response to Public Health Interventions: Some Unintended Consequences in the Alcoholic Beverage Market," *Journal of Consumer Policy. 25,* 27-63.

Snyder, Leslie and Deborah Blood (1992), "Caution: Alcohol Advertising and the Surgeon General's Alcohol Warnings May Have Adverse Effects on Young Adults," *Journal of Applied Communication Research,* 37-53.

Snyder, Leslie, Rances F. Milici, Michael Slater, Helen Sun, and Yulia Strizhakova (2006), "Effects of Alcohol Advertising Exposure on Drinking Among Youth," *Arch Pediatrics Adolescent Medicine,* 160, 18-24.

Short-Term and Long-Term Affective Responses: A Comparison between Emotions and Sentiments

Paulo H M Prado, Federal University of Parana, Brazil

Affective responses have been presented in academic literature as important elements in the study of consumer behavior as they influence the evaluation, memory and judgment processes (Gardner, 1985). Some studies have sought to demonstrate that affective responses have a significant impact on the assessment of consumer satisfaction, revising the theories that are restricted only to cognitive responses (Oliver, 1997; Fournier, 1998). The aim of this study is to compare the difference between affective responses of the consumer in the long and short term concerning consumption, contributing towards providing a more accurate definition of them. As shown in the consumer behavior literature, studies that have been done in this respect treat the different affective responses as just "emotions" in an indistinct and limited way, as they believe that the differences between each of the constructs are very subtle (Oliver, 1989; Prado, 2004). According to the authors of cognitive theories, such as Ortony et al (1988), an emotion can be defined as a short-term affective reaction to a specific object. For Lazarus (1991), emotions reflect a constant change in the environment-person relationship and their origin stems from evaluating a subject according to the level of importance of a particular event to a person's well-being. Bagozzi et al. (1999) define emotions as a mental state of readiness that comes from the cognitive assessments or thoughts about an event. A sentiment represents a disposition to respond emotionally to a specific object in the long term; it is a disposition that transforms non-emotional events into emotionally loaded ones (Frijda; Mesquita, Sonnemans; Van Goozen, 1991). Thus, it consists of an evaluation framework that includes relevant concern with the object. Sentiments are dispositional emotions (Shand, 1922, Arnold, 1960). They are affective schemes, with the same structure as emotions (Fiske, 1922).

In the data collection procedure, the respondents were initially asked to indicate their main webmail provider. They were then asked to indicate their Sentiments about it, in a reduced version of the CES (Higgins, 1997) with 24 items on a 10-point scale (from Nothing to Extremely). They were asked about what happened when they last accessed their webmail provider (in a two line sentence), and then they indicated their emotional state at that moment, using the same scale. Both scales are the same based on the premise of Frijda & Mesquita (2000), in which the dimensionality of the two constructs is the same. Having answered the first part of the questionnaire, the participants were randomly exposed to a stimulus related to their webmail provider, one of low intensity (You must re-enter your personal information because it has been lost. Please re-enter it to continue using our services) and another of strong intensity (All your information has been lost, both your personal information and your stored e-mail messages. Please re-enter your personal information to continue using our services). The stimuli were tested to verify their discrimination power. Once again, the respondents were asked to indicate their emotions and their sentiments, using the same scales. The total sample involved 378 respondents, a suitable number for the necessary tests for the purposes of the study.

The constructs were analyzed initially to examine their dimensionality with an EFA, and their validity with a CFA. The results showed the grouping of positive and negative dimensions for sentiments before and after, with adequate internal consistence in both cases. For emotions, the dimensionality was a little diverse, despite positive and negative being separated. A similar result was found for the emotions reported after the introduction of the stimulus.

The strongest stimulus caused an increase of negative affections and a decrease in positive affections, as expected. In the case of Positive Sentiments, there was a significant fall in the average (X_{before}=4.81 for X_{after}=3.31; t=12.882; p<0.0001). For Negative Sentiments, there was a significant increase on average ($X_{befores}$=2.11 for X_{after}=4.28; t=-15.114; p<0.0001). For Positive Emotions, there was a significant fall in the average (X_{before}=4.04 for X_{after}=2.51; t=13.642; p<0.0001). For Negative Emotions, there was a significant increase in the average (X_{before}=1.99 for X_{after}=6.15; t=-32.832; p<0.0001). The results showed that the variation of the responses for emotions before and after were greater than for sentiments.

For the evaluation of the variation of Negative Sentiments, we saw that the before-after effect was significant (F=92.72, p<0.001). But the relationship between the weak and strong stimuli did not produce statistically different results (F=1.92, p=0.166), as well as the interaction between the two factors (F=2.015, p=0.156).

Considering the variation of negative emotions, we found that the before-after effect was significant (F=910.90. p<0.001). Furthermore, the relationship of the weak and strong stimuli was (F=37.21, 0<0.001). The interaction between them was also significant (F=28.58, 0<0.001).

For the evaluation of the variation of Positive Sentiments, we saw that the before-after effect was significant (F=92.72, p<0.001). But the relationship between the weak and strong stimuli did not produce statistically different results (F=1.92, p=0.166), as well as the interaction between the two factors (F=2.015, p=0.156).

Considering the variation of Positive Emotions, we saw that the before-after effect was significant (F=122.16, p<0.001). Meanwhile, the relationship between the strong and weak stimuli was not shown to be statistically significant (F=0.035, p=0.852), like the interaction between the two factors (F=0.121, p=0.728).

In conclusion, the results showed discrimination in the measurement of emotions and sentiments, as well as variations of these affective responses to applied stimuli. This difference suggested that they are different concepts, although they are grouped under one large category in literature. The results also indicated that sentiments tend to suffer less influence from situational aspects. The variations in negative emotions were more intense than those of negative sentiments. This result was not repeated for the modifications of the positive affective responses. In part, this result may be explained by the nature of the stimulus (mostly negative), and by the asymmetric effect of the losses and gains on the responses of consumers.

References

Clore, Gerald. L.; K. Gasper (2000) Sentiment is believing: Some affective influences on belief. In: Frijda, N.; Manstead, A.S.R.; Bem, S. *Emotions and Beliefs–How sentiments influence thoughts.* Cambridge: Cambridge Press, 45-77.

Fournier, Susan (1998) Consumers and their brands: Developing relationship theory in consumer research. *Journal of Consumer Research*, 24(1), 343-373.

Frijda, Nico; B. Mesquita (2000) Beliefs through Emotions. In: Frijda, N.; Manstead, A.S.R.; Bem, S. *Emotions and Beliefs–How sentiments influence thoughts.* Cambridge: Cambridge University Press, 45-77.

Frijda, Nico; B. Mesquita; J. Sonnemans; S. Van Goozen (1991) The duration of affective phenomena of emotions, sentiments and passions. In: Strongman, K. T. *International review of studies on emotion.* 1, England: Wiley.

Gardner, M. P. (1985) Mood States and Consumer Behavior: A Critical Review, *Journal of Consumer Research*, 12, 281-298.

Lazarus, Richard (1991) Progress on a cognitive-motivational-relational theory of emotion, *American Psychologist*, 46, 819-834

Oliver, Richard L. (1989) Processing of the satisfaction response in consumption: a suggested framework and research propositions. *Journal of Consumer Satisfaction/ Dissatisfaction and Complaining Behavior*. 2, 1-15.

Oliver, Richard L. (1997) *Satisfaction: a behavioral perspective on the consumer*. Nova York: McGraw-Hill.

Ortony, Andrew, Gerald L. Clore, Allan Collins (1988) *The Cognitive Structure of Emotions*. Cambridge: Cambridge Press.

Prado, Paulo H.M. (2004) Relationship Evaluation based on Customer view: A Study in Retail Banks. *Doctoral Dissertation: Getulio Vargas Foundation*, São Paulo.

Richins, Martha. (1997) Measuring emotions in the consumption experience. *Journal of Consumer Research*. 24(1), 127-146.

Shand, A.F. (1922) The relations of complex and sentiment. *Journal of Psychology*, 13, 123-129.

Will Dangling the Carrot Make them Eat it? An Exploration of Children's Perceptions Towards Rewards for Healthy Food

Katherine Prater-Racicot, University of Sydney, Australia
Teresa Davis, University of Sydney, Australia
Catherine Sutton-Brady, University of Sydney, Australia

This study explored children's experiences with and perceptions towards rewards for food. This study explores how children perceived rewards for healthy food. A Consumer Socialization framework (Roedder-John, 1999) was applied to understand how a child's consumer socialization stage influences their perceptions towards the attributes of concrete and abstract rewards. Phenomenological interviews were used to gain understanding of children's perspectives and enabled the identification of the attributes of rewards which are most persuasive in influencing children's healthy food choices.

Reference

Roedder John Deborah (1999) Consumer Socialization of Children: A Retrospective Look At Twenty Five Years of Research, *Journal of Consumer Research*, Vol. 26, December (p.183-213)

The Impact of Mood on Consumer Choice: Compromise or Not?

Cheng Qiu, University of Hong Kong, Hong Kong, China

This research investigates how mood influences consumer choice among a low-end option, a middle (compromise) option, and a high-end option. Previous research suggests that mood may affect consumer judgment through different mechanisms (Schwarz and Clore 2007) which bear different implications for the present research. One possibility is that mood may have motivational impact which drives consumer choice. Happy consumers may wish to maintain their pleasant feelings whereas unhappy consumers may seek mood-lifting opportunities (Isen 1984). In this case, consumers are more likely to choose the compromise option if they are in a good mood than if they are in a bad mood (Lin, Yen, and Chuang 2006). This is because the compromise option is perceived to be a safe choice (Simonson 1989). Such a low-risk choice may contribute to maintaining a good mood while at the same time entail less mood-lifting potential than a high-risk one (Nygren et al. 1996; Raghunathan and Pham 1999).

A second possibility is that mood may signal how benign or problematic the environment is and influence information processing (Schwarz and Clore 2007). Happy consumers tend to process information in a top-down manner, which may facilitate seeing the relationship among the options and their respective mood-management property. Happy consumers may therefore be more attracted by the compromise option than those in a neutral mood. When consumers are in a bad mood, however, they tend to process information in a bottom-up manner based on an assessment of individual product features. When this happens, consumers may be less likely to see the relationship among the options and the corresponding mood-management potential. Rather, they may be more sensitive to negative product features than to positive ones, and give the former more weight in their decisions (Adaval 2001). In this case, the low-end option may be assessed most negatively in terms of quality whereas the high-end option may be assessed most negatively in terms of price. Greater weight given to these negative features may lead unhappy consumers to shun the low-end and high-end options, resulting in choosing the compromise option more often than those in a neutral mood. Thus, consumers in both positive and negative moods may be inclined to choose the compromise option.

Further, this research proposes that the first possibility is more likely to occur when mood clarity is high, whereas the second possibility is more likely to occur when mood clarity is low. This is because for the mood-lifting motivation to guide consumer decision, consumers need to assess their current mood and forecast future mood after choice (Andrade 2005). Thus, when consumers have higher (lower) clarity about their current mood, they may be more (less) likely to act in accordance with a mood-lifting motivation. In the previous research demonstrating the first possibility (Lin, Yen, and Chuang 2006), participants assessed their mood before they made the choice, which may have enhanced mood clarity. In the study reported below, participants did not assess their mood until after making product choices. We expect that the relatively low mood clarity may yield a different pattern of findings as suggested by the second possibility.

Experiment

The experiment had a 3 (mood: positive vs. neutral vs. negative) x 2 (justification for choice: provided vs. not provided) between-subjects design. The latter factor was added to show a boundary condition where the predicted mood effect would diminish if people were induced to deliberate over their decisions and make easily justifiable choices.

Method. First, 194 participants were asked to write a happy, neutral, or sad experience which induced mood. Next, in a product survey, they were asked to imagine that they were going to buy a computer monitor, and were considering three options that differed only in viewable size and price—monitor A (17 in., $119), monitor B (19 in., $159), and monitor C (21 in., $199). After seeing the information, participants in the justification-not-provided condition just indicated their choices, whereas participants in the justification-provided condition wrote down the reasons for choices before indicating their decisions. Next, they were asked to imagine they encountered another set of options—monitor A (19 in., $159), monitor B (21 in., $ 199), and monitor C (23 in., $239), and then completed procedures same as those in the first scenario. These two scenarios together can rule out the possibility that participants preferred a particular product that coincided with the compromise option. In the end, participants indicated their mood.

Main Findings. For the first scenario, when not asked to provide justifications, participants were more likely to choose the compromise option when they were in a positive (50%) or negative mood (53%) than when they were in a neutral mood (24%; *z*-values=2.32 and 2.57, *p*-values<.05). In contrast, when participants explained their choices, they were similarly likely to choose the compromise option regardless of mood (44%, 40%, and 38%). Analyses regarding the second scenario provided converging evidence. When justifications were not required, choice shares of the compromise option were larger when participants were in a positive (50%) or negative (59%) mood than when they were in a neutral mood (24%; *z*-values=2.32 and 3.13, *p*-values<.05). When participants explained the reasons for choices, their choices were likely to be consistent with the decision they made in the first scenario. These findings provide initial evidence that both positive and negative moods may lead to more compromise choices than would a neutral mood under low mood clarity circumstances.

Future Research Plan. More data involving multiple product categories will be collected to validate the robustness of the findings. Whether participants assess their mood before or after the choice will be manipulated, such that a comparison between the two conditions would help further reconcile the present findings with the previous ones. Participants' mood clarity tendency will also be measured (Salovey et al. 1995). If the proposed moderation effect of mood clarity is viable, individuals' chronic differences in mood clarity would also have an impact on the mechanism through which mood influences choice.

References

Adaval, Rashmi (2001), "Sometimes It Just Feels Right: The Differential Weighting of Affect-Consistent Product Information," *Journal of Consumer Research* 28 (1), 1-17.

Andrade, Eduardo B. (2005), "Behavioral Consequences of Affect: Combining Evaluative and Regulatory Mechanisms," *Journal of Consumer Research* 32 (December), 355-62.

Isen, Alice M. (1984), "Toward Understanding the Role of Affect in Cognition," in *Handbook of Social Cognition*, vol. 3, eds. Robert Wyer, Jr. and Thomas Srull, Hillsdale, NJ: Erlbaum,179-236.

Lin, Chien-Huang, HsiuJu Rebecca Yen, and Shin-Chieh Chuang (2006), "The Effects of Emotion and Need for Cognition on Consumer Choice Involving Risk," *Marketing Letters*, 17(1), 47-60.

Nygren, Thomas E., Alice M. Isen, Pamela J. Taylor, and Jessica Dulin (1996), "The Influence of Positive Affect on the Decision Rule in Risky Situations: Focus on Outcome (and Especially Avoidance of Loss) Rather Than Probability," *Organizational Behavior and Human Decision Processes* 66 (1), 59-72.

Raghunathan, Rajagopal, and Michel T. Pham (1999), "All Negative Moods Are Not Equal: Motivational Influences of Anxiety and Sadness on Decision Making," *Organizational Behavior and Human Decision Processes* 79 (1), 56-77.

Salovey, P., Mayer, J. D., Goldman, S. L., Turvey, C., & Palfai, T. P. (1995), "Emotional Attention, Clarity, and Repair: Exploring Emotional Intelligence Using the Trait Meta-Mood Scale," in *Emotion, Disclosure, and Health*, ed. J. W. Pennebaker, Washington, DC: American Psychological Association, 125-54.

Schwarz, Norbert and Gerald L. Clore (2007), "Feelings and Phenomenal Experiences," in *Social Psychology: Handbook of Basic Principles*, 2nd edition, eds. E. Tory Higgins and Arie W. Kruglanski, New York: Guilford, 385-407.

Simonson, Itamar (1989), "Choice Based on Reasons: The Case of Attraction and Compromise Effects," *Journal of Consumer Research*, 16(September), 158-74.

Correlates of Cool Identity: Humor, Need for Uniqueness, Materialism, Status Concern and Brand Consciousness

Kaleel Rahman, American University in Dubai, United Arab Emirates
Helene Cherrier, American University in Dubai, United Arab Emirates

Despite some advances in understanding the meaning and origin of cool (Belk, 2006; Bird and Tapp, 2008; O'Donnel and Wardlow, 2000; Nancarrow et. al 2002), literature uncovering the meaning of cool is still in its infancy in consumer research. However, cool is a heavily used term by marketing practitioners. Advertising, web pages, shirts, music lyrics, book titles, business documents and above all people's conversations are example of places where the word cool is used. For example, a simple search in Amazon.com alone produced over 300 titles of published books which have the word cool as part of their titles, primarily with its slang meaning.

The focus of this paper is to examine the meaning of cool from a marketer's point of view. From literature, we identify possible correlates of cool identity. We conceptualize cool identity as the extent to which consumers consider themselves to be cool. One agreement among the researchers is that they consider the origin of contemporary cool to be the African American culture (Belk, 2006; Moore, 2004). It was basically an attitude adopted by African Americans as a defense mechanism against the prejudice they faced and as a form of detachment from their difficult and often insecure working conditions (*Nancarrow et al., 2002*). However, the meaning of cool has evolved. As Belk (2006, p.7) describes it, cool "refers to a person who is admired because she, or more often he, exhibits a nonchalant control of emotions, a rebellious trickster demeanor, an ironic detachment from the regard of others, and a "cool" style of talking, walking, gesturing, and grooming".

As Nancarrow and colleagues (2002) suggest, the meaning of cool has an inner layer which involves personality characteristics of individuals, as well as an outer layer involving aesthetics and lifestyle. One aspect of inner coolness is linked to irony (Pountain and Robbins, 2000). Irony refers to "a sort of humor, ridicule, or light sarcasm, which adopts a mode of speech the meaning of which is contrary to the literal sense of the words" (Webster's, 2009). For example, one thing is said and its opposite implied, as in the comment, "Beautiful weather, isn't it?" made when it is raining or nasty. As Pountain and Robbins (2000) posits, consumers use cool irony as a weapon in defense and important to maintain a protective cool persona. Irony is also known as sick humor and Jewish humor. Hence we propose that humor is positively related to cool identity.

Another aspect of inner coolness is related to uniqueness. Uniqueness involves a feeling that sets individuals apart from the crowd, but in a manner that is appreciated by others. Tian et al. (2001, p. 52) defined consumers' need for uniqueness (CNFU) as "the trait of pursuing differences relative to others through the acquisition, utilization, and disposition of consumer goods for the purpose of developing and enhancing one's self-image and social image". CNFU is a means for satisfying NFU by using possessions creatively, making unpopular consumption choices, and avoiding buying and consuming commonly used products. According to Tian et al. (2001), all individuals use these consumption behaviors to some extent to establish a unique social image. Several authors have identified concepts of coolness related to uniqueness. Mark of distinction, statement of separateness, refusal to accept norms, anti-authoritarian (Nancarrow et. al., 2002); deviance from the mainstream (Moore, 2004); detachment (Pountain and Robbins, 2000); authenticity (Southgate, 2003). Hence we propose that need for uniqueness is positively related to cool identity

We contend that the outer layer of cool is related to several consumer behavior constructs in general and materialism, status concern, and brand consciousness in particular. As Stephens and colleagues (1975, p. 275) suggested, "the importance of outward appearance–the great importance put upon the conspicuous display of wealth as represented by clothes, flashy cars, and other status conferring material goods" play a key role in defining coolness. In writing of generational shifts in values of cool, Moore (2004, p. 72) posits that "command of fashionable clothing and grooming styles were important in establishing status. Stylishness can be linked to cool not only because stylishness is good (therefore cool in a broad sense) but also because stylishness is based on a kind of knowingness and knowingness is a key feature of cool". As Pountain and Robbins (2002, p. 28) argue once cool was "a form of social deviance and rebellion, but that it is now losing this rebellious status and becoming the dominant ethic of late consumer capitalism". This is consistent with several concepts used to describe coolness by different authors: Nancarrow and colleagues (2002)–dress code, flashy clothes, commodities, aesthetics of designer labels, niche brands, and consumption of performance. Southgate (2003, p. 453)–"cool is the currency of all brands". Hence we propose that: Materialism, Status concern and Brand consciousness are positively related to cool identity

A total of 479 undergraduate students at an English medium university in UAE were asked to complete a questionnaire (in which items were randomized) as part of class exercises. The original content of this questionnaire had diverse objectives and cover more issues than those relevant for the present paper. We believe the cosmopolitan nature of students studying in UAE lends itself to undertaking this research. For example, students on average had traveled to several countries and 80% of them had traveled to a Western country. Fifty four percent were male, median age was 20 years, 59% had his/her own car, 47% had a mobile phone worth over US$ 360.

We used sexual identity scale (Stern et. al., 1987) to develop our four-item cool identity scale: "I FEEL as though I am cool", I LOOK as though I am cool", I DO most things in a manner typical of someone who is cool" and "My INTERESTS are mostly those of a person who is cool" (alpha=.86).

For humor, we used three items from Carbelo-Baquero and colleagues (2006). E.g., "Other people tell me that I say funny things" (alpha=.62). For measuring uniqueness, we used highest loaded three items each on three subscales (creative choice counter-conformity; avoidance of similarity; unpopular choice counter-conformity) of need for uniqueness scale by Tian et al. (2001). E.g., "I'm often on the lookout for new products or brands that will add to my personal uniqueness" (alpha=.69, .62, .68). For materialism, we used material values short form six-item scale developed by Richins (2004). E.g., "I admire people who own expensive homes, cars, and clothes" (alpha=.71). For status concern, we used five items from Eastman and colleagues (1997). E.g., "I would buy a product just because it has status" (alpha=.79). For brand consciousness, we used four items from Shim and Gehrt (1996). E.g., "The more expensive brands are usually my choices" (alpha=.71). All items were measured on 7-point Likert scales.

In analyzing the data, we used correlation analysis in SPSS in order to gain some preliminary insight. We averaged the items under each construct to create a single item measure. Our analysis supports all of our proposed relationships. We briefly list the descriptive statistics and correlation results as follows:

- Cool identity (M=4.53, SD=1.37)
- Humor (M=4.88, SD=1.16) is positively related to cool identity (n= 477, r=.338, p<.01)
- Creative choice counter-conformity (M=4.52, SD=1.37) is positively related to cool identity (n=476, r=.326, p<.01)
- Unpopular choice counter-conformity (M=3.98, SD=1.33) is positively related to cool identity (n=477, r=.349, p<.01)
- Avoidance of similarity (M=3.79, SD=1.35) is positively related to cool identity (n=476, r=.255, p<.01)
- Materialism (M=4.36, SD=1.15) is positively related to cool identity (n= 473, r=.386, p<.01)
- Status concern (M=4.14, SD=1.28) is positively related to cool identity (n=473, r=.326, p<.01)
- Brand consciousness (M=4.07, SD=1.31) is positively related to cool identity (n=475, r=.293, p<.01)

In this paper, we have attempted to examine the meaning of coolness using possible consumer behavior constructs associated to the term. We proposed that humor, need for uniqueness, materialism, status concern and brand consciousness are positively related to coolness. Our preliminary analysis supports all our propositions. Our findings have implications for researchers and practitioners. Given the rich multicultural nature of our sample, we plan to do further analysis such as differences between religion, nationality and gender.

References

Belk, W. R (2006). "Cool Shoes. Cool Self," (in Swedish) in Anne Marie Dahlberg, ed., *Eyes just for Shoes*, Stockholm: Swedish Royal Armoury, pp. 77-90

Bird, S. and Tapp, A. (2008) "Social marketing and the meaning of cool", *Social Marketing Quarterly*, pp. 18-28

Carbelo-Baquero, B.; Alonso-Rodriguez, M. C.; Valero-Garces, C. and Thorson, J. (2006) "A Study of Sense of Humor in Spanish and American Samples", *North American Journal of Psychology,* Vol. 8, No. 3,447-454

Moore, R. (2004). We're cool, mom and dad are swell: Basic slang and generational shifts in values. *American Speech*, *79*(1), 59-86.

Nancarrow, C.; Nancarrow, P. and Page, J. (2002). "An Analysis of the Concept 'Cool' and It's Marketing Implications". *Journal of Consumer Behaviour* 1 (4) p. 311-322

O'Donnell, K. A. and Wardlow, D. L. (2000) A theory on the origins of coolness, Advances in Consumer Research, Vol. 27, pp 13-18

Pountain, D. and Robins, D. (2000b), Cool Rules, Reaktion, London

Marsha L. Richins (2004), "The Material Values Scale: A Re-inquiry into Its Measurement Properties and the Development of a Short Form," *Journal of Consumer Research*, 31 (June), 209-219

Stern, B.B., Barak, B., Gould, S.J. (1987), "Sexual identity scale: a new self-assessment measure", *Sex Roles*, Vol. 17 pp.503-19.

Shim, S. and Gehrt, K. (1996) "Hispanic and native American Adolescents: An exploratory of their approach to shopping", Journal of Retailing, 72 (3), 307-24

Eastman, J., Fredenberger, B, Campbell, D., Calvert, S. (1997) "The relationship between status consumption and materialism: A cross cultural comparison of Chinese, Mexican, and American Students", Journal of Marketing Theory and Practice, 5 (Winter) 52=66

Southgate, N. (2003). Coolhunting with Aristotle. *International Journal of Market Research*, *45*(2), 167-189.

Stephens, R., Levine, S., & Ross, W. (1976). Street addict values: A factor analytic study. *Journal of Social Psychology*, *99*(2), 273.

Tian, K.T., Bearden, W.O., Hunter, G.L. (2001), "Consumers' need for uniqueness: scale development and validation", *Journal of Consumer Research*, Vol. 28 No.1, pp.50-66.

Webster's (2009) Webster's Revised Unabridged Dictionary. Retrieved March 23, 2009, from Dictionary.com website: http://dictionary.reference.com/browse/irony

Social Networking Profiles & Cultural Dimensions: An Empirical Investigation

Carleen Ramlochansingh, St. John's University, USA
Ryall Carroll, St. John's University, USA

In recent years social networking has become very popular and has propelled websites like MySpace, Facebook, and LinkedIn into the mainstream. MySpace, one of the most popular of these social networking sites, was founded just six years ago and already has over 253 million user accounts worldwide (Alexa 2009). As this phenomenon grows and becomes an even larger part of people's lives, it is extremely important for marketers to understand this new medium and currently there is little research on the subject (Wallace, Walker, Lopez, and Jones 2009; Poynter 2008).

Schau and Gilly's (2003) research on motivations, intentions, and strategies for constructing personal Web spaces found that many individuals construct their digital selves referencing only the intangible concepts, things like ideas, beliefs, and values. If *culture* is defined as everything that people in a society learn in relation to values, norms, customs, traditions, and beliefs (Terpstra & Sarathy 2000), then Schau and Gilly's (2003) findings seem to indicate that individuals actually construct their digital selves referencing their culture. Therefore, this research investigates whether an individual's culture is evident in their social networking profiles.

For this study we analyzed profiles from the social networking site MySpace from three different countries with respect to three of Geert Hofstede's Five Cultural Dimensions: individuality, masculinity, and uncertainty avoidance. We reviewed 300 customized profiles by looking at the "About Me" section, where users write their personal information. The three countries under investigation were Australia, Ireland and the United States (US). These countries were chosen because of the US and Australia's similarity on the dimensions Individuality (IDV) and Masculinity (MAS), and their dissimilarity with Ireland on those dimensions, as well as the dissimilarity of the three countries on the dimension of Uncertainty Avoidance (UAI). These similarities and differences will act as our hypothesis of whether or not culture manifests itself in these profiles. If culture does play a role we should expect parallel results in terms of similarities and differences among cultural dimensions in personal profiles as we do among the countries.

The country-specific MySpace sites were used to identify the sample of 300 profiles consisting of 100 Australian, 100 Irish, and 100 US profiles with an equal number of male and female profiles for each country. Each profile page was individually printed and then specially coded on the back to indicate the country of origin. All 300 profile pages were randomized and we ensured the judges were not aware of the country coding on the back during the analysis. The "About me" written description on each profile was then evaluated on all three cultural dimensions.

An individualist (IDV) is one who exists in society only seeking their own self- interest and maybe that of their immediate family (Kale 1991). Therefore profiles were rated high on the IDV dimension if the individual primarily wrote about themselves, including but not limited to their career, hobbies, self description, and their personal likes and dislikes. Profiles were rated low on the IDV dimension if the individual wrote about themselves but also mentioned others in their profile, including but is not limited to family, friends, and/or significant others.

Distinctive Masculine (MAS) traits are assertiveness and competitiveness, and typically dominant masculine societies emphasize wealth and success (Geert-Hofstede.com). Therefore profiles were rated high on the MAS if the writing was very unemotional and the individual wrote about "liking" or "enjoying" their career, cars, and/or school but with little or no mention of or emotion towards family, friends, and/or significant others. Whereas, profiles were rated low on the MAS dimension if the profile section the individual primarily wrote very emotionally, writing about "liking" or "loving" their family, friends, and/or significant others but with little or no mention about "liking" or "enjoying" their career, cars, and/or school.

In strong Uncertainty Avoidance (UAI) societies people attempt to predict the future in order to minimize the possibility of new, unfamiliar, unexpected, unusual circumstances (Kale 1991). Therefore if the individual wrote about their future goals and plans whether it concerned the immediate future, a month, six months and/or a year, or their long term/ life goals they were considered high on UAI. Conversely the individual was considered low on UAI if the person made no mention of any future goals and plans.

To establish reliability, a test of reproducibility was applied to the coding system (Mueller 1987). A total of 90 MySpace profile were selected randomly from the original sample by two new experimenters. Next each of the two new experimenters independently coded their random selection of 90 MySpace profiles (Mueller 1987). The results of the reproducibility test showed that the two new experimenters coded their 90 MySpace profile with an 84.2 percent similarity as the original judge.

As expected, the results showed that the US and Australia's were not significantly different on the dimensions of Individuality and Masculinity ($p's > .2$). Surprisingly, there was also no significant difference on the dimension of Uncertainty Avoidance (UAI) ($p > .2$). When compared to Ireland both the US and Australia showed differences in these cultural dimensions. For Ireland, their Individuality rating was significantly lower ($M = 2.07$) than the US's ($M = 2.44$; $t(198) = 2.918$, $p < .005$) and marginally significant to Australia's profiles ($M = 2.33$; $t(198) = -1.779$, $p < .10$). For Ireland, their Masculinity rating was significantly higher ($M = 1.19$) than the US's ($M = .89$; $t(198) = 2.909$, $p < .005$) and also significantly higher to Australia's profiles ($M = .89$; $t(198) = -2.321$, $p < .5$). Lastly, for Ireland, their Uncertainty Avoidance (UAI) rating was not significantly higher ($M = 1.85$) than the US's ($M = 1.65$; $p > .1$) but was significant to Australia's profiles ($M = 1.61$; $t(198) = 1.973$, $p < .05$).

Since these results, for the most part, paralleled the similarities and differences among cultural dimensions in personal profiles as they do among the countries, these results confirm our expectations that culture is indeed present in individual's personal descriptions. This research helps to build a better understanding of this growing phenomenon of social networking and we hope to build upon this knowledge base in future research.

References

Alexa.com (2009). "MySpace," http://www.alexa.com/data/details/main/myspace.com, Retrieved on March 3, 2009.

Geert-Hofstede.com (2008), "What are Hofstede's five Cultural Dimensions?," http://www.geert-hofstede.com, Retrieved November 16, 2008.

Kale, S. H. (1991), "Culture-specific Marketing Communications: An Analytical Approach," *International Marketing Review, 8 (2)*, 18-30.

Kleine, Susan Schultz, Robert E. Kleine III, and Chris T. Allen (1995), "How Is a Possession 'Me' or 'Not Me'? Characterizing Types and Antecedents of Material Possession Attachment," *Journal of Consumer Research*, Vol. 2 (Dec), 327-343.

Mueller, Barbara (1987), "Reflections of Culture: An Analysis of Japanese and American Advertising Appeals," *Journal of Advertising Research* June/July, 51–59.

Poynter, Ray (2008), "Facebook: the future of networking with customers," *International Journal of Market Research*, Vol. 50 (1), 11-12.

Schau, Hope Jensen, and Mary C. Gilly (2003), "We Are What We Post? Self?Presentation in Personal Web Space," *Journal of Consumer Research*, Vol. 30 (3), 385-404.

Schouten, John W (1991), "Selves in Transition: Symbolic Consumption in Personal Rites of Passage and Identity Reconstruction," *Journal of Consumer Research*, Vol. 17 (4), 412-425.

Terpstra, V., and R. Sarathy (2000), *International Marketing*, 8th Edition, Dryden Press, Sydney.

Wallace, Dawn, Josie Walker, Tará Lopez, and Mike Jones (2009), "Do Word Of Mouth And Advertising Messages On Social Networks Influence The Purchasing Behavior Of College Students?," *Journal of Applied Business Research*, Volume 25 (1), 101-109.

Combining High-Scope and Low-Scope Retail Cues: An Integrative Perspective

Anne L. Roggeveen, Babson College, USA

Dhruv Grewal, Babson College, USA

Ronald Goodstein, Georgetown University, USA

While consumer research has paid significant attention to how product cues signal product quality (e.g., Bakamitsos 2006; Roggeveen, Grewal, and Gotlieb 2006; Zhang and Sood 2002), researchers have allocated fewer resources investigating how cues affect the places where consumers procure these goods. This relative lack of focus is surprising because consumer research into retail cues has a rich history (e.g., Grewal et al. 1998; Gupta and Cooper 1992; Srivastava and Lurie 2001). Yet in the past ten years, the number of publications examining how consumers react to product cues outweighs those on consumers' reactions to retailer cues by a wide margin. The issue becomes even more important when one considers the expanding channels of retail, including the internet, kiosks, and mobile shopping to name but a few. Thus, examining how recent theories and applications in consumer behavior apply to consumers' reactions to retailers is a timely issue. We take on that challenge by integrating research on cue-scope, congruity, and valence to test consumers' reactions to multiple retail cues.

More specifically, our research examines how low-scope cues interact with high-scope cues to affect consumers' evaluations. Previous research in schema-based processing suggests that the manner in which these cues interact in determining evaluations may not be straightforward. For instance, when a stimulus is moderately incongruent with an evoked schema, consumers engage in more extensive processing of the stimulus and often form more extreme evaluations (e.g., Campbell and Goodstein 2001). In our case this suggests that when a low-scope cue is moderately incongruent with a high-scope cue, the low-scope cue may have more impact on evaluations than when it is congruent with the high-scope cue.

In addition, earlier research suggests that the valence of a high-scope cue affects when a low-scope cue is used in attitude formation (e.g., Biswas et al. 2002; Lurie and Srivastava 2005; Miyazaki, Grewal, and Goodstein 2005; Purohit and Srivastava 2001). The results of these studies, however, are equivocal with some research indicating that low-scope cues are used only when the valence of the high-scope cue is positive (Purohit and Srivastava 2001, Miyazaki et al. 2005) and other research indicating that the low-scope cue is only used when the valence of the high-scope cue is negative (Biswas et al. 2002; Lurie and Srivastava 2005). We develop and test a processing model that reconciles these conflicting findings by examining the joint impact of cue-scope, congruity, and valence in a series of related experiments. More specifically we propose and test:

H1: When a low-scope cue is congruent with an accompanying high-scope cue, it will improve evaluations when the high-scope cue is negative but have no impact on evaluations when the high-scope cue is positive.

H2: When a low-scope cue is moderately incongruent with an accompanying high-scope cue, it will improve evaluations when the high-scope cue is positive but have no impact on evaluations when the high-scope cue is negative.

Results of three experiments support these hypotheses indicating that cue congruity affects attitudes and thoughts such that a low-scope cue enhances evaluations of a retailer associated with a positive high-scope cue when the two cues are moderately incongruent. Further, the low-scope cue offsets the effects of a negative high-scope cue when the cues are congruent.

In Experiment 1 (n=320), we paired our low-scope cue (price matching guarantee, PMG) with each of the high-scope cues in order to manipulate congruity. Specifically, a price-based low-scope cue is congruent for a retailer whose reputation is based on price (cf. Srivastava and Lurie 2004), but would be somewhat incongruent for a firm whose reputation is based on service. Thus, we examined two types of reputations (congruent/moderately congruent with PMG), two levels of valence associated with the reputation (poor/excellent), and two levels of PMG (absent/present) in a 2 x 2 x 2 between-subjects design. Each participant was randomly assigned to one of the eight experimental conditions and asked to read a brief scenario describing the reputation of a retailer selling home electronics and they then either read about the retailer's PMG policy or saw nothing about a PMG. After reading the scenario participants rated their perceptions of the retailer in terms of service quality and prices. In support of our hypotheses, the results revealed a three-way interaction for both price and service perceptions.

Experiment 2 followed the same general format as Study 1. However, in this study, the new high-scope reputation cue was related to the retailer's history concerning inventory availability. Following the logic on congruity, the new low-scope cue was an in-stock guarantee (ISG). We again examine two types of congruity (congruent/moderately congruent with ISG), two levels of valence associated with the reputation (poor/excellent), and two levels of ISG (absent/present) in a 2 x 2 x 2 between-subjects design. Participants (n=93) then read a scenario which described the type and valence of the retailer's reputation and either informed them about the retailer's ISG or contained no information about an ISG. Results again supported the hypothesized three-way interaction. Finally, Experiment 3 (n=86) provides evidence as to the process accounting for the results.

In sum, by examining the joint role of cue meaning congruity and the valence of the high-scope cue, our framework provides a more comprehensive understanding of the impact of multiple cues on consumers' evaluations. This framework was supported in three independent studies that manipulated multiple instantiations of each type of cue, as well as two very different retail contexts.

References

Bakamitsos, Georgios A. (2006), "A Cue Alone or a Probe to Think? The Dual Role of Affect in Product Evaluations," *Journal of Consumer Research*, 33 (December), 403-412.

Biswas, Abhijit, Chris Pullig, Mehmet I. Yagci, and Dwane H. Dean (2002), "Consumer Evaluation of Low Price Guarantees: The Moderating Role of Reference Prices and Store Image," *Journal of Consumer Psychology*, 12 (2), 107-18.

Campbell, Margaret and Ronald Goodstein (2001), "The Moderating Effect of Perceived Risk on Consumer's Evaluations of Product Incongruity: Preference for the Norm," *Journal of Consumer Research*, 28 (December), 439-49.

Grewal, Dhruv, R. Krishnan, Julie Baker, and Norm Borin (1998), "The Effect of Store Name, Brand Name and Price Discounts on Consumers' Evaluations and Purchase Intentions," *Journal of Retailing*, 74 (3), 331-352.

Gupta, Sunil and Lee G. Cooper (1992), "The Discounting of Discounts and Promotion Thresholds," *Journal of Consumer Research*, 19 (December), 401-411.

Lurie, Nicholas H. and Joydeep Srivastava (2005), "Price-Matching Guarantees and Consumer Evaluations of Price Information," *Journal of Consumer Psychology*, 15 (2), 149-58.

Miyazaki, Anthony D., Dhruv Grewal, and Ronald C. Goodstein (2005), "The Effect of Multiple Extrinsic Cues on Quality Perceptions: A Matter of Consistency," *Journal of Consumer Research*, 32 (June), 146-53.

Purohit, Devavrat and Joydeep Srivastava (2001), "Effect of Manufacturer Reputation, Retailer Reputation, and Product Warranty on Consumer Judgments of Product Quality: A Cue Diagnosticity Framework," *Journal of Consumer Psychology*, 10 (3), 123-34.

Roggeveen, Anne L., Dhruv Grewal, and Jerry Gotlieb (2006), "Does the Frame of a Comparative Ad Moderate the Effectiveness of Extrinsic Information Cues?" *Journal of Consumer Research*, 33 (June), 115-122.

Srivastava, Joydeep and Nicholas Lurie (2001), "A Consumer Perspective on Price-Matching Refund Policies: Effect on Price Perceptions and Search Behavior," *Journal of Consumer Research*, 28 (September), 296-307.

Zhang, Shi and Sanjay Sood (2002), "'Deep' and 'Surface' Cues: Brand Extension Evaluations by Children and Adults," *Journal of Consumer Research*, 29 (June), 129-141.

Compensatory Consumption When Saying Goodbye

Pilar Rojas Gaviria, Université Libre de Bruxelles (Solvay Brussels School of Economics and Management and Centre Emile Berheim CEB), Belgium
Christian Bluemelhuber, Université Libre de Bruxelles (Solvay Brussels School of Economics and Management and Centre Emile Berheim CEB), Belgium[8]

"Guérit-on jamais des êtres qui nous quittent? [1]"

When choosing the words that best describe developed contemporary societies, specialists seem to agree on a kind of "disruptive" vocabulary. They refer to: liquid, fluid, movement, fragmentation and acceleration (e.g. Lyotard 1978; Marquard 1991; Bauman 2000; Lipovetsky and Charles 2004). These descriptors of an accelerated world capture the continual departure from familiar contexts in which post-modern citizens are embedded.

Continual departures challenge traditional reference points, such as the classic family model, life-long working community or citizenship. The ambiguity and instability of traditional reference points motivate alternative ways of organizing life, contributing to the acceleration of such phenomena as divorce, migration and switching or losing jobs.

In this fast-paced world, our research, studies compensatory consumption in the framework of consumers exposed to the loss of familiar contexts: landscapes, surroundings, and/or significant others. This study is a response to our conviction that investigating human capacity to compensate for the disappearance of familiarity in life through consumption has become an important aspect of consumer research (see for instance, Bonsu and Belk 2003; Curasi et al. 2004 or Schau et al. 2009).

The research method used for this inquiry has been inspired heavily by the bottom-up approach of *Grounded Theory* (Strauss and Corbin 1990)–starting with the data and building the theory from this foundation. This agenda is highlighted by ten case studies of people who have encountered important losses in life. After being shortly debriefed about the idea of lost under investigation, participants shared their stories about their personal loss on four occasions:

1. *A biographical written exercise*: participants were required to identify important losses that had deeply impacted on them.
2. *A lost telling exercise*: participants were recorded during an interview, in which they were asked to describe the details of the loss. Each of these personal telling exercises lasted between one and two hours, during which we interfered as little as possible with the free flow of narrative.
3. *A dialogical experience*: the two first phases enabled us to identify a number of topics common to all participants. We engaged in a dialogical experience (Thompson et al. 1989) during a second round of interviews, with the specific objective of focusing on these particular topics.
4. *Feedback exercise*: participants were invited to provide an individual feedback on the preliminary conclusions that we drew when they modified some of our interpretations and enriched the information we had.

The major results elicited from the data so far can be divided into two groups of strategies in which consumers leverage on consumption, when facing the loss of familiar contexts: *The Teddy Bear Effect* and *The Rebound Effect.*

The Teddy Bear Effect: can be defined as the coercive force that aims at preserving a past that may otherwise be forgotten, in order to ensure the development of a coherent personal narrative. Participants often bring that past closer to themselves as a reassuring strategy, when times become uncertain and challenging (Marquard 1991, p. 81).

This effect can be illustrated with the case of Bruna (32 years old), an Italian citizen who immigrated to Belgium seven years ago. She identifies living overseas as a risk of losing her Italian identity. For instance, she notices that her Italian is becoming less fluent, that she has totally lost track of Italian shops, that she does not know the "new" words used by young Italians, as she no longer watches local television.

Her personal *Teddy Bear* consists of purchasing traditional Italian food at supermarkets, which she feels is consistent with her Italian cooking background. She also travels back to Italy each time she needs to celebrate a professional success. A couple of years ago, after having bought an apartment in Belgium, the risk of losing her identity as Italian increased, she described the purchasing situation as "strange", as she would always have thought of having her own home first in Italy.

Purchasing a house can be seen at first sight as an activity we do in order to live there later on. However, as Martin Heidegger suggests (1958), we already project ourselves dwelling in these places at the time we decide to build or buy them. Residential housing purchase decisions are material signs of our desire to stay in place. In this case, Bruna's decision makes her realize that she was intending to remain in Belgium. Consequently, her reaction was to reinforce her personal *Teddy Bear* by buying most of her furniture in Italy and bringing it by car to Belgium.

The Rebound Effect results from the capacity of the human brain to make up and integrate concepts, and multiple alternative action plans in order to achieve future goals (Ingvar 1985). It consists of consumption-related actions performed to anticipate novelty in life and compensate for past losses. One of our participants, Caroline (28 years old), experienced a *Rebound Effect* after losing a brother in a motorcycle accident.

Her *Rebound* focuses on living a healthier and "carpe-diem" life. After her brother passed away, she became determined to overcome her anorexia, a sickness which had plagued her since she was a teenager. She describes this change in her life as a personal strategy, which obliged her to protect her own life, thus preventing her parents from losing yet another child. She now goes out for meals with friends, without having to search for an excuse for not to eat.

---

[8]Free translation: Do we ever heal from those who leave us?

Her "carpe-diem" *Rebound* acknowledges a new perspective on enjoying life that she and her entire family have adopted. She often consciously reinforces her hedonic consumption, for instance by going on enjoyable outings, allowing herself impulsive purchases of expensive clothes. She visits relatively expensive bars or restaurants from time to time and also bought a new car that satisfies aesthetic criteria more than utilitarian needs.

As the world continues its accelerated innovative path, consumers are exposed more and more to losses of known paths. The speed of change cannot immediately be comprehended by consumers who generally live at a slower speed. This requires "mundane" consumption experiences to compensate for the profound loss of familiarity.

References

Bauman, Zygmunt (2000), *Liquid Modernity*, Cambridge: Polity Press.

Bonsu, Samuel K. and Russell W. Belk (2003), "Do not Go Cheaply into That Good Night: death-Ritual Consumption in Asante, Ghand," *Journal of Consumer Research,* 30, 1, (June), 41-55.

Curasi, Carolyn Folkman, Margaret K. Hogg, Pauline Maclaran (2004), "Identity, Consumption And Loss: The Impact of Women's Experience of Grief and Mourning on Consumption in Empty Nest Households", in *Advances in Consumer Research Volume 31*, eds. Barbara E. Kahn and Mary Frances Luce, Valdosta, GA : Association for Consumer Research, Pages: 615-622.

Escalas, Jennifer Edson and James R. Bettman (2000), "Using Narratives and Autobiographical Memories to Discern Motives." In *The Why of Consumption: Perspectives on Consumer Motives, Goals, and Desires*, ed. S. David Ratneshwar. London: Routledge.

Guignon, Charles (2003) "Meaning in the Work of Art: A Hermeneutic Perspective," *Midwest Studies in Philosophy,* XXVII, 25-44.

Heidegger, Martin (1958), "Batir Habiter Penser," in *Essais et Conférences*, Paris: Gallimard.

Ingvar, D.H. (1985), ""Memory of the future": an essay on the temporal organization of conscious awareness," *Human Neurobiology*, 4, 127-136.

Linde, Charlotte (1993), *Life Stories: The Creation of Coherence*, New York: Oxford University press.

Lipovetsy, Gilles and Sébastian Charles (2004), *Les temps hypermodernes*, Paris : Grasset.

Livingston, Robert and Nicholas Pearce, "The Teddy Bear Effect : Does Babyfaceness Benefit Black CEOs ?, " Psychological Science, Upcoming Issue.

Lyotard, Jean-François (1988), *La condition postmoderne: Rapport sur le savoir*, Paris: Éditions de Minuit.

McAdams, Dan P. (1993), *The Stories we Live by: Personal Myths and the Making of the Self*, New York: The Guilford Press.

______, Ruthellen Josselson, and Amia Lieblich (2005), *Turns in the Road: Narrative Studies of Lives in Transition*, Washington D.C.: American Psychological Association.

McAlexander, James H. (1991), "Divorce, the Disposition of the Relationship, and Everything", in *Advances in Consumer Research Volume 18*, eds. Rebecca H. Holman and Michael R. Solomon, Provo, UT : Association for Consumer Research, Pages: 43-48.

Marquard, Odo (1991), *In Defense of the Accidental*, New York: Oxford University Press.

Ricœur, Paul (1988), "L'identité narrative," *Revue Esprit,* (July), 295-304.

Ricœur, Paul (1990), *Soi-même comme un autre,* Paris: Éditions du Seuil.

Schau, Hope Jensen, Mary C. Gilly and Mary Wolfinbarger (2009), "Consumer Identity Renaissance: The Resurgence of Identity-Inspired Consumption in Retirement," *Journal of Consumer Research*, 36, 2, (August), 255-276.

Strauss, Anselm and Juliet Corbin (1990), *Basics of Qualitative Research: Grounded Theory Procedures and Techniques*, Newbury Park, CA: Sage.

Thompson, Craig J. and Siok Kuan Tambyah (1999) "Trying to Be Cosmopolitan," *Journal of Consumer Research*, 26 ,(3), 214–41.

______, William B. Locander and Howard R. Pollio (1989), "Putting Consumer Experience Back into Consumer Research: The Philosophy and Method of Existential-Phenomenology," *Journal of Consumer Research*, 16, 2, (September), 133-146.

Woodruffe-Burton, Helen, Richard Elliott (2005), "Compensatory Consumption and Narrative Identity Theory", in *Advances in Consumer Research Volume 32*, eds. Geeta Menon and Akshay R. Rao, Duluth, MN : Association for Consumer Research, Pages: 461-465.

High Hopes and Letdowns: The Influence of Self-Esteem on Expectations and Product Failure

Stefanie Rosen, University of South Carolina, USA

Rebecca Naylor, Ohio State University, USA

Cait Poynor, University of Pittsburgh, USA

Self-esteem, defined as how worthwhile one perceives him or herself to be, plays an important role in one's self-concept (Swann et al. 2007). Marketing researchers have explored self-esteem in the context of consumer behavior, showing that it can affect overconsumption (Mandel and Smeesters 2008), perceptions of models (Smeesters and Mandel 2006), brand connections (Escalas and Bettman 2003), and materialism (Chaplin and Roedder-John 2007).

In our research, we explore how product expectations differ by self-esteem. Specifically, we explore the impact of self-esteem on a consumer's expectations of product performance, particularly given other consumers' and professionals' ratings of the product. Our central proposition is that high and low self-esteem consumers will react differently to recommendation information because they differ in their ability to adjust their expectations. Because people with high self-esteem (HSE) are more effective at adjusting their expectations, when they have information (e.g., ratings by other consumers and/or by product experts) indicating lower quality, they adjust their expectations accordingly. However, low self-esteem (LSE) consumers are not as good at making such adjustments. As such, these consumers end up with high hopes for a low quality product. Hence we predict:

H1: Consumers with LSE will have more favorable expectations of an inferior product than consumers with HSE.

We predict hypothesis 1 will hold only in the context of an inferior product. Self-esteem does not shape consumers' expectations of products rated by others as superior because no adjustments to expectations are needed in this case–high expectations are justified for superior products.

What do these differences in expectations by self-esteem and product quality mean for evaluations of the performance of the product? From the satisfaction literature, we know consumers are upset when expectations are not met, per the expectation disconfirmation model (Oliver 1997). People with LSE are putting themselves in a position to experience negative disconfirmation because of their heightened expectations for an objectively worse product. Thus, LSE consumers are likely to judge a lower quality product even more negatively when it performs badly than will HSE consumers. By contrast, HSE people have more realistic expectations of lower quality products. Their expectations might not be met if the lower quality product does not perform, but the gap between expectations and perceived performance will be less than it is for LSE people because the expectations of HSE people are lower a priori. Formally:

H2: Consumers with LSE will have a stronger negative emotional response and will be more likely to complain about their disappointment when an inferior product fails than consumers with HSE.

We test hypothesis 1 in study 1 and hypothesis 2 in study 2. Participants in study 1 (n=174) completed two ostensibly unrelated tasks: indicating their level of agreement/disagreement with the 10 items of the Rosenberg (1965) self-esteem scale (Cronbach's α=.80) and evaluating one of two shampoos. In the superior (inferior) shampoo condition, participants were told that average consumer rating of a hypothetical brand of shampoo was four (two) out of five stars and 75% (25%) of hairstylists recommended the shampoo. The order of the two tasks was counter-balanced for a 2 (shampoo quality) x 2 (order) design. After reading the scenario, participants rated the shampoo on the following dependent variables using nine-point scales: satisfaction, overall impression, and how well they thought it worked. These items were combined into an overall product expectations index (Cronbach's α=.90).

We conducted a 2 (shampoo quality) X measured self-esteem ANOVA. As hypothesized, there was a significant interaction between self-esteem and shampoo quality ($F(1, 170)=6.82, p<.01$). Follow-up analyses in the superior product condition revealed that there was not a significant effect of self-esteem on product expectations ($p=.32$). In the inferior product condition, however, participants with LSE had significantly higher product expectations than participants with HSE ($F(1, 170)=8.58, p<.01$), consistent with hypothesis 1.

In study 2, participants (n=137) indicated their level of agreement/disagreement with the 20 items of the Heatherton and Polivy (1991) self-esteem scale (Cronbach's α=.87) and read a scenario describing a product failure. Participants were asked to imagine that the zipper on a piece of luggage they had owned for five years had broken and that the suitcase was a brand that is considered (or not considered) very high quality. The order of the two tasks was again counter-balanced for a 2 (luggage quality: superior vs. inferior) x 2 (order) design. After reading the scenario, participants rated their anticipated disappointment, anger, and likelihood of complaining to friends/family that the zipper had broken. Disappointment and anger were combined into an emotional response to product failure index (Cronbach's α=.70).

We conducted two 2 (luggage quality) X measured self-esteem ANOVAs, one predicting the emotional response to the product failure and the other predicting likelihood of negative word-of-mouth. As hypothesized, there were significant interactive effects of self-esteem and quality of luggage on both the emotional response to product failure index ($F(1, 136)=8.31, p<.01$) and likelihood of complaining to friends/family ($F(1, 136)=9.93$, p<.01). Follow-up analyses in the superior product condition revealed that participants with both HSE and LSE were equally upset ($p=.12$) and likely to complain when the superior luggage failed ($p=.09$). However, follow-up analyses in the inferior product condition showed that compared to participants with HSE, those with LSE were significantly more upset ($F(1, 136)=6.36, p=.01$) and more likely to complain ($F(1, 136)=7.51, p<.01$) when the zipper broke, supporting hypothesis 2.

Overall, we find that individuals' self-esteem shapes their expectations for products such that LSE consumers have higher expectations of lower quality products than do HSE consumers (study 1). These higher expectations influence subsequent evaluations of product performance, leading LSE consumers to feel more let down when a lower quality product does not perform well than are HSE consumers (study 2).

Selected References

Chaplin, Lan Nguyn and Deborah Roedder-John (2007), " Growing up in a material world: Age Difference in Materialism in Children and Adolescents," *Journal of Consumer Research,* 34(4), 480-93.

Escalas, Jennifer Edson and James R. Bettman (2003), "You are what they eat: The Influence of Reference Groups on Consumers' Connections to Brands," *Journal of Personality and Social Psychology,* 13(3), 339-48.

Heatherton, Todd F. and Janet Polivy (1991), "Development and Validation of a Scale for Measuring State Self-Esteem," *Journal of Personality and Social Psychology,* 60(6), 895-910.

Mandel, Naomi and Dirk Smeesters (2008), "The Sweet Escape: Effects of Mortality Salience on Consumption Quantities for High- and Low- Self-Esteem Consumers," *Journal of Consumer Research,* 35(2), 309-23.

Oliver, Richard L. (1997), *Satisfaction: A Behavioral Perspective on the consumer.* New York, The McGraw-Hill Companies, Inc

Rosenberg, Milton (1965), *Society and the Adolescent Self-image*, Princeton, NJ: Princeton University Press.

Smeesters, Dirk and Naomi Mandel (2006), "Positive and Negative Media Image Effects on the Self," *Journal of Consumer Research,* 32(4), 576-82.

Swann, William B. Jr., Christine Chang-Schneider, and Katie McClarty (2007) Do people's self-views matter? *American Psychologist*, 62(2), 84-94.

A Demonstration of the Influence of Advertising on Brand Choice

J. Edward Russo, Cornell University, USA
Anne-Sophie Chaxel, Cornell University, USA

Advertising influences brand choice (e.g., Mehta, Chen, & Narasimhan, 2008). This is true even for TV commercials that rely mainly on conveying a positive feeling about the brand. Although there is general agreement that such commercials can influence brand choice, there is much less agreement on how they do it. That lack of agreement may reflect the existence of several different ways that commercials succeed, each with its own process through which the viewing of the commercial influences a subsequent brand choice. The purpose of the present work is to demonstrate one such process.

That process requires two steps. First, an effective commercial must install its brand as the initial leader in a choice against a competing brand. This should be straightforward so long as the commercial for the targeted brand is superior to a commercial for the competitor. Not all viewers may see the selected commercial as superior, but it should install its brand as the initial leader for a substantial majority of them.

The second step relies on a phenomenon that occurs during the subsequent product choice. As new information is received, its evaluation tends to be biased toward supporting whichever alternative is currently leading in overall preference (Russo, Meloy and Medvec, 1998). If the superior commercial makes its brand the initial leader, then the distortion of new information during the choice process should enable it to remain in the lead and emerge as the chosen brand for a majority of consumers. Information distortion (ID) is, by now, a well established "predecision" bias (see Brownstein, 2003, for a review). It is frequently observed, difficult to eliminate (Meloy, Russo and Miller, 2006), and quite systematic, increasing linearly with the strength of preference for one option over the other (Russo et al., 1998).

In an experiment, participants were asked to imagine having to decide between two Caribbean resorts for their next vacation. They might see a commercial for each resort, possibly on their websites or on a travel-oriented TV channel. This constitutes Step 1 of our process. Then they might use the internet, books or friends to gather information on several attributes of these two resorts, such as their activities and amenities. This is Step 2.

To track the commercials' influence on each attribute to the eventual brand choice, we used a method known as the stepwise evolution of preference (SEP; Meloy and Russo, 2004). This method requires participants to provide three responses after they have read each product attribute. The first is an evaluation of the attribute. This response is the basis of the measurement of ID. Second, participants are asked which brand they prefer at this point in the process, knowing that more information is coming. This response identifies the current leader. Finally, participants are asked for their confidence in this current leader. This third response captures the strength of their preference for the identified leader. If the superior commercial succeeds in installing its brand for a substantial majority of viewers and if ID is sufficient to preserve enough of that majority in the face of subsequent information, then the targeted brand should be chosen by a majority of participants.

A between-participant design included one experimental and one control condition. In the experimental condition, participants were shown two commercials before they saw five descriptive product attributes and made their choice of resort. A pretest showed one of the commercials (Club Zephyr) to be superior to the other (Club Helios). Neither commercial was designed to convey product information, at least explicitly. None of the five attributes favored one brand over the other (i.e., they were all written and pretested to be "neutral"). In the control group, participants saw no commercials. Their brand choice provided a baseline level of both choice proportion and ID against which the levels observed in the commercial condition could be compared.

Results confirmed our hypothesized process. First, the superior commercial did install Club Zephyr as the initial leader for a clear majority of viewers (80%). In contrast, the control group who saw the first attribute but neither commercial divided their initial preference evenly between the two resorts (50%). Second, enough of the initial effect of the commercials was preserved to enable a significant final preference for the brand with the superior commercial (76%). Third, further analysis demonstrated that the commercial for Club Zephyr resulted in a relatively large mean ID (M=1.25) in the evaluation of information to favor this Club. In comparison, the benchmark level of ID from the control group was only .33. We also computed the confidence in the final choice in each of the two conditions. The greater ID in the advertising condition should have led its participants to be more confident (on a scale from 50 to 100). Confirming this expectation, participants in the advertising group were reliably more confident in their final choice (M=.83) than those in the control group (M =.76). Thus, participants in the commercial condition were more convinced of their choice than participants in the no-advertising condition. This occurred despite there being little information in the advertisement condition and little directional information in any of the five attributes (which were pretested to be neutral).

These results provide one answer to the question: How might advertising influence consumer choice? We showed that a superior commercial can succeed in influencing brand choice by first installing the advertised brand as the initial leader and then letting the subsequent ID help maintain that leadership throughout a subsequent brand choice process. Thus, our findings reveal one specific process through which an advertisement can influence product choice.

References

Brownstein, Aaron L. (2003), "Biased predecision processing", *Psychological Bulletin,* 129 (4) (July), 545-569.

Mehta, Nitin, Xinlei Chen, and Om Narasimhan (2008), "Disentangling the multiple effects of advertising on brand choice decisions", *Marketing Science,* 27(3) (May/June), 334–355.

Meloy, Margaret G. and J. Edward Russo (2004), "Binary Choice under Instructions to Select versus Reject", *Organizational Behavior and Human Decision Processes,* 93 (March), 114-28.

Meloy, Margaret G., J. Edward Russo, and Elizabeth Gelfand Miller (2006), "Monetary Incentives and Mood", *Journal of Marketing Research,* 43, 267-75.

Russo, J. Edward, Margaret G. Meloy, and Victoria Husted Medvec (1998), "Predecisional Distortion of Product Information", *Journal of Marketing Research,* 34 (November), 438-52.

Exposing Consumer Exhibitionists: The Development and Validation of the Consumer Exhibitionism Scale

Christina Saenger, Kent State University, USA
Veronica Thomas, Kent State University, USA
Jennifer Wiggins Johnson, Kent State University, USA
Robert Jewell, Kent State University, USA

Marketing researchers have long recognized phenomena wherein consumers express their self-concepts to others via their consumption activities (Belk 1988; Richins 1994; Escalas and Bettman 2005). Internet technologies, such as social networking sites and blogs, have become more prevalent, enabling consumers to make information about themselves available on a far-reaching scale. They have fundamentally altered the way consumers communicate their consumption activities to others, fostering a culture of exhibitionistic consumer behavior. Consumers are making their consumption activities more publicly available than ever before, from listing their favorite books and music to posting pictures of their lifestyles and experiences for others to see. They update others in their networks' as to their behaviors, plans, and mood through status functionalities, such as those available on Facebook, MySpace, and Twitter. Indeed, some consumers have gone beyond simply utilizing these tools to stay in touch with friends to using these technologies to express themselves to a larger audience. This need to create awareness about one's self has pervaded some individuals' lives, causing them to continually publicize who they are. The purpose of this research is to develop a scale to measure consumer exhibitionism, which we formally define as the tendency to communicate one's consumption activities for the purposes of attracting attention to one's self and informing others about one's self concept in the pursuit of personal satisfaction from making this information public. Using Churchill's (1979) method, we are in the process of refining and validating this scale for future use in consumer research.

The concept of exhibitionism stems from literature in psychology, where exhibitionism is defined as inappropriate self-exposure behavior for the purpose of self-gratification (Blair and Lanyon 1981). Applying the concept to marketing, Holbrook (2001) emphasized exhibitionism as one of the "four E's" of marketing, which focuses on the hedonic, experiential aspects of consumer behavior. Holbrook proposed that consumers use their consumption activities to shape their social images, defining the concept as "the phenomenon wherein consumers use products as signals to convey or express their actual, desired, or ideal self-concepts to others," (p.81). In Holbrook's view, all consumers are exhibitionists; however, we propose it is a tendency that consumers possess in varying amounts, warranting the development of a measurement scale. Further, we broaden Holbrook's definition by specifying two goals beyond the expression of self-concept that consumer exhibitionists seek to attain: attention and satisfaction. Consumer exhibitionism holds a symbiotic relationship with voyeuristic behavior (Holbrook 2001), implying the exhibitionist's desire to gain the attention of others. This is consistent with literature on consumption as an expression of self, where the attention of others to these consumption activities is a necessary component (Belk 1988; Richins 1994; Escalas and Bettman 2005). As a psychological construct, exhibitionistic behavior is engaged in to achieve self-gratification (Blair and Lanyon 1981), indicating that individuals seek satisfaction from exhibitionistic activities.

While consumer exhibitionism has not been previously measured in consumer research, similar constructs have been examined. While market mavens (Feick and Price 1987) and opinion leaders (Katz and Lazarsfeld 1955; Flynn, Goldsmith and Eastman 1996) use their expertise with the goal of helping others better navigate their consumption experiences, consumer exhibitionists behave with the goals of attracting attention to themselves and expressing their self-concepts, seeking personal satisfaction from the act of making information about their consumption activities publicly available. Additionally, brand evangelists "preach the brand's most loved aspects and all positive associations that come with it to people who have so far not acknowledged the wonder of it" (Matzler, Pichler, Hemetsberger 2007, 27). Though consumer exhibitionists do preach about the brands they use, this is done in effort to inform others about their consumption activities, rather than due to a sense of loyalty. Further, consumer exhibitionism is different from conspicuous consumption. While conspicuous consumption (Veblen 1899; O'Cass and McEwen 2007) is concerned with luxury goods, the communication of status, and visible consumption activity, consumer exhibitionists publicize a wide variety of public and private consumption activities that are congruent with who they are. Consumer exhibitionists are more likely to be materialistic (Richins 2004), narcissistic (Raskin and Hall 1979), have high consumer self-confidence (Bearden, Hardesty, and Rose 2001) and be extroverted.

From the literature, we initially developed a set of 27 scale items. We then conducted focus groups with 35 marketing undergraduate students in which we discussed the usage of Internet technology and interpersonal communications, and the ability of each to communicate consumption activities and self-concept related information, generating an additional 25 items for a total of 52. We presented our definition and scale items to the students from our focus groups as a member check to ensure we had accurately captured their input, and revised our items accordingly. We then presented our definition and scale items to 10 experts and colleagues for further refinement, again revising our items per their recommendations. Our current scale contains 32 items.

Our validation plan is as follows: first, we intend to administer the scale to samples from two populations, undergraduate students and MBA students, whom we deem more representative of the average consumer due to age and lifestyle differences from undergraduate students. Based on their responses, we will perform initial exploratory factor analysis and reliability analysis. Next, we will administer our refined scale to a new sample to test its internal validity. At this time, we will include scales representing the related constructs previously discussed to test nomological validity, similar constructs to test discriminant validity, and a measure of the actual behavior to test predictive validity. We will use this data to conduct confirmatory factor analysis and test the relationship between variables using structural equation modeling.

Our research contributes to the consumer behavior literature by providing a conceptual definition and measure of consumer exhibitionism. Our scale will enable researchers to investigate the effects of consumer exhibitionism on consumer behaviors of interest to marketers, such as word of mouth behavior, brand loyalty, brand choice, and online consumer behavior. This research is particularly relevant as Internet technologies that facilitate consumers' abilities to publicly express themselves become increasingly prevalent in society.

References

Bearden, William O., David M. Hardesty, and Randall L. Rose (2001), "Consumer Self-Confidence: Refinements in Conceptualization and Measurement," *Journal of Consumer Research*, 28 (June), 121-34.

Belk, Russell W. (1988), "Possessions and the Extended Self," *Journal of Consumer Research*, 15 (September), 139-68.

Blair, C. David and Richard I. Lanyon (1981). "Exhibitionism: Etiology and Treatment," *Psychological Bulletin*, 89 (May), 439-463.

Churchill Jr., Gilbert A. (1979). "A Paradigm for Developing Better Measures of Marketing Constructs," *Journal of Marketing Research*, 16 (February), 64-73.

Escalas, Jennifer Edson, and James R. Bettman (2005), "Self-Construal, Reference Groups, and Brand Meaning," *Journal of Consumer Research*, 32 (December), 378-89.

Feick, Lawrence F. and Linda L. Price (1987), "The Market Maven: A Diffuser of Marketplace Information," *Journal of Marketing*, 51 (January), 83-97.

Flynn, Leisa Reinecke, Ronald E. Goldsmith, and Jaqueline K. Eastman (1996), "Opinion Leaders and Opinion Seekers: Two New Measurement Scales," *Journal of the Academy of Marketing Science*, 24 (2), 137-47.

Holbrook, Morris B. (2001), "The Millennial Consumer in the Texts of Our Times: Exhibitionism," *Journal of Macromarketing*, 21 (June), 81-95.

Katz, Elihu and Paul F. Lazarsfeld (1955), *Personal Influence*, Glencoe IL: The Free Press.

Matzler, K., E.A. Pichler, and A. Hemetsberger (2007), "Who is Spreading the Word? The Positive Influence of Extraversion on Consumer Passion and Evangelism," ed. A.L. Dixon and K.A. Machliet, San Diego: American Marketing Association, 25-32.

O'Cass, Aron and Hmily McEwen (2004), "Exploring Consumer Status and Conspicuous Consumption," *Journal of Consumer Behaviour*, 4 (October), 25-39.

Raskin, Robert N. and Calvin S. Hall (1979), "A Narcissistic Personality Inventory," *Psychological Reports*, 46, 55-60.

Richins, Marsha L. (1994), "Valuing Things: The Public and Private Meanings of Possessions," *Journal of Consumer Research*, 4 (September), 504-21.

Veblen, Thorstein (1899), *The Theory of the Leisure Class*, New York: The MacMillan Company.

All Positive Emotions Are Not Equal: Cognitive and Motivational Differences between Pride and Surprise

Julian Saint Clair, University of Washington, USA

Abstract

Recent research has begun to explore differences between negative emotions. As for positive emotions, they have generally been lumped into a single homogeneous category when explored in relation to decision making. The study presented here is the first to demonstrate underlying cognitive and motivational differences between distinct positive emotions in the context of decision making. Due to emotional discounting, a recent effect hitherto demonstrated only with negative emotions, these effects are reversed for subjects with high need for cognition (NFC). Emotional discounting, in turn, is shown to be subject to a new boundary condition: self-esteem maintenance.

Background

Decision making is typically studied under the paradigm derived from prospect theory (Khaneman & Tversky, 1979) which seeks to measure subjective utility, likelihood estimations, and risk preference. Subjective utility is most easily understood as the value one attaches to an outcome. The paradigm often obtains these measures using gamble tasks (i.e. Isen & Geva, 1987). For example, subjects are shown a gamble as follows: "Game 3: A 50% chance to win $10 or win nothing." To obtain subjective likelihood estimations, subjects are asked "How likely are you to win this game?" The answer takes the form of a 7-point scale anchored by "Not at all likely" and "Very likely". To obtain risk preferences and subjective utility, subjects are asked "How desirable is this game?" on a 7-point scale anchored by "Not at all desirable" and "Very desirable". The gambles take the form of win/not win and lose/not lose to separate the effects involved with loss avoidance and gain seeking–loss aversion theory shows that, for example, a $10 loss has a stronger effect than a $10 gain.

Predictions

The valence-only hypothesis (Johnson & Tversky, 1983) would predict that subjects in a positive mood are more likely to expect positive events to occur, and subjects in a negative mood are more likely to expect negative events to occur. This would suggest that subjects in any positive mood would report higher likelihood to win a gamble. The beyond-valence perspective (Han et al., 2007), however, is of the opinion that the important predictor of likelihood estimations is the underlying cognitive appraisal dimension of certainty. For example, a highly uncertain negative emotion (fear) should result in lower likelihood estimations than a highly certain negative emotion (anger). Indeed, Lerner and Keltner (2001) find this to be the case. To obtain a similar effect with positive emotions, we must also select two that differ on the underlying cognitive appraisal dimension of certainty. Pride and surprise are two such emotions; pride is highly certain, surprise highly uncertain (Smith & Ellsworth, 1985). Thus, taking the beyond-valence perspective, we predict that:

H1a: Subjects in the *surprise* condition will report lower likelihood to win the 50% gamble than subjects in the *control* condition.

H1b: Subjects in the *pride* condition will report higher likelihood to win the 50% gamble than subjects in the *control* condition.

Research on need for cognition (NFC) has found that those high in NFC, being more analytical thinkers, are typically less subject to emotional primes. They have in fact been shown to actively engage in cognitive discounting of negative emotion during decision making (Kuvaas & Kaufmann, 2004). The present research extends this theory by demonstrating the effect with positive emotions.

H2: The effects predicted under H1a and H1b will be moderated by NFC; the predicted effects will hold true for Low NFC subjects and reverse for High NFC subjects.

No research to date has explored boundary conditions of the emotional discounting done by high NFC subjects. Since pride is a self-focused emotion correlated with self-esteem (Tracy & Robins, 2007), it may be subject to self-esteem regulation motivations. Self-esteem maintenance theory suggests that subjects typically seek an optimal level of self-esteem (i.e., high self-esteem) (Baumeister & Jones, 1978; See Tesser, 2000 for a review). Therefore, subjects with low self-esteem who are experiencing pride may engage in less emotional discounting in an effort to bolster their self-esteem.

H3: The moderation effect of NFC in H2 of subjects in the pride condition reporting higher likelihood to win the 50% gamble will in turn be moderated by Core Self-Evaluations (CSE; a measure of self-esteem); those with low CSE will engage in less emotional discounting of pride than those with high CSE.

Also, because of the nature of the gamble propositions and the study of uncertainty, an Optimism scale is used as a control variable.

Methods

83 subjects at a large US west-coast university participated in the study for course credit. Subjects received the emotion elicitations via a relived emotion task wherein subjects are asked to recount a proud/surprise/control (grocery shopping) event in their lives (Ekman et al., 1983; Levenson, 1992; Lerner & Keltner, 2001). Subjects then received the gambles (see below for gamble descriptions) followed by the NFC scale and an Optimism scale. Subjects already completed the CSE scale prior to this study and that data was matched to the respective subjects. For the dependent variables, subjects were asked to evaluate each gamble independently on desirability and likelihood to win/lose.

Game 1: 10% chance to win $10 or win nothing
Game 2: 50% chance to win $10 or win nothing
Game 3: 90% chance to win $10 or win nothing
Game 4: 10% chance to lose $10 or lose nothing
Game 5: 50% chance to lose $10 or lose nothing
Game 6: 90% chance to lose $10 or lose nothing

Results

All hypotheses are confirmed. Repeated ANOVAs revealed no significant main effect of emotion (p>.1). The predicted two-way interaction of surprise with NFC was, however, significant (p<.05; see Equation 1). The two-way interaction of pride with NFC was not significant (p>.1), however, the predicted three-way interaction of pride, NFC, and CSE achieved significance (p<.05; see Equation 2).

Equation 1–H1a (w/ H2): (F (4, 57)=2.629, p<.05). Y=2.495–4.056 (Condition) + .761 (Optimism) -.639 (NFC) + 1.838 (Condition * NFC). Condition 0=control, 1=surprise.

Equation 2–H1b (w/ H2/H3): (F (5, 50)=3.046, p<.05). Y=-10.778 + 6.658 (Condition) + 6.247 (NFC) -.889 (NFC^2) + 1.080 (CSE)-.692 (Condition*NFC*CSE). Condition 0=control, 1=pride.

Selected References

Baumeister, R. F., Jones, E.E. (1978), "When self-presentation is constrained by the target's knowledge: Consistency and compensation," *Journal of Personality and Social Psychology*, 36, 608-618.

Cryder, C.E., Lerner, J.S., Gross, J.J., Dahl, R.E. (2008), "Misery is not miserly: sad and self-focused individuals spend more," *Psychological Science*, 19, 6, 525-530.

Han, S., Lerner, J.S., Keltner, D. (2007), "Feelings and Consumer Decision making: The Appraisal-Tendency Framework," *Journal of Consumer Psychology*, 17, 3, 158-168.

Isen, A.M., Geva, N. (1987), "The influence of positive affect on acceptable level of risk–The person with a large canoe has a large worry," *Organizational Behavior and Human Decision ProcessesI*, 39, 2, 145-154.

Johar, G.V., Maheswaran, D., Peracchio, L.A. (2006), "MAPping the Frontiers: Theoretical Advances in Consumer Research on Memory, Affect and Persuasion," *Journal of Consumer Research*, 33, 2, 139-149.

Johnson, E.J., & Tversky, A. (1983), "Affect, generalization, and the perception of risk," *Journal of Personality and Social Psychology*, 45, 20-31.

Khaneman, D., Tversky, A. (1979), "Prospect theory: An analysis of decision under risk," *Econometrica*, 47, 2, 263-291.

Kuvass, B., Kaufmann, G. (2004), "Impact of mood, framing, and need for cognition on decision makers' recall and confidence," *Journal of Behavioral Decision Making*, 17, 1, 59-74.

Lerner, J.S., & Keltner, D. (2001), "Fear, anger, and risk," *Journal of Personality and Social Psychology*, 81, 146-159

Lerner, J.S., Small, D.A., Lowewenstein, G. (2004), "Heart strings and purse strings: Carryover effects of emotions on economic decisions," *Psychological Science*, 15, 5, 337-341.

Smith, C.A., Ellsworth, P.C. (1985), "Patterns of Cognitive Appraisal in Emotion," *Journal of Personality and Social Psychology*, 48, 4, 813-838.

Tesser, A. (2000), "On the confluence of self-esteem maintenance mechanisms," *Personality and Social Psychology Review*, 4, 4, 290-299

Tracy, J.L., & Robins, R.W. (2007), "The psychological structure of pride: A tale of two facets," *Journal of Personality and Social Psychology*, 92, 3, 506-525.

"From the Web to the Woods": Connecting the Online to the Offline in Consumers' Play

Daiane Scaraboto, York University, Canada

Current perspectives on play define it as "situational and reliant not simply on abstract rules but also on social networks, attitudes, or events in one's non-game life, technological abilities or limits, structural affordances or limits, local cultures, and personal understandings of leisure." (Taylor 2006, p.156). Despite several efforts directed at defining and exploring different dimensions of play (Grayson 1999; Deighton & Grayson 1995; Holbrook 1994), consumer researchers have focused mainly on the intrinsic motivations of play and the role of marketers in defining playful experiences (Kozinets et al. 2004). We have limited knowledge about other environmental and social conditions that interfere with consumers' playful activities. In this paper, I propose that two major concepts have been overlooked in their relation to play: technology and community.

The rapid expansion of technologies of information and communication promoted major social changes during the last decades (Mick & Fournier 1998). While previous studies have assessed the impact of technology in consumer agency (Kozinets et al. 2004); self-presentation (Schau & Gilly 2003), and dissatisfaction (Ward & Ostrom 2006), the interfaces between technology and play have received partial attention only. Extant theory develops in two streams: play in offline environments (Martin 2004, Holt 1995, Arnould & Price 1993), and online games studies (Mathwick & Rigdon 2004). Attempts to compare both realms have developed in cultural studies and sociology, suggesting that video games and online games serve purposes that are similar to those of offline play (e.g. Jenkins 1998, Taylor 2006). However, manifestations of nature in these two types of worlds may be essentially different. The offline environment can be perceived through all senses. It can be seen and heard, smelled, tasted, and touched. In such environments, players are subject to weather variations and their actions are usually limited to the capacities of their physical bodies. The offline world is one of potentially risky situations where there is constant need to engage all senses in order to cope with the environment (Dreyfus 2001, Tuan 1998). Cyberspace, in contrast, is perceived as "physically safe", decontextualized and aseptic (Wellman & Gulia 1999). While the efforts made so far to understand the particularities of each realm are noteworthy, we lack empirical accounts of the interfaces between the online and offline, technology and nature, in play-related activities enacted by consumers.

I complement prior research by investigating consumer practices in a playful context that involves online and offline activities: geocaching. Geocaching is an increasingly popular game played with the use of GPS devices. Frequently defined as a high-tech version of treasure hunting, it combines technology with outdoor adventure. The basic rule is that individuals hide small containers anywhere in the world and share the geographic coordinates of these caches on the Internet. Players plan a hunt by choosing from a list of caches and their locations on a public website. They download the coordinates to their GPS devices and use them to get to the place where the cache is hidden. When finding a cache, players are asked to sign the notebook, take something from the cache and leave something else to replace what they have taken. When the hunt is over, it is reported on the same website and credit is gained from each cache found. The website geocaching.com has registered over 500,000 players in more than a hundred countries and more than 837,500 active caches worldwide since 2000 (Groundspeak.com).

This investigation of geocaching is an ongoing study initiated in June 2008. I combine netnography (Kozinets 2002) with traditional ethnographic techniques to study geocachers' online and offline activities. I have conducted interviews with geocachers and participant observation in multiple online and offline sites. I gathered field notes, pictures, as well as archival data in the form of podcasts, media texts, and forum discussions.

Preliminary results indicate that the combination of multiple technologies with outdoor activities, nature, and travel attracts and brings together into geocaching individuals with diverse backgrounds, profiles, and motivations. As technology and nature are essential to the game, players need to articulate their incursions into these two apparently opposite fields. While outdoors exploration resonates with the antique "back to nature" sentiment, technology allows for control and safety within the wild and unfamiliar world of nature.

Players also switch between online and offline in order to negotiate the rules of the game, monitor competition, and integrate playful experiences into the space and time of everyday life. It is through online interaction, secured by nicknames and avatars, that players share stories about their hunts for a particular cache, reconstructing them as fantastic, collective experiences. This penetration of offline play into the online realm eventually strengthens the bonds among players and reinforces the communal aspects of play, hence suggesting a fundamental role for technology in shaping communities of play.

These preliminary themes, combined to the growing interest on the communal aspects of consumption (Muniz & O'Guinn 2001) and the increasing pervasiveness of play in current north-American society (Ackerman 1999) suggest that consumer researchers could gain much from an advanced understanding of the communal aspects of play. Although observing that "humans will find community where they will" (Muniz & Schau 2005, p. 746), consumer researchers have recently investigated communities that are mainly related to brands, branded products and the market in general (e.g. Muniz & Schau 2005, Kozinets 2002). Future studies should explore the possibility that play is the central link that brings a community together, helping us understand when and how play and consumption are co-constituted, and extending our knowledge about what sorts of side roles brands and consumption play in constituting communities of practice.

References

Ackerman, Diane (1999), *Deep Play*. New York: Random House.

Arnould, Eric J. and Linda L. Price (1993), "River Magic: Extraordinary Experience and the Extended Service Encounter," *Journal of Consumer Research*, 20 (June), 24-45.

Deighton, John & Grayson, Kent (1995), "Marketing and Seduction: Building Exchange Relationships by Managing Social Consensus", *Journal of Consumer Research, 21*, (March), 518-526.

Delanty, Gerard (2003), *Community*. New York: Routledge.

Dreyfus, H. T. (2001). *On the Internet* [Thinking in Action]. New York: Routledge.

Grayson, Keith (1999), "The Dangers and Opportunities of Playful Consumption" in *Consumer Value: A Framework for Analysis and Research*, ed. Morris B. Holbrook, London: Routledge.

Groundspeak. Available at http://www.geocaching.com

Holbrook, Morris B., Chestnut,R. W., Oliva,T. A., & Greenleaf, E.A. (1984), "Play as Consumption Experience: The Roles of Emotions, Performance, and Personality in the Enjoyment of Games", *Journal of Consumer Research, 11* (September), 728-739.

Holt, Douglas B. (1995), "How Consumers Consume: A Typology of Consumption Practices.", *Journal of Consumer Research, 22* (June), 1-16.

Jenkins, Henry (1998), "'Complete Freedom of Movement': Videogames as Gendered Play Spaces," in Justine Cassell and Henry Jenkins, ed., *From Barbie to Mortal Kombat: Gender and Computer Games*, Cambridge, MA: MIT Press, 262-297.

Kozinets, Robert V. (2002b), "The Field Behind the Screen: Using Netnography for Marketing Research in Online Communities," *Journal of Marketing Research*, 39 (February), 61-72.

Kozinets, Robert V., John F. Sherry, Jr., Diana Storm, Adam Duhachek, Krittinee Nuttavuthisit and Benét DeBerry-Spence (2004), "Ludic Agency and Retail Spectacle," *Journal of Consumer Research*, 31 (December), 658-672.

Martin, Brett, A. S. (2004), "Using the Imagination: Consumer Evoking and Thematizing of the Fantastic Imaginary," *Journal of Consumer Research, 31* (1), 136-149.

Mathwick, Charla & Rigdon, Edward (2004), "Play, Flow, and the Online Search Experience," *Journal of Consumer Research, 31* (2), 324-332.

Mick, David G. & Fournier, Susan (1998), "Paradoxes of Technology: Consumer Cognizance, Emotions, and Coping Strategy," *Journal of Consumer Research, 25* (September), 123-143.

Muniz, Albert M. and & Thomas C. O'Guinn (2001), "Brand Community," *Journal of Consumer Research,* 27 (March), 412-432.

Muniz, Albert M. and Hope Schau (2005), "Religiosity in the Abandoned Apple Newton Brand Community," *Journal of Consumer Research*, 31 (March).

Schau, Hope J. & Gilly, Mary C. (2003), "We are What We Post? Self-presentation in Personal Web Space," *Journal of Consumer Research,* 30 (3), 385-404.

Taylor, T. L. (2006), *Play Between Worlds*. Cambridge, MA: The MIT Press.

Tuan, Yi-Fu (1998), *Escapism*. London: The Johns Hopkins University Press.

Ward, James C. & Ostrom, Amy L. (2006), "Complaining to the Masses: The Role of Protest Framing in Customer-Created Complaint Websites," *Journal of Consumer Research, 33* (September), 220-230.

Wellman, Barry & Gulia, Milena (1999), "Virtual Communities as Communities: Net Surfers Don't Ride Alone" in *Communities in Cyberspace*. Marc A. Smith and Peter Kollock (editors), London. Routledge.

Drawing Association Rules between Purchases and In-Store Behavior: An Extension of the Market Basket Analysis

Julien Schmitt, Loughborough University, UK

Actual observation of shopping behaviors is rarely conducted in marketing research. Behavior is often inferred with a more easily measurable ouput: purchases. Market Basket Analysis (MBA) is one of many techniques used to study shopping behavior through purchases. It aims to identify the associations between product categories based on purchases performed in these categories. Specifically, it answers the following question: if a consumer buys an item from category A, is he more likely to buy an item from category B?

Though this technique is very popular, it has an important limitation. MBA measures associations between categories by using purchases. However, categories may be too closely related in terms of interest that consumers take in, without exhibiting strong purchase associations. To detect such associations not based on purchases, it is necessary to observe actual in-store behavior: the shoppers' paths through the store, the way they behave within product categories to observe shelves, handle products and examine them. This may reveal consumers' interests for product categories.

Using a new data collection allowing to precisely record and time-stamp shoppers' moves and gestures, we extend the classical MBA by integrating in-store physical behavior in the analysis: we draw associations not only from purchases but also from actual in-store behavior. We compare results of our new method with classical MBA results and show a significant improvement.

From purchase associations to behavioral associations

MBA was at first developed in a brick-and-mortar environment. Associations between categories were computed using panel data. Given that the MBA's practicality, it has known a rapid development. Managers consider it as a useful tool to manage cross-promotions or to develop loyalty programs. Researchers use this technique to study multi-category purchase decisions.

MBA has then been used to study cross-buying on the Internet. However, Internet data has an important difference from panel data: it is not limited to purchase behavior. Navigation data is also available, such as web-pages that are viewed, products that are examined, or specific attributes that are investigated. Research uses it to make associations between categories not only based on purchases, but also based on navigation patterns that reveal consumers' interest for categories. More accurate associations have been computed using navigation behavior.

If such associations between behavior within one category and purchases within another exist on the Internet, they are likely to exist also in a real context. Indeed, interests for categories are considered a stronger explanation of association than purchases. Thus, we hypothesize that, in a brick-and-mortar environment, adding information about consumer behavior would lead to better associations between categories.

Research methodology

Data collection

To achieve our research objective, we developed a specially designed program. Implemented with a PDA, this program enables a very accurate data collection: Following the shopper throughout the store, the program user visualizes the store map on a screen and can locate the shopper's position by pinpointing it. This captures and time stamps the entire shopping path. When the shopper stops in front of a shelf, another screen enables the user to capture each shopper's action by clicking on different buttons. Thus, the shopping path and actions are time-stamped and automatically entered in a preformatted database.

For this study, we conducted shopper tracking in a medium-sized store specialized in beaity-care products, and we followed a total of 170 shoppers. To avoid bias, we selected shoppers on a random basis. Shoppers were not aware being followed; this allowed for an unobtrusive tracking process.

Model Development

To draw our model, we consider the variable Z_k describing the behavior adopted by the shopper in the category k. Z_k takes four different values, depending on the interest taken by the shopper at the category k. These values are:

- Z_k="0": the shopper does not stop in the category k. It represents the minimum level of interest.
- Z_k="Stop": the shopper stops within the category k and looks at shelves. It represents the first level of interest.
- Z_k="Examination": the shopper is interested enough to handle a product from category k and investigate it. It represents the second level of interest.
- Z_k="Purchase": the shopper is so interested that he decides to purchase an item. This is the maximum level of interest.

To compare performances between associations based on purchases (classical MBA) and associations based on physical behaviors (Extended MBA), we represent both these models by using Z_k.

To represent Classical MBA, we allow Z_k to take only two values: "0" or "Purchase". Thus we are able to compute the following indicator:

- Confidence (j;i)=P(Z_i=Purchase $\cap$ Z_j=Purchase) / P(Z_i=Purchase)

To represent Extended MBA principle, we allow Z_k to take all its possible values: "0", "Stop", "Examination", and "Purchase". It allows the computation of two additional confidence rules:

- Condidence $_{Stop}$(j;i)=P($Z_{j=}$Purchase $\cap$ Z_i=Stop)/P($_{Zi}$=Stop)
- Condidence$_{Exa}$ (j;i)= P($Z_{j=}$Purchase $\cap$ P$Z_{i=}$Examination) /P(Z_i=Examination)

We then compare the accuracy of associations between categories issued from each of the models.

Results and discussion

Our results show that association rules are stronger when physical behaviors are taken into account simultaneously with purchases. In some cases, associations based on physical behaviors alone are stronger than associations based on purchases. This may be explained by the fact that physical behaviors represent consumers' express interests for product categories that are not taken into account by classical MBA. The better performance of the Extended MBA may also be explained by the fact that it takes into account non-buyers. Indeed, a non-negligible proportion of shoppers leaves the store without buying anything and is therefore not taken into account by classical MBA. However, non-buyers have visited the store, handled some products in different categories, which is valuable information to understand associations between categories.

Our results provide a better understanding of the influence of in-store consumer actions on cross-category decisions: some actions performed in a category may influence a purchase in another category.

References

Agrawal, Rakesh, Tomasz Imienlinski, and Arun Swami (1993), "Mining association rules between sets of items in large databases", *Proceedings of the ACM SIGMOD International Conference on Management of Data*, Washington D.D., 207-216.

Ansari, Asim, Skander Essegaier, and Rajeev Kohli (2000), "Internet recommendation systems", *Journal of Marketing Research*, 37 (August), 363-375.

Bodapati, Anand V. (2008), "Recommendation systems with purchase data", *Journal of Marketing Research*, 45 (February), 77-93.

Danaher, Peter J., Guy W. Mullarkey, and Skander Essegaier (2006), "Factors affecting web site visit duration: a cross-domain analysis", *Journal of Marketing Research*, 43 (May), 182-194.

Linden, G., Smith, B., and York, J. (2003), "Amazon.com recommendations: Item-to-item collaborative filtering", *IEEE Internet Computing*, 7 (1), 76-80.

Moe, Wendy W. (2006), "An empirical two-stage choice model with varying decision rules applied to Internet clickstream data", *Journal of Marketing Research*, 43 (November), 680-692.

Montgomery, Alan L., Li Shibo, Kannan Srinivasan, and John C. Liechty (2004), "Modeling online browsing and path analysis using clickstream data", *Marketing Science*, 23 (Fall), 579-595.

Rossi, Peter E., Robert E. McCulloch, and Greg M. Allenby (1996), "On the value of household purchase history information in target marketing", *Marketing Science*, 15 (4), 321-340.

Russel, Gary J., and Ann Petersen (2000), "Analysis of cross category dependence in market basket selection", *Journal of Retailing*, 76 (3), 367-392.

Russel, Gary J., S. Ratneshwar, Shocker, Allan D., Bell, Anand Bodapati, Alex Degeratu, Lutz Hildebrandt, Namwoon Kim, S. Ramaswani, and H. Shankar (1999), "Multiple-category decision making: review and synthesis", *Marketing Letters*, 10 (August), 319-332.

For a Deeper Understanding of the Sociality that Emanates from Virtual Communities of Consumption

Alexandre Schwob, HEC Paris, France

At a time when the project of reflexive modernization (Beck, Bonss, and Lau 2003) radicalizes modern societies by disembedding the individual from even these "primordial social relations" (Knorr Cetina 2001) which are religious worldviews, previously stable and stratified social hierarchies, and social institutions, consumer researchers have stated that gatherings around specific objects or consumption activities become essential for social ties.

Thus, over the last 15 years, much effort has been dedicated to exploration of various forms and displays of common consumption interests (e.g., Belk and Costa 1998; Cova 1997; Kozinets 2001; McAlexander, Schouten, and Koenig 2002; Muniz and O'Guinn 2001; Schouten and McAlexander 1995; Thompson and Troester 2002). Some authors have strongly advocated that these consumption communities, (sub)cultures, and tribes represent a response to the erosion of traditional forms of sociality (Cova 1997; Firat and Dholakia 1997; Firat and Venkatesh 1995) in which sociality represents "the ways through which actors relate to each other to organise their practices and construe their identities" (Fiske 1998). Whereas more recently some researchers have analyzed deeply the practices of a given tribe (Hewer and Brownlie 2007), strangely enough it has to be acknowledged that very few papers published in consumer research have focused on the social construction of identities of selves in social interaction contexts (Reed 2002), or more specifically on sociality in virtual environments. An attempt to bridge these two gaps has been recently made by Schau and Gilly (2003), but the investigations of these researchers on the different aspects of sociality has not gone beyond revealing the existence of multiple social roles and the self presentations by consumers in cyberspace. I argue that the sociality emanating from Internet deserves to be better understood by considering social sites such as online discussion forums, wherein we get deeper insights into the structural elements that determine consumer identity constructions.

The sociality conveyed by consumption has mainly been conceptualized over the past decades on the individual level through extended self (Belk, 1988) and self presentation (cf. Schau and Gilly 2003), and on the collective level through social practices (Warde, 2005). As Reed (2002) I argue that, although social identity is a rarely used paradigm in consumer research, it is meaningful to conceptualize the role of relations with others and with artefacts in self-conception. I should add that this paradigm can be successfully applied to identity construction processes emanating from technology (Internet) that has a structural potential (DeSanctis and Poole 1994). Following some consumer researchers (Holt and Thompson 2004) and some structuration researchers in Information systems (Whitman and Woszczynski 2003), I chose to direct this paper on the structural focus on the role of agency in social effects. More specifically, this paper is based on traditional "social scientists methods" (Penaloza and Venkatesh 2006) in order to grasp the different ways consumers (as agents) appropriate the online discussion forums of a given virtual community, considered as consumption object and social site (Maignan and Lukas 1997; Presi and al 2006) in which sociality can be investigated. Following Schultz Kleine, Kleine, and Allen (1995), I adopt life narratives to enlighten the importance of others, and the results of personal progression in self-conception.

In order to strengthen the internal validity of the research, I have chosen to investigate forums of one particular virtual community of consumption, www.jeuxvideo.com. It concerns video game players. This website was created in 1997, and members of the community connect on the second most important French Internet forum in terms of volume of activity (measured by posts exchanged). The study proposes a hermeneutical approach applied to consumer experience of discussion forums. The research is inductive and is built upon existential-phenomenological interviews of different forumers at different times.

More specifically, I answer this main research question: "How do consumers appropriate forums of virtual communities of consumption in a sustainable way?" Relationships to forums are the focus of this research, because they constitute the most important part of consumer experience in virtual communities of consumption.

Preliminary results established from interviews of 8 regular members of the community show that, beyond the diversity of perceptions, most consumers agree on the ability of the forums to fullfill evolving needs. Nevertheless, a more precise constitutive analysis reveals elements around which consumer appropriations differ significantly. These are based on routines at the intersection between virtual and real environments, more precisely connexions to the forum, posting activity per se, and socializing from outside (but thanks to) the forums. Interrelationships between these dimensions sustain idiosyncratic knowledge projects (Zwick and Dholakia 2006) that are more or less actively sought by consumers. These knowledge projects are experienced throughout different subject positions related to different practices. Consumers build more or less salient social identities around these positions.

Two fundamental dimensions tend to influence a main "consumption logic" adopted by a given forumer: the degree to which the forum is associated to the knowledge project on a) consumption objects (here, video games) and b) other consumers. According to her/

his personal situation within these two dimensions, a forumer is more or less likely to be situated in "consumer", "expert", "communal", or "social actor" logic. A given consumer can shift from a given logic to another during his/her foruming experience. Interrelationships between these "consumption logics" have now to be more deeply explained and validated with other data and possibly other methods like semiotic squares. Each of these coexisting logics seems to foster subject positions on more or less "locally grounded" and more or less "social" practices (e.g., trolls, polls, games, rankings, conflicts, hacks…) which create the culture of the forum. "Locally grounded" practices are generally deeply tied to the coexistence of different visions of forum "materiality".

In conclusion, beyond extending knowledge on virtual communities of consumption, this research contributes to the Consumer Culture Theory (Arnould and Thompson 2005) stream of research, aiming to anchor consumer research in the sociological paradigm more deeply. As such it opens many perspectives to study the role that consumption plays in social ties.

References

Arnould, Eric J. and Craig J. Thompson (2005), "Consumer Culture Theory (CCT): Twenty Years of Research," *Journal of Consumer Research, 31* (March), 868-82.

Beck, Ulrich, Wolfgang Bonss, and Christoph Lau (2003), "The Theory of Reflexive Modernization," *Theory, Culture & Society 20* (2), 1–33.

Belk, Russell W. (1988), "Possessions and the Extended Self," *Journal of Consumer Research*, 15 (September), 139-68.

Belk, Russell W. and Janeen A. Costa (1998), "The Mountain Man Myth: A Contemporary Consuming Fantasy," *Journal of Consumer Research*, 25 (December), 218-40.

Cova, Bernard (1997), "Community and Consumption: Towards a Definition of the Linking Value of Product or Services," *European Journal of Marketing* 31(3/4), 297-316.

DeSanctis, Gerardine and Marshall Scott Poole (1994), "Capturing the Complexity in Advanced Technology Use: Adaptive Structuration Theory," *Organization Science*, 5 (May), 121-47.

Firat, A. Fuat and Nikhilesh Dholakia (1997), *Consuming People: From Political Economy to Theaters of Consumption*, London and New York: Routledge.

Firat, A. Fuat and Alladi Venkatesh (1995), "Liberatory Postmodernism and the Reenchantment of Consumption," *Journal of Consumer Research*, 22 (December), 239-67.

Fiske, Alan P. (1998), "Human Sociality," *International Society for the Study of Personal Relationships Bulletin*, 14 (2), 4-9.

Hewer, Paul and Douglas Brownlie (2007), "Cultures of Consumption of Car Aficionados: Aesthetics and Consumption Communities," *International Journal of Sociology and Social Policy*, 27 (3/4), 106-119.

Holt, Douglas B. and Craig J. Thompson (2004), "Man-of-Action Heroes: The Pursuit of Heroic Masculinity in Everyday Consumption," *Journal of Consumer Research*, 31 (September), 425-40.

Knorr Cetina, Karin D. (2001), *Postsocial relations: Theorizing Sociality in a Post-Social Environment*, Handbook of social theory, London and Thousand Oaks, CA: Sage.

Kozinets, Robert V. (2001), "Utopian Enterprise: Articulating the Meanings of Star Trek's Culture of Consumption," *Journal of Consumer Research*, 28(June), 67-88.

Maignan Isabelle and Bryan A. Lukas (1997), "The nature and social uses of the Internet: A qualitative investigation," *The Journal of Consumer Affairs*, 31 (2), 346-71

McAlexander, James H., John W. Schouten, and Harold. F. Koenig (2002), "Building brand community," *Journal of Marketing*, 66 (January), 38-54.

Muniz, Albert M. Jr. and Thomas C. O'Guinn (2001), "Brand Community," *Journal of Consumer Research*, 27 (March), 412-32.

Penaloza, Lisa and Alladi Venkatesh (2006), "Further Evolving the New Dominant Logic of Marketing: from Services to the Social Construction of Markets," *Marketing Theory*, Vol. 6 (September) Issue 3, 299-316.

Presi, Caterina, Paul Michell, and Andrew. R. Lock (2006), "Reading Consumers' Identity in Virtual Communities of Consumption: Exploring the Influence of Motive and Focus of Attention," *Association for Consumer Research.* Asia-Pacific Conference Proceedings, 7, 330-338.

Reed, Americus (2002), "Social Identity as a Useful Perspective for Self-Concept-Based Consumer Research," *Psychology and Marketing*, 19 (3), 235-66.

Schouten, John W. and James H. McAlexander (1995), "Subcultures of Consumption: An Ethnography of the New Bikers," *Journal of Consumer Research*, 22 (June), 43-61.

Schultz Kleine, Susan, Robert E. Kleine III, and Chris T. Allen (1994), "How Is a Possession "Me" or "Not Me"? Characterizing Types and an Antecedent of Material Possession Attachment," *Journal of Consumer Research*, 22 (December), 327-43.

Schau, Hope J. and Mary C. Gilly (2003), "We Are What We Post? Self-Presentation in Personal Web Space," *Journal of Consumer Research*, 30 (December), 385-404.

Thompson, Craig J. and Maura Troester (2002), "Consumer Value Systems in the Age of Postmodern Fragmentation: The Case of the Natural Health Microculture," *Journal of Consumer Research*, 28 (March), 550-71.

Warde, Allan (2005), "Consumption and Theories of Practice," *Journal of Consumer Culture*, 5 (2), 131–53.

Whitman, Michael E. and Amy B. Woszczynski (2003), *The Handbook of Information Systems Research,* Idea Group Inc (IGI).

Zwick, Detlev and Nikhilesh Dholakia (2006), "The Epistemic Consumption Object and Postsocial Consumption: Expanding Consumer-Object Theory in Consumer Research," *Consumption, Markets and Culture*, 9 (March), 17-43.

I Shouldn't, or Should I? Distinguishing Shame and Guilt in Goal Pursuit

Rania Semaan, Baruch College CUNY, USA
Stephen Gould, Baruch College CUNY, USA

A goal is a desired outcome which enters the mind of a decision maker as a mental representation associated with affect toward which action may be directed. This research focuses on the emotional reactions to goal progress. Much of this literature has examined these relations at the level of affect. However, two equally valenced but different discrete emotional reactions to goal progress could lead to two different subsequent goal-related behaviors. In this research the focus is on two emotions that arise while evaluating oneself: Shame and Guilt. Tangney (1990) posits that even though shame and guilt might arise from the same situation, they could lead to two different actions. Shame involves negative feelings about the stable, global self; whereas, guilt involves negative feelings about a specific behavior taken by the self. Guilt has been shown to play an important role in choices and self control. However, to the best of our knowledge, there is little research to date that investigates the effect of shame on goal-related behavior.

The goal progress literature offers opposing predictions about goal-directed behavior. On the one hand, when individuals fail to accomplish their goal they are expected to experience negative emotions and negative emotions that signal an unfavorable event reinforce avoidance behaviors and therefore lower goal performance (Ilies and Judge, 2005). On the other hand, negative emotions signal a slower-than-expected progress which in turn leads people to try harder and increase their effort to accomplish their goal (Lawrence, Carver, and Scheier, 2002).

In guilt the object of concern is some specific action or failure to act. Therefore, when guilty, people feel that they did a "bad thing"; their self-concept and identity remain intact and the self remains "able". This causes a motivation for reparative action such as confessing, apologizing, and repairing.

In shame the object of concern is the entire self. When something bad happens it is experienced as a reflection of a bad self where the entire self is negatively evaluated. When experiencing shame, people feel as if they are a "bad person" with a considerable shift in self-perception. When ashamed, people want to remove themselves from the situation that has lead to this experience (Tangney 1990).

Hence, we predict that when people feel guilty towards their goal progress, they would blame it on the behavior rather than the self. Therefore, they would want to repair their wrong deeds by striving harder towards their goal. Whereas when people feel ashamed towards their goal progress, they would blame it on their inability to keep on progressing towards their goal. Their self perception is changed and hence they would have an avoidance reaction and this will lead to goal violation.

However, this effect is moderated by two individual difference factors, shame proneness and guilt proneness. Each individual has the capacity to experience both shame and guilt. However some are more prone to one than the other. Only people high in shame proneness tend to blame the self when failures occur. They actively conceal their negative personal information which may lead to better performance at work. They also tend to experience self-derogation by devaluing the self (Harder, Cutler, and Rockart 1992), whereas people high in guilt proneness tend to blame the failure on the act rather than on the self. Zemack-Rugar et al. (2007) showed that only people who are high in guilt proneness tend to respond to guilt inducing situations and repeatedly link guilt with abstinence. When primed with guilt only those who were high on guilt proneness would show reduced levels of indulgence compared to those who were low on guilt proneness. Therefore, we extend their findings to predict that only those high in shame proneness and low in guilt proneness would respond to a shame inducing situation and when primed with shame they would tend to devalue the self and feel that they are unable to pursue their goal and therefore violate it.

Study 1

Method: 80 subjects participated in the study for course credit. We designed a 2 (Prime: Guilt vs. Shame) x 2 (Guilt proneness: Low vs. High) x 2 (Shame Proneness: Low vs. High) between subjects design.

First, subjects were given the shame versus guilt manipulation. They were then given the manipulation checks followed by a savings goal scenario. They were told to imagine that they have had a saving goal for the past few months. Then they were told that a friend of theirs calls and is going to a concert. Then they were asked to choose whether they would buy the package or not; where choosing to buy the package will be the goal violation. And finally subjects were given the SCAAI scale to assess the level of proneness to shame versus proneness to guilt.

Results: Results showed a significant three-way interaction between prime, guilt proneness and shame proneness ($F(1, 79)=4.2$, $p <0.05$), where those who are high on shame proneness and low on guilt proneness and are primed with shame chose to violate their goal with a mean of 0.752 as opposed to 0.285 (subjects primed with shame but were low on shame proneness and high on guilt proneness). All other effects were not significant ($p>.05$). These results are consistent with the hypothesis that shame leads to avoiding your goal and in turn violating it.

Conclusion

By introducing shame, we were able to address the opposing predictions of goal failures on subsequent behavior. Moreover, we showed that even though shame is more intense and more painful than guilt (Tangney et al 1990), it doesn't necessarily lead to higher goal performance.

In subsequent studies, we aim to address the limitations of the first study. First, we will elicit shame and guilt through goal-related manipulations. Then, we aim to show that the underlying mechanism behind these effects lies in attributing the failure to oneself. Finally, we aim to explore how shame would interact with two regulatory focus orientations (promotion versus prevention; Higgins 2002). In this sense, goal failure could stem from not doing a good thing (e.g. not going to the gym) or doing a bad thing (e.g. eating unhealthy food).

References

Harder, David W., Lisa Cutler, and Leisl Rockart (1992), "Assessment of Shame and Guilt and Their Relationships to Psychopathology," *Journal of Personality Assessment,* 59 (3), 584–604

Tangney, June Price (1990), "Assessing Individual Differences in Proneness to Shame and Guilt: Development of the Self-Conscious Affect and Attribution Inventory," *Journal of Personality and Social Psychology,* 59 (1), 102–11

Social Desirability and Indirect Questioning: New insights from the Implicit Association Test and the Balanced Inventory of Desirable Responding

Hendrik Slabbinck, Ghent University, Belgium
Patrick Van Kenhove, Ghent University, Belgium

Contrary to previous studies that treated Social Desirability Bias (SDB) as a one-dimensional construct, the two-dimensional Balanced Inventory of Desirable Responding, revealed that Indirect Questioning (IQ) is not completely free from SDB. IQ avoids egoistic response tendencies, but not moralistic response tendencies. Furthermore, by combining IQ with the Implicit Association Test (IAT) and behavioural measures, results indicated that IQ assesses individual differences of both the participant and the third-person, used as subject in IQ. The immunity to SDB of the IAT is further confirmed. The study topic was physical concern and designer clothes.

Introduction

When asking socially sensitive or delicate questions, respondents will not always reveal their true thoughts and prefer to respond in a socially correct manner. This discrepancy between someone's true and reported thoughts is called Social Desirability Bias (SDB) and can easily lead to faulty conclusions (Tourangeau & Yan, 2007). SDB is even considered one of the major sources of systematic error in social sciences research (Mick, 1996). Surprisingly, given the importance and omnipresence of SDB, only few marketing researchers have taken SDB into account in their research (Steenkamp et al., in press). Even, if SDB is considered, most researchers applied (a short form of) Marlowe and Crowne's one-dimensional scale (1964). Recent studies, however, indicated that some people are more likely to exhibit SDB in a communion-related context, associated with love, connectedness, ... whereas other people are more likely to exhibit SDB in an agency-related context, associated with power, status, ... These two types of SDB are referred to as moralistic (MRT) and egoistic (ERT) response tendencies (Paulhus & John, 1998). Currently, only Paulhus' Balanced Inventory of Desirable Responding (BIDR: Paulhus, 1992) is able to distinguish between MRT and ERT.

Instead of assessing SDB, different approaches exist to avoid SDB. Two such approaches are Indirect Questioning (IQ) and the Implicit Association Test (IAT: Greenwald et al., 1998).

With IQ, sensitive questions are reformulated in the third-person. As such, while respondents are uninhibitedly describing the opinion of the third-person, they are revealing their own opinion because the respondents' own opinions serve as their reference point. Despite its ability to avoid SDB and its simplicity (Fisher, 1993), the validity of IQ is still questioned because respondents could give estimates of the true answers of the third-person instead of projections of their own thoughts. So far, this question has not yet been fully answered.

The IAT, a response latency task initially developed to measure implicit attitudes, has received a remarkable level of attention to validity concerns. Several studies also concluded that the IAT is rather immune to SDB (Nosek et al., 2007). However, compared to IQ, the IAT requires a complex, time consuming administrative procedure. Moreover, the IAT only produces relative measures with arbitrary zero-points.

Research Objectives and hypotheses

The validity of IQ will be studied by combining an IQ and IAT measure of the same concept. In sum, the first goal of this research is to provide a firm answer to the question whether and under which circumstances IQ is able to avoid SDB. Second, a large collection of validity studies involving the IAT (Greenwald et al., in press), is persuasive evidence that the IAT measures something in the person. Thus, if IQ assesses individual differences of participants and not of the third-person used in IQ, we may expect that the IQ measure will correlate with the IAT measure, notwithstanding many conceptual differences between the two techniques (Sheldon et al, 2007). Finally, to test the predictive validity, IQ and IAT should predict behaviour of participants and not of the third-person.

Research Design

A pretest (n=101) revealed that questioning shopping behaviour of designer clothes was most prone to SDB. As such, participants' physical concern (PhC) was assessed in combination with their possessions of designer clothes (DC). This was done with a 3 X 2 within subjects design. PhC was assessed with a direct measure (Netemeyer, Burton & Liechtenstein, 1995), the IAT and IQ (Netemeyer et al.'s scale, rephrased in the third-person). All measures were counterbalanced. Next, SDB was assessed with the BIDR (Paulhus, 1992). Finally, several questions were asked about the amount of designer clothes participants possessed. These questions were also rephrased in the third-person to obtain an IQ measure. Reliabilities of all measures were satisfactory. Data was collected in the context of a methodological course, resulting in a large sample of 348 undergraduate students.

Results

The first major finding is that IQ is not completely free from SDB. As expected, all direct measures (PhC and DC) were significantly correlated with ERT and/or MRT. Furthermore, IQ was not correlated with ERT ($r_{PhC\text{-}ERT}=.01$, $p>.05$; $r_{DC\text{-}ERT}=-.05$; $p>.05$), but correlated significantly with MRT ($r_{PhC\text{-}MRT}=-.12$, $p<.05$; $r_{DC\text{-}MRT}=-.16$, $p<.01$).

The second major finding is that IQ is weakly, but significantly correlated with the IAT (r=.14, p<0,05). The correlation between direct PhC and IAT is comparable (r=.16, p<.05). This indicates that IQ measures at least something in the person. However, analysing the relation between PhC and DC, reveals that IQ measures also something of the third-person. Indirect PhC correlated only significantly with indirect DC ($r_{PhC\ indirect\text{-}DC\ direct}$=.07, p>.05; $r_{PhC\ indirect\text{-}DC\ indirect}$=.2, p<.01), regardless whether IQ measures were controlled for ERT and MRT. The opposite was true for the direct measures ($r_{PhC\ direct\text{-}DC\ direct}$=.33, p<.001; $r_{PhC\ direct\text{-}DC\ indirect}$=.10, p<.05). The IAT measure of PhC was only correlated with direct DC (r =.228, p<.001) and not with indirect DC (r=.06; p >.05).

Discussion and follow-up research

This study clearly demonstrated the added value of the two-dimensional BIDR. The BIDR revealed that IQ only avoids ERT, but not MRT. Results further confirmed that the IAT is immune to SDB.

Correlation between IQ and IAT indicated that IQ is sensitive to individual differences. However, the lack of correlation between IQ and behavioural variables demonstrated that IQ also measures something of the third-person. Clearly, more research is needed to clarify this duality. Currently, a follow-up study is set up in which possible moderators are included. One of these is the perceived similarity between the participant and the third-person used in IQ (Fisher, 1993). If perceived similarity is low (high), participants could be motivated to differentiate (assimilate) themselves from (with) the third person, resulting in high ERT (MRT). Furthermore, this study did only assess behavioural intentions. Follow-up research will also comprise measures of actual behaviour.

References

Fisher, R. J. (1993), "Social Desirability and the validity of indirect questioning," *Journal of Consumer Research*, 20 (2), 303-315.

Greenwald, A. G., T. A. Poehlman, E. Uhlmann, and M. R. Banaji (in press), "Understanding and using the Implicit Association Test: III. Meta-analysis of predictive validity," *Journal of Personality and Social Psychology*.

Netemeyer, R. G., S. Burton, and D. R. Liechtenstein (1995), "Trait Aspects of Vanity:
Measurement and Relevance to Consumer Behavior," *Journal of Consumer Research*, 20 (4), 612-626.

Nosek, B. A., A . G. Greenwald, and M. R. Banaji (2007), "The Implicit Association Test at age 7: A methodological and conceptual review". In J. A. Bargh (Ed.), *Automatic processes in social thinking and behavior* (pp. 265–292). Philadelphia, PA: Psychology Press.

Paulhus, D. L. (1992), "*Assessing self-deception and impression management in self–reports: The Balanced Inventory of Desirable Responding,*" Vancouver, BC: University of British Columbia.

Paulhus, D. L., and O. P. John (1998), "Egoistic and Moralistic Biases in Self-Perception: The Interplay of Self-Deceptive Styles With Basic Traits and Motives,". *Journal of Personality*, 66 (December), 1025-1060.

Steenkamp, J. B., M. G. De Jong, and H. Baumgartner (in press), "Socially Desirable Response Tendencies in survey research," *Journal of Marketing Research*.

Sheldon, K., L. King, L. Houser-Marko, R. Osbaldiston, and A. Gunz, A. (2007), "Comparing IAT and TAT measures of power versus intimacy motivation," *European Journal of Personality*, 21 (3), 263-280.

Tourangeau, R., and T. Yan (2007), "Sensitive Questions in Surveys," *Psychological Bulletin*, 133 (5), 859-883.

The Scented Winds of Change: Conflicting Notions of Modesty and Vanity among Young Qatari and Emirati Women

Rana Sobh, Qatar University, Qatar
Russell Belk, York University, Canada
Justin Gressell, American University of Sharjah, United Arab Emirates

Individual clothing choices reflect a person's conception of social, gender, and religious identities and are means by which wearers situate themselves socially vis-a-vis established codes of behavior (Gibson 2000; LeBlanc, 2007). Muslim women's clothing is a visible form of public consumption, and has been the subject of much debate within social science literatures (for example, Abu-Odeh, 1994; El-Guindi, 1999a, 1999b; Tarlo, 2005; Ruby, 2006, Gole, 1996, 2002). Modesty in clothing for both men and women is central to Islam. Based on Islamic teachings a woman for instance should be covered in a way that does not reveal her sexuality in public. She should wear clothes that cover the body (except face and hands) and which are loose and opaque, neither revealing what is underneath nor delineating sexually attractive parts of the body (al-Qaradawi 1995:79-87). Other public consumption proscriptions include: perfume, explicit make-up, tattoos, plastic surgery, and wigs or hairpieces (Al-Albani 1994).

The requirement for modesty in women clothing has been translated into different forms and styles of body and hair coverings in different countries and also varies from person to person. A large body of work has looked at the diverse meanings and connotations of the Muslim veil and the practice of *hijab* in Muslim countries where women *decide* whether to observe modest dress, including Egypt (e.g., El-Guindi, 1999a, 1999b), Turkey (Sandikci and Ger, 2001, 2005, 2007; Secor, 2002; Gole, 2002), Mali (Shultz, 2007), Cote D'Ivoire (leBlanc, 2000), Indonesia (Jones 2003), South India (Oseall and Osealla, 2007), and London (Tarlo, 2007a, 2007b). Other work has looked at women's dress in Muslim countries where women *are expected to conform* to a black loose outer gown like the abaya or similar garments worn in Gulf countries, Iran (Balasescu, 2003, 2007), and Yemen (Moors, 2007). However, the black abaya within oil-rich Gulf countries is embedded in a different contemporary local context and is increasingly associated with status and wealth (Abaza, 2007). As a result, it has different meanings and connotations from wearing the chador in Iran, the abaya in Yemen, and purdah in South India. In some Gulf countries like Qatar and Emirates, wearing the black *abaya* and *shayla*[9] and in some cases the burqa or face cover is not necessarily religiously motivated. It is in some cases a social requirement that women are expected to conform to in order to remain loyal to local customs and traditional culture; it is not a legal requirement like it is in Saudi Arabia. Such loyalty is equated with national pride and dignity. Men also are required to conform to a uniform traditional white dress, the *thoub*, and head covering, the *ghatra*, in public.

Studying women clothing practices in Qatar and Emirates (UAE) is particularly interesting because of the social and economic upheaval that these countries have been undergoing and the concomitant shifts in discourses of beauty, religion and modernity in the media, advertising and other forms of local commercial imagery. The gulf region has been known to be the most conservative part of the Arab/ Muslim world where traditional Arab and Muslim values are strictly adhered to and where wearing traditional clothing by both men and women is seen as an essential requirement for cultural integrity and an affirmation of citizenship. However, petrodollar-fueled economic wealth and integration into the global economy have increasingly attracted foreign investment and Westerners to the region, leading to major social changes. In many of the GCC countries, like Qatar and Emirates, the leaderships' desires for modernity and openness to the West has resulted in embracing more western values. This has caused some tensions and concerns that local values and national identities will be diluted and has lead to hot debates between those advocating modernity and those emphasizing the importance of preserving local culture. New clothing styles and adornment practices are increasingly adopted by young women in the region and reflect the conflicting forces of Western values that emphasize display of women's beauty and sexuality in the public sphere and traditional values requiring modesty and promoting a virtuous public domain. This contrast is strikingly evident in shopping malls that house both abaya shops and Western style multinational clothing stores with gigantic posters of provocatively dressed Western women. The abaya itself has been gradually reinvented and has evolved from being a concealing garment that hides women's sexuality and beauty in public to an embellished fashionable, trendy haute couture garment that enhances beauty and reveals sexuality. This has created a thriving abaya fashion industry featuring local and European designers attempting to reinvent the traditional plain costume into a sophisticated and fashionable garment that denotes status and prestige and makes statements about women's affinity for fashion and modernity, all supposedly without undermining the local look.

We seek to explore how women negotiate the conflicting tensions between their desire for fashion, elegance, display of beauty, and expression of individuality in the public sphere on one hand, and their desire to be loyal to local culture and observe proper Muslim dress on the other hand. We look at dress not only as clothing but as including all bodily adornment and beauty enhancement practices (e.g., shoes, purses, watches, jewelry, sunglasses, perfumes, make-up, henna, and cosmetic surgery) that form women's looks in the public sphere. We use insights from in-depth interviews with twenty four Emirati and Qatari female students to ascertain the dynamics underlying these conflicting imperatives of modesty and vanity and to capture some of the ambivalence inherent in these performative constructions of female identity and conceptions of the self.

Preliminary findings reveal that young women resolve conflicting tensions between vanity and modesty on one hand and traditional and modern on the other, through syncreticism rather than forced choice. Thus, many choose a traditional black abaya covered with expensive Swarkovski jewels. The abaya that many young women choose is also more colorful, form-revealing and gives more hints of the outfits they wear beneath. The shayla is also worn sophisticatedly high and exposes some of the hair. The traditional garment is increasingly assuming a modern fashionable appearance accessorized with jewelry, designer handbags and high heel shoes, huge and catchy sunglasses. The look is complemented with flawless make up, nails and strenuous perfumes. The abaya that used to be a unifying garment that expresses women collective religious and cultural identity has evolved into a singularly self-identifying look that is expressive of status, distinctiveness and personal identities. It is used by girls to make statements about their personal tastes and affinities to fashion . Findings also reveal that girls choose different garments, scents, and makeup in different settings. And they find ways to rationalize their own appearance choices while distinguishing it from other practices that they condemn (Bier, 1986; Greenwalt, 1986; Scott and Lyman; 1986). Rather than the dichotomous choices posed by Western authors (Lexus vs. Olive Tree; McWorld vs. Jihad), they have chosen to combine both.

References

Abaza, Mona (2007), "Shifting Landscapes of fashion in Contemporary Egypt", Fashion Theory. 11(2/3), 281-289.

Abu Odeh, Lama (1993), "Post-Colonial Feminism and the Veil: Thinking the Difference", *Feminist Review*. 43 (Spring), 26-37.

Al-Albani, Mohammed Nasr Adeen (2002), "The Jilbab and the Muslim Woman in the Qur'an and Sunnah" [Jilbab almaraa el Muslimah fi al Kitab wa Assunnah], Dar Salam.

Al-Qaradawi, Yusuf (1995) *The Lawful and the Prohibited in Islam* [Al-Halal Wal-Haram Fil Islam], Translators Kamal El-Helbawy, M Moinuddin Siddiqui, Syed Shukry, KUWAIT, Al Faisal Press.

Balasescu, Alexandru (2007), "Haute Couture in Tehran: Two Faces of an Emerging Fashion Scene," *Fashion theory*. 11 (2/3): 299-318.

Balasescu, Alexandru (2003), "Tehran Chic: Islamic headsarves, Fashion Designers, and New Geographies of Modernity", *Fashion Theory*, 7 (1), 39-56

Bier, Kurt (1986), "Justification in Ethics," in *Justification Nomos XXVII*, J. Roland Pennock and John Chapman, ed., New York: New York University Press, 3-27.

Boulanouar, W. Aisha (2006), "Dressing for Success: A background to Muslim Women's Clothing", *New Zealand Journal of Asian Studies*, 2 (12),135-157

El Guindi, Fadwa (1999a). *Veil: Modesty, Privacy and Resistance, Dress, Body and Culture Series*, Oxford and New York, Berg.

---

[9]The black abaya is a long black loose outer garment worn by women in most gulf countries. It is intended to hide the curves of their bodies, while the shayla is a black head cloth used to cover their hair. The abaya is made of two layers of thin material to make sure it is not transparent. Some women also cover their faces with a black veil–niqab- although there is wide agreement amongst Muslim scholars that this is not a religious requirement for physical modesty in Islam but more of a norm for women in some social circles.

El Guindi, Fadwa (1999b), "Veiling Resistance", *Fashion Theory*, 3(1), 51-80.

El Guindi, Fadwa. 1981, "Veiling Infitah with Muslim Ethic: Egypt's Contemporary Islamic Movement", *Social Problems*. 4 (April), 465-485.

Jones, Carla (2007), " Fashion and Faith in Urban Indonesia", 11 (2/3), 211-232.

Gibson, Pamela (2000), "Redressing the Balance: Patriarchy, Postmodernism and Feminism," in *Fashion Cultures: Theories, Explorations and Analysis*. Stella bruzzi and Pamela Gibson, ed., London: Routledge, 349-362.

Gole, Nilufer (2002), "Islam in Public: New Visibilities and New Imageries", *Fashion Theory,* 14 (1), 173-190

Gole, Nilufer (1996), *The Forbidden Modern: Civilisation and Veiling*, Ann Arbor:MI, The University of Michigan Press.

Greenwalt, Kurt (1986), "Distinguishing Justifications from Excuses," *Law and Contemporary Problems*, 49 (Summer), 89-108

LeBlanc, M. Natalie (2000), "Versioning Womanhood and Muslimhood: Fashion and the Life Course in Contemporary Bouake, Cote D'Ivoire", *Africa*. 70(3), 442-480.

Moors, Annelies (2007), "Fashionable Mulsims: Notions of Self, Religion, and Soceity in San'a," *Fashion Theory*. 11(2/3), 319-346.

Osealla, Caroline and Osello, Filippo (2007), "Muslim Style in South India". *Fashion Theory*. 11 (2/3), 233-252.

Ruby, F. Tabassum (2006), "Listening to Voices of Hijab", *Women's Studies International Forum*. 29, 54-66.

Sandikci, Ozlem and Ger, Guliz (2007), "Constructing and Representing the Islamic Consumer in Turkey". *Fashion Theory*. 11 (2/3), 189-210.

Sandikci, Ozlem and Ger, Guliz (2001), " Fundamental Fashions: The Cultural Politics of the Turban and the Levi's" Advances in Consumer Research, 28,146-150.

Sandikci, Ozlem and Ger, Guliz (2005), *Aesthetics, Ethnics and Politics of the Turkish Headscarf*. In Clothing as Material Culture, p 61-82, edited by Susanne Kuchler and Daniel Miller, Oxford and New York, Berg.

Scott, Marvin B. and Stanford B. Lyman (1968), "Accounts," *American Sociological Review*, 33 (February), 46-61.

Secor, J. Anna (2002), "The Veil and Urban Space in Istanbul: Women's Dress Mobility and Islamic Knowledge." *Gender, Place and Culture*. 9(1): 5-22

Shultz, E. Dorothea (2007), "Competing Sartorial Assertions of Femininity and Mali Identity in Mali," *Fashion Theory*. 11(2/3): 253-280.

Tarlo, Emma (2007a), "Islamic Cosmopolitanism: The sartorial Biographies of Three Muslim Women in London", *Fashion Theory*. 11 (2/3), 143-172.

Tarlo, Emma (2007b), "Hijab in London: Metamorphosis, Resonance and Effects", *Journal of Material Culture*. 12(2), 131-156.

Consumer Pride: Emotion as a Social Phenomenon

Katherine Sredl, University of Notre Dame, USA

Consumer emotions are rarely examined from a phenomenological perspective, with few exceptions. One consumer practice that generates emotion and involves consumption is ritual (Ruth, Otnes, and Brunel 1999). According to Collins' Interaction Ritual Chain (2004), elements of sustained rituals elicit emotion in observable ways. This working paper investigates how the elements of consumption-based family rituals elicit pride. It takes an ethnographic approach, using long interviews and participant observation. The focus is on working class, middle class, and upper middle class Sunday family dinners in contemporary Zagreb, Croatia. The findings point to time, aesthetic goods, and family as elements that elicit pride. The paper presents a construct of consumer pride.

Conceptualization

Few articles in the field of consumer behavior research look specifically at pride. Using experimental research, scholars examine pride as a variable to manipulate in persuasive communications (Aaker and Williams 1998) or as a variable in consumer decision-making (Louro, Pieters, and Zeelenberg 2005; Mukhopadhyay and Johar 2007). In a related field, social psychologists note that pride emerges in social contexts and plays a central role in facilitating relationships and in maintaining social hierarchies (Leary 2007). Pride is also distinct from hubris (Tracy and Robins 2007). In spite of the growth of research in the sociology of emotions, there is little research on pride in that field (Turner and Stets 2006). Although emotions arise in ritual, interpretive consumer research on rituals tends to focus on individual practices or on social relationships (Rook 1985; Belk, Wallendorf, and Sherry 1989). Scholarship on specific group rituals, for example, family meals, tends to examine the role of ritual in creating meanings at the group and social levels (Wallendorf and Arnould 1991). Research on consumption-based rituals such as gift-giving argues that individual emotions are an important outcome of these interactions (Ruth, Otnes, and Brunel 1999; Wooten 2000).

I apply Interaction Ritual Chain (IRC), a theory for understanding the relationships between emotions, rituals, and goods, on a micro (small group) as well as a macro-social level (Collins 2004). According to Collins' Interaction Ritual Chain (2004), elements of sustained rituals such as Sunday family dinner reinforce expression of emotion and the status of symbolic goods. My question in this research is: how do consumption-based family rituals elicit pride through the use of aesthetic goods? Overall, this research project will contribute to interpretive consumer research by examining relationships between consumer rituals, aesthetic goods, and family consumption, focusing on three points that, so far, have received little attention in the literature. First, this work aims to provide a means for understanding emotions from a phenomenological perspective. Second, it develops a construct of pride, a specific emotion elicited in rituals. Third, it will consider the ways emotions elicited in ritual influence the consumption of aesthetic and luxury goods (Charters 2006).

This work examines the role of pride and aesthetic goods (i.e. tableware) in consumption-based family rituals in contemporary Zagreb, Croatia, a society that experienced the transition from state socialism as well as war in the 1990s. The mid-day Sunday meal ritual has been practiced among members of working, middle, and upper middle classes in Zagreb through pre-socialist, socialist, and post-socialist (i.e. contemporary) eras. For decades, 2:00pm to 5.30pm on Sunday has been considered a sacred time (Belk et al.) in Zagreb, as all other activity is suspended, while generations of family members gather in the home for lunch.

Globalization has brought many changes, from new suburban shopping centers outside Zagreb, open on Sunday, to new hours for the working week. In the Yugoslav period, the work day ran from 7 a.m. to 3 p.m., providing non-working time in the daylight hours. Sunday was a non-working day. Time outside of work was for leisure and family. Now, the work day runs until 5 p.m. Supermarket chains from Austria and Italy expanded into Zagreb's suburbs and opened on Sunday. Sunday is the second most profitable day of the week for the mega-grocery stores in the suburbs ("Croatian Firms," 2009). The influence of these local and global forces on families and their social function has been significant (Ule 2004). Exploring the elements of the Sunday mid-day, such as emotions elicited, tableware used, time held, group members attending, and place held, is an opportunity better understand the role of ritual in globalization, the role of aesthetic goods in ritual, and the role of emotions in maintaining (or devaluing) rituals.

Method

Conducting depth interviews, small focus groups, and participant-observation of meals allowed this research to move beyond the traditional experimental examination of pride as solely an individual, psychobiological, or cognitive experience (McCracken 1988). In interviews, I used a semi-structured interview format to allow themes to emerge (McCracken). I inquired about informants' meal practices in their families, about their tableware inheritance and use, and about their views on family consumption and, finally, the transformation. I used the snowball method of sampling and recruiting informants who are theoretically representative; I accessed informants through key informants and through friends. A total of 39 informants participated in audio and/or video recorded interviews. Interviews were conducted in Croatian or English and yielded over 17 hours of audio, and about 560 pages of transcripts, translated into English by native Croatian speakers. I participated in 15 family meals over the course of fieldwork, which yielded 100 pages of notes and reflections. Interviews and participant observation were conducted in Zagreb, from October 2006 to July 2007.

Findings

The data analysis applies Interaction Ritual Chain (IRC), a theory developed by Randall Collins (2004), to develop a construct of pride, to understand the phenomenological experience of consumer emotions, and to consider how pride influences the consumption of goods in rituals. The findings indicate three stereotyped components of the ritual-time, aesthetic goods, and family-are integral to eliciting pride. Together, these elements create moments for experiencing pride, influence the use of aesthetic goods to elicit and communicate pride, and reinforce group hierarchies and emotional bonds. The ritual expresses pride in cultural continuity in the context of globalization. Furthermore, cultural norms affirm pride and discourage hubris. A construct of consumer pride is offered, based on the findings, with reference to social psychology scholarship on pride:

Consumer pride is an adaptive, positively valenced, self-conscious emotion, felt in the body, emergent in socially situated action, to which consumers ascribe culturally bound meaning, before, during and after interactions. Consumer pride is bolstered by acknowledgement of the self as responsible for socially valued outcomes, by display and use of goods and services, and by feedback from others. Pride is an enduring emotion, felt at the individual, group and cultural levels, that moderates consumption choices by motivating consumers to perform positive social roles through consumption, and to elicit recognition of individual achievement through consumption and social display. In sum, this working paper argues that consumers experience specific emotions (pride) in rituals. It presents a definition of consumer pride. It also argues that consumers use aesthetic goods to express pride. Future work will further explore the relationships between pride and the ritual elements and processes that elicit emotion: time, aesthetic goods, and family.

References

Aaker, Jennifer L. and Patti Williams (1998), "Empathy versus Pride: The Influence of Emotional Appeals across Cultures," *Journal of Consumer Research*, 25 (December), 241-261.

Belk, Russell W., Melanie Wallendorf, and John F. Sherry Jr. (1989), "The Sacred and the Profane in Consumer Behavior: Theodicy on the Odyssey," *Journal of Consumer Research,* 16, (June), 1-38.

Charters, S. (*2006*). "Aesthetic Products and *Aesthetic* Consumption," *Consumption, Markets and Culture*, 9(3), 235-255.

Collins, Randall (2004). *Interaction Ritual Chains.* Princeton, NJ: Princeton University Press.

"Croatian Firms File Suit against Law Banning Sunday Shopping," (2009), February 19, Retrieved June 15, 2009, http://croatiantimes.com/index.php?id=2824.

Leary, Mark R. (2007), "Motivational and Emotional Aspects of the Self," *Annual Review of Psychology*, 58, 317-344.

Louro, Maria J., Rick Pieters, and Marcel Zeelenberg (2005), "Negative Returns on Positive Emotions: The Influence of Pride and Self-Regulatory Goals on Repurchase Decisions," *Journal of Consumer Research*, 31 (March), 833-840.

McCracken, Grant (1988), *The Long Interview*, Newbury Park, CA: Sage Publications.

Mukhopadhyay, Anirban and Gita Venkataramani Johar (2007), "Tempted or Not? The Effect of Recent Purchase History on Responses to Affective Advertising," Journal of Consumer Research, 33 (March), 445-453.

Rook, Dennis W. (1985), "The Ritual Dimension of Consumer Behavior," *Journal of Consumer Research*, 12 (December), 251-264.

Ruth, Julie, Cele C. Otnes, and Frederic F. Brunel (1999), "Gift Receipt and the Reformulation of Interpersonal Relationships," *Journal of Consumer Research*, 25 (March), 385-402.

Tracy, Jessica L. and Richard W. Robins (2007), "The Psychological Structure of Pride: A Tale of Two Facets," *Journal of Personality and Social Psychology*, vol. 92, 3, 506-525.

Turner, Jonathan H. and Jan E. Stets (2002), *The Sociology of Emotions*, New York: Cambridge Univ. Press.

Ule, Mirjana (2004), "Changes in Family Life Courses in Slovenia," in *Contemporary Perspective in Family Research, vol 5, Families in Eastern Europe*, ed. Mihaela Robil, Oxford, UK: Elsevier Ltd., 87-102.

Wallendorf, Melanie and Eric J. Arnould (1991), "'We Gather Together': Consumption Rituals of Thanksgiving Day," *Journal of Consumer Research*, 18 (June), 13-31.

Wooten, David B. (2000), "Qualitative Steps towards an Expanded Model of Anxiety in Gift-Giving," *Journal of Consumer Research*, 27 (June), 84-95.

Consumer Knowledge as a Moderator of Specificity-Based Product Selection

Jason Stornelli, University of Michigan, USA
Anirban Mukhopadhyay, Hong Kong University of Science and Technology, Hong Kong, China/University of Michigan, USA
Andrew Gershoff, University of Michigan, USA

One way marketers differentiate functionally equivalent or similar offerings is by varying product claim specificity. For example, Wyeth's *Advil* brand is promoted as "the every pain reliever," but *Advil* also offers a specific migraine product. Both contain the same active ingredient (200mg solubilized ibuprofen)–but do migraine sufferers prefer *Advil Migraine* to *Advil Liqui-Gels*? Previous research has shown that consumers favor products with specific claims over those with general positioning strategies. For instance, Chernev (2007) demonstrates that "all-in-one" products offering a number of functional features are perceived as less effective compared to products with one focal feature. However, we argue that preference for specific-use alternatives may depend on the consumer's subjective category knowledge and present a study demonstrating this effect.

Prior research demonstrates that knowledge serves as an influential factor in the type and extent of information search behavior (Brucks 1985; Moorman et al. 2004), the range of choice heuristics available (Bettman, Luce, and Payne 1998), and the formation and recall of category structures (Hutchinson 1983; Alba and Hutchinson 1987). However, the relationship between objective and perceived or subjective knowledge remains unclear (Moorman et al. 2004). Subjective knowledge has been demonstrated to affect consumer choice behavior for new items with which consumers have little familiarity (Park et al. 1988), but to our knowledge, questions remain regarding the impact of subjective knowledge on familiar product categories. Together, this research suggests consumers obtain, interpret, and employ product attribute information differently depending upon both their objective and subjective knowledge, which may affect preferences for high or low product claim specificity.

We performed an experiment to examine whether perceived knowledge influences preferences for specific versus general products. The study employed a 2x2 design (*choice set*: [specific v. all-in-one products] v. [specific v. general products] x *price*: high specific v. low specific) that also measured subjects' self-reported product category knowledge. Subjects were randomly assigned to conditions with stimuli order counterbalanced.

Participants were asked to imagine they had a headache and were at a store to buy medication. They were instructed to choose between two analgesics from the same fictional brand with varied package designs. All subjects saw a specific "headache-relief" product packaged in a box featuring a glowing orange head and a "relieves your TOUGHEST headaches" tagline. Next to this, subjects saw one of two alternatives. In the all-in-one condition, an all-in-one "pain relief" product indicated for multiple uses was presented next to the specific product–these multiple uses were depicted by a glowing orange back, hand, and head on the box. Alternately, in the general condition, a "pain relief" product featuring a body with an all-encompassing orange glow was shown next to the specific product. Both alternative products claimed to relieve "your TOUGHEST pain."

Product prices were varied by condition to determine whether consumers would simply select the less-expensive alternative and to increase generalizability. In the high specific price condition, the "headache relief" medicine was priced at $9.99 while the alternative was priced at $7.99, and vice-versa in the low specific price condition.

After choosing an analgesic, participants' subjective knowledge of the product category was assessed using a continuous self-report measure.

Subjects reporting lower perceived knowledge selected the specific-use headache medication with approximately the same frequency when it was paired with either the general-use or all-in-one products. However, among higher-knowledge participants, choice share of the specific-use product dropped significantly when presented alongside the multiple-use item. Thus, while the majority of consumers preferred the specific-use product, a significant number of higher-knowledge individuals preferred the all-in-one item. All main effects and interactions involving price were non-significant.

These preliminary findings suggest that subjective knowledge influences consumer preference for specific-use products, but additional research is needed to untangle the causes underlying this phenomenon. One possibility is that the specific ailments listed on the all-in-one package could invoke feelings of marketplace metacognition (Wright 2002; Brown and Krishna 2004), such that higher-knowledge consumers may be making choices to counteract perceptions that marketers are encouraging redundant purchases by offering both specific and general alternatives. Alternately, metacognitive perceptions of extensive knowledge may be influencing consumers' propensity to think broadly and consider multiple usage scenarios–past research has demonstrated a broadening effect for high objective knowledge in brand recall tasks (Cowley and Mitchell 2003), but the role of subjective perceptions of knowledge remains unclear.

Alternately, subjective consumer knowledge may be influencing goal-directed purchase inferences. Recall that we gave subjects the specific goal of buying a product for headache relief. Recent research (Labroo and Kim 2009) demonstrates that consumers use increased processing effort as a signal of product instrumentality when engaged in goal-directed situations. Our findings concern the difficulty of matching an appropriate product to a salient need; this difficulty may vary depending upon the consumer's level of knowledge and the level of product claim specificity. Thus, it is possible that the higher effort required to process the all-in-one product leads higher-knowledge participants to prefer it. However, when a general-use product is included in the choice set, and/or when the consumer has a low level of knowledge, the required processing effort may be too great, leading consumers to prefer the "easier" specific product.

Follow-up studies are being considered to analyze these theoretical implications. Future experiments will manipulate the perception of knowledge by employing difficult/easy product tests for greater experimental control. We also plan to vary the level of objective ingredient information provided to further assess the interaction with subjective knowledge perceptions and any resulting inferences regarding similarity. Subsequent tests will also focus upon the specific v. all-in-one choice set as it appears consumers are less able to infer that the general-use product is appropriate for their functional needs. Confidence, risk-perception, and resistance to persuasion will also be assessed, as these constructs are related to consumer knowledge and metacognition (Campbell and Goodstein 2001; Bearden, Hardesty, and Rose 2001; Brown and Krishna 2004).

We are hopeful this research will contribute to a fuller understanding of preference for specific versus more general products, and of inferences consumers form from their subjective and objective knowledge.

References

Alba, Joseph W. and J. Wesley Hutchinson (1987), "Dimensions of Consumer Expertise," *Journal of Consumer Research*, 13(4), 411-454.

Bearden, William O., David M. Hardesty and Randall L. Rose (2001), "Consumer Self-Confidence: Refinements in Conceptualization and Measurement," *Journal of Consumer Research, 28*(June), 121-134.

Bettman, James R., Mary Frances Luce and John W. Payne (1998), "Constructive consumer choice processes," *Journal of Consumer Research*, 25(3), 187-217.

Brown, Christina L. and Aradhna Krishna (2004), "The Skeptical Shopper: A Metacognitive Account for the Effects of Default Options on Choice," *Journal of Consumer Research, 31*(3), 529-539.

Brucks, Merrie (1985), "The Effects of Product Class Knowledge on Information Search Behavior," *Journal of Consumer Research, 12*(1), 1-16.

Campbell, Margaret C. and Ronald C. Goodstein (2001), "The Moderating Effect of Perceived Risk on Consumers' Evaluations of Product Incongruity: Preference for the Norm," *Journal of Consumer Research, 28*(3), 439-449.

Cowley, Elizabeth and Andrew A. Mitchell (2003), "The Moderating Effect of Product Knowledge on the Learning and Organization of Product Information," *Journal of Consumer Research, 30*(December), 443-454.

Chernev, Alexander (2007), "Jack of All Trades or Master of One? Product Differentiation and Compensatory Reasoning in Consumer Choice," *Journal of Consumer Research, 33*(March), 430-444.

Hutchinson, J. Wesley (1983). "Expertise and the Structure of Free Recall," *Advances in Consumer Research, 10*, ed. Richard P. Bagozzi and Alice M. Tybout , 585-589.

Labroo, Aparna A. and Sara Kim (2009), "The Instrumentality Heuristic: Why Metacognitive Difficulty is Desirable During Goal Pursuit," *Psychological Science, 20*(1), 127-134.

Moorman, Christine, Kristin Diehl, David Brinberg and Blair Kidwell (2004), "Subjective Knowledge, Search Locations, and Consumer Choice," *Journal of Consumer Research, 31*(December), 673-680.

Park, C. Whan, Meryl P. Gardner and Vinod K. Thukral (1988), "Self-Perceived Knowledge: Some Effects on Information Processing for a Choice Task," *The American Journal of Psychology, 101*(3), 401-424.

Wright, Peter (2002), "Marketplace Metacognition and Social Intelligence," *Journal of Consumer Research, 28*(4), 677-682.

In the Mind's Eye: Embodied Simulation and Product Judgment

Aner Tal, Duke University, USA

Abstract

Spontaneous mental simulation of product interaction can have systematic effects on product judgment. Two studies demonstrate predictable effects of consumers' physical states on judgment. Physical states affect the simulated experience of products, and consequently judgment of corresponding product attributes. This notion is demonstrated for judgment of product size (study 1) and the energy provided by energy drinks (study 2). Crucially, the effects of physical states relevant to product experience on judgment are shown to depend on conditions supportive of spontaneous simulation (study 2).

Consumers' often engage in mental simulations of future consumption episodes. These simulations have been alternately named mental simulations (Escales 2004), imagery (MacInnis and Price 1987), or consumption visions (Philips 1996). Such simulations have a variety of mostly positive effects on product judgment, including improving consumers' attitude towards products (Escales & Luce 2003; Philips 1996), as well as their consumption experience (Tal, Huber and Lieb 2009).

The Spontaneous Occurrence of Simultion

Interestingly, Keller and McGill (1994) revealed that consumers may engage in imagery spontaneously and without explicit instructions. This corroborates earlier research and speculation (MacInnis and Price 1987). Various factors have been linked to personal and situational propensities to imagine product consumption, including vividness (Keller and McGill 1994; Nowlis et al. 2004), choice mode (Bolton 2003; Shiv and Huber 2000), and product type (Dhar and Werternbroch 2000). Recent work (Tal 2009) builds on this research in suggesting further conditions for the spontaneous occurrence of simulation.

Research in cognitive psychology corroborates wide-spread use of spontaneous simulation of various actions (Barsalou 2003; Jeannerod 2001). People simulate actions and interactions with objects in response to a variety of stimuli, including the observation of others' actions (Gallese and Goldman 1998), words (Tettamanti et al. 2005), and pictures of usable objects (Grafton et al. 1997; Grezes et al. 2003). Importantly, the process of spontaneous simulation is not necessarily conscious, and can consist of brain patterns simulating actions that are not accessible to awareness (Niedenthal et al. 2005).

The prevalence of spontaneous simulation suggests simulation of product interaction might occur even in the absence of explicit instructions to simulate. This makes simulations more general than it would be were it restricted to cases of deliberate imagination, which in turn raises the importance of exploring its effects on judgment.

Simulation Effects on Judgment

Spontaneous simulations are by their nature embodied, in that they involve the consumer acting with their physical body as they are at the moment of simulation (Barsalou 2003). As a consequence, simulation takes into account what actions the consumer can currently engage in. For instance, if a person cannot grasp an object from where they stand, no simulation of grasping will occur (Handy et al. 2003; Fischer and Dahl 2007).

In other words, simulations are sensitive to factors that would affect actual action. Accordingly, simulation will reflect how a product will be experienced given the consumer's current physical state. This may in turn lead to alterations in judgment corresponding to the alterations in simulated experience.

The current work explores some of these effects of spontaneous simulation on judgment. Specifically, the studies reported here show that in situations that support spontaneous simulation (studies 1-2) but not in situations that do not support it (study 2) judgment will reflect the manner in which subjective product experience should be affected by consumers' physical states.

We focus, in particular, on judgment of product size and energy. Subjectively, products provide less sustenance to people who require greater energy to act. Carrying a heavy burden necessitates more energy for action (Proffitt et al. 2003). Hence, products should be experienced as providing less sustenance (i.e., being smaller) and supplying less energy when consumers are burdened. Crucially, we project that this effect will depend on the occurrence of spontaneous simulation, and will therefore occur only in situations supporting simulation.

Study 1

Design. The study was a 2-cell repeated measures design. Participants were randomly assigned to either heavy backpack (15% of body-weight) or light backpack (5 pounds) conditions.

Procedure. Participants (N=14) put on the backpacks at the beginning of the study and walked a distance of approximately 30 feet before beginning so that they could feel the weight of the backpacks. They then answered questions about 21 grocery products. The questions were "how much space each product would consume to store in a pantry relative to other grocery products" (1-9 scale), and "How many days it would last for the average 4 people family" (days).

Results. The data were analyzed using a mixed-model ANOVA with product as a repeated measure. Participants carrying heavy backpacks estimated products as taking up less space (2.49 v. 3.37) and lasting less days (2.98 v. 4.89), $p<.0001$. It appears, then, that conditions supporting simulation lead burdened participants to judge products as smaller, since they would experience them as smaller (i.e., providing less sustenance) in actual experience. This alteration of subjective experience is reflected in simulation, and, consequently, judgment.

Study 2

The second study aimed to provide a conceptual replication of study 1 by demonstrating effects of physical burden on estimated energy provided by energy drinks. The hypothesis was that given that burdened participants require more energy for action, they would estimate energy drinks provide less energy. Importantly, we predicted that such a difference would emerge only when participants could see the energy drinks while answering the question. This is because visual inputs are crucial for the occurrence of spontaneous simulation (Tal 2009).

Methods. Participants (N=72) were randomly assigned to four groups. The design was a 2 (burden) X 2 (drink visibility) repeated measures design. Half the participants could see the drinks during the study, and half could not. Participants estimated how many hours of energy each of 6 energy drinks provided.

Results. There was a significant interaction drink-visibility X estimated-energy interaction (p=.05), such that participant who could see the drinks judged them to provide less energy if burdened by a heavy backpack (2.31 hours) than if not (2.85 hours, contrast p=.05). There was no such effect for participants who did not see the drinks.

Discussion

The studies presented here support the role of spontaneous simulation in determining consumer judgment. Specifically, the studies demonstrate that consumers' physical state can lead to predictable effects on product judgment under conditions that support spontaneous simulation. Future research should add to the generalizability of the phenomena by exploring effects brought about by different physical states and on different judgments, and further explore the process of spontaneous simulation in consumer judgment.

References

Barsalou, Lawrence W. (2003), "Situated Simulation in the Human Conceptual System. *Language and Cognitive Processes, 18*, 513-562.

Bolton, Lisa E. (2003), "Stickier Priors: The Effects of Nonanalytic Versus Analytic Thinking in New Product Forecasting," *Journal of Marketing Research*, 40(1), 65-79.

Dhar, Ravi, & Wertenbroch, Klaus (2000), "Consumer Choice between Hedonic and Utilitarian Goods," *Journal of Marketing Research*, 37(1), 60-71.

Escales , Jennifer Edson (2004), "Imagine Yourself in the Product: Mental Simulation, Narrative Transportation, and Persuasion," *Journal of Advertising*, 33(2), 37-48.

______, Luce, Mary-Francis (2004), "Understanding the Effects of Process versus Outcome-Focused Thought during Advertising," *Journal of Consumer Research*, 31(2), 274-285.

Fischer, Martin H., and Christoph D. Dahl (2007), "The Time Course of Visuo-Motor Affordances," *Experimental Brain Science*, 176, 519-524.

Gallese, V., and A.Goldman (1998), "Mirror Neurons and the Simulation Theory of Mind Reading," *Trends in Cognitive Science*, 12, 493-501.

Grafton, Scott T., Luciano Fadiga, Michael A. Arbib, and Giacomo Rizzolatti (1997), "Premotor Cortex Activation During Observation and Naming of Familiar Tools," *Neuroimage*, 6, 231-236.

Grezes, J., M. Tucker, J. Armony, R. Ellis, and R. E. Passingham (2003), "Objects Automatically Potentiate Action: An fMRI Study of Implicit Processing," *European Journal of Neuroscience*, 17, 2735-2740.

Handy, Tod C., Scott T. Grafton, Neha M. Shroff, Sarah Ketay, and Michael S. Gazzaniga (2003), "Graspable Objects Grab Attention when the Potential for Action is Recognized," *Nature Neuroscience*, 6, 1-7.

Jeannerod, Marc (2001), "Neural Simulation of Action: A Unifying Mechanism for Motor Cognition," *Neuroimage*, 14, S103-109.

Keller, Punam Anand, and Ann L. McGill (1994), "Differences in the Relative Influence of Product Attributes Under Alternative Processing Conditions: Attribute Importance versus Attribute Ease of Imaginability," *Journal of Consumer Psychology*, 3(1), 29-49.

MacInnis, D. J., Price, L. L. (1987), "The Role of Imagery in Information Processing," *Journal of Consumer Research,* 13(3), 473-91

Niedenthal, Paula, Lawrence W. Barsalou, Piotr Winkielman, Silvia Krauth-Gruber, and Francois Ric (2005), "Embodiment in Attitudes, Social Perception, and Emotion," *Personality and Social Psychology Bulletin*. 9(3), 184-211.

Nowlis, Stephen M., Naomi Mandel, and Deborah Brown McCabe (2004), "The Effect of a Delay between Choice and Consumption on Consumption Enjoyment," *Journal of Consumer Research*, 31(3), 502-510.

Philips, Diane (1996), "Anticipating The Future: The Role of Consumption Visions in Consumer Behavior," *Advances in Consumer Research*, 23, 70-75.

Shiv, Baba, and Joel Huber (2000), "The Impact of Anticipating Satisfaction on Consumer Choice," Journal of Consumer Research, 27(2), 202-216.

Tettamanti, Marco, Giovanni Buccino, Maria Cristina Saccuman, Vittorio Gallese, Massimo Danna, Paolo Scifo, Ferruccio Fazio, Giacomo Rizzolatti, Stefano F. Cappa, and Daniela Perani (2005), "Listening to Action-Related Sentences Activates Fronto-Parietal Motor Circuits," *Journal of Cognitive Neuroscience,* 17(2), 273-281.

Tal, Aner (2009), "Action Simulation in Acquisition Cost Estimates," doctoral dissertation, Duke University.

______, Abhijit Guha, Daniel Lieb and Joel Huber (2009), "Mental Simulation and the Evaluation of Hedonic Consumption," working paper.

On Your Mind=On Your Back: How Physical Burden Works as Mental Burden

Aner Tal, Duke University, USA

The current research examines whether physical load acts in a manner that is functionally equivalent to that of mental load. Based on the reliance of both physical and mental drains on a common physical resource, we hypothesize that consumers who are under physical load will function similarly to consumers who are under mental load. This hypothesis is supported in three studies showing that physically burdened participants are willing to spend less effort in a self-control task (study 1), show greater inclination towards unhealthy but tasty foods (study 2), and display greater compromise effects (study 3).

Many tasks in consumers' day to day lives require cognitive resources (Baumeister et al. in press). For instance, some choice tasks are effortful and so require mental resources (Vohs et al. 2008). The exertion of self-control, as in the case of dieting or the renunciation of impulse-shopping, also requires cognitive resources (Baumeister et al. 2007; Vohs and Faber 2007). When sapped of mental resources, consumers may accordingly choose options that are less healthy (Shiv and Fedorikin 1999) and defer choices (Pocheptsova et al. 2007). In sum, then, cognitive resources, also termed regulatory resources, fulfill an important function in many aspects of consumer behavior.

Regulatory resources have by and large tended to be an abstract construct lacking in direct measures. However, recent research has begun to link cognitive regulatory resources to measurable physiological variables. Specifically, Baumeister and his colleagues have shown that the level of glucose in a person's blood corresponds to the level of regulatory resources she possesses at any given point (Galliot and Baumeister 2007; Galliot et al. 2007; Mascicampo and Baumeister 2008). Brain areas responsible for regulatory tasks require and consume energy, and the body's level of energy is indicated by its current level of blood-glucose. Consequently, self-regulatory tasks reduce blood-glucose levels, and, correspondingly, reduced blood-glucose levels correspond to reduced ability to successfully engage in self-control tasks.

Naturally, the level of blood-glucose in one's body is a direct reflection of physical, as well as mental, resources. Thus, it stands to reason that physical exertion, because it reduces the level of blood-glucose, would impact the level of regulatory resources consumers possess, and, consequently, impact their inclination for and capacity to successfully engage in self-control tasks.

Prior work on cognitive load and its effect on consumer behavior has, for understandable reasons, assumed that cognitive load is induced by cognitive tasks. The current work, however, explores the notion that physical exertion can function in a manner equivalent to that of cognitive load and so produce the latter's effects on consumer behavior.

Given the prevalence of physical strains in daily life (e.g., carrying heavy shopping bags), that such strain functions in a manner equivalent to cognitive load would be of considerable importance in marketing research. The studies reported here examine this notion by employing a series of tasks known to be affected by cognitive load, and examining whether physical load in the form of carrying a heavy backpack affects them in the same way as cognitive load.

General Methods

The specific manipulation used to manipulate physical exertion was wearing heavy backpacks (Proffitt et al. 2003). Half the participants in these studies wore heavy backpacks (15% of body-weight), and half the participants wear light backpacks (5 pounds). We expected participants wearing heavy backpack to display effects similar to those of cognitive load.

Study 1: Reading Articles

Participants (N=37) were asked how many articles they would be willing to read for a class presentation. If physical load acts as mental load, we expected high-burden participants to be less inclined to exert considerable effort, and so report a willingness to read a lower number of articles than that low-burden participants are willing to read.

Results supported the hypothesis: high-burden participants were willing to read 4.3 articles, half the number low-burden participants were willing to read (8.6). The effect was significant at the .02 level: $F(1, 35)=5.77$. In other words, physical load seems, in this case, to have acted in a manner functionally equivalent to that of mental load, reducing participants' willingness to engage in a self-control task.

Study 2: Self-Control in Food Choices

Participants (N=73) reported on their preference between unhealthy but attractive foods (chocolate cake, chocolate bar and ice-cream) and healthy but less tasty foods (fruit salad, granola bar, and low-fat frozen yogurt, respectively). Preference for the unhealthy but tasty option was measured on a 9-point scale. Heavy burden participants expressed stronger preference for the less healthy option (adjusted mean 6.89) than low-burden participants (3.7): $F(1,204)=.02$.[10] This provides further support that high physical load functions in a manner equivalent to high mental load, leading to projected lower performance in a self-regulatory task.

Study 3: Compromise Effect

Consumers are known to fall prey to heuristic choice-strategies such as asymmetric dominance and compromise to a greater extent under cognitive load (e.g., Drolet and Luce 2004). If physical load acts as mental load, burdened participants should choose an asymmetrically dominant option to a greater extent than non-burdened participants. To test this, participants in the current study (N=110) chose between three options of both MP3 players and Digital cameras. In both cases one option asymmetrically dominated another. As predicted, high-burden participants chose the compromise option to a greater extent (63.39%) than low-burden participants (49.12%): $F(1, 223)=4.76$, $p=.03$ (tested with mixed model with product type as a repeated measure).

Conclusion

In all three studies participants carrying a heavy physical burden displayed effects equivalent to those high mental-load participants would display: showing lower willingness to exert self-control (studies 1-2) and a greater use of heuristic choice strategies (study 3). This provides initial support for the functional equivalence of physical and mental load.

Further studies should examine whether physical load acts in a manner that is functionally equivalent to mental load in other tasks. In particular, actual, versus predicted or simulated tasks, should be employed. Further, the alternative explanation of burden acting as a simple drain on attention rather than drawing on physical resources should be ruled out. This could be achieved by using a physical drain manipulation that is unlikely to draw attentional resources, such as exercising for ten minutes prior to participation in the study.

References

Baumeister, R. F., Vohs, K. D., & Tice, D. M. (2007), "The Strength Model of Self-Control," *Current Directions in Psychological Science*, 16, 396-403.

Baumeister, R. F., E. A. Sparks, T. F. Stillman, and K. D. Vohs (in press), "Free Will in Consumer Behavior: Self-Control, Ego Depletion, and Choice," *Journal of Consumer Psychology*.

Gailliot, M. T., & R. F. Baumeister (2007), "The Physiology of Willpower: Linking blood glucose to self-control," *Personality and Social Psychology Review*, 11, 303-327.

Gailliot, M.T., R. F. Baumeister, C. N. DeWall, J. K. Maner, E. A. Plant, D. M. Tice, L. E. Brewer, and B. J. Schmeichel (2007), "Self-Control Relies on Glucose as a Limited Energy Source: Willpower is More than a Metaphor," *Journal of Personality and Social Psychology, 92*, 325-336.

Masicampo, E. J., and R. F. Baumeister (2008), "Toward a Physiology of Dual-Process Reasoning and Judgment: Lemonade, Willpower, and Effortful Rule-Based Analysis," *Psychological Science*, 19, 255-260.

Pocheptsova, A., A. On, R. Dhar, and R. F. Baumeister (2009), "Deciding without Resources: Psychological Depletion and Choice in Context", *Journal of Marketing Research*, 46(3), 344-356.

Shiv, B. and Fedorikhin, A. (1999), "Heart and Mind in Conflict: Interplay of Affect and Cognition in Consumer Decision Making," *Journal of Consumer Research*, 26(2), 278-282.

Vohs, K. D. and R. J. Faber (2007), "Spent Resources: Self-Regulatory Resource Availability Affects Impulse Buying," *Journal of Consumer Research*, 33(3), 537-547.

Vohs, K. D., R. F. Baumeister, B. J. Schmeichel, J. M. Twenge, N. M. Nelson, and D. M. Tice (2008), "Making Choices Impairs Subsequent Self-Control: A Limited Resource Account of Decision Making, Self-Regulation, and Active Initiative," *Journal of Personality and Social Psychology, 94*, 883-898.

---

[10]Since some participants in this study breezed through the study, participants who took less than one SD below the mean time to complete the study were eliminated from the sample. There was no difference in completion time between the high and low burden conditions.

Familiarity Hijack: How Morphing Faces with Celebrity Images Can Enhance Trust

Rob Tanner, University of Wisonsin-Madison, USA
Ah-reum Maeng, University of Wisconsin-Madison, USA

Social psychologists have long observed that individuals have a preference for people similar to themselves, judging them as being more attractive (Shanteau and Nagy, 1979), more persuasive (Byrne, 1971), and even being more helpful toward them (Park and Schaller, 2005). More recently, advances in technology have enabled new paradigms for researchers interested in the effects of similarity. For example, researchers specifically interested in the domain of facial similarity have used new graphical technology to morph individual's own faces into the faces of others.

In a series of studies Bailenson et al. (2009) created composite images by morphing the faces of politicians with the faces of experimental participants in a ratio of 65% politician, 35% participant. This ratio is significant as the authors demonstrate that it produces composite faces within which individuals could not perceive their own image. Put differently, participants universally believed they were viewing unaltered pictures of the politicians in question. However, while the composite images may have been identified as being those of the politicians, attitudes toward the composites reflected a different story. In fact, in a series of studies Bailenson et al. showed that individuals consistently demonstrated stronger liking for political candidates when the image of the candidate had been morphed to include 35% of the individual's own face. This effect was especially acute for individuals without a strong prior (i.e., weak partisans and independents) and occurred without any conscious awareness of the facial morphing manipulation.

This fascinating finding raises interesting theoretical questions while also opening the door to possible new methods of persuasion. From a theoretical perspective several key questions remain unanswered. In particular, it is not clear if liking for the composite faces was driven by similarity or familiarity since the two are essentially confounded when morphing an individual's own face into a composite image. From a marketing perspective the possibility that the innate persuasiveness of an agent, for example a decorative model in a print advertisement, could be enhanced by facial morphing is very intriguing. The current work was motivated by both of these issues and explores the effects of morphing the faces of public figures and celebrities into unfamiliar faces. Unlike an individual's own face, which is simultaneously both similar and familiar, the faces of public figures are familiar but not similar to the average individual. As such they provide us with a potential method of teasing apart the previously confounded effects of similarity and familiarity.

In Study 1 (N=81) participants rated the trustworthiness of two faces on a 1-10 scale. We chose to focus on trust both because from a persuasion standpoint it is a key component of source credibility, and because simple liking is a key driver of trust (Nicholson et al. 2001). Face one was a neutral male face while face two (henceforth "Bush morph") consisted of the same neutral male face morphed with 35% of the face of George Bush who we reasoned (especially since the study was carried out around the time of the election) should be highly familiar to participants. While participants rated the neutral face on the midpoint of the scale (M=5.3) they rated the Bush morph as being significantly more trustworthy (M=6.9, t(80)=7.8, p<.001). This result pertained despite 100% of subsequently debriefed participants expressing no recognition of Bush in the composite image. As such, these data support a familiarity explanation as underlying the effect of facial morphing on preference but are inconsistent with a pure similarity explanation as it is hard to imagine how a composite image featuring George Bush would make the resulting face any more similar to our subject population (undergraduate students).

While supporting a familiarity mechanism other explanations could also explain the study 1 data. In particular, a valid alternative explanation would be that individual specific meanings from the minority face in a composite image might be perceived in a morphed face even in the absence of conscious awareness of that face. While one might expect George Bush to represent lack of trust, we can certainly not rule out the possibility that subliminal perception of his identity as a president could increase perceptions of trust. Certainly, assuming that the average individual holds a positive self view, then transfer of individual meaning could potentially explain the Bailenson et al. data, all of which involved participants viewing composite images in which the minority image was their own face. Thus study 2 was designed to disentangle a pure familiarity explanation from an explanation relying on transfer of individual specific meaning.

In study 2 (N=35) participants rated the trustworthiness and athletic ability of one of two faces on a 1-10 scale. Face one was the same neutral male face from study 1 while face two (henceforth "Tiger morph") consisted of the neutral male face morphed with 35% of the face of Tiger Woods. Tiger was chosen both for his high levels of familiarity and popularity, and because he is strongly associated with athletic ability. Thus if individual specific meanings from the minority face are transferred from the morphed face we should expect to see an increase in ratings for athletic ability and trust (via liking). However, if the effects to date are driven purely by familiarity we should expect to see an effect on trust but not one on athletic ability. In fact that is exactly what we found. Consistent with study 1 participants rated the Tiger morph (M=5.33) as being more trustworthy than the neutral face (M=4.0, t(31)=-1.9, p<.07). However, they perceived no difference between the athletic ability of the Tiger morph (M=2.1) and the neutral face (M=2.4, p>0.3). As such these data further support a familiarity explanation as driving the effect on liking and trust and rule out an explanation based on the transfer of individual specific meaning.

References

Bailenson, Jeremy, Shanto Iyengar, Nick Yee and Nathan A. Collins (2009), "Facial Similarity between Voters and Candidates Causes Influence", *Public Opinion Quarterly,* 72(5),935-961.

Byrne, Donn (1971), *The Attraction Paradigm.* New York: Academic Press

Nicholson Carolyn Y., Larry D. Compeau, and Rajesh Sethi, (2001), "The Role of Interpersonal Liking in Building Trust in Long-Term Channel Relationships", *Journal of the Academy of Marketing Science,* 29(1), 3-15.

Park, Justin H. and Mark Schaller, (2005), "Does Attitude Similarity Serve as a Heuristic Cue for Kinship? Evidence of an Implicit Cognitive Association", *Evolution and Human Behavior,* 26, 158-70.

Shanteau, James and Geri F. Nagy, (1979), "Probability of Acceptance in Dating Choice", *Journal of Personality and Social Psychology,* 37, 522-533.

Aided Information Retrieval on Content-Based Websites: Learning Faster or Learning Less?

Dimitrios Tsekouras, Erasmus University Rotterdam, the Netherlands
Benedict Dellaert, Erasmus University Rotterdam, the Netherlands

Consumers are increasingly turning to online based searches to obtain information on a wide variety of subjects. For example, in 2008, 80% of US adult internet users searched at least once for information about products, health issues, or other topics. For almost 60% of internet users, the internet constitutes the main means of searching for information (Jones & Fox 2009).

The key objective of such online information searches for consumers is to learn more about a certain topic. As a result it is very relevant to examine how knowledge formation can best be supported by various information retrieval modes that can be applied by websites. The main research question of this study therefore is how different ways of acquiring information through a given website affect consumers' learning and their intention to revisit the website. Online aids offered by websites help people save time (Peterson & Merino 2003) but the amount of learning remains unclear. Therefore these aids may be beneficial for transactional websites (i.e. when looking for a specific product) but not necessarily for content-based websites where consumers aim to acquire new knowledge.

Research on learning and education suggests a greater effectiveness of active learning practices compared to traditional passive learning techniques (McLeod 2003; Bonwell and Eison 1991). Evidence has shown that active learning practices are more effective in terms of learning outcomes and can lead to better student attitudes and improvements in students' thinking and writing (Bonwell and Eison 1991, Laws et al., 1999). The online environment structure offers an immense opportunity for applying active learning techniques through its interactive capabilities. Many studies on e-learning environments showed that e-learning is more effective than traditional teaching mainly due to the crucial role that interactivity plays in knowledge acquisition and the development of cognitive skills, leading to higher learning outcomes and evaluations of the content and structure of the learning process (Khalifa 2002). There is a difference between e-learning and information search on the internet. E-learning constitutes a structured environment with a specific focus and content which is mainly led by the instructor. Online information search comprises a goal oriented task which is led by an individual's need to solve a recognized problem. Past research so far has been focusing on the importance of knowledge formation modes in teaching environments and the beneficial effects of active learning techniques. We expect that this differential effect between active and passive modes also applies in the case of online information retrieval from a website. Therefore, we propose that the use of different information provision modes (aided or unaided search) can influence the retrieval effectiveness of the visitors on a website.

Since learning leads to goal achievement we also propose that it is a key driver of website evaluation and loyalty. Based on goal setting theories, goal achievement leads to higher degrees of satisfaction and attitude towards the medium (Locke & Latham 1990). Consequently, learning plays an important role in the formation of a positive attitude towards content-based websites as well as on the intention of repeated visits. Previous studies have focused on process-oriented learning and the acquisition of skills that could lead to a state of lock-in due to cognitive barriers (Haubl & Murray 2002) but have largely neglected the role of content-oriented learning (Mittal & Sawhney 2001). In this study, we provide an additional complementary explanation of website loyalty by highlighting the importance of content learning in the context of a content-based website.

Finally, we hypothesize that there is an asymmetric effect of aided versus unaided knowledge formation on mode loyalty. Website visitors who are engaged in unaided (active) search modes are expected to be more willing to remain loyal to their initial search mode because they invested cognitive effort in their initial search task and they are expected to be more reluctant to abandon this investment compared to searchers in the aided (passive) knowledge formation mode where no substantial cognitive effort was endowed. This difference can be attributed to the sunk cost experienced by the visitors of the website (Arkes & Blumer 1985). In addition, differences in mode loyalty could be explained by the increased perceived feeling of control as well as enjoyment that the active search mode offers to the visitors (Dellaert & Dabholkar 2009).

Based on an experimental study using a website for health information, we explore how different ways of acquiring information through a given informational website have a different effect on the intention to revisit the website. We manipulated the ways of acquiring information from a website in aided (passively distributed recommendations) and unaided (actively sought information). Based on process and evaluation data from 190 respondents, we find support for our expectation that active information seeking behavior leads to higher retention effects through the greater learning and positive evaluations towards the website and the search experience. We show that the effect of active knowledge formation on website loyalty is fully mediated by its effect on content learning outcomes. Finally, the hypothesized asymmetric effect of active knowledge formation mode of acquiring the information compared is also confirmed, with a higher lock-in state towards the unaided than to the aided information retrieval mode.

From a consumer behavior perspective, it is insightful to investigate how different knowledge formation modes can lead to differences in terms of learning and loyalty. From an online information provider perspective, it is important to understand the ways that several features of a website can lead to repeated visits over time. There is a trade-off between speed of retrieval and learning. Therefore, it really depends on the objective of the visitors, which type of information retrieval mode will lead to the greatest revisit intention.

References

Arkes, Hal R. and Catherine Blumer (1985), "The Psychology of Sunk Cost," *Organizational Behavior and Human Decision Processes*, 35 (February), 124-40.

Bonwell, Charles C. and James A. Eison (1991), "Active Learning: Creating Excitement in the Classroom," *ASHEERIC Higher Education Report No. 1*, George Washington University, Washington, DC.

Dellaert, Benedict G.C. and Pratibha A. Dabholkar (2009), "Increasing the Attractiveness of Mass Customization: The Role of Complementary On-line Services and Range of Options," *International Journal of Electronic Commerce*, 13 (3), 43-70.

Jones, Sydney and Susannah Fox (2009), "Generations Online in 2009," PEW Internet & American Life Project, http://www.pewinternet.org

Khalifa, Mohamed and Rinky Lam (2002), "Web-Based Learning: Effects on Learning Process and Outcome," *IEEE Transactions on Education*, 45 (November), 350-56.

Laws, Priscilla, David Sokoloff, and Ronald Thornton (1999), "Promoting Active Learning Using the Results of Physics Education Research," *Uni Serve Science News*, 13 (July), 14-19.

Locke, Edwin A. and Gary P. Latham (1990), *A Theory of Goal Setting and Task Performance*, Englewood Cliffs, NJ: Prentice- Hall.

McLeod, Gregory (2003), "Learning Theory and Instructional Design", *Learning Matters*, 2, 35-43.

Mittal, Vikas and Mohanbir S. Sawhney (2001), "Learning and using electronic information products and services: A field study," *Journal of Interactive Marketing*, 15(winter), 2-12.

Murray, Kyle and Gerald Häubl (2007), "Explaining Cognitive Lock-In: The Role of Skill-Based Habits of Use in Consumer Choice," *Journal of Consumer Research*, 34(June), 77-88.

Murray, Kyle B. and Gerald Häubl (2002), "The Fiction of No Friction: A User Skills Approach to Cognitive Lock-In," *Advances in Consumer Research*, 29, 1, 11-18.

Peterson, Robert A. & Maria A. Merino (2003), "Consumer Information Search Behavior and the Internet," *Psychology & Marketing*, 20 (February), 99–122.

A Research of the Spillover Effect of Gift Promotion—Its Forming and Fluctuation

Chung-Hui Tseng, Tamkang Univeristy, Taiwan

Recently, gift promotion is taken as an important issue for firms. Because the gift is free, consumers tend to discount gift's value. Does this discounting evaluation spill to other products belonging to the same category of the gift so that these products also be devaluated by consumers? The research was going to investigate whether the discounting perception toward gift would spill to other product categories with the same brand of the gift, or spill to the same product category with other brands. In this study, we defined the phenomenon as a "spillover effect of gift promotion".

Reviewing relevant literature, spillover effect was discussed in the field of brand extension or brand alliance; however, little discussions about spillover effect of gift promotion were found. Therefore, it is necessary to deeply investigate the forming and fluctuation of spillover effect of gift promotion. In brief, this research consists of two studies. Study one focuses on the forming of spillover effect of gift promotion. Assimilation and contract effect (Herr, Sherman and Fazio, 1983) was taken as the main theory to infer the formation of spillover effect of gift promotion. Study two further examined its fluctuating factors, including an antecedent factor—promotion depth of gift promotion, two consequent factors—perceived value of spillover effect on the same product with other brand and on the same brand with other product category, and two moderating factors—brand awareness and involvement of gift. Anchoring and adjustment theory (Tversky and Kahneman, 1974?Lola, 1982?Yadav, 1994) was taken as the theory to infer the influence of promotion depth on perceived value of spillover effect.

Experiment design was adopted in the two studies. Subjects were college students by convenient sampling. Subjects of the two studies were different. Study one adopted a 2 (gift promotion: present/absent) groups between-subject design. 50 valid questionnaires were gathered. Study two used a 2 (promotion depth of gift promotion: high/low) x 2 (brand awareness of gift: high/low)=4 groups between-subject design. 324 valid questionnaires were analyzed. Besides, involvement of gift were measured and picked out two parts of sample—high and low score of involvement—to test hypotheses.

In the two studies, measurement of perceived value of spillover effect was as below. For example, the gift in the gift promotion was Adidas running shoes, and we would like to measure perceived value of spillover effect on Puma running shoes. In the first step, subjects were asked to answer this question "before" reading an ads of gift promotion: "If you have a budget to buy a pair of running shoes, how much money *(NT$X)* would you like to pay it?" Following, "after " subjects reading an ads of gift promotion, they were asked to answer another question: "if you have a budget to buy a pair of running shoes, how much money *(NT$Y)* would you like to pay a pair of "Puma" running shoes?" Then, the perceived value of spillover effect on Puma running shoes were (Y–X)/X. If the score was negative, spillover effect did appear. This is the measurement method of perceived value of spillover effect on the same product with other brand. And, same method was used to measure perceived value of spillover effect on the same brand with other product category of gift.

After statistical analysis, study one found that when gift promotion presented, it had negative effect on relative products with the gift according to significant result of a t-test. In other word, gift promotion caused negative score of spillover effect on relative product with the gift. This study found out the formation of spillover effect of gift promotion.

Following, study two further found that the spillover effect of gift promotion would show up on other products with the same brand of the gift as well as on the same product category with other brand. In addition, based on results of two three-way ANOVAs, as deeper the promotion depth was, the stronger the spillover effect of gift promotion was. Furthermore, brand awareness of gift did play a moderating role on the spillover effect. That is, under high brand awareness of gift, the difference between spillover effect caused by high and low promotion depth of gift promotion was smaller than the difference under low brand awareness. Finally, involvement of gift also did play a moderating role on the spillover effect. That is, under high involvement of gift, the difference between spillover effect caused by high and low promotion depth of gift promotion was smaller than the difference under low involvement.

Research contributions comprised three points. First, this research discussed background theory of spillover effect of gift promotion and offered a reasonable inference for the phenomenon of spillover effect of gift promotion. Second, finding of this research including two studies make gift promotion research much richer. Moreover, this research, based on experimental results, also offered significant managerial implications for managers.

References

Herr, P. M., S. J. Sherman, and R. H. Fazio (1983), "On the Consequences of Priming: Assimilation and Contrast Effects," *Journal of Experimental Social Psychology*, 19, 323-340.

Lola, L. L. (1982), "Toward a Procedural Theory of Judgment," Working Paper 17, Wisconsin Human Processing Program, Department of Psychology, University of Wisconsin, Madison.

Tversky, A. and D. Kahneman (1974), "Judgment under Uncertainty: Heuristics and Biases," *Science,* 185(Sep.), 1124-1131.

Yadav, M. S. (1994), "How Buyers Evaluate Product Bundles: A Model of Anchoring and Adjustment," *Journal of Consumer Research,* 21(Sep.), 342-353.

Extended Service Encounters and Customer Emotion Management

Gulnur Tumbat, San Francisco State University, USA

The aim of this study is to understand customers' full emotional involvement in service encounters and reveal the emotional nature of their ongoing self-presentation in extended service encounters. This paper presents an exploratory study into customer emotion management in extended service encounters and argues that customers' co-production of the service experience may also include active monitoring and management of their emotions. Such emotion control and resultant display affect the service outcome not only for those customers themselves but also for service providers and other patrons present. Thus, it is important for service marketers to understand and manage their customers' participation in the service experience also through their emotion management in order to provide satisfactory outcomes.

Commercial Construction of Extraordinary Experiences

Gulnur Tumbat, San Francisco State University, USA

The urge for extraordinary experiences is a dominant theme in modern social thought. Although we came to learn a lot about such experiences from various phenomenological accounts that stand in opposition to mundane daily lives, we know very little about how such experiences are strategically constructed and marketed to consumers. In other words, we have a pretty good understanding of such experiences from the consumers' perspective but production side lack such focus with few exceptions and therefore needs more attention The aim of this research is thus to tackle this particular gap. This research addresses the following questions: How do extraordinary experiences in the marketplace are promoted? What are the strategies used by marketers? How do consumers expectations are shaped by marketers' representations?

Exploring the Influence of Spirituality: A New Perspective on Senior Consumers' Behavior

Gaelle Ulvoas-Moal, ESC BRETAGNE Brest, France

Abstract

The interest in spirituality in consumer behaviour is growing. Previous research suggests that consumers' behaviour is influenced by their level of spiritual development and commitment, and that it can be spiritually motivated. This paper explores the influence of spirituality on the consumer behaviour of older adults, as they reach spiritual maturity or undergo intensive spiritual growth toward the end of their life. Responding to a call for conceptual clarification, we define spirituality and differentiate it from religion and religiosity. Spiritual development is explained and the spiritual needs of older adults are described. Research propositions on the influence of spirituality on the consumer behaviour of older adults are presented.

Although spirituality has been a central concept in psychology and sociology for the past ten years, little research has explored its influence on consumer behaviour. The paucity of available research results lies in part from a lack of consensus regarding the definition of spirituality and some confusion between the concepts of spirituality, religion and religiosity (Zinnbauer et Pargament, 2005, McGinn, 1993). Therefore, our study aims at establishing a clear conceptual framework for the study of the influence of spirituality on consumer behaviour, involving a definition of the concept, an explanation of the differences with religion and religiosity and a description of spiritual development.

As the chronological and sequential theory of spiritual development (Fowler, 1981) identifies the last part of life as favourable to increased spiritual development and the achievement of spiritual maturity, thus leading to the display of more salient spiritual characteristics, our second objective is to understand the spirituality of older adults and to identify their spiritual needs.

Our overall objective, therefore, is to draw from the extant literature a research agenda to examine the influence of spirituality on the behaviour of senior consumers. In order to do so, we undertook an extensive inter-disciplinary literature review in the fields of psychology, sociology, psychiatry, gerontology and consumer behaviour, over the last three decades.

Conceptual framework for the study of spirituality in consumer behaviour:

The identification of the characteristics of spirituality (Ulvoas, 2009) leads to the following definition of the concept: "Spirituality is the construction of the meaning of one's life. It appeals to one's ability for transcendence[11] and its objects are the inner self, alterity[12] and the sacred[13]." Spirituality involves a spiritual identity, which can be religious or non religious, and a level of spiritual commitment. Religion, as "a unified system of beliefs and practices related to the sacred" (Delener, 1990), is the most common form of spirituality. It has two dimensions: religious identity (the tradition within which the members of a specific religious group practice their religion, for example Christianity) and religiosity, which is one's level of religious commitment.

The spirituality of older adults:

The spirituality of older adults stems from their cognitive maturity and their ability for gerotranscendence, which Tornstam (1994, 1999) describes as a "shift from a rational and materialist perspective to an increasingly cosmic and transcendent one". Spiritual development is a mechanism which enables older adults to cope with the losses associated with old age (in physical and intellectual capabilities, in body image, of the usual place of residence) and to defend themselves against age related aggressions such as ageism (Mattes, 2005; McFadden, 1996).

Their increasing consciousness of their own mortality can generate strong anxiety (Urien, 2008), which spiritual growth can help reduce, as it involves finding the meaning of one's life and death and a reflection on after life (Ita, 1995). Spiritual needs of older adults involve: restoring personal dignity and transcending the losses and handicaps of old age; reducing death anxiety, accepting to die and preparing for dying; finding the global meaning of one's life, believing in the continuity of life and caring about future generations; establishing positive relationships with others, reducing guilt and reconciling; and establishing an intimate relationship with the sacred (McKinley, 2001; Fry, 2000).

Influences of spirituality on consumer behaviour:

The literature review in the field of consumer behaviour reveals four general types of influence of spirituality. First, spiritual identity and related spiritual values influence the formation of attitude, and erect consumption limits and taboos; the stronger the level of spiritual commitment, the stronger this influence (Homer and Kahle, 1988; Mokhlis, 2006). Spiritual values shape consumption ethics while prescribing the rejection of non compatible consumption behaviours such as the illicit purchase of products, and the adoption of those in line with spiritual values such as purchasing from fair trade distribution channels, or religious prescriptions such as the consumption of Halal food for religious Muslims (Shaw and al., 2005; Mokhlis, 2006). Research propositions directly derived from this, which can be shared by all consumers no matter their age, would be that:

P1a: Spiritually committed consumers, including seniors, have a favourable attitude toward the consumption of products and services in line with their spiritual values.

P1b: Spiritually committed consumers, including seniors, have an unfavourable attitude toward the consumption of products and services opposed to their spiritual values.

Second, spiritual development modifies consumers' identity, which leads to a shift in the orientation of their consumption, from ego satisfaction in early stages of spiritual development to an increasing sensitivity to the impact of their consumption on others in later stages (Ball et al., 2001; Hampton et al., 2002). Hence, as senior consumers have been identified as either spiritually mature or intensively spiritually developing, a research proposition could be stated as follows:

P2a: Spiritually mature senior consumers are more aware of the impact of their consumption on their environment and try to use it to create a positive impact.

P2b: Spiritually developing senior consumers use consumption to fuel their spiritual growth.

Third, a market offering can be entrusted with a spiritual value which contributes to the overall consumption value as perceived by the consumer (Holbrook, 1999).

P3: Senior consumers perceive a market offering including a significant spiritual value as superior to a market offering which includes none.

Finally, spiritual needs generate spiritual motives for consumption (Skousgaard, 2006), which can be intrinsic and aimed at satisfying the spiritual values of the consumer, and extrinsic and aimed at enhancing the comfort level and social prestige of their beholder. Both motivations can coexist (Weaver and Agle, 2002). We formulate our two final propositions as:

P4a: Intrinsically spiritually motivated consumption of seniors is geared at satisfying spiritual needs.

P4b: Extrinsically motivated consumption of seniors is geared at increasing their comfort level and enhancing the way their environment perceives them.

---

[11]Transcendence corresponds to "an individual's capability to step out of his/her immediate perception of time and space and to see life from a wider, more detached angle" (Piedmont, 1999).

[12]Alterity should be understood in a broad sense and includes other human beings, nature and the universe. It is the interconnection of these objects that enables the holistic perspective on life and provides its meaning (Ulvoas, 2009).

[13]The sacred is "a perception of either a divine being or a sense of ultimate reality or truth" (Larson et al., 1998): God, gods, a divine being, the supreme energy, the wholeness of life.

Conclusion and further research

This paper provides a conceptual framework for the study of the influence of spirituality on consumer behaviour. It identifies seniors as consumers with salient spiritual characteristics, including spiritual maturity or intensive spiritual growth, and potentially strong spiritual motivations for consumption. Further research is necessary to examine our research propositions. Given the importance of these growing demographics in most developed economies and the size of certain age-related sectors, including tourism, a better understanding of the influence of spirituality on consumption would appear essential and long overdue.

References

Ball,D.; Hampton,R.; Chronis, A. and Bunker, M. (2001), The development of spirituality and its effect on consumer behaviour, *American Marketing Association Conference Proceedings*, 12, 3-5.

Delener, N. (1990), The effects of religious factors on perceived risk in durable goods purchase decisions, *Journal of Consumer Marketing*, 7 (3), 27-38.

Fowler, J. (1981), *Stages of Faith*, Harper and Row, New York.

Fry, P.S. (2000), Religious involvement, spirituality and personal meaning for life: existential predictors of psychological well-being in community-residing and institutional care elders, *Aging and Mental Health*, 4 (4), 375-387.

Hampton, R.; Ball, D.; Chronis, A. and Bunker, M. (2002), Evidence for the effect of spiritual growth on consumer behaviour, *American Marketing Association Conference Proceedings,* 13, 6-9.

Holbrook, M.B. (1999), *Consumer value: a framework for analysis and research*, London-New York: Routledge.

Homer P.M. and Kahle L.R. (1988), A structural Equation Test of the Value-Attitude-Behavior hierarchy, *Journal of Personality and Social Psychology*, 54, 638-646.

Ita, D.J. (1995-96), Testing a causal model: acceptance of death in hospice patients, *Omega*, 32, 81-92.

Jackson, K.T. (1999), Spirituality as a foundation for freedom and creative imagination in international business ethics, *Journal of Business Ethics*, 19 (1), 663-680.

Larson, D.; Swyers, P. and McCullough, M. (1998), *Scientific Research on Spirituality and Health: a Consensus Report*, National Institute for Healthcare Research, Bethesda.

McFadden, S.H. (1996), Religion, spirituality and aging. In J.E. Birren and K.W. Schaie (Eds), *Handbook of the psychology of aging* (4th ed.). San Diego: Academic Press.

McGinn, B. (1993), The letter and the spirit: Spirituality as an academic discipline, *Christian Spirituality Bulletin*, 1, 1-10.

McKinlay, E. (2001), The spiritual dimension of caring: applying a model for spiritual tasks of ageing, *Journal of Religious Gerontology*, 12, 111-122.

Mattes, R. (2005), Spiritual need one: the aging process: a journey of lifelong spiritual formation, *Journal of Religion, Spirituality and Aging*, 17, 3-4, Special issue: ministering to older adults: the building blocks, 55-72.

Mokhlis, S. (2006), The effect of religiosity on shopping orientation: an exploratory study in Malaysia, *Journal of American Academy of Business*, Cambridge, 9 (1), 64-74.

Piedmont, R. (1999), Does spirituality represent the sixth factor of personality? Spiritual transcendence and the five-factor model, *Journal of Personality*, 67 (6), 986-1013

Shaw, D. and al. (2005), An exploration of values in ethical consumer decision making, *Journal of Consumer Behaviour*, 4 (3), 185-200.

Skousgaard, H. (2006), A Taxonomy of Spiritual Motivations for Consumption, *Advances in Consumer Research*, 33 (1), 294-296.

Tornstam, L. (1999), Late Life Transcendence: A New Developmental Perspective on Aging, in L.E. Thomas and S.A. Eisenhandler (Eds), *Religion, Belief and Spirituality in Late Life,* New York: Springer.

Tornstam, L. (1994), Gero-transcendence: A Theoretical and Empirical Exploration, in L.E. Thomas and S. Eisenhandler (Eds), *Aging and the Religious Dimension* (203-225), Westport, CT: Auburn House.

Ulvoas, G. (2009), Spirituality and the Consumer Behaviour of Older Adults, *Marketing Trends International Conference, 8th Edition*, January 16-17.

Urien, B. and Kilbourne, W. (2008), On the role of materialism in the relationship between death anxiety and quality of life, in *Advances in Consumer Research Volume 35*, eds. Angela Y. Lee and Dilip Soman, Duluth, MN : Association for Consumer Research, 409-415.

Weaver, G.R. and Agle, B.R. (2002), Religiosity and ethical behaviour on organizations: a symbolic interactionist perspective, *The Academy of Management Review*, 27 (1), 77.

Zinnbauer B.J. and Pargament, K.I. (2005), Religiousness and spirituality in *The Handbook for the Psychology of Religion*, Paloutzian, R.F. and Park, C.L. (Editors), The Guilford Press, NY: New York.

Older Adults' Use of New Media

Iris Vermeir, University College Ghent & Ghent University, Belgium

Neal Van Loock, University College Ghent, Belgium

The study of older adults' use of technology has mainly focused on barriers like learning new skills, sensory or cognitive abilities that keep older adults from adopting technological innovations. However, research has shown that some older adults are looking for creative and challenging offers and are active, innovative customers (Szmigin & Carrigan, 2001). The purpose of this research is to investigate which variables determine negative or positive intentions to use new media like the internet and digital TV. The central question is: what are the underlying factors causing different levels of utilization of new technologies? We want to extend previous research on older adults' use of new media technology by combining cognitive, motivational, individual differences and social factors. We use the technology acceptance model (TAM) (Davis, 1986) as a basic framework to test our hypotheses. TAM includes both cognitive factors and motivational factors to investigate technology acceptance and has been successfully used in a wide spectrum of studies (Venkatesh & Davis, 2000). Two important aspects of TAM are perceived ease of use and perceived usefulness which in turn influence –through intentions- acceptance and use of the new technology. Despite vast support for the TAM, additional external variables could influence technology acceptance (Venkatesh, 2000). For example, the impact of user characteristics like individual variables (personality) on perceived ease of use and usefulness as the main factors that influence the behavioral intention to use the system and on behavioral intention as well, is not adequately regarded yet. Previous research already suggested that individual differences are significant factors in explaining both, technology acceptance and user behavior (Arning & Ziefle, 2006)

We extended the TAM in several ways. We included individual differences (risk aversion, innovativeness) and social influences (internalization, identification and compliance) as key determinants that influence new technology's use. Moreover, we investigated the acceptance of new technologies by older adults. Practitioners and researchers need a better understanding of why older people resist or embrace new technologies. Insights in older adults' motivations to accept new technologies could help attune communications to this elderly segment, ultimately leading to higher acceptance of new, helpful technologies. In addition, encouraging older consumers to use the Internet could be valuable for firms, as the sheer number of older consumers gradually increases and they tend to have greater wealth and spending power.

Several hypotheses are postulated. Following Arning and Ziefle (2006), we argue that especially for older adults, ease of use is an important determinant of perceived usefulness of new technologies. We also expect that a higher level of internalization (i.e. the process by which, when one perceives that an important referent thinks one should use a system, one incorporates the referent's belief into one's own belief structure, Malholtra & Galetta, 1999), identification (occurs when system users adopt attitudes and behaviors to achieve a *satisfying, self-defining relationship* with another person or group, Malholtra & Galetta, 1999) and innovativeness are positively related to perception of usefulness, ease of use and use of new technologies. We expect that compliance (occurs when the user adopts particular behaviors to obtain rewards or avoid punishments, Malholtra & Galetta, 1999) and risk aversion are negatively related to perception of usefulness, ease of use and the use of new technologies.

Survey data were collected through self-administered anonymous questionnaires filled in by 179 older adults. Structural equation modeling was performed to analyze the relationships proposed in the hypotheses. Two full structural measurement models (internet/digital TV) were estimated with each scale items used as an indicator of its associated latent variable. The final measurement models had good fit. Next, two structural models were estimated. Results showed adequate model fit for both models. We found no large differences for determinants of intentions to use internet and digital TV. Results show that positive intentions to use both new media are determined by ease of use, identification, compliance and innovativeness. Compliance positively influenced the perceived usefulness and the intention to use internet and digital TV. Ease of use of internet was negatively influenced by compliance. Internalization directly influenced intentions to use digital TV but not Internet. Internalization had an indirect influence on internet use through ease of use and usefulness. Risk aversion did not directly influence use of new media. However, older adults who had higher risk aversion had a lower ease of use perception of internet, indirectly influencing their intention to use the internet. Perception of usefulness did not influence use of new media. Older adults do not need to perceive new media as useful in order to use it. Usefulness was influenced by perceptions of ease of use. Usefulness was also influenced by compliance, internalization and identification (for internet).

In sum, our study not only confirms the importance of perceived ease of use in the basic TAM, but also demonstrates that, in the context of new media use (1) other beliefs (i.e. internalization, identification, and compliance) and (2) individual characteristics (innovativeness, risk aversion) can significantly influence consumer intentions and perceptions of usefulness and ease of use.

Key References

Arning, Katrin and Martina Ziefle (2006), "What older users expect from mobile devices: an empirical survey", in *Proceedings of the Industrial and Engineering Applications of Artificial Intelligence and Expert Systems,* Annecy, France.

Davis, Fred D (1986), *Technology Acceptance Model for Empirically Testing New End- User Information,* Doctoral dissertation, Sloan School of Management, Massachusetts Institute of Technology.

Malhotra, Yogesh and Dennis F. Galletta (1999), "Extending the technology acceptance model for social influence: theoretical bases and empirical validation", in *Proceedings of the 32nd ICSS.*

Szmigin, Isabelle and Marilyn Carrigan (2001), "The older consumer as innovator, does cognitive age hold the key?", *The Journal of Marketing Management, 16(5)* 505-527.

Venkatesh, Viswanath (2000), "Determinants of perceived ease of use: integrating perceived behavioral control, computer anxiety and enjoyment into the technology acceptance model", *Information Systems Research, 11,* 342–365.

Venkatesh, Viswanath and Fred D. Davis (2000), "A theoretical extension of the technology acceptance model: four longitudinal field studies", *Management Science, 46,* 186–204.

Consumers Prefer Television Ads with Dance; Researching the Effects of Dance on Consumer Behavior

Carla Walter, Missouri Southern State University, USA
Loay Altamimi, University of Savoie, France

Prior to 1990, music was considered incidental to the advertising message and its effects on consumer behavior. Importantly, consumer researchers found that music was much more than incidental (Scott 1990). That breakthrough path was facilitated by other researchers examining advertising effects on consumers using theoretical frameworks that borrowed from a variety of disciplines (see McCracken 1986, Scott 1994, Mick and Buhl 1992, McQuarrie and Mick 1999, and Joy and Sherry 2003 for examples). With both this historical yet continual pressing of the frontiers of consumer research as a means of inspiration, this research had multiple purposes. The first was to explore consumers and their relationship with advertisements using dance in them. The second was to evaluate if there were international differences between preferences, and beyond that, what gender preferences existed if any. Finally the research was set to explore what effects an ad with dance in it would have on consumer behavior with respect to the product being advertised. One hundred and one respondents were surveyed in the United States and France in two separate phases to facilitate the research. The two surveys were available to respondents in two versions (English and French) and both were conducted via the internet, using proprietary web-based software (*Sphinx Plus2-Edition Lexica-V5* and SphinxOnline http://www.sphinxonline.com was also utilized in the survey design as well as monitoring data collection and the results analysis). In comparison to traditional methods of survey data collection, web surveys are considered to be a faster and a less expensive way to collect data from a global audience (Schmidt, 1997; Wyatt, 2000; Roztocki and Lahri, 2003; Wright, 2005). Also and more importantly for this study, using the web makes it possible to deliver almost any kind of content (including videos) and to introduce new types of interactivity into the survey process (Baulac, Bolden and Moscarola, 2000; Conrad, Couper and Tourangeau, 2003), such as play/stop video, show/hide or jump to certain elements and questions depending on the respondent's answer.

In the first phase we tested a survey method for examining connections between dance in television advertising, culture, and consumption. The survey incorporated a variety of questions to gather data (i.e., television viewing, search behavior and preference for ads with dance in them online and on television, and demographic information) and utilized open-ended questions based on five interpretive dance premises (Sklar 2001). The assumption was that dance is used in advertising because it communicates nonverbally cultural information and in turn may connect this information to consumption. The three product advertisements using dance in the foreground were Nike, Isenbeck Beer, and MasterCard. The respondents were presented with hyperlinks to the three different television ads to view and rate their preference for. Next they were asked to describe the types of people, dance, and culture presented in their respective preferred ad, and the connection they saw between the type of dance used and the product advertised. The findings suggest that dance in the television ads used in this research communicated information as argued. The findings in phase one make a significant contribution to the literature in demonstrating that dance in television ads influences consumers and their relationship with culture and consumption (Walter et al, accepted, *Consumer Culture Theory 4*, 2009).

In the second round, the same respondents were surveyed again, building on results from the first round. Data from phase two suggests that 67% of respondents preferred ads with dance in them, and the highly significant preference was integral to the advertisement. The main reasons for the enthusiasm for the ads were that dance provided entertainment (65%), a favorable distraction (12%), and hedonic feelings (11%). Preference for all ads was further correlated with respondent's memories of past events. Mainly these centered on a) socialization in educational institutions from childhood through university; b) respondents being reminded of someone else, such as a friend or relative while watching the dance; and c) a social event such as a wedding or party. Two other findings were additionally noteworthy: nearly half of the respondents indicated "Yes", the dance in the ad would influence their desire to buy the product; and just over half stated the opposite. In anticipation of the polarized answers, respondents were queried open endedly on the survey as to their reasons for a "No" or "Yes" response. Respondents who thought the ad would influence their buying indicated they liked the dancing for each of the ads. For the Isenbeck Beer and MasterCard commercial, their view of the dance as humorous was important to the respondents. For Nike and Isenbeck Beer, they also felt the dance made the product interesting. However, for all three of the ads, respondents had "other" reasons for believing the dance would make them buy the product. For those respondents who indicated the dance did not encourage them to buy the product, this was highly significant based on the ad choice. Reasons centered around dislike of credit cards for the MasterCard advertisement. The notion that the advertisement has nothing to do with the product was important for each of the three ads. However again, "other" was given as a large percentage reason for not buying the product for Nike and Isenbeck Beer.

In summary, this exploratory research builds upon dance, advertising, and consumer theories and contributes to the literature in three ways. First, dance may enter the consumer research realms as a viable aspect of television ads, and perhaps ads in hypermedia generally, proving important for understanding consumer behavior in terms of preference or non preference for a product for a variety of cognitive and affective reasons. Secondly, the research method is one that can be adapted to other advertisements that use dance in them, or not, and used for extending the research for example, as in exploring the neurobiological effects on consumers watching dance in advertising. Third, consumer researchers are now sensitized to the use of dance in television advertising, broadening the resources available to evaluate consumers and their behaviors. However, in addition to the neurobiological research agenda, an expanded analysis of consumers' reasons for ad preference with dance in advertisements and measures of the degree to which this preference in different cultures exists can influence consumer behavior is needed. To accomplish this, our research stream includes utilization of in-depth interviews and ethnographic research approaches in addition to the survey methods articulated here.

Partial Bibliography

Baulac, Y., R Bolden, and J. Moscarola (2000) "Interactive research: How internet technology could revolutionize the survey and analysis process," *Association for Survey Computing (ASC) Conference on Survey Research on the Internet*, Imperial College, London

Burrill, D A. (2006) "Check Out My Moves," *Social Semiotics*, 16, 1, 17–38.
Cohen-Stratyner, B. (2001) "Social Dance: Contexts and Definitions" in *Dance Research Journal*, Congress on Research in Dance, 33/2 (Winter), 121-123.
Conrad, F.G., M. P. Couper, and R. Tourangeau (2003) "Interactive Features in Web Surveys," *Joint Meetings of the American Statistical Association,* San Francisco, CA.
Desmond, Jane C. (1997) "Embodying Difference: Issues in Dance and Cultural Studies" in *Meaning in Motion; New Cultural Studies of Dance*, Jane C. Desmond, ed., Durham, NC: Duke UP, 29–54.
Dodds, Sherrill (2004) *Dance on Screen: Genres and Media from Hollywood to Experimental Art*, New York and London: Palgrave MacMillian.
Dunagan, C. (2007) "Performing the Commodity-Sign: Dancing in the Gap," *Dance Research Journal*, 39/2 (Winter), 3–22.
Foster, Susan Leigh (1995) *Choreographing History*, Bloomington and Indianapolis, Indiana UP.
Goellner, Ellen W. and Jacqueline Shea Murphy. 1995. *Bodies of the Text; Dance as Theory, Literature as Dance*, New Jersey: Rutgers UP.
Goulding, C., A. Shankar and R. Elliot (2002) "Working Weeks, Rave Weekends: Identity Fragmentation and the Emergence of New Communities," *Consumption, Markets and Culture*, 5 (4), 261–284.
H'Doubler, Margaret N. (1940) *Dance; A Creative Art Experience*, Wisconsin: University of Wisconsin Press.
Joy A. and J. F. Sherry (2003), "Speaking of Art as Embodied Imagination: A Multisensory Approach to Understanding Aesthetic Experience," *Journal of Consumer Research*, 30 (September), 259–82.
Kaeppler, Adrienne L. (1972) "Method and Theory in Analyzing Dance Structure with an Analysis of Tongan Dance," in *Ethnomusicology*, 16, 2 (May), 173-217.
Lange, Roderyk (1976) *The Nature of Dance; An Anthropological Perspective*, New York: International Publications Service.
Langer, Susanne K. (1953) *Feeling and Form; Theory of Art*, New York: Charles Scribner's Sons.
McCracken, G. (1986) "Culture and Consumption: A Theoretical Account of the Structure and Movement of the Cultural Meaning of Consumer Goods," *Journal of Consumer Research*, 13 (June), 71–84.
McFee, Graham (1992) *Understanding Dance*, London and New York: Routledge.
McQuarrie, E. F. and D. G. Mick (1999) "Visual Rhetoric in Advertising: Text-Interpretive, Experimental, and Reader-Response Analyses, *Journal of Consumer Research*, 26 (June), 37–54.
Mick, D. G. and C. Buhl. (1992) "A Meaning-based Model of Advertising Experiences," *Journal of Consumer Research*, 19 (December), 317–338.
Roztocki, N. and N. Lahri. (2003) "Is the applicability of web-based surveys for academic research limited to the field of information technology?" Proceedings *of the 36th Hawaii International Conference on System Sciences* (HICSS).
Schmidt, W. C. (1997) "World-Wide Web Survey Research: Benefits, Potential Problems, and Solutions," *Behavior Research Methods, Instruments & Computers*, 29(2), 274-279.
Scott, L.M. (1990) "Understanding Jingles and Needledrop: A Rhetorical Approach to Music in Advertising," *Journal of Consumer Research*, 17 (September), 223–236.
Scott, L.M. (1994) Images in Advertising: The Need for a Theory of Visual Rhetoric," *Journal of Consumer Research*, 21 (September), 252–273.
Sklar, Deidre. (2001) "Five Premises for a Culturally Sensitive Approach to Dance," *Moving history/dancing cultures: a dance history reader*, Ann Dils and Ann Cooper Albright, eds., Wesleyan UP: Middltown, CT, 30–22.
Walter, Carla, L.Altamimi, J.J. Moscarola and J. Ibanez-Bueno (2009) "Research Design: Exploring Dance in Advertising and its Influence on Consumption and Culture," *Consumer Culture Theory Conference 4*, presented, Ann Arbor, MI.
Wright, K. B. (2005) "Researching Internet-based populations: Advantages and disadvantages of online survey research, online questionnaire authoring software packages, and web survey services," *Journal of Computer-Mediated Communication*, 10(3).
Wyatt, J. C. (2000) "When to Use Web-Based Surveys," *Journal of the American Medical Informatics Association*, 7(4), 426-430.

Pioneering (Dis)advantage and Later Entrant (Dis)advantage: The Role of Consumer Goals in Pioneer and Later Entrant Brand Advantages

Tor Arne Wanebo, Norwegian University of Life Sciences, Norway
Even J. Lanseng, Norwegian School of Management, Norway

A widely held assumption in consumer research is that there can be only one pioneer brand in a product category and that this pioneer has advantages (i.e. market share and profits) over later entrants. However, most of the brands in a product category are late entrants. This paper investigates whether a late entrant can overcome the pioneer's advantage and achieve one for itself by becoming included in a goal-derived category. The assumption made here is that a favorable position in a goal-derived category simultaneously shields the late entrant from a typicality judgment that would favor the more typical pioneer and places the late entrant closer to a favorable evaluative judgment (i.e. an ideal category member) than the pioneer. Results from two experimental studies suggest that a late entrant strategy capitalizing on consumer's goal-derived categorization is superior to a strategy of adding new and unique attributes in a taxonomic product category. This is true for both the late entrant and for a pioneer that tries to re-position itself when challenged by the later entrant.

The Dynamics of Goal Revision: Updating the Discrepancy-Reducing Model of Self-Regulation

Chen Wang, University of British Columbia, Canada
Anirban Mukhopadhyay, Hong Kong University of Science and Technology, China

Existing research on goal-directed behaviors has largely focused on the process in which people strive for a static goal (Austin and Vancouver 1996; Carver and Scheier 1981; Locke and Latham 1990). However, relatively little attention has been directed toward the dynamic process of goal setting. As Fishbach and colleagues have demonstrated (Fishbach and Dhar 2005; Fishbach, Dhar, and Zhang 2006), goals are not always static. Rather, people frequently revise their goals upward or downward based on the goal-performance discrepancy.

This research examines the dynamics of goal revision by updating the discrepancy-reducing model of self-regulation (Carver and Scheier 1981, 1998). Based on cybernetic control theory (Miller, Galanter, and Pribram 1960), Carver and Scheier's classic model of self-regulation suggests that people continuously monitor the discrepancy between their current state and a desired standard, and that goal-directed behaviors are aimed at reducing such discrepancies.

One limitation of this model is that it treats the goal as a static standard. In this research, we propose instead that the goal is a dynamic function, specifically, an S-shaped function of the goal-performance discrepancy. Based on this proposition, we incorporate an additional element–"Goal Calibrator" –into Carver and Scheier's model. In our revised model, the goal-performance discrepancy serves not only as an input to the system, as suggested by the original model, but also as the input to the goal calibrator. This goal calibrator is directed by an S-shaped function, generating the updated goal for further monitoring. Further, the S-shaped function features the common properties of *proportionality* and *diminishing sensitivity* for both self-set goals and assigned goals, while exhibiting *failure aversion* for self-set goals and *satisficing* for assigned goals.

A series of four experiments provide empirical support for our theorizing. Study 1 provides initial evidence for our hypothesized goal revision for self-set goals. In the context of saving money, we used a one-factor between-subjects design (discrepancy valence: positive vs. negative). The goal-performance discrepancy was manipulated by giving hypothetical feedback. Participants were asked to imagine setting up a financial goal of saving as much money as possible for each of five consecutive months. They were asked to write down their desired saving amount for the first month. Then they were presented with a hypothetical performance outcome (e.g., you saved 15% more vs. less than your goal). Based on the feedback, participants were asked to set up their financial goal for the next month, and the next feedback was presented after that. These procedures were repeated for five iterations. The performance outcomes for each month were random integers between 15% and 19%, always either positive or negative based on feedback condition. A 2 (discrepancy valence) x 5 (month) mixed ANOVA yielded a significant interaction ($F(4,116)=2.57, p<.05$). The pattern was consistent with our prediction. Positive discrepancy resulted in continuous upward goal revision–savings targets for each month were higher than in the previous month. In contrast, negative discrepancy led to the maintenance of the original goal–savings target stayed flat from month to month. This experiment demonstrated (a) the existence of goal revision for self-set goals, and (b) the property of *failure aversion.*

Study 2 replicated the effects in another context, and further investigated the effort exertion under different discrepancy valence. We used a similar design as study 1, but in the context of working out with the goal of burning as many calories as possible on the treadmill for five consecutive days. Consistent with our hypotheses, a 2 (discrepancy valence) x 5 (day) mixed ANOVA yielded a significant interaction ($F(4,40)=6.45, p<.001$), such that those with positive discrepancy indicated the same amount of effort in each trial, whereas those with negative discrepancy indicated increasingly more effort to strive for the goal.

Study 3 further tested the characteristics of the S-shaped function by examining the interaction between the valence and the magnitude of the discrepancy. Specifically, as to self-set goals, we expected *proportionality* and *diminishing sensitivity* for discrepancies with the same valence but differential magnitudes, and *failure aversion* for discrepancies with the same magnitude but opposite valences. We used a 2(discrepancy magnitude: small vs. large) x 2 (discrepancy valence: positive vs. negative) factorial design. Participants were presented a scenario in which they held a goal of burning 200 calories on the treadmill. The goal-performance discrepancy was manipulated by giving hypothetical outcomes (i.e., burning 10 vs. 110 calories more vs. less). Participants were then asked to establish the calorie goal for the next day based on their current performance. As predicted, a 2x2 ANOVA yielded a significant interaction ($F(1,62)=64.64, p<.001$). Consistent with our hypothesized *proportionality*, large discrepancies resulted in greater goal revision than small discrepancies of the same valence. Further, discrepancies had a smaller marginal impact when they were more distant from the origin point, referring to *diminishing sensitivity*. Moreover, positive discrepancies led to larger goal revision than negative discrepancies of the same magnitude, as the predicted *failure aversion.*

Study 4 tested the unique property of *satisficing* for assigned goals. In this study, we utilized a computerized anagram task to establish assigned goals. A similar design as study 1 was used. Participants were first asked to freely set up a goal for the first anagram (i.e., "to find __% of the possible solutions"). Manipulated feedback was presented after participants submitted their answers (i.e., 5% more vs. less than your goal). Since the anagram tasks were cognitively intensive, only three iterations were implemented. A 2 (discrepancy valence) x 3 (iteration) mixed ANOVA yielded a significant interaction ($F(2,39)=10.317, p<.001$). As predicted, those with positive discrepancies initially maintained the original goal, but revised the goal upward as they kept receiving positive feedback. By contrast, those with negative discrepancies revised the goal downward based on the negative feedback. These effects demonstrated the property of *satisficing* for assigned goals.

In sum, the studies reported above provide empirical support for a revised discrepancy-reducing model of self-regulation. This work contributes to the classic discrepancy-reducing model, and therefore the larger goal revision literature.

References

Austin, J. T., and Vancouver, J. B. (1996). Goal constructs in psychology: Structure, process, and content. *Psychological Bulletin, 120,* 338–375.

Carver, C.S., and Scheier, M.F., (1981). *Attention and self-regulation: A control-theory approach to human behavior*. New York: Springer-Verlag.
Carver, C.S., and Scheier, M.F., (1998). *On the Self-Regulation of Behavior*. Cambridge University Press, New York.
Fishbach, Ayelet and Ravi Dhar (2005), "Goals as Excuses or Guides: The Liberating Effect of Perceived Goal Progress on Choice," *Journal of Consumer Research*, 32 (December), 370-77.
Fishbach, Ayelet, Ravi Dhar and Ying Zhang (2006), "Subgoals as Substitutes or Complements: The Role of Goal Accessibility," *Journal of Personality and Social Psychology*, 91 (August), 232-42.
Locke, E. A., and Latham, G. P. (1990). *A theory of goal setting and task performance*. Englewood Cliffs, NJ: Prentice Hall.
Miller,G.A., Galanter,E., and Pribram, K.H. (1960). *Plans and the structure of behavior*. New York: Holt, Rinehart, and Winston.

Social Marketing in Action: Increasing Recycling in a Large Organization

Todd Weaver, Georgia State University, USA

Topic

In recent years, environmental sustainability has become a matter of great concern, prompting individuals, communities, and organizations to take up the difficult task of identifying and reducing their environmental impact. By employing Action Research methodology to intervene in a specific problem situation over time, my research will address the important question of whether grassroots social marketing efforts can successfully increase pro-environmental behavior in a large organization.

Theoretical Frameworks

The majority of research on pro-environmental behavior has employed two related theories: Ajzen's theory of planned behavior (1991) and Schwartz's model of altruistic behavior (1977). Researchers have used these models to examine pro-environmental behavior descriptively by demonstrating the relationship between attitudes, norms and/or intentions and behavior (e.g., Tonglet, Phillips and Bates 2004; Guagnano, Stern and Deitz 1995). However, relatively little research has attempted to identify the processes by which pro-environmental behaviors can be initiated and increased over time. By using Action Research to investigate these behavioral models in a specific context, I hope to gain insight into the behavioral antecedents of pro-environmental behavior as well as the social marketing techniques that can influence these antecedent conditions.

Methodology

Action Research involves a collaboration between the researcher and an organization or community that leads to immediate and ongoing improvements in a problem situation (Susman and Evered 1978). Action Research is particularly appropriate for contributions to transformative consumer research (Ozanne and Saatcioglu 2008), which has been championed by the Association for Consumer Research (Mick 2006). Although there are a variety of Action Research approaches, I am employing Susman and Evered's cycle (1978), which includes the following five steps: diagnosing, action planning, action taking, evaluating, and specifying learning.

The context of this research is a large, southeastern university that is lagging behind other local universities in terms of sustainability efforts. In order to make the scope of this project manageable, I am restricting my focus to recycling, since recycling is a tangible and visible aspect of sustainability that is easily understood by most people. The first step of the Action Research process involves engaging with the community to gain a shared understanding of the problematic situation. I employed a variety of ethnographic methods in this diagnosing stage, including semi-structured interviews with informants that spanned the three focal categories of students, faculty, and staff; an on-line, qualitative survey of the same groups; observations of recycling behavior on campus; and secondary research that included academic journals, publications of the university, and publications of recycling-oriented organizations, such as the Association for the Advancement of Sustainability in Higher Education (AASHE). These sources revealed three important themes that will guide the subsequent steps of the Action Research project.

Initial Findings

The first theme that emerged from my research is that recycling has not been an institutional focus at this university. Unlike many colleges today, there is no person or department tasked with improving sustainability. Although several groups are undertaking a variety of independent efforts to increase recycling, the overall effectiveness of these efforts seems to be limited by their ad-hoc, uncoordinated approach. Different constituencies hear different messages concerning recycling, see different types of recycling bins in different places, and are not sure that recycling bins will be available in a given space or building. This lack of focus has likely suppressed important precursors for recycling, such as social norms and ascriptions of responsibility in Schwartz's (1977) model.

The second theme that emerged is that there is a general lack of awareness of the recycling services available on campus. Community members are not sure which materials can be recycled on campus, nor are they confident that materials placed in bins are actually recycled. If awareness were higher, it would be reasonable to expect that recycling would increase at the university even absent any other changes in current practice. For example, in Ajzen's (1991) model, the lack of awareness would have a detrimental effect on perceived behavioral control over recycling.

Finally, the third theme that emerged from my research is that many students, faculty and staff members do not regard recycling as an important norm. Just as the university's administration has not emphasized recycling and other sustainability initiatives, it seems that many campus constituents do not feel that recycling is a priority. Again, this finding relates to the behavioral antecedents identified in the Schwartz (1977) and Ajzen (1991) models. For example, according to Schwartz (1977), the internalization of social norms regarding recycling would be an important antecedent of recycling behavior. Together, these themes provide an explanation of the low level of recycling at this university, but they also suggest ways in which recycling might be increased via social marketing efforts.

Current Status and Expected Contributions

Currently I am engaging with campus groups in the action planning stage, in which we will use our shared understanding of the problematic situation to develop social marketing campaigns aimed at increasing recycling at the university. These efforts will focus on creating the behavioral antecedents identified by Ajzen (1991) and Schwartz (1977). Furthermore, longitudinal measures of these antecedents will provide evidence of their relationship to recycling behavior. Once complete, I anticipate that this research will not only increase recycling in the focal organization, but it will also provide important insights into the process by which recycling behavior can be initiated and increased over time.

Selected References

Ajzen, Icek (1991), "The Theory of Planned Behavior," *Organizational Behavior and Human Decision Processes*, 50 (2), 179-211.

Eden, Colin and Chris Huxham (1996), "Action Research for Management Research," *British Journal of Management*, 7 (1), 75-86.

Guagnano, Greg, Paul Stern, and Thomas Dietz (1995), "Influences on Attitude-Behavior Relationships: A Natural Experiment with Curbside Recycling," *Environment and Behavior*, 27, 699–718.

Mick, David G (2006), "Meaning and Mattering Through Transformative Consumer Research," Advances in Consumer Research, 33, 1-4.

Ozanne, Julie and Bige Saatcioglu (2008), "Participatory Action Research," *Journal of Consumer Research*, 35 (3), 423-439.

Schwartz, Shalom H. (1977), "Normative Influences on Altruism," in *Advances in Experimental Social Psychology*, Vol. 10, L. Berkowitz, ed. New York: Academic Press, 221-279.

Susman, Gerald I. and Roger D. Evered (1978), "An Assessment of the Scientific Merits of Action Research," *Administrative Science Quarterly*, 23, 582-603.

Tonglet, Michele, Paul S. Phillips, and Margaret P. Bates (2004), "Determining Drivers for Householder Pro-environmental Behaviour: Waste Minimisation Compared to Recycling," *Resources, Conservation and Recycling*, 42, 27-48.

The Influence of Intrinsic and Extrinsic Messages and Benefits on Motivations to Donate

Jennifer Wiggins Johnson, Kent State University, USA
Pamela Grimm, Kent State University, USA
Bret Ellis, Kent State University, USA

It is a common practice for nonprofit organizations to send marketing communications to potential donors that have either intrinsically or extrinsically focused messages. Communications with intrinsically focused messages may emphasize the organization's need, the positive outcomes that the donation will have for the organization and its constituents, and the satisfaction that the donor will feel from having helped the organization. Extrinsically focused messages may emphasize the extrinsic rewards or benefits that the donor will receive in exchange for his or her donation, such as invitations to special events, tangible rewards, or social recognition. The purpose of this research was to determine whether *message focus*, either intrinsic or extrinsic, had an impact on donors' motivation to donate.

Research on motivation has repeatedly found that extrinsic rewards can decrease an individual's intrinsic motivation to engage in a behavior (Deci and Ryan 1985; Harackiewicz, Manderlink, and Sansone 1984; Harackiewicz and Sansone 2000; Lepper, Greene, and Nisbett 1973). This overjustification effect suggests that when individuals experience both intrinsic and extrinsic rewards for a behavior, the behavior is overjustified and the individual attributes the behavior to the extrinsic reward (Deci and Ryan 1985). This results in a drop in intrinsic motivation after the receipt of the rewards. Non-marketing messages have been found to reverse the effects of extrinsic rewards on intrinsic motivations by making intrinsic motivations more salient (Fazio 1981). We believe that the benefits stressed in marketing communications, either intrinsic or extrinsic, will have an impact on motivations to donate that may mitigate the effects of offering a reward for the donation.

An experiment was used to investigate this phenomenon. Three groups of undergraduate students, at three different locations, received different communications messages asking them to participate in a food drive. Messages were delivered verbally by their instructor and through a series of three e-mail messages. One group received intrinsically focused messages, one group received extrinsically focused messages and the third group acted as a control and received no messages, only basic information about the food drive. The intrinsically focused messages emphasized the help that the students would provide for families in need, and the extrinsically focused messages emphasized a promised reward of a pizza party to the students if they reach a predetermined goal for the food drive. While only the extrinsic messages condition emphasized the pizza party, all of the groups were promised and received a pizza party at the conclusion of the food drive if they met a set goal.

Under the cover of a research project on donations being conducted by a friend of the instructor, participants' intrinsic and extrinsic motivations to participate in the food drive were measured three times: once prior to the receipt of any messages, once after the message manipulation, and once after the pizza party. Motivations were measured using two multi-item scales measured on a 1-7 scale with endpoints "strongly agree" and "strongly disagree." Students received extra credit for participating in the research.

A total of 142 students participated in the study: 60 in the intrinsic condition; 54 in the extrinsic condition and 26 in the control group. The items designed to measure motivation were factor analyzed across all three groups. Four items for intrinsic motivation and four items for extrinsic motivation were retained. Factor loadings for the items ranged from .73 to .94, and α=.94 for the intrinsic motivation items and α=.88 for the extrinsic motivation items. The four items for each factor were summed resulting in a mean range of 4 to 28. Manipulation checks indicated that the instructor for the control group had communicated additional messages, compromising the results. Therefore, the control group was dropped from further analysis.

A repeated measures analysis of intrinsic and extrinsic motivation was conducted using message condition as a between subjects factor. We expected to observe an increase in intrinsic motivation from t_1 to t_2 for the group that received intrinsic messages, and not for the group that received extrinsic messages, and the opposite effect for extrinsic motivation. If the overjustification effect occurred, we further expected the intrinsic motivation of both groups to drop from t_2 to t_3, after the receipt of the reward. Our results for the intrinsic messages group were slightly different but theoretically consistent. From t_1 to t_2, the intrinsic messages group did not change their intrinsic motivation, but their extrinsic motivation decreased significantly. From t_2 to t_3, after the reward was administered, the intrinsic messages group's extrinsic motivation increased significantly, consistent with the overjustification effect. However, this increase returned their level of extrinsic motivation to approximately what it was at t_1, suggesting that there may have been some mitigating effect of the messages.

The results for the extrinsic messages group, however, were less clear. From t_1 to t_2, the extrinsic messages group did not significantly change their extrinsic motivation, but their intrinsic motivation increased significantly. The most plausible explanations for this counter-intuitive result was the crash of the economy that took place while the experiment was in progress. The changing economic circumstances, combined with publicity regarding the needs of local food banks in the area, may have influenced the results. It should also be noted that both groups exhibited a very high level of intrinsic motivation to start, suggesting that the results may also reflect a ceiling effect. After the receipt of the reward, however, they experienced the drop in intrinsic motivation associated with the overjustification effect, which again returned them to approximately the same level of intrinsic motivation that they began with at t_1. This again suggests that the messages may have in some way mitigated the overjustification effect, but not in the intended manner.

In order to overcome these limitations, a second study has been planned and will be conducted in May. The second study involves university alumni donations. A single instructor will be responsible for the intrinsic and extrinsic message group, mitigating possible instructor effects. The second study should provide additional insights into the effects of message framing on intrinsic and extrinsic motivations to donate.

References

Deci, Edward L. and Richard M. Ryan (1985), *Intrinsic Motivation and Self-Determination in Human Behavior*: Plenum Press.

Fazio, Russell H. (1981), "On the Self-Perception Explanation of the Overjustification Effect: The Role of the Salience of Initial Attitudes," *Journal of Experimental Social Psychology*, 17, 417-26.

Harackiewicz, Judith M., Manderlink, and Carol Sansone (1984), "Rewarding Pinball Wizardry," *Journal of Personality and Social Psychology*, 47, 287-301.

Harackiewicz, Judith M. and Carol Sansone (2000), *Intrinsic and Extrinsic Motivation: The Search for Optimal Motivation and Performance*, San Diego: Academic Press.

Lepper, Mark R., David Greene, and Richard E. Nisbett (1973), "Undermining Children's Intrinsic Interest with Extrinsic Reward: A Test of the Overjustification Hypothesis," *Journal of Personality and Social Psychology*, 28 (1), 129-37.

Real Men Don't Eat Quiche: Discrepancy Between Automatic and Deliberate Gender-Expressive Choices in Men

Jim Wilkie, Northwestern University, USA
David Gal, Northwestern University, USA

Consumers often purchase products to signal desired identities to their self and others (e.g. Belk 1988; Wernerfelt 1990; Berger & Heath 2007). This paper examined how gender identity considerations affect product choice. What occurs when men and women must choose between a personally appealing, gender-incongruent item and a less appealing, gender-congruent item? Are there gender differences in why certain products are chosen?

Much research has displayed that men and women are faced with pressures to conform to standards set forth by gender norms (e.g. Crocker et al. 1998). Building on research showing that individuals often regulate their impulses in accordance with norms and expectations when they have sufficient cognitive resources to do so (Shiv, Fedorikhin & Nowlis 2005), we posit that individuals will similarly regulate their choices of gender-expressive items. That is, we posit that the availability of cognitive resources will increase the likelihood that individuals choose gender-congruent items that conflict with their automatic preferences.

It is further proposed that men might be more motivated than women to regulate their choices of gender expressive items. This is based on research which has suggested that women and men might face different motivations to conform to gender norms. For instance, women might be more motivated to conform to gender norms when occupying traditional male roles, such as management leadership positions, due to devaluation of women that exhibit "masculine" traits in such roles (Eagly et al. 1992), while men, on the other hand, might be more motivated to conform to gender norms in attempts to maintain their gender identity, due to heightened psychological consequences of gender role deviation for men relative to women (e.g. O'Heron & Orlofsky 1990). Our propositions were supported in three experiments.

Experiment 1: Food Choices

Experiment 1 tested the hypothesis that resource availability would affect choice patterns for products which could be used to signal one's gender identity. Specifically, Experiment 1 examined how gender associations of food items affect the choices of men and women.

Participants made 16 choices from pairs of food items descriptively listed on a menu. For each pair of items provided, subjects chose the food option they most preferred. Each pair consisted of a masculine dish and a feminine dish. The gender of the dish was manipulated through ingredients (e.g. a masculine dish might contain bacon whereas a feminine dish might contain red wine sauce) and food descriptions (e.g. a masculine dish might be described as "hearty" whereas a feminine dish might be described as "luscious"). All subjects were asked to assume that the nutritional content for each item within a pair were roughly equivalent. Participants were randomly assigned to complete this task under high or low cognitive resource availability.

Consistent with our predictions, an ANOVA revealed a significant interaction between gender and cognitive load on menu item choice, $F(1,162)=6.14$, $p<.05$, and that male (but not female) choices were significantly different between cognitive load conditions $F(1,160)=13.51$, $p<.01$. Males in the high load condition (M=.559, SD =.24) chose significantly more (less) feminine (masculine) dishes than males in the low load condition (M=.379, SD=.19), $F(1,160)=13.51$, $p<.001$, $d=.83$. In contrast, females in the high (M=.641, SD=.21) and low (M=.630, SD=.18) load conditions did not differ in their choices $F(1,160)=.05$, $p=.82$, $d=.06$.

Experiment 2: Product Shape

The purpose of experiment 2 was to provide convergent evidence for the role of cognitive resources in gender choice in a different domain.

Building on recent perceptual research which displayed that certain geometric shapes connote affective meaning (e.g. Aronoff 2006), it was hypothesized that angular objects better portray masculine concepts (e.g. aggression) whereas rounded objects better portray feminine concepts (e.g. warmth). Participants were shown a series of two products side by side from twelve different product categories (e.g. beds) and asked to choose the item that they most preferred between the two. For each pair of items there was one option with predominantly rounded features and another option with predominantly angled features (pretests confirmed that the rounded items appeared more feminine and the angular items more masculine). Participants were randomly assigned to complete this task under high or low cognitive load.

Consistent with our proposition that men would be more likely to regulate their choices given sufficient cognitive resources, an ANOVA revealed a significant interaction between gender and cognitive load on product choice, $F(1,273)=4.226$, $p<.05$, and that male (but not female) choices were significantly different between cognitive load conditions, $F(1,271)=5.85$, $p<.05$. Males in the high load condition (M=.477, SD =.18) chose significantly more (less) rounded (angled) products than males in the low load condition (M=.400, SD=.16), $F(1,273)=7.72$, $p<.01$, $d=.45$. In contrast, females in the high (M=.511, SD=.17) and low (M=.514, SD=.14) load conditions did not significantly differ in their choices, $F(1,273)=.11$, $p=.74$, $d=.02$.

Experiment 3: Resource Depletion

The third experiment was developed to provide evidence that the previous results were due to greater gender identity concerns for men (relative to women). It was posited that men would show greater signs of depletion following choices made from a mixed gender choice set (relative to an all-masculine choice set) whereas women would show no difference in depletion between a mixed choice set and all-feminine choice set.

Participants completed two choice tasks similar to experiments 1 and 2 (i.e. food and shape choice tasks) before completing an anagram task designed to measure ego depletion (Baumeister, Bratslavsky, Muraven, and Tice 1998- Experiment 2).

Consistent with our hypothesis that males, but not females, would be particularly depleted by choosing between masculine and feminine options, the interaction between choice sets and gender was significant, $F(1,150)=4.08$, $p<.05$. Planned contrasts for this interaction indicated that males who received mixed gender choice sets (M=5.04, SD=3.86) solved significantly fewer anagrams than males who received masculine choice sets (M=7.45, SD=3.68), $F(1,150)=5.66$, $p<.05$, $d=.64$. Further, there was no difference in the number of anagrams solved for females who received mixed gender choice sets (M=6.73, SD=3.96) and females who received feminine choice sets (M=6.52, SD=3.68), $F(1,150)=.02$, $p=.90$, $d=.05$.

References

Aronoff, J. (2006). How we recognize angry and happy emotion in people, places and things. *Cross-Cultural Research, 401 (1)*, 83-105.

Baumeister, R., Bratslavsky, E., Muraven, M., & Tice, D. (1998). Ego Depletion: Is the Active Self a Limited Resource?, *Journal of Personality and Social Psychology,74 (May),* 1252-1265.

Belk, R. (1988), "Possessions and the Extended Self," *Journal of Consumer Research*, 15 (September), 139-167.

Berger, J. and C. Heath (2007), "Where consumers diverge from others: Identity signaling and product domains," *Journal of Consumer Research*, Vol.34, No.2

Crocker J, Major B, Steele C. 1998. Social stigma. In *Handbook of Social Psychology*, ed. S Fiske, D Gilbert, G Lindzey, vol. 2, pp. 504–53. Boston, MA: McGraw-Hill

Eagly, A., Makhijani, M. & Klonsky, B. (1992). Gender and the Evaluation of Leaders: A Meta-Analysis. *Psychological Bulletin*, 111 (1), 3-22.

O'Heron, C. A., & Orlofsky, J. L. (1990). Stereotypic and nonstereotypic sex role trait and behavior orientations, gender identity, and psychological adjustment. *Journal of Personality and Social Psychology, 58*, 134–143

Shiv, B., Fedorikhin, A., & Nowlis, S. (2005). Interplay of the Heart and Mind in Decision Making. in *Inside Consumption: Frontiers of Research on Consumer Motives, Goals, and Desire*, eds. R. Ratneshwar and D. Mick, Routledge, 166-184.

Wernerfelt, B. (1990), "Advertising Content When Brand Choice is a Signal", *Journal of Business*, 63(1), 91-98.

Examining a Four-Component Model of Consumer Identification Experiences

Chelsea Willness, Brock University, Canada
Katherine White, University of Calgary, Canada
James Agarwal, University of Calgary, Canada

Conceptualization

An emergent theme in the marketing literature is that companies should endeavor to develop long-lasting, deep, and meaningful relationships with their customers (De Wulf et al. 2001; Palmatier et al. 2006). One way these relationships might be cultivated is through the development of a strong sense of identification with the organization (Bhattacharya and Sen 2003). We conceptualize consumer-to-company identification (C-C identification; Bhattacharya and Sen 2003) as when the individual feels a sense of connection with the organization, and these beliefs become self-referential or self-defining in nature (e.g., Ahearne et al. 2005).

We propose that consumer identification experiences are often more complex than existing theories can account for. Thus, we test an expanded model of C-C identification and examine the consequences of differing C-C identification experiences. To do so, we draw on theories of social identity (Tajfel and Turner 1979) and organizational identity (Kreiner and Ashforth 2004) to explicate and test an expanded model of consumer identification with organizations. We extend emerging research on C-C identification by proposing that consumer identification is not a uni-dimensional construct. We make a contribution to the marketing literature by highlighting four distinct identification experiences—identification, disidentification, ambivalent identification, and neutral identification—as they arise in the consumer context. Further, we demonstrate the nomological validity of the expanded model by showing that it predicts company evaluations, perceptions of trustworthiness, in-role behaviors, and extra-role behaviors.

Our proposed two-dimensional model holds that consumers can experience either low or high identification *and* either low or high disidentification, resulting in four consumer identification experiences. Identification (high identification/low disidentification) occurs when the individual feels a sense of connection with the organization and beliefs about the company become self-defining in nature (Dutton et al. 1994). Disidentification (low identification/high disidentification) occurs when the individual actively separates his/her identity from the organization and experiences a negative relational categorization of the self and the organization (Elsbach and Bhattacharya 2001). Ambivalent identification (high identification/high disidentification) toward organizations occurs when an individual simultaneously identifies and disidentifies with an organization (Elsbach 1999). Neutral identification (low identification/low disidentification) involves being low in both identification and disidentification with regard to an organization (Elsbach 1999).

Method

Using a market research company, 9000 people were mailed a letter inviting them to participate (8606 were received after accounting for post office returns). In total, 794 people responded (9.23%) with N=420 complete responses (*Age: M*=47.67, *SD*=11.98). There was no evidence of non-response bias (Armstrong and Overton 1977).

Participants were asked to think of a company that they had patronized in the past, and then completed scale measures to assess the different identification experiences (identification, disidentification, neutral identification, and ambivalent identification; αs=.88, .94, .86, and .88, respectively; adapted from Kreiner and Ashforth, 2004). Respondents also completed measures of company evaluations (White and Dahl 2006; α=.97), trust (e.g., Ganesan 1994; α=.93), and in-role (α=.92) and extra-role (α=.92) behaviors (adapted from Zeithaml et al. 1996). We tested for common method variance (Lindell and Whitney 2001), which was nonsignificant.

Major Findings

We performed confirmatory factor analysis (CFA) to estimate the overall measurement model. Adequate reliability (e.g., *CR*>.70; *AVE*>.50), convergent validity (e.g., loadings>.60), and discriminant validity (e.g., $\sqrt{AVE}>r$) were exhibited. Our proposed four-factor model consisted of 4 items to measure each identification dimension, which demonstrated good fit to the data based on the standard criteria of fit indices (Hu and Bentler 1999). We tested four alternative models, none of which reached acceptable levels of fit compared to our proposed model.

Correlation analysis (controlling for demographics) revealed that each identification experience was related to consumer outcomes in predicted ways (all p<.01): Identification was significantly positively correlated with evaluations of the company (r=.478), trust (r=.492), in-role behaviors (r=.362), and extra-role behaviors (r=.573). Disidentification was strongly negatively correlated with evaluations of the company (r= -.828), trust (r= -.777), in-role behaviors (r= -.786), and extra-role behaviors (r= -.746). Ambivalent identification was weakly to moderately negatively correlated with evaluations of the company (r= -.319), trust (r= -.373), in-role behaviors (r= -.195), and extra-role behaviors (r= -.295). Neutral identification was weakly negatively correlated with evaluations of the company (r= -.277), trust (r= -.311), in-role behaviors (r= -.263), and extra-role behaviors (r= -.320). Regression analyses also supported predictions.

Conclusions

This research reveals the complexity of consumers' identification experiences with the companies they patronize. An expanded four-factor model of C-C identification provides superior fit to the data compared to alternative models, revealing that consumers can experience four distinct organizational identification patterns—identification, disidentification, ambivalent identification, and neutral identification. This finding has important implications for both researchers and practitioners. From a theoretical standpoint, the results show that different forms of organizational identification can and do arise even under conditions where the individual is not a formal group member. From a practical perspective, this research delineates the full range of consumer identification experiences and enables enhanced insight into how customers develop relationships with the companies they patronize. Elucidating the complexity of consumer identification experiences, then, is a step toward further understanding positive consumer-company relationships and resilient consumer loyalty.

Our findings show that identification is associated with the most favorable consumer outcomes, whereas disidentification is associated with the least favorable consumer outcomes. Both neutral and ambivalent identification were related to consumer outcomes in predicted ways—more negative evaluations, perceptions of trust, in-role behaviors, and extra-role behaviors were reported as feelings of neutrality and ambivalence toward the company increased. Ambivalent identification is more strongly related to disidentification than identification and negatively related to consumer outcomes, indicating that it has largely negative consequences. Marketers need to ensure, even with a loyal consumer base that highly identifies with the company, that nothing negative occurs to simultaneously activate feelings of disidentification. The ambivalent consumer also represents an untapped and accessible market that has the potential to be positively swayed to more strongly identify with the company. The current research is an important first step towards elucidating the multi-faceted nature of consumer identification.

Selected References

Ahearne, M. C., Bhattacharya, C. B., and Gruen, T. (2005), "Antecedents and consequences of customer-company identification: Expanding the role of relationship marketing," *Journal of Applied Psychology, 90*, 574-85.

Armstrong, J. S., and Overton, T. S. (1977), "Estimating non-response bias in mail surveys," *Journal of Marketing Research, 14*, 396-402.

Ashforth, B. E., and Mael, F. (1989), "Social Identity Theory and the organization," *Academy of Management Review, 14*, 20-40.

Bhattacharya, C. B., and Sen, S. (2003), "Consumer-company identification: A framework for understanding consumers' relationships with companies," *Journal of Mktg, 67*, 76-88.

De Wulf, K., Odekerken-Schroder, G., and Lacobucci, D. (2001), "Investments in consumer relationships: A cross-country and cross-industry exploration," *Journal of Mktg, 65*, 33-50.

Dutton, J. E., Dukerich, J. M., and Harquail, C. V. (1994), "Organizational images and member identification," *Administrative Science Quarterly, 39*, 239-63.

Elsbach, K. (1999), "An expanded model of organizational identification," *Research in Organizational Behavior, 21*, 163-200.

Elsbach, K., and Bhattacharya, C. B. (2001), "Defining who you are by what you're not: Organizational disidentification and the National Rifle Association," *Organization Science, 12*, 393-413.

Kreiner, G. E., and Ashforth, B. E. (2004), "Evidence toward an expanded model of organizational identification," *Journal of Organizational Behavior, 25*, 1-27.

Palmatier, R. W., Dant, R. P., Grewal, D., and Evans, K. R. (2006), "Factors influencing the effectiveness of relationship marketing: A meta-analysis," *Journal of Marketing, 70, 1*36-53.

Sirdeshmukh, D., Singh, J., and Sabol, B. (2002), "Consumer trust, value, and loyalty in relational exchanges," *Journal of Marketing, 66*, 15-37.

Tajfel, H., and Turner, J. C. (1979), *An Integrative Theory of Intergroup Conflict*, Brooks/Cole.

White, K., and Dahl, D. W. (2007), "Are all outgroups created equal? Consumer identity and dissociative influence," *Journal of Consumer Research, 34*, 525–36.

The Defensive Trust Effect: Consumers' Defensive Use of Belief in a Just World to Cope with Consumption Threat

Andrew Wilson, St. Mary's College of California, USA
Peter Darke, Schulich School of Business, York University, Canada

Consumers cope with many stressful situations: poor service, difficult decisions, and misleading persuasion attempts. Existing evidence suggests that consumers react with distrust towards marketers to avoid being wronged. Campbell and Kirmani (2000) show that consumers respond to salesperson flattery by attending to potential ulterior motives, and lowering trust when such motives are plausible. Darke and Ritchie (2007) show that consumers respond to being misled by an advertiser with generalized suspicion towards all advertisers.

This research examines whether some consumers respond in exactly the opposite way—by displaying increased trust. Our research uses Cognitive Experiential Self Theory (CEST; Epstein & Pacini, 1999) and the notion of secondary control (Rothbaum, Weisz, & Snyder, 1982) to suggest that some consumers respond to threats by evoking basic beliefs about the world, leading to increased trust of the marketer, and reassurance of positive outcomes. This coping strategy is herein termed *defensive trust coping (DTC).*

CEST posits that humans adapt through the development of two systems, termed *rational* and *experiential.* These systems serve multiple goals, including accuracy (maximizing pleasure and minimizing pain) and defense (protecting self-esteem). Individuals hold basic beliefs about the nature of the world, such as the extent to which the world is meaningful vs. chaotic. We use Lerner's (1980) Belief in a Just World (BJW) as a proxy. BJW predicts certain behaviors, especially blaming victims (Rubin & Peplau, 1975). Attributing a victim's fate to his or her own failing reduces the perceived threat to BJW holders. Such coping strategies fit with secondary control (Rothbaum et al., 1982), where individuals adjust their beliefs or perceptions to reduce threat.

Given a choice between differentiable alternatives, threat is greater post-choice. Consumers experience anticipated regret following choice (Brehm, 1956). Moreover, primary control is reduced post-choice because the control exercised through the act of choosing has been lost to the past. Thus, we predict that consumers enlist basic beliefs to a greater extent post-choice than pre-choice.

In study 1, 84 undergraduates were randomly assigned to a between-participants design with choice stage as the experimental factor. Participants imagined themselves interacting with a salesperson while shopping for a digital camera they needed right away. The salesperson presented two alternatives, and recommended one over the other. Product specifications were provided in a comparison matrix, based on the local market.

Marketing agent *trust* was operationalized by adapting Delgado-Ballester's (2004) seven-item benevolence scale (Likert-type; 7 point; α=.92). BJW was measured using the seven item *personal belief in a just world* scale (Dalbert, 1999; also 7-point Likert-type; α=.84). Pre-choice participants (*n*=84) responded to the trust scale, and then chose. Post-choice participants (*n*=86) first chose, and then responded to the trust scale. Then all participants completed the BJW scale and other items.

A median split was performed on BJW (Md=5.00). A 2 (choice stage: pre vs. post) × 2 (BJW: high vs. low) ANOVA on trust revealed no main effects (all p's>.2), but a significant interaction between choice stage and BJW groups (F (1, 80)=4.891, *p*<.05). A complex contrast was calculated by assigning weights of zero to both pre-choice conditions, one to the post-choice/high-BJW condition, and negative one to the post-choice/low-BJW condition (Rosenthal and Rosnow 1984), which was significant (Fψ (1, 80)=5.33, *p*<.05). This was interpreted as support for our theorizing that high-BJW consumers respond to post-choice threat by becoming more trusting whereas low-BJW participants responded in accordance with the more rational view that greater uncertainty should engender greater distrust (Slovic et al. 1991).

Study 2 considers conditions under which the level of pre-choice threat rivals that of post-choice by making the choice more conflicted. Consumers experience pre-decisional conflict in the absence of a clear reason to choose one alternative over the other (Shafir, Simonson, & Tversky, 1993). 195 undergraduates were randomly assigned to a single factor (pre-choice vs. post-choice) between-participants design. As before, participants imagined an interaction with a salesperson, and responded to the same scales. The product comparison matrix was changed such that the alternatives were non-differentiable. Both cameras were priced at $275.

A 2 (choice stage: pre-choice) × 2 (BJW: high vs. low) ANOVA of the trust variable revealed a main effect of BJW, *F*(1, 192)=11.13, *p*<.001; supporting our view that consumers would enlist DTC in the pre-choice stage when the choice involved decision conflict.

Study 3 extended the findings in three important ways: 1) tested whether DTC operates by preconscious processing, by including a manipulation of cognitive load, 2) establish more causal evidence for the role of DTC by manipulating BJW, and 3) investigate whether an obvious, salient ulterior motive on the part of the salesperson represent a boundary condition for the effect. Load was manipulated by a procedure based on Campbell and Kirmani (2000). BJW was manipulated by a memory task in which participants were asked to write a short essay about a time when they received a deserved positive outcome. Ulterior motive was manipulated by varying the recommendation of the salesperson. She recommended the less (more) expensive alternative in the low (high) ulterior motive condition.

242 undergraduate were assigned to 2 (BJW prime) × 2 (load) × 2 (ulterior motive) between participants design. BJW was also a measured factor. Some lower order effects were found, all of which were qualified by a marginal 4-way interaction (F (1, 223)=3.373, *p*=.068). The analysis was split on the ulterior motive factor, which found no effects in the high ulterior motive conditions (all F's<1, all *p's*>.2)–evidence for the boundary condition. In the low ulterior motive conditions, the analysis revealed a 3-way interaction between BJW prime, BJW scores, and load (F (1, 111)=5.883, *p*<.05). Complex contrast suggests that the BJW-primed, high-BJW-score, high load cell (M=4.81) differed from all others (M's range from 3.46 to 4.32; Fψ (1, 111)=12.24, *p*<.001), suggesting that these three factors combined to create elevated trust judgments.

References

Brehm, J. W. (1956). Postdecision changes in the desirability of alternatives. *Journal of Abnormal and Social Psychology, 52*(3), 384-389.

Campbell, M. C., & Kirmani, A. (2000). Consumers' use of persuasion knowledge: The effects of accessibility and cognitive capacity on perceptions of an influence agent. *Journal of Consumer Research, 27*(1), 69-83.

Dalbert, C. (1999). The world is more just for me than generally: About the Personal Belief in a Just World scale's validity. *Social Justice Research, 12*, 79-98.

Darke, P. R., & Ritchie, R. J. B. (2007). The defensive consumer: Advertising deception, defensive processing, and distrust. *Journal of Marketing Research, 44*(1), 114-127.

Delegado-Ballester, E. (2004). Applicability of a brand trust scale across product categories. *European Journal of Marketing, 38*(5/6), 573-592.

Epstein, S., & Pacini, R. (1999). Some basic issues regarding dual-process theories from the perspective of cognitive-experiential self-theory. In S. Chaiken & Y. Trope (Eds.), *Dual Process Theories in Social Psychology* (pp. 462-482). New York and London: The Guilford Press.

Friestad, M., & Wright, P. (1994). The persuasion knowledge model: How people cope with persuasion attempts. *Journal of Consumer Research, 21*(1), 1-31.

Lerner, M. J. (1980). *The belief in a just world: a fundamental delusion.* New York: Plenum Press.

Slovic, Paul, James H. Flynn, and Mark Layman (1991), "Perceived Risk, Trust, and the Politics of Nuclear Waste," Science, 254 (5038), 1603-07.

Rosenthal, Robert and Ralph L. Rosnow (1984), Essentials of Behavioral Research: Methods and Data Analysis, New York: McGraw Hill.

Rothbaum, F., Weisz, J. R., & Snyder, S. S. (1982). Changing the world and changing the self-a two-process model of perceived control. *Journal of Personality and Social Psychology, 42*(1), 5-37.

Rubin, Z., & Peplau, L. A. (1975). Who Believes in a Just World? *Journal of Social Issues, 31*(3), 65-89.

When Does Greenwashing Work? Consumer Perceptions of Corporate Parent and Corporate Societal Marketing Firm Affiliation

Andrew Wilson, St. Mary's College of California, USA
Stacey Robinson, Florida State University, USA
Peter Darke, Schulich School of Business, York University, Canada

This research investigates how the affiliation between a socially responsible marketer firm (corporate societal marketing-CSM) and corporate parent affects consumer perceptions and attitudes. It examines the effects of affiliation when the association is perceived as hidden and subsequently in violation of social norms of openness. The study explores whether any effects impact the parent company and its brands; findings suggest corporate parent affiliation does not automatically lead to negative evaluation of niche marketer brands. However, the openness of the affiliation impacts the positivity or negativity of effect flowing back to the parent company and its affiliated brands.

Corporate societal marketing (CSM) is an increasingly popular brand building technique (Drumwright and Murphy 2001; Hoeffler and Keller 2002). One factor seemingly driving this is an upward trend in consumer expectations of firm social responsibility. A 2004 report found 86% of Americans are likely to switch brands, assuming equivalent price and quality, to one supporting a cause (Cone 2004).

Acquisitions of successful CSM-based firms, serving socially concerned consumers, by conglomerate parent firms is another apparent trend. There are many such examples, recent notable acquisitions include: Green & Black's, a small organic chocolate maker, acquired by Cadbury Schweppes; Coca-Cola acquired premium juice maker Odwalla; Colgate-Palmolive purchased Tom's of Maine, producer of socially-responsible items, and Burt's Bees, an all-natural cosmetic firm, was purchased by chemical giant Clorox Company.

In each case, the parent firm acquired a CSM-based firm built largely on the basis of its corporate societal marketing activities and continued operation of the CSM-based brand(s) more or less unchanged. The apparent strategy of leaving the small organization in place and continuing to market a CSM-oriented brand, assumes consumers will continue to value both brands despite affiliation. This study examines consumer perceptions of the parent firm's brands following acquisition of a CSM-based firm and seeks to appraise consumer evaluations of the parent firm brand(s) when the affiliation between it and the CSM-based firm is known.

Perhaps the acquisition of a CSM-based firm and subsequent operation as independent subsidiaries can be viewed as a persuasion tactic (Friestad and Wright 1994). This work extends investigations of the effectiveness of CSM as a brand building strategy as firm affiliation effects appear unstudied. The study of these effects is important given the trend toward increased consumer expectations of social commitment from marketers and actual acquisitions of CSM-based brands (Harrison 2006).

Additionally, this work considers consumers may infer motives for the CSM-based firm acquisition; such inferences may lead to generalized distrust for the parent firm's products given the circumstances surrounding the acquisition (Campbell 1999; Darke and Ritchie 2007). This work examines the factors that determine whether consumers infer sincere or ulterior motives. Finally, acquisition activity may have effects which spillover to related and unrelated products within the brand portfolio (Roehm and Tybout 2006); this is examined by varying the degree of similarity between brands based upon the consumer's brand schema.

Method & Results

For Study 1, participants reviewed a website of a CSM-based personal products company containing details about its environmental and community activities. Participants were asked about the extent to which the firm was environmentally concerned and engaged in the community. This scale was meant to facilitate brand/firm involvement and evoke attitude commitment towards the brand. Participants read a news article containing an earnings announcement on the parent firm and brief story about an incident resulting in environmental damage. 167 adults were randomly assigned to a between-participants experimental design with disclosure as the experimental factor. Disclosure was manipulated by varying the text of the CSM firm's website. In the disclosure condition, the website mentioned the relationship to the parent firm; the no-disclosure condition did not. Beliefs about the effectiveness of the parent firm's flagship brand were measured. An ANOVA on the effectiveness of the parent firm's product revealed those exposed to the disclosure condition believed the brand was less effective (M=5.11) than did controls (M=5.41; F (1, 165)=3.516, p=.063). It seems when participants learned of the affiliation between the firms, they became suspicious of the parent firm's motives. Such suspicion may generalize to evaluations of the firm's brands.

Study 2 sought to clarify the conditions under which the effects demonstrated in study 1 would be observed and whether the previous study's effects would generalize to other brands in the parent firm's portfolio. The past environment record of the parent firm (track-record) and the level of friendliness/hostility of the transaction in which the CSM-based brand becomes affiliated with the parent are two factors of interest.

Measures of attitude towards the parent brands overlapping CSM-based firm brands (toothpaste) included a functionally related (oral rinse), semantically related (dishwashing liquid), and dissimilar brand (cat food).

270 participants were randomly assigned to a 3 (disclosure: none, open, hidden) X 2 (track record: bad, good) X 2 (hostility of acquisition: hostile, friendly) factorial design. The procedure was identical to study 1, except the news story allowed for manipulation of additional variables. Disclosure, track record and acquisition were manipulated by varying the text of the story. An ANOVA of brand beliefs related to the effectiveness of the parent firm's flagship brand (toothpaste) revealed a significant 3-way interaction (F (1, 253)=5.828, p<.05). Follow up contrasts revealed under a friendly acquisition, with a bad track record, hidden disclosure led to *increased* evaluations (M=5.83) as compared with controls (M=5.15; p<.05). No such effects were observed when the parent had a good track record (all p's>.2).This is consistent with our theorizing when the parent has a bad track record (and thus is motivated to take action to improve) consumers would infer a sincere motive when the acquisition is friendly, as it is reasonable to assume the CSM-based firm has verified the sincerity of corporate parent through their cooperation with the acquisition.

In the hostile acquisition conditions, a different pattern emerged. Hidden disclosure led to *decreased* evaluations (M=5.26) compared with controls (M=5.89; $p<.05$). There are no differences under the good track record condition, it seems consumers infer an impression management (or other insincere) motive for the affiliation with the CSM-firm.

To test our hypothesis on the effects generalizing to related brands, a series of ANOVAs with attitude toward each brand as the dependent variable was conducted, revealing a similar 3-way interaction for the overlapping (toothpaste; $F(1, 253)=4.249$, $p<.05$) and semantically related brand (dishwashing liquid; $F(1, 253)=2.537$, $p=.081$), but not for the functionally related ($F<1$) or dissimilar brand ($F<1$).

References

Campbell, Margaret C. (1999), "Perceptions of Price Unfairness: Antecedents and Consequences," *Journal of Marketing Research,* 36 (May), 187-199.

Cone Inc. (2004), *2004 Cone Corporate Citizenship Study,* Boston: Cone, Inc.

Darke, Peter R. and Robin J.B. Ritchie (2007), "The Defensive Consumer: Advertising Deception, Defensive Processing, and Distrust," *Journal of Marketing Research,* 44 (1), 114-127.

Drumwright, Minette E. and Patrick E. Murphy (2001), "Corporate Societal Marketing," in *Handbook of Marketing and Society,* Paul Bloom and Gregory T. Gundlack, (eds.) Thousand Oaks, CA: Sage Publications, 162-183.

Friestad, Marian and Peter Wright (1994), "The Persuasion Knowledge Model: How People Cope with Persuasion Attempts," *Journal of Consumer Research,* 21 (June), 1-31.

Harrison, Joan, (2006), "Mission-Oriented Firms Change Hands," *Mergers and Acquisitions,* 41(May), 30-31.

Hoeffler, Steve and Kevin Lane Keller (2002), "Building Brand Equity Through Corporate Societal Marketing," *Journal of Public Policy and Marketing,* 21 (1), 78-89.

Roehm, Michelle L. and Alice M. Tybout (2006), "When Will a Brand Scandal Spill Over, and How Should Competitors Respond?," *Journal of Marketing Research,* 43 (3), 366-373.

Naturally Occuring Brands: A New Perspective on Place Marketing

Christine Wright-Isak, Florida Gulf Coast University, USA

This work investigates the intersection of two powerful concepts in marketing research, which have rarely been thought to intersect: brand and community.

Theoretical antecedents:

- *Place Marketing*: Kotler, Heider and Rein (1992) take a primarily macro view of places and their reasons for and tactics used to market themselves. Their focus might be said to take place from the vantage point of the "self-interested place" for it emphasizes economic causes and consequences in which marketing is called on to attract tourists, corporations and industries, or workers on the basis of functional place attributes like tropical climate, low taxes and good schools. Although imagery is acknowledged to be a factor useful in place marketing, they approach it tactically such that accidental benefits of historic or cultural heritage and amenities are communicated to enhance imagery or overcome negative perceptions. Intended audiences include corporations who will be employers and investors in local infrastructure, tourists and conventioneers who will add to local revenue streams, government bodies who can provide aid or residents who constitute a workforce that can be used as an asset.
- *Brand Communities*: O'Guinn and Muniz (1997) focus on communities in marketing but not on the place dimension. They borrowed the sociological concept of community to unpack the underlying symbolic phenomena affecting consumer loyalty to brands. Their work describes episodic community with a very limited number of commitment dimensions. Schouten studied Harley Davidson riders and the community that emerged offers the outlaw spirit of this brand as a benefit. More recently, Holt (2003) applied the idea of belonging to a brand's value set to understanding socio-cultural significance of brand meanings. All of these used the term community to refer to communion of hearts and minds and not geographically. However, O'Guinn and Belk did unite that idea with physical place in their study of Heritage Village (1989).
- *Sociology of Communities*: Sociologists and other consumer researchers have viewed place phenomena as patterned social interactions of individuals that give rise to consistent sets of expectations about how daily life in a given place will occur–culminating in particular characterizations of such places. At one end of a continuum of community studies we find ethnographies of American place like *The Social Order of the Slum* in Chicago (Suttles, 1968) or *Small Town in Mass Society* (Vidich and Bensman 1958). In-between the city and the town have been studies of suburbia like the *Levittowners* (Gans 1967). More episodic but nevertheless place centered is the emergence of norms and periodic social structure centered on consumption in a swap meet studied by Russell Belk, John Sherry and Melanie Wallendorf, (1988) or a flea market (Sherry1990). At the other end we find Perin (1977) specifically examining the intersection of macro level geographic community and micro level behaviors among neighbors in *Everything in its Place: Social Order and Land Use in America.*

Theoretical Synthesis

The intellectual convergence of these perspectives depends on acknowledging that the idea of a symbol that is so central to the concept of brand is a phenomenon of meaning creation. Scholars often view symbols as *existing manifestations of the outcomes of a process of social investment of meaning* in a tangible figure or item. Marketers conceive of brands as *intentionally created clusters of meaning* signified with a mark that can be used to signal consumers about that cluster of meanings. Both perspectives tend to under-acknowledge the continuing interaction of expectation and actual experience associated with a symbol or a brand by consumers. We assert that the "consumer" or the "follower" of a brand has an equal role with its purveyor in determining its significance.

We reason that the three main forms of small town, suburb or city each have a distinct constellation of meanings which makes them symbols. If these three symbols are used by consumers to anticipate what kind of residential community life will take place within them and if these anticipations affect how they choose where to live, then the community forms are potentially "naturally occurring brands." Whereas Kotler et. al. delineated how particular places might purposefully manipulate their features and images as brands (e.g. Chicago, Sarasota), the three archetypal forms of community are not deliberately marketed. Thus the term "naturally occurring." The nature of their significance in consumer decisions adds the term "brands." But for our reasoning to stand, we need to know whether consumers do in fact share a common understanding of the meaning of these types and whether the constellation of meanings is transmitted to subsequent generations within the culture.

This Research consists of two studies conducted 20 years apart. The first is a previously unpublished study comparing small town community to the other two forms to ascertain the role of community stereotype in residence selection. The findings raised interest in the theoretical intersection of place and community and brand as concepts. The second is recent research into whether the relevant images and meanings of town, suburb and city consist of holds true among today's Millennials. Also incorporated into the second study are some measures designed to indicate how such understanding might be transmitted to new generations.

STUDY I: 1985 The study used a three year ethnography, and a set of 6-hour in-depth interviews with 20 newcomers to study the small town form of community. The immediate 50 mile radius around the town in central NJ contained numerous instances of all three types of place-community.

- Findings: a community selection process that perpetuates the typology. Newcomers to a region selected new homes from an array of communities that they characterized using the town-suburbia-city constellation of images and meanings. In choosing a "small town life" they desired the specific social contract of small town neighboring norms they intended to fulfill themselves.
- Identification of the community as a small town by using a commonly understood set of visual cues to the three types of community. In response to unstructured questions respondents explicitly associated images of all three types of community with distinct and separate sets of expectations neighbors would have toward one another.
- Moreover, many had never lived in a small town before, so experience was not how they learned the meaning of this type. Many indicated their understanding arose from portrayals in American literature, cinema and television.

STUDY II: 2009–Investigating the Millennial Generation understanding of the set of community "brands." If community types are "naturally occurring brands" we can expect that each new generation becomes socialized to the meanings associated with them.

- *The broad hypothesis* is that Millennials, being at one or more generations away from the respondents in the original study, and inhabiting a very different social and technological world than 1985 consumers, will *not* assign the same brand labels or meanings to the three types of community in response to visual cues.
- *A second broad hypothesis* is that in addition to interpersonal or familial socialization processes cultural transmission of the constellation of images and meanings associated with each type of community may also occur via television and literature.
- *The research design*: Used survey methodology to investigate how Americans understand these three types of community. Approximately 200 surveys were fielded using both verbal and nonverbal stimuli. 130 were completed with college students up to age 25, another 70 were completed with non-student adults over the age of 35.
- *Study II is limited by region and by number of respondents*, but provides a basis for a larger follow-up study across generations and regions of the U.S.A.

FINDINGS: Analysis indicates the typology is understood by Millennials in the same way as older generations. They link unlabeled pictures of each type of place-community with the "brand" label linked by the older sample consistent with the patterns found by Study I. Briefly:

- *Small towns*–Main Street stores and homes, close-knit, supportive but controlling
- *Suburbia*–cul de sac arrangement of houses, "ticky-tacky," good for kids but conformist
- *Cities*–anonymous, fast and noisy, sophisticated and socially "open" but ruthlessly competitive

Regarding extrafamilial cultural transmission of "brand" meaning, there was considerable overlap in the viewing of the same TV shows, and reading the same books. TV Land network in particular has enabled Millenials to view the same shows (like "Mayberry RFD" or "Ozzie and Harriet" or "Family Ties" as older generations.

References

Belk, Russell, John F. Sherry, Jr., and Melanie Wallendorf (1988). "A Naturalistic Inquiry into Buyer and Seller Behavior at a Swap Meet," in *Journal of Consumer Research*, Vol. 14 (March), 449-470.

Gans, Herbert (1967). *The Levittowners*. New York: Vintage Books.

Holt, Douglas (2003). "What Becomes an Icon Most." Harvard Business Review (March), 43-49.

Kotler, Phillip, Donald H. Haider, and Irving Rein (1996). *Marketing Places*. New York: The Free Press.

O'Guinn, Thomas C., and Russell Belk (1989). "Heaven on Earth: Consumption at Heritage Village, USA," in *Journal of Consumer Research*, Vol. 16 (September), 227-238.

Perin, Constance (1977). *Everything in its Place, Social Order and Land Use in America*. Princeton: Princeton University Press.

Schouten, John W. and James H. McAlexander (1995), "Subcultures of Consumption: An Ethnography of the New Bikers," in *Journal of Consumer Research*, Vol. 22 (June), 43-61.
Sherry, John F., Jr. (1990). "A Sociocultural Analysis of a Midwestern American Flea Market," in *Journal of Consumer Research*, Vol. 17 (June), 13-30.
Suttles, Gerald, D. (1968). *The Social Order of the Slum*. Chicago: University of Chicago Press.
Vidich, Arthur and Joseph Bensman (1968) [1958]. *Small Town in Mass Society*. New York: Prentice-Hall.

Trading between Effort and Money: Consumer Participation and Service Pricing

Lan Xia, Bentley University, USA
Rajneesh Suri, Drexel University, USA

Research in co-production suggests that businesses can treat consumers as partial employees and boost productivity. While some consumers are motivated to do the work by the higher perceived control and convenience, co-production does require consumer effort (i.e., non-monetary input). Little research has examined the process how consumers trade off their effort (i.e., work) with price. In this research we examine factors influencing consumers' tradeoff between work and money. Using 4 experiments, we showed that for the same work, consumers want to save more but pay less. Further, this main effect is moderated by both consumer and service characteristics.

Conditions Under Which "Trivial" Attributes Become Important in Consumer Judgment

Na Xiao, Queen's University, Canada
Peter Dacin, Queen's University, Canada
Laurence Ashworth, Queen's University, Canada

We examine conditions under which attributes that have little or no impact on the performance of a product, known as "trivial attributes", nevertheless have an important impact on product evaluation. Existing work on trivial attributes has shown that they can positively affect product evaluation when they serve to distinguish the product from other comparable options (Carpenter et al., 1994) and when they help justify a particular choice (Brown and Carpenter, 2000; Schlosser and Shavitt, 2002). In a similar vein, attributes that are trivial because the meaning of the attribute is ambiguous or unknown can also positively impact product evaluation, primarily due to conditions, such as a positive brand reputation (Broniarczyk and Gershoff, 2003) or expectations that marketers will adhere to conversational norms, that cause consumers to draw positive inferences about the meaning of the attribute. Inferences based on trivial attributes have also been shown to lower product evaluations when they lower perceptions of the ability of the product to perform its core functions (Meyvis and Janiszewski, 2002).

In short, trivial attributes appear to impact product evaluations for two broad reasons: first, due to the inferences that consumers make based on those attributes; and second, when trivial attributes help consumers make or justify a choice. We suggest that the impact of trivial attributes in the latter case can be attributed more broadly to the ability of the attribute to fulfill contextually activated goals that are not directly related to the performance of the product. In choice contexts, such goals relate primarily to the ease of making a decision (see Bettman et al. 2008 for a discussion of choice goals). However, we argue that different contexts are likely to activate a broad array of different goals that can, under certain circumstances, render a trivial attribute meaningful.

We propose that contextual goals are most likely to cause trivial attributes to become influential when these goals are anxiety-provoking; that is, when they are important, unfulfilled, and their achievement is uncertain (Lazarus 1991). As individuals seek to reduce their anxiety, we expect them to pay special attention to any product information that does, or could, aid in the fulfillment of the anxiety-causing goal. In short, attributes that would ordinarily be ignored may take on special meaning when consumers are in a state of anxiety caused by contextual goals unrelated to the core functions of the product. Finally, we further predicted that this effect should be moderated by consumer self-confidence. Consumers who are particularly confident in their ability to fulfill their goals should be less likely to rely on trivial attributes to help achieve additional contextual goals. We tested this in Study 2.

These hypotheses were investigated in two experiments. We used the same experimental paradigm in both: participants chose between three different bottles of red wine. Four attributes were provided for each brand. Three of those were pretested to be non-trivial: price, vintage, and alcohol content. The forth was pretested to be trivial and included information on whether or not the label displayed the "picking time" of the grapes. Only one brand was said to include picking time information (participants were simply told whether the label included picking time information or not–they were not given specific picking times). Importantly, the brand was counterbalanced across participants, as was the order in which the attributes were presented.

Anxiety was manipulated in both experiments by varying aspects of the choice context designed to inspire impression management concerns. In the low anxiety condition, participants were told that they were choosing a wine to take to an informal party. In the high anxiety condition, the wine was for their future father-in-law. Manipulation checks across experiments showed anxiety levels did indeed vary across these situations.

Study 1: Ninety-seven students participated in a 2-level (anxiety: high, low) between subjects design. We measured how much participants thought about each attribute as they made their decision (along a 5-point scale). Participants also indicated how important each attribute was to their decision by dividing 100 points across the four attributes. Results indicated that participants thought more intensely about the trivial attribute (Ms=3.44 vs. 2.67; $F(1, 95)=7.98, p<.05$) and that the trivial attribute was more important to their decision (Ms

=12.31 vs. 21.87; $F(1, 95)=18.81$, $p<.01$) when anxiety levels were high. Differences in the actual brand chosen, however, failed to reach significance.

Study 2: Ninety-two students participated in a study identical to Study 1 except that we also measured differences in individuals' confidence in their abilities as they pertained to the product at hand (adapted from Bearden et al.'s self-confidence measure; 2001). We predicted that individuals high in self-confidence would be less likely to rely on the trivial attribute as a means to reduce goal-related anxiety. Results replicated findings from Study1: there was a significant main effect of the anxiety manipulation on perceived importance of the trivial attribute ($F(1, 88)=3.84$, $p<.059$). This effect was further replicated on the overall evaluation of brand–consumers evaluated the brand with the higher level of the trivial attribute (counterbalanced across brands) more positively when anxiety was high ($F(1, 88)=7.36$, $p=.01$). Although the predicted interaction did not reach significance in either case, the direction of means did suggest that the effect was primarily driven by consumers low in self-confidence ($ps=.057$ and $.045$ vs. $ps>.50$ and $.08$ for high self-confidence). It is important to note that high self-confidence participants did not experience less anxiety as a result of the manipulation. In other words, the effects of self-confidence were not caused through a reduction in anxiety, but rather perceptions of consumers' ability to fulfill their goals.

To summarize, existing work on trivial attributes has highlighted a number of ways in which such attributes can influence product evaluation. Our research contributes to this literature by demonstrating that the role of trivial attributes is importantly influenced by contextually activated goals–goals that are not related to the core functions of a product but nevertheless can exert an important influence on the way in which consumers interpret the products' attributes. More generally, this suggests that the specific goals activated in any particular product evaluation context are likely to exert an important influence on how each attribute is interpreted and its influence on overall product evaluation and choice.

References

Bearden, WO, DM Hardesty, RL Rose (2001), "Consumer Self-Confidence: Refinements in Conceptualization and Measurement," *The Journal of Consumer Research*, vol.28, 121-133.

Bettman, James R., Mary Frances Luce, and John W Payne (2008), Consumer Decision Making: A Choice Goals Approach, in *Handbook of Consumer Psychology*, Ed. Curtis P. Haugtvedt, Paul M. Herr, Frank R. Kardes, Psychology Press, 589-610

Broniarczyk, Susan M, Andrew D Gershoff (2003), "The reciprocal effects of brand equity and trivial attributes," *Journal of Marketing Research*, 40 (May), 161-175.

Brown, Christina L, Gregory S Carpenter (2000),"Why is the trivial important? A reasons-based account for the effects of trivial attributes on choice," *Journal of Consumer Research*, 26 (Mar), 372-385.

Carpenter, Gregory S, Rashi Glazer, Kent Nakamoto (1994), "Meaningful brands from meaningless differentiation: The dependence on irrelevant attributes," *Journal of Marketing Research*, 31 (Aug), 339-350.

Lazarus, RS. (1991), "Progress on a cognitive-motivational-relational theory of emotion", *American Psychologist*, vol.46, 819-834.

Meyvis, Tom, Chris Janiszewski (2002), "Consumers' beliefs about product benefits: The effect of obviously irrelevant product information," *Journal of Consumer Research*, 28 (Mar), 618-635.

Washing Away Your (Good or Bad) Luck: Superstition, Embodiment, and Gambling Behavior

Alison Jing Xu, University of Illinois at Urbana-Champaign, USA
Rami Zwick, University of California at Riverside, USA
Norbert Schwarz, University of Michigan, USA

Observations of superstitious behavior suggest that gamblers and athletes change their physical appearance after a streak of bad luck, but avoid doing so after a streak of good luck. We test the metaphorical link between changes in physical status and changes in luck in a gambling situation, using hand washing as a manipulation of physical status. Participants who encountered a winning streak bet less in a subsequent round after having than after not having washed their hands. Conversely, participants who encountered a losing streak bet more in a subsequent round after having than after not having washed their hands.

The Effect of Product Familiarity on Price Discount Framing

Ya-Chung Sun, Vanung University, Taiwan
Chiung-Chiao Chang, Vanung University, Taiwan
Shih-Chieh Chuang, National Chung Cheng University, Taiwan
Yin-Hui Cheng , National Taichung University, Taiwan

Consumer knowledge of prices plays an important role in price management since it not only determines how prices are perceived and valued but also influences consumers' purchase decisions (Binkely and Bejnarowicz, 2003; Monroe, 1973, 1992; Simon, 1989; Turley and Cabaniss, 1995). Consumer response to price stimuli may involve cognitive processes such as attention, comprehension, retention and recall, as well as behavioral processes such as the formation of purchase intentions and actual purchase behaviors (Olson and Jacoby 1977).

Product Familiarity

Familiarity has been the focus of recent empirical studies in consumer research that examine information acquisition (Bettman and Park 1980), reactions to advertising (Anderson and Jolson 1980; Edell and Mitchell 1978; Marks and Olson 1981), and the choice of decision rules by consumers (Park 1976).

Familiarity is defined as the number of product-related experiences that have been accumulated by a consumer (Abla and Hutchinson 1987). A consumer's familiarity with a product or brand plays a critical role in his/her information processing and brand evaluation (Abla and Hutchinson 1987; Fazio 1986; Johnson & Russo 1984).

Price Discount Framing

Monroe, Grewal and Compeau (1991, p. 13) noted that "research on the issue of reference price must consider the extent that individuals have different degrees of familiarity with the product category and with the different prices charged for various product alternatives." Similarly, Zeithaml (1988) argued that the price-quality relationship is influenced by consumer price awareness and the ability to detect quality variation in a product class.

Consumers who are more knowledgeable about product and price may make different decisions than consumers who are less knowledgeable. Specifically, those who are knowledgeable should be less willing to pay prices that do not reflect the quality of the product compared to those who lack that knowledge (Rao and Sieben, 1992). Hence, this study examined how consumers with different levels of product familiarity generate different perceptual savings under varied price discount framing presentation forms. As advanced in the previous section, the following hypotheses are offered:

H1: For low-price products, the less familiar consumers are with a product, the higher the likelihood that they will perceive the price reduction when the price reduction is framed in percentage terms instead of dollars.

Study 1 demonstrates that under the low-price product condition, consumers that are more familiar with the product perceive no significant difference in the price reduction whether they are presented in dollar terms or in percentage terms. Furthermore, consumers that are less familiar with the product perceive a more significant difference in the price reduction when it is presented in percentage terms than when it is presented in dollar terms.

Manipulation of Familiarity

The notebook computer was the stimuli. Three indicators were used to measure familiarity, one for the product and the others for the two attributes presented in each product category (Sheng, Parker, & Nakamoto, 2005).

Procedure

The experiment was conducted in a classroom setting. Paper and pencil method was adopted in this study. In the beginning of the experiment, the notebook was adopted to measure the product familiarity of the 166 participants'.

For the notebook computer situation, two price discount scenarios (A and B) with different price discount presentation forms (dollar versus percentage) were used to measure the participants' perceptions of the price discount promotions respectively.

A. Imagine that you had received a direct mail advertisement from your credit card company, offering a NTD 6,250 discount on the purchase of a brand A, AMD Mobile Sempron 3400+ notebook computer regularly priced at NTD 25,000. What degree of perceptual saving does this product bring?
B. Imagine that you had received a direct mail advertisement from your credit card company, offering a 25% discount on the purchase of a brand A, AMD Mobile Sempron 3400+ notebook computer regularly priced at NTD 25,000. What degree of perceptual saving does this product bring?

Results

Measurement of product familiarity

In this experiment, three indicators were used to measure the participants' familiarity with a notebook computer. The median score (=4) was adopted to set the level of high and low familiarity. Under the notebook computer condition, 115 among the 166 participants were in the high familiarity group, while 51 were in the low familiarity group.

Perceived significance of saving

A two-way factorial ANOVA was employed to test the participants' perceptions of the savings. The main effect of the framing price promotion message on the low price notebook computer condition was significant ($F(1,162)=4.301, p<.05$). The participants perceived a price reduction presented in percentage terms ($M=4.47$) as more significant than the same a price reduction presented in dollar terms ($M=3.37$). There was an interaction effect between product familiarity and presentation form on the participants' perceptions of the price promotions ($F(1,162)=8.768, p<.05$).

Under the low-price computer condition, consumers who were more familiar with the product perceived no significant price reduction, whether it was presented in dollar terms ($M=4.58$) or in percentage terms ($M=4.36$) $t(113)=0.77, p> .1$. On the other hand, consumers with a lower level of product familiarity with the product perceived a more significant price reduction when it was presented in percentage terms ($M=4.00$) compared to being presented in dollar terms ($M=2.77$) $t(49)=-3.38, p< .001$. These results support H1.

General Discussion

Study 1demonstrated that under the low-price product condition, those consumers that were more familiar with the product perceived no significant difference in the price reduction whether it was presented in dollar terms or in percentage terms. More importantly, consumers that were less familiar with the product perceived a more significant difference in the price reduction when it was presented in percentage terms compared to being presented in dollar terms. These results supported H1.

Our results show that for the low-price product category conditions, consumers that are less familiar with the product perceived that there was a more significant difference in price reduction when it was presented in percentage terms than presented in dollar terms. Marketers often target their communication efforts to audiences with varying levels of product category familiarity. When forming intentions to purchase, consumers with a high level of product familiarity access and process the different price discount framings. On the other hand, consumers with a low product familiarity rely on fewer but salient price cues to make product judgments and purchase intentions. Hence, marketers must tailor their promotion strategies to affect different familiarity groups

References

Bettman, James R. And C. Whan Park (1980b), "Effects of Prior Knowledge and Experience and Phase of the Choice Process on Consumer Decision Processes: A Protocol Analysis," *Journal of Consumer Research*, 7(December), 234-248.

Binkley, J.K. and Bejnarowicz, J. (2003), "Consumer price awareness in food shopping: the case of quantity surcharges", *Journal of Retailing*, 25(1), 27-35.

Fiske, Susan, Donald Kinder, and W. Michael Larter (1983), "The Novice and the Expert: Knowledge-Based Strategies in Political Cognition," Journal of Experimental Social Psychology, 19(4), 381-400.

Levin, I. P., Schneider, S. L., & Gaeth, G.. J. (1998), "All fames are not created equal: A typology and critical analysis of framing effects," *Organizational Behavior and Human Decision Processes*, 76, 149-188.

Monroe, K.B. (1973), "Buyers' subjective perceptions of price," *Journal of Marketing Research*, 10, 70-80.

Monroe, K.B. (1992), *Politica de Precios*, McGraw-Hill, Madrid.

Simon, H. (1989), *Price Management*, Elsevier, Amsterdam, North-Holland.

Turley, L.W. and Cabaniss, R.F. (1995), "Price Knowledge for services: an empirical investigation", *Journal of Professional Services Marketing*, 12(1), 39-47.

Best Before/Consume More-A Consumer Cultural Exploration into Freshness and Regulations of Contemporary Food Consumption

Carl Yngfalk, Stockholm University, Sweden

Freshness remains a largely unexamined product attribute within consumer research. "Best before dates" printed on products influences food acceptance and has an impact on consumption through subjects' perceptions of freshness and disposal tendencies thereof. This research analyzes this issue by problematizing the relation between discourse constituting subjects' perceptions of freshness in perishable products and subjects' tendencies to dispose these objects. Further, this research should be of interest to both producers and retailers of the food industry as well as regulators.

Introduction and method

Consumer preferences and purchase decisions concerning perishable food products are highly influenced by characteristics concerning price and freshness (International Food Information Council (IFIC) Foundation 2007; Lennernäs et al. 1997; Nordic Council of Ministers 2001). Whilst being a highly individual and perceived characteristic, a most evident source of information intervening with peoples' perceptions of freshness is the "best before" date. Within the European Union, the best-before date label (e.g. best before 01-01-09) is by far the most used and vital source of package information concerning freshness and it is required by federal law to be present on all food products on the market. In Sweden, where this research is conducted, this has been the issue since 1972, creating a peculiar and interesting research environment.

The best before date, communicating freshness, remains a largely unexamined product attribute. In the domains of food science there has been much research conducted on the date label's effects on food quality and nutrition content. In our field–the Journal of Consumer Research community –outside the domains of food science, some scholars, with Brian Wansink as vanguard, have briefly touched upon the psychological and economic impact of freshness dating and expiration dates (Kerley et al. 2008; Wansink and Wright 2006). Shortly put, these scholars have rather briefly illustrated (in controlled environments) that the date label bias human senses by producing stigma and, thus, directly influences consumer perception (Wansink and Wright 2006). In a recent JCR article, also, Sen and Block (2009) problematize the issue concerning the freshness date and describe subjects' willingness to consume products past their freshness dates and how this willingness changes with ownership; in their study, consumers are more likely to consume products out-of-date when they own the products compared to other situations (Sen and Block 2009). While research of this kind focuses largely on the behavioral aspects of the consumer subject concerning their relation to the product attribute, the understanding of discourse intervening with and shaping our perception of freshness in the first place remains quite unclear.

Besides the article by Sen and Block and the brief efforts by Wansink *et al* to problematize the date label's influence on consumer culture there are no efforts made to explore freshness and its impact on food consumption in a larger, social perspective and as powerful control mechanism–organizer of, not only consumption but also production.

Conceptualization and aim

Reasonably, consumers prefer fresh over less fresh food. This research problematizes the relation between discourse constituting subjects' perceptions of freshness in perishable products and subjects' tendencies to dispose these objects. Traditionally, consumer research and marketing have focused largely on product acquisition and value creation processes, as contradictory to peoples' disposal tendencies. It is argued here that by analyzing food product disposal practices among not only consumers, but among *different* actor groups on the market (such as consumers, producers, retailers), a better understanding is gained of socio-cultural, institutional instruments that channel and 'direct' discourse and which, thus, operate as mechanisms of bringing power relations into being. This should be of interest to both producers and regulators.

Through deep interviews with consumers, executive representatives from leading actors in food production, chief state-regulators of food labeling, and retail merchants, this research seeks to further deepen our understanding of how regulative forces in consumer culture and control mechanisms in the supply chain, reach out and intervene with individual subjects' food disposal tendencies.

Further, this research takes as a starting point the discursive power model presented by Denegri-Knott, Zwick, and Schroeder (2006). This model highlights forces which produce discourses and practices and seek to define "normal" consumer behavior in "certain consumption contexts" (Denegri-Knott et al. 2006; see also Thompson 2004). Concerning food freshness one interesting and important question to ask is through which discourses subjects' perception of freshness is constituted and why.

By exploring different subjects' perceptions of freshness and the best before dates, and drawing on high level theoretization of desire (Baudrillard 1998; Deleuze et al. 1988; Deleuze and Guattari 2004; Deleuze 2006), as well as power (e.g. Foucault et al. 1998), *the aim is to illuminate the relation between flows of institutional forces (in a constituting, productive sense, seen from the collective level) and the subjects and objects these adhere to. The aim is also to bring other actor groups into consumer research than merely the consumer while conducting consumer research.*

References

Baudrillard, Jean (1998), *The consumer society : Myths and structures* London: Sage.

Deleuze, Gilles (2006), *Nietzsche and philosophy* New York: Columbia University Press.

Deleuze, Gilles, and Felix Guattari (2004), *A thousand plateaus : Capitalism and schizophrenia* London: Continuum.

Deleuze, Gilles, Seán Hand, and Inc ebrary (1988), *Foucault*Minneapolis: University of Minnesota Press.

Denegri-Knott, Janice, Detlev Zwick, and Jonathan E. Schroeder (2006), "Mapping consumer power: An integrative framework for marketing and consumer research," *European Journal of Marketing,* 40 (9), 950-71.

Foucault, Michel, James D. Faubion, and Paul Rabinow (1998), *Essential works of foucault, 1954-1984* New York; London: New Press; Allen Lane.

International Food Information Council (IFIC) Foundation (2007), "2007 food & health survey: Consumer attitudes toward food, nutrition & health,"

Kerley, Deborah, Kent D. Messer, Brian Wansink, Harry M. Kaiser, and William D. Schulze (2008), "EXPIRATION DATES AND STIGMA: WHY DON'T WE OBSERVE HEDONIC MARKETS FOR PERISHABLE PRODUCTS?" Selected Paper prepared for presentation at the American Agricultural Economics

Lennernäs, M., C. Fjellström, W. Becker, I. Giachetti, A. Schmitt, A. M. R. de Winter, and M. Kearney (1997), "Influences on food choice perceived to be important by nationally-representative samples of adults in the european union," *European Journal of Clinical Nutrition,* 51, S8.

Nordic Council of Ministers (2001), *Food labelling: Nordic consumers' proposals for improvements : A pan-nordic survey of consumer behaviour and attitudes towards food labelling*København: Nordic Council of Ministers.

Sen, Sankar, and Lauren G. Block (2009), "Why my mother never threw anything out: The effect of product freshness on consumption," *Journal of Consumer Research,* 36 (3), 47-55.

Thompson, Craig J. (2004), "Marketplace mythology and discourses of power," *Journal of Consumer Research,* 31 (1), 162-80.

Wansink, Brian, and Alan O. Wright (2006), ""Best if used by ..." how freshness dating influences food acceptance," *Journal of Food Science,* 71 (4), 354.

Scents and Semantics: Do Fragrance Names Influence Consumer Perceptions of Scented Products?

Lauren Yourshaw, University of Pennsylvania, USA

Take a moment and think about the type of products you use or consume throughout your typical day. Now, think about how many of those products are scented. Scent is an integral attribute of numerous consumer products and is used to differentiate products both across and within product categories. The importance of fragrance attributes in the marketing of consumer products is clearly evident by the ever increasing variety of scents being offered. Take for example the laundry detergent category where Tide®, the market leading detergent brand, offers consumers over 15 different scents just for liquid detergent including Mountain Spring, Tropical Clean, Vanilla & Lavender, Soft Ocean Mist and Glacier just to name a few. With all of these fragrance variants inhabiting the marketplace, how do consumers make their choices?

Very little work in consumer research *has focused on how consumers process olfactory attributes that are specific to products. Of the research that has been done with scents in the consumer domain, the main focus has been on how ambient scents (i.e. scents in the environment and do not emanate from a product) influence consumer decision making. Findings from these studies demonstrate that ambient odors can affect both variety seeking and information search (Mitchell, Kahn, and Knasko 1995) as well as overall product judgments (Bosmans, 2006). Moreover, ambient scents can also enhance consumers' ability to recall brands (Morrin and Ratneshwar, 2003). But whether fragrance attributes inherent to a product affect product judgments has received limited attention; therefore, the broad goal of this research is to better understand the factors that shape the perception of olfactory product attributes.*

Previous research in consumer behavior has shown that verbal labels are one factor that plays a role in the processing of sensory information and manipulating these labels can influence consumer evaluations. *Framing of attribute information in either positive or negative terms has been shown to affect taste evaluations (Levin and Gaeth, 1988) and more* recent work by Hoegg and Alba (2007), demonstrates that verbal labels (brand names) can influence taste discrimination. Miller and Kahn (2005) also show that manipulating the typicality and specificity of color and flavor names affects hedonic ratings and ultimately consumer choice decisions. Although verbal labels have been shown to affect the perception of various sensory attributes (i.e. color, flavor etc.) no research has investigated the effect that verbal names of olfactory attributes have on consumer product evaluations.

Work in psychology, however has illustrated the general malleability of odor perception and shows that indeed, semantic framing of a scent can strongly shape a person's perception. The same odor stimuli labeled with a positively or negatively valenced label evokes different hedonic ratings (Herz and von Clef, 2001). For example, the scent of pine needles is rated more pleasant when it is labeled "Christmas tree" compared to when it is presented again to the same subject but labeled "spray disinfectant". Based on this work and findings in consumer research, it is reasonable to hypothesize that the perception of a scented product can be influenced by semantic framing. The work presented here seeks to investigate the effect that changing the descriptiveness of the label given to a scented product has on the overall evaluation of the product.

To test this, a study was conducted in which participants evaluated six different commercially available scented candles. The stimuli were prepared by placing shavings from each candle into 2 ounce plastic cups which were then covered with a lid. Participants were randomly assigned to one of two descriptive label conditions: concrete label condition (e.g. rose) or abstract label condition (e.g. soft floral). Each subject evaluated three candles whose primary odor characteristics were familiar to participants (cinnamon, rose, and powder) as well as three candles whose primary odor characteristics were unfamiliar (citronella, jasmine, and honeysuckle). Pretests were conducted to determine scent familiarity. After smelling each candle, participants made various hedonic evaluations as well as willingness purchase ratings.

Results of the study indicate that verbal labels do influence overall product judgments; however the effect is moderated by odor familiarity. For familiar scents, participants' hedonic ratings were significantly higher when the scent was labeled with an abstract name as compared to a concrete name. However, when the characteristics of the odor were unfamiliar, hedonic ratings were reversed such that odors were evaluated more positively when labeled with a concrete name as compared to an abstract name. A similar pattern of results was also seen with willingness to purchase measures.

In summary, the results from this work demonstrate that scent perceptions are in fact malleable. Whether or not the changes in hedonic judgment are a result of changes in the actual perception of the sensory information needs further investigations. In subsequent studies, we will attempt to understand the mechanisms that underlie these changes in scent evaluations.

Selected References

Bosmans, Anick (2006), "Scents and Sensibility: When Do (In) Congruent Ambient Scents Influence Product Evaluations?" *Journal of Marketing*, 70 (July), 32-43.

Herz, Rachel S. and Julia von Clef (2001), "The Influence of Verbal Labeling on the Perception of Odors: Evidence for Olfactory Illusions," Perception, *30, 381-391.*

Miller, Elizabeth G. and Barbara E. Kahn (2005), "Shades of Meaning: The Effect of Color and Flavor Names on Consumer Choice," *Journal of Consumer Research*, 32 (June), 86-92.

Mitchell, Deborah J., Barbara E. Kahn and Susan C. Knasko (1995), "There's Something in the Air: Effects of Congruent or Incongruent Ambient Odor on Consumer Decision Making," *Journal of Consumer Research*, 22 (September), 229-238.

Morrin, Maureen and S. Ratneshwar (2003), "Does It Make Sense to Use Scents to Enhance Brand Memory?" *Journal of Marketing Research,* 40 (February), 10-25.

Cross Physical Sense: How Weight Influences Consumer Stress and Importance Rating

Meng Zhang, Chinese University of Hong Kong, Hong Kong, China
Xiuping Li, National University of Singapore, Singapore

Weight is an integral part of consumer sensory perception, and a central attribute in product design. For example, to make laptops feel less heavy, colors like white or silver are often used. The location of cookie images on a package could be used to influence how consumers perceive the weight of cookies, which in turn, influence their evaluations of the package (Deng and Kahn 2009).

However, prior consumer research on weight concept has been largely focused on how sensory experience in the other domains influences judgment of weight. In this research, we propose that consumers' physical experience of carrying heavy objects (e.g., carrying a bag of groceries) can influence judgments "irrelevant" to the weight perception. Further, we propose that the experience of carrying heavy weight might influence judgments across domains by two routes (1) activating a physiological state shared by the physical sense of heavy; (2) activating the associated semantic concepts that linked to the weight concept. These two routes, in turn, determine whether these effects are reciprocal: When there is a shared physiological state, the effects are more likely to be bi-directional than when only semantic links are shared.

Specifically, in this study, we investigate how carrying weight influences the judgment of stress and importance. We choose to work on these two kinds of judgments based on the following justifications. First, in daily language, there is ample evidence that we often use sensory experience of weight to describe and understand the emotional experience of stress (heavy steps; my sprits sunk) and the abstract concept of importance (heavily weighted). These may reflect a co-activation of these constructs in our mind. Second, judgments of stress and importance might be differentially linked to "heavy" via one of the above-mentioned routes: Stress, as a basic emotion, is associated with physiological reactions; importance, on the other hand, is primarily a semantic construct. Therefore, these two concepts are good candidates to help us test our theorizing. We predict that for judgments shared a physiological base (i.e., "heavy" and "stress"),[14] the effects are more likely to be reciprocal, however, for the condition when one judgment is physiological (i.e., "heavy"), but the other is an abstract concept (i.e.,"important"), the effects are more likely to be uni-directional (from "heavy" to "importance"). This is because that prior research has found that it is relatively earlier for a physical experience to have effects on an associated abstract concept than the other way around (Boroditsky 2000).

Two experiments were conducted to test our predictions. Experiment 1 provided the first investigation of our hypotheses whereas experiment 2 (on going) further examined the underlying mechanism. Two hundred and fifty-two participants participated in experiment 1. It had a 4 (*Prime*: Heavy, Stress, Importance, Control, between subjects) x 3 (*Target*: Heavy judgment, Stress judgment and Importance judgment, within subjects) mixed design. Upon arrival, participants were told to take part in two unrelated tasks. For the first task, participants in the heavy perception condition were asked to carry a shopping bag with three bottles of water (1.8L each).[15] In the stress condition, participants were asked to recall and briefly describe an event that they felt very stressed, whereas in the importance condition, participants were asked to recall a very important decision they made. In the control condition, participants only completed the second task.

After the first task, participants were given a questionnaire set composed of three tasks: weight estimation, stress levels and important rating (the order was counterbalanced). In weight estimation task, participants estimated the weight of a package (2-item: on a 9-point scale and actual weight estimation in grams). For task related to stress judgment, they were asked to indicate how stressful thinking about class presentation made them feel (on a 9-point scale; 3-item: not at all/very stressful, worried, pressured). For importance judgment, participants needed to rate the importance of a new course on general education (on a 9-point scale; 3-item: not at all/very important, critical, crucial)

The items on stress (α=.87) and importance (α=.91) were averaged. ANOVAs for repeated measures were performed using the averaged ratings on stress and on importance, and subjective weight judgments as dependent variables. The results supported our hypotheses. Data revealed a main effect of judgment types, qualified by the two-way interaction (*ps* <.001). A closer examination of data showed that carrying a heavy bag, as compared to control condition, had an effect on all judgments in the second questionnaire: participants reported a higher weight estimation (M =6.11; 1134.92 g; $M_{control}$=5.30; 603.49g), felt more stressful towards an event (M =6.70; $M_{control}$=6.13) and rated a new subject more important (M =6.07; $M_{control}$=5.13; *ps*< .001). Recalling a stressful event, as compared to control, had significant effects on weight judgment (M=6.05; 776.30; $M_{control}$=5.30; 603.49) and stress feelings (M=6.82; $M_{control}$=6.13; *ps* <.001), but not on importance (M =5.20; $M_{control}$=5.13; p>.1). Finally, importance prime only had effects within the same domain of importance rating (M =5.84; $M_{control}$=5.12, p<.01), but no effects on the other two domains (weight judgment: M =5.37; 621g ; $M_{control}$=5.30; 603g; Stress feeling: M =6.42; $M_{control}$=6.12, p >.1). In other words, these results showed that (1) all the concepts had significant influences within their own domain, consistent with the predictions of priming literature; (2) as we expected, physical sense of carrying heavy objects led people to feel more stressful, and regarded a subject as more important; (c) The link between "heavy" and "stress" were reciprocal, whereas between "heavy" and "importance" was more uni-directional.

In the second experiment (on going), we examined the underlying mechanisms of the asymmetric findings further. If, as we argue, the bi-directional effects depend on whether a physiological state is shared between two domains, then inducing participants with a "physical focus" vs. "thinking focus" should moderate the effects. Specifically, instructing participants to focus on their "physical experience" when doing the task should strengthen the effects between heavy and stress in both directions; however, instructing participants to focus on their "thoughts" should strengthen the effects of "heavy" on "importance". No other effects were predicted. Our on-going experiment 2 had provided some initial support to these predictions.

References

Boroditsky, L. (2000). Metaphoric structuring: Understanding time through spatial metaphors. *Cognition*, *75*, 1–28.

Deng, X., & Kahn, B. E. (2009). Is your product on the right side? The "location effect" on perceived product heaviness and package evaluation. *Journal of Marketing Research*, forthcoming.

Williams L. E., & Bargh, J. A. (2008). Experiencing physical warmth promotes interpersonal warmth. *Science*, 322, 606-607.

Zhong, C.-B., &Leonardelli, G. (2008). Cold and lonely: Does social exclusion literally feel cold? *Psychological Science*, 19, 838-841.

Zhong, C.-B., &Liljenquist, K. (2006). Washing away your sins: Threatened morality and physical cleansing. *Science*, 313, 1451-1452.

Counteractive Construal in Consumer Goal Pursuit

Ying Zhang, University of Texas at Austin, USA
Szu-Chi Huang, University of Texas at Austin, USA
Susan Broniarczyk, University of Texas at Austin, USA

The present research explores a self-control operation, namely counteractive construal, that helps consumers resolve the conflicts between an important goal and a short-term temptation by altering the construal of the temptation. We propose that when experiencing a self-control conflict, consumers intentionally construe temptation as more damaging to the attainment of a long-term goal, and use these

[14] They might also share some semantic links.

[15] A pilot test shows that participants would regard this bag as heavy.

distorted construals to help resolve the conflict in favor of the goals. Four studies in two self-regulatory domains (dieting goal and academic goal) provided converging evidence for the counteractive construal hypothesis. We found that people who were experiencing self-control conflict expected tempting food items to contain more calories, or expected parties to take more time away from studying, and were consequently less interested in consuming these temptations.

Consumers often face temptations in the pursuit of important long-term goals. Because the pursuit of such temptations potentially undermines the attainment of the goal, the presence of both the goal and temptation constitutes a self-control dilemma, which requires individuals to engage in self-control effort in order to maintain their goal pursuit (Aspinwall and Taylor 1997; Fishbach, Friedman, and Kruglanski 2003; Trope and Fishbach 2000). In this research, we propose a self-control mechanism, namely counteractive construal, that consumers employ to help them resist the temptation. Specifically, we propose that whenever consumers experience a conflict between a long-term goal and a short-term temptation, they augment the extent to which the temptation may undermine the goal attainment, thus are more likely to resist the temptation and resolve the self-control conflict in favor of the long-term goal.

Despite consumers' wish to perceive the world in an accurate and objective way, prior research has demonstrated that individuals' motivational states have a profound influence in shaping their perceptions and judgments (Baumeister and Newman 1994; Kunda 1990). Because one's perceptions and judgments are heavily influenced by their motivational states, it is possible that one's motivation to maintain their goal pursuit would potentially alter the construal and assessment of the options in this conflict (Fishbach, Shah, and Kruglanski 2004). In other words, one may help resolve the self-control conflict by augmenting the perceived cost of pursuing the temptation, such that it poses a greater threat to the attainment of the more important goal and would therefore be avoided.

Since we conceptualize counteractive construal as a self-control response designed to help individuals maintain their goal pursuit when facing a dilemma, we expect it to occur only when consumers experience the conflict between a long-term goal and a short-term temptation. The strength of the counteractive operation, accordingly, should depend on the intensity of the conflict: when the conflict is minimal, such as when the goal is unimportant, or the temptation is inaccessible, counteractive construal is unlikely to occur. Based on prior findings in the substitutability between self-control and external control, we further hypothesize that whenever there are externally imposed controls, counteractive construal becomes unnecessary because the external controls would be sufficient to ensure that the long-term goal would not be undermined by the temptation (Kruglanski et al. 2002; Tesser, Martin, and Cornell 1996). Because of the instrumental nature of counteractive construal, we further expect that it should only occur when self-control is effective in helping avoid the temptations. In situations where self-control is of no value in fending off the temptation, we expect no counteractive alterations in the construal of the temptation.

Three studies tested the present predictions. Across all studies, consumers faced a dilemma between succumbing to an immediately gratifying temptation and maintaining their goal pursuit, and we measured their perceptions of the tempting targets to test the counteractive construal hypothesis.

Study 1 and 2 tested whether consumers with (vs. without) an accessible dieting goal would construe tempting food items (cookies and drinks) to contain more calories, depending on whether they expected to have an opportunity to consume the tempting items or not. In study 1, we used a goal strength x temptation availability (available vs. unavailable) two factor design, where the temptation availability was manipulated as a between-subject factor and the strength of the dieting goal was measured as an individual difference factor. The dependent variable was the estimated calorie content in a piece of chocolate-chip cookie. We found that for participants who were told that they would have an option to take one cookie at the end of the study, the strength of their dieting goal positively predicted the amount of calories they perceived the cookie to contain. In contrast, for those who were not offered the option to take a cookie, there was no such relation.

Study 2 directly manipulated the accessibility of the dieting goal for participants and tested their construal of a tempting drink depending on whether they anticipated to have the option to consume the drink or not. We employed a 2 (dieting goal prime: yes vs. no) x 2 (temptation availability: available vs. unavailable) between-subject design. We manipulated the accessibility of participants' dieting goal by changing the settings of the small experiment room with three large posters depicting fit females or natural sceneries. The dependent variable was the estimated calorie content in a cup of sweetened soda. The results confirmed our hypothesis. For participants whose dieting goal was made accessible, they construed the soda to contain more calories when they expected it to be available for consumption than when they did not expect it to be available. However, when participants' dieting goal was not made accessible, the perceived amount of calories in the soda did not differ between those who expected to have an option to consume and those who did not.

Study 3 tested the hypothesis in a different context and included another dependent variable: participants' behavior intentions toward the temptation. We asked undergraduate participants to estimate the duration of a party when shown a flyer that invited them to a party either before or after they reported their desired GPA. We predicted that students who read the party invitation after reporting their desired GPA, in comparison to those who read the flyer before reporting their desired GPA, would experience a self-control conflict and expect the party to be longer, and in turn show lower interest in attending the party. The results showed the predicted goal strength x self-control conflict interaction. When participants viewed the party flyer after answering the school-related questions, their desired GPA positively predicted the anticipated duration of the party. Such relation was not found among participants who viewed the party flyer before answering school related questions. In addition, for participants who experienced the self-control conflict between the academic goal and the tempting party, the estimated duration negatively predicted their intention to attend the party, whereas there was no such relation among participants who did not experience the self-control conflict.

In order to accomplish important long-term goals, consumers need to resist temptations, which are immediately gratifying yet costly to the goal attainment. The present research documented counteractive construal as a self-control mechanism that helps people resolve the conflict between a short-term temptation and a long-term goal. By perceptually increasing the cost of pursuing the temptation when experiencing such dilemma, consumers become more likely to avoid the temptation and maintain their goal pursuit.

References

Aspinwall, Lisa G. and Shelley E. Taylor (1997), "A Stitch in Time: Self-Regulation and Proactive Coping," *Psychological Bulletin*, 121 (3), 417-36.

Baumeister, Roy F. and Leonard S. Newman (1994), "Self-Regulation of Cognitive Inference and Decision Processes," *Personality and Social Psychology Bulletin*, 20 (1), 3-19.

Fishbach, Ayelet, Ronald S. Friedman, and Arie W. Kruglanski (2003), "Leading Us Not Into Temptation: Momentary Allurements Elicit Overriding Goal Activation," *Journal of Personality and Social Psychology*, 84 (2), 296-309.

Fishbach, Ayelet, James Y. Shah, and Arie W. Kruglanski (2004), "Emotional Transfer in Goal Systems," *Journal of Experimental Social Psychology*, 40 (6), 723-38.

Kruglanski, Arie W., James Y. Shah, Ayelet Fishbach, Ron Friedman, Woo Young Chun, and David Sleeth-Keppler (2002), "A Theory of Goal Systems," in *Advances in Experimental Social Psychology, Vol. 34.*, ed. Mark P. Zanna, San Diego, CA US: Academic Press, 331-78.

Kunda, Ziva (1990), "The Case for Motivated Reasoning," *Psychological Bulletin*, 108 (3), 480-98.

Tesser, Abraham, Leonard L. Martin, and David P. Cornell (1996), "On the Substitutability of Self-Protective Mechanisms," in *The Psychology of Action: Linking Cognition and Motivation to Behavior.*, ed. Peter M. Gollwitzer and John A. Bargh, New York, NY US: Guilford Press, 48-68.

Trope, Yaacov and Ayelet Fishbach (2000), "Counteractive Self-Control in Overcoming Temptation," *Journal of Personality and Social Psychology*, 79 (4), 493-506.

Fashion Systems and Historical Culture in the Development of Chinese Global Branding

Wu Zhiyan, University of Exeter, UK
Janet Borgerson, University of Exeter, UK
Jonathan Schroeder, University of Exeter, UK

Global market trends move toward increasing global cultural convergence and, at the same time, a need for local cultural differentiation. To address these contradictory forces, the research investigates processes and practices of marketers and consumers in three related cases: Jay Chou (a well-known Chinese music artist); the Beijing Olympics opening ceremony; and Shanghai Tang (a global fashion brand). The studies reveal strategic processes and mechanisms involved in the creation of a series of texts and codes from Chinese cultural resources. The theoretical and practical significance of studying historical culture, fashion systems and integrating current branding theories in a more holistic manner contributes a new approach to apparent contradictions that clearly must be dealt with simultaneously.

Methodology: multi-sited ethnography studies and ECM Data collection

Multi-sited ethnography is suited for interdisciplinary cultural studies on global and local areas and expresses the diffusion and circulation of cultural meanings, objects and identities in different time and space (Marcus 1998). Interviewing global consumers and marketers in different locations and observing consumption environments and consumers' consumption behaviours, as well as websites and other media resources, reveal the possibility and process of understanding, and engaging, Chinese global branding strategy. An extended case method, a mode of "logical analysis on the data interpretation of field observation, interviews, primary source materials, archived texts" (Holt 2002, p. 73), is employed to illuminate recent global brand culture initiatives from China.

Historical Culture in Branding

From a cultural branding perspective, retro activities and aesthetic fashions, including reproduction (Pearman 1999), retro-servicing (Alexander 1999), retro-styling (Brown 1999), retro retail stores (Maclaran and Stevens 1998), and heritage marketing hybrids, recognize the past's use in brand development. In other words, historical culture is employed to develop brands. Indeed, the presentation of historical culture, or the past, in marketing has been investigated for several decades. Some researchers contend that the prevalence of retroactivities is motivated by consumers' nostalgic desire (e.g. Lowenthal 1985; Belk 1991; Borgerson and Schroeder 2003: Holak and Havlena 1992; Stern 1992; Holbrook 1993; Holbrook and Schindler 1996, 2003).

Others claim that marketing the past is a way of secularizing the sacred historical, cultural, and religious elements and beliefs to enhance marketing activities (e.g. Belk, Wallendorf and Sherry 1989; O'Guinn and Belk 1989). As Eckhardt and Bengtsson suggest in the Chinese case, it may be valuable to engage the past as a strategic brand-signifying practice (2007). Moreover, they demonstrate Chinese branding's emergence in imperial China, marking a long history of attention to these processes.

Brand Development Culture and Fashion Systems

Schroeder and Salzer-Mörling discuss the roles that history and culture play in understanding the cultural codes of branding, expanding recognition of research that taps into what they call brand culture (2006). They write, "If brands exist as cultural, ideological, and political objects, then brand researchers require tools developed to understand culture, politics, and ideology…." (2006, p. 1). Thus, we understand the importance of social, cultural, and historical resources in undertaking branding, marketing, and consumer research.

For purposes of this research, a fashion transformation process model (Cholachatpinyo et al., 2002) allows us to recognize fashion as a system that influences global brand development, engaging fashion branding processes from macro-subjective (economic values/ assumptions that legitimize particular activity); macro-objective (marketplace and economic activities); micro-objective (interaction between individual and variety of fashion objects); and micro-subjective perspectives (psychological phenomena of individual and of the interaction among individuals).

Symbolic production and consumption

Arnould and Thompson (2005) indicate that studies of symbolic production and consumption mainly "draw from semiotic and literary critical theories to analyze the symbolic meanings, cultural ideals, and ideological inducements encoded in popular culture texts and the rhetorical tactics that are used to make these ideological appeals compelling". Studies on symbolic consumption mainly focus on the critical augments about "sign domination" and "sign experimentation." Derivation of sign meaning draws from "sign domination," relying on the social structure and "sign experimentation," focusing on consumers' agency. The notion of symbolic production and consumption in brand culture is grounded in the assumption that non-linguistic sign systems, including aspects of advertising or traditional rituals, are structured like language by means of codes or conventions, yet may demonstrate both aspects of sign derivation.

Global Brand Culture

Cayla and Arnould (2009) adopt a cultural approach to branding in the global marketplace based on different attempts to develop an informed historical and cultural "analysis of brands" (p. 13). Global myths might be targeted to build international brands. Put simply, global brands arouse a global myth and "the global myth of the independent, self-actualizing, decision-making consumer is simultaneously a participant in and citizen of a modernizing world" (p. 102). Holt (2004) posits that a cultural branding approach can "identify the most valuable type of myth for the brand to perform at a particular historical juncture, and then provide specific direction to creative partners on how to compose the myth" (p. 218).

Moreover, Cayla and Eckhardt (2008) evoke the modernity of Asian branding. They found that Asian brand managers highlight universal practices of globalization that simulate "a generic, hyper-urban, and multicultural experience… infused with diverse cultural referents, and therefore contribute to the creation of an imagined Asia as urban, modern and multicultural" (p. 216). For example, Singapore-based fashion brand 77th Street, and Hong Kong–based fashion brand Giordano resolutely emphasize and demonstrate the modernity and fashionableness of Asian brands and its brand development.

Brand culture goes further than recognizing the roles that culture, in various guises, can play for brands and in branding processes. Rather, brands and branding participate in processes of co-creating culture (Schroeder 2009). This research offers a framework to better understand global and local brands' development, exploring consumption and management discourses related to historical culture and fashion in the Chinese context. The findings also address the lack of privileged positions for contemporary Chinese brands in competition with more prominent global brands.

References

Alexander, Gorshanov (1999), "Online Shops Bring Back Haggling," *The Sunday Times*: Business, 11 (April 10).

Arnould, Eric J. and Craig J. Thompson (2005), "Consumer Culture Theory (CCT): Twenty Years of Research,"*Journal of Consumer Research,* **31**(March), 868–881

Belk, Russell. W. (1986), "Art Versus Science as Ways of Generating Knowledge about Materialism" in David Brinberg, Richard J. Lutz (eds) *Perspectives on Methodology in Consumer Research*. New York: Springer-Verlag, 3-36.

Belk, Russell. W (1991), "Possessions and the Sense of Past" in Russell W Belk (eds) *Highways and Buyways: Naturalistic Research From the Consumer Behavior Odyssey*. Provo, UT: Association for Consumer Research,114-30.

Belk, Russell, Melanie Wallendorf, and John F. Sherry, Jr. (1989), "The Sacred and the Profane in Consumer Behavior: Theodicy on the Odyssey," *Journal of Consumer Research*, 16 (June), 1–38.

Bogerson, Janet L. and Jonathan E. Schroeder (2003), "The Lure of Paradise: Marketing the Retro-escape of Hawaii," in Stephen Brown and John F. Sherry, Jr. (eds), *Time, Space and Place: The Rise of Retroscapes*, Armonk, NY: M.E. Sharpe, 219-37.

Brown, Stephen (1999), "Retro-marketing: Yesterday's Tomorrow, Today," *Marketing Intelligence and Planning* 17, 7, 363-76.

Cayla, Julien and Eric Arnould (2009), "A Cultural Approach to Branding in the Global Marketplace," *Journal of International Marketing*, Special Issue on International Branding, 16 (4), 86-112

Cayla, Julien and Giana M. Eckhardt (2008), "Asian Brands and the Shaping of a Transnationalimagined Community,". *Journal of Consumer Research*, 35, 3, 216-30.

Cholachatpinyo, Anothai, Ben Fletcher, Ian Padgett , and Matty Crocker (2002), "A Conceptual Model of the Fashion Process Part 1: The Fashion Transformation Process Model," *Journal of Fashion Marketing and Management*, 6,1, 24-34.

Eckhardt, Giana M. and Anders. Bengtsson (2007), "Pulling the White Rabbit out of the Hat: Consuming Brands in Imperial China," Paper presented at *Association for Consumer Research*, European Conference, July, Milan, Italy.

Holak, Susan L. and William J. Havlena (1992), "Nostalgia: an Exploratory Study of Themes and Emotions in the Nostalgic Experience" in John F. Sherry, Jr. and Brian Sternthal (eds) *Advances in Consumer Research* 19. Provo, UT: Association for Consumer Research, 380-7

Holbrook, Morris B. (1993), "Nostalgia and Consumption Preferences: Some Emerging Patterns of Consumer Tastes," *Journal of Consumer Research* 20 (September), 245-56.

Holbrook, Morris B. (2003), "Nostalgic Bonding: Exploring the Role of Nostalgia in the Consumption Experience," *Journal of Consumer Behavior* 3 (December), 107-27.

Holbrook, Morris B. and Robert M. Schindler, (1996), "Market Segmentation Based on Age and Attitude toward the Past: Concepts, Methods and Findings Concerning Nostalgic Influences on Customer Tastes," *Journal of Business Research* 37, 27-39.

Holt, Douglas B. (2002), "Why Do Brands Cause Trouble? A Dialectical Theory of Consumer Culture and Branding," *Journal of Consumer Research* 29, 1, 70-90.

Holt, Douglas B. (2004), *How Brands Become Icons: The Principles of Cultural Branding*, Cambridge, MA: Harvard Business School Press .

Lowenthal, David (1985), *The Past Is A Foreign Country*, Cambridge: Cambridge University Press.

Maclaran, Pauline and Lorna Stevens (1998), "Romancing the Utopian Marketplace: Dallying with Bakhtin in the Powerscourt Town house centre" in Brown, Stephen., Anne M Doherty, and Bill Clack (eds) *Romancing The Market*. London: Routledge, 172-86.

Marcus, George E (1998), *Ethnography Through Thick and Thin*, Princeton, N.J. : Princeton University Press.

O'Guinn, Thomas C. and Russell W. Belk (1989), "Heaven on Earth: Consumption at Heritage Village, USA," *Journal of Consumer Research*15(September), 227-38.

Pearman, Hugh (1999),"Curiouser and Curiouser," *The Sunday Times*.16 May, 14-15.

Schroeder, Jonathan E. (2009), "The Cultural Codes of Branding," *Marketing Theory*, 9, 123-6.

Schroeder, Jonathan E. and Miriam Salzer-Mörling (eds.) 2006. *Brand Culture*. London: Routledge.

Stern, Barbara B (1992), "Historical and Personal Nostalgia in Advertising Text: the Fin de siecle Effect", *Journal of Advertising* 21, 4, 11-32.

Author Index